SELECTED COMMERCIAL STATUTES

FOR SALES AND CONTRACTS COURSES

2007 Edition

Advisory Panel

Carol L. Chomsky
Professor of Law
University of Minnesota Law School

Christina L. Kunz
Professor of Law
William Mitchell College of Law

Linda J. Rusch
Professor of Law
Gonzaga University School of Law

Elizabeth R. Schiltz
Associate Professor of Law
University of St. Thomas School of Law

THOMSON

WEST

Mat #40573988

ISBN 978-0-314-18000-1

TEXT IS PRINTED ON 10% POST
CONSUMER RECYCLED PAPER

Preface from the Advisory Panel
Selected Commercial Statutes for
Sales and Contracts Courses
2007 Edition

As commercial law professors and users of commercial law supplements in our own teaching, the four of us on the Advisory Panel welcome the opportunity to continue shaping this mainstay of commercial law teaching to better serve the students and teachers who use it. Our aim in this version of Selected Commercial Statutes is to provide a slimmer volume that works effectively for classes focusing on sales and contracts.

Based on our own judgments and surveys of commercial law professors, we made the following decisions:

- The official version of the UCC appears at the front of the book, because it is the Uniform Code as promulgated by NCCUSL and the ALI. Moreover, including all sections of the UCC as promulgated allows students to use section cross-references across articles and to see the consistency and relationship among redrafted provisions (for instance, electronic commerce provisions) across the Code. The same efficiency and consistency results for users of the older versions of the UCC articles by placing them together following the official UCC version—cross-references line up, definitions mesh well, and sections relate well among articles. The arrangement also allows students to more easily remember which version of an article they are using at any given time. Each source is labeled clearly as to its date of enactment or promulgation and the headers for each source are specific, to help users identify the version they are using.

- We have included only selected portions of international sources related to sales and contracts, to keep the book less expensive and less bulky for its users. Some international sources (for instance, UNIDROIT and UNCITRAL material) are readily available online and should be accessed there:
  - *www.uncitral.org*
  - *www.unidroit.org*
  - *www.iccwbo.org*

We believe the supplement will work for most sales and contracts courses, while providing a smaller, more compact set of the necessary materials. We will reconsider these decisions for the 2008 Edition, so we hope that you will let us know how this version served your needs and those of your students.

PREFACE FROM THE ADVISORY PANEL

Advisory Panel:

Prof. Carol L. Chomsky, University of Minnesota Law School, Minneapolis, MN

Prof. Christina L. Kunz, William Mitchell College of Law, St. Paul, MN

Prof. Linda J. Rusch, Gonzaga University School of Law, Spokane, WA

Prof. Elizabeth R. Schiltz, University of St. Thomas School of Law, Minneapolis, MN

June 2007

STUDENT GUIDE:
HOW TO USE THIS COMPILATION OF THE UCC

Suggestions from the Advisory Panel

The 2007 official text of the UCC, as adopted by the American Law Institute (ALI) and the National Conference of Commissioners on Uniform State Laws (NCCUSL), appears first in this volume (pages 1 to 898). The official text includes all revisions and amendments adopted by ALI and NCCUSL, the promulgating bodies for uniform acts. (We use the term "amendment" to refer to changes in language adopted for individual sections. We use the term "revision" to refer to a wholesale rewrite of a UCC Article.) The first page of each article of the official text shows which appendices contain earlier versions, some of which remain enacted law in some jurisdictions. A list of state adoptions of the various articles of the UCC can be found at *www.nccusl.org*.

The appendices contain the following categories of material.

- **Conforming Amendments to Other Articles,** reflecting amendments to the UCC that ALI and NCCUSL recommend be made to ensure that the rest of the UCC remains consistent with a revised or amended Article:

  - Appendix A, containing the conforming amendments that a legislature should enact if it adopts the 2001 revision of Article 1.

  - Appendix B, containing the conforming amendments that a legislature should enact if it adopts the 2003 revision of Article 7.

- **Unamended and unrevised versions of Articles** where revisions have not yet been universally or widely adopted:

  - Appendix C, containing the 2000 version of Article 1 (dated to indicate it does not reflect the 2001 revision).

  - Appendices D and E, containing the 2000 version of Articles 2 and 2A, dated to indicate they do not contain the 2001 conforming amendments accompanying the Article 1 revision or the 2003 and 2005 amendments to Articles 2 and 2A.

  - Appendix I, containing the 2002 unrevised Article 7.

- **Amendments in strikeout/underline format** to selected Articles, included if many states have not yet adopted the amended version:

  - Appendix F, containing the 2003 amendments to Articles 2 and 2A.

  - Appendix J, containing the 2005 amendments to all Articles.

- Selected Commentaries of the Permanent Editorial Board for the UCC (Appendix K).

To facilitate study of earlier versions of certain Articles, we offer some suggestions about how the appendices may be used to do so:

- For a jurisdiction that has adopted neither the 2001 revision of Article 1 nor the 2003 amendments to Articles 2 and 2A, teachers may use the versions of Articles 1, 2, and 2A that appear in Appendices C, D, and E.

- For a jurisdiction that has adopted the 2001 revision of Article 1 but has not adopted the 2003 amendments to Articles 2 and 2A, teachers may use the official text of Article 1, the unamended versions of Articles 2 and 2A (Appendices D and E), and the Conforming Amendments accompanying revised Article 1, in Appendix A (which shows the changes likely made to the unamended versions of Articles 2 and 2A when the 2001 revision of Article 1 was adopted). Alternatively, teachers may use the unrevised version of Article 1 (Appendix C) and depend on the concordance between unrevised Article 1 and the official text (see page 21). In either case, teachers may use the strikeout/underline version of the 2003 amendments to Articles 2 and 2A (Appendix F) to consider the amendments that may be proposed in a jurisdiction based on the adoption by ALI and NCCUSL.

- For jurisdictions that have not incorporated the revisions to Article 7 adopted by ALI and NCCUSL in 2003, teachers may use the version of Article 7 appearing in Appendix I.

- The 2005 amendments in Appendix J have already been incorporated in the official text of the UCC and are included for reference purposes. Under most circumstances, the amendments themselves will not need to be consulted.

For additional source material on the history of the adoption of UCC sections, see

www.nccusl.org
www.ali.org
www.law.upenn.edu/bll/archives/ulc

FOREWORD
TO
OFFICIAL TEXT AND COMMENTS

The Permanent Editorial Board and its constituent organizations, the American Law Institute and the National Conference of Commissioners on Uniform State Laws, have worked for almost two decades to update the Uniform Commercial Code. The effort has been greatly assisted by the American Bar Association, which has provided advisers at each step along the way.

This effort began with two new articles: Article 2A, first promulgated in 1987 and revised in 1990, provides a legal structure for leases of goods, and Article 4A (1989) governs commercial funds transfers. The PEB then directed its attention to the original articles of the Code. The primary goal was not to create new law but rather to bring the articles up to date in terms of modern business practices and technology. Articles 3 and 4, covering negotiable instruments and bank deposits and collections, were thoroughly revised in 1990 (and amendments to a limited number of particular provisions in those articles were recommended in 2002). The PEB then recommended repeal of Article 6 (dealing with bulk sales) as no longer necessary in light of modern commercial realities; as an alternative for jurisdictions that chose not to repeal the article, the PEB drafted a revised version of Article 6. Article 8, dealing with investment securities, was revised in 1994, primarily to provide a full set of rules for the "indirect holding system" that had developed in the securities markets in order to facilitate trades. Article 5, which governs letters of credit, was revised in 1995 to coordinate better with developments in domestic and international letter of credit practice. The modernization of the law of secured credit codified in Article 9, a large undertaking with great commercial significance, was a major achievement.

The state legislatures quickly enacted these revised articles. In the case of Article 9, nationwide enactment was accomplished in just three years, a remarkable achievement. The next step in the modernization process was the promulgation in 2001 of a revised text of Article 1 which, in addition to definitions, contains a limited number of basic substantive rules generally applicable throughout the UCC. Most recently, a set of amendments to sections in Articles 2 and 2A and a revised version of Article 7 were promulgated in 2003. Much of this work, along with the 2002 amendments to Articles 3 and 4, remains on the agenda for enactment in the states. Throughout the modernization project, the PEB and the sponsoring organizations have been cognizant of the need to amend and revise the articles in a manner that comports with modern commercial practices, including the now-prevalent use of electronic methods of doing business. At the same time, the amendments and revisions have exhibited sensitivity to the unique issues that sometimes come into play when transactions involve consumers.

The Conference and the Institute are proud of the modernization of the UCC and grateful to the Reporters and the members of Drafting Committees who devoted long hours to this work, as well as to the many others who participated in the process, especially those who offered constructive criticism and who patiently worked to improve laws so crucial to the economy of the United States.

LANCE. LIEBMAN
Chair
Permanent Editorial Board for
the Uniform Commercial Code

April, 2007

TABLE OF CONTENTS

	Page
Preface	III
Student Guide: How to Use this Compilation of the UCC	V
Uniform Commercial Code	1
UCC Article 1 (2007)	21
UCC Article 2 (2007)	52
UCC Article 2A (2007)	170
UCC Article 3 (2007)	256
UCC Article 4 (2007)	360
UCC Article 4A (2007)	403
UCC Article 5 (2007)	462
UCC Article 6 (2007)	495
UCC Article 7 (2007)	520
UCC Article 8 (2007)	563
UCC Article 9 (2007)	661
Appendix A: Revised UCC Article 1 (2001)—Conforming Amendments to Other Articles	899
Appendix B: Revised UCC Article 7 (2003)—Conforming Amendments to Other Articles	910
Appendix C: 2000 Version of UCC Article 1	937
Appendix D: 2000 Version of UCC Article 2	957
Appendix E: 2000 Version of UCC Article 2A	1061
Appendix F: 2003 Amendments to UCC Articles 2 and 2A—In Strikeout/Underline Format	1137
Appendix G: [omitted]	
Appendix H: [omitted]	
Appendix I: Unrevised Article 7 (2002)	1198
Appendix J: 2005 Amendments to the UCC	1230
Appendix K: PEB Commentaries: #1, #10	1237
Other Uniform Acts	
Uniform Electronic Transactions Act	1247
International Materials	
U.N. Convention on Contracts for the International Sale of Goods (CISG)	1277
Federal Laws	
Electronic Signatures in Global and National Commerce Act (ESIGN)	1293
Magnuson-Moss Warranty Act	1302
Magnuson-Moss Warranty Act Regulations	1310

*

UNIFORM COMMERCIAL CODE*

The American Law Institute
and the
National Conference of
Commissioners on Uniform
State Laws

OFFICIAL TEXT

WITH COMMENTS

UNIFORM COMMERCIAL CODE
ARTICLE, PART, AND
SECTION ANALYSIS

ARTICLE 1. GENERAL PROVISIONS

PART 1. GENERAL PROVISIONS

Section
1–101. Short Titles.
1–102. Scope of Article.
1–103. Construction of [Uniform Commercial Code] to Promote Its Purposes and Policies; Applicability of Supplemental Principles of Law.
1–104. Construction Against Implied Repeal.
1–105. Severability.
1–106. Use of Singular and Plural; Gender.
1–107. Section Captions.
1–108. Relation to Electronic Signatures in Global and National Commerce Act.

PART 2. GENERAL DEFINITIONS AND PRINCIPLES OF INTERPRETATION

1–201. General Definitions.
1–202. Notice; Knowledge.
1–203. Lease Distinguished From Security Interest.
1–204. Value.
1–205. Reasonable Time; Seasonableness.
1–206. Presumptions.

PART 3. TERRITORIAL APPLICABILITY AND GENERAL RULES

1–301. Territorial Applicability; Parties' Power to Choose Applicable Law.
1–302. Variation by Agreement.
1–303. Course of Performance, Course of Dealing, and Usage of Trade.
1–304. Obligation of Good Faith.
1–305. Remedies to Be Liberally Administered.
1–306. Waiver or Renunciation of Claim or Right After Breach.
1–307. Prima Facie Evidence by Third–Party Documents.
1–308. Performance or Acceptance Under Reservation of Rights.
1–309. Option to Accelerate at Will.
1–310. Subordinated Obligations.

ARTICLE 2. SALES

PART 1. SHORT TITLE, GENERAL CONSTRUCTION AND SUBJECT MATTER

2–101. Short Title.
2–102. Scope; Certain Security and Other Transactions Excluded from this Article.
2–103. Definitions and Index of Definitions.
2–104. Definitions: "Merchant"; "Between Merchants"; "Financing Agency".
2–105. Definitions: Transferability; "Future" Goods; "Lot"; "Commercial Unit".
2–106. Definitions: "Contract"; "Agreement"; "Contract for Sale"; "Sale"; "Present Sale"; "Conforming" to Contract; "Termination"; "Cancellation".
2–107. Goods to Be Severed from Realty: Recording.
2–108. Transactions Subject to Other Law.

PART 2. FORM, FORMATION, TERMS AND READJUSTMENT OF CONTRACT; ELECTRONIC CONTRACTING

2–201. Formal Requirements; Statute of Frauds.
2–202. Final Expression in a Record: Parol or Extrinsic Evidence.
2–203. Seals Inoperative.
2–204. Formation in General.
2–205. Firm Offers.
2–206. Offer and Acceptance in Formation of Contract.
2–207. Terms of Contract; Effect of Confirmation.
2–208. Reserved.
2–209. Modification; Rescission and Waiver.
2–210. Delegation of Performance; Assignment of Rights.
2–211. Legal Recognition of Electronic Contracts, Records, and Signatures.
2–212. Attribution.
2–213. Electronic Communication.

PART 3. GENERAL OBLIGATION AND CONSTRUCTION OF CONTRACT

2–301. General Obligations of Parties.

ARTICLE, PART, AND SECTION ANALYSIS

Section

2–302. Unconscionable Contract or Term.

2–303. Allocation or Division of Risks.

2–304. Price Payable in Money, Goods, Realty, or Otherwise.

2–305. Open Price Term.

2–306. Output, Requirements and Exclusive Dealings.

2–307. Delivery in Single Lot or Several.

2–308. Absence of Specified Place for Delivery.

2–309. Absence of Specific Time Provisions; Notice of Termination.

2–310. Open Time for Payment or Running of Credit; Authority to Ship under Reservation.

2–311. Options and Cooperation Respecting Performance.

2–312. Warranty of Title and Against Infringement; Buyer's Obligation Against Infringement.

2–313. Express Warranties by Affirmation, Promise, Description, Sample; Remedial Promise.

2–313A. Obligation to Remote Purchaser Created by Record Packaged with or Accompanying Goods.

2–313B. Obligation to Remote Purchaser Created by Communication to the Public.

2–314. Implied Warranty: Merchantability; Usage of Trade.

2–315. Implied Warranty: Fitness for Particular Purpose.

2–316. Exclusion or Modification of Warranties.

2–317. Cumulation and Conflict of Warranties Express or Implied.

2–318. Third-party Beneficiaries of Warranties and Obligations.

2–319. Reserved.

2–320. Reserved.

2–321. Reserved.

2–322. Reserved.

2–323. Reserved.

2–324. Reserved.

2–325. Failure to Pay by Agreed Letter of Credit.

2–326. Sale on Approval and Sale or Return.

2–327. Special Incidents of Sale on Approval and Sale or Return.

2–328. Sale by Auction.

PART 4. TITLE, CREDITORS, AND GOOD–FAITH PURCHASERS

2–401. Passing of Title; Reservation for Security; Limited Application of this Section.

Section

2–402. Rights of Seller's Creditors Against Sold Goods.

2–403. Power to Transfer; Good Faith Purchase of Goods; "Entrusting".

PART 5. PERFORMANCE

2–501. Insurable Interest in Goods; Manner of Identification of Goods.

2–502. Buyer's Right to Goods on Seller's Insolvency, Repudiation, or Failure to Deliver.

2–503. Manner of Seller's Tender of Delivery.

2–504. Shipment by Seller.

2–505. Seller's Shipment under Reservation.

2–506. Rights of Financing Agency.

2–507. Effect of Seller's Tender; Delivery on Condition.

2–508. Cure by Seller of Improper Tender or Delivery; Replacement.

2–509. Risk of Loss in the Absence of Breach.

2–510. Effect of Breach on Risk of Loss.

2–511. Tender of Payment by Buyer; Payment by Check.

2–512. Payment by Buyer Before Inspection.

2–513. Buyer's Right to Inspection of Goods.

2–514. When Documents Deliverable on Acceptance; When on Payment.

2–515. Preserving Evidence of Goods in Dispute.

PART 6. BREACH, REPUDIATION, AND EXCUSE

2–601. Buyer's Rights on Improper Delivery.

2–602. Manner and Effect of Rejection.

2–603. Merchant Buyer's Duties as to Rejected Goods.

2–604. Buyer's Options as to Salvage of Rejected Goods.

2–605. Waiver of Buyer's Objections by Failure to Particularize.

2–606. What Constitutes Acceptance of Goods.

2–607. Effect of Acceptance; Notice of Breach; Burden of Establishing Breach after Acceptance; Notice of Claim or Litigation to Person Answerable Over.

2–608. Revocation of Acceptance in Whole or in Part.

2–609. Right to Adequate Assurance of Performance.

2–610. Anticipatory Repudiation.

2–611. Retraction of Anticipatory Repudiation.

2–612. "Installment Contract"; Breach.

2–613. Casualty to Identified Goods.

2–614. Substituted Performance.

UNIFORM COMMERCIAL CODE

Section

2–615. Excuse by Failure of Presupposed Conditions.

2–616. Procedure on Notice Claiming Excuse.

PART 7. REMEDIES

2–701. Remedies for Breach of Collateral Contracts Not Impaired.

2–702. Seller's Remedies on Discovery of Buyer's Insolvency.

2–703. Seller's Remedies in General.

2–704. Seller's Right to Identify Goods to the Contract Notwithstanding Breach or to Salvage Unfinished Goods.

2–705. Seller's Stoppage of Delivery in Transit or Otherwise.

2–706. Seller's Resale Including Contract for Resale.

2–707. "Person in the Position of a Seller".

2–708. Seller's Damages for Nonacceptance or Repudiation.

2–709. Action for the Price.

2–710. Seller's Incidental and Consequential Damages.

2–711. Buyer's Remedies in General; Buyer's Security Interest in Rejected Goods.

2–712. "Cover"; Buyer's Procurement of Substitute Goods.

2–713. Buyer's Damages for Nondelivery or Repudiation.

2–714. Buyer's Damages for Breach in Regard to Accepted Goods.

2–715. Buyer's Incidental and Consequential Damages.

2–716. Specific Performance; Buyer's Right to Replevin.

2–717. Deduction of Damages from the Price.

2–718. Liquidation or Limitation of Damages; Deposits.

2–719. Contractual Modification or Limitation of Remedy.

2–720. Effect of "Cancellation" or "Rescission" on Claims for Antecedent Breach.

2–721. Remedies for Fraud.

2–722. Who May Sue Third Parties for Injury to Goods.

2–723. Proof of Market: Time and Place.

2–724. Admissibility of Market Quotations.

2–725. Statute of Limitations in Contracts for Sale.

PART 8. TRANSITIONAL PROVISIONS

2–801. Effective Date.

2–802. Amendment of Existing Article 2.

Section

2–803. Application to Existing Relations.

2–804. Savings Clause.

ARTICLE 2A. LEASES
PART 1. GENERAL PROVISIONS

2A–101. Short Title.

2A–102. Scope.

2A–103. Definitions and Index of Definitions.

2A–104. Leases Subject to Other Law.

2A–105. Territorial Application of Article to Goods Covered by Certificate of Title.

2A–106. Limitation on Power of Parties to Consumer Lease to Choose Applicable Law and Judicial Forum.

2A–107. Waiver or Renunciation of Claim or Right after Default.

2A–108. Unconscionability.

2A–109. Option to Accelerate at Will.

PART 2. FORMATION AND CONSTRUCTION OF LEASE CONTRACT; ELECTRONIC CONTRACTING

2A–201. Statute of Frauds.

2A–202. Final Expression in a Record: Parol or Extrinsic Evidence.

2A–203. Seals Inoperative.

2A–204. Formation in General.

2A–205. Firm Offers.

2A–206. Offer and Acceptance in Formation of Lease Contract.

2A–207. Reserved.

2A–208. Modification, Rescission and Waiver.

2A–209. Lessee under Finance Lease as Beneficiary of Supply Contract.

2A–210. Express Warranties.

2A–211. Warranties Against Interference and Against Infringement; Lessee's Obligation Against Infringement.

2A–212. Implied Warranty of Merchantability.

2A–213. Implied Warranty of Fitness for Particular Purpose.

2A–214. Exclusion or Modification of Warranties.

2A–215. Cumulation and Conflict of Warranties Express or Implied.

2A–216. Third-party Beneficiaries of Express and Implied Warranties.

2A–217. Identification.

2A–218. Insurance and Proceeds.

2A–219. Risk of Loss.

2A–220. Effect of Default on Risk of Loss.

2A–221. Casualty to Identified Goods.

2A–222. Legal Recognition of Electronic Contracts, Records and Signatures.

4

Section

2A–223. Attribution.

2A–224. Electronic Communication.

PART 3. EFFECT OF LEASE CONTRACT

2A–301. Enforceability of Lease Contract.

2A–302. Title to and Possession of Goods.

2A–303. Alienability of Party's Interest under Lease Contract or of Lessor's Residual Interest in Goods; Delegation of Performance; Transfer of Rights.

2A–304. Subsequent Lease of Goods by Lessor.

2A–305. Sale or Sublease of Goods by Lessee.

2A–306. Priority of Certain Liens Arising by Operation of Law.

2A–307. Priority of Liens Arising by Attachment or Levy On, Security Interests In, and Other Claims to Goods.

2A–308. Special Rights of Creditors.

2A–309. Lessor's and Lessee's Rights When Goods Become Fixtures.

2A–310. Lessor's and Lessee's Rights When Goods Become Accessions.

2A–311. Priority Subject to Subordination.

PART 4. PERFORMANCE OF LEASE CONTRACT: REPUDIATED, SUBSTITUTED AND EXCUSED

2A–401. Insecurity: Adequate Assurance of Performance.

2A–402. Anticipatory Repudiation.

2A–403. Retraction of Anticipatory Repudiation.

2A–404. Substituted Performance.

2A–405. Excused Performance.

2A–406. Procedure on Excused Performance.

2A–407. Irrevocable Promises: Finance Leases.

PART 5. DEFAULT

A. IN GENERAL

2A–501. Default: Procedure.

2A–502. Notice after Default.

2A–503. Modification or Impairment of Rights and Remedies.

2A–504. Liquidation of Damages.

2A–505. Cancellation and Termination and Effect of Cancellation, Termination, Rescission, or Fraud on Rights and Remedies.

2A–506. Statute of Limitations.

2A–507. Proof of Market Rent: Time and Place.

2A–507A. Right to Specific Performance or Replevin or the Like.

B. DEFAULT BY LESSOR

2A–508. Lessee's Remedies.

Section

2A–509. Lessee's Rights on Improper Delivery; Manner and Effect of Rejection.

2A–510. Installment Lease Contracts: Rejection and Default.

2A–511. Merchant Lessee's Duties as to Rejected Goods.

2A–512. Lessee's Duties as to Rejected Goods.

2A–513. Cure by Lessor of Improper Tender or Delivery; Replacement.

2A–514. Waiver of Lessee's Objections.

2A–515. Acceptance of Goods.

2A–516. Effect of Acceptance of Goods; Notice of Default; Burden of Establishing Default after Acceptance; Notice of Claim or Litigation to Person Answerable Over.

2A–517. Revocation of Acceptance of Goods.

2A–518. Cover; Substitute Goods.

2A–519. Lessee's Damages for Non-delivery, Repudiation, Default, and Breach of Warranty in Regard to Accepted Goods.

2A–520. Lessee's Incidental and Consequential Damages.

2A–521. Reserved.

2A–522. Lessee's Right to Goods on Lessor's Insolvency.

C. DEFAULT BY LESSEE

2A–523. Lessor's Remedies.

2A–524. Lessor's Right to Identify Goods to Lease Contract.

2A–525. Lessor's Right to Possession of Goods.

2A–526. Lessor's Stoppage of Delivery in Transit or Otherwise.

2A–527. Lessor's Rights to Dispose of Goods.

2A–528. Lessor's Damages for Non-acceptance, Failure to Pay, Repudiation, or Other Default.

2A–529. Lessor's Action for the Rent.

2A–530. Lessor's Incidental and Consequential Damages.

2A–531. Standing to Sue Third Parties for Injury to Goods.

2A–532. Lessor's Rights to Residual Interest.

PART 6. TRANSITIONAL PROVISIONS

2A–601. Effective Date.

2A–602. Amendment of Existing Article 2A.

2A–603. Applicability.

2A–604. Savings Clause.

CONFORMING AMENDMENTS TO ARTICLE 1

ARTICLE 3. NEGOTIABLE INSTRUMENTS

PART 1. GENERAL PROVISIONS AND DEFINITIONS

3–101. Short Title.
3–102. Subject Matter.
3–103. Definitions.
3–104. Negotiable Instrument.
3–105. Issue of Instrument.
3–106. Unconditional Promise or Order.
3–107. Instrument Payable in Foreign Money.
3–108. Payable on Demand or at Definite Time.
3–109. Payable to Bearer or to Order.
3–110. Identification of Person to Whom Instrument Is Payable.
3–111. Place of Payment.
3–112. Interest.
3–113. Date of Instrument.
3–114. Contradictory Terms of Instrument.
3–115. Incomplete Instrument.
3–116. Joint and Several Liability; Contribution.
3–117. Other Agreements Affecting Instrument.
3–118. Statute of Limitations.
3–119. Notice of Right to Defend Action.

PART 2. NEGOTIATION, TRANSFER, AND INDORSEMENT

3–201. Negotiation.
3–202. Negotiation Subject to Rescission.
3–203. Transfer of Instrument; Rights Acquired by Transfer.
3–204. Indorsement.
3–205. Special Indorsement; Blank Indorsement; Anomalous Indorsement.
3–206. Restrictive Indorsement.
3–207. Reacquisition.

PART 3. ENFORCEMENT OF INSTRUMENTS

3–301. Person Entitled to Enforce Instrument.
3–302. Holder in Due Course.
3–303. Value and Consideration.
3–304. Overdue Instrument.
3–305. Defenses and Claims in Recoupment.
3–306. Claims to an Instrument.
3–307. Notice of Breach of Fiduciary Duty.
3–308. Proof of Signatures and Status as Holder in Due Course.
3–309. Enforcement of Lost, Destroyed, or Stolen Instrument.
3–310. Effect of Instrument on Obligation for Which Taken.

Section

3–311. Accord and Satisfaction by Use of Instrument.
3–312. Lost, Destroyed, or Stolen Cashier's Check, Teller's Check, or Certified Check.

PART 4. LIABILITY OF PARTIES

3–401. Signature.
3–402. Signature by Representative.
3–403. Unauthorized Signature.
3–404. Impostors; Fictitious Payees.
3–405. Employer's Responsibility for Fraudulent Indorsement by Employee.
3–406. Negligence Contributing to Forged Signature or Alteration of Instrument.
3–407. Alteration.
3–408. Drawee Not Liable on Unaccepted Draft.
3–409. Acceptance of Draft; Certified Check.
3–410. Acceptance Varying Draft.
3–411. Refusal to Pay Cashier's Checks, Teller's Checks, and Certified Checks.
3–412. Obligation of Issuer of Note or Cashier's Check.
3–413. Obligation of Acceptor.
3–414. Obligation of Drawer.
3–415. Obligation of Indorser.
3–416. Transfer Warranties.
3–417. Presentment Warranties.
3–418. Payment or Acceptance by Mistake.
3–419. Instruments Signed for Accommodation.
3–420. Conversion of Instrument.

PART 5. DISHONOR

3–501. Presentment.
3–502. Dishonor.
3–503. Notice of Dishonor.
3–504. Excused Presentment and Notice of Dishonor.
3–505. Evidence of Dishonor.

PART 6. DISCHARGE AND PAYMENT

3–601. Discharge and Effect of Discharge.
3–602. Payment.
3–603. Tender of Payment.
3–604. Discharge by Cancellation or Renunciation.
3–605. Discharge of Secondary Obligors.

ARTICLE 4. BANK DEPOSITS AND COLLECTIONS

PART 1. GENERAL PROVISIONS AND DEFINITIONS

4–101. Short Title.
4–102. Applicability.

Section

4–103. Variation by Agreement; Measure of Damages; Action Constituting Ordinary Care.

4–104. Definitions and Index of Definitions.

4–105. Definitions of Types of Banks.

4–106. Payable Through or Payable at Bank; Collecting Bank.

4–107. Separate Office of Bank.

4–108. Time of Receipt of Items.

4–109. Delays.

4–110. Electronic Presentment.

4–111. Statute of Limitations.

PART 2. COLLECTION OF ITEMS: DEPOSITARY AND COLLECTING BANKS

4–201. Status of Collecting Bank as Agent and Provisional Status of Credits; Applicability of Article; Item Indorsed "Pay Any Bank".

4–202. Responsibility for Collection or Return; When Action Timely.

4–203. Effect of Instructions.

4–204. Methods of Sending and Presenting; Sending Directly to Payor Bank.

4–205. Depositary Bank Holder of Unindorsed Item.

4–206. Transfer Between Banks.

4–207. Transfer Warranties.

4–208. Presentment Warranties.

4–209. Encoding and Retention Warranties.

4–210. Security Interest of Collecting Bank in Items, Accompanying Documents and Proceeds.

4–211. When Bank Gives Value for Purposes of Holder in Due Course.

4–212. Presentment by Notice of Item Not Payable by, Through, or at Bank; Liability of Drawer or Indorser.

4–213. Medium and Time of Settlement by Bank.

4–214. Right of Charge-Back or Refund; Liability of Collecting Bank; Return of Item.

4–215. Final Payment of Item by Payor Bank; When Provisional Debits and Credits Become Final; When Certain Credits Become Available for Withdrawal.

4–216. Insolvency and Preference.

PART 3. COLLECTION OF ITEMS: PAYOR BANKS

4–301. Deferred Posting; Recovery of Payment by Return of Items; Time of Dishonor; Return of Items by Payor Bank.

Section

4–302. Payor Bank's Responsibility for Late Return of Item.

4–303. When Items Subject to Notice, Stop-Payment Order, Legal Process, or Setoff; Order in Which Items May Be Charged or Certified.

PART 4. RELATIONSHIP BETWEEN PAYOR BANK AND ITS CUSTOMER

4–401. When Bank May Charge Customer's Account.

4–402. Bank's Liability to Customer for Wrongful Dishonor; Time of Determining Insufficiency of Account.

4–403. Customer's Right to Stop Payment; Burden of Proof of Loss.

4–404. Bank Not Obliged to Pay Check More Than Six Months Old.

4–405. Death or Incompetence of Customer.

4–406. Customer's Duty to Discover and Report Unauthorized Signature or Alteration.

4–407. Payor Bank's Right to Subrogation on Improper Payment.

PART 5. COLLECTION OF DOCUMENTARY DRAFTS

4–501. Handling of Documentary Drafts; Duty to Send for Presentment and to Notify Customer of Dishonor.

4–502. Presentment of "On Arrival" Drafts.

4–503. Responsibility of Presenting Bank for Documents and Goods; Report of Reasons for Dishonor; Referee in Case of Need.

4–504. Privilege of Presenting Bank to Deal With Goods; Security Interest for Expenses.

ARTICLE 4A. FUNDS TRANSFERS

PART 1. SUBJECT MATTER AND DEFINITIONS

4A–101. Short Title.

4A–102. Subject Matter.

4A–103. Payment Order—Definitions.

4A–104. Funds Transfer—Definitions.

4A–105. Other Definitions.

4A–106. Time Payment Order Is Received.

4A–107. Federal Reserve Regulations and Operating Circulars.

4A–108. Exclusion of Consumer Transactions Governed by Federal Law.

PART 2. ISSUE AND ACCEPTANCE OF PAYMENT ORDER

4A–201. Security Procedure.

7

Section

4A–202. Authorized and Verified Payment Orders.
4A–203. Unenforceability of Certain Verified Payment Orders.
4A–204. Refund of Payment and Duty of Customer to Report With Respect to Unauthorized Payment Order.
4A–205. Erroneous Payment Orders.
4A–206. Transmission of Payment Order Through Funds—Transfer or Other Communication System.
4A–207. Misdescription of Beneficiary.
4A–208. Misdescription of Intermediary Bank or Beneficiary's Bank.
4A–209. Acceptance of Payment Order.
4A–210. Rejection of Payment Order.
4A–211. Cancellation and Amendment of Payment Order.
4A–212. Liability and Duty of Receiving Bank Regarding Unaccepted Payment Order.

PART 3. EXECUTION OF SENDER'S PAYMENT ORDER BY RECEIVING BANK

4A–301. Execution and Execution Date.
4A–302. Obligations of Receiving Bank in Execution of Payment Order.
4A–303. Erroneous Execution of Payment Order.
4A–304. Duty of Sender to Report Erroneously Executed Payment Order.
4A–305. Liability for Late or Improper Execution or Failure to Execute Payment Order.

PART 4. PAYMENT

4A–401. Payment Date.
4A–402. Obligation of Sender to Pay Receiving Bank.
4A–403. Payment by Sender to Receiving Bank.
4A–404. Obligation of Beneficiary's Bank to Pay and Give Notice to Beneficiary.
4A–405. Payment by Beneficiary's Bank to Beneficiary.
4A–406. Payment by Originator to Beneficiary; Discharge of Underlying Obligation.

PART 5. MISCELLANEOUS PROVISIONS

4A–501. Variation by Agreement and Effect of Funds-Transfer System Rule.
4A–502. Creditor Process Served on Receiving Bank; Set-off by Beneficiary's Bank.
4A–503. Injunction or Restraining Order With Respect to Funds Transfer.

Section

4A–504. Order in Which Items and Payment Orders May Be Charged to Account; Order of Withdrawals From Account.
4A–505. Preclusion of Objection to Debit of Customer's Account.
4A–506. Rate of Interest.
4A–507. Choice of Law.

ARTICLE 5. LETTERS OF CREDIT

5–101. Short Title.
5–102. Definitions.
5–103. Scope.
5–104. Formal Requirements.
5–105. Consideration.
5–106. Issuance, Amendment, Cancellation, and Duration.
5–107. Confirmer, Nominated Person, and Adviser.
5–108. Issuer's Rights and Obligations.
5–109. Fraud and Forgery.
5–110. Warranties.
5–111. Remedies.
5–112. Transfer of Letter of Credit.
5–113. Transfer by Operation of Law.
5–114. Assignment of Proceeds.
5–115. Statute of Limitations.
5–116. Choice of Law and Forum.
5–117. Subrogation of Issuer, Applicant, and Nominated Person.
5–118. Security Interest of Issuer or Nominated Person.

TRANSITION PROVISIONS

[   ]. Effective Date.
[   ]. Repeal.
[   ]. Applicability.
[   ]. Savings Clause.

REPEALER OF ARTICLE 6—BULK TRANSFERS and
[REVISED] ARTICLE 6—BULK SALES
(States To Select One Alternative)

ALTERNATIVE A

1. Repeal.
2. Amendment.
3. Amendment.
4. Savings Clause.

[END OF ALTERNATIVE A]

ALTERNATIVE B

6–101. Short Title.
6–102. Definitions and Index of Definitions.
6–103. Applicability of Article.

Section

6–104. Obligations of Buyer.

6–105. Notice to Claimants.

6–106. Schedule of Distribution.

6–107. Liability for Noncompliance.

6–108. Bulk Sales by Auction; Bulk Sales Conducted by Liquidator.

6–109. What Constitutes Filing; Duties of Filing Officer; Information From Filing Officer.

6–110. Limitation of Actions.

[END OF ALTERNATIVE B]

ARTICLE 7. DOCUMENTS OF TITLE

PART 1. GENERAL

7–101. Short Title.

7–102. Definitions and Index of Definitions.

7–103. Relation of Article to Treaty or Statute.

7–104. Negotiable and Nonnegotiable Document of Title.

7–105. Reissuance in Alternative Medium.

7–106. Control of Electronic Document of Title.

PART 2. WAREHOUSE RECEIPTS:
SPECIAL PROVISIONS

7–201. Person That May Issue a Warehouse Receipt; Storage Under Bond.

7–202. Form of Warehouse Receipt; Effect of Omission.

7–203. Liability for Nonreceipt or Misdescription.

7–204. Duty of Care; Contractual Limitation of Warehouse's Liability.

7–205. Title Under Warehouse Receipt Defeated in Certain Cases.

7–206. Termination of Storage At Warehouse's Option.

7–207. Goods Must Be Kept Separate; Fungible Goods.

7–208. Altered Warehouse Receipts.

7–209. Lien of Warehouse.

7–210. Enforcement of Warehouse's Lien.

PART 3. BILLS OF LADING:
SPECIAL PROVISIONS

7–301. Liability for Nonreceipt or Misdescription; "Said to Contain"; "Shipper's Weight, Load, and Count"; Improper Handling.

7–302. Through Bills of Lading and Similar Documents of Title.

7–303. Diversion; Reconsignment; Change of Instructions.

7–304. Tangible Bills of Lading in a Set.

7–305. Destination Bills.

Section

7–306. Altered Bills of Lading.

7–307. Lien of Carrier.

7–308. Enforcement of Carrier's Lien.

7–309. Duty of Care; Contractual Limitation of Carrier's Liability.

PART 4. WAREHOUSE RECEIPTS AND BILLS
OF LADING: GENERAL OBLIGATIONS

7–401. Irregularities in Issue of Receipt or Bill or Conduct of Issuer.

7–402. Duplicate Document of Title; Overissue.

7–403. Obligation of Bailee to Deliver; Excuse.

7–404. No Liability for Good–Faith Delivery Pursuant to Document of Title 59.

PART 5. WAREHOUSE RECEIPTS AND BILLS OF
LADING: NEGOTIATION AND TRANSFER

7–501. Form of Negotiation and Requirements of Due Negotiation.

7–502. Rights Acquired By Due Negotiation.

7–503. Document of Title to Goods Defeated in Certain Cases.

7–504. Rights Acquired in Absence of Due Negotiation; Effect of Diversion; Stoppage of Delivery.

7–505. Indorser Not Guarantor for Other Parties.

7–506. Delivery Without Indorsement: Right to Compel Indorsement.

7–507. Warranties on Negotiation or Delivery of Document of Title.

7–508. Warranties of Collecting Bank as to Documents of Title.

7–509. Adequate Compliance with Commercial Contract.

PART 6. WAREHOUSE RECEIPTS AND BILLS OF
LADING: MISCELLANEOUS PROVISIONS

7–601. Lost, Stolen, or Destroyed Documents of Title.

7–602. Judicial Process Against Goods Covered by Negotiable Document of Title.

7–603. Conflicting Claims; Interpleader.

PART 7. MISCELLANEOUS PROVISIONS

7–701. Effective Date.

7–702. Repeals.

7–703. Applicability.

7–704. Savings Clause.

ARTICLE 8. INVESTMENT SECURITIES

PART 1. SHORT TITLE AND
GENERAL MATTERS

8–101. Short Title.

UNIFORM COMMERCIAL CODE

Section

8–102. Definitions.

8–103. Rules for Determining Whether Certain Obligations and Interests are Securities or Financial Assets.

8–104. Acquisition of Security or Financial Asset or Interest Therein.

8–105. Notice of Adverse Claim.

8–106. Control.

8–107. Whether Indorsement, Instruction, or Entitlement Order is Effective.

8–108. Warranties in Direct Holding.

8–109. Warranties in Indirect Holding.

8–110. Applicability; Choice of Law.

8–111. Clearing Corporation Rules.

8–112. Creditor's Legal Process.

8–113. Statute of Frauds Inapplicable.

8–114. Evidentiary Rules Concerning Certificated Securities.

8–115. Securities Intermediary and Others Not Liable to Adverse Claimant.

8–116. Securities Intermediary as Purchaser for Value.

PART 2. ISSUE AND ISSUER

8–201. Issuer.

8–202. Issuer's Responsibility and Defenses; Notice of Defect or Defense.

8–203. Staleness as Notice of Defect or Defense.

8–204. Effect of Issuer's Restriction on Transfer.

8–205. Effect of Unauthorized Signature on Security Certificate.

8–206. Completion or Alteration of Security Certificate.

8–207. Rights and Duties of Issuer With Respect to Registered Owners.

8–208. Effect of Signature of Authenticating Trustee, Registrar, or Transfer Agent.

8–209. Issuer's Lien.

8–210. Overissue.

PART 3. TRANSFER OF CERTIFICATED AND UNCERTIFICATED SECURITIES

8–301. Delivery.

8–302. Rights of Purchaser.

8–303. Protected Purchaser.

8–304. Indorsement.

8–305. Instruction.

8–306. Effect of Guaranteeing Signature, Indorsement, or Instruction.

8–307. Purchaser's Right to Requisites for Registration of Transfer.

PART 4. REGISTRATION

8–401. Duty of Issuer to Register Transfer.

8–402. Assurance That Indorsement or Instruction is Effective.

8–403. Demand That Issuer Not Register Transfer.

8–404. Wrongful Registration.

8–405. Replacement of Lost, Destroyed, or Wrongfully Taken Security Certificate.

8–406. Obligation to Notify Issuer of Lost, Destroyed, or Wrongfully Taken Security Certificate.

8–407. Authenticating Trustee, Transfer Agent, and Registrar.

PART 5. SECURITY ENTITLEMENTS

8–501. Securities Account; Acquisition of Security Entitlement From Securities Intermediary.

8–502. Assertion of Adverse Claim Against Entitlement Holder.

8–503. Property Interest of Entitlement Holder in Financial Asset Held by Securities Intermediary.

8–504. Duty of Securities Intermediary to Maintain Financial Asset.

8–505. Duty of Securities Intermediary with Respect to Payments and Distributions.

8–506. Duty of Securities Intermediary to Exercise Rights as Directed by Entitlement Holder.

8–507. Duty of Securities Intermediary to Comply with Entitlement Order.

8–508. Duty of Securities Intermediary to Change Entitlement Holder's Position to Other Form of Security Holding.

8–509. Specification of Duties of Securities Intermediary by Other Statute or Regulation; Manner of Performance of Duties of Securities Intermediary and Exercise of Rights of Entitlement Holder.

8–510. Rights of Purchaser of Security Entitlement From Entitlement Holder.

8–511. Priority Among Security Interests and Entitlement Holders.

PART 6. TRANSITION PROVISIONS FOR REVISED ARTICLE 8

8–601. Effective Date.

8–602. Repeals.

8–603. Savings Clause.

ARTICLE, PART, AND SECTION ANALYSIS

ARTICLE 9. SECURED TRANSACTIONS

PART 1. GENERAL PROVISIONS

[SUBPART 1. SHORT TITLE, DEFINITIONS, AND GENERAL CONCEPTS]

9–101. Short Title.
9–102. Definitions and Index of Definitions.
9–103. Purchase–Money Security Interest; Application of Payments; Burden of Establishing.
9–104. Control of Deposit Account.
9–105. Control of Electronic Chattel Paper.
9–106. Control of Investment Property.
9–107. Control of Letter-of-Credit Right.
9–108. Sufficiency of Description.

[SUBPART 2. APPLICABILITY OF ARTICLE]

9–109. Scope.
9–110. Security Interests Arising Under Article 2 or 2A.

PART 2. EFFECTIVENESS OF SECURITY AGREEMENT; ATTACHMENT OF SECURITY INTEREST; RIGHTS OF PARTIES TO SECURITY AGREEMENT

[SUBPART 1. EFFECTIVENESS AND ATTACHMENT]

9–201. General Effectiveness of Security Agreement.
9–202. Title to Collateral Immaterial.
9–203. Attachment and Enforceability of Security Interest; Proceeds; Supporting Obligations; Formal Requisites.
9–204. After–Acquired Property; Future Advances.
9–205. Use or Disposition of Collateral Permissible.
9–206. Security Interest Arising in Purchase or Delivery of Financial Asset.

[SUBPART 2. RIGHTS AND DUTIES]

9–207. Rights and Duties of Secured Party Having Possession or Control of Collateral.
9–208. Additional Duties of Secured Party Having Control of Collateral.
9–209. Duties of Secured Party if Account Debtor Has Been Notified of Assignment.
9–210. Request for Accounting; Request Regarding List of Collateral or Statement of Account.

PART 3. PERFECTION AND PRIORITY

[SUBPART 1. LAW GOVERNING PERFECTION AND PRIORITY]

9–301. Law Governing Perfection and Priority of Security Interests.

Section
9–302. Law Governing Perfection and Priority of Agricultural Liens.
9–303. Law Governing Perfection and Priority of Security Interests in Goods Covered by a Certificate of Title.
9–304. Law Governing Perfection and Priority of Security Interests in Deposit Accounts.
9–305. Law Governing Perfection and Priority of Security Interests in Investment Property.
9–306. Law Governing Perfection and Priority of Security Interests in Letter-of-Credit Rights.
9–307. Location of Debtor.

[SUBPART 2. PERFECTION]

9–308. When Security Interest or Agricultural Lien Is Perfected; Continuity of Perfection.
9–309. Security Interest Perfected Upon Attachment.
9–310. When Filing Required to Perfect Security Interest or Agricultural Lien; Security Interests and Agricultural Liens to Which Filing Provisions Do Not Apply.
9–311. Perfection of Security Interests in Property Subject to Certain Statutes, Regulations, and Treaties.
9–312. Perfection of Security Interests in Chattel Paper, Deposit Accounts, Documents, Goods Covered by Documents, Instruments, Investment Property, Letter-of-Credit Rights, and Money; Perfection by Permissive Filing; Temporary Perfection Without Filing or Transfer of Possession.
9–313. When Possession by or Delivery to Secured Party Perfects Security Interest Without Filing.
9–314. Perfection by Control.
9–315. Secured Party's Rights on Disposition of Collateral and in Proceeds.
9–316. Continued Perfection of Security Interest Following Change in Governing Law

[SUBPART 3. PRIORITY]

9–317. Interests That Take Priority Over or Take Free of Security Interest or Agricultural Lien.
9–318. No Interest Retained in Right to Payment That Is Sold; Rights and Title of Seller

Section

of Account or Chattel Paper With Respect to Creditors and Purchasers.

9–319. Rights and Title of Consignee With Respect to Creditors and Purchasers.

9–320. Buyer of Goods.

9–321. Licensee of General Intangible and Lessee of Goods in Ordinary Course of Business.

9–322. Priorities Among Conflicting Security Interests in and Agricultural Liens on Same Collateral.

9–323. Future Advances.

9–324. Priority of Purchase–Money Security Interests.

9–325. Priority of Security Interests in Transferred Collateral.

9–326. Priority of Security Interests Created by New Debtor.

9–327. Priority of Security Interests in Deposit Account.

9–328. Priority of Security Interests in Investment Property.

9–329. Priority of Security Interests in Letter-of-Credit Right.

9–330. Priority of Purchaser of Chattel Paper or Instrument.

9–331. Priority of Rights of Purchasers of Instruments, Documents, and Securities Under Other Articles; Priority of Interests in Financial Assets and Security Entitlements Under Article 8.

9–332. Transfer of Money; Transfer of Funds From Deposit Account.

9–333. Priority of Certain Liens Arising by Operation of Law.

9–334. Priority of Security Interests in Fixtures and Crops.

9–335. Accessions.

9–336. Commingled Goods.

9–337. Priority of Security Interests in Goods Covered by Certificate of Title.

9–338. Priority of Security Interest or Agricultural Lien Perfected by Filed Financing Statement Providing Certain Incorrect Information.

9–339. Priority Subject to Subordination.

[SUBPART 4. RIGHTS OF BANK]

9–340. Effectiveness of Right of Recoupment or Set–Off Against Deposit Account.

9–341. Bank's Rights and Duties With Respect to Deposit Account.

Section

9–342. Bank's Right to Refuse to Enter Into or Disclose Existence of Control Agreement.

PART 4. RIGHTS OF THIRD PARTIES

9–401. Alienability of Debtor's Rights.

9–402. Secured Party Not Obligated on Contract of Debtor or in Tort.

9–403. Agreement Not to Assert Defenses Against Assignee.

9–404. Rights Acquired by Assignee; Claims and Defenses Against Assignee.

9–405. Modification of Assigned Contract.

9–406. Discharge of Account Debtor; Notification of Assignment; Identification and Proof of Assignment; Restrictions on Assignment of Accounts, Chattel Paper, Payment Intangibles, and Promissory Notes Ineffective.

9–407. Restrictions on Creation or Enforcement of Security Interest in Leasehold Interest or in Lessor's Residual Interest.

9–408. Restrictions on Assignment of Promissory Notes, Health–Care–Insurance Receivables, and Certain General Intangibles Ineffective.

9–409. Restrictions on Assignment of Letter-of-Credit Rights Ineffective.

PART 5. FILING

[SUBPART 1. FILING OFFICE; CONTENTS AND EFFECTIVENESS OF FINANCING STATEMENT]

9–501. Filing Office.

9–502. Contents of Financing Statement; Record of Mortgage as Financing Statement; Time of Filing Financing Statement.

9–503. Name of Debtor and Secured Party.

9–504. Indication of Collateral.

9–505. Filing and Compliance With Other Statutes and Treaties for Consignments, Leases, Other Bailments, and Other Transactions.

9–506. Effect of Errors or Omissions.

9–507. Effect of Certain Events on Effectiveness of Financing Statement.

9–508. Effectiveness of Financing Statement if New Debtor Becomes Bound by Security Agreement.

9–509. Persons Entitled to File a Record.

9–510. Effectiveness of Filed Record.

9–511. Secured Party of Record.

9–512. Amendment of Financing Statement.

Section

9–513. Termination Statement.

9–514. Assignment of Powers of Secured Party of Record.

9–515. Duration and Effectiveness of Financing Statement; Effect of Lapsed Financing Statement.

9–516. What Constitutes Filing; Effectiveness of Filing.

9–517. Effect of Indexing Errors.

9–518. Claim Concerning Inaccurate or Wrongfully Filed Record.

[SUBPART 2. DUTIES AND OPERATION OF FILING OFFICE]

9–519. Numbering, Maintaining, and Indexing Records; Communicating Information Provided in Records.

9–520. Acceptance and Refusal to Accept Record.

9–521. Uniform Form of Written Financing Statement and Amendment.

9–522. Maintenance and Destruction of Records.

9–523. Information From Filing Office; Sale or License of Records.

9–524. Delay by Filing Office.

9–525. Fees.

9–526. Filing–Office Rules.

9–527. Duty to Report.

PART 6. DEFAULT

[SUBPART 1. DEFAULT AND ENFORCEMENT OF SECURITY INTEREST]

9–601. Rights After Default; Judicial Enforcement; Consignor or Buyer of Accounts, Chattel Paper, Payment Intangibles, or Promissory Notes.

9–602. Waiver and Variance of Rights and Duties.

9–603. Agreement on Standards Concerning Rights and Duties.

9–604. Procedure if Security Agreement Covers Real Property or Fixtures.

9–605. Unknown Debtor or Secondary Obligor.

9–606. Time of Default for Agricultural Lien.

9–607. Collection and Enforcement by Secured Party.

9–608. Application of Proceeds of Collection or Enforcement; Liability for Deficiency and Right to Surplus.

9–609. Secured Party's Right to Take Possession After Default.

9–610. Disposition of Collateral After Default.

9–611. Notification Before Disposition of Collateral.

Section

9–612. Timeliness of Notification Before Disposition of Collateral.

9–613. Contents and Form of Notification Before Disposition of Collateral: General.

9–614. Contents and Form of Notification Before Disposition of Collateral: Consumer–Goods Transaction.

9–615. Application of Proceeds of Disposition; Liability for Deficiency and Right to Surplus.

9–616. Explanation of Calculation of Surplus or Deficiency.

9–617. Rights of Transferee of Collateral.

9–618. Rights and Duties of Certain Secondary Obligors.

9–619. Transfer of Record or Legal Title.

9–620. Acceptance of Collateral in Full or Partial Satisfaction of Obligation; Compulsory Disposition of Collateral.

9–621. Notification of Proposal to Accept Collateral.

9–622. Effect of Acceptance of Collateral.

9–623. Right to Redeem Collateral.

9–624. Waiver.

[SUBPART 2. NONCOMPLIANCE WITH ARTICLE]

9–625. Remedies for Secured Party's Failure to Comply With Article.

9–626. Action in Which Deficiency or Surplus Is in Issue.

9–627. Determination of Whether Conduct Was Commercially Reasonable.

9–628. Nonliability and Limitation on Liability of Secured Party; Liability of Secondary Obligor.

PART 7. TRANSITION

9–701. Effective Date.

9–702. Savings Clause.

9–703. Security Interest Perfected Before Effective Date.

9–704. Security Interest Unperfected Before Effective Date.

9–705. Effectiveness of Action Taken Before Effective Date.

9–706. When Initial Financing Statement Suffices to Continue Effectiveness of Financing Statement.

9–707. Amendment of Pre-Effective-Date Financing Statement.

9–708. Persons Entitled to File Initial Financing Statement or Continuation Statement.

9–709. Priority.

UNIFORM
COMMERCIAL CODE

TITLE

AN ACT

To be known as the Uniform Commercial Code, Relating to Certain Commercial Transactions in or regarding Personal Property and Contracts and other Documents concerning them, including Sales, Commercial Paper, Bank Deposits and Collections, Letters of Credit, Bulk Transfers, Warehouse Receipts, Bills of Lading, other Documents of Title, Investment Securities, and Secured Transactions, including certain Sales of Accounts, Chattel Paper, and Contract Rights; Providing for Public Notice to Third Parties in Certain Circumstances; Regulating Procedure, Evidence and Damages in Certain Court Actions Involving such Transactions, Contracts or Documents; to Make Uniform the Law with Respect Thereto; and Repealing Inconsistent Legislation.

GENERAL COMMENT
of
NATIONAL CONFERENCE OF COMMISSIONERS ON UNIFORM STATE LAWS AND THE AMERICAN LAW INSTITUTE

This Comment covers the development of the Code prior to 1962. Its subsequent history leading to the 1962, 1966, 1972, 1977 and 1987 Official Text and Comment changes is contained in Reports and Forewords of the Permanent Editorial Board for the Uniform Commercial Code, which are set out, supra, this pamphlet.

Uniformity throughout American jurisdictions is one of the main objectives of this Code; and that objective cannot be obtained without substantial uniformity of construction. To aid in uniform construction of this Comment and those which follow the text of each section set forth the purpose of various provisions of this Act to promote uniformity, to aid in viewing the Act as an integrated whole, and to safeguard against misconstruction.

This Act is a revision of the original Uniform Commercial Code promulgated in 1951 and enacted in Pennsylvania in 1953, effective July 1, 1954; and these Comments are a revision of the original comments, which were before the Pennsylvania legislature at the time of its adoption of the Code. Changes from the text enacted in Pennsylvania in 1953 are clearly legitimate legislative history, but without explanation such changes may be misleading, since frequently matters have been omitted as being implicit without statement and language has been changed or added solely for clarity. Accordingly, the changes from the original text were published, under the title "1956 Recommendations of the Editorial Board for the Uniform Commercial Code," early in 1957, with reasons, and revised Comments were then prepared to restate the statutory purpose in the light of the revision of text.

The subsequent history leading to the 1962 Official Text with Comments is set out in detail in Report No. 1 of the Permanent Editorial Board for the Uniform Commercial Code. *** [See Report, supra, this pamphlet.]

Hitherto most commercial transactions have been regulated by a number of Uniform Laws prepared and promulgated by the National Conference of Commissioners on Uniform State Laws. These acts, with the dates of their promulgation by the Conference, are:

Uniform Negotiable Instruments Law.. 1896
Uniform Warehouse Receipts Act 1906
Uniform Sales Act..................... 1906
Uniform Bills of Lading Act 1909
Uniform Stock Transfer Act.......... 1909
Uniform Conditional Sales Act 1918
Uniform Trust Receipts Act 1933

Two of these acts were adopted in every American State and the remaining acts have had wide acceptance. Each of them has become a segment of the statutory law relating to commercial transactions. It has been recognized for some years that these acts needed substantial revision to keep them in step with modern commercial practices and to integrate each of them with the others.

The concept of the present Act is that "commercial transactions" is a single subject of the law, notwithstanding its many facets.

16

A single transaction may very well involve a contract for sale, followed by a sale, the giving of a check or draft for a part of the purchase price, and the acceptance of some form of security for the balance.

The check or draft may be negotiated and will ultimately pass through one or more banks for collection.

If the goods are shipped or stored the subject matter of the sale may be covered by a bill of lading or warehouse receipt or both.

Or it may be that the entire transaction was made pursuant to a letter of credit either domestic or foreign.

Obviously, every phase of commerce involved is but a part of one transaction, namely, the sale of and payment for goods.

If, instead of goods in the ordinary sense, the transaction involved stocks or bonds, some of the phases of the transaction would obviously be different. Others would be the same. In addition, there are certain additional formalities incident to the transfer of stocks and bonds from one owner to another.

This Act purports to deal with all the phases which may ordinarily arise in the handling of a commercial transaction, from start to finish.

Because of the close relationship of each phase of a complete transaction to every other phase, it is believed that each Article of this Act is cognate to the single broad subject "Commercial Transactions", and that this Act is valid under any constitutional provision requiring an act to deal with only one subject. See, for excellent discussions of the meaning of "single subject": House v. Creveling, 147 Tenn. 589, 250 S.W. 357 (1923) and Commonwealth v. Snyder, 279 Pa. 234, 123 A. 792 (1924).

The preparation of the Act (which Section 1–101 denominates the "Uniform Commercial Code") was begun as a joint project of The American Law Institute and the National Conference of Commissioners on Uniform State Laws in 1942. Various drafts were considered by joint committees of both bodies and debated by the full membership of each organization at annual meetings.

In the main, the project was made possible, financially, through a large grant by The Maurice and Laura Falk Foundation of Pittsburgh, Pennsylvania, supplemented by contributions from the Beaumont Foundation of Cleveland, Ohio, and from 98 business and financial concerns and law firms. Additional funds for final revisions and study were received from the Falk Foundation and others.

The original drafting and editorial work which led to the 1952 edition of the Code was in charge of an Editorial Board of which United States Circuit Judge Herbert F. Goodrich of Philadelphia was Chairman. The other members at various times were Professor Karl N. Llewellyn of the University of Chicago Law School, Walter D. Malcolm, Esquire, of Boston, John C. Pryor, Esquire, of Burlington, Iowa, Wm. A. Schnader, Esquire, of Philadelphia, and Harrison Tweed, Esquire, of New York City. In the final stages of work on the Code, certain questions of policy were submitted for consideration to an Enlarged Editorial Board consisting at various times of the foregoing members and Howard L. Barkdull, Esquire, of Cleveland, Joe C. Barrett, Esquire, of Jonesboro, Arkansas, Robert K. Bell, Esquire, of Ocean City, N.J., Robert P. Goldman, Esquire, of Cincinnati, Dean Albert J. Harno of the University of Illinois Law School, Ben W. Heineman, Esquire, of Chicago, Carlos Israels, Esquire, of New York City, Albert E. Jenner, Esquire, of Chicago, Arthur Littleton, Esquire, of Philadelphia, Willard B. Luther, Esquire, of Boston, Kurt F. Pantzer, Esquire, of Indianapolis, Indiana, George Richter, Jr., Esquire, of Los Angeles, R. Jasper Smith, Esquire, of Springfield, Missouri, United States Circuit Judge Sterry Waterman of St. Johnsbury, Vermont, and Charles H. Willard, Esquire, of New York City.

The Chief Reporter of the Code was Professor Llewellyn, and the Associate Chief Reporter was Professor Soia Mentschikoff. Final editorial preparation of the 1952 edition was in the hands of Professor Charles Bunn of the University of Wisconsin Law School. The Coordinators for the revisions leading to this 1962 edition were Professors Robert Braucher and A.E. Sutherland of the Law School of Harvard University, Professor Braucher doing the final editorial preparation for this edition.

The actual drafting was done in some cases by practicing lawyers and in others by teachers of various law schools. The customary procedure required that before a draft was submitted for discussion to the general memberships of The American Law Institute and of the National Conference of Commissioners, it was successively approved by three groups.

The first group were the so-called "advisers", consisting of specially selected judges, practicing lawyers and law teachers. The advisers met with the draftsmen on frequent occasions to debate and iron out, not only the substance but the form and phraseology of the proposed draft.

After the draft was cleared by the advisers, it was meticulously examined by the next two groups—the Council of The American Law Institute and either the Commercial Acts Section or the Property Acts Section of the Conference of Commissioners.

When these bodies had given their approval to the draft, it came before the general membership both of the Institute and of the Conference for consideration.

In addition in the final stages leading to this 1962 edition each article was reviewed and discussed by a special Subcommittee for that article. Recommendations of the Subcommittee were reviewed and acted upon by the Enlarged Editorial Board, pursuant to authority from the sponsoring bodies.

The judges, practicing lawyers and law teachers who originally acted either as advisers or as draftsmen were:

Judges: John T. Loughran, of the New York Court of Appeals; Thomas W. Swan, United States Circuit Judge for the Second Circuit; and the late John D. Wickhem, of the Supreme Court of Wisconsin.

Practicing lawyers: Dana C. Backus, of New York, N.Y.; Howard L. Barkdull, of Cleveland, Ohio; Lawrence G. Bennett, of New York, N.Y.; Harold F. Birnbaum, of Los Angeles, California; William L. Eagleton, of Washington, D.C.; H. Vernon Eney, of Baltimore, Maryland; Fairfax Leary, Jr., of Philadelphia, Pennsylvania; Willard B. Luther, of Boston, Massachusetts; Walter D. Malcolm, of Boston, Massachusetts; Frederic M. Miller, of Des Moines, Iowa; Hiram Thomas, of New York, N.Y.; Sterry R. Waterman, of St. Johnsbury, Vermont; and Cornelius W. Wickersham, of New York, N.Y.

The law teachers were: Ralph J. Baker, of the Harvard Law School; William E. Britton, of the University of Illinois Law School; Charles Bunn, of the University of Wisconsin Law School; Arthur L. Corbin, of Yale University Law School; Allison Dunham, of Columbia University Law School; Grant Gilmore, of Yale University Law School; Albert J. Harno, of the University of Illinois Law School; Friedrich Kessler, of the Yale University Law School; Maurice H. Merrill, of the University of Oklahoma Law School; William L. Prosser, of the University of California School of Law; Louis B. Schwartz, of the University of Pennsylvania Law School; and Bruce Townsend, of the University of Indiana Law School.

The members of the Council of the Institute during the period when the Commercial Code was under consideration were: Dillon Anderson, of Houston, Texas; Fletcher R. Andrews of Cleveland Heights, Ohio; the late Walter P. Armstrong of Memphis, Tennessee; Francis M. Bird, of Atlanta, Georgia; John G. Buchanan, of Pittsburgh, Pennsylvania; Charles Bunn, of Madison, Wisconsin; Howard F. Burns, of Cleveland, Ohio; Herbert W. Clark, of San Francisco, California; R. Ammi Cutter, of Boston, Massachusetts; Norris Darrell, of New York, N.Y.; the late John W. Davis, of New York, N.Y.; Edwin D. Dickinson, of Berkeley, California; Edward J. Dimock, of New York, N.Y.; Arthur Dixon, of Chicago, Illinois; Robert G. Dodge, of Boston, Massachusetts; the late George Donworth, of Seattle, Washington; Charles E. Dunbar, Jr., of New Orleans, Louisiana; William Dean Embree, of New York, N.Y.; Frederick F. Faville, of Des Moines, Iowa; James Alger Fee, of Portland, Oregon; Gerald F. Flood, of Philadelphia, Pennsylvania; H. Eastman Hackney, of Pittsburgh, Pennsylvania; the late Augustus N. Hand, of New York, N.Y.; Learned Hand, of New York, N.Y.; Albert J. Harno, of Urbana, Illinois; the late Earl G. Harrison, of Philadelphia, Pennsylvania; William V. Hodges, of New York, N.Y.; Joseph C. Hutcheson, Jr., of Houston, Texas; Laurence M. Hyde, of Jefferson City, Missouri; William J. Jameson, of Billings, Montana; Joseph F. Johnston, of Birmingham, Alabama; the late William H. Keller, of Lancaster, Pennsylvania; the late Daniel N. Kirby, of St. Louis, Missouri; Monte M. Lemann, of New Orleans, Louisiana; the late William Draper Lewis, of Philadelphia, Pennsylvania; the late Henry T. Lummus, of Swampscott, Massachusetts; William L. Marbury, of Baltimore, Maryland; Robert N. Miller, of Washington, D.C.; the late William D. Mitchell, of New York, N.Y.; John J. Parker, of Charlotte, North Carolina; Thomas I. Parkinson, of New York, N.Y.; George Wharton Pepper, of Philadelphia, Pennsylvania; Timothy N. Pfeiffer, of New York, N.Y.; Orie L. Phillips, of Denver, Colorado; Frederick D.G. Ribble, of Charlottesville, Virginia; William A. Schnader, of Philadelphia, Pennsylvania; Bernard G. Segal, of Philadelphia, Pennsylvania; Austin W. Scott, of Cambridge, Massachusetts; the late Harry Shulman, of New Haven, Connecticut; Henry Upson Sims, of Birmingham, Alabama; the late Sydney Smith, of Jackson, Mississippi; Eugene B. Strassburger, of Pittsburgh, Pennsylvania; Thomas W. Swan, of Guilford, Connecticut; the late Thomas Day Thacher, of New York, N.Y.; Floyd E. Thompson, of Chicago, Illinois; the late Edgar Bronson Tolman, of Chicago, Illinois; the late Robert B. Tunstall, of Norfolk, Virginia; the late Arthur J. Tuttle, of Detroit, Michigan; Harrison Tweed, of New York, N.Y.; Cornelius W. Wickersham, of New York, N.Y.; the late John D. Wickhem, of Madison, Wisconsin; Raymond S. Wilkins, of Boston, Massachusetts; Charles H. Willard, of New York, N.Y.; Laurens Williams, of Washington, D.C.; Edward L. Wright, of Little Rock, Arkansas, and Charles E. Wyzanski, Jr., of Boston, Massachusetts.

The members of the Conference's Commercial Acts Section during the same period were: Howard L. Barkdull, of Cleveland, Ohio; the late William L. Beers, of New Haven, Connecticut; Charles R. Hardin, of Newark, New Jersey; Frank E. Horack, Jr., of Bloomington, Indiana; L. Barrett Jones, of Jackson, Mississippi; Karl N. Llewellyn, now of Chicago, Illinois; Willard B. Luther, of Boston, Massachusetts; William G. McLaren, of Seattle, Washington; Frederic M. Miller, of Des Moines, Iowa; William L. Prosser, of Berkeley, California; Arthur E. Sutherland, Jr., now of Cambridge, Massachusetts; O.H. Thormodsgard, of University, North Dakota; Sterry R. Waterman, of St. Johnsbury, Vermont; and Edward L. Wright, of Little Rock, Arkansas.

The members of the Conference's Property Acts Section during the period when it cooperat-

ed in the consideration of the Code were: Joe C. Barrett, of Jonesboro, Arkansas; the late William L. Beers, of New Haven, Connecticut; Boyd M. Benson, of Huron, South Dakota; George G. Bogert, now of San Francisco, California; C. Walter Cole, of Towson, Maryland; John A. Daly, of Boston, Massachusetts; William L. Eagleton, of Washington, D.C.; H. Vernon Eney, of Baltimore, Maryland; Spencer A. Gard, of Iola, Kansas; Homer B. Harris, of Lincoln, Illinois; W.J. Jameson, of Billings, Montana; the late Sherman R. Moulton, of Burlington, Vermont; J.C. Pryor, of Burlington, Iowa; the late C.M.A. Rogers, of Mobile, Alabama; Murray M. Shoemaker, of Cincinnati, Ohio; and Greenberry Simmons, of Louisville, Kentucky.

The members of the Subcommittees which considered the various articles of the Code in the work leading to the 1958 Edition were:

Article 1: Charles H. Willard, Esquire, Chairman, of New York, New York; Professor Charles Bunn of the University of Wisconsin Law School, Madison, Wisconsin; Mahlon E. Lewis, Esquire, of Pittsburgh, Pennsylvania.

Article 2: Professor Robert Braucher, Chairman, of the Law School of Harvard University, Cambridge, Massachusetts; Professor Karl N. Llewellyn, of the Law School of the University of Chicago, Chicago, Illinois; Bernard D. Broeker, Esquire, of Bethlehem, Pennsylvania; Frank T. Dierson, Esquire, of New York, New York.

Article 3: Professor A.E. Sutherland, Chairman, of the Law School of Harvard University Cambridge, Massachusetts; William R. Emblidge, Esquire, of Buffalo, New York; John J Clarke, Esquire, of the Federal Reserve Bank of New York, New York; James V. Vergari, Esquire, of Federal Reserve Bank of Philadelphia Philadelphia, Pennsylvania.

Article 4: Walter D. Malcolm, Esquire, Chairman, of Boston, Massachusetts; James V. Vergari, Esquire; John J. Clarke, Esquire; Henry J Bailey, III, Esquire, of the Federal Reserve Bank of New York, New York; Rollin C. Huggins Esquire, of Chicago, Illinois; Carl W. Funk, Esquire, of Philadelphia, Pennsylvania.

Article 5: Arthur Littleton, Esquire, Chairman, Philadelphia, Pennsylvania; Mr. Horace M Chadsey, Vice-President of the First National Bank of Boston; Arthur F. McCarthy, Esquire, of Philadelphia, Pennsylvania; Professor Soia

Mentschikoff, of the University of Chicago Law School, Chicago, Illinois. In addition, the following acted as an Advisory Committee to the Article 5 Subcommittee: Ernest A. Carlson, of the Continental Illinois National Bank and Trust Company, Chicago, Illinois; John E. Corrigan, Jr., of the First National Bank of Chicago; Guy A. Crum, of the First National Bank of Chicago; Louis F. Dempsey, of the Northern Trust Company, Chicago, Illinois; Gerard E. Keidel, of the American National Bank and Trust Company of Chicago; Robert W. Maynard, of the Harris Trust and Savings Bank, Chicago, Illinois.

Article 6: Professor Charles Bunn, Chairman; Eugene B. Strassburger, Esquire, of Pittsburgh, Pennsylvania.

Article 7: Professor Robert Braucher, Chairman; John C. Pryor, Esquire, of Burlington, Iowa.

Article 8: Carlos Israels, Esquire, Chairman, of New York, New York; Professor Soia Mentschikoff; Eliot B. Thomas, Esquire, of Philadelphia, Pennsylvania; Fred B. Lund, Esquire, of Boston, Massachusetts.

Article 9: J. Francis Ireton, Esquire, Chairman, of Baltimore, Maryland; Homer L. Kripke, Esquire, of New York, New York; Anthony G. Felix, Jr., Esquire, of Philadelphia, Pennsylvania; Peter F. Coogan, Esquire, of Boston, Massachusetts; Professor Grant Gilmore, of Yale Universi-

ty Law School, New Haven, Connecticut; Harold F. Birnbaum, Esquire, of Los Angeles, California; Richard R. Winters, Esquire, of Pittsburgh, Pennsylvania; Professor John Hanna, of the Law School of Columbia University, New York, New York.

In addition there were informal consultants much too numerous to mention who frequently advised those working on the Code to insure a workable set of laws. In this latter class were included practicing lawyers, hard-headed businessmen and operating bankers, who contributed generously of their time and knowledge so that, not only current business practice, but foreseeable future developments would be covered.

Committees of several Bar Associations, and in particular a committee of the Section of Corporation, Banking and Business Law of the American Bar Association, of which Mr. Walter D. Malcolm of Boston was chairman, considered the various drafts of the Code and made valuable suggestions. After final approval of the Code by the Institute and the Conference, and in accordance with the practice of the Conference, the completed Code was submitted to the American Bar Association and was approved by the House of Delegates of that Association.

* * *

20

UCC ARTICLE 1
GENERAL PROVISIONS

Article 1 was revised in 2001.

2001 conforming amendments to other articles . . . .*Appendix A*
Pre–2001 Article 1 . . . .*Appendix C*
2003 amendments (Article 7 revision) . . . .*Appendix B*
2005 amendments . . . .*Appendix J*

PART 1. GENERAL PROVISIONS

Section
1–101. Short Titles.
1–102. Scope of Article.
1–103. Construction of [Uniform Commercial Code] to Promote Its Purposes and Policies; Applicability of Supplemental Principles of Law.
1–104. Construction Against Implied Repeal.
1–105. Severability.
1–106. Use of Singular and Plural; Gender.
1–107. Section Captions.
1–108. Relation to Electronic Signatures in Global and National Commerce Act.

PART 2. GENERAL DEFINITIONS AND PRINCIPLES OF INTERPRETATION

1–201. General Definitions.
1–202. Notice; Knowledge.
1–203. Lease Distinguished From Security Interest.
1–204. Value.

Section
1–205. Reasonable Time; Seasonableness.
1–206. Presumptions.

PART 3. TERRITORIAL APPLICABILITY AND GENERAL RULES

1–301. Territorial Applicability; Parties' Power to Choose Applicable Law.
1–302. Variation by Agreement.
1–303. Course of Performance, Course of Dealing, and Usage of Trade.
1–304. Obligation of Good Faith.
1–305. Remedies to Be Liberally Administered.
1–306. Waiver or Renunciation of Claim or Right After Breach.
1–307. Prima Facie Evidence by Third–Party Documents.
1–308. Performance or Acceptance Under Reservation of Rights.
1–309. Option to Accelerate at Will.
1–310. Subordinated Obligations.

DRAFTING COMMITTEE TO REVISE UNIFORM COMMERCIAL CODE ARTICLE 1–GENERAL PROVISIONS

BORIS AUERBACH, 332 Ardon Lane, Wyoming, OH 45215, *Chair*

MARION W. BENFIELD, JR., 10 Overlook Circle, New Braunfels, TX 78132

AMELIA H. BOSS, Temple University, School of Law, 1719 N. Broad Street, Philadelphia, PA 19122, *The American Law Institute Representative*

JAMES C. McKAY, JR., Office of Corporation Counsel, 6th Floor South, 441 4th Street, NW, Washington, DC 20001, *Committee on Style Liaison*

H. KATHLEEN PATCHEL, Indiana University–Indianapolis, School of Law, 530 W. New York Street, Indianapolis, IN 46202–5194, *National Conference Associate Reporter*

CURTIS R. REITZ, University of Pennsylvania, School of Law, 3400 Chestnut Street, Philadelphia, PA 19104

CARLYLE C. RING, JR., 1401 H Street NW, Suite 500, Washington, DC 20005, *Enactment Plan Coordinator*

JAMES J. WHITE, University of Michigan Law School, Hutchins Hall, Room 300, 625 S. State Street, Ann Arbor, MI 48109–1215

NEIL B. COHEN, Brooklyn Law School, Room 904A, 250 Joralemon Street, Brooklyn, NY 11201, *Reporter*

EX OFFICIO

JOHN L. McCLAUGHERTY, P.O. Box 553, Charleston, WV 25322, *President*

ROBERT J. TENNESSEN, 3400 City Center, 33 S. 6th Street, Minneapolis, MN 55402–3796, *Division Chair*

AMERICAN BAR ASSOCIATION ADVISORS

HARRY C. SIGMAN, 9717 Cashio Street, Los Angeles, CA 90035, *Advisor*

RICHARD R. GOLDBERG, 51st Floor, 1735 Market Street, Philadelphia, PA 19103, *Real Property, Probate & Trust Law Section Advisor*

WILLIAM J. WOODWARD, JR., Temple University School of Law, 1719 N. Broad Street, Philadelphia, PA 19122, *Business Law Section Advisor*

EXECUTIVE DIRECTOR

FRED H. MILLER, University of Oklahoma, College of Law, 300 Timberdell Rd., Norman, OK 73019, *Executive Director*

WILLIAM J. PIERCE, 1505 Roxbury Road, Ann Arbor, MI 48104, *Executive Director Emeritus*

Concordance of Article 1 Sections

Former Article 1 Section   (Revised Article 1 Section)

Former Article 1 Section	Revised Article 1 Section
1–101	1–101(a)
1–102(1)	1–103(a)
1–102(2)	1–103(a)(1)-(3)
1–102(3)	1–302(a), (b) (1st and 2nd sentences)
1–102(4)	1–302(c)
1–102(5)	1–106
1–103	1–103(b)
1–104	1–104
1–105	1–301 (with significant changes)
1–106	1–305
1–107	1–306
1–108	1–105
1–109	1–107
1–201(1)-(20), (22)-(24), (28-40), (42)-(43), (45-46)	1–201(1)-(20), (22)-(24), (28)-(40), (42)-(43), (45)-(46)
1–201(25)	1–202(a)-(c)
1–201(26)	1–202(d), (e)
1–201(27)	1–202(f)
1–201(37) (all but 1st paragraph)	1–203
1–201(44)	1–204
1–202	1–307
1–203	1–304
1–204(1)	1–302(b) 3rd sentence
1–205	1–303(b)-(e), (g)
1–206	deleted
1–207	1–308
1–208	1–309
1–209	1–310
2–208q	1–303(a), (e), (f)
new	1–101(b)
new	1–102
new	1–108
new	1–201(b)(10a), (30a), (33a), (39a)

PART 1

GENERAL PROVISIONS

§ 1–101. Short Titles.

(a) This [Act] may be cited as the Uniform Commercial Code.

(b) This article may be cited as Uniform Commercial Code–General Provisions.

Official Comment

Source: Former Section 1–101.

Changes from former law: Subsection (b) is new. It is added in order to make the structure of Article 1 parallel with that of the other articles of the Uniform Commercial Code.

1. Each other article of the Uniform Commercial Code (except Articles 10 and 11) may also be cited by its own short title. See Sections 2–101, 2A–101, 3–101, 4–101, 4A–101, 5–101, 6–101, 7–101, 8–101, and 9–101.

§ 1–102. Scope of Article.

This article applies to a transaction to the extent that it is governed by another article of [the Uniform Commercial Code].

Official Comment

Source: New.

1. This section is intended to resolve confusion that has occasionally arisen as to the applicability of the substantive rules in this article. This section makes clear what has always been the case–the rules in Article 1 apply to transactions to the extent that those transactions are governed by one of the other articles of the Uniform Commercial Code. See also Comment 1 to Section 1–301.

§ 1–103. Construction of [Uniform Commercial Code] to Promote Its Purposes and Policies; Applicability of Supplemental Principles of Law.

(a) [The Uniform Commercial Code] must be liberally construed and applied to promote its underlying purposes and policies, which are:

(1) to simplify, clarify, and modernize the law governing commercial transactions;

(2) to permit the continued expansion of commercial practices through custom, usage, and agreement of the parties; and

(3) to make uniform the law among the various jurisdictions.

(b) Unless displaced by the particular provisions of [the Uniform Commercial Code], the principles of law and equity, including the law merchant and the law relative to capacity to contract, principal and agent, estoppel, fraud, misrepresentation, duress, coercion, mistake, bankruptcy, and other validating or invalidating cause supplement its provisions.

Official Comment

Source: Former Section 1–102 (1)-(2); Former Section 1–103.

Changes from former law: This section is derived from subsections (1) and (2) of former Section 1–102 and from former Section 1–103. Subsection (a) of this section combines subsections (1) and (2) of former Section 1–102. Except for changing the form of reference to the Uniform Commercial Code and minor stylistic changes, its language is the same as subsections (1) and (2) of former Section 1–102. Except for changing the form of reference to the Uniform Commercial Code and minor stylistic changes, subsection (b) of this section is identical to former Section 1–103. The provisions have been combined in this section to reflect the interrelationship between them.

1. The Uniform Commercial Code is drawn to provide flexibility so that, since it is intended to be a semi-permanent and infrequently-amended piece of legislation, it will provide its own machinery for expansion of commercial practices. It is intended to make it possible for the law embodied in the Uniform Commercial Code to be applied by the courts in the light of unforeseen and new circumstances and practices. The proper construction of the Uniform Commercial Code requires, of course, that its interpretation and application be limited to its reason.

Even prior to the enactment of the Uniform Commercial Code, courts were careful to keep broad acts from being hampered in their effects by later acts of limited scope. See *Pacific Wool Growers v. Draper & Co.*, 158 Or. 1, 73 P.2d 1391 (1937), and compare Section 1–104. The courts have often recognized that the policies embodied in an act are applicable in reason to subject-matter that was not expressly included in the language of the act, *Commercial Nat. Bank of New Orleans v. Canal–Louisiana Bank & Trust Co.*, 239

U.S. 520, 36 S.Ct. 194, 60 L.Ed. 417 (1916) (bona fide purchase policy of Uniform Warehouse Receipts Act extended to case not covered but of equivalent nature), and did the same where reason and policy so required, even where the subject-matter had been intentionally excluded from the act in general. *Agar v. Orda*, 264 N.Y. 248, 190 N.E. 479 (1934) (Uniform Sales Act change in seller's remedies applied to contract for sale of choses in action even though the general coverage of that Act was intentionally limited to goods "other than things in action.") They implemented a statutory policy with liberal and useful remedies not provided in the statutory text. They disregarded a statutory limitation of remedy where the reason of the limitation did not apply. *Fiterman v. J. N. Johnson & Co.*, 156 Minn. 201, 194 N.W. 399 (1923) (requirement of return of the goods as a condition to rescission for breach of warranty; also, partial rescission allowed). Nothing in the Uniform Commercial Code stands in the way of the continuance of such action by the courts.

The Uniform Commercial Code should be construed in accordance with its underlying purposes and policies. The text of each section should be read in the light of the purpose and policy of the rule or principle in question, as also of the Uniform Commercial Code as a whole, and the application of the language should be construed narrowly or broadly, as the case may be, in conformity with the purposes and policies involved.

2. **Applicability of supplemental principles of law.** Subsection (b) states the basic relationship of the Uniform Commercial Code to supplemental bodies of law. The Uniform Commercial Code was drafted against the backdrop of existing bodies of law, including the common law and equity, and relies on those bodies of law to supplement it provisions in many important ways. At the same time, the Uniform Commercial Code is the primary source of commercial law rules in areas that it governs, and its rules represent choices made by its drafters and the enacting legislatures about the appropriate policies to be furthered in the transactions it covers. Therefore, while principles of common law and equity may *supplement* provisions of the Uniform Commercial Code, they may not be used to *supplant* its provisions, or the purposes and policies those provisions reflect, unless a specific provision of the Uniform Commercial Code provides otherwise. In the absence of such a provision, the Uniform Commercial Code preempts principles of common law and equity that are inconsistent with either its provisions or its purposes and policies.

The language of subsection (b) is intended to reflect both the concept of supplementation and the concept of preemption. Some courts, however, had difficulty in applying the identical language of former Section 1–103 to determine when other law appropriately may be applied to supplement the Uniform Commercial Code, and when that law has been displaced by the Code. Some decisions applied other law in situations in which that application, while not inconsistent with the text of any particular provision of the Uniform Commercial Code, clearly was inconsistent with the underlying purposes and policies reflected in the relevant provisions of the Code. *See, e.g., Sheerbonnet, Ltd. v. American Express Bank, Ltd.*, 951 F. Supp. 403 (S.D.N.Y. 1995). In part, this difficulty arose from Comment 1 to former Section 1–103, which stated that "this section indicates the continued applicability to commercial contracts of all supplemental bodies of law except insofar as they are explicitly displaced by this Act." The "explicitly displaced" language of that Comment did not accurately reflect the proper scope of Uniform Commercial Code preemption, which extends to displacement of other law that is inconsistent with the purposes and policies of the Uniform Commercial Code, as well as with its text.

3. **Application of subsection (b) to statutes.** The primary focus of Section 1–103 is on the relationship between the Uniform Commercial Code and principles of common law and equity as developed by the courts. State law, however, increasingly is statutory. Not only are there a growing number of state statutes addressing specific issues that come within the scope of the Uniform Commercial Code, but in some States many general principles of common law and equity have been codified. When the other law relating to a matter within the scope of the Uniform Commercial Code is a statute, the principles of subsection (b) remain relevant to the court's analysis of the relationship between that statute and the Uniform Commercial Code, but other principles of statutory interpretation that specifically address the interrelationship between statutes will be relevant as well. In some situations, the principles of subsection (b) still will be determinative. For example, the mere fact that an equitable principle is stated in statutory form rather than in judicial decisions should not change the court's analysis of whether the principle can be used to supplement the Uniform Commercial Code–under subsection (b), equitable principles may supplement provisions of the Uniform Commercial Code only if they are consistent with the purposes and policies of the Uniform Commercial Code as well as its text. In other situations, however, other interpretive principles addressing the interrelationship between statutes may lead the court to conclude that the other statute is controlling, even though it con-

flicts with the Uniform Commercial Code. This, for example, would be the result in a situation where the other statute was specifically intended to provide additional protection to a class of individuals engaging in transactions covered by the Uniform Commercial Code.

4. **Listing not exclusive.** The list of sources of supplemental law in subsection (b) is intended to be merely illustrative of the other law that may supplement the Uniform Commercial Code, and is not exclusive. No listing could be exhaustive. Further, the fact that a particular section of the Uniform Commercial Code makes express reference to other law is not intended to suggest the negation of the general application of the principles of subsection (b). Note also that the word "bankruptcy" in subsection (b), continuing the use of that word from former Section 1–103, should be understood not as a specific reference to federal bankruptcy law but, rather, as a reference to general principles of insolvency, whether under federal or state law.

§ 1–104. Construction Against Implied Repeal.

[The Uniform Commercial Code] being a general act intended as a unified coverage of its subject matter, no part of it shall be deemed to be impliedly repealed by subsequent legislation if such construction can reasonably be avoided.

Official Comment

Source: Former Section 1–104.

Changes from former law: Except for changing the form of reference to the Uniform Commercial Code, this section is identical to former Section 1–104.

1. This section embodies the policy that an act that bears evidence of carefully considered permanent regulative intention should not lightly be regarded as impliedly repealed by subsequent legislation. The Uniform Commercial Code, carefully integrated and intended as a uniform codification of permanent character covering an entire "field" of law, is to be regarded as particularly resistant to implied repeal.

§ 1–105. Severability.

If any provision or clause of [the Uniform Commercial Code] or its application to any person or circumstance is held invalid, the invalidity does not affect other provisions or applications of [the Uniform Commercial Code] which can be given effect without the invalid provision or ap-

plication, and to this end the provisions of [the Uniform Commercial Code] are severable.

Official Comment

Source: Former Section 1–108.

Changes from former law: Except for changing the form of reference to the Uniform Commercial Code, this section is identical to former Section 1–108.

1. This is the model severability section recommended by the National Conference of Commissioners on Uniform State Laws for inclusion in all acts of extensive scope.

§ 1–106. Use of Singular and Plural; Gender.

In [the Uniform Commercial Code], unless the statutory context otherwise requires:

(1) words in the singular number include the plural, and those in the plural include the singular; and

(2) words of any gender also refer to any other gender.

Official Comment

Source: Former Section 1–102(5). See also 1 U.S.C. Section 1.

Changes from former law: Other than minor stylistic changes, this section is identical to former Section 1–102(5).

1. This section makes it clear that the use of singular or plural in the text of the Uniform Commercial Code is generally only a matter of drafting style–singular words may be applied in the plural, and plural words may be applied in the singular. Only when it is clear from the statutory context that the use of the singular or plural does not include the other is this rule inapplicable. *See, e.g.,* Section 9–322.

§ 1–107. Section Captions.

Section captions are part of [the Uniform Commercial Code].

Official Comment

Source: Former Section 1–109.

Changes from former law: None.

1. Section captions are a part of the text of the Uniform Commercial Code, and not mere surplusage. This is not the case, however, with respect to subsec-

tion headings appearing in Article 9. See Comment 3 to Section 9–101 ("subsection headings are not a part of the official text itself and have not been approved by the sponsors.").

§1–108. Relation to Electronic Signatures in Global and National Commerce Act.

This article modifies, limits, and supersedes the Federal Electronic Signatures in Global and National Commerce Act, 15 U.S.C. § 7001 *et seq.*, except that nothing in this article modifies, limits, or supersedes section 7001(c) of that act or authorizes electronic delivery of any of the notices described in section 7003(b) of that Act.

Official Comment

Source: New

1. The federal Electronic Signatures in Global and National Commerce Act, 15 U.S.C. Section 7001 *et seq.* became effective in 2000. Section 102(a) of that Act provides that a State statute may modify, limit, or supersede the provisions of section 101 of that Act with respect to state law if such statute, *inter alia*, specifies the alternative procedures or requirements for the use or acceptance (or both) of electronic records or electronic signatures to establish the legal effect, validity, or enforceability of contracts or other records, and (i) such alternative procedures or requirements are consistent with Titles I and II of that Act, (ii) such alternative procedures or requirements do not require, or accord greater legal status or effect to, the implementation or application of a specific technology or technical specification for performing the functions of creating, storing, generating, receiving, communicating, or authenticating electronic records or electronic signatures; and (iii) if enacted or adopted after the date of the enactment of that Act, makes specific reference to that Act. Article 1 fulfills the first two of those three criteria; this Section fulfills the third criterion listed above.

2. As stated in this section, however, Article 1 does not modify, limit, or supersede Section 101(c) of the Electronic Signatures in Global and National Commerce Act (requiring affirmative consent from a consumer to electronic delivery of transactional disclosures that are required by state law to be in writing); nor does it authorize electronic delivery of any of the notices described in Section 103(b) of that Act.

PART 2

GENERAL DEFINITIONS AND PRINCIPLES OF INTERPRETATION

§1–201. General Definitions.

(a) Unless the context otherwise requires, words or phrases defined in this section, or in the additional definitions contained in other articles of [the Uniform Commercial Code] that apply to particular articles or parts thereof, have the meanings stated.

(b) Subject to definitions contained in other articles of [the Uniform Commercial Code] that apply to particular articles or parts thereof:

(1) "Action", in the sense of a judicial proceeding, includes recoupment, counterclaim, set-off, suit in equity, and any other proceeding in which rights are determined.

(2) "Aggrieved party" means a party entitled to pursue a remedy.

(3) "Agreement", as distinguished from "contract", means the bargain of the parties in fact, as found in their language or inferred from other circumstances, including course of performance, course of dealing, or usage of trade as provided in Section 1–303.

(4) "Bank" means a person engaged in the business of banking and includes a savings bank, savings and loan association, credit union, and trust company.

(5) "Bearer" means a person in control of a negotiable electronic document of title or a person in possession of a negotiable instrument, negotiable tangible document of title, or certificated security that is payable to bearer or indorsed in blank.

(6) "Bill of lading" means a document of title evidencing the receipt of goods for shipment issued by a person engaged in the business of directly or indirectly transporting or forwarding goods. The term does not include a warehouse receipt.

(7) "Branch" includes a separately incorporated foreign branch of a bank.

(8) "Burden of establishing" a fact means the burden of persuading the trier of fact that the existence of the fact is more probable than its nonexistence.

(9) "Buyer in ordinary course of business" means a person that buys goods in good faith, without knowledge that the sale violates the rights of another person in the goods, and in the ordinary course from a person, other than a pawnbroker, in the business of selling goods of that kind. A person buys goods in the ordinary course if the sale to the person comports with the usual or customary practices in the kind of business in which the seller is engaged or with the seller's own usual or customary practices. A person that sells oil, gas, or other minerals at the wellhead or mine-head is a person in the business of selling goods of that kind. A buyer in ordinary course of business may buy for cash, by exchange of other property, or on secured or unsecured credit, and may acquire goods or documents of title under a preexisting contract for sale. Only a buyer that takes possession of the goods or has a right to recover the goods from the seller under Article 2 may be a buyer in ordinary course of business. "Buyer in ordinary course of business" does not include a person that acquires goods in a transfer in bulk or as security for or in total or partial satisfaction of a money debt.

(10) "Conspicuous", with reference to a term, means so written, displayed, or presented that a reasonable person against which it is to operate ought to have noticed it. Whether a term is "conspicuous" or not is a decision for the court. Conspicuous terms include the following:

(A) a heading in capitals equal to or greater in size than the surrounding text, or in contrasting type, font, or color to the surrounding text of the same or lesser size; and

(B) language in the body of a record or display in larger type than the surrounding text, or in contrasting type, font, or color to the surrounding text of the same size, or set off from surrounding text of the

same size by symbols or other marks that call attention to the language.

(11) "Consumer" means an individual who enters into a transaction primarily for personal, family, or household purposes.

(12) "Contract", as distinguished from "agreement", means the total legal obligation that results from the parties' agreement as determined by [the Uniform Commercial Code] as supplemented by any other applicable laws.

(13) "Creditor" includes a general creditor, a secured creditor, a lien creditor, and any representative of creditors, including an assignee for the benefit of creditors, a trustee in bankruptcy, a receiver in equity, and an executor or administrator of an insolvent debtor's or assignor's estate.

(14) "Defendant" includes a person in the position of defendant in a counterclaim, cross-claim, or third-party claim.

(15) "Delivery", with respect to an electronic document of title means voluntary transfer of control and with respect to an instrument, a tangible document of title, or chattel paper, means voluntary transfer of possession.

(16) "Document of title" means a record (i) that in the regular course of business or financing is treated as adequately evidencing that the person in possession or control of the record is entitled to receive, control, hold, and dispose of the record and the goods the record covers and (ii) that purports to be issued by or addressed to a bailee and to cover goods in the bailee's possession which are either identified or are fungible portions of an identified mass. The term includes a bill of lading, transport document, dock warrant, dock receipt, warehouse receipt, and order for delivery of goods. An electronic document of title means a document of title evidenced by a record consisting of information stored in an electronic medium. A tangible document of title means a document of title evidenced by a record consisting of information that is inscribed on a tangible medium.

(17) "Fault" means a default, breach, or wrongful act or omission.

(18) "Fungible goods" means:

(A) goods of which any unit, by nature or usage of trade, is the equivalent of any other like unit; or

(B) goods that by agreement are treated as equivalent.

(19) "Genuine" means free of forgery or counterfeiting.

(20) "Good faith," except as otherwise provided in Article 5, means honesty in fact and the observance of reasonable commercial standards of fair dealing.

(21) "Holder" means:

(A) the person in possession of a negotiable instrument that is payable either to bearer or to an identified person that is the person in possession;

(B) the person in possession of a negotiable tangible document of title if the goods are deliverable either to bearer or to the order of the person in possession; or

(C) the person in control of a negotiable electronic document of title.

(22) "Insolvency proceeding" includes an assignment for the benefit of creditors or other proceeding intended to liquidate or rehabilitate the estate of the person involved.

(23) "Insolvent" means:

(A) having generally ceased to pay debts in the ordinary course of business other than as a result of bona fide dispute;

(B) being unable to pay debts as they become due; or

(C) being insolvent within the meaning of federal bankruptcy law.

(24) "Money" means a medium of exchange currently authorized or adopted by a domestic or foreign government. The term includes a monetary unit of account established by an intergovernmental organization or by agreement between two or more countries.

(25) "Organization" means a person other than an individual.

(26) "Party", as distinguished from "third party", means a person that has engaged in a transaction or made an agreement subject to [the Uniform Commercial Code].

(27) "Person" means an individual, corporation, business trust, estate, trust, partnership, limited liability company, association, joint venture, government, governmental subdivision, agency, or instrumentality, public corporation, or any other legal or commercial entity.

(28) "Present value" means the amount as of a date certain of one or more sums payable in the future, discounted to the date certain by use of either an interest rate specified by the parties if that rate is not manifestly unreasonable at the time the transaction is entered into or, if an interest rate is not so specified, a commercially reasonable rate that takes into account the facts and circumstances at the time the transaction is entered into.

(29) "Purchase" means taking by sale, lease, discount, negotiation, mortgage, pledge, lien, security interest, issue or reissue, gift, or any other voluntary transaction creating an interest in property.

(30) "Purchaser" means a person that takes by purchase.

(31) "Record" means information that is inscribed on a tangible medium or that is stored in an electronic or other medium and is retrievable in perceivable form.

(32) "Remedy" means any remedial right to which an aggrieved party is entitled with or without resort to a tribunal.

(33) "Representative" means a person empowered to act for another, including an agent, an officer of a corporation or association, and a trustee, executor, or administrator of an estate.

(34) "Right" includes remedy.

(35) "Security interest" means an interest in personal property or fixtures which secures payment or performance of an obli-

gation. "Security interest" includes any interest of a consignor and a buyer of accounts, chattel paper, a payment intangible, or a promissory note in a transaction that is subject to Article 9. "Security interest" does not include the special property interest of a buyer of goods on identification of those goods to a contract for sale under Section 2–401, but a buyer may also acquire a "security interest" by complying with Article 9. Except as otherwise provided in Section 2–505, the right of a seller or lessor of goods under Article 2 or 2A to retain or acquire possession of the goods is not a "security interest", but a seller or lessor may also acquire a "security interest" by complying with Article 9. The retention or reservation of title by a seller of goods notwithstanding shipment or delivery to the buyer under Section 2–401 is limited in effect to a reservation of a "security interest." Whether a transaction in the form of a lease creates a "security interest" is determined pursuant to Section 1–203.

(36) "Send" in connection with a writing, record, or notice means:

(A) to deposit in the mail or deliver for transmission by any other usual means of communication with postage or cost of transmission provided for and properly addressed and, in the case of an instrument, to an address specified thereon or otherwise agreed, or if there be none to any address reasonable under the circumstances; or

(B) in any other way to cause to be received any record or notice within the time it would have arrived if properly sent.

(37) "Signed" includes using any symbol executed or adopted with present intention to adopt or accept a writing.

(38) "State" means a State of the United States, the District of Columbia, Puerto Rico, the United States Virgin Islands, or any territory or insular possession subject to the jurisdiction of the United States.

(39) "Surety" includes a guarantor or other secondary obligor.

(40) "Term" means a portion of an agreement that relates to a particular matter.

(41) "Unauthorized signature" means a signature made without actual, implied, or apparent authority. The term includes a forgery.

(42) "Warehouse receipt" means a document of title issued by a person engaged in the business of storing goods for hire.

(43) "Writing" includes printing, typewriting, or any other intentional reduction to tangible form. "Written" has a corresponding meaning.

As amended in 2003.

Official Comment

Source: Former Section 1–201.

Changes from former law: In order to make it clear that all definitions in the Uniform Commercial Code (not just those appearing in Article 1, as stated in former Section 1–201, but also those appearing in other Articles) do not apply if the context otherwise requires, a new subsection (a) to that effect has been added, and the definitions now appear in subsection (b). The reference in subsection (a) to the "context" is intended to refer to the context in which the defined term is used in the Uniform Commercial Code. In other words, the definition applies whenever the defined term is used unless the context in which the defined term is used in the statute indicates that the term was not used in its defined sense. Consider, for example, Sections 3–103(a)(9) (defining "promise," in relevant part, as "a written undertaking to pay money signed by the person undertaking to pay") and 3–303(a)(1) (indicating that an instrument is issued or transferred for value if "the instrument is issued or transferred for a promise of performance, to the extent that the promise has been performed"). It is clear from the statutory context of the use of the word "promise" in Section 3–303(a)(1) that the term was not used in the sense of its definition in Section 3–103(a)(9). Thus, the Section 3–103(a)(9) definition should not be used to give meaning to the word "promise" in Section 3–303(a).

Some definitions in former Section 1–201 have been reformulated as substantive provisions and have been moved to other sections. See Sections 1–202 (explicating concepts of notice and knowledge formerly addressed in Sections 1–201(25)-(27)), 1–204 (determining when a person gives value for rights, replacing the definition of "value" in former Section 1–201(44)), and

1–206 (addressing the meaning of presumptions, replacing the definitions of "presumption" and "presumed" in former Section 1–201(31)). Similarly, the portion of the definition of "security interest" in former Section 1–201(37) which explained the difference between a security interest and a lease has been relocated to Section 1–203.

Two definitions in former Section 1–201 have been deleted. The definition of "honor" in former Section 1–201(21) has been moved to Section 2–103(1)(b), inasmuch as the definition only applies to the use of the word in Article 2. The definition of "telegram" in former Section 1–201(41) has been deleted because that word no longer appears in the definition of "conspicuous."

Other than minor stylistic changes and renumbering, the remaining definitions in this section are as in former Article 1 except as noted below.

1. "Action." Unchanged from former Section 1–201, which was derived from similar definitions in Section 191, Uniform Negotiable Instruments Law; Section 76, Uniform Sales Act; Section 58, Uniform Warehouse Receipts Act; Section 53, Uniform Bills of Lading Act.

2. "Aggrieved party." Unchanged from former Section 1–201.

3. "Agreement." Derived from former Section 1–201. As used in the Uniform Commercial Code the word is intended to include full recognition of usage of trade, course of dealing, course of performance and the surrounding circumstances as effective parts thereof, and of any agreement permitted under the provisions of the Uniform Commercial Code to displace a stated rule of law. Whether an agreement has legal consequences is determined by applicable provisions of the Uniform Commercial Code and, to the extent provided in Section 1–103, by the law of contracts.

4. "Bank." Derived from Section 4A–104.

5. "Bearer." Unchanged, except in one respect, from former section 1–201, which was derived from Section 191, Uniform Negotiable Instruments Law. The term bearer applies to negotiable documents of title and has been broadened to include a person in control of an electronic negotiable document of title. Control of an electronic document of title is defined in Article 7 (Section 7–106).

6. "Bill of Lading." Derived from former Section 1–201. The reference to, and definition of, an "airbill" has been deleted as no longer necessary. A bill of lading is one type of document of title as defined in subsection (16). This definition should be read in conjunction with the definition of carrier in Article 7 (Section 7–102).

7. "Branch." Unchanged from former Section 1–201.

8. "Burden of establishing a fact." Unchanged from former Section 1–201.

9. "Buyer in ordinary course of business." Except for minor stylistic changes, identical to former Section 1–201 (as amended in conjunction with the 1999 revisions to Article 9). The major significance of the phrase lies in Section 2–403 and in the Article on Secured Transactions (Article 9).

The first sentence of paragraph (9) makes clear that a buyer from a pawnbroker cannot be a buyer in ordinary course of business. The second sentence explains what it means to buy "in the ordinary course." The penultimate sentence prevents a buyer that does not have the right to possession as against the seller from being a buyer in ordinary course of business. Concerning when a buyer obtains possessory rights, see Sections 2–502 and 2–716. However, the penultimate sentence is not intended to affect a buyer's status as a buyer in ordinary course of business in cases (such as a "drop shipment") involving delivery by the seller to a person buying from the buyer or a donee from the buyer. The requirement relates to whether *as against the seller* the buyer or one taking through the buyer has possessory rights.

10. "Conspicuous." Derived from former Section 1–201(10). This definition states the general standard that to be conspicuous a term ought to be noticed by a reasonable person. Whether a term is conspicuous is an issue for the court. Subparagraphs (A) and (B) set out several methods for making a term conspicuous. Requiring that a term be conspicuous blends a notice function (the term ought to be noticed) and a planning function (giving guidance to the party relying on the term regarding how that result can be achieved). Although these paragraphs indicate some of the methods for making a term attention-calling, the test is whether attention can reasonably be expected to be called to it. The statutory language should not be construed to permit a result that is inconsistent with that test.

11. "Consumer." Derived from Section 9–102(a)(25).

12. "Contract." Except for minor stylistic changes, identical to former Section 1–201.

13. "Creditor." Unchanged from former Section 1–201.

14. "Defendant." Except for minor stylistic changes, identical to former Section 1–201, which was derived from Section 76, Uniform Sales Act.

15. "Delivery." Derived from former Section 1–201. The reference to certificated securities has been deleted in light of the more specific treatment of the matter in Section 8–301. The definition has been revised to accommodate electronic documents of title. Control of an electronic document of title is defined in Article 7 (Section 7–106).

16. "Document of title." Derived from former Section 1–201, which was derived from Section 76, Uniform Sales Act. This definition makes explicit that the obligation or designation of a third party as "bailee" is essential to a document of title and clearly rejects any such result as obtained in Hixson v. Ward, 254 Ill.App. 505 (1929), which treated a conditional sales contract as a document of title. Also the definition is left open so that new types of documents may be included, including documents which gain commercial recognition in the international arena. See UNCITRAL Draft Instrument on the Carriage of Goods By Sea. It is unforeseeable what documents may one day serve the essential purpose now filled by warehouse receipts and bills of lading. The definition is stated in terms of the function of the documents with the intention that any document which gains commercial recognition as accomplishing the desired result shall be included within its scope. Fungible goods are adequately identified within the language of the definition by identification of the mass of which they are a part.

Dock warrants were within the Sales Act definition of document of title apparently for the purpose of recognizing a valid tender by means of such paper. In current commercial practice a dock warrant or receipt is a kind of interim certificate issued by shipping companies upon delivery of the goods at the dock, entitling a designated person to be issued a bill of lading. The receipt itself is invariably nonnegotiable in form although it may indicate that a negotiable bill is to be forthcoming. Such a document is not within the general compass of the definition, although trade usage may in some cases entitle such paper to be treated as a document of title. If the dock receipt actually represents a storage obligation undertaken by the shipping company, then it is a warehouse receipt within this Section regardless of the name given to the instrument.

The goods must be "described," but the description may be by marks or labels and may be qualified in such a way as to disclaim personal knowledge of the issuer regarding contents or condition. However, bag-gage and parcel checks and similar "tokens" of storage which identify stored goods only as those received in exchange for the token are not covered by this Article. The definition is broad enough to include an airway bill.

A document of title may be either tangible or electronic. Tangible documents of title should be construed to mean traditional paper documents. Electronic documents of title are documents that are stored in an electronic medium instead of in tangible form. The concept of an electronic medium should be construed liberally to include electronic, digital, magnetic, optical, electromagnetic, or any other current or similar emerging technologies. As to reissuing a document of title in an alternative medium, see Article 7, Section 7–105. Control for electronic documents of title is defined in Article 7 (Section 7–106).

17. "Fault." Derived from former Section 1–201. "Default" has been added to the list of events constituting fault.

18. "Fungible goods." Derived from former Section 1–201. References to securities have been deleted because Article 8 no longer uses the term "fungible" to describe securities. Accordingly, this provision now defines the concept only in the context of goods.

19. "Genuine." Unchanged from former Section 1–201.

20. "Good faith." Former Section 1–201(19) defined "good faith" simply as honesty in fact; the definition contained no element of commercial reasonableness. Initially, that definition applied throughout the Code with only one exception. Former Section 2–103(1)(b) provided that *"in that Article … good faith in the case of a merchant means honesty in fact and the observance of reasonable commercial standards of fair dealing in the trade."* This alternative definition was limited in applicability though, because it applied only to transactions within the scope of Article 2 and it applied only to merchants.

Over time, however, amendments to the Uniform Commercial Code brought the Article 2 merchant concept of good faith (subjective honesty and objective commercial reasonableness) into other Articles. First, Article 2A explicitly incorporated the Article 2 standard. See Section 2A–103(7). Then, other Articles broadened the applicability of that standard by adopting it for all parties rather than just for merchants. *See, e.g.,* Sections 3–103(a)(4), 4A–105(a)(6), 7–102(a)(6), 8–102(a)(10), and 9–102(a)(43). Finally, Articles 2 and 2A were amended so as to apply the standard to non-merchants as well as merchants. See Sections 2–103(1)(j), 2A–103(1)(m). All of these definitions are comprised of two elements–honesty in fact *and* the observance of reasonable commercial standards of fair dealing. Only revised Article 5 defines "good faith" solely in terms of subjective honesty, and only Article 6 (in the few states that have not chosen to delete the Article) is without definition of good faith. (It should be noted that, while revised Article 6 did not define good faith, Comment 2 to revised Section 6–102 states that "this Article adopts the definition of 'good faith' in Article 1 in all cases, even when the buyer is a merchant.")

Thus, the definition of "good faith" in this section merely confirms what has been the case for a number of years as Articles of the UCC have been amended or revised–the obligation of "good faith," applicable in each Article, is to be interpreted in the context of all Articles except for Article 5 as including both the subjective element of honesty in fact and the objective element of the observance of reasonable commercial standards of fair dealing. As a result, both the subjective and objective elements are part of the standard of "good faith," whether that obligation is specifically referenced in another Article of the Code (other than Article 5) or is provided by this Article.

Of course, as noted in the statutory text, the definition of "good faith" in this section does not apply when the narrower definition of "good faith" in revised Article 5 is applicable.

As noted above, the definition of "good faith" in this section requires not only honesty in fact but also "observance of reasonable commercial standards of fair dealing." Although "fair dealing" is a broad term that must be defined in context, it is clear that it is concerned with the fairness of conduct rather than the care with which an act is performed. This is an entirely different concept than whether a party exercised ordinary care in conducting a transaction. Both concepts are to be determined in the light of reasonable commercial standards, but those standards in each case are directed to different aspects of commercial conduct. See e.g., Sections 3–103(a)(9) and 4–104(c) and Comment 4 to Section 3–103.

21. "Holder." Derived from former Section 1–201. The definition has been reorganized for clarity and amended to provide for electronic negotiable documents of title.

22. "Insolvency proceedings." Unchanged from former Section 1–201.

23. "Insolvent." Derived from former Section 1–201. The three tests of insolvency–"generally ceased to pay debts in the ordinary course of business other than as a result of a bona fide dispute as to them," "unable

to pay debts as they become due," and "insolvent within the meaning of the federal bankruptcy law"–are expressly set up as alternative tests and must be approached from a commercial standpoint.

24. "Money." Substantively identical to former Section 1–201. The test is that of sanction of government, whether by authorization before issue or adoption afterward, which recognizes the circulating medium as a part of the official currency of that government. The narrow view that money is limited to legal tender is rejected.

25. "Organization." The former definition of this word has been replaced with the standard definition used in acts prepared by the National Conference of Commissioners on Uniform State Laws.

26. "Party." Substantively identical to former Section 1–201. Mention of a party includes, of course, a person acting through an agent. However, where an agent comes into opposition or contrast to the principal, particular account is taken of that situation.

27. "Person." The former definition of this word has been replaced with the standard definition used in acts prepared by the National Conference of Commissioners on Uniform State Laws.

28. "Present value." This definition was formerly contained within the definition of "security interest" in former Section 1–201(37).

29. "Purchase." Derived from former Section 1–201. The form of definition has been changed from "includes" to "means."

30. "Purchaser." Unchanged from former Section 1–201.

31. "Record." Derived from Section 9–102(a)(69).

32. "Remedy." Unchanged from former Section 1–201. The purpose is to make it clear that both remedy and right (as defined) include those remedial rights of "self help" which are among the most important bodies of rights under the Uniform Commercial Code, remedial rights being those to which an aggrieved party may resort on its own.

33. "Representative." Derived from former Section 1–201. Reorganized, and form changed from "includes" to "means."

34. "Right." Except for minor stylistic changes, identical to former Section 1–201.

35. "Security Interest." The definition is the first paragraph of the definition of "security interest" in former Section 1–201, with minor stylistic changes. The remaining portion of that definition has been

moved to Section 1–203. Note that, because of the scope of Article 9, the term includes the interest of certain outright buyers of certain kinds of property.

36. "Send." Derived from former Section 1–201. Compare "notifies".

37. "Signed." Derived from former Section 1–201. Former Section 1–201 referred to "intention to authenticate"; because other articles now use the term "authenticate," the language has been changed to "intention to adopt or accept." The latter formulation is derived from the definition of "authenticate" in Section 9–102(a)(7). This provision refers only to writings, because the term "signed," as used in some articles, refers only to writings. This provision also makes it clear that, as the term "signed" is used in the Uniform Commercial Code, a complete signature is not necessary. The symbol may be printed, stamped or written; it may be by initials or by thumbprint. It may be on any part of the document and in appropriate cases may be found in a billhead or letterhead. No catalog of possible situations can be complete and the court must use common sense and commercial experience in passing upon these matters. The question always is whether the symbol was executed or adopted by the party with present intention to adopt or accept the writing.

38. "State." This is the standard definition of the term used in acts prepared by the National Conference of Commissioners on Uniform State Laws.

39. "Surety." This definition makes it clear that "surety" includes all secondary obligors, not just those whose obligation refers to the person obligated as a surety. As to the nature of secondary obligations generally, see Restatement (Third), Suretyship and Guaranty Section 1 (1996).

40. "Term." Unchanged from former Section 1–201.

41. "Unauthorized signature." Unchanged from former Section 1–201.

42. "Warehouse receipt." Derived from former Section 1–201, which was derived from Section 76(1), Uniform Sales Act; Section 1, Uniform Warehouse Receipts Act. Receipts issued by a field warehouse are included, provided the warehouseman and the depositor of the goods are different persons. The definition makes clear that the receipt must qualify as a document of title under subsection (16).

43. "Written" or "writing." Unchanged from former Section 1–201.

As amended in 2003 and 2005.

§ 1–202. Notice; Knowledge.

(a) Subject to subsection (f), a person has "notice" of a fact if the person:

(1) has actual knowledge of it;

(2) has received a notice or notification of it; or

(3) from all the facts and circumstances known to the person at the time in question, has reason to know that it exists.

(b) "Knowledge" means actual knowledge. "Knows" has a corresponding meaning.

(c) "Discover", "learn", or words of similar import refer to knowledge rather than to reason to know.

(d) A person "notifies" or "gives" a notice or notification to another person by taking such steps as may be reasonably required to inform the other person in ordinary course, whether or not the other person actually comes to know of it.

(e) Subject to subsection (f), a person "receives" a notice or notification when:

(1) it comes to that person's attention; or

(2) it is duly delivered in a form reasonable under the circumstances at the place of business through which the contract was made or at another location held out by that person as the place for receipt of such communications.

(f) Notice, knowledge, or a notice or notification received by an organization is effective for a particular transaction from the time it is brought to the attention of the individual conducting that transaction and, in any event, from the time it would have been brought to the individual's attention if the organization had exercised due diligence. An organization exercises due diligence if it maintains reasonable routines for communicating significant information to the person conducting the transaction and there is reasonable compliance with the routines. Due diligence does not require an individual acting for the organization to communicate information unless the communication is part of the individual's regular duties or the individual has reason to know of the transaction and that the transaction would be materially affected by the information.

Official Comment

Source: Derived from former Section 1–201(25)-(27).

Changes from former law: These provisions are substantive rather than purely definitional. Accordingly, they have been relocated from Section 1–201 to this section. The reference to the "forgotten notice" doctrine has been deleted.

1. Under subsection (a), a person has notice of a fact when, *inter alia*, the person has received a notification of the fact in question.

2. As provided in subsection (d), the word "notifies" is used when the essential fact is the proper dispatch of the notice, not its receipt. Compare "Send." When the essential fact is the other party's receipt of the notice, that is stated. Subsection (e) states when a notification is received.

3. Subsection (f) makes clear that notice, knowledge, or a notification, although "received," for instance, by a clerk in Department A of an organization, is effective for a transaction conducted in Department B only from the time when it was or should have been communicated to the individual conducting that transaction.

§ 1–203. Lease Distinguished From Security Interest.

(a) Whether a transaction in the form of a lease creates a lease or security interest is determined by the facts of each case.

(b) A transaction in the form of a lease creates a security interest if the consideration that the lessee is to pay the lessor for the right to possession and use of the goods is an obligation for the term of the lease and is not subject to termination by the lessee, and:

(1) the original term of the lease is equal to or greater than the remaining economic life of the goods;

(2) the lessee is bound to renew the lease for the remaining economic life of the goods or is bound to become the owner of the goods;

(3) the lessee has an option to renew the lease for the remaining economic life of the goods for no additional consideration or for nominal additional consideration upon compliance with the lease agreement; or

(4) the lessee has an option to become the owner of the goods for no additional consideration or for nominal additional consideration upon compliance with the lease agreement.

(c) A transaction in the form of a lease does not create a security interest merely because:

(1) the present value of the consideration the lessee is obligated to pay the lessor for the right to possession and use of the goods is substantially equal to or is greater than the fair market value of the goods at the time the lease is entered into;

(2) the lessee assumes risk of loss of the goods;

(3) the lessee agrees to pay, with respect to the goods, taxes, insurance, filing, recording, or registration fees, or service or maintenance costs;

(4) the lessee has an option to renew the lease or to become the owner of the goods;

(5) the lessee has an option to renew the lease for a fixed rent that is equal to or greater than the reasonably predictable fair market rent for the use of the goods for the term of the renewal at the time the option is to be performed; or

(6) the lessee has an option to become the owner of the goods for a fixed price that is equal to or greater than the reasonably predictable fair market value of the goods at the time the option is to be performed.

(d) Additional consideration is nominal if it is less than the lessee's reasonably predictable cost of performing under the lease agreement if the option is not exercised. Additional consideration is not nominal if:

(1) when the option to renew the lease is granted to the lessee, the rent is stated to be the fair market rent for the use of the goods for the term of the renewal determined at the time the option is to be performed; or

(2) when the option to become the owner of the goods is granted to the lessee, the price is stated to be the fair market value of the goods determined at the time the option is to be performed.

(e) The "remaining economic life of the goods" and "reasonably predictable" fair market rent, fair market value, or cost of performing under the lease agreement must be determined with reference to the facts and circumstances at the time the transaction is entered into.

Official Comment

Source: Former Section 1–201(37).

Changes from former law: This section is substantively identical to those portions of former Section 1–201(37) that distinguished "true" leases from security interests, except that the definition of "present value" formerly embedded in Section 1–201(37) has been placed in Section 1–201(28).

1. An interest in personal property or fixtures which secures payment or performance of an obligation is a "security interest." See Section 1–201(37). Security interests are sometimes created by transactions in the form of leases. Because it can be difficult to distinguish leases that create security interests from those that do not, this section provides rules that govern the determination of whether a transaction in the form of a lease creates a security interest.

2. One of the reasons it was decided to codify the law with respect to leases was to resolve an issue that created considerable confusion in the courts: what is a lease? The confusion existed, in part, due to the last two sentences of the definition of security interest in the 1978 Official Text of the Act, Section 1–201(37). The confusion was compounded by the rather considerable change in the federal, state and local tax laws and accounting rules as they relate to leases of goods. The answer is important because the definition of lease determines not only the rights and remedies of the parties to the lease but also those of third parties. If a transaction creates a lease and not a security interest, the lessee's interest in the goods is limited to its leasehold estate; the residual interest in the goods belongs to the lessor. This has significant implications to the lessee's creditors. "On common law theory, the lessor, since he has not parted with title, is entitled to full protection against the lessee's creditors and trustee in bankruptcy...." 1 G. Gilmore, *Security Interests in Personal Property* Section 3.6, at 76 (1965).

Under pre-UCC chattel security law there was generally no requirement that the lessor file the lease, a financing statement, or the like, to enforce the lease agreement against the lessee or any third party; the Article on Secured Transactions (Article 9) did not change the common law in that respect. Coogan, Leasing and the Uniform Commercial Code, in *Equipment Leasing—Leveraged Leasing* 681, 700 n.25, 729 n.80 (2d ed.1980). The Article on Leases (Article 2A) did not change the law in that respect, except for leases of

fixtures. Section 2A–309. An examination of the common law will not provide an adequate answer to the question of what is a lease. The definition of security interest in Section 1–201(37) of the 1978 Official Text of the Act provided that the Article on Secured Transactions (Article 9) governs security interests disguised as leases, *i.e.*, leases intended as security; however, the definition became vague and outmoded.

Lease is defined in Article 2A as a transfer of the right to possession and use of goods for a term, in return for consideration. Section 2A–103(1)(j). The definition continues by stating that the retention or creation of a security interest is not a lease. Thus, the task of sharpening the line between true leases and security interests disguised as leases continues to be a function of this Article.

This section begins where Section 1–201(35) leaves off. It draws a sharper line between leases and security interests disguised as leases to create greater certainty in commercial transactions.

Prior to enactment of the rules now codified in this section, the 1978 Official Text of Section 1–201(37) provided that whether a lease was intended as security (*i.e.*, a security interest disguised as a lease) was to be determined from the facts of each case; however, (a) the inclusion of an option to purchase did not itself make the lease one intended for security, and (b) an agreement that upon compliance with the terms of the lease the lessee would become, or had the option to become, the owner of the property for no additional consideration, or for a nominal consideration, did make the lease one intended for security.

Reference to the intent of the parties to create a lease or security interest led to unfortunate results. In discovering intent, courts relied upon factors that were thought to be more consistent with sales or loans than leases. Most of these criteria, however, were as applicable to true leases as to security interests. Examples include the typical net lease provisions, a purported lessor's lack of storage facilities or its character as a financing party rather than a dealer in goods. Accordingly, this section contains no reference to the parties' intent.

Subsections (a) and (b) were originally taken from Section 1(2) of the Uniform Conditional Sales Act (act withdrawn 1943), modified to reflect current leasing practice. Thus, reference to the case law prior to the incorporation of those concepts in this article will provide a useful source of precedent. Gilmore, *Security Law, Formalism and Article 9*, 47 Neb.L.Rev. 659, 671 (1968). Whether a transaction creates a lease or a security interest continues to be determined by the facts of each case. Subsection (b) further provides that a transaction creates a security interest if the lessee has an obligation to continue paying consideration for the term of the lease, if the obligation is not terminable by the lessee (thus correcting early statutory gloss, *e.g.*, *In re Royer's Bakery, Inc.*, 1 U.C.C. Rep.Serv. (Callaghan) 342 (Bankr.E.D.Pa.1963)) and if one of four additional tests is met. The first of these four tests, subparagraph (1), is that the original lease term is equal to or greater than the remaining economic life of the goods. The second of these tests, subparagraph (2), is that the lessee is either bound to renew the lease for the remaining economic life of the goods or to become the owner of the goods. *In re Gehrke Enters.*, 1 Bankr. 647, 651–52 (Bankr.W.D.Wis.1979). The third of these tests, subparagraph (3), is whether the lessee has an option to renew the lease for the remaining economic life of the goods for no additional consideration or for nominal additional consideration, which is defined later in this section. *In re Celeryvale Transp.*, 44 Bankr. 1007, 1014–15 (Bankr.E.D.Tenn.1984). The fourth of these tests, subparagraph (4), is whether the lessee has an option to become the owner of the goods for no additional consideration or for nominal additional consideration. All of these tests focus on economics, not the intent of the parties. *In re Berge*, 32 Bankr. 370, 371–73 (Bankr.W.D.Wis.1983).

The focus on economics is reinforced by subsection (c). It states that a transaction does not create a security interest merely because the transaction has certain characteristics listed therein. Subparagraph (1) has no statutory derivative; it states that a full payout lease does not *per se* create a security interest. *Rushton v. Shea*, 419 F.Supp. 1349, 1365 (D.Del.1976). Subparagraphs (2) and (3) provide the same regarding the provisions of the typical net lease. *Compare All–States Leasing Co. v. Ochs*, 42 Or.App. 319, 600 P.2d 899 (Ct.App.1979), *with In re Tillery*, 571 F.2d 1361 (5th Cir.1978). Subparagraph (4) restates and expands the provisions of the 1978 Official Text of Section 1–201(37) to make clear that the option can be to buy or renew. Subparagraphs (5) and (6) treat fixed price options and provide that fair market value must be determined at the time the transaction is entered into. *Compare Arnold Mach. Co. v. Balls*, 624 P.2d 678 (Utah 1981), *with Aoki v. Shepherd Mach. Co.*, 665 F.2d 941 (9th Cir.1982).

The relationship of subsection (b) to subsection (c) deserves to be explored. The fixed price purchase option provides a useful example. A fixed price purchase option in a lease does not of itself create a security interest. This is particularly true if the fixed price is equal to or greater than the reasonably predictable fair market value of the goods at the time the option is to be performed. A security interest is created only if the option price is nominal and the conditions stated in the introduction to the second paragraph of this subsection are met. There is a set of purchase options whose fixed price is less than fair market value but greater than nominal that must be determined on the facts of each case to ascertain whether the transaction in which the option is included creates a lease or a security interest.

It was possible to provide for various other permutations and combinations with respect to options to purchase and renew. For example, this section could have stated a rule to govern the facts of *In re Marhoefer Packing Co.*, 674 F.2d 1139 (7th Cir.1982). This was not done because it would unnecessarily complicate the definition. Further development of this rule is left to the courts.

Subsections (d) and (e) provide definitions and rules of construction.

§ 1–204. Value.

Except as otherwise provided in Articles 3, 4, [and] 5, [and 6], a person gives value for rights if the person acquires them:

(1) in return for a binding commitment to extend credit or for the extension of immediately available credit, whether or not drawn upon and whether or not a chargeback is provided for in the event of difficulties in collection;

(2) as security for, or in total or partial satisfaction of, a preexisting claim;

(3) by accepting delivery under a preexisting contract for purchase; or

(4) in return for any consideration sufficient to support a simple contract.

Official Comment

Source: Former Section 1–201(44).

Changes from former law: Unchanged from former Section 1–201, which was derived from Sections 25, 26, 27, 191, Uniform Negotiable Instruments Law; Section 76, Uniform Sales Act; Section 53, Uniform Bills of Lading Act; Section 58, Uniform Warehouse Receipts Act; Section 22(1), Uniform Stock Transfer Act; Section 1, Uniform Trust Receipts Act. These provisions are substantive rather than purely definitional. Accordingly, they have been relocated from former Section 1–201 to this section.

1. All the Uniform Acts in the commercial law field (except the Uniform Conditional Sales Act) have carried definitions of "value." All those definitions provided that value was any consideration sufficient to support a simple contract, including the taking of property in satisfaction of or as security for a pre-existing claim. Subsections (1), (2), and (4) in substance continue the definitions of "value" in the earlier acts. Subsection (3) makes explicit that "value" is also given in a third situation: where a buyer by taking delivery under a pre-existing contract converts a contingent into a fixed obligation.

This definition is not applicable to Articles 3 and 4, but the express inclusion of immediately available credit as value follows the separate definitions in those Articles. See Sections 4–208, 4–209, 3–303. A bank or other financing agency which in good faith makes advances against property held as collateral becomes a bona fide purchaser of that property even though provision may be made for charge-back in case of trouble. Checking credit is "immediately available" within the meaning of this section if the bank would be subject to an action for slander of credit in case checks drawn against the credit were dishonored, and when a charge-back is not discretionary with the bank, but may only be made when difficulties in collection arise in connection with the specific transaction involved.

§ 1–205. Reasonable Time; Seasonableness.

(a) Whether a time for taking an action required by [the Uniform Commercial Code] is reasonable depends on the nature, purpose, and circumstances of the action.

(b) An action is taken seasonably if it is taken at or within the time agreed or, if no time is agreed, at or within a reasonable time.

Official Comment

Source: Former Section 1–204(2)-(3).

Changes from former law: This section is derived from subsections (2) and (3) of former Section 1–204. Subsection (1) of that section is now incorporated in Section 1–302(b).

1. Subsection (a) makes it clear that requirements that actions be taken within a "reasonable" time are to be applied in the transactional context of the particular action.

2. Under subsection (b), the agreement that fixes the time need not be part of the main agreement, but may occur separately. Notice also that under the definition of "agreement" (Section 1–201) the circumstances of the transaction, including course of dealing or usages of trade or course of performance may be material. On the question what is a reasonable time these matters will often be important.

§ 1–206. Presumptions.

Whenever [the Uniform Commercial Code] creates a "presumption" with respect to a fact, or provides that a fact is "presumed," the trier of fact must find the existence of the fact unless and until evidence is introduced that supports a finding of its nonexistence.

Legislative Note: Former Section 1–206, a Statute of Frauds for sales of "kinds of personal property not otherwise covered," has been deleted. The other articles of the Uniform Commercial Code make individual determinations as to requirements for memorializing transactions within their scope, so that the primary effect of former Section 1–206 was to impose a writing requirement on sales transactions not otherwise governed by the UCC. Deletion of former Section 1–206 does not constitute a recommendation to legislatures as to whether such sales transactions should be covered by a Statute of Frauds; rather, it reflects a determination that there is no need for uniform commercial law to resolve that issue.

Official Comment

Source: Former Section 1–201(31).

Changes from former law. None, other than stylistic changes.

1. Several sections of the Uniform Commercial Code state that there is a "presumption" as to a certain fact, or that the fact is "presumed." This section, derived from the definition appearing in former Section 1–201(31), indicates the effect of those provisions on the proof process.

PART 3

TERRITORIAL APPLICABILITY AND GENERAL RULES

§ 1–301. Territorial Applicability; Parties' Power to Choose Applicable Law.*

(a) In this section:

(1) "Domestic transaction" means a transaction other than an international transaction.

(2) "International transaction" means a transaction that bears a reasonable relation to a country other than the United States.

(b) This section applies to a transaction to the extent that it is governed by another article of the [Uniform Commercial Code].

(c) Except as otherwise provided in this section:

(1) an agreement by parties to a domestic transaction that any or all of their rights and obligations are to be determined by the law of this State or of another State is effective, whether or not the transaction bears a relation to the State designated; and

(2) an agreement by parties to an international transaction that any or all of their rights and obligations are to be determined by the law of this State or of another State or country is effective, whether or not the transaction bears a relation to the State or country designated.

(d) In the absence of an agreement effective under subsection (c), and except as provided in subsections (e) and (g), the rights and obligations of the parties are determined by the law that would be selected by application of this State's conflict of laws principles.

(e) If one of the parties to a transaction is a consumer, the following rules apply:

(1) An agreement referred to in subsection (c) is not effective unless the transaction bears a reasonable relation to the State or country designated.

(2) Application of the law of the State or country determined pursuant to subsection (c) or (d) may not deprive the consumer of the

protection of any rule of law governing a matter within the scope of this section, which both is protective of consumers and may not be varied by agreement:

(A) of the State or country in which the consumer principally resides, unless subparagraph (B) applies; or

(B) if the transaction is a sale of goods, of the State or country in which the consumer both makes the contract and takes delivery of those goods, if such State or country is not the State or country in which the consumer principally resides.

(f) An agreement otherwise effective under subsection (c) is not effective to the extent that application of the law of the State or country designated would be contrary to a fundamental policy of the State or country whose law would govern in the absence of agreement under subsection (d).

(g) To the extent that [the Uniform Commercial Code] governs a transaction, if one of the following provisions of [the Uniform Commercial Code] specifies the applicable law, that provision governs and a contrary agreement is effective only to the extent permitted by the law so specified:

(1) Section 2–402;

(2) Sections 2A–105 and 2A–106;

(3) Section 4–102;

(4) Section 4A–507;

(5) Section 5–116;

[(6) Section 6–103;]

(7) Section 8–110;

(8) Sections 9–301 through 9–307.

Official Comment

Source: Former Section 1–105.

Summary of changes from former law: Section 1–301, which replaces former Section 1–105, represents

---

* Note from the Thomson-West Advisory Panel: As of May 4, 2007, of the 28 jurisdictions that have have adopted revised Article 1, only the Virgin Islands has

revised 1–301. All others have adopted some version of 1–105. For more information, *see* Uniform Laws Annotated.

a significant rethinking of choice of law issues addressed in that section. The new section reexamines both the power of parties to select the jurisdiction whose law will govern their transaction and the determination of the governing law in the absence of such selection by the parties. With respect to the power to select governing law, the draft affords greater party autonomy than former Section 1–105, but with important safeguards protecting consumer interests and fundamental policies.

Section 1–301 addresses contractual designation of governing law somewhat differently than does former Section 1–105. Former law allowed the parties to any transaction to designate a jurisdiction whose law governs if the transaction bears a "reasonable relation" to that jurisdiction. Section 1–301 deviates from this approach by providing different rules for transactions involving a consumer than for non-consumer transactions, such as "business to business" transactions.

In the context of consumer transactions, the language of Section 1–301, unlike that of former Section 1–105, protects consumers against the possibility of losing the protection of consumer protection rules applicable to the aspects of the transaction governed by the Uniform Commercial Code. In most situations, the relevant consumer protection rules will be those of the consumer's home jurisdiction. A special rule, however, is provided for certain face-to-face sales transactions. (See Comment 3.)

In the context of business-to-business transactions, Section 1–301 generally provides the parties with greater autonomy to designate a jurisdiction whose law will govern than did former Section 1–105, but also provides safeguards against abuse that did not appear in former Section 1–105. In the non-consumer context, following emerging international norms, greater autonomy is provided in subsections (c)(1) and (c)(2) by deleting the former requirement that the transaction bear a "reasonable relation" to the jurisdiction. In the case of wholly domestic transactions, however, the jurisdiction designated must be a State. (See Comment 4.)

An important safeguard not present in former Section 1–105 is found in subsection (f). Subsection (f) provides that the designation of a jurisdiction's law is not effective (even if the transaction bears a reasonable relation to that jurisdiction) to the extent that application of that law would be contrary to a fundamental policy of the jurisdiction whose law would govern in the absence of contractual designation. Application of the law designated may be contrary to a fundamental policy of the State or country whose law would otherwise govern either because of the nature of the law designated or because of the "mandatory" nature of the law that would otherwise apply. (See Comment 6.)

In the absence of an effective contractual designation of governing law, former Section 1–105(1) directed the forum to apply its own law if the transaction bore "an appropriate relation to this state." This direction, however, was frequently ignored by courts. Section 1–301(d) provides that, in the absence of an effective contractual designation, the forum should apply the forum's general choice of law principles, subject to certain special rules in consumer transactions. (See Comments 3 and 7).

1. *Applicability of section.* This section is neither a complete restatement of choice of law principles nor a free-standing choice of law statute. Rather, it is a provision of Article 1 of the Uniform Commercial Code. As such, the scope of its application is limited in two significant ways.

First, this section is subject to Section 1–102, which states the scope of Article 1. As that section indicates, Article 1, and the rules contained therein, apply to transactions to the extent that they are governed by one of the other Articles of the Uniform Commercial Code. Thus, this section does not apply to matters outside the scope of the Uniform Commercial Code, such as a services contract, a credit card agreement, or a contract for the sale of real estate. This limitation was implicit in former Section 1–105, and is made explicit in Section 1–301(b).

Second, subsection (g) provides that this section is subject to the specific choice of law provisions contained in other Articles of the Uniform Commercial Code. Thus, to the extent that a transaction otherwise within the scope of this section also is within the scope of one of those provisions, the rules of that specific provision, rather than of this section, apply.

The following cases illustrate these two limitations on the scope of Section 1–301:

Example 1: A, a resident of Indiana, enters into an agreement with Credit Card Company, a Delaware corporation with its chief executive office located in New York, pursuant to which A agrees to pay Credit Card Company for purchases charged to A's credit card. The agreement contains a provision stating that it is governed by the law of South Dakota. The choice of law rules in Section 1–301 do not apply to this agreement because the agreement is not governed by any of the other Articles of the Uniform Commercial Code.

Example 2: A, a resident of Indiana, maintains a checking account with Bank B, an Ohio banking corporation located in Ohio. At the time that the account was established, Bank B and A entered into a "Bank–Customer Agreement" governing their relationship with respect to the account. The Bank–Customer Agreement contains some provisions that purport to limit the liability of Bank B with respect to its decisions whether to honor or dishonor checks purporting to be drawn on A's account. The Bank–Customer Agreement also contains a provision stating that it is governed by the law of Ohio. The provisions purporting to limit the liability of Bank B deal with issues governed by Article 4. Therefore, determination of the law applicable to those issues (including determination of the effectiveness of the choice of law clause as it applies to those issues) is within the scope of Section 1–301 as provided in subsection (b). Nonetheless, the rules of Section 1–301 would not apply to that determination because of subsection (g), which states that the choice of law rules in Section 4–102 govern instead.

2. *Contractual choice of law.* This section allows parties broad autonomy, subject to several important limitations, to select the law governing their transaction, even if the transaction does not bear a relation to the State or country whose law is selected. This recognition of party autonomy with respect to governing law has already been established in several Articles of the Uniform Commercial Code (see Sections 4A–507, 5–116, and 8–110) and is consistent with international norms. See, e.g., Inter–American Convention on the Law Applicable to International Contracts, Article 7 (Mexico City 1994); Convention on the Law Applicable to Contracts for the International Sale of Goods, Article 7(1) (The Hague 1986); EC Convention on the Law Applicable to Contractual Obligations, Article 3(1) (Rome 1980).

There are three important limitations on this party autonomy to select governing law. First, a different, and more protective, rule applies in the context of consumer transactions. (See Comment 3). Second, in an entirely domestic transaction, this section does not validate the selection of foreign law. (See Comment 4.) Third, contractual choice of law will not be given effect to the extent that application of the law designated would be contrary to a fundamental policy of the State or country whose law would be applied in the absence of such contractual designation. (See Comment 6).

This Section does not address the ability of parties to designate non-legal codes such as trade codes as the set of rules governing their transaction. The power of parties to make such a designation as part of their agreement is found in the principles of Section 1–302. That Section, allowing parties broad freedom of contract to structure their relations, is adequate for this purpose. This is also the case with respect to the ability of the parties to designate recognized bodies of rules or principles applicable to commercial transactions that are promulgated by intergovernmental organizations such as UNCITRAL or UNIDROIT. See, e.g., UNIDROIT Principles of International Commercial Contracts.

3. *Consumer transactions.* If one of the parties is a consumer (as defined in Section 1–201(b)(11)), subsection (e) provides the parties less autonomy to designate the State or country whose law will govern.

First, in the case of a consumer transaction, subsection (e)(1) provides that the transaction must bear a reasonable relation to the State or country designated. Thus, the rules of subsection (c) allowing the parties to choose the law of a jurisdiction to which the transaction bears no relation do not apply to consumer transactions.

Second, subsection (e)(2) provides that application of the law of the State or country determined by the rules of this section (whether or not that State or country was designated by the parties) cannot deprive the consumer of the protection of rules of law which govern matters within the scope of Section 1–301, are protective of consumers, and are not variable by agreement. The phrase "rule of law" is intended to refer to case law as well as statutes and administrative regulations. The requirement that the rule of law be one "governing a matter within the scope of this section" means that, consistent with the scope of Section 1–301, which governs choice of law only with regard to the aspects of a transaction governed by the Uniform Commercial Code, the relevant consumer rules are those that govern those aspects of the transaction. Such rules may be found in the Uniform Commercial Code itself, as are the consumer-protective rules in Part 6 of Article 9, or in other law if that other law governs the UCC aspects of the transaction. See, for example, the rule in Section 2.403 of the Uniform Consumer Credit Code which prohibits certain sellers and lessors from taking negotiable instruments other than checks and provides that a holder is not in good faith if the holder takes a negotiable instrument with notice that it is issued in violation of that section.

With one exception (explained in the next paragraph), the rules of law the protection of which the consumer may not be deprived are those of the jurisdiction in which the consumer principally resides. The jurisdiction in which the consumer principally resides is determined at the time relevant to the particular issue involved. Thus, for example, if the issue is one related to formation of a contract, the relevant consumer protective rules are rules of the jurisdiction in which the consumer principally resided at the time the facts relevant to contract formation occurred, even if the consumer no longer principally resides in that jurisdiction at the time the dispute arises or is litigated. If, on the other hand, the issue is one relating to enforcement of obligations, then the relevant consumer protective rules are those of the jurisdiction in which the consumer principally resides at the time enforcement is sought, even if the consumer did not principally reside in that jurisdiction at the time the transaction was entered into.

In the case of a sale of goods to a consumer, in which the consumer both makes the contract and takes possession of the goods in the same jurisdiction and that jurisdiction is not the consumer's principal residence, the rule in subsection (e)(2)(B) applies. In that situation, the relevant consumer protective rules, the protection of which the consumer may not be deprived by the choice of law rules of subsections (c) and (d), are those of the State or country in which both the contract is made and the consumer takes delivery of the goods. This rule, adapted from Section 2A–106 and Article 5 of the EC Convention on the Law Applicable to Contractual Obligations, enables a seller of goods engaging in face-to-face transactions to ascertain the consumer protection rules to which those sales are subject, without the necessity of determining the principal residence of each buyer. The reference in subsection (e)(2)(B) to the State or country in which the consumer makes the contract should not be read to incorporate formalistic concepts of where the last event necessary to conclude the contract took place; rather, the intent is to identify the state in which all material steps necessary to enter into the contract were taken by the consumer.

The following examples illustrate the application of Section 1–301(e)(2) in the context of a contractual choice of law provision:

Example 3: Seller, located in State A, agrees to sell goods to Consumer, whose principal residence is in State B. The parties agree that the law of State A would govern this transaction. Seller ships the goods to Consumer in State B. An issue related to contract formation subsequently arises. Under the law of State A, that issue is governed by State A's uniform version of Article 2. Under the law of State B, that issue is governed by a non-uniform rule, protective of consumers and not variable by agreement, that brings about a different result than would occur

under the uniform version of Article 2. Under Section 1–301(e)(2)(A), the parties' agreement that the law of State A would govern their transaction cannot deprive Consumer of the protection of State B's consumer protective rule. This is the case whether State B's rule is codified in Article 2 of its Uniform Commercial Code or is found elsewhere in the law of State B.

Example 4: Same facts as Example 3, except that (i) Consumer takes all material steps necessary to enter into the agreement to purchase the goods from Seller, and takes delivery of those goods, while on vacation in State A and (ii) the parties agree that the law of State C (in which Seller's chief executive office is located) would govern their transaction. Under subsections (c)(1) and (e)(1), the designation of the law of State C as governing will be effective so long as the transaction is found to bear a reasonable relation to State C (assuming that the relevant law of State C is not contrary to a fundamental policy of the State whose law would govern in the absence of agreement), but that designation cannot deprive Consumer of the protection of any rule of State A that is within the scope of this section and is both protective of consumers and not variable by agreement. State B's consumer protective rule is not relevant because, under Section 1–301(e)(2)(B), the relevant consumer protective rules are those of the jurisdiction in which the consumer both made the contract and took delivery of the goods–here, State A–rather than those of the jurisdiction in which the consumer principally resides.

It is important to note that subsection (e)(2) applies to all determinations of applicable law in transactions in which one party is a consumer, whether that determination is made under subsection (c) (in cases in which the parties have designated the governing law in their agreement) or subsection (d) (in cases in which the parties have not made such a designation). In the latter situation, application of the otherwise-applicable conflict of laws principles of the forum might lead to application of the laws of a State or country other than that of the consumer's principal residence. In such a case, however, subsection (e)(2) applies to preserve the applicability of consumer protection rules for the benefit of the consumer as described above.

4. *Wholly domestic transactions.* While this Section provides parties broad autonomy to select governing law, that autonomy is limited in the case of wholly domestic transactions. In a "domestic transaction," subsection (c)(1) validates only the designation of the law of a State. A "domestic transaction" is a transac-

tion that does not bear a reasonable relation to a country other than the United States. (See subsection (a)). Thus, in a wholly domestic non-consumer transaction, parties may (subject to the limitations set out in subsections (f) and (g)) designate the law of any State but not the law of a foreign country.

5. *International transactions.* This section provides greater autonomy in the context of international transactions. As defined in subsection (a)(2), a transaction is an "international transaction" if it bears a reasonable relation to a country other than the United States. In a non-consumer international transaction, subsection (c)(2) provides that a designation of the law of any State or country is effective (subject, of course, to the limitations set out in subsections (f) and (g)). It is important to note that the transaction need not bear a relation to the State or country designated if the transaction is international. Thus, for example, in a non-consumer lease of goods in which the lessor is located in Mexico and the lessee is located in Louisiana, a designation of the law of Ireland to govern the transaction would be given effect under this section even though the transaction bears no relation to Ireland. The ability to designate the law of any country in non-consumer international transactions is important in light of the common practice in many commercial contexts of designating the law of a "neutral" jurisdiction or of a jurisdiction whose law is well-developed. If a country has two or more territorial units in which different systems of law relating to matters within the scope of this section are applicable (as is the case, for example, in Canada and the United Kingdom), subsection (c)(2) should be applied to designation by the parties of the law of one of those territorial units. Thus, for example, subsection (c)(2) should be applied if the parties to a non-consumer international transaction designate the laws of Ontario or Scotland as governing their transaction.

6. *Fundamental policy.* Subsection (f) provides that an agreement designating the governing law will not be given effect to the extent that application of the designated law would be contrary to a fundamental policy of the State or country whose law would otherwise govern. This rule provides a narrow exception to the broad autonomy afforded to parties in subsection (c). One of the prime objectives of contract law is to protect the justified expectations of the parties and to make it possible for them to foretell with accuracy what will be their rights and liabilities under the contract. In this way, certainty and predictability of result are most likely to be secured. See Restatement (Second) Conflict of Laws, Section 187, comment *e.*

Under the fundamental policy doctrine, a court should not refrain from applying the designated law merely because application of that law would lead to a result different than would be obtained under the local law of the State or country whose law would otherwise govern. Rather, the difference must be contrary to a public policy of that jurisdiction that is so substantial that it justifies overriding the concerns for certainty and predictability underlying modern commercial law as well as concerns for judicial economy generally. Thus, application of the designated law will rarely be found to be contrary to a fundamental policy of the State or country whose law would otherwise govern when the difference between the two concerns a requirement, such as a statute of frauds, that relates to formalities, or general rules of contract law, such as those concerned with the need for consideration.

The opinion of Judge Cardozo in *Loucks v. Standard Oil Co. of New York*, 120 N.E. 198 (1918), regarding the related issue of when a state court may decline to apply the law of another state, is a helpful touchstone here:

Our own scheme of legislation may be different. We may even have no legislation on the subject. That is not enough to show that public policy forbids us to enforce the foreign right. A right of action is property. If a foreign statute gives the right, the mere fact that we do not give a like right is no reason for refusing to help the plaintiff in getting what belongs to him. We are not so provincial as to say that every solution of a problem is wrong because we deal with it otherwise at home. Similarity of legislation has indeed this importance; its presence shows beyond question that the foreign statute does not offend the local policy. But its absence does not prove the contrary. It is not to be exalted into an indispensable condition. The misleading word "comity" has been responsible for much of the trouble. It has been fertile in suggesting a discretion unregulated by general principles.

* * *

The courts are not free to refuse to enforce a foreign right at the pleasure of the judges, to suit the individual notion of expediency or fairness. They do not close their doors, unless help would violate some fundamental principle of justice, some prevalent conception of good morals, some deep-rooted tradition of the common weal.

120 N.E. at 201–02 (citations to authorities omitted).

Application of the designated law may be contrary to a fundamental policy of the State or country whose law would otherwise govern either (i) because the substance of the designated law violates a fundamental principle of justice of that State or country or (ii) because it differs from a rule of that State or country that is "mandatory" in that it *must* be applied in the courts of that State or country without regard to otherwise-applicable choice of law rules of that State or country and without regard to whether the designated law is otherwise offensive. The mandatory rules concept appears in international conventions in this field, *e.g.*, EC Convention on the Law Applicable to Contractual Obligations, although in some cases the concept is applied to authorize the *forum* state to apply *its* mandatory rules, rather than those of the State or country whose law would otherwise govern. The latter situation is not addressed by this section. (See Comment 9.)

It is obvious that a rule that is freely changeable by agreement of the parties under the law of the State or country whose law would otherwise govern cannot be construed as a mandatory rule of that State or country. This does not mean, however, that rules that cannot be changed by agreement under that law are, for that reason alone, mandatory rules. Otherwise, contractual choice of law in the context of the Uniform Commercial Code would be illusory and redundant; the parties would be able to accomplish by choice of law no more than can be accomplished under Section 1–302, which allows variation of otherwise applicable rules by agreement. (Under Section 1–302, the parties could agree to vary the rules that would otherwise govern their transaction by substituting for those rules the rules that would apply if the transaction were governed by the law of the designated State or country without designation of governing law.) Indeed, other than cases in which a mandatory choice of law rule is established by statute (see, *e.g.*, Sections 9–301 through 9–307, explicitly preserved in subsection (g)), cases in which courts have declined to follow the designated law solely because a rule of the State or country whose law would otherwise govern is mandatory are rare.

7. *Choice of law in the absence of contractual designation.* Subsection (d), which replaces the second sentence of former Section 1–105(1), determines which jurisdiction's law governs a transaction in the absence of an effective contractual choice by the parties. Former Section 1–105(1) provided that the law of the forum (*i.e.*, the Uniform Commercial Code) applied if the transaction bore "an appropriate relation to this state." By using an "appropriate relation" test, rather than, for example, a "most significant relationship" test, Section 1–105(1) expressed a bias in favor of applying the forum's law. This bias, while not universally respected by the courts, was justifiable in light of the uncertainty that existed at the time of drafting as to whether the Uniform Commercial Code would be

adopted by all the states; the pro-forum bias would assure that the Uniform Commercial Code would be applied so long as the transaction bore an "appropriate" relation to the forum. Inasmuch as the Uniform Commercial Code has been adopted, at least in part, in all U.S. jurisdictions, the vitality of this point is minimal in the domestic context, and international comity concerns militate against continuing the pro-forum, pro-UCC bias in transnational transactions. Whether the choice is between the law of two jurisdictions that have adopted the Uniform Commercial Code, but whose law differs (because of differences in enacted language or differing judicial interpretations), or between the Uniform Commercial Code and the law of another country, there is no strong justification for directing a court to apply different choice of law principles to that determination than it would apply if the matter were not governed by the Uniform Commercial Code. Similarly, given the variety of choice of law principles applied by the states, it would not be prudent to designate only one such principle as the proper one for transactions governed by the Uniform Commercial Code. Accordingly, in cases in which the parties have not made an effective choice of law, Section 1–301(d) simply directs the forum to apply its ordinary choice of law principles to determine which jurisdiction's law governs, subject to the special rules of Section 1–301(e)(2) with regard to consumer transactions.

8. *Primacy of other Uniform Commercial Code choice of law rules.* Subsection (g), which is essentially identical to former Section 1–105(2), indicates that choice of law rules provided in the other Articles govern when applicable.

9. *Matters not addressed by this section.* As noted in Comment 1, this section is not a complete statement of conflict of laws doctrines applicable in commercial cases. Among the issues this section does not address, and leaves to other law, three in particular deserve mention. First, a forum will occasionally decline to apply the law of a different jurisdiction selected by the parties when application of that law would be contrary to a fundamental policy of the forum jurisdiction, even if it would not be contrary to a fundamental policy of the State or country whose law would govern in the absence of contractual designation. Standards for application of this doctrine relate primarily to concepts of sovereignty rather than commercial law and are thus left to the courts. Second, in determining whether to give effect to the parties' agreement that the law of a particular State or country will govern their relationship, courts must, of necessity, address some issues as to the basic validity of that agreement. These issues might relate, for example, to capacity to contract and

absence of duress. This section does not address these issues. Third, this section leaves to other choice of law principles of the forum the issues of whether, and to what extent, the forum will apply the same law to the non-UCC aspects of a transaction that it applies to the aspects of the transaction governed by the Uniform Commercial Code.

§ 1–302. Variation by Agreement.

(a) Except as otherwise provided in subsection (b) or elsewhere in [the Uniform Commercial Code], the effect of provisions of [the Uniform Commercial Code] may be varied by agreement.

(b) The obligations of good faith, diligence, reasonableness, and care prescribed by [the Uniform Commercial Code] may not be disclaimed by agreement. The parties, by agreement, may determine the standards by which the performance of those obligations is to be measured if those standards are not manifestly unreasonable. Whenever [the Uniform Commercial Code] requires an action to be taken within a reasonable time, a time that is not manifestly unreasonable may be fixed by agreement.

(c) The presence in certain provisions of [the Uniform Commercial Code] of the phrase "unless otherwise agreed", or words of similar import, does not imply that the effect of other provisions may not be varied by agreement under this section.

Official Comment

Source: Former Sections 1–102(3)-(4) and 1–204(1).

Changes: This section combines the rules from subsections (3) and (4) of former Section 1–102 and subsection (1) of former Section 1–204. No substantive changes are made.

1. Subsection (a) states affirmatively at the outset that freedom of contract is a principle of the Uniform Commercial Code: "the effect" of its provisions may be varied by "agreement." The meaning of the statute itself must be found in its text, including its definitions, and in appropriate extrinsic aids; it cannot be varied by agreement. But the Uniform Commercial Code seeks to avoid the type of interference with evolutionary growth found in pre-Code cases such as *Manhattan Co. v. Morgan*, 242 N.Y. 38, 150 N.E. 594 (1926). Thus, private parties cannot make an instrument negotiable within the meaning of Article 3 except as provided in Section 3–104; nor can they change the meaning of such terms as "bona fide purchaser,"

"holder in due course," or "due negotiation," as used in the Uniform Commercial Code. But an agreement can change the legal consequences that would otherwise flow from the provisions of the Uniform Commercial Code. "Agreement" here includes the effect given to course of dealing, usage of trade and course of performance by Sections 1–201 and 1–303; the effect of an agreement on the rights of third parties is left to specific provisions of the Uniform Commercial Code and to supplementary principles applicable under Section 1–103. The rights of third parties under Section 9–317 when a security interest is unperfected, for example, cannot be destroyed by a clause in the security agreement.

This principle of freedom of contract is subject to specific exceptions found elsewhere in the Uniform Commercial Code and to the general exception stated here. The specific exceptions vary in explicitness: the statute of frauds found in Section 2–201, for example, does not explicitly preclude oral waiver of the requirement of a writing, but a fair reading denies enforcement to such a waiver as part of the "contract" made unenforceable; Section 9–602, on the other hand, is a quite explicit limitation on freedom of contract. Under the exception for "the obligations of good faith, diligence, reasonableness and care prescribed by [the Uniform Commercial Code]," provisions of the Uniform Commercial Code prescribing such obligations are not to be disclaimed. However, the section also recognizes the prevailing practice of having agreements set forth standards by which due diligence is measured and explicitly provides that, in the absence of a showing that the standards manifestly are unreasonable, the agreement controls. In this connection, Section 1–303 incorporating into the agreement prior course of dealing and usages of trade is of particular importance.

Subsection (b) also recognizes that nothing is stronger evidence of a reasonable time than the fixing of such time by a fair agreement between the parties. However, provision is made for disregarding a clause which whether by inadvertence or overreaching fixes a time so unreasonable that it amounts to eliminating all remedy under the contract. The parties are not required to fix the most reasonable time but may fix any time which is not obviously unfair as judged by the time of contracting.

2. An agreement that varies the effect of provisions of the Uniform Commercial Code may do so by stating the rules that will govern in lieu of the provisions varied. Alternatively, the parties may vary the effect of such provisions by stating that their relationship will be governed by recognized bodies of rules or principles applicable to commercial transactions. Such bodies of

rules or principles may include, for example, those that are promulgated by intergovernmental authorities such as UNCITRAL or UNIDROIT (*see, e.g.*, UNIDROIT Principles of International Commercial Contracts), or non-legal codes such as trade codes.

3. Subsection (c) is intended to make it clear that, as a matter of drafting, phrases such as "unless otherwise agreed" have been used to avoid controversy as to whether the subject matter of a particular section does or does not fall within the exceptions to subsection (b), but absence of such words contains no negative implication since under subsection (b) the general and residual rule is that the effect of all provisions of the Uniform Commercial Code may be varied by agreement.

§ 1–303. Course of Performance, Course of Dealing, and Usage of Trade.

(a) A "course of performance" is a sequence of conduct between the parties to a particular transaction that exists if:

(1) the agreement of the parties with respect to the transaction involves repeated occasions for performance by a party; and

(2) the other party, with knowledge of the nature of the performance and opportunity for objection to it, accepts the performance or acquiesces in it without objection.

(b) A "course of dealing" is a sequence of conduct concerning previous transactions between the parties to a particular transaction that is fairly to be regarded as establishing a common basis of understanding for interpreting their expressions and other conduct.

(c) A "usage of trade" is any practice or method of dealing having such regularity of observance in a place, vocation, or trade as to justify an expectation that it will be observed with respect to the transaction in question. The existence and scope of such a usage must be proved as facts. If it is established that such a usage is embodied in a trade code or similar record, the interpretation of the record is a question of law.

(d) A course of performance or course of dealing between the parties or usage of trade in the vocation or trade in which they are engaged or of which they are or should be aware is relevant in ascertaining the meaning of the parties' agreement, may give particular meaning to specific terms of the agreement, and may supplement or qualify the terms of the agreement. A usage of trade applicable in the place in which part of the performance under the agreement is to occur may be so utilized as to that part of the performance.

(e) Except as otherwise provided in subsection (f), the express terms of an agreement and any applicable course of performance, course of dealing, or usage of trade must be construed whenever reasonable as consistent with each other. If such a construction is unreasonable:

(1) express terms prevail over course of performance, course of dealing, and usage of trade;

(2) course of performance prevails over course of dealing and usage of trade; and

(3) course of dealing prevails over usage of trade.

(f) Subject to Section 2–209 and Section 2A–208, a course of performance is relevant to show a waiver or modification of any term inconsistent with the course of performance.

(g) Evidence of a relevant usage of trade offered by one party is not admissible unless that party has given the other party notice that the court finds sufficient to prevent unfair surprise to the other party.

Official Comment

Source: Former Sections 1–205, 2–208, and Section 2A–207.

Changes from former law: This section integrates the "course of performance" concept from Articles 2 and 2A into the principles of former Section 1–205, which deals with course of dealing and usage of trade. In so doing, the section slightly modifies the articulation of the course of performance rules to fit more comfortably with the approach and structure of former Section 1–205. There are also slight modifications to be more consistent with the definition of "agreement" in former Section 1–201(3). It should be noted that a course of performance that might otherwise establish a defense to the obligation of a party to a negotiable instrument is not available as a defense against a holder in due course who took the instrument without notice of that course of performance.

1. The Uniform Commercial Code rejects both the "lay-dictionary" and the "conveyancer's" reading of a commercial agreement. Instead the meaning of the agreement of the parties is to be determined by the language used by them and by their action, read and

interpreted in the light of commercial practices and other surrounding circumstances. The measure and background for interpretation are set by the commercial context, which may explain and supplement even the language of a formal or final writing.

2. "Course of dealing," as defined in subsection (b), is restricted, literally, to a sequence of conduct between the parties previous to the agreement. A sequence of conduct after or under the agreement, however, is a "course of performance." "Course of dealing" may enter the agreement either by explicit provisions of the agreement or by tacit recognition.

3. The Uniform Commercial Code deals with "usage of trade" as a factor in reaching the commercial meaning of the agreement that the parties have made. The language used is to be interpreted as meaning what it may fairly be expected to mean to parties involved in the particular commercial transaction in a given locality or in a given vocation or trade. By adopting in this context the term "usage of trade," the Uniform Commercial Code expresses its intent to reject those cases which see evidence of "custom" as representing an effort to displace or negate "established rules of law." A distinction is to be drawn between mandatory rules of law such as the Statute of Frauds provisions of Article 2 on Sales whose very office is to control and restrict the actions of the parties, and which cannot be abrogated by agreement, or by a usage of trade, and those rules of law (such as those in Part 3 of Article 2 on Sales) which fill in points which the parties have not considered and in fact agreed upon. The latter rules hold "unless otherwise agreed" but yield to the contrary agreement of the parties. Part of the agreement of the parties to which such rules yield is to be sought for in the usages of trade which furnish the background and give particular meaning to the language used, and are the framework of common understanding controlling any general rules of law which hold only when there is no such understanding.

4. A usage of trade under subsection (c) must have the "regularity of observance" specified. The ancient English tests for "custom" are abandoned in this connection. Therefore, it is not required that a usage of trade be "ancient or immemorial," "universal," or the like. Under the requirement of subsection (c) full recognition is thus available for new usages and for usages currently observed by the great majority of decent dealers, even though dissidents ready to cut corners do not agree. There is room also for proper recognition of usage agreed upon by merchants in trade codes.

5. The policies of the Uniform Commercial Code controlling explicit unconscionable contracts and clauses (Sections 1-304, 2-302) apply to implicit clauses that rest on usage of trade and carry forward the policy underlying the ancient requirement that a custom or usage must be "reasonable." However, the emphasis is shifted. The very fact of commercial acceptance makes out a *prima facie* case that the usage is reasonable, and the burden is no longer on the usage to establish itself as being reasonable. But the anciently established policing of usage by the courts is continued to the extent necessary to cope with the situation arising if an unconscionable or dishonest practice should become standard.

6. Subsection (d), giving the prescribed effect to usages of which the parties "are or should be aware," reinforces the provision of subsection (c) requiring not universality but only the described "regularity of observance" of the practice or method. This subsection also reinforces the point of subsection (c) that such usages may be either general to trade or particular to a special branch of trade.

7. Although the definition of "agreement" in Section 1-201 includes the elements of course of performance, course of dealing, and usage of trade, the fact that express reference is made in some sections to those elements is not to be construed as carrying a contrary intent or implication elsewhere. Compare Section 1-302(c).

8. In cases of a well established line of usage varying from the general rules of the Uniform Commercial Code where the precise amount of the variation has not been worked out into a single standard, the party relying on the usage is entitled, in any event, to the minimum variation demonstrated. The whole is not to be disregarded because no particular line of detail has been established. In case a dominant pattern has been fairly evidenced, the party relying on the usage is entitled under this section to go to the trier of fact on the question of whether such dominant pattern has been incorporated into the agreement.

9. Subsection (g) is intended to insure that this Act's liberal recognition of the needs of commerce in regard to usage of trade shall not be made into an instrument of abuse.

§ 1-304. Obligation of Good Faith.

Every contract or duty within [the Uniform Commercial Code] imposes an obligation of good faith in its performance and enforcement.

Official Comment

Source: Former Section 1-203.

Changes from former law: Except for changing the form of reference to the Uniform Commercial Code, this section is identical to former Section 1–203.

1. This section sets forth a basic principle running throughout the Uniform Commercial Code. The principle is that in commercial transactions good faith is required in the performance and enforcement of all agreements or duties. While this duty is explicitly stated in some provisions of the Uniform Commercial Code, the applicability of the duty is broader than merely these situations and applies generally, as stated in this section, to the performance or enforcement of every contract or duty within this Act. It is further implemented by Section 1–303 on course of dealing, course of performance, and usage of trade. This section does not support an independent cause of action for failure to perform or enforce in good faith. Rather, this section means that a failure to perform or enforce, in good faith, a specific duty or obligation under the contract, constitutes a breach of that contract or makes unavailable, under the particular circumstances, a remedial right or power. This distinction makes it clear that the doctrine of good faith merely directs a court towards interpreting contracts within the commercial context in which they are created, performed, and enforced, and does not create a separate duty of fairness and reasonableness which can be independently breached.

2. "Performance and enforcement" of contracts and duties within the Uniform Commercial Code include the exercise of rights created by the Uniform Commercial Code.

§ 1–305. Remedies to Be Liberally Administered.

(a) The remedies provided by [the Uniform Commercial Code] must be liberally administered to the end that the aggrieved party may be put in as good a position as if the other party had fully performed but neither consequential or special damages nor penal damages may be had except as specifically provided in [the Uniform Commercial Code] or by other rule of law.

(b) Any right or obligation declared by [the Uniform Commercial Code] is enforceable by action unless the provision declaring it specifies a different and limited effect.

Official Comment

Source: Former Section 1–106.

Changes from former law: Other than changes in the form of reference to the Uniform Commercial Code, this section is identical to former Section 1–106.

1. Subsection (a) is intended to effect three propositions. The first is to negate the possibility of unduly narrow or technical interpretation of remedial provisions by providing that the remedies in the Uniform Commercial Code are to be liberally administered to the end stated in this section. The second is to make it clear that compensatory damages are limited to compensation. They do not include consequential or special damages, or penal damages; and the Uniform Commercial Code elsewhere makes it clear that damages must be minimized. Cf. Sections 1–304, 2–706(1), and 2–712(2). The third purpose of subsection (a) is to reject any doctrine that damages must be calculable with mathematical accuracy. Compensatory damages are often at best approximate: they have to be proved with whatever definiteness and accuracy the facts permit, but no more. Cf. Section 2–204(3).

2. Under subsection (b), any right or obligation described in the Uniform Commercial Code is enforceable by action, even though no remedy may be expressly provided, unless a particular provision specifies a different and limited effect. Whether specific performance or other equitable relief is available is determined not by this section but by specific provisions and by supplementary principles. Cf. Sections 1–103, 2–716.

3. "Consequential" or "special" damages and "penal" damages are not defined in the Uniform Commercial Code; rather, these terms are used in the sense in which they are used outside the Uniform Commercial Code.

§ 1–306. Waiver or Renunciation of Claim or Right After Breach.

A claim or right arising out of an alleged breach may be discharged in whole or in part without consideration by agreement of the aggrieved party in an authenticated record.

Official Comment

Source: Former Section 1–107.

Changes from former law: This section changes former law in two respects. First, former Section 1–107, requiring the "delivery" of a "written waiver or renunciation" merges the separate concepts of the aggrieved party's agreement to forego rights and the manifestation of that agreement. This section separates those concepts, and explicitly requires *agreement* of the aggrieved party. Second, the revised section reflects developments in electronic commerce by providing for memorialization in an authenticated record. In this context, a party may "authenticate" a record by (i) signing a record that is a writing or (ii) attaching to or logically associating with a record that is not a writing an electronic sound, symbol or process with the present intent to adopt or accept the record. See Sections 1–201(b)(37) and 9–102(a)(7).

1. This section makes consideration unnecessary to the effective renunciation or waiver of rights or claims arising out of an alleged breach of a commercial contract where the agreement effecting such renunciation is memorialized in a record authenticated by the aggrieved party. Its provisions, however, must be read in conjunction with the section imposing an obligation of good faith. (Section 1–304).

§ 1–307. Prima Facie Evidence by Third–Party Documents.

A document in due form purporting to be a bill of lading, policy or certificate of insurance, official weigher's or inspector's certificate, consular invoice, or any other document authorized or required by the contract to be issued by a third party is prima facie evidence of its own authenticity and genuineness and of the facts stated in the document by the third party.

Official Comment

Source: Former Section 1–202.

Changes from former law: Except for minor stylistic changes, this Section is identical to former Section 1–202.

1. This section supplies judicial recognition for documents that are relied upon as trustworthy by commercial parties.

2. This section is concerned only with documents that have been given a preferred status by the parties themselves who have required their procurement in the agreement, and for this reason the applicability of the section is limited to actions arising out of the contract that authorized or required the document. The list of documents is intended to be illustrative and not exclusive.

3. The provisions of this section go no further than establishing the documents in question as prima facie evidence and leave to the court the ultimate determination of the facts where the accuracy or authenticity of the documents is questioned. In this connection the section calls for a commercially reasonable interpretation.

4. Documents governed by this section need not be writings if records in another medium are generally relied upon in the context.

§ 1–308. Performance or Acceptance Under Reservation of Rights.

(a) A party that with explicit reservation of rights performs or promises performance or assents to performance in a manner demanded or offered by the other party does not thereby prejudice the rights reserved. Such words as "without prejudice," "under protest," or the like are sufficient.

(b) Subsection (a) does not apply to an accord and satisfaction.

Official Comment

Source: Former Section 1–207.

Changes from former law: This section is identical to former Section 1–207.

1. This section provides machinery for the continuation of performance along the lines contemplated by the contract despite a pending dispute, by adopting the mercantile device of going ahead with delivery, acceptance, or payment "without prejudice," "under protest," "under reserve," "with reservation of all our rights," and the like. All of these phrases completely reserve all rights within the meaning of this section. The section therefore contemplates that limited as well as general reservations and acceptance by a party may be made "subject to satisfaction of our purchaser," "subject to acceptance by our customers," or the like.

2. This section does not add any new requirement of language of reservation where not already required by law, but merely provides a specific measure on which a party can rely as that party makes or concurs in any interim adjustment in the course of performance. It does not affect or impair the provisions of this Act such as those under which the buyer's remedies for defect survive acceptance without being expressly claimed if notice of the defects is given within a reasonable time. Nor does it disturb the policy of those cases which restrict the effect of a waiver of a defect to reasonable limits under the circumstances, even though no such reservation is expressed.

The section is not addressed to the creation or loss of remedies in the ordinary course of performance but rather to a method of procedure where one party is claiming as of right something which the other believes to be unwarranted.

3. Subsection (b) states that this section does not apply to an accord and satisfaction. Section 3–311 governs if an accord and satisfaction is attempted by tender of a negotiable instrument as stated in that section. If Section 3–311 does not apply, the issue of whether an accord and satisfaction has been effected is determined by the law of contract. Whether or not Section 3–311 applies, this section has no application to an accord and satisfaction.

§ 1–309.   Option to Accelerate at Will.

A term providing that one party or that party's successor in interest may accelerate payment or performance or require collateral or additional collateral "at will" or when the party "deems itself insecure," or words of similar import, means that the party has power to do so only if that party in good faith believes that the prospect of payment or performance is impaired. The burden of establishing lack of good faith is on the party against which the power has been exercised.

Official Comment

Source: Former Section 1–208.

Changes from former law: Except for minor stylistic changes, this section is identical to former Section 1–208.

1. The common use of acceleration clauses in many transactions governed by the Uniform Commercial Code, including sales of goods on credit, notes payable at a definite time, and secured transactions, raises an issue as to the effect to be given to a clause that seemingly grants the power to accelerate at the whim and caprice of one party. This section is intended to make clear that despite language that might be so construed and which further might be held to make the agreement void as against public policy or to make the contract illusory or too indefinite for enforcement, the option is to be exercised only in the good faith belief that the prospect of payment or performance is impaired.

Obviously this section has no application to demand instruments or obligations whose very nature permits call at any time with or without reason. This section applies only to an obligation of payment or performance which in the first instance is due at a future date.

§ 1–310.   Subordinated Obligations.

An obligation may be issued as subordinated to performance of another obligation of the person obligated, or a creditor may subordinate its right to performance of an obligation by agreement with either the person obligated or another creditor of the person obligated. Subordination does not create a security interest as against either the common debtor or a subordinated creditor.

Official Comment

Source: Former Section 1–209.

Changes from former law: This section is substantively identical to former Section 1–209. The language in that section stating that it "shall be construed as declaring the law as it existed prior to the enactment of this section and not as modifying it" has been deleted.

1. Billions of dollars of subordinated debt are held by the public and by institutional investors. Commonly, the subordinated debt is subordinated on issue or acquisition and is evidenced by an investment security or by a negotiable or non-negotiable note. Debt is also sometimes subordinated after it arises, either by agreement between the subordinating creditor and the debtor, by agreement between two creditors of the same debtor, or by agreement of all three parties. The subordinated creditor may be a stockholder or other "insider" interested in the common debtor; the subordinated debt may consist of accounts or other rights to payment not evidenced by any instrument. All such cases are included in the terms "subordinated obligation," "subordination," and "subordinated creditor."

2. Subordination agreements are enforceable between the parties as contracts; and in the bankruptcy of the common debtor dividends otherwise payable to the subordinated creditor are turned over to the superior creditor. This "turn-over" practice has on occasion been explained in terms of "equitable lien," "equitable assignment," or "constructive trust," but whatever the label the practice is essentially an equitable remedy and does not mean that there is a transaction "that creates a security interest in personal property ... by contract" or a "sale of accounts, chattel paper, payment intangibles, or promissory notes" within the meaning of Section 9–109. On the other hand, nothing in this section prevents one creditor from assigning his rights to another creditor of the same debtor in such a way as to create a security interest within Article 9, where the parties so intend.

3. The enforcement of subordination agreements is largely left to supplementary principles under Section 1–103. If the subordinated debt is evidenced by a certificated security, Section 8–202(a) authorizes en-

forcement against purchasers on terms stated or referred to on the security certificate. If the fact of subordination is noted on a negotiable instrument, a holder under Sections 3–302 and 3–306 is subject to the term because notice precludes him from taking free of the subordination. Sections 3–302(3)(a), 3–306, and 8–317 severely limit the rights of levying creditors of a subordinated creditor in such cases.

UCC ARTICLE 2
SALES

Pre–2001 Article 2 .... *Appendix D*
2001 amendments (Article 1 revision) .... *Appendix A*
2003 amendments .... *Appendix F*
2003 amendments (Article 7 revision) .... *Appendix B*
2005 amendments .... *Appendix J*

PART 1. SHORT TITLE, GENERAL CONSTRUCTION AND SUBJECT MATTER

Section
2–101. Short Title.
2–102. Scope; Certain Security and Other Transactions Excluded from this Article.
2–103. Definitions and Index of Definitions.
2–104. Definitions: "Merchant"; "Between Merchants"; "Financing Agency".
2–105. Definitions: Transferability; "Future" Goods; "Lot"; "Commercial Unit".
2–106. Definitions: "Contract"; "Agreement"; "Contract for Sale"; "Sale"; "Present Sale"; "Conforming" to Contract; "Termination"; "Cancellation".
2–107. Goods to Be Severed from Realty: Recording.
2–108. Transactions Subject to Other Law.

PART 2. FORM, FORMATION, TERMS AND READJUSTMENT OF CONTRACT; ELECTRONIC CONTRACTING

2–201. Formal Requirements; Statute of Frauds.
2–202. Final Expression in a Record: Parol or Extrinsic Evidence.
2–203. Seals Inoperative.
2–204. Formation in General.
2–205. Firm Offers.
2–206. Offer and Acceptance in Formation of Contract.
2–207. Terms of Contract; Effect of Confirmation.
2–208. Reserved. [Course of Performance or Practical Construction.]
2–209. Modification; Rescission and Waiver.
2–210. Delegation of Performance; Assignment of Rights.

Section
2–211. Legal Recognition of Electronic Contracts, Records, and Signatures.
2–212. Attribution.
2–213. Electronic Communication.

PART 3. GENERAL OBLIGATION AND CONSTRUCTION OF CONTRACT

2–301. General Obligations of Parties.
2–302. Unconscionable Contract or Term.
2–303. Allocation or Division of Risks.
2–304. Price Payable in Money, Goods, Realty, or Otherwise.
2–305. Open Price Term.
2–306. Output, Requirements and Exclusive Dealings.
2–307. Delivery in Single Lot or Several.
2–308. Absence of Specified Place for Delivery.
2–309. Absence of Specific Time Provisions; Notice of Termination.
2–310. Open Time for Payment or Running of Credit; Authority to Ship under Reservation.
2–311. Options and Cooperation Respecting Performance.
2–312. Warranty of Title and Against Infringement; Buyer's Obligation Against Infringement.
2–313. Express Warranties by Affirmation, Promise, Description, Sample; Remedial Promise.
2–313A. Obligation to Remote Purchaser Created by Record Packaged with or Accompanying Goods.
2–313B. Obligation to Remote Purchaser Created by Communication to the Public.
2–314. Implied Warranty: Merchantability; Usage of Trade.

Section

2–315. Implied Warranty: Fitness for Particular Purpose.

2–316. Exclusion or Modification of Warranties.

2–317. Cumulation and Conflict of Warranties Express or Implied.

2–318. Third-party Beneficiaries of Warranties and Obligations.

2–319. Reserved.

2–320. Reserved.

2–321. Reserved.

2–322. Reserved.

2–323. Reserved.

2–324. Reserved.

2–325. Failure to Pay by Agreed Letter of Credit.

2–326. Sale on Approval and Sale or Return.

2–327. Special Incidents of Sale on Approval and Sale or Return.

2–328. Sale by Auction.

PART 4. TITLE, CREDITORS, AND GOOD–FAITH PURCHASERS

2–401. Passing of Title; Reservation for Security; Limited Application of this Section.

2–402. Rights of Seller's Creditors Against Sold Goods.

2–403. Power to Transfer; Good Faith Purchase of Goods; "Entrusting".

PART 5. PERFORMANCE

2–501. Insurable Interest in Goods; Manner of Identification of Goods.

2–502. Buyer's Right to Goods on Seller's Insolvency, Repudiation, or Failure to Deliver.

2–503. Manner of Seller's Tender of Delivery.

2–504. Shipment by Seller.

2–505. Seller's Shipment under Reservation.

2–506. Rights of Financing Agency.

2–507. Effect of Seller's Tender; Delivery on Condition.

2–508. Cure by Seller of Improper Tender or Delivery; Replacement.

2–509. Risk of Loss in the Absence of Breach.

2–510. Effect of Breach on Risk of Loss.

2–511. Tender of Payment by Buyer; Payment by Check.

2–512. Payment by Buyer Before Inspection.

2–513. Buyer's Right to Inspection of Goods.

2–514. When Documents Deliverable on Acceptance; When on Payment.

2–515. Preserving Evidence of Goods in Dispute.

PART 6. BREACH, REPUDIATION, AND EXCUSE

2–601. Buyer's Rights on Improper Delivery.

2–602. Manner and Effect of Rejection.

2–603. Merchant Buyer's Duties as to Rejected Goods.

2–604. Buyer's Options as to Salvage of Rejected Goods.

2–605. Waiver of Buyer's Objections by Failure to Particularize.

2–606. What Constitutes Acceptance of Goods.

2–607. Effect of Acceptance; Notice of Breach; Burden of Establishing Breach after Acceptance; Notice of Claim or Litigation to Person Answerable Over.

2–608. Revocation of Acceptance in Whole or in Part.

2–609. Right to Adequate Assurance of Performance.

2–610. Anticipatory Repudiation.

2–611. Retraction of Anticipatory Repudiation.

2–612. "Installment Contract"; Breach.

2–613. Casualty to Identified Goods.

2–614. Substituted Performance.

2–615. Excuse by Failure of Presupposed Conditions.

2–616. Procedure on Notice Claiming Excuse.

PART 7. REMEDIES

2–701. Remedies for Breach of Collateral Contracts Not Impaired.

2–702. Seller's Remedies on Discovery of Buyer's Insolvency.

2–703. Seller's Remedies in General.

2–704. Seller's Right to Identify Goods to the Contract Notwithstanding Breach or to Salvage Unfinished Goods.

2–705. Seller's Stoppage of Delivery in Transit or Otherwise.

2–706. Seller's Resale Including Contract for Resale.

2–707. "Person in the Position of a Seller".

2–708. Seller's Damages for Nonacceptance or Repudiation.

2–709. Action for the Price.

2–710. Seller's Incidental and Consequential Damages.

2–711. Buyer's Remedies in General; Buyer's Security Interest in Rejected Goods.

2–712. "Cover"; Buyer's Procurement of Substitute Goods.

2–713. Buyer's Damages for Nondelivery or Repudiation.

Section	
2–714.	Buyer's Damages for Breach in Regard to Accepted Goods.
2–715.	Buyer's Incidental and Consequential Damages.
2–716.	Specific Performance; Buyer's Right to Replevin.
2–717.	Deduction of Damages from the Price.
2–718.	Liquidation or Limitation of Damages; Deposits.
2–719.	Contractual Modification or Limitation of Remedy.
2–720.	Effect of "Cancellation" or "Rescission" on Claims for Antecedent Breach.

Section	
2–721.	Remedies for Fraud.
2–722.	Who May Sue Third Parties for Injury to Goods.
2–723.	Proof of Market: Time and Place.
2–724.	Admissibility of Market Quotations.
2–725.	Statute of Limitations in Contracts for Sale.

PART 8. TRANSITIONAL PROVISIONS

2–801.	Effective Date.
2–802.	Amendment of Existing Article 2.
2–803.	Application to Existing Relations.
2–804.	Savings Clause.

PART 1

SHORT TITLE, GENERAL CONSTRUCTION AND SUBJECT MATTER

§ 2–101. Short Title.

This Article shall be known and may be cited as Uniform Commercial Code—Sales.

Official Comment

This Article is a complete revision and modernization of the Uniform Sales Act which was promulgated by the National Conference of Commissioners on Uniform State Laws in 1906 and has been adopted in 34 states and Alaska, the District of Columbia and Hawaii.

The coverage of the present Article is much more extensive than that of the old Sales Act and extends to the various bodies of case law which have been developed both outside of and under the latter.

The arrangement of the present Article is in terms of contract for sale and the various steps of its performance. The legal consequences are stated as following directly from the contract and action taken under it without resorting to the idea of when property or title passed or was to pass as being the determining factor. The purpose is to avoid making practical issues between practical men turn upon the location of an intangible something, the passing of which no man can prove by evidence and to substitute for such abstractions proof of words and actions of a tangible character.

§ 2–102. Scope; Certain Security and Other Transactions Excluded from this Article.

Unless the context otherwise requires, this Article applies to transactions in goods; it does not apply to any transaction which although in the form of an unconditional contract to sell or present sale is intended to operate only as a security transaction nor does this Article impair or repeal any statute regulating sales to consumers, farmers or other specified classes of buyers.

Official Comment

Prior Uniform Statutory Provision: Section 75, Uniform Sales Act.

Changes: Section 75 has been rephrased.

Purposes of Changes and New Matter: To make it clear that:

The Article leaves substantially unaffected the law relating to purchase money security such as conditional sale or chattel mortgage though it regulates the general sales aspects of such transactions. "Security transaction" is used in the same sense as in the Article on Secured Transactions (Article 9).

Cross Reference:
Article 9.

Definitional Cross References:
"Contract". Section 1–201.

ARTICLE 2 § 2–103

"Contract for sale". Section 2–106.
"Goods". Section 2–103.
"Present sale". Section 2–106.
"Sale". Section 2–106.

§ 2–103. Definitions and Index of Definitions.

(1) In this article unless the context otherwise requires:

(a) "Buyer" means a person that buys or contracts to buy goods.

(b) "Conspicuous", with reference to a term, means so written, displayed, or presented that a reasonable person against which it is to operate ought to have noticed it. A term in an electronic record intended to evoke a response by an electronic agent is conspicuous if it is presented in a form that would enable a reasonably configured electronic agent to take it into account or react to it without review of the record by an individual. Whether a term is "conspicuous" or not is a decision for the court. Conspicuous terms include the following:

(i) for a person:

(A) a heading in capitals equal to or greater in size than the surrounding text, or in contrasting type, font, or color to the surrounding text of the same or lesser size; and

(B) language in the body of a record or display in larger type than the surrounding text, or in contrasting type, font, or color to the surrounding text of the same size, or set off from surrounding text of the same size by symbols or other marks that call attention to the language; and

(ii) for a person or an electronic agent, a term that is so placed in a record or display that the person or electronic agent may not proceed without taking action with respect to the particular term.

(c) "Consumer" means an individual who buys or contracts to buy goods that, at the time of contracting, are intended by the individual to be used primarily for personal, family, or household purposes.

(d) "Consumer contract" means a contract between a merchant seller and a consumer.

(e) "Delivery" means, with respect to goods, the voluntary transfer of physical possession or control of goods.

(f) "Electronic" means relating to technology having electrical, digital, magnetic, wireless, optical, electromagnetic, or similar capabilities.

(g) "Electronic agent" means a computer program or an electronic or other automated means used independently to initiate an action or respond to electronic records or performances in whole or in part, without review or action by an individual.

(h) "Electronic record" means a record created, generated, sent, communicated, received, or stored by electronic means.

(i) "Foreign exchange transaction" means a transaction in which one party agrees to deliver a quantity of a specified money or unit of account in consideration of the other party's agreement to deliver another quantity of a different money or unit of account either currently or at a future date, and in which delivery is to be through funds transfer, book entry accounting, or other form of payment order, or other agreed means to transfer a credit balance. The term includes a transaction of this type involving two or more moneys and spot, forward, option, or other products derived from underlying moneys and any combination of these transactions. The term does not include a transaction involving two or more moneys in which one or both of the parties is obligated to make physical delivery, at the time of contracting or in the future, of banknotes, coins, or other form of legal tender or specie.

[(j) Reserved]

[(j) "Good faith" means honesty in fact and the observance of reasonable commercial standards of fair dealing.]

Legislative Note: The definition of "good faith" should not be adopted if the jurisdiction has enacted this definition as part of Article 1.

55

(k) "Goods" means all things that are movable at the time of identification to a contract for sale. The term includes future goods, specially manufactured goods, the unborn young of animals, growing crops, and other identified things attached to realty as described in Section 2–107. The term does not include information, the money in which the price is to be paid, investment securities under Article 8, the subject matter of foreign exchange transactions, or choses in action.

(l) "Receipt of goods" means taking physical possession of goods.

(m) "Record" means information that is inscribed on a tangible medium or that is stored in an electronic or other medium and is retrievable in perceivable form.

Legislative Note: The definition of "record" should not be adopted if the jurisdiction has enacted revised Article 1.

(n) "Remedial promise" means a promise by the seller to repair or replace goods or to refund all or part of the price of goods upon the happening of a specified event.

(o) "Seller" means a person that sells or contracts to sell goods.

(p) "Sign" means, with present intent to authenticate or adopt a record:

(i) to execute or adopt a tangible symbol; or

(ii) to attach to or logically associate with the record an electronic sound, symbol, or process.

(2) Other definitions applying to this Article or to specified Parts thereof, and the sections in which they appear are:

"Acceptance". Section 2–606.
"Between merchants". Section 2–104.
"Cancellation". Section 2–106(4).
"Commercial unit". Section 2–105.
"Conforming to contract". Section 2–106.
"Contract for sale". Section 2–106.
"Cover". Section 2–712.
"Entrusting". Section 2–403.
"Financing agency". Section 2–104.
"Future goods". Section 2–105.
"Identification". Section 2–501.
"Installment contract". Section 2–612.

"Lot". Section 2–105.
"Merchant". Section 2–104.
"Person in position of seller". Section 2–707.
"Present sale". Section 2–106.
"Sale". Section 2–106.
"Sale on approval". Section 2–326.
"Sale or return". Section 2–326.
"Termination". Section 2–106.

(3) "Control" as provided in Section 7–106 and the following definitions in other Articles apply to this Article:

"Check". Section 3–104(f).
"Consignee". Section 7–102(3)
"Consignor". Section 7–102(4)
"Consumer goods". Section 9–102(a)(23).
"Dishonor". Section 3–502.
"Draft". Section 3–104(e).
"Honor". Section 5–102(a)(8).
"Injunction against honor". Section 5–109(b).
"Letter of credit". Section 5–102(a)(10).

(4) In addition Article 1 contains general definitions and principles of construction and interpretation applicable throughout this Article.

As amended in 1994, 1999, 2001, 2003 and 2005.

Official Comment

1. The first sentence of the definition of "conspicuous" is based on Section 1–201(10) but the concept is expanded to include terms in electronic records. The general standard is, that to be conspicuous, a term ought to be noticed by a reasonable person. The second sentence states a special rule for situations where the sender of an electronic record intends to evoke a response from an electronic agent. In that case, the presentation of the term must be capable of evoking a response from a reasonably configured electronic agent. Whether a term is conspicuous is an issue for the court.

Paragraphs (i) and (ii) set out several methods for making a term conspicuous. The requirement that a term be conspicuous functions both as notice (the term ought to be noticed) and as a basis for planning (giving guidance to the party that relies on the term about how that result can be achieved).

Paragraph (i), which relates to the general standard for conspicuousness, is based on original Section 1–201(10) but it is intended to give more guidance than was given in the prior version of this definition. Paragraph (ii) is new and it relates to the special standard for electronic records that are intended to evoke a response from an electronic agent. Although these paragraphs indicate some of the methods for calling attention to a term, the test is whether notice of the term can reasonably be expected. The statutory language should not be construed to permit a result that is inconsistent with that test.

2. A "consumer" is a natural person (*cf.* Section 1–201(27)) who enters into a transaction for a purpose typically associated with consumers–*i.e.*, a personal, family or household purpose. The requirement that the buyer intend that the goods be used "primarily" for personal, family or household purposes is generally consistent with the definition of consumer goods in revised Article 9. *See* Section 9–102(a)(23).

3. The term "consumer contract" is limited to a contract for sale between a seller that is a "merchant" and a buyer that is a "consumer". Thus, neither a sale by a consumer to a consumer nor a sale by a merchant to an individual who intends that the goods be used primarily in a home business qualify as a consumer contract.

4. "Delivery" with respect to documents of title is defined in Section 1–201(15) as the voluntary transfer of possession of the document. This Article defines "delivery" with respect to goods to mean the voluntary transfer of physical possession or control of the goods.

5. The electronic contracting provisions, including the definitions of "electronic," "electronic agent," "electronic record," and "record" are based on the provisions of the Uniform Electronic Transactions Act and are consistent with the federal Electronic Signatures in Global and National Commerce Act (15 U.S.C. § 7001 *et seq.*).

6. The term "foreign exchange transaction" is used in the definition of goods in Section 2–103(1)(k). That definition excludes "the subject matter of foreign exchange transactions."

7. The definition of "goods" in this article has been amended to exclude information not associated with goods. Thus, this article does not directly apply to an electronic transfer of information, such as the transaction involved in *Specht v. Netscape*, 150 F. Supp. 2d 585 (S.D.N.Y. 2001), *aff'd*, 306 F.3d 17 (2d. Cir. 2002). However, transactions often include both goods and information: some are transactions in goods as that term is used in Section 2–102, and some are not. For example, the sale of "smart goods" such as an automobile is a transaction in goods fully within this article even though the automobile contains many computer programs. On the other hand, an architect's provision of architectural plans on a computer disk would not be a transaction in goods. When a transaction includes both the sale of goods and the transfer of rights in information, it is up to the courts to determine whether the transaction is entirely within or outside of this article, or whether or to what extent this article should be applied to a portion of the transaction. While this article may apply to a transaction including information, nothing in this Article alters, creates, or diminishes intellectual property rights.

The definition has also been amended to exclude the subject matter of "foreign exchange transactions." *See* Section 2–103(1)(i). Although a contract in which currency in the commodity exchanged is a sale of goods, an exchange in which delivery is "through funds transfer, book entry accounting, or other form of payment order, or other agreed means to transfer a credit balance" is not a sale of goods and is not governed by this article. In the latter case, Article 4A or other law applies. On the other hand, if the parties agree to a forward transaction where dollars are to be physically delivered in exchange for the delivery of another currency, the transaction is not within the "foreign exchange" exclusion and this article applies.

8. Section 1–202(e) provides rules for determining whether a notice or notification has been received. This Article by contrast defines "receipt of goods" to mean the taking of physical possession of the goods.

9. A "remedial promise" is a promise by the seller to take a certain remedial action upon the happening of a specified event. The types of remedies contemplated by this term as used in this Article are specified in the definition–repair or replacement of the goods, or refund of all or part of the price. No other promise by a seller qualifies as a remedial promise. Furthermore, the seller is entitled to specify precisely the event that will precipitate the obligation. Typical examples include a commitment to repair any parts of the goods that are defective, or a commitment to refund the purchase price if the goods fail to perform in a certain manner. A post-sale promise to correct a problem with the goods that the seller is not obligated to correct that is made to placate a dissatisfied customer is not within the definition of remedial promise. Whether the promised remedy is exclusive, and if so whether it has failed its essential purpose, is determined under Section 2–719.

The distinction between a remedial promise and a warranty that is made in this Article resolves a statute-of-limitations problem. Under original Section 2–725, a right of action for breach of an express warranty accrued at the time the goods were tendered unless the warranty explicitly extended to the future performance of the goods. In that case, the statute of limitations began to run at the time of the discovery of the breach.

By contrast, a right of action for breach of an ordinary (non-warranty) promise accrued when the promise was breached. A number of courts held that commitments by sellers to take remedial action in the event the goods proved to be defective during a specified period of time constituted a warranty, and in theses cases the courts determined that the statute of limitations began to run at the time that the goods were tendered. Other courts used strained reasoning that allowed them to apply the discovery rule even though the promise referred to the future performance of the seller and not the future performance of the goods.

Under this Article, a promise by the seller to take remedial action is not a warranty at all and therefore the statute of limitations for a breach of a remedial promise does not begin to run at either the time the goods are tendered or at the time the breach is discovered. Section 2–725(2)(c) separately addresses the accrual of a right of action for a remedial promise. *See* Official Comment 3 to Section 2–725.

10. The definition of "sign" is broad enough to cover any record that is signed within the meaning of Article 1 or that contains an electronic signature within the meaning of the Uniform Electronic Transactions Act. It is consistent with the federal Electronic Signatures in Global and National Commerce Act (15 U.S.C. § 7001 *et seq.*).

As amended in 2003.

§ 2–104. Definitions: "Merchant"; "Between Merchants"; "Financing Agency".

(1) "Merchant" means a person that deals in goods of the kind or otherwise holds itself out by occupation as having knowledge or skill peculiar to the practices or goods involved in the transaction or to which the knowledge or skill may be attributed by the person's employment of an agent or broker or other intermediary that holds itself out by occupation as having the knowledge or skill.

(2) "Financing agency" means a bank, finance company, or other person that in the ordinary course of business makes advances against goods or documents of title or that by arrangement with either the seller or the buyer intervenes in ordinary course to make or collect payment due or claimed under the contract for sale, as by purchasing or paying the seller's draft or making advances against it or by merely taking it for collection whether or not documents of title ac-

company or are associated with the draft. The term includes also a bank or other person that similarly intervenes between persons that are in the position of seller and buyer in respect to the goods (Section 2–707).

(3) "Between merchants" means in any transaction with respect to which both parties are chargeable with the knowledge or skill of merchants.

As amended in 2003.

Official Comment

Prior Uniform Statutory Provision: None. But see Sections 15(2), (5), 16(c), 45(2) and 71, Uniform Sales Act, and Sections 35 and 37, Uniform Bills of Lading Act for examples of the policy expressly provided for in this Article.

Purposes:

1. This Article assumes that transactions between professionals in a given field require special and clear rules which may not apply to a casual or inexperienced seller or buyer. It thus adopts a policy of expressly stating rules applicable "between merchants" and "as against a merchant", wherever they are needed instead of making them depend upon the circumstances of each case as in the statutes cited above. This section lays the foundation of this policy by defining those who are to be regarded as professionals or "merchants" and by stating when a transaction is deemed to be "between merchants".

2. The term "merchant" as defined here roots in the "law merchant" concept of a professional in business. The professional status under the definition may be based upon specialized knowledge as to the goods, specialized knowledge as to business practices, or specialized knowledge as to both and which kind of specialized knowledge may be sufficient to establish the merchant status is indicated by the nature of the provisions.

The special provisions as to merchants appear only in this Article and they are of three kinds. Sections 2–201(2), 2–205, 2–207 and 2–209 dealing with the statute of frauds, firm offers, confirmatory memoranda and modification rest on normal business practices which are or ought to be typical of and familiar to any person in business. For purposes of these sections almost every person in business would, therefore, be deemed to be a "merchant" under the language "who ... by his occupation holds himself out as having knowledge or skill peculiar to the practices ... involved in the transaction ... " since the practices involved in the transaction are non-specialized business practices such as answering mail. In this type of provision, banks or even universities, for example, well may be "merchants." But even these sections only apply to a merchant in his mercantile capacity; a lawyer or bank president buying fishing tackle for his own use is not a merchant.

On the other hand, in Section 2–314 on the warranty of merchantability, such warranty is implied only "if the seller is a merchant with respect to goods of that kind." Obviously this qualification restricts the implied warranty to a much smaller group than everyone who is engaged in business and requires a professional status as to particular kinds of goods. The exception in Section 2–402(2) for retention of possession by a merchant-seller falls in the same class; as does Section 2–403(2) on entrusting of possession to a merchant "who deals in goods of that kind".

A third group of sections includes 2–103(1)(b), which provides that in the case of a merchant "good faith" includes observance of reasonable commercial standards of fair dealing in the trade; 2–327(1)(c), 2–603 and 2–605, dealing with responsibilities of merchant buyers to follow seller's instructions, etc.; 2–509 on risk of loss, and 2–609 on adequate assurance of performance. This group of sections applies to persons who are merchants under either the "practices" or the "goods" aspect of the definition of merchant.

3. The "or to whom such knowledge or skill may be attributed by his employment of an agent or broker . . . " clause of the definition of merchant means that even persons such as universities, for example, can come within the definition of merchant if they have regular purchasing departments or business personnel who are familiar with business practices and who are equipped to take any action required.

Cross References:

Point 1: Sections 1–102 and 1–203.
Point 2: Sections 2–314, 2–315, and Article 9.

Definitional Cross References:

"Bank". Section 1–201.
"Buyer". Section 2–103.
"Contract for sale". Section 2–106.
"Document of title". Section 1–201.
"Draft". Section 3–104(e).
"Goods". Section 2–103.
"Person". Section 1–201.
"Purchase". Section 1–201.
"Seller". Section 2–103.

§ 2–105. Definitions: Transferability; "Future" Goods; "Lot"; "Commercial Unit".

(1) Goods must be both existing and identified before any interest in them may pass. Goods that are not both existing and identified are "future" goods. A purported present sale of future goods or of any interest therein operates as a contract to sell.

(2) There may be a sale of a part interest in existing identified goods.

(3) An undivided share in an identified bulk of fungible goods is sufficiently identified to be sold although the quantity of the bulk is not determined. Any agreed proportion of the bulk or any quantity thereof agreed upon by number, weight, or other measure may to the extent of the seller's interest in the bulk be sold to the buyer that then becomes an owner in common.

(4) "Lot" means a parcel or a single article which is the subject matter of a separate sale or delivery, whether or not it is sufficient to perform the contract.

(5) "Commercial unit" means such a unit of goods as by commercial usage is a single whole for purposes of sale and division of which materially impairs its character or value on the market or in use. A commercial unit may be a single article (as a machine) or a set of articles (as a suite of furniture or an assortment of sizes) or a quantity (as a bale, gross, or carload) or any other unit treated in use or in the relevant market as a single whole.

As amended in 2003.

Official Comment

Prior Uniform Statutory Provision: Subsections (1), (2), (3) and (4)—Sections 5, 6 and 76, Uniform Sales Act; Subsections (5) and (6)—none.

Changes: Rewritten.

Purposes of Changes and New Matter:

1. Subsection (1) on "goods": The phraseology of the prior uniform statutory provision has been changed so that:

The definition of goods is based on the concept of movability and the term "chattels personal" is not used. It is not intended to deal with things which are not fairly identifiable as movables before the contract is performed.

Growing crops are included within the definition of goods since they are frequently intended for sale. The concept of "industrial" growing crops has been abandoned, for under modern practices fruit, perennial hay, nursery stock and the like must be brought within the scope of this Article. The young of animals are also included expressly in this definition since they, too, are frequently intended for sale and may be contracted for before birth. The period of gestation of domestic animals is such that the provisions of the section on identification can apply as in the case of crops to be planted. The reason of this definition also leads to the inclusion of a wool crop or the like as "goods" subject to identification under this Article.

The exclusion of "money in which the price is to be paid" from the definition of goods does not mean that foreign currency which is included in the definition of money may not be the subject matter of a sales transaction. Goods is intended to cover the sale of money when money is being treated as a commodity but not to include it when money is the medium of payment.

As to contracts to sell timber, minerals, or structures to be removed from the land Section 2–107(1) (Goods to be severed from Realty: recording) controls.

The use of the word "fixtures" is avoided in view of the diversity of definitions of that term. This Article in including within its scope "things attached to realty" adds the further test that they must be capable of severance without material harm thereto. As between the parties any identified things which fall within that definition become "goods" upon the making of the contract for sale.

"Investment securities" are expressly excluded from the coverage of this Article. It is not intended by this exclusion, however, to prevent the application of a particular section of this Article by analogy to securities (as was done with the Original Sales Act in Agar v. Orda, 264 N.Y. 248, 190 N.E. 479, 99 A.L.R. 269 (1934)) when the reason of that section makes such application sensible and the situation involved is not covered by the Article of this Act dealing specifically with such securities (Article 8).

2. References to the fact that a contract for sale can extend to future or contingent goods and that ownership in common follows the sale of a part interest have been omitted here as obvious without need for expression; hence no inference to negate these principles should be drawn from their omission.

3. Subsection (4) does not touch the question of how far an appropriation of a bulk of fungible goods may or may not satisfy the contract for sale.

4. Subsections (5) and (6) on "lot" and "commercial unit" are introduced to aid in the phrasing of later sections.

5. The question of when an identification of goods takes place is determined by the provisions of Section 2–501 and all that this section says is what kinds of goods may be the subject of a sale.

Cross References:

Point 1: Sections 2–107, 2–201, 2–501 and Article 8.
Point 5: Section 2–501.
See also Section 1–201.

Definitional Cross References:

"Buyer". Section 2–103.
"Contract". Section 1–201.
"Contract for sale". Section 2–106.
"Fungible". Section 1–201.
"Money". Section 1–201.
"Present sale". Section 2–106.
"Sale". Section 2–106.
"Seller". Section 2–103.

§ 2–106. Definitions: "Contract"; "Agreement"; "Contract for Sale"; "Sale"; "Present Sale"; "Conforming" to Contract; "Termination"; "Cancellation".

(1) In this Article unless the context otherwise requires "contract" and "agreement" are limited to those relating to the present or future sale of goods. "Contract for sale" includes both a present sale of goods and a contract to sell goods at a future time. A "sale" consists in the passing of title from the seller to the buyer for a price (Section 2–401). A "present sale" means a sale which is accomplished by the making of the contract.

(2) Goods or conduct including any part of a performance are "conforming" or conform to the contract when they are in accordance with the obligations under the contract.

(3) "Termination" occurs when either party pursuant to a power created by agreement or law puts an end to the contract otherwise than for its breach. On "termination" all obligations which are still executory on both sides are discharged but any right based on prior breach or performance survives.

(4) "Cancellation" occurs when either party puts an end to the contract for breach by the other and its effect is the same as that of "termi-

nation" except that the cancelling party also retains any remedy for breach of the whole contract or any unperformed balance.

Official Comment

Prior Uniform Statutory Provision: Subsection (1)—Section 1(1) and (2), Uniform Sales Act; Subsection (2)—none, but subsection generally continues policy of Sections 11, 44 and 69, Uniform Sales Act; Subsections (3) and (4)—none.

Changes: Completely rewritten.

Purposes of Changes and New Matter:

1. Subsection (1): "Contract for sale" is used as a general concept throughout this Article, but the rights of the parties do not vary according to whether the transaction is a present sale or a contract to sell unless the Article expressly so provides.

2. Subsection (2): It is in general intended to continue the policy of requiring exact performance by the seller of his obligations as a condition to his right to require acceptance. However, the seller is in part safeguarded against surprise as a result of sudden technicality on the buyer's part by the provisions of Section 2–508 on seller's cure of improper tender or delivery. Moreover usage of trade frequently permits commercial leeways in performance and the language of the agreement itself must be read in the light of such custom or usage and also, prior course of dealing, and in a long term contract, the course of performance.

3. Subsections (3) and (4): These subsections are intended to make clear the distinction carried forward throughout this Article between termination and cancellation.

Cross References:

Point 2: Sections 1–203, 1–205, and 2–508.

Definitional Cross References:

"Agreement". Section 1–201.
"Buyer". Section 2–103.
"Contract". Section 1–201.
"Goods". Section 2–103.
"Party". Section 1–201.
"Remedy". Section 1–201.
"Rights". Section 1–201.
"Seller". Section 2–103.

§ 2–107. Goods to Be Severed from Realty: Recording.

(1) A contract for the sale of minerals or the like (including oil and gas) or a structure or its materials to be removed from realty is a contract for the sale of goods within this Article if they are to be severed by the seller but until severance a purported present sale thereof which is not effective as a transfer of an interest in land is effective only as a contract to sell.

(2) A contract for the sale apart from the land of growing crops or other things attached to realty and capable of severance without material harm thereto but not described in subsection (1) or of timber to be cut is a contract for the sale of goods within this Article whether the subject matter is to be severed by the buyer or by the seller even though it forms part of the realty at the time of contracting, and the parties can by identification effect a present sale before severance.

(3) The provisions of this section are subject to any third party rights provided by the law relating to realty records, and the contract for sale may be executed and recorded as a document transferring an interest in land and shall then constitute notice to third parties of the buyer's rights under the contract for sale.

As amended in 1972.

Official Comment

Prior Uniform Statutory Provision: See Section 76, Uniform Sales Act on prior policy; Section 7, Uniform Conditional Sales Act.

Purposes:

1. Subsection (1). Notice that this subsection applies only if the minerals or structures "are to be severed by the seller". If the buyer is to sever, such transactions are considered contracts affecting land and all problems of the Statute of Frauds and of the recording of land rights apply to them. Therefore, the Statute of Frauds section of this Article does not apply to such contracts though they must conform to the Statute of Frauds affecting the transfer of interests in land.

2. Subsection (2). "Things attached" to the realty which can be severed without material harm are goods within this Article regardless of who is to effect the severance. The word "fixtures" has been avoided because of the diverse definitions of this term, the test of "severance without material harm" being substituted.

The provision in subsection (3) for recording such contracts is within the purview of this Article since it is a means of preserving the buyer's rights under the contract of sale.

3. The security phases of things attached to or to become attached to realty are dealt with in the Article on Secured Transactions (Article 9) and it is to be noted that the definition of goods in that Article differs from the definition of goods in this Article.

However, both Articles treat as goods growing crops and also timber to be cut under a contract of severance.

Cross References:

Point 1: Section 2–201.
Point 2: Sections 2–103 and 2–105.
Point 3: Articles 9 and 9–105.

Definitional Cross References:

"Buyer". Section 2–103.
"Contract". Section 1–201.
"Contract for sale". Section 2–106.
"Goods". Section 2–103.
"Party". Section 1–201.
"Present sale". Section 2–106.
"Rights". Section 1–201.
"Seller". Section 2–103.

§ 2–108. Transactions Subject to Other Law.

(1) A transaction subject to this article is also subject to any applicable:

(a) [list any certificate of title statutes of this State covering automobiles, trailers, mobile homes, boats, farm tractors, or the like], except with respect to the rights of a buyer in ordinary course of business under Section 2–403(2) which arise before a certificate of title covering the goods is effective in the name of any other buyer;

(b) rule of law that establishes a different rule for consumers; or

(c) statute of this state applicable to the transaction, such as a statute dealing with:

(i) the sale or lease of agricultural products;

(ii) the transfer of human blood, blood products, tissues, or parts;

(iii) the consignment or transfer by artists of works of art or fine prints;

(iv) distribution agreements, franchises, and other relationships through which goods are sold;

(v) the misbranding or adulteration of food products or drugs; and

(vi) dealers in particular products, such as automobiles, motorized wheelchairs, agricultural equipment, and hearing aids.

(2) Except for the rights of a buyer in ordinary course of business under subsection (1)(a), in the event of a conflict between this article and a law referred to in subsection (1), that law governs.

(3) For purposes of this article, failure to comply with a law referred to in subsection (1) has only the effect specified in that law.

(4) This article modifies, limits, and supersedes the federal Electronic Signatures in Global and National Commerce Act, 15 U.S.C. Section 7001 et seq., except that nothing in this article modifies, limits, or supersedes Section 7001(c) of that Act or authorizes electronic delivery of any of the notices described in Section 7003(b) of that Act.

As added in 2003.

Official Comment

1. Section 2–108, which was not in the prior version of this Article, follows the form of Section 2A–104(1).

2. In subsection (1), it is assumed that this article is subject to any applicable federal law, such as the United Nations Convention on Contracts for the International Sale of Goods, 15 U.S.C. App., or the Magnuson–Moss Warranty Act, 15 U.S.C. Sections 2301–2312.

3. Subsection (1)(a) permits the states to list any applicable certificate-of-title statutes. It also provides that Article 2 is subject to their provisions on the transfer and effect of title except for the rights of a buyer in ordinary course of business in certain limited situations. In entrustment situations, the exception in subsection (1)(a) overrides those certificate-of-title statutes that provide that a person cannot qualify as an owner unless a certificate has been issued in the person's name. In those cases where an owner in whose name a certificate has been issued entrusts a titled asset to a dealer that then sells it to a buyer in ordinary course of business, this section provides that the priority issue between the owner and the buyer is to be resolved by reference to the certificate-of-title statute.

Illustration #1. A used car is stolen from the owner by a thief and the thief, by fraud, is able to obtain a clean certificate of title from State X. The thief sells the car to the buyer, a good faith purchaser for value but not a buyer in ordinary course of business, and the thief transfers the certificate of title to the buyer. The exception in subsection (1)(a) does not apply to protect the buyer. Furthermore, under Section 2–403(1), the buyer does not get good title from the thief, regardless of the certificate. The same result follows if the applicable state certificate of title law makes the certificate prima facie evidence of ownership. The buyer will prevail, however, if the applicable certificate of title law conflicts with the result obtained under this Article by making issuance of the certificate conclusive on title.

Illustration #2. The dealer sells a new car to buyer #1 and the dealer signs a form permitting buyer #1 to apply for a certificate of title. Buyer #1 leaves the car with the dealer so that the dealer can finish the preparation work on the car. While the car remains in the dealer's possession and before the state issues a certificate of title in buyer #1's name, buyer #2 makes the dealer a better offer on the car, which the dealer accepts. Buyer #1 entrusted the car to the dealer, and if buyer #2 qualifies as a buyer in ordinary course of business, buyer #2's title to the car will be superior to that of buyer #1.

Illustration #3. An owner in whose name a certificate of title has been issued leaves a car with a dealer for repair. The dealer sells the car to a buyer, who qualifies as a buyer in ordinary course of business. If the certificate-of-title law in the state resolves the priority contest between the owner and the buyer, that solution should be implemented. Otherwise, the buyer prevails under Section 2–403(2).

4. This section also deals with the effect of a conflict or failure to comply with any other state law that might apply to a transaction governed by this Article. Subsection (1) provides that a transaction subject to this Article is also subject to other applicable law, and subsection (2) provides that in the event of a conflict the other law governs (except for the rights of a buyer in ordinary course of business under subsection (1)(a)).

Subsection (1)(b) provides that this Article is also subject to any rule of law that establishes a different rule for consumers. "Rule of law" includes a statute,

an administrative rule properly promulgated under the statute, and a final court decision.

The relationship between Article 2 and federal and state consumer laws will vary from transaction to transaction and from State to State. For example, the Magnuson–Moss Warranty Act, 15 U.S.C.A. §§ 2301 *et. seq.*, may or may not apply to the consumer dispute in question and the applicable state "lemon law" may provide more or less protection than Magnuson–Moss. To the extent that the other law applies and there is a conflict with this Article, that law controls.

Subsection (1)(c) provides an illustrative but not exhaustive list of other applicable state statutes that may preempt all or part of Article 2. For example, franchise contracts may be regulated by state franchise acts, the seller of unmerchantable blood or human tissue may be insulated from warranty liability and disclaimers of the implied warranty of merchantability may be invalidated by non-uniform amendments to Article 2. The existence, scope, and effect of these statutes must be assessed from State to State.

Assuming that there is a conflict, subsection (3) deals with the failure of parties to the contract to comply with the applicable law. The failure has the "effect specified" in the law. Thus, the failure to obtain a required license may make the contract illegal, and therefore unenforceable, while the nonnegligent supply of unmerchantable blood under a "blood shield" statute may mean only that the supplier is insulated from liability for injury to person or property.

5. Subsection (4) takes advantage of a provision of the federal Electronic Signatures in Global and National Commerce Act (E–Sign). E–Sign permits state law to modify, limit or supersede its provisions if the state law is consistent with Titles I and II of E–Sign, gives no special legal effect or validity to and does not require the implementation or application of specific technologies or technical specifications, and if enacted subsequent to E–Sign makes specific reference to E–Sign. Subsection (4) does not apply to section 101(c) of E–Sign, nor does it authorize electronic delivery of the notices described in section 103(b) of E–Sign.

Cross References:

Point 3: Section 2–403.

Definitional Cross References:

"Lease". Section 2A–103.

PART 2

FORM, FORMATION, TERMS AND READJUSTMENT OF CONTRACT; ELECTRONIC CONTRACTING

§ 2–201. Formal Requirements; Statute of Frauds.

(1) A contract for the sale of goods for the price of $5,000 or more is not enforceable by way of action or defense unless there is some record sufficient to indicate that a contract for sale has been made between the parties and signed by the party against which enforcement is sought or by the party's authorized agent or broker. A record is not insufficient because it omits or incorrectly states a term agreed upon, but the contract is not enforceable under this subsection beyond the quantity of goods shown in the record.

(2) Between merchants if within a reasonable time a record in confirmation of the contract and sufficient against the sender is received and the party receiving it has reason to know its contents, it satisfies the requirements of subsection (1) against the recipient unless notice of objection to its contents is given in a record within 10 days after it is received.

(3) A contract that does not satisfy the requirements of subsection (1) but which is valid in other respects is enforceable:

(a) if the goods are to be specially manufactured for the buyer and are not suitable for sale to others in the ordinary course of the seller's business and the seller, before notice of repudiation is received and under circumstances that reasonably indicate that the goods are for the buyer, has made either a substantial beginning of their manufacture or commitments for their procurement;

(b) if the party against which enforcement is sought admits in the party's pleading, or in the party's testimony or otherwise under oath that a contract for sale was made, but the contract is not enforceable under this paragraph beyond the quantity of goods admitted; or

(c) with respect to goods for which payment has been made and accepted or which have been received and accepted (Sec. 2–606).

(4) A contract that is enforceable under this section is not unenforceable merely because it is not capable of being performed within one year or any other period after its making.

As amended in 2003.

Official Comment

1. The record required by subsection (1) need not contain all of the material terms of the contract, and the material terms that are stated need not be precise or accurate. All that is required is that the record afford a reasonable basis to determine that the offered oral evidence rests on a real transaction. The record may be written on a piece of paper or entered into a computer. It need not indicate which party is the buyer and which party is the seller. The only term which must appear is the quantity term. A term indicating the manner by which the quantity is determined is sufficient. Thus, for example, a term indicating that the quantity is based on the output of the seller or the requirements of the buyer satisfies the requirement. *See e.g., Advent Systems v. Unisys*, 925 F.2d 670 (3rd Cir. 1991); *Gestetner Corp. v. Case Equip. Co.*, 815 F.2d 806 (1st Cir. 1987). The same reasoning can be extended to a term that indicates that the contract is similar to, but does not qualify as, an output or requirement contract. *See e.g., PMC Corp. v. Houston Wire and Cable Co.* 797 A.2d 125 (N.H. 2002). Similarly, a term that refers to a master contract that provides a basis for determining a quantity satisfies this requirement. *See e.g., Reigel Fiber Corp. v. Anderson Gin Co.*, 512 F.2d 784 (5th Cir.1975). If a specific amount is stated in the record, even if not accurately stated, recovery is limited to the stated amount. However, the price, time and place of payment or delivery, the general quality of the goods, or any particular warranties need not be included.

Special emphasis must be placed on the permissibility of omitting the price term. In many valid contracts for sale the parties do not mention the price in express terms. The buyer is bound to pay and the seller to accept a reasonable price, which the trier of the fact will determine. Frequently the price is not mentioned at all since the parties have based their agreement on a price list or catalogue known to both of them, and the list or catalogue serves as an efficient safeguard against perjury. Also, "market" prices and valuations that are current in the vicinity constitute a similar check. Of course, if the "price" consists of goods rather than money, the quantity of goods must be stated.

There are only three definite and invariable requirements for the memorandum made by subsection (1). First, the memorandum must evidence a contract for the sale of goods; second, the memorandum must be signed; and third, the memorandum must have a quantity term or a method to determine the quantity.

2. The prior version of subsection (1) began with the phrase "Except as otherwise provided in this section." This language has been deleted. This change was made to provide that the statement of the three statutory exceptions in subsection (3) should not be read as limiting under subsection (1) the possibility that a promisor will be estopped to raise the statute-of-frauds defense in appropriate cases.

3. "Partial performance" as a substitute for the required record can validate the contract only for the goods which have been accepted or for which payment has been made and accepted.

Receipt and acceptance either of goods or of the price constitutes an unambiguous overt admission by both parties that a contract exists. If the court can make a just apportionment, therefore, the agreed price of any goods actually delivered can be recovered without a writing or, if the price has been paid, the seller can be forced to deliver an apportionable part of the goods. The overt actions of the parties make admissible evidence of the other terms of the contract necessary to a just apportionment. This is true even though the actions of the parties are not in themselves inconsistent with a different transaction such as a consignment for resale or a mere loan of money.

Part performance by the buyer requires that the buyer deliver something that is accepted by the seller as the performance. Thus, part payment may be made by money or check accepted by the seller. If the agreed price consists of goods or services, then they must also have been delivered and accepted. When the seller accepts partial payment for a single item the statute is satisfied as to that item. See *Lockwood v. Smigel*, 18 Cal App.3d 800, 99 Cal Rept. 289 (1971).

4. Between merchants, failure to answer a confirmation of a contract in a record that satisfies the requirements of subsection (1) against the sender within ten days of receipt renders the record sufficient against the recipient. The only effect, however, is to take away from the party that fails to answer the defense of the Statute of Frauds. The burden of persuading the trier of fact that a contract was in fact made orally prior to the record confirmation is unaffected.

A merchant includes a person "that by occupation purports to have knowledge or skill peculiar to the *practices* or goods involved in the transaction." Section 2–104(1)(emphasis supplied). Thus, a professional or a farmer should be considered a merchant because the practice of objecting to an improper confirmation ought to be familiar to any person in business.

5. Failure to satisfy the requirements of this section does not render the contract void for all purposes, but merely prevents it from being judicially enforced in favor of a party to the contract. For example, a buyer that takes possession of goods provided for in an oral contract which the seller has not meanwhile repudiated is not a trespasser. Nor would the statute-of-frauds provisions of this section be a defense to a third person that wrongfully induces a party to refuse to perform an oral contract, even though the injured party cannot maintain an action for damages against the party that refuses to perform.

6. It is not necessary that the record be delivered to anybody, nor is this section intended to displace decisions that have given effect to lost records. It need not be signed by both parties, but except as stated in subsection (2), it is not sufficient against a party that has not signed it. Prior to a dispute, no one can determine which party's signature may be necessary, but from the time of contracting each party should be aware that it is the signature of the other which is important.

7. If the making of a contract is admitted in court, either in a written pleading, by stipulation or by oral statement before the court, or is admitted under oath but not in court, as by testimony in a deposition or an affidavit filed with a motion, no additional record is necessary. Subsection (3)(b) makes it impossible to admit the contract in these contexts, and assert that the Statute of Frauds is still a defense. However, in these circumstances, the contract is not conclusively established. The admission is evidential only against the maker and only for the facts admitted. As against the other party, it is not evidential at all.

8. Subsection (4), which was not in prior versions of this Article, repeals the "one year" provision of the Statute of Frauds for contracts for the sale of goods. The phrase "any other applicable period" recognizes that some state statutes apply to periods longer than one year. The confused and contradictory interpretations under the so-called "one year" clause are illustrated by *C.R. Klewin, Inc. v. Flagship Properties, Inc.*, 600 A.2d 772 (Conn. 1991).

Cross References:

See Sections 1–201, 2–202, 2–207, 2–209 and 2–304.
Point 1: Sections 2–211 thru 2–213.
Point 4: Section 2–104

Definitional Cross References:

"Action". Section 1–201.
"Between merchants". Section 2–104.
"Buyer". Section 2–103.
"Contract". Section 1–201.
"Contract for sale". Section 2–106.
"Goods". Section 2–103.
"Notice". Section 1–202.
"Party". Section 1–201.
"Reasonable time". Section 1–205.
"Record". Section 2–103.
"Sale". Section 2–106.
"Seller". Section 2–103.
"Sign". Section 2–103.

As amended in 2003.

§ 2–202. Final Expression in a Record: Parol or Extrinsic Evidence.

(1) Terms with respect to which the confirmatory records of the parties agree or which are otherwise set forth in a record intended by the parties as a final expression of their agreement with respect to such terms as are included therein may not be contradicted by evidence of any prior agreement or of a contemporaneous oral agreement but may be supplemented by evidence of: *consistent*

(a) course of performance, course of dealing, or usage of trade (Section 1–303); and

(b) consistent additional terms unless the court finds the record to have been intended also as a complete and exclusive statement of the terms of the agreement.

(2) Terms in a record may be explained by evidence of course of performance, course of dealing, or usage of trade without a preliminary determination by the court that the language used is ambiguous.

Legislative Note: The cross-references in subsection (1)(a) should not be changed if the jurisdiction has not adopted revised Article 1.

As amended in 2001 and 2003.

Official Comment

1. Subsection (1) codifies the parol evidence rule. The operation of this rule depends on the intention of both parties that the terms in a record are the "final expression of their agreement with respect to the included terms." Without this mutual intention to integrate the record, the parol evidence rule does not apply to exclude evidence of other terms allegedly agreed to prior to or contemporaneously with the record. Unless there is a final record, these alleged terms are provable as part of the agreement by relevant evidence from any credible source. When each party sends a confirmatory record, mutual intention to integrate the agreement is presumed for terms "with respect to which the confirmatory records of the parties agree."

2. Because a record is final for the included terms (an integration), this does not mean that the parties intended that the record contain all the terms of their agreement (a total integration). If a record is final but not complete and exclusive, it cannot be contradicted by evidence of prior agreements reflected in a record or prior or contemporaneous oral agreements, but it can be supplemented by other evidence, drawn from any source, of consistent additional terms. Even if the record is final, complete and exclusive, it can be supplemented by evidence of noncontradictory terms drawn from an applicable course of performance, course of dealing, or usage of trade unless those sources are carefully negated by a term in the record. If the record is final, complete and exclusive it cannot be supplemented by evidence of terms drawn from other sources, even terms that are consistent with the record.

3. Whether a writing is final, and whether a final writing is also complete, are issues for the court. This section rejects any assumption that because a record has been worked out which is final on some matters, it is to be taken as including all the matters agreed upon. If the additional terms are those that, if agreed upon, would certainly have been included in the document in the view of the court, then evidence of their alleged making must be kept from the trier of fact. This section is not intended to suggest what should be the evidentiary strength of a merger clause as evidence of the mutual intent that the record be final and complete. That determination depends upon the particular circumstances of each case.

4. This section does not exclude evidence introduced to show that the contract is avoidable for misrepresentation, mistake, or duress, or that the contract or a term is unenforceable because of unconscionability. This section also does not operate to exclude evi-

dence of a subsequent modification or evidence that, for the purpose of claiming excuse, both parties assumed that a certain event would not occur.

5. Issues of interpretation are generally left to the courts. In interpreting terms in a record, subsection (2) permits either party to introduce evidence drawn from a course of performance, a course of dealing, or a usage of trade without any preliminary determination by the court that the term at issue is ambiguous. This article takes no position on whether a preliminary determination of ambiguity is a condition to the admissibility of evidence drawn from any other source or on whether a contract clause can exclude an otherwise applicable implied-in-fact source.

Cross References:

Point 2: Sections 2-206 and 2-207.
Point 3: Section 2-207.
Point 4: Section 2-302

Definitional Cross References:

"Agreement". Section 1-201.
"Course of dealing". Section 1-303.
"Course of performance". Section 1-303.
"Parties". Section 1-201.
"Record". Section 2-103.
"Term". Section 1-201.
"Usage of trade". Section 1-303.

As amended in 2001 and 2003.

§ 2-203.   Seals Inoperative.

The affixing of a seal to a record evidencing a contract for sale or an offer to buy or sell goods does not constitute the record a sealed instrument. The law with respect to sealed instruments does not apply to such a contract or offer.

As amended in 2003.

Official Comment

Prior Uniform Statutory Provision: Section 3, Uniform Sales Act.

Changes: Portion pertaining to "seals" rewritten.

Purposes of Changes:

1. This section makes it clear that every effect of the seal which relates to "sealed instruments" as such is wiped out insofar as contracts for sale are concerned. However, the substantial effects of a seal, except extension of the period of limitations, may be had by appropriate drafting as in the case of firm offers (see Section 2-205).

2. This section leaves untouched any aspects of a seal which relate merely to signatures or to authentication of execution and the like. Thus, a statute providing that a purported signature gives prima facie evidence of its own authenticity or that a signature gives prima facie evidence of consideration is still applicable to sales transactions even though a seal may be held to be a signature within the meaning of such a statute. Similarly, the authorized affixing of a corporate seal bearing the corporate name to a contractual writing purporting to be made by the corporation may have effect as a signature without any reference to the law of sealed instruments.

Cross Reference:

Point 1: Section 2-205.

Definitional Cross References:

"Contract for sale". Section 2-106.
"Goods". Section 2-103.
"Record". Section 2-103.

§ 2-204.   Formation in General.

(1) A contract for sale of goods may be made in any manner sufficient to show agreement, including offer and acceptance, conduct by both parties which recognizes the existence of a contract, the interaction of electronic agents, and the interaction of an electronic agent and an individual.

(2) An agreement sufficient to constitute a contract for sale may be found even if the moment of its making is undetermined.

(3) Even if one or more terms are left open, a contract for sale does not fail for indefiniteness if the parties have intended to make a contract and there is a reasonably certain basis for giving an appropriate remedy.

(4) Except as otherwise provided in Sections 2-211 through 2-213, the following rules apply:

(a) A contract may be formed by the interaction of electronic agents of the parties, even if no individual was aware of or reviewed the electronic agents' actions or the resulting terms and agreements.

(b) A contract may be formed by the interaction of an electronic agent and an individual acting on the individual's own behalf or for another person. A contract is formed if the individual takes actions that the individual is free to refuse to take or makes a statement, and the individual has reason to know that the actions or statement will:

(i) cause the electronic agent to complete the transaction or performance; or

(ii) indicate acceptance of an offer, regardless of other expressions or actions by the individual to which the electronic agent cannot react.

As amended in 2003.

Official Comment

1. Subsection (1) sets forth the basic policy to recognize any manner of expression of agreement. In addition to traditional contract formation by oral or written agreement, or by performance, subsection (1) provides that an agreement may be made by electronic means. Regardless of how the agreement is formed under this section, the legal effect of the agreement is subject to the other provisions of this Article.

2. Under subsection (1), appropriate conduct by the parties may be sufficient to establish an agreement. Subsection (2) is directed primarily when the correspondence does not disclose the exact point at which the agreement was formed, but the conduct of the parties indicate that a binding obligation has been undertaken.

3. Subsection (3) states the principle for "open terms" which underlies later sections of this Article. If the parties intend to enter into a binding agreement, this subsection recognizes the agreement as valid in law, despite missing terms, if there is any reasonably certain basis for granting a remedy based on commercial standards of indefiniteness. Neither certainty for what the parties were to do nor a finding of the exact amount of damages is required. Neither is the fact that one or more terms are left to be agreed upon enough by itself to defeat an otherwise adequate agreement. This Act makes provision elsewhere for missing terms needed for performance, open price, remedies and the like.

The more terms the parties leave open, the less likely it is that the parties have intended to conclude a binding agreement, but their actions may be conclusive on the matter despite the omissions.

4. Subsections (4)(a) and (b) are derived from Sections 14(a) and (b) of the Uniform Electronic Transactions Act. Subsection (4)(a) confirms that contracts may be formed by machines functioning as electronic agents for the parties to a transaction. This subsection is intended to negate any claim that lack of human intent, at the time of contract formation, prevents contract formation. When machines are involved, the requisite intention to contract flows from the programing and use of the machine. This provision, along with sections 2–211, 2–212, and 2–213, is intended to remove barriers to electronic contract formation.

5. When the requisite intent to enter into a contract exists, subsection (4)(b) validates contracts formed by an individual and an electronic agent. This subsection validates an anonymous click-through transaction. As with subsection (4)(a), the intent to contract by means of an electronic agent comes from the programing and use of the machine. The requisite intent to contract by the individual is found by the acts of the individual that the individual has reason to know will be interpreted by the machine as allowing the machine to complete the transaction or performance, or that will be interpreted by the machine as signifying acceptance on the part of the individual. This intent is only found, though, when the individual is free to refuse to take the actions that the machine will interpret as acceptance or allowance to complete the transaction. For example, if A goes to a website that provides for purchasing goods over the Internet, and after choosing items to be purchased is confronted by a screen which advises her that the transaction will be completed if A clicks "I agree," then A will be bound by the click if A knew or had reason to know that the click would be interpreted as signifying acceptance and A was also free to refuse to take the final action. This provision does not, however, provide for a determination of what terms exist in the agreement. That question is governed by Section 2–207.

6. Nothing in this section is intended to restrict equitable defenses, such as fraud or mistake, in electronic contract formation. However, because the law of electronic mistake is not well developed, and because factual issues may arise that are not easily resolved by legal standards developed for nonelectronic transactions, courts should not automatically apply standards developed in other contexts. The specific differences between electronic and nonelectronic transactions should also be factored in to resolve equitable claims in electronic contracts.

Cross References:

Point 1: Sections 1–103, 2–201, 2–211 through 2–213, and 2–302.
Point 2: Sections 2–205 through 2–209.
Point 3: See Part 3.
Point 4: Sections 2–211 thru 2–213.
Point 5: Sections 2–211 thru 2–213.

Definitional Cross References:

"Agreement". Section 1–201.
"Contract". Section 1–201.

"Contract for sale". Section 2–106.
"Electronic". Section 2–103.
"Electronic agent". Section 2–103.
"Goods". Section 2–103.
"Party". Section 1–201.
"Remedy". Section 1–201.
"Term". Section 1–201.

As amended in 2003.

§ 2–205. Firm Offers.

An offer by a merchant to buy or sell goods in a signed record that by its terms gives assurance that it will be held open is not revocable, for lack of consideration, during the time stated or if no time is stated for a reasonable time, but in no event may the period of irrevocability exceed three months. Any such term of assurance in a form supplied by the offeree must be separately signed by the offeror.

As amended in 2003.

Official Comment

Prior Uniform Statutory Provision: Sections 1 and 3, Uniform Sales Act.

Changes: Completely rewritten by this and other sections of this Article.

Purposes of Changes:

1. This section is intended to modify the former rule which required that "firm offers" be sustained by consideration in order to bind, and to require instead that they must merely be characterized as such and expressed in signed writings.

2. The primary purpose of this section is to give effect to the deliberate intention of a merchant to make a current firm offer binding. The deliberation is shown in the case of an individualized document by the merchant's signature to the offer, and in the case of an offer included on a form supplied by the other party to the transaction by the separate signing of the particular clause which contains the offer. "Signed" here also includes authentication but the reasonableness of the authentication herein allowed must be determined in the light of the purpose of the section. The circumstances surrounding the signing may justify something less than a formal signature or initialing but typically the kind of authentication involved here would consist of a minimum of initialing of the clause involved. A handwritten memorandum on the writer's letterhead purporting in its terms to "confirm" a firm offer already made would be enough to satisfy this section, although not subscribed, since under the circumstances

it could not be considered a memorandum of mere negotiation and it would adequately show its own authenticity. Similarly, an authorized telegram will suffice, and this is true even though the original draft contained only a typewritten signature. However, despite settled courses of dealing or usages of the trade whereby firm offers are made by oral communication and relied upon without more evidence, such offers remain revocable under this Article since authentication by a writing is the essence of this section.

3. This section is intended to apply to current "firm" offers and not to long term options, and an outside time limit of three months during which such offers remain irrevocable has been set. The three month period during which firm offers remain irrevocable under this section need not be stated by days or by date. If the offer states that it is "guaranteed" or "firm" until the happening of a contingency which will occur within the three month period, it will remain irrevocable until that event. A promise made for a longer period will operate under this section to bind the offeror only for the first three months of the period but may of course be renewed. If supported by consideration it may continue for as long as the parties specify. This section deals only with the offer which is not supported by consideration.

4. Protection is afforded against the inadvertent signing of a firm offer when contained in a form prepared by the offeree by requiring that such a clause be separately authenticated. If the offer clause is called to the offeror's attention and he separately authenticates it, he will be bound; Section 2–302 may operate, however, to prevent an unconscionable result which otherwise would flow from other terms appearing in the form.

5. Safeguards are provided to offer relief in the case of material mistake by virtue of the requirement of good faith and the general law of mistake.

Cross References:

Point 1: Section 1–102.
Point 2: Section 1–102.
Point 3: Section 2–201.
Point 5: Section 2–302.

Definitional Cross References:

"Goods". Section 2–103.
"Merchant". Section 2–104.
"Record". Section 2–103.
"Signed". Section 2–103.

§ 2–206. Offer and Acceptance in Formation of Contract.

(1) Unless otherwise unambiguously indicated by the language or circumstances:

(a) an offer to make a contract shall be construed as inviting acceptance in any manner and by any medium reasonable in the circumstances;

(b) an order or other offer to buy goods for prompt or current shipment shall be construed as inviting acceptance either by a prompt promise to ship or by the prompt or current shipment of conforming or nonconforming goods, but the shipment of nonconforming goods is not an acceptance if the seller seasonably notifies the buyer that the shipment is offered only as an accommodation to the buyer.

(2) If the beginning of a requested performance is a reasonable mode of acceptance, an offeror that is not notified of acceptance within a reasonable time may treat the offer as having lapsed before acceptance.

(3) A definite and seasonable expression of acceptance in a record operates as an acceptance even if it contains terms additional to or different from the offer.

As amended in 2003.

Official Comment

1. Subsection (1)(b) deals with a shipment that contains defective goods which is made following an order for the goods. The nonconforming shipment is normally understood as intended to close the bargain even though it constitutes a breach. However, the seller by stating that the shipment is nonconforming and is offered only as an accommodation to the buyer keeps the shipment of from operating as an acceptance.

2. The mirror image rule is rejected in subsection (3), but any responsive record must still be reasonably understood as an "acceptance" and not as a proposal for a different transaction. *See* Official Comment 2 to Section 2–207.

3. Subsection (3) makes it clear that an expression of acceptance can operate as an acceptance (i.e., create a contract) even though it contains terms that are not identical to those in the offer. This rule applies, however, only to an expression of acceptance that is not only seasonable but also "definite." A purported expression of acceptance containing additional or different terms would not be a "definite" acceptance when the offeree's expression clearly communicates to the offeror the offeree's unwillingness to do business unless the offeror assents to those additional or different terms. This is not a definite acceptance since the offeree's expression makes it clear that the offeree is not "accepting" anything; but rather that the offeree is indicating a willingness to do business only on the offeree's terms and that the offeree is awaiting the offeror's assent to those terms. (This result is consistent with the final clause of former Section 2–207(1).) In a situation in which the offer clearly indicates that the offeror is unwilling to do business on any terms other than those contained in the offer, and the offeree responds with an expression of acceptance that contains additional or different terms, a court could also conclude that the offeree's response does not constitute a definite expression of acceptance.

Definitional Cross References:

"Buyer". Section 2–103.
"Conforming". Section 2–106.
"Contract". Section 1–201.
"Goods". Section 2–103.
"Notifies". Section 1–202.
"Reasonable time". Section 1–205.

As amended in 2003.

§ 2–207. Terms of Contract; Effect of Confirmation.

Subject to Section 2–202, if (i) conduct by both parties recognizes the existence of a contract although their records do not otherwise establish a contract, (ii) a contract is formed by an offer and acceptance, or (iii) a contract formed in any manner is confirmed by a record that contains terms additional to or different from those in the contract being confirmed, the terms of the contract are:

(a) terms that appear in the records of both parties;

(b) terms, whether in a record or not, to which both parties agree; and

(c) terms supplied or incorporated under any provision of this Act.

As amended in 2003.

Official Comment

1. This section applies to all contracts for the sale of goods, and it is not limited only to those contracts where there has been a "battle of the forms." The reference in this section to contracts formed by offer

and acceptance includes, *inter alia*, contracts formed by the interaction of electronic agents and by the interaction of an electronic agent of an individual. *See* section 2–204(1).

2. This section applies only when a contract has been created under another section of this Article. The purpose of this section is solely to determine the terms of the contract. When forms are exchanged before or during performance, the result from the application of this section differs from the prior Section 2–207 of this Article and the common law in that this section gives no preference to either the first or the last form; the same test is applied to the terms in each. Terms in a record that insist on all of that record's terms and no other terms as a condition of contract formation have no effect on the operation of this section. When one party insists in that party's record that its own terms are a condition to contract formation, if that party does not subsequently perform or otherwise acknowledge the existence of a contract, if the other party does not agree to those terms, the record's insistence on its own terms will keep a contract from being formed under Sections 2–204 or 2–206, and this section is not applicable. As with original Section 2–207, the courts will have to distinguish between "confirmations" that are addressed in this section and "modifications" that are addressed in Section 2–209.

3. Terms of a contract may be found not only in the consistent terms of records of the parties but also from a straightforward acceptance of an offer, and an expression of acceptance accompanied by one or more additional terms might demonstrate the offeree's agreement to the terms of the offer. If, for example, a buyer sent a purchase order with technical specifications and the seller responded with a record stating "Thank you for your order. We will fill it promptly. Note that we do not make deliveries after 3:00 p.m. on Fridays." it might be reasonable to conclude that both parties agreed to the technical specifications.

Similarly, an offeree's performance is sometimes the acceptance of an offer. If, for example, a buyer sends a purchase order, there is no oral or other agreement, and the seller delivers the goods in response to the purchase order–but the seller does not send the seller's own acknowledgment or acceptance–the seller should normally be treated as having agreed to the terms of the purchase order.

If, however, parties exchange records with conflicting or inconsistent terms, but conduct by both parties recognizes the existence of a contract, subsection (a) provides that the terms of the contract are terms that appear in the records of both parties. But even when both parties send records, there could be nonverbal agreement to additional or different terms that appear in only one of two records. If, for example, both parties' forms called for the sale of 700,000 nuts and bolts but the purchase order or another record of the buyer conditioned the sale on a test of a sample to see if the nuts and bolts would perform properly, the seller's sending a small sample to the buyer might be construed to be an agreement to the buyer's condition. It might also be found that the contract called for arbitration when both forms provided for arbitration but each contained immaterially different arbitration provisions.

In a rare case the terms in the records of both parties might not become part of the contract. This could be the case, for example, when the parties contemplated an agreement to a single negotiated record, and each party submitted to the other party similar proposals and then commenced performance, but the parties never reached a negotiated agreement because of the differences over crucial terms. There is a variety of verbal and nonverbal behavior that may be suggest agreement to another's record. This section leaves the interpretation of that behavior to the discretion of the courts.

4. An "agreement" may include terms derived from a course of performance, a course of dealing, and usage of trade. *See* Sections 1–201(a)(2) and 1–303. If the members of a trade, or if the contracting parties, expect to be bound by a term that appears in the record of only one of the contracting parties, that term is part of the agreement. However, repeated use of a particular term or repeated failure to object to a term on another's record is not normally sufficient in itself to establish a course of performance, a course of dealing or a trade usage.

5. The section omits any specific treatment of terms attached to the goods, or in or on the container in which the goods are delivered. This article takes no position on whether a court should follow the reasoning in Step–Saver Data Systems, Inc. v. Wyse Technology, 939 F.2d 91 (3d Cir. 1991) and Klocek v. Gateway, Inc. 104 F. Supp. 2d 1332 (D. Kan. 2000) (original 2–207 governs) or the contrary reasoning in Hill v. Gateway 2000, 105 F. 3d 1147(7th Cir. 1997) (original 2–207 inapplicable).

Cross References:

Point 1: Sections 2–204 and 2–206.
Point 2: Sections 2–204, 2–206, and 2–209.
Point 3: Sections 1–303, 2–204, 2–206, and 2–209.
Point 4: Sections 1–201, and 1–303.

Definitional Cross References:

"Acceptance". Section 2–206.
"Agree". Section 1–201.
"Contract". Section 1–201.
"Offer". Section 2–204.
"Parties". Section 1–201.
"Records". Section 2–103.
"Terms". Section 1–201.

As amended in 2003.

§ 2–208. Reserved. [Course of Performance or Practical Construction.]

[(1) Where the contract for sale involves repeated occasions for performance by either party with knowledge of the nature of the performance and opportunity for objection to it by the other, any course of performance accepted or acquiesced in without objection shall be relevant to determine the meaning of the agreement.

(2) The express terms of the agreement and any such course of performance, as well as any course of dealing and usage of trade, shall be construed whenever reasonable as consistent with each other; but when such construction is unreasonable, express terms shall control course of performance and course of performance shall control both course of dealing and usage of trade (Section 1–205).

(3) Subject to the provisions of the next section on modification and waiver, such course of performance shall be relevant to show a waiver or modification of any term inconsistent with such course of performance.]

[Official Comment]

[**Prior Uniform Statutory Provision:** No such general provision but concept of this section recognized by terms such as "course of dealing", "the circumstances of the case," "the conduct of the parties," etc., in Uniform Sales Act.

Purposes:

1. The parties themselves know best what they have meant by their words of agreement and their action under that agreement is the best indication of what that meaning was. This section thus rounds out the set of factors which determines the meaning of the "agreement" and therefore also of the "unless otherwise agreed" qualification to various provisions of this Article.

2. Under this section a course of performance is always relevant to determine the meaning of the agreement. Express mention of course of performance elsewhere in this Article carries no contrary implication when there is a failure to refer to it in other sections.

3. Where it is difficult to determine whether a particular act merely sheds light on the meaning of the agreement or represents a waiver of a term of the agreement, the preference is in favor of "waiver" whenever such construction, plus the application of the provisions on the reinstatement of rights waived (see Section 2–209), is needed to preserve the flexible character of commercial contracts and to prevent surprise or other hardship.

4. A single occasion of conduct does not fall within the language of this section but other sections such as the ones on silence after acceptance and failure to specify particular defects can affect the parties' rights on a single occasion (see Sections 2–605 and 2–607).

Cross References:

Point 1: Section 1–201.
Point 2: Section 2–202.
Point 3: Sections 2–209, 2–601 and 2–607.
Point 4: Sections 2–605 and 2–607.]

Legislative Note: This section should not be repealed if the jurisdiction has not adopted revised Article 1.

§ 2–209. Modification; Rescission and Waiver.

(1) An agreement modifying a contract within this Article needs no consideration to be binding.

(2) An agreement in a signed record which excludes modification or rescission except by a signed record may not be otherwise modified or rescinded, but except as between merchants such a requirement in a form supplied by the merchant must be separately signed by the other party.

(3) The requirements of Section 2–201 must be satisfied if the contract as modified is within its provisions.

(4) Although an attempt at modification or rescission does not satisfy the requirements of subsection (2) or (3), it may operate as a waiver.

(5) A party that has made a waiver affecting an executory portion of a contract may retract the waiver by reasonable notification received by the other party that strict performance will be required of any term waived, unless the retrac-

tion would be unjust in view of a material change of position in reliance on the waiver.

As amended in 2003.

Official Comment

Prior Uniform Statutory Provision: Subsection (1)—Compare Section 1, Uniform Written Obligations Act; Subsections (2) to (5)—none.

Purposes of Changes and New Matter:

1. This section seeks to protect and make effective all necessary and desirable modifications of sales contracts without regard to the technicalities which at present hamper such adjustments.

2. Subsection (1) provides that an agreement modifying a sales contract needs no consideration to be binding.

However, modifications made thereunder must meet the test of good faith imposed by this Act. The effective use of bad faith to escape performance on the original contract terms is barred, and the extortion of a "modification" without legitimate commercial reason is ineffective as a violation of the duty of good faith. Nor can a mere technical consideration support a modification made in bad faith.

The test of "good faith" between merchants or as against merchants includes "observance of reasonable commercial standards of fair dealing in the trade" (Section 2–103), and may in some situations require an objectively demonstrable reason for seeking a modification. But such matters as a market shift which makes performance come to involve a loss may provide such a reason even though there is no such unforeseen difficulty as would make out a legal excuse from performance under Sections 2–615 and 2–616.

3. Subsections (2) and (3) are intended to protect against false allegations of oral modifications. "Modification or rescission" includes abandonment or other change by mutual consent, contrary to the decision in Green v. Doniger, 300 N.Y. 238, 90 N.E.2d 56 (1949); it does not include unilateral "termination" or "cancellation" as defined in Section 2–106.

The Statute of Frauds provisions of this Article are expressly applied to modifications by subsection (3). Under those provisions the "delivery and acceptance" test is limited to the goods which have been accepted, that is, to the past. "Modification" for the future cannot therefore be conjured up by oral testimony if the price involved is $500.00 or more since such modification must be shown at least by an authenticated memo. And since a memo is limited in its effect to the quantity of goods set forth in it there is safeguard against oral evidence.

Subsection (2) permits the parties in effect to make their own Statute of Frauds as regards any future modification of the contract by giving effect to a clause in a signed agreement which expressly requires any modification to be by signed writing. But note that if a consumer is to be held to such a clause on a form supplied by a merchant it must be separately signed.

4. Subsection (4) is intended, despite the provisions of subsections (2) and (3), to prevent contractual provisions excluding modification except by a signed writing from limiting in other respects the legal effect of the parties' actual later conduct. The effect of such conduct as a waiver is further regulated in subsection (5).

Cross References:

Point 1: Section 1–203.
Point 2: Sections 1–201, 1–203, 2–615 and 2–616.
Point 3: Sections 2–106, 2–201 and 2–202.
Point 4: Sections 2–202.

Definitional Cross References:

"Agreement". Section 1–201.
"Between merchants". Section 2–104.
"Contract". Section 1–201.
"Merchant". Section 2–104.
"Notification". Section 1–202.
"Signed". Section 1–201.
"Term". Section 1–201.

§ 2–210. Delegation of Performance; Assignment of Rights.

(1) If the seller or buyer assigns rights under a contract, the following rules apply:

(a) Subject to paragraph (b) and except as otherwise provided in Section 9–406 or as otherwise agreed, all rights of the seller or the buyer may be assigned unless the assignment would materially change the duty of the other party, increase materially the burden or risk imposed on that party by the contract, or impair materially that party's chance of obtaining return performance. A right to damages for breach of the whole contract or a right arising out of the assignor's due performance of its entire obligation may be assigned despite an agreement otherwise.

(b) The creation, attachment, perfection, or enforcement of a security interest in the seller's interest under a contract is not an assignment that materially changes the duty of or materially increases the burden or risk imposed on the buyer or materially impairs the buyer's chance of obtaining return performance under paragraph (a) unless, and only to the extent that, enforcement of the security interest results in a delegation of a material performance of the seller. Even in that event, the creation, attachment, perfection, and enforcement of the security interest remain effective. However, the seller is liable to the buyer for damages caused by the delegation to the extent that the damages could not reasonably be prevented by the buyer, and a court may grant other appropriate relief, including cancellation of the contract or an injunction against enforcement of the security interest or consummation of the enforcement.

(2) If the seller or buyer delegates performance of its duties under a contract, the following rules apply:

(a) A party may perform its duties through a delegate unless otherwise agreed or unless the other party has a substantial interest in having the original promisor perform or control the acts required by the contract. Delegation of performance does not relieve the delegating party of any duty to perform or liability for breach.

(b) Acceptance of a delegation of duties by the assignee constitutes a promise to perform those duties. The promise is enforceable by either the assignor or the other party to the original contract.

(c) The other party may treat any delegation of duties as creating reasonable grounds for insecurity and may without prejudice to its rights against the assignor demand assurances from the assignee under Section 2–609.

(d) A contractual term prohibiting the delegation of duties otherwise delegable under paragraph (a) is enforceable, and an attempted delegation is not effective.

(3) An assignment of "the contract" or of "all my rights under the contract" or an assignment in similar general terms is an assignment of rights and unless the language or the circum-

stances, as in an assignment for security, indicate the contrary, it is also a delegation of performance of the duties of the assignor.

(4) Unless the circumstances indicate the contrary, a prohibition of assignment of "the contract" is to be construed as barring only the delegation to the assignee of the assignor's performance.

As amended in 1999 and 2003.

Official Comment

1. This section conforms with revised Article 9.

2. The principles in this section are consistent with the recognition that both the assignment of rights and the delegation of duties are generally normal and permissible incidents of a contract for the sale of goods.

3. Subsection (1)(a) sets out the effect of an assignment by either the seller or the buyer of the rights but not the duties arising under the contract for sale. These rights may effectively be assigned to a third party unless the assignment materially increases the duty, burden or risk, or materially impairs expected performance to the other party, or, subject to subsection (1)(b) and Section 9–406, unless the parties have agreed otherwise. Even then, a right to damages for breach of the whole contract or a right arising out of the assignor's due performance of the assignor's entire obligation can be assigned despite contrary agreement.

An assignment, however, is not effective if it would "materially change the duty of the other party, increase materially the burden or risk imposed on that party by the contract, or increase materially that party's likelihood of obtaining return performance." Subsection (1)(a). The cases where these limitations apply are rare. For example, a seller that has fully performed the contract should always be able to assign the right to payment. This is the basis for most accounts receivable financing. If, however, the contract is still executory, the assignment of the right to payment to a third person might decrease the seller's incentive to perform and, thus, increase the buyer's risk. Similarly, the buyer's assignment of the right to receive a fixed quantity of goods should not usually be objectionable but if the parties have a "requirements" contract, the assignment could increase materially the seller's risk.

Subsection (1)(a) is subject to Section 9–406 of revised Article 9. That provision makes rights to payment for goods sold ("accounts"), whether or not earned, freely alienable notwithstanding a contrary agreement or rule of law.

4. Subsection (1)(a) is subject to subsection (1)(b), which conforms with revised Article 9. If an assignment of rights creates a security interest in the seller's interest under the contract, including a right to future payments, subsection (1)(b) states that there is no material impairment under subsection (1)(a) unless the creation, attachment, perfection and enforcement "results in a delegation of material performance of the seller." This is unlikely in most assignments, and the buyer's basic protection is to demand adequate assurance of due performance from the seller if the assignment creates reasonable grounds for insecurity.

5. Occasionally a seller or buyer will delegate duties under the contract without also assigning rights. For example, a dealer might delegate its duty to procure and deliver a fixed quantity of goods to the buyer to a third party. In these cases, subsection (2) sets the limitations on that power. A contract term prohibiting the delegation of duties renders an attempted delegation ineffective. Subsection (2)(d).

If the third person accepts the delegation, an enforceable promise is made both to the delegator and the person entitled under the contract to perform those duties. Subsection (2)(b). In short, as to the person entitled under the contract a third party beneficiary contract is created. However, the delegator's duty to perform under the contract is not discharged unless the person entitled to performance agrees to substitute the delegatee for the delegator (a novation). *See* subsection (2)(a), last sentence.

The person entitled under the contract may treat any delegation of duties as reasonable grounds for insecurity and may demand adequate assurance of due performance for the assignee-delegatee. Subsection (2)(c).

In any event, a delegation of duties is not effective if the person entitled under the contract has a "substantial interest in having the original promisor perform or control the performance required by the contract." Subsection (2)(a).

6. In the case of ambiguity, subsection (3) provides a rule of interpretation to determine when an assignment of rights should also be considered a delegation of duties. The preference is to construe the language as both a delegation of duties as well as an assignment of rights.

7. This section is not intended as a complete statement of the law of delegation and assignment but is limited to clarifying a few points doubtful under the case law. In particular, neither this section nor this Article touches directly on the questions as the need or effect of notice of the assignment, the rights of succes-

sive assignees, or any question of the form of an assignment, either as between the parties or as against any third parties. Some of these questions are dealt with in Article 9.

Cross References:

Point 1: Article 9.
Point 3: Articles 5 and 9.
Point 4: Article 9.
Point 5: Sections 2–318, 2–609
Point 7: Article 9.

Definitional Cross References:

"Agreement". Section 1–201.
"Buyer". Section 2–103.
"Contract". Section 1–201.
"Party". Section 1–201.
"Rights". Section 1–201.
"Seller". Section 2–103.
"Term". Section 1–201.

As amended in 1999 and 2003.

§ 2–211. Legal Recognition of Electronic Contracts, Records, and Signatures.

(1) A record or signature may not be denied legal effect or enforceability solely because it is in electronic form.

(2) A contract may not be denied legal effect or enforceability solely because an electronic record was used in its formation.

(3) This article does not require a record or signature to be created, generated, sent, communicated, received, stored, or otherwise processed by electronic means or in electronic form.

(4) A contract formed by the interaction of an individual and an electronic agent under Section 2–204(4)(b) does not include terms provided by the individual if the individual had reason to know that the agent could not react to the terms as provided.

As added in 2003.

Official Comment

1. Subsections (1) and (2) are derived from Section 7(a) and (b) of the Uniform Electronic Transactions Act (UETA), and subsection (3) is derived from Section 5(b) of UETA. Subsection (4) is based on Section 206(c) of the Uniform Computer Information Transactions Act (UCITA). Each subsection conforms to the federal Electronic Signatures in Global and National Commerce Act (15 U.S.C. § 7001 *et seq.*).

2. This section sets forth the premise that the medium in which a record, signature, or contract is created, presented or retained does not affect its legal significance. Subsections (1) and (2) are designed to eliminate the single element of medium as a reason to deny effect or enforceability to a record, signature, or contract. The fact that the information is set forth in an electronic, as opposed to paper, medium is irrelevant.

3. A contract may have legal effect and yet be unenforceable. *See* Restatement 2d Contracts Section 8. To the extent that a contract in electronic form may have legal effect but be unenforceable, because it is in electronic form, subsection (2) validates its legality. Likewise, to the extent that a record or signature in electronic form may have legal effect but be unenforceable, because it is in electronic form, subsection (1) validates the legality of the record or signature.

For example, though a contract may be unenforceable, the parties' electronic records may have collateral effects, as in the case of a buyer that insures goods purchased under a contract that is unenforceable under Section 2–201. The insurance company may not deny a claim on the ground that the buyer is not the owner, though the buyer may have no direct remedy against the seller for failure to deliver. *See* Restatement 2d Contracts, Section 8, Illustration 4. Whether an electronic record or signature is valid under other law is not addressed by this Act.

4. While subsection (2) validates the legality of an electronic contract, it does not in any way diminish the requirements for the formation of contracts under Sections 2–204 and 2–206.

Cross References:

Point 3: Section 2–201
Point 4: Section 2–204 and 2–206.

Definitional Cross References:

"Contract". Section 1–201.
"Electronic". Section 2–103.
"Electronic agent". Section 2–103.
"Electronic record". Section 2–103.
"Record". Section 2–103.
"Signature". Section 2–103.

§ 2–212. Attribution.

An electronic record or electronic signature is attributable to a person if it was the act of the person or the person's electronic agent or the person is otherwise legally bound by the act.

As added in 2003.

Official Comment

1. This section is based on Section 9 of the Uniform Electronic Transactions Act (UETA).

2. As long as an electronic record is created by a person or the electronic signature results from a person's action it is attributed to that person. The legal effect of the attribution is derived from other provisions of this Act or from other law. This section simply assures that these rules will be applied in the electronic environment. A person's actions include actions taken by a human agent of the person as well as actions taken by an electronic agent, of the person. Although this section may appear to state the obvious, it assures that the record or signature is not ascribed to a machine, as opposed to the person operating or programming the machine.

3. In each of the following cases, both the electronic record and electronic signature would be attributable to a person under this section:

A. The person types his or her name as part of an e-mail purchase order;

B. The person's employee, pursuant to authority, types the person's name as part of an e-mail purchase order;

C. The person's computer, programmed to order goods upon receipt of inventory information within particular parameters, issues a purchase order which includes the person's name, or other identifying information, as part of the order.

In each of these cases, law other than this Act would ascribe both the signature and the action to the person if done in a paper medium. This section provides that the same result will occur when an electronic medium is used.

4. Nothing in this section affects the use of an electronic signature as a means of attributing a record to a person. Once an electronic signature is attributed to the person, the electronic record with which it is associated would also be attributed to the person unless the person established fraud, forgery, or other invalidating cause. However, an electronic signature is not the only method for attribution of a record.

5. In the context of attribution of records, normally the content of the record will provide the necessary information for a finding of attribution. It is also possible that an established course of dealing between parties may result in a finding of attribution. Just as with a paper record, evidence of forgery or counterfeiting may be introduced to rebut the evidence of attribu-

tion. The use of facsimile transmissions provides a number of examples of attribution using information other than a signature. A facsimile may be attributed to a person because of the information printed across the top of the page that indicates the machine from which it was sent. Similarly, the transmission may contain a letterhead which identifies the sender. Some cases have held that the letterhead actually constituted a signature because it was a symbol adopted by the sender with intent to sign the record. *See Cox Engineering v. Funston Mach. & Supply*, 749 S.W.2d 508, 511 (Tex. App.1988) (plaintiff's letterhead, including address, appearing at top of invoice, provides authentication that identifies the party to be charged and thus satisfies the statute of frauds' signature requirement); *Owen v. Kroger Co.*, 936 F. Supp. 579 (S.D. Ind. 1996)(determining that a letterhead satisfies the signature requirement of the UCC). However, the signature determination resulted from the necessary finding of intention in that case. Other cases have found letterheads not to be signatures because the requisite intention was not present. *See First National Bank in Alamosa v. Ford Motor Credit Co.*, 748 F.Supp. 1464 (D. Colo. 1990)(determining that a pre-printed name on a draft was not a signature for the purpose of accepting a draft). The critical point is that with or without a signature, information within the electronic record may well suffice to provide the facts resulting in attribution of an electronic record to a particular party.

6. Certain information may be present in an electronic environment that does not appear to attribute but which clearly links a person to a particular record. Numerical codes, personal identification numbers, public and private key combinations, all serve to establish the party to which an electronic record should be attributed. Security procedures will be another piece of evidence available to establish attribution.

7. Once it is established that a record or signature is attributable to a particular person, the legal significance of the record or signature is determined by the context and surrounding circumstances in which the recorder signature is created, including the parties' agreement, if any. This will primarily be governed by other sections of this article. *See, e.g.*, Sections 2–201, 2–202, 2–204, 2–206, 2–207, and 2–209.

Cross References:

Point 3: Section 2–201.
Point 5: Section 1–303.
Point 7: Sections 2–201, 2–202, 2–204, 2–206, and 2–209.

Definitional Cross References:

"Electronic". Section 2–103.
"Electronic agent". Section 2–103.
"Electronic record". Section 2–103.
"Record". Section 2–103.
"Signature". Section 2–103.

§ 2–213. Electronic Communication.

(1) If the receipt of an electronic communication has a legal effect, it has that effect even if no individual is aware of its receipt.

(2) Receipt of an electronic acknowledgment of an electronic communication establishes that the communication was received but, in itself, does not establish that the content sent corresponds to the content received.

As added in 2003.

Official Comment

1. This section is adapted from Sections 15(e) and (f) of the Uniform Electronic Transactions Act (UETA).

2. This section deals with electronic communications generally, and it is not limited to electronic records which must be retrievable in perceivable form. The section does not resolve the questions of when or where electronic communications are determined to be sent or received, nor does it indicate that a communication has any particular substantive legal effect.

3. Under subsection (1), receipt is not dependent on a person having notice of the communication. An analogy in a paper based transaction is the recipient that does not read a notice received in the mail. Although "receipt" as defined in Article 1 applies by its terms only to notices, the same concept would apply equally to a communication that is not a notice.

4. Subsection (2) provides legal certainty about the effect of an electronic acknowledgment. This subsection only addresses the fact of the receipt, and it does not set forth the legal significance of the quality of the content, nor whether the electronic communication was read or "opened."

5. This section does not address the question of whether the exchange of electronic communications constitutes the formation of a contract. Those questions are addressed by Sections 2–204 and 2–206.

Cross References:

Point 5: Section 2–204 and 2–206.

Definitional Cross References:

"Electronic". Section 2–103.
"Sent". Section 1–201.

PART 3

GENERAL OBLIGATION AND CONSTRUCTION OF CONTRACT

§ 2–301. General Obligations of Parties.

The obligation of the seller is to transfer and deliver and that of the buyer is to accept and pay in accordance with the contract.

Official Comment

Prior Uniform Statutory Provision: Sections 11 and 41, Uniform Sales Act.

Changes: Rewritten.

Purposes of Changes:

This section uses the term "obligation" in contrast to the term "duty" in order to provide for the "condition" aspects of delivery and payment insofar as they are not modified by other sections of this Article such as those on cure of tender. It thus replaces not only the general provisions of the Uniform Sales Act on the parties' duties, but also the general provisions of that Act on the effect of conditions. In order to determine what is "in accordance with the contract" under this Article usage of trade, course of dealing and performance, and the general background of circumstances must be given due consideration in conjunction with the lay meaning of the words used to define the scope of the conditions and duties.

Cross References:

Section 1–106, 1–205, 2–209, 2–508 and 2–612.

Definitional Cross References:

"Buyer". Section 2–103.
"Contract". Section 1–201.
"Party". Section 1–201.
"Seller". Section 2–103.

§ 2–302. Unconscionable Contract or Term.

(1) If the court as a matter of law finds the contract or any term of the contract to have been unconscionable at the time it was made, the court may refuse to enforce the contract, or it may enforce the remainder of the contract without the unconscionable term, or it may so limit the application of any unconscionable term as to avoid any unconscionable result.

(2) If it is claimed or appears to the court that the contract or any term thereof may be unconscionable, the parties shall be afforded a reasonable opportunity to present evidence as to its commercial setting, purpose, and effect to aid the court in making the determination.

As amended in 2003.

Official Comment

1. This section makes it possible for a court to police explicitly against the contracts or terms which the court finds to be unconscionable instead of attempting to achieve the result by an adverse construction of language, by manipulation of the rules of offer and acceptance, or by a determination that the term is contrary to public policy or to the dominant purpose of the contract. The section allows a court to pass directly on the unconscionability of the contract or a particular term of the contract and to make a conclusion of law as to its unconscionability. Courts have been particularly vigilant when the contract at issue is set forth in a standard form. The principle is one of prevention of oppression and unfair surprise and not of disturbance of allocation of risks because of superior bargaining power. The basic test is whether, in the light of the general commercial background and the commercial needs of the particular trade or case, the term or contract involved is so one-sided as to be unconscionable under the circumstances existing at the time of the making of the contract.

2. Under this section, the court, in its discretion, may refuse to enforce the contract as a whole if the whole contract is determined to be unconscionable, or the court may strike any single term or group of terms which are unconscionable or which are contrary to the essential purpose of the agreement or to material terms to which the parties have expressly agreed, or the court may simply limits the unconscionable results.

3. This section is addressed to the court, and the decision is to be made by the court. The evidence

referred to in subsection (2) is for the court's consideration, not the trier of fact. Only the agreement which results from the court's action on these matters is to be submitted to the general trier of the facts.

Definitional Cross Reference:

"Contract". Section 1–201.
"Term". Section 1–201.

As amended in 2003.

§ 2–303. Allocation or Division of Risks.

Where this Article allocates a risk or a burden as between the parties "unless otherwise agreed", the agreement may not only shift the allocation but may also divide the risk or burden.

Official Comment

Prior Uniform Statutory Provision: None.

Purposes:

1. This section is intended to make it clear that the parties may modify or allocate "unless otherwise agreed" risks or burdens imposed by this Article as they desire, always subject, of course, to the provisions on unconscionability.

Compare Section 1–102(4).

2. The risk or burden may be divided by the express terms of the agreement or by the attending circumstances, since under the definition of "agreement" in this Act the circumstances surrounding the transaction as well as the express language used by the parties enter into the meaning and substance of the agreement.

Cross References:

Point 1: Sections 1–102, 2–302.
Point 2: Section 1–201.

Definitional Cross References:

"Party". Section 1–201.
"Agreement". Section 1–201.

§ 2–304. Price Payable in Money, Goods, Realty, or Otherwise.

(1) The price may be made payable in money or otherwise. If it is payable in whole or in part in goods, each party is a seller of the goods that the party is to transfer.

(2) Even if all or part of the price is payable in an interest in real property the transfer of the goods, and the seller's obligations with reference to them are subject to this Article, but not the transfer of the interest in real property or the transferor's obligations in connection therewith.

As amended in 2003.

Official Comment

Prior Uniform Statutory Provision: Subsections (2) and (3) of Section 9, Uniform Sales Act.

Changes: Rewritten.

Purposes of Changes:

1. This section corrects the phrasing of the Uniform Sales Act so as to avoid misconstruction and produce greater accuracy in commercial result. While it continues the essential intent and purpose of the Uniform Sales Act it rejects any purely verbalistic construction in disregard of the underlying reason of the provisions.

2. Under subsection (1) the provisions of this Article are applicable to transactions where the "price" of goods is payable in something other than money. This does not mean, however, that this whole Article applies automatically and in its entirety simply because an agreed transfer of title to goods is not a gift. The basic purposes and reasons of the Article must always be considered in determining the applicability of any of its provisions.

3. Subsection (2) lays down the general principle that when goods are to be exchanged for realty, the provisions of this Article apply only to those aspects of the transaction which concern the transfer of title to goods but do not affect the transfer of the realty since the detailed regulation of various particular contracts which fall outside the scope of this Article is left to the courts and other legislation. However, the complexities of these situations may be such that each must be analyzed in the light of the underlying reasons in order to determine the applicable principles. Local statutes dealing with realty are not to be lightly disregarded or altered by language of this Article. In contrast, this Article declares definite policies in regard to certain matters legitimately within its scope though concerned with real property situations, and in those instances the provisions of this Article control.

Cross References:

Point 1: Section 1–102.
Point 3: Sections 1–102, 1–103, 1–104 and 2–107.

Definitional Cross References:

"Goods". Section 2–103.

"Money". Section 1–201.
"Party". Section 1–201.
"Seller". Section 2–103.

§ 2–305.   Open Price Term.

(1) The parties if they so intend may conclude a contract for sale even if the price is not settled. In such a case the price is a reasonable price at the time for delivery if:

(a) nothing is said as to price;

(b) the price is left to be agreed by the parties and they fail to agree; or

(c) the price is to be fixed in terms of some agreed market or other standard as set or recorded by a third person or agency and it is not so set or recorded.

(2) A price to be fixed by the seller or by the buyer means a price to be fixed in good faith.

(3) If a price left to be fixed otherwise than by agreement of the parties fails to be fixed through fault of one party, the other may at the party's option treat the contract as canceled or the party may fix a reasonable price.

(4) If, however, the parties intend not to be bound unless the price is fixed or agreed and it is not fixed or agreed, there is no contract. In such a case the buyer must return any goods already received or if unable to do so must pay their reasonable value at the time of delivery and the seller must return any portion of the price paid on account.

As amended in 2003.

Official Comment

Prior Uniform Statutory Provision: Sections 9 and 10, Uniform Sales Act.

Changes: Completely rewritten.

Purposes of Changes:

1. This section applies when the price term is left open on the making of an agreement which is nevertheless intended by the parties to be a binding agreement. This Article rejects in these instances the formula that "an agreement to agree is unenforceable" if the case falls within subsection (1) of this section, and rejects also defeating such agreements on the ground of "indefiniteness". Instead this Article recognizes the dominant intention of the parties to have the deal continue to be binding upon both. As to future performance, since this Article recognizes remedies such as cover (Section 2–712), resale (Section 2–706) and specific performance (Section 2–716) which go beyond any mere arithmetic as between contract price and market price, there is usually a "reasonably certain basis for granting an appropriate remedy for breach" so that the contract need not fail for indefiniteness.

2. Under some circumstances the postponement of agreement on price will mean that no deal has really been concluded, and this is made express in the preamble of subsection (1) ("The parties *if they so intend*") and in subsection (4). Whether or not this is so is, in most cases, a question to be determined by the trier of fact.

3. Subsection (2), dealing with the situation where the price is to be fixed by one party rejects the uncommercial idea that an agreement that the seller may fix the price means that he may fix any price he may wish by the express qualification that the price so fixed must be fixed in good faith. Good faith includes observance of reasonable commercial standards of fair dealing in the trade if the party is a merchant. (Section 2–103). But in the normal case a "posted price" or a future seller's or buyer's "given price," "price in effect," "market price," or the like satisfies the good faith requirement.

4. The section recognizes that there may be cases in which a particular person's judgment is not chosen merely as a barometer or index of a fair price but is an essential condition to the parties' intent to make any contract at all. For example, the case where a known and trusted expert is to "value" a particular painting for which there is no market standard differs sharply from the situation where a named expert is to determine the grade of cotton, and the difference would support a finding that in the one the parties did not intend to make a binding agreement if that expert were unavailable whereas in the other they did so intend. Other circumstances would of course affect the validity of such a finding.

5. Under subsection (3), wrongful interference by one party with any agreed machinery for price fixing in the contract may be treated by the other party as a repudiation justifying cancellation, or merely as a failure to take cooperative action thus shifting to the aggrieved party the reasonable leeway in fixing the price.

6. Throughout the entire section, the purpose is to give effect to the agreement which has been made. That effect, however, is always conditioned by the requirement of good faith action which is made an inherent part of all contracts within this Act. (Section 1–203).

Cross References:

Point 1: Sections 2–204(3), 2–706, 2–712 and 2–716.
Point 3: Section 2–103.
Point 5: Sections 2–311 and 2–610.
Point 6: Section 1–203.

Definitional Cross References:

"Agreement". Section 1–201.
"Burden of establishing". Section 1–201.
"Buyer". Section 2–103.
"Cancellation". Section 2–106.
"Contract". Section 1–201.
"Contract for sale". Section 2–106.
"Fault". Section 1–201.
"Goods". Section 2–103.
"Party". Section 1–201.
"Receipt of goods". Section 2–103.
"Seller". Section 2–103.
"Term". Section 1–201.

§ 2–306. Output, Requirements and Exclusive Dealings.

(1) A term which measures the quantity by the output of the seller or the requirements of the buyer means such actual output or requirements as may occur in good faith, except that no quantity unreasonably disproportionate to any stated estimate or in the absence of a stated estimate to any normal or otherwise comparable prior output or requirements may be tendered or demanded.

(2) A lawful agreement by either the seller or the buyer for exclusive dealing in the kind of goods concerned imposes unless otherwise agreed an obligation by the seller to use best efforts to supply the goods and by the buyer to use best efforts to promote their sale.

Official Comment

Prior Uniform Statutory Provision: None.

Purposes:

1. Subsection (1) of this section, in regard to output and requirements, applies to this specific problem the general approach of this Act which requires the reading of commercial background and intent into the language of any agreement and demands good faith in the performance of that agreement. It applies to such contracts of nonproducing establishments such as dealers or distributors as well as to manufacturing concerns.

2. Under this Article, a contract for output or requirements is not too indefinite since it is held to mean the actual good faith output or requirements of the particular party. Nor does such a contract lack mutuality of obligation since, under this section, the party who will determine quantity is required to operate his plant or conduct his business in good faith and according to commercial standards of fair dealing in the trade so that his output or requirements will approximate a reasonably foreseeable figure. Reasonable elasticity in the requirements is expressly envisaged by this section and good faith variations from prior requirements are permitted even when the variation may be such as to result in discontinuance. A shut-down by a requirements buyer for lack of orders might be permissible when a shut-down merely to curtail losses would not. The essential test is whether the party is acting in good faith. Similarly, a sudden expansion of the plant by which requirements are to be measured would not be included within the scope of the contract as made but normal expansion undertaken in good faith would be within the scope of this section. One of the factors in an expansion situation would be whether the market price had risen greatly in a case in which the requirements contract contained a fixed price. Reasonable variation of an extreme sort is exemplified in Southwest Natural Gas Co. v. Oklahoma Portland Cement Co., 102 F.2d 630 (C.C.A.10, 1939). This Article takes no position as to whether a requirements contract is a provable claim in bankruptcy.

3. If an estimate of output or requirements is included in the agreement, no quantity unreasonably disproportionate to it may be tendered or demanded. Any minimum or maximum set by the agreement shows a clear limit on the intended elasticity. In similar fashion, the agreed estimate is to be regarded as a center around which the parties intend the variation to occur.

4. When an enterprise is sold, the question may arise whether the buyer is bound by an existing output or requirements contract. That question is outside the scope of this Article, and is to be determined on other principles of law. Assuming that the contract continues, the output or requirements in the hands of the new owner continue to be measured by the actual good faith output or requirements under the normal operation of the enterprise prior to sale. The sale itself is not grounds for sudden expansion or decrease.

5. Subsection (2), on exclusive dealing, makes explicit the commercial rule embodied in this Act under which the parties to such contracts are held to have impliedly, even when not expressly, bound themselves to use reasonable diligence as well as good faith in their performance of the contract. Under such contracts the exclusive agent is required, although no

express commitment has been made, to use reasonable effort and due diligence in the expansion of the market or the promotion of the product, as the case may be. The principal is expected under such a contract to refrain from supplying any other dealer or agent within the exclusive territory. An exclusive dealing agreement brings into play all of the good faith aspects of the output and requirement problems of subsection (1). It also raises questions of insecurity and right to adequate assurance under this Article.

Cross References:

Point 4: Section 2–210.
Point 5: Sections 1–203 and 2–609.

Definitional Cross References:

"Agreement". Section 1–201.
"Buyer". Section 2–103.
"Contract for sale". Section 2–106.
"Good faith". Section 2–103.
"Goods". Section 2–103.
"Party". Section 1–201.
"Term". Section 1–201.
"Seller". Section 2–103.

§ 2–307. Delivery in Single Lot or Several Lots.

Unless otherwise agreed all goods called for by a contract for sale must be tendered in a single delivery and payment is due only on such tender but where the circumstances give either party the right to make or demand delivery in lots the price if it can be apportioned may be demanded for each lot.

Official Comment

Prior Uniform Statutory Provision: Section 45(1), Uniform Sales Act.

Changes: Rewritten and expanded.

Purposes of Changes:

1. This section applies where the parties have not specifically agreed whether delivery and payment are to be by lots and generally continues the essential intent of original Act, Section 45(1) by assuming that the parties intended delivery to be in a single lot.

2. Where the actual agreement or the circumstances do not indicate otherwise, delivery in lots is not permitted under this section and the buyer is properly entitled to reject for a deficiency in the tender, subject to any privilege in the seller to cure the tender.

3. The "but" clause of this section goes to the case in which it is not commercially feasible to deliver or to receive the goods in a single lot as for example, where a contract calls for the shipment of ten carloads of coal and only three cars are available at a given time. Similarly, in a contract involving brick necessary to build a building the buyer's storage space may be limited so that it would be impossible to receive the entire amount of brick at once, or it may be necessary to assemble the goods as in the case of cattle on the range, or to mine them.

In such cases, a partial delivery is not subject to rejection for the defect in quantity alone, if the circumstances do not indicate a repudiation or default by the seller as to the expected balance or do not give the buyer ground for suspending his performance because of insecurity under the provisions of Section 2–609. However, in such cases the undelivered balance of goods under the contract must be forthcoming within a reasonable time and in a reasonable manner according to the policy of Section 2–503 on manner of tender of delivery. This is reinforced by the express provisions of Section 2–608 that if a lot has been accepted on the reasonable assumption that its nonconformity will be cured, the acceptance may be revoked if the cure does not seasonably occur. The section rejects the rule of Kelly Construction Co. v. Hackensack Brick Co., 91 N.J.L. 585, 103 A. 417, 2 A.L.R. 685 (1918) and approves the result in Lynn M. Ranger, Inc. v. Gildersleeve, 106 Conn. 372, 138 A. 142 (1927) in which a contract was made for six carloads of coal then rolling from the mines and consigned to the seller but the seller agreed to divert the carloads to the buyer as soon as the car numbers became known to him. He arranged a diversion of two cars and then notified the buyer who then repudiated the contract. The seller was held to be entitled to his full remedy for the two cars diverted because simultaneous delivery of all of the cars was not contemplated by either party.

4. Where the circumstances indicate that a party has a right to delivery in lots, the price may be demanded for each lot if it is apportionable.

Cross References:

Point 1: Section 1–201.
Point 2: Sections 2–508 and 2–601.
Point 3: Sections 2–503, 2–608 and 2–609.

Definitional Cross References:

"Contract for sale". Section 2–106.
"Goods". Section 2–103.
"Lot". Section 2–105.
"Party". Section 1–201.

"Rights". Section 1–201.

§ 2–308. Absence of Specified Place for Delivery.

Unless otherwise agreed:

(a) the place for delivery of goods is the seller's place of business or if none, the seller's residence; but

(b) in a contract for sale of identified goods that to the knowledge of the parties at the time of contracting are in some other place, that place is the place for their delivery; and

(c) documents of title may be delivered through customary banking channels.

As amended in 2003.

Official Comment

Prior Uniform Statutory Provision: Paragraphs (a) and (b)—Section 43(1), Uniform Sales Act; Paragraph (c)—none.

Changes: Slight modification in language.

Purposes of Changes and New Matter:

1. Paragraphs (a) and (b) provide for those noncommercial sales and for those occasional commercial sales where no place or means of delivery has been agreed upon by the parties. Where delivery by carrier is "required or authorized by the agreement", the seller's duties as to delivery of the goods are governed not by this section but by Section 2–504.

2. Under paragraph (b) when the identified goods contracted for are known to both parties to be in some location other than the seller's place of business or residence, the parties are presumed to have intended that place to be the place of delivery. This paragraph also applies (unless, as would be normal, the circumstances show that delivery by way of documents is intended) to a bulk of goods in the possession of a bailee. In such a case, however, the seller has the additional obligation to procure the acknowledgment by the bailee of the buyer's right to possession.

3. Where "customary banking channels" call only for due notification by the banker that the documents are available, leaving the buyer himself to see to the physical receipt of the goods, tender at the buyer's address is not required under paragraph (c). But that paragraph merely eliminates the possibility of a default by the seller if "customary banking channels" have been properly used in giving notice to the buyer. Where the bank has purchased a draft accompanied by or associated with documents or has undertaken its collection on behalf of the seller, Part 5 of Article 4 spells out its duties and relations to its customer. Where the documents move forward under a letter of credit the Article on Letters of Credit spells out the duties and relations between the bank, the seller and the buyer. Delivery in relationship to either tangible or electronic documents of title is defined in Article 1, Section 1–201.

4. The rules of this section apply only "unless otherwise agreed." The surrounding circumstances, usage of trade, course of dealing and course of performance, as well as the express language of the parties, may constitute an "otherwise agreement".

Cross References:

Point 1: Sections 2–504 and 2–505.
Point 2: Section 2–503.
Point 3: Section 2–512, Articles 4, Part 5, and 5.

Definitional Cross References:

"Contract for sale". Section 2–106.
"Delivery". Section 2–103.
"Document of title". Section 1–201.
"Goods". Section 2–103.
"Party". Section 1–201.
"Seller". Section 2–103.

As amended in 2003.

§ 2–309. Absence of Specific Time Provisions; Notice of Termination.

(1) The time for shipment or delivery or any other action under a contract if not provided in this Article or agreed upon shall be a reasonable time.

(2) If the contract provides for successive performances but is indefinite in duration, it is valid for a reasonable time but unless otherwise agreed may be terminated at any time by either party.

(3) Termination of a contract by one party except on the happening of an agreed event requires that reasonable notification be received by the other party and an agreement dispensing with notification is invalid if its operation would be unconscionable. A term specifying standards for the nature and timing of notice is enforceable if the standards are not manifestly unreasonable.

As amended in 2003.

Official Comment

Prior Uniform Statutory Provision: Subsection (1)—see Sections 43(2), 45(2), 47(1) and 48, Uniform Sales Act, for policy continued under this Article; Subsection (2)—none; Subsection (3)—none.

Changes: Completely different in scope.

Purposes of Changes and New Matter:

1. Subsection (1) requires that all actions taken under a sales contract must be taken within a reasonable time where no time has been agreed upon. The reasonable time under this provision turns on the criteria as to "reasonable time" and on good faith and commercial standards set forth in Sections 1–203, 1–204 and 2–103. It thus depends upon what constitutes acceptable commercial conduct in view of the nature, purpose and circumstances of the action to be taken. Agreement as to a definite time, however, may be found in a term implied from the contractual circumstances, usage of trade or course of dealing or performance as well as in an express term. Such cases fall outside of this subsection since in them the time for action is "agreed" by usage.

2. The time for payment, where not agreed upon, is related to the time for delivery; the particular problems which arise in connection with determining the appropriate time of payment and the time for any inspection before payment which is both allowed by law and demanded by the buyer are covered in Section 2–513.

3. The facts in regard to shipment and delivery differ so widely as to make detailed provision for them in the text of this Article impracticable. The applicable principles, however, make it clear that surprise is to be avoided, good faith judgment is to be protected, and notice or negotiation to reduce the uncertainty to certainty is to be favored.

4. When the time for delivery is left open, unreasonably early offers of or demands for delivery are intended to be read under this Article as expressions of desire or intention, requesting the assent or acquiescence of the other party, not as final positions which may amount without more to breach or to create breach by the other side. See Sections 2–207 and 2–609.

5. The obligation of good faith under this Act requires reasonable notification before a contract may be treated as breached because a reasonable time for delivery or demand has expired. This operates both in the case of a contract originally indefinite as to time and of one subsequently made indefinite by waiver.

When both parties let an originally reasonable time go by in silence, the course of conduct under the contract may be viewed as enlarging the reasonable time for tender or demand of performance. The contract may be terminated by abandonment.

6. Parties to a contract are not required in giving reasonable notification to fix, at peril of breach, a time which is in fact reasonable in the unforeseeable judgment of a later trier of fact. Effective communication of a proposed time limit calls for a response, so that failure to reply will make out acquiescence. Where objection is made, however, or if the demand is merely for information as to when goods will be delivered or will be ordered out, demand for assurances on the ground of insecurity may be made under this Article pending further negotiations. Only when a party insists on undue delay or on rejection of the other party's reasonable proposal is there a question of flat breach under the present section.

7. Subsection (2) applies a commercially reasonable view to resolve the conflict which has arisen in the cases as to contracts of indefinite duration. The "reasonable time" of duration appropriate to a given arrangement is limited by the circumstances. When the arrangement has been carried on by the parties over the years, the "reasonable time" can continue indefinitely and the contract will not terminate until notice.

8. Subsection (3) recognizes that the application of principles of good faith and sound commercial practice normally call for such notification of the termination of a going contract relationship as will give the other party reasonable time to seek a substitute arrangement. An agreement dispensing with notification or limiting the time for the seeking of a substitute arrangement is, of course, valid under this subsection unless the results of putting it into operation would be the creation of an unconscionable state of affairs.

9. Justifiable cancellation for breach is a remedy for breach and is not the kind of termination covered by the present subsection.

10. The requirement of notification is dispensed with where the contract provides for termination on the happening of an "agreed event." "Event" is a term chosen here to contrast with "option" or the like.

11. The last sentence of subsection (3) is new and is based on Section 1–302(b). It provides for greater party autonomy. In an appropriate circumstance, the parties may agree that the standard for notice is no notice at all.

Cross References:

Point 1: Sections 1–102, 1–203, 1–204 and 2–103.

Point 2: Sections 2–504, and 2–511 through 2–514.
Point 5: Section 1–203.
Point 6: Section 2–609.
Point 7: Section 2–204.
Point 9: Sections 2–106, 2–318, 2–610 and 2–703.
Point 11: Section 1–102(3).

Definitional Cross References:

"Agreement". Section 1–201.
"Contract". Section 1–201.
"Notification". Section 1–202.
"Party". Section 1–201.
"Reasonable time". Section 1–205.
"Termination". Section 2–106.

As amended in 2003.

§ 2–310. Open Time for Payment or Running of Credit; Authority to Ship under Reservation.

Unless otherwise agreed:

(a) payment is due at the time and place at which the buyer is to receive the goods even though the place of shipment is the place of delivery;

(b) if the seller is required or authorized to send the goods, the seller may ship them under reservation, and may tender the documents of title, but the buyer may inspect the goods after their arrival before payment is due unless the inspection is inconsistent with the terms of the contract (Section 2–513);

(c) if tender of delivery is agreed to be made by way of documents of title otherwise than by paragraph (b), then payment is due regardless of where the goods are to be received (i) at the time and place at which the buyer is to receive delivery of the tangible documents, or (ii) at the time the buyer is to receive delivery of the electronic documents and at the seller's place of business or if none, the seller's residence; and

(d) if the seller is required or authorized to ship the goods on credit, the credit period runs from the time of shipment but postdating the invoice or delaying its dispatch will correspondingly delay the starting of the credit period.

As amended in 2003.

Official Comment

Prior Uniform Statutory Provision: Sections 42 and 47(2), Uniform Sales Act.

Changes: Completely rewritten in this and other sections.

Purposes of Changes: This section is drawn to reflect modern business methods of dealing at a distance rather than face to face. Thus:

1. Paragraph (a) provides that payment is due at the time and place "the buyer is to receive the goods" rather than at the point of delivery except in documentary shipment cases (paragraph (c)). This grants an opportunity for the exercise by the buyer of his preliminary right to inspection before paying even though under the delivery term the risk of loss may have previously passed to him or the running of the credit period has already started.

2. Paragraph (b) while providing for inspection by the buyer before he pays, protects the seller. He is not required to give up possession of the goods until he has received payment, where no credit has been contemplated by the parties. The seller may collect through a bank by a sight draft against an order bill of lading "hold until arrival; inspection allowed." The obligations of the bank under such a provision are set forth in Part 5 of Article 4. Under subsection (c), in the absence of a credit term, the seller is permitted to ship under reservation and if he does payment is then due where and when the buyer is to receive delivery of the tangible documents of title. In the case of an electronic document of title, payment is due when the buyer is to receive delivery of the electronic document and at the seller's place of business, or if none, the seller's residence. Delivery as to documents of title is stated in Article 1, Section 1–201.

3. Unless otherwise agreed, the place for the delivery of the documents and payment is the buyer's city but the time for payment is only after arrival of the goods, since under paragraph (b), and Sections 2–512 and 2–513 the buyer is under no duty to pay prior to inspection. Tender of a document of title requires that the seller be ready, willing and able to transfer possession of a tangible document of title or control of an electronic document of title to the buyer.

4. Where the mode of shipment is such that goods must be unloaded immediately upon arrival, too rapidly to permit adequate inspection before receipt, the seller must be guided by the provisions of this Article on inspection which provide that if the seller wishes to demand payment before inspection, he must put an appropriate term into the contract. Even requiring

payment against documents will not of itself have this desired result if the documents are to be held until the arrival of the goods. But under (b) and (c) if the terms are C.I.F., C.O.D., or cash against documents payment may be due before inspection.

5. Paragraph (d) states the common commercial understanding that an agreed credit period runs from the time of shipment or from that dating of the invoice which is commonly recognized as a representation of the time of shipment. The provision concerning any delay in sending forth the invoice is included because such conduct results in depriving the buyer of his full notice and warning as to when he must be prepared to pay.

Cross References:

Generally: Part 5.
Point 1: Sections 2–504 and 2–509.
Point 2: Sections 2–505, 2–511, 2–512, 2–513 and Article 4.
Point 3: Sections 2–308(b), 2–512 and 2–513.
Point 4: Section 2–513(3)(b).

Definitional Cross References:

"Agreement". Section 1–201.
"Buyer". Section 2–103.
"Delivery". Section 2–103.
"Document of title". Section 1–201.
"Goods". Section 2–103.
"Receipt of goods". Section 2–103.
"Seller". Section 2–103.
"Send". Section 1–201.
"Tender of delivery". Sections 2–503 and 2–507.
"Term". Section 1–201.

As amended in 2003.

§ 2–311. Options and Cooperation Respecting Performance.

(1) An agreement for sale which is otherwise sufficiently definite (Section 2–204(3)) to be a contract is not made invalid by the fact that it leaves particulars of performance to be specified by one of the parties. Any such specification must be made in good faith and within limits set by commercial reasonableness.

(2) Unless otherwise agreed, specifications relating to assortment of the goods are at the buyer's option and specifications or arrangements relating to shipment are at the seller's option.

(3) If the specification would materially affect the other party's performance but is not season-ably made or if one party's cooperation is necessary to the agreed performance of the other but is not seasonably forthcoming, the other party in addition to all other remedies:

(a) is excused for any resulting delay in that party's performance; and

(b) may also either proceed to perform in any reasonable manner or after the time for a material part of that party's performance treat the failure to specify or to cooperate as a breach by failure to deliver or accept the goods.

As amended in 2003.

Official Comment

Prior Uniform Statutory Provision: None.

Purposes:

1. Subsection (1) permits the parties to leave certain detailed particulars of performance to be filled in by either of them without running the risk of having the contract invalidated for indefiniteness. The party to whom the agreement gives power to specify the missing details is required to exercise good faith and to act in accordance with commercial standards so that there is no surprise and the range of permissible variation is limited by what is commercially reasonable. The "agreement" which permits one party so to specify may be found as well in a course of dealing, usage of trade, or implication from circumstances as in explicit language used by the parties.

2. Options as to assortment of goods or shipping arrangements are specifically reserved to the buyer and seller respectively under subsection (2) where no other arrangement has been made. This section rejects the test which mechanically and without regard to usage or the purpose of the option gave the option to the party "first under a duty to move" and applies instead a standard commercial interpretation to these circumstances. The "unless otherwise agreed" provision of this subsection covers not only express terms but the background and circumstances which enter into the agreement.

3. Subsection (3) applies when the exercise of an option or cooperation by one party is necessary to or materially affects the other party's performance, but it is not seasonably forthcoming; the subsection relieves the other party from the necessity for performance or excuses his delay in performance as the case may be. The contract-keeping party may at his option under this subsection proceed to perform in any commercially reasonable manner rather than wait. In addition to the

special remedies provided, this subsection also reserves "all other remedies". The remedy of particular importance in this connection is that provided for insecurity. Request may also be made pursuant to the obligation of good faith for a reasonable indication of the time and manner of performance for which a party is to hold himself ready.

4. The remedy provided in subsection (3) is one which does not operate in the situation which falls within the scope of Section 2–614 on substituted performance. Where the failure to cooperate results from circumstances set forth in that Section, the other party is under a duty to proffer or demand (as the case may be) substitute performance as a condition to claiming rights against the noncooperating party.

Cross References:

Point 1: Sections 1–201, 1–203, 2–204 and 2–708.
Point 3: Sections 1–203 and 2–609.
Point 4: Section 2–614.

Definitional Cross References:

"Agreement". Section 1–201.
"Buyer". Section 2–103.
"Contract for sale". Section 2–106.
"Goods". Section 2–103.
"Party". Section 1–201.
"Remedy". Section 1–201.
"Seasonably". Section 1–205.
"Seller". Section 2–103.

§ 2–312. Warranty of Title and Against Infringement; Buyer's Obligation Against Infringement.

(1) Subject to subsection (3), there is in a contract for sale a warranty by the seller that:

(a) the title conveyed shall be good and its transfer rightful and shall not unreasonably expose the buyer to litigation because of any colorable claim to or interest in the goods; and

(b) the goods shall be delivered free from any security interest or other lien or encumbrance of which the buyer at the time of contracting has no knowledge.

(2) Unless otherwise agreed, a seller that is a merchant regularly dealing in goods of the kind warrants that the goods shall be delivered free of the rightful claim of any third person by way of infringement or the like but a buyer that furnishes specifications to the seller must hold the seller harmless against any such claim that arises out of compliance with the specifications.

(3) A warranty under this section may be disclaimed or modified only by specific language or by circumstances that give the buyer reason to know that the seller does not claim title, that the seller is purporting to sell only the right or title as the seller or a third person may have, or that the seller is selling subject to any claims of infringement or the like.

As amended in 1999 and 2003.

Official Comment

1. Subsection (1) provides for a buyer's basic needs for a title which the buyer in good faith expects to acquire by the purchase, namely, that the buyer receive a good, clean title transferred also in a rightful manner so that the buyer will not be exposed to a lawsuit to protect the title. Under subsection (1), the seller warrants that (1) the title conveyed is good, (2) the transfer is rightful, and (3) the transfer does not unreasonably expose the buyer to litigation because a third person has or asserts a "colorable claim" to or interest in the goods.

In addition to sales in which there is an actual cloud on the title, a warranty that the "title conveyed is good and its transfer rightful" also covers cases when the title is good but the transfer is not rightful. For example, a wrongful transfer with good title occurs where a merchant bailee to which goods are entrusted for repair sells them without authority to a buyer in the ordinary course of business. *See* Section 2–403(2); *Sumner v. Fel–Air, Inc.*, 680 P.2d 1109 (Alaska 1984).

The subsection now expressly states what the courts have long recognized; further protection for the buyer is needed when the title is burdened by colorable claims that affect the value of the goods. *See Frank Arnold KRS, Inc. v. L.S. Meier Auction Co., Inc.*, 806 F.2d 462 (3d Cir. 1986) (two lawsuits contest title); *Jeanneret v. Vichey*, 693 F.2d 259 (2d Cir. 1982) (export restrictions in country from which painting was taken affect value); *Colton v. Decker*, 540 N.W.2d 172 (S.D. 1995) (conflicting vehicle identification numbers). Therefore, not only is the buyer entitled to a good title, but the buyer is also entitled to a marketable title, and until the colorable claim is resolved the market for the goods is impaired. *See Wright v. Vickaryous*, 611 P.2d 20 (Alaska 1980).

The justification for this rule is that the buyer of goods that are warranted for title has a right to rely on the fact that there will be no need later to have to contest ownership. The mere casting of a substantial shadow over the buyer's title, regardless of the ultimate outcome, violates the warranty of good title. *See American Container Corp. v. Hanley Trucking Corp.*, 111 N.J. Super. 322, 268 A.2d 313,318 (1970). It should be noted that not any assertion of a claim by a third party will constitute a breach of the warranty of title. The claim must be reasonable and colorable. *See C.F. Sales, Inc. v. Amfert*, 344 N.W.2d 543 (Iowa 1983).

The warranty of title extends to a buyer whether or not the seller was in possession of the goods at the time the sale or contract to sell was made.

Consistent with original Article 2, this section does not provide for a separate warranty of quiet possession in addition to the warranty of title. Disturbance of quiet possession, although not mentioned specifically, is one way, among many, in which the breach of the warranty of title might be established.

2. "Knowledge" as referred to in subsection (1)(b) is actual knowledge as distinct from notice.

3. The provisions of this Article that require notification to the seller within a reasonable time after the buyer's discovery of a breach (Section 2–607(3)(a)) apply to notice of a breach of the warranty of title when the seller's breach was innocent. However, if the seller's breach were in bad faith, the seller cannot claim prejudice by the delay in giving notice.

4. Subsection (2) provides the warranty against infringement. Unlike the warranty of title, this warranty is limited to sellers that are merchants that "regularly dealing in goods of the kind" sold.

When the goods are part of the seller's normal stock, and are sold in the normal course of business, it is the seller's duty to see that no claim of infringement of a patent or trademark by a third party will impair the buyer's title. A sale by a person other than a dealer, however, raises no implication in its circumstances of the warranty. Nor is there an implication when the buyer orders goods to be assembled, prepared or manufactured on the buyer's own specifications. If, in such a case, the resulting product infringes a patent or trademark, the liability will run from buyer to seller. There is, under these circumstances, a tacit representation on the part of the buyer that the seller will be safe in manufacturing according to the specifications, and the buyer is under an obligation in good faith to indemnify the seller for any loss suffered.

5. Under this section, the cases which recognize the principle that infringements violate the warranty of title but deny the buyer a remedy unless he has been expressly prevented from using the goods are rejected. Under this Article "eviction" is not a necessary condition to the buyer's remedy since the buyer's remedy arises immediately upon receipt of notice of infringement; it is merely one way of establishing the fact of breach.

6. Subsection (3) is concerned with the disclaimer or modification of the warranties of title or against infringement. This is a self-contained provision that govern the modification or disclaimer of warranties under this section. The warranties in this section are not designated as "implied" warranties, and hence these warranties are not subject to the modification and disclaimer provisions of Section 2–316(2) and (3). Unlike Section 2–316, subsection (3) of this section does not create any specific requirements that the disclaimer or modification be contained in a record or be conspicuous.

Under subsection (3), sales by sheriffs, executors, certain foreclosing lienors and persons similarly situated are recognized as possibly being so out of the ordinary commercial course that their peculiar character is immediately apparent to the buyer, and therefore no personal obligation is imposed upon the seller that is purporting to sell only an unknown or limited right. This subsection is not intended to touch upon, and it leaves open, all questions of restitution that arise in these cases, such as when a unique article that is sold is reclaimed by a third party as the rightful owner.

For a foreclosure sale under Article 9, Section 9–610 of revised Article 9 provides that a disposition of collateral under that section includes warranties such as those imposed by this section on a voluntary disposition of property. Consequently, unless properly excluded under subsection (3) or under the special provisions for exclusion in Section 9–610, a disposition under that section of collateral consisting of goods includes the warranties imposed by subsection (1) and, if applicable, subsection (2).

7. The statute of limitations for a breach of warranty under this section is determined under the provisions set out in Section 2–725(1) and (3)(c).

Cross References:

Point 1: Section 2–403.
Point 3: Sections 2–607 and 2–725.
Point 4: Section 1–203.
Point 6: Sections 2–316, 2–609, 2–610 and 2–725.
Point 7: Section 2–316 and 2–725.

Definitional Cross References:

"Agreement". Section 1–201.
"Buyer". Section 2–103.
"Contract for sale". Section 2–106.

"Goods". Section 2–103.
"Merchant". Section 2–104.
"Person". Section 1–201.
"Right". Section 1–201.
"Seller". Section 2–103.

As amended in 1999 and 2003.

§ 2–313. Express Warranties by Affirmation, Promise, Description, Sample; Remedial Promise.

(1) In this section, "immediate buyer" means a buyer that enters into a contract with the seller.

(2) Express warranties by the seller to the immediate buyer are created as follows:

(a) Any affirmation of fact or promise made by the seller which relates to the goods and becomes part of the basis of the bargain creates an express warranty that the goods shall conform to the affirmation or promise.

(b) Any description of the goods which is made part of the basis of the bargain creates an express warranty that the goods shall conform to the description.

(c) Any sample or model that is made part of the basis of the bargain creates an express warranty that the whole of the goods shall conform to the sample or model.

(3) It is not necessary to the creation of an express warranty that the seller use formal words such as "warrant" or "guarantee" or that the seller have a specific intention to make a warranty, but an affirmation merely of the value of the goods or a statement purporting to be merely the seller's opinion or commendation of the goods does not create a warranty.

(4) Any remedial promise made by the seller to the immediate buyer creates an obligation that the promise will be performed upon the happening of the specified event.

As amended in 2003.

Official Comment

1. In subsections (2) and (4) the term "immediate buyer" is used to make clear that the section is limited to express warranties and remedial promises made by a seller to a buyer with which the seller has a contractual relationship. Sections 2–313A and 2–313B address

obligations that run directly from a seller to a remote purchaser.

2. Subsection (4) uses the term "remedial promise," which was not used in original Article 2. This section deals with remedial promises to immediate buyers. Sections 2–313A and 2–313B deal with remedial promises running directly from a seller to a remote purchaser. Remedial promise is defined in Section 2–103(1)(n).

3. "Express" warranties rest on "dickered" aspects of the individual bargain, and go so clearly to the essence of that bargain that words of disclaimer in a form are repugnant to the basic dickered terms. "Implied" warranties rest so clearly on a common factual situation or set of conditions that no particular language or action is necessary to evidence them and they will arise in such a situation unless unmistakably negated. As with original Article 2, warranties of description and sample are designated "express" rather than "implied."

4. This section is limited in its scope and direct purpose to express warranties and remedial promises made by the seller to the immediate buyer as part of a contract for sale. It is not designed in any way to disturb those lines of case law which have recognized that warranties need not be confined to contracts within the scope of this Article.

Under Section 2–313B, a seller may incur an obligation to a remote purchaser through a medium for communication to the public such as advertising. An express warranty to an immediate buyer may also arise through a medium for communication to the public if the elements of this section are satisfied.

The fact that a buyer has rights against an immediate seller under this section does not preclude the buyer from also asserting rights against a remote seller under Section 2–313A or 2–313B.

5. The present section deals with affirmations of fact or promises made by the seller, descriptions of the goods, or exhibitions of samples or models, exactly as it deals with any other part of a negotiation which ends in a contract. No specific intention to make a warranty is necessary if any of these factors is made part of the basis of the bargain. In actual practice affirmations of fact and promises made by the seller about the goods during a bargain are regarded as part of the description of those goods; hence no particular reliance on these statements need be shown in order to weave them into the fabric of the agreement. Rather, any fact which is to take these affirmations or promises, once made, out of the agreement requires clear affirmative proof. The issue normally is one of fact.

6. In view of the principle that the whole purpose of the law of warranty is to determine what it is that the seller has in essence agreed to sell, the policy is adopted of those cases which refuse except in unusual circumstances to recognize a material deletion of the seller's obligation. Thus, a contract is normally a contract for a sale of something describable and described. A clause generally disclaiming "all warranties, express or implied" cannot reduce the seller's obligation for the description and therefore cannot be given literal effect under Section 2–316(1).

This is not intended to mean that the parties, if they consciously desire, cannot make their own bargain as they wish. But in determining what they have agreed upon good faith is a factor and consideration should be given to the fact that the probability is small that a real price is intended to be exchanged for a pseudo-obligation.

7. Subsection (2)(b) makes specific some of the principles set forth above when a description of the goods is given by the seller.

A description need not be by words. Technical specifications, blueprints and the like can afford more exact description than mere language and if made part of the basis of the bargain goods must conform with them. Past deliveries may set the description of quality, either expressly or impliedly by course of dealing. Of course, all descriptions by merchants must be read against the applicable trade usages with the general rules as to merchantability resolving any doubts.

8. The basic situation as to statements affecting the true essence of the bargain is no different when a sample or model is involved in the transaction. This section includes both a "sample" actually drawn from the bulk of goods which is the subject matter of the sale, and a "model" which is offered for inspection when the subject matter is not at hand and which has not been drawn from the bulk of the goods.

Although the underlying principles are unchanged, the facts are often ambiguous when something is shown as illustrative, rather than as a straight sample. In general, the presumption is that any sample or model, just as any affirmation of fact, is intended to become a basis of the bargain. But there is no escape from the question of fact. When the seller exhibits a sample purporting to be drawn from an existing bulk, good faith of course requires that the sample be fairly drawn. But in mercantile experience the mere exhibition of a "sample" does not of itself show whether it is merely intended to "suggest" or to "be" the character of the subject-matter of the contract. The question is whether the seller has so acted with reference to the sample as to become responsible that the whole shall have at least the values shown by it. The circumstances aid in answering this question. If the sample has been drawn from an existing bulk, it must be regarded as describing values of the goods contracted for unless it is accompanied by an unmistakable denial of responsibility. If, on the other hand, a model of merchandise not on hand is offered, the mercantile presumption that it has become a literal description of the subject matter is not so strong, and particularly so if modification on the buyer's initiative impairs any feature of the model.

9. The precise time when words of description or affirmation are made or samples are shown is not material. The sole question is whether the language or samples or models are fairly to be regarded as part of the contract. If language that would otherwise create an obligation under this section is used after the closing of the deal (as when the buyer when taking delivery asks and receives an additional assurance), an obligation will arise if the requirements for a modification are satisfied. *See Downie v. Abex Corp.*, 741 F.2d 1235 (10th Cir. 1984).

10. Concerning affirmations of value or a seller's opinion or commendation under subsection (3), the basic question remains the same: What statements of the seller have in the circumstances and in objective judgment become part of the basis of the bargain? As indicated above, all of the statements of the seller do so unless good reason is shown to the contrary. The provisions of subsection (3) are included, however, since common experience discloses that some statements or predictions cannot fairly be viewed as entering into the bargain. Even as to false statements of value, however, the possibility is left open that a remedy may be provided by the law relating to fraud or misrepresentation.

There are a number of factors relevant to determine whether an expression creates a warranty under this section or is merely puffing. For example, the relevant factors may include whether the seller's representations taken in context, (1) were general rather than specific, (2) related to the consequences of buying rather than the goods themselves, (3) were "hedged" in some way, (4) were related to experimental rather than standard goods, (5) were concerned with some aspects of the goods but not a hidden or unexpected nonconformity, (6) were informal statements made in a formal contracting process, (7) were phrased in terms of opinion rather than fact, or (8) were not capable of objective measurement.

11. The use of the word "promise" in subsection (2)(a) refers to statements about the quality or performance characteristics of the goods. For example, a seller might make an affirmation of fact to the buyer that the goods are of a certain quality, or may promise that the goods when delivered will be of a certain quality, or may promise that the goods will perform in a certain manner after delivery. In normal usage, "promise" refers to a what a person, not goods, will do; that is, a promise is a commitment to act, or refrain from acting, in a certain manner in the future. A promise about the quality or performance characteristics of the goods creates an express warranty if the other elements of a warranty are present whereas a promise by which the seller commits itself to take remedial action upon the happening of a specified event is a remedial promise. The distinction has meaning in the context of the statute of limitations. A right of action for breach of an express warranty accrues when the goods are tendered to the immediate buyer (Section 2–725(3)(a)) unless the warranty consists of a promise that explicitly extends to the future performance of the goods and discovery must await the time for performance, in which case accrual occurs when the immediate buyer discovers or should have discovered the breach (Section 2–725(3)(d)). Section 2–725(2)(c) separately addresses the accrual of a right of action for breach of a remedial promise.

The concept of remedial promise is dealt with in a separate subsection to make clear that it is a concept separate and apart from express warranty and that the elements of an express warranty, such as basis of the bargain, are not applicable.

Cross References:

Point 1: Sections 2–313A and 2–313B.
Point 2: Sections 2–103, 2–313A and 2–313B.
Point 3: Section 2–316(2)(b).
Point 4: Section 2–316.
Point 5: Sections 1–205(4) and 2–314.
Point 6: Section 2–316.
Point 7: Section 2–209.
Point 8: Section 1–103.
Point 11: Section 2–313 and 2–725.

Definitional Cross References:

"Buyer". Section 2–103.
"Conforming". Section 2–106.
"Goods". Section 2–103.
"Remedial promise". Section 2–103.
"Seller". Section 2–103.
"Tender of delivery". Sections 2–503 and 2–507.

As amended in 2003.

§ 2–313A. Obligation to Remote Purchaser Created by Record Packaged with or Accompanying Goods.

(1) In this section:

(a) "Immediate buyer" means a buyer that enters into a contract with the seller.

(b) "Remote purchaser" means a person that buys or leases goods from an immediate buyer or other person in the normal chain of distribution.

(2) This section applies only to new goods and goods sold or leased as new goods in a transaction of purchase in the normal chain of distribution.

(3) If in a record packaged with or accompanying the goods the seller makes an affirmation of fact or promise that relates to the goods, provides a description that relates to the goods, or makes a remedial promise, and the seller reasonably expects the record to be, and the record is, furnished to the remote purchaser, the seller has an obligation to the remote purchaser that:

(a) the goods will conform to the affirmation of fact, promise, or description unless a reasonable person in the position of the remote purchaser would not believe that the affirmation of fact, promise, or description created an obligation; and

(b) the seller will perform the remedial promise.

(4) It is not necessary to the creation of an obligation under this section that the seller use formal words such as "warrant" or "guarantee" or that the seller have a specific intention to undertake an obligation, but an affirmation merely of the value of the goods or a statement purporting to be merely the seller's opinion or commendation of the goods does not create an obligation.

(5) The following rules apply to the remedies for breach of an obligation created under this section:

(a) The seller may modify or limit the remedies available to the remote purchaser if the modification or limitation is furnished to the remote purchaser no later than the time of purchase or if the modification or limitation is contained in the record that contains the affirmation of fact, promise, or description.

(b) Subject to a modification or limitation of remedy, a seller in breach is liable for incidental or consequential damages under Section 2–715, but not for lost profits.

(c) The remote purchaser may recover as damages for breach of a seller's obligation arising under subsection (3) the loss resulting in the ordinary course of events as determined in any reasonable manner.

(6) An obligation that is not a remedial promise is breached if the goods did not conform to the affirmation of fact, promise, or description creating the obligation when the goods left the seller's control.

Legislative Note: To maintain their relative positions in this Act, Sections 2–313A and 2–313B may have to be renumbered according to the convention used by a particular state. For example, in some states they may be designated as 2–313.1 and 2–313.2.

As added in 2003.

Official Comment

1. Sections 2–313A and 2–313B are new, and they follow case law and practice in extending a seller's obligations regarding new goods to remote purchasers. Section 2–313A deals with what are commonly called "pass-through warranties". The usual transaction in which this obligation arises is when a manufacturer sells goods in a package to a retailer and include in the package a record that sets forth the obligations that the manufacturer is willing to undertake in favor of the final party in the distributive chain, who is the person that buys or leases the goods from the retailer. If the manufacturer had sold the goods directly to the final party in the distributive chain, whether the manufacturer would incur liability is determined by Section 2–313 and this section is inapplicable.

No direct contract exists between the seller and the remote purchaser, and thus the seller's obligation under this section is not referred to as an "express warranty." Use of "obligation" rather than "express warranty" avoids any inference that the obligation arises as part of the basis of the bargain as would be required to create an express warranty under section 2–313. The test for whether an obligation other than a remedial promise arises is similar in some respects to the basis of the bargain requirement in section 2–313,

but the test set forth in this section is exclusive. Because "remedial promise" in Section 2–313 is not subject to the requirement that it arise as part of the basis of the bargain, the term is used in this section.

2. The party to which an obligation runs under this section may either buy or lease the goods, and thus the term "remote purchaser" is used. The term is more limited than "purchaser" in Article 1, however, and does not include a donee or any voluntary transferee who is not a buyer or lessee. Moreover, the remote purchaser must be part of the normal chain of distribution for the particular product. That chain will, by definition, include at least three parties and may well include more. For example, the manufacturer might sell first to a wholesaler that would then resell the goods to a retailer for sale or lease to the public. A buyer or lessee from the retailer would qualify as a remote purchaser and could invoke this section against either the manufacturer or the wholesaler (if the wholesaler provided a record to the retailer to be furnished to the final party in the distribution chain), but no subsequent transferee, such as a used-goods buyer or sublessee, would qualify. The law governing assignment and third-party beneficiary, including Section 2–318, should be consulted to determine whether a party other than the remote purchaser can enforce an obligation created under this section.

3. The application of this section is limited to new goods and goods sold or leased as new goods within the normal chain of distribution. It does not apply to goods that are sold outside the normal chain, such as "gray" goods or salvaged goods, nor does it apply if the goods are unused but sold as seconds. The concept is flexible, and to determine whether goods have been sold or leased in the normal chain of distribution requires consideration of the seller's expectations for the manner in which its goods will reach the remote purchaser. For example, a car manufacturer may be aware that certain of its dealers transfer cars among themselves, and under the particular circumstances of the case a court might find that a new car sold initially to one dealer but leased to the remote purchaser by another dealer was leased in the normal chain of distribution. The concept may also include such practices as door-to-door sales and distribution through a nonprofit organization.

The phrase "goods sold or leased as new goods" refers to goods that in the normal course of business would be considered new. There are many instances in which goods might be used for a limited purpose yet be sold or leased in the normal chain of distribution as new goods. For example, goods that have been returned to a dealer by a purchaser and placed back into the dealer's inventory might be sold or leased as new goods in the normal chain of distribution. Other examples might include goods that have been used for the purpose of inspection (*e.g.*, a car that has been test-driven) and goods that have been returned by a sale-or-return buyer (Section 2–326).

4. This section applies only to obligations set forth in a record that is packaged with the goods or otherwise accompanies them (subsection (2)). Examples include a label affixed to the outside of a container, a card inside a container, or a booklet handed to the remote purchaser at the time of purchase. In addition, the seller must be able to anticipate that the remote purchaser will acquire the record, and therefore this section is limited to records that the seller reasonably expects to be furnished, and that are in fact furnished, to the remote purchaser.

Neither this section nor Section 2–313B are intended to overrule cases that impose liability on facts outside the direct scope of one of the sections. For example, the sections are not intended to overrule a decision imposing liability on a seller that distributes a sample to a remote purchaser.

5. Obligations other than remedial promises created under this section are analogous to express warranties and are subject to a test that is akin to the basis of the bargain test of Section 2–313(2). The seller is entitled to shape the scope of the obligation, and the seller's language tending to create an obligation must be considered in context. If a reasonable person in the position of the remote purchaser, reading the seller's language in its entirety, would not believe that an affirmation of fact, promise or description created an obligation, there is no liability under this section.

6. There is no difference between remedial promise as used in this section (and Section 2–313B) and the same term as used in Section 2–313.

7. Subsection (5)(a) makes clear that the seller may employ the provisions of Section 2–719 to modify or limit the remedies available to the remote purchaser for breach of the seller's obligation in this section. The modification or limitation may appear on the same record as the one which creates the obligation, or it may be provided to the remote purchaser separately, but in no event may it be furnished to the remote purchaser any later than the time of purchase.

The requirements and limitations set forth in Section 2–719, such as the requirement of an express statement of exclusivity and the tests for failure of essential purpose (Section 2–719(2)) and unconscionability (Section 2–719(3)) are applicable to a modification or limitation of remedy under this section.

8. As with express warranties, no specific language or intention is necessary to create an obligation, and whether an obligation exists is normally an issue of fact. Subsection (3) is virtually identical to Section 2–313(3), and the tests developed under the common law and under that section to determine whether a statement creates an obligation or is mere puffing are applicable to this section.

Just as a seller can limit the extent to which its language creates an express warranty under Section 2–313 by placing that language in a broader context, a seller under this section or Section 2–313B can limit the extent of its liability to a remote purchaser (subsection(4)(a)). In other words, the seller, in undertaking an obligation under these sections, can control the scope and limits of that obligation.

9. As a rule, a remote purchaser may recover monetary damages measured in the same manner as in the case of an aggrieved buyer under Section 2–714 as well as incidental and consequential damages under Section 2–715 to the extent they would be available to an aggrieved buyer. Subsection (5)(c) parallels Section 2–714(1) in allowing the buyer to recover for loss resulting in the ordinary course of events as determined in any manner which is reasonable. In the case of an obligation that is not a remedial promise, the normal measure of damages would be the difference between the value of the goods if they had conformed to the seller's statements and their actual value, and the normal measure of damages for breach of a remedial promise would be the difference between the value of the promised remedial performance and the value of the actual performance received.

Subsection (5)(b) precludes a remote purchaser from recovering consequential damages in the form of lost profits.

Cross References:

Point 1: Sections 2–313, 2–313A and 2–313B.
Point 2: Section 2–318.
Point 3: Section 2–326.
Point 4: Section 2–313B.
Point 5: Section 2–313.
Point 6: Section 2–313 and 2–313B.
Point 7: Section 2–719.
Point 8: Section 2–313 and 2–313B.
Point 9: Sections 2–714 and 2–715.

Definitional Cross References:

"Buyer". Section 2–103.
"Conforming". Section 2–106.
"Goods". Section 2–103.

"Lease". Section 2A–103.
"Purchase". Section 1–201.
"Record". Section 2–103.
"Remedial promise". Section 2–103.
"Remedy". Section 1–201.
"Sale". Section 2–106.
"Seller". Section 2–103.

As added in 2003.

§ 2–313B. Obligation to Remote Purchaser Created by Communication to the Public.

(1) In this section:

(a) "Immediate buyer" means a buyer that enters into a contract with the seller.

(b) "Remote purchaser" means a person that buys or leases goods from an immediate buyer or other person in the normal chain of distribution.

(2) This section applies only to new goods and goods sold or leased as new goods in a transaction of purchase in the normal chain of distribution.

(3) If in an advertisement or a similar communication to the public a seller makes an affirmation of fact or promise that relates to the goods, provides a description that relates to the goods, or makes a remedial promise, and the remote purchaser enters into a transaction of purchase with knowledge of and with the expectation that the goods will conform to the affirmation of fact, promise, or description, or that the seller will perform the remedial promise, the seller has an obligation to the remote purchaser that:

(a) the goods will conform to the affirmation of fact, promise, or description unless a reasonable person in the position of the remote purchaser would not believe that the affirmation of fact, promise, or description created an obligation; and

(b) the seller will perform the remedial promise.

(4) It is not necessary to the creation of an obligation under this section that the seller use formal words such as "warrant" or "guarantee" or that the seller have a specific intention to undertake an obligation, but an affirmation merely of the value of the goods or a statement purporting to be merely the seller's opinion or commendation of the goods does not create an obligation.

(5) The following rules apply to the remedies for breach of an obligation created under this section:

(a) The seller may modify or limit the remedies available to the remote purchaser if the modification or limitation is furnished to the remote purchaser no later than the time of purchase. The modification or limitation may be furnished as part of the communication that contains the affirmation of fact, promise, or description.

(b) Subject to a modification or limitation of remedy, a seller in breach is liable for incidental or consequential damages under Section 2–715, but not for lost profits.

(c) The remote purchaser may recover as damages for breach of a seller's obligation arising under subsection (3) the loss resulting in the ordinary course of events as determined in any reasonable manner.

(6) An obligation that is not a remedial promise is breached if the goods did not conform to the affirmation of fact, promise, or description creating the obligation when the goods left the seller's control.

Legislative Note: In order to maintain their relative positions in this Act, Sections 2–313A and 2–313B may have to be renumbered according to the convention used by a particular state. For example, in some states they may be designated as 2–313.1 and 2–313.2.

As added in 2003.

Official Comment

1. Sections 2–313B and 2–313A are new, and they follow case law and practice in extending a seller's obligations for new goods to remote purchasers. This section deals with obligations to a remote purchaser created by advertising or a similar communication to the public. The normal situation where this obligation will arise is when a manufacturer engages in an advertising campaign directed towards all or part of the market for its product and will make statements that if made to an immediate buyer would amount to an express warranty or remedial promise under Section 2–313. The goods, however, are sold to someone other than the recipient of the advertising and are then resold or leased to the recipient. By imposing liability

on the seller, this section adopts the approach of cases such as *Randy Knitwear, Inc. v. American Cyanamid Co.*, 11 N.Y.2d 5, 226 N.Y.S.2d 363, 181 N.E.2d 399 (Ct. App. 1962).

If the seller's advertisement is made to an immediate buyer, whether the seller incurs liability is determined by Section 2–313 and this section is inapplicable.

2. This section parallels Section 2–313A in most respects, and the Official Comments to that section should be consulted. In particular, the reasoning of Comment 1 (scope and terminology), Comment 2 (definition of remote purchaser), Comment 3 (new goods and goods sold as new goods in the normal chain of distribution), Comment 4 (reasonable person in the position of the remote purchaser), Comment 7 (modification or limitation of remedy), Comment 8 (puffing and limitations on extent of obligation) and Comment 9 (damages) is adopted here.

3. This section provides an additional test for enforceability not found in Section 2–313A. For the obligation to be created the remote purchaser must, at the time of purchase, have knowledge of the affirmation of fact, promise, description or remedial promise and must also have an expectation that the goods will conform or that the seller will comply. This test is entirely subjective, while the reasonable person test in subsection (3)(a) is objective in nature. Both tests must be met.

Thus, the seller will incur no liability to the remote purchaser if: i) the purchaser did not have knowledge of the seller's statement at the time of purchase; ii) the remote purchaser knew of the seller's statement at the time of purchase but did not expect the goods to conform or the seller to comply; iii) a reasonable person in the position of the remote purchaser would not believe that the seller's statement created an obligation (this test does not apply to remedial promises), or iv) the seller's statement is puffing.

4. To determine whether the tests set forth in this section are satisfied the temporal relationship between the communication and the purchase should be considered by the court. For example, the remote purchaser may acquire the goods years after the seller's advertising campaign. In this circumstance, it would be highly unusual for the advertisement to have created the level of expectation in the remote purchaser or belief in the reasonable person in the position of the remote person necessary for the creation of an obligation under this section.

5. To determine whether an obligation arises under this Section, all information known to the remote purchaser at the time of contracting must be consid-

ered. For example, a news release by a manufacturer limiting the statements made in its advertising and which are known by the remote purchaser, or a communication to the remote purchaser by the immediate seller limiting the statements made in the manufacturer's advertising must be considered to determine whether the expectation requirement applicable to the remote purchaser and the belief requirement applicable to the reasonable person in the position of the remote purchaser are satisfied.

6. The remedies for breach of an obligation arising under this section may be modified or limited as set forth in Section 2–719. The modification or limitation may be contained in the advertisement that creates the obligation, or it may be separately furnished to the remote purchaser no later than the time of purchase.

7. Section 2–318 deals with the extension of obligations to certain third-party beneficiaries. Of course, no extension is necessary if the goods are purchased by an agent. In this case, the knowledge and expectation of the principal, not the agent, are relevant in determining whether an obligation arises under this section. Nothing in this Act precludes a court from determining that a household operates as a buying unit under the law of agency.

Cross References:

Point 1: Sections 2–313, 2–313A and 2–313B.
Point 2: Section 2–313A.
Point 3: Section 2–313A.
Point 6: Section 2–719.
Point 7: Section 2–318.

Definitional Cross References:

"Buyer". Section 2–103.
"Conforming". Section 2–106.
"Goods". Section 2–103.
"Lease". Section 2A–103.
"Purchase". Section 1–201.
"Record". Section 2–103.
"Remedial promise". Section 2–103.
"Remedy". Section 1–201.
"Sale". Section 2–106.
"Seller". Section 2–103.

As added in 2003.

§ 2–314. Implied Warranty: Merchantability; Usage of Trade.

(1) Unless excluded or modified (Section 2–316), a warranty that the goods shall be merchantable is implied in a contract for their sale if

the seller is a merchant with respect to goods of that kind. Under this section the serving for value of food or drink to be consumed either on the premises or elsewhere is a sale.

(2) Goods to be merchantable must be at least such as:

(a) pass without objection in the trade under the contract description;

(b) in the case of fungible goods, are of fair average quality within the description;

(c) are fit for the ordinary purposes for which goods of that description are used;

(d) run, within the variations permitted by the agreement, of even kind, quality and quantity within each unit and among all units involved;

(e) are adequately contained, packaged, and labeled as the agreement may require; and

(f) conform to the promise or affirmations of fact made on the container or label if any.

(3) Unless excluded or modified (Section 2–316) other implied warranties may arise from course of dealing or usage of trade.

As amended in 2003.

Official Comment

1. The phrase "goods of that description" rather than the language from the original Article 2 "for which such goods are used" is used in subsection (2)(c). This change emphasizes the importance of the agreed description in determining fitness for ordinary purposes.

2. The seller's obligation applies to present sales as well as to contracts to sell subject to the effects of any examination of specific goods. *See* Section 2–316(3)(b). The warranty of merchantability also applies to sales for use as well as to sales for resale.

3. The question when the warranty is imposed turns basically on the meaning of the terms of the agreement as recognized in the trade. Goods delivered under an agreement made by a merchant in a given line of trade must be of a quality comparable to that generally acceptable in that line of trade under the description or other designation of the goods used in the agreement. The responsibility imposed rests on any merchant-seller.

4. A specific designation of goods by the buyer does not exclude the seller's obligation that they be fit for the general purposes appropriate to the goods. A contract for the sale of second-hand goods, however, involves only an obligation as is appropriate to the goods according to their contract description. A person making an isolated sale of goods is not a "merchant" within the meaning of the full scope of this section and, thus, no warranty of merchantability would apply. The seller's knowledge of any defects not apparent on inspection would, however, without need for express agreement and in keeping with the underlying reason of the present section and the provisions on good faith, impose an obligation that known material but hidden defects be fully disclosed.

5. Although a seller may not be a "merchant" for the goods in question, if the seller states generally that the goods are "guaranteed," the provisions of this section may furnish a guide to the content of the resulting express warranty. This has particular significance in the case of second-hand sales, and has further significance in limiting the effect of fine-print disclaimer clauses where their effect would be inconsistent with large-print assertions of "guarantee."

6. The second sentence of subsection (1) covers the warranty for food and drink. The serving for value of food or drink for consumption on the premises or elsewhere is treated as a sale.

7. Suppose that an unmerchantable lawn mower causes personal injury to the buyer, who is operating the mower. Without more, the buyer can sue the seller for breach of the implied warranty of merchantability and recover for injury to person "proximately resulting" from the breach. Section 2–715(2)(b).

This opportunity does not resolve the tension between warranty law and tort law where goods cause personal injury or property damage. The primary source of that tension arises from disagreement over whether the concept of defect in tort and the concept of merchantability in Article 2 are coextensive where personal injuries are involved, *i.e.*, if goods are merchantable under warranty law, can they still be defective under tort law, and if goods are not defective under tort law, can they be unmerchantable under warranty law? The answer to both questions should be no, and the tension between merchantability in warranty and defect in tort where personal injury or property damage is involved should be resolved as follows:

When recovery is sought for injury to person or property, whether goods are merchantable is to be determined by applicable state products liability law. When, however, a claim for injury to person or property is based on an implied warranty of fitness under Section 2–315 or an express warranty under

Section 2–313 or an obligation arising under Section 2–313A or 2–313B, this Article determines whether an implied warranty of fitness or an express warranty was made and breached, as well as what damages are recoverable under Section 2–715.

To illustrate, suppose that the seller makes a representation about the safety of a lawn mower that becomes part of the basis of the buyer's bargain. The buyer is injured when the gas tank cracks and a fire breaks out. If the lawnmower without the representation is not defective under applicable tort law, it is not unmerchantable under this section. On the other hand, if the lawnmower did not conform to the representation about safety, the seller made and breached an express warranty and the buyer may sue under Article 2.

8. Subsection (2) does not purport to exhaust the meaning of "merchantable" nor to negate any of its attributes not specifically mentioned in the text of the statute but that arise by usage of trade or through case law. The language used is "must be at least such as . . . ," and the intention is to leave open other possible attributes of merchantability.

9. Paragraphs (a) and (b) of subsection (2) are to be read together. Both refer to the standards of that line of the trade which fits the transaction and the seller's business. "Fair average" is a term directly appropriate to agricultural bulk products and means goods centering around the middle belt of quality, not the least or the worst that can be understood in the particular trade by the designation, but such as can pass "without objection." Of course a fair percentage of the least is permissible but the goods are not "fair average" if they are all of the least or worst quality possible under the description. In cases of doubt about what quality is intended, the price at which a merchant closes a contract is an excellent indication of the nature and scope of the merchant's obligation under the present section.

10. Fitness for the ordinary purposes for which goods of the type are used is a fundamental concept of the present section and is covered in paragraph (2)(c). As stated above, merchantability is also a part of the obligation owing to the buyer for use. Correspondingly, protection, under this aspect of the warranty, of the person buying for resale to the ultimate consumer is equally necessary, and merchantable goods must therefore be "honestly" resalable in the normal course of business because they are what they purport to be.

11. Paragraph (2)(d) on evenness of kind, quality and quantity follows case law. But precautionary language has been added as a remainder of the frequent usages of trade which permit substantial variations both with and without an allowance or an obligation to replace the varying units.

12. Paragraph (2)(e) applies only where the nature of the goods and of the transaction require a certain type of container, package or label. Paragraph (2)(f) applies, on the other hand, wherever there is a label or container on which representations are made, even though the original contract, either by express terms or usage of trade, may not have required either the labeling or the representation. This follows from the general obligation of good faith which requires that a buyer should not be placed in the position of reselling or using goods delivered under false representations appearing on the package or container. No problem of extra consideration arises in this connection since, under this Article, an obligation is imposed by the original contract not to deliver mislabeled articles, and the obligation is imposed where mercantile good faith so requires and without reference to the doctrine of consideration.

13. Exclusion or modification of the warranty of merchantability, or of any part of it, is dealt with in Section 2–316. That section must be read with particular reference to subsection (4) on limitation of remedies. The warranty of merchantability, wherever it is normal, is so commonly taken for granted that its exclusion from the contract is a matter threatening surprise and therefore requiring special precaution.

14. Subsection (3) is to make explicit that usage of trade and course of dealing can create warranties and that they are implied rather than express warranties and thus subject to exclusion or modification under Section 2–316. A typical instance would be the obligation to provide pedigree papers to evidence conformity of the animal to the contract in the case of a pedigreed dog or blooded bull.

15. In an action based on breach of warranty, it is of course necessary to show not only the existence of the warranty but the fact that the warranty was broken and that the breach of the warranty was the proximate cause of the loss sustained. An affirmative showing by the seller that the loss resulted from some action or event following the seller's delivery of the goods can operate as a defense. Equally, evidence indicating that the seller exercised care in the manufacture, processing or selection of the goods is relevant to the issue of whether the warranty was in fact broken. An action by the buyer following an examination of the goods which ought to have indicated the defect complained of can be shown as matter bearing on whether the breach itself was the cause of the injury.

Cross References:

Point 1: Section 2–316.
Point 2: Section 2–316.
Point 3: Sections 1–203 and 2–104.
Point 5: Section 2–315.
Point 7: Section 2–715.
Point 11: Section 2–316.
Point 12: Sections 1–201, 1–205 and 2–316.
Point 13: Section 2–316.
Point 14: Section 2–316.

Definitional Cross References:

"Agreement". Section 1–201.
"Contract". Section 1–201.
"Contract for sale". Section 2–106.
"Goods". Section 2–103.
"Merchant". Section 2–104.
"Seller". Section 2–103.

As amended in 2003.

§ 2–315. Implied Warranty: Fitness for Particular Purpose.

Where the seller at the time of contracting has reason to know any particular purpose for which the goods are required and that the buyer is relying on the seller's skill or judgment to select or furnish suitable goods, there is unless excluded or modified under the next section an implied warranty that the goods shall be fit for such purpose.

Official Comment

Prior Uniform Statutory Provision: Section 15(1), (4), (5), Uniform Sales Act.

Changes: Rewritten.

Purposes of Changes:

1. Whether or not this warranty arises in any individual case is basically a question of fact to be determined by the circumstances of the contracting. Under this section the buyer need not bring home to the seller actual knowledge of the particular purpose for which the goods are intended or of his reliance on the seller's skill and judgment, if the circumstances are such that the seller has reason to realize the purpose intended or that the reliance exists. The buyer, of course, must actually be relying on the seller.

2. A "particular purpose" differs from the ordinary purpose for which the goods are used in that it envisages a specific use by the buyer which is peculiar to the nature of his business whereas the ordinary purposes for which goods are used are those envisaged in

the concept of merchantability and go to uses which are customarily made of the goods in question. For example, shoes are generally used for the purpose of walking upon ordinary ground, but a seller may know that a particular pair was selected to be used for climbing mountains.

A contract may of course include both a warranty of merchantability and one of fitness for a particular purpose.

The provisions of this Article on the cumulation and conflict of express and implied warranties must be considered on the question of inconsistency between or among warranties. In such a case any question of fact as to which warranty was intended by the parties to apply must be resolved in favor of the warranty of fitness for particular purpose as against all other warranties except where the buyer has taken upon himself the responsibility of furnishing the technical specifications.

3. In connection with the warranty of fitness for a particular purpose the provisions of this Article on the allocation or division of risks are particularly applicable in any transaction in which the purpose for which the goods are to be used combines requirements both as to the quality of the goods themselves and compliance with certain laws or regulations. How the risks are divided is a question of fact to be determined, where not expressly contained in the agreement, from the circumstances of contracting, usage of trade, course of performance and the like, matters which may constitute the "otherwise agreement" of the parties by which they may divide the risk or burden.

4. The absence from this section of the language used in the Uniform Sales Act in referring to the seller, "whether he be the grower or manufacturer or not," is not intended to impose any requirement that the seller be a grower or manufacturer. Although normally the warranty will arise only where the seller is a merchant with the appropriate "skill or judgment," it can arise as to non-merchants where this is justified by the particular circumstances.

5. The elimination of the "patent or other trade name" exception constitutes the major extension of the warranty of fitness which has been made by the cases and continued in this Article. Under the present section the existence of a patent or other trade name and the designation of the article by that name, or indeed in any other definite manner, is only one of the facts to be considered on the question of whether the buyer actually relied on the seller, but it is not of itself decisive of the issue. If the buyer himself is insisting on

a particular brand he is not relying on the seller's skill and judgment and so no warranty results. But the mere fact that the article purchased has a particular patent or trade name is not sufficient to indicate nonreliance if the article has been recommended by the seller as adequate for the buyer's purposes.

6. The specific reference forward in the present section to the following section on exclusion or modification of warranties is to call attention to the possibility of eliminating the warranty in any given case. However it must be noted that under the following section the warranty of fitness for a particular purpose must be excluded or modified by a conspicuous writing.

Cross References:

Point 2: Sections 2–314 and 2–317.
Point 3: Section 2–303.
Point 6: Section 2–316.

Definitional Cross References:

"Buyer". Section 2–103.
"Goods". Section 2–103.
"Seller". Section 2–103.

§ 2–316. Exclusion or Modification of Warranties.

(1) Words or conduct relevant to the creation of an express warranty and words or conduct tending to negate or limit warranty shall be construed wherever reasonable as consistent with each other; but subject to Section 2–202, negation or limitation is inoperative to the extent that such construction is unreasonable.

(2) Subject to subsection (3), to exclude or modify the implied warranty of merchantability or any part of it in a consumer contract the language must be in a record, be conspicuous, and state "The seller undertakes no responsibility for the quality of the goods except as otherwise provided in this contract," and in any other contract the language must mention merchantability and in case of a record must be conspicuous. Subject to subsection (3), to exclude or modify the implied warranty of fitness, the exclusion must be in a record and be conspicuous. Language to exclude all implied warranties of fitness in a consumer contract must state "The seller assumes no responsibility that the goods will be fit for any particular purpose for which you may be buying these goods, except as otherwise provided in the contract," and in any other contract the language is sufficient if it states, for example,

that "There are no warranties that extend beyond the description on the face hereof." Language that satisfies the requirements of this subsection for the exclusion or modification of a warranty in a consumer contract also satisfies the requirements for any other contract.

(3) Notwithstanding subsection (2):

(a) unless the circumstances indicate otherwise, all implied warranties are excluded by expressions like "as is", "with all faults" or other language that in common understanding calls the buyer's attention to the exclusion of warranties, makes plain that there is no implied warranty, and, in a consumer contract evidenced by a record, is set forth conspicuously in the record;

(b) if the buyer before entering into the contract has examined the goods or the sample or model as fully as desired or has refused to examine the goods after a demand by the seller there is no implied warranty with regard to defects that an examination in the circumstances should have revealed to the buyer; and

(c) an implied warranty may also be excluded or modified by course of dealing or course of performance or usage of trade.

(4) Remedies for breach of warranty may be limited in accordance with Sections 2–718 and 2–719.

As amended in 2003.

Official Comment

1. Subsection (1) is designed principally to deal with those frequent clauses in sales contracts which seek to exclude "all warranties, express or implied." It seeks to protect a buyer from unexpected and unbargained language of disclaimer by denying effect to this language when inconsistent with language of express warranty and permitting the exclusion of implied warranties only by language or other circumstances which protect the buyer from surprise.

The seller is protected against false allegations of oral warranties by this Article's provisions on parol and extrinsic evidence and against unauthorized representations by the customary "lack of authority" clauses. This Article treats the limitation or avoidance of consequential damages as a matter of limiting remedies for breach, separate from the matter of creation of liability under a warranty. If no warranty exists, there is of course no problem of limiting remedies for breach of warranty. Under subsection (4), the question of limitation of remedy is governed by the sections referred to rather than by this section.

2. The general test for disclaimers of implied warranties remains in subsection (3)(a), and the more specific tests are in subsection (2). A disclaimer that satisfies the requirements of subsection (3)(a) need not also satisfy any of the requirements of subsection (2).

3. Subsection (2) distinguishes between commercial and consumer contracts. In a commercial contract, language that disclaims the implied warranty of merchantability need not be in a record, but if it is in a record it must be conspicuous. Under this subsection, a conspicuous record is required to disclaim the implied warranty of merchantability in a consumer contract and to disclaim the implied warranty of fitness in any contract. Use of the language required by this subsection for consumer contracts satisfies the language requirements for other contracts governed by this subsection.

4. Subsection (2) presupposes that the implied warranty in question exists unless excluded or modified. Whether or not language of disclaimer satisfies the requirements of this section, the language may be relevant under other sections to the question of whether the warranty was ever in fact created. Thus, unless the provisions of this Article on parol and extrinsic evidence prevent its introduction, oral language of a disclaimer may raise issues of fact about whether reliance by the buyer occurred and whether the seller had "reason to know" under the section on implied warranty of fitness for a particular purpose.

5. Subsection (3)(a) deals with general terms such as "as is," "as they stand," "with all faults," and the like. These terms in ordinary commercial usage are understood to mean that the buyer takes the entire risk as to the quality of the goods involved. The terms covered by the subsection are in fact merely a particularization of subsection (3)(c), which provides for exclusion or modification of implied warranties by usage of trade. Nothing in subsection (3)(a) prevents a term such as "there are no implied warranties" from being effective in appropriate circumstances, as when the term is a negotiated term between commercial parties.

Satisfaction of subsection (3)(a) does not require that the language be set forth in a record, but if there is a record the language must be conspicuous if the contract is a consumer contract.

6. The exceptions to the general rule set forth in subsections (3)(b) and (3)(c) are common factual situations in which the circumstances surrounding the transaction are in themselves sufficient to call the buyer's attention to the fact that no implied warranties are made or that a certain implied warranty is being excluded.

Under subsection (3)(b), warranties may be excluded or modified by the circumstances when the buyer examines the goods or a sample or model of them before entering into the contract. "Examination" as used in this paragraph is not synonymous with inspection before acceptance or at any other time after the contract has been made. Of course if the buyer discovers the defect and uses the goods anyway, or if the buyer unreasonably fails to examine the goods before using them, the resulting injuries may be found to have resulted from the buyer's own action rather than have been proximately caused by a breach of warranty. *See* Sections 2–314 and 2–715.

To bring the transaction within the scope of "refused to examine" in subsection (3)(b), it is not sufficient that the goods are available for inspection. There must in addition be an actual examination by the buyer or a demand by the seller that the buyer examine the goods fully. The seller's demand must place the buyer on notice that the buyer is assuming the risk of defects which the examination ought to reveal.

Application of the doctrine of "caveat emptor" in all cases where the buyer examines the goods regardless of statements made by the seller is, however, rejected by this Article. Thus, if the offer of examination is accompanied by words about their merchantability or specific attributes, and the buyer indicates clearly a reliance on those words rather than on the buyer's examination, the words give rise to an "express" warranty. In these cases, the question is one of fact about whether a warranty of merchantability has been expressly incorporated in the agreement.

The particular buyer's skill and the normal method of examining goods in the circumstances determine what defects are excluded by the examination. A failure to notice defects which are obvious cannot excuse the buyer because of the lack of notice. However, an examination under circumstances which do not permit chemical or other testing of the goods does not exclude defects which could be ascertained only by testing. Nor can latent defects be excluded by a simple examination. A professional buyer examining a product in the buyer's field will be held to have assumed the risk for all defects which a professional in the field ought to observe, while a nonprofessional buyer will be held to have assumed the risk only for the defects as a layperson might be expected to observe.

7. The situation in which the buyer gives precise and complete specifications to the seller is not explicitly covered in this section, but this is a frequent circumstance by which the implied warranties may be excluded. The warranty of fitness for a particular purpose would not normally arise since in this situation there is usually no reliance on the seller by the buyer. The warranty of merchantability in a transaction of this type, however, must be considered in connection with the next section on the cumulation and conflict of warranties. Under paragraph(c) of that section in case of an inconsistency the implied warranty of merchantability is displaced by the express warranty that the goods will comply with the specifications. Thus, where the buyer gives detailed specifications as to the goods, neither of the implied warranties as to quality will normally apply to the transaction unless consistent with the specifications.

Cross References:

Point 1: Sections 2–202, 2–718 and 2–719.
Point 6: Sections 1–205, 2–314 and 2–715.

Definitional Cross References:

"Agreement". Section 1–201.
"Buyer". Section 2–103.
"Conspicuous". Section 2–103.
"Consumer contract". Section 2–103.
"Contract". Section 1–201.
"Course of dealing". Section 1–303.
"Goods". Section 2–103.
"Record". Section 2–103.
"Remedy". Section 1–201.
"Seller". Section 2–103.
"Usage of trade". Section 1–303.

As amended in 2003.

§ 2–317. Cumulation and Conflict of Warranties Express or Implied.

Warranties whether express or implied shall be construed as consistent with each other and as cumulative, but if such construction is unreasonable the intention of the parties shall determine which warranty is dominant. In ascertaining that intention the following rules apply:

(a) Exact or technical specifications displace an inconsistent sample or model or general language of description.

(b) A sample from an existing bulk displaces inconsistent general language of description.

(c) Express warranties displace inconsistent implied warranties other than an implied warranty of fitness for a particular purpose.

Official Comment

Prior Uniform Statutory Provision: On cumulation of warranties see Sections 14, 15, and 16, Uniform Sales Act.

Changes: Completely rewritten into one section.

Purposes of Changes:

1. The present section rests on the basic policy of this Article that no warranty is created except by some conduct (either affirmative action or failure to disclose) on the part of the seller. Therefore, all warranties are made cumulative unless this construction of the contract is impossible or unreasonable.

This Article thus follows the general policy of the Uniform Sales Act except that in case of the sale of an article by its patent or trade name the elimination of the warranty of fitness depends solely on whether the buyer has relied on the seller's skill and judgment; the use of the patent or trade name is but one factor in making this determination.

2. The rules of this section are designed to aid in determining the intention of the parties as to which of inconsistent warranties which have arisen from the circumstances of their transaction shall prevail. These rules of intention are to be applied only where factors making for an equitable estoppel of the seller do not exist and where he has in perfect good faith made warranties which later turn out to be inconsistent. To the extent that the seller has led the buyer to believe that all of the warranties can be performed, he is estopped from setting up any essential inconsistency as a defense.

3. The rules in subsections (a), (b) and (c) are designed to ascertain the intention of the parties by reference to the factor which probably claimed the attention of the parties in the first instance. These rules are not absolute but may be changed by evidence showing that the conditions which existed at the time of contracting make the construction called for by the section inconsistent or unreasonable.

Cross Reference:

Point 1: Section 2–315.

Definitional Cross Reference:

"Party". Section 1–201.

§ 2–318. Third–Party Beneficiaries of Warranties and Obligations.

(1) In this section:

(a) "Immediate buyer" means a buyer that enters into a contract with the seller.

(b) "Remote purchaser" means a person that buys or leases goods from an immediate buyer or other person in the normal chain of distribution.

Alternative A to subsection (2)

people (not corp or others)

(2) A seller's warranty to an immediate buyer, whether express or implied, a seller's remedial promise to an immediate buyer, or a seller's obligation to a remote purchaser under Section 2–313A or 2–313B extends to any individual who is in the family or household of the immediate buyer or the remote purchaser or who is a guest in the home of either if it is reasonable to expect that the person may use, consume, or be affected by the goods and who is injured in person by breach of the warranty, remedial promise, or obligation. A seller may not exclude or limit the operation of this section.

Alternative B to subsection (2)

(2) A seller's warranty to an immediate buyer, whether express or implied, a seller's remedial promise to an immediate buyer, or a seller's obligation to a remote purchaser under Section 2–313A or 2–313B extends to any individual who may reasonably be expected to use, consume, or be affected by the goods and who is injured in person by breach of the warranty, remedial promise, or obligation. A seller may not exclude or limit the operation of this section.

Alternative C to subsection (2)

corporations partnerships trusts

(2) A seller's warranty to an immediate buyer, whether express or implied, a seller's remedial promise to an immediate buyer, or a seller's obligation to a remote purchaser under Section 2–313A or 2–313B extends to any person that may reasonably be expected to use, consume, or be affected by the goods and that is injured by breach of the warranty, remedial promise, or obligation. A seller may not exclude or limit the operation of this section with respect to injury to the person of an individual to whom the warranty, remedial promise, or obligation extends.

As amended in 2003.

Official Comment

1. This section retains original Article 2's alternative approaches but expands each alternative to cover obligations arising under Sections 2–313A and 2–313B and remedial promises.

2. The last sentence of each alternative to subsection (2) is not meant to suggest that a seller is precluded from excluding or disclaiming a warranty which might otherwise arise in connection with the sale provided the exclusion or modification is permitted by Section 2–316. Nor is it intended to suggest that the seller is precluded from limiting the remedies of the immediate buyer or remote purchaser in any manner provided in Sections 2–718 or 2–719. *See also* Section 2–313A(4) and Section 2–313B(4). To the extent that the contract of sale contains provisions under which warranties are excluded or modified, or remedies for breach are limited, the provisions are equally operative against beneficiaries of warranties under this section. What this last sentence forbids is exclusion of liability by the seller to the persons to whom the warranties, obligations and remedial promises accruing to the immediate buyer or remote purchaser would extend under this section.

Alternative A extends protection to a third party beneficiary who is a guest in the home of the immediate buyer or remote[] purchaser. The status of "guest in the home" describes the category of beneficiaries covered by this provision, and it does not limit the situs of the breach. Thus, a guest in the home that would otherwise have rights under this section could be injured in the automobile of the immediate buyer or remote purchaser. Beyond this, the section is neutral and is not intended to enlarge or restrict the developed or developing case law on whether the seller's warranties, given to his buyer who resells, extend to other persons in the distributive chain.

The last sentence of Alternative C permits a seller to reduce its obligations to third-party beneficiaries to a level commensurate with that imposed on the seller under Alternative B—that is, to eliminate liability to persons that are not individuals and to eliminate liability for damages other than personal injury.

3. As used in this section, the term "remote purchaser" refers to the party to whom an obligation initially runs under Section 2–313A or 2–313B. It does not refer to any subsequent purchaser of the goods.

4. As applied to warranties and remedial promises arising under Sections 2–313, 2–314 and 2–315, the purpose of this section is to give certain beneficiaries the benefit of the warranties and remedial promises which the immediate buyer received in the contract of sale, thereby freeing any beneficiaries from any technical rules as to "privity." It seeks to accomplish this purpose without any derogation of any right or remedy

arising under the law of torts. Implicit in the section is that any beneficiary of a warranty may bring a direct action for breach of warranty against the seller whose warranty extends to the beneficiary.

Obligations and remedial promises under Sections 2–313A and 2–313B arise initially in a non-privity context but are extended under this section to the same extent as warranties and remedial promises running to a buyer in privity.

Cross References:

Point 1: Sections 2–313A, 2–313B.
Point 2: Sections 2–313A, 2–313B, 2–316, 2–718 and 2–719.
Point 3: Sections 2–313A, 2–313B.
Point 4: Section 2–313, 2–313A, 2–313B, 2–314, 2–315.

Definitional Cross References:

"Buyer". Section 2–103.
"Contract". Section 1–201.
"Goods". Section 2–103.
"Lease". Section 2A–103.
"Remedial promise". Section 2–103.
"Seller". Section 2–103.

As amended in 2003.

§ 2–319. Reserved.

Legislative Note: Sections 2–319 through 2–324 have been eliminated because they are inconsistent with modern commercial practices.

Official Comment

Sections 2–319 through 2–324 have been repealed. The effect of a party's use of shipping terms such as "FOB," "CIF," or the like, absent any express agreement to the meaning of the terms, must be interpreted in light of any applicable usage of trade and any course of performance or course of dealing between the parties.

§ 2–320. Reserved.

§ 2–321. Reserved.

§ 2–322. Reserved.

§ 2–323. Reserved.

§ 2–324. Reserved.

§ 2–325. Failure to Pay by Agreed Letter of Credit.

If the parties agree that the primary method of payment will be by letter of credit, the following rules apply:

(a) The buyer's obligation to pay is suspended by seasonable delivery to the seller of a letter of credit issued or confirmed by a financing agency of good repute in which the issuer and any confirmer undertake to pay against presentation of documents that evidence delivery of the goods.

(b) Failure of a party seasonably to furnish a letter of credit as agreed is a breach of the contract for sale.

(c) If the letter of credit is dishonored or repudiated, the seller, on seasonable notification, may require payment directly from the buyer.

As amended in 2003.

Official Comment

1. This section conforms to revised Article 5.

2. Subsection (c) follows the general policy of this Article and Article 3 (Section 3–310) on conditional payment, under which payment by check or other short-term instrument is not ordinarily final between the parties if the recipient presents the instrument and it is not paid. Thus the furnishing of a letter of credit does not substitute the financing agency's obligation for the buyer's, but the seller must first give the buyer reasonable notice of his intention to demand direct payment from the buyer.

Cross References:

Point 2: Sections 2–403, 2–511(3) and 3–802 and Article 5.

Definitional Cross References:

"Agree". Section 1–201.
"Buyer". Section 2–103.
"Delivery". Section 2–103.
"Dishonored". Section 3–502.
"Financing agency". Section 2–104.
"Letter of credit". Section 5–102(a)(10).
"Notification". Section 1–202.
"Party". Section 1–201.
"Seasonable". Section 1–205.
"Seller". Section 2–103.

As amended in 2003.

§ 2–326. Sale on Approval and Sale or Return.

(1) Unless otherwise agreed, if delivered goods may be returned by the buyer even if they conform to the contract, the transaction is:

(a) a "sale on approval" if the goods are delivered primarily for use; and

(b) a "sale or return" if the goods are delivered primarily for resale.

(2) Goods held on approval are not subject to the claims of the buyer's creditors until acceptance; goods held on sale or return are subject to such claims while in the buyer's possession.

(3) Any "or return" term of a contract for sale is to be treated as a separate contract for sale under Section 2–201 and as contradicting the sale aspect of the contract under Section 2–202.

As amended in 1999 and 2003.

Official Comment

1. Both a "sale on approval" and a "sale or return" should be distinguished from other types of transactions with which they frequently have been confused. A "sale on approval," sometimes also called a "sale on trial" or "on satisfaction," deals with a contract under which the seller undertakes a risk in order to satisfy its prospective buyer with the appearance or performance of the goods that are sold. The goods are delivered to the prospective purchaser but they remain the property of the seller until the buyer accepts them. The price has already been agreed. The buyer's willingness to receive and test the goods is the consideration for the seller's engagement to deliver and sell. A "sale or return," on the other hand, typically is a sale to a merchant whose unwillingness to buy is overcome by the seller's engagement to take back the goods (or any commercial unit of goods) in lieu of payment if they fail to be resold. A "sale or return" is a present sale of goods which may be undone at the buyer's option. Accordingly, subsection (2) provides that goods delivered on approval are not subject to the prospective buyer's creditors until acceptance, and goods delivered in a sale or return are subject to the buyer's creditors while in the buyer's possession.

These two transactions are so strongly delineated in practice and in general understanding that every presumption runs against a delivery to a consumer being a "sale or return" and against a delivery to a merchant for resale being a "sale on approval."

2. The right to return goods for failure to conform to the contract of sale does not make the transaction a "sale on approval" or "sale or return" and has nothing to do with this section or Section 2–327. This section is not concerned with remedies for breach of contract. It deals instead with a power given by the contract to turn back the goods even though they are wholly as

warranted. This section nevertheless presupposes that a contract for sale is contemplated by the parties, although that contract may be of the particular character that this section addresses (*i.e.*, a sale on approval or a sale or return).

If a buyer's obligation as a buyer is conditioned not on its personal approval but on the article's passing a described objective test, the risk of loss by casualty pending the test is properly the seller's and proper return is at its expense. On the point of "satisfaction" as meaning "reasonable satisfaction" when an industrial machine is involved, this Article takes no position.

3. Subsection (3) resolves a conflict in the pre-UCC case law by recognizing that an "or return" provision is so definitely at odds with any ordinary contract for sale of goods that if written agreement is involved the "return" term must be contained in a written memorandum. The "or return" aspect of a sales contract must be treated as a separate contract under the statute of frauds section and as contradicting the sale insofar as questions of parol or extrinsic evidence are concerned.

4. Certain true consignments transactions were dealt with in former Sections 2–326(3) and 9–114. These provisions have been deleted and have been replaced by new provisions of Article 9. *See e.g.*, Sections 9–109(a)(4); 9–103(d); 9–319.

Cross References:

Point 1: Article 9.
Point 2: Sections 2–20, 2–202 and 2–327.
Point 4: Section 2–326 and Article 9.

Definitional Cross References:

"Buyer". Section 2–103.
"Conform to the contract". Section 2–106.
"Creditor". Section 1–201.
"Delivered". Section 2–103.
"Goods". Section 2–103.
"Sale". Section 2–106.
"Sale on approval". Section 2–326.
"Sale on return". Section 2–326.

As amended in 1999, 2000 and 2003.

§ 2–327. Special Incidents of Sale on Approval and Sale or Return.

(1) Under a sale on approval unless otherwise agreed

(a) although the goods are identified to the contract the risk of loss and the title do not pass to the buyer until acceptance; and

(b) use of the goods consistent with the purpose of trial is not acceptance but failure seasonably to notify the seller of election to return the goods is acceptance, and if the goods conform to the contract acceptance of any part is acceptance of the whole; and

(c) after due notification of election to return, the return is at the seller's risk and expense but a merchant buyer must follow any reasonable instructions.

(2) Under a sale or return unless otherwise agreed

(a) the option to return extends to the whole or any commercial unit of the goods while in substantially their original condition, but must be exercised seasonably; and

(b) the return is at the buyer's risk and expense.

Official Comment

Prior Uniform Statutory Provision: Section 19(3), Uniform Sales Act.

Changes: Completely rewritten in preceding and this section.

Purposes of Changes: To make it clear that:

1. In the case of a sale on approval:

If all of the goods involved conform to the contract, the buyer's acceptance of part of the goods constitutes acceptance of the whole. Acceptance of part falls outside the normal intent of the parties in the "on approval" situation and the policy of this Article allowing partial acceptance of a defective delivery has no application here. A case where a buyer takes home two dresses to select one commonly involves two distinct contracts; if not, it is covered by the words "unless otherwise agreed".

2. In the case of a sale or return, the return of any unsold unit merely because it is unsold is the normal intent of the "sale or return" provision, and therefore the right to return for this reason alone is independent of any other action under the contract which would turn on wholly different considerations. On the other hand, where the return of goods is for breach, including return of items resold by the buyer and returned by the ultimate purchasers because of defects, the return procedure is governed not by the present section but by the provisions on the effects and revocation of acceptance.

3. In the case of a sale on approval the risk rests on the seller until acceptance of the goods by the buyer, while in a sale or return the risk remains throughout on the buyer.

4. Notice of election to return given by the buyer in a sale on approval is sufficient to relieve him of any further liability. Actual return by the buyer to the seller is required in the case of a sale or return contract. What constitutes due "giving" of notice, as required in "on approval" sales, is governed by the provisions on good faith and notice. "Seasonable" is used here as defined in Section 1–204. Nevertheless, the provisions of both this Article and of the contract on this point must be read with commercial reason and with full attention to good faith.

Cross References:

Point 1: Sections 2–501, 2–601 and 2–603.
Point 2: Sections 2–607 and 2–608.
Point 4: Sections 1–201 and 1–204.

Definitional Cross References:

"Agreed". Section 1–201.
"Buyer". Section 2–103.
"Commercial unit". Section 2–105.
"Conform". Section 2–106.
"Contract". Section 1–201.
"Goods". Section 2–103.
"Merchant". Section 2–104.
"Notifies". Section 1–202.
"Notification". Section 1–202.
"Sale on approval". Section 2–326.
"Sale or return". Section 2–326.
"Seasonably". Section 1–205.
"Seller". Section 2–103.

§ 2–328.   Sale by Auction.

(1) In a sale by auction, if goods are put up in lots, each lot is the subject of a separate sale.

(2) A sale by auction is complete when the auctioneer so announces by the fall of the hammer or in other customary manner. If a bid is made during the process of completing the sale but before a prior bid is accepted, the auctioneer has discretion to reopen the bidding or to declare the goods sold under the prior bid.

(3) A sale by auction is subject to the seller's right to withdraw the goods unless at the time the goods are put up or during the course of the auction it is announced in express terms that the right to withdraw the goods is not reserved. In an auction in which the right to withdraw the goods is reserved, the auctioneer may withdraw the goods at any time until completion of the sale

is announced by the auctioneer. In an auction in which the right to withdraw the goods is not reserved, after the auctioneer calls for bids on an article or lot, the article or lot may not be withdrawn unless no bid is made within a reasonable time. In either case a bidder may retract a bid until the auctioneer's announcement of completion of the sale, but a bidder's retraction does not revive any previous bid.

(4) If the auctioneer knowingly receives a bid on the seller's behalf or the seller makes or procures such a bid, and notice has not been given that liberty for such bidding is reserved, the buyer may at the buyer's option avoid the sale or take the goods at the price of the last good-faith bid prior to the completion of the sale. This subsection shall not apply to any bid at an auction required by law.

As amended in 2003.

Official Comment

1. The auctioneer may use discretion either in reopening the bidding or closing the sale on a bid made during the process of completing the sale when a bid is made at that moment. The recognition of a bid of this kind by the auctioneer does not mean a closing in favor of the bidder, but only that the bid has been accepted as a continuation of the bidding. If recognized, this bid discharges the bid made during the process of completing the sale.

2. An auction with the right to withdraw the goods is the normal procedure. Because of different usage, the phrases "with reserve" and "without reserve" are no longer used in this section. Nevertheless, auction sales subject to the seller's power to withdraw the goods are known as sales "with reserve," while auction sales where the seller has no power to withdraw the goods are known as sales "without reserve" or "absolute" sales.

3. Suppose, during the course of an auction where the seller reserves power to withdraw the goods, the auctioneer expressly announces that the seller no longer reserves power to withdraw the goods. Original Section 2–328(3) did not recognize this possibility, which exists in practice. Such a conversion, in effect, announces a "reserve bid" in that the goods will not be sold below the last bid before the conversion. A sale "without reserve" can also be converted to a sale "with reserve" during the course of the auction.

Cross Reference:

Point 2: Section 2–205.

Definitional Cross References:

"Buyer". Section 2–103.
"Goods". Section 2–103.
"Lot". Section 2–105.
"Notice". Section 1–202.
"Reasonable time". Section 1–205.
"Sale". Section 2–106.
"Seller". Section 2–103.
"Terms". Section 1–201.

As amended in 2003.

PART 4

TITLE, CREDITORS, AND GOOD–FAITH PURCHASERS

§ 2–401. Passing of Title; Reservation for Security; Limited Application of this Section.

Each provision of this Article with regard to the rights, obligations, and remedies of the seller, the buyer, purchasers, or other third parties applies irrespective of title to the goods except where the provision refers to such title. Insofar as situations are not covered by the other provisions of this Article and matters concerning title become material, the following rules apply:

(1) Title to goods cannot pass under a contract for sale prior to their identification to the contract (Section 2–501), and unless otherwise explicitly agreed, the buyer acquires by their identification a special property as limited by this Act. Any retention or reservation by the seller of the title (property) in goods shipped or delivered to the buyer is limited in effect to a reservation of a security interest. Subject to these provisions and to Article 9, title to goods passes from the seller to the buyer in any manner and on any conditions explicitly agreed on by the parties.

(2) Unless otherwise explicitly agreed title passes to the buyer at the time and place at which the seller completes performance with reference to the delivery of the goods, despite any reservation of a security interest and even if a document of title is to be delivered at a different time or place; and in particular and despite any

reservation of a security interest by the bill of lading:

(a) if the contract requires or authorizes the seller to send the goods to the buyer but does not require the seller to deliver them at destination, title passes to the buyer at the time and place of shipment; but

(b) if the contract requires delivery at destination, title passes on tender there.

(3) Unless otherwise explicitly agreed, if delivery is to be made without moving the goods:

(a) if the seller is to deliver a tangible document of title, title passes at the time when and the place where the seller delivers the document, and if the seller is to deliver an electronic document of title, title passes when the seller delivers the document; or

(b) if the goods are at the time of contracting already identified and no documents of title are to be delivered, title passes at the time and place of contracting.

(4) A rejection or other refusal by the buyer to receive or retain the goods, whether or not justified, or a justified revocation of acceptance revests title to the goods in the seller. Such revesting occurs by operation of law and is not a "sale".

As amended in 2003.

Official Comment

Prior Uniform Statutory Provision: See generally, Sections 17, 18, 19 and 20, Uniform Sales Act.

Purposes: To make it clear that:

1.   This Article deals with the issues between seller and buyer in terms of step by step performance or nonperformance under the contract for sale and not in terms of whether or not "title" to the goods has passed. That the rules of this section in no way alter the rights of either the buyer, seller or third parties declared elsewhere in the Article is made clear by the preamble of this section. This section, however, in no way intends to indicate which line of interpretation should be followed in cases where the applicability of "public" regulation depends upon a "sale" or upon location of "title" without further definition. The basic policy of this Article that known purpose and reason should govern interpretation cannot extend beyond the scope of its own provisions. It is therefore necessary to state what a "sale" is and when title passes under this Article in case the courts deem any public regulation to incorporate the defined term of the "private" law.

2.   "Future" goods cannot be the subject of a present sale. Before title can pass the goods must be identified in the manner set forth in Section 2–501. The parties, however, have full liberty to arrange by specific terms for the passing of title to goods which are existing.

3.   The "special property" of the buyer in goods identified to the contract is excluded from the definition of "security interest"; its incidents are defined in provisions of this Article such as those on the rights of the seller's creditors, on good faith purchase, on the buyer's right to goods on the seller's insolvency, and on the buyer's right to specific performance or replevin.

4.   The factual situations in subsections (2) and (3) upon which passage of title turn actually base the test upon the time when the seller has finally committed himself in regard to specific goods. Thus in a "shipment" contract he commits himself by the act of making the shipment. If shipment is not contemplated subsection (3) turns on the seller's final commitment, i.e. the delivery of documents or the making of the contract. As to delivery of an electronic document of title, see definition of delivery in Article 1, Section 1–201. This Article does not state a rule as to the place of title passage as to goods covered by an electronic document of title.

Cross References:

Point 2: Sections 2–102, 2–501 and 2–502.

Point 3: Sections 1–201, 2–402, 2–403, 2–502 and 2–716.

Definitional Cross References:

"Agreement". Section 1–201.

"Bill of lading". Section 1–201.

"Buyer". Section 2–103.

"Contract". Section 1–201.

"Contract for sale". Section 2–106.

"Delivery". Section 2–103.

"Document of title". Section 1–201.

"Goods". Section 2–103.

"Party". Section 1–201.

"Purchaser". Section 1–201.

"Receipt" of goods. Section 2–103.

"Remedy". Section 1–201.

"Rights". Section 1–201.

"Sale". Section 2–106.

"Security interest". Section 1–201.

"Seller". Section 2–103.

"Send". Section 1–201.

As amended in 2003.

§ 2–402. Rights of Seller's Creditors Against Sold Goods.

(1) Except as provided in subsections (2) and (3), rights of unsecured creditors of the seller with respect to goods that have been identified to a contract for sale are subject to the buyer's rights to recover the goods under Sections 2–502 and 2–716.

(2) A creditor of the seller may treat a sale or an identification of goods to a contract for sale as void if as against the creditor a retention of possession by the seller is fraudulent under any rule of law of the state where the goods are situated. However, retention of possession in good faith and current course of trade by a merchant-seller for a commercially reasonable time after a sale or identification is not fraudulent.

(3) Except as otherwise provided in Section 2–403(2), nothing in this Article shall be deemed to impair the rights of creditors of the seller:

(a) under Article 9; or

(b) if identification to the contract or delivery is made not in current course of trade but in satisfaction of or as security for a preexisting claim for money, security, or the like and is made under circumstances that under any rule of law of the state where the goods are situated would apart from this Article constitute the transaction a fraudulent transfer or voidable preference.

As amended in 2003.

Official Comment

Prior Uniform Statutory Provision: Subsection (2)—Section 26, Uniform Sales Act; Subsections (1) and (3)—none.

Changes: Rephrased.

Purposes of Changes and New Matter: To avoid confusion on ordinary issues between current sellers and buyers and issues in the field of preference and hindrance by making it clear that:

1. Local law on questions of hindrance of creditors by the seller's retention of possession of the goods are outside the scope of this Article, but retention of possession in the current course of trade is legitimate. Transactions which fall within the law's policy against improper preferences are reserved from the protection of this Article.

2. The retention of possession of the goods by a merchant seller for a commercially reasonable time after a sale or identification in current course is exempted from attack as fraudulent. Similarly, the provisions of subsection (3) have no application to identification or delivery made in the current course of trade, as measured against general commercial understanding of what a "current" transaction is.

3. The cross reference in subsection (3) to Section 2–403(2) shows the relationship of these sections and Article 9. A transfer under Section 2–403(2) can cause impairment of the rights of a secured party under Article 9. (Section 9–315(a)).

Cross References:

Point 3: Sections 2–403 and 9–315.

Definitional Cross References:

"Contract for sale". Section 2–106.
"Creditor". Section 1–201.
"Goods". Section 2–103.
"Merchant". Section 2–104.
"Money". Section 1–201.
"Reasonable time". Section 1–205.
"Rights". Section 1–201.
"Sale". Section 2–106.
"Seller". Section 2–103.

As amended in 2003.

§ 2–403. Power to Transfer; Good Faith Purchase of Goods; "Entrusting".

(1) A purchaser of goods acquires all title that the purchaser's transferor had or had power to transfer except that a purchaser of a limited interest acquires rights only to the extent of the interest purchased. A person with voidable title has power to transfer a good title to a good-faith purchaser for value. If goods have been delivered under a transaction of purchase, the purchaser has such power even if:

(a) the transferor was deceived as to the identity of the purchaser;

(b) the delivery was in exchange for a check that is later dishonored;

(c) it was agreed that the transaction was to be a "cash sale"; or

(d) the delivery was procured through criminal fraud.

(2) Any entrusting of goods to a merchant that deals in goods of that kind gives the merchant

power to transfer all of the entruster's rights to the goods and to transfer the goods free of any interest of the entruster to a buyer in ordinary course of business.

(3) "Entrusting" includes any delivery and any acquiescence in retention of possession regardless of any condition expressed between the parties to the delivery or acquiescence and regardless of whether the procurement of the entrusting or the possessor's disposition of the goods was punishable under the criminal law.

[*Legislative Note: If a state adopts the repealer of Article 6—Bulk Transfers (Alternative A), subsection (4) should read as follows:*]

(4) The rights of other purchasers of goods and of lien creditors are governed by Articles 7 and 9.

[*Legislative Note: If a state adopts revised Article 6—Bulk Sales (Alternative B), subsection (4) should read as follows:*]

(4) The rights of other purchasers of goods and of lien creditors are governed by Articles 6, 7, and 9.

As amended in 1998 and 2003.

Official Comment

1. The basic policy that allows the transfer of such title as the transferor has is recognized under subsection (1). In this respect, the provisions of the section are applicable to a person taking by any form of "purchase" as defined by this Act. (Section 1–201(a)(29)). Moreover the policy of this Act expressly providing for the application of supplementary general principles of law to sales transactions wherever appropriate (Section 1–103) joins with the present section to continue unimpaired all rights acquired under the law of agency or of apparent agency or ownership or other estoppel, whether based on statutory provisions or on case law. The section also leaves unimpaired the powers given to selling factors under the earlier Factors Acts. In addition, subsection (1) provides specifically for the protection of the good faith purchaser for value in a number of specific situations which were troublesome under prior law.

On the other hand, the contract of purchase is of course limited by its own terms, as in a case of pledge for a limited amount, or of sale of a fractional interest in goods.

2. The many particular situations in which a buyer in ordinary course of business has been protected against a reservation of a property right or other interest are gathered by subsections (2) and (3) into a single principle protecting persons that buy in ordinary course of business. Consignors have no reason to complain, nor have lenders who hold a security interest in the inventory, since the very purpose of goods in inventory is to be turned into cash by sale. (Section 9–109, which provides that a consignment is within the scope of Article 9; Section 9–315(a), which provides that Article 9 security interests are defeated by the rights of a buyer in ordinary course of business under Section 2–403(2).).

The principle is extended in subsection (3) to fit with the abolition of the old law of "cash sale" by subsection (1)(c). It is freed from any local or specific technicalities, and it extends law to any criminal fraud or conduct punishable under criminal law. The policy is extended, in the interest of simplicity and sense, to any entrusting by a bailor. This is in consonance with the explicit provisions of Section 7–205 on the powers of a warehouse that is also in the business of buying and selling goods of the kind that are warehoused. As to entrusting by a secured party, subsection (2) provides that a buyer in ordinary course of business takes free of the security interest. (*See* Section 9–315(a)).

3. Except as provided in subsection (1), the rights of purchasers other than buyers in ordinary course are left to the Articles on Secured Transactions (Article 9) and Documents of Title (Article 7).

Cross References:

Point 1: Sections 1–103 and 1–201.

Point 2: Sections 2–315, 2–403, 7–205 and Article 9.

Point 3: Sections 1–102, 1–201, 2–104, 2–707 and Articles 6, 7 and 9.

Point 4: Sections 1–102, 1–201, 2–104, 2–707 and Articles 6, 7 and 9.

Definitional Cross References:

"Buyer in ordinary course of business". Section 1–201.

"Delivery". Section 2–103.

"Dishonor". Section 3–502.

"Goods". Section 2–103.

"Person". Section 1–201.

"Purchaser". Section 1–201.

"Term". Section 1–201.

"Value". Section 1–204.

As amended in 2003.

PART 5

PERFORMANCE

§ 2-501.　Insurable Interest in Goods; Manner of Identification of Goods.

(1) The buyer obtains a special property and an insurable interest in goods by identification of existing goods as goods to which the contract refers even if the goods so identified are nonconforming and the buyer has an option to return or reject them. Such identification may be made at any time and in any manner explicitly agreed to by the parties. In the absence of explicit agreement identification occurs:

(a) when the contract is made if it is for the sale of goods already existing and identified;

(b) if the contract is for the sale of future goods other than those described in paragraph (c), when goods are shipped, marked, or otherwise designated by the seller as goods to which the contract refers;

(c) when the crops are planted or otherwise become growing crops or the young are conceived if the contract is for the sale of unborn young to be born within 12 months after contracting or for the sale of crops to be harvested within 12 months or the next normal harvest season after contracting whichever is longer.

(2) The seller retains an insurable interest in goods so long as title to or any security interest in the goods remains in the seller. If the identification is by the seller alone, the seller may until default or insolvency or notification to the buyer that the identification is final substitute other goods for those identified.

(3) Nothing in this section impairs any insurable interest recognized under any other statute or rule of law.

As amended in 2003.

Official Comment

Prior Uniform Statutory Provision: See Sections 17 and 19, Uniform Sales Act.

Purposes:

1. The present section deals with the manner of identifying goods to the contract so that an insurable interest in the buyer and the rights set forth in the next section will accrue. Generally speaking, identification may be made in any manner "explicitly agreed to" by the parties. The rules of paragraphs (a), (b) and (c) apply only in the absence of such "explicit agreement".

2. In the ordinary case identification of particular existing goods as goods to which the contract refers is unambiguous and may occur in one of many ways. It is possible, however, for the identification to be tentative or contingent. In view of the limited effect given to identification by this Article, the general policy is to resolve all doubts in favor of identification.

3. The provision of this section as to "explicit agreement" clarifies the present confusion in the law of sales which has arisen from the fact that under prior uniform legislation all rules of presumption with reference to the passing of title or to appropriation (which in turn depended upon identification) were regarded as subject to the contrary intention of the parties or of the party appropriating. Such uncertainty is reduced to a minimum under this section by requiring "explicit agreement" of the parties before the rules of paragraphs (a), (b) and (c) are displaced—as they would be by a term giving the buyer power to select the goods. An "explicit" agreement, however, need not necessarily be found in the terms used in the particular transaction. Thus, where a usage of the trade has previously been made explicit by reduction to a standard set of "rules and regulations" currently incorporated by reference into the contracts of the parties, a relevant provision of those "rules and regulations" is "explicit" within the meaning of this section.

4. In view of the limited function of identification there is no requirement in this section that the goods be in deliverable state or that all of the seller's duties with respect to the processing of the goods be completed in order that identification occur. For example, despite identification the risk of loss remains on the seller under the risk of loss provisions until completion of his duties as to the goods and all of his remedies remain dependent upon his not defaulting under the contract.

5. Undivided shares in an identified fungible bulk, such as grain in an elevator or oil in a storage tank, can be sold. The mere making of the contract with reference to an undivided share in an identified fungible bulk is enough under subsection (a) to effect an

identification if there is no explicit agreement otherwise. The seller's duty, however, to segregate and deliver according to the contract is not affected by such an identification but is controlled by other provisions of this Article.

6. Identification of crops under paragraph (c) is made upon planting only if they are to be harvested within the year or within the next normal harvest season. The phrase "next normal harvest season" fairly includes nursery stock raised for normally quick "harvest," but plainly excludes a "timber" crop to which the concept of a harvest "season" is inapplicable.

Paragraph (c) is also applicable to a crop of wool or the young of animals to be born within twelve months after contracting. The product of a lumbering, mining or fishing operation, though seasonal, is not within the concept of "growing". Identification under a contract for all or part of the output of such an operation can be effected early in the operation.

Cross References:

Point 1: Section 2–502.
Point 4: Sections 2–509, 2–510 and 2–703.
Point 5: Sections 2–103, 2–105, 2–308, 2–503 and 2–509.
Point 6: Sections 2–103, 2–107(1) and 2–402.

Definitional Cross References:

"Agreement". Section 1–201.
"Buyer". Section 2–103.
"Contract". Section 1–201.
"Contract for sale". Section 2–106.
"Future goods". Section 2–105.
"Goods". Section 2–103.
"Notification". Section 1–202.
"Party". Section 1–201.
"Sale". Section 2–106.
"Security interest". Section 1–201.
"Seller". Section 2–103.

§ 2–502. Buyer's Right to Goods on Seller's Insolvency, Repudiation, or Failure to Deliver.

(1) Subject to subsections (2) and (3) and even if the goods have not been shipped, a buyer that has paid a part or all of the price of goods in which the buyer has a special property under Section 2–501 may on making and keeping good a tender of any unpaid portion of their price recover them from the seller if:

(a) in the case of goods bought by a consumer, the seller repudiates or fails to deliver as required by the contract; or

(b) in all cases, the seller becomes insolvent within 10 days after receipt of the first installment on their price.

(2) The buyer's right to recover the goods under subsection (1) vests upon acquisition of a special property, even if the seller had not then repudiated or failed to deliver.

(3) If the identification creating a special property has been made by the buyer, the buyer acquires the right to recover the goods only if they conform to the contract for sale.

As amended in 1999 and 2003.

Official Comment

1. This section gives an additional right to the buyer as a result of identification of the goods to the contract in the manner provided in Section 2–501. The buyer is given a right to recover the goods, conditioned upon making and keeping good a tender of any unpaid portion of the price, in two limited circumstances. First, a consumer buyer may recover the goods if the seller repudiates the contract or fails to deliver the goods. Second, in any case, the buyer may recover the goods if the seller becomes insolvent within 10 days after the seller receives the first installment on their price. The buyer's right to recover the goods under this section is an exception to the usual rule, under which the disappointed buyer must resort to an action to recover damages.

2. The question of whether the buyer also acquires a security interest in identified goods and has rights to the goods when insolvency takes place after the ten day period provided in this section depends upon compliance with the provisions of the Article on Secured Transactions (Article 9).

3. Under subsection (2), the buyer's right to recover goods under subsection (1) vests upon acquisition of a special property, which occurs upon identification of the goods to the contract. See Section 2–501. Inasmuch as a secured party normally acquires no greater rights in its collateral than its debtor had or had power to convey, see Section 2–403(1)(first sentence), a buyer who acquires a right to recover under this section will take free of a security interest created by the seller if it attaches to the goods after the goods have been identified to the contract. The buyer will take free, even if the buyer does not buy in ordinary course and even if the security interest is perfected. Of course, to the

extent that the buyer pays the price after the security interest attaches, the payments will constitute proceeds of the security interest.

4. Subsection (3) is included to preclude the possibility of unjust enrichment which would exist if the buyer were permitted to recover goods even though they were greatly superior in quality or quantity to that called for by the contract for sale.

Cross References:

Point 1: Sections 1–201 and 2–702.
Point 2: Article 9.

Definitional Cross References:

"Buyer". Section 2–103.
"Consumer". Section 2–103.
"Conform". Section 2–106.
"Contract for sale". Section 2–106.
"Deliver". Section 2–103.
"Goods". Section 2–103.
"Insolvent". Section 1–201.
"Rights". Section 1–201.
"Seller". Section 2–103.

As amended in 1999 and 2003.

§ 2–503. Manner of Seller's Tender of Delivery.

(1) Tender of delivery requires that the seller put and hold conforming goods at the buyer's disposition and give the buyer any notification reasonably necessary to enable the buyer to take delivery. The manner, time, and place for tender are determined by the agreement and this Article, and in particular:

(a) tender must be at a reasonable hour, and if it is of goods they must be kept available for the period reasonably necessary to enable the buyer to take possession; but

(b) unless otherwise agreed the buyer must furnish facilities reasonably suited to the receipt of the goods.

(2) If the case is within Section 2–504, tender requires that the seller comply with its provisions.

(3) If the seller is required to deliver at a particular destination, tender requires that the seller comply with subsection (1) and also in any appropriate case tender documents as described in subsections (4) and (5) of this section.

(4) If goods are in the possession of a bailee and are to be delivered without being moved:

(a) tender requires that the seller either tender a negotiable document of title covering such goods or procure acknowledgment by the bailee to the buyer of the buyer's right to possession of the goods; but

(b) tender to the buyer of a nonnegotiable document of title or of a record directing the bailee to deliver is sufficient tender unless the buyer seasonably objects, and except as otherwise provided in Article 9 receipt by the bailee of notification of the buyer's rights fixes those rights as against the bailee and all third persons; but risk of loss of the goods and of any failure by the bailee to honor the nonnegotiable document of title or to obey the direction remains on the seller until the buyer has had a reasonable time to present the document or direction. Refusal by the bailee to honor the document or to obey the direction defeats the tender.

(5) If the contract requires the seller to deliver documents:

(a) the seller must tender all such documents in correct form; and

(b) tender through customary banking channels is sufficient and dishonor of a draft accompanying or associated with the documents constitutes nonacceptance or rejection.

As amended in 2003.

Official Comment

1. The major general rules governing the manner of proper or due tender of delivery are gathered in this section. The term "tender" is used in this Article in two different senses. In one sense it refers to "due tender," which contemplates an offer coupled with a present ability to fulfill all the conditions that rest on the tendering party, and it must be followed by actual performance if the other party shows readiness to proceed. Unless the context unmistakably indicates otherwise this is the meaning of "tender" in this Article, and the occasional addition of the word "due" is only for clarity and emphasis. At other times it is used to refer to an offer of goods or documents under a contract as if in fulfillment of its conditions even though there is a defect when measured against the contract obligation. Used in either sense, however, "tender" connotes performance by the tendering party

that the other party in default if the other party fails to proceed in some manner. These concepts of tender would apply to tender of either tangible or electronic documents of title.

2. The seller's general duty to tender and deliver is set out in Section 2–301 and more particularly in Section 2–507. The seller's right to a receipt if the seller demands one, if receipts are customary, is governed by Section 1–303.

Subsection (1) of this section sets forth two primary requirements of tender: first, that the seller "put and hold conforming goods at the buyer's disposition" and, second, that the seller "give the buyer any notice reasonably necessary to enable the buyer to take delivery."

In cases in which payment is due and demanded upon delivery, the "buyer's disposition" is qualified by the seller's right to reclaim the goods under Section 2–507(2). However, where the seller is demanding payment on delivery the seller must first allow the buyer to inspect the goods to avoid impairing the tender unless the contract contains standard shipping terms or other terms that would negate the right of inspection before payment. (*See* Section 2–513(3)).

In the case of contracts of sale involving documents, the seller can "put and hold conforming goods at the buyer's disposition" under subsection (1) by tendering documents which give the buyer complete control of the goods under the provisions of Article 7.

3. Under paragraph (a) of subsection (1) usage of the trade and the circumstances of the particular case determine what is a reasonable hour for tender and what constitutes a reasonable period of holding the goods available.

4. The buyer must furnish reasonable facilities for the receipt of the goods tendered by the seller under subsection (1), paragraph (b). This obligation of the buyer is not part of the seller's tender.

5. For the purposes of subsections (2) and (3) there is omitted from this Article the rule under prior uniform legislation that a term requiring the seller to pay the freight or cost of transportation to the buyer is equivalent to an agreement by the seller to deliver to the buyer or at an agreed destination. This omission is with the specific intention of negating the rule, for under this Article a "shipment" contract is regarded as the normal one and a "destination" contract as the variant type. The seller is not obligated to deliver at a named destination and bear the concurrent risk of loss until arrival unless the seller has specifically agreed to deliver or the commercial understanding of the terms used by the parties contemplates a destination contract.

6. Under Subsection (4)(a) the bailee's acknowledgment must be made to the buyer. *See Jason's Foods, Inc. v. Peter Eckrick & Sons, Inc.*, 774 F.2d 214 (7th Cir. 1985) Paragraph (b) of subsection (4) adopts the rule, subject to Article 9, that between the buyer and the seller the risk of loss remains on the seller during a period reasonable for securing acknowledgment of the transfer from the bailee while as against all other parties the buyer's rights are fixed as of the time the bailee receives notice of the transfer.

7. Under subsection (5) documents are never "required" except where there is an express contract term or it is plainly implicit in the peculiar circumstances of the case or in a usage of trade. Documents may, of course, be "authorized" although not required, but these cases are not within the scope of this subsection. When documents are required, there are three main requirements of this subsection: (1) "All": each required document is essential to a proper tender; (2) "Such": the documents must be the ones actually required by the contract in terms of source and substance; (3) "Correct form": All documents must be in correct form. These requirements apply to both tangible and electronic documents of title. When tender is made through customary banking channels, a draft may accompany or be associated with a document of title. The language has been broadened to allow for drafts to be associated with an electronic document of title. Compare Section 2–104(2) definition of financing agency.

When a prescribed document cannot be procured, a question of fact arises under the provision of this Article on substituted performance about whether the agreed manner of delivery is actually commercially impracticable and whether the substitute is commercially reasonable.

Cross References:

Point 2: Sections 1–303, 2–301, 2–310, 2–507 and 2–513 and Article 7.

Point 5: Sections 2–308, 2–310 and 2–509.

Point 7: Section 2–614(1).

Specific matters involving tender are covered in many additional sections of this Article. See Sections 1–205, 2–301, 2–306 to 2–318, 2–504, 2–507(2), 2–511(1), 2–513, 2–612 and 2–614.

Definitional Cross References:

"Agreement". Section 1–201.

"Buyer". Section 2–103.

"Conforming". Section 2–106.

"Contract". Section 1–201.
"Delivery". Section 2–103.
"Dishonor". Section 3–502.
"Document of title". Section 1–201.
"Draft". Section 3–104(e).
"Goods". Section 2–103.
"Notification". Section 1–202.
"Reasonable time". Section 1–205.
"Receipt" of goods. Section 2–103.
"Record". Section 2–103.
"Rights". Section 1–201.
"Seasonably". Section 1–205.
"Seller". Section 2–103.

As amended in 2003.

§ 2–504. Shipment by Seller.

If the seller is required or authorized to send the goods to the buyer and the contract does not require the seller to deliver them at a particular destination, then unless otherwise agreed the seller must:

(a) put conforming goods in the possession of a carrier and make a proper contract for their transportation, having regard to the nature of the goods and other circumstances of the case;

(b) obtain and promptly deliver or tender in due form any document necessary to enable the buyer to obtain possession of the goods or otherwise required by the agreement or by usage of trade; and

(c) promptly notify the buyer of the shipment.

Failure to notify the buyer under paragraph (c) or to make a proper contract under paragraph (a) is a ground for rejection only if material delay or loss ensues.

As amended in 2003.

Official Comment

Prior Uniform Statutory Provision: Section 46, Uniform Sales Act.

Changes: Rewritten.

Purposes of Changes: To continue the general policy of the prior uniform statutory provision while incorporating certain modifications with respect to the requirement that the contract with the carrier be made expressly on behalf of the buyer and as to the necessity of giving notice of the shipment to the buyer, so that:

1. The section is limited to "shipment" contracts as contrasted with "destination" contracts or contracts

for delivery at the place where the goods are located. The general principles embodied in this section cover the special cases of F.O.B. point of shipment contracts and C.I.F. and C. & F. contracts. Under the preceding section on manner of tender of delivery, due tender by the seller requires that he comply with the requirements of this section in appropriate cases.

2. The contract to be made with the carrier under paragraph (a) must conform to all express terms of the agreement, subject to any substitution necessary because of failure of agreed facilities as provided in the later provision on substituted performance. However, under the policies of this Article on good faith and commercial standards and on buyer's rights on improper delivery, the requirements of explicit provisions must be read in terms of their commercial and not their literal meaning. This policy is made express with respect to bills of lading in a set in the provision of this Article on form of bills of lading required in overseas shipment.

3. In the absence of agreement, the provision of this Article on options and cooperation respecting performance gives the seller the choice of any reasonable carrier, routing and other arrangements. Whether or not the shipment is at the buyer's expense the seller must see to any arrangements, reasonable in the circumstances, such as refrigeration, watering of live stock, protection against cold, the sending along of any necessary help, selection of specialized cars and the like for paragraph (a) is intended to cover all necessary arrangements whether made by contract with the carrier or otherwise. There is, however, a proper relaxation of such requirements if the buyer is himself in a position to make the appropriate arrangements and the seller gives him reasonable notice of the need to do so. It is an improper contract under paragraph (a) for the seller to agree with the carrier to a limited valuation below the true value and thus cut off the buyer's opportunity to recover from the carrier in the event of loss, when the risk of shipment is placed on the buyer by his contract with the seller.

4. Both the language of paragraph (b) and the nature of the situation it concerns indicate that the requirement that the seller must obtain and deliver promptly to the buyer in due form any document necessary to enable him to obtain possession of the goods is intended to cumulate with the other duties of the seller such as those covered in paragraph (a).

In this connection, in the case of pool car shipments a delivery order furnished by the seller on the pool car consignee, or on the carrier for delivery out of a larger quantity, satisfies the requirements of paragraph (b) unless the contract requires some other form of document.

5. This Article, unlike the prior uniform statutory provision, makes it the seller's duty to notify the buyer of shipment in all cases. The consequences of his failure to do so, however, are limited in that the buyer may reject on this ground only where material delay or loss ensues.

A standard and acceptable manner of notification in open credit shipments is the sending of an invoice and in the case of documentary contracts is the prompt forwarding of the documents as under paragraph (b) of this section. It is also usual to send on a straight bill of lading but this is not necessary to the required notification. However, should such a document prove necessary or convenient to the buyer, as in the case of loss and claim against the carrier, good faith would require the seller to send it on request.

Frequently the agreement expressly requires prompt notification as by wire or cable. Such a term may be of the essence and the final clause of paragraph (c) does not prevent the parties from making this a particular ground for rejection. To have this vital and irreparable effect upon the seller's duties, such a term should be part of the "dickered" terms written in any "form," or should otherwise be called seasonably and sharply to the seller's attention.

6. Generally, under the final sentence of the section, rejection by the buyer is justified only when the seller's dereliction as to any of the requirements of this section in fact is followed by material delay or damage. It rests on the seller, so far as concerns matters not within the peculiar knowledge of the buyer, to establish that his error has not been followed by events which justify rejection.

Cross References:

Point 1: Section 2–503(2).
Point 2: Sections 1–203, 2–601 and 2–614.
Point 3: Section 2–311(2).
Point 5: Section 1–203.

Definitional Cross References:

"Agreement". Section 1–201.
"Buyer". Section 2–103.
"Conforming". Section 2–106.
"Contract". Section 1–201.
"Delivery". Section 2–103.
"Goods". Section 2–103.
"Notifies". Section 1–202.
"Seller". Section 2–103.
"Send". Section 1–201.
"Usage of trade". Section 1–303.

§ 2–505. Seller's Shipment under Reservation.

(1) If the seller has identified goods to the contract by or before shipment:

(a) The seller's procurement of a negotiable bill of lading to the seller's own order or otherwise reserves in the seller a security interest in the goods. The seller's procurement of the bill to the order of a financing agency or of the buyer indicates in addition only the seller's expectation of transferring that interest to the person named.

(b) A nonnegotiable bill of lading to the seller or the seller's nominee reserves possession of the goods as security. However, unless a seller has a right to reclaim the goods under Section 2–507(2) a nonnegotiable bill of lading naming the buyer as consignee reserves no security interest even if the seller retains possession or control of the bill of lading.

(2) If shipment by the seller with reservation of a security interest is in violation of the contract for sale, it constitutes an improper contract for transportation under Section 2–504 but impairs neither the rights given to the buyer by shipment and identification of the goods to the contract nor the seller's powers as a holder of a negotiable document of title.

As amended in 2003.

Official Comment

1. The security interest reserved to the seller under subsection (1) is restricted to securing payment or performance by the buyer and the seller is strictly limited in the seller's disposition and control of the goods as against the buyer and third parties. Under this Article, the provision as to the passing of a property interest expressly applies "despite any reservation of security title" and also provides that the "rights, obligations and remedies" of the parties are not altered by the incidence of title generally. The security interest, therefore, must be regarded as a means given to the seller to enforce the seller's rights against the buyer which is unaffected by and in turn does not affect the location of title generally. The rules set forth in subsection (1) are not to be altered by any apparent "contrary intent" of the parties as to passing of title, since the rights and remedies of the parties to the contract

115

of sale, as defined in this Article, rest on the contract and its performance or breach and not on presumptions about the location of title.

This Article does not attempt to regulate local procedure for the effective maintenance of the seller's security interest when the action is in replevin by the buyer against the carrier.

2. Every shipment of identified goods under a negotiable bill of lading reserves a security interest in the seller under subsection (1) paragraph (a).

It is frequently convenient for the seller to make the bill of lading to the order of a nominee such as the seller's agent at destination, the financing agency to which the seller expects to negotiate the document or the bank issuing a credit to the seller. In many instances, also, the buyer is made the order party. This Article does not deal directly with the question as to whether a bill of lading made out by the seller to the order of a nominee gives the carrier notice of any rights which the nominee may have so as to limit the carrier's freedom or obligation to honor the bill of lading in the hands of the seller as the original shipper if the expected negotiation fails. This is dealt with in the Article on Documents of Title (Article 7).

3. A non-negotiable bill of lading taken to a party other than the buyer under subsection (1) paragraph (b) reserves possession of the goods as security in the seller but if the seller seeks to withhold the goods improperly the buyer can tender payment and recover them.

4. In the case of a shipment by non-negotiable bill of lading taken to a buyer, the seller, under subsection (1) retains no security interest or possession as against the buyer and by the shipment the seller *de facto* loses control as against the carrier except where he rightfully and effectively stops delivery in transit. (Section 2–705) In cases in which the contract gives the seller the right to payment against delivery, the seller, in appropriate cases, has a right to reclaim the goods under Section 2–507(2), although this right is subject to the claims of a good faith purchaser for value under Section 2–403.

5. Under subsection (2) an improper reservation by the seller which would constitute a breach in no way impairs such of the buyer's rights as result from identification of the goods. The security interest reserved by the seller under subsection (1) does not protect the seller from retaining possession or control of the document or the goods for the purpose of extracting more than is due the seller under the contract.

Cross References:

Point 1: Section 1–201.
Point 2: Article 7.
Point 3: Sections 2–501(2) and 2–504.
Point 4: Sections 2–403, 2–507(2) and 2–705.
Point 5: Sections 2–310, 2–501 and 2–502 and Article 7.

Definitional Cross References:

"Bill of lading". Section 1–201.
"Buyer". Section 2–103.
"Contract". Section 1–201.
"Contract for sale". Section 2–106.
"Delivery". Section 2–103.
"Financing agency". Section 2–104.
"Goods". Section 2–103.
"Holder". Section 1–201.
"Person". Section 1–201.
"Security interest". Section 1–201.
"Seller". Section 2–103.

As amended in 2003.

§ 2–506. Rights of Financing Agency.

(1) Except as otherwise provided in Article 5, a financing agency by paying or purchasing for value a draft that relates to a shipment of goods acquires to the extent of the payment or purchase and in addition to its own rights under the draft and any document of title securing it any rights of the shipper in the goods including the right to stop delivery and the shipper's right to have the draft honored by the buyer.

(2) The right to reimbursement of a financing agency that has in good faith honored or purchased the draft under commitment to or authority from the buyer is not impaired by subsequent discovery of defects with reference to any relevant document that was apparently regular.

As amended in 2003.

Official Comment

Prior Uniform Statutory Provision: None.

Purposes:

1. "Financing agency" is broadly defined in this Article to cover every normal instance in which a party aids or intervenes in the financing of a sales transaction. The term as used in subsection (1) is not in any sense intended as a limitation and covers any other appropriate situation which may arise outside the scope of the definition.

2. "Paying" as used in subsection (1) is typified by the letter of credit, or "authority to pay" situation in which a banker, by arrangement with the buyer or other consignee, pays on his behalf a draft for the price of the goods. It is immaterial whether the draft is formally drawn on the party paying or his principal, whether it is a sight draft paid in cash or a time draft "paid" in the first instance by acceptance, or whether the payment is viewed as absolute or conditional. All of these cases constitute "payment" under this subsection. Similarly, "purchasing for value" is used to indicate the whole area of financing by the seller's banker, and the principle of subsection (1) is applicable without any niceties of distinction between "purchase," "discount," "advance against collection" or the like. But it is important to notice that the only right to have the draft honored that is acquired is that *against the buyer*; if any right against any one else is claimed it will have to be under some separate obligation of that other person. A letter of credit does not necessarily protect *purchasers* of drafts. See Article 5. And for the relations of the parties to documentary drafts see Part 5 of Article 4.

3. Subsection (1) is made applicable to payments or advances against a draft which "relates to" a shipment of goods and this has been chosen as a term of maximum breadth. In particular the term is intended to cover the case of a draft against an invoice or against a delivery order. Further, it is unnecessary that there be an explicit assignment of the invoice attached to the draft to bring the transaction within the reason of this subsection.

4. After shipment, "the rights of the shipper in the goods" are merely security rights and are subject to the buyer's right to force delivery upon tender of the price. The rights acquired by the financing agency are similarly limited and, moreover, if the agency fails to procure any outstanding negotiable document of title, it may find its exercise of these rights hampered or even defeated by the seller's disposition of the document to a third party. This section does not attempt to create any new rights in the financing agency against the carrier which would force the latter to honor a stop order from the agency, a stranger to the shipment, or any new rights against a holder to whom a document of title has been duly negotiated under Article 7.

5. The deletion of the language "on its face" from subsection (2) is designed to accommodate electronic documents of title without changing the requirement of regularity of the document.

Cross References:

Point 1: Section 2–104

Point 2: Part 5 of Article 4 and Article 5.

Point 4: Sections 2–501 and 2–502 and Article 7.

Definitional Cross References:

"Buyer". Section 2–103.

"Document of title". Section 1–201.

"Draft". Section 3–104(e).

"Financing agency". Section 2–104.

"Good faith". Section 2–103.

"Goods". Section 2–103.

"Purchase". Section 1–201.

"Rights". Section 1–201.

"Value". Section 1–204.

As amended in 2003.

§ 2–507. Effect of Seller's Tender; Delivery on Condition.

(1) Tender of delivery is a condition to the buyer's duty to accept the goods and, unless otherwise agreed, to the buyer's duty to pay for them. Tender entitles the seller to acceptance of the goods and to payment according to the contract.

(2) If payment is due and demanded on the delivery to the buyer of goods or documents of title, the seller may reclaim the goods delivered upon a demand made within a reasonable time after the seller discovers or should have discovered that payment was not made.

(3) The seller's right to reclaim under subsection (2) is subject to the rights of a buyer in ordinary course of business or other good-faith purchaser for value under Section 2–403.

As amended in 2003.

Official Comment

1. The provisions of subsection(1), must be read within the framework of the other sections of this Article which bear upon the question of delivery and payment.

2. The "unless otherwise agreed" provision of subsection (1) is directed primarily to cases in which payment in advance has been promised or a letter of credit term has been included. Payment "according to the contract" contemplates immediate payment, payment at the end of an agreed credit term, payment by a time acceptance or the like. Under this Act, "contract" means the total obligation in law which results from the parties' agreement including the effect of this Article. In this context, therefore, there must be considered the effect in law of provisions such as those on

means and manner of payment and on the failure of the agreed means and manner of payment.

3. Subsection (2) provides that the seller has a right to reclamation to recover the goods from the buyer in a cash-sale transaction when the sellers discovers payment has not been made. The phrase "due and demanded" refers to when the seller takes a check that is later dishonored. *See* Section 2–511. This subsection, and subsection (3), make the seller's rights parallel in credit-sale and cash-sale transactions. *See* Section 2–702.

4. Subsection (3) clarifies the rule that the seller's right to reclaim goods under subsection (2) is subject to the right of the buyer in the ordinary course of business or other good faith purchaser.

Cross References:

Point 2: Sections 1–201, 2–511 and 2–614.
Point 3: Sections 2–310, 2–503, 2–511, 2–601, 2–702 and 2–711 to 2–713.

Definitional Cross References:

"Buyer". Section 2–103.
"Contract". Section 1–201.
"Delivery". Section 2–103.
"Document of title". Section 1–201.
"Goods". Section 2–103.
"Good faith". Section 2–103.
"Reasonable time". Section 1–205.
"Rights". Section 1–201.
"Seller". Section 2–103.
"Value". Section 1–204.

As amended in 2003.

§ 2–508. Cure by Seller of Improper Tender or Delivery; Replacement.

(1) If the buyer rejects goods or a tender of delivery under Section 2–601 or 2–612 or, except in a consumer contract, justifiably revokes acceptance under Section 2–608(1)(b) and the agreed time for performance has not expired, a seller that has performed in good faith, upon seasonable notice to the buyer and at the seller's own expense, may cure the breach of contract by making a conforming tender of delivery within the agreed time. The seller shall compensate the buyer for all of the buyer's reasonable expenses caused by the seller's breach of contract and subsequent cure.

(2) If the buyer rejects goods or a tender of delivery under Section 2–601 or 2–612 or, except in a consumer contract, justifiably revokes accep-

tance under Section 2–608(1)(b) and the agreed time for performance has expired, a seller that has performed in good faith, upon seasonable notice to the buyer and at the seller's own expense, may cure the breach of contract, if the cure is appropriate and timely under the circumstances, by making a tender of conforming goods. The seller shall compensate the buyer for all of the buyer's reasonable expenses caused by seller's breach of contract and subsequent cure.

As amended in 2003.

Official Comment

1. Subsection (1) permits a seller that has made a nonconforming tender in any case to make a conforming tender within the contract time upon seasonable notification to the buyer. It presumes that the buyer has rightfully rejected or justifiably revoked acceptance under Section 2–608(1)(b) through timely notification to the seller and has complied with any particularization requirements imposed by Section 2–605(1). This subsection also applies where the seller has taken back the nonconforming goods and refunded the purchase price. The seller may still make a good tender within the contract period. The closer, however, it is to the contract date, the greater is the necessity for extreme promptness on the seller's part in notifying of the intention to cure, if the notification is to be "seasonable" under this subsection.

The rule of this subsection, moreover, is qualified by its underlying reasons. Thus if, after contracting for June delivery, a buyer later makes known to the seller a need for shipment early in the month and the seller ships accordingly, the "contract time" has been cut down by the supervening modification and the time for cure of tender must reflect this modified time term.

2. Cure after a justifiable revocation of acceptance is not available as a matter of right in a consumer contract. Furthermore, even in a nonconsumer contract, cure is not available if the revocation is predicated on Section 2–608(1)(a). If the buyer is revoking because of a known defect that the seller has not been willing or able to cure, there is no justification for giving the seller a second chance to cure.

3. Subsection (2) expands the seller's right to cure after the time for performance has expired. As under subsection (1), the buyer's rightful rejection or in a nonconsumer contract justifiable revocation of acceptance under Section 2–608(1)(b) trigger the seller's right to cure. Original Section 2–508(2) was designed to prevent surprise rejections by requiring the seller to

have "reasonable grounds to believe" the nonconforming tender was acceptable. Although this test has been abandoned, the requirement that the initial tender be made in good faith prevents a seller from deliberately tendering goods that the seller knows the buyer cannot use in order to save the contract and then, upon rejection, insisting on a second right to cure. The good faith standard applies under both subsection (1) and subsection (2).

4. The seller's cure under both subsection (1) and subsection (2) must be of conforming goods. Conforming goods includes not only conformity to the contracted-for quality but also as to quantity or assortment or other similar obligations under the contract. Since the time for performance has expired in a case governed by subsection (2), however, the seller's tender of conforming goods required to effect a cure under this section could not conform to the contracted time for performance. Thus, subsection (1) requires that cure be tendered "within the agreed time" while subsection (2) requires that the tender be "appropriate and timely under the circumstances."

The requirement that the cure be "appropriate and timely under the circumstances" provides important protection for the buyer. If the buyer is acquiring inventory on a just-in-time basis and needs to procure substitute goods from another supplier to keep the buyer's process moving, the cure would not be timely. If the seller knows from the circumstances that strict compliance with the contract obligations is expected, the seller's cure would not be appropriate. If the seller attempts to cure by repair, the cure would not be appropriate if the attempted cure resulted in goods that did not conform in every respect to the requirements of the contract. The standard for quality on the second tender is governed by Section 2–601. Whether a cure is appropriate and timely is based upon the circumstances and needs of the buyer. A seasonable notice to the buyer and timely cure are predicated on the requirement that the notice and offered cure would be untimely if the buyer has reasonably changed its position in good faith reliance on the nonconforming tender.

5. Cure is at the seller's expense, and the seller is obligated to compensate the buyer for all of the buyer's reasonable expenses caused by the breach and the cure. The term "reasonable expenses" is not limited to expenses that would qualify as incidental damages.

The seller's compensation of the buyer's expenses provided in both subsections (1) and (2) is not controlled by remedy limitations that the parties may have agreed to as provided in Section 2–719. A remedy limitation under Section 2–719 is based upon compensation to the aggrieved party for a breach. The reasonable expenses contemplated under this section are designed to cure the breach in conjunction with the seller's provision of a conforming tender or conforming goods. If the seller is not attempting to cure its breach, a remedy limitation agreed to by the parties under Section 2–719 is an effective way to provide compensation for breach.

Cross References:

Point 1: Sections 2–605 and 2–608.
Point 2: Section 2–608.
Point 3: Section 2–608.
Point 4: Section 2–511.
Point 5: Section 2–719.

Definitional Cross References:

"Agreement". Section 1–201.
"Buyer". Section 2–103.
"Conforming". Section 2–106.
"Consumer contract". Section 2–103.
"Contract". Section 1–201.
"Delivery". Section 2–103.
"Goods". Section 2–103.
"Good faith". Section 2–103.
"Notice". Section 1–202.
"Reasonable time". Section 1–205.
"Seasonable". Section 1–205.
"Seller". Section 2–103.

As amended in 2003.

§ 2–509. Risk of Loss in the Absence of Breach.

(1) If the contract requires or authorizes the seller to ship the goods by carrier:

(a) if it does not require the seller to deliver them at a particular destination, the risk of loss passes to the buyer when the goods are delivered to the carrier even if the shipment is under reservation (Section 2–505); but

(b) if it does require the seller to deliver them at a particular destination and the goods are there tendered while in the possession of the carrier, the risk of loss passes to the buyer when the goods are there so tendered as to enable the buyer to take delivery.

(2) If the goods are held by a bailee to be delivered without being moved, the risk of loss passes to the buyer:

(a) on the buyer's receipt of possession or control of a negotiable document of title covering the goods;

(b) on acknowledgment by the bailee to the buyer of the buyer's right to possession of the goods; or

(c) after the buyer's receipt of possession or control of a nonnegotiable document of title or other direction to deliver in a record, as provided in Section 2–503(4)(b).

(3) In any case not within subsection (1) or (2), the risk of loss passes to the buyer on the buyer's receipt of the goods.

(4) The provisions of this section are subject to contrary agreement of the parties and to Sections 2–327 and 2–510.

As amended in 2003.

Official Comment

1. The underlying theory of this section on risk of loss is in conformity with common commercial and insurance practice, to base the risk of loss on the physical location of the goods and not by shifting of the risk with the "property" in the goods.

The scope of the section is limited to those cases where there has been no breach by the seller. When there has been a breach by either party, the risk of loss may be shifted to the breaching party under Section 2–510 if the breaching party did not already bear the risk for any reason the party's delivery or tender fails to conform to the contract, the present section does not apply and the situation is governed by the provisions on effect of breach on risk of loss.

2. In a shipment contract, the risk of loss shifts to the buyer when the goods are delivered to the carrier as required by Section 2–504; in a destination contract, the risk of loss shifts when the goods are tendered to the buyer as required by Section 2–503(3).

3. Unlike prior law, subsection (3) makes no distinction between merchant and non-merchant sellers. In a case not governed by subsection (1) or subsection (2) and not subject to a contrary result under subsection (4), the risk of loss passes to the buyer upon the buyer's receipt of the goods. Receipt requires taking the physical possession of the goods, Section 2–103(1)(l).

4. When the agreement provides for delivery of the goods from seller to the buyer without removal from the physical possession of a bailee, risk of loss passes to the buyer upon receipt of possession or control of the

negotiable document of title, acknowledgment made by the bailee of the buyer's right of possession or the buyer's receipt of possession or control of a non-negotiable document of title or other direction to deliver in a record as provided in Section 2–503. See the definition of control in Article 7, 7–106.

5. Subsections (1) through (3) are subject to subsection (4) which provides for a "contrary agreement" of the parties. This language is intended as the equivalent of the phrase "unless otherwise agreed" used more frequently throughout this Act. "Contrary" is in no way used as a word of limitation, and the buyer and seller are left free to readjust their rights and risks in any manner agreeable to them. Contrary agreement can also be found in the circumstances of the case, a trade usage or practice, or a course of dealing or course of performance.

Cross References:

> Point 1: Section 2–510.
> Point 2: Sections 2–503 and 2–504.
> Point 4: Section 2–503.
> Point 5: Section 2–201.

Definitional Cross References:

> "Agreement". Section 1–201.
> "Buyer". Section 2–103.
> "Contract". Section 1–201.
> "Delivery". Section 2–103.
> "Document of title". Section 1–201.
> "Goods". Section 2–103.
> "Party". Section 1–201.
> "Receipt" of goods. Section 2–103.
> "Sale on approval". Section 2–326.
> "Seller". Section 2–103.

As amended in 2003.

§ 2–510.   Effect of Breach on Risk of Loss.

(1) If a tender or delivery of goods so fails to conform to the contract as to give a right of rejection, the risk of their loss remains on the seller until cure or acceptance.

(2) If the buyer rightfully revokes acceptance, the buyer may to the extent of any deficiency in the buyer's effective insurance coverage treat the risk of loss as having rested on the seller from the beginning.

(3) If the buyer as to conforming goods already identified to the contract for sale repudiates or is otherwise in breach before risk of their loss has passed to the buyer, the seller may to the extent

of any deficiency in the seller's effective insurance coverage treat the risk of loss as resting on the buyer for a commercially reasonable time.

As amended in 2003.

Official Comment

Prior Uniform Statutory Provision: None.

Purposes: To make clear that:

1. Under subsection (1) the seller by his individual action cannot shift the risk of loss to the buyer unless his action conforms with all the conditions resting on him under the contract.

2. The "cure" of defective tenders contemplated by subsection (1) applies only to those situations in which the seller makes changes in goods already tendered, such as repair, partial substitution, sorting out from an improper mixture and the like since "cure" by repossession and new tender has no effect on the risk of loss of the goods originally tendered. The seller's privilege of cure does not shift the risk, however, until the cure is completed.

Where defective documents are involved a cure of the defect by the seller or a waiver of the defects by the buyer will operate to shift the risk under this section. However, if the goods have been destroyed prior to the cure or the buyer is unaware of their destruction at the time he waives the defect in the documents, the risk of the loss must still be borne by the seller, for the risk shifts only at the time of cure, waiver of documentary defects or acceptance of the goods.

3. In cases where there has been a breach of the contract, if the one in control of the goods is the aggrieved party, whatever loss or damage may prove to be uncovered by his insurance falls upon the contract breaker under subsections (2) and (3) rather than upon him. The word "effective" as applied to insurance coverage in those subsections is used to meet the case of supervening insolvency of the insurer. The "deficiency" referred to in the text means such deficiency in the insurance coverage as exists without subrogation. This section merely distributes the risk of loss as stated and is not intended to be disturbed by any subrogation of an insurer.

Cross Reference:

Section 2–509.

Definitional Cross References:

"Buyer". Section 2–103.
"Conform". Section 2–106.
"Contract for sale". Section 2–106.

"Goods". Section 2–103.
"Seller". Section 2–103.

§ 2–511. Tender of Payment by Buyer; Payment by Check.

(1) Unless otherwise agreed tender of payment is a condition to the seller's duty to tender and complete any delivery.

(2) Tender of payment is sufficient when made by any means or in any manner current in the ordinary course of business unless the seller demands payment in legal tender and gives any extension of time reasonably necessary to procure it.

(3) Subject to the provisions of this Act on the effect of an instrument on an obligation (Section 3–310), payment by check is conditional and is defeated as between the parties by dishonor of the check on due presentment.

As amended in 1994.

Official Comment

Prior Uniform Statutory Provision: Section 42, Uniform Sales Act.

Changes: Rewritten by this section and Section 2–507.

Purposes of Changes:

1. The requirement of payment against delivery in subsection (1) is applicable to non-commercial sales generally and to ordinary sales at retail although it has no application to the great body of commercial contracts which carry credit terms. Subsection (1) applies also to documentary contracts in general and to contracts which look to shipment by the seller but contain no term on time and manner of payment, in which situations the payment may, in proper case, be demanded against delivery of appropriate documents.

In the case of specific transactions such as C.O.D. sales or agreements providing for payment against documents, the provisions of this subsection must be considered in conjunction with the special sections of the Article dealing with such terms. The provision that tender of payment is a condition to the seller's duty to tender and complete "any delivery" integrates this section with the language and policy of the section on delivery in several lots which call for separate payment. Finally, attention should be directed to the provision on right to adequate assurance of performance which recognizes, even before the time for tender, an obligation on the buyer not to impair the seller's expectation of receiving payment in due course.

2. Unless there is agreement otherwise the concurrence of the conditions as to tender of payment and tender of delivery requires their performance at a single place or time. This Article determines that place and time by determining in various other sections the place and time for tender of delivery under various circumstances and in particular types of transactions. The sections dealing with time and place of delivery together with the section on right to inspection of goods answer the subsidiary question as to when payment may be demanded before inspection by the buyer.

3. The essence of the principle involved in subsection (2) is avoidance of commercial surprise at the time of performance. The section on substituted performance covers the peculiar case in which legal tender is not available to the commercial community.

4. Subsection (3) is concerned with the rights and obligations as between the parties to a sales transaction when payment is made by check. This Article recognizes that the taking of a seemingly solvent party's check is commercially normal and proper and, if due diligence is exercised in collection, is not to be penalized in any way. The conditional character of the payment under this section refers only to the effect of the transaction "as between the parties" thereto and does not purport to cut into the law of "absolute" and "conditional" payment as applied to such other problems as the discharge of sureties or the responsibilities of a drawee bank which is at the same time an agent for collection.

The phrase "by check" includes not only the buyer's own but any check which does not effect a discharge under Article 3 (Section 3–802). Similarly the reason of this subsection should apply and the same result should be reached where the buyer "pays" by sight draft on a commercial firm which is financing him.

5. Under subsection (3) payment by check is defeated if it is not honored upon due presentment. This corresponds to the provisions of article on Commercial Paper. (Section 3–802). But if the seller procures certification of the check instead of cashing it, the buyer is discharged. (Section 3–411).

6. Where the instrument offered by the buyer is not a payment but a credit instrument such as a note or a check post-dated by even one day, the seller's acceptance of the instrument insofar as third parties are concerned, amounts to a delivery on credit and his remedies are set forth in the section on buyer's insolvency. As between the buyer and the seller, however, the matter turns on the present subsection and the section on conditional delivery and subsequent dishon-

or of the instrument gives the seller rights on it as well as for breach of the contract for sale.

Cross References:

Point 1: Sections 2–307, 2–310, 2–325, 2–503, 2–513 and 2–609.

Point 2: Sections 2–307, 2–310, 2–503, 2–504 and 2–513.

Point 3: Section 2–614.

Point 5: Article 3, esp. Sections 3–802 and 3–411.

Point 6: Sections 2–507, 2–702, and Article 3.

Definitional Cross References:

"Buyer". Section 2–103.

"Check". Section 3–104(f).

"Dishonor". Section 3–502.

"Party". Section 1–201.

"Reasonable time". Section 1–205.

"Seller". Section 2–103.

§ 2–512. Payment by Buyer Before Inspection.

(1) If the contract requires payment before inspection, nonconformity of the goods does not excuse the buyer from so making payment unless:

(a) the nonconformity appears without inspection; or

(b) despite tender of the required documents the circumstances would justify injunction against honor under this Act (Section 5–109(b)).

(2) Payment pursuant to subsection (1) does not constitute an acceptance of goods or impair the buyer's right to inspect or any of the buyer's remedies.

As amended in 1995 and 2003.

Official Comment

Prior Uniform Statutory Provision: None, but see Sections 47 and 49, Uniform Sales Act.

Purposes:

1. Subsection (1) of the present section recognizes that the essence of a contract providing for payment before inspection is the intention of the parties to shift to the buyer the risks which would usually rest upon the seller. The basic nature of the transaction is thus preserved and the buyer is in most cases required to pay first and litigate as to any defects later.

2. "Inspection" under this section is an inspection in a manner reasonable for detecting defects in goods whose surface appearance is satisfactory.

3. Clause (a) of this subsection states an exception to the general rule based on common sense and normal commercial practice. The apparent non-conformity referred to is one which is evident in the mere process of taking delivery.

4. Clause (b) is concerned with contracts for payment against documents and incorporates the general clarification and modification of the case law contained in the section on excuse of a financing agency. Section 5–114.

5. Subsection (2) makes explicit the general policy of the Uniform Sales Act that the payment required before inspection in no way impairs the buyer's remedies or rights in the event of a default by the seller. The remedies preserved to the buyer are all of his remedies, which include as a matter of reason the remedy for total non-delivery after payment in advance.

The provision on performance or acceptance under reservation of rights does not apply to the situations contemplated here in which payment is made in due course under the contract and the buyer need not pay "under protest" or the like in order to preserve his rights as to defects discovered upon inspection.

6. This section applies to cases in which the contract requires payment before inspection either by the express agreement of the parties or by reason of the effect in law of that contract. The present section must therefore be considered in conjunction with the provision on right to inspection of goods which sets forth the instances in which the buyer is not entitled to inspection before payment.

Cross References:

Point 4: Article 5.
Point 5: Section 1–308.
Point 6: Section 2–513(3).

Definitional Cross References:

"Buyer". Section 2–103.
"Conform". Section 2–106.
"Contract". Section 1–201.
"Financing agency". Section 2–104.
"Goods". Section 2–103.
"Remedy". Section 1–201.
"Rights". Section 1–201.

§ 2–513. Buyer's Right to Inspection of Goods.

(1) Unless otherwise agreed and subject to subsection (3), if goods are tendered or delivered or identified to the contract for sale, the buyer has a right before payment or acceptance to inspect them at any reasonable place and time and in any reasonable manner. If the seller is required or authorized to send the goods to the buyer, the inspection may be after their arrival.

(2) Expenses of inspection must be borne by the buyer but may be recovered from the seller if the goods do not conform and are rejected.

(3) Unless otherwise agreed, the buyer is not entitled to inspect the goods before payment of the price if the contract provides:

(a) for delivery on terms that under applicable course of performance, course of dealing, or usage of trade are interpreted to preclude inspection before payment; or

(b) for payment against documents of title, except where the payment is due only after the goods are to become available for inspection.

(4) A place, method, or standard of inspection fixed by the parties is presumed to be exclusive, but unless otherwise expressly agreed it does not postpone identification or shift the place for delivery or for passing the risk of loss. If compliance becomes impossible, inspection shall be as provided in this section unless the place, method, or standard fixed was clearly intended as an indispensable condition failure of which avoids the contract.

As amended in 2003.

Official Comment

Prior Uniform Statutory Provisions: Section 47(2), (3), Uniform Sales Act.

Changes: Rewritten, Subsections (2) and (3) being new.

Purposes of Changes and New Matter: To correspond in substance with the prior uniform statutory provision and to incorporate in addition some of the results of the better case law so that:

1. The buyer is entitled to inspect goods as provided in subsection (1) unless it has been otherwise agreed by the parties. The phrase "unless otherwise agreed" is intended principally to cover such situations as those outlined in subsections (3) and (4) and those

in which the agreement of the parties negates inspection before tender of delivery. However, no agreement by the parties can displace the entire right of inspection except where the contract is simply for the sale of "this thing." Even in a sale of boxed goods "as is" inspection is a right of the buyer, since if the boxes prove to contain some other merchandise altogether the price can be recovered back; nor do the limitations of the provision on effect of acceptance apply in such a case.

2.   The buyer's right of inspection is available to him upon tender, delivery or appropriation of the goods with notice to him. Since inspection is available to him on tender, where payment is due against delivery he may, unless otherwise agreed, make his inspection before payment of the price. It is also available to him after receipt of the goods and so may be postponed after receipt for a reasonable time. Failure to inspect before payment does not impair the right to inspect after receipt of the goods unless the case falls within subsection (4) on agreed and exclusive inspection provisions. The right to inspect goods which have been appropriated with notice to the buyer holds whether or not the sale was by sample.

3.   The buyer may exercise his right of inspection at any reasonable time or place and in any reasonable manner. It is not necessary that he select the most appropriate time, place or manner to inspect or that his selection be the customary one in the trade or locality. Any reasonable time, place or manner is available to him and the reasonableness will be determined by trade usages, past practices between the parties and the other circumstances of the case.

The last sentence of subsection (1) makes it clear that the place of arrival of shipped goods is a reasonable place for their inspection.

4.   Expenses of an inspection made to satisfy the buyer of the seller's performance must be assumed by the buyer in the first instance. Since the rule provides merely for an allocation of expense there is no policy to prevent the parties from providing otherwise in the agreement. Where the buyer would normally bear the expenses of the inspection but the goods are rightly rejected because of what the inspection reveals, demonstrable and reasonable costs of the inspection are part of his incidental damage caused by the seller's breach.

5.   In the case of payment against documents, subsection (3) requires payment before inspection, since shipping documents against which payment is to be made will commonly be tendered while the goods are still in transit. This Article recognizes no exception in any peculiar case in which the goods happen to arrive before the documents are tendered. However, where by the agreement payment is to await the arrival of the goods, inspection before payment becomes proper since the goods are then "available for inspection."

Where by the agreement the documents are to be tendered after arrival of the goods, the buyer is entitled to inspect before payment since the goods are then "available for inspection". Proof of usage is not necessary to establish this right, but if inspection before payment is disputed the contrary must be established by usage or by an explicit contract term to that effect.

For the same reason, that the goods are available for inspection, a term calling for payment against storage documents or a delivery order does not normally bar the buyer's right to inspection before payment under subsection (3)(b). This result is reinforced by the buyer's right under subsection (1) to inspect goods which have been appropriated with notice to him.

6.   Under subsection (4) an agreed place, method or standard of inspection is presumed to be intended as exclusive. However, where compliance with an agreed method or standard becomes impossible, the question is basically one of intention. If the parties clearly intend that the method or standard of inspection is a necessary condition without which the entire agreement should fail, the contract is at an end if that method becomes impossible. On the other hand, if the parties merely seek to indicate a convenient and reliable method or standard but do not intend to give up the agreement in the event of the failure, any reasonable method of inspection may be substituted under this Article.

Since the purpose of an agreed place of inspection is only to make sure at that point whether or not the goods will be rejected, the "exclusive" feature of the named place is satisfied under this Article if the buyer's failure to inspect there is held to be an acceptance with the knowledge of the defects as an inspection would have revealed within the section on waiver of the buyer's objections by failure to particularize. (Section 2–605(1)).

7.   Clauses on time of inspection are commonly clauses which limit the time in which the buyer must inspect and give notice of defects. Such clauses are therefore governed by the section of this Article which requires that such a time limitation must be reasonable.

8.   Inspection under this Article is not to be regarded as a "condition precedent to the passing of title" so that risk until inspection remains on the seller. Under subsection (4) such an approach cannot be sustained.

Issues between the buyer and seller are settled in this Article almost wholly by special provisions and not by the technical determination of the locus of the title. Thus "inspection as a condition to the passing of title" becomes a concept almost without meaning. However, in peculiar circumstances inspection may still have some of the consequences hitherto sought and obtained under that concept.

9. "Inspection" under this section has to do with the buyer's check-up on whether the seller's performance is in accordance with a contract previously made and is not to be confused with the "examination" of the goods or of a sample or model of them at the time of contracting which may affect the warranties involved in the contract.

Cross Reference:

Point 1: Section 2–607.
Point 2: Sections 2–501 and 2–502.
Point 4: Section 2–715.
Point 6: Sections 2–605 to 2–608.
Point 7: Section 1–204.
Point 8: Comment to Section 2–401.
Point 9: Section 2–316(b)(2).

Definitional Cross References:

"Buyer". Section 2–103.
"Conform". Section 2–106.
"Contract". Section 1–201.
"Contract for sale". Section 2–106.
"Course of performance". Section 1–303.
"Document of title". Section 1–201.
"Goods". Section 2–103.
"Party". Section 1–201.
"Presumed". Section 1–201.
"Reasonable time". Section 1–205.
"Rights". Section 1–201.
"Seller". Section 2–103.
"Send". Section 1–201.
"Term". Section 1–201.
"Usage of trade". Section 1–303.

As amended in 2003.

§ 2–514. When Documents Deliverable on Acceptance; When on Payment.

Unless otherwise agreed and except as otherwise provided in Article 5, documents against which a draft is drawn are to be delivered to the drawee on acceptance of the draft if it is payable more than three days after presentment; otherwise, only on payment.

As amended in 2003.

Official Comment

This section, which is consistent with Section 4–503, is subject to Article 5. Under Article 5, because an issuer may have up to seven days to determine compliance of documents (Section 5–108), the delay beyond three days does not necessarily indicate that the draft should be treated as a time draft.

Definitional Cross References:

"Delivery". Section 2–103.
"Draft". Section 3–104(e).

As amended in 2003.

§ 2–515. Preserving Evidence of Goods in Dispute.

In furtherance of the adjustment of any claim or dispute

(a) either party on reasonable notification to the other and for the purpose of ascertaining the facts and preserving evidence has the right to inspect, test and sample the goods including such of them as may be in the possession or control of the other; and

(b) the parties may agree to a third party inspection or survey to determine the conformity or condition of the goods and may agree that the findings shall be binding upon them in any subsequent litigation or adjustment.

Official Comment

Prior Uniform Statutory Provision: None.

Purposes:

1. To meet certain serious problems which arise when there is a dispute as to the quality of the goods and thereby perhaps to aid the parties in reaching a settlement, and to further the use of devices which will promote certainty as to the condition of the goods, or at least aid in preserving evidence of their condition.

2. Under paragraph (a), to afford either party an opportunity for preserving evidence, whether or not agreement has been reached, and thereby to reduce uncertainty in any litigation and, in turn perhaps, to promote agreement.

Paragraph (a) does not conflict with the provisions on the seller's right to resell rejected goods or the buyer's similar right. Apparent conflict between these provisions which will be suggested in certain circumstances is to be resolved by requiring prompt action by the parties. Nor does paragraph (a) impair the effect of a term for payment before inspection. Short of such defects as amount to fraud or substantial failure of consideration, non-conformity is neither an excuse nor a defense to an action for non-acceptance of documents. Normally, therefore, until the buyer has made payment, inspected and rejected the goods, there is no occasion or use for the rights under paragraph (a).

3. Under paragraph (b), to provide for third party inspection upon the agreement of the parties, thereby opening the door to amicable adjustments based upon the findings of such third parties.

The use of the phrase "conformity or condition" makes it clear that the parties' agreement may range from a complete settlement of all aspects of the dispute by a third party to the use of a third party merely to determine and record the condition of the goods so that they can be resold or used to reduce the stake in controversy. "Conformity", at one end of the scale of possible issues, includes the whole question of interpretation of the agreement and its legal effect, the state of the goods in regard to quality and condition, whether any defects are due to factors which operate at the risk of the buyer, and the degree of non-conformity where that may be material. "Condition", at the other end of the scale, includes nothing but the degree of damage or deterioration which the goods show. Paragraph (b) is intended to reach any point in the gamut which the parties may agree upon.

The principle of the section on reservation of rights reinforces this paragraph in simplifying such adjustments as the parties wish to make in partial settlement while reserving their rights as to any further points. Paragraph (b) also suggests the use of arbitration, where desired, of any points left open, but nothing in this section is intended to repeal or amend any statute governing arbitration. Where any question arises as to the extent of the parties' agreement under the paragraph, the presumption should be that it was meant to extend only to the relation between the contract description and the goods as delivered, since that is what a craftsman in the trade would normally be expected to report upon. Finally, a written and authenticated report of inspection or tests by a third party, whether or not sampling has been practicable, is entitled to be admitted as evidence under this Act, for it is a third party document.

Cross References:

Point 2: Sections 2–513(3), 2–706 and 2–711(2) and Article 5.

Point 3: Sections 1–307 and 1–308.

Definitional Cross References:

"Conform". Section 2–106.
"Goods". Section 2–103.
"Notification". Section 1–202.
"Party". Section 1–201.

PART 6

BREACH, REPUDIATION, AND EXCUSE

§ 2–601. Buyer's Rights on Improper Delivery.

Subject to Sections 2–504 and 2–612, and unless otherwise agreed under Sections 2–718 and 2–719, if the goods or the tender of delivery fail in any respect to conform to the contract, the buyer may:

(a) reject the whole;

(b) accept the whole; or

(c) accept any commercial unit or units and reject the rest.

As amended in 2003.

Official Comment

Prior Uniform Statutory Provision: No one general equivalent provision but numerous provisions, dealing with situations of non-conformity where buyer may

accept or reject, including Sections 11, 44 and 69(1), Uniform Sales Act.

Changes: Partial acceptance in good faith is recognized and the buyer's remedies on the contract for breach of warranty and the like, where the buyer has returned the goods after transfer of title, are no longer barred.

Purposes of Changes: To make it clear that:

1. A buyer accepting a non-conforming tender is not penalized by the loss of any remedy otherwise open to him. This policy extends to cover and regulate the acceptance of a part of any lot improperly tendered in any case where the price can reasonably be apportioned. Partial acceptance is permitted whether the part of the goods accepted conforms or not. The only limitation on partial acceptance is that good faith and commercial reasonableness must be used to avoid undue impairment of the value of the remaining portion of the goods. This is the reason for the insistence on

the "commercial unit" in paragraph (c). In this respect, the test is not only what unit has been the basis of contract, but whether the partial acceptance produces so materially adverse an effect on the remainder as to constitute bad faith.

2. Acceptance made with the knowledge of the other party is final. An original refusal to accept may be withdrawn by a later acceptance if the seller has indicated that he is holding the tender open. However, if the buyer attempts to accept, either in whole or in part, after his original rejection has caused the seller to arrange for other disposition of the goods, the buyer must answer for any ensuing damage since the next section provides that any exercise of ownership after rejection is wrongful as against the seller. Further, he is liable even though the seller may choose to treat his action as acceptance rather than conversion, since the damage flows from the misleading notice. Such arrangements for resale or other disposition of the goods by the seller must be viewed as within the normal contemplation of a buyer who has given notice of rejection. However, the buyer's attempts in good faith to dispose of defective goods where the seller has failed to give instructions within a reasonable time are not to be regarded as an acceptance.

3. The right to rejection under this section is subject to the limitations on the right of rejection in installment contracts (Section 2–612) and the standard for rejection in a shipment contract when the seller fails to notify the buyer of the shipment or fails to make a proper contract. (Section 2–504). The right of rejection in this section is also subject to the seller's right to cure (Section 2–508) in appropriate circumstances.

Cross References:

Point 2: Sections 2–602, 2–612, 2–718 and 2–719.
Point 3: Sections 2–504, 2–508 and 2–612.

Definitional Cross References:

"Buyer". Section 2–103.
"Commercial unit". Section 2–105.
"Conform". Section 2–106.
"Contract". Section 1–201.
"Goods". Section 2–103.
"Installment contract". Section 2–612.
"Rights". Section 1–201.
"Seller". Section 2–103.

As amended in 2003.

§ 2–602. Manner and Effect of Rejection.

(1) Rejection of goods must be within a reasonable time after their delivery or tender. It is ineffective unless the buyer seasonably notifies the seller.

(2) Subject to Sections 2–603, 2–604, and Section 2–608(4):

(a) after rejection any exercise of ownership by the buyer with respect to any commercial unit is wrongful as against the seller; and

(b) if the buyer has before rejection taken physical possession of goods in which the buyer does not have a security interest under Section 2–711(3), the buyer is under a duty after rejection to hold them with reasonable care at the seller's disposition for a time sufficient to permit the seller to remove them; but

(c) the buyer has no further obligations with regard to goods rightfully rejected.

(3) The seller's rights with respect to goods wrongfully rejected are governed by the provisions of this Article on Seller's remedies in general (Section 2–703).

As amended in 2003.

Official Comment

Prior Uniform Statutory Provision: Section 50, Uniform Sales Act.

Changes: Rewritten.

Purposes of Changes: To make it clear that:

1. A tender or delivery of goods made pursuant to a contract of sale, even though wholly non-conforming, requires affirmative action by the buyer to avoid acceptance. Under subsection (1), therefore, the buyer is given a reasonable time to notify the seller of his rejection, but without such seasonable notification his rejection is ineffective. The sections of this Article dealing with inspection of goods must be read in connection with the buyer's reasonable time for action under this subsection. Contract provisions limiting the time for rejection fall within the rule of the section on "Time" and are effective if the time set gives the buyer a reasonable time for discovery of defects. What constitutes a due "notifying" of rejection by the buyer to the seller is defined in Section 1–201.

2. Subsection (2) sets forth the duties of the buyer upon rejection. In addition to the duty to hold the goods with reasonable care for the seller's disposition, the buyer also has those duties specified in Sections 2–603, 2–604 and 2–608(4).

3. Elimination of the word "rightful" in the title makes it clear that a buyer can effectively reject goods even though the rejection is wrongful and constitutes a breach. *See* Section 2–703(1). The word "rightful" has also been deleted from the titles to Section 2–603 and 2–604. *See* Official Comments to those sections.

4. The provisions of this section are to be appropriately limited or modified when a negotiation is in process.

Cross References:

Point 1: Sections 1–201, 1–204(1) and (3), 2–512(2), 2–513(1) and 2–606(1)(b).

Point 2: Sections 2–603, 2–604 and 2–608(4).

Point 3: Sections 2–603, 2–604 and 2–703.

Definitional Cross References:

"Buyer". Section 2–103.
"Commercial unit". Section 2–105.
"Goods". Section 2–103.
"Notifies". Section 1–202.
"Reasonable time". Section 1–205.
"Remedy". Section 1–201.
"Rights". Section 1–201.
"Seasonable". Section 1–205.
"Security interest". Section 1–201.
"Seller". Section 2–103.

As amended in 2003.

§ 2–603. Merchant Buyer's Duties as to Rejected Goods.

(1) Subject to any security interest in the buyer under Section 2–711(3), if the seller has no agent or place of business at the market of rejection, a merchant buyer is under a duty after rejection of goods in the buyer's possession or control to follow any reasonable instructions received from the seller with respect to the goods and in the absence of such instructions to make reasonable efforts to sell them for the seller's account if they are perishable or threaten to decline in value speedily. In the case of a rightful rejection, instructions are not reasonable if on demand indemnity for expenses is not forthcoming.

(2) If the buyer sells goods under subsection (1) following a rightful rejection, the buyer is entitled to reimbursement from the seller or out of the proceeds for reasonable expenses of caring for and selling them, and if the expenses include no selling commission then to such commission as is usual in the trade or if there is none to a reasonable sum not exceeding 10 per cent on the gross proceeds.

(3) In complying with this section the buyer is held only to good faith and good-faith conduct under this section is neither acceptance nor conversion nor the basis of an action for damages.

As amended in 2003.

Official Comment

Prior Uniform Statutory Provision: None.

Purposes:

1. This section recognizes the duty imposed upon the merchant buyer by good faith and commercial practice to follow any reasonable instructions of the seller as to reshipping, storing, delivery to a third party, reselling or the like. Subsection (1) goes further and extends the duty to include the making of reasonable efforts to effect a salvage sale where the value of the goods is threatened and the seller's instructions do not arrive in time to prevent serious loss.

2. The limitations on the buyer's duty to resell under subsection (1) are to be liberally construed. The buyer's duty to resell under this section arises from commercial necessity and thus is present only when the seller has "no agent or place of business at the market of rejection". A financing agency which is acting in behalf of the seller in handling the documents rejected by the buyer is sufficiently the seller's agent to lift the burden of salvage resale from the buyer. (See provisions of Sections 4–503 and 5–112 on bank's duties with respect to rejected documents.) The buyer's duty to resell is extended only to goods in his "possession or control", but these are intended as words of wide, rather than narrow, import. In effect, the measure of the buyer's "control" is whether he can practicably effect control without undue commercial burden.

3. The explicit provisions for reimbursement and compensation to the buyer in subsection (2) are applicable and necessary only where he is not acting under instructions from the seller. As provided in subsection (1) the seller's instructions to be "reasonable" must on demand of the buyer include indemnity for expenses.

4. Since this section makes the resale of perishable goods an affirmative duty in contrast to a mere right to sell as under the case law, subsection (3) makes it clear that the buyer is liable only for the exercise of good faith in determining whether the value of the goods is sufficiently threatened to justify a quick resale or whether he has waited a sufficient length of time for instructions, or what a reasonable means and place of resale is.

5. A buyer who fails to make a salvage sale when his duty to do so under this section has arisen is subject to damages pursuant to the section on liberal administration of remedies.

6. Except as otherwise stated in this section, its provisions apply to all effective rejections, including rejections that are wrongful. Thus, any merchant buyer whose rejection is effective is subject to the duties set forth in the first sentence of subsection (1), and a merchant buyer that complies with those duties is entitled to the protection provided by subsection (3). However, the right to indemnity for expenses on demand under the second sentence of subsection (1) and the right to reimbursement for expenses and a commission under subsection (2) are limited to buyers whose rejections are rightful.

Cross References:

Point 2: Sections 4–503 and 5–112.
Point 5: Section 1–106.

Definitional Cross References:

"Buyer". Section 2–103.
"Good faith". Section 2–103.
"Goods". Section 2–103.
"Merchant". Section 2–104.
"Security interest". Section 1–201.
"Seller". Section 2–103.

As amended in 2003.

§ 2–604. Buyer's Options as to Salvage of Rejected Goods.

Subject to the provisions of Section 2–603 on perishables, if the seller gives no instructions within a reasonable time after notification of rejection, the buyer may store the rejected goods for the seller's account or reship them to the seller or resell them for the seller's account with reimbursement as provided in Section 2–603. Such action is not acceptance or conversion.

As amended in 2003.

Official Comment

Prior Uniform Statutory Provision: None.

Purposes:

1. The basic purpose of this section is twofold: on the one hand it aims at reducing the stake in dispute and on the other at avoiding the pinning of a technical "acceptance" on a buyer who has taken steps towards realization on or preservation of the goods in good faith. This section is essentially a salvage section and

the buyer's right to act under it is conditioned upon (1) non-conformity of the goods, (2) due notification of rejection to the seller under the section on manner of rejection, and (3) the absence of any instructions from the seller which the merchant-buyer has a duty to follow under the preceding section.

2. This section no longer refers to "rightful" rejections. Accordingly, its provisions apply to any buyer whose rejection is effective. However, this section is subject to Section 2–603, and the provisions of that section differentiate between rightful and wrongful rejections.

Cross References:

Point 1: Sections 2–602, and 2–603 and 2–706.
Point 2: Section 2–603.

Definitional Cross References:

"Buyer". Section 2–103.
"Goods". Section 2–103.
"Seller". Section 2–103.

As amended in 2003.

§ 2–605. Waiver of Buyer's Objections by Failure to Particularize.

(1) A buyer's failure to state in connection with rejection a particular defect or in connection with revocation of acceptance a defect that justifies revocation precludes the buyer from relying on the unstated defect to justify rejection or revocation of acceptance if the defect is ascertainable by reasonable inspection:

(a) if the seller had a right to cure the defect and could have cured it if stated seasonably; or

(b) between merchants, if the seller has after rejection or revocation of acceptance made a request in a record for a full and final statement in a record of all defects on which the buyer proposes to rely.

(2) A buyer's payment against documents tendered to the buyer made without reservation of rights precludes recovery of the payment for defects apparent in the documents.

As amended in 2003.

Official Comment

1. This section rests upon a policy of permitting the buyer to give a quick and informal notice of defects in

a tender without penalizing the buyer for omissions, while at the same time protecting a seller that is reasonably misled by the buyer's failure to state curable defects. When the defect in a tender is one which could have been cured by the seller, a buyer that merely rejects the delivery without stating any objections to the tender is probably acting in commercial bad faith and is seeking to get out of a agreement which has become unprofitable. Following the general policy of this Article to preserve the deal wherever possible, subsection (1)(a) requires that the seller's right to correct the tender in the circumstances be protected.

Subsection (1) as amended makes three substantive changes. First, the failure to particularize affects only the buyer's right to reject or revoke acceptance. It does not affect the buyer's right to establish a breach of the agreement. Waiver of a right to damages for breach because of a failure properly to notify the seller is governed by Section 2–607(3).

Second, subsection (1) now requires the seller to have had a right to cure under Section 2–508 in addition to having the ability to cure. This point was perhaps implicit in the original provision, but it is now expressly stated to avoid any question of whether this section creates a seller's right to cure independent of the right enumerated in Section 2–508. Thus, if the defect is one that could be cured under Section 2–508, the buyer will have waived that defect as a basis for rejecting the goods or revoking acceptance if the buyer fails to state the defect with sufficient particularity to facilitate the seller's exercise of its right to cure as provided in Section 2–508.

Subsection (1) as revised has been extended to include a notice requirement not only as to rejection but also as to revocation of acceptance. This is necessitated by the expansion of the right to cure (Section 2–508) to cover revocation of acceptance in nonconsumer contracts. The application of the subsection to revocation cases is limited in the following ways: 1) because a revocation under Section 2–608(1)(a) does not activate a right to cure under Section 2–508, the revocation does not activate subsection (1); 2) because Section 2–608(1)(b) involves defects that are by definition difficult to discover, there is no waiver under subsection (1) unless the defect justifies the revocation and the buyer has notice of it; and 3) because the right to cure following revocation of acceptance is restricted under Section 2–508 to nonconsumer contracts, this notice requirement does not apply to a consumer who is seeking to revoke acceptance.

2. When the time for cure has passed, subsection (1)(b) provides that a merchant seller is entitled upon request to a final statement of objections by a merchant buyer upon which the seller can rely. What is needed is a clear statement to the buyer of exactly what is being sought. A formal demand will be sufficient in the case of a merchant-buyer.

3. Subsection (2) has been amended to make clear that a buyer that makes payment upon presentation of the documents to the buyer may waive defects, but that a person that is not the buyer, such as the issuer of a letter of credit that pays as against documents, is not waiving the buyer's right to assert defects in the documents as against the seller.

Subsection (2) applies to documents the same principle contained in Section 2–606(1)(a) for the acceptance of goods; that is, if the buyer accepts documents that have apparent defects, the buyer is presumed to have waived the defects as a basis for rejecting the documents. Subsection (2) is limited to defects which are apparent in the documents. This rule applies to both tangible and electronic documents of title. When payment is required against documents, the documents must be inspected before the payment, and the payment constitutes acceptance of the documents. When the documents are delivered without requiring a contemporary payment by the buyer, the acceptance of the documents by non-objection is postponed until after a reasonable time for the buyer to inspect the documents. In either situation, however, the buyer "waives" only what is apparent in the documents. Moreover, in either case, the acceptance of the documents does not constitute an acceptance of the goods and does not impair any options or remedies of the buyer for improper delivery of the goods. *See* Section 2–512(2).

Cross References:

Point 1: Sections 2–508, 2–607 and 2–608.
Point 3: Sections 2–512, 2–606 and 2–607.

Definitional Cross References:

"Between merchants". Section 2–104.
"Buyer". Section 2–103.
"Record". Section 2–103.
"Seasonably". Section 1–205.
"Seller". Section 2–103.

As amended in 2003.

§ 2–606. What Constitutes Acceptance of Goods.

(1) Acceptance of goods occurs when the buyer:

(a) after a reasonable opportunity to inspect the goods signifies to the seller that the goods are conforming or that the buyer will take or retain them in spite of their non-conformity;

(b) fails to make an effective rejection under Section 2–602(1), but such acceptance does not occur until the buyer has had a reasonable opportunity to inspect them; or

(c) Subject to Section 2–608(4), does any act inconsistent with the seller's ownership.

(2) Acceptance of a part of any commercial unit is acceptance of that entire unit.

As amended in 2003.

Official Comment

Prior Uniform Statutory Provision: Section 48, Uniform Sales Act.

Changes: Rewritten, the qualification in paragraph (c) and subsection (2) being new; otherwise the general policy of the prior legislation is continued.

Purposes of Changes and New Matter: To make it clear that:

1. Under this Article "acceptance" as applied to goods means that the buyer, pursuant to the contract, takes particular goods which have been appropriated to the contract as his own, whether or not he is obligated to do so, and whether he does so by words, action, or silence when it is time to speak. If the goods conform to the contract, acceptance amounts only to the performance by the buyer of one part of his legal obligation.

2. Under this Article acceptance of goods is always acceptance of identified goods which have been appropriated to the contract or are appropriated by the contract. There is no provision for "acceptance of title" apart from acceptance in general, since acceptance of title is not material under this Article to the detailed rights and duties of the parties. (See Section 2–401). The refinements of the older law between acceptance of goods and of title become unnecessary in view of the provisions of the sections on effect and revocation of acceptance, on effects of identification and on risk of loss, and those sections which free the seller's and buyer's remedies from the complications and confusions caused by the question of whether title has or has not passed to the buyer before breach.

3. Under paragraph (a), payment made after tender is always one circumstance tending to signify acceptance of the goods but in itself it can never be more than one circumstance and is not conclusive. Also, a conditional communication of acceptance always remains subject to its expressed conditions.

4. Under paragraph (c), any action taken by the buyer, which is inconsistent with his claim that he has rejected the goods, constitutes an acceptance. However, the provisions of paragraph (c) are subject to the sections dealing with rejection by the buyer which permit the buyer to take certain actions with respect to the goods pursuant to his options and duties imposed by those sections, without effecting an acceptance of the goods. The second clause of paragraph (c) modifies some of the prior case law and makes it clear that "acceptance" in law based on the wrongful act of the acceptor is acceptance only as against the wrongdoer and then only at the option of the party wronged.

In the same manner in which a buyer can bind himself, despite his insistence that he is rejecting or has rejected the goods, by an act inconsistent with the seller's ownership under paragraph (c), he can obligate himself by a communication of acceptance despite a prior rejection under paragraph (a). However, the sections on buyer's rights on improper delivery and on the effect of rightful rejection, make it clear that after he once rejects a tender, paragraph (a) does not operate in favor of the buyer unless the seller has re-tendered the goods or has taken affirmative action indicating that he is holding the tender open. See also Comment 2 to Section 2–601.

5. Subsection (2) supplements the policy of the section on buyer's rights on improper delivery, recognizing the validity of a partial acceptance but insisting that the buyer exercise this right only as to whole commercial units.

Cross References:

Point 2: Sections 2–401, 2–509, 2–510, 2–607, 2–608 and Part 7.
Point 4: Sections 2–601 through 2–604.
Point 5: Section 2–601.

Definitional Cross References:

"Buyer". Section 2–103.
"Commercial unit". Section 2–105.
"Goods". Section 2–103.
"Seller". Section 2–103.

§ 2–607. Effect of Acceptance; Notice of Breach; Burden of Establishing Breach after Acceptance; Notice of Claim or Litigation to Person Answerable Over.

(1) The buyer must pay at the contract rate for any goods accepted.

(2) Acceptance of goods by the buyer precludes rejection of the goods accepted and if made with knowledge of a nonconformity may not be revoked because of it unless the acceptance was on the reasonable assumption that the nonconformity would be seasonably cured, but acceptance does not of itself impair any other remedy provided by this Article for nonconformity.

(3) If a tender has been accepted:

(a) the buyer must within a reasonable time after the buyer discovers or should have discovered any breach notify the seller, but failure to give timely notice bars the buyer from a remedy only to the extent that the seller is prejudiced by the failure; and

(b) if the claim is one for infringement or the like under Section 2–312(2) and the buyer is sued as a result of such a breach, the buyer must so notify the seller within a reasonable time after the buyer receives notice of the litigation or be barred from any remedy over for liability established by the litigation.

(4) The burden is on the buyer to establish any breach with respect to the goods accepted.

(5) If the buyer is sued for indemnity, breach of a warranty, or other obligation for which another party is answerable over:

(a) the buyer may give the other party notice of the litigation in a record, and if the notice states that the other party may come in and defend and that if the other party does not do so the other party will be bound in any action against the other party by the buyer by any determination of fact common to the two litigations, then unless the other party after seasonable receipt of the notice does come in and defend the other party is so bound.

(b) if the claim is one for infringement or the like under Section 2–312(2), the original seller may demand in a record that its buyer turn over to it control of the litigation including settlement or else be barred from any remedy over and if it also agrees to bear all expense and to satisfy any adverse judgment, the buyer is so barred unless the buyer after seasonable receipt of the demand does turn over control.

(6) Subsections (3), (4), and (5) apply to any obligation of a buyer to hold the seller harmless against infringement or the like under Section 2–312(2).

As amended in 2003.

Official Comment

1. Under subsection (1), once the buyer accepts a tender the seller acquires a right to its price on the contract terms. In cases of partial acceptance, the price of any part accepted is, if possible, to be reasonably apportioned. Usually this is to be determined in terms of "the contract rate," which is the rate determined from the agreement based on the rules and policies of this Article.

2. Under subsection (2) acceptance of goods precludes their subsequent rejection of the goods. Any return of the goods thereafter must be by way of revocation of acceptance under Section 2–608. Revocation is unavailable for a non-conformity known to the buyer at the time of acceptance, except where the buyer has accepted on the reasonable assumption that the non-conformity would be seasonably cured.

3. All other remedies of the buyer remain unimpaired under subsection (2). This is intended to include the buyer's full rights for future installments despite the buyer's acceptance of any earlier non-conforming installment.

4. Subsection (3)(a) provides that the buyer must, within a reasonable time of the discovery, or when the buyer should have discovered any breach, give the seller notification of the breach. A failure to give this notice to the seller bars the buyer from a remedy for breach of contract if the seller suffers prejudice due to the failure to notify. *See* Restatement (Second) of Contracts § 229, which provides for an excuse of a condition where the failure is not material and implementation would result in a disproportionate forfeiture.

The time of notification is to be determined by applying commercial standards to a merchant buyer. "A reasonable time" for notification from a retail consumer is to be judged by different standards so that in that case it could be extended beyond what would be a "commercially" reasonable time' in appropriate circumstances because the requirement of notification is meant to defeat commercial bad faith, not to deprive a good faith consumer of a remedy.

The content of the notification need merely be sufficient to let the seller know that the transaction is still troublesome and must be watched. There is no reason to require that the notification which saves the buyer's rights under this section must include a clear statement of all the objections that will be relied on by the buyer, as is required for statements of defects upon rejection (Section 2–605). Nor is there reason to require the notification to be a claim for damages or of any threatened litigation or other resort to a remedy. The notification which preserves the buyer's rights under this Article need only be one that informs the seller that the transaction is claimed to involve a breach, and thus opens the way for normal settlement through negotiation.

5. Under this Article various beneficiaries are given rights for injuries sustained by them because of the seller's breach of warranty. Such a beneficiary does not fall within the reason of the present section in regard to discovery of defects and the giving of notice within a reasonable time after acceptance, since he has nothing to do with acceptance. However, the reason of this section does extend to requiring the beneficiary to notify the seller that an injury has occurred. What is said above, with regard to the extended time for reasonable notification from the lay consumer after the injury is also applicable here; but even a beneficiary can be properly held to the use of good faith in notifying, once he has had time to become aware of the legal situation.

6. Subsection (4) unambiguously places the burden of proof to establish breach on the buyer after acceptance. However, this rule becomes one purely of procedure when the tender accepted was non-conforming and the buyer has given the seller notice of breach under subsection (3). For subsection (2) makes it clear that acceptance leaves unimpaired the buyer's right to be made whole, and that right can be exercised by the buyer not only by way of cross-claim for damages, but also by way of recoupment in diminution or extinction of the price.

7. The vouching-in procedure in subsection (5) includes indemnity actions, and it includes any other party that is answerable over, not just the immediate seller.

Vouching-in does not confer on the notified seller a right to intervene, does not confer jurisdiction of any kind on the court over the seller, and does not create a duty to defend on the part of the seller. Those matters continue to be governed by the applicable rules of civil procedure and substantive law outside this section. Vouching in is based upon the principle that the seller is liable for its contractual obligations for quality or title to the goods which the buyer is being forced to defend.

8. Subsections (3)(b) and (5)(b) give a warrantor against infringement an opportunity to defend or compromise third-party claims or be relieved of liability. Subsection (5)(a) codifies for all warranties the practice of voucher to defend. Subsection (6) makes these provisions applicable to the buyer's liability for infringement under Section 2–312.

9. All of the provisions of this section are subject to any explicit reservation of rights. Section 1–308.

Cross References:

Point 1: Section 1–201.
Point 2: Section 2–608.
Point 4: Sections 1–204 and 2–605.
Point 5: Section 2–318.
Point 6: Sections 2–312 and 3–803.
Point 8: Section 2–312.
Point 9: Section 1–308.

Definitional Cross References:

"Burden of establishing". Section 1–201.
"Buyer". Section 2–103.
"Conform". Section 2–106.
"Contract". Section 1–201.
"Goods". Section 2–103.
"Notice". Section 1–202.
"Reasonable time". Section 1–205.
"Remedy". Section 1–201.
"Seasonably". Section 1–205.

As amended in 2003.

§ 2–608. Revocation of Acceptance in Whole or in Part.

(1) A buyer may revoke acceptance of a lot or commercial unit whose nonconformity substantially impairs its value to the buyer if the buyer has accepted it:

(a) on the reasonable assumption that its nonconformity would be cured and it has not been seasonably cured; or

(b) without discovery of the nonconformity if the buyer's acceptance was reasonably induced either by the difficulty of discovery before acceptance or by the seller's assurances.

(2) Revocation of acceptance must occur within a reasonable time after the buyer discovers or should have discovered the ground for it and before any substantial change in condition of the goods which is not caused by their own defects.

The revocation is not effective until the buyer notifies the seller of it.

(3) A buyer that so revokes has the same rights and duties with regard to the goods involved as if the buyer had rejected them.

(4) If a buyer uses the goods after a rightful rejection or justifiable revocation of acceptance, the following rules apply:

(a) Any use by the buyer that is unreasonable under the circumstances is wrongful as against the seller and is an acceptance only if ratified by the seller.

(b) Any use of the goods that is reasonable under the circumstances is not wrongful as against the seller and is not an acceptance, but in an appropriate case the buyer is obligated to the seller for the value of the use to the buyer.

As amended in 2003.

Official Comment

Prior Uniform Statutory Provision: Section 69(1)(d), (3), (4) and (5), Uniform Sales Act.

Changes: Rewritten.

Purposes of Changes: To make it clear that:

1. Although the prior basic policy is continued, the buyer is no longer required to elect between revocation of acceptance and recovery of damages for breach. Both are now available to him. The non-alternative character of the two remedies is stressed by the terms used in the present section. The section no longer speaks of "rescission," a term capable of ambiguous application either to transfer of title to the goods or to the contract of sale and susceptible also of confusion with cancellation for cause of an executed or executory portion of the contract. The remedy under this section is instead referred to simply as "revocation of acceptance" of goods tendered under a contract for sale and involves no suggestion of "election" of any sort.

2. Revocation of acceptance is possible only where the non-conformity substantially impairs the value of the goods to the buyer. For this purpose the test is not what the seller had reason to know at the time of contracting; the question is whether the non-conformity is such as will in fact cause a substantial impairment of value to the buyer though the seller had no advance knowledge as to the buyer's particular circumstances.

3. "Assurances" by the seller under paragraph (b) of subsection (1) can rest as well in the circumstances or in the contract as in explicit language used at the time of delivery. The reason for recognizing such assurances is that they induce the buyer to delay discovery. These are the only assurances involved in paragraph (b). Explicit assurances may be made either in good faith or bad faith. In either case any remedy accorded by this Article is available to the buyer under the section on remedies for fraud.

4. Subsection (2) requires notification of revocation of acceptance within a reasonable time after discovery of the grounds for such revocation. Since this remedy will be generally resorted to only after attempts at adjustment have failed, the reasonable time period should extend in most cases beyond the time in which notification of breach must be given, beyond the time for discovery of non-conformity after acceptance and beyond the time for rejection after tender. The parties may by their agreement limit the time for notification under this section, but the same sanctions and considerations apply to such agreements as are discussed in the comment on manner and effect of rightful rejection.

5. The content of the notice under subsection (2) is to be determined in this case as in others by considerations of good faith, prevention of surprise, and reasonable adjustment. More will generally be necessary than the mere notification of breach required under the preceding section. On the other hand the requirements of the section on waiver of buyer's objections do not apply here. The fact that quick notification of trouble is desirable affords good ground for being slow to bind a buyer by his first statement. Following the general policy of this Article, the requirements of the content of notification are less stringent in the case of a non-merchant buyer.

6. Under subsection (2) the prior policy is continued of seeking substantial justice in regard to the condition of goods restored to the seller. Thus the buyer may not revoke his acceptance if the goods have materially deteriorated except by reason of their own defects. Worthless goods, however, need not be offered back and minor defects in the articles reoffered are to be disregarded.

7. The policy of the section allowing partial acceptance is carried over into the present section and the buyer may revoke his acceptance, in appropriate cases, as to the entire lot or any commercial unit thereof.

8. Subsection (4) deals with the problem of post-rejection or revocation use of the goods. The courts have developed several alternative approaches. Under original Article 2, a buyer's post-rejection or revocation use of the goods could be treated as an acceptance,

thus undoing the rejection or revocation, could be a violation of the buyer's obligation of reasonable care, or could be a reasonable use for which the buyer must compensate the seller. Subsection (4) adopts the third approach.

In general, a buyer that either rejects or revokes acceptance of the goods should not subsequently use the goods in a manner that is inconsistent with the seller's ownership. In some instances, however, the use may be reasonable. For example, a consumer buyer may have incurred an unavoidable obligation to a third-party financier and, if the seller fails to refund the price as required by this Article, the buyer may have no reasonable alternative but to use the goods (e.g., a rejected mobile home that provides needed shelter). Another example might involve a commercial buyer that is unable immediately to obtain cover and must use the goods to fulfill its obligations to third parties. If circumstances change so that the buyer's use after an effective rejection or a justified revocation of acceptance is no longer reasonable, the continued use of the goods is unreasonable and is wrongful against the seller. This gives the seller the option of ratifying the use, thereby treating it as an acceptance, or pursuing a non-Code remedy for conversion.

If the buyer's use is reasonable under the circumstances, the buyer's actions cannot be treated as an acceptance. The buyer must compensate the seller for the value of the use of the goods to the buyer. Determining the appropriate level of compensation requires a consideration of the buyer's particular circumstances and should take into account the defective condition of the goods. There may be circumstances, such as where the use is solely for the purpose of protecting the buyer's security interest in the goods, where no compensation is due the seller under this section. If the seller has a right to compensation under this section that compensation must be netted out against any right of the buyer to damages for the seller's breach of contract.

Cross References:

Point 3: Section 2–721.
Point 4: Sections 1–204, 2–602 and 2–607.
Point 5: Sections 2–605 and 2–607.
Point 7: Section 2–601.

Definitional Cross References:

"Buyer". Section 2–103.
"Commercial unit". Section 2–105.
"Conform". Section 2–106.
"Goods". Section 2–103.
"Notifies". Section 1–202.

"Reasonable time". Section 1–205.
"Rights". Section 1–201.
"Seasonably". Section 1–205.
"Seller". Section 2–103.
"Value". Section 1–204.

As amended in 2003.

§ 2–609. Right to Adequate Assurance of Performance.

(1) A contract for sale imposes an obligation on each party that the other's expectation of receiving due performance will not be impaired. If reasonable grounds for insecurity arise with respect to the performance of either party, the other may demand in a record adequate assurance of due performance and until the party receives the assurance may if commercially reasonable suspend any performance for which it has not already received the agreed return.

(2) Between merchants, the reasonableness of grounds for insecurity and the adequacy of any assurance offered shall be determined according to commercial standards.

(3) Acceptance of any improper delivery or payment does not prejudice the aggrieved party's right to demand adequate assurance of future performance.

(4) After receipt of a justified demand, failure to provide within a reasonable time not exceeding 30 days such assurance of due performance as is adequate under the circumstances of the particular case is a repudiation of the contract.

As amended in 2003.

Official Comment

Prior Uniform Statutory Provision: See Sections 53, 54(1)(b), 55 and 63(2), Uniform Sales Act.

Purposes:

1. The section rests on the recognition of the fact that the essential purpose of a contract between commercial men is actual performance and they do not bargain merely for a promise, or for a promise plus the right to win a lawsuit and that a continuing sense of reliance and security that the promised performance will be forthcoming when due, is an important feature of the bargain. If either the willingness or the ability of a party to perform declines materially between the time of contracting and the time for performance, the other party is threatened with the loss of a substantial part of what he has bargained for. A seller needs

protection not merely against having to deliver on credit to a shaky buyer, but also against having to procure and manufacture the goods, perhaps turning down other customers. Once he has been given reason to believe that the buyer's performance has become uncertain, it is an undue hardship to force him to continue his own performance. Similarly, a buyer who believes that the seller's deliveries have become uncertain cannot safely wait for the due date of performance when he has been buying to assure himself of materials for his current manufacturing or to replenish his stock of merchandise.

2. Three measures have been adopted to meet the needs of commercial men in such situations. First, the aggrieved party is permitted to suspend his own performance and any preparation therefor, with excuse for any resulting necessary delay, until the situation has been clarified. "Suspend performance" under this section means to hold up performance pending the outcome of the demand, and includes also the holding up of any preparatory action. This is the same principle which governs the ancient law of stoppage and seller's lien, and also of excuse of a buyer from prepayment if the seller's actions manifest that he cannot or will not perform. (Original Act, Section 63(2).)

Secondly, the aggrieved party is given the right to require adequate assurance that the other party's performance will be duly forthcoming. This principle is reflected in the familiar clauses permitting the seller to curtail deliveries if the buyer's credit becomes impaired, which when held within the limits of reasonableness and good faith actually express no more than the fair business meaning of any commercial contract.

Third, and finally, this section provides the means by which the aggrieved party may treat the contract as broken if his reasonable grounds for insecurity are not cleared up within a reasonable time. This is the principle underlying the law of anticipatory breach, whether by way of defective part performance or by repudiation. The present section merges these three principles of law and commercial practice into a single theory of general application to all sales agreements looking to future performance.

3. Subsection (2) of the present section requires that "reasonable" grounds and "adequate" assurance as used in subsection (1) be defined by commercial rather than legal standards. The express reference to commercial standards carries no connotation that the obligation of good faith is not equally applicable here.

Under commercial standards and in accord with commercial practice, a ground for insecurity need not arise from or be directly related to the contract in question. The law as to "dependence" or "independence" of promises within a single contract does not control the application of the present section.

Thus a buyer who falls behind in "his account" with the seller, even though the items involved have to do with separate and legally distinct contracts, impairs the seller's expectation of due performance. Again, under the same test, a buyer who requires precision parts which he intends to use immediately upon delivery, may have reasonable grounds for insecurity if he discovers that his seller is making defective deliveries of such parts to other buyers with similar needs. Thus, too, in a situation such as arose in Jay Dreher Corporation v. Delco Appliance Corporation, 93 F.2d 275 (C.C.A.2, 1937), where a manufacturer gave a dealer an exclusive franchise for the sale of his product but on two or three occasions breached the exclusive dealing clause, although there was no default in orders, deliveries or payments under the separate sales contract between the parties, the aggrieved dealer would be entitled to suspend his performance of the contract for sale under the present section and to demand assurance that the exclusive dealing contract would be lived up to. There is no need for an explicit clause tying the exclusive franchise into the contract for the sale of goods since the situation itself ties the agreements together.

The nature of the sales contract enters also into the question of reasonableness. For example, a report from an apparently trustworthy source that the seller had shipped defective goods or was planning to ship them would normally give the buyer reasonable grounds for insecurity. But when the buyer has assumed the risk of payment before inspection of the goods, as in a sales contract on C.I.F. or similar cash against documents terms, that risk is not to be evaded by a demand for assurance. Therefore no ground for insecurity would exist under this section unless the report went to a ground which would excuse payment by the buyer.

4. What constitutes "adequate" assurance of due performance is subject to the same test of factual conditions. For example, where the buyer can make use of a defective delivery, a mere promise by a seller of good repute that he is giving the matter his attention and that the defect will not be repeated, is normally sufficient. Under the same circumstances, however, a similar statement by a known corner-cutter might well be considered insufficient without the posting of a guaranty or, if so demanded by the buyer, a speedy replacement of the delivery involved. By the same token where a delivery has defects, even though easily curable, which interfere with easy use by the buyer, no

verbal assurance can be deemed adequate which is not accompanied by replacement, repair, money-allowance, or other commercially reasonable cure.

A fact situation such as arose in Corn Products Refining Co. v. Fasola, 94 N.J.L. 181, 109 A. 505 (1920) offers illustration both of reasonable grounds for insecurity and "adequate" assurance. In that case a contract for the sale of oils on 30 days' credit, 2% off for payment within 10 days, provided that credit was to be extended to the buyer only if his financial responsibility was satisfactory to the seller. The buyer had been in the habit of taking advantage of the discount but at the same time that he failed to make his customary 10 day payment, the seller heard rumors, in fact false, that the buyer's financial condition was shaky. Thereupon, the seller demanded cash before shipment or security satisfactory to him. The buyer sent a good credit report from his banker, expressed willingness to make payments when due on the 30 day terms and insisted on further deliveries under the contract. Under this Article the rumors, although false, were enough to make the buyer's financial condition "unsatisfactory" to the seller under the contract clause. Moreover, the buyer's practice of taking the cash discounts is enough, apart from the contract clause, to lay a commercial foundation for suspicion when the practice is suddenly stopped. These matters, however, go only to the justification of the seller's demand for security, or his "reasonable grounds for insecurity".

The adequacy of the assurance given is not measured as in the type of "satisfaction" situation affected with intangibles, such as in personal service cases, cases involving a third party's judgment as final, or cases in which the whole contract is dependent on one party's satisfaction, as in a sale on approval. Here, the seller must exercise good faith and observe commercial standards. This Article thus approves the statement of the court in James B. Berry's Sons Co. of Illinois v. Monark Gasoline & Oil Co., Inc., 32 F.2d 74 (C.C.A.8, 1929), that the seller's satisfaction under such a clause must be based upon reason and must not be arbitrary or capricious; and rejects the purely personal "good faith" test of the Corn Products Refining Co. case, which held that in the seller's sole judgment, if for *any* reason he was dissatisfied, he was entitled to revoke the credit. In the absence of the buyer's failure to take the 2% discount as was his custom, the banker's report given in that case would have been "adequate" assurance under this Act, regardless of the language of the "satisfaction" clause. However, the seller is reasonably entitled to feel insecure at a sudden expansion of the buyer's use of a credit term, and should be entitled either to security or to a satisfactory explanation.

The entire foregoing discussion as to adequacy of assurance by way of explanation is subject to qualification when repeated occasions for the application of this section arise. This Act recognizes that repeated delinquencies must be viewed as cumulative. On the other hand, commercial sense also requires that if repeated claims for assurance are made under this section, the basis for these claims must be increasingly obvious.

5. A failure to provide adequate assurance of performance and thereby to re-establish the security of expectation, results in a breach only "by repudiation" under subsection (4). Therefore, the possibility is continued of retraction of the repudiation under the section dealing with that problem, unless the aggrieved party has acted on the breach in some manner.

The thirty day limit on the time to provide assurance is laid down to free the question of reasonable time from uncertainty in later litigation.

6. Clauses seeking to give the protected party exceedingly wide powers to cancel or readjust the contract when ground for insecurity arises must be read against the fact that good faith is a part of the obligation of the contract and not subject to modification by agreement and includes, in the case of a merchant, the reasonable observance of commercial standards of fair dealing in the trade. Such clauses can thus be effective to enlarge the protection given by the present section to a certain extent, to fix the reasonable time within which requested assurance must be given, or to define adequacy of the assurance in any commercially reasonable fashion. But any clause seeking to set up arbitrary standards for action is ineffective under this Article. Acceleration clauses are treated similarly in the Articles on Commercial Paper and Secured Transactions.

Cross References:

Point 3: Section 1–203.
Point 5: Section 2–611.
Point 6: Sections 1–203, 1–309, Articles 3 and 9.

Definitional Cross References:

"Aggrieved party". Section 1–201.
"Between merchants". Section 2–104.
"Contract". Section 1–201.
"Contract for sale". Section 2–106.
"Party". Section 1–201.
"Reasonable time". Section 1–205.
"Record". Section 2–103.
"Rights". Section 1–201.

§ 2–610. Anticipatory Repudiation.

(1) If either party repudiates the contract with respect to a performance not yet due the loss of which will substantially impair the value of the contract to the other, the aggrieved party may:

(a) for a commercially reasonable time await performance by the repudiating party; or

(b) resort to any remedy for breach (Section 2–703 or Section 2–711), even if the aggrieved party has notified the repudiating party that it would await the latter's performance and has urged retraction; and

(c) in either case suspend performance or proceed in accordance with the provisions of this Article on the seller's right to identify goods to the contract notwithstanding breach or to salvage unfinished goods (Section 2–704).

(2) Repudiation includes language that a reasonable person would interpret to mean that the other party will not or cannot make a performance still due under the contract or voluntary, affirmative conduct that would appear to a reasonable person to make a future performance by the other party impossible.

As amended in 2003.

Official Comment

Prior Uniform Statutory Provision: See Sections 63(2) and 65, Uniform Sales Act.

Purposes: To make it clear that:

1. With the problem of insecurity taken care of by the preceding section and with provision being made in this Article as to the effect of a defective delivery under an installment contract, anticipatory repudiation centers upon an overt communication of intention or an action which renders performance impossible or demonstrates a clear determination not to continue with performance.

Under the present section when such a repudiation substantially impairs the value of the contract, the aggrieved party may at any time resort to his remedies for breach, or he may suspend his own performance while he negotiates with, or awaits performance by, the other party. But if he awaits performance beyond a commercially reasonable time he cannot recover resulting damages which he should have avoided.

2. It is not necessary for repudiation that performance be made literally and utterly impossible. Repudia-

tion can result from action which reasonably indicates a rejection of the continuing obligation. And, a repudiation automatically results under the preceding section on insecurity when a party fails to provide adequate assurance of due future performance within thirty days after a justifiable demand therefor has been made. Under the language of this section, a demand by one or both parties for more than the contract calls for in the way of counter-performance is not in itself a repudiation nor does it invalidate a plain expression of desire for future performance. However, when under a fair reading it amounts to a statement of intention not to perform except on conditions which go beyond the contract, it becomes a repudiation.

3. The test chosen to justify an aggrieved party's action under this section is the same as that in the section on breach in installment contracts—namely the substantial value of the contract. The most useful test of substantial value is to determine whether material inconvenience or injustice will result if the aggrieved party is forced to wait and receive an ultimate tender minus the part or aspect repudiated.

4. After repudiation, the aggrieved party may immediately resort to any remedy he chooses provided he moves in good faith (see Section 1–203). Inaction and silence by the aggrieved party may leave the matter open but it cannot be regarded as misleading the repudiating party. Therefore the aggrieved party is left free to proceed at any time with his options under this section, unless he has taken some positive action which in good faith requires notification to the other party before the remedy is pursued.

5. Subsection (2) provides guidance on when a party can be considered to have repudiated a performance obligation based upon the Restatement (Second) of Contracts § 250 and does not purport to be an exclusive statement of when a repudiation has occurred. Repudiation centers upon an overt communication of intention, actions which render performance impossible, or a demonstration of a clear determination not to perform. Failure to provide adequate assurance of due performance under Section 2–609 also operates as a repudiation.

Cross References:

Point 1: Sections 2–609 and 2–612.
Point 2: Section 2–609.
Point 3: Section 2–612.
Point 4: Section 1–203.
Point 5: Section 2–609.

Definitional Cross References:

"Aggrieved party". Section 1–201.

"Contract". Section 1-201.
"Party". Section 1-201.
"Remedy". Section 1-201.

As amended in 2003.

§ 2-611. Retraction of Anticipatory Repudiation.

(1) Until the repudiating party's next performance is due, that party may retract the repudiation unless the aggrieved party has since the repudiation canceled or materially changed position or otherwise indicated that the repudiation is final.

(2) Retraction may be by any method that clearly indicates to the aggrieved party that the repudiating party intends to perform, but must include any assurance justifiably demanded under Section 2-609.

(3) Retraction reinstates the repudiating party's rights under the contract with due excuse and allowance to the aggrieved party for any delay occasioned by the repudiation.

As amended in 2003.

Official Comment

Prior Uniform Statutory Provision: None.

Purposes: To make it clear that:

1. The repudiating party's right to reinstate the contract is entirely dependent upon the action taken by the aggrieved party. If the latter has cancelled the contract or materially changed his position at any time after the repudiation, there can be no retraction under this section.

2. Under subsection (2) an effective retraction must be accompanied by any assurances demanded under the section dealing with right to adequate assurance. A repudiation is of course sufficient to give reasonable ground for insecurity and to warrant a request for assurance as an essential condition of the retraction. However, after a timely and unambiguous expression of retraction, a reasonable time for the assurance to be worked out should be allowed by the aggrieved party before cancellation.

Cross Reference:

Point 2: Section 2-609.

Definitional Cross References:

"Aggrieved party". Section 1-201.
"Cancellation". Section 2-106.

"Contract". Section 1-201.
"Party". Section 1-201.
"Rights". Section 1-201.

§ 2-612. "Installment Contract"; Breach.

(1) An "installment contract" is one that requires or authorizes the delivery of goods in separate lots to be separately accepted, even if the contract contains a clause "each delivery is a separate contract" or its equivalent.

(2) The buyer may reject any installment that is nonconforming if the nonconformity substantially impairs the value of that installment to the buyer or if nonconformity is a defect in the required documents. However, if the nonconformity does not fall within subsection (3) and the seller gives adequate assurance of its cure the buyer must accept that installment.

(3) If nonconformity or default with respect to one or more installments substantially impairs the value of the whole contract, there is a breach of the whole. But the aggrieved party reinstates the contract if the party accepts a nonconforming installment without seasonably notifying of cancellation or if the party brings an action with respect only to past installments or demands performance as to future installments.

As amended in 2003.

Official Comments

Prior Uniform Statutory Provision: Section 45(2), Uniform Sales Act.

Changes: Rewritten.

Purposes of Changes: To continue prior law but to make explicit the more mercantile interpretation of many of the rules involved, so that:

1. The definition of an installment contract is phrased more broadly in this Article so as to cover installment deliveries tacitly authorized by the circumstances or by the option of either party.

2. In regard to the apportionment of the price for separate payment this Article applies the more liberal test of what can be apportioned rather than the test of what is clearly apportioned by the agreement. This Article also recognizes approximate calculation or apportionment of price subject to subsequent adjustment. A provision for separate payment for each lot delivered ordinarily means that the price is at least roughly calculable by units of quantity, but such a provision is not essential to an "installment contract." If separate

acceptance of separate deliveries is contemplated, no generalized contrast between wholly "entire" and wholly "divisible" contracts has any standing under this Article.

3. This Article rejects any approach which gives clauses such as "each delivery is a separate contract" their legalistically literal effect. Such contracts nonetheless call for installment deliveries. Even where a clause speaks of "a separate contract for all purposes", a commercial reading of the language under the section on good faith and commercial standards requires that the singleness of the document and the negotiation, together with the sense of the situation, prevail over any uncommercial and legalistic interpretation.

4. One of the requirements for rejection under subsection (2) is non-conformity substantially impairing the value of the installment in question. However, an installment agreement may require accurate conformity in quality as a condition to the right to acceptance if the need for the conformity is made clear either by express provision or by the circumstances. In this case the effect of the agreement is to define explicitly what amounts to substantial impairment of value. A clause that requires accurate compliance as a condition to the right to acceptance must, however, have some basis in reason, must avoid imposing hardship by surprise, and it is subject to waiver or to displacement by practical construction.

5. Substantial impairment of the value of an installment can turn not only on the quality of the goods but also on such factors as time, quantity, assortment, and the like. It must be judged in terms of the normal or specifically known purposes of the contract. The defect in required documents refers to such matters as the absence of insurance documents under a contract that requires these documents, falsity of a bill of lading, or one failing to show shipment within the contract period or to the contract destination. Even in these cases, however, the provisions on cure of tender may apply if appropriate documents are readily procurable.

6. Subsection (3) is designed to further the continuance of the contract in the absence of an overt cancellation. The question arising when an action is brought as to a single installment only is resolved by making such action waive the right to cancellation. This involves merely a defect in one or more installments, as contrasted with the situation where there is a true repudiation within the section on anticipatory repudiation. Whether the non-conformity in any given installment justifies cancellation as to the future depends, not on whether such non-conformity indicates an intent or likelihood that the future deliveries will also be defective, but whether the non-conformity substantially impairs the value of the whole contract. If only the seller's security in regard to future installments is impaired, he has the right to demand adequate assurances of proper future performance but has not an immediate right to cancel the entire contract. It is clear under this Article, however, that defects in prior installments are cumulative in effect, so that acceptance does not wash out the defect "waived." Prior policy is continued, putting the rule as to buyer's default on the same footing as that in regard to seller's default.

7. Under the requirement of seasonable notification of cancellation under subsection (3), a buyer who accepts a non-conforming installment which substantially impairs the value of the entire contract should properly be permitted to withhold his decision as to whether or not to cancel pending a response from the seller as to his claim for cure or adjustment. Similarly, a seller may withhold a delivery pending payment for prior ones, at the same time delaying his decision as to cancellation. A reasonable time for notifying of cancellation, judged by commercial standard under the section on good faith, extends of course to include the time covered by any reasonable negotiation in good faith. However, during this period the defaulting party is entitled, on request, to know whether the contract is still in effect, before he can be required to perform further.

8. Subsection (2) makes it clear that the buyer's right in the first instance to reject an installment depends upon whether there has been a substantial impairment of the value of the installment to the buyer and not on the seller's ability to cure the nonconformity. The seller can prevent a rightful rejection by giving adequate assurances of cure. Subsection (2) uses the words "to the buyer" to clarify that the standard for rejecting an installment consistent is the same standard for revoking acceptance under Section 2-608. Therefore, the test is not what the seller had reason to know at the time of contracting; the question is whether the non-conformity is one that will cause a substantial impairment of value to the buyer even though the seller had no knowledge about the buyer's particular circumstances at the time of contracting.

Cross References:

Point 2: Sections 2-307 and 2-607.
Point 3: Section 1-203.
Point 5: Sections 2-208 and 2-609.
Point 6: Section 2-610.
Point 8: Section 2-608.

Definitional Cross References:

"Action". Section 1–201.
"Aggrieved party". Section 1–201.
"Buyer". Section 2–103.
"Cancellation". Section 2–106.
"Conform". Section 2–106.
"Contract". Section 1–201.
"Lot". Section 2–105.
"Notifies". Section 1–202.
"Party". Section 1–201.
"Seasonably". Section 1–205.
"Seller". Section 2–103.

As amended in 2003.

§ 2–613. Casualty to Identified Goods.

If the contract requires for its performance goods identified when the contract is made, and the goods suffer casualty without fault of either party before the risk of loss passes to the buyer, then:

(a) if the loss is total the contract is terminated; and

(b) if the loss is partial or the goods have so deteriorated that they no longer conform to the contract, the buyer may nevertheless demand inspection and at the buyer's option either treat the contract as terminated or accept the goods with due allowance from the contract price for the deterioration or the deficiency in quantity but without further right against the seller.

As amended in 2003.

Official Comment

Prior Uniform Statutory Provision: Sections 7 and 8, Uniform Sales Act.

Changes: Rewritten, the basic policy being continued but the test of a "divisible" or "indivisible" sale or contract being abandoned in favor of adjustment in business terms.

Purposes of Changes:

1. Where goods whose continued existence is presupposed by the agreement are destroyed without fault of either party, the buyer is relieved from his obligation but may at his option take the surviving goods at a fair adjustment. "Fault" is intended to include negligence and not merely wilful wrong. The buyer is expressly given the right to inspect the goods in order to determine whether he wishes to avoid the contract entirely or to take the goods with a price adjustment.

2. The section applies whether the goods were already destroyed at the time of contracting without the knowledge of either party or whether they are destroyed subsequently but before the risk of loss passes to the buyer. Where under the agreement, including of course usage of trade, the risk has passed to the buyer before the casualty, the section has no application. Beyond this, the essential question in determining whether the rules of this section are to be applied is whether the seller has or has not undertaken the responsibility for the continued existence of the goods in proper condition through the time of agreed or expected delivery.

3. The use of the word "terminated" in paragraph (a) clarifies that pre-termination breaches are preserved. *See* Section 2–106(3).

Cross Reference:

Point 4: Section 2–106

Definitional Cross References:

"Buyer". Section 2–103.
"Conform". Section 2–106.
"Contract". Section 1–201.
"Fault". Section 1–201.
"Goods". Section 2–103.
"Party". Section 1–201.
"Rights". Section 1–201.
"Seller". Section 2–103.
"Terminated". Section 2–106.

As amended in 2003.

§ 2–614. Substituted Performance.

(1) If without fault of either party the agreed berthing, loading, or unloading facilities fail or an agreed type of carrier becomes unavailable or the agreed manner of performance otherwise becomes commercially impracticable but a commercially reasonable substitute is available, the substitute performance must be tendered and accepted.

(2) If the agreed means or manner of payment fails because of domestic or foreign governmental regulation, the seller may withhold or stop delivery unless the buyer provides a means or manner of payment which is commercially a substantial equivalent. If delivery has already been taken, payment by the means or in the manner provided by the regulation discharges the buyer's obligation unless the regulation is discriminatory, oppressive, or predatory.

As amended in 2003.

Official Comment

1. Subsection (1) requires the tender of a commercially reasonable substituted performance where agreed to facilities have failed or have become commercially impracticable. Under this Article, in the absence of a specific agreement, the normal or usual facilities enter into the agreement either through the circumstances of the transaction, a usage of trade or a prior course of dealing between the parties.

This section appears between Section 2–613 on casualty to identified goods and Section 2–615 on excuse by failure of presupposed conditions. Those two sections deal with excuse and complete avoidance of the contract when the occurrence or non-occurrence of a contingency which was a basic assumption of the contract makes the expected performance impossible. The distinction between the present section and those sections is whether the failure or impossibility of performance arises in connection with an incidental matter or goes to the very heart of the agreement. The differing lines of solution are contrasted in a comparison of *International Paper Co. v. Rockefeller*, 161 App.Div. 180, 146 N.Y.S. 371 (1914), and *Meyer v. Sullivan*, 40 Cal.App. 723, 181 P. 847 (1919). In the former case, a contract for the sale of spruce to be cut from a particular tract of land was involved. When a fire destroyed the trees growing on that tract the seller was held excused since performance was impossible. In the latter case, the contract called for delivery of wheat "f.o.b. Kosmos Steamer at Seattle." The war led to cancellation of that line's sailing schedule after space had been duly engaged and the buyer was held entitled to demand substituted delivery at the warehouse on the line's loading dock. Under this Article, of course, the seller would also be entitled, had the market gone the other way, to make a substituted tender in that manner.

There must, however, be a true commercial impracticability to excuse the agreed to performance and justify a substituted performance. When this is the case, a reasonable substituted performance tendered by either party should excuse that party from strict compliance with the contract terms which do not go to the essence of the agreement.

2. The substitution provided for in this section as between buyer and seller does not carry over into the obligation of a financing agency under a letter of credit, since the financing agency is entitled to performance which is plainly adequate on its face and without need to look into commercial evidence outside of the documents. *See* Article 5, especially Section 5–108.

3. Under subsection (2), when the contract is still executory on both sides, the seller is permitted to withdraw unless the buyer can provide the seller with a commercially equivalent performance despite the governmental regulation. When, however, only the debt for the price remains, a larger leeway is permitted. The buyer may pay in the manner provided by the regulation, even though this may not be a commercially equivalent performance, provided that the regulation is not "discriminatory, oppressive or predatory."

Cross Reference:

Point 2: Article 5.

Definitional Cross References:

"Buyer". Section 2–103.
"Delivery". Section 2–103.
"Fault". Section 1–201.
"Party". Section 1–201.
"Seller". Section 2–103.

As amended in 2003.

§ 2–615. Excuse by Failure of Presupposed Conditions.

Except to the extent that a seller may have assumed a greater obligation and subject to Section 2–614:

(a) Delay in performance or nonperformance in whole or in part by a seller that complies with paragraphs (b) and (c) is not a breach of the seller's duty under a contract for sale if performance as agreed has been made impracticable by the occurrence of a contingency the nonoccurrence of which was a basic assumption on which the contract was made or by compliance in good faith with any applicable foreign or domestic governmental regulation or order whether or not it later proves to be invalid.

(b) If the causes mentioned in paragraph (a) affect only a part of the seller's capacity to perform, the seller must allocate production and deliveries among its customers but may at its option include regular customers not then under contract as well as its own requirements for further manufacture. The seller may so allocate in any manner that is fair and reasonable.

(c) The seller must notify the buyer seasonably that there will be delay or nonperformance and, if allocation is required under paragraph (b), of the estimated quota thus made available for the buyer.

As amended in 2003.

Official Comment

Prior Uniform Statutory Provision: None.

Purposes:

1. This section excuses a seller from timely delivery of goods contracted for, where his performance has become commercially impracticable because of unforeseen supervening circumstances not within the contemplation of the parties at the time of contracting. The destruction of specific goods and the problem of the use of substituted performance on points other than delay or quantity, treated elsewhere in this Article, must be distinguished from the matter covered by this section.

2. The present section deliberately refrains from any effort at an exhaustive expression of contingencies and is to be interpreted in all cases sought to be brought within its scope in terms of its underlying reason and purpose.

3. The first test for excuse under this Article in terms of basic assumption is a familiar one. The additional test of commercial impracticability (as contrasted with "impossibility," "frustration of performance" or "frustration of the venture") has been adopted in order to call attention to the commercial character of the criterion chosen by this Article.

4. Increased cost alone does not excuse performance unless the rise in cost is due to some unforeseen contingency which alters the essential nature of the performance. Neither is a rise or a collapse in the market in itself a justification, for that is exactly the type of business risk which business contracts made at fixed prices are intended to cover. But a severe shortage of raw materials or of supplies due to a contingency such as war, embargo, local crop failure, unforeseen shutdown of major sources of supply or the like, which either causes a marked increase in cost or altogether prevents the seller from securing supplies necessary to his performance, is within the contemplation of this section. (See Ford & Sons, Ltd., v. Henry Leetham & Sons, Ltd., 21 Com.Cas. 55 (1915, K.B.D.).)

5. Where a particular source of supply is exclusive under the agreement and fails through casualty, the present section applies rather than the provision on destruction or deterioration of specific goods. The same holds true where a particular source of supply is shown by the circumstances to have been contemplated or assumed by the parties at the time of contracting. (See Davis Co. v. Hoffmann–LaRoche Chemical Works, 178 App.Div. 855, 166 N.Y.S. 179 (1917) and International Paper Co. v. Rockefeller, 161 App.Div. 180, 146 N.Y.S. 371 (1914).) There is no excuse under this section, however, unless the seller has employed all due measures to assure himself that his source will not fail. (See Canadian Industrial Alcohol Co., Ltd., v. Dunbar Molasses Co., 258 N.Y. 194, 179 N.E. 383, 80 A.L.R. 1173 (1932) and Washington Mfg. Co. v. Midland Lumber Co., 113 Wash. 593, 194 P. 777 (1921).)

In the case of failure of production by an agreed source for causes beyond the seller's control, the seller should, if possible, be excused since production by an agreed source is without more a basic assumption of the contract. Such excuse should not result in relieving the defaulting supplier from liability nor in dropping into the seller's lap an unearned bonus of damages over. The flexible adjustment machinery of this Article provides the solution under the provision on the obligation of good faith. A condition to his making good the claim of excuse is the turning over to the buyer of his rights against the defaulting source of supply to the extent of the buyer's contract in relation to which excuse is being claimed.

6. In situations in which neither sense nor justice is served by either answer when the issue is posed in flat terms of "excuse" or "no excuse," adjustment under the various provisions of this Article is necessary, especially the sections on good faith, on insecurity and assurance and on the reading of all provisions in the light of their purposes, and the general policy of this Act to use equitable principles in furtherance of commercial standards and good faith.

7. The failure of conditions which go to convenience or collateral values rather than to the commercial practicability of the main performance does not amount to a complete excuse. However, good faith and the reason of the present section and of the preceding one may properly be held to justify and even to require any needed delay involved in a good faith inquiry seeking a readjustment of the contract terms to meet the new conditions.

8. The provisions of this section are made subject to assumption of greater liability by agreement and such agreement is to be found not only in the expressed terms of the contract but in the circumstances surrounding the contracting, in trade usage and the like. Thus the exemptions of this section do not apply when the contingency in question is sufficiently foreshadowed at the time of contracting to be included among the business risks which are fairly to be regard-

ed as part of the dickered terms, either consciously or as a matter of reasonable, commercial interpretation from the circumstances. (See Madeirense Do Brasil, S.A. v. Stulman–Emrick Lumber Co., 147 F.2d 399 (C.C.A., 2 Cir., 1945).) The exemption otherwise present through usage of trade under the present section may also be expressly negated by the language of the agreement. Generally, express agreements as to exemptions designed to enlarge upon or supplant the provisions of this section are to be read in the light of mercantile sense and reason, for this section itself sets up the commercial standard for normal and reasonable interpretation and provides a minimum beyond which agreement may not go.

Agreement can also be made in regard to the consequences of exemption as laid down in paragraphs (b) and (c) and the next section on procedure on notice claiming excuse.

9. The case of a farmer who has contracted to sell crops to be grown on designated land may be regarded as falling either within the section on casualty to identified goods or this section, and he may be excused, when there is a failure of the specific crop, either on the basis of the destruction of identified goods or because of the failure of a basic assumption of the contract.

Exemption of the buyer in the case of a "requirements" contract is covered by the "Output and Requirements" section both as to assumption and allocation of the relevant risks. But when a contract by a manufacturer to buy fuel or raw material makes no specific reference to a particular venture and no such reference may be drawn from the circumstances, commercial understanding views it as a general deal in the general market and not conditioned on any assumption of the continuing operation of the buyer's plant. Even when notice is given by the buyer that the supplies are needed to fill a specific contract of a normal commercial kind, commercial understanding does not see such a supply contract as conditioned on the continuance of the buyer's further contract for outlet. On the other hand, where the buyer's contract is in reasonable commercial understanding conditioned on a definite and specific venture or assumption as, for instance, a war procurement subcontract known to be based on a prime contract which is subject to termination, or a supply contract for a particular construction venture, the reason of the present section may well apply and entitle the buyer to the exemption.

10. Following its basic policy of using commercial practicability as a test for excuse, this section recognizes as of equal significance either a foreign or domestic regulation and disregards any technical distinctions between "law," "regulation," "order" and the like. Nor does it make the present action of the seller depend upon the eventual judicial determination of the legality of the particular governmental action. The seller's good faith belief in the validity of the regulation is the test under this Article and the best evidence of his good faith is the general commercial acceptance of the regulation. However, governmental interference cannot excuse unless it truly "supervenes" in such a manner as to be beyond the seller's assumption of risk. And any action by the party claiming excuse which causes or colludes in inducing the governmental action preventing his performance would be in breach of good faith and would destroy his exemption.

11. An excused seller must fulfill his contract to the extent which the supervening contingency permits, and if the situation is such that his customers are generally affected he must take account of all in supplying one. Subsections (a) and (b), therefore, explicitly permit in any proration a fair and reasonable attention to the needs of regular customers who are probably relying on spot orders for supplies. Customers at different stages of the manufacturing process may be fairly treated by including the seller's manufacturing requirements. A fortiori, the seller may also take account of contracts later in date than the one in question. The fact that such spot orders may be closed at an advanced price causes no difficulty, since any allocation which exceeds normal past requirements will not be reasonable. However, good faith requires, when prices have advanced, that the seller exercise real care in making his allocations, and in case of doubt his contract customers should be favored and supplies prorated evenly among them regardless of price. Save for the extra care thus required by changes in the market, this section seeks to leave every reasonable business leeway to the seller.

Cross References:

Point 1: Sections 2–613 and 2–614.
Point 2: Section 1–201.
Point 5: Sections 1–203 and 2–316.
Point 6: Sections 1–203 and 2–609.
Point 7: Section 2–614.
Point 8: Sections 1–201, 2–302, and 2–616.
Point 9: Sections 1–102, 2–306 and 2–316.

Definitional Cross References:

"Buyer". Section 2–103.
"Contract". Section 1–201.
"Contract for sale". Section 2–106.
"Good faith". Section 2–103.
"Notifies". Section 1–202.

"Seasonably". Section 1–205.
"Seller". Section 2–103.

§ 2–616. Procedure on Notice Claiming Excuse.

(1) If a buyer receives notification of a material or indefinite delay or an allocation justified under Section 2–615, the buyer may by notification in a record to the seller as to any performance concerned, and if the prospective deficiency substantially impairs the value of the whole contract under Section 2–612, then also as to the whole:

   (a) terminate and thereby discharge any unexecuted portion of the contract; or

   (b) modify the contract by agreeing to take the buyer's available quota in substitution.

(2) If after receipt of notification from the seller the buyer fails to modify the contract within a reasonable time not exceeding 30 days, the contract is terminated with respect to any performance affected.

(3) The provisions of this section may not be negated by agreement except in so far as the seller has assumed a greater obligation under Section 2–615.

As amended in 2003.

Official Comment

Prior Uniform Statutory Provision: None.

Purposes:

1. This section seeks to establish simple and workable machinery for providing certainty as to when a supervening and excusing contingency "excuses" the delay, "discharges" the contract, or may result in a waiver of the delay by the buyer. When the seller notifies, in accordance with the preceding section, claiming excuse, the buyer may acquiesce, in which case the contract is so modified. No consideration is necessary in a case of this kind to support such a modification. If the buyer does not elect so to modify the contract, he may terminate it and under subsection (2) his silence after receiving the seller's claim of excuse operates as such a termination. Subsection (3) denies effect to any contract clause made in advance of trouble which would require the buyer to stand ready to take delivery whenever the seller is excused from delivery by unforeseen circumstances.

2. In subsection (2), the term "terminated" conforms with Section 2–613(a) to clarify that pre-termination breaches are preserved and the term "performance" conforms with Section 2–615(a) to specify the broad range of obligation that may be included under this provision.

Cross References:

Point 1: Sections 2–209 and 2–615.
Point 2: Sections 2–613 and 2–615.

Definitional Cross References:

"Buyer". Section 2–103.
"Contract". Section 1–201.
"Installment contract". Section 2–612.
"Notification". Section 1–202.
"Reasonable time". Section 1–205.
"Record". Section 2–103.
"Seller". Section 2–103.
"Termination". Section 2–106.

As amended in 2003.

PART 7

REMEDIES

§ 2–701. Remedies for Breach of Collateral Contracts Not Impaired.

Remedies for breach of any obligation or promise collateral or ancillary to a contract for sale are not impaired by the provisions of this Article.

Official Comment

Prior Uniform Statutory Provision: None.

Purposes:

Whether a claim for breach of an obligation collateral to the contract for sale requires separate trial to avoid confusion of issues is beyond the scope of this Article; but contractual arrangements which as a business matter enter vitally into the contract should be considered a part thereof in so far as cross-claims or defenses are concerned.

Definitional Cross References:

"Contract for sale". Section 2–106.
"Remedy". Section 1–201.

§ 2–702. Seller's Remedies on Discovery of Buyer's Insolvency.

(1) If the seller discovers that the buyer is insolvent, the seller may refuse delivery except

for cash including payment for all goods theretofore delivered under the contract, and stop delivery under Section 2–705.

(2) If the seller discovers that the buyer has received goods on credit while insolvent, the seller may reclaim the goods upon demand made within a reasonable time after the buyer's receipt of the goods. Except as provided in this subsection, the seller may not base a right to reclaim goods on the buyer's fraudulent or innocent misrepresentation of solvency or of intent to pay.

(3) The seller's right to reclaim under subsection (2) is subject to the rights of a buyer in ordinary course of business or other good-faith purchaser for value under Section 2–403. Successful reclamation of goods excludes all other remedies with respect to them.

As amended in 2003.

Official Comment

1. The seller's right to withhold the goods or to stop delivery except for cash when the seller discovers the buyer's insolvency is made explicit in subsection (1) regardless of the passage of title, and the concept of stoppage has been extended to include goods in the possession of any bailee that has not yet attorned to the buyer.

2. Subsection (2) takes as its base line the proposition that any receipt of goods on credit by an insolvent buyer amounts to a tacit business misrepresentation of solvency and therefore is fraudulent as against the particular seller. This section omits the 10–day limitation and the 3–month exception to the 10–day limitation that was in original Article 2. If the buyer is in bankruptcy at the time of reclamation, the seller will have to comply with Section 546(c) of the Bankruptcy Code of 1978, which includes a 10–day limitation.

3. Because the right of the seller to reclaim goods under this section constitutes preferential treatment as against the buyer's other creditors, subsection (3) provides that such reclamation bars all of the seller's other remedies the goods involved.

4. The rights of a seller to reclamation from the buyer under section 2–702 are subordinate to the rights of good faith purchasers from that buyer under Section 2–403. This section takes no position on the seller's claims to proceeds of the goods.

Cross References:

Point 1: Sections 2–401 and 2–705.
Point 4: Sections 2–403 and 2–702.

Definitional Cross References:

"Buyer". Section 2–103.
"Buyer in ordinary course of business". Section 1–201.
"Contract". Section 1–201.
"Good faith". Section 2–103.
"Goods". Section 2–103.
"Insolvent". Section 1–201.
"Person". Section 1–201.
"Purchaser". Section 1–201.
"Reasonable time". Section 1–205.
"Receipt of goods". Section 2–103.
"Remedy". Section 1–201.
"Rights". Section 1–201.
"Seller". Section 2–103.
"Tender of delivery". Sections 2–503 and 2–507.
"Value". Section 1–204.

As amended in 2003.

§ 2–703. Seller's Remedies in General.

(1) A breach of contract by the buyer includes the buyer's wrongful rejection or wrongful attempt to revoke acceptance of goods, wrongful failure to perform a contractual obligation, failure to make a payment when due, and repudiation.

(2) If the buyer is in breach of contract the seller, to the extent provided for by this Act or other law, may:

  (a) withhold delivery of the goods under Section 2–703(4);

  (b) stop delivery of the goods under Section 2–705;

  (c) proceed under Section 2–704 with respect to goods unidentified to the contract or unfinished;

  (d) reclaim the goods under Section 2–507(2) or 2–702(2);

  (e) require payment directly from the buyer under Section 2–325(c);

  (f) cancel under Section 2–703(4);

  (g) resell and recover damages under Section 2–706;

  (h) recover damages for nonacceptance or repudiation under Section 2–708(1);

  (i) recover lost profits under Section 2–708(2);

  (j) recover the price under Section 2–709;

(k) obtain specific performance under Section 2–716;

(l) recover liquidated damages under Section 2–718;

(m) in other cases, recover damages in any manner that is reasonable under the circumstances.

(3) If the buyer becomes insolvent, the seller may:

(a) withhold delivery under Section 2–702(1);

(b) stop delivery of the goods under Section 2–705;

(c) reclaim the goods under Section 2–702(2).

(4) If the buyer wrongfully rejects or revokes acceptance of goods, fails to make a payment when due, or repudiates with respect to a part or the whole, with respect to any goods directly affected and, if the breach is of the whole contract (Section 2–612), with respect to the whole undelivered balance, the aggrieved seller may

(a) withhold delivery of such goods; or

(b) cancel.

As amended in 2003 and 2005.

Official Comment

1. This section is a list of the remedies of the seller available under this Article to remedy any breach by the buyer. It also lists the seller's statutory remedies in the event of the buyer's insolvency. The subsection does not address the extent to which other law provides additional remedies or supplements the statutory remedies in Article 2 (*see* Section 1–103). The remedies available to the seller enumerated in this section may be modified or limited as provided for in Section 2–719.

In addition to the enumerated statutory remedies, the Section also provides for remedies agreed upon by the parties, *see* subsection (2)(l). This section does not cover the remedies that become available to the parties upon demand for adequate assurance under Section 2–609.

This Article rejects any doctrine of election of remedy as a fundamental policy and thus the remedies are essentially cumulative in nature and include all of the available remedies for breach. Whether the pursuit of one remedy bars another depends entirely on the facts of the individual case.

2. The buyer's breach which occasions the use of the remedies under this section may involve only one lot or delivery of goods, or may involve all of the goods

which are the subject matter of the particular contract. The right of the seller to pursue a remedy as to all the goods when the breach is as to only one or more lots is covered by the section on breach in installment contracts. The present section deals only with remedies available after the goods involved in the breach have been determined by that section.

3. In addition to the typical case of refusal to pay or default in payment, the language in subsection (1), "failure to make a payment when due," is intended to cover the dishonor of a check on due presentment, or the non-acceptance of a draft, and the failure to furnish an agreed letter of credit.

4. It should also be noted that this Act requires its provisions to be liberally administered and provides that any right or obligation which it declares is enforceable by action unless a different effect is specifically prescribed (Section 1–103).

Cross References:

Point 2: Section 2–612.
Point 3: Section 2–325.
Point 4: Section 1–103.

Definitional Cross References:

"Buyer". Section 2–103.
"Cancel". Section 2–106.
"Contract". Section 1–201.
"Delivery". Section 2–103.
"Goods". Section 2–103.
"Insolvent". Section 1–201.
"Remedy". Section 1–201.
"Seller". Section 2–103.

As amended in 2003.

§ 2–704. Seller's Right to Identify Goods to the Contract Notwithstanding Breach or to Salvage Unfinished Goods.

(1) An aggrieved seller may in an appropriate case involving breach by the buyer:

(a) identify to the contract conforming goods not already identified if at the time the seller learned of the breach the goods are in the seller's possession or control;

(b) treat as the subject of resale goods that have demonstrably been intended for the particular contract even if those goods are unfinished.

(2) If the goods are unfinished, an aggrieved seller may in the exercise of reasonable commer-

cial judgment for the purposes of avoiding loss and of effective realization either complete the manufacture and wholly identify the goods to the contract or cease manufacture and resell for scrap or salvage value or proceed in any other reasonable manner.

As amended in 2003.

Official Comment

Prior Uniform Statutory Provision: Sections 63(3) and 64(4), Uniform Sales Act.

Changes: Rewritten, the seller's rights being broadened.

Purposes of Changes:

1. This section gives an aggrieved seller the right at the time of breach to identify to the contract any conforming finished goods, regardless of their resalability, and to use reasonable judgment as to completing unfinished goods. It thus makes the goods available for resale under the resale section, the seller's primary remedy, and in the special case in which resale is not practicable, allows the action for the price which would then be necessary to give the seller the value of his contract.

2. Under this Article the seller is given express power to complete manufacture or procurement of goods for the contract unless the exercise of reasonable commercial judgment as to the facts as they appear at the time he learns of the breach makes it clear that such action will result in a material increase in damages. The burden is on the buyer to show the commercially unreasonable nature of the seller's action in completing manufacture.

Cross References:

Sections 2–703 and 2–706.

Definitional Cross References:

"Aggrieved party". Section 1–201.
"Conforming". Section 2–106.
"Contract". Section 1–201.
"Delivery". Section 2–103.
"Goods". Section 2–103.
"Rights". Section 1–201.
"Seller". Section 2–103.

§ 2-705. Seller's Stoppage of Delivery in Transit or Otherwise.

(1) A seller may stop delivery of goods in the possession of a carrier or other bailee if the seller discovers the buyer to be insolvent (Section 2–702) or if the buyer repudiates or fails to make a payment due before delivery or if for any other reason the seller has a right to withhold or reclaim the goods.

(2) As against such buyer the seller may stop delivery until:

(a) receipt of the goods by the buyer;

(b) acknowledgment to the buyer by any bailee of the goods, except a carrier, that the bailee holds the goods for the buyer;

(c) such acknowledgment to the buyer by a carrier by reshipment or as warehouse; or

(d) negotiation to the buyer of any negotiable document of title covering the goods.

(3)(a) To stop delivery the seller must so notify as to enable the bailee by reasonable diligence to prevent delivery of the goods.

(b) After such notification the bailee must hold and deliver the goods according to the directions of the seller but the seller is liable to the bailee for any ensuing charges or damages.

(c) If a negotiable document of title has been issued for goods, the bailee is not obliged to obey a notification to stop until surrender of possession or control of the document.

(d) A carrier that has issued a nonnegotiable bill of lading is not obliged to obey a notification to stop received from a person other than the consignor.

As amended in 2003.

Official Comment

1. Subsection (1) applies when goods are in the possession of a carrier or other bailee. It applies, in addition to a buyer's insolvency, also to any case where the buyer repudiates or fails to make a payment due before delivery or for any other reason the seller has the right to withhold or reclaim the goods. Where stoppage occurs for insecurity, it is merely a suspension of performance, and if assurances are duly forthcoming from the buyer the seller is not entitled to resell or divert.

Improper stoppage is a breach by the seller if it effectively interferes with the buyer's right to due tender under the section on manner of tender of delivery. However, if the bailee obeys an unjustified order to stop the bailee may also be liable to the buyer. The measure of the obligation is dependent on the provisions of the Documents of Title Article (Section 7–303). Subsection 3(b) therefore gives the bailee a right of indemnity as against the seller in this case.

2. "Receipt by the buyer" includes receipt by the buyer's designated representative, the subpurchaser, when shipment is made direct to the subpurchaser and the buyer never receives the goods. As between the buyer and the seller, the seller's right to stop the goods at any time until they reach the place of final delivery is recognized by this section.

Under subsection (3)(c) and (d), the carrier is under no duty to recognize the stop order of a person who is a stranger to the carrier's contract. But the seller's right as against the buyer to stop delivery remains, whether or not the carrier is obligated to recognize the stop order. If the carrier does obey it, the buyer cannot complain merely because of that circumstance; and the seller becomes obligated under subsection (3)(b) to pay the carrier any ensuing damages or charges.

3. A diversion of a shipment is not a "reshipment" under subsection (2)(c) when it is merely an incident to the original contract of transportation, nor is the procurement of "exchange bills" of lading which change only the name of the consignee to that of the buyer's local agent but do not alter the destination of a reshipment.

Acknowledgment by the carrier as a "warehouse" within the meaning of this Article requires a contract of a truly different character from the original shipment, a contract not in extension of transit but as a warehouse.

4. Subsection (3)(c) makes the bailee's obedience of a notification to stop conditional upon the surrender of possession or control of any outstanding negotiable document.

5. The seller is responsible for any charges or losses incurred by the carrier in following the seller's orders, whether or not the carrier was obligated to do so.

6. After an effective stoppage under this section the seller's rights in the goods are the same as if the seller had never made a delivery.

Cross References:

Point 1: Sections 2–503 and 2–609, and Article 7.
Point 2: Section 2–103 and Article 7.

Definitional Cross References:

"Bill of lading". Section 1–201.
"Buyer". Section 2–103.
"Contract for sale". Section 2–106.
"Document of title". Section 1–201.

"Goods". Section 2–103.
"Insolvent". Section 1–201.
"Notification". Section 1–202.
"Receipt of goods". Section 2–103.
"Rights". Section 1–201.

As amended in 2003.

§ 2–706. Seller's Resale Including Contract for Resale.

(1) In an appropriate case involving breach by the buyer, the seller may resell the goods concerned or the undelivered balance thereof. If the resale is made in good faith and in a commercially reasonable manner, the seller may recover the difference between the contract price and the resale price together with any incidental or consequential damages allowed under Section 2–710, but less expenses saved in consequence of the buyer's breach.

(2) Except as otherwise provided in subsection (3) or unless otherwise agreed, resale may be at public or private sale including sale by way of one or more contracts to sell or of identification to an existing contract of the seller. Sale may be as a unit or in parcels and at any time and place, and on any terms, but every aspect of the sale including the method, manner, time, place and terms must be commercially reasonable. The resale must be reasonably identified as referring to the broken contract, but it is not necessary that the goods be in existence or that any or all of them have been identified to the contract before the breach.

(3) If the resale is at private sale, the seller must give the buyer reasonable notification of an intention to resell.

(4) If the resale is at public sale:

(a) only identified goods may be sold unless there is a recognized market for a public sale of futures in goods of the kind;

(b) it must be made at a usual place or market for public sale if one is reasonably available and except in the case of goods which are perishable or threaten to decline in value speedily the seller must give the buyer reasonable notice of the time and place of the resale;

(c) if the goods are not to be within the view of those attending the sale, the notification of sale must state the place where the goods are located and provide for their reasonable inspection by prospective bidders; and

(d) the seller may buy.

(5) A purchaser that buys in good faith at a resale takes the goods free of any rights of the original buyer even if the seller fails to comply with one or more of the requirements of this section.

(6) The seller is not accountable to the buyer for any profit made on any resale. A person in the position of a seller (Section 2–707) or a buyer that has rightfully rejected or justifiably revoked acceptance must account for any excess over the amount of the buyer's security interest under Section 2–711(3).

(7) Failure of a seller to resell under this section does not bar the seller from any other remedy.

As amended in 2003.

Official Comment

1. Consistent with the revision of Section 2–710, this section now provides for consequential as well as incidental damages. Subsection (7) is new, and parallels the provision for buyer cover in 2–713. Original Section 2–706(1) measured damages by the difference between the resale price and the contract price; amended subsection (1) reverses these terms ("difference between the contract price and the resale price") because the contract price must be the larger number for there to be direct damages.

2. The right of resale under this section arises when a seller reclaims goods under Section 2–507 or a buyer repudiates or makes a wrongful but effective rejection. In addition, there is a right of resale if the buyer unjustifiably attempts to revoke acceptance and the seller takes back the goods. However, the seller may choose to ignore the buyer's unjustifiable attempt to revoke acceptance, in which case the appropriate remedy is an action for the price under Section 2–709. Application of the right of resale to cases of buyer repudiation is supplemented by subsection (2), which authorizes a resale of goods which are not in existence or were not identified to the contract before the breach.

Subsection (1) allows the seller to resell the goods after a buyer's breach of contract if the seller has possession or control of the goods. The seller may have possession or control of the goods at the time of the breach or may have regained possession of the goods upon the buyer's wrongful rejection. If the seller has regained possession of the goods from the buyer pursuant to Article 9, that Article controls the seller's rights of resale.

3. Under this Article the seller resells by authority of law, on the seller's own behalf, for the seller's own benefit and for the purpose of setting the seller's damages. The theory of a seller's agency is therefore rejected. The question of whether the title to the goods has or has not passed to the buyer is not relevant for the operation of this section.

4. To recover the damages prescribed in subsection (1), the seller must act "in good faith and in a commercially reasonable manner" in making the resale. If the seller complies with the prescribed standards in making the resale, the seller may recover from the buyer the damages provided for in subsection (1). Evidence of market or current prices at any particular time or place is relevant only for the question of whether the seller acted in a commercially reasonable manner in making the resale.

5. Subsection (2) enables the seller to resell in accordance with reasonable commercial practices so as to realize as high a price as possible in the circumstances. A seller may sell at a public sale or a private sale as long as the choice is commercially reasonable. A "public" sale is one to which members of the public are admitted. A public sale is usually a sale by auction, but all auctions are not public auctions. A private sale may be effected by an auction or by solicitation and negotiation conducted either directly or through a broker. In choosing between a public and private sale, the character of the goods must be considered and relevant trade practices and usages must be observed. A public sale has further requirements stated in subsection (4).

The purpose of subsection (2) is to enable the seller to dispose of the goods to the best advantage, and therefore the seller is permitted in making the resale to depart from the terms and conditions of the original contract for sale to any extent "commercially reasonable" in the circumstances.

As for the place for resale, the focus is on the commercial reasonableness of the seller's choice as to the place for an advantageous resale. This section rejects the theory that the seller should normally resell at the agreed place for delivery and that a resale elsewhere can be permitted only in exceptional cases.

The time for resale is a reasonable time after the buyer's breach. What is a reasonable time depends on the nature of the goods, the condition of the market and the other circumstances of the case; its length cannot be measured by any legal yardstick or divided into degrees. When a seller contemplating resale receives a demand from the buyer for inspection under Section 2–515, the time for resale may be appropriately lengthened.

6. The provision of subsection (2) that the goods need not be in existence to be resold applies when the buyer is guilty of anticipatory repudiation of a contract for future goods before the goods or some of the goods have come into existence. In this case, the seller may exercise the right of resale and fix the damages by "one or more contracts to sell" the quantity of conforming future goods affected by the repudiation.

The companion provision of subsection (2), that resale may be made although the goods were not identified to the contract prior to the buyer's breach, likewise contemplates an anticipatory repudiation by the buyer, but one occurring after the goods are in existence. The seller may identify goods to the contract after the breach, but must identify the goods being sold as pertaining to the breached contract. If the identified goods conform to the contract, their resale will fix the seller's damages as satisfactorily as if the goods had been identified before the breach.

7. If the resale is to be by private sale, subsection (3) requires that reasonable notification of the seller's intention to resell must be given to the buyer. Notification of the time and place of a private resale is not required.

8. Subsection (4) states requirements for a public resale. The requirements of this subsection are in addition to the requirements of subsection (2), which pertain to all resales under this section.

Paragraph (a) of subsection (4) qualifies the last sentence of subsection (2) with respect to resales of unidentified and future goods at public sale. If conforming goods are in existence the seller may identify them to the contract after the buyer's breach and then resell them at public sale. If the goods have not been identified, however, the seller may resell them at public sale only as "future" goods and only if there is a recognized market for public sale of futures in goods of the kind.

Subsection (4)(b) requires that the seller give the buyer reasonable notice of the time and place of a public resale so that the buyer may have an opportunity to bid or to secure the attendance of other bidders. An exception is made in the case of goods "which are perishable or threaten to decline speedily in value."

Since there would be no reasonable prospect of competitive bidding elsewhere, subsection (4)(b) requires that a public resale "must be made at a usual place or market for public sale if one is reasonably available"; *i.e.*, a place or market which prospective bidders may reasonably be expected to attend. The market may still be "reasonably available" under this subsection, although at a considerable distance from the place where the goods are located. In this case, the expense of transporting the goods for resale is recoverable from the buyer as part of the seller's incidental damages under subsection (1). However, the question of availability is one of commercial reasonableness in the circumstances and if such "usual" place or market is not reasonably available, a duly advertised public resale may be held at another place if it is one which prospective bidders may reasonably be expected to attend, as distinguished from a place where there is no demand whatsoever for goods of the kind.

Subsection (4)(c) is designed to permit intelligent bidding. Subsection (4)(d), which permits the seller to bid and, of course, to become the purchaser, benefits the original buyer by tending to increase the resale price and thus decreasing the damages the buyer will have to pay.

9. Subsection (5) allows a purchaser to take the goods free of the rights of the buyer even if the seller has not complied with this section. The policy of resolving any doubts in favor of the resale purchaser operates to the benefit of the buyer by increasing the price the purchaser should be willing to pay.

10. Subsection (6) recognizes that when the seller is entitled to resell under this Article, the goods are the seller's goods and the purpose of resale under this section is to set the seller's damages as against the buyer. However, a person in the position of the seller under Section 2–707 or a buyer asserting a security interest in the goods under Section 2–711(3) has only a limited right in the goods and so must account to the seller for any excess over the limited amount necessary to satisfy that right.

11. Subsection (7) expresses the policy that resale is not a mandatory remedy for the seller. Except as otherwise provided in Section 2–710, the seller is always free to choose between resale and damages for repudiation or nonacceptance under Section 2–708.

Subsection (7) parallels the provision in the cover section, Section 2–712. A seller that fails to comply with the requirements of this section may recover damages under Section 2–708(1). In addition, a seller may recover both incidental and consequential damages under Section 2–710 is the seller's damages have not been liquidated under Section 2–718 or limited under Section 2–719.

Cross References:

Point 1: Section 2–713.

Point 2: Section 2–507, 2–709, Article 9.

Point 4: Section 1–201.

Point 5: Section 2–515.

Point 7: Section 2–104.

Point 8: Sections 2–104 and 2–710.

Point 10: Section 2–707 and 2–711.

Point 11: Sections 2–708, 2–710, 2–712, 2–718 and 2–719.

Definitional Cross References:

"Buyer". Section 2–103.

"Contract". Section 1–201.

"Contract for sale". Section 2–106.

"Good faith". Section 2–103.

"Goods". Section 2–103.

"Notification". Section 1–202.

"Person in position of seller". Section 2–707.

"Purchase". Section 1–201.

"Rights". Section 1–201.

"Sale". Section 2–106.

"Security interest". Section 1–201.

"Seller". Section 2–103.

As amended in 2003.

§ 2–707. "Person in the Position of a Seller".

(1) A "person in the position of a seller" includes as against a principal an agent that has paid or become responsible for the price of goods on behalf of the principal or a person that otherwise holds a security interest or other right in goods similar to that of a seller.

(2) A person in the position of a seller has the same remedies as a seller under this Article.

As amended in 2003.

Official Comment

Unlike original Article 2, which gave a limited range of remedies, subsection (2) now provides that a "person in the position of a seller "has the full range of remedies available to a seller.

Definitional Cross References:

"Goods". Section 2–103.

"Security interest". Section 1–201.

"Seller". Section 2–103.

As amended in 2003.

§ 2–708. Seller's Damages for Nonacceptance or Repudiation.

(1) Subject to subsection (2) and to Section 2–723:

(a) the measure of damages for nonacceptance by the buyer is the difference between the contract price and the market price at the time and place for tender together with any incidental or consequential damages provided in Section 2–710, but less expenses saved in consequence of the buyer's breach; and

(b) the measure of damages for repudiation by the buyer is the difference between the contract price and the market price at the place for tender at the expiration of a commercially reasonable time after the seller learned of the repudiation, but no later than the time stated in paragraph (a), together with any incidental or consequential damages provided in Section 2–710, less expenses saved in consequence of the buyer's breach.

(2) If the measure of damages provided in subsection (1) or in Section 2–706 is inadequate to put the seller in as good a position as performance would have done, the measure of damages is the profit (including reasonable overhead) that the seller would have made from full performance by the buyer, together with any incidental or consequential damages provided in this Article (Section 2–710).

As amended in 2003.

Official Comment

1. This section contains the following changes from original Section 2–708:

a) Consistent with the revision of Section 2–710, this section now provides for consequential as well as incidental damages. Subsection (1) has been divided into two paragraphs. The new paragraph clarifies the measure of damages in anticipatory repudiation. The same approach has taken in Section 2–713 for a buyer's market-based damage claims.

b) Original Section 2–708(1) set the measure of damages as the difference between the market price and the unpaid contract price. The word "unpaid" has been deleted as superfluous and misleading. An aggrieved buyer that has already paid a portion of the price is entitled to recover it in restitution under Section 2–718.

c) Original Section 2–708(1) measured damages by the difference between the market price and the contract price. Subsection (1) reverses the terms ("difference between the contract price and the market price") because the contract price must be the larger number for there to be direct damages. *Compare* Sections 2–712 and 2–713 on buyer's remedies, where the contract price is listed after the cover or market price.

d) Subsection (2) now has the following emphasized language added: "provided in subsection (1) *or in Section 2–706* is inadequate...." Most courts have correctly assumed that original Section 2–708(2) was an alternative to Section 2–706 as well as Section 2–708(1) but still had to ask the question. *See, e.g.,* R.E. Davis *Chemical Corp. v. Diasonics, Inc.,* 826 F.2d 678 (7th Cir. 1987). The change makes this result explicit.

e) In subsection (2), the phrases that appeared in original 2–708(2), "due allowance for costs reasonably incurred" and "due credit for payments or proceeds of resale" have been deleted. As has been noted repeatedly (*see, e.g.,* Harris, A General Theory for Measuring Seller's Damages for Total Breach of Contract, 60 Mich. L. Rev. 577 (1962)), the "due credit" language makes no sense for a seller that has lost a sale not because it ceased manufacture on a buyer's breach but because it has resold a finished product (that was made for its breaching buyer) to one of the seller's existing buyers. When a seller ceases manufacture and resells component parts for scrap or salvage value under Section 2–704(2), a credit for the proceeds is due the buyer to offset the damages under this section. When a seller incurs costs that are not recovered by scrap or salvage, the seller must be given an "allowance" for those costs to measure its loss accurately. *See* E. Farnsworth Contracts Section 12.9 (3rd ed. 1999)(general measure of damages = loss in value + other loss – cost avoided – loss avoided).

2. The right to damages under this section arises when a seller reclaims goods under Section 2–507 or a buyer repudiates or makes a wrongful but effective rejection. In addition, there is a right to damages under this Section if the buyer unjustifiably attempts to revoke acceptance and the seller takes back the goods. However, if the seller refuses to take the goods back in the face of the buyer's unjustifiable attempt to revoke acceptance, the appropriate remedy is an action for the price under Section 2–709.

3. The market price at the time and place for tender is the standard by which damages for nonacceptance are to be determined. The time and place of tender are determined by Section 2–503 on tender of delivery and by the use of common shipping terms. The provisions of Section 2–723 are relevant to determine the market price.

In the event that there is no evidence available of the current market price at the time and place of tender, proof of a substitute market may be made as provided for in Section 2–723. Section 2–723, which is consistent with the admissibility of market quotations, is intended to ease materially the problem of providing competent evidence.

4. Subsection (1)(b) addresses the question of when the market price should be measured in the case of an anticipatory repudiation by the buyer. This section provides that the market price should be measured in a case of repudiation at the place of tender under the agreement at a commercially reasonable time after the seller learned of the repudiation, but no later than the time of tender under the agreement. This time approximates the market price at the time the seller would have resold the goods, even though the seller has not done so under Section 2–706. To determine whether the seller has learned of the repudiation, the court should be sensitive to the rights of the aggrieved party when tactical behavior by the buyer has made the determination difficult. *See Louisiana Power and Light v. Allegheny Ludlow*, 517 F. Supp. 1319 (D.C. La. 1981).

5. Subsection (2) is used in the cases of uncompleted goods, jobbers or middlemen, and other lost-volume sellers. This remedy is an alternative to the remedy under subsection (1) or Section 2–706, and it is available when the damages based upon resale of the goods or market price of the goods do not achieve the goal of full compensation for harm caused by the buyer's breach. No effort has been made to state how lost profits should be calculated because of the variety of situations in which this measurement may be appropriate and the variety of ways in which courts have measured lost profits. This subsection permits the recovery of lost profits in all appropriate cases. Since this section deals with the plaintiff's lost profit on a particular sale, and not with cases where a plaintiff is suing for the "lost profits" from an enterprise as consequential damages, it is not necessary to show a history of earnings; all that is necessary is that the plaintiff shows a loss of the marginal benefit to be gained from performance of the broken contract.

To qualify as a "lost volume" seller, the seller needs to show only that it could have supplied both the breaching purchaser and the resale purchaser with the goods. *Islamic Republic of Iran v. Boeing Co.*, 771 F.2d

1279 (9th Cir. 1985). Where an aggrieved seller has sold goods made for the breaching party to another, courts should consider whether the seller could and would have made a profit on an additional sale in addition to the breached sale. If the seller could not or would not have profitably made another sale in the absence of breach, there is no lost volume and the seller would normally be made whole by a recovery of the incidental costs associated with the substitute transaction.

6. Consequential damages are not recoverable under this section unless the seller has made reasonable attempts to minimize the damages in good faith, either by resale under Section 2–706 or by other reasonable means.

7. When an agreement contains provisions for payment of a liquidated sum of money as an alternative to performance, (such as a take-or-pay contract), it must be determined whether the agreement is truly for alternative performances or whether the alternatives are performance or liquidated damages. Recovery under this section is available when a buyer breaches an alternative performance contract. When the "alternative" is truly liquidated damages and when that damage provision complies with Section 2–718, recovery is under the liquidated damage clause. *See Roye Realty & Developing, Inc. v. Arkla, Inc.*, 863 P.2d 1150, 1154, 22 U.C.C. Rep Serv. 2d 183 (Okl.1993); 5A Corbin, Corbin on Contracts § 1082, at 463–64 (1964).

Cross References:

Point 1: Sections 2–704, 2–710, 2–712, 2–713, 2–718.
Point 2: Section 2–507 and 2–709.
Point 3: Sections 2–503, and 2–723.
Point 4: Section 2–706.
Point 5: Section 2–706.
Point 6: Section 2–706.

Definitional Cross References:

"Buyer". Section 2–103.
"Contract". Section 1–201.
"Reasonable time". Section 1–205.
"Seller". Section 2–103.

As amended in 2003.

§ 2–709. Action for the Price.

(1) If the buyer fails to pay the price as it becomes due, the seller may recover, together with any incidental or consequential damages under Section 2–710, the price:

(a) of goods accepted or of conforming goods lost or damaged within a commercially rea-

sonable time after risk of their loss has passed to the buyer; and

(b) of goods identified to the contract if the seller is unable after reasonable effort to resell them at a reasonable price or the circumstances reasonably indicate that such effort will be unavailing.

(2) If the seller sues for the price, the seller must hold for the buyer any goods that have been identified to the contract and are still in the seller's control. However, if resale becomes possible, the seller may resell them at any time prior to the collection of the judgment. The net proceeds of any such resale must be credited to the buyer, and payment of the judgment entitles the buyer to any goods not resold.

(3) After the buyer has wrongfully rejected or revoked acceptance of the goods or has failed to make a payment due or has repudiated (Section 2–610), a seller that is held not entitled to the price under this section shall nevertheless be awarded damages for nonacceptance under Section 2–708.

As amended in 2003.

Official Comment

Prior Uniform Statutory Provision: Section 63, Uniform Sales Act.

Changes: Rewritten, important commercially needed changes being incorporated.

Purposes of Changes: To make it clear that:

1. Neither the passing of title to the goods nor the appointment of a day certain for payment is now material to a price action.

2. The action for the price is now generally limited to those cases where resale of the goods is impracticable except where the buyer has accepted the goods or where they have been destroyed after risk of loss has passed to the buyer.

3. This section substitutes an objective test by action for the former "not readily resalable" standard. An action for the price under subsection (1)(b) can be sustained only after a "reasonable effort to resell" the goods "at reasonable price" has actually been made or where the circumstances "reasonably indicate" that such an effort will be unavailing.

4. If a buyer is in default not with respect to the price, but on an obligation to make an advance, the seller should recover not under this section for the

price as such, but for the default in the collateral (though coincident) obligation to finance the seller. If the agreement between the parties contemplates that the buyer will acquire, on making the advance, a security interest in the goods, the buyer on making the advance has such an interest as soon as the seller has rights in the agreed collateral. See Section 9–204.

5. "Goods accepted" by the buyer under subsection (1)(a) include only goods as to which there has been no justified revocation of acceptance, for such a revocation means that there has been a default by the seller which bars his rights under this section. "Goods lost or damaged" are covered by the section on risk of loss. "Goods identified to the contract" under subsection (1)(b) are covered by the section on identification and the section on identification notwithstanding breach.

6. This section is intended to be exhaustive in its enumeration of cases where an action for the price lies.

7. If the action for the price fails, the seller may nonetheless have proved a case entitling him to damages for non-acceptance. In such a situation, subsection (3) permits recovery of those damages in the same action.

Cross References:

Point 4: Section 1–106.
Point 5: Sections 2–501, 2–509, 2–510 and 2–704.
Point 7: Section 2–708.

Definitional Cross References:

"Action". Section 1–201.
"Buyer". Section 2–103.
"Conforming". Section 2–106.
"Contract". Section 1–201.
"Goods". Section 2–103.
"Reasonable time". Section 1–205.
"Seller". Section 2–103.

§ 2–710. Seller's Incidental and Consequential Damages.

(1) Incidental damages to an aggrieved seller include any commercially reasonable charges, expenses or commissions incurred in stopping delivery, in the transportation, care, and custody of goods after the buyer's breach, in connection with return or resale of the goods or otherwise resulting from the breach.

(2) Consequential damages resulting from the buyer's breach include any loss resulting from general or particular requirements and needs of which the buyer at the time of contracting had

reason to know and which could not reasonably be prevented by resale or otherwise.

(3) In a consumer contract, a seller may not recover consequential damages from a consumer.

As amended in 2003.

Official Comment

1. Subsection (1) provides for reimbursement by the seller for the expenses reasonably incurred as a result of the buyer's breach. The section sets forth as examples the usual and normal types of damages that may arise from the breach but the provision is intended intends to provide for all commercially reasonable expenditures made by the seller.

2. Subsection (2) permits an aggrieved seller to recover consequential damages. Under this section the loss must result from general or particular requirements of the seller of which the buyer had reason to know at the time of contracting. As with Section 2–715, the "tacit agreement" test is rejected. (*See* Official Comment 2 to Section 2–715). The buyer is not liable for losses that could have been mitigated.

Sellers rarely suffer compensable consequential damages. A buyer's usual default is failure to pay. In normal circumstances, the disappointed seller will be able to sell to another buyer, borrow to replace the breaching buyer's promised payment, or otherwise adjust the seller's affairs to avoid consequential loss. *Cf. Afram Export Corp. v. Metallurgiki Halyps, S.A.*, 772 F.2d 1358, 1368 (7th Cir. 1985).

3. Subsection (3) precludes a seller from recovering consequential damages from a consumer. This is a nonwaivable provision.

Cross References:

Point 1: Section 2–710, 2–711 and 2–715.
Point 2: Section 2–103.

Definitional Cross References:

"Aggrieved party". Section 1–201.
"Buyer". Section 2–103.
"Consumer contract". Section 2–103.
"Delivery". Section 2–103.
"Goods". Section 2–103.
"Seller". Section 2–103.

As amended in 2003.

§ 2–711. Buyer's Remedies in General; Buyer's Security Interest in Rejected Goods.

(1) A breach of contract by the seller includes the seller's wrongful failure to deliver or to per-

form a contractual obligation, making of a non-conforming tender of delivery or performance, and repudiation.

(2) If the seller is in breach of contract, the buyer, to the extent provided for by this Act or other law, may:

(a) in the case of rightful cancellation, rightful rejection, or justifiable revocation of acceptance, recover so much of the price as has been paid;

(b) deduct damages from any part of the price still due under Section 2–717;

(c) cancel under Section 2–711(4);

(d) cover and have damages under Section 2–712 as to all goods affected whether or not they have been identified to the contract;

(e) recover damages for nondelivery or repudiation under Section 2–713;

(f) recover damages for breach with regard to accepted goods or breach with regard to a remedial promise under Section 2–714;

(g) recover identified goods under Section 2–502;

(h) obtain specific performance or obtain the goods by replevin or similar remedy under Section 2–716;

(i) recover liquidated damages under Section 2–718;

(j) in other cases, recover damages in any manner that is reasonable under the circumstances. Consequential damages – 2-715 (2)(a)

(3) On rightful rejection or justifiable revocation of acceptance a buyer has a security interest in goods in the buyer's possession or control for any payments made on their price and any expenses reasonably incurred in their inspection, receipt, transportation, care and custody and may hold such goods and resell them in a like manner as an aggrieved seller (Section 2–706).

(4) If the seller fails to make delivery or repudiates or the buyer rightfully rejects or justifiably revokes acceptance, with respect to any goods involved and with respect to the whole if the breach goes to the whole contract (Section 2–612), the buyer may cancel.

As amended in 2003 and 2005.

Official Comment

1. Despite the seller's breach proper re-tender of delivery as a cure under Section 2–508 effectively precludes the buyer's remedies under this section except for damages for any delay.

2. Under subsection (3), the buyer may hold and resell rejected goods if the buyer has paid a part of the price or incurred expenses of the type specified. "Paid," as used here, includes acceptance of a draft or other time negotiable instrument or the signing of a negotiable note. The buyer's freedom of resale is coextensive with that of a seller under this Article except that the buyer may not keep any profit resulting from the resale and the buyer is limited to retaining only the amount of the price paid and the costs involved in the inspection and handling of the goods. The buyer's security interest in the goods is intended to be limited to the items listed in subsection (3), and the buyer is not permitted to retain funds that the buyer might believe adequate for the damages. The buyer's right to cover, or to have damages for non-delivery, is not impaired by the buyer's exercise of the right of resale.

3. This Act requires its remedies to be liberally administered and provides that any right or obligation which it declares is enforceable by action unless a different effect is specifically prescribed (Section 1–103).

Cross References:

Point 1: Sections 2–502, 2–508, 2–601 and 2–712 through 2–718.
Point 2: Section 2–706.
Point 3: Section 1–103.

Definitional Cross References:

"Aggrieved party". Section 1–201.
"Buyer". Section 2–103.
"Cancellation". Section 2–106.
"Conforming". Section 2–106.
"Contract". Section 1–201.
"Cover". Section 2–712.
"Delivery". Section 2–103.
"Goods". Section 2–103.
"Notifies". Section 1–202.
"Receipt of goods". Section 2–103.
"Remedial promise". Section 2–103.
"Remedy". Section 1–201.
"Security interest". Section 1–201.
"Seller". Section 2–103.

As amended in 2003.

§ 2-712. "Cover"; Buyer's Procurement of Substitute Goods.

(1) If the seller wrongfully fails to deliver or repudiates or the buyer rightfully rejects or justifiably revokes acceptance, the buyer may "cover" by making in good faith and without unreasonable delay any reasonable purchase of or contract to purchase goods in substitution for those due from the seller.

(2) A buyer may recover from the seller as damages the difference between the cost of cover and the contract price together with any incidental or consequential damages under Section 2-715, but less expenses saved in consequence of the seller's breach.

(3) Failure of the buyer to effect cover within this section does not bar the buyer from any other remedy. 2-713 market value

As amended in 2003.

Official Comment

1. The purpose of this section is to provide the buyer with a remedy to enable the buyer to obtain the goods the buyer is entitled to under the contract with the seller. This remedy is the buyer's equivalent of the seller's right to resell.

The buyer is entitled to this remedy if the seller wrongfully fails to deliver the goods or repudiates the contract or if the buyer rightfully rejects or justifiably revokes acceptance. Cover is not available under this section if the buyer accepts the goods and does not rightfully revoke the acceptance.

2. Subsection (1) clarifies the circumstances in which a buyer is entitled to cover, prior language referred to "breach." The language makes it clear that there is a right to cover "[i]f the seller wrongfully fails to deliver or repudiates or the buyer rightfully rejects or justifiably revokes acceptance."

3. Subsection (2) allows a buyer that has appropriately covered to measure damages by the difference between the cover price and the contract price. In addition, the buyer is entitled to incidental damages, and when appropriate, consequential damages under Section 2-715.

4. The definition of "cover" is necessarily flexible, and therefore cover may include a series of contracts or sales as well as a single contract or sale, goods not identical with those involved but commercially usable as reasonable substitutes under the circumstances, and contracts on credit or delivery terms differing from the contract in breach but reasonable under the circum-

stances. The test of a proper cover is whether at the time and place of cover the buyer acted in good faith and in a reasonable manner. It is immaterial that hindsight may later prove that the method of cover used was not the cheapest or most effective.

5. The requirement in subsection (1) that the buyer must cover "without unreasonable delay" is not intended to limit the time necessary for the buyer to examine reasonable options and decide how best to effect cover.

6. Subsection (3) expresses the policy that cover is not a mandatory remedy for the buyer. The buyer is always free to choose between cover and damages for nondelivery under Section 2-713. However, this subsection must be read in conjunction with the section 2-715(2)(a), which limits the recovery of consequential damages to those damages that could not reasonably be prevented by cover or otherwise. Moreover, the operation of Section 2-716(3) on replevin and the like must be considered because the inability to cover is made an express condition to the right of the buyer to replevy the goods.

Cross References:

Point 1: Section 2-706.
Point 4: Section 2-104.
Point 6: Sections 2-713, 2-715 and 2-716.

Definitional Cross References:

"Buyer". Section 2-103.
"Contract". Section 1-201.
"Delivery". Section 2-103.
"Good faith". Section 2-103.
"Goods". Section 2-103.
"Purchase". Section 1-201.
"Reasonable time". Section 1-205.
"Remedy". Section 1-201.
"Seller". Section 2-103.

As amended in 2003.

§ 2-713. Buyer's Damages for Nondelivery or Repudiation.

(1) Subject to Section 2-723, if the seller wrongfully fails to deliver or repudiates or the buyer rightfully rejects or justifiably revokes acceptance:

(a) the measure of damages in the case of wrongful failure to deliver by the seller or rightful rejection or justifiable revocation of acceptance by the buyer is the difference between the market price at the time for tender under the contract and the contract price together with any incidental or consequential damages under Section 2–715, but less expenses saved in consequence of the seller's breach; and

(b) the measure of damages for repudiation by the seller is the difference between the market price at the expiration of a commercially reasonable time after the buyer learned of the repudiation, but no later than the time stated in paragraph (a), and the contract price together with any incidental or consequential damages provided in this Article (Section 2–715), less expenses saved in consequence of the seller's breach.

(2) Market price is to be determined as of the place for tender or, in cases of rejection after arrival or revocation of acceptance, as of the place of arrival.

As amended in 2003.

Official Comment

1. This section provides a rule for anticipatory repudiation cases. This is consistent with the new rule for sellers in Section 2–708(1)(b). In a case not involving repudiation, the buyer's damages will be based on the market price at the time for tender under the agreement. This changes the former rule where the time for measuring damages was at the time the buyer learned of the breach.

2. This section provides for a buyer's expectancy damages when the seller wrongfully fails to deliver the goods or repudiates the contract or the buyer rightfully rejects or justifiably revokes acceptance. This section provides an alternative measure of damages to the cover remedy provided for in Section 2–712.

3. Under subsection (1)(a), the measure of damages for a wrongful failure to deliver the goods by the seller or a rightful rejection or justifiable revocation of acceptance by the buyer is the difference between the market price at the time for tender under the agreement and the contract price.

4. Under subsection (1)(b), in the case of an anticipatory repudiation by the seller the market price should be measured at the place where the buyer would have covered at a commercially reasonable time after the buyer learned of the repudiation, but no later than the time of tender under the agreement. This time approximates the market price at the time the buyer would have covered even though the buyer has

not done so under Section 2–712. This subsection is designed to put the buyer in the position the buyer would have been in if the seller had performed by approximating the harm the buyer has suffered without allowing the buyer an unreasonable time to speculate on the market at the seller's expense.

5. The market price to be used in comparison with the contract price under this section is the price for goods of the same kind and in the same branch of trade.

When the market price under this section is difficult to prove, Section 2–723 on the determination and proof of market price is available to permit a showing of a comparable market price. When no market price is available, evidence of spot sale prices may be used to determine damages under this section. When the unavailability of a market price is caused by a scarcity of goods of the type involved, a good case may be made for specific performance under Section 2–716. *See* the Official Comment to that Section.

6. In addition to the damages provides in this section, the buyer is entitled to incidental and consequential damages under Section 2–715.

7. A buyer that has covered under Section 2–712 may not recover the contract price market price difference under this section, but instead must base the damages on those provided in Section 2–712. To award an additional amount because the buyer could show the market price was higher than the contract price would put the buyer in a better position than performance would have. Of course, the seller would bear the burden of proving that cover had the economic effect of limiting the buyer's actual loss to an amount less than the contract price-market price difference.

An apparent cover, which does not in fact replace the goods contracted for, should not foreclose the use of the contract price-market price measure of damages. If the breaching seller cannot prove that the new purchase is in fact a replacement for the one not delivered under the contract, the "cover" purchase should not foreclose the buyer's recovery under 2–713 of the market contract difference.

Cross References:

Point 2: Section 2–712.
Point 4: Section 2–712.
Point 5: Sections 1–106, 2–708, 2–716 and 2–723.
Point 6: Section 2–715.
Point 7: Section 2–708, 2–712 and 2–713.

Definitional Cross References:

"Buyer". Section 2–103.
"Contract". Section 1–201.
"Delivery". Section 2–103.
"Reasonable time". Section 1–205.
"Seller". Section 2–103.

As amended in 2003.

§ 2–714. Buyer's Damages For Breach in Regard to Accepted Goods.

(1) If the buyer has accepted goods and given notification pursuant to Section 2–607(3), the buyer may recover as damages for any nonconformity of tender the loss resulting in the ordinary course of events from the seller's breach as determined in any reasonable manner.

(2) The measure of damages for breach of warranty is the difference at the time and place of acceptance between the value of the goods accepted and the value they would have had if they had been as warranted, unless special circumstances show proximate damages of a different amount.

(3) In a proper case any incidental and consequential damages under Section 2–715 may also be recovered.

As amended in 2003.

Official Comment

Prior Uniform Statutory Provision: Section 69(6) and (7), Uniform Sales Act.

Changes: Rewritten.

Purposes of Changes:

1. This section deals with the remedies available to the buyer after the goods have been accepted and the time for revocation of acceptance has gone by. In general this section adopts the rule of the prior uniform statutory provision for measuring damages where there has been a breach of warranty as to goods accepted, but goes further to lay down an explicit provision as to the time and place for determining the loss.

The section on deduction of damages from price provides an additional remedy for a buyer who still owes part of the purchase price, and frequently the two remedies will be available concurrently. The buyer's failure to notify of his claim under the section on effects of acceptance, however, operates to bar his remedies under either that section or the present section.

2. The "non-conformity" referred to in subsection (1) includes not only breaches of warranties but also any failure of the seller to perform according to his obligations under the contract. In the case of such non-conformity, the buyer is permitted to recover for his loss "in any manner which is reasonable."

3. Subsection (2) describes the usual, standard and reasonable method of ascertaining damages in the case of breach of warranty but it is not intended as an exclusive measure. It departs from the measure of damages for non-delivery in utilizing the place of acceptance rather than the place of tender. In some cases the two may coincide, as where the buyer signifies his acceptance upon the tender. If, however, the nonconformity is such as would justify revocation of acceptance, the time and place of acceptance under this section is determined as of the buyer's decision not to revoke.

4. The incidental and consequential damages referred to in subsection (3), which will usually accompany an action brought under this section, are discussed in detail in the comment on the next section.

Cross References:

Point 1: Compare Section 2–711; Sections 2–607 and 2–717.
Point 2: Section 2–106.
Point 3: Sections 2–608 and 2–713.
Point 4: Section 2–715.

Definitional Cross References:

"Buyer". Section 2–103.
"Conform". Section 2–106.
"Goods". Section 2–103.
"Notification". Section 1–202.
"Seller". Section 2–103.

§ 2–715. Buyer's Incidental and Consequential Damages.

(1) Incidental damages resulting from the seller's breach include expenses reasonably incurred in inspection, receipt, transportation and care and custody of goods rightfully rejected, any commercially reasonable charges, expenses or commissions in connection with effecting cover and any other reasonable expense incident to the delay or other breach.

(2) Consequential damages resulting from the seller's breach include

(a) any loss resulting from general or particular requirements and needs of which the seller at the time of contracting had reason to know and which could not reasonably be prevented by cover or otherwise; and

(b) injury to person or property proximately resulting from any breach of warranty.

Official Comment

Prior Uniform Statutory Provisions: Subsection (2)(b)—Sections 69(7) and 70, Uniform Sales Act.

Changes: Rewritten.

Purposes of Changes and New Matter:

1. Subsection (1) is intended to provide reimbursement for the buyer who incurs reasonable expenses in connection with the handling of rightfully rejected goods or goods whose acceptance may be justifiably revoked, or in connection with effecting cover where the breach of the contract lies in non-conformity or non-delivery of the goods. The incidental damages listed are not intended to be exhaustive but are merely illustrative of the typical kinds of incidental damage.

2. Subsection (2) operates to allow the buyer, in an appropriate case, any consequential damages which are the result of the seller's breach. The "tacit agreement" test for the recovery of consequential damages is rejected. Although the older rule at common law which made the seller liable for all consequential damages of which he had "reason to know" in advance is followed, the liberality of that rule is modified by refusing to permit recovery unless the buyer could not reasonably have prevented the loss by cover or otherwise. Subparagraph (2) carries forward the provisions of the prior uniform statutory provision as to consequential damages resulting from breach of warranty, but modifies the rule by requiring first that the buyer attempt to minimize his damages in good faith, either by cover or otherwise.

3. In the absence of excuse under the section on merchant's excuse by failure of presupposed conditions, the seller is liable for consequential damages in all cases where he had reason to know of the buyer's general or particular requirements at the time of contracting. It is not necessary that there be a conscious acceptance of an insurer's liability on the seller's part, nor is his obligation for consequential damages limited to cases in which he fails to use due effort in good faith.

Particular needs of the buyer must generally be made known to the seller while general needs must rarely be made known to charge the seller with knowledge.

Any seller who does not wish to take the risk of consequential damages has available the section on contractual limitation of remedy.

4. The burden of proving the extent of loss incurred by way of consequential damage is on the buyer, but the section on liberal administration of remedies rejects any doctrine of certainty which requires almost mathematical precision in the proof of loss. Loss may be determined in any manner which is reasonable under the circumstances.

5. Subsection (2)(b) states the usual rule as to breach of warranty, allowing recovery for injuries "proximately" resulting from the breach. Where the injury involved follows the use of goods without discovery of the defect causing the damage, the question of "proximate" cause turns on whether it was reasonable for the buyer to use the goods without such inspection as would have revealed the defects. If it was not reasonable for him to do so, or if he did in fact discover the defect prior to his use, the injury would not proximately result from the breach of warranty.

6. In the case of sale of wares to one in the business of reselling them, resale is one of the requirements of which the seller has reason to know within the meaning of subsection (2)(a).

Cross References:

Point 1: Section 2–608.
Point 3: Sections 1–203, 2–615 and 2–719.
Point 4: Section 1–106.

Definitional Cross References:

"Cover". Section 2–712.
"Goods". Section 2–103.
"Person". Section 1–201.
"Receipt of goods". Section 2–103.
"Seller". Section 2–103.

§ 2-716. Specific Performance; Buyer's Right to Replevin.

(1) Specific performance may be decreed if the goods are unique or in other proper circumstances. In a contract other than a consumer contract, specific performance may be decreed if the parties have agreed to that remedy. However, even if the parties agree to specific performance, specific performance may not be decreed if the breaching party's sole remaining contractual obligation is the payment of money.

(2) The decree for specific performance may include such terms and conditions as to payment

of the price, damages, or other relief as the court may deem just.

(3) The buyer has a right of replevin or similar remedy for goods identified to the contract if after reasonable effort the buyer is unable to effect cover for such goods or the circumstances reasonably indicate that such effort will be unavailing or if the goods have been shipped under reservation and satisfaction of the security interest in them has been made or tendered.

(4) The buyer's right under subsection (3) vests upon acquisition of a special property, even if the seller had not then repudiated or failed to deliver.

As amended in 1999 and 2003.

Official Comment

1. This section contains the following changes from original Section 2–716:

a) The caption has been amended to make it clear that either party may be entitled to specific performance.

b) The second sentence of subsection (1) explicitly permits parties to bind themselves to specific performance even where it would not otherwise be available.

c) In subsection (3), the phrase "or similar remedy" has been added after "replevin" to reflect the fact that under the governing state law the right may be called "detinue," "sequestration," "claim and delivery," or something else.

d) Subsection (4) corresponds with Section 2–502(2), which in turn is derived from (but broader than) the conforming amendments to Article 9. It provides a vesting rule for cases in which there is a right of replevin.

2. Uniqueness should be determined in light of the total circumstances surrounding the contract and is not limited to goods identified when the contract is formed. The typical specific performance situation today involves an output or requirements contract rather than a contract for the sale of an heirloom or priceless work of art. A buyer's inability to cover is evidence of "other proper circumstances."

3. Subsection (1) provides that a court may decree specific performance if the parties have agreed to that remedy. The parties' agreement to specific performance can be enforced even if legal remedies are entirely adequate. Even in a commercial contract, the third sentence of subsection (1) prevents the aggrieved party from obtaining specific performance if the only obligation of the party in breach is the payment of money.

Whether a buyer is obligated to pay the price is determined by Section 2–709, not by this section.

Nothing in this section constrains the court's exercise of its equitable discretion to decide whether to enter a decree for specific performance or to determine the conditions or terms of the decree. This section assumes that the decree for specific performance is conditioned on a tender of full performance by the party that seeks the remedy.

4. The legal remedy of replevin or a similar remedy is also available for cases in which cover is unavailable and where the goods have been identified to the contract. This is in addition to the prepaying buyer's right to recover identified goods upon the seller's insolvency or, when the goods have been bought for a consumer purpose, upon the seller's repudiation or failure to deliver (Section 2–502). If a negotiable document of title is outstanding, the buyer's right of replevin relates to the document and does not directly relate to the goods. *See* Article 7, especially Section 7–602.

5. Subsection (4) provides that a buyer's right to replevin or a similar remedy vests upon the buyer's acquisition of a special property in the goods (Section 2–501) even if the seller has not at that time repudiated or failed to make a required delivery. This vesting rule assumes application of a "first in time" priority rule. In other words, if the buyer's rights vest under this rule before a creditor acquires an *in rem* right to the goods, including an Article 9 security interest and a lien created by levy, the buyer should prevail.

Cross References:

    Point 1: Section 2–502.
    Point 3: Section 2–709.
    Point 4: Section 2–502 and Article 7.
    Point 5: Section 2–501 and Article 9.

Definitional Cross References:

    "Agreement". Section 1–201.
    "Buyer". Section 2–103.
    "Consumer contract". Section 2–103.
    "Contract". Section 1–201.
    "Deliver". Section 2–201.
    "Goods". Section 2–103.
    "Party". Section 1–201.
    "Remedy". Section 1–201.
    "Rights". Section 1–201.

As amended in 1999 and 2003.

§ 2–717. Deduction of Damages from the Price.

The buyer on notifying the seller of the intention to do so may deduct all or any part of the damages resulting from any breach of the contract from any part of the price still due under the same contract.

As amended in 2003.

Official Comment

Prior Uniform Statutory Provision: See Section 69(1)(a), Uniform Sales Act.

Purposes:

1.   This section permits the buyer to deduct from the price damages resulting from any breach by the seller and does not limit the relief to cases of breach of warranty as did the prior uniform statutory provision. To bring this provision into application the breach involved must be of the same contract under which the price in question is claimed to have been earned.

2.   The buyer, however, must give notice of his intention to withhold all or part of the price if he wishes to avoid a default within the meaning of the section on insecurity and right to assurances. In conformity with the general policies of this Article, no formality of notice is required and any language which reasonably indicates the buyer's reason for holding up his payment is sufficient.

Cross Reference:

Point 2: Section 2–609.

Definitional Cross References:

"Buyer". Section 2–103.
"Contract". Section 1–201.
"Seller". Section 2–103.

§ 2–718. Liquidation or Limitation of Damages; Deposits.

(1)   Damages for breach by either party may be liquidated in the agreement but only at an amount that is reasonable in the light of the anticipated or actual harm caused by the breach and, in a consumer contract, the difficulties of proof of loss, and the inconvenience or nonfeasibility of otherwise obtaining an adequate remedy. Section 2–719 determines the enforceability of a term that limits but does not liquidate damages.

(2)   If the seller justifiably withholds delivery of goods or stops performance because of the buyer's breach or insolvency, the buyer is entitled to restitution of any amount by which the sum of the buyer's payments exceeds the amount to which the seller is entitled by virtue of terms liquidating the seller's damages in accordance with subsection (1).

(3)   The buyer's right to restitution under subsection (2) is subject to offset to the extent that the seller establishes:

(a)   a right to recover damages under the provisions of this Article other than subsection (1); and

(b)   the amount or value of any benefits received by the buyer directly or indirectly by reason of the contract.

(4)   If a seller has received payment in goods, their reasonable value or the proceeds of their resale shall be treated as payments for the purposes of subsection (2). However, if the seller has notice of the buyer's breach before reselling goods received in part performance, the resale is subject to the conditions of this Article on resale by an aggrieved seller (Section 2–706).

As amended in 2003.

Official Comment

1.   The last sentence of subsection (1) clarifies the relationship between this section and Section 2–719.

2.   A valid liquidated damages term may liquidate the amount of all damages, including consequential and incidental damages. As under former law, liquidated damages clauses should be enforced if the amount is reasonable in light of the factors provided in subsection (1). This section thus respects the parties' ability to contract for damages while providing some control by requiring that the term be reasonable under the circumstances of the particular case.

Under original Section 2–718, a party seeking to enforce a liquidated damages term had to demonstrate the difficulty of proving the loss and the inconvenience or nonfeasibility of obtaining an adequate remedy. These requirement have been eliminated in commercial contracts but are retained in consumer contracts.

3.   Original Section 2–718(1) stated that an unreasonably large liquidated damage term was void as a penalty. This language has been eliminated as unnecessary and misleading. If the liquidated damages are reasonable in light of the test of subsection (1), the term should be enforced, thereby rendering the penalty language of the former law redundant. The language was also misleading because of its emphasis on unreasonably large damages. A liquidated damages term that provided for damages that are unreasonably small is likewise unenforceable.

4. If a liquidated damages term is unenforceable, the remedies of this Article become available to the aggrieved party.

5. Under subsection (2), only the buyer's payments that are more than the amount of an enforceable liquidated damages term need to be returned to the buyer. If the buyer has made payment by virtue of a trade-in or other goods deposited with the seller, subsection (4) provides that the reasonable value of the goods or the goods' resale price should be used to determine what the buyer has paid, not the value the seller allowed the buyer in the trade-in. To assure that the seller obtains a reasonable price for the goods, the seller must comply with the resale provisions of Section 2–706 if the seller knows of the buyer's breach before the seller has otherwise resold them.

Subsection (2) expands the situations in which restitution was available under prior law. Original Section 2–718(2) was limited to circumstances in which the seller justifiably withheld delivery because of the buyer's breach. Subsection (2) extends the right to situations where the seller stops performance because of the buyer's breach or insolvency.

6. Subsection (3) continues the rule from the former law without change. If there is no enforceable liquidated damages term, under subsection (2) the buyer is entitled to restitution subject to a right of set off by the seller for any damages to which the seller is otherwise entitled to under this Article.

Cross References:

Point 1: Section 2–719.
Point 2: Section 2–302.
Point 3: Section 2–718.
Point 5: Sections 2–706 and 2–718.

Definitional Cross References:

"Aggrieved party". Section 1–201.
"Agreement". Section 1–201.
"Buyer". Section 2–103.
"Consumer contract". Section 2–103.
"Contract". Section 1–201.
"Goods". Section 2–103.
"Insolvent". Section 1–201.
"Notice". Section 1–202.
"Party". Section 1–201.
"Remedy". Section 1–201.
"Seller". Section 2–103.
"Term". Section 1–201.

As amended in 2003.

§ 2–719. Contractual Modification or Limitation of Remedy.

(1) Subject to the provisions of subsections (2) and (3) of this section and of the preceding section on liquidation and limitation of damages,

    (a) the agreement may provide for remedies in addition to or in substitution for those provided in this Article and may limit or alter the measure of damages recoverable under this Article, as by limiting the buyer's remedies to return of the goods and repayment of the price or to repair and replacement of non-conforming goods or parts; and

    (b) resort to a remedy as provided is optional unless the remedy is expressly agreed to be exclusive, in which case it is the sole remedy.

(2) Where circumstances cause an exclusive or limited remedy to fail of its essential purpose, remedy may be had as provided in this Act.

(3) Consequential damages may be limited or excluded unless the limitation or exclusion is unconscionable. Limitation of consequential damages for injury to the person in the case of consumer goods is prima facie unconscionable but limitation of damages where the loss is commercial is not.

Official Comment

Prior Uniform Statutory Provision: None.

Purposes:

1. Under this section parties are left free to shape their remedies to their particular requirements and reasonable agreements limiting or modifying remedies are to be given effect.

However, it is of the very essence of a sales contract that at least minimum adequate remedies be available. If the parties intend to conclude a contract for sale within this Article they must accept the legal consequence that there be at least a fair quantum of remedy for breach of the obligations or duties outlined in the contract. Thus any clause purporting to modify or limit the remedial provisions of this Article in an unconscionable manner is subject to deletion and in that event the remedies made available by this Article are applicable as if the stricken clause had never existed. Similarly, under subsection (2), where an apparently fair and reasonable clause because of circumstances fails in its purpose or operates to deprive either party of the substantial value of the bargain, it must give way to the general remedy provisions of this Article.

2. Subsection (1)(b) creates a presumption that clauses prescribing remedies are cumulative rather than exclusive. If the parties intend the term to describe the sole remedy under the contract, this must be clearly expressed.

3. Subsection (3) recognizes the validity of clauses limiting or excluding consequential damages but makes it clear that they may not operate in an unconscionable manner. Actually such terms are merely an allocation of unknown or undeterminable risks. The seller in all cases is free to disclaim warranties in the manner provided in Section 2–316.

Cross References:

Point 1: Section 2–302.
Point 3: Section 2–316.

Definitional Cross References:

"Agreement". Section 1–201.
"Buyer". Section 2–103.
"Conforming". Section 2–106.
"Contract". Section 1–201.
"Goods". Section 2–103.
"Remedy". Section 1–201.
"Seller". Section 2–103.

§ 2–720. Effect of "Cancellation" or "Rescission" on Claims for Antecedent Breach.

Unless the contrary intention clearly appears, expressions of "cancellation" or "rescission" of the contract or the like shall not be construed as a renunciation or discharge of any claim in damages for an antecedent breach.

Official Comment

Prior Uniform Statutory Provision: None.

Purpose:

This section is designed to safeguard a person holding a right of action from any unintentional loss of rights by the ill-advised use of such terms as "cancellation", "rescission", or the like. Once a party's rights have accrued they are not to be lightly impaired by concessions made in business decency and without intention to forego them. Therefore, unless the cancellation of a contract expressly declares that it is "without reservation of rights", or the like, it cannot be considered to be a renunciation under this section.

Cross Reference:

Section 1–107.

Definitional Cross References:

"Cancellation". Section 2–106.
"Contract". Section 1–201.

§ 2–721. Remedies for Fraud.

Remedies for material misrepresentation or fraud include all remedies available under this Article for non-fraudulent breach. Neither rescission or a claim for rescission of the contract for sale nor rejection or return of the goods shall bar or be deemed inconsistent with a claim for damages or other remedy.

Official Comment

Prior Uniform Statutory Provision: None.

Purposes: To correct the situation by which remedies for fraud have been more circumscribed than the more modern and mercantile remedies for breach of warranty. Thus the remedies for fraud are extended by this section to coincide in scope with those for non-fraudulent breach. This section thus makes it clear that neither rescission of the contract for fraud nor rejection of the goods bars other remedies unless the circumstances of the case make the remedies incompatible.

Definitional Cross References:

"Contract for sale". Section 2–106.
"Goods". Section 2–103.
"Remedy". Section 1–201.

§ 2–722. Who May Sue Third Parties for Injury to Goods.

If a third party so deals with goods that have been identified to a contract for sale as to cause actionable injury to a party to that contract:

(a) a right of action against the third party is in either party to the contract for sale that has title to or a security interest or a special property or an insurable interest in the goods, and if the goods have been destroyed or converted, a right of action is also in the party that either bore the risk of loss under the contract for sale or has since the injury assumed that risk as against the other;

(b) if at the time of the injury the party plaintiff did not bear the risk of loss as against the other party to the contract for sale and there is no arrangement between them for disposition of the recovery, the party plaintiff's suit or settlement is, subject to its own interest, as a fiduciary for the other party to the contract; and

(c) either party may with the consent of the other sue for the benefit of whom it may concern.

As amended in 2003.

Official Comment

Prior Uniform Statutory Provision: None.

Purposes: To adopt and extend somewhat the principle of the statutes which provide for suit by the real party in interest. The provisions of this section apply only after identification of the goods. Prior to that time only the seller has a right of action. During the period between identification and final acceptance (except in the case of revocation of acceptance) it is possible for both parties to have the right of action. Even after final acceptance both parties may have the right of action if the seller retains possession or otherwise retains an interest.

Definitional Cross References:

"Action". Section 1–201.
"Buyer". Section 2–103.
"Contract for sale". Section 2–106.
"Goods". Section 2–103.
"Party". Section 1–201.
"Rights". Section 1–201.
"Security interest". Section 1–201.

§ 2–723. Proof of Market: Time and Place.

(1) If evidence of a price prevailing at the times or places described in this Article is not readily available, the price prevailing within any reasonable time before or after the time described or at any other place that in commercial judgment or under usage of trade would serve as a reasonable substitute for the one described may be used, making any proper allowance for the cost of transporting the goods to or from the other place.

(2) Evidence of a relevant price prevailing at a time or place other than the one described in this Article offered by one party is not admissible unless and until the party has given the other party such notice as the court finds sufficient to prevent unfair surprise.

As amended in 2003.

Official Comment

Prior Uniform Statutory Provision: None.

Purposes: To eliminate the most obvious difficulties arising in connection with the determination of market price, when that is stipulated as a measure of damages by some provision of this Article. Where the appropriate market price is not readily available the court is here granted reasonable leeway in receiving evidence of prices current in other comparable markets or at other times comparable to the one in question. In accordance with the general principle of this Article against surprise, however, a party intending to offer evidence of such a substitute price must give suitable notice to the other party.

1. This section is not intended to exclude the use of any other reasonable method of determining market price or of measuring damages if the circumstances of the case make this necessary.

2. In the case of repudiation Sections 2–708(1)(b) and 2–713(1)(b) provide the rule for the proper measure of damages.

Cross Reference:

Point 2: Section 2–708 and 2–713.

Definitional Cross References:

"Notifies". Section 1–202.
"Party". Section 1–201.
"Reasonable time". Section 1–205.
"Usage of trade". Section 1–303.

As amended in 2003.

§ 2–724. Admissibility of Market Quotations.

If the prevailing price or value of any goods regularly bought and sold in any established commodity market is in issue, reports in official publications or trade journals or in newspapers, periodicals or other means of communication in general circulation published as the reports of the market are admissible in evidence. The circumstances of the preparation of such a report may be shown to affect its weight but not its admissibility.

As amended in 2003.

Official Comment

Prior Uniform Statutory Provision: None.

Purposes: To make market quotations admissible in evidence while providing for a challenge of the material by showing the circumstances of its preparation.

No explicit provision as to the weight to be given to market quotations is contained in this section, but such quotations, in the absence of compelling challenge, offer an adequate basis for a verdict.

Market quotations are made admissible when the price or value of goods traded "in any established market" is in issue. The reason of the section does not require that the market be closely organized in the manner of a produce exchange. It is sufficient if transactions in the commodity are frequent and open enough to make a market established by usage in which one price can be expected to affect another and in which an informed report of the range and trend of prices can be assumed to be reasonably accurate.

This section does not in any way intend to limit or negate the application of similar rules of admissibility to other material, whether by action of the courts or by statute. The purpose of the present section is to assure a minimum of mercantile administration in this important situation and not to limit any liberalizing trend in modern law.

Definitional Cross Reference:
"Goods". Section 2–103.

§ 2–725. Statute of Limitations in Contracts for Sale.

(1) Except as otherwise provided in this section, an action for breach of any contract for sale must be commenced within the later of four years after the right of action has accrued under subsection (2) or (3) or one year after the breach was or should have been discovered, but no longer than five years after the right of action accrued. By the original agreement the parties may reduce the period of limitation to not less than one year but may not extend it. However, in a consumer contract, the period of limitation may not be reduced.

(2) Except as otherwise provided in subsection (3), the following rules apply:

(a) Except as otherwise provided in this subsection, a right of action for breach of a contract accrues when the breach occurs, even if the aggrieved party did not have knowledge of the breach.

(b) For breach of a contract by repudiation, a right of action accrues at the earlier of when the aggrieved party elects to treat the repudiation as a breach or when a commercially reasonable time for awaiting performance has expired.

(c) For breach of a remedial promise, a right of action accrues when the remedial promise is not performed when performance is due.

(d) In an action by a buyer against a person that is answerable over to the buyer for a claim asserted against the buyer, the buyer's right of action against the person answerable over accrues at the time the claim was originally asserted against the buyer.

(3) If a breach of a warranty arising under Section 2–312, 2–313(2), 2–314, or 2–315, or a breach of an obligation, other than a remedial promise, arising under Section 2–313A or 2–313B, is claimed, the following rules apply:

(a) Except as otherwise provided in paragraph (c), a right of action for breach of a warranty arising under Section 2–313(2), 2–314, or 2–315 accrues when the seller has tendered delivery to the immediate buyer, as defined in Section 2–313, and has completed performance of any agreed installation or assembly of the goods.

(b) Except as otherwise provided in paragraph (c), a right of action for breach of an obligation, other than a remedial promise, arising under Section 2–313A or 2–313B accrues when the remote purchaser, as defined in Section 2–313A or 2–313B, receives the goods.

(c) If a warranty arising under Section 2–313(2) or an obligation, other than a remedial promise, arising under Section 2–313A or 2–313B explicitly extends to future performance of the goods and discovery of the breach must await the time for performance, the right of action accrues when the immediate buyer as defined in Section 2–313 or the remote purchaser as defined in Section 2–313A or 2–313B discovers or should have discovered the breach.

(d) A right of action for breach of warranty arising under Section 2–312 accrues when the aggrieved party discovers or should have discovered the breach. However, an action for breach of the warranty of noninfringement may not be commenced more than six years after tender of delivery of the goods to the aggrieved party.

(4) If an action commenced within the time limited by subsection (1) is so terminated as to leave available a remedy by another action for the same breach, the other action may be commenced after the expiration of the time limited and within six months after the termination of the first action unless the termination resulted from voluntary discontinuance or from dismissal for failure or neglect to prosecute.

(5) This section does not alter the law on tolling of the statute of limitations nor does it apply to causes of action that accrued before this Act becomes effective.

As amended in 2003.

Official Comment

1. Original Section 2–725 has been changed as follows: 1) The basic four-year limitation period in subsection (1) has been supplemented by a discovery rule that permits a cause of action to be brought within one year after the breach was or should have been discovered, although no later than five years after the time the cause would otherwise have accrued; 2) The applicable limitation period cannot be reduced in a consumer contract (subsection (1)); 3) Subsection (2) contains specific rules for cases of repudiation, breach of a remedial promise, and actions where another person is answerable over; 4) Subsection (3)(a) provides that the limitation period for breach of warranty accrues when tender of delivery has occurred and the seller has completed any agreed installation or assembly of the goods; 5) Subsection (3) contains specific rules for breach of an obligation arising under Section 2–313A or 2–313B, for breach of a warranty arising under Section 2–312, and for breach of a warranty against infringement.

2. Subsection (1) continues the four-year limitation period of original Article 2 but provides for a possible one-year extension to accommodate a discovery of the breach late in the four year period after accrual. The four year period under this Article is shorter than many other statutes of limitation for breach of contract and it provides a period which is appropriate given the nature of the contracts under this Article and modern business practices. As under original Article 2, the period of limitation can be reduced to one year by an agreement in a commercial contract, but the amended section does not permit this reduction in consumer contracts.

3. Subsections (2) and (3) provide rules for accrual of the various types of action that this Article allows. Certainty of commercial relationships is advanced when the rules are clearly set forth. Subsection (2) sets out the accrual rules for actions other than for breach of a warranty, which includes actions based on repudiation or breach of a remedial promise and actions where another person is answerable over. Subsection (3) sets out the accrual rules for the various claims based on a warranty, including a warranty of title and a warranty against infringement, or on an obligation other than a remedial promise arising under Section 2–313A or 2–313B.

Subsection (2)(a) states the general rule from prior law that a right of action for breach of contract accrues when the breach occurs without regard to the aggrieved party's knowledge of the breach. This general rule is then subject to the three more explicit rules in subsection (2) and to the rules for breach of warranty stated in subsection (3).

Subsection (2)(b) provides an explicit rule for repudiation. In a repudiation, the aggrieved party may await performance for a commercially reasonable time or resort to any remedy for breach. Section 2–610. The accrual rule for breach of contract in a repudiation case is based on the earlier of those two time periods.

Subsection (2)(c) provides that a cause of action for breach of a remedial promise accrues when the promise is not performed at the time performance is due.

Subsection (2)(d) addresses the problem that has arisen in the cases when an intermediary party is sued for a breach of obligation for which its seller or another person is answerable over, but the limitations period in the upstream lawsuit has already expired. This subsection allows a party four years, or if reduced in the agreement, not less than one year, from when the claim is originally asserted against the buyer for the buyer to sue the person that is answerable over. Whether a party is in fact answerable over to the buyer is not addressed in this section.

4. Subsection (3) addresses the accrual rules for breach of a warranty arising under Section 2–312, 2–313(2), 2–314 or 2–315, or of an obligation other than a remedial promise arising under Section 2–313A or 2–313B. The subsection does not apply to remedial promises arising under Section 2–313(4); the limitation for all remedial promises are governed by subsection 2(c). The accrual rules explicitly incorporate the definitions of "immediate buyer" and "remote purchaser" in Sections 2–313, 2–313A and 2–313B. Any cause of action brought by another person to which the warranty or

obligation extends is <u>derivative</u> in nature. Thus, the time period applicable to the immediate buyer or remote purchaser governs even if the action is brought by a person to which the warranty or obligation extends under Section 2–318.

Subsection (3)(a) continues the general rule that an action for breach of warranty accrues in the case of an express or implied warranty to an immediate buyer upon completion of tender of delivery of nonconforming goods to the immediate buyer but makes explicit that accrual is deferred until the completion of any installation or assembly that the seller has agreed to undertake. This extension of the time of accrual in the case of installation or assembly applies only in the case of a seller that promises to install or assemble and not in the case of a third party, independent of the seller, undertaking the action.

Subsection (3)(b) addresses the accrual of a cause of action for breach of an obligation other than a remedial promise arising under Section 2–313A or 2–313B. In these cases, the cause of action accrues when the remote purchaser (as defined in those sections) receives the goods. This accrual rule balances the rights of the remote buyer or remote lessee to be able to have a cause of action based upon the warranty obligation the seller has created against the rights of the seller to have some limit on the length of time the seller is liable.

Both of these accrual rules are subject to the exception in subsection (3)(c) for a warranty or obligation that explicitly extends to the future performance of the goods and discovery of the breach must await the time for performance. In this case, the cause of action does not accrue until the buyer or remote purchaser discovers or should have discovered the breach.

For a warranty of title or a warranty of non-infringement under Section 2–312, subsection (3)(d) provides that a cause of action accrues when the aggrieved party discovers or should have discovered the breach. In a typical case, the aggrieved party will not discover the breach until it is sued by a party that asserts title to the goods or that asserts an infringement, either event

which could be many years after the buyer acquired the goods. This accrual rule allows the aggrieved party appropriate leeway to then bring a claim against the person that made the warranty. In recognition of a need to have a time of repose in an infringement case, a party may not bring an action based upon a warranty of non-infringement more than six years after tender of delivery.

5. Subsection (4) states the saving provision included in many state statutes and permits an additional short period for bringing new actions where suits begun within the four year period have been terminated so as to leave a remedy still available for the same breach.

6. Subsection (5) makes it clear that this Article does not purport to alter or modify in any respect the law on tolling of the Statute of Limitations as it now prevails in the various jurisdictions.

Cross References:

Point 1: Sections 2–312, 2–313A, and 2–313B.
Point 3: Sections 2–313A, 2–313B, and 2–610.
Point 4: Sections 2–312, 2–313,2–313A, 2–313B, 2–314, 2–315 and 2–318.

Definitional Cross References:

"Action". Section 1–201.
"Aggrieved party". Section 1–201.
"Agreement". Section 1–201.
"Buyer". Section 2–103.
"Consumer contract". Section 2–103.
"Contract". Section 1–201.
"Contract for sale". Section 2–106.
"Delivery". Section 2–103.
"Goods". Section 2–103.
"Party". Section 1–201.
"Reasonable time". Section 1–205.
"Remedial promise". Section 2–103.
"Remedy". Section 1–201.
"Term". Section 1–201.
"Termination". Section 2–106.

As amended in 2003.

PART 8

TRANSITIONAL PROVISIONS

§ 2–801.　Effective Date.

This [Act] takes effect on _____, 20__ .

As added in 2003.

§ 2–802.　Amendment of Existing Article 2.

This [Act] amends [insert citation to existing Article 2].

As added in 2003.

§ 2–803. Application to Existing Relations.

(1) This [Act] applies to a transaction within its scope that is entered into on or after the effective date of this [Act].

(2) This [Act] does not apply to a transaction that is entered into before the effective date of this [Act] even if the transaction would be subject to this [Act] if it had been entered into after the effective date of this [Act].

(3) This [Act] does not apply to a right of action that accrued before the effective date of this [Act].

(4) Section 2–313B of this [Act] does not apply to an advertisement or similar communication made before the effective date of this [Act].

As added in 2003.

§ 2–804. Savings Clause.

A transaction entered into before the effective date of this [Act], and the rights, obligations, and interests flowing from that transaction, are governed by any statute or other law amended or repealed by this [Act] as if amendment or repeal had not occurred and may be terminated, completed, consummated, or enforced under that statute or other law.

As added in 2003.

UCC ARTICLE 2A

LEASES

Pre–2001 Article 2A . . . .*Appendix E*
2001 amendments (Article 1 revision) . . . .*Appendix A*
2003 amendments . . . .*Appendix F*
2003 amendments (Article 7 revision) . . . .*Appendix B*
2005 amendments . . . .*Appendix J*

PART 1. GENERAL PROVISIONS

Section
2A–101. Short Title.
2A–102. Scope.
2A–103. Definitions and Index of Definitions.
2A–104. Leases Subject to Other Law.
2A–105. Territorial Application of Article to Goods Covered by Certificate of Title.
2A–106. Limitation on Power of Parties to Consumer Lease to Choose Applicable Law and Judicial Forum.
2A–107. Waiver or Renunciation of Claim or Right after Default.
2A–108. Unconscionability.
2A–109. Option to Accelerate at Will.

PART 2. FORMATION AND CONSTRUCTION OF LEASE CONTRACT; ELECTRONIC CONTRACTING

2A–201. Statute of Frauds.
2A–202. Final Expression in a Record: Parol or Extrinsic Evidence.
2A–203. Seals Inoperative.
2A–204. Formation in General.
2A–205. Firm Offers.
2A–206. Offer and Acceptance in Formation of Lease Contract.
2A–207. Reserved. [Course of Performance or Practical Construction.]
2A–208. Modification, Rescission and Waiver.
2A–209. Lessee under Finance Lease as Beneficiary of Supply Contract.
2A–210. Express Warranties.
2A–211. Warranties Against Interference and Against Infringement; Lessee's Obligation Against Infringement.
2A–212. Implied Warranty of Merchantability.

Section
2A–213. Implied Warranty of Fitness for Particular Purpose.
2A–214. Exclusion or Modification of Warranties.
2A–215. Cumulation and Conflict of Warranties Express or Implied.
2A–216. Third-party Beneficiaries of Express and Implied Warranties.
2A–217. Identification.
2A–218. Insurance and Proceeds.
2A–219. Risk of Loss.
2A–220. Effect of Default on Risk of Loss.
2A–221. Casualty to Identified Goods.
2A–222. Legal Recognition of Electronic Contracts, Records and Signatures.
2A–223. Attribution.
2A–224. Electronic Communication.

PART 3. EFFECT OF LEASE CONTRACT

2A–301. Enforceability of Lease Contract.
2A–302. Title to and Possession of Goods.
2A–303. Alienability of Party's Interest under Lease Contract or of Lessor's Residual Interest in Goods; Delegation of Performance; Transfer of Rights.
2A–304. Subsequent Lease of Goods by Lessor.
2A–305. Sale or Sublease of Goods by Lessee.
2A–306. Priority of Certain Liens Arising by Operation of Law.
2A–307. Priority of Liens Arising by Attachment or Levy On, Security Interests In, and Other Claims to Goods.
2A–308. Special Rights of Creditors.
2A–309. Lessor's and Lessee's Rights When Goods Become Fixtures.
2A–310. Lessor's and Lessee's Rights When Goods Become Accessions.
2A–311. Priority Subject to Subordination.

PART 4. PERFORMANCE OF LEASE CONTRACT: REPUDIATED, SUBSTITUTED AND EXCUSED

2A–401. Insecurity: Adequate Assurance of Performance.
2A–402. Anticipatory Repudiation.
2A–403. Retraction of Anticipatory Repudiation.
2A–404. Substituted Performance.
2A–405. Excused Performance.
2A–406. Procedure on Excused Performance.
2A–407. Irrevocable Promises: Finance Leases.

PART 5. DEFAULT

A. IN GENERAL

2A–501. Default: Procedure.
2A–502. Notice after Default.
2A–503. Modification or Impairment of Rights and Remedies.
2A–504. Liquidation of Damages.
2A–505. Cancellation and Termination and Effect of Cancellation, Termination, Rescission, or Fraud on Rights and Remedies.
2A–506. Statute of Limitations.
2A–507. Proof of Market Rent: Time and Place.
2A–507A Right to Specific Performance or Replevin or the Like.

B. DEFAULT BY LESSOR

2A–508. Lessee's Remedies.
2A–509. Lessee's Rights on Improper Delivery; Manner and Effect of Rejection.
2A–510. Installment Lease Contracts: Rejection and Default.
2A–511. Merchant Lessee's Duties as to Rejected Goods.
2A–512. Lessee's Duties as to Rejected Goods.
2A–513. Cure by Lessor of Improper Tender or Delivery; Replacement.
2A–514. Waiver of Lessee's Objections.
2A–515. Acceptance of Goods.

2A–516. Effect of Acceptance of Goods; Notice of Default; Burden of Establishing Default after Acceptance; Notice of Claim or Litigation to Person Answerable Over.
2A–517. Revocation of Acceptance of Goods.
2A–518. Cover; Substitute Goods.
2A–519. Lessee's Damages for Non-delivery, Repudiation, Default, and Breach of Warranty in Regard to Accepted Goods.
2A–520. Lessee's Incidental and Consequential Damages.
2A–521. Reserved.
2A–522. Lessee's Right to Goods on Lessor's Insolvency.

C. DEFAULT BY LESSEE

2A–523. Lessor's Remedies.
2A–524. Lessor's Right to Identify Goods to Lease Contract.
2A–525. Lessor's Right to Possession of Goods.
2A–526. Lessor's Stoppage of Delivery in Transit or Otherwise.
2A–527. Lessor's Rights to Dispose of Goods.
2A–528. Lessor's Damages for Non-acceptance, Failure to Pay, Repudiation, or Other Default.
2A–529. Lessor's Action for the Rent.
2A–530. Lessor's Incidental and Consequential Damages.
2A–531. Standing to Sue Third Parties for Injury to Goods.
2A–532. Lessor's Rights to Residual Interest.

PART 6. TRANSITIONAL PROVISIONS

2A–601. Effective Date.
2A–602. Amendment of Existing Article 2A.
2A–603. Applicability.
2A–604. Savings Clause.

Conforming Amendments to Article 1.

PART 1

GENERAL PROVISIONS

§ 2A–101. Short Title.

This Article shall be known and may be cited as the Uniform Commercial Code—Leases.

Official Comment

Rationale for Codification:

There are several reasons for codifying the law with respect to leases of goods. An analysis of the case law as it applies to leases of goods suggests at least three significant issues to be resolved by codification. First, what is a lease? It is necessary to define lease to determine whether a transaction creates a lease or a security interest disguised as a lease. If the transaction creates a security interest disguised as a lease, the lessor will be required to file a financing statement or take other action to perfect its interest in the goods against third parties. There is no such requirement with respect to leases. Yet the distinction between a lease and a security interest disguised as a lease is not clear. Second, will the lessor be deemed to have made warranties to the lessee? If the transaction is a sale the express and implied warranties of Article 2 of the Uniform Commercial Code apply. However, the warranty law with respect to leases is uncertain. Third, what remedies are available to the lessor upon the lessee's default? If the transaction is a security interest disguised as a lease, the answer is stated in Part 5 of the Article on Secured Transactions (Article 9). There is no clear answer with respect to leases.

There are reasons to codify the law with respect to leases of goods in addition to those suggested by a review of the reported cases. The answer to this important question should not be limited to the issues raised in these cases. Is it not also proper to determine the remedies available to the lessee upon the lessor's default? It is, but that issue is not reached through a review of the reported cases. This is only one of the many issues presented in structuring, negotiating and documenting a lease of goods.

Statutory Analogue:

After it was decided to proceed with the codification project, the drafting committee of the National Conference of Commissioners on Uniform State Laws looked for a statutory analogue, gradually narrowing the focus to the Article on Sales (Article 2) and the Article on Secured Transactions (Article 9). A review of the literature with respect to the sale of goods reveals that Article 2 is predicated upon certain assumptions: Parties to the sales transaction frequently are without counsel; the agreement of the parties often is oral or evidenced by scant writings; obligations between the parties are bilateral; applicable law is influenced by the need to preserve freedom of contract. A review of the literature with respect to personal property security law reveals that Article 9 is predicated upon very different assumptions: Parties to a secured transaction regularly are represented by counsel; the agreement of the parties frequently is reduced to a writing, extensive in scope; the obligations between the parties are essentially unilateral; and applicable law seriously limits freedom of contract.

The lease is closer in spirit and form to the sale of goods than to the creation of a security interest. While parties to a lease are sometimes represented by counsel and their agreement is often reduced to a writing, the obligations of the parties are bilateral and the common law of leasing is dominated by the need to preserve freedom of contract. Thus the drafting committee concluded that Article 2 was the appropriate statutory analogue.

Issues:

The drafting committee then identified and resolved several issues critical to codification:

Scope: The scope of the Article was limited to leases (Section 2A-102). There was no need to include leases intended as security, *i.e.*, security interests disguised as leases, as they are adequately treated in Article 9. Further, even if leases intended as security were included, the need to preserve the distinction would remain, as policy suggests treatment significantly different from that accorded leases.

Definition of Lease: Lease was defined to exclude leases intended as security (Section 2A-103(1)(j)). Given the litigation to date a revised definition of security interest was suggested for inclusion in the Act. (Section 1-201(37)). This revision sharpens the distinction between leases and security interests disguised as leases.

Filing: The lessor was not required to file a financing statement against the lessee or take any other action to protect the lessor's interest in the goods (Section 2A-301). The refined definition of security interest will more clearly signal the need to file to potential lessors of goods. Those lessors who are concerned will file a protective financing statement (Section 9-408).

Warranties: All of the express and implied warranties of the Article on Sales (Article 2) were included (Sections 2A-210 through 2A-216), revised to reflect differences in lease transactions. The lease of goods is sufficiently similar to the sale of goods to justify this decision. Further, many courts have reached the same decision.

Certificate of Title Laws: Many leasing transactions involve goods subject to certificate of title statutes. To avoid conflict with those statutes, this Article is subject to them (Section 2A-104(1)(a)).

Consumer Leases: Many leasing transactions involve parties subject to consumer protection statutes or decisions. To avoid conflict with those laws this Article is subject to them to the extent provided in

(Section 2A–104(1)(c) and (2)). Further, certain consumer protections have been incorporated in the Article.

Finance Leases: Certain leasing transactions substitute the supplier of the goods for the lessor as the party responsible to the lessee with respect to warranties and the like. The definition of finance lease (Section 2A–103(1)(g)) was developed to describe these transactions. Various sections of the Article implement the substitution of the supplier for the lessor, including Sections 2A–209 and 2A–407. No attempt was made to fashion a special rule where the finance lessor is an affiliate of the supplier of goods; this is to be developed by the courts, case by case.

Sale and Leaseback: Sale and leaseback transactions are becoming increasingly common. A number of state statutes treat transactions where possession is retained by the seller as fraudulent *per se* or *prima facie* fraudulent. That position is not in accord with modern practice and thus is changed by the Article "if the buyer bought for value and in good faith" (Section 2A–308(3)).

Remedies: The Article has not only provided for lessor's remedies upon default by the lessee (Sections 2A–523 through 2A–531), but also for lessee's remedies upon default by the lessor (Sections 2A–508 through 2A–522). This is a significant departure from Article 9, which provides remedies only for the secured party upon default by the debtor. This difference is compelled by the bilateral nature of the obligations between the parties to a lease.

Damages: Many leasing transactions are predicated on the parties' ability to stipulate an appropriate measure of damages in the event of default. The rule with respect to sales of goods (Section 2–718) is not sufficiently flexible to accommodate this practice. Consistent with the common law emphasis upon freedom to contract, the Article has created a revised rule that allows greater flexibility with respect to leases of goods (Section 2A–504(1)).

History:

This Article is a revision of the Uniform Personal Property Leasing Act, which was approved by the National Conference of Commissioners on Uniform State Laws in August, 1985. However, it was believed that the subject matter of the Uniform Personal Property Leasing Act would be better treated as an article of this Act. Thus, although the Conference promulgated the Uniform Personal Property Leasing Act as a Uniform Law, activity was held in abeyance to allow time to restate the Uniform Personal Property Leasing Act as Article 2A.

In August, 1986 the Conference approved and recommended this Article (including conforming amendments to Article 1 and Article 9) for promulgation as an amendment to this Act. In December, 1986 the Council of the American Law Institute approved and recommended this Article (including conforming amendments to Article 1 and Article 9), with official comments, for promulgation as an amendment to this Act. In March, 1987 the Permanent Editorial Board for the Uniform Commercial Code approved and recommended this Article (including conforming amendments to Article 1 and Article 9), with official comments, for promulgation as an amendment to this Act. In May, 1987 the American Law Institute approved and recommended this Article (including conforming amendments to Article 1 and Article 9), with official comments, for promulgation as an amendment to this Act. In August, 1987 the Conference confirmed its approval of the final text of this Article.

Upon its initial promulgation, Article 2A was rapidly enacted in several states, was introduced in a number of other states, and underwent bar association, law revision commission and legislative study in still further states. In that process debate emerged, principally sparked by the study of Article 2A by the California Bar Association, California's non-uniform amendments to Article 2A, and articles appearing in a symposium on Article 2A published after its promulgation in the Alabama Law Review. The debate chiefly centered on whether Article 2A had struck the proper balance or was clear enough concerning the ability of a lessor to grant a security interest in its leasehold interest and in the residual, priority between a secured party and the lessee, and the lessor's remedy structure under Article 2A.

This debate over issues on which reasonable minds could and did differ began to affect the enactment effort for Article 2A in a deleterious manner. Consequently, the Standby Committee for Article 2A, composed predominantly of the former members of the drafting committee, reviewed the legislative actions and studies in the various states, and opened a dialogue with the principal proponents of the non-uniform amendments. Negotiations were conducted in conjunction with, and were facilitated by, a study of the uniform Article and the non-uniform Amendments by the New York Law Revision Commission. Ultimately, a consensus was reached, which has been approved by the membership of the Conference, the Permanent Editorial Board, and the Council of the Institute. Rapid and uniform enactment of Article 2A is expected as a result of the completed amendments. The Article 2A experience reaffirms the essential viability of the procedures of the Conference and the Institute for creating and updating uniform state law in the commercial law area.

Relationship of Article 2A to Other Articles:

The Article on Sales provided a useful point of reference for codifying the law of leases. Many of the provisions of that Article were carried over, changed to reflect differences in style, leasing terminology or leasing practices. Thus, the official comments to those sections of Article 2 whose provisions were carried over are incorporated by reference in Article 2A, as well; further, any case law interpreting those provisions should be viewed as persuasive but not binding on a court when deciding a similar issue with respect to leases. Any change in the sequence that has been made when carrying over a provision from Article 2 should be viewed as a matter of style, not substance. This is not to suggest that in other instances Article 2A did not also incorporate substantially revised provisions of Article 2, Article 9 or otherwise where the revision was driven by a concern over the substance; but for the lack of a mandate, the drafting committee might well have made the same or a similar change in the statutory analogue. Those sections in Article 2A include Sections 2A–104, 2A–105, 2A–106, 2A–108(2) and (4), 2A–109(2), 2A–208, 2A–214(2) and (3)(a), 2A–216, 2A–303, 2A–306, 2A–503, 2A–504(3)(b), 2A–506(2), and 2A–515. For lack of relevance or significance not all of the provisions of Article 2 were incorporated in Article 2A.

This codification was greatly influenced by the fundamental tenet of the common law as it has developed with respect to leases of goods: freedom of the parties to contract. Note that, like all other Articles of this Act, the principles of construction and interpretation contained in Article 1 are applicable throughout Article 2A (Section 2A–103(4)). These principles include the ability of the parties to vary the effect of the provisions of Article 2A, subject to certain limitations including those that relate to the obligations of good faith, diligence, reasonableness and care (Section 1–102(3)). Consistent with those principles no negative inference is to be drawn by the episodic use of the phrase "unless otherwise agreed" in certain provisions of Article 2A. Section 1–102(4). Indeed, the contrary is true, as the general rule in the Act, including this Article, is that the effect of the Act's provisions may be varied by agreement. Section 1–102(3). This conclusion follows even where the statutory analogue contains the phrase and the correlative provision in Article 2A does not.

2003 AMENDMENTS TO

UNIFORM COMMERCIAL CODE
ARTICLE 2A–LEASES

The Drafting Committee was charged with making changes to Article 2A where appropriate to incorporate amendments to Article 2, also being considered at this time, and also with making changes to the Article necessitated by the recent revision of Article 9. It is anticipated that the amendments to Articles 2 and 2A will be presented to the state legislatures as a single package.

As with original Article 2A, these amendments are intended to reflect the distinctive nature of leasing as a commercial transaction. Therefore the following principles should be considered in applying this Article:

Leasing is Distinctive From Other Commercial Transactions

Leasing is a distinct commercial transaction which is different in many respects from either the sale or the secured financing of goods. A true lease of goods involves the payment for the temporary possession, use and enjoyment of goods, and a lease is entered into with an expectation that the goods will be returned to the owner at the end of the lease term. In contrast, a sale of goods involves a transfer of title for a price, and a security interest involves an interest in the goods that is limited to the remaining secured debt. The separation of ownership and possession in a lease of goods as well as other considerations can result in many differences between the law of leases and the law for the sale of goods. These differences include remedies and, to some extent, contract formation and warranties.

Lease Contract Formation

Leases often involve complex, on-going, multi-faceted obligations. Ownership of the residual remains with the lessor, and for that reason the lessor has a continuing economic interest in the goods that is not present in a sale. Therefore, lease contracts commonly cover many matters other than the lessor's duty to provide the goods and the lessee's duty to pay rent. These include where and when the goods will be returned to the lessor; options to renew the lease or purchase the goods; maintenance and repairs; restrictions on use of the goods; taxes, insurance; and record keeping. For these reasons, leasing custom and practice favors formal, structured rules of contract formation and greater usage, particularly in commercial leases, of a record of the parties' agreement embodying their understanding.

Warranties

Because of the manner in which leased goods are promoted and distributed–for example, lessors generally do not engage in mass-market advertising aimed at, or make representations in materials to be delivered to, remote lessees–amended Article 2A does not contain provisions analogous to Sections 2–313A and 2–313B of amended Article 2. Though nothing in this Article precludes, in an appropriate case, the application of the principles contained in those sections to a lease transaction, a lessor is responsible only for the lessor's representations and those of the lessor's agents and the lessor is not for the representations made by a third party, such as the supplier or manufacturer of the goods. In addition, a lessee may have the right as a "remote purchaser" under Article 2 to assert claims under Sections 2–313A and 2–313B directly against a manufacturer or supplier that has engaged in advertising.

Damages

The typical measure of damages for breach of a lease differs from that applied in the law that governs the sale of goods in that, for breach of a lease contract by the lessee, the present value of an ongoing stream of rental payments normally must be taken into consideration as well as the lessor's rights to return of the goods with a certain residual value. As a result, if the goods are sold following a default by the lessee, in calculating the lessee's deficiency, the value of the lessor's residual interest should be excluded from the disposition proceeds that are credited to the lessee.

As amended in 1990, 2003 and 2005.

§ 2A–102. Scope.

This Article applies to any transaction, regardless of form, that creates a lease.

Official Comment

Uniform Statutory Source: Section 9–102(1). Throughout this Article, unless otherwise stated, references to "Section" are to other sections of this Act.

Changes: Substantially revised.

Purposes: This Article governs transactions as diverse as the lease of a hand tool to an individual for a few hours and the leveraged lease of a complex line of industrial equipment to a multi-national organization for a number of years.

To achieve that end it was necessary to provide that this Article applies to any transaction, regardless of form, that creates a lease. Since lease is defined as a transfer of an interest in goods (Section 2A–103(1)(j))

and goods is defined to include fixtures (Section 2A–103(1)(h)), application is limited to the extent the transaction relates to goods, including fixtures. Further, since the definition of lease does not include a sale (Section 2–106(1)) or retention or creation of a security interest (Section 1–201(37)), application is further limited; sales and security interests are governed by other Articles of this Act.

Finally, in recognition of the diversity of the transactions to be governed, the sophistication of many of the parties to these transactions, and the common law tradition as it applies to the bailment for hire or lease, freedom of contract has been preserved. DeKoven, Proceedings After Default by the Lessee Under a True Lease of Equipment, in 1C P. Coogan, W. Hogan, D. Vagts, *Secured Transactions Under the Uniform Commercial Code*, § 29B.02[2] (1986). Thus, despite the extensive regulatory scheme established by this Article, the parties to a lease will be able to create private rules to govern their transaction. Sections 2A–103(4) and 1–102(3). However, there are special rules in this Article governing consumer leases, as well as other state and federal statutes, that may further limit freedom of contract with respect to consumer leases.

A court may apply this Article by analogy to any transaction, regardless of form, that creates a lease of personal property other than goods, taking into account the expressed intentions of the parties to the transaction and any differences between a lease of goods and a lease of other property. Such application has precedent as the provisions of the Article on Sales (Article 2) have been applied by analogy to leases of goods. *E.g.*, Hawkland, *The Impact of the Uniform Commercial Code on Equipment Leasing*, 1972 Ill.L.F. 446; Murray, *Under the Spreading Analogy of Article 2 of the Uniform Commercial Code*, 39 Fordham L.Rev. 447 (1971). Whether such application would be appropriate for other bailments of personal property, gratuitous or for hire, should be determined by the facts of each case. *See Mieske v. Bartell Drug Co.*, 92 Wash.2d 40, 46–48, 593 P.2d 1308, 1312 (1979).

Further, parties to a transaction creating a lease of personal property other than goods, or a bailment of personal property may provide by agreement that this Article applies. Upholding the parties' choice is consistent with the spirit of this Article.

Definitional Cross Reference:

"Lease". Section 2A–103(1)(p).

§ 2A–103. Definitions and Index of Definitions.

(1) In this Article, unless the context otherwise requires:

(a) "Cancellation" occurs when either party puts an end to the lease contract for default by the other party.

(b) "Commercial unit" means such a unit of goods as by commercial usage is a single whole for purposes of lease and division of which materially impairs its character or value on the market or in use. A commercial unit may be a single article, as a machine, or a set of articles, as a suite of furniture or a line of machinery, or a quantity, as a gross or carload, or any other unit treated in use or in the relevant market as a single whole.

(c) "Conforming" goods or performance under a lease contract means goods or performance that are in accordance with the obligations under the lease contract.

(d) "Conspicuous", with reference to a term, means so written, displayed, or presented that a reasonable person against which it is to operate ought to have noticed it. A term in an electronic record intended to evoke a response by an electronic agent is conspicuous if it is presented in a form that would enable a reasonably configured electronic agent to take it into account or react to it without review of the record by an individual. Whether a term is "conspicuous" or not is a decision for the court. Conspicuous terms include the following:

(i) for a person:

(A) a heading in capitals equal to or greater in size than the surrounding text, or in contrasting type, font, or color to the surrounding text of the same or lesser size; and

(B) language in the body of a record or display in larger type than the surrounding text, or in contrasting type, font, or color to the surrounding text of the same size, or set off from surrounding text of the same size by symbols or other marks that call attention to the language; and

(ii) for a person or an electronic agent, a term that is so placed in a record or display that the person or electronic agent cannot proceed without taking action with respect to the particular term.

(e) "Consumer" means an individual who leases or contracts to lease goods that, at the time of contracting, are intended by the individual to be used primarily for personal, family, or household purposes.

(f) "Consumer lease" means a lease that a lessor regularly engaged in the business of leasing or selling makes to a consumer.

Legislative Note: Present Article 2A has a bracketed provision allowing States to insert a dollar cap on leases designated as consumer leases, amended Article 2 defines "consumer contract" and does not include a dollar cap in the definition. Some States have not included a dollar cap in present Article 2A and States which have adopted a dollar cap have stated varying amounts. If a State wishes to include a dollar cap, the cap should be inserted here. Any cap probably should be set high enough to bring within the definition most automobile leasing transactions for personal, family, or household use.

(g) "Delivery" means the voluntary transfer of physical possession or control of goods.

(h) "Electronic" means relating to technology having electrical, digital, magnetic, wireless, optical, electromagnetic, or similar capabilities.

(i) "Electronic agent" means a computer program or an electronic or other automated means used independently to initiate an action or respond to electronic records or performances in whole or in part, without review or action by an individual.

(j) "Electronic record" means a record created, generated, sent, communicated, received, or stored by electronic means.

(k) "Fault" means wrongful act, omission, breach, or default.

(l) "Finance lease" means a lease with respect to which:

(i) the lessor does not select, manufacture, or supply the goods;

(ii) the lessor acquires the goods or the right to possession and use of the goods in connection with the lease or, in the case of goods that have been leased previously by the lessor and are not being leased to a consumer, in connection with another lease; and

(iii) one of the following occurs:

(A) the lessee receives a copy of the agreement by which the lessor acquired, or proposes to acquire, the goods or the right to possession and use of the goods before signing the lease agreement;

(B) the lessee's approval of the agreement or of the general contractual terms under which the lessor acquired or proposes to acquire the goods or the right to possession and use of the goods is a condition to the effectiveness of the lease contract;

(C) the lessee, before signing the lease agreement, receives an accurate and complete statement designating the promises and warranties, and any disclaimers of warranties, limitations or modifications of remedies, or liquidated damages, including those of a third party, such as the manufacturer of the goods, provided to the lessor by the person supplying the goods in connection with or as part of the contract by which the lessor acquired the goods or the right to possession and use of the goods; or

(D) if the lease is not a consumer lease, before the lessee signs the lease agreement, the lessor informs the lessee in a record:

(I) of the identity of the person supplying the goods to the lessor, unless the lessee has selected that person and directed the lessor to acquire the goods or the right to possession and use of the goods from that person;

(II) that the lessee is entitled under this article to the promises and warranties, including those of any third party, provided to the lessor by the person supplying the goods in connection with or as part of the contract by which the lessor acquired

the goods or the right to possession and use of the goods; and

(III) that the lessee may communicate with the person supplying the goods to the lessor and receive an accurate and complete statement of those promises and warranties, including any disclaimers and limitations of them, or a statement of remedies.

[(m) "Good faith" means honesty in fact and the observance of reasonable commercial standards of fair dealing.]

Legislative Note: Definition (m) should not be adopted if the jurisdiction has enacted the equivalent provision in the 2001 Revised Article 1.

(n) "Goods" means all things that are movable at the time of identification to a lease contract or that are fixtures (Section 2A–309). The term includes future goods, specially manufactured goods, and the unborn young of animals. The term does not include information, the money in which the price is to be paid, investment securities under Article 8, or choses in action.

(o) "Installment lease contract" means a lease contract that authorizes or requires the delivery of goods in separate lots to be separately accepted, even though the lease contract contains a clause "each delivery is a separate lease" or its equivalent.

(p) "Lease" means a transfer of the right to possession and use of goods for a period in return for consideration, but a sale, including a sale on approval or a sale or return, retention or creation of a security interest, or license of information is not a lease. Unless the context clearly indicates otherwise, the term includes a sublease.

(q) "Lease agreement", as distinguished from "lease contract", means the bargain, with respect to the lease, of the lessor and the lessee in fact as found in their language or inferred from other circumstances including course of performance, course of dealing , or usage of trade as provided in Section 1–303. Unless the context clearly indicates otherwise, the term includes a sublease agreement.

(r) "Lease contract", as distinguished from "lease agreement", means the total legal obligation that results from the lease agreement as determined by the [Uniform Commercial Code] as supplemented by any other applicable rules of law. Unless the context clearly indicates otherwise, the term includes a sublease contract.

(s) "Leasehold interest" means the interest of the lessor or the lessee under a lease contract.

(t) "Lessee" means a person that acquires the right to possession and use of goods under a lease. Unless the context clearly indicates otherwise, the term includes a sublessee.

(u) "Lessee in ordinary course of business" means a person that leases goods in good faith, without knowledge that the lease violates the rights of another person, and in the ordinary course from a person, other than a pawnbroker, in the business of selling or leasing goods of that kind. A person leases in ordinary course if the lease to the person comports with the usual or customary practices in the kind of business in which the lessor is engaged or with the lessor's own usual or customary practices. A lessee in ordinary course of business may lease for cash, by exchange of other property, or on secured or unsecured credit, and may acquire goods or documents of title under a preexisting lease contract. Only a lessee that takes possession of the goods or has a right to recover the goods from the lessor under this article may be a lessee in ordinary course of business. A person that acquires goods in a transfer in bulk or as security for or in total or partial satisfaction of a money debt is not a lessee in ordinary course of business.

(v) "Lessor" means a person that transfers the right to possession and use of goods under a lease. Unless the context clearly indicates otherwise, the term includes a sublessor.

(w) "Lessor's residual interest" means the lessor's interest in the goods after expiration, termination, or cancellation of the lease contract.

(x) "Lien" means a charge against or interest in goods to secure payment of a debt or

performance of an obligation. The term does not include a security interest.

(y) "Lot" means a parcel or a single article that is the subject matter of a separate lease or delivery, whether or not it is sufficient to perform the lease contract.

(z) "Merchant lessee" means a lessee that is a merchant with respect to goods of the kind subject to the lease.

(aa) "Present value" means the amount as of a date certain of one or more sums payable in the future, discounted to the date certain by use of either an interest rate specified by the parties if that rate is not manifestly unreasonable at the time the transaction is entered into or, if an interest rate is not so specified, a commercially reasonable rate that takes into account the facts and circumstances at the time the transaction is entered into.

Legislative Note: Definition (aa) should not be adopted if the jurisdiction has enacted the equivalent provision in the 2001 Revised Article 1.

(bb) "Purchase" includes taking by sale, lease, mortgage, security interest, pledge, gift, or any other voluntary transaction creating an interest in goods.

Legislative Note: Definition (bb) should not be adopted if the jurisdiction has enacted the equivalent provision in the 2001 Revised Article 1.

(cc) "Record" means information that is inscribed on a tangible medium or that is stored in an electronic or other medium and is retrievable in perceivable form.

Legislative Note: Definition (cc) should not be adopted if the jurisdiction has enacted the equivalent provision in the 2001 Revised Article 1.

(dd) "Sign" means, with present intent to authenticate or adopt a record,

(i) to execute or adopt a tangible symbol; or

(ii) to attach to or logically associate with the record an electronic sound, symbol, or process.

(ee) "Sublease" means a lease of goods the right to possession and use of which was acquired by the lessor as a lessee under an existing lease.

(ff) "Supplier" means a person from which a lessor buys or leases goods to be leased under a finance lease.

(gg) "Supply contract" means a contract under which a lessor buys or leases goods to be leased.

(hh) "Termination" occurs when either party pursuant to a power created by agreement or law puts an end to the lease contract otherwise than for default.

(2) Other definitions applying to this Article and the sections in which they appear are:
"Accessions". Section 2A–310(1).
"Construction mortgage". Section 2A–309(1)(d).
"Encumbrance". Section 2A–309(1)(e).
"Fixtures". Section 2A–309(1)(a).
"Fixture filing". Section 2A–309(1)(b).
"Purchase money lease". Section 2A–309(1)(c).

(3) The following definitions in other Articles apply to this Article:
"Between merchants". Section 2–104(3).
"Buyer". Section 2–103(1)(a).
"Consumer goods". Section 9–109(1).
"Entrusting". Section 2–403(3).
"Letter of credit". Section 5–102(a)(10).
"Merchant". Section 2–104(1).
"Receipt of goods". Section 2–103(1)(c).
"Sale". Section 2–106(1).
"Sale on approval". Section 2–326.
"Sale or return". Section 2–326.
"Seller". Section 2–103(1)(n).

(4) In addition Article 1 contains general definitions and principles of construction and interpretation applicable throughout this Article.

As amended in 1990, 1999, 2001 and 2003.

Official Comment

Note from Advisory Panel: The Official Comment was not amended to conform to all of the 2003 changes in text.

(a) The definition of "Buyer in ordinary course of business" is in Article 1 (Section 1–201(9)). It was amended as part of the Article 9 revision process, and revised Article 1 is consistent with the Article 9 amendment.

(b) "Cancellation". Section 2–106(4). The effect of a cancellation is provided in Section 2A–505(1).

(c) "Commercial unit". Section 2–105(6).

(d) "Conforming". Section 2–106(2).

(e) "Consumer lease". New. This Article includes a subset of rules that applies only to consumer leases. Sections 2A–106, 2A–108(2), 2A–108(4), 2A–109(2), 2A–221, 2A–309, 2A–406, 2A–407, 2A–504(3)(b), and 2A–516(3)(b).

For a transaction to qualify as a consumer lease it must first qualify as a lease. Section 2A–103(1)(j). Note that this Article regulates the transactional elements of a lease, including a consumer lease; consumer protection statutes, present and future, and existing consumer protection decisions are unaffected by this Article. Section 2A–104(1)(c) and (2). Of course, Article 2A as state law also is subject to federal consumer protection law.

This definition is modeled after the definition of consumer lease in the Consumer Leasing Act, 15 U.S.C. § 1667 (1982), and in the Unif. Consumer Credit Code § 1.301(14), 7A U.L.A. 43 (1974). However, this definition of consumer lease differs from its models in several respects: the lessor can be a person regularly engaged either in the business of leasing or of selling goods, the lease need not be for a term exceeding four months, a lease primarily for an agricultural purpose is not covered, and whether there should be a limitation by dollar amount and its amount is left up to the individual states.

This definition focuses on the parties as well as the transaction. If a lease is within this definition, the lessor must be regularly engaged in the business of leasing or selling, and the lessee must be an individual, not an organization; note that a lease to two or more individuals having a common interest through marriage or the like is not excluded as a lease to an organization under Section 1–201(28). The lessee must take the interest primarily for a personal, family or household purpose. If required by the enacting state, total payments under the lease contract, excluding payments for options to renew or buy, cannot exceed the figure designated.

(f) "Fault". Section 1–201(16).

(g) For a transaction to qualify as a finance lease it must first qualify as a lease. Unless the lessor is comfortable that the transaction will qualify as a finance lease, the lease agreement should include provisions giving the lessor the benefits created by the subset of rules applicable to the transaction that qualifies as a finance lease under this Article.

A finance lease is the product of a three party transaction. The supplier manufactures or supplies the goods pursuant to the lessee's specification, perhaps even pursuant to a purchase order, sales agreement or lease agreement between the supplier and the lessee. After the prospective finance lease is negotiated, a purchase order, sales agreement, or lease agreement is entered into by the lessor (as buyer or prime lessee) or an existing order, agreement or lease is assigned by the lessee to the lessor, and the lessor and the lessee then enter into a lease or sublease of the goods. Due to the limited function usually performed by the lessor, the lessee looks almost entirely to the supplier for representations, covenants and warranties. If a manufacturer's warranty carries through, the lessee may also look to that. Yet, this definition does not restrict the lessor's function solely to the supply of funds; if the lessor undertakes or performs other functions, express warranties, covenants and the common law will protect the lessee.

This definition focuses on the transaction, not the status of the parties; to avoid confusion it is important to note that in other contexts, *e.g.*, tax and accounting, the term finance lease has been used to connote different types of lease transactions, including leases that are disguised secured transactions. M. Rice, *Equipment Financing*, 62–71 (1981). A lessor who is a merchant with respect to goods of the kind subject to the lease may be a lessor under a finance lease. Many leases that are leases back to the seller of goods (Section 2A–308(3)) will be finance leases. This conclusion is easily demonstrated by a hypothetical. Assume that B has bought goods from C pursuant to a sales contract. After delivery to and acceptance of the goods by B, B negotiates to sell the goods to A and simultaneously to lease the goods back from A, on terms and conditions that, we assume, will qualify the transaction as a lease. In documenting the sale and lease back, B assigns the original sales contract between B, as buyer, and C, as seller, to A. A review of these facts leads to the conclusion that the lease from A to B qualifies as a finance lease, as all three conditions of the definition are satisfied. Subparagraph (i) is satisfied as A, the lessor, had nothing to do with the selection, manufacture, or supply of the equipment. Subparagraph (ii) is satisfied as A, the lessor, bought the equipment at the same time that A leased the equipment to B, which certainly is in connection with the lease. Finally, subparagraph (iii)(A) is satisfied as A entered into the sales contract with B at the same time that A leased the equipment back to B. B, the lessee, will have received a copy of the sales contract in a timely fashion.

Subparagraph (i) requires the lessor to remain outside the selection, manufacture and supply of the goods; that is the rationale for releasing the lessor from most of its traditional liability. The lessor is not prohibited from possession, maintenance or operation of the goods, as policy does not require such prohibition. To insure the lessee's reliance on the supplier, and not on the lessor, subparagraph (ii) requires that the goods (where the lessor is the buyer of the goods) or that the right to possession and use of the goods (where the lessor is the prime lessee and the sublessor of the goods) be acquired in connection with the lease (or sublease) to qualify as a finance lease. The scope of the phrase "in connection with" is to be developed by the courts, case by case. Finally, as the lessee generally relies almost entirely upon the supplier for representations and covenants, and upon the supplier or a manufacturer, or both, for warranties with respect to the goods, subparagraph (iii) requires that one of the following occur: (A) the lessee receive a copy of the supply contract before signing the lease contract; (B) the lessee's approval of the supply contract is a condition to the effectiveness of the lease contract; (C) the lessee receive a statement describing the promises and warranties and any limitations relevant to the lessee before signing the lease contract; or (D) before signing the lease contract and except in a consumer lease, the lessee receive a writing identifying the supplier (unless the supplier was selected and required by the lessee) and the rights of the lessee under Section 2A–303, and advising the lessee a statement of promises and warranties is available from the supplier. Thus, even where oral supply orders or computer placed supply orders are compelled by custom and usage the transaction may still qualify as a finance lease if the lessee approves the supply contract before the lease contract is effective and such approval was a condition to the effectiveness of the lease contract. Moreover, where the lessor does not want the lessee to see the entire supply contract, including price information, the lessee may be provided with a separate statement of the terms of the supply contract relevant to the lessee; promises between the supplier and the lessor that do not affect the lessee need not be included. The statement can be a restatement of those terms or a copy of portions of the supply contract with the relevant terms clearly designated. Any implied warranties need not be designated, but a disclaimer or modification of remedy must be designated. A copy of any manufacturer's warranty is sufficient if that is the warranty provided. However, a copy of any Regulation M disclosure given pursuant to 12 C.F.R. § 213.4(g) concerning warranties in itself is not sufficient since those disclosures need only briefly identify express warranties and need not include any disclaimer of warranty.

Under subparagraphs (ii) and (iii), except when the new lease is to a consumer lessee, a finance lessor can have that status on re-leasing the property after it is returned from an original lease. However, in that case, the other elements required for the lease to be a finance lessee must be complied with.

If a transaction does not qualify as a finance lease, the parties may achieve the same result by agreement; no negative implications are to be drawn if the transaction does not qualify. Further, absent the application of special rules (fraud, duress, and the like), a lease that qualifies as a finance lease and is assigned by the lessor or the lessee to a third party does not lose its status as a finance lease under this Article. Finally, this Article creates no special rule where the lessor is an affiliate of the supplier; whether the transaction qualifies as a finance lease will be determined by the facts of each case.

(h) "Goods". Section 9–105(1)(h). See Section 2A–103(3) for reference to the definition of "Account", "Chattel paper", "Document", "General intangibles" and "Instrument". See Section 2A–217 for determination of the time and manner of identification.

(i) "Installment lease contract". Section 2–612(1).

(j) "Lease". New. There are several reasons to codify the law with respect to leases of goods. An analysis of the case law as it applies to leases of goods suggests at least several significant issues to be resolved by codification. First and foremost is the definition of a lease. It is necessary to define lease to determine whether a transaction creates a lease or a security interest disguised as a lease. If the transaction creates a security interest disguised as a lease, the transaction will be governed by the Article on Secured Transactions (Article 9) and the lessor will be required to file a financing statement or take other action to perfect its interest in the goods against third parties. There is no such requirement with respect to leases under the common law and, except with respect to leases of fixtures (Section 2A–309), this Article imposes no such requirement. Yet the distinction between a lease and a security interest disguised as a lease is not clear from the case law at the time of the promulgation of this Article. DeKoven, *Leases of Equipment: Puritan Leasing Company v. August, A Dangerous Decision*, 12 U.S.F. L.Rev. 257 (1978).

At common law a lease of personal property is a bailment for hire. While there are several definitions of bailment for hire, all require a thing to be let and a price for the letting. Thus, in modern terms and as

provided in this definition, a lease is created when the lessee agrees to furnish consideration for the right to the possession and use of goods over a specified period of time. Mooney, *Personal Property Leasing: A Challenge*, 36 Bus.Law. 1605, 1607 (1981). Further, a lease is neither a sale (Section 2–106(1)) nor a retention or creation of a security interest (Section 1–201(37)). Due to extensive litigation to distinguish true leases from security interests, an amendment to Section 1–201(37) has been promulgated with this Article to create a sharper distinction.

This section as well as Section 1–201(37) must be examined to determine whether the transaction in question creates a lease or a security interest. The following hypotheticals indicate the perimeters of the issue. Assume that A has purchased a number of copying machines, new, for $1,000 each; the machines have an estimated useful economic life of three years. A advertises that the machines are available to rent for a minimum of one month and that the monthly rental is $100.00. A intends to enter into leases where A provides all maintenance, without charge to the lessee. Further, the lessee will rent the machine, month to month, with no obligation to renew. At the end of the lease term the lessee will be obligated to return the machine to A's place of business. This transaction qualifies as a lease under the first half of the definition, for the transaction includes a transfer by A to a prospective lessee of possession and use of the machine for a stated term, month to month. The machines are goods (Section 2A–103(1)(h)). The lessee is obligated to pay consideration in return, $100.00 for each month of the term.

However, the second half of the definition provides that a sale or a security interest is not a lease. Since there is no passing of title, there is no sale. Sections 2A–103(3) and 2–106(1). Under pre-Act security law this transaction would have created a bailment for hire or a true lease and not a conditional sale. *Da Rocha v. Macomber*, 330 Mass. 611, 614–15, 116 N.E.2d 139, 142 (1953). Under Section 1–201(37), as amended with the promulgation of this Article, the same result would follow. While the lessee is obligated to pay rent for the one month term of the lease, one of the other four conditions of the second paragraph of Section 1–201(37) must be met and none is. The term of the lease is one month and the economic life of the machine is 36 months; thus, subparagraph (a) of Section 1–201(37) is not now satisfied. Considering the amount of the monthly rent, absent economic duress or coercion, the lessee is not bound either to renew the lease for the remaining economic life of the goods or to become the owner. If the lessee did lease the machine for 36 months, the lessee would have paid the lessor $3,600 for a machine that could have been purchased for $1,000; thus, subparagraph (b) of Section 1–201(37) is not satisfied. Finally, there are no options; thus, subparagraphs (c) and (d) of Section 1–201(37) are not satisfied. This transaction creates a lease, not a security interest. However, with each renewal of the lease the facts and circumstances at the time of each renewal must be examined to determine if that conclusion remains accurate, as it is possible that a transaction that first creates a lease, later creates a security interest.

Assume that the facts are changed and that A requires each lessee to lease the goods for 36 months, with no right to terminate. Under pre-Act security law this transaction would have created a conditional sale, and not a bailment for hire or true lease. *Hervey v. Rhode Island Locomotive Works*, 93 U.S. 664, 672–73 (1876). Under this subsection, and Section 1–201(37), as amended with the inclusion of this Article in the Act, the same result would follow. The lessee's obligation for the term is not subject to termination by the lessee and the term is equal to the economic life of the machine.

Between these extremes there are many transactions that can be created. Some of the transactions have not been properly categorized by the courts in applying the 1978 and earlier Official Texts of Section 1–201(37). This subsection, together with Section 1–201(37), as amended with the promulgation of this Article, draws a brighter line, which should create a clearer signal to the professional lessor and lessee.

(k) "Lease agreement". This definition is derived from the first sentence of Section 1–201(3). Because the definition of lease is broad enough to cover future transfers, lease agreement includes an agreement contemplating a current or subsequent transfer. Thus it was not necessary to make an express reference to an agreement for the future lease of goods (Section 2–106(1)). This concept is also incorporated in the definition of lease contract. Note that the definition of lease does not include transactions in ordinary building materials that are incorporated into an improvement on land. Section 2A–309(2).

The provisions of this Article, if applicable, determine whether a lease agreement has legal consequences; otherwise the law of bailments and other applicable law determine the same. Sections 2A–103(4) and 1–103.

(l) "Lease contract". This definition is derived from the definition of contract in Section 1–201(11). Note

that a lease contract may be for the future lease of goods, since this notion is included in the definition of lease.

(m) "Leasehold interest". New.

(n) "Lessee". New.

(o) The definition of "Lessee in ordinary course of business" conforms with amendments to Section 1–201(9)(buyer in ordinary course of business) that were part of the Article 9 revision process (with the omission of the reference to sales of minerals).

(p) "Lessor". New.

(q) "Lessor's residual interest". New.

(r) "Lien". New. This term is used in Section 2A–307 (Priority of Liens Arising by Attachment or Levy on, Security Interests in, and Other Claims to Goods).

(s) "Lot". Section 2–105(5).

(t) "Merchant lessee". New. This term is used in Section 2A–511 (Merchant Lessee's Duties as to Rightfully Rejected Goods). A person may satisfy the requirement of dealing in goods of the kind subject to the lease as lessor, lessee, seller, or buyer.

(u) "Present value". New. Authorities agree that present value should be used to determine fairly the damages payable by the lessor or the lessee on default. *E.g., Taylor v. Commercial Credit Equip. Corp.*, 170 Ga.App. 322, 316 S.E.2d 788 (1984). Present value is defined to mean an amount that represents the discounted value as of a date certain of one or more sums payable in the future. This is a function of the economic principle that a dollar today is more valuable to the holder than a dollar payable in two years. While there is no question as to the principle, reasonable people would differ as to the rate of discount to apply in determining the value of that future dollar today. To minimize litigation, this Article allows the parties to specify the discount or interest rate, if the rate was not manifestly unreasonable at the time the transaction was entered into. In all other cases, the interest rate will be a commercially reasonable rate that takes into account the facts and circumstances of each case, as of the time the transaction was entered into.

(v) "Purchase". Section 1–201(32). This definition omits the reference to lien contained in the definition of purchase in Article 1 (Section 1–201(32)). This should not be construed to exclude consensual liens from the definition of purchase in this Article; the exclusion was mandated by the scope of the definition of lien in Section 2A–103(1)(r). Further, the definition of purchaser in this Article adds a reference to lease; as purchase is defined in Section 1–201(32) to include any other voluntary transaction creating an interest in property, this addition is not substantive.

(w) "Sublease". New.

(x) "Supplier". New.

(y) "Supply contract". New.

(z) "Termination". Section 2–106(3). The effect of a termination is provided in Section 2A–505(2).

As amended in 2001, 2003 and 2005.

§ 2A–104. Leases Subject to Other Law.

(1) A lease subject to this Article, is also subject to any applicable:

(a) [list any certificate of title statutes covering automobiles, trailers, mobile homes, boats, farm tractors, or the like;]

(b) certificate of title statute of another jurisdiction (Section 2A–105); or

(c) rule of law that establishes a different rule for consumers.

(2) To the extent there is a conflict between this Article, other than Sections 2A–105, 2A–304(3), and 2A–305(3), and a law referred to in subsection (1), that law governs.

(3) For purposes of this Article, failure to comply with a law referred to in subsection (1) has only the effect specified in that law.

(4) This article modifies, limits, and supersedes the federal Electronic Signatures in Global and National Commerce Act, 15 U.S.C. Section 7001 et seq., except that nothing in this article modifies, limits, or supersedes Section 7001(c) of that Act or authorizes electronic delivery of any of the notices described in Section 7003(b) of that Act.

As amended in 1990 and 2003.

Official Comment

Uniform Statutory Source: Sections 9–203(4) and 9–302(3)(b) and (c).

Changes: Substantially revised.

Purposes:

1. This Article creates a comprehensive scheme for the regulation of transactions that create leases. Section 2A–102. Thus, the Article supersedes all prior legislation dealing with leases, except to the extent set forth in this Section.

2. Subsection (1) states the general rule that a lease, although governed by the scheme of this Article, also may be governed by certain other applicable laws. This may occur in the case of a consumer lease. Section 2A–103(1)(e). Those laws may be state statutes existing prior to enactment of Article 2A or passed afterward. In this case, it is desirable for this Article to specify which statute controls. Or the law may be a pre-existing consumer protection decision. This Article preserves such decisions. Or the law may be a statute of the United States. Such a law controls without any statement in this Article under applicable principles of preemption.

An illustration of a statute of the United States that governs consumer leases is the Consumer Leasing Act, 15 U.S.C. §§ 1667–1667(e) (1982) and its implementing regulation, Regulation M, 12 C.F.R. § 213 (1986); the statute mandates disclosures of certain lease terms, delimits the liability of a lessee in leasing personal property, and regulates the advertising of lease terms. An illustration of a state statute that governs consumer leases and which if adopted in the enacting state prevails over this Article is the Unif. Consumer Credit Code, which includes many provisions similar to those of the Consumer Leasing Act, e.g. Unif. Consumer Credit Code §§ 3.202, 3.209, 3.401, 7A U.L.A. 108–09, 115, 125 (1974), as well as provisions in addition to those of the Consumer Leasing Act, e.g., Unif. Consumer Credit Code §§ 5.109–.111, 7A U.L.A. 171–76 (1974) (the right to cure a default). Such statutes may define consumer lease so as to govern transactions within and without the definition of consumer lease under this Article.

3. Under subsection (2), subject to certain limited exclusions, in case of conflict a statute or a decision described in subsection (1) prevails over this Article. For example, a provision like Unif. Consumer Credit Code § 5.112, 7A U.L.A. 176 (1974), limiting self-help repossession, prevails over Section 2A–525(3). A consumer protection decision rendered after the effective date of this Article may supplement its provisions. For example, in relation to Article 9 a court might conclude that an acceleration clause may not be enforced against an individual debtor after late payments have been accepted unless a prior notice of default is given. To the extent the decision establishes a general principle applicable to transactions other than secured transactions, it may supplement Section 2A–502.

4. Consumer protection in lease transactions is primarily left to other law. However, several provisions of this Article do contain special rules that may not be varied by agreement in the case of a consumer lease. *E.g.*, Sections 2A–106, 2A–108, and 2A–109(2). Were

that not so, the ability of the parties to govern their relationship by agreement together with the position of the lessor in a consumer lease too often could result in a one-sided lease agreement.

5. In construing this provision the reference to statute should be deemed to include applicable regulations. A consumer protection decision is "final" on the effective date of this Article if it is not subject to appeal on that date or, if subject to appeal, is not later reversed on appeal. Of course, such a decision can be overruled by a later decision or superseded by a later statute.

6. Subsection (4) takes advantage of a provision of the federal Electronic Signatures in Global and National Commerce Act (E-Sign). E-Sign permits state law to modify, limit or supersede its provisions if the state law is consistent with Titles I and II of E-Sign, gives no special legal effect or validity to and does not require the implementation or application of specific technologies or technical specifications, and if enacted subsequent to E-Sign makes specific reference to E-Sign. Subsection (4) does not apply to section 101(c) of E-Sign, nor does it authorize electronic delivery of the notices described in section 103(b) of E-Sign.

Cross References:

Point 3: Section 2A-525.
Point 4: Sections 2A-106, 2A-108 and 2A-109.

Definitional Cross Reference:

"Lease". Section 2A-103(1)(p).

As amended in 2003.

§ 2A-105.   Territorial Application of Article to Goods Covered by Certificate of Title.

(1) This section applies to goods covered by a certificate of title, even if there is no other relationship between the jurisdiction under whose certificate of title the goods are covered and the goods or the lessee or lessor.

(2) Goods become covered by a certificate of title when a valid application for the certificate of title and the application fee are delivered to the appropriate authority. Goods cease to be covered by a certificate of title at the earlier of the time the certificate of title ceases to be effective under the law of the issuing jurisdiction or the time the goods become covered subsequently by a certificate of title issued by another jurisdiction.

(3) Subject to Sections 2A-304(3) and 2A-305(3), with respect to goods covered by a certificate of title under a statute of this State or of another jurisdiction, compliance and the effect of compliance or noncompliance with the certificate-of-title statute are governed by the local law of the jurisdiction whose certificate of title covers the goods from the time the goods become covered by the certificate until the goods cease to be covered by the certificate of title.

As amended in 2003.

Official Comment

Uniform Statutory Source: Former Section 9-103(2)(a) and (b) (now codified as Sections 9-303 and 9-316).

Changes: Substantially revised. The provisions of the last sentence of former Section 9-103(2)(b) were not incorporated as they are superfluous in this context. The provisions of former Section 9-103(2)(d) were not incorporated because the problems dealt with are adequately addressed by this section and Sections 2A-304(3) and 305(3)

Purposes: The new certificate referred to in (2) must be permanent, not temporary. Generally, the lessor or creditor whose interest is indicated on the most recently issued certificate of title will prevail over interests indicated on certificates issued previously by other jurisdictions. This provision reflects a policy that it is reasonable to require holders of interests in goods covered by a certificate of title to police the goods or risk losing their interests when a new certificate of title is issued by another jurisdiction.

Cross References:

Sections 2A-304(3), 2A-305(3), and Sections 9-303, 9-316 and 9-337.

Definitional Cross Reference:

"Goods". Section 2A-103(1)(n).

As amended in 2003.

§ 2A-106.   Limitation on Power of Parties to Consumer Lease to Choose Applicable Law and Judicial Forum.

(1) If the law chosen by the parties to a consumer lease is that of a jurisdiction other than a jurisdiction in which the lessee resides at the time the lease agreement becomes enforceable or within 30 days thereafter or in which the goods are to be used, the choice is not enforceable.

(2) If the judicial forum chosen by the parties to a consumer lease is a forum that would not otherwise have jurisdiction over the lessee, the choice is not enforceable.

Official Comment

Uniform Statutory Source: Uniform Consumer Credit Code § 1.201(8). 1974.

Changes: Substantially Revised.

Purposes: There is a real danger that a lessor may induce a consumer lessee to agree that the applicable law will be a jurisdiction that has little effective consumer protection, or to agree that the applicable forum will be a forum that is inconvenient for the lessee in the event of litigation. As a result, this section invalidates these choice of law or forum clauses, except where the law chosen is that of the state of the consumer's residence or where the goods will be kept, or the forum chosen is one that otherwise would have jurisdiction over the lessee. However, the jurisdiction in which the goods are to be used may include the jurisdiction in which they are physically delivered to the lessee. Thus, a term selecting the law of the jurisdiction of delivery normally is enforceable under this section.

Subsection (1) limits potentially abusive choice of law clauses in consumer leases. This section has no effect on choice of law clauses in leases that are not consumer leases and those clauses would be governed by other law.

Subsection (2) prevents enforcement of potentially abusive jurisdictional consent clauses in consumer leases. By using the term judicial forum, this section does not limit selection of a nonjudicial forum, such as arbitration. This section has no effect on choice of forum clauses in leases that are not consumer leases; such clauses are, as a matter of current law, "prima facie valid". *The Bremen v. Zapata Off–Shore Co.*, 407 U.S. 1, 10 (1972) and these clauses would be governed by other law.

Cross Reference:

Section 9–103(1)(c).

Definitional Cross References:

"Consumer lease". Section 2A–103(1)(f).
"Lease agreement". Section 2A–103(1)(k).
"Lessee". Section 2A–103(1)(t).
"Goods". Section 2A–103(1)(n).
"Party". Section 1–201.

As amended in 2003.

§ 2A–107. Waiver or Renunciation of Claim or Right after Default.

A claim or right arising out of an alleged default or breach of warranty may be discharged in whole or in part without consideration by the aggrieved party in a signed record.

As amended in 2003.

Official Comment

Uniform Statutory Source: Section 1–107.

Changes: Revised to reflect leasing practices and terminology. This clause is used throughout the official comments to this Article to indicate the scope of change in the provisions of the Uniform Statutory Source included in the section; these changes range from one extreme, *e.g.*, a significant difference in practice (a warranty as to merchantability is not implied in a finance lease (Section 2A–212)) to the other extreme, *e.g.*, a modest difference in style or terminology (the transaction governed is a lease not a sale (Section 2A–103)).

Definitional Cross References:

"Record". Section 2A–103(1)(p).
"Signed". Section 2A–103(1)(dd).

§ 2A–108. Unconscionability.

(1) If the court as a matter of law finds a lease contract or any clause of a lease contract to have been unconscionable at the time it was made the court may refuse to enforce the lease contract, or it may enforce the remainder of the lease contract without the unconscionable clause, or it may so limit the application of any unconscionable clause as to avoid any unconscionable result.

(2) With respect to a consumer lease, if the court as a matter of law finds that a lease contract or any clause of a lease contract has been induced by unconscionable conduct or that unconscionable conduct has occurred in the collection of a claim arising from a lease contract, the court may grant appropriate relief.

(3) Before making a finding of unconscionability under subsection (1) or (2), the court, on its own motion or that of a party, shall afford the parties a reasonable opportunity to present evidence as to the setting, purpose, and effect of the lease contract or clause thereof, or of the conduct.

(4) In an action in which the lessee claims unconscionability with respect to a consumer lease:

    (a) If the court finds unconscionability under subsection (1) or (2), the court shall award reasonable attorney's fees to the lessee.

    (b) If the court does not find unconscionability and the lessee claiming unconscionability has brought or maintained an action the lessee knew to be groundless, the court shall award reasonable attorney's fees to the party against which the claim is made.

    (c) In determining attorney's fees, the amount of the recovery on behalf of the claimant under subsections (1) and (2) is not controlling.

As amended in 2003.

Official Comment

Uniform Statutory Source: Section 2–302 and Uniform Consumer Credit Code § 5.108.

Changes: Subsection (1) is taken almost verbatim from the provisions of Section 2–302(1). Subsection (2) is suggested by the provisions of Uniform Consumer Credit Code § 5.108(1), (2). Subsection (3), taken from the provisions of Section 2–302(2), has been expanded to cover unconscionable conduct. Uniform Consumer Credit Code § 5.108(3). The provision for the award of attorney's fees to consumers, subsection (4), covers unconscionability under subsection (1) as well as (2). Subsection (4) is modeled on the provisions of Uniform Consumer Credit Code § 5.108(6).

Purposes: Subsections (1) and (3) of this section apply the concept of unconscionability reflected in the provisions of Section 2–302 to leases. *See Dillman & Assocs. v. Capitol Leasing Co.,* 110 Ill.App.3d 335, 342, 442 N.E.2d 311, 316 (App.Ct.1982). Subsection (3) omits the adjective "commercial" found in subsection 2–302(2) because subsection (3) is concerned with all leases and the relevant standard of conduct is determined by the context.

The balance of the section is modeled on the provisions of Uniform Consumer Credit Code § 5.108. Thus subsection (2) recognizes that a consumer lease or a clause in a consumer lease may not itself be unconscionable but that the agreement would never have been entered into if unconscionable means had not been employed to induce the consumer to agree. To make a statement to induce the consumer to lease the goods, in the expectation of invoking an integration clause in the lease to exclude the statement's admissibility in a subsequent dispute, may be unconscionable. Subsection (2) also provides a consumer remedy for unconscionable conduct, such as using or threatening to use force or violence, in the collection of a claim arising from a lease contract. These provisions are not exclusive. The remedies of this section are in addition to remedies otherwise available for the same conduct under other law, for example, an action in tort for abusive debt collection or under another statute of this State for such conduct. The reference to appropriate relief in subsection (2) is intended to foster liberal administration of this remedy. Sections 2A–103(4) and 1–106(1).

Subsection (4) authorizes an award of reasonable attorney's fees if the court finds unconscionability with respect to a consumer lease under subsection (1) or (2). Provision is also made for recovery by the party against whom the claim was made if the court does not find unconscionability and does find that the consumer knew the action to be groundless. Further, subsection (4)(b) is independent of, and thus will not override, a term in the lease agreement that provides for the payment of attorney's fees.

Cross References:

Section 1–106(1), Section 2–302 and Section 2A–103(4).

Definitional Cross References:

    "Action". Section 1–201.
    "Consumer lease". Section 2A–103(1)(f).
    "Lease contract". Section 2A–103(1)(r).
    "Lessee". Section 2A–103(1)(t).
    "Party". Section 1–201.

§ 2A–109. Option to Accelerate at Will.

(1) A term providing that one party or that party's successor in interest may accelerate payment or performance or require collateral or additional collateral "at will" or "when the party deems itself insecure" or words of similar import means that the party has power to do so only if that party in good faith believes that the prospect of payment or performance is impaired.

(2) With respect to a consumer lease, the burden of establishing good faith under subsection (1) is on the party that has exercised the power; otherwise the burden of establishing lack of good faith is on the party against which the power has been exercised.

As amended in 2003.

Official Comment

Uniform Statutory Source: Section 1–208 and Uniform Consumer Credit Code § 5.109(2).

Purposes: Subsection (1) reflects modest changes in style to the provisions of the first sentence of Section 1–208.

Subsection (2), however, reflects a significant change in the provisions of the second sentence of Section 1–208 by creating a new rule with respect to a consumer lease. A lease provision allowing acceleration at the will of the lessor or when the lessor deems itself insecure is of critical importance to the lessee. In a consumer lease it is a provision that is not usually agreed to by the parties but is usually mandated by the lessor. Therefore, where its invocation depends not on specific criteria but on the discretion of the lessor, its use should be regulated to prevent abuse. Subsection (1) imposes a duty of good faith upon its exercise. Subsection (2) shifts the burden of establishing good faith to the lessor in the case of a consumer lease, but not otherwise.

Cross Reference:

Section 1–208.

Definitional Cross References:

"Burden of establishing". Section 1–201.
"Consumer lease". Section 2A–103(1)(f).
"Good faith". Sections 2A–103(1)(m).
"Party". Section 1–201.
"Term". Section 1–201.

PART 2

FORMATION AND CONSTRUCTION OF LEASE CONTRACT; ELECTRONIC CONTRACTING

§ 2A–201. Statute of Frauds.

(1) A lease contract is not enforceable by way of action or defense unless:

(a) the total payments to be made under the lease contract, excluding payments for options to renew or buy, are less than $1,000; or

(b) there is a record, signed by the party against which enforcement is sought or by that party's authorized agent, sufficient to indicate that a lease contract has been made between the parties and to describe the goods leased and the lease term.

(2) Any description of leased goods or of the lease term is sufficient and satisfies subsection (1)(b), whether or not it is specific, if it reasonably identifies what is described.

(3) A record is not insufficient because it omits or incorrectly states a term agreed upon, but the lease contract is not enforceable under subsection (1)(b) beyond the lease term and the quantity of goods shown in the record.

(4) A lease contract that does not satisfy the requirements of subsection (1), but which is valid in other respects, is enforceable:

(a) if the goods are to be specially manufactured or obtained for the lessee and are not suitable for lease or sale to others in the ordinary course of the lessor's business, and the lessor, before notice of repudiation is received and under circumstances that reasonably indicate that the goods are for the lessee, has made either a substantial beginning of their manufacture or commitments for their procurement;

(b) if the party against which enforcement is sought admits in the party's pleading, or in the party's testimony or otherwise under oath that a lease contract was made, but the lease contract is not enforceable under this paragraph beyond the quantity of goods admitted; or

(c) with respect to goods that have been received and accepted by the lessee.

(5) The lease term under a lease contract referred to in subsection (4) is:

(a) if there is a record signed by the party against which enforcement is sought or by that party's authorized agent specifying the lease term, the term so specified;

(b) if the party against which enforcement is sought admits in the party's pleading, or in the party's testimony or otherwise under oath a lease term, the term so admitted; or

(c) a reasonable lease term.

(6) A lease contract that is enforceable under this section is not unenforceable merely because

it is not capable of being performed within one year or any other period after its making.

As amended in 2003.

Official Comment

1. This section, although closely parallel to Article 2–201, conforms to custom and usage in lease transactions. Section 2–201(2), which has a special rule for sales between merchants, is not included in this section as the number of those transactions that involve leases, as opposed to sales, is modest. Subsection (4) creates no exception for transactions where payment has been made and accepted. This is a departure from Section 2–201(3)(c). The reason for the departure is grounded in the distinction between sales and leases. Unlike a buyer in a sales transaction, the lessee does not tender payment in full for goods delivered, but only payment of rent for one or more months. Therefore, as a matter of policy, this act of payment is not a sufficient substitute for the required memorandum.

2. Amended Article 2A retains the requirements of original Article 2A that lease contracts for $1,000 or more must satisfy the requirements of this section. Leases often involve a complex, on-going relationship between the lessor and lessee, and it is often important that there be a record that affords a basis to believe that the proffered evidence rests on a real transaction unless, as in Article 2, a substitute for a record described in subsection (4) fulfills the same function.

3. Subsection (5) establishes the criteria for supplying the lease term if it is omitted, as the lease contract may still be enforceable under subsection (4).

4. Subsection (6), which was not in prior versions of this Article, repeals the "one year" provision of the Statute of Frauds for contracts for the lease of goods. The phrase "any other applicable period" recognizes that some state statutes apply to periods longer than one year. The confused and contradictory interpretations under the so-called "one year" clause are illustrated in *C.R. Klewin, Inc. v. Flagship Properties, Inc.*, 600 A.2d 772 (Conn. 1991).

Cross References:

Point 1: Sections 2–201, 9–110 and 9–203(1)(a).

Definitional Cross References:

"Action". Section 1–201.
"Agreed". Section 1–201.
"Buying". Section 2A–103(1)(a).
"Goods". Section 2A–103(1)(n).
"Lease". Section 2A–103(1)(p).
"Lease contract". Section 2A–103(1)(r).

"Lessee". Section 2A–103(1)(t).
"Lessor". Section 2A–103(1)(v).
"Notice". Section 1–202.
"Party". Section 1–201.
"Record". Section 2A–201(1)(cc).
"Sale". Section 2–106(1).
"Signed". Section 2A–103(1)(dd).
"Term". Section 1–201.

As amended in 2003.

§ 2A–202. Final Expression in a Record: Parol or Extrinsic Evidence.

(1) Terms with respect to which the confirmatory memoranda of the parties agree or which are otherwise set forth in a record intended by the parties as a final expression of their agreement with respect to such terms as are included therein may not be contradicted by evidence of any prior agreement or of a contemporaneous oral agreement but may be supplemented by evidence of :

  (a) course of performance, course of dealing, or usage of trade (Section 1–303); and

  (b) consistent additional terms unless the court finds the record to have been intended also as a complete and exclusive statement of the terms of the agreement.

(2) Terms in a record may be explained by evidence of course of performance, course of dealing, or usage of trade without a preliminary determination by the court that the language used is ambiguous.

As amended in 2003.

Official Comment

Uniform Statutory Source: Section 2–202.

This section is based on and conforms to amended Article 2, Section 2–202. The official commentary to that Section may be of aid in the interpretation of this section.

Cross Reference:

Section 2–202

Definitional Cross References:

"Agreement". Section 1–201.
"Course of dealing". Section 1–303.
"Party". Section 1–201.
"Term". Section 1–201.
"Record". Section 2A–103(1)(cc).

"Usage of trade". Section 1–303.

As amended in 2003.

§ 2A–203. Seals Inoperative.

The affixing of a seal to a record evidencing a lease contract or an offer to enter into a lease contract does not render the record a sealed instrument and the law with respect to sealed instruments does not apply to the lease contract or offer.

As amended in 2003.

Official Comment

Uniform Statutory Source: Section 2–203.

Changes: Revised to reflect leasing practices and terminology.

Definitional Cross References:

"Lease contract". Section 2A–103(1)(r).
"Record". Section 2A–103(1)(cc).

§ 2A–204. Formation in General.

(1) A lease contract may be made in any manner sufficient to show agreement, including offer and acceptance, conduct by both parties which recognizes the existence of a lease contract, the interaction of electronic agents, and the interaction of an electronic agent and an individual.

(2) An agreement sufficient to constitute a lease contract may be found although the moment of its making is undetermined.

(3) Even if one or more terms are left open, a lease contract does not fail for indefiniteness if the parties have intended to make a lease contract and there is a reasonably certain basis for giving an appropriate remedy.

(4) Except as otherwise provided in Sections 2A–222 through 2A–224, the following rules apply:

(a) A lease contract may be formed by the interaction of electronic agents of the parties, even if no individual was aware of or reviewed the electronic agents' actions or the resulting terms and agreements.

(b) A lease contract may be formed by the interaction of an electronic agent and an individual acting on the individual's own behalf or for another person. A lease contract is formed if the individual takes actions that the individual is free to refuse to take or makes a statement, and the individual has reason to know that the actions or statement will:

(i) cause the electronic agent to complete the transaction or performance; or

(ii) indicate acceptance of an offer, regardless of other expressions or actions by the individual to which the electronic agent cannot react.

As amended in 2003.

Official Comment

Uniform Statutory Source: Section 2–204.

Changes: Revised to reflect leasing practices and terminology.

This section is based on and conforms to amended Article 2, Section 2–204. The official commentary to that Section may be of aid in the interpretation of this section.

Cross Reference:

Section 2–204.

Definitional Cross References:

"Agreement". Section 1–201.
"Electronic" Section 2A–103(1)(h).
"Electronic Agent". Section 2A–103(1)(i).
"Electronic Record". Section 2A–103(1)(j).
"Lease contract". Section 2A–103(1)(r).
"Party". Section 1–201.
"Record". Section 2A–103(1)(cc).
"Remedy". Section 1–201.
"Term". Section 1–201.

As amended in 2003.

§ 2A–205. Firm Offers.

An offer by a merchant to lease goods to or from another person in a signed record that by its terms gives assurance it will be held open is not revocable, for lack of consideration, during the time stated or, if no time is stated, for a reasonable time, but in no event may the period of irrevocability exceed three months. Any such term of assurance in a form supplied by the offeree must be separately signed by the offeror.

As amended in 2003.

Official Comment

Uniform Statutory Source: Section 2–205.

Changes: Revised to reflect leasing practices and terminology.

Definitional Cross References:

"Goods". Section 2A–103(1)(n).
"Lease". Section 2A–103(1)(p).
"Merchant". Section 2–104(1).
"Person". Section 1–201.
"Reasonable time". Section 1–205.
"Record". Section 2A–103(1)(cc).
"Signed". Section 2A–103(1)(dd).
"Term". Section 1–201.

§ 2A–206.　Offer and Acceptance in Formation of Lease Contract.

(1) Unless otherwise unambiguously indicated by the language or circumstances, an offer to make a lease contract must be construed as inviting acceptance in any manner and by any medium reasonable in the circumstances.

(2) If the beginning of a requested performance is a reasonable mode of acceptance, an offeror who is not notified of acceptance within a reasonable time may treat the offer as having lapsed before acceptance.

Official Comment

Uniform Statutory Source: Section 2–206(1)(a) and (2).

Changes: Revised to reflect leasing practices and terminology.

Definitional Cross References:

"Lease contract". Section 2A–103(1)(r).
"Notifies". Section 1–201.
"Reasonable time". Section 1–205.

§ 2A–207.　Reserved. [Course of Performance or Practical Construction]

[(1) If a lease contract involves repeated occasions for performance by either party with knowledge of the nature of the performance and opportunity for objection to it by the other, any course of performance accepted or acquiesced in without objection is relevant to determine the meaning of the lease agreement.

(2) The express terms of a lease agreement and any course of performance, as well as any course of dealing and usage of trade, must be construed whenever reasonable as consistent with each other; but if that construction is un-

reasonable, express terms control course of performance, course of performance controls both course of dealing and usage of trade, and course of dealing controls usage of trade.

(3) Subject to the provisions of Section 2A–208 on modification and waiver, course of performance is relevant to show a waiver or modification of any term inconsistent with the course of performance.]

[Official Comment]

[Uniform Statutory Source: Sections 2–208 and 1–205(4).

Changes: Revised to reflect leasing practices and terminology, except that subsection (2) was further revised to make the subsection parallel the provisions of Section 1–205(4) by adding that course of dealing controls usage of trade.

Purposes: The section should be read in conjunction with Section 2A–208. In particular, although a specific term may control over course of performance as a matter of lease construction under subsection (2), subsection (3) allows the same course of dealing to show a waiver or modification, if Section 2A–208 is satisfied.]

Legislative Note: Section 2A–207 should not be repealed if a jurisdiction has not enacted the 2001 Revised Article 1.

§ 2A–208.　Modification, Rescission and Waiver.

(1) An agreement modifying a lease contract needs no consideration to be binding.

(2) A signed lease agreement that excludes modification or rescission except by a signed record may not be otherwise modified or rescinded, but, except as between merchants, such a requirement in a form supplied by a merchant must be separately signed by the other party.

(3) Although an attempt at modification or rescission does not satisfy the requirements of subsection (2), it may operate as a waiver.

(4) A party that has made a waiver affecting an executory portion of a lease contract may retract the waiver by reasonable notification received by the other party that strict performance will be required of any term waived, unless the retraction would be unjust in view of a material change of position in reliance on the waiver.

As amended in 2003.

Official Comment

Uniform Statutory Source: Section 2–209.

Changes: Revised to reflect leasing practices and terminology, except that the provisions of subsection 2–209(3) were omitted.

Purposes: Section 2–209(3) provides that "the requirements of the statute of frauds section of this Article (Section 2–201) must be satisfied if the contract as modified is within its provisions." This provision was not incorporated as it is unfair to allow an oral modification to make the entire lease contract unenforceable, *e.g.* if the modification takes it a few dollars over the dollar limit. At the same time, the problem could not be solved by providing that the lease contract would still be enforceable in its pre-modification state (if it then satisfied the statute of frauds) since in some cases that might be worse than no enforcement at all. Resolution of the issue is left to the courts based on the facts of each case.

Cross References:

Sections 2–201 and 2–209.

Definitional Cross References:

"Agreement". Section 1–201.
"Between merchants". Section 2–104(3).
"Lease agreement". Section 2A–103(1)(k).
"Lease contract". Section 2A–103(1)(r).
"Merchant". Section 2–104(1).
"Notification". Section 1–202.
"Party". Section 1–201.
"Record". Section 2A–103(1)(cc).
"Signed". Section 2A–103(1)(dd).
"Term". Section 1–201.

§ 2A–209. Lessee under Finance Lease as Beneficiary of Supply Contract.

(1) The benefit of a supplier's promises to the lessor under the supply contract and of all warranties, whether express or implied, including those of any third party provided in connection with or as part of the supply contract, extends to the lessee to the extent of the lessee's leasehold interest under a finance lease related to the supply contract, but is subject to the terms of the warranty and of the supply contract and all defenses or claims arising therefrom.

(2) The extension of the benefit of a supplier's promises and of warranties to the lessee (Section 2A–209(1)) does not: (i) modify the rights and obligations of the parties to the supply contract, whether arising therefrom or otherwise, or (ii) impose any duty or liability under the supply contract on the lessee.

(3) Any modification or rescission of the supply contract by the supplier and the lessor is effective between the supplier and the lessee unless, before the modification or rescission, the supplier has received notice that the lessee has entered into a finance lease related to the supply contract. If the modification or rescission is effective between the supplier and the lessee, the lessor is deemed to have assumed, in addition to the obligations of the lessor to the lessee under the lease contract, promises of the supplier to the lessor and warranties that were so modified or rescinded as they existed and were available to the lessee before modification or rescission.

(4) In addition to the extension of the benefit of the supplier's promises and of warranties to the lessee under subsection (1), the lessee retains all rights that the lessee may have against the supplier which arise from an agreement between the lessee and the supplier or under other law.

As amended in 1990.

Official Comment

Uniform Statutory Source: None.

Changes: This section is modeled on Section 9–318, the Restatement (Second) of Contracts §§ 302–315 (1981), and leasing practices. *See Earman Oil Co. v. Burroughs Corp.*, 625 F.2d 1291, 1296–97 (5th Cir. 1980).

Purposes:

1. The function performed by the lessor in a finance lease is extremely limited. Section 2A–103(1)(g). The lessee looks to the supplier of the goods for warranties and the like or, in some cases as to warranties, to the manufacturer if a warranty made by that person is passed on. That expectation is reflected in subsection (1), which is self-executing. As a matter of policy, the operation of this provision may not be excluded, modified or limited; however, an exclusion, modification, or limitation of any term of the supply contract or warranty, including any with respect to rights and remedies, and any defense or claim such as a statute of limitations, effective against the lessor as the acquiring party under the supply contract, is also effective against the lessee as the beneficiary designated under this provision. For example, the supplier is not precluded from excluding or modifying an express or implied warranty under a supply contract. Sections 2–312(2) and 2–316, or Section 2A–214. Further, the supplier is

not precluded from limiting the rights and remedies of the lessor and from liquidating damages. Sections 2–718 and 2–719 or Sections 2A–503 and 2A–504. If the supply contract excludes or modifies warranties, limits remedies, or liquidates damages with respect to the lessor, such provisions are enforceable against the lessee as beneficiary. Thus, only selective discrimination against the beneficiaries designated under this section is precluded, i.e., exclusion of the supplier's liability to the lessee with respect to warranties made to the lessor. This section does not affect the development of other law with respect to products liability.

2. Enforcement of this benefit is by action. Sections 2A–103(4) and 1–106(2).

3. The benefit extended by these provisions is not without a price, as this Article also provides in the case of a finance lease that is not a consumer lease that the lessee's promises to the lessor under the lease contract become irrevocable and independent upon the lessee's acceptance of the goods. Section 2A–407.

4. Subsection (2) limits the effect of subsection (1) on the supplier and the lessor by preserving, notwithstanding the transfer of the benefits of the supply contract to the lessee, all of the supplier's and the lessor's rights and obligations with respect to each other and others; it further absolves the lessee of any duties with respect to the supply contract that might have been inferred from the extension of the benefits thereof.

5. Subsections (2) and (3) also deal with difficult issues related to modification or rescission of the supply contract. Subsection (2) states a rule that determines the impact of the statutory extension of benefit contained in subsection (1) upon the relationship of the parties to the supply contract and, in a limited respect, upon the lessee. This statutory extension of benefit, like that contained in Sections 2A–216 and 2–318, is not a modification of the supply contract by the parties. Thus, subsection (3) states the rules that apply to a modification or rescission of the supply contract by the parties. Subsection (3) provides that a modification or rescission is not effective between the supplier and the lessee if, before the modification or rescission occurs, the supplier received notice that the lessee has entered into the finance lease. On the other hand, if the modification or rescission is effective, then to the extent of the modification or rescission of the benefit or warranty, the lessor by statutory dictate assumes an obligation to provide to the lessee that which the lessee would otherwise lose. For example, assume a reduction in an express warranty from four years to one year. No prejudice to the lessee may occur if the goods perform as agreed. If, however, there is a breach of the express warranty after one year and before four years pass, the lessor is liable. A remedy for any prejudice to the lessee because of the bifurcation of the lessee's recourse resulting from the action of the supplier and the lessor is left to resolution by the courts based on the facts of each case.

6. Subsection (4) makes it clear that the rights granted to the lessee by this section do not displace any rights the lessee otherwise may have against the supplier.

Cross References:

Point 1: Sections 2–313, 2–316, 2–718, and 2–719 and Sections 2A–103(1)(g), 2A–214, 2A–503, and 2A–504.

Point 2: Section 1–106 and Sections 2A–103.

Point 3: Section 2A–407

Point 5: Section 2–318 and Section 2A–216.

Definitional Cross References:

"Action". Section 1–201.

"Finance lease". Section 2A–103(1)(l).

"Leasehold interest". Section 2A–103(1)(s).

"Lessee". Section 2A–103(1)(t).

"Lessor". Section 2A–103(1)(v).

"Notice". Section 1–202.

"Party". Section 1–201.

"Rights". Section 1–201.

"Supplier". Section 2A–103(1)(ff).

"Supply contract". Section 2A–103(1)(gg).

"Term". Section 1–201.

§ 2A–210. Express Warranties.

(1) Express warranties by the lessor are created as follows:

    (a) Any affirmation of fact or promise made by the lessor to the lessee which relates to the goods and becomes part of the basis of the bargain creates an express warranty that the goods will conform to the affirmation or promise.

    (b) Any description of the goods which is made part of the basis of the bargain creates an express warranty that the goods will conform to the description.

    (c) Any sample or model that is made part of the basis of the bargain creates an express warranty that the whole of the goods will conform to the sample or model.

(2) It is not necessary to the creation of an express warranty that the lessor use formal

words, such as "warrant" or "guarantee," or that the lessor have a specific intention to make a warranty, but an affirmation merely of the value of the goods or a statement purporting to be merely the lessor's opinion or commendation of the goods does not create a warranty.

Official Comment

Uniform Statutory Source: Section 2–313.

Changes: Revised to reflect leasing practices and terminology.

Purposes: All of the express and implied warranties of the Article on Sales (Article 2) are included in this Article, revised to reflect the differences between a sale of goods and a lease of goods. Sections 2A–210 through 2A–216. The lease of goods is sufficiently similar to the sale of goods to justify this decision. Hawkland, *The Impact of the Uniform Commercial Code on Equipment Leasing*, 1972 Ill.L.F. 446, 459–60. Many state and federal courts have reached the same conclusion.

Value of the goods, as used in subsection (2), includes rental value.

Cross References:

Section 2–313, and Sections 2A–210 through 2A–216.

Definitional Cross References:

"Conforming". Section 2A–103(1)(c).
"Goods". Section 2A–103(1)(n).
"Lessee". Section 2A–103(1)(t).
"Lessor". Section 2A–103(1)(v).
"Value". Section 1–204.

§ 2A–211. Warranties Against Interference and Against Infringement; Lessee's Obligation Against Infringement.

(1) Except in a finance lease, a lessor in a lease contract warrants that, except for claims by any person by way of infringement or the like, for the duration of the lease no person holds:

  (a) a claim to or interest in the goods not attributable to the lessee's own act or omission which will interfere with the lessee's enjoyment of its leasehold interest; or

  (b) a colorable claim to or interest in the goods which will unreasonably expose the lessee to litigation.

(2) A finance lessor warrants that, except for claims by way of infringement or the like, for the duration of the lease no person holds:

  (a) a claim or interest in the goods that arose from an act or omission of the lessor which will interfere with the lessee's enjoyment of its leasehold interest; or

  (b) a colorable claim to or interest in the goods that arose from an act or omission of the lessor which will unreasonably expose the lessee to litigation.

(3) Except in a finance lease, a lessor that is a merchant regularly dealing in goods of the kind warrants that the goods will be delivered free of the rightful claim of a third party by way of infringement or the like. However, a lessee that furnishes specifications to a lessor or a supplier holds the lessor and the supplier harmless against any claim of infringement or the like that arises out of compliance with the specifications.

(4) A warranty under this section may be excluded or modified only by specific language that is conspicuous and contained in a record, or by circumstances, including course of performance, course of dealing, or usage of trade, that give the lessee reason to know that the lessor is leasing the goods subject to a claim or interest of any person, or that it is leasing subject to any claims of infringement or the like.

As amended in 2003 and 2005.

Official Comment

1. Scope of warranty of title. Unlike other warranties in Part 5, the warranty made by a lessor in subsections (1), (2), and (3) is standardized but can be disclaimed or modified under subsection (4).

The lessor, other than a finance lessor, warrants that (1) that no person holds an interest that interfere with the lessee's enjoyment of its leasehold, (a warranty of quite enjoyment) and (2) the transfer does not unreasonably expose the lessee to litigation. An unreasonable exposure to litigation occurs when a third person has or asserts a "colorable" claim to or interest in the goods.

The following cases illustrate the concept of colorable claims: *Frank Arnold KRS, Inc. v. L.S. Meier Auction Co., Inc.*, 806 F.2d 462 (3d Cir. 1986) (two law suits contest title); *Jeanneret v. Vichey*, 693 F.2d 259 (2d Cir. 1982) (export restrictions in country from which painting was taken affect value); *Colton v. Decker*, 540 N.W.2d 172 (S.D. 1995) (conflicting vehicle identification numbers). As one court put it, there "need not be an actual encumbrance of the purchaser's title or actual disturbance of possession to permit a purchaser to recover for a breach of warranty of title when he demonstrates the existence of a cloud on his title, regardless of whether it eventually develops that a third party's title is superior." The policy is that a purchaser "should not be required to engage in a contest over the validity of his ownership." *Maroon Chevrolet, Inc. v. Nordstrom*, 587 So.2d 514, 518 (Fla. App. 1991) (conflicting vehicle identification numbers). Amended Article 2A follows this principle.

2. A finance lessor is essentially a middle-man between a supplier and the lessee. The lessee, therefore, looks to the supplier (seller or lessor) for warranty protection, including warranties of title. Section 2A–209. Therefore, a finance lessor warrants only against its own acts. Subsection (2).

3. Unlike the warranty of title, for the warranty against infringement the lessor must be a merchant who "regularly deals in goods of the kind sold." The warranty can be disclaimed or modified under subsection (4). *See Bonneau Co. v. AG Industries, Inc.*, 116 F.3d 155 (5th Cir. 1997), which holds that if the buyer furnishes specifications to a seller who follows them, there is no warranty against infringement under Section 2–312(3). Moreover, although a lessor warrants against claims or interests, the lessor is not responsible for safeguarding the lessee against claims or encumbrances that might arise because of the lessee's own acts (*e.g.*, an act that would be a default under the lease) or omissions (*e.g.*, a city impounds a leased car and refuses to release it until the lessee pays delinquent parking fines).

4. Disclaimers. Subsection (4), which has been moved from original 2A–214(4), deals with the disclaimer or modification of the warranty of title or against infringement, and it states the general standard that must be met to disclaim or modify against an immediate lessee. The language needs to be conspicuous and in a record.

Cross References:

Point 2: Section 2A–209
Point 3: Section 2–312 and Section 2A–211.
Point 4: Section 2A–414.

Definitional Cross References:

"Delivery". Section 2A–103(1)(g).
"Finance lease". Section 2A–103(1)(l).
"Goods". Section 2A–103(1)(n).
"Lease". Section 2A–103(1)(p).
"Lease contract". Section 2A–103(1)(r).
"Leasehold interest". Section 2A–103(1)(s).
"Lessee". Section 2A–103(1)(t).

"Lessor". Section 2A–103(1)(v).
"Merchant". Section 2–104(1).
"Person". Section 1–201.
"Record". Section 2A–103(1)(cc).
"Supplier". Section 2A–103(1)(ff).

As amended in 2003.

§ 2A–212. Implied Warranty of Merchantability.

(1) Except in a finance lease, a warranty that the goods will be merchantable is implied in a lease contract if the lessor is a merchant with respect to goods of that kind.

(2) Goods to be merchantable must be at least such as

(a) pass without objection in the trade under the description in the lease agreement;

(b) in the case of fungible goods, are of fair average quality within the description;

(c) are fit for the ordinary purposes for which goods of that description are used;

(d) run, within the variation permitted by the lease agreement, of even kind, quality, and quantity within each unit and among all units involved;

(e) are adequately contained, packaged, and labeled as the lease agreement may require; and

(f) conform to any promises or affirmations of fact made on the container or label.

(3) Other implied warranties may arise from course of dealing or usage of trade.

As amended in 2003.

Official Comment

1. The question when the warranty is imposed turns basically on the meaning of the terms of the agreement as recognized in the trade. Goods delivered under an agreement made by a merchant in a given line of trade must be of a quality comparable to that generally acceptable in that line of trade under the description or other designation of the goods used in the agreement. The responsibility imposed rests on any merchant-lessor.

2. If an unmerchantable good causes personal injury to the lessee who is injured while using the good, the lessee can sue the lessor for breach of the implied warranty of merchantability and recover for injury to

person "proximately resulting" from the breach. Section 2A–520(2)(b). Because the lessee has an action for breach of warranty and probably an action in tort as well, there is a tension between warranty law and tort law where goods cause personal injury or property damage. The primary source of that tension comes from the disagreement over whether the concept of defect in tort and the concept of merchantability in Article 2A are coextensive when a personal injury is caused by the defective good: *i.e.*, if goods are merchantable under warranty law can they still be defective under tort law, and if goods are not defective under tort law can they be unmerchantable under warranty law? The answer to both questions should be no, and the tension between merchantability in warranty and defect in tort where personal injury or property damage is involved should be resolved as follows:

When recovery is sought for injury to person or property, whether goods are merchantable is to be determined by applicable state products liability law. When, however, a claim for injury to person or property is based on an implied warranty of fitness under Section 2A–213 or an express warranty under Section 2A–210 this Article determines whether an implied warranty of fitness or an express warranty was made and breached, as well as what damages are recoverable under Section 2A–530.

Thus, if a lessor makes a representation about the safety of a product that becomes part of the basis of the lessee's bargain and the lessee is injured by the product, the product without the representation is not defective under applicable tort law, it is not unmerchantable under this section. On the other hand, if the product did not conform to the representation about safety, then the lessor made and breached an express warranty and the lessee may recover under Article 2A.

3. Subsection (2) does not purport to exhaust the meaning of "merchantable" nor to negate any of its attributes not specifically mentioned in the text of the statute but that arise by usage of trade or through case law. The language used is "must be at least such as . . . ," and the intention is to leave open other possible attributes of merchantability.

4. Paragraphs (a) and (b) of subsection (2) are to be read together. Both refer to the standards of that line of the trade which fits the transaction and the lessor's business. "Fair average" is a term directly appropriate to agricultural bulk products and means goods centering around the middle belt of quality, not the least or the worst that can be understood in the particular trade by the designation, but such as can pass "with-

out objection." Of course a fair percentage of the least is permissible but the goods are not "fair average" if they are all of the least or worst quality possible under the description. In cases of doubt about what quality is intended, the price at which a merchant closes a contract is an excellent indication of the nature and scope of the merchant's obligation under the present section.

5. Fitness for the ordinary purposes for which goods of the type are used is a fundamental concept of the present section and is covered in paragraph (2)(c). The phrase "goods of that description" rather than the language from the original Article 2A "for which goods of that type are used" is used in subsection (2)(c). This change emphasizes the importance of the agreed description to determine fitness for ordinary purposes.

6. Paragraph (2)(d) on evenness of kind, quality and quantity follows case law. But precautionary language has been added as a reminder of the frequent usages of trade which permit substantial variations both with and without an allowance or an obligation to replace the varying units.

7. Paragraph (2)(e) applies only where the nature of the goods and of the transaction require a certain type of container, package or label. Paragraph (2)(f) applies, on the other hand, wherever there is a label or container on which representations are made, even though the original contract, either by express terms or usage of trade, may not have required either the labeling or the representation. This follows from the general obligation of good faith which requires that a lessee should not be placed in the position of using goods delivered under false representations that appear on the package or container. No problem of extra consideration arises in this connection since, under this Article, an obligation is imposed by the original contract not to deliver mislabeled articles, and the obligation is imposed where mercantile good faith requires and without reference to the doctrine of consideration.

8. Exclusion or modification of the warranty of merchantability, or of any part of it, is dealt with in Section 2A–214. That section must be read with particular reference to its subsection (6) on limitation of remedies. The warranty of merchantability, wherever it is normal, is so commonly taken for granted that its exclusion from the contract is a matter threatening surprise and therefore requiring special precaution.

9. Subsection (3) makes explicit that usage of trade and course of dealing can create warranties, and that they are implied rather than express warranties, and thus subject to exclusion or modification under Section 2A–214.

10. In an action based on breach of warranty, it is of course necessary to show not only the existence of the warranty but the fact that the warranty was broken and that the breach of the warranty was the proximate cause of the loss sustained. An affirmative showing by the lessor that the loss resulted from some action or event following the lessor's delivery of the goods can operate as a defense. Equally, evidence that indicates that the lessor exercised care in the manufacture, processing or selection of the goods is relevant to the issue of whether the warranty was in fact broken. An action by the lessee following an examination of the goods which ought to have indicated the defect complained of can be shown as matter bearing on whether the breach itself was the cause of the injury.

Cross References:

Point 2: Sections 2A-210, 2A-520 and 2A-530.
Point 8: Section 2A-214.
Point 9: Section 2A-214.

Definitional Cross References:

"Conforming". Section 2A-103(1)(c).
"Course of dealing". Section 1-303.
"Finance lease". Section 2A-103(1)(l).
"Fungible". Section 1-201.
"Goods". Section 2A-103(1)(n).
"Lease agreement". Section 2A-103(1)(k).
"Lease contract". Section 2A-103(1)(r).
"Lessor". Section 2A-103(1)(v).
"Merchant". Section 2-104(1).
"Usage of trade". Section 1-303.

As amended in 2003.

§ 2A-213. Implied Warranty of Fitness for Particular Purpose.

Except in a finance lease, if the lessor at the time the lease contract is made has reason to know of any particular purpose for which the goods are required and that the lessee is relying on the lessor's skill or judgment to select or furnish suitable goods, there is in the lease contract an implied warranty that the goods will be fit for that purpose.

Official Comment

Uniform Statutory Source: Section 2-315.

Changes: Revised to reflect leasing practices and terminology. *E.g., All-States Leasing Co. v. Bass*, 96 Idaho 873, 879, 538 P.2d 1177, 1183 (1975) (implied warranty of fitness for a particular purpose (Article 2) extends to lease transactions).

Definitional Cross References:

"Finance lease". Section 2A-103(1)(l).
"Goods". Section 2A-103(1)(n).
"Knows". Section 1-201.
"Lease contract". Section 2A-103(1)(r).
"Lessee". Section 2A-103(1)(t).
"Lessor". Section 2A-103(1)(v).

§ 2A-214. Exclusion or Modification of Warranties.

(1) Words or conduct relevant to the creation of an express warranty and words or conduct tending to negate or limit a warranty must be construed wherever reasonable as consistent with each other; but, subject to Section 2A-202, negation or limitation is inoperative to the extent that the construction is unreasonable.

(2) Subject to subsection (3), to exclude or modify the implied warranty of merchantability or any part of it the language must be in a record and be conspicuous. In a consumer lease the language must state "The lessor undertakes no responsibility for the quality of the goods except as otherwise provided in this contract," and in any other contract the language must mention "merchantability". Subject to subsection (3), to exclude or modify the implied warranty of fitness the exclusion must be in a record and be conspicuous. Language to exclude all implied warranties of fitness in a consumer lease must state "The lessor assumes no responsibility that the goods will be fit for any particular purpose for which you may be leasing these goods, except as otherwise provided in the contract," and in any other contract the language is sufficient if it states, for example, that "There are no warranties that extend beyond the description on the face hereof." Language that satisfies the requirements of this subsection for a consumer lease also satisfies its requirements for any other lease contract.

(3) Notwithstanding subsection (2):

(a) unless the circumstances indicate otherwise, all implied warranties are excluded by expressions like "as is", "with all faults", or other language that in common understanding calls the lessee's attention to the exclusion of warranties and makes plain that there is no implied warranty, if in a record and conspicuous;

(b) if the lessee before entering into the lease contract has examined the goods or the sample or model as fully as desired or has refused to examine the goods, after a demand by the lessor there is no implied warranty with regard to defects that an examination ought in the circumstances to have revealed to the lessee; and

(c) an implied warranty may also be excluded or modified by course of dealing, or course of performance, or usage of trade.

(4) Remedies for breach of warranty can be limited in accordance with Section 2A–503 and 2A–504.

As amended in 2003.

Official Comment

The changes conform to amended Article 2. Former subsection (4) has been moved to Section 2–211.

1. Subsection (1) deals with clauses in lease contracts that seek to exclude "all warranties, express or implied." This section protects a lessee from unexpected and unbargained language of disclaimer by denying effect to this language when it is inconsistent with language of express warranty, and permits the exclusion of implied warranties only by language or other circumstances which protect the lessee from surprise.

The lessor is protected against false allegations of oral warranties by this Article's provisions on parol and extrinsic evidence and against unauthorized representations by the customary "lack of authority" clauses. This Article treats the limitation or avoidance of consequential damages as a matter of limiting remedies for breach, separate from the matter of creation of liability under a warranty. If no warranty exists, there is of course no problem of limiting remedies for breach of warranty. Under subsection (4), the question of limitation of remedy is governed by the sections referred to rather than by this section.

2. The general test for disclaimers of implied warranties remains in subsection (3)(a), and the more specific tests are in subsection (2). A disclaimer that satisfies the requirements of subsection (3)(a) need not also satisfy any of the requirements of subsection (2).

3. Subsection (2) distinguishes between commercial and consumer leases. However, unlike the parallel provision in Article 2 (Section 2–316), under this section all exclusions under subsection (2) must be in a record and the language must be conspicuous, unlike Article 2 which only makes this mandatory for consumer contracts. Thus in both commercial and consumer leases,

language that disclaims the implied warranty of merchantability must be in a record, and must be conspicuous. Subsection (2) presupposes that the implied warranty in question exists unless excluded or modified.

4. Subsection (3)(a) deals with general terms such as "as is," "as they stand," "with all faults," and the like. These terms in ordinary commercial usage are understood to mean that the lessee takes the entire risk as to the quality of the goods involved. The terms covered by the subsection are in fact merely a particularization of subsection (3)(c), which provides for exclusion or modification of implied warranties by usage of trade. Nothing in subsection (3)(a) prevents a term such as "there are no implied warranties" from being effective in appropriate circumstances, as when the term is a negotiated term between commercial parties.

Satisfaction of subsection (3)(a) requires that the language be set forth in a record and the language must be conspicuous. This is a variance with the parallel provision in Article 2 that makes these requirements mandatory only in consumer contracts.

5. The exceptions to the general rule set forth in subsections (3)(b) and (3)(c) are common factual situations in which the circumstances surrounding the transaction are in themselves sufficient to call the lessee's attention to the fact that no implied warranties are made or that a certain implied warranty is being excluded.

Under subsection (3)(b), warranties may be excluded or modified by the circumstances when the lessee examines the goods or a sample or model of them before entering into the contract. "Examination" as used in this paragraph is not synonymous with inspection before acceptance or at any other time after the lease has been made. Of course if the lessee discovers the defect and uses the goods anyway, or if the lessee unreasonably fails to examine the goods before using them, the resulting injuries may be found to have resulted from the lessee's own action rather than have been proximately caused by a breach of warranty.

To bring the transaction within the scope of "refused to examine" in subsection (3)(a), it is not sufficient that the goods are available for inspection. There must in addition be an actual examination by the lessee or a demand by the lessor that the lessee examine the goods fully. The lessor's demand must place the lessee on notice that the lessee is assuming the risk of defects which the examination ought to reveal.

The particular lessee's skill and the normal method of examining goods in the circumstances determine what defects are excluded by the examination. A failure to notice defects which are obvious cannot excuse the lessee because of the lack of notice. However, an examination under circumstances which do not permit chemical or other testing of the goods does not exclude defects which could be ascertained only by testing. Nor can latent defects be excluded by a simple examination. A professional lessee examining a product in the lessee's field will be held to have assumed the risk for all defects which a professional in the field ought to observe, while a nonprofessional lessee will be held to have assumed the risk only for the defects as a layperson might be expected to observe.

Definitional Cross References:

"Conspicuous". Section 2A–103(1)(d).
"Course of dealing". Section 1–303.
"Fault". Section 2A–103(1)(k).
"Goods". Section 2A–103(1)(n).
"Knows". Section 1–201.
"Lease". Section 2A–103(1)(p).
"Lease contract". Section 2A–103(1)(r).
"Lessee". Section 2A–103(1)(t).
"Person". Section 1–201.
"Record". Section 2A–103(1)(cc).
"Usage of trade". Section 1–303.

As amended in 2003.

§ 2A–215. Cumulation and Conflict of Warranties Express or Implied.

Warranties, whether express or implied, must be construed as consistent with each other and as cumulative, but if that construction is unreasonable, the intention of the parties determines which warranty is dominant. In ascertaining that intention the following rules apply:

(a) Exact or technical specifications displace an inconsistent sample or model or general language of description.

(b) A sample from an existing bulk displaces inconsistent general language of description.

(c) Express warranties displace inconsistent implied warranties other than an implied warranty of fitness for a particular purpose.

Official Comment

Uniform Statutory Source: Section 2–317.

Definitional Cross Reference:

"Party". Section 1–201.

§ 2A–216. Third-party Beneficiaries of Express and Implied Warranties.

ALTERNATIVE A

A warranty to or for the benefit of a lessee under this Article, whether express or implied, extends to any natural person who is in the family or household of the lessee or who is a guest in the lessee's home if it is reasonable to expect that such person may use, consume, or be affected by the goods and who is injured in person by breach of the warranty. This section does not displace principles of law and equity that extend a warranty to or for the benefit of a lessee to other persons. The operation of this section may not be excluded, modified, or limited, but an exclusion, modification, or limitation of the warranty, including any with respect to rights and remedies, effective against the lessee is also effective against any beneficiary designated under this section.

ALTERNATIVE B

A warranty to or for the benefit of a lessee under this Article, whether express or implied, extends to any natural person who may reasonably be expected to use, consume, or be affected by the goods and who is injured in person by breach of the warranty. This section does not displace principles of law and equity that extend a warranty to or for the benefit of a lessee to other persons. The operation of this section may not be excluded, modified, or limited, but an exclusion, modification, or limitation of the warranty, including any with respect to rights and remedies, effective against the lessee is also effective against the beneficiary designated under this section.

ALTERNATIVE C

A warranty to or for the benefit of a lessee under this Article, whether express or implied, extends to any person who may reasonably be expected to use, consume, or be affected by the goods and who is injured by breach of the warranty. The operation of this section may not be excluded, modified, or limited with respect to injury to the person of an individual to whom the warranty extends, but an exclusion, modification, or limitation of the warranty, including any with respect to rights and remedies, effective against the lessee is also effective against the beneficiary designated under this section.

Official Comment

Uniform Statutory Source: Section 2–318.

Changes: The provisions of Section 2–318 have been included in this section, modified in two respects: first, to reflect leasing practice, including the special practices of the lessor under a finance lease; second, to reflect and thus codify elements of the official comment to Section 2–318 with respect to the effect of disclaimers and limitations of remedies against third parties.

Purposes: Alternative A is based on the 1962 version of Section 2–318 and is least favorable to the injured person as the doctrine of privity imposed by other law is abrogated to only a limited extent. Alternatives B and C are based on later additions to Section 2–318 and are more favorable to the injured person. In determining which alternative to select, the state legislature should consider making its choice parallel to the choice it made with respect to Section 2–318, as interpreted by the courts.

The last sentence of each of Alternatives A, B and C does not preclude the lessor from excluding or modifying an express or implied warranty under a lease. Section 2A–214. Further, that sentence does not preclude the lessor from limiting the rights and remedies of the lessee and from liquidating damages. Sections 2A–503 and 2A–504. If the lease excludes or modifies warranties, limits remedies for breach, or liquidates damages with respect to the lessee, such provisions are enforceable against the beneficiaries designated under this section. However, this last sentence forbids selective discrimination against the beneficiaries designated under this section, *i.e.*, exclusion of the lessor's liability to the beneficiaries with respect to warranties made by the lessor to the lessee.

Other law, including the Article on Sales (Article 2), may apply in determining the extent to which a warranty to or for the benefit of the lessor extends to the lessee and third parties. This is in part a function of whether the lessor has bought or leased the goods.

This Article does not purport to change the development of the relationship of the common law, with respect to products liability, including strict liability in tort (as restated in Restatement (Second) of Torts, § 402A (1965)), to the provisions of this Act. *Compare Cline v. Prowler Indus. of Maryland*, 418 A.2d 968 (Del.1980) and *Hawkins Constr. Co. v. Matthews Co.*, 190 Neb. 546, 209 N.W.2d 643 (1973) with *Dippel v. Sciano*, 37 Wis.2d 443, 155 N.W.2d 55 (1967).

Cross References:

Section 2–318, and Sections 2A–214, 2A–503 and 2A–504.

Definitional Cross References:

"Goods". Section 2A–103(1)(n).
"Lessee". Section 2A–103(1)(t).
"Person". Section 1–201.
"Remedy". Section 1–201.
"Rights". Section 1–201.

§ 2A–217. Identification.

Identification of goods as goods to which a lease contract refers may be made at any time and in any manner explicitly agreed to by the parties. In the absence of explicit agreement, identification occurs:

(a) when the lease contract is made if the lease contract is for a lease of goods that are existing and identified;

(b) when the goods are shipped, marked, or otherwise designated by the lessor as goods to which the lease contract refers, if the lease contract is for a lease of goods that are not existing and identified; or

(c) when the young are conceived, if the lease contract is for a lease of unborn young of animals.

Official Comment

Uniform Statutory Source: Section 2–501.

Changes: This section, together with Section 2A–218, is derived from the provisions of Section 2–501, with changes to reflect lease terminology; however, this section omits as irrelevant to leasing practice the treatment of special property.

Purposes: With respect to subsection (b) there is a certain amount of ambiguity in the reference to when goods are designated, *e.g.*, when the lessor is both selling and leasing goods to the same lessee/buyer and has marked goods for delivery but has not distinguished between those related to the lease contract and those related to the sales contract. As in Section 2–501(1)(b), this issue has been left to be resolved by the courts, case by case.

Cross References:

Section 2–501 and Section 2A–218.

Definitional Cross References:

"Agreement". Section 1–201.
"Goods". Section 2A–103(1)(n).
"Lease". Section 2A–103(1)(p).
"Lease contract". Section 2A–103(1)(r).
"Lessor". Section 2A–103(1)(v).
"Party". Section 1–201.

§ 2A–218. Insurance and Proceeds.

(1) A lessee obtains an insurable interest when existing goods are identified to the lease contract even though the goods identified are nonconforming and the lessee has an option to reject them.

(2) If a lessee has an insurable interest only by reason of the lessor's identification of the goods, the lessor, until default or insolvency or notification to the lessee that identification is final, may substitute other goods for those identified.

(3) Notwithstanding a lessee's insurable interest under subsections (1) and (2), the lessor retains an insurable interest until an option to buy has been exercised by the lessee and risk of loss has passed to the lessee.

(4) Nothing in this section impairs any insurable interest recognized under any other statute or rule of law.

(5) The parties by agreement may determine that one or more parties have an obligation to obtain and pay for insurance covering the goods and by agreement may determine the beneficiary of the proceeds of the insurance.

Official Comment

Uniform Statutory Source: Section 2–501.

Changes: This section, together with Section 2A–217, is derived from the provisions of Section 2–501, with changes and additions to reflect leasing practices and terminology.

Purposes: Subsection (2) states a rule allowing substitution of goods by the lessor under certain circumstances, until default or insolvency of the lessor, or until notification to the lessee that identification is final. Subsection (3) states a rule regarding the lessor's insurable interest that, by virtue of the difference between a sale and a lease, necessarily is different from the rule stated in Section 2–501(2) regarding the seller's insurable interest. For this purpose the option to buy shall be deemed to have been exercised by the lessee when the resulting sale is closed, not when the lessee gives notice to the lessor. Further, subsection (5)

is new and reflects the common practice of shifting the responsibility and cost of insuring the goods between the parties to the lease transaction.

Cross References:

Sections 2–501, 2–501(2) and Section 2A–217.

Definitional Cross References:

"Agreement". Section 1–201.
"Buying". Section 2A–103(1)(a).
"Conforming". Section 2A–103(1)(c).
"Goods". Section 2A–103(1)(n).
"Insolvent". Section 1–201.
"Lease contract". Section 2A–103(1)(r).
"Lessee". Section 2A–103(1)(t).
"Lessor". Section 2A–103(1)(v).
"Notification". Section 1–202.
"Party". Section 1–201.

§ 2A–219. Risk of Loss.

(1) Except in the case of a finance lease, risk of loss is retained by the lessor and does not pass to the lessee. In the case of a finance lease, risk of loss passes to the lessee.

(2) Subject to Section 2A–220, if risk of loss is to pass to the lessee and the time of passage is not stated, the following rules apply:

(a) If the lease contract requires or authorizes the goods to be shipped by carrier

(i) and it does not require delivery at a particular destination, the risk of loss passes to the lessee when the goods are delivered to the carrier; but

(ii) if it does require delivery at a particular destination and the goods are there tendered while in the possession of the carrier, the risk of loss passes to the lessee when the goods are there so tendered as to enable the lessee to take delivery.

(b) If the goods are held by a bailee to be delivered without being moved, the risk of loss passes to the lessee on acknowledgment by the bailee to the lessee of the lessee's right to possession of the goods.

(c) In any case not within subsection (a) or (b), the risk of loss passes to the lessee on the lessee's receipt of the goods.

As amended in 2003.

Official Comment

Uniform Statutory Source: Section 2–509(1) through (3).

Changes: Subsection (1) is new. The introduction to subsection (2) is new, but subparagraph (a) incorporates the provisions of Section 2–509(1); subparagraph (b) incorporates the provisions of Section 2–509(2) only in part, reflecting current practice in lease transactions.

Purposes: Subsection (1) states rules related to retention or passage of risk of loss consistent with current practice in lease transactions. The provisions of subsection (4) of Section 2–509 are not incorporated as they are not necessary. This section does not deal with responsibility for loss caused by the wrongful act of either the lessor or the lessee.

Cross References:

Sections 2–509(1), 2–509(2) and 2–509(4).

Definitional Cross References:

"Delivery". Section 2A–103(1)(g).
"Finance lease". Section 2A–103(1)(l).
"Goods". Section 2A–103(1)(n).
"Lease contract". Section 2A–103(1)(r).
"Lessee". Section 2A–103(1)(t).
"Lessor". Section 2A–103(1)(v).
"Merchant". Section 2–104(1).
"Receipt". Section 2–103(1)(c).
"Rights". Section 1–201.
"Supplier". Section 2A–103(1)(ff).

§ 2A–220. Effect of Default on Risk of Loss.

(1) Where risk of loss is to pass to the lessee and the time of passage is not stated:

(a) If a tender or delivery of goods so fails to conform to the lease contract as to give a right of rejection, the risk of their loss remains with the lessor, or, in the case of a finance lease, the supplier, until cure or acceptance.

(b) If the lessee rightfully revokes acceptance, the lessee, to the extent of any deficiency in its effective insurance coverage, may treat the risk of loss as having remained with the lessor from the beginning.

(2) Whether or not risk of loss is to pass to the lessee, if the lessee as to conforming goods already identified to a lease contract repudiates or is otherwise in default under the lease contract, the lessor, or, in the case of a finance lease, the supplier, to the extent of any deficiency in its effective insurance coverage may treat the risk of loss as resting on the lessee for a commercially reasonable time.

As amended in 2003.

Official Comment

Uniform Statutory Source: Section 2–510.

Changes: Revised to reflect leasing practices and terminology. The rule in Section (1)(b) does not allow the lessee under a finance lease to treat the risk of loss as having remained with the supplier from the beginning. This is appropriate given the limited circumstances under which the lessee under a finance lease is allowed to revoke acceptance. Section 2A–517 and Section 2A–516 official comment.

Cross Reference

Section 2A–516 and 2A–517.

Definitional Cross References:

"Conforming". Section 2A–103(1)(c).
"Delivery". Section 2A–103(1)(g).
"Finance lease". Section 2A–103(1)(l).
"Goods". Section 2A–103(1)(n).
"Lease contract". Section 2A–103(1)(r).
"Lessee". Section 2A–103(1)(t).
"Lessor". Section 2A–103(1)(v).
"Reasonable time". Section 1–205.
"Rights". Section 1–201.
"Supplier". Section 2A–103(1)(ff).

§ 2A–221. Casualty to Identified Goods.

If a lease contract requires goods identified when the lease contract is made, and the goods suffer casualty without fault of the lessee, the lessor or the supplier before delivery, or the goods suffer casualty before risk of loss passes to the lessee pursuant to the lease agreement or Section 2A–219:

(a) if the loss is total, the lease contract is terminated; and

(b) if the loss is partial or the goods have so deteriorated as to no longer conform to the lease contract, the lessee may nevertheless demand inspection and at the lessee's option either treat the lease contract as terminated or, except in a finance lease that is not a consumer lease, accept the goods with due allowance from the rent payable for the balance of the lease term for the deterioration or the deficiency in quantity but without further right against the lessor.

As amended in 2003.

Official Comment

Uniform Statutory Source: Section 2–613.

Changes: Revised to reflect leasing practices and terminology.

Purpose: Due to the vagaries of determining the amount of due allowance (Section 2–613(b)), no attempt was made in subsection (b) to treat a problem unique to lease contracts and installment sales contracts: determining how to recapture the allowance, *e.g.*, application to the first or last rent payments or allocation, *pro rata*, to all rent payments.

Cross References:

Section 2–613.

Definitional Cross References:

"Conforming". Section 2A–103(1)(c).
"Consumer lease". Section 2A–103(1)(f).
"Delivery". Section 2A–103(1)(g).
"Fault". Section 2A–103(1)(k).
"Finance lease". Section 2A–103(1)(l).
"Goods". Section 2A–103(1)(n).
"Lease". Section 2A–103(1)(p).
"Lease agreement". Section 2A–103(1)(k).
"Lease contract". Section 2A–103(1)(r).
"Lessee". Section 2A–103(1)(t).
"Lessor". Section 2A–103(1)(v).
"Rights". Section 1–201.
"Supplier". Section 2A–103(1)(ff).

§ 2A–222. Legal Recognition of Electronic Contracts, Records and Signatures.

(1) A record or signature may not be denied legal effect or enforceability solely because it is in electronic form.

(2) A contract may not be denied legal effect or enforceability solely because an electronic record was used in its formation.

(3) This article does not require a record or signature to be created, generated, sent, communicated, received, stored, or otherwise processed by electronic means or in electronic form.

(4) A contract formed by the interaction of an individual and an electronic agent under Section 2A–204(4)(b) does not include terms provided by the individual if the individual had reason to know that the agent could not react to the terms as provided.

As added in 2003.

Official Comment

1. Subsections (1) and (2) are derived from Section 7(a) and (b) of the Uniform Electronic Transactions Act (UETA), and subsection (3) is derived from Section 5(a) of UETA. Subsection (4) is based on Section 206(c) of the Uniform Computer Information Transactions Act (UCITA). Each subsection conforms to the federal Electronic Signatures in Global and National Commerce Act (15 U.S.C. § 7001 *et seq.*).

2. This section sets forth the premise that the medium in which a record, signature, or contract is created, presented or retained does not affect its legal significance. Subsections (1) and (2) are designed to eliminate the single element of medium as a reason to deny effect or enforceability to a record, signature, or contract. The fact that the information is set forth in an electronic, as opposed to paper, medium is irrelevant.

3. A contract may have legal effect and yet be unenforceable. *See* Restatement 2d Contracts Section 8. To the extent that a contract in electronic form may have legal effect but be unenforceable, because it is in electronic form, subsection (2) validates its legality. Likewise, to the extent that a record or signature in electronic form may have legal effect but be unenforceable, because it is in electronic form, subsection (1) validates the legality of the record or signature. Whether an electronic record or signature is valid under other law is not addressed by this Act.

4. While subsection (2) validates the legality of an electronic contract, it does not in any way diminish the requirements for the formation of contracts under Sections 2A–204 and 2A–206.

5. Paper leases are tangible chattel paper under Article 9, and lease financiers and syndicators often perfect security interests in the paper by taking physical possession of it. Sections 9–102(a)(11), (78), 9–310(b)(6), 9–313(a). Article 9 provides for "control" as an analogue to possession for electronic chattel paper. Sections 9–102(a)(11), (31), 9–105, 9–310(b)(8), 9–314(a). To acquire control, a secured party must comply with each of the requirements of Section 9–105.

Cross References:

Point 3: Section 2–201
Point 4: Sections 2A–204 and 2A–206.

Definitional Cross References:

"Electronic" Section 2A–103(1)(h).

"Electronic Agent". Section 2A–103(1)(i).

"Electronic Record". Section 2A–103(1)(j).

"Record". Section 2A–103 (1)(cc).

"Sign". Section 2A–103(1)(dd).

As added in 2003.

§ 2A–223. Attribution.

An electronic record or electronic signature is attributed to a person if it was the act of the person or the person's electronic agent or the person is otherwise legally bound by the act.

As added in 2003.

Official Comment

1. This section is based on Section 9 of the Uniform Electronic Transactions Act (UETA).

2. As long as an electronic record is created by a person or the electronic signature results from a person's action it is attributed to that person. The legal effect of the attribution is derived from other provisions of this Act or from other law. This section simply assures that these rules will be applied in the electronic environment. A person's actions include actions taken by a human agent of the person as well as actions taken by an electronic agent, of the person. Although this section may appear to state the obvious, it assures that the record or signature is not ascribed to a machine, as opposed to the person operating or programming the machine.

3. Nothing in this section affects the use of an electronic signature as a means of attributing a record to a person. Once an electronic signature is attributed to the person, the electronic record with which it is associated would also be attributed to the person unless the person established fraud, forgery, or other invalidating cause. However, an electronic signature is not the only method for attribution of a record.

4. In the context of attribution of records, normally the content of the record will provide the necessary information for a finding of attribution. It is also possible that an established course of dealing between parties may result in a finding of attribution. Just as with a paper record, evidence of forgery or counterfeiting may be introduced to rebut the evidence of attribution. The use of facsimile transmissions provides a number of examples of attribution using information other than a signature. A facsimile may be attributed to a person because of the information printed across the top of the page that indicates the machine from which it was sent. Similarly, the transmission may contain a letterhead which identifies the sender. Some cases have held that the letterhead actually constituted a signature because it was a symbol adopted by the sender with intent to sign the record. *See* Cox Engineering v. Funston Mach. & Supply, 749 S.W.2d 508, 511 (Tex.App.1988) (plaintiff's letterhead, including address, appearing at top of invoice, provides authentication that identifies the party to be charged and thus satisfies the statute of frauds' signature requirement); Owen v. Kroger Co., 936 F. Supp. 579 (S.D. Ind. 1996)(determining that a letterhead satisfies the signature requirement of the UCC). However, the signature determination resulted from the necessary finding of intention in that case. Other cases have found letterheads NOT to be signatures because the requisite intention was not present. *See* First National Bank in Alamosa v. Ford Motor Credit Co., 748 F. Supp. 1464 (D. Colo. 1990)(determining that a pre-printed name on a draft was not a signature for the purpose of accepting a draft). The critical point is that with or without a signature, information within the electronic record may well suffice to provide the facts resulting in attribution of an electronic record to a particular party.

5. Certain information may be present in an electronic environment that does not appear to attribute but which clearly links a person to a particular record. Numerical codes, personal identification numbers, public and private key combinations, all serve to establish the party to which an electronic record should be attributed. Security procedures will be another piece of evidence available to establish attribution.

6. Once it is established that a record or signature is attributable to a particular person, the legal significance of the record or signature is determined by the context and surrounding circumstances in which the recorder signature is created, including the parties' agreement, if any. This will primarily be governed by other sections of this article. *See, e.g.*, sections 2–201, 2–202, 2–204, 2–206, and 2–209 and Sections 2A–201, 2A–202, 2A–204, 2A–206 and 2A–209.

Cross References:

Point 6: Sections 2–201, 2–202, 2–204, 2–206, and 2–209 and Sections 2A–201, 2A–202, 2A–204, 2A–206 and 2A–209.

Definitional Cross References:

"Electronic" Section 2A–103(1)(h).

"Electronic Agent". Section 2A–103(1)(i).

"Electronic Record". Section 2A–103(1)(j).

"Record". Section 2A–103 (1)(cc).

"Sign". Section 2A–103(1)(dd).

As added in 2003.

§ 2A-224. Electronic Communication.

(1) If the receipt of an electronic communication has a legal effect, it has that effect even if no individual is aware of its receipt.

(2) Receipt of an electronic acknowledgment of an electronic communication establishes that the communication was received but, in itself, does not establish that the content sent corresponds to the content received.

As added in 2003.

Official Comment

1. This section is adapted from Sections 15(e) and (f) of the Uniform Electronic Transactions Act (UETA).

2. This section deals with electronic communications generally, and it is not limited to electronic records which must be retrievable in perceivable form. The section does not resolve the questions of when or where electronic communications are determined to be sent or received, nor does it indicate that a communication has any particular substantive legal effect.

3. Under subsection (1), receipt is not dependent on a person having notice communication. An analogy in a paper based transaction is the recipient that does not read a notice received in the mail.

4. Subsection (2) provides legal certainty about the effect of an electronic acknowledgment. This subsection only addresses the fact of the receipt, and it does not set forth the legal significance of the quality of the content, nor whether the electronic communication was read or "opened."

5. This section does not address the question of whether the exchange of electronic communications constitutes the formation of a contract. Those questions are addressed by Sections 2A-204 and 2A-206.

Cross References:

Point 5: Section 2A-204 and 2A-206.

Definitional Cross References:

"Electronic" Section 2A-103(1)(h).
"Electronic Agent". Section 2A-103(1)(i).
"Electronic Record". Section 2A-103(1)(j).
"Record". Section 2A-103 (1)(cc).
"Sign". Section 2A-103(1)(dd).

As added in 2003.

PART 3

EFFECT OF LEASE CONTRACT

§ 2A-301. Enforceability Of Lease Contract.

Except as otherwise provided in this Article, a lease contract is effective and enforceable according to its terms between the parties, against purchasers of the goods and against creditors of the parties.

Official Comment

Uniform Statutory Source: Section 9-201.

Changes: The first sentence of Section 9-201 was incorporated, modified to reflect leasing terminology. The second sentence of Section 9-201 was eliminated as not relevant to leasing practices.

Purposes:

1. This section establishes a general rule regarding the validity and enforceability of a lease contract. The lease contract is effective and enforceable between the parties and against third parties. Exceptions to this general rule arise where there is a specific rule to the contrary in this Article. Enforceability is, thus, depen-

dent upon the lease contract meeting the requirements of the Statute of Frauds provisions of Section 2A-201. Enforceability is also a function of the lease contract conforming to the principles of construction and interpretation contained in the Article on General Provisions (Article 1). Section 2A-103(4).

2. The effectiveness or enforceability of the lease contract is not dependent upon the lease contract or any financing statement or the like being filed or recorded; however, the priority of the interest of a lessor of fixtures with respect to the interests of certain third parties in such fixtures is subject to the provisions of the Article on Secured Transactions (Article 9). Section 2A-309. Prior to the adoption of this Article filing or recording was not required with respect to leases, only leases intended as security. The definition of security interest, as amended concurrently with the adoption of this Article, more clearly delineates leases and leases intended as security and thus signals the need to file. Section 1-201(37). Those lessors who are concerned about whether the transaction creates a lease or a security interest will continue to

file a protective financing statement. Section 9–408. Coogan, Leasing and the Uniform Commercial Code, in *Equipment Leasing–Leveraged Leasing* 681, 744–46 (2d ed. 1980).

3. Hypothetical:

(a) In construing this section it is important to recognize its relationship to other sections in this Article. This is best demonstrated by reference to a hypothetical. Assume that on February 1 A, a manufacturer of combines and other farm equipment, leased a fleet of six combines to B, a corporation engaged in the business of farming, for a 12 month term. Under the lease agreement between A and B, A agreed to defer B's payment of the first two months' rent to April 1. On March 1 B recognized that it would need only four combines and thus subleased two combines to C for an 11 month term.

(b) This hypothetical raises a number of issues that are answered by the sections contained in this part. Since lease is defined to include sublease (Section 2A–103(1)(j) and (w)), this section provides that the prime lease between A and B and the sublease between B and C are enforceable in accordance with their terms, except as otherwise provided in this Article; that exception, in this case, is one of considerable scope.

(c) The separation of ownership, which is in A, and possession, which is in B with respect to four combines and which is in C with respect to two combines, is not relevant. Section 2A–302. A's interest in the six combines cannot be challenged simply because A parted with possession to B, who in turn parted with possession of some of the combines to C. Yet it is important to note that by the terms of Section 2A–302 this conclusion is subject to change if otherwise provided in this Article.

(d) B's entering the sublease with C raises an issue that is treated by this part. In a dispute over the leased combines A may challenge B's right to sublease. The rule is permissive as to transfers of interests under a lease contract, including subleases. Section 2A–303(2). However, the rule has two significant qualifications. If the prime lease contract between A and B prohibits B from subleasing the combines, or makes such a sublease an event of default, Section 2A–303(2) applies; thus, while B's interest under the prime lease may be transferred under the sublease to C, A may have a remedy pursuant to Section 2A–303(5). Absent a prohibition or default provision in the prime lease contract A might be able to argue that the sublease to C materially increases A's risk; thus, while B's interest

under the prime lease may be transferred under the sublease to C, A may have a remedy pursuant to Section 2A–303(5). Section 2A–303(5)(b)(ii).

(e) Resolution of this issue is also a function of the section dealing with the sublease of goods by a prime lessee (Section 2A–305). Subsection (1) of Section 2A–305, which is subject to the rules of Section 2A–303 stated above, provides that C takes subject to the interest of A under the prime lease between A and B. However, there are two exceptions. First, if B is a merchant (Sections 2A–103(3) and 2–104(1)) dealing in goods of that kind and C is a sublessee in the ordinary course of business (Sections 2A–103(1)(o) and 2A–103(1)(n)), C takes free of the prime lease between A and B. Second, if B has rejected the six combines under the prime lease with A, and B disposes of the goods by sublease to C, C takes free of the prime lease if C can establish good faith. Section 2A–511(4).

(f) If the facts of this hypothetical are expanded and we assume that the prime lease obligated B to maintain the combines, an additional issue may be presented. Prior to entering the sublease, B, in satisfaction of its maintenance covenant, brought the two combines that it desired to sublease to a local independent dealer of A's. The dealer did the requested work for B. C inspected the combines on the dealer's lot after the work was completed. C signed the sublease with B two days later. C, however, was prevented from taking delivery of the two combines as B refused to pay the dealer's invoice for the repairs. The dealer furnished the repair service to B in the ordinary course of the dealer's business. If under applicable law the dealer has a lien on repaired goods in the dealer's possession, the dealer's lien will take priority over B's and C's interests and also should take priority over A's interest, depending upon the terms of the lease contract and the applicable law. Section 2A–306.

(g) Now assume that C is in financial straits and one of C's creditors obtains a judgment against C. If the creditor levies on C's subleasehold interest in the two combines, who will prevail? Unless the levying creditor also holds a lien covered by Section 2A–306, discussed above, the judgment creditor will take its interest subject to B's rights under the sublease and A's rights under the prime lease. Section 2A–307(1). The hypothetical becomes more complicated if we assume that B is in financial straits and B's creditor holds the judgment. Here the judgment creditor takes subject to the sublease unless the lien attached to the two combines before the sublease contract became enforceable. Section 2A–307(2)(a). However, B's judgment creditor cannot prime A's interest in the goods because, with respect to A, the judgment creditor is a creditor of B in its capacity as lessee under the prime lease between A and B. Thus, here the judgment creditor's interest is subject to the lease between A and B. Section 2A–307(1).

(h) Finally, assume that on April 1 B is unable to pay A the deferred rent then due under the prime lease, but that C is current in its payments under the sublease from B. What effect will B's default under the prime lease between A and B have on C's rights under the sublease between B and C? Section 2A–301 provides that a lease contract is effective against the creditors of either party. Since a lease contract includes a sublease contract (Section 2A–103(1)(*l*)), the sublease contract between B and C arguably could be enforceable against A, a prime lessor who has extended unsecured credit to B, the prime lessee/sublessor, if the sublease contract meets the requirements of Section 2A–201. However, the rule stated in Section 2A–301 is subject to other provisions in this Article. Under Section 2A–305, C, as sublessee, would take subject to the prime lease contract in most cases. Thus, B's default under the prime lease will in most cases lead to A's recovery of the goods from C. Section 2A–523. A and C could provide otherwise by agreement. Section 2A–311. C's recourse will be to assert a claim for damages against B. Sections 2A–211(1) and 2A–508.

4.   Relationship Between Sections:

(a) As the analysis of the hypothetical demonstrates, Part 3 of the Article focuses on issues that relate to the enforceability of the lease contract (Sections 2A–301, 2A–302 and 2A–303) and to the priority of various claims to the goods subject to the lease contract (Sections 2A–304, 2A–305, 2A–306, 2A–307, 2A–308, 2A–309, 2A–310, and 2A–311).

(b) This section states a general rule of enforceability, which is subject to specific rules to the contrary stated elsewhere in the Article. Section 2A–302 negates any notion that the separation of title and possession is fraudulent as a rule of law. Finally, Section 2A–303 states rules with respect to the transfer of the lessor's interest (as well as the residual interest in the goods) or the lessee's interest under the lease contract. Qualifications are imposed as a function of various issues, including whether the transfer is the creation or enforcement of a security interest or one that is material to the other party to the lease contract. In addition, a system of rules is created to deal with the rights and duties among assignor, assignee and the other party to the lease contract.

(c) Sections 2A–304 and 2A–305 are twins that deal with good faith transferees of goods subject to the lease contract. Section 2A–304 creates a set of rules with respect to transfers by the lessor of goods subject to a lease contract; the transferee considered is a subsequent lessee of the goods. The priority dispute covered here is between the subsequent lessee and the original lessee of the goods (or persons claiming through the original lessee). Section 2A–305 creates a set of rules with respect to transfers by the lessee of goods subject to a lease contract; the transferees considered are buyers of the goods or sublessees of the goods. The priority dispute covered here is between the transferee and the lessor of the goods (or persons claiming through the lessor).

(d) Section 2A–306 creates a rule with respect to priority disputes between holders of liens for services or materials furnished with respect to goods subject to a lease contract and the lessor or the lessee under that contract. Section 2A–307 creates a rule with respect to priority disputes between the lessee and creditors of the lessor and priority disputes between the lessor and creditors of the lessee.

(e) Section 2A–308 creates a series of rules relating to allegedly fraudulent transfers and preferences. The most significant rule is that set forth in subsection (3) which validates sale-leaseback transactions if the buyer-lessor can establish that he or she bought for value and in good faith.

(f) Sections 2A–309 and 2A–310 create a series of rules with respect to priority disputes between various third parties and a lessor of fixtures or accessions, respectively, with respect thereto.

(g) Finally, Section 2A–311 allows parties to alter the statutory priorities by agreement.

Cross References:

Point 1: Section 2A–201
Point 2: Sections 1–201 and 1–203, Section 2A–309 and Article 9.
Point 3: Sections 2A–103, 2A–201, 2A–211, 2A–303, 2A–305, 2A–306, 2A–307 2A–511, 2A–523.
Point 4: Sections 2A–301 through 2A–311.

Definitional Cross References:

"Creditor". Section 1–201.
"Goods". Section 2A–103(1)(n).
"Lease contract". Section 2A–103(1)(r).
"Party". Section 1–201.
"Purchaser". Section 1–201.

"Term". Section 1–201.

As amended in 1990.

§ 2A-302. Title to and Possession of Goods.

Except as otherwise provided in this Article, each provision of this Article applies whether the lessor or a third party has title to the goods, and whether the lessor, the lessee, or a third party has possession of the goods, notwithstanding any statute or rule of law that possession or the absence of possession is fraudulent.

Official Comment

Uniform Statutory Source: Section 9–202.

Changes: Section 9–202 was modified to reflect leasing terminology and to clarify the law of leases with respect to fraudulent conveyances or transfers.

Purposes: The separation of ownership and possession of goods between the lessor and the lessee (or a third party) has created problems under certain fraudulent conveyance statutes. *See, e.g., In re Ludlum Enters.,* 510 F.2d 996 (5th Cir. 1975); *Suburbia Fed. Sav. & Loan Ass'n v. Bel–Air Conditioning Co.,* 385 So.2d 1151 (Fla.Dist.Ct.App.1980). This section provides, among other things, that separation of ownership and possession *per se* does not affect the enforceability of the lease contract. Sections 2A–301 and 2A–308.

Cross References:

Sections 2A–301, 2A–308 and Section 9–202.

Definitional Cross References:

"Goods". Section 2A–103(1)(n).
"Lessee". Section 2A–103(1)(t).
"Lessor". Section 2A–103(1)(v).

§ 2A-303. Alienability of Party's Interest under Lease Contract or of Lessor's Residual Interest in Goods; Delegation of Performance; Transfer of Rights.

(1) As used in this section, "creation of a security interest" includes the sale of a lease contract that is subject to Article 9 by reason of Section 9–109(a)(3).

(2) Subject to subsection (3) and except as otherwise provided in Section 9–407 or as otherwise agreed, a provision in a lease agreement which (i) prohibits the voluntary or involuntary transfer, including a transfer by sale, sublease, creation or enforcement of a security interest, or attachment, levy, or other judicial process, of an interest of a party under the lease contract or of the lessor's residual interest in the goods, or (ii) makes such a transfer an event of default, gives rise to the rights and remedies provided in subsection (4). However, a transfer that is prohibited or is an event of default under the lease agreement is otherwise effective.

(3) A provision in a lease agreement which (i) prohibits a transfer of a right to damages for default with respect to the whole lease contract or of a right to payment arising out of the transferor's due performance of the transferor's entire obligation, or (ii) makes such a transfer an event of default, is not enforceable, and such a transfer is not a transfer that materially impairs the prospect of obtaining return performance by, materially changes the duty of, or materially increases the burden or risk imposed on, the other party to the lease contract within subsection (4).

(4) Subject to subsection (3) and Section 9–407:

(a) if a transfer is made that is an event of default under a lease agreement, the party to the lease contract not making the transfer, unless that party waives the default or otherwise agrees, has the rights and remedies described in Section 2A–501(2);

(b) if paragraph (a) is not applicable and if a transfer is made that (i) is prohibited under a lease agreement or (ii) materially impairs the prospect of obtaining return performance by, materially changes the duty of, or materially increases the burden or risk imposed on, the other party to the lease contract, unless the party not making the transfer agrees at any time to the transfer in the lease contract or otherwise, then, except as limited by contract, (i) the transferor is liable to the party not making the transfer for damages caused by the transfer to the extent that the damages could not reasonably be prevented by the party not making the transfer and (ii) a court having jurisdiction may grant other appropriate relief, including cancellation of the lease contract or an injunction against the transfer.

(5) A transfer of "the lease" or of "all my rights under the lease", or a transfer in similar general terms, is a transfer of rights and, unless the language or the circumstances, as in a transfer for security, indicate the contrary, the transfer is a delegation of duties by the transferor to the transferee. Acceptance by the transferee constitutes a promise by the transferee to perform those duties. The promise is enforceable by either the transferor or the other party to the lease contract.

(6) Unless otherwise agreed by the lessor and the lessee, a delegation of performance does not relieve the transferor as against the other party of any duty to perform or of any liability for default.

(7) In a consumer lease, to prohibit the transfer of an interest of a party under the lease contract or to make a transfer an event of default, the language must be specific, by a record, and conspicuous.

As amended in 1990, 1999 and 2003.

Official Comment

1. Subsection (2) states a rule, consistent with Section 9–401(b), that voluntary and involuntary transfers of an interest of a party under the lease contract or of the lessor's residual interest, including by way of the creation or enforcement of a security interest, are effective, notwithstanding a provision in the lease agreement prohibiting the transfer or making the transfer an event of default. Although the transfers are effective, the provision in the lease agreement is nevertheless enforceable, but only as provided in subsection (4). Under subsection (4) the prejudiced party is limited to the remedies on "default under the lease contract" in this Article and, except as limited by this Article, as provided in the lease agreement, if the transfer has been made an event of default. Section 2A–501(2). Usually, there will be a specific provision to this effect or a general provision making a breach of a covenant an event of default. In those cases where the transfer is prohibited, but not made an event of default, the prejudiced party may recover damages; or, if the damage remedy would be ineffective adequately to protect that party, the court can order cancellation of the lease contract or enjoin the transfer. This rule that such provisions generally are enforceable is subject to subsection (3) and Section 9–407, which make such provisions unenforceable in certain instances.

2. Under Section 9–407, a provision in a lease agreement which prohibits the creation or enforcement of a security interest, including sales of lease contracts subject to Article 9 (Section 9–109(a)(3)), or makes it an event of default is generally not enforceable, reflecting the policy of Section 9–406 and former Section 9–318(4).

3. Subsection (3) is based upon Section 2–210(2) and Section 9–406. It makes unenforceable a prohibition against transfers of certain rights to payment or a provision making the transfer an event of default. It also provides that such transfers do not materially impair the prospect of obtaining return performance by, materially change the duty of, or materially increase the burden or risk imposed on, the other party to the lease contract so as to give rise to the rights and remedies stated in subsection (4). Accordingly, a transfer of a right to payment cannot be prohibited or made an event of default, or be one that materially impairs performance, changes duties or increases risk, if the right is already due or will become due without further performance being required by the party to receive payment. Thus, a lessor can transfer the right to future payments under the lease contract, including by way of a grant of a security interest, and the transfer will not give rise to the rights and remedies stated in subsection (4) if the lessor has no remaining performance under the lease contract. The mere fact that the lessor is obligated to allow the lessee to remain in possession and to use the goods as long as the lessee is not in default does not mean that there is remaining performance on the part of the lessor. Likewise, the fact that the lessor has potential liability under a "non-operating" lease contract for breaches of warranty does not mean that there is remaining performance. In contrast, the lessor would have remaining performance under a lease contract requiring the lessor to regularly maintain and service the goods or to provide "upgrades" of the equipment on a periodic basis in order to avoid obsolescence. The basic distinction is between a mere potential duty to respond which is not remaining performance, and an affirmative duty to render stipulated performance. Although the distinction may be difficult to draw in some cases, it is instructive to focus on the difference between "operating" and "non-operating" leases as generally understood in the marketplace. Even if there is "remaining performance" under a lease contract, a transfer for security of a right to payment that is made an event of default or that is in violation of a prohibition against transfer does not give rise to the rights and remedies under subsection (4) if it does not constitute an actual delegation of a material performance under Section 9–407.

4. The application of either the rule of Section 9–407 or the rule of subsection (3) to the grant by the

lessor of a security interest in the lessor's right to future payment under the lease contract may produce the same result. Both provisions generally protect security transfers by the lessor in particular because the creation by the lessor of a security interest or the enforcement of that interest generally will not prejudice the lessee's rights if it does not result in a delegation of the lessor's duties. To the contrary, the receipt of loan proceeds or relief from the enforcement of an antecedent debt normally should enhance the lessor's ability to perform its duties under the lease contract. Nevertheless, there are circumstances where relief might be justified. For example, if ownership of the goods is transferred pursuant to enforcement of a security interest to a party whose ownership would prevent the lessee from continuing to possess the goods, relief might be warranted. See 49 U.S.C. § 1401(a) and (b) which places limitations on the operation of aircraft in the United States based on the citizenship or corporate qualification of the registrant.

5. Relief on the ground of material prejudice when the lease agreement does not prohibit the transfer or make it an event of default should be afforded only in extreme circumstances, considering the fact that the party asserting material prejudice did not insist upon a provision in the lease agreement that would protect against such a transfer.

6. Subsection (4) implements the rule of subsection (2). Subsection (2) provides that, even though a transfer is effective, a provision in the lease agreement prohibiting it or making it an event of default may be enforceable as provided in subsection (4). See Brummond v. First National Bank of Clovis, 656 P.2d 884, 35 U.C.C.Rep.Serv. (Callaghan) 1311 (N.Mex.1983), stating the analogous rule for Section 9–311. If the transfer prohibited by the lease agreement is made an event of default, then, under subsection (4)(a), unless the default is waived or there is an agreement otherwise, the aggrieved party has the rights and remedies referred to in Section 2A–501(2), viz. those in this Article and, except as limited in the Article, those provided in the lease agreement. In the unlikely circumstance that the lease agreement prohibits the transfer without making a violation of the prohibition an event of default or, even if there is no prohibition against the transfer, and the transfer is one that materially impairs performance, changes duties, or increases risk (for example, a sublease or assignment to a party using the goods improperly or for an illegal purpose), then subsection (4)(b) is applicable. In that circumstance, unless the party aggrieved by the transfer has otherwise agreed in the lease contract, such as by assenting to a particular transfer or to transfers in

general, or agrees in some other manner, the aggrieved party has the right to recover damages from the transferor and a court may, in appropriate circumstances, grant other relief, such as cancellation of the lease contract or an injunction against the transfer.

7. If a transfer gives rise to the rights and remedies provided in subsection (4), the transferee as an alternative may propose, and the other party may accept, adequate cure or compensation for past defaults and adequate assurance of future due performance under the lease contract. Subsection (4) does not preclude any other relief that may be available to a party to the lease contract aggrieved by a transfer subject to an enforceable prohibition, such as an action for interference with contractual relations.

8. Subsection (7) requires that a provision in a consumer lease prohibiting a transfer, or making it an event of default, must be specific, written and conspicuous. See Section 1–201(10). This assists in protecting a consumer lessee against surprise assertions of default.

9. Subsection (5) is taken almost verbatim from the provisions of Section 2–210(5). The subsection states a rule of construction that distinguishes a commercial assignment, which substitutes the assignee for the assignor as to rights and duties, and an assignment for security or financing assignment, which substitutes the assignee for the assignor only as to rights. Note that the assignment for security or financing assignment is a subset of all security interests. Security interest is defined to include "any interest of a buyer of ___ chattel paper". Section 1–201(37). Chattel paper is defined to include a lease. Section 9–102. Thus, a buyer of leases is the holder of a security interest in the leases. That conclusion should not influence this issue, as the policy is quite different. Whether a buyer of leases is the holder of a commercial assignment, or an assignment for security or financing assignment should be determined by the language of the assignment or the circumstances of the assignment.

Cross References:

Point 1: Section 2A–501 and Sections 9–401 and 9–407.
Point 2: Sections 9–109, 9–318, 9–416 and 9–417.
Point 3: Section 2–210 and Sections 9–406 and 9–407.
Point 4: Section 9–407.
Point 6: Section 2A–501 and Section 9–311.
Point 8: Section 1–201.
Point 9: Section 1–201 and Section 2–210 and Section 9–102.

Definitional Cross References:

"Agreed" and "Agreement". Section 1–201.
"Conspicuous". Section 2A–103(1)(d).
"Goods". Section 2A–103(1)(n).
"Lease". Section 2A–103(1)(p).
"Lease contract". Section 2A–103(1)(r).
"Lessee". Section 2A–103(1)(t).
"Lessor". Section 2A–103(1)(v).
"Lessor's residual interest". Section 2A–103(1)(w).
"Notice". Section 1–202.
"Party". Section 1–201.
"Person". Section 1–201.
"Reasonable time". Section 1–205.
"Record". Section 2A–103(1)(cc).
"Rights". Section 1–201.
"Term". Section 1–201.

As amended in 1999.

§ 2A–304. Subsequent Lease of Goods by Lessor.

(1) Subject to Section 2A–303, a subsequent lessee from a lessor of goods under an existing lease contract obtains, to the extent of the lease-hold interest transferred, the leasehold interest in the goods that the lessor had or had power to transfer, and except as provided in subsection (2) and Section 2A–527(4), takes subject to the existing lease contract. A lessor with voidable title has power to transfer a good leasehold interest to a good faith subsequent lessee for value, but only to the extent set forth in the preceding sentence. If goods have been delivered under a transaction of purchase, the lessor has that power even if:

(a) the lessor's transferor was deceived as to the identity of the lessor;

(b) the delivery was in exchange for a check which is later dishonored;

(c) it was agreed that the transaction was to be a "cash sale"; or

(d) the delivery was procured through criminal fraud.

(2) A subsequent lessee in ordinary course of business from a lessor that is a merchant dealing in goods of that kind to which the goods were entrusted by the existing lessee of that lessor before the interest of the subsequent lessee became enforceable against that lessor obtains, to the extent of the leasehold interest transferred, all of that lessor's and the existing lessee's rights

to the goods, and takes free of the existing lease contract.

(3) A subsequent lessee from the lessor of goods that are subject to an existing lease contract and are covered by a certificate of title issued under a statute of this State or of another jurisdiction takes no greater rights than those provided both by this section and by the certificate of title statute.

As amended in 1990 and 2003.

Official Comment

Uniform Statutory Source: Section 2–403.

Changes: While Section 2–403 was used as a model for this section, the provisions of Section 2–403 were significantly revised to reflect leasing practices and to integrate this Article with certificate of title statutes.

Purposes:

1. This section must be read in conjunction with, as it is subject to, the provisions of Section 2A–303, which govern voluntary and involuntary transfers of rights and duties under a lease contract, including the lessor's residual interest in the goods.

2. This section must also be read in conjunction with Section 2–403. This section and Section 2A–305 are derived from Section 2–403, which states a unified policy on good faith purchases of goods. Given the scope of the definition of purchaser (Section 1–201(33)), a person who bought goods to lease as well as a person who bought goods subject to an existing lease from a lessor will take pursuant to Section 2–403. Further, a person who leases such goods from the person who bought them should also be protected under Section 2–403, first because the lessee's rights are derivative and second because the definition of purchaser should be interpreted to include one who takes by lease; no negative implication should be drawn from the inclusion of lease in the definition of purchase in this Article. Section 2A–103(1)(v).

3. There are hypotheticals that relate to an entrustee's unauthorized lease of entrusted goods to a third party that are outside the provisions of Sections 2–403, 2A–304 and 2A–305. Consider a sale of goods by M, a merchant, to B, a buyer. After paying for the goods B allows M to retain possession of the goods as B is short of storage. Before B calls for the goods M leases the goods to L, a lessee. This transaction is not governed by Section 2–403(2) as L is not a buyer in the ordinary course of business. Section 1–201(9). Further, this transaction is not governed by Section 2A–304(2) as B is not an existing lessee. Finally, this transaction is not

governed by Section 2A–305(2) as B is not M's lessor. Section 2A–307(2) resolves the potential dispute between B, M and L. By virtue of B's entrustment of the goods to M and M's lease of the goods to L, B has a cause of action against M under the common law. Sections 2A–103(4) and 1–103. *See, e.g.,* Restatement (Second) of Torts §§ 222A–243. Thus, B is a creditor of M. Sections 2A–103(4) and 1–201(12). Section 2A–307(2) provides that B, as M's creditor, takes subject to M's lease to L. Thus, if L does not default under the lease, L's enjoyment and possession of the goods should be undisturbed. However, B is not without recourse. B's action should result in a judgment against M providing, among other things, a turnover of all proceeds arising from M's lease to L, as well as a transfer of all of M's right, title and interest as lessor under M's lease to L, including M's residual interest in the goods. Section 2A–103(1)(q).

4. Subsection (1) states a rule with respect to the leasehold interest obtained by a subsequent lessee from a lessor of goods under an existing lease contract. The interest will include such leasehold interest as the lessor has in the goods as well as the leasehold interest that the lessor had the power to transfer. Thus, the subsequent lessee obtains unimpaired all rights acquired under the law of agency, apparent agency, ownership or other estoppel, whether based upon statutory provisions or upon case law principles. Sections 2A–103(4) and 1–103. In general, the subsequent lessee takes subject to the existing lease contract, including the existing lessee's rights thereunder. Furthermore, the subsequent lease contract is, of course, limited by its own terms, and the subsequent lessee takes only to the extent of the leasehold interest transferred thereunder.

5. Subsection (1) further provides that a lessor with voidable title has power to transfer a good leasehold interest to a good faith subsequent lessee for value. In addition, subsections (1)(a) through (d) provide specifically for the protection of the good faith subsequent lessee for value in a number of specific situations which have been troublesome under prior law.

6. The position of an existing lessee who entrusts leased goods to its lessor is not distinguishable from the position of other entrusters. Thus, subsection (2) provides that the subsequent lessee in the ordinary course of business takes free of the existing lease contract between the lessor entrustee and the lessee entruster, if the lessor is a merchant dealing in goods of that kind. Further, the subsequent lessee obtains all of the lessor entrustee's and the lessee entruster's rights to the goods, but only to the extent of the leasehold interest transferred by the lessor entrustee.

Thus, the lessor entrustee retains the residual interest in the goods. Section 2A–103(1)(q). However, entrustment by the existing lessee must have occurred before the interest of the subsequent lessee became enforceable against the lessor. Entrusting is defined in Section 2–403(3) and that definition applies here. Section 2A–103(3).

7. Subsection (3) states a rule with respect to a transfer of goods from a lessor to a subsequent lessee where the goods are subject to an existing lease and covered by a certificate of title. The subsequent lessee's rights are no greater than those provided by this section and the applicable certificate of title statute, including any applicable case law construing such statute. Where the relationship between the certificate of title statute and Section 2–403, the statutory analogue to this section, has been construed by a court, that construction is incorporated here. Sections 2A–103(4) and 1–102(1) and (2). The better rule is that the certificate of title statutes are in harmony with Section 2–403 and thus would be in harmony with this section. *E.g., Atwood Chevrolet–Olds v. Aberdeen Mun. School Dist.,* 431 So.2d 926, 928 (Miss.1983); *Godfrey v. Gilsdorf,* 476 P.2d 3, 6, 86 Nev. 714, 718 (1970); *Martin v. Nager,* 192 N.J.Super. 189, 197–98, 469 A.2d 519, 523 (Super.Ct.Ch.Div.1983). Where the certificate of title statute is silent on this issue of transfer, this section will control.

Cross References:

Point 1: Section 2A–303.

Point 2: Sections 2–201 and 2–403 and Sections 2A–103 and 2A–305.

Point 3: Section 1–201 and Section 2–403 and Sections 2A–103, 2A–304, 2A–305, 2A–307.

Point 4: Section 1–103 and Section 2A–103.

Point 6: Section 1–102 and Section 2–403 and Sections 2A–103.

Point 7: Section 1–201 and Section 2–403 and Sections 2A–103.

Definitional Cross References:

"Agreed". Section 1–201.

"Delivery". Section 2A–103(1)(g).

"Entrusting". Section 2–403(3).

"Good faith". Sections 2A–103(1)(m).

"Goods". Section 2A–103(1)(n).

"Lease". Section 2A–103(1)(p).

"Lease contract". Section 2A–103(1)(r).

"Leasehold interest". Section 2A–103(1)(s).

"Lessee". Section 2A–103(1)(t).

"Lessee in the ordinary course of business". Section 2A–103(1)(o).

"Lessor". Section 2A–103(1)(v).
"Merchant". Section 2–104(1).
"Purchase". Section 2A–103(1)(bb).
"Rights". Section 1–201.
"Value". Section 1–204.

§ 2A–305.   Sale or Sublease of Goods by Lessee.

(1) Subject to Section 2A–303, a buyer or sublessee from the lessee of goods under an existing lease contract obtains, to the extent of the interest transferred, the leasehold interest in the goods that the lessee had or had power to transfer, and except as provided in subsection (2) and Section 2A–511(4), takes subject to the existing lease contract. A lessee with a voidable leasehold interest has power to transfer a good leasehold interest to a good faith buyer for value or a good faith sublessee for value, but only to the extent set forth in the preceding sentence. If goods have been delivered under a transaction of lease the lessee has that power even if:

(a) the lessor was deceived as to the identity of the lessee;

(b) the delivery was in exchange for a check which is later dishonored; or

(c) the delivery was procured through criminal fraud.

(2) A buyer in ordinary course of business or a sublessee in ordinary course of business from a lessee that is a merchant dealing in goods of that kind to which the goods were entrusted by the lessor obtains, to the extent of the interest transferred, all of the lessor's and lessee's rights to the goods, and takes free of the existing lease contract.

(3) A buyer or sublessee from the lessee of goods that are subject to an existing lease contract and are covered by a certificate of title issued under a statute of this State or of another jurisdiction takes no greater rights than those provided both by this section and by the certificate of title statute.

As amended in 2003.

Official Comment

Uniform Statutory Source: Section 2–403.

Changes: While Section 2–403 was used as a model for this section, the provisions of Section 2–403 were significantly revised to reflect leasing practice and to integrate this Article with certificate of title statutes.

Purposes: This section, a companion to Section 2A–304, states the rule with respect to the leasehold interest obtained by a buyer or sublessee from a lessee of goods under an existing lease contract. *Cf.* Section 2A–304 official comment. Note that this provision is consistent with existing case law, which prohibits the bailee's transfer of title to a good faith purchaser for value under Section 2–403(1). *Rohweder v. Aberdeen Product. Credit Ass'n*, 765 F.2d 109 (8th Cir. 1985).

Subsection (2) is also consistent with existing case law. *American Standard Credit, Inc. v. National Cement Co.*, 643 F.2d 248, 269–70 (5th Cir. 1981); *but cf. Exxon Co., U.S.A. v. TLW Computer Indus.*, 37 U.C.C.Rep.Serv. (Callaghan) 1052, 1057–58 (D.Mass. 1983). Unlike Section 2A–304(2), this subsection does not contain any requirement with respect to the time that the goods were entrusted to the merchant. In Section 2A–304(2) the competition is between two customers of the merchant lessor; the time of entrusting was added as a criterion to create additional protection to the customer who was first in time: the existing lessee. In subsection (2) the equities between the competing interests were viewed as balanced.

There appears to be some overlap between Section 2–403(2) and Section 2A–305(2) with respect to a buyer in the ordinary course of business. However, an examination of this Article's definition of buyer in the ordinary course of business (Section 2A–103(1)(a)) makes clear that this reference was necessary to treat entrusting in the context of a lease.

Subsection (3) states a rule of construction with respect to a transfer of goods from a lessee to a buyer or sublessee, where the goods are subject to an existing lease and covered by a certificate of title. *Cf.* Section 2A–304 official comment.

Cross References:

Sections 2–403, 2A–103(1)(a), 2A–304 and 2A–305(2).

Definitional Cross References:

"Buyer". Section 2–103(1)(a).
"Buyer in the ordinary course of business". Section 2A–103(1)(a).
"Delivery". Section 2A–103(1)(g).
"Entrusting". Section 2–403(3).
"Good faith". Sections 2A–103(1)(m).
"Goods". Section 2A–103(1)(n).
"Lease". Section 2A–103(1)(p).
"Lease contract". Section 2A–103(1)(r).
"Leasehold interest." Section 2A–103(1)(s).

"Lessee". Section 2A–103(1)(t).

"Lessee in the ordinary course of business". Section 2A–103(1)(o).

"Lessor". Section 2A–103(1)(v).

"Merchant". Section 2–104(1).

"Rights". Section 1–201.

"Sale". Section 2–106(1).

"Sublease". Section 2A–103(1)(ee).

"Value". Section 1–204.

§ 2A–306. Priority of Certain Liens Arising by Operation of Law.

If a person in the ordinary course of its business furnishes services or materials with respect to goods subject to a lease contract, a lien upon those goods in the possession of that person given by statute or rule of law for those materials or services takes priority over any interest of the lessor or lessee under the lease contract or this Article unless the lien is created by statute and the statute provides otherwise or unless the lien is created by rule of law and the rule of law provides otherwise.

As amended in 2003.

Official Comment

Uniform Statutory Source: Section 9–310.

Changes: The approach reflected in the provisions of Section 9–310 was included, but revised to conform to leasing terminology and to expand the exception to the special priority granted to protected liens to cover liens created by rule of law as well as those created by statute.

Purposes: This section should be interpreted to allow a qualified lessor or a qualified lessee to be the competing lienholder if the statute or rule of law so provides. The reference to statute includes applicable regulations and cases; these sources must be reviewed in resolving a priority dispute under this section.

Cross Reference:

Section 9–333.

Definitional Cross References:

"Goods". Section 2A–103(1)(n).

"Lease contract". Section 2A–103(1)(r).

"Lessee". Section 2A–103(1)(t).

"Lessor". Section 2A–103(1)(v).

"Lien". Section 2A–103(1)(x).

"Person". Section 1–201.

§ 2A–307. Priority of Liens Arising by Attachment or Levy On, Security Interests In, and Other Claims to Goods.

(1) Except as otherwise provided in Section 2A–306, a creditor of a lessee takes subject to the lease contract.

(2) Except as otherwise provided in subsection (3) and Sections 2A–306 and 2A–308, a creditor of a lessor takes subject to the lease contract unless the creditor holds a lien that attached to the goods before the lease contract became enforceable.

(3) Except as otherwise provided in Sections 9–317, 9–321, and 9–323, a lessee takes a leasehold interest subject to a security interest held by a creditor of the lessor.

As amended in 1990, 1999 and 2003.

Official Comment

1. Subsection (1) states a general rule of priority that a creditor of the lessee takes subject to the lease contract. The term lessee (Section 2A–102(a)(25)) includes sublessee. Therefore, this subsection not only covers disputes between the prime lessor and a creditor of the prime lessee but also disputes between the prime lessor, or the sublessor, and a creditor of the sublessee. Furthermore, by using the term "creditor" (Section 1–201(13)), this subsection covers disputes with a general creditor, a secured creditor, a lien creditor and any representative of creditors.

2. Subsection (2) states a general rule of priority that a creditor of a lessor takes subject to the lease contract. Thus, the section only covers disputes between the prime lessee and a creditor of the prime lessor but also disputes between the prime lessee, or the sublessee, and a creditor of the sublessor.

3. To take priority over the lease contract, and the interests derived from the lease contract the creditor's lien must have attached before the lease contract became enforceable.

4. The rules of this section operate in favor of whichever party to the lease contract can enforce it, even if one party may not, *e.g.*, because of Section 2A–201(1)(b).

5. The provisions of the predecessor of this section, original Section 2A–307, which dealt with the relationship between a secured creditor of the lessor and a lessee have been moved to revised Article 9 in Sections 9–317, 9–321, and 9–323.

Cross References:

Point 1: Section 1–201.
Point 4: Section 2A–201.
Point 5: Section 2A–307 and Sections 9–317, 9–321 and 9–323.

Definitional Cross References:

"Creditor". Section 1–201.
"Goods". Section 2A–103(1)(n).
"Knowledge". Section 1–202.
"Lease". Section 2A–103(1)(p).
"Lease contract". Section 2A–103(1)(r).
"Leasehold interest". Section 2A–103(1)(s).
"Lessee". Section 2A–103(1)(t).
"Lessee in the ordinary course of business". Section 2A–103(1)(o).
"Lessor". Section 2A–103(1)(v).
"Lien". Section 2A–103(1)(x).
"Party". Section 1–201.
"Pursuant to commitment". Section 2A–103(3).
"Security interest". Section 1–201.

As amended in 1999 and 2003.

§ 2A–308. Special Rights of Creditors.

(1) A creditor of a lessor in possession of goods subject to a lease contract may treat the lease contract as void if as against the creditor retention of possession by the lessor is fraudulent under any statute or rule of law, but retention of possession in good faith and current course of trade by the lessor for a commercially reasonable time after the lease contract becomes enforceable is not fraudulent.

(2) Nothing in this Article impairs the rights of creditors of a lessor if the lease contract (a) becomes enforceable, not in current course of trade but in satisfaction of or as security for a pre-existing claim for money, security, or the like, and (b) is made under circumstances which under any statute or rule of law apart from this Article would constitute the transaction a fraudulent transfer or voidable preference.

(3) A creditor of a seller may treat a sale or an identification of goods to a contract for sale as void if as against the creditor retention of possession by the seller is fraudulent under any statute or rule of law, but retention of possession of the goods pursuant to a lease contract entered into by the seller as lessee and the buyer as lessor in connection with the sale or identification of the goods is not fraudulent if the buyer bought for value and in good faith.

Official Comment

Uniform Statutory Source: Section 2–402(2) and (3)(b).

Changes: Rephrased and new material added to conform to leasing terminology and practice.

Purposes: Subsection (1) states a general rule of avoidance where the lessor has retained possession of goods if such retention is fraudulent under any statute or rule of law. However, the subsection creates an exception under certain circumstances for retention of possession of goods for a commercially reasonable time after the lease contract becomes enforceable.

Subsection (2) also preserves the possibility of an attack on the lease by creditors of the lessor if the lease was made in satisfaction of or as security for a pre-existing claim, and would constitute a fraudulent transfer or voidable preference under other law.

Finally, subsection (3) states a new rule with respect to sale-leaseback transactions, *i.e.*, transactions where the seller sells goods to a buyer but possession of the goods is retained by the seller pursuant to a lease contract between the buyer as lessor and the seller as lessee. Notwithstanding any statute or rule of law that would treat such retention as fraud, whether *per se*, *prima facie*, or otherwise, the retention is not fraudulent if the buyer bought for value (Section 1–201(44)) and in good faith (Sections 1–201(19) and 2–103(1)(b)). Section 2A–103(3) and (4). This provision overrides Section 2–402(2) to the extent it would otherwise apply to a sale-leaseback transaction.

Cross References:

Section 1–201, Section 2–402(2) and Section 2A–103(4).

Definitional Cross References:

"Buyer". Section 2–103(1)(a).
"Contract". Section 1–201.
"Creditor". Section 1–201.
"Good faith". Sections 2A–103(1)(m).
"Goods". Section 2A–103(1)(n).
"Lease contract". Section 2A–103(1)(r).
"Lessee". Section 2A–103(1)(t).
"Lessor". Section 2A–103(1)(v).
"Money". Section 1–201.
"Reasonable time". Section 1–205.
"Rights". Section 1–201.
"Sale". Section 2–106(1).
"Seller". Section 2–103(1)(o).
"Value". Section 1–204.

§ 2A-309.   Lessor's and Lessee's Rights When Goods Become Fixtures.

(1) In this section:

(a) goods are "fixtures" if they become so related to particular real property that an interest in them arises under real property law;

(b) a "fixture filing" is the filing, in the office where a mortgage on the real property would be filed or recorded, of a financing statement covering goods that are or are to become fixtures and conforming to the requirements of Section 9-502(a) and (b);

(c) a lease is a "purchase money lease" unless the lessee has possession or use of the goods or the right to possession or use of the goods before the lease agreement is enforceable;

(d) a mortgage is a "construction mortgage" to the extent it secures an obligation incurred for the construction of an improvement on land, including the acquisition cost of the land, if a recorded record of the mortgage so indicates; and

(e) "encumbrance" includes real property mortgages and other liens on real property and all other rights in real property that are not ownership interests.

(2) Under this Article a lease may be of goods that are fixtures or may continue in goods that become fixtures, but no lease exists under this Article of ordinary building materials incorporated into an improvement on land.

(3) This Article does not prevent creation of a lease of fixtures pursuant to real property law.

(4) The perfected interest of a lessor of fixtures has priority over a conflicting interest of an encumbrancer or owner of the real property if:

(a) the lease is a purchase money lease, the conflicting interest of the encumbrancer or owner arises before the goods become fixtures, the interest of the lessor is perfected by a fixture filing before the goods become fixtures or within 10 days thereafter, and the lessee has an interest of record in the real property or is in possession of the real property; or

(b) the interest of the lessor is perfected by a fixture filing before the interest of the en-

cumbrancer or owner is of record, the lessor's interest has priority over any conflicting interest of a predecessor in title of the encumbrancer or owner, and the lessee has an interest of record in the real property or is in possession of the real property.

(5) The interest of a lessor of fixtures, whether or not perfected, has priority over the conflicting interest of an encumbrancer or owner of the real property if:

(a) the fixtures are readily removable factory or office machines, readily removable equipment that is not primarily used or leased for use in the operation of the real property, or readily removable replacements of domestic appliances that are goods subject to a consumer lease, and before the goods become fixtures the lease contract is enforceable; or

(b) the conflicting interest is a lien on the real property obtained by legal or equitable proceedings after the lease contract is enforceable; or

(c) the encumbrancer or owner has consented in a record to the lease or has disclaimed an interest in the goods as fixtures; or

(d) the lessee has a right to remove the goods as against the encumbrancer or owner, but if the lessee's right to remove terminates, the priority of the interest of the lessor continues for a reasonable time.

(6) Notwithstanding subsection (4)(a) but otherwise subject to subsections (4) and (5), the interest of a lessor of fixtures, including the lessor's residual interest, is subordinate to the conflicting interest of an encumbrancer of the real property under a construction mortgage recorded before the goods become fixtures if the goods become fixtures before the completion of the construction. To the extent given to refinance a construction mortgage, the conflicting interest of an encumbrancer of the real property under a mortgage has this priority to the same extent as the encumbrancer of the real property under the construction mortgage.

(7) In cases not covered by subsections (3) through (6), priority between the interest of a lessor of fixtures, including the lessor's residual interest, and the conflicting interest of an encumbrancer or owner of the real property that is

not the lessee is determined by the priority rules governing conflicting interests in real property.

(8) If the interest of a lessor of fixtures, including the lessor's residual interest, has priority over all conflicting interests of all owners and encumbrancers of the real property, the lessor or the lessee may (i) on default, expiration, termination, or cancellation of the lease agreement but subject to the agreement and this Article, or (ii) if necessary to enforce other rights and remedies of the lessor or lessee under this Article, remove the goods from the real property, free and clear of all conflicting interests of all owners and encumbrancers of the real property, but the lessor or lessee must reimburse any encumbrancer or owner of the real property that is not the lessee and that has not otherwise agreed for the cost of repair of any physical injury, but not for any diminution in value of the real property caused by the absence of the goods removed or by any necessity of replacing them. A person entitled to reimbursement may refuse permission to remove until the party seeking removal gives adequate security for the performance of this obligation.

(9) Even if the lease agreement does not create a security interest, the interest of a lessor of fixtures, including the lessor's residual interest, is perfected by filing a financing statement as a fixture filing for leased goods that are or are to become fixtures in accordance with the relevant provisions of Article 9.

As amended in 1990, 1999 and 2003.

Official Comment

Uniform Statutory Source: Section 9–313.

Changes: Revised to reflect leasing terminology and to add new material.

Purposes:

1. While Section 9–313 provided a model for this section, certain provisions were substantially revised.

2. Section 2A–309(1)(c), which is new, defines purchase money lease to exclude leases where the lessee had possession or use of the goods or the right thereof before the lease agreement became enforceable. This term is used in subsection (4)(a) as one of the conditions that must be satisfied to obtain priority over the conflicting interest of an encumbrancer or owner of the real estate.

3. Section 2A–309(4), which states one of several priority rules found in this section, deletes reference to

office machines and the like (Section 9–313(4)(c)) as well as certain liens (Section 9–313(4)(d)). However, these items are included in subsection (5), another priority rule that is more permissive than the rule found in subsection (4) as it applies whether or not the interest of the lessor is perfected. In addition, subsection (5)(a) expands the scope of the provisions of Section 9–313(4)(c) to include readily removable equipment not primarily used or leased for use in the operation of real estate; the qualifier is intended to exclude from the expanded rule equipment integral to the operation of real estate, *e.g.*, heating and air conditioning equipment.

4. The rule stated in subsection (7) is more liberal than the rule stated in Section 9–313(7) in that issues of priority not otherwise resolved in this subsection are left for resolution by the priority rules governing conflicting interests in real estate, as opposed to the Section 9–313(7) automatic subordination of the security interest in fixtures. Note that, for the purpose of this section, where the interest of an encumbrancer or owner of the real estate is paramount to the interest of the lessor, the latter term includes the residual interest of the lessor.

5. The rule stated in subsection (8) is more liberal than the rule stated in Section 9–313(8) in that the right of removal is extended to both the lessor and the lessee and the occasion for removal includes expiration, termination or cancellation of the lease agreement, and enforcement of rights and remedies under this Article, as well as default. The new language also provides that upon removal the goods are free and clear of conflicting interests of owners and encumbrancers of the real estate.

6. Finally, subsection (9) provides a mechanism for the lessor of fixtures to perfect its interest by filing a financing statement under the provisions of the Article on Secured Transactions (Article 9), even though the lease agreement does not create a security interest. Section 1–201(37). The relevant provisions of Article 9 must be interpreted permissively to give effect to this mechanism as it implicitly expands the scope of Article 9 so that its filing provisions apply to transactions that create a lease of fixtures, even though the lease agreement does not create a security interest. This mechanism is similar to that provided in Section 2–326(3)(c) for the seller of goods on consignment, even though the consignment is not "intended as security". Section 1–201(37). Given the lack of litigation with respect to the mechanism created for consignment sales, this new mechanism should prove effective.

Cross References:

Point 1: Section 9–313, 9–334 and 9–604.
Point 3: Section 9–334.
Point 4: Section 9–334.
Point 5: Section 9–604.
Point 6: Section 1–201 and Section 2–326.

Definitional Cross References:

"Agreed". Section 1–201.
"Cancellation". Section 2A–103(1)(a).
"Conforming". Section 2A–103(1)(c).
"Consumer lease". Section 2A–103(1)(f).
"Goods". Section 2A–103(1)(n).
"Lease". Section 2A–103(1)(p).
"Lease agreement". Section 2A–103(1)(k).
"Lease contract". Section 2A–103(1)(r).
"Lessee". Section 2A–103(1)(t).
"Lessor". Section 2A–103(1)(v).
"Lien". Section 2A–103(1)(x).
"Mortgage". Section 9–105(1)(j).
"Party". Section 1–201.
"Person". Section 1–201.
"Reasonable time". Section 1–205.
"Record". Section 2A–103(1)(cc).
"Remedy". Section 1–201.
"Rights". Section 1–201.
"Security interest". Section 1–201.
"Termination". Section 2A–103(1)(hh).
"Value". Section 1–204.

§ 2A–310. Lessor's and Lessee's Rights When Goods Become Accessions.

(1) Goods are "accessions" when they are installed in or affixed to other goods.

(2) The interest of a lessor or a lessee under a lease contract entered into before the goods became accessions is superior to all interests in the whole except as stated in subsection (4).

(3) The interest of a lessor or a lessee under a lease contract entered into at the time or after the goods became accessions is superior to all subsequently acquired interests in the whole except as stated in subsection (4) but is subordinate to interests in the whole existing at the time the lease contract was made unless the holders of such interests in the whole have in a record consented to the lease or disclaimed an interest in the goods as part of the whole.

(4) The interest of a lessor or a lessee under a lease contract described in subsection (2) or (3) is subordinate to the interest of

(a) a buyer in the ordinary course of business or a lessee in the ordinary course of busi-

ness of any interest in the whole acquired after the goods became accessions; or

(b) a creditor with a security interest in the whole perfected before the lease contract was made to the extent that the creditor makes subsequent advances without knowledge of the lease contract.

(5) When under subsections (2) or (3) and (4) a lessor or a lessee of accessions holds an interest that is superior to all interests in the whole, the lessor or the lessee may (a) on default, expiration, termination, or cancellation of the lease contract by the other party but subject to the provisions of the lease contract and this Article, or (b) if necessary to enforce other rights and remedies under this Article, remove the goods from the whole, free and clear of all interests in the whole, but the lessor or the lessee must reimburse any holder of an interest in the whole who is not the lessee and who has not otherwise agreed for the cost of repair of any physical injury but not for any diminution in value of the whole caused by the absence of the goods removed or by any necessity for replacing them. A person entitled to reimbursement may refuse permission to remove until the party seeking removal gives adequate security for the performance of this obligation.

As amended in 2003.

Official Comment

Uniform Statutory Source: Section 9–314.

Changes: Revised to reflect leasing terminology and to add new material.

Purposes: Subsections (1) and (2) restate the provisions of subsection (1) of Section 9–314 to clarify the definition of accession and to add leasing terminology to the priority rule that applies when the lease is entered into before the goods become accessions. Subsection (3) restates the provisions of subsection (2) of Section 9–314 to add leasing terminology to the priority rule that applies when the lease is entered into on or after the goods become accessions. Unlike the rule with respect to security interests, the lease is merely subordinate, not invalid.

Subsection (4) creates two exceptions to the priority rules stated in subsections (2) and (3). Subsection (4) deletes the special priority rule found in the provisions of Section 9–314(3)(b) as the interests of the lessor and lessee are entitled to greater protection.

Finally, subsection (5) is modeled on the provisions of Section 9–314(4) with respect to removal of accessions, restated to reflect the parallel changes in Section 2A–309(8).

Neither this section nor Section 9–314 governs where the accession to the goods is not subject to the interest of a lessor or a lessee under a lease contract and is not subject to the interest of a secured party under a security agreement. This issue is to be resolved by the courts, case by case.

Unlike the rules governing a security interest under Article 9, there is never a requirement in this Article that a lessor make a public filing to fully protect its interest in the leased goods against third party claims. Similarly, a lessor need not make a public filing to protect any interest in accessions to those leased goods. Accordingly, priority rules involving leased accessions should not be resolved by reference to Article 9's filing rules.

Cross References:

Section 2A–309(8), and Sections 9–102 and 9–335.

Definitional Cross References:

"Agreed". Section 1–201.
"Buyer in the ordinary course of business". Section 2A–103(1)(a).
"Cancellation". Section 2A–103(1)(a).
"Creditor". Section 1–201.
"Goods". Section 2A–103(1)(n).
"Holder". Section 1–201.
"Knowledge". Section 1–202.
"Lease". Section 2A–103(1)(p).
"Lease contract". Section 2A–103(1)(r).
"Lessee". Section 2A–103(1)(t).
"Lessee in the ordinary course of business". Section 2A–103(1)(o).

"Lessor". Section 2A–103(1)(v).
"Party". Section 1–201.
"Person". Section 1–201.
"Remedy". Section 1–201.
"Rights". Section 1–201.
"Security interest". Section 1–201.
"Termination". Section 2A–103(1)(hh).
"Value". Section 1–204.
"Writing". Section 1–201.

As amended in 2003.

§ 2A–311. Priority Subject to Subordination.

Nothing in this Article prevents subordination by agreement by any person entitled to priority.

As added in 1990.

Official Comment

Uniform Statutory Source: Section 9–316.

Purposes: The several preceding sections deal with questions of priority. This section is inserted to make it entirely clear that a person entitled to priority may effectively agree to subordinate the claim. Only the person entitled to priority may make such an agreement: the rights of such a person cannot be adversely affected by an agreement to which that person is not a party.

Cross References:

Section 1–102 and Sections 2A–304 through 2A–310.

Definitional Cross References:

"Agreement". Section 1–201.
"Person". Section 1–201.

PART 4

PERFORMANCE OF LEASE CONTRACT: REPUDIATED, SUBSTITUTED AND EXCUSED

§ 2A–401. Insecurity: Adequate Assurance of Performance.

(1) A lease contract imposes an obligation on each party that the other's expectation of receiving due performance will not be impaired.

(2) If reasonable grounds for insecurity arise with respect to the performance of either party, the insecure party may demand in a record adequate assurance of due performance. Until the insecure party receives that assurance, if commercially reasonable the insecure party may suspend any performance for which the insecure party has not already received the agreed return.

(3) A repudiation of the lease contract occurs if assurance of due performance adequate under the circumstances of the particular case is not provided to the insecure party within a reasonable time, not to exceed 30 days after receipt of a demand by the other party.

(4) Between merchants, the reasonableness of grounds for insecurity and the adequacy of any assurance offered must be determined according to commercial standards.

(5) Acceptance of any nonconforming delivery or payment does not prejudice the aggrieved party's right to demand adequate assurance of future performance.

As amended in 2003.

Official Comment

Uniform Statutory Source: Section 2–609.

Changes: Revised to reflect leasing practices and terminology. Note that in the analogue to subsection (3) (Section 2–609(4)), the adjective "justified" modifies demand. The adjective was deleted here as unnecessary, implying no substantive change.

Definitional Cross References:

"Aggrieved party". Section 1–201.
"Agreed". Section 1–201.
"Between merchants". Section 2–104(3).
"Conforming". Section 2A–103(1)(c).
"Delivery". Section 2A–103(1)(g).
"Lease contract". Section 2A–103(1)(r).
"Party". Section 1–201.
"Reasonable time". Section 1–205.
"Receipt". Section 2–103(1)(c).
"Record". Section 2A–103(1)(cc).
"Rights". Section 1–201.

§ 2A–402.   Anticipatory Repudiation.

(1) If either party repudiates a lease contract with respect to a performance not yet due under the lease contract, the loss of which performance will substantially impair the value of the lease contract to the other, the aggrieved party may:

(a) for a commercially reasonable time, await retraction of repudiation and performance by the repudiating party;

(b) make demand pursuant to Section 2A–401 and await assurance of future performance adequate under the circumstances of the particular case; or

(c) resort to any right or remedy upon default under the lease contract or this Article, even if the aggrieved party has notified the repudiating party that the aggrieved party would await the repudiating party's performance and assurance and has urged retraction. In addition, whether or not the aggrieved party is pursuing one of the foregoing remedies, the aggrieved party may suspend performance or, if the aggrieved party is the lessor, proceed in accordance with the provisions of this Article on the lessor's right to identify goods to the lease contract notwithstanding default or to salvage unfinished goods under Section 2A–524.

(2) Repudiation includes language that a reasonable person would interpret to mean that the other person will not or cannot make a performance still due under the contract or voluntary, affirmative conduct that would appear to a reasonable party to make a future performance by the other party impossible.

As amended in 2003.

Official Comment

Uniform Statutory Source: Section 2–610.

Changes: Revised to reflect leasing practices and terminology.

Subsection (2), provides guidance on when a party can be considered to have repudiated a performance obligation based upon the Restatement (Second) of Contracts § 250 and does not purport to be an exclusive statement of when a repudiation has occurred. Repudiation centers upon an overt communication of intention, actions which render performance impossible, or a demonstration of a clear determination not to perform. Repudiation does not require that performance be made utterly impossible, rather, actions which reasonably indicate rejection of the performance obligation suffice. Failure to provide adequate assurance of due performance under Section 2A–401 also operates as a repudiation.

Cross Reference:

Section 2A–401.

Definitional Cross References:

"Aggrieved party". Section 1–201.
"Goods". Section 2A–103(1)(n).
"Lease contract". Section 2A–103(1)(r).
"Lessor". Section 2A–103(1)(v).
"Notifies". Section 1–201.
"Party". Section 1–201.
"Reasonable time". Section 1–205.
"Remedy". Section 1–201.
"Rights". Section 1–201.
"Value". Section 1–204.

As amended in 2003.

§ 2A–403. Retraction of Anticipatory Repudiation.

(1) Until the repudiating party's next performance is due, the repudiating party can retract the repudiation unless, since the repudiation, the aggrieved party has cancelled the lease contract or materially changed the aggrieved party's position or otherwise indicated that the aggrieved party considers the repudiation final.

(2) Retraction may be by any method that clearly indicates to the aggrieved party that the repudiating party intends to perform under the lease contract and includes any assurance demanded under Section 2A–401.

(3) Retraction reinstates a repudiating party's rights under a lease contract with due excuse and allowance to the aggrieved party for any delay occasioned by the repudiation.

Official Comment

Uniform Statutory Source: Section 2–611.

Changes: Revised to reflect leasing practices and terminology. Note that in the analogue to subsection (2) (Section 2–611(2)) the adjective "justifiably" modifies demanded. The adjective was deleted here (as it was in Section 2A–401) as unnecessary, implying no substantive change.

Definitional Cross References:

"Aggrieved party". Section 1–201.
"Cancellation". Section 2A–103(1)(a).
"Lease contract". Section 2A–103(1)(r).
"Party". Section 1–201.
"Rights". Section 1–201.

§ 2A–404. Substituted Performance.

(1) If without fault of the lessee, the lessor and the supplier, the agreed berthing, loading, or unloading facilities fail or the agreed type of carrier becomes unavailable or the agreed manner of performance otherwise becomes commercially impracticable, but a commercially reasonable substitute is available, the substitute performance must be tendered and accepted.

(2) If the agreed means or manner of payment fails because of domestic or foreign governmental regulation:

(a) the lessor may withhold or stop delivery or cause the supplier to withhold or stop delivery unless the lessee provides a means or manner of payment that is commercially a substantial equivalent; and

(b) if delivery has already been taken, payment by the means or in the manner provided by the regulation discharges the lessee's obligation unless the regulation is discriminatory, oppressive, or predatory.

As amended in 2003.

Official Comment

Uniform Statutory Source: Section 2–614.

Changes: Revised to reflect leasing practices and terminology.

Definitional Cross References:

"Agreed". Section 1–201.
"Delivery". Section 2A–103(1)(g).
"Fault". Section 2A–103(1)(k).
"Lessee". Section 2A–103(1)(t).
"Lessor". Section 2A–103(1)(v).
"Supplier". Section 2A–103(1)(ff).

§ 2A–405. Excused Performance.

Subject to Section 2A–404 on substituted performance, the following rules apply:

(a) Delay in performance or nonperformance in whole or in part by a lessor or a supplier that complies with paragraphs (b) and (c) is not a default under the lease contract if performance as agreed has been made impracticable by the occurrence of a contingency the nonoccurrence of which was a basic assumption on which the lease contract was made or by compliance in good faith with any applicable foreign or domestic governmental regulation or order, whether or not the regulation or order later proves to be invalid.

(b) If the causes mentioned in paragraph (a) affect only part of the lessor's or the supplier's capacity to perform, the lessor or supplier shall allocate production and deliveries among customers but at the lessor's or supplier's option may include regular customers not then under contract for sale or lease as well as the lessor's or supplier's own requirements for further manufacture.

The lessor or supplier may so allocate in any manner that is fair and reasonable.

(c) The lessor seasonably shall notify the lessee and in the case of a finance lease the supplier seasonably shall notify the lessor and the lessee, if known, that there will be delay or nonperformance and, if allocation is required under paragraph (b), of the estimated quota thus made available for the lessee.

As amended in 2003.

Official Comment

Uniform Statutory Source: Section 2–615.

Changes: Revised to reflect leasing practices and terminology.

Although the section has been expanded beyond the context of delivery to apply to delay in performance or nonperformance, it does not apply unless the lessor's delay or nonperformance would otherwise constitute a default under the lease contract.

The section by its terms applies only to lessors, although the rationale might in an appropriate case apply and entitle a lessee to an excuse. In a finance lease that is not a consumer lease, however, the statutory "hell or high water" provision of Section 2A–407 precludes the lessee from claiming the excuse.

Definitional Cross References:

"Agreed". Section 1–201.
"Contract". Section 1–201.
"Delivery". Section 2A–103(1)(g).
"Finance lease". Section 2A–103(1)(l).
"Good faith". Sections 2A–103(1)(m).
"Knows". Section 1–201.
"Lease". Section 2A–103(1)(p).
"Lease contract". Section 2A–103(1)(r).
"Lessee". Section 2A–103(1)(t).
"Lessor". Section 2A–103(1)(v).
"Notifies". Section 1–201.
"Sale". Section 2–106(1).
"Seasonably". Section 1–204(3).
"Supplier". Section 2A–103(1)(ff).

As amended in 2003.

§ 2A–406. Procedure on Excused Performance.

(1) If the lessee receives notification of a material or indefinite delay or an allocation justified under Section 2A–405, the lessee may by notification in a record to the lessor as to any goods involved, and with respect to all of the goods if under an installment lease contract the value of the whole lease contract is substantially impaired (Section 2A–510):

(a) terminate the lease contract (Section 2A–505(2)); or

(b) except in a finance lease that is not a consumer lease, modify the lease contract by accepting the available quota in substitution, with due allowance from the rent payable for the balance of the lease term for the deficiency but without further right against the lessor.

(2) If, after receipt of a notification from the lessor under Section 2A–405, the lessee fails so to modify the lease agreement within a reasonable time not exceeding 30 days, the lease contract is terminated with respect to any performance affected.

As amended in 2003.

Official Comment

Uniform Statutory Source: Section 2–616(1) and (2).

Changes: Revised to reflect leasing practices and terminology. Note that subsection 1(a) allows the lessee under a lease, including a finance lease, the right to terminate the lease for excused performance (Sections 2A–404 and 2A–405). However, subsection 1(b), which allows the lessee the right to modify the lease for excused performance, excludes a finance lease that is not a consumer lease. This exclusion is compelled by the same policy that led to codification of provisions with respect to irrevocable promises. Section 2A–407.

Definitional Cross References:

"Consumer lease". Section 2A–103(1)(f).
"Delivery". Section 2A–103(1)(g).
"Finance lease". Section 2A–103(1)(l).
"Goods". Section 2A–103(1)(n).
"Installment lease contract". Section 2A–103(1)(o).
"Lease agreement". Section 2A–103(1)(q).
"Lease contract". Section 2A–103(1)(r).
"Lessee". Section 2A–103(1)(t).
"Lessor". Section 2A–103(1)(v).
"Notice". Section 1–202.
"Reasonable time". Section 1–205.
"Receipt". Section 2–103(1)(c).
"Record". Section 2A–103(1)(cc).
"Rights". Section 1–201.
"Termination". Section 2A–103(1)(hh).

"Value". Section 1–204.

§ 2A–407. Irrevocable Promises: Finance Leases.

(1) In the case of a finance lease that is not a consumer lease the lessee's promises under the lease contract become irrevocable and independent upon the lessee's acceptance of the goods.

(2) A promise that has become irrevocable and independent under subsection (1):

(a) is effective and enforceable between the parties, and by or against third parties including assignees of the parties; and

(b) is not subject to cancellation, termination, modification, repudiation, excuse, or substitution without the consent of the party to whom the promise runs.

(3) This section does not affect the validity under any other law of a covenant in any lease contract making the lessee's promises irrevocable and independent upon the lessee's acceptance of the goods.

Official Comment

Uniform Statutory Source: None.

Purposes:

1. This section extends the benefits of the classic "hell or high water" clause to a finance lease that is not a consumer lease. This section is self-executing; no special provision need be added to the contract. This section makes covenants in a finance lease irrevocable and independent due to the function of the finance lessor in a three party relationship: the lessee is looking to the supplier to perform the essential covenants and warranties. Section 2A–209. Thus, upon the lessee's acceptance of the goods the lessee's promises to the lessor under the lease contract become irrevocable and independent. The provisions of this section remain subject to the obligation of good faith (Sections 2A–103(4) and 1–203), and the lessee's revocation of acceptance (Section 2A–517).

2. The section requires the lessee to perform even if the lessor's performance after the lessee's acceptance is not in accordance with the lease contract; the lessee may, however, have and pursue a cause of action against the lessor, e.g., breach of certain limited warranties (Sections 2A–210 and 2A–211(1)). This is appropriate because the benefit of the supplier's promises and warranties to the lessor under the supply contract and, in some cases, the warranty of a manufacturer who is not the supplier, is extended to the lessee under

the finance lease. Section 2A–209. Despite this balance, this section excludes a finance lease that is a consumer lease. That a consumer be obligated to pay notwithstanding defective goods or the like is a principle that is not tenable under case law (Unico v. Owen, 50 N.J. 101, 232 A.2d 405 (1967)), state statute (Unif.Consumer Credit Code §§ 3.403–.405, 7A U.L.A. 126–31 (1974)), or federal statute (15 U.S.C. § 1666i (1982)).

3. The relationship of the three parties to a transaction that qualifies as a finance lease is best demonstrated by a hypothetical. A, the potential lessor, has been contacted by B, the potential lessee, to discuss the lease of an expensive line of equipment that B has recently placed an order for with C, the manufacturer of such goods. The negotiation is completed and A, as lessor, and B, as lessee, sign a lease of the line of equipment for a 60–month term. B, as buyer, assigns the purchase order with C to A. If this transaction creates a lease (Section 2A–103(1)(j)), this transaction should qualify as a finance lease. Section 2A–103(1)(g).

4. The line of equipment is delivered by C to B's place of business. After installation by C and testing by B, B accepts the goods by signing a certificate of delivery and acceptance, a copy of which is sent by B to A and C. One year later the line of equipment malfunctions and B falls behind in its manufacturing schedule.

5. Under this Article, because the lease is a finance lease, no warranty of fitness or merchantability is extended by A to B. Sections 2A–212(1) and 2A–213. Absent an express provision in the lease agreement, application of Section 2A–210 or Section 2A–211(1), or application of the principles of law and equity, including the law with respect to fraud, duress, or the like (Sections 2A–103(4) and 1–103), B has no claim against A. B's obligation to pay rent to A continues as the obligation became irrevocable and independent when B accepted the line of equipment (Section 2A–407(1)). B has no right of set-off with respect to any part of the rent still due under the lease. Section 2A–508(6). However, B may have another remedy. Despite the lack of privity between B and C (the purchase order with C having been assigned by B to A), B may have a claim against C. Section 2A–209(1).

6. This section does not address whether a "hell or high water" clause, *i.e.*, a clause that is to the effect of this section, is enforceable if included in a finance lease that is a consumer lease or a lease that is not a finance lease. That issue will continue to be determined by the facts of each case and other law which this section does not affect. Sections 2A–104, 2A–103(4), 9–206 and 9–318. However, with respect to finance leases that are not consumer leases courts have enforced "hell or high

water" clauses. *In re O.P.M. Leasing Servs.*, 21 Bankr. 993, 1006 (Bankr.S.D.N.Y.1982).

7. Subsection (2) further provides that a promise that has become irrevocable and independent under subsection (1) is enforceable not only between the parties but also against third parties. Thus, the finance lease can be transferred or assigned without disturbing enforceability. Further, subsection (2) also provides that the promise cannot, among other things, be cancelled or terminated without the consent of the lessor.

Cross References:

Point 1: Sections 1–203 and Sections 2A–103, 2A–209, and 2A–517.

Point 2: Sections 2A–209, 2A–210, and 2A–211.

Point 3: Section 2A–103.

Point 5: Section 1–203 and Sections 2A–209, 2A–210, 2A–211, 2A–212, 2A–213, 2A–407, 2A–508.

Point 6: Sections 2A–103, 2A–104 and Sections 9–403 and 9–404.

Definitional Cross References:

"Cancellation". Section 2A–103(1)(a).

"Consumer lease". Section 2A–103(1)(f).

"Finance lease". Section 2A–103(1)(l).

"Goods". Section 2A–103(1)(n).

"Lease contract". Section 2A–103(1)(r).

"Lessee". Section 2A–103(1)(t).

"Party". Section 1–201.

"Termination". Section 2A–103(1)(hh).

PART 5

DEFAULT

A. IN GENERAL

§ 2A–501. Default: Procedure.

(1) Whether the lessor or the lessee is in default under a lease contract is determined by the lease agreement and this Article.

(2) If the lessor or the lessee is in default under the lease contract, the party seeking enforcement has rights and remedies as provided in this Article and, except as limited by this Article, as provided in the lease agreement.

(3) If the lessor or the lessee is in default under the lease contract, the party seeking enforcement may reduce the party's claim to judgment, or otherwise enforce the lease contract by self-help or any available judicial procedure or nonjudicial procedure, including administrative proceeding, arbitration, or the like, in accordance with this Article.

(4) Except as otherwise provided in Section 1–305(a) or this Article or the lease agreement, the rights and remedies referred to in subsections (2) and (3) are cumulative.

(5) If the lease agreement covers both real property and goods, the party seeking enforcement may proceed under this Part as to the goods, or under other applicable law as to both the real property and the goods in accordance with that party's rights and remedies in respect of the real property, in which case this Part does not apply.

As amended in 2001 and 2005.

Official Comment

Uniform Statutory Source: Section 9–501.

Changes: Substantially revised.

Purposes:

1. Subsection (1) is new and represents a departure from the Article on Secured Transactions (Article 9) as the subsection makes clear that whether a party to the lease agreement is in default is determined by this Article as well as the agreement. Sections 2A–508 and 2A–523. It further departs from Article 9 in recognizing the potential default of either party, a function of the bilateral nature of the obligations between the parties to the lease contract.

2. Subsection (2) is a version of the first sentence of Section 9–501(1), revised to reflect leasing terminology.

3. Subsection (3), an expansive version of the second sentence of Section 9–501(1), lists the procedures that may be followed by the party seeking enforcement; in effect, the scope of the procedures listed in subsection (3) is consistent with the scope of the procedures available to the foreclosing secured party.

4. Subsection (4) establishes that the parties' rights and remedies are cumulative. DeKoven, *Leases of Equipment: Puritan Leasing Company v. August, A Dangerous Decision*, 12 U.S.F.L.Rev. 257, 276–80 (1978). Cumulation, and largely unrestricted selection, of remedies is allowed in furtherance of the general policy of the Commercial Code, stated in Section 1–106, that remedies be liberally administered to put the aggrieved party in as good a position as if the other

party had fully performed. Therefore, cumulation of, or selection among, remedies is available to the extent necessary to put the aggrieved party in as good a position as it would have been in had there been full performance. However, cumulation of, or selection among, remedies is not available to the extent that the cumulation or selection would put the aggrieved party in a better position than it would have been in had there been full performance by the other party.

5. Section 9–501(3), which, among other things, states that certain rules, to the extent they give rights to the debtor and impose duties on the secured party, may not be waived or varied, was not incorporated in this Article. Given the significance of freedom of contract in the development of the common law as it applies to bailments for hire and the lessee's lack of an equity of redemption, there was no reason to impose that restraint.

Cross References:

Point 1: Sections 2A–508 and 2A–532.
Point 2: Section 9–601.
Point 3: Section 9–601.
Point 4: Section 1–103.
Point 5: Section 9–602.

Definitional Cross References:

"Goods". Section 2A–103(1)(n).
"Lease agreement". Section 2A–103(1)(q).
"Lease contract". Section 2A–103(1)(r).
"Lessee". Section 2A–103(1)(t).
"Lessor". Section 2A–103(1)(v).
"Party". Section 1–201.
"Remedy". Section 1–201.
"Rights". Section 1–201.

As amended in 2001.

§ 2A–502. Notice after Default.

Except as otherwise provided in this Article or the lease agreement, the lessor or lessee in default under the lease contract is not entitled to notice of default or notice of enforcement from the other party to the lease agreement.

Official Comment

Uniform Statutory Source: None.

Purposes: This section makes clear that absent agreement to the contrary or provision in this Article to the contrary, e.g., Section 2A–516(3)(a), the party in default is not entitled to notice of default or enforcement. While a review of Part 5 of Article 9 leads to the same conclusion with respect to giving notice of default to

the debtor, it is never stated. Although Article 9 requires notice of disposition and strict foreclosure, the different scheme of lessors' and lessees' rights and remedies developed under the common law, and codified by this Article, generally does not require notice of enforcement; furthermore, such notice is not mandated by due process requirements. However, certain sections of this Article do require notice. E.g., Section 2A–517(2) 2A–517(4). *Previous incorrect cross reference corrected by Permanent Editorial Board, November 1992.*

Cross References:

Sections 2A–516(3)(a), 2A–517(4), and Article 9.

Definitional Cross References:

"Lease agreement". Section 2A–103(1)(q).
"Lease contract". Section 2A–103(1)(r).
"Lessee". Section 2A–103(1)(t).
"Lessor". Section 2A–103(1)(v).
"Notice". Section 1–202.
"Party". Section 1–201.

§ 2A–503. Modification or Impairment of Rights and Remedies.

(1) Except as otherwise provided in this Article, the lease agreement may include rights and remedies for default in addition to or in substitution for those provided in this Article and may limit or alter the measure of damages recoverable under this Article.

(2) Resort to a remedy provided under this Article or in the lease agreement is optional unless the remedy is expressly agreed to be exclusive. If circumstances cause an exclusive or limited remedy to fail of its essential purpose, or provision for an exclusive remedy is unconscionable, remedy may be had as provided in this Article.

(3) Consequential damages may be liquidated under Section 2A–504, or may otherwise be limited, altered, or excluded unless the limitation, alteration, or exclusion is unconscionable. Limitation, alteration, or exclusion of consequential damages for injury to the person in the case of consumer goods is prima facie unconscionable but limitation, alteration, or exclusion of damages where the loss is commercial is not prima facie unconscionable.

(4) Rights and remedies on default by the lessor or the lessee with respect to any obligation or

promise collateral or ancillary to the lease contract are not impaired by this Article.

Official Comment

Uniform Statutory Source: Sections 2–719 and 2–701.

Changes: Rewritten to reflect lease terminology and to clarify the relationship between this section and Section 2A–504.

Purposes:

1. A significant purpose of this Part is to provide rights and remedies for those parties to a lease who fail to provide them by agreement or whose rights and remedies fail of their essential purpose or are unenforceable. However, it is important to note that this implies no restriction on freedom to contract. Sections 2A–103(4) and 1–102(3). Thus, subsection (1), a revised version of the provisions of Section 2–719(1), allows the parties to the lease agreement freedom to provide for rights and remedies in addition to or in substitution for those provided in this Article and to alter or limit the measure of damages recoverable under this Article. Except to the extent otherwise provided in this Article (*e.g.*, Sections 2A–105, 106 and 108(1) and (2)), this Part shall be construed neither to restrict the parties' ability to provide for rights and remedies or to limit or alter the measure of damages by agreement, nor to imply disapproval of rights and remedy schemes other than those set forth in this Part.

2. Subsection (2) makes explicit with respect to this Article what is implicit in Section 2–719 with respect to the Article on Sales (Article 2): if an exclusive remedy is held to be unconscionable, remedies under this Article are available. Section 2–719 official comment 1.

3. Subsection (3), a revision of Section 2–719(3), makes clear that consequential damages may also be liquidated. Section 2A–504(1).

4. Subsection (4) is a revision of the provisions of Section 2–701. This subsection leaves the treatment of default with respect to obligations or promises collateral or ancillary to the lease contract to other law. Sections 2A–103(4) and 1–103. An example of such an obligation would be that of the lessor to the secured creditor which has provided the funds to leverage the lessor's lease transaction; an example of such a promise would be that of the lessee, as seller, to the lessor, as buyer, in a sale-leaseback transaction.

Cross References:

Point 1: Sections 1–102, 1–103, Section 2–719 and Sections 2A–103, 2A–105, 2A–106, 2A–108.

Point 2: Section 2–719.

Point 3: Section 2–719 and Section 2A–504.

Point 4: Section 1–103, Section 2–701 and Section 2A–103.

Definitional Cross References:

"Agreed". Section 1–201.

"Consumer goods". Section 9–109(1).

"Lease agreement". Section 2A–103(1)(q).

"Lease contract". Section 2A–103(1)(r).

"Lessee". Section 2A–103(1)(t).

"Lessor". Section 2A–103(1)(v).

"Person". Section 1–201.

"Remedy". Section 1–201.

"Rights". Section 1–201.

§ 2A–504. Liquidation of Damages.

(1) Damages payable by either party for default, or any other act or omission, including indemnity for loss or diminution of anticipated tax benefits or loss or damage to lessor's residual interest, may be liquidated in the lease agreement but only at an amount or by a formula that is reasonable in light of the then anticipated harm caused by the default or other act or omission. Section 2A–503 determines the enforceability of a term that limits but does not liquidate damages.

(2) If the lease agreement provides for liquidation of damages, and such provision does not comply with subsection (1), or such provision is an exclusive or limited remedy that circumstances cause to fail of its essential purpose, remedy may be had as provided in this Article.

(3) If the lessor justifiably withholds delivery of goods or stops performance because of the lessee's default or insolvency, the lessee is entitled to restitution of any amount by which the sum of the lessee's payments exceeds the amount to which the lessor is entitled by virtue of terms liquidating the lessor's damages in accordance with subsection (1).

(4) A lessee's right to restitution under subsection (3) is subject to offset to the extent the lessor establishes:

(a) a right to recover damages under the provisions of this Article other than subsection (1); and

(b) the amount or value of any benefits received by the lessee directly or indirectly by reason of the lease contract.

As amended in 2003.

Official Comment

1. Many leasing transactions are predicated on the parties' ability to agree to an appropriate amount of damages or formula for damages in the event of default or other act or omission. The rule with respect to sales of goods (Section 2–718) may not be sufficiently flexible to accommodate this practice. Thus, consistent with the common law emphasis upon freedom to contract with respect to bailments for hire, this section has created a revised rule that allows greater flexibility with respect to leases of goods.

2. Subsection (1), also in variance to the provisions of Section 2–718(1), provides for liquidation of damages in the lease agreement not only at a stated amount but also by a formula. Section 2–718(1) does not by its express terms include liquidation by a formula; this difference was compelled by modern leasing practice. Subsection (1), also in variance with Section 2–718(1), provides for liquidation of damages for default as well as any other act or omission.

3. A liquidated damages formula that is common in leasing practice provides that the sum of lease payments past due, accelerated future lease payments, and the lessor's estimated residual interest, less the net proceeds of disposition (whether by sale or re-lease) of the leased goods is the lessor's damages. Tax indemnities, costs, interest and attorney's fees are also added to determine the lessor's damages. Another common liquidated damages formula utilizes a periodic depreciation allocation as a credit to the aforesaid amount in mitigation of a lessor's damages. A third formula provides for a fixed number of periodic payments as a means of liquidating damages. Stipulated loss or stipulated damage schedules are also common. Whether these formulae are enforceable will be determined in the context of each case by applying a standard of reasonableness in light of the harm anticipated when the formula was agreed to. Whether the inclusion of these formulae will affect the classification of the transaction as a lease or a security interest is to be determined by the facts of each case. Section 1–201(37). *E.g., In re Noack*, 44 Bankr. 172, 174–75 (Bankr.E.D.Wis.1984).

4. This section does not incorporate two other tests that under sales law determine enforceability of liquidated damages in a consumer sale, *i.e.*, difficulties of proof of loss and inconvenience or nonfeasibility of otherwise obtaining an adequate remedy. The ability to liquidate damages is critical to modern leasing practice; given the parties' freedom to contract at common law, the policy behind retaining these two additional requirements here was thought to be outweighed. Further, given the expansion of subsection (1) to enable the parties to liquidate the amount payable with respect to an indemnity for loss or diminution of anticipated tax benefits resulted in another change: the last sentence of Section 2–718(1), providing that a term fixing unreasonably large liquidated damages is void as a penalty, was also not incorporated. The impact of local, state and federal tax laws on a leasing transaction can result in an amount payable with respect to the tax indemnity many times greater than the original purchase price of the goods. By deleting the reference to unreasonably large liquidated damages the parties are free to negotiate a formula, restrained by the rule of reasonableness in this section. These changes should invite the parties to liquidate damages. Peters, *Remedies for Breach of Contracts Relating to the Sale of Goods Under the Uniform Commercial Code: A Roadmap for Article Two*, 73 Yale L.J. 199, 278 (1963).

5. Subsection (2), a revised version of Section 2–719(2), provides that if the liquidated damages provision is not enforceable or fails of its essential purpose, remedy may be had as provided in this Article.

6. The lessee is entitled to restitution to the extent the lessee's payments exceed the amounts to which the lessor is entitled under a term limiting or liquidating damages that is enforceable under subsection (1). In the absence of such a term, pursuant to subsection (4), a lessor that withholds or stops performance under subsection (3) may retain payments made by the lessee, which would include any deposit or down payment, but only to the extent the lessor is able to prove damages.

Cross References:

Point 1: Sections 2–718.
Point 2: Section 2–718.
Point 4: Section 2–718.
Point 5: Section 2–719.

Definitional Cross References:

"Consumer lease". Section 2A–103(1)(f).
"Delivery". Section 2A–103(1)(g).
"Goods". Section 2A–103(1)(n).
"Insolvent". Section 1–201.
"Lease agreement". Section 2A–103(1)(q).
"Lease contract". Section 2A–103(1)(r).
"Lessee". Section 2A–103(1)(t).

"Lessor". Section 2A–103(1)(v).

"Lessor's residual interest". Section 2A–103(1)(w).

"Party". Section 1–201.

"Present value". Section 2A–103(1)(aa).

"Remedy". Section 1–201.

"Rights". Section 1–201.

"Term". Section 1–201.

"Value". Section 1–204.

As amended in 2003.

§ 2A–505. Cancellation and Termination and Effect of Cancellation, Termination, Rescission, or Fraud on Rights and Remedies.

(1) On cancellation of the lease contract, all obligations that are still executory on both sides are discharged, but any right based on prior default or performance survives, and the cancelling party also retains any remedy for default of the whole lease contract or any unperformed balance.

(2) On termination of the lease contract, all obligations that are still executory on both sides are discharged but any right based on prior default or performance survives.

(3) Unless the contrary intention clearly appears, expressions of "cancellation," "rescission," or the like of the lease contract may not be construed as a renunciation or discharge of any claim in damages for an antecedent default.

(4) Rights and remedies for material misrepresentation or fraud include all rights and remedies available under this Article for default.

(5) Neither rescission nor a claim for rescission of the lease contract nor rejection or return of the goods may bar or be deemed inconsistent with a claim for damages or other right or remedy.

Official Comment

Uniform Statutory Source: Sections 2–106(3) and (4), 2–720 and 2–721.

Changes: Revised to reflect leasing practices and terminology.

Definitional Cross References:

"Cancellation". Section 2A–103(1)(a).

"Goods". Section 2A–103(1)(n).

"Lease contract". Section 2A–103(1)(r).

"Party". Section 1–201.

"Remedy". Section 1–201.

"Rights". Section 1–201.

"Termination". Section 2A–103(1)(hh).

§ 2A–506. Statute of Limitations.

(1) An action for default under a lease contract, including breach of warranty or indemnity, must be commenced within four years after the cause of action accrued. Except in a consumer lease or an action for indemnity, the original lease agreement may reduce the period of limitations to not less than one year.

(2) A cause of action for default accrues when the act or omission on which the default or breach of warranty is based is or should have been discovered by the aggrieved party, or when the default occurs, whichever is later. A cause of action for indemnity accrues when the act or omission on which the claim for indemnity is based is or should have been discovered by the indemnified party, whichever is later.

(3) If an action commenced within the time limited by subsection (1) is so terminated as to leave available a remedy by another action for the same default or breach of warranty or indemnity, the other action may be commenced after the expiration of the time limited and within six months after the termination of the first action unless the termination resulted from voluntary discontinuance or from dismissal for failure or neglect to prosecute.

(4) This section does not alter the law on tolling of the statute of limitations nor does it apply to causes of action that have accrued before this Article becomes effective.

As amended in 2003.

Official Comment

1. Subsection (1) does not incorporate the limitation found in Section 2–725(1) prohibiting the parties from extending the period of limitation. Breach of warranty and indemnity claims often arise in a lease transaction; with the passage of time such claims often diminish or are eliminated. To encourage the parties to commence litigation under these circumstances makes little sense.

2. As amended, subsection (1) now contains the similar limitations contained in amended Section 2–725, which restricts the parties right to reduce the four year limitation period in the consumer lease.

3. Subsection (2) states two rules for determining when a cause of action accrues. With respect to default,

the rule of Section 2–725(2) is not incorporated in favor of a more liberal rule of the later of the date when the default occurs or when the act or omission on which it is based is or should have been discovered. With respect to indemnity, a similarly liberal rule is adopted.

Cross References:

Point 1: Sections 2–725.
Point 2: Sections 2–725.
Point 3: Sections 2–725.

Definitional Cross References:

"Action". Section 1–201.
"Aggrieved party". Section 1–201.
"Lease contract". Section 2A–103(1)(r).
"Party". Section 1–201.
"Remedy". Section 1–201.
"Termination". Section 2A–103(1)(hh).

As amended in 2003.

§ 2A–507. Proof of Market Rent: Time and Place.

(1) Damages based on market rent (Section 2A–519 or 2A–528) are determined according to the rent for the use of the goods concerned for a lease term identical to the remaining lease term of the original lease agreement and prevailing at the times specified in Sections 2A–519 and 2A–528.

(2) If evidence of rent for the use of the goods concerned for a lease term identical to the remaining lease term of the original lease agreement and prevailing at the times or places described in this Article is not readily available, the rent prevailing within any reasonable time before or after the time described or at any other place or for a different lease term which in commercial judgment or under usage of trade would serve as a reasonable substitute for the one described may be used, making any proper allowance for the difference, including the cost of transporting the goods to or from the other place.

(3) Evidence of a relevant rent prevailing at a time or place or for a lease term other than the one described in this Article offered by one party is not admissible unless and until he [or she] has given the other party notice the court finds sufficient to prevent unfair surprise.

(4) If the prevailing rent or value of any goods regularly leased in any established market is in issue, reports in official publications or trade journals or in newspapers or periodicals of general circulation published as the reports of that market are admissible in evidence. The circumstances of the preparation of the report may be shown to affect its weight but not its admissibility.

Official Comment

Uniform Statutory Source: Sections 2–723 and 2–724.

Changes: Revised to reflect leasing practices and terminology. Sections 2A–519 and 2A–528 specify the times as of which market rent is to be determined.

Definitional Cross References:

"Goods". Section 2A–103(1)(h).
"Lease". Section 2A–103(1)(j).
"Lease agreement". Section 2A–103(1)(k).
"Notice". Section 1–201(25).
"Party". Section 1–201(29).
"Reasonable time". Section 1–204(1) and (2).
"Usage of trade". Section 1–205.
"Value". Section 1–201(44).

§ 2A–507A. Right to Specific Performance or Replevin or the Like.

(1) Specific performance may be decreed if the goods are unique or in other proper circumstances. In a contract other than a consumer lease, specific performance may be decreed if the parties have agreed to that remedy. However, even if the parties agree to specific performance, specific performance may not be decreed if the breaching party's sole remaining contractual obligation is the payment of money.

(2) A decree for specific performance may include any terms and conditions as to payment of the rent, damages, or other relief that the court deems just.

(3) A lessee has a right of replevin or similar remedy for goods identified to the lease contract if after reasonable effort the lessee is unable to effect cover for those goods or the circumstances reasonably indicate that the effort will be unavailing.

Legislative Note: To maintain its relative position in this Act, Section 2A–507A may have to be renumbered according to the convention used by a particular state. For example, in some states it may be designated as 2A–507.1.

As added in 2003 and amended in 2005.

Official Comment

1. This provision has been moved from its former location, Section 2A–521, because it has been amended to give rights to both lessors and lessees. Section 2A–521 is in Part B (Default by Lessor). This provision is now placed in the general default provisions.

2. Subsection (1) provides that a court may decree specific performance if the parties have agreed to that remedy. The parties' agreement to specific performance can be enforced even if legal remedies are entirely adequate. Even in a commercial contract, the third sentence of subsection (1) prevents the aggrieved party from obtaining specific performance if the only obligation of the party in breach is the payment of money. Whether a lessee is obligated to pay the price is determined by Section 2A–529, not by this section.

Nothing in this section constrains the court's exercise of its equitable discretion to decide whether to enter a decree for specific performance or to determine the conditions or terms of the decree. This section assumes that the decree for specific performance is conditioned on a tender of full performance by the party that seeks the remedy.

Cross References:

Point 1: Section 2A–521.
Point 2: Section 2–709.

Definitional Cross References:

"Goods". Section 2A–103(1)(n).
"Lease". Section 2A–103(1)(p).
"Lease agreement". Section 2A–103(1)(q).
"Notice". Section 1–202.
"Party". Section 1–201.
"Reasonable time". Section 1–205.
"Usage of trade". Section 1–303.
"Value". Section 1–204.

As added in 2003.

B. DEFAULT BY LESSOR

§ 2A–508. Lessee's Remedies.

(1) If a lessor fails to deliver the goods in conformity to the lease contract or repudiates the contract, or a lessee rightfully rejects the goods or justifiably revokes acceptance of the goods, the lessor is in default under the lease contract, and the lessee may do one or more of the following:

(a) cancel the lease contract;

(b) recover so much of the rent and security as has been paid and is just under the circumstances;

(c) cover and obtain damages under Section 2A–518;

(d) recover damages for nondelivery under Section 2A–519(1);

(e) if an acceptance of goods has not been justifiably revoked, recover damages for default with regard to accepted goods under Section 2A–519(3) and (4);

(f) enforce a security interest under subsection (4);

(g) recover identified goods under Section 2A–522;

(h) obtain specific performance or obtain the goods by replevin or similar remedy under Section 2A–507A;

(i) recover liquidated damages under Section 2A–504;

(j) enforce limited remedies under Section 2A–503;

(k) exercise any other right or pursue any other remedy as provided in the lease contract.

(2) If a lessor is otherwise in default under a lease contract, the lessee may exercise the rights and pursue the remedies provided in the lease contract, which may include a right to cancel the lease, and in Section 2A–519(3).

(3) If a lessor has breached a warranty, whether express or implied, the lessee may recover damages (Section 2A–519(4)).

(4) On rightful rejection or justifiable revocation of acceptance, a lessee has a security interest in goods in the lessee's possession or control for any rent and security that has been paid and any expenses reasonably incurred in their inspection, receipt, transportation, and care and custody and may hold those goods and dispose of them in good faith and in a commercially reasonable manner, subject to Section 2A–527(5).

(5) Subject to the provisions of Section 2A–407, a lessee, on notifying the lessor of the lessee's intention to do so, may deduct all or any part of the damages resulting from any default under the lease contract from any part of the rent still due under the same lease contract.

As amended in 2003 and 2005.

Official Comment

1. This section is an index to Sections 2A–503 through 2A–505 and 2A–509 through 2A–522 which set out the lessee's rights and remedies after the lessor's default. The lessor and the lessee can agree to modify the rights and remedies available under this Article; they can, among other things, provide that for defaults other than those specified in subsection (1) the lessee can exercise the rights and remedies referred to in subsection (1); and they can create a new scheme of rights and remedies triggered by the occurrence of the default. Sections 2A–103(4) and 1–302.

2. Subsection (1), a substantially rewritten version of the provisions of Section 2–711(1), lists the cumulative remedies of the lessee where the lessor has failed to deliver conforming goods or has repudiated the contract, or the lessee has rightfully rejected or justifiably revoked. Sections 2A–501(2) and (4). Subsection (1) also allows the lessee to exercise any contractual remedy. This Article rejects any general doctrine of election of remedy. To determine if one remedy bars another in a particular case is a function of whether the lessee has been put in as good a position as if the lessor had fully performed the lease agreement. Use of multiple remedies is barred only if the effect is to put the lessee in a better position than it would have been in had the lessor fully performed under the lease. Sections 2A–103(4), 2A–501(4). Subsection (1)(b), in recognition that no bright line can be created that would operate fairly in all installment lease cases and in recognition of the fact that a lessee may be able to cancel the lease (revoke acceptance of the goods) after the goods have been in use for some period of time, does not require that all lease payments made by the lessee under the lease be returned upon cancellation. Rather, only such portion as is just of the rent and security payments made may be recovered. If a defect in the goods is discovered immediately upon tender to the lessee and the goods are rejected immediately, then the lessee should recover all payments made. If, however, for example, a 36–month equipment lease is terminated in the 12th month because the lessor has materially breached the contract by failing to perform its maintenance obligations, it may be just to return only a small part or none of the rental payments already made.

3. Subsection (2) covers defaults which do not deprive the lessee of the goods and which are not so serious as to justify rejection or revocation of acceptance under subsection (1). It also covers defaults for which the lessee could have rejected or revoked acceptance of the goods but elects not to do so and retains the goods. In either case, a lessee which retains the goods is entitled to recover damages as stated in Section 2A–519(3). That measure of damages is "the loss resulting in the ordinary course of events from the lessor's default as determined in any manner that is reasonable together with incidental and consequential damages, less expenses saved in consequence of the lessor's breach."

4. Subsection (1)(k) and subsection (2) recognize that the lease agreement may provide rights and remedies in addition to or different from those which Article 2A provides. In particular, subsection (2) provides that the lease agreement may give the remedy of cancellation of the lease for defaults by the lessor that would not otherwise be material defaults which would justify cancellation under subsection (1). If there is a right to cancel, there is, of course, a right to reject or revoke acceptance of the goods.

5. Subsection (3) adds to the completeness of the index by including a reference to the lessee's recovery of damages upon the lessor's breach of warranty. This breach may not rise to the level of a default by the lessor justifying revocation of acceptance. If the lessee properly rejects or revokes acceptance of the goods because of a breach of warranty, the rights and remedies are those provided in subsection (1) rather than those in Section 2A–519(4).

6. Subsection (4), a revised version of the provisions of Section 2–711(3), recognizes, on rightful rejection or justifiable revocation, the lessee's security interest in goods in its possession and control. Section 9–110 recognizes security interests arising under that Article. Pursuant to Section 2A–511(4), a purchaser who purchases goods from the lessee in good faith takes free of any rights of the lessor, or in the case of a finance lease, the supplier. These goods, however, must have been rightfully rejected and disposed of pursuant to Section 2A–511 or 2A–512. However, Section 2A–517(5) provides that the lessee will have the same rights and duties with respect to goods where acceptance has been revoked as with respect to goods rejected. Thus, Section 2A–511(4) will apply to the lessee's disposition of the goods.

7. Pursuant to Section 2A–527(5), the lessee must account to the lessor for the excess proceeds of such disposition, after satisfaction of the claim secured by the lessee's security interest.

8. Subsection (5) sanctions a right of set-off by the lessee, subject to the rule of Section 2A–407 with respect to irrevocable promises in a finance lease that is not a consumer lease, and further subject to an

enforceable "hell or high water" clause in the lease agreement. Section 2A–407 official comment. No attempt is made to state how the set-off should occur. This is to be determined by the facts of each case.

9. There is no special treatment of the finance lease in this section. Absent supplemental principles of law and equity to the contrary, in the case of most finance leases, following the lessee's acceptance of the goods, the lessee will have no rights or remedies against the lessor, because the lessor's obligations to the lessee are minimal. Sections 2A–210 and 2A–211(1). Since the lessee will look to the supplier for performance, this is appropriate. Section 2A–209.

Cross References:

Point 1: Section 1–302 and Sections 2A–103, 2A-503 through 2A–505 and 2A–509 through 2A–522.
Point 2: Section 2–711 and Section 2A–501.
Point 3: Section 2A–519.
Point 5: Section 2A–519.
Point 6: Section 2–711 and Sections 2A–511, 2A–512, 2A–517 and Section 9–110.
Point 7: Section 2A–527.
Point 8: Section 2A–407.
Point 9: Sections 2A–209, 2A–210 and 2A–211.

Definitional Cross References:

"Conforming". Section 2A–103(1)(c).
"Delivery". Section 2A–103(1)(g).
"Good faith". Sections 2A–103(1)(m).
"Goods". Section 2A–103(1)(n).
"Installment lease contract". Section 2A–103(1)(o).
"Lease contract". Section 2A–103(1)(r).
"Lessee". Section 2A–103(1)(t).
"Lessor". Section 2A–103(1)(v).
"Notifies". Section 1–201.
"Receipt". Section 2–103(1)(c).
"Remedy". Section 1–201.
"Rights". Section 1–201.
"Security interest". Section 1–201.
"Value". Section 1–204.

As amended in 2003.

§ **2A–509.** Lessee's Rights on Improper Delivery; Manner and Effect of Rejection.

(1) Subject to Sections 2A–503, 2A–504, and 2A–510, if the goods or the tender of delivery fail in any respect to conform to the contract, the lessee may:
(a) reject the whole;
(b) accept the whole; or

(c) accept any commercial unit or units and reject the rest.

(2) Rejection of goods must be within a reasonable time after their delivery or tender. It is ineffective unless the lessee seasonably notifies the lessor or supplier.

(3) Subject to Sections 2A–511, 2A–512, and 2A–517(6):
(a) after rejection any use by the lessee with respect to any commercial unit is wrongful as against the lessor or supplier; and
(b) if the lessee has before rejection taken physical possession of goods in which the lessee does not have a security interest under Section 2A–508(4), the lessee is under a duty after rejection to hold them with reasonable care at the lessor's or supplier's disposition for a time sufficient to permit the lessor or supplier to remove them; but
(c) the lessee has no further obligations with regard to goods rightfully rejected.
(d) The lessor's or supplier's remedies with respect to goods wrongfully rejected are governed by Section 2A–523.

As amended in 2003.

Official Comment

Uniform Statutory Source: Sections 2–601 and 2–602(1).

Changes: Revised to reflect leasing practices and terminology.

1. This section, which conforms with amended Article 2, contains the parallel rules for a sales contract that are contained in Section 2–601 and 2–602. The amendments clarify that this section is subject not only to Section 2A–510, but also Sections 2A–503 and 2A–504.

2. Subsection (3) was originally contained in the prior version of 2A–512, and this has been moved for logical clarity. This subsection sets forth the duties of the lessee upon rejection. In addition to the duty to hold the goods with reasonable care for the lessor's disposition, the lessee also has those duties, as appropriate, specified in Sections 2A–511, 2A–512 and 2A–517(6).

3. Elimination of the word "rightful" in the title makes it clear that a lessee can effectively reject goods even though the rejection is wrongful and constitutes a

breach. The word "rightfully" has also been deleted from the titles to Section 2A–511 and 2A–512.

Cross References:

Point 1: Section 2–601 and 2–602 and Section 2A–510, 2A–503 and 2A–504.

Point 2: Section 2–603, 2–604 and 2–608(4).

Point 3: Section 2–603, 2–604 and 2–703.

Definitional Cross References:

"Commercial unit". Section 2A–103(1)(b).

"Conforming". Section 2A–103(1)(c).

"Delivery". Section 2A–103(1)(g).

"Goods". Section 2A–103(1)(n).

"Installment lease contract". Section 2A–103(1)(o).

"Lease contract". Section 2A–103(1)(r).

"Lessee". Section 2A–103(1)(t).

"Lessor". Section 2A–103(1)(v).

"Notifies". Section 1–201.

"Reasonable time". Section 1–205.

"Rights". Section 1–201.

"Seasonably". Section 1–204(3).

As amended in 2003 and 2005.

§ 2A–510. Installment Lease Contracts: Rejection and Default.

(1) Under an installment lease contract a lessee may reject any delivery that is nonconforming if the nonconformity substantially impairs the value of that delivery to the lessee or the nonconformity is a defect in the required documents; but if the nonconformity does not fall within subsection (2) and the lessor or the supplier gives adequate assurance of its cure, the lessee must accept that delivery.

(2) If a nonconformity or default with respect to one or more deliveries substantially impairs the value of the installment lease contract as a whole there is a default with respect to the whole. But, the aggrieved party reinstates the installment lease contract as a whole if the aggrieved party accepts a nonconforming delivery without seasonably notifying of cancellation or brings an action with respect only to past deliveries or demands performance as to future deliveries.

As amended in 2003.

Official Comment

Uniform Statutory Source: Section 2–612.

Changes: Revised to reflect leasing practices and terminology.

Subsection (1) makes it clear that the lessee's right in the first instance to reject an installment depends upon whether there has been a substantial impairment of the value of the installment to the lessee and not on the lessor's ability to cure the nonconformity. The lessor can prevent a rightful rejection by giving adequate assurances of cure. Subsection (1) uses the words "to the lessee" to clarify the standard for rejecting an installment consistent is the same standard for revoking acceptance under Section 2A–517. Therefore, the test is not what the lessor had reason to know at the time of the lease agreement; the question is whether the non-conformity is one that will cause a substantial impairment of value to the lessee even though the lessor had no knowledge about the lessee's particular circumstances at the time of the lease agreement.

Cross Reference:

Section 2A–517.

Definitional Cross References:

"Action". Section 1–201(b)(1).

"Aggrieved party". Section 1–201(b)(2).

"Cancellation". Section 2A–103(1)(a).

"Conforming". Section 2A–103(1)(c).

"Delivery". Section 2A–103(1)(g).

"Installment lease contract". Section 2A–103(1)(o).

"Lessee". Section 2A–103(1)(t).

"Lessor". Section 2A–103(1)(v).

"Notifies". Section 1–201.

"Seasonably". Section 1–204(3).

"Supplier". Section 2A–103(1)(ff).

"Value". Section 1–204.

As amended in 2003.

§ 2A–511. Merchant Lessee's Duties as to Rejected Goods.

(1) Subject to any security interest of a lessee (Section 2A–508(4)), if a lessor or a supplier has no agent or place of business at the market of rejection, a merchant lessee, after rejection of goods in the lessee's possession or control, shall follow any reasonable instructions received from the lessor or the supplier with respect to the goods. In the absence of those instructions, a merchant lessee shall make reasonable efforts to sell, lease, or otherwise dispose of the goods for the lessor's account if they threaten to decline in value speedily. In the case of a rightful rejection

instructions are not reasonable if on demand indemnity for expenses is not forthcoming.

(2) If a merchant lessee (subsection (1)) or any other lessee (Section 2A–512) disposes of goods following a rightful rejection, the lessee is entitled to reimbursement either from the lessor or the supplier or out of the proceeds for reasonable expenses of caring for and disposing of the goods and, if the expenses include no disposition commission, to such commission as is usual in the trade, or if there is none, to a reasonable sum not exceeding 10 percent of the gross proceeds.

(3) In complying with this section or Section 2A–512, the lessee is held only to good faith. Good faith conduct hereunder is neither acceptance or conversion nor the basis of an action for damages.

(4) A purchaser that purchases in good faith from a lessee pursuant to this section or Section 2A–512 takes the goods free of any rights of the lessor and the supplier even if the lessee fails to comply with one or more of the requirements of this Article.

As amended in 2003.

Official Comment

Uniform Statutory Source: Sections 2–603 and 2–706(5).

Changes: Revised to reflect leasing practices and terminology. This section, by its terms, applies to merchants as well as others. Thus, in construing the section it is important to note that under this Act the term good faith is defined differently for merchants (Section 2–103(1)(b)) than for others (Section 1–201(19)). Section 2A–103(3) and (4).

Definitional Cross References:

"Action". Section 1–201.
"Good faith". Sections 2A–103(1)(m).
"Goods". Section 2A–103(1)(n).
"Lease". Section 2A–103(1)(p).
"Lessee". Section 2A–103(1)(t).
"Lessor". Section 2A–103(1)(v).
"Merchant lessee". Section 2A–103(1)(z).
"Purchaser". Section 1–201.
"Rights". Section 1–201.
"Security interest". Section 1–201.
"Supplier". Section 2A–103(1)(ff).
"Value". Section 1–204.

§ 2A–512. Lessee's Duties as to Rejected Goods.

(1) If the lessor or the supplier gives no instructions within a reasonable time after notification of rejection, the lessee may store the rejected goods for the lessor's or the supplier's account or ship them to the lessor or the supplier or dispose of them for the lessor's or the supplier's account with reimbursement in the manner provided in Section 2A–511.

(2) Action by the lessee pursuant to subsection (1) is not acceptance or conversion.

As amended in 2003.

Official Comment

Changes: The change in the title conforms to amended Article 2. Original subsections (1)(a) and (c) have been moved to Section 2A–509(3).

Cross References:

Section 2A–509.

Definitional Cross References:

"Action". Section 1–201.
"Goods". Section 2A–103(1)(n).
"Lessee". Section 2A–103(1)(t).
"Lessor". Section 2A–103(1)(v).
"Notification". Section 1–202.
"Reasonable time". Section 1–205.
"Seasonably". Section 1–204(3).
"Security interest". Section 1–201.
"Supplier". Section 2A–103(1)(ff).
"Value". Section 1–204.

As amended in 2003.

§ 2A–513. Cure by Lessor of Improper Tender or Delivery; Replacement.

(1) If the lessee rejects goods or a tender of delivery under Section 2A–509 or 2A–510 or, except in a consumer contract, justifiably revokes acceptance under Section 2A–517(1)(b) and the agreed time for performance has not expired, a lessor or a supplier that has performed in good faith, upon seasonable notice to the lessee, and at the lessor's or supplier's own expense, may cure the default by making a conforming tender of delivery within the agreed time. The lessor or supplier shall compensate the lessee for all of the lessee's reasonable expenses caused by the lessor's or supplier's default and subsequent cure.

(2) If the lessee rejects goods or a tender of delivery under Section 2A–509 or 2A–510 or, except in a consumer lease, justifiably revokes acceptance under Section 2A–517(1)(b) and the agreed time for performance has expired, a lessor or supplier that has performed in good faith may, upon seasonable notice to the lessee and at the lessor's or supplier's own expense, cure the default, if the cure is appropriate and timely under the circumstances, by making a tender of conforming goods. The lessor or supplier shall compensate the lessee for all of the lessee's reasonable expenses caused by the lessor's or supplier's default and subsequent cure.

As amended in 2003.

Official Comment

Uniform Statutory Source: Section 2–508.

Changes: Revised to reflect leasing practices and terminology.

This section is based on and conforms to amended Article 2, Section 2–508. The official commentary to that Section may be of aid in the interpretation of this section.

Definitional Cross References:

"Conforming". Section 2A–103(1)(c).
"Delivery". Section 2A–103(1)(g).
"Lease contract". Section 2A–103(1)(r).
"Lessee". Section 2A–103(1)(t).
"Lessor". Section 2A–103(1)(v).
"Money". Section 1–201.
"Notifies". Section 1–201.
"Reasonable time". Section 1–205.
"Seasonably". Section 1–204(3).
"Supplier". Section 2A–103(1)(ff).

As amended in 2003.

§ 2A–514. Waiver of Lessee's Objections.

(1) A lessee's failure to state in connection with rejection a particular defect or in connection with revocation of acceptance a defect that justifies revocation precludes the lessee from relying on the unstated defect to justify rejection or revocation of acceptance if the defect is ascertainable by reasonable inspection

(a) if the lessor or supplier had a right to cure the defect and could have cured it if stated seasonably; or

(b) between merchants if the lessor or the supplier after rejection or revocation of acceptance has made a request in a record for a full and final statement in a record of all defects on which the lessee proposes to rely.

(2) A lessee's failure to reserve rights when paying rent or other consideration against documents presented to the lessee precludes recovery of the payment for defects apparent in the documents.

As amended in 2003 and 2005.

Official Comment

Uniform Statutory Source: Section 2–605.

Changes: Revised to reflect leasing practices and terminology.

Purposes: This section is based on and conforms to amended Article 2 Section 2–605. The official commentary to that Section may aid in the interpretation of this section.

Cross Reference:

Section 2–605 official comment 4.

Definitional Cross References:

"Between merchants". Section 2–104(3).
"Goods". Section 2A–103(1)(n).
"Lessee". Section 2A–103(1)(t).
"Lessor". Section 2A–103(1)(v).
"Record". Section 2A–103(1)(cc).
"Rights". Section 1–201.
"Seasonably". Section 1–204(3).
"Supplier". Section 2A–103(1)(ff).

As amended in 2003.

§ 2A–515. Acceptance of Goods.

(1) Acceptance of goods occurs when the lessee:

(a) after a reasonable opportunity to inspect the goods signifies to the lessor or supplier that the goods are conforming or will be taken or retained in spite of their nonconformity;

(b) fails to make an effective rejection under Section 2A–509(2), but such acceptance does not occur until the lessee has had a reasonable opportunity to inspect them; or

(c) subject to Section 2A–517(6), uses the goods in any manner that is inconsistent with the lessor's or supplier's rights.

(2) Acceptance of a part of any commercial unit is acceptance of that entire unit.

As amended in 2003.

Official Comment

This section parallels the rules for acceptance under Article 2 (Section 2–606).

Cross Reference:

Section 2–608.

Definitional Cross References:

"Commercial unit". Section 2A–103(1)(b).
"Conforming". Section 2A–103(1)(c).
"Goods". Section 2A–103(1)(n).
"Lessee". Section 2A–103(1)(t).
"Lessor". Section 2A–103(1)(v).
"Supplier". Section 2A–103(1)(ff).

As amended in 2003.

§ 2A–516. Effect of Acceptance of Goods; Notice of Default; Burden of Establishing Default after Acceptance; Notice of Claim or Litigation to Person Answerable Over.

(1) A lessee must pay rent for any goods accepted in accordance with the lease contract

(2) A lessee's acceptance of goods precludes rejection of the goods accepted. In the case of a finance lease, if made with knowledge of a nonconformity, acceptance may not be revoked because of it. In any other case, if made with knowledge of a nonconformity, acceptance may not be revoked because of it unless the acceptance was on the reasonable assumption that the nonconformity would be seasonably cured. Acceptance does not of itself impair any other remedy provided by this Article or the lease agreement for nonconformity.

(3) If a tender has been accepted:

(a) within a reasonable time after the lessee discovers or should have discovered any default, the lessee shall notify the lessor and the supplier, if any; however, failure to give timely notice bars the lessee from a remedy only to the extent that the lessor or supplier is prejudiced by the failure;

(b) except in the case of a consumer lease, within a reasonable time after the lessee receives notice of litigation for infringement or the like (Section 2A–211) the lessee shall notify the lessor or be barred from any remedy over for liability established by the litigation; and

(c) the burden is on the lessee to establish any default.

(4) If a lessee is sued for indemnity, breach of a warranty or other obligation for which another party is answerable over the following rules apply:

(a) The lessee may give the other party notice of the litigation in a record. If the notice states that the person notified may come in and defend and that if the person notified does not do so that person will be bound in any action against that person by the lessee by any determination of fact common to the two litigations, then unless the person notified after seasonable receipt of the notice does come in and defend that person is so bound.

(b) The other party may demand in a record that the lessee turn over control of the litigation including settlement if the claim is one for infringement or the like (Section 2A–211) or else be barred from any remedy over. If the demand states that the other party agrees to bear all expense and to satisfy any adverse judgment, then unless the lessee after seasonable receipt of the demand does turn over control the lessee is so barred.

(5) Subsections (3) and (4) apply to any obligation of a lessee to hold the lessor or the supplier harmless against infringement or the like (Section 2A–211).

As amended in 2003.

Official Comment

Uniform Statutory Source: Section 2–607.

Changes: Substantially revised.

Purposes:

1. Subsection (2) creates a special rule for finance leases, precluding revocation if acceptance is made with knowledge of nonconformity with respect to the lease agreement, as opposed to the supply agreement;

this is not inequitable as the lessee has a direct claim against the supplier. Section 2A–209(1). Revocation of acceptance of a finance lease is permitted if the lessee's acceptance was without discovery of the nonconformity (with respect to the lease agreement, not the supply agreement) and was reasonably induced by the lessor's assurances. Section 2A–517(1)(b). Absent exclusion or modification, the lessor under a finance lease makes certain warranties to the lessee. Sections 2A–210 and 2A–211(1). Revocation of acceptance is not prohibited even after the lessee's promise has become irrevocable and independent. Section 2A–407 official comment. Where the finance lease creates a security interest, the rule may be to the contrary. *General Elec. Credit Corp. of Tennessee v. Ger–Beck Mach. Co.*, 806 F.2d 1207 (3rd Cir. 1986).

2. Subsection (3)(a) requires the lessee to give notice of default within a reasonable time after the lessee discovered or should have discovered the default. Failure to provide the notice bars the lessee from any remedy to the extent that the lessor or supplier is prejudiced by the lack of notice. In a finance lease, notice may be given either to the supplier, the lessor, or both, but remedy is barred against either party if that party is not notified and that party is prejudiced by the lack of notice. In a finance lease, the lessor is usually not liable for defects in the goods and the essential notice is to the supplier. While notice to the finance lessor will often not give any additional rights to the lessee, it would be good practice to give the notice since the finance lessor has an interest in the goods. Subsection (3)(a) does not use the term finance lease, but the definition of supplier is a person from whom a lessor buys or leases goods to be leased under a finance lease. Section 2A–103(1)(x). Therefore, there can be a "supplier" only in a finance lease. Subsection (4) applies similar notice rules if a lessee is sued for a breach of warranty or other obligation for which another party is answerable over.

3. Subsection (3)(b) requires the lessee to give the lessor notice of litigation for infringement or the like. There is an exception created for a consumer lease. While the exception was considered for a finance lease, it was not created because it was not necessary—the lessor in a finance lease does not give a warranty against infringement. Section 2A–211(2). Even though not required under subsection (3)(b), the lessee who takes under a finance lease should consider giving notice of litigation for infringement or the like to the supplier, because the lessee obtains the benefit of the suppliers' promises subject to the suppliers' defenses or claims. Sections 2A–209(1) and 2–607(3)(b).

Cross References:

Point 1: Section 2A–209, 2A–210, 2A–211 2A–407, 2A–517.
Point 2: Sections 2A–103.
Point 3: Section 2–607 and 2A–209, 2A–211.

Definitional Cross References:

"Action". Section 1–201.
"Agreement". Section 1–201.
"Burden of establishing". Section 1–201.
"Conforming". Section 2A–103(1)(c).
"Consumer lease". Section 2A–103(1)(f).
"Delivery". Section 2A–103(1)(g).
"Discover". Section 1–201.
"Finance lease". Section 2A–103(1)(l).
"Goods". Section 2A–103(1)(n).
"Knowledge". Section 1–202.
"Lease agreement". Section 2A–103(1)(q).
"Lease contract". Section 2A–103(1)(r).
"Lessee". Section 2A–103(1)(t).
"Lessor". Section 2A–103(1)(v).
"Notice". Section 1–202.
"Notifies". Section 1–202.
"Person". Section 1–201.
"Reasonable time". Section 1–205.
"Receipt". Section 2–103(1)(c).
"Record". Section 2A–103(1)(cc).
"Remedy". Section 1–201.
"Seasonably". Section 1–204(3).
"Supplier". Section 2A–103(1)(ff).

As amended in 2003.

§ 2A–517. Revocation of Acceptance of Goods.

(1) A lessee may revoke acceptance of a lot or commercial unit whose nonconformity substantially impairs its value to the lessee if the lessee has accepted it:

   (a) except in the case of a finance lease, on the reasonable assumption that its nonconformity would be cured and it has not been seasonably cured; or

   (b) without discovery of the nonconformity if the lessee's acceptance was reasonably induced either by the lessor's assurances or, except in the case of a finance lease, by the difficulty of discovery before acceptance.

(2) Except in the case of a finance lease that is not a consumer lease, a lessee may revoke acceptance of a lot or commercial unit if the lessor defaults under the lease contract and the default

substantially impairs the value of that lot or commercial unit to the lessee.

(3) If the lease agreement so provides, the lessee may revoke acceptance of a lot or commercial unit because of other defaults by the lessor.

(4) Revocation of acceptance must occur within a reasonable time after the lessee discovers or should have discovered the ground for it and before any substantial change in condition of the goods which is not caused by the nonconformity. Revocation is not effective until the lessee notifies the lessor.

(5) A lessee that so revokes has the same rights and duties with regard to the goods involved as if the lessee had rejected them.

(6) If a lessee uses the goods after a rightful rejection or justifiable revocation of acceptance, the following rules apply:

(a) Any use by the lessee which is unreasonable under the circumstances is wrongful as against the lessor or supplier and is an acceptance only if ratified by the lessor or supplier.

(b) Any use of the goods which is reasonable under the circumstances is not wrongful as against the lessor or supplier and is not an acceptance, but in an appropriate case the lessee shall be obligated to the lessor or supplier for the value of the use to the lessee.

As amended in 2003 and 2005.

Official Comment

Uniform Statutory Source: Section 2–608.

Changes: Revised to reflect leasing practices and terminology. Note that in the case of a finance lease the lessee retains a limited right to revoke acceptance. Sections 2A–517(1)(b) and 2A–516 official comment. New subsections (2) and (3) added.

Purposes:

1. The section states the situations under which the lessee may return the goods to the lessor and cancel the lease. Subsection (2) recognizes that the lessor may have continuing obligations under the lease and that a default as to those obligations may be sufficiently material to justify revocation of acceptance of the leased items and cancellation of the lease by the lessee. For example, a failure by the lessor to fulfill its obligation to maintain leased equipment or to supply other goods which are necessary for the operation of the leased equipment may justify revocation of acceptance and cancellation of the lease.

2. Subsection (3) specifically provides that the lease agreement may provide that the lessee can revoke acceptance for defaults by the lessor which in the absence of such an agreement might not be considered sufficiently serious to justify revocation. That is, the parties are free to contract on the question of what defaults are so material that the lessee can cancel the lease.

3. Subsection (6) deals with the problem of post-rejection or revocation use of the goods. If the lessee's use after an effective rejection or a justified revocation of acceptance is unreasonable under the circumstances, it is inconsistent with the rejection or revocation of acceptance and is wrongful as against the lessor. This gives the lessor the option of ratifying the use, thereby treating it as an acceptance, or pursuing a non-Code remedy for conversion.

If the lessee's use is reasonable under the circumstances, the lessee's actions cannot be treated as an acceptance. The lessee must, in appropriate circumstances, compensate the lessor for the value of the use of the goods to the lessee. Determining the appropriate level of compensation requires a consideration of the lessee's particular circumstances and should take into account the defective condition of the goods. There may be circumstances, such as where the use is solely for the purpose of protecting the lessee's security interest in the goods, where no compensation is due the lessor. In other circumstances, the lessor's right to compensation must be netted out against any right of the lessee to damages.

In general, a lessee that either rejects or revokes acceptance of the goods should not subsequently use the goods in a manner that is inconsistent with the lessor's interest. In some instances, however, the use may be reasonable. An example might involve a commercial lessee that is unable immediately to obtain cover and must use the goods to fulfill the lessee's obligations to third parties. If circumstances change so that the lessee's use is no longer reasonable, the continued use of the goods is unreasonable and is wrongful against the lessor. Of course, a lessee's rejection must be rightful, or its revocation must be justified; a lessee cannot make a false claim of nonconformity and limit the obligation to pay rent to the value of the use to the lessee.

Cross Reference:

Section 2A–516 official comment.

Definitional Cross References:

"Commercial unit". Section 2A–103(1)(b).
"Conforming". Section 2A–103(1)(c).
"Discover". Section 1–201.
"Finance lease". Section 2A–103(1)(l).
"Goods". Section 2A–103(1)(n).
"Lessee". Section 2A–103(1)(t).
"Lessor". Section 2A–103(1)(v).
"Lot". Section 2A–103(1)(y).
"Notifies". Section 1–201.
"Reasonable time". Section 1–205.
"Rights". Section 1–201.
"Seasonably". Section 1–204(3).
"Value". Section 1–204.

As amended in 2003 and 2005.

§ 2A–518. Cover; Substitute Goods.

(1) After a default by a lessor under the lease contract of the type described in Section 2A–508(1), or, if agreed, after other default by the lessor, the lessee may cover by making any purchase or lease of or contract to purchase or lease goods in substitution for those due from the lessor.

(2) Except as otherwise provided with respect to damages liquidated in the lease agreement (Section 2A–504) or otherwise determined pursuant to agreement of the parties (Sections 1–102(3) and 2A–503), if a lessee's cover is by a lease agreement substantially similar to the original lease agreement and the new lease agreement is made in good faith and in a commercially reasonable manner, the lessee may recover from the lessor as damages (i) the present value, as of the date of the commencement of the term of the new lease agreement, of the rent under the new lease agreement applicable to that period of the new lease term which is comparable to the then remaining term of the original lease agreement minus the present value as of the same date of the total rent for the then remaining lease term of the original lease agreement, and (ii) any incidental or consequential damages, less expenses saved in consequence of the lessor's default.

(3) If a lessee's cover is by lease agreement that for any reason does not qualify for treatment under subsection (2), or is by purchase or otherwise, the lessee may recover from the lessor as if the lessee had elected not to cover and Section 2A–519 governs.

As amended in 2001.

Official Comment

Uniform Statutory Source: Section 2–712.

Changes: Substantially revised.

Purposes:

1. Subsection (1) allows the lessee to take action to fix its damages after default by the lessor. Such action may consist of the lease of goods. The decision to cover is a function of commercial judgment, not a statutory mandate replete with sanctions for failure to comply. *Cf.* Section 9–507.

2. Subsection (2) states a rule for determining the amount of lessee's damages provided that there is no agreement to the contrary. The lessee's damages will be established using the new lease agreement as a measure if the following three criteria are met: (i) the lessee's cover is by lease agreement, (ii) the lease agreement is substantially similar to the original lease agreement, and (iii) such cover was effected in good faith, and in a commercially reasonable manner. Thus, the lessee will be entitled to recover from the lessor the present value, as of the date of commencement of the term of the new lease agreement, of the rent under the new lease agreement applicable to that period which is comparable to the then remaining term of the original lease agreement less the present value of the rent reserved for the remaining term under the original lease, together with incidental or consequential damages less expenses saved in consequence of the lessor's default. Consequential damages may include loss suffered by the lessee because of deprivation of the use of the goods during the period between the default and the acquisition of the goods under the new lease agreement. If the lessee's cover does not satisfy the criteria of subsection (2), Section 2A–519 governs.

3. Two of the three criteria to be met by the lessee are familiar, but the concept of the new lease agreement being substantially similar to the original lease agreement is not. Given the many variables facing a party who intends to lease goods and the rapidity of change in the market place, the policy decision was made not to draft with specificity. It was thought unwise to seek to establish certainty at the cost of fairness. Thus, the decision of whether the new lease agreement is substantially similar to the original will be determined case by case.

4. While the section does not draw a bright line, it is possible to describe some of the factors that should be considered in finding that a new lease agreement is substantially similar to the original. First, the goods

subject to the new lease agreement should be examined. For example, in a lease of computer equipment the new lease might be for more modern equipment. However, it may be that at the time of the lessor's breach it was not possible to obtain the same type of goods in the market place. Because the lessee's remedy under Section 2A–519 is intended to place the lessee in essentially the same position as if he had covered, if goods similar to those to have been delivered under the original lease are not available, then the computer equipment in this hypothetical should qualify as a commercially reasonable substitute. *See* Section 2–712(1).

5. Second, the various elements of the new lease agreement should also be examined. Those elements include the presence or absence of options to purchase or release; the lessor's representations, warranties and covenants to the lessee, as well as those to be provided by the lessee to the lessor; and the services, if any, to be provided by the lessor or by the lessee. All of these factors allocate cost and risk between the lessor and the lessee and thus affect the amount of rent to be paid. If the differences between the original lease and the new lease can be easily valued, it would be appropriate for a court to adjust the difference in rental to take account of the difference between the two leases, find that the new lease is substantially similar to the old lease, and award cover damages under this section. If, for example, the new lease requires the lessor to insure the goods in the hands of the lessee, while the original lease required the lessee to insure, the usual cost of such insurance could be deducted from the rent due under the new lease before determining the difference in rental between the two leases.

6. Having examined the goods and the agreement, the test to be applied is whether, in light of these comparisons, the new lease agreement is substantially similar to the original lease agreement. These findings should not be made with scientific precision, as they are a function of economics, nor should they be made independently with respect to the goods and each element of the agreement, as it is important that a sense of commercial judgment pervade the finding. To establish the new lease as a proper measure of damage under subsection (2), these factors, taken as a whole, must result in a finding that the new lease agreement is substantially similar to the original.

7. A new lease can be substantially similar to the original lease even though its term extends beyond the remaining term of the original lease, so long as both (a) the lease terms are commercially comparable (e.g., it is highly unlikely that a one-month rental and a five-year lease would reflect similar commercial realities), and

(b) the court can fairly apportion a part of the rental payments under the new lease to that part of the term of the new lease which is comparable to the remaining lease term under the original lease. Also, the lease term of the new lease may be comparable to the term of the original lease even though the beginning and ending dates of the two leases are not the same. For example, a two-month lease of agricultural equipment for the months of August and September may be comparable to a two-month lease running from the 15th of August to the 15th of October if in the particular location two-month leases beginning on August 15th are basically interchangeable with two-month leases beginning August 1st. Similarly, the term of a one-year truck lease beginning on the 15th of January may be comparable to the term of a one-year truck lease beginning January 2d. If the lease terms are found to be comparable, the court may base cover damages on the entire difference between the costs under the two leases.

Cross References:

Point 1: Section 9–625 and 9–626.
Point 2: Section 2A–519.
Point 4: Section 2–712 and Section 2A–519.

Definitional Cross References:

"Agreement". Section 1–201.
"Contract". Section 1–201.
"Good faith". Sections 2A–103(1)(m).
"Goods". Section 2A–103(1)(n).
"Lease". Section 2A–103(1)(p).
"Lease agreement". Section 2A–103(1)(q).
"Lease contract". Section 2A–103(1)(r).
"Lessee". Section 2A–103(1)(t).
"Lessor". Section 2A–103(1)(v).
"Party". Section 1–201.
"Present value". Section 2A–103(1)(aa).
"Purchase". Section 2A–103(1)(bb).

As amended in 2001.

§ 2A–519. Lessee's Damages for Non-delivery, Repudiation, Default, and Breach of Warranty in Regard to Accepted Goods.

(1) Except as otherwise provided with respect to damages liquidated in the lease agreement (Section 2A–504) or otherwise determined pursuant to agreement of the parties (Sections 1–102(3) and 2A–503), if a lessee elects not to cover or a lessee elects to cover and the cover is by lease agreement that for any reason does not

qualify for treatment under Section 2A–518(2), or is by purchase or otherwise, the measure of damages for non-delivery or repudiation by the lessor or for rejection or revocation of acceptance by the lessee is the present value, as of the date of the default, of the then market rent minus the present value as of the same date of the original rent, computed for the remaining lease term of the original lease agreement, together with incidental and consequential damages, less expenses saved in consequence of the lessor's default.

(2) Market rent is to be determined as of the place for tender or, in cases of rejection after arrival or revocation of acceptance, as of the place of arrival.

(3) Except as otherwise agreed, if the lessee has accepted goods and given notification (Section 2A–516(3)), the measure of damages for non-conforming tender or delivery or other default by a lessor is the loss resulting in the ordinary course of events from the lessor's default as determined in any manner that is reasonable together with incidental and consequential damages, less expenses saved in consequence of the lessor's default.

(4) Except as otherwise agreed, the measure of damages for breach of warranty is the present value at the time and place of acceptance of the difference between the value of the use of the goods accepted and the value if they had been as warranted for the lease term, unless special circumstances show proximate damages of a different amount, together with incidental and consequential damages, less expenses saved in consequence of the lessor's default or breach of warranty.

As amended in 2001.

Official Comment

Uniform Statutory Source: Sections 2–713 and 2–714.

Changes: Substantially revised.

Purposes:

1. Subsection (1), a revised version of the provisions of Section 2–713(1), states the basic rule governing the measure of lessee's damages for non-delivery or repudiation by the lessor or for rightful rejection or revocation of acceptance by the lessee. This measure will apply, absent agreement to the contrary, if the lessee does not cover or if the cover does not qualify

under Section 2A–518. There is no sanction for cover that does not qualify.

2. The measure of damage is the present value, as of the date of default, of the market rent for the remaining term of the lease less the present value of the original rent for the remaining term of the lease, plus incidental and consequential damages less expenses saved in consequence of the default. Note that the reference in Section 2A–519(1) is to the date of default not to the date of an event of default. An event of default under a lease agreement becomes a default under a lease agreement only after the expiration of any relevant period of grace and compliance with any notice requirements under this Article and the lease agreement. American Bar Foundation, *Commentaries on Indentures*, § 5–1, at 216–217 (1971). Section 2A–501(1). This conclusion is also a function of whether, as a matter of fact or law, the event of default has been waived, suspended or cured. Sections 2A–103(4) and 1–103.

3. Subsection (2), a revised version of the provisions of Section 2–713(2), states the rule with respect to determining market rent.

4. Subsection (3), a revised version of the provisions of Section 2–714(1) and (3), states the measure of damages where goods have been accepted and acceptance is not revoked. The subsection applies both to defaults which occur at the inception of the lease and to defaults which occur subsequently, such as failure to comply with an obligation to maintain the leased goods. The measure in essence is the loss, in the ordinary course of events, flowing from the default.

5. Subsection (4), a revised version of the provisions of Section 2–714(2), states the measure of damages for breach of warranty. The measure in essence is the present value of the difference between the value of the goods accepted and of the goods if they had been as warranted.

6. Subsections (1), (3) and (4) specifically state that the parties may by contract vary the damages rules stated in those subsections.

Cross References:

  Point 1: Section 2–713 and Section 2A–518.
  Point 2: Sections 2A–501 and 2A–519.
  Point 3: Section 2–713.
  Point 4: Section 2–714.
  Point 5: Section 2–714.

Definitional Cross References:

  "Conforming". Section 2A–103(1)(c).
  "Delivery". Section 2A–103(1)(g).

"Goods". Section 2A–103(1)(n).
"Lease". Section 2A–103(1)(p).
"Lease agreement". Section 2A–103(1)(q).
"Lessee". Section 2A–103(1)(t).
"Lessor". Section 2A–103(1)(v).
"Notification". Section 1–202.
"Present value". Section 2A–103(1)(aa).
"Value". Section 1–204.

As amended in 2001.

§ 2A–520. Lessee's Incidental and Consequential Damages.

(1) Incidental damages resulting from a lessor's default include expenses reasonably incurred in inspection, receipt, transportation, and care and custody of goods rightfully rejected or goods the acceptance of which is justifiably revoked, any commercially reasonable charges, expenses or commissions in connection with effecting cover, and any other reasonable expense incident to the default.

(2) Consequential damages resulting from a lessor's default include:

(a) any loss resulting from general or particular requirements and needs of which the lessor at the time of contracting had reason to know and which could not reasonably be prevented by cover or otherwise; and

(b) injury to person or property proximately resulting from any breach of warranty.

Official Comment

Uniform Statutory Source: Section 2–715.

Changes: Revised to reflect leasing terminology and practices.

Purposes: Subsection (1), a revised version of the provisions of Section 2–715(1), lists some examples of incidental damages resulting from a lessor's default; the list is not exhaustive. Subsection (1) makes clear that it applies not only to rightful rejection, but also to justifiable revocation.

Subsection (2), a revised version of the provisions of Section 2–715(2), lists some examples of consequential damages resulting from a lessor's default; the list is not exhaustive.

Cross Reference:

Section 2–715.

Definitional Cross References:

"Goods". Section 2A–103(1)(n).
"Knows". Section 1–201.
"Lessee". Section 2A–103(1)(t).
"Lessor". Section 2A–103(1)(v).
"Person". Section 1–201.
"Receipt". Section 2–103(1)(c).

§ 2A–521. Reserved.

Legislative Note: The section on specific performance has been moved to Section 2A–507A because it has been amended so that the remedy is available to both lessors and lessees.

§ 2A–522. Lessee's Right to Goods on Lessor's Insolvency.

(1) Subject to subsection (2) and even if the goods have not been shipped, a lessee that has paid a part or all of the rent and security for goods identified to a lease contract (Section 2A–217) on making and keeping good a tender of any unpaid portion of the rent and security due under the lease contract may recover the goods identified from the lessor if

(a) in the case of goods leased by a consumer, the lessor repudiates or fails to deliver as required by the lease contract; or

(b) in all cases, the lessor becomes insolvent within 10 days after receipt of the first installment on their rent and security.

(2) A lessee acquires the right to recover goods identified to a lease contract only if they conform to the lease contract.

As amended in 2003.

Official Comment

Uniform Statutory Source: Section 2–502.

Changes: Revised to reflect leasing practices and terminology.

1. This section gives the lessee the goods identified under Section 2A–217 upon making and keeping good a tender of any unpaid portion of the rent and security, in two limited circumstances. First, a consumer lessee may recover the goods if the lessor repudiates the contract or fails to deliver the goods. Second, in any case, the lessee may recover the goods if the lessor becomes insolvent within 10 days after the lessor receives the first installment on their price. The lessee's right to recover the goods under this section is an exception to the usual rule, under which the disap-

241

pointed lessee must resort to an action to recover damages.

2. The lessee's right to recover goods to a lease contract is dependent upon the goods conforming to the lease contract.

Cross Reference:

Point 1: Sections 2A–217.

Definitional Cross References:

"Conforming". Section 2A–103(1)(c).
"Goods". Section 2A–103(1)(n).
"Insolvent". Section 1–201.
"Lease contract". Section 2A–103(1)(r).
"Lessee". Section 2A–103(1)(t).
"Lessor". Section 2A–103(1)(v).
"Receipt". Section 2–103(1)(c).
"Rights". Section 1–201.

As amended in 2003.

C. DEFAULT BY LESSEE

§ 2A–523. Lessor's Remedies.

(1) If the lessee wrongfully rejects or attempts to revoke acceptance of goods or fails to make a payment when due or repudiates with respect to a part or the whole, the lessee is in default under the lease contract with respect to any goods involved and the lessor may do one or more of the following:

(a) withhold delivery of the goods and take possession of goods previously delivered under Section 2A–525;

(b) stop delivery of the goods by any carrier or bailee under Section 2A–526;

(c) proceed under Section 2A–524 with respect to goods still unidentified to the lease contract or unfinished;

(d) obtain specific performance under Section 2A–507A or recover the rent under Section 2A–529;

(e) dispose of the goods and recover damages under Section 2A–527 or retain the goods and recover damages under Section 2A–528;

(f) cancel the lease contract;

(g) recover liquidated damages under Section 2A–504;

(h) enforce limited remedies under Section 2A–503;

(i) exercise any other rights or pursue any other remedies provided in the lease agreement.

(2) If a lessee becomes insolvent but is not in default of the lease contract under subsections (1) or (4), the lessor may:

(a) refuse to deliver the goods under Section 2A–525(1);

(b) take possession of the goods under Section 2A–525(2);

(c) stop delivery of the goods by any bailee or carrier under Section 2A–526(1).

(3) If a lessor does not fully exercise a right or obtain a remedy to which the lessor is entitled under subsection (1), the lessor may recover the loss resulting in the ordinary course of events from the lessee's default as determined in any reasonable manner, together with incidental or consequential damages allowed under Section 2A–530, less expenses saved in consequence of the lessee's default.

(4) If a lessee is otherwise in default under a lease contract, the lessor may exercise the rights and pursue the remedies provided in the lease contract, which may include a right to cancel the lease. In addition, unless otherwise provided in the lease contract:

(a) if the default substantially impairs the value of the lease contract to the lessor, the lessor may exercise the rights and pursue the remedies provided in subsections (1) or (2); or

(b) if the default does not substantially impair the value of the lease contract to the lessor, the lessor may recover as provided in subsection (2).

As amended in 2003 and 2005.

Official Comment

1. Subsection (1) is an index to Sections 2A-503 through 2A-505, Section 2A-507 and Sections 2A-524 through 2A-531 and states that the remedies provided in those sections are available for the defaults referred to in subsection (1): wrongful rejection or revocation of acceptance, failure to make a payment when due, or repudiation. In addition, remedies provided in the lease contract are available. Subsection (3) sets out a remedy if the lessor does not pursue to completion a right or

actually obtain a remedy available under subsection (1), and subsection (4) sets out statutory remedies for defaults not specifically referred to in subsection (1). Subsection (4) provides that, if any default by the lessee other than those specifically referred to in subsection (1) is material, the lessor can exercise the remedies provided in subsection (1) or (3); otherwise the available remedy is as provided in subsection (4). A lessor who has brought an action seeking or has nonjudicially pursued one or more of the remedies available under subsection (1) may amend so as to claim or may nonjudicially pursue a remedy under subsection (3) unless the right or remedy first chosen has been pursued to an extent actually inconsistent with the new course of action. The intent of the provision is to reject the doctrine of election of remedies and to permit an alteration of course by the lessor unless such alteration would actually have an effect on the lessee that would be unreasonable under the circumstances. Furthermore, the lessor may pursue remedies under both subsections (1) and (3) unless doing so would put the lessor in a better position than it would have been in had the lessee fully performed.

2. The lessor and the lessee can agree to modify the rights and remedies available under the Article; they can, among other things, provide that for defaults other than those specified in subsection (1) the lessor can exercise the rights and remedies referred to in subsection (1), whether or not the default would otherwise be held to substantially impair the value of the lease contract to the lessor; they can also create a new scheme of rights and remedies triggered by the occurrence of the default. Sections 2A–103(4) and 1–302.

3. This Article rejects any general doctrine of election of remedy. Whether, in a particular case, one remedy bars another, is a function of whether lessor has been put in as good a position as if the lessee had fully performed the lease contract. Multiple remedies are barred only if the effect is to put the lessor in a better position than it would have been in had the lessee fully performed under the lease. Sections 2A–103(4), 2A–501(4), and 1–305(a).

4. Hypothetical: To better understand the application of subsection (1) it is useful to review a hypothetical. Assume that A is a merchant in the business of selling and leasing new bicycles of various types. B is about to engage in the business of subleasing bicycles to summer residents of and visitors to an island resort. A, as lessor, has agreed to lease 60 bicycles to B. While there is one master lease, deliveries and terms are staggered. 20 bicycles are to be delivered by A to B's island location on June 1; the term of the lease of these bicycles is four months. 20 bicycles are to be delivered

by A to B's island location on July 1; the term of the lease of these bicycles is three months. Finally, 20 bicycles are to be delivered by A to B's island location on August 1; the term of the lease of these bicycles is two months. B is obligated to pay rent to A on the 15th day of each month during the term for the lease. Rent is $50 per month, per bicycle. B has no option to purchase or release and must return the bicycles to A at the end of the term, in good condition, reasonable wear and tear excepted. Since the retail price of each bicycle is $400 and bicycles used in the retail rental business have a useful economic life of 36 months, this transaction creates a lease. Sections 2A–103(1)(j) and 1–302.

5. A's current inventory of bicycles is not large. Thus, upon signing the lease with B in February, A agreed to purchase 60 new bicycles from A's principal manufacturer, with special instructions to drop ship the bicycles to B's island location in accordance with the delivery schedule set forth in the lease.

6. The first shipment of 20 bicycles was received by B on May 21. B inspected the bicycles, accepted the same as conforming to the lease and signed a receipt of delivery and acceptance. However, due to poor weather that summer, business was terrible and B was unable to pay the rent due on June 15. Pursuant to the lease A sent B notice of default and proceeded to enforce his rights and remedies against B.

7. A's counsel first advised A that under Section 2A–510(2) and the terms of the lease B's failure to pay was a default with respect to the whole. Thus, to minimize A's continued exposure, A was advised to take possession of the bicycles. If A had possession of the goods A could refuse to deliver. Section 2A–525(1). However, the facts here are different. With respect to the bicycles in B's possession, A has the right to take possession of the bicycles, without breach of the peace. Section 2A–525(2). If B refuses to allow A access to the bicycles, A can proceed by action, including replevin or injunctive relief.

8. With respect to the 40 bicycles that have not been delivered, this Article provides various alternatives. First, assume that 20 of the remaining 40 bicycles have been manufactured and delivered by the manufacturer to a carrier for shipment to B. Given the size of the shipment, the carrier was using a small truck for the delivery and the truck had not yet reached the island ferry when the manufacturer (at the request of A) instructed the carrier to divert the shipment to A's place of business. A's right to stop delivery is recognized under these circumstances. Section 2A–526(1). Second, assume that the 20 remaining bicycles

were in the process of manufacture when B defaulted. A retains the right (as between A as lessor and B as lessee) to exercise reasonable commercial judgment whether to complete manufacture or to dispose of the unfinished goods for scrap. Since A is not the manufacturer and A has a binding contract to buy the bicycles, A elected to allow the manufacturer to complete the manufacture of the bicycles, but instructed the manufacturer to deliver the completed bicycles to A's place of business. Section 2A–524(2).

9. Thus, so far A has elected to exercise the remedies referred to in subparagraphs (b) through (d) in subsection (1). None of these remedies bars any of the others because A's election and enforcement merely resulted in A's possession of the bicycles. Had B performed A would have recovered possession of the bicycles. Thus A is in the process of obtaining the benefit of his bargain. Note that A could exercise any other rights or pursue any other remedies provided in the lease contract (Section 2A–523(1)(f)), or elect to recover his loss due to the lessee's default under Section 2A–523(2).

10. A's counsel next would determine what action, if any, should be taken with respect to the goods. As stated in subparagraph (e) and as discussed fully in Section 2A–527(1) the lessor may, but has no obligation to, dispose of the goods by a substantially similar lease (indeed, the lessor has no obligation whatsoever to dispose of the goods at all) and recover damages based on that action, but lessor will not be able to recover damages which put it in a better position than performance would have done, nor will it be able to recover damages for losses which it could have reasonably avoided. In this case, since A is in the business of leasing and selling bicycles, A will probably inventory the 60 bicycles for its retail trade.

11. A's counsel then will determine which of the various means of ascertaining A's damages against B are available. Subparagraph (e) catalogues each relevant section. First, under Section 2A–527(2) the amount of A's claim is computed by comparing the original lease between A and B with any subsequent lease of the bicycles but only if the subsequent lease is substantially similar to the original lease contract. While the section does not define this term, the official comment does establish some parameters. If, however, A elects to lease the bicycles to his retail trade, it is unlikely that the resulting lease will be substantially similar to the original, as leases to retail customers are considerably different from leases to wholesale customers like B. If, however, the leases were substantially similar, the damage claim is for accrued and unpaid rent to the beginning of the new lease, plus the present value as of the same date, of the rent reserved under the original lease for the balance of its term less the present value as of the same date of the rent reserved under the replacement lease for a term comparable to the balance of the term of the original lease, together with incidental damages less expenses saved in consequence of the lessee's default.

12. If the new lease is not substantially similar or if A elects to sell the bicycles or to hold the bicycles, damages are computed under Section 2A–528 or 2A–529.

13. If A elects to pursue his claim under Section 2A–528(1) the damage rule is the same as that stated in Section 2A–528(2) except that damages are measured from default if the lessee never took possession of the goods or from the time when the lessor did or could have regained possession and that the standard of comparison is not the rent reserved under a substantially similar lease entered into by the lessor but a market rent, as defined in Section 2A–507. Further, if the facts of this hypothetical were more elaborate A may be able to establish that the measure of damage under subsection (1) is inadequate to put him in the same position that B's performance would have, in which case A can claim the present value of his lost profits.

14. Yet another alternative for computing A's damage claim against B which will be available in some situations is recovery of the present value, as of entry of judgment, of the rent for the then remaining lease term under Section 2A–529. However, this formulation is not available if the goods have been repossessed or tendered back to A. For the 20 bicycles repossessed and the remaining 40 bicycles, A will be able to recover the present value of the rent only if A is unable to dispose of them, or circumstances indicate the effort will be unavailing. If A has prevailed in an action for the rent, at any time up to collection of a judgment by A against B, A might dispose of the bicycles. In such case A's claim for damages against B is governed by Section 2A–527 or 2A–528. Section 2A–529(3). The resulting recalculation of claim should reduce the amount recoverable by A against B and the lessor is required to cause an appropriate credit to be entered against the earlier judgment. However, the nature of the post-judgment proceedings to resolve this issue, and the sanctions for a failure to comply, if any, will be determined by other law.

15. Finally, if the lease agreement had so provided pursuant to subparagraph (f), A's claim against B would not be determined under any of these statutory

formulae, but pursuant to a liquidated damages clause. Section 2A–504(1).

16. These various methods of computing A's damage claim against B are alternatives subject to Section 2A–501(4). However, the pursuit of any one of these alternatives is not a bar to, nor has it been barred by, A's earlier action to obtain possession of the 60 bicycles. These formulae, which vary as a function of an overt or implied mitigation of damage theory, focus on allowing A a recovery of the benefit of his bargain with B. Had B performed, A would have received the rent as well as the return of the 60 bicycles at the end of the term.

17. Finally, A's counsel should also advise A of his right to cancel the lease contract under subparagraph (a). Section 2A–505(1). Cancellation will discharge all existing obligations but preserve A's rights and remedies.

18. Subsection (2) recognizes that a lessor who is entitled to exercise the rights or to obtain a remedy granted by subsection (1) may choose not to do so. In such cases, the lessor can recover damages as provided in subsection (2). For example, for non-payment of rent, the lessor may decide not to take possession of the goods and cancel the lease, but rather to merely sue for the unpaid rent as it comes due plus lost interest or other damages "determined in any reasonable manner." Subsection (2) also negates any loss of alternative rights and remedies by reason of having invoked or commenced the exercise or pursuit of any one or more rights or remedies.

19. Subsection (3) allows the lessor access to a remedy scheme provided in this Article as well as that contained in the lease contract if the lessee is in default for reasons other than those stated in subsection (1). Note that the reference to this Article includes supplementary principles of law and equity, e.g., fraud, misrepresentation and duress. Sections 2A–103(4) and 1–103.

20. There is no special treatment of the finance lease in this section. Absent supplementary principles of law to the contrary, in most cases the supplier will have no rights or remedies against the defaulting lessee. Section 2A–209(2)(ii). Given that the supplier will look to the lessor for payment, this is appropriate. However, there is a specific exception to this rule with respect to the right to identify goods to the lease contract. Section 2A–524(2). The parties are free to create a different result in a particular case. Sections 2A–103(4) and 1–302.

Cross References:

Point 1: Section 2A–524, 2A–531.
Point 2: Section 1–302 and Section 2A–103.
Point 3: Section 1–106 and Sections 2A–103 and 2A–501.
Point 4: Section 1–302 and Section 2A–103.
Point 7: Section 2A–510, 2A–525.
Point 8: Sections 2A–524 and 2A–526.
Point 9: Section 2A–523.
Point 10: Section 2A–527.
Point 11: Section 2A–527.
Point 12: Section 2A–528 and 2A–529.
Point 13: 2A–507 and 2A–528.
Point 14: Section 2A–527, 2A–528 and 2A–529.
Point 15: Section 2A–504.
Point 16: 2A–501.
Point 17: Section 2A–505.
Point 19: Section 1–103 and Section 2A–103.
Point 20: Section 1–302 and Section 2A–103, 2A–209, 2A–524.

Definitional Cross References:

"Delivery". Section 2A–103(1)(g).
"Goods". Section 2A–103(1)(n).
"Installment lease contract". Section 2A–103(1)(o).
"Lease contract". Section 2A–103(1)(r).
"Lessee". Section 2A–103(1)(t).
"Lessor". Section 2A–103(1)(v).
"Remedy". Section 1–201.
"Rights". Section 1–201.
"Value". Section 1–204.

As amended in 2003.

§ 2A–524. Lessor's Right to Identify Goods to Lease Contract.

(1) After default by the lessee under the lease contract of the type described in Section 2A–523(1) or 2A–523(4)(a) or, if agreed, after other default by the lessee, the lessor may:

(a) identify to the lease contract conforming goods not already identified if at the time the lessor learned of the default they were in the lessor's or the supplier's possession or control; and

(b) dispose of goods (Section 2A–527(1)) that demonstrably have been intended for the particular lease contract even though those goods are unfinished.

(2) If the goods are unfinished, in the exercise of reasonable commercial judgment for the purposes of avoiding loss and of effective realization, an aggrieved lessor or the supplier may either

§ 2A–524

complete manufacture and wholly identify the goods to the lease contract or cease manufacture and lease, sell, or otherwise dispose of the goods for scrap or salvage value or proceed in any other reasonable manner.

As amended in 2005.

Official Comment

Uniform Statutory Source: Section 2–704.

Changes: Revised to reflect leasing practices and terminology.

Purposes: The remedies provided by this section are available to the lessor (i) if there has been a default by the lessee which falls within Section 2A–523(1) or 2A–523(3)(a), or (ii) if there has been any other default for which the lease contract gives the lessor the remedies provided by this section. Under "(ii)", the lease contract may give the lessor the remedies of identification and disposition provided by this section in various ways. For example, a lease provision might specifically refer to the remedies of identification and disposition, or it might refer to this section by number (*i.e.,* 2A–524), or it might do so by a more general reference such as "all rights and remedies provided by Article 2A for default by the lessee."

Cross References:

Section 2A–523.

Definitional Cross References:

"Aggrieved party". Section 1–201.
"Conforming". Section 2A–103(1)(c).
"Goods". Section 2A–103(1)(n).
"Learn". Section 1–201.
"Lease". Section 2A–103(1)(p).
"Lease contract". Section 2A–103(1)(r).
"Lessor". Section 2A–103(1)(v).
"Rights". Section 1–201.
"Supplier". Section 2A–103(1)(ff).
"Value". Section 1–204.

§ 2A–525. Lessor's Right to Possession of Goods.

(1) If a lessor discovers the lessee to be insolvent, the lessor may refuse to deliver the goods.

(2) After a default by the lessee under the lease contract of the type described in Section 2A–523(1) or 2A–523(4)(a) or, if agreed, after other default by the lessee, the lessor has the right to take possession of the goods. If the lease contract so provides, the lessor may require the lessee to assemble the goods and make them available to the lessor at a place to be designated by the lessor which is reasonably convenient to both parties. Without removal, the lessor may render unusable any goods employed in trade or business, and may dispose of goods on the lessee's premises (Section 2A–527).

(3) The lessor may proceed under subsection (2) without judicial process if it can be done without breach of the peace or the lessor may proceed by action.

As amended in 2005.

Official Comment

Uniform Statutory Source: Sections 2–702(1) and 9–503.

Changes: Substantially revised.

Purposes:

1. Subsection (1), a revised version of the provisions of Section 2–702(1), allows the lessor to refuse to deliver goods if the lessee is insolvent. Note that the provisions of Section 2–702(2), granting the unpaid seller certain rights of reclamation, were not incorporated in this section. Subsection (2) made this unnecessary.

2. Subsection (2), a revised version of the provisions of Section 9–503, allows the lessor, on a Section 2A–523(1) or 2A–523(3)(a) default by the lessee, the right to take possession of or reclaim the goods. Also, the lessor can contract for the right to take possession of the goods for other defaults by the lessee. Therefore, since the lessee's insolvency is an event of default in a standard lease agreement, subsection (2) is the functional equivalent of Section 2–702(2). Further, subsection (2) sanctions the classic crate and delivery clause obligating the lessee to assemble the goods and to make them available to the lessor. Finally, the lessor may leave the goods in place, render them unusable (if they are goods employed in trade or business), and dispose of them on the lessee's premises.

3. Subsection (3), a revised version of the provisions of Section 9–503, allows the lessor to proceed under subsection (2) without judicial process, absent breach of the peace, or by action. Sections 2A–501(3), 2A–103(4) and 1–201(1). In the appropriate case action includes injunctive relief. *Clark Equip. Co. v. Armstrong Equip. Co.*, 431 F.2d 54 (5th Cir.1970), *cert. denied,* 402 U.S. 909 (1971). This Section, as well as a number of other Sections in this Part, are included in the Article to codify the lessor's common law right to protect the lessor's reversionary interest in the goods.

Section 2A–103(1)(q). These Sections are intended to supplement and not displace principles of law and equity with respect to the protection of such interest. Sections 2A–103(4) and 1–103. Such principles apply in many instances, *e.g.*, loss or damage to goods if risk of loss passes to the lessee, failure of the lessee to return goods to the lessor in the condition stipulated in the lease, and refusal of the lessee to return goods to the lessor after termination or cancellation of the lease. See also Section 2A–532.

Cross References:

Point 1: Section 2–702.

Point 2: Section 2–702, Section 2A–523 and Section 9–503, 9–609.

Point 3: Section 1–201, Sections 2A-103, 2A–501, 2A–532 and Section 9–503.

Definitional Cross References:

"Action". Section 1–201.
"Delivery". Section 2A–103(1)(g).
"Discover". Section 1–201.
"Goods". Section 2A–103(1)(n).
"Insolvent". Section 1–201.
"Lease contract". Section 2A–103(1)(r).
"Lessee". Section 2A–103(1)(t).
"Lessor". Section 2A–103(1)(v).
"Party". Section 1–201.
"Rights". Section 1–201.

§ 2A–526. Lessor's Stoppage of Delivery in Transit or Otherwise.

(1) A lessor may stop delivery of goods in the possession of a carrier or other bailee if the lessor discovers the lessee to be insolvent or if the lessee repudiates or fails to make a payment due before delivery, whether for rent, security or otherwise under the lease contract, or for any other reason the lessor has a right to withhold or take possession of the goods.

(2) In pursuing its remedies under subsection (1), the lessor may stop delivery until

(a) receipt of the goods by the lessee;

(b) acknowledgment to the lessee by any bailee of the goods, except a carrier, that the bailee holds the goods for the lessee; or

(c) such an acknowledgment to the lessee by a carrier via reshipment or as a warehouse.

(3)(a) To stop delivery, a lessor shall so notify as to enable the bailee by reasonable diligence to prevent delivery of the goods.

(b) After notification, the bailee shall hold and deliver the goods according to the directions of the lessor, but the lessor is liable to the bailee for any ensuing charges or damages.

(c) A carrier that has issued a nonnegotiable bill of lading is not obliged to obey a notification to stop received from a person other than the consignor.

As amended in 2003.

Official Comment

Uniform Statutory Source: Section 2–705.

Changes: Revised to reflect leasing practices and terminology.

Definitional Cross References:

"Bill of lading". Section 1–201.
"Delivery". Section 2A–103(1)(g).
"Discover". Section 1–201.
"Goods". Section 2A–103(1)(n).
"Insolvent". Section 1–201.
"Lease contract". Section 2A–103(1)(r).
"Lessee". Section 2A–103(1)(t).
"Lessor". Section 2A–103(1)(v).
"Notifies" and "Notification". Section 1–202.
"Person". Section 1–201.
"Receipt". Section 2–103(1)(c).
"Remedy". Section 1–201.
"Rights". Section 1–201.

§ 2A–527. Lessor's Rights to Dispose of Goods.

(1) After a default by a lessee under the lease contract of the type described in Section 2A–523(1) or 2A–523(4)(a) or after the lessor refuses to deliver or takes possession of goods (Section 2A–525 or 2A–526), or, if agreed, after other default by a lessee, the lessor may dispose of the goods concerned or the undelivered balance thereof by lease, sale, or otherwise.

(2) Except as otherwise provided with respect to damages liquidated in the lease agreement (Section 2A–504) or otherwise determined pursuant to agreement of the parties (Section 1–302 and 2A–503), if the disposition is by lease agreement substantially similar to the original lease agreement and the new lease agreement is made in good faith and in a commercially reasonable manner, the lessor may recover from the lessee as damages (i) accrued and unpaid rent as of the

date of the commencement of the term of the new lease agreement, (ii) the present value, as of the same date, of the total rent for the then remaining lease term of the original lease agreement minus the present value, as of the same date, of the rent under the new lease agreement applicable to that period of the new lease term which is comparable to the then remaining term of the original lease agreement, and (iii) any incidental or consequential damages allowed under Section 2A–530, less expenses saved in consequence of the lessee's default.

(3) If the lessor's disposition is by lease agreement that for any reason does not qualify for treatment under subsection (2), or is by sale or otherwise, the lessor may recover from the lessee as if the lessor had elected not to dispose of the goods and Section 2A–528 governs.

(4) A subsequent buyer or lessee that buys or leases from the lessor in good faith for value as a result of a disposition under this section takes the goods free of the original lease contract and any rights of the original lessee even if the lessor fails to comply with one or more of the requirements of this Article.

(5) The lessor is not accountable to the lessee for any profit made on any disposition. A lessee that has rightfully rejected or justifiably revoked acceptance shall account to the lessor for any excess over the amount of the lessee's security interest (Section 2A–508(4)).

Legislative Note: The cross-reference in subsection (2) should not be changed if the jurisdiction has not adopted the 2001 Revised Article 1.

As amended in 2001 and 2003.

Official Comment

Uniform Statutory Source: Section 2–706(1), (5) and (6).

Changes: Substantially revised.

Purposes:

1. Subsection (1), a revised version of the first sentence of subsection 2–706(1), allows the lessor the right to dispose of goods after a statutory or other material default by the lessee (even if the goods remain in the lessee's possession—Section 2A–525(2)), after the lessor refuses to deliver or takes possession of the goods, or, if agreed, after other contractual default. The lessor's decision to exercise this right is a function of a commercial judgment, not a statutory mandate replete with sanctions for failure to comply. Cf. Section 9–507. As the owner of the goods, in the case of a lessor, or as the prime lessee of the goods, in the case of a sublessor, compulsory disposition of the goods is inconsistent with the nature of the interest held by the lessor or the sublessor and is not necessary because the interest held by the lessee or the sublessee is not protected by a right of redemption under the common law or this Article. Subsection 2A–527(5).

2. The rule for determining the measure of damages recoverable by the lessor against the lessee is a function of several variables. If the lessor has elected to effect disposition under subsection (1) and such disposition is by lease that qualifies under subsection (2), the measure of damages set forth in subsection (2) will apply, absent agreement to the contrary. Sections 2A–504, 2A–103(4) and 1–102(3).

3. The lessor's damages will be established using the new lease agreement as a measure if the following three criteria are satisfied: (i) the lessor disposed of the goods by lease, (ii) the lease agreement is substantially similar to the original lease agreement, and (iii) such disposition was in good faith, and in a commercially reasonable manner. Thus, the lessor will be entitled to recover from the lessee the accrued and unpaid rent as of the date of commencement of the term of the new lease, and the present value, as of the same date, of the rent, under the original lease for the then remaining term less the present value as of the same date of the rent under the new lease agreement applicable to the period of the new lease comparable to the remaining term under the original lease, together with incidental damages less expenses saved in consequence of the lessee's default. If the lessor's disposition does not satisfy the criteria of subsection (2), the lessor may calculate its claim against the lessee pursuant to Section 2A–528. Section 2A–523(1)(e).

4. Two of the three criteria to be met by the lessor are familiar, but the concept of the new lease agreement that is substantially similar to the original lease agreement is not. Given the many variables facing a party who intends to lease goods and the rapidity of change in the market place, the policy decision was made not to draft with specificity. It was thought unwise to seek to establish certainty at the cost of fairness. The decision of whether the new lease agreement is substantially similar to the original will be determined case by case.

5. While the section does not draw a bright line, it is possible to describe some of the factors that should be considered in a finding that a new lease agreement is substantially similar to the original. The various

elements of the new lease agreement should be examined. Those elements include the options to purchase or release; the lessor's representations, warranties and covenants to the lessee as well as those to be provided by the lessee to the lessor; and the services, if any, to be provided by the lessor or by the lessee. All of these factors allocate cost and risk between the lessor and the lessee and thus affect the amount of rent to be paid. These findings should not be made with scientific precision, as they are a function of economics, nor should they be made independently, as it is important that a sense of commercial judgment pervade the finding. See Section 2A–507(2). To establish the new lease as a proper measure of damage under subsection (2), these various factors, taken as a whole, must result in a finding that the new lease agreement is substantially similar to the original. If the differences between the original lease and the new lease can be easily valued, it would be appropriate for a court to find that the new lease is substantially similar to the old lease, adjust the difference in the rent between the two leases to take account of the differences, and award damages under this section. If, for example, the new lease requires the lessor to insure the goods in the hands of the lessee, while the original lease required the lessee to insure, the usual cost of such insurance could be deducted from rent due under the new lease before the difference in rental between the two leases is determined.

6. The following hypothetical illustrates the difficulty of providing a bright line. Assume that A buys a jumbo tractor for $1 million and then leases the tractor to B for a term of 36 months. The tractor is delivered to and is accepted by B on May 1. On June 1 B fails to pay the monthly rent to A. B returns the tractor to A, who immediately releases the tractor to C for a term identical to the term remaining under the lease between A and B. All terms and conditions under the lease between A and C are identical to those under the original lease between A and B, except that C does not provide any property damage or other insurance coverage, and B agreed to provide complete coverage. Coverage is expensive and difficult to obtain. It is a question of fact whether it is so difficult to adjust the recovery to take account of the difference between the two leases as to insurance that the second lease is not substantially similar to the original.

7. A new lease can be substantially similar to the original lease even though its term extends beyond the remaining term of the original lease, so long as both (a) the lease terms are commercially comparable (e.g., it is highly unlikely that a one-month rental and a five-year lease would reflect similar realities), and (b) the court can fairly apportion a part of the rental payments

under the new lease to that part of the term of the new lease which is comparable to the remaining lease term under the original lease. Also, the lease term of the new lease may be comparable to the remaining term of the original lease even though the beginning and ending dates of the two leases are not the same. For example, a two-month lease of agricultural equipment for the months of August and September may be comparable to a two-month lease running from the 15th of August to the 15th of October if in the particular location two-month leases beginning on August 15th are basically interchangeable with two-month leases beginning August 1st. Similarly, the term of a one-year truck lease beginning on the 15th of January may be comparable to the term of a one-year truck lease beginning January 2d. If the lease terms are found to be comparable, the court may base cover damages on the entire difference between the costs under the two leases.

8. Subsection (3), which is new, provides that if the lessor's disposition is by lease that does not qualify under subsection (2), or is by sale or otherwise, Section 2A–528 governs.

9. Subsection (4), a revised version of subsection 2–706(5), applies to protect a subsequent buyer or lessee who buys or leases from the lessor in good faith and for value, pursuant to a disposition under this section. Note that by its terms, the rule in subsection 2A–304(1), which provides that the subsequent lessee takes subject to the original lease contract, is controlled by the rule stated in this subsection.

10. Subsection (5), a revised version of subsection 2–706(6), provides that the lessor is not accountable to the lessee for any profit made by the lessor on a disposition. This rule follows from the fundamental premise of the bailment for hire that the lessee under a lease of goods has no equity of redemption to protect.

Cross References:

Point 1: Section 2–706, Section 2A–525 and 2A–527 and Section 9–625 and 9–627.

Point 2: Section 1–302 and Section 2A–103 and 2A–504.

Point 3: Sections 2A–523 and 2A–528.

Point 5: Section 2A–507.

Point 8: Section 2A–528.

Point 9: Section 2–706 and Section 2A–304.

Point 10: Section 2–706.

Definitional Cross References:

"Buyer" and "Buying". Section 2–103(1)(a).

"Delivery". Section 2A–103(1)(g).

"Good faith". Sections 2A–103(1)(m).

"Goods". Section 2A–103(1)(n).
"Lease". Section 2A–103(1)(p).
"Lease contract". Section 2A–103(1)(r).
"Lessee". Section 2A–103(1)(t).
"Lessor". Section 2A–103(1)(v).
"Present value". Section 2A–103(1)(aa).
"Rights". Section 1–201.
"Sale". Section 2–106(1).
"Security interest". Section 1–201.
"Value". Section 1–204.

As amended in 2001.

§ 2A–528. Lessor's Damages for Non-acceptance, Failure to Pay, Repudiation, or Other Default.

(1) Except as otherwise provided with respect to damages liquidated in the lease agreement (Section 2A–504) or otherwise determined pursuant to agreement of the parties (Sections 1–302 and 2A–503), if a lessor elects to retain the goods or a lessor elects to dispose of the goods and the disposition is by lease agreement that for any reason does not qualify for treatment under Section 2A–527(2), or is by sale or otherwise, the lessor may recover from the lessee as damages for a default of the type described in Section 2A–523(1) or 2A–523(4)(a), or, if agreed, for other default of the lessee, (i) accrued and unpaid rent as of the date of default if the lessee has never taken possession of the goods, or, if the lessee has taken possession of the goods, as of the date the lessor repossesses the goods or an earlier date on which the lessee makes a tender of the goods to the lessor, (ii) the present value as of the date determined under clause (i) of the total rent for the then remaining lease term of the original lease agreement minus the present value as of the same date of the market rent at the place where the goods are located computed for the same lease term, and (iii) any incidental or consequential damages allowed under Section 2A–530, less expenses saved in consequence of the lessee's default.

(2) If the measure of damages provided in subsection (1) is inadequate to put a lessor in as good a position as performance would have, the measure of damages is the present value of the profit, including reasonable overhead, the lessor would have made from full performance by the lessee, together with any incidental or consequential damages allowed under Section 2A–530.

As amended in 2001 and 2003.

Official Comment

1. Subsection (1), a substantially revised version of Section 2–708(1), states the basic rule governing the measure of lessor's damages for a default described in Section 2A–523(1) or (3)(a), and, if agreed, for a contractual default. This measure will apply if the lessor elects to retain the goods (whether undelivered, returned by the lessee, or repossessed by the lessor after acceptance and default by the lessee) or if the lessor's disposition does not qualify under subsection 2A–527(2). Section 2A–527(3). Note that under some of these conditions, the lessor may recover damages from the lessee pursuant to the rule set forth in Section 2A–529. There is no sanction for disposition that does not qualify under subsection 2A–527(2). Application of the rule set forth in this section is subject to agreement to the contrary. Sections 2A–504, 2A–103(4) and 1–302.

2. If the lessee has never taken possession of the goods, the measure of damage is the accrued and unpaid rent as of the date of default together with the present value, as of the date of default, of the original rent for the remaining term of the lease less the present value as of the same date of market rent, and incidental damages, less expenses saved in consequence of the default. Note that the reference in Section 2A–528(1)(i) and (ii) is to the date of default not to the date of an event of default. An event of default under a lease agreement becomes a default under a lease agreement only after the expiration of any relevant period of grace and compliance with any notice requirements under this Article and the lease agreement. American Bar Foundation, *Commentaries on Indentures*, § 5–1, at 216–217 (1971). Section 2A–501(1). This conclusion is also a function of whether, as a matter of fact or law, the event of default has been waived, suspended or cured. Sections 2A–103(4) and 1–103. If the lessee has taken possession of the goods, the measure of damages is the accrued and unpaid rent as of the earlier of the time the lessor repossesses the goods or the time the lessee tenders the goods to the lessor plus the difference between the present value, as of the same time, of the rent under the lease for the remaining lease term and the present value, as of the same time, of the market rent.

3. Market rent is computed pursuant to Section 2A–507.

4. Subsection (2), a somewhat revised version of the provisions of subsection 2–708(2), states a measure of damages which applies if the measure of damages in subsection (1) is inadequate to put the lessor in as good

a position as performance would have. The measure of damage is the lessor's profit, including overhead, together with incidental damages and consequential damages.

5. In calculating profit, a court should include any expected appreciation of the goods, *e.g.* the foal of a leased brood mare. Because this subsection is intended to give the lessor the benefit of the bargain, a court should consider any reasonable benefit or profit expected by the lessor from the performance of the lease agreement. *See Honeywell, Inc. v. Lithonia Lighting, Inc.*, 317 F.Supp. 406, 413 (N.D.Ga.1970); *Locks v. Wade*, 36 N.J.Super. 128, 131, 114 A.2d 875, 877 (Super.Ct.App.Div.1955). Further, in calculating profit the concept of present value must be given effect. *Taylor v. Commercial Credit Equip. Corp.*, 170 Ga.App. 322, 316 S.E.2d 788 (Ct.App.1984). *See generally* Section 2A–103(1)(u).

Cross References:

Point 1: Section 1–302, Section 2–708 and Sections 2A–103, 2A–504, 2A–523, 2A–527 and 2A–529.

Point 2: Section 1–103 and Sections 2A–103, 2A–501, 2A–528.

Point 3: Section 2A–507.

Point 4: Section 2–708.

Point 5: Section 2A–103.

Definitional Cross References:

"Agreement". Section 1–201.

"Goods". Section 2A–103(1)(n).

"Lease". Section 2A–103(1)(p).

"Lease agreement". Section 2A–103(1)(q).

"Lessee". Section 2A–103(1)(t).

"Lessor". Section 2A–103(1)(v).

"Party". Section 1–201.

"Present value". Section 2A–103(1)(aa).

"Sale". Section 2–106(1).

As amended in 2001 and 2003.

§ 2A–529. Lessor's Action for the Rent.

(1) After default by the lessee under the lease contract of the type described in Section 2A–523(1) or 2A–523(4)(a) or, if agreed, after other default by the lessee, if the lessor complies with subsection (2), the lessor may recover from the lessee as damages:

(a) for goods accepted by the lessee and not repossessed by or tendered to the lessor, and for conforming goods lost or damaged within a commercially reasonable time after risk of loss passes to the lessee (Section 2A–219), (i) accrued and unpaid rent as of the date of entry of judgment in favor of the lessor, (ii) the present value as of the same date of the rent for the then remaining lease term of the lease agreement, and (iii) any incidental or consequential damages allowed under Section 2A–530, less expenses saved in consequence of the lessee's default; and

(b) for goods identified to the lease contract if the lessor is unable after reasonable effort to dispose of them at a reasonable price or the circumstances reasonably indicate that effort will be unavailing, (i) accrued and unpaid rent as of the date of entry of judgment in favor of the lessor, (ii) the present value as of the same date of the rent for the then remaining lease term of the lease agreement, and (iii) any incidental or consequential damages allowed under Section 2A–530, less expenses saved in consequence of the lessee's default.

(2) Except as provided in subsection (3), the lessor shall hold for the lessee for the remaining lease term of the lease agreement any goods that have been identified to the lease contract and are in the lessor's control.

(3) The lessor may dispose of the goods at any time before collection of the judgment for damages obtained pursuant to subsection (1). If the disposition is before the end of the remaining lease term of the lease agreement, the lessor's recovery against the lessee for damages is governed by Section 2A–527 or 2A–528, and the lessor will cause an appropriate credit to be provided against a judgment for damages to the extent that the amount of the judgment exceeds the recovery available pursuant to Section 2A–527 or 2A–528.

(4) Payment of the judgment for damages obtained pursuant to subsection (1) entitles the lessee to the use and possession of the goods not then disposed of for the remaining lease term of and in accordance with the lease agreement.

(5) After default by the lessee under the lease contract of the type described in Section 2A–523(1) or 2A–523(4)(a) or, if agreed, after other default by the lessee, a lessor that is held not entitled to rent under this section must nevertheless be awarded damages for nonacceptance under Section 2A–527 or 2A–528.

As amended in 2003.

Official Comment

Uniform Statutory Source: Section 2–709.

Changes: Substantially revised.

Purposes:

1. Absent a lease contract provision to the contrary, an action for the full unpaid rent (discounted to present value as of the time of entry of judgment as to rent due after that time) is available as to goods not lost or damaged only if the lessee retains possession of the goods or the lessor is or apparently will be unable to dispose of them at a reasonable price after reasonable effort. There is no general right in a lessor to recover the full rent from the lessee upon holding the goods for the lessee. If the lessee tenders goods back to the lessor, and the lessor refuses to accept the tender, the lessor will be limited to the damages it would have suffered had it taken back the goods. The rule in Article 2 that the seller can recover the price of accepted goods is rejected here. In a lease, the lessor always has a residual interest in the goods which the lessor usually realizes upon at the end of a lease term by either sale or a new lease. Therefore, it is not a substantial imposition on the lessor to require it to take back and dispose of the goods if the lessee chooses to tender them back before the end of the lease term: the lessor will merely do earlier what it would have done anyway, sell or relet the goods. Further, the lessee will frequently encounter substantial difficulties if the lessee attempts to sublet the goods for the remainder of the lease term. In contrast to the buyer who owns the entire interest in goods and can easily dispose of them, the lessee is selling only the right to use the goods under the terms of the lease and the sublessee must assume a relationship with the lessor. In that situation, it is usually more efficient to eliminate the original lessee as a middleman by allowing the lessee to return the goods to the lessor who can then redispose of them.

2. In some situations even where possession of the goods is reacquired, a lessor will be able to recover as damages the present value of the full rent due, not under this section, but under 2A–528(2) which allows a lost profit recovery if necessary to put the lessor in the position it would have been in had the lessee performed. Following is an example of such a case. A is a lessor of construction equipment and maintains a substantial inventory. B leases from A a backhoe for a period of two weeks at a rental of $1,000. After three days, B returns the backhoe and refuses to pay the rent. A has five backhoes in inventory, including the one returned by B. During the next 11 days after the

return by B of the backhoe, A rents no more than three backhoes at any one time and, therefore, always has two on hand. If B had kept the backhoe for the full rental period, A would have earned the full rental on that backhoe, plus the rental on the other backhoes it actually did rent during that period. Getting this backhoe back before the end of the lease term did not enable A to make any leases it would not otherwise have made. The only way to put A in the position it would have been in had the lessee fully performed is to give the lessor the full rentals. A realized no savings at all because the backhoe was returned early and might even have incurred additional expense if it was paying for parking space for equipment in inventory. A has no obligation to relet the backhoe for the benefit of B rather than leasing that backhoe or any other in inventory for its own benefit. Further, it is probably not reasonable to expect A to dispose of the backhoe by sale when it is returned in an effort to reduce damages suffered by B. Ordinarily, the loss of a two-week rental would not require A to reduce the size of its backhoe inventory. Whether A would similarly be entitled to full rentals as lost profit in a one-year lease of a backhoe is a question of fact: in any event the lessor, subject to mitigation of damages rules, is entitled to be put in as good a position as it would have been had the lessee fully performed the lease contract.

3. Under subsection (2) a lessor who is able and elects to sue for the rent due under a lease must hold goods not lost or damaged for the lessee. Subsection (3) creates an exception to the subsection (2) requirement. If the lessor disposes of those goods prior to collection of the judgment (whether as a matter of law or agreement), the lessor's recovery is governed by the measure of damages in Section 2A–527 if the disposition is by lease that is substantially similar to the original lease, or otherwise by the measure of damages in Section 2A–528. Section 2A–523 official comment.

4. Subsection (4), which is new, further reinforces the requisites of Subsection (2). In the event the judgment for damages obtained by the lessor against the lessee pursuant to subsection (1) is satisfied, the lessee regains the right to use and possession of the remaining goods for the balance of the original lease term; a partial satisfaction of the judgment creates no right in the lessee to use and possession of the goods.

5. The relationship between subsections (2) and (4) is important to understand. Subsection (2) requires the lessor to hold for the lessee identified goods in the lessor's possession. Absent agreement to the contrary, whether in the lease or otherwise, under most circumstances the requirement that the lessor hold the goods

for the lessee for the term will mean that the lessor is not allowed to use them. Sections 2A–103(4) and 1–203. Further, the lessor's use of the goods could be viewed as a disposition of the goods that would bar the lessor from recovery under this section, remitting the lessor to the two preceding sections for a determination of the lessor's claim for damages against the lessee.

6. Subsection (5), the analogue of subsection 2–709(3), further reinforces the thrust of subsection (3) by stating that a lessor who is held not entitled to rent under this section has not elected a remedy; the lessor must be awarded damages under Sections 2A–527 and 2A–528. This is a function of two significant policies of this Article—that resort to a remedy is optional, unless expressly agreed to be exclusive (Section 2A–503(2)) and that rights and remedies provided in this Article generally are cumulative. (Section 2A–501(2) and (4)).

Cross References:

Point 2: Section 2A–528.
Point 3: Section 2A–523, 2A–527 and 2A–528.
Point 5: Section 1–203 and Section 2A–103.
Point 6: Section 2–709 and Sections 2A–501, 2A–503, 2A–527, 2A–528.

Definitional Cross References:

"Action". Section 1–201.
"Conforming". Section 2A–103(1)(c).
"Goods". Section 2A–103(1)(n).
"Lease". Section 2A–103(1)(j).
"Lease agreement". Section 2A–103(1)(q).
"Lease contract". Section 2A–103(1)(r).
"Lessee". Section 2A–103(1)(t).
"Lessor". Section 2A–103(1)(v).
"Present value". Section 2A–103(1)(aa).
"Reasonable time". Section 1–205.

§ 2A–530. Lessor's Incidental and Consequential Damages.

(1) Incidental damages to an aggrieved lessor include any commercially reasonable charges, expenses, or commissions incurred in stopping delivery, in the transportation, care and custody of goods after the lessee's default, in connection with return or disposition of the goods, or otherwise resulting from the default.

(2) Consequential damages resulting from a lessee's default include any loss resulting from general or particular requirements and needs of which the lessee at the time of contracting had reason to know and which could not reasonably

be prevented by disposition under Section 2A–527 or otherwise.

(3) In a consumer lease contract, a lessor may not recover consequential damages from a consumer.

As amended in 2003.

Official Comment

Uniform Statutory Source: Section 2–710.

Changes: Revised to reflect leasing practices and terminology.

1. Subsection (1) provides for reimbursement by the lessor for the expenses reasonably incurred as a result of the lessee's breach. The section sets forth as examples the usual and normal types of damages that may arise from the breach but the provision is intended intends to provide for all commercially reasonable expenditures made by the lessor.

2. Subsection (2), permits an aggrieved lessor to recover consequential damages. Under this section the loss must result from general or particular requirements of the lessor of which the lessee had reason to know at the time of contracting. The lessee is not liable for losses that could have been mitigated.

3. Subsection (3) precludes a lessor from recovering consequential damages from a consumer. This is a non-waivable provision.

Definitional Cross References:

"Aggrieved party". Section 1–201.
"Delivery". Section 2A–103(1)(g).
"Goods". Section 2A–103(1)(n).
"Lessee". Section 2A–103(1)(t).
"Lessor". Section 2A–103(1)(v).

As amended in 2003.

§ 2A–531. Standing to Sue Third Parties for Injury to Goods.

(1) If a third party so deals with goods that have been identified to a lease contract as to cause actionable injury to a party to the lease contract (a) the lessor has a right of action against the third party, and (b) the lessee also has a right of action against the third party if the lessee:

(a) has a security interest in the goods;

(b) has an insurable interest in the goods; or

(c) bears the risk of loss under the lease contract or has since the injury assumed that risk as against the lessor and the goods have been converted or destroyed.

(2) If at the time of the injury the party plaintiff did not bear the risk of loss as against the other party to the lease contract and there is no arrangement between them for disposition of the recovery, the party plaintiff's suit or settlement, subject to the party plaintiff's own interest, is as a fiduciary for the other party to the lease contract.

(3) Either party with the consent of the other may sue for the benefit of which it may concern.

As amended in 2003.

Official Comment

Uniform Statutory Source: Section 2–722.

Changes: Revised to reflect leasing practices and terminology.

Definitional Cross References:

"Action". Section 1–201.
"Goods". Section 2A–103(1)(n).
"Lease contract". Section 2A–103(1)(r).
"Lessee". Section 2A–103(1)(t).

"Lessor". Section 2A–103(1)(v).
"Party". Section 1–201.
"Rights". Section 1–201.
"Security interest". Section 1–201.

§ 2A–532. Lessor's Rights to Residual Interest.

In addition to any other recovery permitted by this Article or other law, the lessor may recover from the lessee an amount that will fully compensate the lessor for any loss of or damage to the lessor's residual interest in the goods caused by the default of the lessee.

Official Comment

Uniform Statutory Source: None.

Purposes: This section recognizes the right of the lessor to recover under this Article (as well as under other law) from the lessee for failure to comply with the lease obligations as to the condition of leased goods when returned to the lessor, for failure to return the goods at the end of the lease, or for any other default which causes loss or injury to the lessor's residual interest in the goods.

PART 6

TRANSITIONAL PROVISIONS

§ 2A–601. Effective Date.

This [Act] takes effect on _____, 20__.

As added in 2003.

§ 2A–602. Amendment of Existing Article 2A.

This [Act] amends [insert citation to existing Article 2A].

As added in 2003.

§ 2A–603. Applicability.

(1) This [Act] applies to a transaction within its scope that is entered into on or after the effective date of this [Act].

(2) This [Act] does not apply to a transaction that is entered into before the effective date of this [Act] even if the transaction would be sub-ject to this [Act] if it had been entered into after the effective date of this [Act].

(3) This [Act] does not apply to a cause of action that has accrued before the effective date of this [Act].

As added in 2003.

§ 2A–604. Savings Clause.

A transaction entered into before the effective date of this [Act] and the rights, obligations, and interests flowing from that transaction are governed by any statute or other law amended or repealed by this [Act] as if amendment or repeal had not occurred and may be terminated, completed, consummated, or enforced under that statute or other law.

As added in 2003.

CONFORMING AMENDMENT TO ARTICLE 1

§ 1–303.   Course of Performance, Course of Dealing, and Usage of Trade.

* * *

(f) Subject to Section 2–209 <u>and Section 2A–208</u>, a course of performance is relevant to show a waiver or modification of any term inconsistent with the course of performance.

UCC ARTICLE 3
NEGOTIABLE INSTRUMENTS

Article 3 was revised in 1990.

Pre–1990 revision . . . . *Appendix G*
2001 amendments (Article 1 revision) . . . . *Appendix A*
2002 amendments . . . . *Appendix H*
2005 amendments . . . . *Appendix J*

PART 1.   GENERAL PROVISIONS AND DEFINITIONS

Section
3–101. Short Title.
3–102. Subject Matter.
3–103. Definitions.
3–104. Negotiable Instrument.
3–105. Issue of Instrument.
3–106. Unconditional Promise or Order.
3–107. Instrument Payable in Foreign Money.
3–108. Payable on Demand or at Definite Time.
3–109. Payable to Bearer or to Order.
3–110. Identification of Person to Whom Instrument Is Payable.
3–111. Place of Payment.
3–112. Interest.
3–113. Date of Instrument.
3–114. Contradictory Terms of Instrument.
3–115. Incomplete Instrument.
3–116. Joint and Several Liability; Contribution.
3–117. Other Agreements Affecting Instrument.
3–118. Statute of Limitations.
3–119. Notice of Right to Defend Action.

PART 2.   NEGOTIATION, TRANSFER, AND INDORSEMENT

3–201. Negotiation.
3–202. Negotiation Subject to Rescission.
3–203. Transfer of Instrument; Rights Acquired by Transfer.
3–204. Indorsement.
3–205. Special Indorsement; Blank Indorsement; Anomalous Indorsement.
3–206. Restrictive Indorsement.
3–207. Reacquisition.

PART 3.   ENFORCEMENT OF INSTRUMENTS

3–301. Person Entitled to Enforce Instrument.
3–302. Holder in Due Course.
3–303. Value and Consideration.
3–304. Overdue Instrument.
3–305. Defenses and Claims in Recoupment.
3–306. Claims to an Instrument.
3–307. Notice of Breach of Fiduciary Duty.
3–308. Proof of Signatures and Status as Holder in Due Course.
3–309. Enforcement of Lost, Destroyed, or Stolen Instrument.
3–310. Effect of Instrument on Obligation for Which Taken.
3–311. Accord and Satisfaction by Use of Instrument.
3–312. Lost, Destroyed, or Stolen Cashier's Check, Teller's Check, or Certified Check.

PART 4.   LIABILITY OF PARTIES

3–401. Signature.
3–402. Signature by Representative.
3–403. Unauthorized Signature.
3–404. Impostors; Fictitious Payees.
3–405. Employer's Responsibility for Fraudulent Indorsement by Employee.
3–406. Negligence Contributing to Forged Signature or Alteration of Instrument.
3–407. Alteration.
3–408. Drawee Not Liable on Unaccepted Draft.
3–409. Acceptance of Draft; Certified Check.
3–410. Acceptance Varying Draft.
3–411. Refusal to Pay Cashier's Checks, Teller's Checks, and Certified Checks.
3–412. Obligation of Issuer of Note or Cashier's Check.
3–413. Obligation of Acceptor.

ARTICLE 3

Section

3–414. Obligation of Drawer.
3–415. Obligation of Indorser.
3–416. Transfer Warranties.
3–417. Presentment Warranties.
3–418. Payment or Acceptance by Mistake.
3–419. Instruments Signed for Accommodation.
3–420. Conversion of Instrument.

PART 5. DISHONOR

3–501. Presentment.
3–502. Dishonor.

Section

3–503. Notice of Dishonor.
3–504. Excused Presentment and Notice of Dishonor.
3–505. Evidence of Dishonor.

PART 6. DISCHARGE AND PAYMENT

3–601. Discharge and Effect of Discharge.
3–602. Payment.
3–603. Tender of Payment.
3–604. Discharge by Cancellation or Renunciation.
3–605. Discharge of Secondary Obligors.

National Conference of Commissioners on Uniform State Laws

REPORTERS

Robert L. Jordan, Los Angeles, California

William D. Warren, Los Angeles, California

DRAFTING COMMITTEE
CO–CHAIRMEN

Robert Haydock, Jr., Boston, Massachusetts

Carlyle C. Ring, Jr., Alexandria, Virginia

MEMBERS

Boris Auerbach, Cincinnati, Ohio

William M. Burke, Los Angeles, California

William E. Hogan, New York, New York

Charles W. Joiner, Ann Arbor, Michigan

Frederick H. Miller, Norman, Oklahoma

Donald J. Rapson, Livingston, New Jersey, *The American Law Institute Representative*

Lawrence J. Bugge, Madison, Wisconsin, *President (Member Ex Officio)*

Neal Ossen, Hartford, Connecticut, *Chairman, Division C (Member Ex Officio)*

REVIEW COMMITTEE
CHAIRMAN

Frank F. Jestrab, Chevy Chase, Maryland

MEMBERS

Rupert R. Bullivant, Portland, Oregon

Michael Franck, Lansing, Michigan

CONSULTANT

Fairfax Leary, Jr., Villanova, Pennsylvania

ADVISORS

Thomas C. Baxter, Jr., *Federal Reserve Bank of New York*

Roland E. Brandel, *American Bar Association*

Leon P. Ciferni, *National Westminster Bank USA*

William B. Davenport, *American Bar Association, Section of Business Law, Ad Hoc Committee on Payment Systems*

Carl Felsenfeld, *Association of the Bar of the City of New York*

Thomas J. Greco, *American Bankers Association*

Oliver I. Ireland, *Board of Governors of Federal Reserve System*

John R.H. Kimball, *Federal Reserve Bank of Boston*

John F. Lee, *New York Clearing House Association*

Norman R. Nelson, *New York Clearing House Association*

Ernest T. Patrikis, *Federal Reserve Bank of New York*

Anne B. Pope, *National Corporate Cash Management Association*

Paul S. Turner, *Occidental Petroleum Corporation* and *National Corporate Cash Management Association*

Stanley M. Walker, *Exxon Company, U.S.A.* and *National Corporate Cash Management Association*

ADDITIONAL PARTICIPANTS

Henry N. Dyhouse, *U.S. Central Credit Union*

Robert Egan, *Chemical Bank*

Paul T. Even, *National Gypsum Company*

James Foorman, *First Chicago Corporation*

J. Kevin French, *Exxon Company, U.S.A.*

Richard M. Gottlieb, *Manufacturers Hanover Trust Company*

Douglas E. Harris, *Morgan Guaranty Trust Company of New York*

Arthur L. Herold, *National Corporate Cash Management Association*

Shirley Holder, *Atlantic Richfield Company*

Paul E. Homrighausen, *Bankers Clearing House Association* and *National Automated Clearing House Association*

Gail M. Inaba, *Morgan Guaranty Trust Company of New York*

Richard P. Kessler, Jr., *Credit Union National Association*

James W. Kopp, *Shell Oil Company*

Donald R. Lawrence, *Citibank N.A.*

Robert M. MacAllister, *Chase Manhattan Bank NA*

Thomas E. Montgomery, *California Bankers Association*

W. Robert Moore, *American Bankers Association*

Samuel Newman, *Manufacturers Hanover Trust Company*

Nena Nodge, *National Corporate Cash Management Association*

Robert J. Pisapia, *Occidental Petroleum Corporation*

Deborah S. Prutzman, *Arnold & Porter*

James S. Rogers, Professor of Law, Newton, Massachusetts

Robert M. Rosenblith, *Manufacturers Hanover Trust Company*

Jamileh Soufan, *American General Corporation*

Irma Villarreal, *Aon Corporation*

PREFATORY NOTE

Revised Article 3 (with miscellaneous and conforming amendments to Articles 1 and 4) is a companion undertaking to Article 4A on funds transfers. Both efforts were undertaken for the purpose of accommodating modern technologies and practices in payment systems and with respect to negotiable instruments. Both efforts were drafted by the same committee over essentially the same period of time. The work on Article 4A was accorded priority and completed in 1989, and revised Article 3 was completed in 1990.

Revised Article 3 may, not inappropriately, be regarded as the latest effort in the progressive codification of the common law of negotiable instruments that began with the English Bills of Exchange Act enacted by Parliament in 1882. The Uniform Negotiable Instruments Law was promulgated by the Conference in 1896, and it in turn was reorganized and modernized by original Article 3—Commercial Paper as part of the Uniform Commercial Code jointly promulgated in 1952 by the Conference and the American Law Institute. Revised Article 3 in 1990 modernizes, reorganizes and clarifies the law.

Purpose of Drafting Effort

The original Articles 3 and 4 and their predecessors were based upon a paper payment system. Literally, there has been an explosion in the volume of paper to process since Articles 3 and 4 were first promulgated. In the early '50s, around 7 billion checks were processed annually. Correctly anticipating an increase in check volume as the result of a retail approach taken by bankers at that time, the American Bankers Association in 1954 placed a team on a research and development project to identify the most efficient method of processing checks mechanically. The eminently successful MICR line technology was the result. Upon its implementation, checks were processed at high rates of speed. In major part as a result of this technology, a seven-fold explosion in check volume has occurred between the '50s and 1988. In 1988, the Federal Reserve estimated check volume at 48 billion written annually. In 1987, Congress enacted the Expedited Funds Availability Act, and the Federal Reserve Board implemented it in 1988 with Regulation CC. Regulation CC covers many aspects of the forward check collection process and all aspects of the return process.

Present Articles 3 and 4, written for a paper-based system, do not adequately address the issues of responsibility and liability as they relate to modern technologies now employed and the procedures required by the current volume of checks and by the "Expedited Funds Availability Act" and Regulation CC. While agreements among parties to particular transactions have provided some relief, such stop-gap measures are no longer adequate.

In addition, practices have developed which are not easily accommodated within existing Article 3. For example, variable rate notes were unknown when Article 3 first was promulgated; they are common today. Questions about the "cash equivalency" of cashier's checks and money orders have arisen as banks have sought to raise defenses to the payment of these instruments.

The revision of Article 3 and Article 4 to update, improve and maintain the viability of it is necessary to accommodate these changing practices and modern technologies, the needs of a rapidly expanding national and international economy, the requirement for more rapid funds availability, and the need for more clarity and certainty. Absent such an update, further Federal preemption of state law may likely occur.

Uniformity is Essential

Traditionally, the legal structures for payments have been regulated by state law through the Uniform Commercial Code. In recent years, however, the Federal government has established regulations for credit and debit cards, and for the availability of funds in a way that regulates much of the check collection process.

With respect to wholesale funds transfers, on an average day two trillion dollars is transferred. Article 4A of the UCC promulgated in 1989 provides the governing comprehensive rules. In 1990, 12 states enacted Article 4A including California, New York and Illinois. In 1991, Article 4A has been introduced in the legislatures of most of the other states, and it is anticipated that most, if not all, will enact Article 4A uniformly. Within a short time, perhaps by 1992, the law of wholesale funds transfers should be uniform throughout the 50 states.

The law for payments through checks and which governs other negotiable instruments similarly should be uniform and up-to-date, either through state enactments or Federal preemption. Otherwise, checks as a viable payment system in international and national transactions will be severely hampered and the utility of other negotiable instruments impaired.

Process of Achieving Uniformity

The essence of uniform law revision is to obtain a sufficient consensus and balance among the interests of the various participants so that universal and uniform adoption by the legislatures of all 50 states may be achieved. As is the practice of the Conference, announcement of the drafting undertaking for Articles 3, 4 and 4A was widely circulated in 1985. Anyone who so requested, received notice of all meetings and was invited to attend. Upon request, names were put on a mailing list to receive copies of drafts as they progressed. In addition, the American Bar Association Ad Hoc Committee on Payments Systems closely followed the work of the Conference and widely circulated the drafts.

The Drafting Committee had 3 or 4 meetings each year and, by August 1990, had held 20 meetings. The drafting meetings began on Friday morning and ended on Sunday at noon. All the meetings were well attended, and the average attendance was 50 or more. The discussion of the drafts was open for comment by all those who attended. In addition, the reporters received a substantial amount of comment and suggestions by written and other communications between meetings of the drafting committee. The work product was read line for line at the annual meetings of the Conference three different years. In addition, the American Law Institute circulated the drafts two or three times to its entire membership. The ALI consultative group also held a meeting to comment and make suggestions on the draft. In addition, progress reports were published annually in *The Business Lawyer* from 1985 through 1990.

The consensus, balance and quality achieved in this lengthy deliberative process is a product not only of the fine work of the reporters and the drafting committee, but also the faithful and energetic participation of the advisors and participants in the drafting meetings. The advisors representing a variety of interests were:

Thomas C. Baxter, Jr., Federal Reserve Bank of New York

Roland E. Brandel, American Bar Association

Leon P. Ciferni, National Westminster Bank USA

William B. Davenport, American Bar Association, Section of Business Law, Ad Hoc Committee on Payment Systems

Carl Felsenfeld, Association of the Bar of the City of New York

Thomas J. Greco, American Bankers Association

Oliver I. Ireland, Board of Governors of Federal Reserve System

John R. H. Kimball, Federal Reserve Bank of Boston

John F. Lee, New York Clearing House Association

Norman R. Nelson, New York Clearing House Association

Ernest T. Patrikis, Federal Reserve Bank of New York

Anne B. Pope, National Corporate Cash Management Association

Paul S. Turner, Occidental Petroleum Corporation and National Corporate Cash Management Association

Stanley M. Walker, Exxon Company, U.S.A. and National Corporate Cash Management Association

Other participants who regularly attended drafting meetings were:

Henry N. Dyhouse, U.S. Central Credit Union

Robert Egan, Chemical Bank

Paul T. Even, National Gypsum Corporation

James Foorman, First Chicago Corporation

J. Kevin French, Exxon Company, U.S.A.

Richard M. Gottlieb, Manufacturers Hanover Trust Company

Douglas E. Harris, National Corporate Cash Management Association

Arthur L. Herold, National Corporate Cash Management Association

Shirley Holder, Atlantic Richfield Company

Paul E. Homrighausen, Bankers Clearing House Association

Gail M. Inaba, Morgan Guaranty Trust Company of New York

Richard P. Kessler, Jr., Credit Union National Association

James W. Kopp, Shell Oil Company

Donald R. Lawrence, Citibank, N.A.

Robert M. McAllister, Chase Manhattan Bank, N.A.

Thomas E. Montgomery, California Bankers Association

W. Robert Moore, American Bankers Association

Samuel Newman, Manufacturers Hanover Trust Company

Nena Nodge, National Corporate Cash Management Association

Robert J. Pisapia, Occidental Petroleum Corporation

Deborah S. Prutzman, Arnold & Porter

James S. Rogers, Professor of Law, Newton, Massachusetts

Robert M. Rosenblith, Manufacturers Hanover Trust Company

Jamileh Soufan, American General Corporation

Irma Villarreal, Aon Corporation

Balance Achieved

The consensus reflected in Revised Article 3 and in the conforming amendments to Articles 1 and 4 is supported by the participants from the banking community, the users, and the Federal regulators because it reflects a balance that each interest can reasonably embrace. Some of the benefits of the Revision include:

A. Benefits in the Public Interest

Certainty—Revised Articles 3 and 4 remove numerous uncertainties that exist in the current provisions and thus reduce risk to the payment system and allow appropriate planning by its users and operators.

Speed and Reliability—The Revision removes impediments to the use of automation, and better conforms to Regulation CC to expedite the availability of funds to customers and to reduce risks to banks.

Lower Costs—The Revision by providing for modern technologies, lowers costs to banks and thus to their customers.

Reduced Litigation—By clarification of troublesome issues, and by the provisions of Sections 3–404 through 3–406 which reform rules for allocation of loss from forgeries and alterations, the Revision should significantly reduce litigation.

B. Benefits to Users

"Good Faith"—The definition of good faith under Sections 3–103(a)(4) and 4–104(c) is expanded to include observance of reasonable commercial standards of fair dealing. This objective standard for good faith applies to the performance of all duties and obligations established under Articles 3 and 4.

Fiduciary Provisions—Section 3–307 protects drawers and persons owed a fiduciary responsibility by imposing stricter standards for obtaining holder in due course rights by a person dealing with the defaulting agent or fiduciary. It also spells out the circumstances under which a person receiving funds has notice of a breach of fiduciary duty, and resulting liability.

Accord and Satisfaction—Under Section 3–311 payees can avoid the unintentional accord and satisfaction by returning the funds or by giving a notice that requires checks to be sent to a particular office where such proposals can be handled. On the other hand, the drawer of a full settlement check is protected from the instrument being indorsed with protest and thus losing the money and being liable on the balance of the claim.

Cashier's Checks—Section 3–411 and related provisions considerably improve the acceptability of bank obligations like cashier's checks as cash equivalents by providing disincentives to wrongful dishonor, such as the possible recovery of consequential damages.

Indorser Liability—Section 3–415 gives more time to hold a check before the user loses indorser liability.

Reporting Forgeries—Section 4–406 increases the outside time a customer has to report forged checks or alterations to thirty days. It also requires a bank truncating checks to retain the item or the capacity to furnish legible copies for seven years.

Individual Agent and Corporate Liability—Section 3–402, as to corporate instruments signed by agents without adequate indication and representation, (except as against a holder in due course), allows a representative to show the parties did not intend individual liability. It affords full protection to the agent that signs a corporate check, even though the check does not show representative status. Also, Section 3–403(b) makes it clear that a signature of an organization is considered unauthorized if more than one signature is required and it is missing.

Direct Suits—Section 3–420 allows a person whose indorsement is forged to sue the depositary bank directly, rather than each drawee of the checks involved.

C. Benefits to the Banking Community

Certainty—Section 3–104 and related provisions clarify what types of contracts are within Article 3 and how they are to be treated, thus promoting certainty of legal rules and reducing litigation costs and risks. Checks that may omit "words of negotiability" are included as fully negotiable; confusion over travelers checks is eliminated; variable rate instruments are included; and there is clarification of the impact of the FTC "Holder" Rule, clarification of the ability of parties to an instrument that is not included in Article 3 to contract for the application of its rules to their contract; and clarification of ordinary money orders as checks rather than bank obligations.

"Ordinary Care"—In Sections 3–103(a)(7) and 4–104(c), ordinary care is defined, making clear that financial institutions taking checks for processing or for payment by automated means need not manually handle each instrument if that is consistent with the institution's procedures and the procedures used do not vary unreasonably from the general usage of banks. This clarification is designed to accommodate and facilitate efficiency, thus lowering costs and lowering expedited funds availability risks. The definition of ordinary care relates to those specif-

Table of Disposition of Sections in Former Article 3

The reference to a section in Revised Article 3 is to the section that refers to the issue addressed by the section in Former Article 3. If there is no comparable section in Revised Article 3 to a section in Former Article 3, that fact is indicated by the word "Omitted."

Former Article 3 Section	Revised Article 3 or 4 Section
3–101	3–101
3–102(1)(a)	3–105(a)
3–102(1)(b)	3–103(a)(6)
3–102(1)(c)	3–103(a)(9)
3–102(1)(d)	Omitted. See Comment 2 to 3–414.
3–102(1)(e)	3–104(b)
3–102(2)	3–103(b)
3–102(3)	3–103(c)
3–102(4)	3–103(d)
3–103(1)	3–102(a)
3–103(2)	3–102(b)
3–104(1)	3–104(a)
3–104(2)(a)	3–104(e)
3–104(2)(b)	3–104(f)
3–104(2)(c)	3–104(j)
3–104(2)(d)	3–104(e)
3–104(3)	Omitted.
3–105(1)(a)	3–106(a)
3–105(1)(b)	Omitted. See Comment 1 to 3–106.
3–105(1)(c)	Omitted. See Comment 1 to 3–106.
3–105(1)(d)	Omitted. See Comment 1 to 3–106.
3–105(1)(e)	Omitted. See Comment 1 to 3–106.
3–105(1)(f)	3–106(b)(ii)
3–105(1)(g)	3–106(b)(ii)
3–105(1)(h)	3–106(b)(ii)
3–105(2)(a)	3–106(a)(ii)
3–105(2)(b)	3–106(b)(ii)
3–106(1)	3–104(a)
3–106(2)	Omitted.
3–107(1)	Omitted. See Comment to 3–107.
3–107(2)	3–107
3–108	3–108(a)
3–109(1)	3–108(b)
3–109(2)	Omitted.
3–110(1)	3–109(b)
3–110(1)(a)	Omitted.
3–110(1)(b)	Omitted.
3–110(1)(c)	Omitted.
3–110(1)(d)	3–110(d)
3–110(1)(e)	3–110(c)(2)(i)
3–110(1)(f)	3–110(c)(2)(iv)
3–110(1)(g)	Omitted.
3–110(2)	Omitted.
3–110(3)	3–109(b)
3–111(a)	3–109(a)(1)
3–111(b)	3–109(a)(1)
3–111(c)	3–109(a)(3) and 3–205(b)
3–112(1)(a)	Omitted.
3–112(1)(b)	3–104(a)(3)(i)
3–112(1)(c)	3–104(a)(3)(i)

Former Article 3 Section	Revised Article 3 or 4 Section
3–112(1)(d)	3–104(a)(3)(ii)
3–112(1)(e)	3–104(a)(3)(iii)
3–112(1)(f)	3–311
3–112(1)(g)	Omitted.
3–112(2)	Omitted.
3–113	Omitted.
3–114(1)	Omitted. See Comment to 3–113.
3–114(2)	3–113(a)
3–114(3)	Omitted. See Comment to 3–113.
3–115	3–115
3–116(a)	3–110(d)
3–116(b)	3–110(d)
3–117(a)	3–110(c)(2)(ii)
3–117(b)	3–110(c)(2)(i)
3–117(c)	Omitted.
3–118(a)	3–104(e) and 3–103(a)(6)
3–118(b)	3–114
3–118(c)	3–114
3–118(d)	3–112
3–118(e)	3–116(a)
3–118(f)	Omitted.
3–119	3–117 and 3–106(a) and (b)
3–120	4–106(a)
3–121	4–106(b)
3–122	Omitted. See Comment 1 to 3–118.
3–201(1)	3–203(b)
3–201(2)	3–204(c)
3–201(3)	3–203(c)
3–202(1)	3–201(a)
3–202(2)	3–204(a)
3–202(3)	3–203(d)
3–202(4)	Omitted.
3–203	3–204(d)
3–204(1)	3–205(a)
3–204(2)	3–205(b)
3–204(3)	3–205(c)
3–205	Omitted.
3–206(1)	3–206(a)
3–206(2)	3–206(c)(4) and (d)
3–206(3)	3–206(b), (c), and (e)
3–206(4)	3–206(d) and (e)
3–207(1)(a)	3–202(a)(i)
3–207(1)(b)	3–202(a)(ii)
3–207(1)(c)	3–202(a)(iii)
3–207(1)(d)	3–202(a)(iii)
3–207(2)	3–202(b)
3–208	3–207
3–301	Omitted. See Comment to 3–301.
3–302(1)	3–302(a)
3–302(2)	Omitted. See Comment 4 to 3–302.
3–302(3)(a)	3–302(c)(i)
3–302(3)(b)	3–302(c)(iii)
3–302(3)(c)	3–302(c)(ii)
3–302(4)	3–302(e)
3–303(a)	3–303(a)(1) and (2)
3–303(b)	3–303(a)(3)

Former Article 3 Section	Revised Article 3 or 4 Section
3–303(c)	3–303(a)(4) and (5)
3–304(1)(a)	3–302(a)(1)
3–304(1)(b)	Omitted.
3–304(2)	3–307(b)
3–304(3)(a)	3–302(a)(2)(iii); 3–304(b)(1)
3–304(3)(b)	3–304(b)(3)
3–304(3)(c)	3–304(a)(1), (2) and (3)
3–304(4)(a)	Omitted.
3–304(4)(b)	Omitted.
3–304(4)(c)	Omitted.
3–304(4)(d)	Omitted.
3–304(4)(e)	3–307
3–304(4)(f)	3–304(c)
3–304(5)	3–302(b)
3–304(6)	Omitted.
3–305(1)	3–306
3–305(2)(a)	3–305(a)(1)(i)
3–305(2)(b)	3–305(a)(1)(ii)
3–305(2)(c)	3–305(a)(1)(iii)
3–305(2)(d)	3–305(a)(1)(iv)
3–305(2)(e)	3–601(b)
3–306(a)	3–306
3–306(b)	3–305(a)(2)
3–306(c)	3–305(a)(2); 3–303(b); 3–105(b)
3–306(d)	3–305(c)
3–307(1)(a)	3–308(a)
3–307(1)(b)	3–308(a)
3–307(2)	3–308(b)
3–307(3)	3–308(b)
3–401(1)	3–401(a)
3–401(2)	3–401(b)
3–402	3–204(a)
3–403(1)	3–402(a)
3–403(2)(a)	3–402(b)(2)
3–403(2)(b)	3–402(b)(2)
3–403(3)	3–402(b)(1)
3–404(1)	3–403(a)
3–404(2)	3–403(a)
3–405(1)(a)	3–404(a)
3–405(1)(b)	3–404(b)(i)
3–405(1)(c)	3–405
3–405(2)	3–403(c)
3–406	3–406
3–407(1)(a)	3–407(a)(i)
3–407(1)(b)	3–407(a)(ii)
3–407(1)(c)	3–407(a)(i)
3–407(2)(a)	3–407(b)
3–407(2)(b)	3–407(b)
3–407(3)	3–407(c)
3–408	3–303(b)
3–409(1)	3–408
3–409(2)	Omitted. See Comment 1 to 3–408.
3–410(1)	3–409(a)
3–410(2)	3–409(b)
3–410(3)	3–409(c)
3–411(1)	3–409(d); 3–414(c); 3–415(d)

Former Article 3 Section	Revised Article 3 or 4 Section
3–411(2)	3–409(d)
3–411(3)	Omitted.
3–412(1)	3–410(a)
3–412(2)	3–410(b)
3–412(3)	3–410(c)
3–413(1)	3–412; 3–413(a)
3–413(2)	3–414(b) and (e)
3–413(3)	Omitted.
3–414(1)	3–415(a) and (b)
3–414(2)	Omitted.
3–415(1)	3–419(a)
3–415(2)	3–419(b)
3–415(3)	Omitted. See 3–605(h)
3–415(4)	3–419(c)
3–415(5)	3–419(e)
3–416(1)	Omitted.
3–416(2)	3–419(d)
3–416(3)	Omitted.
3–416(4)	3–419(c)
3–416(5)	Omitted.
3–416(6)	Omitted.
3–417(1)	3–417
3–417(2)	3–416
3–417(3)	Omitted.
3–417(4)	Omitted.
3–418	3–418
3–419(1)	3–420(a)
3–419(2)	3–420(b)
3–419(3)	3–420(c)
3–419(4)	3–206(c)(4) and (d)
3–501(1)(a)	3–414(b); 3–502(b)(3) and (4)
3–501(1)(b)	3–415(a); 3–502(a)(1) and (2); 3–502(b), (c), (d) and (e)
3–501(1)(c)	3–414(f); 3–415(e)
3–501(2)(a)	3–503(a)
3–501(2)(b)	Omitted. See Comment 2 to 3–414.
3–501(3)	Omitted. See Comment to 3–505.
3–501(4)	Omitted.
3–502(1)(a)	3–415(e)
3–502(1)(b)	3–414(f)
3–502(2)	Omitted. See Comment to 3–505.
3–503	Omitted. See Comment to 3–502.
3–504(1)	3–501(a)
3–504(2)(a)	3–501(b)(1)
3–504(2)(b)	3–501(b)(1)
3–504(2)(c)	3–501(b)(1); 3–111
3–504(3)(a)	3–501(b)(1)
3–504(3)(b)	Omitted.
3–504(4)	3–501(b)(1)
3–504(5)	Omitted.
3–505(1)(a)	3–501(b)(2)(i)
3–505(1)(b)	3–501(b)(2)(ii)
3–505(1)(c)	Omitted.
3–505(1)(d)	3–501(b)(2)(iii)
3–505(2)	Omitted.
3–506(1)	Omitted.

ARTICLE 3

Former Article 3 Section	Revised Article 3 or 4 Section
3–506(2)	Omitted.
3–507(1)	3–502
3–507(2)	Omitted.
3–507(3)	3–501(b)(3)(i)
3–507(4)	Omitted.
3–508(1)	3–503(b)
3–508(2)	3–503(c)
3–508(3)	3–503(b)
3–508(4)	Omitted.
3–508(5)	Omitted.
3–508(6)	Omitted.
3–508(7)	Omitted.
3–508(8)	3–503(b)
3–509(1)	3–505(b)
3–509(2)	3–505(b)
3–509(3)	3–505(b)
3–509(4)	Omitted.
3–509(5)	Omitted.
3–510(a)	3–505(a)(1)
3–510(b)	3–505(a)(2)
3–510(c)	3–505(a)(3)
3–511(1)	Omitted.
3–511(2)(a)	3–504(a)(iv)
3–511(2)(b)	3–504(a)(ii), (iv), and (v); 3–504(b)
3–511(2)(c)	3–504(a)(i)
3–511(3)(a)	3–504(a)(ii)
3–511(3)(b)	3–504(a)(ii)
3–511(4)	3–502(f)
3–511(5)	Omitted.
3–511(6)	Omitted.
3–601(1)	3–601(a)
3–601(2)	3–601(a)
3–601(3)	Omitted.
3–602	3–601(b)
3–603(1)	3–602(a) and (b)
3–603(1)(a)	3–602(b)(2)
3–603(1)(b)	Omitted. See 3–206(c)(3).
3–603(2)	Omitted.
3–604(1)	3–603(c)
3–604(2)	3–603(b)
3–604(3)	3–603(c)
3–605(1)(a)	3–604(a)(i)
3–605(1)(b)	3–604(a)(ii)
3–605(2)	3–604(b)
3–606(1)(a)	3–605(b) and (c)
3–606(1)(b)	3–605(e)
3–606(2)	Omitted.
3–701(1)	Omitted.
3–701(2)	Omitted.
3–701(3)	Omitted.
3–801(1)	Omitted.
3–801(2)	Omitted.
3–801(3)	Omitted.
3–801(4)	Omitted.
3–802(1)(a)	3–310(a) and (c)
3–802(1)(b)	3–310(b) and (c)

Former Article 3 Section	Revised Article 3 or 4 Section
3–802(2)	Omitted.
3–803	3–119
3–804	3–309
3–805	Omitted. See Comment 2 to 3–104.

PART 1

GENERAL PROVISIONS AND DEFINITIONS

§ 3–101. Short Title.

This Article may be cited as Uniform Commercial Code—Negotiable Instruments.

§ 3–102. Subject Matter.

(a) This Article applies to negotiable instruments. It does not apply to money, to payment orders governed by Article 4A, or to securities governed by Article 8.

(b) If there is conflict between this Article and Article 4 or 9, Articles 4 and 9 govern.

(c) Regulations of the Board of Governors of the Federal Reserve System and operating circulars of the Federal Reserve Banks supersede any inconsistent provision of this Article to the extent of the inconsistency.

Official Comment

1. Former Article 3 had no provision affirmatively stating its scope. Former Section 3–103 was a limitation on scope. In revised Article 3, Section 3–102 states that Article 3 applies to "negotiable instruments," defined in Section 3–104. Section 3–104(b) also defines the term "instrument" as a synonym for "negotiable instrument." In most places Article 3 uses the shorter term "instrument." This follows the convention used in former Article 3.

2. The reference in former Section 3–103(1) to "documents of title" is omitted as superfluous because these documents contain no promise to pay money. The definition of "payment order" in Section 4A–103(a)(1)(iii) excludes drafts which are governed by Article 3. Section 3–102(a) makes clear that a payment order governed by Article 4A is not governed by Article 3. Thus, Article 3 and Article 4A are mutually exclusive.

Article 8 states in Section 8–103(d) that "A writing that is a security certificate is governed by this Article and not by Article 3, even though it also meets the requirements of that Article." Section 3–102(a) conforms to this provision. With respect to some promises or orders to pay money, there may be a question whether the promise or order is an instrument under Section 3–104(a) or a certificated security under Section 8–102(a)(4) and (15). Whether a writing is covered by Article 3 or Article 8 has important consequences. Among other things, under Section 8–207, the issuer of a certificated security may treat the registered owner as the owner for all purposes until the presentment for registration of a transfer. The issuer of a negotiable instrument, on the other hand, may discharge its obligation to pay the instrument only by paying a person entitled to enforce under Section 3–301. There are also important consequences to an indorser. An indorser of a security does not undertake the issuer's obligation or make any warranty that the issuer will honor the underlying obligation, while an indorser of a negotiable instrument becomes secondarily liable on the underlying obligation.

Ordinarily the distinction between instruments and certificated securities in non-bearer form should be relatively clear. A certificated security under Article 8 must be in registered form (Section 8–102(a)(13)) so that it can be registered on the issuer's records. By contrast, registration plays no part in Article 3. The distinction between an instrument and a certificated security in bearer form may be somewhat more difficult and will generally lie in the economic functions of the two writings. Ordinarily, negotiable instruments under Article 3 will be separate and distinct instruments, while certificated securities under Article 8 will be either one of a class or series or by their terms divisible into a class or series (Section 8–102(a)(15)(ii)). Thus, a promissory note in bearer form could come under either Article 3 if it were simply an individual note, or under Article 8 if it were one of a series of notes or divisible into a series. An additional distinction is whether the instrument is of the type commonly dealt in on securities exchanges or markets or commonly recognized as a medium for investment (Section 8–102(a)(15)(iii)). Thus, a check written in bearer form (i.e., a check made payable to "cash") would not be a certificated security within Article 8 of the Uniform Commercial Code.

Occasionally, a particular writing may fit the definition of both a negotiable instrument under Article 3 and of an investment security under Article 8. In such cases, the instrument is subject exclusively to the requirements of Article 8. Section 8–103(d) and Section 3–102(a).

3. Although the terms of Article 3 apply to transactions by Federal Reserve Banks, federal preemption would make ineffective any Article 3 provision that conflicts with federal law. The activities of the Federal Reserve Banks are governed by regulations of the Federal Reserve Board and by operating circulars issued by the Reserve Banks themselves. In some instances, the operating circulars are issued pursuant to a Federal Reserve Board regulation. In other cases, the Reserve Bank issues the operating circular under its own authority under the Federal Reserve Act, subject to review by the Federal Reserve Board. Section 3–102(c) states that Federal Reserve Board regulations and operating circulars of the Federal Reserve Banks supersede any inconsistent provision of Article 3 to the extent of the inconsistency. Federal Reserve Board regulations, being valid exercises of regulatory authority pursuant to a federal statute, take precedence over state law if there is an inconsistency. Childs v. Federal Reserve Bank of Dallas, 719 F.2d 812 (5th Cir.1983), reh. den. 724 F.2d 127 (5th Cir.1984). Section 3–102(c) treats operating circulars as having the same effect whether issued under the Reserve Bank's own authority or under a Federal Reserve Board regulation. Federal statutes may also preempt Article 3. For example, the Expedited Funds Availability Act, 12 U.S.C. § 4001 et seq., provides that the Act and the regulations issued pursuant to the Act supersede any inconsistent provisions of the UCC. 12 U.S.C. § 4007(b).

4. In Clearfield Trust Co. v. United States, 318 U.S. 363 (1943), the Court held that if the United States is a party to an instrument, its rights and duties are governed by federal common law in the absence of a specific federal statute or regulation. In United States v. Kimbell Foods, Inc., 440 U.S. 715 (1979), the Court stated a three-pronged test to ascertain whether the federal common-law rule should follow the state rule. In most instances courts under the *Kimbell* test have shown a willingness to adopt UCC rules in formulating federal common law on the subject. In *Kimbell* the Court adopted the priorities rules of Article 9.

5. In 1989 the United Nations Commission on International Trade Law completed a Convention on International Bills of Exchange and International Promissory Notes. If the United States becomes a party to this Convention, the Convention will preempt state law with respect to international bills and notes governed by the Convention. Thus, an international bill of exchange or promissory note that meets the definition of instrument in Section 3–104 will not be governed by Article 3 if it is governed by the Convention. That Convention applies only to bills and notes that indicate on their face that they involve cross-border transactions. It does not apply at all to checks. Convention Articles 1(3), 2(1), 2(2). Moreover, because it applies only if the bill or note specifically calls for application of the Convention, Convention Article 1, there is little chance that the Convention will apply accidentally to a transaction that the parties intended to be governed by this Article.

As amended in 1995 and 2002.

§ 3–103. Definitions.

(a) In this Article:
 (1) "Acceptor" means a drawee who has accepted a draft.
 (2) "Consumer account" means an account established by an individual primarily for personal, family, or household purposes.
 (3) "Consumer transaction" means a transaction in which an individual incurs an obligation primarily for personal, family, or household purposes.
 (4) "Drawee" means a person ordered in a draft to make payment.
 (5) "Drawer" means a person who signs or is identified in a draft as a person ordering payment.
 (6) ["Good faith" means honesty in fact and the observance of reasonable commercial standards of fair dealing.]*
 (7) "Maker" means a person who signs or is identified in a note as a person undertaking to pay.
 (8) "Order" means a written instruction to pay money signed by the person giving the instruction. The instruction may be

* Note from the Thomson-West Advisory Panel: Subsection was deleted by Revised Article 1 (2001).

addressed to any person, including the person giving the instruction, or to one or more persons jointly or in the alternative but not in succession. An authorization to pay is not an order unless the person authorized to pay is also instructed to pay.

(9) "Ordinary care" in the case of a person engaged in business means observance of reasonable commercial standards, prevailing in the area in which the person is located, with respect to the business in which the person is engaged. In the case of a bank that takes an instrument for processing for collection or payment by automated means, reasonable commercial standards do not require the bank to examine the instrument if the failure to examine does not violate the bank's prescribed procedures and the bank's procedures do not vary unreasonably from general banking usage not disapproved by this Article or Article 4.

(10) "Party" means a party to an instrument.

(11) "Principal obligor," with respect to an instrument, means the accommodated party or any other party to the instrument against whom a secondary obligor has recourse under this article.

(12) "Promise" means a written undertaking to pay money signed by the person undertaking to pay. An acknowledgment of an obligation by the obligor is not a promise unless the obligor also undertakes to pay the obligation.

(13) "Prove" with respect to a fact means to meet the burden of establishing the fact (Section 1–201(b)(8)).

(14) ["Record" means information that is inscribed on a tangible medium or that is stored in an electronic or other medium and is retrievable in perceivable form.]

(15) "Remitter" means a person who purchases an instrument from its issuer if the instrument is payable to an identified person other than the purchaser.

(16) "Remotely-created consumer item" means an item drawn on a consumer account, which is not created by the payor bank and does not bear a handwritten signature purporting to be the signature of the drawer.

(17) "Secondary obligor," with respect to an instrument, means (a) an indorser or an accommodation party, (b) a drawer having the obligation described in Section 3–414(d), or (c) any other party to the instrument that has recourse against another party to the instrument pursuant to Section 3–116(b).

(b) Other definitions applying to this Article and the sections in which they appear are:

"Acceptance" Section 3–409
"Accommodated party" Section 3–419
"Accommodation party" Section 3–419
"Account" Section 4–104
"Alteration" Section 3–407
"Anomalous indorsement" Section 3–205
"Blank indorsement" Section 3–205
"Cashier's check" Section 3–104
"Certificate of deposit" Section 3–104
"Certified check" Section 3–409
"Check" Section 3–104
"Consideration" Section 3–303
"Draft" Section 3–104
"Holder in due course" Section 3–302
"Incomplete instrument" Section 3–115
"Indorsement" Section 3–204
"Indorser" Section 3–204
"Instrument" Section 3–104
"Issue" Section 3–105
"Issuer" Section 3–105
"Negotiable instrument" Section 3–104
"Negotiation" Section 3–201
"Note" Section 3–104
"Payable at a definite time" Section 3–108
"Payable on demand" Section 3–108
"Payable to bearer" Section 3–109
"Payable to order" Section 3–109
"Payment" Section 3–602
"Person entitled to enforce" Section 3–301
"Presentment" Section 3–501
"Reacquisition" Section 3–207
"Special indorsement" Section 3–205
"Teller's check" Section 3–104
"Transfer of instrument" Section 3–203

"Traveler's check" Section 3–104

"Value" Section 3–303

(c) The following definitions in other Articles apply to this Article:

"Banking day" Section 4–104

"Clearing house" Section 4–104

"Collecting bank" Section 4–105

"Depositary bank" Section 4–105

"Documentary draft" Section 4–104

"Intermediary bank" Section 4–105

"Item" Section 4–104

"Payor bank" Section 4–105

"Suspends payments" Section 4–104

(d) In addition, Article 1 contains general definitions and principles of construction and interpretation applicable throughout this Article.

Legislative Note. A jurisdiction that enacts this statute that has not yet enacted the revised version of UCC Article 1 should add to Section 3–103 the definition of "good faith" that appears in the official version of Section 1–201(b)(20) and the definition of "record" that appears in the official version of Section 1–201(b)(31). Sections 3–103(a)(6) and (14) are reserved for that purpose. A jurisdiction that already has adopted or simultaneously adopts the revised Article 1 should not add those definitions, but should leave those numbers "reserved." If jurisdictions follow the numbering suggested here, the subsections will have the same numbering in all jurisdictions that have adopted these amendments (whether they have or have not adopted the revised version of UCC Article 1).

As amended in 2001 and 2002.

Official Comment

1. Subsection (a) defines some common terms used throughout the Article that were not defined by former Article 3 and adds the definitions of "order" and "promise" found in former Section 3–102(1)(b) and (c).

2. The definition of "order" includes an instruction given by the signer to itself. The most common example of this kind of order is a cashier's check: a draft with respect to which the drawer and drawee are the same bank or branches of the same bank. Former Section 3–118(a) treated a cashier's check as a note. It stated "a draft drawn on the drawer is effective as a note." Although it is technically more correct to treat a cashier's check as a promise by the issuing bank to pay rather than an order to pay, a cashier's check is in the form of a check and it is normally referred to as a check. Thus, revised Article 3 follows banking practice in referring to a cashier's check as both a draft and a check rather than a note. Some insurance companies also follow the practice of issuing drafts in which the drawer draws on itself and makes the draft payable at or through a bank. These instruments are also treated as drafts. The obligation of the drawer of a cashier's check or other draft drawn on the drawer is stated in Section 3–412.

An order may be addressed to more than one person as drawee either jointly or in the alternative. The authorization of alternative drawees follows former Section 3–102(1)(b) and recognizes the practice of drawers, such as corporations issuing dividend checks, who for commercial convenience name a number of drawees, usually in different parts of the country. Section 3–501(b)(1) provides that presentment may be made to any one of multiple drawees. Drawees in succession are not permitted because the holder should not be required to make more than one presentment. Dishonor by any drawee named in the draft entitles the holder to rights of recourse against the drawer or indorsers.

3. The last sentence of subsection (a)(12) is intended to make it clear that an I.O.U. or other written acknowledgment of indebtedness is not a note unless there is also an undertaking to pay the obligation.

4. This Article now uses the broadened definition of good faith in revised Article 1. The definition requires not only honesty in fact but also "observance of reasonable commercial standards of fair dealing." Although fair dealing is a broad term that must be defined in context, it is clear that it is concerned with the fairness of conduct rather than the care with which an act is performed. Failure to exercise ordinary care in conducting a transaction is an entirely different concept than failure to deal fairly in conducting the transaction. Both fair dealing and ordinary care, which is defined in Section 3–103(a)(7), are to be judged in the light of reasonable commercial standards, but those standards in each case are directed to different aspects of commercial conduct.

5. Subsection (a)(9) is a definition of ordinary care which is applicable not only to Article 3 but to Article 4 as well. See Section 4–104(c). The general rule is stated in the first sentence of subsection (a)(9) and it applies both to banks and to persons engaged in businesses other than banking. Ordinary care means observance of reasonable commercial standards of the relevant businesses prevailing in the area in which the person is located. The second sentence of subsection (a)(9) is a particular rule limited to the duty of a bank

to examine an instrument taken by a bank for processing for collection or payment by automated means. This particular rule applies primarily to Section 4–406 and it is discussed in Comment 4 to that section. Nothing in Section 3–103(a)(9) is intended to prevent a customer from proving that the procedures followed by a bank are unreasonable, arbitrary, or unfair.

6. The definition of consumer account includes a joint account established by more than one individual. See Section 1–106(1).

As amended in 2001 and 2002.

§ 3–104. Negotiable Instrument.

(a) Except as provided in subsections (c) and (d), "negotiable instrument" means an unconditional promise or order to pay a fixed amount of money, with or without interest or other charges described in the promise or order, if it:

(1) is payable to bearer or to order at the time it is issued or first comes into possession of a holder;

(2) is payable on demand or at a definite time; and

(3) does not state any other undertaking or instruction by the person promising or ordering payment to do any act in addition to the payment of money, but the promise or order may contain (i) an undertaking or power to give, maintain, or protect collateral to secure payment, (ii) an authorization or power to the holder to confess judgment or realize on or dispose of collateral, or (iii) a waiver of the benefit of any law intended for the advantage or protection of an obligor.

(b) "Instrument" means a negotiable instrument.

(c) An order that meets all of the requirements of subsection (a), except paragraph (1), and otherwise falls within the definition of "check" in subsection (f) is a negotiable instrument and a check.

(d) A promise or order other than a check is not an instrument if, at the time it is issued or first comes into possession of a holder, it contains a conspicuous statement, however expressed, to the effect that the promise or order is not negotiable or is not an instrument governed by this Article.

(e) An instrument is a "note" if it is a promise and is a "draft" if it is an order. If an instrument falls within the definition of both "note" and "draft," a person entitled to enforce the instrument may treat it as either.

(f) "Check" means (i) a draft, other than a documentary draft, payable on demand and drawn on a bank or (ii) a cashier's check or teller's check. An instrument may be a check even though it is described on its face by another term, such as "money order."

(g) "Cashier's check" means a draft with respect to which the drawer and drawee are the same bank or branches of the same bank.

(h) "Teller's check" means a draft drawn by a bank (i) on another bank, or (ii) payable at or through a bank.

(i) "Traveler's check" means an instrument that (i) is payable on demand, (ii) is drawn on or payable at or through a bank, (iii) is designated by the term "traveler's check" or by a substantially similar term, and (iv) requires, as a condition to payment, a countersignature by a person whose specimen signature appears on the instrument.

(j) "Certificate of deposit" means an instrument containing an acknowledgment by a bank that a sum of money has been received by the bank and a promise by the bank to repay the sum of money. A certificate of deposit is a note of the bank.

Official Comment

1. The definition of "negotiable instrument" defines the scope of Article 3 since Section 3–102 states: "This Article applies to negotiable instruments." The definition in Section 3–104(a) incorporates other definitions in Article 3. An instrument is either a "promise," defined in Section 3–103(a)(12), or "order," defined in Section 3–103(a)(8). A promise is a written undertaking to pay money signed by the person undertaking to pay. An order is a written instruction to pay money signed by the person giving the instruction. Thus, the term "negotiable instrument" is limited to a signed writing that orders or promises payment of money. "Money" is defined in Section 1–201(24) and is not limited to United States dollars. It also includes a medium of exchange established by a foreign government or monetary units of account established by an intergovernmental organization or by agreement between two or more nations. Five other requirements are stated in Section 3–104(a): First, the promise or

order must be "unconditional." The quoted term is explained in Section 3–106. Second, the amount of money must be "a fixed amount *** with or without interest or other charges described in the promise or order." Section 3–112(b) relates to "interest." Third, the promise or order must be "payable to bearer or to order." The quoted phrase is explained in Section 3–109. An exception to this requirement is stated in subsection (c). Fourth, the promise or order must be payable "on demand or at a definite time." The quoted phrase is explained in Section 3–108. Fifth, the promise or order may not state "any other undertaking or instruction by the person promising or ordering payment to do any act in addition to the payment of money" with three exceptions. The quoted phrase is based on the first sentence of N.I.L. Section 5 which is the precursor of "no other promise, order, obligation or power given by the maker or drawer" appearing in former Section 3–104(1)(b). The words "instruction" and "undertaking" are used instead of "order" and "promise" that are used in the N.I.L. formulation because the latter words are defined terms that include only orders or promises to pay money. The three exceptions stated in Section 3–104(a)(3) are based on and are intended to have the same meaning as former Section 3–112(1)(b), (c), (d), and (e), as well as N.I.L. § 5(1), (2), and (3). Subsection (b) states that "instrument" means a "negotiable instrument." This follows former Section 3–102(1)(e) which treated the two terms as synonymous.

2. Unless subsection (c) applies, the effect of subsection (a)(1) and Section 3–102(a) is to exclude from Article 3 any promise or order that is not payable to bearer or to order. There is no provision in revised Article 3 that is comparable to former Section 3–805. The comment to former Section 3–805 states that the typical example of a writing covered by that section is a check reading "Pay John Doe." Such a check was governed by former Article 3 but there could not be a holder in due course of the check. Under Section 3–104(c) such a check is governed by revised Article 3 and there can be a holder in due course of the check. But subsection (c) applies only to checks. The comment to former Section 3–805 does not state any example other than the check to illustrate that section. Subsection (c) is based on the belief that it is good policy to treat checks, which are payment instruments, as negotiable instruments whether or not they contain the words "to the order of". These words are almost always pre-printed on the check form. Occasionally the drawer of a check may strike out these words before issuing the check. In the past some credit unions used check forms that did not contain the quoted words. Such check forms may still be in use

but they are no longer common. Absence of the quoted words can easily be overlooked and should not affect the rights of holders who may pay money or give credit for a check without being aware that it is not in the conventional form.

Total exclusion from Article 3 of other promises or orders that are not payable to bearer or to order serves a useful purpose. It provides a simple device to clearly exclude a writing that does not fit the pattern of typical negotiable instruments and which is not intended to be a negotiable instrument. If a writing could be an instrument despite the absence of "to order" or "to bearer" language and a dispute arises with respect to the writing, it might be argued that the writing is a negotiable instrument because the other requirements of subsection (a) are somehow met. Even if the argument is eventually found to be without merit it can be used as a litigation ploy. Words making a promise or order payable to bearer or to order are the most distinguishing feature of a negotiable instrument and such words are frequently referred to as "words of negotiability." Article 3 is not meant to apply to contracts for the sale of goods or services or the sale or lease of real property or similar writings that may contain a promise to pay money. The use of words of negotiability in such contracts would be an aberration. Absence of the words precludes any argument that such contracts might be negotiable instruments.

An order or promise that is excluded from Article 3 because of the requirements of Section 3–104(a) may nevertheless be similar to a negotiable instrument in many respects. Although such a writing cannot be made a negotiable instrument within Article 3 by contract or conduct of its parties, nothing in Section 3–104 or in Section 3–102 is intended to mean that in a particular case involving such a writing a court could not arrive at a result similar to the result that would follow if the writing were a negotiable instrument. For example, a court might find that the obligor with respect to a promise that does not fall within Section 3–104(a) is precluded from asserting a defense against a bona fide purchaser. The preclusion could be based on estoppel or ordinary principles of contract. It does not depend upon the law of negotiable instruments. An example is stated in the paragraph following Case # 2 in Comment 4 to Section 3–302.

Moreover, consistent with the principle stated in Section 1–102(2)(b), the immediate parties to an order or promise that is not an instrument may provide by agreement that one or more of the provisions of Article 3 determine their rights and obligations under the writing. Upholding the parties' choice is not inconsistent with Article 3. Such an agreement may bind a transferee of the writing if the transferee has notice of it or the agreement arises from usage of trade and the agreement does not violate other law or public policy. An example of such an agreement is a provision that a transferee of the writing has the rights of a holder in due course stated in Article 3 if the transferee took rights under the writing in good faith, for value, and without notice of a claim or defense.

Even without an agreement of the parties to an order or promise that is not an instrument, it may be appropriate, consistent with the principles stated in Section 1–102(2), for a court to apply one or more provisions of Article 3 to the writing by analogy, taking into account the expectations of the parties and the differences between the writing and an instrument governed by Article 3. Whether such application is appropriate depends upon the facts of each case.

3. Subsection (d) allows exclusion from Article 3 of a writing that would otherwise be an instrument under subsection (a) by a statement to the effect that the writing is not negotiable or is not governed by Article 3. For example, a promissory note can be stamped with the legend NOT NEGOTIABLE. The effect under subsection (d) is not only to negate the possibility of a holder in due course, but to prevent the writing from being a negotiable instrument for any purpose. Subsection (d) does not, however, apply to a check. If a writing is excluded from Article 3 by subsection (d), a court could, nevertheless, apply Article 3 principles to it by analogy as stated in Comment 2.

4. Instruments are divided into two general categories: drafts and notes. A draft is an instrument that is an order. A note is an instrument that is a promise. Section 3–104(e). The term "bill of exchange" is not used in Article 3. It is generally understood to be a synonym for the term "draft." Subsections (f) through (j) define particular instruments that fall within the categories of draft and note. The term "draft," defined in subsection (e), includes a "check" which is defined in subsection (f). "Check" includes a share draft drawn on a credit union payable through a bank because the definition of bank (Section 4–105) includes credit unions. However, a draft drawn on an insurance company payable through a bank is not a check because it is not drawn on a bank. "Money orders" are sold both by banks and non-banks. They vary in form and their form determines how they are treated in Article 3. The most common form of money order sold by banks is that of an ordinary check drawn by the purchaser except that the amount is machine impressed. That kind of money order is a check under Article 3 and is subject to a stop order by the purchas-

er-drawer as in the case of ordinary checks. The seller bank is the drawee and has no obligation to a holder to pay the money order. If a money order falls within the definition of a teller's check, the rules applicable to teller's checks apply. Postal money orders are subject to federal law. "Teller's check" is separately defined in subsection (h). A teller's check is always drawn by a bank and is usually drawn on another bank. In some cases a teller's check is drawn on a nonbank but is made payable at or through a bank. Article 3 treats both types of teller's check identically, and both are included in the definition of "check." A cashier's check, defined in subsection (g), is also included in the definition of "check." Traveler's checks are issued both by banks and nonbanks and may be in the form of a note or draft. Subsection (i) states the essential characteristics of a traveler's check. The requirement that the instrument be "drawn on or payable at or through a bank" may be satisfied without words on the instrument that identify a bank as drawee or paying agent so long as the instrument bears an appropriate routing number that identifies a bank as paying agent.

The definitions in Regulation CC § 229.2 of the terms "check," "cashier's check," "teller's check," and "traveler's check" are different from the definitions of those terms in Article 3.

Certificates of deposit are treated in former Article 3 as a separate type of instrument. In revised Article 3, Section 3–104(j) treats them as notes.

5. There are some differences between the requirements of Article 3 and the requirements included in Article 3 of the Convention on International Bills of Exchange and International Promissory Notes. Most obviously, the Convention does not include the limitation on extraneous undertakings set forth in Section 3–104(a)(3), and does not permit documents payable to bearer that would be permissible under Section 3–104(a)(1) and Section 3–109. See Convention Article 3. In most respects, however, the requirements of Section 3–104 and Article 3 of the Convention are quite similar.

As amended in 2002.

§ 3–105. Issue of Instrument.

(a) "Issue" means the first delivery of an instrument by the maker or drawer, whether to a holder or nonholder, for the purpose of giving rights on the instrument to any person.

(b) An unissued instrument, or an unissued incomplete instrument that is completed, is binding on the maker or drawer, but nonissuance is a defense. An instrument that is conditionally issued or is issued for a special purpose is binding on the maker or drawer, but failure of the condition or special purpose to be fulfilled is a defense.

(c) "Issuer" applies to issued and unissued instruments and means a maker or drawer of an instrument.

Official Comment

1. Under former Section 3–102(1)(a) "issue" was defined as the first delivery to a "holder or a remitter" but the term "remitter" was neither defined nor otherwise used. In revised Article 3, Section 3–105(a) defines "issue" more broadly to include the first delivery to anyone by the drawer or maker for the purpose of giving rights to anyone on the instrument. "Delivery" with respect to instruments is defined in Section 1–201(14) as meaning "voluntary transfer of possession."

2. Subsection (b) continues the rule that nonissuance, conditional issuance or issuance for a special purpose is a defense of the maker or drawer of an instrument. Thus, the defense can be asserted against a person other than a holder in due course. The same rule applies to nonissuance of an incomplete instrument later completed.

3. Subsection (c) defines "issuer" to include the signer of an unissued instrument for convenience of reference in the statute.

§ 3–106. Unconditional Promise or Order.

(a) Except as provided in this section, for the purposes of Section 3–104(a), a promise or order is unconditional unless it states (i) an express condition to payment, (ii) that the promise or order is subject to or governed by another record, or (iii) that rights or obligations with respect to the promise or order are stated in another record. A reference to another record does not of itself make the promise or order conditional.

(b) A promise or order is not made conditional (i) by a reference to another record for a statement of rights with respect to collateral, prepayment, or acceleration, or (ii) because payment is limited to resort to a particular fund or source.

(c) If a promise or order requires, as a condition to payment, a countersignature by a person whose specimen signature appears on the promise or order, the condition does not make the promise or order conditional for the purposes of Section 3–104(a). If the person whose specimen signature appears on an instrument fails to countersign the instrument, the failure to countersign is a defense to the obligation of the issuer, but the failure does not prevent a transferee of the instrument from becoming a holder of the instrument.

(d) If a promise or order at the time it is issued or first comes into possession of a holder contains a statement, required by applicable statutory or administrative law, to the effect that the rights of a holder or transferee are subject to claims or defenses that the issuer could assert against the original payee, the promise or order is not thereby made conditional for the purposes of Section 3–104(a); but if the promise or order is an instrument, there cannot be a holder in due course of the instrument.

As amended in 2002.

Official Comment

1. This provision replaces former Section 3–105. Its purpose is to define when a promise or order fulfills the requirement in Section 3–104(a) that it be an "unconditional" promise or order to pay. Under Section 3–106(a) a promise or order is deemed to be unconditional unless one of the two tests of the subsection make the promise or order conditional. If the promise or order states an express condition to payment, the promise or order is not an instrument. For example, a promise states, "I promise to pay $100,000 to the order of John Doe if he conveys title to Blackacre to me." The promise is not an instrument because there is an express condition to payment. However, suppose a promise states, "In consideration of John Doe's promise to convey title to Blackacre I promise to pay $100,000 to the order of John Doe." That promise can be an instrument if Section 3–104 is otherwise satisfied. Although the recital of the executory promise of Doe to convey Blackacre might be read as an implied condition that the promise be performed, the condition is not an express condition as required by Section 3–106(a)(i). This result is consistent with former Section 3–105(1)(a) and (b). Former Section 3–105(1)(b) is not repeated in Section 3–106 because it is not necessary. It is an example of an implied condition. Former Section 3–105(1)(d), (e), and (f) and the first clause of former Section 3–105(1)(c) are other examples of implied conditions. They are not repeated in Section 3–106 because they are not necessary. The law is not changed.

Section 3–106(a)(ii) and (iii) carry forward the substance of former Section 3–105(2)(a). The only change is the use of "writing" instead of "agreement" and a broadening of the language that can result in conditionality. For example, a promissory note is not an instrument defined by Section 3–104 if it contains any of the following statements: 1. "This note is subject to a contract of sale dated April 1, 1990 between the payee and maker of this note." 2. "This note is subject to a loan and security agreement dated April 1, 1990 between the payee and maker of this note." 3. "Rights and obligations of the parties with respect to this note are stated in an agreement dated April 1, 1990 between the payee and maker of this note." It is not relevant whether any condition to payment is or is not stated in the writing to which reference is made. The rationale is that the holder of a negotiable instrument should not be required to examine another document to determine rights with respect to payment. But subsection (b)(i) permits reference to a separate writing for information with respect to collateral, prepayment, or acceleration.

Many notes issued in commercial transactions are secured by collateral, are subject to acceleration in the event of default, or are subject to prepayment. A statement of rights and obligations concerning collateral, prepayment, or acceleration does not prevent the note from being an instrument if the statement is in the note itself. See Section 3–104(a)(3) and Section 3–108(b). In some cases it may be convenient not to include a statement concerning collateral, prepayment, or acceleration in the note, but rather to refer to an accompanying loan agreement, security agreement or mortgage for that statement. Subsection (b)(i) allows a reference to the appropriate writing for a statement of these rights. For example, a note would not be made conditional by the following statement: "This note is secured by a security interest in collateral described in a security agreement dated April 1, 1990 between the payee and maker of this note. Rights and obligations with respect to the collateral are [stated in] [governed by] the security agreement." The bracketed words are alternatives, either of which complies.

Subsection (b)(ii) addresses the issues covered by former Section 3–105(1)(f), (g), and (h) and Section 3–105(2)(b). Under Section 3–106(a) a promise or order is not made conditional because payment is limited to payment from a particular source or fund. This reverses the result of former Section 3–105(2)(b). There is no cogent reason why the general credit of a legal entity must be pledged to have a negotiable instrument. Market forces determine the marketability of instruments of this kind. If potential buyers don't want promises or orders that are payable only from a particular source or fund, they won't take them, but Article 3 should apply.

2. Subsection (c) applies to traveler's checks or other instruments that may require a countersignature. Although the requirement of a countersignature is a condition to the obligation to pay, traveler's checks are treated in the commercial world as money substitutes and therefore should be governed by Article 3. The first sentence of subsection (c) allows a traveler's check to meet the definition of instrument by stating that the countersignature condition does not make it conditional for the purposes of Section 3–104. The second sentence states the effect of a failure to meet the condition. Suppose a thief steals a traveler's check and cashes it by skillfully imitating the specimen signature so that the countersignature appears to be authentic. The countersignature is for the purpose of identification of the owner of the instrument. It is not an indorsement. Subsection (c) provides that the failure of the owner to countersign does not prevent a transferee from becoming a holder. Thus, the merchant or bank that cashed the traveler's check becomes a holder when the traveler's check is taken. The forged countersignature is a defense to the obligation of the issuer to pay the instrument, and is included in defenses under Section 3–305(a)(2). These defenses may not be asserted against a holder in due course. Whether a holder has notice of the defense is a factual question. If the countersignature is a very bad forgery, there may be notice. But if the merchant or bank cashed a traveler's check and the countersignature appeared to be similar to the specimen signature, there might not be notice that the countersignature was forged. Thus, the merchant or bank could be a holder in due course.

3. Subsection (d) concerns the effect of a statement to the effect that the rights of a holder or transferee are subject to claims and defenses that the issuer could assert against the original payee. The subsection applies only if the statement is required by statutory or administrative law. The prime example is the Federal Trade Commission Rule (16 C.F.R. Part 433) preserving consumers' claims and defenses in consumer credit sales. The intent of the FTC rule is to make it impossible for there to be a holder in due course of a note bearing the FTC legend and undoubtedly that is the result. But, under former Article 3, the legend may also have had the unintended effect of making the note conditional, thus excluding the note from former Article 3 altogether. Subsection (d) is designed to make it possible to preclude the possibility of a holder in due course without excluding the instrument from Article 3. Most of the provisions of Article 3 are not

affected by the holder-in-due-course doctrine and there is no reason why Article 3 should not apply to a note bearing the FTC legend if holder-in-due-course rights are not involved. Under subsection (d) the statement does not make the note conditional. If the note otherwise meets the requirements of Section 3–104(a) it is a negotiable instrument for all purposes except that there cannot be a holder in due course of the note. No particular form of legend or statement is required by subsection (d). The form of a particular legend or statement may be determined by the other statute or administrative law. For example, the FTC legend required in a note taken by the seller in a consumer sale of goods or services is tailored to that particular transaction and therefore uses language that is somewhat different from that stated in subsection (d), but the difference in expression does not affect the essential similarity of the message conveyed. The effect of the FTC legend is to make the rights of a holder or transferee subject to claims or defenses that the issuer could assert against the original payee of the note.

§ 3–107. Instrument Payable in Foreign Money.

Unless the instrument otherwise provides, an instrument that states the amount payable in foreign money may be paid in the foreign money or in an equivalent amount in dollars calculated by using the current bank-offered spot rate at the place of payment for the purchase of dollars on the day on which the instrument is paid.

Official Comment

The definition of instrument in Section 3–104 requires that the promise or order be payable in "money." That term is defined in Section 1–201(24) and is not limited to United States dollars. Section 3–107 states than an instrument payable in foreign money may be paid in dollars if the instrument does not prohibit it. It also states a conversion rate which applies in the absence of a different conversion rate stated in the instrument. The reference in former Section 3–107(1) to instruments payable in "currency" or "current funds" has been dropped as superfluous.

§ 3–108. Payable on Demand or at Definite Time.

(a) A promise or order is "payable on demand" if it (i) states that it is payable on demand or at sight, or otherwise indicates that it is payable at the will of the holder, or (ii) does not state any time of payment.

(b) A promise or order is "payable at a definite time" if it is payable on elapse of a definite period of time after sight or acceptance or at a fixed date or dates or at a time or times readily ascertainable at the time the promise or order is issued, subject to rights of (i) prepayment, (ii) acceleration, (iii) extension at the option of the holder, or (iv) extension to a further definite time at the option of the maker or acceptor or automatically upon or after a specified act or event.

(c) If an instrument, payable at a fixed date, is also payable upon demand made before the fixed date, the instrument is payable on demand until the fixed date and, if demand for payment is not made before that date, becomes payable at a definite time on the fixed date.

Official Comment

This section is a restatement of former Section 3–108 and Section 3–109. Subsection (b) broadens former Section 3–109 somewhat by providing that a definite time includes a time readily ascertainable at the time the promise or order is issued. Subsection (b)(iii) and (iv) restates former Section 3–109(1)(d). It adopts the generally accepted rule that a clause providing for extension at the option of the holder, even without a time limit, does not affect negotiability since the holder is given only a right which the holder would have without the clause. If the extension is to be at the option of the maker or acceptor or is to be automatic, a definite time limit must be stated or the time of payment remains uncertain and the order or promise is not a negotiable instrument. If a definite time limit is stated, the effect upon certainty of time of payment is the same as if the instrument were made payable at the ultimate date with a term providing for acceleration.

§ 3–109. Payable to Bearer or to Order.

(a) A promise or order is payable to bearer if it:

(1) states that it is payable to bearer or to the order of bearer or otherwise indicates that the person in possession of the promise or order is entitled to payment;

(2) does not state a payee; or

(3) states that it is payable to or to the order of cash or otherwise indicates that it is not payable to an identified person.

(b) A promise or order that is not payable to bearer is payable to order if it is payable (i) to the order of an identified person or (ii) to an identified person or order. A promise or order that is payable to order is payable to the identified person.

(c) An instrument payable to bearer may become payable to an identified person if it is specially indorsed pursuant to Section 3–205(a). An instrument payable to an identified person may become payable to bearer if it is indorsed in blank pursuant to Section 3–205(b).

Official Comment

1. Under Section 3–104(a), a promise or order cannot be an instrument unless the instrument is payable to bearer or to order when it is issued or unless Section 3–104(c) applies. The terms "payable to bearer" and "payable to order" are defined in Section 3–109. The quoted terms are also relevant in determining how an instrument is negotiated. If the instrument is payable to bearer it can be negotiated by delivery alone. Section 3–201(b). An instrument that is payable to an identified person cannot be negotiated without the indorsement of the identified person. Section 3–201(b). An instrument payable to order is payable to an identified person. Section 3–109(b). Thus, an instrument payable to order requires the indorsement of the person to whose order the instrument is payable.

2. Subsection (a) states when an instrument is payable to bearer. An instrument is payable to bearer if it states that it is payable to bearer, but some instruments use ambiguous terms. For example, check forms usually have the words "to the order of" printed at the beginning of the line to be filled in for the name of the payee. If the drawer writes in the word "bearer" or "cash," the check reads "to the order of bearer" or "to the order of cash." In each case the check is payable to bearer. Sometimes the drawer will write the name of the payee "John Doe" but will add the words "or bearer." In that case the check is payable to bearer. Subsection (a). Under subsection (b), if an instrument is payable to bearer it can't be payable to order. This is different from former Section 3–110(3). An instrument that purports to be payable both to order and bearer states contradictory terms. A transferee of the instrument should be able to rely on the bearer term and acquire rights as a holder without obtaining the indorsement of the identified payee. An instrument is also payable to bearer if it does not state a payee. Instruments that do not state a payee are in most cases incomplete instruments. In some cases the drawer of a check may deliver or mail it to the person to be paid without filling in the line for the name of the payee. Under subsection (a) the check is payable to bearer when it is sent or delivered. It is also an incomplete instrument. This case is discussed in Comment 2 to Section 3–115. Subsection (a)(3) contains the words "otherwise indicates that it is not payable to an identified person." The quoted words are meant to cover uncommon cases in which an instrument indicates that it is not meant to be payable to a specific person. Such an instrument is treated like a check payable to "cash." The quoted words are not meant to apply to an instrument stating that it is payable to an identified person such as "ABC Corporation" if ABC Corporation is a nonexistent company. Although the holder of the check cannot be the nonexistent company, the instrument is not payable to bearer. Negotiation of such an instrument is governed by Section 3–404(b).

§ 3–110. Identification of Person to Whom Instrument Is Payable.

(a) The person to whom an instrument is initially payable is determined by the intent of the person, whether or not authorized, signing as, or in the name or behalf of, the issuer of the instrument. The instrument is payable to the person intended by the signer even if that person is identified in the instrument by a name or other identification that is not that of the intended person. If more than one person signs in the name or behalf of the issuer of an instrument and all the signers do not intend the same person as payee, the instrument is payable to any person intended by one or more of the signers.

(b) If the signature of the issuer of an instrument is made by automated means, such as a check-writing machine, the payee of the instrument is determined by the intent of the person who supplied the name or identification of the payee, whether or not authorized to do so.

(c) A person to whom an instrument is payable may be identified in any way, including by name, identifying number, office, or account number. For the purpose of determining the holder of an instrument, the following rules apply:

(1) If an instrument is payable to an account and the account is identified only by number, the instrument is payable to the person to whom the account is payable. If an instrument is payable to an account identified by number and by the name of

a person, the instrument is payable to the named person, whether or not that person is the owner of the account identified by number.

(2) If an instrument is payable to:

(i) a trust, an estate, or a person described as trustee or representative of a trust or estate, the instrument is payable to the trustee, the representative, or a successor of either, whether or not the beneficiary or estate is also named;

(ii) a person described as agent or similar representative of a named or identified person, the instrument is payable to the represented person, the representative, or a successor of the representative;

(iii) a fund or organization that is not a legal entity, the instrument is payable to a representative of the members of the fund or organization; or

(iv) n office or to a person described as holding an office, the instrument is payable to the named person, the incumbent of the office, or a successor to the incumbent.

(d) If an instrument is payable to two or more persons alternatively, it is payable to any of them and may be negotiated, discharged, or enforced by any or all of them in possession of the instrument. If an instrument is payable to two or more persons not alternatively, it is payable to all of them and may be negotiated, discharged, or enforced only by all of them. If an instrument payable to two or more persons is ambiguous as to whether it is payable to the persons alternatively, the instrument is payable to the persons alternatively.

Official Comment

1. Section 3–110 states rules for determining the identity of the person to whom an instrument is initially payable if the instrument is payable to an identified person. This issue usually arises in a dispute over the validity of an indorsement in the name of the payee. Subsection (a) states the general rule that the person to whom an instrument is payable is determined by the intent of "the person, whether or not authorized, signing as, or in the name or behalf of, the issuer of the instrument." "Issuer" means the maker or drawer of

the instrument. Section 3–105(c). If X signs a check as drawer of a check on X's account, the intent of X controls. If X, as President of Corporation, signs a check as President in behalf of Corporation as drawer, the intent of X controls. If X forges Y's signature as drawer of a check, the intent of X also controls. Under Section 3–103(a)(5), Y is referred to as the drawer of the check because the signing of Y's name identifies Y as the drawer. But since Y's signature was forged Y has no liability as drawer (Section 3–403(a)) unless some other provision of Article 3 or Article 4 makes Y liable. Since X, even though unauthorized, signed in the name of Y as issuer, the intent of X determines to whom the check is payable.

In the case of a check payable to "John Smith," since there are many people in the world named "John Smith" it is not possible to identify the payee of the check unless there is some further identification or the intention of the drawer is determined. Name alone is sufficient under subsection (a), but the intention of the drawer determines which John Smith is the person to whom the check is payable. The same issue is presented in cases of misdescriptions of the payee. The drawer intends to pay a person known to the drawer as John Smith. In fact that person's name is James Smith or John Jones or some other entirely different name. If the check identifies the payee as John Smith, it is nevertheless payable to the person intended by the drawer. That person may indorse the check in either the name John Smith or the person's correct name or in both names. Section 3–204(d). The intent of the drawer is also controlling in fictitious payee cases. Section 3–404(b). The last sentence of subsection (a) refers to rare cases in which the signature of an organization requires more than one signature and the persons signing on behalf of the organization do not all intend the same person as payee. Any person intended by a signer for the organization is the payee and an indorsement by that person is an effective indorsement.

Subsection (b) recognizes the fact that in a large number of cases there is no human signer of an instrument because the instrument, usually a check, is produced by automated means such as a check-writing machine. In that case, the relevant intent is that of the person who supplied the name of the payee. In most cases that person is an employee of the drawer, but in some cases the person could be an outsider who is committing a fraud by introducing names of payees of checks into the system that produces the checks. A check-writing machine is likely to be operated by means of a computer in which is stored information as to name and address of the payee and the amount of the check. Access to the computer may allow production of fraudulent checks without knowledge of the organization that is the issuer of the check. Section 3–404(b) is also concerned with this issue. See Case # 4 in Comment 2 to Section 3–404.

2. Subsection (c) allows the payee to be identified in any way including the various ways stated. Subsection (c)(1) relates to instruments payable to bank accounts. In some cases the account might be identified by name and number, and the name and number might refer to different persons. For example, a check is payable to "X Corporation Account No. 12345 in Bank of Podunk." Under the last sentence of subsection (c)(1), this check is payable to X Corporation and can be negotiated by X Corporation even if Account No. 12345 is some other person's account or the check is not deposited in that account. In other cases the payee is identified by an account number and the name of the owner of the account is not stated. For example, Debtor pays Creditor by issuing a check drawn on Payor Bank. The check is payable to a bank account owned by Creditor but identified only by number. Under the first sentence of subsection (c)(1) the check is payable to Creditor and, under Section 1–201(20), Creditor becomes the holder when the check is delivered. Under Section 3–201(b), further negotiation of the check requires the indorsement of Creditor. But under Section 4–205(a), if the check is taken by a depositary bank for collection, the bank may become a holder without the indorsement. Under Section 3–102(b), provisions of Article 4 prevail over those of Article 3. The depositary bank warrants that the amount of the check was credited to the payee's account.

3. Subsection (c)(2) replaces former Section 3–117 and subsection (1)(e), (f), and (g) of former Section 3–110. This provision merely determines who can deal with an instrument as a holder. It does not determine ownership of the instrument or its proceeds. Subsection (c)(2)(i) covers trusts and estates. If the instrument is payable to the trust or estate or to the trustee or representative of the trust or estate, the instrument is payable to the trustee or representative or any successor. Under subsection (c)(2)(ii), if the instrument states that it is payable to Doe, President of X Corporation, either Doe or X Corporation can be holder of the instrument. Subsection (c)(2)(iii) concerns informal organizations that are not legal entities such as unincorporated clubs and the like. Any representative of the members of the organization can act as holder. Subsection (c)(2)(iv) applies principally to instruments

payable to public offices such as a check payable to County Tax Collector.

4. Subsection (d) replaces former Section 3–116. An instrument payable to X or Y is governed by the first sentence of subsection (d). An instrument payable to X and Y is governed by the second sentence of subsection (d). If an instrument is payable to X or Y, either is the payee and if either is in possession that person is the holder and the person entitled to enforce the instrument. Section 3–301. If an instrument is payable to X and Y, neither X nor Y acting alone is the person to whom the instrument is payable. Neither person, acting alone, can be the holder of the instrument. The instrument is "payable to an identified person." The "identified person" is X and Y acting jointly. Section 3–109(b) and Section 1–102(5)(a). Thus, under Section 1–201(20) X or Y, acting alone, cannot be the holder or the person entitled to enforce or negotiate the instrument because neither, acting alone, is the identified person stated in the instrument.

The third sentence of subsection (d) is directed to cases in which it is not clear whether an instrument is payable to multiple payees alternatively. In the case of ambiguity persons dealing with the instrument should be able to rely on the indorsement of a single payee. For example, an instrument payable to X and/or Y is treated like an instrument payable to X or Y.

§ 3–111.   Place of Payment.

Except as otherwise provided for items in Article 4, an instrument is payable at the place of payment stated in the instrument. If no place of payment is stated, an instrument is payable at the address of the drawee or maker stated in the instrument. If no address is stated, the place of payment is the place of business of the drawee or maker. If a drawee or maker has more than one place of business, the place of payment is any place of business of the drawee or maker chosen by the person entitled to enforce the instrument. If the drawee or maker has no place of business, the place of payment is the residence of the drawee or maker.

Official Comment

If an instrument is payable at a bank in the United States, Section 3–501(b)(1) states that presentment must be made at the place of payment, i.e. the bank. The place of presentment of a check is governed by Regulation CC § 229.36.

§ 3–112. Interest.

(a) Unless otherwise provided in the instrument, (i) an instrument is not payable with interest, and (ii) interest on an interest-bearing instrument is payable from the date of the instrument.

(b) Interest may be stated in an instrument as a fixed or variable amount of money or it may be expressed as a fixed or variable rate or rates. The amount or rate of interest may be stated or described in the instrument in any manner and may require reference to information not contained in the instrument. If an instrument provides for interest, but the amount of interest payable cannot be ascertained from the description, interest is payable at the judgment rate in effect at the place of payment of the instrument and at the time interest first accrues.

Official Comment

1. Under Section 3–104(a) the requirement of a "fixed amount" applies only to principal. The amount of interest payable is that described in the instrument. If the description of interest in the instrument does not allow for the amount of interest to be ascertained, interest is payable at the judgment rate. Hence, if an instrument calls for interest, the amount of interest will always be determinable. If a variable rate of interest is prescribed, the amount of interest is ascertainable by reference to the formula or index described or referred to in the instrument. The last sentence of subsection (b) replaces subsection (d) of former Section 3–118.

2. The purpose of subsection (b) is to clarify the meaning of "interest" in the introductory clause of Section 3–104(a). It is not intended to validate a provision for interest in an instrument if that provision violates other law.

§ 3–113. Date of Instrument.

(a) An instrument may be antedated or postdated. The date stated determines the time of payment if the instrument is payable at a fixed period after date. Except as provided in Section 4–401(c), an instrument payable on demand is not payable before the date of the instrument.

(b) If an instrument is undated, its date is the date of its issue or, in the case of an unissued instrument, the date it first comes into possession of a holder.

Official Comment

This section replaces former Section 3–114. Subsections (1) and (3) of former Section 3–114 are deleted as unnecessary. Section 3–113(a) is based in part on subsection (2) of former Section 3–114. The rule that a demand instrument is not payable before the date of the instrument is subject to Section 4–401(c) which allows the payor bank to pay a postdated check unless the drawer has notified the bank of the postdating pursuant to a procedure prescribed in that subsection. With respect to an undated instrument, the date is the date of issue.

§ 3–114. Contradictory Terms of Instrument.

If an instrument contains contradictory terms, typewritten terms prevail over printed terms, handwritten terms prevail over both, and words prevail over numbers.

Official Comment

Section 3–114 replaces subsections (b) and (c) of former Section 3–118.

§ 3–115. Incomplete Instrument.

(a) "Incomplete instrument" means a signed writing, whether or not issued by the signer, the contents of which show at the time of signing that it is incomplete but that the signer intended it to be completed by the addition of words or numbers.

(b) Subject to subsection (c), if an incomplete instrument is an instrument under Section 3–104, it may be enforced according to its terms if it is not completed, or according to its terms as augmented by completion. If an incomplete instrument is not an instrument under Section 3–104, but, after completion, the requirements of Section 3–104 are met, the instrument may be enforced according to its terms as augmented by completion.

(c) If words or numbers are added to an incomplete instrument without authority of the signer, there is an alteration of the incomplete instrument under Section 3–407.

(d) The burden of establishing that words or numbers were added to an incomplete instrument without authority of the signer is on the person asserting the lack of authority.

Official Comment

1. This section generally carries forward the rules set out in former Section 3–115. The term "incomplete instrument" applies both to an "instrument," i.e. a writing meeting all the requirements of Section 3–104, and to a writing intended to be an instrument that is signed but lacks some element of an instrument. The test in both cases is whether the contents show that it is incomplete and that the signer intended that additional words or numbers be added.

2. If an incomplete instrument meets the requirements of Section 3–104 and is not completed it may be enforced in accordance with its terms. Suppose, in the following two cases, that a note delivered to the payee is incomplete solely because a space on the pre-printed note form for the due date is not filled in:

Case # 1. If the incomplete instrument is never completed, the note is payable on demand. Section 3–108(a)(ii). However, if the payee and the maker agreed to a due date, the maker may have a defense under Section 3–117 if demand for payment is made before the due date agreed to by the parties.

Case # 2. If the payee completes the note by filling in the due date agreed to by the parties, the note is payable on the due date stated. However, if the due date filled in was not the date agreed to by the parties there is an alteration of the note. Section 3–407 governs the case.

Suppose Debtor pays Creditor by giving Creditor a check on which the space for the name of the payee is left blank. The check is an instrument but it is incomplete. The check is enforceable in its incomplete form and it is payable to bearer because it does not state a payee. Section 3–109(a)(2). Thus, Creditor is a holder of the check. Normally in this kind of case Creditor would simply fill in the space with Creditor's name. When that occurs the check becomes payable to the Creditor.

3. In some cases the incomplete instrument does not meet the requirements of Section 3–104. An example is a check with the amount not filled in. The check cannot be enforced until the amount is filled in. If the payee fills in an amount authorized by the drawer the check meets the requirements of Section 3–104 and is enforceable as completed. If the payee fills in an unauthorized amount there is an alteration of the check and Section 3–407 applies.

4. Section 3–302(a)(1) also bears on the problem of incomplete instruments. Under that section a person cannot be a holder in due course of the instrument if it is so incomplete as to call into question its validity.

Subsection (d) of Section 3–115 is based on the last clause of subsection (2) of former Section 3–115.

§ 3–116. Joint and Several Liability; Contribution.

(a) Except as otherwise provided in the instrument, two or more persons who have the same liability on an instrument as makers, drawers, acceptors, indorsers who indorse as joint payees, or anomalous indorsers are jointly and severally liable in the capacity in which they sign.

(b) Except as provided in Section 3–419(f) or by agreement of the affected parties, a party having joint and several liability who pays the instrument is entitled to receive from any party having the same joint and several liability contribution in accordance with applicable law.

As amended in 2002.

Official Comment

1. Subsection (a) replaces subsection (e) of former Section 3–118. Subsection (b) states contribution rights of parties with joint and several liability by referring to applicable law. But subsection (b) is subject to Section 3–419(f). If one of the parties with joint and several liability is an accommodation party and the other is the accommodated party, Section 3–419(f) applies. Because one of the joint and several obligors may have recourse against the other joint and several obligor under subsection (b), each party that is jointly and severally liable under subsection (a) is a secondary obligor in part and a principal obligor in part, as those terms are defined in Section 3–103(a). Accordingly, Section 3–605 determines the effect of a release, an extension of time, or a modification of the obligation of one of the joint and several obligors, as well as the effect of an impairment of collateral provided by one of those obligors.

2. Indorsers normally do not have joint and several liability. Rather, an earlier indorser has liability to a later indorser. But indorsers can have joint and several liability in two cases. If an instrument is payable to two payees jointly, both payees must indorse. The indorsement is a joint indorsement and the indorsers have joint and several liability and subsection (b) applies. The other case is that of two or more anomalous indorsers. The term is defined in Section 3–205(d). An anomalous indorsement normally indicates that the indorser signed as an accommodation party. If more than one accommodation party indorses a note as an accommodation to the maker, the indorsers have joint and several liability and subsection (b) applies.

As amended in 2002.

§ 3–117. Other Agreements Affecting Instrument.

Subject to applicable law regarding exclusion of proof of contemporaneous or previous agreements, the obligation of a party to an instrument to pay the instrument may be modified, supplemented, or nullified by a separate agreement of the obligor and a person entitled to enforce the instrument, if the instrument is issued or the obligation is incurred in reliance on the agreement or as part of the same transaction giving rise to the agreement. To the extent an obligation is modified, supplemented, or nullified by an agreement under this section, the agreement is a defense to the obligation.

Official Comment

1. The separate agreement might be a security agreement or mortgage or it might be an agreement that contradicts the terms of the instrument. For example, a person may be induced to sign an instrument under an agreement that the signer will not be liable on the instrument unless certain conditions are met. Suppose X requested credit from Creditor who is willing to give the credit only if an acceptable accommodation party will sign the note of X as co-maker. Y agrees to sign as co-maker on the condition that Creditor also obtain the signature of Z as co-maker. Creditor agrees and Y signs as co-maker with X. Creditor fails to obtain the signature of Z on the note. Under Sections 3–412 and 3–419(b), Y is obliged to pay the note, but Section 3–117 applies. In this case, the agreement modifies the terms of the note by stating a condition to the obligation of Y to pay the note. This case is essentially similar to a case in which a maker of a note is induced to sign the note by fraud of the holder. Although the agreement that Y not be liable on the note unless Z also signs may not have been fraudulently made, a subsequent attempt by Creditor to require Y to pay the note in violation of the agreement is a bad faith act. Section 3–117, in treating the agreement as a defense, allows Y to assert the agreement against Creditor, but the defense would not be good against a subsequent holder in due course of the note that took it without notice of the agreement. If there cannot be a holder in due course because of Section 3–106(d), a subsequent holder that took the note in good faith, for value and without knowledge of the agreement would not be able to enforce the liability of Y. This result is consistent with the risk that a holder not in due course takes with respect to fraud in inducing issuance of an instrument.

2. The effect of merger or integration clauses to the effect that a writing is intended to be the complete and exclusive statement of the terms of the agreement or that the agreement is not subject to conditions is left to the supplementary law of the jurisdiction pursuant to Section 1–103. Thus, in the case discussed in Comment 1, whether Y is permitted to prove the condition to Y's obligation to pay the note is determined by that law. Moreover, nothing in this section is intended to validate an agreement which is fraudulent or void as against public policy, as in the case of a note given to deceive a bank examiner.

§ 3–118. Statute of Limitations.

(a) Except as provided in subsection (e), an action to enforce the obligation of a party to pay a note payable at a definite time must be commenced within six years after the due date or dates stated in the note or, if a due date is accelerated, within six years after the accelerated due date.

(b) Except as provided in subsection (d) or (e), if demand for payment is made to the maker of a note payable on demand, an action to enforce the obligation of a party to pay the note must be commenced within six years after the demand. If no demand for payment is made to the maker, an action to enforce the note is barred if neither principal nor interest on the note has been paid for a continuous period of 10 years.

(c) Except as provided in subsection (d), an action to enforce the obligation of a party to an unaccepted draft to pay the draft must be commenced within three years after dishonor of the draft or 10 years after the date of the draft, whichever period expires first.

(d) An action to enforce the obligation of the acceptor of a certified check or the issuer of a teller's check, cashier's check, or traveler's check must be commenced within three years after demand for payment is made to the acceptor or issuer, as the case may be.

(e) An action to enforce the obligation of a party to a certificate of deposit to pay the instrument must be commenced within six years after demand for payment is made to the maker, but if the instrument states a due date and the maker is not required to pay before that date, the six-year period begins when a demand for payment is in effect and the due date has passed.

(f) An action to enforce the obligation of a party to pay an accepted draft, other than a certified check, must be commenced (i) within six years after the due date or dates stated in the draft or acceptance if the obligation of the acceptor is payable at a definite time, or (ii) within six years after the date of the acceptance if the obligation of the acceptor is payable on demand.

(g) Unless governed by other law regarding claims for indemnity or contribution, an action (i) for conversion of an instrument, for money had and received, or like action based on conversion, (ii) for breach of warranty, or (iii) to enforce an obligation, duty, or right arising under this Article and not governed by this section must be commenced within three years after the [cause of action] accrues.

Official Comment

1. Section 3–118 differs from former Section 3–122, which states when a cause of action accrues on an instrument. Section 3–118 does not define when a cause of action accrues. Accrual of a cause of action is stated in other sections of Article 3 such as those that state the various obligations of parties to an instrument. The only purpose of Section 3–118 is to define the time within which an action to enforce an obligation, duty, or right arising under Article 3 must be commenced. Section 3–118 does not attempt to state all rules with respect to a statute of limitations. For example, the circumstances under which the running of a limitations period may be tolled is left to other law pursuant to Section 1–103.

2. The first six subsections apply to actions to enforce an obligation of any party to an instrument to pay the instrument. This changes present law in that indorsers who may become liable on an instrument after issue are subject to a period of limitations running from the same date as that of the maker or drawer. Subsections (a) and (b) apply to notes. If the note is payable at a definite time, a six-year limitations period starts at the due date of the note, subject to prior acceleration. If the note is payable on demand, there are two limitations periods. Although a note payable on demand could theoretically be called a day after it was issued, the normal expectation of the parties is that the note will remain outstanding until there is some reason to call it. If the law provides that the limitations period does not start until demand is made, the cause of action to enforce it may never be barred. On the other hand, if the limitations period starts when demand for payment may be made, i.e. at any time after the note was issued, the payee of a note on which interest or portions of principal are being paid could lose the right to enforce the note even though it was treated as a continuing obligation by the parties. Some demand notes are not enforced because the payee has forgiven the debt. This is particularly true in family and other noncommercial transactions. A demand note found after the death of the payee may be presented for payment many years after it was issued. The maker may be a relative and it may be difficult to determine whether the note represents a real or a forgiven debt. Subsection (b) is designed to bar notes that no longer represent a claim to payment and to require reasonably prompt action to enforce notes on which there is default. If a demand for payment is made to the maker, a six-year limitations period starts to run when demand is made. The second sentence of subsection (b) bars an action to enforce a demand note if no demand has been made on the note and no payment of interest or principal has been made for a continuous period of 10 years. This covers the case of a note that does not bear interest or a case in which interest due on the note has not been paid. This kind of case is likely to be a family transaction in which a failure to demand payment may indicate that the holder did not intend to enforce the obligation but neglected to destroy the note. A limitations period that bars stale claims in this kind of case is appropriate if the period is relatively long.

3. Subsection (c) applies primarily to personal uncertified checks. Checks are payment instruments rather than credit instruments. The limitations period expires three years after the date of dishonor or 10 years after the date of the check, whichever is earlier. Teller's checks, cashier's checks, certified checks, and traveler's checks are treated differently under subsection (d) because they are commonly treated as cash equivalents. A great delay in presenting a cashier's check for payment in most cases will occur because the check was mislaid during that period. The person to whom traveler's checks are issued may hold them indefinitely as a safe form of cash for use in an emergency. There is no compelling reason for barring the claim of the owner of the cashier's check or traveler's check. Under subsection (d) the claim is never barred because the three-year limitations period does not start to run until demand for payment is made. The limitations period in subsection (d) in effect applies only to cases in which there is a dispute about the legitimacy of the claim of the person demanding payment.

4. Subsection (e) covers certificates of deposit. The limitations period of six years doesn't start to run until the depositor demands payment. Most certificates of deposit are payable on demand even if they state a due date. The effect of a demand for payment before maturity is usually that the bank will pay, but that a penalty will be assessed against the depositor in the form of a reduction in the amount of interest that is paid. Subsection (e) also provides for cases in which the bank has no obligation to pay until the due date. In that case the limitations period doesn't start to run until there is a demand for payment in effect and the due date has passed.

5. Subsection (f) applies to accepted drafts other than certified checks. When a draft is accepted it is in effect turned into a note of the acceptor. In almost all cases the acceptor will agree to pay at a definite time. Subsection (f) states that in that case the six-year limitations period starts to run on the due date. In the rare case in which the obligation of the acceptor is payable on demand, the six-year limitations period starts to run at the date of the acceptance.

6. Subsection (g) covers warranty and conversion cases and other actions to enforce obligations or rights arising under Article 3. A three-year period is stated and subsection (g) follows general law in stating that the period runs from the time the cause of action accrues. Since the traditional term "cause of action" may have been replaced in some states by "claim for relief" or some equivalent term, the words "cause of action" have been bracketed to indicate that the words

may be replaced by an appropriate substitute to conform to local practice.

7. One of the most significant differences between this Article and the Convention on International Bills of Exchange and International Promissory Notes is that the statute of limitation under the Convention generally is only four years, rather than the six years provided by this section. See Convention Article 84.

As amended in 2002.

§ 3–119. Notice of Right to Defend Action.

In an action for breach of an obligation for which a third person is answerable over pursuant to this Article or Article 4, the defendant may give the third person notice of the litigation in a record, and the person notified may then give similar notice to any other person who is answerable over. If the notice states (i) that the person notified may come in and defend and (ii) that failure to do so will bind the person notified in an action later brought by the person giving the notice as to any determination of fact common to the two litigations, the person notified is so bound unless after seasonable receipt of the notice the person notified does come in and defend.

As amended in 2002.

Official Comment

This section is a restatement of former Section 3–803.

PART 2

NEGOTIATION, TRANSFER, AND INDORSEMENT

§ 3–201. Negotiation.

(a) "Negotiation" means a transfer of possession, whether voluntary or involuntary, of an instrument by a person other than the issuer to a person who thereby becomes its holder.

(b) Except for negotiation by a remitter, if an instrument is payable to an identified person, negotiation requires transfer of possession of the instrument and its indorsement by the holder. If an instrument is payable to bearer, it may be negotiated by transfer of possession alone.

Official Comment

1. Subsections (a) and (b) are based in part on subsection (1) of former Section 3–202. A person can

become holder of an instrument when the instrument is issued to that person, or the status of holder can arise as the result of an event that occurs after issuance. "Negotiation" is the term used in Article 3 to describe this post-issuance event. Normally, negotiation occurs as the result of a voluntary transfer of possession of an instrument by a holder to another person who becomes the holder as a result of the transfer. Negotiation always requires a change in possession of the instrument because nobody can be a holder without possessing the instrument, either directly or through an agent. But in some cases the transfer of possession is involuntary and in some cases the person transferring possession is not a holder. In defining "negotiation" former Section 3–202(1) used the word "transfer," an undefined term, and "delivery," defined in Section 1–201(14) to mean voluntary change of possession. Instead, subsections (a) and (b) use the term "transfer of possession" and, subsection (a) states that negotiation can occur by an involuntary transfer of possession. For example, if an instrument is payable to bearer and it is stolen by Thief or is found by Finder, Thief or Finder becomes the holder of the instrument when possession is obtained. In this case there is an involuntary transfer of possession that results in negotiation to Thief or Finder.

2. In most cases negotiation occurs by a transfer of possession by a holder or remitter. Remitter transactions usually involve a cashier's or teller's check. For example, Buyer buys goods from Seller and pays for them with a cashier's check of Bank that Buyer buys from Bank. The check is issued by Bank when it is delivered to Buyer, regardless of whether the check is payable to Buyer or to Seller. Section 3–105(a). If the check is payable to Buyer, negotiation to Seller is done by delivery of the check to Seller after it is indorsed by Buyer. It is more common, however, that the check when issued will be payable to Seller. In that case Buyer is referred to as the "remitter." Section 3–103(a)(15). The remitter, although not a party to the check, is the owner of the check until ownership is transferred to Seller by delivery. This transfer is a negotiation because Seller becomes the holder of the check when Seller obtains possession. In some cases Seller may have acted fraudulently in obtaining possession of the check. In those cases Buyer may be entitled to rescind the transfer to Seller because of the fraud and assert a claim of ownership to the check under Section 3–306 against Seller or a subsequent transferee of the check. Section 3–202(b) provides for rescission of negotiation, and that provision applies to rescission by a remitter as well as by a holder.

3. Other sections of Article 3 may modify the rule stated in the first sentence of subsection (b). See for example, Sections 3–404, 3–405 and 3–406.

§ 3–202. Negotiation Subject to Rescission.

(a) Negotiation is effective even if obtained (i) from an infant, a corporation exceeding its powers, or a person without capacity, (ii) by fraud, duress, or mistake, or (iii) in breach of duty or as part of an illegal transaction.

(b) To the extent permitted by other law, negotiation may be rescinded or may be subject to other remedies, but those remedies may not be asserted against a subsequent holder in due course or a person paying the instrument in good faith and without knowledge of facts that are a basis for rescission or other remedy.

Official Comment

1. This section is based on former Section 3–207. Subsection (2) of former Section 3–207 prohibited rescission of a negotiation against holders in due course. Subsection (b) of Section 3–202 extends this protection to payor banks.

2. Subsection (a) applies even though the lack of capacity or the illegality, is of a character which goes to the essence of the transaction and makes it entirely void. It is inherent in the character of negotiable instruments that any person in possession of an instrument which by its terms is payable to that person or to bearer is a holder and may be dealt with by anyone as a holder. The principle finds its most extreme application in the well settled rule that a holder in due course may take the instrument even from a thief and be protected against the claim of the rightful owner. The policy of subsection (a) is that any person to whom an instrument is negotiated is a holder until the instrument has been recovered from that person's possession. The remedy of a person with a claim to an instrument is to recover the instrument by replevin or otherwise; to impound it or to enjoin its enforcement, collection or negotiation; to recover its proceeds from the holder; or to intervene in any action brought by the holder against the obligor. As provided in Section 3–305(c), the claim of the claimant is not a defense to the obligor unless the claimant defends the action.

3. There can be no rescission or other remedy against a holder in due course or a person who pays in good faith and without notice, even though the prior negotiation may have been fraudulent or illegal in its essence and entirely void. As against any other party the claimant may have any remedy permitted by law. This section is not intended to specify what that remedy may be, or to prevent any court from imposing conditions or limitations such as prompt action or return of the consideration received. All such questions are left to the law of the particular jurisdiction. Section 3–202 gives no right that would not otherwise exist. The section is intended to mean that any remedies afforded by other law are cut off only by a holder in due course.

§ 3–203. Transfer of Instrument; Rights Acquired by Transfer.

(a) An instrument is transferred when it is delivered by a person other than its issuer for the purpose of giving to the person receiving delivery the right to enforce the instrument.

(b) Transfer of an instrument, whether or not the transfer is a negotiation, vests in the transferee any right of the transferor to enforce the instrument, including any right as a holder in due course, but the transferee cannot acquire rights of a holder in due course by a transfer, directly or indirectly, from a holder in due course if the transferee engaged in fraud or illegality affecting the instrument.

(c) Unless otherwise agreed, if an instrument is transferred for value and the transferee does not become a holder because of lack of indorsement by the transferor, the transferee has a specifically enforceable right to the unqualified indorsement of the transferor, but negotiation of the instrument does not occur until the indorsement is made.

(d) If a transferor purports to transfer less than the entire instrument, negotiation of the instrument does not occur. The transferee obtains no rights under this Article and has only the rights of a partial assignee.

Official Comment

1. Section 3-203 is based on former Section 3-201 which stated that a transferee received such rights as the transferor had. The former section was confusing because some rights of the transferor are not vested in the transferee unless the transfer is a negotiation. For example, a transferee that did not become the holder could not negotiate the instrument, a right that the transferor had. Former Section 3-201 did not define "transfer." Subsection (a) defines transfer by limiting it to cases in which possession of the instrument is delivered for the purpose of giving to the person receiving delivery the right to enforce the instrument.

Although transfer of an instrument might mean in a particular case that title to the instrument passes to the transferee, that result does not follow in all cases. The right to enforce an instrument and ownership of the instrument are two different concepts. A thief who steals a check payable to bearer becomes the holder of the check and a person entitled to enforce it, but does not become the owner of the check. If the thief transfers the check to a purchaser the transferee obtains the right to enforce the check. If the purchaser is not a holder in due course, the owner's claim to the check may be asserted against the purchaser. Ownership rights in instruments may be determined by principles of the law of property, independent of

Article 3, which do not depend upon whether the instrument was transferred under Section 3-203. Moreover, a person who has an ownership right in an instrument might not be a person entitled to enforce the instrument. For example, suppose X is the owner and holder of an instrument payable to X. X sells the instrument to Y but is unable to deliver immediate possession to Y. Instead, X signs a document conveying all of X's right, title, and interest in the instrument to Y. Although the document may be effective to give Y a claim to ownership of the instrument, Y is not a person entitled to enforce the instrument until Y obtains possession of the instrument. No transfer of the instrument occurs under Section 3-203(a) until it is delivered to Y.

An instrument is a reified right to payment. The right is represented by the instrument itself. The right to payment is transferred by delivery of possession of the instrument "by a person other than its issuer for the purpose of giving to the person receiving delivery the right to enforce the instrument." The quoted phrase excludes issue of an instrument, defined in Section 3-105, and cases in which a delivery of possession is for some purpose other than transfer of the right to enforce. For example, if a check is presented for payment by delivering the check to the drawee, no transfer of the check to the drawee occurs because there is no intent to give the drawee the right to enforce the check.

2. Subsection (b) states that transfer vests in the transferee any right of the transferor to enforce the instrument "including any right as a holder in due course." If the transferee is not a holder because the transferor did not indorse, the transferee is nevertheless a person entitled to enforce the instrument under Section 3-301 if the transferor was a holder at the time of transfer. Although the transferee is not a holder, under subsection (b) the transferee obtained the rights of the transferor as holder. Because the transferee's rights are derivative of the transferor's rights, those rights must be proved. Because the transferee is not a holder, there is no presumption under Section 3-308 that the transferee, by producing the instrument, is entitled to payment. The instrument, by its terms, is not payable to the transferee and the transferee must account for possession of the unindorsed instrument by proving the transaction through which the transferee acquired it. Proof of a transfer to the transferee by a holder is proof that the transferee has acquired the rights of a holder. At that point the transferee is entitled to the presumption under Section 3-308.

Under subsection (b) a holder in due course that transfers an instrument transfers those rights as a holder in due course to the purchaser. The policy is to assure the holder in due course a free market for the instrument. There is one exception to this rule stated in the concluding clause of subsection (b). A person who is party to fraud or illegality affecting the instrument is not permitted to wash the instrument clean by passing it into the hands of a holder in due course and then repurchasing it.

3. Subsection (c) applies only to a transfer for value. It applies only if the instrument is payable to order or specially indorsed to the transferor. The transferee acquires, in the absence of a contrary agreement, the specifically enforceable right to the indorsement of the transferor. Unless otherwise agreed, it is a right to the general indorsement of the transferor with full liability as indorser, rather than to an indorsement without recourse. The question may arise if the transferee has paid in advance and the indorsement is omitted fraudulently or through oversight. A transferor who is willing to indorse only without recourse or unwilling to indorse at all should make those intentions clear before transfer. The agreement of the transferee to take less than an unqualified indorsement need not be an express one, and the understanding may be implied from conduct, from past practice, or from the circumstances of the transaction. Subsection (c) provides that there is no negotiation of the instrument until the indorsement by the transferor is made. Until that time the transferee does not become a holder, and if earlier notice of a defense or claim is received, the transferee does not qualify as a holder in due course under Section 3–302.

4. The operation of Section 3–203 is illustrated by the following cases. In each case Payee, by fraud, induced Maker to issue a note to Payee. The fraud is a defense to the obligation of Maker to pay the note under Section 3–305(a)(2).

Case # 1. Payee negotiated the note to X who took as a holder in due course. After the instrument became overdue X negotiated the note to Y who had notice of the fraud. Y succeeds to X's rights as a holder in due course and takes free of Maker's defense of fraud.

Case # 2. Payee negotiated the note to X who took as a holder in due course. Payee then repurchased the note from X. Payee does not succeed to X's rights as a holder in due course and is subject to Maker's defense of fraud.

Case # 3. Payee negotiated the note to X who took as a holder in due course. X sold the note to

Purchaser who received possession. The note, however, was indorsed to X and X failed to indorse it. Purchaser is a person entitled to enforce the instrument under Section 3–301 and succeeds to the rights of X as holder in due course. Purchaser is not a holder, however, and under Section 3–308 Purchaser will have to prove the transaction with X under which the rights of X as holder in due course were acquired.

Case # 4. Payee sold the note to Purchaser who took for value, in good faith and without notice of the defense of Maker. Purchaser received possession of the note but Payee neglected to indorse it. Purchaser became a person entitled to enforce the instrument but did not become the holder because of the missing indorsement. If Purchaser received notice of the defense of Maker before obtaining the indorsement of Payee, Purchaser cannot become a holder in due course because at the time notice was received the note had not been negotiated to Purchaser. If indorsement by Payee was made after Purchaser received notice, Purchaser had notice of the defense when it became the holder.

5. Subsection (d) restates former Section 3–202(3). The cause of action on an instrument cannot be split. Any indorsement which purports to convey to any party less than the entire amount of the instrument is not effective for negotiation. This is true of either "Pay A one-half," or "Pay A two-thirds and B one-third." Neither A nor B becomes a holder. On the other hand an indorsement reading merely "Pay A and B" is effective, since it transfers the entire cause of action to A and B as tenants in common. An indorsement purporting to convey less than the entire instrument does, however, operate as a partial assignment of the cause of action. Subsection (d) makes no attempt to state the legal effect of such an assignment, which is left to other law. A partial assignee of an instrument has rights only to the extent the applicable law gives rights, either at law or in equity, to a partial assignee.

6. The rules for transferring instruments set out in this section are similar to the rules in Article 13 of the Convention on International Bills of Exchange and International Promissory Notes.

As amended in 2002.

§ 3–204. Indorsement.

(a) "Indorsement" means a signature, other than that of a signer as maker, drawer, or acceptor, that alone or accompanied by other words is made on an instrument for the purpose of (i) negotiating the instrument, (ii) restricting payment of the instrument, or (iii) incurring indorser's liability on the instrument, but regardless of the intent of the signer, a signature and its accompanying words is an indorsement unless the accompanying words, terms of the instrument, place of the signature, or other circumstances unambiguously indicate that the signature was made for a purpose other than indorsement. For the purpose of determining whether a signature is made on an instrument, a paper affixed to the instrument is a part of the instrument.

(b) "Indorser" means a person who makes an indorsement.

(c) For the purpose of determining whether the transferee of an instrument is a holder, an indorsement that transfers a security interest in the instrument is effective as an unqualified indorsement of the instrument.

(d) If an instrument is payable to a holder under a name that is not the name of the holder, indorsement may be made by the holder in the name stated in the instrument or in the holder's name or both, but signature in both names may be required by a person paying or taking the instrument for value or collection.

Official Comment

1. Subsection (a) is a definition of "indorsement," a term which was not defined in former Article 3. Indorsement is defined in terms of the purpose of the signature. If a blank or special indorsement is made to give rights as a holder to a transferee the indorsement is made for the purpose of negotiating the instrument. Subsection (a)(i). If the holder of a check has an account in the drawee bank and wants to be sure that payment of the check will be made by credit to the holder's account, the holder can indorse the check by signing the holder's name with the accompanying words "for deposit only" before presenting the check for payment to the drawee bank. In that case the purpose of the quoted words is to restrict payment of the instrument. Subsection (a)(ii). If X wants to guarantee payment of a note signed by Y as maker, X can do so by signing X's name to the back of the note as an indorsement. This indorsement is known as an anomalous indorsement (Section 3–205(d)) and is made for the purpose of incurring indorser's liability on the note. Subsection (a)(iii). In some cases an indorsement may serve more than one purpose. For example, if the holder of a check deposits it to the holder's

account in a depositary bank for collection and indorses the check by signing the holder's name with the accompanying words "for deposit only" the purpose of the indorsement is both to negotiate the check to the depositary bank and to restrict payment of the check.

The "but" clause of the first sentence of subsection (a) elaborates on former Section 3–402. In some cases it may not be clear whether a signature was meant to be that of an indorser, a party to the instrument in some other capacity such as drawer, maker or acceptor, or a person who was not signing as a party. The general rule is that a signature is an indorsement if the instrument does not indicate an unambiguous intent of the signer not to sign as an indorser. Intent may be determined by words accompanying the signature, the place of signature, or other circumstances. For example, suppose a depositary bank gives cash for a check properly indorsed by the payee. The bank requires the payee's employee to sign the back of the check as evidence that the employee received the cash. If the signature consists only of the initials of the employee it is not reasonable to assume that it was meant to be an indorsement. If there was a full signature but accompanying words indicated that it was meant as a receipt for the cash given for the check, it is not an indorsement. If the signature is not qualified in any way and appears in the place normally used for indorsements, it may be an indorsement even though the signer intended the signature to be a receipt. To take another example, suppose the drawee of a draft signs the draft on the back in the space usually used for indorsements. No words accompany the signature. Since the drawee has no reason to sign a draft unless the intent is to accept the draft, the signature is effective as an acceptance. Custom and usage may be used to determine intent. For example, by long-established custom and usage, a signature in the lower right hand corner of an instrument indicates an intent to sign as the maker of a note or the drawer of a draft. Any similar clear indication of an intent to sign in some other capacity or for some other purpose may establish that a signature is not an indorsement. For example, if the owner of a traveler's check countersigns the check in the process of negotiating it, the countersignature is not an indorsement. The countersignature is a condition to the issuer's obligation to pay and its purpose is to provide a means of verifying the identify of the person negotiating the traveler's check by allowing comparison of the specimen signature and the countersignature. The countersignature is not necessary for negotiation and the signer does not incur indorser's liability. See Comment 2 to Section 3–106.

The last sentence of subsection (a) is based on subsection (2) of former Section 3–202. An indorsement on an allonge is valid even though there is sufficient space on the instrument for an indorsement.

2. Assume that Payee indorses a note to Creditor as security for a debt. Under subsection (b) of Section 3–203 Creditor takes Payee's rights to enforce or transfer the instrument subject to the limitations imposed by Article 9. Subsection (c) of Section 3–204 makes clear that Payee's indorsement to Creditor, even though it mentions creation of a security interest, is an unqualified indorsement that gives to Creditor the right to enforce the note as its holder.

3. Subsection (d) is a restatement of former Section 3–203. Section 3–110(a) states that an instrument is payable to the person intended by the person signing as or in the name or behalf of the issuer even if that person is identified by a name that is not the true name of the person. In some cases the name used in the instrument is a misspelling of the correct name and in some cases the two names may be entirely different. The payee may indorse in the name used in the instrument, in the payee's correct name, or in both. In each case the indorsement is effective. But because an indorsement in a name different from that used in the instrument may raise a question about its validity and an indorsement in a name that is not the correct name of the payee may raise a problem of identifying the indorser, the accepted commercial practice is to indorse in both names. Subsection (d) allows a person paying or taking the instrument for value or collection to require indorsement in both names.

§ 3–205. Special Indorsement; Blank Indorsement; Anomalous Indorsement.

(a) If an indorsement is made by the holder of an instrument, whether payable to an identified person or payable to bearer, and the indorsement identifies a person to whom it makes the instrument payable, it is a "special indorsement." When specially indorsed, an instrument becomes payable to the identified person and may be negotiated only by the indorsement of that person. The principles stated in Section 3–110 apply to special indorsements.

(b) If an indorsement is made by the holder of an instrument and it is not a special indorsement, it is a "blank indorsement." When indorsed in blank, an instrument becomes payable to bearer and may be negotiated by transfer of possession alone until specially indorsed.

(c) The holder may convert a blank indorsement that consists only of a signature into a special indorsement by writing, above the signature of the indorser, words identifying the person to whom the instrument is made payable.

(d) "Anomalous indorsement" means an indorsement made by a person who is not the holder of the instrument. An anomalous indorsement does not affect the manner in which the instrument may be negotiated.

Official Comment

1. Subsection (a) is based on subsection (1) of former Section 3–204. It states the test of a special indorsement to be whether the indorsement identifies a person to whom the instrument is payable. Section 3–110 states rules for identifying the payee of an instrument. Section 3–205(a) incorporates the principles stated in Section 3–110 in identifying an indorsee. The language of Section 3–110 refers to language used by the issuer of the instrument. When that section is used with respect to an indorsement, Section 3–110 must be read as referring to the language used by the indorser.

2. Subsection (b) is based on subsection (2) of former Section 3–204. An indorsement made by the holder is either a special or blank indorsement. If the indorsement is made by a holder and is not a special indorsement, it is a blank indorsement. For example, the holder of an instrument, intending to make a special indorsement, writes the words "Pay to the order of" without completing the indorsement by writing the name of the indorsee. The holder's signature appears under the quoted words. The indorsement is not a special indorsement because it does not identify a person to whom it makes the instrument payable. Since it is not a special indorsement it is a blank indorsement and the instrument is payable to bearer. The result is analogous to that of a check in which the name of the payee is left blank by the drawer. In that case the check is payable to bearer. See the last paragraphs of Comment 2 to Section 3–115.

A blank indorsement is usually the signature of the indorser on the back of the instrument without other words. Subsection (c) is based on subsection (3) of former Section 3–204. A "restrictive indorsement" described in Section 3–206 can be either a blank indorsement or a special indorsement. "Pay to T, in trust for B" is a restrictive indorsement. It is also a special indorsement because it identifies T as the person to whom the instrument is payable. "For deposit only" followed by the signature of the payee of a check is a restrictive indorsement. It is also a blank indorsement because it does not identify the person to whom the instrument is payable.

3. The only effect of an "anomalous indorsement," defined in subsection (d), is to make the signer liable on the instrument as an indorser. Such an indorsement is normally made by an accommodation party. Section 3–419.

4. Articles 14 and 16 of the Convention on International Bills of Exchange and International Promissory Notes includes similar rules for blank and special indorsements.

As amended in 2002.

§ 3–206. Restrictive Indorsement.

(a) An indorsement limiting payment to a particular person or otherwise prohibiting further transfer or negotiation of the instrument is not effective to prevent further transfer or negotiation of the instrument.

(b) An indorsement stating a condition to the right of the indorsee to receive payment does not affect the right of the indorsee to enforce the instrument. A person paying the instrument or taking it for value or collection may disregard the condition, and the rights and liabilities of that person are not affected by whether the condition has been fulfilled.

(c) If an instrument bears an indorsement (i) described in Section 4–201(b), or (ii) in blank or to a particular bank using the words "for deposit," "for collection," or other words indicating a purpose of having the instrument collected by a bank for the indorser or for a particular account, the following rules apply:

(1) A person, other than a bank, who purchases the instrument when so indorsed converts the instrument unless the amount paid for the instrument is received by the indorser or applied consistently with the indorsement.

(2) A depositary bank that purchases the instrument or takes it for collection when so indorsed converts the instrument unless the amount paid by the bank with respect to the instrument is received by the indorser or applied consistently with the indorsement.

(3) A payor bank that is also the depositary bank or that takes the instrument for immediate payment over the counter from a person other than a collecting bank converts the instrument unless the proceeds of the instrument are received by the indorser or applied consistently with the indorsement.

(4) Except as otherwise provided in paragraph (3), a payor bank or intermediary bank may disregard the indorsement and is not liable if the proceeds of the instrument are not received by the indorser or applied consistently with the indorsement.

(d) Except for an indorsement covered by subsection (c), if an instrument bears an indorsement using words to the effect that payment is to be made to the indorsee as agent, trustee, or other fiduciary for the benefit of the indorser or another person, the following rules apply:

(1) Unless there is notice of breach of fiduciary duty as provided in Section 3–307, a person who purchases the instrument from the indorsee or takes the instrument from the indorsee for collection or payment may pay the proceeds of payment or the value given for the instrument to the indorsee without regard to whether the indorsee violates a fiduciary duty to the indorser.

(2) A subsequent transferee of the instrument or person who pays the instrument is neither given notice nor otherwise affected by the restriction in the indorsement unless the transferee or payor knows that the fiduciary dealt with the instrument or its proceeds in breach of fiduciary duty.

(e) The presence on an instrument of an indorsement to which this section applies does not prevent a purchaser of the instrument from becoming a holder in due course of the instrument unless the purchaser is a converter under subsection (c) or has notice or knowledge of breach of fiduciary duty as stated in subsection (d).

(f) In an action to enforce the obligation of a party to pay the instrument, the obligor has a defense if payment would violate an indorsement to which this section applies and the payment is not permitted by this section.

Official Comment

1. This section replaces former Sections 3–205 and 3–206 and clarifies the law of restrictive indorsements.

2. Subsection (a) provides that an indorsement that purports to limit further transfer or negotiation is ineffective to prevent further transfer or negotiation. If a payee indorses "Pay A only," A may negotiate the instrument to subsequent holders who may ignore the restriction on the indorsement. Subsection (b) provides that an indorsement that states a condition to the right of a holder to receive payment is ineffective to condition payment. Thus if a payee indorses "Pay A if A ships goods complying with our contract," the right of A to enforce the instrument is not affected by the condition. In the case of a note, the obligation of the maker to pay A is not affected by the indorsement. In the case of a check, the drawee can pay A without regard to the condition, and if the check is dishonored the drawer is liable to pay A. If the check was negotiated by the payee to A in return for a promise to perform a contract and the promise was not kept, the payee would have a defense or counterclaim against A if the check were dishonored and A sued the payee as indorser, but the payee would have that defense or counterclaim whether or not the condition to the right of A was expressed in the indorsement. Former Section 3–206 treated a conditional indorsement like indorsements for deposit or collection. In revised Article 3, Section 3–206(b) rejects that approach and makes the conditional indorsement ineffective with respect to parties other than the indorser and indorsee. Since the indorsements referred to in subsections (a) and (b) are not effective as restrictive indorsements, they are no longer described as restrictive indorsements.

3. The great majority of restrictive indorsements are those that fall within subsection (c) which continues previous law. The depositary bank or the payor bank, if it takes the check for immediate payment over the counter, must act consistently with the indorsement, but an intermediary bank or payor bank that takes the check from a collecting bank is not affected by the indorsement. Any other person is also bound by the indorsement. For example, suppose a check is payable to X, who indorses in blank but writes above the signature the words "For deposit only." The check is stolen and is cashed at a grocery store by the thief. The grocery store indorses the check and deposits it in Depositary Bank. The account of the grocery store is credited and the check is forwarded to Payor Bank which pays the check. Under subsection (c), the grocery store and Depositary Bank are converters of the check because X did not receive the amount paid for the check. Payor Bank and any intermediary bank

in the collection process are not liable to X. This Article does not displace the law of waiver as it may apply to restrictive indorsements. The circumstances under which a restrictive indorsement may be waived by the person who made it is not determined by this Article.

4. Subsection (d) replaces subsection (4) of former Section 3–206. Suppose Payee indorses a check "Pay to T in trust for B." T indorses in blank and delivers it to (a) Holder for value; (b) Depositary Bank for collection; or (c) Payor Bank for payment. In each case these takers can safely pay T so long as they have no notice under Section 3–307 of any breach of fiduciary duty that T may be committing. For example, under subsection (b)* of Section 3–307 these takers have notice of a breach of trust if the check was taken in any transaction known by the taker to be for T's personal benefit. Subsequent transferees of the check from Holder or Depositary Bank are not affected by the restriction unless they have knowledge that T dealt with the check in breach of trust.

5. Subsection (f) allows a restrictive indorsement to be used as a defense by a person obliged to pay the instrument if that person would be liable for paying in violation of the indorsement.

Previous incorrect cross reference corrected by Permanent Editorial Board action November 1992.

§ 3–207. Reacquisition.

Reacquisition of an instrument occurs if it is transferred to a former holder, by negotiation or otherwise. A former holder who reacquires the instrument may cancel indorsements made after the reacquirer first became a holder of the instrument. If the cancellation causes the instrument to be payable to the reacquirer or to bearer, the reacquirer may negotiate the instrument. An indorser whose indorsement is canceled is discharged, and the discharge is effective against any subsequent holder.

Official Comment

Section 3–207 restates former Section 3–208. Reacquisition refers to cases in which a former holder reacquires the instrument either by negotiation from the present holder or by a transfer other than negotiation. If the reacquisition is by negotiation, the former holder reacquires the status of holder. Although Section 3–207 allows the holder to cancel all indorsements made after the holder first acquired holder status, cancellation is not necessary. Status of holder is not affected whether or not cancellation is made. But if the reacquisition is not the result of negotiation the former holder can obtain holder status only by striking the former holder's indorsement and any subsequent indorsements. The latter case is an exception to the general rule that if an instrument is payable to an identified person, the indorsement of that person is necessary to allow a subsequent transferee to obtain the status of holder. Reacquisition without indorsement by the person to whom the instrument is payable is illustrated by two examples:

Case # 1. X, a former holder, buys the instrument from Y, the present holder. Y delivers the instrument to X but fails to indorse it. Negotiation does not occur because the transfer of possession did not result in X's becoming holder. Section 3–201(a). The instrument by its terms is payable to Y, not to X. But X can obtain the status of holder by striking X's indorsement and all subsequent indorsements. When these indorsements are struck, the instrument by its terms is payable either to X or to bearer, depending upon how X originally became holder. In either case X becomes holder. Section 1–201(20).

Case # 2. X, the holder of an instrument payable to X, negotiates it to Y by special indorsement. The negotiation is part of an underlying transaction between X and Y. The underlying transaction is rescinded by agreement of X and Y, and Y returns the instrument without Y's indorsement. The analysis is the same as that in Case # 1. X can obtain holder status by cancelling X's indorsement to Y.

In Case # 1 and Case # 2, X acquired ownership of the instrument after reacquisition, but X's title was clouded because the instrument by its terms was not payable to X. Normally, X can remedy the problem by obtaining Y's indorsement, but in some cases X may not be able to conveniently obtain that indorsement. Section 3–207 is a rule of convenience which relieves X of the burden of obtaining an indorsement that serves no substantive purpose. The effect of cancellation of any indorsement under Section 3–207 is to nullify it. Thus, the person whose indorsement is canceled is relieved of indorser's liability. Since cancellation is notice of discharge, discharge is effective even with respect to the rights of a holder in due course. Sections 3–601 and 3–604.

PART 3

ENFORCEMENT OF INSTRUMENTS

§ 3–301. Person Entitled to Enforce Instrument.

"Person entitled to enforce" an instrument means (i) the holder of the instrument, (ii) a nonholder in possession of the instrument who has the rights of a holder, or (iii) a person not in possession of the instrument who is entitled to enforce the instrument pursuant to Section 3–309 or 3–418(d). A person may be a person entitled to enforce the instrument even though the person is not the owner of the instrument or is in wrongful possession of the instrument.

Official Comment

This section replaces former Section 3–301 that stated the rights of a holder. The rights stated in former Section 3–301 to transfer, negotiate, enforce, or discharge an instrument are stated in other sections of Article 3. In revised Article 3, Section 3–301 defines "person entitled to enforce" an instrument. The definition recognizes that enforcement is not limited to holders. The quoted phrase includes a person enforcing a lost or stolen instrument. Section 3–309. It also includes a person in possession of an instrument who

is not a holder. A nonholder in possession of an instrument includes a person that acquired rights of a holder by subrogation or under Section 3–203(a). It also includes both a remitter that has received an instrument from the issuer but has not yet transferred or negotiated the instrument to another person and also any other person who under applicable law is a successor to the holder or otherwise acquires the holder's rights.

As amended in 2002.

§ 3–302. Holder in Due Course.

(a) Subject to subsection (c) and Section 3–106(d), "holder in due course" means the holder of an instrument if: 3–104(a)–(d)   3–201, 3

(1) the instrument when issued or negotiated to the holder does not bear such apparent evidence of forgery or alteration or is not otherwise so irregular or incomplete as to call into question its authenticity; and

(2) the holder took the instrument (i) for value, (ii) in good faith, (iii) without no-

3–303   3–103(a)(6)   1–202(a)
A–210   1–201(b)(20)
A–211

tice that the instrument is overdue or has been dishonored or that there is an uncured default with respect to payment of another instrument issued as part of the same series, (iv) without notice that the instrument contains an unauthorized signature or has been altered, (v) without notice of any claim to the instrument described in Section 3–306, and (vi) without notice that any party has a defense or claim in recoupment described in Section 3–305(a).

(b) Notice of discharge of a party, other than discharge in an insolvency proceeding, is not notice of a defense under subsection (a), but discharge is effective against a person who became a holder in due course with notice of the discharge. Public filing or recording of a document does not of itself constitute notice of a defense, claim in recoupment, or claim to the instrument.

(c) Except to the extent a transferor or predecessor in interest has rights as a holder in due course, a person does not acquire rights of a holder in due course of an instrument taken (i) by legal process or by purchase in an execution, bankruptcy, or creditor's sale or similar proceeding, (ii) by purchase as part of a bulk transaction not in ordinary course of business of the transferor, or (iii) as the successor in interest to an estate or other organization.

(d) If, under Section 3–303(a)(1), the promise of performance that is the consideration for an instrument has been partially performed, the holder may assert rights as a holder in due course of the instrument only to the fraction of the amount payable under the instrument equal to the value of the partial performance divided by the value of the promised performance.

(e) If (i) the person entitled to enforce an instrument has only a security interest in the instrument and (ii) the person obliged to pay the instrument has a defense, claim in recoupment, or claim to the instrument that may be asserted against the person who granted the security interest, the person entitled to enforce the instrument may assert rights as a holder in due course only to an amount payable under the instrument which, at the time of enforcement of the instrument, does not exceed the amount of the unpaid obligation secured.

(f) To be effective, notice must be received at a time and in a manner that gives a reasonable opportunity to act on it.

(g) This section is subject to any law limiting status as a holder in due course in particular classes of transactions.

Official Comment

1. Subsection (a)(1) is a return to the N.I.L. rule that the taker of an irregular or incomplete instrument is not a person the law should protect against defenses of the obligor or claims of prior owners. This reflects a policy choice against extending the holder in due course doctrine to an instrument that is so incomplete or irregular "as to call into question its authenticity." The term "authenticity" is used to make it clear that the irregularity or incompleteness must indicate that the instrument may not be what it purports to be. Persons who purchase or pay such instruments should do so at their own risk. Under subsection (1) of former Section 3–304, irregularity or incompleteness gave a purchaser notice of a claim or defense. But it was not clear from that provision whether the claim or defense had to be related to the irregularity or incomplete aspect of the instrument. This ambiguity is not present in subsection (a)(1).

2. Subsection (a)(2) restates subsection (1) of former Section 3–302. Section 3–305(a) makes a distinction between defenses to the obligation to pay an instrument and claims in recoupment by the maker or drawer that may be asserted to reduce the amount payable on the instrument. Because of this distinction, which was not made in former Article 3, the reference in subsection (a)(2)(vi) is to both a defense and a claim in recoupment. Notice of forgery or alteration is stated separately because forgery and alteration are not technically defenses under subsection (a) of Section 3–305.

3. Discharge is also separately treated in the first sentence of subsection (b). Except for discharge in an insolvency proceeding, which is specifically stated to be a real defense in Section 3–305(a)(1), discharge is not expressed in Article 3 as a defense and is not included in Section 3–305(a)(2). Discharge is effective against anybody except a person having rights of a holder in due course who took the instrument without notice of the discharge. Notice of discharge does not disqualify a person from becoming a holder in due course. For example, a check certified after it is negotiated by the payee may subsequently be negotiated to a holder. If the holder had notice that the certification occurred after negotiation by the payee, the holder necessarily

had notice of the discharge of the payee as indorser. Section 3–415(d). Notice of that discharge does not prevent the holder from becoming a holder in due course, but the discharge is effective against the holder. Section 3–601(b). Notice of a defense under Section 3–305(a)(1) of a maker, drawer or acceptor based on a bankruptcy discharge is different. There is no reason to give holder in due course status to a person with notice of that defense. The second sentence of subsection (b) is from former Section 3–304(5).

4. Professor Britton in his treatise Bills and Notes 309 (1961) stated: "A substantial number of decisions before the [N.I.L.] indicates that at common law there was nothing in the position of the payee as such which made it impossible for him to be a holder in due course." The courts were divided, however, about whether the payee of an instrument could be a holder in due course under the N.I.L.. Some courts read N.I.L. § 52(4) to mean that a person could be a holder in due course only if the instrument was "negotiated" to that person. N.I.L. § 30 stated that "an instrument is negotiated when it is transferred from one person to another in such manner as to constitute the transferee the holder thereof." Normally, an instrument is "issued" to the payee; it is not transferred to the payee. N.I.L. § 191 defined "issue" as the "first delivery of the instrument *** to a person who takes it as a holder." Thus, some courts concluded that the payee never could be a holder in due course. Other courts concluded that there was no evidence that the N.I.L. was intended to change the common law rule that the payee could be a holder in due course. Professor Britton states on p. 318: "The typical situations which raise the [issue] are those where the defense of a maker is interposed because of fraud by a [maker who is] principal debtor *** against a surety co-maker, or where the defense of fraud by a purchasing remitter is interposed by the drawer of the instrument against the good faith purchasing payee."

Former Section 3–302(2) stated: "A payee may be a holder in due course." This provision was intended to resolve the split of authority under the N.I.L.. It made clear that there was no intent to change the common-law rule that allowed a payee to become a holder in due course. See Comment 2 to former Section 3–302. But there was no need to put subsection (2) in former Section 3–302 because the split in authority under the N.I.L. was caused by the particular wording of N.I.L. § 52(4). The troublesome language in that section was not repeated in former Article 3 nor is it repeated in revised Article 3. Former Section 3–302(2) has been omitted in revised Article 3 because it is surplusage and may be misleading. The payee of an instrument

can be a holder in due course, but use of the holder-in-due-course doctrine by the payee of an instrument is not the normal situation.

The primary importance of the concept of holder in due course is with respect to assertion of defenses or claims in recoupment (Section 3–305) and of claims to the instrument (Section 3–306). The holder-in-due-course doctrine assumes the following case as typical. Obligor issues a note or check to Obligee. Obligor is the maker of the note or drawer of the check. Obligee is the payee. Obligor has some defense to Obligor's obligation to pay the instrument. For example, Obligor issued the instrument for goods that Obligee promised to deliver. Obligee never delivered the goods. The failure of Obligee to deliver the goods is a defense. Section 3–303(b). Although Obligor has a defense against Obligee, if the instrument is negotiated to Holder and the requirements of subsection (a) are met, Holder may enforce the instrument against Obligor free of the defense. Section 3–305(b). In the typical case the holder in due course is not the payee of the instrument. Rather, the holder in due course is an immediate or remote transferee of the payee. If Obligor in our example is the only obligor on the check or note, the holder-in-due-course doctrine is irrelevant in determining rights between Obligor and Obligee with respect to the instrument.

But in a small percentage of cases it is appropriate to allow the payee of an instrument to assert rights as a holder in due course. The cases are like those referred to in the quotation from Professor Britton referred to above, or other cases in which conduct of some third party is the basis of the defense of the issuer of the instrument. The following are examples:

Case # 1. Buyer pays for goods bought from Seller by giving to Seller a cashier's check bought from Bank. Bank has a defense to its obligation to pay the check because Buyer bought the check from Bank with a check known to be drawn on an account with insufficient funds to cover the check. If Bank issued the check to Buyer as payee and Buyer indorsed it over to Seller, it is clear that Seller can be a holder in due course taking free of the defense if Seller had no notice of the defense. Seller is a transferee of the check. There is no good reason why Seller's position should be any different if Bank drew the check to the order of Seller as payee. In that case, when Buyer took delivery of the check from Bank, Buyer became the owner of the check even though Buyer was not the holder. Buyer was a remitter. Section 3–103(a)(15). At that point nobody was the holder. When Buyer delivered the check to Seller, ownership of the check was transferred to Seller who also became the holder. This is a negotiation. Section 3–201. The rights of Seller should not be affected by the fact that in one case the negotiation to Seller was by a holder and in the other case the negotiation was by a remitter. Moreover, it should be irrelevant whether Bank delivered the check to Buyer and Buyer delivered it to Seller or whether Bank delivered it directly to Seller. In either case Seller can be a holder in due course that takes free of Bank's defense.

Case # 2. X fraudulently induces Y to join X in a spurious venture to purchase a business. The purchase is to be financed by a bank loan for part of the price. Bank lends money to X and Y by deposit in a joint account of X and Y who sign a note payable to Bank for the amount of the loan. X then withdraws the money from the joint account and absconds. Bank acted in good faith and without notice of the fraud of X against Y. Bank is payee of the note executed by Y, but its right to enforce the note against Y should not be affected by the fact that Y was induced to execute the note by the fraud of X. Bank can be a holder in due course that takes free of the defense of Y. Case # 2 is similar to Case # 1. In each case the payee of the instrument has given value to the person committing the fraud in exchange for the obligation of the person against whom the fraud was committed. In each case the payee was not party to the fraud and had no notice of it.

Suppose in Case # 2 that the note does not meet the requirements of Section 3–104(a) and thus is not a negotiable instrument covered by Article 3. In that case, Bank cannot be a holder in due course but the result should be the same. Bank's rights are determined by general principles of contract law. Restatement Second, Contracts § 164(2) governs the case. If Y is induced to enter into a contract with Bank by a fraudulent misrepresentation by X, the contract is voidable by Y unless Bank "in good faith and without reason to know of the misrepresentation either gives value or relies materially on the transaction." Comment e to § 164(2) states:

"This is the same principle that protects an innocent person who purchases goods or commercial paper in good faith, without notice and for value from one who obtained them from the original owner by a misrepresentation. See Uniform Commercial Code §§ 2–403(1), 3–305. In the cases that fall within [§ 164(2)], however, the innocent person deals directly with the recipient of the misrepresentation, which is made by one not a party to the contract."

The same result follows in Case # 2 if Y had been induced to sign the note as an accommodation party (Section 3–419). If Y signs as co-maker of a note for the benefit of X, Y is a surety with respect to the obligation of X to pay the note but is liable as maker of the note to pay Bank. Section 3–419(b). If Bank is a holder in due course, the fraud of X cannot be asserted against Bank under Section 3–305(b). But the result is the same without resort to holder-in-due-course doctrine. If the note is not a negotiable instrument governed by Article 3, general rules of suretyship apply. Restatement, Security § 119 states that the surety (Y) cannot assert a defense against the creditor (Bank) based on the fraud of the principal (X) if the creditor "without knowledge of the fraud *** extended credit to the principal on the security of the surety's promise ***." The underlying principle of § 119 is the same as that of § 164(2) of Restatement Second, Contracts.

Case # 3. Corporation draws a check payable to Bank. The check is given to an officer of Corporation who is instructed to deliver it to Bank in payment of a debt owed by Corporation to Bank. Instead, the officer, intending to defraud Corporation, delivers the check to Bank in payment of the officer's personal debt, or the check is delivered to Bank for deposit to the officer's personal account. If Bank obtains payment of the check, Bank has received funds of Corporation which have been used for the personal benefit of the officer. Corporation in this case will assert a claim to the proceeds of the check against Bank. If Bank was a holder in due course of the check it took the check free of Corporation's claim. Section 3–306. The issue in this case is whether Bank had notice of the claim when it took the check. If Bank knew that the officer was a fiduciary with respect to the check, the issue is governed by Section 3–307.

Case # 4. Employer, who owed money to X, signed a blank check and delivered it to Secretary with instructions to complete the check by typing in X's name and the amount owed to X. Secretary fraudulently completed the check by typing in the name of Y, a creditor to whom Secretary owed money. Secretary then delivered the check to Y in payment of Secretary's debt. Y obtained payment of the check. This case is similar to Case # 3. Since Secretary was authorized to complete the check, Employer is bound by Secretary's act in making the check payable to Y. The drawee bank properly paid the check. Y received funds of Employer which were used for the personal benefit of Secretary. Employer asserts a claim to these funds against Y. If Y is a holder in due course, Y takes free of the claim. Whether Y is a holder in due course depends upon whether Y had notice of Employer's claim.

5. Subsection (c) is based on former Section 3–302(3). Like former Section 3–302(3), subsection (c) is intended to state existing case law. It covers a few situations in which the purchaser takes an instrument under unusual circumstances. The purchaser is treated as a successor in interest to the prior holder and can acquire no better rights. But if the prior holder was a holder in due course, the purchaser obtains rights of a holder in due course.

Subsection (c) applies to a purchaser in an execution sale or sale in bankruptcy. It applies equally to an attaching creditor or any other person who acquires the instrument by legal process or to a representative, such as an executor, administrator, receiver or assignee for the benefit of creditors, who takes the instrument as part of an estate. Subsection (c) applies to bulk purchases lying outside of the ordinary course of business of the seller. For example, it applies to the purchase by one bank of a substantial part of the paper held by another bank which is threatened with insolvency and seeking to liquidate its assets. Subsection (c) would also apply when a new partnership takes over for value all of the assets of an old one after a new member has entered the firm, or to a reorganized or consolidated corporation taking over the assets of a predecessor.

In the absence of controlling state law to the contrary, subsection (c) applies to a sale by a state bank commissioner of the assets of an insolvent bank. However, subsection (c) may be preempted by federal law if the Federal Deposit Insurance Corporation takes over an insolvent bank. Under the governing federal law, the FDIC and similar financial institution insurers are given holder in due course status and that status is also acquired by their assignees under the shelter doctrine.

6. Subsections (d) and (e) clarify two matters not specifically addressed by former Article 3:

Case # 5. Payee negotiates a $1,000 note to Holder who agrees to pay $900 for it. After paying $500, Holder learns that Payee defrauded Maker in the transaction giving rise to the note. Under subsection (d) Holder may assert rights as a holder in due course to the extent of $555.55 ($500 ÷ $900 = .555 × $1,000 = $555.55). This formula rewards Holder with a ratable portion of the bargained for profit.

Case # 6. Payee negotiates a note of Maker for $1,000 to Holder as security for payment of Payee's debt to Holder of $600. Maker has a defense which is good against Payee but of which Holder has no notice. Subsection (e) applies. Holder may assert rights as a holder in due course only to the extent of $600. Payee does not get the benefit of the holder-in-due-course status of Holder. With respect to $400 of the note, Maker may assert any rights that Maker has against Payee. A different result follows if the payee of a note negotiated it to a person who took it as a holder in due course and that person pledged the note as security for a debt. Because the defense cannot be asserted against the pledgor, the pledgee can assert rights as a holder in due course for the full amount of the note for the benefit of both the pledgor and the pledgee.

7. There is a large body of state statutory and case law restricting the use of the holder in due course doctrine in consumer transactions as well as some business transactions that raise similar issues. Subsection (g) subordinates Article 3 to that law and any other similar law that may evolve in the future. Section 3–106(d) also relates to statutory or administrative law intended to restrict use of the holder-in-due-course doctrine. See Comment 3 to Section 3–106.

8. The status of holder in due course resembles the status of protected holder under Article 29 of the Convention on International Bills of Exchange and International Promissory Notes. The requirements for being a protected holder under Article 29 generally track those of Section 3–302.

As amended in 2002.

§ 3–303. Value and Consideration.

(a) An instrument is issued or transferred for value if:

    (1) the instrument is issued or transferred for a promise of performance, to the extent the promise has been performed;

    (2) the transferee acquires a security interest or other lien in the instrument other than a lien obtained by judicial proceeding;

    (3) the instrument is issued or transferred as payment of, or as security for, an antecedent claim against any person, whether or not the claim is due;

    (4) the instrument is issued or transferred in exchange for a negotiable instrument; or

(5) the instrument is issued or transferred in exchange for the incurring of an irrevocable obligation to a third party by the person taking the instrument.

(b) "Consideration" means any consideration sufficient to support a simple contract. The drawer or maker of an instrument has a defense if the instrument is issued without consideration. If an instrument is issued for a promise of performance, the issuer has a defense to the extent performance of the promise is due and the promise has not been performed. If an instrument is issued for value as stated in subsection (a), the instrument is also issued for consideration.

Official Comment

1. Subsection (a) is a restatement of former Section 3–303 and subsection (b) replaces former Section 3–408. The distinction between value and consideration in Article 3 is a very fine one. Whether an instrument is taken for value is relevant to the issue of whether a holder is a holder in due course. If an instrument is not issued for consideration the issuer has a defense to the obligation to pay the instrument. Consideration is defined in subsection (b) as "any consideration sufficient to support a simple contract." The definition of value in Section 1–201(44), which doesn't apply to Article 3, includes "any consideration sufficient to support a simple contract." Thus, outside Article 3, anything that is consideration is also value. A different rule applies in Article 3. Subsection (b) of Section 3–303 states that if an instrument is issued for value it is also issued for consideration.

Case # 1. X owes Y $1,000. The debt is not represented by a note. Later X issues a note to Y for the debt. Under subsection (a)(3) X's note is issued for value. Under subsection (b) the note is also issued for consideration whether or not, under contract law, Y is deemed to have given consideration for the note.

Case # 2. X issues a check to Y in consideration of Y's promise to perform services in the future. Although the executory promise is consideration for issuance of the check it is value only to the extent the promise is performed. Subsection (a)(1).

Case # 3. X issues a note to Y in consideration of Y's promise to perform services. If at the due date of the note Y's performance is not yet due, Y may enforce the note because it was issued for consideration. But if at the due date of the note, Y's

performance is due and has not been performed, X has a defense. Subsection (b).

2. Subsection (a), which defines value, has primary importance in cases in which the issue is whether the holder of an instrument is a holder in due course and particularly to cases in which the issuer of the instrument has a defense to the instrument. Suppose Buyer and Seller signed a contract on April 1 for the sale of goods to be delivered on May 1. Payment of 50% of the price of the goods was due upon signing of the contract. On April 1 Buyer delivered to Seller a check in the amount due under the contract. The check was drawn by X to Buyer as payee and was indorsed to Seller. When the check was presented for payment to the drawee on April 2, it was dishonored because X had stopped payment. At that time Seller had not taken any action to perform the contract with Buyer. If X has a defense on the check, the defense can be asserted against Seller who is not a holder in due course because Seller did not give value for the check. Subsection (a)(1). The policy basis for subsection (a)(1) is that the holder who gives an executory promise of performance will not suffer an out-of-pocket loss to the extent the executory promise is unperformed at the time the holder learns of dishonor of the instrument. When Seller took delivery of the check on April 1, Buyer's obligation to pay 50% of the price on that date was suspended, but when the check was dishonored on April 2 the obligation revived. Section 3–310(b). If payment for goods is due at or before delivery and the buyer fails to make the payment, the seller is excused from performing the promise to deliver the goods. Section 2–703. Thus, Seller is protected from an out-of-pocket loss even if the check is not enforceable. Holder-in-due-course status is not necessary to protect Seller.

3. Subsection (a)(2) equates value with the obtaining of a security interest or a nonjudicial lien in the instrument. The term "security interest" covers Article 9 cases in which an instrument is taken as collateral as well as bank collection cases in which a bank acquires a security interest under Section 4–210. The acquisition of a common-law or statutory banker's lien is also value under subsection (a)(2). An attaching creditor or other person who acquires a lien by judicial proceedings does not give value for the purposes of subsection (a)(2).

4. Subsection (a)(3) follows former Section 3–303(b) in providing that the holder takes for value if the instrument is taken in payment of or as security for an antecedent claim, even though there is no extension of time or other concession, and whether or not the claim is due. Subsection (a)(3) applies to any claim against

any person; there is no requirement that the claim arise out of contract. In particular the provision is intended to apply to an instrument given in payment of or as security for the debt of a third person, even though no concession is made in return.

5. Subsection (a)(4) and (5) restate former Section 3–303(c). They state generally recognized exceptions to the rule that an executory promise is not value. A negotiable instrument is value because it carries the possibility of negotiation to a holder in due course, after which the party who gives it is obliged to pay. The same reasoning applies to any irrevocable commitment to a third person, such as a letter of credit issued when an instrument is taken.

6. The term "promise" in paragraph (a)(1) is used in the phrase "promise of performance" and for that reason does not have the specialized meaning given that term in Section 3–103(a)(12). See Section 1–201 ("Changes from Former Law"). No inference should be drawn from the decision to use the phrase "promise of performance," although the phrase does include the word "promise," which has the specialized definition set forth in Section 3–103. Indeed, that is true even though "undertaking" is used instead of "promise" in Section 3–104(a)(3). See Section 3–104 comment 1 (explaining the use of the term "undertaking" in Section 3–104 to avoid use of the defined term "promise").

As amended in 2002.

§ 3–304. Overdue Instrument.

(a) An instrument payable on demand becomes overdue at the earliest of the following times:

    (1) on the day after the day demand for payment is duly made;

    (2) if the instrument is a check, 90 days after its date; or

    (3) if the instrument is not a check, when the instrument has been outstanding for a period of time after its date which is unreasonably long under the circumstances of the particular case in light of the nature of the instrument and usage of the trade.

(b) With respect to an instrument payable at a definite time the following rules apply:

    (1) If the principal is payable in installments and a due date has not been accelerated, the instrument becomes overdue upon default under the instrument for non-payment of an installment, and the in-

strument remains overdue until the default is cured.

    (2) If the principal is not payable in installments and the due date has not been accelerated, the instrument becomes overdue on the day after the due date.

    (3) If a due date with respect to principal has been accelerated, the instrument becomes overdue on the day after the accelerated due date.

(c) Unless the due date of principal has been accelerated, an instrument does not become overdue if there is default in payment of interest but no default in payment of principal.

Official Comment

1. To be a holder in due course, one must take without notice that an instrument is overdue. Section 3–302(a)(2)(iii). Section 3–304 replaces subsection (3) of former Section 3–304. For the sake of clarity it treats demand and time instruments separately. Subsection (a) applies to demand instruments. A check becomes stale after 90 days.

Under former Section 3–304(3)(c), a holder that took a demand note had notice that it was overdue if it was taken "more than a reasonable length of time after its issue." In substitution for this test, subsection (a)(3) requires the trier of fact to look at both the circumstances of the particular case and the nature of the instrument and trade usage. Whether a demand note is stale may vary a great deal depending on the facts of the particular case.

2. Subsections (b) and (c) cover time instruments. They follow the distinction made under former Article 3 between defaults in payment of principal and interest. In subsection (b) installment instruments and single payment instruments are treated separately. If an installment is late, the instrument is overdue until the default is cured.

§ 3–305. Defenses and Claims in Recoupment.

(a) Except as otherwise provided in this section, the right to enforce the obligation of a party to pay an instrument is subject to the following:

    (1) a defense of the obligor based on (i) infancy of the obligor to the extent it is a defense to a simple contract, (ii) duress, lack of legal capacity, or illegality of the transaction which, under other law, nul-

[handwritten annotation: the whole thing overdue if one installment overdue]

lifies the obligation of the obligor, (iii) fraud that induced the obligor to sign the instrument with neither knowledge nor reasonable opportunity to learn of its character or its essential terms, or (iv) discharge of the obligor in insolvency proceedings;

(2) a defense of the obligor stated in another section of this Article or a defense of the obligor that would be available if the person entitled to enforce the instrument were enforcing a right to payment under a simple contract; and

(3) a claim in recoupment of the obligor against the original payee of the instrument if the claim arose from the transaction that gave rise to the instrument; but the claim of the obligor may be asserted against a transferee of the instrument only to reduce the amount owing on the instrument at the time the action is brought.

(b) The right of a holder in due course to enforce the obligation of a party to pay the instrument is subject to defenses of the obligor stated in subsection (a)(1), but is not subject to defenses of the obligor stated in subsection (a)(2) or claims in recoupment stated in subsection (a)(3) against a person other than the holder.

(c) Except as stated in subsection (d), in an action to enforce the obligation of a party to pay the instrument, the obligor may not assert against the person entitled to enforce the instrument a defense, claim in recoupment, or claim to the instrument (Section 3–306) of another person, but the other person's claim to the instrument may be asserted by the obligor if the other person is joined in the action and personally asserts the claim against the person entitled to enforce the instrument. An obligor is not obliged to pay the instrument if the person seeking enforcement of the instrument does not have rights of a holder in due course and the obligor proves that the instrument is a lost or stolen instrument.

(d) In an action to enforce the obligation of an accommodation party to pay an instrument, the accommodation party may assert against the person entitled to enforce the instrument any defense or claim in recoupment under subsection (a) that the accommodated party could assert against the person entitled to enforce the instrument, except the defenses of discharge in insolvency proceedings, infancy, and lack of legal capacity.

(e) In a consumer transaction, if law other than this article requires that an instrument include a statement to the effect that the rights of a holder or transferee are subject to a claim or defense that the issuer could assert against the original payee, and the instrument does not include such a statement:

(1) the instrument has the same effect as if the instrument included such a statement;

(2) the issuer may assert against the holder or transferee all claims and defenses that would have been available if the instrument included such a statement; and

(3) the extent to which claims may be asserted against the holder or transferee is determined as if the instrument included such a statement.

(f) This section is subject to law other than this article that establishes a different rule for consumer transactions.

Legislative Note: *If a consumer protection law in this state addresses the same issue as subsection (g), it should be examined for consistency with subsection (g) and, if inconsistent, should be amended.*

As amended in 2002.

Official Comment

1. Subsection (a) states the defenses to the obligation of a party to pay the instrument. Subsection (a)(1) states the "real defenses" that may be asserted against any person entitled to enforce the instrument.

Subsection (a)(1)(i) allows assertion of the defense of infancy against a holder in due course, even though the effect of the defense is to render the instrument voidable but not void. The policy is one of protection of the infant even at the expense of occasional loss to an innocent purchaser. No attempt is made to state when infancy is available as a defense or the conditions under which it may be asserted. In some jurisdictions it is held that an infant cannot rescind the transaction or set up the defense unless the holder is restored to the position held before the instrument was taken which, in the case of a holder in due course, is normally impossible. In other states an infant who has misrepresented age may be estopped to assert infancy. Such questions are left to other law, as an integral part of the policy of each state as to the protection of infants.

Subsection (a)(1)(ii) covers mental incompetence, guardianship, ultra vires acts or lack of corporate capacity to do business, or any other incapacity apart from infancy. Such incapacity is largely statutory. Its existence and effect is left to the law of each state. If under the state law the effect is to render the obligation of the instrument entirely null and void, the defense may be asserted against a holder in due course. If the effect is merely to render the obligation voidable at the election of the obligor, the defense is cut off.

Duress, which is also covered by subsection (a)(ii), is a matter of degree. An instrument signed at the point of a gun is void, even in the hands of a holder in due course. One signed under threat to prosecute the son of the maker for theft may be merely voidable, so that the defense is cut off. Illegality is most frequently a matter of gambling or usury, but may arise in other forms under a variety of statutes. The statutes differ in their provisions and the interpretations given them. They are primarily a matter of local concern and local policy. All such matters are therefore left to the local law. If under that law the effect of the duress or the illegality is to make the obligation entirely null and void, the defense may be asserted against a holder in due course. Otherwise it is cut off.

Subsection (a)(1)(iii) refers to "real" or "essential" fraud, sometimes called fraud in the essence or fraud in the factum, as effective against a holder in due course. The common illustration is that of the maker who is tricked into signing a note in the belief that it is merely a receipt or some other document. The theory of the defense is that the signature on the instrument is ineffective because the signer did not intend to sign such an instrument at all. Under this provision the defense extends to an instrument signed with knowledge that it is a negotiable instrument, but without knowledge of its essential terms. The test of the defense is that of excusable ignorance of the contents of the writing signed. The party must not only have been in ignorance, but must also have had no reasonable opportunity to obtain knowledge. In determining what is a reasonable opportunity all relevant factors are to be taken into account, including the intelligence, education, business experience, and ability to read or understand English of the signer. Also relevant is the nature of the representations that were made, whether the signer had good reason to rely on the representations or to have confidence in the person making them,

the presence or absence of any third person who might read or explain the instrument to the signer, or any other possibility of obtaining independent information, and the apparent necessity, or lack of it, for acting without delay. Unless the misrepresentation meets this test, the defense is cut off by a holder in due course.

Subsection (a)(1)(iv) states specifically that the defense of discharge in insolvency proceedings is not cut off when the instrument is purchased by a holder in due course. "Insolvency proceedings" is defined in Section 1–201(22) and it includes bankruptcy whether or not the debtor is insolvent. Subsection (2)(e) of former Section 3–305 is omitted. The substance of that provision is stated in Section 3–601(b).

2. Subsection (a)(2) states other defenses that, pursuant to subsection (b), are cut off by a holder in due course. These defenses comprise those specifically stated in Article 3 and those based on common law contract principles. Article 3 defenses are nonissuance of the instrument, conditional issuance, and issuance for a special purpose (Section 3–105(b)); failure to countersign a traveler's check (Section 3–106(c)); modification of the obligation by a separate agreement (Section 3–117); payment that violates a restrictive indorsement (Section 3–206(f)); instruments issued without consideration or for which promised performance has not been given (Section 3–303(b)), and breach of warranty when a draft is accepted (Section 3–417(b)). The most prevalent common law defenses are fraud, misrepresentation or mistake in the issuance of the instrument. In most cases the holder in due course will be an immediate or remote transferee of the payee of the instrument. In most cases the holder-in-due-course doctrine is irrelevant if defenses are being asserted against the payee of the instrument, but in a small number of cases the payee of the instrument may be a holder in due course. Those cases are discussed in Comment 4 to Section 3–302.

Assume Buyer issues a note to Seller in payment of the price of goods that Seller fraudulently promises to deliver but which are never delivered. Seller negotiates the note to Holder who has no notice of the fraud. If Holder is a holder in due course, Holder is not subject to Buyer's defense of fraud. But in some cases an original party to the instrument is a holder in due course. For example, Buyer fraudulently induces Bank to issue a cashier's check to the order of Seller. The check is delivered by Bank to Seller, who has no notice of the fraud. Seller can be a holder in due course and can take the check free of Bank's defense of fraud. This case is discussed as Case # 1 in Comment

4 to Section 3–302. Former Section 3–305 stated that a holder in due course takes free of defenses of "any party to the instrument with whom the holder has not dealt." The meaning of this language was not at all clear and if read literally could have produced the wrong result. In the hypothetical case, it could be argued that Seller "dealt" with Bank because Bank delivered the check to Seller. But it is clear that Seller should take free of Bank's defense against Buyer regardless of whether Seller took delivery of the check from Buyer or from Bank. The quoted language is not included in Section 3–305. It is not necessary. If Buyer issues an instrument to Seller and Buyer has a defense against Seller, that defense can obviously be asserted. Buyer and Seller are the only people involved. The holder-in-due-course doctrine has no relevance. The doctrine applies only to cases in which more than two parties are involved. Its essence is that the holder in due course does not have to suffer the consequences of a defense of the obligor on the instrument that arose from an occurrence with a third party.

3. Subsection (a)(3) is concerned with claims in recoupment which can be illustrated by the following example. Buyer issues a note to the order of Seller in exchange for a promise of Seller to deliver specified equipment. If Seller fails to deliver the equipment or delivers equipment that is rightfully rejected, Buyer has a defense to the note because the performance that was the consideration for the note was not rendered. Section 3–303(b). This defense is included in Section 3–305(a)(2). That defense can always be asserted against Seller. This result is the same as that reached under former Section 3–408.

But suppose Seller delivered the promised equipment and it was accepted by Buyer. The equipment, however, was defective. Buyer retained the equipment and incurred expenses with respect to its repair. In this case, Buyer does not have a defense under Section 3–303(b). Seller delivered the equipment and the equipment was accepted. Under Article 2, Buyer is obliged to pay the price of the equipment which is represented by the note. But Buyer may have a claim against Seller for breach of warranty. If Buyer has a warranty claim, the claim may be asserted against Seller as a counterclaim or as a claim in recoupment to reduce the amount owing on the note. It is not relevant whether Seller is or is not a holder in due course of the note or whether Seller knew or had notice that Buyer had the warranty claim. It is obvious that holder-in-due-course doctrine cannot be used to allow Seller to cut off a warranty claim that Buyer has against Seller. Subsection (b) specifically covers this point by stating that a holder in due course is not subject to a "claim in recoupment *** against a person other than the holder."

Suppose Seller negotiates the note to Holder. If Holder had notice of Buyer's warranty claim at the time the note was negotiated to Holder, Holder is not a holder in due course (Section 3–302(a)(2)(iv)) and Buyer may assert the claim against Holder (Section 3–305(a)(3)) but only as a claim in recoupment, i.e. to reduce the amount owed on the note. If the warranty claim is $1,000 and the unpaid note is $10,000, Buyer owes $9,000 to Holder. If the warranty claim is more than the unpaid amount of the note, Buyer owes nothing to Holder, but Buyer cannot recover the unpaid amount of the warranty claim from Holder. If Buyer had already partially paid the note, Buyer is not entitled to recover the amounts paid. The claim can be used only as an offset to amounts owing on the note. If Holder had no notice of Buyer's claim and otherwise qualifies as a holder in due course, Buyer may not assert the claim against Holder. Section 3–305(b).

The result under Section 3–305 is consistent with the result reached under former Article 3, but the rules for reaching the result are stated differently. Under former Article 3 Buyer could assert rights against Holder only if Holder was not a holder in due course, and Holder's status depended upon whether Holder had notice of a defense by Buyer. Courts have held that Holder had that notice if Holder had notice of Buyer's warranty claim. The rationale under former Article 3 was "failure of consideration." This rationale does not distinguish between cases in which the seller fails to perform and those in which the buyer accepts the performance of seller but makes a claim against the seller because the performance is faulty. The term "failure of consideration" is subject to varying interpretations and is not used in Article 3. The use of the term "claim in recoupment" in Section 3–305(a)(3) is a more precise statement of the nature of Buyer's right against Holder. The use of the term does not change the law because the treatment of a defense under subsection (a)(2) and a claim in recoupment under subsection (a)(3) is essentially the same.

Under former Article 3, case law was divided on the issue of the extent to which an obligor on a note could assert against a transferee who is not a holder in due course a debt or other claim that the obligor had against the original payee of the instrument. Some courts limited claims to those that arose in the transaction that gave rise to the note. This is the approach taken in Section 3–305(a)(3). Other courts allowed the obligor on the note to use any debt or other claim, no matter how unrelated to the note, to offset the amount owed on the note. Under current judicial authority and non–UCC statutory law, there will be many cases in which a transferee of a note arising from a sale transaction will not qualify as a holder in due course. For example, applicable law may require the use of a note to which there cannot be a holder in due course. See Section 3–106(d) and Comment 3 to Section 3–106. It is reasonable to provide that the buyer should not be denied the right to assert claims arising out of the sale transaction. Subsection (a)(3) is based on the belief that it is not reasonable to require the transferee to bear the risk that wholly unrelated claims may also be asserted. The determination of whether a claim arose from the transaction that gave rise to the instrument is determined by law other than this Article and thus may vary as local law varies.

4. Subsection (c) concerns claims and defenses of a person other than the obligor on the instrument. It applies principally to cases in which an obligation is paid with the instrument of a third person. For example, Buyer buys goods from Seller and negotiates to Seller a cashier's check issued by Bank in payment of the price. Shortly after delivering the check to Seller, Buyer learns that Seller had defrauded Buyer in the sale transaction. Seller may enforce the check against Bank even though Seller is not a holder in due course. Bank has no defense to its obligation to pay the check and it may not assert defenses, claims in recoupment, or claims to the instrument of Buyer, except to the extent permitted by the "but" clause of the first sentence of subsection (c). Buyer may have a claim to the instrument under Section 3–306 based on a right to rescind the negotiation to Seller because of Seller's fraud. Section 3–202(b) and Comment 2 to Section 3–201. Bank cannot assert that claim unless Buyer is joined in the action in which Seller is trying to enforce payment of the check. In that case Bank may pay the amount of the check into court and the court will decide whether that amount belongs to Buyer or Seller. The last sentence of subsection (c) allows the issuer of an instrument such as a cashier's check to refuse payment in the rare case in which the issuer can prove that the instrument is a lost or stolen instrument and the person seeking enforcement does not have rights of a holder in due course.

5. Subsection (d) applies to instruments signed for accommodation (Section 3–419) and this subsection equates the obligation of the accommodation party to that of the accommodated party. The accommodation party can assert whatever defense or claim the accommodated party had against the person enforcing the instrument. The only exceptions are discharge in bankruptcy, infancy and lack of capacity. The same

rule does not apply to an indorsement by a holder of the instrument in negotiating the instrument. The indorser, as transferor, makes a warranty to the indorsee, as transferee, that no defense or claim in recoupment is good against the indorser. Section 3–416(a)(4). Thus, if the indorsee sues the indorser because of dishonor of the instrument, the indorser may not assert the defense or claim in recoupment of the maker or drawer against the indorsee.

Section 3–305(d) must be read in conjunction with Section 3–605, which provides rules (usually referred to as suretyship defenses) for determining when the obligation of an accommodation party is discharged, in whole or in part, because of some act or omission of a person entitled to enforce the instrument. To the extent a rule stated in Section 3–605 is inconsistent with Section 3–305(d), the Section 3–605 rule governs. For example, Section 3–605(a) provides rules for determining when and to what extent a discharge of the accommodated party under Section 3–604 will discharge the accommodation party. As explained in Comment 2 to Section 3–605, discharge of the accommodated party is normally part of a settlement under which the holder of a note accepts partial payment from an accommodated party who is financially unable to pay the entire amount of the note. If the holder then brings an action against the accommodation party to recover the remaining unpaid amount of the note, the accommodation party cannot use Section 3–305(d) to nullify Section 3–605(a) by asserting the discharge of the accommodated party as a defense. On the other hand, suppose the accommodated party is a buyer of goods who issued the note to the seller who took the note for the buyer's obligation to pay for the goods. Suppose the buyer has a claim for breach of warranty with respect to the goods against the seller and the warranty claim may be asserted against the holder of the note. The warranty claim is a claim in recoupment. If the holder and the accommodated party reach a settlement under which the holder accepts payment less than the amount of the note in full satisfaction of the note and the warranty claim, the accommodation party could defend an action on the note by the holder by asserting the accord and satisfaction under Section 3–305(d). There is no conflict with Section 3–605(a) because that provision is not intended to apply to settlement of disputed claims.

6. Subsection (e) is added to clarify the treatment of an instrument that omits the notice currently required by the Federal Trade Commission Rule related to certain consumer credit sales and consumer purchase money loans (16 C.F.R. Part 433). This subsection adopts the view that the instrument should be

treated as if the language required by the FTC Rule were present. It is based on the language describing that rule in Section 3–106(d) and the analogous provision in Section 9–404(d).

7. Subsection (f) is modeled on Sections 9–403(e) and 9–404(c). It ensures that Section 3–305 is interpreted to accommodate relevant consumer-protection laws. The absence of such a provision from other sections in Article 3 should not justify any inference about the meaning of those sections.

8. Articles 28 and 30 of the Convention on International Bills of Exchange and International Promissory Notes includes a similar dichotomy, with a narrower group of defenses available against a protected holder under Articles 28(1) and 30 than are available under Article 28(2) against a holder that is not a protected holder.

As amended in 2002.

§ 3–306. Claims to an Instrument.

A person taking an instrument, other than a person having rights of a holder in due course, is subject to a claim of a property or possessory right in the instrument or its proceeds, including a claim to rescind a negotiation and to recover the instrument or its proceeds. A person having rights of a holder in due course takes free of the claim to the instrument.

Official Comment

This section expands on the reference to "claims to" the instrument mentioned in former Sections 3–305 and 3–306. Claims covered by the section include not only claims to ownership but also any other claim of a property or possessory right. It includes the claim to a lien or the claim of a person in rightful possession of an instrument who was wrongfully deprived of possession. Also included is a claim based on Section 3–202(b) for rescission of a negotiation of the instrument by the claimant. Claims to an instrument under Section 3–306 are different from claims in recoupment referred to in Section 3–305(a)(3). The rule of this section is similar to the rule of Article 30(2) of the Convention on International Bills of Exchange and International Promissory Notes.

As amended in 2002.

§ 3–307. Notice of Breach of Fiduciary Duty.

(a) In this section:

(1) "Fiduciary" means an agent, trustee, partner, corporate officer or director, or other representative owing a fiduciary duty with respect to an instrument.

(2) "Represented person" means the principal, beneficiary, partnership, corporation, or other person to whom the duty stated in paragraph (1) is owed.

(b) If (i) an instrument is taken from a fiduciary for payment or collection or for value, (ii) the taker has knowledge of the fiduciary status of the fiduciary, and (iii) the represented person makes a claim to the instrument or its proceeds on the basis that the transaction of the fiduciary is a breach of fiduciary duty, the following rules apply:

(1) Notice of breach of fiduciary duty by the fiduciary is notice of the claim of the represented person.

(2) In the case of an instrument payable to the represented person or the fiduciary as such, the taker has notice of the breach of fiduciary duty if the instrument is (i) taken in payment of or as security for a debt known by the taker to be the personal debt of the fiduciary, (ii) taken in a transaction known by the taker to be for the personal benefit of the fiduciary, or (iii) deposited to an account other than an account of the fiduciary, as such, or an account of the represented person.

(3) If an instrument is issued by the represented person or the fiduciary as such, and made payable to the fiduciary personally, the taker does not have notice of the breach of fiduciary duty unless the taker knows of the breach of fiduciary duty.

(4) If an instrument is issued by the represented person or the fiduciary as such, to the taker as payee, the taker has notice of the breach of fiduciary duty if the instrument is (i) taken in payment of or as security for a debt known by the taker to be the personal debt of the fiduciary, (ii) taken in a transaction known by the taker to be for the personal benefit of the fiduciary, or (iii) deposited to an account other than an account of the fiduciary, as

such, or an account of the represented person.

Official Comment

1.   This section states rules for determining when a person who has taken an instrument from a fiduciary has notice of a breach of fiduciary duty that occurs as a result of the transaction with the fiduciary. Former Section 3–304(2) and (4)(e) related to this issue, but those provisions were unclear in their meaning. Section 3–307 is intended to clarify the law by stating rules that comprehensively cover the issue of when the taker of an instrument has notice of breach of a fiduciary duty and thus notice of a claim to the instrument or its proceeds.

2.   Subsection (a) defines the terms "fiduciary" and "represented person" and the introductory paragraph of subsection (b) describes the transaction to which the section applies. The basic scenario is one in which the fiduciary in effect embezzles money of the represented person by applying the proceeds of an instrument that belongs to the represented person to the personal use of the fiduciary. The person dealing with the fiduciary may be a depositary bank that takes the instrument for collection or a bank or other person that pays value for the instrument. The section also covers a transaction in which an instrument is presented for payment to a payor bank that pays the instrument by giving value to the fiduciary. Subsections (b)(2), (3), and (4) state rules for determining when the person dealing with the fiduciary has notice of breach of fiduciary duty. Subsection (b)(1) states that notice of breach of fiduciary duty is notice of the represented person's claim to the instrument or its proceeds.

Under Section 3–306, a person taking an instrument is subject to a claim to the instrument or its proceeds, unless the taker has rights of a holder in due course. Under Section 3–302(a)(2)(v), the taker cannot be a holder in due course if the instrument was taken with notice of a claim under Section 3–306. Section 3–307 applies to cases in which a represented person is asserting a claim because a breach of fiduciary duty resulted in a misapplication of the proceeds of an instrument. The claim of the represented person is a claim described in Section 3–306. Section 3–307 states rules for determining when a person taking an instrument has notice of the claim which will prevent assertion of rights as a holder in due course. It also states rules for determining when a payor bank pays an instrument with notice of breach of fiduciary duty.

Section 3–307(b) applies only if the person dealing with the fiduciary "has knowledge of the fiduciary status of the fiduciary." Notice which does not amount to knowledge is not enough to cause Section 3–307 to apply. "Knowledge" is defined in Section 1–201(25). In most cases, the "taker" referred to in Section 3–307 will be a bank or other organization. Knowledge of an organization is determined by the rules stated in Section 1–201(27). In many cases, the individual who receives and processes an instrument on behalf of the organization that is the taker of the instrument "for payment or collection or for value" is a clerk who has no knowledge of any fiduciary status of the person from whom the instrument is received. In such cases, Section 3–307 doesn't apply because, under Section 1–201(27), knowledge of the organization is determined by the knowledge of the "individual conducting that transaction," i.e. the clerk who receives and processes the instrument. Furthermore, paragraphs (2) and (4) each require that the person acting for the organization have knowledge of facts that indicate a breach of fiduciary duty. In the case of an instrument taken for deposit to an account, the knowledge is found in the fact that the deposit is made to an account other than that of the represented person or a fiduciary account for benefit of that person. In other cases the person acting for the organization must know that the instrument is taken in payment or as security for a personal debt of the fiduciary or for the personal benefit of the fiduciary. For example, if the instrument is being used to buy goods or services, the person acting for the organization must know that the goods or services are for the personal benefit of the fiduciary. The requirement that the taker have knowledge rather than notice is meant to limit Section 3–307 to relatively uncommon cases in which the person who deals with the fiduciary knows all the relevant facts: the fiduciary status and that the proceeds of the instrument are being used for the personal debt or benefit of the fiduciary or are being paid to an account that is not an account of the represented person or of the fiduciary, as such. Mere notice of these facts is not enough to put the taker on notice of the breach of fiduciary duty and does not give rise to any duty of investigation by the taker.

3.   Subsection (b)(2) applies to instruments payable to the represented person or the fiduciary as such. For example, a check payable to Corporation is indorsed in the name of Corporation by Doe as its President. Doe gives the check to Bank as partial repayment of a personal loan that Bank had made to Doe. The check was indorsed either in blank or to Bank. Bank collects the check and applies the proceeds to reduce the amount owed on Doe's loan. If the person acting for Bank in the transaction knows that Doe is a fiduciary and that the check is being used to

pay a personal obligation of Doe, subsection (b)(2) applies. If Corporation has a claim to the proceeds of the check because the use of the check by Doe was a breach of fiduciary duty, Bank has notice of the claim and did not take the check as a holder in due course. The same result follows if Doe had indorsed the check to himself before giving it to Bank. Subsection (b)(2) follows Uniform Fiduciaries Act § 4 in providing that if the instrument is payable to the fiduciary, as such, or to the represented person, the taker has notice of a claim if the instrument is negotiated for the fiduciary's personal debt. If fiduciary funds are deposited to a personal account of the fiduciary or to an account that is not an account of the represented person or of the fiduciary, as such, there is a split of authority concerning whether the bank is on notice of a breach of fiduciary duty. Subsection (b)(2)(iii) states that the bank is given notice of breach of fiduciary duty because of the deposit. The Uniform Fiduciaries Act § 9 states that the bank is not on notice unless it has knowledge of facts that makes its receipt of the deposit an act of bad faith.

The rationale of subsection (b)(2) is that it is not normal for an instrument payable to the represented person or the fiduciary, as such, to be used for the personal benefit of the fiduciary. It is likely that such use reflects an unlawful use of the proceeds of the instrument. If the fiduciary is entitled to compensation from the represented person for services rendered or for expenses incurred by the fiduciary the normal mode of payment is by a check drawn on the fiduciary account to the order of the fiduciary.

4. Subsection (b)(3) is based on Uniform Fiduciaries Act § 6 and applies when the instrument is drawn by the represented person or the fiduciary as such to the fiduciary personally. The term "personally" is used as it is used in the Uniform Fiduciaries Act to mean that the instrument is payable to the payee as an individual and not as a fiduciary. For example, Doe as President of Corporation writes a check on Corporation's account to the order of Doe personally. The check is then indorsed over to Bank as in Comment 3. In this case there is no notice of breach of fiduciary duty because there is nothing unusual about the transaction. Corporation may have owed Doe money for salary, reimbursement for expenses incurred for the benefit of Corporation, or for any other reason. If Doe is authorized to write checks on behalf of Corporation to pay debts of Corporation, the check is a normal way of paying a debt owed to Doe. Bank may assume that Doe may use the instrument for his personal benefit.

5. Subsection (b)(4) can be illustrated by a hypothetical case. Corporation draws a check payable to an organization. X, an officer or employee of Corporation, delivers the check to a person acting for the organization. The person signing the check on behalf of Corporation is X or another person. If the person acting for the organization in the transaction knows that X is a fiduciary, the organization is on notice of a claim by Corporation if it takes the instrument under the same circumstances stated in subsection (b)(2). If the organization is a bank and the check is taken in repayment of a personal loan of the bank to X, the case is like the case discussed in Comment 3. It is unusual for Corporation, the represented person, to pay a personal debt of Doe by issuing a check to the bank. It is more likely that the use of the check by Doe reflects an unlawful use of the proceeds of the check. The same analysis applies if the check is made payable to an organization in payment of goods or services. If the person acting for the organization knew of the fiduciary status of X and that the goods or services were for X's personal benefit, the organization is on notice of a claim by Corporation to the proceeds of the check. See the discussion in the last paragraph of Comment 2.

§ 3–308. Proof of Signatures and Status as Holder in Due Course.

(a) In an action with respect to an instrument, the authenticity of, and authority to make, each signature on the instrument is admitted unless specifically denied in the pleadings. If the validity of a signature is denied in the pleadings, the burden of establishing validity is on the person claiming validity, but the signature is presumed to be authentic and authorized unless the action is to enforce the liability of the purported signer and the signer is dead or incompetent at the time of trial of the issue of validity of the signature. If an action to enforce the instrument is brought against a person as the undisclosed principal of a person who signed the instrument as a party to the instrument, the plaintiff has the burden of establishing that the defendant is liable on the instrument as a represented person under Section 3–402(a).

(b) If the validity of signatures is admitted or proved and there is compliance with subsection (a), a plaintiff producing the instrument is entitled to payment if the plaintiff proves entitlement to enforce the instrument under Section 3–301, unless the defendant proves a defense or claim in recoupment. If a defense or claim in recoupment is proved, the right to payment of the plaintiff is subject to the defense or claim, except to the extent the plaintiff proves that the plaintiff has rights of a holder in due course which are not subject to the defense or claim.

Official Comment

1. Section 3–308 is a modification of former Section 3–307. The first two sentences of subsection (a) are a restatement of former Section 3–307(1). The purpose of the requirement of a specific denial in the pleadings is to give the plaintiff notice of the defendant's claim of forgery or lack of authority as to the particular signature, and to afford the plaintiff an opportunity to investigate and obtain evidence. If local rules of pleading permit, the denial may be on information and belief, or it may be a denial of knowledge or information sufficient to form a belief. It need not be under oath unless the local statutes or rules require verification. In the absence of such specific denial the signature stands admitted, and is not in issue. Nothing in this section is intended, however, to prevent amendment of the pleading in a proper case.

The question of the burden of establishing the signature arises only when it has been put in issue by specific denial. "Burden of establishing" is defined in Section 1–201. The burden is on the party claiming under the signature, but the signature is presumed to be authentic and authorized except as stated in the second sentence of subsection (a). "Presumed" is defined in Section 1–201 and means that until some evidence is introduced which would support a finding that the signature is forged or unauthorized, the plaintiff is not required to prove that it is valid. The presumption rests upon the fact that in ordinary experience forged or unauthorized signatures are very uncommon, and normally any evidence is within the control of, or more accessible to, the defendant. The defendant is therefore required to make some sufficient showing of the grounds for the denial before the plaintiff is required to introduce evidence. The defendant's evidence need not be sufficient to require a directed verdict, but it must be enough to support the denial by permitting a finding in the defendant's favor. Until introduction of such evidence the presumption requires a finding for the plaintiff. Once such evidence is introduced the burden of establishing the signature by a preponderance of the total evidence is on the plaintiff. The presumption does not arise if the action is to enforce the obligation of a purported signer who has died or become incompetent before the evidence is required, and so is disabled from obtaining or introducing it. "Action" is defined in Section 1–201 and includes a claim asserted against the estate of a deceased or an incompetent.

The last sentence of subsection (a) is a new provision that is necessary to take into account Section 3–402(a) that allows an undisclosed principal to be liable on an instrument signed by an authorized representative. In that case the person enforcing the instrument must prove that the undisclosed principal is liable.

2. Subsection (b) restates former Section 3–307(2) and (3). Once signatures are proved or admitted a holder, by mere production of the instrument, proves "entitlement to enforce the instrument" because under Section 3–301 a holder is a person entitled to enforce the instrument. Any other person in possession of an instrument may recover only if that person has the rights of a holder. Section 3–301. That person must prove a transfer giving that person such rights under Section 3–203(b) or that such rights were obtained by subrogation or succession.

If a plaintiff producing the instrument proves entitlement to enforce the instrument, either as a holder or a person with rights of a holder, the plaintiff is entitled to recovery unless the defendant proves a defense or claim in recoupment. Until proof of a defense or claim in recoupment is made, the issue as to whether the plaintiff has rights of a holder in due course does not arise. In the absence of a defense or claim in recoupment, any person entitled to enforce the instrument is entitled to recover. If a defense or claim in recoupment is proved, the plaintiff may seek to cut off the defense or claim in recoupment by proving that the plaintiff is a holder in due course or that the plaintiff has rights of a holder in due course under Section 3–203(b) or by subrogation or succession. All elements of Section 3–302(a) must be proved.

Nothing in this section is intended to say that the plaintiff must necessarily prove rights as a holder in due course. The plaintiff may elect to introduce no further evidence, in which case a verdict may be directed for the plaintiff or the defendant, or the issue of the defense or claim in recoupment may be left to the trier of fact, according to the weight and sufficiency of the defendant's evidence. The plaintiff may elect to rebut the defense or claim in recoupment by proof to the contrary, in which case a verdict may be directed for either party or the issue may be for the trier of fact. Subsection (b) means only that if the plaintiff claims the rights of a holder in due course against the defense or claim in recoupment, the plaintiff has the burden of proof on that issue.

§ 3–309. Enforcement of Lost, Destroyed, or Stolen Instrument.

(a) A person not in possession of an instrument is entitled to enforce the instrument if:

(1) the person seeking to enforce the instrument:

(A) was entitled to enforce the instrument when loss of possession occurred; or

(B) has directly or indirectly acquired ownership of the instrument from a person who was entitled to enforce the instrument when loss of possession occurred;

(2) the loss of possession was not the result of a transfer by the person or a lawful seizure; and

(3) the person cannot reasonably obtain possession of the instrument because the instrument was destroyed, its whereabouts cannot be determined, or it is in the wrongful possession of an unknown person or a person that cannot be found or is not amenable to service of process.

(b) A person seeking enforcement of an instrument under subsection (a) must prove the terms of the instrument and the person's right to enforce the instrument. If that proof is made, Section 3–308 applies to the case as if the person seeking enforcement had produced the instrument. The court may not enter judgment in favor of the person seeking enforcement unless it finds that the person required to pay the instrument is adequately protected against loss that might occur by reason of a claim by another person to enforce the instrument. Adequate protection may be provided by any reasonable means.

As amended in 2002.

Official Comment

1. Section 3–309 is a modification of former Section 3–804. The rights stated are those of "a person entitled to enforce the instrument" at the time of loss rather than those of an "owner" as in former Section 3–804. Under subsection (b), judgment to enforce the instrument cannot be given unless the court finds that the defendant will be adequately protected against a claim to the instrument by a holder that may appear at some later time. The court is given discretion in determining how adequate protection is to be assured. Former Section 3–804 allowed the court to "require security indemnifying the defendant against loss." Under Section 3–309 adequate protection is a flexible concept. For example, there is substantial risk that a holder in due course may make a demand for payment if the instrument was payable to bearer when it was lost or stolen. On the other hand if the instrument was payable to the person who lost the instrument and that person did not indorse the instrument, no other person could be a holder of the instrument. In some cases there is risk of loss only if there is doubt about whether the facts alleged by the person who lost the instrument are true. Thus, the type of adequate protection that is reasonable in the circumstances may depend on the degree of certainty about the facts in the case.

2. Subsection (a) is intended to reject the result in Dennis Joslin Co. v. Robinson Broadcasting Corp., 977 F. Supp. 491 (D.D.C. 1997). A transferee of a lost instrument need prove only that its transferor was entitled to enforce, not that the transferee was in possession at the time the instrument was lost. The protections of subsection (a) should also be available when instruments are lost during transit, because whatever the precise status of ownership at the point of loss, either the sender or the receiver ordinarily would have been entitled to enforce the instrument during the course of transit. The amendments to subsection (a) are not intended to alter in any way the rules that apply to the preservation of checks in connection with truncation or any other expedited method of check collection or processing.

3. A security interest may attach to the right of a person not in possession of an instrument to enforce the instrument. Although the secured party may not be the owner of the instrument, the secured party may nevertheless be entitled to exercise its debtor's right to enforce the instrument by resorting to its collection rights under the circumstances described in Section 9–607. This section does not address whether the person required to pay the instrument owes any duty to a secured party that is not itself the owner of the instrument.

As amended in 2002.

§ 3–310. Effect of Instrument on Obligation for Which Taken.

(a) Unless otherwise agreed, if a certified check, cashier's check, or teller's check is taken for an obligation, the obligation is discharged to the same extent discharge would result if an amount of money equal to the amount of the instrument were taken in payment of the obligation. Discharge of the obligation does not affect any liability that the obligor may have as an indorser of the instrument.

(b) Unless otherwise agreed and except as provided in subsection (a), if a note or an uncertified check is taken for an obligation, the obligation is suspended to the same extent the obligation would be discharged if an amount of money equal to the amount of the instrument were taken, and the following rules apply:

(1) In the case of an uncertified check, suspension of the obligation continues until dishonor of the check or until it is paid or certified. Payment or certification of the check results in discharge of the obligation to the extent of the amount of the check.

(2) In the case of a note, suspension of the obligation continues until dishonor of the note or until it is paid. Payment of the note results in discharge of the obligation to the extent of the payment.

(3) Except as provided in paragraph (4), if the check or note is dishonored and the obligee of the obligation for which the instrument was taken is the person entitled to enforce the instrument, the obligee may enforce either the instrument or the obligation. In the case of an instrument of a third person which is negotiated to the obligee by the obligor, discharge of the obligor on the instrument also discharges the obligation.

(4) If the person entitled to enforce the instrument taken for an obligation is a person other than the obligee, the obligee may not enforce the obligation to the extent the obligation is suspended. If the obligee is the person entitled to enforce the instrument but no longer has possession of it because it was lost, stolen, or destroyed, the obligation may not be enforced to the extent of the amount payable on the instrument, and to that extent the obligee's rights against the obligor are limited to enforcement of the instrument.

(c) If an instrument other than one described in subsection (a) or (b) is taken for an obligation, the effect is (i) that stated in subsection (a) if the instrument is one on which a bank is liable as maker or acceptor, or (ii) that stated in subsection (b) in any other case.

Official Comment

1. Section 3–310 is a modification of former Section 3–802. As a practical matter, application of former Section 3–802 was limited to cases in which a check or a note was given for an obligation. Subsections (a) and (b) of Section 3–310 are therefore stated in terms of checks and notes in the interests of clarity. Subsection (c) covers the rare cases in which some other instrument is given to pay an obligation.

2. Subsection (a) deals with the case in which a certified check, cashier's check or teller's check is given in payment of an obligation. In that case the obligation is discharged unless there is an agreement to the contrary. Subsection (a) drops the exception in former Section 3–802 for cases in which there is a right of recourse on the instrument against the obligor. Under former Section 3–802(1)(a) the obligation was not discharged if there was a right of recourse on the instrument against the obligor. Subsection (a) changes this result. The underlying obligation is discharged, but any right of recourse on the instrument is preserved.

3. Subsection (b) concerns cases in which an uncertified check or a note is taken for an obligation. The typical case is that in which a buyer pays for goods or services by giving the seller the buyer's personal check, or in which the buyer signs a note for the purchase price. Subsection (b) also applies to the uncommon cases in which a check or note of a third person is given in payment of the obligation. Subsection (b) preserves the rule under former Section 3–802(1)(b) that the buyer's obligation to pay the price is suspended, but subsection (b) spells out the effect more precisely. If the check or note is dishonored, the seller may sue on either the dishonored instrument or the contract of sale if the seller has possession of the instrument and is the person entitled to enforce it. If the right to enforce the instrument is held by somebody other than the seller, the seller can't enforce the right to payment of the price under the sales contract because that right is represented by the instrument which is enforceable by somebody else. Thus, if the seller sold the note or the check to a holder and has not reacquired it after dishonor, the only right that survives is the right to enforce the instrument. What that means is that even though the suspension of the obligation may end upon dishonor under paragraph (b)(1), the obligation is not revived in the circumstances described in paragraph (b)(4).

The last sentence of subsection (b)(3) applies to cases in which an instrument of another person is indorsed over to the obligee in payment of the obligation. For example, Buyer delivers an uncertified personal check of X payable to the order of Buyer to Seller in payment of the price of goods. Buyer indorses the check over to Seller. Buyer is liable on the check as indorser. If Seller neglects to present the check for payment or to deposit it for collection within 30 days of the indorsement, Buyer's liability as indorser is discharged. Section 3–415(e). Under the last sentence of Section 3–310(b)(3) Buyer is also discharged on the obligation to pay for the goods.

4. There was uncertainty concerning the applicability of former Section 3–802 to the case in which the check given for the obligation was stolen from the payee, the payee's signature was forged, and the forger obtained payment. The last sentence of subsection (b)(4) addresses this issue. If the payor bank pays a holder, the drawer is discharged on the underlying obligation because the check was paid. Subsection (b)(1). If the payor bank pays a person not entitled to enforce the instrument, as in the hypothetical case, the suspension of the underlying obligation continues because the check has not been paid. Section 3–602(a). The payee's cause of action is against the depositary bank or payor bank in conversion under Section 3–420 or against the drawer under Section 3–309. In the latter case, the drawer's obligation under Section 3–414(b) is triggered by dishonor which occurs because the check is unpaid. Presentment for payment to the drawee is excused under Section 3–504(a)(i) and, under Section 3–502(e), dishonor occurs without presentment if the check is not paid. The payee cannot merely ignore the instrument and sue the drawer on the underlying contract. This would impose on the drawer the risk that the check when stolen was indorsed in blank or to bearer.

A similar analysis applies with respect to lost instruments that have not been paid. If a creditor takes a check of the debtor in payment of an obligation, the obligation is suspended under the introductory paragraph of subsection (b). If the creditor then loses the check, what are the creditor's rights? The creditor can request the debtor to issue a new check and in many cases, the debtor will issue a replacement check after stopping payment on the lost check. In that case both the debtor and creditor are protected. But the debtor is not obliged to issue a new check. If the debtor refuses to issue a replacement check, the last sentence of subsection (b)(4) applies. The creditor may not enforce the obligation of debtor for which the check was taken. The creditor may assert only rights on the

check. The creditor can proceed under Section 3–309 to enforce the obligation of the debtor, as drawer, to pay the check.

5. Subsection (c) deals with rare cases in which other instruments are taken for obligations. If a bank is the obligor on the instrument, subsection (a) applies and the obligation is discharged. In any other case subsection (b) applies.

As amended in 2002.

§ 3–311. Accord and Satisfaction by Use of Instrument.

(a) If a person against whom a claim is asserted proves that (i) that person in good faith tendered an instrument to the claimant as full satisfaction of the claim, (ii) the amount of the claim was unliquidated or subject to a bona fide dispute, and (iii) the claimant obtained payment of the instrument, the following subsections apply.

(b) Unless subsection (c) applies, the claim is discharged if the person against whom the claim is asserted proves that the instrument or an accompanying written communication contained a conspicuous statement to the effect that the instrument was tendered as full satisfaction of the claim.

(c) Subject to subsection (d), a claim is not discharged under subsection (b) if either of the following applies:

(1) The claimant, if an organization, proves that (i) within a reasonable time before the tender, the claimant sent a conspicuous statement to the person against whom the claim is asserted that communications concerning disputed debts, including an instrument tendered as full satisfaction of a debt, are to be sent to a designated person, office, or place, and (ii) the instrument or accompanying communication was not received by that designated person, office, or place.

(2) The claimant, whether or not an organization, proves that within 90 days after payment of the instrument, the claimant tendered repayment of the amount of the instrument to the person against whom the claim is asserted. This paragraph does not apply if the claimant is an organization that sent a statement complying with paragraph (1)(i).

(d) A claim is discharged if the person against whom the claim is asserted proves that within a reasonable time before collection of the instrument was initiated, the claimant, or an agent of the claimant having direct responsibility with respect to the disputed obligation, knew that the instrument was tendered in full satisfaction of the claim.

Official Comment

1. This section deals with an informal method of dispute resolution carried out by use of a negotiable instrument. In the typical case there is a dispute concerning the amount that is owed on a claim.

Case # 1. The claim is for the price of goods or services sold to a consumer who asserts that he or she is not obliged to pay the full price for which the consumer was billed because of a defect or breach of warranty with respect to the goods or services.

Case # 2. A claim is made on an insurance policy. The insurance company alleges that it is not liable under the policy for the amount of the claim.

In either case the person against whom the claim is asserted may attempt an accord and satisfaction of the disputed claim by tendering a check to the claimant for some amount less than the full amount claimed by the claimant. A statement will be included on the check or in a communication accompanying the check to the effect that the check is offered as full payment or full satisfaction of the claim. Frequently, there is also a statement to the effect that obtaining payment of the check is an agreement by the claimant to a settlement of the dispute for the amount tendered. Before enactment of revised Article 3, the case law was in conflict over the question of whether obtaining payment of the check had the effect of an agreement to the settlement proposed by the debtor. This issue was governed by a common law rule, but some courts hold that the common law was modified by former Section 1–207 which they interpreted as applying to full settlement checks.

2. Comment d. to Restatement of Contracts, Section 281 discusses the full satisfaction check and the applicable common law rule. In a case like Case # 1, the buyer can propose a settlement of the disputed bill by a clear notation on the check indicating that the check is tendered as full satisfaction of the bill. Under the common law rule the seller, by obtaining payment of the check accepts the offer of compromise by the buyer. The result is the same if the seller adds a notation to the check indicating that the check is accepted under protest or in only partial satisfaction of the claim. Under the common law rule the seller can refuse the check or can accept it subject to the condition stated by the buyer, but the seller can't accept the check and refuse to be bound by the condition. The rule applies only to an unliquidated claim or a claim disputed in good faith by the buyer. The dispute in the courts was whether Section 1–207 changed the common law rule. The Restatement states that section "need not be read as changing this well-established rule."

3. As part of the revision of Article 3, Section 1–207 has been amended to add subsection (2) stating that Section 1–207 "does not apply to an accord and satisfaction." Because of that amendment and revised Article 3, Section 3–311 governs full satisfaction checks. Section 3–311 follows the common law rule with some minor variations to reflect modern business conditions. In cases covered by Section 3–311 there will often be an individual on one side of the dispute and a business organization on the other. This section is not designed to favor either the individual or the business organization. In Case # 1 the person seeking the accord and satisfaction is an individual. In Case # 2 the person seeking the accord and satisfaction is an insurance company. Section 3–311 is based on a belief that the common law rule produces a fair result and that informal dispute resolution by full satisfaction checks should be encouraged.

4. Subsection (a) states three requirements for application of Section 3–311. "Good faith" in subsection (a)(i) is defined in Section 3–103(a)(6) as not only honesty in fact, but the observance of reasonable commercial standards of fair dealing. The meaning of "fair dealing" will depend upon the facts in the particular case. For example, suppose an insurer tenders a check in settlement of a claim for personal injury in an accident clearly covered by the insurance policy. The claimant is necessitous and the amount of the check is very small in relationship to the extent of the injury and the amount recoverable under the policy. If the trier of fact determines that the insurer was taking unfair advantage of the claimant, an accord and satisfaction would not result from payment of the check because of the absence of good faith by the insurer in making the tender. Another example of lack of good faith is found in the practice of some business debtors in routinely printing full satisfaction language on their check stocks so that all or a large part of the debts of the debtor are paid by checks bearing the full satisfaction language, whether or not there is any dispute with the creditor. Under such a practice the claimant cannot be sure whether a tender in full satisfaction is or is not being made. Use of a check on which full satisfac-

tion language was affixed routinely pursuant to such a business practice may prevent an accord and satisfaction on the ground that the check was not tendered in good faith under subsection (a)(i).

Section 3-311 does not apply to cases in which the debt is a liquidated amount and not subject to a bona fide dispute. Subsection (a)(ii). Other law applies to cases in which a debtor is seeking discharge of such a debt by paying less than the amount owed. For the purpose of subsection (a)(iii) obtaining acceptance of a check is considered to be obtaining payment of the check.

The person seeking the accord and satisfaction must prove that the requirements of subsection (a) are met. If that person also proves that the statement required by subsection (b) was given, the claim is discharged unless subsection (c) applies. Normally the statement required by subsection (b) is written on the check. Thus, the canceled check can be used to prove the statement as well as the fact that the claimant obtained payment of the check. Subsection (b) requires a "conspicuous" statement that the instrument was tendered in full satisfaction of the claim. "Conspicuous" is defined in Section 1-201(10). The statement is conspicuous if "it is so written that a reasonable person against whom it is to operate ought to have noticed it." If the claimant can reasonably be expected to examine the check, almost any statement on the check should be noticed and is therefore conspicuous. In cases in which the claimant is an individual the claimant will receive the check and will normally indorse it. Since the statement concerning tender in full satisfaction normally will appear above the space provided for the claimant's indorsement of the check, the claimant "ought to have noticed" the statement.

5. Subsection (c)(1) is a limitation on subsection (b) in cases in which the claimant is an organization. It is designed to protect the claimant against inadvertent accord and satisfaction. If the claimant is an organization payment of the check might be obtained without notice to the personnel of the organization concerned with the disputed claim. Some business organizations have claims against very large numbers of customers. Examples are department stores, public utilities and the like. These claims are normally paid by checks sent by customers to a designated office at which clerks employed by the claimant or a bank acting for the claimant process the checks and record the amounts paid. If the processing office is not designed to deal with communications extraneous to recording the amount of the check and the account number of the customer, payment of a full satisfaction check can easily be obtained without knowledge by the claimant

of the existence of the full satisfaction statement. This is particularly true if the statement is written on the reverse side of the check in the area in which indorsements are usually written. Normally, the clerks of the claimant have no reason to look at the reverse side of checks. Indorsement by the claimant normally is done by mechanical means or there may be no indorsement at all. Section 4-205(a). Subsection (c)(1) allows the claimant to protect itself by advising customers by a conspicuous statement that communications regarding disputed debts must be sent to a particular person, office, or place. The statement must be given to the customer within a reasonable time before the tender is made. This requirement is designed to assure that the customer has reasonable notice that the full satisfaction check must be sent to a particular place. The reasonable time requirement could be satisfied by a notice on the billing statement sent to the customer. If the full satisfaction check is sent to the designated destination and the check is paid, the claim is discharged. If the claimant proves that the check was not received at the designated destination the claim is not discharged unless subsection (d) applies.

6. Subsection (c)(2) is also designed to prevent inadvertent accord and satisfaction. It can be used by a claimant other than an organization or by a claimant as an alternative to subsection (c)(1). Some organizations may be reluctant to use subsection (c)(1) because it may result in confusion of customers that causes checks to be routinely sent to the special designated person, office, or place. Thus, much of the benefit of rapid processing of checks may be lost. An organization that chooses not to send a notice complying with subsection (c)(1)(i) may prevent an inadvertent accord and satisfaction by complying with subsection (c)(2). If the claimant discovers that it has obtained payment of a full satisfaction check, it may prevent an accord and satisfaction if, within 90 days of the payment of the check, the claimant tenders repayment of the amount of the check to the person against whom the claim is asserted.

7. Subsection (c) is subject to subsection (d). If a person against whom a claim is asserted proves that the claimant obtained payment of a check known to have been tendered in full satisfaction of the claim by "the claimant or an agent of the claimant having direct responsibility with respect to the disputed obligation," the claim is discharged even if (i) the check was not sent to the person, office, or place required by a notice complying with subsection (c)(1), or (ii) the claimant tendered repayment of the amount of the check in compliance with subsection (c)(2).

A claimant knows that a check was tendered in full satisfaction of a claim when the claimant "has actual knowledge" of that fact. Section 1–201(25). Under Section 1–201(27), if the claimant is an organization, it has knowledge that a check was tendered in full satisfaction of the claim when that fact is

"brought to the attention of the individual conducting that transaction, and in any event when it would have been brought to his attention if the organization had exercised due diligence. An organization exercises due diligence if it maintains reasonable routines for communicating significant information to the person conducting the transaction and there is reasonable compliance with the routines. Due diligence does not require an individual acting for the organization to communicate information unless such communication is part of his regular duties or unless he has reason to know of the transaction and that the transaction would be materially affected by the information."

With respect to an attempted accord and satisfaction the "individual conducting that transaction" is an employee or other agent of the organization having direct responsibility with respect to the dispute. For example, if the check and communication are received by a collection agency acting for the claimant to collect the disputed claim, obtaining payment of the check will result in an accord and satisfaction even if the claimant gave notice, pursuant to subsection (c)(1), that full satisfaction checks be sent to some other office. Similarly, if a customer asserting a claim for breach of warranty with respect to defective goods purchased in a retail outlet of a large chain store delivers the full satisfaction check to the manager of the retail outlet at which the goods were purchased, obtaining payment of the check will also result in an accord and satisfaction. On the other hand, if the check is mailed to the chief executive officer of the chain store subsection (d) would probably not be satisfied. The chief executive officer of a large corporation may have general responsibility for operations of the company, but does not normally have direct responsibility for resolving a small disputed bill to a customer. A check for a relatively small amount mailed to a high executive officer of a large organization is not likely to receive the executive's personal attention. Rather, the check would normally be routinely sent to the appropriate office for deposit and credit to the customer's account. If the check does receive the personal attention of the high executive officer and the officer is aware of the full-satisfac-

tion language, collection of the check will result in an accord and satisfaction because subsection (d) applies. In this case the officer has assumed direct responsibility with respect to the disputed transaction.

If a full satisfaction check is sent to a lock box or other office processing checks sent to the claimant, it is irrelevant whether the clerk processing the check did or did not see the statement that the check was tendered as full satisfaction of the claim. Knowledge of the clerk is not imputed to the organization because the clerk has no responsibility with respect to an accord and satisfaction. Moreover, there is no failure of "due diligence" under Section 1–201(27) if the claimant does not require its clerks to look for full satisfaction statements on checks or accompanying communications. Nor is there any duty of the claimant to assign that duty to its clerks. Section 3–311(c) is intended to allow a claimant to avoid an inadvertent accord and satisfaction by complying with either subsection (c)(1) or (2) without burdening the check-processing operation with extraneous and wasteful additional duties.

8. In some cases the disputed claim may have been assigned to a finance company or bank as part of a financing arrangement with respect to accounts receivable. If the account debtor was notified of the assignment, the claimant is the assignee of the account receivable and the "agent of the claimant" in subsection (d) refers to an agent of the assignee.

§ 3–312. Lost, Destroyed, or Stolen Cashier's Check, Teller's Check, or Certified Check.*

(a) In this section:

(1) "Check" means a cashier's check, teller's check, or certified check.

(2) "Claimant" means a person who claims the right to receive the amount of a cashier's check, teller's check, or certified check that was lost, destroyed, or stolen.

(3) "Declaration of loss" means a statement, made in a record under penalty of perjury, to the effect that (i) the declarer lost possession of a check, (ii) the declarer is the drawer or payee of the check, in the case of a certified check, or the remitter

---

* [Section 3–312 was not adopted as part of the 1990 Official Text of Revised Article 3. It was officially approved and recommended for enactment in all states in

August 1991 by the National Conference of Commissioners on Uniform State Laws.]

or payee of the check, in the case of a cashier's check or teller's check, (iii) the loss of possession was not the result of a transfer by the declarer or a lawful seizure, and (iv) the declarer cannot reasonably obtain possession of the check because the check was destroyed, its whereabouts cannot be determined, or it is in the wrongful possession of an unknown person or a person that cannot be found or is not amenable to service of process.

(4) "Obligated bank" means the issuer of a cashier's check or teller's check or the acceptor of a certified check.

(b) A claimant may assert a claim to the amount of a check by a communication to the obligated bank describing the check with reasonable certainty and requesting payment of the amount of the check, if (i) the claimant is the drawer or payee of a certified check or the remitter or payee of a cashier's check or teller's check, (ii) the communication contains or is accompanied by a declaration of loss of the claimant with respect to the check, (iii) the communication is received at a time and in a manner affording the bank a reasonable time to act on it before the check is paid, and (iv) the claimant provides reasonable identification if requested by the obligated bank. Delivery of a declaration of loss is a warranty of the truth of the statements made in the declaration. If a claim is asserted in compliance with this subsection, the following rules apply:

(1) The claim becomes enforceable at the later of (i) the time the claim is asserted, or (ii) the 90th day following the date of the check, in the case of a cashier's check or teller's check, or the 90th day following the date of the acceptance, in the case of a certified check.

(2) Until the claim becomes enforceable, it has no legal effect and the obligated bank may pay the check or, in the case of a teller's check, may permit the drawee to pay the check. Payment to a person entitled to enforce the check discharges all liability of the obligated bank with respect to the check.

(3) If the claim becomes enforceable before the check is presented for payment, the obligated bank is not obliged to pay the check.

(4) When the claim becomes enforceable, the obligated bank becomes obliged to pay the amount of the check to the claimant if payment of the check has not been made to a person entitled to enforce the check. Subject to Section 4-302(a)(1), payment to the claimant discharges all liability of the obligated bank with respect to the check.

(c) If the obligated bank pays the amount of a check to a claimant under subsection (b)(4) and the check is presented for payment by a person having rights of a holder in due course, the claimant is obliged to (i) refund the payment to the obligated bank if the check is paid, or (ii) pay the amount of the check to the person having rights of a holder in due course if the check is dishonored.

(d) If a claimant has the right to assert a claim under subsection (b) and is also a person entitled to enforce a cashier's check, teller's check, or certified check which is lost, destroyed, or stolen, the claimant may assert rights with respect to the check either under this section or Section 3-309.

As added in 1991 and amended in 2002.

Official Comment

1. This section applies to cases in which a cashier's check, teller's check, or certified check is lost, destroyed, or stolen. In one typical case a customer of a bank closes his or her account and takes a cashier's check or teller's check of the bank as payment of the amount of the account. The customer may be moving to a new area and the check is to be used to open a bank account in that area. In such a case the check will normally be payable to the customer. In another typical case a cashier's check or teller's check is bought from a bank for the purpose of paying some obligation of the buyer of the check. In such a case the check may be made payable to the customer and then negotiated to the creditor by indorsement. But often, the payee of the check is the creditor. In the latter case the customer is a remitter. The section covers loss of the check by either the remitter or the payee. The section also covers loss of a certified check by either the drawer or payee.

Under Section 3-309 a person seeking to enforce a lost, destroyed, or stolen cashier's check or teller's check may be required by the court to give adequate protection to the issuing bank against loss that might occur by reason of the claim by another person to enforce the check. This might require the posting of an expensive bond for the amount of the check. The purpose of Section 3-312 is to offer a person who loses such a check a means of getting refund of the amount of the check within a reasonable period of time without the expense of posting a bond and with full protection of the obligated bank.

2. A claim to the amount of a lost, destroyed, or stolen cashier's check, teller's check, or certified check may be made under subsection (b) if the following requirements of that subsection are met. First, a claim may be asserted only by the drawer or payee of a certified check or the remitter or payee of a cashier's check or teller's check. An indorsee of a check is not covered because the indorsee is not an original party to the check or a remitter. Limitation to an original party or remitter gives the obligated bank the ability to determine, at the time it becomes obligated on the check, the identity of the person or persons who can assert a claim with respect to the check. The bank is not faced with having to determine the rights of some person who was not a party to the check at that time or with whom the bank had not dealt. If a cashier's check is issued to the order of the person who purchased it from the bank and that person indorses it over to a third person who loses the check, the third person may assert rights to enforce the check under Section 3-309 but has no rights under Section 3-312.

Second, the claim must be asserted by a communication to the obligated bank describing the check with reasonable certainty and requesting payment of the amount of the check. "Obligated bank" is defined in subsection (a)(4). Third, the communication must be received in time to allow the obligated bank to act on the claim before the check is paid, and the claimant must provide reasonable identification if requested. Subsections (b)(iii) and (iv). Fourth, the communication must contain or be accompanied by a declaration of loss described in subsection (b). This declaration is an affidavit or other writing made under penalty of perjury alleging the loss, destruction, or theft of the check and stating that the declarer is a person entitled to assert a claim, i.e. the drawer or payee of a certified check or the remitter or payee of a cashier's check or teller's check.

A claimant who delivers a declaration of loss makes a warranty of the truth of the statements made in the declaration. The warranty is made to the obligated bank and anybody who has a right to enforce the check. If the declaration of loss falsely alleges loss of a cashier's check that did not in fact occur, a holder of the check who was unable to obtain payment because subsection (b)(3) and (4) caused the obligated bank to dishonor the check would have a cause of action against the declarer for breach of warranty.

The obligated bank may not impose additional requirements on the claimant to assert a claim under subsection (b). For example, the obligated bank may not require the posting of a bond or other form of security. Section 3-312(b) states the procedure for asserting claims covered by the section. Thus, procedures that may be stated in other law for stating claims to property do not apply and are displaced within the meaning of Section 1-103.

3. A claim asserted under subsection (b) does not have any legal effect, however, until the date it becomes enforceable, which cannot be earlier than 90 days after the date of a cashier's check or teller's check or 90 days after the date of acceptance of a certified check. Thus, if a lost check is presented for payment within the 90-day period, the bank may pay a person entitled to enforce the check without regard to the claim and is discharged of all liability with respect to the check. This ensures the continued utility of cashier's checks, teller's checks, and certified checks as cash equivalents. Virtually all such checks are presented for payment within 90 days.

If the claim becomes enforceable and payment has not been made to a person entitled to enforce the check, the bank becomes obligated to pay the amount of the check to the claimant. Subsection (b)(4). When the bank becomes obligated to pay the amount of the check to the claimant, the bank is relieved of its obligation to pay the check. Subsection (b)(3). Thus, any person entitled to enforce the check, including even a holder in due course, loses the right to enforce the check after a claim under subsection (b) becomes enforceable.

If the obligated bank pays the claimant under subsection (b)(4), the bank is discharged of all liability with respect to the check. The only exception is the unlikely case in which the obligated bank subsequently incurs liability under Section 4-302(a)(1) with respect to the check. For example, Obligated Bank is the issuer of a cashier's check and, after a claim becomes enforceable, it pays the claimant under subsection (b)(4). Later the check is presented to Obligated Bank for payment over the counter. Under subsection (b)(3), Obligated Bank is not obliged to pay the check and may dishonor the check by returning it to the person who presented it for payment. But the normal rules of check collection are not affected by Section 3–312. If Obligated Bank retains the check beyond midnight of the day of presentment without settling for it, it becomes accountable for the amount of the check under Section 4–302(a)(1) even though it had no obligation to pay the check.

An obligated bank that pays the amount of a check to a claimant under subsection (b)(4) is discharged of all liability on the check so long as the assertion of the claim meets the requirements of subsection (b) discussed in Comment 2. This is important in cases of fraudulent declarations of loss. For example, if the claimant falsely alleges a loss that in fact did not occur, the bank, subject to Section 1–203, may rely on the declaration of loss. On the other hand, a claim may be asserted only by a person described in subsection (b)(i). Thus, the bank is discharged under subsection (a)(4) only if it pays such a person. Although it is highly unlikely, it is possible that more than one person could assert a claim under subsection (b) to the amount of a check. Such a case could occur if one of the claimants makes a false declaration of loss. The obligated bank is not required to determine whether a claimant who complies with subsection (b) is acting wrongfully. The bank may utilize procedures outside this Article, such as interpleader, under which the conflicting claims may be adjudicated.

Although it is unlikely that a lost check would be presented for payment after the claimant was paid by the bank under subsection (b)(4), it is possible for it to happen. Suppose the declaration of loss by the claimant fraudulently alleged a loss that in fact did not occur. If the claimant negotiated the check, presentment for payment would occur shortly after negotiation in almost all cases. Thus, a fraudulent declaration of loss is not likely to occur unless the check is negotiated after the 90–day period has already expired or shortly before expiration. In such a case the holder of the check, who may not have noticed the date of the check, is not entitled to payment from the obligated bank if the check is presented for payment after the claim becomes enforceable. Subsection (b)(3). The remedy of the holder who is denied payment in that case is an action against the claimant under subsection (c) if the holder is a holder in due course, or for breach of warranty under subsection (b). The holder would also have common law remedies against the claimant under the law of restitution or fraud.

4. The following cases illustrate the operation of Section 3–312:

Case # 1. Obligated Bank (OB) certified a check drawn by its customer, Drawer (D), payable to Payee (P). Two days after the check was certified, D lost the check and then asserted a claim pursuant to subsection (b). The check had not been presented for payment when D's claim became enforceable 90 days after the check was certified. Under subsection (b)(4), at the time D's claim became enforceable OB became obliged to pay D the amount of the check. If the check is later presented for payment, OB may refuse to pay the check and has no obligation to anyone to pay the check. Any obligation owed by D to P, for which the check was intended as payment, is unaffected because the check was never delivered to P.

Case # 2. Obligated Bank (OB) issued a teller's check to Remitter (R) payable to Payee (P). R delivered the check to P in payment of an obligation. P lost the check and then asserted a claim pursuant to subsection (b). To carry out P's order, OB issued an order pursuant to Section 4–403(a) to the drawee of the teller's check to stop payment of the check effective on the 90th day after the date of the teller's check. The check was not presented for payment. On the 90th day after the date of the teller's check P's claim becomes enforceable and OB becomes obliged to pay P the amount of the check. As in Case # 1, OB has no further liability with respect to the check to anyone. When R delivered the check to P, R's underlying obligation to P was discharged under Section 3–310. Thus, R suffered no loss. Since P received the amount of the check, P also suffered no loss except with respect to the delay in receiving the amount of the check.

Case # 3. Obligated Bank (OB) issued a cashier's check to its customer, Payee (P). Two days after issue, the check was stolen from P who then asserted a claim pursuant to subsection (b). Ten days after issue, the check was deposited by X in an account in Depositary Bank (DB). X had found the check and forged the indorsement of P. DB promptly presented the check to OB and obtained payment on behalf of X. On the 90th day after the date of the check P's claim becomes enforceable and P is entitled to receive the amount of the check from OB. Subsection (b)(4). Although the check was presented for payment before P's claim becomes enforceable, OB is not discharged. Because of the forged indorsement X was not a holder and neither was DB. Thus, neither is a person entitled to enforce the check (Section 3–301) and OB is not discharged under Section 3–602(a). Thus, under subsection (b)(4), because OB did not pay a person entitled to enforce the check, OB must pay P. OB's remedy is against DB for breach of warranty under Section 4–208(a)(1). As an alternative to the remedy under Section 3–312, P could recover from DB for conversion under Section 3–420(a).

Case # 4. Obligated Bank (OB) issued a cashier's check to its customer, Payee (P). P made an unrestricted blank indorsement of the check and mailed the check to P's bank for deposit to P's account. The check was never received by P's bank. When P discovered the loss, P asserted a claim pursuant to subsection (b). X found the check and deposited it in X's account in Depositary Bank (DB) after indorsing the check. DB presented the check for payment before the end of the 90–day period after its date. OB paid the check. Because of the unrestricted blank indorsement by P, X became a holder of the check. DB also became a holder. Since the check was paid before P's claim became enforceable and payment was made to a person entitled to enforce the check, OB is discharged of all liability with respect to the check. Subsection (b)(2). Thus, P is not entitled to payment from OB. Subsection (b)(4) doesn't apply.

Case # 5. Obligated Bank (OB) issued a cashier's check to its customer, Payee (P). P made an unrestricted blank indorsement of the check and mailed the check to P's bank for deposit to P's account. The check was never received by P's bank. When P discovered the loss, P asserted a claim pursuant to subsection (b). At the end of the 90–day period after the date of the check, OB paid the amount of the check to P under subsection (b)(4). X then found the check and deposited it to X's account in Depositary Bank (DB). DB presented the check to OB for payment. OB is not obliged to pay the check. Subsection (b)(4). If OB dishonors the check, DB's remedy is to charge back X's account. Section 4–214(a). Although P, as an indorser, would normally

have liability to DB under Section 3–415(a) because the check was dishonored, P is released from that liability under Section 3–415(e) because collection of the check was initiated more than 30 days after the indorsement. DB has a remedy only against X. A depositary bank that takes a cashier's check that cannot be presented for payment before expiration of the 90–day period after its date is on notice that the check might not be paid because of the possibility of a claim asserted under subsection (b) which would excuse the issuer of the check from paying the check. Thus, the depositary bank cannot safely release funds with respect to the check until it has assurance that the check has been paid. DB cannot be a holder in due course of the check because it took the check when the check was overdue. Section 3–304(a)(2). Thus, DB has no action against P under subsection (c).

Case # 6. Obligated Bank (OB) issued a cashier's check payable to bearer and delivered it to its customer, Remitter (R). R held the check for 90 days and then wrongfully asserted a claim to the amount of the check under subsection (b). The declaration of loss fraudulently stated that the check was lost. R received payment from OB under subsection (b)(4). R then negotiated the check to X for value. X presented the check to OB for payment. Although OB, under subsection (b)(2), was not obliged to pay the check, OB paid X by mistake. OB's teller did not notice that the check was more than 90 days old and was not aware that OB was not obliged to pay the check. If X took the check in good faith, OB may not recover from X. Section 3–418(c). OB's remedy is to recover from R for fraud or for breach of warranty in making a false declaration of loss. Subsection (b).

As amended in 2004.

PART 4

LIABILITY OF PARTIES

§ 3–401. Signature.

(a) A person is not liable on an instrument unless (i) the person signed the instrument, or (ii) the person is represented by an agent or representative who signed the instrument and the signature is binding on the represented person under Section 3–402.

(b) A signature may be made (i) manually or by means of a device or machine, and (ii) by the

use of any name, including a trade or assumed name, or by a word, mark, or symbol executed or adopted by a person with present intention to authenticate a writing.

Official Comment

1. Obligation on an instrument depends on a signature that is binding on the obligor. The signature may be made by the obligor personally or by an agent

authorized to act for the obligor. Signature by agents is covered by Section 3–402. It is not necessary that the name of the obligor appear on the instrument, so long as there is a signature that binds the obligor. Signature includes an indorsement.

2. A signature may be handwritten, typed, printed or made in any other manner. It need not be subscribed, and may appear in the body of the instrument, as in the case of "I, John Doe, promise to pay ***" without any other signature. It may be made by mark, or even by thumbprint. It may be made in any name, including any trade name or assumed name, however false and fictitious, which is adopted for the purpose. Parol evidence is admissible to identify the signer, and when the signer is identified the signature is effective. Indorsement in a name other than that of the indorser is governed by Section 3–204(d).

This section is not intended to affect any other law requiring a signature by mark to be witnessed, or any signature to be otherwise authenticated, or requiring any form of proof.

§ 3–402. Signature by Representative.

(a) If a person acting, or purporting to act, as a representative signs an instrument by signing either the name of the represented person or the name of the signer, the represented person is bound by the signature to the same extent the represented person would be bound if the signature were on a simple contract. If the represented person is bound, the signature of the representative is the "authorized signature of the represented person" and the represented person is liable on the instrument, whether or not identified in the instrument.

(b) If a representative signs the name of the representative to an instrument and the signature is an authorized signature of the represented person, the following rules apply:

(1) If the form of the signature shows unambiguously that the signature is made on behalf of the represented person who is identified in the instrument, the representative is not liable on the instrument.

(2) Subject to subsection (c), if (i) the form of the signature does not show unambiguously that the signature is made in a representative capacity or (ii) the represented person is not identified in the instrument, the representative is liable on the instrument to a holder in due

course that took the instrument without notice that the representative was not intended to be liable on the instrument. With respect to any other person, the representative is liable on the instrument unless the representative proves that the original parties did not intend the representative to be liable on the instrument.

(c) If a representative signs the name of the representative as drawer of a check without indication of the representative status and the check is payable from an account of the represented person who is identified on the check, the signer is not liable on the check if the signature is an authorized signature of the represented person.

Official Comment

1. Subsection (a) states when the represented person is bound on an instrument if the instrument is signed by a representative. If under the law of agency the represented person would be bound by the act of the representative in signing either the name of the represented person or that of the representative, the signature is the authorized signature of the represented person. Former Section 3–401(1) stated that "no person is liable on an instrument unless his signature appears thereon." This was interpreted as meaning that an undisclosed principal is not liable on an instrument. This interpretation provided an exception to ordinary agency law that binds an undisclosed principal on a simple contract.

It is questionable whether this exception was justified by the language of former Article 3 and there is no apparent policy justification for it. The exception is rejected by subsection (a) which returns to ordinary rules of agency. If P, the principal, authorized A, the agent, to borrow money on P's behalf and A signed A's name to a note without disclosing that the signature was on behalf of P, A is liable on the instrument. But if the person entitled to enforce the note can also prove that P authorized A to sign on P's behalf, why shouldn't P also be liable on the instrument? To recognize the liability of P takes nothing away from the utility of negotiable instruments. Furthermore, imposing liability on P has the merit of making it impossible to have an instrument on which nobody is liable even though it was authorized by P. That result could occur under former Section 3–401(1) if an authorized agent signed "as agent" but the note did not identify the principal. If the dispute was between the agent and the payee of the note, the agent could escape liability on the note by proving that the agent and the payee did not intend that the agent be liable on the note when the note was issued. Former Section 3–403(2)(b). Under the prevailing interpretation of former Section 3–401(1), the principal was not liable on the note under former 3–401(1) because the principal's name did not appear on the note. Thus, nobody was liable on the note even though all parties knew that the note was signed by the agent on behalf of the principal. Under Section 3–402(a) the principal would be liable on the note.

2. Subsection (b) concerns the question of when an agent who signs an instrument on behalf of a principal is bound on the instrument. The approach followed by former Section 3–403 was to specify the form of signature that imposed or avoided liability. This approach was unsatisfactory. There are many ways in which there can be ambiguity about a signature. It is better to state a general rule. Subsection (b)(1) states that if the form of the signature unambiguously shows that it is made on behalf of an identified represented person (for example, "P, by A, Treasurer") the agent is not liable. This is a workable standard for a court to apply. Subsection (b)(2) partly changes former Section 3–403(2). Subsection (b)(2) relates to cases in which the agent signs on behalf of a principal but the form of the signature does not fall within subsection (b)(1). The following cases are illustrative. In each case John Doe is the authorized agent of Richard Roe and John Doe signs a note on behalf of Richard Roe. In each case the intention of the original parties to the instrument is that Roe is to be liable on the instrument but Doe is not to be liable.

Case # 1. Doe signs "John Doe" without indicating in the note that Doe is signing as agent. The note does not identify Richard Roe as the represented person.

Case # 2. Doe signs "John Doe, Agent" but the note does not identify Richard Roe as the represented person.

Case # 3. The name "Richard Roe" is written on the note and immediately below that name Doe signs "John Doe" without indicating that Doe signed as agent.

In each case Doe is liable on the instrument to a holder in due course without notice that Doe was not intended to be liable. In none of the cases does Doe's signature unambiguously show that Doe was signing as agent for an identified principal. A holder in due course should be able to resolve any ambiguity against Doe.

But the situation is different if a holder in due course is not involved. In each case Roe is liable on the note. Subsection (a). If the original parties to the note did not intend that Doe also be liable, imposing liability on Doe is a windfall to the person enforcing the note. Under subsection (b)(2) Doe is prima facie liable because his signature appears on the note and the form of the signature does not unambiguously refute personal liability. But Doe can escape liability by proving that the original parties did not intend that he be liable on the note. This is a change from former Section 3–403(2)(a).

A number of cases under former Article 3 involved situations in which an agent signed the agent's name to a note, without qualification and without naming the person represented, intending to bind the principal but not the agent. The agent attempted to prove that the other party had the same intention. Some of these cases involved mistake, and in some there was evidence that the agent may have been deceived into signing in that manner. In some of the cases the court refused to allow proof of the intention of the parties and imposed liability on the agent based on former Section 3–403(2)(a) even though both parties to the instrument may have intended that the agent not be liable. Subsection (b)(2) changes the result of those cases, and is consistent with Section 3–117 which allows oral or written agreements to modify or nullify apparent obligations on the instrument.

Former Section 3–403 spoke of the represented person being "named" in the instrument. Section 3–402 speaks of the represented person being "identified" in the instrument. This change in terminology is intended to reject decisions under former Section 3–403(2) requiring that the instrument state the legal name of the represented person.

3. Subsection (c) is directed at the check cases. It states that if the check identifies the represented person the agent who signs on the signature line does not have to indicate agency status. Virtually all checks used today are in personalized form which identify the person on whose account the check is drawn. In this case, nobody is deceived into thinking that the person signing the check is meant to be liable. This subsection is meant to overrule cases decided under former Article 3 such as Griffin v. Ellinger, 538 S.W.2d 97 (Texas 1976).

§ 3–403. Unauthorized Signature.

(a) Unless otherwise provided in this Article or Article 4, an unauthorized signature is ineffective except as the signature of the unauthorized signer in favor of a person who in good faith pays the instrument or takes it for value. An unauthorized signature may be ratified for all purposes of this Article.

(b) If the signature of more than one person is required to constitute the authorized signature of an organization, the signature of the organization is unauthorized if one of the required signatures is lacking.

(c) The civil or criminal liability of a person who makes an unauthorized signature is not affected by any provision of this Article which makes the unauthorized signature effective for the purposes of this Article.

Official Comment

1. "Unauthorized" signature is defined in Section 1–201(43) as one that includes a forgery as well as a signature made by one exceeding actual or apparent authority. Former Section 3–404(1) stated that an unauthorized signature was inoperative as the signature of the person whose name was signed unless that person "is precluded from denying it." Under former Section 3–406 if negligence by the person whose name was signed contributed to an unauthorized signature, that person "is precluded from asserting the *** lack of authority." Both of these sections were applied to cases in which a forged signature appeared on an instrument and the person asserting rights on the instrument alleged that the negligence of the purported signer contributed to the forgery. Since the standards for liability between the two sections differ, the overlap between the sections caused confusion. Section 3–403(a) deals with the problem by removing the preclusion language that appeared in former Section 3–404.

2. The except clause of the first sentence of subsection (a) states the generally accepted rule that the unauthorized signature, while it is wholly inoperative as that of the person whose name is signed, is effective to impose liability upon the signer or to transfer any rights that the signer may have in the instrument. The signer's liability is not in damages for breach of warranty of authority, but is full liability on the instrument in the capacity in which the signer signed. It is, however, limited to parties who take or pay the instrument in good faith; and one who knows that the signature is unauthorized cannot recover from the signer on the instrument.

3. The last sentence of subsection (a) allows an unauthorized signature to be ratified. Ratification is a retroactive adoption of the unauthorized signature by the person whose name is signed and may be found

from conduct as well as from express statements. For example, it may be found from the retention of benefits received in the transaction with knowledge of the unauthorized signature. Although the forger is not an agent, ratification is governed by the rules and principles applicable to ratification of unauthorized acts of an agent.

Ratification is effective for all purposes of this Article. The unauthorized signature becomes valid so far as its effect as a signature is concerned. Although the ratification may relieve the signer of liability on the instrument, it does not of itself relieve the signer of liability to the person whose name is signed. It does not in any way affect the criminal law. No policy of the criminal law prevents a person whose name is forged to assume liability to others on the instrument by ratifying the forgery, but the ratification cannot affect the rights of the state. While the ratification may be taken into account with other relevant facts in determining punishment, it does not relieve the signer of criminal liability.

4. Subsection (b) clarifies the meaning of "unauthorized" in cases in which an instrument contains less than all of the signatures that are required as authority to pay a check. Judicial authority was split on the issue whether the one-year notice period under former Section 4–406(4) (now Section 4–406(f)) barred a customer's suit against a payor bank that paid a check containing less than all of the signatures required by the customer to authorize payment of the check. Some cases took the view that if a customer required that a check contain the signatures of both A and B to authorize payment and only A signed, there was no unauthorized signature within the meaning of that term in former Section 4–406(4) because A's signature was neither unauthorized nor forged. The other cases correctly pointed out that it was the customer's signature at issue and not that of A; hence, the customer's signature was unauthorized if all signatures required to authorize payment of the check were not on the check. Subsection (b) follows the latter line of cases. The same analysis applies if A forged the signature of B. Because the forgery is not effective as a signature of B, the required signature of B is lacking.

Subsection (b) refers to "the authorized signature of an organization." The definition of "organization" in Section 1–201(28) is very broad. It covers not only commercial entities but also "two or more persons having a joint or common interest." Hence subsection (b) would apply when a husband and wife are both required to sign an instrument.

§ 3–404. Impostors; Fictitious Payees.

(a) If an impostor, by use of the mails or otherwise, induces the issuer of an instrument to issue the instrument to the impostor, or to a person acting in concert with the impostor, by impersonating the payee of the instrument or a person authorized to act for the payee, an indorsement of the instrument by any person in the name of the payee is effective as the indorsement of the payee in favor of a person who, in good faith, pays the instrument or takes it for value or for collection.

(b) If (i) a person whose intent determines to whom an instrument is payable (Section 3–110(a) or (b)) does not intend the person identified as payee to have any interest in the instrument, or (ii) the person identified as payee of an instrument is a fictitious person, the following rules apply until the instrument is negotiated by special indorsement:

(1) Any person in possession of the instrument is its holder.

(2) An indorsement by any person in the name of the payee stated in the instrument is effective as the indorsement of the payee in favor of a person who, in good faith, pays the instrument or takes it for value or for collection.

(c) Under subsection (a) or (b), an indorsement is made in the name of a payee if (i) it is made in a name substantially similar to that of the payee or (ii) the instrument, whether or not indorsed, is deposited in a depositary bank to an account in a name substantially similar to that of the payee.

(d) With respect to an instrument to which subsection (a) or (b) applies, if a person paying the instrument or taking it for value or for collection fails to exercise ordinary care in paying or taking the instrument and that failure substantially contributes to loss resulting from payment of the instrument, the person bearing the loss may recover from the person failing to exercise ordinary care to the extent the failure to exercise ordinary care contributed to the loss.

Official Comment

1. Under former Article 3, the impostor cases were governed by former Section 3–405(1)(a) and the fictitious payee cases were governed by Section 3–405(1)(b). Section 3–404 replaces former Section 3–405(1)(a) and (b) and modifies the previous law in some respects. Former Section 3–405 was read by some courts to require that the indorsement be in the exact name of the named payee. Revised Article 3 rejects this result. Section 3–404(c) requires only that the indorsement be made in a name "substantially similar" to that of the payee. Subsection (c) also recognizes the fact that checks may be deposited without indorsement. Section 4–205(a).

Subsection (a) changes the former law in a case in which the impostor is impersonating an agent. Under former Section 3–405(1)(a), if Impostor impersonated Smith and induced the drawer to draw a check to the order of Smith, Impostor could negotiate the check. If Impostor impersonated Smith, the president of Smith Corporation, and the check was payable to the order of Smith Corporation, the section did not apply. See the last paragraph of Comment 2 to former Section 3–405. In revised Article 3, Section 3–404(a) gives Impostor the power to negotiate the check in both cases.

2. Subsection (b) is based in part on former Section 3–405(1)(b) and in part on N.I.L. § 9(3). It covers cases in which an instrument is payable to a fictitious or nonexisting person and to cases in which the payee is a real person but the drawer or maker does not intend the payee to have any interest in the instrument. Subsection (b) applies to any instrument, but its primary importance is with respect to checks of corporations and other organizations. It also applies to forged check cases. The following cases illustrate subsection (b):

Case # 1. Treasurer is authorized to draw checks in behalf of Corporation. Treasurer fraudulently draws a check of Corporation payable to Supplier Co., a non-existent company. Subsection (b) applies because Supplier Co. is a fictitious person and because Treasurer did not intend Supplier Co. to have any interest in the check. Under subsection (b)(1) Treasurer, as the person in possession of the check, becomes the holder of the check. Treasurer indorses the check in the name "Supplier Co." and deposits it in Depositary Bank. Under subsection (b)(2) and (c)(i), the indorsement is effective to make Depositary Bank the holder and therefore a person entitled to enforce the instrument. Section 3–301.

Case # 2. Same facts as Case # 1 except that Supplier Co. is an actual company that does business with Corporation. If Treasurer intended to steal the check when the check was drawn, the result in Case # 2 is the same as the result in Case # 1. Subsection (b) applies because Treasurer did not intend

Supplier Co. to have any interest in the check. It does not make any difference whether Supplier Co. was or was not a creditor of Corporation when the check was drawn. If Treasurer did not decide to steal the check until after the check was drawn, the case is covered by Section 3–405 rather than Section 3–404(b), but the result is the same. See Case # 6 in Comment 3 to Section 3–405.

Case # 3. Checks of Corporation must be signed by two officers. President and Treasurer both sign a check of Corporation payable to Supplier Co., a company that does business with Corporation from time to time but to which Corporation does not owe any money. Treasurer knows that no money is owed to Supplier Co. and does not intend that Supplier Co. have any interest in the check. President believes that money is owed to Supplier Co. Treasurer obtains possession of the check after it is signed. Subsection (b) applies because Treasurer is "a person whose intent determines to whom an instrument is payable" and Treasurer does not intend Supplier Co. to have any interest in the check. Treasurer becomes the holder of the check and may negotiate it by indorsing it in the name "Supplier Co."

Case # 4. Checks of Corporation are signed by a check-writing machine. Names of payees of checks produced by the machine are determined by information entered into the computer that operates the machine. Thief, a person who is not an employee or other agent of Corporation, obtains access to the computer and causes the check-writing machine to produce a check payable to Supplier Co., a nonexistent company. Subsection (b)(ii) applies. Thief then obtains possession of the check. At that point Thief becomes the holder of the check because Thief is the person in possession of the instrument. Subsection (b)(1). Under Section 3–301 Thief, as holder, is the "person entitled to enforce the instrument" even though Thief does not have title to the check and is in wrongful possession of it. Thief indorses the check in the name "Supplier Co." and deposits it in an account in Depositary Bank which Thief opened in the name "Supplier Co." Depositary Bank takes the check in good faith and credits the "Supplier Co." account. Under subsection (b)(2) and (c)(i), the indorsement is effective. Depositary Bank becomes the holder and the person entitled to enforce the check. The check is presented to the drawee bank for payment and payment is made. Thief then withdraws the credit to the account. Although the check was issued without authority given by Corporation, the drawee bank is entitled to pay the check and charge Corporation's account if

there was an agreement with Corporation allowing the bank to debit Corporation's account for payment of checks produced by the check-writing machine whether or not authorized. The indorsement is also effective if Supplier Co. is a real person. In that case subsection (b)(i) applies. Under Section 3–110(b) Thief is the person whose intent determines to whom the check is payable, and Thief did not intend Supplier Co. to have any interest in the check. When the drawee bank pays the check, there is no breach of warranty under Section 3–417(a)(1) or 4–208(a)(1) because Depositary Bank was a person entitled to enforce the check when it was forwarded for payment.

Case # 5. Thief, who is not an employee or agent of Corporation, steals check forms of Corporation. John Doe is president of Corporation and is authorized to sign checks on behalf of Corporation as drawer. Thief draws a check in the name of Corporation as drawer by forging the signature of Doe. Thief makes the check payable to the order of Supplier Co. with the intention of stealing it. Whether Supplier Co. is a fictitious person or a real person, Thief becomes the holder of the check and the person entitled to enforce it. The analysis is the same as that in Case # 4. Thief deposits the check in an account in Depositary Bank which Thief opened in the name "Supplier Co." Thief either indorses the check in a name other than "Supplier Co." or does not indorse the check at all. Under Section 4–205(a) a depositary bank may become holder of a check deposited to the account of a customer if the customer was a holder, whether or not the customer indorses. Subsection (c)(ii) treats deposit to an account in a name substantially similar to that of the payee as the equivalent of indorsement in the name of the payee. Thus, the deposit is an effective indorsement of the check. Depositary Bank becomes the holder of the check and the person entitled to enforce the check. If the check is paid by the drawee bank, there is no breach of warranty under Section 3–417(a)(1) or 4–208(a)(1) because Depositary Bank was a person entitled to enforce the check when it was forwarded for payment and, unless Depositary Bank knew about the forgery of Doe's signature, there is no breach of warranty under Section 3–417(a)(3) or 4–208(a)(3). Because the check was a forged check the drawee bank is not entitled to charge Corporation's account unless Section 3–406 or Section 4–406 applies.

3. In cases governed by subsection (a) the dispute will normally be between the drawer of the check that was obtained by the impostor and the drawee bank

that paid it. The drawer is precluded from obtaining recredit of the drawer's account by arguing that the check was paid on a forged indorsement so long as the drawee bank acted in good faith in paying the check. Cases governed by subsection (b) are illustrated by Cases #1 through #5 in Comment 2. In Cases #1, #2, and #3 there is no forgery of the check, thus the drawer of the check takes the loss if there is no lack of good faith by the banks involved. Cases #4 and #5 are forged check cases. Depositary Bank is entitled to retain the proceeds of the check if it didn't know about the forgery. Under Section 3–418 the drawee bank is not entitled to recover from Depositary Bank on the basis of payment by mistake because Depositary Bank took the check in good faith and gave value for the check when the credit given for the check was withdrawn. And there is no breach of warranty under Section 3–417(a)(1) or (3) or 4–208(a)(1) or (3). Unless Section 3–406 applies the loss is taken by the drawee bank if a forged check is paid, and that is the result in Case #5. In Case #4 the loss is taken by Corporation, the drawer, because an agreement between Corporation and the drawee bank allowed the bank to debit Corporation's account despite the unauthorized use of the check-writing machine.

If a check payable to an impostor, fictitious payee, or payee not intended to have an interest in the check is paid, the effect of subsections (a) and (b) is to place the loss on the drawer of the check rather than on the drawee or the depositary bank that took the check for collection. Cases governed by subsection (a) always involve fraud, and fraud is almost always involved in cases governed by subsection (b). The drawer is in the best position to avoid the fraud and thus should take the loss. This is true in Case #1, Case #2, and Case #3. But in some cases the person taking the check might have detected the fraud and thus have prevented the loss by the exercise of ordinary care. In those cases, if that person failed to exercise ordinary care, it is reasonable that that person bear loss to the extent the failure contributed to the loss. Subsection (d) is intended to reach that result. It allows the person who suffers loss as a result of payment of the check to recover from the person who failed to exercise ordinary care. In Case #1, Case #2, and Case #3, the person suffering the loss is Corporation, the drawer of the check. In each case the most likely defendant is the depositary bank that took the check and failed to exercise ordinary care. In those cases, the drawer has a cause of action against the offending bank to recover a portion of the loss. The amount of loss to be allocated to each party is left to the trier of fact. Ordinary care is defined in Section 3–103(a)(9). An example of the type of conduct by a depositary bank

that could give rise to recovery under subsection (d) is discussed in Comment 4 to Section 3–405. That comment addresses the last sentence of Section 3–405(b) which is similar to Section 3–404(d).

In Case #1, Case #2, and Case #3, there was no forgery of the drawer's signature. But cases involving checks payable to a fictitious payee or a payee not intended to have an interest in the check are often forged check cases as well. Examples are Case #4 and Case #5. Normally, the loss in forged check cases is on the drawee bank that paid the check. Case #5 is an example. In Case #4 the risk with respect to the forgery is shifted to the drawer because of the agreement between the drawer and the drawee bank. The doctrine that prevents a drawee bank from recovering payment with respect to a forged check if the payment was made to a person who took the check for value and in good faith is incorporated into Section 3–418 and Sections 3–417(a)(3) and 4–208(a)(3). This doctrine is based on the assumption that the depositary bank normally has no way of detecting the forgery because the drawer is not that bank's customer. On the other hand, the drawee bank, at least in some cases, may be able to detect the forgery by comparing the signature on the check with the specimen signature that the drawee has on file. But in some forged check cases the depositary bank is in a position to detect the fraud. Those cases typically involve a check payable to a fictitious payee or a payee not intended to have an interest in the check. Subsection (d) applies to those cases. If the depositary bank failed to exercise ordinary care and the failure substantially contributed to the loss, the drawer in Case #4 or the drawee bank in Case #5 has a cause of action against the depositary bank under subsection (d). Comment 4 to Section 3–405 can be used as a guide to the type of conduct that could give rise to recovery under Section 3–404(d).

§ 3–405. Employer's Responsibility for Fraudulent Indorsement by Employee.

(a) In this section:

(1) "Employee" includes an independent contractor and employee of an independent contractor retained by the employer.

(2) "Fraudulent indorsement" means (i) in the case of an instrument payable to the employer, a forged indorsement purporting to be that of the employer, or (ii) in the case of an instrument with respect to which the employer is the issuer, a

forged indorsement purporting to be that of the person identified as payee.

(3) "Responsibility" with respect to instruments means authority (i) to sign or indorse instruments on behalf of the employer, (ii) to process instruments received by the employer for bookkeeping purposes, for deposit to an account, or for other disposition, (iii) to prepare or process instruments for issue in the name of the employer, (iv) to supply information determining the names or addresses of payees of instruments to be issued in the name of the employer, (v) to control the disposition of instruments to be issued in the name of the employer, or (vi) to act otherwise with respect to instruments in a responsible capacity. "Responsibility" does not include authority that merely allows an employee to have access to instruments or blank or incomplete instrument forms that are being stored or transported or are part of incoming or outgoing mail, or similar access.

(b) For the purpose of determining the rights and liabilities of a person who, in good faith, pays an instrument or takes it for value or for collection, if an employer entrusted an employee with responsibility with respect to the instrument and the employee or a person acting in concert with the employee makes a fraudulent indorsement of the instrument, the indorsement is effective as the indorsement of the person to whom the instrument is payable if it is made in the name of that person. If the person paying the instrument or taking it for value or for collection fails to exercise ordinary care in paying or taking the instrument and that failure substantially contributes to loss resulting from the fraud, the person bearing the loss may recover from the person failing to exercise ordinary care to the extent the failure to exercise ordinary care contributed to the loss.

(c) Under subsection (b), an indorsement is made in the name of the person to whom an instrument is payable if (i) it is made in a name substantially similar to the name of that person or (ii) the instrument, whether or not indorsed, is deposited in a depositary bank to an account in a name substantially similar to the name of that person.

Official Comment

1. Section 3–405 is addressed to fraudulent indorsements made by an employee with respect to instruments with respect to which the employer has given responsibility to the employee. It covers two categories of fraudulent indorsements: indorsements made in the name of the employer to instruments payable to the employer and indorsements made in the name of payees of instruments issued by the employer. This section applies to instruments generally but normally the instrument will be a check. Section 3–405 adopts the principle that the risk of loss for fraudulent indorsements by employees who are entrusted with responsibility with respect to checks should fall on the employer rather than the bank that takes the check or pays it, if the bank was not negligent in the transaction. Section 3–405 is based on the belief that the employer is in a far better position to avoid the loss by care in choosing employees, in supervising them, and in adopting other measures to prevent forged indorsements on instruments payable to the employer or fraud in the issuance of instruments in the name of the employer. If the bank failed to exercise ordinary care, subsection (b) allows the employer to shift loss to the bank to the extent the bank's failure to exercise ordinary care contributed to the loss. "Ordinary care" is defined in Section 3–103(a)(9). The provision applies regardless of whether the employer is negligent.

The first category of cases governed by Section 3–405 are those involving indorsements made in the name of payees of instruments issued by the employer. In this category, Section 3–405 includes cases that were covered by former Section 3–405(1)(c). The scope of Section 3–405 in revised Article 3 is, however, somewhat wider. It covers some cases not covered by former Section 3–405(1)(c) in which the entrusted employee makes a forged indorsement to a check drawn by the employer. An example is Case # 6 in Comment 3. Moreover, a larger group of employees is included in revised Section 3–405. The key provision is the definition of "responsibility" in subsection (a)(1) which identifies the kind of responsibility delegated to an employee which will cause the employer to take responsibility for the fraudulent acts of that employee. An employer can insure this risk by employee fidelity bonds.

The second category of cases governed by Section 3–405—fraudulent indorsements of the name of the employer to instruments payable to the employer—were covered in former Article 3 by Section 3–406. Under former Section 3–406, the employer took the loss only if negligence of the employer could be proved. Under revised Article 3, Section 3–406 need not be used with respect to forgeries of the employer's indorsement. Section 3–405 imposes the loss on the employer without proof of negligence.

2. With respect to cases governed by former Section 3–405(1)(c), Section 3–405 is more favorable to employers in one respect. The bank was entitled to the preclusion provided by former Section 3–405(1)(c) if it took the check in good faith. The fact that the bank acted negligently did not shift the loss to the bank so long as the bank acted in good faith. Under revised Section 3–405 the loss may be recovered from the bank to the extent the failure of the bank to exercise ordinary care contributed to the loss.

3. Section 3–404(b) and Section 3–405 both apply to cases of employee fraud. Section 3–404(b) is not limited to cases of employee fraud, but most of the cases to which it applies will be cases of employee fraud. The following cases illustrate the application of Section 3–405. In each case it is assumed that the bank that took the check acted in good faith and was not negligent.

Case # 1. Janitor, an employee of Employer, steals a check for a very large amount payable to Employer after finding it on a desk in one of Employer's offices. Janitor forges Employer's indorsement on the check and obtains payment. Since Janitor was not entrusted with "responsibility" with respect to the check, Section 3–405 does not apply. Section 3–406 might apply to this case. The issue would be whether Employer was negligent in safeguarding the check. If not, Employer could assert that the indorsement was forged and bring an action for conversion against the depositary or payor bank under Section 3–420.

Case # 2. X is Treasurer of Corporation and is authorized to write checks on behalf of Corporation by signing X's name as Treasurer. X draws a check in the name of Corporation and signs X's name as Treasurer. The check is made payable to X. X then indorses the check and obtains payment. Assume that Corporation did not owe any money to X and did not authorize X to write the check. Although the writing of the check was not authorized, Corporation is bound as drawer of the check because X had authority to sign checks on behalf of Corporation. This result follows from agency law and Section 3–402(a). Section 3–405 does not apply in this case because there is no forged indorsement. X was payee of the check so the indorsement is valid. Section 3–110(a).

Case # 3. The duties of Employee, a bookkeeper, include posting the amounts of checks payable to Employer to the accounts of the drawers of the checks. Employee steals a check payable to Employer which was entrusted to Employee and forges Employer's indorsement. The check is deposited by Employee to an account in Depositary Bank which Employee opened in the same name as Employer, and the check is honored by the drawee bank. The indorsement is effective as Employer's indorsement because Employee's duties include processing checks for bookkeeping purposes. Thus, Employee is entrusted with "responsibility" with respect to the check. Neither Depositary Bank nor the drawee bank is liable to Employer for conversion of the check. The same result follows if Employee deposited the check in the account in Depositary Bank without indorsement. Section 4–205(a). Under subsection (c) deposit in a depositary bank in an account in a name substantially similar to that of Employer is the equivalent of an indorsement in the name of Employer.

Case # 4. Employee's duties include stamping Employer's unrestricted blank indorsement on checks received by Employer and depositing them in Employer's bank account. After stamping Employer's unrestricted blank indorsement on a check, Employee steals the check and deposits it in Employee's personal bank account. Section 3–405 doesn't apply because there is no forged indorsement. Employee is authorized by Employer to indorse Employer's checks. The fraud by Employee is not the indorsement but rather the theft of the indorsed check. Whether Employer has a cause of action against the bank in which the check was deposited is determined by whether the bank had notice of the breach of fiduciary duty by Employee. The issue is determined under Section 3–307.

Case # 5. The computer that controls Employer's check-writing machine was programmed to cause a check to be issued to Supplier Co. to which money was owed by Employer. The address of Supplier Co. was included in the information in the computer. Employee is an accounts payable clerk whose duties include entering information into the computer. Employee fraudulently changed the address of Supplier Co. in the computer data bank to an address of Employee. The check was subsequently produced by the check-writing machine and mailed to the address that Employee had entered into the computer. Employee obtained possession of the check, indorsed it in the name of Supplier Co, and deposited it to an account in Depositary Bank which Employee opened in the name "Supplier Co." The check was honored by the drawee bank. The indorsement is effective under Section 3–405(b) because Employee's duties allowed Employee to supply information determining the address of the payee of the check. An employee that is entrusted with duties that enable the employee to determine the address to which a check is to be sent controls the disposition of the check and facilitates forgery of the indorsement. The employer is held responsible. The drawee may debit the account of Employer for the amount of the check. There is no breach of warranty by Depositary Bank under Section 3–417(a)(1) or 4–208(a)(1).

Case # 6. Treasurer is authorized to draw checks in behalf of Corporation. Treasurer draws a check of Corporation payable to Supplier Co., a company that sold goods to Corporation. The check was issued to pay the price of these goods. At the time the check was signed Treasurer had no intention of stealing the check. Later, Treasurer stole the check, indorsed it in the name "Supplier Co." and obtained payment by depositing it to an account in Depositary Bank which Treasurer opened in the name "Supplier Co.". The indorsement is effective under Section 3–405(b). Section 3–404(b) does not apply to this case.

Case # 7. Checks of Corporation are signed by Treasurer in behalf of Corporation as drawer. Clerk's duties include the preparation of checks for issue by Corporation. Clerk prepares a check payable to the order of Supplier Co. for Treasurer's signature. Clerk fraudulently informs Treasurer that the check is needed to pay a debt owed to Supplier Co, a company that does business with Corporation. No money is owed to Supplier Co. and Clerk intends to steal the check. Treasurer signs it and returns it to Clerk for mailing. Clerk does not indorse the check but deposits it to an account in Depositary Bank which Clerk opened in the name "Supplier Co.". The check is honored by the drawee bank. Section 3–404(b)(i) does not apply to this case because Clerk, under Section 3–110(a), is not the person whose intent determines to whom the check is payable. But Section 3–405 does apply and it treats the deposit by Clerk as an effective indorsement by Clerk because Clerk was entrusted with responsibility with respect to the check. If Supplier Co. is a fictitious person Section 3–404(b)(ii) applies. But the result is the same. Clerk's deposit is treated as an effective indorsement of the check whether Supplier Co. is a fictitious or a real person or whether money was or was not owing to Supplier Co. The drawee bank may debit the account of Corporation for the amount of the check and there is no breach of warranty by Depositary Bank under Section 3–417(1)(a).

4. The last sentence of subsection (b) is similar to subsection (d) of Section 3–404 which is discussed in Comment 3 to Section 3–404. In Case # 5, Case # 6, or Case # 7 the depositary bank may have failed to exercise ordinary care when it allowed the employee to open an account in the name "Supplier Co.," to deposit checks payable to "Supplier Co." in that account, or to withdraw funds from that account that were proceeds of checks payable to Supplier Co. Failure to exercise ordinary care is to be determined in the context of all the facts relating to the bank's conduct with respect to the bank's collection of the check. If the trier of fact finds that there was such a failure and that the failure substantially contributed to loss, it could find the depositary bank liable to the extent the failure contributed to the loss. The last sentence of subsection (b) can be illustrated by an example. Suppose in Case # 5 that the check is not payable to an obscure "Supplier Co." but rather to a well-known national corporation. In addition, the check is for a very large amount of money. Before depositing the check, Employee opens an account in Depositary Bank in the name of the corporation and states to the person conducting the transaction for the bank that Employee is manager of a new office being opened by the corporation. Depositary Bank opens the account without requiring Employee to produce any resolutions of the corporation's board of directors or other evidence of authorization of Employee to act for the corporation. A few days later, the check is deposited, the account is credited, and the check is presented for payment. After Depositary Bank receives payment, it allows Employee to withdraw the credit by a wire transfer to an account in a bank in a foreign country. The trier of fact could find that Depositary Bank did not exercise ordinary care and that the failure to exercise ordinary care contributed to the loss suffered by Employer. The trier of fact could allow recovery by Employer from Depositary Bank for all or part of the loss suffered by Employer.

As amended in 2005.

§ 3–406. Negligence Contributing to Forged Signature or Alteration of Instrument.

(a) A person whose failure to exercise ordinary care substantially contributes to an alteration of an instrument or to the making of a forged signature on an instrument is precluded from asserting the alteration or the forgery against a person who, in good faith, pays the instrument or takes it for value or for collection.

(b) Under subsection (a), if the person asserting the preclusion fails to exercise ordinary care in paying or taking the instrument and that failure substantially contributes to loss, the loss is allocated between the person precluded and the person asserting the preclusion according to the extent to which the failure of each to exercise ordinary care contributed to the loss.

(c) Under subsection (a), the burden of proving failure to exercise ordinary care is on the person asserting the preclusion. Under subsection (b), the burden of proving failure to exercise ordinary care is on the person precluded.

Official Comment

1. Section 3–406(a) is based on former Section 3–406. With respect to alteration, Section 3–406 adopts the doctrine of Young v. Grote, 4 Bing. 253 (1827), which held that a drawer who so negligently draws an instrument as to facilitate its material alteration is liable to a drawee who pays the altered instrument in good faith. Under Section 3–406 the doctrine is expanded to apply not only to drafts but to all instruments. It includes in the protected class any "person who, in good faith, pays the instrument or takes it for value or for collection." Section 3–406 rejects decisions holding that the maker of a note owes no duty of care to the holder because at the time the instrument is issued there is no contract between them. By issuing the instrument and "setting it afloat upon a sea of strangers" the maker or drawer voluntarily enters into a relation with later holders which justifies imposition of a duty of care. In this respect an instrument so negligently drawn as to facilitate alteration does not differ in principle from an instrument containing blanks which may be filled. Under Section 3–407 a person paying an altered instrument or taking it for value, in good faith and without notice of the alteration may enforce rights with respect to the instrument according to its original terms. If negligence of the obligor substantially contributes to an alteration, this section gives the holder or the payor the alternative right to treat the altered instrument as though it had been issued in the altered form.

No attempt is made to define particular conduct that will constitute "failure to exercise ordinary care [that] substantially contributes to an alteration." Rather, "ordinary care" is defined in Section 3–103(a)(9) in general terms. The question is left to the court or the jury for decision in the light of the circumstances in the particular case including reasonable commercial standards that may apply.

Section 3–406 does not make the negligent party liable in tort for damages resulting from the alteration. If the negligent party is estopped from asserting the alteration the person taking the instrument is fully protected because the taker can treat the instrument as having been issued in the altered form.

2. Section 3–406 applies equally to a failure to exercise ordinary care that substantially contributes to the making of a forged signature on an instrument. Section 3–406 refers to "forged signature" rather than "unauthorized signature" that appeared in former Section 3–406 because it more accurately describes the scope of the provision. Unauthorized signature is a broader concept that includes not only forgery but also the signature of an agent which does not bind the principal under the law of agency. The agency cases are resolved independently under agency law. Section 3–406 is not necessary in those cases.

The "substantially contributes" test of former Section 3–406 is continued in this section in preference to a "direct and proximate cause" test. The "substantially contributes" test is meant to be less stringent than a "direct and proximate cause" test. Under the less stringent test the preclusion should be easier to establish. Conduct "substantially contributes" to a material alteration or forged signature if it is a contributing cause of the alteration or signature and a substantial factor in bringing it about. The analysis of "substantially contributes" in former Section 3–406 by the court in Thompson Maple Products v. Citizens National Bank of Corry, 234 A.2d 32 (Pa.Super.Ct.1967), states what is intended by the use of the same words in revised Section 3–406(b). Since Section 3–404(d) and Section 3–405(b) also use the words "substantially contributes" the analysis of these words also applies to those provisions.

3. The following cases illustrate the kind of conduct that can be the basis of a preclusion under Section 3–406(a):

Case # 1. Employer signs checks drawn on Employer's account by use of a rubber stamp of Employer's signature. Employer keeps the rubber stamp along with Employer's personalized blank check forms in an unlocked desk drawer. An unauthorized person fraudulently uses the check forms to write checks on Employer's account. The checks are signed by use of the rubber stamp. If Employer demands that Employer's account in the drawee bank be recredited because the forged check was not properly payable, the drawee bank may defend by asserting that Employer is precluded from asserting the forgery. The trier of fact could find that Employer failed to exercise ordinary care to safeguard the rubber stamp and the check forms and that the failure substantially contributed to the forgery of Employer's signature by the unauthorized use of the rubber stamp.

Case # 2. An insurance company draws a check to the order of Sarah Smith in payment of a claim of a policyholder, Sarah Smith, who lives in Alabama. The insurance company also has a policyholder with the same name who lives in Illinois. By mistake, the insurance company mails the check to the Illinois Sarah Smith who indorses the check and obtains payment. Because the payee of the check is the Alabama Sarah Smith, the indorsement by the Illinois Sarah Smith is a forged indorsement. Section 3-110(a). The trier of fact could find that the insurance company failed to exercise ordinary care when it mailed the check to the wrong person and that the failure substantially contributed to the making of the forged indorsement. In that event the insurance company could be precluded from asserting the forged indorsement against the drawee bank that honored the check.

Case # 3. A company writes a check for $10. The figure "10" and the word "ten" are typewritten in the appropriate spaces on the check form. A large blank space is left after the figure and the word. The payee of the check, using a typewriter with a typeface similar to that used on the check, writes the word "thousand" after the word "ten" and a comma and three zeros after the figure "10". The drawee bank in good faith pays $10,000 when the check is presented for payment and debits the account of the drawer in that amount. The trier of fact could find that the drawer failed to exercise ordinary care in writing the check and that the failure substantially contributed to the alteration. In that case the drawer is precluded from asserting the alteration against the drawee if the check was paid in good faith.

4. Subsection (b) differs from former Section 3-406 in that it adopts a concept of comparative negligence. If the person precluded under subsection (a) proves that the person asserting the preclusion failed to exercise ordinary care and that failure substantially contributed to the loss, the loss may be allocated between the two parties on a comparative negligence basis. In the case of a forged indorsement the litigation is usually between the payee of the check and the depositary bank that took the check for collection. An example is a case like Case # 1 of Comment 3 to Section 3-405. If the trier of fact finds that Employer failed to exercise

ordinary care in safeguarding the check and that the failure substantially contributed to the making of the forged indorsement, subsection (a) of Section 3-406 applies. If Employer brings an action for conversion against the depositary bank that took the checks from the forger, the depositary bank could assert the preclusion under subsection (a). But suppose the forger opened an account in the depositary bank in a name identical to that of Employer, the payee of the check, and then deposited the check in the account. Subsection (b) may apply. There may be an issue whether the depositary bank should have been alerted to possible fraud when a new account was opened for a corporation shortly before a very large check payable to a payee with the same name is deposited. Circumstances surrounding the opening of the account may have suggested that the corporation to which the check was payable may not be the same as the corporation for which the account was opened. If the trier of fact finds that collecting the check under these circumstances was a failure to exercise ordinary care, it could allocate the loss between the depositary bank and Employer, the payee.

§ 3-407. Alteration.

(a) "Alteration" means (i) an unauthorized change in an instrument that purports to modify in any respect the obligation of a party, or (ii) an unauthorized addition of words or numbers or other change to an incomplete instrument relating to the obligation of a party.

(b) Except as provided in subsection (c), an alteration fraudulently made discharges a party whose obligation is affected by the alteration unless that party assents or is precluded from asserting the alteration. No other alteration discharges a party, and the instrument may be enforced according to its original terms.

(c) A payor bank or drawee paying a fraudulently altered instrument or a person taking it for value, in good faith and without notice of the alteration, may enforce rights with respect to the instrument (i) according to its original terms, or (ii) in the case of an incomplete instrument altered by unauthorized completion, according to its terms as completed.

Official Comment

1. This provision restates former Section 3-407. Former Section 3-407 defined a "material" alteration as any alteration that changes the contract of the

parties in any respect. Revised Section 3–407 refers to such a change as an alteration. As under subsection (2) of former Section 3–407, discharge because of alteration occurs only in the case of an alteration fraudulently made. There is no discharge if a blank is filled in the honest belief that it is authorized or if a change is made with a benevolent motive such as a desire to give the obligor the benefit of a lower interest rate. Changes favorable to the obligor are unlikely to be made with any fraudulent intent, but if such an intent is found the alteration may operate as a discharge.

Discharge is a personal defense of the party whose obligation is modified and anyone whose obligation is not affected is not discharged. But if an alteration discharges a party there is also discharge of any party having a right of recourse against the discharged party because the obligation of the party with the right of recourse is affected by the alteration. Assent to the alteration given before or after it is made will prevent the party from asserting the discharge. The phrase "or is precluded from asserting the alteration" in subsection (b) recognizes the possibility of an estoppel or other ground barring the defense which does not rest on assent.

2. Under subsection (c) a person paying a fraudulently altered instrument or taking it for value, in good faith and without notice of the alteration, is not affected by a discharge under subsection (b). The person paying or taking the instrument may assert rights with respect to the instrument according to its original terms or, in the case of an incomplete instrument that is altered by unauthorized completion, according to its terms as completed. If blanks are filled or an incomplete instrument is otherwise completed, subsection (c) places the loss upon the party who left the instrument incomplete by permitting enforcement in its completed form. This result is intended even though the instrument was stolen from the issuer and completed after the theft.

§ 3–408. Drawee Not Liable on Unaccepted Draft.

A check or other draft does not of itself operate as an assignment of funds in the hands of the drawee available for its payment, and the drawee is not liable on the instrument until the drawee accepts it.

Official Comment

1. This section is a restatement of former Section 3–409(1). Subsection (2) of former Section 3–409 is deleted as misleading and superfluous. Comment 3

says of subsection (2): "It is intended to make it clear that this section does not in any way affect any liability which may arise apart from the instrument." In reality subsection (2) did not make anything clear and was a source of confusion. If all it meant was that a bank that has not certified a check may engage in other conduct that might make it liable to a holder, it stated the obvious and was superfluous. Section 1–103 is adequate to cover those cases.

2. Liability with respect to drafts may arise under other law. For example, Section 4–302 imposes liability on a payor bank for late return of an item.

§ 3–409. Acceptance of Draft; Certified Check.

(a) "Acceptance" means the drawee's signed agreement to pay a draft as presented. It must be written on the draft and may consist of the drawee's signature alone. Acceptance may be made at any time and becomes effective when notification pursuant to instructions is given or the accepted draft is delivered for the purpose of giving rights on the acceptance to any person.

(b) A draft may be accepted although it has not been signed by the drawer, is otherwise incomplete, is overdue, or has been dishonored.

(c) If a draft is payable at a fixed period after sight and the acceptor fails to date the acceptance, the holder may complete the acceptance by supplying a date in good faith.

(d) "Certified check" means a check accepted by the bank on which it is drawn. Acceptance may be made as stated in subsection (a) or by a writing on the check which indicates that the check is certified. The drawee of a check has no obligation to certify the check, and refusal to certify is not dishonor of the check.

Official Comment

1. The first three subsections of Section 3–409 are a restatement of former Section 3–410. Subsection (d) adds a definition of certified check which is a type of accepted draft.

2. Subsection (a) states the generally recognized rule that the mere signature of the drawee on the instrument is a sufficient acceptance. Customarily the signature is written vertically across the face of the instrument, but since the drawee has no reason to sign for any other purpose a signature in any other place, even on the back of the instrument, is sufficient. It need not be accompanied by such words as "Accepted,"

"Certified," or "Good." It must not, however, bear any words indicating an intent to refuse to honor the draft. The last sentence of subsection (a) states the generally recognized rule that an acceptance written on the draft takes effect when the drawee notifies the holder or gives notice according to instructions.

3. The purpose of subsection (c) is to provide a definite date of payment if none appears on the instrument. An undated acceptance of a draft payable "thirty days after sight" is incomplete. Unless the acceptor writes in a different date the holder is authorized to complete the acceptance according to the terms of the draft by supplying a date of acceptance. Any date supplied by the holder is effective if made in good faith.

4. The last sentence of subsection (d) states the generally recognized rule that in the absence of agreement a bank is under no obligation to certify a check. A check is a demand instrument calling for payment rather than acceptance. The bank may be liable for breach of any agreement with the drawer, the holder, or any other person by which it undertakes to certify. Its liability is not on the instrument, since the drawee is not so liable until acceptance. Section 3–408. Any liability is for breach of the separate agreement.

§ 3–410. Acceptance Varying Draft.

(a) If the terms of a drawee's acceptance vary from the terms of the draft as presented, the holder may refuse the acceptance and treat the draft as dishonored. In that case, the drawee may cancel the acceptance.

(b) The terms of a draft are not varied by an acceptance to pay at a particular bank or place in the United States, unless the acceptance states that the draft is to be paid only at that bank or place.

(c) If the holder assents to an acceptance varying the terms of a draft, the obligation of each drawer and indorser that does not expressly assent to the acceptance is discharged.

Official Comment

1. This section is a restatement of former Section 3–412. It applies to conditional acceptances, acceptances for part of the amount, acceptances to pay at a different time from that required by the draft, or to the acceptance of less than all of the drawees. It applies to any other engagement changing the essential terms of the draft. If the drawee makes a varied acceptance the holder may either reject it or assent to it. The holder may reject by insisting on acceptance of the draft as presented. Refusal by the drawee to accept the draft

as presented is dishonor. In that event the drawee is not bound by the varied acceptance and is entitled to have it canceled.

If the holder assents to the varied acceptance, the drawee's obligation as acceptor is according to the terms of the varied acceptance. Under subsection (c) the effect of the holder's assent is to discharge any drawer or indorser who does not also assent. The assent of the drawer or indorser must be affirmatively expressed. Mere failure to object within a reasonable time is not assent which will prevent the discharge.

2. Under subsection (b) an acceptance does not vary from the terms of the draft if it provides for payment at any particular bank or place in the United States unless the acceptance states that the draft is to be paid only at such bank or place. Section 3–501(b)(1) states that if an instrument is payable at a bank in the United States presentment must be made at the place of payment (Section 3–111) which in this case is at the designated bank.

§ 3–411. Refusal to Pay Cashier's Checks, Teller's Checks, and Certified Checks.

(a) In this section, "obligated bank" means the acceptor of a certified check or the issuer of a cashier's check or teller's check bought from the issuer.

(b) If the obligated bank wrongfully (i) refuses to pay a cashier's check or certified check, (ii) stops payment of a teller's check, or (iii) refuses to pay a dishonored teller's check, the person asserting the right to enforce the check is entitled to compensation for expenses and loss of interest resulting from the nonpayment and may recover consequential damages if the obligated bank refuses to pay after receiving notice of particular circumstances giving rise to the damages.

(c) Expenses or consequential damages under subsection (b) are not recoverable if the refusal of the obligated bank to pay occurs because (i) the bank suspends payments, (ii) the obligated bank asserts a claim or defense of the bank that it has reasonable grounds to believe is available against the person entitled to enforce the instrument, (iii) the obligated bank has a reasonable doubt whether the person demanding payment is the person entitled to enforce the instrument, or (iv) payment is prohibited by law.

Official Comment

1. In some cases a creditor may require that the debt be paid by an obligation of a bank. The debtor may comply by obtaining certification of the debtor's check, but more frequently the debtor buys from a bank a cashier's check or teller's check payable to the creditor. The check is taken by the creditor as a cash equivalent on the assumption that the bank will pay the check. Sometimes, the debtor wants to retract payment by inducing the obligated bank not to pay. The typical case involves a dispute between the parties to the transaction in which the check is given in payment. In the case of a certified check or cashier's check, the bank can safely pay the holder of the check despite notice that there may be an adverse claim to the check (Section 3–602). It is also clear that the bank that sells a teller's check has no duty to order the bank on which it is drawn not to pay it. A debtor using any of these types of checks has no right to stop payment. Nevertheless, some banks will refuse payment as an accommodation to a customer. Section 3–411 is designed to discourage this practice.

2. The term "obligated bank" refers to the issuer of the cashier's check or teller's check and the acceptor of the certified check. If the obligated bank wrongfully refuses to pay, it is liable to pay for expenses and loss of interest resulting from the refusal to pay. There is no express provision for attorney's fees, but attorney's fees are not meant to be necessarily excluded. They could be granted because they fit within the language "expenses *** resulting from the nonpayment." In addition the bank may be liable to pay consequential damages if it has notice of the particular circumstances giving rise to the damages.

3. Subsection (c) provides that expenses or consequential damages are not recoverable if the refusal to pay is because of the reasons stated. The purpose is to limit that recovery to cases in which the bank refuses to pay even though its obligation to pay is clear and it is able to pay. Subsection (b) applies only if the refusal to honor the check is wrongful. If the bank is not obliged to pay there is no recovery. The bank may assert any claim or defense that it has, but normally the bank would not have a claim or defense. In the usual case it is a remitter that is asserting a claim to the check on the basis of a rescission of negotiation to the payee under Section 3–202. See Comment 2 to Section 3–201. The bank can assert that claim if there is compliance with Section 3–305(c), but the bank is not protected from damages under subsection (b) if the claim of the remitter is not upheld. In that case, the bank is insulated from damages only if payment is enjoined under Section 3–602(b)(1). Subsection (c)(iii) refers to cases in which the bank may have a reasonable doubt about the identity of the person demanding payment. For example, a cashier's check is payable to "Supplier Co." The person in possession of the check presents it for payment over the counter and claims to be an officer of Supplier Co. The bank may refuse payment until it has been given adequate proof that the presentment in fact is being made for Supplier Co., the person entitled to enforce the check.

§ 3–412. Obligation of Issuer of Note or Cashier's Check.

The issuer of a note or cashier's check or other draft drawn on the drawer is obliged to pay the instrument (i) according to its terms at the time it was issued or, if not issued, at the time it first came into possession of a holder, or (ii) if the issuer signed an incomplete instrument, according to its terms when completed, to the extent stated in Sections 3–115 and 3–407. The obligation is owed to a person entitled to enforce the instrument or to an indorser who paid the instrument under Section 3–415.

Official Comment

1. The obligations of the maker, acceptor, drawer, and indorser are stated in four separate sections. Section 3–412 states the obligation of the maker of a note and is consistent with former Section 3–413(1). Section 3–412 also applies to the issuer of a cashier's check or other draft drawn on the drawer. Under former Section 3–118(a), since a cashier's check or other draft drawn on the drawer was "effective as a note," the drawer was liable under former Section 3–413(1) as a maker. Under Sections 3–103(a)(8) and 3–104(f) a cashier's check or other draft drawn on the drawer is treated as a draft to reflect common commercial usage, but the liability of the drawer is stated by Section 3–412 as being the same as that of the maker of a note rather than that of the drawer of a draft. Thus, Section 3–412 does not in substance change former law.

2. Under Section 3–105(b) nonissuance of either a complete or incomplete instrument is a defense by a maker or drawer against a person that is not a holder in due course.

3. The obligation of the maker may be modified in the case of alteration if, under Section 3–406, the maker is precluded from asserting the alteration.

4. The rule of this section is similar to the rule of Article 39 of the Convention on International Bills of Exchange and International Promissory Notes.

As amended in 2002.

§ 3-413. Obligation of Acceptor.

(a) The acceptor of a draft is obliged to pay the draft (i) according to its terms at the time it was accepted, even though the acceptance states that the draft is payable "as originally drawn" or equivalent terms, (ii) if the acceptance varies the terms of the draft, according to the terms of the draft as varied, or (iii) if the acceptance is of a draft that is an incomplete instrument, according to its terms when completed, to the extent stated in Sections 3-115 and 3-407. The obligation is owed to a person entitled to enforce the draft or to the drawer or an indorser who paid the draft under Section 3-414 or 3-415.

(b) If the certification of a check or other acceptance of a draft states the amount certified or accepted, the obligation of the acceptor is that amount. If (i) the certification or acceptance does not state an amount, (ii) the amount of the instrument is subsequently raised, and (iii) the instrument is then negotiated to a holder in due course, the obligation of the acceptor is the amount of the instrument at the time it was taken by the holder in due course.

Official Comment

Subsection (a) is consistent with former Section 3-413(1). Subsection (b) has primary importance with respect to certified checks. It protects the holder in due course of a certified check that was altered after certification and before negotiation to the holder in due course. A bank can avoid liability for the altered amount by stating on the check the amount the bank agrees to pay. The subsection applies to other accepted drafts as well. The rule of this section is similar to the rule of Articles 41 of the Convention on International Bills of Exchange and International Promissory Notes. Articles 42 and 43 of the Convention include more detailed rules that in many respects do not have parallels in this Article.

As amended in 2002.

§ 3-414. Obligation of Drawer.

(a) This section does not apply to cashier's checks or other drafts drawn on the drawer.

(b) If an unaccepted draft is dishonored, the drawer is obliged to pay the draft (i) according to its terms at the time it was issued or, if not issued, at the time it first came into possession of a holder, or (ii) if the drawer signed an incomplete instrument, according to its terms when completed, to the extent stated in Sections 3-115 and 3-407. The obligation is owed to a person entitled to enforce the draft or to an indorser who paid the draft under Section 3-415.

(c) If a draft is accepted by a bank, the drawer is discharged, regardless of when or by whom acceptance was obtained.

(d) If a draft is accepted and the acceptor is not a bank, the obligation of the drawer to pay the draft if the draft is dishonored by the acceptor is the same as the obligation of an indorser under Section 3-415(a) and (c).

(e) If a draft states that it is drawn "without recourse" or otherwise disclaims liability of the drawer to pay the draft, the drawer is not liable under subsection (b) to pay the draft if the draft is not a check. A disclaimer of the liability stated in subsection (b) is not effective if the draft is a check.

(f) If (i) a check is not presented for payment or given to a depositary bank for collection within 30 days after its date, (ii) the drawee suspends payments after expiration of the 30-day period without paying the check, and (iii) because of the suspension of payments, the drawer is deprived of funds maintained with the drawee to cover payment of the check, the drawer to the extent deprived of funds may discharge its obligation to pay the check by assigning to the person entitled to enforce the check the rights of the drawer against the drawee with respect to the funds.

Official Comment

1. Subsection (a) excludes cashier's checks because the obligation of the issuer of a cashier's check is stated in Section 3-412.

2. Subsection (b) states the obligation of the drawer on an unaccepted draft. It replaces former Section 3-413(2). The requirement under former Article 3 of notice of dishonor or protest has been eliminated. Under revised Article 3, notice of dishonor is necessary only with respect to indorser's liability. The liability of the drawer of an unaccepted draft is treated as a primary liability. Under former Section 3-102(1)(d) the term "secondary party" was used to refer to a

drawer or indorser. The quoted term is not used in revised Article 3. The effect of a draft drawn without recourse is stated in subsection (e).

3. Under subsection (c) the drawer is discharged of liability on a draft accepted by a bank regardless of when acceptance was obtained. This changes former Section 3–411(1) which provided that the drawer is discharged only if the holder obtains acceptance. Holders that have a bank obligation do not normally rely on the drawer to guarantee the bank's solvency. A holder can obtain protection against the insolvency of a bank acceptor by a specific guaranty of payment by the drawer or by obtaining an indorsement by the drawer. Section 3–205(d).

4. Subsection (d) states the liability of the drawer if a draft is accepted by a drawee other than a bank and the acceptor dishonors. The drawer of an unaccepted draft is the only party liable on the instrument. The drawee has no liability on the draft. Section 3–408. When the draft is accepted, the obligations change. The drawee, as acceptor, becomes primarily liable and the drawer's liability is that of a person secondarily liable as a guarantor of payment. The drawer's liability is identical to that of an indorser, and subsection (d) states the drawer's liability that way. The drawer is liable to pay the person entitled to enforce the draft or any indorser that pays pursuant to Section 3–415. The drawer in this case is discharged if notice of dishonor is required by Section 3–503 and is not given in compliance with that section. A drawer that pays has a right of recourse against the acceptor. Section 3–413(a).

5. Subsection (e) does not permit the drawer of a check to avoid liability under subsection (b) by drawing the check without recourse. There is no legitimate purpose served by issuing a check on which nobody is liable. Drawing without recourse is effective to disclaim liability of the drawer if the draft is not a check. Suppose, in a documentary sale, Seller draws a draft on Buyer for the price of goods shipped to Buyer. The draft is payable upon delivery to the drawee of an order bill of lading covering the goods. Seller delivers the draft with the bill of lading to Finance Company that is named as payee of the draft. If Seller draws without recourse Finance Company takes the risk that Buyer will dishonor. If Buyer dishonors, Finance Company has no recourse against Seller but it can obtain reimbursement by selling the goods which it controls through the bill of lading.

6. Subsection (f) is derived from former Section 3–502(1)(b). It is designed to protect the drawer of a check against loss resulting from suspension of pay-

ments by the drawee bank when the holder of the check delays collection of the check. For example, X writes a check payable to Y for $1,000. The check is covered by funds in X's account in the drawee bank. Y delays initiation of collection of the check for more than 30 days after the date of the check. The drawee bank suspends payments after the 30–day period and before the check is presented for payment. If the $1,000 of funds in X's account have not been withdrawn, X has a claim for those funds against the drawee bank and, if subsection (e) were not in effect, X would be liable to Y on the check because the check was dishonored. Section 3–502(e). If the suspension of payments by the drawee bank will result in payment to X of less than the full amount of the $1,000 in the account or if there is a significant delay in payment to X, X will suffer a loss which would not have been suffered if Y had promptly initiated collection of the check. In most cases, X will not suffer any loss because of the existence of federal bank deposit insurance that covers accounts up to $100,000. Thus, subsection (e) has relatively little importance. There might be some cases, however, in which the account is not fully insured because it exceeds $100,000 or because the account doesn't qualify for deposit insurance. Subsection (f) retains the phrase "deprived of funds maintained with the drawee" appearing in former Section 3–502(1)(b). The quoted phrase applies if the suspension of payments by the drawee prevents the drawer from receiving the benefit of funds which would have paid the check if the holder had been timely in initiating collection. Thus, any significant delay in obtaining full payment of the funds is a deprivation of funds. The drawer can discharge drawer's liability by assigning rights against the drawee with respect to the funds to the holder.

7. The obligation of the drawer under this section is similar to the obligation of the drawer under Article 38 of the Convention on International Bills of Exchange and International Promissory Notes.

As amended in 2002.

§ 3–415. Obligation of Indorser.

(a) Subject to subsections (b), (c), (d), (e) and to Section 3–419(d), if an instrument is dishonored, an indorser is obliged to pay the amount due on the instrument (i) according to the terms of the instrument at the time it was indorsed, or (ii) if the indorser indorsed an incomplete instrument, according to its terms when completed, to the extent stated in Sections 3–115 and 3–407. The obligation of the indorser is owed to a person entitled to enforce the instrument or to a subsequent indorser who paid the instrument under this section.

(b) If an indorsement states that it is made "without recourse" or otherwise disclaims liability of the indorser, the indorser is not liable under subsection (a) to pay the instrument.

(c) If notice of dishonor of an instrument is required by Section 3–503 and notice of dishonor complying with that section is not given to an indorser, the liability of the indorser under subsection (a) is discharged.

(d) If a draft is accepted by a bank after an indorsement is made, the liability of the indorser under subsection (a) is discharged.

(e) If an indorser of a check is liable under subsection (a) and the check is not presented for payment, or given to a depositary bank for collection, within 30 days after the day the indorsement was made, the liability of the indorser under subsection (a) is discharged.

As amended in 1993.

Official Comment

1. Subsections (a) and (b) restate the substance of former Section 3–414(1). Subsection (2) of former Section 3–414 has been dropped because it is superfluous. Although notice of dishonor is not mentioned in subsection (a), it must be given in some cases to charge an indorser. It is covered in subsection (c). Regulation CC § 229.35(b) provides that a bank handling a check for collection or return is liable to a bank that subsequently handles the check to the extent the latter bank does not receive payment for the check. This liability applies whether or not the bank incurring the liability indorsed the check.

2. Section 3–503 states when notice of dishonor is required and how it must be given. If required notice of dishonor is not given in compliance with Section 3–503, subsection (c) of Section 3–415 states that the effect is to discharge the indorser's obligation.

3. Subsection (d) is similar in effect to Section 3–414(c) if the draft is accepted by a bank after the indorsement is made. See Comment 3 to Section 3–414. If a draft is accepted by a bank before the indorsement is made, the indorser incurs the obligation stated in subsection (a).

4. Subsection (e) modifies former Sections 3–503(2)(b) and 3–502(1)(a) by stating a 30–day rather than a seven-day period, and stating it as an absolute rather than a presumptive period.

5. As stated in subsection (a), the obligation of an indorser to pay the amount due on the instrument is generally owed not only to a person entitled to enforce the instrument but also to a subsequent indorser who paid the instrument. But if the prior indorser and the subsequent indorser are both anomalous indorsers, this rule does not apply. In that case, Section 3–116 applies. Under Section 3–116(a), the anomalous indorsers are jointly and severally liable and if either pays the instrument the indorser who pays has a right of contribution against the other. Section 3–116(b). The right to contribution in Section 3–116(b) is subject to "agreement of the affected parties." Suppose the subsequent indorser can prove an agreement with the prior indorser under which the prior indorser agreed to treat the subsequent indorser as a guarantor of the obligation of the prior indorser. Rights of the two indorsers between themselves would be governed by the agreement. Under suretyship law, the subsequent indorser under such an agreement is referred to as a sub-surety. Under the agreement, if the subsequent indorser pays the instrument there is a right to reimbursement from the prior indorser; if the prior indorser pays the instrument, there is no right of recourse against the subsequent indorser. See PEB Commentary No. 11, dated February 10, 1994 [Appendix V, infra].

6. The rule of this section is similar to the rule of Article 44 of the Convention on International Bills of Exchange and International Promissory Notes.

As amended in 2002.

§ 3–416. Transfer Warranties.

(a) A person who transfers an instrument for consideration warrants to the transferee and, if the transfer is by indorsement, to any subsequent transferee that:

(1) the warrantor is a person entitled to enforce the instrument;

(2) all signatures on the instrument are authentic and authorized;

(3) the instrument has not been altered;

(4) the instrument is not subject to a defense or claim in recoupment of any party which can be asserted against the warrantor;

(5) the warrantor has no knowledge of any insolvency proceeding commenced with respect to the maker or acceptor or, in

the case of an unaccepted draft, the drawer; and

(6) with respect to a remotely-created consumer item, that the person on whose account the item is drawn authorized the issuance of the item in the amount for which the item is drawn.

(b) A person to whom the warranties under subsection (a) are made and who took the instrument in good faith may recover from the warrantor as damages for breach of warranty an amount equal to the loss suffered as a result of the breach, but not more than the amount of the instrument plus expenses and loss of interest incurred as a result of the breach.

(c) The warranties stated in subsection (a) cannot be disclaimed with respect to checks. Unless notice of a claim for breach of warranty is given to the warrantor within 30 days after the claimant has reason to know of the breach and the identity of the warrantor, the liability of the warrantor under subsection (b) is discharged to the extent of any loss caused by the delay in giving notice of the claim.

(d) A [cause of action] for breach of warranty under this section accrues when the claimant has reason to know of the breach.

As amended in 2002.

Official Comment

1. Subsection (a) is taken from subsection (2) of former Section 3–417. Subsections (3) and (4) of former Section 3–417 are deleted. Warranties under subsection (a) in favor of the immediate transferee apply to all persons who transfer an instrument for consideration whether or not the transfer is accompanied by indorsement. Any consideration sufficient to support a simple contract will support those warranties. If there is an indorsement the warranty runs with the instrument and the remote holder may sue the indorser-warrantor directly and thus avoid a multiplicity of suits.

2. Since the purpose of transfer (Section 3–203(a)) is to give the transferee the right to enforce the instrument, subsection (a)(1) is a warranty that the transferor is a person entitled to enforce the instrument (Section 3–301). Under Section 3–203(b) transfer gives the transferee any right of the transferor to enforce the instrument. Subsection (a)(1) is in effect a warranty that there are no unauthorized or missing indorse-

ments that prevent the transferor from making the transferee a person entitled to enforce the instrument.

3. The rationale of subsection (a)(4) is that the transferee does not undertake to buy an instrument that is not enforceable in whole or in part, unless there is a contrary agreement. Even if the transferee takes as a holder in due course who takes free of the defense or claim in recoupment, the warranty gives the transferee the option of proceeding against the transferor rather than litigating with the obligor on the instrument the issue of the holder-in-due-course status of the transferee. Subsection (3) of former Section 3–417 which limits this warranty is deleted. The rationale is that while the purpose of a "no recourse" indorsement is to avoid a guaranty of payment, the indorsement does not clearly indicate an intent to disclaim warranties.

4. Under subsection (a)(5) the transferor does not warrant against difficulties of collection, impairment of the credit of the obligor or even insolvency. The transferee is expected to determine such questions before taking the obligation. If insolvency proceedings as defined in Section 1–201(22) have been instituted against the party who is expected to pay and the transferor knows it, the concealment of that fact amounts to a fraud upon the transferee, and the warranty against knowledge of such proceedings is provided accordingly.

5. Transfer warranties may be disclaimed with respect to any instrument except a check. Between the immediate parties disclaimer may be made by agreement. In the case of an indorser, disclaimer of transferor's liability, to be effective, must appear in the indorsement with words such as "without warranties" or some other specific reference to warranties. But in the case of a check, subsection (c) of Section 3–416 provides that transfer warranties cannot be disclaimed at all. In the check collection process the banking system relies on these warranties.

6. Subsection (b) states the measure of damages for breach of warranty. There is no express provision for attorney's fees, but attorney's fees are not meant to be necessarily excluded. They could be granted because they fit within the phrase "expenses *** incurred as a result of the breach." The intention is to leave to other state law the issue as to when attorney's fees are recoverable.

7. Since the traditional term "cause of action" may have been replaced in some states by "claim for relief" or some equivalent term, the words "cause of action" in subsection (d) have been bracketed to indicate that

the words may be replaced by an appropriate substitute to conform to local practice.

8. Subsection (a)(6) is based on a number of nonuniform amendments designed to address concerns about certain kinds of check fraud. The provision implements a limited rejection of Price v. Neal, 97 Eng. Rep. 871 (K.B. 1762), so that in certain circumstances (those involving remotely-created consumer items) the payor bank can use a warranty claim to absolve itself of responsibility for honoring an unauthorized item. The provision rests on the premise that monitoring by depositary banks can control this type of fraud more effectively than any practices readily available to payor banks. The provision expressly includes both the case in which the consumer does not authorize the item at all and also the case in which the consumer authorizes the item but in an amount different from the amount in which the item is drawn. Similar provisions appear in Sections 3–417, 4–207, and 4–208.

The provision supplements applicable federal law, which requires telemarketers who submit instruments for payment to obtain the customer's "express verifiable authorization," which may be either in writing or tape recorded and must be made available upon request to the customer's bank. Federal Trade Commission's Telemarketing Sales Rule, 16 C.F.R. § 310.3(a)(3), implementing the Telemarketing and Consumer Fraud and Abuse Prevention Act, 15 U.S.C. §§ 6101–6108. Some states also have consumer-protection laws governing authorization of instruments in telemarketing transactions. *See, e.g.,* 9 Vt. Stat. Ann. § 2464.

9. Article 45 of the Convention on International Bills of Exchange and International Promissory Notes includes warranties that are similar (except for the warranty in subsection (a)(6)).

As amended in 2002.

§ 3–417. Presentment Warranties.

(a) If an unaccepted draft is presented to the drawee for payment or acceptance and the drawee pays or accepts the draft, (i) the person obtaining payment or acceptance, at the time of presentment, and (ii) a previous transferor of the draft, at the time of transfer, warrant to the drawee making payment or accepting the draft in good faith that:

    (1) the warrantor is, or was, at the time the warrantor transferred the draft, a person entitled to enforce the draft or authorized to obtain payment or acceptance of

the draft on behalf of a person entitled to enforce the draft;

    (2) the draft has not been altered;

    (3) the warrantor has no knowledge that the signature of the drawer of the draft is unauthorized; and

    (4) with respect to any remotely-created consumer item, that the person on whose account the item is drawn authorized the issuance of the item in the amount for which the item is drawn.

(b) A drawee making payment may recover from any warrantor damages for breach of warranty equal to the amount paid by the drawee less the amount the drawee received or is entitled to receive from the drawer because of the payment. In addition, the drawee is entitled to compensation for expenses and loss of interest resulting from the breach. The right of the drawee to recover damages under this subsection is not affected by any failure of the drawee to exercise ordinary care in making payment. If the drawee accepts the draft, breach of warranty is a defense to the obligation of the acceptor. If the acceptor makes payment with respect to the draft, the acceptor is entitled to recover from any warrantor for breach of warranty the amounts stated in this subsection.

(c) If a drawee asserts a claim for breach of warranty under subsection (a) based on an unauthorized indorsement of the draft or an alteration of the draft, the warrantor may defend by proving that the indorsement is effective under Section 3–404 or 3–405 or the drawer is precluded under Section 3–406 or 4–406 from asserting against the drawee the unauthorized indorsement or alteration.

(d) If (i) a dishonored draft is presented for payment to the drawer or an indorser or (ii) any other instrument is presented for payment to a party obliged to pay the instrument, and (iii) payment is received, the following rules apply:

    (1) The person obtaining payment and a prior transferor of the instrument warrant to the person making payment in good faith that the warrantor is, or was, at the time the warrantor transferred the instrument, a person entitled to enforce the instrument or authorized to obtain

payment on behalf of a person entitled to enforce the instrument.

(2) The person making payment may recover from any warrantor for breach of warranty an amount equal to the amount paid plus expenses and loss of interest resulting from the breach.

(e) The warranties stated in subsections (a) and (d) cannot be disclaimed with respect to checks. Unless notice of a claim for breach of warranty is given to the warrantor within 30 days after the claimant has reason to know of the breach and the identity of the warrantor, the liability of the warrantor under subsection (b) or (d) is discharged to the extent of any loss caused by the delay in giving notice of the claim.

(f) A [cause of action] for breach of warranty under this section accrues when the claimant has reason to know of the breach.

As amended in 2002.

Official Comment

1. This section replaces subsection (1) of former Section 3–417. The former provision was difficult to understand because it purported to state in one subsection all warranties given to any person paying any instrument. The result was a provision replete with exceptions that could not be readily understood except after close scrutiny of the language. In revised Section 3–417, presentment warranties made to drawees of uncertified checks and other unaccepted drafts are stated in subsection (a). All other presentment warranties are stated in subsection (d).

2. Subsection (a) states three warranties. Subsection (a)(1) in effect is a warranty that there are no unauthorized or missing indorsements. "Person entitled to enforce" is defined in Section 3–301. Subsection (a)(2) is a warranty that there is no alteration. Subsection (a)(3) is a warranty of no knowledge that there is a forged drawer's signature. Subsection (a) states that the warranties are made to the drawee and subsections (b) and (c) identify the drawee as the person entitled to recover for breach of warranty. There is no warranty made to the drawer under subsection (a) when presentment is made to the drawee. Warranty to the drawer is governed by subsection (d) and that applies only when presentment for payment is made to the drawer with respect to a dishonored draft. In Sun 'N Sand, Inc. v. United California Bank, 582 P.2d 920 (Cal.1978), the court held that under former Section 3–417(1) a warranty was made to the drawer of

a check when the check was presented to the drawee for payment. The result in that case is rejected.

3. Subsection (a)(1) retains the rule that the drawee does not admit the authenticity of indorsements and subsection (a)(3) retains the rule of Price v. Neal, 3 Burr. 1354 (1762), that the drawee takes the risk that the drawer's signature is unauthorized unless the person presenting the draft has knowledge that the drawer's signature is unauthorized. Under subsection (a)(3) the warranty of no knowledge that the drawer's signature is unauthorized is also given by prior transferors of the draft.

4. Subsection (d) applies to presentment for payment in all cases not covered by subsection (a). It applies to presentment of notes and accepted drafts to any party obliged to pay the instrument, including an indorser, and to presentment of dishonored drafts if made to the drawer or an indorser. In cases covered by subsection (d), there is only one warranty and it is the same as that stated in subsection (a)(1). There are no warranties comparable to subsections (a)(2) and (a)(3) because they are appropriate only in the case of presentment to the drawee of an unaccepted draft. With respect to presentment of an accepted draft to the acceptor, there is no warranty with respect to alteration or knowledge that the signature of the drawer is unauthorized. Those warranties were made to the drawee when the draft was presented for acceptance (Section 3–417(a)(2) and (3)) and breach of that warranty is a defense to the obligation of the drawee as acceptor to pay the draft. If the drawee pays the accepted draft the drawee may recover the payment from any warrantor who was in breach of warranty when the draft was accepted. Section 3–417(b). Thus, there is no necessity for these warranties to be repeated when the accepted draft is presented for payment. Former Section 3–417(1)(b)(iii) and (c)(iii) are not included in revised Section 3–417 because they are unnecessary. Former Section 3–417(1)(c)(iv) is not included because it is also unnecessary. The acceptor should know what the terms of the draft were at the time acceptance was made.

If presentment is made to the drawer or maker, there is no necessity for a warranty concerning the signature of that person or with respect to alteration. If presentment is made to an indorser, the indorser had itself warranted authenticity of signatures and that the instrument was not altered. Section 3–416(a)(2) and (3).

5. The measure of damages for breach of warranty under subsection (a) is stated in subsection (b). There is no express provision for attorney's fees, but attor-

ney's fees are not meant to be necessarily excluded. They could be granted because they fit within the language "expenses *** resulting from the breach." Subsection (b) provides that the right of the drawee to recover for breach of warranty is not affected by a failure of the drawee to exercise ordinary care in paying the draft. This provision follows the result reached under former Article 3 in Hartford Accident & Indemnity Co. v. First Pennsylvania Bank, 859 F.2d 295 (3d Cir.1988).

6. Subsection (c) applies to checks and other unaccepted drafts. It gives to the warrantor the benefit of rights that the drawee has against the drawer under Section 3-404, 3-405, 3-406, or 4-406. If the drawer's conduct contributed to a loss from forgery or alteration, the drawee should not be allowed to shift the loss from the drawer to the warrantor.

7. The first sentence of subsection (e) recognizes that checks are normally paid by automated means and that payor banks rely on warranties in making payment. Thus, it is not appropriate to allow disclaimer or warranties appearing on checks that normally will not be examined by the payor bank. The second sentence requires a breach of warranty claim to be asserted within 30 days after the drawee learns of the breach and the identity of the warrantor.

8. Since the traditional term "cause of action" may have been replaced in some states by "claim for relief" or some equivalent term, the words "cause of action" in subsection (f) have been bracketed to indicate that the words may be replaced by an appropriate substitute to conform to local practice.

9. For discussion of subsection (a)(4), see Comment 8 to Section 3-416.

As amended in 2002.

§ 3-418. Payment or Acceptance by Mistake.

(a) Except as provided in subsection (c), if the drawee of a draft pays or accepts the draft and the drawee acted on the mistaken belief that (i) payment of the draft had not been stopped pursuant to Section 4-403 or (ii) the signature of the drawer of the draft was authorized, the drawee may recover the amount of the draft from the person to whom or for whose benefit payment was made or, in the case of acceptance, may revoke the acceptance. Rights of the drawee under this subsection are not affected by failure of the drawee to exercise ordinary care in paying or accepting the draft.

(b) Except as provided in subsection (c), if an instrument has been paid or accepted by mistake and the case is not covered by subsection (a), the person paying or accepting may, to the extent permitted by the law governing mistake and restitution, (i) recover the payment from the person to whom or for whose benefit payment was made or (ii) in the case of acceptance, may revoke the acceptance.

(c) The remedies provided by subsection (a) or (b) may not be asserted against a person who took the instrument in good faith and for value or who in good faith changed position in reliance on the payment or acceptance. This subsection does not limit remedies provided by Section 3-417 or 4-407.

(d) Notwithstanding Section 4-215, if an instrument is paid or accepted by mistake and the payor or acceptor recovers payment or revokes acceptance under subsection (a) or (b), the instrument is deemed not to have been paid or accepted and is treated as dishonored, and the person from whom payment is recovered has rights as a person entitled to enforce the dishonored instrument.

Official Comment

1. This section covers payment or acceptance by mistake and replaces former Section 3-418. Under former Article 3, the remedy of a drawee that paid or accepted a draft by mistake was based on the law of mistake and restitution, but that remedy was not specifically stated. It was provided by Section 1-103. Former Section 3-418 was simply a limitation on the unstated remedy under the law of mistake and restitution. Under revised Article 3, Section 3-418 specifically states the right of restitution in subsections (a) and (b). Subsection (a) allows restitution in the two most common cases in which the problem is presented: payment or acceptance of forged checks and checks on which the drawer has stopped payment. If the drawee acted under a mistaken belief that the check was not forged or had not been stopped, the drawee is entitled to recover the funds paid or to revoke the acceptance whether or not the drawee acted negligently. But in each case, by virtue of subsection (c), the drawee loses the remedy if the person receiving payment or acceptance was a person who took the check in good faith and for value or who in good faith changed position in reliance on the payment or acceptance. Subsections (a) and (c) are consistent with former Section 3-418 and the rule of Price v. Neal. The result in the two

cases covered by subsection (a) is that the drawee in most cases will not have a remedy against the person paid because there is usually a person who took the check in good faith and for value or who in good faith changed position in reliance on the payment or acceptance.

2. If a check has been paid by mistake and the payee receiving payment did not give value for the check or did not change position in reliance on the payment, the drawee bank is entitled to recover the amount of the check under subsection (a) regardless of how the check was paid. The drawee bank normally pays a check by a credit to an account of the collecting bank that presents the check for payment. The payee of the check normally receives the payment by a credit to the payee's account in the depositary bank. But in some cases the payee of the check may have received payment directly from the drawee bank by presenting the check for payment over the counter. In those cases the payee is entitled to receive cash, but the payee may prefer another form of payment such as a cashier's check or teller's check issued by the drawee bank. Suppose Seller contracted to sell goods to Buyer. The contract provided for immediate payment by Buyer and delivery of the goods 20 days after payment. Buyer paid by mailing a check for $10,000 drawn on Bank payable to Seller. The next day Buyer gave a stop payment order to Bank with respect to the check Buyer had mailed to Seller. A few days later Seller presented Buyer's check to Bank for payment over the counter and requested a cashier's check as payment. Bank issued and delivered a cashier's check for $10,000 payable to Seller. The teller failed to discover Buyer's stop order. The next day Bank discovered the mistake and immediately advised Seller of the facts. Seller refused to return the cashier's check and did not deliver any goods to Buyer.

Under Section 4–215, Buyer's check was paid by Bank at the time it delivered its cashier's check to Seller. See Comment 3 to Section 4–215. Bank is obliged to pay the cashier's check and has no defense to that obligation. The cashier's check was issued for consideration because it was issued in payment of Buyer's check. Although Bank has no defense on its cashier's check it may have a right to recover $10,000, the amount of Buyer's check, from Seller under Section 3–418(a). Bank paid Buyer's check by mistake. Seller did not give value for Buyer's check because the promise to deliver goods to Buyer was never performed. Section 3–303(a)(1). And, on these facts, Seller did not change position in reliance on the payment of Buyer's check. Thus, the first sentence of Section 3–418(c) does not apply and Seller is obliged to

return $10,000 to Bank. Bank is obliged to pay the cashier's check but it has a counterclaim against Seller based on its rights under Section 3–418(a). This claim can be asserted against Seller, but it cannot be asserted against some other person with rights of a holder in due course of the cashier's check. A person without rights of a holder in due course of the cashier's check would take subject to Bank's claim against Seller because it is a claim in recoupment. Section 3–305(a)(3).

If Bank recovers from Seller under Section 3–418(a), the payment of Buyer's check is treated as unpaid and dishonored. Section 3–418(d). One consequence is that Seller may enforce Buyer's obligation as drawer to pay the check. Section 3–414. Another consequence is that Seller's rights against Buyer on the contract of sale are also preserved. Under Section 3–310(b) Buyer's obligation to pay for the goods was suspended when Seller took Buyer's check and remains suspended until the check is either dishonored or paid. Under Section 3–310(b)(2) 3–310(b)(1) * the obligation is discharged when the check is paid. Since Section 3–418(d) treats Buyer's check as unpaid and dishonored, Buyer's obligation is not discharged and suspension of the obligation terminates. Under Section 3–310(b)(3), Seller may enforce either the contract of sale or the check subject to defenses and claims of Buyer.

If Seller had released the goods to Buyer before learning about the stop order, Bank would have no recovery against Seller under Section 3–418(a) because Seller in that case gave value for Buyer's check. Section 3–418(c). In this case Bank's sole remedy is under Section 4–407 by subrogation.

3. Subsection (b) covers cases of payment or acceptance by mistake that are not covered by subsection (a). It directs courts to deal with those cases under the law governing mistake and restitution. Perhaps the most important class of cases that falls under subsection (b), because it is not covered by subsection (a), is that of payment by the drawee bank of a check with respect to which the bank has no duty to the drawer to pay either because the drawer has no account with the bank or because available funds in the drawer's account are not sufficient to cover the amount of the check. With respect to such a case, under Restatement of Restitution § 29, if the bank paid because of a mistaken belief that there were available funds in the drawer's account sufficient to cover the amount of the check, the bank is entitled to restitution. But § 29 is subject to Restatement of Restitution § 33 which denies restitution if the holder of the check receiving payment paid value in good faith for the check and had no reason to know that the

check was paid by mistake when payment was received.

The result in some cases is clear. For example, suppose Father gives Daughter a check for $10,000 as a birthday gift. The check is drawn on Bank in which both Father and Daughter have accounts. Daughter deposits the check in her account in Bank. An employee of Bank, acting under the belief that there were available funds in Father's account to cover the check, caused Daughter's account to be credited for $10,000. In fact, Father's account was overdrawn and Father did not have overdraft privileges. Since Daughter received the check gratuitously there is clear unjust enrichment if she is allowed to keep the $10,000 and Bank is unable to obtain reimbursement from Father. Thus, Bank should be permitted to reverse the credit to Daughter's account. But this case is not typical. In most cases the remedy of restitution will not be available because the person receiving payment of the check will have given value for it in good faith.

In some cases, however, it may not be clear whether a drawee bank should have a right of restitution. For example, a check-kiting scheme may involve a large number of checks drawn on a number of different banks in which the drawer's credit balances are based on uncollected funds represented by fraudulently drawn checks. No attempt is made in Section 3–418 to state rules for determining the conflicting claims of the various banks that may be victimized by such a scheme. Rather, such cases are better resolved on the basis of general principles of law and the particular facts presented in the litigation.

4. The right of the drawee to recover a payment or to revoke an acceptance under Section 3–418 is not affected by the rules under Article 4 that determine when an item is paid. Even though a payor bank may have paid an item under Section 4–215, it may have a right to recover the payment under Section 3–418. National Savings & Trust Co. v. Park Corp., 722 F.2d 1303 (6th Cir.1983), cert. denied, 466 U.S. 939 (1984), correctly states the law on the issue under former Article 3. Revised Article 3 does not change the previous law.

* *Previous incorrect cross reference corrected by Permanent Editorial Board action November 1992.*

§ 3–419. Instruments Signed for Accommodation.

(a) If an instrument is issued for value given for the benefit of a party to the instrument ("accommodated party") and another party to the instrument ("accommodation party") signs the instrument for the purpose of incurring liability on the instrument without being a direct beneficiary of the value given for the instrument, the instrument is signed by the accommodation party "for accommodation."

(b) An accommodation party may sign the instrument as maker, drawer, acceptor, or indorser and, subject to subsection (d), is obliged to pay the instrument in the capacity in which the accommodation party signs. The obligation of an accommodation party may be enforced notwithstanding any statute of frauds and whether or not the accommodation party receives consideration for the accommodation.

(c) A person signing an instrument is presumed to be an accommodation party and there is notice that the instrument is signed for accommodation if the signature is an anomalous indorsement or is accompanied by words indicating that the signer is acting as surety or guarantor with respect to the obligation of another party to the instrument. Except as provided in Section 3–605, the obligation of an accommodation party to pay the instrument is not affected by the fact that the person enforcing the obligation had notice when the instrument was taken by that person that the accommodation party signed the instrument for accommodation.

(d) If the signature of a party to an instrument is accompanied by words indicating unambiguously that the party is guaranteeing collection rather than payment of the obligation of another party to the instrument, the signer is obliged to pay the amount due on the instrument to a person entitled to enforce the instrument only if (i) execution of judgment against the other party has been returned unsatisfied, (ii) the other party is insolvent or in an insolvency proceeding, (iii) the other party cannot be served with process, or (iv) it is otherwise apparent that payment cannot be obtained from the other party.

(e) If the signature of a party to an instrument is accompanied by words indicating that the party guarantees payment or the signer signs the instrument as an accommodation party in some other manner that does not unambiguously indicate an intention to guarantee collection rather than payment, the signer is obliged to pay the amount due on the instrument to a person entitled to enforce the instrument in the same circumstances as the accommodated party would be obliged, without prior resort to the accommodated party by the person entitled to enforce the instrument.

(f) An accommodation party who pays the instrument is entitled to reimbursement from the accommodated party and is entitled to enforce the instrument against the accommodated party. In proper circumstances, an accommodation party may obtain relief that requires the accommodated party to perform its obligations on the instrument. An accommodated party that pays the instrument has no right of recourse against, and is not entitled to contribution from, an accommodation party.

As amended in 2002.

Official Comment

1. Section 3–419 replaces former Section 3–415 and 3–416. An accommodation party is a person who signs an instrument to benefit the accommodated party either by signing at the time value is obtained by the accommodated party or later, and who is not a direct beneficiary of the value obtained. An accommodation party will usually be a co-maker or anomalous indorser. Subsection (a) distinguishes between direct and indirect benefit. For example, if X cosigns a note of Corporation that is given for a loan to Corporation, X is an accommodation party if no part of the loan was paid to X or for X's direct benefit. This is true even though X may receive indirect benefit from the loan because X is employed by Corporation or is a stockholder of Corporation, or even if X is the sole stockholder so long as Corporation and X are recognized as separate entities.

2. It does not matter whether an accommodation party signs gratuitously either at the time the instrument is issued or after the instrument is in the possession of a holder. Subsection (b) of Section 3–419 takes the view stated in Comment 3 to former Section 3–415 that there need be no consideration running to the accommodation party: "The obligation of the accommodation party is supported by any consideration for which the instrument is taken before it is due. Subsection (2) is intended to change occasional decisions holding that there is no sufficient consideration where an accommodation party signs a note after it is in the hands of a holder who has given value. The [accommodation] party is liable to the holder in such a case even though there is no extension of time or other concession."

3. As stated in Comment 1, whether a person is an accommodation party is a question of fact. But it is almost always the case that a co-maker who signs with words of guaranty after the signature is an accommodation party. The same is true of an anomalous indorser. In either case a person taking the instrument is put on notice of the accommodation status of the co-maker or indorser. This is relevant to Section 3–605(e). But, under subsection (c), signing with words of guaranty or as an anomalous indorser also creates a presumption that the signer is an accommodation party. A party challenging accommodation party status would have to rebut this presumption by producing evidence that the signer was in fact a direct beneficiary of the value given for the instrument.

An accommodation party is always a surety. A surety who is not a party to the instrument, however, is not an accommodation party. For example, if M issues a note payable to the order of P, and S signs a separate contract in which S agrees to pay P the amount of the instrument if it is dishonored, S is a surety but is not an accommodation party. In such a case, S's rights and duties are determined under the general law of suretyship. In unusual cases two parties to an instrument may have a surety relationship that is not governed by Article 3 because the requirements of Section 3–419(a) are not met. In those cases the general law of suretyship applies to the relationship. See PEB Commentary No. 11, dated February 10, 1994 [Appendix V, infra].

4. Subsection (b) states that an accommodation party is liable on the instrument in the capacity in which the party signed the instrument. In most cases that capacity will be either that of a maker or indorser of a note. But subsection (d) provides a limitation on subsection (b). If the signature of the accommodation party is accompanied by words indicating unambiguously that the party is guaranteeing collection rather than payment of the instrument, liability is limited to that stated in subsection (d), which is based on former Section 3–416(2).

Former Article 3 was confusing because the obligation of a guarantor was covered both in Section 3–415 and in Section 3–416. The latter section suggested that a signature accompanied by words of guaranty created an obligation distinct from that of an accommodation party. Revised Article 3 eliminates that confusion by stating in Section 3–419 the obligation of a person who uses words of guaranty. Portions of former Section 3–416 are preserved. Former Section 3–416(2) is reflected in Section 3–419(d) and former Section 3–416(4) is reflected in Section 3–419(c). Words added to an anomalous indorsement indicating that payment of the instrument is guaranteed by the indorser do not change the liability of the indorser as stated in Section 3–415. This is a change from former Section 3–416(5). See PEB Commentary No. 11, supra.

5. Subsection (e) like former Section 3–415(5), provides that an accommodation party that pays the instrument is entitled to enforce the instrument against the accommodated party. Since the accommodation party that pays the instrument is entitled to enforce the instrument against the accommodated party, the accommodation party also obtains rights to any security interest or other collateral that secures payment of the instrument. Subsection (e) also provides that an accommodation party that pays the instrument is entitled to reimbursement from the accommodated party. See PEB Commentary No. 11, supra.

6. In occasional cases, the accommodation party might pay the instrument even though the accommodated party had a defense to its obligation that was available to the accommodation party under Section 3–305(d). In such cases, the accommodation party's right to reimbursement may conflict with the accommodated party's right to raise its defense. For example, suppose the accommodation party pays the instrument without being aware of the defense. In that case the accommodation party should be entitled to reimbursement. Suppose the accommodation party paid the instrument with knowledge of the defense. In that case, to the extent of the defense, reimbursement ordinarily would not be justified, but under some circumstances reimbursement may be justified depending upon the facts of the case. The resolution of this conflict is left to the general law of suretyship. Section 1–103. See PEB Commentary No. 11, supra.

7. Section 3–419, along with Section 3–116(a) and (b), Section 3–305(d) and Section 3–605, provides rules governing the rights of accommodation parties. In addition, except to the extent that it is displaced by provisions of this Article, the general law of suretyship also applies to the rights of accommodation parties. Section 1–103. See PEB Commentary No. 11, supra.

As amended in 2002.

§ 3–420. Conversion of Instrument.

(a) The law applicable to conversion of personal property applies to instruments. An instrument is also converted if it is taken by transfer, other than a negotiation, from a person not entitled to enforce the instrument or a bank makes or obtains payment with respect to the instrument for a person not entitled to enforce the instrument or receive payment. An action for conversion of an instrument may not be brought by (i) the issuer or acceptor of the instrument or (ii) a payee or indorsee who did not receive delivery of the instrument either directly or through delivery to an agent or a co-payee.

(b) In an action under subsection (a), the measure of liability is presumed to be the amount payable on the instrument, but recovery may not exceed the amount of the plaintiff's interest in the instrument.

(c) A representative, other than a depositary bank, who has in good faith dealt with an instrument or its proceeds on behalf of one who was not the person entitled to enforce the instrument is not liable in conversion to that person beyond the amount of any proceeds that it has not paid out.

Official Comment

1. Section 3–420 is a modification of former Section 3–419. The first sentence of Section 3–420(a) states a general rule that the law of conversion applicable to personal property also applies to instruments. Paragraphs (a) and (b) of former Section 3–419(1) are deleted as inappropriate in cases of noncash items that may be delivered for acceptance or payment in collection letters that contain varying instructions as to what to do in the event of nonpayment on the day of delivery. It is better to allow such cases to be governed by the general law of conversion that would address the issue of when, under the circumstances prevailing, the presenter's right to possession has been denied. The second sentence of Section 3–420(a) states that an instrument is converted if it is taken by transfer other than a negotiation from a person not entitled to enforce the instrument or taken for collection or payment from a person not entitled to enforce the instrument or receive payment. This covers cases in which a depositary or payor bank takes an instrument bearing a forged indorsement. It also covers cases in which an instrument is payable to two persons and the two persons are not alternative payees, e.g. a check payable to John and Jane Doe. Under Section 3–110(d) the check can be negotiated or enforced only by both persons acting jointly. Thus, neither payee acting without the consent of the other, is a person entitled to enforce the instrument. If John indorses the check and Jane does not, the indorsement is not effective to allow negotiation of the check. If Depositary Bank takes the check for deposit to John's account, Depositary Bank is liable to Jane for conversion

of the check if she did not consent to the transaction. John, acting alone, is not the person entitled to enforce the check because John is not the holder of the check. Section 3–110(d) and Comment 4 to Section 3–110. Depositary Bank does not get any greater rights under Section 4–205(1). If it acted for John as its customer, it did not become holder of the check under that provision because John, its customer, was not a holder.

Under former Article 3, the cases were divided on the issue of whether the drawer of a check with a forged indorsement can assert rights against a depositary bank that took the check. The last sentence of Section 3–420(a) resolves the conflict by following the rule stated in Stone & Webster Engineering Corp. v. First National Bank & Trust Co., 184 N.E.2d 358 (Mass.1962). There is no reason why a drawer should have an action in conversion. The check represents an obligation of the drawer rather than property of the drawer. The drawer has an adequate remedy against the payor bank for recredit of the drawer's account for unauthorized payment of the check.

There was also a split of authority under former Article 3 on the issue of whether a payee who never received the instrument is a proper plaintiff in a conversion action. The typical case was one in which a check was stolen from the drawer or in which the check was mailed to an address different from that of the payee and was stolen after it arrived at that address. The thief forged the indorsement of the payee and obtained payment by depositing the check to an account in a depositary bank. The issue was whether the payee could bring an action in conversion against the depositary bank or the drawee bank. In revised Article 3, under the last sentence of Section 3–420(a), the payee has no conversion action because the check was never delivered to the payee. Until delivery, the payee does not have any interest in the check. The payee never became the holder of the check nor a person entitled to enforce the check. Section 3–301. Nor is the payee injured by the fraud. Normally the drawer of a check intends to pay an obligation owed to the payee. But if the check is never delivered to the payee, the obligation owed to the payee is not affected. If the check falls into the hands of a thief who obtains payment after forging the signature of the payee as an indorsement, the obligation owed to the payee continues to exist after the thief receives payment. Since the payee's right to enforce the underlying obligation is unaffected by the fraud of the thief, there is no reason to give any additional remedy to the payee. The drawer of the check has no conversion remedy, but the drawee is not entitled to charge the drawer's account when the drawee wrongfully honored the check. The

remedy of the drawee is against the depositary bank for breach of warranty under Section 3–417(a)(1) or 4–208(a)(1). The loss will fall on the person who gave value to the thief for the check.

The situation is different if the check is delivered to the payee. If the check is taken for an obligation owed to the payee, the last sentence of Section 3–310(b)(4) provides that the obligation may not be enforced to the extent of the amount of the check. The payee's rights are restricted to enforcement of the payee's rights in the instrument. In this event the payee is injured by the theft and has a cause of action for conversion.

The payee receives delivery when the check comes into the payee's possession, as for example when it is put into the payee's mailbox. Delivery to an agent is delivery to the payee. If a check is payable to more than one payee, delivery to one of the payees is deemed to be delivery to all of the payees. Occasionally, the person asserting a conversion cause of action is an indorsee rather than the original payee. If the check is stolen before the check can be delivered to the indorsee and the indorsee's indorsement is forged, the analysis is similar. For example, a check is payable to the order of A. A indorses it to B and puts it into an envelope addressed to B. The envelope is never delivered to B. Rather, Thief steals the envelope, forges B's indorsement to the check and obtains payment. Because the check was never delivered to B, the indorsee, B has no cause of action for conversion, but A does have such an action. A is the owner of the check. B never obtained rights in the check. If A intended to negotiate the check to B in payment of an obligation, that obligation was not affected by the conduct of Thief. B can enforce that obligation. Thief stole A's property not B's.

2. Subsection (2) of former Section 3–419 is amended because it is not clear why the former law distinguished between the liability of the drawee and that of other converters. Why should there be a conclusive presumption that the liability is face amount if a drawee refuses to pay or return an instrument or makes payment on a forged indorsement, while the liability of a maker who does the same thing is only presumed to be the face amount? Moreover, it was not clear under former Section 3–419(2) what face amount meant. If a note for $10,000 is payable in a year at 10% interest, it is common to refer to $10,000 as the face amount, but if the note is converted the loss to the owner also includes the loss of interest. In revised Article 3, Section 3–420(b), by referring to "amount payable on the instrument," allows the full amount due under the instrument to be recovered.

The "but" clause in subsection (b) addresses the problem of conversion actions in multiple payee checks. Section 3–110(d) states that an instrument cannot be enforced unless all payees join in the action. But an action for conversion might be brought by a payee having no interest or a limited interest in the proceeds of the check. This clause prevents such a plaintiff from receiving a windfall. An example is a check payable to a building contractor and a supplier of building material. The check is not payable to the payees alternatively. Section 3–110(d). The check is delivered to the contractor by the owner of the building. Suppose the contractor forges supplier's signature as an indorsement of the check and receives the entire proceeds of the check. The supplier should not, without qualification, be able to recover the entire amount of the check from the bank that converted the check. Depending upon the contract between the contractor and the supplier, the amount of the check may be due entirely to the contractor, in which case there should be no recovery, entirely to the supplier, in which case recovery should be for the entire amount, or part may be due to one and the rest to the other, in which case recovery should be limited to the amount due to the supplier.

3. Subsection (3) of former Section 3–419 drew criticism from the courts, that saw no reason why a depositary bank should have the defense stated in the subsection. See Knesz v. Central Jersey Bank & Trust Co., 477 A.2d 806 (N.J.1984). The depositary bank is ultimately liable in the case of a forged indorsement check because of its warranty to the payor bank under Section 4–208(a)(1) and it is usually the most convenient defendant in cases involving multiple checks drawn on different banks. There is no basis for requiring the owner of the check to bring multiple actions against the various payor banks and to require those banks to assert warranty rights against the depositary bank. In revised Article 3, the defense provided by Section 3–420(c) is limited to collecting banks other than the depositary bank. If suit is brought against both the payor bank and the depositary bank, the owner, of course, is entitled to but one recovery.

PART 5

DISHONOR

§ 3–501. Presentment.

(a) "Presentment" means a demand made by or on behalf of a person entitled to enforce an instrument (i) to pay the instrument made to the drawee or a party obliged to pay the instrument or, in the case of a note or accepted draft payable at a bank, to the bank, or (ii) to accept a draft made to the drawee.

(b) The following rules are subject to Article 4, agreement of the parties, and clearing-house rules and the like:

(1) Presentment may be made at the place of payment of the instrument and must be made at the place of payment if the instrument is payable at a bank in the United States; may be made by any commercially reasonable means, including an oral, written, or electronic communication; is effective when the demand for payment or acceptance is received by the person to whom presentment is made; and is effective if made to any one of two or more makers, acceptors, drawees, or other payors.

(2) Upon demand of the person to whom presentment is made, the person making presentment must (i) exhibit the instrument, (ii) give reasonable identification and, if presentment is made on behalf of another person, reasonable evidence of authority to do so, and (iii) sign a receipt on the instrument for any payment made or surrender the instrument if full payment is made.

(3) Without dishonoring the instrument, the party to whom presentment is made may (i) return the instrument for lack of a necessary indorsement, or (ii) refuse payment or acceptance for failure of the presentment to comply with the terms of the instrument, an agreement of the parties, or other applicable law or rule.

(4) The party to whom presentment is made may treat presentment as occurring on the next business day after the day of presentment if the party to whom presentment is made has established a cut-off hour not earlier than 2 p.m. for the receipt and processing of instruments presented for payment or acceptance and

presentment is made after the cut-off hour.

Official Comment

Subsection (a) defines presentment. Subsection (b)(1) states the place and manner of presentment. Electronic presentment is authorized. The communication of the demand for payment or acceptance is effective when received. Subsection (b)(2) restates former Section 3–505. Subsection (b)(2)(i) allows the person to whom presentment is made to require exhibition of the instrument, unless the parties have agreed otherwise as in an electronic presentment agreement. Former Section 3–507(3) is the antecedent of subsection (b)(3)(i). Since a payor must decide whether to pay or accept on the day of presentment, subsection (b)(4) allows the payor to set a cut-off hour for receipt of instruments presented.

§ 3–502. Dishonor.

(a) Dishonor of a note is governed by the following rules:

(1) If the note is payable on demand, the note is dishonored if presentment is duly made to the maker and the note is not paid on the day of presentment.

(2) If the note is not payable on demand and is payable at or through a bank or the terms of the note require presentment, the note is dishonored if presentment is duly made and the note is not paid on the day it becomes payable or the day of presentment, whichever is later.

(3) If the note is not payable on demand and paragraph (2) does not apply, the note is dishonored if it is not paid on the day it becomes payable.

(b) Dishonor of an unaccepted draft other than a documentary draft is governed by the following rules:

(1) If a check is duly presented for payment to the payor bank otherwise than for immediate payment over the counter, the check is dishonored if the payor bank makes timely return of the check or sends timely notice of dishonor or nonpayment under Section 4–301 or 4–302, or becomes accountable for the amount of the check under Section 4–302.

(2) If a draft is payable on demand and paragraph (1) does not apply, the draft is dishonored if presentment for payment is duly made to the drawee and the draft is not paid on the day of presentment.

(3) If a draft is payable on a date stated in the draft, the draft is dishonored if (i) presentment for payment is duly made to the drawee and payment is not made on the day the draft becomes payable or the day of presentment, whichever is later, or (ii) presentment for acceptance is duly made before the day the draft becomes payable and the draft is not accepted on the day of presentment.

(4) If a draft is payable on elapse of a period of time after sight or acceptance, the draft is dishonored if presentment for acceptance is duly made and the draft is not accepted on the day of presentment.

(c) Dishonor of an unaccepted documentary draft occurs according to the rules stated in subsection (b)(2), (3), and (4), except that payment or acceptance may be delayed without dishonor until no later than the close of the third business day of the drawee following the day on which payment or acceptance is required by those paragraphs.

(d) Dishonor of an accepted draft is governed by the following rules:

(1) If the draft is payable on demand, the draft is dishonored if presentment for payment is duly made to the acceptor and the draft is not paid on the day of presentment.

(2) If the draft is not payable on demand, the draft is dishonored if presentment for payment is duly made to the acceptor and payment is not made on the day it becomes payable or the day of presentment, whichever is later.

(e) In any case in which presentment is otherwise required for dishonor under this section and presentment is excused under Section 3–504, dishonor occurs without presentment if the instrument is not duly accepted or paid.

(f) If a draft is dishonored because timely acceptance of the draft was not made and the person entitled to demand acceptance consents to a late acceptance, from the time of acceptance the draft is treated as never having been dishonored.

Official Comment

1. Section 3–415 provides that an indorser is obliged to pay an instrument if the instrument is dishonored and is discharged if the indorser is entitled to notice of dishonor and notice is not given. Under Section 3–414, the drawer is obliged to pay an unaccepted draft if it is dishonored. The drawer, however, is not entitled to notice of dishonor except to the extent required in a case governed by Section 3–414(d). Part 5 tells when an instrument is dishonored (Section 3–502) and what it means to give notice of dishonor (Section 3–503). Often dishonor does not occur until presentment (Section 3–501), and frequently presentment and notice of dishonor are excused (Section 3–504).

2. In the great majority of cases presentment and notice of dishonor are waived with respect to notes. In most cases a formal demand for payment to the maker of the note is not contemplated. Rather, the maker is expected to send payment to the holder of the note on the date or dates on which payment is due. If payment is not made when due, the holder usually makes a demand for payment, but in the normal case in which presentment is waived, demand is irrelevant and the holder can proceed against indorsers when payment is not received. Under former Article 3, in the small minority of cases in which presentment and dishonor were not waived with respect to notes, the indorser was discharged from liability (former Section 3–502(1)(a)) unless the holder made presentment to the maker on the exact day the note was due (former Section 3–503(1)(c)) and gave notice of dishonor to the indorser before midnight of the third business day after dishonor (former Section 3–508(2)). These provisions are omitted from Revised Article 3 as inconsistent with practice which seldom involves face-to-face dealings.

3. Subsection (a) applies to notes. Subsection (a)(1) applies to notes payable on demand. Dishonor requires presentment, and dishonor occurs if payment is not made on the day of presentment. There is no change from previous Article 3. Subsection (a)(2) applies to notes payable at a definite time if the note is payable at or through a bank or, by its terms, presentment is required. Dishonor requires presentment, and dishonor occurs if payment is not made on the due date or the day of presentment if presentment is made after the due date. Subsection (a)(3) applies to all other notes. If the note is not paid on its due date it is dishonored. This allows holders to collect notes in

ways that make sense commercially without having to be concerned about a formal presentment on a given day.

4. Subsection (b) applies to unaccepted drafts other than documentary drafts. Subsection (b)(1) applies to checks. Except for checks presented for immediate payment over the counter, which are covered by subsection (b)(2), dishonor occurs according to rules stated in Article 4. Those rules contemplate four separate situations that warrant discussion. The first two situations arise in the normal course of affairs, in which the drawee bank makes settlement for the amount of the check to the presenting bank. In the first situation, the drawee bank under Section 4–301 recovers this settlement if it returns the check by its midnight deadline (Section 4–104). In that case the check is not paid and dishonor occurs under Section 3–502(b)(1). The second situation arises if the drawee bank has made such a settlement and does not return the check or give notice of dishonor or nonpayment within the midnight deadline. In that case, the settlement becomes final payment of the check under Section 4–215. Because the drawee bank already has paid such an item, it cannot be "accountable" for the item under the terms of Section 4–302(a)(1). Thus, no dishonor occurs regardless of whether the drawee bank retains the check indefinitely or for some reason returns the check after its midnight deadline.

The third and fourth situations arise less commonly, in cases in which the drawee bank does not settle for the check when it is received. Under Section 4–302 if the drawee bank is not also the depositary bank and retains the check without settling for it beyond midnight of the day it is presented for payment, the bank at that point becomes "accountable" for the amount of the check, i.e., it is obliged to pay the amount of the check. If the drawee bank is also the depositary bank, the bank becomes accountable for the amount of the check if the bank does not pay the check or return it or send notice of dishonor by its midnight deadline. Hence, if the drawee bank is also the depositary bank and does not either settle for the check when it is received (a settlement that would ripen into final payment if the drawee bank failed to take action to recover the settlement by its midnight deadline) or return the check or an appropriate notice by its midnight deadline, the drawee bank will become accountable for the amount of the check under Section 4–302. Thus, in all cases in which the drawee bank becomes accountable under Section 4–302, the check has not been paid (either by a settlement that became unrecoverable or otherwise) and thus, under Section 3–502(b)(1), the check is dishonored.

The fact that a bank that is accountable for the amount of the check under Section 4–302 is obliged to pay the check does not mean that the check has been paid. Indeed, because each of the paragraphs of Section 4–302(b) is limited by its terms to situations in which a bank has not paid the item, a drawee bank will be accountable under Section 4–302 only in situations in which it has not previously paid the check. Section 3–502(b)(1) reflects the view that a person presenting a check is entitled to payment, not just the ability to hold the drawee accountable under Section 4–302. If that payment is not made in a timely manner, the check is dishonored.

Regulation CC Section 229.36(d) provides that settlement between banks for the forward collection of checks is final. The relationship of that section to Articles 3 and 4 is discussed in the Commentary to that section.

Subsection (b)(2) applies to demand drafts other than those governed by subsection (b)(1). It covers checks presented for immediate payment over the counter and demand drafts other than checks. Dishonor occurs if presentment for payment is made and payment is not made on the day of presentment.

Subsection (b)(3) and (4) applies to time drafts. An unaccepted time draft differs from a time note. The maker of a note knows that the note has been issued, but the drawee of a draft may not know that a draft has been drawn on it. Thus, with respect to drafts, presentment for payment or acceptance is required. Subsection (b)(3) applies to drafts payable on a date stated in the draft. Dishonor occurs if presentment for payment is made and payment is not made on the day the draft becomes payable or the day of presentment if presentment is made after the due date. The holder of an unaccepted draft payable on a stated date has the option of presenting the draft for acceptance before the day the draft becomes payable to establish whether the drawee is willing to assume liability by accepting. Under subsection (b)(3)(ii) dishonor occurs when the draft is presented and not accepted. Subsection (b)(4) applies to unaccepted drafts payable on elapse of a period of time after sight or acceptance. If the draft is payable 30 days after sight, the draft must be presented for acceptance to start the running of the 30–day period. Dishonor occurs if it is not accepted. The rules in subsection (b)(3) and (4) follow former Section 3–501(1)(a).

5. Subsection (c) gives drawees an extended period to pay documentary drafts because of the time that may be needed to examine the documents. The period prescribed is that given by Section 5–112 in cases in which a letter of credit is involved.

6. Subsection (d) governs accepted drafts. If the acceptor's obligation is to pay on demand the rule, stated in subsection (d)(1), is the same as for that of a demand note stated in subsection (a)(1). If the acceptor's obligation is to pay at a definite time the rule, stated in subsection (d)(2), is the same as that of a time note payable at a bank stated in subsection (b)(2).

7. Subsection (e) is a limitation on subsection (a)(1) and (2), subsection (b), subsection (c), and subsection (d). Each of those provisions states dishonor as occurring after presentment. If presentment is excused under Section 3–504, dishonor occurs under those provisions without presentment if the instrument is not duly accepted or paid.

8. Under subsection (b)(3)(ii) and (4) if a draft is presented for acceptance and the draft is not accepted on the day of presentment, there is dishonor. But after dishonor, the holder may consent to late acceptance. In that case, under subsection (f), the late acceptance cures the dishonor. The draft is treated as never having been dishonored. If the draft is subsequently presented for payment and payment is refused dishonor occurs at that time.

As amended in 2002.

§ 3–503. Notice of Dishonor.

(a) The obligation of an indorser stated in Section 3–415(a) and the obligation of a drawer stated in Section 3–414(d) may not be enforced unless (i) the indorser or drawer is given notice of dishonor of the instrument complying with this section or (ii) notice of dishonor is excused under Section 3–504(b).

(b) Notice of dishonor may be given by any person; may be given by any commercially reasonable means, including an oral, written, or electronic communication; and is sufficient if it reasonably identifies the instrument and indicates that the instrument has been dishonored or has not been paid or accepted. Return of an instrument given to a bank for collection is sufficient notice of dishonor.

(c) Subject to Section 3–504(c), with respect to an instrument taken for collection by a collecting bank, notice of dishonor must be given (i) by the bank before midnight of the next banking day following the banking day on which the bank receives notice of dishonor of the instrument, or (ii) by any other person within 30 days following the day on which the person receives notice of dishonor. With respect to any other instrument, notice of dishonor must be given within 30 days following the day on which dishonor occurs.

Official Comment

1. Subsection (a) is consistent with former Section 3–501(2)(a), but notice of dishonor is no longer relevant to the liability of a drawer except for the case of a draft accepted by an acceptor other than a bank. Comments 2 and 4 to Section 3–414. There is no reason why drawers should be discharged on instruments they draw until payment or acceptance. They are entitled to have the instrument presented to the drawee and dishonored (Section 3–414(b)) before they are liable to pay, but no notice of dishonor need be made to them as a condition of liability. Subsection (b), which states how notice of dishonor is given, is based on former Section 3–508(3).

2. Subsection (c) replaces former Section 3–508(2). It differs from that section in that it provides a 30–day period for a person other than a collecting bank to give notice of dishonor rather than the three-day period allowed in former Article 3. Delay in giving notice of dishonor may be excused under Section 3–504(c).

§ 3–504. Excused Presentment and Notice of Dishonor.

(a) Presentment for payment or acceptance of an instrument is excused if (i) the person entitled to present the instrument cannot with reasonable diligence make presentment, (ii) the maker or acceptor has repudiated an obligation to pay the instrument or is dead or in insolvency proceedings, (iii) by the terms of the instrument presentment is not necessary to enforce the obligation of indorsers or the drawer, (iv) the drawer or indorser whose obligation is being enforced has waived presentment or otherwise has no reason to expect or right to require that the instrument be paid or accepted, or (v) the drawer instructed the drawee not to pay or accept the draft or the drawee was not obligated to the drawer to pay the draft.

(b) Notice of dishonor is excused if (i) by the terms of the instrument notice of dishonor is not necessary to enforce the obligation of a party to pay the instrument, or (ii) the party whose obligation is being enforced waived notice of dishon-

or. A waiver of presentment is also a waiver of notice of dishonor.

(c) Delay in giving notice of dishonor is excused if the delay was caused by circumstances beyond the control of the person giving the notice and the person giving the notice exercised reasonable diligence after the cause of the delay ceased to operate.

Official Comment

Section 3–504 is largely a restatement of former Section 3–511. Subsection (4) of former Section 3–511 is replaced by Section 3–502(f).

§ 3–505. Evidence of Dishonor.

(a) The following are admissible as evidence and create a presumption of dishonor and of any notice of dishonor stated:

    (1) a document regular in form as provided in subsection (b) which purports to be a protest;

    (2) a purported stamp or writing of the drawee, payor bank, or presenting bank on or accompanying the instrument stating that acceptance or payment has been refused unless reasons for the refusal are stated and the reasons are not consistent with dishonor;

    (3) a book or record of the drawee, payor bank, or collecting bank, kept in the usual course of business which shows dishonor, even if there is no evidence of who made the entry.

(b) A protest is a certificate of dishonor made by a United States consul or vice consul, or a notary public or other person authorized to administer oaths by the law of the place where dishonor occurs. It may be made upon information satisfactory to that person. The protest must identify the instrument and certify either that presentment has been made or, if not made, the reason why it was not made, and that the instrument has been dishonored by nonacceptance or nonpayment. The protest may also certify that notice of dishonor has been given to some or all parties.

Official Comment

Protest is no longer mandatory and must be requested by the holder. Even if requested, protest is not a condition to the liability of indorsers or drawers. Protest is a service provided by the banking system to establish that dishonor has occurred. Like other services provided by the banking system, it will be available if market incentives, inter-bank agreements, or governmental regulations require it, but liabilities of parties no longer rest on it. Protest may be a requirement for liability on international drafts governed by foreign law which this Article cannot affect.

PART 6

DISCHARGE AND PAYMENT

§ 3–601. Discharge and Effect of Discharge.

(a) The obligation of a party to pay the instrument is discharged as stated in this Article or by an act or agreement with the party which would discharge an obligation to pay money under a simple contract.

(b) Discharge of the obligation of a party is not effective against a person acquiring rights of a holder in due course of the instrument without notice of the discharge.

Official Comment

Subsection (a) replaces subsections (1) and (2) of former Section 3–601. Subsection (b) restates former Section 3–602. Notice of discharge is not treated as notice of a defense that prevents holder in due course status. Section 3–302(b). Discharge is effective against a holder in due course only if the holder had notice of the discharge when holder in due course status was acquired. For example, if an instrument bearing a canceled indorsement is taken by a holder, the holder has notice that the indorser has been discharged. Thus, the discharge is effective against the holder even if the holder is a holder in due course.

§ 3–602. Payment.

(a) Subject to subsection (e), an instrument is paid to the extent payment is made by or on behalf of a party obliged to pay the instrument, and to a person entitled to enforce the instrument.

(b) Subject to subsection (e), a note is paid to the extent payment is made by or on behalf of a party obliged to pay the note to a person that formerly was entitled to enforce the note only if at the time of the payment the party obliged to pay has not received adequate notification that the note has been transferred and that payment is to be made to the transferee. A notification is adequate only if it is signed by the transferor or the transferee; reasonably identifies the trans-

ferred note; and provides an address at which payments subsequently are to be made. Upon request, a transferee shall seasonably furnish reasonable proof that the note has been transferred. Unless the transferee complies with the request, a payment to the person that formerly was entitled to enforce the note is effective for purposes of subsection (c) even if the party obliged to pay the note has received a notification under this paragraph.

(c) Subject to subsection (e), to the extent of a payment under subsections (a) and (b), the obligation of the party obliged to pay the instrument is discharged even though payment is made with knowledge of a claim to the instrument under Section 3–306 by another person.

(d) Subject to subsection (e), a transferee, or any party that has acquired rights in the instrument directly or indirectly from a transferee, including any such party that has rights as a holder in due course, is deemed to have notice of any payment that is made under subsection (b) after the date that the note is transferred to the transferee but before the party obliged to pay the note receives adequate notification of the transfer.

(e) The obligation of a party to pay the instrument is not discharged under subsections (a) through (d) if:

(1) a claim to the instrument under Section 3–306 is enforceable against the party receiving payment and (i) payment is made with knowledge by the payor that payment is prohibited by injunction or similar process of a court of competent jurisdiction, or (ii) in the case of an instrument other than a cashier's check, teller's check, or certified check, the party making payment accepted, from the person having a claim to the instrument, indemnity against loss resulting from refusal to pay the person entitled to enforce the instrument; or

(2) the person making payment knows that the instrument is a stolen instrument and pays a person it knows is in wrongful possession of the instrument.

(f) As used in this section, "signed," with respect to a record that is not a writing, includes the attachment to or logical association with the record of an electronic symbol, sound, or process with the present intent to adopt or accept the record.

As amended in 2002.

Official Comment

1. This section replaces former Section 3–603(1). The phrase "claim to the instrument" in subsection (a) means, by reference to Section 3–306, a claim of ownership or possession and not a claim in recoupment. Subsection (e)(1)(ii) is added to conform to Section 3–411. Section 3–411 is intended to discourage an obligated bank from refusing payment of a cashier's check, certified check or dishonored teller's check at the request of a claimant to the check who provided the bank with indemnity against loss. See Comment 1 to Section 3–411. An obligated bank that refuses payment under those circumstances not only remains liable on the check but may also be liable to the holder of the check for consequential damages. Section 3–602(e)(1)(ii) and Section 3–411, read together, change the rule of former Section 3–603(1) with respect to the obligation of the obligated bank on the check. Payment to the holder of a cashier's check, teller's check, or certified check discharges the obligation of the obligated bank on the check to both the holder and the claimant even though indemnity has been given by the person asserting the claim. If the obligated bank pays the check in violation of an agreement with the claimant in connection with the indemnity agreement, any liability that the bank may have for violation of the agreement is not governed by Article 3, but is left to other law. This section continues the rule that the obligor is not discharged on the instrument if payment is made in violation of an injunction against payment. See Section 3–411(c)(iv).

2. Subsection (a) covers payments made in a traditional manner, to the person entitled to enforce the instrument. Subsection (b), which provides an alternative method of payment, deals with the situation in which a person entitled to enforce the instrument transfers the instrument without giving notice to parties obligated to pay the instrument. If that happens and one of those parties subsequently makes a payment to the transferor, the payment is effective even

though it is not made to the person entitled to enforce the instrument. Unlike the earlier version of Section 3–602, this rule is consistent with Section 9–406(a), Restatement of Mortgages § 5.5, and Restatement of Contracts § 338(1).

3. In determining the party to whom a payment is made for purposes of this section, courts should look to traditional rules of agency. Thus, if the original payee of a note transfers ownership of the note to a third party but continues to service the obligation, the law of agency might treat payments made to the original payee as payments made to the third party.

4. Subsection (d) assures that the discharge provided by subsection (c) is effective against the transferee and those whose rights derive from the transferee. By deeming those persons to have notice of any payment made under subsection (b), subsection (d) gives those persons "notice of the discharge" within the meaning of Section 3–302(b). Accordingly, the discharge is effective against those persons, even if any of them has the rights of a holder in due course. Compare Section 3–601(b). The deemed notice provided by subsection (d) does not, however, prevent a person from becoming or acquiring the rights of, a holder in due course. See Section 3–302(b). Thus, such a person does not become subject to other defenses described in Section 3–305(a)(2), claims in recoupment described in Section 3–305(a)(3), or claims to the instrument under Section 3–306. A transferee can prevent payment to the transferor from discharging the obligation on the note by assuring that each person who is obligated on the note receives adequate notification pursuant to subsection (b) prior to making a payment.

As amended in 2002 and 2003.

§ 3–603. Tender of Payment.

(a) If tender of payment of an obligation to pay an instrument is made to a person entitled to enforce the instrument, the effect of tender is governed by principles of law applicable to tender of payment under a simple contract.

(b) If tender of payment of an obligation to pay an instrument is made to a person entitled to enforce the instrument and the tender is refused, there is discharge, to the extent of the amount of the tender, of the obligation of an indorser or accommodation party having a right of recourse with respect to the obligation to which the tender relates.

(c) If tender of payment of an amount due on an instrument is made to a person entitled to enforce the instrument, the obligation of the obligor to pay interest after the due date on the amount tendered is discharged. If presentment is required with respect to an instrument and the obligor is able and ready to pay on the due date at every place of payment stated in the instrument, the obligor is deemed to have made tender of payment on the due date to the person entitled to enforce the instrument.

Official Comment

Section 3-603 replaces former Section 3-604. Subsection (a) generally incorporates the law of tender of payment applicable to simple contracts. Subsections (b) and (c) state particular rules. Subsection (b) replaces former Section 3-604(2). Under subsection (b) refusal of a tender of payment discharges any indorser or accommodation party having a right of recourse against the party making the tender. Subsection (c) replaces former Section 3-604(1) and (3).

§ 3-604. Discharge by Cancellation or Renunciation.

(a) A person entitled to enforce an instrument, with or without consideration, may discharge the obligation of a party to pay the instrument (i) by an intentional voluntary act, such as surrender of the instrument to the party, destruction, mutilation, or cancellation of the instrument, cancellation or striking out of the party's signature, or the addition of words to the instrument indicating discharge, or (ii) by agreeing not to sue or otherwise renouncing rights against the party by a signed record.

(b) Cancellation or striking out of an indorsement pursuant to subsection (a) does not affect the status and rights of a party derived from the indorsement.

(c) In this section, "signed," with respect to a record that is not a writing, includes the attachment to or logical association with the record of an electronic symbol, sound, or process with the present intent to adopt or accept the record.

As amended in 2002.

Official Comment

Section 3-604 replaces former Section 3-605.

§ 3-605. Discharge of Secondary Obligors.

(a) If a person entitled to enforce an instrument releases the obligation of a principal obligor in whole or in part, and another party to the instrument is a secondary obligor with respect to the obligation of that principal obligor, the following rules apply:

(1) Any obligations of the principal obligor to the secondary obligor with respect to any previous payment by the secondary obligor are not affected. Unless the terms of the release preserve the secondary obligor's recourse, the principal obligor is discharged, to the extent of the release, from any other duties to the secondary obligor under this article.

(2) Unless the terms of the release provide that the person entitled to enforce the instrument retains the right to enforce the instrument against the secondary obligor, the secondary obligor is discharged to the same extent as the principal obligor from any unperformed portion of its obligation on the instrument. If the instrument is a check and the obligation of the secondary obligor is based on an indorsement of the check, the secondary obligor is discharged without regard to the language or circumstances of the discharge or other release.

(3) If the secondary obligor is not discharged under paragraph (2), the secondary obligor is discharged to the extent of the value of the consideration for the release, and to the extent that the release would otherwise cause the secondary obligor a loss.

(b) If a person entitled to enforce an instrument grants a principal obligor an extension of the time at which one or more payments are due on the instrument and another party to the instrument is a secondary obligor with respect to the obligation of that principal obligor, the following rules apply:

(1) Any obligations of the principal obligor to the secondary obligor with respect to any previous payment by the secondary obligor are not affected. Unless the terms of the extension preserve the secondary obligor's recourse, the extension correspondingly extends the time for performance of any other duties owed to the secondary obligor by the principal obligor under this article.

(2) The secondary obligor is discharged to the extent that the extension would otherwise cause the secondary obligor a loss.

(3) To the extent that the secondary obligor is not discharged under paragraph (2), the secondary obligor may perform its obligations to a person entitled to enforce the instrument as if the time for payment had not been extended or, unless the terms of the extension provide that the person entitled to enforce the instrument retains the right to enforce the instrument against the secondary obligor as if the time for payment had not been extended, treat the time for performance of its obligations as having been extended correspondingly.

(c) If a person entitled to enforce an instrument agrees, with or without consideration, to a modification of the obligation of a principal obligor other than a complete or partial release or an extension of the due date and another party to the instrument is a secondary obligor with respect to the obligation of that principal obligor, the following rules apply:

(1) Any obligations of the principal obligor to the secondary obligor with respect to any previous payment by the secondary obligor are not affected. The modification correspondingly modifies any other duties owed to the secondary obligor by the principal obligor under this article.

(2) The secondary obligor is discharged from any unperformed portion of its obligation to the extent that the modification would otherwise cause the secondary obligor a loss.

(3) To the extent that the secondary obligor is not discharged under paragraph (2), the secondary obligor may satisfy its obligation on the instrument as if the modification had not occurred, or treat its obligation on the instrument as having been modified correspondingly.

(d) If the obligation of a principal obligor is secured by an interest in collateral, another party to the instrument is a secondary obligor with respect to that obligation, and a person entitled to enforce the instrument impairs the value of the interest in collateral, the obligation of the secondary obligor is discharged to the extent of the impairment. The value of an interest in collateral is impaired to the extent the value of the interest is reduced to an amount less than the amount of the recourse of the secondary obligor, or the reduction in value of the interest causes

an increase in the amount by which the amount of the recourse exceeds the value of the interest. For purposes of this subsection, impairing the value of an interest in collateral includes failure to obtain or maintain perfection or recordation of the interest in collateral, release of collateral without substitution of collateral of equal value or equivalent reduction of the underlying obligation, failure to perform a duty to preserve the value of collateral owed, under Article 9 or other law, to a debtor or other person secondarily liable, and failure to comply with applicable law in disposing of or otherwise enforcing the interest in collateral.

(e) A secondary obligor is not discharged under subsections (a)(3), (b), (c), or (d) unless the person entitled to enforce the instrument knows that the person is a secondary obligor or has notice under Section 3–419(c) that the instrument was signed for accommodation.

(f) A secondary obligor is not discharged under this section if the secondary obligor consents to the event or conduct that is the basis of the discharge, or the instrument or a separate agreement of the party provides for waiver of discharge under this section specifically or by general language indicating that parties waive defenses based on suretyship or impairment of collateral. Unless the circumstances indicate otherwise, consent by the principal obligor to an act that would lead to a discharge under this section constitutes consent to that act by the secondary obligor if the secondary obligor controls the principal obligor or deals with the person entitled to enforce the instrument on behalf of the principal obligor.

(g) A release or extension preserves a secondary obligor's recourse if the terms of the release or extension provide that:

(1) the person entitled to enforce the instrument retains the right to enforce the instrument against the secondary obligor; and

(2) the recourse of the secondary obligor continues as if the release or extension had not been granted.

(h) Except as otherwise provided in subsection (i), a secondary obligor asserting discharge under this section has the burden of persuasion both with respect to the occurrence of the acts alleged to harm the secondary obligor and loss or prejudice caused by those acts.

(i) If the secondary obligor demonstrates prejudice caused by an impairment of its recourse, and the circumstances of the case indicate that the amount of loss is not reasonably susceptible of calculation or requires proof of facts that are not ascertainable, it is presumed that the act impairing recourse caused a loss or impairment equal to the liability of the secondary obligor on the instrument. In that event, the burden of persuasion as to any lesser amount of the loss is on the person entitled to enforce the instrument.

As amended in 2002.

Official Comment

1. This section contains rules that are applicable when a secondary obligor (as defined in Section 3–103(a)(17)) is a party to an instrument. These rules essentially parallel modern interpretations of the law of suretyship and guaranty that apply when a secondary obligor is not a party to an instrument. See generally *Restatement of the Law, Third, Suretyship and Guaranty* (1996). Of course, the rules in this section do not resolve all possible issues concerning the rights and duties of the parties. In the event that a situation is presented that is not resolved by this section (or the other related sections of this Article), the resolution may be provided by the general law of suretyship because, pursuant to Section 1–103, that law is applicable unless displaced by provisions of this Act.

2. Like the law of suretyship and guaranty, Section 3–605 provides secondary obligors with defenses that are not available to other parties to instruments. The general operation of Section 3–605, and its relationship to the law of suretyship and guaranty, can be illustrated by an example. Bank agrees to lend $10,000 to Borrower, but only if Backer also is liable for repayment of the loan. The parties could consummate that transaction in three different ways. First, if Borrower and Backer incurred those obligations with contracts not governed by this Article (such as a note that is not an instrument for purposes of this Article), the general law of suretyship and guaranty would be applicable. Under modern nomenclature, Bank is the "obligee," Borrower is the "principal obligor," and Backer is the "secondary obligor." See *Restatement of Suretyship and Guaranty* § 1. Then assume that Bank and Borrower agree to a modification of their rights and obligations after the note is signed. For example, they might agree that Borrower may repay the loan at some date after the due date, or that Borrower may dis-

charge its repayment obligation by paying Bank $3,000 rather than $10,000. Alternatively, suppose that Bank releases collateral that Borrower has given to secure the loan. Under the law of suretyship and guaranty, the secondary obligor may be discharged under certain circumstances if these modifications of the obligations between Bank (the obligee) and Borrower (the principal obligor) are made without the consent of Backer (the secondary obligor). The rights that the secondary obligor has to a discharge of its liability in such cases commonly are referred to as suretyship defenses. The extent of the discharge depends upon the particular circumstances. See *Restatement of Suretyship and Guaranty* §§ 37, 39–44.

A second possibility is that the parties might decide to evidence the loan by a negotiable instrument. In that scenario, Borrower signs a note under which Borrower is obliged to pay $10,000 to the order of Bank on a due date stated in the note. Backer becomes liable for the repayment obligation by signing the note as a co-maker or indorser. In either case the note is signed for accommodation, Backer is an accommodation party, and Borrower is the accommodated party. See Section 3–419 (describing the obligations of accommodation parties). For purposes of Section 3–605, Backer is also a "secondary obligor" and Borrower is a "principal obligor," as those terms are defined in Section 3–103. Because Backer is a party to the instrument, its rights to a discharge based on any modification of obligations between Bank and Borrower are governed by Section 3–605 rather than by the general law of suretyship and guaranty. Within Section 3–605, subsection (a) describes the consequences of a release of Borrower, subsection (b) describes the consequences of an extension of time, and subsection (c) describes the consequences of other modifications.

The third possibility is that Borrower would use an instrument governed by this Article to evidence its repayment obligation, but Backer's obligation would be created in some way other than by becoming party to that instrument. In that case, Backer's rights are determined by suretyship and guaranty law rather than by this Article. See Comment 3 to Section 3–419.

A person also can acquire secondary liability without having been a secondary obligor at the time that the principal obligation was created. For example, a transferee of real or personal property that assumes the obligation of the transferor as maker of a note secured by the property becomes by operation of law a principal obligor, with the transferor becoming a secondary obligor. *Restatement of Suretyship and Guaranty* § 2(e); *Restatement of Mortgages* § 5.1. Article 3 does not determine the effect of the release of the transferee in that case because the assuming transferee is not a "party" to the instrument as defined in Section 3–103(a)(10). Section 3–605(a) does not apply then because the holder has not discharged the obligation of a "principal obligor," a term defined in Section 3–103(a)(11). Thus, the resolution of that question is governed by the law of suretyship. See *Restatement of Suretyship and Guaranty* § 39.

3. Section 3–605 is not, however, limited to the conventional situation of the accommodation party discussed in Comment 2. It also applies in four other situations. First, it applies to indorsers of notes who are not accommodation parties. Unless an indorser signs without recourse, the indorser's liability under Section 3–415(a) is functionally similar to that of a guarantor of payment. For example, if Bank in the second hypothetical discussed in Comment 2 indorsed the note and transferred it to Second Bank, Bank is liable to Second Bank in the event of dishonor of the note by Borrower. Section 3–415(a). Because of that secondary liability as indorser, Bank qualifies as a "secondary obligor" under Section 3–103(a)(17) and has the same rights under Section 3–605 as an accommodation party.

Second, a similar analysis applies to the drawer of a draft that is accepted by a party that is not a bank. Under Section 3–414(d), that drawer has liability on the same terms as an indorser under Section 3–415(a). Thus, the drawer in that case is a "secondary obligor" under Section 3–103(a)(17) and has rights under Section 3–605 to that extent.

Third, a similar principle justifies application of Section 3–605 to persons who indorse a check. Assume that Drawer draws a check to the order of Payee. Payee then indorses the check and transfers it to Transferee. If Transferee presents the check and it is dishonored, Transferee may recover from Drawer under Section 3–414 or Payee under Section 3–415. Because of that secondary liability as an indorser, Payee is a secondary obligor under Section 3–103(a)(17). Drawer is a "principal obligor" under Section 3–103(a)(11). As noted in Comment 4, below, however, Section 3–605(a)(3) will discharge indorsers of checks in some cases in which other secondary obligors will not be discharged by this section.

Fourth, this section also deals with the rights of co-makers of instruments, even when those co-makers do not qualify as accommodation parties. The co-makers' rights of contribution under Section 3–116 make each co-maker a secondary obligor to the extent of that right of contribution.

4. Subsection (a) is based on *Restatement of Suretyship and Guaranty* § 39. It addresses the effects of a release of the principal obligor by the person entitled to enforce the instrument. Paragraph (a)(1) governs the effect of that release on the principal obligor's duties to the secondary obligor; paragraphs (a)(2) and (a)(3) govern the effect of that release on the secondary obligor's duties to the person entitled to enforce the instrument.

With respect to the duties of the principal obligor, the release of course cannot affect obligations of the principal obligor with respect to payments that the secondary obligor already has made. But with respect to future payments by the secondary obligor, paragraph (a)(1) (based on *Restatement of Suretyship and Guaranty* § 39(a)) provides that the principal obligor is discharged, to the extent of the release, from any other duties to the secondary obligor. That rule is appropriate because otherwise the discharge granted to the principal obligor would be illusory: it would have obtained a release from a person entitled to enforce that instrument, but it would be directly liable for the same sum to the secondary obligor if the secondary obligor later complied with its secondary obligation to pay the instrument. This discharge does not occur, though, if the terms of the release effect a "preservation of recourse" as described in subsection (g). See Comment 10, below.

The discharge under paragraph (a)(1) of the principal obligor's duties to the secondary obligor is broad, applying to all duties under this article. This includes not only the principal obligor's liability as a party to an instrument (as a maker, drawer or indorser under Sections 3–412 through 3–415) but also obligations under Sections 3–116 and 3–419.

Paragraph (a)(2) is based closely on *Restatement of Suretyship and Guaranty* § 39(b). It articulates a default rule that the release of a principal obligor also discharges the secondary obligor, to the extent of the release granted to the principal obligor, from any unperformed portion of its obligation on the instrument. The discharge of the secondary obligor under paragraph (a)(2) is phrased more narrowly than the discharge of the principal obligor is phrased under paragraph (a)(1) because, unlike principal obligors, the only obligations of secondary obligors in Article 3 are "on the instrument" as makers or indorsers.

The parties can opt out of that rule by including a contrary statement in the terms of the release. The provision does not contemplate that any "magic words" are necessary. Thus, discharge of the secondary obligor under paragraph (a)(2) is avoided not only if the terms of the release track the statutory language (e.g., the person entitled to enforce the instrument "retains the right to enforce the instrument" against the secondary obligor), or if the terms of the release effect a preservation of recourse under subsection (g), but also if the terms of the release include a simple statement that the parties intend to "release the principal obligor but not the secondary obligor" or that the person entitled to enforce the instrument "reserves its rights" against the secondary obligor. At the same time, because paragraph (a)(2) refers to the "terms of the release," extrinsic circumstances cannot be used to establish that the parties intended the secondary obligor to remain obligated. If a release of the principal obligor includes such a provision, the secondary obligor is, nonetheless, discharged to the extent of the consideration that is paid for the release; that consideration is treated as a payment in partial satisfaction of the instrument.

Notwithstanding language in the release that prevents discharge of the secondary obligor under paragraph (a)(2), paragraph (a)(3) discharges the secondary obligor from its obligation to a person entitled to enforce the instrument to the extent that the release otherwise would cause the secondary obligor a loss. The rationale for that provision is that a release of the principal obligor changes the economic risk for which the secondary obligor contracted. This risk may be increased in two ways. First, by releasing the principal obligor, the person entitled to enforce the instrument has eliminated the likelihood of future payments by the principal obligor that would lessen the obligation of the secondary obligor. Second, unless the release effects a preservation of the secondary obligor's recourse, the release eliminates the secondary obligor's claims against the principal obligor with respect to any future payment by the secondary obligor. The discharge provided by this paragraph prevents that increased risk from causing the secondary obligor a loss. Moreover, permitting releases to be negotiated between the principal obligor and the person entitled to enforce the instrument without regard to the consequences to the secondary obligor would create an undue risk of opportunistic behavior by the obligee and principal obligor. That concern is lessened, and the discharge is not provided by paragraph (a)(3), if the secondary obligor has consented to the release or is deemed to have consented to it under subsection (f) (which presumes consent by a secondary obligor to actions taken by a principal obligor if the secondary obligor controls the principal obligor or deals with the person entitled to enforce the instrument on behalf of the principal obligor). See Comment 9, below.

Subsection (a) (and Restatement Section 39(b), the concepts of which it follows quite closely) is designed to facilitate negotiated workouts between a creditor and a principal obligor, so long as they are not at the expense of a secondary obligor who has not consented to the arrangement (either specifically or by waiving its rights to discharge under this section). Thus, for example, the provision facilitates an arrangement in which the principal obligor pays some portion of a guaranteed obligation, the person entitled to enforce the instrument grants a release to the principal obligor in exchange for that payment, and the person entitled to enforce the instrument pursues the secondary obligor for the remainder of the obligation. Under paragraph (a)(2), the person entitled to enforce the instrument may pursue the secondary obligor despite the release of the principal obligor so long as the terms of the release provide for this result. Under paragraph (a)(3), though, the secondary obligor will be protected against any loss it might suffer by reason of that release (if the secondary obligor has not waived discharge under subsection (f)). It should be noted that the obligee may be able to minimize the risk of such loss (and, thus, of the secondary obligor's discharge) by giving the secondary obligor prompt notice of the release even though such notice is not required.

The foregoing principles are illustrated by the following cases:

Case 1. D borrows $1000 from C. The repayment obligation is evidenced by a note issued by D, payable to the order of C. S is an accommodation indorser of the note. As the due date of the note approaches, it becomes obvious that D cannot pay the full amount of the note and may soon be facing bankruptcy. C, in order to collect as much as possible from D and lessen the need to seek recovery from S, agrees to release D from its obligation under the note in exchange for $100 in cash. The agreement to release D is silent as to the effect of the release on S. Pursuant to Section 3–605(a)(2), the release of D discharges S from its obligations to C on the note.

Case 2. Same facts as Case 1, except that the terms of the release provide that C retains its rights to enforce the instrument against S. D is discharged from its obligations to S pursuant to Section 3–605(a)(1), but S is not discharged from its obligations to C pursuant to Section 3–605(a)(2). However, if S could have recovered from D any sum it paid to C (had D not been discharged from its obligation to S), S has been harmed by the release and is discharged pursuant to Section 3–605(a)(3) to the extent of that harm.

Case 3. Same facts as Case 1, except that the terms of the release provide that C retains its rights to enforce the instrument against S and that S retains its recourse against D. Under subsection (g), the release effects a preservation of recourse. Thus, S is not discharged from its obligations to C pursuant to Section 3–605(a)(2) and D is not discharged from its obligations to S pursuant to Section 3–605(a)(1). Because S's claims against D are preserved, S will not suffer the kind of loss described in Case 2. If no other loss is suffered by S as a result of the release, S is not discharged pursuant to this section.

Case 4. Same facts as Case 3, except that D had made arrangements to work at a second job in order to earn the money to fulfill its obligations on the note. When C released D, however, D canceled the plans for the second job. While S still retains its recourse against D, S may be discharged from its obligation under the instrument to the extent that D's decision to forgo the second job causes S a loss because forgoing the job renders D unable to fulfill its obligations to S under Section 3–419.

Subsection (a) reflects a change from former Section 3–605(b), which provided categorically that the release of a principal obligor by the person entitled to enforce the instrument did not discharge a secondary obligor's obligation on the instrument and assumed that the release also did not discharge the principal obligor's obligations to the secondary obligor under Section 3–419. The rule under subsection (a) is much closer to the policy of the *Restatement of Suretyship and Guaranty* than was former Section 3–605(b). The change, however, is likely to affect only a narrow category of cases. First, as discussed above, Section 3–605 applies only to transactions in which the payment obligation is represented by a negotiable instrument, and, within that set of transactions, only to those transactions in which the secondary obligation is incurred by indorsement or cosigning, not to transactions that involve a separate document of guaranty. See Comment 2, above. Second, as provided in subsection (f), secondary obligors cannot obtain a discharge under subsection (a) in any transaction in which they have consented to the challenged conduct. Thus, subsection (a) will not apply to any transaction that includes a provision waiving suretyship defenses (a provision that is almost universally included in commercial loan documentation) or to any transaction in which the creditor obtains the consent of the secondary obligor at the time of the release.

The principal way in which subsection (a) goes beyond the policy of *Restatement* § 39 is with respect to the liability of indorsers of checks. Specifically, the last sentence of paragraph (a)(2) provides that a release of a principal obligor grants a complete discharge to the indorser of a check, without requiring the indorser to prove harm. In that particular context, it seems likely that continuing responsibility for the indorser often would be so inconsistent with the expectations of the parties as to create a windfall for the creditor and an unfair surprise for the indorser. Thus, the statute implements a simple rule that grants a complete discharge. The creditor, of course, can avoid that rule by contracting with the secondary obligor for a different result at the time that the creditor grants the release to the principal obligor.

5.   Subsection (b) is based on *Restatement of Suretyship and Guaranty* § 40 and relates to extensions of the due date of the instrument. An extension of time to pay a note is often beneficial to the secondary obligor because the additional time may enable the principal obligor to obtain the funds to pay the instrument. In some cases, however, the extension may cause loss to the secondary obligor, particularly if deterioration of the financial condition of the principal obligor reduces the amount that the secondary obligor is able to recover on its right of recourse when default occurs. For example, suppose that the instrument is an installment note and the principal debtor is temporarily short of funds to pay a monthly installment. The payee agrees to extend the due date of the installment for a month or two to allow the debtor to pay when funds are available. Paragraph (b)(2) provides that an extension of time results in a discharge of the secondary obligor, but only to the extent that the secondary obligor proves that the extension caused loss. See subsection (h) (discussing the burden of proof under Section 3–605). Thus, if the extension is for a long period, the secondary obligor might be able to prove that during the period of extension the principal obligor became insolvent, reducing the value of the right of recourse of the secondary obligor. In such a case, paragraph (b)(2) discharges the secondary obligor to the extent of that harm. Although not required to notify the secondary obligor of the extension, the payee can minimize the risk of loss by the secondary obligor by giving the secondary obligor prompt notice of the extension; prompt notice can enhance the likelihood that the secondary obligor's right of recourse can remain valuable, and thus can limit the likelihood that the secondary obligor will suffer a loss because of the extension. See *Restatement of Suretyship and Guaranty* Section 38 comment b.

If the secondary obligor is not discharged under paragraph (b)(2) (either because it would not suffer a loss by reason of the extension or because it has waived its right to discharge pursuant to subsection (f)), it is important to understand the effect of the extension on the rights and obligations of the secondary obligor. Consider the following cases:

Case 5. A borrows money from Lender and issues a note payable to the order of Lender that is due on April 1, 2002. B signs the note for accommodation at the request of Lender. B signed the note either as co-maker or as an anomalous indorser. In either case Lender subsequently makes an agreement with A extending the due date of A's obligation to pay the note to July 1, 2002. In either case B did not agree to the extension, and the extension did not address Lender's rights against B. Under paragraph (b)(1), A's obligations to B under this article are also extended to July 1, 2002. Under paragraph (b)(3), if B is not discharged, B may treat its obligations to Lender as also extended, or may pay the instrument on the original due date.

Case 6. Same facts as Case 5, except that the extension agreement includes a statement that the Lender retains its right to enforce the note against B on its original terms. Under paragraph (b)(3), B is liable on the original due date, but under paragraph (b)(1), A's obligations to B under Section 3–419 are not due until July 1, 2002.

Case 7. Same facts as Case 5, except that the extension agreement includes a statement that the Lender retains its right to enforce the note against B on its original terms and B retains its recourse against A as though no extension had been granted. Under paragraph (b)(3), B is liable on the original due date. Under paragraph (b)(1), A's obligations to B under Section 3–419 are not extended.

Under section 3–605(b), the results in Case 5 and Case 7 are identical to the results that follow from the law of suretyship and guaranty. See *Restatement of Suretyship and Guaranty* § 40. The situation in Case 6 is not specifically addressed in the Restatement, but the resolution in this Section is consistent with the concepts of suretyship and guaranty law as reflected in the Restatement. If the secondary obligor is called upon to pay on the due date, it may be difficult to quantify the extent to which the extension has impaired the right of recourse of the secondary obligor at that time. Still, the secondary obligor does have a right to make a claim against the obligee at that time. As a practical matter a suit making such a claim should establish the facts relevant to the extent of the impairment. *See Restatement of Suretyship and Guaranty* § 37(4).

As a practical matter, an extension of the due date will normally occur only when the principal obligor is unable to pay on the due date. The interest of the secondary obligor normally is to acquiesce in the willingness of the person entitled to enforce the instrument to wait for payment from the principal obligor rather than to pay right away and rely on an action against the principal obligor that may have little or no value. But in unusual cases the secondary obligor may prefer to pay the holder on the original due date so as to avoid continuing accrual of interest. In such cases, the secondary obligor may do so. See paragraph (b)(3). If the terms of the extension provide that the person entitled to enforce the instrument retains its right to enforce the instrument against the secondary obligor on the original due date, though, those terms are effective and the secondary obligor may not delay payment until the extended due date. Unless the extension agreement effects a preservation of recourse, however, the secondary obligor may not proceed against the principal obligor under Section 3–419 until the extended due date. See paragraph (b)(1). To the extent that delay causes loss to the secondary obligor it is discharged under paragraph (b)(2).

Even in those cases in which a secondary obligor does not have a duty to pay the instrument on the original due date, it always has the right to pay the instrument on that date, and perhaps minimize its loss by doing so. The secondary obligor is not precluded, however, from asserting its rights to discharge under Section 3–605(b)(2) if it does not exercise that option. The critical issue is whether the extension caused the secondary obligor a loss by increasing the difference between its cost of performing its obligation on the instrument and the amount recoverable from the principal obligor under this Article. The decision by the secondary obligor not to exercise its option to pay on the original due date may, under the circumstances, be a factor to be considered in the determination of that issue, especially if the secondary obligor has been given prompt notice of the extension (as discussed above).

6. Subsection (c) is based on *Restatement of Suretyship and Guaranty* § 41. It is a residual provision, which applies to modifications of the obligation of the principal obligor that are not covered by subsections (a) and (b). Under subsection (c)(1), a modification of the obligation of the principal obligor on the instrument (other than a release covered by subsection (a) or an extension of the due date covered by subsection (b)), will correspondingly modify the duties of the principal obligor to the secondary obligor. Under subsection (c)(2), such a modification also will result in discharge of the secondary obligor to the extent the modification causes loss to the secondary obligor. To the extent that the secondary obligor is not discharged and the obli-

gation changes the amount of money payable on the instrument, or the timing of such payment, subsection (c)(3) provides the secondary obligor with a choice: it may satisfy its obligation on the instrument as if the modification had not occurred, or it may treat its obligation to pay the instrument as having been modified in a manner corresponding to the modification of the principal obligor's obligation.

The following cases illustrate the application of subsection (c):

Case 8. Corporation borrows money from Lender and issues a note payable to Lender. X signs the note as an accommodation party for Corporation. The note refers to a loan agreement under which the note was issued, which states various events of default that allow Lender to accelerate the due date of the note. Among the events of default are breach of covenants not to incur debt beyond specified limits and not to engage in any line of business substantially different from that currently carried on by Corporation. Without consent of X, Lender agrees to modify the covenants to allow Corporation to enter into a new line of business that X considers to be risky, and to incur debt beyond the limits specified in the loan agreement to finance the new venture. This modification discharges X to the extent that the modification otherwise would cause X a loss.

Case 9. Corporation borrows money from Lender and issues a note payable to Lender in the amount of $100,000. X signs the note as an accommodation party for Corporation. The note calls for 60 equal monthly payments of interest and principal. Before the first payment is made, Corporation and Lender agree to modify the note by changing the repayment schedule to require four annual payments of interest only, followed by a fifth payment of interest and the entire $100,000 principal balance. To the extent that the modification does not discharge X, X has the option of fulfilling its obligation on the note in accordance with the original terms or the modified terms.

7. Subsection (d) is based on *Restatement of Suretyship and Guaranty* § 42 and deals with the discharge of secondary obligors by impairment of collateral. The last sentence of subsection (d) states four common examples of what is meant by impairment. Because it uses the term "includes," the provision allows a court to find impairment in other cases as well. There is extensive case law on impairment of collateral. The secondary obligor is discharged to the extent that the secondary obligor proves that impairment was caused by a person entitled to enforce the instrument. For example, assume that the payee of a secured note fails to perfect the security interest. The collateral is owned by the principal obligor who subsequently files in bankruptcy. As a result of the failure to perfect, the security interest is not enforceable in bankruptcy. If the payee were to obtain payment from the secondary obligor, the secondary obligor would be subrogated to the payee's security interest in the collateral under Section 3–419 and general principles of suretyship law. See *Restatement of Suretyship and Guaranty § 28(1)(c)*. In this situation, though, the value of the security interest is impaired completely because the security interest is unenforceable. Thus, the secondary obligor is discharged from its obligation on the note to the extent of that impairment. If the value of the collateral impaired is as much or more than the amount of the note, and if there will be no recovery on the note as an unsecured claim, there is a complete discharge. Subsection (d) applies whether the collateral is personalty or realty, whenever the obligation in question is in the form of a negotiable instrument.

8. Subsection (e) is based on the former Section 3–605(h). The requirement of knowledge in the first clause is consistent with Section 9–628. The requirement of notice in the second clause is consistent with Section 3–419(c).

9. The importance of the suretyship defenses provided in Section 3–605 is greatly diminished by the fact that the right to discharge can be waived as provided in subsection (f). The waiver can be effectuated by a provision in the instrument or in a separate agreement. It is standard practice to include such a waiver of suretyship defenses in notes prepared by financial institutions or other commercial creditors. Thus, Section 3–605 will result in the discharge of an accommodation party on a note only in the occasional case in which the note does not include such a waiver clause and the person entitled to enforce the note nevertheless takes actions that would give rise to a discharge under this section without obtaining the consent of the secondary obligor.

Because subsection (f) by its terms applies only to a discharge "under this section," subsection (f) does not operate to waive a defense created by other law (such as the law governing enforcement of security interests under Article 9) that cannot be waived under that law. See, e.g., Section 9–602.

The last sentence of subsection (f) creates an inference of consent on the part of the secondary obligor whenever the secondary obligor controls the principal obligor or deals with the creditor on behalf of the principal obligor. That sentence is based on *Restatement of Suretyship and Guaranty* § 48(2).

10. Subsection (g) explains the criteria for determining whether the terms of a release or extension preserve the secondary obligor's recourse, a concept of importance in the application of subsections (a) and (b). First, the terms of the release or extension must provide that the person entitled to enforce the instrument retains the right to enforce the instrument against the secondary obligor. Second, the terms of the release or extension must provide that the recourse of the secondary obligor against the principal obligor continues as though the release or extension had not been granted. Those requirements are drawn from *Restatement of Suretyship and Guaranty* § 38.

11. Subsections (h) and (i) articulate rules for the burden of persuasion under Section 3–605. Those rules are based on *Restatement of Suretyship and Guaranty* § 49.

As amended in 2002.

ADDENDUM TO REVISED ARTICLE 3

Notes to Legislative Counsel

1. If revised Article 3 is adopted in your state, the reference in Section 2–511 to Section 3–802 should be changed to Section 3–310.

2. If revised Article 3 is adopted in your state and the Uniform Fiduciaries Act is also in effect in your state, you may want to consider amending Uniform Fiduciaries Act § 9 to conform to Section 3–307(b)(2)(iii) and (4)(iii). See Official Comment 3 to Section 3–307.

UCC ARTICLE 4

BANK DEPOSITS AND COLLECTIONS

Pre–1990 Article 4 . . . .*Appendix G*
2001 amendments (Article 1 revision) . . . .*Appendix A*
2002 amendments . . . .*Appendix H*
2003 amendments (Article 7 revision) . . . .*Appendix B*

PART 1. GENERAL PROVISIONS AND DEFINITIONS

Section
4–101. Short Title.
4–102. Applicability.
4–103. Variation by Agreement; Measure of Damages; Action Constituting Ordinary Care.
4–104. Definitions and Index of Definitions.
4–105. Definitions of Types of Banks.
4–106. Payable Through or Payable at Bank; Collecting Bank.
4–107. Separate Office of Bank.
4–108. Time of Receipt of Items.
4–109. Delays.
4–110. Electronic Presentment.
4–111. Statute of Limitations.

PART 2. COLLECTION OF ITEMS: DEPOSITARY AND COLLECTING BANKS

4–201. Status of Collecting Bank as Agent and Provisional Status of Credits; Applicability of Article; Item Indorsed "Pay Any Bank".
4–202. Responsibility for Collection or Return; When Action Timely.
4–203. Effect of Instructions.
4–204. Methods of Sending and Presenting; Sending Directly to Payor Bank.
4–205. Depositary Bank Holder of Unindorsed Item.
4–206. Transfer Between Banks.
4–207. Transfer Warranties.
4–208. Presentment Warranties.
4–209. Encoding and Retention Warranties.
4–210. Security Interest of Collecting Bank in Items, Accompanying Documents and Proceeds.
4–211. When Bank Gives Value for Purposes of Holder in Due Course.

Section
4–212. Presentment by Notice of Item Not Payable by, Through, or at Bank; Liability of Drawer or Indorser.
4–213. Medium and Time of Settlement by Bank.
4–214. Right of Charge–Back or Refund; Liability of Collecting Bank; Return of Item.
4–215. Final Payment of Item by Payor Bank; When Provisional Debits and Credits Become Final; When Certain Credits Become Available for Withdrawal.
4–216. Insolvency and Preference.

PART 3. COLLECTION OF ITEMS: PAYOR BANKS

4–301. Deferred Posting; Recovery of Payment by Return of Items; Time of Dishonor; Return of Items by Payor Bank.
4–302. Payor Bank's Responsibility for Late Return of Item.
4–303. When Items Subject to Notice, Stop-Payment Order, Legal Process, or Setoff; Order in Which Items May Be Charged or Certified.

PART 4. RELATIONSHIP BETWEEN PAYOR BANK AND ITS CUSTOMER

4–401. When Bank May Charge Customer's Account.
4–402. Bank's Liability to Customer for Wrongful Dishonor; Time of Determining Insufficiency of Account.
4–403. Customer's Right to Stop Payment; Burden of Proof of Loss.
4–404. Bank Not Obliged to Pay Check More Than Six Months Old.
4–405. Death or Incompetence of Customer.
4–406. Customer's Duty to Discover and Report Unauthorized Signature or Alteration.

Section

4–407. Payor Bank's Right to Subrogation on Improper Payment.

PART 5. COLLECTION OF DOCUMENTARY DRAFTS

4–501. Handling of Documentary Drafts; Duty to Send for Presentment and to Notify Customer of Dishonor.

Section

4–502. Presentment of "On Arrival" Drafts.

4–503. Responsibility of Presenting Bank for Documents and Goods; Report of Reasons for Dishonor; Referee in Case of Need.

4–504. Privilege of Presenting Bank to Deal With Goods; Security Interest for Expenses.

PART 1

GENERAL PROVISIONS AND DEFINITIONS

§ 4–101. Short Title.

This Article may be cited as Uniform Commercial Code—Bank Deposits and Collections.

As amended in 1990.

Official Comment

1. The great number of checks handled by banks and the country-wide nature of the bank collection process require uniformity in the law of bank collections. There is needed a uniform statement of the principal rules of the bank collection process with ample provision for flexibility to meet the needs of the large volume handled and the changing needs and conditions that are bound to come with the years. This Article meets that need.

2. In 1950 at the time Article 4 was drafted, 6.7 billion checks were written annually. By the time of the 1990 revision of Article 4 annual volume was estimated by the American Bankers Association to be about 50 billion checks. The banking system could not have coped with this increase in check volume had it not developed in the late 1950s and early 1960s an automated system for check collection based on encoding checks with machine-readable information by Magnetic Ink Character Recognition (MICR). An important goal of the 1990 revision of Article 4 is to promote the efficiency of the check collection process by making the provisions of Article 4 more compatible with the needs of an automated system and, by doing so, increase the speed and lower the cost of check collection for those who write and receive checks. An additional goal of the 1990 revision of Article 4 is to remove any statutory barriers in the Article to the ultimate adoption of programs allowing the presentment of checks to payor banks by electronic transmission of information captured from the MICR line on the checks. The potential of these programs for saving the time and expense of transporting the huge volume of checks from depositary to payor banks is evident.

3. Article 4 defines rights between parties with respect to bank deposits and collections. It is not a regulatory statute. It does not regulate the terms of the bank-customer agreement, nor does it prescribe what constraints different jurisdictions may wish to impose on that relationship in the interest of consumer protection. The revisions in Article 4 are intended to create a legal framework that accommodates automation and truncation for the benefit of all bank customers. This may raise consumer problems which enacting jurisdictions may wish to address in individual legislation. For example, with respect to Section 4–401(c), jurisdictions may wish to examine their unfair and deceptive practices laws to determine whether they are adequate to protect drawers who postdate checks from unscrupulous practices that may arise on the part of persons who induce drawers to issue postdated checks in the erroneous belief that the checks will not be immediately payable. Another example arises from the fact that under various truncation plans customers will no longer receive their cancelled checks and will no longer have the cancelled check to prove payment. Individual legislation might provide that a copy of a bank statement along with a copy of the check is prima facie evidence of payment.

§ 4–102. Applicability.

(a) To the extent that items within this Article are also within Articles 3 and 8, they are subject to those Articles. If there is conflict, this Article governs Article 3, but Article 8 governs this Article.

(b) The liability of a bank for action or nonaction with respect to an item handled by it for purposes of presentment, payment, or collection is governed by the law of the place where the bank is located. In the case of action or non-action by or at a branch or separate office of a bank, its liability is governed by the law of the place where the branch or separate office is located.

As amended in 1990.

Official Comment

1. The rules of Article 3 governing negotiable instruments, their transfer, and the contracts of the parties thereto apply to the items collected through banking channels wherever no specific provision is found in this Article. In the case of conflict, this Article governs. See Section 3–102(b).

Bonds and like instruments constituting investment securities under Article 8 may also be handled by banks for collection purposes. Various sections of Article 8 prescribe rules of transfer some of which (see Sections 8–304 and 8–306 Sections 8–108 and 8–304) may conflict with provisions of this Article (Sections 4–205, 4–207, and 4–208). In the case of conflict, Article 8 governs. *Amendments approved by the Permanent Editorial Board for Uniform Commercial Code November 4, 1995.*

Section 4–210 deals specifically with overlapping problems and possible conflicts between this Article and Article 9. However, similar reconciling provisions are not necessary in the case of Articles 5 and 7. Sections 4–301 and 4–302 are consistent with Section 5–112. In the case of Article 7 documents of title frequently accompany items but they are not themselves items. See Section 4–104(a)(9).

In Clearfield Trust Co. v. United States, 318 U.S. 363 (1943), the Court held that if the United States is a party to an instrument, its rights and duties are governed by federal common law in the absence of a specific federal statute or regulation. In United States v. Kimbell Foods, Inc., 440 U.S. 715 (1979), the Court stated a three-pronged test to ascertain whether the federal common-law rule should follow the state rule. In most instances courts under the *Kimbell* test have shown a willingness to adopt UCC rules in formulating federal common law on the subject. In *Kimbell* the Court adopted the priorities rules of Article 9.

In addition, applicable federal law may supersede provisions of this Article. One federal law that does so is the Expedited Funds Availability Act, 12 U.S.C. § 4001 et seq., and its implementing Regulation CC, 12 CFR Pt. 229. In some instances this law is alluded to in the statute, e.g., Section 4–215(e) and (f). In other instances, although not referred to in this Article, the provisions of the EFAA and Regulation CC control with respect to checks. For example, except between the depositary bank and its customer, all settlements are final and not provisional (Regulation CC, Section 229.36(d)), and the midnight deadline may be extended (Regulation CC, Section 229.30(c)). The comments to this Article suggest in most instances the relevant Regulation CC provisions.

2. Subsection (b) is designed to state a workable rule for the solution of otherwise vexatious problems of the conflicts of laws:

a. The routine and mechanical nature of bank collections makes it imperative that one law govern the activities of one office of a bank. The requirement found in some cases that to hold an indorser notice must be given in accordance with the law of the place of indorsement, since that method of notice became an implied term of the indorser's contract, is more theoretical than practical.

b. Adoption of what is in essence a tort theory of the conflict of laws is consistent with the general theory of this Article that the basic duty of a collecting bank is one of good faith and the exercise of ordinary care. Justification lies in the fact that, in using an ambulatory instrument, the drawer, payee, and indorsers must know that action will be taken with respect to it in other jurisdictions. This is especially pertinent with respect to the law of the place of payment.

c. The phrase "action or non-action with respect to any item handled by it for purposes of presentment, payment, or collection" is intended to make the conflicts rule of subsection (b) apply from the inception of the collection process of an item through all phases of deposit, forwarding, presentment, payment and remittance or credit of proceeds. Specifically the subsection applies to the initial act of a depositary bank in receiving an item and to the incidents of such receipt. The conflicts rule of Weissman v. Banque De Bruxelles, 254 N.Y. 488, 173 N.E. 835 (1930), is rejected. The subsection applies to questions of possible vicarious liability of a bank for action or non-action of sub-agents (see Section 4–202(c)), and tests these questions by the law of the state of the location of the bank which uses the sub-agent. The conflicts rule of St. Nicholas Bank of New York v. State Nat. Bank, 128 N.Y. 26, 27 N.E. 849, 13 L.R.A. 241 (1891), is rejected. The subsection applies to action or non-action of a payor bank in connection with handling an item (see Sections 4–215(a), 4–301, 4–302, 4–303) as well as action or non-action of a collecting bank (Sections 4–201 through 4–216); to action or non-action of a bank which suspends payment or is affected by another bank suspending payment (Section 4–216); to action or non-action of a bank with respect to an item under the rule of Part 4 of Article 4.

d. In a case in which subsection (b) makes this Article applicable, Section 4–103(a) leaves open the possibility of an agreement with respect to applicable law. This freedom of agreement follows the general policy of Section 1–105.

§ 4–103. Variation by Agreement; Measure of Damages; Action Constituting Ordinary Care.

(a) The effect of the provisions of this Article may be varied by agreement, but the parties to the agreement cannot disclaim a bank's responsibility for its lack of good faith or failure to exercise ordinary care or limit the measure of damages for the lack or failure. However, the parties may determine by agreement the standards by which the bank's responsibility is to be measured if those standards are not manifestly unreasonable.

(b) Federal Reserve regulations and operating circulars, clearing-house rules, and the like have the effect of agreements under subsection (a), whether or not specifically assented to by all parties interested in items handled.

(c) Action or non-action approved by this Article or pursuant to Federal Reserve regulations or operating circulars is the exercise of ordinary care and, in the absence of special instructions, action or non-action consistent with clearing-house rules and the like or with a general banking usage not disapproved by this Article, is prima facie the exercise of ordinary care.

(d) The specification or approval of certain procedures by this Article is not disapproval of other procedures that may be reasonable under the circumstances.

(e) The measure of damages for failure to exercise ordinary care in handling an item is the amount of the item reduced by an amount that could not have been realized by the exercise of ordinary care. If there is also bad faith it includes any other damages the party suffered as a proximate consequence.

As amended in 1990.

Official Comment

1. Section 1–102 states the general principles and rules for variation of the effect of this Act by agreement and the limitations to this power. Section 4–103 states the specific rules for variation of Article 4 by agreement and also certain standards of ordinary care. In view of the technical complexity of the field of bank collections, the enormous number of items handled by banks, the certainty that there will be variations from the normal in each day's work in each bank, the certainty of changing conditions and the possibility of developing improved methods of collection to speed the process, it would be unwise to freeze present methods of operation by mandatory statutory rules. This section, therefore, permits within wide limits variation of the effect of provisions of the Article by agreement.

2. Subsection (a) confers blanket power to vary all provisions of the Article by agreements of the ordinary kind. The agreements may not disclaim a bank's responsibility for its own lack of good faith or failure to exercise ordinary care and may not limit the measure of damages for the lack or failure, but this subsection like Section 1–102(3) approves the practice of parties determining by agreement the standards by which the responsibility is to be measured. In the absence of a showing that the standards manifestly are unreasonable, the agreement controls. Owners of items and other interested parties are not affected by agreements under this subsection unless they are parties to the agreement or are bound by adoption, ratification, estoppel or the like.

As here used "agreement" has the meaning given to it by Section 1–201(3). The agreement may be direct, as between the owner and the depositary bank; or indirect, as in the case in which the owner authorizes a particular type of procedure and any bank in the collection chain acts pursuant to such authorization. It may be with respect to a single item; or to all items handled for a particular customer, e.g., a general agreement between the depositary bank and the customer at the time a deposit account is opened. Legends on deposit tickets, collection letters and acknowledgments of items, coupled with action by the affected party constituting acceptance, adoption, ratification, estoppel or the like, are agreements if they meet the tests of the definition of "agreement." See Section 1–201(3). First Nat. Bank of Denver v. Federal Reserve Bank, 6 F.2d 339 (8th Cir.1925) (deposit slip); Jefferson County Bldg. Ass'n v. Southern Bank & Trust Co., 225 Ala. 25, 142 So. 66 (1932) (signature card and deposit slip); Semingson v. Stock Yards Nat. Bank, 162 Minn. 424, 203 N.W. 412 (1925) (passbook); Farmers State Bank v. Union Nat. Bank, 42 N.D. 449, 454, 173 N.W. 789, 790 (1919) (acknowledgment of receipt of item).

3. Subsection (a) (subject to its limitations with respect to good faith and ordinary care) goes far to meet the requirements of flexibility. However, it does not by itself confer fully effective flexibility. Since it is recognized that banks handle a great number of items every business day and that the parties interested in each item include the owner of the item, the drawer (if it is a check), all nonbank indorsers, the payor bank and from one to five or more collecting banks, it is obvious that it is impossible, practically, to obtain direct agreements from all of these parties on all items. In total, the interested parties constitute virtually every adult person and business organization in the United States. On the other hand they may become bound to agreements on the principle that collecting banks acting as agents have authority to make binding agreements with respect to items being handled. This conclusion was assumed but was not flatly decided in Federal Reserve Bank of Richmond v. Malloy, 264 U.S. 160, at 167, 44 S.Ct. 296, at 298, 68 L.Ed. 617, 31 A.L.R. 1261 (1924).

To meet this problem subsection (b) provides that official or quasi-official rules of collection, that is Federal Reserve regulations and operating circulars, clearing-house rules, and the like, have the effect of agreements under subsection (a), whether or not specifically assented to by all parties interested in items handled. Consequently, such official or quasi-official rules may, standing by themselves but subject to the good faith and ordinary care limitations, vary the effect of the provisions of Article 4.

Federal Reserve regulations. Various sections of the Federal Reserve Act (12 U.S.C. § 221 et seq.) authorize the Board of Governors of the Federal Reserve System to direct the Federal Reserve banks to exercise bank collection functions. For example, Section 16 (12 U.S.C. § 248(o)) authorizes the Board to require each Federal Reserve bank to exercise the functions of a clearing house for its members and Section 13 (12 U.S.C. § 342) authorizes each Federal Reserve bank to receive deposits from nonmember banks solely for the purposes of exchange or of collection. Under this statutory authorization the Board has issued Regulation J (Subpart A—Collection of Checks and Other Items). Under the supremacy clause of the Constitution, federal regulations prevail over state statutes. Moreover, the Expedited Funds Availability Act, 12 U.S.C. Section 4007(b) provides that the Act and Regulation CC, 12 CFR 229, supersede "any provision of the law of any State, including the Uniform Commercial Code as in effect in such State, which is inconsistent with this chapter or such regulations." See Comment 1 to Section 4–102.

Federal Reserve operating circulars. The regulations of the Federal Reserve Board authorize the Federal Reserve banks to promulgate operating circulars covering operating details. Regulation J, for example, provides that "Each Reserve Bank shall receive and handle items in accordance with this subpart, and shall issue operating circulars governing the details of its handling of items and other matters deemed appropriate by the Reserve Bank." This Article recognizes that "operating circulars" issued pursuant to the regulations and concerned with operating details as appropriate may, within their proper sphere, vary the effect of the Article.

Clearing–House Rules. Local clearing houses have long issued rules governing the details of clearing; hours of clearing, media of remittance, time for return of mis-sent items and the like. The case law has recognized these rules, within their proper sphere, as binding on affected parties and as appropriate sources for the courts to look to in filling out details of bank collection law. Subsection (b) in recognizing clearing-house rules as a means of preserving flexibility continues the sensible approach indicated in the cases. Included in the term "clearing houses" are county and regional clearing houses as well as those within a single city or town. There is, of course, no intention of authorizing a local clearing house or a group of clearing houses to rewrite the basic law generally. The term "clearing-house rules" should be understood in the light of functions the clearing houses have exercised in the past.

And the like. This phrase is to be construed in the light of the foregoing. "Federal Reserve regulations and operating circulars" cover rules and regulations issued by public or quasi-public agencies under statutory authority. "Clearing-house rules" cover rules issued by a group of banks which have associated themselves to perform through a clearing house some of their collection, payment and clearing functions. Other agencies or associations of this kind may be established in the future whose rules and regulations could be appropriately looked on as constituting means of avoiding absolute statutory rigidity. The phrase "and the like" leaves open possibilities for future development. An agreement between a number of banks or even all the banks in an area simply because they are banks, would not of itself, by virtue of the phrase "and the like," meet the purposes and objectives of subsection (b).

4. Under this Article banks come under the general obligations of the use of good faith and the exercise of ordinary care. "Good faith" is defined in Section 1–

201(b)(20). The term "ordinary care" is defined in Section 3–103(a)(9). These definitions are made to apply to Article 4 by Section 4–104(c). Section 4–202 states respects in which collecting banks must use ordinary care. Subsection (c) of Section 4–103 provides that action or non-action approved by the Article or pursuant to Federal Reserve regulations or operating circulars constitutes the exercise of ordinary care. Federal Reserve regulations and operating circulars constitute an affirmative standard of ordinary care equally with the provisions of Article 4 itself.

Subsection (c) further provides that, absent special instructions, action or non-action consistent with clearing-house rules and the like or with a general banking usage not disapproved by the Article, prima facie constitutes the exercise of ordinary care. Clearing-house rules and the phrase "and the like" have the significance set forth above in these Comments. The term "general banking usage" is not defined but should be taken to mean a general usage common to banks in the area concerned. See Section 1–205(2). In a case in which the adjective "general" is used, the intention is to require a usage broader than a mere practice between two or three banks but it is not intended to require a usage broader than a mere practice between two or three banks but it is not intended to require anything as broad as a country-wide usage. A usage followed generally throughout a state, a substantial portion of a state, a metropolitan area or the like would certainly be sufficient. Consistently with the principle of Section 1–205(3), action or non-action consistent with clearing-house rules or the like or with banking usages prima facie constitutes the exercise of ordinary care. However, the phrase "in the absence of special instructions" affords owners of items an opportunity to prescribe other standards and although there may be no direct supervision or control of clearing houses or banking usages by official supervisory authorities, the confirmation of ordinary care by compliance with these standards is prima facie only, thus conferring on the courts the ultimate power to determine ordinary care in any case in which it should appear desirable to do so. The prima facie rule does, however, impose on the party contesting the standards to establish that they are unreasonable, arbitrary or unfair as used by the particular bank.

5. Subsection (d), in line with the flexible approach required for the bank collection process is designed to make clear that a novel procedure adopted by a bank is not to be considered unreasonable merely because that procedure is not specifically contemplated by this Article or by agreement, or because it has not yet been generally accepted as a bank usage. Changing conditions constantly call for new procedures and someone has to use the new procedure first. If this procedure is found to be reasonable under the circumstances, provided, of course, that it is not inconsistent with any provision of the Article or other law or agreement, the bank which has followed the new procedure should not be found to have failed in the exercise of ordinary care.

6. Subsection (e) sets forth a rule for determining the measure of damages for failure to exercise ordinary care which, under subsection (a), cannot be limited by agreement. In the absence of bad faith the maximum recovery is the amount of the item concerned. The term "bad faith" is not defined; the connotation is the absence of good faith (Section 3–103). When it is established that some part or all of the item could not have been collected even by the use of ordinary care the recovery is reduced by the amount that would have been in any event uncollectible. This limitation on recovery follows the case law. Finally, if bad faith is established the rule opens to allow the recovery of other damages, whose "proximateness" is to be tested by the ordinary rules applied in comparable cases. Of course, it continues to be as necessary under subsection (e) as it has been under ordinary common law principles that, before the damage rule of the subsection becomes operative, liability of the bank and some loss to the customer or owner must be established.

As amended in 2002.

§ 4–104. Definitions and Index of Definitions.

(a) In this Article, unless the context otherwise requires:

(1) "Account" means any deposit or credit account with a bank, including a demand, time, savings, passbook, share draft, or like account, other than an account evidenced by a certificate of deposit;

(2) "Afternoon" means the period of a day between noon and midnight;

(3) "Banking day" means the part of a day on which a bank is open to the public for carrying on substantially all of its banking functions;

(4) "Clearing house" means an association of banks or other payors regularly clearing items;

(5) "Customer" means a person having an account with a bank or for whom a bank has

agreed to collect items, including a bank that maintains an account at another bank;

(6) "Documentary draft" means a draft to be presented for acceptance or payment if specified documents, certificated securities (Section 8–102) or instructions for uncertificated securities (Section 8–102), or other certificates, statements, or the like are to be received by the drawee or other payor before acceptance or payment of the draft;

(7) "Draft" means a draft as defined in Section 3–104 or an item, other than an instrument, that is an order;

(8) "Drawee" means a person ordered in a draft to make payment;

(9) "Item" means an instrument or a promise or order to pay money handled by a bank for collection or payment. The term does not include a payment order governed by Article 4A or a credit or debit card slip;

(10) "Midnight deadline" with respect to a bank is midnight on its next banking day following the banking day on which it receives the relevant item or notice or from which the time for taking action commences to run, whichever is later;

(11) "Settle" means to pay in cash, by clearing-house settlement, in a charge or credit or by remittance, or otherwise as agreed. A settlement may be either provisional or final;

(12) "Suspends payments" with respect to a bank means that it has been closed by order of the supervisory authorities, that a public officer has been appointed to take it over, or that it ceases or refuses to make payments in the ordinary course of business.

(b) Other definitions applying to this Article and the sections in which they appear are:

"Agreement for electronic presentment" Section 4–110.

"Collecting bank" Section 4–105.

"Depositary bank" Section 4–105.

"Intermediary bank" Section 4–105.

"Payor bank" Section 4–105.

"Presenting bank" Section 4–105.

"Presentment notice" Section 4–110.

(c) "Control" as provided in Section 7–106 and the following definitions in other Articles apply to this Article:

"Acceptance" Section 3–409.

"Alteration" Section 3–407.

"Cashier's check" Section 3–104.

"Certificate of deposit" Section 3–104.

"Certified check" Section 3–409.

"Check" Section 3–104.

["Good Faith" Section 3–103.]*

"Holder in due course" Section 3–302.

"Instrument" Section 3–104.

"Notice of dishonor" Section 3–503.

"Order" Section 3–103.

"Ordinary care" Section 3–103.

"Person entitled to enforce" Section 3–301.

"Presentment" Section 3–501.

"Promise" Section 3–103.

"Prove" Section 3–103.

"Record" Section 3–103.

"Remotely–Created consumer item" Section 3–103.

"Teller's check" Section 3–104.

"Unauthorized signature" Section 3–403.

(d) In addition, Article 1 contains general definitions and principles of construction and interpretation applicable throughout this Article.

As amended in 1990, 1994, 2001, 2002 and 2003.

Official Comment

1. Paragraph (a)(1): "Account" is defined to include both asset accounts in which a customer has deposited money and accounts from which a customer may draw on a line of credit. The limiting factor is that the account must be in a bank.

2. Paragraph (a)(3): "Banking day." Under this definition that part of a business day when a bank is open only for limited functions, e.g., to receive deposits and cash checks, but with loan, bookkeeping and other departments closed, is not part of a banking day.

3. Paragraph (a)(4): "Clearing house." Occasionally express companies, governmental agencies and other nonbanks deal directly with a clearing house; hence the definition does not limit the term to an association of banks.

4. Paragraph (a)(5): "Customer." It is to be noted that this term includes a bank carrying an account

* Note from Thomson-West Advisory Panel: The definition of good faith in 3–103 was deleted by Revised Article 1 (2001).

with another bank as well as the more typical nonbank customer or depositor.

5. Paragraph (a)(6): "Documentary draft" applies even though the documents do not accompany the draft but are to be received by the drawee or other payor before acceptance or payment of the draft. Documents may be either in electronic or tangible form. See Article 5, Section 5–102, Comment 2 and Article 1, Section 1–201 (definition of "document of title").

6. Paragraph (a)(7): "Draft" is defined in Section 3–104 as a form of instrument. Since Article 4 applies to items that may not fall within the definition of instrument, the term is defined here to include an item that is a written order to pay money, even though the item may not qualify as an instrument. The term "order" is defined in Section 3–103.

7. Paragraph (a)(8): "Drawee" is defined in Section 3–103 in terms of an Article 3 draft which is a form of instrument. Here "drawee" is defined in terms of an Article 4 draft which includes items that may not be instruments.

8. Paragraph (a)(9): "Item" is defined broadly to include an instrument, as defined in Section 3–104, as well as promises or orders that may not be within the definition of "instrument." The terms "promise" and "order" are defined in Section 3–103. A promise is a written undertaking to pay money. An order is a written instruction to pay money. But see Section 4–110(c). Since bonds and other investment securities under Article 8 may be within the term "instrument" or "promise," they are items and when handled by banks for collection are subject to this Article. See Comment 1 to Section 4–102. The functional limitation on the meaning of this term is the willingness of the banking system to handle the instrument, undertaking or instruction for collection or payment.

9. Paragraph (a)(10): "Midnight deadline." The use of this phrase is an example of the more mechanical approach used in this Article. Midnight is selected as a termination point or time limit to obtain greater uniformity and definiteness than would be possible from other possible terminating points, such as the close of the banking day or business day.

10. Paragraph (a)(11): The term "settle" has substantial importance throughout Article 4. In the American Bankers Association Bank Collection Code, in deferred posting statutes, in Federal Reserve regulations and operating circulars, in clearing-house rules, in agreements between banks and customers and in legends on deposit tickets and collection letters, there is repeated reference to "conditional" or "provisional" credits or payments. Tied in with this concept of

creditors or payments being in some way tentative, has been a related but somewhat different problem as to when an item is "paid" or "finally paid" either to determine the relative priority of the item as against attachments, stop-payment orders and the like or in insolvency situations. There has been extensive litigation in the various states on these problems. To a substantial extent the confusion, the litigation and even the resulting court decisions fail to take into account that in the collection process some debits or credits are provisional or tentative and others are final and that very many debits or credits are provisional or tentative for awhile but later become final. Similarly, some cases fail to recognize that within a single bank, particularly a payor bank, each item goes through a series of processes and that in a payor bank most of these processes are preliminary to the basic act of payment or "final payment."

The term "settle" is used as a convenient term to characterize a broad variety of conditional, provisional, tentative and also final payments of items. Such a comprehensive term is needed because it is frequently difficult or unnecessary to determine whether a particular action is tentative or final or when a particular credit shifts from the tentative class to the final class. Therefore, its use throughout the Article indicates that in that particular context it is unnecessary or unwise to determine whether the debit or the credit or the payment is tentative or final. However, if qualified by the adjective "provisional" its tentative nature is intended, and if qualified by the adjective "final" its permanent nature is intended.

Examples of the various types of settlement contemplated by the term include payments in cash; the efficient but somewhat complicated process of payment through the adjustment and offsetting of balances through clearing houses; debit or credit entries in accounts between banks; the forwarding of various types of remittance instruments, sometimes to cover a particular item but more frequently to cover an entire group of items received on a particular day.

11. Paragraph (a)(12): "Suspends payments." This term is designed to afford an objective test to determine when a bank is no longer operating as a part of the banking system.

As amended in 2003.

§ 4–105. **Definitions of Types of Banks.**

In this Article:

(1) ["Bank" means a person engaged in the business of banking, including a savings bank,

savings and loan association, credit union, or trust company;]

(2) "Depositary bank" means the first bank to take an item even though it is also the payor bank, unless the item is presented for immediate payment over the counter;

(3) "Payor bank" means a bank that is the drawee of a draft;

(4) "Intermediary bank" means a bank to which an item is transferred in course of collection except the depositary or payor bank;

(5) "Collecting bank" means a bank handling an item for collection except the payor bank;

(6) "Presenting bank" means a bank presenting an item except a payor bank.

Legislative Note: A jurisdiction that enacts this statute that has not yet enacted the revised version of UCC Article 1 should leave the definition of "Bank" in Section 4–105(1). Section 4–105(1) is reserved for that purpose. A jurisdiction that has adopted or simultaneously adopts the revised Article 1 should delete the definition of "Bank" from Section 4–105(1), but should leave those numbers "reserved." If jurisdictions follow the numbering suggested here, the subsections will have the same numbering in all jurisdictions that have adopted these amendments (whether they have or have not adopted the revised version of UCC Article 1). In either case, they should change the title of the section, as indicated in these revisions, so that all jurisdictions will have the same title for the section.

As amended in 1990 and 2002.

Official Comment

1. The definitions in general exclude a bank to which an item is issued, as this bank does not take by transfer except in the particular case covered in which the item is issued to a payee for collection, as in the case in which a corporation is transferring balances from one account to another. Thus, the definition of "depositary bank" does not include the bank to which a check is made payable if a check is given in payment of a mortgage. This bank has the status of a payee under Article 3 on Negotiable Instruments and not that of a collecting bank.

2. Paragraph (1): "Bank" is defined in Section 1–201(4) as meaning "any person engaged in the business of banking." The definition in paragraph (1) makes clear that "bank" includes savings banks, sav-

ings and loan associations, credit unions and trust companies, in addition to the commercial banks commonly denoted by use of the term "bank."

3. Paragraph (2): A bank that takes an "on us" item for collection, for application to a customer's loan, or first handles the item for other reasons is a depositary bank even though it is also the payor bank. However, if the holder presents the item for immediate payment over the counter, the payor bank is not a depositary bank.

4. Paragraph (3): The definition of "payor bank" is clarified by use of the term "drawee." That term is defined in Section 4–104 as meaning "a person ordered in a draft to make payment." An "order" is defined in Section 3–103 as meaning "a written instruction to pay money.... An authorization to pay is not an order unless the person authorized to pay is also instructed to pay." The definition of order is incorporated into Article 4 by Section 4–104(c). Thus a payor bank is one instructed to pay in the item. A bank does not become a payor bank by being merely authorized to pay or by being given an instruction to pay not contained in the item.

5. Paragraph (4): The term "intermediary bank" includes the last bank in the collection process if the drawee is not a bank. Usually the last bank is also a presenting bank.

§ 4–106. Payable Through or Payable at Bank: Collecting Bank.

(a) If an item states that it is "payable through" a bank identified in the item, (i) the item designates the bank as a collecting bank and does not by itself authorize the bank to pay the item, and (ii) the item may be presented for payment only by or through the bank.

ALTERNATIVE A

(b) If an item states that it is "payable at" a bank identified in the item, the item is equivalent to a draft drawn on the bank.

ALTERNATIVE B

(b) If an item states that it is "payable at" a bank identified in the item, (i) the item designates the bank as a collecting bank and does not by itself authorize the bank to pay the item, and (ii) the item may be presented for payment only by or through the bank.

(c) If a draft names a nonbank drawee and it is unclear whether a bank named in the draft is a co-drawee or a collecting bank, the bank is a collecting bank.

As added in 1990.

Official Comment

1. This section replaces former Sections 3–120 and 3–121. Some items are made "payable through" a particular bank. Subsection (a) states that such language makes the bank a collecting bank and not a payor bank. An item identifying a "payable through" bank can be presented for payment to the drawee only by the "payable through" bank. The item cannot be presented to the drawee over the counter for immediate payment or by a collecting bank other than the "payable through" bank.

2. Subsection (b) retains the alternative approach of the present law. Under Alternative A a note payable at a bank is the equivalent of a draft drawn on the bank and the midnight deadline provisions of Sections 4–301 and 4–302 apply. Under Alternative B a "payable at" bank is in the same position as a "payable through" bank under subsection (a).

3. Subsection (c) rejects the view of some cases that a bank named below the name of a drawee is itself a drawee. The commercial understanding is that this bank is a collecting bank and is not accountable under Section 4–302 for holding an item beyond its deadline. The liability of the bank is governed by Sections 4–202(a) and 4–103(e).

§ 4–107. Separate Office of Bank.

A branch or separate office of a bank is a separate bank for the purpose of computing the time within which and determining the place at or to which action may be taken or notices or orders shall be given under this Article and under Article 3.

As amended in 1962 and 1990.

Official Comment

1. A rule with respect to the status of a branch or separate office of a bank as a part of any statute on bank collections is highly desirable if not absolutely necessary. However, practices in the operations of branches and separate offices vary substantially in the different states and it has not been possible to find any single rule that is logically correct, fair in all situations and workable under all different types of practices. The decision not to draft the section with greater specificity leaves to the courts the resolution of the issues arising under this section on the basis of the facts of each case.

2. In many states and for many purposes a branch or separate office of the bank should be treated as a separate bank. Many branches function as separate banks in the handling and payment of items and require time for doing so similar to that of a separate bank. This is particularly true if branch banking is permitted throughout a state or in different towns and cities. Similarly, if there is this separate functioning a particular branch or separate office is the only proper place for various types of action to be taken or orders or notices to be given. Examples include the drawing of a check on a particular branch by a customer whose account is carried at that branch; the presentment of that same check at that branch; the issuance of an order to the branch to stop payment on the check.

3. Section 1 of the American Bankers Association Bank Collection Code provided simply: "A branch or office of any such bank shall be deemed a bank." Although this rule appears to be brief and simple, as applied to particular sections of the ABA Code it produces illogical and, in some cases, unreasonable results. For example, under Section 11 of the ABA Code it seems anomalous for one branch of a bank to have charged an item to the account of the drawer and another branch to have the power to elect to treat the item as dishonored. Similar logical problems would flow from applying the same rule to Article 4. Warranties by one branch to another branch under Sections 4–207 and 4–208 (each considered a separate bank) do not make sense.

4. Assuming that it is not desirable to make each branch a separate bank for all purposes, this section provides that a branch or separate office is a separate bank for certain purposes. In so doing the single legal entity of the bank as a whole is preserved, thereby carrying with it the liability of the institution as a whole on such obligations as it may be under. On the other hand, in cases in which the Article provides a number of time limits for different types of action by banks, if a branch functions as a separate bank, it should have the time limits available to a separate bank. Similarly if in its relations to customers a branch functions as a separate bank, notices and orders with respect to accounts of customers of the branch should be given at the branch. For example, whether a branch has notice sufficient to affect its status as a holder in due course of an item taken by it should depend upon what notice that branch has received with respect to the item. Similarly the receipt of a stop-payment order at one branch should not be

notice to another branch so as to impair the right of the second branch to be a holder in due course of the item, although in circumstances in which ordinary care requires the communication of a notice or order to the proper branch of a bank, the notice or order would be effective at the proper branch from the time it was or should have been received. See Section 1–201(27).

5. The bracketed language ("maintaining its own deposit ledger") in former Section 4–106 is deleted. Today banks keep records on customer accounts by electronic data storage. This has led most banks with branches to centralize to some degree their record keeping. The place where records are kept has little meaning if the information is electronically stored and is instantly retrievable at all branches of the bank. Hence, the inference to be drawn from the deletion of the bracketed language is that where record keeping is done is no longer an important factor in determining whether a branch is a separate bank.

§ 4–108. Time of Receipt of Items.

(a) For the purpose of allowing time to process items, prove balances, and make the necessary entries on its books to determine its position for the day, a bank may fix an afternoon hour of 2 P.M. or later as a cutoff hour for the handling of money and items and the making of entries on its books.

(b) An item or deposit of money received on any day after a cutoff hour so fixed or after the close of the banking day may be treated as being received at the opening of the next banking day.

As amended in 1990.

Official Comment

1. Each of the huge volume of checks processed each day must go through a series of accounting procedures that consume time. Many banks have found it necessary to establish a cutoff hour to allow time for these procedures to be completed within the time limits imposed by Article 4. Subsection (a) approves a cutoff hour of this type provided it is not earlier than 2 P.M. Subsection (b) provides that if such a cutoff hour is fixed, items received after the cutoff hour may be treated as being received at the opening of the next banking day. If the number of items received either through the mail or over the counter tends to taper off radically as the afternoon hours progress, a 2 P.M. cutoff hour does not involve a large portion of the items received but at the same time permits a bank using such a cutoff hour to leave its doors open later in

the afternoon without forcing into the evening the completion of its settling and proving process.

2. The provision in subsection (b) that items or deposits received after the close of the banking day may be treated as received at the opening of the next banking day is important in cases in which a bank closes at twelve or one o'clock, e.g., on a Saturday, but continues to receive some items by mail or over the counter if, for example, it opens Saturday evening for the limited purpose of receiving deposits and cashing checks.

§ 4–109. Delays.

(a) Unless otherwise instructed, a collecting bank in a good faith effort to secure payment of a specific item drawn on a payor other than a bank, and with or without the approval of any person involved, may waive, modify, or extend time limits imposed or permitted by this [Act] for a period not exceeding two additional banking days without discharge of drawers or indorsers or liability to its transferor or a prior party.

(b) Delay by a collecting bank or payor bank beyond time limits prescribed or permitted by this [Act] or by instructions is excused if (i) the delay is caused by interruption of communication or computer facilities, suspension of payments by another bank, war, emergency conditions, failure of equipment, or other circumstances beyond the control of the bank, and (ii) the bank exercises such diligence as the circumstances require.

As amended in 1990.

Official Comment

1. Sections 4–202(b), 4–214, 4–301, and 4–302 prescribe various time limits for the handling of items. These are the limits of time within which a bank, in fulfillment of its obligation to exercise ordinary care, must handle items entrusted to it for collection or payment. Under Section 4–103 they may be varied by agreement or by Federal Reserve regulations or operating circular, clearing-house rules, or the like. Subsection (a) permits a very limited extension of these time limits. It authorizes a collecting bank to take additional time in attempting to collect drafts drawn on nonbank payors with or without the approval of any interested party. The right of a collecting bank to waive time limits under subsection (a) does not apply to checks. The two-day extension can only be granted in a good faith effort to secure payment and only with respect to specific items. It cannot be exercised if the customer instructs otherwise. Thus limited the escape

provision should afford a limited degree of flexibility in special cases but should not interfere with the overall requirement and objective of speedy collections.

2. An extension granted under subsection (a) is without discharge of drawers or indorsers. It therefore extends the times for presentment or payment as specified in Article 3.

3. Subsection (b) is another escape clause from time limits. This clause operates not only with respect to time limits imposed by the Article itself but also time limits imposed by special instructions, by agreement or by Federal regulations or operating circulars, clearing-house rules or the like. The latter time limits are "permitted" by the Code. For example, a payor bank that fails to make timely return of a dishonored item may be accountable for the amount of the item. Subsection (b) excuses a bank from this liability when its failure to meet its midnight deadline resulted from, for example, a computer breakdown that was beyond the control of the bank, so long as the bank exercised the degree of diligence that the circumstances required. In Port City State Bank v. American National Bank, 486 F.2d 196 (10th Cir.1973), the court held that a bank exercised sufficient diligence to be excused under this subsection. If delay is sought to be excused under this subsection, the bank has the burden of proof on the issue of whether it exercised "such diligence as the circumstances require." The subsection is consistent with Regulation CC, Section 229.38(e).

§ 4–110. Electronic Presentment.

(a) "Agreement for electronic presentment" means an agreement, clearing-house rule, or Federal Reserve regulation or operating circular, providing that presentment of an item may be made by transmission of an image of an item or information describing the item ("presentment notice") rather than delivery of the item itself. The agreement may provide for procedures governing retention, presentment, payment, dishonor, and other matters concerning items subject to the agreement.

(b) Presentment of an item pursuant to an agreement for presentment is made when the presentment notice is received.

(c) If presentment is made by presentment notice, a reference to "item" or "check" in this Article means the presentment notice unless the context otherwise indicates.

As added in 1990.

Official Comment

1. "An agreement for electronic presentment" refers to an agreement under which presentment may be made to a payor bank by a presentment notice rather than by presentment of the item. Under imaging technology now under development, the presentment notice might be an image of the item. The electronic presentment agreement may provide that the item may be retained by a depositary bank, other collecting bank, or even a customer of the depositary bank, or it may provide that the item will follow the presentment notice. The identifying characteristic of an electronic presentment agreement is that presentment occurs when the presentment notice is received. "An agreement for electronic presentment" does not refer to the common case of retention of items by payor banks because the item itself is presented to the payor bank in these cases. Payor bank check retention is a matter of agreement between payor banks and their customers. Provisions on payor bank check retention are found in Section 4–406(b).

2. The assumptions under which the electronic presentment amendments are based are as follows: No bank will participate in an electronic presentment program without an agreement. These agreements may be either bilateral (Section 4–103(a)), under which two banks that frequently do business with each other may agree to depositary bank check retention, or multilateral (Section 4–103(b)), in which large segments of the banking industry may participate in such a program. In the latter case, federal or other uniform regulatory standards would likely supply the substance of the electronic presentment agreement, the application of which could be triggered by the use of some form of identifier on the item. Regulation CC, Section 229.36(c) authorizes truncation agreements but forbids them from extending return times or otherwise varying requirements of the part of Regulation CC governing check collection without the agreement of all parties interested in the check. For instance, an extension of return time could damage a depositary bank which must make funds available to its customers under mandatory availability schedules. The Expedited Funds Availability Act, 12 U.S.C. Section 4008(b)(2), directs the Federal Reserve Board to consider requiring that banks provide for check truncation.

3. The parties affected by an agreement for electronic presentment, with the exception of the customer, can be expected to protect themselves. For example, the payor bank can probably be expected to limit its risk of loss from drawer forgery by limiting the dollar amount of eligible items (Federal Reserve pro-

gram), by reconcilement agreements (ABA Safekeeping program), by insurance (credit union share draft program), or by other means. Because agreements will exist, only minimal amendments are needed to make clear that the UCC does not prohibit electronic presentment.

§ 4-111. Statute of Limitations.

An action to enforce an obligation, duty, or right arising under this Article must be commenced within three years after the [cause of action] accrues.

As added in 1990.

Official Comment

This section conforms to the period of limitations set by Section 3–118(g) for actions for breach of warranty and to enforce other obligations, duties or rights arising under Article 3. Bracketing "cause of action" recognizes that some states use a different term, such as "claim for relief."

PART 2

COLLECTION OF ITEMS: DEPOSITARY AND COLLECTING BANKS

§ 4-201. Status of Collecting Bank as Agent and Provisional Status of Credits; Applicability of Article; Item Indorsed "Pay Any Bank".

(a) Unless a contrary intent clearly appears and before the time that a settlement given by a collecting bank for an item is or becomes final, the bank, with respect to an item, is an agent or sub-agent of the owner of the item and any settlement given for the item is provisional. This provision applies regardless of the form of indorsement or lack of indorsement and even though credit given for the item is subject to immediate withdrawal as of right or is in fact withdrawn; but the continuance of ownership of an item by its owner and any rights of the owner to proceeds of the item are subject to rights of a collecting bank, such as those resulting from outstanding advances on the item and rights of recoupment or setoff. If an item is handled by banks for purposes of presentment, payment, collection, or return, the relevant provisions of this Article apply even though action of the parties clearly establishes that a particular bank has purchased the item and is the owner of it.

(b) After an item has been indorsed with the words "pay any bank" or the like, only a bank may acquire the rights of a holder until the item has been:

(1) returned to the customer initiating collection; or

(2) specially indorsed by a bank to a person who is not a bank.

As amended in 1990.

Official Comment

1. This section states certain basic rules of the bank collection process. One basic rule, appearing in the last sentence of subsection (a), is that, to the extent applicable, the provisions of the Article govern without regard to whether a bank handling an item owns the item or is an agent for collection. Historically, much time has been spent and effort expended in determining or attempting to determine whether a bank was a purchaser of an item or merely an agent for collection. See discussion of this subject and cases cited in 11 A.L.R. 1043, 16 A.L.R. 1084, 42 A.L.R. 492, 68 A.L.R. 725, 99 A.L.R. 486. See also Section 4 of the American Bankers Association Bank Collection Code. The general approach of Article 4, similar to that of other articles, is to provide, within reasonable limits, rules or answers to major problems known to exist in the bank collection process without regard to questions of status and ownership but to keep general principles such as status and ownership available to cover residual areas not covered by specific rules. In line with this approach, the last sentence of subsection (a) says in effect that Article 4 applies to practically every item moving through banks for the purpose of presentment, payment or collection.

2. Within this general rule of broad coverage, the first two sentences of subsection (a) state a rule of agency status. "Unless a contrary intent clearly appears" the status of a collecting bank is that of an agent or sub-agent for the owner of the item. Although as indicated in Comment 1 it is much less important under Article 4 to determine status than has been the case heretofore, status may have importance in some residual areas not covered by specific rules. Further, since status has been considered so important

in the past, to omit all reference to it might cause confusion. The status of agency "applies regardless of the form of indorsement or lack of indorsement and even though credit given for the item is subject to immediate withdrawal as of right or is in fact withdrawn." Thus questions heretofore litigated as to whether ordinary indorsements "for deposit," "for collection" or in blank have the effect of creating an agency status or a purchase, no longer have significance in varying the prima facie rule of agency. Similarly, the nature of the credit given for an item or whether it is subject to immediate withdrawal as of right or is in fact withdrawn, does not alter the agency status. See A.L.R. references supra in Comment 1.

A contrary intent can change agency status but this must be clear. An example of a clear contrary intent would be if collateral papers established or the item bore a legend stating that the item was sold absolutely to the depositary bank.

3. The prima facie agency status of collecting banks is consistent with prevailing law and practice today. Section 2 of the American Bankers Association Bank Collection Code so provided. Legends on deposit tickets, collection letters and acknowledgments of items and Federal Reserve operating circulars consistently so provide. The status is consistent with rights of charge-back (Section 4–214 and Section 11 of the ABA Code) and risk of loss in the event of insolvency (Section 4–216 and Section 13 of the ABA Code). The right of charge-back with respect to checks is limited by Regulation CC, Section 226.36(d).

4. Affirmative statement of a prima facie agency status for collecting banks requires certain limitations and qualifications. Under current practices substantially all bank collections sooner or later merge into bank credits, at least if collection is effected. Usually, this takes place within a few days of the initiation of collection. An intermediary bank receives final collection and evidences the result of its collection by a "credit" on its books to the depositary bank. The depositary bank evidences the results of its collection by a "credit" in the account of its customer. As used in these instances the term "credit" clearly indicates a debtor-creditor relationship. At some stage in the bank collection process the agency status of a collecting bank changes to that of debtor, a debtor of its customer. Usually at about the same time it also becomes a creditor for the amount of the item, a creditor of some intermediary, payor or other bank. Thus the collection is completed, all agency aspects are terminated and the identity of the item has become completely merged in bank accounts, that of the customer with

the depositary bank and that of one bank with another.

Although Section 4–215(a) provides that an item is finally paid when the payor bank takes or fails to take certain action with respect to the item, the final payment of the item may or may not result in the simultaneous final settlement for the item in the case of all prior parties. If a series of provisional debits and credits for the item have been entered in accounts between banks, the final payment of the item by the payor bank may result in the automatic firming up of all these provisional debits and credits under Section 4–215(c), and the consequent receipt of final settlement for the item by each collecting bank and the customer of the depositary bank simultaneously with such action of the payor bank. However, if the payor bank or some intermediary bank accounts for the item with a remittance draft, the next prior bank usually does not receive final settlement for the item until the remittance draft finally clears. See Section 4–213(c). The first sentence of subsection (a) provides that the agency status of a collecting bank (whether intermediary or depositary) continues until the settlement given by it for the item is or becomes final. In the case of the series of provisional credits covered by Section 4–215(c), this could be simultaneously with the final payment of the item by the payor bank. In cases in which remittance drafts are used or in straight non-cash collections, this would not be until the times specified in Sections 4–213(c) and 4–215(d). With respect to checks Regulation CC Sections 229.31(c), 229.32(b) and 229.36(d) provide that all settlements between banks are final in both the forward collection and return of checks.

Under Section 4–213(a) settlements for items may be made by any means agreed to by the parties. Since it is impossible to contemplate all the kinds of settlements that will be utilized, no attempt is made in Article 4 to provide when settlement is final in all cases. The guiding principle is that settlements should be final when the presenting person has received usable funds. Section 4–213(c) and (d) and Section 4–215(c) provide when final settlement occurs with respect to certain kinds of settlement, but these provisions are not intended to be exclusive.

A number of practical results flow from the rule continuing the agency status of a collecting bank until its settlement for the item is or becomes final, some of which are specifically set forth in this Article. One is that risk of loss continues in the owner of the item rather than the agent bank. See Section 4–214. Offsetting rights favorable to the owner are that pending such final settlement, the owner has the preference rights of Section 4–216 and the direct rights of Section 4–302 against the payor bank. It also follows from this rule that the dollar limitations of Federal Deposit Insurance are measured by the claim of the owner of the item rather than that of the collecting bank. With respect to checks, rights of the parties in insolvency are determined by Regulation CC Section 229.39 and the liability of a bank handling a check to a subsequent bank that does not receive payment because of suspension of payments by another bank is stated in Regulation CC Section 229.35(b).

5. In those cases in which some period of time elapses between the final payment of the item by the payor bank and the time that the settlement of the collecting bank is or becomes final, e.g., if the payor bank or an intermediary bank accounts for the item with a remittance draft or in straight noncash collections, the continuance of the agency status of the collecting bank necessarily carries with it the continuance of the owner's status as principal. The second sentence of subsection (a) provides that whatever rights the owner has to proceeds of the item are subject to the rights of collecting banks for outstanding advances on the item and other valid rights, if any. The rule provides a sound rule to govern cases of attempted attachment of proceeds of a non-cash item in the hands of the payor bank as property of the absent owner. If a collecting bank has made an advance on an item which is still outstanding, its right to obtain reimbursement for this advance should be superior to the rights of the owner to the proceeds or to the rights of a creditor of the owner. An intentional crediting of proceeds of an item to the account of a prior bank known to be insolvent, for the purpose of acquiring a right of setoff, would not produce a valid setoff. See 8 Zollman, Banks and Banking (1936) Sec. 5443.

6. This section and Article 4 as a whole represent an intentional abandonment of the approach to bank collection problems appearing in Section 4 of the American Bankers Association Bank Collection Code. Because the tremendous volume of items handled makes impossible the examination by all banks of all indorsements on all items and thus in fact this examination is not made, except perhaps by depositary banks, it is unrealistic to base the rights and duties of all banks in the collection chain on variations in the form of indorsements. It is anomalous to provide throughout the ABA Code that the prima facie status of collecting banks is that of agent or sub-agent but in Section 4 to provide that subsequent holders (sub-agents) shall have the right to rely on the presumption that the bank of deposit (the primary agent) is the owner of the item. It is unrealistic, particularly in this background, to base rights and duties on status of agent or owner. Thus Section 4–201 makes the pertinent provisions of Article 4 applicable to substantially all items handled by banks for presentment, payment or collection, recognizes the prima facie status of most banks as agents, and then seeks to state appropriate limits and some attributes to the general rules so expressed.

7. Subsection (b) protects the ownership rights with respect to an item indorsed "pay any bank or banker" or in similar terms of a customer initiating collection or of any bank acquiring a security interest under Section 4–210, in the event the item is subsequently acquired under improper circumstances by a person who is not a bank and transferred by that person to another person, whether or not a bank. Upon return to the customer initiating collection of an item so indorsed, the indorsement may be cancelled (Section 3–207). A bank holding an item so indorsed may transfer the item out of banking channels by special indorsement; however, under Section 4–103(e), the bank would be liable to the owner of the item for any loss resulting therefrom if the transfer had been made in bad faith or with lack of ordinary care. If briefer and more simple forms of bank indorsements are developed under Section 4–206 (e.g., the use of bank transit numbers in lieu of present lengthy forms of bank indorsements), a depositary bank having the transit number "X100" could make subsection (b) operative by indorsements such as "Pay any bank—X100." Regulation CC Section 229.35(c) states the effect of an indorsement on a check by a bank.

§ 4–202. Responsibility for Collection or Return; When Action Timely.

(a) A collecting bank must exercise ordinary care in:

(1) presenting an item or sending it for presentment;

(2) sending notice of dishonor or nonpayment or returning an item other than a documentary draft to the bank's transferor after learning that the item has not been paid or accepted, as the case may be;

(3) settling for an item when the bank receives final settlement; and

(4) notifying its transferor of any loss or delay in transit within a reasonable time after discovery thereof.

(b) A collecting bank exercises ordinary care under subsection (a) by taking proper action before its midnight deadline following receipt of an item, notice, or settlement. Taking proper action within a reasonably longer time may constitute the exercise of ordinary care, but the bank has the burden of establishing timeliness.

(c) Subject to subsection (a)(1), a bank is not liable for the insolvency, neglect, misconduct, mistake, or default of another bank or person or for loss or destruction of an item in the possession of others or in transit.

As amended in 1990.

Official Comment

1. Subsection (a) states the basic responsibilities of a collecting bank. Of course, under Section 1–203 a collecting bank is subject to the standard requirement of good faith. By subsection (a) it must also use ordinary care in the exercise of its basic collection tasks. By Section 4–103(a) neither requirement may be disclaimed.

2. If the bank makes presentment itself, subsection (a)(1) requires ordinary care with respect both to the time and manner of presentment. (Sections 3–501 and 4–212.) If it forwards the item to be presented the subsection requires ordinary care with respect to routing (Section 4–204), and also in the selection of intermediary banks or other agents.

3. Subsection (a) describes types of basic action with respect to which a collecting bank must use ordinary care. Subsection (b) deals with the time for taking action. It first prescribes the general standard for timely action, namely, for items received on Monday, proper action (such as forwarding or presenting) on Monday or Tuesday is timely. Although under current "production line" operations banks customarily move items along on regular schedules substantially briefer than two days, the subsection states an outside time within which a bank may know it has taken timely action. To provide flexibility from this standard norm, the subsection further states that action within a reasonably longer time may be timely but the bank has the burden of proof. In the case of time items, action after the midnight deadline, but sufficiently in advance of maturity for proper presentation, is a clear example of a "reasonably longer time" that is timely. The standard of requiring action not later than Tuesday in the case of Monday items is also subject to possibilities of variation under the general provisions of Section 4–103, or under the special provisions regarding time of receipt of items (Section 4–108), and regarding delays (Section 4–109). This subsection (b) deals only with collecting banks. The time

limits applicable to payor banks appear in Sections 4–301 and 4–302.

4. At common law the so-called New York collection rule subjected the initial collecting bank to liability for the actions of subsequent banks in the collection chain; the so-called Massachusetts rule was that each bank, subject to the duty of selecting proper intermediaries, was liable only for its own negligence. Subsection (c) adopts the Massachusetts rule. But since this is stated to be subject to subsection (a)(1) a collecting bank remains responsible for using ordinary care in selecting properly qualified intermediary banks and agents and in giving proper instructions to them. Regulation CC Section 229.36(d) states the liability of a bank during the forward collection of checks.

§ 4–203. Effect of Instructions.

Subject to Article 3 concerning conversion of instruments (Section 3–420) and restrictive indorsements (Section 3–206), only a collecting bank's transferor can give instructions that affect the bank or constitute notice to it, and a collecting bank is not liable to prior parties for any action taken pursuant to the instructions or in accordance with any agreement with its transferor.

As amended in 1990.

Official Comment

This section adopts a "chain of command" theory which renders it unnecessary for an intermediary or collecting bank to determine whether its transferor is "authorized" to give the instructions. Equally the bank is not put on notice of any "revocation of authority" or "lack of authority" by notice received from any other person. The desirability of speed in the collection process and the fact that, by reason of advances made, the transferor may have the paramount interest in the item requires the rule.

The section is made subject to the provisions of Article 3 concerning conversion of instruments (Section 3–420) and restrictive indorsements (Section 3–206). Of course instructions from or an agreement with its transferor does not relieve a collecting bank of its general obligation to exercise good faith and ordinary care. See Section 4–103(a). If in any particular case a bank has exercised good faith and ordinary care and is relieved of responsibility by reason of instructions of or an agreement with its transferor, the owner of the item may still have a remedy for loss against the transferor (another bank) if such transferor has given wrongful instructions.

The rules of the section are applied only to collecting banks. Payor banks always have the problem of making proper payment of an item; whether such payment is proper should be based upon all of the rules of Articles 3 and 4 and all of the facts of any particular case, and should not be dependent exclusively upon instructions from or an agreement with a person presenting the item.

§ 4–204. Methods of Sending and Presenting; Sending Directly to Payor Bank.

(a) A collecting bank shall send items by a reasonably prompt method, taking into consideration relevant instructions, the nature of the item, the number of those items on hand, the cost of collection involved, and the method generally used by it or others to present those items.

(b) A collecting bank may send:

(1) an item directly to the payor bank;

(2) an item to a nonbank payor if authorized by its transferor; and

(3) an item other than documentary drafts to a nonbank payor, if authorized by Federal Reserve regulation or operating circular, clearing-house rule, or the like.

(c) Presentment may be made by a presenting bank at a place where the payor bank or other payor has requested that presentment be made.

As amended in 1962 and 1990.

Official Comment

1. Subsection (a) prescribes the general standards applicable to proper sending or forwarding of items. Because of the many types of methods available and the desirability of preserving flexibility any attempt to prescribe limited or precise methods is avoided.

2. Subsection (b)(1) codifies the practice of direct mail, express, messenger or like presentment to payor banks. The practice is now country-wide and is justified by the need for speed, the general responsibility of banks, Federal Deposit Insurance protection and other reasons.

3. Full approval of the practice of direct sending is limited to cases in which a bank is a payor. Since nonbank drawees or payors may be of unknown responsibility, substantial risks may be attached to placing in their hands the instruments calling for payments from them. This is obviously so in the case of documentary drafts. However, in some cities practices

have long existed under clearing-house procedures to forward certain types of items to certain nonbank payors. Examples include insurance loss drafts drawn by field agents on home offices. For the purpose of leaving the door open to legitimate practices of this kind, subsection (b)(3) affirmatively approves direct sending of any item other than documentary drafts to any nonbank payor, if authorized by Federal Reserve regulation or operating circular, clearing-house rule or the like.

On the other hand subsection (b)(2) approves sending any item directly to a nonbank payor if authorized by a collecting bank's transferor. This permits special instructions or agreements out of the norm and is consistent with the "chain of command" theory of Section 4–203. However, if a transferor other than the owner of the item, e.g., a prior collecting bank, authorizes a direct sending to a nonbank payor, such transferor assumes responsibility for the propriety or impropriety of such authorization.

4. Section 3–501(b) provides where presentment may be made. This provision is expressly subject to Article 4. Section 4–204(c) specifically approves presentment by a presenting bank at any place requested by the payor bank or other payor. The time when a check is received by a payor bank for presentment is governed by Regulation CC Section 229.36(b).

§ 4–205. Depositary Bank Holder of Unindorsed Item.

If a customer delivers an item to a depositary bank for collection:

(1) the depositary bank becomes a holder of the item at the time it receives the item for collection if the customer at the time of delivery was a holder of the item, whether or not the customer indorses the item, and, if the bank satisfies the other requirements of Section 3–302, it is a holder in due course; and

(2) the depositary bank warrants to collecting banks, the payor bank or other payor, and the drawer that the amount of the item was paid to the customer or deposited to the customer's account.

As amended in 1990.

Official Comment

Section 3–201(b) provides that negotiation of an instrument payable to order requires indorsement by the holder. The rule of former Section 4–205(1) was that the depositary bank may supply a missing indorsement of its customer unless the item contains the words "payee's indorsement required" or the like. The cases have differed on the status of the depositary bank as a holder if it fails to supply its customer's indorsement. Marine Midland Bank, N.A. v. Price, Miller, Evans & Flowers, 446 N.Y.S.2d 797 (N.Y.App.Div. 4th Dept. 1981), *rev'd*, 455 N.Y.S.2d 565 (N.Y.1982). It is common practice for depositary banks to receive unindorsed checks under so-called "lock-box" agreements from customers who receive a high volume of checks. No function would be served by requiring a depositary bank to run these items through a machine that would supply the customer's indorsement except to afford the drawer and the subsequent banks evidence that the proceeds of the item reached the customer's account. Paragraph (1) provides that the depositary bank becomes a holder when it takes the item for deposit if the depositor is a holder. Whether it supplies the customer's indorsement is immaterial. Paragraph (2) satisfies the need for a receipt of funds by the depositary bank by imposing on that bank a warranty that it paid the customer or deposited the item to the customer's account. This warranty runs not only to collecting banks and to the payor bank or nonbank drawee but also to the drawer, affording protection to these parties that the depositary bank received the item and applied it to the benefit of the holder.

§ 4–206.   Transfer Between Banks.

Any agreed method that identifies the transferor bank is sufficient for the item's further transfer to another bank.

As amended in 1990.

Official Comment

This section is designed to permit the simplest possible form of transfer from one bank to another, once an item gets in the bank collection chain, provided only identity of the transferor bank is preserved. This is important for tracing purposes and if recourse is necessary. However, since the responsibilities of the various banks appear in the Article it becomes unnecessary to have liability or responsibility depend on more formal indorsements. Simplicity in the form of transfer is conducive to speed. If the transfer is between banks, this section takes the place of the more formal requirements of Section 3–201.

§ 4–207.   Transfer Warranties.

(a) A customer or collecting bank that transfers an item and receives a settlement or other consideration warrants to the transferee and to any subsequent collecting bank that:

(1) the warrantor is a person entitled to enforce the item;

(2) all signatures on the item are authentic and authorized;

(3) the item has not been altered;

(4) the item is not subject to a defense or claim in recoupment (Section 3–305(a)) of any party that can be asserted against the warrantor;

(5) the warrantor has no knowledge of any insolvency proceeding commenced with respect to the maker or acceptor or, in the case of an unaccepted draft, the drawer; and

(6) with respect to any remotely-created consumer item, that the person on whose account the item is drawn authorized the issuance of the item in the amount for which the item is drawn.

(b) If an item is dishonored, a customer or collecting bank transferring the item and receiving settlement or other consideration is obliged to pay the amount due on the item (i) according to the terms of the item at the time it was transferred, or (ii) if the transfer was of an incomplete item, according to its terms when completed as stated in Sections 3–115 and 3–407. The obligation of a transferor is owed to the transferee and to any subsequent collecting bank that takes the item in good faith. A transferor cannot disclaim its obligation under this subsection by an indorsement stating that it is made "without recourse" or otherwise disclaiming liability.

(c) A person to whom the warranties under subsection (a) are made and who took the item in good faith may recover from the warrantor as damages for breach of warranty an amount equal to the loss suffered as a result of the breach, but not more than the amount of the item plus expenses and loss of interest incurred as a result of the breach.

(d) The warranties stated in subsection (a) cannot be disclaimed with respect to checks. Unless notice of a claim for breach of warranty is given to the warrantor within 30 days after the claimant has reason to know of the breach and the identity of the warrantor, the warrantor is discharged to the extent of any loss caused by the delay in giving notice of the claim.

(e) A cause of action for breach of warranty under this section accrues when the claimant has reason to know of the breach.

As added in 1990 and amended in 2002.

Official Comment

1. Except for subsection (b), this section conforms to Section 3–416 and extends its coverage to items. The substance of this section is discussed in the Comment to Section 3–416. Subsection (b) provides that customers or collecting banks that transfer items, whether by indorsement or not, undertake to pay the item if the item is dishonored. This obligation cannot be disclaimed by a "without recourse" indorsement or otherwise. With respect to checks, Regulation CC Section 229.34 states the warranties made by paying and returning banks.

2. For an explanation of subsection (a)(6), see comment 8 to Section 3–416.

As amended in 2002.

§ 4–208. Presentment Warranties.

(a) If an unaccepted draft is presented to the drawee for payment or acceptance and the drawee pays or accepts the draft, (i) the person obtaining payment or acceptance, at the time of presentment, and (ii) a previous transferor of the draft, at the time of transfer, warrant to the drawee that pays or accepts the draft in good faith that:

(1) the warrantor is, or was, at the time the warrantor transferred the draft, a person entitled to enforce the draft or authorized to obtain payment or acceptance of the draft on behalf of a person entitled to enforce the draft;

(2) the draft has not been altered; and

(3) the warrantor has no knowledge that the signature of the purported drawer of the draft is unauthorized; and

(4) with respect to any remotely-created consumer item, that the person on whose account the item is drawn authorized the issuance of the item in the amount for which the item is drawn.

(b) A drawee making payment may recover from a warrantor damages for breach of warranty equal to the amount paid by the drawee less the amount the drawee received or is entitled to receive from the drawer because of the payment. In addition, the drawee is entitled to compensation for expenses and loss of interest resulting from the breach. The right of the drawee to recover damages under this subsection is not affected by any failure of the drawee to exercise ordinary care in making payment. If the drawee accepts the draft (i) breach of warranty is a defense to the obligation of the acceptor, and (ii) if the acceptor makes payment with respect to the draft, the acceptor is entitled to recover from a warrantor for breach of warranty the amounts stated in this subsection.

(c) If a drawee asserts a claim for breach of warranty under subsection (a) based on an unauthorized indorsement of the draft or an alteration of the draft, the warrantor may defend by proving that the indorsement is effective under Section 3–404 or 3–405 or the drawer is precluded under Section 3–406 or 4–406 from asserting against the drawee the unauthorized indorsement or alteration.

(d) If (i) a dishonored draft is presented for payment to the drawer or an indorser or (ii) any other item is presented for payment to a party obliged to pay the item, and the item is paid, the person obtaining payment and a prior transferor of the item warrant to the person making payment in good faith that the warrantor is, or was, at the time the warrantor transferred the item, a person entitled to enforce the item or authorized to obtain payment on behalf of a person entitled to enforce the item. The person making payment may recover from any warrantor for breach of warranty an amount equal to the amount paid plus expenses and loss of interest resulting from the breach.

(e) The warranties stated in subsections (a) and (d) cannot be disclaimed with respect to checks. Unless notice of a claim for breach of warranty is given to the warrantor within 30 days after the claimant has reason to know of the breach and the identity of the warrantor, the warrantor is discharged to the extent of any loss caused by the delay in giving notice of the claim.

(f) A cause of action for breach of warranty under this section accrues when the claimant has reason to know of the breach.

As added in 1990 and amended in 2002.

Official Comment

1. This section conforms to Section 3–417 and extends its coverage to items. The substance of this section is discussed in the Comment to Section 3–417. "Draft" is defined in Section 4–104 as including an item that is an order to pay so as to make clear that the term "draft" in Article 4 may include items that are not instruments within Section 3–104.

2. For an explanation of subsection (a)(4), see comment 8 to Section 3–416.

As amended in 2002.

§ 4–209. Encoding and Retention Warranties.

(a) A person who encodes information on or with respect to an item after issue warrants to any subsequent collecting bank and to the payor bank or other payor that the information is correctly encoded. If the customer of a depositary bank encodes, that bank also makes the warranty.

(b) A person who undertakes to retain an item pursuant to an agreement for electronic presentment warrants to any subsequent collecting bank and to the payor bank or other payor that retention and presentment of the item comply with the agreement. If a customer of a depositary bank undertakes to retain an item, that bank also makes this warranty.

(c) A person to whom warranties are made under this section and who took the item in good faith may recover from the warrantor as damages for breach of warranty an amount equal to the loss suffered as a result of the breach, plus expenses and loss of interest incurred as a result of the breach.

As added in 1990.

Official Comment

1. Encoding and retention warranties are included in Article 4 because they are unique to the bank collection process. These warranties are breached only by the person doing the encoding or retaining the item and not by subsequent banks handling the item. Encoding and check retention may be done by customers who are payees of a large volume of checks; hence, this section imposes warranties on customers as well as banks. If a customer encodes or retains, the depositary bank is also liable for any breach of this warranty.

2. A misencoding of the amount on the MICR line is not an alteration under Section 3–407(a) which defines alteration as changing the contract of the parties. If a drawer wrote a check for $2,500 and the depositary bank encoded $25,000 on the MICR line, the payor bank could debit the drawer's account for only $2,500. This subsection would allow the payor bank to hold the depositary bank liable for the amount paid out over $2,500 without first pursuing the person who received payment. Intervening collecting banks would not be liable to the payor bank for the depositary bank's error. If a drawer wrote a check for $25,000 and the depositary bank encoded $2,500, the payor bank becomes liable for the full amount of the check. The payor bank's rights against the depositary bank depend on whether the payor bank has suffered a loss. Since the payor bank can debit the drawer's account for $25,000, the payor bank has a loss only to the extent that the drawer's account is less than the full amount of the check. There is no requirement that the payor bank pursue collection against the drawer beyond the amount in the drawer's account as a condition to the payor bank's action against the depositary bank for breach of warranty. See Georgia Railroad Bank & Trust Co. v. First National Bank & Trust, 229 S.E.2d 482 (Ga.App.1976), aff'd, 235 S.E.2d 1 (Ga. 1977), and First National Bank of Boston v. Fidelity Bank, National Association, 724 F.Supp. 1168 (E.D.Pa. 1989).

3. A person retaining items under an electronic presentment agreement (Section 4–110) warrants that it has complied with the terms of the agreement regarding its possession of the item and its sending a proper presentment notice. If the keeper is a customer, its depositary bank also makes this warranty.

§ 4–210. Security Interest of Collecting Bank in Items, Accompanying Documents and Proceeds.

(a) A collecting bank has a security interest in an item and any accompanying documents or the proceeds of either:

(1) in case of an item deposited in an account, to the extent to which credit given for the item has been withdrawn or applied;

(2) in case of an item for which it has given credit available for withdrawal as of right, to the extent of the credit given, whether or not the credit is drawn upon or there is a right of charge-back; or

(3) if it makes an advance on or against the item.

(b) If credit given for several items received at one time or pursuant to a single agreement is withdrawn or applied in part, the security interest remains upon all the items, any accompanying documents or the proceeds of either. For the purpose of this section, credits first given are first withdrawn.

(c) Receipt by a collecting bank of a final settlement for an item is a realization on its security interest in the item, accompanying documents, and proceeds. So long as the bank does not receive final settlement for the item or give up possession of the item or possession or control of the accompanying documents for purposes other than collection, the security interest continues to that extent and is subject to Article 9, but:

(1) no security agreement is necessary to make the security interest enforceable (Section 9–203(b)(3)(A));

(2) no filing is required to perfect the security interest; and

(3) the security interest has priority over conflicting perfected security interests in the item, accompanying documents, or proceeds.

As amended in 1999 and 2003.

Official Comment

1. Subsection (a) states a rational rule for the interest of a bank in an item. The customer of the depositary bank is normally the owner of the item and the several collecting banks are agents of the customer (Section 4–201). A collecting agent may properly make advances on the security of paper held for collection, and acquires at common law a possessory lien for these advances. Subsection (a) applies an analogous principle to a bank in the collection chain which extends credit on items in the course of collection. The bank has a security interest to the extent stated in this section. To the extent of its security interest it is a holder for value (Sections 3–303, 4–211) and a holder in due course if it satisfies the other requirements for that status (Section 3–302). Subsection (a) does not derogate from the banker's general common law lien or right of setoff against indebtedness owing in deposit accounts. See Section 1–103. Rather subsection (a) specifically implements and extends the principle as a part of the bank collection process.

2. Subsection (b) spreads the security interest of the bank over all items in a single deposit or received under a single agreement and a single giving of credit. It also adopts the "first-in, first-out" rule.

3. Collection statistics establish that the vast majority of items handled for collection are in fact collected. The first sentence of subsection (c) reflects the fact that in the normal case the bank's security interest is self-liquidating. The remainder of the subsection correlates the security interest with the provisions of Article 9, particularly for use in the cases of noncollection in which the security interest may be important.

§ 4–211. When Bank Gives Value for Purposes of Holder in Due Course.

For purposes of determining its status as a holder in due course, a bank has given value to the extent it has a security interest in an item, if the bank otherwise complies with the requirements of Section 3–302 on what constitutes a holder in due course.

As amended in 1990.

Official Comment

The section completes the thought of the previous section and makes clear that a security interest in an item is "value" for the purpose of determining the holder's status as a holder in due course. The provision is in accord with the prior law (N.I.L. Section 27) and with Article 3 (Section 3–303). The section does not prescribe a security interest under Section 4–210 as a test of "value" generally because the meaning of "value" under other Articles is adequately defined in Section 1–201.

§ 4–212. Presentment by Notice of Item Not Payable by, Through, or at Bank; Liability of Drawer or Indorser.

(a) Unless otherwise instructed, a collecting bank may present an item not payable by, through, or at a bank by sending to the party to accept or pay a record providing notice that the bank holds the item for acceptance or payment. The notice must be sent in time to be received on or before the day when presentment is due and the bank must meet any requirement of the party to accept or pay under Section 3–501 by the close of the bank's next banking day after it knows of the requirement.

(b) If presentment is made by notice and payment, acceptance, or request for compliance with a requirement under Section 3–501 is not received by the close of business on the day after maturity or, in the case of demand items, by the close of business on the third banking day after notice was sent, the presenting bank may treat the item as dishonored and charge any drawer or indorser by sending it notice of the facts.

As amended in 1990 and 2002.

Official Comment

1. This section codifies a practice extensively followed in presentation of trade acceptances and documentary and other drafts drawn on nonbank payors. It imposes a duty on the payor to respond to the notice of the item if the item is not to be considered dishonored. Notice of such a dishonor charges drawers and indorsers. Presentment under this section is good presentment under Article 3. See Section 3–501.

2. A drawee not receiving notice is not, of course, liable to the drawer for wrongful dishonor.

3. A bank so presenting an instrument must be sufficiently close to the drawee to be able to exhibit the instrument on the day it is requested to do so or the next business day at the latest.

§ 4–213. Medium and Time of Settlement by Bank.

(a) With respect to settlement by a bank, the medium and time of settlement may be prescribed by Federal Reserve regulations or circulars, clearing-house rules, and the like, or agreement. In the absence of such prescription:

(1) the medium of settlement is cash or credit to an account in a Federal Reserve bank of or specified by the person to receive settlement; and

(2) the time of settlement, is:

(i) with respect to tender of settlement by cash, a cashier's check, or teller's check, when the cash or check is sent or delivered;

(ii) with respect to tender of settlement by credit in an account in a Federal Reserve Bank, when the credit is made;

(iii) with respect to tender of settlement by a credit or debit to an account in a bank, when the credit or debit is made or, in the case of tender of settlement by authority to charge an account, when the authority is sent or delivered; or

(iv) with respect to tender of settlement by a funds transfer, when payment is made pursuant to Section 4A–406(a) to the person receiving settlement.

(b) If the tender of settlement is not by a medium authorized by subsection (a) or the time of settlement is not fixed by subsection (a), no settlement occurs until the tender of settlement is accepted by the person receiving settlement.

(c) If settlement for an item is made by cashier's check or teller's check and the person receiving settlement, before its midnight deadline:

(1) presents or forwards the check for collection, settlement is final when the check is finally paid; or

(2) fails to present or forward the check for collection, settlement is final at the midnight deadline of the person receiving settlement.

(d) If settlement for an item is made by giving authority to charge the account of the bank giving settlement in the bank receiving settlement, settlement is final when the charge is made by the bank receiving settlement if there are funds available in the account for the amount of the item.

As amended in 1990.

Official Comment

1. Subsection (a) sets forth the medium of settlement that the person receiving settlement must accept. In nearly all cases the medium of settlement will be determined by agreement or by Federal Reserve regulations and circulars, clearing-house rules, and the like. In the absence of regulations, rules or agreement, the person receiving settlement may demand cash or credit in a Federal Reserve bank. If the person receiving settlement does not have an account in a Federal Reserve bank, it may specify the account of another bank in a Federal Reserve bank. In the unusual case in which there is no agreement on the medium of settlement and the bank making settlement tenders settlement other than cash or Federal Reserve bank credit, no settlement has occurred under subsection (b) unless the person receiving settlement accepts the settlement tendered. For example, if a payor bank, without agreement, tenders a teller's check, the bank receiving the settlement may reject the check and return it to the payor bank or it may accept the check as settlement.

2. In several provisions of Article 4 the time that a settlement occurs is relevant. Subsection (a) sets out a general rule that the time of settlement, like the means of settlement, may be prescribed by agreement.

In the absence of agreement, the time of settlement for tender of the common agreed media of settlement is that set out in subsection (a)(2). The time of settlement by cash, cashier's or teller's check or authority to charge an account is the time the cash, check or authority is sent, unless presentment is over the counter in which case settlement occurs upon delivery to the presenter. If there is no agreement on the time of settlement and the tender of settlement is not made by one of the media set out in subsection (a), under subsection (b) the time of settlement is the time the settlement is accepted by the person receiving settlement.

3. Subsections (c) and (d) are special provisions for settlement by remittance drafts and authority to charge an account in the bank receiving settlement. The relationship between final settlement and final payment under Section 4–215 is addressed in subsection (b) of Section 4–215. With respect to settlement by cashier's checks or teller's checks, other than in response to over-the-counter presentment, the bank receiving settlement can keep the risk that the check will not be paid on the bank tendering the check in settlement by acting to initiate collection of the check within the midnight deadline of the bank receiving settlement. If the bank fails to initiate settlement before its midnight deadline, final settlement occurs at the midnight deadline, and the bank receiving settlement assumes the risk that the check will not be paid. If there is no agreement that permits the bank tendering settlement to tender a cashier's or teller's check, subsection (b) allows the bank receiving the check to reject it, and, if it does, no settlement occurs. However, if the bank accepts the check, settlement occurs and the time of final settlement is governed by subsection (c).

With respect to settlement by tender of authority to charge the account of the bank making settlement in the bank receiving settlement, subsection (d) provides that final settlement does not take place until the account charged has available funds to cover the amount of the item. If there is no agreement that permits the bank tendering settlement to tender an authority to charge an account as settlement, subsection (b) allows the bank receiving the tender to reject it. However, if the bank accepts the authority, settlement occurs and the time of final settlement is governed by subsection (d).

§ 4–214. Right of Charge–Back or Refund; Liability of Collecting Bank: Return of Item.

(a) If a collecting bank has made provisional settlement with its customer for an item and fails

by reason of dishonor, suspension of payments by a bank, or otherwise to receive settlement for the item which is or becomes final, the bank may revoke the settlement given by it, charge back the amount of any credit given for the item to its customer's account, or obtain refund from its customer, whether or not it is able to return the item, if by its midnight deadline or within a longer reasonable time after it learns the facts it returns the item or sends notification of the facts. If the return or notice is delayed beyond the bank's midnight deadline or a longer reasonable time after it learns the facts, the bank may revoke the settlement, charge back the credit, or obtain refund from its customer, but it is liable for any loss resulting from the delay. These rights to revoke, charge back, and obtain refund terminate if and when a settlement for the item received by the bank is or becomes final.

(b) A collecting bank returns an item when it is sent or delivered to the bank's customer or transferor or pursuant to its instructions.

(c) A depositary bank that is also the payor may charge back the amount of an item to its customer's account or obtain refund in accordance with the section governing return of an item received by a payor bank for credit on its books (Section 4–301).

(d) The right to charge back is not affected by:

(1) previous use of a credit given for the item; or

(2) failure by any bank to exercise ordinary care with respect to the item, but a bank so failing remains liable.

(e) A failure to charge back or claim refund does not affect other rights of the bank against the customer or any other party.

(f) If credit is given in dollars as the equivalent of the value of an item payable in foreign money, the dollar amount of any charge-back or refund must be calculated on the basis of the bank-offered spot rate for the foreign money prevailing on the day when the person entitled to the charge-back or refund learns that it will not receive payment in ordinary course.

As amended in 1990.

Official Comment

1. Under current bank practice, in a major portion of cases banks make provisional settlement for items

when they are first received and then await subsequent determination of whether the item will be finally paid. This is the principal characteristic of what are referred to in banking parlance as "cash items." Statistically, this practice of settling provisionally first and then awaiting final payment is justified because the vast majority of such cash items are finally paid, with the result that in this great preponderance of cases it becomes unnecessary for the banks making the provisional settlements to make any further entries. In due course the provisional settlements become final simply with the lapse of time. However, in those cases in which the item being collected is not finally paid or if for various reasons the bank making the provisional settlement does not itself receive final payment, provision is made in subsection (a) for the reversal of the provisional settlements, charge-back of provisional credits and the right to obtain refund.

2. Various causes of a bank's not receiving final payment, with the resulting right of charge-back or refund, are stated or suggested in subsection (a). These include dishonor of the original item; dishonor of a remittance instrument given for it; reversal of a provisional credit for the item; suspension of payments by another bank. The causes stated are illustrative; the right of charge-back or refund is stated to exist whether the failure to receive final payment in ordinary course arises through one of them "or otherwise."

3. The right of charge-back or refund exists if a collecting bank has made a provisional settlement for an item with its customer but terminates if and when a settlement received by the bank for the item is or becomes final. If the bank fails to receive such a final settlement the right of charge-back or refund must be exercised promptly after the bank learns the facts. The right exists (if so promptly exercised) whether or not the bank is able to return the item. The second sentence of subsection (a) adopts the view of Appliance Buyers Credit Corp. v. Prospect National Bank, 708 F.2d 290 (7th Cir.1983), that if the midnight deadline for returning an item or giving notice is not met, a collecting bank loses its rights only to the extent of damages for any loss resulting from the delay.

4. Subsection (b) states when an item is returned by a collecting bank. Regulation CC, Section 229.31 preempts this subsection with respect to checks by allowing direct return to the depositary bank. Because a returned check may follow a different path than in forward collection, settlement given for the check is final and not provisional except as between the depositary bank and its customer. Regulation CC Section 229.36(d). See also Regulations CC Sections 229.31(c)

and 229.32(b). Thus owing to the federal preemption, this subsection applies only to noncheck items.

5. The rule of subsection (d) relating to charge-back (as distinguished from claim for refund) applies irrespective of the cause of the nonpayment, and of the person ultimately liable for nonpayment. Thus charge-back is permitted even if nonpayment results from the depositary bank's own negligence. Any other rule would result in litigation based upon a claim for wrongful dishonor of other checks of the customer, with potential damages far in excess of the amount of the item. Any other rule would require a bank to determine difficult questions of fact. The customer's protection is found in the general obligation of good faith (Sections 1–203 and 4–103). If bad faith is established the customer's recovery "includes other damages, if any, suffered by the party as a proximate consequence" (Section 4–103(e); see also Section 4–402).

6. It is clear that the charge-back does not relieve the bank from any liability for failure to exercise ordinary care in handling the item. The measure of damages for such failure is stated in Section 4–103(e).

7. Subsection (f) states a rule fixing the time for determining the rate of exchange if there is a charge-back or refund of a credit given in dollars for an item payable in a foreign currency. Compare Section 3–107. Fixing such a rule is desirable to avoid disputes. If in any case the parties wish to fix a different time for determining the rate of exchange, they may do so by agreement.

§ 4–215. Final Payment of Item by Payor Bank; When Provisional Debits and Credits Become Final; When Certain Credits Become Available for Withdrawal.

(a) An item is finally paid by a payor bank when the bank has first done any of the following:

(1) paid the item in cash;

(2) settled for the item without having a right to revoke the settlement under statute, clearing-house rule, or agreement; or

(3) made a provisional settlement for the item and failed to revoke the settlement in the time and manner permitted by statute, clearing-house rule, or agreement.

(b) If provisional settlement for an item does not become final, the item is not finally paid.

(c) If provisional settlement for an item between the presenting and payor banks is made through a clearing house or by debits or credits in an account between them, then to the extent that provisional debits or credits for the item are entered in accounts between the presenting and payor banks or between the presenting and successive prior collecting banks seriatim, they become final upon final payment of the item by the payor bank.

(d) If a collecting bank receives a settlement for an item which is or becomes final, the bank is accountable to its customer for the amount of the item and any provisional credit given for the item in an account with its customer becomes final.

(e) Subject to (i) applicable law stating a time for availability of funds and (ii) any right of the bank to apply the credit to an obligation of the customer, credit given by a bank for an item in a customer's account becomes available for withdrawal as of right:

(1) if the bank has received a provisional settlement for the item, when the settlement becomes final and the bank has had a reasonable time to receive return of the item and the item has not been received within that time;

(2) if the bank is both the depositary bank and the payor bank, and the item is finally paid, at the opening of the bank's second banking day following receipt of the item.

(f) Subject to applicable law stating a time for availability of funds and any right of a bank to apply a deposit to an obligation of the depositor, a deposit of money becomes available for withdrawal as of right at the opening of the bank's next banking day after receipt of the deposit.

As amended in 1990.

Official Comment

1. By the definition and use of the term "settle" (Section 4–104(a)(11)) this Article recognizes that various debits or credits, remittances, settlements or payments given for an item may be either provisional or final, that settlements sometimes are provisional and sometimes are final and sometimes are provisional for awhile but later become final. Subsection (a) defines when settlement for an item constitutes final payment.

Final payment of an item is important for a number of reasons. It is one of several factors determining the relative priorities between items and notices, stop-payment orders, legal process and setoffs (Section 4–

303). It is the "end of the line" in the collection process and the "turn around" point commencing the return flow of proceeds. It is the point at which many provisional settlements become final. See Section 4–215(c). Final payment of an item by the payor bank fixes preferential rights under Section 4–216.

2. If an item being collected moves through several states, e.g., is deposited for collection in California, moves through two or three California banks to the Federal Reserve Bank of San Francisco, to the Federal Reserve Bank of Boston, to a payor bank in Maine, the collection process involves the eastward journey of the item from California to Maine and the westward journey of the proceeds from Maine to California. Subsection (a) recognizes that final payment does not take place, in this hypothetical case, on the journey of the item eastward. It also adopts the view that neither does final payment occur on the journey westward because what in fact is journeying westward are *proceeds* of the item.

3. Traditionally and under various decisions payment in cash of an item by a payor bank has been considered final payment. Subsection (a)(1) recognizes and provides that payment of an item in cash by a payor bank is final payment.

4. Section 4–104(a)(11) defines "settle" as meaning "to pay in cash, by clearing-house settlement, in a charge or credit or by remittance, or otherwise as agreed. A settlement may be either provisional or final." Subsection (a)(2) of Section 4–215 provides that an item is finally paid by a payor bank when the bank has "settled for the item without having a right to revoke the settlement under statute, clearing-house rule or agreement." Former subsection (1)(b) is modified by subsection (a)(2) to make clear that a payor bank cannot make settlement provisional by unilaterally reserving a right to revoke the settlement. The right must come from a statute (e.g., Section 4–301), clearing-house rule or other agreement. Subsection (a)(2) provides in effect that if the payor bank finally settles for an item this constitutes final payment of the item. The subsection operates if nothing has occurred and no situation exists making the settlement provisional. If under statute, clearing-house rule or agreement, a right of revocation of the settlement exists, the settlement is provisional. Conversely, if there is an absence of a right to revoke under statute, clearing-house rule or agreement, the settlement is final and such final settlement constitutes final payment of the item.

A primary example of a statutory right on the part of the payor bank to revoke a settlement is the right to revoke conferred by Section 4–301. The underlying theory and reason for deferred posting statutes (Section 4–301) is to require a settlement on the date of receipt of an item but to keep that settlement provisional with the right to revoke prior to the midnight deadline. In any case in which Section 4–301 is applicable, any settlement by the payor bank is provisional solely by virtue of the statute, subsection (a)(2) of Section 4–215 does not operate, and such provisional settlement does not constitute final payment of the item. With respect to checks, Regulation CC Section 229.36(d) provides that settlement between banks for the forward collection of checks is final. The relationship of this provision to Article 4 is discussed in the Commentary to that section.

A second important example of a right to revoke a settlement is that arising under clearing-house rules. It is very common for clearing-house rules to provide that items exchanged and settled for in a clearing (e.g., before 10:00 a.m. on Monday) may be returned and the settlements revoked up to but not later than 2:00 p.m. on the same day (Monday) or under deferred posting at some hour on the next business day (e.g., 2:00 p.m. Tuesday). Under this type of rule the Monday morning settlement is provisional and being provisional does not constitute a final payment of the item.

An example of an agreement allowing the payor bank to revoke a settlement is a case in which the payor bank is also the depositary bank and has signed a receipt or duplicate deposit ticket or has made an entry in a passbook acknowledging receipt, for credit to the account of A, of a check drawn on it by B. If the receipt, deposit ticket, passbook or other agreement with A is to the effect that any credit so entered is provisional and may be revoked pending the time required by the payor bank to process the item to determine if it is in good form and there are funds to cover it, the agreement keeps the receipt or credit provisional and avoids its being either final settlement or final payment.

The most important application of subsection (a)(2) is that in which presentment of an item has been made over the counter for immediate payment. In this case Section 4–301(a) does not apply to make the settlement provisional, and final payment has occurred unless a rule or agreement provides otherwise.

5. Former Section 4–213(1)(c) provided that final payment occurred when the payor bank completed the "process of posting." The term was defined in former Section 4–109. In the present Article, Section 4–109 has been deleted and the process-of-posting test has been abandoned in Section 4–215(a) for determining when final payment is made. Difficulties in determining when the events described in former Section 4–109 take place make the process-of-posting test unsuitable for a system of automated check collection or electronic presentment.

6. The last sentence of former Section 4–213(1) is deleted as an unnecessary source of confusion. Initially the view that payor bank may be accountable for, that is, liable for the amount of, an item that it has already paid seems incongruous. This is particularly true in the light of the language formerly found in Section 4–302 stating that the payor bank can defend against liability for accountability by showing that it has already settled for the item. But, at least with respect to former Section 4–213(1)(c), such a provision was needed because under the process-of-posting test a payor bank may have paid an item without settling for it. Now that Article 4 has abandoned the process-of-posting test, the sentence is no longer needed. If the payor bank has neither paid the item nor returned it within its midnight deadline, the payor bank is accountable under Section 4–302.

7. Subsection (a)(3) covers the situation in which the payor bank makes a provisional settlement for an item, and this settlement becomes final at a later time by reason of the failure of the payor bank to revoke it in the time and manner permitted by statute, clearing-house rule or agreement. An example of this type of situation is the clearing-house settlement referred to in Comment 4. In the illustration there given if the time limit for the return of items received in the Monday morning clearing is 2:00 p.m. on Tuesday and the provisional settlement has not been revoked at that time in a manner permitted by the clearing-house rules, the provisional settlement made on Monday morning becomes final at 2:00 p.m. on Tuesday. Subsection (a)(3) provides specifically that in this situation the item is finally paid at 2:00 p.m. Tuesday. If on the other hand a payor bank receives an item in the mail on Monday and makes some provisional settlement for the item on Monday, it has until midnight on Tuesday to return the item or give notice and revoke any settlement under Section 4–301. In this situation subsection (a)(3) of Section 4–215 provides that if the provisional settlement made on Monday is not revoked before midnight on Tuesday as permitted by Section 4–301, the item is finally paid at midnight on Tuesday. With respect to checks, Regulation CC Section 229.30(c) allows an extension of the midnight deadline under certain circumstances. If a bank does not expeditiously return a check liability may accrue under Regulation CC Section 229.38. For the relationship of

that liability to responsibility under this Article, see Regulation CC Sections 229.30 and 229.38.

8. Subsection (b) relates final settlement to final payment under Section 4–215. For example, if a payor bank makes provisional settlement for an item by sending a cashier's or teller's check and that settlement fails to become final under Section 4–213(c), subsection (b) provides that final payment has not occurred. If the item is not paid, the drawer remains liable, and under Section 4–302(a) the payor bank is accountable unless it has returned the item before its midnight deadline. In this regard, subsection (b) is an exception to subsection (a)(3). Even if the payor bank has not returned an item by its midnight deadline there is still no final payment if provisional settlement had been made and settlement failed to become final. However, if presentment of the item was over the counter for immediate payment, final payment has occurred under Section 4–215(a)(2). Subsection (b) does not apply because the settlement was not provisional. Section 4–301(a). In this case the presenting person, often the payee of the item, has the right to demand cash or the cash equivalent of federal reserve credit. If the presenting person accepts another medium of settlement such as a cashier's or teller's check, the presenting person takes the risk that the payor bank may fail to pay a cashier's check because of insolvency or that the drawee of a teller's check may dishonor it.

9. Subsection (c) states the country-wide usage that when the item is finally paid by the payor bank under subsection (a) this final payment automatically without further action "firms up" other provisional settlements made for it. However, the subsection makes clear that this "firming up" occurs only if the settlement between the presenting and payor banks was made either through a clearing house or by debits and credits in accounts between them. It does not take place if the payor bank remits for the item by sending some form of remittance instrument. Further, the "firming up" continues only to the extent that provisional debits and credits are entered seriatim in accounts between banks which are successive to the presenting bank. The automatic "firming up" is broken at any time that any collecting bank remits for the item by sending a remittance draft, because final payment to the remittee then usually depends upon final payment of the remittance draft.

10. Subsection (d) states the general rule that if a collecting bank receives settlement for an item which is or becomes final, the bank is accountable to its customer for the amount of the item. One means of accounting is to remit to its customer the amount it has

received on the item. If previously it gave to its customer a provisional credit for the item in an account its receipt of final settlement for the item "firms up" this provisional credit and makes it final. When this credit given by it so becomes final, in the usual case its agency status terminates and it becomes a debtor to its customer for the amount of the item. See Section 4–201(a). If the accounting is by a remittance instrument or authorization to charge further time will usually be required to complete its accounting (Section 4–213).

11. Subsection (e) states when certain credits given by a bank to its customer become available for withdrawal as of right. Subsection (e)(1) deals with the situation in which a bank has given a credit (usually provisional) for an item to its customer and in turn has received a provisional settlement for the item from an intermediary or payor bank to which it has forwarded the item. In this situation before the provisional credit entered by the collecting bank in the account of its customer becomes available for withdrawal as of right, it is not only necessary that the provisional settlement received by the bank for the item becomes final but also that the collecting bank has a reasonable time to receive return of the item and the item has not been received within that time. How much time is "reasonable" for these purposes will of course depend on the distance the item has to travel and the number of banks through which it must pass (having in mind not only travel time by regular lines of transmission but also the successive midnight deadlines of the several banks) and other pertinent facts. Also, if the provisional settlement received is some form of a remittance instrument or authorization to charge, the "reasonable" time depends on the identity and location of the payor of the remittance instrument, the means for clearing such instrument, and other pertinent facts. With respect to checks Regulation CC Sections 229.10–229.13 or similar applicable state law (Section 229.20) control. This is also time for the situation described in Comment 12.

12. Subsection (e)(2) deals with the situation of a bank that is both a depositary bank and a payor bank. The subsection recognizes that if A and B are both customers of a depositary-payor bank and A deposits B's check on the depositary-payor in A's account on Monday, time must be allowed to permit the check under the deferred posting rules of Section 4–301 to reach the bookkeeper for B's account at some time on Tuesday, and, if there are insufficient funds in B's account, to reverse or charge back the provisional

credit in A's account. Consequently this provisional credit in A's account does not become available for withdrawal as of right until the opening of business on Wednesday. If it is determined on Tuesday that there are insufficient funds in B's account to pay the check, the credit to A's account can be reversed on Tuesday. On the other hand if the item is in fact paid on Tuesday, the rule of subsection (e)(2) is desirable to avoid uncertainty and possible disputes between the bank and its customer as to exactly what hour within the day the credit is available.

§ 4–216. Insolvency and Preference.

(a) If an item is in or comes into the possession of a payor or collecting bank that suspends payment and the item has not been finally paid, the item must be returned by the receiver, trustee, or agent in charge of the closed bank to the presenting bank or the closed bank's customer.

(b) If a payor bank finally pays an item and suspends payments without making a settlement for the item with its customer or the presenting bank which settlement is or becomes final, the owner of the item has a preferred claim against the payor bank.

(c) If a payor bank gives or a collecting bank gives or receives a provisional settlement for an item and thereafter suspends payments, the suspension does not prevent or interfere with the settlement's becoming final if the finality occurs automatically upon the lapse of certain time or the happening of certain events.

(d) If a collecting bank receives from subsequent parties settlement for an item, which settlement is or becomes final and the bank suspends payments without making a settlement for the item with its customer which settlement is or becomes final, the owner of the item has a preferred claim against the collecting bank.

As amended in 1990.

Official Comment

1. The underlying purpose of the provisions of this section is not to confer upon banks, holders of items or anyone else preferential positions in the event of bank failures over general depositors or any other creditors of the failed banks. The purpose is to fix as definitely as possible the cut-off point of time for the completion or cessation of the collection process in the case of items that happen to be in the process at the time a particular bank suspends payments. It must be remembered that in bank collections as a whole and in the handling of items by an individual bank, items go through a whole series of processes. It must also be remembered that at any particular point of time a particular bank (at least one of any size) is functioning as a depositary bank for some items, as an intermediary bank for others, as a presenting bank for still others and as a payor bank for still others, and that when it suspends payments it will have close to its normal load of items working through its various processes. For the convenience of receivers, owners of items, banks, and in fact substantially everyone concerned, it is recognized that at the particular moment of time that a bank suspends payment, a certain portion of the items being handled by it have progressed far enough in the bank collection process that it is preferable to permit them to continue the remaining distance, rather than to send them back and reverse the many entries that have been made or the steps that have been taken with respect to them. Therefore, having this background and these purposes in mind, the section states what items must be turned backward at the moment suspension intervenes and what items have progressed far enough that the collection process with respect to them continues, with the resulting necessary statement of rights of various parties flowing from this prescription of the cut-off time.

2. The rules stated are similar to those stated in the American Bankers Association Bank Collection Code, but with the abandonment of any theory of trust. On the other hand, some law previous to this Act may be relevant. See Note, Uniform Commercial Code: Stopping Payment of an Item Deposited with an Insolvent Depositary Bank, 40 Okla.L.Rev. 689 (1987). Although for practical purposes Federal Deposit Insurance affects materially the result of bank failures on holders of items and banks, no attempt is made to vary the rules of the section by reason of such insurance.

3. It is recognized that in view of Jennings v. United States Fidelity & Guaranty Co., 294 U.S. 216, 55 S.Ct. 394, 79 L.Ed. 869, 99 A.L.R. 1248 (1935), amendment of the National Bank Act would be necessary to have this section apply to national banks. But there is no reason why it should not apply to others. See Section 1–108.

PART 3

COLLECTION OF ITEMS: PAYOR BANKS

§ 4–301. Deferred Posting; Recovery of Payment by Return of Items; Time of Dishonor; Return of Items by Payor Bank.

(a) If a payor bank settles for a demand item other than a documentary draft presented otherwise than for immediate payment over the counter before midnight of the banking day of receipt, the payor bank may revoke the settlement and recover the settlement if, before it has made final payment and before its midnight deadline, it

(1) returns the item;

(2) returns an image of the item, if the party to which the return is made has entered into an agreement to accept an image as a return of the item and the image is returned in accordance with that agreement; or

(3) sends a record providing notice of dishonor or nonpayment if the item is unavailable for return.

(b) If a demand item is received by a payor bank for credit on its books, it may return the item or send notice of dishonor and may revoke any credit given or recover the amount thereof withdrawn by its customer, if it acts within the time limit and in the manner specified in subsection (a).

(c) Unless previous notice of dishonor has been sent, an item is dishonored at the time when for purposes of dishonor it is returned or notice sent in accordance with this section.

(d) An item is returned:

(1) as to an item presented through a clearing house, when it is delivered to the presenting or last collecting bank or to the clearing house or is sent or delivered in accordance with clearing-house rules; or

(2) in all other cases, when it is sent or delivered to the bank's customer or transferor or pursuant to instructions.

As amended in 1990 and 2002.

Official Comment

1. The term "deferred posting" appears in the caption of Section 4–301. This refers to the practice permitted by statute in most of the states before the UCC under which a payor bank receives items on one day but does not post the items to the customer's account until the next day. Items dishonored were then returned after the posting on the day after receipt. Under Section 4–301 the concept of "deferred posting" merely allows a payor bank that has settled for an item on the day of receipt to return a dishonored item on the next day before its midnight deadline, without regard to when the item was actually posted. With respect to checks Regulation CC Section 229.30(c) extends the midnight deadline under the UCC under certain circumstances. See the Commentary to Regulation CC Section 229.38(d) on the relationship between the UCC and Regulation CC on settlement.

2. The function of this section is to provide the circumstances under which a payor bank that has made timely settlement for an item may return the item and revoke the settlement so that it may recover any settlement made. These circumstances are: (1) the item must be a demand item other than a documentary draft; (2) the item must be presented otherwise than for immediate payment over the counter; and (3) the payor bank must return the item (or give notice if the item is unavailable for return) before its midnight deadline and before it has paid the item. With respect to checks, see Regulation CC Section 229.31(f) on notice in lieu of return and Regulation CC Section 229.33 as to the different requirement of notice of nonpayment. An instance of when an item may be unavailable for return arises under a collecting bank check retention plan under which presentment is made by a presentment notice and the item is retained by the collecting bank. Section 4–215(a)(2) provides that final payment occurs if the payor bank has settled for an item without a right to revoke the settlement under statute, clearing-house rule or agreement. In any case in which Section 4–301(a) is applicable, the payor bank has a right to revoke the settlement by statute; therefore, Section 4–215(a)(2) is inoperable, and the settlement is provisional. Hence, if the settlement is not over the counter and the payor bank settles in a manner that does not constitute final payment, the payor bank can revoke the settlement by returning the item before its midnight deadline.

3. The relationship of Section 4–301(a) to final settlement and final payment under Section 4–215 is illustrated by the following case. Depositary Bank

sends by mail an item to Payor Bank with instructions to settle by remitting a teller's check drawn on a bank in the city where Depositary Bank is located. Payor Bank sends the teller's check on the day the item was presented. Having made timely settlement, under the deferred posting provisions of Section 4–301(a), Payor Bank may revoke that settlement by returning the item before its midnight deadline. If it fails to return the item before its midnight deadline, it has finally paid the item if the bank on which the teller's check was drawn honors the check. But if the teller's check is dishonored there has been no final settlement under Section 4–213(c) and no final payment under Section 4–215(b). Since the Payor Bank has neither paid the item nor made timely return, it is accountable for the item under Section 4–302(a).

4. The time limits for action imposed by subsection (a) are adopted by subsection (b) for cases in which the payor bank is also the depositary bank, but in this case the requirement of a settlement on the day of receipt is omitted.

5. Subsection (c) fixes a base point from which to measure the time within which notice of dishonor must be given. See Section 3–503.

6. Subsection (d) leaves banks free to agree upon the manner of returning items but establishes a precise time when an item is "returned." For definition of "sent" as used in paragraphs (1) and (2) see Section 1–201(38). Obviously the subsection assumes that the item has not been "finally paid" under Section 4–215(a). If it has been, this provision has no operation.

7. The fact that an item has been paid under proposed Section 4–215 does not preclude the payor bank from asserting rights of restitution or revocation under Section 3–418. National Savings and Trust Co. v. Park Corp., 722 F.2d 1303 (6th Cir.1983), cert. denied, 466 U.S. 939 (1984), is the correct interpretation of the present law on this issue.

8. Paragraph (a)(2) is designed to facilitate electronic check-processing by authorizing the payor bank to return an image of the item instead of the actual item. It applies only when the payor bank and the party to which the return has been made have agreed that the payor bank can make such a return and when the return complies with the agreement. The purpose of the paragraph is to prevent third parties (such as the depositor of the check) from contending that the payor bank missed its midnight deadline because it failed to return the actual item in a timely manner. If the payor bank missed its midnight deadline, payment would have become final under Section 4–215 and the depositary bank would have lost its right of chargeback

under Section 4–214. Of course, the depositary bank might enter into an agreement with its depositor to resolve that problem, but it is not clear that agreements by banks with their customers can resolve all such issues. In any event, paragraph (a)(2) should eliminate the need for such agreements. The provision rests on the premise that it is inappropriate to penalize a payor bank simply because it returns the actual item a few business days after the midnight deadline of the payor bank sent notice before that deadline to a collecting bank that had agreed to accept such notices.

Nothing in paragraph (a)(2) authorizes the payor bank to destroy the check.

As amended in 2002.

§ 4–302. Payor Bank's Responsibility for Late Return of Item.

(a) If an item is presented to and received by a payor bank, the bank is accountable for the amount of:

(1) a demand item, other than a documentary draft, whether properly payable or not, if the bank, in any case in which it is not also the depositary bank, retains the item beyond midnight of the banking day of receipt without settling for it or, whether or not it is also the depositary bank, does not pay or return the item or send notice of dishonor until after its midnight deadline; or

(2) any other properly payable item unless, within the time allowed for acceptance or payment of that item, the bank either accepts or pays the item or returns it and accompanying documents.

(b) The liability of a payor bank to pay an item pursuant to subsection (a) is subject to defenses based on breach of a presentment warranty (Section 4–208) or proof that the person seeking enforcement of the liability presented or transferred the item for the purpose of defrauding the payor bank.

As amended in 1990.

Official Comment

1. Subsection (a)(1) continues the former law distinguishing between cases in which the payor bank is not also the depositary bank and those in which the payor bank is also the depositary bank ("on us" items). For "on us" items the payor bank is accountable if it retains the item beyond its midnight deadline without

settling for it. If the payor bank is not the depositary bank it is accountable if it retains the item beyond midnight of the banking day of receipt without settling for it. It may avoid accountability either by settling for the item on the day of receipt and returning the item before its midnight deadline under Section 4–301 or by returning the item on the day of receipt. This rule is consistent with the deferred posting practice authorized by Section 4–301 which allows the payor bank to make provisional settlement for an item on the day of receipt and to revoke that settlement by returning the item on the next day. With respect to checks, Regulation CC Section 229.36(d) provides that settlements between banks for forward collection of checks are final when made. See the Commentary on that provision for its effect on the UCC.

2. If the settlement given by the payor bank does not become final, there has been no payment under Section 4–215(b), and the payor bank giving the failed settlement is accountable under subsection (a)(1) of Section 4–302. For instance, the payor bank makes provisional settlement by sending a teller's check that is dishonored. In such a case settlement is not final under Section 4–213(c) and no payment occurs under Section 4–215(b). Payor bank is accountable on the item. The general principle is that unless settlement provides the presenting bank with usable funds, settlement has failed and the payor bank is accountable for the amount of the item. On the other hand, if the payor bank makes a settlement for the item that becomes final under Section 4–215, the item has been paid and thus the payor bank is not accountable for the item under this Section. *Amendments approved by the Permanent Editorial Board for Uniform Commercial Code November 2, 2002.*

3. Subsection (b) is an elaboration of the deleted introductory language of former Section 4–302: "In the absence of a valid defense such as breach of a presentment warranty (subsection (1) of Section 4–207), settlement effected or the like...." A payor bank can defend an action against it based on accountability by showing that the item contained a forged indorsement or a fraudulent alteration. Subsection (b) drops the ambiguous "or the like" language and provides that the payor bank may also raise the defense of fraud. Decisions that hold an accountable bank's liability to be "absolute" are rejected. A payor bank that makes a late return of an item should not be liable to a defrauder operating a check kiting scheme. In Bank of Leumi Trust Co. v. Bally's Park Place Inc., 528 F.Supp. 349 (S.D.N.Y.1981), and American National Bank v. Foodbasket, 497 P.2d 546 (Wyo.1972), banks that were accountable under Section 4–302 for missing their mid-

night deadline were successful in defending against parties who initiated collection knowing that the check would not be paid. The "settlement effected" language is deleted as unnecessary. If a payor bank is accountable for an item it is liable to pay it. If it has made final payment for an item, it is no longer accountable for the item.

§ 4–303. When Items Subject to Notice, Stop-Payment Order, Legal Process, or Setoff; Order in Which Items May Be Charged or Certified.

(a) Any knowledge, notice, or stop-payment order received by, legal process served upon, or setoff exercised by a payor bank comes too late to terminate, suspend, or modify the bank's right or duty to pay an item or to charge its customer's account for the item if the knowledge, notice, stop-payment order, or legal process is received or served and a reasonable time for the bank to act thereon expires or the setoff is exercised after the earliest of the following:

(1) the bank accepts or certifies the item;

(2) the bank pays the item in cash;

(3) the bank settles for the item without having a right to revoke the settlement under statute, clearing-house rule, or agreement;

(4) the bank becomes accountable for the amount of the item under Section 4–302 dealing with the payor bank's responsibility for late return of items; or

(5) with respect to checks, a cutoff hour no earlier than one hour after the opening of the next banking day after the banking day on which the bank received the check and no later than the close of that next banking day or, if no cutoff hour is fixed, the close of the next banking day after the banking day on which the bank received the check.

(b) Subject to subsection (a), items may be accepted, paid, certified, or charged to the indicated account of its customer in any order.

As amended in 1990.

Official Comment

1. While a payor bank is processing an item presented for payment, it may receive knowledge or a legal notice affecting the item, such as knowledge or a notice that the drawer has filed a petition in bankruptcy or made an assignment for the benefit of creditors;

may receive an order of the drawer stopping payment on the item; may have served on it an attachment of the account of the drawer; or the bank itself may exercise a right of setoff against the drawer's account. Each of these events affects the account of the drawer and may eliminate or freeze all or part of whatever balance is available to pay the item. Subsection (a) states the rule for determining the relative priorities between these various legal events and the item.

2. The rule is that if any one of several things has been done to the item or if it has reached any one of several stages in its processing at the time the knowledge, notice, stop-payment order or legal process is received or served and a reasonable time for the bank to act thereon expires or the setoff is exercised, the knowledge, notice, stop-payment order, legal process or setoff comes too late, the item has priority and a charge to the customer's account may be made and is effective. With respect to the effect of the customer's bankruptcy, the bank's rights are governed by Bankruptcy Code Section 542(c) which codifies the result of Bank of Marin v. England, 385 U.S. 99 (1966). Section 4–405 applies to the death or incompetence of the customer.

3. Once a payor bank has accepted or certified an item or has paid the item in cash, the event has occurred that determines priorities between the item and the various legal events usually described as the "four legals." Paragraphs (1) and (2) of subsection (a) so provide. If a payor bank settles for an item presented over the counter for immediate payment by a cashier's check or teller's check which the presenting person agrees to accept, paragraph (3) of subsection (a) would control and the event determining priority has occurred. Because presentment was over the counter, Section 4–301(a) does not apply to give the payor bank the statutory right to revoke the settlement. Thus the requirements of paragraph (3) have been met unless a clearing-house rule or agreement of the parties provides otherwise.

4. In the usual case settlement for checks is by entries in bank accounts. Since the process-of-posting test has been abandoned as inappropriate for automated check collection, the determining event for priorities is a given hour on the day after the item is received. (Paragraph (5) of subsection (a).) The hour may be fixed by the bank no earlier than one hour after the opening on the next banking day after the bank received the check and no later than the close of that banking day. If an item is received after the payor bank's regular Section 4–108 cutoff hour, it is treated as received the next banking day. If a bank receives

an item after its regular cutoff hour on Monday and an attachment is levied at noon on Tuesday, the attachment is prior to the item if the bank had not before that hour taken the action described in paragraphs (1), (2), and (3) of subsection (a). The Commentary to Regulation CC Section 229.36(d) explains that even though settlement by a paying bank for a check is final for Regulation CC purposes, the paying bank's right to return the check before its midnight deadline under the UCC is not affected.

5. Another event conferring priority for an item and a charge to the customer's account based upon the item is stated by the language "become accountable for the amount of the item under Section 4–302 dealing with the payor bank's responsibility for late return of items." Expiration of the deadline under Section 4–302 with resulting accountability by the payor bank for the amount of the item, establishes priority of the item over notices, stop-payment orders, legal process or setoff.

6. In the case of knowledge, notice, stop-payment orders and legal process the effective time for determining whether they were received too late to affect the payment of an item and a charge to the customer's account by reason of such payment, is receipt plus a reasonable time for the bank to act on any of these communications. Usually a relatively short time is required to communicate to the accounting department advice of one of these events but certainly some time is necessary. Compare Sections 1–201(27) and 4–403. In the case of setoff the effective time is when the setoff is actually made.

7. As between one item and another no priority rule is stated. This is justified because of the impossibility of stating a rule that would be fair in all cases, having in mind the almost infinite number of combinations of large and small checks in relation to the available balance on hand in the drawer's account; the possible methods of receipt; and other variables. Further, the drawer has drawn all the checks, the drawer should have funds available to meet all of them and has no basis for urging one should be paid before another; and the holders have no direct right against the payor bank in any event, unless of course, the bank has accepted, certified or finally paid a particular item, or has become liable for it under Section 4–302. Under subsection (b) the bank has the right to pay items for which it is itself liable ahead of those for which it is not.

PART 4

RELATIONSHIP BETWEEN PAYOR
BANK AND ITS CUSTOMER

§ 4–401. When Bank May Charge Customer's Account.

(a) A bank may charge against the account of a customer an item that is properly payable from the account even though the charge creates an overdraft. An item is properly payable if it is authorized by the customer and is in accordance with any agreement between the customer and bank.

(b) A customer is not liable for the amount of an overdraft if the customer neither signed the item nor benefited from the proceeds of the item.

(c) A bank may charge against the account of a customer a check that is otherwise properly payable from the account, even though payment was made before the date of the check, unless the customer has given notice to the bank of the postdating describing the check with reasonable certainty. The notice is effective for the period stated in Section 4–403(b) for stop-payment orders, and must be received at such time and in such manner as to afford the bank a reasonable opportunity to act on it before the bank takes any action with respect to the check described in Section 4–303. If a bank charges against the account of a customer a check before the date stated in the notice of postdating, the bank is liable for damages for the loss resulting from its act. The loss may include damages for dishonor of subsequent items under Section 4–402.

(d) A bank that in good faith makes payment to a holder may charge the indicated account of its customer according to:

(1) the original terms of the altered item; or

(2) the terms of the completed item, even though the bank knows the item has been completed unless the bank has notice that the completion was improper.

As amended in 1990.

Official Comment

1. An item is properly payable from a customer's account if the customer has authorized the payment and the payment does not violate any agreement that may exist between the bank and its customer. For an example of a payment held to violate an agreement with a customer, see Torrance National Bank v. Enesco Federal Credit Union, 285 P.2d 737 (Cal.App.1955). An item drawn for more than the amount of a customer's account may be properly payable. Thus under subsection (a) a bank may charge the customer's account for an item even though payment results in an overdraft. An item containing a forged drawer's signature or forged indorsement is not properly payable. Concern has arisen whether a bank may require a customer to execute a stop-payment order when the customer notifies the bank of the loss of an unindorsed or specially indorsed check. Since such a check cannot be properly payable from the customer's account, it is inappropriate for a bank to require stop-payment order in such a case.

2. Subsection (b) adopts the view of case authority holding that if there is more than one customer who can draw on an account, the nonsigning customer is not liable for an overdraft unless that person benefits from the proceeds of the item.

3. Subsection (c) is added because the automated check collection system cannot accommodate postdated checks. A check is usually paid upon presentment without respect to the date of the check. Under the former law, if a payor bank paid a postdated check before its stated date, it could not charge the customer's account because the check was not "properly payable." Hence, the bank might have been liable for wrongfully dishonoring subsequent checks of the drawer that would have been paid had the postdated check not been prematurely paid. Under subsection (c) a customer wishing to postdate a check must notify the payor bank of its postdating in time to allow the bank to act on the customer's notice before the bank has to commit itself to pay the check. If the bank fails to act on the customer's timely notice, it may be liable for damages for the resulting loss which may include damages for dishonor of subsequent items. This Act does not regulate fees that banks charge their customers for a notice of postdating or other services covered by the Act, but under principles of law such as unconscionability or good faith and fair dealing, courts have reviewed fees and the bank's exercise of a discretion to set fees. Perdue v. Crocker National Bank, 38 Cal.3d 913 (1985) (unconscionability); Best v. United Bank of Oregon, 739 P.2d 554, 562–566 (1987) (good faith and

fair dealing). In addition, Section 1–203 provides that every contract or duty within this Act imposes an obligation of good faith in its performance or enforcement.

4. Section 3–407(c) states that a payor bank or drawee which pays a fraudulently altered instrument in good faith and without notice of the alteration may enforce rights with respect to the instrument according to its original terms or, in the case of an incomplete instrument altered by unauthorized completion, according to its terms as completed. Section 4–401(d) follows the rule stated in Section 3–407(c) by applying it to an altered item and allows the bank to enforce rights with respect to the altered item by charging the customer's account.

§ 4–402. Bank's Liability to Customer for Wrongful Dishonor; Time of Determining Insufficiency of Account.

(a) Except as otherwise provided in this Article, a payor bank wrongfully dishonors an item if it dishonors an item that is properly payable, but a bank may dishonor an item that would create an overdraft unless it has agreed to pay the overdraft.

(b) A payor bank is liable to its customer for damages proximately caused by the wrongful dishonor of an item. Liability is limited to actual damages proved and may include damages for an arrest or prosecution of the customer or other consequential damages. Whether any consequential damages are proximately caused by the wrongful dishonor is a question of fact to be determined in each case.

(c) A payor bank's determination of the customer's account balance on which a decision to dishonor for insufficiency of available funds is based may be made at any time between the time the item is received by the payor bank and the time that the payor bank returns the item or gives notice in lieu of return, and no more than one determination need be made. If, at the election of the payor bank, a subsequent balance determination is made for the purpose of reevaluating the bank's decision to dishonor the item, the account balance at that time is determinative of whether a dishonor for insufficiency of available funds is wrongful.

As amended in 1990.

Official Comment

1. Subsection (a) states positively what has been assumed under the original Article: that if a bank fails to honor a properly payable item it may be liable to its customer for wrongful dishonor. Under subsection (b) the payor bank's wrongful dishonor of an item gives rise to a statutory cause of action. Damages may include consequential damages. Confusion has resulted from the attempts of courts to reconcile the first and second sentences of former Section 4–402. The second sentence implied that the bank was liable for some form of damages other than those proximately caused by the dishonor if the dishonor was other than by mistake. But nothing in the section described what these noncompensatory damages might be. Some courts have held that in distinguishing between mistaken dishonors and nonmistaken dishonors, the so-called "trader" rule has been retained that allowed a "merchant or trader" to recover substantial damages for wrongful dishonor without proof of damages actually suffered. Comment 3 to former Section 4–402 indicated that this was not the intent of the drafters. White & Summers, Uniform Commercial Code, Section 18–4 (1988), states: "The negative implication is that when wrongful dishonors occur not 'through mistake' but willfully, the court may impose damages greater than 'actual damages'.... Certainly the reference to 'mistake' in the second sentence of 4–402 invites a court to adopt the relevant pre-Code distinction." Subsection (b) by deleting the reference to mistake in the second sentence precludes any inference that Section 4–402 retains the "trader" rule. Whether a bank is liable for noncompensatory damages, such as punitive damages, must be decided by Section 1–103 and Section 1–106 ("by other rule of law").

2. Wrongful dishonor is different from "failure to exercise ordinary care in handling an item," and the measure of damages is that stated in this section, not that stated in Section 4–103(e). By the same token, if a dishonor comes within this section, the measure of damages of this section applies and not another measure of damages. If the wrongful refusal of the beneficiary's bank to make funds available from a funds transfer causes the beneficiary's check to be dishonored, no specific guidance is given as to whether recovery is under this section or Article 4A. In each case this issue must be viewed in its factual context, and it was thought unwise to seek to establish certainty at the cost of fairness.

3. The second and third sentences of subsection (b) reject decisions holding that as a matter of law the dishonor of a check is not the "proximate cause" of the arrest and prosecution of the customer and leave to determination in each case as a question of fact whether the dishonor is or may be the "proximate cause."

4. Banks commonly determine whether there are sufficient funds in an account to pay an item after the close of banking hours on the day of presentment when they post debit and credit items to the account. The determination is made on the basis of credits available for withdrawal as of right or made available for withdrawal by the bank as an accommodation to its customer. When it is determined that payment of the item would overdraw the account, the item may be returned at any time before the bank's midnight deadline the following day. Before the item is returned new credits that are withdrawable as of right may have been added to the account. Subsection (c) eliminates uncertainty under Article 4 as to whether the failure to make a second determination before the item is returned on the day following presentment is a wrongful dishonor if new credits were added to the account on that day that would have covered the amount of the check.

5. Section 4–402 has been construed to preclude an action for wrongful dishonor by a plaintiff other than the bank's customer. Loucks v. Albuquerque National Bank, 418 P.2d 191 (N.Mex.1966). Some courts have allowed a plaintiff other than the customer to sue when the customer is a business entity that is one and the same with the individual or individuals operating it. Murdaugh Volkswagen, Inc. v. First National Bank, 801 F.2d 719 (4th Cir.1986) and Karsh v. American City Bank, 113 Cal.App.3d 419, 169 Cal.Rptr. 851 (1980). However, where the wrongful dishonor impugns the reputation of an operator of the business, the issue is not merely, as the court in Koger v. East First National Bank, 443 So.2d 141 (Fla.App.1983), put it, one of a literal versus a liberal interpretation of Section 4–402. Rather the issue is whether the statutory cause of action in Section 4–402 displaces, in accordance with Section 1–103, any cause of action that existed at common law in a person who is not the customer whose reputation was damaged. See Marcum v. Security Trust and Savings Co., 221 Ala. 419, 129 So. 74 (1930). While Section 4–402 should not be interpreted to displace the latter cause of action, the section itself gives no cause of action to other than a "customer," however that definition is construed, and thus confers no cause of action on the holder of a dishonored item. First American National Bank v. Commerce Union Bank, 692 S.W.2d 642 (Tenn.App. 1985).

§ 4–403. Customer's Right to Stop Payment; Burden of Proof of Loss.

(a) A customer or any person authorized to draw on the account if there is more than one person may stop payment of any item drawn on the customer's account or close the account by an order to the bank describing the item or account with reasonable certainty received at a time and in a manner that affords the bank a reasonable opportunity to act on it before any action by the bank with respect to the item described in Section 4–303. If the signature of more than one person is required to draw on an account, any of these persons may stop payment or close the account.

(b) A stop-payment order is effective for six months, but it lapses after 14 calendar days if the original order was oral and was not confirmed in a record within that period. A stop-payment order may be renewed for additional six-month periods by a record given to the bank within a period during which the stop-payment order is effective.

(c) The burden of establishing the fact and amount of loss resulting from the payment of an item contrary to a stop-payment order or order to close an account is on the customer. The loss from payment of an item contrary to a stop-payment order may include damages for dishonor of subsequent items under Section 4–402.

As amended in 1990 and 2002.

Official Comment

1. The position taken by this section is that stopping payment or closing an account is a service which depositors expect and are entitled to receive from banks notwithstanding its difficulty, inconvenience and expense. The inevitable occasional losses through failure to stop or close should be borne by the banks as a cost of the business of banking.

2. Subsection (a) follows the decisions holding that a payee or indorsee has no right to stop payment. This is consistent with the provision governing payment or satisfaction. See Section 3–602. The sole exception to this rule is found in Section 4–405 on payment after notice of death, by which any person claiming an interest in the account can stop payment.

3. Payment is commonly stopped only on checks; but the right to stop payment is not limited to checks, and extends to any item payable by any bank. If the maker of a note payable at a bank is in a position analogous to that of a drawer (Section 4–106) the maker may stop payment of the note. By analogy the rule extends to drawees other than banks.

4. A cashier's check or teller's check purchased by a customer whose account is debited in payment for the check is not a check drawn on the customer's account within the meaning of subsection (a); hence, a customer purchasing a cashier's check or teller's check has no right to stop payment of such a check under subsection (a). If a bank issuing a cashier's check or teller's check refuses to pay the check as an accommodation to its customer or for other reasons, its liability on the check is governed by Section 3–411. There is no right to stop payment after certification of a check or other acceptance of a draft, and this is true no matter who procures the certification. See Sections 3–411 and 4–303. The acceptance is the drawee's own engagement to pay, and it is not required to impair its credit by refusing payment for the convenience of the drawer.

5. Subsection (a) makes clear that if there is more than one person authorized to draw on a customer's account any one of them can stop payment of any check drawn on the account or can order the account closed. Moreover, if there is a customer, such as a corporation, that requires its checks to bear the signatures of more than one person, any of these persons may stop payment on a check. In describing the item, the customer, in the absence of a contrary agreement, must meet the standard of what information allows the bank under the technology then existing to identify the item with reasonable certainty.

6. Under subsection (b), a stop-payment order is effective after the order, whether written or oral, is received by the bank and the bank has a reasonable opportunity to act on it. If the order is written it remains in effect for six months from that time. If the order is oral it lapses after 14 days unless there is written confirmation. If there is written confirmation within the 14–day period, the six-month period dates from the giving of the oral order. A stop-payment order may be renewed any number of times by written notice given during a six-month period while a stop order is in effect. A new stop-payment order may be given after a six-month period expires, but such a notice takes effect from the date given. When a stop-payment order expires it is as though the order had never been given, and the payor bank may pay the item in good faith under Section 4–404 even though a stop-payment order had once been given.

7. A payment in violation of an effective direction to stop payment is an improper payment, even though it is made by mistake or inadvertence. Any agreement to the contrary is invalid under Section 4–103(a) if in paying the item over the stop-payment order the bank has failed to exercise ordinary care. An agreement to the contrary which is imposed upon a customer as part

of a standard form contract would have to be evaluated in the light of the general obligation of good faith. Sections 1–203 and 4–104(c). The drawee is, however, entitled to subrogation to prevent unjust enrichment (Section 4–407); retains common law defenses, e.g., that by conduct in recognizing the payment the customer has ratified the bank's action in paying over a stop-payment order (Section 1–103); and retains common law rights, e.g., to recover money paid under a mistake under Section 3–418. It has sometimes been said that payment cannot be stopped against a holder in due course, but the statement is inaccurate. The payment can be stopped but the drawer remains liable on the instrument to the holder in due course (Sections 3–305, 3–414) and the drawee, if it pays, becomes subrogated to the rights of the holder in due course against the drawer. Section 4–407. The relationship between Sections 4–403 and 4–407 is discussed in the comments to Section 4–407. Any defenses available against a holder in due course remain available to the drawer, but other defenses are cut off to the same extent as if the holder were bringing the action.

§ 4–404. Bank Not Obliged to Pay Check More Than Six Months Old.

A bank is under no obligation to a customer having a checking account to pay a check, other than a certified check, which is presented more than six months after its date, but it may charge its customer's account for a payment made thereafter in good faith.

Official Comment

This section incorporates a type of statute that had been adopted in 26 jurisdictions before the Code. The time limit is set at six months because banking and commercial practice regards a check outstanding for longer than that period as stale, and a bank will normally not pay such a check without consulting the depositor. It is therefore not required to do so, but is given the option to pay because it may be in a position to know, as in the case of dividend checks, that the drawer wants payment made.

Certified checks are excluded from the section because they are the primary obligation of the certifying bank (Sections 3–409 and 3–413). The obligation runs directly to the holder of the check. The customer's account was presumably charged when the check was certified.

§ 4–405. Death or Incompetence of Customer.

(a) A payor or collecting bank's authority to accept, pay, or collect an item or to account for proceeds of its collection, if otherwise effective, is not rendered ineffective by incompetence of a customer of either bank existing at the time the item is issued or its collection is undertaken if the bank does not know of an adjudication of incompetence. Neither death nor incompetence of a customer revokes the authority to accept, pay, collect, or account until the bank knows of the fact of death or of an adjudication of incompetence and has reasonable opportunity to act on it.

(b) Even with knowledge, a bank may for 10 days after the date of death pay or certify checks drawn on or before that date unless ordered to stop payment by a person claiming an interest in the account.

As amended in 1990.

Official Comment

1. Subsection (a) follows existing decisions holding that a drawee (payor) bank is not liable for the payment of a check before it has notice of the death or incompetence of the drawer. The justice and necessity of the rule are obvious. A check is an order to pay which the bank must obey under penalty of possible liability for dishonor. Further, with the tremendous volume of items handled any rule that required banks to verify the continued life and competency of drawers would be completely unworkable.

One or both of these same reasons apply to other phases of the bank collection and payment process and the rule is made wide enough to apply to these other phases. It applies to all kinds of "items"; to "customers" who own items as well as "customers" who draw or make them; to the function of collecting items as well as the function of accepting or paying them; to the carrying out of instructions to account for proceeds even though these may involve transfers to third parties; to depositary and intermediary banks as well as payor banks; and to incompetency existing at the time of the issuance of an item or the commencement of the collection or payment process as well as to incompetency occurring thereafter. Further, the requirement of actual knowledge makes inapplicable the rule of some cases that an adjudication of incompetency is constructive notice to all the world because obviously it is as impossible for banks to keep posted on such adjudications (in the absence of actual knowledge) as it is to keep posted as to death of immediate or remote customers.

2. Subsection (b) provides a limited period after death during which a bank may continue to pay checks

(as distinguished from other items) even though it has notice. The purpose of the provision, as of the existing statutes, is to permit holders of checks drawn and issued shortly before death to cash them without the necessity of filing a claim in probate. The justification is that these checks normally are given in immediate payment of an obligation, that there is almost never any reason why they should not be paid, and that filing in probate is a useless formality, burdensome to the holder, the executor, the court and the bank.

This section does not prevent an executor or administrator from recovering the payment from the holder of the check. It is not intended to affect the validity of any gift causa mortis or other transfer in contemplation of death, but merely to relieve the bank of liability for the payment.

3. Any surviving relative, creditor or other person who claims an interest in the account may give a direction to the bank not to pay checks, or not to pay a particular check. Such notice has the same effect as a direction to stop payment. The bank has no responsibility to determine the validity of the claim or even whether it is "colorable." But obviously anyone who has an interest in the estate, including the person named as executor in a will, even if the will has not yet been admitted to probate, is entitled to claim an interest in the account.

§ 4–406. Customer's Duty to Discover and Report Unauthorized Signature or Alteration.

(a) A bank that sends or makes available to a customer a statement of account showing payment of items for the account shall either return or make available to the customer the items paid or provide information in the statement of account sufficient to allow the customer reasonably to identify the items paid. The statement of account provides sufficient information if the item is described by item number, amount, and date of payment.

(b) If the items are not returned to the customer, the person retaining the items shall either retain the items or, if the items are destroyed, maintain the capacity to furnish legible copies of the items until the expiration of seven years after receipt of the items. A customer may request an item from the bank that paid the item, and that bank must provide in a reasonable time either the item or, if the item has been destroyed or is not otherwise obtainable, a legible copy of the item.

(c) If a bank sends or makes available a statement of account or items pursuant to subsection (a), the customer must exercise reasonable promptness in examining the statement or the items to determine whether any payment was not authorized because of an alteration of an item or because a purported signature by or on behalf of the customer was not authorized. If, based on the statement or items provided, the customer should reasonably have discovered the unauthorized payment, the customer must promptly notify the bank of the relevant facts.

(d) If the bank proves that the customer failed, with respect to an item, to comply with the duties imposed on the customer by subsection (c), the customer is precluded from asserting against the bank:

(1) the customer's unauthorized signature or any alteration on the item, if the bank also proves that it suffered a loss by reason of the failure; and

(2) the customer's unauthorized signature or alteration by the same wrongdoer on any other item paid in good faith by the bank if the payment was made before the bank received notice from the customer of the unauthorized signature or alteration and after the customer had been afforded a reasonable period of time, not exceeding 30 days, in which to examine the item or statement of account and notify the bank.

(e) If subsection (d) applies and the customer proves that the bank failed to exercise ordinary care in paying the item and that the failure substantially contributed to loss, the loss is allocated between the customer precluded and the bank asserting the preclusion according to the extent to which the failure of the customer to comply with subsection (c) and the failure of the bank to exercise ordinary care contributed to the loss. If the customer proves that the bank did not pay the item in good faith, the preclusion under subsection (d) does not apply.

(f) Without regard to care or lack of care of either the customer or the bank, a customer who does not within one year after the statement or items are made available to the customer (subsection (a)) discover and report the customer's unauthorized signature on or any alteration on the item is precluded from asserting against the bank the unauthorized signature or alteration. If there is a preclusion under this subsection, the payor bank may not recover for breach of warranty under Section 4–208 with respect to the unauthorized signature or alteration to which the preclusion applies.

As amended in 1990.

Revised Official Comment

1. Under subsection (a), if a bank that has paid a check or other item for the account of a customer makes available to the customer a statement of account showing payment of the item, the bank must either return the item to the customer or provide a description of the item sufficient to allow the customer to identify it. Under subsection (c), the customer has a duty to exercise reasonable promptness in examining the statement or the returned item to discover any unauthorized signature of the customer or any alteration and to promptly notify the bank if the customer should reasonably have discovered the unauthorized signature or alteration.

The duty stated in subsection (c) becomes operative only if the "bank sends or makes available a statement of account or items pursuant to subsection (a)." A bank is not under a duty to send a statement of account or the paid items to the customer; but, if it does not do so, the customer does not have any duties under subsection (c).

Under subsection (a), a statement of account must provide information "sufficient to allow the customer reasonably to identify the items paid." If the bank supplies its customer with an image of the paid item, it complies with this standard. But a safe harbor rule is provided. The bank complies with the standard of providing "sufficient information" if "the item is described by item number, amount, and date of payment." This means that the customer's duties under subsection (c) are triggered if the bank sends a statement of account complying with the safe harbor rule without returning the paid items. A bank does not have to return the paid items unless it has agreed with the customer to do so. Whether there is such an agreement depends upon the particular circumstances. See Section 1–201(3). If the bank elects to provide the minimum information that is "sufficient" under subsection (a) and, as a consequence, the customer could not "reasonably have discovered the unauthorized payment," there is no preclusion under subsection (d). If the customer made a record of the issued checks on the check stub or carbonized copies furnished by the bank in the checkbook, the customer should usually be able to verify the paid items shown on the statement of account and discover any unauthorized or altered checks. But there could be exceptional circumstances. For example, if a check is altered by changing the name of the payee, the customer could not normally detect the fraud unless the customer is given the paid check or the statement of account discloses the name of the payee of the altered check. If the customer could not "reasonably have discovered the unauthorized payment" under subsection (c) there would not be a preclusion under subsection (d).

The safe harbor provided by subsection (a) serves to permit a bank, based on the state of existing technology, to trigger the customer's duties under subsection (c) by providing a "statement of account showing payment of items" without having to return the paid items, in any case in which the bank has not agreed with the customer to return the paid items. The safe harbor does not, however, preclude a customer under subsection (d) from asserting its unauthorized signature or an alteration against a bank in those circumstances in which under subsection (c) the customer should not "reasonably have discovered the unauthorized payment." Whether the customer has failed to comply with its duties under subsection (c) is determined on a case-by-case basis.

The provision in subsection (a) that a statement of account contains "sufficient information if the item is described by item number, amount, and date of payment" is based upon the existing state of technology. This information was chosen because it can be obtained by the bank's computer from the check's MICR line without examination of the items involved. The other two items of information that the customer would normally want to know—the name of the payee and the date of the item—cannot currently be obtained from the MICR line. The safe harbor rule is important in determining the feasibility of payor or collecting bank check retention plans. A customer who keeps a record of checks written, e.g., on the check stubs or carbonized copies of the checks supplied by the bank in the checkbook, will usually have sufficient information to identify the items on the basis of item number, amount, and date of payment. But customers who do not utilize these record-keeping methods may not. The policy decision is that accommodating customers who do not keep adequate records is not as desirable as accommodating customers who keep more careful records. This policy results in less cost to the check collection system and thus to all customers of the system. It is expected that technological advances such as image processing may make it possi-

ble for banks to give customers more information in the future in a manner that is fully compatible with automation or truncation systems. At that time the Permanent Editorial Board may wish to make recommendations for an amendment revising the safe harbor requirements in the light of those advances.

2. Subsection (d) states the consequences of a failure by the customer to perform its duty under subsection (c) to report an alteration or the customer's unauthorized signature. Subsection (d)(1) applies to the unauthorized payment of the item to which the duty to report under subsection (c) applies. If the bank proves that the customer "should reasonably have discovered the unauthorized payment" (See Comment 1) and did not notify the bank, the customer is precluded from asserting against the bank the alteration or the customer's unauthorized signature if the bank proves that it suffered a loss as a result of the failure of the customer to perform its subsection (c) duty. Subsection (d)(2) applies to cases in which the customer fails to report an unauthorized signature or alteration with respect to an item in breach of the subsection (c) duty (See Comment 1) and the bank subsequently pays other items of the customer with respect to which there is an alteration or unauthorized signature of the customer and the same wrongdoer is involved. If the payment of the subsequent items occurred after the customer has had a reasonable time (not exceeding 30 days) to report with respect to the first item and before the bank received notice of the unauthorized signature or alteration of the first item, the customer is precluded from asserting the alteration or unauthorized signature with respect to the subsequent items.

If the customer is precluded in a single or multiple item unauthorized payment situation under subsection (d), but the customer proves that the bank failed to exercise ordinary care in paying the item or items and that the failure substantially contributed to the loss, subsection (e) provides a comparative negligence test for allocating loss between the customer and the bank. Subsection (e) also states that, if the customer proves that the bank did not pay the item in good faith, the preclusion under subsection (d) does not apply.

Subsection (d)(2) changes former subsection (2)(b) by adopting a 30-day period in place of a 14-day period. Although the 14-day period may have been sufficient when the original version of Article 4 was drafted in the 1950s, given the much greater volume of checks at the time of the revision, a longer period was viewed as more appropriate. The rule of subsection (d)(2) follows pre-Code case law that payment of an additional item or items bearing an unauthorized signature or alteration by the same wrongdoer is a loss suffered by the bank traceable to the customer's failure to exercise reasonable care (See Comment 1) in examining the statement and notifying the bank of objections to it. One of the most serious consequences of failure of the customer to comply with the requirements of subsection (c) is the opportunity presented to the wrongdoer to repeat the misdeeds. Conversely, one of the best ways to keep down losses in this type of situation is for the customer to promptly examine the statement and notify the bank of an unauthorized signature or alteration so that the bank will be alerted to stop paying further items. Hence, the rule of subsection (d)(2) is prescribed, and to avoid dispute a specific time limit, 30 days, is designated for cases to which the subsection applies. These considerations are not present if there are no losses resulting from the payment of additional items. In these circumstances, a reasonable period for the customer to comply with its duties under subsection (c) would depend on the circumstances (Section 1–204(2)) and the subsection (d)(2) time limit should not be imported by analogy into subsection (c).

3. Subsection (b) applies if the items are not returned to the customer. Check retention plans may include a simple payor bank check retention plan or the kind of check retention plan that would be authorized by a truncation agreement in which a collecting bank or the payee may retain the items. Even after agreeing to a check retention plan, a customer may need to see one or more checks for litigation or other purposes. The customer's request for the check may always be made to the payor bank. Under subsection (b) retaining banks may destroy items but must maintain the capacity to furnish legible copies for seven years. A legible copy may include an image of an item. This Act does not define the length of the reasonable period of time for a bank to provide the check or copy of the check. What is reasonable depends on the capacity of the bank and the needs of the customer. This Act does not specify sanctions for failure to retain or furnish the items or legible copies; this is left to other laws regulating banks. See Comment 3 to Section 4–101. Moreover, this Act does not regulate fees that banks charge their customers for furnishing items or copies or other services covered by the Act, but under principles of law such as unconscionability or good faith and fair dealing, courts have reviewed fees and the bank's exercise of a discretion to set fees. Perdue v. Crocker National Bank, 38 Cal.3d 913 (1985) (unconscionability); Best v. United Bank of Oregon, 739 P.2d 554, 562–566 (1987) (good faith and fair dealing). In addition, Section 1–203 provides that every contract or duty within this Act imposes an obligation of good faith in its performance or enforcement.

4. Subsection (e) replaces former subsection (3) and poses a modified comparative negligence test for determining liability. See the discussion on this point in the Comments to Sections 3–404, 3–405, and 3–406. The term "good faith" is defined in Section 1–201(b)(20) as including "observance of reasonable commercial standards of fair dealing." The connotation of this standard is fairness and not absence of negligence.

The term "ordinary care" used in subsection (e) is defined in Section 3–103(a)(7), made applicable to Article 4 by Section 4–104(c), to provide that sight examination by a payor bank is not required if its procedure is reasonable and is commonly followed by other comparable banks in the area. The case law is divided on this issue. The definition of "ordinary care" in Section 3–103 rejects those authorities that hold, in effect, that failure to use sight examination is negligence as a matter of law. The effect of the definition of "ordinary care" on Section 4–406 is only to provide that in the small percentage of cases in which a customer's failure to examine its statement or returned items has led to loss under subsection (d) a bank should not have to share that loss solely because it has adopted an automated collection or payment procedure in order to deal with the great volume of items at a lower cost to all customers.

5. Several changes are made in former Section 4–406(5). First, former subsection (5) is deleted and its substance is made applicable only to the one-year notice preclusion in former subsection (4) (subsection (f)). Thus if a drawer has not notified the payor bank of an unauthorized check or material alteration within the one-year period, the payor bank may not choose to recredit the drawer's account and pass the loss to the collecting banks on the theory of breach of warranty. Second, the reference in former subsection (4) to unauthorized indorsements is deleted. Section 4–406 imposes no duties on the drawer to look for unauthorized indorsements. Section 4–111 sets out a statute of limitations allowing a customer a three-year period to seek a credit to an account improperly charged by payment of an item bearing an unauthorized indorsement. Third, subsection (c) is added to Section 4–208 to assure that if a depositary bank is sued for breach of a presentment warranty, it can defend by showing that the drawer is precluded by Section 3–406 or Section 4–406(c) and (d). *Revisions approved by the Permanent Editorial Board for the Uniform Commercial Code, March 16, 1991.*

As amended in 2002.

§ 4–407. Payor Bank's Right to Subrogation on Improper Payment.

If a payor bank has paid an item over the order of the drawer or maker to stop payment, or after an account has been closed, or otherwise under circumstances giving a basis for objection by the drawer or maker, to prevent unjust enrichment and only to the extent necessary to prevent loss to the bank by reason of its payment of the item, the payor bank is subrogated to the rights

(1) of any holder in due course on the item against the drawer or maker;

(2) of the payee or any other holder of the item against the drawer or maker either on the item or under the transaction out of which the item arose; and

(3) of the drawer or maker against the payee or any other holder of the item with respect to the transaction out of which the item arose.

As amended in 1990.

Official Comment

1. Section 4–403 states that a stop-payment order or an order to close an account is binding on a bank. If a bank pays an item over such an order it is prima facie liable, but under subsection (c) of Section 4–403 the burden of establishing the fact and amount of loss from such payment is on the customer. A defense frequently interposed by a bank in an action against it for wrongful payment over a stop-payment order is that the drawer or maker suffered no loss because it would have been liable to a holder in due course in any event. On this argument some cases have held that payment cannot be stopped against a holder in due course. Payment can be stopped, but if it is, the drawer or maker is liable and the sound rule is that the bank is subrogated to the rights of the holder in due course. The preamble and paragraph (1) of this section state this rule.

2. Paragraph (2) also subrogates the bank to the rights of the payee or other holder against the drawer or maker either on the item or under the transaction out of which it arose. It may well be that the payee is not a holder in due course but still has good rights against the drawer. These may be on the check but also may not be as, for example, where the drawer buys goods from the payee and the goods are partially defective so that the payee is not entitled to the full price, but the goods are still worth a portion of the contract price. If the drawer retains the goods it is obligated to pay a part of the agreed price. If the bank has paid the check it should be subrogated to this claim of the payee against the drawer.

3. Paragraph (3) subrogates the bank to the rights of the drawer or maker against the payee or other holder with respect to the transaction out of which the item arose. If, for example, the payee was a fraudulent salesman inducing the drawer to issue a check for defective securities, and the bank pays the check over a stop-payment order but reimburses the drawer for such payment, the bank should have a basis for getting the money back from the fraudulent salesman.

4. The limitations of the preamble prevent the bank itself from getting any double recovery or benefits out of its subrogation rights conferred by the section.

5. The spelling out of the affirmative rights of the bank in this section does not destroy other existing rights (Section 1–103). Among others these may include the defense of a payor bank that by conduct in recognizing the payment a customer has ratified the bank's action in paying in disregard of a stop-payment order or right to recover money paid under a mistake.

PART 5

COLLECTION OF DOCUMENTARY DRAFTS

§ 4–501. Handling of Documentary Drafts; Duty to Send for Presentment and to Notify Customer of Dishonor.

A bank that takes a documentary draft for collection shall present or send the draft and accompanying documents for presentment and, upon learning that the draft has not been paid or accepted in due course, shall seasonably notify its customer of the fact even though it may have discounted or bought the draft or extended credit available for withdrawal as of right.

As amended in 1990.

Official Comment

This section states the duty of a bank handling a documentary draft for a customer. "Documentary draft" is defined in Section 4–104. The duty stated exists even if the bank has bought the draft. This is because to the customer the draft normally represents an underlying commercial transaction, and if that is not going through as planned the customer should know it promptly. An electronic document of title may be presented through allowing access to the document or delivery of the document. Article 1, Section 1–201 (definition of "delivery").

As amended in 2003.

§ 4–502. Presentment of "On Arrival" Drafts.

If a draft or the relevant instructions require presentment "on arrival", "when goods arrive" or the like, the collecting bank need not present until in its judgment a reasonable time for arrival of the goods has expired. Refusal to pay or accept because the goods have not arrived is not dishonor; the bank must notify its transferor of the refusal but need not present the draft again until it is instructed to do so or learns of the arrival of the goods.

As amended in 1990.

Official Comment

The section is designed to establish a definite rule for "on arrival" drafts. The term includes not only drafts drawn payable "on arrival" but also drafts forwarded with instructions to present "on arrival." The term refers to the arrival of the relevant goods. Unless a bank has actual knowledge of the arrival of the goods, as for example, when it is the "notify" party on the bill of lading, the section only requires the exercise of such judgment in estimating time as a bank may be expected to have. Commonly the buyer-drawee will want the goods and will therefore call for the documents and take up the draft when they do arrive.

§ 4–503. Responsibility of Presenting Bank for Documents and Goods; Report of Reasons for Dishonor; Referee in Case of Need.

Unless otherwise instructed and except as provided in Article 5, a bank presenting a documentary draft:

(1) must deliver the documents to the drawee on acceptance of the draft if it is payable more than three days after presentment; otherwise, only on payment; and

(2) upon dishonor, either in the case of presentment for acceptance or presentment for payment, may seek and follow instructions from any referee in case of need designated in the draft or, if the presenting bank does not choose to utilize the referee's services, it must use diligence and good faith to ascertain the reason for dishonor, must notify its transferor of the dishonor and of the results of its effort to ascertain the reasons therefor, and must request instructions.

However the presenting bank is under no obligation with respect to goods represented by the documents except to follow any reasonable instructions seasonably received; it has a right to reimbursement for any expense incurred in following instructions and to prepayment of or indemnity for those expenses.

As amended in 1990.

Official Comment

1. This section states the rules governing, in the absence of instructions, the duty of the presenting bank in case either of honor or of dishonor of a documentary draft. The section should be read in connection with Section 2–514 on when documents are deliverable on acceptance, when on payment. In the case of a dishonor of the draft, the bank, subject to Section 4–504, must return possession or control of the documents to its principal.

2. If the draft is drawn under a letter of credit, Article 5 controls. See Sections 5–109 through 5–114.

As amended in 2003.

§ 4–504. Privilege of Presenting Bank to Deal With Goods; Security Interest for Expenses.

(a) A presenting bank that, following the dishonor of a documentary draft, has seasonably requested instructions but does not receive them within a reasonable time may store, sell, or otherwise deal with the goods in any reasonable manner.

(b) For its reasonable expenses incurred by action under subsection (a) the presenting bank has a lien upon the goods or their proceeds, which may be foreclosed in the same manner as an unpaid seller's lien.

As amended in 1990.

Official Comment

The section gives the presenting bank, after dishonor, a privilege to deal with the goods in any commercially reasonable manner pending instructions from its transferor and, if still unable to communicate with its principal after a reasonable time, a right to realize its expenditures as if foreclosing on an unpaid seller's lien (Section 2–706). The provision includes situations in which storage of goods or other action becomes commercially necessary pending receipt of any requested instructions, even if the requested instructions are later received.

The "reasonable manner" referred to means one reasonable in the light of business factors and the judgment of a business man.

UCC ARTICLE 4A

FUNDS TRANSFERS

2001 amendments (Article 1 revision) . . . .*Appendix A*

PART 1. SUBJECT MATTER AND DEFINITIONS

Section

4A–101. Short Title.
4A–102. Subject Matter.
4A–103. Payment Order—Definitions.
4A–104. Funds Transfer—Definitions.
4A–105. Other Definitions.
4A–106. Time Payment Order Is Received.
4A–107. Federal Reserve Regulations and Operating Circulars.
4A–108. Exclusion of Consumer Transactions Governed by Federal Law.

PART 2. ISSUE AND ACCEPTANCE OF PAYMENT ORDER

4A–201. Security Procedure.
4A–202. Authorized and Verified Payment Orders.
4A–203. Unenforceability of Certain Verified Payment Orders.
4A–204. Refund of Payment and Duty of Customer to Report With Respect to Unauthorized Payment Order.
4A–205. Erroneous Payment Orders.
4A–206. Transmission of Payment Order Through Funds-Transfer or Other Communication System.
4A–207. Misdescription of Beneficiary.
4A–208. Misdescription of Intermediary Bank or Beneficiary's Bank.
4A–209. Acceptance of Payment Order.
4A–210. Rejection of Payment Order.
4A–211. Cancellation and Amendment of Payment Order.
4A–212. Liability and Duty of Receiving Bank Regarding Unaccepted Payment Order.

PART 3. EXECUTION OF SENDER'S PAYMENT ORDER BY RECEIVING BANK

4A–301. Execution and Execution Date.
4A–302. Obligations of Receiving Bank in Execution of Payment Order.

Section

4A–303. Erroneous Execution of Payment Order.
4A–304. Duty of Sender to Report Erroneously Executed Payment Order.
4A–305. Liability for Late or Improper Execution or Failure to Execute Payment Order.

PART 4. PAYMENT

4A–401. Payment Date.
4A–402. Obligation of Sender to Pay Receiving Bank.
4A–403. Payment by Sender to Receiving Bank.
4A–404. Obligation of Beneficiary's Bank to Pay and Give Notice to Beneficiary.
4A–405. Payment by Beneficiary's Bank to Beneficiary.
4A–406. Payment by Originator to Beneficiary; Discharge of Underlying Obligation.

PART 5. MISCELLANEOUS PROVISIONS

4A–501. Variation by Agreement and Effect of Funds-Transfer System Rule.
4A–502. Creditor Process Served on Receiving Bank; Set-off by Beneficiary's Bank.
4A–503. Injunction or Restraining Order With Respect to Funds Transfer.
4A–504. Order in Which Items and Payment Orders May Be Charged to Account; Order of Withdrawals From Account.
4A–505. Preclusion of Objection to Debit of Customer's Account.
4A–506. Rate of Interest.
4A–507. Choice of Law.

National Conference of Commissioners on Uniform State Laws

REPORTER

Robert L. Jordan, Los Angeles, California

William D. Warren, Los Angeles, California

DRAFTING COMMITTEE
CO–CHAIRMEN

Carlyle C. Ring, Jr., Alexandria, Virginia

Robert Haydock, Jr., Boston, Massachusetts

MEMBERS

Boris Auerbach, Cincinnati, Ohio

Richard F. Dole, Jr., Houston, Texas

William E. Hogan, New York, New York

Charles W. Joiner, Ann Arbor, Michigan

Frederick H. Miller, Norman, Oklahoma

Donald J. Rapson, Livingston, New Jersey, *The American Law Institute Representative*

Michael P. Sullivan, Minneapolis, Minnesota, *President, (Member Ex Officio)*

Neal Ossen, Hartford, Connecticut, *Chairman, Division C, (Member Ex Officio)*

REVIEW COMMITTEE
CHAIRMAN

Frank F. Jestrab, Chevy Chase, Maryland

MEMBERS

Rupert R. Bullivant, Portland, Oregon

Michael Franck, Lansing, Michigan

CONSULTANT

Fairfax Leary, Jr., Villanova, Pennsylvania

ADVISORS

Thomas C. Baxter, Jr., Federal Reserve Bank of New York

Roland E. Brandel, American Bar Association

Leon P. Ciferni, National Westminster Bank, U.S.A.

William B. Davenport, American Bar Association, Section of Business Law, Ad Hoc Committee on Payment Systems

Carl Felsenfeld, Association of the Bar of the City of New York

J. Kevin French, Exxon Company, U.S.A.

Thomas J. Greco, American Bankers Association

Arthur L. Herold, National Corporate Cash Management Association

John R. H. Kimball, Federal Reserve Bank of Boston

John F. Lee, New York Clearing House Association

W. Robert Moore, American Bankers Association

Ernest T. Patrikis, Federal Reserve Bank of New York

Richard B. Wagner, General Motors Corporation

ADDITIONAL PARTICIPANTS

Dean Bitner, Sears, Roebuck & Company

Henry N. Dyhouse, U.S. Central Credit Union

James Foorman, First Chicago Corporation

Richard M. Gottlieb, Manufacturers Hanover Trust Company

Shirley Holder, Atlantic Richfield Company

Paul E. Homrighausen, Bankers Clearing House Association and National Automated Clearing House Association

Gail M. Inaba, Morgan Guaranty Trust Company of New York

Oliver I. Ireland, Board of Governors of Federal Reserve System

Richard P. Kessler, Jr., Credit Union National Association

James W. Kopp, Shell Oil Company

Robert M. MacAllister, Chase Manhattan Bank NA

Thomas E. Montgomery, California Bankers Association

Norman R. Nelson, New York Clearing House Association

Samuel Newman, Manufacturers Hanover Trust Company

Nena Nodge, National Corporate Cash Management Association

Robert J. Pisapia, Occidental Petroleum Corporation

Deborah S. Prutzman, Arnold & Porter

Robert M. Rosenblith, Manufacturers Hanover Trust Company

Paul S. Turner, Occidental Petroleum Corporation

ARTICLE 4A

Irma Villarreal, Aon Corporation

Suzanne Weakley, Atlantic Richfield Company

PREFATORY NOTE

The National Conference of Commissioners on Uniform State laws and The American Law Institute have approved a new Article 4A to the Uniform Commercial Code. Comments that follow each of the sections of the statute are intended as official comments. They explain in detail the purpose and meaning of the various sections and the policy considerations on which they are based.

Description of transaction covered by Article 4A.

There are a number of mechanisms for making payments through the banking system. Most of these mechanisms are covered in whole or part by state or federal statutes. In terms of number of transactions, payments made by check or credit card are the most common payment methods. Payment by check is covered by Articles 3 and 4 of the UCC and some aspects of payment by credit card are covered by federal law. In recent years electronic funds transfers have been increasingly common in consumer transactions. For example, in some cases a retail customer can pay for purchases by use of an access or debit card inserted in a terminal at the retail store that allows the bank account of the customer to be instantly debited. Some aspects of these point-of-sale transactions and other consumer payments that are effected electronically are covered by a federal statute, the Electronic Fund Transfer Act (EFTA). If any part of a funds transfer is covered by EFTA, the entire funds transfer is excluded from Article 4A.

Another type of payment, commonly referred to as a wholesale wire transfer, is the primary focus of Article 4A. Payments that are covered by Article 4A are overwhelmingly between business or financial institutions. The dollar volume of payments made by wire transfer far exceeds the dollar volume of payments made by other means. The volume of payments by wire transfer over the two principal wire payment systems—the Federal Reserve wire transfer network (Fedwire) and the New York Clearing House Interbank Payments Systems (CHIPS)—exceeds one trillion dollars per day. Most payments carried out by use of automated clearing houses are consumer payments covered by EFTA and therefore not covered by Article 4A. There is, however, a significant volume of nonconsumer ACH payments that closely resemble wholesale wire transfers. These payments are also covered by Article 4A.

There is some resemblance between payments made by wire transfer and payments made by other means such as paper-based checks and credit cards or electronically-based consumer payments, but there are also many differences. Article 4A excludes from its coverage these other payment mechanisms. Article 4A follows a policy of treating the transaction that it covers—a "funds transfer"—as a unique method of payment that is governed by unique principles of law that address the operational and policy issues presented by this kind of payment.

The funds transfer that is covered by Article 4A is not a complex transaction and can be illustrated by the following example which is used throughout the Prefatory Note as a basis for discussion. X, a debtor, wants to pay an obligation owed to Y. Instead of delivering to Y a negotiable instrument such as a check or some other writing such as a credit card slip that enables Y to obtain payment from a bank, X transmits an instruction to X's bank to credit a sum of money to the bank account of Y. In most cases X's bank and Y's bank are different banks. X's bank may carry out X's instruction by instructing Y's bank to credit Y's account in the amount that X requested. The instruction that X issues to its bank is a "payment order." X is the "sender" of the payment order and X's bank is the "receiving bank" with respect to X's order. Y is the "beneficiary" of X's order. When X's bank issues an instruction to Y's bank to carry out X's payment order, X's bank "executes" X's order. The instruction of X's bank to Y's bank is also a payment order. With respect to that order, X's bank is the sender, Y's bank is the receiving bank, and Y is the beneficiary. The

405

entire series of transactions by which X pays Y is knows as the "funds transfer." With respect to the funds transfer, X is the "originator," X's bank is the "originator's bank," Y is the "beneficiary" and Y's bank is the "beneficiary's bank." In more complex transactions there are one or more additional banks known as "intermediary banks" between X's bank and Y's bank. In the funds transfer the instruction contained in the payment order of X to its bank is carried out by a series of payment orders by each bank in the transmission chain to the next bank in the chain until Y's bank receives a payment order to make the credit to Y's account. In most cases, the payment order of each bank to the next bank in the chain is transmitted electronically, and often the payment order of X to its bank is also transmitted electronically, but the means of transmission does not have any legal significance. A payment order may be transmitted by any means, and in some cases the payment order is transmitted by a slow means such as first class mail. To reflect this fact, the broader term "funds transfer" rather than the narrower term "wire transfer" is used in Article 4A to describe the overall payment transaction.

Funds transfers are divided into two categories determined by whether the instruction to pay is given by the person making payment or the person receiving payment. If the instruction is given by the person making the payment, the transfer is commonly referred to as a "credit transfer." If the instruction is given by the person receiving payment, the transfer is commonly referred to as a "debit transfer." Article 4A governs credit transfers and excludes debit transfers.

Why is Article 4A needed?

There is no comprehensive body of law that defines the rights and obligations that arise from wire transfers. Some aspects of wire transfers are governed by rules of the principal transfer systems. Transfers made by Fedwire are governed by Federal Reserve Regulation J and transfers over CHIPS are governed by the CHIPS rules. Transfers made by means of automated clearing houses are governed by uniform rules adopted by various associations of banks in various parts of the nation or by Federal Reserve rules or operating circulars. But the various

funds transfer system rules apply to only limited aspects of wire transfer transactions. The resolution of the many issues that are not covered by funds transfer system rules depends on contracts of the parties, to the extent that they exist, or principles of law applicable to other payment mechanisms that might be applied by analogy. The result is a great deal of uncertainty. There is no consensus about the juridical nature of a wire transfer and consequently of the rights and obligations that are created. Article 4A is intended to provide the comprehensive body of law that we do not have today.

Characteristics of a funds transfer.

There are a number of characteristics of funds transfers covered by Article 4A that have influenced the drafting of the statute. The typical funds transfer involves a large amount of money. Multimillion dollar transactions are commonplace. The originator of the transfer and the beneficiary are typically sophisticated business or financial organizations. High speed is another predominant characteristic. Most funds transfers are completed on the same day, even in complex transactions in which there are several intermediary banks in the transmission chain. A funds transfer is a highly efficient substitute for payments made by the delivery of paper instruments. Another characteristic is extremely low cost. A transfer that involves many millions of dollars can be made for a price of a few dollars. Price does not normally vary very much or at all with the amount of the transfer. This system of pricing may not be feasible if the bank is exposed to very large liabilities in connection with the transaction. The pricing system assumes that the price reflects primarily the cost of the mechanical operation performed by the bank, but in fact, a bank may have more or less potential liability with respect to a funds transfer depending upon the amount of the transfer. Risk of loss to banks carrying out a funds transfer may arise from a variety of causes. In some funds transfers, there may be extensions of very large amounts of credit for short periods of time by the banks that carry out a funds transfer. If a payment order is issued to the beneficiary's bank, it is normal for the bank to release funds to the beneficiary immediately. Sometimes, payment to the beneficiary's bank by the bank that issued the order to the beneficiary's bank is delayed until the end of the day. If that payment is not received because of the insolvency of the bank that is obliged to pay, the beneficiary's bank may suffer a loss. There is also risk of loss if a bank fails to execute the payment order of a customer, or if the order is executed late. There also may be an error in the payment order issued by a bank that is executing the payment order of its customer. For example, the error might relate to the amount to be paid or to the identity of the person to be paid. Because the dollar amounts involved in funds transfers are so large, the risk of loss if something goes wrong in a transaction may also be very large. A major policy issue in the drafting of Article 4A is that of determining how risk of loss is to be allocated given the price structure in the industry.

Concept of acceptance and effect of acceptance by the beneficiary's bank.

Rights and obligations under Article 4A arise as the result of "acceptance" of a payment order by the bank to which the order is addressed. Section 4A–209. The effect of acceptance varies depending upon whether the payment order is issued to the beneficiary's bank or to a bank other than the beneficiary's bank. Acceptance by the beneficiary's bank is particularly important because it defines when the beneficiary's bank becomes obligated to the beneficiary to pay the amount of the payment order. Although Article 4A follows convention in using the term "funds transfer" to identify the payment from X to Y that is described above, no money or property right of X is actually transferred to Y. X pays Y by causing Y's bank to become indebted to Y in the amount of the payment. This debt arises when Y's bank accepts the payment order that X's bank issued to Y's bank to execute X's order. If the funds transfer was carried out by use of one or more intermediary banks between X's bank and Y's bank, Y's bank becomes indebted to Y when Y's bank accepts the payment order issued to it by an intermediary bank. The funds transfer is completed when this debt is incurred. Acceptance, the event that determines when the debt of Y's bank to Y arises, occurs (i) when Y's bank pays Y or notifies Y of receipt of the payment order, or (ii) when Y's bank receives pay-

ment from the bank that issued a payment order to Y's bank.

The only obligation of the beneficiary's bank that results from acceptance of a payment order is to pay the amount of the order to the beneficiary. No obligation is owed to either the sender of the payment order accepted by the beneficiary's bank or to the originator of the funds transfer. The obligation created by acceptance by the beneficiary's bank is for the benefit of the beneficiary. The purpose of the sender's payment order is to effect payment by the originator to the beneficiary and that purpose is achieved when the beneficiary's bank accepts the payment order. Section 4A–405 states rules for determining when the obligation of the beneficiary's bank to the beneficiary has been paid.

Acceptance by a bank other than the beneficiary's bank.

In the funds transfer described above, what is the obligation of X's bank when it receives X's payment order? Funds transfers by a bank on behalf of its customer are made pursuant to an agreement or arrangement that may or may not be reduced to a formal document signed by the parties. It is probably true that in most cases there is either no express agreement or the agreement addresses only some aspects of the transaction. Substantial risk is involved in funds transfers and a bank may not be willing to give this service to all customers, and may not be willing to offer it to any customer unless certain safeguards against loss such as security procedures are in effect. Funds transfers often involve the giving of credit by the receiving bank to the customer, and that also may involve an agreement. These considerations are reflected in Article 4A by the principle that, in the absence of a contrary agreement, a receiving bank does not incur liability with respect to a payment order until it accepts it. If X and X's bank in the hypothetical case had an agreement that obliged the bank to act on X's payment orders and the bank failed to comply with the agreement, the bank can be held liable for breach of the agreement. But apart from any obligation arising by agreement, the bank does not incur any liability with respect to X's payment order until the bank accepts the order. X's payment order is treated by Article 4A as a request by X to the bank to take action that will cause X's payment order to be carried out. That request can be accepted by X's bank by "executing" X's payment order. Execution occurs when X's bank sends a payment order to Y's bank intended by X's bank to carry out the payment order of X. X's bank could also execute X's payment order by issuing a payment order to an intermediary bank instructing the intermediary bank to instruct Y's bank to make the credit to Y's account. In that case execution and acceptance of X's order occur when the payment order of X's bank is sent to the intermediary bank. When X's bank executes X's payment order the bank is entitled to receive payment from X and may debit an authorized account of X. If X's bank does not execute X's order and the amount of the order is covered by a withdrawable credit balance in X's authorized account, the bank must pay X interest on the money represented by X's order unless X is given prompt notice of rejection of the order. Section 4A–210(b).

Bank error in funds transfers.

If a bank, other than the beneficiary's bank, accepts a payment order, the obligations and liabilities are owed to the originator of the funds transfer. Assume in the example stated above, that X's bank executes X's payment order by issuing a payment order to an intermediary bank that executes the order of X's bank by issuing a payment order to Y's bank. The obligations of X's bank with respect to execution are owed to X. The obligations of the intermediary bank with respect to execution are also owed to X. Section 4A–302 states standards with respect to the time and manner of execution of payment orders. Section 4A–305 states the measure of damages for improper execution. It also states that a receiving bank is liable for damages if it fails to execute a payment order that it was obliged by express agreement to execute. In each case consequential damages are not recoverable unless an express agreement of the receiving bank provides for them. The policy basis for this limitation is discussed in Comment 2 to Section 4A–305.

Error in the consummation of a funds transfer is not uncommon. There may be a discrepancy in the amount that the originator orders to be paid to the beneficiary and the amount that the beneficiary's bank is ordered to pay. For example, if the originator's payment order instructs payment of $100,000 and the payment order of the originator's bank instructs payment of $1,000,000, the originator's bank is entitled to receive only $100,000 from the originator and has the burden of recovering the additional $900,000 paid to the beneficiary by mistake. In some cases the originator's bank or an intermediary bank instructs payment to a beneficiary other than the beneficiary stated in the originator's payment order. If the wrong beneficiary is paid the bank that issued the erroneous payment order is not entitled to receive payment of the payment order that it executed and has the burden of recovering the mistaken payment. The originator is not obliged to pay its payment order. Section 4A–303 and Section 4A–207 state rules for determining the rights and obligations of the various parties to the funds transfer in these cases and in other typical cases in which error is made.

Pursuant to Section 4A–402(c) the originator is excused from the obligation to pay the originator's bank if the funds transfer is not completed, i.e. payment by the originator to the beneficiary is not made. Payment by the originator to the beneficiary occurs when the beneficiary's bank accepts a payment order for the benefit of the beneficiary of the originator's payment order. Section 4A–406. If for any reason that acceptance does not occur, the originator is not required to pay the payment order that it issued or, if it already paid, is entitled to refund of the payment with interest. This "money-back guarantee" is an important protection of the originator of a funds transfer. The same rule applies to any other sender in the funds transfer. Each sender's obligation to pay is excused if the beneficiary's bank does not accept a payment order for the benefit of the beneficiary of that sender's order. There is an important exception to this rule. It is common practice for the originator of a funds transfer to designate the intermediary bank or banks through which the funds transfer is to be routed. The originator's bank is required by Section 4A–302 to follow the instruction of the originator with respect to intermediary banks. If the originator's bank sends a payment order to the intermediary bank designated in the originator's order and the intermediary bank causes the funds transfer to miscarry by failing to execute the payment order or by instructing payment to the wrong beneficiary, the originator's bank is not required to pay its payment order and if it has already paid it is entitled to recover payment from the intermediary bank. This remedy is normally adequate, but if the originator's bank already paid its order and the intermediary bank has suspended payments or is not permitted by law to refund payment, the originator's bank will suffer a loss. Since the originator required the originator's bank to use the failed intermediary bank, Section 4A–402(e) provides that in this case the originator is obliged to pay its payment order and has a claim against the intermediary bank for the amount of the order. The same principle applies to any other sender that designates a subsequent intermediary bank.

Unauthorized payment orders.

An important issue addressed in Section 4A–202 and Section 4A–203 is how the risk of loss from unauthorized payment orders is to be allocated. In a large percentage of cases, the payment order of the originator of the funds transfer is transmitted electronically to the originator's bank. In these cases it may not be possible for the bank to know whether the electronic message has been authorized by its customer. To ensure that no unauthorized person is transmitting messages to the bank, the normal practice is to establish security procedures that usually involve the use of codes or identifying numbers or words. If the bank accepts a payment order that purports to be that of its customer after verifying its authenticity by complying with a security procedure agreed to by the customer and the bank, the customer is bound to pay the order even if it was not authorized. But there is an important limitation on this rule. The bank is entitled to payment in the case of an unauthorized order only if the court finds that the security procedure was a commercially reasonable method of providing security against unauthorized payment orders. The customer can also avoid liability if it can prove that the unauthorized order was not initiated by an employee or other agent of the customer having access to confidential security information or by a person who obtained that information from a source controlled by the customer. The policy issues are discussed in the comments following Section 4A–203. If the bank accepts an unauthorized payment order without verifying it in compliance with a security procedure, the loss falls on the bank.

Security procedures are also important in cases of error in the transmission of payment orders. There may be an error by the sender in the amount of the order, or a sender may transmit a payment order and then erroneously transmit a duplicate of the order. Normally, the sender is bound by the payment order even if it is issued by mistake. But in some cases an error of this kind can be detected by a security procedure. Although the receiving bank is not obliged to provide a security procedure for the detection of error, if such a procedure is agreed to by the bank Section 4A–205 provides that if the error is not detected because the receiving bank does not comply with the procedure, any resulting loss is borne by the bank failing to comply with the security procedure.

Insolvency losses.

Some payment orders do not involve the granting of credit to the sender by the receiving bank. In those cases, the receiving bank accepts the sender's order at the same time the bank receives payment of the order. This is true of a transfer of funds by Fedwire or of cases in which the receiving bank can debit a funded account of the sender. But in some cases the granting of credit is the norm. This is true of a payment order over CHIPS. In a CHIPS transaction the receiving bank usually will accept the order before receiving payment from the sending bank. Payment is delayed until the end of the day when settlement is made through the Federal Reserve System. If the receiving bank is an intermediary bank, it will accept by issuing a payment order to another bank and the intermediary bank is obliged to pay that payment order. If the receiving bank is the beneficiary's bank, the bank usually will accept by releasing funds to the beneficiary before the bank has received payment. If a sending bank suspends payments before settling its liabilities at the end of the day, the financial stability of banks that are net creditors of the insolvent bank may also be put into jeopardy, because the dollar volume of funds transfers between the banks may be extremely large. With respect to two banks that are dealing with each other in a series of transactions in which each bank is sometimes a receiving bank and sometimes a sender, the risk of insolvency can be managed if amounts payable as a sender and amounts receivable as a receiving bank are roughly equal. But if these amounts are significantly out of balance, a net creditor bank may have a very significant credit risk during the day before settlement occurs. The Federal Reserve System and the banking community are greatly concerned with this risk, and various measures have been instituted to reduce this credit exposure. Article 4A also addresses this problem. A receiving bank can always avoid this risk by delaying acceptance of a payment order until after the bank has received payment. For example, if the beneficiary's bank credits the beneficiary's account it can avoid acceptance by not notifying the beneficiary of the receipt of the order or by notifying the beneficiary that the credit may not be withdrawn until the beneficiary's bank receives payment. But if the beneficiary's bank releases funds to the beneficiary before receiving settlement, the result in a funds transfer other than a transfer by means of an automated clearing house or similar provisional settlement system is that the beneficiary's bank may not recover the funds if it fails to receive settlement. This rule encourages the banking system to impose credit limitations on banks that issue payment orders. These limitations are already in effect. CHIPS has also proposed a loss-sharing plan to be adopted for implementation in the second half of 1990 under which CHIPS participants will be required to provide funds necessary to complete settlement of the obligations of one or more participants that are unable to meet settlement obligations. Under this plan, it will be a virtual certainty that there will be settlement on CHIPS in the event of failure by a single bank. Section 4A–403(b) and (c) are also addressed to reducing risks of insolvency. Under these provisions the amount owed by a failed bank with respect to payment orders it issued is the net amount owing after setting off amounts owed to the failed bank with respect to payment orders it received. This rule allows credit exposure to be managed by limitations on the net debit position of a bank.

International transfers.

The major international legal document dealing with the subject of electronic funds transfers is the Model Law on International Credit Transfers adopted in 1992 by the United Nations Commission on International Trade Law. It covers basically the same type of transaction as does Article 4A, although it requires the funds transferred to have an international component. The Model Law and Article 4A basically live together in harmony, but to the extent there are differences they must be recognized and, to the extent possible, avoided or adjusted by agreement. See PEB Commentary No. 13, dated February 16, 1994 [Appendix V, infra].

PART 1

SUBJECT MATTER AND DEFINITIONS

§ 4A–101. Short Title.

This Article may be cited as Uniform Commercial Code—Funds Transfers.

§ 4A–102. Subject Matter.

Except as otherwise provided in Section 4A–108, this Article applies to funds transfers defined in Section 4A–104.

Official Comment

Article 4A governs a specialized method of payment referred to in the Article as a funds transfer but also commonly referred to in the commercial community as a wholesale wire transfer. A funds transfer is made by means of one or more payment orders. The scope of Article 4A is determined by the definitions of "payment order" and "funds transfer" found in Section 4A–103 and Section 4A–104.

The funds transfer governed by Article 4A is in large part a product of recent and developing technological changes. Before this Article was drafted there was no comprehensive body of law—statutory or judicial—that defined the juridical nature of a funds transfer or the rights and obligations flowing from payment orders. Judicial authority with respect to funds transfers is sparse, undeveloped and not uniform. Judges have had to resolve disputes by referring to general principles of common law or equity, or they have sought guidance in statutes such as Article 4 which are applicable to other payment methods. But attempts to define rights and obligations in funds transfers by general principles or by analogy to rights and obligations in negotiable instrument law or the law of check collection have not been satisfactory.

In the drafting of Article 4A, a deliberate decision was made to write on a clean slate and to treat a funds transfer as a unique method of payment to be governed by unique rules that address the particular issues raised by this method of payment. A deliberate decision was also made to use precise and detailed rules to assign responsibility, define behavioral norms, allocate risks and establish limits on liability, rather than to rely on broadly stated, flexible principles. In the drafting of these rules, a critical consideration was that the various parties to funds transfers need to be able to predict risk with certainty, to insure against risk, to adjust operational and security procedures, and to price funds transfer services appropriately. This consideration is particularly important given the very large amounts of money that are involved in funds transfers.

Funds transfers involve competing interests—those of the banks that provide funds transfer services and the commercial and financial organizations that use the services, as well as the public interest. These competing interests were represented in the drafting process and they were thoroughly considered. The rules that emerged represent a careful and delicate balancing of those interests and are intended to be the exclusive means of determining the rights, duties and liabilities of the affected parties in any situation covered by particular provisions of the Article. Consequently, resort to principles of law or equity outside of Article 4A is not appropriate to create rights, duties and liabilities inconsistent with those stated in this Article.

§ 4A–103. Payment Order—Definitions.

(a) In this Article:

(1) "Payment order" means an instruction of a sender to a receiving bank, transmitted orally, electronically, or in writing, to pay, or to cause another bank to pay, a fixed or determinable amount of money to a beneficiary if:

   (i) the instruction does not state a condition to payment to the beneficiary other than time of payment,

   (ii) the receiving bank is to be reimbursed by debiting an account of, or otherwise receiving payment from, the sender, and

   (iii) the instruction is transmitted by the sender directly to the receiving bank or to an agent, funds-transfer system, or communication system for transmittal to the receiving bank.

(2) "Beneficiary" means the person to be paid by the beneficiary's bank.

(3) "Beneficiary's bank" means the bank identified in a payment order in which an account of the beneficiary is to be credited pursuant to the order or which otherwise is to make payment to the beneficiary if the order does not provide for payment to an account.

(4) "Receiving bank" means the bank to which the sender's instruction is addressed.

(5) "Sender" means the person giving the instruction to the receiving bank.

(b) If an instruction complying with subsection (a)(1) is to make more than one payment to a beneficiary, the instruction is a separate payment order with respect to each payment.

(c) A payment order is issued when it is sent to the receiving bank.

Official Comment

This section is discussed in the Comment following Section 4A–104.

§ 4A–104. Funds Transfer—Definitions.

In this Article:

(a) "Funds transfer" means the series of transactions, beginning with the originator's payment order, made for the purpose of making payment to the beneficiary of the order. The term includes any payment order issued by the originator's bank or an intermediary bank intended to carry out the originator's payment order. A funds transfer is completed by acceptance by the beneficiary's bank of a payment order for the benefit of the beneficiary of the originator's payment order.

(b) "Intermediary bank" means a receiving bank other than the originator's bank or the beneficiary's bank.

(c) "Originator" means the sender of the first payment order in a funds transfer.

(d) "Originator's bank" means (i) the receiving bank to which the payment order of the originator is issued if the originator is not a bank, or (ii) the originator if the originator is a bank.

Official Comment

1. Article 4A governs a method of payment in which the person making payment (the "originator") directly transmits an instruction to a bank either to make payment to the person receiving payment (the "beneficiary") or to instruct some other bank to make payment to the beneficiary. The payment from the originator to the beneficiary occurs when the bank that is to pay the beneficiary becomes obligated to pay the beneficiary. There are two basic definitions: "Payment order" stated in Section 4A–103 and "Funds transfer" stated in Section 4A–104. These definitions, other related definitions, and the scope of Article 4A can best be understood in the context of specific fact situations. Consider the following cases:

Case #1. X, which has an account in Bank A, instructs that bank to pay $1,000,000 to Y's account in Bank A. Bank A carries out X's instruction by making a credit of $1,000,000 to Y's account and notifying Y that the credit is available for immediate withdrawal. The instruction by X to Bank A is a "payment order" which was issued when it was sent to Bank A. Section 4A–103(a)(1) and (c). X is the "sender" of the payment order and Bank A is the "receiving bank." Section 4A–103(a)(5) and (a)(4). Y is the "beneficiary" of the payment order and Bank A is the "beneficiary's bank." Section 4A–103(a)(2) and (a)(3). When Bank A notified Y of receipt of the payment order, Bank A "accepted" the payment order. Section 4A–209(b)(1). When Bank A accepted the order it incurred an obligation to Y to pay the amount of the order. Section 4A–404(a). When Bank A accepted X's order, X incurred an obligation to pay Bank A the amount of the order. Section 4A–402(b). Payment from X to Bank A would normally be made by a debit to X's account in Bank A. Section 4A–403(a)(3). At the time Bank A incurred the obligation to pay Y, payment of $1,000,000 by X to Y was also made. Section 4A–406(a). Bank A paid Y when it gave notice to Y of a withdrawable credit of $1,000,000 to Y's account. Sec-

tion 4A–405(a). The overall transaction, which comprises the acts of X and Bank A, in which the payment by X to Y is accomplished is referred to as the "funds transfer." Section 4A–104(a). In this case only one payment order was involved in the funds transfer. A one-payment-order funds transfer is usually referred to as a "book transfer" because the payment is accomplished by the receiving bank's debiting the account of the sender and crediting the account of the beneficiary in the same bank. X, in addition to being the sender of the payment order to Bank A, is the "originator" of the funds transfer. Section 4A–104(c). Bank A is the "originator's bank" in the funds transfer as well as the beneficiary's bank. Section 4A–104(d).

Case #2. Assume the same facts as in Case #1 except that X instructs Bank A to pay $1,000,000 to Y's account in Bank B. With respect to this payment order, X is the sender, Y is the beneficiary, and Bank A is the receiving bank. Bank A carries out X's order by instructing Bank B to pay $1,000,000 to Y's account. This instruction is a payment order in which Bank A is the sender, Bank B is the receiving bank, and Y is the beneficiary. When Bank A issued its payment order to Bank B, Bank A "executed" X's order. Section 4A–301(a). In the funds transfer, X is the originator, Bank A is the originator's bank, and Bank B is the beneficiary's bank. When Bank A executed X's order, X incurred an obligation to pay Bank A the amount of the order. Section 4A–402(c). When Bank B accepts the payment order issued to it by Bank A, Bank B incurs an obligation to Y to pay the amount of the order (Section 4A–404(a)) and Bank A incurs an obligation to pay Bank B. Section 4A–402(b). Acceptance by Bank B also results in payment of $1,000,000 by X to Y. Section 4A–406(a). In this case two payment orders are involved in the funds transfer.

Case #3. Assume the same facts as in Case #2 except that Bank A does not execute X's payment order by issuing a payment order to Bank B. One bank will not normally act to carry out a funds transfer for another bank unless there is a preexisting arrangement between the banks for transmittal of payment orders and settlement of accounts. For example, if Bank B is a foreign bank with which Bank A has no relationship, Bank A can utilize a bank that is a correspondent of both Bank A and Bank B. Assume Bank A issues a payment order to Bank C to pay $1,000,000 to Y's account in Bank B. With respect to this order, Bank A is the sender, Bank C is the receiving bank, and Y is the beneficiary. Bank C will execute the payment order of Bank A by issuing a payment order to Bank B to pay $1,000,000 to Y's account in Bank B. With respect to Bank C's payment order, Bank C is the sender, Bank B is the receiving bank, and Y is the beneficiary. Payment of $1,000,000 by X to Y occurs when Bank B accepts the payment order issued to it by Bank C. In this case the funds transfer involves three payment orders. In the funds transfer, X is the originator, Bank A is the originator's bank, Bank B is the beneficiary's bank, and Bank C is an "intermediary bank." Section 4A–104(b). In some cases there may be more than one intermediary bank, and in those cases each intermediary bank is treated like Bank C in Case #3.

As the three cases demonstrate, a payment under Article 4A involves an overall transaction, the funds transfer, in which the originator, X, is making payment to the beneficiary, Y, but the funds transfer may encompass a series of payment orders that are issued in order to effect the payment initiated by the originator's payment order.

In some cases the originator and the beneficiary may be the same person. This will occur, for example, when a corporation orders a bank to transfer funds from an account of the corporation in that bank to another account of the corporation in that bank or in some other bank. In some funds transfers the first bank to issue a payment order is a bank that is executing a payment order of a customer that is not a bank. In this case the customer is the originator. In other cases, the first bank to issue a payment order is not acting for a customer, but is making a payment for its own account. In that event the first bank to issue a payment order is the originator as well as the originator's bank.

2. "Payment order" is defined in Section 4A–103(a)(1) as an instruction to a bank to pay, or to cause another bank to pay, a fixed or determinable amount of money. The bank to which the instruction is addressed is known as the "receiving bank." Section 4A–103(a)(4). "Bank" is defined in Section 4A–105(a)(2). The effect of this definition is to limit Article 4A to payments made through the banking system. A transfer of funds made by an entity outside the banking system is excluded. A transfer of funds through an entity other than a bank is usually a consumer transaction involving relatively small amounts of money and a single contract carried out by transfers of cash or a cash equivalent such as a check. Typically, the transferor delivers cash or a check to the company making the transfer, which agrees to pay a like amount to a person designated by the transferor. Transactions covered by Article 4A typically involve very large amounts of money in which several transactions involving several banks may be necessary to carry out the payment. Payments are normally made by debits or credits to bank accounts. Originators and beneficiaries are almost always business organizations and the transfers are usually made to pay obligations. Moreover, these transactions are frequently done on the basis of very short-term credit granted by the receiving bank to the sender of the payment order. Wholesale wire transfers involve policy questions that are distinct from those involved in consumer-based transactions by nonbanks.

3. Further limitations on the scope of Article 4A are found in the three requirements found in subparagraphs (i), (ii), and (iii) of Section 4A–103(a)(1). Subparagraph (i) states that the instruction to pay is a payment order only if it "does not state a condition to payment to the beneficiary other than time of payment." An instruction to pay a beneficiary sometimes is subject to a requirement that the beneficiary perform some act such as delivery of documents. For example, a New York bank may have issued a letter of credit in favor of X, a California seller of goods to be shipped to the New York bank's customer in New York. The terms of the letter of credit provide for payment to X if documents are presented to prove shipment of the goods. Instead of providing for presentment of the documents to the New York bank, the letter of credit states that they may be presented to a California bank that acts as an agent for payment. The New York bank sends an instruction to the California bank to pay X upon presentation of the required documents. The instruction is not covered by Article 4A because payment to the beneficiary is conditional upon receipt of shipping documents. The function of banks in a funds transfer under Article 4A is comparable to the role of banks in the collection and payment of checks in that it is essentially mechanical in nature. The low price and high speed that characterize funds transfers reflect this fact. Conditions to payment by the California bank other than time of payment impose responsibilities on that bank that go beyond those in Article 4A funds transfers. Although the payment by the New York bank to X under the letter of credit is not covered by Article 4A, if X is paid by the California bank, payment of the obligation of the New York bank to reimburse the California bank could be made by an Article 4A funds transfer. In such a case there is a distinction between the payment by the New York bank to X under the letter of credit and the payment by the New York bank to the California bank. For example, if the New York bank pays its reimbursement obligation to the California bank by a Fedwire naming the California bank as beneficiary (see Comment 1 to Section 4A–107), payment is made to the California

bank rather than to X. That payment is governed by Article 4A and it could be made either before or after payment by the California bank to X. The payment by the New York bank to X under the letter of credit is not governed by Article 4A and it occurs when the California bank, as agent of the New York bank, pays X. No payment order was involved in that transaction. In this example, if the New York bank had erroneously sent an instruction to the California bank unconditionally instructing payment to X, the instruction would have been an Article 4A payment order. If the payment order was accepted (Section 4A–209(b)) by the California bank, a payment by the New York bank to X would have resulted (Section 4A–406(a)). But Article 4A would not prevent recovery of funds from X on the basis that X was not entitled to retain the funds under the law of mistake and restitution, letter of credit law or other applicable law.

4. Transfers of funds made through the banking system are commonly referred to as either "credit" transfers or "debit" transfers. In a credit transfer the instruction to pay is given by the person making payment. In a debit transfer the instruction to pay is given by the person receiving payment. The purpose of subparagraph (ii) of subsection (a)(1) of Section 4A–103 is to include credit transfers in Article 4A and to exclude debit transfers. All of the instructions to pay in the three cases described in Comment 1 fall within subparagraph (ii). Take Case #2 as an example. With respect to X's instruction given to Bank A, Bank A will be reimbursed by debiting X's account or otherwise receiving payment from X. With respect to Bank A's instruction to Bank B, Bank B will be reimbursed by receiving payment from Bank A. In a debit transfer, a creditor, pursuant to authority from the debtor, is enabled to draw on the debtor's bank account by issuing an instruction to pay to the debtor's bank. If the debtor's bank pays, it will be reimbursed by the debtor rather than by the person giving the instruction. For example, the holder of an insurance policy may pay premiums by authorizing the insurance company to order the policyholder's bank to pay the insurance company. The order to pay may be in the form of a draft covered by Article 3, or it might be an instruction to pay that is not an instrument under that Article. The bank receives reimbursement by debiting the policyholder's account. Or, a subsidiary corporation may make payments to its parent by authorizing the parent to order the subsidiary's bank to pay the parent from the subsidiary's account. These transactions are not covered by Article 4A because subparagraph (2) is not satisfied. Article 4A is limited to transactions in which the account to be debited by the receiving bank is that of the person in whose name the instruction is given.

If the beneficiary of a funds transfer is the originator of the transfer, the transfer is governed by Article 4A if it is a credit transfer in form. If it is in the form of a debit transfer it is not governed by Article 4A. For example, Corporation has accounts in Bank A and Bank B. Corporation instructs Bank A to pay to Corporation's account in Bank B. The funds transfer is governed by Article 4A. Sometimes, Corporation will authorize Bank B to draw on Corporation's account in Bank A for the purpose of transferring funds into Corporation's account in Bank B. If Corporation also makes an agreement with Bank A under which Bank A is authorized to follow instructions of Bank B, as agent of Corporation, to transfer funds from Customer's account in Bank A, the instruction of Bank B is a payment order of Customer and is governed by Article 4A. This kind of transaction is known in the wire-transfer business as a "drawdown transfer." If Corporation does not make such an agreement with Bank A and Bank B instructs Bank A to make the transfer, the order is in form a debit transfer and is not governed by Article 4A. These debit transfers are normally ACH transactions in which Bank A relies on Bank B's warranties pursuant to ACH rules, including the warranty that the transfer is authorized.

5. The principal effect of subparagraph (iii) of subsection (a) of Section 4A–103 is to exclude from Article 4A payments made by check or credit card. In those cases the instruction of the debtor to the bank on which the check is drawn or to which the credit card slip is to be presented is contained in the check or credit card slip signed by the debtor. The instruction is not transmitted by the debtor directly to the debtor's bank. Rather, the instruction is delivered or otherwise transmitted by the debtor to the creditor who then presents it to the bank either directly or through bank collection channels. These payments are governed by Articles 3 and 4 and federal law. There are, however, limited instances in which the paper on which a check is printed can be used as the means of transmitting a payment order that is covered by Article 4A. Assume that Originator instructs Originator's Bank to pay $10,000 to the account of Beneficiary in Beneficiary's Bank. Since the amount of Originator's payment order is small, if Originator's Bank and Beneficiary's Bank do not have an account relationship, Originator's Bank may execute Originator's order by issuing a teller's check payable to Beneficiary's Bank for $10,000 along with instructions to credit Beneficiary's account in that amount. The instruction to Beneficiary's Bank to credit Beneficiary's account is a payment order.

The check is the means by which Originator's Bank pays its obligation as sender of the payment order. The instruction of Originator's Bank to Beneficiary's Bank might be given in a letter accompanying the check or it may be written on the check itself. In either case the instruction to Beneficiary's Bank is a payment order but the check itself (which is an order to pay addressed to the drawee rather than to Beneficiary's Bank) is an instrument under Article 3 and is not a payment order. The check can be both the means by which Originator's Bank pays its obligation under § 4A-402(b) to Beneficiary's Bank and the means by which the instruction to Beneficiary's Bank is transmitted.

6. Most payments covered by Article 4A are commonly referred to as wire transfers and usually involve some kind of electronic transmission, but the applicability of Article 4A does not depend upon the means used to transmit the instruction of the sender. Transmission may be by letter or other written communication, oral communication or electronic communication. An oral communication is normally given by telephone. Frequently the message is recorded by the receiving bank to provide evidence of the transaction, but apart from problems of proof there is no need to record the oral instruction. Transmission of an instruction may be a direct communication between the sender and the receiving bank or through an intermediary such as an agent of the sender, a communication system such as international cable, or a funds transfer system such as CHIPS, SWIFT or an automated clearing house.

§ 4A-105. Other Definitions.

(a) In this Article:

(1) "Authorized account" means a deposit account of a customer in a bank designated by the customer as a source of payment of payment orders issued by the customer to the bank. If a customer does not so designate an account, any account of the customer is an authorized account if payment of a payment order from that account is not inconsistent with a restriction on the use of that account.

(2) "Bank" means a person engaged in the business of banking and includes a savings bank, savings and loan association, credit union, and trust company. A branch or separate

office of a bank is a separate bank for purposes of this Article.

(3) "Customer" means a person, including a bank, having an account with a bank or from whom a bank has agreed to receive payment orders.

(4) "Funds-transfer business day" of a receiving bank means the part of a day during which the receiving bank is open for the receipt, processing, and transmittal of payment orders and cancellations and amendments of payment orders.

(5) "Funds-transfer system" means a wire transfer network, automated clearing house, or other communication system of a clearing house or other association of banks through which a payment order by a bank may be transmitted to the bank to which the order is addressed.

(6) ["Good faith" means honesty in fact and the observance of reasonable commercial standards of fair dealing.]*

(7) "Prove" with respect to a fact means to meet the burden of establishing the fact (Section 1-201(b)(8)).

(b) Other definitions applying to this Article and the sections in which they appear are:
"Acceptance" Section 4A-209
"Beneficiary" Section 4A-103
"Beneficiary's bank" Section 4A-103
"Executed" Section 4A-301
"Execution date" Section 4A-301
"Funds transfer" Section 4A-104
"Funds-transfer system rule" Section 4A-501
"Intermediary bank" Section 4A-104
"Originator" Section 4A-104
"Originator's bank" Section 4A-104
"Payment by beneficiary's bank to beneficiary" Section 4A-405
"Payment by originator to beneficiary" Section 4A-406
"Payment by sender to receiving bank" Section 4A-403
"Payment date" Section 4A-401
"Payment order" Section 4A-103
"Receiving bank" Section 4A-103
"Security procedure" Section 4A-201

* Note from to Thomson-West Advisory Panel: The definition of good faith was deleted by Revised Article 1 (2001).

"Sender" Section 4A–103

(c) The following definitions in Article 4 apply to this Article:

"Clearing house" Section 4–104

"Item" Section 4–104

"Suspends payments" Section 4–104

(d) In addition Article 1 contains general definitions and principles of construction and interpretation applicable throughout this Article.

As amended in 2001.

Official Comment

1. The definition of "bank" in subsection (a)(2) includes some institutions that are not commercial banks. The definition reflects the fact that many financial institutions now perform functions previously restricted to commercial banks, including acting on behalf of customers in funds transfers. Since many funds transfers involve payment orders to or from foreign countries the definition also covers foreign banks. The definition also includes Federal Reserve Banks. Funds transfers carried out by Federal Reserve Banks are described in Comments 1 and 2 to Section 4A–107.

2. Funds transfer business is frequently transacted by banks outside of general banking hours. Thus, the definition of banking day in Section 4–104(1)(c) cannot be used to describe when a bank is open for funds transfer business. Subsection (a)(4) defines a new term, "funds transfer business day," which is applicable to Article 4A. The definition states, "is open for the receipt, processing, and transmittal of payment orders and cancellations and amendments of payment orders." In some cases it is possible to electronically transmit payment orders and other communications to a receiving bank at any time. If the receiving bank is not open for the processing of an order when it is received, the communication is stored in the receiving bank's computer for retrieval when the receiving bank is open for processing. The use of the conjunctive makes clear that the defined term is limited to the period during which all functions of the receiving bank can be performed, i.e., receipt, processing, and transmittal of payment orders, cancellations and amendments.

3. Subsection (a)(5) defines "funds transfer system." The term includes a system such as CHIPS which provides for transmission of a payment order as well as settlement of the obligation of the sender to pay the order. It also includes automated clearing houses, operated by a clearing house or other association of banks, which process and transmit payment orders of

banks to other banks. In addition the term includes organizations that provide only transmission services such as SWIFT. The definition also includes the wire transfer network and automated clearing houses of Federal Reserve Banks. Systems of the Federal Reserve Banks, however, are treated differently from systems of other associations of banks. Funds transfer systems other than systems of the Federal Reserve Banks are treated in Article 4A as a means of communication of payment orders between participating banks. Section 4A–206. The Comment to that section and the Comment to Section 4A–107 explain how Federal Reserve Banks function under Article 4A. Funds transfer systems are also able to promulgate rules binding on participating banks that, under Section 4A–501, may supplement or in some cases may even override provisions of Article 4A.

4. Subsection (d) incorporates definitions stated in Article 1 as well as principles of construction and interpretation stated in that Article. Included is Section 1–103. The last paragraph of the Comment to Section 4A–102 is addressed to the issue of the extent to which general principles of law and equity should apply to situations covered by provisions of Article 4A.

§ 4A–106. Time Payment Order Is Received.

(a) The time of receipt of a payment order or communication cancelling or amending a payment order is determined by the rules applicable to receipt of a notice stated in Section 1–202. A receiving bank may fix a cut-off time or times on a funds-transfer business day for the receipt and processing of payment orders and communications cancelling or amending payment orders. Different cut-off times may apply to payment orders, cancellations, or amendments, or to different categories of payment orders, cancellations, or amendments. A cut-off time may apply to senders generally or different cut-off times may apply to different senders or categories of payment orders. If a payment order or communication cancelling or amending a payment order is received after the close of a funds-transfer business day or after the appropriate cut-off time on a funds-transfer business day, the receiving bank may treat the payment order or communication as received at the opening of the next funds-transfer business day.

(b) If this Article refers to an execution date or payment date or states a day on which a receiving bank is required to take action, and the date or day does not fall on a funds-transfer business day, the next day that is a funds-transfer business day is treated as the date or day stated, unless the contrary is stated in this Article.

As amended in 2001.

Official Comment

The time that a payment order is received by a receiving bank usually defines the payment date or the execution date of a payment order. Section 4A–401 and Section 4A–301. The time of receipt of a payment order, or communication cancelling or amending a payment order is defined in subsection (a) by reference to the rules stated in Section 1–202. Thus, time of receipt is determined by the same rules that determine when a notice is received. Time of receipt, however, may be altered by a cut-off time.

As amended in 2001.

§ 4A–107. Federal Reserve Regulations and Operating Circulars.

Regulations of the Board of Governors of the Federal Reserve System and operating circulars of the Federal Reserve Banks supersede any inconsistent provision of this Article to the extent of the inconsistency.

Official Comment

1. Funds transfers under Article 4A may be made, in whole or in part, by payment orders through a Federal Reserve Bank in what is usually referred to as a transfer by Fedwire. If Bank A, which has an account in Federal Reserve Bank X, wants to pay $1,000,000 to Bank B, which has an account in Federal Reserve Bank Y, Bank A can issue an instruction to Reserve Bank X requesting a debit of $1,000,000 to Bank A's Reserve account and an equal credit to Bank B's Reserve account. Reserve Bank X will debit Bank A's account and will credit the account of Reserve Bank Y. Reserve Bank X will issue an instruction to Reserve Bank Y requesting a debit of $1,000,000 to the account of Reserve Bank X and an equal credit to Bank B's account in Reserve Bank Y. Reserve Bank Y will make the requested debit and credit and will give Bank B an advice of credit. The definition of "bank" in Section 4A–105(a)(2) includes both Reserve Bank X and Reserve Bank Y. Bank A's instruction to Reserve Bank X to pay money to Bank B is a payment order under Section 4A–103(a)(1). Bank A is the sender and Reserve Bank X is the receiving bank. Bank B is the beneficiary of Bank A's order and of the funds transfer.

Bank A is the originator of the funds transfer and is also the originator's bank. Section 4A–104(c) and (d). Reserve Bank X, an intermediary bank under Section 4A–104(b), executes Bank A's order by sending a payment order to Reserve Bank Y instructing that bank to credit the Federal Reserve account of Bank B. Reserve Bank Y is the beneficiary's bank.

Suppose the transfer of funds from Bank A to Bank B is part of a larger transaction in which Originator, a customer of Bank A, wants to pay Beneficiary, a customer of Bank B. Originator issues a payment order to Bank A to pay $1,000,000 to the account of Beneficiary in Bank B. Bank A may execute Originator's order by means of Fedwire which simultaneously transfers $1,000,000 from Bank A to Bank B and carries a message instructing Bank B to pay $1,000,000 to the account of Y. The Fedwire transfer is carried out as described in the previous paragraph, except that the beneficiary of the funds transfer is Beneficiary rather than Bank B. Reserve Bank X and Reserve Bank Y are intermediary banks. When Reserve Bank Y advises Bank B of the credit to its Federal Reserve account it will also instruct Bank B to pay to the account of Beneficiary. The instruction is a payment order to Bank B which is the beneficiary's bank. When Reserve Bank Y advises Bank B of the credit to its Federal Reserve account Bank B receives payment of the payment order issued to it by Reserve Bank Y. Section 4A–403(a)(1). The payment order is automatically accepted by Bank B at the time it receives the payment order of Reserve Bank Y. Section 4A–209(b)(2). At the time of acceptance by Bank B payment by Originator to Beneficiary also occurs. Thus, in a Fedwire transfer, payment to the beneficiary's bank, acceptance by the beneficiary's bank and payment by the originator to the beneficiary all occur simultaneously by operation of law at the time the payment order to the beneficiary's bank is received.

If Originator orders payment to the account of Beneficiary in Bank C rather than Bank B, the analysis is somewhat modified. Bank A may not have any relationship with Bank C and may not be able to make payment directly to Bank C. In that case, Bank A could send a Fedwire instructing Bank B to instruct Bank C to pay Beneficiary. The analysis is the same as the previous case except that Bank B is an intermediary bank and Bank C is the beneficiary's bank.

2. A funds transfer can also be made through a Federal Reserve Bank in an automated clearing house transaction. In a typical case, Originator instructs Originator's Bank to pay to the account of Beneficiary in Beneficiary's Bank. Originator's instruction to pay a particular beneficiary is transmitted to Originator's

Bank along with many other instructions for payment to other beneficiaries by many different beneficiary's banks. All of these instructions are contained in a magnetic tape or other electronic device. Transmission of instructions to the various beneficiary's banks requires that Originator's instructions be processed and repackaged with instructions of other originators so that all instructions to a particular beneficiary's bank are transmitted together to that bank. The repackaging is done in processing centers usually referred to as automated clearing houses. Automated clearing houses are operated either by Federal Reserve Banks or by other associations of banks. If Originator's Bank chooses to execute Originator's instructions by transmitting them to a Federal Reserve Bank for processing by the Federal Reserve Bank, the transmission to the Federal Reserve Bank results in the issuance of payment orders by Originator's Bank to the Federal Reserve Bank, which is an intermediary bank. Processing by the Federal Reserve Bank will result in the issuance of payment orders by the Federal Reserve Bank to Beneficiary's Bank as well as payment orders to other beneficiary's banks making payments to carry out Originator's instructions.

3. Although the terms of Article 4A apply to funds transfers involving Federal Reserve Banks, federal preemption would make ineffective any Article 4A provision that conflicts with federal law. The payments activities of the Federal Reserve Banks are governed by regulations of the Federal Reserve Board and by operating circulars issued by the Reserve Banks themselves. In some instances, the operating circulars are issued pursuant to a Federal Reserve Board regulation. In other cases, the Reserve Bank issues the operating circular under its own authority under the Federal Reserve Act, subject to review by the Federal Reserve Board. Section 4A–107 states that Federal Reserve Board regulations and operating circulars of the Federal Reserve Banks supersede any inconsistent provision of Article 4A to the extent of the inconsistency. Federal Reserve Board regulations, being valid exercises of

regulatory authority pursuant to a federal statute, take precedence over state law if there is an inconsistency. Childs v. Federal Reserve Bank of Dallas, 719 F.2d 812 (5th Cir.1983), reh. den. 724 F.2d 127 (5th Cir.1984). Section 4A–107 treats operating circulars as having the same effect whether issued under the Reserve Bank's own authority or under a Federal Reserve Board regulation.

§ 4A–108. Exclusion of Consumer Transactions Governed by Federal Law

This Article does not apply to a funds transfer any part of which is governed by the Electronic Fund Transfer Act of 1978 (Title XX, Public Law 95–630, 92 Stat. 3728, 15 U.S.C. § 1693 et seq.) as amended from time to time.

Official Comment

The Electronic Fund Transfer Act of 1978 is a federal statute that covers a wide variety of electronic funds transfers involving consumers. The types of transfers covered by the federal statute are essentially different from the wholesale wire transfers that are the primary focus of Article 4A. Section 4A–108 excludes a funds transfer from Article 4A if any part of the transfer is covered by the federal law. Existing procedures designed to comply with federal law will not be affected by Article 4A. The effect of Section 4A–108 is to make Article 4A and EFTA mutually exclusive. For example, if a funds transfer is to a consumer account in the beneficiary's bank and the funds transfer is made in part by use of Fedwire and in part by means of an automated clearing house, EFTA applies to the ACH part of the transfer but not to the Fedwire part. Under Section 4A–108, Article 4A does not apply to any part of the transfer. However, in the absence of any law to govern the part of the funds transfer that is not subject to EFTA, a court might apply appropriate principles from Article 4A by analogy.

PART 2

ISSUE AND ACCEPTANCE OF PAYMENT ORDER

§ 4A–201. Security Procedure.

"Security procedure" means a procedure established by agreement of a customer and a receiving bank for the purpose of (i) verifying that a payment order or communication amending or cancelling a payment order is that of the customer, or (ii) detecting error in the transmis-

sion or the content of the payment order or communication. A security procedure may require the use of algorithms or other codes, identifying words or numbers, encryption, callback procedures, or similar security devices. Comparison of a signature on a payment order or communication with an authorized specimen signature of the customer is not by itself a security procedure.

Official Comment

A large percentage of payment orders and communications amending or cancelling payment orders are transmitted electronically and it is standard practice to use security procedures that are designed to assure the authenticity of the message. Security procedures can also be used to detect error in the content of messages or to detect payment orders that are transmitted by mistake as in the case of multiple transmission of the same payment order. Security procedures might also apply to communications that are transmitted by telephone or in writing. Section 4A–201 defines these security procedures. The definition of security procedure limits the term to a procedure "established by agreement of a customer and a receiving bank." The term does not apply to procedures that the receiving bank may follow unilaterally in processing payment orders. The question of whether loss that may result from the transmission of a spurious or erroneous payment order will be borne by the receiving bank or the sender or purported sender is affected by whether a security procedure was or was not in effect and whether there was or was not compliance with the procedure. Security procedures are referred to in Sections 4A–202 and 4A–203, which deal with authorized and verified payment orders, and Section 4A–205, which deals with erroneous payment orders.

§ 4A–202. Authorized and Verified Payment Orders.

(a) A payment order received by the receiving bank is the authorized order of the person identified as sender if that person authorized the order or is otherwise bound by it under the law of agency.

(b) If a bank and its customer have agreed that the authenticity of payment orders issued to the bank in the name of the customer as sender will be verified pursuant to a security procedure, a payment order received by the receiving bank is effective as the order of the customer, whether or not authorized, if (i) the security procedure is a commercially reasonable method of providing security against unauthorized payment orders, and (ii) the bank proves that it accepted the payment order in good faith and in compliance with the security procedure and any written agreement or instruction of the customer restricting acceptance of payment orders issued in

the name of the customer. The bank is not required to follow an instruction that violates a written agreement with the customer or notice of which is not received at a time and in a manner affording the bank a reasonable opportunity to act on it before the payment order is accepted.

(c) Commercial reasonableness of a security procedure is a question of law to be determined by considering the wishes of the customer expressed to the bank, the circumstances of the customer known to the bank, including the size, type, and frequency of payment orders normally issued by the customer to the bank, alternative security procedures offered to the customer, and security procedures in general use by customers and receiving banks similarly situated. A security procedure is deemed to be commercially reasonable if (i) the security procedure was chosen by the customer after the bank offered, and the customer refused, a security procedure that was commercially reasonable for that customer, and (ii) the customer expressly agreed in writing to be bound by any payment order, whether or not authorized, issued in its name and accepted by the bank in compliance with the security procedure chosen by the customer.

(d) The term "sender" in this Article includes the customer in whose name a payment order is issued if the order is the authorized order of the customer under subsection (a), or it is effective as the order of the customer under subsection (b).

(e) This section applies to amendments and cancellations of payment orders to the same extent it applies to payment orders.

(f) Except as provided in this section and in Section 4A–203(a)(1), rights and obligations arising under this section or Section 4A–203 may not be varied by agreement.

Official Comment

This section is discussed in the Comment following Section 4A–203.

§ 4A–203. Unenforceability of Certain Verified Payment Orders.

(a) If an accepted payment order is not, under Section 4A–202(a), an authorized order of a customer identified as sender, but is effective as an order of the customer pursuant to Section 4A–202(b), the following rules apply:

(1) By express written agreement, the receiving bank may limit the extent to which it is entitled to enforce or retain payment of the payment order.

(2) The receiving bank is not entitled to enforce or retain payment of the payment order if the customer proves that the order was not caused, directly or indirectly, by a person (i) entrusted at any time with duties to act for the customer with respect to payment orders or the security procedure, or (ii) who obtained access to transmitting facilities of the customer or who obtained, from a source controlled by the customer and without authority of the receiving bank, information facilitating breach of the security procedure, regardless of how the information was obtained or whether the customer was at fault. Information includes any access device, computer software, or the like.

(b) This section applies to amendments of payment orders to the same extent it applies to payment orders.

Official Comment

1. Some person will always be identified as the sender of a payment order. Acceptance of the order by the receiving bank is based on a belief by the bank that the order was authorized by the person identified as the sender. If the receiving bank is the beneficiary's bank acceptance means that the receiving bank is obliged to pay the beneficiary. If the receiving bank is not the beneficiary's bank, acceptance means that the receiving bank has executed the sender's order and is obliged to pay the bank that accepted the order issued in execution of the sender's order. In either case the receiving bank may suffer a loss unless it is entitled to enforce payment of the payment order that it accepted. If the person identified as the sender of the order refuses to pay on the ground that the order was not authorized by that person, what are the rights of the receiving bank? In the absence of a statute or agreement that specifically addresses the issue, the question usually will be resolved by the law of agency. In some cases, the law of agency works well. For example, suppose the receiving bank executes a payment order given by means of a letter apparently written by a corporation that is a customer of the bank and appar-

ently signed by an officer of the corporation. If the receiving bank acts solely on the basis of the letter, the corporation is not bound as the sender of the payment order unless the signature was that of the officer and the officer was authorized to act for the corporation in the issuance of payment orders, or some other agency doctrine such as apparent authority or estoppel causes the corporation to be bound. Estoppel can be illustrated by the following example. Suppose P is aware that A, who is unauthorized to act for P, has fraudulently misrepresented to T that A is authorized to act for P. T believes A and is about to rely on the misrepresentation. If P does not notify T of the true facts although P could easily do so, P may be estopped from denying A's lack of authority. A similar result could follow if the failure to notify T is the result of negligence rather than a deliberate decision. Restatement, Second, Agency § 8B. Other equitable principles such as subrogation or restitution might also allow a receiving bank to recover with respect to an unauthorized payment order that it accepted. In Gatoil (U.S.A.), Inc. v. Forest Hill State Bank, 1 U.C.C.Rep.Serv.2d 171 (D.Md.1986), a joint venturer not authorized to order payments from the account of the joint venture, ordered a funds transfer from the account. The transfer paid a bona fide debt of the joint venture. Although the transfer was unauthorized the court refused to require recredit of the account because the joint venture suffered no loss. The result can be rationalized on the basis of subrogation of the receiving bank to the right of the beneficiary of the funds transfer to receive the payment from the joint venture.

But in most cases these legal principles give the receiving bank very little protection in the case of an authorized payment order. Cases like those just discussed are not typical of the way that most payment orders are transmitted and accepted, and such cases are likely to become even less common. Given the large amount of the typical payment order, a prudent receiving bank will be unwilling to accept a payment order unless it has assurance that the order is what it purports to be. This assurance is normally provided by security procedures described in Section 4A–201.

In a very large percentage of cases covered by Article 4A, transmission of the payment order is made electronically. The receiving bank may be required to act on the basis of a message that appears on a computer screen. Common law concepts of authority of agent to bind principal are not helpful. There is no way of determining the identity or the authority of the person who caused the message to be sent. The receiving bank is not relying on the authority of any particular person to act for the purported sender. The case is not comparable to payment of a check by the drawee bank on the basis of a signature that is forged. Rather, the receiving bank relies on a security procedure pursuant to which the authenticity of the message can be "tested" by various devices which are designed to provide certainty that the message is that of the sender identified in the payment order. In the wire transfer business the concept of "authorized" is different from that found in agency law. In that business a payment order is treated as the order of the person in whose name it is issued if it is properly tested pursuant to a security procedure and the order passes the test.

Section 4A–202 reflects the reality of the wire transfer business. A person in whose name a payment order is issued is considered to be the sender of the order if the order is "authorized" as stated in subsection (a) or if the order is "verified" pursuant to a security procedure in compliance with subsection (b). If subsection (b) does not apply, the question of whether the customer is responsible for the order is determined by the law of agency. The issue is one of actual or apparent authority of the person who caused the order to be issued in the name of the customer. In some cases the law of agency might allow the customer to be bound by an unauthorized order if conduct of the customer can be used to find an estoppel against the customer to deny that the order was unauthorized. If the customer is bound by the order under any of these agency doctrines, subsection (a) treats the order as authorized and thus the customer is deemed to be the sender of the order. In most cases, however, subsection (b) will apply. In that event there is no need to make an agency law analysis to determine authority. Under Section 4A–202, the issue of liability of the purported sender of the payment order will be determined by agency law only if the receiving bank did not comply with subsection (b).

2. The scope of Section 4A–202 can be illustrated by the following cases. *Case #1.* A payment order purporting to be that of Customer is received by Receiving Bank but the order was fraudulently transmitted by a person who had no authority to act for Customer. *Case #2.* An authentic payment order was sent by Customer, but before the order was received by Receiving Bank the order was fraudulently altered by an unauthorized person to change the beneficiary. *Case #3.* An authentic payment order was received by Receiving Bank, but before the order was executed by Receiving Bank a person who had no authority to act for Customer fraudulently sent a communication purporting to amend the order by changing the beneficiary. In each case Receiving Bank acted on the fraudu-

lent communication by accepting the payment order. These cases are all essentially similar and they are treated identically by Section 4A–202. In each case Receiving Bank acted on a communication that it thought was authorized by Customer when in fact the communication was fraudulent. No distinction is made between Case #1 in which Customer took no part at all in the transaction and Case #2 and Case #3 in which an authentic order was fraudulently altered or amended by an unauthorized person. If subsection (b) does not apply, each case is governed by subsection (a). If there are no additional facts on which an estoppel might be found, Customer is not responsible in Case #1 for the fraudulently issued payment order, in Case #2 for the fraudulent alteration or in Case #3 for the fraudulent amendment. Thus, in each case Customer is not liable to pay the order and Receiving Bank takes the loss. The only remedy of Receiving Bank is to seek recovery from the person who received payment as beneficiary of the fraudulent order. If there was verification in compliance with subsection (b), Customer will take the loss unless Section 4A–203 applies.

3. Subsection (b) of Section 4A–202 is based on the assumption that losses due to fraudulent payment orders can best be avoided by the use of commercially reasonable security procedures, and that the use of such procedures should be encouraged. The subsection is designed to protect both the customer and the receiving bank. A receiving bank needs to be able to rely on objective criteria to determine whether it can safely act on a payment order. Employees of the bank can be trained to "test" a payment order according to the various steps specified in the security procedure. The bank is responsible for the acts of these employees. Subsection (b)(ii) requires the bank to prove that it accepted the payment order in good faith and "in compliance with the security procedure." If the fraud was not detected because the bank's employee did not perform the acts required by the security procedure, the bank has not complied. Subsection (b)(ii) also requires the bank to prove that it complied with any agreement or instruction that restricts acceptance of payment orders issued in the name of the customer. A customer may want to protect itself by imposing limitations on acceptance of payment orders by the bank. For example, the customer may prohibit the bank from accepting a payment order that is not payable from an authorized account, that exceeds the credit balance in specified accounts of the customer, or that exceeds some other amount. Another limitation may relate to the beneficiary. The customer may provide the bank with a list of authorized beneficiaries and

prohibit acceptance of any payment order to a beneficiary not appearing on the list. Such limitations may be incorporated into the security procedure itself or they may be covered by a separate agreement or instruction. In either case, the bank must comply with the limitations if the conditions stated in subsection (b) are met. Normally limitations on acceptance would be incorporated into an agreement between the customer and the receiving bank, but in some cases the instruction might be unilaterally given by the customer. If standing instructions or an agreement state limitations on the ability of the receiving bank to act, provision must be made for later modification of the limitations. Normally this would be done by an agreement that specifies particular procedures to be followed. Thus, subsection (b) states that the receiving bank is not required to follow an instruction that violates a written agreement. The receiving bank is not bound by an instruction unless it has adequate notice of it. Subsections (25), (26) and (27) of Section 1–201 apply.

Subsection (b)(i) assures that the interests of the customer will be protected by providing an incentive to a bank to make available to the customer a security procedure that is commercially reasonable. If a commercially reasonable security procedure is not made available to the customer, subsection (b) does not apply. The result is that subsection (a) applies and the bank acts at its peril in accepting a payment order that may be unauthorized. Prudent banking practice may require that security procedures be utilized in virtually all cases except for those in which personal contact between the customer and the bank eliminates the possibility of an unauthorized order. The burden of making available commercially reasonable security procedures is imposed on receiving banks because they generally determine what security procedures can be used and are in the best position to evaluate the efficacy of procedures offered to customers to combat fraud. The burden on the customer is to supervise its employees to assure compliance with the security procedure and to safeguard confidential security information and access to transmitting facilities so that the security procedure cannot be breached.

4. The principal issue that is likely to arise in litigation involving subsection (b) is whether the security procedure in effect when a fraudulent payment order was accepted was commercially reasonable. The concept of what is commercially reasonable in a given case is flexible. Verification entails labor and equipment costs that can vary greatly depending upon the degree of security that is sought. A customer that transmits very large numbers of payment orders in

very large amounts may desire and may reasonably expect to be provided with state-of-the-art procedures that provide maximum security. But the expense involved may make use of a state-of-the-art procedure infeasible for a customer that normally transmits payment orders infrequently or in relatively low amounts. Another variable is the type of receiving bank. It is reasonable to require large money center banks to make available state-of-the-art security procedures. On the other hand, the same requirement may not be reasonable for a small country bank. A receiving bank might have several security procedures that are designed to meet the varying needs of different customers. The type of payment order is another variable. For example, in a wholesale wire transfer, each payment order is normally transmitted electronically and individually. A testing procedure will be individually applied to each payment order. In funds transfers to be made by means of an automated clearing house many payment orders are incorporated into an electronic device such as a magnetic tape that is physically delivered. Testing of the individual payment orders is not feasible. Thus, a different kind of security procedure must be adopted to take into account the different mode of transmission.

The issue of whether a particular security procedure is commercially reasonable is a question of law. Whether the receiving bank complied with the procedure is a question of fact. It is appropriate to make the finding concerning commercial reasonability a matter of law because security procedures are likely to be standardized in the banking industry and a question of law standard leads to more predictability concerning the level of security that a bank must offer to its customers. The purpose of subsection (b) is to encourage banks to institute reasonable safeguards against fraud but not to make them insurers against fraud. A security procedure is not commercially unreasonable simply because another procedure might have been better or because the judge deciding the question would have opted for a more stringent procedure. The standard is not whether the security procedure is the best available. Rather it is whether the procedure is reasonable for the particular customer and the particular bank, which is a lower standard. On the other hand, a security procedure that fails to meet prevailing standards of good banking practice applicable to the particular bank should not be held to be commercially reasonable. Subsection (c) states factors to be considered by the judge in making the determination of commercial reasonableness. Sometimes an informed customer refuses a security procedure that is commercially reasonable and suitable for that customer and insists on using a higher-risk procedure because it is more convenient or cheaper. In that case, under the last sentence of subsection (c), the customer has voluntarily assumed the risk of failure of the procedure and cannot shift the loss to the bank. But this result follows only if the customer expressly agrees in writing to assume that risk. It is implicit in the last sentence of subsection (c) that a bank that accedes to the wishes of its customer in this regard is not acting in bad faith by so doing so long as the customer is made aware of the risk. In all cases, however, a receiving bank cannot get the benefit of subsection (b) unless it has made available to the customer a security procedure that is commercially reasonable and suitable for use by that customer. In most cases, the mutual interest of bank and customer to protect against fraud should lead to agreement to a security procedure which is commercially reasonable.

5. The effect of Section 4a-202(b) is to place the risk of loss on the customer if an unauthorized payment order is accepted by the receiving bank after verification by the bank in compliance with a commercially reasonable security procedure. An exception to this result is provided by Section 4A-203(a)(2). The customer may avoid the loss resulting from such a payment order if the customer can prove that the fraud was not committed by a person described in that subsection. Breach of a commercially reasonable security procedure requires that the person committing the fraud have knowledge of how the procedure works and knowledge of codes, identifying devices, and the like. That person may also need access to transmitting facilities through an access device or other software in order to breach the security procedure. This confidential information must be obtained either from a source controlled by the customer or from a source controlled by the receiving bank. If the customer can prove that the person committing the fraud did not obtain the confidential information from an agent or former agent of the customer or from a source controlled by the customer, the loss is shifted to the bank. "Prove" is defined in Section 4A-105(a)(7). Because of bank regulation requirements, in this kind of case there will always be a criminal investigation as well as an internal investigation of the bank to determine the probable explanation for the breach of security. Because a funds transfer fraud usually will involve a very large amount of money, both the criminal investigation and the internal investigation are likely to be thorough. In some cases there may be an investigation by bank examiners as well. Frequently, these investigations will develop evidence of who is at fault and the cause of the loss. The customer will have access to evidence developed in these investigations and that evidence can be used by the customer in meeting its burden of proof.

6. The effect of Section 4A-202(b) may also be changed by an agreement meeting the requirements of Section 4A-203(a)(1). Some customers may be unwilling to take all or part of the risk of loss with respect to unauthorized payment orders even if all of the requirements of Section 4A-202(b) are met. By virtue of Section 4A-203(a)(1), a receiving bank may assume all of the risk of loss with respect to unauthorized payment orders or the customer and bank may agree that losses from unauthorized payment orders are to be divided as provided in the agreement.

7. In a large majority of cases the sender of a payment order is a bank. In many cases in which there is a bank sender, both the sender and the receiving bank will be members of a funds transfer system over which the payment order is transmitted. Since Section 4A-202(f) does not prohibit a funds transfer system rule from varying rights and obligations under Section 4A-202, a rule of the funds transfer system can determine how loss due to an unauthorized payment order from a participating bank to another participating bank is to be allocated. A funds transfer system rule, however, cannot change the rights of a customer that is not a participating bank. § 4A-501(b). Section 4A-202(f) also prevents variation by agreement except to the extent stated.

§ 4A-204. Refund of Payment and Duty of Customer to Report With Respect to Unauthorized Payment Order.

(a) If a receiving bank accepts a payment order issued in the name of its customer as sender which is (i) not authorized and not effective as the order of the customer under Section 4A-202, or (ii) not enforceable, in whole or in part, against the customer under Section 4A-203, the bank shall refund any payment of the payment order received from the customer to the extent the bank is not entitled to enforce payment and shall pay interest on the refundable amount calculated from the date the bank received payment to the date of the refund. However, the customer is not entitled to interest from the bank on the amount to be refunded if the customer fails to exercise ordinary care to determine that the order was not authorized by the customer and to notify the bank of the relevant facts within a reasonable time not exceeding 90 days after the date the customer received notification from the bank that the order was accepted or that the customer's account was debited with respect to the order. The bank is not entitled to any recovery from the customer on account of a failure by the customer to give notification as stated in this section.

(b) Reasonable time under subsection (a) may be fixed by agreement as stated in Section 1–302(b), but the obligation of a receiving bank to refund payment as stated in subsection (a) may not otherwise be varied by agreement.

As amended in 2001.

Official Comment

1. With respect to unauthorized payment orders, in a very large percentage of cases a commercially reasonable security procedure will be in effect. Section 4A–204 applies only to cases in which (i) no commercially reasonable security procedure is in effect, (ii) the bank did not comply with a commercially reasonable security procedure that was in effect, (iii) the sender can prove, pursuant to Section 4A–203(a)(2), that the culprit did not obtain confidential security information controlled by the customer, or (iv) the bank, pursuant to Section 4A–203(a)(1) agreed to take all or part of the loss resulting from an unauthorized payment order. In each of these cases the bank takes the risk of loss with respect to an unauthorized payment order because the bank is not entitled to payment from the customer with respect to the order. The bank normally debits the customer's account or otherwise receives payment from the customer shortly after acceptance of the payment order. Subsection (a) of Section 4A–204 states that the bank must recredit the account or refund payment to the extent the bank is not entitled to enforce payment.

2. Section 4A–204 is designed to encourage a customer to promptly notify the receiving bank that it has accepted an unauthorized payment order. Since cases of unauthorized payment orders will almost always involve fraud, the bank's remedy is normally to recover from the beneficiary of the unauthorized order if the beneficiary was party to the fraud. This remedy may not be worth very much and it may not make any difference whether or not the bank promptly learns about the fraud. But in some cases prompt notification may make it easier for the bank to recover some part of its loss from the culprit. The customer will routinely be notified of the debit to its account with respect to an unauthorized order or will otherwise be notified of acceptance of the order. The customer has a duty to exercise ordinary care to determine that the order was unauthorized after it has received notification from the bank, and to advise the bank of the

relevant facts within a reasonable time not exceeding 90 days after receipt of notification. Reasonable time is not defined and it may depend on the facts of the particular case. If a payment order for $1,000,000 is wholly unauthorized, the customer should normally discover it in far less than 90 days. If a $1,000,000 payment order was authorized but the name of the beneficiary was fraudulently changed, a much longer period may be necessary to discover the fraud. But in any event, if the customer delays more than 90 days the customer's duty has not been met. The only consequence of a failure of the customer to perform this duty is a loss of interest on the refund payable by the bank. A customer that acts promptly is entitled to interest from the time the customer's account was debited or the customer otherwise made payment. The rate of interest is stated in Section 4A–506. If the customer fails to perform the duty, no interest is recoverable for any part of the period before the bank learns that it accepted an unauthorized order. But the bank is not entitled to any recovery from the customer based on negligence for failure to inform the bank. Loss of interest is in the nature of a penalty on the customer designed to provide an incentive for the customer to police its account. There is no intention to impose a duty on the customer that might result in shifting loss from the unauthorized order to the customer.

§ 4A–205.   Erroneous Payment Orders.

(a) If an accepted payment order was transmitted pursuant to a security procedure for the detection of error and the payment order (i) erroneously instructed payment to a beneficiary not intended by the sender, (ii) erroneously instructed payment in an amount greater than the amount intended by the sender, or (iii) was an erroneously transmitted duplicate of a payment order previously sent by the sender, the following rules apply:

(1) If the sender proves that the sender or a person acting on behalf of the sender pursuant to Section 4A–206 complied with the security procedure and that the error would have been detected if the receiving bank had also complied, the sender is not obliged to pay the order to the extent stated in paragraphs (2) and (3).

(2) If the funds transfer is completed on the basis of an erroneous payment order described in clause (i) or (iii) of subsection (a), the sender is not obliged to pay the order and the receiv-

ing bank is entitled to recover from the beneficiary any amount paid to the beneficiary to the extent allowed by the law governing mistake and restitution.

(3) If the funds transfer is completed on the basis of a payment order described in clause (ii) of subsection (a), the sender is not obliged to pay the order to the extent the amount received by the beneficiary is greater than the amount intended by the sender. In that case, the receiving bank is entitled to recover from the beneficiary the excess amount received to the extent allowed by the law governing mistake and restitution.

(b) If (i) the sender of an erroneous payment order described in subsection (a) is not obliged to pay all or part of the order, and (ii) the sender receives notification from the receiving bank that the order was accepted by the bank or that the sender's account was debited with respect to the order, the sender has a duty to exercise ordinary care, on the basis of information available to the sender, to discover the error with respect to the order and to advise the bank of the relevant facts within a reasonable time, not exceeding 90 days, after the bank's notification was received by the sender. If the bank proves that the sender failed to perform that duty, the sender is liable to the bank for the loss the bank proves it incurred as a result of the failure, but the liability of the sender may not exceed the amount of the sender's order.

(c) This section applies to amendments to payment orders to the same extent it applies to payment orders.

Official Comment

1. This section concerns error in the content or in the transmission of payment orders. It deals with three kinds of error. *Case #1.* The order identifies a beneficiary not intended by the sender. For example, Sender intends to wire funds to a beneficiary identified only by an account number. The wrong account number is stated in the order. *Case #2.* The error is in the amount of the order. For example, Sender intends to wire $1,000 to Beneficiary. Through error, the payment order instructs payment of $1,000,000. *Case #3.* A payment order is sent to the receiving bank and then, by mistake, the same payment order is sent to the receiving bank again. In Case #3, the receiving bank may have no way of knowing whether the second

order is a duplicate of the first or is another order. Similarly, in Case #1 and Case #2, the receiving bank may have no way of knowing that the error exists. In each case, if this section does not apply and the funds transfer is completed, Sender is obliged to pay the order. Section 4A–402. Sender's remedy, based on payment by mistake, is to recover from the beneficiary that received payment.

Sometimes, however, transmission of payment orders of the sender to the receiving bank is made pursuant to a security procedure designed to detect one or more of the errors described above. Since "security procedure" is defined by Section 4A–201 as "a procedure established by agreement of a customer and a receiving bank for the purpose of * * * detecting error * * *," Section 4A–205 does not apply if the receiving bank and the customer did not agree to the establishment of a procedure for detecting error. A security procedure may be designed to detect an account number that is not one to which Sender normally makes payment. In that case, the security procedure may require a special verification that payment to the stated account number was intended. In the case of dollar amounts, the security procedure may require different codes for different dollar amounts. If a $1,000,000 payment order contains a code that is inappropriate for that amount, the error in amount should be detected. In the case of duplicate orders, the security procedure may require that each payment order be identified by a number or code that applies to no other order. If the number or code of each payment order received is registered in a computer base, the receiving bank can quickly identify a duplicate order. The three cases covered by this section are essentially similar. In each, if the error is not detected, some beneficiary will receive funds that the beneficiary was not intended to receive. If this section applies, the risk of loss with respect to the error of the sender is shifted to the bank which has the burden of recovering the funds from the beneficiary. The risk of loss is shifted to the bank only if the sender proves that the error would have been detected if there had been compliance with the procedure and that the sender (or an agent under Section 4A–206) complied. In the case of a duplicate order or a wrong beneficiary, the sender doesn't have to pay the order. In the case of an overpayment, the sender does not have to pay the order to the extent of the overpayment. If subsection (a)(1) applies, the position of the receiving bank is comparable to that of a receiving bank that erroneously executes a payment order as stated in Section 4A–303. However, failure of the sender to timely report the error is covered by Section 4A–205(b) rather than by Section 4A–304 which applies only to erroneous execution under Section 4A–303. A receiving bank to which the risk of loss is shifted by subsection (a)(1) or (2) is entitled to recover the amount erroneously paid to the beneficiary to the extent allowed by the law of mistake and restitution. Rights of the receiving bank against the beneficiary are similar to those of a receiving bank that erroneously executes a payment order as stated in Section 4A–303. Those rights are discussed in Comment 2 to Section 4A–303.

2. A security procedure established for the purpose of detecting error is not effective unless both sender and receiving bank comply with the procedure. Thus, the bank undertakes a duty of complying with the procedure for the benefit of the sender. This duty is recognized in subsection (a)(1). The loss with respect to the sender's error is shifted to the bank if the bank fails to comply with the procedure and the sender (or an agent under Section 4A–206) does comply. Although the customer may have been negligent in transmitting the erroneous payment order, the loss is put on the bank on a last-clear-chance theory. A similar analysis applies to subsection (b). If the loss with respect to an error is shifted to the receiving bank and the sender is notified by the bank that the erroneous payment order was accepted, the sender has a duty to exercise ordinary care to discover the error and notify the bank of the relevant facts within a reasonable time not exceeding 90 days. If the bank can prove that the sender failed in this duty it is entitled to compensation for the loss incurred as a result of the failure. Whether the bank is entitled to recover from the sender depends upon whether the failure to give timely notice would have made any difference. If the bank could not have recovered from the beneficiary that received payment under the erroneous payment order even if timely notice had been given, the sender's failure to notify did not cause any loss of the bank.

3. Section 4A–205 is subject to variation by agreement under Section 4A–501. Thus, if a receiving bank and its customer have agreed to a security procedure for detection of error, the liability of the receiving bank for failing to detect an error of the customer as provided in Section 4A–205 may be varied as provided in an agreement of the bank and the customer.

§ 4A–206. Transmission of Payment Order Through Funds-Transfer or Other Communication System.

(a) If a payment order addressed to a receiving bank is transmitted to a funds-transfer system or other third-party communication system for transmittal to the bank, the system is deemed to be an agent of the sender for the purpose of transmitting the payment order to the bank. If there is a discrepancy between the terms of the payment order transmitted to the system and the terms of the payment order transmitted by the system to the bank, the terms of the payment order of the sender are those transmitted by the system. This section does not apply to a funds-transfer system of the Federal Reserve Banks.

(b) This section applies to cancellations and amendments of payment orders to the same extent it applies to payment orders.

Official Comment

1. A payment order may be issued to a receiving bank directly by delivery of a writing or electronic device or by an oral or electronic communication. If an agent of the sender is employed to transmit orders on behalf of the sender, the sender is bound by the order transmitted by the agent on the basis of agency law. Section 4A–206 is an application of that principle to cases in which a funds transfer or communication system acts as an intermediary in transmitting the sender's order to the receiving bank. The intermediary is deemed to be an agent of the sender for the purpose of transmitting payment orders and related messages for the sender. Section 4A–206 deals with error by the intermediary.

2. Transmission by an automated clearing house of an association of banks other than the Federal Reserve Banks is an example of a transaction covered by Section 4A–206. Suppose Originator orders Originator's Bank to cause a large number of payments to be made to many accounts in banks in various parts of the country. These payment orders are electronically transmitted to Originator's Bank and stored in an electronic device that is held by Originator's Bank. Or, transmission of the various payment orders is made by delivery to Originator's Bank of an electronic device containing the instruction to the bank. In either case the terms of the various payment orders by Originator are determined by the information contained in the electronic device. In order to execute the various orders, the information in the electronic device must be processed. For example, if some of the orders are for payments to accounts in Bank X and some to accounts in Bank Y, Originator's Bank will execute these orders of Originator by issuing a series of payment orders to Bank X covering all payments to accounts in that bank, and by issuing a series of payment orders to Bank Y covering all payments to accounts in that bank. The orders to Bank X may be transmitted

together by means of an electronic device, and those to Bank Y may be included in another electronic device. Typically, this processing is done by an automated clearing house acting for a group of banks including Originator's Bank. The automated clearing house is a funds transfer system. Section 4A–105(a)(5). Originator's Bank delivers Originator's electronic device or transmits the information contained in the device to the funds transfer system for processing into payment orders of Originator's Bank to the appropriate beneficiary's banks. The processing may result in an erroneous payment order. Originator's Bank, by use of Originator's electronic device, may have given information to the funds transfer system instructing payment of $100,000 to an account in Bank X, but because of human error or an equipment malfunction the processing may have converted that instruction into an instruction to Bank X to make a payment of $1,000,000. Under Section 4A–206, Originator's Bank issued a payment order for $1,000,000 to Bank X when the erroneous information was sent to Bank X. Originator's Bank is responsible for the error of the automated clearing house. The liability of the funds transfer system that made the error is not governed by Article 4A. It is left to the law of contract, a funds transfer system rule, or other applicable law.

In the hypothetical case just discussed, if the automated clearing house is operated by a Federal Reserve Bank, the analysis is different. Section 4A–206 does not apply. Originator's Bank will execute Originator's payment orders by delivery or transmission of the electronic information to the Federal Reserve Bank for processing. The result is that Originator's Bank has issued payment orders to the Federal Reserve Bank which, in this case, is acting as an intermediary bank. When the Federal Reserve Bank has processed the information given to it by Originator's Bank it will issue payment orders to the various beneficiary's banks. If the processing results in an erroneous payment order, the Federal Reserve Bank has erroneously executed the payment order of Originator's Bank and the case is governed by Section 4A–303.

§ 4A–207. Misdescription of Beneficiary.

(a) Subject to subsection (b), if, in a payment order received by the beneficiary's bank, the name, bank account number, or other identification of the beneficiary refers to a nonexistent or unidentifiable person or account, no person has rights as a beneficiary of the order and acceptance of the order cannot occur.

(b) If a payment order received by the beneficiary's bank identifies the beneficiary both by name and by an identifying or bank account number and the name and number identify different persons, the following rules apply:

(1) Except as otherwise provided in subsection (c), if the beneficiary's bank does not know that the name and number refer to different persons, it may rely on the number as the proper identification of the beneficiary of the order. The beneficiary's bank need not determine whether the name and number refer to the same person.

(2) If the beneficiary's bank pays the person identified by name or knows that the name and number identify different persons, no person has rights as beneficiary except the person paid by the beneficiary's bank if that person was entitled to receive payment from the originator of the funds transfer. If no person has rights as beneficiary, acceptance of the order cannot occur.

(c) If (i) a payment order described in subsection (b) is accepted, (ii) the originator's payment order described the beneficiary inconsistently by name and number, and (iii) the beneficiary's bank pays the person identified by number as permitted by subsection (b)(1), the following rules apply:

(1) If the originator is a bank, the originator is obliged to pay its order.

(2) If the originator is not a bank and proves that the person identified by number was not entitled to receive payment from the originator, the originator is not obliged to pay its order unless the originator's bank proves that the originator, before acceptance of the originator's order, had notice that payment of a payment order issued by the originator might be made by the beneficiary's bank on the basis of an identifying or bank account number even if it identifies a person different from the named beneficiary. Proof of notice may be made by any admissible evidence. The originator's bank satisfies the burden of proof if it proves that the originator, before the payment order was accepted, signed a writing stating the information to which the notice relates.

(d) In a case governed by subsection (b)(1), if the beneficiary's bank rightfully pays the person identified by number and that person was not entitled to receive payment from the originator, the amount paid may be recovered from that person to the extent allowed by the law governing mistake and restitution as follows:

    (1) If the originator is obliged to pay its payment order as stated in subsection (c), the originator has the right to recover.

    (2) If the originator is not a bank and is not obliged to pay its payment order, the originator's bank has the right to recover.

Official Comment

1. Subsection (a) deals with the problem of payment orders issued to the beneficiary's bank for payment to nonexistent or unidentifiable persons or accounts. Since it is not possible in that case for the funds transfer to be completed, subsection (a) states that the order cannot be accepted. Under Section 4A–402(c), a sender of a payment order is not obliged to pay its order unless the beneficiary's bank accepts a payment order instructing payment to the beneficiary of that sender's order. Thus, if the beneficiary of a funds transfer is nonexistent or unidentifiable, each sender in the funds transfer that has paid its payment order is entitled to get its money back.

2. Subsection (b), which takes precedence over subsection (a), deals with the problem of payment orders in which the description of the beneficiary does not allow identification of the beneficiary because the beneficiary is described by name and by an identifying number or an account number and the name and number refer to different persons. A very large percentage of payment orders issued to the beneficiary's bank by another bank are processed by automated means using machines capable of reading orders on standard formats that identify the beneficiary by an identifying number or the number of a bank account. The processing of the order by the beneficiary's bank and the crediting of the beneficiary's account are done by use of the identifying or bank account number without human reading of the payment order itself. The process is comparable to that used in automated payment of checks. The standard format, however, may also allow the inclusion of the name of the beneficiary and other information which can be useful to the beneficiary's bank and the beneficiary but which plays no part in the process of payment. If the beneficiary's bank has both the account number and name of the beneficiary supplied by the originator of the funds

transfer, it is possible for the beneficiary's bank to determine whether the name and number refer to the same person, but if a duty to make that determination is imposed on the beneficiary's bank the benefits of automated payment are lost. Manual handling of payment orders is both expensive and subject to human error. If payment orders can be handled on an automated basis there are substantial economies of operation and the possibility of clerical error is reduced. Subsection (b) allows banks to utilize automated processing by allowing banks to act on the basis of the number without regard to the name if the bank does not know that the name and number refer to different persons. "Know" is defined in Section 1–201(25) to mean actual knowledge, and Section 1–201(27) states rules for determining when an organization has knowledge of information received by the organization. The time of payment is the pertinent time at which knowledge or lack of knowledge must be determined.

Although the clear trend is for beneficiary's banks to process payment orders by automated means, Section 4A–207 is not limited to cases in which processing is done by automated means. A bank that processes by semi-automated means or even manually may rely on number as stated in Section 4A–207.

In cases covered by subsection (b) the erroneous identification would in virtually all cases be the identifying or bank account number. In the typical case the error is made by the originator of the funds transfer. The originator should know the name of the person who is to receive payment and can further identify that person by an address that would normally be known to the originator. It is not unlikely, however, that the originator may not be sure whether the identifying or account number refers to the person the originator intends to pay. Subsection (b)(1) deals with the typical case in which the beneficiary's bank pays on the basis of the account number and is not aware at the time of payment that the named beneficiary is not the holder of the account which was paid. In some cases the false number will be the result of error by the originator. In other cases fraud is involved. For example, Doe is the holder of shares in Mutual Fund. Thief, impersonating Doe, requests redemption of the shares and directs Mutual Fund to wire the redemption proceeds to Doe's account #12345 in Beneficiary's Bank. Mutual Fund originates a funds transfer by issuing a payment order to Originator's Bank to make the payment to Doe's account #12345 in Beneficiary's Bank. Originator's Bank executes the order by issuing a conforming payment order to Beneficiary's Bank which makes payment to account #12345. That account is the account of Roe rather than Doe. Roe might be a person acting in concert with Thief or Roe might be an innocent third party. Assume that Roe is a gem merchant that agreed to sell gems to Thief who agreed to wire the purchase price to Roe's account in Beneficiary's Bank. Roe believed that the credit to Roe's account was a transfer of funds from Thief and released the gems to Thief in good faith in reliance on the payment. The case law is unclear on the responsibility of a beneficiary's bank in carrying out a payment order in which the identification of the beneficiary by name and number is conflicting. See Securities Fund Services, Inc. v. American National Bank, 542 F.Supp. 323 (N.D.Ill.1982) and Bradford Trust Co. v. Texas American Bank, 790 F.2d 407 (5th Cir.1986). Section 4A-207 resolves the issue.

If Beneficiary's Bank did not know about the conflict between the name and number, subsection (b)(1) applies. Beneficiary's Bank has no duty to determine whether there is a conflict and it may rely on the number as the proper identification of the beneficiary of the order. When it accepts the order, it is entitled to payment from Originator's Bank. Section 4A-402(b). On the other hand, if Beneficiary's Bank knew about the conflict between the name and number and nevertheless paid Roe, subsection (b)(2) applies. Under that provision, acceptance of the payment order of Originator's Bank did not occur because there is no beneficiary of that order. Since acceptance did not occur Originator's Bank is not obliged to pay Beneficiary's Bank. Section 4A-402(b). Similarly, Mutual Fund is excused from its obligation to pay Originator's Bank. Section 4A-402(c). Thus, Beneficiary's Bank takes the loss. Its only cause of action is against Thief. Roe is not obliged to return the payment to the beneficiary's bank because Roe received the payment in good faith and for value. Article 4A makes irrelevant the issue of whether Mutual Fund was or was not negligent in issuing its payment order.

3. Normally, subsection (b)(1) will apply to the hypothetical case discussed in Comment 2. Beneficiary's Bank will pay on the basis of the number without knowledge of the conflict. In that case subsection (c) places the loss on either Mutual Fund or Originator's Bank. It is not unfair to assign the loss to Mutual Fund because it is the person who dealt with the imposter and it supplied the wrong account number. It could have avoided the loss if it had not used an account number that it was not sure was that of Doe. Mutual Fund, however, may not have been aware of the risk involved in giving both name and number. Subsection (c) is designed to protect the originator, Mutual Fund, in this case. Under that subsection, the originator is responsible for the inconsistent descrip-

tion of the beneficiary if it had notice that the order might be paid by the beneficiary's bank on the basis of the number. If the originator is a bank, the originator always has that responsibility. The rationale is that any bank should know how payment orders are processed and paid. If the originator is not a bank, the originator's bank must prove that its customer, the originator, had notice. Notice can be proved by any admissible evidence, but the bank can always prove notice by providing the customer with a written statement of the required information and obtaining the customer's signature to the statement. That statement will then apply to any payment order accepted by the bank thereafter. The information need not be supplied more than once.

In the hypothetical case if Originator's Bank made the disclosure stated in the last sentence of subsection (c)(2), Mutual Fund must pay Originator's Bank. Under subsection (d)(1), Mutual Fund has an action to recover from Roe if recovery from Roe is permitted by the law governing mistake and restitution. Under the assumed facts Roe should be entitled to keep the money as a person who took it in good faith and for value since it was taken as payment for the gems. In that case, Mutual Fund's only remedy is against Thief. If Roe was not acting in good faith, Roe has to return the money to Mutual Fund. If Originator's Bank does not prove that Mutual Fund had notice as stated in subsection (c)(2), Mutual Fund is not required to pay Originator's Bank. Thus, the risk of loss falls on Originator's Bank whose remedy is against Roe or Thief as stated above. Subsection (d)(2).

§ 4A-208. Misdescription of Intermediary Bank or Beneficiary's Bank.

(a) This subsection applies to a payment order identifying an intermediary bank or the beneficiary's bank only by an identifying number.

(1) The receiving bank may rely on the number as the proper identification of the intermediary or beneficiary's bank and need not determine whether the number identifies a bank.

(2) The sender is obliged to compensate the receiving bank for any loss and expenses incurred by the receiving bank as a result of its reliance on the number in executing or attempting to execute the order.

(b) This subsection applies to a payment order identifying an intermediary bank or the beneficiary's bank both by name and an identifying number if the name and number identify different persons.

(1) If the sender is a bank, the receiving bank may rely on the number as the proper identification of the intermediary or beneficiary's bank if the receiving bank, when it executes the sender's order, does not know that the name and number identify different persons. The receiving bank need not determine whether the name and number refer to the same person or whether the number refers to a bank. The sender is obliged to compensate the receiving bank for any loss and expenses incurred by the receiving bank as a result of its reliance on the number in executing or attempting to execute the order.

(2) If the sender is not a bank and the receiving bank proves that the sender, before the payment order was accepted, had notice that the receiving bank might rely on the number as the proper identification of the intermediary or beneficiary's bank even if it identifies a person different from the bank identified by name, the rights and obligations of the sender and the receiving bank are governed by subsection (b)(1), as though the sender were a bank. Proof of notice may be made by any admissible evidence. The receiving bank satisfies the burden of proof if it proves that the sender, before the payment order was accepted, signed a writing stating the information to which the notice relates.

(3) Regardless of whether the sender is a bank, the receiving bank may rely on the name as the proper identification of the intermediary or beneficiary's bank if the receiving bank, at the time it executes the sender's order, does not know that the name and number identify different persons. The receiving bank need not determine whether the name and number refer to the same person.

(4) If the receiving bank knows that the name and number identify different persons, reliance on either the name or the number in executing the sender's payment order is a breach of the obligation stated in Section 4A–302(a)(1).

Official Comment

1. This section addresses an issue similar to that addressed by Section 4A–207. Because of automation in the processing of payment orders, a payment order may identify the beneficiary's bank or an intermediary bank by an identifying number. The bank identified by number might or might not also be identified by name. The following two cases illustrate Section 4A–208(a) and (b):

Case #1. Originator's payment order to Originator's Bank identifies the beneficiary's bank as Bank A and instructs payment to Account #12345 in that bank. Originator's Bank executes Originator's order by issuing a payment order to Intermediary Bank. In the payment order of Originator's Bank the beneficiary's bank is identified as Bank A but is also identified by number, #67890. The identifying number refers to Bank B rather than Bank A. If processing by Intermediary Bank of the payment order of Originator's Bank is done by automated means, Intermediary Bank, in executing the order, will rely on the identifying number and will issue a payment order to Bank B rather than Bank A. If there is an Account #12345 in Bank B, the payment order of Intermediary Bank would normally be accepted and payment would be made to a person not intended by Originator. In this case, Section 4A–208(b)(1) puts the risk of loss on Originator's Bank. Intermediary Bank may rely on the number #67890 as the proper identification of the beneficiary's bank. Intermediary Bank has properly executed the payment order of Originator's Bank. By using the wrong number to describe the beneficiary's bank, Originator's Bank has improperly executed Originator's payment order because the payment order of Originator's Bank provides for payment to the wrong beneficiary, the holder of Account #12345 in Bank B rather than the holder of Account #12345 in Bank A. Section 4A–302(a)(1) and Section 4A–303(c). Originator's Bank is not entitled to payment from Originator but is required to pay Intermediary Bank. Section 4A–303(c) and Section 4A–402(c). Intermediary Bank is also entitled to compensation for any loss and expenses resulting from the error by Originator's Bank.

If there is no Account #12345 in Bank B, the result is that there is no beneficiary of the payment order issued by Originator's Bank and the funds transfer will not be completed. Originator's Bank is not entitled to payment from Originator and Intermediary Bank is not entitled to payment from Originator's Bank. Section 4A–402(c). Since Originator's Bank improperly executed Originator's payment order it may be liable for damages under Section 4A–305. As stated above, Intermediary Bank is entitled to compensation for loss and expenses resulting from the error by Originator's Bank.

Case #2. Suppose the same payment order by Originator to Originator's Bank as in Case #1. In executing the payment order Originator's Bank issues a payment order to Intermediary Bank in which the beneficiary's bank is identified only by number, #67890. That number does not refer to Bank A. Rather, it identifies a person that is not a bank. If processing by Intermediary Bank of the payment order of Originator's Bank is done by automated means, Intermediary Bank will rely on the number #67890 to identify the beneficiary's bank. Intermediary Bank has no duty to determine whether the number identifies a bank. The funds transfer cannot be completed in this case because no bank is identified as the beneficiary's bank. Subsection (a) puts the risk of loss on Originator's Bank. Originator's Bank is not entitled to payment from Originator. Section 4A–402(c). Originator's Bank has improperly executed Originator's payment order and may be liable for damages under Section 4A–305. Originator's Bank is obliged to compensate Intermediary Bank for loss and expenses resulting from the error by Originator's Bank.

Subsection (a) also applies if #67890 identifies a bank, but the bank is not Bank A. Intermediary Bank may rely on the number as the proper identification of the beneficiary's bank. If the bank to which Intermediary Bank sends its payment order accepts the order, Intermediary Bank is entitled to payment from Originator's Bank, but Originator's Bank is not entitled to payment from Originator. The analysis is similar to that in Case #1.

2. Subsection (b)(2) of Section 4A–208 addresses cases in which an erroneous identification of a beneficiary's bank or intermediary bank by name and number is made in a payment order of a sender that is not a bank. Suppose Originator issues a payment order to Originator's Bank that instructs that bank to use an intermediary bank identified as Bank A and by an identifying number, #67890. The identifying number refers to Bank B. Originator intended to identify Bank A as intermediary bank. If Originator's Bank relied on the number and issued a payment order to Bank B the rights of Originator's Bank depend upon whether the proof of notice stated in subsection (b)(2) is made by Originator's Bank. If proof is made, Originator's Bank's rights are governed by subsection (b)(1) of Section 4A–208. Originator's Bank is not liable for breach of Section 4A–302(a)(1) and is entitled to compensation from Originator for any loss and expenses resulting from Originator's error. If notice is not proved, Originator's Bank may not rely on the number in executing Originator's payment order. Since Originator's Bank does not get the benefit of subsection

(b)(1) in that case, Originator's Bank improperly executed Originator's payment order and is in breach of the obligation stated in Section 4A–302(a)(1). If notice is not given, Originator's Bank can rely on the name if it is not aware of the conflict in name and number. Subsection (b)(3).

3. Although the principal purpose of Section 4A–208 is to accommodate automated processing of payment orders, Section 4A–208 applies regardless of whether processing is done by automation, semiautomated means or manually.

§ 4A–209. Acceptance of Payment Order.

(a) Subject to subsection (d), a receiving bank other than the beneficiary's bank accepts a payment order when it executes the order.

(b) Subject to subsections (c) and (d), a beneficiary's bank accepts a payment order at the earliest of the following times:

(1) when the bank (i) pays the beneficiary as stated in Section 4A–405(a) or 4A–405(b), or (ii) notifies the beneficiary of receipt of the order or that the account of the beneficiary has been credited with respect to the order unless the notice indicates that the bank is rejecting the order or that funds with respect to the order may not be withdrawn or used until receipt of payment from the sender of the order;

(2) when the bank receives payment of the entire amount of the sender's order pursuant to Section 4A–403(a)(1) or 4A–403(a)(2); or

(3) the opening of the next funds-transfer business day of the bank following the payment date of the order if, at that time, the amount of the sender's order is fully covered by a withdrawable credit balance in an authorized account of the sender or the bank has otherwise received full payment from the sender, unless the order was rejected before that time or is rejected within (i) one hour after that time, or (ii) one hour after the opening of the next business day of the sender following the payment date if that time is later. If notice of rejection is received by the sender after the payment date and the authorized account of the sender does not bear interest, the bank is obliged to pay interest to the sender on the amount of the order for the

number of days elapsing after the payment date to the day the sender receives notice or learns that the order was not accepted, counting that day as an elapsed day. If the withdrawable credit balance during that period falls below the amount of the order, the amount of interest payable is reduced accordingly.

(c) Acceptance of a payment order cannot occur before the order is received by the receiving bank. Acceptance does not occur under subsection (b)(2) or (b)(3) if the beneficiary of the payment order does not have an account with the receiving bank, the account has been closed, or the receiving bank is not permitted by law to receive credits for the beneficiary's account.

(d) A payment order issued to the originator's bank cannot be accepted until the payment date if the bank is the beneficiary's bank, or the execution date if the bank is not the beneficiary's bank. If the originator's bank executes the originator's payment order before the execution date or pays the beneficiary of the originator's payment order before the payment date and the payment order is subsequently canceled pursuant to Section 4A–211(b), the bank may recover from the beneficiary any payment received to the extent allowed by the law governing mistake and restitution.

Official Comment

1. This section treats the sender's payment order as a request by the sender to the receiving bank to execute or pay the order and that request can be accepted or rejected by the receiving bank. Section 4A–209 defines when acceptance occurs. Section 4A–210 covers rejection. Acceptance of the payment order imposes an obligation on the receiving bank to the sender if the receiving bank is not the beneficiary's bank, or to the beneficiary if the receiving bank is the beneficiary's bank. These obligations are stated in Section 4A–302 and Section 4A–404.

2. Acceptance by a receiving bank other than the beneficiary's bank is defined in Section 4A–209(a). That subsection states the only way that a bank other than the beneficiary's bank can accept a payment order. A payment order to a bank other than the beneficiary's bank is, in effect, a request that the receiving bank execute the sender's order by issuing a payment order to the beneficiary's bank or to an intermediary bank. Normally, acceptance occurs at the time of execution, but there is an exception stated

in subsection (d) and discussed in Comment 9. Execution occurs when the receiving bank "issues a payment order intended to carry out" the sender's order. Section 4A–301(a). In some cases the payment order issued by the receiving bank may not conform to the sender's order. For example, the receiving bank might make a mistake in the amount of its order, or the order might be issued to the wrong beneficiary's bank or for the benefit of the wrong beneficiary. In all of these cases there is acceptance of the sender's order by the bank when the receiving bank issues its order intended to carry out the sender's order, even though the bank's payment order does not in fact carry out the instruction of the sender. Improper execution of the sender's order may lead to liability to the sender for damages or it may mean that the sender is not obliged to pay its payment order. These matters are covered in Section 4A–303, Section 4A–305, and Section 4A–402.

3. A receiving bank has no duty to accept a payment order unless the bank makes an agreement, either before or after issuance of the payment order, to accept it, or acceptance is required by a funds transfer system rule. If the bank makes such an agreement it incurs a contractual obligation based on the agreement and may be held liable for breach of contract if a failure to execute violates the agreement. In many cases a bank will enter into an agreement with its customer to govern the rights and obligations of the parties with respect to payment orders issued to the bank by the customer or, in cases in which the sender is also a bank, there may be a funds transfer system rule that governs the obligations of a receiving bank with respect to payment orders transmitted over the system. Such agreements or rules can specify the circumstances under which a receiving bank is obliged to execute a payment order and can define the extent of liability of the receiving bank for breach of the agreement or rule. Section 4A–305(d) states the liability for breach of an agreement to execute a payment order.

4. In the case of a payment order issued to the beneficiary's bank, acceptance is defined in Section 4A–209(b). The function of a beneficiary's bank that receives a payment order is different from that of a receiving bank that receives a payment order for execution. In the typical case, the beneficiary's bank simply receives payment from the sender of the order, credits the account of the beneficiary and notifies the beneficiary of the credit. Acceptance by the beneficiary's bank does not create any obligation to the sender. Acceptance by the beneficiary's bank means that the bank is liable to the beneficiary for the amount of the

order. Section 4A–404(a). There are three ways in which the beneficiary's bank can accept a payment order which are described in the following comments.

5. Under Section 4A–209(b)(1), the beneficiary's bank can accept a payment order by paying the beneficiary. In the normal case of crediting an account of the beneficiary, payment occurs when the beneficiary is given notice of the right to withdraw the credit, the credit is applied to a debt of the beneficiary, or "funds with respect to the order" are otherwise made available to the beneficiary. Section 4A–405(a). The quoted phrase covers cases in which funds are made available to the beneficiary as a result of receipt of a payment order for the benefit of the beneficiary but the release of funds is not expressed as payment of the order. For example, the beneficiary's bank might express a release of funds equal to the amount of the order as a "loan" that will be automatically repaid when the beneficiary's bank receives payment by the sender of the order. If the release of funds is designated as a loan pursuant to a routine practice of the bank, the release is conditional payment of the order rather than a loan, particularly if normal incidents of a loan such as the signing of a loan agreement or note and the payment of interest are not present. Such a release of funds is payment to the beneficiary under Section 4A–405(a). Under Section 4A–405(c) the bank cannot recover the money from the beneficiary if the bank does not receive payment from the sender of the payment order that it accepted. Exceptions to this rule are stated in § 4A–405(d) and (e). The beneficiary's bank may also accept by notifying the beneficiary that the order has been received. "Notifies" is defined in Section 1–201(26). In some cases a beneficiary's bank will receive a payment order during the day but settlement of the sender's obligation to pay the order will not occur until the end of the day. If the beneficiary's bank wants to defer incurring liability to the beneficiary until the beneficiary's bank receives payment, it can do so. The beneficiary's bank incurs no liability to the beneficiary with respect to a payment order that it receives until it accepts the order. If the bank does not accept pursuant to subsection (b)(1), acceptance does not occur until the end of the day when the beneficiary's bank receives settlement. If the sender settles, the payment order will be accepted under subsection (b)(2) and the funds will be released to the beneficiary the next morning. If the sender doesn't settle, no acceptance occurs. In either case the beneficiary's bank suffers no loss.

6. In most cases the beneficiary's bank will receive a payment order from another bank. If the sender is a bank and the beneficiary's bank receives payment from the sender by final settlement through the Federal Reserve System or a funds transfer system (Section 4A–403(a)(1)) or, less commonly, through credit to an account of the beneficiary's bank with the sender or another bank (Section 4A–403(a)(2)), acceptance by the beneficiary's bank occurs at the time payment is made. Section 4A–209(b)(2). A minor exception to this rule is stated in Section 4A–209(c). Section 4A–209(b)(2) results in automatic acceptance of payment orders issued to a beneficiary's bank by means of Fedwire because the Federal Reserve account of the beneficiary's bank is credited and final payment is made to that bank when the payment order is received.

Subsection (b)(2) would also apply to cases in which the beneficiary's bank mistakenly pays a person who is not the beneficiary of the payment order issued to the beneficiary's bank. For example, suppose the payment order provides for immediate payment to Account #12345. The beneficiary's bank erroneously credits Account #12346 and notifies the holder of that account of the credit. No acceptance occurs in this case under subsection (b)(1) because the beneficiary of the order has not been paid or notified. The holder of Account #12345 is the beneficiary of the order issued to the beneficiary's bank. But acceptance will normally occur if the beneficiary's bank takes no other action, because the bank will normally receive settlement with respect to the payment order. At that time the bank has accepted because the sender paid its payment order. The bank is liable to pay the holder of Account #12345. The bank has paid the holder of Account #12346 by mistake, and has a right to recover the payment if the credit is withdrawn, to the extent provided in the law governing mistake and restitution.

7. Subsection (b)(3) covers cases of inaction by the beneficiary's bank. It applies whether or not the sender is a bank and covers a case in which the sender and the beneficiary both have accounts with the receiving bank and payment will be made by debiting the account of the sender and crediting the account of the beneficiary. Subsection (b)(3) is similar to subsection (b)(2) in that it bases acceptance by the beneficiary's bank on payment by the sender. Payment by the sender is effected by a debit to the sender's account if the account balance is sufficient to cover the amount of the order. On the payment date (Section 4A–401) of the order the beneficiary's bank will normally credit the beneficiary's account and notify the beneficiary of receipt of the order if it is satisfied that the sender's account balance covers the order or is willing to give credit to the sender. In some cases, however, the bank may not be willing to give credit to the sender and it may not be possible for the bank to determine until the

end of the day on the payment date whether there are sufficient good funds in the sender's account. There may be various transactions during the day involving funds going into and out of the account. Some of these transactions may occur late in the day or after the close of the banking day. To accommodate this situation, subsection (b)(3) provides that the status of the account is determined at the opening of the next funds transfer business day of the beneficiary's bank after the payment date of the order. If the sender's account balance is sufficient to cover the order, the beneficiary's bank has a source of payment and the result in almost all cases is that the bank accepts the order at that time if it did not previously accept under subsection (b)(1). In rare cases, a bank may want to avoid acceptance under subsection (b)(3) by rejecting the order as discussed in Comment 8.

8. Section 4A–209 is based on a general principle that a receiving bank is not obliged to accept a payment order unless it has agreed or is bound by a funds transfer system rule to do so. Thus, provision is made to allow the receiving bank to prevent acceptance of the order. This principle is consistently followed if the receiving bank is not the beneficiary's bank. If the receiving bank is not the beneficiary's bank, acceptance is in the control of the receiving bank because it occurs only if the order is executed. But in the case of the beneficiary's bank acceptance can occur by passive receipt of payment under subsection (b)(2) or (3). In the case of a payment made by Fedwire acceptance cannot be prevented. In other cases the beneficiary's bank can prevent acceptance by giving notice of rejection to the sender before payment occurs under Section 4A–403(a)(1) or (2). A minor exception to the ability of the beneficiary's bank to reject is stated in Section 4A–502(c)(3).

Under subsection (b)(3) acceptance occurs at the opening of the next funds transfer business day of the beneficiary's bank following the payment date unless the bank rejected the order before that time or it rejects within one hour after that time. In some cases the sender and the beneficiary's bank may not be in the same time zone or the beginning of the business day of the sender and the funds transfer business day of the beneficiary's bank may not coincide. For example, the sender may be located in California and the beneficiary's bank in New York. Since in most cases notice of rejection would be communicated electronically or by telephone, it might not be feasible for the bank to give notice before one hour after the opening of the funds transfer business day in New York because at that hour, the sender's business day may not have started in California. For that reason, there are alter-

native deadlines stated in subsection (b)(3). In the case stated, the bank acts in time if it gives notice within one hour after the opening of the business day of the sender. But if the notice of rejection is received by the sender after the payment date, the bank is obliged to pay interest to the sender if the sender's account does not bear interest. In that case the bank had the use of funds of the sender that the sender could reasonably assume would be used to pay the beneficiary. The rate of interest is stated in Section 4A–506. If the sender receives notice on the day after the payment date the sender is entitled to one day's interest. If receipt of notice is delayed for more than one day, the sender is entitled to interest for each additional day of delay.

9. Subsection (d) applies only to a payment order by the originator of a funds transfer to the originator's bank and it refers to the following situation. On April 1, Originator instructs Bank A to make a payment on April 15 to the account of Beneficiary in Bank B. By mistake, on April 1, Bank A executes Originator's payment order by issuing a payment order to Bank B instructing immediate payment to Beneficiary. Bank B credited Beneficiary's account and immediately released the funds to Beneficiary. Under subsection (d) no acceptance by Bank A occurred on April 1 when Originator's payment order was executed because acceptance cannot occur before the execution date which in this case would be April 15 or shortly before that date. Section 4A–301(b). Under Section 4A–402(c), Originator is not obliged to pay Bank A until the order is accepted and that can't occur until the execution date. But Bank A is required to pay Bank B when Bank B accepted Bank A's order on April 1. Unless Originator and Beneficiary are the same person, in almost all cases Originator is paying a debt owed to Beneficiary and early payment does not injure Originator because Originator does not have to pay Bank A until the execution date. Section 4A–402(c). Bank A takes the interest loss. But suppose that on April 3, Originator concludes that no debt was owed to Beneficiary or that the debt was less than the amount of the payment order. Under Section 4A–211(b) Originator can cancel its payment order if Bank A has not accepted. If early execution of Originator's payment order is acceptance, Originator can suffer a loss because cancellation after acceptance is not possible without the consent of Bank A and Bank B. Section 4A–211(c). If Originator has to pay Bank A, Originator would be required to seek recovery of the money from Beneficiary. Subsection (d) prevents this result and puts the risk of loss on Bank A by providing that the early execution does not result in acceptance until the execu-

tion date. Since on April 3 Originator's order was not yet accepted, Originator can cancel it under Section 4A–211(b). The result is that Bank A is not entitled to payment from Originator but is obliged to pay Bank B. Bank A has paid Beneficiary by mistake. If Originator's payment order is cancelled, Bank A becomes the originator of an erroneous funds transfer to Beneficiary. Bank A has the burden of recovering payment from Beneficiary on the basis of a payment by mistake. If Beneficiary received the money in good faith in payment of a debt owed to Beneficiary by Originator, the law of mistake and restitution may allow Beneficiary to keep all or part of the money received. If Originator owed money to Beneficiary, Bank A has paid Originator's debt and, under the law of restitution, which applies pursuant to Section 1–103, Bank A is subrogated to Beneficiary's rights against Originator on the debt.

If Bank A is the Beneficiary's bank and Bank A credited Beneficiary's account and released the funds to Beneficiary on April 1, the analysis is similar. If Originator's order is cancelled, Bank A has paid Beneficiary by mistake. The right of Bank A to recover the payment from Beneficiary is similar to Bank A's rights in the preceding paragraph.

§ 4A–210.   Rejection of Payment Order.

(a) A payment order is rejected by the receiving bank by a notice of rejection transmitted to the sender orally, electronically, or in writing. A notice of rejection need not use any particular words and is sufficient if it indicates that the receiving bank is rejecting the order or will not execute or pay the order. Rejection is effective when the notice is given if transmission is by a means that is reasonable in the circumstances. If notice of rejection is given by a means that is not reasonable, rejection is effective when the notice is received. If an agreement of the sender and receiving bank establishes the means to be used to reject a payment order, (i) any means complying with the agreement is reasonable and (ii) any means not complying is not reasonable unless no significant delay in receipt of the notice resulted from the use of the noncomplying means.

(b) This subsection applies if a receiving bank other than the beneficiary's bank fails to execute a payment order despite the existence on the execution date of a withdrawable credit balance in an authorized account of the sender sufficient to cover the order. If the sender does not receive notice of rejection of the order on the execution date and the authorized account of the sender does not bear interest, the bank is obliged to pay interest to the sender on the amount of the order for the number of days elapsing after the execution date to the earlier of the day the order is canceled pursuant to Section 4A–211(d) or the day the sender receives notice or learns that the order was not executed, counting the final day of the period as an elapsed day. If the withdrawable credit balance during that period falls below the amount of the order, the amount of interest is reduced accordingly.

(c) If a receiving bank suspends payments, all unaccepted payment orders issued to it are deemed rejected at the time the bank suspends payments.

(d) Acceptance of a payment order precludes a later rejection of the order. Rejection of a payment order precludes a later acceptance of the order.

Official Comment

1. With respect to payment orders issued to a receiving bank other than the beneficiary's bank, notice of rejection is not necessary to prevent acceptance of the order. Acceptance can occur only if the receiving bank executes the order. Section 4A–209(a). But notice of rejection will routinely be given by such a bank in cases in which the bank cannot or is not willing to execute the order for some reason. There are many reasons why a bank doesn't execute an order. The payment order may not clearly instruct the receiving bank because of some ambiguity in the order or an internal inconsistency. In some cases, the receiving bank may not be able to carry out the instruction because of equipment failure, credit limitations on the receiving bank, or some other factor which makes proper execution of the order infeasible. In those cases notice of rejection is a means of informing the sender of the facts so that a corrected payment order can be transmitted or the sender can seek alternate means of completing the funds transfer. The other major reason for not executing an order is that the sender's account is insufficient to cover the order and the receiving bank is not willing to give credit to the sender. If the sender's account is sufficient to cover the order and the receiving bank chooses not to execute the order, notice of rejection is necessary to prevent liability to pay interest to the sender if the case falls within Section 4A–210(b) which is discussed in Comment 3.

2. A payment order to the beneficiary's bank can be accepted by inaction of the bank. Section 4A–209(b)(2) and (3). To prevent acceptance under those provisions it is necessary for the receiving bank to send notice of rejection before acceptance occurs. Subsection (a) of Section 4A–210 states the rule that rejection is accomplished by giving notice of rejection. This incorporates the definitions in Section 1–201(26). Rejection is effective when notice is given if it is given by a means that is reasonable in the circumstances. Otherwise, it is effective when the notice is received. The question of when rejection is effective is important only in the relatively few cases under subsection (b)(2) and (3) in which a notice of rejection is necessary to prevent acceptance. The question of whether a particular means is reasonable depends on the facts in a particular case. In a very large percentage of cases the sender and the receiving bank will be in direct electronic contact with each other and in those cases a notice of rejection can be transmitted instantaneously. Since time is of the essence in a large proportion of funds transfers, some quick means of transmission would usually be required, but this is not always the case. The parties may specify by agreement the means by which communication between the parties is to be made.

3. Subsection (b) deals with cases in which a sender does not learn until after the execution date that the sender's order has not been executed. It applies only to cases in which the receiving bank was assured of payment because the sender's account was sufficient to cover the order. Normally, the receiving bank will accept the sender's order if it is assured of payment, but there may be some cases in which the bank chooses to reject. Unless the receiving bank had obligated itself by agreement to accept, the failure to accept is not wrongful. There is no duty of the receiving bank to accept the payment order unless it is obliged to accept by express agreement. Section 4A–212. But even if the bank has not acted wrongfully, the receiving bank had the use of the sender's money that the sender could reasonably assume was to be the source of payment of the funds transfer. Until the sender learns that the order was not accepted the sender is denied the use of that money. Subsection (b) obliges the receiving bank to pay interest to the sender as restitution unless the sender receives notice of rejection on the execution date. The time of receipt of notice is determined pursuant to § 1–201(27). The rate of interest is stated in Section 4A–506. If the sender receives notice on the day after the execution date, the sender is entitled to one day's interest. If receipt of notice is delayed for more than one day, the sender is entitled to interest for each additional day of delay.

4. Subsection (d) treats acceptance and rejection as mutually exclusive. If a payment order has been accepted, rejection of that order becomes impossible. If a payment order has been rejected it cannot be accepted later by the receiving bank. Once notice of rejection has been given, the sender may have acted on the notice by making the payment through other channels. If the receiving bank wants to act on a payment order that it has rejected it has to obtain the consent of the sender. In that case the consent of the sender would amount to the giving of a second payment order that substitutes for the rejected first order. If the receiving bank suspends payments (Section 4–104(1)(k)), subsection (c) provides that unaccepted payment orders are deemed rejected at the time suspension of payments occurs. This prevents acceptance by passage of time under Section 4A–209(b)(3).

§ 4A–211. Cancellation and Amendment of Payment Order.

(a) A communication of the sender of a payment order cancelling or amending the order may be transmitted to the receiving bank orally, electronically, or in writing. If a security procedure is in effect between the sender and the receiving bank, the communication is not effective to cancel or amend the order unless the communication is verified pursuant to the security procedure or the bank agrees to the cancellation or amendment.

(b) Subject to subsection (a), a communication by the sender cancelling or amending a payment order is effective to cancel or amend the order if notice of the communication is received at a time and in a manner affording the receiving bank a reasonable opportunity to act on the communication before the bank accepts the payment order.

(c) After a payment order has been accepted, cancellation or amendment of the order is not effective unless the receiving bank agrees or a funds-transfer system rule allows cancellation or amendment without agreement of the bank.

(1) With respect to a payment order accepted by a receiving bank other than the beneficiary's bank, cancellation or amendment is not effective unless a conforming cancellation or amendment of the payment order issued by the receiving bank is also made.

(2) With respect to a payment order accepted by the beneficiary's bank, cancellation or amendment is not effective unless the order was issued in execution of an unauthorized payment order, or because of a mistake by a sender in the funds transfer which resulted in the issuance of a payment order (i) that is a duplicate of a payment order previously issued by the sender, (ii) that orders payment to a beneficiary not entitled to receive payment from the originator, or (iii) that orders payment in an amount greater than the amount the beneficiary was entitled to receive from the originator. If the payment order is canceled or amended, the beneficiary's bank is entitled to recover from the beneficiary any amount paid to the beneficiary to the extent allowed by the law governing mistake and restitution.

(d) An unaccepted payment order is canceled by operation of law at the close of the fifth funds-transfer business day of the receiving bank after the execution date or payment date of the order.

(e) A canceled payment order cannot be accepted. If an accepted payment order is canceled, the acceptance is nullified and no person has any right or obligation based on the acceptance. Amendment of a payment order is deemed to be cancellation of the original order at the time of amendment and issue of a new payment order in the amended form at the same time.

(f) Unless otherwise provided in an agreement of the parties or in a funds-transfer system rule, if the receiving bank, after accepting a payment order, agrees to cancellation or amendment of the order by the sender or is bound by a funds-transfer system rule allowing cancellation or amendment without the bank's agreement, the sender, whether or not cancellation or amendment is effective, is liable to the bank for any loss and expenses, including reasonable attorney's fees, incurred by the bank as a result of the cancellation or amendment or attempted cancellation or amendment.

(g) A payment order is not revoked by the death or legal incapacity of the sender unless the receiving bank knows of the death or of an adjudication of incapacity by a court of competent jurisdiction and has reasonable opportunity to act before acceptance of the order.

(h) A funds-transfer system rule is not effective to the extent it conflicts with subsection (c)(2).

Official Comment

1. This section deals with cancellation and amendment of payment orders. It states the conditions under which cancellation or amendment is both effective and rightful. There is no concept of wrongful cancellation or amendment of a payment order. If the conditions stated in this section are not met the attempted cancellation or amendment is not effective. If the stated conditions are met the cancellation or amendment is effective and rightful. The sender of a payment order may want to withdraw or change the order because the sender has had a change of mind about the transaction or because the payment order was erroneously issued or for any other reason. One common situation is that of multiple transmission of the same order. The sender that mistakenly transmits the same order twice wants to correct the mistake by cancelling the duplicate order. Or, a sender may have intended to order a payment of $1,000,000 but mistakenly issued an order to pay $10,000,000. In this case the sender might try to correct the mistake by cancelling the order and issuing another order in the proper amount. Or, the mistake could be corrected by amending the order to change it to the proper amount. Whether the error is corrected by amendment or cancellation and reissue the net result is the same. This result is stated in the last sentence of subsection (e).

2. Subsection (a) allows a cancellation or amendment of a payment order to be communicated to the receiving bank "orally, electronically, or in writing." The quoted phrase is consistent with the language of Section 4A–103(a) applicable to payment orders. Cancellations and amendments are normally subject to verification pursuant to security procedures to the same extent as payment orders. Subsection (a) recognizes this fact by providing that in cases in which there is a security procedure in effect between the sender and the receiving bank the bank is not bound by a communication cancelling or amending an order unless verification has been made. This is necessary to protect the bank because under subsection (b) a cancellation or amendment can be effective by unilateral action of the sender. Without verification the bank cannot be sure whether the communication was or was not effective to cancel or amend a previously verified payment order.

3. If the receiving bank has not yet accepted the order, there is no reason why the sender should not be able to cancel or amend the order unilaterally so long

as the requirements of subsections (a) and (b) are met. If the receiving bank has accepted the order, it is possible to cancel or amend but only if the requirements of subsection (c) are met.

First consider the case of a receiving bank other than the beneficiary's bank. If the bank has not yet accepted the order, the sender can unilaterally cancel or amend. The communication amending or cancelling the payment order must be received in time to allow the bank to act on it before the bank issues its payment order in execution of the sender's order. The time that the sender's communication is received is governed by Section 4a–106. If a payment order does not specify a delayed payment date or execution date, the order will normally be executed shortly after receipt. Thus, as a practical matter, the sender will have very little time in which to instruct cancellation or amendment before acceptance. In addition, a receiving bank will normally have cut-off times for receipt of such communications, and the receiving bank is not obliged to act on communications received after the cut-off hour. Cancellation by the sender after execution of the order by the receiving bank requires the agreement of the bank unless a funds transfer rule otherwise provides. Subsection (c). Although execution of the sender's order by the receiving bank does not itself impose liability on the receiving bank (under Section 4A–402 no liability is incurred by the receiving bank to pay its order until it is accepted), it would commonly be the case that acceptance follows shortly after issuance. Thus, as a practical matter, a receiving bank that has executed a payment order will incur a liability to the next bank in the chain before it would be able to act on the cancellation request of its customer. It is unreasonable to impose on the receiving bank a risk of loss with respect to a cancellation request without the consent of the receiving bank.

The statute does not state how or when the agreement of the receiving bank must be obtained for cancellation after execution. The receiving bank's consent could be obtained at the time cancellation occurs or it could be based on a preexisting agreement. Or, a funds transfer system rule could provide that cancellation can be made unilaterally by the sender. By virtue of that rule any receiving bank covered by the rule is bound. Section 4A–501. If the receiving bank has already executed the sender's order, the bank would not consent to cancellation unless the bank to which the receiving bank has issued its payment order consents to cancellation of that order. It makes no sense to allow cancellation of a payment order unless all subsequent payment orders in the funds transfer that were issued because of the cancelled payment order are

also cancelled. Under subsection (c)(1), if a receiving bank consents to cancellation of the payment order after it has executed, the cancellation is not effective unless the receiving bank also cancels the payment order issued by the bank.

4. With respect to a payment order issued to the beneficiary's bank, acceptance is particularly important because it creates liability to pay the beneficiary, it defines when the originator pays its obligation to the beneficiary, and it defines when any obligation for which the payment is made is discharged. Since acceptance affects the rights of the originator and the beneficiary it is not appropriate to allow the beneficiary's bank to agree to cancellation or amendment except in unusual cases. Except as provided in subsection (c)(2), cancellation or amendment after acceptance by the beneficiary's bank is not possible unless all parties affected by the order agree. Under subsection (c)(2), cancellation or amendment is possible only in the four cases stated. The following examples illustrate subsection (c)(2):

Case #1. Originator's Bank executed a payment order issued in the name of its customer as sender. The order was not authorized by the customer and was fraudulently issued. Beneficiary's Bank accepted the payment order issued by Originator's Bank. Under subsection (c)(2) Originator's Bank can cancel the order if Beneficiary's Bank consents. It doesn't make any difference whether the payment order that Originator's Bank accepted was or was not enforceable against the customer under Section 4A–202(b). Verification under that provision is important in determining whether Originator's Bank or the customer has the risk of loss, but it has no relevance under Section 4A–211(c)(2). Whether or not verified, the payment order was not authorized by the customer. Cancellation of the payment order to Beneficiary's Bank causes the acceptance of Beneficiary's Bank to be nullified. Subsection (e). Beneficiary's Bank is entitled to recover payment from the beneficiary to the extent allowed by the law of mistake and restitution. In this kind of case the beneficiary is usually a party to the fraud who has no right to receive or retain payment of the order.

Case #2. Originator owed Beneficiary $1,000,000 and ordered Bank A to pay that amount to the account of Beneficiary in Bank B. Bank A issued a complying order to Bank B, but by mistake issued a duplicate order as well. Bank B accepted both orders. Under subsection (c)(2)(i) cancellation of the duplicate order could be made by Bank A with the consent of Bank B. Beneficiary has no right to receive or retain payment of the duplicate payment order if only $1,000,000 was owed by Originator to Beneficiary. If Originator owed

$2,000,000 to Beneficiary, the law of restitution might allow Beneficiary to retain the $1,000,000 paid by Bank B on the duplicate order. In that case Bank B is entitled to reimbursement from Bank A under subsection (f).

Case #3. Originator owed $1,000,000 to X. Intending to pay X, Originator ordered Bank A to pay $1,000,000 to Y's account in Bank B. Bank A issued a complying payment order to Bank B which Bank B accepted by releasing the $1,000,000 to Y. Under subsection (c)(2)(ii) Bank A can cancel its payment order to Bank B with the consent of Bank B if Y was not entitled to receive payment from Originator. Originator can also cancel its order to Bank A with Bank A's consent. Subsection (c)(1). Bank B may recover the $1,000,000 from Y unless the law of mistake and restitution allows Y to retain some or all of the amount paid. If no debt was owed to Y, Bank B should have a right of recovery.

Case #4. Originator owed Beneficiary $10,000. By mistake Originator ordered Bank A to pay $1,000,000 to the account of Beneficiary in Bank B. Bank A issued a complying order to Bank B which accepted by notifying Beneficiary of its right to withdraw $1,000,000. Cancellation is permitted in this case under subsection (c)(2)(iii). If Bank B paid Beneficiary it is entitled to recover the payment except to the extent the law of mistake and restitution allows Beneficiary to retain payment. In this case Beneficiary might be entitled to retain $10,000, the amount of the debt owed to Beneficiary. If Beneficiary may retain $10,000, Bank B would be entitled to $10,000 from Bank A pursuant to subsection (f). In this case Originator also cancelled its order. Thus Bank A would be entitled to $10,000 from Originator pursuant to subsection (f).

5. Unless constrained by a funds transfer system rule, a receiving bank may agree to cancellation or amendment of the payment order under subsection (c) but is not required to do so regardless of the circumstances. If the receiving bank has incurred liability as a result of its acceptance of the sender's order, there are substantial risks in agreeing to cancellation or amendment. This is particularly true for a beneficiary's bank. Cancellation or amendment after acceptance by the beneficiary's bank can be made only in the four cases stated and the beneficiary's bank may not have any way of knowing whether the requirements of subsection (c) have been met or whether it will be able to recover payment from the beneficiary that received payment. Even with indemnity the beneficiary's bank may be reluctant to alienate its customer, the beneficiary, by denying the customer the funds. Subsection (c) leaves the decision to the beneficiary's

bank unless the consent of the beneficiary's bank is not required under a funds transfer system rule or other interbank agreement. If a receiving bank agrees to cancellation or amendment under subsection (c)(1) or (2), it is automatically entitled to indemnification from the sender under subsection (f). The indemnification provision recognizes that a sender has no right to cancel a payment order after it is accepted by the receiving bank. If the receiving bank agrees to cancellation, it is doing so as an accommodation to the sender and it should not incur a risk of loss in doing so.

6. Acceptance by the receiving bank of a payment order issued by the sender is comparable to acceptance of an offer under the law of contracts. Under that law the death or legal incapacity of an offeror terminates the offer even though the offeree has no notice of the death or incapacity. Restatement Second, Contracts § 48. Comment a. to that section states that the "rule seems to be a relic of the obsolete view that a contract requires a 'meeting of minds,' and it is out of harmony with the modern doctrine that a manifestation of assent is effective without regard to actual mental assent." Subsection (g), which reverses the Restatement rule in the case of a payment order, is similar to Section 4–405(1) which applies to checks. Subsection (g) does not address the effect of the bankruptcy of the sender of a payment order before the order is accepted, but the principle of subsection (g) has been recognized in Bank of Marin v. England, 385 U.S. 99 (1966). Although Bankruptcy Code Section 542(c) may not have been drafted with wire transfers in mind, its language can be read to allow the receiving bank to charge the sender's account for the amount of the payment order if the receiving bank executed it in ignorance of the bankruptcy.

7. Subsection (d) deals with stale payment orders. Payment orders normally are executed on the execution date or the day after. An order issued to the beneficiary's bank is normally accepted on the payment date or the day after. If a payment order is not accepted on its execution or payment date or shortly thereafter, it is probable that there was some problem with the terms of the order or the sender did not have sufficient funds or credit to cover the amount of the order. Delayed acceptance of such an order is normally not contemplated, but the order may not have been cancelled by the sender. Subsection (d) provides for cancellation by operation of law to prevent an unexpected delayed acceptance.

8. A funds transfer system rule can govern rights and obligations between banks that are parties to payment orders transmitted over the system even if

the rule conflicts with Article 4A. In some cases, however, a rule governing a transaction between two banks can affect a third party in an unacceptable way. Subsection (h) deals with such a case. A funds transfer system rule cannot allow cancellation of a payment order accepted by the beneficiary's bank if the rule conflicts with subsection (c)(2). Because rights of the beneficiary and the originator are directly affected by acceptance, subsection (c)(2) severely limits cancellation. These limitations cannot be altered by funds transfer system rule.

§ 4A–212. Liability and Duty of Receiving Bank Regarding Unaccepted Payment Order.

If a receiving bank fails to accept a payment order that it is obliged by express agreement to accept, the bank is liable for breach of the agreement to the extent provided in the agreement or in this Article, but does not otherwise have any duty to accept a payment order or, before acceptance, to take any action, or refrain from taking action, with respect to the order except as provided in this Article or by express agreement. Liability based on acceptance arises only when acceptance occurs as stated in Section 4A–209, and liability is limited to that provided in this Article. A receiving bank is not the agent of the sender or beneficiary of the payment order it accepts, or of any other party to the funds transfer, and the bank owes no duty to any party to the funds transfer except as provided in this Article or by express agreement.

Official Comment

With limited exceptions stated in this Article, the duties and obligations of receiving banks that carry out a funds transfer arise only as a result of acceptance of payment orders or of agreements made by receiving banks. Exceptions are stated in Section 4A–209(b)(3) and Section 4A–210(b). A receiving bank is not like a collecting bank under Article 4. No receiving bank, whether it be an originator's bank, an intermediary bank or a beneficiary's bank, is an agent for any other party in the funds transfer.

PART 3

EXECUTION OF SENDER'S PAYMENT ORDER BY RECEIVING BANK

§ 4A–301. Execution and Execution Date.

(a) A payment order is "executed" by the receiving bank when it issues a payment order intended to carry out the payment order received by the bank. A payment order received by the beneficiary's bank can be accepted but cannot be executed.

(b) "Execution date" of a payment order means the day on which the receiving bank may properly issue a payment order in execution of the sender's order. The execution date may be determined by instruction of the sender but cannot be earlier than the day the order is received and, unless otherwise determined, is the day the order is received. If the sender's instruction states a payment date, the execution date is the payment date or an earlier date on which execution is reasonably necessary to allow payment to the beneficiary on the payment date.

Official Comment

1. The terms "executed," "execution" and "execution date" are used only with respect to a payment order to a receiving bank other than the beneficiary's bank. The beneficiary's bank can accept the payment order that it receives, but it does not execute the order. Execution refers to the act of the receiving bank in issuing a payment order "intended to carry out" the payment order that the bank received. A receiving bank has executed an order even if the order issued by the bank does not carry out the order received by the bank. For example, the bank may have erroneously issued an order to the wrong beneficiary, or in the wrong amount or to the wrong beneficiary's bank. In each of these cases execution has occurred but the execution is erroneous. Erroneous execution is covered in Section 4A–303.

2. "Execution date" refers to the time a payment order should be executed rather than the day it is actually executed. Normally the sender will not specify an execution date, but most payment orders are meant to be executed immediately. Thus, the execution date is normally the day the order is received by the receiving bank. It is common for the sender to

specify a "payment date" which is defined in Section 4A–401 as "the day on which the amount of the order is payable to the beneficiary by the beneficiary's bank." Except for automated clearing house transfers, if a funds transfer is entirely within the United States and the payment is to be carried out electronically, the execution date is the payment date unless the order is received after the payment date. If the payment is to be carried out through an automated clearing house, execution may occur before the payment date. In an ACH transfer the beneficiary is usually paid one or two days after issue of the originator's payment order. The execution date is determined by the stated payment date and is a day before the payment date on which execution is reasonably necessary to allow payment on the payment date. A funds transfer system rule could also determine the execution date of orders received by the receiving bank if both the sender and the receiving bank are participants in the funds transfer system. The execution date can be determined by the payment order itself or by separate instructions of the sender or an agreement of the sender and the receiving bank. The second sentence of subsection (b) must be read in the light of Section 4A–106 which states that if a payment order is received after the cut-off time of the receiving bank it may be treated by the bank as received at the opening of the next funds transfer business day.

3. Execution on the execution date is timely, but the order can be executed before or after the execution date. Section 4A–209(d) and Section 4A–402(c) state the consequences of early execution and Section 4A–305(a) states the consequences of late execution.

§ 4A–302. Obligations of Receiving Bank in Execution of Payment Order.

(a) Except as provided in subsections (b) through (d), if the receiving bank accepts a payment order pursuant to Section 4A–209(a), the bank has the following obligations in executing the order:

(1) The receiving bank is obliged to issue, on the execution date, a payment order complying with the sender's order and to follow the sender's instructions concerning (i) any intermediary bank or funds-transfer system to be used in carrying out the funds transfer, or (ii) the means by which payment orders are to be transmitted in the funds transfer. If the originator's bank issues a payment order to an intermediary bank, the originator's bank is obliged to instruct the intermediary bank ac-

cording to the instruction of the originator. An intermediary bank in the funds transfer is similarly bound by an instruction given to it by the sender of the payment order it accepts.

(2) If the sender's instruction states that the funds transfer is to be carried out telephonically or by wire transfer or otherwise indicates that the funds transfer is to be carried out by the most expeditious means, the receiving bank is obliged to transmit its payment order by the most expeditious available means, and to instruct any intermediary bank accordingly. If a sender's instruction states a payment date, the receiving bank is obliged to transmit its payment order at a time and by means reasonably necessary to allow payment to the beneficiary on the payment date or as soon thereafter as is feasible.

(b) Unless otherwise instructed, a receiving bank executing a payment order may (i) use any funds-transfer system if use of that system is reasonable in the circumstances, and (ii) issue a payment order to the beneficiary's bank or to an intermediary bank through which a payment order conforming to the sender's order can expeditiously be issued to the beneficiary's bank if the receiving bank exercises ordinary care in the selection of the intermediary bank. A receiving bank is not required to follow an instruction of the sender designating a funds-transfer system to be used in carrying out the funds transfer if the receiving bank, in good faith, determines that it is not feasible to follow the instruction or that following the instruction would unduly delay completion of the funds transfer.

(c) Unless subsection (a)(2) applies or the receiving bank is otherwise instructed, the bank may execute a payment order by transmitting its payment order by first class mail or by any means reasonable in the circumstances. If the receiving bank is instructed to execute the sender's order by transmitting its payment order by a particular means, the receiving bank may issue its payment order by the means stated or by any means as expeditious as the means stated.

(d) Unless instructed by the sender, (i) the receiving bank may not obtain payment of its charges for services and expenses in connection with the execution of the sender's order by issuing a payment order in an amount equal to the amount of the sender's order less the amount of the charges, and (ii) may not instruct a subsequent receiving bank to obtain payment of its charges in the same manner.

Official Comment

1. In the absence of agreement, the receiving bank is not obliged to execute an order of the sender. Section 4A–212. Section 4A–302 states the manner in which the receiving bank may execute the sender's order if execution occurs. Subsection (a)(1) states the residual rule. The payment order issued by the receiving bank must comply with the sender's order and, unless some other rule is stated in the section, the receiving bank is obliged to follow any instruction of the sender concerning which funds transfer system is to be used, which intermediary banks are to be used, and what means of transmission is to be used. The instruction of the sender may be incorporated in the payment order itself or may be given separately. For example, there may be a master agreement between the sender and receiving bank containing instructions governing payment orders to be issued from time to time by the sender to the receiving bank. In most funds transfers, speed is a paramount consideration. A sender that wants assurance that the funds transfer will be expeditiously completed can specify the means to be used. The receiving bank can follow the instructions literally or it can use an equivalent means. For example, if the sender instructs the receiving bank to transmit by telex, the receiving bank could use telephone instead. Subsection (c). In most cases the sender will not specify a particular means but will use a general term such as "by wire" or "wire transfer" or "as soon as possible." These words signify that the sender wants a same-day transfer. In these cases the receiving bank is required to use a telephonic or electronic communication to transmit its order and is also required to instruct any intermediary bank to which it issues its order to transmit by similar means. Subsection (a)(2). In other cases, such as an automated clearing house transfer, a same-day transfer is not contemplated. Normally the sender's instruction or the context in which the payment order is received makes clear the type of funds transfer that is appropriate. If the sender states a payment date with respect to the payment order, the receiving bank is obliged to execute the order at a time and in a manner to meet the payment date if that is feasible. Subsection (a)(2). This provision would apply to many ACH transfers made to pay recurring debts of the sender. In other cases, involving relatively small amounts, time may not be an important factor and cost may be a more important element. Fast means, such as telephone or elec-

tronic transmission, are more expensive than slow means such as mailing. Subsection (c) states that in the absence of instructions the receiving bank is given discretion to decide. It may issue its payment order by first class mail or by any means reasonable in the circumstances. Section 4A–305 states the liability of a receiving bank for breach of the obligations stated in Section 4A–302.

2. Subsection (b) concerns the choice of intermediary banks to be used in completing the funds transfer, and the funds transfer system to be used. If the receiving bank is not instructed about the matter, it can issue an order directly to the beneficiary's bank or can issue an order to an intermediary bank. The receiving bank also has discretion concerning use of a funds transfer system. In some cases it may be reasonable to use either an automated clearing house system or a wire transfer system such as Fedwire or CHIPS. Normally, the receiving bank will follow the instruction of the sender in these matters, but in some cases it may be prudent for the bank not to follow instructions. The sender may have designated a funds transfer system to be used in carrying out the funds transfer, but it may not be feasible to use the designated system because of some impediment such as a computer breakdown which prevents prompt execution of the order. The receiving bank is permitted to use an alternate means of transmittal in a good faith effort to execute the order expeditiously. The same leeway is not given to the receiving bank if the sender designates an intermediary bank through which the funds transfer is to be routed. The sender's designation of that intermediary bank may mean that the beneficiary's bank is expecting to obtain a credit from that intermediary bank and may have relied on that anticipated credit. If the receiving bank uses another intermediary bank the expectations of the beneficiary's bank may not be realized. The receiving bank could choose to route the transfer to another intermediary bank and then to the designated intermediary bank if there were some reason such as a lack of a correspondent-bank relationship or a bilateral credit limitation, but the designated intermediary bank cannot be circumvented. To do so violates the sender's instructions.

3. The normal rule, under subsection (a)(1), is that the receiving bank, in executing a payment order, is required to issue a payment order that complies as to amount with that of the sender's order. In most cases the receiving bank issues an order equal to the amount of the sender's order and makes a separate charge for services and expenses in executing the sender's order. In some cases, particularly if it is an intermediary bank that is executing an order, charges are collected by

deducting them from the amount of the payment order issued by the executing bank. If that is done, the amount of the payment order accepted by the beneficiary's bank will be slightly less than the amount of the originator's payment order. For example, Originator, in order to pay an obligation of $1,000,000 owed to Beneficiary, issues a payment order to Originator's Bank to pay $1,000,000 to the account of Beneficiary in Beneficiary's Bank. Originator's Bank issues a payment order to Intermediary Bank for $1,000,000 and debits Originator's account for $1,000,010. The extra $10 is the fee of Originator's Bank. Intermediary Bank executes the payment order of Originator's Bank by issuing a payment order to Beneficiary's Bank for $999,990, but under § 4A–402(c) is entitled to receive $1,000,000 from Originator's Bank. The $10 difference is the fee of Intermediary Bank. Beneficiary's Bank credits Beneficiary's account for $999,990. When Beneficiary's Bank accepts the payment order of Intermediary Bank the result is a payment of $999,990 from Originator to Beneficiary. Section 4A–406(a). If that payment discharges the $1,000,000 debt, the effect is that Beneficiary has paid the charges of Intermediary Bank and Originator has paid the charges of Originator's Bank. Subsection (d) of Section 4A–302 allows Intermediary Bank to collect its charges by deducting them from the amount of the payment order, but only if instructed to do so by Originator's Bank. Originator's Bank is not authorized to give that instruction to Intermediary Bank unless Originator authorized the instruction. Thus, Originator can control how the charges of Originator's Bank and Intermediary Bank are to be paid. Subsection (d) does not apply to charges of Beneficiary's Bank to Beneficiary.

In the case discussed in the preceding paragraph the $10 charge is trivial in relation to the amount of the payment and it may not be important to Beneficiary how the charge is paid. But it may be very important if the $1,000,000 obligation represented the price of exercising a right such as an option favorable to Originator and unfavorable to Beneficiary. Beneficiary might well argue that it was entitled to receive $1,000,000. If the option was exercised shortly before its expiration date, the result could be loss of the option benefit because the required payment of $1,000,000 was not made before the option expired. Section 4A–406(c) allows Originator to preserve the option benefit. The amount received by Beneficiary is deemed to be $1,000,000 unless Beneficiary demands the $10 and Originator does not pay it.

§ 4A–303. Erroneous Execution of Payment Order.

(a) A receiving bank that (i) executes the payment order of the sender by issuing a payment

order in an amount greater than the amount of the sender's order, or (ii) issues a payment order in execution of the sender's order and then issues a duplicate order, is entitled to payment of the amount of the sender's order under Section 4A–402(c) if that subsection is otherwise satisfied. The bank is entitled to recover from the beneficiary of the erroneous order the excess payment received to the extent allowed by the law governing mistake and restitution.

(b) A receiving bank that executes the payment order of the sender by issuing a payment order in an amount less than the amount of the sender's order is entitled to payment of the amount of the sender's order under Section 4A–402(c) if (i) that subsection is otherwise satisfied and (ii) the bank corrects its mistake by issuing an additional payment order for the benefit of the beneficiary of the sender's order. If the error is not corrected, the issuer of the erroneous order is entitled to receive or retain payment from the sender of the order it accepted only to the extent of the amount of the erroneous order. This subsection does not apply if the receiving bank executes the sender's payment order by issuing a payment order in an amount less than the amount of the sender's order for the purpose of obtaining payment of its charges for services and expenses pursuant to instruction of the sender.

(c) If a receiving bank executes the payment order of the sender by issuing a payment order to a beneficiary different from the beneficiary of the sender's order and the funds transfer is completed on the basis of that error, the sender of the payment order that was erroneously executed and all previous senders in the funds transfer are not obliged to pay the payment orders they issued. The issuer of the erroneous order is entitled to recover from the beneficiary of the order the payment received to the extent allowed by the law governing mistake and restitution.

Official Comment

1. Section 4A–303 states the effect of erroneous execution of a payment order by the receiving bank. Under Section 4A–402(c) the sender of a payment order is obliged to pay the amount of the order to the receiving bank if the bank executes the order, but the

obligation to pay is excused if the beneficiary's bank does not accept a payment order instructing payment to the beneficiary of the sender's order. If erroneous execution of the sender's order causes the wrong beneficiary to be paid, the sender is not required to pay. If erroneous execution causes the wrong amount to be paid the sender is not obliged to pay the receiving bank an amount in excess of the amount of the sender's order. Section 4A–303 takes precedence over Section 4A–402(c) and states the liability of the sender and the rights of the receiving bank in various cases of erroneous execution.

2. Subsections (a) and (b) deal with cases in which the receiving bank executes by issuing a payment order in the wrong amount. If Originator ordered Originator's Bank to pay $1,000,000 to the account of Beneficiary in Beneficiary's Bank, but Originator's Bank erroneously instructed Beneficiary's Bank to pay $2,000,000 to Beneficiary's account, subsection (a) applies. If Beneficiary's Bank accepts the order of Originator's Bank, Beneficiary's Bank is entitled to receive $2,000,000 from Originator's Bank, but Originator's Bank is entitled to receive only $1,000,000 from Originator. Originator's Bank is entitled to recover the overpayment from Beneficiary to the extent allowed by the law governing mistake and restitution. Originator's Bank would normally have a right to recover the overpayment from Beneficiary, but in unusual cases the law of restitution might allow Beneficiary to keep all or part of the overpayment. For example, if Originator owed $2,000,000 to Beneficiary and Beneficiary received the extra $1,000,000 in good faith in discharge of the debt, Beneficiary may be allowed to keep it. In this case Originator's Bank has paid an obligation of Originator and under the law of restitution, which applies through Section 1–103, Originator's Bank would be subrogated to Beneficiary's rights against Originator on the obligation paid by Originator's Bank.

If Originator's Bank erroneously executed Originator's order by instructing Beneficiary's Bank to pay less than $1,000,000, subsection (b) applies. If Originator's Bank corrects its error by issuing another payment order to Beneficiary's Bank that results in payment of $1,000,000 to Beneficiary, Originator's Bank is entitled to payment of $1,000,000 from Originator. If the mistake is not corrected, Originator's Bank is entitled to payment from Originator only in the amount of the order issued by Originator's Bank.

3. Subsection (a) also applies to duplicate payment orders. Assume Originator's Bank properly executes Originator's $1,000,000 payment order and then by mistake issues a second $1,000,000 payment order in execution of Originator's order. If Beneficiary's Bank accepts both orders issued by Originator's Bank, Beneficiary's Bank is entitled to receive $2,000,000 from Originator's Bank but Originator's Bank is entitled to receive only $1,000,000 from Originator. The remedy of Originator's Bank is the same as that of a receiving bank that executes by issuing an order in an amount greater than the sender's order. It may recover the overpayment from Beneficiary to the extent allowed by the law governing mistake and restitution and in a proper case as stated in Comment 2 may have subrogation rights if it is not entitled to recover from Beneficiary.

4. Suppose Originator instructs Originator's Bank to pay $1,000,000 to Account #12345 in Beneficiary's Bank. Originator's Bank erroneously instructs Beneficiary's Bank to pay $1,000,000 to Account #12346 and Beneficiary's Bank accepted. Subsection (c) covers this case. Originator is not obliged to pay its payment order, but Originator's Bank is required to pay $1,000,000 to Beneficiary's Bank. The remedy of Originator's Bank is to recover $1,000,000 from the holder of Account #12346 that received payment by mistake. Recovery based on the law of mistake and restitution is described in Comment 2.

§ 4A–304. Duty of Sender to Report Erroneously Executed Payment Order.

If the sender of a payment order that is erroneously executed as stated in Section 4A–303 receives notification from the receiving bank that the order was executed or that the sender's account was debited with respect to the order, the sender has a duty to exercise ordinary care to determine, on the basis of information available to the sender, that the order was erroneously executed and to notify the bank of the relevant facts within a reasonable time not exceeding 90 days after the notification from the bank was received by the sender. If the sender fails to perform that duty, the bank is not obliged to pay interest on any amount refundable to the sender under Section 4A–402(d) for the period before the bank learns of the execution error. The bank is not entitled to any recovery from the sender on account of a failure by the sender to perform the duty stated in this section.

Official Comment

This section is identical in effect to Section 4A–204 which applies to unauthorized orders issued in the name of a customer of the receiving bank. The rationale is stated in Comment 2 to Section 4A–204.

§ 4A–305. Liability for Late or Improper Execution or Failure to Execute Payment Order.

(a) If a funds transfer is completed but execution of a payment order by the receiving bank in breach of Section 4A–302 results in delay in payment to the beneficiary, the bank is obliged to pay interest to either the originator or the beneficiary of the funds transfer for the period of delay caused by the improper execution. Except as provided in subsection (c), additional damages are not recoverable.

(b) If execution of a payment order by a receiving bank in breach of Section 4A–302 results in (i) noncompletion of the funds transfer, (ii) failure to use an intermediary bank designated by the originator, or (iii) issuance of a payment order that does not comply with the terms of the payment order of the originator, the bank is liable to the originator for its expenses in the funds transfer and for incidental expenses and interest losses, to the extent not covered by subsection (a), resulting from the improper execution. Except as provided in subsection (c), additional damages are not recoverable.

(c) In addition to the amounts payable under subsections (a) and (b), damages, including consequential damages, are recoverable to the extent provided in an express written agreement of the receiving bank.

(d) If a receiving bank fails to execute a payment order it was obliged by express agreement to execute, the receiving bank is liable to the sender for its expenses in the transaction and for incidental expenses and interest losses resulting from the failure to execute. Additional damages, including consequential damages, are recoverable to the extent provided in an express written agreement of the receiving bank, but are not otherwise recoverable.

(e) Reasonable attorney's fees are recoverable if demand for compensation under subsection (a) or (b) is made and refused before an action is brought on the claim. If a claim is made for breach of an agreement under subsection (d) and the agreement does not provide for damages, reasonable attorney's fees are recoverable if demand for compensation under subsection (d) is made and refused before an action is brought on the claim.

(f) Except as stated in this section, the liability of a receiving bank under subsections (a) and (b) may not be varied by agreement.

Official Comment

1. Subsection (a) covers cases of delay in completion of a funds transfer resulting from an execution by a receiving bank in breach of Section 4A–302(a). The receiving bank is obliged to pay interest on the amount of the order for the period of the delay. The rate of interest is stated in Section 4A–506. With respect to wire transfers (other than ACH transactions) within the United States, the expectation is that the funds transfer will be completed the same day. In those cases, the originator can reasonably expect that the originator's account will be debited on the same day as the beneficiary's account is credited. If the funds transfer is delayed, compensation can be paid either to the originator or to the beneficiary. The normal practice is to compensate the beneficiary's bank to allow that bank to compensate the beneficiary by back-valuing the payment by the number of days of delay. Thus, the beneficiary is in the same position that it would have been in if the funds transfer had been completed on the same day. Assume on Day 1, Originator's Bank issues its payment order to Intermediary Bank which is received on that day. Intermediary Bank does not execute that order until Day 2 when it issues an order to Beneficiary's Bank which is accepted on that day. Intermediary Bank complies with subsection (a) by paying one day's interest to Beneficiary's Bank for the account of Beneficiary.

2. Subsection (b) applies to cases of breach of Section 4A–302 involving more than mere delay. In those cases the bank is liable for damages for improper execution but they are limited to compensation for interest losses and incidental expenses of the sender resulting from the breach, the expenses of the sender in the funds transfer and attorney's fees. This subsection reflects the judgment that imposition of consequential damages on a bank for commission of an error is not justified.

The leading common law case on the subject of consequential damages is Evra Corp. v. Swiss Bank Corp., 673 F.2d 951 (7th Cir.1982), in which Swiss Bank, an intermediary bank, failed to execute a payment order. Because the beneficiary did not receive timely payment the originator lost a valuable ship charter. The lower court awarded the originator $2.1

million for lost profits even though the amount of the payment order was only $27,000. The Seventh Circuit reversed, in part on the basis of the common law rule of Hadley v. Baxendale that consequential damages may not be awarded unless the defendant is put on notice of the special circumstances giving rise to them. Swiss Bank may have known that the originator was paying the shipowner for the hire of a vessel but did not know that a favorable charter would be lost if the payment was delayed. "Electronic payments are not so unusual as to automatically place a bank on notice of extraordinary consequences if such a transfer goes awry. Swiss Bank did not have enough information to infer that if it lost a $27,000 payment order it would face liability in excess of $2 million." 673 F.2d at 956.

If *Evra* means that consequential damages can be imposed if the culpable bank has notice of particular circumstances giving rise to the damages, it does not provide an acceptable solution to the problem of bank liability for consequential damages. In the typical case transmission of the payment order is made electronically. Personnel of the receiving bank that process payment orders are not the appropriate people to evaluate the risk of liability for consequential damages in relation to the price charged for the wire transfer service. Even if notice is received by higher level management personnel who could make an appropriate decision whether the risk is justified by the price, liability based on notice would require evaluation of payment orders on an individual basis. This kind of evaluation is inconsistent with the high-speed, low-price, mechanical nature of the processing system that characterizes wire transfers. Moreover, in *Evra* the culpable bank was an intermediary bank with which the originator did not deal. Notice to the originator's bank would not bind the intermediary bank, and it seems impractical for the originator's bank to convey notice of this kind to intermediary banks in the funds transfer. The success of the wholesale wire transfer industry has largely been based on its ability to effect payment at low cost and great speed. Both of these essential aspects of the modern wire transfer system would be adversely affected by a rule that imposed on banks liability for consequential damages. A banking industry amicus brief in *Evra* stated: "Whether banks can continue to make EFT services available on a widespread basis, by charging reasonable rates, depends on whether they can do so without incurring unlimited consequential risks. Certainly, no bank would handle for $3.25 a transaction entailing potential liability in the millions of dollars."

As the court in *Evra* also noted, the originator of the funds transfer is in the best position to evaluate the risk that a funds transfer will not be made on time and to manage that risk by issuing a payment order in time to allow monitoring of the transaction. The originator, by asking the beneficiary, can quickly determine if the funds transfer has been completed. If the originator has sent the payment order at a time that allows a reasonable margin for correcting error, no loss is likely to result if the transaction is monitored. The other published cases on this issue reach the *Evra* result. Central Coordinates, Inc. v. Morgan Guaranty Trust Co., 40 U.C.C.Rep.Serv. 1340 (N.Y.Sup.Ct.1985), and Gatoil (U.S.A.), Inc. v. Forest Hill State Bank, 1 U.C.C.Rep.Serv.2d 171 (D.Md.1986).

Subsection (c) allows the measure of damages in subsection (b) to be increased by an express written agreement of the receiving bank. An originator's bank might be willing to assume additional responsibilities and incur additional liability in exchange for a higher fee.

3. Subsection (d) governs cases in which a receiving bank has obligated itself by express agreement to accept payment orders of a sender. In the absence of such an agreement there is no obligation by a receiving bank to accept a payment order. Section 4A–212. The measure of damages for breach of an agreement to accept a payment order is the same as that stated in subsection (b). As in the case of subsection (b), additional damages, including consequential damages, may be recovered to the extent stated in an express written agreement of the receiving bank.

4. Reasonable attorney's fees are recoverable only in cases in which damages are limited to statutory damages stated in subsections (a), (b) and (d). If additional damages are recoverable because provided for by an express written agreement, attorney's fees are not recoverable. The rationale is that there is no need for statutory attorney's fees in the latter case, because the parties have agreed to a measure of damages which may or may not provide for attorney's fees.

5. The effect of subsection (f) is to prevent reduction of a receiving bank's liability under Section 4A–305.

PART 4

PAYMENT

§ 4A–401. Payment Date.

"Payment date" of a payment order means the day on which the amount of the order is payable to the beneficiary by the beneficiary's bank. The payment date may be determined by instruction of the sender but cannot be earlier than the day the order is received by the beneficiary's bank and, unless otherwise determined, is the day the order is received by the beneficiary's bank.

Official Comment

"Payment date" refers to the day the beneficiary's bank is to pay the beneficiary. The payment date may be expressed in various ways so long as it indicates the day the beneficiary is to receive payment. For example, in ACH transfers the payment date is the equivalent of "settlement date" or "effective date." Payment date applies to the payment order issued to the beneficiary's bank, but a payment order issued to a receiving bank other than the beneficiary's bank may also state a date for payment to the beneficiary. In the latter case, the statement of a payment date is to instruct the receiving bank concerning time of execution of the sender's order. Section 4A–301(b).

§ 4A–402. Obligation of Sender to Pay Receiving Bank.

(a) This section is subject to Sections 4A–205 and 4A–207.

(b) With respect to a payment order issued to the beneficiary's bank, acceptance of the order by the bank obliges the sender to pay the bank the amount of the order, but payment is not due until the payment date of the order.

(c) This subsection is subject to subsection (e) and to Section 4A–303. With respect to a payment order issued to a receiving bank other than the beneficiary's bank, acceptance of the order by the receiving bank obliges the sender to pay the bank the amount of the sender's order. Payment by the sender is not due until the execution date of the sender's order. The obligation of that sender to pay its payment order is excused if the funds transfer is not completed by acceptance by the beneficiary's bank of a payment order instructing payment to the beneficiary of that sender's payment order.

(d) If the sender of a payment order pays the order and was not obliged to pay all or part of the amount paid, the bank receiving payment is obliged to refund payment to the extent the sender was not obliged to pay. Except as provided in Sections 4A–204 and 4A–304, interest is payable on the refundable amount from the date of payment.

(e) If a funds transfer is not completed as stated in subsection (c) and an intermediary bank is obliged to refund payment as stated in subsection (d) but is unable to do so because not permitted by applicable law or because the bank suspends payments, a sender in the funds transfer that executed a payment order in compliance with an instruction, as stated in Section 4A–302(a)(1), to route the funds transfer through that intermediary bank is entitled to receive or retain payment from the sender of the payment order that it accepted. The first sender in the funds transfer that issued an instruction requiring routing through that intermediary bank is subrogated to the right of the bank that paid the intermediary bank to refund as stated in subsection (d).

(f) The right of the sender of a payment order to be excused from the obligation to pay the order as stated in subsection (c) or to receive refund under subsection (d) may not be varied by agreement.

Official Comment

1. Subsection (b) states that the sender of a payment order to the beneficiary's bank must pay the order when the beneficiary's bank accepts the order. At that point the beneficiary's bank is obliged to pay the beneficiary. Section 4A–404(a). The last clause of subsection (b) covers a case of premature acceptance by the beneficiary's bank. In some funds transfers, notably automated clearing house transfers, a beneficiary's bank may receive a payment order with a payment date after the day the order is received. The beneficiary's bank might accept the order before the payment date by notifying the beneficiary of receipt of the order. Although the acceptance obliges the beneficiary's bank to pay the beneficiary, payment is not due until the

447

payment date. The last clause of subsection (b) is consistent with that result. The beneficiary's bank is also not entitled to payment from the sender until the payment date.

2. Assume that Originator instructs Bank A to order immediate payment to the account of Beneficiary in Bank B. Execution of Originator's payment ordered by Bank A is acceptance under Section 4A–209(a). Under the second sentence of Section 4A–402(c) the acceptance creates an obligation of Originator to pay Bank A the amount of the order. The last clause of that sentence deals with attempted funds transfers that are not completed. In that event the obligation of the sender to pay its payment order is excused. Originator makes payment to Beneficiary when Bank B, the beneficiary's bank, accepts a payment order for the benefit of Beneficiary. Section 4A–406(a). If that acceptance by Bank B does not occur, the funds transfer has miscarried because Originator has not paid Beneficiary. Originator doesn't have to pay its payment order, and if it has already paid it is entitled to refund of the payment with interest. The rate of interest is stated in Section 4A–506. This "money-back guarantee" is an important protection of Originator. Originator is assured that it will not lose its money if something goes wrong in the transfer. For example, risk of loss resulting from payment to the wrong beneficiary is borne by some bank, not by Originator. The most likely reason for noncompletion is a failure to execute or an erroneous execution of a payment order by Bank A or an intermediary bank. Bank A may have issued its payment order to the wrong bank or it may have identified the wrong beneficiary in its order. The money-back guarantee is particularly important to Originator if noncompletion of the funds transfer is due to the fault of an intermediary bank rather than Bank A. In that case Bank A must refund payment to Originator, and Bank A has the burden of obtaining refund from the intermediary bank that it paid.

Subsection (c) can result in loss if an intermediary bank suspends payments. Suppose Originator instructs Bank A to pay to Beneficiary's account in Bank B and to use Bank C as an intermediary bank. Bank A executes Originator's order by issuing a payment order to Bank C. Bank A pays Bank C. Bank C fails to execute the order of Bank A and suspends payments. Under subsections (c) and (d), Originator is not obliged to pay Bank A and is entitled to refund from Bank A of any payment that it may have made. Bank A is entitled to a refund from Bank C, but Bank C is insolvent. Subsection (e) deals with this case. Bank A was required to issue its payment order to

Bank C because Bank C was designated as an intermediary bank by Originator. Section 4A–302(a)(1). In this case Originator takes the risk of insolvency of Bank C. Under subsection (e), Bank A is entitled to payment from Originator and Originator is subrogated to the right of Bank A under subsection (d) to refund of payment from Bank C.

3. A payment order is not like a negotiable instrument on which the drawer or maker has liability. Acceptance of the order by the receiving bank creates an obligation of the sender to pay the receiving bank the amount of the order. That is the extent of the sender's liability to the receiving bank and no other person has any rights against the sender with respect to the sender's order.

§ 4A–403. Payment by Sender to Receiving Bank.

(a) Payment of the sender's obligation under Section 4A–402 to pay the receiving bank occurs as follows:

(1) If the sender is a bank, payment occurs when the receiving bank receives final settlement of the obligation through a Federal Reserve Bank or through a funds-transfer system.

(2) If the sender is a bank and the sender (i) credited an account of the receiving bank with the sender, or (ii) caused an account of the receiving bank in another bank to be credited, payment occurs when the credit is withdrawn or, if not withdrawn, at midnight of the day on which the credit is withdrawable and the receiving bank learns of that fact.

(3) If the receiving bank debits an account of the sender with the receiving bank, payment occurs when the debit is made to the extent the debit is covered by a withdrawable credit balance in the account.

(b) If the sender and receiving bank are members of a funds-transfer system that nets obligations multilaterally among participants, the receiving bank receives final settlement when settlement is complete in accordance with the rules of the system. The obligation of the sender to pay the amount of a payment order transmitted through the funds-transfer system may be satisfied, to the extent permitted by the rules of the system, by setting off and applying against the sender's obligation the right of the sender to receive payment from the receiving bank of the amount of any other payment order transmitted to the sender by the receiving bank through the funds-transfer system. The aggregate balance of obligations owed by each sender to each receiving bank in the funds-transfer system may be satisfied, to the extent permitted by the rules of the system, by setting off and applying against that balance the aggregate balance of obligations owed to the sender by other members of the system. The aggregate balance is determined after the right of setoff stated in the second sentence of this subsection has been exercised.

(c) If two banks transmit payment orders to each other under an agreement that settlement of the obligations of each bank to the other under Section 4A-402 will be made at the end of the day or other period, the total amount owed with respect to all orders transmitted by one bank shall be set off against the total amount owed with respect to all orders transmitted by the other bank. To the extent of the setoff, each bank has made payment to the other.

(d) In a case not covered by subsection (a), the time when payment of the sender's obligation under Section 4A-402(b) or 4A-402(c) occurs is governed by applicable principles of law that determine when an obligation is satisfied.

Official Comment

1. This section defines when a sender pays the obligation stated in Section 4A-402. If a group of two or more banks engage in funds transfers with each other, the participating banks will sometimes be senders and sometimes be receiving banks. With respect to payment orders other than Fedwires, the amounts of the various payment orders may be credited and debited to accounts of one bank with another or to a clearing house account of each bank and amounts owed and amounts due are netted. Settlement is made through a Federal Reserve Bank by charges to the Federal Reserve accounts of the net debtor banks and credits to the Federal Reserve accounts of the net creditor banks. In the case of Fedwires the sender's obligation is settled by a debit to the Federal Reserve account of the sender and a credit to the Federal Reserve account of the receiving bank at the time the receiving bank receives the payment order. Both of these cases are covered by subsection (a)(1). When the Federal Reserve settlement becomes final the obligation of the sender under Section 4A-402 is paid.

2. In some cases a bank does not settle an obligation owed to another bank through a Federal Reserve Bank. This is the case if one of the banks is a foreign bank without access to the Federal Reserve payment system. In this kind of case, payment is usually made by credits or debits to accounts of the two banks with each other or to accounts of the two banks in a third bank. Suppose Bank B has an account in Bank A. Bank A advises Bank B that its account in Bank A has been credited $1,000,000 and that the credit is immediately withdrawable. Bank A also instructs Bank B to pay $1,000,000 to the account of Beneficiary in Bank B. This case is covered by subsection (a)(2). Bank B may want to immediately withdraw this credit. For example, it might do so by instructing Bank A to debit the account and pay some third party. Payment by Bank A to Bank B of Bank A's payment order occurs when the withdrawal is made. Suppose Bank B does not withdraw the credit. Since Bank B is the beneficiary's bank, one of the effects of receipt of payment by Bank B is that acceptance of Bank A's payment order automatically occurs at the time of payment. Section 4A-209(b)(2). Acceptance means that Bank B is obliged to pay $1,000,000 to Beneficiary. Section 4A-404(a). Subsection (a)(2) of Section 4A-403 states that payment does not occur until midnight if the credit is not withdrawn. This allows Bank B an opportunity to reject the order if it does not have time to withdraw the credit to its account and it is not willing to incur the liability to Beneficiary before it has use of the funds represented by the credit.

3. Subsection (a)(3) applies to a case in which the sender (bank or nonbank) has a funded account in the receiving bank. If Sender has an account in Bank and issues a payment order to Bank, Bank can obtain payment from Sender by debiting the account of Sender, which pays its Section 4A-402 obligation to Bank when the debit is made.

4. Subsection (b) deals with multilateral settlements made through a funds transfer system and is based on the CHIPS settlement system. In a funds transfer system such as CHIPS, which allows the various banks that transmit payment orders over the system to settle obligations at the end of each day, settlement is not based on individual payment orders. Each bank using the system engages in funds transfers with many other banks using the system. Settlement for any participant is based on the net credit or debit position of that participant with all other banks using the system. Subsection (b) is designed to make clear that the obligations of any sender are paid when the net position of that sender is settled in accordance with

the rules of the funds transfer system. This provision is intended to invalidate any argument, based on common-law principles, that multilateral netting is not valid because mutuality of obligation is not present. Subsection (b) dispenses with any mutuality of obligation requirements. Subsection (c) applies to cases in which two banks send payment orders to each other during the day and settle with each other at the end of the day or at the end of some other period. It is similar to subsection (b) in that it recognizes that a sender's obligation to pay a payment order is satisfied by a setoff. The obligations of each bank as sender to the other as receiving bank are obligations of the bank itself and not as representative of customers. These two sections are important in the case of insolvency of a bank. They make clear that liability under Section 4A–402 is based on the net position of the insolvent bank after setoff.

5. Subsection (d) relates to the uncommon case in which the sender doesn't have an account relationship with the receiving bank and doesn't settle through a Federal Reserve Bank. An example would be a customer that pays over the counter for a payment order that the customer issues to the receiving bank. Payment would normally be by cash, check or bank obligation. When payment occurs is determined by law outside Article 4A.

§ 4A–404. Obligation of Beneficiary's Bank to Pay and Give Notice to Beneficiary.

(a) Subject to Sections 4A–211(e), 4A–405(d), and 4A–405(e), if a beneficiary's bank accepts a payment order, the bank is obliged to pay the amount of the order to the beneficiary of the order. Payment is due on the payment date of the order, but if acceptance occurs on the payment date after the close of the funds-transfer business day of the bank, payment is due on the next funds-transfer business day. If the bank refuses to pay after demand by the beneficiary and receipt of notice of particular circumstances that will give rise to consequential damages as a result of nonpayment, the beneficiary may recover damages resulting from the refusal to pay to the extent the bank had notice of the damages, unless the bank proves that it did not pay because of a reasonable doubt concerning the right of the beneficiary to payment.

(b) If a payment order accepted by the beneficiary's bank instructs payment to an account of the beneficiary, the bank is obliged to notify the beneficiary of receipt of the order before midnight of the next funds-transfer business day following the payment date. If the payment order does not instruct payment to an account of the beneficiary, the bank is required to notify the beneficiary only if notice is required by the order. Notice may be given by first class mail or any other means reasonable in the circumstances. If the bank fails to give the required notice, the bank is obliged to pay interest to the beneficiary on the amount of the payment order from the day notice should have been given until the day the beneficiary learned of receipt of the payment order by the bank. No other damages are recoverable. Reasonable attorney's fees are also recoverable if demand for interest is made and refused before an action is brought on the claim.

(c) The right of a beneficiary to receive payment and damages as stated in subsection (a) may not be varied by agreement or a funds-transfer system rule. The right of a beneficiary to be notified as stated in subsection (b) may be varied by agreement of the beneficiary or by a funds-transfer system rule if the beneficiary is notified of the rule before initiation of the funds transfer.

Official Comment

1. The first sentence of subsection (a) states the time when the obligation of the beneficiary's bank arises. The second and third sentences state when the beneficiary's bank must make funds available to the beneficiary. They also state the measure of damages for failure, after demand, to comply. Since the Expedited Funds Availability Act, 12 U.S.C. 4001 et seq., also governs funds availability in a funds transfer, the second and third sentences of subsection (a) may be subject to preemption by that Act.

2. Subsection (a) provides that the beneficiary of an accepted payment order may recover consequential damages if the beneficiary's bank refuses to pay the order after demand by the beneficiary if the bank at that time had notice of the particular circumstances giving rise to the damages. Such damages are recoverable only to the extent the bank had "notice of the damages." The quoted phrase requires that the bank have notice of the general type or nature of the damages that will be suffered as a result of the refusal to pay and their general magnitude. There is no requirement that the bank have notice of the exact or even the approximate amount of the damages, but if the

amount of damages is extraordinary the bank is entitled to notice of that fact. For example, in Evra Corp. v. Swiss Bank Corp., 673 F.2d 951 (7th Cir.1982), failure to complete a funds transfer of only $27,000 required to retain rights to a very favorable ship charter resulted in a claim for more than $2,000,000 of consequential damages. Since it is not reasonably foreseeable that a failure to make a relatively small payment will result in damages of this magnitude, notice is not sufficient if the beneficiary's bank has notice only that the $27,000 is necessary to retain rights on a ship charter. The bank is entitled to notice that an exceptional amount of damages will result as well. For example, there would be adequate notice if the bank had been made aware that damages of $1,000,000 or more might result.

3. Under the last clause of subsection (a) the beneficiary's bank is not liable for damages if its refusal to pay was "because of a reasonable doubt concerning the right of the beneficiary to payment." Normally there will not be any question about the right of the beneficiary to receive payment. Normally, the bank should be able to determine whether it has accepted the payment order and, if it has been accepted, the first sentence of subsection (a) states that the bank is obliged to pay. There may be uncommon cases, however, in which there is doubt whether acceptance occurred. For example, if acceptance is based on receipt of payment by the beneficiary's bank under Section 4A–403(a)(1) or (2), there may be cases in which the bank is not certain that payment has been received. There may also be cases in which there is doubt about whether the person demanding payment is the person identified in the payment order as beneficiary of the order.

The last clause of subsection (a) does not apply to cases in which a funds transfer is being used to pay an obligation and a dispute arises between the originator and the beneficiary concerning whether the obligation is in fact owed. For example, the originator may try to prevent payment to the beneficiary by the beneficiary's bank by alleging that the beneficiary is not entitled to payment because of fraud against the originator or a breach of contract relating to the obligation. The fraud or breach of contract claim of the originator may be grounds for recovery by the originator from the beneficiary after the beneficiary is paid, but it does not affect the obligation of the beneficiary's bank to pay the beneficiary. Unless the payment order has been cancelled pursuant to Section 4A–211(c), there is no excuse for refusing to pay the beneficiary and, in a proper case, the refusal may result in consequential damages. Except in the case of a book transfer, in

which the beneficiary's bank is also the originator's bank, the originator of a funds transfer cannot cancel a payment order to the beneficiary's bank, with or without the consent of that bank, because the originator is not the sender of that order. Thus, the beneficiary's bank may safely ignore any instruction by the originator to withhold payment to the beneficiary.

4. Subsection (b) states the duty of the beneficiary's bank to notify the beneficiary of receipt of the order. If acceptance occurs under Section 4A–209(b)(1) the beneficiary is normally notified. Thus, subsection (b) applies primarily to cases in which acceptance occurs under Section 4A–209(b)(2) or (3). Notice under subsection (b) is not required if the person entitled to the notice agrees or a funds transfer system rule provides that notice is not required and the beneficiary is given notice of the rule. In ACH transactions the normal practice is not to give notice to the beneficiary unless notice is requested by the beneficiary. This practice can be continued by adoption of a funds transfer system rule. Subsection (a) is not subject to variation by agreement or by a funds transfer system rule.

§ 4A–405. Payment by Beneficiary's Bank to Beneficiary.

(a) If the beneficiary's bank credits an account of the beneficiary of a payment order, payment of the bank's obligation under Section 4A–404(a) occurs when and to the extent (i) the beneficiary is notified of the right to withdraw the credit, (ii) the bank lawfully applies the credit to a debt of the beneficiary, or (iii) funds with respect to the order are otherwise made available to the beneficiary by the bank.

(b) If the beneficiary's bank does not credit an account of the beneficiary of a payment order, the time when payment of the bank's obligation under Section 4A–404(a) occurs is governed by principles of law that determine when an obligation is satisfied.

(c) Except as stated in subsections (d) and (e), if the beneficiary's bank pays the beneficiary of a payment order under a condition to payment or agreement of the beneficiary giving the bank the right to recover payment from the beneficiary if the bank does not receive payment of the order, the condition to payment or agreement is not enforceable.

(d) A funds-transfer system rule may provide that payments made to beneficiaries of funds transfers made through the system are provisional until receipt of payment by the beneficiary's bank of the payment order it accepted. A beneficiary's bank that makes a payment that is provisional under the rule is entitled to refund from the beneficiary if (i) the rule requires that both the beneficiary and the originator be given notice of the provisional nature of the payment before the funds transfer is initiated, (ii) the beneficiary, the beneficiary's bank and the originator's bank agreed to be bound by the rule, and (iii) the beneficiary's bank did not receive payment of the payment order that it accepted. If the beneficiary is obliged to refund payment to the beneficiary's bank, acceptance of the payment order by the beneficiary's bank is nullified and no payment by the originator of the funds transfer to the beneficiary occurs under Section 4A–406.

(e) This subsection applies to a funds transfer that includes a payment order transmitted over a funds-transfer system that (i) nets obligations multilaterally among participants, and (ii) has in effect a loss-sharing agreement among participants for the purpose of providing funds necessary to complete settlement of the obligations of one or more participants that do not meet their settlement obligations. If the beneficiary's bank in the funds transfer accepts a payment order and the system fails to complete settlement pursuant to its rules with respect to any payment order in the funds transfer, (i) the acceptance by the beneficiary's bank is nullified and no person has any right or obligation based on the acceptance, (ii) the beneficiary's bank is entitled to recover payment from the beneficiary, (iii) no payment by the originator to the beneficiary occurs under Section 4A–406, and (iv) subject to Section 4A–402(e), each sender in the funds transfer is excused from its obligation to pay its payment order under Section 4A–402(c) because the funds transfer has not been completed.

Official Comment

1. This section defines when the beneficiary's bank pays the beneficiary and when the obligation of the beneficiary's bank under Section 4A–404 to pay the beneficiary is satisfied. In almost all cases the bank will credit an account of the beneficiary when it receives a payment order. In the typical case the beneficiary is paid when the beneficiary is given notice of the right to withdraw the credit. Subsection (a)(i). In some cases payment might be made to the beneficiary not by releasing funds to the beneficiary, but by apply-

ing the credit to a debt of the beneficiary. Subsection (a)(ii). In this case the beneficiary gets the benefit of the payment order because a debt of the beneficiary has been satisfied. The two principal cases in which payment will occur in this manner are setoff by the beneficiary's bank and payment of the proceeds of the payment order to a garnishing creditor of the beneficiary. These cases are discussed in Comment 2 to Section 4A–502.

2. If a beneficiary's bank releases funds to the beneficiary before it receives payment from the sender of the payment order, it assumes the risk that the sender may not pay the sender's order because of suspension of payments or other reason. Subsection (c). As stated in Comment 5 to Section 4A–209, the beneficiary's bank can protect itself against this risk by delaying acceptance. But if the bank accepts the order it is obliged to pay the beneficiary. If the beneficiary's bank has given the beneficiary notice of the right to withdraw a credit made to the beneficiary's account, the beneficiary has received payment from the bank. Once payment has been made to the beneficiary with respect to an obligation incurred by the bank under Section 4A–404(a), the payment cannot be recovered by the beneficiary's bank unless subsection (d) or (e) applies. Thus, a right to withdraw a credit cannot be revoked if the right to withdraw constituted payment of the bank's obligation. This principle applies even if funds were released as a "loan" (see Comment 5 to Section 4A–209), or were released subject to a condition that they would be repaid in the event the bank does not receive payment from the sender of the payment order, or the beneficiary agreed to return the payment if the bank did not receive payment from the sender.

3. Subsection (c) is subject to an exception stated in subsection (d) which is intended to apply to automated clearing house transfers. ACH transfers are made in batches. A beneficiary's bank will normally accept, at the same time and as part of a single batch, payment orders with respect to many different originator's banks. Comment 2 to Section 4A–206. The custom in ACH transactions is to release funds to the beneficiary early on the payment date even though settlement to the beneficiary's bank does not occur until later in the day. The understanding is that payments to beneficiaries are provisional until the beneficiary's bank receives settlement. This practice is similar to what happens when a depositary bank releases funds with respect to a check forwarded for collection. If the check is dishonored the bank is entitled to recover the funds from the customer. ACH transfers are widely

perceived as check substitutes. Section 4A–405(d) allows the funds transfer system to adopt a rule making payments to beneficiaries provisional. If such a rule is adopted, a beneficiary's bank that releases funds to the beneficiary will be able to recover the payment if it doesn't receive payment of the payment order that it accepted. There are two requirements with respect to the funds transfer system rule. The beneficiary, the beneficiary's bank and the originator's bank must all agree to be bound by the rule and the rule must require that both the beneficiary and the originator be given notice of the provisional nature of the payment before the funds transfer is initiated. There is no requirement that the notice be given with respect to a particular funds transfer. Once notice of the provisional nature of the payment has been given, the notice is effective for all subsequent payments to or from the person to whom the notice was given. Subsection (d) provides only that the funds transfer system rule must require notice to the beneficiary and the originator. The beneficiary's bank will know what the rule requires, but it has no way of knowing whether the originator's bank complied with the rule. Subsection (d) does not require proof that the originator received notice. If the originator's bank failed to give the required notice and the originator suffered as a result, the appropriate remedy is an action by the originator against the originator's bank based on that failure. But the beneficiary's bank will not be able to get the benefit of subsection (d) unless the beneficiary had notice of the provisional nature of the payment because subsection (d) requires an agreement by the beneficiary to be bound by the rule. Implicit in an agreement to be bound by a rule that makes a payment provisional is a requirement that notice be given of what the rule provides. The notice can be part of the agreement or separately given. For example, notice can be given by providing a copy of the system's operating rules.

With respect to ACH transfers made through a Federal Reserve Bank acting as an intermediary bank, the Federal Reserve Bank is obliged under Section 4A–402(b) to pay a beneficiary's bank that accepts the payment order. Unlike Fedwire transfers, under current ACH practice a Federal Reserve Bank that processes a payment order does not obligate itself to pay if the originator's bank fails to pay the Federal Reserve Bank. It is assumed that the Federal Reserve will use its right of preemption which is recognized in Section 4A–107 to disclaim the Section 4A–402(b) obligation in ACH transactions if it decides to retain the provisional payment rule.

4. Subsection (e) is another exception to subsection (c). It refers to funds transfer systems having loss-sharing rules described in the subsection. CHIPS has proposed a rule that fits the description. Under the CHIPS loss-sharing rule the CHIPS banks will have agreed to contribute funds to allow the system to settle for payment orders sent over the system during the day in the event that one or more banks are unable to meet their settlement obligations. Subsection (e) applies only if CHIPS fails to settle despite the loss-sharing rule. Since funds under the loss-sharing rule will be instantly available to CHIPS and will be in an amount sufficient to cover any failure that can be reasonably anticipated, it is extremely unlikely that CHIPS would ever fail to settle. Thus, subsection (e) addresses an event that should never occur. If that event were to occur, all payment orders made over the system would be cancelled under the CHIPS rule. Thus, no bank would receive settlement, whether or not a failed bank was involved in a particular funds transfer. Subsection (e) provides that each funds transfer in which there is a payment order with respect to which there is a settlement failure is unwound. Acceptance by the beneficiary's bank in each funds transfer is nullified. The consequences of nullification are that the beneficiary has no right to receive or retain payment by the beneficiary's bank, no payment is made by the originator to the beneficiary and each sender in the funds transfer is, subject to Section 4A–402(e), not obliged to pay its payment order and is entitled to refund under Section 4A–402(d) if it has already paid.

§ 4A–406. Payment by Originator to Beneficiary; Discharge of Underlying Obligation.

(a) Subject to Sections 4A–211(e), 4A–405(d), and 4A–405(e), the originator of a funds transfer pays the beneficiary of the originator's payment order (i) at the time a payment order for the benefit of the beneficiary is accepted by the beneficiary's bank in the funds transfer and (ii) in an amount equal to the amount of the order accepted by the beneficiary's bank, but not more than the amount of the originator's order.

(b) If payment under subsection (a) is made to satisfy an obligation, the obligation is discharged to the same extent discharge would result from payment to the beneficiary of the same amount in money, unless (i) the payment under subsection (a) was made by a means prohibited by the contract of the beneficiary with respect to the obligation, (ii) the beneficiary, within a reasonable time after receiving notice of receipt of the order by the beneficiary's bank, notified the originator of the beneficiary's refusal of the payment, (iii) funds with respect to the order were not withdrawn by the beneficiary or applied to a debt of the beneficiary, and (iv) the beneficiary would suffer a loss that could reasonably have been avoided if payment had been made by a means complying with the contract. If payment by the originator does not result in discharge under this section, the originator is subrogated to the rights of the beneficiary to receive payment from the beneficiary's bank under Section 4A–404(a).

(c) For the purpose of determining whether discharge of an obligation occurs under subsection (b), if the beneficiary's bank accepts a payment order in an amount equal to the amount of the originator's payment order less charges of one or more receiving banks in the funds transfer, payment to the beneficiary is deemed to be in the amount of the originator's order unless upon demand by the beneficiary the originator does not pay the beneficiary the amount of the deducted charges.

(d) Rights of the originator or of the beneficiary of a funds transfer under this section may be varied only by agreement of the originator and the beneficiary.

Official Comment

1. Subsection (a) states the fundamental rule of Article 4A that payment by the originator to the beneficiary is accomplished by providing to the beneficiary the obligation of the beneficiary's bank to pay. Since this obligation arises when the beneficiary's bank accepts a payment order, the originator pays the beneficiary at the time of acceptance and in the amount of the payment order accepted.

2. In a large percentage of funds transfers, the transfer is made to pay an obligation of the originator. Subsection (a) states that the beneficiary is paid by the originator when the beneficiary's bank accepts a payment order for the benefit of the beneficiary. When that happens the effect under subsection (b) is to substitute the obligation of the beneficiary's bank for the obligation of the originator. The effect is similar to that under Article 3 if a cashier's check payable to the beneficiary had been taken by the beneficiary. Normally, payment by funds transfer is sought by the beneficiary because it puts money into the hands of the beneficiary more quickly. As a practical matter the beneficiary and the originator will nearly always agree to the funds transfer in advance. Under subsection (b)

acceptance by the beneficiary's bank will result in discharge of the obligation for which payment was made unless the beneficiary had made a contract with respect to the obligation which did not permit payment by the means used. Thus, if there is no contract of the beneficiary with respect to the means of payment of the obligation, acceptance by the beneficiary's bank of a payment order to the account of the beneficiary can result in discharge.

3. Suppose Beneficiary's contract stated that payment of an obligation owed by Originator was to be made by a cashier's check of Bank A. Instead, Originator paid by a funds transfer to Beneficiary's account in Bank B. Bank B accepted a payment order for the benefit of Beneficiary by immediately notifying Beneficiary that the funds were available for withdrawal. Before Beneficiary had a reasonable opportunity to withdraw the funds Bank B suspended payments. Under the unless clause of subsection (b) Beneficiary is not required to accept the payment as discharging the obligation owed by Originator to Beneficiary if Beneficiary's contract means that Beneficiary was not required to accept payment by wire transfer. Beneficiary could refuse the funds transfer as payment of the obligation and could resort to rights under the underlying contract to enforce the obligation. The rationale is that Originator cannot impose the risk of Bank B's insolvency on Beneficiary if Beneficiary had specified another means of payment that did not entail that risk. If Beneficiary is required to accept Originator's payment, Beneficiary would suffer a loss that would not have occurred if payment had been made by a cashier's check on Bank A, and Bank A has not suspended payments. In this case Originator will have to pay twice. It is obliged to pay the amount of its payment order to the bank that accepted it and has to pay the obligation it owes to Beneficiary which has not been discharged. Under the last sentence of subsection (b) Originator is subrogated to Beneficiary's right to receive payment from Bank B under Section 4A–404(a).

4. Suppose Beneficiary's contract called for payment by a Fedwire transfer to Bank B, but the payment order accepted by Bank B was not a Fedwire transfer. Before the funds were withdrawn by Beneficiary, Bank B suspended payments. The sender of the payment order to Bank B paid the amount of the order to Bank B. In this case the payment by Originator did not comply with Beneficiary's contract, but the noncompliance did not result in a loss to Beneficiary as required by subsection (b)(iv). A Fedwire transfer avoids the risk of insolvency of the sender of the payment order to Bank B, but it does not affect the

risk that Bank B will suspend payments before withdrawal of the funds by Beneficiary. Thus, the unless clause of subsection (b) is not applicable and the obligation owed to Beneficiary is discharged.

5. Charges of receiving banks in a funds transfer normally are nominal in relationship to the amount being paid by the originator to the beneficiary. Wire transfers are normally agreed to in advance and the parties may agree concerning how these charges are to be divided between the parties. Subsection (c) states a rule that applies in the absence of agreement. In some funds transfers charges of banks that execute payment orders are collected by deducting the charges from the amount of the payment order issued by the bank, i.e. the bank issues a payment order that is slightly less than the amount of the payment order that is being executed. The process is described in Comment 3 to

Section 4A–302. The result in such a case is that the payment order accepted by the beneficiary's bank will be slightly less than the amount of the originator's order. Subsection (c) recognizes the principle that a beneficiary is entitled to full payment of a debt paid by wire transfer as a condition to discharge. On the other hand, subsection (c) prevents a beneficiary from denying the originator the benefit of the payment by asserting that discharge did not occur because deduction of bank charges resulted in less than full payment. The typical case is one in which the payment is made to exercise a valuable right such as an option which is unfavorable to the beneficiary. Subsection (c) allows discharge notwithstanding the deduction unless the originator fails to reimburse the beneficiary for the deducted charges after demand by the beneficiary.

PART 5

MISCELLANEOUS PROVISIONS

§ 4A–501. Variation by Agreement and Effect of Funds-Transfer System Rule.

(a) Except as otherwise provided in this Article, the rights and obligations of a party to a funds transfer may be varied by agreement of the affected party.

(b) "Funds-transfer system rule" means a rule of an association of banks (i) governing transmission of payment orders by means of a funds-transfer system of the association or rights and obligations with respect to those orders, or (ii) to the extent the rule governs rights and obligations between banks that are parties to a funds transfer in which a Federal Reserve Bank, acting as an intermediary bank, sends a payment order to the beneficiary's bank. Except as otherwise provided in this Article, a funds-transfer system rule governing rights and obligations between participating banks using the system may be effective even if the rule conflicts with this Article and indirectly affects another party to the funds transfer who does not consent to the rule. A funds-transfer system rule may also govern rights and obligations of parties other than participating banks using the system to the extent stated in Sections 4A–404(c), 4A–405(d), and 4A–507(c).

Official Comment

1. This section is designed to give some flexibility to Article 4A. Funds transfer system rules govern

rights and obligations between banks that use the system. They may cover a wide variety of matters such as form and content of payment orders, security procedures, cancellation rights and procedures, indemnity rights, compensation rules for delays in completion of a funds transfer, time and method of settlement, credit restrictions with respect to senders of payment orders and risk allocation with respect to suspension of payments by a participating bank. Funds transfer system rules can be very effective in supplementing the provisions of Article 4A and in filling gaps that may be present in Article 4A. To the extent they do not conflict with Article 4A there is no problem with respect to their effectiveness. In that case they merely supplement Article 4A. Section 4A–501 goes further. It states that unless the contrary is stated, funds transfer system rules can override provisions of Article 4A. Thus, rights and obligations of a sender bank and a receiving bank with respect to each other can be different from that stated in Article 4A to the extent a funds transfer system rule applies. Since funds transfer system rules are defined as those governing the relationship between participating banks, a rule can have a direct effect only on participating banks. But a rule that affects the conduct of a participating bank may indirectly affect the rights of nonparticipants such as the originator or beneficiary of a funds transfer, and such a rule can be effective even though it may affect nonparticipants without their consent. For example, a rule might prevent execution of a payment order or might allow cancellation of a payment order with the result that a funds transfer is not completed or is delayed. But a rule purporting to define rights and obligations of nonparticipants in the system would not be effective to alter Article 4A rights because the rule is not within the definition of funds transfer system rule. Rights and obligations arising under Article 4A may also be varied by agreement of the affected parties, except to the extent Article 4A otherwise provides. Rights and obligations arising under Article 4A can also be changed by Federal Reserve regulations and operating circulars of Federal Reserve Banks. Section 4A–107.

2. Subsection (b)(ii) refers to ACH transfers. Whether an ACH transfer is made through an automated clearing house of a Federal Reserve Bank or through an automated clearing house of another association of banks, the rights and obligations of the originator's bank and the beneficiary's bank are governed by uniform rules adopted by various associations of banks in various parts of the nation. With respect to transfers in which a Federal Reserve Bank acts as intermediary bank these rules may be incorporated, in whole or in part, in operating circulars of the Federal Reserve Bank. Even if not so incorporated these rules can still be binding on the association banks. If a transfer is made through a Federal Reserve Bank, the rules are effective under subsection (b)(ii). If the transfer is not made through a Federal Reserve Bank, the association rules are effective under subsection (b)(i).

§ 4A–502. Creditor Process Served on Receiving Bank; Setoff by Beneficiary's Bank.

(a) As used in this section, "creditor process" means levy, attachment, garnishment, notice of lien, sequestration, or similar process issued by or on behalf of a creditor or other claimant with respect to an account.

(b) This subsection applies to creditor process with respect to an authorized account of the sender of a payment order if the creditor process is served on the receiving bank. For the purpose of determining rights with respect to the creditor process, if the receiving bank accepts the payment order the balance in the authorized account is deemed to be reduced by the amount of the payment order to the extent the bank did not otherwise receive payment of the order, unless the creditor process is served at a time and in a manner affording the bank a reasonable opportu-

nity to act on it before the bank accepts the payment order.

(c) If a beneficiary's bank has received a payment order for payment to the beneficiary's account in the bank, the following rules apply:

(1) The bank may credit the beneficiary's account. The amount credited may be set off against an obligation owed by the beneficiary to the bank or may be applied to satisfy creditor process served on the bank with respect to the account.

(2) The bank may credit the beneficiary's account and allow withdrawal of the amount credited unless creditor process with respect to the account is served at a time and in a manner affording the bank a reasonable opportunity to act to prevent withdrawal.

(3) If creditor process with respect to the beneficiary's account has been served and the bank has had a reasonable opportunity to act on it, the bank may not reject the payment order except for a reason unrelated to the service of process.

(d) Creditor process with respect to a payment by the originator to the beneficiary pursuant to a funds transfer may be served only on the beneficiary's bank with respect to the debt owed by that bank to the beneficiary. Any other bank served with the creditor process is not obliged to act with respect to the process.

Official Comment

1. When a receiving bank accepts a payment order, the bank normally receives payment from the sender by debiting an authorized account of the sender. In accepting the sender's order the bank may be relying on a credit balance in the account. If creditor process is served on the bank with respect to the account before the bank accepts the order but the bank employee responsible for the acceptance was not aware of the creditor process at the time the acceptance occurred, it is unjust to the bank to allow the creditor process to take the credit balance on which the bank may have relied. Subsection (b) allows the bank to obtain payment from the sender's account in this case. Under that provision, the balance in the sender's account to which the creditor process applies is deemed to be reduced by the amount of the payment order unless there was sufficient time for notice of the service of creditor process to be received by personnel of the bank responsible for the acceptance.

2. Subsection (c) deals with payment orders issued to the beneficiary's bank. The bank may credit the beneficiary's account when the order is received, but under Section 4A–404(a) the bank incurs no obligation to pay the beneficiary until the order is accepted pursuant to Section 4A–209(b). Thus, before acceptance, the credit to the beneficiary's account is provisional. But under Section 4A–209(b) acceptance occurs if the beneficiary's bank pays the beneficiary pursuant to Section 4A–405(a). Under that provision, payment occurs if the credit to the beneficiary's account is applied to a debt of the beneficiary. Subsection (c)(1) allows the bank to credit the beneficiary's account with respect to a payment order and to accept the order by setting off the credit against an obligation owed to the bank or applying the credit to creditor process with respect to the account.

Suppose a beneficiary's bank receives a payment order for the benefit of a customer. Before the bank accepts the order, the bank learns that creditor process has been served on the bank with respect to the customer's account. Normally there is no reason for a beneficiary's bank to reject a payment order, but if the beneficiary's account is garnished, the bank may be faced with a difficult choice. If it rejects the order, the garnishing creditor's potential recovery of funds of the beneficiary is frustrated. It may be faced with a claim by the creditor that the rejection was a wrong to the creditor. If the bank accepts the order, the effect is to allow the creditor to seize funds of its customer, the beneficiary. Subsection (c)(3) gives the bank no choice in this case. It provides that it may not favor its customer over the creditor by rejecting the order. The beneficiary's bank may rightfully reject only if there is an independent basis for rejection.

3. Subsection (c)(2) is similar to subsection (b). Normally the beneficiary's bank will release funds to the beneficiary shortly after acceptance or it will accept by releasing funds. Since the bank is bound by a garnishment order served before funds are released to the beneficiary, the bank might suffer a loss if funds were released without knowledge that a garnishment order had been served. Subsection (c)(2) protects the bank if it did not have adequate notice of the garnishment when the funds were released.

4. A creditor may want to reach funds involved in a funds transfer. The creditor may try to do so by serving process on the originator's bank, an intermediary bank or the beneficiary's bank. The purpose of subsection (d) is to guide the creditor and the court as to the proper method of reaching the funds involved in a funds transfer. A creditor of the originator can levy on the account of the originator in the originator's

bank before the funds transfer is initiated, but that levy is subject to the limitations stated in subsection (b). The creditor of the originator cannot reach any other funds because no property of the originator is being transferred. A creditor of the beneficiary cannot levy on property of the originator and until the funds transfer is completed by acceptance by the beneficiary's bank of a payment order for the benefit of the beneficiary, the beneficiary has no property interest in the funds transfer which the beneficiary's creditor can reach. A creditor of the beneficiary that wants to reach the funds to be received by the beneficiary must serve creditor process on the beneficiary's bank to reach the obligation of the beneficiary's bank to pay the beneficiary which arises upon acceptance by the beneficiary's bank under Section 4A–404(a).

5. "Creditor process" is defined in subsection (a) to cover a variety of devices by which a creditor of the holder of a bank account or a claimant to a bank account can seize the account. Procedure and nomenclature varies widely from state to state. The term used in Section 4A–502 is a generic term.

§ 4A–503. Injunction or Restraining Order With Respect to Funds Transfer.

For proper cause and in compliance with applicable law, a court may restrain (i) a person from issuing a payment order to initiate a funds transfer, (ii) an originator's bank from executing the payment order of the originator, or (iii) the beneficiary's bank from releasing funds to the beneficiary or the beneficiary from withdrawing the funds. A court may not otherwise restrain a person from issuing a payment order, paying or receiving payment of a payment order, or otherwise acting with respect to a funds transfer.

Official Comment

This section is related to Section 4A–502(d) and to Comment 4 to Section 4A–502. It is designed to prevent interruption of a funds transfer after it has been set in motion. The initiation of a funds transfer can be prevented by enjoining the originator or the originator's bank from issuing a payment order. After the funds transfer is completed by acceptance of a payment order by the beneficiary's bank, that bank can be enjoined from releasing funds to the beneficiary or the beneficiary can be enjoined from withdrawing the funds. No other injunction is permitted. In particular, intermediary banks are protected, and injunctions against the originator and the originator's bank are limited to issuance of a payment order. Except for the beneficiary's bank, nobody can be enjoined from paying a payment order, and no receiving bank can be enjoined from receiving payment from the sender of the order that it accepted.

§ 4A–504. Order in Which Items and Payment Orders May Be Charged to Account; Order of Withdrawals From Account.

(a) If a receiving bank has received more than one payment order of the sender or one or more payment orders and other items that are payable from the sender's account, the bank may charge the sender's account with respect to the various orders and items in any sequence.

(b) In determining whether a credit to an account has been withdrawn by the holder of the account or applied to a debt of the holder of the account, credits first made to the account are first withdrawn or applied.

Official Comment

1. Subsection (a) concerns priority among various obligations that are to be paid from the same account. A customer may have written checks on its account with the receiving bank and may have issued one or more payment orders payable from the same account. If the account balance is not sufficient to cover all of the checks and payment orders, some checks may be dishonored and some payment orders may not be accepted. Although there is no concept of wrongful dishonor of a payment order in Article 4A in the absence of an agreement to honor by the receiving bank, some rights and obligations may depend on the amount in the customer's account. Section 4A–209(b)(3) and Section 4A–210(b). Whether dishonor of a check is wrongful also may depend upon the balance in the customer's account. Under subsection (a), the bank is not required to consider the competing items and payment orders in any particular order. Rather it may charge the customer's account for the various items and orders in any order. Suppose there is $12,000 in the customer's account. If a check for $5,000 is presented for payment and the bank receives a $10,000 payment order from the customer, the bank could dishonor the check and accept the payment order. Dishonor of the check is not wrongful because the account balance was less than the amount of the check after the bank charged the account $10,000 on account of the payment order. Or, the bank could pay the check and not execute the payment order because

the amount of the order is not covered by the balance in the account.

2. Subsection (b) follows Section 4–208(b) in using the first-in-first-out rule for determining the order in which credits to an account are withdrawn.

§ 4A–505. Preclusion of Objection to Debit of Customer's Account.

If a receiving bank has received payment from its customer with respect to a payment order issued in the name of the customer as sender and accepted by the bank, and the customer received notification reasonably identifying the order, the customer is precluded from asserting that the bank is not entitled to retain the payment unless the customer notifies the bank of the customer's objection to the payment within one year after the notification was received by the customer.

Official Comment

This section is in the nature of a statute of repose for objecting to debits made to the customer's account. A receiving bank that executes payment orders of a customer may have received payment from the customer by debiting the customer's account with respect to a payment order that the customer was not required to pay. For example, the payment order may not have been authorized or verified pursuant to Section 4A–202 or the funds transfer may not have been completed. In either case the receiving bank is obliged to refund the payment to the customer and this obligation to refund payment cannot be varied by agreement. Section 4A–204 and Section 4A–402. Refund may also be required if the receiving bank is not entitled to payment from the customer because the bank erroneously executed a payment order. Section 4A–303. A similar analysis applies to that case. Section 4A–402(d) and (f) require refund and the obligation to refund may not be varied by agreement. Under 4A–505, however, the obligation to refund may not be asserted by the customer if the customer has not objected to the debiting of the account within one year after the customer received notification of the debit.

§ 4A–506. Rate of Interest.

(a) If, under this Article, a receiving bank is obliged to pay interest with respect to a payment order issued to the bank, the amount payable may be determined (i) by agreement of the sender and receiving bank, or (ii) by a funds-transfer system rule if the payment order is transmitted through a funds-transfer system.

(b) If the amount of interest is not determined by an agreement or rule as stated in subsection (a), the amount is calculated by multiplying the applicable Federal Funds rate by the amount on which interest is payable, and then multiplying the product by the number of days for which interest is payable. The applicable Federal Funds rate is the average of the Federal Funds rates published by the Federal Reserve Bank of New York for each of the days for which interest is payable divided by 360. The Federal Funds rate for any day on which a published rate is not available is the same as the published rate for the next preceding day for which there is a published rate. If a receiving bank that accepted a payment order is required to refund payment to the sender of the order because the funds transfer was not completed, but the failure to complete was not due to any fault by the bank, the interest payable is reduced by a percentage equal to the reserve requirement on deposits of the receiving bank.

Official Comment

1. A receiving bank is required to pay interest on the amount of a payment order received by the bank in a number of situations. Sometimes the interest is payable to the sender and in other cases it is payable to either the originator or the beneficiary of the funds transfer. The relevant provisions are Section 4A–204(a), Section 4A–209(b)(3), Section 4A–210(b), Section 4A–305(a), Section 4A–402(d) and Section 4A–404(b). The rate of interest may be governed by a funds transfer system rule or by agreement as stated in subsection (a). If subsection (a) doesn't apply, the rate is determined under subsection (b). Subsection (b) is illustrated by the following example. A bank is obliged to pay interest on $1,000,000 for three days, July 3, July 4, and July 5. The published Fed Funds rate is .082 for July 3 and .081 for July 5. There is no published rate for July 4 because that day is not a banking day. The rate for July 3 applies to July 4. The applicable Fed Funds rate is .08167 (the average of .082, .082, and .081) divided by 360 which equals .0002268. The amount of interest payable is $1,000,000 × .0002268 × 3 = $680.40.

2. In some cases, interest is payable in spite of the fact that there is no fault by the receiving bank. The last sentence of subsection (b) applies to those cases. For example, a funds transfer might not be completed

because the beneficiary's bank rejected the payment order issued to it by the originator's bank or an intermediary bank. Section 4A–402(c) provides that the originator is not obliged to pay its payment order and Section 4A–402(d) provides that the originator's bank must refund any payment received plus interest. The requirement to pay interest in this case is not based on fault by the originator's bank. Rather, it is based on restitution. Since the originator's bank had the use of the originator's money, it is required to pay the originator for the value of that use. The value of that use is not determined by multiplying the interest rate by the refundable amount because the originator's bank is required to deposit with the Federal Reserve a percentage of the bank's deposits as a reserve requirement. Since that deposit does not bear interest, the bank had use of the refundable amount reduced by a percentage equal to the reserve requirement. If the reserve requirement is 12%, the amount of interest payable by the bank under the formula stated in subsection (b) is reduced by 12%.

§ 4A–507. Choice of Law.

(a) The following rules apply unless the affected parties otherwise agree or subsection (c) applies:

(1) The rights and obligations between the sender of a payment order and the receiving bank are governed by the law of the jurisdiction in which the receiving bank is located.

(2) The rights and obligations between the beneficiary's bank and the beneficiary are governed by the law of the jurisdiction in which the beneficiary's bank is located.

(3) The issue of when payment is made pursuant to a funds transfer by the originator to the beneficiary is governed by the law of the jurisdiction in which the beneficiary's bank is located.

(b) If the parties described in each paragraph of subsection (a) have made an agreement selecting the law of a particular jurisdiction to govern rights and obligations between each other, the law of that jurisdiction governs those rights and obligations, whether or not the payment order or the funds transfer bears a reasonable relation to that jurisdiction.

(c) A funds-transfer system rule may select the law of a particular jurisdiction to govern (i) rights and obligations between participating banks with respect to payment orders transmitted or processed through the system, or (ii) the rights and obligations of some or all parties to a funds transfer any part of which is carried out by means of the system. A choice of law made pursuant to clause (i) is binding on participating banks. A choice of law made pursuant to clause (ii) is binding on the originator, other sender, or a receiving bank having notice that the funds-transfer system might be used in the funds transfer and of the choice of law by the system when the originator, other sender, or receiving bank issued or accepted a payment order. The beneficiary of a funds transfer is bound by the choice of law if, when the funds transfer is initiated, the beneficiary has notice that the funds-transfer system might be used in the funds transfer and of the choice of law by the system. The law of a jurisdiction selected pursuant to this subsection may govern, whether or not that law bears a reasonable relation to the matter in issue.

(d) In the event of inconsistency between an agreement under subsection (b) and a choice-of-law rule under subsection (c), the agreement under subsection (b) prevails.

(e) If a funds transfer is made by use of more than one funds-transfer system and there is inconsistency between choice-of-law rules of the systems, the matter in issue is governed by the law of the selected jurisdiction that has the most significant relationship to the matter in issue.

Official Comment

1. Funds transfers are typically interstate or international in character. If part of a funds transfer is governed by Article 4A and another part is governed by other law, the rights and obligations of parties to the funds transfer may be unclear because there is no clear consensus in various jurisdictions concerning the juridical nature of the transaction. Unless all of a funds transfer is governed by a single law it may be very difficult to predict the result if something goes wrong in the transfer. Section 4A–507 deals with this problem. Subsection (b) allows parties to a funds transfer to make a choice-of-law agreement. Subsection (c) allows a funds transfer system to select the law of a particular jurisdiction to govern funds transfers carried out by means of the system. Subsection (a) states residual rules if no choice of law has occurred under subsection (b) or subsection (c).

2. Subsection (a) deals with three sets of relationships. Rights and obligations between the sender of a payment order and the receiving bank are governed by the law of the jurisdiction in which the receiving bank is located. If the receiving bank is the beneficiary's bank the rights and obligations of the beneficiary are also governed by the law of the jurisdiction in which the receiving bank is located. Suppose Originator, located in Canada, sends a payment order to Originator's Bank located in a state in which Article 4A has been enacted. The order is for payment to an account of Beneficiary in a bank in England. Under subsection (a)(1), the rights and obligations of Originator and Originator's Bank toward each other are governed by Article 4A if an action is brought in a court in the Article 4A state. If an action is brought in a Canadian court, the conflict of laws issue will be determined by Canadian law which might or might not apply the law of the state in which Originator's Bank is located. If that law is applied, the execution of Originator's order will be governed by Article 4A, but with respect to the payment order of Originator's Bank to the English bank, Article 4A may or may not be applied with respect to the rights and obligations between the two banks. The result may depend upon whether action is brought in a court in the state in which Originator's Bank is located or in an English court. Article 4A is binding only on a court in a state that enacts it. It can have extraterritorial effect only to the extent courts of another jurisdiction are willing to apply it. Subsection (c) also bears on the issues discussed in this Comment.

Under Section 4A–406 payment by the originator to the beneficiary of the funds transfer occurs when the beneficiary's bank accepts a payment order for the benefit of the beneficiary. A jurisdiction in which Article 4A is not in effect may follow a different rule or it may not have a clear rule. Under Section 4A–507(a)(3) the issue is governed by the law of the jurisdiction in which the beneficiary's bank is located. Since the payment to the beneficiary is made through the beneficiary's bank it is reasonable that the issue of when payment occurs be governed by the law of the jurisdiction in which the bank is located. Since it is difficult in many cases to determine where a beneficiary is located, the location of the beneficiary's bank provides a more certain rule.

3. Subsection (b) deals with choice-of-law agreements and it gives maximum freedom of choice. Since the law of funds transfers is not highly developed in the case law there may be a strong incentive to choose the law of a jurisdiction in which Article 4A is in effect because it provides a greater degree of certainty with respect to the rights of various parties. With respect to commercial transactions, it is often said that "[u]ni-

formity and predictability based upon commercial convenience are the prime considerations in making the choice of governing law ...." R. Leflar, American Conflicts Law, § 185 (1977). Subsection (b) is derived in part from recently enacted choice-of-law rules in the States of New York and California. N.Y.Gen. Obligations Law 5–1401 (McKinney's 1989 Supp.) and California Civil Code § 1646.5. This broad endorsement of freedom of contract is an enhancement of the approach taken by Restatement (Second) of Conflict of Laws § 187(b) (1971). The Restatement recognizes the basic right of freedom of contract, but the freedom granted the parties may be more limited than the freedom granted here. Under the formulation of the Restatement, if there is no substantial relationship to the jurisdiction whose law is selected and there is no "other" reasonable basis for the parties' choice, then the selection of the parties need not be honored by a court. Further, if the choice is violative of a fundamental policy of a state which has a materially greater interest than the chosen state, the selection could be disregarded by a court. Those limitations are not found in subsection (b).

4. Subsection (c) may be the most important provision in regard to creating uniformity of law in funds transfers. Most rights stated in Article 4A regard parties who are in privity of contract such as originator and beneficiary, sender and receiving bank, and beneficiary's bank and beneficiary. Since they are in privity they can make a choice of law by agreement. But that is not always the case. For example, an intermediary bank that improperly executes a payment order is not in privity with either the originator or the beneficiary. The ability of a funds transfer system to make a choice of law by rule is a convenient way of dispensing with individual agreements and to cover cases in which agreements are not feasible. It is probable that funds transfer systems will adopt a governing law to increase the certainty of commercial transactions that are ef-

fected over such systems. A system rule might adopt the law of an Article 4A state to govern transfers on the system in order to provide a consistent, unitary, law governing all transfers made on the system. To the extent such system rules develop, individual choice-of-law agreements become unnecessary.

Subsection (c) has broad application. A system choice of law applies not only to rights and obligations between banks that use the system, but may also apply to other parties to the funds transfer so long as some part of the transfer was carried out over the system. The originator and any other sender or receiving bank in the funds transfer is bound if at the time it issues or accepts a payment order it had notice that the funds transfer involved use of the system and that the system chose the law of a particular jurisdiction. Under Section 4A–107, the Federal Reserve by regulation could make a similar choice of law to govern funds transfers carried out by use of Federal Reserve Banks. Subsection (d) is a limitation on subsection (c). If parties have made a choice-of-law agreement that conflicts with a choice of law made under subsection (c), the agreement prevails.

5. Subsection (e) addresses the case in which a funds transfer involves more than one funds transfer system and the systems adopt conflicting choice-of-law rules. The rule that has the most significant relationship to the matter at issue prevails. For example, each system should be able to make a choice of law governing payment orders transmitted over that system with regard to a choice of law made by another system.

TECHNICAL AMENDMENT TO ARTICLE 1

A state enacting Article 4A should amend Section 1–105(2) by adding the following:

"Governing law in the Article on Funds Transfers. Section 4A–507."

UCC ARTICLE 5

LETTERS OF CREDIT

Article 5 was revised in 1995.

2001 amendments (Article 1 revision) ....*Appendix A*
2003 amendments (Article 7 revision) ....*Appendix B*

Section
5–101. Short Title.
5–102. Definitions.
5–103. Scope.
5–104. Formal Requirements.
5–105. Consideration.
5–106. Issuance, Amendment, Cancellation, and Duration.
5–107. Confirmer, Nominated Person, and Adviser.
5–108. Issuer's Rights and Obligations.
5–109. Fraud and Forgery.
5–110. Warranties.
5–111. Remedies.
5–112. Transfer of Letter of Credit.

Section
5–113. Transfer by Operation of Law.
5–114. Assignment of Proceeds.
5–115. Statute of Limitations.
5–116. Choice of Law and Forum.
5–117. Subrogation of Issuer, Applicant, and Nominated Person.
5–118. Security Interest of Issuer or Nominated Person.

TRANSITION PROVISIONS
[   ]. Effective Date.
[   ]. Repeal.
[   ]. Applicability.
[   ]. Savings Clause.

National Conference of Commissioners on Uniform State Laws

REPORTER

James J. White, Ann Arbor, Michigan

DRAFTING COMMITTEE

CHAIRMAN

Carlyle C. Ring, Jr., Vienna, Virginia

MEMBERS

Marion W. Benfield, Jr., Winston–Salem, North Carolina

John P. Burton, Santa Fe, New Mexico, *National Conference Representative and The American Law Institute Representative*

Bruce A. Coggeshall, Portland, Maine

William C. Hillman, Boston, Massachusetts

Edwin E. Huddleson, III, Washington, District of Columbia, *The American Law Institute Representative*

Jeremiah Marsh, Chicago, Illinois

Richard L. Morningstar, Washington, District of Columbia

Edwin E. Smith, Boston, Massachusetts

Sandra S. Stern, Scarsdale, New York

Richard C. Hite, Wichita, Kansas, *President (Member Ex Officio)*

Neal Ossen, Hartford, Connecticut, *Chairman, Division C (Member Ex Officio)*

REVIEW COMMITTEE

CHAIRMAN

William M. Burke, Los Angeles, California

MEMBERS

Boris Auerbach, Wyoming, Ohio

Robert J. Desiderio, Albuquerque, New Mexico

PREFATORY NOTE

Reason for Revision

When the original Article 5 was drafted 40 years ago, it was written for paper transactions and before many innovations in letters of credit. Now electronic and other media are used extensively. Since the 50's, standby letters of credit have developed and now nearly $500 billion standby letters of credit are issued annually worldwide, of which $250 billion are issued in the United States. The use of deferred payment letters of credit has also greatly increased. The customs and practices for letters of credit have evolved and are reflected in the Uniform Customs and Practice (UCP), usually incorporated into letters of credit, particularly international letters of credit, which have seen four revisions since the 1950's; the current version became effective in 1994 (UCP 500). Lastly, in a number of areas, court decisions have resulted in conflicting rules.

Prior to the appointment of a drafting committee, the ABA UCC Committee appointed a Task Force composed of knowledgeable practitioners and academics. The ABA Task Force studied the case law, evolving technologies and the changes in customs and practices. The Task Force identified a large number of issues which they discussed at some length, and made recommendations for revisions to Article 5. The Task Force stated in a foreword:

"As a result of these increases and changes in usage, practice, players, and pressure, it comes as no surprise that there has been a sizable increase in litigation. Indeed, the approximately 62 cases reported in the United States in 1987 constituted double the cumulative reported cases up to 1965....

Moreover, almost forty years of hard use have revealed weaknesses, gaps and errors in the original statute which compromise its rele-

vance. U.C.C. Article 5 was one of the few areas of the Uniform Commercial Code which did not benefit from prior codification and it should come as no surprise that it may require some revision....

Measured in terms of these areas which are vital to any system of commercial law, the current combination of statute and case law is found wanting in major respects both as to predictability and certainty. What is at issue here are not matters of sophistry but important issues of substance which have not been resolved by the current case law/code method and which admit of little likelihood of such resolution." (45 Bus. Lawyer 1521, at 1532, 1535–6)[1]

The Drafting Committee began its deliberations with the Task Force Report in hand. The final work of the Drafting Committee varies from many of the suggestions of the Task Force.

Need for Uniformity

Letters of Credit are a major instrument in international trade, as well as domestic transactions. To facilitate its usefulness and competitiveness, it is essential that U.S. law be in harmony with international rules and practices, as well as flexible enough to accommodate changes in technology and practices that have, and are, evolving. Not only should the rules be consistent within the United States, but they need to be substantively and procedurally consistent with international practices.

Thus, the goals of the drafting effort were:

- conforming the Article 5 rules to current customs and practices;

- accommodating new forms of Letters of Credit, changes in customs and practices, and evolving technology, particularly the use of electronic media;

- maintaining Letters of Credit as an inexpensive and efficient instrument facilitating trade; and

- resolving conflicts among reported decisions.

1. The Task Force members were: Professor James E. Byrne (George Mason University School of Law) Chair; Professor Boris Kozolchyk (University of Arizona College of Law); Michael Evan Avidon (Moses & Singer); James G. Barnes (Baker & McKenzie); Arthur G. Lloyd (Citi-bank N.A.); Janis S. Penton (Rosen, Wachtell & Gilbert); Richard F. Purcell (Connell, Rice & Sugar Co.); Alan L. Bloodgood (Morgan Guaranty Trust Co.); Charles del Busto (Manufacturers Hanover Trust Co.); Vincent Maulella (Manufacturers Hanover Trust Co.).

Process of Achieving Uniformity

The essence of uniform law revision is to obtain a sufficient consensus and balance among the interests of the various participants so that universal and uniform enactment by the various States may be achieved.

In part this is accomplished by extensive consultation on and broad circulation of the drafts from 1990, when the project began, until approval of the final draft by the American law Institute (ALI) and the National Conference of Commissioners on Uniform State Laws (NCCUSL).

Hundreds of groups were invited to participate in the drafting process. Twenty Advisors were appointed, representing a cross-section of interested parties. In addition 20 Observers regularly attended drafting meetings and over 100 were on the mailing list to receive all drafts of the revision.

The Drafting Committee meetings were open and all those who attended were afforded full opportunity to express their views and participate in the dialogue. The Advisors and Observers were a balanced group with ten representatives of users (Beneficiaries and Applicants); five representatives of governmental agencies; five representatives of the U.S. Council on International Banking (USCIB); seven from major banks in letter of credit transactions; eight from regional banks; and seven law professors who teach and write on Letters of Credit.

Nine Drafting Committee meetings were held that began Friday morning and ended Sunday noon. In addition, the draft was twice debated in full by NCCUSL, once by the ALI Council, once considered by the ALI Consultative Group and once by an ad hoc Committee of the Council; and reviewed and discussed by the ABA Subcommittee on Letters of Credit semi-annually and by several state and city bar association committees.

The drafts were regularly reviewed and discussed in *The Business Lawyer*, *Letter of Credit Update*, and in other publications.

The consensus, balance and quality achieved in this lengthy deliberative process is a product of not only its Reporter and the Drafting Committee, but also the faithful and energetic participation of the following Advisors and active participants:

Advisors

Professor Gerald T. McLaughlin, Loyola Law School, ABA, Section of Business Law

James G. Barnes, Baker & McKenzie/U.S. Council on International Banking, Inc.

Harold S. Burman, U.S. Department of State

James E. Byrne, George Mason University, Institute of International Banking Law and Practice Inc.

Professor John Dolan, original ABA Advisor

Henry N. Dyhouse, U.S. Central Credit Union

David P. Goch, Treasury Management Association

Thomas J. Greco, American Bankers Association

Henry Harfield, Shearman & Sterling

Oliver I. Ireland, Board of Governors of Federal Reserve Board

James W. Kopp, Shell Oil Company/Treasury Management Association

Professor Boris Kozolchyk, University of Arizona/National Law Center for Inter–American Free Trade, U.S. Council on International Banking, Inc.

Vincent M. Maulella, Manufacturers Hanover Trust Co./U.S.Council on International Banking, Inc.

Robert M. Rosenblith, National Westminster Bank

Bradley K. Sabel, Federal Reserve Bank of New York

Joseph H. Sommer, Federal Reserve Bank of New York

Jamileh Soufan, American General Corporation/Treasury Management Association

Dan Taylor, U.S. Council on International Banking, Inc.

William H. Thornton, Security Pacific National Bank/California Bankers Association

Paul S. Turner, Occidental Petroleum Corporation/Treasury Management Association

Stanley M. Walker, Exxon Company U.S.A./Treasury Management Association

Active Participants

Michael E. Avidon, Moses & Singer/N.Y. State Bar Association, Banking Law Committee, Subcommittee on Letters of Credit

Walter B. Baker, ABN AMRO Bank, N.V.

Thomas C. Baxter, Jr., Federal Reserve Bank of New York

Professor Amelia H. Boss, Pennsylvania Bar Association, Section of Corporation, Banking & Business Law, Commercial Law Committee

Maria A. Chanco, Bank of America, N.T. & S.A.

Frank P. Curran, Treasury Management Association

Carol R. Dennis, Office of Federal Procurement Policy, OFMB

Albert J. Givray, Oklahoma Bar Association, Section of Banking & Commercial Law

Sidney S. Goldstein, New York State Bar Association

Professor Egon Guttman, The American University

George A. Hisert, State Bar of California, Section of Business Law, Committee on UCC, Subcommittee on Letters of Credit

Larry J. Jones, Mobil Oil Credit Corporation

Carter H. Klein, Jenner & Block

Arthur G. Lloyd, ABA, Section of Business Law, Committee on UCC, Subcommittee on Letters of Credit, Working Group on UCC Article 5 Revision

Rebecca S. McCulloch, ABN AMRO Bank, N.V.

Dennis L. Noah, First National Bank of Maryland/U.S. Council on International Banking, Inc.

James Purvis, The Bank of California

James E. Roselle, First National Bank of Chicago

R. David Whitaker, ABA, Section of Business Law, Committee on UCC, Subcommittee on ECP, Working Group on EDC

Brooke Wunnicke, ABA, Section of Business Law, Committee on UCC, Subcommittee on Letters of Credit

Balance of Benefits

Uniform laws can be enacted only if there is a consensus that the benefits achieved advance the public interest in a manner that can be embraced by all users of the law. It appears that as drafted, Revised Article 5 will enjoy substantial support by the participating interests in letter of credit transactions.

Benefits of Revised Article 5 in General

Independence Principle. Revised Article 5 clearly and forcefully states the independence of the letter of credit obligations from the underlying transactions that was unexpressed in, but was a fundamental predicate for, the original Article 5 (Sections 5–103(d) and 5–108(f)). Certainty of payment, independent of other claims, setoffs or other causes of action, is a core element of the commercial utility of letters of credit.

Clarifications. The revision authorizes the use of electronic technology (Sections 5–102(a)(14) and 5–104); expressly permits deferred payment letters of credit (Section 5–102(a)(8)) and two party letters of credit (Section 5–102(a)(10)); provides rules for unstated expiry dates (Section 5–106(c)), perpetual letters of credit (Section 5–106(d)), and non-documentary conditions (Section 5–108(g)); clarifies and establishes rules for successors by operation of law (Sections 5–102(a)(15) and 5–113); conforms to existing practice for assignment of proceeds (Section 5–114); and clarifies the rules where decisions have been in conflict (Section 5–106, Comment 1; Section 5–108, Comments 1, 3, 4, 7, and 9; Section 5–109, Comments 1 and 3; Section 5–113, Comment 1; and Section 5–117, Comment 1).

Harmonizes with International Practice

The UCP is used in most international letters of credit and in many domestic letters of credit. These international practices are well known and employed by the major issuers and users of letters of credit. Revisions have been made to Article 5 to coordinate the Article 5 rules with current international practice (e.g., deferred payment obligations, reasonable time to examine documents, preclusion, non-documentary conditions, return of documents, and irrevocable unless stated to be revocable).

Benefits of Revised Article 5 to Issuers

Consequential Damages. Section 5–111 precludes consequential and punitive damages. It, however, provides strong incentives for Issuers to honor, including provisions for attorneys fees and expenses of litigation, interest, and specific performance. If consequential and punitive damages were allowed, the cost of letters of credit could rise substantially.

Statute of Limitation. Section 5–115 establishes a one year statute of limitation from the expiration date or from accrual of the cause of action, whichever occurs later. Because it is usually obvious to all when there has been a breach, a short limitation period is fair to potential plaintiffs.

Choice of Law. Section 5–116 permits the issuer (or nominated party or adviser) to choose the law of the jurisdiction that will govern even if that law bears no relation to the transaction. Absent agreement, Section 5–116 states choice of law rules.

Assignment of Proceeds. Section 5–114 conforms more fully to existing practice and provides an orderly procedure for recording and accommodating assignments by consent of the issuer (or nominated party).

Subrogation. Section 5–117 clarifies the subrogation rights of an Issuer who has honored a letter of credit. These rights of subrogation also extend to an applicant who reimburses and a nominated party who pays or gives value.

Recognition of UCP. Section 5–116(c) expressly recognizes that if the UCP is incorporated by reference into the letter of credit, the agreement varies the provisions of Article 5 with which it may conflict except for the non-variable provisions of Article 5.

Benefits of Revised Article 5 to Applicants

Warranties. Section 5–110 specifies the warranties made by a beneficiary. It gives the applicant on a letter of credit which has been honored a direct cause of action if a drawing is fraudulent or forged or if a drawing violates any agreement augmented by a letter of credit.

Strict Compliance. Absent agreement to the contrary, the issuer must dishonor a presentation that does not strictly comply under standard practice with the terms and conditions of the letter of credit (Section 5–108).

Subrogation. New Section 5–117 clarifies the parties' rights of subrogation if the letter of credit is honored.

Limitations on General Disclaimers and Waivers. Section 5–103(c) limits the effect of general disclaimers and waivers in a letter of credit, or reimbursement or other agreement.

Benefits of Revised Article 5 to Beneficiaries

Irrevocable. A letter of credit is irrevocable unless the letter of credit expressly provides it is revocable (Section 5–106(a)).

Preclusion. Section 5–108(c) now provides that the Issuer is precluded from asserting any discrepancy not stated in its notice timely given, except for fraud, forgery or expiration.

Timely Examination. Section 5–108(b) requires examination and notice of any discrepancies within a reasonable time not to exceed the 7th business day after presentation of the documents.

Transfers by Operation of Law. New Section 5–113 allows a successor to a beneficiary by operation of law to make presentation and receive payment or acceptance.

Damages. The damages provided are expanded and clarified. They include attorneys fees and expenses of litigation and payment of the full amount of the wrongfully dishonored or repudiated demand, with interest, without an obligation of the beneficiary to mitigate damages (Section 5–111).

Revisions for Article 9 and Transition Provisions

The draft includes suggested revisions to conform Article 9 to the Article 5 changes. Article 9 itself is under revision and the interface with Revised Article 5 will be more fully examined by the Article 9 drafting committee, as well, in light of changes to Article 9. The Article 9 revisions will probably not be completed until 1998–9. Revised Article 8 (1994) also makes changes to Article 9 so care should be taken to coordinate the changes of both Revised Articles 5 and 8 within each State.

The draft also includes transition provisions and some cross reference changes in other Articles of the UCC.

ARTICLE 5

Lastly, there follows a table showing the changes from the original Article 5 made by the revisions to Article 5.

Table of Disposition of Sections in Former Article 5

The reference to a section in revised Article 5 is to the section that refers to the issue addressed by the section in former Article 5. If there is no comparable section in Revised Article 5 to a section in former Article 5, that fact is indicated by the word "Omitted" and a reason is stated.

Former Article 5 Section	Revised Article 5 Section
5–101	5–101
5–102(1)	5–103(a)
5–102(2)	Omitted (inherent in 5–103(a) and definitions)
5–103(3)	(first sentence omitted) 5–103(b)
5–103(1)(a)	5–102(a)(10); 5–106(a); 5–102(a)(8)
5–103(1)(b)	5–102(a)(6)("Document"), and 5–102(a)(14)("Record"); "Documentary" draft or demand not used
5–103(1)(c)	5–102(a)(9)
5–103(1)(d)	5–102(a)(3)
5–103(1)(e)	5–102(a)(1)
5–103(1)(f)	5–102(a)(4)
5–103(1)(g)	("Applicant" rather than "Customer") 5–102(a)(2)
5–103(2)	Omitted as not applicable
5–103(3)	5–102(b)
5–103(4)	5–102(c)
5–104	5–104 and 5–102(6) and (14)
5–105	5–105
5–106(1)	5–106(a)
5–106(2)	5–106(b)
5–106(3)	5–106(b)
5–106(4)	5–106(b)
5–107(1)	5–107(c)
5–107(2)	5–107(a)
5–107(3)	5–107(c)
5–107(4)	Omitted as inadvisable default rule
5–108	Omitted (as outdated)
5–109(1)	5–108
5–109(2)	5–108
5–109(3)	Omitted (all issuers required to observe standard practices)
5–110(1)	Omitted (covered in definitions and comments)
5–110(2)	Omitted (covered in definitions and comments)
5–111(1)	5–110(a)
5–111(2)	5–110(b)
5–112(1)	5–108(b) and (c)
5–112(2)	5–108(h)
5–112(3)	5–102(a)(12)
5–113	Omitted (covered by other contract law)
5–114(1)	5–108(a)
5–114(2)(a)	5–109(a)(1)
5–114(2)(b)	5–109(a)(2)
5–114(3)	5–108(i)
5–114(4), (5)	Omitted; were optional
5–115(1)	5–111
5–115(2)	5–111
5–116(1)	5–112
5–116(2)	5–114
5–116(3)	5–114
5–117	Omitted (covered by other law)

ARTICLE 5

Table of New Provisions

(Provisions which were not included in former Article 5 and subjects not addressed in former Article 5.)

Subject	Revised Article 5 Section
"Successor to a beneficiary"	5–102(15)
Non-variable terms	5–103(c)
Independence principle	5–103(d)
Unstated expiry date	5–106(c)
Perpetual letter of credit	5–106(d)
Preclusion of unstated deficiencies	5–108(c)
Standard practice	5–108(e)
Independence of obligation	5–108(f)
Non-documentary conditions	5–108(g)
Standards for issuing injunction	5–109(b)
Transfer by operation of law	5–113
Statute of Limitation	5–115
Choice of law	5–116
Subrogation	5–117

§ 5–101.   Short Title.

This article may be cited as Uniform Commercial Code—Letters of Credit.

Official Comment

The Official Comment to the original Section 5–101 was a remarkably brief inaugural address. Noting that letters of credit had not been the subject of statutory enactment and that the law concerning them had been developed in the cases, the Comment stated that Article 5 was intended "within its limited scope" to set an independent theoretical frame for the further development of letters of credit. That statement addressed accurately conditions as they existed when the statement was made, nearly half a century ago. Since Article 5 was originally drafted, the use of letters of credit has expanded and developed, and the case law concerning these developments is, in some respects, discordant.

Revision of Article 5 therefore has required reappraisal both of the statutory goals and of the extent to which particular statutory provisions further or adversely affect achievement of those goals.

The statutory goal of Article 5 was originally stated to be: (1) to set a substantive theoretical frame that describes the function and legal nature of letters of credit; and (2) to preserve procedural flexibility in order to accommodate further development of the efficient use of letters of credit. A letter of credit is an idiosyncratic form of undertaking that supports performance of an obligation incurred in a separate financial, mercantile, or other transaction or arrangement. The objectives of the original and revised Article 5 are best achieved (1) by defining the peculiar characteristics of a letter of credit that distinguish it and the legal consequences of its use from other forms of assurance such as secondary guarantees, performance bonds, and insurance policies, and from ordinary contracts, fiduciary engagements, and escrow arrangements; and (2) by preserving flexibility through variation by agreement in order to respond to and accommodate developments in custom and usage that are not inconsistent with the essential definitions and substantive mandates of the statute. No statute can, however, prescribe the manner in which such substantive rights and duties are to be enforced or imposed without risking stultification of wholesome developments in the letter of credit mechanism. Letter of credit law should remain responsive to commercial reality and in particular to the customs and expectations of the international banking and mercantile community. Courts should read the terms of this article in a manner consistent with these customs and expectations.

The subject matter in Article 5, letters of credit, may also be governed by an international convention that is now being drafted by UNCITRAL, the draft Convention on Independent Guarantees and Standby Letters of Credit. The Uniform Customs and Practice is an international body of trade practice that is commonly adopted by international and domestic letters of credit and as such is the "law of the transaction" by agreement of the parties. Article 5 is consistent with and was influenced by the rules in the existing version of the UCP. In addition to the UCP and the international convention, other bodies of law apply to letters of credit. For example, the federal bankruptcy law applies to letters of credit with respect to applicants and beneficiaries that are in bankruptcy; regulations of the Federal Reserve Board and the Comptroller of the Currency lay out requirements for banks that issue letters of credit and describe how letters of credit are to be treated for calculating asset risk and for the purpose of loan limitations. In addition there is an array of anti-boycott and other similar laws that may affect the issuance and performance of letters of credit. All of these laws are beyond the scope of Article 5, but in certain circumstances they will override Article 5.

§ 5–102.   Definitions.

(a) In this article:

(1) "Adviser" means a person who, at the request of the issuer, a confirmer, or another adviser, notifies or requests another adviser to notify the beneficiary that a letter of credit has been issued, confirmed, or amended.

(2) "Applicant" means a person at whose request or for whose account a letter of credit is issued. The term includes a person who requests an issuer to issue a letter of credit on behalf of another if the person making the request undertakes an obligation to reimburse the issuer.

(3) "Beneficiary" means a person who under the terms of a letter of credit is entitled to have its complying presentation honored. The term includes a person to whom drawing rights have been transferred under a transferable letter of credit.

(4) "Confirmer" means a nominated person who undertakes, at the request or with the consent of the issuer, to honor a presenta-

tion under a letter of credit issued by another.

(5) "Dishonor" of a letter of credit means failure timely to honor or to take an interim action, such as acceptance of a draft, that may be required by the letter of credit.

(6) "Document" means a draft or other demand, document of title, investment security, certificate, invoice, or other record, statement, or representation of fact, law, right, or opinion (i) which is presented in a written or other medium permitted by the letter of credit or, unless prohibited by the letter of credit, by the standard practice referred to in Section 5–108(e) and (ii) which is capable of being examined for compliance with the terms and conditions of the letter of credit. A document may not be oral.

(7) "Good faith" means honesty in fact in the conduct or transaction concerned.

(8) "Honor" of a letter of credit means performance of the issuer's undertaking in the letter of credit to pay or deliver an item of value. Unless the letter of credit otherwise provides, "honor" occurs

(i) upon payment,

(ii) if the letter of credit provides for acceptance, upon acceptance of a draft and, at maturity, its payment, or

(iii) if the letter of credit provides for incurring a deferred obligation, upon incurring the obligation and, at maturity, its performance.

(9) "Issuer" means a bank or other person that issues a letter of credit, but does not include an individual who makes an engagement for personal, family, or household purposes.

(10) "Letter of credit" means a definite undertaking that satisfies the requirements of Section 5–104 by an issuer to a beneficiary at the request or for the account of an applicant or, in the case of a financial institution, to itself or for its own account, to honor a documentary presentation by payment or delivery of an item of value.

(11) "Nominated person" means a person whom the issuer (i) designates or authorizes to pay, accept, negotiate, or otherwise give value under a letter of credit and (ii) undertakes by agreement or custom and practice to reimburse.

(12) "Presentation" means delivery of a document to an issuer or nominated person for honor or giving of value under a letter of credit.

(13) "Presenter" means a person making a presentation as or on behalf of a beneficiary or nominated person.

(14) "Record" means information that is inscribed on a tangible medium, or that is stored in an electronic or other medium and is retrievable in perceivable form.

(15) "Successor of a beneficiary" means a person who succeeds to substantially all of the rights of a beneficiary by operation of law, including a corporation with or into which the beneficiary has been merged or consolidated, an administrator, executor, personal representative, trustee in bankruptcy, debtor in possession, liquidator, and receiver.

(b) Definitions in other Articles applying to this article and the sections in which they appear are:

"Accept" or "Acceptance" Section 3–409

"Value" Sections 3–303, 4–211

(c) Article 1 contains certain additional general definitions and principles of construction and interpretation applicable throughout this article.

Official Comment

1. Since no one can be a confirmer unless that person is a nominated person as defined in Section 5–102(a)(11), those who agree to "confirm" without the designation or authorization of the issuer are not confirmers under Article 5. Nonetheless, the undertakings to the beneficiary of such persons may be enforceable by the beneficiary as letters of credit issued by the "confirmer" for its own account or as guarantees or contracts outside of Article 5.

2. The definition of "document" contemplates and facilitates the growing recognition of electronic and other nonpaper media as "documents," however, for the time being, data in those media constitute docu-

ments only in certain circumstances. For example, a facsimile received by an issuer would be a document only if the letter of credit explicitly permitted it, if the standard practice authorized it and the letter did not prohibit it, or the agreement of the issuer and beneficiary permitted it. The fact that data transmitted in a nonpaper (unwritten) medium can be recorded on paper by a recipient's computer printer, facsimile machine, or the like does not under current practice render the data so transmitted a "document." A facsimile or S.W.I.F.T. message received directly by the issuer is in an electronic medium when it crosses the boundary of the issuer's place of business. One wishing to make a presentation by facsimile (an electronic medium) will have to procure the explicit agreement of the issuer (assuming that the standard practice does not authorize it). Article 5 contemplates that electronic documents may be presented under a letter of credit and the provisions of this Article should be read to apply to electronic documents as well as tangible documents. An electronic document of title is delivered through the voluntary transfer of control. Article 1, Section 1–201 (definition of "delivery"). See Article 7, Section 7–106 on control of an electronic document. Where electronic transmissions are authorized neither by the letter of credit nor by the practice, the beneficiary may transmit the data electronically to its agent who may be able to put it in written form and make a conforming presentation. Cf. Article 7, Section 7–105 on reissuing an electronic document in a tangible medium.

3. "Good faith" continues in revised Article 5 to be defined as "honesty in fact." "Observance of reasonable standards of fair dealing" has not been added to the definition. The narrower definition of "honesty in fact" reinforces the "independence principle" in the treatment of "fraud," "strict compliance," "preclusion," and other tests affecting the performance of obligations that are unique to letters of credit. This narrower definition—which does not include "fair dealing"—is appropriate to the decision to honor or dishonor a presentation of documents specified in a letter of credit. The narrower definition is also appropriate for other parts of revised Article 5 where greater certainty of obligations is necessary and is consistent with the goals of speed and low cost. It is important that U.S. letters of credit have continuing vitality and competitiveness in international transactions.

For example, it would be inconsistent with the "independence" principle if any of the following occurred: (i) the beneficiary's failure to adhere to the standard of "fair dealing" in the underlying transaction or otherwise in presenting documents were to provide appli-

cants and issuers with an "unfairness" defense to dishonor even when the documents complied with the terms of the letter of credit; (ii) the issuer's obligation to honor in "strict compliance in accordance with standard practice" were changed to "reasonable compliance" by use of the "fair dealing" standard, or (iii) the preclusion against the issuer (Section 5–108(d)) were modified under the "fair dealing" standard to enable the issuer later to raise additional deficiencies in the presentation. The rights and obligations arising from presentation, honor, dishonor and reimbursement, are independent and strict, and thus "honesty in fact" is an appropriate standard.

The contract between the applicant and beneficiary is not governed by Article 5, but by applicable contract law, such as Article 2 or the general law of contracts. "Good faith" in that contract is defined by other law, such as Section 2–103(1)(b) or Restatement of Contracts 2d, § 205, which incorporate the principle of "fair dealing" in most cases, or a State's common law or other statutory provisions that may apply to that contract.

The contract between the applicant and the issuer (sometimes called the "reimbursement" agreement) is governed in part by this article (e.g., Sections 5–108(i), 5–111(b), and 5–103(c)) and partly by other law (e.g., the general law of contracts). The definition of good faith in Section 5–102(a)(7) applies only to the extent that the reimbursement contract is governed by provisions in this article; for other purposes good faith is defined by other law.

4. Payment and acceptance are familiar modes of honor. A third mode of honor, incurring an unconditional obligation, has legal effects similar to an acceptance of a time draft but does not technically constitute an acceptance. The practice of making letters of credit available by "deferred payment undertaking" as now provided in UCP 500 has grown up in other countries and spread to the United States. The definition of "honor" will accommodate that practice.

5. The exclusion of consumers from the definition of "issuer" is to keep creditors from using a letter of credit in consumer transactions in which the consumer might be made the issuer and the creditor would be the beneficiary. If that transaction were recognized under Article 5, the effect would be to leave the consumer without defenses against the creditor. That outcome would violate the policy behind the Federal Trade Commission Rule in 16 CFR Part 433. In a consumer transaction, an individual cannot be an issuer where that person would otherwise be either the principal debtor or a guarantor.

6. The label on a document is not conclusive; certain documents labelled "guarantees" in accordance with European (and occasionally, American) practice are letters of credit. On the other hand, even documents that are labelled "letter of credit" may not constitute letters of credit under the definition in Section 5–102(a). When a document labelled a letter of credit requires the issuer to pay not upon the presentation of documents, but upon the determination of an extrinsic fact such as applicant's failure to perform a construction contract, and where that condition appears on its face to be fundamental and would, if ignored, leave no obligation to the issuer under the document labelled letter of credit, the issuer's undertaking is not a letter of credit. It is probably some form of suretyship or other contractual arrangement and may be enforceable as such. See Sections 5–102(a)(10) and 5–103(d). Therefore, undertakings whose fundamental term requires an issuer to look beyond documents and beyond conventional reference to the clock, calendar, and practices concerning the form of various documents are not governed by Article 5. Although Section 5–108(g) recognizes that certain nondocumentary conditions can be included in a letter of credit without denying the undertaking the status of letter of credit, that section does not apply to cases where the nondocumentary condition is fundamental to the issuer's obligation. The rules in Sections 5–102(a)(10), 5–103(d), and 5–108(g) approve the conclusion in Wichita Eagle & Beacon Publishing Co. v. Pacific Nat. Bank, 493 F.2d 1285 (9th Cir.1974).

The adjective "definite" is taken from the UCP. It approves cases that deny letter of credit status to documents that are unduly vague or incomplete. See, e.g., *Transparent Products Corp. v. Paysaver Credit Union,* 864 F.2d 60 (7th Cir.1988). Note, however, that no particular phrase or label is necessary to establish a letter of credit. It is sufficient if the undertaking of the issuer shows that it is intended to be a letter of credit. In most cases the parties' intention will be indicated by a label on the undertaking itself indicating that it is a "letter of credit," but no such language is necessary.

A financial institution may be both the issuer and the applicant or the issuer and the beneficiary. Such letters are sometimes issued by a bank in support of the bank's own lease obligations or on behalf of one of its divisions as an applicant or to one of its divisions as beneficiary, such as an overseas branch. Because wide use of letters of credit in which the issuer and the applicant or the issuer and the beneficiary are the same would endanger the unique status of letters of credit, only financial institutions are authorized to issue them.

In almost all cases the ultimate performance of the issuer under a letter of credit is the payment of money. In rare cases the issuer's obligation is to deliver stock certificates or the like. The definition of letter of credit in Section 5–102(a)(10) contemplates those cases.

7. Under the UCP any bank is a nominated bank where the letter of credit is "freely negotiable." A letter of credit might also nominate by the following: "We hereby engage with the drawer, indorsers, and bona fide holders of drafts drawn under and in compliance with the terms of this credit that the same will be duly honored on due presentation" or "available with any bank by negotiation." A restricted negotiation credit might be "available with x bank by negotiation" or the like.

Several legal consequences may attach to the status of nominated person. First, when the issuer nominates a person, it is authorizing that person to pay or give value and is authorizing the beneficiary to make presentation to that person. Unless the letter of credit provides otherwise, the beneficiary need not present the documents to the issuer before the letter of credit expires; it need only present those documents to the nominated person. Secondly, a nominated person that gives value in good faith has a right to payment from the issuer despite fraud. Section 5–109(a)(1).

8. A "record" must be in or capable of being converted to a perceivable form. For example, an electronic message recorded in a computer memory that could be printed from that memory could constitute a record. Similarly, a tape recording of an oral conversation could be a record.

9. Absent a specific agreement to the contrary, documents of a beneficiary delivered to an issuer or nominated person are considered to be presented under the letter of credit to which they refer, and any payment or value given for them is considered to be made under that letter of credit. As the court held in Alaska Textile Co. v. Chase Manhattan Bank, N.A., 982 F.2d 813, 820 (2d Cir.1992), it takes a "significant showing" to make the presentation of a beneficiary's documents for "collection only" or otherwise outside letter of credit law and practice.

10. Although a successor of a beneficiary is one who succeeds "by operation of law," some of the successions contemplated by Section 5–102(a)(15) will have resulted from voluntary action of the beneficiary such as merger of a corporation. Any merger makes the successor corporation the "successor of a beneficia-

ry'' even though the transfer occurs partly by operation of law and partly by the voluntary action of the parties. The definition excludes certain transfers, where no part of the transfer is "by operation of law"—such as the sale of assets by one company to another.

11. "Draft" in Article 5 does not have the same meaning it has in Article 3. For example, a document may be a draft under Article 5 even though it would not be a negotiable instrument, and therefore would not qualify as a draft under Section 3–104(e).

As amended in 2003.

§ 5–103. Scope.

(a) This article applies to letters of credit and to certain rights and obligations arising out of transactions involving letters of credit.

(b) The statement of a rule in this article does not by itself require, imply, or negate application of the same or a different rule to a situation not provided for, or to a person not specified, in this article.

(c) With the exception of this subsection, subsections (a) and (d), Sections 5–102(a)(9) and (10), 5–106(d), and 5–114(d), and except to the extent prohibited in Sections 1–302 and 5–117(d), the effect of this article may be varied by agreement or by a provision stated or incorporated by reference in an undertaking. A term in an agreement or undertaking generally excusing liability or generally limiting remedies for failure to perform obligations is not sufficient to vary obligations prescribed by this article.

(d) Rights and obligations of an issuer to a beneficiary or a nominated person under a letter of credit are independent of the existence, performance, or nonperformance of a contract or arrangement out of which the letter of credit arises or which underlies it, including contracts or arrangements between the issuer and the applicant and between the applicant and the beneficiary.

As amended in 2001.

Official Comment

1. Sections 5–102(a)(10) and 5–103 are the principal limits on the scope of Article 5. Many undertakings in commerce and contract are similar, but not identical to the letter of credit. Principal among those are "secondary," "accessory," or "suretyship" guarantees. Although the word "guarantee" is sometimes used to describe an independent obligation like that of the issuer of a letter of credit (most often in the case of European bank undertakings but occasionally in the case of undertakings of American banks), in the United States the word "guarantee" is more typically used to describe a suretyship transaction in which the "guarantor" is only secondarily liable and has the right to assert the underlying debtor's defenses. This article does not apply to secondary or accessory guarantees and it is important to recognize the distinction between letters of credit and those guarantees. It is often a defense to a secondary or accessory guarantor's liability that the underlying debt has been discharged or that the debtor has other defenses to the underlying liability. In letter of credit law, on the other hand, the independence principle recognized throughout Article 5 states that the issuer's liability is independent of the underlying obligation. That the beneficiary may have breached the underlying contract and thus have given a good defense on that contract to the applicant against the beneficiary is no defense for the issuer's refusal to honor. Only staunch recognition of this principle by the issuers and the courts will give letters of credit the continuing vitality that arises from the certainty and speed of payment under letters of credit. To that end, it is important that the law not carry into letter of credit transactions rules that properly apply only to secondary guarantees or to other forms of engagement.

2. Like all of the provisions of the Uniform Commercial Code, Article 5 is supplemented by Section 1–103 and, through it, by many rules of statutory and common law. Because this article is quite short and has no rules on many issues that will affect liability with respect to a letter of credit transaction, law beyond Article 5 will often determine rights and liabilities in letter of credit transactions. Even within letter of credit law, the article is far from comprehensive; it deals only with "certain" rights of the parties. Particularly with respect to the standards of performance that are set out in Section 5–108, it is appropriate for the parties and the courts to turn to customs and practice such as the Uniform Customs and Practice for Documentary Credits, currently published by the International Chamber of Commerce as I.C.C. Pub. No. 500 (hereafter UCP). Many letters of credit specifically adopt the UCP as applicable to the particular transaction. Where the UCP are adopted but conflict with Article 5 and except where variation is prohibited, the UCP terms are permissible contractual modifications under Sections 1–302 and 5–103(c). See Section 5–116(c). Normally Article 5 should not be considered to conflict with practice except when a rule explicitly

stated in the UCP or other practice is different from a rule explicitly stated in Article 5.

Except by choosing the law of a jurisdiction that has not adopted the Uniform Commercial Code, it is not possible entirely to escape the Uniform Commercial Code. Since incorporation of the UCP avoids only "conflicting" Article 5 rules, parties who do not wish to be governed by the nonconflicting provisions of Article 5 must normally either adopt the law of a jurisdiction other than a State of the United States or state explicitly the rule that is to govern. When rules of custom and practice are incorporated by reference, they are considered to be explicit terms of the agreement or undertaking.

Neither the obligation of an issuer under Section 5–108 nor that of an adviser under Section 5–107 is an obligation of the kind that is invariable under Section 1–102(3). Section 5–103(c) and Comment 1 to Section 5–108 make it clear that the applicant and the issuer may agree to almost any provision establishing the obligations of the issuer to the applicant. The last sentence of subsection (c) limits the power of the issuer to achieve that result by a nonnegotiated disclaimer or limitation of remedy.

What the issuer could achieve by an explicit agreement with its applicant or by a term that explicitly defines its duty, it cannot accomplish by a general disclaimer. The restriction on disclaimers in the last sentence of subsection (c) is based more on procedural than on substantive unfairness. Where, for example, the reimbursement agreement provides explicitly that the issuer need not examine any documents, the applicant understands the risk it has undertaken. A term in a reimbursement agreement which states generally that an issuer will not be liable unless it has acted in "bad faith" or committed "gross negligence" is ineffective under Section 5–103(c). On the other hand, less general terms such as terms that permit issuer reliance on an oral or electronic message believed in good faith to have been received from the applicant or terms that entitle an issuer to reimbursement when it honors a "substantially" though not "strictly" complying presentation, are effective. In each case the question is whether the disclaimer or limitation is sufficiently clear and explicit in reallocating a liability or risk that is allocated differently under a variable Article 5 provision.

Of course, no term in a letter of credit, whether incorporated by reference to practice rules or stated specifically, can free an issuer from a conflicting contractual obligation to its applicant. If, for example, an issuer promised its applicant that it would pay only

against an inspection certificate of a particular company but failed to require such a certificate in its letter of credit or made the requirement only a nondocumentary condition that had to be disregarded, the issuer might be obliged to pay the beneficiary even though its payment might violate its contract with its applicant.

3. Parties should generally avoid modifying the definitions in Section 5–102. The effect of such an agreement is almost inevitably unclear. To say that something is a "guarantee" in the typical domestic transaction is to say that the parties intend that particular legal rules apply to it. By acknowledging that something is a guarantee, but asserting that it is to be treated as a "letter of credit," the parties leave a court uncertain about where the rules on guarantees stop and those concerning letters of credit begin.

4. Section 5–102(2) and (3) of Article 5 are omitted as unneeded; the omission does not change the law.

As amended in 2001.

§ 5–104. Formal Requirements.

A letter of credit, confirmation, advice, transfer, amendment, or cancellation may be issued in any form that is a record and is authenticated (i) by a signature or (ii) in accordance with the agreement of the parties or the standard practice referred to in Section 5–108(e).

Official Comment

1. Neither Section 5–104 nor the definition of letter of credit in Section 5–102(a)(10) requires inclusion of all the terms that are normally contained in a letter of credit in order for an undertaking to be recognized as a letter of credit under Article 5. For example, a letter of credit will typically specify the amount available, the expiration date, the place where presentation should be made, and the documents that must be presented to entitle a person to honor. Undertakings that have the formalities required by Section 5–104 and meet the conditions specified in Section 5–102(a)(10) will be recognized as letters of credit even though they omit one or more of the items usually contained in a letter of credit.

2. The authentication specified in this section is authentication only of the identity of the issuer, confirmer, or adviser.

An authentication agreement may be by system rule, by standard practice, or by direct agreement between the parties. The reference to practice is intended to incorporate future developments in the UCP and other practice rules as well as those that may arise spontaneously in commercial practice.

3. Many banking transactions, including the issuance of many letters of credit, are now conducted mostly by electronic means. For example, S.W.I.F.T. is currently used to transmit letters of credit from issuing to advising banks. The letter of credit text so transmitted may be printed at the advising bank, stamped "original" and provided to the beneficiary in that form. The printed document may then be used as a way of controlling and recording payments and of recording and authorizing assignments of proceeds or transfers of rights under the letter of credit. Nothing in this section should be construed to conflict with that practice.

To be a record sufficient to serve as a letter of credit or other undertaking under this section, data must have a durability consistent with that function. Because consideration is not required for a binding letter of credit or similar undertaking (Section 5–105) yet those undertakings are to be strictly construed (Section 5–108), parties to a letter of credit transaction are especially dependent on the continued availability of the terms and conditions of the letter of credit or other undertaking. By declining to specify any particular medium in which the letter of credit must be established or communicated, Section 5–104 leaves room for future developments.

§ 5–105. Consideration.

Consideration is not required to issue, amend, transfer, or cancel a letter of credit, advice, or confirmation.

Official Comment

It is not to be expected that any issuer will issue its letter of credit without some form of remuneration. But it is not expected that the beneficiary will know what the issuer's remuneration was or whether in fact there was any identifiable remuneration in a given case. And it might be difficult for the beneficiary to prove the issuer's remuneration. This section dispenses with this proof and is consistent with the position of Lord Mansfield in *Pillans v. Van Mierop*, 97 Eng.Rep. 1035 (K.B. 1765) in making consideration irrelevant.

§ 5–106. Issuance, Amendment, Cancellation, and Duration.

(a) A letter of credit is issued and becomes enforceable according to its terms against the issuer when the issuer sends or otherwise trans-

mits it to the person requested to advise or to the beneficiary. A letter of credit is revocable only if it so provides.

(b) After a letter of credit is issued, rights and obligations of a beneficiary, applicant, confirmer, and issuer are not affected by an amendment or cancellation to which that person has not consented except to the extent the letter of credit provides that it is revocable or that the issuer may amend or cancel the letter of credit without that consent.

(c) If there is no stated expiration date or other provision that determines its duration, a letter of credit expires one year after its stated date of issuance or, if none is stated, after the date on which it is issued.

(d) A letter of credit that states that it is perpetual expires five years after its stated date of issuance, or if none is stated, after the date on which it is issued.

Official Comment

1. This section adopts the position taken by several courts, namely that letters of credit that are silent as to revocability are irrevocable. See, e.g., *Weyerhaeuser Co. v. First Nat. Bank*, 27 UCC Rep.Serv. 777 (S.D. Iowa 1979); West Va. Hous. Dev. Fund v. Sroka, 415 F.Supp. 1107 (W.D.Pa.1976). This is the position of the current UCP (500). Given the usual commercial understanding and purpose of letters of credit, revocable letters of credit offer unhappy possibilities for misleading the parties who deal with them.

2. A person can consent to an amendment by implication. For example, a beneficiary that tenders documents for honor that conform to an amended letter of credit but not to the original letter of credit has probably consented to the amendment. By the same token an applicant that has procured the issuance of a transferable letter of credit has consented to its transfer and to performance under the letter of credit by a person to whom the beneficiary's rights are duly transferred. If some, but not all of the persons involved in a letter of credit transaction consent to performance that does not strictly conform to the original letter of credit, those persons assume the risk that other nonconsenting persons may insist on strict compliance with the original letter of credit. Under subsection (b) those not consenting are not bound. For example, an issuer might agree to amend its letter of credit or honor documents presented after the expiration date in the belief that the applicant has consented or will consent to the amendment or will waive presentation

after the original expiration date. If that belief is mistaken, the issuer is bound to the beneficiary by the terms of the letter of credit as amended or waived, even though it may be unable to recover from the applicant.

In general, the rights of a recognized transferee beneficiary cannot be altered without the transferee's consent, but the same is not true of the rights of assignees of proceeds from the beneficiary. When the beneficiary makes a complete transfer of its interest that is effective under the terms for transfer established by the issuer, adviser, or other party controlling transfers, the beneficiary no longer has an interest in the letter of credit, and the transferee steps into the shoes of the beneficiary as the one with rights under the letter of credit. Section 5–102(a)(3). When there is a partial transfer, both the original beneficiary and the transferee beneficiary have an interest in performance of the letter of credit and each expects that its rights will not be altered by amendment unless it consents.

The assignee of proceeds under a letter of credit from the beneficiary enjoys no such expectation. Notwithstanding an assignee's notice to the issuer of the assignment of proceeds, the assignee is not a person protected by subsection (b). An assignee of proceeds should understand that its rights can be changed or completely extinguished by amendment or cancellation of the letter of credit. An assignee's claim is precarious, for it depends entirely upon the continued existence of the letter of credit and upon the beneficiary's preparation and presentation of documents that would entitle the beneficiary to honor under Section 5–108.

3. The issuer's right to cancel a revocable letter of credit does not free it from a duty to reimburse a nominated person who has honored, accepted, or undertaken a deferred obligation prior to receiving notice of the amendment or cancellation. Compare UCP Article 8.

4. Although all letters of credit should specify the date on which the issuer's engagement expires, the failure to specify an expiration date does not invalidate the letter of credit, or diminish or relieve the obligation of any party with respect to the letter of credit. A letter of credit that may be revoked or terminated at the discretion of the issuer by notice to the beneficiary is not "perpetual."

§ 5–107. Confirmer, Nominated Person, and Adviser.

(a) A confirmer is directly obligated on a letter of credit and has the rights and obligations of an issuer to the extent of its confirmation. The confirmer also has rights against and obligations to the issuer as if the issuer were an applicant and the confirmer had issued the letter of credit at the request and for the account of the issuer.

(b) A nominated person who is not a confirmer is not obligated to honor or otherwise give value for a presentation.

(c) A person requested to advise may decline to act as an adviser. An adviser that is not a confirmer is not obligated to honor or give value for a presentation. An adviser undertakes to the issuer and to the beneficiary accurately to advise the terms of the letter of credit, confirmation, amendment, or advice received by that person and undertakes to the beneficiary to check the apparent authenticity of the request to advise. Even if the advice is inaccurate, the letter of credit, confirmation, or amendment is enforceable as issued.

(d) A person who notifies a transferee beneficiary of the terms of a letter of credit, confirmation, amendment, or advice has the rights and obligations of an adviser under subsection (c). The terms in the notice to the transferee beneficiary may differ from the terms in any notice to the transferor beneficiary to the extent permitted by the letter of credit, confirmation, amendment, or advice received by the person who so notifies.

Official Comment

1. A confirmer has the rights and obligations identified in Section 5–108. Accordingly, unless the context otherwise requires, the terms "confirmer" and "confirmation" should be read into this article wherever the terms "issuer" and "letter of credit" appear.

A confirmer that has paid in accordance with the terms and conditions of the letter of credit is entitled to reimbursement by the issuer even if the beneficiary committed fraud (see Section 5–109(a)(1)(ii)) and, in that sense, has greater rights against the issuer than the beneficiary has. To be entitled to reimbursement from the issuer under the typical confirmed letter of credit, the confirmer must submit conforming documents, but the confirmer's presentation to the issuer need not be made before the expiration date of the letter of credit.

A letter of credit confirmation has been analogized to a guarantee of issuer performance, to a parallel letter of credit issued by the confirmer for the account of the issuer or the letter of credit applicant or both, and to a back-to-back letter of credit in which the confirmer is a kind of beneficiary of the original issuer's letter of credit. Like letter of credit undertakings, confirmations are both unique and flexible, so that no one of these analogies is perfect, but unless otherwise indicated in the letter of credit or confirmation, a confirmer should be viewed by the letter of credit issuer and the beneficiary as an issuer of a parallel letter of credit for the account of the original letter of credit issuer. Absent a direct agreement between the applicant and a confirmer, normally the obligations of a confirmer are to the issuer not the applicant, but the applicant might have a right to injunction against a confirmer under Section 5–109 or warranty claim under Section 5–110, and either might have claims against the other under Section 5–117.

2. No one has a duty to advise until that person agrees to be an adviser or undertakes to act in accordance with the instructions of the issuer. Except where there is a prior agreement to serve or where the silence of the adviser would be an acceptance of an offer to contract, a person's failure to respond to a request to advise a letter of credit does not in and of itself create any liability, nor does it establish a relationship of issuer and adviser between the two. Since there is no duty to advise a letter of credit in the absence of a prior agreement, there can be no duty to advise it timely or at any particular time. When the adviser manifests its agreement to advise by actually doing so (as is normally the case), the adviser cannot have violated any duty to advise in a timely way. This analysis is consistent with the result of Sound of Market Street v. Continental Bank International, 819 F.2d 384 (3d Cir.1987) which held that there is no such duty. This section takes no position on the reasoning of that case, but does not overrule the result. By advising or agreeing to advise a letter of credit, the adviser assumes a duty to the issuer and to the beneficiary accurately to report what it has received from the issuer, but, beyond determining the apparent authenticity of the letter, an adviser has no duty to investigate the accuracy of the message it has received from the issuer. "Checking" the apparent authenticity of the request to advise means only that the prospective adviser must attempt to authenticate the message (e.g., by "testing" the telex that comes from the purported issuer), and if it is unable to authenticate the message must report that fact to the issuer and, if it chooses to advise the message, to the beneficiary. By proper agreement, an adviser may disclaim its obligation under this section.

3. An issuer may issue a letter of credit which the adviser may advise with different terms. The issuer may then believe that it has undertaken a certain engagement, yet the text in the hands of the beneficiary will contain different terms, and the beneficiary would not be entitled to honor if the documents it submitted did not comply with the terms of the letter of credit as originally issued. On the other hand, if the adviser also confirmed the letter of credit, then as a confirmer it will be independently liable on the letter of credit as advised and confirmed. If in that situation the beneficiary's ultimate presentation entitled it to honor under the terms of the confirmation but not under those in the original letter of credit, the confirmer would have to honor but might not be entitled to reimbursement from the issuer.

4. When the issuer nominates another person to "pay," "negotiate," or otherwise to take up the documents and give value, there can be confusion about the legal status of the nominated person. In rare cases the person might actually be an agent of the issuer and its act might be the act of the issuer itself. In most cases the nominated person is not an agent of the issuer and has no authority to act on the issuer's behalf. Its "nomination" allows the beneficiary to present to it and earns it certain rights to payment under Section 5–109 that others do not enjoy. For example, when an issuer issues a "freely negotiable credit," it contemplates that banks or others might take up documents under that credit and advance value against them, and it is agreeing to pay those persons but only if the presentation to the issuer made by the nominated person complies with the credit. Usually there will be no agreement to pay, negotiate, or to serve in any other capacity by the nominated person, therefore the nominated person will have the right to decline to take the documents. It may return them or agree merely to act as a forwarding agent for the documents but without giving value against them or taking any responsibility for their conformity to the letter of credit.

§ 5–108. Issuer's Rights and Obligations.

(a) Except as otherwise provided in Section 5–109, an issuer shall honor a presentation that, as determined by the standard practice referred to in subsection (e), appears on its face strictly to comply with the terms and conditions of the letter of credit. Except as otherwise provided in Section 5–113 and unless otherwise agreed with the applicant, an issuer shall dishonor a presentation that does not appear so to comply.

(b) An issuer has a reasonable time after presentation, but not beyond the end of the seventh business day of the issuer after the day of its receipt of documents:

(1) to honor,

(2) if the letter of credit provides for honor to be completed more than seven business days after presentation, to accept a draft or incur a deferred obligation, or

(3) to give notice to the presenter of discrepancies in the presentation.

(c) Except as otherwise provided in subsection (d), an issuer is precluded from asserting as a basis for dishonor any discrepancy if timely notice is not given, or any discrepancy not stated in the notice if timely notice is given.

(d) Failure to give the notice specified in subsection (b) or to mention fraud, forgery, or expiration in the notice does not preclude the issuer from asserting as a basis for dishonor fraud or forgery as described in Section 5–109(a) or expiration of the letter of credit before presentation.

(e) An issuer shall observe standard practice of financial institutions that regularly issue letters of credit. Determination of the issuer's observance of the standard practice is a matter of interpretation for the court. The court shall offer the parties a reasonable opportunity to present evidence of the standard practice.

(f) An issuer is not responsible for:

(1) the performance or nonperformance of the underlying contract, arrangement, or transaction,

(2) an act or omission of others, or

(3) observance or knowledge of the usage of a particular trade other than the standard practice referred to in subsection (e).

(g) If an undertaking constituting a letter of credit under Section 5–102(a)(10) contains nondocumentary conditions, an issuer shall disregard the nondocumentary conditions and treat them as if they were not stated.

(h) An issuer that has dishonored a presentation shall return the documents or hold them at the disposal of, and send advice to that effect to, the presenter.

(i) An issuer that has honored a presentation as permitted or required by this article:

(1) is entitled to be reimbursed by the applicant in immediately available funds not later than the date of its payment of funds;

(2) takes the documents free of claims of the beneficiary or presenter;

(3) is precluded from asserting a right of recourse on a draft under Sections 3–414 and 3–415;

(4) except as otherwise provided in Sections 5–110 and 5–117, is precluded from restitution of money paid or other value given by mistake to the extent the mistake concerns discrepancies in the documents or tender which are apparent on the face of the presentation; and

(5) is discharged to the extent of its performance under the letter of credit unless the issuer honored a presentation in which a required signature of a beneficiary was forged.

Official Comment

1. This section combines some of the duties previously included in Sections 5–114 and 5–109. Because a confirmer has the rights and duties of an issuer, this section applies equally to a confirmer and an issuer. See Section 5–107(a).

The standard of strict compliance governs the issuer's obligation to the beneficiary and to the applicant. By requiring that a "presentation" appear strictly to comply, the section requires not only that the documents themselves appear on their face strictly to comply, but also that the other terms of the letter of credit such as those dealing with the time and place of presentation are strictly complied with. Typically, a letter of credit will provide that presentation is timely if made to the issuer, confirmer, or any other nominated person prior to expiration of the letter of credit. Accordingly, a nominated person that has honored a demand or otherwise given value before expiration will have a right to reimbursement from the issuer even though presentation to the issuer is made after the expiration of the letter of credit. Conversely, where the beneficiary negotiates documents to one who is not a nominated person, the beneficiary or that person acting on behalf of the beneficiary must make presentation to a nominated person, confirmer, or issuer prior to the expiration date.

This section does not impose a bifurcated standard under which an issuer's right to reimbursement might be broader than a beneficiary's right to honor. However, the explicit deference to standard practice in Section 5–108(a) and (e) and elsewhere expands issuers' rights of reimbursement where that practice so provides. Also, issuers can and often do contract with their applicants for expanded rights of reimbursement. Where that is done, the beneficiary will have to meet a more stringent standard of compliance as to the issuer than the issuer will have to meet as to the applicant. Similarly, a nominated person may have reimbursement and other rights against the issuer based on this article, the UCP, bank-to-bank reimbursement rules, or other agreement or undertaking of the issuer. These rights may allow the nominated person to recover from the issuer even when the nominated person would have no right to obtain honor under the letter of credit.

The section adopts strict compliance, rather than the standard that commentators have called "substantial compliance," the standard arguably applied in *Banco Español de Credito v. State Street Bank and Trust Company,* 385 F.2d 230 (1st Cir.1967) and *Flagship Cruises Ltd. v. New England Merchants Nat. Bank,* 569 F.2d 699 (1st Cir.1978). Strict compliance does not mean slavish conformity to the terms of the letter of credit. For example, standard practice (what issuers do) may recognize certain presentations as complying that an unschooled layman would regard as discrepant. By adopting standard practice as a way of measuring strict compliance, this article indorses the conclusion of the court in *New Braunfels Nat. Bank v. Odiorne,* 780 S.W.2d 313 (Tex.Ct.App. 1989) (beneficiary could collect when draft requested payment on 'Letter of Credit No. 86-122-5' and letter of credit specified 'Letter of Credit No. 86-122-S' holding strict compliance does not demand oppressive perfectionism). The section also indorses the result in *Tosco Corp. v. Federal Deposit Insurance Corp.,* 723 F.2d 1242 (6th Cir.1983). The letter of credit in that case called for "drafts Drawn under Bank of Clarksville Letter of Credit Number 105." The draft presented stated "drawn under Bank of Clarksville, Clarksville, Tennessee letter of Credit No. 105." The court correctly found that despite the change of upper case "L" to a lower case "l" and the use of the word "No." instead of "Number," and despite the addition of the words "Clarksville, Tennessee," the presentation conformed. Similarly a document addressed by a foreign person to General Motors as "Jeneral Motors" would strictly conform in the absence of other defects.

Identifying and determining compliance with standard practice are matters of interpretation for the court, not for the jury. As with similar rules in Sections 4A-202(c) and 2-302, it is hoped that there will be more consistency in the outcomes and speedier resolution of disputes if the responsibility for determining the nature and scope of standard practice is grant-ed to the court, not to a jury. Granting the court authority to make these decisions will also encourage the salutary practice of courts' granting summary judgment in circumstances where there are no significant factual disputes. The statute encourages outcomes such as *American Coleman Co. v. Intrawest Bank,* 887 F.2d 1382 (10th Cir.1989), where summary judgment was granted.

In some circumstances standards may be established between the issuer and the applicant by agreement or by custom that would free the issuer from liability that it might otherwise have. For example, an applicant might agree that the issuer would have no duty whatsoever to examine documents on certain presentations (e.g., those below a certain dollar amount). Where the transaction depended upon the issuer's payment in a very short time period (e.g., on the same day or within a few hours of presentation), the issuer and the applicant might agree to reduce the issuer's responsibility for failure to discover discrepancies. By the same token, an agreement between the applicant and the issuer might permit the issuer to examine documents exclusively by electronic or electro-optical means. Neither those agreements nor others like them explicitly made by issuers and applicants violate the terms of Section 5-108(a) or (b) or Section 5-103(c).

2. Section 5-108(a) balances the need of the issuer for time to examine the documents against the possibility that the examiner (at the urging of the applicant or for fear that it will not be reimbursed) will take excessive time to search for defects. What is a "reasonable time" is not extended to accommodate an issuer's procuring a waiver from the applicant. See Article 14c of the UCP.

Under both the UCC and the UCP the issuer has a reasonable time to honor or give notice. The outside limit of that time is measured in business days under the UCC and in banking days under the UCP, a difference that will rarely be significant. Neither business nor banking days are defined in Article 5, but a court may find useful analogies in Regulation CC, 12 CFR 229.2, in state law outside of the Uniform Commercial Code, and in Article 4.

Examiners must note that the seven-day period is not a safe harbor. The time within which the issuer must give notice is the lesser of a reasonable time or seven business days. Where there are few documents (as, for example, with the mine run standby letter of credit), the reasonable time would be less than seven days. If more than a reasonable time is consumed in examination, no timely notice is possible. What is a "reasonable time" is to be determined by examining the behavior of those in the business of examining documents, mostly banks. Absent prior agreement of the issuer, one could not expect a bank issuer to examine documents while the beneficiary waited in the lobby if the normal practice was to give the documents to a person who had the opportunity to examine those together with many others in an orderly process. That the applicant has not yet paid the issuer or that the applicant's account with the issuer is insufficient to cover the amount of the draft is not a basis for extension of the time period.

This section does not preclude the issuer from contacting the applicant during its examination; however, the decision to honor rests with the issuer, and it has no duty to seek a waiver from the applicant or to notify the applicant of receipt of the documents. If the issuer dishonors a conforming presentation, the beneficiary will be entitled to the remedies under Section 5–111, irrespective of the applicant's views.

Even though the person to whom presentation is made cannot conduct a reasonable examination of documents within the time after presentation and before the expiration date, presentation establishes the parties' rights. The beneficiary's right to honor or the issuer's right to dishonor arises upon presentation at the place provided in the letter of credit even though it might take the person to whom presentation has been made several days to determine whether honor or dishonor is the proper course. The issuer's time for honor or giving notice of dishonor may be extended or shortened by a term in the letter of credit. The time for the issuer's performance may be otherwise modified or waived in accordance with Section 5–106.

The issuer's time to inspect runs from the time of its "receipt of documents." Documents are considered to be received only when they are received at the place specified for presentation by the issuer or other party to whom presentation is made. "Receipt of documents" when documents of title are presented must be read in light of the definition of "delivery" in Article 1, Section 1–201 and the definition of "presentment" in Section 5–102(a)(12).

Failure of the issuer to act within the time permitted by subsection (b) constitutes dishonor. Because of the preclusion in subsection (c) and the liability that the issuer may incur under Section 5–111 for wrongful dishonor, the effect of such a silent dishonor may ultimately be the same as though the issuer had honored, i.e., it may owe damages in the amount drawn but unpaid under the letter of credit.

3. The requirement that the issuer send notice of the discrepancies or be precluded from asserting discrepancies is new to Article 5. It is taken from the similar provision in the UCP and is intended to promote certainty and finality.

The section thus substitutes a strict preclusion principle for the doctrines of waiver and estoppel that might otherwise apply under Section 1–103. It rejects the reasoning in *Flagship Cruises Ltd. v. New England Merchants' Nat. Bank,* 569 F.2d 699 (1st Cir.1978) and *Wing On Bank Ltd. v. American Nat. Bank & Trust Co.,* 457 F.2d 328 (5th Cir.1972) where the issuer was held to be estopped only if the beneficiary relied on the issuer's failure to give notice.

Assume, for example, that the beneficiary presented documents to the issuer shortly before the letter of credit expired, in circumstances in which the beneficiary could not have cured any discrepancy before expiration. Under the reasoning of *Flagship* and *Wing On,* the beneficiary's inability to cure, even if it had received notice, would absolve the issuer of its failure to give notice. The virtue of the preclusion obligation adopted in this section is that it forecloses litigation about reliance and detriment.

Even though issuers typically give notice of the discrepancy of tardy presentation when presentation is made after the expiration of a credit, they are not required to give that notice and the section permits them to raise late presentation as a defect despite their failure to give that notice.

4. To act within a reasonable time, the issuer must normally give notice without delay after the examining party makes its decision. If the examiner decides to dishonor on the first day, it would be obliged to notify the beneficiary shortly thereafter, perhaps on the same business day. This rule accepts the reasoning in cases such as *Datapoint Corp. v. M & I Bank,* 665 F.Supp. 722 (W.D.Wis.1987) and *Esso Petroleum Canada, Div. of Imperial Oil, Ltd. v. Security Pacific Bank,* 710 F.Supp. 275 (D.Or.1989).

The section deprives the examining party of the right simply to sit on a presentation that is made within seven days of expiration. The section requires the examiner to examine the documents and make a decision and, having made a decision to dishonor, to communicate promptly with the presenter. Nevertheless, a beneficiary who presents documents shortly before the expiration of a letter of credit runs the risk that it will never have the opportunity to cure any discrepancies.

5. Confirmers, other nominated persons, and collecting banks acting for beneficiaries can be presenters and, when so, are entitled to the notice provided in

subsection (b). Even nominated persons who have honored or given value against an earlier presentation of the beneficiary and are themselves seeking reimbursement or honor need notice of discrepancies in the hope that they may be able to procure complying documents. The issuer has the obligations imposed by this section whether the issuer's performance is characterized as "reimbursement" of a nominated person or as "honor."

6. In many cases a letter of credit authorizes presentation by the beneficiary to someone other than the issuer. Sometimes that person is identified as a "payor" or "paying bank," or as an "acceptor" or "accepting bank," in other cases as a "negotiating bank," and in other cases there will be no specific designation. The section does not impose any duties on a person other than the issuer or confirmer, however a nominated person or other person may have liability under this article or at common law if it fails to perform an express or implied agreement with the beneficiary.

7. The issuer's obligation to honor runs not only to the beneficiary but also to the applicant. It is possible that an applicant who has made a favorable contract with the beneficiary will be injured by the issuer's wrongful dishonor. Except to the extent that the contract between the issuer and the applicant limits that liability, the issuer will have liability to the applicant for wrongful dishonor under Section 5–111 as a matter of contract law. A good faith extension of the time in Section 5–108(b) by agreement between the issuer and beneficiary binds the applicant even if the applicant is not consulted or does not consent to the extension.

The issuer's obligation to dishonor when there is no apparent compliance with the letter of credit runs only to the applicant. No other party to the transaction can complain if the applicant waives compliance with terms or conditions of the letter of credit or agrees to a less stringent standard for compliance than that supplied by this article. Except as otherwise agreed with the applicant, an issuer may dishonor a noncomplying presentation despite an applicant's waiver.

Waiver of discrepancies by an issuer or an applicant in one or more presentations does not waive similar discrepancies in a future presentation. Neither the issuer nor the beneficiary can reasonably rely upon honor over past waivers as a basis for concluding that a future defective presentation will justify honor. The reasoning of *Courtaulds of North America Inc. v. North Carolina Nat. Bank,* 528 F.2d 802 (4th Cir.1975) is accepted and that expressed in *Schweibish v. Pontchartrain State Bank,* 389 So.2d 731 (La.App.1980) and

Titanium Metals Corp. v. Space Metals, Inc., 529 P.2d 431 (Utah 1974) is rejected.

8. The standard practice referred to in subsection (e) includes (i) international practice set forth in or referenced by the Uniform Customs and Practice, (ii) other practice rules published by associations of financial institutions, and (iii) local and regional practice. It is possible that standard practice will vary from one place to another. Where there are conflicting practices, the parties should indicate which practice governs their rights. A practice may be overridden by agreement or course of dealing. See Section 1–205(4).

9. The responsibility of the issuer under a letter of credit is to examine documents and to make a prompt decision to honor or dishonor based upon that examination. Nondocumentary conditions have no place in this regime and are better accommodated under contract or suretyship law and practice. In requiring that nondocumentary conditions in letters of credit be ignored as surplusage, Article 5 remains aligned with the UCP (see UCP 500 Article 13c), approves cases like *Pringle-Associated Mortgage Corp. v. Southern National Bank,* 571 F.2d 871, 874 (5th Cir.1978), and rejects the reasoning in cases such as *Sherwood & Roberts, Inc. v. First Security Bank,* 682 P.2d 149 (Mont. 1984).

Subsection (g) recognizes that letters of credit sometimes contain nondocumentary terms or conditions. Conditions such as a term prohibiting "shipment on vessels more than 15 years old," are to be disregarded and treated as surplusage. Similarly, a requirement that there be an award by a "duly appointed arbitrator" would not require the issuer to determine whether the arbitrator had been "duly appointed." Likewise a term in a standby letter of credit that provided for differing forms of certification depending upon the particular type of default does not oblige the issuer independently to determine which kind of default has occurred. These conditions must be disregarded by the issuer. Where the nondocumentary conditions are central and fundamental to the issuer's obligation (as for example a condition that would require the issuer to determine in fact whether the beneficiary had performed the underlying contract or whether the applicant had defaulted) their inclusion may remove the undertaking from the scope of Article 5 entirely. See Section 5–102(a)(10) and Comment 6 to Section 5–102.

Subsection (g) would not permit the beneficiary or the issuer to disregard terms in the letter of credit such as place, time, and mode of presentation. The rule in subsection (g) is intended to prevent an issuer from deciding or even investigating extrinsic facts, but not from consulting the clock, the calendar, the relevant law and practice, or its own general knowledge of documentation or transactions of the type underlying a particular letter of credit.

Even though nondocumentary conditions must be disregarded in determining compliance of a presentation (and thus in determining the issuer's duty to the beneficiary), an issuer that has promised its applicant that it will honor only on the occurrence of those nondocumentary conditions may have liability to its applicant for disregarding the conditions.

10. Subsection (f) condones an issuer's ignorance of "any usage of a particular trade"; that trade is the trade of the applicant, beneficiary, or others who may be involved in the underlying transaction. The issuer is expected to know usage that is commonly encountered in the course of document examination. For example, an issuer should know the common usage with respect to documents in the maritime shipping trade but would not be expected to understand synonyms used in a particular trade for product descriptions appearing in a letter of credit or an invoice.

11. Where the issuer's performance is the delivery of an item of value other than money, the applicant's reimbursement obligation would be to make the "item of value" available to the issuer.

12. An issuer is entitled to reimbursement from the applicant after honor of a forged or fraudulent drawing if honor was permitted under Section 5–109(a).

13. The last clause of Section 5–108(i)(5) deals with a special case in which the fraud is not committed by the beneficiary, but is committed by a stranger to the transaction who forges the beneficiary's signature. If the issuer pays against documents on which a required signature of the beneficiary is forged, it remains liable to the true beneficiary. This principle is applicable to both electronic and tangible documents.

As amended in 2003.

§ 5–109. Fraud and Forgery.

(a) If a presentation is made that appears on its face strictly to comply with the terms and conditions of the letter of credit, but a required document is forged or materially fraudulent, or honor of the presentation would facilitate a material fraud by the beneficiary on the issuer or applicant:

(1) the issuer shall honor the presentation, if honor is demanded by (i) a nominated person who has given value in good faith and without notice of forgery or material fraud, (ii) a confirmer who has honored its confir-

mation in good faith, (iii) a holder in due course of a draft drawn under the letter of credit which was taken after acceptance by the issuer or nominated person, or (iv) an assignee of the issuer's or nominated person's deferred obligation that was taken for value and without notice of forgery or material fraud after the obligation was incurred by the issuer or nominated person; and

(2) the issuer, acting in good faith, may honor or dishonor the presentation in any other case.

(b) If an applicant claims that a required document is forged or materially fraudulent or that honor of the presentation would facilitate a material fraud by the beneficiary on the issuer or applicant, a court of competent jurisdiction may temporarily or permanently enjoin the issuer from honoring a presentation or grant similar relief against the issuer or other persons only if the court finds that:

(1) the relief is not prohibited under the law applicable to an accepted draft or deferred obligation incurred by the issuer;

(2) a beneficiary, issuer, or nominated person who may be adversely affected is adequately protected against loss that it may suffer because the relief is granted;

(3) all of the conditions to entitle a person to the relief under the law of this State have been met; and

(4) on the basis of the information submitted to the court, the applicant is more likely than not to succeed under its claim of forgery or material fraud and the person demanding honor does not qualify for protection under subsection (a)(1).

Official Comment

1. This recodification makes clear that fraud must be found either in the documents or must have been committed by the beneficiary on the issuer or applicant. See *Cromwell v. Commerce & Energy Bank*, 464 So.2d 721 (La.1985).

Secondly, it makes clear that fraud must be "material." Necessarily courts must decide the breadth and width of "materiality." The use of the word requires that the fraudulent aspect of a document be material to a purchaser of that document or that the fraudulent act be significant to the participants in the underlying transaction. Assume, for example, that the beneficiary has a contract to deliver 1,000 barrels of salad oil. Knowing that it has delivered only 998, the beneficiary nevertheless submits an invoice showing 1,000 barrels. If two barrels in a 1,000 barrel shipment would be an insubstantial and immaterial breach of the underlying contract, the beneficiary's act, though possibly fraudulent, is not materially so and would not justify an injunction. Conversely, the knowing submission of those invoices upon delivery of only five barrels would be materially fraudulent. The courts must examine the underlying transaction when there is an allegation of material fraud, for only by examining that transaction can one determine whether a document is fraudulent or the beneficiary has committed fraud and, if so, whether the fraud was material.

Material fraud by the beneficiary occurs only when the beneficiary has no colorable right to expect honor and where there is no basis in fact to support such a right to honor. The section indorses articulations such as those stated in *Intraworld Indus. v. Girard Trust Bank*, 336 A.2d 316 (Pa.1975), *Roman Ceramics Corp. v. People's Nat. Bank*, 714 F.2d 1207 (3d Cir.1983), and similar decisions and embraces certain decisions under Section 5–114 that relied upon the phrase "fraud in the transaction." Some of these decisions have been summarized as follows in *Ground Air Transfer v. Westate's Airlines*, 899 F.2d 1269, 1272–73 (1st Cir.1990):

> We have said throughout that courts may not *"normally"* issue an injunction because of an important exception to the general "no injunction" rule. The exception, as we also explained in Itek, 730 F.2d at 24–25, concerns "fraud" so serious as to make it obviously pointless and unjust to permit the beneficiary to obtain the money. Where the circumstances *"plainly"* show that the underlying contract forbids the beneficiary to call a letter of credit, Itek, 730 F.2d at 24; where they show that the contract deprives the beneficiary of even a *"colorable"* right to do so, id., at 25; where the contract and circumstances reveal that the beneficiary's demand for payment has "absolutely no basis in fact," id.; see Dynamics Corp. of America, 356 F.Supp. at 999; where the beneficiary's conduct has "so vitiated the entire transaction that the legitimate purposes of the independence of the issuer's obligation would no longer be served," Itek, 730 F.2d at 25 (quoting *Roman Ceramics Corp. v. Peoples National Bank*, 714 F.2d 1207, 1212 n.12, 1215 (3d Cir.1983)(quoting Intraworld Indus., 336 A.2d at 324–25)); *then* a court may enjoin payment.

2. Subsection (a)(2) makes clear that the issuer may honor in the face of the applicant's claim of fraud. The subsection also makes clear what was not stated in former Section 5–114, that the issuer may dishonor and defend that dishonor by showing fraud or forgery of the kind stated in subsection (a). Because issuers may be liable for wrongful dishonor if they are unable to prove forgery or material fraud, presumably most issuers will choose to honor despite applicant's claims of fraud or forgery unless the applicant procures an injunction. Merely because the issuer has a right to dishonor and to defend that dishonor by showing forgery or material fraud does not mean it has a duty to the applicant to dishonor. The applicant's normal recourse is to procure an injunction, if the applicant is unable to procure an injunction, it will have a claim against the issuer only in the rare case in which it can show that the issuer did not honor in good faith.

3. Whether a beneficiary can commit fraud by presenting a draft under a clean letter of credit (one calling only for a draft and no other documents) has been much debated. Under the current formulation it would be possible but difficult for there to be fraud in such a presentation. If the applicant were able to show that the beneficiary were committing material fraud on the applicant in the underlying transaction, then payment would facilitate a material fraud by the beneficiary on the applicant and honor could be enjoined. The courts should be skeptical of claims of fraud by one who has signed a "suicide" or clean credit and thus granted a beneficiary the right to draw by mere presentation of a draft.

4. The standard for injunctive relief is high, and the burden remains on the applicant to show, by evidence and not by mere allegation, that such relief is warranted. Some courts have enjoined payments on letters of credit on insufficient showing by the applicant. For example, in *Griffin Cos. v. First Nat. Bank*, 374 N.W.2d 768 (Minn.App.1985), the court enjoined payment under a standby letter of credit, basing its decision on plaintiff's allegation, rather than competent evidence, of fraud.

There are at least two ways to prohibit injunctions against honor under this section after acceptance of a draft by the issuer. First is to define honor (see Section 5–102(a)(8)) in the particular letter of credit to occur upon acceptance and without regard to later payment of the acceptance. Second is explicitly to agree that the applicant has no right to an injunction after acceptance—whether or not the acceptance constitutes honor.

5. Although the statute deals principally with injunctions against honor, it also cautions against granting "similar relief" and the same principles apply when the applicant or issuer attempts to achieve the same legal outcome by injunction against presentation (see *Ground Air Transfer Inc. v. Westates Airlines, Inc.*, 899 F.2d 1269 (1st Cir.1990)), interpleader, declaratory judgment, or attachment. These attempts should face the same obstacles that face efforts to enjoin the issuer from paying. Expanded use of any of these devices could threaten the independence principle just as much as injunctions against honor. For that reason courts should have the same hostility to them and place the same restrictions on their use as would be applied to injunctions against honor. Courts should not allow the "sacred cow of equity to trample the tender vines of letter of credit law."

6. Section 5–109(a)(1) also protects specified third parties against the risk of fraud. By issuing a letter of credit that nominates a person to negotiate or pay, the issuer (ultimately the applicant) induces that nominated person to give value and thereby assumes the risk that a draft drawn under the letter of credit will be transferred to one with a status like that of a holder in due course who deserves to be protected against a fraud defense.

7. The "loss" to be protected against—by bond or otherwise under subsection (b)(2)—includes incidental damages. Among those are legal fees that might be incurred by the beneficiary or issuer in defending against an injunction action.

§ 5–110. Warranties.

(a) If its presentation is honored, the beneficiary warrants:

(1) to the issuer, any other person to whom presentation is made, and the applicant that there is no fraud or forgery of the kind described in Section 5–109(a); and

(2) to the applicant that the drawing does not violate any agreement between the applicant and beneficiary or any other agreement intended by them to be augmented by the letter of credit.

(b) The warranties in subsection (a) are in addition to warranties arising under Article 3, 4, 7, and 8 because of the presentation or transfer of documents covered by any of those articles.

Official Comment

1. Since the warranties in subsection (a) are not given unless a letter of credit has been honored, no breach of warranty under this subsection can be a defense to dishonor by the issuer. Any defense must be based on Section 5–108 or 5–109 and not on this section. Also, breach of the warranties by the beneficiary in subsection (a) cannot excuse the applicant's duty to reimburse.

2. The warranty in Section 5–110(a)(2) assumes that payment under the letter of credit is final. It does not run to the issuer, only to the applicant. In most cases the applicant will have a direct cause of action for breach of the underlying contract. This warranty has primary application in standby letters of credit or other circumstances where the applicant is not a party to an underlying contract with the beneficiary. It is not a warranty that the statements made on the presentation of the documents presented are truthful nor is it a warranty that the documents strictly comply under Section 5–108(a). It is a warranty that the beneficiary has performed all the acts expressly and implicitly necessary under any underlying agreement to entitle the beneficiary to honor. If, for example, an underlying sales contract authorized the beneficiary to draw only upon "due performance" and the beneficiary drew even though it had breached the underlying contract by delivering defective goods, honor of its draw would break the warranty. By the same token, if the underlying contract authorized the beneficiary to draw only upon actual default or upon its or a third party's determination of default by the applicant and if the beneficiary drew in violation of its authorization, then upon honor of its draw the warranty would be breached. In many cases, therefore, the documents presented to the issuer will contain inaccurate statements (concerning the goods delivered or concerning default or other matters), but the breach of warranty arises not because the statements are untrue but because the beneficiary's drawing violated its express or implied obligations in the underlying transaction.

3. The damages for breach of warranty are not specified in Section 5–111. Courts may find damage analogies in Section 2–714 in Article 2 and in warranty decisions under Articles 3 and 4.

Unlike wrongful dishonor cases—where the damages usually equal the amount of the draw—the damages for breach of warranty will often be much less than the amount of the draw, sometimes zero. Assume a seller entitled to draw only on proper performance of its sales contract. Assume it breaches the sales contract in a way that gives the buyer a right to damages but no right to reject. The applicant's damages for breach of the warranty in subsection (a)(2) are limited to the damages it could recover for breach of the contract of sale. Alternatively assume an underlying agreement that authorizes a beneficiary to draw only the "amount in default." Assume a default of $200,000 and a draw of $500,000. The damages for breach of warranty would be no more than $300,000.

§ 5–111.   Remedies.

(a) If an issuer wrongfully dishonors or repudiates its obligation to pay money under a letter of credit before presentation, the beneficiary, successor, or nominated person presenting on its own behalf may recover from the issuer the amount that is the subject of the dishonor or repudiation. If the issuer's obligation under the letter of credit is not for the payment of money, the claimant may obtain specific performance or, at the claimant's election, recover an amount equal to the value of performance from the issuer. In either case, the claimant may also recover incidental but not consequential damages. The claimant is not obligated to take action to avoid damages that might be due from the issuer under this subsection. If, although not obligated to do so, the claimant avoids damages, the claimant's recovery from the issuer must be reduced by the amount of damages avoided. The issuer has the burden of proving the amount of damages avoided. In the case of repudiation the claimant need not present any document.

(b) If an issuer wrongfully dishonors a draft or demand presented under a letter of credit or honors a draft or demand in breach of its obligation to the applicant, the applicant may recover damages resulting from the breach, including incidental but not consequential damages, less any amount saved as a result of the breach.

(c) If an adviser or nominated person other than a confirmer breaches an obligation under this article or an issuer breaches an obligation not covered in subsection (a) or (b), a person to whom the obligation is owed may recover damages resulting from the breach, including incidental but not consequential damages, less any amount saved as a result of the breach. To the extent of the confirmation, a confirmer has the liability of an issuer specified in this subsection and subsections (a) and (b).

(d) An issuer, nominated person, or adviser who is found liable under subsection (a), (b), or

(c) shall pay interest on the amount owed thereunder from the date of wrongful dishonor or other appropriate date.

(e) Reasonable attorney's fees and other expenses of litigation must be awarded to the prevailing party in an action in which a remedy is sought under this article.

(f) Damages that would otherwise be payable by a party for breach of an obligation under this article may be liquidated by agreement or undertaking, but only in an amount or by a formula that is reasonable in light of the harm anticipated.

Official Comment

1. The right to specific performance is new. The express limitation on the duty of the beneficiary to mitigate damages adopts the position of certain courts and commentators. Because the letter of credit depends upon speed and certainty of payment, it is important that the issuer not be given an incentive to dishonor. The issuer might have an incentive to dishonor if it could rely on the burden of mitigation falling on the beneficiary, (to sell goods and sue only for the difference between the price of the goods sold and the amount due under the letter of credit). Under the scheme contemplated by Section 5–111(a), the beneficiary would present the documents to the issuer. If the issuer wrongfully dishonored, the beneficiary would have no further duty to the issuer with respect to the goods covered by documents that the issuer dishonored and returned. The issuer thus takes the risk that the beneficiary will let the goods rot or be destroyed. Of course the beneficiary may have a duty of mitigation to the applicant arising from the underlying agreement, but the issuer would not have the right to assert that duty by way of defense or setoff. See Section 5–117(d). If the beneficiary sells the goods covered by dishonored documents or if the beneficiary sells a draft after acceptance but before dishonor by the issuer, the net amount so gained should be subtracted from the amount of the beneficiary's damages—at least where the damage claim against the issuer equals or exceeds the damage suffered by the beneficiary. If, on the other hand, the beneficiary suffers damages in an underlying transaction in an amount that exceeds the amount of the wrongfully dishonored demand (e.g., where the letter of credit does not cover 100 percent of the underlying obligation), the damages avoided should not necessarily be deducted from the beneficiary's claim against the issuer. In such a case, the damages would be the lesser

of (i) the amount recoverable in the absence of mitigation (that is, the amount that is subject to the dishonor or repudiation plus any incidental damages) and (ii) the damages remaining after deduction for the amount of damages actually avoided.

A beneficiary need not present documents as a condition of suit for anticipatory repudiation, but if a beneficiary could never have obtained documents necessary for a presentation conforming to the letter of credit, the beneficiary cannot recover for anticipatory repudiation of the letter of credit. *Doelger v. Battery Park Bank,* 201 A.D. 515, 194 N.Y.S. 582 (1922) and *Decor by Nikkei Int'l, Inc. v. Federal Republic of Nigeria,* 497 F.Supp. 893 (S.D.N.Y.1980), *aff'd,* 647 F.2d 300 (2d Cir.1981), *cert. denied,* 454 U.S. 1148 (1982). The last sentence of subsection (c) does not expand the liability of a confirmer to persons to whom the confirmer would not otherwise be liable under Section 5–107.

Almost all letters of credit, including those that call for an acceptance, are "obligations to pay money" as that term is used in Section 5–111(a).

2. What damages "result" from improper honor is for the courts to decide. Even though an issuer pays a beneficiary in violation of Section 5–108(a) or of its contract with the applicant, it may have no liability to an applicant. If the underlying contract has been fully performed, the applicant may not have been damaged by the issuer's breach. Such a case would occur when A contracts for goods at $100 per ton, but, upon delivery, the market value of conforming goods has decreased to $25 per ton. If the issuer pays over discrepancies, there should be no recovery by A for the price differential if the issuer's breach did not alter the applicant's obligation under the underlying contract, i.e., to pay $100 per ton for goods now worth $25 per ton. On the other hand, if the applicant intends to resell the goods and must itself satisfy the strict compliance requirements under a second letter of credit in connection with its sale, the applicant may be damaged by the issuer's payment despite discrepancies because the applicant itself may then be unable to procure honor on the letter of credit where it is the beneficiary, and may be unable to mitigate its damages by enforcing its rights against others in the underlying transaction. Note that an issuer found liable to its applicant may have recourse under Section 5–117 by subrogation to the applicant's claim against the beneficiary or other persons.

One who inaccurately advises a letter of credit breaches its obligation to the beneficiary, but may cause no damage. If the beneficiary knows the terms of the letter of credit and understands the advice to be inaccurate, the beneficiary will have suffered no damage as a result of the adviser's breach.

3. Since the confirmer has the rights and duties of an issuer, in general it has an issuer's liability, see subsection (c). The confirmer is usually a confirming bank. A confirming bank often also plays the role of an adviser. If it breaks its obligation to the beneficiary, the confirming bank may have liability as an issuer or, depending upon the obligation that was broken, as an adviser. For example, a wrongful dishonor would give it liability as an issuer under Section 5–111(a). On the other hand a confirming bank that broke its obligation to advise the credit but did not commit wrongful dishonor would be treated under Section 5–111(c).

4. Consequential damages for breach of obligations under this article are excluded in the belief that these damages can best be avoided by the beneficiary or the applicant and out of the fear that imposing consequential damages on issuers would raise the cost of the letter of credit to a level that might render it uneconomic. *A fortiori* punitive and exemplary damages are excluded, however, this section does not bar recovery of consequential or even punitive damages for breach of statutory or common law duties arising outside of this article.

5. The section does not specify a rate of interest. It leaves the setting of the rate to the court. It would be appropriate for a court to use the rate that would normally apply in that court in other situations where interest is imposed by law.

6. The court must award attorney's fees to the prevailing party, whether that party is an applicant, a beneficiary, an issuer, a nominated person, or adviser. Since the issuer may be entitled to recover its legal fees and costs from the applicant under the reimbursement agreement, allowing the issuer to recover those fees from a losing beneficiary may also protect the applicant against undeserved losses. The party entitled to attorneys' fees has been described as the "prevailing party." Sometimes it will be unclear which party "prevailed," for example, where there are multiple issues and one party wins on some and the other party wins on others. Determining which is the prevailing party is in the discretion of the court. Subsection (e) authorizes attorney's fees in all actions where a remedy is sought "under this article." It applies even when the remedy might be an injunction under Section 5–109 or when the claimed remedy is otherwise outside of Section 5–111. Neither an issuer nor a confirmer should be treated as a "losing" party when an injunction is granted to the applicant over the objection of

the issuer or confirmer; accordingly neither should be liable for fees and expenses in that case.

"Expenses of litigation" is intended to be broader than "costs." For example, expense of litigation would include travel expenses of witnesses, fees for expert witnesses, and expenses associated with taking depositions.

7. For the purposes of Section 5–111(f) "harm anticipated" must be anticipated at the time when the agreement that includes the liquidated damage clause is executed or at the time when the undertaking that includes the clause is issued. See Section 2A–504.

§ 5–112.   Transfer of Letter of Credit.

(a) Except as otherwise provided in Section 5–113, unless a letter of credit provides that it is transferable, the right of a beneficiary to draw or otherwise demand performance under a letter of credit may not be transferred.

(b) Even if a letter of credit provides that it is transferable, the issuer may refuse to recognize or carry out a transfer if:

(1) the transfer would violate applicable law; or

(2) the transferor or transferee has failed to comply with any requirement stated in the letter of credit or any other requirement relating to transfer imposed by the issuer which is within the standard practice referred to in Section 5–108(e) or is otherwise reasonable under the circumstances.

Official Comment

1. In order to protect the applicant's reliance on the designated beneficiary, letter of credit law traditionally has forbidden the beneficiary to convey to third parties its right to draw or demand payment under the letter of credit. Subsection (a) codifies that rule. The term "transfer" refers to the beneficiary's conveyance of that right. Absent incorporation of the UCP (which make elaborate provision for partial transfer of a commercial letter of credit) or similar trade practice and absent other express indication in the letter of credit that the term is used to mean something else, a term in the letter of credit indicating that the beneficiary has the right to transfer should be taken to mean that the beneficiary may convey to a third party its right to draw or demand payment. Even in that case, the issuer or other person controlling the transfer may make the beneficiary's right to transfer subject to conditions, such as timely notification, payment of a fee, delivery of the letter of credit to the issuer or other person controlling the transfer, or execution of appropriate forms to document the transfer. A nominated person who is not a confirmer has no obligation to recognize a transfer.

The power to establish "requirements" does not include the right absolutely to refuse to recognize transfers under a transferable letter of credit. An issuer who wishes to retain the right to deny all transfers should not issue transferable letters of credit or should incorporate the UCP. By stating its requirements in the letter of credit an issuer may impose any requirement without regard to its conformity to practice or reasonableness. Transfer requirements of issuers and nominated persons must be made known to potential transferors and transferees to enable those parties to comply with the requirements. A common method of making such requirements known is to use a form that indicates the information that must be provided and the instructions that must be given to enable the issuer or nominated person to comply with a request to transfer.

2. The issuance of a transferable letter of credit with the concurrence of the applicant is *ipso facto* an agreement by the issuer and applicant to permit a beneficiary to transfer its drawing right and permit a nominated person to recognize and carry out that transfer without further notice to them. In international commerce, transferable letters of credit are often issued under circumstances in which a nominated person or adviser is expected to facilitate the transfer from the original beneficiary to a transferee and to deal with that transferee. In those circumstances it is the responsibility of the nominated person or adviser to establish procedures satisfactory to protect itself against double presentation or dispute about the right to draw under the letter of credit. Commonly such a person will control the transfer by requiring that the original letter of credit be given to it or by causing a paper copy marked as an original to be issued where the original letter of credit was electronic. By keeping possession of the original letter of credit the nominated person or adviser can minimize or entirely exclude the possibility that the original beneficiary could properly procure payment from another bank. If the letter of credit requires presentation of the original letter of credit itself, no other payment could be procured. In addition to imposing whatever requirements it considers appropriate to protect itself against double payment the person that is facilitating the transfer has a right to charge an appropriate fee for its activity.

"Transfer" of a letter of credit should be distinguished from "assignment of proceeds." The former is analogous to a novation or a substitution of beneficiaries. It contemplates not merely payment to but also performance by the transferee. For example, under the typical terms of transfer for a commercial letter of credit, a transferee could comply with a letter of credit transferred to it by signing and presenting its own draft and invoice. An assignee of proceeds, on the other hand, is wholly dependent on the presentation of a draft and invoice signed by the beneficiary.

By agreeing to the issuance of a transferable letter of credit, which is not qualified or limited, the applicant may lose control over the identity of the person whose performance will earn payment under the letter of credit.

§ 5–113. Transfer by Operation of Law.

(a) A successor of a beneficiary may consent to amendments, sign and present documents, and receive payment or other items of value in the name of the beneficiary without disclosing its status as a successor.

(b) A successor of a beneficiary may consent to amendments, sign and present documents, and receive payment or other items of value in its own name as the disclosed successor of the beneficiary. Except as otherwise provided in subsection (e), an issuer shall recognize a disclosed successor of a beneficiary as beneficiary in full substitution for its predecessor upon compliance with the requirements for recognition by the issuer of a transfer of drawing rights by operation of law under the standard practice referred to in Section 5–108(e) or, in the absence of such a practice, compliance with other reasonable procedures sufficient to protect the issuer.

(c) An issuer is not obliged to determine whether a purported successor is a successor of a beneficiary or whether the signature of a purported successor is genuine or authorized.

(d) Honor of a purported successor's apparently complying presentation under subsection (a) or (b) has the consequences specified in Section 5–108(i) even if the purported successor is not the successor of a beneficiary. Documents signed in the name of the beneficiary or of a disclosed successor by a person who is neither the beneficiary nor the successor of the beneficiary are forged documents for the purposes of Section 5–109.

(e) An issuer whose rights of reimbursement are not covered by subsection (d) or substantially

similar law and any confirmer or nominated person may decline to recognize a presentation under subsection (b).

(f) A beneficiary whose name is changed after the issuance of a letter of credit has the same rights and obligations as a successor of a beneficiary under this section.

Official Comment

This section affirms the result in *Pastor v. Nat. Republic Bank of Chicago,* 76 Ill.2d 139, 390 N.E.2d 894 (Ill.1979) and *Federal Deposit Insurance Co. v. Bank of Boulder,* 911 F.2d 1466 (10th Cir.1990). Both electronic and tangible documents may be signed.

An issuer's requirements for recognition of a successor's status might include presentation of a certificate of merger, a court order appointing a bankruptcy trustee or receiver, a certificate of appointment as bankruptcy trustee, or the like. The issuer is entitled to rely upon such documents which on their face demonstrate that presentation is made by a successor of a beneficiary. It is not obliged to make an independent investigation to determine the fact of succession.

As amended in 2003.

§ 5–114. Assignment of Proceeds.

(a) In this section, "proceeds of a letter of credit" means the cash, check, accepted draft, or other item of value paid or delivered upon honor or giving of value by the issuer or any nominated person under the letter of credit. The term does not include a beneficiary's drawing rights or documents presented by the beneficiary.

(b) A beneficiary may assign its right to part or all of the proceeds of a letter of credit. The beneficiary may do so before presentation as a present assignment of its right to receive proceeds contingent upon its compliance with the terms and conditions of the letter of credit.

(c) An issuer or nominated person need not recognize an assignment of proceeds of a letter of credit until it consents to the assignment.

(d) An issuer or nominated person has no obligation to give or withhold its consent to an assignment of proceeds of a letter of credit, but consent may not be unreasonably withheld if the assignee possesses and exhibits the letter of credit and presentation of the letter of credit is a condition to honor.

(e) Rights of a transferee beneficiary or nominated person are independent of the beneficiary's assignment of the proceeds of a letter of credit and are superior to the assignee's right to the proceeds.

(f) Neither the rights recognized by this section between an assignee and an issuer, transferee beneficiary, or nominated person nor the issuer's or nominated person's payment of proceeds to an assignee or a third person affect the rights between the assignee and any person other than the issuer, transferee beneficiary, or nominated person. The mode of creating and perfecting a security interest in or granting an assignment of a beneficiary's rights to proceeds is governed by Article 9 or other law. Against persons other than the issuer, transferee beneficiary, or nominated person, the rights and obligations arising upon the creation of a security interest or other assignment of a beneficiary's right to proceeds and its perfection are governed by Article 9 or other law.

Official Comment

1. Subsection (b) expressly validates the beneficiary's present assignment of letter of credit proceeds if made after the credit is established but before the proceeds are realized. This section adopts the prevailing usage—"assignment of proceeds"—to an assignee. That terminology carries with it no implication, however, that an assignee acquires no interest until the proceeds are paid by the issuer. For example, an "assignment of the right to proceeds" of a letter of credit for purposes of security that meets the requirements of Section 9–203(b) would constitute the present creation of a security interest in a "letter-of-credit right." This security interest can be perfected by control (Section 9–107). Although subsection (a) explains the meaning of " 'proceeds' of a letter of credit," it should be emphasized that those proceeds also may be Article 9 proceeds of other collateral. For example, if a seller of inventory receives a letter of credit to support the account that arises upon the sale, payments made under the letter of credit are Article 9 proceeds of the inventory, account, and any document of title covering the inventory. Thus, the secured party who had a perfected security interest in that inventory, account, or document has a perfected security interest in the proceeds collected under the letter of credit, so long as they are identifiable cash proceeds (Section 9–315(a), (d)). This perfection is continuous, regardless of whether the secured party perfected a security interest in the right to letter of credit proceeds.

2. An assignee's rights to enforce an assignment of proceeds against an issuer and the priority of the assignee's rights against a nominated person or transferee beneficiary are governed by Article 5. Those rights and that priority are stated in subsections (c), (d), and (e). Note also that Section 4–210 gives first priority to a collecting bank that has given value for a documentary draft.

3. By requiring that an issuer or nominated person consent to the assignment of proceeds of a letter of credit, subsections (c) and (d) follow more closely recognized national and international letter of credit practices than did prior law. In most circumstances, it has always been advisable for the assignee to obtain the consent of the issuer in order better to safeguard its right to the proceeds. When notice of an assignment has been received, issuers normally have required signatures on a consent form. This practice is reflected in the revision. By unconditionally consenting to such an assignment, the issuer or nominated person becomes bound, subject to the rights of the superior parties specified in subsection (e), to pay to the assignee the assigned letter of credit proceeds that the issuer or nominated person would otherwise pay to the beneficiary or another assignee.

Where the letter of credit must be presented as a condition to honor and the assignee holds and exhibits the letter of credit to the issuer or nominated person, the risk to the issuer or nominated person of having to pay twice is minimized. In such a situation, subsection (d) provides that the issuer or nominated person may not unreasonably withhold its consent to the assignment.

§ 5–115.   Statute of Limitations.

An action to enforce a right or obligation arising under this article must be commenced within one year after the expiration date of the relevant letter of credit or one year after the [claim for relief] [cause of action] accrues, whichever occurs later. A [claim for relief] [cause of action] accrues when the breach occurs, regardless of the aggrieved party's lack of knowledge of the breach.

Official Comment

1. This section is based upon Sections 4–111 and 2–725(2).

2. This section applies to all claims for which there are remedies under Section 5–111 and to other claims made under this article, such as claims for breach of

warranty under Section 5–110. Because it covers all claims under Section 5–111, the statute of limitations applies not only to wrongful dishonor claims against the issuer but also to claims between the issuer and the applicant arising from the reimbursement agreement. These might be for reimbursement (issuer v. applicant) or for breach of the reimbursement contract by wrongful honor (applicant v. issuer).

3. The statute of limitations, like the rest of the statute, applies only to a letter of credit issued on or after the effective date and only to transactions, events, obligations, or duties arising out of or associated with such a letter. If a letter of credit was issued before the effective date and an obligation on that letter of credit was breached after the effective date, the complaining party could bring its suit within the time that would have been permitted prior to the adoption of Section 5–115 and would not be limited by the terms of Section 5–115.

§ 5–116. Choice of Law and Forum.

(a) The liability of an issuer, nominated person, or adviser for action or omission is governed by the law of the jurisdiction chosen by an agreement in the form of a record signed or otherwise authenticated by the affected parties in the manner provided in Section 5–104 or by a provision in the person's letter of credit, confirmation, or other undertaking. The jurisdiction whose law is chosen need not bear any relation to the transaction.

(b) Unless subsection (a) applies, the liability of an issuer, nominated person, or adviser for action or omission is governed by the law of the jurisdiction in which the person is located. The person is considered to be located at the address indicated in the person's undertaking. If more than one address is indicated, the person is considered to be located at the address from which the person's undertaking was issued. For the purpose of jurisdiction, choice of law, and recognition of interbranch letters of credit, but not enforcement of a judgment, all branches of a bank are considered separate juridical entities and a bank is considered to be located at the place where its relevant branch is considered to be located under this subsection.

(c) Except as otherwise provided in this subsection, the liability of an issuer, nominated person, or adviser is governed by any rules of custom or practice, such as the Uniform Customs and Practice for Documentary Credits, to which

the letter of credit, confirmation, or other undertaking is expressly made subject. If (i) this article would govern the liability of an issuer, nominated person, or adviser under subsection (a) or (b), (ii) the relevant undertaking incorporates rules of custom or practice, and (iii) there is conflict between this article and those rules as applied to that undertaking, those rules govern except to the extent of any conflict with the nonvariable provisions specified in Section 5–103(c).

(d) If there is conflict between this article and Article 3, 4, 4A, or 9, this article governs.

(e) The forum for settling disputes arising out of an undertaking within this article may be chosen in the manner and with the binding effect that governing law may be chosen in accordance with subsection (a).

Official Comment

1. Although it would be possible for the parties to agree otherwise, the law normally chosen by agreement under subsection (a) and that provided in the absence of agreement under subsection (b) is the substantive law of a particular jurisdiction not including the choice of law principles of that jurisdiction. Thus, two parties, an issuer and an applicant, both located in Oklahoma might choose the law of New York. Unless they agree otherwise, the section anticipates that they wish the substantive law of New York to apply to their transaction and they do not intend that a New York choice of law principle might direct a court to Oklahoma law. By the same token, the liability of an issuer located in New York is governed by New York substantive law—in the absence of agreement—even in circumstances in which choice of law principles found in the common law of New York might direct one to the law of another State. Subsection (b) states the relevant choice of law principles and it should not be subordinated to some other choice of law rule. Within the States of the United States *renvoi* will not be a problem once every jurisdiction has enacted Section 5–116 because every jurisdiction will then have the same choice of law rule and in a particular case all choice of law rules will point to the same substantive law.

Subsection (b) does not state a choice of law rule for the "liability of an applicant." However, subsection (b) does state a choice of law rule for the liability of an issuer, nominated person, or adviser, and since some of the issues in suits by applicants against those persons involve the "liability of an issuer, nominated person, or adviser," subsection (b) states the choice of law rule for those issues. Because an issuer may have liability to a confirmer both as an issuer (Section 5–108(a), Comment 5 to Section 5–108) and as an applicant (Section 5–107(a), Comment 1 to Section 5–107, Section 5–108(i)), subsection (b) may state the choice of law rule for some but not all of the issuer's liability in a suit by a confirmer.

2. Because the confirmer or other nominated person may choose different law from that chosen by the issuer or may be located in a different jurisdiction and fail to choose law, it is possible that a confirmer or nominated person may be obligated to pay (under their law) but will not be entitled to payment from the issuer (under its law). Similarly, the rights of an unreimbursed issuer, confirmer, or nominated person against a beneficiary under Section 5–109, 5–110, or 5–117, will not necessarily be governed by the same law that applies to the issuer's or confirmer's obligation upon presentation. Because the UCP and other practice are incorporated in most international letters of credit, disputes arising from different legal obligations to honor have not been frequent. Since Section 5–108 incorporates standard practice, these problems should be further minimized—at least to the extent that the same practice is and continues to be widely followed.

3. This section does not permit what is now authorized by the nonuniform Section 5–102(4) in New York. Under the current law in New York a letter of credit that incorporates the UCP is not governed in any respect by Article 5. Under revised Section 5–116 letters of credit that incorporate the UCP or similar practice will still be subject to Article 5 in certain respects. First, incorporation of the UCP or other practice does not override the nonvariable terms of Article 5. Second, where there is no conflict between Article 5 and the relevant provision of the UCP or other practice, both apply. Third, practice provisions incorporated in a letter of credit will not be effective if they fail to comply with Section 5–103(c). Assume, for example, that a practice provision purported to free a party from any liability unless it were "grossly negligent" or that the practice generally limited the remedies that one party might have against another. Depending upon the circumstances, that disclaimer or limitation of liability might be ineffective because of Section 5–103(c).

Even though Article 5 is generally consistent with UCP 500, it is not necessarily consistent with other rules or with versions of the UCP that may be adopted after Article 5's revision, or with other practices that may develop. Rules of practice incorporated in the letter of credit or other undertaking are those in effect when the letter of credit or other undertaking is issued. Except in the unusual cases discussed in the immediately preceding paragraph, practice adopted in a letter of credit will override the rules of Article 5 and the parties to letter of credit transactions must be familiar with practice (such as future versions of the UCP) that is explicitly adopted in letters of credit.

4. In several ways Article 5 conflicts with and overrides similar matters governed by Articles 3 and 4. For example, "draft" is more broadly defined in letter of credit practice than under Section 3–104. The time allowed for honor and the required notification of reasons for dishonor are different in letter of credit practice than in the handling of documentary and other drafts under Articles 3 and 4.

5. Subsection (e) must be read in conjunction with existing law governing subject matter jurisdiction. If the local law restricts a court to certain subject matter jurisdiction not including letter of credit disputes, subsection (e) does not authorize parties to choose that forum. For example, the parties' agreement under Section 5–116(e) would not confer jurisdiction on a probate court to decide a letter of credit case.

If the parties choose a forum under subsection (e) and if—because of other law—that forum will not take jurisdiction, the parties' agreement or undertaking should then be construed (for the purpose of forum selection) as though it did not contain a clause choosing a particular forum. That result is necessary to avoid sentencing the parties to eternal purgatory where neither the chosen State nor the State which would have jurisdiction but for the clause will take jurisdiction—the former in disregard of the clause and the latter in honor of the clause.

§ 5–117. Subrogation of Issuer, Applicant, and Nominated Person.

(a) An issuer that honors a beneficiary's presentation is subrogated to the rights of the beneficiary to the same extent as if the issuer were a secondary obligor of the underlying obligation owed to the beneficiary and of the applicant to the same extent as if the issuer were the secondary obligor of the underlying obligation owed to the applicant.

(b) An applicant that reimburses an issuer is subrogated to the rights of the issuer against any beneficiary, presenter, or nominated person to the same extent as if the applicant were the secondary obligor of the obligations owed to the issuer and has the rights of subrogation of the issuer to the rights of the beneficiary stated in subsection (a).

(c) A nominated person who pays or gives value against a draft or demand presented under a letter of credit is subrogated to the rights of:

(1) the issuer against the applicant to the same extent as if the nominated person were a secondary obligor of the obligation owed to the issuer by the applicant;

(2) the beneficiary to the same extent as if the nominated person were a secondary obligor of the underlying obligation owed to the beneficiary; and

(3) the applicant to same extent as if the nominated person were a secondary obligor of the underlying obligation owed to the applicant.

(d) Notwithstanding any agreement or term to the contrary, the rights of subrogation stated in subsections (a) and (b) do not arise until the issuer honors the letter of credit or otherwise pays and the rights in subsection (c) do not arise until the nominated person pays or otherwise gives value. Until then, the issuer, nominated person, and the applicant do not derive under this section present or prospective rights forming the basis of a claim, defense, or excuse.

Official Comment

1. By itself this section does not grant any right of subrogation. It grants only the right that would exist if the person seeking subrogation "were a secondary obligor." (The term "secondary obligor" refers to a surety, guarantor, or other person against whom or whose property an obligee has recourse with respect to the obligation of a third party. See Restatement of the Law Third, Suretyship and Guaranty § 1 (1996).) If the secondary obligor would not have a right to subrogation in the circumstances in which one is claimed under this section, none is granted by this section. In effect, the section does no more than to remove an impediment that some courts have found to subrogation because they conclude that the issuer's or other claimant's rights are "independent" of the underlying obligation. If, for example, a secondary obligor would not have a subrogation right because its payment did not fully satisfy the underlying obligation, none would be available under this section. The section indorses the position of Judge Becker in *Tudor Development Group, Inc. v. United States Fidelity and Guaranty,* 968 F.2d 357 (3rd Cir.1991).

2. To preserve the independence of the letter of credit obligation and to insure that subrogation not be used as an offensive weapon by an issuer or others, the admonition in subsection (d) must be carefully observed. Only one who has completed its performance in a letter of credit transaction can have a right to subrogation. For example, an issuer may not dishonor and then defend its dishonor or assert a setoff on the ground that it is subrogated to another person's rights. Nor may the issuer complain after honor that its subrogation rights have been impaired by any good faith dealings between the beneficiary and the applicant or any other person. Assume, for example, that the beneficiary under a standby letter of credit is a mortgagee. If the mortgagee were obliged to issue a release of the mortgage upon payment of the underlying debt (by the issuer under the letter of credit), that release might impair the issuer's rights of subrogation, but the beneficiary would have no liability to the issuer for having granted that release.

§ 5–118. Security Interest of Issuer or Nominated Person.

(a) An issuer or nominated person has a security interest in a document presented under a letter of credit to the extent that the issuer or nominated person honors or gives value for the presentation.

(b) So long as and to the extent that an issuer or nominated person has not been reimbursed or has not otherwise recovered the value given with respect to a security interest in a document under subsection (a), the security interest continues and is subject to Article 9, but:

(1) a security agreement is not necessary to make the security interest enforceable under Section 9–203(b)(3);

(2) if the document is presented in a medium other than a written or other tangible medium, the security interest is perfected; and

(3) if the document is presented in a written or other tangible medium and is not a certificated security, chattel paper, a document of title, an instrument, or a letter of credit, the security interest is perfected and has priority over a conflicting security interest in the document so long as the debtor does not have possession of the document.

As added in 1999.

Official Comment

1. This section gives the issuer of a letter of credit or a nominated person thereunder an automatic perfected security interest in a "document" (as that term is defined in Section 5–102(a)(6)). The security interest arises only if the document is presented to the issuer or nominated person under the letter of credit and only to the extent of the value that is given. This security interest is analogous to that awarded to a collecting bank under Section 4–210. Subsection (b) contains special rules governing the security interest arising under this section. In all other respects, a security interest arising under this section is subject to Article 9. See Section 9–109. Thus, for example, a security interest arising under this section may give rise to a security interest in proceeds under Section 9–315.

2. Subsection (b)(1) makes a security agreement unnecessary to the creation of a security interest under this section. Under subsection (b)(2), a security interest arising under this section is perfected if the document is presented in a medium other than a written or tangible medium. Documents that are written and that are not an otherwise-defined type of collateral under Article 9 (e.g., an invoice or inspection certificate) may be goods, in which an issuer or nominated person could perfect its security interest by possession. Because the definition of document in Section 5–102(a)(6) includes records (e.g., electronic records) that may not be goods, subsection (b)(2) provides for automatic perfection (i.e., without filing or possession).

Under subsection (b)(3), if the document (i) is in a written or tangible medium, (ii) is not a certificated security, chattel paper, a document of title, an instrument, or a letter of credit, and (iii) is not in the debtor's possession, the security interest is perfected and has priority over a conflicting security interest. If the document is a type of tangible collateral that subsection (b)(3) excludes from its perfection and priority rules, the issuer or nominated person must comply with the normal method of perfection (e.g., possession of an instrument) and is subject to the applicable Article 9 priority rules. Documents to which subsection (b)(3) applies may be important to an issuer or nominated person. For example, a confirmer who pays the beneficiary must be assured that its rights to all documents are not impaired. It will find it necessary to present all of the required documents to the issuer in order to be reimbursed. Moreover, when a nominated person sends documents to an issuer in connection with the nominated person's reimbursement, that activity is not a collection, enforcement, or disposition of collateral under Article 9.

One purpose of this section is to protect an issuer or nominated person from claims of a beneficiary's creditors. It is a fallback provision inasmuch as issuers and nominated persons frequently may obtain and perfect security interests under the usual Article 9 rules, and, in many cases, the documents will be owned by the issuer, nominated person, or applicant.

As added in 1999.

Transition Provisions

§ [   ]. **Effective Date.**

This [Act] shall become effective on _____, 199__.

§ [   ]. **Repeal.**

This [Act] [repeals] [amends] [insert citation to existing Article 5].

§ [   ]. **Applicability.**

This [Act] applies to a letter of credit that is issued on or after the effective date of this [Act]. This [Act] does not apply to a transaction, event, obligation, or duty arising out of or associated with a letter of credit that was issued before the effective date of this [Act].

§ [   ]. **Savings Clause.**

A transaction arising out of or associated with a letter of credit that was issued before the effective date of this [Act] and the rights, obligations, and interests flowing from that transaction are governed by any statute or other law amended or repealed by this [Act] as if repeal or amendment had not occurred and may be terminated, completed, consummated, or enforced under that statute or other law.

UCC ARTICLE 6

ALTERNATIVE A: BULK TRANSFERS REPEALER

ALTERNATIVE B: BULK SALES

Article 6 was revised in 1989.

(States To Select One Alternative)

ALTERNATIVE A

Section
1. Repeal.
2. Amendment.
3. Amendment.
4. Savings Clause.

[END OF ALTERNATIVE A]

ALTERNATIVE B

6–101. Short Title.
6–102. Definitions and Index of Definitions.

Section
6–103. Applicability of Article.
6–104. Obligations of Buyer.
6–105. Notice to Claimants.
6–106. Schedule of Distribution.
6–107. Liability for Noncompliance.
6–108. Bulk Sales by Auction; Bulk Sales Conducted by Liquidator.
6–109. What Constitutes Filing; Duties of Filing Officer; Information From Filing Officer.
6–110. Limitation of Actions.

[END OF ALTERNATIVE B]

National Conference of Commissioners on Uniform State Laws

CO–REPORTERS

Steven L. Harris, Champaign, Illinois

William D. Hawkland, Baton Rouge, Louisiana

DRAFTING COMMITTEE CHAIRMAN

Gerald L. Bepko, Indianapolis, Indiana

MEMBERS

William C. Hillman, Providence, Rhode Island

Frederick H. Miller, Norman, Oklahoma

Raymond P. Pepe, Harrisburg, Pennsylvania

Donald J. Rapson, Livingston, New Jersey, *The American Law Institute Representative*

Curtis R. Reitz, Philadelphia, Pennsylvania

Millard H. Ruud, Austin, Texas, *Drafting Liaison*

Hiroshi Sakai, Honolulu, Hawaii

Michael P. Sullivan, Minneapolis, Minnesota, *President (Member Ex Officio)*

Neal Ossen, Hartford, Connecticut, *Chairman, Division C (Member Ex Officio)*

REVIEW COMMITTEE CHAIRMAN

John A. Chanin, Honolulu, Hawaii

MEMBERS

Stephen E. Cicilline, Providence, Rhode Island

Morris W. Macey, Atlanta, Georgia

Robert G. Pugh, Shreveport, Louisiana

ABA ADVISOR, SECTION OF CORPORATION, BANKING, AND BUSINESS LAW

Howard Ruda, New York, New York

ADDITIONAL ADVISORS

Don L. Baker, Commercial Law League of America

William Z. Fox, National Auctioneers Association

Thomas J. Greco, American Bankers Association

Frank R. Kennedy, National Bankruptcy Conference

James E. Snider, National Association of Credit Management

Douglas H. Williams, National Commercial Finance Association

PREFATORY NOTE

Background. Bulk sale legislation originally was enacted in response to a fraud perceived to be common around the turn of the century: a merchant would acquire his stock in trade on credit, then sell his entire inventory ("in bulk") and abscond with the proceeds, leaving creditors unpaid. The creditors had a right to sue the merchant on the unpaid debts, but that right often was of little practical value. Even if the merchant-debtor was found, in personam jurisdiction over him might not have been readily available. Those creditors who succeeded in obtaining a judgment often were unable to satisfy it because the defrauding seller had spent or hidden the sale proceeds. Nor did the creditors ordinarily have recourse to the merchandise sold. The transfer of the inventory to an innocent buyer effectively immunized the goods from the reach of the seller's creditors. The creditors of a bulk seller thus might be left without a means to satisfy their claims.

To a limited extent, the law of fraudulent conveyances ameliorated the creditors' plight. When the buyer in bulk was in league with the seller or paid less than full value for the inventory, fraudulent conveyance law enabled the defrauded creditors to avoid the sale and apply the transferred inventory toward the satisfaction of their claims against the seller. But fraudulent conveyance law provided no remedy against persons who bought in good faith, without reason to know of the seller's intention to pocket the proceeds and disappear, and for adequate value. In those cases, the only remedy for the seller's creditors was to attempt to recover from the absconding seller.

State legislatures responded to this perceived "bulk sale risk" with a variety of legislative enactments. Common to these statutes was the imposition of a duty on the buyer in bulk to notify the seller's creditors of the impending sale. The buyer's failure to comply with these and any other statutory duties generally afforded the seller's creditors a remedy analogous to the remedy for fraudulent conveyances: the creditors acquired the right to set aside the sale and reach the transferred inventory in the hands of the buyer.

Like its predecessors, Article 6 (1987 Official Text) is remarkable in that it obligates buyers in bulk to incur costs to protect the interests of the seller's creditors, with whom they usually have no relationship. Even more striking is that Article 6 affords creditors a remedy against a good faith purchaser for full value without notice of any wrongdoing on the part of the seller. The Article thereby impedes normal business transactions, many of which can be expected to benefit the seller's creditors. For this reason, Article 6 has been subjected to serious criticism. See, e.g., Rapson, *U.C.C. Article 6: Should It Be Revised or "Deep-Sixed"?* 38 Bus.Law. 1753 (1983).

In the legal context in which Article 6 (1987 Official Text) and its nonuniform predecessors were enacted, the benefits to creditors appeared to justify the costs of interfering with good faith transactions. Today, however, creditors are better able than ever to make informed decisions about whether to extend credit. Changes in technology have enabled credit reporting services to provide fast, accurate, and more complete credit histories at relatively little cost. A search of the public real estate and personal property records will disclose most encumbrances on a debtor's property with little inconvenience.

In addition, changes in the law now afford creditors greater opportunities to collect their debts. The development of "minimum contacts" with the forum state as a basis for *in personam* jurisdiction and the universal promulgation of state long-arm statutes and rules have greatly improved the possibility of obtaining personal jurisdiction over a debtor who flees to another state. Widespread enactment of the Uniform Enforcement of Foreign Judgments Act has facilitated nation-wide collection of judgments. And to the extent that a bulk sale is fraudulent and the buyer is a party to fraud, aggrieved creditors have a remedy under the Uniform Fraudulent Transfer Act. Moreover, creditors of a merchant no longer face the choice of extending unsecured credit or no credit at all. Retaining an interest in inventory to secure its price has become relatively simple and inexpensive under Article 9.

Finally, there is no evidence that, in today's economy, fraudulent bulk sales are frequent enough, or engender credit losses significant enough, to require regulation of all bulk sales, including the vast majority that are conducted in good faith. Indeed, the experience of the Canadian Province of British Columbia, which repealed its Sale of Goods in Bulk Act in 1985, and of the United Kingdom, which never has enacted bulk sales legislation, suggests that regulation of bulk sales no longer is necessary.

Recommendation. The National Conference of Commissioners on Uniform State Laws and the American Law Institute believe that changes in the business and legal contexts in which sales are conducted have made regulation of bulk sales unnecessary. The Conference and the Institute therefore withdraw their support for Article 6 of the Uniform Commercial Code and encourage those states that have enacted the Article to repeal it.

The Conference and the Institute recognize that bulk sales may present a particular problem in some states and that some legislatures may wish to continue to regulate bulk sales. They believe that existing Article 6 has become inadequate for that purpose. For those states that are disinclined to repeal Article 6, they have promulgated a revised version of Article 6. The revised Article is designed to afford better protection to creditors while minimizing the impediments to good-faith transactions.

The Official Comment to Section 6–101 explains the rationale underlying the revisions and highlights the major substantive changes reflected in them. Of particular interest is Section 6–103(1)(a), which limits the application of the revised Article to bulk sales by sellers whose principal business is the sale of inventory from stock. In approving this provision, the Conference and the Institute were mindful that some states have expanded the coverage of existing Article 6 to include bulk sales conducted by sellers whose principal business is the operation of a restaurant or tavern. Expansion of the scope of revised Article 6 is inconsistent with the recommendation that Article 6 be repealed. Nevertheless, the inclusion of restaurants and taverns within the scope of the revised Article as it is enacted in particular jurisdictions would not disturb the internal logic and structure of the revised Article.

ALTERNATIVE A

Section
1. Repeal.
2. Amendment.
3. Amendment.
4. Savings Clause.

[§ 1. Repeal.

Article 6 and Section 9–111 of the Uniform Commercial Code are hereby repealed, effective ————.

§ 2. Amendment.

Section 1–105(2) of the Uniform Commercial Code is hereby amended to read as follows:

(2) Where one of the following provisions of this Act specifies the applicable law, that provision governs and a contrary agreement is effective only to the extent permitted by the law (including the conflict of laws rules) so specified:

Rights of creditors against sold goods. Section 2–402.

Applicability of the Article on Leases. Sections 2A–105 and 2A–106.

Applicability of the Article on Bank Deposits and Collections. Section 4–102.

Bulk transfers subject to the Article on Bulk Transfers. Section 6–102.

Applicability of the Article on Investment Securities. Section 8–106.

Perfection provisions of the Article on Secured Transactions. Section 9–103.

§ 3. Amendment.

Section 2–403(4) of the Uniform Commercial Code is hereby amended to read as follows:

(4) The rights of other purchasers of goods and of lien creditors are governed by the Articles on Secured Transactions (Article 9), ~~Bulk Transfers (Article 6)~~ and Documents of Title (Article 7).

§ 4. Savings Clause.

Rights and obligations that arose under Article 6 and Section 9–111 of the Uniform Commercial Code before their repeal remain valid and may be enforced as though those statutes had not been repealed.]

Legislative Note: To take account of differences between former Article 9 and revised Article 9, a State that repeals Article 6 after revised Article 9 takes effect must make the following changes to Alternative A. First, inasmuch as revised Article 9 contains no counterpart of former Section 9– 111, the reference to that section in Section 1 of the repealer should be deleted, and Section 4 of the repeal bill should allude to former Section 9– 111. Second, the last entry in Section 1–105(2) should be amended as shown above in this Appendix.

[END OF ALTERNATIVE A]

ALTERNATIVE B

Section
6–101. Short Title.
6–102. Definitions and Index of Definitions.
6–103. Applicability of Article.
6–104. Obligations of Buyer.
6–105. Notice to Claimants.
6–106. Schedule of Distribution.
6–107. Liability for Noncompliance.
6–108. Bulk Sales by Auction; Bulk Sales Conducted by Liquidator.
6–109. What Constitutes Filing; Duties of Filing Officer; Information From Filing Officer.
6–110. Limitation of Actions.

[§ 6–101.   Short Title.

This Article shall be known and may be cited as Uniform Commercial Code—Bulk Sales.

Official Comment

Prior Uniform Statutory Provision: Section 6–101 (1987 Official Text).

Change: This Article applies only to sales, as defined in Section 2–103(1), and not to other transfers.

Purpose of Change: Transfers other than sales, *e.g.*, grants of security interests, do not present risks to creditors necessitating advance notice in accordance with the provisions of this Article. The Uniform Fraudulent Transfer Act affords a remedy to creditors who are injured by donative transfers.

Rationale for Revision of the Article:

Article 6 (1987 Official Text) imposes upon transferees in bulk several duties toward creditors of the transferor. These duties include the duty to notify the creditors of the impending bulk transfer and, in those jurisdictions that have adopted optional Section 6–106, the duty to assure that the new consideration for the transfer is applied to pay debts of the transferor.

Compliance with the provisions of Article 6 can be burdensome, particularly when the transferor has a large number of creditors. When the transferor is actively engaged in business at a number of locations, assembling a current list of creditors may not be possible. Mailing a notice to each creditor may prove costly. When the goods that are the subject of the transfer are located in several jurisdictions, the transferor may be obligated to comply with Article 6 as enacted in each jurisdiction. The widespread enactment of nonuniform amendments makes compliance with Article 6 in multiple-state transactions problematic. Moreover, the Article requires compliance even when there is no reason to believe that the transferor is conducting a fraudulent transfer, *e.g.*, when the transferor is scaling down the business but remaining available to creditors.

Article 6 imposes strict liability for noncompliance. Failure to comply with the provisions of the Article renders the transfer ineffective, even when the transferor has attempted compliance in good faith, and even when no creditor has been injured by the noncompliance. The potential liability for minor noncompliance may be high. If the transferor should enter bankruptcy before the expiration of the limitation period, Bankruptcy Code §§ 544(b), 550(a), 11 U.S.C. §§ 544(b), 550(a), may enable the transferor's bankruptcy trustee to set aside the entire transaction and recover from the noncomplying transferee all the goods transferred or their value. The trustee has this power even though the noncompliance was with respect to only a single creditor holding a small claim.

The benefits that compliance affords to creditors do not justify the substantial burdens and risks that the Article imposes upon good faith purchasers of business assets. The Article requires that notice be sent only ten days before the transferee takes possession of the goods or pays for them, whichever happens first. Given the delay between sending the notice and its receipt, creditors have scant opportunity to avail themselves of a judicial or nonjudicial remedy before the transfer has been consummated.

In some cases Article 6 may have the unintended effect of injuring, rather than aiding, creditors of the transferor. Those transferees who recognize the burdens and risks that Article 6 imposes upon them sometimes agree to purchase only at a reduced price. Others refuse to purchase at all, leaving the creditors to realize only the liquidation value, rather than the going concern value, of the business goods.

As a response to these inadequacies and others, the National Conference of Commissioners on Uniform State Laws has completely revised Article 6. This revision is designed to reduce the burdens and risks imposed upon good-faith buyers of business assets while increasing the protection afforded to creditors. Among the major changes it makes are the following:

—this Article applies only when the buyer has notice, or after reasonable inquiry would have had notice, that the seller will not continue to operate the same or a similar kind of business after the sale (Section 6–102(1)(c)).

—this Article does not apply to sales in which the value of the property otherwise available to creditors is less than $10,000 or those in which the value of the property is greater than $25,000,000 (Section 6–103(3)(l)).

—the choice-of-law provision (Sections 6–103(1)(b) and 6–103(2)) limits the applicable law to that of one jurisdiction.

—when the seller is indebted to a large number of persons, the buyer need neither obtain a list of those persons nor send individual notices to each person but instead may give notice by filing (Sections 6–105(2) and 6–104(2)).

—the notice period is increased from 10 days to 45 days (Section 6–105(5)), and the statute of limitations is extended from six months to one year (Section 6–110).

—the notice must include a copy of a "schedule of distribution," which sets forth how the net contract price is to be distributed (Sections 6–105(3) and 6–106(1)).

—a buyer who makes a good faith effort to comply with the requirements of this Article or to exclude the sale from the application of this Article, or who acts on the good faith belief that this Article does not apply to the sale, is not liable for noncompliance (Section 6–107(3)).

—a buyer's noncompliance does not render the sale ineffective or otherwise affect the buyer's title to the goods; rather, the liability of a noncomplying buyer is for damages caused by the noncompliance (Sections 6–107(1) and 6–107(8)).

In addition to making these and other major substantive changes, revised Article 6 resolves the ambiguities that three decades of law practice, judicial construction, and scholarly inquiry have disclosed.

§ 6–102. Definitions and Index of Definitions.

(1) In this Article, unless the context otherwise requires:

(a) "Assets" means the inventory that is the subject of a bulk sale and any tangible and intangible personal property used or held for use primarily in, or arising from, the seller's business and sold in connection with that inventory, but the term does not include:

(i) fixtures (section 9–102(a)(41)) other than readily removable factory and office machines;

(ii) the lessee's interest in a lease of real property; or

(iii) property to the extent it is generally exempt from creditor process under nonbankruptcy law.

(b) "Auctioneer" means a person whom the seller engages to direct, conduct, control, or be responsible for a sale by auction.

(c) "Bulk sale" means:

(i) in the case of a sale by auction or a sale or series of sales conducted by a liquidator on the seller's behalf, a sale or series of sales not in the ordinary course of the seller's business of more than half of the seller's inventory, as measured by value on the date of the bulk-sale agreement, if on that date the auctioneer or liquidator has notice, or after reasonable inquiry would have had notice, that the seller will not continue to operate the same or a similar kind of business after the sale or series of sales; and

(ii) in all other cases, a sale not in the ordinary course of the seller's business of more than half the seller's inventory, as measured by value on the date of the bulk-sale agreement, if on that date the buyer has notice, or after reasonable inquiry would have had notice, that the seller will not continue to operate the same or a similar kind of business after the sale.

(d) "Claim" means a right to payment from the seller, whether or not the right is reduced to judgment, liquidated, fixed, matured, disputed, secured, legal, or equitable. The term includes costs of collection and attorney's fees only to the extent that the laws of this state permit the holder of the claim to recover them in an action against the obligor.

(e) "Claimant" means a person holding a claim incurred in the seller's business other than:

(i) an unsecured and unmatured claim for employment compensation and benefits, including commissions and vacation, severance, and sick-leave pay;

(ii) a claim for injury to an individual or to property, or for breach of warranty, unless:

(A) a right of action for the claim has accrued;

(B) the claim has been asserted against the seller; and

(C) the seller knows the identity of the person asserting the claim and the basis upon which the person has asserted it; and

(States To Select One Alternative)

ALTERNATIVE A

[(iii) a claim for taxes owing to a governmental unit.]

ALTERNATIVE B

[(iii) a claim for taxes owing to a governmental unit, if:

(A) a statute governing the enforcement of the claim permits or requires notice of the bulk sale to be given to the governmental unit in a manner other than by compliance with the requirements of this Article; and

(B) notice is given in accordance with the statute.]

(f) "Creditor" means a claimant or other person holding a claim.

(g)(i) "Date of the bulk sale" means:

(A) if the sale is by auction or is conducted by a liquidator on the seller's behalf, the date on which more than ten percent of the net proceeds is paid to or for the benefit of the seller; and

(B) in all other cases, the later of the date on which:

(I) more than ten percent of the net contract price is paid to or for the benefit of the seller; or

(II) more than ten percent of the assets, as measured by value, are transferred to the buyer.

(ii) For purposes of this subsection:

(A) Delivery of a negotiable instrument (Section 3–104(1)) to or for the benefit of the seller in exchange for assets constitutes payment of the contract price pro tanto;

(B) To the extent that the contract price is deposited in an escrow, the contract price is paid to or for the benefit of the seller when the seller acquires the unconditional right to receive the deposit or when the deposit is delivered to the seller or for the benefit of the seller, whichever is earlier; and

(C) An asset is transferred when a person holding an unsecured claim can no longer obtain through judicial proceedings rights to the asset that are superior to those of the buyer arising as a result of the bulk sale. A person holding an unsecured claim can obtain those superior rights to a tangible asset at least until the buyer has an unconditional right, under the bulk-sale agreement, to possess the asset, and a person holding an unsecured claim can obtain those superior rights to an intangible asset at least until the buyer has an unconditional right, under the bulk-sale agreement, to use the asset.

(h) "Date of the bulk-sale agreement" means:

(i) in the case of a sale by auction or conducted by a liquidator (subsection (c)(i)), the date on which the seller engages the auctioneer or liquidator; and

(ii) in all other cases, the date on which a bulk-sale agreement becomes enforceable between the buyer and the seller.

(i) "Debt" means liability on a claim.

(j) "Liquidator" means a person who is regularly engaged in the business of disposing of assets for businesses contemplating liquidation or dissolution.

(k) "Net contract price" means the new consideration the buyer is obligated to pay for the assets less:

(i) he amount of any proceeds of the sale of an asset, to the extent the proceeds are applied in partial or total satisfaction of a debt secured by the asset; and

(ii) the amount of any debt to the extent it is secured by a security interest or lien that is enforceable against the asset before and after it has been sold to a buyer. If a debt is secured by an asset and other property of the seller, the amount of the debt secured by a security interest or lien that is enforceable against the asset is determined by multiplying the debt by a fraction, the numerator of which is the value of the new consideration for the asset on the date of the bulk sale and the denominator of which is the value of all property securing the debt on the date of the bulk sale.

(l) "Net proceeds" means the new consideration received for assets sold at a sale by auction or a sale conducted by a liquidator on the seller's behalf less:

(i) commissions and reasonable expenses of the sale;

(ii) the amount of any proceeds of the sale of an asset, to the extent the proceeds are applied in partial or total satisfaction of a debt secured by the asset; and

(iii) the amount of any debt to the extent it is secured by a security interest or lien that is enforceable against the asset before and after it has been sold to a buyer. If a debt is secured by an asset and other property of the seller, the amount of the debt secured by a security interest or lien that is enforceable against the asset is determined by multiplying the debt by a fraction, the numerator of which is the value of the new consideration for the asset on the date of the bulk sale and the denominator of which is the value of all property securing the debt on the date of the bulk sale.

(m) A sale is "in the ordinary course of the seller's business" if the sale comports with usual or customary practices in the kind of business in which the seller is engaged or with the seller's own usual or customary practices.

(n) "United States" includes its territories and possessions and the Commonwealth of Puerto Rico.

(o) "Value" means fair market value.

(p) "Verified" means signed and sworn to or affirmed.

(2) The following definitions in other Articles apply to this Article:

(a) "Buyer." Section 2–103(1)(a).

(b) "Equipment." Section 9–102(a)(33).

(c) "Inventory." Section 9–102(a)(48).

(d) "Sale." Section 2–106(1).

(e) "Seller." Section 2–103(1)(d).

(3) In addition, Article 1 contains general definitions and principles of construction and interpretation applicable throughout this Article.

As amended in 1999.

Official Comment

1. (a) "Assets". New. The term generally includes only "personal property." Whether particular property is "personal property" is to be determined by

law outside this Article; however, for purposes of this Article, (i) the term includes "readily removable factory and office machines" (compare Section 9–334(e)(2)(A)), even if they are covered by applicable real estate law and thus are "fixtures" as defined in Section 9–102(a)(41); (ii) the term does not include the lessee's interest in a lease of real property, even if that interest is considered to be personal property under other applicable law; and (iii) the term does not include property to the extent that it is "generally exempt from creditor process under nonbankruptcy law."

(b) "Auctioneer". Compare Section 6–108(3) (1987 Official Text).

(c) "Bulk Sale". Bulk sales are of two kinds. Subsection (1)(c)(i) describes bulk sales conducted by a professional intermediary (i.e., an auctioneer or liquidator), as to which sales Section 6–108 applies. If these indirect sales occur as a series of related sales, then the entire series is treated as a single "bulk sale" and the term applies to the sales in the aggregate. Sales made directly by the seller to the buyer, described in subsection (1)(c)(ii), include sales conducted by an auctioneer or liquidator for its own account.

The elements of both direct and indirect sales are the same. Some of these elements have been borrowed from the 1987 Official Text of Article 6 and restated. For example, the term includes only sales that are not "in the ordinary course of the seller's business" (subsection (1)(m)). The sale must be of "more than half of the seller's inventory, as measured by value [subsection (1)(o)] on the date of the bulk-sale agreement [subsection (1)(h)]." All inventory owned by the seller should be included in the calculation, regardless of where it is located. Inventory that is encumbered by a security interest or lien should be counted at its gross value, although the fact that it is encumbered may affect the applicability of this Article to the sale.

The determination whether a sale is a "bulk sale" and thus subject to this Article is not affected by whether other types of property are sold in connection with inventory. However, other provisions of this Article take account of the fact that other property may be sold in connection with inventory. For example, the availability of the exclusion in Section 6–103(3)(l) turns on the value of all the "assets," not just the inventory. Similarly, the notice required by Section 6–105 must describe the "assets," not just the inventory. And Section 6–107(4) measures the buyer's maximum cumulative liability for noncompliance by the value of the inventory and equipment sold in the bulk sale.

In an effort to limit its coverage to sales posing the greatest risks to creditors, this Article adds an additional element to the definition of "bulk sale." A sale is not a "bulk sale" unless the buyer, auctioneer, or liquidator has notice, or after a reasonable inquiry would have had notice, that the seller will not continue to operate the same or a similar kind of business after the sale. Whether a person has "notice" depends upon what the person knows and what the person would have known had the person conducted a reasonable inquiry. The issue of whether a transaction was a bulk sale is likely to be litigated only when the seller has absconded with the sale proceeds. This Article requires that the matters as to which the buyer, auctioneer, or liquidator had notice be determined only by reference to facts that the person knew or would have known at the date of the bulk-sale agreement. Reference to what actually occurred is inappropriate.

Whether an inquiry is "reasonable" depends on the facts and circumstances of each case. These facts and circumstances may include the identities of the buyer and seller and the type of assets being sold. In some cases, a reasonable inquiry may consist of no inquiry at all concerning the seller's future.

Not every change in business operations poses a substantial enough risk to creditors to justify the costs of compliance with this Article. Thus, in determining whether post-sale business is of a kind that is "the same" or "similar" to the business conducted before the sale, a court should consider whether, viewed from the perspective of the creditors of the seller, the change poses extraordinary risks or whether the change is a normal risk that creditors can be assumed to take. In particular, when the post-bulk sale business differs from the pre-bulk sale business only in the size of the business conducted, the seller should be considered to be continuing in the same or a similar kind of business and the sale should not be considered a bulk sale.

The seller must "continue to operate" the same or a similar kind of business as owner. If the owner sells the business assets to a buyer and continues to manage the business as an employee of the buyer, the seller is not continuing to operate the business within the meaning of this Article.

(d) "Claim". New. The first sentence derives from Bankruptcy Code § 101(4), 11 U.S.C. § 101(4). Changes, including the deletion of Section 101(4)(B), were made for stylistic purposes only.

(e) "Claimant". New. This term defines the category of claim holders who are the primary beneficiaries of the duties that this Article imposes. Compare "Creditor" (subsection (1)(f)).

States that choose not to afford taxing authorities the benefits of this Article should adopt Alternative A. Adoption of Alternative B would afford the benefits of this Article to taxing authorities except with respect to those taxes as to which there has been compliance with another statute requiring that notice of the bulk sale be given to the taxing authority.

(f) "Creditor". New. The term includes all holders of claims against the seller, even holders of claims arising from consumer transactions. Compare "Claimant" (subsection (1)(e)).

(g) "Date of the bulk sale". New. The parties are able to control the date of the bulk sale in several ways. They can keep the proceeds of the sale in escrow, thereby delaying the date of payment, or they can specifically agree that the assets remain subject to the reach of the seller's creditors, thereby delaying the date that the assets are transferred. By adjusting the time that the buyer acquires an unconditional right to possess tangible assets and the time the buyer acquires an unconditional right to use intangible assets, the parties may affect the substantive rights of creditors and thereby control the date the assets are transferred.

The connection between the time of transfer and the buyer's rights under the bulk-sale agreement appears only for purposes of sales to which this Article applies. Subsection (1)(g) does not purport to affect the rights of creditors of a seller of property for other purposes or under other circumstances.

(h) "Date of the bulk-sale agreement". New. Law outside this Article, including the provisions of Article 2, determines when an agreement for a bulk sale becomes enforceable between the buyer and the seller and when an auctioneer or liquidator is engaged.

(i) "Debt". New. This subsection is borrowed from Bankruptcy Code Section 101(11).

(j) "Liquidator". New. Although the definition of "liquidator" is quite broad, the term is used with respect to sales that are "conducted" by a liquidator on behalf of the seller. See subsection (1)(c)(i). Thus only those liquidators that "conduct" sales will be affected by this Article.

(k) "Net contract price". New. Consideration is not "new consideration" to the extent that it consists of the partial or total satisfaction of an antecedent debt owed to the buyer by the seller. When the buyer buys assets along with property other than assets, the "net contract price" is that portion of the new consideration allocable to the assets.

(l) "Net proceeds". New. The term appears, without definition, in Section 6–108 (1987 Official Text).

(m) "In the ordinary course of the seller's business". New.

(n) "United States". New. This subsection derives from former Section 9–103(3)(c).

(o) "Value". New. The definition in Section 1–201(44) is not appropriate in the context of this Article.

(p) "Verified". New.

2. "Good faith". This Article adopts the definition of "good faith" in Article 1 in all cases, even when the buyer is a merchant.

Cross-References:

Point 1(a): Sections 9–102, 9–334.
Point 1(c): Sections 1–201 and 6–103.
Point 1(g): Article 2 generally.
Point 1(h): Section 2–201 and Article 2 generally.

§ 6–103. Applicability of Article.

(1) Except as otherwise provided in subsection (3), this Article applies to a bulk sale if:

(a) the seller's principal business is the sale of inventory from stock; and

(b) on the date of the bulk-sale agreement the seller is located in this state or, if the seller is located in a jurisdiction that is not a part of the United States, the seller's major executive office in the United States is in this state.

(2) A seller is deemed to be located at his [or her] place of business. If a seller has more than one place of business, the seller is deemed located at his [or her] chief executive office.

(3) This Article does not apply to:

(a) a transfer made to secure payment or performance of an obligation;

(b) a transfer of collateral to a secured party pursuant to Section 9–609;

(c) a disposition of collateral pursuant to Section 9–610;

(d) retention of collateral pursuant to Section 9–620;

(e) a sale of an asset encumbered by a security interest or lien if (i) all the proceeds of the sale are applied in partial or total satisfaction of the debt secured by the security interest or lien or (ii) the security interest or lien is enforceable against the asset after it has been sold to the buyer and the net contract price is zero;

(f) a general assignment for the benefit of creditors or to a subsequent transfer by the assignee;

(g) a sale by an executor, administrator, receiver, trustee in bankruptcy, or any public officer under judicial process;

(h) a sale made in the course of judicial or administrative proceedings for the dissolution or reorganization of an organization;

(i) a sale to a buyer whose principal place of business is in the United States and who:

  (i) not earlier than 21 days before the date of the bulk sale, (A) obtains from the seller a verified and dated list of claimants of whom the seller has notice three days before the seller sends or delivers the list to the buyer or (B) conducts a reasonable inquiry to discover the claimants;

  (ii) assumes in full the debts owed to claimants of whom the buyer has knowledge on the date the buyer receives the list of claimants from the seller or on the date the buyer completes the reasonable inquiry, as the case may be;

  (iii) is not insolvent after the assumption; and

  (iv) gives written notice of the assumption not later than 30 days after the date of the bulk sale by sending or delivering a notice to the claimants identified in subparagraph (ii) or by filing a notice in the office of the [Secretary of State];

(j) a sale to a buyer whose principal place of business is in the United States and who:

  (i) assumes in full the debts that were incurred in the seller's business before the date of the bulk sale;

  (ii) is not insolvent after the assumption; and

  (iii) gives written notice of the assumption not later than 30 days after the date of the bulk sale by sending or delivering a notice to each creditor whose debt is assumed or by filing a notice in the office of the [Secretary of State];

(k) a sale to a new organization that is organized to take over and continue the business of the seller and that has its principal place of business in the United States if:

  (i) the buyer assumes in full the debts that were incurred in the seller's business before the date of the bulk sale;

  (ii) the seller receives nothing from the sale except an interest in the new organization that is subordinate to the claims against the organization arising from the assumption; and

  (iii) the buyer gives written notice of the assumption not later than 30 days after the date of the bulk sale by sending or delivering a notice to each creditor whose debt is assumed or by filing a notice in the office of the [Secretary of State];

(l) a sale of assets having:

  (i) a value, net of liens and security interests, of less than $10,000. If a debt is secured by assets and other property of the seller, the net value of the assets is determined by subtracting from their value an amount equal to the product of the debt multiplied by a fraction, the numerator of which is the value of the assets on the date of the bulk sale and the denominator of which is the value of all property securing the debt on the date of the bulk sale; or

  (ii) a value of more than $25,000,000 on the date of the bulk-sale agreement; or

(m) a sale required by, and made pursuant to, statute.

(4) The notice under subsection (3)(i)(iv) must state: (i) that a sale that may constitute a bulk sale has been or will be made; (ii) the date or prospective date of the bulk sale; (iii) the individual, partnership, or corporate names and the addresses of the seller and buyer; (iv) the address to which inquiries about the sale may be made, if different from the seller's address; and (v) that the buyer has assumed or will assume in full the debts owed to claimants of whom the

buyer has knowledge on the date the buyer receives the list of claimants from the seller or completes a reasonable inquiry to discover the claimants.

(5) The notice under subsections (3)(j)(iii) and (3)(k)(iii) must state: (i) that a sale that may constitute a bulk sale has been or will be made; (ii) the date or prospective date of the bulk sale; (iii) the individual, partnership, or corporate names and the addresses of the seller and buyer; (iv) the address to which inquiries about the sale may be made, if different from the seller's address; and (v) that the buyer has assumed or will assume the debts that were incurred in the seller's business before the date of the bulk sale.

(6) For purposes of subsection (3)(*l*), the value of assets is presumed to be equal to the price the buyer agrees to pay for the assets. However, in a sale by auction or a sale conducted by a liquidator on the seller's behalf, the value of assets is presumed to be the amount the auctioneer or liquidator reasonably estimates the assets will bring at auction or upon liquidation.

As amended in 1999.

Official Comment

Prior Uniform Statutory Provision: Sections 6–102 and 6–103 (1987 Official Text).

Changes: New choice-of-law provision; exclusions from the Article clarified, revised, and expanded.

Purposes of Changes and New Matter:

1. Subsection (1)(a) follows Section 6–102(3) of the 1987 Official Text and makes Article 6 applicable only when the seller's principal business is the sale of inventory from stock. This Article does not apply to a sale by a seller whose principal business is the sale of goods other than inventory, e.g., a farmer, is the sale of inventory not from stock, e.g., a manufacturer who produces goods to order, or is the sale of services, e.g., a dry cleaner, barber, or operator of a hotel, tavern, or restaurant.

2. The choice-of-law rule in subsections (1)(b) and (2) derives from former Section 9–103(3) (now codified as Sections 9–301 and 9–307). Any agreement between the buyer and the seller with regard to the law governing a bulk sale does not affect the choice-of-law rule in this Article.

3. Some of the transactions excluded by subsection (3), e.g., those excluded by subsection (3)(a), may not be bulk sales. This Article nevertheless specifically

excludes them in order to allay any doubts about the Article's applicability. Certain transactions, e.g., the sale of fully encumbered inventory that remains subject to a security interest, may be excluded by more than one subsection.

4. Subsections (3)(a), (b), (c), (d), and (e) derive from subsections (1) and (3) of Section 6–103 (1987 Official Text).

5. Subsections (3)(f), (g), and (h) restate subsections (2), (4), and (5) of Section 6–103 with minor changes.

6. Subsections (3)(i), (j), and (k) relate to sales in which the buyer assumes specified debts of the seller. A bulk sale does not fall within any of these subsections unless the buyer's assumption of debts is binding and irrevocable.

Subsection (3)(j) derives from subsection (6) of Section 6–103 (1987 Official Text) and is available to buyers who are not insolvent (as defined in Section 1–201(23)), assume all the seller's business debts in full, and give notice of the assumption. Subsection (3)(k) derives from subsection (7) of Section 6–103 (1987 Official Text) and excludes transactions in which the risks to creditors are minimal. Like subsection (3)(j), this subsection applies only if the buyer assumes all the seller's business debts in full and gives notice of the assumption. In addition, the buyer must be a new organization that is organized to take over and continue the seller's business, the seller must receive nothing from the sale other than an interest in the new organization, and the seller's interest must be subordinate to the claims arising from the assumption. Sales that may qualify for the exclusion include the incorporation of a partnership or sole proprietorship.

Buyers often are reluctant to assume debts of which they have no knowledge. Subsection (3)(i), which is new, permits a qualifying buyer to exclude a sale from this Article by assuming only those debts owed to claimants of whom the buyer has knowledge after the buyer either conducts a reasonable inquiry to discover claimants or obtains a list of claimants from the seller. A buyer who takes a verified list from the seller is held to have knowledge of the claimants on the list and is entitled to rely in good faith on the list without making further inquiry. The protection afforded by the assumption of these debts, while not perfect, is sufficiently great to eliminate the need for compliance with Article 6.

7. Subsection (3)(*l*) is new. Although the bulk sale of even a very small business may be of concern to some creditors, losses to creditors from sales of assets

in which the seller's equity is less than $10,000 are not likely to justify the costs of complying with this Article. Sales of assets having a value of more than $25,000,000 have not presented serious risks to creditors. Publicity normally attends sales of that magnitude, and the sellers are unlikely to be able successfully to remove the proceeds from the reach of creditors. As used in this subsection, "price" includes all consideration for the assets, not only new consideration. Compare "Net contract price" (Section 6–102(1)(k)). If the auctioneer or liquidator does not make an estimation, then no presumption arises.

8. Subsection (3)(m) is new. This Article assumes that creditors are aware of statutes that may require their debtors to conduct bulk sales under specified circumstances, *e.g.*, upon the termination of a franchise or of a contract between a dealer and supplier, and are able to take account of any risk that those sales may impose.

Cross-References:

Point 1: Sections 9–102(a)(23), (33), (34), (44), (48).
Point 2: Sections 1–105, 9–301, and 9–307.
Point 3: Section 6–102.
Point 4: Sections 9–609, 9–610, and 9–620.
Point 6: Sections 1–201 and 1–203.
Point 7: Section 6–102.

Definitional Cross-References:

"Asset". Section 6–102.
"Auctioneer". Section 6–102.
"Bulk sale". Section 6–102.
"Buyer". Section 2–103.
"Claimant". Section 6–102.
"Collateral". Section 9–102(a)(12).
"Date of the bulk sale". Section 6–102.
"Date of the bulk-sale agreement". Section 6–102.
"Debt". Section 6–102.
"Insolvent". Section 1–201.
"Inventory". Section 9–102(a)(48).
"Knowledge". Section 1–201.
"Liquidator". Section 6–102.
"Net contract price". Section 6–102.
"Notice". Section 1–201.
"Organization". Section 1–201.
"Presumed". Section 1–201.
"Proceeds". Section 9–102(a)(64).
"Sale". Section 2–106.
"Secured party". Section 9–102(a)(72).
"Security interest". Section 1–201.
"Seller". Section 2–103.
"Send". Section 1–201.
"United States". Section 6–102.
"Value". Section 6–102.
"Verified". Section 6–102.

§ 6–104. Obligations of Buyer.

(1) In a bulk sale as defined in Section 6–102(1)(c)(ii) the buyer shall:

(a) obtain from the seller a list of all business names and addresses used by the seller within three years before the date the list is sent or delivered to the buyer;

(b) unless excused under subsection (2), obtain from the seller a verified and dated list of claimants of whom the seller has notice three days before the seller sends or delivers the list to the buyer and including, to the extent known by the seller, the address of and the amount claimed by each claimant;

(c) obtain from the seller or prepare a schedule of distribution (Section 6–106(1));

(d) give notice of the bulk sale in accordance with Section 6–105;

(e) unless excused under Section 6–106(4), distribute the net contract price in accordance with the undertakings of the buyer in the schedule of distribution; and

(f) unless excused under subsection (2), make available the list of claimants (subsection (1)(b)) by:

(i) promptly sending or delivering a copy of the list without charge to any claimant whose written request is received by the buyer no later than six months after the date of the bulk sale;

(ii) permitting any claimant to inspect and copy the list at any reasonable hour upon request received by the buyer no later than six months after the date of the bulk sale; or

(iii) filing a copy of the list in the office of the [Secretary of State] no later than the time for giving a notice of the bulk sale (Section 6–105(5)). A list filed in accordance with this subparagraph must state the individual, partnership, or corporate name and a mailing address of the seller.

(2) A buyer who gives notice in accordance with Section 6–105(2) is excused from complying

with the requirements of subsections (1)(b) and (1)(f).

Official Comment

Prior Uniform Statutory Provision: Section 6–104 (1987 Official Text).

Changes: Revised and rewritten.

Purposes of Changes and New Matter:

1. Subsection (1) sets forth the buyer's duties in a bulk sale conducted by the seller. The buyer's failure to perform these duties may result in liability under Section 6–107. An auctioneer in a bulk sale by auction and a liquidator in a bulk sale that the liquidator conducts on the seller's behalf have similar duties but may face somewhat different liability. See Section 6–108(1). The buyer's duties are designed to afford the seller's claimants the opportunity to learn of the bulk sale before the seller has removed the assets from their reach and has received payment that is easily secreted.

2. Section 6–104(3) (1987 Official Text) provides that "[r]esponsibility for the completeness and accuracy of the list of creditors rests on the transferor, and the transfer is not rendered ineffective by errors or omissions therein unless the transferee is shown to have had knowledge." This sentence has been deleted as superfluous. Nothing in this Article suggests that the buyer is responsible for the completeness or accuracy of the list of claimants. The buyer's only obligations with respect to the list are to obtain it from the seller and to make it available. A buyer who sends or delivers notice of the bulk sale in accordance with Section 6–105(1) may rely in good faith on the list supplied by the seller unless, at the time the notice is sent or delivered, the buyer has knowledge of a claimant not on the list. A buyer who knows of a claimant not on the list is obligated to send notice of the bulk sale to that claimant.

3. The buyer's only obligation with respect to the net contract price is to comply with the schedule of distribution. The schedule may provide for the buyer to pay the entire net contract price to the seller. If so, the buyer complies with the requirements of Section 6–104(1)(e) by paying the entire net contract price to the seller.

4. The purpose of the list of claimants is to enable the buyer to give claimants notice of the bulk sale. If the buyer gives notice by filing in a public office (Section 6–105(2)), then the buyer need not obtain or preserve a list of the seller's claimants.

Cross-References:

Point 1: Sections 6–107 and 6–108.
Point 2: Sections 6–105 and 1–203.
Point 3: Section 6–106.
Point 4: Section 6–105.

Definitional Cross-References:

"Buyer". Section 2–103.
"Bulk sale". Section 6–102.
"Claimant". Section 6–102.
"Date of the bulk sale". Section 6–102.
"Net contract price". Section 6–102.
"Notice". Section 1–201.
"Seller". Section 2–103.
"Verified". Section 6–102.

§ 6–105. Notice to Claimants.

(1) Except as otherwise provided in subsection (2), to comply with Section 6–104(1)(d), the buyer shall send or deliver a written notice of the bulk sale to each claimant on the list of claimants (Section 6–104(1)(b)) and to any other claimant of whom the buyer has knowledge at the time the notice of the bulk sale is sent or delivered.

(2) A buyer may comply with Section 6–104(1)(d) by filing a written notice of the bulk sale in the office of the [Secretary of State] if:

(a) on the date of the bulk-sale agreement the seller has 200 or more claimants, exclusive of claimants holding secured or matured claims for employment compensation and benefits, including commissions and vacation, severance, and sick-leave pay; or

(b) the buyer has received a verified statement from the seller stating that, as of the date of the bulk-sale agreement, the number of claimants, exclusive of claimants holding secured or matured claims for employment compensation and benefits, including commissions and vacation, severance, and sick-leave pay, is 200 or more.

(3) The written notice of the bulk sale must be accompanied by a copy of the schedule of distribution (Section 6–106(1)) and state at least:

(a) that the seller and buyer have entered into an agreement for a sale that may constitute a bulk sale under the laws of the State of _____;

(b) the date of the agreement;

(c) the date on or after which more than ten percent of the assets were or will be transferred;

(d) the date on or after which more than ten percent of the net contract price was or will be paid, if the date is not stated in the schedule of distribution;

(e) the name and a mailing address of the seller;

(f) any other business name and address listed by the seller pursuant to Section 6–104(1)(a);

(g) the name of the buyer and an address of the buyer from which information concerning the sale can be obtained;

(h) a statement indicating the type of assets or describing the assets item by item;

(i) the manner in which the buyer will make available the list of claimants (Section 6–104(1)(f)), if applicable; and

(j) if the sale is in total or partial satisfaction of an antecedent debt owed by the seller, the amount of the debt to be satisfied and the name of the person to whom it is owed.

(4) For purposes of subsections (3)(e) and (3)(g), the name of a person is the person's individual, partnership, or corporate name.

(5) The buyer shall give notice of the bulk sale not less than 45 days before the date of the bulk sale and, if the buyer gives notice in accordance with subsection (1), not more than 30 days after obtaining the list of claimants.

(6) A written notice substantially complying with the requirements of subsection (3) is effective even though it contains minor errors that are not seriously misleading.

(7) A form substantially as follows is sufficient to comply with subsection (3):

Notice of Sale

(1) _____, whose address is _____, is described in this notice as the "seller."

(2) _____, whose address is _____, is described in this notice as the "buyer."

(3) The seller has disclosed to the buyer that within the past three years the seller has used other business names, operated at other addresses, or both, as follows: _____.

(4) The seller and the buyer have entered into an agreement dated _____, for a sale that may constitute a bulk sale under the laws of the state of _____.

(5) The date on or after which more than ten percent of the assets that are the subject of the sale were or will be transferred is _____, and [if not stated in the schedule of distribution] the date on or after which more than ten percent of the net contract price was or will be paid is _____.

(6) The following assets are the subject of the sale: _____.

(7) [If applicable] The buyer will make available to claimants of the seller a list of the seller's claimants in the following manner: _____.

(8) [If applicable] The sale is to satisfy $_____ of an antecedent debt owed by the seller to _____.

(9) A copy of the schedule of distribution of the net contract price accompanies this notice.

[End of Notice]

Official Comment

Prior Uniform Statutory Provision: Sections 6–105 and 6–107 (1987 Official Text).

Changes: Revised, alternative method of giving notice added, and form of notice added.

Purposes of Changes and New Matter:

1. Subsection (1) sets forth the method by which the buyer may discharge the duty to notify the seller's claimants of the impending sale. The buyer "has knowledge" of a claimant only if the buyer has actual knowledge sufficient to enable the buyer to send a notice to the claimant. A buyer who knows only that the seller has other, unidentified claimants complies with this subsection by giving notice to the claimants on the seller's list.

2. Subsection (2) is new. It affords the buyer the opportunity to publish notice in cases in which the number of claimants—and thus the costs of compliance and risk of inadvertent noncompliance—are large. Although a filed notice will not inform every claimant of the impending sale, a filed notice is expected to inform a sufficient number of claimants (perhaps through credit reporting services) to enable them to stop an unfair or fraudulent transaction before it occurs.

The buyer may give notice by filing if the seller actually has 200 or more claimants or if the buyer receives a verified statement that the seller has 200 or more claimants. Claimants who hold secured or ma-tured claims for employment compensation and bene-fits are not counted in determining the number of claimants for this purpose; however, they are entitled to receive notice of the bulk sale.

The duty to give notice must be performed in good faith. A buyer who receives a verified statement from the seller but knows the statement to be false does not act in good faith and thus does not comply with subsec-tion (2)(b).

3. Subsection (3) prescribes the contents of the notice. The contents are the same regardless of whether notice is sent to each claimant or filed, except that the information in subsection (3)(i) is required only when notice is sent. The requirements of subsec-tion (3) are the minimum; a notice that includes additional information is effective. The requirement in subsection (3)(h) for the description of assets is modeled on former Section 9–402(1) (now codified as Sections 9–108, 9–502, and 9–504). Neither the identi-fication of assets by serial number nor an item-by-item list of assets is required.

Subsection (3)(j) applies when the sale satisfies a debt owed by the seller to the buyer or to a third party. Section 6–103(3) excludes certain sales of this kind from the application of this Article.

4. Subsection (4) requires that a notice give the proper name of the seller and the buyer. A trade name is insufficient. See Section 9–503(c). However, subsection (3)(f) requires that trade names be added when the seller has provided them to the buyer. The list need not include trade names or other names that the seller has used but not listed, even if the buyer knows of the names.

5. Subsection (5) requires that notice be given not less than 45 days before the date of the bulk sale. The period was extended from the 10 days afforded by the 1987 Official Text to provide ample time for claimants to receive or discover the notice and to take any action that the law permits to collect their claims from the seller. For example, depending upon the facts of each case and upon applicable law, claimants might seek to enjoin the sale, acquire a judicial lien on the assets or the proceeds, threaten to refuse to deal with the buyer unless the seller's debt is paid, or file an involuntary bankruptcy petition against the seller. The "date of the bulk sale" is defined in such a way as to permit the seller to transfer the assets to the buyer or the buyer to pay the price to the seller (but not both) before or during the 45 days.

6. Subsection (6) derives from former Section 9–402(8) (now codified as Section 9–506). The purpose

of filing is to give notice to claimants. Whether an error in the seller's name is seriously misleading should depend upon whether a claimant searching under the seller's correct name could have found the filing. Whether an error other than in the seller's name is seriously misleading should depend upon whether the error prejudiced the ability of claimants to assert their rights.

Cross-References:

Point 1: Sections 1–201 and 6–104.
Point 2: Sections 1–203 and 6–104.
Point 3: Sections 6–102, 6–104, 9–108, 9–502 and 9–504.
Point 4: Sections 6–104 and 9–503.
Point 5: Sections 6–102.
Point 6: Sections 6–107 and 9–506.

Definitional Cross-References:

"Asset". Section 6–102.
"Bulk sale". Section 6–102.
"Buyer". Section 2–103.
"Claim". Section 6–102.
"Claimant". Section 6–102.
"Date of the bulk sale". Section 6–102.
"Date of the bulk-sale agreement". Section 6–102.
"Debt". Section 6–102.
"Knowledge". Section 1–201.
"Net contract price". Section 6–102.
"Seller". Section 2–103.
"Send". Section 1–201.
"Verified". Section 6–102.
"Written". Section 1–201.

§ 6–106. Schedule of Distribution.

(1) The seller and buyer shall agree on how the net contract price is to be distributed and set forth their agreement in a written schedule of distribution.

(2) The schedule of distribution may provide for distribution to any person at any time, in-cluding distribution of the entire net contract price to the seller.

(3) The buyer's undertakings in the schedule of distribution run only to the seller. However, a buyer who fails to distribute the net contract price in accordance with the buyer's undertak-ings in the schedule of distribution is liable to a creditor only as provided in Section 6–107(1).

(4) If the buyer undertakes in the schedule of distribution to distribute any part of the net contract price to a person other than the seller, and, after the buyer has given notice in accor-

dance with Section 6–105, some or all of the anticipated net contract price is or becomes unavailable for distribution as a consequence of the buyer's or seller's having complied with an order of court, legal process, statute, or rule of law, the buyer is excused from any obligation arising under this Article or under any contract with the seller to distribute the net contract price in accordance with the buyer's undertakings in the schedule if the buyer:

(a) distributes the net contract price remaining available in accordance with any priorities for payment stated in the schedule of distribution and, to the extent that the price is insufficient to pay all the debts having a given priority, distributes the price pro rata among those debts shown in the schedule as having the same priority;

(b) distributes the net contract price remaining available in accordance with an order of court;

(c) commences a proceeding for interpleader in a court of competent jurisdiction and is discharged from the proceeding; or

(d) reaches a new agreement with the seller for the distribution of the net contract price remaining available, sets forth the new agreement in an amended schedule of distribution, gives notice of the amended schedule, and distributes the net contract price remaining available in accordance with the buyer's undertakings in the amended schedule.

(5) The notice under subsection (4)(d) must identify the buyer and the seller, state the filing number, if any, of the original notice, set forth the amended schedule, and be given in accordance with subsection (1) or (2) of Section 6–105, whichever is applicable, at least 14 days before the buyer distributes any part of the net contract price remaining available.

(6) If the seller undertakes in the schedule of distribution to distribute any part of the net contract price, and, after the buyer has given notice in accordance with Section 6–105, some or all of the anticipated net contract price is or becomes unavailable for distribution as a consequence of the buyer's or seller's having complied with an order of court, legal process, statute, or rule of law, the seller and any person in control

of the seller are excused from any obligation arising under this Article or under any agreement with the buyer to distribute the net contract price in accordance with the seller's undertakings in the schedule if the seller:

(a) distributes the net contract price remaining available in accordance with any priorities for payment stated in the schedule of distribution and, to the extent that the price is insufficient to pay all the debts having a given priority, distributes the price pro rata among those debts shown in the schedule as having the same priority;

(b) distributes the net contract price remaining available in accordance with an order of court;

(c) commences a proceeding for interpleader in a court of competent jurisdiction and is discharged from the proceeding; or

(d) prepares a written amended schedule of distribution of the net contract price remaining available for distribution, gives notice of the amended schedule, and distributes the net contract price remaining available in accordance with the amended schedule.

(7) The notice under subsection (6)(d) must identify the buyer and the seller, state the filing number, if any, of the original notice, set forth the amended schedule, and be given in accordance with subsection (1) or (2) of Section 6–105, whichever is applicable, at least 14 days before the seller distributes any part of the net contract price remaining available.

Official Comment

Purposes:

1. A principal purpose of bulk sales legislation has been to impair the ability of a seller to liquidate inventory and abscond with the proceeds, leaving creditors unpaid. Toward this end, a significant minority of jurisdictions adopted optional Section 6–106 (1987 Official Text), which imposes upon a transferee in bulk the duty to apply the new consideration for the transfer to the debts of the transferor pro rata. When one or more of these debts is unliquidated, disputed, or allegedly secured, making a pro rata distribution may prove quite difficult and distribution of the consideration may be delayed considerably. In addition, since preferences generally are permitted under state law, the

appropriateness of mandating a pro rata distribution is questionable. Accordingly, this Article does not require the buyer to apply the consideration to payment of the seller's debts.

This Article recognizes, however, that the seller's claimants have an interest in learning what will happen to the net contract price. If the contemplated distribution is objectionable, claimants should be able to avail themselves of whatever remedies state law or federal law allows to prevent the sale or tie up the price. On the other hand, if the price is to be distributed in a manner that is favorable to creditors, then advance knowledge of that fact will facilitate the sale by obviating any need for claimants to interfere with it.

To afford advance notice of the intended distribution of the contract price, Section 6–105(3) requires the buyer to include with the notice of the sale a copy of the "schedule of distribution"—i.e., of the agreement between the buyer and the seller on how the net contract price is to be distributed.

2. This Article does not require the net contract price to be applied in any particular fashion. Rather, the buyer and the seller may agree to whatever they wish. They must, however, disclose their agreement in ample time before the date of the bulk sale. See Section 6–105(5). The terms of the schedule of distribution in any given sale will be a function of the negotiations between buyer and seller as affected by any applicable non-Code law (e.g., corporate dissolution statutes) imposing distribution requirements in sales of the kind conducted.

In formulating the schedule, the parties may be well advised to consider the likely reaction of claimants to the schedule. For example, a schedule that contemplates the distribution of the entire net contract price to the seller or to a single creditor may prompt the filing of an involuntary bankruptcy petition. A schedule that contemplates paying the net contract price into an escrow established for the benefit of the seller's claimants may be more favorably received.

The seller may incur additional debt between the time the schedule is published and the time the net contract price is paid. The schedule may provide for payment of those debts from the net contract price.

3. Unless otherwise agreed, the buyer's only liability to creditors for failure to comply with his undertakings in the schedule of distribution is set forth in Section 6–107(1). A creditor named in the schedule may not rely on the creation or publication of the schedule as the basis for imposing liability against the buyer on any other theory, including that of estoppel or third-party beneficiary.

The seller may wish to undertake to pay some of the price to creditors. The seller may, but need not, include this undertaking in the schedule of distribution. The buyer is not responsible for performance of the seller's undertakings. Thus, if the seller makes an undertaking with respect to payment of the net contract price and fails to perform in accordance with it, the buyer faces no liability. However, certain persons in control of the seller may be liable under those circumstances. See Section 6–107(11).

4. In some cases, the precise amount of the net contract price may be unknown at the time that the schedule of distribution is formulated and notice of the bulk sale is given. In other cases, the net contract price may prove to be less than originally anticipated. Parties who fail to provide for these contingencies in the schedule of distribution and are unable to abide by the original schedule may be required to give a new notice with a new schedule.

The inability to abide by the schedule may be due to an external legal event, e.g., the suffering of a garnishment lien on the net contract price, the filing of a bankruptcy petition, or compliance with a corporate dissolution statute. If so, subsection (4), which applies to the extent that the net contract price is within the control of the buyer, may afford relief to the buyer, and subsection (6), which applies to the extent the net contract price is within the control of the seller, may afford relief to a person in control of the seller. Although this Article imposes no obligation on sellers with respect to distribution of the net contract price (or otherwise), a seller may incur an obligation of this kind by agreement with the buyer. Accordingly, subsection (6) provides the means by which the seller as well as a person in control of the seller may be excused from any such obligation.

Subsections (4)(a) and (6)(a) permit the buyer or seller respectively to distribute the net contract price remaining available in accordance with any priorities for payment. A schedule need not afford priority to particular debts. If the schedule contains no priorities, then the debts are treated as if they are all of the same priority, and the buyer or seller, as the case may be, may distribute the price pro rata in partial satisfaction of the debts set forth in the schedule. Law other than this Article determines whether a court order or a proceeding for interpleader is available for purposes of subsections (4)(b), (4)(c), (6)(b), and (6)(c).

Cross-References:

Point 1: Sections 6–104 and 6–105.
Point 2: Sections 6–105.
Point 3: Sections 1–102 and 6–107.

Definitional Cross-References:

"Buyer". Section 2–103.
"Contract". Section 1–201.
"Creditor". Section 1–201.
"Debt". Section 6–102.
"Net contract price". Section 6–102.
"Person". Section 1–201.
"Seller". Section 2–103.
"Written". Section 1–201.

§ 6–107.   Liability for Noncompliance.

(1) Except as provided in subsection (3), and subject to the limitation in subsection (4):

(a) a buyer who fails to comply with the requirements of Section 6–104(1)(e) with respect to a creditor is liable to the creditor for damages in the amount of the claim, reduced by any amount that the creditor would not have realized if the buyer had complied; and

(b) a buyer who fails to comply with the requirements of any other subsection of Section 6–104 with respect to a claimant is liable to the claimant for damages in the amount of the claim, reduced by any amount that the claimant would not have realized if the buyer had complied.

(2) In an action under subsection (1), the creditor has the burden of establishing the validity and amount of the claim, and the buyer has the burden of establishing the amount that the creditor would not have realized if the buyer had complied.

(3) A buyer who:

(a) made a good faith and commercially reasonable effort to comply with the requirements of Section 6–104(1) or to exclude the sale from the application of this Article under Section 6–103(3); or

(b) on or after the date of the bulk-sale agreement, but before the date of the bulk sale, held a good faith and commercially reasonable belief that this Article does not apply to the particular sale is not liable to creditors for failure to comply with the requirements of Section 6–104. The buyer has the burden of establishing the good faith and commercial reasonableness of the effort or belief.

(4) In a single bulk sale the cumulative liability of the buyer for failure to comply with the requirements of Section 6–104(1) may not exceed an amount equal to:

(a) if the assets consist only of inventory and equipment, twice the net contract price, less the amount of any part of the net contract price paid to or applied for the benefit of the seller or a creditor; or

(b) if the assets include property other than inventory and equipment, twice the net value of the inventory and equipment less the amount of the portion of any part of the net contract price paid to or applied for the benefit of the seller or a creditor which is allocable to the inventory and equipment.

(5) For the purposes of subsection (4)(b), the "net value" of an asset is the value of the asset less (i) the amount of any proceeds of the sale of an asset, to the extent the proceeds are applied in partial or total satisfaction of a debt secured by the asset and (ii) the amount of any debt to the extent it is secured by a security interest or lien that is enforceable against the asset before and after it has been sold to a buyer. If a debt is secured by an asset and other property of the seller, the amount of the debt secured by a security interest or lien that is enforceable against the asset is determined by multiplying the debt by a fraction, the numerator of which is the value of the asset on the date of the bulk sale and the denominator of which is the value of all property securing the debt on the date of the bulk sale. The portion of a part of the net contract price paid to or applied for the benefit of the seller or a creditor that is "allocable to the inventory and equipment" is the portion that bears the same ratio to that part of the net contract price as the net value of the inventory and equipment bears to the net value of all of the assets.

(6) A payment made by the buyer to a person to whom the buyer is, or believes he [or she] is, liable under subsection (1) reduces pro tanto the buyer's cumulative liability under subsection (4).

(7) No action may be brought under subsection (1)(b) by or on behalf of a claimant whose claim is unliquidated or contingent.

(8) A buyer's failure to comply with the requirements of Section 6–104(1) does not (i) impair the buyer's rights in or title to the assets, (ii) render the sale ineffective, void, or voidable, (iii) entitle a creditor to more than a single satisfaction of his [or her] claim, or (iv) create liability other than as provided in this Article.

(9) Payment of the buyer's liability under subsection (1) discharges pro tanto the seller's debt to the creditor.

(10) Unless otherwise agreed, a buyer has an immediate right of reimbursement from the seller for any amount paid to a creditor in partial or total satisfaction of the buyer's liability under subsection (1).

(11) If the seller is an organization, a person who is in direct or indirect control of the seller, and who knowingly, intentionally, and without legal justification fails, or causes the seller to fail, to distribute the net contract price in accordance with the schedule of distribution is liable to any creditor to whom the seller undertook to make payment under the schedule for damages caused by the failure.

Official Comment

Prior Uniform Statutory Provision: None.

Purposes:

1. This section sets forth the consequences of noncompliance with the requirements of Section 6–104. Although other legal consequences may result from a bulk sale—e.g., the buyer may be liable to the seller under Article 2 or to the seller's creditors under the Uniform Fraudulent Transfer Act—no other consequences may be imposed by reason of the buyer's failure to comply with the requirements of this Article.

The two subsections of Section 6–107(1) reflect the duties set forth in Section 6–104. The duties generally run only to claimants, but the duty to distribute the net contract price in accordance with the schedule of distribution (Section 6–104(1)(e)) may run also to certain creditors.

2. Article 6 (1987 Official Text), like many of its nonuniform predecessors, makes a noncomplying transfer ineffective against aggrieved creditors. In contrast, noncompliance with this Article neither renders the sale ineffective nor otherwise affects the buyer's rights in or title to the assets.

Liability under this Article is for breach of a statutory duty. The buyer's only liability is personal (in personam) liability. Aggrieved creditors may only recover money damages. In rem remedies, which are available upon noncompliance with Article 6 (1987 Official Text), are not available under this Article. Thus, aggrieved creditors no longer may treat the sale as if it had not occurred and use the judicial process to apply assets purchased by the buyer toward the satisfaction of their claims against the seller.

The change in the theory of liability and in the available remedy should be of particular significance if the seller enters bankruptcy after the sale is consummated. When an aggrieved creditor of the transferor has a nonbankruptcy right to avoid a transfer in whole or in part, as may be the case under Article 6 (1987 Official Text), the transferor's bankruptcy trustee may avoid the entire transfer. See Bankruptcy Code § 544(b), 11 U.S.C. § 544(b). Under this Article, a person who is aggrieved by the buyer's noncompliance may not avoid the sale. Rather, the person is entitled only to recover damages as provided in this section. Because no creditor has the right to avoid the transaction or to assert a remedy that is the functional equivalent of avoidance, the seller's bankruptcy trustee likewise should be unable to do so.

3. This Article makes explicit what is implicit in Article 6 (1987 Official Text): only those persons as to whom there has been noncompliance are entitled to a remedy. For example, if notices are sent to each claimant other than claimant A, claimant B cannot recover. Similarly, a creditor who acquires a claim after notice is given has no remedy unless the buyer undertakes in the schedule of distribution to pay that creditor and the buyer fails to meet the obligation.

4. Unlike Article 6 (1987 Official Text), which imposes strict liability upon a noncomplying transferee, this Article imposes liability for noncompliance only when the failure to comply actually has injured a creditor and only to the extent of the injury. Each creditor's damages are measured by the injury that the particular creditor sustained as a consequence of the buyer's failure to comply. This measure is stated as the amount of the debt reduced by any amount that the person would not have realized if the buyer had complied. Compare Section 4–103(5).

5. A buyer is liable only for the buyer's own noncompliance with the requirements of Section 6–104. Under that section, the only step the buyer must take to discover the identity of the seller's claimants is to

obtain a list of claimants from the seller. If the seller's list is incomplete and the buyer lacks knowledge of claimant C, then claimant C has no remedy under subsection (1)(b) of this section.

6. The creditor has the burden of establishing the validity and amount of the debt owed by the seller as well as the fact of the buyer's noncompliance. In contesting the allegation of noncompliance, the buyer may introduce evidence tending to show either that the sale was not a bulk sale or that the sale was a bulk sale to which this Article does not apply. In contesting the validity and amount of the debt, the buyer may introduce evidence tending to show that the seller had a defense to the debt. The buyer has the burden of establishing the amount that the creditor would not have realized even if the buyer had complied. Implicit in subsection (2) is that certain failures to comply with the requirements of this Article will cause no injury and thus result in no liability.

The following examples illustrate the operation of subsection (2):

Example 1: The buyer fails to give notice of the bulk sale. Claimant D, who appears on seller's list of claimants, admits to having had actual knowledge of the impending sale two months before it occurred. The buyer is likely to be able to meet the burden of establishing that even had the buyer given notice of the sale, claimant D would not have recovered any more than the claimant actually recovered.

Example 2: The buyer failed to obtain a list of seller's business names (Section 6–104(1)(a)) or to make available the list of claimants (Section 6–104(1)(f)). In many cases, the buyer may be able to meet the burden of establishing that compliance with those subsections would not have enabled claimants to recover any more than they actually recovered.

7. Subsection (3) may afford a complete defense to a noncomplying buyer. This defense is available to buyers who establish that they made a good faith effort to comply with the requirements of this Article or made a good faith effort to exclude the sale from the application of this Article (e.g., by assuming debts and attempting to comply with the notice requirements of Section 6–103(3)(i), (j), or (k)). When a buyer makes a good faith effort to comply with this Article or to exclude the transaction from its coverage, the injury caused by noncompliance is likely to be *de minimis*. In any event, the primary responsibility for satisfying claims rests with the creditors, and this Article imposes no greater duty upon buyers who attempt to comply

with this Article or to exclude a sale from its application than to make a good faith effort to do so.

The defense of subsection (3) also is available to buyers who act on the good faith belief that this Article does not apply to the sale (e.g., because the sale is not a bulk sale or is excluded under Section 6–103). The good-faith-belief defense is an acknowledgement that reasonable people may disagree over whether a given transaction is or is not a bulk sale and over whether Section 6–103 excludes a particular transaction. A buyer acting in good faith should be protected from the liability that this Article otherwise would impose on buyers who may be completely innocent of wrongdoing. A buyer who is unaware of the requirements of this Article holds no belief concerning the applicability of the Article and so may not use the defense.

8. Even a buyer who completely fails to comply with this Article may not be liable in an amount equal to sum of the seller's debts. Subsection (4) limits the aggregate recovery for "any one bulk sale," which term includes a series of sales by a liquidator. The maximum cumulative liability for noncompliance with this Article parallels the maximum recovery generally available to creditors under the 1987 Official Text of Article 6. Under that Article, the noncomplying transferee may have to "pay twice" for the goods. First, the transferee may pay the purchase price to the transferor; then, the transferee may lose the goods to aggrieved creditors.

Under this Article, the maximum cumulative liability is an amount equal to twice the net contract price of the inventory and equipment (i.e., twice the amount that would be available to unsecured creditors from the inventory and equipment), less the amount of any portion of that net contract price paid to or applied for the benefit of the seller or a creditor of the seller. Unless the buyer receives credit for amounts paid to the seller (which amounts the creditors have a right to apply to payment of their claims), the buyer might wind up paying an amount equal to the net contract price three times (once to the seller and twice to aggrieved creditors). The grant of credit for amounts paid to the seller's creditors recognizes that ordinarily the seller has no obligation to pay creditors pro rata.

When the assets sold consist of only inventory and equipment, calculation of the maximum cumulative liability is relatively simple. But when the assets sold include property in addition to inventory and equipment, the calculation becomes more difficult. When inventory or equipment secures a debt that also is secured by other collateral and the aggregate value of the collateral exceeds the secured debt, a determination of the amount in clause (ii) of subsection (5) may require an allocation of the collateral to the debt in accordance with the statutory formula. In addition, one may need to determine which portion of payments of the net contract price is allocable to inventory and equipment. Subsection (5) directs that this allocation be made by multiplying the part of the net contract price paid to or applied for the benefit of the seller or a creditor by a fraction whose nominator is the net value of the inventory and equipment and whose denominator is the net value of all the assets.

Sometimes the seller may receive the net contract price and pay some or all of it to one or more creditors. In determining whether a payment to a creditor was made from the net contract price or from another source, courts are free to employ tracing rules. Amounts paid to secured parties usually are taken into account in determining the net contract price; if so, the buyer should not receive credit for them.

9. The buyer need not wait for judgment to be entered before paying a person believed to be a creditor of the seller. Indeed, the buyer is entitled to credit for amounts paid to persons who in fact may not be creditors of the seller, as long as the buyer acts with the belief that the seller is so indebted. As is the case with respect to all obligations under the Code, the buyer's belief must be held in good faith.

10. Any amounts paid by the buyer in satisfaction of the liability created by Section 6–107(1) reduce the seller's liability to the recipient pro tanto. Consequently, the buyer is entitled to immediate reimbursement of those amounts from the seller. The right of reimbursement is available only for amounts paid to actual creditors. Amounts paid to those whom the buyer incorrectly believes to be creditors ordinarily are not recoverable from the seller, although the buyer is entitled to credit for those amounts against the aggregate liability in subsection (4). Of course, the buyer and seller may vary the seller's reimbursement obligation by agreement.

11. Because of the difficulty in valuing claims that are unliquidated or contingent, persons holding claims of that kind may not bring an action under subsection (1)(b). If the claim remains unliquidated or contingent throughout the limitation period in Section 6–110, then these creditors have no remedy for noncompliance under that subsection. They may, however, be entitled to a remedy under subsection (1)(a) of (11) for failure to distribute the net contract price in accordance with the schedule of distribution.

12. In certain circumstances, subsection (11) imposes liability on a person in direct or indirect control of a

seller that is an organization. Excuse under Section 6–106(6) is a "legal justification" that prevents liability from attaching under subsection (11). No special provision applies to the seller who fails to comply with the schedule. The seller already owes the debt to the creditor, and other law governs the consequences of a debtor who fails to pay a debt when promised.

Cross-References:

Point 1: Section 6–104.
Point 4: Section 4–103.
Point 5: Sections 6–104 and 6–105.
Point 6: Sections 1–201, 6–102, 6–103, and 6–104.
Point 7: Sections 1–102, 1–201, 6–102 and 6–103.
Point 8: Section 6–102.
Point 9: Section 1–203.
Point 10: Section 1–102.
Point 11: Sections 6–102 and 6–110.
Point 12: Section 6–106.

Definitional Cross-References:

"Assets". Section 6–102.
"Bulk sale". Section 6–102.
"Burden of establishing". Section 1–201.
"Buyer". Section 2–103.
"Claim". Section 6–102.
"Claimant". Section 6–102.
"Creditor". Section 6–102.
"Date of the bulk sale". Section 6–102.
"Equipment". Section 6–102.
"Good faith". Section 6–102.
"Inventory". Section 9–102(a)(48).
"Net contract price". Section 6–102.
"Organization". Section 1–201.
"Person". Section 1–201.
"Proceeds". Section 9–102(a)(64).
"Security interest". Section 1–201.
"Seller". Section 2–103.
"Written". Section 1–201.

§ 6–108. Bulk Sales by Auction; Bulk Sales Conducted by Liquidator.

(1) Sections 6–104, 6–105, 6–106, and 6–107 apply to a bulk sale by auction and a bulk sale conducted by a liquidator on the seller's behalf with the following modifications:

    (a) "buyer" refers to auctioneer or liquidator, as the case may be;

    (b) "net contract price" refers to net proceeds of the auction or net proceeds of the sale, as the case may be;

    (c) the written notice required under Section 6–105(3) must be accompanied by a copy of the schedule of distribution (Section 6–106(1)) and state at least:

(i) that the seller and the auctioneer or liquidator have entered into an agreement for auction or liquidation services that may constitute an agreement to make a bulk sale under the laws of the State of _____;

(ii) the date of the agreement;

(iii) the date on or after which the auction began or will begin or the date on or after which the liquidator began or will begin to sell assets on the seller's behalf;

(iv) the date on or after which more than ten percent of the net proceeds of the sale were or will be paid, if the date is not stated in the schedule of distribution;

(v) the name and a mailing address of the seller;

(vi) any other business name and address listed by the seller pursuant to Section 6–104(1)(a);

(vii) the name of the auctioneer or liquidator and an address of the auctioneer or liquidator from which information concerning the sale can be obtained;

(viii) a statement indicating the type of assets or describing the assets item by item;

(ix) the manner in which the auctioneer or liquidator will make available the list of claimants (Section 6–104(1)(f)), if applicable; and

(x) if the sale is in total or partial satisfaction of an antecedent debt owed by the seller, the amount of the debt to be satisfied and the name of the person to whom it is owed; and

(d) in a single bulk sale the cumulative liability of the auctioneer or liquidator for failure to comply with the requirements of this section may not exceed the amount of the net proceeds of the sale allocable to inventory and equipment sold less the amount of the portion of any part of the net proceeds paid to or applied for the benefit of a creditor which is allocable to the inventory and equipment.

(2) A payment made by the auctioneer or liquidator to a person to whom the auctioneer or liquidator is, or believes he [or she] is, liable under this section reduces pro tanto the auctioneer's or liquidator's cumulative liability under subsection (1)(d).

(3) A form substantially as follows is sufficient to comply with subsection (1)(c):

Notice of Sale

(1) _____, whose address is _____, is described in this notice as the "seller."

(2) _____, whose address is _____, is described in this notice as the "auctioneer" or "liquidator."

(3) The seller has disclosed to the auctioneer or liquidator that within the past three years the seller has used other business names, operated at other addresses, or both, as follows: _____.

(4) The seller and the auctioneer or liquidator have entered into an agreement dated _____ for auction or liquidation services that may constitute an agreement to make a bulk sale under the laws of the State of _____.

(5) The date on or after which the auction began or will begin or the date on or after which the liquidator began or will begin to sell assets on the seller's behalf is _____, and [if not stated in the schedule of distribution] the date on or after which more than ten percent of the net proceeds of the sale were or will be paid is _____.

(6) The following assets are the subject of the sale: _____.

(7) [If applicable] The auctioneer or liquidator will make available to claimants of the seller a list of the seller's claimants in the following manner: _____.

(8) [If applicable] The sale is to satisfy $_____ of an antecedent debt owed by the seller to _____.

(9) A copy of the schedule of distribution of the net proceeds accompanies this notice.

[End of Notice]

(4) A person who buys at a bulk sale by auction or conducted by a liquidator need not comply with the requirements of Section 6–104(1)

and is not liable for the failure of an auctioneer or liquidator to comply with the requirements of this section.

Official Comment

Prior Uniform Statutory Provision: Section 6–108.

Changes: Revised, expanded to include sales conducted by a liquidator on the seller's behalf, and form of notice added.

Purposes of Changes and New Matter:

1. This section applies only to bulk sales by auction or conducted by a liquidator on the seller's behalf, as defined in Section 6–102(1)(c). Bulk sales conducted by an auctioneer or liquidator on its own behalf are treated as ordinary bulk sales and are not subject to this section.

2. Regardless of whether the assets are sold directly from the seller to the buyer, are sold to a variety of buyers at auction, or are sold on the seller's behalf by a liquidator to one or more buyers, a going-out-of-business sale of inventory presents similar risks to claimants. Auctioneers and liquidators are likely to be in a better position to ascertain whether the sale they are conducting is, or is part of, a bulk sale than are their customers. Accordingly, buyers at auctions and from liquidators selling assets of others need not be concerned with complying with this Article. Instead, this section imposes upon auctioneers and liquidators duties and liabilities that are similar, but not always identical, to those of a buyer under Sections 6–104(1) and 6–107. Except to the extent that this section treats bulk sales by auctioneers and liquidators differently from those conducted by the seller on its own behalf, the Official Comments to Sections 6–104(1) and 6–107, as well as the Comments to Sections 6–105 and 6–106, which those sections incorporate by reference, are applicable to sales to which this section applies.

3. Subsection (1)(d) sets forth the maximum cumulative liability for auctioneers and liquidators "in any one bulk sale," which term includes a series of sales by a liquidator. This liability is to be calculated in a manner similar to that set forth in Sections 6–107(4) and 6–107(5). The term "net proceeds of the auction or sale allocable to inventory and equipment" is analogous to the term "net value of the inventory and equipment"; however, the former takes into account the reasonable expenses of the auction or sale whereas the latter does not. Also, the latter is doubled whereas the former is not. The "amount of the portion of any part of the net proceeds paid to or applied for the benefit of a creditor which is allocable to inventory and equipment" is determined by multiplying the part of the net proceeds paid to or applied for the benefit of a creditor by a fraction whose numerator is the net proceeds of the sale allocable to inventory and equipment and whose denominator is the total net proceeds of the auction or sale. Because the amount of the net proceeds allocable to inventory and equipment is not doubled, the auctioneer or liquidator is not entitled to credit for payments made to the seller.

4. Section 6–107(3) applies to all bulk sales. Accordingly, an auctioneer or liquidator who makes a good faith effort to comply with the requirements of this Article or to exclude the sale from this Article or who acts under a good faith belief that this Article does not apply to the sale faces no liability whatsoever.

Cross-References:

Point 1: Section 6–102.
Point 2: Sections 6–102, 6–104, 6–105, 6–106, and 6–107.
Point 3: Sections 6–102 and 6–107.
Point 4: Section 6–107.

Definitional Cross-References:

"Assets". Section 6–102.
"Auctioneer". Section 6–102.
"Bulk sale". Section 6–102.
"Claimants". Section 6–102.
"Creditor". Section 6–102.
"Debt". Section 6–102.
"Equipment". Section 9–102(a)(33).
"Inventory". Section 9–102(a)(48).
"Liquidator". Section 6–102.
"Net proceeds". Section 6–102.
"Person". Section 1–201.
"Seller". Section 2–103.
"Written". Section 1–201.

§ 6–109. What Constitutes Filing; Duties of Filing Officer; Information From Filing Officer.

(1) Presentation of a notice or list of claimants for filing and tender of the filing fee or acceptance of the notice or list by the filing officer constitutes filing under this Article.

(2) The filing officer shall:

(a) mark each notice or list with a file number and with the date and hour of filing;

(b) hold the notice or list or a copy for public inspection;

(c) index the notice or list according to each name given for the seller and for the buyer; and

(d) note in the index the file number and the addresses of the seller and buyer given in the notice or list.

(3) If the person filing a notice or list furnishes the filing officer with a copy, the filing officer upon request shall note upon the copy the file number and date and hour of the filing of the original and send or deliver the copy to the person.

(4) The fee for filing and indexing and for stamping a copy furnished by the person filing to show the date and place of filing is $_____ for the first page and $_____ for each additional page. The fee for indexing each name more than two is $_____.

(5) Upon request of any person, the filing officer shall issue a certificate showing whether any notice or list with respect to a particular seller or buyer is on file on the date and hour stated in the certificate. If a notice or list is on file, the certificate must give the date and hour of filing of each notice or list and the name and address of each seller, buyer, auctioneer, or liquidator. The fee for the certificate is $_____ if the request for the certificate is in the standard form prescribed by the [Secretary of State] and otherwise is $_____. Upon request of any person, the filing officer shall furnish a copy of any filed notice or list for a fee of $_____.

(6) The filing officer shall keep each notice or list for two years after it is filed.

Official Comment

Prior Uniform Statutory Provision: None.

Purposes of New Matter:

This Article contemplates public filing of bulk sale notices and lists of claimants in a single filing office in each state. This section, which derives substantially from former Sections 9–403 and 9–407 (now codified as Sections 9–515, 9–516, 9–519, 9–522, 9–523, and 9–525), governs filing. The filing system is designed to enable one seeking information about a sale to discover any filed notices or lists by searching under either the seller's or the buyer's (but not the auctioneer's or liquidator's) individual, partnership, or corporate name.

Cross-References:

Sections 6–103, 6–105, 9–403, and 9–407.

Definitional Cross-References:

"Auctioneer". Section 6–102.
"Buyer". Section 2–103.
"Liquidator". Section 6–102.
"Person". Section 1–201.
"Seller". Section 2–103.
"Send". Section 1–201.

§ 6–110. Limitation of Actions.

(1) Except as provided in subsection (2), an action under this Article against a buyer, auctioneer, or liquidator must be commenced within one year after the date of the bulk sale.

(2) If the buyer, auctioneer, or liquidator conceals the fact that the sale has occurred, the limitation is tolled and an action under this Article may be commenced within the earlier of (i) one year after the person bringing the action discovers that the sale has occurred or (ii) one year after the person bringing the action should have discovered that the sale has occurred, but no later than two years after the date of the bulk sale. Complete noncompliance with the requirements of this Article does not of itself constitute concealment.

(3) An action under Section 6–107(11) must be commenced within one year after the alleged violation occurs.

Official Comment

Prior Uniform Statutory Provision: Section 6–111 (1987 Official Text).

Changes: Statute of limitations extended and clarified.

Purposes of Changes and New Matter:

1. This Article imposes liability upon only those who do not make a good faith and commercially reasonable effort to comply with the requirements of the Article or to exclude the sale from the application of the Article and who do not hold a good faith and commercially reasonable belief that the Article is inapplicable to the sale. Consequently, it extends the six-month limitation period of the 1987 Official Text, which applies to good faith transferees as well as those not in good faith, to one year. The period commences with the date of the bulk sale.

2. Cases decided under the 1987 Official Text of Article 6 disagree over whether the complete failure to comply with the requirements of that Article constitutes a concealment that tolls the limitation. This Article adopts the view that noncompliance does not of itself constitute concealment.

3. This Article does not contemplate tolling the limitation for actions against a person in control of the seller who fails to distribute the net contract price in accordance with the schedule of distribution. Those actions must be commenced within one year after the alleged violation occurs.

Cross-References:

Point 1: Sections 1–201, 6–102, 6–107 and 6–108.
Point 3: Section 6–107.

Definitional Cross-References:

"Action". Section 1–201.
"Auctioneer". Section 6–102.
"Buyer". Section 2–103.
"Date of the bulk sale". Section 6–102.
"Liquidator". Section 6–102.]

[END OF ALTERNATIVE B]

CONFORMING AMENDMENT TO SECTION 1–105

States adopting Alternative B should amend Section 1–105(2) of the Uniform Commercial Code to read as follows:

(2) Where one of the following provisions of this Act specifies the applicable law, that provision governs and a contrary agreement is effective only to the extent permitted by the law (including the conflict of laws rules) so specified:

Rights of creditors against sold goods. Section 2–402.

Applicability of the Article on Leases. Sections 2A–105 and 2A–106.

Applicability of the Article on Bank Deposits and Collections. Section 4–102.

Bulk ~~transfers~~ sales subject to the Article on Bulk ~~Transfers~~ Sales. Section ~~6–102~~ 6–103.

Applicability of the Article on Investment Securities. Section 8–106.

Perfection provisions of the Article on Secured Transactions. Section 9–103.

CONFORMING AMENDMENT TO SECTION 2–403

States adopting Alternative B should amend Section 2–403(4) of the Uniform Commercial Code to read as follows:

(4) The rights of other purchasers of goods and of lien creditors are governed by the Articles on Secured Transactions (Article 9), Bulk ~~Transfers~~ Sales (Article 6) and Documents of Title (Article 7).

UCC ARTICLE 7

DOCUMENTS OF TITLE

Article 7 was revised in 2003.

2003 conforming amendments to other articles .... *Appendix B*
Pre–2003 Article 7 .... *Appendix I*

PART 1. GENERAL

Section
7–101. Short Title.
7–102. Definitions and Index of Definitions.
7–103. Relation of Article to Treaty or Statute.
7–104. Negotiable and Nonnegotiable Document of Title.
7–105. Reissuance in Alternative Medium.
7–106. Control of Electronic Document of Title.

PART 2. WAREHOUSE RECEIPTS: SPECIAL PROVISIONS

7–201. Person That May Issue a Warehouse Receipt; Storage Under Bond.
7–202. Form of Warehouse Receipt; Effect of Omission.
7–203. Liability for Nonreceipt or Misdescription.
7–204. Duty of Care; Contractual Limitation of Warehouse's Liability.
7–205. Title Under Warehouse Receipt Defeated in Certain Cases.
7–206. Termination of Storage at Warehouse's Option.
7–207. Goods Must Be Kept Separate; Fungible Goods.
7–208. Altered Warehouse Receipts.
7–209. Lien of Warehouse.
7–210. Enforcement of Warehouse's Lien.

PART 3. BILLS OF LADING: SPECIAL PROVISIONS

7–301. Liability for Nonreceipt or Misdescription; "Said to Contain"; "Shipper's Weight, Load, and Count"; Improper Handling.
7–302. Through Bills of Lading and Similar Documents of Title.

Section
7–303. Diversion; Reconsignment; Change of Instructions.
7–304. Tangible Bills of Lading in a Set.
7–305. Destination Bills.
7–306. Altered Bills of Lading.
7–307. Lien of Carrier.
7–308. Enforcement of Carrier's Lien.
7–309. Duty of Care; Contractual Limitation of Carrier's Liability.

PART 4. WAREHOUSE RECEIPTS AND BILLS OF LADING: GENERAL OBLIGATIONS

7–401. Irregularities in Issue of Receipt or Bill or Conduct of Issuer.
7–402. Duplicate Document of Title; Overissue.
7–403. Obligation of Bailee to Deliver; Excuse.
7–404. No Liability for Good–Faith Delivery Pursuant to Document of Title.

PART 5. WAREHOUSE RECEIPTS AND BILLS OF LADING: NEGOTIATION AND TRANSFER

7–501. Form of Negotiation and Requirements of Due Negotiation.
7–502. Rights Acquired by Due Negotiation.
7–503. Document of Title to Goods Defeated in Certain Cases.
7–504. Rights Acquired in Absence of Due Negotiation; Effect of Diversion; Stoppage of Delivery.
7–505. Indorser Not Guarantor for Other Parties.
7–506. Delivery Without Indorsement: Right to Compel Indorsement.
7–507. Warranties on Negotiation or Delivery of Document of Title.
7–508. Warranties of Collecting Bank as to Documents of Title.

7–509. Adequate Compliance with Commercial Contract.

PART 6. WAREHOUSE RECEIPTS AND BILLS OF LADING: MISCELLANEOUS PROVISIONS

7–601. Lost, Stolen, or Destroyed Documents of Title.

7–602. Judicial Process Against Goods Covered by Negotiable Document of Title.
7–603. Conflicting Claims; Interpleader.

PART 7. MISCELLANEOUS PROVISIONS

7–701. Effective Date.
7–702. Repeals.
7–703. Applicability.
7–704. Savings Clause.

DRAFTING COMMITTEE TO REVISE UNIFORM COMMERCIAL CODE ARTICLE 7, DOCUMENTS OF TITLE

The Committee acting for the National Conference of Commissioners on Uniform State Laws and the American Law Institute in preparing the Revised Uniform Commercial Code Article 7 is as follows:

HENRY DEEB GABRIEL, JR., Loyola University, School of Law, 526 Pine St., New Orleans, LA 70118, *Chair*

EDWARD V. CATTELL, JR., Suite 2000, 1628 John F. Kennedy Blvd., Philadelphia, PA 19103, *The American Law Institute Representative*

PATRICIA BRUMFIELD FRY, University of Missouri–Columbia, School of Law, Missouri Ave. & Conley Ave., Columbia, MO 65211

SANDRA S. STERN, 909 Third Ave., 5th Floor, New York, New York 10022

NEAL OSSEN, 21 Oak St., Suite 201, Hartford, CT 06106, *Enactment Plan Coordinator*

DREW KERSHEN, University of Oklahoma, College of Law, 300 Timberdell Road, Norman, OK 73019, *Co-Reporter*

LINDA J. RUSCH, Hamline University, School of Law, 1536 Hewitt Ave., St. Paul, MN 55104, *The American Law Institute Representative and Co-Reporter*

EX OFFICIO

K. KING BURNETT, P.O. Box 910, Salisbury, MD 21803–0910, *President*

JOSEPH P. MAZUREK, Box 797, Helena, MT 59624, *Division Chair*

AMERICAN BAR ASSOCIATION ADVISOR

WILLIAM H. TOWLE, P.O. Box 3267, Missoula, MT 59806–3267, *American Bar Association Advisor*

EXECUTIVE DIRECTOR

WILLIAM H. HENNING, University of Alabama, School of Law, Box 870382, Tuscaloosa, AL 35487–0382, *Executive Director*

WILLIAM J. PIERCE, 1505 Roxbury Road, Ann Arbor, MI 48104, *Executive Director Emeritus*

PREFATORY NOTE

Article 7 is the last of the articles of the Uniform Commercial Code to be revised. The genesis of this project is twofold: to provide a framework for the further development of electronic documents of title and to update the article for modern times in light of state, federal and international developments. Each section has been reviewed to determine its suitability given modern practice, the need for medium and gender neutrality, and modern statutory drafting.

To provide for electronic documents of title, several definitions in Article 1 were revised including "bearer," "bill of lading," "delivery," "document of title," "holder," and "warehouse receipt." The concept of an electronic document of title allows for commercial practice to determine whether records issued by bailees are "in the regular course of business or financing" and are "treated as adequately evidencing that the person in possession or control of the record is entitled to receive, control, hold, and dispose of the record and the goods the record covers." Rev. Section 1–201(b)(16). Such records in electronic form are electronic documents of title and in tangible form are tangible documents of title. Conforming amendments to other Articles of the UCC are also necessary to fully integrate electronic documents of title into the UCC. Conform-

521

ing amendments to other Articles of the UCC are contained in Appendix I.

Key to the integration of the electronic document of title scheme is the concept of "control" defined in Section 7–106. This definition is adapted from the Uniform Electronic Transactions Act § 16 on Transferrable Records and from Uniform Commercial Code § 9–105 concerning control of electronic chattel paper. Control of an electronic document of title is the conceptual equivalent to possession and indorsement of a tangible document of title. Of equal importance is the acknowledgment that parties may desire to substitute an electronic document of title for an already-issued paper document and vice versa. Section 7–105 sets forth the minimum requirements that need to be fulfilled in order to give effect to the substitute document issued in the alternate medium. To the extent possible, the rules for electronic documents of title are the same or as similar as possible to the rules for tangible documents of title. If a rule is meant to be limited to one medium or the other, that is clearly stated. Rules that reference documents of title, warehouse receipts, or bills of lading without a designation to "electronic" or "tangible" apply to documents of title in either medium. As with tangible negotiable documents of title, electronic negotiable documents of title may be negotiated and duly negotiated. Section 7–501.

Other changes that have been made are:

1. New definitions of "carrier," "good faith," "record", "sign" and "shipper" in Section 7–102.

2. Deletion of references to tariffs or filed classifications given the deregulation of the affected industries. See e.g. section 7–103 and 7–309,

3. Clarifying the rules regarding when a document is nonnegotiable. Section 7–104.

4. Making clear when rules apply just to warehouse receipts or bills of lading, thus eliminating the need for former section 7–105.

5. Clarifying that particular terms need not be included in order to have a valid warehouse receipt. Section 7–202.

6. Broadening the ability of the warehouse to make an effective limitation of liability in its warehouse receipt or storage agreement in accord with commercial practice. Section 7–204.

7. Allowing a warehouse to have a lien on goods covered by a storage agreement and clarifying the priority rules regarding the claim of a warehouse lien as against other interests. Section 7–209.

8. Conforming language usage to modern shipping practice. Sections 7–301 and 7–302.

9. Clarifying the extent of the carrier's lien. Section 7–307.

10. Adding references to Article 2A when appropriate. See e.g. Sections 7–503, 7–504, 7–509.

11. Clarifying that the warranty made by negotiation or delivery of a document of title should apply only in the case of a voluntary transfer of possession or control of the document. Section 7–507.

12. Providing greater flexibility to a court regarding adequate protection against loss when ordering delivery of the goods or issuance of a substitute document. Section 7–601.

13. Providing conforming amendments to the other Articles of the Uniform Commercial Code to accommodate electronic documents of title.

Legislative Note: All cross-references in this draft to Article 1 are to Revised Article 1 (2001). In the event a state has not enacted Revised Article 1, the cross-references should be changed to refer to the relevant sections in former Article 1.

PART 1

GENERAL

§ 7–101. Short Title.

This article may be cited as Uniform Commercial Code–Documents of Title.

Official Comment

Prior Uniform Statutory Provision: Former Section 7–101.

Changes: Revised for style only.

This Article is a revision of the 1962 Official Text with Comments as amended since 1962. The 1962 Official Text was a consolidation and revision of the Uniform Warehouse Receipts Act and the Uniform Bills of Lading Act, and embraced the provisions of the Uniform Sales Act relating to negotiation of documents of title.

This Article does not contain the substantive criminal provisions found in the Uniform Warehouse Receipts and Bills of Lading Acts. These criminal provisions are inappropriate to a Commercial Code, and for the most part duplicate portions of the ordinary criminal law relating to frauds. This revision deletes the former Section 7–105 that provided that courts could apply a rule from Parts 2 and 3 by analogy to a situation not explicitly covered in the provisions on warehouse receipts or bills of lading when it was appropriate. This is, of course, an unexceptional proposition and need not be stated explicitly in the statute. Thus former Section 7–105 has been deleted. Whether applying a rule by analogy to a situation is appropriate depends upon the facts of each case.

The Article does not attempt to define the tort liability of bailees, except to hold certain classes of bailees to a minimum standard of reasonable care. For important classes of bailees, liabilities in case of loss, damages or destruction, as well as other legal questions associated with particular documents of title, are governed by federal statutes, international treaties, and in some cases regulatory state laws, which supersede the provisions of this Article in case of inconsistency. See Section 7–103.

§ 7–102. Definitions and Index of Definitions.

(a) In this article, unless the context otherwise requires:

(1) "Bailee" means a person that by a warehouse receipt, bill of lading, or other document of title acknowledges possession of goods and contracts to deliver them.

(2) "Carrier" means a person that issues a bill of lading.

(3) "Consignee" means a person named in a bill of lading to which or to whose order the bill promises delivery.

(4) "Consignor" means a person named in a bill of lading as the person from which the goods have been received for shipment.

(5) "Delivery order" means a record that contains an order to deliver goods directed to a warehouse, carrier, or other person that in the ordinary course of business issues warehouse receipts or bills of lading.

(6) "Good faith" means honesty in fact and the observance of reasonable commercial standards of fair dealing.

(7) "Goods" means all things that are treated as movable for the purposes of a contract for storage or transportation.

(8) "Issuer" means a bailee that issues a document of title or, in the case of an unaccepted delivery order, the person that orders the possessor of goods to deliver. The term includes a person for which an agent or employee purports to act in issuing a document if the agent or employee has real or apparent authority to issue documents, even if the issuer did not receive any goods, the goods were misdescribed, or in any other respect the agent or employee violated the issuer's instructions.

(9) "Person entitled under the document" means the holder, in the case of a negotiable document of title, or the person to which delivery of the goods is to be made by the terms of, or pursuant to instructions in a record under, a nonnegotiable document of title.

(10) "Record" means information that is inscribed on a tangible medium or that is stored in an electronic or other medium and is retrievable in perceivable form.

(11) "Sign" means, with present intent to authenticate or adopt a record:

(A) to execute or adopt a tangible symbol; or

(B) to attach to or logically associate with the record an electronic sound, symbol, or process.

(12) "Shipper" means a person that enters into a contract of transportation with a carrier.

(13) "Warehouse" means a person engaged in the business of storing goods for hire.

(b) Definitions in other articles applying to this article and the sections in which they appear are:

(1) "Contract for sale", Section 2–106.

(2) "Lessee in ordinary course", Section 2A–103.

(3) "Receipt" of goods, Section 2–103.

(c) In addition, Article 1 contains general definitions and principles of construction and interpretation applicable throughout this article.

Legislative Note: If the state has enacted Revised Article 1, the definitions of "good faith" in subsection (a)(6) and "record" in (a)(10) need not be enacted in this section as they are contained in Article 1, Section 1–201. These subsections should be marked as "reserved" in order to provide for uniform numbering of subsections.

Official Comment

Prior Uniform Statutory Provision: Former Section 7–102.

Changes: New definitions of "carrier," "good faith," "record," "sign," and "shipper." Other definitions revised to accommodate electronic mediums.

Purposes:

1. "Bailee" is used in this Article as a blanket term to designate carriers, warehousemen and others who normally issue documents of title on the basis of goods which they have received. The definition does not, however, require actual possession of the goods. If a bailee acknowledges possession when it does not have possession, the bailee is bound by sections of this Article which declare the "bailee's" obligations. (See definition of "Issuer" in this section and Sections 7–203 and 7–301 on liability in case of non-receipt.) A "carrier" is one type of bailee and is defined as a person that issues a bill of lading. A "shipper" is a person who enters into the contract of transportation with the carrier. The definitions of "bailee," "consignee," "consignor," "goods", and "issuer", are unchanged in substance from prior law. "Document of title" is defined in Article 1, and may be in either tangible or electronic form.

2. The definition of warehouse receipt contained in the general definitions section of this Act (Section 1–201) does not require that the issuing warehouse be "lawfully engaged" in business or for profit. The warehouse's compliance with applicable state regulations such as the filing of a bond has no bearing on the substantive issues dealt with in this Article. Certainly the issuer's violations of law should not diminish its responsibility on documents the issuer has put in commercial circulation. But it is still essential that the business be storing goods "for hire" (Section 1–201

and this section). A person does not become a warehouse by storing its own goods.

3. When a delivery order has been accepted by the bailee it is for practical purposes indistinguishable from a warehouse receipt. Prior to such acceptance there is no basis for imposing obligations on the bailee other than the ordinary obligation of contract which the bailee may have assumed to the depositor of the goods. Delivery orders may be either electronic or tangible documents of title. See definition of "document of title" in Section 1–201.

4. The obligation of good faith imposed by this Article and by Article 1, Section 1–304 includes the observance of reasonable commercial standards of fair dealing.

5. The definitions of "record" and "sign" are included to facilitate electronic mediums. See comment 9 to Section 9–102 discussing "record" and the comment to amended Section 2–103 discussing "sign."

6. "Person entitled under the document" is moved from former Section 7–403.

7. These definitions apply in this Article unless the context otherwise requires. The "context" is intended to refer to the context in which the defined term is used in the Uniform Commercial Code. The definition applies whenever the defined term is used unless the context in which the defined term is used in the statute indicates that the term was not used in its defined sense. See comment to Section 1–201.

Cross References:

Point 1: Sections 1–201, 7–203 and 7–301.
Point 2: Sections 1–201 and 7–203.
Point 3: Section 1–201.
Point 4: Section 1–304.
Point 5: Section 9–102 and 2–103.
See general comment to document of title in Section 1–201.

Definitional Cross References:

"Bill of lading". Section 1–201.
"Contract". Section 1–201.
"Contract for sale". Section 2–106.
"Delivery". Section 1–201.
"Document of title". Section 1–201.
"Person". Section 1–201.
"Purchase". Section 1–201.
"Receipt of goods". Section 2–103.
"Right". Section 1–201.
"Warehouse receipt". Section 1–201.

§ 7–103. Relation of Article to Treaty or Statute.

(a) This article is subject to any treaty or statute of the United States or regulatory statute of this state to the extent the treaty, statute, or regulatory statute is applicable.

(b) This article does not modify or repeal any law prescribing the form or content of a document of title or the services or facilities to be afforded by a bailee, or otherwise regulating a bailee's business in respects not specifically treated in this article. However, violation of such a law does not affect the status of a document of title that otherwise is within the definition of a document of title.

(c) This [act] modifies, limits, and supersedes the federal Electronic Signatures in Global and National Commerce Act (15 U.S.C. Section 7001, et. seq.) but does not modify, limit, or supersede Section 101(c) of that act (15 U.S.C. Section 7001(c)) or authorize electronic delivery of any of the notices described in Section 103(b) of that act (15 U.S.C. Section 7003(b)).

(d) To the extent there is a conflict between [the Uniform Electronic Transactions Act] and this article, this article governs.

Legislative Note: In states that have not enacted the Uniform Electronic Transactions Act in some form, states should consider their own state laws to determine whether there is a conflict between the provisions of this article and those laws particularly as those other laws may affect electronic documents of title.

Official Comment

Prior Uniform Statutory Provision: Former Sections 7–103 and 10–104.

Changes: Deletion of references to tariffs and classifications; incorporation of former Section 10–104 into subsection (b), provide for intersection with federal and state law governing electronic transactions.

Purposes:

1. To make clear what would of course be true without the Section, that applicable Federal law is paramount.

2. To make clear also that regulatory state statutes (such as those fixing or authorizing a commission to fix rates and prescribe services, authorizing different charges for goods of different values, and limiting liability for loss to the declared value on which the charge was based) are not affected by the Article and are controlling on the matters which they cover unless preempted by federal law. The reference in former Section 7–103 to tariffs, classifications, and regulations filed or issued pursuant to regulatory state statutes has been deleted as inappropriate in the modern era of diminished regulation of carriers and warehouses. If a regulatory scheme requires a carrier or warehouse to issue a tariff or classification, that tariff or classification would be given effect via the state regulatory scheme that this Article recognizes as controlling. Permissive tariffs or classifications would not displace the provisions of this act, pursuant to this section, but may be given effect through the ability of parties to incorporate those terms by reference into their agreement.

3. The document of title provisions of this act supplement the federal law and regulatory state law governing bailees. This Article focuses on the commercial importance and usage of documents of title. State ex. rel Public Service Commission v. Gunkelman & Sons, Inc., 219 N.W.2d 853 (N.D. 1974).

4. Subsection (c) is included to make clear the interrelationship between the federal Electronic Signatures in Global and National Commerce Act and this article and the conforming amendments to other articles of the Uniform Commercial Code promulgated as part of the revision of this article. Section 102 of the federal act allows a State statute to modify, limit, or supersede the provisions of Section 101 of the federal act. See the comments to Revised Article 1, Section 1–108.

5. Subsection (d) makes clear that once this article is in effect, its provisions regarding electronic commerce and regarding electronic documents of title control in the event there is a conflict with the provisions of the Uniform Electronic Transactions Act or other applicable state law governing electronic transactions.

Cross References:

Sections 1–108, 7–201, 7–202, 7–204, 7–206, 7–309, 7–401, 7–403.

Definitional Cross Reference:

"Bill of lading". Section 1–201.

§ 7–104. Negotiable and Nonnegotiable Document of Title.

(a) Except as otherwise provided in subsection (c), a document of title is negotiable if by its terms the goods are to be delivered to bearer or to the order of a named person.

(b) A document of title other than one described in subsection (a) is nonnegotiable. A bill of lading that states that the goods are consigned to a named person is not made negotiable by a provision that the goods are to be delivered only against an order in a record signed by the same or another named person.

(c) A document of title is nonnegotiable if, at the time it is issued, the document has a conspicuous legend, however expressed, that it is nonnegotiable.

Official Comment

Prior Uniform Statutory Provision: Former Section 7–104.

Changes: Subsection (a) is revised to reflect modern style and trade practice. Subsection (b) is revised for style and medium neutrality. Subsection (c) is new.

Purposes:

1. This Article deals with a class of commercial paper representing commodities in storage or transportation. This "commodity paper" is to be distinguished from what might be called "money paper" dealt with in the Article of this Act on Commercial Paper (Article 3) and "investment paper" dealt with in the Article of this Act on Investment Securities (Article 8). The class of "commodity paper" is designated "document of title" following the terminology of the Uniform Sales Act Section 76. Section 1–201. The distinctions between negotiable and nonnegotiable documents in this section makes the most important subclassification employed in the Article, in that the holder of negotiable documents may acquire more rights than its transferor had (See Section 7–502). The former Section 7–104, which provided that a document of title was negotiable if it runs to a named person or assigns if such designation was recognized in overseas trade, has been deleted as not necessary in light of current commercial practice.

A document of title is negotiable only if it satisfies this section. "Deliverable on proper indorsement and surrender of this receipt" will not render a document negotiable. Bailees often include such provisions as a means of insuring return of nonnegotiable receipts for record purposes. Such language may be regarded as insistence by the bailee upon a particular kind of receipt in connection with delivery of the goods. Subsection (a) makes it clear that a document is not negotiable which provides for delivery to order or bearer only if written instructions to that effect are given by a named person. Either tangible or electronic docu-ments of title may be negotiable if the document meets the requirement of this section.

2. Subsection (c) is derived from Section 3–104(d). Prior to issuance of the document of title, an issuer may stamp or otherwise provide by a notation on the document that it is nonnegotiable even if the document would otherwise comply with the requirement of subsection (a). Once issued as a negotiable document of title, the document cannot be changed from a negotiable document to a nonnegotiable document. A document of title that is nonnegotiable cannot be made negotiable by stamping or providing a notation that the document is negotiable. The only way to make a document of title negotiable is to comply with subsection (a). A negotiable document of title may fail to be duly negotiated if the negotiation does not comply with the requirements for "due negotiation" stated in Section 7–501.

Cross Reference:

Sections 7–501 and 7–502.

Definitional Cross References:

"Bearer". Section 1–201.
"Bill of lading". Section 1–201.
"Delivery". Section 1–201.
"Document of title". Section 1–201.
"Person". Section 1–201.
"Sign". Section 7–102
"Warehouse receipt". Section 1–201.

§ 7–105. Reissuance in Alternative Medium.

(a) Upon request of a person entitled under an electronic document of title, the issuer of the electronic document may issue a tangible document of title as a substitute for the electronic document if:

(1) the person entitled under the electronic document surrenders control of the document to the issuer; and

(2) the tangible document when issued contains a statement that it is issued in substitution for the electronic document.

(b) Upon issuance of a tangible document of title in substitution for an electronic document of title in accordance with subsection (a):

(1) the electronic document ceases to have any effect or validity; and

(2) the person that procured issuance of the tangible document warrants to all subse-

quent persons entitled under the tangible document that the warrantor was a person entitled under the electronic document when the warrantor surrendered control of the electronic document to the issuer.

(c) Upon request of a person entitled under a tangible document of title, the issuer of the tangible document may issue an electronic document of title as a substitute for the tangible document if:

(1) the person entitled under the tangible document surrenders possession of the document to the issuer; and

(2) the electronic document when issued contains a statement that it is issued in substitution for the tangible document.

(d) Upon issuance of an electronic document of title in substitution for a tangible document of title in accordance with subsection (c):

(1) the tangible document ceases to have any effect or validity; and

(2) the person that procured issuance of the electronic document warrants to all subsequent persons entitled under the electronic document that the warrantor was a person entitled under the tangible document when the warrantor surrendered possession of the tangible document to the issuer.

Official Comment

Prior Uniform Statutory Provisions: None.

Other relevant law: UNCITRAL Draft Instrument on the Carriage of Goods by Sea Transport Law.

Purpose:

1. This section allows for documents of title issued in one medium to be reissued in another medium. This section applies to both negotiable and nonnegotiable documents. This section sets forth minimum requirements for giving the reissued document effect and validity. The issuer is not required to issue a document in an alternative medium and if the issuer chooses to do so, it may impose additional requirements. Because a document of title imposes obligations on the issuer of the document, it is imperative for the issuer to be the one who issues the substitute document in order for the substitute document to be effective and valid.

2. The request must be made to the issuer by the person entitled to enforce the document of title (Section 7–102(a)(9)) and that person must surrender pos-

session or control of the original document to the issuer. The reissued document must have a notation that it has been issued as a substitute for the original document. These minimum requirements must be met in order to give the substitute document effect and validity. If these minimum requirements are not met for issuance of a substitute document of title, the original document of title continues to be effective and valid. Section 7–402. However, if the minimum requirements imposed by this section are met, in addition to any other requirements that the issuer may impose, the substitute document will be the document that is effective and valid.

3. To protect parties who subsequently take the substitute document of title, the person who procured issuance of the substitute document warrants that it was a person entitled under the original document at the time it surrendered possession or control of the original document to the issuer. This warranty is modeled after the warranty found in Section 4–209.

Cross Reference:

Sections 7–106, 7–402 and 7–601.

Definitional Cross Reference:

"Person entitled to enforce," Section 7–102.

§ 7–106. Control of Electronic Document of Title.

(a) A person has control of an electronic document of title if a system employed for evidencing the transfer of interests in the electronic document reliably establishes that person as the person to which the electronic document was issued or transferred.

(b) A system satisfies subsection (a), and a person is deemed to have control of an electronic document of title, if the document is created, stored, and assigned in such a manner that:

(1) a single authoritative copy of the document exists which is unique, identifiable, and, except as otherwise provided in paragraphs (4), (5), and (6), unalterable;

(2) the authoritative copy identifies the person asserting control as:

(A) the person to which the document was issued; or

(B) if the authoritative copy indicates that the document has been transferred, the person to which the document was most recently transferred;

(3) the authoritative copy is communicated to and maintained by the person asserting control or its designated custodian;

(4) copies or amendments that add or change an identified assignee of the authoritative copy can be made only with the consent of the person asserting control;

(5) each copy of the authoritative copy and any copy of a copy is readily identifiable as a copy that is not the authoritative copy; and

(6) any amendment of the authoritative copy is readily identifiable as authorized or unauthorized.

Official Comment

Prior Uniform Statutory Provision: Uniform Electronic Transactions Act Section 16.

Purpose:

1. The section defines "control" for electronic documents of title and derives its rules from the Uniform Electronic Transactions Act § 16 on transferrable records. Unlike UETA § 16, however, a document of title may be reissued in an alternative medium pursuant to Section 7–105. At any point in time in which a document of title is in electronic form, the control concept of this section is relevant. As under UETA § 16, the control concept embodied in this section provides the legal framework for developing systems for electronic documents of title.

2. Control of an electronic document of title substitutes for the concept of indorsement and possession in the tangible document of title context. See Section 7–501. A person with a tangible document of title delivers the document by voluntarily transferring possession and a person with an electronic document of title delivers the document by voluntarily transferring control. (Delivery is defined in Section 1–201).

3. Subsection (a) sets forth the general rule that the "system employed for evidencing the transfer of interests in the electronic document reliably establishes that person as the person to which the electronic document was issued or transferred." The key to having a system that satisfies this test is that identity of *the* person to which the document was issued or transferred must be reliably established. Of great importance to the functioning of the control concept is to be able to demonstrate, at any point in time, *the person* entitled under the electronic document. For example, a carrier may issue an electronic bill of lading by having the required information in a database that is encrypted and accessible by virtue of a password. If the computer system in which the required information is maintained identifies the person as *the* person to which the electronic bill of lading was issued or transferred, that person has control of the electronic document of title. That identification may be by virtue of passwords or other encryption methods. Registry systems may satisfy this test. For example, see the electronic warehouse receipt system established pursuant to 7 C.F.R. Part 735. This Article leaves to the market place the development of sufficient technologies and business practices that will meet the test.

An electronic document of title is evidenced by a record consisting of information stored in an electronic medium. Section 1–201. For example, a record in a computer database could be an electronic document of title assuming that it otherwise meets the definition of document of title. To the extent that third parties wish to deal in paper mediums, Section 7–105 provides a mechanism for exiting the electronic environment by having the issuer reissue the document of title in a tangible medium. Thus if a person entitled to enforce an electronic document of title causes the information in the record to be printed onto paper without the issuer's involvement in issuing the document of title pursuant to Section 7–105, that paper is not a document of title.

4. Subsection (a) sets forth the general test for control. Subsection (b) sets forth a safe harbor test that if satisfied, results in control under the general test in subsection (a). The test in subsection (b) is also used in Section 9–105 although Section 9–105 does not include the general test of subsection (a). Under subsection (b), at any point in time, a party should be able to identify the single authoritative copy which is unique and identifiable as the authoritative copy. This does not mean that once created that the authoritative copy need be static and never moved or copied from its original location. To the extent that backup systems exist which result in multiple copies, the key to this idea is that at any point in time, the one authoritative copy needs to be unique and identifiable.

Parties may not by contract provide that control exists. The test for control is a factual test that depends upon whether the general test in subsection (a) or the safe harbor in subsection (b) is satisfied.

5. Article 7 has historically provided for rights under documents of title and rights of transferees of documents of title as those rights relate to the goods covered by the document. Third parties may possess or have control of documents of title. While misfeasance or negligence in failure to transfer or misdelivery of the document by those third parties may create serious

issues, this Article has never dealt with those issues as it relates to tangible documents of title, preferring to leave those issues to the law of contracts, agency and tort law. In the electronic document of title regime, third party registry systems are just beginning to develop. It is very difficult to write rules regulating those third parties without some definitive sense of how the third party registry systems will be structured. Systems that are evolving to date tend to be "closed" systems in which all participants must sign on to the master agreement which provides for rights as against the registry system as well as rights among the members. In those closed systems, the document of title never leaves the system so the parties rely upon the master agreement as to rights against the registry for its failures in dealing with the document. This article contemplates that those "closed" systems will continue to evolve and that the control mechanism in this statute provides a method for the participants in the closed system to achieve the benefits of obtaining control allowed by this article.

This article also contemplates that parties will evolve open systems where parties need not be subject to a master agreement. In an open system a party that is expecting to obtain rights through an electronic document may not be a party to the master agreement. To the extent that open systems evolve by use of the control concept contained in this section, the law of contracts, agency, and torts as it applies to the registry's misfeasance or negligence concerning the transfer of control of the electronic document will allocate the risks and liabilities of the parties as that other law now does so for third parties who hold tangible documents and fail to deliver the documents.

Cross Reference:

Sections 7–105 and 7–501.

Definitional Cross–References:

"Delivery", 1–201.
"Document of title", 1–201.

PART 2

WAREHOUSE RECEIPTS: SPECIAL PROVISIONS

§ 7–201. Person That May Issue a Warehouse Receipt; Storage Under Bond.

(a) A warehouse receipt may be issued by any warehouse.

(b) If goods, including distilled spirits and agricultural commodities, are stored under a statute requiring a bond against withdrawal or a license for the issuance of receipts in the nature of warehouse receipts, a receipt issued for the goods is deemed to be a warehouse receipt even if issued by a person that is the owner of the goods and is not a warehouse.

Official Comment

Prior Uniform Statutory Provision: Former Section 7–201.

Changes: Update for style only.

Purposes:

It is not intended by re-enactment of subsection (a) to repeal any provisions of special licensing or other statutes regulating who may become a warehouse. Limitations on the transfer of the receipts and criminal sanctions for violation of such limitations are not impaired. Section 7–103. Compare Section 7–401(4) on the liability of the issuer in such cases. Subsection (b) covers receipts issued by the owner for whiskey or

other goods stored in bonded warehouses under such statutes as 26 U.S.C. Chapter 51.

Cross References:

Sections 7–103, 7–401.

Definitional Cross References:

"Warehouse receipt". Section 1–201.
"Warehouse". Section 7–102.

§ 7–202. Form of Warehouse Receipt; Effect of Omission.

(a) A warehouse receipt need not be in any particular form.

(b) Unless a warehouse receipt provides for each of the following, the warehouse is liable for damages caused to a person injured by its omission:

(1) a statement of the location of the warehouse facility where the goods are stored;

(2) the date of issue of the receipt;

(3) the unique identification code of the receipt;

(4) a statement whether the goods received will be delivered to the bearer, to a named person, or to a named person or its order;

(5) the rate of storage and handling charges, unless goods are stored under a field warehousing arrangement, in which case a statement of that fact is sufficient on a nonnegotiable receipt;

(6) a description of the goods or the packages containing them;

(7) the signature of the warehouse or its agent;

(8) if the receipt is issued for goods that the warehouse owns, either solely, jointly, or in common with others, a statement of the fact of that ownership; and

(9) a statement of the amount of advances made and of liabilities incurred for which the warehouse claims a lien or security interest, unless the precise amount of advances made or liabilities incurred, at the time of the issue of the receipt, is unknown to the warehouse or to its agent that issued the receipt, in which case a statement of the fact that advances have been made or liabilities incurred and the purpose of the advances or liabilities is sufficient.

(c) A warehouse may insert in its receipt any terms that are not contrary to [the Uniform Commercial Code] and do not impair its obligation of delivery under Section 7–403 or its duty of care under Section 7–204. Any contrary provision is ineffective.

Official Comment

Prior Uniform Statutory Provision: Former Section 7–202.

Changes: Language is updated to accommodate electronic commerce and to reflect modern style.

Purposes:

1. This section does not displace any particular legislation that requires other terms in a warehouse receipt or that may require a particular form of a warehouse receipt. This section does not require that a warehouse receipt be issued. A warehouse receipt that is issued need not contain any of the terms listed in subsection (b) in order to qualify as a warehouse receipt as long as the receipt falls within the definition of "warehouse receipt" in Article 1. Thus the title has been changed to eliminate the phrase "essential terms" as provided in prior law. The only consequence of a warehouse receipt not containing any term listed

in subsection (b) is that a person injured by a term's omission has a right as against the warehouse for harm caused by the omission. Cases, such as In re Celotex Corp., 134 B. R. 993 (Bankr. M.D. Fla. 1991), that held that in order to have a valid warehouse receipt all of the terms listed in this section must be contained in the receipt, are disapproved.

2. The unique identification code referred to in subsection (b)(3) can include any combination of letters, number, signs, and/or symbols that provide a unique identification. Whether an electronic or tangible warehouse receipt contains a signature will be resolved with the definition of sign in Section 7–102.

Cross References:

Sections 7–103 and 7–401.

Definitional Cross References:

"Bearer". Section 1–201.
"Delivery". Section 1–201.
"Goods". Section 7–102.
"Person". Section 1–201.
"Security interest". Section 1–201.
"Sign". Section 7–102.
"Term". Section 1–201.
"Warehouse receipt". Section 1–201.
"Warehouse". Section 7–102.

§ 7–203. Liability for Nonreceipt or Misdescription.

A party to or purchaser for value in good faith of a document of title, other than a bill of lading, that relies upon the description of the goods in the document may recover from the issuer damages caused by the nonreceipt or misdescription of the goods, except to the extent that:

(1) the document conspicuously indicates that the issuer does not know whether all or part of the goods in fact were received or conform to the description, such as a case in which the description is in terms of marks or labels or kind, quantity, or condition, or the receipt or description is qualified by "contents, condition, and quality unknown", "said to contain", or words of similar import, if the indication is true; or

(2) the party or purchaser otherwise has notice of the nonreceipt or misdescription.

Official Comment

Prior Uniform Statutory Provision: Former Section 7–203.

Changes: Changes to this section are for style only.

Purpose:

This section is a simplified restatement of existing law as to the method by which a bailee may avoid responsibility for the accuracy of descriptions which are made by or in reliance upon information furnished by the depositor. The issuer is liable on documents issued by an agent, contrary to instructions of its principal, without receiving goods. No disclaimer of the latter liability is permitted.

Cross Reference:

Section 7–301.

Definitional Cross References:

"Conspicuous". Section 1–201.
"Document of title". Section 1–201.
"Goods". Section 7–102.
"Good Faith". Section 1–201. [7–102]
"Issuer". Section 7–102.
"Notice". Section 1–202.
"Party". Section 1–201.
"Purchaser". Section 1–201.
"Receipt of goods". Section 2–103.
"Value". Section 1–204.

§ 7–204. Duty Of Care; Contractual Limitation of Warehouse's Liability.

(a) A warehouse is liable for damages for loss of or injury to the goods caused by its failure to exercise care with regard to the goods that a reasonably careful person would exercise under similar circumstances. Unless otherwise agreed, the warehouse is not liable for damages that could not have been avoided by the exercise of that care.

(b) Damages may be limited by a term in the warehouse receipt or storage agreement limiting the amount of liability in case of loss or damage beyond which the warehouse is not liable. Such a limitation is not effective with respect to the warehouse's liability for conversion to its own use. On request of the bailor in a record at the time of signing the storage agreement or within a reasonable time after receipt of the warehouse receipt, the warehouse's liability may be increased on part or all of the goods covered by the storage agreement or the warehouse receipt. In this event, increased rates may be charged based on an increased valuation of the goods.

(c) Reasonable provisions as to the time and manner of presenting claims and commencing actions based on the bailment may be included in the warehouse receipt or storage agreement.

[(d) This section does not modify or repeal [Insert reference to any statute that imposes a higher responsibility upon the warehouse or invalidates a contractual limitation that would be permissible under this Article].]

Legislative Note: Insert in subsection (d) a reference to any statute which imposes a higher responsibility upon the warehouse or invalidates a contractual limitation that would be permissible under this Article. If no such statutes exist, this section should be deleted.

Official Comment

Prior Uniform Statutory Provision: Former Section 7–204.

Changes: Updated to reflect modern, standard commercial practices.

Purposes of Changes:

1. Subsection (a) continues the rule without change from former Section 7–204 on the warehouse's obligation to exercise reasonable care.

2. Former Section 7–204(2) required that the term limiting damages do so by setting forth a specific liability per article or item or of a value per unit of weight. This requirement has been deleted as out of step with modern industry practice. Under subsection (b) a warehouse may limit its liability for damages for loss of or damage to the goods by a term in the warehouse receipt or storage agreement without the term constituting an impermissible disclaimer of the obligation of reasonable care. The parties cannot disclaim by contract the warehouse's obligation of care. Section 1–302. For example, limitations based upon per unit of weight, per package, per occurrence, or per receipt as well as limitations based upon a multiple of the storage rate may be commercially appropriate. As subsection (d) makes clear, the states or the federal government may supplement this section with more rigid standards of responsibility for some or all bailees.

3. Former Section 7–204(2) also provided that an increased rate can not be charged if contrary to a tariff. That language has been deleted. If a tariff is required under state or federal law, pursuant to Section 7–103(a), the tariff would control over the rule of this section allowing an increased rate. The provisions of a non-mandatory tariff may be incorporated by reference in the parties' agreement. See Comment 2 to Section 7–103. Subsection (c) deletes the reference to

tariffs for the same reason that the reference has been omitted in subsection (b).

4. As under former Section 7–204(2), subsection (b) provides that a limitation of damages is ineffective if the warehouse has converted the goods to its own use. A mere failure to redeliver the goods is not conversion to the warehouse's own use. See Adams v. Ryan & Christie Storage, Inc., 563 F. Supp. 409 (E.D. Pa. 1983) aff'd 725 F.2d 666 (3rd Cir. 1983). Cases such as I.C.C. Metals Inc. v. Municipal Warehouse Co., 409 N.E. 2d 849 (N.Y. Ct. App. 1980) holding that mere failure to redeliver results in a presumption of conversion to the warehouse's own use are disapproved. "Conversion to its own use" is narrower than the idea of conversion generally. Cases such as Lipman v. Peterson, 575 P.2d 19 (Kan. 1978) holding to the contrary are disapproved.

5. Storage agreements commonly establish the contractual relationship between warehouses and depositors who have an on-going relationship. The storage agreement may allow for the movement of goods into and out of a warehouse without the necessity of issuing or amending a warehouse receipt upon each entry or exit of goods from the warehouse.

Cross References:

Sections 1–302, 7–103, 7–309 and 7–403.

Definitional Cross References:

"Goods". Section 7–102.
"Reasonable time". Section 1–204.
"Sign". Section 7–102.
"Term". Section 1–201.
"Value". Section 1–204.
"Warehouse receipt". Section 1–201.
"Warehouse". Section 7–102.

§ 7–205. Title Under Warehouse Receipt Defeated in Certain Cases.

A buyer in ordinary course of business of fungible goods sold and delivered by a warehouse that is also in the business of buying and selling such goods takes the goods free of any claim under a warehouse receipt even if the receipt is negotiable and has been duly negotiated.

Official Comment

Prior Uniform Statutory Provision: Former Section 7–205.

Changes: Changes for style only.

Purposes:

1. The typical case covered by this section is that of the warehouse-dealer in grain, and the substantive question at issue is whether in case the warehouse becomes insolvent the receipt holders shall be able to trace and recover grain shipped to farmers and other purchasers from the elevator. This was possible under the old acts, although courts were eager to find estoppels to prevent it. The practical difficulty of tracing fungible grain means that the preservation of this theoretical right adds little to the commercial acceptability of negotiable grain receipts, which really circulate on the credit of the warehouse. Moreover, on default of the warehouse, the receipt holders at least share in what grain remains, whereas retaking the grain from a good faith cash purchaser reduces the purchaser completely to the status of general creditor in a situation where there was very little the purchaser could do to guard against the loss. Compare 15 U.S.C. Section 714p enacted in 1955.

2. This provision applies to both negotiable and nonnegotiable warehouse receipts. The concept of due negotiation is provided for in 7–501. The definition of "buyer in ordinary course" is in Article 1 and provides, among other things, that a buyer must either have possession or a right to obtain the goods under Article 2 in order to be a buyer in ordinary course. This section requires actual delivery of the fungible goods to the buyer in ordinary course. Delivery requires voluntary transfer of possession of the fungible goods to the buyer. See amended Section 2–103. This section is not satisfied by the delivery of the document of title to the buyer in ordinary course.

Cross References:

Sections 2–403 and 9–320.

Definitional Cross References:

"Buyer in ordinary course of business". Section 1–201.
"Delivery". Section 1–201.
"Duly negotiate". Section 7–501.
"Fungible" goods. Section 1–201.
"Goods". Section 7–102.
"Value". Section 1–204.
"Warehouse receipt". Section 1–201.
"Warehouse". Section 7–102.

§ 7–206. Termination of Storage at Warehouse's Option.

(a) A warehouse, by giving notice to the person on whose account the goods are held and any other person known to claim an interest in the goods, may require payment of any charges and removal of the goods from the warehouse at the termination of the period of storage fixed by the document of title or, if a period is not fixed, within a stated period not less than 30 days after the warehouse gives notice. If the goods are not removed before the date specified in the notice, the warehouse may sell them pursuant to Section 7–210.

(b) If a warehouse in good faith believes that goods are about to deteriorate or decline in value to less than the amount of its lien within the time provided in subsection (a) and Section 7–210, the warehouse may specify in the notice given under subsection (a) any reasonable shorter time for removal of the goods and, if the goods are not removed, may sell them at public sale held not less than one week after a single advertisement or posting.

(c) If, as a result of a quality or condition of the goods of which the warehouse did not have notice at the time of deposit, the goods are a hazard to other property, the warehouse facilities, or other persons, the warehouse may sell the goods at public or private sale without advertisement or posting on reasonable notification to all persons known to claim an interest in the goods. If the warehouse, after a reasonable effort, is unable to sell the goods, it may dispose of them in any lawful manner and does not incur liability by reason of that disposition.

(d) A warehouse shall deliver the goods to any person entitled to them under this article upon due demand made at any time before sale or other disposition under this section.

(e) A warehouse may satisfy its lien from the proceeds of any sale or disposition under this section but shall hold the balance for delivery on the demand of any person to which the warehouse would have been bound to deliver the goods.

Official Comment

Prior Uniform Statutory Provision: Former Section 7–206.

Changes: Changes for style.

Purposes:

1. This section provides for three situations in which the warehouse may terminate storage for reasons other then enforcement of its lien as permitted by Section 7–210. Most warehousing is for an indefinite term, the bailor being entitled to delivery on reasonable demand. It is necessary to define the warehouse's power to terminate the bailment, since it would be commercially intolerable to allow warehouses to order removal of the goods on short notice. The thirty day period provided where the document does not carry its own period of termination corresponds to commercial practice of computing rates on a monthly basis. The right to terminate under subsection (a) includes a right to require payment of "any charges", but does not depend on the existence of unpaid charges.

2. In permitting expeditious disposition of perishable and hazardous goods the pre-Code Uniform Warehouse Receipts Act, Section 34, made no distinction between cases where the warehouse knowingly undertook to store such goods and cases where the goods were discovered to be of that character subsequent to storage. The former situation presents no such emergency as justifies the summary power of removal and sale. Subsections (b) and (c) distinguish between the two situations. The reason of this section should apply if the goods become hazardous during the course of storage. The process for selling the goods described in Section 7–210 governs the sale of goods under this section except as provided in subsections (b) and (c) for the situations described in those subsections respectively.

3. Protection of its lien is the only interest which the warehouse has to justify summary sale of perishable goods which are not hazardous. This same interest must be recognized when the stored goods, although not perishable, decline in market value to a point which threatens the warehouse's security.

4. The right to order removal of stored goods is subject to provisions of the public warehousing laws of some states forbidding warehouses from discriminating among customers. Nor does the section relieve the warehouse of any obligation under the state laws to secure the approval of a public official before disposing of deteriorating goods. Such regulatory statutes and the regulations under them remain in force and operative. Section 7–103.

Cross References:

Sections 7–103 and 7–403.

Definitional Cross References:

"Delivery". Section 1–201.
"Document of title". Section 1–102.
"Good faith". Section 1–201 [7–102].
"Goods". Section 7–102.
"Notice". Section 1–202.
"Notification". Section 1–202.

"Person". Section 1–201.
"Reasonable time". Section 1–205.
"Value". Section 1–204.
"Warehouse". Section 7–102.

§ 7–207. Goods Must Be Kept Separate; Fungible Goods.

(a) Unless the warehouse receipt provides otherwise, a warehouse shall keep separate the goods covered by each receipt so as to permit at all times identification and delivery of those goods. However, different lots of fungible goods may be commingled.

(b) If different lots of fungible goods are commingled, the goods are owned in common by the persons entitled thereto and the warehouse is severally liable to each owner for that owner's share. If, because of overissue, a mass of fungible goods is insufficient to meet all the receipts the warehouse has issued against it, the persons entitled include all holders to which overissued receipts have been duly negotiated.

Official Comment

Prior Uniform Statutory Provision: Former Section 7–207.

Changes: Changes for style only.

Purposes:

No change of substance is made from former Section 7–207. Holders to whom overissued receipts have been duly negotiated shall share in a mass of fungible goods. Where individual ownership interests are merged into claims on a common fund, as is necessarily the case with fungible goods, there is no policy reason for discriminating between successive purchasers of similar claims.

Definitional Cross References:

"Delivery". Section 1–201.
"Duly negotiate". Section 7–501.
"Fungible goods". Section 1–201.
"Goods". Section 7–102.
"Holder". Section 1–201.
"Person". Section 1–201.
"Warehouse receipt". Section 1–201.
"Warehouse". Section 7–102.

§ 7–208. Altered Warehouse Receipts.

If a blank in a negotiable tangible warehouse receipt has been filled in without authority, a good-faith purchaser for value and without notice of the lack of authority may treat the insertion as authorized. Any other unauthorized alteration leaves any tangible or electronic warehouse receipt enforceable against the issuer according to its original tenor.

Official Comment

Prior Uniform Statutory Provision: Former Section 7–208.

Changes: To accommodate electronic documents of title.

Purpose:

1. The execution of tangible warehouse receipts in blank is a dangerous practice. As between the issuer and an innocent purchaser the risks should clearly fall on the former. The purchaser must have purchased the tangible negotiable warehouse receipt in good faith and for value to be protected under the rule of the first sentence which is a limited exception to the general rule in the second sentence. Electronic document of title systems should have protection against unauthorized access and unauthorized changes. See 7–106. Thus the protection for good faith purchasers found in the first sentence is not necessary in the context of electronic documents.

2. Under the second sentence of this section, an unauthorized alteration whether made with or without fraudulent intent does not relieve the issuer of its liability on the warehouse receipt as originally executed. The unauthorized alteration itself is of course ineffective against the warehouse. The rule stated in the second sentence applies to both tangible and electronic warehouse receipts.

Definitional Cross References:

"Good faith". Section 1–201 [7–102].
"Issuer". Section 7–102.
"Notice". Section 1–202.
"Purchaser". Section 1–201.
"Value". Section 1–204.
"Warehouse receipt". Section 1–201.

§ 7–209. Lien of Warehouse.

(a) A warehouse has a lien against the bailor on the goods covered by a warehouse receipt or storage agreement or on the proceeds thereof in its possession for charges for storage or transportation, including demurrage and terminal charges, insurance, labor, or other charges, present or future, in relation to the goods, and for expenses necessary for preservation of the goods or reasonably incurred in their sale pursuant to law. If the person on whose account the goods are held is liable for similar charges or expenses in relation to other goods whenever deposited and it is stated in the warehouse receipt or storage agreement that a lien is claimed for charges and expenses in relation to other goods, the warehouse also has a lien against the goods covered by the warehouse receipt or storage agreement or on the proceeds thereof in its possession for those charges and expenses, whether or not the other goods have been delivered by the warehouse. However, as against a person to which a negotiable warehouse receipt is duly negotiated, a warehouse's lien is limited to charges in an amount or at a rate specified in the warehouse receipt or, if no charges are so specified, to a reasonable charge for storage of the specific goods covered by the receipt subsequent to the date of the receipt.

(b) A warehouse may also reserve a security interest against the bailor for the maximum amount specified on the receipt for charges other than those specified in subsection (a), such as for money advanced and interest. The security interest is governed by Article 9.

(c) A warehouse's lien for charges and expenses under subsection (a) or a security interest under subsection (b) is also effective against any person that so entrusted the bailor with possession of the goods that a pledge of them by the bailor to a good-faith purchaser for value would have been valid. However, the lien or security interest is not effective against a person that before issuance of a document of title had a legal interest or a perfected security interest in the goods and that did not:

(1) deliver or entrust the goods or any document of title covering the goods to the bailor or the bailor's nominee with:

(A) actual or apparent authority to ship, store, or sell;

(B) power to obtain delivery under Section 7–403; or

(C) power of disposition under Sections 2–403, 2A–304(2), 2A–305(2), 9–320, or 9–321(c) or other statute or rule of law; or

(2) acquiesce in the procurement by the bailor or its nominee of any document.

(d) A warehouse's lien on household goods for charges and expenses in relation to the goods under subsection (a) is also effective against all persons if the depositor was the legal possessor of the goods at the time of deposit. In this subsection, "household goods" means furniture, furnishings, or personal effects used by the depositor in a dwelling.

(e) A warehouse loses its lien on any goods that it voluntarily delivers or unjustifiably refuses to deliver.

Official Comment

Prior Uniform Statutory Provision: Former Sections 7–209 and 7–503.

Changes: Expanded to recognize warehouse lien when a warehouse receipt is not issued but goods are covered by a storage agreement.

Purposes:

1. Subsection (a) defines the warehouse's statutory lien. Other than allowing a warehouse to claim a lien under this section when there is a storage agreement and not a warehouse receipt, this section remains unchanged in substance from former Section 7–209(1). Under the first sentence, a specific lien attaches automatically without express notation on the receipt or storage agreement with regard to goods stored under the receipt or the storage agreement. That lien is limited to the usual charges arising out of a storage transaction.

Example 1: Bailor stored goods with a warehouse and the warehouse issued a warehouse receipt. A lien against those goods arose as set forth in subsection (a), the first sentence, for the charges for storage and the other expenses of those goods. The warehouse may enforce its lien under Section 7–210 as against the bailor. Whether the warehouse receipt is negotiable or nonnegotiable is not important to the warehouse's rights as against the bailor.

Under the second sentence, by notation on the receipt or storage agreement, the lien can be made a general lien extending to like charges in relation to other goods. Both the specific lien and general lien are as to goods in the possession of the warehouse and extend to proceeds from the goods as long as the proceeds are in the possession of the warehouse. The same rules apply whether the receipt is negotiable or non-negotiable.

Example 2: Bailor stored goods (lot A) with a warehouse and the warehouse issued a warehouse receipt for those goods. In the warehouse receipt it is stated that the warehouse will also have a lien on goods covered by the warehouse receipt for storage charges and the other expenses for any other goods that are stored with the warehouse by the bailor. The statement about the lien on other goods does not specify an amount or a rate. Bailor then stored other goods (lot B) with the warehouse. Under subsection (a), first sentence, the warehouse has a lien on the specific goods (lot A) covered by the warehouse receipt. Under subsection (a), second sentence, the warehouse has a lien on the goods in lot A for the storage charges and the other expenses arising from the goods in lot B. That lien is enforceable as against the bailor regardless of whether the receipt is negotiable or nonnegotiable.

Under the third sentence, if the warehouse receipt is negotiable, the lien as against a holder of that receipt by due negotiation is limited to the amount or rate specified on the receipt for the specific lien or the general lien, or, if none is specified, to a reasonable charge for storage of the specific goods covered by the receipt for storage after the date of the receipt.

Example 3: Same facts as Example 1 except that the warehouse receipt is negotiable and has been duly negotiated (Section 7–501) to a person other than the bailor. Under the last sentence of subsection (a), the warehouse may enforce its lien against the bailor's goods stored in the warehouse as against the person to whom the negotiable warehouse receipt has been duly negotiated. Section 7–502. That lien is limited to the charges or rates specified in the receipt or a reasonable charge for storage as stated in the last sentence of subsection (a).

Example 4: Same facts as Example 2 except that the warehouse receipt is negotiable and has been duly negotiated (Section 7–501) to a person other than the bailor. Under the last sentence of subsection (a), the lien on lot A goods for the storage charges and the other expenses arising from storage of lot B goods is not enforceable as against the person to whom the receipt has been duly negotiated. Without a statement of a specified amount or rate for the general lien, the warehouse's general lien is not enforceable as against the person to whom the negotiable document has been duly negotiated. However, the warehouse lien for charges and expenses related to storage of lot A goods is still enforceable as against the person to whom the receipt was duly negotiated.

Example 5. Same facts as Examples 2 and 4 except the warehouse had stated on the negotiable warehouse receipt a specified amount or rate for the

general lien on other goods (lot B). Under the last sentence of subsection (a), the general lien on lot A goods for the storage charges and the other expenses arising from storage of lot B goods is enforceable as against the person to whom the receipt has been duly negotiated.

2. Subsection (b) provides for a security interest based upon agreement. Such a security interest arises out of relations between the parties other than bailment for storage or transportation, as where the bailee assumes the role of financier or performs a manufacturing operation, extending credit in reliance upon the goods covered by the receipt. Such a security interest is not a statutory lien. Compare Sections 9–109 and 9–333. It is governed in all respects by Article 9, except that subsection (b) requires that the receipt specify a maximum amount and limits the security interest to the amount specified. A warehouse could also take a security interest to secure its charges for storage and the other expenses listed in subsection (a) to protect these claims upon the loss of the statutory possessory warehouse lien if the warehouse loses possession of the goods as provided in subsection (e).

Example 6: Bailor stores goods with a warehouse and the warehouse issues a warehouse receipt that states that the warehouse is taking a security interest in the bailed goods for charges of storage, expenses, for money advanced, for manufacturing services rendered, and all other obligations that the bailor may owe the warehouse. That is a security interest covered in all respects by Article 9. Subsection (b). As allowed by this section, a warehouse may rely upon its statutory possessory lien to protect its charges for storage and the other expenses related to storage. For those storage charges covered by the statutory possessory lien, the warehouse is not required to use a security interest under subsection (b).

3. Subsections (a) and (b) validate the lien and security interest "against the bailor." Under basic principles of derivative rights as provided in Section 7–504, the warehouse lien is also valid as against parties who obtain their rights from the bailor except as otherwise provided in subsection (a), third sentence, or subsection (c).

Example 7: Bailor stores goods with a warehouse and the warehouse issues a nonnegotiable warehouse receipt that also claims a general lien in other goods stored with the warehouse. A lien on the bailed goods for the charges for storage and the other expenses arises under subsection (a). Bailor notifies the warehouse that the goods have been sold to

Buyer and the bailee acknowledges that fact to the Buyer. Section 2–503. The warehouse lien for storage of those goods is effective against Buyer for both the specific lien and the general lien. Section 7–504.

Example 8: Bailor stores goods with a warehouse and the warehouse issues a nonnegotiable warehouse receipt. A lien on the bailed goods for the charges for storage and the other expenses arises under subsection (a). Bailor grants a security interest in the goods while the goods are in the warehouse's possession to Secured Party (SP) who properly perfects a security interest in the goods. See Revised 9–312(d). The warehouse lien is superior in priority over SP's security interest. See Revised 9–203(b)(2) (debtor can grant a security interest to the extent of debtor's rights in the collateral).

Example 9: Bailor stores goods with a warehouse and the warehouse issues a negotiable warehouse receipt. A lien on the bailed goods for the charges for storage and the other expenses arises under subsection (a). Bailor grants a security interest in the negotiable document to SP. SP properly perfects its interest in the negotiable document by taking possession through a 'due negotiation.' Revised 9–312(c). SP's security interest is subordinate to the warehouse lien. Section 7–209(a), third sentence. Given that bailor's rights are subject to the warehouse lien, the bailor cannot grant to the SP greater rights than the bailor has under Section 9–203(b)(2), perfection of the security interest in the negotiable document and the goods covered by the document through SP's filing of a financing statement should not give a different result.

As against third parties who have interests in the goods prior to the storage with the warehouse, subsection (c) continues the rule under the prior uniform statutory provision that to validate the lien or security interest of the warehouse, the owner must have entrusted the goods to the depositor, and that the circumstances must be such that a pledge by the depositor to a good faith purchaser for value would have been valid. Thus the owner's interest will not be subjected to a lien or security interest arising out of a deposit of its goods by a thief. The warehouse may be protected because of the actual, implied or apparent authority of the depositor, because of a Factor's Act, or because of other circumstances which would protect a bona fide pledgee, unless those circumstances are denied effect under the second sentence of subsection (c). The language of Section 7–503 is brought into subsection (c) for purposes of clarity. The comments to Section 7–503 are helpful in interpreting delivery, entrustment or acquiescence.

Where the third party is the holder of a security interest, obtained prior to the issuance of a negotiable warehouse receipt, the rights of the warehouse depend on the priority given to a hypothetical bona fide pledgee by Article 9, particularly Section 9–322. Thus the special priority granted to statutory liens by Section 9–333 does not apply to liens under subsection (a) of this section, since subsection (c), second sentence, "expressly provides otherwise" within the meaning of Section 9–333.

As to household goods, however, subsection (d) makes the warehouse's lien "for charges and expenses in relation to the goods" effective against all persons if the depositor was the legal possessor. The purpose of the exception is to permit the warehouse to accept household goods for storage in sole reliance on the value of the goods themselves, especially in situations of family emergency.

Example 10: Bailor grants a perfected security interest in the goods to SP prior to storage of the goods with the warehouse. Bailor then stores goods with the warehouse and the warehouse issues a warehouse receipt for the goods. A warehouse lien on the bailed goods for the charges for storage or other expenses arises under subsection (a). The warehouse lien is not effective as against SP unless SP entrusted the goods to the bailor with actual or apparent authority to ship store, or sell the goods or with power of disposition under subsection (c)(1) or acquiesced in the bailor's procurement of a document of title under subsection (c)(2). This result obtains whether the receipt is negotiable or nonnegotiable.

Example 11: Sheriff who had lawfully repossessed household goods in an eviction action stored the goods with a warehouse. A lien on the bailed goods arises under subsection (a). The lien is effective as against the owner of the goods. Subsection (d).

4. As under previous law, this section creates a statutory possessory lien in favor of the warehouse on the goods stored with the warehouse or on the proceeds of the goods. The warehouse loses its lien if it loses possession of the goods or the proceeds. Subsection (e).

5. Where goods have been stored under a nonnegotiable warehouse receipt and are sold by the person to whom the receipt has been issued, frequently the goods are not withdrawn by the new owner. The obligations of the seller of the goods in this situation are set forth in Section 2–503(4) on tender of delivery and include procurement of an acknowledgment by the bailee of the buyer's right to possession of the goods. If

a new receipt is requested, such an acknowledgment can be withheld until storage charges have been paid or provided for. The statutory lien for charges on the goods sold, granted by the first sentence of subsection (a), continues valid unless the bailee gives it up. See Section 7–403. But once a new receipt is issued to the buyer, the buyer becomes "the person on whose account the goods are held" under the second sentence of subsection (a); unless the buyer undertakes liability for charges in relation to other goods stored by the seller, there is no general lien against the buyer for such charges. Of course, the bailee may preserve the general lien in such a case either by an arrangement by which the buyer "is liable for" such charges, or by reserving a security interest under subsection (b).

6. A possessory warehouse lien arises as provided under subsection (a) if the parties to the bailment have a storage agreement or a warehouse receipt is issued. In the modern warehouse, the bailor and the bailee may enter into a master contract governing the bailment with the bailee and bailor keeping track of the goods stored pursuant to the master contract by notation on their respective books and records and the parties send notification via electronic communication as to what goods are covered by the master contract. Warehouse receipts are not issued. See Comment 4 to Section 7–204. There is no particular form for a warehouse receipt and failure to contain any of the terms listed in Section 7–202 does not deprive the warehouse of its lien that arises under subsection (a). See the comment to Section 7–202.

Cross References:

Point 1: Sections 7–501 and 7–502.
Point 2: Sections 9–109 and 9–333.
Point 3: Sections 2–503, 7–503, 7–504, 9–203, 9–312, and 9–322 .
Point 4: Sections 2–503, 7–501, 7–502, 7–504, 9–312, 9–331, 9–333, 9–401.
Point 5: Sections 2–503 and 7–403.
Point 6: Sections 7–202 and 7–204.

Definitional Cross References:

"Delivery". Section 1–201.
"Document of Title". Section 1–201
"Goods". Section 7–102.
"Money". Section 1–201.
"Person". Section 1–201.
"Purchaser". Section 1–201.
"Right". Section 1–201.
"Security interest". Section 1–201.
"Value". Section 1–204.
"Warehouse receipt". Section 1–201.
"Warehouse". Section 7–102.

§ 7–210. Enforcement of Warehouse's Lien.

(a) Except as otherwise provided in subsection (b), a warehouse's lien may be enforced by public or private sale of the goods, in bulk or in packages, at any time or place and on any terms that are commercially reasonable, after notifying all persons known to claim an interest in the goods. The notification must include a statement of the amount due, the nature of the proposed sale, and the time and place of any public sale. The fact that a better price could have been obtained by a sale at a different time or in a method different from that selected by the warehouse is not of itself sufficient to establish that the sale was not made in a commercially reasonable manner. The warehouse sells in a commercially reasonable manner if the warehouse sells the goods in the usual manner in any recognized market therefor, sells at the price current in that market at the time of the sale, or otherwise sells in conformity with commercially reasonable practices among dealers in the type of goods sold. A sale of more goods than apparently necessary to be offered to ensure satisfaction of the obligation is not commercially reasonable, except in cases covered by the preceding sentence.

(b) A warehouse may enforce its lien on goods, other than goods stored by a merchant in the course of its business, only if the following requirements are satisfied:

(1) All persons known to claim an interest in the goods must be notified.

(2) The notification must include an itemized statement of the claim, a description of the goods subject to the lien, a demand for payment within a specified time not less than 10 days after receipt of the notification, and a conspicuous statement that unless the claim is paid within that time the goods will be advertised for sale and sold by auction at a specified time and place.

(3) The sale must conform to the terms of the notification.

(4) The sale must be held at the nearest suitable place to where the goods are held or stored.

(5) After the expiration of the time given in the notification, an advertisement of the

sale must be published once a week for two weeks consecutively in a newspaper of general circulation where the sale is to be held. The advertisement must include a description of the goods, the name of the person on whose account the goods are being held, and the time and place of the sale. The sale must take place at least 15 days after the first publication. If there is no newspaper of general circulation where the sale is to be held, the advertisement must be posted at least 10 days before the sale in not fewer than six conspicuous places in the neighborhood of the proposed sale.

(c) Before any sale pursuant to this section, any person claiming a right in the goods may pay the amount necessary to satisfy the lien and the reasonable expenses incurred in complying with this section. In that event, the goods may not be sold but must be retained by the warehouse subject to the terms of the receipt and this article.

(d) A warehouse may buy at any public sale held pursuant to this section.

(e) A purchaser in good faith of goods sold to enforce a warehouse's lien takes the goods free of any rights of persons against which the lien was valid, despite the warehouse's noncompliance with this section.

(f) A warehouse may satisfy its lien from the proceeds of any sale pursuant to this section but shall hold the balance, if any, for delivery on demand to any person to which the warehouse would have been bound to deliver the goods.

(g) The rights provided by this section are in addition to all other rights allowed by law to a creditor against a debtor.

(h) If a lien is on goods stored by a merchant in the course of its business, the lien may be enforced in accordance with subsection (a) or (b).

(i) A warehouse is liable for damages caused by failure to comply with the requirements for sale under this section and, in case of willful violation, is liable for conversion.

Official Comment

Prior Uniform Statutory Provision: Former Section 7–210.

Changes: Update to accommodate electronic commerce and for style.

Purposes:

1. Subsection (a) makes "commercial reasonableness" the standard for foreclosure proceedings in all cases except non-commercial storage with a warehouse. The latter category embraces principally storage of household goods by private owners; and for such cases the detailed provisions as to notification, publication and public sale are retained in subsection (b) with one change. The requirement in former Section 7–210(2)(b) that the notification must be sent in person or by registered or certified mail has been deleted. Notification may be sent by any reasonable means as provided in Section 1–202. The swifter, more flexible procedure of subsection (a) is appropriate to commercial storage. Compare seller's power of resale on breach by buyer under the provisions of the Article on Sales (Section 2–706). Commercial reasonableness is a flexible concept that allows for a wide variety of actions to satisfy the rule of this section, including electronic means of posting and sale.

2. The provisions of subsections (d) and (e) permitting the bailee to bid at public sales and confirming the title of purchasers at foreclosure sales are designed to secure more bidding and better prices and remain unchanged from former Section 7–210.

3. A warehouses may have recourse to an interpleader action in appropriate circumstances. See Section 7–603.

4. If a warehouse has both a warehouse lien and a security interest, the warehouse may enforce both the lien and the security interest simultaneously by using the procedures of Article 9. Section 7–210 adopts as its touchstone "commercial reasonableness" for the enforcement of a warehouse lien. Following the procedures of Article 9 satisfies "commercial reasonableness."

Cross Reference:

Sections 2–706, 7–403, 7–603 and Part 6 of Article 9.

Definitional Cross References:

"Bill of lading". Section 1–201.
"Conspicuous". Section 1–201.
"Creditor". Section 1–201.
"Delivery". Section 1–201.
"Document of Title". Section 1–201.
"Good faith". Section 1–201 [7–102].
"Goods". Section 7–102.
"Notification". Section 1–202.
"Notifies". Section 1–202.
"Person". Section 1–201.
"Purchaser". Section 1–201.

"Rights". Section 1–201.
"Term". Section 1–201.
"Warehouse". Section 7–102.

PART 3

BILLS OF LADING: SPECIAL PROVISIONS

§ 7–301. Liability for Nonreceipt or Misdescription; "Said to Contain"; "Shipper's Weight, Load, and Count"; Improper Handling.

(a) A consignee of a nonnegotiable bill of lading which has given value in good faith, or a holder to which a negotiable bill has been duly negotiated, relying upon the description of the goods in the bill or upon the date shown in the bill, may recover from the issuer damages caused by the misdating of the bill or the nonreceipt or misdescription of the goods, except to the extent that the bill indicates that the issuer does not know whether any part or all of the goods in fact were received or conform to the description, such as in a case in which the description is in terms of marks or labels or kind, quantity, or condition or the receipt or description is qualified by "contents or condition of contents of packages unknown", "said to contain", "shipper's weight, load, and count," or words of similar import, if that indication is true.

(b) If goods are loaded by the issuer of a bill of lading;

(1) the issuer shall count the packages of goods if shipped in packages and ascertain the kind and quantity if shipped in bulk; and

(2) words such as "shipper's weight, load, and count," or words of similar import indicating that the description was made by the shipper are ineffective except as to goods concealed in packages.

(c) If bulk goods are loaded by a shipper that makes available to the issuer of a bill of lading adequate facilities for weighing those goods, the issuer shall ascertain the kind and quantity within a reasonable time after receiving the shipper's request in a record to do so. In that case, "shipper's weight" or words of similar import are ineffective.

(d) The issuer of a bill of lading, by including in the bill the words "shipper's weight, load, and count," or words of similar import, may indicate that the goods were loaded by the shipper, and, if that statement is true, the issuer is not liable for damages caused by the improper loading. However, omission of such words does not imply liability for damages caused by improper loading.

(e) A shipper guarantees to an issuer the accuracy at the time of shipment of the description, marks, labels, number, kind, quantity, condition, and weight, as furnished by the shipper, and the shipper shall indemnify the issuer against damage caused by inaccuracies in those particulars. This right of indemnity does not limit the issuer's responsibility or liability under the contract of carriage to any person other than the shipper.

Official Comment

Prior Uniform Statutory Provision: Former Section 7–301.

Changes: Changes for clarity, style and to recognize deregulation in the transportation industry.

Purposes:

1. This section continues the rules from former Section 7–301 with one substantive change. The obligations of the issuer of the bill of lading under former subsections (2) and (3) were limited to issuers who were common carriers. Subsections (b) and (c) apply the same rules to all issuers not just common carriers. This section is compatible with the policies stated in the federal Bills of Lading Act, 49 U.S.C. § 80113 (2000).

2. The language of the pre-Code Uniform Bills of Lading Act suggested that a carrier is ordinarily liable for damage caused by improper loading, but may relieve itself of liability by disclosing on the bill that shipper actually loaded. A more accurate statement of the law is that the carrier is not liable for losses caused by act or default of the shipper, which would include improper loading. D. H. Overmyer Co. v. Nelson Brantley Glass Go., 168 S.E.2d 176 (Ga. Ct. App. 1969). There was some question whether under pre-Code law a carrier was liable even to a good faith purchaser of a

negotiable bill for such losses, if the shipper's faulty loading in fact caused the loss. Subsection (d) permits the carrier to bar, by disclosure of shipper's loading, liability to a good faith purchaser. There is no implication that decisions such as Modern Tool Corp. v. Pennsylvania R. Co., 100 F.Supp. 595 (D.N.J.1951), are disapproved.

3. This section is a restatement of existing law as to the method by which a bailee may avoid responsibility for the accuracy of descriptions which are made by or in reliance upon information furnished by the depositor or shipper. The wording in this section–"contents or condition of contents of packages unknown" or "shipper's weight, load and count"–to indicate that the shipper loaded the goods or that the carrier does not know the description, condition, or contents of the loaded packages continues to be appropriate as commonly understood in the transportation industry. The reasons for this wording are as important in 2002 as when the prior section initially was approved. The issuer is liable on documents issued by an agent, contrary to instructions of his principal, without receiving goods. No disclaimer of this liability is permitted since it is not a matter either of the care of the goods or their description.

4. The shipper's erroneous report to the carrier concerning the goods may cause damage to the carrier. Subsection (e) therefore provides appropriate indemnity.

5. The word "freight" in the former Section 7–301 has been changed to "goods" to conform to international and domestic land transport usage in which "freight" means the price paid for carriage of the goods and not the goods themselves. Hence, changing the word "freight" to the word "goods" is a clarifying change that fits both international and domestic practice.

Cross References:

Sections 7–203, 7–309 and 7–501.

Definitional Cross References:

"Bill of lading". Section 1–201.
"Consignee". Section 7–102.
"Document of Title". Section 1–201.
"Duly negotiate". Section 7–501.
"Good faith". Section 1–201. [7–102].
"Goods". Section 7–102.
"Holder". Section 1–201.
"Issuer". Section 7–102.
"Notice". Section 1–202.
"Party". Section 1–201.
"Purchaser." Section 1–201.

"Receipt of Goods". Section 2–103.
"Value". Section 1–204.

§ 7–302. Through Bills of Lading and Similar Documents of Title.

(a) The issuer of a through bill of lading, or other document of title embodying an undertaking to be performed in part by a person acting as its agent or by a performing carrier, is liable to any person entitled to recover on the bill or other document for any breach by the other person or the performing carrier of its obligation under the bill or other document. However, to the extent that the bill or other document covers an undertaking to be performed overseas or in territory not contiguous to the continental United States or an undertaking including matters other than transportation, this liability for breach by the other person or the performing carrier may be varied by agreement of the parties.

(b) If goods covered by a through bill of lading or other document of title embodying an undertaking to be performed in part by a person other than the issuer are received by that person, the person is subject, with respect to its own performance while the goods are in its possession, to the obligation of the issuer. The person's obligation is discharged by delivery of the goods to another person pursuant to the bill or other document and does not include liability for breach by any other person or by the issuer.

(c) The issuer of a through bill of lading or other document of title described in subsection (a) is entitled to recover from the performing carrier, or other person in possession of the goods when the breach of the obligation under the bill or other document occurred:

(1) the amount it may be required to pay to any person entitled to recover on the bill or other document for the breach, as may be evidenced by any receipt, judgment, or transcript of judgment; and

(2) the amount of any expense reasonably incurred by the issuer in defending any action commenced by any person entitled to recover on the bill or other document for the breach.

Official Comment

Prior Uniform Statutory Provision: Former Section 7–302.

Changes: To conform to current terminology and for style.

Purposes:

1. This section continues the rules from former Section 7–302 without substantive change. The term "performing carrier" is substituted for the term "connecting carrier" to conform the terminology of this section with terminology used in recent UNCITRAL and OAS proposals concerning transportation and through bills of lading. This change in terminology is not substantive. This section is compatible with liability on carriers under federal law. See 49 U.S.C. §§ 11706, 14706 and 15906.

The purpose of this section is to subject the initial carrier under a through bill to suit for breach of the contract of carriage by any performing carrier and to make it clear that any such performing carrier holds the goods on terms which are defined by the document of title even though such performing carrier did not issue the document. Since the performing carrier does hold the goods on the terms of the document, it must honor a proper demand for delivery or a diversion order just as the original bailee would have to. Similarly it has the benefits of the excuses for non-delivery and limitations of liability provided for the original bailee who issued the bill. Unlike the original bailee-issuer, the performing carrier's responsibility is limited to the period while the goods are in its possession. The section does not impose any obligation to issue through bills.

2. The reference to documents other than through bills looks to the possibility that multi-purpose documents may come into use, e.g., combination warehouse receipts and bills of lading. As electronic documents of title come into common usage, storage documents (e.g. warehouse receipts) and transportation documents (e.g. bills of lading) may merge seamlessly into one electronic document that can serve both the storage and transportation segments of the movement of goods.

3. Under subsection (a) the issuer of a through bill of lading may become liable for the fault of another person. Subsection (c) gives the issuer appropriate rights of recourse.

4. Despite the broad language of subsection (a), Section 7–302 is subject to preemption by federal laws and treaties. Section 7–103. The precise scope of federal preemption in the transportation sector is a question determined under federal law.

Cross reference:

Section 7–103

Definitional Cross References:

"Agreement". Section 1–201.
"Bailee". Section 7–102.
"Bill of lading". Section 1–201.
"Delivery". Section 1–201.
"Document of title". Section 1–201.
"Goods". Section 7–102.
"Issuer". Section 7–102.
"Party". Section 1–201.
"Person". Section 1–201.

§ 7–303. Diversion; Reconsignment; Change of Instructions.

(a) Unless the bill of lading otherwise provides, a carrier may deliver the goods to a person or destination other than that stated in the bill or may otherwise dispose of the goods, without liability for misdelivery, on instructions from:

(1) the holder of a negotiable bill;

(2) the consignor on a nonnegotiable bill, even if the consignee has given contrary instructions;

(3) the consignee on a nonnegotiable bill in the absence of contrary instructions from the consignor, if the goods have arrived at the billed destination or if the consignee is in possession of the tangible bill or in control of the electronic bill; or

(4) the consignee on a nonnegotiable bill, if the consignee is entitled as against the consignor to dispose of the goods.

(b) Unless instructions described in subsection (a) are included in a negotiable bill of lading, a person to which the bill is duly negotiated may hold the bailee according to the original terms.

Official Comment

Prior Uniform Statutory Provision: Former Section 7–303.

Changes: To accommodate electronic documents and for style.

Purposes:

1. Diversion is a very common commercial practice which defeats delivery to the consignee originally named in a bill of lading. This section continues former Section 7–303's safe harbor rules for carriers in situations involving diversion and adapts those rules to electronic documents of title. This section works com-

patibly with Section 2–705. Carriers may as a business matter be willing to accept instructions from consignees in which case the carrier will be liable for misdelivery if the consignee was not the owner or otherwise empowered to dispose of the goods under subsection (a)(4). The section imposes no duty on carriers to undertake diversion. The carrier is of course subject to the provisions of mandatory filed tariffs as provided in Section 7–103.

2. It should be noted that the section provides only an immunity for carriers against liability for "misdelivery." It does not, for example, defeat the title to the goods which the consignee-buyer may have acquired from the consignor-seller upon delivery of the goods to the carrier under a non-negotiable bill of lading. Thus if the carrier, upon instructions from the consignor, returns the goods to the consignor, the consignee may recover the goods from the consignor or the consignor's insolvent estate. However, under certain circumstances, the consignee's title may be defeated by diversion of the goods in transit to a different consignee. The rights that arise between the consignor-seller and the consignee-buyer out of a contract for the sale of goods are governed by Article 2.

Cross References:

Point 1: Sections 2–705 and 7–103.
Point 2: Article 2, Sections 7–403 and 7–504(3).

Definitional Cross References:

"Bailee". Section 7–102.
"Bill of lading". Section 1–201.
"Carrier". Section 7–102
"Consignee". Section 7–102.
"Consignor". Section 7–102.
"Delivery". Section 1–201.
"Goods". Section 7–102.
"Holder". Section 1–201.
"Notice". Section 1–202.
"Person". Section 1–201.
"Purchaser". Section 1–201.
"Term". Section 1–201.

§ 7–304. Tangible Bills of Lading in a Set.

(a) Except as customary in international transportation, a tangible bill of lading may not be issued in a set of parts. The issuer is liable for damages caused by violation of this subsection.

(b) If a tangible bill of lading is lawfully issued in a set of parts, each of which contains an identification code and is expressed to be valid only if the goods have not been delivered against

any other part, the whole of the parts constitutes one bill.

(c) If a tangible negotiable bill of lading is lawfully issued in a set of parts and different parts are negotiated to different persons, the title of the holder to which the first due negotiation is made prevails as to both the document of title and the goods even if any later holder may have received the goods from the carrier in good faith and discharged the carrier's obligation by surrendering its part.

(d) A person that negotiates or transfers a single part of a tangible bill of lading issued in a set is liable to holders of that part as if it were the whole set.

(e) The bailee shall deliver in accordance with Part 4 against the first presented part of a tangible bill of lading lawfully issued in a set. Delivery in this manner discharges the bailee's obligation on the whole bill.

Official Comment

Prior Uniform Statutory Provision: Former Section 7–304.

Changes: To limit bills in a set to tangible bills of lading and to use terminology more consistent with modern usage.

Purposes:

1. Tangible bills of lading in a set are still used in some nations in international trade. Consequently, a tangible bill of lading part of a set could be at issue in a lawsuit that might come within Article 7. The statement of the legal effect of a lawfully issued set is in accord with existing commercial law relating to maritime and other international tangible bills of lading. This law has been codified in the Hague and Warsaw Conventions and in the Carriage of Goods by Sea Act, the provisions of which would ordinarily govern in situations where bills in a set are recognized by this Article. Tangible bills of lading in a set are prohibited in domestic trade.

2. Electronic bills of lading in domestic or international trade will not be issued in a set given the requirements of control necessary to deliver the bill to another person. An electronic bill of lading will be a single, authoritative copy. Section 7–106. Hence, this section differentiates between electronic bills of lading and tangible bills of lading. This section does not prohibit electronic data messages about goods in transit because these electronic data messages are not the issued bill of lading. Electronic data messages contain

information for the carrier's management and handling of the cargo but this information for the carrier's use is not the issued bill of lading.

Cross Reference:

Section 7–103, 7–303 and 7–106.

Definitional Cross References:

"Bailee". Section 7–102.
"Bill of lading". Section 1–201.
"Delivery". Section 1–201.
"Document of title". Section 1–201.
"Duly negotiate". Section 7–501.
"Good faith". Section 1–201. [7–102].
"Goods". Section 7–102.
"Holder". Section 1–201.
"Issuer". Section 7–102.
"Person". Section 1–201.
"Receipt of goods". Section 2–103.

§ 7–305.   Destination Bills.

(a) Instead of issuing a bill of lading to the consignor at the place of shipment, a carrier, at the request of the consignor, may procure the bill to be issued at destination or at any other place designated in the request.

(b) Upon request of any person entitled as against a carrier to control the goods while in transit and on surrender of possession or control of any outstanding bill of lading or other receipt covering the goods, the issuer, subject to Section 7–105, may procure a substitute bill to be issued at any place designated in the request.

Official Comment

Prior Uniform Statutory Provision: Former Section 7–305.

Changes: To accommodate electronic bills of lading and for style.

Purposes:

1. Subsection (a) continues the rules of former Section 7–305(1) without substantive change. This proposal is designed to facilitate the use of order bills in connection with fast shipments. Use of order bills on high speed shipments is impeded by the fact that the goods may arrive at destination before the documents, so that no one is ready to take delivery from the carrier. This is especially inconvenient for carriers by

truck and air, who do not have terminal facilities where shipments can be held to await the consignee's appearance. Order bills would be useful to take advantage of bank collection. This may be preferable to C.O.D. shipment in which the carrier, e.g. a truck driver, is the collecting and remitting agent. Financing of shipments under this plan would be handled as follows: seller at San Francisco delivers the goods to an airline with instructions to issue a bill in New York to a named bank. Seller receives a receipt embodying this undertaking to issue a destination bill. Airline wires its New York freight agent to issue the bill as instructed by the seller. Seller wires the New York bank a draft on buyer. New York bank indorses the bill to buyer when the buyer honors the draft. Normally seller would act through its own bank in San Francisco, which would extend credit in reliance on the airline's contract to deliver a bill to the order of its New York correspondent. This section is entirely permissive; it imposes no duty to issue such bills. Whether a performing carrier will act as issuing agent is left to agreement between carriers.

2. Subsection (b) continues the rule from former Section 7–305(2) with accommodation for electronic bills of lading. If the substitute bill changes from an electronic to a tangible medium or vice versa, the issuance of the substitute bill must comply with Section 7–105 to give the substitute bill validity and effect.

Cross Reference:

Section 7–105.

Definitional Cross References:

"Bill of lading". Section 1–201.
"Consignor". Section 7–102.
"Goods". Section 7–102.
"Issuer". Section 7–102.
"Receipt of goods". Section 2–103.

§ 7–306.   Altered Bills of Lading.

An unauthorized alteration or filling in of a blank in a bill of lading leaves the bill enforceable according to its original tenor.

Official Comment

Prior Uniform Statutory Provision: Former Section 7–306.

Changes: None

Purposes:

An unauthorized alteration or filling in of a blank, whether made with or without fraudulent intent, does not relieve the issuer of its liability on the document as originally executed. This section applies to both tangible and electronic bills of lading, applying the same rule to both types of bills of lading. The control concept of Section 7–106 requires that any changes to the electronic document of title be readily identifiable as authorized or unauthorized. Section 7–306 should be compared to Section 7–208 where a different rule applies to the unauthorized filling in of a blank for tangible warehouse receipts.

Cross Reference:

Sections 7–106 and 7–208.

Definitional Cross References:

"Bill of lading". Section 1–201.
"Issuer". Section 7–102.

§ 7–307.   Lien of Carrier.

(a) A carrier has a lien on the goods covered by a bill of lading or on the proceeds thereof in its possession for charges after the date of the carrier's receipt of the goods for storage or transportation, including demurrage and terminal charges, and for expenses necessary for preservation of the goods incident to their transportation or reasonably incurred in their sale pursuant to law. However, against a purchaser for value of a negotiable bill of lading, a carrier's lien is limited to charges stated in the bill or the applicable tariffs or, if no charges are stated, a reasonable charge.

(b) A lien for charges and expenses under subsection (a) on goods that the carrier was required by law to receive for transportation is effective against the consignor or any person entitled to the goods unless the carrier had notice that the consignor lacked authority to subject the goods to those charges and expenses. Any other lien under subsection (a) is effective against the consignor and any person that permitted the bailor to have control or possession of the goods unless the carrier had notice that the bailor lacked authority.

(c) A carrier loses its lien on any goods that it voluntarily delivers or unjustifiably refuses to deliver.

Official Comment

Prior Uniform Statutory Provision: Former Section 7–307.

Changes: Expanded to cover proceeds of the goods transported.

Purposes:

1.   The section is intended to give carriers a specific statutory lien for charges and expenses similar to that given to warehouses by the first sentence of Section 7–209(a) and extends that lien to the proceeds of the goods as long as the carrier has possession of the proceeds. But because carriers do not commonly claim a lien for charges in relation to other goods or lend money on the security of goods in their hands, provisions for a general lien or a security interest similar to those in Section 7–209(a) and (b) are omitted. Carriers may utilize Article 9 to obtain a security interest and become a secured party or a carrier may agree to limit its lien rights in a transportation agreement with the shipper. As the lien given by this section is specific, and the storage or transportation often preserves or increases the value of the goods, subsection (b) validates the lien against anyone who permitted the bailor to have possession of the goods. Where the carrier is required to receive the goods for transportation, the owner's interest may be subjected to charges and expenses arising out of deposit of his goods by a thief. The crucial mental element is the carrier's knowledge or reason to know of the bailor's lack of authority. If the carrier does not know or have reason to know of the bailor's lack of authority, the carrier has a lien under this section against any person so long as the conditions of subsection (b) are satisfied. In light of the crucial mental element, Sections 7–307 and 9–333 combine to give priority to a carrier's lien over security interests in the goods. In this regard, the judicial decision in In re Sharon Steel Corp., 25 U.C.C. Rep.2d 503, 176 B.R. 384 (W.D. Pa. 1995) is correct and is the controlling precedent.

2.   The reference to charges in this section means charges relating to the bailment relationship for transportation. Charges does not mean that the bill of lading must state a specific rate or a specific amount. However, failure to state a specific rate or a specific amount has legal consequences under the second sentence of subsection (a).

3.   The carrier's specific lien under this section is a possessory lien. See subsection (c). Part 3 of Article 7 does not require any particular form for a bill of

lading. The carrier's lien arises when the carrier has issued a bill of lading.

Cross References:

Point 1: Sections 7-209, 9-109 and 9-333.
Point 3. Section 7-202 and 7-209.

Definitional Cross References:

"Bill of lading". Section 1-201.
"Carrier". Section 7-102.
"Consignor". Section 7-102.
"Delivery". Section 1-201.
"Goods". Section 7-102.
"Person". Section 1-201.
"Purchaser". Section 1-201.
"Value". Section 1-204.

§ 7-308. Enforcement of Carrier's Lien.

(a) A carrier's lien on goods may be enforced by public or private sale of the goods, in bulk or in packages, at any time or place and on any terms that are commercially reasonable, after notifying all persons known to claim an interest in the goods. The notification must include a statement of the amount due, the nature of the proposed sale, and the time and place of any public sale. The fact that a better price could have been obtained by a sale at a different time or in a method different from that selected by the carrier is not of itself sufficient to establish that the sale was not made in a commercially reasonable manner. The carrier sells goods in a commercially reasonable manner if the carrier sells the goods in the usual manner in any recognized market therefor, sells at the price current in that market at the time of the sale, or otherwise sells in conformity with commercially reasonable practices among dealers in the type of goods sold. A sale of more goods than apparently necessary to be offered to ensure satisfaction of the obligation is not commercially reasonable, except in cases covered by the preceding sentence.

(b) Before any sale pursuant to this section, any person claiming a right in the goods may pay the amount necessary to satisfy the lien and the reasonable expenses incurred in complying with this section. In that event, the goods may not be sold but must be retained by the carrier, subject to the terms of the bill of lading and this article.

(c) A carrier may buy at any public sale pursuant to this section.

(d) A purchaser in good faith of goods sold to enforce a carrier's lien takes the goods free of any rights of persons against which the lien was valid, despite the carrier's noncompliance with this section.

(e) A carrier may satisfy its lien from the proceeds of any sale pursuant to this section but shall hold the balance, if any, for delivery on demand to any person to which the carrier would have been bound to deliver the goods.

(f) The rights provided by this section are in addition to all other rights allowed by law to a creditor against a debtor.

(g) A carrier's lien may be enforced pursuant to either subsection (a) or the procedure set forth in Section 7-210(b).

(h) A carrier is liable for damages caused by failure to comply with the requirements for sale under this section and, in case of willful violation, is liable for conversion.

Official Comment

Prior Uniform Statutory Provision: Former Section 7-308.

Changes: To conform language to modern usage and for style.

Purposes:

This section is intended to give the carrier an enforcement procedure of its lien coextensive with that given the warehouse in cases other than those covering noncommercial storage by the warehouse. See Section 7-210 and comments.

Cross Reference:

Section 7-210.

Definitional Cross References:

"Bill of lading". Section 1-201.
"Carrier". Section 7-102.
"Creditor". Section 1-201.
"Delivery". Section 1-201.
"Good faith". Section 1-201. [7-102]
"Goods". Section 7-102.
"Notification". Section 1-202.
"Notifies". Section 1-202.
"Person". Section 1-201.
"Purchaser". Section 1-201.
"Rights". Section 1-201.
"Term". Section 1-201.

§ 7–309. Duty of Care; Contractual Limitation of Carrier's Liability.

(a) A carrier that issues a bill of lading, whether negotiable or nonnegotiable, shall exercise the degree of care in relation to the goods which a reasonably careful person would exercise under similar circumstances. This subsection does not affect any statute, regulation, or rule of law that imposes liability upon a common carrier for damages not caused by its negligence.

(b) Damages may be limited by a term in the bill of lading or in a transportation agreement that the carrier's liability may not exceed a value stated in the bill or transportation agreement if the carrier's rates are dependent upon value and the consignor is afforded an opportunity to declare a higher value and the consignor is advised of the opportunity. However, such a limitation is not effective with respect to the carrier's liability for conversion to its own use.

(c) Reasonable provisions as to the time and manner of presenting claims and commencing actions based on the shipment may be included in a bill of lading or a transportation agreement.

Official Comment

Prior Uniform Statutory Provision: Former Section 7–309.

Changes: References to tariffs eliminated because of deregulation, adding reference to transportation agreements, and for style.

Purposes:

1. A bill of lading may also serve as the contract between the carrier and the bailor. Parties in their contract should be able to limit the amount of damages for breach of that contract including breach of the duty to take reasonable care of the goods. The parties cannot disclaim by contract the carrier's obligation of care. Section 1–302.

Federal statutes and treaties for air, maritime and rail transport may alter the standard of care. These federal statutes and treaties preempt this section when applicable. Section 7–103. Subsection (a) does not impair any rule of law imposing the liability of an insurer on a common carrier in intrastate commerce. Subsection (b), however, applies to the common carrier's liability as an insurer as well as to liability based on negligence. Subsection (b) allows the term limiting

damages to appear either in the bill of lading or in the parties' transportation agreement. Compare 7–204(b). Subsection (c) allows the parties to agree to provisions regarding time and manner of presenting claims or commencing actions if the provisions are either in the bill of lading or the transportation agreement. Compare 7–204(c). Transportation agreements are commonly used to establish agreed terms between carriers and shippers that have an on-going relationship.

2. References to public tariffs in former Section 7–309(2) and (3) have been deleted in light of the modern era of deregulation. See Comment 2 to Section 7–103. If a tariff is required under state or federal law, pursuant to Section 7–103(a), the tariff would control over the rule of this section. As governed by contract law, parties may incorporate by reference the limits on the amount of damages or the reasonable provisions as to the time and manner of presenting claims set forth in applicable tariffs, e.g. a maximum unit value beyond which goods are not taken or a disclaimer of responsibility for undeclared articles of extraordinary value.

3. As under former Section 7–309(2), subsection (b) provides that a limitation of damages is ineffective if the carrier has converted the goods to its own use. A mere failure to redeliver the goods is not conversion to the carrier's own use. "Conversion to its own use" is narrower than the idea of conversion generally. Art Masters Associates, Ltd. v. United Parcel Service, 77 N.Y.2d 200, 567 N.E.2d 226 (1990); See, Kemper Ins. Co. v. Fed. Ex. Corp., 252 F.3d 509 (1st Cir.), *cert. denied* 534 U.S. 1020 (2001) (opinion interpreting federal law).

4. As used in this section, damages may include damages arising from delay in delivery. Delivery dates and times are often specified in the parties' contract. See Section 7–403.

Cross Reference:

Sections 1–302, 7–103, 7–204, 7–403.

Definitional Cross References:

"Action". Section 1–201.
"Bill of lading". Section 1–201.
"Carrier". Section 7–102.
"Consignor". Section 7–102.
"Document of Title". Section 1–102.
"Goods". Section 7–102.
"Value". Section 1–204.

PART 4

WAREHOUSE RECEIPTS AND BILLS OF LADING: GENERAL OBLIGATIONS

§ 7–401. Irregularities in Issue of Receipt or Bill or Conduct of Issuer.

The obligations imposed by this article on an issuer apply to a document of title even if:

(1) the document does not comply with the requirements of this article or of any other statute, rule, or regulation regarding its issuance, form, or content;

(2) the issuer violated laws regulating the conduct of its business;

(3) the goods covered by the document were owned by the bailee when the document was issued; or

(4) the person issuing the document is not a warehouse but the document purports to be a warehouse receipt.

Official Comment

Prior Uniform Statutory Provision: Former Section 7–401.

Changes: Changes for style only.

Purposes:

The bailee's liability on its document despite non-receipt or misdescription of the goods is affirmed in Sections 7–203 and 7–301. The purpose of this section is to make it clear that regardless of irregularities a document which falls within the definition of document of title imposes on the issuer the obligations stated in this Article. For example, a bailee will not be permitted to avoid its obligation to deliver the goods (Section 7–403) or its obligation of due care with respect to them (Sections 7–204 and 7–309) by taking the position that no valid "document" was issued because it failed to file a statutory bond or did not pay stamp taxes or did not disclose the place of storage in the document. Tate v. Action Moving & Storage, Inc., 383 S.E.2d 229 (N.C. App. 1989), *rev. denied* 389 S.E.2d 104 (N.C. 1990). Sanctions against violations of statutory or administrative duties with respect to documents should be limited to revocation of license or other measures prescribed by the regulation imposing the duty. See Section 7–103.

Cross References:

Sections 7–103, 7–203, 7–204, 7–301, 7–309.

Definitional Cross References:

"Bailee". Section 7–102.
"Document of title". Section 1–201.
"Goods". Section 7–102.
"Issuer". Section 7–102.
"Person". Section 1–201.
"Warehouse receipt". Section 1–201.
"Warehouse". Section 7–102.

§ 7–402. Duplicate Document of Title; Overissue.

A duplicate or any other document of title purporting to cover goods already represented by an outstanding document of the same issuer does not confer any right in the goods, except as provided in the case of tangible bills of lading in a set of parts, overissue of documents for fungible goods, substitutes for lost, stolen, or destroyed documents, or substitute documents issued pursuant to Section 7–105. The issuer is liable for damages caused by its overissue or failure to identify a duplicate document by a conspicuous notation.

Official Comment

Prior Uniform Statutory Provision: Former Section 7–402.

Changes: Changes to accommodate electronic documents.

Purposes:

1. This section treats a duplicate which is not properly identified as a duplicate like any other overissue of documents: a purchaser of such a document acquires no title but only a cause of action for damages against the person that made the deception possible, except in the cases noted in the section. But parts of a tangible bill lawfully issued in a set of parts are not "overissue" (Section 7–304). Of course, if the issuer has clearly indicated that a document is a duplicate so that no one can be deceived by it, and in fact the duplicate is a correct copy of the original, the issuer is not liable for preparing and delivering such a duplicate copy.

Section 7–105 allows documents of title to be reissued in another medium. Re-issuance of a document in an alternative medium under Section 7–105 requires that the original document be surrendered to the issuer in order to make the substitute document the effective document. If the substitute document is not issued in compliance with section 7–105, then the document should be treated as a duplicate under this section.

2. The section applies to nonnegotiable documents to the extent of providing an action for damages for one who acquires an unmarked duplicate from a transferor who knew the facts and would therefore have had no cause of action against the issuer of the duplicate. Ordinarily the transferee of a nonnegotiable document acquires only the rights of its transferor.

3. Overissue is defined so as to exclude the common situation where two valid documents of different issuers are outstanding for the same goods at the same time. Thus freight forwarders commonly issue bills of lading to their customers for small shipments to be combined into carload shipments for which the railroad will issue a bill of lading to the forwarder. So also a warehouse receipt may be outstanding against goods, and the holder of the receipt may issue delivery orders against the same goods. In these cases dealings with the subsequently issued documents may be effective to transfer title; e.g. negotiation of a delivery order will effectively transfer title in the ordinary case where no dishonesty has occurred and the goods are available to satisfy the orders. Section 7–503 provides for cases of conflict between documents of different issuers.

Cross References:

Point 1: Sections 7–105, 7–207, 7–304, and 7–601.
Point 3: Section 7–503.

Definitional Cross References:

"Bill of lading". Section 1–201.
"Conspicuous". Section 1–201.
"Document of title". Section 1–201.
"Fungible goods." Section 1–201.
"Goods". Section 7–102.
"Issuer". Section 7–102.
"Right". Section 1–201.

§ 7–403. Obligation of Bailee to Deliver; Excuse.

(a) A bailee shall deliver the goods to a person entitled under a document of title if the person complies with subsections (b) and (c), unless and to the extent that the bailee establishes any of the following:

(1) delivery of the goods to a person whose receipt was rightful as against the claimant;

(2) damage to or delay, loss, or destruction of the goods for which the bailee is not liable;

(3) previous sale or other disposition of the goods in lawful enforcement of a lien or on a warehouse's lawful termination of storage;

(4) the exercise by a seller of its right to stop delivery pursuant to Section 2–705 or by a lessor of its right to stop delivery pursuant to Section 2A–526;

(5) a diversion, reconsignment, or other disposition pursuant to Section 7–303;

(6) release, satisfaction, or any other personal defense against the claimant; or

(7) any other lawful excuse.

(b) A person claiming goods covered by a document of title shall satisfy the bailee's lien if the bailee so requests or if the bailee is prohibited by law from delivering the goods until the charges are paid.

(c) Unless a person claiming the goods is a person against which the document of title does not confer a right under Section 7–503(a):

(1) the person claiming under a document shall surrender possession or control of any outstanding negotiable document covering the goods for cancellation or indication of partial deliveries; and

(2) the bailee shall cancel the document or conspicuously indicate in the document the partial delivery or the bailee is liable to any person to which the document is duly negotiated.

Official Comment

Prior Uniform Statutory Provision: Former Section 7–403.

Changes: Definition in former Section 7–403(4) moved to Section 7–102; bracketed language in former Section 7–403(1)(b) deleted; added cross reference to Section 2A–526; changes for style.

Purposes:

1. The present section, following former Section 7–403, is constructed on the basis of stating what previous deliveries or other circumstances operate to excuse

the bailee's normal obligation on the document. Accordingly, "justified" deliveries under the pre-Code uniform acts now find their place as "excuse" under subsection (a).

2. The principal case covered by subsection (a)(1) is delivery to a person whose title is paramount to the rights represented by the document. For example, if a thief deposits stolen goods in a warehouse facility and takes a negotiable receipt, the warehouse is not liable on the receipt if it has surrendered the goods to the true owner, even though the receipt is held by a good faith purchaser. See Section 7–503(a). However, if the owner entrusted the goods to a person with power of disposition, and that person deposited the goods and took a negotiable document, the owner receiving delivery would not be rightful as against a holder to whom the negotiable document was duly negotiated, and delivery to the owner would not give the bailee a defense against such a holder. See Sections 7–502(a)(2), 7–503(a)(1).

3. Subsection (a)(2) amounts to a cross reference to all the tort law that determines the varying responsibilities and standards of care applicable to commercial bailees. A restatement of this tort law would be beyond the scope of this Act. Much of the applicable law as to responsibility of bailees for the preservation of the goods and limitation of liability in case of loss has been codified for particular classes of bailees in interstate and foreign commerce by federal legislation and treaty and for intrastate carriers and other bailees by the regulatory state laws preserved by Section 7–103. In the absence of governing legislation the common law will prevail subject to the minimum standard of reasonable care prescribed by Sections 7–204 and 7–309 of this Article.

The bracketed language found in former Section 7–403(1)(b) has been deleted thereby leaving the allocations of the burden of going forward with the evidence and the burden of proof to the procedural law of the various states.

Subsection (a)(4) contains a cross reference to both the seller's and the lessor's rights to stop delivery under Article 2 and Article 2A respectively.

4. As under former Section 7–403, there is no requirement that a request for delivery must be accompanied by a formal tender of the amount of the charges due. Rather, the bailee must request payment of the amount of its lien when asked to deliver, and only in case this request is refused is it justified in declining to deliver because of nonpayment of charges. Where delivery without payment is forbidden by law, the request is treated as implicit. Such a prohibition reflects a policy of uniformity to prevent discrimination by failure to request payment in particular cases. Subsection (b) must be read in conjunction with the priorities given to the warehouse lien and the carrier lien under Section 7–209 and 7–307, respectively. If the parties are in dispute about whether the request for payment of the lien is legally proper, the bailee may have recourse to interpleader. See Section 7–603.

5. Subsection (c) states the obvious duty of a bailee to take up a negotiable document or note partial deliveries conspicuously thereon, and the result of failure in that duty. It is subject to only one exception, that stated in subsection (a)(1) of this section and in Section 7–503(a). Subsection (c) is limited to cases of delivery to a claimant; it has no application, for example, where goods held under a negotiable document are lawfully sold to enforce the bailee's lien.

6. When courts are considering subsection (a)(7), "any other lawful excuse," among others, refers to compliance with court orders under Sections 7–601, 7–602 and 7–603.

Cross References:

Point 2: Sections 7–502 and 7–503.
Point 3: Sections 2–705, 2A–526, 7–103, 7–204, and 7–309 and 10–103.
Point 4: Sections 7–209, 7–307 and 7–603.
Point 5: Section 7–503(1).
Point 6: Sections 7–601, 7–602, and 7–603.

Definitional Cross References:

"Bailee". Section 7–102.
"Conspicuous". Section 1–201.
"Delivery". Section 1–201.
"Document of title". Section 1–201.
"Duly negotiate". Section 7–501.
"Goods". Section 7–102.
"Lessor". Section 2A–103.
"Person". Section 1–201.
"Receipt of goods". Section 2–103.
"Right". Section 1–201.
"Terms". Section 1–201.
"Warehouse". Section 7–102.

§ 7–404. No Liability for Good–Faith Delivery Pursuant to Document of Title.

A bailee that in good faith has received goods and delivered or otherwise disposed of the goods according to the terms of a document of title or pursuant to this article is not liable for the goods even if:

(1) the person from which the bailee received the goods did not have authority to procure the document or to dispose of the goods; or

(2) the person to which the bailee delivered the goods did not have authority to receive the goods.

Official Comment

Prior Uniform Statutory Provision: Former Section 7–404.

Changes: Changes reflect the definition of good faith in Section 1–201 [7–102] and for style .

Purposes:

This section uses the test of good faith, as defined in Section 1–201 [7–102], to continue the policy of former Section 7–404. Good faith now means "honesty in fact and the observance of reasonable commercial standards of fair dealing." The section states explicitly that the common law rule of "innocent conversion" by unauthorized "intermeddling" with another's property is inapplicable to the operations of commercial carriers

and warehousemen that in good faith perform obligations that they have assumed and that generally they are under a legal compulsion to assume. The section applies to delivery to a fraudulent holder of a valid document as well as to delivery to the holder of an invalid document. Of course, in appropriate circumstances, a bailee may use interpleader or other dispute resolution process. See Section 7–603.

Cross Reference:

Section 7–603.

Definitional Cross References:

"Bailee". Section 7–102.
"Delivery". Section 1–201.
"Document of title". Section 1–201.
"Good faith". Section 1–201. [7–102].
"Goods". Section 7–102.
"Person". Section 1–201.
"Receipt of goods". Section 2–103.
"Term". Section 1–201.

PART 5

WAREHOUSE RECEIPTS AND BILLS OF LADING: NEGOTIATION AND TRANSFER

§ 7–501. Form of Negotiation and Requirements of Due Negotiation.

(a) The following rules apply to a negotiable tangible document of title:

(1) If the document's original terms run to the order of a named person, the document is negotiated by the named person's indorsement and delivery. After the named person's indorsement in blank or to bearer, any person may negotiate the document by delivery alone.

(2) If the document's original terms run to bearer, it is negotiated by delivery alone.

(3) If the document's original terms run to the order of a named person and it is delivered to the named person, the effect is the same as if the document had been negotiated.

(4) Negotiation of the document after it has been indorsed to a named person requires indorsement by the named person and delivery.

(5) A document is duly negotiated if it is negotiated in the manner stated in this subsec-

tion to a holder that purchases it in good faith, without notice of any defense against or claim to it on the part of any person, and for value, unless it is established that the negotiation is not in the regular course of business or financing or involves receiving the document in settlement or payment of a monetary obligation.

(b) The following rules apply to a negotiable electronic document of title:

(1) If the document's original terms run to the order of a named person or to bearer, the document is negotiated by delivery of the document to another person. Indorsement by the named person is not required to negotiate the document.

(2) If the document's original terms run to the order of a named person and the named person has control of the document, the effect is the same as if the document had been negotiated.

(3) A document is duly negotiated if it is negotiated in the manner stated in this subsec-

tion to a holder that purchases it in good faith, without notice of any defense against or claim to it on the part of any person, and for value, unless it is established that the negotiation is not in the regular course of business or financing or involves taking delivery of the document in settlement or payment of a monetary obligation.

(c) Indorsement of a nonnegotiable document of title neither makes it negotiable nor adds to the transferee's rights.

(d) The naming in a negotiable bill of lading of a person to be notified of the arrival of the goods does not limit the negotiability of the bill or constitute notice to a purchaser of the bill of any interest of that person in the goods.

Official Comment

Prior Uniform Statutory Provision: Former Section 7–501.

Changes: To accommodate negotiable electronic documents of title.

Purpose:

1. Subsection (a) has been limited to tangible negotiable documents of title but otherwise remains unchanged in substance from the rules in former Section 7–501. Subsection (b) is new and applies to negotiable electronic documents of title. Delivery of a negotiable electronic document is through voluntary transfer of control. Section 1–201 definition of "delivery." The control concept as applied to negotiable electronic documents of title is the substitute for both possession and indorsement as applied to negotiable tangible documents of title. Section 7–106.

Article 7 does not separately define the term "duly negotiated." However, the elements of "duly negotiated" are set forth in subsection (a)(5) for tangible documents and (b)(3) for electronic documents. As under former Section 7–501, in order to effect a "due negotiation" the negotiation must be in the "regular course of business or financing" in order to transfer greater rights than those held by the person negotiating. The foundation of the mercantile doctrine of good faith purchase for value has always been, as shown by the case situations, the furtherance and protection of the regular course of trade. The reason for allowing a person, in bad faith or in error, to convey away rights which are not its own has from the beginning been to make possible the speedy handling of that great run of commercial transactions which are patently usual and normal.

There are two aspects to the usual and normal course of mercantile dealings, namely, the person making the transfer and the nature of the transaction itself. The first question which arises is: Is the transferor a person with whom it is reasonable to deal as having full powers? In regard to documents of title the only holder whose possession or control appears, commercially, to be in order is almost invariably a person in the trade. No commercial purpose is served by allowing a tramp or a professor to "duly negotiate" an order bill of lading for hides or cotton not their own, and since such a transfer is obviously not in the regular course of business, it is excluded from the scope of the protection of subsections (a)(5) or (b)(3).

The second question posed by the "regular course" qualification is: Is the transaction one which is normally proper to pass full rights without inquiry, even though the transferor itself may not have such rights to pass, and even though the transferor may be acting in breach of duty? In raising this question the "regular course" criterion has the further advantage of limiting, the effective wrongful disposition to transactions whose protection will really further trade. Obviously, the snapping up of goods for quick resale at a price suspiciously below the market deserves no protection as a matter of policy: it is also clearly outside the range of regular course.

Any notice on the document sufficient to put a merchant on inquiry as to the "regular course" quality of the transaction will frustrate a "due negotiation". Thus irregularity of the document or unexplained staleness of a bill of lading may appropriately be recognized as negating a negotiation in "regular" course.

A pre-existing claim constitutes value, and "due negotiation" does not require "new value." A usual and ordinary transaction in which documents are received as security for credit previously extended may be in "regular" course, even though there is a demand for additional collateral because the creditor "deems himself insecure." But the matter has moved out of the regular course of financing if the debtor is thought to be insolvent, the credit previously extended is in effect cancelled, and the creditor snatches a plank in the shipwreck under the guise of a demand for additional collateral. Where a money debt is "paid" in commodity paper, any question of "regular" course disappears, as the case is explicitly excepted from "due negotiation".

2. Negotiation under this section may be made by any holder no matter how the holder acquired possession or control of the document.

3. Subsections (a)(3) and (b)(2) make explicit a matter upon which the intent of the pre-Code law was clear but the language somewhat obscure: a negotiation results from a delivery to a banker or buyer to whose order the document has been taken by the person making the bailment. There is no presumption of irregularity in such a negotiation; it may very well be in "regular course."

4. This Article does not contain any provision creating a presumption of due negotiation to, and full rights in, a holder of a document of title akin to that created by Uniform Commercial Code Article 3. But the reason of the provisions of this Act (Section 1–307) on the prima facie authenticity and accuracy of third party documents, joins with the reason of the present section to work such a presumption in favor of any person who has power to make a due negotiation. It would not make sense for this Act to authorize a purchaser to indulge the presumption of regularity if the courts were not also called upon to do so. Allocations of the burden of going forward with the evidence and the burden of proof are left to the procedural law of the various states.

5. Subsections (c) and (d) are unchanged from prior law and apply to both tangible and electronic documents of title.

Cross References:

Sections 1–307, 7–502 and 7–503.

Definitional Cross References:

"Bearer". Section 1–201.
"Control". Section 7–106.
"Delivery". Section 1–201.
"Document of title". Section 1–201.
"Good faith". Section 1–201 [7–102].
"Holder". Section 1–201.
"Notice". Section 1–202.
"Person". Section 1–201.
"Purchase". Section 1–201.
"Rights". Section 1–201.
"Term". Section 1–201.
"Value". Section 1–204.

§ 7–502. Rights Acquired by Due Negotiation.

(a) Subject to Sections 7–205 and 7–503, a holder to which a negotiable document of title has been duly negotiated acquires thereby:

(1) title to the document;

(2) title to the goods;

(3) all rights accruing under the law of agency or estoppel, including rights to goods delivered to the bailee after the document was issued; and

(4) the direct obligation of the issuer to hold or deliver the goods according to the terms of the document free of any defense or claim by the issuer except those arising under the terms of the document or under this article, but in the case of a delivery order, the bailee's obligation accrues only upon the bailee's acceptance of the delivery order and the obligation acquired by the holder is that the issuer and any indorser will procure the acceptance of the bailee.

(b) Subject to Section 7–503, title and rights acquired by due negotiation are not defeated by any stoppage of the goods represented by the document of title or by surrender of the goods by the bailee and are not impaired even if:

(1) the due negotiation or any prior due negotiation constituted a breach of duty;

(2) any person has been deprived of possession of a negotiable tangible document or control of a negotiable electronic document by misrepresentation, fraud, accident, mistake, duress, loss, theft, or conversion; or

(3) a previous sale or other transfer of the goods or document has been made to a third person.

Official Comment

Prior Uniform Statutory Provision: Former Section 7–502.

Changes: To accommodate electronic documents of title and for style.

Purpose:

1. This section applies to both tangible and electronic documents of title. The elements of duly negotiated, which constitutes a due negotiation, are set forth in Section 7–501. The several necessary qualifications of the broad principle that the holder of a document acquired in a due negotiation is the owner of the document and the goods have been brought together in the next section (Section 7–503).

2. Subsection (a)(3) covers the case of "feeding" of a duly negotiated document by subsequent delivery to the bailee of such goods as the document falsely pur-

ported to cover; the bailee in such case is estopped as against the holder of the document.

3. The explicit statement in subsection (a)(4) of the bailee's direct obligation to the holder precludes the defense that the document in question was "spent" after the carrier had delivered the goods to a previous holder. But the holder is subject to such defenses as non-negligent destruction even though not apparent on the document. The sentence on delivery orders applies only to delivery orders in negotiable form which have been duly negotiated. On delivery orders, see also Section 7–503(b) and Comment.

4. Subsection (b) continues the law which gave full effect to the issuance or due negotiation of a negotiable document. The subsection adds nothing to the effect of the rules stated in subsection (a), but it has been included since such explicit reference was provided under former Section 7–502 to preserve the right of a purchaser by due negotiation. The listing is not exhaustive. The language "any stoppage" is included lest an inference be drawn that a stoppage of the goods before or after transit might cut off or otherwise impair the purchaser's rights.

Cross References:

Sections 7–103, 7–205, 7–403, 7–501, and 7–503.

Definitional Cross References:

"Bailee". Section 7–102.
"Control". Section 7–106.
"Delivery". Section 1–201.
"Delivery order". Section 7–102.
"Document of title". Section 1–201.
"Duly negotiate". Section 7–501.
"Fungible". Section 1–201.
"Goods". Section 7–102.
"Holder". Section 1–201.
"Issuer". Section 7–102.
"Person". Section 1–201.
"Rights". Section 1–201.
"Term". Section 1–201.
"Warehouse receipt". Section 1–201.

§ 7–503. Document of Title to Goods Defeated in Certain Cases.

(a) A document of title confers no right in goods against a person that before issuance of the document had a legal interest or a perfected security interest in the goods and that did not:

(1) deliver or entrust the goods or any document of title covering the goods to the bailor or the bailor's nominee with:

(A) actual or apparent authority to ship, store, or sell;

(B) power to obtain delivery under Section 7–403; or

(C) power of disposition under Section 2–403, 2A–304(2), 2A–305(2), 9–320, or 9–321(c) or other statute or rule of law; or

(2) acquiesce in the procurement by the bailor or its nominee of any document.

(b) Title to goods based upon an unaccepted delivery order is subject to the rights of any person to which a negotiable warehouse receipt or bill of lading covering the goods has been duly negotiated. That title may be defeated under Section 7–504 to the same extent as the rights of the issuer or a transferee from the issuer.

(c) Title to goods based upon a bill of lading issued to a freight forwarder is subject to the rights of any person to which a bill issued by the freight forwarder is duly negotiated. However, delivery by the carrier in accordance with Part 4 pursuant to its own bill of lading discharges the carrier's obligation to deliver.

Official Comment

Prior Uniform Statutory Provision: Former Section 7–503.

Changes: Changes to cross-reference to Article 2A and for style.

Purposes:

1. In general it may be said that the title of a purchaser by due negotiation prevails over almost any interest in the goods which existed prior to the procurement of the document of title if the possession of the goods by the person obtaining the document derived from any action by the prior claimant which introduced the goods into the stream of commerce or carried them along that stream. A thief of the goods cannot indeed by shipping or storing them to the thief's own order acquire power to transfer them to a good faith purchaser. Nor can a tenant or mortgagor defeat any rights of a landlord or mortgagee which have been perfected under the local law merely by wrongfully shipping or storing a portion of the crop or other goods. However, "acquiescence" by the landlord or mortgagee does not require active consent under subsection (a)(2) and knowledge of the likelihood of storage or shipment with no objection or effort to control it is sufficient to defeat the landlord's or the mortgagee's rights as against one who takes by due

negotiation of a negotiable document. In re Sharon Steel, 176 B.R. 384 (Bankr. W.D. Pa. 1995); In re R.V. Segars Co, 54 B.R. 170 (Bankr. S.C. 1985); In re Jamestown Elevators, Inc., 49 B.R. 661 (Bankr. N.D. 1985).

On the other hand, where goods are delivered to a factor for sale, even though the factor has made no advances and is limited in its duty to sell for cash, the goods are "entrusted" to the factor "with actual ... authority ... to sell" under subsection (a)(1), and if the factor procures a negotiable document of title it can transfer the owner's interest to a purchaser by due negotiation. Further, where the factor is in the business of selling, goods entrusted to it simply for safekeeping or storage may be entrusted under circumstances which give the factor "apparent authority to ship, store or sell" under subsection (a)(1), or power of disposition under Section 2–403, 2A–304(2), 2A–305(2), 7–205, 9–320, or 9–321(c) or under a statute such as the earlier Factors Acts, or under a rule of law giving effect to apparent ownership. See Section 1–103.

Persons having an interest in goods also frequently deliver or entrust them to agents or servants other than factors for the purpose of shipping or warehousing or under circumstances reasonably contemplating such action. This Act is clear that such persons assume full risk that the agent to whom the goods are so delivered may ship or store in breach of duty, take a document to the agent's own order and then proceed to misappropriate the negotiable document of title that embodies the goods. This Act makes no distinction between possession or mere custody in such situations and finds no exception in the case of larceny by a bailee or the like. The safeguard in such situations lies in the requirement that a due negotiation can occur only "in the regular course of business or financing" and that the purchase be in good faith and without notice. See Section 7–501. Documents of title have no market among the commercially inexperienced and the commercially experienced do not take them without inquiry from persons known to be truck drivers or petty clerks even though such persons purport to be operating in their own names.

Again, where the seller allows a buyer to receive goods under a contract for sale, though as a "conditional delivery" or under "cash sale" terms and on explicit agreement for immediate payment, the buyer thereby acquires power to defeat the seller's interest by transfer of the goods to certain good faith purchasers. See Section 2–403. Both in policy and under the language of subsection (a)(1) that same power must be extended to accomplish the same result if the buyer procures a negotiable document of title to the goods and duly negotiates it.

This comment 1 should be considered in interpreting delivery, entrustment or acquiescence in application of Section 7–209.

2. Under subsection (a) a delivery order issued by a person having no right in or power over the goods is ineffective unless the owner acts as provided in subsection (a)(1) or (2). Thus the rights of a transferee of a non-negotiable warehouse receipt can be defeated by a delivery order subsequently issued by the transferor only if the transferee "delivers or entrusts" to the "person procuring" the delivery order or "acquiesces" in that person's procurement. Similarly, a second delivery order issued by the same issuer for the same goods will ordinarily be subject to the first, both under this section and under Section 7–402. After a delivery order is validly issued but before it is accepted, it may nevertheless be defeated under subsection (b) in much the same way that the rights of a transferee may be defeated under Section 7–504. For example, a buyer in ordinary course from the issuer may defeat the rights of the holder of a prior delivery order if the bailee receives notification of the buyer's rights before notification of the holder's rights. Section 7–504(b)(2). But an accepted delivery order has the same effect as a document issued by the bailee.

3. Under subsection (c) a bill of lading issued to a freight forwarder is subordinated to the freight forwarder's document of title, since the bill on its face gives notice of the fact that a freight forwarder is in the picture and the freight forwarder has in all probability issued a document of title. But the carrier is protected in following the terms of its own bill of lading.

Cross References:

Point 1: Sections 1–103, 2–403, 2A–304(2), 2A–305(2), 7–205, 7–209, 7–501, 9–320, 9–321(c), and 9–331.

Point 2: Sections 7–402 and 7–504.

Point 3: Sections 7–402, 7–403 and 7–404.

Definitional Cross References:

"Bill of lading". Section 1–201.

"Contract for sale". Section 2–106.

"Delivery". Section 1–201.

"Delivery order". Section 7–102.

"Document of title". Section 1–201.

"Duly negotiate". Section 7–501.

"Goods". Section 7–102.

"Person". Section 1–201.

"Right". Section 1–201.

"Warehouse receipt". Section 1–201.

§ 7–504. Rights Acquired in Absence of Due Negotiation; Effect of Diversion; Stoppage of Delivery.

(a) A transferee of a document of title, whether negotiable or nonnegotiable, to which the document has been delivered but not duly negotiated, acquires the title and rights that its transferor had or had actual authority to convey.

(b) In the case of a transfer of a nonnegotiable document of title, until but not after the bailee receives notice of the transfer, the rights of the transferee may be defeated:

(1) by those creditors of the transferor which could treat the transfer as void under Section 2–402 or 2A–308 ;

(2) by a buyer from the transferor in ordinary course of business if the bailee has delivered the goods to the buyer or received notification of the buyer's rights;

(3) by a lessee from the transferor in ordinary course of business if the bailee has delivered the goods to the lessee or received notification of the lessee's rights; or

(4) as against the bailee, by good-faith dealings of the bailee with the transferor.

(c) A diversion or other change of shipping instructions by the consignor in a nonnegotiable bill of lading which causes the bailee not to deliver the goods to the consignee defeats the consignee's title to the goods if the goods have been delivered to a buyer in ordinary course of business or a lessee in ordinary course of business and, in any event, defeats the consignee's rights against the bailee.

(d) Delivery of the goods pursuant to a nonnegotiable document of title may be stopped by a seller under Section 2–705 or a lessor under Section 2A–526, subject to the requirements of due notification in those sections. A bailee that honors the seller's or lessor's instructions is entitled to be indemnified by the seller or lessor against any resulting loss or expense.

Official Comment

Prior Uniform Statutory Provision: Former Section 7–504.

Changes: To include cross-references to Article 2A and for style.

Purposes:

1. Under the general principles controlling negotiable documents, it is clear that in the absence of due negotiation a transferor cannot convey greater rights than the transferor has, even when the negotiation is formally perfect. This section recognizes the transferor's power to transfer rights which the transferor has or has "actual authority to convey." Thus, where a negotiable document of title is being transferred the operation of the principle of estoppel is not recognized, as contrasted with situations involving the transfer of the goods themselves. (Compare Section 2–403 on good faith purchase of goods.) This section applies to both tangible and electronic documents of title.

A necessary part of the price for the protection of regular dealings with negotiable documents of title is an insistence that no dealing which is in any way irregular shall be recognized as a good faith purchase of the document or of any rights pertaining to it. So, where the transfer of a negotiable document fails as a negotiation because a requisite indorsement is forged or otherwise missing, the purchaser in good faith and for value may be in the anomalous position of having less rights, in part, than if the purchaser had purchased the goods themselves. True, the purchaser's rights are not subject to defeat by attachment of the goods or surrender of them to the purchaser's transferor (contrast subsection (b)); but on the other hand, the purchaser cannot acquire enforceable rights to control or receive the goods over the bailee's objection merely by giving notice to the bailee. Similarly, a consignee who makes payment to its consignor against a straight bill of lading can thereby acquire the position of a good faith purchaser of goods under provisions of the Article of this Act on Sales (Section 2–403), whereas the same payment made in good faith against an unendorsed order bill would not have such effect. The appropriate remedy of a purchaser in such a situation is to regularize its status by compelling indorsement of the document (see Section 7–506).

2. As in the case of transfer—as opposed to "due negotiation"—of negotiable documents, subsection (a) empowers the transferor of a nonnegotiable document to transfer only such rights as the transferor has or has "actual authority" to convey. In contrast to situations involving the goods themselves the operation of estoppel or agency principles is not here recognized to enable the transferor to convey greater rights than the transferor actually has. Subsection (b) makes it clear, however, that the transferee of a nonnegotiable docu-

ment may acquire rights greater in some respects than those of his transferor by giving notice of the transfer to the bailee. New subsection (b)(3) provides for the rights of a lessee in the ordinary course.

Subsection (b)(2) & (3) require delivery of the goods. Delivery of the goods means the voluntary transfer of physical possession of the goods. See amended 2–103.

3. Subsection (c) is in part a reiteration of the carrier's immunity from liability if it honors instructions of the consignor to divert, but there is added a provision protecting the title of the substituted consignee if the latter is a buyer in ordinary course of business. A typical situation would be where a manufacturer, having shipped a lot of standardized goods to A on nonnegotiable bill of lading, diverts the goods to customer B who pays for them. Under pre-Code passage-of-title-by-appropriation doctrine A might reclaim the goods from B. However, no consideration of commercial policy supports this involvement of an innocent third party in the default of the manufacturer on his contract to A; and the common commercial practice of diverting goods in transit suggests a trade understanding in accordance with this subsection. The same result should obtain if the substituted consignee is a lessee in ordinary course. The extent of the lessee's interest in the goods is less than a buyer's interest in the goods. However, as against the first consignee and the lessee in ordinary course as the substituted consignee, the lessee's rights in the goods as granted under the lease are superior to the first consignee's rights.

4. Subsection (d) gives the carrier an express right to indemnity where the carrier honors a seller's request to stop delivery.

5. Section 1–202 gives the bailee protection, if due diligence is exercised where the bailee's organization has not had time to act on a notification.

Cross References:

Point 1: Sections 2–403 and 7–506.
Point 2: Sections 2–403 and 2A–304.
Point 3: Sections 7–303, 7–403(a)(5) and 7–404.
Point 4: Sections 2–705 and 7–403(a)(4).
Point 5: Section 1–202.

Definitional Cross References:

"Bailee". Section 7–102.
"Bill of lading". Section 1–201.
"Buyer in ordinary course of business". Section 1–201.
"Consignee". Section 7–102.
"Consignor". Section 7–102.
"Creditor". Section 1–201.
"Delivery". Section 1–201.

"Document of Title". Section 1–201.
"Duly negotiate". Section 7–501.
"Good faith". Section 1–201. [7–102].
"Goods". Section 7–102.
"Honor". Section 1–201.
"Lessee in ordinary course". Section 2A–103.
"Notification" Section 1–202.
"Purchaser". Section 1–201.
"Rights". Section 1–201.

§ 7–505. Indorser not Guarantor for Other Parties.

The indorsement of a tangible document of title issued by a bailee does not make the indorser liable for any default by the bailee or previous indorsers.

Official Comment

Prior Uniform Statutory Provision: Former Section 7–505.

Changes: Limited to tangible documents of title.

Purposes:

This section is limited to tangible documents of title as the concept of indorsement is irrelevant to electronic documents of title. Electronic documents of title will be transferred by delivery of control. Section 7–106. The indorsement of a tangible document of title is generally understood to be directed towards perfecting the transferee's rights rather than towards assuming additional obligations. The language of the present section, however, does not preclude the one case in which an indorsement given for value guarantees future action, namely, that in which the bailee has not yet become liable upon the document at the time of the indorsement. Under such circumstances the indorser, of course, engages that appropriate honor of the document by the bailee will occur. See Section 7–502(a)(4) as to negotiable delivery orders. However, even in such a case, once the bailee attorns to the transferee, the indorser's obligation has been fulfilled and the policy of this section excludes any continuing obligation on the part of the indorser for the bailee's ultimate actual performance.

Cross Reference:

Sections 7–106 and 7–502.

Definitional Cross References:

"Bailee". Section 7–102.
"Document of title". Section 1–201.
"Party". Section 1–201.

§ 7–506. Delivery Without Indorsement: Right to Compel Indorsement.

The transferee of a negotiable tangible document of title has a specifically enforceable right to have its transferor supply any necessary indorsement, but the transfer becomes a negotiation only as of the time the indorsement is supplied.

Official Comment

Prior Uniform Statutory Provision: Former Section 7–506.

Changes: Limited to tangible documents of title.

Purposes:

1. This section is limited to tangible documents of title as the concept of indorsement is irrelevant to electronic documents of title. Electronic documents of title will be transferred by delivery of control. Section 7–106. From a commercial point of view the intention to transfer a tangible negotiable document of title which requires an indorsement for its transfer, is incompatible with an intention to withhold such indorsement and so defeat the effective use of the document. Further, the preceding section and the Comment thereto make it clear that an indorsement generally imposes no responsibility on the indorser.

2. Although this section provides that delivery of a tangible document of title without the necessary indorsement is effective as a transfer, the transferee, of course, has not regularized its position until such indorsement is supplied. Until this is done the transferee cannot claim rights under due negotiation within the requirements of this Article (Section 7–501(a)(5)) on "due negotiation". Similarly, despite the transfer to the transferee of the transferor's title, the transferee cannot demand the goods from the bailee until the negotiation has been completed and the document is in proper form for surrender. See Section 7–403(c).

Cross References:

Point 1: Sections 7–106 and 7–505.
Point 2: Sections 7–501(a)(5) and 7–403(c).

Definitional Cross References:

"Document of title". Section 1–201.
"Rights". Section 1–201.

§ 7–507. Warranties on Negotiation or Delivery of Document of Title.

If a person negotiates or delivers a document of title for value, otherwise than as a mere intermediary under Section 7–508, unless otherwise agreed, the transferor, in addition to any warranty made in selling or leasing the goods, warrants to its immediate purchaser only that:

(1) the document is genuine;

(2) the transferor does not have knowledge of any fact that would impair the document's validity or worth; and

(3) the negotiation or delivery is rightful and fully effective with respect to the title to the document and the goods it represents.

Official Comment

Prior Uniform Statutory Provision: Former Section 7–507.

Changes: Substitution of the word "delivery" for the word "transfer," reference leasing transactions and style.

Purposes:

1. Delivery of goods by use of a document of title does not limit or displace the ordinary obligations of a seller or lessor as to any warranties regarding the goods that arises under other law. If the transfer of documents attends or follows the making of a contract for the sale or lease of goods, the general obligations on warranties as to the goods (Sections 2–312 through 2–318 and Sections 2A–210 through 2A–316) are brought to bear as well as the special warranties under this section.

2. The limited warranties of a delivering or collecting intermediary, including a collecting bank, are stated in Section 7–508.

Cross References:

Point 1: Sections 2–312 through 2–318 and 2A–310–through 2A–316.
Point 2: Section 7–508.

Definitional Cross References:

"Delivery". Section 1–201.
"Document of title". Section 1–201.
"Genuine". Section 1–201.
"Goods". Section 7–102.
"Person". Section 1–201.
"Purchaser". Section 1–201.
"Value". Section 1–204.

§ 7–508. Warranties of Collecting Bank as to Documents of Title.

A collecting bank or other intermediary known to be entrusted with documents of title on behalf of another or with collection of a draft or other claim against delivery of documents warrants by the delivery of the documents only its own good faith and authority even if the collecting bank or other intermediary has purchased or made advances against the claim or draft to be collected.

Official Comment

Prior Uniform Statutory Provision: Former Section 7–508.

Changes: Changes for style only.

Purposes:

1. To state the limited warranties given with respect to the documents accompanying a documentary draft.

2. In warranting its authority a collecting bank or other intermediary only warrants its authority from its transferor. See Section 4–203. It does not warrant the genuineness or effectiveness of the document. Compare Section 7–507.

3. Other duties and rights of banks handling documentary drafts for collection are stated in Article 4, Part 5. On the meaning of draft, see Section 4–104 and Section 5–102, comment 11.

Cross References:

Sections 4–104, 4–203, 4–501 through 4–504, 5–102, and 7–507.

Definitional Cross References:

"Collecting bank". Section 4–105.

"Delivery". Section 1–201.
"Document of title". Section 1–102.
"Documentary draft". Section 4–104.
"Intermediary bank". Section 4–105.
"Good faith". Section 1–201 [7–102.]

§ 7–509. Adequate Compliance with Commercial Contract.

Whether a document of title is adequate to fulfill the obligations of a contract for sale, a contract for lease, or the conditions of a letter of credit is determined by Article 2, 2A, or 5.

Official Comment

Prior Uniform Statutory Provision: Former Section 7–509.

Changes: To reference Article 2A.

Purposes:

To cross-refer to the Articles of this Act which deal with the substantive issues of the type of document of title required under the contract entered into by the parties.

Cross References:

Articles 2, 2A and 5.

Definitional Cross References:

"Contract for sale". Section 2–106.
"Document of title". Section 1–201.
"Lease". Section 2A–103.

PART 6

WAREHOUSE RECEIPTS AND BILLS OF LADING: MISCELLANEOUS PROVISIONS

§ 7–601. Lost, Stolen, or Destroyed Documents of Title.

(a) If a document of title is lost, stolen, or destroyed, a court may order delivery of the goods or issuance of a substitute document and the bailee may without liability to any person comply with the order. If the document was negotiable, a court may not order delivery of the goods or issuance of a substitute document without the claimant's posting security unless it finds that any person that may suffer loss as a result of nonsurrender of possession or control of the document is adequately protected against the loss. If the document was nonnegotiable, the

court may require security. The court may also order payment of the bailee's reasonable costs and attorney's fees in any action under this subsection.

(b) A bailee that, without a court order, delivers goods to a person claiming under a missing negotiable document of title is liable to any person injured thereby. If the delivery is not in good faith, the bailee is liable for conversion. Delivery in good faith is not conversion if the claimant posts security with the bailee in an amount at least double the value of the goods at the time of posting to indemnify any person injured by the delivery which files a notice of claim within one year after the delivery.

Official Comment

Prior Uniform Statutory Provision: Former Section 7-601.

Changes: To accommodate electronic documents; to provide flexibility to courts similar to the flexibility in Section 3-309; to update to the modern era of deregulation; and for style.

Purposes:

1. Subsection (a) authorizes courts to order compulsory delivery of the goods or compulsory issuance of a substitute document. Compare Section 7-402. Using language similar to that found in Section 3-309, courts are given discretion as to what is adequate protection when the lost, stolen or destroyed document was negotiable or whether security should be required when the lost, stolen or destroyed document was nonnegotiable. In determining whether a party is adequately protected against loss in the case of a negotiable document, the court should consider the likelihood that the party will suffer a loss. The court is also given discretion as to the bailee's costs and attorney fees. The rights and obligations of a bailee under this section depend upon whether the document of title is lost, stolen or destroyed and is in addition to the ability of the bailee to bring an action for interpleader. See Section 7-603.

2. Courts have the authority under this section to order a substitute document for either tangible or electronic documents. If the substitute document will be in a different medium than the original document, the court should fashion its order in light of the requirements of Section 7-105.

3. Subsection (b) follows prior Section 7-601 in recognizing the legality of the well established commercial practice of bailees making delivery in good faith when they are satisfied that the claimant is the person entitled under a missing (i.e. lost , stolen, or destroyed) negotiable document. Acting without a court order, the bailee remains liable on the original negotiable document and, to avoid conversion liability, the bailee may insist that the claimant provide an indemnity bond. Cf. Section 7-403.

4. Claimants on non-negotiable instruments are permitted to avail themselves of the subsection (a) procedure because straight (non-negotiable) bills of lading sometimes contain provisions that the goods shall not be delivered except upon production of the bill. If the carrier should choose to insist upon production of the bill, the consignee should have some means

of compelling delivery on satisfactory proof of entitlement. Without a court order, a bailee may deliver, subject to Section 7-403, to a person claiming goods under a non-negotiable document that the same person claims is lost, stolen, or destroyed.

5. The bailee's lien should be protected when a court orders delivery of the goods pursuant to this section.

Cross References:

Point 1: Sections 3-309, 7-402 and 7-603.
Point 2: Section 7-105.
Point 3: Section 7-403.
Point 4: Section 7-403.
Point 5: Sections 7-209 and 7-307.

Definitional Cross References:

"Bailee". Section 7-102.
"Delivery". Section 1-201.
"Document of title". Section 1-201.
"Good faith". Section 1-201 [7-102].
"Goods". Section 7-102.
"Person". Section 1-201.

§ 7-602. Judicial Process Against Goods Covered by Negotiable Document of Title.

Unless a document of title was originally issued upon delivery of the goods by a person that did not have power to dispose of them, a lien does not attach by virtue of any judicial process to goods in the possession of a bailee for which a negotiable document of title is outstanding unless possession or control of the document is first surrendered to the bailee or the document's negotiation is enjoined. The bailee may not be compelled to deliver the goods pursuant to process until possession or control of the document is surrendered to the bailee or to the court. A purchaser of the document for value without notice of the process or injunction takes free of the lien imposed by judicial process.

Official Comment

Prior Uniform Statutory Provisions: Former Section 7-602.

Changes: Changes to accommodate electronic documents of title and for style.

Purposes:

1. The purpose of the section is to protect the bailee from conflicting claims of the document of title

holder and the judgment creditors of the person who deposited the goods. The rights of the former prevail unless, in effect, the judgment creditors immobilize the negotiable document of title through the surrender of possession of a tangible document or control of an electronic document. However, if the document of title was issued upon deposit of the goods by a person who had no power to dispose of the goods so that the document is ineffective to pass title, judgment liens are valid to the extent of the debtor's interest in the goods.

2. The last sentence covers the possibility that the holder of a document who has been enjoined from negotiating it will violate the injunction by negotiating to an innocent purchaser for value. In such case the lien will be defeated.

Cross Reference:

Sections 7–106 and 7–501 through 7–503.

Definitional Cross References:

"Bailee". Section 7–102.
"Delivery". Section 1–201.
"Document of title". Section 1–201.
"Goods". Section 7–102.
"Notice". Section 1–202.
"Person". Section 1–201.
"Purchase". Section 1–201.
"Value". Section 1–204.

§ 7–603.   Conflicting Claims; Interpleader.

If more than one person claims title to or possession of the goods, the bailee is excused from delivery until the bailee has a reasonable time to ascertain the validity of the adverse claims or to commence an action for interpleader. The bailee may assert an interpleader either in defending an action for nondelivery of the goods or by original action.

Official Comment

Prior Uniform Statutory Provisions: Former Section 7–603.

Changes: Changes for style only.

Purposes:

1. The section enables a bailee faced with conflicting claims to the goods to compel the claimants to litigate their claims with each other rather than with the bailee. The bailee is protected from legal liability when the bailee complies with court orders from the interpleader. *See e.g.* Northwestern National Sales, Inc. v. Commercial Cold Storage, Inc., 162 Ga. App. 741, 293 S.E.2d 30 (1982).

2. This section allows the bailee to bring an interpleader action but does not provide an exclusive basis for allowing interpleader. If either state or federal procedural rules allow an interpleader in other situations, the bailee may commence an interpleader under those rules. Even in an interpleader to which this section applies, the state or federal process of interpleader applies to the bailee's action for interpleader. For example, state or federal interpleader statutes or rules may permit a bailee to protect its lien or to seek attorney's fees and costs in the interpleader action.

Cross reference:

Point 1: Section 7–403.

Definitional Cross References:

"Action". Section 1–201.
"Bailee". Section 7–102.
"Delivery". Section 1–201.
"Goods". Section 7–102.
"Person". Section 1–201.
"Reasonable time". Section 1–205.

PART 7

MISCELLANEOUS PROVISIONS

LEGISLATIVE NOTE: The following provisions should be used to apply to both the Article 7 provisions and the conforming amendments to other articles of the Uniform Commercial Code found in Appendix B.

§ 7–701.   Effective Date.

This [Act] takes effect on [ ].

§ 7–702.   Repeals.

[Existing Article 7] and [Section 10–104 of the Uniform Commercial Code] are repealed.

Official Comment

A state should repeal its prior version of Uniform Commercial Code Article 7 on documents of title and Uniform Commercial Code section 10–204. The substance of Section 10–104 has been incorporated into Section 7–103(b).

§ 7–703. Applicability.

This [Act] applies to a document of title that is issued or a bailment that arises on or after the effective date of this [Act]. This [Act] does not apply to a document of title that is issued or a bailment that arises before the effective date of this [Act] even if the document of title or bailment would be subject to this [Act] if the document of title had been issued or bailment had arisen on or after the effective date of this [Act]. This [Act] does not apply to a right of action that has accrued before the effective date of this [Act].

Official Comment

This Act will apply prospectively only to documents of title issued or bailments that arise after the effective date of the Act.

§ 7–704. Savings Clause.

A document of title issued or a bailment that arises before the effective date of this [Act] and the rights, obligations, and interests flowing from that document or bailment are governed by any statute or other rule amended or repealed by this [Act] as if amendment or repeal had not occurred and may be terminated, completed, consummated, or enforced under that statute or other rule.

Official Comment

This Act will apply prospectively only to documents of title issued or bailments that arise after the effective date of the Act. To the extent that issues arise based upon documents of title or rights or obligations that arise prior to the effective date of this Act, prior law will apply to resolve those issues.

UCC ARTICLE 8

INVESTMENT SECURITIES

Article 8 was revised in 1994.

2001 amendments (Article 1 revision) . . . .*Appendix A*
2003 amendments (Article 7 revision) . . . .*Appendix B*

PART 1. SHORT TITLE AND GENERAL MATTERS

Section
8–101. Short Title.
8–102. Definitions.
8–103. Rules for Determining Whether Certain Obligations and Interests are Securities or Financial Assets.
8–104. Acquisition of Security or Financial Asset or Interest Therein.
8–105. Notice of Adverse Claim.
8–106. Control.
8–107. Whether Indorsement, Instruction, or Entitlement Order is Effective.
8–108. Warranties in Direct Holding.
8–109. Warranties in Indirect Holding.
8–110. Applicability; Choice of Law.
8–111. Clearing Corporation Rules.
8–112. Creditor's Legal Process.
8–113. Statute of Frauds Inapplicable.
8–114. Evidentiary Rules Concerning Certificated Securities.
8–115. Securities Intermediary and Others Not Liable to Adverse Claimant.
8–116. Securities Intermediary as Purchaser for Value.

PART 2. ISSUE AND ISSUER

8–201. Issuer.
8–202. Issuer's Responsibility and Defenses; Notice of Defect or Defense.
8–203. Staleness as Notice of Defect or Defense.
8–204. Effect of Issuer's Restriction on Transfer.
8–205. Effect of Unauthorized Signature on Security Certificate.
8–206. Completion or Alteration of Security Certificate.

Section
8–207. Rights and Duties of Issuer with Respect to Registered Owners.
8–208. Effect of Signature of Authenticating Trustee, Registrar, or Transfer Agent.
8–209. Issuer's Lien.
8–210. Overissue.

PART 3. TRANSFER OF CERTIFICATED AND UNCERTIFICATED SECURITIES

8–301. Delivery.
8–302. Rights of Purchaser.
8–303. Protected Purchaser.
8–304. Indorsement.
8–305. Instruction.
8–306. Effect of Guaranteeing Signature, Indorsement, or Instruction.
8–307. Purchaser's Right to Requisites for Registration of Transfer.

PART 4. REGISTRATION

8–401. Duty of Issuer to Register Transfer.
8–402. Assurance that Indorsement or Instruction is Effective.
8–403. Demand that Issuer Not Register Transfer.
8–404. Wrongful Registration.
8–405. Replacement of Lost, Destroyed, or Wrongfully Taken Security Certificate.
8–406. Obligation to Notify Issuer of Lost, Destroyed, or Wrongfully Taken Security Certificate.
8–407. Authenticating Trustee, Transfer Agent, and Registrar.

PART 5. SECURITY ENTITLEMENTS

8–501. Securities Account; Acquisition of Security Entitlement from Securities Intermediary.
8–502. Assertion of Adverse Claim Against Entitlement Holder.

Section

8–503. Property Interest of Entitlement Holder in Financial Asset Held by Securities Intermediary.

8–504. Duty of Securities Intermediary to Maintain Financial Asset.

8–505. Duty of Securities Intermediary with Respect to Payments and Distributions.

8–506. Duty of Securities Intermediary to Exercise Rights as Directed by Entitlement Holder.

8–507. Duty of Securities Intermediary to Comply with Entitlement Order.

8–508. Duty of Securities Intermediary to Change Entitlement Holder's Position to Other Form of Security Holding.

Section

8–509. Specification of Duties of Securities Intermediary by Other Statute or Regulation; Manner of Performance of Duties of Securities Intermediary and Exercise of Rights of Entitlement Holder.

8–510. Rights of Purchaser of Security Entitlement from Entitlement Holder.

8–511. Priority Among Security Interests and Entitlement Holders.

PART 6. TRANSITION PROVISIONS FOR REVISED ARTICLE 8

8–601. Effective Date.

8–602. Repeals.

8–603. Savings Clause.

National Conference of Commissioners on Uniform State Laws

REPORTER

James Steven Rogers, Newton, Massachusetts

DRAFTING COMMITTEE

CHAIRMAN

Curtis R. Reitz, Philadelphia, Pennsylvania

MEMBERS

Ann E. Conaway Anker, Wilmington, Delaware

John Fox Arnold, St. Louis, Missouri

Robert J. Desiderio, Albuquerque, New Mexico

Egon Guttman, Washington, District of Columbia, *The American Law Institute Representative*

Howard T. Rosen, Millburn, New Jersey

Richard B. Smith, New York, New York, *The American Law Institute Representative* and *American Bar Association Advisor*

Howard J. Swibel, Chicago, Illinois

Justin L. Vigdor, Rochester, New York

Richard C. Hite, Wichita, Kansas, *President (Member Ex Officio)*

K. King Burnett, Salisbury, Maryland, *Chairman, Division A (Member Ex Officio)*

REVIEW COMMITTEE

CHAIRMAN

Michael P. Sullivan, Minneapolis, Minnesota

MEMBERS

Gerald L. Bepko, Indianapolis, Indiana

Reed L. Martineau, Salt Lake City, Utah

ADVISORS

Charles W. Mooney, Jr., *American Bar Association, Section of Business Law*

Thomas J. Greco, *American Bankers Association*

CONSULTANTS

Jonathan Kallman, *United States Securities and Exchange Commission*

Calvin Ninomiya and Cynthia E. Reese, *United States Department of the Treasury*

Lawranne Stewart, *Board of Governors, Federal Reserve System*

Debra W. Cook and MarySue Fisher, *Federal Reserve Bank of New York*

PREFATORY NOTE

The present version of Article 8 is the product of a major revision made necessary by the fact that the prior version of Article 8 did not adequately deal with the system of securities holding through securities intermediaries that has developed in the past few decades. Although the prior version of Article 8 did contain some provisions dealing with securities holding through securities intermediaries, these were engrafted onto a structure designed for securities practices of earlier times. The resulting legal uncertainties adversely affected all participants. The revision is intended to eliminate these uncertainties by providing a modern legal structure for current securities holding practices.

I. EVOLUTION OF SECURITIES HOLDING SYSTEMS

A. The Traditional Securities Holding System

The original version of Article 8, drafted in the 1940s and 1950s, was based on the assumption that possession and delivery of physical certificates are the key elements in the securities holding system. Ownership of securities was traditionally evidenced by possession of the certificates, and changes were accomplished by delivery of the certificates.

Transfer of securities in the traditional certificate-based system was a complicated, labor-intensive process. Each time securities were traded, the physical certificates had to be delivered from the seller to the buyer, and in the case of registered securities the certificates had to be surrendered to the issuer or its transfer agent for registration of transfer. As is well known, the mechanical problems of processing the paperwork for securities transfers reached crisis proportions in the late 1960s, leading to calls for the elimination of the physical certificate and development of modern electronic systems for recording ownership of securities and transfers of ownership. That was the focus of the revision effort that led to the promulgation of the 1978 amendments to Article 8 concerning uncertificated securities.

B. The Uncertificated Securities System Envisioned by the 1978 Amendments

In 1978, amendments to Article 8 were approved to establish the commercial law rules that were thought necessary to permit the evolution of a system in which issuers would no longer issue certificates. The Drafting Committee that produced the 1978 amendments was given a fairly limited charge. It was to draft the revisions that would be needed for uncertificated securities, but otherwise leave the Article 8 rules unchanged. Accordingly, the 1978 amendments primarily took the form of adding parallel provisions dealing with uncertificated securities to the existing rules of Article 8 on certificated securities.

The system of securities holding contemplated by the 1978 amendments differed from the traditional system only in that ownership of securities would not be evidenced by physical certificates. It was contemplated that changes in ownership would continue to be reflected by changes in the records of the issuer. The main difference would be that instead of surrendering an indorsed certificate for registration of transfer, an instruction would be sent to the issuer directing it to register the transfer. Although a system of the sort contemplated by the 1978 amendments may well develop in the coming decades, this has not yet happened for most categories of securities. Mutual funds shares have long been issued in uncertificated form, but virtually all other forms of publicly traded corporate securities are still issued in certificated form. Individual investors who wish to be recorded as registered owners on the issuers' books still obtain and hold physical certificates. The certificates representing the largest portion of the shares of publicly traded companies, however, are not held by the beneficial owners, but by clearing corporations. Settlement of securities trading occurs not by delivery of certificates or by registration of transfer on the records of the issuers or their transfer agents, but by computer entries in the records of clearing corporations and securities intermediaries. That is quite different from the system envisioned by the 1978 amendments.

C. Evolution of the Indirect Holding System

At the time of the "paperwork crunch" in the late 1960s, the trading volume on the New York Stock Exchange that so seriously strained the capacities of the clearance and settlement system was in the range of 10 million shares per day. Today, the system can easily handle trading volume on routine days of hundreds of millions of shares. This processing capacity could have been achieved only by the application of modern electronic information processing systems. Yet the legal rules under which the system operates are *not* the uncertificated securities provisions of Article 8. To understand why this is so, one must delve at least a bit deeper into the operations of the current system.

If one examines the shareholder records of large corporations whose shares are publicly traded on the exchanges or in the over the counter market, one would find that one entity—Cede & Co.—is listed as the shareholder of record of somewhere in the range of sixty to eighty per cent of the outstanding shares of all publicly traded companies. Cede & Co. is the nominee name used by The Depository Trust Company ("DTC"), a limited purpose trust company organized under New York law for the purpose of acting as a depository to hold securities for the benefit of its participants, some 600 or so broker-dealers and banks. Essentially all of the trading in publicly held companies is executed through the broker-dealers who are participants in DTC, and the great bulk of public securities—the sixty to eighty per cent figure noted above—are held by these broker-dealers and banks on behalf of their customers. If all of these broker-dealers and banks held physical certificates, then as trades were executed each day it would be necessary to deliver the certificates back and forth among these broker-dealers and banks. By handing all of their securities over to a common depository all of these deliveries can be eliminated. Transfers can be accomplished by adjustments to the participants' DTC accounts.

Although the use of a common depository eliminates the needs for physical deliveries, an enormous number of entries would still have to be made on DTC's books if each transaction between its participants were recorded one by one on DTC's books. Any two major broker-dealers may have executed numerous trades with each other in a given security on a single day. Significant processing efficiency has been achieved by netting all of the transactions among the participants that occur each day, so that entries need be made on the depository's books only for the net changes in the positions of each participant at the end of each day. This clearance and netting function might well be performed by the securities exchanges or by the same institution that acts as the depository, as is the case in many other securities markets around the world. In the United States, however, this clearance and netting function is carried out by a separate corporation, National Securities Clearing Corporation ("NSCC"). All that needs to be done to settle each day's trading is for NSCC to compute the net receive and deliver obligations and to instruct DTC to make the corresponding adjustments in the participants' accounts.

The broker-dealers and banks who are participants in the DTC–NSCC system in turn provide analogous clearance and settlement functions to their own customers. If Customer A buys 100 shares of XYZ Co. through Broker, and Customer B sells 100 shares of XYZ Co. through the same Broker, the trade can be settled by entries on Broker's books. Neither DTC's books showing Broker's total position in XYZ Co., nor XYZ Co.'s books showing DTC's total position in XYZ Co., need be changed to reflect the settlement of this trade. One can readily appreciate the significance of the settlement function performed at this level if one considers that a single major bank may be acting as securities custodian for hundreds or thousands of mutual funds, pension funds, and other institutional investors. On any given day, the customers of that bank may have entered into an enormous number of trades, yet it is possible that relatively little of this trading activity will result in any net change in the custodian bank's positions on the books of DTC.

Settlement of market trading in most of the major U.S. securities markets is now effected primarily through some form of netted clearance and depository system. Virtually all publicly traded corporate equity securities, corporate debt securities, and municipal debt securities are now eligible for deposit in the DTC system. Recently, DTC has implemented a similar depository settlement system for the commercial paper market, and could, but for limitations in present Article 8, handle other forms of short-term money market securities such as bankers' acceptances. For trading in mortgage-backed securities, such as Ginnie Mae's, a similar depository settlement system has been developed by Participants Trust Company. For trading in U.S. Treasury securities, a somewhat analogous book-entry system is operated under Treasury rules by the Federal Reserve System.

D. Need for Different Legal Rules for the Direct and Indirect Holding Systems

Both the traditional paper-based system, and the uncertificated system contemplated by the 1978 amendments, can be described as "direct" securities holding systems; that is, the beneficial owners of securities have a direct relationship with the issuer of the securities. For securities in bearer form, whoever has possession of the certificate thereby has a direct claim against the issuer. For registered securities, the registered owner, whether of certificated or uncertificated securities, has a direct relationship with the issuer by virtue of being recorded as the owner on the records maintained by the issuer or its transfer agent.

By contrast, the DTC depository system for corporate equity and debt securities can be described as an "indirect holding" system, that is, the issuer's records do not show the identity of all of the beneficial owners. Instead, a large portion of the outstanding securities of any given issue are recorded on the issuer's records as belonging to a depository. The depository's records in turn show the identity of the banks or brokers who are its members, and the records of those securities intermediaries show the identity of their customers.

Even after the 1978 amendments, the rules of Article 8 did not deal effectively with the indirect holding system. The rules of the 1978 version of Article 8 were based on the assumption that changes in ownership of securities would still be effected either by delivery of physical certificates or by registration of transfer on the books of the issuer. Yet in the indirect holding system, settlement of the vast majority of securities trades does not involve either of these events. For most, if not all, of the securities held through DTC, physical certificates representing DTC's total position do exist. These "jumbo certificates," however, are never delivered from person to person. Just as nothing ever happens to these certificates, virtually nothing happens to the official registry of stockholders maintained by the issuers or their transfer agents to reflect the great bulk of the changes in ownership of shares that occur each day.

The principal mechanism through which securities trades are settled today is not delivery of certificates or registration of transfers on the issuer's books, but netted settlement arrangements and accounting entries on the books of a multi-tiered pyramid of securities intermediaries. Herein is the basic problem. Virtually all of the rules of the prior version of Article 8 specifying how changes in ownership of securities are effected, and what happens if something goes awry in the process, were keyed to the concepts of a

transfer of physical certificates or registration of transfers on the books of the issuers, yet that is not how changes in ownership are actually reflected in the modern securities holding system.

II. BRIEF OVERVIEW OF REVISED ARTICLE 8

A. Drafting Approach— Neutrality Principle

One of the objectives of the revision of Article 8 is to devise a structure of commercial law rules for investment securities that will be sufficiently flexible to respond to changes in practice over the next few decades. If it were possible to predict with confidence how the securities holding and trading system would develop, one could produce a statute designed specifically for the system envisioned. Recent experience, however, shows the danger of that approach. The 1978 amendments to Article 8 were based on the assumption that the solution to the problems that plagued the paper-based securities trading system of the 1960s would be the development of uncertificated securities. Instead, the solution thus far has been the development of the indirect holding system.

If one thought that the indirect holding system would come to dominate securities holding, one might draft Article 8 rules designed primarily for the indirect holding system, giving limited attention to the traditional direct holding system of security certificates or any uncertificated version of a direct holding system that might develop in the future. It is, however, by no means clear whether the long-term evolution will be toward decreased or increased use of direct holdings. At present, investors in most equity securities can either hold their securities through brokers or request that certificates be issued in their own name. For the immediate future it seems likely that that situation will continue. One can imagine many plausible scenarios for future evolution. Direct holding might become less and less common as investors become more familiar and comfortable with book-entry systems and/or as market or regulatory pressures develop that discourage direct holding. One might note, for example, that major brokerage firms are beginning to impose fees for having certificates issued and that some observers have suggested that acceleration of the cycle for settlement of securities trades might be facilitated by discouraging customers from obtaining certificates. On the other hand, other observers feel that it is important for investors to retain the option of holding securities in certificated form, or at least in some form that gives them a direct relationship with the issuer and does not require them to hold through brokers or other securities intermediaries. Some groups within the securities industry are beginning to work on development of uncertificated systems that would preserve this option.

Revised Article 8 takes a neutral position on the evolution of securities holding practices. The revision was based on the assumption that the path of development will be determined by market and regulatory forces and that the Article 8 rules should not seek to influence that development in any specific direction. Although various drafting approaches were considered, it became apparent early in the revision process that the differences between the direct holding system and the indirect holding system are sufficiently significant that it is best to treat them as separate systems requiring different legal concepts. Accordingly, while the rules of the prior version of Article 8 have, in large measure, been retained for the direct holding system, a new Part 5 has been added, setting out the commercial law rules for the indirect securities holding system. The principle of neutrality does carry some implications for the design of specific Article 8 rules. At the very least, the Article 8 rules for all securities holding systems should be sufficiently clear and predictable that uncertainty about the governing law does not itself operate as a constraint on market developments. In addition, an effort has been made to identify and eliminate any Article 8 rules that might act as impediments to any of the foreseeable paths of development.

B. Direct Holding System

With respect to securities held directly, Revised Article 8 retains the basic conceptual structure and rules of present law. Part 2, which is largely unchanged from former law, deals with certain aspects of the obligations of issuers. The primary purpose of the rules of Part 2 is to apply to investment securities the principles of negotiable instruments law that preclude the issuers of negotiable instruments from asserting defenses against subsequent purchasers. Part 3 deals

with transfer for securities held directly. One of its principal purposes is to apply to investment securities the principles of negotiable instruments law that protect purchasers of negotiable instruments against adverse claims. Part 4 deals with the process of registration of transfer by the issuer or transfer agent.

Although the basic concepts of the direct holding system rules have been retained, there are significant changes in terminology, organization, and statement of the rules. Some of the major changes are as follows:

Simplification of Part 3. The addition of the new Part 5 on the indirect holding system makes unnecessary the rather elaborate provisions of former law, such as those in Section 8–313, that sought to fit the indirect holding system into the conceptual structure of the direct holding system. Thus, Part 3 of Revised Article 8 is, in many respects, more similar to the original version of Article 8 than to the 1978 version.

Protected purchaser. The prior version of Article 8 used the term "bona fide purchaser" to refer to those purchasers who took free from adverse claims, and it used the phrase "good faith" in stating the requirements for such status. In order to promote clarity, Revised Article 8 states the rules that protect purchasers against adverse claims without using the phrase "good faith" and uses the new term "protected purchaser" to refer to purchasers in the direct holding system who are protected against adverse claims. See Sections 8–105 and 8–303.

Certificated versus uncertificated securities. The rules of the 1978 version of Article 8 concerning uncertificated securities have been simplified considerably. The 1978 version added provisions on uncertificated securities parallel to the provisions of the original version of Article 8 dealing with securities represented by certificates. Thus, virtually every section had one set of rules on "certificated securities" and another on "uncertificated securities." The constant juxtaposition of "certificated securities" and "uncertificated securities" has probably led readers to overemphasize the differences. Revised Article 8 has a unitary definition of "security" in Section 8–102(a)(15) which refers to the underlying intangible interest or obligation. In Revised Article 8, the difference between certificated and uncertificated is treated not as an inherent attribute of the security but as a difference in the means by which ownership is evidenced. The terms "certificated" and "uncertificated" security are used in those sections where it is important to distinguish between these two means of evidencing ownership. Revised Article 8 also deletes the provisions of the 1978 version concerning "transaction statements" and "registered pledges." These changes are explained in the Revision Notes 3, 4, and 5, below.

Scope of Parts 2, 3, and 4. The rules of Parts 2, 3, and 4 deal only with the rights of persons who hold securities directly. In typical securities holding arrangements in the modern depository system, only the clearing corporation would be a direct holder of the securities. Thus, while the rules of Parts 2, 3, and 4 would apply to the relationship between the issuer and the clearing corporation, they have no application to relationships below the clearing corporation level. Under Revised Article 8, a person who holds a security through a broker or securities custodian has a security entitlement governed by the Part 5 rules but is not the direct holder of the security. Thus, the rules of Revised Section 8–303 on the rights of "protected purchasers," which are the analog of the bona fide purchaser rules of former Article 8, do not apply to persons who hold securities through brokers or securities custodians. Instead, Part 5 contains its own rules to protect investors in the indirect holding system against adverse claims. See Revised Section 8–502.

C. Indirect Holding System

Although the Revised Article 8 provisions for the indirect holding system are somewhat complex, the basic approach taken can be summarized rather briefly. Revised Article 8 abandons the attempt to describe all of the complex relationships in the indirect holding system using the simple concepts of the traditional direct holding system. Instead, new rules specifically designed for the indirect holding system are added as Part 5 of Article 8. In a nutshell, the approach is to describe the core of the package of rights of a person who holds a security through a securities intermediary and then give that package of rights a name.

The starting point of Revised Article 8's treatment of the indirect holding system is the concept of "security entitlement." The term is defined in Section 8–102(a)(17) as "the rights and property interest of an entitlement holder with respect to a financial asset specified in Part 5." Like many legal concepts, however, the meaning of "security entitlement" is to be found less in any specific definition than in the matrix of rules that use the term. In a sense, then, the entirety of Part 5 is the definition of "security entitlement" because the Part 5 rules specify the rights and property interest that comprise a security entitlement.

Part 5 begins by specifying, in Section 8–501, when an entitlement holder acquires a security entitlement. The basic rule is very simple. A person acquires a security entitlement when the securities intermediary credits the financial asset to the person's account. The remaining sections of Part 5 specify the content of the security entitlement concept. Section 8–504 provides that a securities intermediary must maintain a sufficient quantity of financial assets to satisfy the claims of all of its entitlement holders. Section 8–503 provides that these financial assets are held by the intermediary for the entitlement holders, are not the property of the securities intermediary, and are not subject to claims of the intermediary's general creditors. Thus, a security entitlement is itself a form of property interest not merely an *in personam* claim against the intermediary. The concept of a security entitlement does, however, include a package of *in personam* rights against the intermediary. Other Part 5 rules identify the core of this package of rights, subject to specification by agreement and regulatory law. See Sections 8–505 through 8–509.

To illustrate the basic features of the new rules, consider a simple example of two investors, John and Mary, each of whom owns 1000 shares of Acme, Inc., a publicly traded company. John has a certificate representing his 1000 shares and is registered on the books maintained by Acme's transfer agent as the holder of record of those 1000 shares. Accordingly, he has a direct claim against the issuer, he receives dividends and distributions directly from the issuer, and he receives proxies directly from the issuer for purposes of voting his shares. Mary has chosen to hold her securities through her broker. She does not have a certificate and is not registered on Acme's stock books as a holder of record. She enjoys the economic and corporate benefits of ownership but does so through her broker and any other intermediaries in the chain back to the issuer. John's interest in Acme common stock would be described under Revised Article 8 as a direct interest in a "security." Thus, if John grants a security interest in his investment position, the collateral would be described as a "security." Mary's interest in Acme common stock would be described under Revised Article 8 as a "security entitlement." Thus, if Mary grants a security interest in her investment position, the collateral would be described as a "security entitlement."

For many purposes, there is no need to differentiate among the various ways that an investor might hold securities. For example, for purposes of financial accounting, John and Mary would each be described as the owner of 1000 shares of Acme common stock. For those purposes it is irrelevant that John is the registered owner and has physical possession of a certificate, while Mary holds her position through an intermediary. Revised Article 8 recognizes this point in Section 8–104 which provides that acquiring a security entitlement and acquiring a security certificate are different ways of acquiring an interest in the underlying security.

D. Security Interests

Along with the revision of Article 8, significant changes have been made in the rules concerning security interests in securities. The revision returns to the pre–1978 structure in which the rules on security interests in investment securities are set out in Article 9, rather than in Article 8. The changes in Article 9 are, in part, conforming changes to adapt Article 9 to the new concept of a security entitlement. The Article 9 changes, however, go beyond that to establish a simplified structure for the creation and perfection of security interests in investment securities, whether held directly or indirectly.

The Revised Article 9 rules continue the long-established principle that a security interest in a security represented by a certificate can be perfected by a possessory pledge. The revised rules, however, do not require that all security interests in investment securities be implemented by procedures based on the conceptual structure of the common law pledge. Under the revised Article 9 rules, a security interest in securities can be created pursuant to Section 9–203 in the same fashion as a security interest in any other form of property, that is, by agreement between the debtor and secured party. There is no requirement of a "transfer," "delivery," or any similar action, physical or metaphysical, for the creation of an effective security interest. A security interest in securities is, of course, a form of property interest, but the only requirements for creation of this form of property interest are those set out in Section 9–203.

The perfection methods for security interests in investment securities are set out in Sections 9–309, 9–312, 9–313, and 9–314. The basic rule is that a security interest may be perfected by "control." The concept of control, defined in Section 8–106, plays an important role in both Article 8 and Article 9. In general, obtaining control means taking the steps necessary to place the lender in a position where it can have the collateral sold off without the further cooperation of the debtor. Thus, for certificated securities, a lender obtains control by taking possession of the certificate with any necessary indorsement. For securities held through a securities intermediary, the lender can obtain control in two ways. First, the lender obtains control if it becomes the entitlement holder; that is, has the securities positions transferred to an account in its own name. Second, the lender obtains control if the securities intermediary agrees to act on instructions from the secured party to dispose of the positions, even though the debtor remains the entitlement holder. Such an arrangement suffices to give the lender control even though the debtor retains the right to trade and exercise other ordinary rights of an entitlement holder.

Except where the debtor is itself a securities firm, filing of an ordinary Article 9 financing statement is also a permissible alternative method of perfection. However, filing with respect to investment property does not assure the lender the same protections as for other forms of collateral, since the priority rules provide that a secured party who obtains control has priority over a secured party who does not obtain control.

The details of the new rules on security interests, as applied both to the retail level and to arrangements for secured financing of securities dealers, are explained in the Official Comments to Sections 9–309, 9–312, 9–313, and 9–314.

III. SCOPE AND APPLICATION OF ARTICLE 8

A. Terminology

To understand the scope and application of the rules of Revised Article 8, and the related security interest rules of Article 9, it is necessary to understand some of the key defined terms:

Security, defined in Section 8–102(a)(15), has essentially the same meaning as under the prior version of Article 8. The difference in Revised Article 8 is that the definition of security does not determine the coverage of all of Article 8. Although the direct holding system rules in Parts 2, 3, and 4 apply only to securities, the indirect holding system rules of Part 5 apply to the broader category of "financial assets."

Financial asset, defined in Section 8–103(a)(9), is the term used to describe the forms of property to which the indirect holding system rules of Part 5 apply. The term includes not only "securities," but also other interests, obligations, or property that are held through securities accounts. The best illustration of the broader scope of the term financial asset is the treatment of money market instruments, discussed below.

Security entitlement, defined in Section 8–103(a)(17), is the term used to describe the property interest of a person who holds a security or other financial asset through a securities intermediary.

Securities intermediary, defined in Section 8–103(a)(14), is the term used for those who hold securities for others in the indirect holding system. It covers clearing corporations, banks acting as securities custodians, and brokers holding securities for their customers.

Entitlement holder, defined in Section 8–103(a)(7), is the term used for those who hold securities through intermediaries.

Securities account, defined in Section 8–501(a), describes the form of arrangement between a securities intermediary and an entitlement holder that gives rise to a security entitlement. As explained below, the definition of securities account plays a key role in setting the scope of the indirect holding system rules of Part 5.

Investment property, defined in Section 9–102(a)(49), determines the application of the new Article 9 rules for secured transactions. In addition to securities and security entitlements, the Article 9 term "investment property" is defined to include "securities account" in order to simplify the drafting of the Article 9 rules that permit debtors to grant security interests either in specific security entitlements or in an entire securities account. The other difference between the coverage of the Article 8 and Article 9 terms is that commodity futures contracts are excluded from Article 8, but are included within the Article 9 definition of "investment property." Thus, the new Article 9 rules apply to security interests in commodity futures positions as well as security interests in securities positions.

B. Notes on Scope of Article 8

Article 8 is in no sense a comprehensive codification of the law governing securities or transactions in securities. Although Article 8 deals with some aspects of the rights of securities holders against issuers, most of that relationship is governed not by Article 8, but by corporation, securities, and contract law. Although Article 8 deals with some aspects of the rights and duties of parties who transfer securities, it is not a codification of the law of contracts for the purchase or sale of securities. (The prior version of Article 8 did include a few miscellaneous rules on contracts for the sale of securities, but these have not been included in Revised Article 8). Although the new indirect holding system rules of Part 5 deal with some aspects of the relationship between brokers or other securities professionals and their customers, Article 8 is still not in any sense a comprehensive code of the law governing the relationship between broker-dealers or other securities intermediaries and their customers. Most of the law governing that relationship is the common law of contract and agency, supplemented or supplanted by regulatory law.

The distinction between the aspects of the broker-customer relationship that are and are not dealt with in this Article may be illuminated by considering the differing roles of the broker in a typical securities transaction, in which the broker acts as agent for the customer. When a customer directs a broker to buy or sell securities for the customer, and the broker executes that trade on a securities exchange or in the over the counter market, the broker is entering into a contract for the purchase or sale of the securities as agent of the customer. The rules of the exchange, practices of the market, or regulatory law will specify when and how that contract is to be performed. For example, today the terms of the standard contract for trades in most corporate securities require the seller to deliver the securities, and the buyer to pay for them, five business days after the date that the contract was made, although the SEC has recently promulgated a rule that will accelerate the cycle to require settlement in three business days. In the common speech of the industry, the transaction in which the broker enters into a contract for the purchase or sale of the securities is referred to as executing the trade, and the transaction in which the securities are delivered and paid for is referred to as settlement. Thus, the current settlement cycle is known as $T + 5$, that is, settlement is required on the fifth business day after the date of the trade, and the new SEC rule will change it to $T + 3$. One must be careful in moving from the jargon of the securities industry to the jargon of the legal profession. For most practical economic purposes, the trade date is the date that counts, because that is the time at which the price is set, the risk of price changes shifts, and the parties become bound to perform. For purposes of precise legal analysis, however, the securities phrase "trade" or "execute a trade" means enter into a contract for the purchase or sale of the securities. The transfer of property interests occurs not at the time the contract is made but at the time it is performed, that is, at settlement.

The distinction between trade and settlement is important in understanding the scope of Article 8. Article 8 deals with the settlement phase of securities transactions. It deals with the mechanisms by which interests in securities are transferred, and the rights and duties of those who are involved in the transfer process. It does not deal with the process of entering into contracts for the transfer of securities or regulate the rights and duties of those involved in the contracting process. To use securities parlance, Article 8 deals not with the trade, but with settlement of the trade. Indeed, Article 8 does not even deal with all aspects of settlement. In a netted clearance and settlement system such as the NSCC–DTC system, individual trades are not settled one-by-one by corresponding entries on the books of any depository. Rather, settlement

of the individual trades occurs through the clearing arrangements, in accordance with the rules and agreements that govern those arrangements.

In the rules dealing with the indirect holding system, one must be particularly careful to bear in mind the distinction between trade and settlement. Under Revised Article 8, the property interest of a person who holds securities through an intermediary is described as a "security entitlement," which is defined in Revised Section 8–102(a)(17) as the package of rights and property interest of an entitlement holder specified in Part 5. Saying that the security entitlement is a package of rights against the broker does not mean that all of the customer's rights against the broker are part of the security entitlement and hence part of the subject matter of Article 8. The distinction between trade and settlement remains fundamental. The rules of this Article on the indirect holding system deal with brokers and other intermediaries as media through which investors hold their financial assets. Brokers are also media through which investors buy and sell their financial assets, but that aspect of their role is not the subject of this Article.

The principal goal of the Article 8 revision project is to provide a satisfactory framework for analysis of the indirect holding system. The technique used in Revised Article 8 is to acknowledge explicitly that the relationship between a securities intermediary and its entitlement holders is sui generis, and to state the applicable commercial law rules directly, rather than by inference from a categorization of the relationship based on legal concepts of a different era. One of the consequences of this drafting technique is that in order to provide content to the concept of security entitlement it becomes necessary to identify the core of the package of rights that make up a security entitlement. Sections 8–504 through 8–508 cover such basic matters as the duty of the securities intermediary to maintain a sufficient quantity of securities to satisfy all of its entitlement holders, the duty of the securities intermediary to pass through to entitlement holder the economic and corporate law rights of ownership of the security, and the duty of the securities intermediary to comply with authorized entitlement orders originated by the entitlement holder. These sections are best thought of as definitional; that is, a relationship which does not include these rights is not the kind of relationship that Revised Article 8 deals with. Because these sections take the form of statements of the duties of an intermediary toward its entitlement holders, one must be careful to avoid a distorted perspective on what Revised Article 8 is and is not designed to do. Revised Article 8 is not, and should not be, a comprehensive body of private law governing the relationship between brokers and their customers, nor a body of regulatory law to police against improper conduct by brokers or other intermediaries. Many, if not most, aspects of the relationship between brokers and customers are governed by the common law of contract and agency, supplemented or supplanted by federal and state regulatory law. Revised Article 8 does not take the place of this body of private and regulatory law. If there are gaps in the regulatory law, they should be dealt with as such; Article 8 is not the place to address them. Article 8 deals with how interests in securities are evidenced and how they are transferred. By way of a rough analogy, one might think of Article 8 as playing the role for the securities markets that real estate recording acts play for the real estate markets. Real estate recording acts do not regulate the conduct of parties to real estate transactions; Article 8 does not regulate the conduct of parties to securities transactions.

C. Application of Revised Articles 8 and 9 to Common Investments and Investment Arrangements

It may aid understanding to sketch briefly the treatment under Revised Articles 8 and 9 of a variety of relatively common products and arrangements.

1. Publicly traded stocks and bonds.

"Security" is defined in Revised Section 8–102(a)(15) in substantially the same terms as in the prior version of Article 8. It covers the ordinary publicly traded investment securities, such as corporate stocks and bonds. Parts 2, 3, and 4 govern the interests of persons who hold securities directly, and Part 5 governs the interest of those who hold securities indirectly.

Ordinary publicly traded securities provide a good illustration of the relationship between the direct and indirect holding system rules. The distinction between the direct and indirect holding systems is not an attribute of the securities

themselves but of the way in which a particular person holds the securities. Thus, whether one looks to the direct holding system rules of Parts 2, 3, and 4 or the indirect holding system rules of Part 5 will depend on the level in the securities holding system being analyzed.

Consider, for example, corporate stock which is held through a depository, such as DTC. The clearing corporation, or its nominee, is the registered owner of all of the securities it holds on behalf of all of its participants. Thus the rules of Parts 2, 3, and 4 of Revised Article 8 apply to the relationship between the issuer and the clearing corporation. If, as is typically the case today, the securities are still represented by certificates, the clearing corporation will be the holder of the security certificate or certificates representing its total holdings. So far as Article 8 is concerned, the relationship between the issuer and the clearing corporation is no different from the relationship between the issuer and any other registered owner.

The relationship between the clearing corporation and its participants is governed by the indirect holding system rules of Part 5. At that level, the clearing corporation is the securities intermediary and the participant is the entitlement holder. If the participant is itself a securities intermediary, such as a broker holding for its customers or a bank acting as a securities custodian, the Part 5 rules apply to its relationship to its own customers. At that level the broker or bank custodian is the securities intermediary and the customer is the entitlement holder. Note that the broker or bank custodian is both an entitlement holder and a securities intermediary—but is so with respect to different security entitlements. For purposes of Article 8 analysis, the customer's security entitlement against the broker or bank custodian is a different item of property from the security entitlement of the broker or bank custodian against the clearing corporation.

For investors who hold their securities directly, it makes no difference that some other investors hold their interests indirectly. Many investors today choose to hold their securities directly, becoming the registered owners on the books of the issuer and obtaining certificates registered in their names. For such investors, the addition of the new indirect holding system rules to Article 8 is entirely irrelevant. They will continue to deal directly with the issuers, or their transfer agents, under essentially the same rules as in the prior version of Article 8.

The securities holding options available to investors in a particular form of security may depend on the terms of the security. For example, direct holding is frequently not available for new issues of state and local government bonds. At one time, state and local government bonds were commonly issued in bearer form. Today, however, new issues of state and local government bonds must be in registered form and most are issued in what is known as "book-entry only" form; that is, the issuer specifies that the only person it will directly register as the registered owner is a clearing corporation. Thus, one of the inherent terms of the security is that investors can hold only in the indirect holding system.

2. Treasury securities.

U.S. government securities fall within the definition of security in Article 8 and therefore are governed by Article 8 in the same fashion as any other publicly held debt security, except insofar as Article 8 is preempted by applicable federal law or regulation.

New Treasury securities are no longer issued in certificated form; they can be held only through the book-entry systems established by the Treasury and Federal Reserve Banks. The Treasury offers a book-entry system, known as "Treasury Direct" which enables individual investors to have their positions recorded directly on the books of a Federal Reserve Bank, in a fashion somewhat similar to the uncertificated direct holding system contemplated by the 1978 version of Article 8. The governing law for the Treasury Direct system, however, is set out in the applicable Treasury regulations. The Treasury Direct system is not designed for active trading.

The great bulk of Treasury securities are held not through the Treasury Direct system but through a multi-tiered indirect holding system. The Federal Reserve Banks, acting as fiscal agent for the Treasury, maintain records of the holdings of member banks of the Federal Reserve System, and those banks in turn maintain records showing the extent to which they are holding for themselves or their own customers, including government securities dealers, institutional investors, or smaller banks who in turn

may act as custodians for investors. The indirect holding system for Treasury securities was established under federal regulations promulgated in the 1970s. In the 1980s, Treasury released the proposed TRADES regulations that would have established a more comprehensive body of federal commercial law for the Treasury holding system. During the Article 8 revision process, Treasury withdrew these regulations, anticipating that once Revised Article 8 is enacted, it will be possible to base the law for the Treasury system on the new Article 8 rules.

3. Broker-customer relationships.

Whether the relationship between a broker and its customer is governed by the Article 8 Part 5 rules depends on the nature of the services that the broker performs for the customer.

Some investors use brokers only to purchase and sell securities. These customers take delivery of certificates representing the securities they purchase and hold them in their own names. When they wish to sell, they deliver the certificates to the brokers. The Article 8 Part 5 rules would not affect such customers, because the Part 5 rules deal with arrangements in which investors hold securities through securities intermediaries. The transaction between the customer and broker might be the traditional agency arrangement in which the broker buys or sells on behalf of the customer as agent for an undisclosed principal, or it might be a dealer transaction in which the "broker" as principal buys from or sells to the customer. In either case, if the customer takes delivery and holds the securities directly, she will become the "purchaser" of a "security" whose interest therein is governed by the rules of Parts 2, 3, and 4 of Article 8. If the customer meets the other requirements of Section 8–303(a), the customer who takes delivery can qualify as a "protected purchaser" who takes free from any adverse claims under Section 8–303(b). The broker's role in such transactions is primarily governed by non-Article 8 law. There are only a few provisions of Article 8 that affect the relationship between the customer and broker in such cases. See Section 8–108 (broker makes to the customer the warranties of a transferor) and 8–115 (broker not liable in conversion if customer was acting wrongfully against a third party in selling securities).

Many investors use brokers not only to purchase and sell securities, but also as the custodians through whom they hold their securities. The indirect holding system rules of Part 5 apply to the custodial aspect of this relationship. If a customer purchases a security through a broker and directs the broker to hold the security in an account for the customer, the customer will never become a "purchaser" of a "security" whose interest therein is governed by the rules of Parts 2, 3, and 4 of Article 8. Accordingly, the customer does not become a "protected purchaser" under Section 8–303. Rather, the customer becomes an "entitlement holder" who has a "security entitlement" to the security against the broker as "securities intermediary." See Section 8–501. It would make no sense to say that the customer in such a case takes an interest in the security free from all other claims, since the nature of the relationship is that the customer has an interest in common with other customers who hold positions in the same security through the same broker. Section 8–502, however, does protect an entitlement holder against adverse claims, in the sense that once the entitlement holder has acquired the package of rights that comprise a security entitlement no one else can take that package of rights away by arguing that the transaction that resulted in the customer's acquisition of the security entitlement was the traceable product of a transfer or transaction that was wrongful as against the claimant.

4. Bank deposit accounts; brokerage asset management accounts.

An ordinary bank deposit account would not fall within the definition of "security" in Section 8–102(a)(15), so the rules of Parts 2, 3, and 4 of Article 8 do not apply to deposit accounts. Nor would the relationship between a bank and its depositors be governed by the rules of Part 5 of Article 8. The Part 5 rules apply to "security entitlements." Section 8–501(b) provides that a person has a security entitlement when a securities intermediary credits a financial asset to the person's "securities account." "Securities account" is defined in Section 8–501(a) as "an account to which a financial asset is or may be credited in accordance with an agreement under which the person maintaining the account undertakes to treat the person for whom the account is maintained as entitled to exercise the rights that comprise the financial asset." The definition of

securities account plays a key role in setting the scope of Part 5 of Article 8. A person has a security entitlement governed by Part 5 only if the relationship in question falls within the definition of "securities account." The definition of securities account in Section 8–501(a) excludes deposit accounts from the Part 5 rules of Article 8. One of the basic elements of the relationship between a securities intermediary and an entitlement holder is that the securities intermediary has the duty to hold exactly the quantity of securities that it carries for the account of its customers. See Section 8–504. The assets that a securities intermediary holds for its entitlement holder are not assets that the securities intermediary can use in its own proprietary business. See Section 8–503. A deposit account is an entirely different arrangement. A bank is not required to hold in its vaults or in deposit accounts with other banks a sum of money equal to the claims of all of its depositors. Banks are permitted to use depositors' funds in their ordinary lending business; indeed, that is a primary function of banks. A deposit account, unlike a securities account, is simply a debtor-creditor relationship. Thus a bank or other financial institution maintaining deposit accounts is not covered by Part 5 of Article 8.

Today, it is common for brokers to maintain securities accounts for their customers which include arrangements for the customers to hold liquid "cash" assets in the form of money market mutual fund shares. Insofar as the broker is holding money market mutual fund shares for its customer, the customer has a security entitlement to the money market mutual fund shares. It is also common for brokers to offer their customers an arrangement in which the customer has access to those liquid assets via a deposit account with a bank, whereby shares of the money market fund are redeemed to cover checks drawn on the account. Article 8 applies only to the securities account; the linked bank account remains an account covered by other law. Thus the rights and duties of the customer and the bank are governed not by Article 8, but by the relevant payment system law, such as Article 4 or Article 4A.

5. Trusts.

The indirect holding system rules of Part 5 of Article 8 are not intended to govern all relationships in which one person holds securities "on behalf of" another. Rather, the Part 5 rules come into play only if the relationship in question falls within the definition of securities account in Section 8–501(a). The definition of securities account serves the important function of ensuring that ordinary trust arrangements are not inadvertently swept into Part 5 of Article 8. Suppose that Bank serves as trustee of a trust for the benefit of Beneficiary. The corpus of the trust is invested in securities and other financial assets. Although Bank is, in some senses, holding securities for Beneficiary, the arrangement would not fall within the definition of securities account. Bank, as trustee, has not undertaken to treat Beneficiary as entitled to exercise all of the rights that comprise the portfolio securities. For instance, although Beneficiary receives the economic benefit of the portfolio securities, Beneficiary does not have the right to direct dispositions of individual trust assets or to exercise voting or other corporate law rights with respect to the individual securities. Thus Bank's obligations to Beneficiary as trustee are governed by ordinary trust law, not by Part 5 of Article 8. Of course, if Bank, as trustee, holds the securities through an intermediary, Part 5 of Revised Article 8 would govern the relationship between Bank, as entitlement holder, and the intermediary through which Bank holds the securities. It is also possible that a different department of Bank acts as the intermediary through which Bank, as trustee, holds the securities. Bank, *qua* securities custodian, might be holding securities for a large number of customers, including Bank's own trust department. Insofar as Bank may be regarded as acting in different capacities, Part 5 of Article 8 may be relevant to the relationship between the two sides of Bank's business. However, the relationship between Bank as trustee and the beneficiaries of the trust would remain governed by trust law, not Article 8.

6. Mutual fund shares.

Shares of mutual funds are Article 8 securities, whether the fund is organized as a corporation, business trust, or other form of entity. See Sections 8–102(a)(15) and 8–103(b). Mutual funds commonly do not issue certificates. Thus, mutual fund shares are typically uncertificated securities under Article 8.

Although a mutual fund is, in a colloquial sense, holding the portfolio securities on behalf of the fund's shareholders, the indirect holding system rules of Part 5 do not apply to the relationship between the fund and its shareholders. The Part 5 rules apply to "security entitlements." Section 8–501(e) provides that issuance of a security is not establishment of a security entitlement. Thus, because mutual funds shares do fit within the Article 8 definition of security, the relationship between the fund and its shareholders is automatically excluded from the Part 5 rules.

Of course, a person might hold shares in a mutual fund through a brokerage account. Because mutual fund shares are securities, they automatically fall within the broader term "financial asset," so the Part 5 indirect holding system rules apply to mutual fund shares that are held through securities accounts. That is, a person who holds mutual fund shares through a brokerage account could have a security entitlement to the mutual fund shares, just as the person would have a security entitlement to any other security carried in the brokerage account.

7. Stock of closely held corporations.

Ordinary corporate stock falls within the Article 8 definition of security, whether or not it is publicly traded. See Sections 8–102(a)(15) and 8–103(a). There is nothing in the new indirect holding system rules of Article 8 that would preclude their application to shares of companies that are not publicly traded. The indirect holding system rules, however, would come into play only if the shares were in fact held through a securities account with a securities intermediary. Since that is typically not the case with respect to shares of closely held corporations, transactions involving those shares will continue to be governed by the traditional rules, as amended, that are set out in Parts 2, 3, and 4 of Article 8, and the corresponding provisions of Article 9. The simplification of the Article 8 rules on uncertificated securities may, however, make the alternative of dispensing with certificates more attractive for closely held corporations.

8. Partnership interests and limited liability company shares.

Interests in partnerships or shares of limited liability companies are not Article 8 securities unless they are in fact dealt in or traded on securities exchanges or in securities markets.

See Section 8–103(c). The issuers, however, may if they wish explicitly "opt-in" by specifying that the interests or shares are securities governed by Article 8. Even though interests in partnerships or shares of limited liability companies do not generally fall within the category of "security" in Article 8, they would fall within the broader term "financial asset." Accordingly, if such interests are held through a securities account with a securities intermediary, the indirect holding system rules of Part 5 apply, and the interest of a person who holds them through such an account is a security entitlement.

9. Bankers' acceptances, commercial paper, and other money market instruments.

Money market instruments, such as commercial paper, bankers' acceptances, and certificates of deposit, are good examples of a form of property that may fall within the definition of "financial asset," even though they may not fall within the definition of "security." Section 8–103(d) provides that a writing that meets the definition of security certificate under Section 8–102(a)(15) is governed by Article 8, even though it also fits within the definition of "negotiable instrument" in Article 3.

Some forms of short term money market instruments may meet the requirements of an Article 8 security, while others may not. For example, the Article 8 definition of security requires that the obligation be in registered or bearer form. Bankers' acceptances are typically payable "to order," and thus do not qualify as Article 8 securities. Thus, the obligations of the immediate parties to a bankers' acceptance are governed by Article 3, rather than Article 8. That is an entirely appropriate classification, even for those bankers' acceptance that are handled as investment media in the securities markets, because Article 8, unlike Article 3, does not contain rules specifying the standardized obligations of parties to instruments. For example, the Article 3 rules on the obligations of acceptors and drawers of drafts are necessary to specify the obligations represented by bankers' acceptances, but Article 8 contains no provisions dealing with these issues.

Immobilization through a depository system is, however, just as important for money market instruments as for traditional securities. Under the prior version of Article 8, the rules on the depository system, set out in Section 8–320, applied only to Article 8 securities. Although some forms of money market instruments could be fitted within the language of the Article 8 definition of "security," this is not true for bankers' acceptances. Accordingly, it was not thought feasible to make bankers' acceptances eligible for deposit in clearing corporations under the prior version of Article 8. Revised Article 8 solves this problem by separating the coverage of the Part 5 rules from the definition of security. Even though a bankers' acceptance or other money market instrument is an Article 3 negotiable instrument rather than an Article 8 security, it would still fall within the definition of financial asset in Section 8–102(a)(9). Accordingly, if the instrument is held through a clearing corporation or other securities intermediary, the rules of Part 5 of Article 8 apply.

10. Repurchase agreement transactions.

Repurchase agreements are an important form of transaction in the securities business, particularly in connection with government securities. Repos and reverse repos can be used for a variety of purposes. The one that is of particular concern for purposes of commercial law rules is the use of repurchase agreements as a form of financing transaction for government securities dealers. Government securities dealers typically obtain intra-day financing from their clearing banks, and then at the end of the trading day seek overnight financing from other sources to repay that day's advances from the clearing bank. Repos are the principal source of this financing. The dealer ("repo seller") sells securities to the financing source ("repo buyer") for cash, and at the same time agrees to repurchase the same or like securities the following day, or at some other brief interval. The sources of the financing include a variety of entities seeking short term investments for surplus cash, such as pension funds, business corporations, money market funds, and banks. The pricing may be computed in various ways, but in essence the price at which the dealer agrees to repurchase the securities exceeds the price paid to the dealer by an amount equivalent to interest on the funds.

The transfer of the securities from a securities dealer as repo seller to a provider of funds as repo buyer can be effected in a variety of ways. The repo buyer might be willing to allow the repo

577

seller to keep the securities "in its hands," relying on the dealer's representation that it will hold them on behalf of the repo buyer. In the jargon of the trade, these are known as "hold-in-custody repos" or "HIC repos." At the other extreme, the repo buyer might insist that the dealer "hand over" the securities so that in the event that the dealer fails and is unable to perform its obligation to repurchase them, the repo buyer will have the securities "in its hands." The jargon for these is "delivered-out repos." A wide variety of arrangements between these two extremes might be devised, in which the securities are "handed over" to a third party with powers concerning their disposition allocated between the repo seller and repo buyer in a variety of ways.

Specification of the rights of repo buyers is complicated by the fact that the transfer of the interest in securities from the repo seller to the repo buyer might be characterized as an outright sale or as the creation of a security interest. Article 8 does not attempt to specify any categorical rules on that issue.

Article 8 sets out rules on the rights of parties who have implemented securities transactions in certain ways. It does not, however, deal with the legal characterization of the transactions that are implemented through the Article 8 mechanisms. Rather, the Article 8 rules apply without regard to the characterization of transactions for other purposes. For example, the Article 8 rules for the direct holding system provide that a person who takes delivery of a duly indorsed security certificate for value and without notice of adverse claims takes free from any adverse claims. That rule applies without regard to the character of the transaction in which the security certificate was delivered. It applies both to delivery upon original issue and to delivery upon transfer. It applies to transfers in settlement of sales and to transfers in pledge. Similarly, the Article 8 indirect holding system rules, such as the adverse claim cut-off rules in Sections 8–502 and 8–510, apply to the transactions that fall within their terms, whether those transactions were sales, secured transactions, or something else.

Repos involve transfers of interests in securities. The Article 8 rules apply to transfers of securities in repos, just as they apply to transfers of securities in any other form of transaction. The transfer of the interest in securities from the

repo seller to the repo buyer might be characterized as an outright sale or as the creation of a security interest. Article 8 does not determine that question. The rules of Revised Article 8 have, however, been drafted to minimize the possibility that disputes over the characterization of the transfer in a repo would affect substantive questions that are governed by Article 8. See, e.g., Section 8–510 and Comment 4 thereto.

11. Securities lending transactions.

In a typical securities lending transaction, the owner of securities lends them to another person who needs the securities to satisfy a delivery obligation. For example, when a customer of a broker sells a security short, the broker executes an ordinary trade as seller and so must deliver the securities at settlement. The customer is "short" against the broker because the customer has an open obligation to deliver the securities to the broker, which the customer hopes to be able to satisfy by buying in the securities at a lower price. If the short seller's broker does not have the securities in its own inventory, the broker will borrow them from someone else. The securities lender delivers the securities to the borrowing broker, and the borrowing broker becomes contractually obligated to redeliver a like quantity of the same security. Securities borrowers are required to provide collateral, usually government securities, to assure performance of their redelivery obligation.

The securities lender does not retain any property interest in the securities that are delivered to the borrower. The transaction is an outright transfer in which the borrower obtains full title. The whole point of securities lending is that the borrower needs the securities to transfer them to someone else. It would make no sense to say that the lender retains any property interest in the securities it has lent. Accordingly, even if the securities borrower defaults on its redelivery obligation, the securities lender has no property interest in the original securities that could be asserted against any person to whom the securities borrower may have transferred them. One need not look to adverse claim cut-off rules to reach that result; the securities lender never had an adverse claim. The securities borrower's default is no different from any other breach of contract. The securities lender's protection is its right to foreclose on the collateral given to secure the borrower's redelivery obligation. Perhaps the best way to understand securities lending is to note that the word "loan" in securities lending transactions is used in the sense it carries in loans of money, as distinguished from loans of specific identifiable chattels. Someone who lends money does not retain any property interest in the money that is handed over to the borrower. To use civil law terminology, securities lending is *mutuum,* rather than *commodatum.* See Story on Bailments, §§ 6 and 47.

12. Traded stock options.

Stock options issued and cleared through the Options Clearing Corporation ("OCC") are a good example of a form of investment vehicle that is treated as a financial asset to which the Part 5 rules apply, but not as an Article 8 security to which Parts 2, 3, and 4 apply. OCC carries on its books the options positions of the brokerage firms which are clearing members of OCC. The clearing members in turn carry on their books the options positions of their customers. The arrangements are structurally similar to the securities depository system. In the options structure, however, there is no issuer separate from the clearing corporation. The financial assets held through the system are standardized contracts entitling the holder to purchase or sell a certain security at a set price. Rather than being an interest in or obligation of a separate issuer, an option is a contractual right against the counter-party. In order to assure performance of the options, OCC interposes itself as counter-party to each options trade. The rules of Parts 2, 3, and 4 of this Article, however, do not well describe the obligations and rights of OCC. On the other hand, the rules of Part 5, and the related Article 9 rules on security interests and priorities, do provide a workable legal framework for the commercial law analysis of the rights of the participants in the options market. Accordingly, publicly traded securities options are included within the definition of "financial asset," but not "security." See Section 8–103(e). Thus, although OCC would not be an issuer of a security for purposes of this Article, it would be a clearing corporation, against whom its clearing members have security entitlements to the options positions. Similarly, the clearing members' customers have security entitlements against the clearing members. Traded stock options are also a good illustration of the point that the classifica-

tion issues under Article 8 are very different from classification under other law, such as the federal securities laws. See Section 8–102(d). Stock options are treated as securities for purposes of federal securities laws, but not for purposes of Article 8.

13. Commodity futures.

Section 8–103(f) provides that a "commodity contract" is not a security or a financial asset. Section 9–102(a)(15) defines commodity contract to include commodity futures contracts, commodity options, and options on commodity futures contracts that are traded on or subject to the rules of a board of trade that has been designated as a contract market for that contract pursuant to the federal commodities laws. Thus, commodity contracts themselves are not Article 8 securities to which the rules of Parts 2, 3, and 4 apply, nor is the relationship between a customer and a commodity futures commission merchant governed by the Part 5 rules of Article 8. Commodity contracts, however, are included within the Article 9 definition of "investment property." Thus security interests in commodity positions are governed by essentially the same set of rules as security interests in security entitlements.

14. "Whatever else they have or may devise."

The classification question posed by the above-captioned category of investment products and arrangements is among the most difficult—and important—issue raised by the Article 8 revision process. Rapid innovation is perhaps the only constant characteristic of the securities and financial markets. The rules of Revised Article 8 are intended to be sufficiently flexible to accommodate new developments.

A common mechanism by which new financial instruments are devised is that a financial institution that holds some security, financial instrument, or pool thereof, creates interests in that asset or pool which are sold to others. It is not possible to answer in the abstract the question of how such interests are treated under Article 8, because the variety of such products is limited only by human imagination and current regulatory structures. At this general level, however, one can note that there are at least three possible treatments under Article 8 of the relationship between the institution which creates the interests and the persons who hold them. (Again, it must be borne in mind that the Article 8 classification issue may be different from the classification question posed by federal securities law or other regulation.) First, creation of the new interests in the underlying assets may constitute issuance of a new Article 8 security. In that case the relationship between the institution that created the interest and the persons who hold them is not governed by the Part 5 rules, but by the rules of Parts 2, 3, and 4. See Section 8–501(e). That, for example, is the structure of issuance of mutual fund shares. Second, the relationship between the entity creating the interests and those holding them may fit within the Part 5 rules, so that the persons are treating as having security entitlements against the institution with respect to the underlying assets. That, for example, is the structure used for stock options. Third, it may be that the creation of the new interests in the underlying assets does not constitute issuance of a new Article 8 security, nor does the relationship between the entity creating the interests and those holding them fit within the Part 5 rules. In that case, the relationship is governed by other law, as in the case of ordinary trusts.

The first of these three possibilities—that the creation of the new interest is issuance of a new security for Article 8 purposes—is a fairly common pattern. For example, an American depositary receipt facility does not maintain securities accounts but issues securities called ADRs in respect of foreign securities deposited in such facility. Similarly, custodians of government securities which issue receipts, certificates, or the like representing direct interests in those securities (sometimes interests split between principal and income) do not maintain securities accounts but issue securities representing those interests. Trusts holding assets, in a variety of structured and securitized transactions, which issue certificates or the like representing "pass-through" or undivided beneficial interests in the trust assets, do not maintain securities accounts but issue securities representing those interests.

In analyzing these classification questions, courts should take care to avoid mechanical jurisprudence based solely upon exegesis of the wording of definitions in Article 8. The result of classification questions is that different sets of rules come into play. In order to decide the classification question it is necessary to understand fully the commercial setting and consider which set of rules best fits the transaction. Rather than letting the choice of rules turn on interpretation of the words of the definitions, the interpretation of the words of the definitions should turn on the suitability of the application of the substantive rules.

IV. CHANGES FROM PRIOR (1978) VERSION OF ARTICLE 8

A. Table of Disposition of Sections in Prior Version

Article 8 (1978)	Revised Articles 8 and 9
8–101	8–101
8–102(1)(a)	8–102(a)(4) & (15)
8–102(1)(b)	8–102(a)(15) & (18)
8–102(1)(c)	8–102(a)(15)
8–102(1)(d)	8–102(a)(13)
8–102(1)(e)	8–102(a)(2)
8–102(2)	8–202(b)(1)
8–102(3)	8–102(a)(5)
8–102(4)	omitted, see Revision Note 1
8–102(5)	8–102(b)
8–102(6)	8–102(c)
8–103	8–209
8–104	8–210
8–105(1)	omitted, see Revision Note 8
8–105(2)	omitted, see Revision Note 4
8–105(3)	8–114
8–106	8–110
8–107	omitted, see Revision Note 8
8–108	omitted, see Revision Note 5

Article 8 (1978)	Revised Articles 8 and 9
8–201	8–201
8–202	8–202; transaction statement provisions omitted, see Revision Note 4
8–203	8–203
8–204	8–204; transaction statement provisions omitted, see Revision Note 4
8–205	8–205; transaction statement provisions omitted, see Revision Note 4
8–206	8–206; transaction statement provisions omitted, see Revision Note 4
8–207	8–207; registered pledge provisions omitted, see Revision Note 5
8–208	8–208; transaction statement provisions omitted, see Revision Note 4
8–301	8–302(a) & (b)
8–302(1)	8–303(a)
8–302(2)	8–102(a)(1)
8–302(3)	8–303(b)
8–302(4)	8–302(c)
8–303	8–102(a)(3)
8–304(1)	8–105(d)
8–304(2)	omitted, see Revision Note 4
8–304(3)	8–105(b)
8–305	8–105(c)
8–306(1)	8–108(f)
8–306(2)	8–108(a)
8–306(3)	8–108(g)
8–306(4)	8–108(h)
8–306(5)	8–108(e)
8–306(6)	8–306(h)
8–306(7)	8–108(b), 8–306(h)
8–306(8)	omitted, see Revision Note 5
8–306(9)	8–108(c)
8–306(10)	8–108(i)
8–307	8–304(d)
8–308(1)	8–102(a)(11), 8–107
8–308(2)	8–304(a)
8–308(3)	8–304(b)
8–308(4)	8–102(a)(12)
8–308(5)	8–107 & 8–305(a)
8–308(6)	8–107
8–308(7)	8–107
8–308(8)	8–107
8–308(9)	8–304(f) & 8–305(b)
8–308(10)	8–107
8–308(11)	8–107
8–309	8–304(c)
8–310	8–304(e)
8–311(a)	omitted, see 8–106(b)(2), 8–301(b)(1), 8–303
8–311(b)	8–404
8–312	8–306
8–313(1)(a)	omitted, see Revision Note 2; see also 8–301(a)(1) & (2)
8–313(1)(b)	omitted, see Revision Note 2; see also 8–301(b)(1) & (2)

Article 8 (1978)	Revised Articles 8 and 9
8–313(1)(c)	omitted, see Revision Note 2; see also 8–301(a)(3)
8–313(1)(d)	omitted, see Revision Note 2; see also 8–501(b)
8–313(1)(e)	omitted, see Revision Note 2; see also 8–301(a)(2)
8–313(1)(f)	omitted, see Revision Note 2; see also 8–301(b)(2)
8–313(1)(g)	omitted, see Revision Notes 1 & 2; see also 8–501(b), 8–111
8–313(1)(h)–(j)	omitted, see Revision Note 2; see also 9–203
8–313(2)	omitted, see Revision Note 2; see also 8–503
8–313(3)	omitted, see Revision Note 2
8–313(4)	8–102(a)(14)
8–314	omitted, see Revision Note 8
8–315	omitted, see Revision Note 8
8–316	8–307
8–317	8–112
8–318	8–115
8–319	omitted, see 8–113 and Revision Note 7
8–320	omitted, see Revision Note 1
8–321	omitted, see 9–203, 9–309, 9–312, 9–314
8–401	8–401
8–402	8–402, see Revision Note 6
8–403	8–403, see Revision Note 6
8–404	8–404
8–405(1)	8–406
8–405(2)	8–405(a)
8–405(3)	8–405(b)
8–406	8–407
8–407	omitted, see Revision Note 8
8–408	omitted, see Revision Note 4

B. Revision Notes

1. Provisions of former Article 8 on clearing corporations.

The keystone of the treatment of the indirect holding system in the prior version of Article 8 was the special provision on clearing corporations in Section 8–320. Section 8–320 was added to Article 8 in 1962, at the very end of the process that culminated in promulgation and enactment of the original version of the Code. The key concepts of the original version of Article 8 were "bona fide purchaser" and "delivery." Under Section 8–302 (1962) one could qualify as a "bona fide purchaser" only if one had taken delivery of a security, and Section 8–313 (1962) specified what counted as a delivery.

Section 8–320 was added to take account of the development of the system in which trades can be settled by netted book-entry movements at a depository without physical deliveries of certificates. Rather than reworking the basic concepts, however, Section 8–320 brought the depository system within Article 8 by definitional fiat. Subsection (a) of Section 8–320 (1962) stated that a transfer or pledge could be effected by entries on the books of a central depository, and subsection (b) stated that such an entry "has the effect of a delivery of a security in bearer form or duly indorsed in blank." In 1978, Section 8–320 was revised to conform it to the general substitution of the concept of "transfer" for "delivery," but the basic structure remained the same. Under the 1978 version of Article 8, the only book-entry transfers that qualified the transferee for bona fide purchaser rights were those made on the books of a clearing corporation. See Sections 8–302(1)(c), 8–313(1)(g), and 8–320. Thus, for practical purposes, the indirect holding system rules of the prior version of Article 8 required that the securities be held by a clearing corporation in accordance with the central depository rules of Section 8–320.

Some of the definitional provisions concerning clearing corporation in the prior version of Article 8 seem to have conflated the commercial law rules on the effect of book-entry transactions with issues about the regulation of entities that are acting as clearing corporations. For example, the Section 8–320 rules that gave effect to book-entry transfers applied only if the security was "in the custody of the clearing corporation, another clearing corporation, [or] a custodian bank." "Custodian bank" was defined in Section 8–102(4) as "a bank or trust company that is supervised and examined by state or federal authority having supervision over banks and is acting as custodian for a clearing corporation." Although this was probably inadvertent, these definitional provisions have operated as an obstacle to the development of clearing arrangements for global trading, since they effectively precluded clearing corporations from using foreign banks as custodians.

Revised Article 8 is based on the view that Article 8 is not the proper place for regulatory decisions about whether certain sorts of financial institutions should or should not be permitted to engage in a particular aspect of the securities business, such as acting as a clearing corporation, or how they should be permitted to conduct that business. Rather, Article 8 should deal only with the commercial law questions of what duties and rights flow from doing business as a clearing corporation, leaving it to other regulatory law to decide which entities should be permitted to act as clearing corporations, and to regulate their activities. Federal securities laws now establish a detailed regulatory structure for clearing corporations; there is no need for Article 8 to duplicate parts of that structure. Revised Article 8 deletes all provision of the prior version which had the effect of specifying how clearing corporations should conduct their operations. For example, Revised Article 8 deletes the definition of "custodian bank," which operated in the prior version only as a regulatory restriction on how clearing corporations could hold securities.

In general, the structure of Revised Article 8 is such that there is relatively little need for special provisions on clearing corporations. Book-entry transactions effected through clearing corporations are treated under the same rules in Part 5 as book-entry transactions effected through any other securities intermediary. Accordingly, Revised Article 8 has no direct analog of the special provisions in Section 8–320 on transfers on the books of clearing corporations.

2. Former Section 8–313—"Transfer."

Section 8–313 of the 1978 version of Article was extremely complicated, because it attempted to cover many different issues. The following account of the evolution of Section 8–313 may assist in understanding why a different approach is taken in Revised Article 8. This explanation is, however, intended not as an actual account of historical events, but as a conceptual reconstruction, devised from the perspective of, and with the benefit of, hindsight.

The original objective of Article 8 was to ensure that certificates representing investment securities would be "negotiable" in the sense that purchasers would be protected by the bona fide purchaser rules. The requirements for bona fide purchaser status were that the purchaser had to (i) take delivery of the security and (ii) give value in good faith and without notice of adverse claims. Section 8–313 specified what counted as a "delivery," and Section 8–302 specified the other requirements.

The 1978 amendments added provisions on uncertificated securities, but the basic organizational pattern was retained. Section 8–302 continued to state the requirements of value, good faith, and lack of notice for good faith purchase, and Section 8–313 stated the mechanism by which the purchase had to be implemented. Delivery as defined in the original version of Section 8–313 had a meaning similar to the concept known in colloquial securities jargon as "good delivery"; that is, physical delivery with any necessary indorsement. Although the word "delivery" has now come to be used in securities parlance in a broader sense than physical delivery, when the provisions for uncertificated securities were added it was thought preferable to use another word. Thus, the word "transfer" was substituted for "delivery" in Section 8–313.

The 1978 amendments also moved the rules governing security interests in securities from Article 9 to Article 8, though the basic conceptual structure of the common law of pledge was retained. Since a pledge required a delivery, and since the term transfer had been substituted for delivery, the 1978 amendments provided that in order to create a security interest there must be a "transfer," in the defined Article 8 sense, from the debtor to the secured party. Accordingly, provisions had to be added to Section 8–313 so that any of the steps that should suffice to create a perfected security interest would be deemed to constitute a "transfer" within the meaning of Section 8–313. Thus, the Section 8–313 rules on "transfer," which had in the previous version dealt only with what counted as a delivery that qualified one for bona fide purchaser status, became the statutory locus for all of the rules on creation and perfection of security interests in securities. Accordingly the rather elaborate rules of subsections (1)(h), (1)(i), and (1)(j) were added.

Having expanded Section 8–313 to the point that it served as the rule specifying the formal requirements for transfer of all significant forms of interests in securities, it must have seemed only logical to take the next step and make the Section 8–313 rules the exclusive means of transferring interests in securities. Thus, while the prior version had stated that "Delivery to a purchaser occurs when ...", the 1978 version stated that "Transfer of a security or a limited interest (including a security interest) therein to a purchaser occurs *only* ...." Having taken that step, however, it then became necessary to ensure that anyone who should be regarded as having an interest in a security would be covered by some provision of Section 8–313. Thus, the provisions of subsection (1)(d)(ii) and (iii) were added to make it possible to say that the customers of a securities intermediary who hold interests in securities held by the intermediary in fungible bulk received "transfers."

Section 8–313(1)(d) was the key provision in the 1978 version dealing with the indirect holding system at the level below securities depositories. It operated in essentially the same fashion as Section 8–320; that is, it stated that when a broker or bank holding securities in fungible bulk makes entries on its books identifying a quantity of the fungible bulk as belonging to the customer, that action is treated as a "transfer"— in the special Section 8–313 sense—of an interest in the security from the intermediary to the customer.

Revised Article 8 has no direct analog of the 1978 version of Section 8–313. The rules on secured transactions have been returned to Article 9, so subsections of Section 8–313 (1978) dealing with security interests are deleted from Article 8. Insofar as portions of Section 8–313 (1978) were designed to specify the formal requirements for transferees to qualify for protection against adverse claims, their place is taken by Revised Section 8–301, which defines "delivery," in a fashion somewhat akin to the pre–1978 version of Section 8–313. The descendant of the provisions of Section 8–313 (1978) dealing with the indirect holding system is Revised Section 8–501 which specifies when a person acquires a security entitlement. Section 8–501, however, is based on a different analysis of the transaction in which a customer acquires a position in the indirect holding system. The transaction is not described as a "transfer" of an interest in some portion of a fungible bulk of securities held by the securities intermediary but as the creation of a security entitlement. Accordingly, just as Revised Article 8 has no direct analog of the Section 8–320 rules on clearing corporation transfers, it has no direct analog of the Section 8–313(1) rules on "transfers" of interests in securities held in fungible bulk.

3. Uncertificated securities provisions.

Given the way that securities holding practices have evolved, the sharp distinction that the 1978 version of Article 8 drew between certificated securities and uncertificated securities has become somewhat misleading. Since many provisions of the 1978 version had separate subsections dealing first with certificated securities and then with uncertificated securities, and since people intuitively realize that the volume of trading in the modern securities markets could not possibly be handled by pushing around certificates, it was only natural for a reader of the statute to conclude that the uncertificated securities provisions of Article 8 were the basis of the book-entry system. That, however, is not the case. Although physical delivery of certificates plays little role in the settlement system, most publicly traded securities are still, in legal theory, certificated securities. To use clearance and settlement jargon, the book-entry securities holding system has used "immobilization" rather than "dematerialization."

584

The important legal and practical difference is between the direct holding system, in which the beneficial owners have a direct relationship with the issuer, and the indirect holding system, in which securities are held through tiers of securities intermediaries. Accordingly, in Revised Article 8 the contrast between certificated securities and uncertificated securities has been minimized or eliminated as much as possible in stating the substantive provisions.

4. Transaction statements.

Although the 1978 provisions on uncertificated securities contemplated a system in which there would be no definitive certificates as reifications of the underlying interests or obligations, the 1978 amendments did not really dispense with all requirements of paper evidence of securities holding. The 1978 amendments required issuers of uncertificated securities to send paper "transaction statements" upon registration of transfer. Section 8–408 regulated the content and format of these transaction statements in considerable detail. The statements had to be in writing, include specific information, and contain a conspicuous legend stating that "This statement is merely a record of the rights of the addressee as of the time of its issuance. Delivery of this statement, of itself, confers no rights on the recipient. This statement is neither a negotiable instrument nor a security." Issuers were required to send statements when any transfer was registered (known as "initial transaction statements") and also were required to send periodic statements at least annually and also upon any security holder's reasonable request. Fees were regulated to some extent, in that Section 8–408(8) specified that if periodic statements were sent at least quarterly, the issuer could charge for statements requested by security holders at other times.

The detailed specification of reporting requirements for issuers of uncertificated securities was quite different from the treatment of securities intermediaries. Though the prior version of Article 8 did require non-clearing corporation securities intermediaries to send confirmations of transfers—a requirement deleted in Revised Article 8—it did not regulate their content or format. Article 8 has never imposed periodic reporting requirements on securities intermediaries. Thus, reporting requirements for the indirect holding system were left to agreements and regulatory authorities, while reporting requirements for a book-entry direct holding system were imposed by statute.

Securities holding systems based on transaction statements of the sort contemplated by the 1978 amendments have not yet evolved to any major extent—indeed, the statutory specification of the details of the information system may itself have acted as an impediment to the evolution of a book-entry direct system. Accordingly, Revised Article 8 drops the statutory requirements concerning transaction statements. The record keeping and reporting obligations of issuers of uncertificated securities would be left to agreement and other law, as is the case today for securities intermediaries.

In the 1978 version, the Part 2 rules concerning transfer restrictions, issuers' defenses, and the like were based on the assumption that transaction statements would be used in a fashion analogous to traditional security certificates. For example, Sections 8–202 and 8–204 specified that the terms of a security, or any restrictions on transfer imposed by the issuer, had to be noted on the transaction statement. Revised Article 8 deletes all such references to transaction statements. The terms of securities, or of restrictions of transfer, would be governed by whatever law or agreement specifies these matters, just as is the case for various other forms of business entities, such as partnerships, that have never issued certificates representing interests. Other Part 2 rules, such as Sections 8–205, 8–206, and 8–208, attempted to state rules on forgery and related matters for transactions statements. Since Revised Article 8 does not specify the format for information systems for uncertificated securities, there is no point in attempting to state rules on the consequences of wrongful information transmission in the particular format of written statements authenticated by signatures.

5. Deletion of provisions on registered pledges.

The 1978 version of Article 8 also added detailed provisions concerning "registered pledges" of uncertificated securities. Revised Article 8 adopts a new system of rules for security interests in securities, for both the direct and indirect holding systems that make it unnecessary to

585

have special statutory provisions for registered pledges of uncertificated securities.

The reason that the 1978 version of Article 8 created this concept was that if the only means of creating security interests was the pledge, it seemed necessary to provide some substitute for the pledge in the absence of a certificate. The point of the registered pledge was, presumably, that it permitted a debtor to grant a perfected security interest in securities, yet still keep the securities in the debtor's own name for purposes of dividends, voting, and the like. The concept of registered pledge has, however, been thought troublesome by many legal commentators and securities industry participants. For example, in Massachusetts where many mutual funds have their headquarters, a non-uniform amendment was enacted to permit the issuer of an uncertificated security to refuse to register a pledge and instead issue a certificate to the owner that the owner could then pledge by ordinary means.

Under the 1978 version of Article 8, if an issuer chose to issue securities in uncertificated form, it was also required by statute to offer a registered pledge program. Revised Articles 8 and 9 take a different approach. All of the provisions dealing with registered pledges have been deleted. This does not mean, however, that issuers cannot offer such a service. The control rules of Revised Section 8–106 and the related priority provisions in Article 9 establish a structure that permits issuers to develop systems akin to the registered pledge device, without mandating that they do so, or legislating the details of the system. In essence, the registered pledge or control device amounts to a record keeping service. A debtor can always transfer securities to its lender. In a registered pledge or control agreement arrangement, the issuer keeps track of which securities the secured party holds for its own account outright, and which securities it holds in pledge from its debtors.

Under the rules of Revised Articles 8 and 9, the registered pledge issue can easily be left to resolution by the market. The concept of control is defined in such fashion that if an issuer or securities intermediary wishes to offer a service akin to the registered pledge device it can do so. The issuer or securities intermediary would offer to enter into agreements with the debtor and secured party under which it would hold the securities for the account of the debtor, but sub-

ject to instructions from the secured party. The secured party would thereby obtain control assuring perfection and priority of its lien.

Even if such arrangements are not offered by issuers, persons who hold uncertificated securities will have several options for using them as collateral for secured loans. Under the new rules, filing is a permissible method of perfection, for debtors other than securities firms. A secured party who relies on filing is, of course, exposed to the risk that the debtor will double finance and grant a later secured lender a security interest under circumstances that give that lender control and hence priority. If the lender is unwilling to run that risk, the debtor can transfer the securities outright to the lender on the books of the issuer, though between the parties the debtor would be the owner and the lender only a secured party. That, of course, requires that the debtor trust the secured party not to dispose of the collateral wrongfully, and the debtor may also need to make arrangements with the secured party to exercise benefits of ownership such as voting and receiving distributions.

It may well be that both lenders and borrowers would prefer to have some arrangement, such as the registered pledge device of current law, that permits the debtor to remain as the registered owner entitled to vote and receive dividends but gives the lender exclusive power to order their disposition. The approach taken in this revision is that if there is a genuine demand for such arrangements, it can be met by the market. The difficulty with the approach of present Article 8 is that it mandates that any issuer that wishes to issue securities in uncertificated form must also offer this record keeping service. That obligation may well have acted as a disincentive to the development of uncertificated securities. Thus, the deletion of the mandated registered pledge provisions is consistent with the principle of neutrality toward the evolution of securities holding practices.

6. Former Section 8–403—Issuer's Duty as to Adverse Claims.

Section 8–403 of the prior version of Article 8 dealt with the obligations of issuers to adverse claimants. The starting point of American law on issuers' liability in such circumstances is the old case of *Lowry v. Commercial & Farmers'*

Bank, 15 F.Cas. 1040 (C.C.D.Md.1848) (No. 8551), under which issuers could be held liable for registering a transfer at the direction of a registered owner who was acting wrongfully as against a third person in making the transfer. The *Lowry* principle imposed onerous liability on issuers, particularly in the case of transfers by fiduciaries, such as executors and trustees. To protect against risk of such liability, issuers developed the practice of requiring extensive documentation for fiduciary stock transfers to assure themselves that the fiduciaries were acting rightfully. As a result, fiduciary stock transfers were cumbersome and time consuming.

In the present century, American law has gradually moved away from the *Lowry* principle. Statutes such as the Uniform Fiduciaries Act, the Model Fiduciary Stock Transfer Act, and the Uniform Act for the Simplification of Fiduciary Security Transfers sought to avoid the delays in stock transfers that could result from issuers' demands for documentation by limiting the issuer's responsibility for transfers in breach of the registered owner's duty to others. Although these statutes provided that issuers had no duty of inquiry to determine whether a fiduciary was acting rightfully, they all provided that an issuer could be liable if the issuer acted with notice of third party claims.

The prior version of Article 8 followed the same approach as the various fiduciary transfer statutes. Issuers were not required to seek out information from which they could determine whether a fiduciary was acting properly, but they were liable if they registered a transfer with notice that the fiduciary was acting improperly. Former Section 8–308(11) said that the failure of a fiduciary to comply with a controlling instrument or failure to obtain a court approval required under local law did not render the indorsement or instruction unauthorized. However, if a fiduciary was in fact acting improperly, then the beneficiary would be treated as an adverse claimant. See Section 8–302(2) (1978) and Comment 4. Former Section 8–403 specified that if written notice of an adverse claim had been sent to the issuer, the issuer "shall inquire into the adverse claim" before registering a transfer on the indorsement or instruction of the registered owner. The issuer could "discharge any duty of inquiry by any reasonable means," including by notifying the

adverse claimant that the transfer would be registered unless the adverse claimant obtained a court order or gave an indemnity bond.

Revised Article 8 rejects the *Lowry* principle altogether. It provides that an issuer is not liable for wrongful registration if it acts on an effective indorsement or instruction, even though the issuer may have notice of adverse claims, so long as the issuer has not been served with legal process and is not acting in collusion with the wrongdoer in registering the transfer. See Revised Section 8–404 and Comments thereto. The provisions of prior Section 8–403 specifying that issuers had a duty to investigate adverse claims of which they had notice are deleted.

Revised Article 8 also deletes the provisions set out in Section 8–403(3) of prior law specifying that issuers did not have a duty to inquire into the rightfulness of transfers by fiduciaries. The omission of the rules formerly in Section 8–403(3) does not, of course, mean that issuers would be liable for acting on the instruction of fiduciaries in the circumstances covered by former Section 8–403(3). Former Section 8–403(3) assumed that issuers would be liable if they registered a transfer with notice of an adverse claim. Former Section 8–403(3) was necessary only to negate any inference that knowledge that a transfer was initiated by a fiduciary might give constructive notice of adverse claims. Under Section 8–404 of Revised Article 8, mere notice of adverse claims does not impose duties on the issuer. Accordingly the provisions included in former Section 8–403(3) are unnecessary.

Although the prior version of Article 8 included provisions similar or identical to those set out in the Uniform Act for the Simplification of Fiduciary Security Transfers and similar statutes, most states retained these statutes at the time the Uniform Commercial Code was adopted. These statutes are based on a premise different from Revised Article 8. The fiduciary simplification acts are predicated on the assumption that an issuer would be liable to an adverse claimant if the issuer had notice. These statutes seek only to preclude any inference that issuers have such notice when they register transfers on the instructions of a fiduciary. Revised Article 8 is based on the view that a third party should not be able to interfere with the relationship between an issuer and its registered shareholders unless the claimant obtains legal process. Since notice of an adverse claim does not impose duties on an issuer under Revised Article 8, the Uniform Act for the Simplification of Fiduciary Security Transfers, or similar statutes, should be repealed upon enactment of Revised Article 8.

7. Former Section 8–319—Statute of Frauds.

Revised Article 8 deletes the special statute of frauds provision for securities contracts that was set out in former Section 8–319. See Revised Section 8–113. Most of the litigation involving the statute of frauds rule of the prior version of Article 8 involved informal transactions, rather than transactions on the organized securities markets. Typical cases were those in which an employee or former employee of a small enterprise sued to enforce an alleged promise that he or she would receive an equity interest in the business. The usual commercial policies relating to writings in contracts for the sale of personal property are at most tangentially implicated in such cases. There was a rather large and complex body of case law dealing with the applicability of Section 8–319 to cases of this sort. It seems doubtful that the cost of litigating these issues was warranted by whatever protections the statute of frauds offered against fraudulent claims.

Subsection (c) of former Section 8–319 provided that the statute of frauds bar did not apply if a written confirmation was sent and the recipient did not seasonably send an objection. That provision, however, presumably would not have had the effect of binding a broker's customer to the terms of a trade for which confirmation had been sent though the customer had not objected within 10 days. In the first place, the relationship between a broker and customer is ordinarily that of agent and principal; thus the broker is not seeking to enforce a contract for sale of a security, but to bind its principal for action taken by the broker as agent. Former Section 8–319 did not by its terms apply to the agency relationship. Moreover, even if former Section 8–319(c) applied, it is doubtful that it, of its own force, had the effect of precluding the customer from disputing whether there was a contract or what the terms of the contract were. Former Section 8–319(c) only removed the statute of frauds as a bar to enforcement; it did not say that there was a contract or that the confirmation had the effect of excluding other evidence of its terms. Thus,

deletion of former Section 8–319 does not change the law one way or the other on whether a customer who fails to object to a written confirmation is precluded from denying the trade described in the confirmation, because that issue was never governed by former Section 8–319(c).

8. Miscellaneous.

Prior Section 8–105. Revised Article 8 deletes the statement found in Section 8–105(1) of the prior version that certificated securities "are negotiable instruments." This provision was added very late in the drafting process of the original Uniform Commercial Code. Apparently the thought was that it might be useful in dealing with potential transition problems arising out of the fact that bonds were then treated as negotiable instruments under the Uniform Negotiable Instruments Law. During that era, many other statutes, such as those specifying permissible categories of investments for regulated entities, might have used such phrases as "negotiable securities" or "negotiable instruments." Section 8–105 seems to have been included in the original version of Article 8 to avoid unfortunate interpretations of those other statutes once securities were moved from the Uniform Negotiable Instruments Law to UCC Article 8. Whether or not Section 8–105 was necessary at that time, it has surely outlived its purpose. The statement that securities "are negotiable instruments" is very confusing. As used in the Uniform Commercial Code, the term "negotiable instrument" means an instrument that is governed by Article 3; yet Article 8 securities are not governed by Article 3. Courts have occasionally cited Section 8–105(1) of prior law for the proposition that the rules that are generally thought of as characteristic of negotiability, such as the rule that bona fide purchasers take free from adverse claims, apply to certificated securities. Section 8–105(1), however, is unnecessary for that purpose, since the relevant rules are set out in specific provisions of Article 8.

Prior Sections 8–107 and 8–314. Article 8 has never been, and should not be, a comprehensive codification of the law of contracts for the purchase and sale of securities. The prior version of Article 8 did contain, however, a number of provisions dealing with miscellaneous aspects of the law of contracts as applied to contracts for the sale of securities. Section 8–107 dealt with one remedy for breach, and Section 8–314 dealt with certain aspects of performance. Revised Article 8 deletes these on the theory that inclusion of a few sections on issues of contract law is likely to cause more harm than good since inferences might be drawn from the failure to cover related issues. The deletion of these sections is not, however, intended as a rejection of the rules of contract law and interpretation that they expressed.

Prior Section 8–315. It is not entirely clear what the function of Section 8–315 of prior law was. The section specified that the owner of a security could recover it from a person to whom it had been transferred, if the transferee did not qualify as a bona fide purchaser. It seems to have been intended only to recognize that securities, like any other form of personal property, are governed by the general principle of property law that an owner can recover property from a person to whom it has been transferred under circumstances that did not cut off the owner's claim. Although many other Articles of the UCC deal with cut-off rules, Article 8 was the only one that included an affirmative statement of the rights of an owner to recover her property. It seems wiser to adopt the same approach as in Articles 2, 3, 7, and 9, and leave this point to other law. Accordingly, Section 8–315 is deleted in Revised Article 8, without, of course, implying rejection of the nearly self-evident rule that it sought to express.

Prior Section 8–407. This section, entitled "Exchangeability of Securities," seemed to say that holders of securities had the right to cause issuers to convert them back and forth from certificated to uncertificated form. The provision, however, applied only if the issuer "regularly maintains a system for issuing the class of securities involved under which both certificated and uncertificated securities are regularly issued to the category of owners, which includes the person in whose name the new security is to be registered." The provision seems unnecessary, since it applied only if the issuer decided that it should. The matter can be covered by agreement or corporate charter or by-laws.

V. ACKNOWLEDGMENTS

On behalf of the National Conference of Commissioners on Uniform State Laws and the American Law Institute, the Drafting Committee and the Reporter acknowledge with deep appreciation the dedicated and helpful assistance of a great many individuals and organizations. Among the large number of individuals who participated in the development of Revised Article 8, special mention should be made of a few whose contributions were extraordinary.

Preceding the preparation of Revised Article 8, the topic was carefully studied by the Advisory Committee on Settlement of Market Transactions of the American Bar Association Section of Business Law, under the chairmanship of Robert Haydock, Jr., of Boston, MA. Martin Aronstein, of Philadelphia, PA, reporter for the 1977 revision of Article 8, served on the Haydock Committee and continued to advise the Drafting Committee. Robert C. Mendelson, New York, NY, who also served on the Haydock Committee, is chair of the Market Transactions Advisory Committee set up by the Securities and Exchange Commission; Bob Mendelson's considerable contribution to the preparation of Revised Article 8 was most important. Other members of the Haydock Committee had continuing roles either as members of the Drafting Committee or as sources of valuable advice to that committee.

The revision of Article 8 is the culmination of a successful federal-state collaboration among the American Law Institute and the National Conference of Commissioners on Uniform State Laws, sponsors of the Uniform Commercial Code, and representatives of the United States Department of the Treasury, the Securities and Exchange Commission, the Federal Reserve System, and other federal bodies. The product reflects the assistance of many people, and particularly of Jonathan Kallman and Ari Burstein on behalf of the SEC, Calvin Ninomiya, Cynthia E. Reese, and Virginia S. Rutledge of Treasury, Lawranne Stewart of the Board of Governors of the Federal Reserve System, Debra W. Cook and MarySue Fisher of the Federal Reserve Bank of New York, and George Wilder and Carla Behnfeldt of the Commodity Futures Trading Commission.

Representatives of organizations in the securities and banking industry and their counsel gave generously of their time and knowledge. Special mention should be made of Norman R. Nelson, New York Clearing House, R. May Lee, Public Securities Association, Robert J. Woldow and Karen Saperstein, National Securities Clearing

Corporation, Leopold S. Rassnick, Participants Trust Company, Robert Wittie and Patricia Louie, Investment Company Institute, Thomas A. Williams, Richard B. Nesson and Carl Urist, Depository Trust Company, Dennis A. Dutterer, Board of Trade Clearing Corporation, Evalyn Lipton Fishbein, State Street Bank and Trust Company, Robert P. DeGregorie, Chemical Bank, Gail M. Inaba, Morgan Guaranty Trust Company of New York, Anthony J. Leitner, Goldman, Sachs & Company, Robert M. MacAllister, The Chase Manhattan Bank, N.A., Kevin J. Moynihan, Merrill Lynch, Pierce, Fenner & Smith Inc., Lois J. Radisch, J.P. Morgan & Co., James J. Volpe, First Chicago Trust Company of New York, and Richard E. Smith, Securities Transfer Association.

Many lawyers and law professors contributed to the work of the Drafting Committee. Special appreciation is due to Sandra M. Rocks, New York, NY, who participated on behalf of the ABA UCC Investment Securities Subcommittee and ABA Task Force on TRADES Regulations. Others who participated included Steven Harris and James R. McDaniel, Chicago, IL, Kenneth B. Davis, Jr., Madison, WI, David M. Huggins and Bradley Y. Smith, New York, NY, David J. Schraa, Brussels, Belgium, and Randall D. Guynn, London, England. The Reporter and Drafting Committee also received assistance from the dedicated work of lawyers, not themselves experts in securities law, who reviewed and commented upon drafts and participated in the revision process through meetings of the Members Consultative Group of the American Law Institute and at various national, state, and local bar association programs.

PART 1

SHORT TITLE AND GENERAL MATTERS

§ 8–101. Short Title.

This Article may be cited as Uniform Commercial Code—Investment Securities.

§ 8–102. Definitions.

(a) In this Article:

(1) "Adverse claim" means a claim that a claimant has a property interest in a financial asset and that it is a violation of the rights of the claimant for another person to hold, transfer, or deal with the financial asset.

(2) "Bearer form," as applied to a certificated security, means a form in which the security is payable to the bearer of the security certificate according to its terms but not by reason of an indorsement.

(3) "Broker" means a person defined as a broker or dealer under the federal securities laws, but without excluding a bank acting in that capacity.

(4) "Certificated security" means a security that is represented by a certificate.

(5) "Clearing corporation" means:

(i) a person that is registered as a "clearing agency" under the federal securities laws;

(ii) a federal reserve bank; or

(iii) any other person that provides clearance or settlement services with respect to financial assets that would require it to register as a clearing agency under the federal securities laws but for an exclusion or exemption from the registration requirement, if its activities as a clearing corporation, including promulgation of rules, are subject to regulation by a federal or state governmental authority.

(6) "Communicate" means to:

(i) send a signed writing; or

(ii) transmit information by any mechanism agreed upon by the persons transmitting and receiving the information.

(7) "Entitlement holder" means a person identified in the records of a securities intermediary as the person having a security entitlement against the securities in-

termediary. If a person acquires a security entitlement by virtue of Section 8–501(b)(2) or (3), that person is the entitlement holder.

(8) "Entitlement order" means a notification communicated to a securities intermediary directing transfer or redemption of a financial asset to which the entitlement holder has a security entitlement.

(9) "Financial asset," except as otherwise provided in Section 8–103, means:

(i) a security;

(ii) an obligation of a person or a share, participation, or other interest in a person or in property or an enterprise of a person, which is, or is of a type, dealt in or traded on financial markets, or which is recognized in any area in which it is issued or dealt in as a medium for investment; or

(iii) any property that is held by a securities intermediary for another person in a securities account if the securities intermediary has expressly agreed with the other person that the property is to be treated as a financial asset under this Article.

As context requires, the term means either the interest itself or the means by which a person's claim to it is evidenced, including a certificated or uncertificated security, a security certificate, or a security entitlement.

(10) [[reserved] "Good faith," for purposes of the obligation of good faith in the performance or enforcement of contracts or duties within this Article, means honesty in fact and the observance of reasonable commercial standards of fair dealing.] *Deleted by Revised Art. 1 (2001).*

(11) "Indorsement" means a signature that alone or accompanied by other words is made on a security certificate in registered form or on a separate document for the purpose of assigning, transferring, or redeeming the security or granting a power to assign, transfer, or redeem it.

(12) "Instruction" means a notification communicated to the issuer of an uncertificat-

ed security which directs that the transfer of the security be registered or that the security be redeemed.

(13) "Registered form," as applied to a certificated security, means a form in which:

(i) the security certificate specifies a person entitled to the security; and

(ii) a transfer of the security may be registered upon books maintained for that purpose by or on behalf of the issuer, or the security certificate so states.

(14) "Securities intermediary" means:

(i) a clearing corporation; or

(ii) a person, including a bank or broker, that in the ordinary course of its business maintains securities accounts for others and is acting in that capacity.

(15) "Security," except as otherwise provided in Section 8–103, means an obligation of an issuer or a share, participation, or other interest in an issuer or in property or an enterprise of an issuer:

(i) which is represented by a security certificate in bearer or registered form, or the transfer of which may be registered upon books maintained for that purpose by or on behalf of the issuer;

(ii) which is one of a class or series or by its terms is divisible into a class or series of shares, participations, interests, or obligations; and

(iii) which:

(A) is, or is of a type, dealt in or traded on securities exchanges or securities markets; or

(B) is a medium for investment and by its terms expressly provides that it is a security governed by this Article.

(16) "Security certificate" means a certificate representing a security.

(17) "Security entitlement" means the rights and property interest of an entitlement holder with respect to a financial asset specified in Part 5.

(18) "Uncertificated security" means a security that is not represented by a certificate.

(b) Other definitions applying to this Article and the sections in which they appear are:

Appropriate person Section 8–107
Control Section 8–106
Delivery Section 8–301
Investment company security Section 8–103
Issuer Section 8–201
Overissue Section 8–210
Protected purchaser Section 8–303
Securities account Section 8–501

(c) In addition, Article 1 contains general definitions and principles of construction and interpretation applicable throughout this Article.

(d) The characterization of a person, business, or transaction for purposes of this Article does not determine the characterization of the person, business, or transaction for purposes of any other law, regulation, or rule.

As amended in 2001.

Official Comment

1. "Adverse claim." The definition of the term "adverse claim" has two components. First, the term refers only to property interests. Second, the term means not merely that a person has a property interest in a financial asset but that it is a violation of the claimant's property interest for the other person to hold or transfer the security or other financial asset.

The term adverse claim is not, of course, limited to ownership rights, but extends to other property interests established by other law. A security interest, for example, would be an adverse claim with respect to a transferee from the debtor since any effort by the secured party to enforce the security interest against the property would be an interference with the transferee's interest.

The definition of adverse claim in the prior version of Article 8 might have been read to suggest that any wrongful action concerning a security, even a simple breach of contract, gave rise to an adverse claim. Insofar as such cases as *Fallon v. Wall Street Clearing Corp.*, 586 N.Y.S.2d 953, 182 A.D.2d 245, (1992) and *Pentech Intl. v. Wall St. Clearing Co.*, 983 F.2d 441 (2d Cir.1993), were based on that view, they are rejected by the new definition which explicitly limits the term adverse claim to property interests. Suppose, for example, that A contracts to sell or deliver securities to B, but fails to do so and instead sells or pledges the securities to C. B, the promisee, has an action against A for breach of contract, but absent unusual circumstances the action for breach would not give rise to a property interest in the securities. Accordingly, B does not have an adverse claim. An adverse claim might, however, be based upon principles of equitable remedies that give rise to property claims. It would, for example, cover a right established by other law to rescind a transaction in which securities were transferred. Suppose, for example, that A holds securities and is induced by B's fraud to transfer them to B. Under the law of contract or restitution, A may have a right to rescind the transfer, which gives A a property claim to the securities. If so, A has an adverse claim to the securities in B's hands. By contrast, if B had committed no fraud, but had merely committed a breach of contract in connection with the transfer from A to B, A may have only a right to damages for breach, not a right to rescind. In that case, A would not have an adverse claim to the securities in B's hands.

2. "Bearer form." The definition of "bearer form" has remained substantially unchanged since the early drafts of the original version of Article 8. The requirement that the certificate be payable to bearer by its terms rather than by an indorsement has the effect of preventing instruments governed by other law, such as chattel paper or Article 3 negotiable instruments, from being inadvertently swept into the Article 8 definition of security merely by virtue of blank indorsements. Although the other elements of the definition of security in Section 8–102(a)(14) probably suffice for that purpose in any event, the language used in the prior version of Article 8 has been retained.

3. "Broker." Broker is defined by reference to the definitions of broker and dealer in the federal securities laws. The only difference is that banks, which are excluded from the federal securities law definition, are included in the Article 8 definition when they perform functions that would bring them within the federal securities law definition if it did not have the clause excluding banks. The definition covers both those who act as agents ("brokers" in securities parlance) and those who act as principals ("dealers" in securities parlance). Since the definition refers to persons "defined" as brokers or dealers under the federal securities law, rather than to persons required to "register" as brokers or dealers under the federal securities law, it covers not only registered brokers and dealers but also those exempt from the registration requirement, such as purely intrastate brokers. The only substantive rules that turn on the defined term broker are one provision of the section on warranties, Section 8–108(i), and the special perfection rule in Article 9 for security interests granted by brokers or securities intermediaries, Section 9–309(10).

4. "Certificated security." The term "certificated security" means a security that is represented by a security certificate.

5. "Clearing corporation." The definition of clearing corporation limits its application to entities that are subject to a rigorous regulatory framework. Accordingly, the definition includes only federal reserve banks, persons who are registered as "clearing agencies" under the federal securities laws (which impose a comprehensive system of regulation of the activities and rules of clearing agencies), and other entities subject to a comparable system of regulatory oversight.

6. "Communicate." The term "communicate" assures that the Article 8 rules will be sufficiently flexible to adapt to changes in information technology. Sending a signed writing always suffices as a communication, but the parties can agree that a different means of transmitting information is to be used. Agreement is defined in Section 1–201(3) as "the bargain of the parties in fact as found in their language or by implication from other circumstances including course of dealing or usage of trade or course of performance." Thus, use of an information transmission method might be found to be authorized by agreement, even though the parties have not explicitly so specified in a formal agreement. The term communicate is used in Sections 8–102(a)(7) (definition of entitlement order), 8–102(a)(11) (definition of instruction), and 8–403 (demand that issuer not register transfer).

7. "Entitlement holder." This term designates those who hold financial assets through intermediaries in the indirect holding system. Because many of the rules of Part 5 impose duties on securities intermediaries in favor of entitlement holders, the definition of entitlement holder is, in most cases, limited to the person specifically designated as such on the records of the intermediary. The last sentence of the definition covers the relatively unusual cases where a person may acquire a security entitlement under Section 8–501 even though the person may not be specifically designated as an entitlement holder on the records of the securities intermediary.

A person may have an interest in a security entitlement, and may even have the right to give entitlement orders to the securities intermediary with respect to it, even though the person is not the entitlement holder. For example, a person who holds securities through a securities account in its own name may have given discretionary trading authority to another person, such as an investment adviser. Similarly, the control provisions in Section 8–106 and the related provisions in Article 9 are designed to facilitate transactions in which a person who holds securities through a securities account uses them as collateral in an arrangement where the securities intermediary has agreed that if the secured party so directs the intermediary will dispose of the positions. In such arrangements, the debtor remains the entitlement holder but has agreed that the secured party can initiate entitlement orders. Moreover, an entitlement holder may be acting for another person as a nominee, agent, trustee, or in another capacity. Unless the entitlement holder is itself acting as a securities intermediary for the other person, in which case the other person would be an entitlement holder with respect to the securities entitlement, the relationship between an entitlement holder and another person for whose benefit the entitlement holder holds a securities entitlement is governed by other law.

8. "Entitlement order." This term is defined as a notification communicated to a securities intermediary directing transfer or redemption of the financial asset to which an entitlement holder has a security entitlement. The term is used in the rules for the indirect holding system in a fashion analogous to the use of the terms "indorsement" and "instruction" in the rules for the direct holding system. If a person directly holds a certificated security in registered form and wishes to transfer it, the means of transfer is an indorsement. If a person directly holds an uncertificated security and wishes to transfer it, the means of transfer is an instruction. If a person holds a security entitlement, the means of disposition is an entitlement order. An entitlement order includes a direction under Section 8–508 to the securities intermediary to transfer a financial asset to the account of the entitlement holder at another financial intermediary or to cause the financial asset to be transferred to the entitlement holder in the direct holding system (e.g., the delivery of a securities certificate registered in the name of the former entitlement holder). As noted in Comment 7, an entitlement order need not be initiated by the entitlement holder in order to be effective, so long as the entitlement holder has authorized the other party to initiate entitlement orders. See Section 8–107(b).

9. "Financial asset." The definition of "financial asset," in conjunction with the definition of "securities account" in Section 8–501, sets the scope of the indirect holding system rules of Part 5 of Revised Article 8. The Part 5 rules apply not only to securities held through intermediaries, but also to other financial assets held through intermediaries. The term financial asset is defined to include not only securities but also a broader category of obligations, shares, participations, and interests.

Having separate definitions of security and financial asset makes it possible to separate the question of the proper scope of the traditional Article 8 rules from the question of the proper scope of the new indirect holding system rules. Some forms of financial assets should be covered by the indirect holding system rules of Part 5, but not by the rules of Parts 2, 3, and 4. The term financial asset is used to cover such property. Because the term security entitlement is defined in terms of financial assets rather than securities, the rules concerning security entitlements set out in Part 5 of Article 8 and in Revised Article 9 apply to the broader class of financial assets.

The fact that something does or could fall within the definition of financial asset does not, without more, trigger Article 8 coverage. The indirect holding system rules of Revised Article 8 apply only if the financial asset is in fact held in a securities account, so that the interest of the person who holds the financial asset through the securities account is a security entitlement. Thus, questions of the scope of the indirect holding system rules cannot be framed as "Is such-and-such a 'financial asset' under Article 8?" Rather, one must analyze whether the relationship between an institution and a person on whose behalf the institution holds an asset falls within the scope of the term securities account as defined in Section 8–501. That question turns in large measure on whether it makes sense to apply the Part 5 rules to the relationship.

The term financial asset is used to refer both to the underlying asset and the particular means by which ownership of that asset is evidenced. Thus, with respect to a certificated security, the term financial asset may, as context requires, refer either to the interest or obligation of the issuer or to the security certificate representing that interest or obligation. Similarly, if a person holds a security or other financial asset through a securities account, the term financial asset may, as context requires, refer either to the underlying asset or to the person's security entitlement.

10. "Good faith." Section 1–203 provides that "Every contract or duty within [the Uniform Commercial Code] imposes an obligation of good faith in its performance or enforcement." Section 1–201(b)(20) defines "good faith" as "honesty in fact and the observance of reasonable commercial standards of fair dealing." The reference to commercial standards makes clear that assessments of conduct are to be made in light of the commercial setting. The substantive rules of Article 8 have been drafted to take account of the commercial circumstances of the securities holding and processing system. For example, Section 8–115 provides that a securities intermediary acting on an effective entitlement order, or a broker or other agent acting as a conduit in a securities transaction, is not liable to an adverse claimant, unless the claimant obtained legal process or the intermediary acted in collusion with the wrongdoer. This, and other similar provisions, see Sections 8–404 and 8–503(e), do not depend on notice of adverse claims, because it would impair rather than advance the interest of investors in having a sound and efficient securities clearance and settlement system to require intermediaries to investigate the propriety of the transactions they are processing. The good faith obligation does not supplant the standards of conduct established in provisions of this kind.

In Revised Article 8, the definition of good faith is not germane to the question whether a purchaser takes free from adverse claims. The rules on such questions as whether a purchaser who takes in suspicious circumstances is disqualified from protected purchaser status are treated not as an aspect of good faith but directly in the rules of Section 8–105 on notice of adverse claims.

11. "Indorsement" is defined as a signature made on a security certificate or separate document for purposes of transferring or redeeming the security. The definition is adapted from the language of Section 8–308(1) of the prior version and from the definition of indorsement in the Negotiable Instruments Article, see Section 3–204(a). The definition of indorsement does not include the requirement that the signature be made by an appropriate person or be authorized. Those questions are treated in the separate substantive provision on whether the indorsement is effective, rather than in the definition of indorsement. See Section 8–107.

12. "Instruction" is defined as a notification communicated to the issuer of an uncertificated security directing that transfer be registered or that the security be redeemed. Instructions are the analog for uncertificated securities of indorsements of certificated securities.

13. "Registered form." The definition of "registered form" is substantially the same as in the prior version of Article 8. Like the definition of bearer form, it serves primarily to distinguish Article 8 securities from instruments governed by other law, such as Article 3.

14. "Securities intermediary." A "securities intermediary" is a person that in the ordinary course of its business maintains securities accounts for others and is acting in that capacity. The most common examples

of securities intermediaries would be clearing corporations holding securities for their participants, banks acting as securities custodians, and brokers holding securities on behalf of their customers. Clearing corporations are listed separately as a category of securities intermediary in subparagraph (i) even though in most circumstances they would fall within the general definition in subparagraph (ii). The reason is to simplify the analysis of arrangements such as the NSCC–DTC system in which NSCC performs the comparison, clearance, and netting function, while DTC acts as the depository. Because NSCC is a registered clearing agency under the federal securities laws, it is a clearing corporation and hence a securities intermediary under Article 8, regardless of whether it is at any particular time or in any particular aspect of its operations holding securities on behalf of its participants.

The terms securities intermediary and broker have different meanings. Broker means a person engaged in the business of buying and selling securities, as agent for others or as principal. Securities intermediary means a person maintaining securities accounts for others. A stockbroker, in the colloquial sense, may or may not be acting as a securities intermediary.

The definition of securities intermediary includes the requirement that the person in question is "acting in the capacity" of maintaining securities accounts for others. This is to take account of the fact that a particular entity, such as a bank, may act in many different capacities in securities transactions. A bank may act as a transfer agent for issuers, as a securities custodian for institutional investors and private investors, as a dealer in government securities, as a lender taking securities as collateral, and as a provider of general payment and collection services that might be used in connection with securities transactions. A bank that maintains securities accounts for its customers would be a securities intermediary with respect to those accounts; but if it takes a pledge of securities from a borrower to secure a loan, it is not thereby acting as a securities intermediary with respect to the pledged securities, since it holds them for its own account rather than for a customer. In other circumstances, those two functions might be combined. For example, if the bank is a government securities dealer it may maintain securities accounts for customers and also provide the customers with margin credit to purchase or carry the securities, in much the same way that brokers provide margin loans to their customers.

15. "Security." The definition of "security" has three components. First, there is the subparagraph (i) test that the interest or obligation be fully transferable, in the sense that the issuer either maintains transfer books or the obligation or interest is represented by a certificate in bearer or registered form. Second, there is the subparagraph (ii) test that the interest or obligation be divisible, that is, one of a class or series, as distinguished from individual obligations of the sort governed by ordinary contract law or by Article 3. Third, there is the subparagraph (iii) functional test, which generally turns on whether the interest or obligation is, or is of a type, dealt in or traded on securities markets or securities exchanges. There is, however, an "opt-in" provision in subparagraph (iii) which permits the issuer of any interest or obligation that is "a medium of investment" to specify that it is a security governed by Article 8.

The divisibility test of subparagraph (ii) applies to the security—that is, the underlying intangible interest—not the means by which that interest is evidenced. Thus, securities issued in book-entry only form meet the divisibility test because the underlying intangible interest is divisible via the mechanism of the indirect holding system. This is so even though the clearing corporation is the only eligible direct holder of the security.

The third component, the functional test in subparagraph (iii), provides flexibility while ensuring that the Article 8 rules do not apply to interests or obligations in circumstances so unconnected with the securities markets that parties are unlikely to have thought of the possibility that Article 8 might apply. Subparagraph (iii)(A) covers interests or obligations that either are dealt in or traded on securities exchanges or securities markets, or are of a type dealt in or traded on securities exchanges or securities markets. The "is dealt in or traded on" phrase eliminates problems in the characterization of new forms of securities which are to be traded in the markets, even though no similar type has previously been dealt in or traded in the markets. Subparagraph (iii)(B) covers the broader category of media for investment, but it applies only if the terms of the interest or obligation specify that it is an Article 8 security. This opt-in provision allows for deliberate expansion of the scope of Article 8.

Section 8–103 contains additional rules on the treatment of particular interests as securities or financial assets.

16. "Security certificate." The term "security" refers to the underlying asset, e.g., 1000 shares of common stock of Acme, Inc. The term "security certificate" refers to the paper certificates that have traditionally been used to embody the underlying intangible interest.

17. "Security entitlement" means the rights and property interest of a person who holds securities or other financial assets through a securities intermediary. A security entitlement is both a package of personal rights against the securities intermediary and an interest in the property held by the securities intermediary. A security entitlement is not, however, a specific property interest in any financial asset held by the securities intermediary or by the clearing corporation through which the securities intermediary holds the financial asset. See Sections 8–104(c) and 8–503. The formal definition of security entitlement set out in subsection (a)(16) of this section is a cross-reference to the rules of Part 5. In a sense, then, the entirety of Part 5 is the definition of security entitlement. The Part 5 rules specify the rights and property interest that comprise a security entitlement.

18. "Uncertificated security." The term "uncertificated security" means a security that is not represented by a security certificate. For uncertificated securities, there is no need to draw any distinction between the underlying asset and the means by which a direct holder's interest in that asset is evidenced. Compare "certificated security" and "security certificate."

Definitional Cross References:

"Agreement". Section 1–201(b)(3).
"Bank". Section 1–201(b)(4).
"Person". Section 1–201(b)(27).
"Send". Section 1–201(b)(36).
"Signed". Section 1–201(b)(37).
"Writing". Section 1–201(b)(43).

As amended in 1999 and 2001.

§ 8–103. Rules for Determining Whether Certain Obligations and Interests are Securities or Financial Assets.

(a) A share or similar equity interest issued by a corporation, business trust, joint stock company, or similar entity is a security.

(b) An "investment company security" is a security. "Investment company security" means a share or similar equity interest issued by an entity that is registered as an investment company under the federal investment company laws, an interest in a unit investment trust that is so registered, or a face-amount certificate issued by a face-amount certificate company that is so registered. Investment company security does not include an insurance policy or endowment policy or annuity contract issued by an insurance company.

(c) An interest in a partnership or limited liability company is not a security unless it is dealt in or traded on securities exchanges or in securities markets, its terms expressly provide that it is a security governed by this Article, or it is an investment company security. However, an interest in a partnership or limited liability company is a financial asset if it is held in a securities account.

(d) A writing that is a security certificate is governed by this Article and not by Article 3, even though it also meets the requirements of that Article. However, a negotiable instrument governed by Article 3 is a financial asset if it is held in a securities account.

(e) An option or similar obligation issued by a clearing corporation to its participants is not a security, but is a financial asset.

(f) A commodity contract, as defined in Section 9–102(a)(15), is not a security or a financial asset.

(g) A document of title is not a financial asset unless Section 8–102(a)(9)(iii) applies.

As amended in 1999 and 2003.

Official Comment

1. This section contains rules that supplement the definitions of "financial asset" and "security" in Section 8–102. The Section 8–102 definitions are worded in general terms, because they must be sufficiently comprehensive and flexible to cover the wide variety of investment products that now exist or may develop. The rules in this section are intended to foreclose interpretive issues concerning the application of the general definitions to several specific investment products. No implication is made about the application of the Section 8–102 definitions to investment products not covered by this section.

2. Subsection (a) establishes an unconditional rule that ordinary corporate stock is a security. That is so whether or not the particular issue is dealt in or traded on securities exchanges or in securities markets. Thus, shares of closely held corporations are Article 8 securities.

3. Subsection (b) establishes that the Article 8 term "security" includes the various forms of the investment vehicles offered to the public by investment companies registered as such under the federal Investment Company Act of 1940, as amended. This clarification is prompted principally by the fact that the typical transaction in shares of open-end investment compa-

nies is an issuance or redemption, rather than a transfer of shares from one person to another as is the case with ordinary corporate stock. For similar reasons, the definitions of indorsement, instruction, and entitlement order in Section 8–102 refer to "redemptions" as well as "transfers," to ensure that the Article 8 rules on such matters as signature guaranties, Section 8–306, assurances, Sections 8–402 and 8–507, and effectiveness, Section 8–107, apply to directions to redeem mutual fund shares. The exclusion of insurance products is needed because some insurance company separate accounts are registered under the Investment Company Act of 1940, but these are not traded under the usual Article 8 mechanics.

4. Subsection (c) is designed to foreclose interpretive questions that might otherwise be raised by the application of the "of a type" language of Section 8–102(a)(15)(iii) to partnership interests. Subsection (c) establishes the general rule that partnership interests or shares of limited liability companies are not Article 8 securities unless they are in fact dealt in or traded on securities exchanges or in securities markets. The issuer, however, may explicitly "opt-in" by specifying that the interests or shares are securities governed by Article 8. Partnership interests or shares of limited liability companies are included in the broader term "financial asset." Thus, if they are held through a securities account, the indirect holding system rules of Part 5 apply, and the interest of a person who holds them through such an account is a security entitlement.

5. Subsection (d) deals with the line between Article 3 negotiable instruments and Article 8 investment securities. It continues the rule of the prior version of Article 8 that a writing that meets the Article 8 definition is covered by Article 8 rather than Article 3, even though it also meets the definition of negotiable instrument. However, subsection (d) provides that an Article 3 negotiable instrument is a "financial asset" so that the indirect holding system rules apply if the instrument is held through a securities intermediary. This facilitates making items such as money market instruments eligible for deposit in clearing corporations.

6. Subsection (e) is included to clarify the treatment of investment products such as traded stock options, which are treated as financial assets but not securities. Thus, the indirect holding system rules of Part 5 apply, but the direct holding system rules of Parts 2, 3, and 4 do not.

7. Subsection (f) excludes commodity contracts from all of Article 8. However, under Article 9, commodity contracts are included in the definition of "investment property." Therefore, the Article 9 rules on security interests in investment property do apply to security interests in commodity positions. See Section 9–102 and Comment 6 thereto. "Commodity contract" is defined in Section 9–102(a)(15).

8. Subsection (g) allows a document of title to be a financial asset and thus subject to the indirect holding system rules of Part 5 only to the extent that the intermediary and the person entitled under the document agree to do so. This is to prevent the inadvertent application of the Part 5 rules to intermediaries who may hold either electronic or tangible documents of title.

Definitional Cross References:

"Clearing corporation". Section 8–102(a)(5).
"Commodity contract". Section 9–102(a)(15).
"Financial asset". Section 8–102(a)(9).
"Security". Section 8–102(a)(15).
"Security certificate". Section 8–102(a)(16).

As amended in 2003.

§ 8–104. Acquisition of Security or Financial Asset or Interest Therein.

(a) A person acquires a security or an interest therein, under this Article, if:

(1) the person is a purchaser to whom a security is delivered pursuant to Section 8–301; or

(2) the person acquires a security entitlement to the security pursuant to Section 8–501.

(b) A person acquires a financial asset, other than a security, or an interest therein, under this Article, if the person acquires a security entitlement to the financial asset.

(c) A person who acquires a security entitlement to a security or other financial asset has the rights specified in Part 5, but is a purchaser of any security, security entitlement, or other financial asset held by the securities intermediary only to the extent provided in Section 8–503.

(d) Unless the context shows that a different meaning is intended, a person who is required by other law, regulation, rule, or agreement to transfer, deliver, present, surrender, exchange, or otherwise put in the possession of another person a security or financial asset satisfies that requirement by causing the other person to acquire an interest in the security or financial asset pursuant to subsection (a) or (b).

Official Comment

1. This section lists the ways in which interests in securities and other financial assets are acquired under Article 8. In that sense, it describes the scope of Article 8. Subsection (a) describes the two ways that a person may acquire a security or interest therein under this Article: (1) by delivery (Section 8–301), and (2) by acquiring a security entitlement. Each of these methods is described in detail in the relevant substantive provisions of this Article. Part 3, beginning with the definition of "delivery" in Section 8–301, describes how interests in securities are acquired in the direct holding system. Part 5, beginning with the rules of Section 8–501 on how security entitlements are acquired, describes how interests in securities are acquired in the indirect holding system.

Subsection (b) specifies how a person may acquire an interest under Article 8 in a financial asset other than a security. This Article deals with financial assets other than securities only insofar as they are held in the indirect holding system. For example, a bankers' acceptance falls within the definition of "financial asset," so if it is held through a securities account the entitlement holder's right to it is a security entitlement governed by Part 5. The bankers' acceptance itself, however, is a negotiable instrument governed by Article 3, not by Article 8. Thus, the provisions of Parts 2, 3, and 4 of this Article that deal with the rights of direct holders of securities are not applicable. Article 3, not Article 8, specifies how one acquires a direct interest in a bankers' acceptance. If a bankers' acceptance is delivered to a clearing corporation to be held for the account of the clearing corporation's participants, the clearing corporation becomes the holder of the bankers' acceptance under the Article 3 rules specifying how negotiable instruments are transferred. The rights of the clearing corporation's participants, however, are governed by Part 5 of this Article.

2. The distinction in usage in Article 8 between the term "security" (and its correlatives "security certificate" and "uncertificated security") on the one hand, and "security entitlement" on the other, corresponds to the distinction between the direct and indirect holding systems. For example, with respect to certificated securities that can be held either directly or through intermediaries, obtaining possession of a security certificate and acquiring a security entitlement are both means of holding the underlying security. For many other purposes, there is no need to draw a distinction between the means of holding. For purposes of commercial law analysis, however, the form of holding may make a difference. Where an item of property can be held in different ways, the rules on how one deals with it, including how one transfers it or how one grants a security interest in it, differ depending on the form of holding.

Although a security entitlement is means of holding the underlying security or other financial asset, a person who has a security entitlement does not have any direct claim to a specific asset in the possession of the securities intermediary. Subsection (c) provides explicitly that a person who acquires a security entitlement is a "purchaser" of any security, security entitlement, or other financial asset held by the securities intermediary only in the sense that under Section 8–503 a security entitlement is treated as a *sui generis* form of property interest.

3. Subsection (d) is designed to ensure that parties will retain their expected legal rights and duties under Revised Article 8. One of the major changes made by the revision is that the rules for the indirect holding system are stated in terms of the "security entitlements" held by investors, rather than speaking of them as holding direct interests in securities. Subsection (d) is designed as a translation rule to eliminate problems of co-ordination of terminology, and facilitate the continued use of systems for the efficient handling of securities and financial assets through securities intermediaries and clearing corporations. The efficiencies of a securities intermediary or clearing corporation are, in part, dependent on the ability to transfer securities credited to securities accounts in the intermediary or clearing corporation to the account of an issuer, its agent, or other person by book entry in a manner that permits exchanges, redemptions, conversions, and other transactions (which may be governed by pre-existing or new agreements, constitutional documents, or other instruments) to occur and to avoid the need to withdraw from immobilization in an intermediary or clearing corporation physical securities in order to deliver them for such purposes. Existing corporate charters, indentures and like documents may require the "presentation," "surrender," "delivery," or "transfer" of securities or security certificates for purposes of exchange, redemption, conversion or other reason. Likewise, documents may use a wide variety of terminology to describe, in the context for example of a tender or exchange offer, the means of putting the offeror or the issuer or its agent in possession of the security. Subsection (d) takes the place of provisions of prior law which could be used to reach the legal conclusion that book-entry transfers are equivalent to physical delivery to the person to whose account the book entry is credited.

Definitional Cross References:

"Delivery". Section 8–301.
"Financial asset". Section 8–102(a)(9).
"Person". Section 1–201(30).
"Purchaser". Sections 1–201(33) & 8–116.
"Security". Section 8–102(a)(15).
"Security entitlement". Section 8–102(a)(17).

§ 8–105. Notice of Adverse Claim.

(a) A person has notice of an adverse claim if:

(1) the person knows of the adverse claim;

(2) the person is aware of facts sufficient to indicate that there is a significant probability that the adverse claim exists and deliberately avoids information that would establish the existence of the adverse claim; or

(3) the person has a duty, imposed by statute or regulation, to investigate whether an adverse claim exists, and the investigation so required would establish the existence of the adverse claim.

(b) Having knowledge that a financial asset or interest therein is or has been transferred by a representative imposes no duty of inquiry into the rightfulness of a transaction and is not notice of an adverse claim. However, a person who knows that a representative has transferred a financial asset or interest therein in a transaction that is, or whose proceeds are being used, for the individual benefit of the representative or otherwise in breach of duty has notice of an adverse claim.

(c) An act or event that creates a right to immediate performance of the principal obligation represented by a security certificate or sets a date on or after which the certificate is to be presented or surrendered for redemption or exchange does not itself constitute notice of an adverse claim except in the case of a transfer more than:

(1) one year after a date set for presentment or surrender for redemption or exchange; or

(2) six months after a date set for payment of money against presentation or surrender of the certificate, if money was available for payment on that date.

(d) A purchaser of a certificated security has notice of an adverse claim if the security certificate:

(1) whether in bearer or registered form, has been indorsed "for collection" or "for surrender" or for some other purpose not involving transfer; or

(2) is in bearer form and has on it an unambiguous statement that it is the property of a person other than the transferor, but the mere writing of a name on the certificate is not such a statement.

(e) Filing of a financing statement under Article 9 is not notice of an adverse claim to a financial asset.

Official Comment

1. The rules specifying whether adverse claims can be asserted against persons who acquire securities or security entitlements, Sections 8–303, 8–502, and 8–510, provide that one is protected against an adverse claim only if one takes without notice of the claim. This section defines notice of an adverse claim.

The general Article 1 definition of "notice" in Section 1–201(25)—which provides that a person has notice of a fact if "from all the facts and circumstances known to him at the time in question he has reason to know that it exists"—does not apply to the interpretation of "notice of adverse claims." The Section 1–201(25) definition of "notice" does, however, apply to usages of that term and its cognates in Article 8 in contexts other than notice of adverse claims.

2. This section must be interpreted in light of the definition of "adverse claim" in Section 8–102(a)(1). "Adverse claim" does not include all circumstances in which a third party has a property interest in securities, but only those situations where a security is transferred in violation of the claimant's property interest. Therefore, awareness that someone other than the transferor has a property interest is not notice of an adverse claim. The transferee must be aware that the transfer violates the other party's property interest. If A holds securities in which B has some form of property interest, and A transfers the securities to C, C may know that B has an interest, but infer that A is acting in accordance with A's obligations to B. The mere fact that C knew that B had a property interest does not mean that C had notice of an adverse claim. Whether C had notice of an adverse claim depends on whether C had sufficient awareness that A was acting

in violation of B's property rights. The rule in subsection (b) is a particularization of this general principle.

3. Paragraph (a)(1) provides that a person has notice of an adverse claim if the person has knowledge of the adverse claim. Knowledge is defined in Section 1–201(25) as actual knowledge.

4. Paragraph (a)(2) provides that a person has notice of an adverse claim if the person is aware of a significant probability that an adverse claim exists and deliberately avoids information that might establish the existence of the adverse claim. This is intended to codify the "willful blindness" test that has been applied in such cases. See *May v. Chapman,* 16 M. & W. 355, 153 Eng.Rep. 1225 (1847); *Goodman v. Simonds,* 61 U.S. 343 (1857).

The first prong of the willful blindness test of paragraph (a)(2) turns on whether the person is aware facts sufficient to indicate that there is a significant probability that an adverse claim exists. The "awareness" aspect necessarily turns on the actor's state of mind. Whether facts known to a person make the person aware of a "significant probability" that an adverse claim exists turns on facts about the world and the conclusions that would be drawn from those facts, taking account of the experience and position of the person in question. A particular set of facts might indicate a significant probability of an adverse claim to a professional with considerable experience in the usual methods and procedures by which securities transactions are conducted, even though the same facts would not indicate a significant probability of an adverse claim to a non-professional.

The second prong of the willful blindness test of paragraph (a)(2) turns on whether the person "deliberately avoids information" that would establish the existence of the adverse claim. The test is the character of the person's response to the information the person has. The question is whether the person deliberately failed to seek further information because of concern that suspicions would be confirmed.

Application of the "deliberate avoidance" test to a transaction by an organization focuses on the knowledge and the actions of the individual or individuals conducting the transaction on behalf of the organization. Thus, an organization that purchases a security is not willfully blind to an adverse claim unless the officers or agents who conducted that purchase transaction are willfully blind to the adverse claim. Under the two prongs of the willful blindness test, the individual or individuals conducting a transaction must know of facts indicating a substantial probability that the adverse claim exists and deliberately fail to seek further information that might confirm or refute the indication. For this purpose, information known to individuals within an organization who are not conducting or aware of a transaction, but not forwarded to the individuals conducting the transaction, is not pertinent in determining whether the individuals conducting the transaction had knowledge of a substantial probability of the existence of the adverse claim. Cf. Section 1–201(27). An organization may also "deliberately avoid information" if it acts to preclude or inhibit transmission of pertinent information to those individuals responsible for the conduct of purchase transactions.

5. Paragraph (a)(3) provides that a person has notice of an adverse claim if the person would have learned of the adverse claim by conducting an investigation that is required by other statute or regulation. This rule applies only if there is some other statute or regulation that explicitly requires persons dealing with securities to conduct some investigation. The federal securities laws require that brokers and banks, in certain specified circumstances, check with a stolen securities registry to determine whether securities offered for sale or pledge have been reported as stolen. If securities that were listed as stolen in the registry are taken by an institution that failed to comply with requirement to check the registry, the institution would be held to have notice of the fact that they were stolen under paragraph (a)(3). Accordingly, the institution could not qualify as a protected purchaser under Section 8–303. The same result has been reached under the prior version of Article 8. See *First Nat'l Bank of Cicero v. Lewco Securities,* 860 F.2d 1407 (7th Cir.1988).

6. Subsection (b) provides explicitly for some situations involving purchase from one described or identifiable as a representative. Knowledge of the existence of the representative relation is not enough in itself to constitute "notice of an adverse claim" that would disqualify the purchaser from protected purchaser status. A purchaser may take a security on the inference that the representative is acting properly. Knowledge that a security is being transferred to an individual account of the representative or that the proceeds of the transaction will be paid into that account is not sufficient to constitute "notice of an adverse claim," but knowledge that the proceeds will be applied to the personal indebtedness of the representative is. See *State Bank of Binghamton v. Bache,* 162 Misc. 128, 293 N.Y.S. 667 (1937).

7. Subsection (c) specifies whether a purchaser of a "stale" security is charged with notice of adverse

claims, and therefore disqualified from protected purchaser status under Section 8–303. The fact of "staleness" is viewed as notice of certain defects after the lapse of stated periods, but the maturity of the security does not operate automatically to affect holders' rights. The periods of time here stated are shorter than those appearing in the provisions of this Article on staleness as notice of defects or defenses of an issuer (Section 8–203) since a purchaser who takes a security after funds or other securities are available for its redemption has more reason to suspect claims of ownership than issuer's defenses. An owner will normally turn in a security rather than transfer it at such a time. Of itself, a default never constitutes notice of a possible adverse claim. To provide otherwise would not tend to drive defaulted securities home and would serve only to disrupt current financial markets where many defaulted securities are actively traded. Unpaid or overdue coupons attached to a bond do not bring it within the operation of this subsection, though they may be relevant under the general test of notice of adverse claims in subsection (a).

8. Subsection (d) provides the owner of a certificated security with a means of protection while a security certificate is being sent in for redemption or exchange. The owner may endorse it "for collection" or "for surrender," and this constitutes notice of the owner's claims, under subsection (d).

Definitional Cross References:

"Adverse claim". Section 8–102(a)(1).
"Bearer form". Section 8–102(a)(2).
"Certificated security". Section 8–102(a)(4).
"Financial asset". Section 8–102(a)(9).
"Knowledge". Section 1–201(25).
"Person". Section 1–201(30).
"Purchaser". Sections 1–201(33) & 8–116.
"Registered form". Section 8–102(a)(13).
"Representative". Section 1–201(35).
"Security certificate". Section 8–102(a)(16).

§ 8–106. Control.

(a) A purchaser has "control" of a certificated security in bearer form if the certificated security is delivered to the purchaser.

(b) A purchaser has "control" of a certificated security in registered form if the certificated security is delivered to the purchaser, and:

(1) the certificate is indorsed to the purchaser or in blank by an effective indorsement; or

(2) the certificate is registered in the name of the purchaser, upon original issue or registration of transfer by the issuer.

(c) A purchaser has "control" of an uncertificated security if:

(1) the uncertificated security is delivered to the purchaser; or

(2) the issuer has agreed that it will comply with instructions originated by the purchaser without further consent by the registered owner.

(d) A purchaser has "control" of a security entitlement if:

(1) the purchaser becomes the entitlement holder;

(2) the securities intermediary has agreed that it will comply with entitlement orders originated by the purchaser without further consent by the entitlement holder; or

(3) another person has control of the security entitlement on behalf of the purchaser or, having previously acquired control of the security entitlement, acknowledges that it has control on behalf of the purchaser.

(e) If an interest in a security entitlement is granted by the entitlement holder to the entitlement holder's own securities intermediary, the securities intermediary has control.

(f) A purchaser who has satisfied the requirements of subsection (c) or (d) has control, even if the registered owner in the case of subsection (c) or the entitlement holder in the case of subsection (d) retains the right to make substitutions for the uncertificated security or security entitlement, to originate instructions or entitlement orders to the issuer or securities intermediary, or otherwise to deal with the uncertificated security or security entitlement.

(g) An issuer or a securities intermediary may not enter into an agreement of the kind described in subsection (c)(2) or (d)(2) without the consent of the registered owner or entitlement holder, but an issuer or a securities intermediary is not required to enter into such an agreement even though the registered owner or entitlement holder so directs. An issuer or securities intermediary that has entered into such an agreement is not required to confirm the existence of the agreement to another party unless requested to do so by the registered owner or entitlement holder.

As amended in 1999.

Official Comment

1. The concept of "control" plays a key role in various provisions dealing with the rights of purchasers, including secured parties. See Sections 8–303 (protected purchasers); 8–503(e) (purchasers from securities intermediaries); 8–510 (purchasers of security entitlements from entitlement holders); 9–314 (perfection of security interests); 9–328 (priorities among conflicting security interests).

Obtaining "control" means that the purchaser has taken whatever steps are necessary, given the manner in which the securities are held, to place itself in a position where it can have the securities sold, without further action by the owner.

2. Subsection (a) provides that a purchaser obtains "control" with respect to a certificated security in bearer form by taking "delivery," as defined in Section 8–301. Subsection (b) provides that a purchaser obtains "control" with respect to a certificated security in registered form by taking "delivery," as defined in Section 8–301, provided that the security certificate has been indorsed to the purchaser or in blank. Section 8–301 provides that delivery of a certificated security occurs when the purchaser obtains possession of the security certificate, or when an agent for the purchaser (other than a securities intermediary) either acquires possession or acknowledges that the agent holds for the purchaser.

3. Subsection (c) specifies the means by which a purchaser can obtain control over uncertificated securities which the transferor holds directly. Two mechanisms are possible.

Under subsection (c)(1), securities can be "delivered" to a purchaser. Section 8–301(b) provides that "delivery" of an uncertificated security occurs when the purchaser becomes the registered holder. So far as the issuer is concerned, the purchaser would then be entitled to exercise all rights of ownership. See Section 8–207. As between the parties to a purchase transaction, however, the rights of the purchaser are determined by their contract. Cf. Section 9–202. Arrangements covered by this paragraph are analogous to arrangements in which bearer certificates are delivered to a secured party—so far as the issuer or any other parties are concerned, the secured party appears to be the outright owner, although it is in fact holding as collateral property that belongs to the debtor.

Under subsection (c)(2), a purchaser has control if the issuer has agreed to act on the instructions of the purchaser, even though the owner remains listed as the registered owner. The issuer, of course, would be acting wrongfully against the registered owner if it

entered into such an agreement without the consent of the registered owner. Subsection (g) makes this point explicit. The subsection (c)(2) provision makes it possible for issuers to offer a service akin to the registered pledge device of the 1978 version of Article 8, without mandating that all issuers offer that service.

4. Subsection (d) specifies the means by which a purchaser can obtain control of a security entitlement. Three mechanisms are possible, analogous to those provided in subsection (c) for uncertificated securities. Under subsection (d)(1), a purchaser has control if it is the entitlement holder. This subsection would apply whether the purchaser holds through the same intermediary that the debtor used, or has the securities position transferred to its own intermediary. Subsection (d)(2) provides that a purchaser has control if the securities intermediary has agreed to act on entitlement orders originated by the purchaser if no further consent by the entitlement holder is required. Under subsection (d)(2), control may be achieved even though the original entitlement holder remains as the entitlement holder. Finally, a purchaser may obtain control under subsection (d)(3) if another person has control and the person acknowledges that it has control on the purchaser's behalf. Control under subsection (d)(3) parallels the delivery of certificated securities and uncertificated securities under Section 8–301. Of course, the acknowledging person cannot be the debtor.

This section specifies only the minimum requirements that such an arrangement must meet to confer "control"; the details of the arrangement can be specified by agreement. The arrangement might cover all of the positions in a particular account or subaccount, or only specified positions. There is no requirement that the control party's right to give entitlement orders be exclusive. The arrangement might provide that only the control party can give entitlement orders, or that either the entitlement holder or the control party can give entitlement orders. See subsection (f).

The following examples illustrate the application of subsection (d):

Example 1. Debtor grants Alpha Bank a security interest in a security entitlement that includes 1000 shares of XYZ Co. stock that Debtor holds through an account with Able & Co. Alpha also has an account with Able. Debtor instructs Able to transfer the shares to Alpha, and Able does so by crediting the shares to Alpha's account. Alpha has control of the 1000 shares under subsection (d)(1). Although Debtor may have become the beneficial owner of the new securities entitlement, as between Debtor and Alpha, Able has agreed to act on Alpha's entitlement orders because, as between Able and Alpha, Alpha has become the entitlement holder. See Section 8–506.

Example 2. Debtor grants Alpha Bank a security interest in a security entitlement that includes 1000 shares of XYZ Co. stock that Debtor holds through an account with Able & Co. Alpha does not have an account with Able. Alpha uses Beta as its securities custodian. Debtor instructs Able to transfer the shares to Beta, for the account of Alpha, and Able does so. Alpha has control of the 1000 shares under subsection (d)(1). As in Example 1, although Debtor may have become the beneficial owner of the new securities entitlement, as between Debtor and Alpha, Beta has agreed to act on Alpha's entitlement orders because, as between Beta and Alpha, Alpha has become the entitlement holder.

Example 3. Debtor grants Alpha Bank a security interest in a security entitlement that includes 1000 shares of XYZ Co. stock that Debtor holds through an account with Able & Co. Debtor, Able, and Alpha enter into an agreement under which Debtor will continue to receive dividends and distributions, and will continue to have the right to direct dispositions, but Alpha also has the right to direct dispositions. Alpha has control of the 1000 shares under subsection (d)(2).

Example 4. Able & Co., a securities dealer, grants Alpha Bank a security interest in a security entitlement that includes 1000 shares of XYZ Co. stock that Able holds through an account with Clearing Corporation. Able causes Clearing Corporation to transfer the shares into Alpha's account at Clearing Corporation. As in Example 1, Alpha has control of the 1000 shares under subsection (d)(1).

Example 5. Able & Co., a securities dealer, grants Alpha Bank a security interest in a security entitlement that includes 1000 shares of XYZ Co. stock that Able holds through an account with Clearing Corporation. Alpha does not have an account with Clearing Corporation. It holds its securities through Beta Bank, which does have an account with Clearing Corporation. Able causes Clearing Corporation to transfer the shares into Beta's account at Clearing Corporation. Beta credits the position to Alpha's account with Beta. As in Example 2, Alpha has control of the 1000 shares under subsection (d)(1).

Example 6. Able & Co., a securities dealer, grants Alpha Bank a security interest in a security entitlement that includes 1000 shares of XYZ Co. stock that Able holds through an account with Clearing Corporation. Able causes Clearing Corporation to transfer the shares into a pledge account, pursuant to an agreement under which Able will continue to receive dividends, distributions, and the like, but Alpha has the right to direct dispositions. As in Example 3, Alpha has control of the 1000 shares under subsection (d)(2).

Example 7. Able & Co., a securities dealer, grants Alpha Bank a security interest in a security entitlement that includes 1000 shares of XYZ Co. stock that Able holds through an account with Clearing Corporation. Able, Alpha, and Clearing Corporation enter into an agreement under which Clearing Corporation will act on instructions from Alpha with respect to the XYZ Co. stock carried in Able's account, but Able will continue to receive dividends, distributions, and the like, and will also have the right to direct dispositions. As in Example 3, Alpha has control of the 1000 shares under subsection (d)(2).

Example 8. Able & Co., a securities dealer, holds a wide range of securities through its account at Clearing Corporation. Able enters into an arrangement with Alpha Bank pursuant to which Alpha provides financing to Able secured by securities identified as the collateral on lists provided by Able to Alpha on a daily or other periodic basis. Able, Alpha, and Clearing Corporation enter into an agreement under which Clearing Corporation agrees that if at any time Alpha directs Clearing Corporation to do so, Clearing Corporation will transfer any securities from Able's account at Alpha's instructions. Because Clearing Corporation has agreed to act on Alpha's instructions with respect to any securities carried in Able's account, at the moment that Alpha's security interest attaches to securities listed by Able, Alpha obtains control of those securities under subsection (d)(2). There is no requirement that Clearing Corporation be informed of which securities Able has pledged to Alpha.

Example 9. Debtor grants Alpha Bank a security interest in a security entitlement that includes 1000 shares of XYZ Co. stock that Debtor holds through an account with Able & Co. Beta Bank agrees with Alpha to act as Alpha's collateral agent with respect to the security entitlement. Debtor, Able, and Beta enter into an agreement under which Debtor will continue to receive dividends and distributions, and will continue to have the right to direct dispositions, but Beta also has the right to direct dispositions. Because Able has agreed that it will comply with entitlement orders originated by Beta without further consent by Debtor, Beta has control of the security entitlement (see Example 3). Because Beta has control on behalf of Alpha, Alpha also has control under subsection (d)(3). It is not necessary for Able to enter into an agreement directly with Alpha or for Able to be aware of Beta's agency relationship with Alpha.

5. For a purchaser to have "control" under subsection (c)(2) or (d)(2), it is essential that the issuer or securities intermediary, as the case may be, actually be a party to the agreement. If a debtor gives a secured party a power of attorney authorizing the secured party to act in the name of the debtor, but the issuer or securities intermediary does not specifically agree to this arrangement, the secured party does not have "control" within the meaning of subsection (c)(2) or (d)(2) because the issuer or securities intermediary is not a party to the agreement. The secured party does not have control under subsection (c)(1) or (d)(1) because, although the power of attorney might give the secured party authority to act on the debtor's behalf as an agent, the secured party has not actually become the registered owner or entitlement holder.

6. Subsection (e) provides that if an interest in a security entitlement is granted by an entitlement holder to the securities intermediary through which the security entitlement is maintained, the securities intermediary has control. A common transaction covered by this provision is a margin loan from a broker to its customer.

7. The term "control" is used in a particular defined sense. The requirements for obtaining control are set out in this section. The concept is not to be interpreted by reference to similar concepts in other bodies of law. In particular, the requirements for "possession" derived from the common law of pledge are not to be used as a basis for interpreting subsection (c)(2) or (d)(2). Those provisions are designed to supplant the concepts of "constructive possession" and the like. A principal purpose of the "control" concept is to eliminate the uncertainty and confusion that results from attempting to apply common law possession concepts to modern securities holding practices.

The key to the control concept is that the purchaser has the ability to have the securities sold or transferred without further action by the transferor. There is no requirement that the powers held by the purchaser be exclusive. For example, in a secured lending arrangement, if the secured party wishes, it can allow the debtor to retain the right to make substitutions, to

direct the disposition of the uncertificated security or security entitlement, or otherwise to give instructions or entitlement orders. (As explained in Section 8–102, Comment 8, an entitlement order includes a direction under Section 8–508 to the securities intermediary to transfer a financial asset to the account of the entitlement holder at another financial intermediary or to cause the financial asset to be transferred to the entitlement holder in the direct holding system (e.g., by delivery of a securities certificate registered in the name of the former entitlement holder).) Subsection (f) is included to make clear the general point stated in subsections (c) and (d) that the test of control is whether the purchaser has obtained the requisite power, not whether the debtor has retained other powers. There is no implication that retention by the debtor of powers other than those mentioned in subsection (f) is inconsistent with the purchaser having control. Nor is there a requirement that the purchaser's powers be unconditional, provided that further consent of the entitlement holder is not a condition.

Example 10. Debtor grants to Alpha Bank and to Beta Bank a security interest in a security entitlement that includes 1000 shares of XYZ Co. stock that Debtor holds through an account with Able & Co. By agreement among the parties, Alpha's security interest is senior and Beta's is junior. Able agrees to act on the entitlement orders of either Alpha or Beta. Alpha and Beta each has control under subsection (d)(2). Moreover, Beta has control notwithstanding a term of Able's agreement to the effect that Able's obligation to act on Beta's entitlement orders is conditioned on Alpha's consent. The crucial distinction is that Able's agreement to act on Beta's entitlement orders is not conditioned on Debtor's further consent.

Example 11. Debtor grants to Alpha Bank a security interest in a security entitlement that includes 1000 shares of XYZ Co. stock that Debtor holds through an account with Able & Co. Able agrees to act on the entitlement orders of Alpha, but Alpha's right to give entitlement orders to the securities intermediary is conditioned on the Debtor's default. Alternatively, Alpha's right to give entitlement orders is conditioned upon Alpha's statement to Able that Debtor is in default. Because Able's agreement to act on ~~Beta's~~ *Alpha's**[*]* entitlement orders is not conditioned on Debtor's further consent, Alpha has

* *Amendments in italics approved by the Permanent Editorial Board for Uniform Commercial Code January 15, 2000.*

control of the securities entitlement under either alternative.

In many situations, it will be better practice for both the securities intermediary and the purchaser to insist that any conditions relating in any way to the entitlement holder be effective only as between the purchaser and the entitlement holder. That practice would avoid the risk that the securities intermediary could be caught between conflicting assertions of the entitlement holder and the purchaser as to whether the conditions in fact have been met. Nonetheless, the existence of unfulfilled conditions effective against the intermediary would not preclude the purchaser from having control.

Definitional Cross References:

"Bearer form". Section 8–102(a)(2).
"Certificated security". Section 8–102(a)(4).
"Delivery". Section 8–301.
"Effective". Section 8–107.
"Entitlement holder". Section 8–102(a)(7).
"Entitlement order". Section 8–102(a)(8).
"Indorsement". Section 8–102(a)(11).
"Instruction". Section 8–102(a)(12).
"Purchaser". Sections 1–201(33) & 8–116.
"Registered form". Section 8–102(a)(13).
"Securities intermediary". Section 8–102(a)(14).
"Security entitlement". Section 8–102(a)(17).
"Uncertificated security". Section 8–102(a)(18).

As amended in 1999 and 2000.

§ 8–107. Whether Indorsement, Instruction, or Entitlement Order is Effective.

(a) "Appropriate person" means:

(1) with respect to an indorsement, the person specified by a security certificate or by an effective special indorsement to be entitled to the security;

(2) with respect to an instruction, the registered owner of an uncertificated security;

(3) with respect to an entitlement order, the entitlement holder;

(4) if the person designated in paragraph (1), (2), or (3) is deceased, the designated person's successor taking under other law or the designated person's personal representative acting for the estate of the decedent; or

(5) if the person designated in paragraph (1), (2), or (3) lacks capacity, the designated person's guardian, conservator, or other

similar representative who has power under other law to transfer the security or financial asset.

(b) An indorsement, instruction, or entitlement order is effective if:

(1) it is made by the appropriate person;

(2) it is made by a person who has power under the law of agency to transfer the security or financial asset on behalf of the appropriate person, including, in the case of an instruction or entitlement order, a person who has control under Section 8–106(c)(2) or (d)(2); or

(3) the appropriate person has ratified it or is otherwise precluded from asserting its ineffectiveness.

(c) An indorsement, instruction, or entitlement order made by a representative is effective even if:

(1) the representative has failed to comply with a controlling instrument or with the law of the State having jurisdiction of the representative relationship, including any law requiring the representative to obtain court approval of the transaction; or

(2) the representative's action in making the indorsement, instruction, or entitlement order or using the proceeds of the transaction is otherwise a breach of duty.

(d) If a security is registered in the name of or specially indorsed to a person described as a representative, or if a securities account is maintained in the name of a person described as a representative, an indorsement, instruction, or entitlement order made by the person is effective even though the person is no longer serving in the described capacity.

(e) Effectiveness of an indorsement, instruction, or entitlement order is determined as of the date the indorsement, instruction, or entitlement order is made, and an indorsement, instruction, or entitlement order does not become ineffective by reason of any later change of circumstances.

Official Comment

1. This section defines two concepts, "appropriate person" and "effective." Effectiveness is a broader concept than appropriate person. For example, if a security or securities account is registered in the name

of Mary Roe, Mary Roe is the "appropriate person," but an indorsement, instruction, or entitlement order made by John Doe is "effective" if, under agency or other law, Mary Roe is precluded from denying Doe's authority. Treating these two concepts separately facilitates statement of the rules of Article 8 that state the legal effect of an indorsement, instruction, or entitlement order. For example, a securities intermediary is protected against liability if it acts on an effective entitlement order, but has a duty to comply with an entitlement order only if it is originated by an appropriate person. See Sections 8–115 and 8–507.

One important application of the "effectiveness" concept is in the direct holding system rules on the rights of purchasers. A purchaser of a certificated security in registered form can qualify as a protected purchaser who takes free from adverse claims under Section 8–303 only if the purchaser obtains "control." Section 8–106 provides that a purchaser of a certificated security in registered form obtains control if there has been an "effective" indorsement.

2. Subsection (a) provides that the term "appropriate person" covers two categories: (1) the person who is actually designated as the person entitled to the security or security entitlement, and (2) the successor or legal representative of that person if that person has died or otherwise lacks capacity. Other law determines who has power to transfer a security on behalf of a person who lacks capacity. For example, if securities are registered in the name of more than one person and one of the designated persons dies, whether the survivor is the appropriate person depends on the form of tenancy. If the two were registered joint tenants with right of survivorship, the survivor would have that power under other law and thus would be the "appropriate person." If securities are registered in the name of an individual and the individual dies, the law of decedents' estates determines who has power to transfer the decedent's securities. That would ordinarily be the executor or administrator, but if a "small estate statute" permits a widow to transfer a decedent's securities without administration proceedings, she would be the appropriate person. If the registration of a security or a securities account contains a designation of a death beneficiary under the Uniform Transfer on Death Security Registration Act or comparable legislation, the designated beneficiary would, under that law, have power to transfer upon the person's death and so would be the appropriate person. Article 8 does not contain a list of such representatives, because any list is likely to become outdated by developments in other law.

3. Subsection (b) sets out the general rule that an indorsement, instruction, or entitlement order is effective if it is made by the appropriate person or by a person who has power to transfer under agency law or if the appropriate person is precluded from denying its effectiveness. The control rules in Section 8–106 provide for arrangements where a person who holds securities through a securities intermediary, or holds uncertificated securities directly, enters into a control agreement giving the secured party the right to initiate entitlement orders of instructions. Paragraph 2 of subsection (b) states explicitly that an entitlement order or instruction initiated by a person who has obtained such a control agreement is "effective."

Subsections (c), (d), and (e) supplement the general rule of subsection (b) on effectiveness. The term "representative," used in subsections (c) and (d), is defined in Section 1–201(35).

4. Subsection (c) provides that an indorsement, instruction, or entitlement order made by a representative is effective even though the representative's action is a violation of duties. The following example illustrates this subsection:

> Example 1. Certificated securities are registered in the name of John Doe. Doe dies and Mary Roe is appointed executor. Roe indorses the security certificate and transfers it to a purchaser in a transaction that is a violation of her duties as executor.

Roe's indorsement is effective, because Roe is the appropriate person under subsection (a)(4). This is so even though Roe's transfer violated her obligations as executor. The policies of free transferability of securities that underlie Article 8 dictate that neither a purchaser to whom Roe transfers the securities nor the issuer who registers transfer should be required to investigate the terms of the will to determine whether Roe is acting properly. Although Roe's indorsement is effective under this section, her breach of duty may be such that her beneficiary has an adverse claim to the securities that Roe transferred. The question whether that adverse claim can be asserted against purchasers is governed not by this section but by Section 8–303. Under Section 8–404, the issuer has no duties to an adverse claimant unless the claimant obtains legal process enjoining the issuer from registering transfer.

5. Subsection (d) deals with cases where a security or a securities account is registered in the name of a person specifically designated as a representative. The following example illustrates this subsection:

> Example 2. Certificated securities are registered in the name of "John Jones, trustee of the Smith Family Trust." John Jones is removed as trustee

and Martha Moe is appointed successor trustee. The securities, however, are not reregistered, but remain registered in the name of "John Jones, trustee of the Smith Family Trust." Jones indorses the security certificate and transfers it to a purchaser.

Subsection (d) provides that an indorsement by John Jones as trustee is effective even though Jones is no longer serving in that capacity. Since the securities were registered in the name of "John Jones, trustee of the Smith Family Trust," a purchaser, or the issuer when called upon to register transfer, should be entitled to assume without further inquiry that Jones has the power to act as trustee for the Smith Family Trust.

Note that subsection (d) does not apply to a case where the security or securities account is registered in the name of principal rather than the representative as such. The following example illustrates this point:

Example 3. Certificated securities are registered in the name of John Doe. John Doe dies and Mary Roe is appointed executor. The securities are not reregistered in the name of Mary Roe as executor. Later, Mary Roe is removed as executor and Martha Moe is appointed as her successor. After being removed, Mary Roe indorses the security certificate that is registered in the name of John Doe and transfers it to a purchaser.

Mary Roe's indorsement is not made effective by subsection (d), because the securities were not registered in the name of Mary Roe as representative. A purchaser or the issuer registering transfer should be required to determine whether Roe has power to act for John Doe. Purchasers and issuers can protect themselves in such cases by requiring signature guaranties. See Section 8–306.

6. Subsection (e) provides that the effectiveness of an indorsement, instruction, or entitlement order is determined as of the date it is made. The following example illustrates this subsection:

Example 4. Certificated securities are registered in the name of John Doe. John Doe dies and Mary Roe is appointed executor. Mary Roe indorses the security certificate that is registered in the name of John Doe and transfers it to a purchaser. After the indorsement and transfer, but before the security certificate is presented to the issuer for registration of transfer, Mary Roe is removed as executor and Martha Moe is appointed as her successor.

Mary Roe's indorsement is effective, because at the time Roe indorsed she was the appropriate person under subsection (a)(4). Her later removal as executor does not render the indorsement ineffective. Accord-

ingly, the issuer would not be liable for registering the transfer. See Section 8–404.

Definitional Cross References:

"Entitlement order". Section 8–102(a)(8).
"Financial asset". Section 8–102(a)(9).
"Indorsement". Section 8–102(a)(11).
"Instruction". Section 8–102(a)(12).
"Representative". Section 1–201(35).
"Securities account". Section 8–501.
"Security". Section 8–102(a)(15).
"Security certificate". Section 8–102(a)(16).
"Security entitlement". Section 8–102(a)(17).
"Uncertificated security". Section 8–102(a)(18).

§ 8–108. Warranties in Direct Holding.

(a) A person who transfers a certificated security to a purchaser for value warrants to the purchaser, and an indorser, if the transfer is by indorsement, warrants to any subsequent purchaser, that:

(1) the certificate is genuine and has not been materially altered;

(2) the transferor or indorser does not know of any fact that might impair the validity of the security;

(3) there is no adverse claim to the security;

(4) the transfer does not violate any restriction on transfer;

(5) if the transfer is by indorsement, the indorsement is made by an appropriate person, or if the indorsement is by an agent, the agent has actual authority to act on behalf of the appropriate person; and

(6) the transfer is otherwise effective and rightful.

(b) A person who originates an instruction for registration of transfer of an uncertificated security to a purchaser for value warrants to the purchaser that:

(1) the instruction is made by an appropriate person, or if the instruction is by an agent, the agent has actual authority to act on behalf of the appropriate person;

(2) the security is valid;

(3) there is no adverse claim to the security; and

(4) at the time the instruction is presented to the issuer:

(i) the purchaser will be entitled to the registration of transfer;

(ii) the transfer will be registered by the issuer free from all liens, security interests, restrictions, and claims other than those specified in the instruction;

(iii) the transfer will not violate any restriction on transfer; and

(iv) the requested transfer will otherwise be effective and rightful.

(c) A person who transfers an uncertificated security to a purchaser for value and does not originate an instruction in connection with the transfer warrants that:

(1) the uncertificated security is valid;

(2) there is no adverse claim to the security;

(3) the transfer does not violate any restriction on transfer; and

(4) the transfer is otherwise effective and rightful.

(d) A person who indorses a security certificate warrants to the issuer that:

(1) there is no adverse claim to the security; and

(2) the indorsement is effective.

(e) A person who originates an instruction for registration of transfer of an uncertificated security warrants to the issuer that:

(1) the instruction is effective; and

(2) at the time the instruction is presented to the issuer the purchaser will be entitled to the registration of transfer.

(f) A person who presents a certificated security for registration of transfer or for payment or exchange warrants to the issuer that the person is entitled to the registration, payment, or exchange, but a purchaser for value and without notice of adverse claims to whom transfer is registered warrants only that the person has no knowledge of any unauthorized signature in a necessary indorsement.

(g) If a person acts as agent of another in delivering a certificated security to a purchaser, the identity of the principal was known to the person to whom the certificate was delivered, and the certificate delivered by the agent was received by the agent from the principal or received by the agent from another person at the direction of the principal, the person delivering the security certificate warrants only that the delivering person has authority to act for the principal and does not know of any adverse claim to the certificated security.

(h) A secured party who redelivers a security certificate received, or after payment and on order of the debtor delivers the security certificate to another person, makes only the warranties of an agent under subsection (g).

(i) Except as otherwise provided in subsection (g), a broker acting for a customer makes to the issuer and a purchaser the warranties provided in subsections (a) through (f). A broker that delivers a security certificate to its customer, or causes its customer to be registered as the owner of an uncertificated security, makes to the customer the warranties provided in subsection (a) or (b), and has the rights and privileges of a purchaser under this section. The warranties of and in favor of the broker acting as an agent are in addition to applicable warranties given by and in favor of the customer.

Official Comment

1. Subsections (a), (b), and (c) deal with warranties by security transferors to purchasers. Subsections (d) and (e) deal with warranties by security transferors to issuers. Subsection (f) deals with presentment warranties.

2. Subsection (a) specifies the warranties made by a person who transfers a certificated security to a purchaser for value. Paragraphs (3), (4), and (5) make explicit several key points that are implicit in the general warranty of paragraph (6) that the transfer is effective and rightful. Subsection (b) sets forth the warranties made to a purchaser for value by one who originates an instruction. These warranties are quite similar to those made by one transferring a certificated security, subsection (a), the principal difference being the absolute warranty of validity. If upon receipt of the instruction the issuer should dispute the validity of the security, the burden of proving validity is upon the transferor. Subsection (c) provides for the limited circumstances in which an uncertificated security could be transferred without an instruction, see Section 8–301(b)(2). Subsections (d) and (e) give the issuer the benefit of the warranties of an indorser or originator on those matters not within the issuer's knowledge.

3. Subsection (f) limits the warranties made by a purchaser for value without notice whose presentation

of a security certificate is defective in some way but to whom the issuer does register transfer. The effect is to deny the issuer a remedy against such a person unless at the time of presentment the person had knowledge of an unauthorized signature in a necessary indorsement. The issuer can protect itself by refusing to make the transfer or, if it registers the transfer before it discovers the defect, by pursuing its remedy against a signature guarantor.

4. Subsection (g) eliminates all substantive warranties in the relatively unusual case of a delivery of certificated security by an agent of a disclosed principal where the agent delivers the exact certificate that it received from or for the principal. Subsection (h) limits the warranties given by a secured party who redelivers a certificate. Subsection (i) specifies the warranties of brokers in the more common scenarios.

5. Under Section 1–102(3) the warranty provisions apply "unless otherwise agreed" and the parties may enter into express agreements to allocate the risks of possible defects. Usual estoppel principles apply with respect to transfers of both certificated and uncertificated securities whenever the purchaser has knowledge of the defect, and these warranties will not be breached in such a case.

Definitional Cross References:

"Adverse claim". Section 8–102(a)(1).
"Appropriate person". Section 8–107.
"Broker". Section 8–102(a)(3).
"Certificated security". Section 8–102(a)(4).
"Indorsement". Section 8–102(a)(11).
"Instruction". Section 8–102(a)(12).
"Issuer". Section 8–201.
"Person". Section 1–201(30).
"Purchaser". Sections 1–201(33) & 8–116.
"Secured party". Section 9–102(a)(72).
"Security". Section 8–102(a)(15).
"Security certificate". Section 8–102(a)(16).
"Uncertificated security". Section 8–102(a)(18).
"Value". Sections 1–201(44) & 8–116.

§ 8–109. Warranties in Indirect Holding.

(a) A person who originates an entitlement order to a securities intermediary warrants to the securities intermediary that:

(1) the entitlement order is made by an appropriate person, or if the entitlement order is by an agent, the agent has actual authority to act on behalf of the appropriate person; and

(2) there is no adverse claim to the security entitlement.

(b) A person who delivers a security certificate to a securities intermediary for credit to a securities account or originates an instruction with respect to an uncertificated security directing that the uncertificated security be credited to a securities account makes to the securities intermediary the warranties specified in Section 8–108(a) or (b).

(c) If a securities intermediary delivers a security certificate to its entitlement holder or causes its entitlement holder to be registered as the owner of an uncertificated security, the securities intermediary makes to the entitlement holder the warranties specified in Section 8–108(a) or (b).

Official Comment

1. Subsection (a) provides that a person who originates an entitlement order warrants to the securities intermediary that the order is authorized, and warrants the absence of adverse claims. Subsection (b) specifies the warranties that are given when a person who holds securities directly has the holding converted into indirect form. A person who delivers a certificate to a securities intermediary or originates an instruction for an uncertificated security gives to the securities intermediary the transfer warranties under Section 8–108. If the securities intermediary in turn delivers the certificate to a higher level securities intermediary, it gives the same warranties.

2. Subsection (c) states the warranties that a securities intermediary gives when a customer who has been holding securities in an account with the securities intermediary requests that certificates be delivered or that uncertificated securities be registered in the customer's name. The warranties are the same as those that brokers make with respect to securities that the brokers sell to or buy on behalf of the customers. See Section 8–108(i).

3. As with the Section 8–108 warranties, the warranties specified in this section may be modified by agreement under Section 1–102(3).

Definitional Cross References:

"Adverse claim". Section 8–102(a)(1).
"Appropriate person". Section 8–107.
"Entitlement holder". Section 8–102(a)(7).
"Entitlement order". Section 8–102(a)(8).
"Instruction". Section 8–102(a)(12).
"Person". Section 1–201(30).

"Securities account". Section 8–501.
"Securities intermediary". Section 8–102(a)(14).
"Security certificate". Section 8–102(a)(16).
"Uncertificated security". Section 8–102(a)(18).

§ 8–110. Applicability; Choice of Law.

(a) The local law of the issuer's jurisdiction, as specified in subsection (d), governs:

(1) the validity of a security;

(2) the rights and duties of the issuer with respect to registration of transfer;

(3) the effectiveness of registration of transfer by the issuer;

(4) whether the issuer owes any duties to an adverse claimant to a security; and

(5) whether an adverse claim can be asserted against a person to whom transfer of a certificated or uncertificated security is registered or a person who obtains control of an uncertificated security.

(b) The local law of the securities intermediary's jurisdiction, as specified in subsection (e), governs:

(1) acquisition of a security entitlement from the securities intermediary;

(2) the rights and duties of the securities intermediary and entitlement holder arising out of a security entitlement;

(3) whether the securities intermediary owes any duties to an adverse claimant to a security entitlement; and

(4) whether an adverse claim can be asserted against a person who acquires a security entitlement from the securities intermediary or a person who purchases a security entitlement or interest therein from an entitlement holder.

(c) The local law of the jurisdiction in which a security certificate is located at the time of delivery governs whether an adverse claim can be asserted against a person to whom the security certificate is delivered.

(d) "Issuer's jurisdiction" means the jurisdiction under which the issuer of the security is organized or, if permitted by the law of that jurisdiction, the law of another jurisdiction specified by the issuer. An issuer organized under the law of this State may specify the law of another jurisdiction as the law governing the matters specified in subsection (a)(2) through (5).

(e) The following rules determine a "securities intermediary's jurisdiction" for purposes of this section:

(1) If an agreement between the securities intermediary and its entitlement holder governing the securities account expressly provides that a particular jurisdiction is the securities intermediary's jurisdiction for purposes of this part, this article, or this [Act], that jurisdiction is the securities intermediary's jurisdiction.

(2) If paragraph (1) does not apply and an agreement between the securities intermediary and its entitlement holder governing the securities account expressly provides that the agreement is governed by the law of a particular jurisdiction, that jurisdiction is the securities intermediary's jurisdiction.

(3) If neither paragraph (1) nor paragraph (2) applies and an agreement between the securities intermediary and its entitlement holder governing the securities account expressly provides that the securities account is maintained at an office in a particular jurisdiction, that jurisdiction is the securities intermediary's jurisdiction.

(4) If none of the preceding paragraphs applies, the securities intermediary's jurisdiction is the jurisdiction in which the office identified in an account statement as the office serving the entitlement holder's account is located.

(5) If none of the preceding paragraphs applies, the securities intermediary's jurisdiction is the jurisdiction in which the chief executive office of the securities intermediary is located.

(f) A securities intermediary's jurisdiction is not determined by the physical location of certificates representing financial assets, or by the jurisdiction in which is organized the issuer of the financial asset with respect to which an entitlement holder has a security entitlement, or by the location of facilities for data processing or other record keeping concerning the account.

As amended in 1999.

Official Comment

1. This section deals with applicability and choice of law issues concerning Article 8. The distinction between the direct and indirect holding systems plays a significant role in determining the governing law. An investor in the direct holding system is registered on the books of the issuer and/or has possession of a security certificate. Accordingly, the jurisdiction of incorporation of the issuer or location of the certificate determine the applicable law. By contrast, an investor in the indirect holding system has a security entitlement, which is a bundle of rights against the securities intermediary with respect to a security, rather than a direct interest in the underlying security. Accordingly, in the rules for the indirect holding system, the jurisdiction of incorporation of the issuer of the underlying security or the location of any certificates that might be held by the intermediary or a higher tier intermediary, do not determine the applicable law.

The phrase "local law" refers to the law of a jurisdiction other than its conflict of laws rules. See Restatement (Second) of Conflict of Laws § 4.

2. Subsection (a) provides that the law of an issuer's jurisdiction governs certain issues where the substantive rules of Article 8 determine the issuer's rights and duties. Paragraph (1) of subsection (a) provides that the law of the issuer's jurisdiction governs the validity of the security. This ensures that a single body of law will govern the questions addressed in Part 2 of Article 8, concerning the circumstances in which an issuer can and cannot assert invalidity as a defense against purchasers. Similarly, paragraphs (2), (3), and (4) of subsection (a) ensure that the issuer will be able to look to a single body of law on the questions addressed in Part 4 of Article 8, concerning the issuer's duties and liabilities with respect to registration of transfer.

Paragraph (5) of subsection (a) applies the law of an issuer's jurisdiction to the question whether an adverse claim can be asserted against a purchaser to whom transfer has been registered, or who has obtained control over an uncertificated security. Although this issue deals with the rights of persons other than the issuer, the law of the issuer's jurisdiction applies because the purchasers to whom the provision applies are those whose protection against adverse claims depends on the fact that their interests have been recorded on the books of the issuer.

The principal policy reflected in the choice of law rules in subsection (a) is that an issuer and others should be able to look to a single body of law on the matters specified in subsection (a), rather than having to look to the law of all of the different jurisdictions in which security holders may reside. The choice of law policies reflected in this subsection do not require that the body of law governing all of the matters specified in subsection (a) be that of the jurisdiction in which the issuer is incorporated. Thus, subsection (d) provides that the term "issuer's jurisdiction" means the jurisdiction in which the issuer is organized, or, if permitted by that law, the law of another jurisdiction selected by the issuer. Subsection (d) also provides that issuers organized under the law of a State which adopts this Article may make such a selection, except as to the validity issue specified in paragraph (1). The question whether an issuer can assert the defense of invalidity may implicate significant policies of the issuer's jurisdiction of incorporation. See, e.g., Section 8–202 and Comments thereto.

Although subsection (a) provides that the issuer's rights and duties concerning registration of transfer are governed by the law of the issuer's jurisdiction, other matters related to registration of transfer, such as appointment of a guardian for a registered owner or the existence of agency relationships, might be governed by another jurisdiction's law. Neither this section nor Section 1–105 deals with what law governs the appointment of the administrator or executor; that question is determined under generally applicable choice of law rules.

3. Subsection (b) provides that the law of the securities intermediary's jurisdiction governs the issues concerning the indirect holding system that are dealt with in Article 8. Paragraphs (1) and (2) cover the matters dealt with in the Article 8 rules defining the concept of security entitlement and specifying the duties of securities intermediaries. Paragraph (3) provides that the law of the security intermediary's jurisdiction determines whether the intermediary owes any duties to an adverse claimant. Paragraph (4) provides that the law of the security intermediary's jurisdiction determines whether adverse claims can be asserted against entitlement holders and others.

Subsection (e) determines what is a "securities intermediary's jurisdiction." The policy of subsection (b) is to ensure that a securities intermediary and all of its entitlement holders can look to a single, readily-identifiable body of law to determine their rights and duties. Accordingly, subsection (e) sets out a sequential series of tests to facilitate identification of that body of law. Paragraph (1) of subsection (e) permits specification of the securities intermediary's jurisdiction by agreement. In the absence of such a specification, the law chosen by the parties to govern the securities account determines the securities intermediary's jurisdiction. See paragraph (2). Because the policy of this section is to enable parties to determine, in advance and with certainty, what law will apply to transactions governed by this Article, the validation of the parties' selection of governing law by agreement is not conditioned upon a determination that the jurisdiction whose law is chosen bear a "reasonable relation" to the transaction. See Section 4A–507; compare Section 1–105(1). That is also true with respect to the similar provisions in subsection (d) of this section and in Section 9–305. The remaining paragraphs in subsection (e) contain additional default rules for determining the securities intermediary's jurisdiction.

Subsection (f) makes explicit a point that is implicit in the Article 8 description of a security entitlement as a bundle of rights against the intermediary with respect to a security or other financial asset, rather than as a direct interest in the underlying security or other financial asset. The governing law for relationships in the indirect holding system is not determined by such matters as the jurisdiction of incorporation of the issuer of the securities held through the intermediary, or the location of any physical certificates held by the intermediary or a higher tier intermediary.

4. Subsection (c) provides a choice of law rule for adverse claim issues that may arise in connection with delivery of security certificates in the direct holding system. It applies the law of the place of delivery. If a certificated security issued by an Idaho corporation is sold, and the sale is settled by physical delivery of the certificate from Seller to Buyer in New York, under subsection (c), New York law determines whether Buyer takes free from adverse claims. The domicile of Seller, Buyer, and any adverse claimant is irrelevant.

5. The following examples illustrate how a court in a jurisdiction which has enacted this section would determine the governing law:

Example 1. John Doe, a resident of Kansas, maintains a securities account with Able & Co. Able is incorporated in Delaware. Its chief executive offices are located in Illinois. The office where Doe transacts business with Able is located in Missouri. The agreement between Doe and Able specifies that Illinois is the securities intermediary's (Able's) jurisdiction. Through the account, Doe holds securities of a Colorado corporation, which Able holds through Clearing Corporation. The rules of Clearing Corporation provide that the rights and duties of Clearing Corporation and its participants are governed by New York law. Subsection (a) specifies that a controversy concerning the rights and duties as between the issuer

and Clearing Corporation is governed by Colorado law. Subsections (b) and (e) specify that a controversy concerning the rights and duties as between the Clearing Corporation and Able is governed by New York law, and that a controversy concerning the rights and duties as between Able and Doe is governed by Illinois law.

Example 2. Same facts as to Doe and Able as in Example 1. Through the account, Doe holds securities of a Senegalese corporation, which Able holds through Clearing Corporation. Clearing Corporation's operations are located in Belgium, and its rules and agreements with its participants provide that they are governed by Belgian law. Clearing Corporation holds the securities through a custodial account at the Paris branch office of Global Bank, which is organized under English law. The agreement between Clearing Corporation and Global Bank provides that it is governed by French law. Subsection (a) specifies that a controversy concerning the rights and duties as between the issuer and Global Bank is governed by Senegalese law. Subsections (b) and (e) specify that a controversy concerning the rights and duties as between Global Bank and Clearing Corporation is governed by French law, that a controversy concerning the rights and duties as between Clearing Corporation and Able is governed by Belgian law, and that a controversy concerning the rights and duties as between Able and Doe is governed by Illinois law.

6. To the extent that this section does not specify the governing law, general choice of law rules apply. For example, suppose that in either of the examples in the preceding Comment, Doe enters into an agreement with Roe, also a resident of Kansas, in which Doe agrees to transfer all of his interests in the securities held through Able to Roe. Article 8 does not deal with whether such an agreement is enforceable or whether it gives Roe some interest in Doe's security entitlement. This section specifies what jurisdiction's law governs the issues that are dealt with in Article 8. Article 8, however, does specify that securities intermediaries have only limited duties with respect to adverse claims. See Section 8–115. Subsection (b)(3) of this section provides that Illinois law governs whether Able owes any duties to an adverse claimant. Thus, if Illinois has adopted Revised Article 8, Section 8–115 as enacted in Illinois determines whether Roe has any rights against Able.

7. The choice of law provisions concerning security interests in securities and security entitlements are set out in Section 9–305.

Definitional Cross References:

"Adverse claim". Section 8–102(a)(1).
"Agreement". Section 1–201(3).
"Certificated security". Section 8–102(a)(4).
"Entitlement holder". Section 8–102(a)(7).
"Financial asset". Section 8–102(a)(9).
"Issuer". Section 8–201.
"Person". Section 1–201(30).
"Purchase". Section 1–201(32).
"Securities intermediary". Section 8–102(a)(14).
"Security". Section 8–102(a)(15).
"Security certificate". Section 8–102(a)(16).
"Security entitlement". Section 8–102(a)(17).
"Uncertificated security". Section 8–102(a)(18).

As amended in 1999.

§ 8–111. Clearing Corporation Rules.

A rule adopted by a clearing corporation governing rights and obligations among the clearing corporation and its participants in the clearing corporation is effective even if the rule conflicts with this [Act] and affects another party who does not consent to the rule.

Official Comment

1. The experience of the past few decades shows that securities holding and settlement practices may develop rapidly, and in unforeseeable directions. Accordingly, it is desirable that the rules of Article 8 be adaptable both to ensure that commercial law can conform to changing practices and to ensure that commercial law does not operate as an obstacle to developments in securities practice. Even if practices were unchanging, it would not be possible in a general statute to specify in detail the rules needed to provide certainty in the operations of the clearance and settlement system.

The provisions of this Article and Article 1 on the effect of agreements provide considerable flexibility in the specification of the details of the rights and obligations of participants in the securities holding system by agreement. See Sections 8–504 through 8–509, and Section 1–102(3) and (4). Given the magnitude of the exposures involved in securities transactions, however, it may not be possible for the parties in developing practices to rely solely on private agreements, particularly with respect to matters that might affect others, such as creditors. For example, in order to be fully effective, rules of clearing corporations on the finality or reversibility of securities settlements must not only bind the participants in the clearing corporation but also be effective against their creditors. Section 8–111

provides that clearing corporation rules are effective even if they indirectly affect third parties, such as creditors of a participant. This provision does not, however, permit rules to be adopted that would govern the rights and obligations of third parties other than as a consequence of rules that specify the rights and obligations of the clearing corporation and its participants.

2. The definition of clearing corporation in Section 8–102 covers only federal reserve banks, entities registered as clearing agencies under the federal securities laws, and others subject to comparable regulation. The rules of registered clearing agencies are subject to regulatory oversight under the federal securities laws.

Definitional Cross References:

"Clearing corporation". Section 8–102(a)(5).

§ 8–112. Creditor's Legal Process.

(a) The interest of a debtor in a certificated security may be reached by a creditor only by actual seizure of the security certificate by the officer making the attachment or levy, except as otherwise provided in subsection (d). However, a certificated security for which the certificate has been surrendered to the issuer may be reached by a creditor by legal process upon the issuer.

(b) The interest of a debtor in an uncertificated security may be reached by a creditor only by legal process upon the issuer at its chief executive office in the United States, except as otherwise provided in subsection (d).

(c) The interest of a debtor in a security entitlement may be reached by a creditor only by legal process upon the securities intermediary with whom the debtor's securities account is maintained, except as otherwise provided in subsection (d).

(d) The interest of a debtor in a certificated security for which the certificate is in the possession of a secured party, or in an uncertificated security registered in the name of a secured party, or a security entitlement maintained in the name of a secured party, may be reached by a creditor by legal process upon the secured party.

(e) A creditor whose debtor is the owner of a certificated security, uncertificated security, or security entitlement is entitled to aid from a court of competent jurisdiction, by injunction or otherwise, in reaching the certificated security, uncertificated security, or security entitlement or in satisfying the claim by means allowed at law or in equity in regard to property that cannot readily be reached by other legal process.

Official Comment

1. In dealing with certificated securities the instrument itself is the vital thing, and therefore a valid levy cannot be made unless all possibility of the certificate's wrongfully finding its way into a transferee's hands has been removed. This can be accomplished only when the certificate is in the possession of a public officer, the issuer, or an independent third party. A debtor who has been enjoined can still transfer the security in contempt of court. See *Overlock v. Jerome–Portland Copper Mining Co.,* 29 Ariz. 560, 243 P. 400 (1926). Therefore, although injunctive relief is provided in subsection (e) so that creditors may use this method to gain control of the certificated security, the security certificate itself must be reached to constitute a proper levy whenever the debtor has possession.

2. Subsection (b) provides that when the security is uncertificated and registered in the debtor's name, the debtor's interest can be reached only by legal process upon the issuer. The most logical place to serve the issuer would be the place where the transfer records are maintained, but that location might be difficult to identify, especially when the separate elements of a computer network might be situated in different places. The chief executive office is selected as the appropriate place by analogy to Section 9–307(b)(3). See Comment 2 to that section. This section indicates only how attachment is to be made, not when it is legally justified. For that reason there is no conflict between this section and *Shaffer v. Heitner,* 433 U.S. 186 (1977).

3. Subsection (c) provides that a security entitlement can be reached only by legal process upon the debtor's security intermediary. Process is effective only if directed to the debtor's own security intermediary. If Debtor holds securities through Broker, and Broker in turn holds through Clearing Corporation, Debtor's property interest is a security entitlement against Broker. Accordingly, Debtor's creditor cannot reach Debtor's interest by legal process directed to the Clearing Corporation. See also Section 8–115.

4. Subsection (d) provides that when a certificated security, an uncertificated security, or a security entitlement is controlled by a secured party, the debtor's interest can be reached by legal process upon the secured party. This section does not attempt to provide for rights as between the creditor and the secured party, as, for example, whether or when the secured party must liquidate the security.

Definitional Cross References:

"Certificated security". Section 8–102(a)(4).
"Issuer". Section 8–201.
"Secured party". Section 9–102(a)(72).
"Securities intermediary". Section 8–102(a)(14).
"Security certificate". Section 8–102(a)(16).
"Security entitlement". Section 8–102(a)(17).
"Uncertificated security". Section 8–102(a)(18).

§ 8–113.   Statute of Frauds Inapplicable.

A contract or modification of a contract for the sale or purchase of a security is enforceable whether or not there is a writing signed or record authenticated by a party against whom enforcement is sought, even if the contract or modification is not capable of performance within one year of its making.

Official Comment

This section provides that the statute of frauds does not apply to contracts for the sale of securities, reversing prior law which had a special statute of frauds in Section 8–319 (1978). With the increasing use of electronic means of communication, the statute of frauds is unsuited to the realities of the securities business. For securities transactions, whatever benefits a statute of frauds may play in filtering out fraudulent claims are outweighed by the obstacles it places in the development of modern commercial practices in the securities business.

Definitional Cross References:

"Action". Section 1–201(1).
"Contract". Section 1–201(11).
"Writing". Section 1–201(46).

§ 8–114.   Evidentiary Rules Concerning Certificated Securities.

The following rules apply in an action on a certificated security against the issuer:

(1) Unless specifically denied in the pleadings, each signature on a security certificate or in a necessary indorsement is admitted.

(2) If the effectiveness of a signature is put in issue, the burden of establishing effectiveness is on the party claiming under the signature, but the signature is presumed to be genuine or authorized.

(3) If signatures on a security certificate are admitted or established, production of the certificate entitles a holder to recover on it unless the defendant establishes a defense or a defect going to the validity of the security.

(4) If it is shown that a defense or defect exists, the plaintiff has the burden of establishing that the plaintiff or some person under whom the plaintiff claims is a person against whom the defense or defect cannot be asserted.

Official Comment

This section adapts the rules of negotiable instruments law concerning procedure in actions on instruments, see Section 3–308, to actions on certificated securities governed by this Article. An "action on a security" includes any action or proceeding brought against the issuer to enforce a right or interest that is part of the security, such as an action to collect principal or interest or a dividend, or to establish a right to vote or to receive a new security under an exchange offer or plan of reorganization. This section applies only to certificated securities; actions on uncertificated securities are governed by general evidentiary principles.

Definitional Cross References:

"Action". Section 1–201(1).
"Burden of establishing". Section 1–201(8).
"Certificated security". Section 8–102(a)(4).
"Indorsement". Section 8–102(a)(11).
"Issuer". Section 8–201.
"Presumed". Section 1–201(31).
"Security". Section 8–102(a)(15).
"Security certificate". Section 8–102(a)(16).

§ 8–115. Securities Intermediary and Others Not Liable to Adverse Claimant.

A securities intermediary that has transferred a financial asset pursuant to an effective entitlement order, or a broker or other agent or bailee that has dealt with a financial asset at the direction of its customer or principal, is not liable to a person having an adverse claim to the financial asset, unless the securities intermediary, or broker or other agent or bailee:

(1) took the action after it had been served with an injunction, restraining order, or other legal process enjoining it from doing so, issued by a court of competent jurisdic-

tion, and had a reasonable opportunity to act on the injunction, restraining order, or other legal process; or

(2) acted in collusion with the wrongdoer in violating the rights of the adverse claimant; or

(3) in the case of a security certificate that has been stolen, acted with notice of the adverse claim.

Official Comment

1. Other provisions of Article 8 protect certain purchasers against adverse claims, both for the direct holding system and the indirect holding system. See Sections 8–303 and 8–502. This section deals with the related question of the possible liability of a person who acted as the "conduit" for a securities transaction. It covers both securities intermediaries—the "conduits" in the indirect holding system—and brokers or other agents or bailees—the "conduits" in the direct holding system. The following examples illustrate its operation:

Example 1. John Doe is a customer of the brokerage firm of Able & Co. Doe delivers to Able a certificate for 100 shares of XYZ Co. common stock, registered in Doe's name and properly indorsed, and asks the firm to sell it for him. Able does so. Later, John Doe's spouse Mary Doe brings an action against Able asserting that Able's action was wrongful against her because the XYZ Co. stock was marital property in which she had an interest, and John Doe was acting wrongfully against her in transferring the securities.

Example 2. Mary Roe is a customer of the brokerage firm of Baker & Co. and holds her securities through a securities account with Baker. Roe instructs Baker to sell 100 shares of XYZ Co. common stock that she carried in her account. Baker does so. Later, Mary Roe's spouse John Roe brings an action against Baker asserting that Baker's action was wrongful against him because the XYZ Co. stock was marital property in which he had an interest, and Mary Roe was acting wrongfully against him in transferring the securities.

Under common law conversion principles, Mary Doe might be able to assert that Able & Co. is liable to her in Example 1 for exercising dominion over property inconsistent with her rights in it. On that or some similar theory John Roe might assert that Baker is liable to him in Example 2. Section 8–115 protects both Able and Baker from liability.

2. The policy of this section is similar to that of many other rules of law that protect agents and bailees from liability as innocent converters. If a thief steals property and ships it by mail, express service, or carrier, to another person, the recipient of the property does not obtain good title, even though the recipient may have given value to the thief and had no notice or knowledge that the property was stolen. Accordingly, the true owner can recover the property from the recipient or obtain damages in a conversion or similar action. An action against the postal service, express company, or carrier presents entirely different policy considerations. Accordingly, general tort law protects agents or bailees who act on the instructions of their principals or bailors. See Restatement (Second) of Torts § 235. See also UCC Section 7-404.

3. Except as provided in paragraph 3, this section applies even though the securities intermediary, or the broker or other agent or bailee, had notice or knowledge that another person asserts a claim to the securities. Consider the following examples:

Example 3.   Same facts as in Example 1, except that before John Doe brought the XYZ Co. security certificate to Able for sale, Mary Doe telephoned or wrote to the firm asserting that she had an interest in all of John Doe's securities and demanding that they not trade for him.

Example 4.   Same facts as in Example 2, except that before Mary Roe gave an entitlement order to Baker to sell the XYZ Co. securities from her account, John Doe telephoned or wrote to the firm asserting that he had an interest in all of Mary Roe's securities and demanding that they not trade for her.

Section 8-115 protects Able and Baker from liability. The protections of Section 8-115 do not depend on the presence or absence of notice of adverse claims. It is essential to the securities settlement system that brokers and securities intermediaries be able to act promptly on the directions of their customers. Even though a firm has notice that someone asserts a claim to a customer's securities or security entitlements, the firm should not be placed in the position of having to make a legal judgment about the validity of the claim at the risk of liability either to its customer or to the third party for guessing wrong. Under this section, the broker or securities intermediary is privileged to act on the instructions of its customer or entitlement holder, unless it has been served with a restraining order or other legal process enjoining it from doing so. This is already the law in many jurisdictions. For example a section of the New York Banking Law provides that banks need not recognize any adverse claim to funds or securities on deposit with them unless they have been served with legal process. N.Y. Banking Law § 134. Other sections of the UCC embody a similar policy. See Sections 3-602, 5-114(2)(b).

Paragraph (1) of this section refers only to a court order enjoining the securities intermediary or the broker or other agent or bailee from acting at the instructions of the customer. It does not apply to cases where the adverse claimant tells the intermediary or broker that the customer has been enjoined, or shows the intermediary or broker a copy of a court order binding the customer.

Paragraph (3) takes a different approach in one limited class of cases, those where a customer sells stolen certificated securities through a securities firm. Here the policies that lead to protection of securities firms against assertions of other sorts of claims must be weighed against the desirability of having securities firms guard against the disposition of stolen securities. Accordingly, paragraph (3) denies protection to a broker, custodian, or other agent or bailee who receives a stolen security certificate from its customer, if the broker, custodian, or other agent or bailee had notice of adverse claims. The circumstances that give notice of adverse claims are specified in Section 8-105. The result is that brokers, custodians, and other agents and bailees face the same liability for selling stolen certificated securities that purchasers face for buying them.

4. As applied to securities intermediaries, this section embodies one of the fundamental principles of the Article 8 indirect holding system rules—that a securities intermediary owes duties only to its own entitlement holders. The following examples illustrate the operation of this section in the multi-tiered indirect holding system:

Example 5.   Able & Co., a broker-dealer, holds 50,000 shares of XYZ Co. stock in its account at Clearing Corporation. Able acquired the XYZ shares from another firm, Baker & Co., in a transaction that Baker contends was tainted by fraud, giving Baker a right to rescind the transaction and recover the XYZ shares from Able. Baker sends notice to Clearing Corporation stating that Baker has a claim to the 50,000 shares of XYZ Co. in Able's account. Able then initiates an entitlement order directing Clearing Corporation to transfer the 50,000 shares of XYZ Co. to another firm in settlement of a trade. Under Section 8-115, Clearing Corporation is privileged to comply with Able's entitlement order, without fear of liability to Baker. This is so even though Clearing Corporation has notice of Baker's claim, unless Baker obtains a court order enjoining Clearing Corporation from acting on Able's entitlement order.

Example 6. Able & Co., a broker-dealer, holds 50,000 shares of XYZ Co. stock in its account at Clearing Corporation. Able initiates an entitlement order directing Clearing Corporation to transfer the 50,000 shares of XYZ Co. to another firm in settlement of a trade. That trade was made by Able for its own account, and the proceeds were devoted to its own use. Able becomes insolvent, and it is discovered that Able has a shortfall in the shares of XYZ Co. stock that it should have been carrying for its customers. Able's customers bring an action against Clearing Corporation asserting that Clearing Corporation acted wrongfully in transferring the XYZ shares on Able's order because those were shares that should have been held by Able for its customers. Under Section 8–115, Clearing Corporation is not liable to Able's customers, because Clearing Corporation acted on an effective entitlement order of its own entitlement holder, Able. Clearing Corporation's protection against liability does not depend on the presence or absence of notice or knowledge of the claim by Clearing Corporation.

5. If the conduct of a securities intermediary or a broker or other agent or bailee rises to a level of complicity in the wrongdoing of its customer or principal, the policies that favor protection against liability do not apply. Accordingly, paragraph (2) provides that the protections of this section do not apply if the securities intermediary or broker or other agent or bailee acted in collusion with the customer or principal in violating the rights of another person. The collusion test is intended to adopt a standard akin to the tort rules that determine whether a person is liable as an aider or abettor for the tortious conduct of a third party. See Restatement (Second) of Torts § 876.

Knowledge that the action of the customer is wrongful is a necessary but not sufficient condition of the collusion test. The aspect of the role of securities intermediaries and brokers that Article 8 deals with is the clerical or ministerial role of implementing and recording the securities transactions that their customers conduct. Faithful performance of this role consists of following the instructions of the customer. It is not the role of the record-keeper to police whether the transactions recorded are appropriate, so mere awareness that the customer may be acting wrongfully does not itself constitute collusion. That, of course, does not insulate an intermediary or broker from responsibility in egregious cases where its action goes beyond the ordinary standards of the business of implementing and recording transactions, and reaches a level of

affirmative misconduct in assisting the customer in the commission of a wrong.

Definitional Cross References:

"Broker". Section 8–102(a)(3).
"Effective". Section 8–107.
"Entitlement order". Section 8–102(a)(8).
"Financial asset". Section 8–102(a)(9).
"Securities intermediary". Section 8–102(a)(14).
"Security certificate". Section 8–102(a)(16).

§ 8–116. Securities Intermediary as Purchaser For Value.

A securities intermediary that receives a financial asset and establishes a security entitlement to the financial asset in favor of an entitlement holder is a purchaser for value of the financial asset. A securities intermediary that acquires a security entitlement to a financial asset from another securities intermediary acquires the security entitlement for value if the securities intermediary acquiring the security entitlement establishes a security entitlement to the financial asset in favor of an entitlement holder.

Official Comment

1. This section is intended to make explicit two points that, while implicit in other provisions, are of sufficient importance to the operation of the indirect holding system that they warrant explicit statement. First, it makes clear that a securities intermediary that receives a financial asset and establishes a security entitlement in respect thereof in favor of an entitlement holder is a "purchaser" of the financial asset that the securities intermediary received. Second, it makes clear that by establishing a security entitlement in favor of an entitlement holder a securities intermediary gives value for any corresponding financial asset that the securities intermediary receives or acquires from another party, whether the intermediary holds directly or indirectly.

In many cases a securities intermediary that receives a financial asset will also be transferring value to the person from whom the financial asset was received. That, however, is not always the case. Payment may occur through a different system than settlement of the securities side of the transaction, or the securities might be transferred without a corresponding payment, as when a person moves an account from one securities intermediary to another. Even though the securities intermediary does not give value to the transferor, it does give value by incurring obligations to its own entitlement holder. Although the general definition of value in Section 1–201(44)(d) should be interpreted to cover the point, this section is included to make this point explicit.

2. The following examples illustrate the effect of this section:

Example 1. Buyer buys 1000 shares of XYZ Co. common stock through Buyer's broker Able & Co. to be held in Buyer's securities account. In settlement of the trade, the selling broker delivers to Able a security certificate in street name, indorsed in blank, for 1000 shares XYZ Co. stock, which Able holds in its vault. Able credits Buyer's account for securities in that amount. Section 8–116 specifies that Able is a purchaser of the XYZ Co. stock certificate, and gave value for it. Thus, Able can obtain the benefit of Section 8–303, which protects purchasers for value, if it satisfies the other requirements of that section.

Example 2. Buyer buys 1000 shares XYZ Co. common stock through Buyer's broker Able & Co. to be held in Buyer's securities account. The trade is settled by crediting 1000 shares XYZ Co. stock to Able's account at Clearing Corporation. Able credits Buyer's account for securities in that amount. When Clearing Corporation credits Able's account, Able acquires a security entitlement under Section 8–501. Section 8–116 specifies that Able acquired this security entitlement for value. Thus, Able can obtain the benefit of Section 8–502, which protects persons who acquire security entitlements for value, if it satisfies the other requirements of that section.

Example 3. Thief steals a certificated bearer bond from Owner. Thief sends the certificate to his broker Able & Co. to be held in his securities account, and Able credits Thief's account for the bond. Section 8–116 specifies that Able is a purchaser of the bond and gave value for it. Thus, Able can obtain the benefit of Section 8–303, which protects purchasers for value, if it satisfies the other requirements of that section.

Definitional Cross References:

"Financial asset". Section 8–102(a)(9).
"Securities intermediary". Section 8–102(a)(14).
"Security entitlement". Section 8–102(a)(17).
"Entitlement holder". Section 8–102(a)(7).

PART 2

ISSUE AND ISSUER

§ 8–201. Issuer.

(a) With respect to an obligation on or a defense to a security, an "issuer" includes a person that:

(1) places or authorizes the placing of its name on a security certificate, other than as authenticating trustee, registrar, transfer agent, or the like, to evidence a share, participation, or other interest in its property or in an enterprise, or to evidence its duty to perform an obligation represented by the certificate;

(2) creates a share, participation, or other interest in its property or in an enterprise, or undertakes an obligation, that is an uncertificated security;

(3) directly or indirectly creates a fractional interest in its rights or property, if the fractional interest is represented by a security certificate; or

(4) becomes responsible for, or in place of, another person described as an issuer in this section.

(b) With respect to an obligation on or defense to a security, a guarantor is an issuer to the extent of its guaranty, whether or not its obligation is noted on a security certificate.

(c) With respect to a registration of a transfer, issuer means a person on whose behalf transfer books are maintained.

Official Comment

1. The definition of "issuer" in this section functions primarily to describe the persons whose defenses may be cut off under the rules in Part 2. In large measure it simply tracks the language of the definition of security in Section 8–102(a)(15).

2. Subsection (b) distinguishes the obligations of a guarantor as issuer from those of the principal obligor. However, it does not exempt the guarantor from the impact of subsection (d) of Section 8–202. Whether or not the obligation of the guarantor is noted on the security is immaterial. Typically, guarantors are parent corporations, or stand in some similar relationship to the principal obligor. If that relationship existed at

the time the security was originally issued the guaranty would probably have been noted on the security. However, if the relationship arose afterward, e.g., through a purchase of stock or properties, or through merger or consolidation, probably the notation would not have been made. Nonetheless, the holder of the security is entitled to the benefit of the obligation of the guarantor.

3. Subsection (c) narrows the definition of "issuer" for purposes of Part 4 of this Article (registration of transfer). It is supplemented by Section 8–407.

Definitional Cross References:

"Person". Section 1–201(30).
"Security". Section 8–102(a)(15).
"Security certificate". Section 8–102(a)(16).
"Uncertificated security". Section 8–102(a)(18).

§ 8–202. Issuer's Responsibility and Defenses; Notice of Defect or Defense.

(a) Even against a purchaser for value and without notice, the terms of a certificated security include terms stated on the certificate and terms made part of the security by reference on the certificate to another instrument, indenture, or document or to a constitution, statute, ordinance, rule, regulation, order, or the like, to the extent the terms referred to do not conflict with terms stated on the certificate. A reference under this subsection does not of itself charge a purchaser for value with notice of a defect going to the validity of the security, even if the certificate expressly states that a person accepting it admits notice. The terms of an uncertificated security include those stated in any instrument, indenture, or document or in a constitution, statute, ordinance, rule, regulation, order, or the like, pursuant to which the security is issued.

(b) The following rules apply if an issuer asserts that a security is not valid:

(1) A security other than one issued by a government or governmental subdivision, agency, or instrumentality, even though issued with a defect going to its validity, is valid in the hands of a purchaser for value and without notice of the particular defect unless the defect involves a violation of a constitutional provision. In that case, the security is valid in the hands of a purchaser for value and without notice of the defect, other than one who takes by original issue.

(2) Paragraph (1) applies to an issuer that is a government or governmental subdivision, agency, or instrumentality only if there has been substantial compliance with the legal requirements governing the issue or the issuer has received a substantial consideration for the issue as a whole or for the particular security and a stated purpose of the issue is one for which the issuer has power to borrow money or issue the security.

(c) Except as otherwise provided in Section 8–205, lack of genuineness of a certificated security is a complete defense, even against a purchaser for value and without notice.

(d) All other defenses of the issuer of a security, including nondelivery and conditional delivery of a certificated security, are ineffective against a purchaser for value who has taken the certificated security without notice of the particular defense.

(e) This section does not affect the right of a party to cancel a contract for a security "when, as and if issued" or "when distributed" in the event of a material change in the character of the security that is the subject of the contract or in the plan or arrangement pursuant to which the security is to be issued or distributed.

(f) If a security is held by a securities intermediary against whom an entitlement holder has a security entitlement with respect to the security, the issuer may not assert any defense that the issuer could not assert if the entitlement holder held the security directly.

Official Comment

1. In this Article the rights of the purchaser for value without notice are divided into two aspects, those against the issuer, and those against other claimants to the security. Part 2 of this Article, and especially this section, deal with rights against the issuer.

Subsection (a) states, in accordance with the prevailing case law, the right of the issuer (who prepares the text of the security) to include terms incorporated by adequate reference to an extrinsic source, so long as the terms so incorporated do not conflict with the stated terms. Thus, the standard practice of referring in a bond or debenture to the trust indenture under which it is issued without spelling out its necessarily complex and lengthy provisions is approved. Every stock certificate refers in some manner to the charter or articles of incorporation of the issuer. At least where there is more than one class of stock authorized applicable corporation codes specifically require a statement or summary as to preferences, voting powers and the like. References to constitutions, statutes, ordinances, rules, regulations or orders are not so common, except in the obligations of governments or governmental agencies or units; but where appropriate they fit into the rule here stated.

Courts have generally held that an issuer is estopped from denying representations made in the text of a security. *Delaware–New Jersey Ferry Co. v. Leeds*, 21 Del.Ch. 279, 186 A. 913 (1936). Nor is a defect in form or the invalidity of a security normally available to the issuer as a defense. *Bonini v. Family Theatre Corporation*, 327 Pa. 273, 194 A. 498 (1937); *First National Bank of Fairbanks v. Alaska Airmotive*, 119 F.2d 267 (C.C.A.Alaska 1941).

2. The rule in subsection (a) requiring that the terms of a security be noted or referred to on the certificate is based on practices and expectations in the direct holding system for certificated securities. This rule does not express a general rule or policy that the terms of a security are effective only if they are communicated to beneficial owners in some particular fashion. Rather, subsection (a) is based on the principle that a purchaser who does obtain a certificate is entitled to assume that the terms of the security have been noted or referred to on the certificate. That policy does not come into play in a securities holding system in which purchasers do not take delivery of certificates.

The provisions of subsection (a) concerning notation of terms on security certificates are necessary only because paper certificates play such an important role for certificated securities that a purchaser should be protected against assertion of any defenses or rights that are not noted on the certificate. No similar problem exists with respect to uncertificated securities. The last sentence of subsection (a) is, strictly speaking, unnecessary, since it only recognizes the fact that the terms of an uncertificated security are determined by whatever other law or agreement governs the security. It is included only to preclude any inference that uncertificated securities are subject to any requirement analogous to the requirement of notation of terms on security certificates.

The rule of subsection (a) applies to the indirect holding system only in the sense that if a certificated security has been delivered to the clearing corporation or other securities intermediary, the terms of the security should be noted or referred to on the certificate.

If the security is uncertificated, that principle does not apply even at the issuer-clearing corporation level. The beneficial owners who hold securities through the clearing corporation are bound by the terms of the security, even though they do not actually see the certificate. Since entitlement holders in an indirect holding system have not taken delivery of certificates, the policy of subsection (a) does not apply.

3. The penultimate sentence of subsection (a) and all of subsection (b) embody the concept that it is the duty of the issuer, not of the purchaser, to make sure that the security complies with the law governing its issue. The penultimate sentence of subsection (a) makes clear that the issuer cannot, by incorporating a reference to a statute or other document, charge the purchaser with notice of the security's invalidity. Subsection (b) gives to a purchaser for value without notice of the defect the right to enforce the security against the issuer despite the presence of a defect that otherwise would render the security invalid. There are three circumstances in which a purchaser does not gain such rights: first, if the defect involves a violation of constitutional provisions, these rights accrue only to a subsequent purchaser, that is, one who takes other than by original issue. This Article leaves to the law of each particular State the rights of a purchaser on original issue of a security with a constitutional defect. No negative implication is intended by the explicit grant of rights to a subsequent purchaser.

Second, governmental issuers are distinguished in subsection (b) from other issuers as a matter of public policy, and additional safeguards are imposed before governmental issues are validated. Governmental issuers are estopped from asserting defenses only if there has been substantial compliance with the legal requirements governing the issue or if substantial consideration has been received and a stated purpose of the issue is one for which the issuer has power to borrow money or issue the security. The purpose of the substantial compliance requirement is to make certain that a mere technicality as, e.g., in the manner of publishing election notices, shall not be a ground for depriving an innocent purchaser of rights in the security. The policy is here adopted of such cases as *Tommie v. City of Gadsden*, 229 Ala. 521, 158 So. 763 (1935), in which minor discrepancies in the form of the election ballot used were overlooked and the bonds were declared valid since there had been substantial compliance with the statute.

A long and well established line of federal cases recognizes the principle of estoppel in favor of purchasers for value without notices where municipalities issue bonds containing recitals of compliance with governing constitutional and statutory provisions, made by the municipal authorities entrusted with determining such compliance. *Chaffee County v. Potter,* 142 U.S. 355 (1892); *Oregon v. Jennings,* 119 U.S. 74 (1886); *Gunnison County Commissioners v. Rollins,* 173 U.S. 255 (1898). This rule has been qualified, however, by requiring that the municipality have power to issue the security. *Anthony v. County of Jasper,* 101 U.S. 693 (1879); *Town of South Ottawa v. Perkins,* 94 U.S. 260 (1876). This section follows the case law trend, simplifying the rule by setting up two conditions for an estoppel against a governmental issuer: (1) substantial consideration given, and (2) power in the issuer to borrow money or issue the security for the stated purpose. As a practical matter the problem of policing governmental issuers has been alleviated by the present practice of requiring legal opinions as to the validity of the issue. The bulk of the case law on this point is nearly 100 years old and it may be assumed that the question now seldom arises.

Section 8–210, regarding overissue, provides the third exception to the rule that an innocent purchase for value takes a valid security despite the presence of a defect that would otherwise give rise to invalidity. See that section and its Comment for further explanation.

4. Subsection (e) is included to make clear that this section does not affect the presently recognized right of either party to a "when, as and if" or "when distributed" contract to cancel the contract on substantial change.

5. Subsection (f) has been added because the introduction of the security entitlement concept requires some adaptation of the Part 2 rules, particularly those that distinguish between purchasers who take by original issue and subsequent purchasers. The basic concept of Part 2 is to apply to investment securities the principle of negotiable instruments law that an obligor is precluded from asserting most defenses against purchasers for value without notice. Section 8–202 describes in some detail which defenses issuers can raise against purchasers for value and subsequent purchasers for value. Because these rules were drafted with the direct holding system in mind, some interpretive problems might be presented in applying them to the indirect holding. For example, if a municipality issues a bond in book-entry only form, the only direct "purchaser" of that bond would be the clearing corporation. The policy of precluding the issuer from asserting defenses is, however, equally applicable. Subsection (f) is designed to ensure that the defense preclusion rules developed for the direct holding system will also apply to the indirect holding system.

Definitional Cross References:

"Certificated security". Section 8–102(a)(4).
"Notice". Section 1–201(25).
"Purchaser". Sections 1–201(33) & 8–116.
"Security". Section 8–102(a)(15).
"Uncertificated security". Section 8–102(a)(18).
"Value". Sections 1–201(44) & 8–116.

§ 8–203. Staleness as Notice of Defect or Defense.

After an act or event, other than a call that has been revoked, creating a right to immediate performance of the principal obligation represented by a certificated security or setting a date on or after which the security is to be presented or surrendered for redemption or exchange, a purchaser is charged with notice of any defect in its issue or defense of the issuer, if the act or event:

(1) requires the payment of money, the delivery of a certificated security, the registration of transfer of an uncertificated security, or any of them on presentation or surrender of the security certificate, the money or security is available on the date set for payment or exchange, and the purchaser takes the security more than one year after that date; or

(2) is not covered by paragraph (1) and the purchaser takes the security more than two years after the date set for surrender or presentation or the date on which performance became due.

Official Comment

1. The problem of matured or called securities is here dealt with in terms of the effect of such events in giving notice of the issuer's defenses and not in terms of "negotiability". The substance of this section applies only to certificated securities because certificates may be transferred to a purchaser by delivery after the security has matured, been called, or become redeemable or exchangeable. It is contemplated that uncertificated securities which have matured or been called will merely be canceled on the books of the issuer and the proceeds sent to the registered owner. Uncertificated securities which have become redeemable or exchangeable, at the option of the owner, may be transferred to a purchaser, but the transfer is effectuated only by registration of transfer, thus necessitating communication with the issuer. If defects or defenses in such

securities exist, the issuer will necessarily have the opportunity to bring them to the attention of the purchaser.

2. The fact that a security certificate is in circulation long after it has been called for redemption or exchange must give rise to the question in a purchaser's mind as to why it has not been surrendered. After the lapse of a reasonable period of time a purchaser can no longer claim "no reason to know" of any defects or irregularities in its issue. Where funds are available for the redemption the security certificate is normally turned in more promptly and a shorter time is set as the "reasonable period" than is set where funds are not available.

Defaulted certificated securities may be traded on financial markets in the same manner as unmatured and undefaulted instruments and a purchaser might not be placed upon notice of irregularity by the mere fact of default. An issuer, however, should at some point be placed in a position to determine definitely its liability on an invalid or improper issue, and for this purpose a security under this section becomes "stale" two years after the default. A different rule applies when the question is notice not of issuer's defenses but of claims of ownership. Section 8–105 and Comment.

3. Nothing in this section is designed to extend the life of preferred stocks called for redemption as "shares of stock" beyond the redemption date. After such a call, the security represents only a right to the funds set aside for redemption.

Definitional Cross References:

"Certificated security". Section 8–102(a)(4).
"Notice". Section 1–201(25).
"Purchaser". Sections 1–201(33) & 8–116.
"Security". Section 8–102(a)(15).
"Security certificate". Section 8–102(a)(16).
"Uncertificated security". Section 8–102(a)(18).

§ 8–204. Effect of Issuer's Restriction on Transfer.

A restriction on transfer of a security imposed by the issuer, even if otherwise lawful, is ineffective against a person without knowledge of the restriction unless:

(1) the security is certificated and the restriction is noted conspicuously on the security certificate; or

(2) the security is uncertificated and the registered owner has been notified of the restriction.

Official Comment

1. Restrictions on transfer of securities are imposed by issuers in a variety of circumstances and for a variety of purposes, such as to retain control of a close corporation or to ensure compliance with federal securities laws. Other law determines whether such restrictions are permissible. This section deals only with the consequences of failure to note the restriction on a security certificate.

This section imposes no bar to enforcement of a restriction on transfer against a person who has actual knowledge of it.

2. A restriction on transfer of a certificated security is ineffective against a person without knowledge of the restriction unless the restriction is noted conspicuously on the certificate. The word "noted" is used to make clear that the restriction need not be set forth in full text. Refusal by an issuer to register a transfer on the basis of an unnoted restriction would be a violation of the issuer's duty to register under Section 8–401.

3. The policy of this section is the same as in Section 8–202. A purchaser who takes delivery of a certificated security is entitled to rely on the terms stated on the certificate. That policy obviously does not apply to uncertificated securities. For uncertificated securities, this section requires only that the registered owner has been notified of the restriction. Suppose, for example, that A is the registered owner of an uncertificated security, and that the issuer has notified A of a restriction on transfer. A agrees to sell the security to B, in violation of the restriction. A completes a written instruction directing the issuer to register transfer to B, and B pays A for the security at the time A delivers the instruction to B. A does not inform B of the restriction, and B does not otherwise have notice or knowledge of it at the time B pays and receives the instruction. B presents the instruction to the issuer, but the issuer refuses to register the transfer on the grounds that it would violate the restriction. The issuer has complied with this section, because it did notify the registered owner A of the restriction. The issuer's refusal to register transfer is not wrongful. B has an action against A for breach of transfer warranty, see Section 8–108(b)(4)(iii). B's mistake was treating an uncertificated security transaction in the fashion appropriate only for a certificated security. The mechanism for transfer of uncertificated securities is registration of transfer on the books of the issuer; handing over an instruction only initiates the process. The purchaser should make arrangements to ensure that the price is not paid until it knows that the issuer has or will register transfer.

4. In the indirect holding system, investors neither take physical delivery of security certificates nor have uncertificated securities registered in their names. So long as the requirements of this section have been satisfied at the level of the relationship between the issuer and the securities intermediary that is a direct holder, this section does not preclude the issuer from enforcing a restriction on transfer. See Section 8–202(a) and Comment 2 thereto.

5. This section deals only with restrictions imposed by the issuer. Restrictions imposed by statute are not affected. See *Quiner v. Marblehead Social Co.,* 10 Mass. 476 (1813); *Madison Bank v. Price,* 79 Kan. 289, 100 P. 280 (1909); *Healey v. Steele Center Creamery Ass'n,* 115 Minn. 451, 133 N.W. 69 (1911). Nor does it deal with private agreements between stockholders containing restrictive covenants as to the sale of the security.

Definitional Cross References:

"Certificated security". Section 8–102(a)(4).
"Conspicuous". Section 1–201(10).
"Issuer". Section 8–201.
"Knowledge". Section 1–201(25).
"Notify". Section 1–201(25).
"Purchaser". Sections 1–201(33) & 8–116.
"Security". Section 8–102(a)(15).
"Security certificate". Section 8–102(a)(16).
"Uncertificated security". Section 8–102(a)(18).

§ 8–205. Effect of Unauthorized Signature on Security Certificate.

An unauthorized signature placed on a security certificate before or in the course of issue is ineffective, but the signature is effective in favor of a purchaser for value of the certificated security if the purchaser is without notice of the lack of authority and the signing has been done by:

(1) an authenticating trustee, registrar, transfer agent, or other person entrusted by the issuer with the signing of the security certificate or of similar security certificates, or the immediate preparation for signing of any of them; or

(2) an employee of the issuer, or of any of the persons listed in paragraph (1), entrusted with responsible handling of the security certificate.

Official Comment

1. The problem of forged or unauthorized signatures may arise where an employee of the issuer, transfer agent, or registrar has access to securities which the employee is required to prepare for issue by affixing the corporate seal or by adding a signature necessary for issue. This section is based upon the issuer's duty to avoid the negligent entrusting of securities to such persons. Issuers have long been held responsible for signatures placed upon securities by parties whom they have held out to the public as authorized to prepare such securities. See *Fifth Avenue Bank of New York v. The Forty–Second & Grand Street Ferry Railroad Co.,* 137 N.Y. 231, 33 N.E. 378, 19 L.R.A. 331, 33 Am.St.Rep. 712 (1893); *Jarvis v. Manhattan Beach Co.,* 148 N.Y. 652, 43 N.E. 68, 31 L.R.A. 776, 51 Am.St.Rep. 727 (1896). The "apparent authority" concept of some of the case-law, however, is here extended and this section expressly rejects the technical distinction, made by courts reluctant to recognize forged signatures, between cases where forgers sign signatures they are authorized to sign under proper circumstances and those in which they sign signatures they are never authorized to sign. *Citizens' & Southern National Bank v. Trust Co. of Georgia,* 50 Ga.App. 681, 179 S.E. 278 (1935). Normally the purchaser is not in a position to determine which signature a forger, entrusted with the preparation of securities, has "apparent authority" to sign. The issuer, on the other hand, can protect itself against such fraud by the careful selection and bonding of agents and employees, or by action over against transfer agents and registrars who in turn may bond their personnel.

2. The issuer cannot be held liable for the honesty of employees not entrusted, directly or indirectly, with the signing, preparation, or responsible handling of similar securities and whose possible commission of forgery it has no reason to anticipate. The result in such cases as *Hudson Trust Co. v. American Linseed Co.,* 232 N.Y. 350, 134 N.E. 178 (1922), and *Dollar Savings Fund & Trust Co. v. Pittsburgh Plate Glass Co.,* 213 Pa. 307, 62 A. 916, 5 Ann.Cas. 248 (1906) is here adopted.

3. This section is not concerned with forged or unauthorized indorsements, but only with unauthorized signatures of issuers, transfer agents, etc., placed upon security certificates during the course of their issue. The protection here stated is available to all purchasers for value without notice and not merely to subsequent purchasers.

Definitional Cross References:

"Certificated security". Section 8–102(a)(4).
"Issuer". Section 8–201.
"Notice". Section 1–201(25).
"Purchaser". Sections 1–201(33) & 8–116.

"Security certificate". Section 8–102(a)(14).

"Unauthorized signature". Section 1–201(43).

§ 8–206. Completion of Alteration of Security Certificate.

(a) If a security certificate contains the signatures necessary to its issue or transfer but is incomplete in any other respect:

(1) any person may complete it by filling in the blanks as authorized; and

(2) even if the blanks are incorrectly filled in, the security certificate as completed is enforceable by a purchaser who took it for value and without notice of the incorrectness.

(b) A complete security certificate that has been improperly altered, even if fraudulently, remains enforceable, but only according to its original terms.

Official Comment

1. The problem of forged or unauthorized signatures necessary for the issue or transfer of a security is not involved here, and a person in possession of a blank certificate is not, by this section, given authority to fill in blanks with such signatures. Completion of blanks left in a transfer instruction is dealt with elsewhere (Section 8–305(a)).

2. Blanks left upon issue of a security certificate are the only ones dealt with here, and a purchaser for value without notice is protected. A purchaser is not in a good position to determine whether blanks were completed by the issuer or by some person not authorized to complete them. On the other hand the issuer can protect itself by not placing its signature on the writing until the blanks are completed or, if it does sign before all blanks are completed, by carefully selecting the agents and employees to whom it entrusts the writing after authentication. With respect to a security certificate that is completed by the issuer but later is altered, the issuer has done everything it can to protect the purchaser and thus is not charged with the terms as altered. However, it is charged according to the original terms, since it is not thereby prejudiced. If the completion or alteration is obviously irregular, the purchaser may not qualify as a purchaser who took without notice under this section.

3. Only the purchaser who physically takes the certificate is directly protected. However, a transferee may receive protection indirectly through Section 8–302(a).

4. The protection granted a purchaser for value without notice under this section is modified to the extent that an overissue may result where an incorrect amount is inserted into a blank (Section 8–210).

Definitional Cross References:

"Notice". Section 1–201(25).

"Purchaser". Sections 1–201(33) & 8–116.

"Security certificate". Section 8–102(a)(16).

"Unauthorized signature". Section 1–201(43).

"Value". Sections 1–201(44) & 8–116.

§ 8–207. Rights and Duties of Issuer with Respect to Registered Owners.

(a) Before due presentment for registration of transfer of a certificated security in registered form or of an instruction requesting registration of transfer of an uncertificated security, the issuer or indenture trustee may treat the registered owner as the person exclusively entitled to vote, receive notifications, and otherwise exercise all the rights and powers of an owner.

(b) This Article does not affect the liability of the registered owner of a security for a call, assessment, or the like.

Official Comment

1. Subsection (a) states the issuer's right to treat the registered owner of a security as the person entitled to exercise all the rights of an owner. This right of the issuer is limited by the provisions of Part 4 of this article. Once there has been due presentation for registration of transfer, the issuer has a duty to register ownership in the name of the transferee. Section 8–401. Thus its right to treat the old registered owner as exclusively entitled to the rights of ownership must cease.

The issuer may under this section make distributions of money or securities to the registered owners of securities without requiring further proof of ownership, provided that such distributions are distributable to the owners of all securities of the same issue and the terms of the security do not require surrender of a security certificate as a condition of payment or exchange. Any such distribution shall constitute a defense against a claim for the same distribution by a person, even if that person is in possession of the security certificate and is a protected purchaser of the security. See PEB Commentary No. 4, dated March 10, 1990.

2. Subsection (a) is permissive and does not require that the issuer deal exclusively with the registered owner. It is free to require proof of ownership before paying out dividends or the like if it chooses to. *Barbato v. Breeze Corporation,* 128 N.J.L. 309, 26 A.2d 53 (1942).

3. This section does not operate to determine who is finally entitled to exercise voting and other rights or to receive payments and distributions. The parties are still free to incorporate their own arrangements as to these matters in seller-purchaser agreements which may be definitive as between them.

4. No change in existing state laws as to the liability of registered owners for calls and assessments is here intended; nor is anything in this section designed to estop record holders from denying ownership when assessments are levied if they are otherwise entitled to do so under state law. See *State ex rel. Squire v. Murfey, Blosson & Co.,* 131 Ohio St. 289, 2 N.E.2d 866 (1936); *Willing v. Delaplaine,* 23 F.Supp. 579 (1937).

5. No interference is intended with the common practice of closing the transfer books or taking a record date for dividend, voting, and other purposes, as provided for in by-laws, charters, and statutes.

Definitional Cross References:

"Certificated security". Section 8–102(a)(4).
"Instruction". Section 8–102(a)(12).
"Issuer". Section 8–201.
"Registered form". Section 8–102(a)(13).
"Security". Section 8–102(a)(15).
"Uncertificated security". Section 8–102(a)(18).

§ 8–208. Effect of Signature of Authenticating Trustee, Registrar, or Transfer Agent.

(a) A person signing a security certificate as authenticating trustee, registrar, transfer agent, or the like, warrants to a purchaser for value of the certificated security, if the purchaser is without notice of a particular defect, that:

(1) the certificate is genuine;

(2) the person's own participation in the issue of the security is within the person's capacity and within the scope of the authority received by the person from the issuer; and

(3) the person has reasonable grounds to believe that the certificated security is in the form and within the amount the issuer is authorized to issue.

(b) Unless otherwise agreed, a person signing under subsection (a) does not assume responsibility for the validity of the security in other respects.

Official Comment

1. The warranties here stated express the current understanding and prevailing case law as to the effect of the signatures of authenticating trustees, transfer agents, and registrars. See *Jarvis v. Manhattan Beach Co.,* 148 N.Y. 652, 43 N.E. 68, 31 L.R.A. 776, 51 Am.St.Rep. 727 (1896). Although it has generally been regarded as the particular obligation of the transfer agent to determine whether securities are in proper form as provided by the by-laws and Articles of Incorporation, neither a registrar nor an authenticating trustee should properly place a signature upon a certificate without determining whether it is at least regular on its face. The obligations of these parties in this respect have therefore been made explicit in terms of due care. See *Feldmeier v. Mortgage Securities, Inc.,* 34 Cal.App.2d 201, 93 P.2d 593 (1939).

2. Those cases which hold that an authenticating trustee is not liable for any defect in the mortgage or property which secures the bond or for any fraudulent misrepresentations made by the issuer are not here affected since these matters do not involve the genuineness or proper form of the security. *Ainsa v. Mercantile Trust Co.,* 174 Cal. 504, 163 P. 898 (1917); *Tschetinian v. City Trust Co.,* 186 N.Y. 432, 79 N.E. 401 (1906); *Davidge v. Guardian Trust Co. of New York,* 203 N.Y. 331, 96 N.E. 751 (1911).

3. The charter or an applicable statute may affect the capacity of a bank or other corporation undertaking to act as an authenticating trustee, registrar, or transfer agent. See, for example, the Federal Reserve Act (U.S.C.A., Title 12, Banks and Banking, Section 248) under which the Board of Governors of the Federal Reserve Bank is authorized to grant special permits to National Banks permitting them to act as trustees. Such corporations are therefore held to certify as to their legal capacity to act as well as to their authority.

4. Authenticating trustees, registrars, and transfer agents have normally been held liable for an issue in excess of the authorized amount. *Jarvis v. Manhattan Beach Co.,* supra; *Mullen v. Eastern Trust & Banking Co.,* 108 Me. 498, 81 A. 948 (1911). In imposing upon these parties a duty of due care with respect to the amount they are authorized to help issue, this section does not necessarily validate the security, but merely

holds persons responsible for the excess issue liable in damages for any loss suffered by the purchaser.

5. Aside from questions of genuineness and excess issue, these parties are not held to certify as to the validity of the security unless they specifically undertake to do so. The case law which has recognized a unique responsibility on the transfer agent's part to testify as to the validity of any security which it countersigns is rejected.

6. This provision does not prevent a transfer agent or issuer from agreeing with a registrar of stock to protect the registrar in respect of the genuineness and proper form of a security certificate signed by the issuer or the transfer agent or both. Nor does it interfere with proper indemnity arrangements between the issuer and trustees, transfer agents, registrars, and the like.

7. An unauthorized signature is a signature for purposes of this section if and only if it is made effective by Section 8–205.

Definitional Cross References:

"Certificated security". Section 8–102(a)(4).
"Genuine". Section 1–201(18).
"Issuer". Section 8–201.
"Notice". Section 1–201(25).
"Purchaser". Sections 1–201(33) & 8–116.
"Security". Section 8–102(a)(15).
"Security certificate". Section 8–102(a)(16).
"Uncertificated security". Section 8–102(a)(18).
"Value". Sections 1–201(44) & 8–116.

§ 8–209. Issuer's Lien.

A lien in favor of an issuer upon a certificated security is valid against a purchaser only if the right of the issuer to the lien is noted conspicuously on the security certificate.

Official Comment

This section is similar to Sections 8–202 and 8–204 which require that the terms of a certificated security and any restriction on transfer imposed by the issuer be noted on the security certificate. This section differs from those two sections in that the purchaser's knowledge of the issuer's claim is irrelevant. "Noted" makes clear that the text of the lien provisions need not be set forth in full. However, this would not override a provision of an applicable corporation code requiring statement in haec verba. This section does not apply to uncertificated securities. It applies to the indirect holding system in the same fashion as Sections 8–202 and 8–204, see Comment 2 to Section 8–202.

Definitional Cross References:

"Certificated security". Section 8–102(a)(4).
"Issuer". Section 8–201.
"Purchaser". Sections 1–201(33) & 8–116.
"Security". Section 8–102(a)(15).
"Security certificate". Section 8–102(a)(16).

§ 8–210. Overissue.

(a) In this section, "overissue" means the issue of securities in excess of the amount the issuer has corporate power to issue, but an overissue does not occur if appropriate action has cured the overissue.

(b) Except as otherwise provided in subsections (c) and (d), the provisions of this Article which validate a security or compel its issue or reissue do not apply to the extent that validation, issue, or reissue would result in overissue.

(c) If an identical security not constituting an overissue is reasonably available for purchase, a person entitled to issue or validation may compel the issuer to purchase the security and deliver it if certificated or register its transfer if uncertificated, against surrender of any security certificate the person holds.

(d) If a security is not reasonably available for purchase, a person entitled to issue or validation may recover from the issuer the price the person or the last purchaser for value paid for it with interest from the date of the person's demand.

Official Comment

1. Deeply embedded in corporation law is the conception that "corporate power" to issue securities stems from the statute, either general or special, under which the corporation is organized. Corporation codes universally require that the charter or articles of incorporation state, at least as to capital shares, maximum limits in terms of number of shares or total dollar capital. Historically, special incorporation statutes are similarly drawn and sometimes similarly limit the face amount of authorized debt securities. The theory is that issue of securities in excess of the authorized amounts is prohibited. See, for example, *McWilliams v. Geddes & Moss Undertaking Co.*, 169 So. 894 (1936, La.); *Crawford v. Twin City Oil Co.*, 216 Ala. 216, 113 So. 61 (1927); *New York and New Haven R.R. Co. v. Schuyler*, 34 N.Y. 30 (1865). This conception persists despite modern corporation codes under which, by action of directors and stockholders, additional shares can be authorized by charter amendment and thereaf-

ter issued. This section does not give a person entitled to validation, issue, or reissue of a security, the right to compel amendment of the charter to authorize additional shares. Therefore, in a case where issue of an additional security would require charter amendment, the plaintiff is limited to the two alternate remedies set forth in subsections (c) and (d). The last clause of subsection (a), which is added in Revised Article 8, does, however, recognize that under modern conditions, overissue may be a relatively minor technical problem that can be cured by appropriate action under governing corporate law.

2. Where an identical security is reasonably available for purchase, whether because traded on an organized market, or because one or more security owners may be willing to sell at a not unreasonable price, the issuer, although unable to issue additional shares, will be able to purchase them and may be compelled to follow that procedure. *West v. Tintic Standard Mining Co.*, 71 Utah 158, 263 P. 490 (1928).

3. The right to recover damages from an issuer who has permitted an overissue to occur is well settled.

New York and New Haven R.R. Co. v. Schuyler, 34 N.Y. 30 (1865). The measure of such damages, however, has been open to question, some courts basing them upon the value of stock at the time registration is refused; some upon the value at the time of trial; and some upon the highest value between the time of refusal and the time of trial. *Allen v. South Boston Railroad*, 150 Mass. 200, 22 N.E. 917, 5 L.R.A. 716, 15 Am.St.Rep. 185 (1889); *Commercial Bank v. Kortright*, 22 Wend. (N.Y.) 348 (1839). The purchase price of the security to the last purchaser who gave value for it is here adopted as being the fairest means of reducing the possibility of speculation by the purchaser. Interest may be recovered by the best available measure of compensation for delay.

Definitional Cross References:

"Issuer". Section 8–201.
"Security". Section 8–102(a)(15).
"Security certificate". Section 8–102(a)(16).
"Uncertificated security". Section 8–102(a)(18).

PART 3

TRANSFER OF CERTIFICATED AND UNCERTIFICATED SECURITIES

§ 8–301. Delivery.

(a) Delivery of a certificated security to a purchaser occurs when:

(1) the purchaser acquires possession of the security certificate;

(2) another person, other than a securities intermediary, either acquires possession of the security certificate on behalf of the purchaser or, having previously acquired possession of the certificate, acknowledges that it holds for the purchaser; or

(3) a securities intermediary acting on behalf of the purchaser acquires possession of the security certificate, only if the certificate is in registered form and is (i) registered in the name of the purchaser, (ii) payable to the order of the purchaser, or (iii) specially indorsed to the purchaser by an effective indorsement and has not been indorsed to the securities intermediary or in blank.

(b) Delivery of an uncertificated security to a purchaser occurs when:

(1) the issuer registers the purchaser as the registered owner, upon original issue or registration of transfer; or

(2) another person, other than a securities intermediary, either becomes the registered owner of the uncertificated security on behalf of the purchaser or, having previously become the registered owner, acknowledges that it holds for the purchaser.

As amended in 1999.

Official Comment

1. This section specifies the requirements for "delivery" of securities. Delivery is used in Article 8 to describe the formal steps necessary for a purchaser to acquire a direct interest in a security under this Article. The concept of delivery refers to the implementation of a transaction, not the legal categorization of the transaction which is consummated by delivery. Issuance and transfer are different kinds of transaction, though both may be implemented by delivery. Sale and pledge are different kinds of transfers, but both may be implemented by delivery.

2. Subsection (a) defines delivery with respect to certificated securities. Paragraph (1) deals with sim-

ple cases where purchasers themselves acquire physical possession of certificates. Paragraphs (2) and (3) of subsection (a) specify the circumstances in which delivery to a purchaser can occur although the certificate is in the possession of a person other than the purchaser. Paragraph (2) contains the general rule that a purchaser can take delivery through another person, so long as the other person is actually acting on behalf of the purchaser or acknowledges that it is holding on behalf of the purchaser. Paragraph (2) does not apply to acquisition of possession by a securities intermediary, because a person who holds securities through a securities account acquires a security entitlement, rather than having a direct interest. See Section 8–501. Subsection (a)(3) specifies the limited circumstances in which delivery of security certificates to a securities intermediary is treated as a delivery to the customer. Note that delivery is a method of perfecting a security interest in a certificated security. See Section 9–313(a), (e).

3. Subsection (b) defines delivery with respect to uncertificated securities. Use of the term "delivery" with respect to uncertificated securities, does, at least on first hearing, seem a bit solecistic. The word "delivery" is, however, routinely used in the securities business in a broader sense than manual tradition. For example, settlement by entries on the books of a clearing corporation is commonly called "delivery," as in the expression "delivery versus payment." The diction of this section has the advantage of using the same term for uncertificated securities as for certificated securities, for which delivery is conventional usage. Paragraph (1) of subsection (b) provides that delivery occurs when the purchaser becomes the registered owner of an uncertificated security, either upon original issue or registration of transfer. Paragraph (2) provides for delivery of an uncertificated security through a third person, in a fashion analogous to subsection (a)(2).

Definitional Cross References:

"Certificated security". Section 8–102(a)(4).
"Effective". Section 8–107.
"Issuer". Section 8–201.
"Purchaser". Sections 1–201(33) & 8–116.
"Registered form". Section 8–102(a)(13).
"Securities intermediary". Section 8–102(a)(14).
"Security certificate". Section 8–102(a)(16).
"Special indorsement". Section 8–304(a).
"Uncertificated security". Section 8–102(a)(18).

Amendments in italics approved by the Permanent Editorial Board for Uniform Commercial Code January 15, 2000.

As amended in 1999.

§ 8–302.   Rights of Purchaser.

(a) Except as otherwise provided in subsections (b) and (c), a purchaser of a certificated or uncertificated security acquires all rights in the security that the transferor had or had power to transfer.

(b) A purchaser of a limited interest acquires rights only to the extent of the interest purchased.

(c) A purchaser of a certificated security who as a previous holder had notice of an adverse claim does not improve its position by taking from a protected purchaser.

As amended in 1999.

Official Comment

1. Subsection (a) provides that a purchaser of a certificated or uncertificated security acquires all rights that the transferor had or had power to transfer. This statement of the familiar "shelter" principle is qualified by the exceptions that a purchaser of a limited interest acquires only that interest, subsection (b), and that a person who does not qualify as a protected purchaser cannot improve its position by taking from a subsequent protected purchaser, subsection (c).

2. Although this section provides that a purchaser acquires a property interest in a certificated or uncertificated security, it does not state that a person can acquire an interest in a security only by purchase. Article 8 also is not a comprehensive codification of all of the law governing the creation or transfer of interests in securities *by purchase*.* For example, the grant of a security interest is a transfer of a property interest, but the formal steps necessary to effectuate such a transfer are governed by Article 9, not by Article 8. Under the Article 9 rules, a security interest in a certificated or uncertificated security can be created by execution of a security agreement under Section 9–203 and can be perfected by filing. A transfer of an Article 9 security interest can be implemented by an Article 8 delivery, but need not be.

Similarly, Article 8 does not determine whether a property interest in certificated or uncertificated security is acquired under other law, such as the law of gifts, trusts, or equitable remedies. Nor does Article 8 deal with transfers by operation of law. For example, transfers from decedent to administrator, from ward to guardian, and from bankrupt to trustee in bankruptcy are governed by other law as to both the time they occur and the substance of the transfer. The Article 8 rules do, however, determine whether the issuer is obligated to recognize the rights that a third party, such as a transferee, may acquire under other law. See Sections 8–207, 8–401, and 8–404.

Definitional Cross References:

"Certificated security". Section 8–102(a)(4).
"Notice of adverse claim". Section 8–105.
"Protected purchaser". Section 8–303.
"Purchaser". Sections 1–201(33) & 8–116.
"Uncertificated security". Section 8–102(a)(18).
"Delivery". Section 8–301.

As amended in 1999 and 2000.

§ 8–303. Protected Purchaser.

(a) "Protected purchaser" means a purchaser of a certificated or uncertificated security, or of an interest therein, who:

(1) gives value;

(2) does not have notice of any adverse claim to the security; and

(3) obtains control of the certificated or uncertificated security.

(b) In addition to acquiring the rights of a purchaser, a protected purchaser also acquires its interest in the security free of any adverse claim.

Official Comment

1. Subsection (a) lists the requirements that a purchaser must meet to qualify as a "protected purchaser." Subsection (b) provides that a protected purchaser takes its interest free from adverse claims. "Purchaser" is defined broadly in Section 1–201. A secured party as well as an outright buyer can qualify as a protected purchaser. Also, "purchase" includes taking by issue, so a person to whom a security is originally issued can qualify as a protected purchaser.

2. To qualify as a protected purchaser, a purchaser must give value, take without notice of any adverse claim, and obtain control. Value is used in the broad sense defined in Section 1–201(44). See also Section 8–116 (securities intermediary as purchaser for value). Adverse claim is defined in Section 8–102(a)(1). Section 8–105 specifies whether a purchaser has notice of an adverse claim. Control is defined in Section 8–106.

To qualify as a protected purchaser there must be a time at which all of the requirements are satisfied. Thus if a purchaser obtains notice of an adverse claim before giving value or satisfying the requirements for control, the purchaser cannot be a protected purchaser. See also Section 8–304(d).

The requirement that a protected purchaser obtain control expresses the point that to qualify for the adverse claim cut-off rule a purchaser must take through a transaction that is implemented by the appropriate mechanism. By contrast, the rules in Part 2 provide that any purchaser for value of a security without notice of a defense may take free of the issuer's defense based on that defense. See Section 8–202.

3. The requirements for control differ depending on the form of the security. For securities represented by bearer certificates, a purchaser obtains control by delivery. See Sections 8–106(a) and 8–301(a). For securities represented by certificates in registered form, the requirements for control are: (1) delivery as defined in Section 8–301(b), plus (2) either an effective indorsement or registration of transfer by the issuer. See Section 8–106(b). Thus, a person who takes through a forged indorsement does not qualify as a protected purchaser by virtue of the delivery alone. If, however, the purchaser presents the certificate to the issuer for registration of transfer, and the issuer registers transfer over the forged indorsement, the purchaser can qualify as a protected purchaser of the new certificate. If the issuer registers transfer on a forged indorsement, the true owner will be able to recover from the issuer for wrongful registration, see Section 8–404, unless the owner's delay in notifying the issuer of a loss or theft of the certificate results in preclusion under Section 8–406.

For uncertificated securities, a purchaser can obtain control either by delivery, see Sections 8–106(c)(1) and 8–301(b), or by obtaining an agreement pursuant to which the issuer agrees to act on instructions from the purchaser without further consent from the registered owner, see Section 8–106(c)(2). The control agreement device of Section 8–106(c)(2) takes the place of the "registered pledge" concept of the 1978 version of Article 8. A secured lender who obtains a control agreement under Section 8–106(c)(2) can qualify as a protected purchaser of an uncertificated security.

4. This section states directly the rules determining whether one takes free from adverse claims without using the phrase "good faith." Whether a person who takes under suspicious circumstances is disqualified is determined by the rules of Section 8–105 on notice of

adverse claims. The term "protected purchaser," which replaces the term "bona fide purchaser" used in the prior version of Article 8, is derived from the term "protected holder" used in the Convention on International Bills and Notes prepared by the United Nations Commission on International Trade Law ("UNCITRAL").

Definitional Cross References:

"Adverse claim". Section 8–102(a)(1).
"Certificated security". Section 8–102(a)(4).
"Control". Section 8–106.
"Notice of adverse claim". Section 8–105.
"Purchaser". Sections 1–201(33) & 8–116.
"Uncertificated security". Section 8–102(a)(18).
"Value". Sections 1–201(44) & 8–116.

§ 8–304. Indorsement.

(a) An indorsement may be in blank or special. An indorsement in blank includes an indorsement to bearer. A special indorsement specifies to whom a security is to be transferred or who has power to transfer it. A holder may convert a blank indorsement to a special indorsement.

(b) An indorsement purporting to be only of part of a security certificate representing units intended by the issuer to be separately transferable is effective to the extent of the indorsement.

(c) An indorsement, whether special or in blank, does not constitute a transfer until delivery of the certificate on which it appears or, if the indorsement is on a separate document, until delivery of both the document and the certificate.

(d) If a security certificate in registered form has been delivered to a purchaser without a necessary indorsement, the purchaser may become a protected purchaser only when the indorsement is supplied. However, against a transferor, a transfer is complete upon delivery and the purchaser has a specifically enforceable right to have any necessary indorsement supplied.

(e) An indorsement of a security certificate in bearer form may give notice of an adverse claim to the certificate, but it does not otherwise affect a right to registration that the holder possesses.

(f) Unless otherwise agreed, a person making an indorsement assumes only the obligations provided in Section 8–108 and not an obligation that the security will be honored by the issuer.

Official Comment

1. By virtue of the definition of indorsement in Section 8–102 and the rules of this section, the simplified method of indorsing certificated securities previously set forth in the Uniform Stock Transfer Act is continued. Although more than one special indorsement on a given security certificate is possible, the desire for dividends or interest, as the case may be, should operate to bring the certificate home for registration of transfer within a reasonable period of time. The usual form of assignment which appears on the back of a stock certificate or in a separate "power" may be filled up either in the form of an assignment, a power of attorney to transfer, or both. If it is not filled up at all but merely signed, the indorsement is in blank. If filled up either as an assignment or as a power of attorney to transfer, the indorsement is special.

2. Subsection (b) recognizes the validity of a "partial" indorsement, e.g., as to fifty shares of the one hundred represented by a single certificate. The rights of a transferee under a partial indorsement to the status of a protected purchaser are left to the case law.

3. Subsection (c) deals with the effect of an indorsement without delivery. There must be a voluntary parting with control in order to effect a valid transfer of a certificated security as between the parties. *Levey v. Nason,* 279 Mass. 268, 181 N.E. 193 (1932), and *National Surety Co. v. Indemnity Insurance Co. of North America,* 237 App.Div. 485, 261 N.Y.S. 605 (1933). The provision in Section 10 of the Uniform Stock Transfer Act that an attempted transfer without delivery amounts to a promise to transfer is omitted. Even under that Act the effect of such a promise was left to the applicable law of contracts, and this Article by making no reference to such situations intends to achieve a similar result. With respect to delivery there is no counterpart to subsection (d) on right to compel indorsement, such as is envisaged in *Johnson v. Johnson,* 300 Mass. 24, 13 N.E.2d 788 (1938), where the transferee under a written assignment was given the right to compel a transfer of the certificate.

4. Subsection (d) deals with the effect of delivery without indorsement. As between the parties the transfer is made complete upon delivery, but the transferee cannot become a protected purchaser until indorsement is made. The indorsement does not operate retroactively, and notice may intervene between delivery and indorsement so as to prevent the transferee from becoming a protected purchaser. Although a purchaser taking without a necessary indorsement may

be subject to claims of ownership, any issuer's defense of which the purchaser had no notice at the time of delivery will be cut off, since the provisions of this Article protect all purchasers for value without notice (Section 8–202).

The transferee's right to compel an indorsement where a security certificate has been delivered with intent to transfer is recognized in the case law. See *Coats v. Guaranty Bank & Trust Co.,* 170 La. 871, 129 So. 513 (1930). A proper indorsement is one of the requisites of transfer which a purchaser of a certificated security has a right to obtain (Section 8–307). A purchaser may not only compel an indorsement under that section but may also recover for any reasonable expense incurred by the transferor's failure to respond to the demand for an indorsement.

5. Subsection (e) deals with the significance of an indorsement on a security certificate in bearer form. The concept of indorsement applies only to registered securities. A purported indorsement of bearer paper is normally of no effect. An indorsement "for collection," "for surrender" or the like, charges a purchaser with notice of adverse claims (Section 8–105(d)) but does not operate beyond this to interfere with any right the holder may otherwise possess to have the security registered.

6. Subsection (f) makes clear that the indorser of a security certificate does not warrant that the issuer will honor the underlying obligation. In view of the nature of investment securities and the circumstances under which they are normally transferred, a transferor cannot be held to warrant as to the issuer's actions. As a transferor the indorser, of course, remains liable for breach of the warranties set forth in this Article (Section 8–108).

Definitional Cross References:

"Bearer form". Section 8–102(a)(2).
"Certificated security". Section 8–102(a)(4).
"Indorsement". Section 8–102(a)(11).
"Purchaser". Sections 1–201(33) & 8–116.
"Registered form". Section 8–102(a)(13).
"Security certificate". Section 8–102(a)(16).

§ 8–305. Instruction.

(a) If an instruction has been originated by an appropriate person but is incomplete in any other respect, any person may complete it as authorized and the issuer may rely on it as completed, even though it has been completed incorrectly.

(b) Unless otherwise agreed, a person initiating an instruction assumes only the obligations imposed by Section 8–108 and not an obligation that the security will be honored by the issuer.

Official Comment

1. The term instruction is defined in Section 8–102(a)(12) as a notification communicated to the issuer of an uncertificated security directing that transfer be registered. Section 8–107 specifies who may initiate an effective instruction.

Functionally, presentation of an instruction is quite similar to the presentation of an indorsed certificate for registration. Note that instruction is defined in terms of "communicate," see Section 8–102(a)(6). Thus, the instruction may be in the form of a writing signed by the registered owner or in any other form agreed upon by the issuer and the registered owner. Allowing nonwritten forms of instructions will permit the development and employment of means of transmitting instructions electronically.

When a person who originates an instruction leaves a blank and the blank later is completed, subsection (a) gives the issuer the same rights it would have had against the originating person had that person completed the blank. This is true regardless of whether the person completing the instruction had authority to complete it. Compare Section 8–206 and its Comment, dealing with blanks left upon issue.

2. Subsection (b) makes clear that the originator of an instruction, like the indorser of a security certificate, does not warrant that the issuer will honor the underlying obligation, but does make warranties as a transferor under Section 8–108.

Definitional Cross References:

"Appropriate person". Section 8–107.
"Instruction". Section 8–102(a)(12).
"Issuer". Section 8–201.

§ 8–306. Effect of Guaranteeing Signature, Indorsement, or Instruction.

(a) A person who guarantees a signature of an indorser of a security certificate warrants that at the time of signing:

(1) the signature was genuine;

(2) the signer was an appropriate person to indorse, or if the signature is by an agent, the agent had actual authority to act on behalf of the appropriate person; and

(3) the signer had legal capacity to sign.

(b) A person who guarantees a signature of the originator of an instruction warrants that at the time of signing:

(1) the signature was genuine;

(2) the signer was an appropriate person to originate the instruction, or if the signature is by an agent, the agent had actual authority to act on behalf of the appropriate person, if the person specified in the instruction as the registered owner was, in fact, the registered owner, as to which fact the signature guarantor does not make a warranty; and

(3) the signer had legal capacity to sign.

(c) A person who specially guarantees the signature of an originator of an instruction makes the warranties of a signature guarantor under subsection (b) and also warrants that at the time the instruction is presented to the issuer:

(1) the person specified in the instruction as the registered owner of the uncertificated security will be the registered owner; and

(2) the transfer of the uncertificated security requested in the instruction will be registered by the issuer free from all liens, security interests, restrictions, and claims other than those specified in the instruction.

(d) A guarantor under subsections (a) and (b) or a special guarantor under subsection (c) does not otherwise warrant the rightfulness of the transfer.

(e) A person who guarantees an indorsement of a security certificate makes the warranties of a signature guarantor under subsection (a) and also warrants the rightfulness of the transfer in all respects.

(f) A person who guarantees an instruction requesting the transfer of an uncertificated security makes the warranties of a special signature guarantor under subsection (c) and also warrants the rightfulness of the transfer in all respects.

(g) An issuer may not require a special guaranty of signature, a guaranty of indorsement, or a guaranty of instruction as a condition to registration of transfer.

(h) The warranties under this section are made to a person taking or dealing with the security in reliance on the guaranty, and the guarantor is liable to the person for loss resulting from their breach. An indorser or originator of an instruction whose signature, indorsement, or instruction has been guaranteed is liable to a guarantor for any loss suffered by the guarantor as a result of breach of the warranties of the guarantor.

Official Comment

1. Subsection (a) provides that a guarantor of the signature of the indorser of a security certificate warrants that the signature is genuine, that the signer is an appropriate person or has actual authority to indorse on behalf of the appropriate person, and that the signer has legal capacity. Subsection (b) provides similar, though not identical, warranties for the guarantor of a signature of the originator of an instruction for transfer of an uncertificated security.

Appropriate person is defined in Section 8–107(a) to include a successor or person who has power under other law to act for a person who is deceased or lacks capacity. Thus if a certificate registered in the name of Mary Roe is indorsed by Jane Doe as executor of Mary Roe, a guarantor of the signature of Jane Doe warrants that she has power to act as executor.

Although the definition of appropriate person in Section 8–107(a) does not itself include an agent, an indorsement by an agent is effective under Section 8–107(b) if the agent has authority to act for the appropriate person. Accordingly, this section provides an explicit warranty of authority for agents.

2. The rationale of the principle that a signature guarantor warrants the authority of the signer, rather than simply the genuineness of the signature, was explained in the leading case of *Jennie Clarkson Home for Children v. Missouri, K. & T.R. Co.*, 182 N.Y. 47, 74 N.E. 571, 70 A.L.R. 787 (1905), which dealt with a guaranty of the signature of a person indorsing on behalf of a corporation. "If stock is held by an individual who is executing a power of attorney for its transfer, the member of the exchange who signs as a witness thereto guaranties not only the genuineness of the signature affixed to the power of attorney, but that the person signing is the individual in whose name the stock stands. With reference to stock standing in the name of a corporation, which can only sign a power of attorney through its authorized officers or agents, a different situation is presented. If the witnessing of the signature of the corporation is only that of the signature of a person who signs for the corporation, then the guaranty is of no value, and there is nothing to protect purchasers or the companies who are called

upon to issue new stock in the place of that transferred from the frauds of persons who have signed the names of corporations without authority. If such is the only effect of the guaranty, purchasers and transfer agents must first go to the corporation in whose name the stock stands and ascertain whether the individual who signed the power of attorney had authority to do so. This will require time, and in many cases will necessitate the postponement of the completion of the purchase by the payment of the money until the facts can be ascertained. The broker who is acting for the owner has an opportunity to become acquainted with his customer, and may readily before sale ascertain, in case of a corporation, the name of the officer who is authorized to execute the power of attorney. It was therefore, we think, the purpose of the rule to cast upon the broker who witnesses the signature the duty of ascertaining whether the person signing the name of the corporation had authority to do so, and making the witness a guarantor that it is the signature of the corporation in whose name the stock stands."

3. Subsection (b) sets forth the warranties that can reasonably be expected from the guarantor of the signature of the originator of an instruction, who, though familiar with the signer, does not have any evidence that the purported owner is in fact the owner of the subject uncertificated security. This is in contrast to the position of the person guaranteeing a signature on a certificate who can see a certificate in the signer's possession in the name of or indorsed to the signer or in blank. Thus, the warranty in paragraph (2) of subsection (b) is expressly conditioned on the actual registration's conforming to that represented by the originator. If the signer purports to be the owner, the guarantor under paragraph (2), warrants only the identity of the signer. If, however, the signer is acting in a representative capacity, the guarantor warrants both the signer's identity and authority to act for the purported owner. The issuer needs no warranty as to the facts of registration because those facts can be ascertained from the issuer's own records.

4. Subsection (c) sets forth a "special guaranty of signature" under which the guarantor additionally warrants both registered ownership and freedom from undisclosed defects of record. The guarantor of the signature of an indorser of a security certificate effectively makes these warranties to a purchaser for value on the evidence of a clean certificate issued in the name of the indorser, indorsed to the indorser or indorsed in blank. By specially guaranteeing under subsection (c), the guarantor warrants that the instruction will, when presented to the issuer, result in

the requested registration free from defects not specified.

5. Subsection (d) makes clear that the warranties of a signature guarantor are limited to those specified in this section and do not include a general warranty of rightfulness. On the other hand subsections (e) and (f) provide that a person guaranteeing an indorsement or an instruction does warrant that the transfer is rightful in all respects.

6. Subsection (g) makes clear what can be inferred from the combination of Sections 8–401 and 8–402, that the issuer may not require as a condition to transfer a guaranty of the indorsement or instruction nor may it require a special signature guaranty.

7. Subsection (h) specifies to whom the warranties in this section run, and also provides that a person who gives a guaranty under this section has an action against the indorser or originator for any loss suffered by the guarantor.

Definitional Cross References:

"Appropriate person". Section 8–107.
"Genuine". Section 1–201(18).
"Indorsement". Section 8–102(a)(11).
"Instruction". Section 8–102(a)(12).
"Issuer". Section 8–201.
"Security certificate". Section 8–102(a)(16).
"Uncertificated security". Section 8–102(a)(18).

§ 8–307. Purchaser's Right to Requisites for Registration of Transfer.

Unless otherwise agreed, the transferor of a security on due demand shall supply the purchaser with proof of authority to transfer or with any other requisite necessary to obtain registration of the transfer of the security, but if the transfer is not for value, a transferor need not comply unless the purchaser pays the necessary expenses. If the transferor fails within a reasonable time to comply with the demand, the purchaser may reject or rescind the transfer.

Official Comment

1. Because registration of the transfer of a security is a matter of vital importance, a purchaser is here provided with the means of obtaining such formal requirements for registration as signature guaranties, proof of authority, transfer tax stamps and the like. The transferor is the one in a position to supply most conveniently whatever documentation may be requisite for registration of transfer, and the duty to do so upon demand within a reasonable time is here stated affirmatively. If an essential item is peculiarly within the

province of the transferor so that the transferor is the only one who can obtain it, the purchaser may specifically enforce the right to obtain it. Compare Section 8–304(d). If a transfer is not for value the transferor need not pay expenses.

2. If the transferor's duty is not performed the transferee may reject or rescind the contract to trans-fer. The transferee is not bound to do so. An action for damages for breach of contract may be preferred.

Definitional Cross References:

"Purchaser". Sections 1–201(33) & 8–116.
"Security". Section 8–102(a)(15).
"Value". Sections 1–201(44) & 8–116.

PART 4

REGISTRATION

§ 8–401. Duty of Issuer to Register Transfer.

(a) If a certificated security in registered form is presented to an issuer with a request to register transfer or an instruction is presented to an issuer with a request to register transfer of an uncertificated security, the issuer shall register the transfer as requested if:

(1) under the terms of the security the person seeking registration of transfer is eligible to have the security registered in its name;

(2) the indorsement or instruction is made by the appropriate person or by an agent who has actual authority to act on behalf of the appropriate person;

(3) reasonable assurance is given that the indorsement or instruction is genuine and authorized (Section 8–402);

(4) any applicable law relating to the collection of taxes has been complied with;

(5) the transfer does not violate any restriction on transfer imposed by the issuer in accordance with Section 8–204;

(6) a demand that the issuer not register transfer has not become effective under Section 8–403, or the issuer has complied with Section 8–403(b) but no legal process or indemnity bond is obtained as provided in Section 8–403(d); and

(7) the transfer is in fact rightful or is to a protected purchaser.

(b) If an issuer is under a duty to register a transfer of a security, the issuer is liable to a person presenting a certificated security or an instruction for registration or to the person's principal for loss resulting from unreasonable delay in registration or failure or refusal to register the transfer.

Official Comment

1. This section states the duty of the issuer to register transfers. A duty exists only if certain preconditions exist. If any of the preconditions do not exist, there is no duty to register transfer. If an indorsement on a security certificate is a forgery, there is no duty. If an instruction to transfer an uncertificated security is not originated by an appropriate person, there is no duty. If there has not been compliance with applicable tax laws, there is no duty. If a security certificate is properly indorsed but nevertheless the transfer is in fact wrongful, there is no duty unless the transfer is to a protected purchaser (and the other preconditions exist).

This section does not constitute a mandate that the issuer must establish that all preconditions are met before the issuer registers a transfer. The issuer may waive the reasonable assurances specified in paragraph (a)(3). If it has confidence in the responsibility of the persons requesting transfer, it may ignore questions of compliance with tax laws. Although an issuer has no duty if the transfer is wrongful, the issuer has no duty to inquire into adverse claims, see Section 8–404.

2. By subsection (b) the person entitled to registration may not only compel it but may hold the issuer liable in damages for unreasonable delay.

3. Section 8–201(c) provides that with respect to registration of transfer, "issuer" means the person on whose behalf transfer books are maintained. Transfer agents, registrars or the like within the scope of their respective functions have rights and duties under this Part similar to those of the issuer. See Section 8–407.

Definitional Cross References:

"Appropriate person". Section 8–107.
"Certificated security". Section 8–102(a)(4).

"Genuine". Section 1–201(18).
"Indorsement". Section 8–102(a)(11).
"Instruction". Section 8–102(a)(12).
"Issuer". Section 8–201.
"Protected purchaser". Section 8–303.
"Registered form". Section 8–102(a)(13).
"Uncertificated security". Section 8–102(a)(18).

§ 8–402. Assurance that Indorsement or Instruction is Effective.

(a) An issuer may require the following assurance that each necessary indorsement or each instruction is genuine and authorized:

(1) in all cases, a guaranty of the signature of the person making an indorsement or originating an instruction including, in the case of an instruction, reasonable assurance of identity;

(2) if the indorsement is made or the instruction is originated by an agent, appropriate assurance of actual authority to sign;

(3) if the indorsement is made or the instruction is originated by a fiduciary pursuant to Section 8–107(a)(4) or (a)(5), appropriate evidence of appointment or incumbency;

(4) if there is more than one fiduciary, reasonable assurance that all who are required to sign have done so; and

(5) if the indorsement is made or the instruction is originated by a person not covered by another provision of this subsection, assurance appropriate to the case corresponding as nearly as may be to the provisions of this subsection.

(b) An issuer may elect to require reasonable assurance beyond that specified in this section.

(c) In this section:

(1) "Guaranty of the signature" means a guaranty signed by or on behalf of a person reasonably believed by the issuer to be responsible. An issuer may adopt standards with respect to responsibility if they are not manifestly unreasonable.

(2) "Appropriate evidence of appointment or incumbency" means:

(i) in the case of a fiduciary appointed or qualified by a court, a certificate issued by or under the direction or supervision of the court or an officer thereof and dated within 60 days before the date of presentation for transfer; or

(ii) in any other case, a copy of a document showing the appointment or a certificate issued by or on behalf of a person reasonably believed by an issuer to be responsible or, in the absence of that document or certificate, other evidence the issuer reasonably considers appropriate.

Official Comment

1. An issuer is absolutely liable for wrongful registration of transfer if the indorsement or instruction is ineffective. See Section 8–404. Accordingly, an issuer is entitled to require such assurance as is reasonable under the circumstances that all necessary indorsements are effective, and thus to minimize its risk. This section establishes the requirements the issuer may make in terms of documentation which, except in the rarest of instances, should be easily furnished. Subsection (b) provides that an issuer may require additional assurances if that requirement is reasonable under the circumstances, but if the issuer demands more than reasonable assurance that the instruction or the necessary indorsements are genuine and authorized, the presenter may refuse the demand and sue for improper refusal to register. Section 8–401(b).

2. Under subsection (a)(1), the issuer may require in all cases a guaranty of signature. See Section 8–306. When an instruction is presented the issuer always may require reasonable assurance as to the identity of the originator. Subsection (c) allows the issuer to require that the person making these guaranties be one reasonably believed to be responsible, and the issuer may adopt standards of responsibility which are not manifestly unreasonable. Regulations under the federal securities laws, however, place limits on the requirements transfer agents may impose concerning the responsibility of eligible signature guarantors. See 17 CFR 240.17Ad–15.

3. This section, by paragraphs (2) through (5) of subsection (a), permits the issuer to seek confirmation that the indorsement or instruction is genuine and authorized. The permitted methods act as a double check on matters which are within the warranties of the signature guarantor. See Section 8–306. Thus, an agent may be required to submit a power of attorney, a corporation to submit a certified resolution evidencing the authority of its signing officer to sign, an executor or administrator to submit the usual "shortform certificate," etc. But failure of a fiduciary to obtain court approval of the transfer or to comply with other re-

quirements does not make the fiduciary's signature ineffective. Section 8–107(c). Hence court orders and other controlling instruments are omitted from subsection (a).

Subsection (a)(3) authorizes the issuer to require "appropriate evidence" of appointment or incumbency, and subsection (c) indicates what evidence will be "appropriate". In the case of a fiduciary appointed or qualified by a court that evidence will be a court certificate dated within sixty days before the date of presentation, subsection (c)(2)(i). Where the fiduciary is not appointed or qualified by a court, as in the case of a successor trustee, subsection (c)(2)(ii) applies. In that case, the issuer may require a copy of a trust instrument or other document showing the appointment, or it may require the certificate of a responsible person. In the absence of such a document or certificate, it may require other appropriate evidence. If the security is registered in the name of the fiduciary as such, the person's signature is effective even though the person is no longer serving in that capacity, see Section 8–107(d), hence no evidence of incumbency is needed.

4. Circumstances may indicate that a necessary signature was unauthorized or was not that of an appropriate person. Such circumstances would be ignored at risk of absolute liability. To minimize that risk the issuer may properly exercise the option given by subsection (b) to require assurance beyond that specified in subsection (a). On the other hand, the facts at hand may reflect only on the rightfulness of the transfer. Such facts do not create a duty of inquiry, because the issuer is not liable to an adverse claimant unless the claimant obtains legal process. See Section 8–404.

Definitional Cross References:

"Appropriate person". Section 8–107.
"Genuine". Section 1–201(18).
"Indorsement". Section 8–102(a)(11).
"Instruction". Section 8–102(a)(12).
"Issuer". Section 8–201.

§ 8–403. Demand that Issuer Not Register Transfer.

(a) A person who is an appropriate person to make an indorsement or originate an instruction may demand that the issuer not register transfer of a security by communicating to the issuer a notification that identifies the registered owner and the issue of which the security is a part and provides an address for communications directed to the person making the demand. The demand is effective only if it is received by the issuer at a time and in a manner affording the issuer reasonable opportunity to act on it.

(b) If a certificated security in registered form is presented to an issuer with a request to register transfer or an instruction is presented to an issuer with a request to register transfer of an uncertificated security after a demand that the issuer not register transfer has become effective, the issuer shall promptly communicate to (i) the person who initiated the demand at the address provided in the demand and (ii) the person who presented the security for registration of transfer or initiated the instruction requesting registration of transfer a notification stating that:

(1) the certificated security has been presented for registration of transfer or the instruction for registration of transfer of the uncertificated security has been received;

(2) a demand that the issuer not register transfer had previously been received; and

(3) the issuer will withhold registration of transfer for a period of time stated in the notification in order to provide the person who initiated the demand an opportunity to obtain legal process or an indemnity bond.

(c) The period described in subsection (b)(3) may not exceed 30 days after the date of communication of the notification. A shorter period may be specified by the issuer if it is not manifestly unreasonable.

(d) An issuer is not liable to a person who initiated a demand that the issuer not register transfer for any loss the person suffers as a result of registration of a transfer pursuant to an effective indorsement or instruction if the person who initiated the demand does not, within the time stated in the issuer's communication, either:

(1) obtain an appropriate restraining order, injunction, or other process from a court of competent jurisdiction enjoining the issuer from registering the transfer; or

(2) file with the issuer an indemnity bond, sufficient in the issuer's judgment to protect the issuer and any transfer agent, registrar, or other agent of the issuer involved from any loss it or they may suffer by refusing to register the transfer.

(e) This section does not relieve an issuer from liability for registering transfer pursuant to an indorsement or instruction that was not effective.

Official Comment

1. The general rule under this Article is that if there has been an effective indorsement or instruction, a person who contends that registration of the transfer would be wrongful should not be able to interfere with the registration process merely by sending notice of the assertion to the issuer. Rather, the claimant must obtain legal process. See Section 8–404. Section 8–403 is an exception to this general rule. It permits the registered owner—but not third parties—to demand that the issuer not register a transfer.

2. This section is intended to alleviate the problems faced by registered owners of certificated securities who lose or misplace their certificates. A registered owner who realizes that a certificate may have been lost or stolen should promptly report that fact to the issuer, lest the owner be precluded from asserting a claim for wrongful registration. See Section 8–406. The usual practice of issuers and transfer agents is that when a certificate is reported as lost, the owner is notified that a replacement can be obtained if the owner provides an indemnity bond. See Section 8–405. If the registered owner does not plan to transfer the securities, the owner might choose not to obtain a replacement, particularly if the owner suspects that the certificate has merely been misplaced.

Under this section, the owner's notification that the certificate has been lost would constitute a demand that the issuer not register transfer. No indemnity bond or legal process is necessary. If the original certificate is presented for registration of transfer, the issuer is required to notify the registered owner of that fact, and defer registration of transfer for a stated period. In order to prevent undue delay in the process of registration, the stated period may not exceed thirty days. This gives the registered owner an opportunity to either obtain legal process or post an indemnity bond and thereby prevent the issuer from registering transfer.

3. Subsection (e) makes clear that this section does not relieve an issuer from liability for registering a transfer pursuant to an ineffective indorsement. An issuer's liability for wrongful registration in such cases does not depend on the presence or absence of notice that the indorsement was ineffective. Registered owners who are confident that they neither indorsed the certificates, nor did anything that would preclude them from denying the effectiveness of another's indorsement, see Sections 8–107(b) and 8–406, might prefer to pursue their rights against the issuer for wrongful registration rather than take advantage of the opportunity to post a bond or seek a restraining order when notified by the issuer under this section that their lost certificates have been presented for registration in apparently good order.

Definitional Cross References:

"Appropriate person". Section 8–107.
"Certificated security". Section 8–102(a)(4).
"Communicate". Section 8–102(a)(6).
"Effective". Section 8–107.
"Indorsement". Section 8–102(a)(11).
"Instruction". Section 8–102(a)(12).
"Issuer". Section 8–201.
"Registered form". Section 8–102(a)(13).
"Uncertificated security". Section 8–102(a)(18).

§ 8–404. Wrongful Registration.

(a) Except as otherwise provided in Section 8–406, an issuer is liable for wrongful registration of transfer if the issuer has registered a transfer of a security to a person not entitled to it, and the transfer was registered:

(1) pursuant to an ineffective indorsement or instruction;

(2) after a demand that the issuer not register transfer became effective under Section 8–403(a) and the issuer did not comply with Section 8–403(b);

(3) after the issuer had been served with an injunction, restraining order, or other legal process enjoining it from registering the transfer, issued by a court of competent jurisdiction, and the issuer had a reasonable opportunity to act on the injunction, restraining order, or other legal process; or

(4) by an issuer acting in collusion with the wrongdoer.

(b) An issuer that is liable for wrongful registration of transfer under subsection (a) on demand shall provide the person entitled to the security with a like certificated or uncertificated security, and any payments or distributions that the person did not receive as a result of the wrongful registration. If an overissue would result, the issuer's liability to provide the person with a like security is governed by Section 8–210.

(c) Except as otherwise provided in subsection (a) or in a law relating to the collection of taxes, an issuer is not liable to an owner or other person suffering loss as a result of the registration of a transfer of a security if registration was made pursuant to an effective indorsement or instruction.

Official Comment

1. Subsection (a)(1) provides that an issuer is liable if it registers transfer pursuant to an indorsement or instruction that was not effective. For example, an issuer that registers transfer on a forged indorsement is liable to the registered owner. The fact that the issuer had no reason to suspect that the indorsement was forged or that the issuer obtained the ordinary assurances under Section 8–402 does not relieve the issuer from liability. The reason that issuers obtain signature guaranties and other assurances is that they are liable for wrongful registration.

Subsection (b) specifies the remedy for wrongful registration. Pre–Code cases established the registered owner's right to receive a new security where the issuer had wrongfully registered a transfer, but some cases also allowed the registered owner to elect between an equitable action to compel issue of a new security and an action for damages. Cf. *Casper v. Kalt–Zimmers Mfg. Co.*, 159 Wis. 517, 149 N.W. 754 (1914). Article 8 does not allow such election. The true owner of a certificated security is required to take a new security except where an overissue would result and a similar security is not reasonably available for purchase. See Section 8–210. The true owner of an uncertificated security is entitled and required to take restoration of the records to their proper state, with a similar exception for overissue.

2. Read together, subsections (c) and (a) have the effect of providing that an issuer has no duties to an adverse claimant unless the claimant serves legal process on the issuer to enjoin registration. Issuers, or their transfer agents, perform a record-keeping function for the direct holding system that is analogous to the functions performed by clearing corporations and securities intermediaries in the indirect holding system. This section applies to the record-keepers for the direct holding system the same standard that Section 8–115 applies to the record-keepers for the indirect holding system. Thus, issuers are not liable to adverse claimants merely on the basis of notice. As in the case of the analogous rules for the indirect holding system, the policy of this section is to protect the right of investors to have their securities transfers processed without the disruption or delay that might result if the record-keepers risked liability to third parties. It would be undesirable to apply different standards to the direct and indirect holding systems, since doing so might operate as a disincentive to the development of a book-entry direct holding system.

3. This section changes prior law under which an issuer could be held liable, even though it registered transfer on an effective indorsement or instruction, if the issuer had in some fashion been notified that the transfer might be wrongful against a third party, and the issuer did not appropriately discharge its duty to inquire into the adverse claim. See Section 8–403 (1978).

The rule of former Section 8–403 was anomalous inasmuch as Section 8–207 provides that the issuer is entitled to "treat the registered owner as the person exclusively entitled to vote, receive notifications, and otherwise exercise all the rights and powers of an owner." Under Section 8–207, the fact that a third person notifies the issuer of a claim does not preclude the issuer from treating the registered owner as the person entitled to the security. See *Kerrigan v. American Orthodontics Corp.*, 960 F.2d 43 (7th Cir.1992). The change made in the present version of Section 8–404 ensures that the rights of registered owners and the duties of issuers with respect to registration of transfer will be protected against third-party interference in the same fashion as other rights of registered ownership.

Definitional Cross References:

"Certificated security". Section 8–102(a)(4).
"Effective". Section 8–107.
"Indorsement". Section 8–102(a)(11).
"Instruction". Section 8–102(a)(12).
"Issuer". Section 8–201.
"Security". Section 8–102(a)(15).
"Uncertificated security". Section 8–102(a)(18).

§ 8–405. Replacement of Lost, Destroyed, or Wrongfully Taken Security Certificate.

(a) If an owner of a certificated security, whether in registered or bearer form, claims that the certificate has been lost, destroyed, or wrongfully taken, the issuer shall issue a new certificate if the owner:

(1) so requests before the issuer has notice that the certificate has been acquired by a protected purchaser;

(2) files with the issuer a sufficient indemnity bond; and

(3) satisfies other reasonable requirements imposed by the issuer.

(b) If, after the issue of a new security certificate, a protected purchaser of the original certificate presents it for registration of transfer, the issuer shall register the transfer unless an overissue would result. In that case, the issuer's liability is governed by Section 8–210. In addition to any rights on the indemnity bond, an issuer may recover the new certificate from a person to whom it was issued or any person taking under that person, except a protected purchaser.

Official Comment

1. This section enables the owner to obtain a replacement of a lost, destroyed or stolen certificate, provided that reasonable requirements are satisfied and a sufficient indemnity bond supplied.

2. Where an "original" security certificate has reached the hands of a protected purchaser, the registered owner—who was in the best position to prevent the loss, destruction or theft of the security certificate—is now deprived of the new security certificate issued as a replacement. This changes the pre-UCC law under which the original certificate was ineffective after the issue of a replacement except insofar as it might represent an action for damages in the hands of a purchaser for value without notice. *Keller v. Eureka Brick Mach. Mfg. Co.,* 43 Mo.App. 84, 11 L.R.A. 472 (1890). Where both the original and the new certificate have reached protected purchasers the issuer is required to honor both certificates unless an overissue would result and the security is not reasonably available for purchase. See Section 8–210. In the latter case alone, the protected purchaser of the original certificate is relegated to an action for damages. In either case, the issuer itself may recover on the indemnity bond.

Definitional Cross References:

"Bearer form". Section 8–102(a)(2).
"Certificated security". Section 8–102(a)(4).
"Issuer". Section 8–201.
"Notice". Section 1–201(25).
"Overissue". Section 8–210.
"Protected purchaser". Section 8–303.
"Registered form". Section 8–102(a)(13).
"Security certificate". Section 8–102(a)(16).

§ 8–406. Obligation to Notify Issuer of Lost, Destroyed, or Wrongfully Taken Security Certificate.

If a security certificate has been lost, apparently destroyed, or wrongfully taken, and the owner fails to notify the issuer of that fact within a reasonable time after the owner has notice of it and the issuer registers a transfer of the security before receiving notification, the owner may not assert against the issuer a claim for registering the transfer under Section 8–404 or a claim to a new security certificate under Section 8–405.

Official Comment

An owner who fails to notify the issuer within a reasonable time after the owner knows or has reason to know of the loss or theft of a security certificate is estopped from asserting the ineffectiveness of a forged or unauthorized indorsement and the wrongfulness of the registration of the transfer. If the lost certificate was indorsed by the owner, then the registration of the transfer was not wrongful under Section 8–404, unless the owner made an effective demand that the issuer not register transfer under Section 8–403.

Definitional Cross References:

"Issuer". Section 8–201.
"Notify". Section 1–201(25).
"Security certificate". Section 8–102(a)(16).

§ 8–407. Authenticating Trustee, Transfer Agent, and Registrar.

A person acting as authenticating trustee, transfer agent, registrar, or other agent for an issuer in the registration of a transfer of its securities, in the issue of new security certificates or uncertificated securities, or in the cancellation of surrendered security certificates has the same obligation to the holder or owner of a certificated or uncertificated security with regard to the particular functions performed as the issuer has in regard to those functions.

Official Comment

1. Transfer agents, registrars, and the like are here expressly held liable both to the issuer and to the owner for wrongful refusal to register a transfer as well as for wrongful registration of a transfer in any case within the scope of their respective functions where the issuer would itself be liable. Those cases which have regarded these parties solely as agents of

the issuer and have therefore refused to recognize their liability to the owner for mere nonfeasance, i.e., refusal to register a transfer, are rejected. *Hulse v. Consolidated Quicksilver Mining Corp.,* 65 Idaho 768, 154 P.2d 149 (1944); *Nicholson v. Morgan,* 119 Misc. 309, 196 N.Y.Supp. 147 (1922); *Lewis v. Hargadine–McKittrick Dry Goods Co.,* 305 Mo. 396, 274 S.W. 1041 (1924).

2. The practice frequently followed by authenticating trustees of issuing certificates of indebtedness rather than authenticating duplicate certificates where securities have been lost or stolen became obsolete in

view of the provisions of Section 8–405, which makes express provision for the issue of substitute securities. It is not a breach of trust or lack of due diligence for trustees to authenticate new securities. Cf. *Switzerland General Ins. Co. v. N.Y.C. & H.R.R. Co.,* 152 App.Div. 70, 136 N.Y.S. 726 (1912).

Definitional Cross References:

"Certificated security". Section 8–102(a)(4).
"Issuer". Section 8–201.
"Security". Section 8–102(a)(15).
"Security certificate". Section 8–102(a)(16).
"Uncertificated security". Section 8–102(a)(18).

PART 5

SECURITY ENTITLEMENTS

§ 8–501. Securities Account; Acquisition of Security Entitlement from Securities Intermediary.

(a) "Securities account" means an account to which a financial asset is or may be credited in accordance with an agreement under which the person maintaining the account undertakes to treat the person for whom the account is maintained as entitled to exercise the rights that comprise the financial asset.

(b) Except as otherwise provided in subsections (d) and (e), a person acquires a security entitlement if a securities intermediary:

(1) indicates by book entry that a financial asset has been credited to the person's securities account;

(2) receives a financial asset from the person or acquires a financial asset for the person and, in either case, accepts it for credit to the person's securities account; or

(3) becomes obligated under other law, regulation, or rule to credit a financial asset to the person's securities account.

(c) If a condition of subsection (b) has been met, a person has a security entitlement even though the securities intermediary does not itself hold the financial asset.

(d) If a securities intermediary holds a financial asset for another person, and the financial asset is registered in the name of, payable to the order of, or specially indorsed to the other person, and has not been indorsed to the securities intermediary or in blank, the other person is

treated as holding the financial asset directly rather than as having a security entitlement with respect to the financial asset.

(e) Issuance of a security is not establishment of a security entitlement.

Official Comment

1. Part 5 rules apply to security entitlements, and Section 8–501(b) provides that a person has a security entitlement when a financial asset has been credited to a "securities account." Thus, the term "securities account" specifies the type of arrangements between institutions and their customers that are covered by Part 5. A securities account is a consensual arrangement in which the intermediary undertakes to treat the customer as entitled to exercise the rights that comprise the financial asset. The consensual aspect is covered by the requirement that the account be established pursuant to agreement. The term agreement is used in the broad sense defined in Section 1–201(3). There is no requirement that a formal or written agreement be signed.

As the securities business is presently conducted, several significant relationships clearly fall within the definition of a securities account, including the relationship between a clearing corporation and its participants, a broker and customers who leave securities with the broker, and a bank acting as securities custodian and its custodial customers. Given the enormous variety of arrangements concerning securities that exist today, and the certainty that new arrangements will evolve in the future, it is not possible to specify all of the arrangements to which the term does and does not apply.

Whether an arrangement between a firm and another person concerning a security or other financial asset is a "securities account" under this Article depends on whether the firm has undertaken to treat the other person as entitled to exercise the rights that comprise the security or other financial asset. Section 1–102, however, states the fundamental principle of interpretation that the Code provisions should be construed and applied to promote their underlying purposes and policies. Thus, the question whether a given arrangement is a securities account should be decided not by dictionary analysis of the words of the definition taken out of context, but by considering whether it promotes the objectives of Article 8 to include the arrangement within the term securities account.

The effect of concluding that an arrangement is a securities account is that the rules of Part 5 apply. Accordingly, the definition of "securities account" must be interpreted in light of the substantive provisions in Part 5, which describe the core features of the type of relationship for which the commercial law rules of Revised Article 8 concerning security entitlements were designed. There are many arrangements between institutions and other persons concerning securities or other financial assets which do not fall within the definition of "securities account" because the institutions have not undertaken to treat the other persons as entitled to exercise the ordinary rights of an entitlement holder specified in the Part 5 rules. For example, the term securities account does not cover the relationship between a bank and its depositors or the relationship between a trustee and the beneficiary of an ordinary trust, because those are not relationships in which the holder of a financial asset has undertaken to treat the other as entitled to exercise the rights that comprise the financial asset in the fashion contemplated by the Part 5 rules.

In short, the primary factor in deciding whether an arrangement is a securities account is whether application of the Part 5 rules is consistent with the expectations of the parties to the relationship. Relationships not governed by Part 5 may be governed by other parts of Article 8 if the relationship gives rise to a new security, or may be governed by other law entirely.

2. Subsection (b) of this section specifies what circumstances give rise to security entitlements. Paragraph (1) of subsection (b) sets out the most important rule. It turns on the intermediary's conduct, reflecting a basic operating assumption of the indirect holding system that once a securities intermediary has acknowledged that it is carrying a position in a financial asset for its customer or participant, the intermediary is obligated to treat the customer or participant as entitled to the financial asset. Paragraph (1) does not attempt to specify exactly what accounting, record-keeping, or information transmission steps suffice to indicate that the intermediary has credited the account. That is left to agreement, trade practice, or rule in order to provide the flexibility necessary to accommodate varying or changing accounting and information processing systems. The point of paragraph (1) is that once an intermediary has acknowledged that it is carrying a position for the customer or participant, the customer or participant has a security entitlement. The precise form in which the intermediary manifests that acknowledgment is left to private ordering.

Paragraph (2) of subsection (b) sets out a different operational test, turning not on the intermediary's accounting system but on the facts that accounting systems are supposed to represent. Under paragraph (b)(2) a person has a security entitlement if the intermediary has received and accepted a financial asset for credit to the account of its customer or participant. For example, if a customer of a broker or bank custodian delivers a security certificate in proper form to the broker or bank to be held in the customer's account, the customer acquires a security entitlement. Paragraph (b)(2) also covers circumstances in which the intermediary receives a financial asset from a third person for credit to the account of the customer or participant. Paragraph (b)(2) is not limited to circumstances in which the intermediary receives security certificates or other financial assets in physical form. Paragraph (b)(2) also covers circumstances in which the intermediary acquires a security entitlement with respect to a financial asset which is to be credited to the account of the intermediary's own customer. For example, if a customer transfers her account from Broker A to Broker B, she acquires security entitlements against Broker B once the clearing corporation has credited the positions to Broker B's account. It should be noted, however, that paragraph (b)(2) provides that a person acquires a security entitlement when the intermediary not only receives but also accepts the financial asset for credit to the account. This limitation is included to take account of the fact that there may be circumstances in which an intermediary has received a financial asset but is not willing to undertake the obligations that flow from establishing a security entitlement. For example, a security certificate which is sent to an intermediary may not be in proper form, or may represent a type of financial asset which the intermediary is not willing to carry for others. It should be noted that in all but extremely unusual cases, the circumstances covered by paragraph (2) will also be covered by paragraph (1), because the intermediary will have credited the positions to the customer's account.

Paragraph (3) of subsection (b) sets out a residual test, to avoid any implication that the failure of an intermediary to make the appropriate entries to credit a position to a customer's securities account would prevent the customer from acquiring the rights of an entitlement holder under Part 5. As is the case with the paragraph (2) test, the paragraph (3) test would not be needed for the ordinary cases, since they are covered by paragraph (1).

3. In a sense, Section 8–501(b) is analogous to the rules set out in the provisions of Sections 8–313(1)(d) and 8–320 of the prior version of Article 8 that specified what acts by a securities intermediary or clearing corporation sufficed as a transfer of securities held in fungible bulk. Unlike the prior version of Article 8, however, this section is not based on the idea that an entitlement holder acquires rights only by virtue of a "transfer" from the securities intermediary to the entitlement holder. In the indirect holding system, the significant fact is that the securities intermediary has undertaken to treat the customer as entitled to the financial asset. It is up to the securities intermediary to take the necessary steps to ensure that it will be able to perform its undertaking. It is, for example, entirely possible that a securities intermediary might make entries in a customer's account reflecting that customer's acquisition of a certain security at a time when the securities intermediary did not itself happen to hold any units of that security. The person from whom the securities intermediary bought the security might have failed to deliver and it might have taken some time to clear up the problem, or there may have been an operational gap in time between the crediting of a customer's account and the receipt of securities from another securities intermediary. The entitlement holder's rights against the securities intermediary do not depend on whether or when the securities intermediary acquired its interests. Subsection (c) is intended to make this point clear. Subsection (c) does not mean that the intermediary is free to create security entitlements without itself holding sufficient financial assets to satisfy its entitlement holders. The duty of a securities intermediary to maintain sufficient assets is governed by Section 8–504 and regulatory law. Subsection (c) is included only to make it clear the question whether a person has acquired a security entitlement does not depend on whether the intermediary has complied with that duty.

4. Part 5 of Article 8 sets out a carefully designed system of rules for the indirect holding system. Persons who hold securities through brokers or custodians have security entitlements that are governed by Part 5, rather than being treated as the direct holders of securities. Subsection (d) specifies the limited circumstance in which a customer who leaves a financial asset with a broker or other securities intermediary has a direct interest in the financial asset, rather than a security entitlement.

The customer can be a direct holder only if the security certificate, or other financial asset, is registered in the name of, payable to the order of, or specially indorsed to the customer, and has not been indorsed by the customer to the securities intermediary or in blank. The distinction between those circumstances where the customer can be treated as direct owner and those where the customer has a security entitlement is essentially the same as the distinction drawn under the federal bankruptcy code between customer name securities and customer property. The distinction does not turn on any form of physical identification or segregation. A customer who delivers certificates to a broker with blank indorsements or stock powers is not a direct holder but has a security entitlement, even though the broker holds those certificates in some form of separate safe-keeping arrangement for that particular customer. The customer remains the direct holder only if there is no indorsement or stock power so that further action by the customer is required to place the certificates in a form where they can be transferred by the broker.

The rule of subsection (d) corresponds to the rule set out in Section 8–301(a)(3) specifying when acquisition of possession of a certificate by a securities intermediary counts as "delivery" to the customer.

5. Subsection (e) is intended to make clear that Part 5 does not apply to an arrangement in which a security is issued representing an interest in underlying assets, as distinguished from arrangements in which the underlying assets are carried in a securities account. A common mechanism by which new financial instruments are devised is that a financial institution that holds some security, financial instrument, or pool thereof, creates interests in that asset or pool which are sold to others. In many such cases, the interests so created will fall within the definition of "security" in Section 8–102(a)(15). If so, then by virtue of subsection (e) of Section 8–501, the relationship between the institution that creates the interests and the persons who hold them is not a security entitlement to which the Part 5 rules apply. Accordingly, an arrangement such as an American depositary receipt facility which creates freely transferable interests in underlying securities will be issuance of a

security under Article 8 rather than establishment of a security entitlement to the underlying securities.

The subsection (e) rule can be regarded as an aspect of the definitional rules specifying the meaning of securities account and security entitlement. Among the key components of the definition of security in Section 8–102(a)(15) are the "transferability" and "divisibility" tests. Securities, in the Article 8 sense, are fungible interests or obligations that are intended to be tradable. The concept of security entitlement under Part 5 is quite different. A security entitlement is the package of rights that a person has against the person's own intermediary with respect to the positions carried in the person's securities account. That package of rights is not, as such, something that is traded. When a customer sells a security that she had held through a securities account, her security entitlement is terminated; when she buys a security that she will hold through her securities account, she acquires a security entitlement. In most cases, settlement of a securities trade will involve termination of one person's security entitlement and acquisition of a security entitlement by another person. That transaction, however, is not a "transfer" of the same entitlement from one person to another. That is not to say that an entitlement holder cannot transfer an interest in her security entitlement as such; granting a security interest in a security entitlement is such a transfer. On the other hand, the nature of a security entitlement is that the intermediary is undertaking duties only to the person identified as the entitlement holder.

Definitional Cross References:

"Financial asset". Section 8–102(a)(9).
"Indorsement". Section 8–102(a)(11).
"Securities intermediary". Section 8–102(a)(14).
"Security". Section 8–102(a)(15).
"Security entitlement". Section 8–102(a)(17).

§ 8–502. Assertion of Adverse Claim Against Entitlement Holder.

An action based on an adverse claim to a financial asset, whether framed in conversion, replevin, constructive trust, equitable lien, or other theory, may not be asserted against a person who acquires a security entitlement under Section 8–501 for value and without notice of the adverse claim.

Official Comment

1. The section provides investors in the indirect holding system with protection against adverse claims by specifying that no adverse claim can be asserted against a person who acquires a security entitlement under Section 8–501 for value and without notice of the adverse claim. It plays a role in the indirect holding system analogous to the rule of the direct holding system that protected purchasers take free from adverse claims (Section 8–303).

This section does not use the locution "takes free from adverse claims" because that could be confusing as applied to the indirect holding system. The nature of indirect holding system is that an entitlement holder has an interest in common with others who hold positions in the same financial asset through the same intermediary. Thus, a particular entitlement holder's interest in the financial assets held by its intermediary is necessarily "subject to" the interests of others. See Section 8–503. The rule stated in this section might have been expressed by saying that a person who acquires a security entitlement under Section 8–501 for value and without notice of adverse claims takes "that security entitlement" free from adverse claims. That formulation has not been used, however, for fear that it would be misinterpreted as suggesting that the person acquires a right to the underlying financial assets that could not be affected by the competing rights of others claiming through common or higher tier intermediaries. A security entitlement is a complex bundle of rights. This section does not deal with the question of what rights are in the bundle. Rather, this section provides that once a person has acquired the bundle, someone else cannot take it away on the basis of assertion that the transaction in which the security entitlement was created involved a violation of the claimant's rights.

2. Because securities trades are typically settled on a net basis by book-entry movements, it would ordinarily be impossible for anyone to trace the path of any particular security, no matter how the interest of parties who hold through intermediaries is described. Suppose, for example, that S has a 1000 share position in XYZ common stock through an account with a broker, Able & Co. S's identical twin impersonates S and directs Able to sell the securities. That same day, B places an order with Baker & Co., to buy 1000 shares of XYZ common stock. Later, S discovers the wrongful act and seeks to recover "her shares." Even if S can show that, at the stage of the trade, her sell order was matched with B's buy order, that would not suffice to show that "her shares" went to B. Settlement between Able and Baker occurs on a net basis for all trades in XYZ that day; indeed Able's net position may have been such that it received rather than delivered shares in XYZ through the settlement system.

In the unlikely event that this was the only trade in XYZ common stock executed in the market that day, one could follow the shares from S's account to B's account. The plaintiff in an action in conversion or similar legal action to enforce a property interest must show that the defendant has an item of property that belongs to the plaintiff. In this example, B's security entitlement is not the same item of property that formerly was held by S, it is a new package of rights that B acquired against Baker under Section 8–501. Principles of equitable remedies might, however, provide S with a basis for contending that if the position B received was the traceable product of the wrongful taking of S's property by S's twin, a constructive trust should be imposed on B's property in favor of S. See G. Palmer, The Law of Restitution § 2.14. Section 8–502 ensures that no such claims can be asserted against a person, such as B in this example, who acquires a security entitlement under Section 8–501 for value and without notice, regardless of what theory of law or equity is used to describe the basis of the assertion of the adverse claim.

In the above example, S would ordinarily have no reason to pursue B unless Able is insolvent and S's claim will not be satisfied in the insolvency proceedings. Because S did not give an entitlement order for the disposition of her security entitlement, Able must recredit her account for the 1000 shares of XYZ common stock. See Section 8–507(b).

3. The following examples illustrate the operation of Section 8–502.

Example 1. Thief steals bearer bonds from Owner. Thief delivers the bonds to Broker for credit to Thief's securities account, thereby acquiring a security entitlement under Section 8–501(b). Under other law, Owner may have a claim to have a constructive trust imposed on the security entitlement as the traceable product of the bonds that Thief misappropriated. Because Thief was himself the wrongdoer, Thief obviously had notice of Owner's adverse claim. Accordingly, Section 8–502 does not preclude Owner from asserting an adverse claim against Thief.

Example 2. Thief steals bearer bonds from Owner. Thief owes a personal debt to Creditor. Creditor has a securities account with Broker. Thief agrees to transfer the bonds to Creditor as security for or in satisfaction of his debt to Creditor. Thief does so by sending the bonds to Broker for credit to Creditor's securities account. Creditor thereby acquires a security entitlement under Section 8–501(b). Under other law, Owner may have a claim to have a constructive trust imposed on the security entitle-

ment as the traceable product of the bonds that Thief misappropriated. Creditor acquired the security entitlement for value, since Creditor acquired it as security for or in satisfaction of Thief's debt to Creditor. See Section 1–201(44). If Creditor did not have notice of Owner's claim, Section 8–502 precludes any action by Owner against Creditor, whether framed in constructive trust or other theory. Section 8–105 specifies what counts as notice of an adverse claim.

Example 3. Father, as trustee for Son, holds XYZ Co. shares in a securities account with Able & Co. In violation of his fiduciary duties, Father sells the XYZ Co. shares and uses the proceeds for personal purposes. Father dies, and his estate is insolvent. Assume—implausibly—that Son is able to trace the XYZ Co. shares and show that the "same shares" ended up in Buyer's securities account with Baker & Co. Section 8–502 precludes any action by Son against Buyer, whether framed in constructive trust or other theory, provided that Buyer acquired the security entitlement for value and without notice of adverse claims.

Example 4. Debtor holds XYZ Co. shares in a securities account with Able & Co. As collateral for a loan from Bank, Debtor grants Bank a security interest in the security entitlement to the XYZ Co. shares. Bank perfects by a method which leaves Debtor with the ability to dispose of the shares. See Section 9–312. In violation of the security agreement, Debtor sells the XYZ Co. shares and absconds with the proceeds. Assume—implausibly—that Bank is able to trace the XYZ Co. shares and show that the "same shares" ended up in Buyer's securities account with Baker & Co. Section 8–502 precludes any action by Bank against Buyer, whether framed in constructive trust or other theory, provided that Buyer acquired the security entitlement for value and without notice of adverse claims.

Example 5. Debtor owns controlling interests in various public companies, including Acme and Ajax. Acme owns 60% of the stock of another public company, Beta. Debtor causes the Beta stock to be pledged to Lending Bank as collateral for Ajax's debt. Acme holds the Beta stock through an account with a securities custodian, C Bank, which in turn holds through Clearing Corporation. Lending Bank is also a Clearing Corporation participant. The pledge of the Beta stock is implemented by Acme instructing C Bank to instruct Clearing Corporation to debit C Bank's account and credit Lending Bank's account. Acme and Ajax both become insolvent. The Beta stock is still valuable. Acme's liquidator asserts that the pledge of the Beta stock for Ajax's debt was wrongful as against Acme and seeks to recover the Beta stock from Lending Bank. Because the pledge was implemented by an outright transfer into Lending Bank's account at Clearing Corporation, Lending Bank acquired a security entitlement to the Beta stock under Section 8–501. Lending Bank acquired the security entitlement for value, since it acquired it as security for a debt. See Section 1–201(44). If Lending Bank did not have notice of Acme's claim, Section 8–502 will preclude any action by Acme against Lending Bank, whether framed in constructive trust or other theory.

Example 6. Debtor grants Alpha Co. a security interest in a security entitlement that includes 1000 shares of XYZ Co. stock that Debtor holds through an account with Able & Co. Alpha also has an account with Able. Debtor instructs Able to transfer the shares to Alpha, and Able does so by crediting the shares to Alpha's account. Alpha has control of the 1000 shares under Section 8–106(d). (The facts to this point are identical to those in Section 8–106, Comment 4, Example 1, except that Alpha Co. was Alpha Bank.) Alpha next grants Beta Co. a security interest in the 1000 shares included in Alpha's security entitlement. See Section 9–207(c)(3). Alpha instructs Able to transfer the shares to Gamma Co., Beta's custodian. Able does so, and Gamma credits the 1000 shares to Beta's account. Beta now has control under Section 8–106(d). By virtue of Debtor's explicit permission or by virtue of the permission inherent in Debtor's creation of a security interest in favor of Alpha and Alpha's resulting power to grant a security interest under Section 9–207, Debtor has no adverse claim to assert against Beta, assuming implausibly that Debtor could "trace" an interest to the Gamma account. Moreover, even if Debtor did hold an adverse claim, if Beta did not have notice of Debtor's claim, Section 8–502 will preclude any action by Debtor against Beta, whether framed in constructive trust or other theory.

4. Although this section protects entitlement holders against adverse claims, it does not protect them against the risk that their securities intermediary will not itself have sufficient financial assets to satisfy the claims of all of its entitlement holders. Suppose that Customer A holds 1000 shares of XYZ Co. stock in an account with her broker, Able & Co. Able in turn holds 1000 shares of XYZ Co. through its account with Clearing Corporation, but has no other positions in XYZ Co. shares, either for other customers or for its own proprietary account. Customer B places an order with Able for the purchase of 1000 shares of XYZ Co.

stock, and pays the purchase price. Able credits B's account with a 1000 share position in XYZ Co. stock, but Able does not itself buy any additional XYZ Co. shares. Able fails, having only 1000 shares to satisfy the claims of A and B. Unless other insolvency law establishes a different distributional rule, A and B would share the 1000 shares held by Able pro rata, without regard to the time that their respective entitlements were established. See Section 8–503(b). Section 8–502 protects entitlement holders, such as A and B, against adverse claimants. In this case, however, the problem that A and B face is not that someone is trying to take away their entitlements, but that the entitlements are not worth what they thought. The only role that Section 8–502 plays in this case is to preclude any assertion that A has some form of claim against B by virtue of the fact that Able's establishment of an entitlement in favor of B diluted A's rights to the limited assets held by Able.

Definitional Cross References:

"Adverse claim". Section 8–102(a)(1).
"Financial asset". Section 8–102(a)(9).
"Notice of adverse claim". Section 8–105.
"Security entitlement". Section 8–102(a)(17).
"Value". Sections 1–201(44) & 8–116.

As amended in 1999.

§ **8–503. Property Interest of Entitlement Holder in Financial Asset Held By Securities Intermediary.**

(a) To the extent necessary for a securities intermediary to satisfy all security entitlements with respect to a particular financial asset, all interests in that financial asset held by the securities intermediary are held by the securities intermediary for the entitlement holders, are not property of the securities intermediary, and are not subject to claims of creditors of the securities intermediary, except as otherwise provided in Section 8–511.

(b) An entitlement holder's property interest with respect to a particular financial asset under subsection (a) is a pro rata property interest in all interests in that financial asset held by the securities intermediary, without regard to the time the entitlement holder acquired the security entitlement or the time the securities intermediary acquired the interest in that financial asset.

(c) An entitlement holder's property interest with respect to a particular financial asset under subsection (a) may be enforced against the securities intermediary only by exercise of the entitlement holder's rights under Sections 8–505 through 8–508.

(d) An entitlement holder's property interest with respect to a particular financial asset under subsection (a) may be enforced against a purchaser of the financial asset or interest therein only if:

(1) insolvency proceedings have been initiated by or against the securities intermediary;

(2) the securities intermediary does not have sufficient interests in the financial asset to satisfy the security entitlements of all of its entitlement holders to that financial asset;

(3) the securities intermediary violated its obligations under Section 8–504 by transferring the financial asset or interest therein to the purchaser; and

(4) the purchaser is not protected under subsection (e).

The trustee or other liquidator, acting on behalf of all entitlement holders having security entitlements with respect to a particular financial asset, may recover the financial asset, or interest therein, from the purchaser. If the trustee or other liquidator elects not to pursue that right, an entitlement holder whose security entitlement remains unsatisfied has the right to recover its interest in the financial asset from the purchaser.

(e) An action based on the entitlement holder's property interest with respect to a particular financial asset under subsection (a), whether framed in conversion, replevin, constructive trust, equitable lien, or other theory, may not be asserted against any purchaser of a financial asset or interest therein who gives value, obtains control, and does not act in collusion with the securities intermediary in violating the securities intermediary's obligations under Section 8–504.

Official Comment

1. This section specifies the sense in which a security entitlement is an interest in the property held by the securities intermediary. It expresses the ordinary understanding that securities that a firm holds for its customers are not general assets of the firm subject to the claims of creditors. Since securities intermediaries generally do not segregate securities in such fashion that one could identify particular securities as the ones held for customers, it would not be realistic for this section to state that "customers' securities" are not subject to creditors' claims. Rather subsection (a) provides that to the extent necessary to satisfy all customer claims, all units of that security held by the firm are held for the entitlement holders, are not property of the securities intermediary, and are not subject to creditors' claims, except as otherwise provided in Section 8–511.

An entitlement holder's property interest under this section is an interest with respect to a specific issue of securities or financial assets. For example, customers of a firm who have positions in XYZ common stock have security entitlements with respect to the XYZ common stock held by the intermediary, while other customers who have positions in ABC common stock have security entitlements with respect to the ABC common stock held by the intermediary.

Subsection (b) makes clear that the property interest described in subsection (a) is an interest held in common by all entitlement holders who have entitlements to a particular security or other financial asset. Temporal factors are irrelevant. One entitlement holder cannot claim that its rights to the assets held by the intermediary are superior to the rights of another entitlement holder by virtue of having acquired those rights before, or after, the other entitlement holder. Nor does it matter whether the intermediary had sufficient assets to satisfy all entitlement holders' claims at one point, but no longer does. Rather, all entitlement holders have a pro rata interest in whatever positions in that financial asset the intermediary holds.

Although this section describes the property interest of entitlement holders in the assets held by the intermediary, it does not necessarily determine how property held by a failed intermediary will be distributed in insolvency proceedings. If the intermediary fails and its affairs are being administered in an insolvency proceeding, the applicable insolvency law governs how the various parties having claims against the firm are treated. For example, the distributional rules for stockbroker liquidation proceedings under the Bankruptcy Code and Securities Investor Protection Act ("SIPA") provide that all customer property is distributed pro rata among all customers in proportion to the dollar value of their total positions, rather than dividing the property on an issue by issue basis. For intermediaries that are not subject to the Bankruptcy Code and SIPA, other insolvency law would determine what distributional rule is applied.

2. Although this section recognizes that the entitlement holders of a securities intermediary have a property interest in the financial assets held by the intermediary, the incidents of this property interest are established by the rules of Article 8, not by common law property concepts. The traditional Article 8 rules on certificated securities were based on the idea that a paper certificate could be regarded as a nearly complete reification of the underlying right. The rules on transfer and the consequences of wrongful transfer could then be written using the same basic concepts as the rules for physical chattels. A person's claim of ownership of a certificated security is a right to a specific identifiable physical object, and that right can be asserted against any person who ends up in possession of that physical certificate, unless cut off by the rules protecting purchasers for value without notice. Those concepts do not work for the indirect holding system. A security entitlement is not a claim to a specific identifiable thing; it is a package of rights and interests that a person has against the person's securities intermediary and the property held by the intermediary. The idea that discrete objects might be traced through the hands of different persons has no place in the Revised Article 8 rules for the indirect holding system. The fundamental principles of the indirect holding system rules are that an entitlement holder's own intermediary has the obligation to see to it that the entitlement holder receives all of the economic and corporate rights that comprise the financial asset, and that the entitlement holder can look only to that intermediary for performance of the obligations. The entitlement holder cannot assert rights directly against other persons, such as other intermediaries through whom the intermediary holds the positions, or third parties to whom the intermediary may have wrongfully transferred interests, except in extremely unusual circumstances where the third party was itself a participant in the wrongdoing. Subsections (c) through (e) reflect these fundamental principles.

Subsection (c) provides that an entitlement holder's property interest can be enforced against the intermediary only by exercise of the entitlement holder's rights under Sections 8–505 through 8–508. These are the provisions that set out the duty of an intermediary to see to it that the entitlement holder receives all of the economic and corporate rights that comprise the security. If the intermediary is in insolvency proceedings and can no longer perform in accordance with the ordinary Part 5 rules, the applicable insolvency law will determine how the intermediary's assets are to be distributed.

Subsections (d) and (e) specify the limited circumstances in which an entitlement holder's property interest can be asserted against a third person to whom the intermediary transferred a financial asset that was subject to the entitlement holder's claim when held by the intermediary. Subsection (d) provides that the property interest of entitlement holders cannot be asserted against any transferee except in the circumstances therein specified. So long as the intermediary is solvent, the entitlement holders must look to the intermediary to satisfy their claims. If the intermediary does not hold financial assets corresponding to the entitlement holders' claims, the intermediary has the duty to acquire them. See Section 8–504. Thus, paragraphs (1), (2), and (3) of subsection (d) specify that the only occasion in which the entitlement holders can pursue transferees is when the intermediary is unable to perform its obligation, and the transfer to the transferee was a violation of those obligations. Even in that case, a transferee who gave value and obtained control is protected by virtue of the rule in subsection (e), unless the transferee acted in collusion with the intermediary.

Subsections (d) and (e) have the effect of protecting transferees from an intermediary against adverse claims arising out of assertions by the intermediary's entitlement holders that the intermediary acted wrongfully in transferring the financial assets. These rules, however, operate in a slightly different fashion than traditional adverse claim cut-off rules. Rather than specifying that a certain class of transferee takes free from all claims, subsections (d) and (e) specify the circumstances in which this particular form of claim can be asserted against a transferee. Revised Article 8 also contains general adverse claim cut-off rules for the indirect holding system. See Sections 8–502 and 8–510. The rule of subsections (d) and (e) takes precedence over the general cut-off rules of those sections, because Section 8–503 itself defines and sets limits on the assertion of the property interest of entitlement holders. Thus, the question whether entitlement holders' property interest can be asserted as an adverse claim against a transferee from the intermediary is governed by the collusion test of Section 8–503(e), rather than by the "without notice" test of Sections 8–502 and 8–510.

3. The limitations that subsections (c) through (e) place on the ability of customers of a failed intermediary to recover securities or other financial assets from transferees are consistent with the fundamental policies of investor protection that underlie this Article and other bodies of law governing the securities business. The commercial law rules for the securities

holding and transfer system must be assessed from the forward-looking perspective of their impact on the vast number of transactions in which no wrongful conduct occurred or will occur, rather than from the *post hoc* perspective of what rule might be most advantageous to a particular class of persons in litigation that might arise out of the occasional case in which someone has acted wrongfully. Although one can devise hypothetical scenarios where particular customers might find it advantageous to be able to assert rights against someone other than the customers' own intermediary, commercial law rules that permitted customers to do so would impair rather than promote the interest of investors and the safe and efficient operation of the clearance and settlement system. Suppose, for example, that Intermediary A transfers securities to B, that Intermediary A acted wrongfully as against its customers in so doing, and that after the transaction Intermediary A did not have sufficient securities to satisfy its obligations to its entitlement holders. Viewed solely from the standpoint of the customers of Intermediary A, it would seem that permitting the property to be recovered from B, would be good for investors. That, however, is not the case. B may itself be an intermediary with its own customers, or may be some other institution through which individuals invest, such as a pension fund or investment company. There is no reason to think that rules permitting customers of an intermediary to trace and recover securities that their intermediary wrongfully transferred work to the advantage of investors in general. To the contrary, application of such rules would often merely shift losses from one set of investors to another. The uncertainties that would result from rules permitting such recoveries would work to the disadvantage of all participants in the securities markets.

The use of the collusion test in Section 8–503(e) furthers the interests of investors generally in the sound and efficient operation of the securities holding and settlement system. The effect of the choice of this standard is that customers of a failed intermediary must show that the transferee from whom they seek to recover was affirmatively engaged in wrongful conduct, rather than casting on the transferee any burden of showing that the transferee had no awareness of wrongful conduct by the failed intermediary. The rule of Section 8–503(e) is based on the long-standing policy that it is undesirable to impose upon purchasers of securities any duty to investigate whether their sellers may be acting wrongfully.

Rather than imposing duties to investigate, the general policy of the commercial law of the securities holding and transfer system has been to eliminate legal rules that might induce participants to conduct investigations of the authority of persons transferring securities on behalf of others for fear that they might be held liable for participating in a wrongful transfer. The rules in Part 4 of Article 8 concerning transfers by fiduciaries provide a good example. Under *Lowry v. Commercial & Farmers' Bank,* 15 F.Cas. 1040 (C.C.D.Md.1848) (No. 8581), an issuer could be held liable for wrongful transfer if it registered transfer of securities by a fiduciary under circumstances where it had any reason to believe that the fiduciary may have been acting improperly. In one sense that seems to be advantageous for beneficiaries who might be harmed by wrongful conduct by fiduciaries. The consequence of the *Lowry* rule, however, was that in order to protect against risk of such liability, issuers developed the practice of requiring extensive documentation for fiduciary stock transfers, making such transfers cumbersome and time consuming. Accordingly, the rules in Part 4 of Article 8, and in the prior fiduciary transfer statutes, were designed to discourage transfer agents from conducting investigations into the rightfulness of transfers by fiduciaries.

The rules of Revised Article 8 implement for the indirect holding system the same policies that the rules on protected purchasers and registration of transfer adopt for the direct holding system. A securities intermediary is, by definition, a person who is holding securities on behalf of other persons. There is nothing unusual or suspicious about a transaction in which a securities intermediary sells securities that it was holding for its customers. That is exactly what securities intermediaries are in business to do. The interests of customers of securities intermediaries would not be served by a rule that required counterparties to transfers from securities intermediaries to investigate whether the intermediary was acting wrongfully against its customers. Quite the contrary, such a rule would impair the ability of securities intermediaries to perform the function that customers want.

The rules of Section 8–503(c) through (e) apply to transferees generally, including pledgees. The reasons for treating pledgees in the same fashion as other transferees are discussed in the Comments to Section 8–511. The statement in subsection (a) that an intermediary holds financial assets for customers and not as its own property does not, of course, mean that the intermediary lacks power to transfer the financial assets to others. For example, although Article 9 provides that for a security interest to attach the debtor must either have "rights" in the collateral or the power to transfer "rights" in the collateral to a secured party, see Section 9–203, the fact that an intermediary is holding a financial asset in a form that permits ready transfer means that it has such rights, even if the intermediary is acting wrongfully against its entitlement holders in granting the security interest. The question whether the secured party takes subject to the entitlement holder's claim in such a case is governed by Section 8–511, which is an application to secured transactions of the general principles expressed in subsections (d) and (e) of this section.

Definitional Cross References:

"Control". Section 8–106.
"Entitlement holder". Section 8–102(a)(7).
"Financial asset". Section 8–102(a)(9).
"Insolvency proceedings". Section 1–201(22).
"Purchaser". Sections 1–201(33) & 8–116.
"Securities intermediary". Section 8–102(a)(14).
"Security entitlement". Section 8–102(a)(17).
"Value". Sections 1–201(44) & 8–116.

§ 8–504. Duty of Securities Intermediary to Maintain Financial Asset.

(a) A securities intermediary shall promptly obtain and thereafter maintain a financial asset in a quantity corresponding to the aggregate of all security entitlements it has established in favor of its entitlement holders with respect to that financial asset. The securities intermediary may maintain those financial assets directly or through one or more other securities intermediaries.

(b) Except to the extent otherwise agreed by its entitlement holder, a securities intermediary may not grant any security interests in a financial asset it is obligated to maintain pursuant to subsection (a).

(c) A securities intermediary satisfies the duty in subsection (a) if:

(1) the securities intermediary acts with respect to the duty as agreed upon by the entitlement holder and the securities intermediary; or

(2) in the absence of agreement, the securities intermediary exercises due care in accordance with reasonable commercial standards to obtain and maintain the financial asset.

(d) This section does not apply to a clearing corporation that is itself the obligor of an option or similar obligation to which its entitlement holders have security entitlements.

Official Comment

1. This section expresses one of the core elements of the relationships for which the Part 5 rules were designed, to wit, that a securities intermediary undertakes to hold financial assets corresponding to the security entitlements of its entitlement holders. The locution "shall promptly obtain and shall thereafter maintain" is taken from the corresponding regulation under federal securities law, 17 C.F.R. § 240.15c3–3. This section recognizes the reality that as the securities business is conducted today, it is not possible to identify particular securities as belonging to customers as distinguished from other particular securities that are the firm's own property. Securities firms typically keep all securities in fungible form, and may maintain their inventory of a particular security in various locations and forms, including physical securities held in vaults or in transit to transfer agents, and book entry positions at one or more clearing corporations. Accordingly, this section states that a securities intermediary shall maintain a quantity of financial assets corresponding to the aggregate of all security entitlements it has established. The last sentence of subsection (a) provides explicitly that the securities intermediary may hold directly or indirectly. That point is implicit in the use of the term "financial asset," inasmuch as Section 8–102(a)(9) provides that the term "financial asset" may refer either to the underlying asset or the means by which it is held, including both security certificates and security entitlements.

2. Subsection (b) states explicitly a point that is implicit in the notion that a securities intermediary must maintain financial assets corresponding to the security entitlements of its entitlement holders, to wit, that it is wrongful for a securities intermediary to grant security interests in positions that it needs to satisfy customers' claims, except as authorized by the customers. This statement does not determine the rights of a secured party to whom a securities intermediary wrongfully grants a security interest; that issue is governed by Sections 8–503 and 8–511.

Margin accounts are common examples of arrangements in which an entitlement holder authorizes the securities intermediary to grant security interests in the positions held for the entitlement holder. Securities firms commonly obtain the funds needed to provide margin loans to their customers by "rehypothecating" the customers' securities. In order to facilitate rehypothecation, agreements between margin customers and their brokers commonly authorize the broker to commingle securities of all margin customers for rehypothecation to the lender who provides the financing. Brokers commonly rehypothecate customer securities having a value somewhat greater than the amount of the loan made to the customer, since the lenders who provide the necessary financing to the broker need some cushion of protection against the risk of decline in the value of the rehypothecated securities. The extent and manner in which a firm may rehypothecate customers' securities are determined by the agreement between the intermediary and the entitlement holder and by applicable regulatory law. Current regulations under the federal securities laws require that brokers obtain the explicit consent of customers before pledging customer securities or commingling different customers' securities for pledge. Federal regulations also limit the extent to which a broker may rehypothecate customer securities to 110% of the aggregate amount of the borrowings of all customers.

3. The statement in this section that an intermediary must obtain and maintain financial assets corresponding to the aggregate of all security entitlements it has established is intended only to capture the general point that one of the key elements that distinguishes securities accounts from other relationships, such as deposit accounts, is that the intermediary undertakes to maintain a direct correspondence between the positions it holds and the claims of its customers. This section is not intended as a detailed specification of precisely how the intermediary is to perform this duty, nor whether there may be special circumstances in which an intermediary's general duty is excused. Accordingly, the general statement of the duties of a securities intermediary in this and the following sections is supplemented by two other provisions. First, each of Sections 8–504 through 8–508 contains an "agreement/due care" provision. Second, Section 8–509 sets out general qualifications on the duties stated in these sections, including the important point that compliance with corresponding regulatory provisions constitutes compliance with the Article 8 duties.

4. The "agreement/due care" provision in subsection (c) of this section is necessary to provide sufficient flexibility to accommodate the general duty stated in subsection (a) to the wide variety of circumstances that may be encountered in the modern securities holding system. For the most common forms of publicly traded securities, the modern depository-based indirect holding system has made the likelihood of an actual loss of securities remote, though correctable errors in accounting or temporary interruptions of data processing facilities may occur. Indeed, one of the reasons for the evolution of book-entry systems is to eliminate the risk of loss or destruction of physical certificates.

There are, however, some forms of securities and other financial assets which must still be held in physical certificated form, with the attendant risk of loss or destruction. Risk of loss or delay may be a more significant consideration in connection with foreign securities. An American securities intermediary may well be willing to hold a foreign security in a securities account for its customer, but the intermediary may have relatively little choice of or control over foreign intermediaries through which the security must in turn be held. Accordingly, it is common for American securities intermediaries to disclaim responsibility for custodial risk of holding through foreign intermediaries.

Subsection (c)(1) provides that a securities intermediary satisfies the duty stated in subsection (a) if the intermediary acts with respect to that duty in accordance with the agreement between the intermediary and the entitlement holder. Subsection (c)(2) provides that if there is no agreement on the matter, the intermediary satisfies the subsection (a) duty if the intermediary exercises due care in accordance with reasonable commercial standards to obtain and maintain the financial asset in question. This formulation does not state that the intermediary has a universally applicable statutory duty of due care. Section 1–102(3) provides that statutory duties of due care cannot be disclaimed by agreement, but the "agreement/due care" formula contemplates that there may be particular circumstances where the parties do not wish to create a specific duty of due care, for example, with respect to foreign securities. Under subsection (c)(1), compliance with the agreement constitutes satisfaction of the subsection (a) duty, whether or not the agreement provides that the intermediary will exercise due care.

In each of the sections where the "agreement/due care" formula is used, it provides that entering into an agreement and performing in accordance with that agreement is a method by which the securities intermediary may satisfy the statutory duty stated in that section. Accordingly, the general obligation of good faith performance of statutory and contract duties, see Sections 1–203 and 8–102(a)(10), would apply to such an agreement. It would not be consistent with the obligation of good faith performance for an agreement to purport to establish the usual sort of arrangement between an intermediary and entitlement holder, yet disclaim altogether one of the basic elements that define that relationship. For example, an agreement stating that an intermediary assumes no responsibilities whatsoever for the safekeeping any of the entitlement holder's securities positions would not be consistent with good faith performance of the intermediary's duty to obtain and maintain financial assets corresponding to the entitlement holder's security entitlements.

To the extent that no agreement under subsection (c)(1) has specified the details of the intermediary's performance of the subsection (a) duty, subsection (c)(2) provides that the intermediary satisfies that duty if it exercises due care in accordance with reasonable commercial standards. The duty of care includes both care in the intermediary's own operations and care in the selection of other intermediaries through whom the intermediary holds the assets in question. The statement of the obligation of due care is meant to incorporate the principles of the common law under which the specific actions or precautions necessary to meet the obligation of care are determined by such factors as the nature and value of the property, the customs and practices of the business, and the like.

5. This section necessarily states the duty of a securities intermediary to obtain and maintain financial assets only at the very general and abstract level. For the most part, these matters are specified in great detail by regulatory law. Broker-dealers registered under the federal securities laws are subject to detailed regulation concerning the safeguarding of customer securities. See 17 C.F.R. § 240.15c3–3. Section 8–509(a) provides explicitly that if a securities intermediary complies with such regulatory law, that constitutes compliance with Section 8–503. In certain circumstances, these rules permit a firm to be in a position where it temporarily lacks a sufficient quantity of financial assets to satisfy all customer claims. For example, if another firm has failed to make a delivery to the firm in settlement of a trade, the firm is permitted a certain period of time to clear up the problem before it is obligated to obtain the necessary securities from some other source.

6. Subsection (d) is intended to recognize that there are some circumstances, where the duty to maintain a sufficient quantity of financial assets does not apply because the intermediary is not holding anything on behalf of others. For example, the Options Clearing Corporation is treated as a "securities intermediary" under this Article, although it does not itself hold options on behalf of its participants. Rather, it becomes the issuer of the options, by virtue of guaranteeing the obligations of participants in the clearing corporation who have written or purchased the options cleared through it. See Section 8–103(e). Accordingly, the general duty of an intermediary under subsection (a) does not apply, nor would other provisions of Part 5 that depend upon the existence of a requirement that

the securities intermediary hold financial assets, such as Sections 8–503 and 8–508.

Definitional Cross References:

"Agreement". Section 1–201(3).
"Clearing corporation". Section 8–102(a)(5).
"Entitlement holder". Section 8–102(a)(7).
"Financial asset". Section 8–102(a)(9).
"Securities intermediary". Section 8–102(a)(14).
"Security entitlement". Section 8–102(a)(17).

§ 8–505. Duty of Securities Intermediary with Respect to Payments and Distributions.

(a) A securities intermediary shall take action to obtain a payment or distribution made by the issuer of a financial asset. A securities intermediary satisfies the duty if:

(1) the securities intermediary acts with respect to the duty as agreed upon by the entitlement holder and the securities intermediary; or

(2) in the absence of agreement, the securities intermediary exercises due care in accordance with reasonable commercial standards to attempt to obtain the payment or distribution.

(b) A securities intermediary is obligated to its entitlement holder for a payment or distribution made by the issuer of a financial asset if the payment or distribution is received by the securities intermediary.

Official Comment

1. One of the core elements of the securities account relationships for which the Part 5 rules were designed is that the securities intermediary passes through to the entitlement holders the economic benefit of ownership of the financial asset, such as payments and distributions made by the issuer. Subsection (a) expresses the ordinary understanding that a securities intermediary will take appropriate action to see to it that any payments or distributions made by the issuer are received. One of the main reasons that investors make use of securities intermediaries is to obtain the services of a professional in performing the record-keeping and other functions necessary to ensure that payments and other distributions are received.

2. Subsection (a) incorporates the same "agreement/due care" formula as the other provisions of Part 5 dealing with the duties of a securities intermediary.

651

See Comment 4 to Section 8–504. This formulation permits the parties to specify by agreement what action, if any, the intermediary is to take with respect to the duty to obtain payments and distributions. In the absence of specification by agreement, the intermediary satisfies the duty if the intermediary exercises due care in accordance with reasonable commercial standards. The provisions of Section 8–509 also apply to the Section 8–505 duty, so that compliance with applicable regulatory requirements constitutes compliance with the Section 8–505 duty.

3. Subsection (b) provides that a securities intermediary is obligated to its entitlement holder for those payments or distributions made by the issuer that are in fact received by the intermediary. It does not deal with the details of the time and manner of payment. Moreover, as with any other monetary obligation, the obligation to pay may be subject to other rights of the obligor, by way of set-off counterclaim or the like. Section 8–509(c) makes this point explicit.

Definitional Cross References:

"Agreement". Section 1–201(3).
"Entitlement holder". Section 8–102(a)(7).
"Financial asset". Section 8–102(a)(9).
"Securities intermediary". Section 8–102(a)(14).
"Security entitlement". Section 8–102(a)(17).

§ 8–506. Duty of Securities Intermediary to Exercise Rights as Directed by Entitlement Holder.

A securities intermediary shall exercise rights with respect to a financial asset if directed to do so by an entitlement holder. A securities intermediary satisfies the duty if:

(1) the securities intermediary acts with respect to the duty as agreed upon by the entitlement holder and the securities intermediary; or

(2) in the absence of agreement, the securities intermediary either places the entitlement holder in a position to exercise the rights directly or exercises due care in accordance with reasonable commercial standards to follow the direction of the entitlement holder.

Official Comment

1. Another of the core elements of the securities account relationships for which the Part 5 rules were designed is that although the intermediary may, by virtue of the structure of the indirect holding system, be the party who has the power to exercise the corporate and other rights that come from holding the security, the intermediary exercises these powers as representative of the entitlement holder rather than at its own discretion. This characteristic is one of the things that distinguishes a securities account from other arrangements where one person holds securities "on behalf of" another, such as the relationship between a mutual fund and its shareholders or a trustee and its beneficiary.

2. The fact that the intermediary exercises the rights of security holding as representative of the entitlement holder does not, of course, preclude the entitlement holder from conferring discretionary authority upon the intermediary. Arrangements are not uncommon in which investors do not wish to have their intermediaries forward proxy materials or other information. Thus, this section provides that the intermediary shall exercise corporate and other rights "if directed to do so" by the entitlement holder. Moreover, as with the other Part 5 duties, the "agreement/due care" formulation is used in stating how the intermediary is to perform this duty. This section also provides that the intermediary satisfies the duty if it places the entitlement holder in a position to exercise the rights directly. This is to take account of the fact that some of the rights attendant upon ownership of the security, such as rights to bring derivative and other litigation, are far removed from the matters that intermediaries are expected to perform.

3. This section, and the two that follow, deal with the aspects of securities holding that are related to investment decisions. For example, one of the rights of holding a particular security that would fall within the purview of this section would be the right to exercise a conversion right for a convertible security. It is quite common for investors to confer discretionary authority upon another person, such as an investment adviser, with respect to these rights and other investment decisions. Because this section, and the other sections of Part 5, all specify that a securities intermediary satisfies the Part 5 duties if it acts in accordance with the entitlement holder's agreement, there is no inconsistency between the statement of duties of a securities intermediary and these common arrangements.

4. Section 8–509 also applies to the Section 8–506 duty, so that compliance with applicable regulatory requirements constitutes compliance with this duty. This is quite important in this context, since the federal securities laws establish a comprehensive system of regulation of the distribution of proxy materials and

exercise of voting rights with respect to securities held through brokers and other intermediaries. By virtue of Section 8–509(a), compliance with such regulatory requirement constitutes compliance with the Section 8–506 duty.

Definitional Cross References:

"Agreement". Section 1–201(3).
"Entitlement holder". Section 8–102(a)(7).
"Financial asset". Section 8–102(a)(9).
"Securities intermediary". Section 8–102(a)(14).
"Security entitlement". Section 8–102(a)(17).

§ 8–507. Duty of Securities Intermediary to Comply With Entitlement Order.

(a) A securities intermediary shall comply with an entitlement order if the entitlement order is originated by the appropriate person, the securities intermediary has had reasonable opportunity to assure itself that the entitlement order is genuine and authorized, and the securities intermediary has had reasonable opportunity to comply with the entitlement order. A securities intermediary satisfies the duty if:

(1) the securities intermediary acts with respect to the duty as agreed upon by the entitlement holder and the securities intermediary; or

(2) in the absence of agreement, the securities intermediary exercises due care in accordance with reasonable commercial standards to comply with the entitlement order.

(b) If a securities intermediary transfers a financial asset pursuant to an ineffective entitlement order, the securities intermediary shall reestablish a security entitlement in favor of the person entitled to it, and pay or credit any payments or distributions that the person did not receive as a result of the wrongful transfer. If the securities intermediary does not reestablish a security entitlement, the securities intermediary is liable to the entitlement holder for damages.

Official Comment

1. Subsection (a) of this section states another aspect of duties of securities intermediaries that make up security entitlements—the securities intermediary's duty to comply with entitlement orders. One of the main reasons for holding securities through securities intermediaries is to enable rapid transfer in settlement of trades. Thus the right to have one's orders for disposition of the security entitlement honored is an inherent part of the relationship. Subsection (b) states the correlative liability of a securities intermediary for transferring a financial asset from an entitlement holder's account pursuant to an entitlement order that was not effective.

2. The duty to comply with entitlement orders is subject to several qualifications. The intermediary has a duty only with respect to an entitlement order that is in fact originated by the appropriate person. Moreover, the intermediary has a duty only if it has had reasonable opportunity to assure itself that the order is genuine and authorized, and reasonable opportunity to comply with the order. The same "agreement/due care" formula is used in this section as in the other Part 5 sections on the duties of intermediaries, and the rules of Section 8–509 apply to the Section 8–507 duty.

3. Appropriate person is defined in Section 8–107. In the usual case, the appropriate person is the entitlement holder, see Section 8–107(a)(3). Entitlement holder is defined in Section 8–102(a)(7) as the person "identified in the records of a securities intermediary as the person having a security entitlement." Thus, the general rule is that an intermediary's duty with respect to entitlement orders runs only to the person with whom the intermediary has established a relationship. One of the basic principles of the indirect holding system is that securities intermediaries owe duties only to their own customers. See also Section 8–115. The only situation in which a securities intermediary has a duty to comply with entitlement orders originated by a person other than the person with whom the intermediary established a relationship is covered by Section 8–107(a)(4) and (a)(5), which provide that the term "appropriate person" includes the successor or personal representative of a decedent, or the custodian or guardian of a person who lacks capacity. If the entitlement holder is competent, another person does not fall within the defined term "appropriate person" merely by virtue of having power to act as an agent for the entitlement holder. Thus, an intermediary is not required to determine at its peril whether a person who purports to be authorized to act for an entitlement holder is in fact authorized to do so. If an entitlement holder wishes to be able to act through agents, the entitlement holder can establish appropriate arrangements in advance with the securities intermediary.

One important application of this principle is that if an entitlement holder grants a security interest in its security entitlements to a third-party lender, the intermediary owes no duties to the secured party, unless the intermediary has entered into a "control" agreement in which it agrees to act on entitlement orders originated by the secured party. See Section 8–106. Even though the security agreement or some other document may give the secured party authority to act as agent for the debtor, that would not make the secured party an "appropriate person" to whom the security intermediary owes duties. If the entitlement holder and securities intermediary have agreed to such a control arrangement, then the intermediary's action in following instructions from the secured party would satisfy the subsection (a) duty. Although an agent, such as the secured party in this example, is not an "appropriate person," an entitlement order is "effective" if originated by an authorized person. See Section 8–107(a) and (b). Moreover, Section 8–507(a) provides that the intermediary satisfies its duty if it acts in accordance with the entitlement holder's agreement.

4. Subsection (b) provides that an intermediary is liable for a wrongful transfer if the entitlement order was "ineffective." Section 8–107 specifies whether an entitlement order is effective. An "effective entitlement order" is different from an "entitlement order originated by an appropriate person." An entitlement order is effective under Section 8–107(b) if it is made by the appropriate person, or by a person who has power to act for the appropriate person under the law of agency, or if the appropriate person has ratified the entitlement order or is precluded from denying its effectiveness. Thus, although a securities intermediary does not have a duty to act on an entitlement order originated by the entitlement holder's agent, the intermediary is not liable for wrongful transfer if it does so.

Subsection (b), together with Section 8–107, has the effect of leaving to other law most of the questions of the sort dealt with by Article 4A for wire transfers of funds, such as allocation between the securities intermediary and the entitlement holder of the risk of fraudulent entitlement orders.

5. The term entitlement order does not cover all directions that a customer might give a broker concerning securities held through the broker. Article 8 is not a codification of all of the law of customers and stockbrokers. Article 8 deals with the settlement of securities trades, not the trades. The term entitlement order does not refer to instructions to a broker to make trades, that is, enter into contracts for the purchase or sale of securities. Rather, the entitlement order is the mechanism of transfer for securities held through intermediaries, just as indorsements and instructions are the mechanism for securities held directly. In the ordinary case the customer's direction to

the broker to deliver the securities at settlement is implicit in the customer's instruction to the broker to sell. The distinction is, however, significant in that this section has no application to the relationship between the customer and broker with respect to the trade itself. For example, assertions by a customer that it was damaged by a broker's failure to execute a trading order sufficiently rapidly or in the proper manner are not governed by this Article.

Definitional Cross References:

"Agreement". Section 1–201(3).
"Appropriate person". Section 8–107.
"Effective". Section 8–107.
"Entitlement holder". Section 8–102(a)(7).
"Entitlement order". Section 8–102(a)(8).
"Financial asset". Section 8–102(a)(9).
"Securities intermediary". Section 8–102(a)(14).
"Security entitlement". Section 8–102(a)(17).

§ 8–508. Duty of Securities Intermediary to Change Entitlement Holder's Position to Other Form of Security Holding.

A securities intermediary shall act at the direction of an entitlement holder to change a security entitlement into another available form of holding for which the entitlement holder is eligible, or to cause the financial asset to be transferred to a securities account of the entitlement holder with another securities intermediary. A securities intermediary satisfies the duty if:

(1) the securities intermediary acts as agreed upon by the entitlement holder and the securities intermediary; or

(2) in the absence of agreement, the securities intermediary exercises due care in accordance with reasonable commercial standards to follow the direction of the entitlement holder.

Official Comment

1. This section states another aspect of the duties of securities intermediaries that make up security entitlements—the obligation of the securities intermediary to change an entitlement holder's position into any other form of holding for which the entitlement holder is eligible or to transfer the entitlement holder's position to an account at another intermediary. This section does not state unconditionally that the securities intermediary is obligated to turn over a certificate

to the customer or to cause the customer to be registered on the books of the issuer, because the customer may not be eligible to hold the security directly. For example, municipal bonds are now commonly issued in "book-entry only" form, in which the only entity that the issuer will register on its own books is a depository.

If security certificates in registered form are issued for the security, and individuals are eligible to have the security registered in their own name, the entitlement holder can request that the intermediary deliver or cause to be delivered to the entitlement holder a certificate registered in the name of the entitlement holder or a certificate indorsed in blank or specially indorsed to the entitlement holder. If security certificates in bearer form are issued for the security, the entitlement holder can request that the intermediary deliver or cause to be delivered a certificate in bearer form. If the security can be held by individuals directly in uncertificated form, the entitlement holder can request that the security be registered in its name. The specification of this duty does not determine the pricing terms of the agreement in which the duty arises.

2. The same "agreement/due care" formula is used in this section as in the other Part 5 sections on the duties of intermediaries. So too, the rules of Section 8–509 apply to the Section 8–508 duty.

Definitional Cross References:

"Agreement". Section 1–201(3).
"Entitlement holder". Section 8–102(a)(7).
"Financial asset". Section 8–102(a)(9).
"Securities intermediary". Section 8–102(a)(14).
"Security entitlement". Section 8–102(a)(17).

§ 8–509. Specification of Duties of Securities Intermediary by Other Statute or Regulation; Manner of Performance of Duties of Securities Intermediary and Exercise of Rights of Entitlement Holder.

(a) If the substance of a duty imposed upon a securities intermediary by Sections 8–504 through 8–508 is the subject of other statute, regulation, or rule, compliance with that statute, regulation, or rule satisfies the duty.

(b) To the extent that specific standards for the performance of the duties of a securities intermediary or the exercise of the rights of an entitlement holder are not specified by other statute, regulation, or rule or by agreement between the securities intermediary and entitlement holder, the securities intermediary shall perform its duties and the entitlement holder shall exercise its rights in a commercially reasonable manner.

(c) The obligation of a securities intermediary to perform the duties imposed by Sections 8–504 through 8–508 is subject to:

(1) rights of the securities intermediary arising out of a security interest under a security agreement with the entitlement holder or otherwise; and

(2) rights of the securities intermediary under other law, regulation, rule, or agreement to withhold performance of its duties as a result of unfulfilled obligations of the entitlement holder to the securities intermediary.

(d) Sections 8–504 through 8–508 do not require a securities intermediary to take any action that is prohibited by other statute, regulation, or rule.

Official Comment

This Article is not a comprehensive statement of the law governing the relationship between broker-dealers or other securities intermediaries and their customers. Most of the law governing that relationship is the common law of contract and agency, supplemented or supplanted by regulatory law. This Article deals only with the most basic commercial/property law principles governing the relationship. Although Sections 8–504 through 8–508 specify certain duties of securities intermediaries to entitlement holders, the point of these sections is to identify what it means to have a security entitlement, not to specify the details of performance of these duties.

For many intermediaries, regulatory law specifies in great detail the intermediary's obligations on such matters as safekeeping of customer property, distribution of proxy materials, and the like. To avoid any conflict between the general statement of duties in this Article and the specific statement of intermediaries' obligations in such regulatory schemes, subsection (a) provides that compliance with applicable regulation constitutes compliance with the duties specified in Sections 8–504 through 8–508.

Definitional Cross References:

"Agreement". Section 1–201(3).
"Entitlement holder". Section 8–102(a)(7).
"Securities intermediary". Section 8–102(a)(14).
"Security agreement". Section 9–102(a)(73).

"Security interest". Section 1–201(37).

§ 8–510. Rights of Purchaser of Security Entitlement from Entitlement Holder.

(a) In a case not covered by the priority rules in Article 9 or the rules stated in subsection (c), an action based on an adverse claim to a financial asset or security entitlement, whether framed in conversion, replevin, constructive trust, equitable lien, or other theory, may not be asserted against a person who purchases a security entitlement, or an interest therein, from an entitlement holder if the purchaser gives value, does not have notice of the adverse claim, and obtains control.

(b) If an adverse claim could not have been asserted against an entitlement holder under Section 8–502, the adverse claim cannot be asserted against a person who purchases a security entitlement, or an interest therein, from the entitlement holder.

(c) In a case not covered by the priority rules in Article 9, a purchaser for value of a security entitlement, or an interest therein, who obtains control has priority over a purchaser of a security entitlement, or an interest therein, who does not obtain control. Except as otherwise provided in subsection (d), purchasers who have control rank according to priority in time of:

(1) the purchaser's becoming the person for whom the securities account, in which the security entitlement is carried, is maintained, if the purchaser obtained control under Section 8–106(d)(1);

(2) the securities intermediary's agreement to comply with the purchaser's entitlement orders with respect to security entitlements carried or to be carried in the securities account in which the security entitlement is carried, if the purchaser obtained control under Section 8–106(d)(2); or

(3) if the purchaser obtained control through another person under Section 8–106(d)(3), the time on which priority would be based under this subsection if the other person were the secured party.

(d) A securities intermediary as purchaser has priority over a conflicting purchaser who has control unless otherwise agreed by the securities intermediary.

As amended in 1999.

Official Comment

1. This section specifies certain rules concerning the rights of persons who purchase interests in security entitlements from entitlement holders. The rules of this section are provided to take account of cases where the purchaser's rights are derivative from the rights of another person who is and continues to be the entitlement holder.

2. Subsection (a) provides that no adverse claim can be asserted against a purchaser of an interest in a security entitlement if the purchaser gives value, obtains control, and does not have notice of the adverse claim. The primary purpose of this rule is to give adverse claim protection to persons who take security interests in security entitlements and obtain control, but do not themselves become entitlement holders.

The following examples illustrate subsection (a):

Example 1. X steals a certificated bearer bond from Owner. X delivers the certificate to Able & Co. for credit to X's securities account. Later, X borrows from Bank and grants bank a security interest in the security entitlement. Bank obtains control under Section 8–106(d)(2) by virtue of an agreement in which Able agrees to comply with entitlement orders originated by Bank. X absconds.

Example 2. Same facts as in Example 1, except that Bank does not obtain a control agreement. Instead, Bank perfects by filing a financing statement.

In both of these examples, when X deposited the bonds X acquired a security entitlement under Section 8–501. Under other law, Owner may be able to have a constructive trust imposed on the security entitlement as the traceable product of the bonds that X misappropriated. X granted a security interest in that entitlement to Bank. Bank was a purchaser of an interest in the security entitlement from X. In Example 1, although Bank was not a person who acquired a security entitlement from the intermediary, Bank did obtain control. If Bank did not have notice of Owner's claim, Section 8–510(a) precludes Owner from asserting an adverse claim against Bank. In Example 2, Bank had a perfected security interest, but did not obtain control. Accordingly, Section 8–510(a) does not preclude Owner from asserting its adverse claim against Bank.

3. Subsection (b) applies to the indirect holding system a limited version of the "shelter principle." The following example illustrates the relatively limited class of cases for which it may be needed:

Example 3. Thief steals a certificated bearer bond from Owner. Thief delivers the certificate to Able & Co. for credit to Thief's securities account. Able forwards the certificate to a clearing corporation for credit to Able's account. Later Thief instructs Able to sell the positions in the bonds. Able sells to Baker & Co., acting as broker for Buyer. The trade is settled by book-entries in the accounts of Able and Baker at the clearing corporation, and in the accounts of Thief and Buyer at Able and Baker respectively. Owner may be able to reconstruct the trade records to show that settlement occurred in such fashion that the "same bonds" that were carried in Thief's account at Able are traceable into Buyer's account at Baker. Buyer later decides to donate the bonds to Alma Mater University and executes an assignment of its rights as entitlement holder to Alma Mater.

Buyer had a position in the bonds, which Buyer held in the form of a security entitlement against Baker. Buyer then made a gift of the position to Alma Mater. Although Alma Mater is a purchaser, Section 1–201(33), it did not give value. Thus, Alma Mater is a person who purchased a security entitlement, or an interest therein, from an entitlement holder (Buyer). Buyer was protected against Owner's adverse claim by the Section 8–502 rule. Thus, by virtue of Section 8–510(b), Owner is also precluded from asserting an adverse claim against Alma Mater.

4. Subsection (c) specifies a priority rule for cases where an entitlement holder transfers conflicting interests in the same security entitlement to different purchasers. It follows the same principle as the Article 9 priority rule for investment property, that is, control trumps non-control. Indeed, the most significant category of conflicting "purchasers" may be secured parties. Priority questions for security interests, however, are governed by the rules in Article 9. Subsection (c) applies only to cases not covered by the Article 9 rules. It is intended primarily for disputes over conflicting claims arising out of repurchase agreement transactions that are not covered by the other rules set out in Articles 8 and 9.

The following example illustrates subsection (c):

Example 4. Dealer holds securities through an account at Alpha Bank. Alpha Bank in turns holds through a clearing corporation account. Dealer transfers securities to RP1 in a "hold in custody" repo transaction. Dealer then transfers the same securities to RP2 in another repo transaction. The repo to RP2 is implemented by transferring the securities from Dealer's regular account at Alpha Bank to a special account maintained by Alpha Bank for Dealer and RP2. The agreement among Dealer, RP2, and Alpha Bank provides that Dealer can make substitutions for the securities but RP2 can direct Alpha Bank to sell any securities held in the special account. Dealer becomes insolvent. RP1 claims a prior interest in the securities transferred to RP2.

In this example Dealer remained the entitlement holder but agreed that RP2 could initiate entitlement orders to Dealer's security intermediary, Alpha Bank. If RP2 had become the entitlement holder, the adverse claim rule of Section 8–502 would apply. Even if RP2 does not become the entitlement holder, the arrangement among Dealer, Alpha Bank, and RP2 does suffice to give RP2 control. Thus, under Section 8–510(c), RP2 has priority over RP1, because RP2 is a purchaser who obtained control, and RP1 is a purchaser who did not obtain control. The same result could be reached under Section 8–510(a) which provides that RP1's earlier in time interest cannot be asserted as an adverse claim against RP2. The same result would follow under the Article 9 priority rules if the interests of RP1 and RP2 are characterized as "security interests," see Section 9–328(1). The main point of the rules of Section 8–510(c) is to ensure that there will be clear rules to cover the conflicting claims of RP1 and RP2 without characterizing their interests as Article 9 security interests.

The priority rules in Article 9 for conflicting security interests also include a default temporal priority rule for cases where multiple secured parties have obtained control but omitted to specify their respective rights by agreement. See Section 9–328(2) and Comment 5 to Section 9–328. Because the purchaser priority rule in Section 8–510(c) is intended to track the Article 9 priority rules, it too has a temporal priority rule for cases where multiple non-secured party purchasers have obtained control but omitted to specify their respective rights by agreement. The rule is patterned on Section 9–328(2).

5. If a securities intermediary itself is a purchaser, subsection (d) provides that it has priority over the interest of another purchaser who has control. Article 9 contains a similar rule. See Section 9–328(3).

Definitional Cross References:

"Adverse claim". Section 8–102(a)(1).
"Control". Section 8–106.
"Entitlement holder". Section 8–102(a)(7).
"Notice of adverse claim". Section 8–105.
"Purchase". Section 1–201(32).
"Purchaser". Sections 1–201(33) & 8–116.
"Securities intermediary". Section 8–102(a)(14).

"Security entitlement".   Section 8–102(a)(17).
"Value".   Sections 1–201(44) & 8–116.

As amended in 1999.

§ 8–511.   Priority Among Security Interests and Entitlement Holders.

(a) Except as otherwise provided in subsections (b) and (c), if a securities intermediary does not have sufficient interests in a particular financial asset to satisfy both its obligations to entitlement holders who have security entitlements to that financial asset and its obligation to a creditor of the securities intermediary who has a security interest in that financial asset, the claims of entitlement holders, other than the creditor, have priority over the claim of the creditor.

(b) A claim of a creditor of a securities intermediary who has a security interest in a financial asset held by a securities intermediary has priority over claims of the securities intermediary's entitlement holders who have security entitlements with respect to that financial asset if the creditor has control over the financial asset.

(c) If a clearing corporation does not have sufficient financial assets to satisfy both its obligations to entitlement holders who have security entitlements with respect to a financial asset and its obligation to a creditor of the clearing corporation who has a security interest in that financial asset, the claim of the creditor has priority over the claims of entitlement holders.

Official Comment

1. This section sets out priority rules for circumstances in which a securities intermediary fails leaving an insufficient quantity of securities or other financial assets to satisfy the claims of its entitlement holders and the claims of creditors to whom it has granted security interests in financial assets held by it. Subsection (a) provides that entitlement holders' claims have priority except as otherwise provided in subsection (b), and subsection (b) provides that the secured creditor's claim has priority if the secured creditor obtains control, as defined in Section 8–106. The following examples illustrate the operation of these rules.

Example 1.   Able & Co., a broker, borrows from Alpha Bank and grants Alpha Bank a security interest pursuant to a written agreement which identifies certain securities that are to be collateral for the loan, either specifically or by category. Able holds these securities in a clearing corporation account. Able becomes insolvent and it is discovered that Able holds insufficient securities to satisfy the claims of customers who have paid for securities that they held in accounts with Able and the collateral claims of Alpha Bank. Alpha Bank's security interest in the security entitlements that Able holds through the clearing corporation account may be perfected under the automatic perfection rule of Section 9–309(10), but Alpha Bank did not obtain control under Section 8–106. Thus, under Section 8–511(a) the entitlement holders' claims have priority over Alpha Bank's claim.

Example 2.   Able & Co., a broker, borrows from Beta Bank and grants Beta Bank a security interest in securities that Able holds in a clearing corporation account. Pursuant to the security agreement, the securities are debited from Alpha's account and credited to Beta's account in the clearing corporation account. Able becomes insolvent and it is discovered that Able holds insufficient securities to satisfy the claims of customers who have paid for securities that they held in accounts with Able and the collateral claims of Alpha Bank. Although the transaction between Able and Beta took the form of an outright transfer on the clearing corporation's books, as between Able and Beta, Able remains the owner and Beta has a security interest. In that respect the situation is no different than if Able had delivered bearer bonds to Beta in pledge to secure a loan. Beta's security interest is perfected, and Beta obtained control. See Sections 8–106 and 9–314. Under Section 8–511(b), Beta Bank's security interest has priority over claims of Able's customers.

The result in Example 2 is an application to this particular setting of the general principle expressed in Section 8–503, and explained in the Comments thereto, that the entitlement holders of a securities intermediary cannot assert rights against third parties to whom the intermediary has wrongfully transferred interests, except in extremely unusual circumstances where the third party was itself a participant in the transferor's wrongdoing. Under subsection (b) the claim of a secured creditor of a securities intermediary has priority over the claims of entitlement holders if the secured creditor has obtained control. If, however, the secured creditor acted in collusion with the intermediary in violating the intermediary's obligation to its entitlement holders, then under Section 8–503(e), the entitlement holders, through their representative in insolvency proceedings, could recover the interest from the secured creditor, that is, set aside the security interest.

2. The risk that investors who hold through an intermediary will suffer a loss as a result of a wrongful pledge by the intermediary is no different than the risk that the intermediary might fail and not have the securities that it was supposed to be holding on behalf of its customers, either because the securities were never acquired by the intermediary or because the intermediary wrongfully sold securities that should have been kept to satisfy customers' claims. Investors are protected against that risk by the regulatory regimes under which securities intermediaries operate. Intermediaries are required to maintain custody, through clearing corporation accounts or in other approved locations, of their customers' securities and are prohibited from using customers' securities in their own business activities. Securities firms who are carrying both customer and proprietary positions are not permitted to grant blanket liens to lenders covering all securities which they hold, for their own account or for their customers. Rather, securities firms designate specifically which positions they are pledging. Under SEC Rules 8c–1 and 15c2–1, customers' securities can be pledged only to fund loans to customers, and only with the consent of the customers. Customers' securities cannot be pledged for loans for the firm's proprietary business; only proprietary positions can be pledged for proprietary loans. SEC Rule 15c3–3 implements these prohibitions in a fashion tailored to modern securities firm accounting systems by requiring brokers to maintain a sufficient inventory of securities, free from any liens, to satisfy the claims of all of their customers for fully paid and excess margin securities. Revised Article 8 mirrors that requirement, specifying in Section 8–504 that a securities intermediary must maintain a sufficient quantity of investment property to satisfy all security entitlements, and may not grant security interests in the positions it is required to hold for customers, except as authorized by the customers.

If a failed brokerage has violated the customer protection regulations and does not have sufficient securities to satisfy customers' claims, its customers are protected against loss from a shortfall by the Securities Investor Protection Act ("SIPA"). Securities firms required to register as brokers or dealers are also required to become members of the Securities Investor Protection Corporation ("SIPC"), which provides their customers with protection somewhat similar to that provided by FDIC and other deposit insurance programs for bank depositors. When a member firm fails, SIPC is authorized to initiate a liquidation proceeding under the provisions of SIPA. If the assets of the securities firm are insufficient to satisfy all customer claims, SIPA makes contributions to the estate from a fund financed by assessments on its members to protect customers against losses up to $500,000 for cash and securities held at member firms.

Article 8 is premised on the view that the important policy of protecting investors against the risk of wrongful conduct by their intermediaries is sufficiently treated by other law.

3. Subsection (c) sets out a special rule for secured financing provided to enable clearing corporations to complete settlement. In order to permit clearing corporations to establish liquidity facilities where necessary to ensure completion of settlement, subsection (c) provides a priority for secured lenders to such clearing corporations. Subsection (c) does not turn on control because the clearing corporation may be the top tier securities intermediary for the securities pledged, so that there may be no practicable method for conferring control on the lender.

Definitional Cross References:

"Clearing corporation". Section 8–102(a)(5).
"Control". Section 8–106.
"Entitlement holder". Section 8–102(a)(7).
"Financial asset". Section 8–102(a)(9).
"Securities intermediary". Section 8–102(a)(14).
"Security entitlement". Section 8–102(a)(17).
"Security interest". Section 1–201(37).
"Value". Sections 1–201(44) & 8–116.

PART 6

TRANSITION PROVISIONS FOR REVISED ARTICLE 8

§ 8–601. Effective Date.

This [Act] takes effect . . . .

§ 8–602. Repeals.

This [Act] repeals . . . .

Official Comment

If the State has adopted the Uniform Act for the Simplification of Fiduciary Security Transfers, or similar legislation, it should be repealed.

§ 8-603. Savings Clause.

(a) This [Act] does not affect an action or proceeding commenced before this [Act] takes effect.

(b) If a security interest in a security is perfected at the date this [Act] takes effect, and the action by which the security interest was perfected would suffice to perfect a security interest under this [Act], no further action is required to continue perfection. If a security interest in a security is perfected at the date this [Act] takes effect but the action by which the security interest was perfected would not suffice to perfect a security interest under this [Act], the security interest remains perfected for a period of four months after the effective date and continues perfected thereafter if appropriate action to perfect under this [Act] is taken within that period. If a security interest is perfected at the date this [Act] takes effect and the security interest can be perfected by filing under this [Act], a financing statement signed by the secured party instead of the debtor may be filed within that period to continue perfection or thereafter to perfect.

Official Comment

The revision of Article 8 should present few significant transition problems. Although the revision involves significant changes in terminology and analysis, the substantive rules are, in large measure, based upon the current practices and are consistent with results that could be reached, albeit at times with some struggle, by proper interpretation of the rules of present law. Thus, the new rules can be applied, without significant dislocations, to transactions and events that occurred prior to enactment.

The enacting provisions should not, whether by applicability, transition, or savings clause language, attempt to provide that old Article 8 continues to apply to "transactions," "events," "rights," "duties," "liabilities," or the like that occurred or accrued before the effective date and that new Article 8 applies to those that occur or accrue after the effective date. The reason for revising Article 8 and corresponding provisions of Article 9 is the concern that the provisions of old Article 8 could be interpreted or misinterpreted to yield results that impede the safe and efficient operation of the national system for the clearance and settlement of securities transactions. Accordingly, it is not the case that any effort should be made to preserve the applicability of old Article 8 to transactions and events that occurred before the effective date.

Only two circumstances seem to warrant continued application of rules of old Article 8. First, to avoid disruption in the conduct of litigation, it may make sense to provide for continued application of the old Article 8 rules to lawsuits pending before the effective date. Second, there are some limited circumstances in which prior law permitted perfection of security interests by methods that are not provided for in the revised version. Section 8–313(1)(h) (1978) permitted perfection of security interests in securities held through intermediaries by notice to the intermediary. Under Revised Articles 8 and 9, security interests can be perfected in such cases by control, which requires the agreement of the intermediary, or by filing. It is likely that secured parties who relied strongly on such collateral under prior law did not simply send notices but obtained agreements from the intermediaries that would suffice for control under the new rules. However, it seems appropriate to include a provision that gives a secured creditor some opportunity after the effective date to perfect in this or any other case in which there is doubt whether the method of perfection used under prior law would be sufficient under the new version.

UCC ARTICLE 9

SECURED TRANSACTIONS

Article 9 was revised in 1999.

2001 amendments (Article 1 revision)....................................*Appendix A*
2003 amendments (Article 7 revision)...............................*Appendix B*

Table of Disposition of Sections in Former Article 9 and Other Code Sections.

Table Indicating Sources or Derivations of New Article 9 Sections and Conforming Amendments.

PART 1. GENERAL PROVISIONS

[SUBPART 1. SHORT TITLE, DEFINITIONS, AND GENERAL CONCEPTS]

Section
9–101. Short Title.
9–102. Definitions and Index of Definitions.
9–103. Purchase-Money Security Interest; Application of Payments; Burden of Establishing.
9–104. Control of Deposit Account.
9–105. Control of Electronic Chattel Paper.
9–106. Control of Investment Property.
9–107. Control of Letter-of-Credit Right.
9–108. Sufficiency of Description.

[SUBPART 2. APPLICABILITY OF ARTICLE]

9–109. Scope.
9–110. Security Interests Arising Under Article 2 or 2A.

PART 2. EFFECTIVENESS OF SECURITY AGREEMENT; ATTACHMENT OF SECURITY INTEREST; RIGHTS OF PARTIES TO SECURITY AGREEMENT

[SUBPART 1. EFFECTIVENESS AND ATTACHMENT]

9–201. General Effectiveness of Security Agreement.
9–202. Title to Collateral Immaterial.
9–203. Attachment and Enforceability of Security Interest; Proceeds; Supporting Obligations; Formal Requisites.

Section
9–204. After-Acquired Property; Future Advances.
9–205. Use or Disposition of Collateral Permissible.
9–206. Security Interest Arising in Purchase or Delivery of Financial Asset.

[SUBPART 2. RIGHTS AND DUTIES]

9–207. Rights and Duties of Secured Party Having Possession or Control of Collateral.
9–208. Additional Duties of Secured Party Having Control of Collateral.
9–209. Duties of Secured Party if Account Debtor Has Been Notified of Assignment.
9–210. Request for Accounting; Request Regarding List of Collateral or Statement of Account.

PART 3. PERFECTION AND PRIORITY

[SUBPART 1. LAW GOVERNING PERFECTION AND PRIORITY]

9–301. Law Governing Perfection and Priority of Security Interests.
9–302. Law Governing Perfection and Priority of Agricultural Liens.
9–303. Law Governing Perfection and Priority of Security Interests in Goods Covered by a Certificate of Title.
9–304. Law Governing Perfection and Priority of Security Interests in Deposit Accounts.
9–305. Law Governing Perfection and Priority of Security Interests in Investment Property.
9–306. Law Governing Perfection and Priority of Security Interests in Letter-of-Credit Rights.
9–307. Location of Debtor.

[SUBPART 2. PERFECTION]

9–308. When Security Interest or Agricultural Lien Is Perfected; Continuity of Perfection.

9–309. Security Interest Perfected Upon Attachment.

9–310. When Filing Required to Perfect Security Interest or Agricultural Lien; Security Interests and Agricultural Liens to Which Filing Provisions Do Not Apply.

9–311. Perfection of Security Interests in Property Subject to Certain Statutes, Regulations, and Treaties.

9–312. Perfection of Security Interests in Chattel Paper, Deposit Accounts, Documents, Goods Covered by Documents, Instruments, Investment Property, Letter-of-Credit Rights, and Money; Perfection by Permissive Filing; Temporary Perfection Without Filing or Transfer of Possession.

9–313. When Possession by or Delivery to Secured Party Perfects Security Interest Without Filing.

9–314. Perfection by Control.

9–315. Secured Party's Rights on Disposition of Collateral and in Proceeds.

9–316. Continued Perfection of Security Interest Following Change in Governing Law.

[SUBPART 3. PRIORITY]

9–317. Interests That Take Priority Over or Take Free of Security Interest or Agricultural Lien.

9–318. No Interest Retained in Right to Payment That Is Sold; Rights and Title of Seller of Account or Chattel Paper With Respect to Creditors and Purchasers.

9–319. Rights and Title of Consignee With Respect to Creditors and Purchasers.

9–320. Buyer of Goods.

9–321. Licensee of General Intangible and Lessee of Goods in Ordinary Course of Business.

9–322. Priorities Among Conflicting Security Interests in and Agricultural Liens on Same Collateral.

9–323. Future Advances.

9–324. Priority of Purchase-Money Security Interests.

9–325. Priority of Security Interests in Transferred Collateral.

Section

9–326. Priority of Security Interests Created by New Debtor.

9–327. Priority of Security Interests in Deposit Account.

9–328. Priority of Security Interests in Investment Property.

9–329. Priority of Security Interests in Letter-of-Credit Right.

9–330. Priority of Purchaser of Chattel Paper or Instrument.

9–331. Priority of Rights of Purchasers of Instruments, Documents, and Securities Under Other Articles; Priority of Interests in Financial Assets and Security Entitlements Under Article 8.

9–332. Transfer of Money; Transfer of Funds From Deposit Account.

9–333. Priority of Certain Liens Arising by Operation of Law.

9–334. Priority of Security Interests in Fixtures and Crops.

9–335. Accessions.

9–336. Commingled Goods.

9–337. Priority of Security Interests in Goods Covered by Certificate of Title.

9–338. Priority of Security Interest or Agricultural Lien Perfected by Filed Financing Statement Providing Certain Incorrect Information.

9–339. Priority Subject to Subordination.

[SUBPART 4. RIGHTS OF BANK]

9–340. Effectiveness of Right of Recoupment or Set-Off Against Deposit Account.

9–341. Bank's Rights and Duties With Respect to Deposit Account.

9–342. Bank's Right to Refuse to Enter Into or Disclose Existence of Control Agreement.

PART 4. RIGHTS OF THIRD PARTIES

9–401. Alienability of Debtor's Rights.

9–402. Secured Party Not Obligated on Contract of Debtor or in Tort.

9–403. Agreement Not to Assert Defenses Against Assignee.

9–404. Rights Acquired by Assignee; Claims and Defenses Against Assignee.

9–405. Modification of Assigned Contract.

9–406. Discharge of Account Debtor; Notification of Assignment; Identification and Proof of Assignment; Restrictions on Assignment of Accounts, Chattel Pa-

Section

per, Payment Intangibles, and Promissory Notes Ineffective.

9–407. Restrictions on Creation or Enforcement of Security Interest in Leasehold Interest or in Lessor's Residual Interest.

9–408. Restrictions on Assignment of Promissory Notes, Health-Care-Insurance Receivables, and Certain General Intangibles Ineffective.

9–409. Restrictions on Assignment of Letter-of-Credit Rights Ineffective.

PART 5. FILING

[SUBPART 1. FILING OFFICE; CONTENTS AND EFFECTIVENESS OF FINANCING STATEMENT]

9–501. Filing Office.

9–502. Contents of Financing Statement; Record of Mortgage as Financing Statement; Time of Filing Financing Statement.

9–503. Name of Debtor and Secured Party.

9–504. Indication of Collateral.

9–505. Filing and Compliance With Other Statutes and Treaties for Consignments, Leases, Other Bailments, and Other Transactions.

9–506. Effect of Errors or Omissions.

9–507. Effect of Certain Events on Effectiveness of Financing Statement.

9–508. Effectiveness of Financing Statement if New Debtor Becomes Bound by Security Agreement.

9–509. Persons Entitled to File a Record.

9–510. Effectiveness of Filed Record.

9–511. Secured Party of Record.

9–512. Amendment of Financing Statement.

9–513. Termination Statement.

9–514. Assignment of Powers of Secured Party of Record.

9–515. Duration and Effectiveness of Financing Statement; Effect of Lapsed Financing Statement.

9–516. What Constitutes Filing; Effectiveness of Filing.

9–517. Effect of Indexing Errors.

9–518. Claim Concerning Inaccurate or Wrongfully Filed Record.

[SUBPART 2. DUTIES AND OPERATION OF FILING OFFICE]

9–519. Numbering, Maintaining, and Indexing Records; Communicating Information Provided in Records.

Section

9–520. Acceptance and Refusal to Accept Record.

9–521. Uniform Form of Written Financing Statement and Amendment.

9–522. Maintenance and Destruction of Records.

9–523. Information From Filing Office; Sale or License of Records.

9–524. Delay by Filing Office.

9–525. Fees.

9–526. Filing–Office Rules.

9–527. Duty to Report.

PART 6. DEFAULT

[SUBPART 1. DEFAULT AND ENFORCEMENT OF SECURITY INTEREST]

9–601. Rights After Default; Judicial Enforcement; Consignor or Buyer of Accounts, Chattel Paper, Payment Intangibles, or Promissory Notes.

9–602. Waiver and Variance of Rights and Duties.

9–603. Agreement on Standards Concerning Rights and Duties.

9–604. Procedure if Security Agreement Covers Real Property or Fixtures.

9–605. Unknown Debtor or Secondary Obligor.

9–606. Time of Default for Agricultural Lien.

9–607. Collection and Enforcement by Secured Party.

9–608. Application of Proceeds of Collection or Enforcement; Liability for Deficiency and Right to Surplus.

9–609. Secured Party's Right to Take Possession After Default.

9–610. Disposition of Collateral After Default.

9–611. Notification Before Disposition of Collateral.

9–612. Timeliness of Notification Before Disposition of Collateral.

9–613. Contents and Form of Notification Before Disposition of Collateral: General.

9–614. Contents and Form of Notification Before Disposition of Collateral: Consumer-Goods Transaction.

9–615. Application of Proceeds of Disposition; Liability for Deficiency and Right to Surplus.

9–616. Explanation of Calculation of Surplus or Deficiency.

9–617. Rights of Transferee of Collateral.

9–618. Rights and Duties of Certain Secondary Obligors.

Section

9-619. Transfer of Record or Legal Title.

9-620. Acceptance of Collateral in Full or Partial Satisfaction of Obligation; Compulsory Disposition of Collateral.

9-621. Notification of Proposal to Accept Collateral.

9-622. Effect of Acceptance of Collateral.

9-623. Right to Redeem Collateral.

9-624. Waiver.

[SUBPART 2. NONCOMPLIANCE WITH ARTICLE]

9-625. Remedies for Secured Party's Failure to Comply With Article.

9-626. Action in Which Deficiency or Surplus Is in Issue.

9-627. Determination of Whether Conduct Was Commercially Reasonable.

Section

9-628. Nonliability and Limitation on Liability of Secured Party; Liability of Secondary Obligor.

PART 7. TRANSITION

9-701. Effective Date.

9-702. Savings Clause.

9-703. Security Interest Perfected Before Effective Date.

9-704. Security Interest Unperfected Before Effective Date.

9-705. Effectiveness of Action Taken Before Effective Date.

9-706. When Initial Financing Statement Suffices to Continue Effectiveness of Financing Statement.

9-707. Amendment of Pre-Effective-Date Financing Statement.

9-708. Persons Entitled to File Initial Financing Statement or Continuation Statement.

9-709. Priority.

AMERICAN BAR ASSOCIATION ADVISORS

ROBERT BAUER, 1300 N. 17th Street, #1800, Arlington, VA 22209, *Intellectual Property Law Section Advisor*

RICHARD E. CHERIN, 1 Riverfront Plaza, Newark, NJ 07102, *Business Law Section Advisor*

RICHARD R. GOLDBERG, 51st Floor, 1735 Market Street, Philadelphia, PA 19103, *Real Property, Probate & Trust Law Section Advisor*

LAWRENCE A. MANZANARES, City & County Building, 1437 Bannock Street, Courtroom 303W, Denver, CO 80202, *Judicial Administration Division, National Conference of Special Court Judges Advisor*

STEVEN O. WEISE, 40th Floor, 601 S. Figueroa Street, Los Angeles, CA 90017, *Advisor*

EXECUTIVE DIRECTOR

FRED H. MILLER, University of Oklahoma, College of Law, 300 Timberdell Road, Norman, OK 73019, *Executive Director*

WILLIAM J. PIERCE, 1505 Roxbury Road, Ann Arbor, MI 48104, *Executive Director Emeritus*

Table of Disposition of Sections in Former
Article 9 and Other Code Sections

Old Article 9	New Article 9
9–101	9–101
9–102	9–109
9–103(1)(a), (b); (c) omitted	9–301
9–103(1)(d)	9–316
9–103(2)(a), (b); (c) omitted	9–303, 9–316
9–103(2)(d)	9–337
9–103(3)(a), (b); (c) omitted	9–301
9–103(3)(d)	9–307
9–103(3)(e)	9–316
9–103(4)	9–301
9–103(5)	9–301
9–103(6)	9–304, 9–305, 9–306
9–104	9–109
9–105	9–102
9–106	9–102
9–107	9–103
9–108	Omitted as no longer needed
9–109	9–102
9–110	9–108
9–111	Deleted as unnecessary
9–112	Omitted—see 9–102(a)(28)
9–113	9–110
9–114	Omitted—see 9–103 and 9–324
9–115(1)	9–102, 9–106
9–115(2)	9–203, 9–308
9–115(3)	9–108
9–115(4)	9–309, 9–312, 9–314
9–115(5)	9–327, 9–328, 9–329
9–115(6)	9–203, 9–313
9–115(e)	9–106
9–116	9–206, 9–309
9–201	9–201
9–202	9–202
9–203(1)-(3)	9–203
9–203(4)	9–201
9–204	9–204
9–205	9–205
9–206	9–403
9–207	9–207
9–208	9–210
9–301(1)-(2)	9–317
9–301(3)	9–102
9–301(4)	9–323
9–302(1)	9–309, 9–310
9–302(2)	9–310
9–302(3), (4)	9–311
9–303	9–308
9–304	9–312
9–305	9–306, 9–313
9–306	9–315

ARTICLE 9

Old Article 9	New Article 9
9–307(1)-(2)	9–320
9–307(3)	9–323
9–308	9–330
9–309	9–331
9–310	9–333
9–311	9–401
9–312(1)	9–322
9–312(2) omitted	See Appendix II
9–312(3), (4)	9–324
9–312(5), (6)	9–322
9–312(7)	9–323
9–313(1)-(7)	9–334
9–313(8)	9–604
9–314	9–335
9–315	9–336
9–316	9–339
9–317	9–402
9–318(1)	9–404
9–318(2)	9–405
9–318(3), (4)	9–406
9–401	9–501
9–402(1)	9–504, 9–502
9–402(2)	Omitted as unnecessary
9–402(3)	9–521
9–402(4)	9–512
9–402(5), (6)	9–502
9–402(7)	9–503(a)(4), 9–507
9–402(8)	9–506
9–403(1)	9–516(a)
9–403(2)	9–515
9–403(3)	9–515, 9–522
9–403(4)	9–519
9–403(5)	9–525
9–403(6)	9–515
9–403(7)	9–519
9–404	9–513
9–405	9–514, 9–519
9–406	9–512
9–407	9–523
9–408	9–505
9–501(1), (2)	9–601
9–501(3)	9–602, 9–603
9–501(4)	9–604
9–501 (5)	9–601
9–502	9–607, 9–608
9–503	9–609
9–504(1)	9–610, 9–615
9–504(2)	9–615
9–504(3)	9–610, 9–611, 9–624
9–504(4)	9–617
9–504(5)	9–618
9–505	9–620, 9–621, 9–624
9–506	9–623, 9–624
9–507	9–625, 9–627
Other Code Sections	**New Article 9**
2–326(3)	9–102

Other Code Sections	New Article 9
2A–303(3)	9–407
2A–307(2)(b) and (c)	9–317
2A–307(3)	9–321
2A–307(4)	9–323

TABLE INDICATING SOURCES OR DERIVATIONS
OF NEW ARTICLE 9 SECTIONS
AND CONFORMING AMENDMENTS

New Article 9 Sections (Note: many sections contain some new coverage)	Primary Old Article 9 and Other Code Sections
9–101	9–101
9–102	9–105, 9–106, 9–109, 9–301(3), 9–306 (1), 9–115, 2–326(3)
9–103	9–107
9–104 (New)	Derived from 8–106
9–105 (New)	Derived from 8–106
9–106	8–106 and 9–115(e)
9–107 (New)	Derived from 8–106
9–108	9–110, 9–115(3)
9–109	9–102, 9–104
9–110	9–113
9–201	9–201, 9–203(4)
9–202	9–202
9–203	9–203, 9–115(2), (6)
9–204	9–204
9–205	9–205
9–206	9–116
9–207	9–207
9–208 (New)	
9–209 (New)	
9–210	9–208
9–301	9–103(1)(a), (b), 9–103(3)(a), (b),9–103(4) 9–103(5) substantially modified
9–302 (New)	
9–303	9–103(2)(a), (b), substantially revised
9–304 (New)	Derived from 8–110(e) and former 9–103(6)
9–305	9–103(6)
9–306 (New)	Derived in part from 8–110(e) and 9–305 and former 9–103(6)
9–307	9–103(3)(d), as substantially revised
9–308	9–303, 9–115(2)
9–309	9–302(1), 9–115(4)(c), (d), 9–116
9–310	9–302(1), (2)
9–311	9–302(3), (4)
9–312	9–115(4) and 9–304, with additions and some changes
9–313	9–305, 9–115(6)
9–314 (New in part)	9–115(4) and derived from 8–106
9–315	9–306
9–316	9–103(1)(d), (2)(b), (3)(e), as modified
9–317	9–301, 2A–307(2)
9–318 (New)	
9–319 (New)	
9–320	9–307

ARTICLE 9

New Article 9 Sections (Note: many sections contain some new coverage)	Primary Old Article 9 and Other Code Sections
9–321	2A–103(1)(o), 2A–307(3)
9–322	9–312(5), (6)
9–323	9–312(7), 9–301(4), 9–307(3), 2A–307(4)
9–324	9–312(3), (4)
9–325 (New)	But see 9–402(7)
9–326 (New)	But see 9–402(7)
9–327	Derived from 9–115(5)
9–328	9–115(5)
9–329 (New) Loosely modeled after former 9–115(5). See also 5–114 and 5–118	
9–330	9–308
9–331	9–309
9–332 (New)	But see Comment 2(c) to 9–306
9–333	9–310
9–334	9–313
9–335 (New)	Section replaces former 9–314
9–336 (New)	Section replaces former 9–315
9–337	Derived from 9–103(2)(d)
9–338 (New)	
9–339	9–316
9–340 (New)	
9–341 (New)	
9–342 (New)	Derived from 8–106(g)
9–401	9–311
9–402	9–317
9–403	9–206
9–404	9–318(1)
9–405	9–318(2)
9–406	9–318(3), (4)
9–407	2A–303
9–408 (New)	
9–409 (New)	See also 5–114
9–501	Derived from former 9–401
9–502	9–402(1), (5), (6)
9–503 (New) Subsection (a)(4),(b) and (c) derive from former 9–402(7); otherwise, new	
9–504	9–402(1)
9–505	9–408
9–506	9–402(8)
9–507	9–402(7)
9–508 (New)	But see 9–402(7)
9–509 (New)	
9–510 (New)	
9–511 (New)	
9–512	9–402(4)
9–513	9–404
9–514	9–405
9–515	9–403(2), (3), (6)
9–516 (Basically New) Subsection (a) is former 9–403(1); the remainder is new	
9–517 (New)	
9–518 (New)	

669

New Article 9 Sections (**Note:** many sections contain some new coverage)	Primary Old Article 9 and Other Code Sections
9–519	9–403(4), (7); 9–405(2)
9–520 (New)	
9–521 (New)	
9–522	9–403(3), revised substantially
9–523	9–407; subsections (d) and (e) are new
9–524 (New)	Derived from 4–109
9–525	Various sections of former Part 4
9–526 (New)	Subsection (b) derives in part from the Uniform Consumer Credit Code (1974)
9–527 (New)	Derived in part from the Uniform Consumer Credit Code (1974)
9–601	9–501(1), (2), (5)
9–602	9–501(3)
9–603	9–501(3)
9–604	9–501(4), 9–313(8)
9–605 (New)	
9–606 (New)	
9–607	9–502, subsections (b), (d), and (e) are new
9–608	Subsection (a) is new. Subsection (b) derives from former 9–502(2)
9–609	9–503
9–610	9–504(1), (3)
9–611	9–504(3)
9–612 (New)	
9–613 (New)	
9–614 (New)	
9–615	9–504(1), (2)
9–616 (New)	
9–617	9–504(4)
9–618	9–504(5)
9–619 (New)	
9–620	9–505
9–621	9–505
9–622 (New)	
9–623	9–506
9–624	9–504(3), 9–505, 9–506
9–625	9–507
9–626 (New)	
9–627	9–507(2)
9–628 (New)	
9–701	No comparable provision in Article 9 (See Article 10)
9–702	No comparable provision in Article 9 (See Article 10)
9–703	No comparable provision in Article 9 (See Article 10)
9–704	No comparable provision in Article 9 (See Article 10)
9–705	No comparable provision in Article 9 (See Article 10)
9–706	No comparable provision in Article 9 (See Article 10)

New Article 9 Sections (Note: many sections contain some new coverage)	Primary Old Article 9 and Other Code Sections
9–707	No comparable provision in Article 9 (See Article 10)
9–708	No comparable provision in Article 9 (See Article 10)
9–709	No comparable provision in Article 9 (See Article 10)

Conforming Amendments to Other Code Sections and Comments

1–105(2)	4–210
1–201(9), (32), (37)	5–118 (New)
2–103(3)	Article 6 (unless repealed)
2–210; New subsection (3) added	7–503
2–312; Comment	8–102 Comment
2–326(3)	8–103 (f)
2–502 (1) and (2)	8–106 and Comment
2–716(3)	8–110
2A–103(3)	8–301 (3)
2A–303	8–302 (a)
2A–307	8–502 Comment
2A–309	8–510

PART 1

GENERAL PROVISIONS

[SUBPART 1. SHORT TITLE, DEFINITIONS, AND GENERAL CONCEPTS]

§ 9–101. Short Title.

This article may be cited as Uniform Commercial Code–Secured Transactions.

Official Comment

1. **Source.** This Article supersedes former Uniform Commercial Code (UCC) Article 9. As did its predecessor, it provides a comprehensive scheme for the regulation of security interests in personal property and fixtures. For the most part this Article follows the general approach and retains much of the terminology of former Article 9. In addition to describing many aspects of the operation and interpretation of this Article, these Comments explain the material changes that this Article makes to former Article 9. Former Article 9 superseded the wide variety of pre-UCC security devices. Unlike the Comments to former Article 9, however, these Comments dwell very little on the pre-UCC state of the law. For that reason, the Comments to former Article 9 will remain of substantial historical value and interest. They also will remain useful in understanding the background and general conceptual approach of this Article.

Citations to "Bankruptcy Code Section ____ " in these Comments are to Title 11 of the United States Code as in effect on December 31, 1998.

2. **Background and History.** In 1990, the Permanent Editorial Board for the UCC with the support of its sponsors, The American Law Institute and the National Conference of Commissioners on Uniform State Laws, established a committee to study Article 9 of the UCC. The study committee issued its report as of December 1, 1992, recommending the creation of a drafting committee for the revision of Article 9 and also recommending numerous specific changes to Article 9. Organized in 1993, a drafting committee met fifteen times from 1993 to 1998. This Article was approved by its sponsors in 1998.

3. **Reorganization and Renumbering; Captions; Style.** This Article reflects a substantial reorganization of former Article 9 and renumbering of most sections. New Part 4 deals with several aspects of third-party rights and duties that are unrelated to perfection and priority. Some of these were covered by Part 3 of former Article 9. Part 5 deals with filing (covered by former Part 4) and Part 6 deals with default and enforcement (covered by former Part 5). Appendix I contains conforming revisions to other articles of the UCC, and Appendix II contains model provisions for production-money priority.

This Article also includes headings for the subsections as an aid to readers. Unlike section captions, which are part of the UCC, see Section 1–109, subsection headings are not a part of the official text itself and have not been approved by the sponsors. Each jurisdiction in which this Article is introduced may consider whether to adopt the headings as a part of the statute and whether to adopt a provision clarifying the effect, if any, to be given to the headings. This Article also has been conformed to current style conventions.

4. **Summary of Revisions.** Following is a brief summary of some of the more significant revisions of Article 9 that are included in this Article.

a. **Scope of Article 9.** This Article expands the scope of Article 9 in several respects.

Deposit accounts. Section 9–109 includes within this Article's scope deposit accounts as original collateral, except in consumer transactions. Former Article 9 dealt with deposit accounts only as proceeds of other collateral.

Sales of payment intangibles and promissory notes. Section 9–109 also includes within the scope of this Article most sales of "payment intangibles" (defined in Section 9–102 as general intangibles under which an account debtor's principal obligation is monetary) and "promissory notes" (also defined in Section 9–102). Former Article 9 included sales of accounts and chattel paper, but not sales of payment intangibles or promissory notes. In its inclusion of sales of payment intangibles and promissory notes, this Article continues the drafting convention found in former Article 9; it provides that the sale of accounts, chattel paper, payment intangibles, or promissory notes creates a "security interest." The definition of "account" in Section 9–102 also has been expanded to include various rights to payment that were general intangibles under former Article 9.

Health-care-insurance receivables. Section 9–109 narrows Article 9's exclusion of transfers of interests in insurance policies by carving out of the exclusion

"health-care-insurance receivables" (defined in Section 9–102). A health-care-insurance receivable is included within the definition of "account" in Section 9–102.

Nonpossessory statutory agricultural liens. Section 9–109 also brings nonpossessory statutory agricultural liens within the scope of Article 9.

Consignments. Section 9–109 provides that "true" consignments-bailments for the purpose of sale by the bailee are security interests covered by Article 9, with certain exceptions. See Section 9–102 (defining "consignment"). Currently, many consignments are subject to Article 9's filing requirements by operation of former Section 2–326.

Supporting obligations and property securing rights to payment. This Article also addresses explicitly (i) obligations, such as guaranties and letters of credit, that support payment or performance of collateral such as accounts, chattel paper, and payment intangibles, and (ii) any property (including real property) that secures a right to payment or performance that is subject to an Article 9 security interest. See Sections 9–203, 9–308.

Commercial tort claims. Section 9–109 expands the scope of Article 9 to include the assignment of commercial tort claims by narrowing the exclusion of tort claims generally. However, this Article continues to exclude tort claims for bodily injury and other non-business tort claims of a natural person. See Section 9–102 (defining "commercial tort claim").

Transfers by States and governmental units of States. Section 9–109 narrows the exclusion of transfers by States and their governmental units. It excludes only transfers covered by another statute (other than a statute generally applicable to security interests) to the extent the statute governs the creation, perfection, priority, or enforcement of security interests.

Nonassignable general intangibles, promissory notes, health-care-insurance receivables, and letter-of-credit rights. This Article enables a security interest to attach to letter-of-credit rights, health-care-insurance receivables, promissory notes, and general intangibles, including contracts, permits, licenses, and franchises, notwithstanding a contractual or statutory prohibition against or limitation on assignment. This Article explicitly protects third parties against any adverse effect of the creation or attempted enforcement of the security interest. See Sections 9–408, 9–409.

Subject to Sections 9–408 and 9–409 and two other exceptions (Sections 9406, concerning accounts, chattel paper, and payment intangibles, and 9407, concerning interests in leased goods), Section 9–401 establishes a baseline rule that the inclusion of transactions and collateral within the scope of Article 9 has no effect on non-Article 9 law dealing with the alienability or inalienability of property. For example, if a commercial tort claim is nonassignable under other applicable law, the fact that a security interest in the claim is within the scope of Article 9 does not override the other applicable law's effective prohibition of assignment.

b. **Duties of Secured Party.** This Article provides for expanded duties of secured parties.

Release of control. Section 9–208 imposes upon a secured party having control of a deposit account, investment property, or a letter-of-credit right the duty to release control when there is no secured obligation and no commitment to give value. Section 9–209 contains analogous provisions when an account debtor has been notified to pay a secured party.

Information. Section 9–210 expands a secured party's duties to provide the debtor with information concerning collateral and the obligations that it secures.

Default and enforcement. Part 6 also includes some additional duties of secured parties in connection with default and enforcement. See, e.g., Section 9–616 (duty to explain calculation of deficiency or surplus in a consumer-goods transaction).

c. **Choice of Law.** The choice-of-law rules for the law governing perfection, the effect of perfection or nonperfection, and priority are found in Part 3, Subpart 1 (Sections 9–301 through 9–307). See also Section 9–316.

Where to file: Location of debtor. This Article changes the choice-of-law rule governing perfection (i.e., where to file) for most collateral to the law of the jurisdiction where the debtor is located. See Section 9–301. Under former Article 9, the jurisdiction of the debtor's location governed only perfection and priority of a security interest in accounts, general intangibles, mobile goods, and, for purposes of perfection by filing, chattel paper and investment property.

Determining debtor's location. As a baseline rule, Section 9–307 follows former Section 9–103, under which the location of the debtor is the debtor's place of business (or chief executive office, if the debtor has more than one place of business). Section 9–307 contains three major exceptions. First, a "registered organization," such as a corporation or limited liability company, is located in the State under whose law the debtor is organized, e.g., a corporate debtor's State of incorporation. Second, an individual debtor is located at his or her principal residence. Third, there are

special rules for determining the location of the United States and registered organizations organized under the law of the United States.

Location of non-U.S. debtors. If, applying the foregoing rules, a debtor is located in a jurisdiction whose law does not require public notice as a condition of perfection of a nonpossessory security interest, the entity is deemed located in the District of Columbia. See Section 9307. Thus, to the extent that this Article applies to non-U.S. debtors, perfection could be accomplished in many cases by a domestic filing.

Priority. For tangible collateral such as goods and instruments, Section 9–301 provides that the law applicable to priority and the effect of perfection or nonperfection will remain the law of the jurisdiction where the collateral is located, as under former Section 9–103 (but without the confusing "last event" test). For intangible collateral, such as accounts, the applicable law for priority will be that of the jurisdiction in which the debtor is located.

Possessory security interests; agricultural liens. Perfection, the effect of perfection or nonperfection, and priority of a possessory security interest or an agricultural lien are governed by the law of the jurisdiction where the collateral subject to the security interest or lien is located. See Sections 9–301, 9302.

Goods covered by certificates of title; deposit accounts; letter-of-credit rights; investment property. This Article includes several refinements to the treatment of choice-of-law matters for goods covered by certificates of title. See Section 9–303. It also provides special choice-of-law rules, similar to those for investment property under current Articles 8 and 9, for deposit accounts (Section 9–304), investment property (Section 9–305), and letter-of-credit rights (Section 9306).

Change in applicable law. Section 9–316 addresses perfection following a change in applicable law.

d. **Perfection.** The rules governing perfection of security interests and agricultural liens are found in Part 3, Subpart 2 (Sections 9–308 through 9–316).

Deposit accounts; letter-of-credit rights. With certain exceptions, this Article provides that a security interest in a deposit account or a letter-of-credit right may be perfected *only* by the secured party's acquiring "control" of the deposit account or letter-of-credit right. See Sections 9–312, 9–314. Under Section 9–104, a secured party has "control" of a deposit account when, with the consent of the debtor, the secured party obtains the depositary bank's agreement to act on the secured party's instructions (including when the secured party becomes the account holder) or when the secured party is itself the depositary bank. The control requirements are patterned on Section 8106, which specifies the requirements for control of investment property. Under Section 9–107, "control" of a letter-of-credit right occurs when the issuer or nominated person consents to an assignment of proceeds under Section 5114.

Electronic chattel paper. Section 9–102 includes a new defined term: "electronic chattel paper." Electronic chattel paper is a record or records consisting of information stored in an electronic medium (i.e., it is not written). Perfection of a security interest in electronic chattel paper may be by control or filing. See Sections 9–105 (*sui generis* definition of control of electronic chattel paper), 9312 (perfection by filing), 9314 (perfection by control).

Investment property. The perfection requirements for "investment property" (defined in Section 9–102), including perfection by control under Section 9–106, remain substantially unchanged. However, a new provision in Section 9–314 is designed to ensure that a secured party retains control in "repledge" transactions that are typical in the securities markets.

Instruments, agricultural liens, and commercial tort claims. This Article expands the types of collateral in which a security interest may be perfected by filing to include instruments. See Section 9–312. Agricultural liens and security interests in commercial tort claims also are perfected by filing, under this Article. See Sections 9–308, 9–310.

Sales of payment intangibles and promissory notes. Although former Article 9 covered the outright sale of accounts and chattel paper, sales of most other types of receivables also are financing transactions to which Article 9 should apply. Accordingly, Section 9–102 expands the definition of "account" to include many types of receivables (including "health-care-insurance receivables," defined in Section 9–102) that former Article 9 classified as "general intangibles." It thereby subjects to Article 9's filing system sales of more types of receivables than did former Article 9. Certain sales of payment intangibles-primarily bank loan participation transactions-should not be subject to the Article 9 filing rules. These transactions fall in a residual category of collateral, "payment intangibles" (general intangibles under which the account debtor's principal obligation is monetary), the sale of which is exempt from the filing requirements of Article 9. See Sections 9–102, 9–109, 9–309 (perfection upon attachment). The perfection rules for sales of promissory notes are the same as those for sales of payment intangibles.

Possessory security interests. Several provisions of this Article address aspects of security interests involving a secured party or a third party who is in possession of the collateral. In particular, Section 9–313 resolves a number of uncertainties under former Section 9–305. It provides that a security interest in collateral in the possession of a third party is perfected when the third party acknowledges in an authenticated record that it holds for the secured party's benefit. Section 9–313 also provides that a third party need not so acknowledge and that its acknowledgment does not impose any duties on it, unless it otherwise agrees. A special rule in Section 9–313 provides that if a secured party already is in possession of collateral, its security interest remains perfected by possession if it delivers the collateral to a third party and the collateral is accompanied by instructions to hold it for the secured party or to redeliver it to the secured party. Section 9–313 also clarifies the limited circumstances under which a security interest in goods covered by a certificate of title may be perfected by the secured party's taking possession.

Automatic perfection. Section 9–309 lists various types of security interests as to which no public-notice step is required for perfection (e.g., purchase-money security interests in consumer goods other than automobiles). This automatic perfection also extends to a transfer of a health-care-insurance receivable *to* a health-care provider. Those transfers normally will be made by natural persons who receive health-care services; there is little value in requiring filing for perfection in that context. Automatic perfection also applies to security interests created by sales of payment intangibles and promissory notes. Section 9–308 provides that a perfected security interest in collateral supported by a "supporting obligation" (such as an account supported by a guaranty) also is a perfected security interest in the supporting obligation, and that a perfected security interest in an obligation secured by a security interest or lien on property (e.g., a real-property mortgage) also is a perfected security interest in the security interest or lien.

e. Priority; Special Rules for Banks and Deposit Accounts. The rules governing priority of security interests and agricultural liens are found in Part 3, Subpart 3 (Sections 9–317 through 9–342). This Article includes several new priority rules and some special rules relating to banks and deposit accounts (Sections 9–340 through 9–342).

Purchase-money security interests: General; consumer-goods transactions; inventory. Section 9–103 substantially rewrites the definition of purchase-money security interest (PMSI) (although the term is not formally "defined"). The substantive changes, however, apply only to non-consumer-goods transactions. (Consumer transactions and consumer-goods transactions are discussed below in Comment 4.j.) For non-consumer-goods transactions, Section 9–103 makes clear that a security interest in collateral may be (to some extent) both a PMSI as well as a non-PMSI, in accord with the "dual status" rule applied by some courts under former Article 9 (thereby rejecting the "transformation" rule). The definition provides an even broader conception of a PMSI in inventory, yielding a result that accords with private agreements entered into in response to the uncertainty under former Article 9. It also treats consignments as purchase-money security interests in inventory. Section 9–324 revises the PMSI priority rules, but for the most part without material change in substance. Section 9–324 also clarifies the priority rules for competing PMSIs in the same collateral.

Purchase-money security interests in livestock; agricultural liens. Section 9–324 provides a special PMSI priority, similar to the inventory PMSI priority rule, for livestock. Section 9–322 (which contains the baseline first-to-file-or-perfect priority rule) also recognizes special non-Article 9 priority rules for agricultural liens, which can override the baseline first-in-time rule.

Purchase-money security interests in software. Section 9–324 contains a new priority rule for a software purchase-money security interest. (Section 9–102 includes a definition of "software.") Under Section 9–103, a software PMSI includes a PMSI in software that is used in goods that are also subject to a PMSI. (Note also that the definition of "chattel paper" has been expanded to include records that evidence a monetary obligation and a security interest in specific goods and software used in the goods.)

Investment property. The priority rules for investment property are substantially similar to the priority rules found in former Section 9–115, which was added in conjunction with the 1994 revisions to UCC Article 8. Under Section 9–328, if a secured party has control of investment property (Sections 8106, 9106), its security interest is senior to a security interest perfected in another manner (e.g., by filing). Also under Section 9328, security interests perfected by control generally rank according to the time that control is obtained or, in the case of a security entitlement or a commodity contract carried in a commodity account, the time when the control arrangement is entered into. This is a change from former Section 9–115, under which the security interests ranked equally. However, as between a securities intermediary's security interest in a security entitlement that it maintains for the debtor and a security interest held by another secured party, the securities intermediary's security interest is senior.

Deposit accounts. This Article's priority rules applicable to deposit accounts are found in Section 9–327. They are patterned on and are similar to those for investment property in former Section 9–115 and Section 9–328 of this Article. Under Section 9–327, if a secured party has control of a deposit account, its security interest is senior to a security interest perfected in another manner (i.e., as cash proceeds). Also under Section 9327, security interests perfected by control rank according to the time that control is obtained. However, as between a depositary bank's security interest and one held by another secured party, the depositary bank's security interest is senior. A corresponding rule in Section 9–340 makes a depositary bank's right of set-off generally senior to a security interest held by another secured party. However, if the other secured party becomes the depositary bank's customer with respect to the deposit account, then its security interest is senior to the depositary bank's security interest and right of set-off. Sections 9–327, 9–340.

Letter-of-credit rights. The priority rules for security interests in letter-of-credit rights are found in Section 9–329. They are somewhat analogous to those for deposit accounts. A security interest perfected by control has priority over one perfected in another manner (i.e., as a supporting obligation for the collateral in which a security interest is perfected). Security interests in a letter-of-credit right perfected by control rank according to the time that control is obtained. However, the rights of a transferee beneficiary or a nominated person are independent and superior to the extent provided in Section 5–114. See Section 9–109(c)(4).

Chattel paper and instruments. Section 9–330 is the successor to former Section 9–308. As under former Section 9–308, differing priority rules apply to purchasers of chattel paper who give new value and take possession (or, in the case of electronic chattel paper, obtain control) of the collateral depending on whether a conflicting security interest in the collateral is claimed merely as proceeds. The principal change relates to the role of knowledge and the effect of an indication of a previous assignment of the collateral. Section 9–330 also affords priority to purchasers of instruments who take possession in good faith and without knowledge that the purchase violates the rights of the competing secured party. In addition, to qualify for priority, purchasers of chattel paper, but not of instruments, must purchase in the ordinary course of business.

Proceeds. Section 9–322 contains new priority rules that clarify when a special priority of a security interest in collateral continues or does not continue with respect to proceeds of the collateral. Other refinements to the priority rules for proceeds are included in Sections 9–324 (purchase-money security interest priority) and 9–330 (priority of certain purchasers of chattel paper and instruments).

Miscellaneous priority provisions. This Article also includes (i) clarifications of selected good-faith-purchase and similar issues (Sections 9–317, 9–331); (ii) new priority rules to deal with the "double debtor" problem arising when a debtor creates a security interest in collateral acquired by the debtor subject to a security interest created by another person (Section 9–325); (iii) new priority rules to deal with the problems created when a change in corporate structure or the like results in a new entity that has become bound by the original debtor's after-acquired property agreement (Section 9–326); (iv) a provision enabling most transferees of funds from a deposit account or money to take free of a security interest (Section 9–332); (v) substantially rewritten and refined priority rules dealing with accessions and commingled goods (Sections 9–335, 9–336); (vi) revised priority rules for security interests in goods covered by a certificate of title (Section 9–337); and (vii) provisions designed to ensure that security interests in deposit accounts will not extend to most transferees of funds on deposit or payees from deposit accounts and will not otherwise "clog" the payments system (Sections 9–341, 9–342).

Model provisions relating to production-money security interests. Appendix II to this Article contains model definitions and priority rules relating to "production-money security interests" held by secured parties who give new value used in the production of crops. Because no consensus emerged on the wisdom of these provisions during the drafting process, the sponsors make no recommendation on whether these model provisions should be enacted.

f. **Proceeds.** Section 9–102 contains an expanded definition of "proceeds" of collateral which includes additional rights and property that arise out of collateral, such as distributions on account of collateral and claims arising out of the loss or nonconformity of, defects in, or damage to collateral. The term also includes collections on account of "supporting obligations," such as guarantees.

g. **Part 4: Additional Provisions Relating to Third–Party Rights.** New Part 4 contains several provisions relating to the relationships between certain third parties and the parties to secured transactions. It contains new Sections 9–401 (replacing former Section 9–311) (alienability of debtor's rights), 9–402 (replacing former Section 9–317) (secured party not obligated on debtor's contracts), 9–403 (replacing former Section 9–206) (agreement not to assert defenses against assignee), 9–404, 9–405, and 9–406 (replacing former Section 9–318) (rights acquired by assignee, modification of assigned contract, discharge of account debtor, restrictions on assignment of account, chattel paper, promissory note, or payment intangible ineffective), 9–407 (replacing some provisions of former Section 2A–303) (restrictions on creation or enforcement of security interest in leasehold interest or lessor's residual interest ineffective). It also contains new Sections 9–408 (restrictions on assignment of promissory notes, health-care-insurance receivables ineffective, and certain general intangibles ineffective) and 9–409 (restrictions on assignment of letter-of-credit rights ineffective), which are discussed above.

h. **Filing.** Part 5 (formerly Part 4) of Article 9 has been substantially rewritten to simplify the statutory text and to deal with numerous problems of interpretation and implementation that have arisen over the years.

Medium-neutrality. This Article is "medium-neutral"; that is, it makes clear that parties may file and otherwise communicate with a filing office by means of records communicated and stored in media other than on paper.

Identity of person who files a record; authorization. Part 5 is largely indifferent as to the person who effects a filing. Instead, it addresses whose authorization is necessary for a person to file a record with a filing office. The filing scheme does not contemplate that the identity of a "filer" will be a part of the searchable records. This approach is consistent with, and a necessary aspect of, eliminating signatures or other evidence of authorization from the system (except to the extent that filing offices may choose to employ authentication procedures in connection with electronic communications). As long as the appropriate person authorizes the filing, or, in the case of a termination statement, the debtor is entitled to the termination, it is largely insignificant whether the secured party or another person files any given record.

Section 9–509 collects in one place most of the rules that determine when a record may be filed. In general, the debtor's authorization is required for the filing of an initial financing statement or an amendment that adds collateral. With one further exception, a secured party of record's authorization is required for the filing of other amendments. The exception arises if a secured party has failed to provide a termination statement that is required because there is no outstanding secured obligation or commitment to give value. In that situation, a debtor is authorized to file a termination statement indicating that it has been filed by the debtor.

Financing statement formal requisites. The formal requisites for a financing statement are set out in Section 9–502. A financing statement must provide the name of the debtor and the secured party and an indication of the collateral that it covers. Sections 9–503 and 9–506 address the sufficiency of a name provided on a financing statement and clarify when a debtor's name is correct and when an incorrect name is insufficient. Section 9–504 addresses the indication of collateral covered. Under Section 9–504, a super-generic description (e.g., "all assets" or "all personal property") in a financing statement is a sufficient indication of the collateral. (Note, however, that a super-generic description is inadequate for purposes of a security agreement. See Sections 9–108, 9–203.) To facilitate electronic filing, this Article does not require that the debtor's signature or other authorization appear on a financing statement. Instead, it prohibits the filing of unauthorized financing statements and imposes liability upon those who violate the prohibition. See Sections 9–509, 9–626.

Filing-office operations. Part 5 contains several provisions governing filing operations. First, it prohibits the filing office from rejecting an initial financing statement or other record for a reason other than one of the few that are specified. See Sections 9–520, 9–516. Second, the filing office is obliged to link all subsequent records (e.g., assignments, continuation statements, etc.) to the initial financing statement to which they relate. See Section 9–519. Third, the filing office may delete a financing statement and related records from the files no earlier than one year after lapse (lapse normally is five years after the filing date), and then only if a continuation statement has not been filed. See Sections 9–515, 9–519, 9–522. Thus, a financing statement and related records would be discovered by a search of the files even after the filing of a termination statement. This approach helps eliminate filing-office discretion and also eases problems associated with multiple secured parties and multiple partial assignments. Fourth, Part 5 mandates performance standards for filing offices. See Sections 9–519, 9–520, 9–523. Fifth, it provides for the promulgation of filing-office rules to deal with details best left out of the statute and requires the filing office to submit periodic reports. See Sections 9–526, 9–527.

Correction of records: Defaulting or missing secured parties and fraudulent filings. In some areas of the country, serious problems have arisen from fraudulent financing statements that are filed against public officials and other persons. This Article addresses the fraud problem by providing the opportunity for a debtor to file a termination statement when a secured party wrongfully refuses or fails to provide a termination statement. See Section 9–509. This opportunity also addresses the problem of secured parties that simply disappear through mergers or liquidations. In addition, Section 9–518 affords a statutory method by which a debtor who believes that a filed record is inaccurate or was wrongfully filed may indicate that fact in the files by filing a correction statement, albeit without affecting the efficacy, if any, of the challenged record.

Extended period of effectiveness for certain financing statements. Section 9–515 contains an exception to the usual rule that financing statements are effective for five years unless a continuation statement is filed to continue the effectiveness for another five years. Under that section, an initial financing statement filed in connection with a "public-finance transaction" or a "manufactured-home transaction" (terms defined in Section 9–102) is effective for 30 years.

National form of financing statement and related forms. Section 9–521 provides for uniform, national written forms of financing statements and related written records that must be accepted by a filing office that accepts written records.

i. Default and Enforcement. Part 6 of Article 9 extensively revises former Part 5. Provisions relating to enforcement of consumer-goods transactions and consumer transactions are discussed in Comment 4.j.

Debtor, secondary obligor; waiver. Section 9–602 clarifies the identity of persons who have rights and persons to whom a secured party owes specified duties under Part 6. Under that section, the rights and duties are enjoyed by and run to the "debtor," defined in Section 9–102 to mean any person with a non-lien property interest in collateral, and to any "obligor." However, with one exception (Section 9–616, as it relates to a consumer obligor), the rights and duties concerned affect non-debtor obligors only if they are "secondary obligors." "Secondary obligor" is defined in Section 9–102 to include one who is secondarily obligated on the secured obligation, e.g., a guarantor, or one who has a right of recourse against the debtor or another obligor with respect to an obligation secured by collateral. However, under Section 9–628, the secured party is relieved from any duty or liability to any person unless the secured party knows that the person is a debtor or obligor. Resolving an issue on which courts disagreed under former Article 9, this Article generally prohibits waiver by a secondary obligor of its rights and a secured party's duties under Part 6. See Section 9–602. However, Section 9–624 permits a secondary obligor or debtor to waive the right to notification of disposition of collateral and, in a non-consumer transaction, the right to redeem collateral, if the secondary obligor or debtor agrees to do so after default.

Rights of collection and enforcement of collateral. Section 9–607 explains in greater detail than former 9–502 the rights of a secured party who seeks to collect or enforce collateral, including accounts, chattel paper, and payment intangibles. It also sets forth the enforcement rights of a depositary bank holding a security interest in a deposit account maintained with the depositary bank. Section 9–607 relates solely to the rights of a secured party vis-a-vis a debtor with respect to collections and enforcement. It does not affect the rights or duties of third parties, such as account debtors on collateral, which are addressed elsewhere (e.g., Section 9–406). Section 9–608 clarifies the manner in which proceeds of collection or enforcement are to be applied.

Disposition of collateral: Warranties of title. Section 9–610 imposes on a secured party who disposes of collateral the warranties of title, quiet possession, and the like that are otherwise applicable under other law. It also provides rules for the exclusion or modification of those warranties.

Disposition of collateral: Notification, application of proceeds, surplus and deficiency, other effects. Section 9–611 requires a secured party to give notification of a disposition of collateral to other secured parties and lienholders who have filed financing statements against the debtor covering the collateral. (That duty was eliminated by the 1972 revisions to Article 9.) However, that section relieves the secured party from that duty when the secured party undertakes a search of the records and a report of the results is unreasonably delayed. Section 9–613, which applies only to non-consumer transactions, specifies the contents of a sufficient notification of disposition and provides that a notification sent 10 days or more before the earliest time for disposition is sent within a reasonable time. Section 9–615 addresses the application of proceeds of disposition, the entitlement of a debtor to any surplus, and the liability of an obligor for any deficiency. Section 9–619 clarifies the effects of a disposition by a secured party, including the rights of transferees of the collateral.

Rights and duties of secondary obligor. Section 9–618 provides that a secondary obligor obtains the rights and assumes the duties of a secured party if the secondary obligor receives an assignment of a secured obligation, agrees to assume the secured party's rights and duties upon a transfer to it of collateral, or becomes subrogated to the rights of the secured party with respect to the collateral. The assumption, transfer, or subrogation is not a disposition of collateral under Section 9–610, but it does relieve the former secured party of further duties. Former Section 9–504(5) did not address whether a secured party was relieved of its duties in this situation.

Transfer of record or legal title. Section 9–619 contains a new provision making clear that a transfer of record or legal title to a secured party is not of itself a disposition under Part 6. This rule applies regardless of the circumstances under which the transfer of title occurs.

Strict foreclosure. Section 9–620, unlike former Section 9–505, permits a secured party to accept collateral in partial satisfaction, as well as full satisfaction, of the obligations secured. This right of strict foreclosure extends to intangible as well as tangible property. Section 9–622 clarifies the effects of an acceptance of collateral on the rights of junior claimants. It rejects the approach taken by some courts–deeming a secured party to have constructively retained collateral in satisfaction of the secured obligations–in the case of a secured party's unreasonable delay in the disposition of collateral. Instead, unreasonable delay is relevant when determining whether a disposition under Section 9–610 is commercially reasonable.

Effect of noncompliance: "Rebuttable presumption" test. Section 9–626 adopts the "rebuttable presumption" test for the failure of a secured party to proceed in accordance with certain provisions of Part 6. (As discussed in Comment 4.j., the test does not necessarily apply to consumer transactions.) Under this approach, the deficiency claim of a noncomplying secured party is calculated by crediting the obligor with the greater of the actual net proceeds of a disposition and the amount of net proceeds that would have been realized if the disposition had been conducted in accordance with Part 6 (e.g., in a commercially reasonable manner). For non-consumer transactions, Section 9–626 rejects the "absolute bar" test that some courts have imposed; that approach bars a noncomplying secured party from recovering any deficiency, regardless of the loss (if any) the debtor suffered as a consequence of the noncompliance.

"Low-price" dispositions: Calculation of deficiency and surplus. Section 9–615(f) addresses the problem of procedurally regular dispositions that fetch a low price. Subsection (f) provides a special method for calculating a deficiency if the proceeds of a disposition of collateral to a secured party, a person related to the secured party, or a secondary obligor are "significantly below the range of proceeds that a complying disposition to a person other than the secured party, a person related to the secured party, or a secondary obligor would have brought." ("Person related to" is defined in Section 9–102.) In these situations there is reason to suspect that there may be inadequate incentives to obtain a better price. Consequently, instead of calculating a deficiency (or surplus) based on the actual net proceeds, the deficiency (or surplus) would be calculated based on the proceeds that would have been received in a disposition to a person other than the secured party, a person related to the secured party, or a secondary obligor.

j. **Consumer Goods, Consumer–Goods Transactions, and Consumer Transactions.** This Article (including the accompanying conforming revisions (see Appendix I)) includes several special rules for "consumer goods," "consumer transactions," and "consumer-goods transactions." Each term is defined in Section 9–102.

(i) Revised Sections 2–502 and 2–716 provide a buyer of consumer goods with enhanced rights to possession of the goods, thereby accelerating the opportunity to achieve "buyer in ordinary course of business" status under Section 1–201.

(ii) Section 9–103(e) (allocation of payments for determining extent of purchase-money status), (f) (purchase-money status not affected by cross-collateralization, refinancing, restructuring, or the like), and (g) (secured party has burden of establishing extent of purchase-money status) do not apply to consumer-goods transactions. Sections 9–103 also provides that the limitation of those provisions to transactions other than consumer-goods transactions leaves to the courts the proper rules for consumer-goods transactions and prohibits the courts from drawing inferences from that limitation.

(iii) Section 9–108 provides that in a consumer transaction a description of consumer goods, a security entitlement, securities account, or commodity account "only by [UCC-defined] type of collateral" is not a sufficient collateral description in a security agreement.

(iv) Sections 9–403 and 9–404 make effective the Federal Trade Commission's anti-holder-in-due-course rule (when applicable), 16 C.F.R. Part 433, even in the absence of the required legend.

(v) The 10–day safe-harbor for notification of a disposition provided by Section 9–612 does not apply in a consumer transaction.

(vi) Section 9–613 (contents and form of notice of disposition) does not apply to a consumer-goods transaction.

(vii) Section 9–614 contains special requirements for the contents of a notification of disposition and a safe-harbor, "plain English" form of notification, for consumer-goods transactions.

(viii) Section 9–616 requires a secured party in a consumer-goods transaction to provide a debtor with a notification of how it calculated a deficiency at the time it first undertakes to collect a deficiency.

(ix) Section 9–620 prohibits partial strict foreclosure with respect to consumer goods collateral and, unless the debtor agrees to waive the requirement in an authenticated record after default, in certain cases requires the secured party to dispose of consumer goods collateral which has been repossessed.

(x) Section 9–626 ("rebuttable presumption" rule) does not apply to a consumer transaction. Section 9–626 also provides that its limitation to transactions other than consumer transactions leaves to the courts the proper rules for consumer transactions and prohibits the courts from drawing inferences from that limitation.

k. **Good Faith.** Section 9–102 contains a new definition of "good faith" that includes not only "honesty in fact" but also "the observance of reasonable commercial standards of fair dealing." The definition is similar to the ones adopted in connection with other, recently completed revisions of the UCC.

l. **Transition Provisions.** Part 7 (Sections 9–701 through 9–709) contains transition provisions. Transition from former Article 9 to this Article will be particularly challenging in view of its expanded scope, its modification of choice-of-law rules for perfection and priority, and its expansion of the methods of perfection.

m. **Conforming and Related Amendments to Other UCC Articles.** Appendix I contains several proposed revisions to the provisions and Comments of other UCC articles. For the most part the revisions are explained in the Comments to the proposed revisions. Cross-references in other UCC articles to sections of Article 9 also have been revised.

Article 1. Revised Section 1–201 contains revisions to the definitions of "buyer in ordinary course of business," "purchaser," and "security interest."

Articles 2 and 2A. Sections 2–210, 2–326, 2–502, 2–716, 2A–303, and 2A–307 have been revised to address the intersection between Articles 2 and 2A and Article 9.

Article 5. New Section 5–118 is patterned on Section 4–210. It provides for a security interest in documents presented under a letter of credit in favor of the issuer and a nominated person on the letter of credit.

Article 8. Revisions to Section 8–106, which deals with "control" of securities and security entitlements, conform it to Section 8–302, which deals with "delivery." Revisions to Section 8–110, which deals with a "securities intermediary's jurisdiction," conform it to the revised treatment of a "commodity intermediary's jurisdiction" in Section 9–305. Sections 8–301 and 8–302 have been revised for clarification. Section 8–510 has been revised to conform it to the revised priority rules of Section 9–328. Several Comments in Article 8 also have been revised.

§ 9–102. Definitions and Index of Definitions.

(a) **[Article 9 definitions.]** In this article:

(1) "Accession" means goods that are physically united with other goods in such a manner that the identity of the original goods is not lost.

(2) "Account", except as used in "account for", means a right to payment of a monetary obligation, whether or not earned by performance, (i) for property that has been or is to be sold, leased, licensed, assigned, or otherwise disposed of, (ii) for services rendered or to be rendered, (iii) for a policy of insurance issued or to be issued, (iv) for a secondary obligation incurred or to be incurred, (v) for energy provided or to be provided, (vi) for the use or hire of a vessel under a charter or other contract, (vii) arising out of the use of a credit or charge card or information contained on or for use with the card, or (viii) as winnings in a lottery or other game of chance operated or sponsored by a State, governmental unit of a State, or person licensed or authorized to operate the game by a State or governmental unit of a State. The term includes health-care-insurance receivables. The term does not include (i) rights to payment evidenced by chattel paper or an instrument, (ii) commercial tort claims, (iii) deposit accounts, (iv) investment property, (v) letter-of-credit rights or letters of credit, or (vi) rights to payment for money or funds advanced or sold, other than rights arising out of the use of a credit or charge card or information contained on or for use with the card.

(3) "Account debtor" means a person obligated on an account, chattel paper, or general intangible. The term does not include persons obligated to pay a negotiable instrument, even if the instrument constitutes part of chattel paper.

(4) "Accounting", except as used in "accounting for", means a record:

(A) authenticated by a secured party;

(B) indicating the aggregate unpaid secured obligations as of a date not more than 35 days earlier or 35 days later than the date of the record; and

(C) identifying the components of the obligations in reasonable detail.

(5) "Agricultural lien" means an interest in farm products:

(A) which secures payment or performance of an obligation for:

(i) goods or services furnished in connection with a debtor's farming operation; or

(ii) rent on real property leased by a debtor in connection with its farming operation;

(B) which is created by statute in favor of a person that:

(i) in the ordinary course of its business furnished goods or services to a debtor in connection with a debtor's farming operation; or

(ii) leased real property to a debtor in connection with the debtor's farming operation; and

(C) whose effectiveness does not depend on the person's possession of the personal property.

(6) "As-extracted collateral" means:

(A) oil, gas, or other minerals that are subject to a security interest that:

(i) is created by a debtor having an interest in the minerals before extraction; and

(ii) attaches to the minerals as extracted; or

(B) accounts arising out of the sale at the wellhead or minehead of oil, gas, or other minerals in which the debtor had an interest before extraction.

(7) "Authenticate" means:

(A) to sign; or

(B) to execute or otherwise adopt a symbol, or encrypt or similarly process a record in whole or in part, with the present intent of the authenticating person to identify the person and adopt or accept a record.

(8) "Bank" means an organization that is engaged in the business of banking. The term includes savings banks, savings and loan associations, credit unions, and trust companies.

(9) "Cash proceeds" means proceeds that are money, checks, deposit accounts, or the like.

(10) "Certificate of title" means a certificate of title with respect to which a statute provides for the security interest in question to be indicated on the certificate as a condition or result of the security interest's obtaining priority over the rights of a lien creditor with respect to the collateral.

(11) "Chattel paper" means a record or records that evidence both a monetary obligation and a security interest in specific goods, a security interest in specific goods and software used in the goods, a security interest in specific goods and license of software used in the goods, a lease of specific goods, or a lease of specific goods and license of software used in the goods. In this paragraph, "monetary obligation" means a monetary obligation secured by the goods or owed under a lease of the goods and includes a monetary obligation with respect to software used in the goods. The term does not include (i) charters or other contracts involving the use or hire of a vessel or (ii) records that evidence a right to payment arising out of the use of a credit or charge card or information contained on or for use with the card. If a transaction is evidenced by records that include an instrument or series of instruments, the group of records taken together constitutes chattel paper.

(12) "Collateral" means the property subject to a security interest or agricultural lien. The term includes:

(A) proceeds to which a security interest attaches;

(B) accounts, chattel paper, payment intangibles, and promissory notes that have been sold; and

(C) goods that are the subject of a consignment.

(13) "Commercial tort claim" means a claim arising in tort with respect to which:

(A) the claimant is an organization; or

(B) the claimant is an individual and the claim:

(i) arose in the course of the claimant's business or profession; and

(ii) does not include damages arising out of personal injury to or the death of an individual.

(14) "Commodity account" means an account maintained by a commodity intermediary in which a commodity contract is carried for a commodity customer.

(15) "Commodity contract" means a commodity futures contract, an option on a commodity futures contract, a commodity option, or another contract if the contract or option is:

(A) traded on or subject to the rules of a board of trade that has been designated as a contract market for such a contract pursuant to federal commodities laws; or

(B) traded on a foreign commodity board of trade, exchange, or market, and is carried on the books of a commodity intermediary for a commodity customer.

(16) "Commodity customer" means a person for which a commodity intermediary carries a commodity contract on its books.

(17) "Commodity intermediary" means a person that:

(A) is registered as a futures commission merchant under federal commodities law; or

(B) in the ordinary course of its business provides clearance or settlement services for a board of trade that has been designated as a contract market pursuant to federal commodities law.

(18) "Communicate" means:

(A) to send a written or other tangible record;

(B) to transmit a record by any means agreed upon by the persons sending and receiving the record; or

(C) in the case of transmission of a record to or by a filing office, to transmit a record by any means prescribed by filing-office rule.

(19) "Consignee" means a merchant to which goods are delivered in a consignment.

(20) "Consignment" means a transaction, regardless of its form, in which a person delivers goods to a merchant for the purpose of sale and:

(A) the merchant:

(i) deals in goods of that kind under a name other than the name of the person making delivery;

(ii) is not an auctioneer; and

(iii) is not generally known by its creditors to be substantially engaged in selling the goods of others;

(B) with respect to each delivery, the aggregate value of the goods is $1,000 or more at the time of delivery;

(C) the goods are not consumer goods immediately before delivery; and

(D) the transaction does not create a security interest that secures an obligation.

(21) "Consignor" means a person that delivers goods to a consignee in a consignment.

(22) "Consumer debtor" means a debtor in a consumer transaction.

(23) "Consumer goods" means goods that are used or bought for use primarily for personal, family, or household purposes.

(24) "Consumer-goods transaction" means a consumer transaction in which:

(A) an individual incurs an obligation primarily for personal, family, or household purposes; and

(B) a security interest in consumer goods secures the obligation.

(25) "Consumer obligor" means an obligor who is an individual and who incurred the obligation as part of a transaction entered into primarily for personal, family, or household purposes.

(26) "Consumer transaction" means a transaction in which (i) an individual incurs an obligation primarily for personal, family, or household purposes, (ii) a security interest secures the obligation, and (iii) the collateral is held or acquired primarily for personal, family, or household purposes. The term includes consumer-goods transactions.

(27) "Continuation statement" means an amendment of a financing statement which:

(A) identifies, by its file number, the initial financing statement to which it relates; and

(B) indicates that it is a continuation statement for, or that it is filed to continue the effectiveness of, the identified financing statement.

(28) "Debtor" means:

(A) a person having an interest, other than a security interest or other lien, in the collateral, whether or not the person is an obligor;

(B) a seller of accounts, chattel paper, payment intangibles, or promissory notes; or

(C) a consignee.

(29) "Deposit account" means a demand, time, savings, passbook, or similar account maintained with a bank. The term does not include investment property or accounts evidenced by an instrument.

(30) "Document" means a document of title or a receipt of the type described in Section 7–201(b).

(31) "Electronic chattel paper" means chattel paper evidenced by a record or records consisting of information stored in an electronic medium.

(32) "Encumbrance" means a right, other than an ownership interest, in real property. The term includes mortgages and other liens on real property.

(33) "Equipment" means goods other than inventory, farm products, or consumer goods.

(34) "Farm products" means goods, other than standing timber, with respect to which the debtor is engaged in a farming operation and which are:

(A) crops grown, growing, or to be grown, including:

(i) crops produced on trees, vines, and bushes; and

(ii) aquatic goods produced in aquacultural operations;

(B) livestock, born or unborn, including aquatic goods produced in aquacultural operations;

(C) supplies used or produced in a farming operation; or

(D) products of crops or livestock in their unmanufactured states.

(35) "Farming operation" means raising, cultivating, propagating, fattening, grazing, or any other farming, livestock, or aquacultural operation.

(36) "File number" means the number assigned to an initial financing statement pursuant to Section 9–519(a).

(37) "Filing office" means an office designated in Section 9–501 as the place to file a financing statement.

(38) "Filing-office rule" means a rule adopted pursuant to Section 9–526.

(39) "Financing statement" means a record or records composed of an initial financing statement and any filed record relating to the initial financing statement.

(40) "Fixture filing" means the filing of a financing statement covering goods that are or are to become fixtures and satisfying Section 9–502(a) and (b). The term includes the filing of a financing statement covering goods of a transmitting utility which are or are to become fixtures.

(41) "Fixtures" means goods that have become so related to particular real property that an interest in them arises under real property law.

(42) "General intangible" means any personal property, including things in action, other than accounts, chattel paper, commercial tort claims, deposit accounts, documents, goods, instruments, investment property, letter-of-credit rights, letters of credit, money, and oil, gas, or other minerals before extraction. The term includes payment intangibles and software.

(43) [reserved] ["Good faith" means honesty in fact and the observance of reasonable commercial standards of fair dealing.] *Deleted by Revised Art. 1 (2001).*

(44) "Goods" means all things that are movable when a security interest attaches. The term includes (i) fixtures, (ii) standing timber that is to be cut and removed under a conveyance or contract for sale, (iii) the unborn young of animals, (iv) crops grown, growing, or to be grown, even if the crops are produced on trees, vines, or bushes, and (v) manufactured homes. The term also includes a computer program embedded in goods and any supporting information provided in connec-

tion with a transaction relating to the program if (i) the program is associated with the goods in such a manner that it customarily is considered part of the goods, or (ii) by becoming the owner of the goods, a person acquires a right to use the program in connection with the goods. The term does not include a computer program embedded in goods that consist solely of the medium in which the program is embedded. The term also does not include accounts, chattel paper, commercial tort claims, deposit accounts, documents, general intangibles, instruments, investment property, letter-of-credit rights, letters of credit, money, or oil, gas, or other minerals before extraction.

(45) "Governmental unit" means a subdivision, agency, department, county, parish, municipality, or other unit of the government of the United States, a State, or a foreign country. The term includes an organization having a separate corporate existence if the organization is eligible to issue debt on which interest is exempt from income taxation under the laws of the United States.

(46) "Health-care-insurance receivable" means an interest in or claim under a policy of insurance which is a right to payment of a monetary obligation for health-care goods or services provided or to be provided.

(47) "Instrument" means a negotiable instrument or any other writing that evidences a right to the payment of a monetary obligation, is not itself a security agreement or lease, and is of a type that in ordinary course of business is transferred by delivery with any necessary indorsement or assignment. The term does not include (i) investment property, (ii) letters of credit, or (iii) writings that evidence a right to payment arising out of the use of a credit or charge card or information contained on or for use with the card.

(48) "Inventory" means goods, other than farm products, which:

(A) are leased by a person as lessor;

(B) are held by a person for sale or lease or to be furnished under a contract of service;

(C) are furnished by a person under a contract of service; or

(D) consist of raw materials, work in process, or materials used or consumed in a business.

(49) "Investment property" means a security, whether certificated or uncertificated, security entitlement, securities account, commodity contract, or commodity account.

(50) "Jurisdiction of organization", with respect to a registered organization, means the jurisdiction under whose law the organization is organized.

(51) "Letter-of-credit right" means a right to payment or performance under a letter of credit, whether or not the beneficiary has demanded or is at the time entitled to demand payment or performance. The term does not include the right of a beneficiary to demand payment or performance under a letter of credit.

(52) "Lien creditor" means:

(A) a creditor that has acquired a lien on the property involved by attachment, levy, or the like;

(B) an assignee for benefit of creditors from the time of assignment;

(C) a trustee in bankruptcy from the date of the filing of the petition; or

(D) a receiver in equity from the time of appointment.

(53) "Manufactured home" means a structure, transportable in one or more sections, which, in the traveling mode, is eight body feet or more in width or 40 body feet or more in length, or, when erected on site, is 320 or more square feet, and which is built on a permanent chassis and designed to be used as a dwelling with or without a permanent foundation when connected to the required utilities, and includes the plumbing, heating, air-conditioning, and electrical systems contained therein. The term includes any structure

that meets all of the requirements of this paragraph except the size requirements and with respect to which the manufacturer voluntarily files a certification required by the United States Secretary of Housing and Urban Development and complies with the standards established under Title 42 of the United States Code.

(54) "Manufactured-home transaction" means a secured transaction:

(A) that creates a purchase-money security interest in a manufactured home, other than a manufactured home held as inventory; or

(B) in which a manufactured home, other than a manufactured home held as inventory, is the primary collateral.

(55) "Mortgage" means a consensual interest in real property, including fixtures, which secures payment or performance of an obligation.

(56) "New debtor" means a person that becomes bound as debtor under Section 9–203(d) by a security agreement previously entered into by another person.

(57) "New value" means (i) money, (ii) money's worth in property, services, or new credit, or (iii) release by a transferee of an interest in property previously transferred to the transferee. The term does not include an obligation substituted for another obligation.

(58) "Noncash proceeds" means proceeds other than cash proceeds.

(59) "Obligor" means a person that, with respect to an obligation secured by a security interest in or an agricultural lien on the collateral, (i) owes payment or other performance of the obligation, (ii) has provided property other than the collateral to secure payment or other performance of the obligation, or (iii) is otherwise accountable in whole or in part for payment or other performance of the obligation. The term does not include issuers or nominated persons under a letter of credit.

(60) "Original debtor", except as used in Section 9–310(c), means a person that, as

debtor, entered into a security agreement to which a new debtor has become bound under Section 9–203(d).

(61) "Payment intangible" means a general intangible under which the account debtor's principal obligation is a monetary obligation.

(62) "Person related to", with respect to an individual, means:

(A) the spouse of the individual;

(B) a brother, brother-in-law, sister, or sister-in-law of the individual;

(C) an ancestor or lineal descendant of the individual or the individual's spouse; or

(D) any other relative, by blood or marriage, of the individual or the individual's spouse who shares the same home with the individual.

(63) "Person related to", with respect to an organization, means:

(A) a person directly or indirectly controlling, controlled by, or under common control with the organization;

(B) an officer or director of, or a person performing similar functions with respect to, the organization;

(C) an officer or director of, or a person performing similar functions with respect to, a person described in subparagraph (A);

(D) the spouse of an individual described in subparagraph (A), (B), or (C); or

(E) an individual who is related by blood or marriage to an individual described in subparagraph (A), (B), (C), or (D) and shares the same home with the individual.

(64) "Proceeds", except as used in Section 9–609(b), means the following property:

(A) whatever is acquired upon the sale, lease, license, exchange, or other disposition of collateral;

(B) whatever is collected on, or distributed on account of, collateral;

(C) rights arising out of collateral;

(D) to the extent of the value of collateral, claims arising out of the loss, nonconformity, or interference with the use of, defects or infringement of rights in, or damage to, the collateral; or

(E) to the extent of the value of collateral and to the extent payable to the debtor or the secured party, insurance payable by reason of the loss or nonconformity of, defects or infringement of rights in, or damage to, the collateral.

(65) "Promissory note" means an instrument that evidences a promise to pay a monetary obligation, does not evidence an order to pay, and does not contain an acknowledgment by a bank that the bank has received for deposit a sum of money or funds.

(66) "Proposal" means a record authenticated by a secured party which includes the terms on which the secured party is willing to accept collateral in full or partial satisfaction of the obligation it secures pursuant to Sections 9–620, 9–621, and 9–622.

(67) "Public-finance transaction" means a secured transaction in connection with which:

(A) debt securities are issued;

(B) all or a portion of the securities issued have an initial stated maturity of at least 20 years; and

(C) the debtor, obligor, secured party, account debtor or other person obligated on collateral, assignor or assignee of a secured obligation, or assignor or assignee of a security interest is a State or a governmental unit of a State.

(68) "Pursuant to commitment", with respect to an advance made or other value given by a secured party, means pursuant to the secured party's obligation, whether or not a subsequent event of default or other event not within the secured party's control has relieved or may relieve the secured party from its obligation.

(69) "Record", except as used in "for record", "of record", "record or legal title", and

"record owner", means information that is inscribed on a tangible medium or which is stored in an electronic or other medium and is retrievable in perceivable form.

(70) "Registered organization" means an organization organized solely under the law of a single State or the United States and as to which the State or the United States must maintain a public record showing the organization to have been organized.

(71) "Secondary obligor" means an obligor to the extent that:

(A) the obligor's obligation is secondary; or

(B) the obligor has a right of recourse with respect to an obligation secured by collateral against the debtor, another obligor, or property of either.

(72) "Secured party" means:

(A) a person in whose favor a security interest is created or provided for under a security agreement, whether or not any obligation to be secured is outstanding;

(B) a person that holds an agricultural lien;

(C) a consignor;

(D) a person to which accounts, chattel paper, payment intangibles, or promissory notes have been sold;

(E) a trustee, indenture trustee, agent, collateral agent, or other representative in whose favor a security interest or agricultural lien is created or provided for; or

(F) a person that holds a security interest arising under Section 2–401, 2–505, 2–711(3), 2A–508(5), 4–210, or 5–118.

(73) "Security agreement" means an agreement that creates or provides for a security interest.

(74) "Send", in connection with a record or notification, means:

(A) to deposit in the mail, deliver for transmission, or transmit by any other usual means of communication, with postage or cost of transmission provided for, addressed to any address reasonable under the circumstances; or

(B) to cause the record or notification to be received within the time that it would have been received if properly sent under subparagraph (A).

(75) "Software" means a computer program and any supporting information provided in connection with a transaction relating to the program. The term does not include a computer program that is included in the definition of goods.

(76) "State" means a State of the United States, the District of Columbia, Puerto Rico, the United States Virgin Islands, or any territory or insular possession subject to the jurisdiction of the United States.

(77) "Supporting obligation" means a letter-of-credit right or secondary obligation that supports the payment or performance of an account, chattel paper, a document, a general intangible, an instrument, or investment property.

(78) "Tangible chattel paper" means chattel paper evidenced by a record or records consisting of information that is inscribed on a tangible medium.

(79) "Termination statement" means an amendment of a financing statement which:

(A) identifies, by its file number, the initial financing statement to which it relates; and

(B) indicates either that it is a termination statement or that the identified financing statement is no longer effective.

(80) "Transmitting utility" means a person primarily engaged in the business of:

(A) operating a railroad, subway, street railway, or trolley bus;

(B) transmitting communications electrically, electromagnetically, or by light;

(C) transmitting goods by pipeline or sewer; or

(D) transmitting or producing and transmitting electricity, steam, gas, or water.

(b) [Definitions in other articles.] "Control" as provided in Section 7–106 and the following definitions in other articles apply to this article:

"Applicant". Section 5–102.
"Beneficiary". Section 5–102.
"Broker". Section 8–102.
"Certificated security". Section 8–102.
"Check". Section 3–104.
"Clearing corporation". Section 8–102.
"Contract for sale". Section 2–106.
"Customer". Section 4–104.
"Entitlement holder". Section 8–102.
"Financial asset". Section 8–102.
"Holder in due course". Section 3–302.
"Issuer" (with respect to a letter of credit or letter-of-credit right). Section 5–102.
"Issuer" (with respect to a security). Section 8–201.
"Issuer" (with respect to documents of title). Section 7–102.
"Lease". Section 2A–103.
"Lease agreement". Section 2A–103.
"Lease contract". Section 2A–103.
"Leasehold interest". Section 2A–103.
"Lessee". Section 2A–103.
"Lessee in ordinary course of business". Section 2A–103.
"Lessor". Section 2A–103.
"Lessor's residual interest". Section 2A–103.
"Letter of credit". Section 5–102.
"Merchant". Section 2–104.
"Negotiable instrument". Section 3–104.
"Nominated person". Section 5–102.
"Note". Section 3–104.
"Proceeds of a letter of credit". Section 5–114.
"Prove". Section 3–103.
"Sale". Section 2–106.
"Securities account". Section 8–501.
"Securities intermediary". Section 8–102.
"Security". Section 8–102.
"Security certificate". Section 8–102.
"Security entitlement". Section 8–102.
"Uncertificated security". Section 8–102.

(c) [Article 1 definitions and principles.] Article 1 contains general definitions and principles of construction and interpretation applicable throughout this article.

As amended in 1999, 2000, 2001 and 2003.

Official Comment

1. **Source.** All terms that are defined in Article 9 and used in more than one section are consolidated in this section. Note that the definition of "security interest" is found in Section 1–201, not in this Article, and

has been revised. See Appendix I. Many of the definitions in this section are new; many others derive from those in former Section 9–105. The following Comments also indicate other sections of former Article 9 that defined (or explained) terms.

2. **Parties to Secured Transactions.**

a. **"Debtor"; "Obligor"; "Secondary Obligor."** Determining whether a person was a "debtor" under former Section 9–105(1)(d) required a close examination of the context in which the term was used. To reduce the need for this examination, this Article redefines "debtor" and adds new defined terms, "secondary obligor" and "obligor." In the context of Part 6 (default and enforcement), these definitions distinguish among three classes of persons: (i) those persons who may have a stake in the proper enforcement of a security interest by virtue of their non-lien property interest (typically, an ownership interest) in the collateral, (ii) those persons who may have a stake in the proper enforcement of the security interest because of their obligation to pay the secured debt, and (iii) those persons who have an obligation to pay the secured debt but have no stake in the proper enforcement of the security interest. Persons in the first class are debtors. Persons in the second class are secondary obligors if any portion of the obligation is secondary or if the obligor has a right of recourse against the debtor or another obligor with respect to an obligation secured by collateral. One must consult the law of suretyship to determine whether an obligation is secondary. The Restatement (3d), Suretyship and Guaranty § 1 (1996), contains a useful explanation of the concept. Obligors in the third class are neither debtors nor secondary obligors. With one exception (Section 9–616, as it relates to a consumer obligor), the rights and duties provided by Part 6 affect non-debtor obligors only if they are "secondary obligors."

By including in the definition of "debtor" all persons with a property interest (other than a security interest in or other lien on collateral), the definition includes transferees of collateral, whether or not the secured party knows of the transfer or the transferee's identity. Exculpatory provisions in Part 6 protect the secured party in that circumstance. See Sections 9–605 and 9–628. The definition renders unnecessary former Section 9–112, which governed situations in which collateral was not owned by the debtor. The definition also includes a "consignee," as defined in this section, as well as a seller of accounts, chattel paper, payment intangibles, or promissory notes.

Secured parties and other lienholders are excluded from the definition of "debtor" because the interests of those parties normally derive from and encumber a debtor's interest. However, if in a *separate* secured transaction a secured party grants, *as debtor*, a security interest in its own interest (i.e., its security interest and any obligation that it secures), the secured party is a debtor *in that transaction*. This typically occurs when a secured party with a security interest in specific goods assigns chattel paper.

Consider the following examples:

Example 1: Behnfeldt borrows money and grants a security interest in her Miata to secure the debt. Behnfeldt is a debtor and an obligor.

Example 2: Behnfeldt borrows money and grants a security interest in her Miata to secure the debt. Bruno co-signs a negotiable note as maker. As before, Behnfeldt is the debtor and an obligor. As an accommodation party (see Section 3–419), Bruno is a secondary obligor. Bruno has this status even if the note states that her obligation is a primary obligation and that she waives all suretyship defenses.

Example 3: Behnfeldt borrows money on an unsecured basis. Bruno co-signs the note and grants a security interest in her Honda to secure her obligation. Inasmuch as Behnfeldt does not have a property interest in the Honda, Behnfeldt is not a debtor. Having granted the security interest, Bruno is the debtor. Because Behnfeldt is a principal obligor, she is not a secondary obligor. Whatever the outcome of enforcement of the security interest against the Honda or Bruno's secondary obligation, Bruno will look to Behnfeldt for her losses. The enforcement will not affect Behnfeldt's aggregate obligations.

When the principal obligor (borrower) and the secondary obligor (surety) each has granted a security interest in different collateral, the status of each is determined by the collateral involved.

Example 4: Behnfeldt borrows money and grants a security interest in her Miata to secure the debt. Bruno co-signs the note and grants a security interest in her Honda to secure her obligation. When the secured party enforces the security interest in Behnfeldt's Miata, Behnfeldt is the debtor, and Bruno is a secondary obligor. When the secured party enforces the security interest in the Honda, Bruno is the "debtor." As in Example 3, Behnfeldt is an obligor, but not a secondary obligor.

b. **"Secured Party."** The secured party is the person in whose favor the security interest has been created, as determined by reference to the security agreement. This definition controls, among other things, which person has the duties and potential lia-

688

bility that Part 6 imposes upon a secured party. The definition of "secured party" also includes a "consignor," a person to which accounts, chattel paper, payment intangibles, or promissory notes have been sold, and the holder of an agricultural lien.

The definition of "secured party" clarifies the status of various types of representatives. Consider, for example, a multi-bank facility under which Bank A, Bank B, and Bank C are lenders and Bank A serves as the collateral agent. If the security interest is granted to the banks, then they are the secured parties. If the security interest is granted to Bank A as collateral agent, then Bank A is the secured party.

c. **Other Parties.** A "consumer obligor" is defined as the obligor in a consumer transaction. Definitions of "new debtor" and "original debtor" are used in the special rules found in Sections 9–326 and 9–508.

3. **Definitions Relating to Creation of a Security Interest.**

a. **"Collateral."** As under former Section 9–105, "collateral" is the property subject to a security interest and includes accounts and chattel paper that have been sold. It has been expanded in this Article. The term now explicitly includes proceeds subject to a security interest. It also reflects the broadened scope of the Article. It includes property subject to an agricultural lien as well as payment intangibles and promissory notes that have been sold.

b. **"Security Agreement."** The definition of "security agreement" is substantially the same as under former Section 9–105—an agreement that creates or provides for a security interest. However, the term frequently was used colloquially in former Article 9 to refer to the document or writing that contained a debtor's security agreement. This Article eliminates that usage, reserving the term for the more precise meaning specified in the definition.

Whether an agreement creates a security interest depends not on whether the parties intend that the law *characterize* the transaction as a security interest but rather on whether the transaction falls within the definition of "security interest" in Section 1–201. Thus, an agreement that the parties characterize as a "lease" of goods may be a "security agreement," notwithstanding the parties' stated intention that the law treat the transaction as a lease and not as a secured transaction. See Section 1–203.

4. **Goods-Related Definitions.**

a. **"Goods"; "Consumer Goods"; "Equipment"; "Farm Products"; "Farming Operation"; "Inventory."** The definition of "goods" is substantial-

ly the same as the definition in former Section 9–105. This Article also retains the four mutually-exclusive "types" of collateral that consist of goods: "consumer goods," "equipment," "farm products," and "inventory." The revisions are primarily for clarification.

The classes of goods are mutually exclusive. For example, the same property cannot simultaneously be both equipment and inventory. In borderline cases—a physician's car or a farmer's truck that might be either consumer goods or equipment—the principal use to which the property is put is determinative. Goods can fall into different classes at different times. For example, a radio may be inventory in the hands of a dealer and consumer goods in the hands of a consumer. As under former Article 9, goods are "equipment" if they do not fall into another category.

The definition of "consumer goods" follows former Section 9–109. The classification turns on whether the debtor uses or bought the goods for use "primarily for personal, family, or household purposes."

Goods are inventory if they are leased by a lessor or held by a person for sale or lease. The revised definition of "inventory" makes clear that the term includes goods leased by the debtor to others as well as goods held for lease. (The same result should have obtained under the former definition.) Goods to be furnished or furnished under a service contract, raw materials, and work in process also are inventory. Implicit in the definition is the criterion that the sales or leases are or will be in the ordinary course of business. For example, machinery used in manufacturing is equipment, not inventory, even though it is the policy of the debtor to sell machinery when it becomes obsolete or worn. Inventory also includes goods that are consumed in a business (e.g., fuel used in operations). In general, goods used in a business are equipment if they are fixed assets or have, as identifiable units, a relatively long period of use, but are inventory, even though not held for sale or lease, if they are used up or consumed in a short period of time in producing a product or providing a service.

Goods are "farm products" if the debtor is engaged in farming operations with respect to the goods. Animals in a herd of livestock are covered whether the debtor acquires them by purchase or as a result of natural increase. Products of crops or livestock remain farm products as long as they have not been subjected to a manufacturing process. The terms "crops" and "livestock" are not defined. The new definition of "farming operations" is for clarification only.

Crops, livestock, and their products cease to be "farm products" when the debtor ceases to be engaged in farming operations with respect to them. If, for example, they come into the possession of a marketing agency for sale or distribution or of a manufacturer or processor as raw materials, they become inventory. Products of crops or livestock, even though they remain in the possession of a person engaged in farming operations, lose their status as farm products if they are subjected to a manufacturing process. What is and what is not a manufacturing operation is not specified in this Article. At one end of the spectrum, some processes are so closely connected with farming—such as pasteurizing milk or boiling sap to produce maple syrup or sugar—that they would not constitute manufacturing. On the other hand an extensive canning operation would be manufacturing. Once farm products have been subjected to a manufacturing operation, they normally become inventory.

The revised definition of "farm products" clarifies the distinction between crops and standing timber and makes clear that aquatic goods produced in aquacultural operations may be either crops or livestock. Although aquatic goods that are vegetable in nature often would be crops and those that are animal would be livestock, this Article leaves the courts free to classify the goods on a case-by-case basis. See Section 9–324, Comment 11.

The definitions of "goods" and "software" are also mutually exclusive. Computer programs usually constitute "software," and, as such, are not "goods" as this Article uses the terms. However, under the circumstances specified in the definition of "goods," computer programs embedded in goods are part of the "goods" and are not "software."

b. **"Accession"; "Manufactured Home"; "Manufactured–Home Transaction."** Other specialized definitions of goods include "accession" (see the special priority and enforcement rules in Section 9–335), and "manufactured home" (see Section 9–515, permitting a financing statement in a "manufactured-home transaction" to be effective for 30 years). The definition of "manufactured home" borrows from the federal Manufactured Housing Act, 42 U.S.C. §§ 5401 *et seq.*, and is intended to have the same meaning.

c. **"As–Extracted Collateral."** Under this Article, oil, gas, and other minerals that have not been extracted from the ground are treated as real property, to which this Article does not apply. Upon extraction, minerals become personal property (goods) and eligible to be collateral under this Article. See the definition of "goods," which excludes "oil, gas, and other minerals before extraction." To take account of financing practices reflecting the shift from real to personal property,

this Article contains special rules for perfecting security interests in minerals which attach upon extraction and in accounts resulting from the sale of minerals at the wellhead or minehead. See, e.g., Sections 9–301(4) (law governing perfection and priority); 9–501 (place of filing), 9–502 (contents of financing statement), 9–519 (indexing of records). The new term, "as-extracted collateral," refers to the minerals and related accounts to which the special rules apply. The term "at the wellhead" encompasses arrangements based on a sale of the produce at the moment that it issues from the ground and is measured, without technical distinctions as to whether title passes at the "Christmas tree" of a well, the far side of a gathering tank, or at some other point. The term "at . . . the minehead" is comparable.

The following examples explain the operation of these provisions.

Example 5: Debtor owns an interest in oil that is to be extracted. To secure Debtor's obligations to Lender, Debtor enters into an authenticated agreement granting Lender an interest in the oil. Although Lender may acquire an interest in the oil under real-property law, Lender does not acquire a security interest under this Article until the oil becomes personal property, i.e., until is extracted and becomes "goods" to which this Article applies. Because Debtor had an interest in the oil before extraction and Lender's security interest attached to the oil as extracted, the oil is "as-extracted collateral."

Example 6: Debtor owns an interest in oil that is to be extracted and contracts to sell the oil to Buyer at the wellhead. In an authenticated agreement, Debtor agrees to sell to Lender the right to payment from Buyer. This right to payment is an account that constitutes "as-extracted collateral." If Lender then resells the account to Financer, Financer acquires a security interest. However, inasmuch as the debtor-seller in that transaction, Lender, had no interest in the oil before extraction, Financer's collateral (the account it owns) is not "as-extracted collateral."

Example 7: Under the facts of Example 6, before extraction, Buyer grants a security interest in the oil to Bank. Although Bank's security interest attaches when the oil is extracted, Bank's security interest is not in "as-extracted collateral," inasmuch as its debtor, Buyer, did not have an interest in the oil before extraction.

5. **Receivables-related Definitions.**

a. **"Account"; "Health–Care–Insurance Receivable"; "As–Extracted Collateral."** The definition of "account" has been expanded and reformulated. It is no longer limited to rights to payment relating to goods or services. Many categories of rights to payment that were classified as general intangibles under former Article 9 are accounts under this Article. Thus, if they are sold, a financing statement must be filed to perfect the buyer's interest in them. Among the types of property that are expressly excluded from the definition is "a right to payment for money or funds advanced or sold." As defined in Section 1–201, "money" is limited essentially to currency. As used in the exclusion from the definition of "account," however, "funds" is a broader concept (although the term is not defined). For example, when a bank-lender credits a borrower's deposit account for the amount of a loan, the bank's advance of funds is not a transaction giving rise to an account.

The definition of "health-care-insurance receivable" is new. It is a subset of the definition of "account." However, the rules generally applicable to account debtors on accounts do not apply to insurers obligated on health-care-insurance receivables. See Sections 9–404(e), 9–405(d), 9–406(i).

Note that certain accounts also are "as-extracted collateral." See Comment 4.c., Examples 6 and 7.

b. **"Chattel Paper"; "Electronic Chattel Paper"; "Tangible Chattel Paper."** "Chattel paper" consists of a monetary obligation together with a security interest in or a lease of specific goods if the obligation and security interest or lease are evidenced by "a record or records." The definition has been expanded from that found in former Article 9 to include records that evidence a monetary obligation and a security interest in specific goods and software used in the goods, *a security interest in specific goods and license of software used in the goods, or a lease of specific goods and license of software used in the goods. The expanded definition covers transactions in which the debtor's or lessee's monetary obligation includes amounts owed with respect to software used in the goods. The monetary obligation with respect to the software need not be owed under a license from the secured party or lessor, and the secured party or lessor need not be a party to the license transaction itself. Among the types of monetary obligations that are included in "chattel paper" are amounts that have been advanced by the secured party or lessor to enable the debtor or lessee to acquire or obtain financing for a license of the software used in the goods.** The definition also makes clear that rights to payment arising out of credit-card transactions are not chattel paper.

* Amendments in italics approved by the Permanent Editorial Board for Uniform Commercial Code October 20, 1999.

Charters of vessels are expressly excluded from the definition of chattel paper; they are accounts. The term "charter" as used in this section includes bareboat charters, time charters, successive voyage charters, contracts of affreightment, contracts of carriage, and all other arrangements for the use of vessels. Under former Section 9–105, only if the evidence of an obligation consisted of "a writing or writings" could an obligation qualify as chattel paper. In this Article, traditional, written chattel paper is included in the definition of "tangible chattel paper." "Electronic chattel paper" is chattel paper that is stored in an electronic medium instead of in tangible form. The concept of an electronic medium should be construed liberally to include electrical, digital, magnetic, optical, electromagnetic, or any other current or similar emerging technologies.

The definition of electronic chattel paper does not dictate that it be created in any particular fashion. For example, a record consisting of a tangible writing may be converted to electronic form (e.g., by creating electronic images of a signed writing). Or, records may be initially created and executed in electronic form (e.g., a lessee might authenticate an electronic record of a lease that is then stored in electronic form). In either case the resulting records are electronic chattel paper.

c. **"Instrument"; "Promissory Note."** The definition of "instrument" includes a negotiable instrument. As under former Section 9–105, it also includes any other right to payment of a monetary obligation that is evidenced by a writing of a type that in ordinary course of business is transferred by delivery (and, if necessary, an indorsement or assignment). Except in the case of chattel paper, the fact that an instrument is secured by a security interest or encumbrance on property does not change the character of the instrument as such or convert the combination of the instrument and collateral into a separate classification of personal property. The definition makes clear that rights to payment arising out of credit-card transactions are not instruments. The definition of "promissory note" is new, necessitated by the inclusion of sales of promissory notes within the scope of Article 9. It explicitly excludes obligations arising out of "orders" to pay (e.g., checks) as opposed to "promises" to pay. See Section 3–104.

d. **"General Intangible"; "Payment Intangible."** "General intangible" is the residual category of personal property, including things in action, that is not included in the other defined types of collateral. Examples are various categories of intellectual property and the right to payment of a loan of funds that is not evidenced by chattel paper or an instrument. As used in the definition of "general intangible," "things in action" includes rights that arise under a license of intellectual property, including the right to exploit the intellectual property without liability for infringement. The definition has been revised to exclude commercial tort claims, deposit accounts, and letter-of-credit rights. Each of the three is a separate type of collateral. One important consequence of this exclusion is that tortfeasors (commercial tort claims), banks (deposit accounts), and persons obligated on letters of credit (letter-of-credit rights) are not "account debtors" having the rights and obligations set forth in Sections 9-404, 9-405, and 9-406. In particular, tortfeasors, banks, and persons obligated on letters of credit are not obligated to pay an assignee (secured party) upon receipt of the notification described in Section 9-404(a). See Comment 5.h. Another important consequence relates to the adequacy of the description in the security agreement. See Section 9-108.

"Payment intangible" is a subset of the definition of "general intangible." The sale of a payment intangible is subject to this Article. See Section 9-109(a)(3). Virtually any intangible right could give rise to a right to payment of money once one hypothesizes, for example, that the account debtor is in breach of its obligation. The term "payment intangible," however, embraces only those general intangibles "under which the account debtor's *principal* obligation is a monetary obligation." (Emphasis added.)

In classifying intangible collateral, a court should begin by identifying the particular rights that have been assigned. The account debtor (promisor) under a particular contract may owe several types of monetary obligations as well as other, nonmonetary obligations. If the promisee's right to payment of money is assigned separately, the right is an account or payment intangible, depending on how the account debtor's obligation arose. When all the promisee's rights are assigned together, an account, a payment intangible, and a general intangible all may be involved, depending on the nature of the rights.

A right to the payment of money is frequently buttressed by ancillary covenants, such as covenants in a purchase agreement, note, or mortgage requiring insurance on the collateral or forbidding removal of the collateral, or covenants to preserve the creditworthiness of the promisor, such as covenants restricting dividends and the like. This Article does not treat these ancillary rights separately from the rights to payment to which they relate. For example, attachment and perfection of an assignment of a right to payment of a monetary obligation, whether it be an account or payment intangible, also carries these ancillary rights.

Every "payment intangible" is also a "general intangible." Likewise, "software" is a "general intangible" for purposes of this Article. See Comment 25. Accordingly, except as otherwise provided, statutory provisions applicable to general intangibles apply to payment intangibles and software.

e. **"Letter-of-Credit Right."** The term "letter-of-credit right" embraces the rights to payment and performance under a letter of credit (defined in Section 5-102). However, it does not include a beneficiary's right to demand payment or performance. Transfer of those rights to a transferee beneficiary is governed by Article 5. See Sections 9-107, Comment 4, and 9-329, Comments 3 and 4.

f. **"Supporting Obligation."** This new term covers the most common types of credit enhancements—suretyship obligations (including guarantees) and letter-of-credit rights that support one of the types of collateral specified in the definition. As explained in Comment 2.a., suretyship law determines whether an obligation is "secondary" for purposes of this definition. Section 9-109 generally excludes from this Article transfers of interests in insurance policies. However, the regulation of a secondary obligation as an insurance product does not necessarily mean that it is a "policy of insurance" for purposes of the exclusion in Section 9-109. Thus, this Article may cover a secondary obligation (as a supporting obligation), even if the obligation is issued by a regulated insurance company and the obligation is subject to regulation as an "insurance" product.

This Article contains rules explicitly governing attachment, perfection, and priority of security interests in supporting obligations. See Sections 9-203, 9-308, 9-310, and 9-322. These provisions reflect the principle that a supporting obligation is an incident of the collateral it supports.

Collections of or other distributions under a supporting obligation are "proceeds" of the supported collateral as well as "proceeds" of the supporting obligation itself. See Section 9-102 (defining "proceeds") and Comment 13.b. As such, the collections and distributions are subject to the priority rules applicable to proceeds generally. See Section 9-322. However, under the special rule governing security interests in a letter-of-credit right, a secured party's failure to obtain control (Section 9–107) of a letter-of-credit right supporting collateral may leave its security interest exposed to a priming interest of a party who does take control. See Section 9–329 (security interest in a letter-of-credit right perfected by control has priority over a conflicting security interest).

g. **"Commercial Tort Claim."** This term is new. A tort claim may serve as original collateral under this Article only if it is a "commercial tort claim." See Section 9–109(d). Although security interests in commercial tort claims are within its scope, this Article does not override other applicable law restricting the assignability of a tort claim. See Section 9–401. A security interest in a tort claim also may exist under this Article if the claim is proceeds of other collateral.

h. **"Account Debtor."** An "account debtor" is a person obligated on an account, chattel paper, or general intangible. The account debtor's obligation often is a monetary obligation; however, this is not always the case. For example, if a franchisee uses its rights under a franchise agreement (a general intangible) as collateral, then the franchisor is an "account debtor." As a general matter, Article 3, and not Article 9, governs obligations on negotiable instruments. Accordingly, the definition of "account debtor" excludes obligors on negotiable instruments constituting part of chattel paper. The principal effect of this change from the definition in former Article 9 is that the rules in Sections 9–403, 9–404, 9–405, and 9–406, dealing with the rights of an assignee and duties of an account debtor, do not apply to an assignment of chattel paper in which the obligation to pay is evidenced by a negotiable instrument. (Section 9–406(d), however, does apply to promissory notes, including negotiable promissory notes.) Rather, the assignee's rights are governed by Article 3. Similarly, the duties of an obligor on a nonnegotiable instrument are governed by non-Article 9 law unless the nonnegotiable instrument is a part of chattel paper, in which case the obligor is an account debtor.

i. **Receivables Under Government Entitlement Programs**. This Article does not contain a defined term that encompasses specifically rights to payment or performance under the many and varied government entitlement programs. Depending on the nature of a right under a program, it could be an account, a payment intangible, a general intangible other than a payment intangible, or another type of collateral. The right also might be proceeds of collateral (e.g., crops).

6. **Investment–Property–Related Definitions: "Commodity Account"; "Commodity Contract"; "Commodity Customer"; "Commodity Interme-** diary"; **"Investment Property."** These definitions are substantially the same as the corresponding definitions in former Section 9–115. "Investment property" includes securities, both certificated and uncertificated, securities accounts, security entitlements, commodity accounts, and commodity contracts. The term investment property includes a "securities account" in order to facilitate transactions in which a debtor wishes to create a security interest in all of the investment positions held through a particular account rather than in particular positions carried in the account. Former Section 9–115 was added in conjunction with Revised Article 8 and contained a variety of rules applicable to security interests in investment property. These rules have been relocated to the appropriate sections of Article 9. See, e.g., Sections 9–203 (attachment), 9–314 (perfection by control), 9–328 (priority).

The terms "security," "security entitlement," and related terms are defined in Section 8–102, and the term "securities account" is defined in Section 8–501. The terms "commodity account," "commodity contract," "commodity customer," and "commodity intermediary" are defined in this section. Commodity contracts are not "securities" or "financial assets" under Article 8. See Section 8–103(f). Thus, the relationship between commodity intermediaries and commodity customers is not governed by the indirect-holding-system rules of Part 5 of Article 8. For securities, Article 9 contains rules on security interests, and Article 8 contains rules on the rights of transferees, including secured parties, on such matters as the rights of a transferee if the transfer was itself wrongful and gives rise to an adverse claim. For commodity contracts, Article 9 establishes rules on security interests, but questions of the sort dealt with in Article 8 for securities are left to other law.

The indirect-holding-system rules of Article 8 are sufficiently flexible to be applied to new developments in the securities and financial markets, where that is appropriate. Accordingly, the definition of "commodity contract" is narrowly drafted to ensure that it does not operate as an obstacle to the application of the Article 8 indirect-holding-system rules to new products. The term "commodity contract" covers those contracts that are traded on or subject to the rules of a designated contract market and foreign commodity contracts that are carried on the books of American commodity intermediaries. The effect of this definition is that the category of commodity contracts that are excluded from Article 8 but governed by Article 9 is essentially the same as the category of contracts that fall within the exclusive regulatory jurisdiction of the federal Commodity Futures Trading Commission.

Commodity contracts are different from securities or other financial assets. A person who enters into a commodity futures contract is not buying an asset having a certain value and holding it in anticipation of increase in value. Rather the person is entering into a contract to buy or sell a commodity at set price for delivery at a future time. That contract may become advantageous or disadvantageous as the price of the commodity fluctuates during the term of the contract. The rules of the commodity exchanges require that the contracts be marked to market on a daily basis; that is, the customer pays or receives any increment attributable to that day's price change. Because commodity customers may incur obligations on their contracts, they are required to provide collateral at the outset, known as "original margin," and may be required to provide additional amounts, known as "variation margin," during the term of the contract.

The most likely setting in which a person would want to take a security interest in a commodity contract is where a lender who is advancing funds to finance an inventory of a physical commodity requires the borrower to enter into a commodity contract as a hedge against the risk of decline in the value of the commodity. The lender will want to take a security interest in both the commodity itself and the hedging commodity contract. Typically, such arrangements are structured as security interests in the entire commodity account in which the borrower carries the hedging contracts, rather than in individual contracts.

One important effect of including commodity contracts and commodity accounts in Article 9 is to provide a clearer legal structure for the analysis of the rights of commodity clearing organizations against their participants and futures commission merchants against their customers. The rules and agreements of commodity clearing organizations generally provide that the clearing organization has the right to liquidate any participant's positions in order to satisfy obligations of the participant to the clearing corporation. Similarly, agreements between futures commission merchants and their customers generally provide that the futures commission merchant has the right to liquidate a customer's positions in order to satisfy obligations of the customer to the futures commission merchant.

The main property that a commodity intermediary holds as collateral for the obligations that the commodity customer may incur under its commodity contracts is not other commodity contracts carried by the customer but the other property that the customer has posted as margin. Typically, this property will be securities. The commodity intermediary's security interest

in such securities is governed by the rules of this Article on security interests in securities, not the rules on security interests in commodity contracts or commodity accounts.

Although there are significant analytic and regulatory differences between commodities and securities, the development of commodity contracts on financial products in the past few decades has resulted in a system in which the commodity markets and securities markets are closely linked. The rules on security interests in commodity contracts and commodity accounts provide a structure that may be essential in times of stress in the financial markets. Suppose, for example that a firm has a position in a securities market that is hedged by a position in a commodity market, so that payments that the firm is obligated to make with respect to the securities position will be covered by the receipt of funds from the commodity position. Depending upon the settlement cycles of the different markets, it is possible that the firm could find itself in a position where it is obligated to make the payment with respect to the securities position before it receives the matching funds from the commodity position. If cross-margining arrangements have not been developed between the two markets, the firm may need to borrow funds temporarily to make the earlier payment. The rules on security interests in investment property would facilitate the use of positions in one market as collateral for loans needed to cover obligations in the other market.

7. **Consumer-Related Definitions: "Consumer Debtor"; "Consumer Goods"; "Consumer-goods transaction"; "Consumer Obligor"; "Consumer Transaction."** The definition of "consumer goods" (discussed above) is substantially the same as the definition in former Section 9–109. The definitions of "consumer debtor," "consumer obligor," "consumer-goods transaction," and "consumer transaction" have been added in connection with various new (and old) consumer-related provisions and to designate certain provisions that are inapplicable in consumer transactions.

"Consumer-goods transaction" is a subset of "consumer transaction." Under each definition, both the obligation secured and the collateral must have a personal, family, or household purpose. However, "mixed" business and personal transactions also may be characterized as a consumer-goods transaction or consumer transaction. Subparagraph (A) of the definition of consumer-goods transactions and clause (i) of the definition of consumer transaction are primary purpose tests. Under these tests, it is necessary to determine the primary purpose of the obligation or obligations secured. Subparagraph (B) and clause (iii) of these definitions are satisfied if any of the collateral is consumer goods, in the case of a consumer-goods transaction, or "is held or acquired primarily for personal, family, or household purposes," in the case of a consumer transaction. The fact that some of the obligations secured or some of the collateral for the obligation does not satisfy the tests (e.g., some of the collateral is acquired for a business purpose) does not prevent a transaction from being a "consumer transaction" or "consumer-goods transaction."

8. **Filing-Related Definitions: "Continuation Statement"; "File Number"; "Filing Office"; "Filing-office Rule"; "Financing Statement"; "Fixture Filing"; "Manufactured–Home Transaction"; "New Debtor"; "Original Debtor"; "Public–Finance Transaction"; "Termination Statement"; "Transmitting Utility."** These definitions are used exclusively or primarily in the filing-related provisions in Part 5. Most are self-explanatory and are discussed in the Comments to Part 5. A financing statement filed in a manufactured-home transaction or a public-finance transaction may remain effective for 30 years instead of the 5 years applicable to other financing statements. See Section 9–515(b). The definitions relating to medium neutrality also are significant for the filing provisions. See Comment 9.

The definition of "transmitting utility" has been revised to embrace the business of transmitting communications generally to take account of new and future types of communications technology. The term designates a special class of debtors for whom separate filing rules are provided in Part 5, thereby obviating the many local fixture filings that would be necessary under the rules of Section 9–501 for a far-flung public-utility debtor. A transmitting utility will not necessarily be regulated by or operating as such in a jurisdiction where fixtures are located. For example, a utility might own transmission lines in a jurisdiction, although the utility generates no power and has no customers in the jurisdiction.

9. **Definitions Relating to Medium Neutrality.**

a. **"Record."** In many, but not all, instances, the term "record" replaces the term "writing" and "written." A "record" includes information that is in intangible form (e.g., electronically stored) as well as tangible form (e.g., written on paper). Given the rapid development and commercial adoption of modern communication and storage technologies, requirements that documents or communications be "written," "in writing," or otherwise in tangible form do not necessarily reflect or aid commercial practices.

A "record" need not be permanent or indestructible, but the term does not include any oral or other communication that is not stored or preserved by any means. The information must be stored on paper or in some other medium. Information that has not been retained other than through human memory does not qualify as a record. Examples of current technologies commercially used to communicate or store information include, but are not limited to, magnetic media, optical discs, digital voice messaging systems, electronic mail, audio tapes, and photographic media, as well as paper. "Record" is an inclusive term that includes all of these methods of storing or communicating information. Any "writing" is a record. A record may be authenticated. See Comment 9.b. A record may be created without the knowledge or intent of a particular person.

Like the terms "written" or "in writing," the term "record" does not establish the purposes, permitted uses, or legal effect that a record may have under any particular provision of law. Whatever is filed in the Article 9 filing system, including financing statements, continuation statements, and termination statements, whether transmitted in tangible or intangible form, would fall within the definition. However, in some instances, statutes or filing-office rules may require that a paper record be filed. In such cases, even if this Article permits the filing of an electronic record, compliance with those statutes or rules is necessary. Similarly, a filer must comply with a statute or rule that requires a particular type of encoding or formatting for an electronic record.

This Article sometimes uses the terms "for record," "of record," "record or legal title," and "record owner." Some of these are terms traditionally used in real-property law. The definition of "record" in this Article now explicitly excepts these usages from the defined term. Also, this Article refers to a record that is filed or recorded in real-property recording systems to record a mortgage as a "record of a mortgage." This usage recognizes that the defined term "mortgage" means an interest in real property; it does not mean the record that evidences, or is filed or recorded with respect to, the mortgage.

b. **"Authenticate"; "Communicate"; "Send."** The terms "authenticate" and "authenticated" generally replace "sign" and "signed." "Authenticated" replaces and broadens the definition of "signed," in Section 1–201, to encompass authentication of all records, not just writings. (References to authentication of, e.g., an agreement, demand, or notification mean, of course, authentication of a record containing an agreement, demand, or notification.) The terms "communicate" and "send" also contemplate the possibility of communication by nonwritten media. These definitions include the act of transmitting both tangible and intangible records. The definition of "send" replaces, for purposes of this Article, the corresponding term in Section 1–201. The reference to "usual means of communication" in that definition contemplates an inquiry into the appropriateness of the method of transmission used in the particular circumstances involved.

10. **Scope-Related Definitions.**

a. **Expanded Scope of Article: "Agricultural Lien"; "Consignment"; "Payment Intangible"; "Promissory Note."** These new definitions reflect the expanded scope of Article 9, as provided in Section 9–109(a).

b. **Reduced Scope of Exclusions: "Governmental Unit"; "Health–Care–Insurance Receivable"; "Commercial Tort Claims."** These new definitions reflect the reduced scope of the exclusions, provided in Section 9–109(c) and (d), of transfers by governmental debtors and assignments of interests in insurance policies and commercial tort claims.

11. **Choice-of-Law–Related Definitions: "Certificate of Title"; "Governmental Unit"; "Jurisdiction of Organization"; "Registered Organization"; "State."** These new definitions reflect the changes in the law governing perfection and priority of security interests and agricultural liens provided in Part 3, Subpart 1.

Not every organization that may provide information about itself in the public records is a "registered organization." For example, a general partnership is not a "registered organization," even if it files a statement of partnership authority under Section 303 of the Uniform Partnership Act (1994) or an assumed name ("dba") certificate. This is because the State under whose law the partnership is organized is not required to maintain a public record showing that the partnership has been organized. In contrast, corporations, limited liability companies, and limited partnerships are "registered organizations."

12. **Deposit–Account–Related   Definitions: "Deposit Account"; "Bank."** The revised definition of "deposit account" incorporates the definition of "bank," which is new. The definition derives from the definitions of "bank" in Sections 4–105(1) and 4A–105(a)(2), which focus on whether the organization is "engaged in the business of banking."

Deposit accounts evidenced by Article 9 "instruments" are excluded from the term "deposit account."

In contrast, former Section 9–105 excluded from the former definition "an account evidenced by a certificate of deposit." The revised definition clarifies the proper treatment of nonnegotiable or uncertificated certificates of deposit. Under the definition, an uncertificated certificate of deposit would be a deposit account (assuming there is no writing evidencing the bank's obligation to pay) whereas a nonnegotiable certificate of deposit would be a deposit account only if it is not an "instrument" as defined in this section (a question that turns on whether the nonnegotiable certificate of deposit is "of a type that in ordinary course of business is transferred by delivery with any necessary indorsement or assignment.")

A deposit account evidenced by an instrument is subject to the rules applicable to instruments generally. As a consequence, a security interest in such an instrument cannot be perfected by "control" (see Section 9–104), and the special priority rules applicable to deposit accounts (see Sections 9–327 and 9–340) do not apply.

The term "deposit account" does not include "investment property," such as securities and security entitlements. Thus, the term also does not include shares in a money-market mutual fund, even if the shares are redeemable by check.

13. **Proceeds-Related Definitions: "Cash Proceeds"; "Noncash Proceeds"; "Proceeds."** The revised definition of "proceeds" expands the definition beyond that contained in former Section 9–306 and resolves ambiguities in the former section.

a. **Distributions on Account of Collateral.** The phrase "whatever is collected on, or distributed on account of, collateral," in subparagraph (B), is broad enough to cover cash or stock dividends distributed on account of securities or other investment property that is original collateral. Compare former Section 9–306 ("Any payments or distributions made with respect to investment property collateral are proceeds."). This section rejects the holding of *FDIC v. Hastie*, 2 F.3d 1042 (10th Cir. 1993) (postpetition cash dividends on stock subject to a prepetition pledge are not "proceeds" under Bankruptcy Code Section 552(b)), to the extent the holding relies on the Article 9 definition of "proceeds."

b. **Distributions on Account of Supporting Obligations.** Under subparagraph (B), collections on and distributions on account of collateral consisting of various credit-support arrangements ("supporting obligations," as defined in Section 9–102) also are proceeds. Consequently, they are afforded treatment identical to proceeds collected from or distributed by the obligor on the underlying (supported) right to payment or other collateral. Proceeds of supporting obligations also are proceeds of the underlying rights to payment or other collateral.

c. **Proceeds of Proceeds.** The definition of "proceeds" no longer provides that proceeds of proceeds are themselves proceeds. That idea is expressed in the revised definition of "collateral" in Section 9–102. No change in meaning is intended.

d. **Proceeds Received by Person Who Did Not Create Security Interest.** When collateral is sold subject to a security interest and the buyer then resells the collateral, a question arose under former Article 9 concerning whether the "debtor" had "received" what the buyer received on resale and, therefore, whether those receipts were "proceeds" under former Section 9–306(2). This Article contains no requirement that property be "received" by the debtor for the property to qualify as proceeds. It is necessary only that the property be traceable, directly or indirectly, to the original collateral.

e. **Cash Proceeds and Noncash Proceeds.** The definition of "cash proceeds" is substantially the same as the corresponding definition in former Section 9–306. The phrase "and the like" covers property that is functionally equivalent to "money, checks, or deposit accounts," such as some money-market accounts that are securities or part of securities entitlements. Proceeds other than cash proceeds are noncash proceeds.

14. **Consignment-Related Definitions: "Consignee"; "Consignment"; "Consignor."** The definition of "consignment" excludes, in subparagraphs (B) and (C), transactions for which filing would be inappropriate or of insufficient benefit to justify the costs. A consignment excluded from the application of this Article by one of those subparagraphs may still be a true consignment; however, it is governed by non-Article 9 law. The definition also excludes, in subparagraph (D), what have been called "consignments intended for security." These "consignments" are not bailments but secured transactions. Accordingly, all of Article 9 applies to them. See Sections 1–201(b)(35), 9–109(a)(1). The "consignor" is the person who delivers goods to the "consignee" in a consignment.

The definition of "consignment" requires that the goods be delivered "to a merchant for the purpose of sale." If the goods are delivered for another purpose as well, such as milling or processing, the transaction is a consignment nonetheless because a purpose of the delivery is "sale." On the other hand, if a merchant-processor-bailee will not be selling the goods itself but will be delivering to buyers to which the owner-bailor

agreed to sell the goods, the transaction would not be a consignment.

15. **"Accounting."** This definition describes the record and information that a debtor is entitled to request under Section 9–210.

16. **"Document."** The definition of "document" incorporates both tangible and electronic documents of title. See Section 1–201(15)[1–201(b)16] and Comment 15 [16].

Legislative Note: Former Article 1 defined document of title in section 1–201(15) and accompanying comment 15. Revised Article 1 defines document of title in Section 1–201(b)(16) and accompanying comment 16. Cross references should be adapted depending upon which version of Article 1 is in force in the jurisdiction.

18. **"Fixtures."** This definition is unchanged in substance from the corresponding definition in former Section 9–313. See Section 9–334 (priority of security interests in fixtures and crops).

19. **"Good Faith."** This Article expands the definition of "good faith" to include "the observance of reasonable commercial standards of fair dealing." The definition in this section applies when the term is used in this Article, and the same concept applies in the context of this Article for purposes of the obligation of good faith imposed by Section 1–203. See subsection (c).

20. **"Lien Creditor"** This definition is unchanged in substance from the corresponding definition in former Section 9–301.

21. **"New Value."** This Article deletes former Section 9–108. Its broad formulation of new value, which embraced the taking of after-acquired collateral for a pre-existing claim, was unnecessary, counterintuitive, and ineffective for its original purpose of sheltering after-acquired collateral from attack as a voidable preference in bankruptcy. The new definition derives from Bankruptcy Code Section 547(a). The term is used with respect to temporary perfection of security interests in instruments, certificated securities, or negotiable documents under Section 9–312(e) and with respect to chattel paper priority in Section 9–330.

22. **"Person Related To."** Section 9–615 provides a special method for calculating a deficiency or surplus when "the secured party, a person related to the secured party, or a secondary obligor" acquires the collateral at a foreclosure disposition. Separate definitions of the term are provided with respect to an individual secured party and with respect to a secured party that is an organization. The definitions are patterned on the corresponding definition in Section

1.301(32) of the Uniform Consumer Credit Code (1974).

23. **"Proposal."** This definition describes a record that is sufficient to propose to retain collateral in full or partial satisfaction of a secured obligation. See Sections 9–620, 9–621, 9–622.

24. **"Pursuant to Commitment."** This definition is unchanged in substance from the corresponding definition in former Section 9–105. It is used in connection with special priority rules applicable to future advances. See Section 9–323.

25. **"Software."** The definition of "software" is used in connection with the priority rules applicable to purchase-money security interests. See Sections 9–103, 9–324. Software, like a payment intangible, is a type of general intangible for purposes of this Article. See Comment 4.a., above, regarding the distinction between "goods" and "software."

26. **Terminology: "Assignment" and "Transfer."** In numerous provisions, this Article refers to the "assignment" or the "transfer" of property interests. These terms and their derivatives are not defined. This Article generally follows common usage by using the terms "assignment" and "assign" to refer to transfers of rights to payment, claims, and liens and other security interests. It generally uses the term "transfer" to refer to other transfers of interests in property. Except when used in connection with a letter-of-credit transaction (see Section 9–107, Comment 4), no significance should be placed on the use of one term or the other. Depending on the context, each term may refer to the assignment or transfer of an outright ownership interest or to the assignment or transfer of a limited interest, such as a security interest.

As amended in 1999, 2000, 2001 and 2003.

§ 9–103. Purchase-Money Security Interest; Application of Payments; Burden of Establishing.

(a) **[Definitions.]** In this section:
(1) "purchase-money collateral" means goods or software that secures a purchase-money obligation incurred with respect to that collateral; and
(2) "purchase-money obligation" means an obligation of an obligor incurred as all or part of the price of the collateral or for value given to enable the debtor to acquire rights in or the use of the collateral if the value is in fact so used.

(b) **[Purchase-money security interest in goods.]** A security interest in goods is a purchase-money security interest:
(1) to the extent that the goods are purchase-money collateral with respect to that security interest;
(2) if the security interest is in inventory that is or was purchase-money collateral, also to the extent that the security interest secures a purchase-money obligation incurred with respect to other inventory in which the secured party holds or held a purchase-money security interest; and
(3) also to the extent that the security interest secures a purchase-money obligation incurred with respect to software in which the secured party holds or held a purchase-money security interest.

(c) **[Purchase-money security interest in software.]** A security interest in software is a purchase-money security interest to the extent that the security interest also secures a purchase-money obligation incurred with respect to goods in which the secured party holds or held a purchase-money security interest if:
(1) the debtor acquired its interest in the software in an integrated transaction in which it acquired an interest in the goods; and
(2) the debtor acquired its interest in the software for the principal purpose of using the software in the goods.

(d) **[Consignor's inventory purchase-money security interest.]** The security interest of a consignor in goods that are the subject of a consignment is a purchase-money security interest in inventory.

(e) **[Application of payment in non-consumer-goods transaction.]** In a transaction other than a consumer-goods transaction, if the extent to which a security interest is a purchase-money security interest depends on the application of a payment to a particular obligation, the payment must be applied:
(1) in accordance with any reasonable method of application to which the parties agree;
(2) in the absence of the parties' agreement to a reasonable method, in accordance with any intention of the obligor manifested at or before the time of payment; or

(3) in the absence of an agreement to a reasonable method and a timely manifestation of the obligor's intention, in the following order:

(A) to obligations that are not secured; and

(B) if more than one obligation is secured, to obligations secured by purchase-money security interests in the order in which those obligations were incurred.

(f) **[No loss of status of purchase-money security interest in non-consumer-goods transaction.]** In a transaction other than a consumer-goods transaction, a purchase-money security interest does not lose its status as such, even if:

(1) the purchase-money collateral also secures an obligation that is not a purchase-money obligation;

(2) collateral that is not purchase-money collateral also secures the purchase-money obligation; or

(3) the purchase-money obligation has been renewed, refinanced, consolidated, or restructured.

(g) **[Burden of proof in non-consumer-goods transaction.]** In a transaction other than a consumer-goods transaction, a secured party claiming a purchase-money security interest has the burden of establishing the extent to which the security interest is a purchase-money security interest.

(h) **[Non-consumer-goods transactions; no inference.]** The limitation of the rules in subsections (e), (f), and (g) to transactions other than consumer-goods transactions is intended to leave to the court the determination of the proper rules in consumer-goods transactions. The court may not infer from that limitation the nature of the proper rule in consumer-goods transactions and may continue to apply established approaches.

Official Comment

1. **Source.** Former Section 9–107.

2. **Scope of This Section.** Under Section 9–309(1), a purchase-money security interest in consumer goods is perfected when it attaches. Sections 9–317 and 9–324 provide special priority rules for purchase-money security interests in a variety of contexts. This

section explains when a security interest enjoys purchase-money status.

3. **"Purchase-Money Collateral"; "Purchase-Money Obligation"; "Purchase-Money Security Interest."** Subsection (a) defines "purchase-money collateral" and "purchase-money obligation." These terms are essential to the description of what constitutes a purchase-money security interest under subsection (b). As used in subsection (a)(2), the definition of "purchase-money obligation," the "price" of collateral or the "value given to enable" includes obligations for expenses incurred in connection with acquiring rights in the collateral, sales taxes, duties, finance charges, interest, freight charges, costs of storage in transit, demurrage, administrative charges, expenses of collection and enforcement, attorney's fees, and other similar obligations.

The concept of "purchase-money security interest" requires a close nexus between the acquisition of collateral and the secured obligation. Thus, a security interest does not qualify as a purchase-money security interest if a debtor acquires property on unsecured credit and subsequently creates the security interest to secure the purchase price.

4. **Cross-Collateralization of Purchase-Money Security Interests in Inventory.** Subsection (b)(2) deals with the problem of cross-collateralized purchase-money security interests in inventory. Consider a simple example:

Example: Seller (S) sells an item of inventory (Item–1) to Debtor (D), retaining a security interest in Item–1 to secure Item–1's price and all other obligations, existing and future, of D to S. S then sells another item of inventory to D (Item–2), again retaining a security interest in Item–2 to secure Item–2's price as well as all other obligations of D to S. D then pays to S Item–1's price. D then sells Item–2 to a buyer in ordinary course of business, who takes Item–2 free of S's security interest.

Under subsection (b)(2), S's security interest in *Item–1* securing *Item–2's unpaid price* would be a purchase-money security interest. This is so because S has a purchase-money security interest in Item–1, Item–1 secures the price of (a "purchase-money obligation incurred with respect to") Item–2 ("other inventory"), and Item–2 itself was subject to a purchase-money security interest. Note that, to the extent Item–1 secures the price of Item–2, S's security interest in Item–1 would not be a purchase-money security interest under subsection (b)(1). The security interest in Item–1 is a purchase-money security interest under subsection (b)(1) only to the extent that Item–1 is "purchase-money collateral," i.e., only to the extent that Item–1 "secures a purchase-money obligation incurred with respect to that collateral" (i.e., Item–1). See subsection (a)(1).

5. **Purchase-Money Security Interests in Goods and Software.** Subsections (b) and (c) limit purchase-money security interests to security interests in goods, including fixtures, and software. Otherwise, no change in meaning from former Section 9–107 is intended. The second sentence of former Section 9–115(5)(f) made the purchase-money priority rule (former Section 9–312(4)) inapplicable to investment property. This section's limitation makes that provision unnecessary.

Subsection (c) describes the limited circumstances under which a security interest in goods may be accompanied by a purchase-money security interest in software. The software must be acquired by the debtor in a transaction integrated with the transaction in which the debtor acquired the goods, and the debtor must acquire the software for the principal purpose of using the software in the goods. "Software" is defined in Section 9–102.

6. **Consignments.** Under former Section 9–114, the priority of the consignor's interest is similar to that of a purchase-money security interest. Subsection (d) achieves this result more directly, by defining the interest of a "consignor," defined in Section 9–102, to be a purchase-money security interest in inventory for purposes of this Article. This drafting convention obviates any need to set forth special priority rules applicable to the interest of a consignor. Rather, the priority of the consignor's interest as against the rights of lien creditors of the consignee, competing secured parties, and purchasers of the goods from the consignee can be determined by reference to the priority rules generally applicable to inventory, such as Sections 9–317, 9–320, 9–322, and 9–324. For other purposes, including the rights and duties of the consignor and consignee as between themselves, the consignor would remain the owner of goods under a bailment arrangement with the consignee. See Section 9–319.

7. **Provisions Applicable Only to Non–Consumer–Goods Transactions.**

a. **"Dual-Status" Rule.** For transactions other than consumer-goods transactions, this Article approves what some cases have called the "dual-status" rule, under which a security interest may be a purchase-money security interest to some extent and a non-purchase-money security interest to some extent. (Concerning consumer-goods transactions, see subsection (h) and Comment 8.) Some courts have found this rule to be explicit or implicit in the words "to the extent," found in former Section 9–107 and continued in subsections (b)(1) and (b)(2). The rule is made explicit in subsection (e). For non-consumer-goods transactions, this Article rejects the "transformation" rule adopted by some cases, under which any cross-collateralization, refinancing, or the like destroys the purchase-money status entirely.

Consider, for example, what happens when a $10,000 loan secured by a purchase-money security interest is refinanced by the original lender, and, as part of the transaction, the debtor borrows an additional $2,000 secured by the collateral. Subsection (f) resolves any doubt that the security interest remains a purchase-money security interest. Under subsection (b), however, it enjoys purchase-money status only to the extent of $10,000.

b. **Allocation of Payments.** Continuing with the example, if the debtor makes a $1,000 payment on the $12,000 obligation, then one must determine the extent to which the security interest remains a purchase-money security interest—$9,000 or $10,000. Subsection (e)(1) expresses the overriding principle, applicable in cases other than consumer-goods transactions, for determining the extent to which a security interest is a purchase-money security interest under these circumstances: freedom of contract, as limited by principle of reasonableness. An unconscionable method of application, for example, is not a reasonable one and so would not be given effect under subsection (e)(1). In the absence of agreement, subsection (e)(2) permits the obligor to determine how payments should be allocated. If the obligor fails to manifest its intention, obligations that are not secured will be paid first. (As used in this Article, the concept of "obligations that are not secured" means obligations for which the debtor has not created a security interest. This concept is different from and should not be confused with the concept of an "unsecured claim" as it appears in Bankruptcy Code Section 506(a).) The obligor may prefer this approach, because unsecured debt is likely to carry a higher interest rate than secured debt. A creditor who would prefer to be secured rather than unsecured also would prefer this approach.

After the unsecured debt is paid, payments are to be applied first toward the obligations secured by purchase-money security interests. In the event that there is more than one such obligation, payments first received are to be applied to obligations first incurred. See subsection (e)(3). Once these obligations are paid, there are no purchase-money security interests and no additional allocation rules are needed.

Subsection (f) buttresses the dual-status rule by making it clear that (in a transaction other than a consumer-goods transaction) cross-collateralization and renewals, refinancings, and restructurings do not cause a purchase-money security interest to lose its status as such. The statutory terms "renewed," "refinanced," and "restructured" are not defined. Whether the terms encompass a particular transaction depends upon whether, under the particular facts, the purchase-money character of the security interest fairly can be said to survive. Each term contemplates that an identifiable portion of the purchase-money obligation could be traced to the new obligation resulting from a renewal, refinancing, or restructuring.

c. **Burden of Proof.** As is the case when the extent of a security interest is in issue, under subsection (g) the secured party claiming a purchase-money security interest in a transaction other than a consumer-goods transaction has the burden of establishing whether the security interest retains its purchase-money status. This is so whether the determination is to be made following a renewal, refinancing, or restructuring or otherwise.

8. **Consumer-Goods Transactions; Characterization Under Other Law.** Under subsection (h), the limitation of subsections (e), (f), and (g) to transactions other than consumer-goods transactions leaves to the court the determination of the proper rules in consumer-goods transactions. Subsection (h) also instructs the court not to draw any inference from this limitation as to the proper rules for consumer-goods transactions and leaves the court free to continue to apply established approaches to those transactions.

This section addresses only whether a security interest is a "purchase-money security interest" under this Article, primarily for purposes of perfection and priority. See, e.g., Sections 9–317, 9–324. In particular, its adoption of the dual-status rule, allocation of payments rules, and burden of proof standards for non-consumer-goods transactions is not intended to affect or influence characterizations under other statutes. Whether a security interest is a "purchase-money security interest" under other law is determined by that law. For example, decisions under Bankruptcy Code Section 522(f) have applied both the dual-status and the transformation rules. The Bankruptcy Code does not expressly adopt the state law definition of "purchase-money security interest." Where federal law does not defer to this Article, this Article does not, and could not, determine a question of federal law.

§ 9–104.   Control of Deposit Account.

(a) **[Requirements for control.]** A secured party has control of a deposit account if:

(1) the secured party is the bank with which the deposit account is maintained;

(2) the debtor, secured party, and bank have agreed in an authenticated record that the bank will comply with instructions originated by the secured party directing disposition of the funds in the deposit account without further consent by the debtor; or

(3) the secured party becomes the bank's customer with respect to the deposit account.

(b) **[Debtor's right to direct disposition.]** A secured party that has satisfied subsection (a) has control, even if the debtor retains the right to direct the disposition of funds from the deposit account.

Official Comment

1. **Source.** New; derived from Section 8–106.

2. **Why "Control" Matters.** This section explains the concept of "control" of a deposit account. "Control" under this section may serve two functions. First, "control . . . pursuant to the debtor's agreement" may substitute for an authenticated security agreement as an element of attachment. See Section 9–203(b)(3)(D). Second, when a deposit account is taken as original collateral, the only method of perfection is obtaining control under this section. See Section 9–312(b)(1).

3. **Requirements for "Control."** This section derives from Section 8–106 of Revised Article 8, which defines "control" of securities and certain other investment property. Under subsection (a)(1), the bank with which the deposit account is maintained has control. The effect of this provision is to afford the bank automatic perfection. No other form of public notice is necessary; all actual and potential creditors of the debtor are always on notice that the bank with which the debtor's deposit account is maintained may assert a claim against the deposit account.

Under subsection (a)(2), a secured party may obtain control by obtaining the bank's authenticated agreement that it will comply with the secured party's instructions without further consent by the debtor. The analogous provision in Section 8–106 does not require that the agreement be authenticated. An agreement to comply with the secured party's instructions suffices for "control" of a deposit account under this section even if the bank's agreement is subject to specified conditions, e.g., that the secured party's instructions are accompanied by a certification that the debtor is in default. (Of course, if the condition is the *debtor's* further consent, the statute explicitly provides that the agreement would *not* confer control.) See revised Section 8–106, Comment 7.

Under subsection (a)(3), a secured party may obtain control by becoming the bank's "customer," as defined in Section 4–104. As the customer, the secured party would enjoy the right (but not necessarily the exclusive right) to withdraw funds from, or close, the deposit account. See Sections 4–401(a), 4–403(a).

Although the arrangements giving rise to control may themselves prevent, or may enable the secured party at its discretion to prevent, the debtor from reaching the funds on deposit, subsection (b) makes clear that the debtor's ability to reach the funds is not inconsistent with "control."

Perfection by control is not available for bank accounts evidenced by an instrument (e.g., certain certificates of deposit), which by definition are "instruments" and not "deposit accounts." See Section 9–102 (defining "deposit account" and "instrument").

§ 9–105. Control of Electronic Chattel Paper.

A secured party has control of electronic chattel paper if the record or records comprising the chattel paper are created, stored, and assigned in such a manner that:

(1) a single authoritative copy of the record or records exists which is unique, identifiable and, except as otherwise provided in paragraphs (4), (5), and (6), unalterable;

(2) the authoritative copy identifies the secured party as the assignee of the record or records;

(3) the authoritative copy is communicated to and maintained by the secured party or its designated custodian;

(4) copies or revisions that add or change an identified assignee of the authoritative copy can be made only with the participation of the secured party;

(5) each copy of the authoritative copy and any copy of a copy is readily identifiable as a copy that is not the authoritative copy; and

(6) any revision of the authoritative copy is readily identifiable as an authorized or unauthorized revision.

Official Comment

1. **Source.** New.

2. **"Control" of Electronic Chattel Paper.** This Article covers security interests in "electronic chattel paper," a new term defined in Section 9–102. This section governs how "control" of electronic chattel paper may be obtained. A secured party's control of electronic chattel paper (i) may substitute for an authenticated security agreement for purposes of attachment under Section 9–203, (ii) is a method of perfection under Section 9–314, and (iii) is a condition for obtaining special, non-temporal priority under Section 9–330. Because electronic chattel paper cannot be transferred, assigned, or possessed in the same manner as tangible chattel paper, a special definition of control is necessary. In descriptive terms, this section provides that control of electronic chattel paper is the functional equivalent of possession of "tangible chattel paper" (a term also defined in Section 9–102).

3. **"Authoritative Copy" of Electronic Chattel Paper.** One requirement for establishing control is that a particular copy be an "authoritative copy." Although other copies may exist, they must be distinguished from the authoritative copy. This may be achieved, for example, through the methods of authentication that are used or by business practices involving the marking of any additional copies. When tangible chattel paper is converted to electronic chattel paper, in order to establish that a copy of the electronic chattel paper is the authoritative copy it may be necessary to show that the tangible chattel paper no longer exists or has been permanently marked to indicate that it is not the authoritative copy.

4. **Development of Control Systems.** This Article leaves to the marketplace the development of systems and procedures, through a combination of suitable technologies and business practices, for dealing with control of electronic chattel paper in a commercial context. However, achieving control under this section requires more than the agreement of interested persons that the elements of control are satisfied. For example, paragraph (4) contemplates that control requires that it be a physical impossibility (or sufficiently unlikely or implausible so as to approach practical impossibility) to add or change an identified assignee without the participation of the secured party (or its authorized representative). It would not be enough for the assignor merely to agree that it will not change the identified assignee without the assignee-secured party's consent. However, the standards applied to determine whether a party is in control of electronic chattel paper should not be more stringent than the standards

now applied to determine whether a party is in possession of tangible chattel paper. Control of electronic chattel paper contemplates systems or procedures such that the secured party must take some action (either directly or through its designated custodian) to effect a change or addition to the authoritative copy. But just as a secured party does not lose possession of tangible chattel paper merely by virtue of the possibility that a person acting on its behalf *could* wrongfully redeliver the chattel paper to the debtor, so control of electronic chattel paper would not be defeated by the possibility that the secured party's interest *could* be subverted by the wrongful conduct of a person (such as a custodian) acting on its behalf.

Systems that evolve for control of electronic chattel paper may or may not involve a third party custodian of the relevant records. However, this section and the concept of control of electronic chattel paper are not based on the same concepts as are control of deposit accounts (Section 9–104), security entitlements, a type of investment property (Section 9–106), and letter-of-credit rights (Section 9–107). The rules for control of that collateral are based on existing market practices and legal and regulatory regimes for institutions such as banks and securities intermediaries. Analogous practices for electronic chattel paper are developing nonetheless. The flexible approach adopted by this section, moreover, should not impede the development of these practices and, eventually, legal and regulatory regimes, which may become analogous to those for, e.g., investment property.

§ 9–106. Control of Investment Property.

(a) **[Control under Section 8–106.]** A person has control of a certificated security, uncertificated security, or security entitlement as provided in Section 8–106.

(b) **[Control of commodity contract.]** A secured party has control of a commodity contract if:

(1) the secured party is the commodity intermediary with which the commodity contract is carried; or

(2) the commodity customer, secured party, and commodity intermediary have agreed that the commodity intermediary will apply any value distributed on account of the commodity contract as directed by the secured party without further consent by the commodity customer.

(c) **[Effect of control of securities account or commodity account.]** A secured party having control of all security entitlements or commodity contracts carried in a securities account or commodity account has control over the securities account or commodity account.

Official Comment

1. **Source.** Former Section 9–115(e).

2. **"Control" Under Article 8.** For an explanation of "control" of securities and certain other investment property, see Section 8–106, Comments 4 and 7.

3. **"Control" of Commodity Contracts.** This section, as did former Section 9–115(1)(e), contains provisions relating to control of commodity contracts which are analogous to those in Section 8–106 for other types of investment property.

4. **Securities Accounts and Commodity Accounts.** For drafting convenience, control with respect to a securities account or commodity account is defined in terms of obtaining control over the security entitlements or commodity contracts. Of course, an agreement that provides that (without further consent of the debtor) the securities intermediary or commodity intermediary will honor instructions from the secured party concerning a securities account or commodity account described as such is sufficient. Such an agreement necessarily implies that the intermediary will honor instructions concerning all security entitlements or commodity contracts carried in the account and thus affords the secured party control of all the security entitlements or commodity contracts.

§ 9–107. Control of Letter-of-Credit Right.

A secured party has control of a letter-of-credit right to the extent of any right to payment or performance by the issuer or any nominated person if the issuer or nominated person has consented to an assignment of proceeds of the letter of credit under Section 5–114(c) or otherwise applicable law or practice.

Official Comment

1. **Source.** New.

2. **"Control" of Letter-of-Credit Right.** Whether a secured party has control of a letter-of-credit right may determine the secured party's priority as against competing secured parties. See Section 9–329. This section provides that a secured party acquires control

of a letter-of-credit right by receiving an assignment if the secured party obtains the consent of the issuer or any nominated person, such as a confirmer or negotiating bank, under Section 5–114 or other applicable law or practice. Because both issuers and nominated persons may give or be obligated to give value under a letter of credit, this section contemplates that a secured party obtains control of a letter-of-credit right with respect to the issuer or a particular nominated person only to the extent that the issuer or that nominated person consents to the assignment. For example, if a secured party obtains control to the extent of an issuer's obligation but fails to obtain the consent of a nominated person, the secured party does not have control to the extent that the nominated person gives value. In many cases the person or persons who will give value under a letter of credit will be clear from its terms. In other cases, prudence may suggest obtaining consent from more than one person. The details of the consenting issuer's or nominated person's duties to pay or otherwise render performance to the secured party are left to the agreement of the parties.

3. **"Proceeds of a Letter of Credit."** Section 5–114 follows traditional banking terminology by referring to a letter of credit beneficiary's assignment of its right to receive payment thereunder as an assignment of the "proceeds of a letter of credit." However, as the seller of goods can assign its right to receive payment (an "account") before it has been earned by delivering the goods to the buyer, so the beneficiary of a letter of credit can assign its contingent right to payment before the letter of credit has been honored. See Section 5–114(b). If the assignment creates a security interest, the security interest can be perfected at the time it is created. An assignment of, including the creation of a security interest in, a letter-of-credit right is an assignment of a present interest.

4. **"Transfer" vs. "Assignment."** Letter-of-credit law and practice distinguish the "transfer" of a letter of credit from an "assignment." Under a transfer, the transferee itself becomes the beneficiary and acquires the right to draw. Whether a new, substitute credit is issued or the issuer advises the transferee of its status as such, the transfer constitutes a novation under which the transferee is the new, substituted beneficiary (but only to the extent of the transfer, in the case of a partial transfer).

Section 5–114(e) provides that the rights of a transferee beneficiary or nominated person are independent of the beneficiary's assignment of the proceeds of a letter of credit and are superior to the assignee's right to the proceeds. For this reason, transfer does not appear in this Article as a means of control or perfection. Section 9–109(c)(4) recognizes the independent and superior rights of a transferee beneficiary under Section 5–114(e); this Article does not apply to the rights of a transferee beneficiary or nominated person to the extent that those rights are independent and superior under Section 5–114.

5. **Supporting Obligation: Automatic Attachment and Perfection.** A letter-of-credit right is a type of "supporting obligation," as defined in Section 9–102. Under Sections 9–203 and 9–308, a security interest in a letter-of-credit right automatically attaches and is automatically perfected if the security interest in the supported obligation is a perfected security interest. However, unless the secured party has control of the letter-of-credit right or itself becomes a transferee beneficiary, it cannot obtain any rights against the issuer or a nominated person under Article 5. Consequently, as a practical matter, the secured party's rights would be limited to its ability to locate and identify proceeds distributed by the issuer or nominated person under the letter of credit.

§ 9–108.   Sufficiency of Description.

(a) **[Sufficiency of description.]** Except as otherwise provided in subsections (c), (d), and (e), a description of personal or real property is sufficient, whether or not it is specific, if it reasonably identifies what is described.

(b) **[Examples of reasonable identification.]** Except as otherwise provided in subsection (d), a description of collateral reasonably identifies the collateral if it identifies the collateral by:

(1) specific listing;

(2) category;

(3) except as otherwise provided in subsection (e), a type of collateral defined in [the Uniform Commercial Code];

(4) quantity;

(5) computational or allocational formula or procedure; or

(6) except as otherwise provided in subsection (c), any other method, if the identity of the collateral is objectively determinable.

(c) **[Supergeneric description not sufficient.]** A description of collateral as "all the debtor's assets" or "all the debtor's personal property" or using words of similar import does not reasonably identify the collateral.

(d) **[Investment property.]** Except as otherwise provided in subsection (e), a description of a security entitlement, securities account, or commodity account is sufficient if it describes:

(1) the collateral by those terms or as investment property; or

(2) the underlying financial asset or commodity contract.

(e) **[When description by type insufficient.]** A description only by type of collateral defined in [the Uniform Commercial Code] is an insufficient description of:

(1) a commercial tort claim; or

(2) in a consumer transaction, consumer goods, a security entitlement, a securities account, or a commodity account.

Official Comment

1. **Source.** Former Sections 9–110, 9–115(3).

2. **General Rules.** Subsection (a) retains substantially the same formulation as former Section 9–110. Subsection (b) expands upon subsection (a) by indicating a variety of ways in which a description might reasonably identify collateral. Whereas a provision similar to subsection (b) was applicable only to investment property under former Section 9–115(3), subsection (b) applies to all types of collateral, subject to the limitation in subsection (d). Subsection (b) is subject to subsection (c), which follows prevailing case law and adopts the view that an "all assets" or "all personal property" description for purposes of a *security agreement* is *not* sufficient. Note, however, that under Section 9–504, a *financing statement* sufficiently indicates the collateral if it "covers all assets or all personal property."

The purpose of requiring a description of collateral in a security agreement under Section 9–203 is evidentiary. The test of sufficiency of a description under this section, as under former Section 9–110, is that the description do the job assigned to it: make possible the identification of the collateral described. This section rejects any requirement that a description is insufficient unless it is exact and detailed (the so-called "serial number" test).

3. **After-Acquired Collateral.** Much litigation has arisen over whether a description in a security agreement is sufficient to include after-acquired collateral if the agreement does not explicitly so provide. This question is one of contract interpretation and is not susceptible to a statutory rule (other than a rule to the effect that it is a question of contract interpretation). Accordingly, this section contains no reference to descriptions of after-acquired collateral.

4. **Investment Property.** Under subsection (d), the use of the wrong Article 8 terminology does not render a description invalid (e.g., a security agreement intended to cover a debtor's "security entitlements" is sufficient if it refers to the debtor's "securities"). Note also that given the broad definition of "securities account" in Section 8–501, a security interest in a securities account also includes all other rights of the debtor against the securities intermediary arising out of the securities account. For example, a security interest in a securities account would include credit balances due to the debtor from the securities intermediary, whether or not they are proceeds of a security entitlement. Moreover, describing collateral as a securities account is a simple way of describing all of the security entitlements carried in the account.

5. **Consumer Investment Property; Commercial Tort Claims.** Subsection (e) requires greater specificity of description in order to prevent debtors from inadvertently encumbering certain property. Subsection (e) requires that a description by defined "type" of collateral alone of a commercial tort claim or, in a consumer transaction, of a security entitlement, securities account, or commodity account, is not sufficient. For example, "all existing and after-acquired investment property" or "all existing and after-acquired security entitlements," without more, would be insufficient in a consumer transaction to describe a security entitlement, securities account, or commodity account. The reference to "*only* by type" in subsection (e) means that a description is sufficient if it satisfies subsection (a) and contains a descriptive component beyond the "type" alone. Moreover, if the collateral consists of a securities account or commodity account, a description of the account is sufficient to cover all existing and future security entitlements or commodity contracts carried in the account. See Section 9–203(h), (i).

Under Section 9–204, an after-acquired collateral clause in a security agreement will not reach future commercial tort claims. It follows that when an effective security agreement covering a commercial tort claim is entered into the claim already will exist. Subsection (e) does not require a description to be specific. For example, a description such as "all tort claims arising out of the explosion of debtor's factory" would suffice, even if the exact amount of the claim, the theory on which it may be based, and the identity of the tortfeasor(s) are not described. (Indeed, those facts may not be known at the time.)

[SUBPART 2. APPLICABILITY OF ARTICLE]

§ 9–109. Scope.

(a) **[General scope of article.]** Except as otherwise provided in subsections (c) and (d), this article applies to:

(1) a transaction, regardless of its form, that creates a security interest in personal property or fixtures by contract;

(2) an agricultural lien;

(3) a sale of accounts, chattel paper, payment intangibles, or promissory notes;

(4) a consignment;

(5) a security interest arising under Section 2–401, 2–505, 2–711(3), or 2A–508(5), as provided in Section 9–110; and

(6) a security interest arising under Section 4–210 or 5–118.

(b) **[Security interest in secured obligation.]** The application of this article to a security interest in a secured obligation is not affected by the fact that the obligation is itself secured by a transaction or interest to which this article does not apply.

(c) **[Extent to which article does not apply.]** This article does not apply to the extent that:

(1) a statute, regulation, or treaty of the United States preempts this article;

(2) another statute of this State expressly governs the creation, perfection, priority, or enforcement of a security interest created by this State or a governmental unit of this State;

(3) a statute of another State, a foreign country, or a governmental unit of another State or a foreign country, other than a statute generally applicable to security interests, expressly governs creation, perfection, priority, or enforcement of a security interest created by the State, country, or governmental unit; or

(4) the rights of a transferee beneficiary or nominated person under a letter of credit are independent and superior under Section 5–114.

(d) **[Inapplicability of article.]** This article does not apply to:

(1) a landlord's lien, other than an agricultural lien;

(2) a lien, other than an agricultural lien, given by statute or other rule of law for services or materials, but Section 9–333 applies with respect to priority of the lien;

(3) an assignment of a claim for wages, salary, or other compensation of an employee;

(4) a sale of accounts, chattel paper, payment intangibles, or promissory notes as part of a sale of the business out of which they arose;

(5) an assignment of accounts, chattel paper, payment intangibles, or promissory notes which is for the purpose of collection only;

(6) an assignment of a right to payment under a contract to an assignee that is also obligated to perform under the contract;

(7) an assignment of a single account, payment intangible, or promissory note to an assignee in full or partial satisfaction of a preexisting indebtedness;

(8) a transfer of an interest in or an assignment of a claim under a policy of insurance, other than an assignment by or to a health-care provider of a health-care-insurance receivable and any subsequent assignment of the right to payment, but Sections 9–315 and 9–322 apply with respect to proceeds and priorities in proceeds;

(9) an assignment of a right represented by a judgment, other than a judgment taken on a right to payment that was collateral;

(10) a right of recoupment or set-off, but:

(A) Section 9–340 applies with respect to the effectiveness of rights of recoupment or set-off against deposit accounts; and

(B) Section 9–404 applies with respect to defenses or claims of an account debtor;

706

(11) the creation or transfer of an interest in or lien on real property, including a lease or rents thereunder, except to the extent that provision is made for:

(A) liens on real property in Sections 9–203 and 9–308;

(B) fixtures in Section 9–334;

(C) fixture filings in Sections 9–501, 9–502, 9–512, 9–516, and 9–519; and

(D) security agreements covering personal and real property in Section 9–604;

(12) an assignment of a claim arising in tort, other than a commercial tort claim, but Sections 9–315 and 9–322 apply with respect to proceeds and priorities in proceeds; or

(13) an assignment of a deposit account in a consumer transaction, but Sections 9–315 and 9–322 apply with respect to proceeds and priorities in proceeds.

Official Comment

1. **Source.** Former Sections 9–102, 9–104.

2. **Basic Scope Provision.** Subsection (a)(1) derives from former Section 9–102(1) and (2). These subsections have been combined and shortened. No change in meaning is intended. Under subsection (a)(1), all consensual security interests in personal property and fixtures are covered by this Article, except for transactions excluded by subsections (c) and (d). As to which transactions give rise to a "security interest," the definition of that term in Section 1–201 must be consulted. When a security interest is created, this Article applies regardless of the form of the transaction or the name that parties have given to it.

3. **Agricultural Liens.** Subsection (a)(2) is new. It expands the scope of this Article to cover agricultural liens, as defined in Section 9–102.

4. **Sales of Accounts, Chattel Paper, Payment Intangibles, Promissory Notes, and Other Receivables.** Under subsection (a)(3), as under former Section 9–102, this Article applies to sales of accounts and chattel paper. This approach generally has been successful in avoiding difficult problems of distinguishing between transactions in which a receivable secures an obligation and those in which the receivable has been sold outright. In many commercial financing transactions the distinction is blurred.

Subsection (a)(3) expands the scope of this Article by including the sale of a "payment intangible" (defined in Section 9–102 as "a general intangible under which the account debtor's principal obligation is a monetary obligation") and a "promissory note" (also defined in Section 9–102). To a considerable extent, this Article affords these transactions treatment identical to that given sales of accounts and chattel paper. In some respects, however, sales of payment intangibles and promissory notes are treated differently from sales of other receivables. See, e.g., Sections 9–309 (automatic perfection upon attachment), 9–408 (effect of restrictions on assignment). By virtue of the expanded definition of "account" (defined in Section 9–102), this Article now covers sales of (and other security interests in) "health-care-insurance receivables" (also defined in Section 9–102). Although this Article occasionally distinguishes between outright sales of receivables and sales that secure an obligation, neither this Article nor the definition of "security interest" (Section 1–201(37)) delineates how a particular transaction is to be classified. That issue is left to the courts.

5. **Transfer of Ownership in Sales of Receivables.** A "sale" of an account, chattel paper, a promissory note, or a payment intangible includes a sale of a right in the receivable, such as a sale of a participation interest. The term also includes the sale of an enforcement right. For example, a "[p]erson entitled to enforce" a negotiable promissory note (Section 3–301) may sell its ownership rights in the instrument. See Section 3–203, Comment 1 ("Ownership rights in instruments may be determined by principles of the law of property, independent of Article 3, which do not depend upon whether the instrument was transferred under Section 3–203."). Also, the right under Section 3–309 to enforce a lost, destroyed, or stolen negotiable promissory note may be sold to a purchaser who could enforce that right by causing the seller to provide the proof required under that section. This Article rejects decisions reaching a contrary result, e.g., *Dennis Joslin Co. v. Robinson Broadcasting*, 977 F. Supp. 491 (D.D.C. 1997).

Nothing in this section or any other provision of Article 9 prevents the transfer of full and complete ownership of an account, chattel paper, an instrument, or a payment intangible in a transaction of sale. However, as mentioned in Comment 4, neither this Article nor the definition of "security interest" in Section 1–201 provides rules for distinguishing sales transactions from those that create a security interest securing an obligation. This Article applies to both types of transactions. The principal effect of this coverage is to apply this Article's perfection and priority rules to these sales transactions. Use of terminology such as "security interest," "debtor," and "collateral" is merely a drafting convention adopted to reach this end, and its use has no relevance to distinguishing sales from other transactions. See PEB Commentary No. 14.

Following a debtor's outright sale and transfer of ownership of a receivable, the debtor-seller retains no legal or equitable rights in the receivable that has been sold. See Section 9–318(a). This is so whether or not the buyer's security interest is perfected. (A security interest arising from the sale of a promissory note or payment intangible is perfected upon attachment without further action. See Section 9–309.) However, if the buyer's interest in accounts or chattel paper is unperfected, a subsequent lien creditor, perfected secured party, or qualified buyer can reach the sold receivable and achieve priority over (or take free of) the buyer's unperfected security interest under Section 9–317. This is so not because the seller of a receivable retains rights in the property sold; it does not. Nor is this so because the seller of a receivable is a "debtor" and the buyer of a receivable is a "secured party" under this Article (they are). It is so for the simple reason that Sections 9–318(b), 9–317, and 9–322 make it so, as did former Sections 9–301 and 9–312. Because the buyer's security interest is unperfected, for purposes of determining the rights of creditors of and purchasers for value from the debtor-seller, under Section 9–318(b) the debtor-seller is deemed to have the rights and title it sold. Section 9–317 subjects the buyer's unperfected interest in accounts and chattel paper to that of the debtor-seller's lien creditor and other persons who qualify under that section.

6. **Consignments.** Subsection (a)(4) is new. This Article applies to every "consignment." The term, defined in Section 9–102, includes many but not all "true" consignments (i.e., bailments for the purpose of sale). If a transaction is a "sale or return," as defined in revised Section 2–326, it is not a "consignment." In a "sale or return" transaction, the buyer becomes the owner of the goods, and the seller may obtain an enforceable security interest in the goods only by satisfying the requirements of Section 9–203.

Under common law, creditors of a bailee were unable to reach the interest of the bailor (in the case of a consignment, the consignor-owner). Like former Section 2–326 and former Article 9, this Article changes the common-law result; however, it does so in a different manner. For purposes of determining the rights and interests of third-party creditors of, and purchasers of the goods from, the consignee, but not for other purposes, such as remedies of the consignor, the consignee is deemed to acquire under this Article whatev-

er rights and title the consignor had or had power to transfer. See Section 9–319. The interest of a consignor is defined to be a security interest under revised Section 1–201(37), more specifically, a purchase-money security interest in the consignee's inventory. See Section 9–103(d). Thus, the rules pertaining to lien creditors, buyers, and attachment, perfection, and priority of competing security interests apply to consigned goods. The relationship between the consignor and consignee is left to other law. Consignors also have no duties under Part 6. See Section 9–601(g).

Sometimes parties characterize transactions that secure an obligation (other than the bailee's obligation to returned bailed goods) as "consignments." These transactions are not "consignments" as contemplated by Section 9–109(a)(4). See Section 9–102. This Article applies also to these transactions, by virtue of Section 9–109(a)(1). They create a security interest within the meaning of the first sentence of Section 1–201(37).

This Article does not apply to bailments for sale that fall outside the definition of "consignment" in Section 9–102 and that do not create a security interest that secures an obligation.

7. **Security Interest in Obligation Secured by Non–Article 9 Transaction.** Subsection (b) is unchanged in substance from former Section 9–102(3). The following example provides an illustration.

Example 1: O borrows $10,000 from M and secures its repayment obligation, evidenced by a promissory note, by granting to M a mortgage on O's land. This Article does not apply to the creation of the real-property mortgage. However, if M sells the promissory note to X or gives a security interest in the note to secure M's own obligation to X, this Article applies to the security interest thereby created in favor of X. The security interest in the promissory note is covered by this Article even though the note is secured by a real-property mortgage. Also, X's security interest in the note gives X an attached security interest in the mortgage lien that secures the note and, if the security interest in the note is perfected, the security interest in the mortgage lien likewise is perfected. See Sections 9–203, 9–308.

It also follows from subsection (b) that an attempt to obtain or perfect a security interest in a secured obligation by complying with non-Article 9 law, as by an assignment of record of a real-property mortgage, would be ineffective. Finally, it is implicit from subsection (b) that one cannot obtain a security interest in a lien, such as a mortgage on real property, that is not also coupled with an equally effective security interest

708

in the secured obligation. This Article rejects cases such as In re *Maryville Savings & Loan Corp.*, 743 F.2d 413 (6th Cir. 1984), clarified on reconsideration, 760 F.2d 119 (1985).

8. **Federal Preemption.** Former Section 9–104(a) excluded from Article 9 "a security interest subject to any statute of the United States, to the extent that such statute governs the rights of parties to and third parties affected by transactions in particular types of property." Some (erroneously) read the former section to suggest that Article 9 sometimes deferred to federal law even when federal law did not preempt Article 9. Subsection (c)(1) recognizes explicitly that this Article defers to federal law only when and to the extent that it must—i.e., when federal law preempts it.

9. **Governmental Debtors.** Former Section 9–104(e) excluded transfers by governmental debtors. It has been revised and replaced by the exclusions in new paragraphs (2) and (3) of subsection (c). These paragraphs reflect the view that Article 9 should apply to security interests created by a State, foreign country, or a "governmental unit" (defined in Section 9–102) of either except to the extent that another statute governs the issue in question. Under paragraph (2), this Article defers to all statutes of the forum State. (A forum cannot determine whether it should consult the choice-of-law rules in the forum's UCC unless it first determines that its UCC applies to the transaction before it.) Paragraph (3) defers to statutes of another State or a foreign country only to the extent that those statutes contain rules applicable specifically to security interests created by the governmental unit in question.

Example 2: A New Jersey state commission creates a security interest in favor of a New York bank. The validity of the security interest is litigated in New York. The relevant security agreement provides that it is governed by New York law. To the extent that a New Jersey statute contains rules peculiar to creation of security interests by governmental units generally, to creation of security interests by state commissions, or to creation of security interests by this particular state commission, then that law will govern. On the other hand, to the extent that New Jersey law provides that security interests created by governmental units, state commissions, or this state commission are governed by the law generally applicable to secured transactions (i.e., New Jersey's Article 9), then New York's Article 9 will govern.

Example 3: An airline that is an instrumentality of a foreign country creates a security interest in favor of a New York bank. The analysis used in the previous example would apply here. That is, if the

matter is litigated in New York, New York law would govern except to the extent that the foreign country enacted a statute applicable to security interests created by governmental units generally or by the airline specifically.

The fact that New York law applies does not necessarily mean that perfection is accomplished by filing in New York. Rather, it means that the court should apply New York's Article 9, including its choice-of-law provisions. Under New York's Section 9–301, perfection is governed by the law of the jurisdiction in which the debtor is located. Section 9–307 determines the debtor's location for choice-of-law purposes.

If a transaction does not bear an appropriate relation to the forum State, then that State's Article 9 will not apply, regardless of whether the transaction would be excluded by paragraph (3).

Example 4: A Belgian governmental unit grants a security interest in its equipment to a Swiss secured party. The equipment is located in Belgium. A dispute arises and, for some reason, an action is brought in a New Mexico state court. Inasmuch as the transaction bears no "appropriate relation" to New Mexico, New Mexico's UCC, including its Article 9, is inapplicable. See Section 1–105(1). New Mexico's Section 9–109(c) on excluded transactions should not come into play. Even if the parties agreed that New Mexico law would govern, the parties' agreement would not be effective because the transaction does not bear a "reasonable relation" to New Mexico. See Section 1–105(1).

Conversely, Article 9 will come into play only if the litigation arises in a UCC jurisdiction or if a foreign choice-of-law rule leads a foreign court to apply the law of a UCC jurisdiction. For example, if issues concerning a security interest granted by a foreign airline to a New York bank are litigated overseas, the court may be bound to apply the law of the debtor's jurisdiction and not New York's Article 9.

10. **Certain Statutory and Common–Law Liens; Interests in Real Property.** With few exceptions (nonconsensual agricultural liens being one), this Article applies only to consensual security interests in personal property. Following former Section 9–104(b) and (j), paragraphs (1) and (11) of subsection (d) exclude landlord's liens and leases and most other interests in or liens on real property. These exclusions generally reiterate the limitations on coverage (i.e., "by contract," "in personal property and fixtures") made explicit in subsection (a)(1). Similarly, most jurisdictions provide special liens to suppliers of many types of services and materials, either by statute or by common

law. With the exception of agricultural liens, it is not necessary for this Article to provide general codification of this lien structure, which is determined in large part by local conditions and which is far removed from ordinary commercial financing. As under former Section 9–104(c), subsection (d)(2) excludes these suppliers' liens (other than agricultural liens) from this Article. However, Section 9–333 provides a rule for determining priorities between certain possessory suppliers' liens and security interests covered by this Article.

11. **Wage and Similar Claims.** As under former Section 9–104(d), subsection (d)(3) excludes assignments of claims for wages and the like from this Article. These assignments present important social issues that other law addresses. The Federal Trade Commission has ruled that, with some exceptions, the taking of an assignment of wages or other earnings is an unfair act or practice under the Federal Trade Commission Act. See 16 C.F.R. Part 444. State statutes also may regulate such assignments.

12. **Certain Sales and Assignments of Receivables; Judgments.** In general this Article covers security interests in (including sales of) accounts, chattel paper, payment intangibles, and promissory notes. Paragraphs (4), (5), (6), and (7) of subsection (d) exclude from the Article certain sales and assignments of receivables that, by their nature, do not concern commercial financing transactions. These paragraphs add to the exclusions in former Section 9–104(f) analogous sales and assignments of payment intangibles and promissory notes. For similar reasons, subsection (d)(9) retains the exclusion of assignments of judgments under former Section 9–104(h) (other than judgments taken on a right to payment that itself was collateral under this Article).

13. **Insurance.** Subsection (d)(8) narrows somewhat the broad exclusion of interests in insurance policies under former Section 9–104(g). This Article now covers assignments by or to a health-care provider of "health-care-insurance receivables" (defined in Section 9–102).

14. **Set-Off.** Subsection (d)(10) adds two exceptions to the general exclusion of set-off rights from Article 9 under former Section 9–104(i). The first takes account of new Section 9–340, which regulates the effectiveness of a set-off against a deposit account that stands as collateral. The second recognizes Section 9–404, which affords the obligor on an account, chattel paper, or general intangible the right to raise claims and defenses against an assignee (secured party).

15. **Tort Claims.** Subsection (d)(12) narrows somewhat the broad exclusion of transfers of tort claims under former Section 9–104(k). This Article now applies to assignments of "commercial tort claims" (defined in Section 9–102) as well as to security interests in tort claims that constitute proceeds of other collateral (e.g., a right to payment for negligent destruction of the debtor's inventory). Note that once a claim arising in tort has been settled and reduced to a contractual obligation to pay, the right to payment becomes a payment intangible and ceases to be a claim arising in tort.

This Article contains two special rules governing creation of a security interest in tort claims. First, a description of collateral in a security agreement as "all tort claims" is insufficient to meet the requirement for attachment. See Section 9–108(e). Second, no security interest attaches under an after-acquired property clause to a tort claim. See Section 9–204(b). In addition, this Article does not determine whom the tortfeasor must pay to discharge its obligation. Inasmuch as a tortfeasor is not an "account debtor," the rules governing waiver of defenses and discharge of an obligation by an obligor (Sections 9–403, 9–404, 9–405, and 9–406) are inapplicable to tort-claim collateral.

16. **Deposit Accounts.** Except in consumer transactions, deposit accounts may be taken as original collateral under this Article. Under former Section 9–104(*l*), deposit accounts were excluded as original collateral, leaving security interests in deposit accounts to be governed by the common law. The common law is nonuniform, often difficult to discover and comprehend, and frequently costly to implement. As a consequence, debtors who wished to use deposit accounts as collateral sometimes were precluded from doing so as a practical matter. By excluding deposit accounts from the Article's scope as original collateral in consumer transactions, subsection (d)(13) leaves those transactions to law other than this Article. However, in both consumer and non-consumer transactions, sections 9–315 and 9–322 apply to deposit accounts as proceeds and with respect to priorities in proceeds.

This Article contains several safeguards to protect debtors against inadvertently encumbering deposit accounts and to reduce the likelihood that a secured party will realize a windfall from a debtor's deposit accounts. For example, because "deposit account" is a separate type of collateral, a security agreement covering general intangibles will not adequately describe deposit accounts. Rather, a security agreement must reasonably identify the deposit accounts that are the subject of a security interest, e.g., by using the term "deposit accounts." See Section 9–108. To perfect a security interest in a deposit account as original collateral, a secured party (other than the bank with which the deposit account is maintained) must obtain "control" of the account either by obtaining the bank's authenticated agreement or by becoming the bank's customer with respect to the deposit account. See Sections 9–312(b)(1), 9–104. Either of these steps requires the debtor's consent.

This Article also contains new rules that determine which State's law governs perfection and priority of a security interest in a deposit account (Section 9–304), priority of conflicting security interests in and set-off rights against a deposit account (Sections 9–327, 9–340), the rights of transferees of funds from an encumbered deposit account (Section 9–332), the obligations of the bank (Section 9–341), enforcement of security interests in a deposit account (Section 9–607(c)), and the duty of a secured party to terminate control of a deposit account (Section 9–208(b)).

As amended in 2000.

§ 9–110. Security Interests Arising Under Article 2 or 2A.

A security interest arising under Section 2–401, 2–505, 2–711(3), or 2A–508(5) is subject to this article. However, until the debtor obtains possession of the goods:

(1) the security interest is enforceable, even if Section 9–203(b)(3) has not been satisfied;

(2) filing is not required to perfect the security interest;

(3) the rights of the secured party after default by the debtor are governed by Article 2 or 2A; and

(4) the security interest has priority over a conflicting security interest created by the debtor.

Official Comments

1. **Source.** Former Section 9–113.

2. **Background.** Former Section 9–113, from which this section derives, referred generally to security interests "arising solely under the Article on Sales (Article 2) or the Article on Leases (Article 2A)." Views differed as to the precise scope of that section. In contrast, Section 9–110 specifies the security interests to which it applies.

3. **Security Interests Under Articles 2 and 2A.** Section 2–505 explains how a seller of goods may reserve a security interest in them. Section 2–401 indicates that a reservation of title by the seller of

goods, despite delivery to the buyer, is limited to reservation of a security interest. As did former Article 9, this Article governs a security interest arising solely under one of those sections; however, until the buyer obtains possession of the goods, the security interest is enforceable even in the absence of a security agreement, filing is not necessary to perfect the security interest, and the seller-secured party's rights on the buyer's default are governed by Article 2.

Sections 2–711(3) and 2A–508(5) create a security interest in favor of a buyer or lessee in possession of goods that were rightfully rejected or as to which acceptance was justifiably revoked. As did former Article 9, this Article governs a security interest arising solely under one of those sections; however, until the seller or lessor obtains possession of the goods, the security interest is enforceable even in the absence of a security agreement, filing is not necessary to perfect the security interest, and the secured party's (buyer's or lessee's) rights on the debtor's (seller's or lessor's) default are governed by Article 2 or 2A, as the case may be.

4. **Priority.** This section adds to former Section 9–113 a priority rule. Until the debtor obtains possession of the goods, a security interest arising under one of the specified sections of Article 2 or 2A has priority over conflicting security interests created by the debtor. Thus, a security interest arising under Section 2–401 or 2–505 has priority over a conflicting security interest in the buyer's after-acquired goods, even if the goods in question are inventory. Arguably, the same result would obtain under Section 9–322, but even if it would not, a purchase-money-like priority is appropriate. Similarly, a security interest under Section 2–711(3) or 2A–508(5) has priority over security interests claimed by the seller's or lessor's secured lender. This result is appropriate, inasmuch as the payments giving rise to the debt secured by the Article 2 or 2A security interest are likely to be included among the lender's proceeds.

Example: Seller owns equipment subject to a security interest created by Seller in favor of Lender. Buyer pays for the equipment, accepts the goods, and then justifiably revokes acceptance. As long as Seller does not recover possession of the equipment, Buyer's security interest under Section 2–711(3) is senior to that of Lender.

In the event that a security interest referred to in this section conflicts with a security interest that is created by a person other than the debtor, Section 9–325 applies. Thus, if Lender's security interest in the example was created not by Seller but by the person from whom Seller acquired the goods, Section 9–325 would govern.

5. **Relationship to Other Rights and Remedies Under Articles 2 and 2A.** This Article does not specifically address the conflict between (i) a security interest created by a buyer or lessee and (ii) the seller's or lessor's right to withhold delivery under Section 2–702(1), 2–703(a), or 2A–525, the seller's or lessor's right to stop delivery under Section 2–705 or 2A–526, or the seller's right to reclaim under Section 2–507(2) or 2–702(2). These conflicts are governed by the first sentence of Section 2–403(1), under which the buyer's secured party obtains no greater rights in the goods than the buyer had or had power to convey, or Section 2A–307(1), under which creditors of the lessee take subject to the lease contract.

PART 2

EFFECTIVENESS OF SECURITY AGREEMENT; ATTACHMENT OF SECURITY INTEREST; RIGHTS OF PARTIES TO SECURITY AGREEMENT

[SUBPART 1. EFFECTIVENESS AND ATTACHMENT]

§ 9–201. General Effectiveness of Security Agreement.

(a) **[General effectiveness.]** Except as otherwise provided in [the Uniform Commercial Code], a security agreement is effective according to its terms between the parties, against purchasers of the collateral, and against creditors.

(b) **[Applicable consumer laws and other law.]** A transaction subject to this article is subject to any applicable rule of law which establishes a different rule for consumers and [insert reference to (i) any other statute or regulation that regulates the rates, charges, agreements, and practices for loans, credit sales, or other extensions of credit and (ii) any consumer-protection statute or regulation].

(c) **[Other applicable law controls.]** In case of conflict between this article and a rule of law, statute, or regulation described in subsection (b), the rule of law, statute, or regulation controls. Failure to comply with a statute or regulation described in subsection (b) has only the effect the statute or regulation specifies.

(d) **[Further deference to other applicable law.]** This article does not:

(1) validate any rate, charge, agreement, or practice that violates a rule of law, statute, or regulation described in subsection (b); or

(2) extend the application of the rule of law, statute, or regulation to a transaction not otherwise subject to it.

Official Comment

1. **Source.** Former Sections 9–201, 9–203(4).

2. **Effectiveness of Security Agreement.** Subsection (a) provides that a security agreement is generally effective. With certain exceptions, a security agreement is effective between the debtor and secured party and is likewise effective against third parties. Note that "security agreement" is used here (and elsewhere in this Article) as it is defined in Section 9–102: "an agreement that creates or provides for a security interest." It follows that subsection (a) does not provide that every term or provision contained in a record that contains a security agreement or that is so labeled is effective. Properly read, former Section 9–201 was to the same effect. Exceptions to the general rule of subsection (a) arise where there is an overriding provision in this Article or any other Article of the UCC. For example, Section 9–317 subordinates unperfected security interests to lien creditors and certain buyers, and several provisions in Part 3 subordinate some security interests to other security interests and interests of purchasers.

3. **Law, Statutes, and Regulations Applicable to Certain Transactions.** Subsection (b) makes clear that certain transactions, although subject to this Article, also are subject to other applicable laws relating to consumers or specified in that subsection. Subsection (c) provides that the other law is controlling in the event of a conflict, and that a violation of other law does not *ipso facto* constitute a violation of this Article. Subsection (d) provides that this Article does not validate violations under or extend the application of the other applicable laws.

§ 9–202. Title to Collateral Immaterial.

Except as otherwise provided with respect to consignments or sales of accounts, chattel paper, payment intangibles, or promissory notes, the provisions of this article with regard to rights and obligations apply whether title to collateral is in the secured party or the debtor.

Official Comment

1. **Source.** Former Section 9–202.

2. **Title Immaterial.** The rights and duties of parties to a secured transaction and affected third parties are provided in this Article without reference to the location of "title" to the collateral. For example, the characteristics of a security interest that secures the purchase price of goods are the same whether the secured party appears to have retained title or the debtor appears to have obtained title and then conveyed title or a lien to the secured party.

3. **When Title Matters.**

a. **Under This Article.** This section explicitly acknowledges two circumstances in which the effect of certain Article 9 provisions turns on ownership (title). First, in some respects sales of accounts, chattel paper, payment intangibles, and promissory notes receive special treatment. See, e.g., Sections 9–207(a), 9–210(b), 9–615(e). Buyers of receivables under former Article 9 were treated specially, as well. See, e.g., former Section 9–502(2). Second, the remedies of a consignor under a true consignment and, for the most part, the remedies of a buyer of accounts, chattel paper, payment intangibles, or promissory notes are determined by other law and not by Part 6. See Section 9–601(g).

b. **Under Other Law.** This Article does not determine which line of interpretation (e.g., title theory or lien theory, retained title or conveyed title) should be followed in cases in which the applicability of another rule of law depends upon who has title. If, for example, a revenue law imposes a tax on the "legal" owner of goods or if a corporation law makes a vote of the stockholders prerequisite to a corporation "giving" a security interest but not if it acquires property "subject" to a security interest, this Article does not attempt to define whether the secured party is a "legal" owner or whether the transaction "gives" a security interest for the purpose of such laws. Other rules of law or the agreement of the parties determines the location and source of title for those purposes.

§ 9–203. Attachment and Enforceability of Security Interest; Proceeds; Supporting Obligations; Formal Requisites.

(a) **[Attachment.]** A security interest attaches to collateral when it becomes enforceable against the debtor with respect to the collateral, unless an agreement expressly postpones the time of attachment.

(b) **[Enforceability.]** Except as otherwise provided in subsections (c) through (i), a security interest is enforceable against the debtor and third parties with respect to the collateral only if :

(1) value has been given;

(2) the debtor has rights in the collateral or the power to transfer rights in the collateral to a secured party; and

(3) one of the following conditions is met:

(A) the debtor has authenticated a security agreement that provides a description of the collateral and, if the security interest covers timber to be cut, a description of the land concerned;

(B) the collateral is not a certificated security and is in the possession of the secured party under Section 9–313 pursuant to the debtor's security agreement;

(C) the collateral is a certificated security in registered form and the security certificate has been delivered to the secured party under Section 8–301 pursuant to the debtor's security agreement; or

(D) the collateral is deposit accounts, electronic chattel paper, investment property, letter-of-credit rights, or electronic documents, and the secured party has control under Section 7–106, 9–104, 9–105, 9–106, or 9–107 pursuant to the debtor's security agreement.

(c) **[Other UCC provisions.]** Subsection (b) is subject to Section 4–210 on the security interest of a collecting bank, Section 5–118 on the security interest of a letter-of-credit issuer or nominated person, Section 9–110 on a security interest arising under Article 2 or 2A, and Section 9–206 on security interests in investment property.

(d) **[When person becomes bound by another person's security agreement.]** A person becomes bound as debtor by a security agreement entered into by another person if, by operation of law other than this article or by contract:

(1) the security agreement becomes effective to create a security interest in the person's property; or

(2) the person becomes generally obligated for the obligations of the other person, including the obligation secured under the security agreement, and acquires or succeeds to all or substantially all of the assets of the other person.

(e) **[Effect of new debtor becoming bound.]** If a new debtor becomes bound as debtor by a security agreement entered into by another person:

(1) the agreement satisfies subsection (b)(3) with respect to existing or after-acquired property of the new debtor to the extent the property is described in the agreement; and

(2) another agreement is not necessary to make a security interest in the property enforceable.

(f) **[Proceeds and supporting obligations.]** The attachment of a security interest in collateral gives the secured party the rights to proceeds provided by Section 9–315 and is also attachment of a security interest in a supporting obligation for the collateral.

(g) **[Lien securing right to payment.]** The attachment of a security interest in a right to payment or performance secured by a security interest or other lien on personal or real property is also attachment of a security interest in the security interest, mortgage, or other lien.

(h) **[Security entitlement carried in securities account.]** The attachment of a security interest in a securities account is also attachment of a security interest in the security entitlements carried in the securities account.

(i) **[Commodity contracts carried in commodity account.]** The attachment of a security interest in a commodity account is also attachment of a security interest in the commodity contracts carried in the commodity account.

As amended in 2003.

Official Comment

1. **Source.** Former Sections 9–203, 9–115(2), (6).

2. **Creation, Attachment, and Enforceability.** Subsection (a) states the general rule that a security interest attaches to collateral only when it becomes enforceable against the debtor. Subsection (b) specifies the circumstances under which a security interest becomes enforceable. Subsection (b) states three basic prerequisites to the existence of a security interest: value (paragraph (1)), rights or power to transfer rights in collateral (paragraph (2)), and agreement plus satisfaction of an evidentiary requirement (paragraph (3)). When all of these elements exist, a security interest becomes enforceable between the parties and attaches under subsection (a). Subsection (c) identifies certain exceptions to the general rule of subsection (b).

3. **Security Agreement; Authentication.** Under subsection (b)(3), enforceability requires the debtor's security agreement and compliance with an evidentiary requirement in the nature of a Statute of Frauds. Paragraph (3)(A) represents the most basic of the evidentiary alternatives, under which the debtor must authenticate a security agreement that provides a description of the collateral. Under Section 9–102, a "security agreement" is "an agreement that creates or provides for a security interest." Neither that definition nor the requirement of paragraph (3)(A) rejects the deeply rooted doctrine that a bill of sale, although absolute in form, may be shown in fact to have been given as security. Under this Article, as under prior law, a debtor may show by parol evidence that a transfer purporting to be absolute was in fact for security. Similarly, a self-styled "lease" may serve as a security agreement if the agreement creates a security interest. See Section 1–201(37) (distinguishing security interest from lease).

4. **Possession, Delivery, or Control Pursuant to Security Agreement.** The other alternatives in subsection (b)(3) dispense with the requirement of an authenticated security agreement and provide alternative evidentiary tests. Under paragraph (3)(B), the secured party's possession substitutes for the debtor's authentication under paragraph (3)(A) if the secured party's possession is "pursuant to the debtor's security agreement." That phrase refers to the debtor's agreement to the secured party's possession for the purpose of creating a security interest. The phrase should not be confused with the phrase "debtor has authenticated a security agreement," used in paragraph (3)(A), which contemplates the debtor's authentication of a record. In the unlikely event that possession is obtained without the debtor's agreement, possession would not suffice as a substitute for an authenticated security agreement. However, once the security interest has become enforceable and has attached, it is not impaired by the fact that the secured party's possession is maintained without the agreement of a subse-

quent debtor (e.g., a transferee). Possession as contemplated by Section 9–313 is possession for purposes of subsection (b)(3)(B), even though it may not constitute possession "pursuant to the debtor's agreement" and consequently might not serve as a substitute for an authenticated security agreement under subsection (b)(3)(A). Subsection (b)(3)(C) provides that delivery of a certificated security to the secured party under Section 8–301 pursuant to the debtor's security agreement is sufficient as a substitute for an authenticated security agreement. Similarly, under subsection (b)(3)(D), control of investment property, a deposit account, electronic chattel paper, a letter-of-credit right, or electronic documents satisfies the evidentiary test if control is pursuant to the debtor's security agreement.

5. **Collateral Covered by Other Statute or Treaty.** One evidentiary purpose of the formal requisites stated in subsection (b) is to minimize the possibility of future disputes as to the terms of a security agreement (e.g., as to the property that stands as collateral for the obligation secured). One should distinguish the evidentiary functions of the formal requisites of attachment and enforceability (such as the requirement that a security agreement contain a description of the collateral) from the more limited goals of "notice filing" for financing statements under Part 5, explained in Section 9–502, Comment 2. When perfection is achieved by compliance with the requirements of a statute or treaty described in Section 9–311(a), such as a federal recording act or a certificate-of-title statute, the manner of describing the collateral in a registry imposed by the statute or treaty may or may not be adequate for purposes of this section and Section 9–108. However, the description contained in the security agreement, not the description in a public registry or on a certificate of title, controls for purposes of this section.

6. **Debtor's Rights; Debtor's Power to Transfer Rights.** Subsection (b)(2) conditions attachment on the debtor's having "rights in the collateral or the power to transfer rights in the collateral to a secured party." A debtor's limited rights in collateral, short of full ownership, are sufficient for a security interest to attach. However, in accordance with basic personal property conveyancing principles, the baseline rule is that a security interest attaches only to whatever rights a debtor may have, broad or limited as those rights may be.

Certain exceptions to the baseline rule enable a debtor to transfer, and a security interest to attach to, greater rights than the debtor has. See Part 3, Subpart 3 (priority rules). The phrase, "or the power to trans-

fer rights in the collateral to a secured party," accommodates those exceptions. In some cases, a debtor may have power to transfer another person's rights only to a class of transferees that excludes secured parties. See, e.g., Section 2–403(2) (giving certain merchants power to transfer an entruster's rights to a buyer in ordinary course of business). Under those circumstances, the debtor would not have the power to create a security interest in the other person's rights, and the condition in subsection (b)(2) would not be satisfied.

7. **New Debtors.** Subsection (e) makes clear that the enforceability requirements of subsection (b)(3) are met when a new debtor becomes bound under an original debtor's security agreement. If a new debtor becomes bound as debtor by a security agreement entered into by another person, the security agreement satisfies the requirement of subsection (b)(3) as to the existing and after-acquired property of the new debtor to the extent the property is described in the agreement.

Subsection (d) explains when a new debtor becomes bound. Persons who become bound under paragraph (2) are limited to those who both become primarily liable for the original debtor's obligations and succeed to (or acquire) its assets. Thus, the paragraph excludes sureties and other secondary obligors as well as persons who become obligated through veil piercing and other non-successorship doctrines. In many cases, paragraph (2) will exclude successors to the assets and liabilities of a division of a debtor. See also Section 9–508, Comment 3.

8. **Supporting Obligations.** Under subsection (f), a security interest in a "supporting obligation" (defined in Section 9–102) automatically follows from a security interest in the underlying, supported collateral. This result was implicit under former Article 9. Implicit in subsection (f) is the principle that the secured party's interest in a supporting obligation extends to the supporting obligation only to the extent that it supports the collateral in which the secured party has a security interest. Complex issues may arise, however, if a supporting obligation supports many separate obligations of a particular account debtor and if the supported obligations are separately assigned as security to several secured parties. The problems may be exacerbated if a supporting obligation is limited to an aggregate amount that is less than the aggregate amount of the obligations it supports. This Article does not contain provisions dealing with competing claims to a limited supporting obligation. As under former Article 9, the law of suretyship and the agreements of the parties will control.

9. **Collateral Follows Right to Payment or Performance.** Subsection (g) codifies the common-law rule that a transfer of an obligation secured by a security interest or other lien on personal or real property also transfers the security interest or lien. See Restatement (3d), Property (Mortgages) § 5.4(a) (1997). See also Section 9–308(e) (analogous rule for perfection).

10. **Investment Property.** Subsections (h) and (i) make clear that attachment of a security interest in a securities account or commodity account is also attachment in security entitlements or commodity contracts carried in the accounts.

As amended in 2003.

§ 9–204. After-Acquired Property; Future Advances.

(a) **[After-acquired collateral.]** Except as otherwise provided in subsection (b), a security agreement may create or provide for a security interest in after-acquired collateral.

(b) **[When after-acquired property clause not effective.]** A security interest does not attach under a term constituting an after-acquired property clause to:

(1) consumer goods, other than an accession when given as additional security, unless the debtor acquires rights in them within 10 days after the secured party gives value; or

(2) a commercial tort claim.

(c) **[Future advances and other value.]** A security agreement may provide that collateral secures, or that accounts, chattel paper, payment intangibles, or promissory notes are sold in connection with, future advances or other value, whether or not the advances or value are given pursuant to commitment.

Official Comment

1. **Source.** Former Section 9–204.

2. **After-Acquired Property; Continuing General Lien.** Subsection (a) makes clear that a security interest arising by virtue of an after-acquired property clause is no less valid than a security interest in collateral in which the debtor has rights at the time value is given. A security interest in after-acquired property is not merely an "equitable" interest; no further action by the secured party—such as a supplemental agreement covering the new collateral—is required. This section adopts the principle of a "continuing general lien" or "floating lien." It validates a security interest in the debtor's existing and (upon acquisition) future assets, even though the debtor has liberty to use or dispose of collateral without being required to account for proceeds or substitute new collateral. See Section 9–205. Subsection (a), together with subsection (c), also validates "cross-collateral" clauses under which collateral acquired at any time secures advances whenever made.

3. **After-Acquired Consumer Goods.** Subsection (b)(1) makes ineffective an after-acquired property clause covering consumer goods (defined in Section 9–109), except as accessions (see Section 9–335), acquired more than 10 days after the secured party gives value. Subsection (b)(1) is unchanged in substance from the corresponding provision in former Section 9–204(2).

4. **Commercial Tort Claims.** Subsection (b)(2) provides that an after-acquired property clause in a security agreement does not reach future commercial tort claims. In order for a security interest in a tort claim to attach, the claim must be in existence when the security agreement is authenticated. In addition, the security agreement must describe the tort claim with greater specificity than simply "all tort claims." See Section 9–108(e).

5. **Future Advances; Obligations Secured.** Under subsection (c) collateral may secure future as well as past or present advances if the security agreement so provides. This is in line with the policy of this Article toward security interests in after-acquired property under subsection (a). Indeed, the parties are free to agree that a security interest secures any obligation whatsoever. Determining the obligations secured by collateral is solely a matter of construing the parties' agreement under applicable law. This Article rejects the holdings of cases decided under former Article 9 that applied other tests, such as whether a future advance or other subsequently incurred obligation was of the same or a similar type or class as earlier advances and obligations secured by the collateral.

6. **Sales of Receivables.** Subsections (a) and (c) expressly validate after-acquired property and future advance clauses not only when the transaction is for security purposes but also when the transaction is the sale of accounts, chattel paper, payment intangibles, or

promissory notes .. This result was implicit under former Article 9.

7. **Financing Statements.** The effect of after-acquired property and future advance clauses as components of a security agreement should not be confused with the requirements applicable to financing statements under this Article's system of perfection by notice filing. The references to after-acquired property clauses and future advance clauses in this section are limited to security agreements. There is no need to refer to after-acquired property or future advances or other obligations secured in a financing statement. See Section 9–502, Comment 2.

As amended in 2000.

§ 9–205. Use or Disposition of Collateral Permissible.

(a) **[When security interest not invalid or fraudulent.]** A security interest is not invalid or fraudulent against creditors solely because:

(1) the debtor has the right or ability to:

(A) use, commingle, or dispose of all or part of the collateral, including returned or repossessed goods;

(B) collect, compromise, enforce, or otherwise deal with collateral;

(C) accept the return of collateral or make repossessions; or

(D) use, commingle, or dispose of proceeds; or

(2) the secured party fails to require the debtor to account for proceeds or replace collateral.

(b) **[Requirements of possession not relaxed.]** This section does not relax the requirements of possession if attachment, perfection, or enforcement of a security interest depends upon possession of the collateral by the secured party.

Official Comment

1. **Source.** Former Section 9–205.

2. **Validity of Unrestricted "Floating Lien."** This Article expressly validates the "floating lien" on shifting collateral. See Sections 9–201, 9–204 and Comment 2. This section provides that a security interest is not invalid or fraudulent by reason of the debtor's

liberty to dispose of the collateral without being required to account to the secured party for proceeds or substitute new collateral. As did former Section 9–205, this section repeals the rule of *Benedict v. Ratner*, 268 U.S. 353 (1925), and other cases which held such arrangements void as a matter of law because the debtor was given unfettered dominion or control over collateral. The *Benedict* rule did not effectively discourage or eliminate security transactions in inventory and receivables. Instead, it forced financing arrangements to be self-liquidating. Although this section repeals *Benedict*, the filing and other perfection requirements (see Part 3, Subpart 2, and Part 5) provide for public notice that overcomes any potential misleading effects of a debtor's use and control of collateral. Moreover, nothing in this section prevents the debtor and secured party from agreeing to procedures by which the secured party polices or monitors collateral or to restrictions on the debtor's dominion. However, this Article leaves these matters to agreement based on business considerations, not on legal requirements.

3. **Possessory Security Interests.** Subsection (b) makes clear that this section does not relax the requirements for perfection by possession under Section 9–313. If a secured party allows the debtor access to and control over collateral its security interest may be or become unperfected.

4. **Permissible Freedom for Debtor to Enforce Collateral.** Former Section 9–205 referred to a debtor's "liberty. .to collect or compromise accounts or chattel paper." This section recognizes the broader rights of a debtor to "enforce," as well as to "collect" and "compromise" collateral. This section's reference to collecting, compromising, and enforcing "collateral" instead of "accounts or chattel paper" contemplates the many other types of collateral that a debtor may wish to "collect, compromise, or enforce": e.g., deposit accounts, documents, general intangibles, instruments, investment property, and letter-of-credit rights.

§ 9–206. Security Interest Arising in Purchase or Delivery of Financial Asset.

(a) **[Security interest when person buys through securities intermediary.]** A security interest in favor of a securities intermediary attaches to a person's security entitlement if:

(1) the person buys a financial asset through the securities intermediary in a transaction in which the person is obligated to pay the

purchase price to the securities intermediary at the time of the purchase; and

(2) the securities intermediary credits the financial asset to the buyer's securities account before the buyer pays the securities intermediary.

(b) **[Security interest secures obligation to pay for financial asset.]** The security interest described in subsection (a) secures the person's obligation to pay for the financial asset.

(c) **[Security interest in payment against delivery transaction.]** A security interest in favor of a person that delivers a certificated security or other financial asset represented by a writing attaches to the security or other financial asset if:

(1) the security or other financial asset:

(A) in the ordinary course of business is transferred by delivery with any necessary indorsement or assignment; and

(B) is delivered under an agreement between persons in the business of dealing with such securities or financial assets; and

(2) the agreement calls for delivery against payment.

(d) **[Security interest secures obligation to pay for delivery.]** The security interest described in subsection (c) secures the obligation to make payment for the delivery.

Official Comment

1. **Source.** Former 9–116.

2. **Codification of "Broker's Lien."** Depending upon a securities intermediary's arrangements with its entitlement holders, the securities intermediary may treat the entitlement holder as entitled to financial assets before the entitlement holder has actually made payment for them. For example, many brokers permit retail customers to pay for financial assets by check. The broker may not receive final payment of the check until several days after the broker has credited the customer's securities account for the financial assets. Thus, the customer will have acquired a security entitlement prior to payment. Subsection (a) provides that, in such circumstances, the securities intermediary has

a security interest in the entitlement holder's security entitlement. Under subsection (b) the security interest secures the customer's obligation to pay for the financial asset in question. Subsections (a) and (b) codify and adapt to the indirect holding system the so-called "broker's lien," which has long been recognized. See Restatement, Security § 12.

3. **Financial Assets Delivered Against Payment.** Subsection (c) creates a security interest in favor of persons who deliver certificated securities or other financial assets in physical form, such as money market instruments, if the agreed payment is not received. In some arrangements for settlement of transactions in physical financial assets, the seller's securities custodian will deliver physical certificates to the buyer's securities custodian and receive a time-stamped delivery receipt. The buyer's securities custodian will examine the certificate to ensure that it is in good order, and that the delivery matches a trade in which the buyer has instructed the seller to deliver to that custodian. If all is in order, the receiving custodian will settle with the delivering custodian through whatever funds settlement system has been agreed upon or is used by custom and usage in that market. The understanding of the trade, however, is that the delivery is conditioned upon payment, so that if payment is not made for any reason, the security will be returned to the deliverer. Subsection (c) clarifies the rights of persons making deliveries in such circumstances. It provides the person making delivery with a security interest in the securities or other financial assets; under subsection (d), the security interest secures the seller's right to receive payment for the delivery. Section 8–301 specifies when delivery of a certificated security occurs; that section should be applied as well to other financial assets as well for purposes of this section.

4. **Automatic Attachment and Perfection.** Subsections (a) and (c) refer to attachment of a security interest. Attachment under this section has the same incidents (enforceability, right to proceeds, etc.) as attachment under Section 9–203. This section overrides the general attachment rules in Section 9–203. See Section 9–203(c). A securities intermediary's security interest under subsection (a) is perfected by control without further action. See Section 8–106 (control); 9–314 (perfection). Security interests arising under subsection (c) are automatically perfected. See Section 9–309(9).

[SUBPART 2. RIGHTS AND DUTIES]

§ 9–207. Rights and Duties of Secured Party Having Possession or Control of Collateral.

(a) **[Duty of care when secured party in possession.]** Except as otherwise provided in subsection (d), a secured party shall use reasonable care in the custody and preservation of collateral in the secured party's possession. In the case of chattel paper or an instrument, reasonable care includes taking necessary steps to preserve rights against prior parties unless otherwise agreed.

(b) **[Expenses, risks, duties, and rights when secured party in possession.]** Except as otherwise provided in subsection (d), if a secured party has possession of collateral:

(1) reasonable expenses, including the cost of insurance and payment of taxes or other charges, incurred in the custody, preservation, use, or operation of the collateral are chargeable to the debtor and are secured by the collateral;

(2) the risk of accidental loss or damage is on the debtor to the extent of a deficiency in any effective insurance coverage;

(3) the secured party shall keep the collateral identifiable, but fungible collateral may be commingled; and

(4) the secured party may use or operate the collateral:

(A) for the purpose of preserving the collateral or its value;

(B) as permitted by an order of a court having competent jurisdiction; or

(C) except in the case of consumer goods, in the manner and to the extent agreed by the debtor.

(c) **[Duties and rights when secured party in possession or control.]** Except as otherwise provided in subsection (d), a secured party having possession of collateral or control of collateral under Section 7–106, 9–104, 9–105, 9–106, or 9–107:

(1) may hold as additional security any proceeds, except money or funds, received from the collateral;

(2) shall apply money or funds received from the collateral to reduce the secured obligation, unless remitted to the debtor; and

(3) may create a security interest in the collateral.

(d) **[Buyer of certain rights to payment.]** If the secured party is a buyer of accounts, chattel paper, payment intangibles, or promissory notes or a consignor:

(1) subsection (a) does not apply unless the secured party is entitled under an agreement:

(A) to charge back uncollected collateral; or

(B) otherwise to full or limited recourse against the debtor or a secondary obligor based on the nonpayment or other default of an account debtor or other obligor on the collateral; and

(2) subsections (b) and (c) do not apply.

As amended in 2003.

Official Comment

1. **Source.** Former Section 9–207.

2. **Duty of Care for Collateral in Secured Party's Possession.** Like former section 9–207, subsection (a) imposes a duty of care, similar to that imposed on a pledgee at common law, on a secured party in possession of collateral. See Restatement, Security §§ 17, 18. In many cases a secured party in possession of collateral may satisfy this duty by notifying the debtor of action that should be taken and allowing the debtor to take the action itself. If the secured party itself takes action, its reasonable expenses may be added to the secured obligation. The revised definitions of "collateral," "debtor," and "secured party" in Section 9–102 make this section applicable to collateral subject to an agricultural lien if the collateral is in the lienholder's possession. Under Section 1–102 the duty to exercise reasonable care may not be disclaimed by agreement, although under that section the parties remain free to determine by agreement standards that are not manifestly unreasonable as to what constitutes reasonable care. Unless otherwise agreed, for a secured party in possession of chattel paper or an instrument, reasonable care includes the preservation of rights against prior parties. The secured party's right to have

instruments or documents indorsed or transferred to it or its order is dealt with in the relevant sections of Articles 3, 7, and 8. See Sections 3–201, 7–506, 8–304(d).

3. Specific Rules When Secured Party in Possession or Control of Collateral. Subsections (b) and (c) provide rules following common-law precedents which apply unless the parties otherwise agree. The rules in subsection (b) apply to typical issues that may arise while a secured party is in possession of collateral, including expenses, insurance, and taxes, risk of loss or damage, identifiable and fungible collateral, and use or operation of collateral. Subsection (c) contains rules that apply in certain circumstances that may arise when a secured party is in either possession or control of collateral. These circumstances include the secured party's receiving proceeds from the collateral and the secured party's creation of a security interest in the collateral.

4. Applicability Following Default. This section applies when the secured party has possession of collateral either before or after default. See Sections 9–601(b), 9–609. Subsection (b)(4)(C) limits agreements concerning the use or operation of collateral to collateral other than consumer goods. Under Section 9–602(1), a debtor cannot waive or vary that limitation.

5. "Repledges" and Right of Redemption. Subsection (c)(3) eliminates the qualification in former Section 9–207 to the effect that the terms of a "repledge" may not "impair" a debtor's "right to redeem" collateral. The change is primarily for clarification. There is no basis on which to draw from subsection (c)(3) any inference concerning the debtor's right to redeem the collateral. The debtor enjoys that right under Section 9–623; this section need not address it. For example, if the collateral is a negotiable note that the secured party (SP–1) repledges to SP–2, nothing in this section suggests that the debtor (D) does not retain the right to redeem the note upon payment to SP–1 of all obligations secured by the note. But, as explained below, the debtor's unimpaired right to redeem as against the debtor's original secured party nevertheless may not be enforceable as against the new secured party.

In resolving questions that arise from the creation of a security interest by SP–1, one must take care to distinguish D's rights against SP–1 from D's rights against SP–2. Once D discharges the secured obligation, D becomes entitled to the note; SP–1 has no legal basis upon which to withhold it. If, as a practical matter, SP–1 is unable to return the note because SP–

2 holds it as collateral for SP–1's unpaid debt, then SP–1 is liable to D under the law of conversion.

Whether SP–2 would be liable to D depends on the relative priority of SP–2's security interest and D's interest. By permitting SP–1 to create a security interest in the collateral (repledge), subsection (c)(3) provides a statutory power for SP–1 to give SP–2 a security interest (subject, of course, to any agreement by SP–1 not to give a security interest). In the vast majority of cases where repledge rights are significant, the security interest of the second secured party, SP–2 in the example, will be senior to the debtor's interest. By virtue of the debtor's consent or applicable legal rules, SP–2 typically would cut off D's rights in investment property or be immune from D's claims. See Sections 9–331, 3–306 (holder in due course), 8–303 (protected purchaser), 8–502 (acquisition of a security entitlement), 8–503(e) (action by entitlement holder). Moreover, the expectations and business practices in some markets, such as the securities markets, are such that D's consent to SP–2's taking free of D's rights inheres in D's creation of SP–1's security interest which gives rise to SP–1's power under this section. In these situations, D would have no right to recover the collateral or recover damages from SP–2. Nevertheless, D would have a damage claim against SP–1 if SP–1 had given a security interest to SP–2 in breach of its agreement with D. Moreover, if SP–2's security interest secures an amount that is less than the amount secured by SP–1's security interest (granted by D), then D's exercise of its right to redeem would provide value sufficient to discharge SP–1's obligations to SP–2.

For the most part this section does not change the law under former Section 9–207, although eliminating the reference to the debtor's right of redemption may alter the secured party's right to repledge in one respect. Former Section 9–207 could have been read to limit the secured party's statutory right to repledge collateral to repledge transactions in which the collateral did not secure a greater obligation than that of the original debtor. Inasmuch as this is a matter normally dealt with by agreement between the debtor and secured party, any change would appear to have little practical effect.

6. "Repledges" of Investment Property. The following example will aid the discussion of "repledges" of investment property.

Example. Debtor grants Alpha Bank a security interest in a security entitlement that includes 1000 shares of XYZ Co. stock that Debtor holds through an account with Able & Co. Alpha does not have an account with Able. Alpha uses Beta Bank as its securities custodian. Debtor instructs Able to transfer the shares to Beta, for the account of Alpha, and Able does so. Beta then credits Alpha's account. Alpha has control of the security entitlement for the 1000 shares under Section 8–106(d). (These are the facts of Example 2, Section 8–106, Comment 4.) Although, as between Debtor and Alpha, Debtor may have become the beneficial owner of the new securities entitlement with Beta, Beta has agreed to act on Alpha's entitlement orders because, as between Beta and Alpha, Alpha has become the entitlement holder.

Next, Alpha grants Gamma Bank a security interest in the security entitlement with Beta that includes the 1000 shares of XYZ Co. stock. In order to afford Gamma control of the entitlement, Alpha instructs Beta to transfer the stock to Gamma's custodian, Delta Bank, which credits Gamma's account for 1000 shares. At this point Gamma holds its securities entitlement for its benefit as well as that of its debtor, Alpha. Alpha's derivative rights also are for the benefit of Debtor.

In many, probably most, situations and at any particular point in time, it will be impossible for Debtor or Alpha to "trace" Alpha's "repledge" to any particular securities entitlement or financial asset of Gamma or anyone else. Debtor would retain, of course, a right to redeem the collateral from Alpha upon satisfaction of the secured obligation. However, in the absence of a traceable interest, Debtor would retain only a personal claim against Alpha in the event Alpha failed to restore the security entitlement to Debtor. Moreover, even in the unlikely event that Debtor could trace a property interest, in the context of the financial markets, normally the operation of this section, Debtor's explicit agreement to permit Alpha to create a senior security interest, or legal rules permitting Gamma to cut off Debtor's rights or become immune from Debtor's claims would effectively subordinate Debtor's interest to the holder of a security interest created by Alpha. And, under the shelter principle, all subsequent transferees would obtain interests to which Debtor's interest also would be subordinate.

7. **Buyers of Chattel Paper and Other Receivables; Consignors.** This section has been revised to reflect the fact that a seller of accounts, chattel paper, payment intangibles, or promissory notes retains no interest in the collateral and so is not disadvantaged by the secured party's noncompliance with the requirements of this section. Accordingly, subsection (d) provides that subsection (a) applies only to security interests that secure an obligation and to sales of receivables in which the buyer has recourse against the debtor. (Of course, a buyer of accounts or payment intangibles could not have "possession" of original collateral, but might have possession of proceeds, such as promissory notes or checks.) The meaning of "recourse" in this respect is limited to recourse arising out of the account debtor's failure to pay or other default.

Subsection (d) makes subsections (b) and (c) inapplicable to buyers of accounts, chattel paper, payment intangibles, or promissory notes and consignors. Of course, there is no reason to believe that a buyer of receivables or a consignor could not, for example, create a security interest or otherwise transfer an interest in the collateral, regardless of who has possession of the collateral. However, this section leaves the rights of those owners to law other than Article 9.

As amended in 2000.

§ 9–208. Additional Duties of Secured Party Having Control of Collateral.

(a) **[Applicability of section.]** This section applies to cases in which there is no outstanding secured obligation and the secured party is not committed to make advances, incur obligations, or otherwise give value.

(b) **[Duties of secured party after receiving demand from debtor.]** Within 10 days after receiving an authenticated demand by the debtor:

(1) a secured party having control of a deposit account under Section 9–104(a)(2) shall send to the bank with which the deposit account is maintained an authenticated statement that releases the bank from any further obligation to comply with instructions originated by the secured party;

(2) a secured party having control of a deposit account under Section 9–104(a)(3) shall:

(A) pay the debtor the balance on deposit in the deposit account; or

(B) transfer the balance on deposit into a deposit account in the debtor's name;

(3) a secured party, other than a buyer, having control of electronic chattel paper under Section 9–105 shall:

(A) communicate the authoritative copy of the electronic chattel paper to the debtor or its designated custodian;

(B) if the debtor designates a custodian that is the designated custodian with which the authoritative copy of the electronic chattel paper is maintained for the secured party, communicate to the custodian an authenticated record releasing the designated custodian from any further obligation to comply with instructions originated by the secured party and instructing the custodian to comply with instructions originated by the debtor; and

(C) take appropriate action to enable the debtor or its designated custodian to make copies of or revisions to the authoritative copy which add or change an identified assignee of the authoritative copy without the consent of the secured party;

(4) a secured party having control of investment property under Section 8–106(d)(2) or 9–106(b) shall send to the securities intermediary or commodity intermediary with which the security entitlement or commodity contract is maintained an authenticated record that releases the securities intermediary or commodity intermediary from any further obligation to comply with entitlement orders or directions originated by the secured party;

(5) a secured party having control of a letter-of-credit right under Section 9–107 shall send to each person having an unfulfilled obligation to pay or deliver proceeds of the letter of credit to the secured party an authenticated release from any further obligation to pay or deliver proceeds of the letter of credit to the secured party; and

(6) a secured party having control of an electronic document shall:

(A) give control of the electronic document to the debtor or its designated custodian;

(B) if the debtor designates a custodian that is the designated custodian with which the authoritative copy of the electronic document is maintained for the secured party, communicate to the custodian an authenticated record releasing the designated custodian from any further obligation to comply with instruc-

tions originated by the secured party and instructing the custodian to comply with instructions originated by the debtor; and

(C) take appropriate action to enable the debtor or its designated custodian to make copies of or revisions to the authoritative copy which add or change an identified assignee of the authoritative copy without the consent of the secured party.

As amended in 2003.

Official Comment

1. **Source.** New.

2. **Scope and Purpose.** This section imposes duties on a secured party who has control of a deposit account, electronic chattel paper, investment property, a letter-of-credit right, or electronic documents of title. The duty to terminate the secured party's control is analogous to the duty to file a termination statement, imposed by Section 9–513. Under subsection (a), it applies only when there is no outstanding secured obligation and the secured party is not committed to give value. The requirements of this section can be varied by agreement under Section 1–102(3). For example, a debtor could by contract agree that the secured party may comply with subsection (b) by releasing control more than 10 days after demand. Also, duties under this section should not be read to conflict with the terms of the collateral itself. For example, if the collateral is a time deposit account, subsection (b)(2) should not require a secured party with control to make an early withdrawal of the funds (assuming that were possible) in order to pay them over to the debtor or put them in an account in the debtor's name.

3. **Remedy for Failure to Relinquish Control.** If a secured party fails to comply with the requirements of subsection (b), the debtor has the remedy set forth in Section 9–625(e). This remedy is identical to that applicable to failure to provide or file a termination statement under Section 9–513.

4. **Duty to Relinquish Possession.** Although Section 9–207 addresses directly the duties of a secured party in possession of collateral, that section does not require the secured party to relinquish possession when the secured party ceases to hold a security interest. Under common law, absent agreement to the contrary, the failure to relinquish possession of collateral upon satisfaction of the secured obligation would con-

stitute a conversion. Inasmuch as problems apparently have not surfaced in the absence of statutory duties under former Article 9 and the common-law duty appears to have been sufficient, this Article does not impose a statutory duty to relinquish possession.

As amended in 2000 and 2003.

§ 9–209. Duties of Secured Party if Account Debtor Has Been Notified of Assignment.

(a) **[Applicability of section.]** Except as otherwise provided in subsection (c), this section applies if:

(1) there is no outstanding secured obligation; and

(2) the secured party is not committed to make advances, incur obligations, or otherwise give value.

(b) **[Duties of secured party after receiving demand from debtor.]** Within 10 days after receiving an authenticated demand by the debtor, a secured party shall send to an account debtor that has received notification of an assignment to the secured party as assignee under Section 9–406(a) an authenticated record that releases the account debtor from any further obligation to the secured party.

(c) **[Inapplicability to sales.]** This section does not apply to an assignment constituting the sale of an account, chattel paper, or payment intangible.

Official Comment

1. **Source.** New.

2. **Scope and Purpose.** Like Sections 9–208 and 9–513, which require a secured party to relinquish control of collateral and to file or provide a termination statement for a financing statement, this section requires a secured party to free up collateral when there no longer is any outstanding secured obligation or any commitment to give value in the future. This section addresses the case in which account debtors have been notified to pay a secured party to whom the receivables have been assigned. It requires the secured party (assignee) to inform the account debtors that they no longer are obligated to make payment to the secured party. See subsection (b). It does not apply to account debtors whose obligations on an account, chattel paper, or payment intangible have been sold. See subsection (c).

§ 9–210. Request for Accounting; Request Regarding List of Collateral or Statement of Account.

(a) **[Definitions.]** In this section:

(1) "Request" means a record of a type described in paragraph (2), (3), or (4).

(2) "Request for an accounting" means a record authenticated by a debtor requesting that the recipient provide an accounting of the unpaid obligations secured by collateral and reasonably identifying the transaction or relationship that is the subject of the request.

(3) "Request regarding a list of collateral" means a record authenticated by a debtor requesting that the recipient approve or correct a list of what the debtor believes to be the collateral securing an obligation and reasonably identifying the transaction or relationship that is the subject of the request.

(4) "Request regarding a statement of account" means a record authenticated by a debtor requesting that the recipient approve or correct a statement indicating what the debtor believes to be the aggregate amount of unpaid obligations secured by collateral as of a specified date and reasonably identifying the transaction or relationship that is the subject of the request.

(b) **[Duty to respond to requests.]** Subject to subsections (c), (d), (e), and (f), a secured party, other than a buyer of accounts, chattel paper, payment intangibles, or promissory notes or a consignor, shall comply with a request within 14 days after receipt:

(1) in the case of a request for an accounting, by authenticating and sending to the debtor an accounting; and

(2) in the case of a request regarding a list of collateral or a request regarding a statement of account, by authenticating and sending to the debtor an approval or correction.

(c) **[Request regarding list of collateral; statement concerning type of collateral.]** A secured party that claims a security interest in all of a particular type of collateral owned by the debtor may comply with a request regarding a list of collateral by sending to the debtor an authenticated record including a statement to that effect within 14 days after receipt.

(d) **[Request regarding list of collateral; no interest claimed.]** A person that receives a request regarding a list of collateral, claims no interest in the collateral when it receives the request, and claimed an interest in the collateral at an earlier time shall comply with the request within 14 days after receipt by sending to the debtor an authenticated record:

(1) disclaiming any interest in the collateral; and

(2) if known to the recipient, providing the name and mailing address of any assignee of or successor to the recipient's interest in the collateral.

(e) **[Request for accounting or regarding statement of account; no interest in obligation claimed.]** A person that receives a request for an accounting or a request regarding a statement of account, claims no interest in the obligations when it receives the request, and claimed an interest in the obligations at an earlier time shall comply with the request within 14 days after receipt by sending to the debtor an authenticated record:

(1) disclaiming any interest in the obligations; and

(2) if known to the recipient, providing the name and mailing address of any assignee of or successor to the recipient's interest in the obligations.

(f) **[Charges for responses.]** A debtor is entitled without charge to one response to a request under this section during any six-month period. The secured party may require payment of a charge not exceeding $25 for each additional response.

As amended in 1999.

Official Comment

1. **Source.** Former Section 9–208.

2. **Scope and Purpose.** This section provides a procedure whereby a debtor may obtain from a secured party information about the secured obligation and the collateral in which the secured party may claim a security interest. It clarifies and resolves some of the issues that arose under former Section 9–208 and makes information concerning the secured indebtedness readily available to debtors, both before and after default. It applies to agricultural lien transactions (see the definitions of "debtor," "secured party," and "collateral" in Section 9–102), but generally not to sales of receivables. See subsection (b).

3. **Requests by Debtors Only.** A financing statement filed under Part 5 may disclose only that a secured party may have a security interest in specified types of collateral. In most cases the financing statement will contain no indication of the obligation (if any) secured, whether any security interest actually exists, or the particular property subject to a security interest. Because creditors of and prospective purchasers from a debtor may have legitimate needs for more detailed information, it is necessary to provide a procedure under which the secured party will be required to provide information. On the other hand, the secured party should not be under a duty to disclose any details of the debtor's financial affairs to any casual inquirer or competitor who may inquire. For this reason, this section gives the right to request information to the debtor only. The debtor may submit a request in connection with negotiations with subsequent creditors and purchasers, as well as for the purpose of determining the status of its credit relationship or demonstrating which of its assets are free of a security interest.

4. **Permitted Types of Requests for Information.** Subsection (a) contemplates that a debtor may request three types of information by submitting three types of "requests" to the secured party. First, the debtor may request the secured party to prepare and send an "accounting" (defined in Section 9–102). Second, the debtor may submit to the secured party a list of collateral for the secured party's approval or correction. Third, the debtor may submit to the secured party for its approval or correction a statement of the aggregate amount of unpaid secured obligations. Inasmuch as a secured party may have numerous transactions and relationships with a debtor, each request must identify the relevant transactions or relationships. Subsections (b) and (c) require the secured party to respond to a request within 14 days following receipt of the request.

5. **Recipients Claiming No Interest in the Transaction.** A debtor may be unaware that a creditor with whom it has dealt has assigned its security interest or the secured obligation. Subsections (d) and (e) impose upon recipients of requests under this section the duty to inform the debtor that they claim no interest in the collateral or secured obligation, respectively, and to inform the debtor of the name and

mailing address of any known assignee or successor. As under subsections (b) and (c), a response to a request under subsection (d) or (e) is due 14 days following receipt.

6. **Waiver; Remedy for Failure to Comply.** The debtor's rights under this section may not be waived or varied. See Section 9–602(2). Section 9–625 sets forth the remedies for noncompliance with the requirements of this section.

7. **Limitation on Free Responses to Requests.** Under subsection (f), during a six-month period a debtor is entitled to receive from the secured party one free response to a request. The debtor is not entitled to a free response to *each* type of request (i.e., three free responses) during a six-month period.

As amended in 2000.

PART 3

PERFECTION AND PRIORITY

[SUBPART 1. LAW GOVERNING PERFECTION AND PRIORITY]

§ 9–301. Law Governing Perfection and Priority of Security Interests.

Except as otherwise provided in Sections 9–303 through 9–306, the following rules determine the law governing perfection, the effect of perfection or nonperfection, and the priority of a security interest in collateral:

(1) Except as otherwise provided in this section, while a debtor is located in a jurisdiction, the local law of that jurisdiction governs perfection, the effect of perfection or nonperfection, and the priority of a security interest in collateral.

(2) While collateral is located in a jurisdiction, the local law of that jurisdiction governs perfection, the effect of perfection or nonperfection, and the priority of a possessory security interest in that collateral.

(3) Except as otherwise provided in paragraph (4), while tangible negotiable documents, goods, instruments, money, or tangible chattel paper is located in a jurisdiction, the local law of that jurisdiction governs:

(A) perfection of a security interest in the goods by filing a fixture filing;

(B) perfection of a security interest in timber to be cut; and

(C) the effect of perfection or nonperfection and the priority of a nonpossessory security interest in the collateral.

(4) The local law of the jurisdiction in which the wellhead or minehead is located governs perfection, the effect of perfection or nonperfection, and the priority of a security interest in as-extracted collateral.

As amended in 2003.

Official Comment

1. **Source.** Former Sections 9–103(1)(a), (b), 9–103(3)(a), (b), 9–103(5), substantially modified.

2. **Scope of This Subpart.** Part 3, Subpart 1 (Sections 9–301 through 9–307) contains choice-of-law rules similar to those of former Section 9–103. Former Section 9–103 generally addresses which State's law governs "perfection and the effect of perfection or non-perfection of" security interests. See, e.g., former Section 9–103(1)(b). This Article follows the broader and more precise formulation in former Section 9–103(6)(b), which was revised in connection with the promulgation of Revised Article 8 in 1994: "perfection, the effect of perfection or non-perfection, and the priority of" security interests. Priority, in this context, subsumes all of the rules in Part 3, including "cut off" or "take free" rules such as Sections 9–317(b), (c), and (d), 9–320(a), (b), and (d), and 9–332. This subpart does not address choice of law for other purposes. For example, the law applicable to issues such as attachment, validity, characterization (e.g., true lease or security interest), and enforcement is governed by the rules in Section 1–105; that governing law typically is specified in the same agreement that contains the security agreement. And, another jurisdiction's law may govern other third-party matters addressed in this Article. See Section 9–401, Comment 3.

3. **Scope of Referral.** In designating the jurisdiction whose law governs, this Article directs the court to apply only the substantive ("local") law of a particular jurisdiction and not its choice-of-law rules.

Example 1: Litigation over the priority of a security interest in accounts arises in State X. State X has adopted the official text of this Article, which provides that priority is determined by the local law of the jurisdiction in which the debtor is located. See Section 9–301(1). The debtor is located in State Y. Even if State Y has retained former Article 9 or enacted a nonuniform choice-of-law rule (e.g., one that provides that perfection is governed by the law of State Z), a State X court should look only to the substantive law of State Y and disregard State Y's choice-of-law rule. State Y's substantive law (e.g., its Section 9–501) provides that financing statements should be filed in a filing office in State Y. Note, however, that if the identical perfection issue were to be litigated in State Y, the court would look to State Y's former Section 9–103 or nonuniform 9–301 and conclude that a filing in State Y is ineffective.

Example 2: In the preceding Example, assume that State X has adopted the official text of this Article, and State Y has adopted a nonuniform Section 9–301(1) under which perfection is governed by the whole law of State X, including its choice-of-law rules. If litigation occurs in State X, the court should look to the substantive law of State Y, which provides that financing statements are to be filed in a filing office in State Y. If litigation occurs in State Y, the court should look to the law of State X, whose choice-of-law rule requires that the court apply the substantive law of State Y. Thus, regardless of the jurisdiction in which the litigation arises, the financing statement should be filed in State Y.

4. **Law Governing Perfection: General Rule.** Paragraph (1) contains the general rule: the law governing perfection of security interests in both tangible and intangible collateral, whether perfected by filing or automatically, is the law of the jurisdiction of the debtor's location, as determined under Section 9–307.

Paragraph (1) substantially simplifies the choice-of-law rules. Former Section 9–103 contained different choice-of-law rules for different types of collateral. Under Section 9–301(1), the law of a single jurisdiction governs perfection with respect to most types of collateral, both tangible and intangible. Paragraph (1) eliminates the need for former Section 9–103(1)(c), which concerned purchase-money security interests in tangible collateral that is intended to move from one jurisdiction to the other. It is likely to reduce the frequency of cases in which the governing law changes after a financing statement is properly filed. (Presumably, debtors change their own location less frequently than they change the location of their collateral.) The approach taken in paragraph (1) also eliminates some difficult priority issues and the need to distinguish between "mobile" and "ordinary" goods, and it reduces the number of filing offices in which secured parties must file or search when collateral is located in several jurisdictions.

5. **Law Governing Perfection: Exceptions.** The general rule is subject to several exceptions. It does not apply to goods covered by a certificate of title (see Section 9–303), deposit accounts (see Section 9–304), investment property (see Section 9–305), or letter-of-credit rights (see Section 9–306). Nor does it apply to possessory security interests, i.e., security interests that the secured party has perfected by taking possession of the collateral (see paragraph (2)), security interests perfected by filing a fixture filing (see subparagraph (3)(A)), security interests in timber to be cut (subparagraph (3)(B)), or security interests in as-extracted collateral (see paragraph (4)).

a. **Possessory Security Interests.** Paragraph (2) applies to possessory security interests and provides that perfection is governed by the local law of the jurisdiction in which the collateral is located. This is the rule of former Section 9–103(1)(b), except paragraph (2) eliminates the troublesome "last event" test of former law.

The distinction between nonpossessory and possessory security interests creates the potential for the same jurisdiction to apply two different choice-of-law rules to determine perfection in the same collateral. For example, were a secured party in possession of an instrument or a tangible document to relinquish possession in reliance on temporary perfection, the applicable law immediately would change from that of the location of the collateral to that of the location of the debtor. The applicability of two different choice-of-law rules for perfection is unlikely to lead to any material practical problems. The perfection rules of one Article 9 jurisdiction are likely to be identical to those of another. Moreover, under paragraph (3), the relative priority of competing security interests in tangible collateral is resolved by reference to the law of the jurisdiction in which the collateral is located, regardless of how the security interests are perfected.

b. **Fixtures.** Application of the general rule in paragraph (1) to perfection of a security interest in fixtures would yield strange results. For example, perfection of a security interest in fixtures located in Arizona and owned by a Delaware corporation would be governed by the law of Delaware. Although Delaware law would send one to a filing office in Arizona for the place to file a financing statement as a fixture filing, see Section 9–501, Delaware law would not take account of local, nonuniform, real-property filing and recording requirements that Arizona law might impose. For this reason, paragraph (3)(A) contains a special rule for security interests perfected by a fixture filing; the law of the jurisdiction in which the fixtures are located governs perfection, including the formal requisites of a fixture filing. Under paragraph (3)(C), the same law governs priority. Fixtures are "goods" as defined in Section 9–102.

c. **Timber to Be Cut.** Application of the general rule in paragraph (1) to perfection of a security interest in timber to be cut would yield undesirable results analogous to those described with respect to fixtures. Paragraph (3)(B) adopts a similar solution: perfection is governed by the law of the jurisdiction in which the timber is located. As with fixtures, under paragraph (3)(C), the same law governs priority. Timber to be cut also is "goods" as defined in Section 9–102.

Paragraph (3)(B) applies only to "timber to be cut," not to timber that has been cut. Consequently, once the timber is cut, the general choice-of-law rule in paragraph (1) becomes applicable. To ensure continued perfection, a secured party should file in both the jurisdiction in which the timber to be cut is located and in the state where the debtor is located. The former filing would be with the office in which a real property mortgage would be filed, and the latter would be a central filing. See Section 9–501.

d. **As-Extracted Collateral.** Paragraph (4) adopts the rule of former Section 9–103(5) with respect to certain security interests in minerals and related accounts. Like security interests in fixtures perfected by filing a fixture filing, security interests in minerals that are as-extracted collateral are perfected by filing in the office designated for the filing or recording of a mortgage on the real property. For the same reasons, the law governing perfection and priority is the law of the jurisdiction in which the wellhead or minehead is located.

6. **Change in Law Governing Perfection.** When the debtor changes its location to another jurisdiction, the jurisdiction whose law governs perfection under paragraph (1) changes, as well. Similarly, the law governing perfection of a possessory security interest in collateral under paragraph (2) changes when the collateral is removed to another jurisdiction. Nevertheless, these changes will not result in an immediate loss of perfection. See Section 9–316(a), (b).

7. **Law Governing Effect of Perfection and Priority: Goods, Documents, Instruments, Money, Negotiable Documents, and Tangible Chattel Paper.** Under former Section 9–103, the law of a

single jurisdiction governed both questions of perfection and those of priority. This Article generally adopts that approach. See paragraph (1). But the approach may create problems if the debtor and collateral are located in different jurisdictions. For example, assume a security interest in equipment located in Pennsylvania is perfected by filing in Illinois, where the debtor is located. If the law of the jurisdiction in which the debtor is located were to govern priority, then the priority of an execution lien on goods located in Pennsylvania would be governed by rules enacted by the Illinois legislature.

To address this problem, paragraph (3)(C) divorces questions of perfection from questions of "the effect of perfection or nonperfection and the priority of a security interest." Under paragraph (3)(C), the rights of competing claimants to tangible collateral are resolved by reference to the law of the jurisdiction in which the collateral is located. A similar bifurcation applied to security interests in investment property under former Section 9–103(6). See Section 9–305.

Paragraph (3)(C) applies the law of the situs to determine priority only with respect to goods (including fixtures), instruments, money, tangible negotiable documents, and tangible chattel paper. Compare former Section 9–103(1), which applied the law of the location of the collateral to documents, instruments, and "ordinary" (as opposed to "mobile") goods. This Article does not distinguish among types of goods. The ordinary/mobile goods distinction appears to address concerns about where to file and search, rather than concerns about priority. There is no reason to preserve this distinction under the bifurcated approach.

Particularly serious confusion may arise when the choice-of-law rules of a given jurisdiction result in each of two competing security interests in the same collateral being governed by a different priority rule. The potential for this confusion existed under former Section 9–103(4) with respect to chattel paper: Perfection by possession was governed by the law of the location of the paper, whereas perfection by filing was governed by the law of the location of the debtor. Consider the mess that would have been created if the language or interpretation of former Section 9–308 were to differ in the two relevant States, or if one of the relevant jurisdictions (e.g., a foreign country) had not adopted Article 9. The potential for confusion could have been exacerbated when a secured party perfected both by taking possession in the State where the collateral is located (State A) and by filing in the State where the debtor is located (State B)—a common practice for some chattel paper financers. By providing that the law of the jurisdiction in which the collateral is located governs priority, paragraph (3) substantially diminishes this problem.

8. **Non-U.S. Debtors.** This Article applies the same choice-of-law rules to all debtors, foreign and domestic. For example, it adopts the bifurcated approach for determining the law applicable to security interests in goods and other tangible collateral. See Comment 5.a., above. The Article contains a new rule specifying the location of non-U.S. debtors for purposes of this Part. The rule appears in Section 9–307 and is explained in the Comments to that section. Former Section 9–103(3)(c), which contained a special choice-of-law rule governing security interests created by debtors located in a non-U.S. jurisdiction, proved unsatisfactory and was deleted.

As amended in 2003.

§ 9–302. Law Governing Perfection and Priority of Agricultural Liens.

While farm products are located in a jurisdiction, the local law of that jurisdiction governs perfection, the effect of perfection or nonperfection, and the priority of an agricultural lien on the farm products.

Official Comment

1. **Source.** New.

2. **Agricultural Liens.** This section provides choice-of-law rules for agricultural liens on farm products. Perfection, the effect of perfection or nonperfection, and priority all are governed by the law of the jurisdiction in which the farm products are located. Other choice-of-law rules, including Section 1–105, determine which jurisdiction's law governs other matters, such as the secured party's rights on default. See Section 9–301, Comment 2. Inasmuch as no agricultural lien on proceeds arises under this Article, this section does not expressly apply to proceeds of agricultural liens. However, if another statute creates an agricultural lien on proceeds, it may be appropriate for courts to apply the choice-of-law rule in this section to determine priority in the proceeds.

§ 9–303. Law Governing Perfection and Priority of Security Interests in Goods Covered by a Certificate of Title.

(a) **[Applicability of section.]** This section applies to goods covered by a certificate of title, even if there is no other relationship between the jurisdiction under whose certificate of title the goods are covered and the goods or the debtor.

(b) **[When goods covered by certificate of title.]** Goods become covered by a certificate of title when a valid application for the certificate of title and the applicable fee are delivered to the appropriate authority. Goods cease to be covered by a certificate of title at the earlier of the time the certificate of title ceases to be effective under the law of the issuing jurisdiction or the time the goods become covered subsequently by a certificate of title issued by another jurisdiction.

(c) **[Applicable law.]** The local law of the jurisdiction under whose certificate of title the goods are covered governs perfection, the effect of perfection or nonperfection, and the priority of a security interest in goods covered by a certificate of title from the time the goods become covered by the certificate of title until the goods cease to be covered by the certificate of title.

Official Comment

1. **Source.** Former Section 9–103(2)(a), (b), substantially revised.

2. **Scope of This Section.** This section applies to "goods covered by a certificate of title." The new definition of "certificate of title" in Section 9–102 makes clear that this section applies not only to certificate-of-title statutes under which perfection occurs upon notation of the security interest on the certificate but also to those that contemplate notation but provide that perfection is achieved by another method, e.g., delivery of designated documents to an official. Subsection (a), which is new, makes clear that this section applies to certificates of a jurisdiction having no other contacts with the goods or the debtor. This result comports with most of the reported cases on the subject and with contemporary business practices in the trucking industry.

3. **Law Governing Perfection and Priority.** Subsection (c) is the basic choice-of-law rule for goods covered by a certificate of title. Perfection and priority of a security interest are governed by the law of the jurisdiction under whose certificate of title the goods are covered from the time the goods become covered by the certificate of title until the goods cease to be covered by the certificate of title.

Normally, under the law of the relevant jurisdiction, the perfection step would consist of compliance with that jurisdiction's certificate-of-title statute and a resulting notation of the security interest on the certificate of title. See Section 9–311(b). In the typical case of an automobile or over-the-road truck, a person who wishes to take a security interest in the vehicle can ascertain whether it is subject to any security interests by looking at the certificate of title. But certificates of title cover certain types of goods in some States but not in others. A secured party who does not realize this may extend credit and attempt to perfect by filing in the jurisdiction in which the debtor is located. If the goods had been titled in another jurisdiction, the lender would be unperfected.

Subsection (b) explains when goods become covered by a certificate of title and when they cease to be covered. Goods may become covered by a certificate of title, even though no certificate of title has issued. Former Section 9–103(2)(b) provided that the law of the jurisdiction issuing the certificate ceases to apply upon "surrender" of the certificate. This Article eliminates the concept of "surrender." However, if the certificate is surrendered in conjunction with an appropriate application for a certificate to be issued by another jurisdiction, the law of the original jurisdiction ceases to apply because the goods became covered subsequently by a certificate of title from another jurisdiction. Alternatively, the law of the original jurisdiction ceases to apply when the certificate "ceases to be effective" under the law of that jurisdiction. Given the diversity in certificate-of-title statutes, the term "effective" is not defined.

4. **Continued Perfection.** The fact that the law of one State ceases to apply under subsection (b) does not mean that a security interest perfected under that law becomes unperfected automatically. In most cases, the security interest will remain perfected. See Section 9–316(d), (e). Moreover, a perfected security interest may be subject to defeat by certain buyers and secured parties. See Section 9–337.

5. **Inventory.** Compliance with a certificate-of-title statute generally is *not* the method of perfecting security interests in inventory. Section 9–311(d) provides that a security interest created in inventory held by a person in the business of selling goods of that kind is subject to the normal filing rules; compliance with a certificate-of-title statute is not necessary or effective to perfect the security interest. Most certificate-of-title statutes are in accord.

The following example explains the subtle relationship between this rule and the choice-of-law rules in Section 9–303 and former Section 9–103(2):

Example: Goods are located in State A and covered by a certificate of title issued under the law of State A. The State A certificate of title is "clean"; it does not reflect a security interest. Owner takes the goods to State B and sells (trades in) the goods to Dealer, who is in the business of selling goods of that kind and is located (within the meaning of Section 9–307) in State B. As is customary, Dealer retains the duly assigned State A certificate of title pending resale of the goods. Dealer's inventory financer, SP, obtains a security interest in the goods under its after-acquired property clause.

Under Section 9–311(d) of both State A and State B, Dealer's inventory financer, SP, must perfect by filing instead of complying with a certificate-of-title statute. If Section 9–303 were read to provide that the law applicable to perfection of SP's security interest is that of State A, because the goods are covered by a State A certificate, then SP would be required to file in State A under State A's Section 9–501. That result would be anomalous, to say the least, since the principle underlying Section 9–311(d) is that the inventory should be treated as ordinary goods.

Section 9–303 (and former Section 9–103(2)) should be read as providing that the law of State B, not State A, applies. A court looking to the forum's Section 9–303(a) would find that Section 9–303 applies only if two conditions are met: (i) the goods are covered by the certificate as explained in Section 9–303(b), i.e., application had been made for a State (here, State A) to issue a certificate of title covering the goods and (ii) the certificate is a "certificate of title" as defined in Section 9–102, i.e., "a statute provides for the security interest in question to be indicated on the certificate as a condition or result of the security interest's obtaining priority over the rights of a lien creditor." Stated otherwise, Section 9–303 applies only when compliance with a certificate-of-title statute, and not filing, is the appropriate method of perfection. Under the law of State A, *for purposes of perfecting SP's security interest in the dealer's inventory*, the proper method of perfection is filing—not compliance with State A's certificate-of-title statute. For that reason, the goods are not covered by a "certificate of title," and the second condition is not met. Thus, Section 9–303 does not apply to the goods. Instead, Section 9–301 applies, and the applicable law is that of State B, where the debtor (dealer) is located.

6. **External Constraints on This Section.** The need to coordinate Article 9 with a variety of nonuniform certificate-of-title statutes, the need to provide rules to take account of situations in which multiple certificates of title are outstanding with respect to

particular goods, and the need to govern the transition from perfection by filing in one jurisdiction to perfection by notation in another all create pressure for a detailed and complex set of rules. In an effort to minimize complexity, this Article does not attempt to coordinate Article 9 with the entire array of certificate-of-title statutes. In particular, Sections 9–303, 9–311, and 9–316(d) and (e) assume that the certificate-of-title statutes to which they apply do not have relation-back provisions (i.e., provisions under which perfection is deemed to occur at a time earlier than when the perfection steps actually are taken). A Legislative Note to Section 9–311 recommends the elimination of relation-back provisions in certificate-of-title statutes affecting perfection of security interests.

Ideally, at any given time, only one certificate of title is outstanding with respect to particular goods. In fact, however, sometimes more than one jurisdiction issues more than one certificate of title with respect to the same goods. This situation results from defects in certificate-of-title laws and the interstate coordination of those laws, not from deficiencies in this Article. As long as the possibility of multiple certificates of title remains, the potential for innocent parties to suffer losses will continue. At best, this Article can identify clearly which innocent parties will bear the losses in familiar fact patterns.

As amended in 2000.

§ 9–304. Law Governing Perfection and Priority of Security Interests in Deposit Accounts.

(a) **[Law of bank's jurisdiction governs.]** The local law of a bank's jurisdiction governs perfection, the effect of perfection or nonperfection, and the priority of a security interest in a deposit account maintained with that bank.

(b) **[Bank's jurisdiction.]** The following rules determine a bank's jurisdiction for purposes of this part:

(1) If an agreement between the bank and its customer governing the deposit account expressly provides that a particular jurisdiction is the bank's jurisdiction for purposes of this part, this article, or [the Uniform Commercial Code], that jurisdiction is the bank's jurisdiction.

(2) If paragraph (1) does not apply and an agreement between the bank and its customer governing the deposit account expressly provides that the agreement is

governed by the law of a particular jurisdiction, that jurisdiction is the bank's jurisdiction.

(3) If neither paragraph (1) nor paragraph (2) applies and an agreement between the bank and its customer governing the deposit account expressly provides that the deposit account is maintained at an office in a particular jurisdiction, that jurisdiction is the bank's jurisdiction.

(4) If none of the preceding paragraphs applies, the bank's jurisdiction is the jurisdiction in which the office identified in an account statement as the office serving the customer's account is located.

(5) If none of the preceding paragraphs applies, the bank's jurisdiction is the jurisdiction in which the chief executive office of the bank is located.

Official Comment

1. **Source.** New; derived from Section 8–110(e) and former Section 9–103(6).

2. **Deposit Accounts.** Under this section, the law of the "bank's jurisdiction" governs perfection and priority of a security interest in deposit accounts. Subsection (b) contains rules for determining the "bank's jurisdiction." The substance of these rules is substantially similar to that of the rules determining the "security intermediary's jurisdiction" under former Section 8–110(e), except that subsection (b)(1) provides more flexibility than the analogous provision in former Section 8–110(e)(1). Subsection (b)(1) permits the parties to choose the law of one jurisdiction to govern perfection and priority of security interests and a different governing law for other purposes. The parties' choice is effective, even if the jurisdiction whose law is chosen bears no relationship to the parties or the transaction. Section 8–110(e)(1) has been conformed to subsection (b)(1) of this section, and Section 9–305(b)(1), concerning a commodity intermediary's jurisdiction, makes a similar departure from former Section 9–103(6)(e)(i).

3. **Change in Law Governing Perfection.** When the bank's jurisdiction changes, the jurisdiction whose law governs perfection under subsection (a) changes, as well. Nevertheless, the change will not result in an immediate loss of perfection. See Section 9–316(f), (g).

§ 9–305. Law Governing Perfection and Priority of Security Interests in Investment Property.

(a) **[Governing law: general rules.]** Except as otherwise provided in subsection (c), the following rules apply:

(1) While a security certificate is located in a jurisdiction, the local law of that jurisdiction governs perfection, the effect of perfection or nonperfection, and the priority of a security interest in the certificated security represented thereby.

(2) The local law of the issuer's jurisdiction as specified in Section 8–110(d) governs perfection, the effect of perfection or nonperfection, and the priority of a security interest in an uncertificated security.

(3) The local law of the securities intermediary's jurisdiction as specified in Section 8–110(e) governs perfection, the effect of perfection or nonperfection, and the priority of a security interest in a security entitlement or securities account.

(4) The local law of the commodity intermediary's jurisdiction governs perfection, the effect of perfection or nonperfection, and the priority of a security interest in a commodity contract or commodity account.

(b) **[Commodity intermediary's jurisdiction.]** The following rules determine a commodity intermediary's jurisdiction for purposes of this part:

(1) If an agreement between the commodity intermediary and commodity customer governing the commodity account expressly provides that a particular jurisdiction is the commodity intermediary's jurisdiction for purposes of this part, this article, or [the Uniform Commercial Code], that jurisdiction is the commodity intermediary's jurisdiction.

(2) If paragraph (1) does not apply and an agreement between the commodity intermediary and commodity customer governing the commodity account expressly provides that the agreement is governed by the law of a particular jurisdiction, that jurisdiction is the commodity intermediary's jurisdiction.

(3) If neither paragraph (1) nor paragraph (2) applies and an agreement between the commodity intermediary and commodity customer governing the commodity account expressly provides that the commodity account is maintained at an office in a particular jurisdiction, that jurisdiction is the commodity intermediary's jurisdiction.

(4) If none of the preceding paragraphs applies, the commodity intermediary's jurisdiction is the jurisdiction in which the office identified in an account statement as the office serving the commodity customer's account is located.

(5) If none of the preceding paragraphs applies, the commodity intermediary's jurisdiction is the jurisdiction in which the chief executive office of the commodity intermediary is located.

(c) **[When perfection governed by law of jurisdiction where debtor located.]** The local law of the jurisdiction in which the debtor is located governs:

(1) perfection of a security interest in investment property by filing;

(2) automatic perfection of a security interest in investment property created by a broker or securities intermediary; and

(3) automatic perfection of a security interest in a commodity contract or commodity account created by a commodity intermediary.

Official Comment

1. **Source.** Former Section 9–103(6).

2. **Investment Property: General Rules.** This section specifies choice-of-law rules for perfection and priority of security interests in investment property. Subsection (a)(1) covers security interests in certificated securities. Subsection (a)(2) covers security interests in uncertificated securities. Subsection (a)(3) covers security interests in security entitlements and securities accounts. Subsection (a)(4) covers security interests in commodity contracts and commodity accounts. The approach of each of these paragraphs is essentially the same. They identify the jurisdiction's law that governs questions of perfection and priority by using the same principles that Article 8 uses to determine other questions concerning that form of investment property. Thus, for certificated securities, the law of

the jurisdiction in which the certificate is located governs. Cf. Section 8–110(c). For uncertificated securities, the law of the issuer's jurisdiction governs. Cf. Section 8–110(a). For security entitlements and securities accounts, the law of the securities intermediary's jurisdiction governs. Cf. Section 8–110(b). For commodity contracts and commodity accounts, the law of the commodity intermediary's jurisdiction governs. Because commodity contracts and commodity accounts are not governed by Article 8, subsection (b) contains rules that specify the commodity intermediary's jurisdiction. These are analogous to the rules in Section 8–110(e) specifying a securities intermediary's jurisdiction. Subsection (b)(1) affords the parties greater flexibility than did former Section 9–103(6)(3). See also Section 9–304(b) (bank's jurisdiction); Revised Section 8–110(e)(1) (securities intermediary's jurisdiction).

3. **Investment Property: Exceptions.** Subsection (c) establishes an exception to the general rules set out in subsection (a). It provides that perfection of a security interest by filing, automatic perfection of a security interest in investment property created by a debtor who is a broker or securities intermediary (see Section 9–309(10)), and automatic perfection of a security interest in a commodity contract or commodity account of a debtor who is a commodity intermediary (see Section 9–309(11)) are governed by the law of the jurisdiction in which the debtor is located, as determined under Section 9–307.

4. **Examples:** The following examples illustrate the rules in this section:

Example 1: A customer residing in New Jersey maintains a securities account with Able & Co. The agreement between the customer and Able specifies that it is governed by Pennsylvania law but expressly provides that the law of California is Able's jurisdiction for purposes of the Uniform Commercial Code. Through the account the customer holds securities of a Massachusetts corporation, which Able holds through a clearing corporation located in New York. The customer obtains a margin loan from Able. Subsection (a)(3) provides that California law—the law of the securities intermediary's jurisdiction—governs perfection and priority of the security interest, even if California has no other relationship to the parties or the transaction.

Example 2: A customer residing in New Jersey maintains a securities account with Able & Co. The agreement between the customer and Able specifies that it is governed by Pennsylvania law. Through the account the customer holds securities of a Massachusetts corporation, which Able holds through a clear-

ing corporation located in New York. The customer obtains a loan from a lender located in Illinois. The lender takes a security interest and perfects by obtaining an agreement among the debtor, itself, and Able, which satisfies the requirement of Section 8–106(d)(2) to give the lender control. Subsection (a)(3) provides that Pennsylvania law—the law of the securities intermediary's jurisdiction—governs perfection and priority of the security interest, even if Pennsylvania has no other relationship to the parties or the transaction.

Example 3: A customer residing in New Jersey maintains a securities account with Able & Co. The agreement between the customer and Able specifies that it is governed by Pennsylvania law. Through the account, the customer holds securities of a Massachusetts corporation, which Able holds through a clearing corporation located in New York. The customer borrows from SP–1, and SP–1 files a financing statement in New Jersey. Later, the customer obtains a loan from SP–2. SP–2 takes a security interest and perfects by obtaining an agreement among the debtor, itself, and Able, which satisfies the requirement of Section 8–106(d)(2) to give the SP–2 control. Subsection (c) provides that perfection of SP–1's security interest by filing is governed by the location of the debtor, so the filing in New Jersey was appropriate. Subsection (a)(3), however, provides that Pennsylvania law—the law of the securities intermediary's jurisdiction—governs all other questions of perfection and priority. Thus, Pennsylvania law governs perfection of SP–2's security interest, and Pennsylvania law also governs the priority of the security interests of SP–1 and SP–2.

5. **Change in Law Governing Perfection.** When the issuer's jurisdiction, the securities intermediary's jurisdiction, or commodity intermediary's jurisdiction changes, the jurisdiction whose law governs perfection under subsection (a) changes, as well. Similarly, the law governing perfection of a possessory security interest in a certificated security changes when the collateral is removed to another jurisdiction, see subsection (a)(1), and the law governing perfection by filing changes when the debtor changes its location. See subsection (c). Nevertheless, these changes will not result in an immediate loss of perfection. See Section 9–316.

§ 9–306.   Law Governing Perfection and Priority of Security Interests in Letter-of-Credit Rights.

(a) **[Governing law: issuer's or nominated person's jurisdiction.]** Subject to subsection (c), the local law of the issuer's jurisdiction or a nominated person's jurisdiction governs perfection, the effect of perfection or nonperfection, and the priority of a security interest in a letter-of-credit right if the issuer's jurisdiction or nominated person's jurisdiction is a State.

(b) **[Issuer's or nominated person's jurisdiction.]** For purposes of this part, an issuer's jurisdiction or nominated person's jurisdiction is the jurisdiction whose law governs the liability of the issuer or nominated person with respect to the letter-of-credit right as provided in Section 5–116.

(c) **[When section not applicable.]** This section does not apply to a security interest that is perfected only under Section 9–308(d).

Official Comment

1. **Source.** New; derived in part from Section 8–110(e) and former Section 9–103(6).

2. **Sui Generis Treatment.** This section governs the applicable law for perfection and priority of security interests in letter-of-credit rights, other than a security interest perfected only under Section 9–308(d) (i.e., as a supporting obligation). The treatment differs substantially from that provided in Section 9–304 for deposit accounts. The basic rule is that the law of the issuer's or nominated person's (e.g., confirmer's) jurisdiction, derived from the terms of the letter of credit itself, controls perfection and priority, but only if the issuer's or nominated person's jurisdiction is a State, as defined in Section 9–102. If the issuer's or nominated person's jurisdiction is not a State, the baseline rule of Section 9–301 applies—perfection and priority are governed by the law of the debtor's location, determined under Section 9–307. Export transactions typically involve a foreign issuer and a domestic nominated person, such as a confirmer, located in a State. The principal goal of this section is to reduce the likelihood that perfection and priority would be governed by the law of a foreign jurisdiction in a transaction that is essentially domestic from the standpoint of the debtor-beneficiary, its creditors, and a domestic nominated person.

3. **Issuer's or Nominated Person's Jurisdiction.** Subsection (b) defers to the rules established under Section 5–116 for determination of an issuer's or nominated person's jurisdiction.

Example: An Italian bank issues a letter of credit that is confirmed by a New York bank. The beneficiary is a Connecticut corporation. The letter of credit provides that the issuer's liability is governed by Italian law, and the confirmation provides that the confirmer's liability is governed by the law of New York. Under Sections 9–306(b) and 5–116(a), Italy is the issuer's jurisdiction and New York is the confirmer's (nominated person's) jurisdiction. Because the confirmer's jurisdiction is a State, the law of New York governs perfection and priority of a security interest in the beneficiary's letter-of-credit right against the confirmer. See Section 9–306(a). However, because the issuer's jurisdiction is not a State, the law of that jurisdiction does not govern. See Section 9–306(a). Rather, the choice-of-law rule in Section 9–301(1) applies to perfection and priority of a security interest in the beneficiary's letter-of-credit right against the issuer. Under that section, perfection and priority are governed by the law of the jurisdiction in which the debtor (beneficiary) is located. That jurisdiction is Connecticut. See Section 9–307.

4. **Scope of this Section.** This section specifies only the law governing perfection, the effect of perfection or nonperfection, and priority of security interests. Section 5–116 specifies the law governing the liability of, and Article 5 (or other applicable law) deals with the rights and duties of, an issuer or nominated person. Perfection, nonperfection, and priority have no effect on those rights and duties.

5. **Change in Law Governing Perfection.** When the issuer's jurisdiction, or nominated person's jurisdiction changes, the jurisdiction whose law governs perfection under subsection (a) changes, as well. Nevertheless, this change will not result in an immediate loss of perfection. See Section 9–316(f), (g).

§ 9–307. Location of Debtor.

(a) **["Place of business."]** In this section, "place of business" means a place where a debtor conducts its affairs.

(b) **[Debtor's location: general rules.]** Except as otherwise provided in this section, the following rules determine a debtor's location:

(1) A debtor who is an individual is located at the individual's principal residence.

(2) A debtor that is an organization and has only one place of business is located at its place of business.

(3) A debtor that is an organization and has more than one place of business is located at its chief executive office.

(c) **[Limitation of applicability of subsection (b).]** Subsection (b) applies only if a debtor's residence, place of business, or chief executive office, as applicable, is located in a jurisdiction whose law generally requires information concerning the existence of a nonpossessory security interest to be made generally available in a filing, recording, or registration system as a condition or result of the security interest's obtaining priority over the rights of a lien creditor with respect to the collateral. If subsection (b) does not apply, the debtor is located in the District of Columbia.

(d) **[Continuation of location: cessation of existence, etc.]** A person that ceases to exist, have a residence, or have a place of business continues to be located in the jurisdiction specified by subsections (b) and (c).

(e) **[Location of registered organization organized under State law.]** A registered organization that is organized under the law of a State is located in that State.

(f) **[Location of registered organization organized under federal law; bank branches and agencies.]** Except as otherwise provided in subsection (i), a registered organization that is organized under the law of the United States and a branch or agency of a bank that is not organized under the law of the United States or a State are located:

(1) in the State that the law of the United States designates, if the law designates a State of location;

(2) in the State that the registered organization, branch, or agency designates, if the law of the United States authorizes the registered organization, branch, or agency to designate its State of location; or

(3) in the District of Columbia, if neither paragraph (1) nor paragraph (2) applies.

(g) **[Continuation of location: change in status of registered organization.]** A registered organization continues to be located in the jurisdiction specified by subsection (e) or (f) notwithstanding:

(1) the suspension, revocation, forfeiture, or lapse of the registered organization's status as such in its jurisdiction of organization; or

(2) the dissolution, winding up, or cancellation of the existence of the registered organization.

(h) **[Location of United States.]** The United States is located in the District of Columbia.

(i) **[Location of foreign bank branch or agency if licensed in only one state.]** A branch or agency of a bank that is not organized under the law of the United States or a State is located in the State in which the branch or agency is licensed, if all branches and agencies of the bank are licensed in only one State.

(j) **[Location of foreign air carrier.]** A foreign air carrier under the Federal Aviation Act of 1958, as amended, is located at the designated office of the agent upon which service of process may be made on behalf of the carrier.

(k) **[Section applies only to this part.]** This section applies only for purposes of this part.

Official Comment

1. **Source.** Former Section 9-103(3)(d), substantially revised.

2. **General Rules.** As a general matter, the location of the debtor determines the jurisdiction whose law governs perfection of a security interest. See Sections 9-301(1), 9-305(c). It also governs priority of a security interest in certain types of intangible collateral, such as accounts, electronic chattel paper, and general intangibles. This section determines the location of the debtor for choice-of-law purposes, but not for other purposes. See subsection (k).

Subsection (b) states the general rules: An individual debtor is deemed to be located at the individual's principal residence with respect to both personal and business assets. Any other debtor is deemed to be located at its place of business if it has only one, or at its chief executive office if it has more than one place of business.

As used in this section, a "place of business" means a place where the debtor conducts its affairs. See subsection (a). Thus, every organization, even eleemosynary institutions and other organizations that do not conduct "for profit" business activities, has a "place of business." Under subsection (d), a person who ceases to exist, have a residence, or have a place of business continues to be located in the jurisdiction determined by subsection (b).

The term "chief executive office" is not defined in this Section or elsewhere in the Uniform Commercial

Code. "Chief executive office" means the place from which the debtor manages the main part of its business operations or other affairs. This is the place where persons dealing with the debtor would normally look for credit information, and is the appropriate place for filing. With respect to most multi-state debtors, it will be simple to determine which of the debtor's offices is the "chief executive office." Even when a doubt arises, it would be rare that there could be more than two possibilities. A secured party in such a case may protect itself by perfecting under the law of each possible jurisdiction.

Similarly, the term "principal residence" is not defined. If the security interest in question is a purchase-money security interest in consumer goods which is perfected upon attachment, see Section 9–309(1), the choice of law may make no difference. In other cases, when a doubt arises, prudence may dictate perfecting under the law of each jurisdiction that might be the debtor's "principal residence."

The general rule is subject to several exceptions, each of which is discussed below.

3. **Non-U.S. Debtors.** Under the general rules of this section, a non-U.S. debtor normally would be located in a foreign jurisdiction and, as a consequence, foreign law would govern perfection. When foreign law affords no public notice of security interests, the general rule yields unacceptable results.

Accordingly, subsection (c) provides that the normal rules for determining the location of a debtor (i.e., the rules in subsection (b)) apply only if they yield a location that is "a jurisdiction whose law generally requires information concerning the existence of a nonpossessory security interest to be made generally available in a filing, recording, or registration system as a condition or result of the security interest's obtaining priority over the rights of a lien creditor with respect to the collateral." The phrase "generally requires" is meant to include legal regimes that generally require notice in a filing or recording system as a condition of perfecting nonpossessory security interests, but which permit perfection by another method (e.g., control, automatic perfection, temporary perfection) in limited circumstances. A jurisdiction that has adopted this Article or an earlier version of this Article is such a jurisdiction. If the rules in subsection (b) yield a jurisdiction whose law does not generally require notice in a filing or registration system, the debtor is located in the District of Columbia.

Example 1: Debtor is an English corporation with 7 offices in the United States and its chief executive office in London, England. Debtor creates a security interest in its accounts. Under subsection (b)(3), Debtor would be located in England. However, subsection (c) provides that subsection (b) applies only if English law generally conditions perfection on giving public notice in a filing, recording, or registration system. Otherwise, Debtor is located in the District of Columbia. Under Section 9–301(1), perfection, the effect of perfection, and priority are governed by the law of the jurisdiction of the debtor's location—here, England or the District of Columbia (depending on the content of English law).

Example 2: Debtor is an English corporation with 7 offices in the United States and its chief executive office in London, England. Debtor creates a security interest in equipment located in London. Under subsection (b)(3) Debtor would be located in England. However, subsection (c) provides that subsection (b) applies only if English law generally conditions perfection on giving public notice in a filing, recording, or registration system. Otherwise, Debtor is located in the District of Columbia. Under Section 9–301(1), perfection is governed by the law of the jurisdiction of the debtor's location, whereas, under Section 9–301(3), the law of the jurisdiction in which the collateral is located—here, England—governs priority.

The foregoing discussion assumes that each transaction bears an appropriate relation to the forum State. In the absence of an appropriate relation, the forum State's entire UCC, including the choice-of-law provisions in Article 9 (Sections 9–301 through 9–307), will not apply. See Section 9–109, Comment 9.

4. **Registered Organizations Organized Under Law of a State.** Under subsection (e), a registered organization (e.g., a corporation or limited partnership) organized under the law of a "State" (defined in Section 9–102) is located in its State of organization. Subsection (g) makes clear that events affecting the status of a registered organization, such as the dissolution of a corporation or revocation of its charter, do not affect its location for purposes of subsection (e). However, certain of these events may result in, or be accompanied by, a transfer of collateral from the registered organization to another debtor. This section does not determine whether a transfer occurs, nor does it determine the legal consequences of any transfer.

Determining the registered organization-debtor's location by reference to the jurisdiction of organization could provide some important side benefits for the filing systems. A jurisdiction could structure its filing system so that it would be impossible to make a mistake in a registered organization-debtor's name on a financing statement. For example, a filer would be informed if a filed record designated an incorrect corporate name for the debtor. Linking filing to the jurisdiction of organization also could reduce pressure on the system imposed by transactions in which registered organizations cease to exist—as a consequence of merger or consolidation, for example. The jurisdiction of organization might prohibit such transactions unless steps were taken to ensure that existing filings were refiled against a successor or terminated by the secured party.

5. **Registered Organizations Organized Under Law of United States; Branches and Agencies of Banks Not Organized Under Law of United States.** Subsection (f) specifies the location of a debtor that is a registered organization organized under the law of the United States. It defers to the law of the United States, to the extent that that law determines, or authorizes the debtor to determine, the debtor's location. Thus, if the law of the United States designates a particular State as the debtor's location, that State is the debtor's location for purposes of this Article's choice-of-law rules. Similarly, if the law of the United States authorizes the registered organization to designate its State of location, the State that the registered organization designates is the State in which it is located for purposes of this Article's choice-of-law

rules. In other cases, the debtor is located in the District of Columbia.

In some cases, the law of the United States authorizes the registered organization to designate a main office, home office, or other comparable office. See, e.g., 12 U.S.C. §§ 22 and 1464(a); 12 C.F.R. § 552.3. Designation of such an office constitutes the designation of the State of location for purposes of Section 9-307(f)(2).

In cases not governed by subsection (f) or (i), the location of a foreign bank is determined by subsections (b) and (c).

6. **United States.** To the extent that Article 9 governs (see Sections 1-105, 9-109(c)), the United States is located in the District of Columbia for purposes of this Article's choice-of-law rules. See subsection (h).

7. **Foreign Air Carriers.** Subsection (j) follows former Section 9-103(3)(d). To the extent that it is applicable, the Convention on the International Recognition of Rights in Aircraft (Geneva Convention) supersedes state legislation on this subject, as set forth in Section 9-311(b), but some nations are not parties to that Convention.

[SUBPART 2. PERFECTION]

§ 9-308. When Security Interest or Agricultural Lien Is Perfected; Continuity of Perfection.

(a) **[Perfection of security interest.]** Except as otherwise provided in this section and Section 9-309, a security interest is perfected if it has attached and all of the applicable requirements for perfection in Sections 9-310 through 9-316 have been satisfied. A security interest is perfected when it attaches if the applicable requirements are satisfied before the security interest attaches.

(b) **[Perfection of agricultural lien.]** An agricultural lien is perfected if it has become effective and all of the applicable requirements for perfection in Section 9-310 have been satisfied. An agricultural lien is perfected when it becomes effective if the applicable requirements are satisfied before the agricultural lien becomes effective.

(c) **[Continuous perfection; perfection by different methods.]** A security interest or agricultural lien is perfected continuously if it is

originally perfected by one method under this article and is later perfected by another method under this article, without an intermediate period when it was unperfected.

(d) **[Supporting obligation.]** Perfection of a security interest in collateral also perfects a security interest in a supporting obligation for the collateral.

(e) **[Lien securing right to payment.]** Perfection of a security interest in a right to payment or performance also perfects a security interest in a security interest, mortgage, or other lien on personal or real property securing the right.

(f) **[Security entitlement carried in securities account.]** Perfection of a security interest in a securities account also perfects a security interest in the security entitlements carried in the securities account.

(g) **[Commodity contract carried in commodity account.]** Perfection of a security interest in a commodity account also perfects a security interest in the commodity contracts carried in the commodity account.

Legislative Note: Any statute conflicting with subsection (e) must be made expressly subject to that subsection.

Official Comment

1. **Source.** Former Sections 9–303, 9–115(2).

2. **General Rule.** This Article uses the term "attach" to describe the point at which property becomes subject to a security interest. The requisites for attachment are stated in Section 9–203. When it attaches, a security interest may be either perfected or unperfected. "Perfected" means that the security interest has attached and the secured party has taken all the steps required by this Article as specified in Sections 9–310 through 9–316. A perfected security interest may still be or become subordinate to other interests. See, e.g., Sections 9–320, 9–322. However, in general, after perfection the secured party is protected against creditors and transferees of the debtor and, in particular, against any representative of creditors in insolvency proceedings instituted by or against the debtor. See, e.g., Section 9–317.

Subsection (a) explains that the time of perfection is when the security interest has attached and any necessary steps for perfection, such as taking possession or filing, have been taken. The "except" clause refers to the perfection-upon-attachment rules appearing in Section 9–309. It also reflects that other subsections of this section, e.g., subsection (d), contain automatic-perfection rules. If the steps for perfection have been taken in advance, as when the secured party files a financing statement before giving value or before the debtor acquires rights in the collateral, then the security interest is perfected when it attaches.

3. **Agricultural Liens.** Subsection (b) is new. It describes the elements of perfection of an agricultural lien.

4. **Continuous Perfection.** The following example illustrates the operation of subsection (c):

Example 1: Debtor, an importer, creates a security interest in goods that it imports and the documents of title that cover the goods. The secured party, Bank, takes possession of a tangible negotiable bill of lading covering certain imported goods and thereby perfects its security interest in the bill of lading and the goods. See Sections 9–313(a), 9–312(c)(1). Bank releases the bill of lading to the debtor for the purpose of procuring the goods from the carrier and selling them. Under Section 9–312(f), Bank contin-

ues to have a perfected security interest in the document and goods for 20 days. Bank files a financing statement covering the collateral before the expiration of the 20–day period. Its security interest now continues perfected for as long as the filing is good.

If the successive stages of Bank's security interest succeed each other without an intervening gap, the security interest is "perfected continuously," and the date of perfection is when the security interest first became perfected (i.e., when Bank received possession of the tangible bill of lading). If, however, there is a gap between stages—for example, if Bank does not file until after the expiration of the 20–day period specified in Section 9–312(f) and leaves the collateral in the debtor's possession—then, the chain being broken, the perfection is no longer continuous. The date of perfection would now be the date of filing (after expiration of the 20–day period). Bank's security interest would be vulnerable to any interests arising during the gap period which under Section 9–317 take priority over an unperfected security interest.

5. **Supporting Obligations.** Subsection (d) is new. It provides for automatic perfection of a security interest in a supporting obligation for collateral if the security interest in the collateral is perfected. This is unlikely to effect any change in the law prior to adoption of this Article.

Example 2: Buyer is obligated to pay Debtor for goods sold. Buyer's president guarantees the obligation. Debtor creates a security interest in the right to payment (account) in favor of Lender. Under Section 9–203(f), the security interest attaches to Debtor's rights under the guarantee (supporting obligation). Under subsection (d), perfection of the security interest in the account constitutes perfection of the security interest in Debtor's rights under the guarantee.

6. **Rights to Payment Secured by Lien.** Subsection (e) is new. It deals with the situation in which a security interest is created in a right to payment that is secured by a security interest, mortgage, or other lien.

Example 3: Owner gives to Mortgagee a mortgage on Blackacre to secure a loan. Owner's obligation to pay is evidenced by a promissory note. In need of working capital, Mortgagee borrows from Financer and creates a security interest in the note in favor of Financer. Section 9–203(g) adopts the traditional view that the mortgage follows the note; i.e., the transferee of the note acquires the mortgage, as well. This subsection adopts a similar principle: perfection of a security interest in the right to payment constitutes perfection of a security interest in the mortgage securing it.

An important consequence of the rules in Section 9–203(g) and subsection (e) is that, by acquiring a perfected security interest in a mortgage (or other secured) note, the secured party acquires a security interest in the mortgage (or other lien) that is senior to the rights of a person who becomes a lien creditor of the mortgagee (Article 9 debtor). See Section 9–317(a)(2). This result helps prevent the separation of the mortgage (or other lien) from the note.

Under this Article, attachment and perfection of a security interest in a secured right to payment do not of themselves affect the obligation to pay. For example, if the obligation is evidenced by a negotiable note, then Article 3 dictates the person whom the maker must pay to discharge the note and any lien securing it. See Section 3–602. If the right to payment is a payment intangible, then Section 9–406 determines whom the account debtor must pay.

Similarly, this Article does not determine who has the power to release a mortgage of record. That issue is determined by real-property law.

7. **Investment Property.** Subsections (f) and (g) follow former Section 9–115(2).

As amended in 2003.

§ 9–309. Security Interest Perfected Upon Attachment.

The following security interests are perfected when they attach:

(1) a purchase-money security interest in consumer goods, except as otherwise provided in Section 9–311(b) with respect to consumer goods that are subject to a statute or treaty described in Section 9–311(a);

(2) an assignment of accounts or payment intangibles which does not by itself or in conjunction with other assignments to the same assignee transfer a significant part of the assignor's outstanding accounts or payment intangibles;

(3) a sale of a payment intangible;

(4) a sale of a promissory note;

(5) a security interest created by the assignment of a health-care-insurance receivable to the provider of the health-care goods or services;

(6) a security interest arising under Section 2–401, 2–505, 2–711(3), or 2A–508(5), until the debtor obtains possession of the collateral;

(7) a security interest of a collecting bank arising under Section 4–210;

(8) a security interest of an issuer or nominated person arising under Section 5–118;

(9) a security interest arising in the delivery of a financial asset under Section 9–206(c);

(10) a security interest in investment property created by a broker or securities intermediary;

(11) a security interest in a commodity contract or a commodity account created by a commodity intermediary;

(12) an assignment for the benefit of all creditors of the transferor and subsequent transfers by the assignee thereunder;

(13) a security interest created by an assignment of a beneficial interest in a decedent's estate; and

(14) a sale by an individual of an account that is a right to payment of winnings in a lottery or other game of chance.

Official Comment

1. **Source.** Derived from former Sections 9–302(1), 9–115(4)(c), (d), 9–116.

2. **Automatic Perfection.** This section contains the perfection-upon-attachment rules previously located in former Sections 9–302(1), 9–115(4)(c), (d), and 9–116. Rather than continue to state the rule by indirection, this section explicitly provides for perfection upon attachment.

3. **Purchase-Money Security Interest in Consumer Goods.** Former Section 9–302(1)(d) has been revised and appears here as paragraph (1). No filing or other step is required to perfect a purchase-money security interest in consumer goods, other than goods, such as automobiles, that are subject to a statute or treaty described in Section 9–311(a). However, filing is required to perfect a non-purchase-money security interest in consumer goods and is necessary to prevent a buyer of consumer goods from taking free of a security interest under Section 9–320(b). A fixture filing is required for priority over conflicting interests in fixtures to the extent provided in Section 9–334.

4. **Rights to Payment.** Paragraph (2) expands upon former Section 9–302(1)(e) by affording automatic perfection to certain assignments of payment intangibles as well as accounts. The purpose of paragraph (2) is to save from *ex post facto* invalidation casual or isolated assignments—assignments which no one would think of filing. Any person who regularly takes assignments of any debtor's accounts or payment in-

tangibles should file. In this connection Section 9–109(d)(4) through (7), which excludes certain transfers of accounts, chattel paper, payment intangibles, and promissory notes from this Article, should be consulted.

Paragraphs (3) and (4), which are new, afford automatic perfection to sales of payment intangibles and promissory notes, respectively. They reflect the practice under former Article 9. Under that Article, filing a financing statement did not affect the rights of a buyer of payment intangibles or promissory notes, inasmuch as the former Article did not cover those sales. To the extent that the exception in paragraph (2) covers outright sales of payment intangibles, which automatically are perfected under paragraph (3), the exception is redundant.

Paragraph (14), which is new, affords automatic perfection to sales by individuals of an "account" (as defined in Section 9–102) consisting of the right to winnings in a lottery or other game of chance. Payments on these accounts typically extend for periods of twenty years or more. It would be unduly burdensome for the secured party, who would have no other reason to maintain contact with the seller, to monitor the the seller's whereabouts for such a length of time. This paragraph was added in 2001. It applies to a sale of an account described in it, even if the sale was entered into before the effective date of the paragraph. However, if the relative priorities of conflicting claims to the account were established before the paragraph took effect, Article 9 as in effect immediately prior to the date the paragraph took effect determines priority.

5. **Health-Care-Insurance Receivables.** Paragraph (5) extends automatic perfection to assignments of health-care-insurance receivables if the assignment is made to the health-care provider that provided the health-care goods or services. The primary effect is that, when an individual assigns a right to payment under an insurance policy to the person who provided health-care goods or services, the provider has no need to file a financing statement against the individual. The normal filing requirements apply to other assignments of health-care-insurance receivables covered by this Article, e.g., assignments from the health-care provider to a financer.

6. **Investment Property.** Paragraph (9) replaces the last clause of former Section 9–116(2), concerning security interests that arise in the delivery of a financial asset.

Paragraphs (10) and (11) replace former Section 9–115(4)(c) and (d), concerning secured financing of securities and commodity firms and clearing corporations.

The former sections indicated that, with respect to certain security interests created by a securities intermediary or commodity intermediary, "[t]he filing of a financing statement ... has no effect for purposes of perfection or priority with respect to that security interest." No change in meaning is intended by the deletion of the quoted phrase.

Secured financing arrangements for securities firms are currently implemented in various ways. In some circumstances, lenders may require that the transactions be structured as "hard pledges," where the securities are transferred on the books of a clearing corporation from the debtor's account to the lender's account or to a special pledge account for the lender where they cannot be disposed of without the specific consent of the lender. In other circumstances, lenders are content with so-called "agreement to pledge" or "agreement to deliver" arrangements, where the debtor retains the positions in its own account, but reflects on its books that the positions have been hypothecated and promises that the securities will be transferred to the secured party's account on demand.

The perfection and priority rules of this Article are designed to facilitate current secured financing arrangements for securities firms as well as to provide sufficient flexibility to accommodate new arrangements that develop in the future. Hard pledge arrangements are covered by the concept of control. See Sections 9–314, 9–106, 8–106. Non-control secured financing arrangements for securities firms are covered by the automatic perfection rule of paragraph (10). Before the 1994 revision of Articles 8 and 9, agreement to pledge arrangements could be implemented under a provision that a security interest in securities given for new value under a written security agreement was perfected without filing or possession for a period of 21 days. Although the security interests were temporary in legal theory, the financing arrangements could, in practice, be continued indefinitely by rolling over the loans at least every 21 days. Accordingly, a knowledgeable creditor of a securities firm realizes that the firm's securities may be subject to security interests that are not discoverable from any public records. The automatic-perfection rule of paragraph (10) makes it unnecessary to engage in the purely formal practice of rolling over these arrangements every 21 days.

In some circumstances, a clearing corporation may be the debtor in a secured financing arrangement. For example, a clearing corporation that settles delivery-versus-payment transactions among its participants on a net, same-day basis relies on timely payments from all participants with net obligations due to the system. If a participant that is a net debtor were to default on its payment obligation, the clearing corporation would not receive some of the funds needed to settle with participants that are net creditors to the system. To complete end-of-day settlement after a payment default by a participant, a clearing corporation that settles on a net, same-day basis may need to draw on credit lines and pledge securities of the defaulting participant or other securities pledged by participants in the clearing corporation to secure such drawings. The clearing corporation may be the top-tier securities intermediary for the securities pledged, so that it would not be practical for the lender to obtain control. Even where the clearing corporation holds some types of securities through other intermediaries, however, the clearing corporation is unlikely to be able to complete the arrangements necessary to convey "control" over the securities to be pledged in time to complete settlement in a timely manner. However, the term "securities intermediary" is defined in Section 8–102(a)(14) to include clearing corporations. Thus, the perfection rule of paragraph (10) applies to security interests in investment property granted by clearing corporations.

7. **Beneficial Interests in Trusts.** Under former Section 9–302(1)(c), filing was not required to perfect a security interest created by an assignment of a beneficial interest in a trust. Because beneficial interests in trusts are now used as collateral with greater frequency in commercial transactions, under this Article filing is required to perfect a security interest in a beneficial interest.

8. **Assignments for Benefit of Creditors.** No filing or other action is required to perfect an assignment for the benefit of creditors. These assignments are not financing transactions, and the debtor ordinarily will not be engaging in further credit transactions.

§ 9–310. When Filing Required to Perfect Security Interest or Agricultural Lien; Security Interests and Agricultural Liens to Which Filing Provisions Do Not Apply.

(a) **[General rule: perfection by filing.]** Except as otherwise provided in subsection (b) and Section 9–312(b), a financing statement must be filed to perfect all security interests and agricultural liens.

(b) **[Exceptions: filing not necessary.]** The filing of a financing statement is not necessary to perfect a security interest:

(1) that is perfected under Section 9–308(d), (e), (f), or (g);

(2) that is perfected under Section 9–309 when it attaches;

(3) in property subject to a statute, regulation, or treaty described in Section 9–311(a);

(4) in goods in possession of a bailee which is perfected under Section 9–312(d)(1) or (2);

(5) in certificated securities, documents, goods, or instruments which is perfected without filing, control, or possession under Section 9–312(e), (f), or (g);

(6) in collateral in the secured party's possession under Section 9–313;

(7) in a certificated security which is perfected by delivery of the security certificate to the secured party under Section 9–313;

(8) in deposit accounts, electronic chattel paper, electronic documents, investment property, or letter-of-credit rights which is perfected by control under Section 9–314;

(9) in proceeds which is perfected under Section 9–315; or

(10) that is perfected under Section 9–316.

(c) **[Assignment of perfected security interest.]** If a secured party assigns a perfected security interest or agricultural lien, a filing under this article is not required to continue the perfected status of the security interest against creditors of and transferees from the original debtor.

As amended in 2003.

Official Comment

1. **Source.** Former Section 9–302(1), (2).

2. **General Rule.** Subsection (a) establishes a central Article 9 principle: Filing a financing statement is necessary for perfection of security interests and agricultural liens. However, filing is not necessary to perfect a security interest that is perfected by another permissible method, see subsection (b), nor does filing ordinarily perfect a security interest in a deposit account, letter-of-credit right, or money. See Section 9–312(b). Part 5 of the Article deals with the office in which to file, mechanics of filing, and operations of the filing office.

3. **Exemptions from Filing.** Subsection (b) lists the security interests for which filing is not required as

a condition of perfection, because they are perfected automatically upon attachment (subsections (b)(2) and (b)(9)) or upon the occurrence of another event (subsections (b)(1), (b)(5), and (b)(9)), because they are perfected under the law of another jurisdiction (subsection (b)(10)), or because they are perfected by another method, such as by the secured party's taking possession or control (subsections (b)(3), (b)(4), (b)(5), (b)(6), (b)(7), and (b)(8)).

4. **Assignments of Perfected Security Interests.** Subsection (c) concerns assignment of a perfected security interest or agricultural lien. It provides that no filing is necessary in connection with an assignment by a secured party to an assignee in order to maintain perfection as against creditors of and transferees from the original debtor.

Example 1: Buyer buys goods from Seller, who retains a security interest in them. After Seller perfects the security interest by filing, Seller assigns the perfected security interest to X. The security interest, in X's hands and without further steps on X's part, continues perfected against *Buyer's* transferees and creditors.

Example 2: Dealer creates a security interest in specific equipment in favor of Lender. After Lender perfects the security interest in the equipment by filing, Lender assigns the chattel paper (which includes the perfected security interest in Dealer's equipment) to X. The security interest in the equipment, in X's hands and without further steps on X's part, continues perfected against *Dealer's* transferees and creditors. However, regardless of whether Lender made the assignment to secure Lender's obligation to X or whether the assignment was an outright sale of the chattel paper, the assignment creates a security interest in the chattel paper in favor of X. Accordingly, X must take whatever steps may be required for perfection in order to be protected against *Lender's* transferees and creditors with respect to the chattel paper.

Subsection (c) applies not only to an assignment of a security interest perfected by filing but also to an assignment of a security interest perfected by a method other than by filing, such as by control or by possession. Although subsection (c) addresses explicitly only the absence of an additional filing requirement, the same result normally will follow in the case of an assignment of a security interest perfected by a method other than by filing. For example, as long as possession of collateral is maintained by an assignee or by the assignor or another person on behalf of the assignee, no further perfection steps need be taken on account of

the assignment to continue perfection as against creditors and transferees of the original debtor. Of course, additional action may be required for perfection of the assignee's interest as against creditors and transferees of the *assignor*.

Similarly, subsection (c) applies to the assignment of a security interest perfected by compliance with a statute, regulation, or treaty under Section 9–311(b), such as a certificate-of-title statute. Unless the statute expressly provides to the contrary, the security interest will remain perfected against creditors of and transferees from the original debtor, even if the assignee takes no action to cause the certificate of title to reflect the assignment or to cause its name to appear on the certificate of title. See PEB Commentary No. 12, which discusses this issue under former Section 9–302(3). Compliance with the statute is "equivalent to filing" under Section 9–311(b).

§ 9–311. Perfection of Security Interests in Property Subject to Certain Statutes, Regulations, and Treaties.

(a) **[Security interest subject to other law.]** Except as otherwise provided in subsection (d), the filing of a financing statement is not necessary or effective to perfect a security interest in property subject to:

(1) a statute, regulation, or treaty of the United States whose requirements for a security interest's obtaining priority over the rights of a lien creditor with respect to the property preempt Section 9–310(a);

(2) [list any certificate-of-title statute covering automobiles, trailers, mobile homes, boats, farm tractors, or the like, which provides for a security interest to be indicated on the certificate as a condition or result of perfection, and any non-Uniform Commercial Code central filing statute]; or

(3) a certificate-of-title statute of another jurisdiction which provides for a security interest to be indicated on the certificate as a condition or result of the security interest's obtaining priority over the rights of a lien creditor with respect to the property.

(b) **[Compliance with other law.]** Compliance with the requirements of a statute, regulation, or treaty described in subsection (a) for obtaining priority over the rights of a lien creditor is equivalent to the filing of a financing statement under this article. Except as otherwise provided in subsection (d) and Sections 9–313 and 9–316(d) and (e) for goods covered by a certificate of title, a security interest in property subject to a statute, regulation, or treaty described in subsection (a) may be perfected only by compliance with those requirements, and a security interest so perfected remains perfected notwithstanding a change in the use or transfer of possession of the collateral.

(c) **[Duration and renewal of perfection.]** Except as otherwise provided in subsection (d) and Section 9–316(d) and (e), duration and renewal of perfection of a security interest perfected by compliance with the requirements prescribed by a statute, regulation, or treaty described in subsection (a) are governed by the statute, regulation, or treaty. In other respects, the security interest is subject to this article.

(d) **[Inapplicability to certain inventory.]** During any period in which collateral subject to a statute specified in subsection (a)(2) is inventory held for sale or lease by a person or leased by that person as lessor and that person is in the business of selling goods of that kind, this section does not apply to a security interest in that collateral created by that person.

Legislative Note: This Article contemplates that perfection of a security interest in goods covered by a certificate of title occurs upon receipt by appropriate State officials of a properly tendered application for a certificate of title on which the security interest is to be indicated, without a relation back to an earlier time. States whose certificate-of-title statutes provide for perfection at a different time or contain a relation-back provision should amend the statutes accordingly.

As amended in 2000.

Official Comment

1. **Source.** Former Section 9–302(3), (4).

2. **Federal Statutes, Regulations, and Treaties.** Subsection (a)(1) exempts from the filing provisions of this Article transactions as to which a system of filing—state or federal—has been established under federal law. Subsection (b) makes clear that when such a system exists, perfection of a relevant security interest can be achieved only through compliance with that system (i.e., filing under this Article is not a permissible alternative).

An example of the type of federal statute referred to in subsection (a)(1) is 49 U.S.C. §§ 44107–11, for civil aircraft of the United States. The Assignment of Claims Act of 1940, as amended, provides for notice to contracting and disbursing officers and to sureties on bonds but does not establish a national filing system and therefore is not within the scope of subsection (a)(1). An assignee of a claim against the United States may benefit from compliance with the Assignment of Claims Act. But regardless of whether the assignee complies with that Act, the assignee must file under this Article in order to perfect its security interest against creditors and transferees of its assignor.

Subsection (a)(1) provides explicitly that the filing requirement of this Article defers only to federal statutes, regulations, or treaties whose requirements for a security interest's obtaining priority over the rights of a lien creditor preempt Section 9–310(a). The provision eschews reference to the term "perfection," inasmuch as Section 9–308 specifies the meaning of that term and a preemptive rule may use other terminology.

3. **State Statutes.** Subsections (a)(2) and (3) exempt from the filing requirements of this Article transactions covered by State certificate-of-title statutes covering motor vehicles and the like. The description of certificate-of-title statutes in subsections (a)(2) and (a)(3) tracks the language of the definition of "certificate of title" in Section 9–102. For a discussion of the operation of state certificate-of-title statutes in interstate contexts, see the Comments to Section 9–303.

Some states have enacted central filing statutes with respect to secured transactions in kinds of property that are of special importance in the local economy. Subsection (a)(2) defers to these statutes with respect to filing for that property.

4. **Inventory Covered by Certificate of Title.** Under subsection (d), perfection of a security interest in the inventory of a person in the business of selling goods of that kind is governed by the normal perfection rules, even if the inventory is subject to a certificate-of-title statute. Compliance with a certificate-of-title statute is both unnecessary and ineffective to perfect a security interest in inventory to which this subsection applies. Thus, a secured party who finances an automobile dealer that is in the business of selling and leasing its inventory of automobiles can perfect a security interest in all the automobiles by filing a financing statement but not by compliance with a certificate-of-title statute.

Subsection (d), and thus the filing and other perfection provisions of this Article, does not apply to inventory that is subject to a certificate-of-title statute and is of a kind that the debtor is not in the business of selling. For example, if goods are subject to a certificate-of-title statute and the debtor is in the business of leasing but not of selling, goods of that kind, the other subsections of this section govern perfection of a security interest in the goods. The fact that the debtor eventually sells the goods does not, of itself, mean that the debtor "is in the business of selling goods of that kind."

The filing and other perfection provisions of this Article apply to goods subject to a certificate-of-title statute only "during any period in which collateral is inventory held for sale or lease or leased." If the debtor takes goods of this kind out of inventory and uses them, say, as equipment, a filed financing statement would not remain effective to perfect a security interest.

5. Compliance with Perfection Requirements of Other Statute. Subsection (b) makes clear that compliance with the perfection requirements (i.e., the requirements for obtaining priority over a lien creditor), but not other requirements, of a statute, regulation, or treaty described in subsection (a) is sufficient for perfection under this Article. Perfection of a security interest under such a statute, regulation, or treaty has all the consequences of perfection under this Article.

The interplay of this section with certain certificate-of-title statutes may create confusion and uncertainty. For example, statutes under which perfection does not occur until a certificate of title is issued will create a gap between the time that the goods are covered by the certificate under Section 9–303 and the time of perfection. If the gap is long enough, it may result in turning some unobjectionable transactions into avoidable preferences under Bankruptcy Code Section 547. (The preference risk arises if more than 10 days (or 20 days, in the case of a purchase-money security interest) passes between the time a security interest attaches (or the debtor receives possession of the collateral, in the case of a purchase-money security interest) and the time it is perfected.) Accordingly, the Legislative Note to this section instructs the legislature to amend the applicable certificate-of-title statute to provide that perfection occurs upon receipt by the appropriate State official of a properly tendered application for a certificate of title on which the security interest is to be indicated.

Under some certificate-of-title statutes, including the Uniform Motor Vehicle Certificate of Title and Anti–Theft Act, perfection generally occurs upon delivery of specified documents to a state official but may, under certain circumstances, relate back to the time of at-tachment. This relation-back feature can create great difficulties for the application of the rules in Sections 9–303 and 9–311(b). Accordingly, the Legislative Note also recommends to legislatures that they remove any relation-back provisions from certificate-of-title statutes affecting security interests.

6. Compliance with Perfection Requirements of Other Statute as Equivalent to Filing. Under Subsection (b), compliance with the perfection requirements (i.e., the requirements for obtaining priority over a lien creditor) of a statute, regulation, or treaty described in subsection (a) "is equivalent to the filing of a financing statement."

The quoted phrase appeared in former Section 9–302(3). Its meaning was unclear, and many questions arose concerning the extent to which and manner in which Article 9 rules referring to "filing" were applicable to perfection by compliance with a certificate-of-title statute. This Article takes a variety of approaches for applying Article 9's filing rules to compliance with other statutes and treaties. First, as discussed above in Comment 5, it leaves the determination of some rules, such as the rule establishing time of perfection (Section 9–516(a)), to the other statutes themselves. Second, this Article explicitly applies some Article 9 filing rules to perfection under other statutes or treaties. See, e.g., Section 9–505. Third, this Article makes other Article 9 rules applicable to security interests perfected by compliance with another statute through the "equivalent to . . . filing" provision in the first sentence of Section 9–311(b). The third approach is reflected for the most part in occasional Comments explaining how particular rules apply when perfection is accomplished under Section 9–311(b). See, e.g., Section 9–310, Comment 4; Section 9–315, Comment 6; Section 9–317, Comment 8. The absence of a Comment indicating that a particular filing provision applies to perfection pursuant to Section 9–311(b) does not mean the provision is inapplicable.

7. Perfection by Possession of Goods Covered by Certificate-of-Title Statute. A secured party who holds a security interest perfected under the law of State A in goods that subsequently are covered by a State B certificate of title may face a predicament. Ordinarily, the secured party will have four months under State B's Section 9–316(c) and (d) in which to (re)perfect as against a purchaser of the goods by having its security interest noted on a State B certificate. This procedure is likely to require the cooperation of the debtor and any competing secured party whose security interest has been noted on the certificate. Comment 4(e) to former Section 9–103 observed that "that cooperation is not likely to be forthcoming from an owner who wrongfully procured the issuance of a new certificate not showing the out-of-state security interest, or from a local secured party finding himself in a priority contest with the out-of-state secured party." According to that Comment, "[t]he only solution for the out-of-state secured party under present certificate of title statutes seems to be to reperfect by possession, i.e., by repossessing the goods." But the "solution" may not have worked: Former Section 9–302(4) provided that a security interest in property subject to a certificate-of-title statute "can be perfected only by compliance therewith."

Sections 9–316(d) and (e), 9–311(c), and 9–313(b) of this Article resolve the conflict by providing that a security interest that remains perfected solely by virtue of Section 9–316(e) can be (re)perfected by the secured party's taking possession of the collateral. These sections contemplate only that taking possession of goods covered by a certificate of title will work as a method of perfection. None of these sections creates a right to take possession. Section 9–609 and the agreement of the parties define the secured party's right to take possession.

As amended in 2000.

§ 9–312. Perfection of Security Interests in Chattel Paper, Deposit Accounts, Documents, Goods Covered by Documents, Instruments, Investment Property, Letter-of-Credit Rights, and Money; Perfection by Permissive Filing; Temporary Perfection Without Filing or Transfer of Possession.

(a) **[Perfection by filing permitted.]** A security interest in chattel paper, negotiable documents, instruments, or investment property may be perfected by filing.

(b) **[Control or possession of certain collateral.]** Except as otherwise provided in Section 9–315(c) and (d) for proceeds:

(1) a security interest in a deposit account may be perfected only by control under Section 9–314;

(2) and except as otherwise provided in Section 9–308(d), a security interest in a letter-of-credit right may be perfected only by control under Section 9–314; and

(3) a security interest in money may be perfected only by the secured party's taking possession under Section 9–313.

(c) **[Goods covered by negotiable document.]** While goods are in the possession of a bailee that has issued a negotiable document covering the goods:

(1) a security interest in the goods may be perfected by perfecting a security interest in the document; and

(2) a security interest perfected in the document has priority over any security interest that becomes perfected in the goods by another method during that time.

(d) **[Goods covered by nonnegotiable document.]** While goods are in the possession of a bailee that has issued a nonnegotiable document covering the goods, a security interest in the goods may be perfected by:

(1) issuance of a document in the name of the secured party;

(2) the bailee's receipt of notification of the secured party's interest; or

(3) filing as to the goods.

(e) **[Temporary perfection: new value.]** A security interest in certificated securities, negotiable documents, or instruments is perfected without filing or the taking of possession or control for a period of 20 days from the time it attaches to the extent that it arises for new value given under an authenticated security agreement.

(f) **[Temporary perfection: goods or documents made available to debtor.]** A perfected security interest in a negotiable document or goods in possession of a bailee, other than one that has issued a negotiable document for the goods, remains perfected for 20 days without filing if the secured party makes available to the debtor the goods or documents representing the goods for the purpose of:

(1) ultimate sale or exchange; or

(2) loading, unloading, storing, shipping, transshipping, manufacturing, processing, or otherwise dealing with them in a manner preliminary to their sale or exchange.

(g) **[Temporary perfection: delivery of security certificate or instrument to debtor.]** A perfected security interest in a certificated security or instrument remains perfected for 20 days without filing if the secured party delivers the security certificate or instrument to the debtor for the purpose of:

(1) ultimate sale or exchange; or

(2) presentation, collection, enforcement, renewal, or registration of transfer.

(h) **[Expiration of temporary perfection.]** After the 20-day period specified in subsection (e), (f), or (g) expires, perfection depends upon compliance with this article.

As amended in 2003.

Official Comment

1. **Source.** Former Section 9–304, with additions and some changes.

2. **Instruments.** Under subsection (a), a security interest in instruments may be perfected by filing. This rule represents an important change from former Article 9, under which the secured party's taking possession of an instrument was the only method of achieving long-term perfection. The rule is likely to be particularly useful in transactions involving a large number of notes that a debtor uses as collateral but continues to collect from the makers. A security interest perfected by filing is subject to defeat by certain subsequent purchasers (including secured parties). Under Section 9–330(d), purchasers for value who take possession of an instrument without knowledge that the purchase violates the rights of the secured party generally would achieve priority over a security interest in the instrument perfected by filing. In addition, Section 9–331 provides that filing a financing statement does not constitute notice that would preclude a subsequent purchaser from becoming a holder in due course and taking free of all claims under Section 3–306.

3. **Chattel Paper; Negotiable Documents.** Subsection (a) further provides that filing is available as a method of perfection for security interests in chattel paper and negotiable documents. Tangible chattel paper is sometimes delivered to the assignee, and sometimes left in the hands of the assignor for collection. Subsection (a) allows the assignee to perfect its security interest by filing in the latter case. Alternatively, the assignee may perfect by taking possession. See Section 9–313(a). An assignee of electronic chattel paper may perfect by taking control. See Sections 9–314(a), 9–105. The security interest of an assignee who takes possession or control may qualify for priority over a competing security interest perfected by filing. See Section 9–330.

Negotiable documents may be, and usually are, delivered to the secured party. See Article 1, Section 1–201 (definition of "delivery"). The secured party's taking possession of a tangible document or control of an electronic document will suffice as a perfection step. See Sections 9–313(a), 9–314 and 7–106. However, as is the case with chattel paper, a security interest in a negotiable document may be perfected by filing.

4. **Investment Property.** A security interest in investment property, including certificated securities, uncertificated securities, security entitlements, and securities accounts, may be perfected by filing. However, security interests created by brokers, securities intermediaries, or commodity intermediaries are automatically perfected; filing is of no effect. See Section 9–309(10), (11). A security interest in all kinds of investment property also may be perfected by control, see Sections 9–314, 9–106, and a security interest in a certificated security also may be perfected by the secured party's taking delivery under Section 8–301. See Section 9–313(a). A security interest perfected only by filing is subordinate to a conflicting security interest perfected by control or delivery. See Section 9–328(1), (5). Thus, although filing is a permissible method of perfection, a secured party who perfects by filing takes the risk that the debtor has granted or will grant a security interest in the same collateral to another party who obtains control. Also, perfection by filing would not give the secured party protection against other types of adverse claims, since the Article 8 adverse claim cut-off rules require control. See Section 8–510.

5. **Deposit Accounts.** Under new subsection (b)(1), the only method of perfecting a security interest in a deposit account as original collateral is by control. Filing is ineffective, except as provided in Section 9–315 with respect to proceeds. As explained in Section 9–104, "control" can arise as a result of an agreement among the secured party, debtor, and bank, whereby the bank agrees to comply with instructions of the secured party with respect to disposition of the funds on deposit, even though the debtor retains the right to direct disposition of the funds. Thus, subsection (b)(1) takes an intermediate position between certain non-UCC law, which conditions the effectiveness of a security interest on the secured party's enjoyment of such dominion and control over the deposit account that the debtor is unable to dispose of the funds, and the approach this Article takes to securities accounts, under which a secured party who is unable to reach the collateral without resort to judicial process may perfect by filing. By conditioning perfection on "control," rather than requiring the secured party to enjoy absolute

dominion to the exclusion of the debtor, subsection (b)(1) permits perfection in a wide variety of transactions, including those in which the secured party actually relies on the deposit account in extending credit and maintains some meaningful dominion over it, but does not wish to deprive the debtor of access to the funds altogether.

6. **Letter-of-Credit Rights.** Letter-of-credit rights commonly are "supporting obligations," as defined in Section 9–102. Perfection as to the related account, chattel paper, document, general intangible, instrument, or investment property will perfect as to the letter-of-credit rights. See Section 9–308(d). Subsection (b)(2) provides that, in other cases, a security interest in a letter-of-credit right may be perfected only by control. "Control," for these purposes, is explained in Section 9–107.

7. **Goods Covered by Document of Title.** Subsection (c) applies to goods in the possession of a bailee who has issued a negotiable document covering the goods. Subsection (d) applies to goods in the possession of a bailee who has issued a nonnegotiable document of title, including a document of title that is "non-negotiable" under Section 7–104. Section 9–313 governs perfection of a security interest in goods in the possession of a bailee who has not issued a document of title.

Subsection (c) clarifies the perfection and priority rules in former Section 9–304(2). Consistently with the provisions of Article 7, subsection (c) takes the position that, as long as a negotiable document covering goods is outstanding, title to the goods is, so to say, locked up in the document. Accordingly, a security interest in goods covered by a negotiable document may be perfected by perfecting a security interest in the document. The security interest also may be perfected by another method, e.g., by filing. The priority rule in subsection (c) governs only priority between (i) a security interest in goods which is perfected by perfecting in the document and (ii) a security interest in the goods which becomes perfected by another method while the goods are covered by the document.

Example 1: While wheat is in a grain elevator and covered by a negotiable warehouse receipt, Debtor creates a security interest in the wheat in favor of SP–1 and SP–2. SP–1 perfects by filing a financing statement covering "wheat." Thereafter, SP–2 perfects by filing a financing statement describing the warehouse receipt. Subsection (c)(1) provides that SP–2's security interest is perfected. Subsection (c)(2) provides that SP–2's security interest is senior to SP–1's.

Example 2: The facts are as in Example 1, but SP–1's security interest attached and was perfected before the goods were delivered to the grain elevator. Subsection (c)(2) does not apply, because SP–1's security interest did not become perfected during the time that the wheat was in the possession of a bailee. Rather, the first-to-file-or-perfect priority rule applies. See Sections 9–322 and 7–503.

A secured party may become "a holder to whom a negotiable document of title has been duly negotiated" under Section 7–501. If so, the secured party acquires the rights specified by Article 7. Article 9 does not limit those rights, which may include the right to priority over an earlier-perfected security interest. See Section 9–331(a).

Subsection (d) takes a different approach to the problem of goods covered by a nonnegotiable document. Here, title to the goods is not looked on as being locked up in the document, and the secured party may perfect its security interest directly in the goods by filing as to them. The subsection provides two other methods of perfection: issuance of the document in the secured party's name (as consignee of a straight bill of lading or the person to whom delivery would be made under a non-negotiable warehouse receipt) and receipt of notification of the secured party's interest by the bailee. Perfection under subsection (d) occurs when the bailee receives notification of the secured party's interest in the goods, regardless of who sends the notification. Receipt of notification is effective to perfect, regardless of whether the bailee responds. Unlike former Section 9–304(3), from which it derives, subsection (d) does not apply to goods in the possession of a bailee who has not issued a document of title. Section 9–313(c) covers that case and provides that perfection by possession as to goods not covered by a document requires the bailee's acknowledgment.

8. **Temporary Perfection Without Having First Otherwise Perfected.** Subsection (e) follows former Section 9–304(4) in giving perfected status to security interests in certificated securities, instruments, and negotiable documents for a short period (reduced from 21 to 20 days, which is the time period generally applicable in this Article), although there has been no filing and the collateral is in the debtor's possession or control. The 20–day temporary perfection runs from the date of attachment. There is no limitation on the purpose for which the debtor is in possession, but the secured party must have given "new value" (defined in Section 9–102) under an authenticated security agreement.

9. Maintaining Perfection After Surrendering Possession. There are a variety of legitimate reasons—many of them are described in subsections (f) and (g)—why certain types of collateral must be released temporarily to a debtor. No useful purpose would be served by cluttering the files with records of such exceedingly short term transactions.

Subsection (f) affords the possibility of 20–day perfection in negotiable documents and goods in the possession of a bailee but not covered by a negotiable document. Subsection (g) provides for 20–day perfection in certificated securities and instruments. These subsections derive from former Section 9–305(5). However, the period of temporary perfection has been reduced from 21 to 20 days, which is the time period generally applicable in this Article, and "enforcement" has been added in subsection (g) as one of the special and limited purposes for which a secured party can release an instrument or certificated security to the debtor and still remain perfected. The period of temporary perfection runs from the date a secured party who already has a perfected security interest turns over the collateral to the debtor. There is no new value requirement, but the turnover must be for one or more of the purposes stated in subsection (f) or (g). The 20–day period may be extended by perfecting as to the collateral by another method before the period expires. However, if the security interest is not perfected by another method until after the 20–day period expires, there will be a gap during which the security interest is unperfected.

Temporary perfection extends only to the negotiable document or goods under subsection (f) and only to the certificated security or instrument under subsection (g). It does not extend to proceeds. If the collateral is sold, the security interest will continue in the proceeds for the period specified in Section 9–315.

Subsections (f) and (g) deal only with perfection. Other sections of this Article govern the priority of a security interest in goods after surrender of possession or control of the document covering them. In the case of a purchase-money security interest in inventory, priority may be conditioned upon giving notification to a prior inventory financer. See Section 9–324.

As amended in 2003.

§ 9–313. When Possession by or Delivery to Secured Party Perfects Security Interest Without Filing.

(a) **[Perfection by possession or delivery.]** Except as otherwise provided in subsection (b), a secured party may perfect a security interest in tangible negotiable documents, goods, instruments, money, or tangible chattel paper by taking possession of the collateral. A secured party may perfect a security interest in certificated securities by taking delivery of the certificated securities under Section 8–301.

(b) **[Goods covered by certificate of title.]** With respect to goods covered by a certificate of title issued by this State, a secured party may perfect a security interest in the goods by taking possession of the goods only in the circumstances described in Section 9–316(d).

(c) **[Collateral in possession of person other than debtor.]** With respect to collateral other than certificated securities and goods covered by a document, a secured party takes possession of collateral in the possession of a person other than the debtor, the secured party, or a lessee of the collateral from the debtor in the ordinary course of the debtor's business, when:

(1) the person in possession authenticates a record acknowledging that it holds possession of the collateral for the secured party's benefit; or

(2) the person takes possession of the collateral after having authenticated a record acknowledging that it will hold possession of collateral for the secured party's benefit.

(d) **[Time of perfection by possession; continuation of perfection.]** If perfection of a security interest depends upon possession of the collateral by a secured party, perfection occurs no earlier than the time the secured party takes possession and continues only while the secured party retains possession.

(e) **[Time of perfection by delivery; continuation of perfection.]** A security interest in a certificated security in registered form is perfected by delivery when delivery of the certificated security occurs under Section 8–301 and remains perfected by delivery until the debtor obtains possession of the security certificate.

(f) **[Acknowledgment not required.]** A person in possession of collateral is not required to acknowledge that it holds possession for a secured party's benefit.

(g) **[Effectiveness of acknowledgment; no duties or confirmation.]** If a person acknowledges that it holds possession for the secured party's benefit:

(1) the acknowledgment is effective under subsection (c) or Section 8–301(a), even if the acknowledgment violates the rights of a debtor; and

(2) unless the person otherwise agrees or law other than this article otherwise provides, the person does not owe any duty to the secured party and is not required to confirm the acknowledgment to another person.

(h) **[Secured party's delivery to person other than debtor.]** A secured party having possession of collateral does not relinquish possession by delivering the collateral to a person other than the debtor or a lessee of the collateral from the debtor in the ordinary course of the debtor's business if the person was instructed before the delivery or is instructed contemporaneously with the delivery:

(1) to hold possession of the collateral for the secured party's benefit; or

(2) to redeliver the collateral to the secured party.

(i) **[Effect of delivery under subsection (h); no duties or confirmation.]** A secured party does not relinquish possession, even if a delivery under subsection (h) violates the rights of a debtor. A person to which collateral is delivered under subsection (h) does not owe any duty to the secured party and is not required to confirm the delivery to another person unless the person otherwise agrees or law other than this article otherwise provides.

As amended in 2003.

Official Comment

1. **Source.** Former Sections 9–305, 9–115(6).

2. **Perfection by Possession.** As under the common law of pledge, no filing is required by this Article to perfect a security interest if the secured party takes possession of the collateral. See Section 9–310(b)(6).

This section permits a security interest to be perfected by the taking of possession only when the collateral is goods, instruments, tangible negotiable documents, money, or tangible chattel paper. Accounts, commercial tort claims, deposit accounts, investment property, letter-of-credit rights, letters of credit, and oil, gas, or other minerals before extraction are excluded. (But see Comment 6, below, regarding certificated securities.) A security interest in accounts and payment intangibles—property not ordinarily represented by any writing whose delivery operates to transfer the right to payment—may under this Article be perfected only by filing. This rule would not be affected by the fact that a security agreement or other record described the assignment of such collateral as a "pledge." Section 9–309(2) exempts from filing certain assignments of accounts or payment intangibles which are out of the ordinary course of financing. These exempted assignments are perfected when they attach. Similarly, under Section 9–309(3), sales of payment intangibles are automatically perfected.

3. **"Possession."** This section does not define "possession." It adopts the general concept as it developed under former Article 9. As under former Article 9, in determining whether a particular person has possession, the principles of agency apply. For example, if the collateral is in possession of an agent of the secured party for the purposes of possessing on behalf of the secured party, and if the agent is not also an agent of the debtor, the secured party has taken actual possession, and subsection (c) does not apply. Sometimes a person holds collateral both as an agent of the secured party and as an agent of the debtor. The fact of dual agency is not of itself inconsistent with the secured party's having taken possession (and thereby having rendered subsection (c) inapplicable). The debtor cannot qualify as an agent for the secured party for purposes of the secured party's taking possession. And, under appropriate circumstances, a court may determine that a person in possession is so closely connected to or controlled by the debtor that the debtor has retained effective possession, even though the person may have agreed to take possession on behalf of the secured party. If so, the person's taking possession would not constitute the secured party's taking possession and would not be sufficient for perfection. See also Section 9–205(b). In a typical escrow arrangement, where the escrowee has possession of collateral as agent for both the secured party and the debtor, the debtor's relationship to the escrowee is not such as to constitute retention of possession by the debtor.

4. **Goods in Possession of Third Party: Perfection.** Former Section 9–305 permitted perfection of a security interest by notification to a bailee in possession of collateral. This Article distinguishes between goods in the possession of a bailee who has issued a document of title covering the goods and goods in the possession of a third party who has not issued a document. Section 9–312(c) or (d) applies to the former, depending on whether the document is negotiable. Section 9–313(c) applies to the latter. It provides a

method of perfection by possession when the collateral is possessed by a third person who is not the secured party's agent.

Notification of a third person does not suffice to perfect under Section 9–313(c). Rather, perfection does not occur unless the third person authenticates an acknowledgment that it holds possession of the collateral for the secured party's benefit. Compare Section 9–312(d), under which receipt of notification of the security party's interest by a bailee holding goods covered by a nonnegotiable document is sufficient to perfect, even if the bailee does not acknowledge receipt of the notification. A third person may acknowledge that it will hold for the secured party's benefit goods to be received in the future. Under these circumstances, perfection by possession occurs when the third person obtains possession of the goods.

Under subsection (c), acknowledgment of notification by a "lessee . . . in . . . ordinary course of . . . business" (defined in Section 2A–103) does not suffice for possession. The section thus rejects the reasoning of *In re Atlantic Systems, Inc.*, 135 B.R. 463 (Bankr. S.D.N.Y. 1992) (holding that notification to debtor-lessor's lessee sufficed to perfect security interest in leased goods). See Steven O. Weise, *Perfection by Possession: The Need for an Objective Test*, 29 Idaho Law Rev. 705 (1992–93) (arguing that lessee's possession in ordinary course of debtor-lessor's business does not provide adequate public notice of possible security interest in leased goods). Inclusion of a per se rule concerning lessees is not meant to preclude a court, under appropriate circumstances, from determining that a third person is so closely connected to or controlled by the debtor that the debtor has retained effective possession. If so, the third person's acknowledgment would not be sufficient for perfection.

In some cases, it may be uncertain whether a person who has possession of collateral is an agent of the secured party or a non-agent bailee. Under those circumstances, prudence might suggest that the secured party obtain the person's acknowledgment to avoid litigation and ensure perfection by possession regardless of how the relationship between the secured party and the person is characterized.

5. **No Relation Back.** Former Section 9–305 provided that a security interest is perfected by possession from the time possession is taken "without a relation back." As the Comment to former Section 9–305 observed, the relation-back theory, under which the taking of possession was deemed to relate back to the date of the original security agreement, has had little vitality since the 1938 revision of the Federal Bankruptcy Act. The theory is inconsistent with former Article 9 and with this Article. See Section 9–313(d). Accordingly, this Article deletes the quoted phrase as unnecessary. Where a pledge transaction is contemplated, perfection dates only from the time possession is taken, although a security interest may attach, unperfected. The only exceptions to this rule are the short, 20–day periods of perfection provided in Section 9–312(e), (f), and (g), during which a debtor may have possession of specified collateral in which there is a perfected security interest.

6. **Certificated Securities.** The second sentence of subsection (a) reflects the traditional rule for perfection of a security interest in certificated securities. Compare Section 9–115(6) (1994 Official Text); Sections 8–321, 8–313(1)(a) (1978 Official Text); Section 9–305 (1972 Official Text). It has been modified to refer to "delivery" under Section 8–301. Corresponding changes appear in Section 9–203(b).

Subsection (e), which is new, applies to a secured party in possession of security certificates or another person who has taken delivery of security certificates and holds them for the secured party's benefit under Section 8–301. See Comment 8.

Under subsection (e), a possessory security interest in a certificated security remains perfected until the debtor obtains possession of the security certificate. This rule is analogous to that of Section 9–314(c), which deals with perfection of security interests in investment property by control. See Section 9–314, Comment 3.

7. **Goods Covered by Certificate of Title.** Subsection (b) is necessary to effect changes to the choice-of-law rules governing goods covered by a certificate of title. These changes are described in the Comments to Section 9–311. Subsection (b), like subsection (a), does not create a right to take possession. Rather, it indicates the circumstances under which the secured party's taking possession of goods covered by a certificate of title is effective to perfect a security interest in the goods: the goods become covered by a certificate of title issued by this State at a time when the security interest is perfected by any method under the law of another jurisdiction.

8. **Goods in Possession of Third Party: No Duty to Acknowledge; Consequences of Acknowledgment.** Subsections (f) and (g) are new and address matters as to which former Article 9 was silent. They derive in part from Section 8–106(g). Subsection (f) provides that a person in possession of collateral is not required to acknowledge that it holds for a secured party. Subsection (g)(1) provides that an acknowledg-

ment is effective even if wrongful as to the debtor. Subsection (g)(2) makes clear that an acknowledgment does not give rise to any duties or responsibilities under this Article. Arrangements involving the possession of goods are hardly standardized. They include bailments for services to be performed on the goods (such as repair or processing), for use (leases), as security (pledges), for carriage, and for storage. This Article leaves to the agreement of the parties and to any other applicable law the imposition of duties and responsibilities upon a person who acknowledges under subsection (c). For example, by acknowledging, a third party does not become obliged to act on the secured party's direction or to remain in possession of the collateral unless it agrees to do so or other law so provides.

9. **Delivery to Third Party by Secured Party.** New subsections (h) and (i) address the practice of mortgage warehouse lenders. These lenders typically send mortgage notes to prospective purchasers under cover of letters advising the prospective purchasers that the lenders hold security interests in the notes. These lenders relied on notification to maintain perfection under former 9–305. Requiring them to obtain authenticated acknowledgments from each prospective purchaser under subsection (c) could be unduly burdensome and disruptive of established practices. Under subsection (h), when a secured party in possession itself delivers the collateral to a third party, instructions to the third party would be sufficient to maintain perfection by possession; an acknowledgment would not be necessary. Under subsection (i), the secured party does not relinquish possession by making a delivery under subsection (h), even if the delivery violates the rights of the debtor. That subsection also makes clear that a person to whom collateral is delivered under subsection (h) does not owe any duty to the secured party and is not required to confirm the delivery to another person unless the person otherwise agrees or law other than this Article provides otherwise.

As amended in 2000 and 2003.

§ 9–314.   Perfection by Control.

(a) **[Perfection by control.]** A security interest in investment property, deposit accounts, letter-of-credit rights, electronic chattel paper, or electronic documents may be perfected by control of the collateral under Section 7–106, 9–104, 9–105, 9–106, or 9–107.

(b) **[Specified collateral: time of perfection by control; continuation of perfection.]**

A security interest in deposit accounts, electronic chattel paper, letter-of-credit rights, or electronic documents is perfected by control under Section 7–106, 9–104, 9–105, or 9–107 when the secured party obtains control and remains perfected by control only while the secured party retains control.

(c) **[Investment property: time of perfection by control; continuation of perfection.]** A security interest in investment property is perfected by control under Section 9–106 from the time the secured party obtains control and remains perfected by control until:

(1) the secured party does not have control; and

(2) one of the following occurs:

(A) if the collateral is a certificated security, the debtor has or acquires possession of the security certificate;

(B) if the collateral is an uncertificated security, the issuer has registered or registers the debtor as the registered owner; or

(C) if the collateral is a security entitlement, the debtor is or becomes the entitlement holder.

As amended in 2003.

Official Comment

1. **Source.** Substantially new; derived in part from former Section 9–115(4).

2. **Control.** This section provides for perfection by control with respect to investment property, deposit accounts, letter-of-credit rights, electronic chattel paper, and electronic documents. For explanations of how a secured party takes control of these types of collateral, see Sections 9–104 through 9–107 and Section 7–106. Subsection (b) explains when a security interest is perfected by control and how long a security interest remains perfected by control. Like Section 9–313(d) and for the same reasons, subsection (b) makes no reference to the doctrine of "relation back." See Section 9–313, Comment 5. As to an electronic document that is reissued in a tangible medium, Section 7–105, a secured party that is perfected by control in the electronic document should file as to the document before relinquishing control in order to maintain continuous perfection in the document. See Section 9–308.

3. **Investment Property.** Subsection (c) provides a special rule for investment property. Once a secured

party has control, its security interest remains perfected by control until the secured party ceases to have control and the debtor receives possession of collateral that is a certificated security, becomes the registered owner of collateral that is an uncertificated security, or becomes the entitlement holder of collateral that is a security entitlement. The result is particularly important in the "repledge" context. See Section 9–207, Comment 5.

In a transaction in which a secured party who has control grants a security interest in investment property or sells outright the investment property, by virtue of the debtor's consent or applicable legal rules, a purchaser from the secured party typically will cut off the debtor's rights in the investment property or be immune from the debtor's claims. See Section 9–207, Comments 5 and 6. If the investment property is a security, the debtor normally would retain no interest in the security following the purchase from the secured party, and a claim of the debtor against the secured party for redemption (Section 9–623) or otherwise with respect to the security would be a purely personal claim. If the investment property transferred by the secured party is a financial asset in which the debtor had a security entitlement credited to a securities account maintained with the secured party as a securities intermediary, the debtor's claim against the secured party could arise as a part of its securities account notwithstanding its personal nature. (This claim would be analogous to a "credit balance" in the securities account, which is a component of the securities account even though it is a personal claim against the intermediary.) In the case in which the debtor may retain an interest in investment property notwithstanding a repledge or sale by the secured party, subsection (c) makes clear that the security interest will remain perfected by control.

As amended in 2003.

§ 9–315. Secured Party's Rights on Disposition of Collateral and in Proceeds.

(a) **[Disposition of collateral: continuation of security interest or agricultural lien; proceeds.]** Except as otherwise provided in this article and in Section 2–403(2):

(1) a security interest or agricultural lien continues in collateral notwithstanding sale, lease, license, exchange, or other disposition thereof unless the secured party authorized the disposition free of the security interest or agricultural lien; and

(2) a security interest attaches to any identifiable proceeds of collateral.

(b) **[When commingled proceeds identifiable.]** Proceeds that are commingled with other property are identifiable proceeds:

(1) if the proceeds are goods, to the extent provided by Section 9–336; and

(2) if the proceeds are not goods, to the extent that the secured party identifies the proceeds by a method of tracing, including application of equitable principles, that is permitted under law other than this article with respect to commingled property of the type involved.

(c) **[Perfection of security interest in proceeds.]** A security interest in proceeds is a perfected security interest if the security interest in the original collateral was perfected.

(d) **[Continuation of perfection.]** A perfected security interest in proceeds becomes unperfected on the 21st day after the security interest attaches to the proceeds unless:

(1) the following conditions are satisfied:

(A) a filed financing statement covers the original collateral;

(B) the proceeds are collateral in which a security interest may be perfected by filing in the office in which the financing statement has been filed; and

(C) the proceeds are not acquired with cash proceeds;

(2) the proceeds are identifiable cash proceeds; or

(3) the security interest in the proceeds is perfected other than under subsection (c) when the security interest attaches to the proceeds or within 20 days thereafter.

(e) **[When perfected security interest in proceeds becomes unperfected.]** If a filed financing statement covers the original collateral, a security interest in proceeds which remains perfected under subsection (d)(1) becomes unperfected at the later of:

(1) when the effectiveness of the filed financing statement lapses under Section 9–515 or is terminated under Section 9–513; or

(2) the 21st day after the security interest attaches to the proceeds.

Official Comment

1. **Source.** Former Section 9–306.

2. **Continuation of Security Interest or Agricultural Lien Following Disposition of Collateral.** Subsection (a)(1), which derives from former Section 9–306(2), contains the general rule that a security interest survives disposition of the collateral. In these cases, the secured party may repossess the collateral from the transferee or, in an appropriate case, maintain an action for conversion. The secured party may claim both any proceeds and the original collateral but, of course, may have only one satisfaction.

In many cases, a purchaser or other transferee of collateral will take free of a security interest, and the secured party's only right will be to proceeds. For example, the general rule does not apply, and a security interest does not continue in collateral, if the secured party authorized the disposition, in the agreement that contains the security agreement or otherwise. Subsection (a)(1) adopts the view of PEB Commentary No. 3 and makes explicit that the authorized disposition to which it refers is an authorized disposition "free of" the security interest or agricultural lien. The secured party's right to proceeds under this section or under the express terms of an agreement does not in itself constitute an authorization of disposition. The change in language from former Section 9–306(2) is not intended to address the frequently litigated situation in which the effectiveness of the secured party's consent to a disposition is conditioned upon the secured party's receipt of the proceeds. In that situation, subsection (a) leaves the determination of authorization to the courts, as under former Article 9.

This Article contains several provisions under which a transferee takes free of a security interest or agricultural lien. For example, Section 9–317 states when transferees take free of unperfected security interests; Sections 9–320 and 9–321 on goods, 9–321 on general intangibles, 9–330 on chattel paper and instruments, and 9–331 on negotiable instruments, negotiable documents, and securities state when purchasers of such collateral take free of a security interest, even though perfected and even though the disposition was not authorized. Section 9–332 enables most transferees (including non-purchasers) of funds from a deposit account and most transferees of money to take free of a perfected security interest in the deposit account or money.

Likewise, the general rule that a security interest survives disposition does not apply if the secured party entrusts goods collateral to a merchant who deals in goods of that kind and the merchant sells the collateral to a buyer in ordinary course of business. Section 2–403(2) gives the merchant the power to transfer all the secured party's rights to the buyer, even if the sale is wrongful as against the secured party. Thus, under subsection (a)(1), an entrusting secured party runs the same risk as any other entruster.

3. **Secured Party's Right to Identifiable Proceeds.** Under subsection (a)(2), which derives from former Section 9–306(2), a security interest attaches to any identifiable "proceeds," as defined in Section 9–102. See also Section 9–203(f). Subsection (b) is new. It indicates when proceeds commingled with other property are identifiable proceeds and permits the use of whatever methods of tracing other law permits with respect to the type of property involved. Among the "equitable principles" whose use other law may permit is the "lowest intermediate balance rule." See Restatement (2d), Trusts § 202.

4. **Automatic Perfection in Proceeds: General Rule.** Under subsection (c), a security interest in proceeds is a perfected security interest if the security interest in the original collateral was perfected. This Article extends the period of automatic perfection in proceeds from 10 days to 20 days. Generally, a security interest in proceeds becomes unperfected on the 21st day after the security interest attaches to the proceeds. See subsection (d). The loss of perfected status under subsection (d) is prospective only. Compare, e.g., Section 9–515(c) (deeming security interest unperfected retroactively).

5. **Automatic Perfection in Proceeds: Proceeds Acquired with Cash Proceeds.** Subsection (d)(1) derives from former Section 9–306(3)(a). It carries forward the basic rule that a security interest in proceeds remains perfected beyond the period of automatic perfection if a filed financing statement covers the original collateral (e.g., inventory) and the proceeds are collateral in which a security interest may be perfected by filing in the office where the financing statement has been filed (e.g., equipment). A different rule applies if the proceeds are acquired with cash proceeds, as is the case if the original collateral (inventory) is sold for cash (cash proceeds) that is used to purchase equipment (proceeds). Under these circumstances, the security interest in the equipment proceeds remains perfected only if the description in the filed financing indicates the type of property constituting the proceeds (e.g., "equipment").

This section reaches the same result but takes a different approach. It recognizes that the treatment of proceeds acquired with cash proceeds under former

752

Section 9–306(3)(a) essentially was superfluous. In the example, had the filing covered "equipment" as well as "inventory," the security interest in the proceeds would have been perfected under the usual rules governing after-acquired equipment (see former Sections 9–302, 9–303); paragraph (3)(a) added only an exception to the general rule. Subsection (d)(1)(C) of this section takes a more direct approach. It makes the general rule of continued perfection inapplicable to proceeds acquired with cash proceeds, leaving perfection of a security interest in those proceeds to the generally applicable perfection rules under subsection (d)(3).

Example 1: Lender perfects a security interest in Debtor's inventory by filing a financing statement covering "inventory." Debtor sells the inventory and deposits the buyer's check into a deposit account. Debtor draws a check on the deposit account and uses it to pay for equipment. Under the "lowest intermediate balance rule," which is a permitted method of tracing in the relevant jurisdiction, see Comment 3, the funds used to pay for the equipment were identifiable proceeds of the inventory. Because the proceeds (equipment) were acquired with cash proceeds (deposit account), subsection (d)(1) does not extend perfection beyond the 20–day automatic period.

Example 2: Lender perfects a security interest in Debtor's inventory by filing a financing statement covering "all debtor's property." As in Example 1, Debtor sells the inventory, deposits the buyer's check into a deposit account, draws a check on the deposit account, and uses the check to pay for equipment. Under the "lowest intermediate balance rule," which is a permitted method of tracing in the relevant jurisdiction, see Comment 3, the funds used to pay for the equipment were identifiable proceeds of the inventory. Because the proceeds (equipment) were acquired with cash proceeds (deposit account), subsection (d)(1) does not extend perfection beyond the 20–day automatic period. However, because the financing statement is sufficient to perfect a security interest in debtor's equipment, under subsection (d)(3) the security interest in the equipment proceeds remains perfected beyond the 20–day period.

6. **Automatic Perfection in Proceeds: Lapse or Termination of Financing Statement During 20–Day Period; Perfection Under Other Statute or Treaty.** Subsection (e) provides that a security interest in proceeds perfected under subsection (d)(1) ceases to be perfected when the financing statement covering the original collateral lapses or is terminated. If the lapse or termination occurs before the 21st day after

the security interest attaches, however, the security interest in the proceeds remains perfected until the 21st day. Section 9–311(b) provides that compliance with the perfection requirements of a statute or treaty described in Section 9–311(a) "is equivalent to the filing of a financing statement." It follows that collateral subject to a security interest perfected by such compliance under Section 9–311(b) is covered by a "filed financing statement" within the meaning of Section 9–315(d) and (e).

7. **Automatic Perfection in Proceeds: Continuation of Perfection in Cash Proceeds.** Former Section 9–306(3)(b) provided that if a filed financing statement covered original collateral, a security interest in identifiable cash proceeds of the collateral remained perfected beyond the ten-day period of automatic perfection. Former Section 9–306(3)(c) contained a similar rule with respect to identifiable cash proceeds of investment property. Subsection (d)(2) extends the benefits of former Sections 9–306(3)(b) and (3)(c) to identifiable cash proceeds of all types of original collateral in which a security interest is perfected by any method. Under subsection (d)(2), if the security interest in the original collateral was perfected, a security interest in identifiable cash proceeds will remain perfected indefinitely, regardless of whether the security interest in the original collateral remains perfected. In many cases, however, a purchaser or other transferee of the cash proceeds will take free of the perfected security interest. See, e.g., Sections 9–330(d) (purchaser of check), 9–331 (holder in due course of check), 9–332 (transferee of money or funds from a deposit account).

8. **Insolvency Proceedings; Returned and Repossessed Goods.** This Article deletes former Section 9–306(4), which dealt with proceeds in insolvency proceedings. Except as otherwise provided by the Bankruptcy Code, the debtor's entering into bankruptcy does not affect a secured party's right to proceeds.

This Article also deletes former Section 9–306(5), which dealt with returned and repossessed goods. Section 9–330, Comments 9 to 11 explain and clarify the application of priority rules to returned and repossessed goods as proceeds of chattel paper.

9. **Proceeds of Collateral Subject to Agricultural Lien.** This Article does not determine whether a lien extends to proceeds of farm products encumbered by an agricultural lien. If, however, the proceeds are themselves farm products on which an "agricultural lien" (defined in Section 9–102) arises under other law, then the agricultural-lien provisions of this Article apply to the agricultural lien on the proceeds in the

same way in which they would apply had the farm products not been proceeds.

§ 9–316. Continued Perfection of Security Interest Following Change in Governing Law.

(a) [**General rule: effect on perfection of change in governing law.**] A security interest perfected pursuant to the law of the jurisdiction designated in Section 9–301(1) or 9–305(c) remains perfected until the earliest of:

(1) the time perfection would have ceased under the law of that jurisdiction;

(2) the expiration of four months after a change of the debtor's location to another jurisdiction; or

(3) the expiration of one year after a transfer of collateral to a person that thereby becomes a debtor and is located in another jurisdiction.

(b) [**Security interest perfected or unperfected under law of new jurisdiction.**] If a security interest described in subsection (a) becomes perfected under the law of the other jurisdiction before the earliest time or event described in that subsection, it remains perfected thereafter. If the security interest does not become perfected under the law of the other jurisdiction before the earliest time or event, it becomes unperfected and is deemed never to have been perfected as against a purchaser of the collateral for value.

(c) [**Possessory security interest in collateral moved to new jurisdiction.**] A possessory security interest in collateral, other than goods covered by a certificate of title and as-extracted collateral consisting of goods, remains continuously perfected if:

(1) the collateral is located in one jurisdiction and subject to a security interest perfected under the law of that jurisdiction;

(2) thereafter the collateral is brought into another jurisdiction; and

(3) upon entry into the other jurisdiction, the security interest is perfected under the law of the other jurisdiction.

(d) [**Goods covered by certificate of title from this state.**] Except as otherwise provided in subsection (e), a security interest in goods covered by a certificate of title which is perfected by any method under the law of another jurisdiction when the goods become covered by a certificate of title from this State remains perfected until the security interest would have become unperfected under the law of the other jurisdiction had the goods not become so covered.

(e) [**When subsection (d) security interest becomes unperfected against purchasers.**] A security interest described in subsection (d) becomes unperfected as against a purchaser of the goods for value and is deemed never to have been perfected as against a purchaser of the goods for value if the applicable requirements for perfection under Section 9–311(b) or 9–313 are not satisfied before the earlier of:

(1) the time the security interest would have become unperfected under the law of the other jurisdiction had the goods not become covered by a certificate of title from this State; or

(2) the expiration of four months after the goods had become so covered.

(f) [**Change in jurisdiction of bank, issuer, nominated person, securities intermediary, or commodity intermediary.**] A security interest in deposit accounts, letter-of-credit rights, or investment property which is perfected under the law of the bank's jurisdiction, the issuer's jurisdiction, a nominated person's jurisdiction, the securities intermediary's jurisdiction, or the commodity intermediary's jurisdiction, as applicable, remains perfected until the earlier of:

(1) the time the security interest would have become unperfected under the law of that jurisdiction; or

(2) the expiration of four months after a change of the applicable jurisdiction to another jurisdiction.

(g) [**Subsection (f) security interest perfected or unperfected under law of new jurisdiction.**] If a security interest described in subsection (f) becomes perfected under the law of the other jurisdiction before the earlier of the time or the end of the period described in that subsection, it remains perfected thereafter. If the security interest does not become perfected under the law of the other jurisdiction before the earlier of that time or the end of that period, it becomes unperfected and is deemed never to have been perfected as against a purchaser of the collateral for value.

Official Comment

1. **Source.** Former Section 9–103(1)(d), (2)(b), (3)(e), as modified.

2. **Continued Perfection.** This section deals with continued perfection of security interests that have been perfected under the law of another jurisdiction. The fact that the law of a particular jurisdiction ceases to govern perfection under Sections 9–301 through 9–307 does not necessarily mean that a security interest perfected under that law automatically becomes unperfected. To the contrary: This section generally provides that a security interest perfected under the law of one jurisdiction remains perfected for a fixed period of time (four months or one year, depending on the circumstances), even though the jurisdiction whose law governs perfection changes. However, cessation of perfection under the law of the original jurisdiction cuts short the fixed period. The four-month and one-year periods are long enough for a secured party to discover in most cases that the law of a different jurisdiction governs perfection and to reperfect (typically by filing) under the law of that jurisdiction. If a secured party properly reperfects a security interest before it becomes unperfected under subsection (a), then the security interest remains perfected continuously thereafter. See subsection (b).

Example 1: Debtor is a general partnership whose chief executive office is in Pennsylvania. Lender perfects a security interest in Debtor's equipment by filing in Pennsylvania on May 15, 2002. On April 1, 2005, without Lender's knowledge, Debtor moves its chief executive office to New Jersey. Lender's security interest remains perfected for four months after the move. See subsection (a)(2).

Example 2: Debtor is a general partnership whose chief executive office is in Pennsylvania. Lender perfects a security interest in Debtor's equipment by filing in Pennsylvania on May 15, 2002. On April 1, 2007, without Lender's knowledge, Debtor moves its chief executive office to New Jersey. Lender's security interest remains perfected only through May 14, 2007, when the effectiveness of the filed financing statement lapses. See subsection (a)(1). Although, under these facts, Lender would have only a short period of time to discover that Debtor had relocated and to reperfect under New Jersey law, Lender could have protected itself by filing a continuation statement in Pennsylvania before Debtor relocated. By doing so, Lender would have prevented lapse and

allowed itself the full four months to discover Debtor's new location and refile there or, if Debtor is in default, to perfect by taking possession of the equipment.

Example 3: Under the facts of Example 2, Lender files a financing statement in New Jersey before the effectiveness of the Pennsylvania financing statement lapses. Under subsection (b), Lender's security interest is continuously perfected beyond May 14, 2007, for a period determined by New Jersey's Article 9.

Subsection (a)(3) allows a one-year period in which to reperfect. The longer period is necessary, because, even with the exercise of due diligence, the secured party may be unable to discover that the collateral has been transferred to a person located in another jurisdiction.

Example 4: Debtor is a Pennsylvania corporation. Lender perfects a security interest in Debtor's equipment by filing in Pennsylvania. Debtor's shareholders decide to "reincorporate" in Delaware. They form a Delaware corporation (Newcorp) into which they merge Debtor. The merger effectuates a transfer of the collateral from Debtor to Newcorp, which thereby becomes a debtor and is located in another jurisdiction. Under subsection (a)(3), the security interest remains perfected for one year after the merger. If a financing statement is filed in Delaware against Newcorp within the year following the merger, then the security interest remains perfected thereafter for a period determined by Delaware's Article 9.

Note that although Newcorp is a "new debtor" as defined in Section 9–102, the application of subsection (a)(3) is not limited to transferees who are new debtors. Note also that, under Section 9–507, the financing statement naming Debtor remains effective even though Newcorp has become the debtor.

This section addresses security interests that are perfected (i.e., that have attached and as to which any required perfection step has been taken) before the debtor changes its location. As the following example explains, this section does not apply to security interests that have not attached before the location changes.

Example 5: Debtor is a Pennsylvania corporation. Debtor grants to Lender a security interest in Debtor's existing and after-acquired inventory. Lender perfects by filing in Pennsylvania. Debtor's shareholders decide to "reincorporate" in Delaware. They form a Delaware corporation (Newcorp) into which they merge Debtor. By virtue of the merger, Newcorp becomes bound by Debtor's security agreement. See Section 9–203. After the merger, Newcorp acquires inventory to which Lender's security interest attaches. Because Newcorp is located in Delaware, Delaware law governs perfection of a security interest in Newcorp's inventory. See Sections 9–301, 9–307. Having failed to perfect under Delaware law, Lender holds an unperfected security interest in the inventory acquired by Newcorp after the merger. The same result follows regardless of the name of the Delaware corporation (i.e., even if the Delaware corporation and Debtor have the same name). A different result would occur if Debtor and Newcorp were incorporated in the same state. See Section 9–508, Comment 4.

3. **Retroactive Unperfection.** Subsection (b) sets forth the consequences of the failure to reperfect before perfection ceases under subsection (a): the security interest becomes unperfected prospectively and, as against purchasers for value, including buyers and secured parties, but not as against donees or lien creditors, retroactively. The rule applies to agricultural liens, as well. See also Section 9–515 (taking the same approach with respect to lapse). Although this approach creates the potential for circular priorities, the alternative—retroactive unperfection against lien creditors—would create substantial and unjustifiable preference risks.

Example 6: Under the facts of Example 4, six months after the merger, Buyer bought from Newcorp some equipment formerly owned by Debtor. At the time of the purchase, Buyer took subject to Lender's perfected security interest, of which Buyer was unaware. See Section 9–315(a)(1). However, subsection (b) provides that if Lender fails to reperfect in Delaware within a year after the merger, its security interest becomes unperfected and is deemed never to have been perfected against Buyer. Having given value and received delivery of the equipment without knowledge of the security interest and before it was perfected, Buyer would take free of the security interest. See Section 9–317(b).

Example 7: Under the facts of Example 4, one month before the merger, Debtor created a security interest in certain equipment in favor of Financer, who perfected by filing in Pennsylvania. At that time, Financer's security interest is subordinate to Lender's. See Section 9–322(a)(1). Financer reperfects by filing in Delaware within a year after the merger, but Lender fails to do so. Under subsection (b), Lender's security interest is deemed never to have been perfected against Financer, a purchaser

for value. Consequently, under Section 9–322(a)(2), Financer's security interest is now senior.

Of course, the expiration of the time period specified in subsection (a) does not of itself prevent the secured party from later reperfecting under the law of the new jurisdiction. If the secured party does so, however, there will be a gap in perfection, and the secured party may lose priority as a result. Thus, in Example 7, if Lender perfects by filing in Delaware more than one year under the merger, it will have a new date of filing and perfection for purposes of Section 9–322(a)(1). Financer's security interest, whose perfection dates back to the filing in Pennsylvania under subsection (b), will remain senior.

4. **Possessory Security Interests.** Subsection (c) deals with continued perfection of possessory security interests. It applies not only to security interests perfected solely by the secured party's having taken possession of the collateral. It also applies to security interests perfected by a method that includes as an element of perfection the secured party's having taken possession, such as perfection by taking delivery of a certificated security in registered form, see Section 9–313(a), and perfection by obtaining control over a certificated security. See Section 9–314(a).

5. **Goods Covered by Certificate of Title.** Subsections (d) and (e) address continued perfection of a security interest in goods covered by a certificate of title. The following examples explain the operation of those subsections.

Example 8: Debtor's automobile is covered by a certificate of title issued by Illinois. Lender perfects a security interest in the automobile by complying with Illinois' certificate-of-title statute. Thereafter, Debtor applies for a certificate of title in Indiana. Six months thereafter, Creditor acquires a judicial lien on the automobile. Under Section 9–303(b), Illinois law ceases to govern perfection; rather, once Debtor delivers the application and applicable fee to the appropriate Indiana authority, Indiana law governs. Nevertheless, under Indiana's Section 9–316(d), Lender's security interest remains perfected until it would become unperfected under Illinois law had no certificate of title been issued by Indiana. (For example, Illinois' certificate-of-title statute may provide that the surrender of an Illinois certificate of title in connection with the issuance of a certificate of title by another jurisdiction causes a security interest noted thereon to become unperfected.) If Lender's security interest remains perfected, it is senior to Creditor's judicial lien.

Example 9: Under the facts in Example 8, five months after Debtor applies for an Indiana certificate of title, Debtor sells the automobile to Buyer. Under subsection (e)(2), because Lender did not reperfect within the four months after the goods became covered by the Indiana certificate of title, Lender's security interest is deemed never to have been perfected against Buyer. Under Section 9–317(b), Buyer is likely to take free of the security interest. Lender could have protected itself by perfecting its security interest either under Indiana's certificate-of-title statute, see Section 9–311, or, if it had a right to do so under an agreement or Section 9–609, by taking possession of the automobile. See Section 9–313(b).

The results in Examples 8 and 9 do not depend on the fact that the original perfection was achieved by notation on a certificate of title. Subsection (d) applies regardless of the method by which a security interest is perfected under the law of another jurisdiction when the goods became covered by a certificate of title from this State.

Section 9–337 affords protection to a limited class of persons buying or acquiring a security interest in the goods while a security interest is perfected under the law of another jurisdiction but after this State has issued a clean certificate of title.

6. **Deposit Accounts, Letter-of-Credit Rights, and Investment Property.** Subsections (f) and (g) address changes in the jurisdiction of a bank, issuer of an uncertificated security, issuer of or nominated person under a letter of credit, securities intermediary, and commodity intermediary. The provisions are analogous to those of subsections (a) and (b).

7. **Agricultural Liens.** This section does not apply to agricultural liens.

Example 10: Supplier holds an agricultural lien on corn. The lien arises under an Iowa statute. Supplier perfects by filing a financing statement in Iowa, where the corn is located. See Section 9–302. Debtor stores the corn in Missouri. Assume the Iowa agricultural lien survives or an agricultural lien arises under Missouri law (matters that this Article does not govern). Once the corn is located in Missouri, Missouri becomes the jurisdiction whose law governs perfection. See Section 9–302. Thus, the agricultural lien will not be perfected unless Supplier files a financing statement in Missouri.

As amended in 2000.

[SUBPART 3. PRIORITY]

§ 9–317. Interests That Take Priority Over or Take Free of Security Interest or Agricultural Lien.

(a) **[Conflicting security interests and rights of lien creditors.]** A security interest or agricultural lien is subordinate to the rights of:

(1) a person entitled to priority under Section 9–322; and

(2) except as otherwise provided in subsection (e), a person that becomes a lien creditor before the earlier of the time:

(A) the security interest or agricultural lien is perfected; or

(B) one of the conditions specified in Section 9–203(b)(3) is met and a financing statement covering the collateral is filed.

(b) **[Buyers that receive delivery.]** Except as otherwise provided in subsection (e), a buyer, other than a secured party, of tangible chattel paper, tangible documents, goods, instruments, or a security certificate takes free of a security interest or agricultural lien if the buyer gives value and receives delivery of the collateral without knowledge of the security interest or agricultural lien and before it is perfected.

(c) **[Lessees that receive delivery.]** Except as otherwise provided in subsection (e), a lessee of goods takes free of a security interest or agricultural lien if the lessee gives value and receives delivery of the collateral without knowledge of the security interest or agricultural lien and before it is perfected.

(d) **[Licensees and buyers of certain collateral.]** A licensee of a general intangible or a buyer, other than a secured party, of accounts, electronic chattel paper, electronic documents, general intangibles, or investment property other than a certificated security takes free of a security interest if the licensee or buyer gives value without knowledge of the security interest and before it is perfected.

(e) **[Purchase-money security interest.]** Except as otherwise provided in Sections 9–320 and 9–321, if a person files a financing statement with respect to a purchase-money security interest before or within 20 days after the debtor receives delivery of the collateral, the security interest takes priority over the rights of a buyer, lessee, or lien creditor which arise between the time the security interest attaches and the time of filing.

As amended in 2000 and 2003.

Official Comment

1. **Source.** Former Sections 9–301, 2A–307(2).

2. **Scope of This Section.** As did former Section 9–301, this section lists the classes of persons who take priority over, or take free of, an unperfected security interest. Section 9–308 explains when a security interest or agricultural lien is "perfected." A security interest that has attached (see Section 9–203) but as to which a required perfection step has not been taken is "unperfected." Certain provisions have been moved from former Section 9–301. The definition of "lien creditor" now appears in Section 9–102, and the rules governing priority in future advances are found in Section 9–323.

3. **Competing Security Interests.** Section 9–322 states general rules for determining priority among conflicting security interests and refers to other sections that state special rules of priority in a variety of situations. The security interests given priority under Section 9–322 and the other sections to which it refers take priority in general even over a perfected security interest. *A fortiori* they take priority over an unperfected security interest. *Paragraph (a)(1) of this section so states.**

4. **Filed but Unattached Security Interest vs. Lien Creditor.** Under former Section 9–301(1)(b), a lien creditor's rights had priority over an unperfected security interest. Perfection required attachment (former Section 9–303), and attachment required the giving of value (former Section 9–203). It followed that, if a secured party had filed a financing statement, but the debtor had not entered into a security agreement and value had not yet been given, an intervening lien creditor whose lien arose after filing but before attachment of the security interest acquired rights that are senior to those of the secured party who later gives value. This result comported with the *nemo dat* concept: When the security interest attached, the collateral was already subject to the judicial lien.

* Amendments in italics approved by the Permanent Editorial Board for Uniform Commercial Code Oct. 20, 1999.

On the other hand, this approach treated the first secured advance differently from all other advances, even in circumstances in which a security agreement covering the collateral had been entered into before the judicial lien attached. The special rule for future advances in former Section 9–301(4) (substantially reproduced in Section 9–323(b)) afforded priority to a discretionary advance made by a secured party within 45 days after the lien creditor's rights arose as long as the secured party was "perfected" when the lien creditor's lien arose–i.e., as long as the advance was not the first one and an earlier advance had been made.

Subsection (a)(2) revises former Section 9–301(1)(b) and, in appropriate cases, treats the first advance the same as subsequent advances. More specifically, a judicial lien that arises after the security-agreement condition of Section 9–203(b)(3) is satisfied and a financing statement is filed, but before the security interest attaches and becomes perfected, is subordinate to all advances secured by the security interest, even the first advance, except as otherwise provided in Section 9–323(b). However, if the security interest becomes unperfected (e.g., because the effectiveness of the filed financing statement lapses) before the judicial lien arises, the security interest is subordinate. If a financing statement is filed but a security interest does not attach, then no priority contest arises. The lien creditor has the only enforceable claim to the property.

5. **Security Interest of Consignor or Receivables Buyer vs. Lien Creditor.** Section 1–201(37) defines "security interest" to include the interest of most true consignors of goods and the interest of most buyers of certain receivables (accounts, chattel paper, payment intangibles, and promissory notes). A consignee of goods or a seller of accounts or chattel paper each is deemed to have rights in the collateral which a lien creditor may reach, as long as the competing security interest of the consignor or buyer is unperfected. This is so even though, as between the consignor and the debtor-consignee, the latter has only limited rights, and, as between the buyer and debtor-seller, the latter does not have any rights in the collateral. See Sections 9–318 (seller), 9–319 (consignee). Security interests arising from sales of payment intangibles and promissory notes are automatically perfected. See Section 9–309. Accordingly, a subsequent judicial lien always would be subordinate to the rights of a buyer of those types of receivables.

6. **Purchasers Other Than Secured Parties.** Subsections (b), (c), and (d) afford priority over an unperfected security interest to certain purchasers (other than secured parties) of collateral. They derive from former Sections 9–301(1)(c), 2A–307(2), and 9–301(d). Former Section 9–301(1)(c) and (1)(d) provided that unperfected security interests are "subordinate" to the rights of certain purchasers. But, as former Comment 9 suggested, the practical effect of subordination in this context is that the purchaser takes free of the security interest. To avoid any possible misinterpretation, subsections (b) and (d) of this section use the phrase "takes free."

Subsection (b) governs goods, as well as intangibles of the type whose transfer is effected by physical delivery of the representative piece of paper (tangible chattel paper, tangible documents, instruments, and security certificates). To obtain priority, a buyer must both give value and receive delivery of the collateral without knowledge of the existing security interest and before perfection. Even if the buyer gave value without knowledge and before perfection, the buyer would take subject to the security interest if perfection occurred before physical delivery of the collateral to the buyer. Subsection (c) contains a similar rule with respect to lessees of goods. Note that a lessee of goods in ordinary course of business takes free of all security interests created by the lessor, even if perfected. See Section 9–321.

Normally, there will be no question when a buyer of tangible chattel paper, tangible documents, instruments, or security certificates "receives delivery" of the property. See Section 1–201 (defining "delivery"). However, sometimes a buyer or lessee of goods, such as complex machinery, takes delivery of the goods in stages and completes assembly at its own location. Under those circumstances, the buyer or lessee "receives delivery" within the meaning of subsections (b) and (c) when, after an inspection of the portion of the goods remaining with the seller or lessor, it would be apparent to a potential lender to the seller or lessor that another person might have an interest in the goods.

The rule of subsection (b) obviously is not appropriate where the collateral consists of intangibles and there is no representative piece of paper whose physical delivery is the only or the customary method of transfer. Therefore, with respect to such intangibles (accounts, electronic chattel paper, electronic documents, general intangibles, and investment property other than certificated securities), subsection (d) gives priority to any buyer who gives value without knowledge, and before perfection, of the security interest. A licensee of a general intangible takes free of an unperfected security interest in the general intangible under the same circumstances. Note that a licensee of a general intangible in ordinary course of business takes rights under a nonexclusive license free of security interests created by the licensor, even if perfected. See Section 9–321.

Unless Section 9–109 excludes the transaction from this Article, a buyer of accounts, chattel paper, payment intangibles, or promissory notes is a "secured party" (defined in Section 9–102), and subsections (b) and (d) do not determine priority of the security interest created by the sale. Rather, the priority rules generally applicable to competing security interests apply. See Section 9–322.

7. **Agricultural Liens.** Subsections (a), (b), and (c) subordinate unperfected agricultural liens in the same manner in which they subordinate unperfected security interests.

8. **Purchase-Money Security Interests.** Subsection (e) derives from former Section 9–301(2). It provides that, if a purchase-money security interest is perfected by filing no later than 20 days after the debtor receives delivery of the collateral, the security interest takes priority over the rights of buyers, lessees, or lien creditors which arise between the time the security interest attaches and the time of filing. Subsection (e) differs from former Section 9–301(2) in two significant respects. First, subsection (e) protects a purchase-money security interest against all buyers and lessees, not just against transferees in bulk. Second, subsection (e) conditions this protection on filing within 20, as opposed to ten, days after delivery.

Section 9–311(b) provides that compliance with the perfection requirements of a statute or treaty described in Section 9–311(a) "is equivalent to the filing of a financing statement." It follows that a person who perfects a security interest in goods covered by a certificate of title by complying with the perfection requirements of an applicable certificate-of-title statute "files a financing statement" within the meaning of subsection(e).

As amended in 1999, 2000 and 2003.

§ 9–318. No Interest Retained in Right to Payment That Is Sold; Rights and Title of Seller of Account or Chattel Paper With Respect to Creditors and Purchasers.

(a) **[Seller retains no interest.]** A debtor that has sold an account, chattel paper, payment intangible, or promissory note does not retain a legal or equitable interest in the collateral sold.

(b) **[Deemed rights of debtor if buyer's security interest unperfected.]** For purposes of determining the rights of creditors of, and purchasers for value of an account or chattel paper from, a debtor that has sold an account or chattel paper, while the buyer's security interest is unperfected, the debtor is deemed to have rights and title to the account or chattel paper identical to those the debtor sold.

Official Comment

1. **Source.** New.

2. **Sellers of Accounts, Chattel Paper, Payment Intangibles, and Promissory Notes.** Section 1–201(37) defines "security interest" to include the interest of a buyer of accounts, chattel paper, payment intangibles, or promissory notes. See also Section 9–109(a) and Comment 5. Subsection (a) makes explicit what was implicit, but perfectly obvious, under former Article 9: The fact that a sale of an account or chattel paper gives rise to a "security interest" does not imply that the seller retains an interest in the property that has been sold. To the contrary, a seller of an account or chattel paper retains no interest whatsoever in the property to the extent that it has been sold. Subsection (a) also applies to sales of payment intangibles and promissory notes, transactions that were not covered by former Article 9. Neither this Article nor the definition of "security interest" in Section 1–201 provides rules for distinguishing sales transactions from those that create a security interest securing an obligation.

3. **Buyers of Accounts and Chattel Paper.** Another aspect of sales of accounts and chattel paper also was implicit, and equally obvious, under former Article 9: If the buyer's security interest is unperfected, then for purposes of determining the rights of certain third parties, the seller (debtor) is deemed to have all rights and title that the seller sold. The seller is deemed to have these rights even though, as between the parties, it has sold all its rights to the buyer. Subsection (b) makes this explicit. As a consequence of subsection (b), if the buyer's security interest is unperfected, the seller can transfer, and the creditors of the seller can reach, the account or chattel paper as if it had not been sold.

Example: Debtor sells accounts or chattel paper to Buyer–1 and retains no interest in them. Buyer–1 does not file a financing statement. Debtor then sells the same receivables to Buyer–2. Buyer–2 files a proper financing statement. Having sold the receivables to Buyer–1, Debtor would not have any rights

in the collateral so as to permit Buyer–2's security (ownership) interest to attach. Nevertheless, under this section, for purposes of determining the rights of purchasers for value from Debtor, Debtor is deemed to have the rights that Debtor sold. Accordingly, Buyer–2's security interest attaches, is perfected by the filing, and, under Section 9–322, is senior to Buyer–1's interest.

4. **Effect of Perfection.** If the security interest of a buyer of accounts or chattel paper is perfected the usual result would take effect: transferees from and creditors of the seller could not acquire an interest in the sold accounts or chattel paper. The same result generally would occur if payment intangibles or promissory notes were sold, inasmuch as the buyer's security interest is automatically perfected under Section 9–309. However, in certain circumstances a purchaser who takes possession of a promissory note will achieve priority, under Sections 9–330 or 9–331, over the security interest of an earlier buyer of the promissory note. It necessarily follows that the seller in those circumstances retains the power to transfer the promissory note, as if it had not been sold, to a purchaser who obtains priority under either of those sections. See Section 9–203(b)(3), Comment 6.

§ 9–319.   Rights and Title of Consignee With Respect to Creditors and Purchasers.

(a) **[Consignee has consignor's rights.]** Except as otherwise provided in subsection (b), for purposes of determining the rights of creditors of, and purchasers for value of goods from, a consignee, while the goods are in the possession of the consignee, the consignee is deemed to have rights and title to the goods identical to those the consignor had or had power to transfer.

(b) **[Applicability of other law.]** For purposes of determining the rights of a creditor of a consignee, law other than this article determines the rights and title of a consignee while goods are in the consignee's possession if, under this part, a perfected security interest held by the consignor would have priority over the rights of the creditor.

Official Comment

1. **Source.** New.

2. **Consignments.** This section takes an approach to consignments similar to that taken by Section 9–318 with respect to buyers of accounts and chattel paper.

Revised Section 1–201(37) defines "security interest" to include the interest of a consignor of goods under many true consignments. Section 9–319(a) provides that, for purposes of determining the rights of certain third parties, the consignee is deemed to acquire all rights and title that the consignor had, if the consignor's security interest is unperfected. The consignee acquires these rights even though, as between the parties, it purchases a limited interest in the goods (as would be the case in a true consignment, under which the consignee acquires only the interest of a bailee). As a consequence of this section, creditors of the consignee can acquire judicial liens and security interests in the goods.

Insofar as creditors of the consignee are concerned, this Article to a considerable extent reformulates the former law, which appeared in former Sections 2–326 and 9–114, without changing the results. However, neither Article 2 nor former Article 9 specifically addresses the rights of non-ordinary course buyers from the consignee. Former Section 9–114 contained priority rules applicable to security interests in consigned goods. Under this Article, the priority rules for purchase-money security interests in inventory apply to consignments. See Section 9–103(d). Accordingly, a special section containing priority rules for consignments no longer is needed. Section 9–317 determines whether the rights of a judicial lien creditor are senior to the interest of the consignor, Sections 9–322 and 9–324 govern competing security interests in consigned goods, and Sections 9–317, 9–315, and 9–320 determine whether a buyer takes free of the consignor's interest.

The following example explains the operation of this section:

Example 1: SP–1 delivers goods to Debtor in a transaction constituting a "consignment" as defined in Section 9–102. SP–1 does not file a financing statement. Debtor then grants a security interest in the goods to SP–2. SP–2 files a proper financing statement. Assuming Debtor is a mere bailee, as in a "true" consignment, Debtor would not have any rights in the collateral (beyond those of a bailee) so as to permit SP–2's security interest to attach to any greater rights. Nevertheless, under this section, for purposes of determining the rights of Debtor's creditors, Debtor is deemed to acquire SP–1's rights. Accordingly, SP–2's security interest attaches, is perfected by the filing, and, under Section 9–322, is senior to SP–1's interest.

3. **Effect of Perfection.** Subsection (b) contains a special rule with respect to consignments that are perfected. If application of this Article would result in

the consignor having priority over a competing creditor, then other law determines the rights and title of the consignee.

Example 2: SP–1 delivers goods to Debtor in a transaction constituting a "consignment" as defined in Section 9–102. SP–1 files a proper financing statement. Debtor then grants a security interest in the goods to SP–2. Under Section 9–322, SP–1's security interest is senior to SP–2's. Subsection (b) indicates that, for purposes of determining SP–2's rights, other law determines the rights and title of the consignee. If, for example, a consignee obtains only the special property of a bailee, then SP–2's security interest would attach only to that special property.

Example 3: SP–1 obtains a security interest in all Debtor's existing and after-acquired inventory. SP–1 perfects its security interest with a proper filing. Then SP–2 delivers goods to Debtor in a transaction constituting a "consignment" as defined in Section 9–102. SP–2 files a proper financing statement but does not send notification to SP–1 under Section 9–324(b). Accordingly, SP–2's security interest is junior to SP–1's under Section 9–322(a). Under Section 9–319(a), Debtor is deemed to have the consignor's rights and title, so that SP–1's security interest attaches to SP–2's ownership interest in the goods. Thereafter, Debtor grants a security interest in the goods to SP–3, and SP–3 perfects by filing. Because SP–2's perfected security interest is senior to SP–3's under Section 9–322(a), Section 9–319(b) applies: Other law determines Debtor's rights and title to the goods insofar as SP–3 is concerned, and SP–3's security interest attaches to those rights.

§ 9–320. Buyer of Goods.

(a) **[Buyer in ordinary course of business.]** Except as otherwise provided in subsection (e), a buyer in ordinary course of business, other than a person buying farm products from a person engaged in farming operations, takes free of a security interest created by the buyer's seller, even if the security interest is perfected and the buyer knows of its existence.

(b) **[Buyer of consumer goods.]** Except as otherwise provided in subsection (e), a buyer of goods from a person who used or bought the goods for use primarily for personal, family, or household purposes takes free of a security interest, even if perfected, if the buyer buys:

(1) without knowledge of the security interest;

(2) for value;

§9–320

§9–320

(3) primarily for the buyer's personal, family, or household purposes; and

(4) before the filing of a financing statement covering the goods.

(c) **[Effectiveness of filing for subsection (b).]** To the extent that it affects the priority of a security interest over a buyer of goods under subsection (b), the period of effectiveness of a filing made in the jurisdiction in which the seller is located is governed by Section 9–316(a) and (b).

(d) **[Buyer in ordinary course of business at wellhead or minehead.]** A buyer in ordinary course of business buying oil, gas, or other minerals at the wellhead or minehead or after extraction takes free of an interest arising out of an encumbrance.

(e) **[Possessory security interest not affected.]** Subsections (a) and (b) do not affect a security interest in goods in the possession of the secured party under Section 9–313.

Official Comment

1. **Source.** Former Section 9–307.

2. **Scope of This Section.** This section states when buyers of goods take free of a security interest even though perfected. Of course, a buyer who takes free of a perfected security interest takes free of an unperfected one. Section 9–317 should be consulted to determine what purchasers, in addition to the buyers covered in this section, take free of an unperfected security interest. Article 2 states general rules on purchase of goods from a seller with defective or voidable title (Section 2–403).

3. **Buyers in Ordinary Course.** Subsection (a) derives from former Section 9–307(1). The definition of "buyer in ordinary course of business" in Section 1–201 restricts its application to buyers "from a person, other than a pawnbroker, in the business of selling goods of that kind." Thus subsection (a) applies primarily to inventory collateral. The subsection further excludes from its operation buyers of "farm products"(defined in Section 9–102) from a person engaged in farming operations. The buyer in ordinary course of business is defined as one who buys goods "in good faith, without knowledge that the sale violates the rights of another person and in the ordinary course." Subsection (a) provides that such a buyer takes free of a security interest, even though perfected, and even though the buyer knows the security interest exists. Reading the definition together with the rule of law

results in the buyer's taking free if the buyer merely knows that a security interest covers the goods but taking subject if the buyer knows, in addition, that the sale violates a term in an agreement with the secured party.

As did former Section 9–307(1), subsection (a) applies only to security interests created by the seller of the goods to the buyer in ordinary course. However, under certain circumstances a buyer in ordinary course who buys goods that were encumbered with a security interest created by a person other than the seller may take free of the security interest, as Example 2 explains. See also Comment 6, below.

Example 1: Manufacturer, who is in the business of manufacturing appliances, owns manufacturing equipment subject to a perfected security interest in favor of Lender. Manufacturer sells the equipment to Dealer, who is in the business of buying and selling used equipment. Buyer buys the equipment from Dealer. Even if Buyer qualifies as a buyer in the ordinary course of business, Buyer does not take free of Lender's security interest under subsection (a), because Dealer did not create the security interest; Manufacturer did.

Example 2: Manufacturer, who is in the business of manufacturing appliances, owns manufacturing equipment subject to a perfected security interest in favor of Lender. Manufacturer sells the equipment to Dealer, who is in the business of buying and selling used equipment. Lender learns of the sale but does nothing to assert its security interest. Buyer buys the equipment from Dealer. Inasmuch as Lender's acquiescence constitutes an "entrusting" of the goods to Dealer within the meaning of Section 2–403(3) Buyer takes free of Lender's security interest under Section 2–403(2) if Buyer qualifies as a buyer in ordinary course of business.

4. **Buyers of Farm Products.** This section does not enable a buyer of farm products to take free of a security interest created by the seller, even if the buyer is a buyer in ordinary course of business. However, a buyer of farm products may take free of a security interest under Section 1324 of the Food Security Act of 1985, 7 U.S.C. § 1631.

5. **Buyers of Consumer Goods.** Subsection (b), which derives from former Section 9–307(2), deals with buyers of collateral that the debtor-seller holds as "consumer goods" (defined in Section 9–102). Under Section 9–309(1), a purchase-money interest in consumer goods, except goods that are subject to a statute or treaty described in Section 9–311(a) (such as automobiles that are subject to a certificate-of-title statute),

is perfected automatically upon attachment. There is no need to file to perfect. Under subsection (b) a buyer of consumer goods takes free of a security interest, even though perfected, if the buyer buys (1) without knowledge of the security interest, (2) for value, (3) primarily for the buyer's own personal, family, or household purposes, and (4) before a financing statement is filed.

As to purchase money-security interests which are perfected without filing under Section 9–309(1): A secured party may file a financing statement, although filing is not required for perfection. If the secured party does file, all buyers take subject to the security interest. If the secured party does not file, a buyer who meets the qualifications stated in the preceding paragraph takes free of the security interest.

As to security interests for which a perfection step is required: This category includes all non-purchase-money security interests, and all security interests, whether or not purchase-money, in goods subject to a statute or treaty described in Section 9–311(a), such as automobiles covered by a certificate-of-title statute. As long as the required perfection step has not been taken and the security interest remains unperfected, not only the buyers described in subsection (b) but also the purchasers described in Section 9–317 will take free of the security interest. After a financing statement has been filed or the perfection requirements of the applicable certificate-of-title statute have been complied with (compliance is the equivalent of filing a financing statement; see Section 9–311(b)), all subsequent buyers, under the rule of subsection (b), are subject to the security interest.

The rights of a buyer under subsection (b) turn on whether a financing statement has been filed against consumer goods. Occasionally, a debtor changes his or her location after a filing is made. Subsection (c), which derives from former Section 9–103(1)(d)(iii), deals with the continued effectiveness of the filing under those circumstances. It adopts the rules of Sections 9–316(a) and (b). These rules are explained in the Comments to that section.

6. **Authorized Dispositions.** The limitations that subsections (a) and (b) impose on the persons who may take free of a security interest apply of course only to unauthorized sales by the debtor. If the secured party authorized the sale in an express agreement or otherwise, the buyer takes free under Section 9–315(a) without regard to the limitations of this section. (That section also states the right of a secured party to the proceeds of a sale, authorized or unauthorized.) Moreover, the buyer also takes free if the secured party

waived or otherwise is precluded from asserting its security interest against the buyer. See Section 1–103.

7. **Oil, Gas, and Other Minerals.** Under subsection (d), a buyer in ordinary course of business of minerals at the wellhead or minehead or after extraction takes free of a security interest created by the seller. Specifically, it provides that qualified buyers take free not only of Article 9 security interests but also of interests "arising out of an encumbrance." As defined in Section 9–102, the term "encumbrance" means "a right, other than an ownership interest, in real property." Thus, to the extent that a mortgage encumbers minerals not only before but also after extraction, subsection (d) enables a buyer in ordinary course of the minerals to take free of the mortgage. This subsection does not, however, enable these buyers to take free of interests arising out of ownership interests in the real property. This issue is significant only in a minority of states. Several of them have adopted special statutes and nonuniform amendments to Article 9 to provide special protections to mineral owners, whose interests often are highly fractionalized in the case of oil and gas. See Terry I. Cross, *Oil and Gas Product Liens—Statutory Security Interests for Producers and Royalty Owners Under the Statutes of Kansas, New Mexico, Oklahoma, Texas and Wyoming*, 50 Consumer Fin. L. Q. Rep. 418 (1996). Inasmuch as a complete resolution of the issue would require the addition of complex provisions to this Article, and there are good reasons to believe that a uniform solution would not be feasible, this Article leaves its resolution to other legislation.

8. **Possessory Security Interests.** Subsection (e) is new. It rejects the holding of *Tanbro Fabrics Corp. v. Deering Milliken, Inc.*, 350 N.E.2d 590 (N.Y. 1976) and, together with Section 9–317(b), prevents a buyer of goods collateral from taking free of a security interest if the collateral is in the possession of the secured party. "The secured party" referred in subsection (e) is the holder of the security interest referred to in subsection (a) or (b). Section 9–313 determines whether a secured party is in possession for purposes of this section. Under some circumstances, Section 9–313 provides that a secured party is in possession of collateral even if the collateral is in the physical possession of a third party.

§ 9–321. Licensee of General Intangible and Lessee of Goods in Ordinary Course of Business.

(a) **["Licensee in ordinary course of business."]** In this section, "licensee in ordinary course of business" means a person that becomes a licensee of a general intangible in good faith, without knowledge that the license violates the rights of another person in the general intangible, and in the ordinary course from a person in the business of licensing general intangibles of that kind. A person becomes a licensee in the ordinary course if the license to the person comports with the usual or customary practices in the kind of business in which the licensor is engaged or with the licensor's own usual or customary practices.

(b) **[Rights of licensee in ordinary course of business.]** A licensee in ordinary course of business takes its rights under a nonexclusive license free of a security interest in the general intangible created by the licensor, even if the security interest is perfected and the licensee knows of its existence.

(c) **[Rights of lessee in ordinary course of business.]** A lessee in ordinary course of business takes its leasehold interest free of a security interest in the goods created by the lessor, even if the security interest is perfected and the lessee knows of its existence.

Official Comment

1. **Source.** Derived from Sections 2A–103(1)(o), 2A–307(3).

2. **Licensee in Ordinary Course.** Like the analogous rules in Section 9–320(a) with respect to buyers in ordinary course and subsection (c) with respect to lessees in ordinary course, the new rule in subsection (b) reflects the expectations of the parties and the marketplace: a licensee under a nonexclusive license takes subject to a security interest unless the secured party authorizes the license free of the security interest or other, controlling law such as that of this section (protecting ordinary-course licensees) dictates a contrary result. See Sections 9–201, 9–315. The definition of "licensee in ordinary course of business" in subsection (a) is modeled upon that of "buyer in ordinary course of business."

3. **Lessee in Ordinary Course.** Subsection (c) contains the rule formerly found in Section 2A–307(3). The rule works in the same way as that of Section 9–320(a).

§ 9–322. Priorities Among Conflicting Security Interests in and Agricultural Liens on Same Collateral.

(a) **[General priority rules.]** Except as otherwise provided in this section, priority among conflicting security interests and agricultural liens in the same collateral is determined according to the following rules:

(1) Conflicting perfected security interests and agricultural liens rank according to priority in time of filing or perfection. Priority dates from the earlier of the time a filing covering the collateral is first made or the security interest or agricultural lien is first perfected, if there is no period thereafter when there is neither filing nor perfection.

(2) A perfected security interest or agricultural lien has priority over a conflicting unperfected security interest or agricultural lien.

(3) The first security interest or agricultural lien to attach or become effective has priority if conflicting security interests and agricultural liens are unperfected.

(b) **[Time of perfection: proceeds and supporting obligations.]** For the purposes of subsection (a)(1):

(1) the time of filing or perfection as to a security interest in collateral is also the time of filing or perfection as to a security interest in proceeds; and

(2) the time of filing or perfection as to a security interest in collateral supported by a supporting obligation is also the time of filing or perfection as to a security interest in the supporting obligation.

(c) **[Special priority rules: proceeds and supporting obligations.]** Except as otherwise provided in subsection (f), a security interest in collateral which qualifies for priority over a conflicting security interest under Section 9–327, 9–328, 9–329, 9–330, or 9–331 also has priority over a conflicting security interest in:

(1) any supporting obligation for the collateral; and

(2) proceeds of the collateral if:

(A) the security interest in proceeds is perfected;

(B) the proceeds are cash proceeds or of the same type as the collateral; and

(C) in the case of proceeds that are proceeds of proceeds, all intervening proceeds are cash proceeds, proceeds of the same type as the collateral, or an account relating to the collateral.

(d) **[First-to-file priority rule for certain collateral.]** Subject to subsection (e) and except as otherwise provided in subsection (f), if a security interest in chattel paper, deposit accounts, negotiable documents, instruments, investment property, or letter-of-credit rights is perfected by a method other than filing, conflicting perfected security interests in proceeds of the collateral rank according to priority in time of filing.

(e) **[Applicability of subsection (d).]** Subsection (d) applies only if the proceeds of the collateral are not cash proceeds, chattel paper, negotiable documents, instruments, investment property, or letter-of-credit rights.

(f) **[Limitations on subsections (a) through (e).]** Subsections (a) through (e) are subject to:

(1) subsection (g) and the other provisions of this part;

(2) Section 4–210 with respect to a security interest of a collecting bank;

(3) Section 5–118 with respect to a security interest of an issuer or nominated person; and

(4) Section 9–110 with respect to a security interest arising under Article 2 or 2A.

(g) **[Priority under agricultural lien statute.]** A perfected agricultural lien on collateral has priority over a conflicting security interest in or agricultural lien on the same collateral if the statute creating the agricultural lien so provides.

Official Comment

1. **Source.** Former Section 9–312(5), (6).

2. **Scope of This Section.** In a variety of situations, two or more people may claim a security interest in the same collateral. This section states general rules of priority among conflicting security interests. As subsection (f) provides, the general rules in subsections (a) through (e) are subject to the rule in subsection (g) governing perfected agricultural liens and to the other rules in this Part of this Article. Rules that override this section include those applicable to purchase-money security interests (Section 9–324) and those qualifying for special priority in particular types of collateral. See, e.g., Section 9–327 (deposit accounts); Section 9–328 (investment property); Section 9–329 (letter-of-credit rights); Section 9–330 (chattel paper and instruments);

Section 9–334 (fixtures). In addition, the general rules of sections (a) through (e) are subject to priority rules governing security interests arising under Articles 2, 2A, 4, and 5.

3. **General Rules.** Subsection (a) contains three general rules. Subsection (a)(1) governs the priority of competing perfected security interests. Subsection (a)(2) governs the priority of competing security interests if one is perfected and the other is not. Subsection (a)(3) governs the priority of competing unperfected security interests. The rules may be regarded as adaptations of the idea, deeply rooted at common law, of a race of diligence among creditors. The first two rules are based on precedence in the time as of which the competing secured parties either filed their financing statements or obtained perfected security interests. Under subsection (a)(1), the first secured party who files or perfects has priority. Under subsection (a)(2), which is new, a perfected security interest has priority over an unperfected one. Under subsection (a)(3), if both security interests are unperfected, the first to attach has priority. Note that Section 9–709(b) may affect the application of subsection (a) to a filing that occurred before the effective date of this Article and which would be ineffective to perfect a security interest under former Article 9 but effective under this Article.

4. **Competing Perfected Security Interests.** When there is more than one perfected security interest, the security interests rank according to priority in time of filing or perfection. "Filing," of course, refers to the filing of an effective financing statement. "Perfection" refers to the acquisition of a perfected security interest, i.e., one that has attached and as to which any required perfection step has been taken. See Sections 9–308 and 9–309.

Example 1: On February 1, A files a financing statement covering a certain item of Debtor's equipment. On March 1, B files a financing statement covering the same equipment. On April 1, B makes a loan to Debtor and obtains a security interest in the equipment. On May 1, A makes a loan to Debtor and obtains a security interest in the same collateral. A has priority even though B's loan was made earlier and was perfected when made. It makes no difference whether A knew of B's security interest when A made its advance.

The problem stated in Example 1 is peculiar to a notice-filing system under which filing may occur before the security interest attaches (see Section 9–502). The justification for determining priority by order of filing lies in the necessity of protecting the filing system—that is, of allowing the first secured party who has filed to make subsequent advances without each time having to check for subsequent filings as a condition of protection. Note, however, that this first-to-file protection is not absolute. For example, Section 9–324 affords priority to certain purchase-money security interests, even if a competing secured party was the first to file or perfect.

Example 2: A and B make non-purchase-money advances secured by the same collateral. The collateral is in Debtor's possession, and neither security interest is perfected when the second advance is made. Whichever secured party first perfects its security interest (by taking possession of the collateral or by filing) takes priority. It makes no difference whether that secured party knows of the other security interest at the time it perfects its own.

The rule of subsection (a)(1), affording priority to the first to file or perfect, applies to security interests that are perfected by any method, including temporarily (Section 9–312) or upon attachment (Section 9–309), even though there may be no notice to creditors or subsequent purchasers and notwithstanding any common-law rule to the contrary. The form of the claim to priority, i.e., filing or perfection, may shift from time to time, and the rank will be based on the first filing or perfection as long as there is no intervening period without filing or perfection. See Section 9–308(c).

Example 3: On October 1, A acquires a temporarily perfected (20–day) security interest, unfiled, in a tangible negotiable document in the debtor's possession under Section 9–312(e). On October 5, B files and thereby perfects a security interest that previously had attached to the same document. On October 10, A files. A has priority, even after the 20–day period expires, regardless of whether A knows of B's security interest when A files. A was the first to perfect and maintained continuous perfection or filing since the start of the 20–day period. However, the perfection of A's security interest extends only "to the extent it arises for new value given." To the extent A's security interest secures advances made by A beyond the 20–day period, its security interest would be subordinate to B's, inasmuch as B was the first to file.

In general, the rule in subsection (a)(1) does not distinguish among various advances made by a secured party. The priority of every advance dates from the earlier of filing or perfection. However, in rare instances, the priority of an advance dates from the time the advance is made. See Example 3 and Section 9–323.

5. **Priority in After-Acquired Property.** The application of the priority rules to after-acquired property

must be considered separately for each item of collateral. Priority does not depend only on time of perfection but may also be based on priority in filing before perfection.

Example 4: On February 1, A makes advances to Debtor under a security agreement covering "all Debtor's machinery, both existing and after-acquired." A promptly files a financing statement. On April 1, B takes a security interest in all Debtor's machinery, existing and after-acquired, to secure an outstanding loan. The following day, B files a financing statement. On May 1, Debtor acquires a new machine. When Debtor acquires rights in the new machine, both A and B acquire security interests in the machine simultaneously. Both security interests are perfected simultaneously. However, A has priority because A filed before B.

When after-acquired collateral is encumbered by more than one security interest, one of the security interests often is a purchase-money security interest that is entitled to special priority under Section 9–324.

6. **Priority in Proceeds: General Rule.** Subsection (b)(1) follows former Section 9–312(6). It provides that the baseline rules of subsection (a) apply generally to priority conflicts in proceeds except where otherwise provided (e.g., as in subsections (c) through (e)). Under Section 9–203, attachment cannot occur (and therefore, under Section 9–308, perfection cannot occur) as to particular collateral until the collateral itself comes into existence and the debtor has rights in it. Thus, a security interest in proceeds of original collateral does not attach and is not perfected until the proceeds come into existence and the debtor acquires rights in them.

Example 5: On April 1, Debtor authenticates a security agreement granting to A a security interest in all Debtor's existing and after-acquired inventory. The same day, A files a financing statement covering inventory. On May 1, Debtor authenticates a security agreement granting B a security interest in all Debtor's existing and future accounts. On June 1, Debtor sells inventory to a customer on 30–day unsecured credit. When Debtor acquires the account, B's security interest attaches to it and is perfected by B's financing statement. At the very same time, A's security interest attaches to the account as proceeds of the inventory and is automatically perfected. See Section 9–315. Under subsection (b) of this section, for purposes of determining A's priority in the account, the time of filing as to the original collateral (April 1, as to inventory) is also the time of filing as to proceeds (account). Accordingly, A's security interest in the account has priority over B's. Of course, had B filed its financing statement before A filed (e.g., on March 1), then B would have priority in the accounts.

Section 9–324 governs the extent to which a special purchase-money priority in goods or software carries over into the proceeds of the original collateral.

7. **Priority in Proceeds: Special Rules.** Subsections (c), (d), and (e), which are new, provide additional priority rules for proceeds of collateral in situations where the temporal (first-in-time) rules of subsection (a)(1) are not appropriate. These new provisions distinguish what these Comments refer to as "non-filing collateral" from what they call "filing collateral." As used in these Comments, non-filing collateral is collateral of a type for which perfection may be achieved by a method other than filing (possession or control, mainly) and for which secured parties who so perfect generally do not expect or need to conduct a filing search. More specifically, non-filing collateral is chattel paper, deposit accounts, negotiable documents, instruments, investment property, and letter-of-credit rights. Other collateral—accounts, commercial tort claims, general intangibles, goods, nonnegotiable documents, and payment intangibles–is filing collateral.

8. **Proceeds of Non-Filing Collateral: Non-Temporal Priority.** Subsection (c)(2) provides a baseline priority rule for proceeds of non-filing collateral which applies if the secured party has taken the steps required for non-temporal priority over a conflicting security interest in non-filing collateral (e.g., control, in the case of deposit accounts, letter-of-credit rights, investment property, and in some cases, electronic negotiable documents, section 9–331). This rule determines priority in proceeds of non-filing collateral whether or not there exists an actual conflicting security interest in the original non-filing collateral. Under subsection (c)(2), the priority in the original collateral continues in proceeds if the security interest in proceeds is perfected and the proceeds are cash proceeds or non-filing proceeds "of the same type" as the original collateral. As used in subsection (c)(2), "type" means a type of collateral defined in the Uniform Commercial Code and should be read broadly. For example, a security is "of the same type" as a security entitlement (i.e., investment property), and a promissory note is "of the same type" as a draft (i.e., an instrument).

Example 6: SP–1 perfects its security interest in investment property by filing. SP–2 perfects subsequently by taking control of a certificated security. Debtor receives cash proceeds of the security (e.g., dividends deposited into Debtor's deposit account). If the first-to-file-or-perfect rule of subsection (a)(1) were applied, SP–1's security interest in the cash proceeds would be senior, although SP–2's security interest continues perfected under Section 9–315 beyond the 20–day period of automatic perfection. This was the result under former Article 9. Under subsection (c), however, SP–2's security interest is senior.

Note that a different result would obtain in Example 6 (i.e., SP–1's security interest would be senior) if SP–1 were to obtain control of the deposit-account proceeds. This is so because subsection (c) is subject to subsection (f), which in turn provides that the priority rules under subsections (a) through (e) are subject to "the other provisions of this part." One of those "other provisions" is Section 9–327, which affords priority to a security interest perfected by control. See Section 9–327(1).

Example 7: SP–1 perfects its security interest in investment property by filing. SP–2 perfects subsequently by taking control of a certificated security. Debtor receives proceeds of the security consisting of a new certificated security issued as a stock dividend on the original collateral. Although the new security is of the same type as the original collateral (i.e., investment property), once the 20–day period of automatic perfection expires (see Section 9–315(d)), SP–2's security interest is unperfected. (SP–2 has not filed or taken delivery or control, and no temporary-perfection rule applies.) Consequently, once the 20–day period expires, subsection (c) does not confer priority, and, under subsection (a)(2), SP–1's security interest in the security is senior. This was the result under former Article 9.

Example 8: SP–1 perfects its security interest in investment property by filing. SP–2 perfects subsequently by taking control of a certificated security and also by filing against investment property. Debtor receives proceeds of the security consisting of a new certificated security issued as a stock dividend of the collateral. Because the new security is of the same type as the original collateral (i.e., investment property) and (unlike Example 7) SP–2's security interest is perfected by filing, SP–2's security interest is senior under subsection (c). If the new security were redeemed by the issuer upon surrender and yet another security were received by Debtor, SP–2's security interest would continue to enjoy priority under subsection (c). The new security would be proceeds of proceeds.

Example 9: SP–1 perfects its security interest in investment property by filing. SP–2 subsequently perfects its security interest in investment property by taking control of a certificated security and also by filing against investment property. Debtor receives proceeds of the security consisting of a dividend check that it deposits to a deposit account. Because the check and the deposit account are cash proceeds, SP–1's and SP–2's security interests in the cash proceeds are perfected under Section 9–315 beyond the 20–day period of automatic perfection. However, SP–2's security interest is senior under subsection (c).

Example 10: SP–1 perfects its security interest in investment property by filing. SP–2 perfects subsequently by taking control of a certificated security and also by filing against investment property. Debtor receives an instrument as proceeds of the security. (Assume that the instrument is not cash proceeds.) Because the instrument is not of the same type as the original collateral (i.e., investment property), SP–2's security interest, although perfected by filing, does not achieve priority under subsection (c). Under the first-to-file-or-perfect rule of subsection (a)(1), SP–1's security interest in the proceeds is senior.

The proceeds of proceeds are themselves proceeds. See Section 9–102 (defining "proceeds" and "collateral"). Sometimes competing security interests arise in proceeds that are several generations removed from the original collateral. As the following example explains, the applicability of subsection (c) may turn on the nature of the intervening proceeds.

Example 11: SP–1 perfects its security interest in Debtor's deposit account by obtaining control. Thereafter, SP–2 files against inventory, (presumably) searches, finds no indication of a conflicting security interest, and advances against Debtor's existing and after-acquired inventory. Debtor uses funds from the deposit account to purchase inventory, which SP–1 can trace as identifiable proceeds of its security interest in Debtor's deposit account, and which SP–2 claims as original collateral. The inventory is sold and the proceeds deposited into *another* deposit account, as to which SP–1 has not obtained control. Subsection (c) does not govern priority in this other deposit account. This deposit account is cash proceeds and is also the same type of collateral as SP–1's original collateral, as required by subsections (c)(2)(A) and (B). However, SP–1's security interest does not satisfy subsection (c)(2)(C) because the inventory proceeds, which intervened between the original deposit account and the deposit account constituting the proceeds at issue, are not cash proceeds, proceeds of the same type as the collateral (original deposit account), or an account relating to the collateral. Stated otherwise, once proceeds other

than cash proceeds, proceeds of the same type as the original collateral, or an account relating to the original collateral intervene in the chain of proceeds, priority under subsection (c) is thereafter unavailable. The special priority rule in subsection (d) also is inapplicable to this case. See Comment 9, Example 13, below. Instead, the general first-to-file-or-perfect rule of subsections (a) and (b) apply. Under that rule, SP–1 has priority unless its security interest in the inventory proceeds became unperfected under Section 9–315(d). Had SP–2 filed against inventory before SP–1 obtained control of the original deposit account, the SP–2 would have had priority even if SP–1's security interest in the inventory proceeds remained perfected.

9. **Proceeds of Non–Filing Collateral: Special Temporal Priority.** Under subsections (d) and (e), if a security interest in non-filing collateral is perfected by a method other than filing (e.g., control or possession), it does not retain its priority over a conflicting security interest in proceeds that are filing collateral. Moreover, it is not entitled to priority in proceeds under the first-to file-or-perfect rule of subsections (a)(1) and (b). Instead, under subsection (d), priority is determined by a new first-to-file rule.

Example 12: SP–1 perfects its security interest in Debtor's deposit account by obtaining control. Thereafter, SP–2 files against equipment, (presumably) searches, finds no indication of a conflicting security interest, and advances against Debtor's equipment. SP–1 then files against Debtor's equipment. Debtor uses funds from the deposit account to purchase equipment, which SP–1 can trace as proceeds of its security interest in Debtor's deposit account. If the first-to-file-or-perfect rule were applied, SP–1's security interest would be senior under subsections (a)(1) and (b), because it was the first to perfect in the original collateral and there was no period during which its security interest was unperfected. Under subsection (d), however, SP–2's security interest would be senior because it filed first. This corresponds with the likely expectations of the parties.

Note that under subsection (e), the first-to-file rule of subsection (d) applies only if the proceeds in question are other than non-filing collateral (i.e., if the proceeds are filing collateral). If the proceeds are non-filing collateral, either the first-to-file-or-perfect rule under subsections (a) and (b) or the non-temporal priority rule in subsection (c) would apply, depending on the facts.

Example 13: SP–1 perfects its security interest in Debtor's deposit account by obtaining control. Thereafter, SP–2 files against inventory, (presumably) searches, finds no indication of a conflicting security interest, and advances against Debtor's existing and after-acquired inventory. Debtor uses funds from the deposit account to purchase inventory, which SP–1 can trace as identifiable proceeds of its security interest in Debtor's deposit account, and which SP–2 claims as original collateral. The inventory is sold and the proceeds deposited into *another* deposit account, as to which SP–1 has not obtained control. As discussed above in Comment 8, Example 11, subsection (c) does not govern priority in this deposit account. Subsection (d) also does not govern, because the proceeds at issue (the deposit account) are cash proceeds. See subsection (e). Rather, the general rules of subsections (a) and (b) govern.

10. **Priority in Supporting Obligations.** Under subsections (b)(2) and (c)(1), a security interest having priority in collateral also has priority in a supporting obligation for that collateral. However, the rules in these subsections are subject to the special rule in Section 9–329 governing the priority of security interests in a letter-of-credit right. See subsection (f). Under Section 9–329, a secured party's failure to obtain control (Section 9–107) of a letter-of-credit right that serves as supporting collateral leaves its security interest exposed to a priming interest of a party who does take control.

11. **Unperfected Security Interests.** Under subsection (a)(3), if conflicting security interests are unperfected, the first to attach has priority. This rule may be of merely theoretical interest, inasmuch as it is hard to imagine a situation where the case would come into litigation without either secured party's having perfected its security interest. If neither security interest had been perfected at the time of the filing of a petition in bankruptcy, ordinarily neither would be good against the trustee in bankruptcy under the Bankruptcy Code.

12. **Agricultural Liens.** Statutes other than this Article may purport to grant priority to an agricultural lien as against a conflicting security interest or agricultural lien. Under subsection (g), if another statute grants priority to an agricultural lien, the agricultural lien has priority only if the same statute creates the agricultural lien and the agricultural lien is perfected. Otherwise, subsection (a) applies the same priority rules to an agricultural lien as to a security interest, regardless of whether the agricultural lien conflicts with another agricultural lien or with a security interest.

Inasmuch as no agricultural lien on proceeds arises under this Article, subsections (b) through (e) do not apply to proceeds of agricultural liens. However, if an agricultural lien has priority under subsection (g) and the statute creating the agricultural lien gives the secured party a lien on proceeds of the collateral subject to the lien, a court should apply the principle of subsection (g) and award priority in the proceeds to the holder of the perfected agricultural lien.

As amended in 2000 and 2003.

§ 9–323. Future Advances.

(a) **[When priority based on time of advance.]** Except as otherwise provided in subsection (c), for purposes of determining the priority of a perfected security interest under Section 9–322(a)(1), perfection of the security interest dates from the time an advance is made to the extent that the security interest secures an advance that:

(1) is made while the security interest is perfected only:

(A) under Section 9–309 when it attaches; or

(B) temporarily under Section 9–312(e), (f), or (g); and

(2) is not made pursuant to a commitment entered into before or while the security interest is perfected by a method other than under Section 9–309 or 9–312(e), (f), or (g).

(b) **[Lien creditor.]** Except as otherwise provided in subsection (c), a security interest is subordinate to the rights of a person that becomes a lien creditor to the extent that the security interest secures an advance made more than 45 days after the person becomes a lien creditor unless the advance is made:

(1) without knowledge of the lien; or

(2) pursuant to a commitment entered into without knowledge of the lien.

(c) **[Buyer of receivables.]** Subsections (a) and (b) do not apply to a security interest held by a secured party that is a buyer of accounts, chattel paper, payment intangibles, or promissory notes or a consignor.

(d) **[Buyer of goods.]** Except as otherwise provided in subsection (e), a buyer of goods other than a buyer in ordinary course of business takes free of a security interest to the extent that it secures advances made after the earlier of:

   (1) the time the secured party acquires knowledge of the buyer's purchase; or

   (2) 45 days after the purchase.

   (e) **[Advances made pursuant to commitment: priority of buyer of goods.]** Subsection (d) does not apply if the advance is made pursuant to a commitment entered into without knowledge of the buyer's purchase and before the expiration of the 45–day period.

   (f) **[Lessee of goods.]** Except as otherwise provided in subsection (g), a lessee of goods, other than a lessee in ordinary course of business, takes the leasehold interest free of a security interest to the extent that it secures advances made after the earlier of:

   (1) the time the secured party acquires knowledge of the lease; or

   (2) 45 days after the lease contract becomes enforceable.

   (g) **[Advances made pursuant to commitment: priority of lessee of goods.]** Subsection (f) does not apply if the advance is made pursuant to a commitment entered into without knowledge of the lease and before the expiration of the 45–day period.

As amended in 1999.

Official Comment

   1. **Source.** Former Sections 9–312(7), 9–301(4), 9–307(3), 2A–307(4).

   2. **Scope of This Section.** A security agreement may provide that collateral secures future advances. See Section 9–204(c). This section collects all of the special rules dealing with the priority of advances made by a secured party after a third party acquires an interest in the collateral. Subsection (a) applies when the third party is a competing secured party. It replaces and clarifies former Section 9–312(7). Subsection (b) deals with lien creditors and replaces former Section 9–301(4). Subsections (d) and (e) deal with buyers and replace former Section 9–307(3). Subsections (f) and (g) deal with lessees and replace former Section 2A–307(4).

   3. **Competing Security Interests.** Under a proper reading of the first-to-file-or-perfect rule of Section 9–322(a)(1) (and former Section 9–312(5)), it is abundantly clear that the time when an advance is made plays no role in determining priorities among conflicting security interests except when a financing statement was not filed and the advance is the giving of value as the last step for attachment and perfection. Thus, a secured party takes subject to all advances secured by a competing security interest having priority under Section 9–322(a)(1). This result generally obtains regardless of how the competing security interest is perfected and regardless of whether the advances are made "pursuant to commitment" (Section 9–102). Subsection (a) of this section states the only other instance when the time of an advance figures in the priority scheme in Section 9–322: when the security interest is perfected only automatically under Section 9–309 or temporarily under Section 9–312(e), (f), or (g), and the advance is not made pursuant to a commitment entered into while the security interest was perfected by another method. Thus, an advance has priority from the date it is made only in the rare case in which it is made without commitment and while the security interest is perfected only temporarily under Section 9–312.

   The new formulation in subsection (a) clarifies the result when the initial advance is paid and a new ("future") advance is made subsequently. Under former Section 9–312(7), the priority of the new advance turned on whether it was "made while a security interest is perfected." This section resolves any ambiguity by omitting the quoted phrase.

   Example 1: On February 1, A makes an advance secured by machinery in the debtor's possession and files a financing statement. On March 1, B makes an advance secured by the same machinery and files a financing statement. On April 1, A makes a further advance, under the original security agreement, against the same machinery. A was the first to file and so, under the first-to-file-or-perfect rule of Section 9–322(a)(1), A's security interest has priority over B's, both as to the February 1 and as to the April 1 advance. It makes no difference whether A knows of B's intervening advance when A makes the second advance. Note that, as long as A was the first to file or perfect, A would have priority with respect to both advances if either A or B had perfected by taking possession of the collateral. Likewise, A would have priority if A's April 1 advance was not made under the original agreement with the debtor, but was under a new agreement.

   Example 2: On October 1, A acquires a temporarily perfected (20–day) security interest, unfiled, in a tangible negotiable document in the debtor's possession under Section 9–312(e) or (f). The security interest secures an advance made on that day as well as future advances. On October 5, B files and thereby perfects a security interest that previously had attached to the same document. On October 8, A makes an additional advance. On October 10, A files. Under Section 9–322(a)(1), because A was the first to perfect and maintained continuous perfection or filing since the start of the 20–day period, A has priority, even after the 20–day period expires. See Section 9–322, Comment 4, Example 3. However, under this section, for purposes of Section 9–322(a)(1), to the extent A's security interest secures the October 8 advance, the security interest was perfected on October 8. Inasmuch as B perfected on October 5, B has priority over the October 8 advance.

The rule in subsection (a) is more liberal toward the priority of future advances than the corresponding rules applicable to intervening lien creditors (subsection (b)), buyers (subsections (d) and (e)), and lessees (subsections (f) and (g)).

4. **Competing Lien Creditors.** Subsection (b) replaces former Section 9–301(4). *It addresses the problem considered by PEB Commentary No. 2 and removes the ambiguity that necessitated the Commentary. Former Section 9–301(4) appeared to state a general rule that a lien creditor has priority over a perfected security interest and is "subject to" the security interest "only" in specified circumstances. Because that section spoke to the making of an "advance," it arguably implied that to the extent a security interest secured non-advances (expenses, interest, etc.), it was junior to the lien creditor's interest* and addresses the rights of a "lien creditor," as defined in Section 9–102. Under Section 9–317(a)(2), a *perfected* security interest is senior to the rights of ~~a subsequent lien creditor~~ *a person who becomes a lien creditor, unless the person becomes a lien creditor before the security interest is perfected and before a financing statement covering the collateral is filed* and Section 9–203(b)(3) is satisfied. Subsection (b) of this section ~~eliminates the erroneous implication of former law by providing that a perfected~~ *provides that a* security interest is subordinate ~~only~~ *to those rights* to the extent that the specified circumstances occur. *Subsection (b) does not elevate the priority of a security interest*

*that is subordinate to the rights of a lien creditor under Section 9–317(a)(2); it only subordinates.**

As under former Section 9–301(4), a secured party's knowledge does not cut short the 45–day period during which future advances can achieve priority over an intervening lien creditor's interest. Rather, because of the impact of the rule in subsection (b) on the question whether the security interest for future advances is "protected" under Section 6323(c)(2) and (d) of the Internal Revenue Code as amended by the Federal Tax Lien Act of 1966, the priority of the security interest for future advances over a lien creditor is made absolute for 45 days regardless of knowledge of the secured party concerning the lien. If, however, the advance is made after the 45 days, the advance will not have priority unless it was made or committed without knowledge of the lien.

5. **Sales of Receivables; Consignments.** Subsections (a) and (b) do not apply to outright sales of accounts, chattel paper, payment intangibles, or promissory notes, nor do they apply to consignments.

6. **Competing Buyers and Lessees.** Under subsections (d) and (e), a buyer will not take subject to a security interest to the extent it secures advances made after the secured party has knowledge that the buyer has purchased the collateral or more than 45 days after the purchase unless the advances were made pursuant to a commitment entered into before the expiration of the 45–day period and without knowledge of the purchase. Subsections (f) and (g) provide an analogous rule for lessees. Of course, a buyer in ordinary course who takes free of the security interest under Section 9–320 and a lessee in ordinary course who takes free under Section 9–321 are not subject to any future advances. Subsections (d) and (e) replace former Section 9–307(3), and subsections (f) and (g) replace former Section 2A–307(4). No change in meaning is intended.

As amended in 1999, 2000 and 2003.

§ 9–324. Priority of Purchase-Money Security Interests.

(a) **[General rule: purchase-money priority.]** Except as otherwise provided in subsection (g), a perfected purchase-money security interest in goods other than inventory or livestock has priority over a conflicting security interest in the same goods, and, except as otherwise provided in

---

* Amendments in italics approved by the Permanent Editorial Board for Uniform Commercial Code Oct. 20, 1999.

Section 9–327, a perfected security interest in its identifiable proceeds also has priority, if the purchase-money security interest is perfected when the debtor receives possession of the collateral or within 20 days thereafter.

(b) **[Inventory purchase-money priority.]** Subject to subsection (c) and except as otherwise provided in subsection (g), a perfected purchase-money security interest in inventory has priority over a conflicting security interest in the same inventory, has priority over a conflicting security interest in chattel paper or an instrument constituting proceeds of the inventory and in proceeds of the chattel paper, if so provided in Section 9–330, and, except as otherwise provided in Section 9–327, also has priority in identifiable cash proceeds of the inventory to the extent the identifiable cash proceeds are received on or before the delivery of the inventory to a buyer, if:

(1) the purchase-money security interest is perfected when the debtor receives possession of the inventory;

(2) the purchase-money secured party sends an authenticated notification to the holder of the conflicting security interest;

(3) the holder of the conflicting security interest receives the notification within five years before the debtor receives possession of the inventory; and

(4) the notification states that the person sending the notification has or expects to acquire a purchase-money security interest in inventory of the debtor and describes the inventory.

(c) **[Holders of conflicting inventory security interests to be notified.]** Subsections (b)(2) through (4) apply only if the holder of the conflicting security interest had filed a financing statement covering the same types of inventory:

(1) if the purchase-money security interest is perfected by filing, before the date of the filing; or

(2) if the purchase-money security interest is temporarily perfected without filing or possession under Section 9–312(f), before the beginning of the 20–day period thereunder.

(d) **[Livestock purchase-money priority.]** Subject to subsection (e) and except as otherwise provided in subsection (g), a perfected purchase-money security interest in livestock that are farm products has priority over a conflicting security interest in the same livestock, and, except as otherwise provided in Section 9–327, a perfected security interest in their identifiable proceeds and identifiable products in their unmanufactured states also has priority, if:

(1) the purchase-money security interest is perfected when the debtor receives possession of the livestock;

(2) the purchase-money secured party sends an authenticated notification to the holder of the conflicting security interest;

(3) the holder of the conflicting security interest receives the notification within six months before the debtor receives possession of the livestock; and

(4) the notification states that the person sending the notification has or expects to acquire a purchase-money security interest in livestock of the debtor and describes the livestock.

(e) **[Holders of conflicting livestock security interests to be notified.]** Subsections (d)(2) through (4) apply only if the holder of the conflicting security interest had filed a financing statement covering the same types of livestock:

(1) if the purchase-money security interest is perfected by filing, before the date of the filing; or

(2) if the purchase-money security interest is temporarily perfected without filing or possession under Section 9–312(f), before the beginning of the 20–day period thereunder.

(f) **[Software purchase-money priority.]** Except as otherwise provided in subsection (g), a perfected purchase-money security interest in software has priority over a conflicting security interest in the same collateral, and, except as otherwise provided in Section 9–327, a perfected security interest in its identifiable proceeds also has priority, to the extent that the purchase-money security interest in the goods in which the software was acquired for use has priority in the goods and proceeds of the goods under this section.

(g) **[Conflicting purchase-money security interests.]** If more than one security interest qualifies for priority in the same collateral under subsection (a), (b), (d), or (f):

(1) a security interest securing an obligation incurred as all or part of the price of the collateral has priority over a security interest securing an obligation incurred for value given to enable the debtor to acquire rights in or the use of collateral; and

(2) in all other cases, Section 9–322(a) applies to the qualifying security interests.

Official Comment

1. **Source.** Former Section 9–312(3), (4).

2. **Priority of Purchase-Money Security Interests.** This section contains the priority rules applicable to purchase-money security interests, as defined in Section 9–103. It affords a special, non-temporal priority to those purchase-money security interests that satisfy the statutory conditions. In most cases, priority will be over a security interest asserted under an after-acquired property clause. See Section 9–204 on the extent to which security interests in after-acquired property are validated.

A purchase-money security interest can be created only in goods and software. See Section 9–103. Section 9–324(a), which follows former Section 9–312(4), contains the general rule for purchase-money security interests in goods. It is subject to subsections (b) and (c), which derive from former Section 9–312(3) and apply to purchase-money security interests in inventory, and subsections (d) and (e), which apply to purchase-money security interests in livestock that are farm products. Subsection (f) applies to purchase-money security interests in software. Subsection (g) deals with the relatively unusual case in which a debtor creates two purchase-money security interests in the same collateral and both security interests qualify for special priority under one of the other subsections.

Former Section 9–312(2) contained a rule affording special priority to those who provided secured credit that enabled a debtor to produce crops. This rule proved unworkable and has been eliminated from this Article. Instead, model Section 9–324A contains a revised production-money priority rule. That section is a model, not uniform, provision. The sponsors of the UCC have taken no position as to whether it should be enacted, instead leaving the matter for state legislatures to consider if they are so inclined.

3. **Purchase-Money Priority in Goods Other Than Inventory and Livestock.** Subsection (a) states a general rule applicable to all types of goods except inventory and farm-products livestock: the purchase-money interest takes priority if it is perfected when the debtor receives possession of the collateral or within 20 days thereafter. (As to the 20–day "grace period," compare Section 9–317(e). Former Sections 9–312(4) and 9–301(2) contained a 10–day grace period.) The perfection requirement means that the purchase-money secured party either has filed a financing statement before that time or has a temporarily perfected security interest in goods covered by documents under Section 9–312(e) and (f) which is continued in a perfected status by filing before the expiration of the 20–day period specified in that section. A purchase-money security interest qualifies for priority under subsection (a), even if the purchase-money secured party knows that a conflicting security interest has been created and/or that the holder of the conflicting interest has filed a financing statement covering the collateral.

Normally, there will be no question when "the debtor receives possession of the collateral" for purposes of subsection (a). However, sometimes a debtor buys goods and takes possession of them in stages, and then assembly and testing are completed (by the seller or debtor-buyer) at the debtor's location. Under those circumstances, the buyer "takes possession" within the meaning of subsection (a) when, after an inspection of the portion of the goods in the debtor's possession, it would be apparent to a potential lender to the debtor that the debtor has acquired an interest in the goods taken as a whole.

A similar issue concerning the time when "the debtor receives possession" arises when a person acquires possession of goods under a transaction that is not governed by this Article and then later agrees to buy the goods on secured credit. For example, a person may take possession of goods as lessee under a lease contract and then exercise an option to purchase the goods from the lessor on secured credit. Under Section 2A–307(1), creditors of the lessee generally take subject to the lease contract; filing a financing statement against the lessee is unnecessary to protect the lessor's leasehold or residual interest. Once the lease is converted to a security interest, filing a financing statement is necessary to protect the seller's (former lessor's) security interest. Accordingly, the 20–day period in subsection (a) does not commence until the goods become "collateral" (defined in Section 9–102), i.e., until they are subject to a security interest.

4. **Purchase-Money Security Interests in Inventory.** Subsections (b) and (c) afford a means by which a purchase-money security interest in inventory can achieve priority over an earlier-filed security interest in the same collateral. To achieve priority, the purchase-money security interest must be perfected when the debtor receives possession of the inventory.

For a discussion of when "the debtor receives possession," see Comment 3, above. The 20–day grace period of subsection (a) does not apply.

The arrangement between an inventory secured party and its debtor typically requires the secured party to make periodic advances against incoming inventory or periodic releases of old inventory as new inventory is received. A fraudulent debtor may apply to the secured party for advances even though it has already given a purchase-money security interest in the inventory to another secured party. For this reason, subsections (b)(2) through (4) and (c) impose a second condition for the purchase-money security interest's achieving priority: the purchase-money secured party must give notification to the holder of a conflicting security interest who filed against the same item or type of inventory before the purchase-money secured party filed or its security interest became perfected temporarily under Section 9–312(e) or (f). The notification requirement protects the non-purchase-money inventory secured party in such a situation: if the inventory secured party has received notification, it presumably will not make an advance; if it has not received notification (or if the other security interest does not qualify as purchase-money), any advance the inventory secured party may make ordinarily will have priority under Section 9–322. Inasmuch as an arrangement for periodic advances against incoming goods is unusual outside the inventory field, subsection (a) does not contain a notification requirement.

5. **Notification to Conflicting Inventory Secured Party: Timing.** Under subsection (b)(3), the perfected purchase-money security interest achieves priority over a conflicting security interest only if the holder of the conflicting security interest receives a notification within five years before the debtor receives possession of the purchase-money collateral. If the debtor never receives possession, the five-year period never begins, and the purchase-money security interest has priority, even if notification is not given. However, where the purchase-money inventory financing began by the purchase-money secured party's possession of a negotiable document of title, to retain priority the secured party must give the notification required by subsection (b) at or before the usual time, i.e., when the debtor gets possession of the inventory, even though the security interest remains perfected for 20 days under Section 9–312(e) or (f).

Some people have mistakenly read former Section 9–312(3)(b) to require, as a condition of purchase-money priority in inventory, that the purchase-money secured party give the notification before it files a financing statement. Read correctly, the "before" clauses compare (i) the time when the holder of the conflicting security interest filed a financing statement with (ii) the time when the purchase-money security interest becomes perfected by filing or automatically perfected temporarily. Only if (i) occurs before (ii) must notification be given to the holder of the conflicting security interest. Subsection (c) has been rewritten to clarify this point.

6. **Notification to Conflicting Inventory Secured Party: Address.** Inasmuch as the address provided as that of the secured party on a filed financing statement is an "address that is reasonable under the circumstances," the holder of a purchase-money security interest may satisfy the requirement to "send" notification to the holder of a conflicting security interest in inventory by sending a notification to that address, even if the address is or becomes incorrect. See Section 9–102 (definition of "send"). Similarly, because the address is "held out by [the holder of the conflicting security interest] as the place for receipt of such communications [i.e., communications relating to security interests]," the holder is deemed to have "received" a notification delivered to that address. See Section 1–201(26).

7. **Consignments.** Subsections (b) and (c) also determine the priority of a consignor's interest in consigned goods as against a security interest in the goods created by the consignee. Inasmuch as a consignment subject to this Article is defined to be a purchase-money security interest, see Section 9–103(d), no inference concerning the nature of the transaction should be drawn from the fact that a consignor uses the term "security interest" in its notice under subsection (b)(4). Similarly, a notice stating that the consignor has delivered or expects to deliver goods, properly described, "on consignment" meets the requirements of subsection (b)(4), even if it does not contain the term "security interest," and even if the transaction subsequently is determined to be a security interest. Cf. Section 9–505 (use of "consignor" and "consignee" in financing statement).

8. **Priority in Proceeds: General.** When the purchase-money secured party has priority over another secured party, the question arises whether this priority extends to the proceeds of the original collateral. Subsections (a), (d), and (f) give an affirmative answer, but only as to proceeds in which the security interest is perfected (see Section 9–315). Although this qualification did not appear in former Section 9–312(4), it was implicit in that provision.

In the case of inventory collateral under subsection (b), where financing frequently is based on the resulting accounts, chattel paper, or other proceeds, the special priority of the purchase-money secured interest carries over into only certain types of proceeds. As under former Section 9–312(3), the purchase-money priority in inventory under subsection (b) carries over into identifiable cash proceeds (defined in Section 9–102) received on or before the delivery of the inventory to a buyer.

As a general matter, also like former Section 9–312(3), the purchase-money priority in inventory does *not* carry over into proceeds consisting of accounts or chattel paper. Many parties financing inventory are quite content to protect their first-priority security interest in the inventory itself. They realize that when the inventory is sold, someone else will be financing the resulting receivables (accounts or chattel paper), and the priority for inventory will not run forward to the receivables constituting the proceeds. Indeed, the cash supplied by the receivables financer often will be used to pay the inventory financing. In some situations, the party financing the inventory on a purchase-money basis makes contractual arrangements that the proceeds of receivables financing by another be devoted to paying off the inventory security interest.

However, the purchase-money priority in inventory *does* carry over to proceeds consisting of chattel paper and its proceeds (and also to instruments) to the extent provided in Section 9–330. Under Section 9–330(e), the holder of a purchase-money security interest in inventory is deemed to give new value for proceeds consisting of chattel paper. Taken together, Sections 9–324(b) and 9–330(e) enable a purchase-money inventory secured party to obtain priority in chattel paper constituting proceeds of the inventory, even if the secured party does not actually give new value for the chattel paper, provided the purchase-money secured party satisfies the other conditions for achieving priority.

When the proceeds of original collateral (goods or software) consist of a deposit account, Section 9–327 governs priority to the extent it conflicts with the priority rules of this section.

9. **Priority in Accounts Constituting Proceeds of Inventory.** The application of the priority rules in subsection (b) is shown by the following examples:

Example 1: Debtor creates a security interest in its existing and after-acquired inventory in favor of SP–1, who files a financing statement covering inventory. SP–2 subsequently takes a purchase-money security interest in certain inventory and, under subsection (b), achieves priority in this inventory over SP–1. This inventory is then sold, producing accounts. Accounts are not cash proceeds, and so the special purchase-money priority in the inventory does not control the priority in the accounts. Rather, the first-to-file-or-perfect rule of Section 9–322(a)(1) applies. The time of SP–1's filing as to the inventory is also the time of filing as to the accounts under Section 9–322(b). Assuming that each security interest in the accounts proceeds remains perfected under Section 9–315, SP–1 has priority as to the accounts.

Example 2: In Example 1, if SP–2 had filed directly against accounts, the date of that filing as to accounts would be compared with the date of SP–1's filing as to the inventory. The first filed would prevail under Section 9–322(a)(1).

Example 3: If SP–3 had filed against accounts in Example 1 before either SP–1 or SP–2 filed against inventory, SP–3's filing against accounts would have priority over the filings of SP–1 and SP–2. This result obtains even though the filings against inventory are effective to continue the perfected status of SP–1's and SP–2's security interest in the accounts beyond the 20–day period of automatic perfection. See Section 9–315. SP–1's and SP–2's position as to the inventory does not give them a claim to accounts (as proceeds of the inventory) which is senior to someone who has filed earlier against accounts. If, on the other hand, either SP–1's or SP–2's filing against the inventory preceded SP–3's filing against accounts, SP–1 or SP–2 would outrank SP–3 as to the accounts.

10. **Purchase-Money Security Interests in Livestock.** New subsections (d) and (e) provide a purchase-money priority rule for farm-products livestock. They are patterned on the purchase-money priority rule for inventory found in subsections (b) and (c) and include a requirement that the purchase-money secured party notify earlier-filed parties. Two differences between subsections (b) and (d) are noteworthy. First, unlike the purchase-money inventory lender, the purchase-money livestock lender enjoys priority in *all* proceeds of the collateral. Thus, under subsection (d), the purchase-money secured party takes priority in accounts over an earlier-filed accounts financer. Second, subsection (d) affords priority in certain products of the collateral as well as proceeds.

11. **Purchase-Money Security Interests in Aquatic Farm Products.** Aquatic goods produced in aquacultural operations (e.g., catfish raised on a catfish farm) are farm products. See Section 9–102 (definition of "farm products"). The definition does not indicate whether aquatic goods are "crops," as to which the model production money security interest priority in Section 9–324A applies, or "livestock," as to which the

purchase-money priority in subsection (d) of this section applies. This Article leaves courts free to determine the classification of particular aquatic goods on a case-by-case basis, applying whichever priority rule makes more sense in the overall context of the debtor's business.

12. **Purchase-Money Security Interests in Software.** Subsection (f) governs the priority of purchase-money security interests in software. Under Section 9–103(c), a purchase-money security interest arises in software only if the debtor acquires its interest in the software for the principal purpose of using the software in goods subject to a purchase-money security interest. Under subsection (f), a purchase-money security interest in software has the same priority as the purchase-money security interest in the goods in which the software was acquired for use. This priority is determined under subsections (b) and (c) (for inventory) or (a) (for other goods).

13. **Multiple Purchase-Money Security Interests.** New subsection (g) governs priority among multiple purchase-money security interests in the same collateral. It grants priority to purchase-money security interests securing the price of collateral (i.e., created in favor of the seller) over purchase-money security interests that secure enabling loans. Section 7.2(c) of the Restatement (3d) of the Law of Property (Mortgages) (1997) adopts this rule with respect to real property mortgages. As Comment *d* to that section explains:

the equities favor the vendor. Not only does the vendor part with specific real estate rather than money, but the vendor would never relinquish it at all except on the understanding that the vendor will be able to use it to satisfy the obligation to pay the price. This is the case even though the vendor may know that the mortgagor is going to finance the transaction in part by borrowing from a third party and giving a mortgage to secure that obligation. In the final analysis, the law is more sympathetic to the vendor's hazard of losing real estate previously owned than to the third party lender's risk of being unable to collect from an interest in real estate that never previously belonged to it.

The first-to-file-or-perfect rule of Section 9–322 applies to multiple purchase-money security interests securing enabling loans.

§ 9–325. Priority of Security Interests in Transferred Collateral.

(a) **[Subordination of security interest in transferred collateral.]** Except as otherwise provided in subsection (b), a security interest created by a debtor is subordinate to a security interest in the same collateral created by another person if:

(1) the debtor acquired the collateral subject to the security interest created by the other person;

(2) the security interest created by the other person was perfected when the debtor acquired the collateral; and

(3) there is no period thereafter when the security interest is unperfected.

(b) **[Limitation of subsection (a) subordination.]** Subsection (a) subordinates a security interest only if the security interest:

(1) otherwise would have priority solely under Section 9–322(a) or 9–324; or

(2) arose solely under Section 2–711(3) or 2A–508(5).

Official Comment

1. **Source.** New.

2. **"Double Debtor Problem."** This section addresses the "double debtor" problem, which arises when a debtor acquires property that is subject to a security interest created by another debtor.

3. **Taking Subject to Perfected Security Interest.** Consider the following scenario:

Example 1: A owns an item of equipment subject to a perfected security interest in favor of SP–A. A sells the equipment to B, not in the ordinary course of business. B acquires its interest subject to SP–A's security interest. See Sections 9–201, 9–315(a)(1). Under this section, if B creates a security interest in the equipment in favor of SP–B, SP–B's security interest is subordinate to SP–A's security interest, even if SP–B filed against B before SP–A filed against A, and even if SP–B took a purchase-money security interest. Normally, SP–B could have investigated the source of the equipment and discovered SP–A's filing before making an advance against the equipment, whereas SP–A had no reason to search the filings against someone other than its debtor, A.

4. **Taking Subject to Unperfected Security Interest.** This section applies only if the security interest in the transferred collateral was perfected when the transferee acquired the collateral. See subsection (a)(2). If this condition is not met, then the normal priority rules apply.

Example 2: A owns an item of equipment subject to an unperfected security interest in favor of SP–A. A sells the equipment to B, who gives value and takes delivery of the equipment without knowledge of the security interest. B takes free of the security interest. See Section 9–317(b). If B then creates a security interest in favor of SP–B, no priority issue arises; SP–B has the only security interest in the equipment.

Example 3: The facts are as in Example 2, except that B knows of SP–A's security interest and therefore takes the equipment subject to it. If B creates a security interest in the equipment in favor of SP–B, this section does not determine the relative priority of the security interests. Rather, the normal priority rules govern. If SP–B perfects its security interest, then, under Section 9–322(a)(2), SP–A's unperfected security interest will be junior to SP–B's perfected security interest. The award of priority to SP–B is premised on the belief that SP–A's failure to file could have misled SP–B.

5. **Taking Subject to Perfected Security Interest that Becomes Unperfected.** This section applies only if the security interest in the transferred collateral did not become unperfected at any time after the transferee acquired the collateral. See subsection (a)(3). If this condition is not met, then the normal priority rules apply.

Example 4: As in Example 1, A owns an item of equipment subject to a perfected security interest in favor of SP–A. A sells the equipment to B, not in the ordinary course of business. B acquires its interest subject to SP–A's security interest. See Sections 9–201, 9–315(a)(1). B creates a security interest in favor of SP–B, and SP–B perfects its security interest. This section provides that SP–A's security interest is senior to SP–B's. However, if SP–A's financing statement lapses while SP–B's security interest is perfected, then the normal priority rules would apply, and SP–B's security interest would become senior to SP–A's security interest. See Sections 9–322(a)(2), 9–515(c).

6. **Unusual Situations.** The appropriateness of the rule of subsection (a) is most apparent when it works to subordinate security interests having priority under the basic priority rules of Section 9–322(a) or the purchase-money priority rules of Section 9–324. The rule also works properly when applied to the security interest of a buyer under Section 2–711(3) or a lessee under Section 2A–508(5). However, subsection (a) may provide an inappropriate resolution of the "double debtor" problem in some of the wide variety of

other contexts in which the problem may arise. Although subsection (b) limits the application of subsection (a) to those cases in which subordination is known to be appropriate, courts should apply the rule in other settings, if necessary to promote the underlying purposes and policies of the Uniform Commercial Code. See Section 1–103(a).

As amended in 2005.

§ 9–326. Priority of Security Interests Created by New Debtor.

(a) **[Subordination of security interest created by new debtor.]** Subject to subsection (b), a security interest created by a new debtor which is perfected by a filed financing statement that is effective solely under Section 9–508 in collateral in which a new debtor has or acquires rights is subordinate to a security interest in the same collateral which is perfected other than by a filed financing statement that is effective solely under Section 9–508.

(b) **[Priority under other provisions; multiple original debtors.]** The other provisions of this part determine the priority among conflicting security interests in the same collateral perfected by filed financing statements that are effective solely under Section 9–508. However, if the security agreements to which a new debtor became bound as debtor were not entered into by the same original debtor, the conflicting security interests rank according to priority in time of the new debtor's having become bound.

Official Comment

1. **Source.** New.

2. **Subordination of Security Interests Created by New Debtor.** This section addresses the priority contests that may arise when a new debtor becomes bound by the security agreement of an original debtor and each debtor has a secured creditor.

Subsection (a) subordinates the original debtor's secured party's security interest perfected against the new debtor solely under Section 9–508. The security interest is subordinated to security interests in the same collateral perfected by another method, e.g., by filing against the new debtor. As used in this section, "a filed financing statement that is effective solely under Section 9–508" refers to a financing statement filed against the *original debtor* that continues to be effective under Section 9–508. It does not encompass a new initial financing statement providing the name of the new debtor, even if the initial financing statement is filed to maintain the effectiveness of a financing statement under the circumstances described in Section 9–508(b). Nor does it encompass a financing statement filed against the original debtor which remains effective against collateral transferred by the original debtor to the new debtor. See Section 9–508(c). Concerning priority contests involving transferred collateral, see Sections 9–325 and 9–507.

Example 1: SP–X holds a perfected-by-filing security interest in X Corp's existing and after-acquired inventory, and SP–Z holds a perfected-by-possession security interest in an item of Z Corp's inventory. Z Corp becomes bound as debtor by X Corp's security agreement (e.g., Z Corp buys X Corp's assets and assumes its security agreement). See Section 9–203(d). Under Section 9–508, SP–X's financing statement is effective to perfect a security interest in the item of inventory in which Z Corp has rights. However, subsection (a) provides that SP–X's security interest is subordinate to SP–Z's, regardless of whether SP–X's financing statement was filed before SP–Z perfected its security interest.

Example 2: SP–X holds a perfected-by-filing security interest in X Corp's existing and after-acquired inventory, and SP–Z holds a perfected-by-filing security interest in Z Corp's existing and after-acquired inventory. Z Corp becomes bound as debtor by X Corp's security agreement. Subsequently, Z Corp acquires a new item of inventory. Under Section 9–508, SP–X's financing statement is effective to perfect a security interest in the new item of inventory in which Z Corp has rights. However, because SP–Z's security interest was perfected by another method, subsection (a) provides that SP–X's security interest is subordinate to SP–Z's, regardless of which financing statement was filed first. This would be the case even if SP–Z filed after Z Corp became bound by X Corp's security agreement.

3. **Other Priority Rules.** Subsection (b) addresses the priority among security interests created by the original debtor (X Corp). By invoking the other priority rules of this subpart, as applicable, subsection (b) preserves the relative priority of security interests created by the original debtor.

Example 3: Under the facts of Example 2, SP–Y also holds a perfected-by-filing security interest in X Corp's existing and after-acquired inventory. SP–Y filed after SP–X. Inasmuch as both SP–X's and SP–Y's security interests in inventory acquired by Z Corp after it became bound are perfected solely under Section 9–508, the normal priority rules determine their relative priorities. Under the "first-to-file-or-perfect" rule of Section 9–322(a)(1), SP–X has priority over SP–Y.

Example 4: Under the facts of Example 3, after Z Corp became bound by X Corp's security agreement, SP–Y promptly filed a new initial financing statement against Z Corp. At that time, SP–X's security interest was perfected only by virtue of its original filing against X Corp which was "effective solely under Section 9–508." Because SP–Y's security interest no longer is perfected by a financing statement that is "effective solely under Section 9–508," this section does not apply to the priority contest. Rather, the normal priority rules apply. Under Section 9–322, because SP–Y's financing statement was filed *against Z Corp*, the new debtor, before SP–X's, SP–Y's security interest is senior to that of SP–X. Similarly, the normal priority rules would govern priority between SP–Y and SP–Z.

The second sentence of subsection (b) effectively limits the applicability of the first sentence to situations in which a new debtor has become bound by more than one security agreement entered into by the *same* original debtor. When the new debtor has become bound by security agreements entered into by *different* original debtors, the second sentence provides that priority is based on priority in time of the new debtor's becoming bound.

Example 5: Under the facts of Example 2, SP–W holds a perfected-by-filing security interest in W Corp's existing and after-acquired inventory. After Z Corp became bound by X Corp's security agreement in favor of SP–X, Z Corp became bound by W Corp's security agreement. Under subsection (b), SP–W's security interest in inventory acquired by Z Corp is subordinate to that of SP–X, because Z Corp became bound under SP–X's security agreement before it became bound under SP–W's security agreement. This is the result regardless of which financing statement (SP–X's or SP–W's) was filed first.

The second sentence of subsection (b) reflects the generally accepted view that priority based on the first-to-file rule is inappropriate for resolving priority disputes when the filings were made against different debtors. Like subsection (a) and the first sentence of subsection (b), however, the second sentence of subsection (b) relates only to priority conflicts among security interests perfected by filed financing statements that are "effective solely under Section 9–508."

Example 6: Under the facts of Example 5, after Z Corp became bound by W Corp's security agreement, SP–W promptly filed a new initial financing statement against Z Corp. At that time, SP–X's security interest was perfected only pursuant to its original filing against X Corp which was "effective solely under Section 9–508." Because SP–W's security interest is not perfected by a financing statement that is "effective solely under Section 9–508," this section does not apply to the priority contest. Rather, the normal priority rules apply. Under Section 9–322, because SP–W's financing statement was the first to be filed *against Z Corp*, the new debtor, SP–W's security interest is senior to that of SP–X. Similarly, the normal priority rules would govern priority between SP–W and SP–Z.

§ 9–327. Priority of Security Interests in Deposit Account.

The following rules govern priority among conflicting security interests in the same deposit account:

(1) A security interest held by a secured party having control of the deposit account under Section 9–104 has priority over a conflicting security interest held by a secured party that does not have control.

(2) Except as otherwise provided in paragraphs (3) and (4), security interests perfected by control under Section 9–314 rank according to priority in time of obtaining control.

(3) Except as otherwise provided in paragraph (4), a security interest held by the bank with which the deposit account is maintained has priority over a conflicting security interest held by another secured party.

(4) A security interest perfected by control under Section 9–104(a)(3) has priority over a security interest held by the bank with which the deposit account is maintained.

Official Comment

1. **Source.** New; derived from former Section 9–115(5).

2. **Scope of This Section.** This section contains the rules governing the priority of conflicting security interests in deposit accounts. It overrides conflicting priority rules. See Sections 9–322(f)(1), 9–324(a), (b), (d), (f). This section does not apply to accounts evidenced by an instrument (e.g., certain certificates of deposit), which by definition are not "deposit accounts."

3. **Control.** Under paragraph (1), security interests perfected by control (Sections 9–314, 9–104) take prior-

ity over those perfected otherwise, e.g., as identifiable cash proceeds under Section 9–315. Secured parties for whom the deposit account is an integral part of the credit decision will, at a minimum, insist upon the right to immediate access to the deposit account upon the debtor's default (i.e., control). Those secured parties for whom the deposit account is less essential will not take control, thereby running the risk that the debtor will dispose of funds on deposit (either outright or for collateral purposes) after default but before the account can be frozen by court order or the secured party can obtain control.

Paragraph (2) governs the case (expected to be very rare) in which a bank enters into a Section 9–104(a)(2) control agreement with more than one secured party. It provides that the security interests rank according to time of obtaining control. If the bank is solvent and the control agreements are well drafted, the bank will be liable to each secured party, and the priority rule will have no practical effect.

4. **Priority of Bank.** Under paragraph (3), the security interest of the bank with which the deposit account is maintained normally takes priority over all other conflicting security interests in the deposit account, regardless of whether the deposit account constitutes the competing secured party's original collateral or its proceeds. A rule of this kind enables banks to extend credit to their depositors without the need to examine either the public record or their own records to determine whether another party might have a security interest in the deposit account.

A secured party who takes a security interest in the deposit account as original collateral can protect itself against the results of this rule in one of two ways. It can take control of the deposit account by becoming the bank's customer. Under paragraph (4), this arrangement operates to subordinate the bank's security interest. Alternatively, the secured party can obtain a subordination agreement from the bank. See Section 9–339.

A secured party who claims the deposit account as proceeds of other collateral can reduce the risk of becoming junior by obtaining the debtor's agreement to deposit proceeds into a specific cash-collateral account and obtaining the agreement of that bank to subordinate all its claims to those of the secured party. But if the debtor violates its agreement and deposits funds into a deposit account other than the cash-collateral account, the secured party risks being subordinated.

5. **Priority in Proceeds of, and Funds Transferred from, Deposit Account.** The priority afforded

by this section does not extend to proceeds of a deposit account. Rather, Section 9–322(c) through (e) and the provisions referred to in Section 9–322(f) govern priorities in proceeds of a deposit account. Section 9–315(d) addresses continuation of perfection in proceeds of deposit accounts. As to funds transferred from a deposit account that serves as collateral, see Section 9–332.

§ 9–328. Priority of Security Interests in Investment Property.

The following rules govern priority among conflicting security interests in the same investment property:

(1) A security interest held by a secured party having control of investment property under Section 9–106 has priority over a security interest held by a secured party that does not have control of the investment property.

(2) Except as otherwise provided in paragraphs (3) and (4), conflicting security interests held by secured parties each of which has control under Section 9–106 rank according to priority in time of:

(A) if the collateral is a security, obtaining control;

(B) if the collateral is a security entitlement carried in a securities account and:

  (i) if the secured party obtained control under Section 8–106(d)(1), the secured party's becoming the person for which the securities account is maintained;

  (ii) if the secured party obtained control under Section 8–106(d)(2), the securities intermediary's agreement to comply with the secured party's entitlement orders with respect to security entitlements carried or to be carried in the securities account; or

  (iii) if the secured party obtained control through another person under Section 8–106(d)(3), the time on which priority would be based under this paragraph if the other person were the secured party; or

(C) if the collateral is a commodity contract carried with a commodity intermediary, the satisfaction of the requirement for control specified in Section 9–106(b)(2) with respect to commodity contracts carried or

to be carried with the commodity intermediary.

(3) A security interest held by a securities intermediary in a security entitlement or a securities account maintained with the securities intermediary has priority over a conflicting security interest held by another secured party.

(4) A security interest held by a commodity intermediary in a commodity contract or a commodity account maintained with the commodity intermediary has priority over a conflicting security interest held by another secured party.

(5) A security interest in a certificated security in registered form which is perfected by taking delivery under Section 9–313(a) and not by control under Section 9–314 has priority over a conflicting security interest perfected by a method other than control.

(6) Conflicting security interests created by a broker, securities intermediary, or commodity intermediary which are perfected without control under Section 9–106 rank equally.

(7) In all other cases, priority among conflicting security interests in investment property is governed by Sections 9–322 and 9–323.

Official Comment

1. **Source.** Former Section 9–115(5).

2. **Scope of This Section.** This section contains the rules governing the priority of conflicting security interests in investment property. Paragraph (1) states the most important general rule—that a secured party who obtains control has priority over a secured party who does not obtain control. Paragraphs (2) through (4) deal with conflicting security interests each of which is perfected by control. Paragraph (5) addresses the priority of a security interest in a certificated security which is perfected by delivery but not control. Paragraph (6) deals with the relatively unusual circumstance in which a broker, securities intermediary, or commodity intermediary has created conflicting security interests none of which is perfected by control. Paragraph (7) provides that the general priority rules of Sections 9–322 and 9–323 apply to cases not covered by the specific rules in this section. The principal application of this residual rule is that the usual first in time of filing rule applies to conflicting security interests that are perfected only by filing. Because the control priority rule of paragraph (1) provides for the ordinary cases in which persons purchase securities on margin credit from their brokers, there is no need for special rules for purchase-money security interests. See

also Section 9–103 (limiting purchase-money collateral to goods and software).

3. **General Rule: Priority of Security Interest Perfected by Control.** Under paragraph (1), a secured party who obtains control has priority over a secured party who does not obtain control. The control priority rule does not turn on either temporal sequence or awareness of conflicting security interests. Rather, it is a structural rule, based on the principle that a lender should be able to rely on the collateral without question if the lender has taken the necessary steps to assure itself that it is in a position where it can foreclose on the collateral without further action by the debtor. The control priority rule is necessary because the perfection rules provide considerable flexibility in structuring secured financing arrangements. For example, at the "retail" level, a secured lender to an investor who wants the full measure of protection can obtain control, but the creditor may be willing to accept the greater measure of risk that follows from perfection by filing. Similarly, at the "wholesale" level, a lender to securities firms can leave the collateral with the debtor and obtain a perfected security interest under the automatic perfection rule of Section 9–309(10), but a lender who wants to be entirely sure of its position will want to obtain control. The control priority rule of paragraph (1) is an essential part of this system of flexibility. It is feasible to provide more than one method of perfecting security interests only if the rules ensure that those who take the necessary steps to obtain the full measure of protection do not run the risk of subordination to those who have not taken such steps. A secured party who is unwilling to run the risk that the debtor has granted or will grant a conflicting control security interest should not make a loan without obtaining control of the collateral.

As applied to the retail level, the control priority rule means that a secured party who obtains control has priority over a conflicting security interest perfected by filing without regard to inquiry into whether the control secured party was aware of the filed security interest. Prior to the 1994 revisions to Articles 8 and 9, Article 9 did not permit perfection of security interests in securities by filing. Accordingly, parties who deal in securities never developed a practice of searching the UCC files before conducting securities transactions. Although filing is now a permissible method of perfection, in order to avoid disruption of existing practices in this business it is necessary to give perfection by filing a different and more limited effect for securities than for some other forms of collateral. The priority rules are not based on the assumption that parties who perfect by the usual method of obtaining control will search the files. Quite the contrary, the control priority rule is intended to ensure that, with respect to investment property, secured parties who do obtain control are entirely unaffected by filings. To state the point another way, perfection by filing is intended to affect only general creditors or other secured creditors who rely on filing. The rule that a security interest perfected by filing can be primed by a control security interest, without regard to awareness, is a consequence of the system of perfection and priority rules for investment property. These rules are designed to take account of the circumstances of the securities markets, where filing is not given the same effect as for some other forms of property. No implication is made about the effect of filing with respect to security interests in other forms of property, nor about other Article 9 rules, e.g., Section 9–330, which govern the circumstances in which security interests in other forms of property perfected by filing can be primed by subsequent perfected security interests.

The following examples illustrate the application of the priority rule in paragraph (1):

Example 1: Debtor borrows from Alpha and grants Alpha a security interest in a variety of collateral, including all of Debtor's investment property. At that time Debtor owns 1000 shares of XYZ Co. stock for which Debtor has a certificate. Alpha perfects by filing. Later, Debtor borrows from Beta and grants Beta a security interest in the 1000 shares of XYZ Co. stock. Debtor delivers the certificate, properly indorsed, to Beta. Alpha and Beta both have perfected security interests in the XYZ Co. stock. Beta has control, see Section 8–106(b)(1), and hence has priority over Alpha.

Example 2: Debtor borrows from Alpha and grants Alpha a security interest in a variety of collateral, including all of Debtor's investment property. At that time Debtor owns 1000 shares of XYZ Co. stock, held through a securities account with Able & Co. Alpha perfects by filing. Later, Debtor borrows from Beta and grants Beta a security interest in the 1000 shares of XYZ Co. stock. Debtor instructs Able to have the 1000 shares transferred through the clearing corporation to Custodian Bank, to be credited to Beta's account with Custodian Bank. Alpha and Beta both have perfected security interests in the XYZ Co. stock. Beta has control, see Section 8–106(d)(1), and hence has priority over Alpha.

Example 3: Debtor borrows from Alpha and grants Alpha a security interest in a variety of collateral, including all of Debtor's investment property. At that time Debtor owns 1000 shares of XYZ Co. stock, which is held through a securities account with Able & Co. Alpha perfects by filing. Later, Debtor borrows from Beta and grants Beta a security interest in the 1000 shares of XYZ Co. stock. Debtor, Able, and Beta enter into an agreement under which Debtor will continue to receive dividends and distributions, and will continue to have the right to direct dispositions, but Beta will also have the right to direct dispositions and receive the proceeds. Alpha and Beta both have perfected security interests in the XYZ Co. stock (more precisely, in the Debtor's security entitlement to the financial asset consisting of the XYZ Co. stock). Beta has control, see Section 8–106(d)(2), and hence has priority over Alpha.

Example 4: Debtor borrows from Alpha and grants Alpha a security interest in a variety of collateral, including all of Debtor's investment property. At that time Debtor owns 1000 shares of XYZ Co. stock, held through a securities account with Able & Co. Alpha perfects by filing. Debtor's agreement with Able & Co. provides that Able has a security interest in all securities carried in the account as security for any obligations of Debtor to Able. Debtor incurs obligations to Able and later defaults on the obligations to Alpha and Able. Able has control by virtue of the rule of Section 8–106(e) that if a customer grants a security interest to its own intermediary, the intermediary has control. Since Alpha does not have control, Able has priority over Alpha under the general control priority rule of paragraph (1).

4. Conflicting Security Interests Perfected by Control: Priority of Securities Intermediary or Commodity Intermediary. Paragraphs (2) through (4) govern the priority of conflicting security interests each of which is perfected by control. The following example explains the application of the rules in paragraphs (3) and (4):

Example 5: Debtor holds securities through a securities account with Able & Co. Debtor's agreement with Able & Co. provides that Able has a security interest in all securities carried in the account as security for any obligations of Debtor to Able. Debtor borrows from Beta and grants Beta a security interest in 1000 shares of XYZ Co. stock carried in the account. Debtor, Able, and Beta enter into an agreement under which Debtor will continue to receive dividends and distributions and will continue to have the right to direct dispositions, but Beta will also have the right to direct dispositions and receive the proceeds. Debtor incurs obligations to Able and later defaults on the obligations to Beta and Able. Both Beta and Able have control, so the general control priority rule of paragraph (1) does not apply. Com-

pare Example 4. Paragraph (3) provides that a security interest held by a securities intermediary in positions of its own customer has priority over a conflicting security interest of an external lender, so Able has priority over Beta. (Paragraph (4) contains a parallel rule for commodity intermediaries.) The agreement among Able, Beta, and Debtor could, of course, determine the relative priority of the security interests of Able and Beta, see Section 9–339, but the fact that the intermediary has agreed to act on the instructions of a secured party such as Beta does not itself imply any agreement by the intermediary to subordinate.

5. Conflicting Security Interests Perfected by Control: Temporal Priority. Former Section 9–115 introduced into Article 9 the concept of conflicting security interests that rank equally. Paragraph (2) of this section governs priority in those circumstances in which more than one secured party (other than a broker, securities intermediary, or commodity intermediary) has control. It replaces the equal-priority rule for conflicting security interests in investment property with a temporal rule. For securities, both certificated and uncertificated, under paragraph (2)(A) priority is based on the time that control is obtained. For security entitlements carried in securities accounts, the treatment is more complex. Paragraph (2)(B) bases priority on the timing of the steps taken to achieve control. The following example illustrates the application of paragraph (2).

Example 6: Debtor borrows from Alpha and grants Alpha a security interest in a variety of collateral, including all of Debtor's investment property. At that time Debtor owns a security entitlement that includes 1000 shares of XYZ Co. stock that Debtor holds through a securities account with Able & Co. Debtor, Able, and Alpha enter into an agreement under which Debtor will continue to receive dividends and distributions, and will continue to have the right to direct dispositions, but Alpha will also have the right to direct dispositions and receive the proceeds. Later, Debtor borrows from Beta and grants Beta a security interest in all its investment property, existing and after-acquired. Debtor, Able, and Beta enter into an agreement under which Debtor will continue to receive dividends and distributions, and will continue to have the right to direct dispositions, but Beta will also have the right to direct dispositions and receive the proceeds. Alpha and Beta both have perfected-by-control security interests in the security entitlement to the XYZ Co. stock by virtue of their agreements with Able. See Sections 9–314(a), 9–106(a), 8–106(d)(2). Under paragraph (2)(B)(ii), the priority of each security interest dates from the time of the secured party's agreement with Able. Because Alpha's agreement was first in time, Alpha has priority. This priority applies equally to security entitlements to financial assets credited to the account after the agreement was entered into.

The priority rule is analogous to "first-to-file" priority under Section 9–322 with respect to after-acquired collateral. Paragraphs (2)(B)(i) and (2)(B)(iii) provide similar rules for security entitlements as to which control is obtained by other methods, and paragraph (2)(C) provides a similar rule for commodity contracts carried in a commodity account. Section 8–510 also has been revised to provide a temporal priority conforming to paragraph (2)(B).

6. **Certificated Securities.** A long-standing practice has developed whereby secured parties whose collateral consists of a security evidenced by a security certificate take possession of the security certificate. If the security certificate is in bearer form, the secured party's acquisition of possession constitutes "delivery" under Section 8–301(a)(1), and the delivery constitutes "control" under Section 8–106(a). Comment 5 discusses the priority of security interests perfected by control of investment property.

If the security certificate is in registered form, the secured party will not achieve control over the security unless the security certificate contains an appropriate indorsement or is (re)registered in the secured party's name. See Section 8–106(b). However, the secured party's acquisition of possession constitutes "delivery" of the security certificate under Section 8–301 and serves to perfect the security interest under Section 9–313(a), even if the security certificate has not been appropriately indorsed and has not been (re)registered in the secured party's name. A security interest perfected by this method has priority over a security interest perfected other than by control (e.g., by filing). See paragraph (5).

The priority rule stated in paragraph (5) may seem anomalous, in that it can afford less favorable treatment to purchasers who buy collateral outright that to those who take a security interest in it. For example, a buyer of a security certificate would cut off a security interest perfected by filing only if the buyer achieves the status of a protected purchaser under Section 8–303. The buyer would not be a protected purchaser, for example, if it does not obtain "control" under Section 8–106 (e.g., if it fails to obtain a proper indorsement of the certificate) or if it had notice of an adverse claim under Section 8–105. The apparent anomaly disappears, however, when one understands the priority rule not as one intended to protect careless or guilty parties, but as one that eliminates the need to conduct a search of the public records only insofar as necessary to serve the needs of the securities markets.

7. **Secured Financing of Securities Firms.** Priority questions concerning security interests granted by brokers and securities intermediaries are governed by the general control-beats-non-control priority rule of paragraph (1), as supplemented by the special rules set out in paragraphs (2) (temporal priority—first to control), (3) (special priority for securities intermediary), and (6) (equal priority for non-control). The following examples illustrate the priority rules as applied to this setting. (In all cases it is assumed that the debtor retains sufficient other securities to satisfy all customers' claims. This section deals with the relative rights of secured lenders to a securities firm. Disputes between a secured lender and the firm's own customers are governed by Section 8–511.)

Example 7: Able & Co., a securities dealer, enters into financing arrangements with two lenders, Alpha Bank and Beta Bank. In each case the agreements provide that the lender will have a security interest in the securities identified on lists provided to the lender on a daily basis, that the debtor will deliver the securities to the lender on demand, and that the debtor will not list as collateral any securities which the debtor has pledged to any other lender. Upon Able's insolvency it is discovered that Able has listed the same securities on the collateral lists provided to both Alpha and Beta. Alpha and Beta both have perfected security interests under the automatic-perfection rule of Section 9–309(10). Neither Alpha nor Beta has control. Paragraph (6) provides that the security interests of Alpha and Beta rank equally, because each of them has a non-control security interest granted by a securities firm. They share pro-rata.

Example 8: Able enters into financing arrangements, with Alpha Bank and Beta Bank as in Example 7. At some point, however, Beta decides that it is unwilling to continue to provide financing on a non-control basis. Able directs the clearing corporation where it holds its principal inventory of securities to move specified securities into Beta's account. Upon Able's insolvency it is discovered that a list of collateral provided to Alpha includes securities that had been moved to Beta's account. Both Alpha and Beta have perfected security interests; Alpha under the automatic-perfection rule of Section 9–309(10), and Beta under that rule and also the perfection-by-control rule in Section 9–314(a). Beta has control but

Alpha does not. Beta has priority over Alpha under paragraph (1).

Example 9: Able & Co. carries its principal inventory of securities through Clearing Corporation, which offers a "shared control" facility whereby a participant securities firm can enter into an arrangement with a lender under which the securities firm will retain the power to trade and otherwise direct dispositions of securities carried in its account, but Clearing Corporation agrees that, at any time the lender so directs, Clearing Corporation will transfer any securities from the firm's account to the lender's account or otherwise dispose of them as directed by the lender. Able enters into financing arrangements with two lenders, Alpha and Beta, each of which obtains such a control agreement from Clearing Corporation. The agreement with each lender provides that Able will designate specific securities as collateral on lists provided to the lender on a daily or other periodic basis, and that it will not pledge the same securities to different lenders. Upon Able's insolvency, it is discovered that Able has listed the same securities on the collateral lists provided to both Alpha and Beta. Both Alpha and Beta have control over the disputed securities. Paragraph (2) awards priority to whichever secured party first entered into the agreement with Clearing Corporation.

8. **Relation to Other Law.** Section 1–103 provides that "unless displaced by particular provisions of this Act, the principles of law and equity ... shall supplement its provisions." There may be circumstances in which a secured party's action in acquiring a security interest that has priority under this section constitutes conduct that is wrongful under other law. Though the possibility of such resort to other law may provide an appropriate "escape valve" for cases of egregious conduct, care must be taken to ensure that this does not impair the certainty and predictability of the priority rules. Whether a court may appropriately look to other law to impose liability upon or estop a secured party from asserting its Article 9 priority depends on an assessment of the secured party's conduct under the standards established by such other law as well as a determination of whether the particular application of such other law is displaced by the UCC.

Some circumstances in which other law is clearly displaced by the UCC rules are readily identifiable. Common law "first in time, first in right" principles, or correlative tort liability rules such as common law conversion principles under which a purchaser may incur liability to a person with a prior property interest without regard to awareness of that claim, are necessarily displaced by the priority rules set out in this section since these rules determine the relative ranking of security interests in investment property. So too, Article 8 provides protections against adverse claims to certain purchasers of interests in investment property. In circumstances where a secured party not only has priority under Section 9–328, but also qualifies for protection against adverse claims under Section 8–303, 8–502, or 8–510, resort to other law would be precluded.

In determining whether it is appropriate in a particular case to look to other law, account must also be taken of the policies that underlie the commercial law rules on securities markets and security interests in securities. A principal objective of the 1994 revision of Article 8 and the provisions of Article 9 governing investment property was to ensure that secured financing transactions can be implemented on a simple, timely, and certain basis. One of the circumstances that led to the revision was the concern that uncertainty in the application of the rules on secured transactions involving securities and other financial assets could contribute to systemic risk by impairing the ability of financial institutions to provide liquidity to the markets in times of stress. The control priority rule is designed to provide a clear and certain rule to ensure that lenders who have taken the necessary steps to establish control do not face a risk of subordination to other lenders who have not done so.

The control priority rule does not turn on an inquiry into the state of a secured party's awareness of potential conflicting claims because a rule under which a person's rights depended on that sort of after-the-fact inquiry could introduce an unacceptable measure of uncertainty. If an inquiry into awareness could provide a complete and satisfactory resolution of the problem in all cases, the priority rules of this section would have incorporated that test. The fact that they do not necessarily means that resort to other law based solely on that factor is precluded, though the question whether a control secured party induced or encouraged its financing arrangement with actual knowledge that the debtor would be violating the rights of another secured party may, in some circumstances, appropriately be treated as a factor in determining whether the control party's action is the kind of egregious conduct for which resort to other law is appropriate.

§ 9–329. Priority of Security Interests in Letter-of-Credit Right.

The following rules govern priority among conflicting security interests in the same letter-of-credit right:

(1) A security interest held by a secured party having control of the letter-of-credit right under Section 9–107 has priority to the extent of its control over a conflicting security interest held by a secured party that does not have control.

(2) Security interests perfected by control under Section 9–314 rank according to priority in time of obtaining control.

Official Comment

1. **Source.** New; loosely modeled after former Section 9–115(5).

2. **General Rule.** Paragraph (1) awards priority to a secured party who perfects a security interest directly in letter-of-credit rights (i.e., one that takes an assignment of proceeds and obtains consent of the issuer or any nominated person under Section 5–114(c)) over another conflicting security interest (i.e., one that is perfected automatically in the letter-of-credit rights as supporting obligations under Section 9–308(d)). This is consistent with international letter-of-credit practice and provides finality to payments made to recognized assignees of letter-of-credit proceeds. If an issuer or nominated person recognizes multiple security interests in a letter-of-credit right, resulting in multiple parties having control (Section 9–107), under paragraph (2) the security interests rank according to the time of obtaining control.

3. **Drawing Rights; Transferee Beneficiaries.** Drawing under a letter of credit is personal to the beneficiary and requires the beneficiary to perform the conditions for drawing under the letter of credit. Accordingly, a beneficiary's grant of a security interest in a letter of credit includes the beneficiary's "letter-of-credit right" as defined in Section 9–102 and the right to "proceeds of [the] letter of credit" as defined in Section 5–114(a), but does not include the right to demand payment under the letter of credit.

Section 5–114(e) provides that the "[r]ights of a transferee beneficiary or nominated person are independent of the beneficiary's assignment of the proceeds of a letter of credit and are superior to the assignee's right to the proceeds." To the extent the rights of a transferee beneficiary or nominated person are independent and superior, this Article does not apply. See Section 9–109(c).

Under Article 5, there is in effect a novation upon the transfer with the issuer becoming bound on a new, independent obligation to the transferee. The rights of nominated persons and transferee beneficiaries under a letter of credit include the right to demand payment from the issuer. Under Section 5–114(e), their rights to

payment are independent of their obligations to the beneficiary (or original beneficiary) and superior to the rights of assignees of letter-of-credit proceeds (Section 5–114(c)) and others claiming a security interest in the beneficiary's (or original beneficiary's) letter-of-credit rights.

A transfer of drawing rights under a transferable letter of credit establishes independent Article 5 rights in the transferee and does not create or perfect an Article 9 security interest in the transferred drawing rights. The definition of "letter-of-credit right" in Section 9–102 excludes a beneficiary's drawing rights. The exercise of drawing rights by a transferee beneficiary may breach a contractual obligation of the transferee to the original beneficiary concerning when and how much the transferee may draw or how it may use the funds received under the letter of credit. If, for example, drawing rights are transferred to support a sale or loan from the transferee to the original beneficiary, then the transferee would be obligated to the original beneficiary under the sale or loan agreement to account for any drawing and for the use of any funds received. The transferee's obligation would be governed by the applicable law of contracts or restitution.

4. **Secured Party-Transferee Beneficiaries.** As described in Comment 3, drawing rights under letters of credit are transferred in many commercial contexts in which the transferee is not a secured party claiming a security interest in an underlying receivable supported by the letter of credit. Consequently, a transfer of a letter of credit is not a method of "perfection" of a security interest. The transferee's independent right to draw under the letter of credit and to receive and retain the value thereunder (in effect, priority) is not based on Article 9 but on letter-of-credit law and the terms of the letter of credit. Assume, however, that a secured party does hold a security interest in a receivable that is owned by a beneficiary-debtor and supported by a transferable letter of credit. Assume further that the beneficiary-debtor causes the letter of credit to be transferred to the secured party, the secured party draws under the letter of credit, and, upon the issuer's payment to the secured party-transferee, the underlying account debtor's obligation to the original beneficiary-debtor is satisfied. In this situation, the payment to the secured party-transferee is proceeds of the receivable collected by the secured party-transferee. Consequently, the secured party-transferee would have certain duties to the debtor and third parties under Article 9. For example, it would be obliged to collect under the letter of credit in a commercially

reasonable manner and to remit any surplus pursuant to Sections 9–607 and 9–608.

This scenario is problematic under letter-of-credit law and practice, inasmuch as a transferee beneficiary collects in its own right arising from its own performance. Accordingly, under Section 5–114, the independent and superior rights of a transferee control over any inconsistent duties under Article 9. A transferee beneficiary may take a transfer of drawing rights to avoid reliance on the original beneficiary's credit and collateral, and it may consider any Article 9 rights superseded by its Article 5 rights. Moreover, it will not always be clear (i) whether a transferee beneficiary has a security interest in the underlying collateral, (ii) whether any security interest is senior to the rights of others, or (iii) whether the transferee beneficiary is aware that it holds a security interest. There will be clear cases in which the role of a transferee beneficiary as such is merely incidental to a conventional secured financing. There also will be cases in which the existence of a security interest may have little to do with the position of a transferee beneficiary as such. In dealing with these cases and less clear cases involving the possible application of Article 9 to a nominated person or a transferee beneficiary, the right to demand payment under a letter of credit should be distinguished from letter-of-credit rights. The courts also should give appropriate consideration to the policies and provisions of Article 5 and letter-of-credit practice as well as Article 9.

§ 9–330.   Priority of Purchaser of Chattel Paper or Instrument.

(a) **[Purchaser's priority: security interest claimed merely as proceeds.]** A purchaser of chattel paper has priority over a security interest in the chattel paper which is claimed merely as proceeds of inventory subject to a security interest if:

(1) in good faith and in the ordinary course of the purchaser's business, the purchaser gives new value and takes possession of the chattel paper or obtains control of the chattel paper under Section 9–105; and

(2) the chattel paper does not indicate that it has been assigned to an identified assignee other than the purchaser.

(b) **[Purchaser's priority: other security interests.]** A purchaser of chattel paper has priority over a security interest in the chattel paper which is claimed other than merely as

proceeds of inventory subject to a security interest if the purchaser gives new value and takes possession of the chattel paper or obtains control of the chattel paper under Section 9–105 in good faith, in the ordinary course of the purchaser's business, and without knowledge that the purchase violates the rights of the secured party.

(c) **[Chattel paper purchaser's priority in proceeds.]** Except as otherwise provided in Section 9–327, a purchaser having priority in chattel paper under subsection (a) or (b) also has priority in proceeds of the chattel paper to the extent that:

(1) Section 9–322 provides for priority in the proceeds; or

(2) the proceeds consist of the specific goods covered by the chattel paper or cash proceeds of the specific goods, even if the purchaser's security interest in the proceeds is unperfected.

(d) **[Instrument purchaser's priority.]** Except as otherwise provided in Section 9–331(a), a purchaser of an instrument has priority over a security interest in the instrument perfected by a method other than possession if the purchaser gives value and takes possession of the instrument in good faith and without knowledge that the purchase violates the rights of the secured party.

(e) **[Holder of purchase-money security interest gives new value.]** For purposes of subsections (a) and (b), the holder of a purchase-money security interest in inventory gives new value for chattel paper constituting proceeds of the inventory.

(f) **[Indication of assignment gives knowledge.]** For purposes of subsections (b) and (d), if chattel paper or an instrument indicates that it has been assigned to an identified secured party other than the purchaser, a purchaser of the chattel paper or instrument has knowledge that the purchase violates the rights of the secured party.

Official Comment

1. **Source.** Former Section 9–308.

2. **Non-Temporal Priority.** This Article permits a security interest in chattel paper or instruments to be perfected either by filing or by the secured party's taking possession. This section enables secured parties

and other purchasers of chattel paper (both electronic and tangible) and instruments to obtain priority over earlier-perfected security interests.

3. **Chattel Paper.** Subsections (a) and (b) follow former Section 9–308 in distinguishing between earlier-perfected security interests in chattel paper that is claimed merely as proceeds of inventory subject to a security interest and chattel paper that is claimed other than merely as proceeds. Like former Section 9–308, this section does not elaborate upon the phrase "merely as proceeds." For an elaboration, see PEB Commentary No. 8.

This section makes explicit the "good faith" requirement and retains the requirements of "the ordinary course of the purchaser's business" and the giving of "new value" as conditions for priority. Concerning the last, this Article deletes former Section 9–108 and adds to Section 9–102 a completely different definition of the term "new value." Under subsection (e), the holder of a purchase-money security interest in inventory is deemed to give "new value" for chattel paper constituting the proceeds of the inventory. Accordingly, the purchase-money secured party may qualify for priority in the chattel paper under subsection (a) or (b), whichever is applicable, even if it does not make an additional advance against the chattel paper.

If a possessory security interest in tangible chattel paper or a perfected-by-control security interest in electronic chattel paper does not qualify for priority under this section, it may be subordinate to a perfected-by-filing security interest under Section 9–322(a)(1).

4. **Possession.** The priority afforded by this section turns in part on whether a purchaser "takes possession" of tangible chattel paper. Similarly, the governing law provisions in Section 9–301 address both "possessory" and "nonpossessory" security interests. Two common practices have raised particular concerns. First, in some cases the parties create more than one copy or counterpart of chattel paper evidencing a single secured obligation or lease. This practice raises questions as to which counterpart is the "original" and whether it is necessary for a purchaser to take possession of all counterparts in order to "take possession" of the chattel paper. Second, parties sometimes enter into a single "master" agreement. The master agreement contemplates that the parties will enter into separate "schedules" from time to time, each evidencing chattel paper. Must a purchaser of an obligation or lease evidenced by a single schedule also take possession of the master agreement as well as the schedule in order to "take possession" of the chattel paper?

The problem raised by the first practice is easily solved. The parties may in the terms of their agreement and by designation on the chattel paper identify only one counterpart as the original chattel paper for purposes of taking possession of the chattel paper. Concerns about the second practice also are easily solved by careful drafting. Each schedule should provide that it incorporates the terms of the master agreement, not the other way around. This will make it clear that each schedule is a "stand alone" document.

5. **Chattel Paper Claimed Merely as Proceeds.** Subsection (a) revises the rule in former Section 9–308(b) to eliminate reference to what the purchaser knows. Instead, a purchaser who meets the possession or control, ordinary course, and new value requirements takes priority over a competing security interest unless the chattel paper itself indicates that it has been assigned to an identified assignee other than the purchaser. Thus subsection (a) recognizes the common practice of placing a "legend" on chattel paper to indicate that it has been assigned. This approach, under which the chattel paper purchaser who gives new value in ordinary course can rely on possession of unlegended, tangible chattel paper without any concern for other facts that it may know, comports with the expectations of both inventory and chattel paper financers.

6. **Chattel Paper Claimed Other Than Merely as Proceeds.** Subsection (b) eliminates the requirement that the purchaser take without knowledge that the "specific paper" is subject to the security interest and substitutes for it the requirement that the purchaser take "without knowledge that the purchase violates the rights of the secured party." This standard derives from the definition of "buyer in ordinary course of business" in Section 1–201(9). The source of the purchaser's knowledge is irrelevant. Note, however, that "knowledge" means "actual knowledge." Section 1–201(25).

In contrast to a junior secured party in accounts, who may be required in some special circumstances to undertake a search under the "good faith" requirement, see Comment 5 to Section 9–331, a purchaser of chattel paper under this section is not required as a matter of good faith to make a search in order to determine the existence of prior security interests. There may be circumstances where the purchaser undertakes a search nevertheless, either on its own volition or because other considerations make it advisable to do so, e.g., where the purchaser also is purchasing accounts. Without more, a purchaser of chattel paper who has seen a financing statement covering the chattel paper or who knows that the chattel paper is encumbered with a security interest, does not have knowledge that its purchase violates the secured party's rights. However, if a purchaser sees a statement in a financing statement to the effect that a purchase of chattel paper from the debtor would violate the rights of the filed secured party, the purchaser would have such knowledge. Likewise, under new subsection (f), if the chattel paper itself indicates that it had been assigned to an identified secured party other than the purchaser, the purchaser would have wrongful knowledge for purposes of subsection (b), thereby preventing the purchaser from qualifying for priority under that subsection, even if the purchaser did not have actual knowledge. In the case of tangible chattel paper, the indication normally would consist of a written legend on the chattel paper. In the case of electronic chattel paper, this Article leaves to developing market and technological practices the manner in which the chattel paper would indicate an assignment.

7. **Instruments.** Subsection (d) contains a special priority rule for instruments. Under this subsection, a purchaser of an instrument has priority over a security interest perfected by a method other than possession (e.g., by filing, temporarily under Section 9–312(e) or (g), as proceeds under Section 9–315(d), or automatically upon attachment under Section 9–309(4) if the security interest arises out of a sale of the instrument) if the purchaser gives value and takes possession of the instrument in good faith and without knowledge that the purchase violates the rights of the secured party. Generally, to the extent subsection (d) conflicts with Section 3–306, subsection (d) governs. See Section 3–102(b). For example, notice of a conflicting security interest precludes a purchaser from becoming a holder in due course under Section 3–302 and thereby taking free of all claims to the instrument under Section 3–306. However, a purchaser who takes even with knowledge of the security interest qualifies for priority under subsection (d) if it takes without knowledge that the purchase violates the rights of the holder of the security interest. Likewise, a purchaser qualifies for priority under subsection (d) if it takes for "value" as defined in Section 1–201, even if it does not take for "value" as defined in Section 3–303.

Subsection (d) is subject to Section 9–331(a), which provides that Article 9 does not limit the rights of a holder in due course under Article 3. Thus, in the rare case in which the purchaser of an instrument qualifies for priority under subsection (d), but another person has the rights of a holder in due course of the instrument, the other person takes free of the purchaser's claim. See Section 3–306.

The rule in subsection (d) is similar to the rules in subsections (a) and (b), which govern priority in chattel paper. The observations in Comment 6 concerning the requirement of good faith and the phrase "without knowledge that the purchase violates the rights of the secured party" apply equally to purchasers of instruments. However, unlike a purchaser of chattel paper, to qualify for priority under this section a purchaser of an instrument need only give "value" as defined in Section 1–201; it need not give "new value." Also, the purchaser need not purchase the instrument in the ordinary course of its business.

Subsection (d) applies to checks as well as notes. For example, to collect and retain checks that are proceeds (collections) of accounts free of a senior secured party's claim to the same checks, a junior secured party must satisfy the good-faith requirement (honesty in fact and the observance of reasonable commercial standards of fair dealing) of this subsection. This is the same good-faith requirement applicable to holders in due course. See Section 9–331, Comment 5.

8. **Priority in Proceeds of Chattel Paper.** Subsection (c) sets forth the two circumstances under which the priority afforded to a purchaser of chattel paper under subsection (a) or (b) extends also to proceeds of the chattel paper. The first is if the purchaser would have priority under the normal priority rules applicable to proceeds. The second, which the following Comments discuss in greater detail, is if the proceeds consist of the specific goods covered by the chattel paper. Former Article 9 generally was silent as to the priority of a security interest in proceeds when a purchaser qualifies for priority under Section 9–308 (but see former Section 9–306(5)(b), concerning returned and repossessed goods).

9. **Priority in Returned and Repossessed Goods.** Returned and repossessed goods may constitute proceeds of chattel paper. The following Comments explain the treatment of returned and repossessed goods as proceeds of chattel paper. The analysis is consistent with that of PEB Commentary No. 5, which these Comments replace, and is based upon the following example:

Example: SP–1 has a security interest in all the inventory of a dealer in goods (Dealer); SP–1's security interest is perfected by filing. Dealer sells some of its inventory to a buyer in the ordinary course of business (BIOCOB) pursuant to a conditional sales contract (chattel paper) that does not indicate that it has been assigned to SP–1. SP–2 purchases the chattel paper from Dealer and takes possession of the paper in good faith, in the ordinary course of business, and without knowledge that the purchase violates the rights of SP–1. Subsequently, BIOCOB returns the goods to Dealer because they are defective. Alternatively, Dealer acquires possession of the goods following BIOCOB's default.

10. **Assignment of Non-Lease Chattel Paper.**

a. **Loan by SP–2 to Dealer Secured by Chattel Paper (or Functional Equivalent Pursuant to Recourse Arrangement).**

(1) **Returned Goods.** If BIOCOB returns the goods to Dealer for repairs, Dealer is merely a bailee and acquires thereby no meaningful rights in the goods to which SP–1's security interest could attach. (Although SP–1's security interest could attach to Dealer's interest as a bailee, that interest is not likely to be of any particular value to SP–1.) Dealer is the owner of the *chattel paper* (i.e., the owner of a right to payment secured by a security interest in the goods); SP–2 has a security interest in the chattel paper, as does SP–1 (as proceeds of the goods under Section 9–315). Under Section 9–330, SP–2's security interest in the chattel paper is senior to that of SP–1. SP–2 enjoys this priority regardless of whether, or when, SP–2 filed a financing statement covering the chattel paper. Because chattel paper and goods represent different types of collateral, Dealer does not have any meaningful interest in *goods* to which either SP–1's or SP–2's security interest could attach in order to secure Dealer's obligations to either creditor. See Section 9–102 (defining "chattel paper" and "goods").

Now assume that BIOCOB returns the goods to Dealer under circumstances whereby Dealer once again becomes the owner of the goods. This would be the case, for example, if the goods were defective and BIOCOB was entitled to reject or revoke acceptance of the goods. See Sections 2–602 (rejection), 2–608 (revocation of acceptance). Unless BIOCOB has waived its defenses as against assignees of the chattel paper, SP–1's and SP–2's rights against BIOCOB would be subject to BIOCOB's claims and defenses. See Sections 9–403, 9–404. SP–1's security interest would attach again because the returned goods would be proceeds of the chattel paper. Dealer's acquisition of the goods easily can be characterized as "proceeds" consisting of an "in kind" collection on or distribution on account of the chattel paper. See Section 9–102 (definition of "proceeds"). Assuming that SP–1's security interest is perfected by filing against the goods and that the filing is made in the same office where a filing would be made against the chattel paper, SP–1's security interest in the goods would remain perfected beyond the 20–day period of automatic perfection. See Section 9–315(d).

Because Dealer's newly reacquired interest in the goods is proceeds of the chattel paper, SP–2's security interest also would attach in the goods as proceeds. If SP–2 had perfected its security interest in the chattel paper by filing (again, assuming that filing against the chattel paper was made in the same office where a filing would be made against the goods), SP–2's security interest in the reacquired goods would be perfected beyond 20 days. See Section 9–315(d). However, if SP–2 had relied only on its possession of the chattel paper for perfection and had not filed against the chattel paper or the goods, SP–2's security interest would be unperfected after the 20–day period. See Section 9–315(d). Nevertheless, SP–2's unperfected security interest in the goods would be senior to SP–1's security interest under Section 9–330(c). The result in this priority contest is not affected by SP–2's acquiescence or non-acquiescence in the return of the goods to Dealer.

(2) **Repossessed Goods.** As explained above, Dealer owns the chattel paper covering the goods, subject to security interests in favor of SP–1 and SP–2. In Article 9 parlance, Dealer has an interest in chattel paper, not goods. If Dealer, SP–1, or SP–2 repossesses the goods upon BIOCOB's default, whether the repossession is rightful or wrongful as among Dealer, SP–1, or SP–2, Dealer's interest will not change. The location of goods and the party who possesses them does not affect the fact that Dealer's interest is in chattel paper, not goods. The goods continue to be owned by BIOCOB. SP–1's security interest in the goods does not attach until such time as Dealer reacquires an interest (other than a bare possessory interest) in the goods. For example, Dealer might buy the goods at a foreclosure sale from SP–2 (whose security interest in the chattel paper is senior to that of SP–1); that disposition would cut off BIOCOB's rights in the goods. Section 9–617.

In many cases the matter would end upon sale of the goods to Dealer at a foreclosure sale and there would be no priority contest between SP–1 and SP–2; Dealer would be unlikely to buy the goods under circumstances whereby SP–2 would retain its security interest. There can be exceptions, however. For example, Dealer may be obliged to purchase the goods from SP–2 and SP–2 may be obliged to convey the goods to Dealer, but Dealer may fail to pay SP–2. Or, one could imagine that SP–2, like SP–1, has a general security interest in the inventory of Dealer. In the latter case, SP–2 should not receive the benefit of any special priority rule, since its interest in no way derives from priority under Section 9–330. In the former case, SP–2's security interest in the goods reacquired by Dealer is senior to SP–1's security interest under Section 9–330.

b. **Dealer's Outright Sale of Chattel Paper to SP–2.** Article 9 also applies to a transaction whereby SP–2 buys the chattel paper in an outright sale transaction without recourse against Dealer. Sections 1–201(37), 9–109(a). Although Dealer does not, in such a transaction, retain any residual ownership interest in the chattel paper, the chattel paper constitutes proceeds of the goods to which SP–1's security interest will attach and continue following the sale of the goods. Section 9–315(a). Even though Dealer has not retained any interest in the chattel paper, as discussed above BIOCOB subsequently may return the goods to Dealer under circumstances whereby Dealer reacquires an interest in the goods. The priority contest between SP–1 and SP–2 will be resolved as discussed above; Section 9–330 makes no distinction among purchasers of chattel paper on the basis of whether the purchaser is an outright buyer of chattel paper or one whose security interest secures an obligation of Dealer.

11. **Assignment of Lease Chattel Paper.** As defined in Section 9–102, "chattel paper" includes not only writings that evidence security interests in specific goods but also those that evidence true leases of goods.

The analysis with respect to lease chattel paper is similar to that set forth above with respect to non-lease chattel paper. It is complicated, however, by the fact that, unlike the case of chattel paper arising out of a sale, Dealer retains a residual interest in the *goods*. See Section 2A–103(1)(q) (defining "lessor's residual interest"); *In re Leasing Consultants, Inc.*, 486 F.2d 367 (2d Cir. 1973) (lessor's residual interest under true lease is an interest in goods and is a separate type of collateral from lessor's interest in the lease). If Dealer leases goods to a "lessee in ordinary course of business" (LIOCOB), then LIOCOB takes its interest under the lease (i.e., its "leasehold interest") free of the security interest of SP–1. See Sections 2A–307(3), 2A–103(1)(m) (defining "leasehold interest"), (1)(o) (defining "lessee in ordinary course of business"). SP–1 would, however, retain its security interest in the residual interest. In addition, SP–1 would acquire an interest in the lease chattel paper as proceeds. If Dealer then assigns the lease chattel paper to SP–2, Section 9–330 gives SP–2 priority over SP–1 with respect to the chattel paper, *but not* with respect to the residual interest in the *goods*. Consequently, assignees of lease chattel paper typically take a security interest in and file against the lessor's residual interest in goods, expecting their priority in the goods to be governed by the first-to-file-or-perfect rule of Section 9–322.

If the goods are returned to Dealer, other than upon expiration of the lease term, then the security interests of both SP–1 and SP–2 normally would attach to the goods as proceeds of the chattel paper. (If the goods are returned to Dealer at the expiration of the lease term and the lessee has made all payments due under the lease, however, then Dealer no longer has any rights under the chattel paper. Dealer's interest in the goods consists solely of its residual interest, as to which SP–2 has no claim.) This would be the case, for example, when the lessee rescinds the lease or when the lessor recovers possession in the exercise of its remedies under Article 2A. See, e.g., Section 2A–525. If SP–2 enjoyed priority in the chattel paper under Section 9–330, then SP–2 likewise would enjoy priority in the returned goods as proceeds. This does not mean that SP–2 necessarily is entitled to the entire value of the returned goods. The value of the goods represents the sum of the present value of (i) the value of their use for the term of the lease and (ii) the value of the residual interest. SP–2 has priority in the former, but SP–1 ordinarily would have priority in the latter. Thus, an allocation of a portion of the value of the goods to each component may be necessary. Where, as here, one secured party has a security interest in the lessor's residual interest and another has a priority security interest in the chattel paper, it may be advisable for the conflicting secured parties to establish a method for making such an allocation and otherwise to determine their relative rights in returned goods by agreement.

As amended in 2000.

§ 9–331. Priority of Rights of Purchasers of Instruments, Documents, and Securities Under Other Articles; Priority of Interests in Financial Assets and Security Entitlements Under Article 8.

(a) **[Rights under Articles 3, 7, and 8 not limited.]** This article does not limit the rights of a holder in due course of a negotiable instrument, a holder to which a negotiable document of title has been duly negotiated, or a protected purchaser of a security. These holders or purchasers take priority over an earlier security interest, even if perfected, to the extent provided in Articles 3, 7, and 8.

(b) **[Protection under Article 8.]** This article does not limit the rights of or impose liability on a person to the extent that the person is protected against the assertion of a claim under Article 8.

(c) **[Filing not notice.]** Filing under this article does not constitute notice of a claim or defense to the holders, or purchasers, or persons described in subsections (a) and (b).

Official Comment

1. **Source.** Former Section 9–309.

2. **"Priority."** In some provisions, this Article distinguishes between claimants that take collateral free of a security interest (in the sense that the security interest no longer encumbers the collateral) and those that take an interest in the collateral that is senior to a surviving security interest. See, e.g., Section 9–317. Whether a holder or purchaser referred to in this section takes free or is senior to a security interest depends on whether the purchaser is a buyer of the collateral or takes a security interest in it. The term "priority" is meant to encompass both scenarios, as it does in Section 9–330.

3. **Rights Acquired by Purchasers.** The rights to which this section refers are set forth in Sections 3–305 and 3–306 (holder in due course), 7–502 (holder to whom a negotiable document of title has been duly negotiated), and 8–303 (protected purchaser). The holders and purchasers referred to in this section do not always take priority over a security interest. See, e.g., Section 7–503 (affording paramount rights to certain owners and secured parties as against holder to whom a negotiable document of title has been duly negotiated). Accordingly, this section adds the clause, "to the extent provided in Articles 3, 7, and 8" to former Section 9–309.

4. **Financial Assets and Security Entitlements.** New subsection (b) provides explicit protection for those who deal with financial assets and security entitlements and who are immunized from liability under Article 8. See, e.g., Sections 8–502, 8–503(e), 8–510, 8–511. The new subsection makes explicit in Article 9 what is implicit in former Article 9 and explicit in several provisions of Article 8. It does not change the law.

5. **Collections by Junior Secured Party.** Under this section, a secured party with a junior security interest in receivables (accounts, chattel paper, promissory notes, or payment intangibles) may collect and retain the proceeds of those receivables free of the claim of a senior secured party to the same receivables, if the junior secured party is a holder in due course of the proceeds. In order to qualify as a holder in due course, the junior must satisfy the requirements of Section 3–302, which include taking in "good faith." This means that the junior not only must act "honestly" but also must observe "reasonable commercial standards of fair dealing" under the particular circumstances. See Section 9–102(a). Although "good faith" does not impose a general duty of inquiry, e.g., a search of the records in filing offices, there may be circumstances in which "reasonable commercial standards of fair dealing" would require such a search.

Consider, for example, a junior secured party in the business of financing or buying accounts who fails to undertake a search to determine the existence of prior security interests. Because a search, under the usages of trade of that business, would enable it to know or learn upon reasonable inquiry that collecting the accounts violated the rights of a senior secured party, the junior may fail to meet the good-faith standard. See Utility Contractors Financial Services, Inc. v. Amsouth Bank, NA, 985 F.2d 1554 (11th Cir. 1993). Likewise, a junior secured party who collects accounts when it knows or should know under the particular circumstances that doing so would violate the rights of a senior secured party, because the debtor had agreed not to grant a junior security interest in, or sell, the accounts, may not meet the good-faith test. Thus, if a junior secured party conducted or should have conducted a search and a financing statement filed on behalf of the senior secured party states such a restriction, the junior's collection would not meet the good-faith standard. On the other hand, if there was a course of performance between the senior secured party and the debtor which placed no such restrictions on the debtor and allowed the debtor to collect and use the proceeds without any restrictions, the junior secured party may then satisfy the requirements for being a holder in due course. This would be more likely in those circumstances where the junior secured party was providing additional financing to the debtor on an on-going basis by lending against or buying the accounts and had no notice of any restrictions against doing so. Generally, the senior secured party would not be prejudiced because the practical effect of such payment to the junior secured party is little different than if the debtor itself had made the collections and subsequently paid the secured party from the debtor's general funds. Absent collusion, the junior secured party would take the funds free of the senior security interests. See Section 9–332. In contrast, the senior secured party is likely to be prejudiced if the debtor is going out of business and the junior secured party collects the accounts by notifying the account debtors to make payments directly to the junior. Those collections may not be consistent with "reasonable commercial standards of fair dealing."

Whether the junior secured party qualifies as a holder in due course is fact-sensitive and should be decided on a case-by-case basis in the light of those circumstances. Decisions such as Financial Management Services, Inc. v. Familian, 905 P.2d 506 (Ariz. App. Div. 1995) (finding holder in due course status) could be determined differently under this application of the good-faith requirement.

The concepts addressed in this Comment are also applicable to junior secured parties as purchasers of instruments under Section 9–330(d). See Section 9–330, Comment 7.

§ 9–332. Transfer of Money; Transfer of Funds From Deposit Account.

(a) **[Transferee of money.]** A transferee of money takes the money free of a security interest unless the transferee acts in collusion with the debtor in violating the rights of the secured party.

(b) **[Transferee of funds from deposit account.]** A transferee of funds from a deposit account takes the funds free of a security interest in the deposit account unless the transferee acts in collusion with the debtor in violating the rights of the secured party.

Official Comment

1. **Source.** New.

2. **Scope of This Section.** This section affords broad protection to transferees who take funds from a deposit account and to those who take money. The term "transferee" is not defined; however, the debtor itself is not a transferee. Thus this section does not cover the case in which a debtor withdraws money (currency) from its deposit account or the case in which a bank debits an encumbered account and credits another account it maintains for the debtor.

A transfer of funds from a deposit account, to which subsection (b) applies, normally will be made by check, by funds transfer, or by debiting the debtor's deposit account and crediting another depositor's account.

Example 1: Debtor maintains a deposit account with Bank A. The deposit account is subject to a perfected security interest in favor of Lender. Debtor draws a check on the account, payable to Payee. Inasmuch as the check is not the proceeds of the deposit account (it is an order to pay funds from the deposit account), Lender's security interest in the

deposit account does not give rise to a security interest in the check. Payee deposits the check into its own deposit account, and Bank A pays it. Unless Payee acted in collusion with Debtor in violating Lender's rights, Payee takes the funds (the credits running in favor of Payee) free of Lender's security interest. This is true regardless of whether Payee is a holder in due course of the check and even if Payee gave no value for the check.

Example 2: Debtor maintains a deposit account with Bank A. The deposit account is subject to a perfected security interest in favor of Lender. At Bank B's suggestion, Debtor moves the funds from the account at Bank A to Debtor's deposit account with Bank B. Unless Bank B acted in collusion with Debtor in violating Lender's rights, Bank B takes the funds (the credits running in favor of Bank B) free from Lender's security interest. See subsection (b). However, inasmuch as the deposit account maintained with Bank B constitutes the proceeds of the deposit account at Bank A, Lender's security interest would attach to that account as proceeds. See Section 9–315.

Subsection (b) also would apply if, in the example, Bank A debited Debtor's deposit account in exchange for the issuance of Bank A's cashier's check. Lender's security interest would attach to the cashier's check as proceeds of the deposit account, and the rules applicable to instruments would govern any competing claims to the cashier's check. See, e.g., Sections 3–306, 9–322, 9–330, 9–331.

If Debtor withdraws money (currency) from an encumbered deposit account and transfers the money to a third party, then subsection (a), to the extent not displaced by federal law relating to money, applies. It contains the same rule as subsection (b).

Subsection (b) applies to *transfers of funds from* a deposit account; it does not apply to *transfers of the deposit account* itself or of an interest therein. For example, this section does not apply to the creation of a security interest in a deposit account. Competing claims to the deposit account itself are dealt with by other Article 9 priority rules. See Sections 9–317(a), 9–327, 9–340, 9–341. Similarly, a corporate merger normally would not result in a transfer of funds from a deposit account. Rather, it might result in a transfer of the deposit account itself. If so, the normal rules applicable to transferred collateral would apply; this section would not.

3. **Policy.** Broad protection for transferees helps to ensure that security interests in deposit accounts do

not impair the free flow of funds. It also minimizes the likelihood that a secured party will enjoy a claim to whatever the transferee purchases with the funds. Rules concerning recovery of payments traditionally have placed a high value on finality. The opportunity to upset a completed transaction, or even to place a completed transaction in jeopardy by bringing suit against the transferee of funds, should be severely limited. Although the giving of value usually is a prerequisite for receiving the ability to take free from third-party claims, where payments are concerned the law is even more protective. Thus, Section 3–418(c) provides that, even where the law of restitution otherwise would permit recovery of funds paid by mistake, no recovery may be had from a person "who in good faith changed position in reliance on the payment." Rather than adopt this standard, this section eliminates all reliance requirements whatsoever. Payments made by mistake are relatively rare, but payments of funds from encumbered deposit accounts (e.g., deposit accounts containing collections from accounts receivable) occur with great regularity. In most cases, unlike payment by mistake, no one would object to these payments. In the vast proportion of cases, the transferee probably would be able to show a change of position in reliance on the payment. This section does not put the transferee to the burden of having to make this proof.

4. **"Bad Actors."** To deal with the question of the "bad actor," this section borrows "collusion" language from Article 8. See, e.g., Sections 8–115, 8–503(e). This is the most protective (i.e., least stringent) of the various standards now found in the UCC. Compare, e.g., Section 1–201(9) ("without knowledge that the sale ... is in violation of the ... security interest"); Section 1–201(19) ("honesty in fact in the conduct or transaction concerned"); Section 3–302(a)(2)(v) ("without notice of any claim").

5. **Transferee Who Does Not Take Free.** This section sets forth the circumstances under which certain transferees of money or funds take free of security interests. It does not determine the rights of a transferee who does not take free of a security interest.

Example 3: The facts are as in Example 2, but, in wrongfully moving the funds from the deposit account at Bank A to Debtor's deposit account with Bank B, Debtor acts in collusion with Bank B. Bank B does not take the funds free of Lender's security interest under this section. If Debtor grants a security interest to Bank B, Section 9–327 governs the relative priorities of Lender and Bank B. Under Section 9–327(3), Bank B's security interest in the Bank B deposit account is senior to Lender's security

interest in the deposit account as proceeds. However, Bank B's senior security interest does not protect Bank B against any liability to Lender that might arise from Bank B's wrongful conduct.

§ 9–333. Priority of Certain Liens Arising by Operation of Law.

(a) **["Possessory lien."]** In this section, "possessory lien" means an interest, other than a security interest or an agricultural lien:

(1) which secures payment or performance of an obligation for services or materials furnished with respect to goods by a person in the ordinary course of the person's business;

(2) which is created by statute or rule of law in favor of the person; and

(3) whose effectiveness depends on the person's possession of the goods.

(b) **[Priority of possessory lien.]** A possessory lien on goods has priority over a security interest in the goods unless the lien is created by a statute that expressly provides otherwise.

Official Comment

1. **Source.** Former Section 9–310.

2. **"Possessory Liens."** This section governs the relative priority of security interests arising under this Article and "possessory liens," i.e., common-law and statutory liens whose effectiveness depends on the lienor's possession of goods with respect to which the lienor provided services or furnished materials in the ordinary course of its business. As under former Section 9–310, the possessory lien has priority over a security interest unless the possessory lien is created by a statute that expressly provides otherwise. If the statute creating the possessory lien is silent as to its priority relative to a security interest, this section provides a rule of interpretation that the possessory lien takes priority, even if the statute has been construed judicially to make the possessory lien subordinate.

§ 9–334. Priority of Security Interests in Fixtures and Crops.

(a) **[Security interest in fixtures under this article.]** A security interest under this article may be created in goods that are fixtures or may continue in goods that become fixtures. A security interest does not exist under this article in ordinary building materials incorporated into an improvement on land.

(b) **[Security interest in fixtures under real-property law.]** This article does not prevent creation of an encumbrance upon fixtures under real property law.

(c) **[General rule: subordination of security interest in fixtures.]** In cases not governed by subsections (d) through (h), a security interest in fixtures is subordinate to a conflicting interest of an encumbrancer or owner of the related real property other than the debtor.

(d) **[Fixtures purchase-money priority.]** Except as otherwise provided in subsection (h), a perfected security interest in fixtures has priority over a conflicting interest of an encumbrancer or owner of the real property if the debtor has an interest of record in or is in possession of the real property and:

(1) the security interest is a purchase-money security interest;

(2) the interest of the encumbrancer or owner arises before the goods become fixtures; and

(3) the security interest is perfected by a fixture filing before the goods become fixtures or within 20 days thereafter.

(e) **[Priority of security interest in fixtures over interests in real property.]** A perfected security interest in fixtures has priority over a conflicting interest of an encumbrancer or owner of the real property if:

(1) the debtor has an interest of record in the real property or is in possession of the real property and the security interest:

(A) is perfected by a fixture filing before the interest of the encumbrancer or owner is of record; and

(B) has priority over any conflicting interest of a predecessor in title of the encumbrancer or owner;

(2) before the goods become fixtures, the security interest is perfected by any method permitted by this article and the fixtures are readily removable:

(A) factory or office machines;

(B) equipment that is not primarily used or leased for use in the operation of the real property; or

(C) replacements of domestic appliances that are consumer goods;

(3) the conflicting interest is a lien on the real property obtained by legal or equitable proceedings after the security interest was perfected by any method permitted by this article; or

(4) the security interest is:

(A) created in a manufactured home in a manufactured-home transaction; and

(B) perfected pursuant to a statute described in Section 9–311(a)(2).

(f) **[Priority based on consent, disclaimer, or right to remove.]** A security interest in fixtures, whether or not perfected, has priority over a conflicting interest of an encumbrancer or owner of the real property if:

(1) the encumbrancer or owner has, in an authenticated record, consented to the security interest or disclaimed an interest in the goods as fixtures; or

(2) the debtor has a right to remove the goods as against the encumbrancer or owner.

(g) **[Continuation of paragraph (f)(2) priority.]** The priority of the security interest under paragraph (f)(2) continues for a reasonable time if the debtor's right to remove the goods as against the encumbrancer or owner terminates.

(h) **[Priority of construction mortgage.]** A mortgage is a construction mortgage to the extent that it secures an obligation incurred for the construction of an improvement on land, including the acquisition cost of the land, if a recorded record of the mortgage so indicates. Except as otherwise provided in subsections (e) and (f), a security interest in fixtures is subordinate to a construction mortgage if a record of the mortgage is recorded before the goods become fixtures and the goods become fixtures before the completion of the construction. A mortgage has this priority to the same extent as a construction mortgage to the extent that it is given to refinance a construction mortgage.

(i) **[Priority of security interest in crops.]** A perfected security interest in crops growing on real property has priority over a conflicting interest of an encumbrancer or owner of the real property if the debtor has an interest of record in or is in possession of the real property.

(j) **[Subsection (i) prevails.]** Subsection (i) prevails over any inconsistent provisions of the following statutes:

[List here any statutes containing provisions inconsistent with subsection (i).]

Legislative Note: States that amend statutes to remove provisions inconsistent with subsection (i) need not enact subsection (j).

Official Comment

1. **Source.** Former Section 9–313.

2. **Scope of This Section.** This section contains rules governing the priority of security interests in fixtures and crops as against persons who claim an interest in real property. Priority contests with other Article 9 security interests are governed by the other priority rules of this Article. The provisions with respect to fixtures follow those of former Section 9–313. However, they have been rewritten to conform to Section 2A–309 and to prevailing style conventions. Subsections (i) and (j), which apply to crops, are new.

3. **Security Interests in Fixtures.** Certain goods that are the subject of personal-property (chattel) financing become so affixed or otherwise so related to real property that they become part of the real property. These goods are called "fixtures." See Section 9–102 (definition of "fixtures"). Some fixtures retain their personal-property nature: a security interest under this Article may be created in fixtures and may continue in goods that become fixtures. See subsection (a). However, if the goods are ordinary building materials incorporated into an improvement on land, no security interest in them exists. Rather, the priority of claims to the building materials are determined by the law governing claims to real property. (Of course, the fact that no security interest exists in ordinary building materials incorporated into an improvement on land does not prejudice any rights the secured party may have against the debtor or any other person who violated the secured party's rights by wrongfully incorporating the goods into real property.)

Thus, this section recognizes three categories of goods: (1) those that retain their chattel character entirely and are not part of the real property; (2) ordinary building materials that have become an integral part of the real property and cannot retain their chattel character for purposes of finance; and (3) an intermediate class that has become real property for certain purposes, but as to which chattel financing may be preserved.

To achieve priority under certain provisions of this section, a security interest must be perfected by making a "fixture filing" (defined in Section 9–102) in the real-property records. Because the question whether goods have become fixtures often is a difficult one under applicable real-property law, a secured party may make a fixture filing as a precaution. Courts should not infer from a fixture filing that the secured party concedes that the goods are or will become fixtures.

4. **Priority in Fixtures: General.** In considering priority problems under this section, one must first determine whether real-property claimants per se have an interest in the crops or fixtures as part of real property. If not, it is immaterial, so far as concerns real property parties as such, whether a security interest arising under this Article is perfected or unperfected. In no event does a real-property claimant (e.g., owner or mortgagee) acquire an interest in a "pure" chattel just because a security interest therein is unperfected. If on the other hand real-property law gives real-property parties an interest in the goods, a conflict arises and this section states the priorities.

5. **Priority in Fixtures: Residual Rule.** Subsection (c) states the residual priority rule, which applies only if one of the other rules does not: A security interest in fixtures is subordinate to a conflicting interest of an encumbrancer or owner of the related real property other than the debtor.

6. **Priority in Fixtures: First to File or Record.** Subsection (e)(1), which follows former Section 9–313(4)(b), contains the usual priority rule of conveyancing, that is, the first to file or record prevails. In order to achieve priority under this rule, however, the security interest must be perfected by a "fixture filing" (defined in Section 9–102), i.e., a filing for record in the real property records and indexed therein, so that it will be found in a real-property search .. The condition in subsection (e)(1)(B), that the security interest must have had priority over any conflicting interest of a predecessor in title of the conflicting encumbrancer or owner, appears to limit to the first-in-time principle. However, this apparent limitation is nothing other than an expression of the usual rule that a person must be entitled to transfer what he has. Thus, if the fixture security interest is subordinate to a mortgage, it is subordinate to an interest of an assignee of the mortgage, even though the assignment is a later recorded instrument. Similarly if the fixture security interest is subordinate to the rights of an owner, it is subordinate to a subsequent grantee of the owner and

likewise subordinate to a subsequent mortgagee of the owner.

7. Priority in Fixtures: Purchase-Money Security Interests. Subsection (d), which follows former Section 9–313(4)(a), contains the principal exception to the first-to-file-or-record rule of subsection (e)(1). It affords priority to purchase-money security interests in fixtures as against *prior* recorded real-property interests, provided that the purchase-money security interest is filed as a fixture filing in the real-property records before the goods become fixtures or within 20 days thereafter. This priority corresponds to the purchase-money priority under Section 9–324(a). (Like other 10–day periods in former Article 9, the 10–day period in this section has been changed to 20 days.)

It should be emphasized that this purchase-money priority with the 20–day grace period for filing is limited to rights against real-property interests that arise *before* the goods become fixtures. There is no such priority with the 20–day grace period as against real-property interests that arise subsequently. The fixture security interest can defeat subsequent real-property interests only if it is filed first and prevails under the usual conveyancing rule in subsection (e)(1) or one of the other rules in this section.

8. Priority in Fixtures: Readily Removable Goods. Subsection (e)(2), which derives from Section 2A–309 and former Section 9–313(4)(d), contains another exception to the usual first-to-file-or-perfect rule. It affords priority to the holders of security interests in certain types of readily removable goods—factory and office machines, equipment that is not primarily used or leased for use in the operation of the real property, and (as discussed below) certain replacements of domestic appliances. This rule is made necessary by the confusion in the law as to whether certain machinery, equipment, and appliances become fixtures. It protects a secured party who, perhaps in the mistaken belief that the readily removable goods will not become fixtures, makes a UCC filing (or otherwise perfects under this Article) rather than making a fixture filing.

Frequently, under applicable law, goods of the type described in subsection (e)(2) will not be considered to have become part of the real property. In those cases, the fixture security interest does not conflict with a real-property interest, and resort to this section is unnecessary. However, if the goods have become part of the real property, subsection (e)(2) enables a fixture secured party to take priority over a conflicting real-property interest if the fixture security interest is perfected by a fixture filing or by any other method permitted by this Article. If perfection is by fixture filing, the fixture security interest would have priority over subsequently recorded real-property interests under subsection (e)(1) and, if the fixture security interest is a purchase-money security interest (a likely scenario), it would also have priority over most real property interests under the purchase-money priority of subsection (d). Note, however, that unlike the purchase-money priority rule in subsection (d), the priority rules in subsection (e) override the priority given to a construction mortgage under subsection (h).

The rule in subsection (e)(2) is limited to readily removable replacements of domestic appliances. It does not apply to original installations. Moreover, it is limited to appliances that are "consumer goods" (defined in Section 9–102) in the hands of the debtor. The principal effect of the rule is to make clear that a secured party financing occasional replacements of domestic appliances in noncommercial, owner-occupied contexts need not concern itself with real-property descriptions or records; indeed, for a purchase-money replacement of consumer goods, perfection without any filing will be possible. See Section 9–309(1).

9. Priority in Fixtures: Judicial Liens. Subsection (e)(3), which follows former Section 9–313(4)(d), adopts a first-in-time rule applicable to conflicts between a fixture security interest and a lien on the real property obtained by legal or equitable proceedings. Such a lien is subordinate to an earlier-perfected security interest, regardless of the method by which the security interest was perfected. Judgment creditors generally are not reliance creditors who search real-property records. Accordingly, a perfected fixture security interest takes priority over a subsequent judgment lien or other lien obtained by legal or equitable proceedings, even if no evidence of the security interest appears in the relevant real-property records. Subsection (e)(3) thus protects a perfected fixture security interest from avoidance by a trustee in bankruptcy under Bankruptcy Code Section 544(a), regardless of the method of perfection.

10. Priority in Fixtures: Manufactured Homes. A manufactured home may become a fixture. New subsection (e)(4) contains a special rule granting priority to certain security interests created in a "manufactured home" as part of a "manufactured-home transaction" (both defined in Section 9–102). Under this rule, a security interest in a manufactured home that becomes a fixture has priority over a conflicting interest of an encumbrancer or owner of the real property if the security interest is perfected under a certificate-of-title statute (see Section 9–311). Subsection (e)(4) is only one of the priority rules applicable to security interests in a manufactured home that becomes a fixture. Thus, a security interest in a manufactured home which does not qualify for priority under this subsection may qualify under another.

11. **Priority in Fixtures: Construction Mortgages.** The purchase-money priority presents a difficult problem in relation to construction mortgages. The latter ordinarily will have been recorded even before the commencement of delivery of materials to the job, and therefore would take priority over fixture security interests were it not for the purchase-money priority. However, having recorded first, the holder of a construction mortgage reasonably expects to have first priority in the improvement built using the mortgagee's advances. Subsection (g) expressly gives priority to the construction mortgage recorded before the filing of the purchase-money security interest in fixtures. A refinancing of a construction mortgage has the same priority as the construction mortgage itself. The phrase "an obligation incurred for the construction of an improvement" covers both optional advances and advances pursuant to commitment. Both types of advances have the same priority under subsection (g).

The priority under this subsection applies only to goods that become fixtures during the construction period leading to the completion of the improvement. The construction priority will not apply to additions to the building made long after completion of the improvement, even if the additions are financed by the real-property mortgagee under an open-end clause of the construction mortgage. In such case, subsections (d), (e), and (f) govern.

Although this subsection affords a construction mortgage priority over a purchase-money security interest that otherwise would have priority under subsection (d), the subsection is subject to the priority rules in subsections (e) and (f). Thus, a construction mortgage may be junior to a fixture security interest perfected by a fixture filing before the construction mortgage was recorded. See subsection (e)(1).

12. **Crops.** Growing crops are "goods" in which a security interest may be created and perfected under this Article. In some jurisdictions, a mortgage of real property may cover crops, as well. In the event that crops are encumbered by both a mortgage and an Article 9 security interest, subsection (i) provides that the security interest has priority. States whose real-property law provides otherwise should either amend that law directly or override it by enacting subsection (j).

§ 9–335. Accessions.

(a) **[Creation of security interest in accession.]** A security interest may be created in an accession and continues in collateral that becomes an accession.

(b) **[Perfection of security interest.]** If a security interest is perfected when the collateral becomes an accession, the security interest remains perfected in the collateral.

(c) **[Priority of security interest.]** Except as otherwise provided in subsection (d), the other provisions of this part determine the priority of a security interest in an accession.

(d) **[Compliance with certificate-of-title statute.]** A security interest in an accession is subordinate to a security interest in the whole which is perfected by compliance with the requirements of a certificate-of-title statute under Section 9–311(b).

(e) **[Removal of accession after default.]** After default, subject to Part 6, a secured party may remove an accession from other goods if the security interest in the accession has priority over the claims of every person having an interest in the whole.

(f) **[Reimbursement following removal.]** A secured party that removes an accession from other goods under subsection (e) shall promptly reimburse any holder of a security interest or other lien on, or owner of, the whole or of the other goods, other than the debtor, for the cost of repair of any physical injury to the whole or the other goods. The secured party need not reimburse the holder or owner for any diminution in value of the whole or the other goods caused by the absence of the accession removed or by any necessity for replacing it. A person entitled to reimbursement may refuse permission to remove until the secured party gives adequate assurance for the performance of the obligation to reimburse.

Official Comment

1. **Source.** Former Section 9–314.

2. **"Accession."** This section applies to an "accession," as defined in Section 9–102, regardless of the cost or difficulty of removing the accession from the other goods, and regardless of whether the original goods have come to form an integral part of the other goods. This section does not apply to goods whose identity has been lost. Goods of that kind are "commingled goods" governed by Section 9–336. Neither this section nor the following one addresses the case of

collateral that changes form without the addition of other goods.

3. **"Accession" vs. "Other Goods."** This section distinguishes among the "accession," the "other goods," and the "whole." The last term refers to the combination of the "accession" and the "other goods." If one person's collateral becomes physically united with another person's collateral, each is an "accession."

Example 1: SP–1 holds a security interest in the debtor's tractors (which are not subject to a certificate-of-title statute), and SP–2 holds a security interest in a particular tractor engine. The engine is installed in a tractor. From the perspective of SP–1, the tractor becomes an "accession" and the engine is the "other goods." From the perspective of SP–2, the engine is the "accession" and the tractor is the "other goods." The completed tractor—tractor cum engine—constitutes the "whole."

4. **Scope.** This section governs only a few issues concerning accessions. Subsection (a) contains rules governing continuation of a security interest in an accession. Subsection (b) contains a rule governing continued perfection of a security interest in goods that become an accession. Subsection (d) contains a special priority rule governing accessions that become part of a whole covered by a certificate of title. Subsections (e) and (f) govern enforcement of a security interest in an accession.

5. **Matters Left to Other Provisions of This Article: Attachment and Perfection.** Other provisions of this Article often govern accession-related issues. For example, this section does not address whether a secured party acquires a security interest in the whole if its collateral becomes an accession. Normally this will turn on the description of the collateral in the security agreement.

Example 2: Debtor owns a computer subject to a perfected security interest in favor of SP–1. Debtor acquires memory and installs it in the computer. Whether SP–1's security interest attaches to the memory depends on whether the security agreement covers it.

Similarly, this section does not determine whether perfection against collateral that becomes an accession is effective to perfect a security interest in the whole. Other provisions of this Article, including the requirements for indicating the collateral covered by a financing statement, resolve that question.

6. **Matters Left to Other Provisions of This Article: Priority.** With one exception, concerning goods covered by a certificate of title (see subsection (d)), the other provisions of this Part, including the rules governing purchase-money security interests, determine the priority of most security interests in an accession, including the relative priority of a security interest in an accession and a security interest in the whole. See subsection (c).

Example 3: Debtor owns an office computer subject to a security interest in favor of SP–1. Debtor acquires memory and grants a perfected security interest in the memory to SP–2. Debtor installs the memory in the computer, at which time (one assumes) SP–1's security interest attaches to the memory. The first-to-file-or-perfect rule of Section 9–322 governs priority in the memory. If, however, SP–2's security interest is a purchase-money security interest, Section 9–324(a) would afford priority in the memory to SP–2, regardless of which security interest was perfected first.

7. **Goods Covered by Certificate of Title.** This section does govern the priority of a security interest in an accession that is or becomes part of a whole that is subject to a security interest perfected by compliance with a certificate-of-title statute. Subsection (d) provides that a security interest in the whole, perfected by compliance with a certificate-of-title statute, takes priority over a security interest in the accession. It enables a secured party to rely upon a certificate of title without having to check the UCC files to determine whether any components of the collateral may be encumbered. The subsection imposes a corresponding risk upon those who finance goods that may become part of goods covered by a certificate of title. In doing so, it reverses the priority that appeared reasonable to most pre-UCC courts.

Example 4: Debtor owns an automobile subject to a security interest in favor of SP–1. The security interest is perfected by notation on the certificate of title. Debtor buys tires subject to a perfected-by-filing purchase-money security interest in favor of SP–2 and mounts the tires on the automobile's wheels. If the security interest in the automobile attaches to the tires, then SP–1 acquires priority over SP–2. The same result would obtain if SP–1's security interest attached to the automobile and was perfected after the tires had been mounted on the wheels.

§ 9–336. Commingled Goods.

(a) **["Commingled goods."]** In this section, "commingled goods" means goods that are physically united with other goods in such a manner that their identity is lost in a product or mass.

(b) **[No security interest in commingled goods as such.]** A security interest does not exist in commingled goods as such. However, a security interest may attach to a product or mass that results when goods become commingled goods.

(c) **[Attachment of security interest to product or mass.]** If collateral becomes commingled goods, a security interest attaches to the product or mass.

(d) **[Perfection of security interest.]** If a security interest in collateral is perfected before the collateral becomes commingled goods, the security interest that attaches to the product or mass under subsection (c) is perfected.

(e) **[Priority of security interest.]** Except as otherwise provided in subsection (f), the other provisions of this part determine the priority of a security interest that attaches to the product or mass under subsection (c).

(f) **[Conflicting security interests in product or mass]** If more than one security interest attaches to the product or mass under subsection (c), the following rules determine priority:

(1) A security interest that is perfected under subsection (d) has priority over a security interest that is unperfected at the time the collateral becomes commingled goods.

(2) If more than one security interest is perfected under subsection (d), the security interests rank equally in proportion to the value of the collateral at the time it became commingled goods.

Official Comment

1. **Source.** Former Section 9–315.

2. **"Commingled Goods."** Subsection (a) defines "commingled goods." It is meant to include not only goods whose identity is lost through manufacturing or production (e.g., flour that has become part of baked goods) but also goods whose identity is lost by commingling with other goods from which they cannot be distinguished (e.g., ball bearings).

3. **Consequences of Becoming "Commingled Goods."** By definition, the identity of the original collateral cannot be determined once the original collateral becomes commingled goods. Consequently, the security interest in the specific original collateral alone is lost once the collateral becomes commingled goods, and no security interest in the original collateral can

be created thereafter except as a part of the resulting product or mass. See subsection (b).

Once collateral becomes commingled goods, the secured party's security interest is transferred from the original collateral to the product or mass. See subsection (c). If the security interest in the original collateral was perfected, the security interest in the product or mass is a perfected security interest. See subsection (d). This perfection continues until lapse.

4. **Priority of Perfected Security Interests That Attach Under This Section.** This section governs the priority of competing security interests in a product or mass only when both security interests arise under this section. In that case, if both security interests are perfected by operation of this section (see subsections (c) and (d)), then the security interests rank equally, in proportion to the value of the collateral at the time it became commingled goods. See subsection (f)(2).

Example 1: SP–1 has a perfected security interest in Debtor's eggs, which have a value of $300 and secure a debt of $400, and SP–2 has a perfected security interest in Debtor's flour, which has a value of $500 and secures a debt of $700. Debtor uses the flour and eggs to make cakes, which have a value of $1000. The two security interests rank equally and share in the ratio of 3:5. Applying this ratio to the entire value of the product, SP–1 would be entitled to $375 (i.e., 3/8 x $1000), and SP–2 would be entitled to $625 (i.e., 5/8 x $1000).

Example 2: Assume the facts of Example 1, except that SP–1's collateral, worth $300, secures a debt of $200. Recall that, if the cake is worth $1000, then applying the ratio of 3:5 would entitle SP–1 to $375 and SP–2 to $625. However, SP–1 is not entitled to collect from the product more than it is owed. Accordingly, SP–1's share would be only $200, SP–2 would receive the remaining value, up to the amount it is owed ($700).

Example 3: Assume that the cakes in the previous examples have a value of only $600. Again, the parties share in the ratio of 3:5. If, as in Example 1, SP–1 is owed $400, then SP–1 is entitled to $225 (i.e., 3/8 x $600), and SP–2 is entitled to $375 (i.e., 5/8 x $600). Debtor receives nothing. If, however, as in Example 2, SP–1 is owed only $200, then SP–2 receives $400.

The results in the foregoing examples remain the same, regardless of whether SP–1 or SP–2 (or each) has a purchase-money security interest.

5. **Perfection: Unperfected Security Interests.** The rule explained in the preceding Comment applies only when both security interests in original collateral are perfected when the goods become commingled goods. If a security interest in original collateral is unperfected at the time the collateral becomes commingled goods, subsection (f)(1) applies.

Example 4: SP–1 has a perfected security interest in the debtor's eggs, and SP–2 has an unperfected security interest in the debtor's flour. Debtor uses the flour and eggs to make cakes. Under subsection (c), both security interests attach to the cakes. But since SP–1's security interest was perfected at the time of commingling and SP–2's was not, only SP–1's security interest in the cakes is perfected. See subsection (d). Under subsection (f)(1) and Section 9–322(a)(2), SP–1's perfected security interest has priority over SP–2's unperfected security interest.

If both security interests are unperfected, the rule of Section 9–322(a)(3) would apply.

6. **Multiple Security Interests.** On occasion, a single input may be encumbered by more than one security interest. In those cases, the multiple secured parties should be treated like a single secured party for purposes of determining their collective share under subsection (f)(2). The normal priority rules would determine how that share would be allocated between them. Consider the following example, which is a variation on Example 1 above:

Example 5: SP–1A has a perfected, first-priority security interest in Debtor's eggs. SP–1B has a perfected, second-priority security interest in the same collateral. The eggs have a value of $300. Debtor owes $200 to SP–1A and $200 to SP–1B. SP–2 has a perfected security interest in Debtor's flour, which has a value of $500 and secures a debt of $600. Debtor uses the flour and eggs to make cakes, which have a value of $1000.

For purposes of subsection (f)(2), SP–1A and SP–1B should be treated like a single secured party. The collective security interest would rank equally with that of SP–2. Thus, the secured parties would share in the ratio of 3 (for SP–1A and SP–1B combined) to 5 (for SP–2). Applying this ratio to the entire value of the product, SP–1A and SP–1B in the aggregate would be entitled to $375 (i.e., 3/8 x $1000), and SP–2 would be entitled to $625 (i.e., 5/8 x $1000).

SP–1A and SP–1B would share the $375 in accordance with their priority, as established under other rules. Inasmuch as SP–1A has first priority, it would receive $200, and SP–1B would receive $175.

7. **Priority of Security Interests That Attach Other Than by Operation of This Section.** Under subsection (e), the normal priority rules determine the priority of a security interest that attaches to the product or mass other than by operation of this section. For example, assume that SP–1 has a perfected security interest in Debtor's existing and after-acquired baked goods, and SP–2 has a perfected security interest in Debtor's flour. When the flour is processed into cakes, subsections (c) and (d) provide that SP–2 acquires a perfected security interest in the cakes. If SP–1 filed against the baked goods before SP–2 filed against the flour, then SP–1 will enjoy priority in the cakes. See Section 9–322 (first-to-file-or-perfect). But if SP–2 filed against the flour before SP–1 filed against the baked goods, then SP–2 will enjoy priority in the cakes to the extent of its security interest.

§ 9–337. Priority of Security Interests in Goods Covered by Certificate of Title.

If, while a security interest in goods is perfected by any method under the law of another jurisdiction, this State issues a certificate of title that does not show that the goods are subject to the security interest or contain a statement that they may be subject to security interests not shown on the certificate:

(1) a buyer of the goods, other than a person in the business of selling goods of that kind, takes free of the security interest if the buyer gives value and receives delivery of the goods after issuance of the certificate and without knowledge of the security interest; and

(2) the security interest is subordinate to a conflicting security interest in the goods that attaches, and is perfected under Section 9–311(b), after issuance of the certificate and without the conflicting secured party's knowledge of the security interest.

Official Comment

1. **Source.** Derived from former Section 9–103(2)(d).

2. **Protection for Buyers and Secured Parties.** This section affords protection to certain good-faith purchasers for value who are likely to have relied on a "clean" certificate of title, i.e., one that neither shows that the goods are subject to a particular security interest nor contains a statement that they may be subject to security interests not shown on the certificate. Under this section, a buyer can take free of, and

the holder of a conflicting security interest can acquire priority over, a security interest that is perfected by any method under the law of another jurisdiction. The fact that the security interest has been reperfected by possession under Section 9–313 does not of itself disqualify the holder of a conflicting security interest from protection under paragraph (2).

§ 9–338. Priority of Security Interest or Agricultural Lien Perfected by Filed Financing Statement Providing Certain Incorrect Information.

If a security interest or agricultural lien is perfected by a filed financing statement providing information described in Section 9–516(b)(5) which is incorrect at the time the financing statement is filed:

(1) the security interest or agricultural lien is subordinate to a conflicting perfected security interest in the collateral to the extent that the holder of the conflicting security interest gives value in reasonable reliance upon the incorrect information; and

(2) a purchaser, other than a secured party, of the collateral takes free of the security interest or agricultural lien to the extent that, in reasonable reliance upon the incorrect information, the purchaser gives value and, in the case of tangible chattel paper, tangible documents, goods, instruments, or a security certificate, receives delivery of the collateral.

As amended in 2003.

Official Comment

1. **Source.** New.

2. **Effect of Incorrect Information in Financing Statement.** Section 9–520(a) requires the filing office to reject financing statements that do not contain information concerning the debtor as specified in Section 9–516(b)(5). An error in this information does not render the financing statement ineffective. On rare occasions, a subsequent purchaser of the collateral (i.e., a buyer or secured party) may rely on the misinformation to its detriment. This section subordinates a security interest or agricultural lien perfected by an effective, but flawed, financing statement to the rights of a buyer or holder of a perfected security interest to the extent that, in reasonable reliance on the incorrect information, the purchaser gives value and, in the case of tangible collateral, receives delivery of the collateral. A purchaser who has not made itself aware of the information in the filing office with respect to the debtor cannot act in "reasonable reliance" upon incorrect information.

3. **Relationship to Section 9–507.** This section applies to financing statements that contain information that is incorrect at the time of filing and imposes a small risk of subordination on the filer. In contrast, Section 9–507 deals with financing statements containing information that is correct at the time of filing but which becomes incorrect later. Except as provided in Section 9–507 with respect to changes in the debtor's name, an otherwise effective financing statement does not become ineffective if the information contained in it becomes inaccurate.

§ 9–339. Priority Subject to Subordination.

This article does not preclude subordination by agreement by a person entitled to priority.

Official Comment

1. **Source.** Former Section 9–316.

2. **Subordination by Agreement.** The preceding sections deal elaborately with questions of priority. This section makes it entirely clear that a person entitled to priority may effectively agree to subordinate its claim. Only the person entitled to priority may make such an agreement: a person's rights cannot be adversely affected by an agreement to which the person is not a party.

[SUBPART 4. RIGHTS OF BANK]

§ 9–340. Effectiveness of Right of Recoupment or Set-Off Against Deposit Account.

(a) **[Exercise of recoupment or set-off.]** Except as otherwise provided in subsection (c), a bank with which a deposit account is maintained may exercise any right of recoupment or set-off against a secured party that holds a security interest in the deposit account.

(b) **[Recoupment or set-off not affected by security interest.]** Except as otherwise provided in subsection (c), the application of this article to a security interest in a deposit account does not affect a right of recoupment or set-off of the secured party as to a deposit account maintained with the secured party.

(c) **[When set-off ineffective.]** The exercise by a bank of a set-off against a deposit account is ineffective against a secured party that holds a security interest in the deposit account which is perfected by control under Section 9–104(a)(3), if the set-off is based on a claim against the debtor.

Official Comment

1. **Source.** New; subsection (b) is based on a non-uniform Illinois amendment.

2. **Set-off vs. Security Interest.** This section resolves the conflict between a security interest in a deposit account and the bank's rights of recoupment and set-off.

Subsection (a) states the general rule and provides that the bank may effectively exercise rights of recoupment and set-off against the secured party. Subsection (c) contains an exception: if the secured party has control under Section 9–104(a)(3) (i.e., if it has become the bank's customer), then any set-off exercised by the bank against a debt owed by the debtor (as opposed to a debt owed to the bank by the secured party) is ineffective. The bank may, however, exercise its recoupment rights effectively. This result is consistent with the priority rule in Section 9–327(4), under which the security interest of a bank in a deposit account is subordinate to that of a secured party who has control under Section 9–104(a)(3).

This section deals with rights of set-off and recoupment that a bank may have under other law. It does not create a right of set-off or recoupment, nor is it intended to override any limitations or restrictions that other law imposes on the exercise of those rights.

3. **Preservation of Set-Off Right.** Subsection (b) makes clear that a bank may hold both a right of set-off against, and an Article 9 security interest in, the same deposit account. By holding a security interest in a deposit account, a bank does not impair any right of set-off it would otherwise enjoy. This subsection does not pertain to accounts evidenced by an instrument (e.g., certain certificates of deposit), which are excluded from the definition of "deposit accounts."

§ 9–341. Bank's Rights and Duties With Respect to Deposit Account.

Except as otherwise provided in Section 9–340(c), and unless the bank otherwise agrees in an authenticated record, a bank's rights and duties with respect to a deposit account main-

tained with the bank are not terminated, suspended, or modified by:

(1) the creation, attachment, or perfection of a security interest in the deposit account;

(2) the bank's knowledge of the security interest; or

(3) the bank's receipt of instructions from the secured party.

Official Comment

1. **Source.** New.

2. **Free Flow of Funds.** This section is designed to prevent security interests in deposit accounts from impeding the free flow of funds through the payment system. Subject to two exceptions, it leaves the bank's rights and duties with respect to the deposit account and the funds on deposit unaffected by the creation or perfection of a security interest or by the bank's knowledge of the security interest. In addition, the section permits the bank to ignore the instructions of the secured party unless it had agreed to honor them or unless other law provides to the contrary. A secured party who wishes to deprive the debtor of access to funds on deposit or to appropriate those funds for itself needs to obtain the agreement of the bank, utilize the judicial process, or comply with procedures set forth in other law. Section 4–303(a), concerning the effect of notice on a bank's right and duty to pay items, is not to the contrary. That section addresses only whether an otherwise effective notice comes too late; it does not determine whether a timely notice is otherwise effective.

3. **Operation of Rule.** The general rule of this section is subject to Section 9–340(c), under which a bank's right of set-off may not be exercised against a deposit account in the secured party's name if the right is based on a claim against the debtor. This result reflects current law in many jurisdictions and does not appear to have unduly disrupted banking practices or the payments system. The more important function of this section, which is not impaired by Section 9–340, is the bank's right to follow the debtor's (customer's) instructions (e.g., by honoring checks, permitting withdrawals, etc.) until such time as the depository institution is served with judicial process or receives instructions with respect to the funds on deposit from a secured party who has control over the deposit account.

4. **Liability of Bank.** This Article does not determine whether a bank that pays out funds from an encumbered deposit is liable to the holder of a security interest. Although the fact that a secured party has control over the deposit account and the manner by which control was achieved may be relevant to the

imposition of liability, whatever rule applies generally when a bank pays out funds in which a third party has an interest would determine liability to a secured party. Often, this rule is found in a non-UCC adverse claim statute.

5. **Certificates of Deposit.** This section does not address the obligations of banks that issue instruments evidencing deposits (e.g., certain certificates of deposit).

§ 9–342. Bank's Right to Refuse to Enter Into or Disclose Existence of Control Agreement.

This article does not require a bank to enter into an agreement of the kind described in Section 9–104(a)(2), even if its customer so requests or directs. A bank that has entered into such an agreement is not required to confirm the existence of the agreement to another person unless requested to do so by its customer.

Official Comment

1. **Source.** New; derived from Section 8–106(g).

2. **Protection for Bank.** This section protects banks from the need to enter into agreements against their will and from the need to respond to inquiries from persons other than their customers.

PART 4

RIGHTS OF THIRD PARTIES

§ 9–401. Alienability of Debtor's Rights.

(a) **[Other law governs alienability; exceptions.]** Except as otherwise provided in subsection (b) and Sections 9–406, 9–407, 9–408, and 9–409, whether a debtor's rights in collateral may be voluntarily or involuntarily transferred is governed by law other than this article.

(b) **[Agreement does not prevent transfer.]** An agreement between the debtor and secured party which prohibits a transfer of the debtor's rights in collateral or makes the transfer a default does not prevent the transfer from taking effect.

Official Comment

1. **Source.** Former Section 9–311.

2. **Scope of This Part.** This Part deals with several issues affecting third parties (i.e., parties other than the debtor and the secured party). These issues are not addressed in Part 3, Subpart 3, which deals with priorities. This Part primarily addresses the rights and duties of account debtors and other persons obligated on collateral who are not, themselves, parties to a secured transaction.

3. **Governing Law.** There was some uncertainty under former Article 9 as to which jurisdiction's law (usually, which jurisdiction's version of Article 9) applied to the matters that this Part addresses. Part 3, Subpart 1, does not determine the law governing these matters because they do not relate to perfection, the effect of perfection or nonperfection, or priority. However, it might be inappropriate for a designation of

applicable law by a debtor and secured party under Section 1–105 to control the law applicable to an independent transaction or relationship between the debtor and an account debtor.

Consider an example under Section 9–408.

Example 1: State X has adopted this Article; former Article 9 is the law of State Y. A general intangible (e.g., a franchise agreement) between a debtor-franchisee, D, and an account debtor-franchisor, AD, is governed by the law of State Y. D grants to SP a security interest in its rights under the franchise agreement. The franchise agreement contains a term prohibiting D's assignment of its rights under the agreement. D and SP agree that their secured transaction is governed by the law of State X. Under State X's Section 9–408, the restriction on D's assignment is ineffective to prevent the creation, attachment, or perfection of SP's security interest. State Y's former Section 9–318(4), however, does not address restrictions on the creation of security interests in general intangibles other than general intangibles for money due or to become due. Accordingly, it does not address restrictions on the assignment to SP of D's rights under the franchise agreement. The non-Article–9 law of State Y, which does address restrictions, provides that the prohibition on assignment is effective.

This Article does not provide a specific answer to the question of which State's law applies to the restriction on assignment in the example. However, assuming that under non-UCC choice-of-law principles the effectiveness of the restriction would be governed by the law of State Y, which governs the franchise agreement, the fact that State X's Article 9 governs the secured transaction between SP and D would not override the otherwise applicable law governing the agreement. Of course, to the extent that jurisdictions eventually adopt identical versions of this Article and courts interpret it consistently, the inability to identify the applicable law in circumstances such as those in the example may be inconsequential.

4. **Inalienability Under Other Law.** Subsection (a) addresses the question whether property necessarily is transferable by virtue of its inclusion (i.e., its eligibility as collateral) within the scope of Article 9. It gives a negative answer, subject to the identified exceptions. The substance of subsection (a) was implicit under former Article 9.

5. **Negative Pledge Covenant.** Subsection (b) is an exception to the general rule in subsection (a). It makes clear that in secured transactions under this Article the debtor has rights in collateral (whether legal title or equitable) which it can transfer and which its creditors can reach. It is best explained with an example.

> **Example 2:** A debtor, D, grants to SP a security interest to secure a debt in excess of the value of the collateral. D agrees with SP that it will not create a subsequent security interest in the collateral and that any security interest purportedly granted in violation of the agreement will be void. Subsequently, in violation of its agreement with SP, D purports to grant a security interest in the same collateral to another secured party.

Subsection (b) validates D's creation of the subsequent (prohibited) security interest, which might even achieve priority over the earlier security interest. See Comment 7. However, unlike some other provisions of this Part, such as Section 9–406, subsection (b) does not provide that the agreement restricting assignment itself is "ineffective." Consequently, the debtor's breach may create a default.

6. **Rights of Lien Creditors.** Difficult problems may arise with respect to attachment, levy, and other judicial procedures under which a debtor's creditors may reach collateral subject to a security interest. For example, an obligation may be secured by collateral worth many times the amount of the obligation. If a lien creditor has caused all or a portion of the collateral to be seized under judicial process, it may be difficult to determine the amount of the debtor's "equity" in the collateral that has been seized. The section leaves

resolution of this problem to the courts. The doctrine of marshaling may be appropriate.

7. **Sale of Receivables.** If a debtor sells an account, chattel paper, payment intangible, or promissory note outright, as against the buyer the debtor has no remaining rights to transfer. If, however, the buyer fails to perfect its interest, then solely insofar as the rights of certain third parties are concerned, the debtor is deemed to retain its rights and title. See Section 9–318. The debtor has the power to convey these rights to a subsequent purchaser. If the subsequent purchaser (buyer or secured lender) perfects its interest, it will achieve priority over the earlier, unperfected purchaser. See Section 9–322(a)(1).

§ 9–402. Secured Party Not Obligated on Contract of Debtor or in Tort.

The existence of a security interest, agricultural lien, or authority given to a debtor to dispose of or use collateral, without more, does not subject a secured party to liability in contract or tort for the debtor's acts or omissions.

Official Comment

1. **Source.** Former Section 9–317.

2. **Nonliability of Secured Party.** This section, like former Section 9–317, rejects theories on which a secured party might be held liable on a debtor's contracts or in tort merely because a security interest exists or because the debtor is entitled to dispose of or use collateral. This section expands former Section 9–317 to cover agricultural liens.

§ 9–403. Agreement Not to Assert Defenses Against Assignee.

(a) **["Value."]** In this section, "value" has the meaning provided in Section 3–303(a).

(b) **[Agreement not to assert claim or defense.]** Except as otherwise provided in this section, an agreement between an account debtor and an assignor not to assert against an assignee any claim or defense that the account debtor may have against the assignor is enforceable by an assignee that takes an assignment:

(1) for value;

(2) in good faith;

(3) without notice of a claim of a property or possessory right to the property assigned; and

(4) without notice of a defense or claim in recoupment of the type that may be asserted against a person entitled to enforce a negotiable instrument under Section 3–305(a).

(c) **[When subsection (b) not applicable.]** Subsection (b) does not apply to defenses of a type that may be asserted against a holder in due course of a negotiable instrument under Section 3–305(b).

(d) **[Omission of required statement in consumer transaction.]** In a consumer transaction, if a record evidences the account debtor's obligation, law other than this article requires that the record include a statement to the effect that the rights of an assignee are subject to claims or defenses that the account debtor could assert against the original obligee, and the record does not include such a statement:

(1) the record has the same effect as if the record included such a statement; and

(2) the account debtor may assert against an assignee those claims and defenses that would have been available if the record included such a statement.

(e) **[Rule for individual under other law.]** This section is subject to law other than this article which establishes a different rule for an account debtor who is an individual and who incurred the obligation primarily for personal, family, or household purposes.

(f) **[Other law not displaced.]** Except as otherwise provided in subsection (d), this section does not displace law other than this article which gives effect to an agreement by an account debtor not to assert a claim or defense against an assignee.

Official Comment

1. **Source.** Former Section 9–206.

2. **Scope and Purpose.** Subsection (b), like former Section 9–206, generally validates an agreement between an account debtor and an assignor that the account debtor will not assert against an assignee claims and defenses that it may have against the assignor. These agreements are typical in installment sale agreements and leases. However, this section expands former Section 9–206 to apply to all account debtors; it is not limited to account debtors that have bought or leased goods. This section applies only to the obligations of an "account debtor," as defined in Section 9–102. Thus, it does not determine the circumstances under which and the extent to which a person who is obligated on a negotiable instrument is disabled from asserting claims and defenses. Rather, Article 3 must be consulted. See, e.g., Sections 3–305, 3–306. Article 3 governs even when the negotiable instrument constitutes part of chattel paper. See Section 9–102 (an obligor on a negotiable instrument constituting part of chattel paper is not an "account debtor").

3. **Conditions of Validation; Relationship to Article 3.** Subsection (b) validates an account debtor's agreement only if the assignee takes an assignment for value, in good faith, and without notice of conflicting claims to the property assigned or of certain claims or defenses of the account debtor. Like former Section 9–206, this section is designed to put the assignee in a position that is no better and no worse than that of a holder in due course of a negotiable instrument under Article 3. However, former Section 9–206 left open certain issues, e.g., whether the section incorporated the special Article 3 definition of "value" in Section 3–303 or the generally applicable definition in Section 1–201(44). Subsection (a) addresses this question; it provides that "value" has the meaning specified in Section 3–303(a). Similarly, subsection (c) provides that subsection (b) does not validate an agreement with respect to defenses that could be asserted against a holder in due course under Section 3–305(b) (the so-called "real" defenses). In 1990, the definition of "holder in due course" (Section 3–302) and the articulation of the rights of a holder in due course (Sections 3–305 and 3–306) were revised substantially. This section tracks more closely the rules of Sections 3–302, 3–305, and 3–306.

4. **Relationship to Terms of Assigned Property.** Former Section 9–206(2), concerning warranties accompanying the sale of goods, has been deleted as unnecessary. This Article does not regulate the terms of the account, chattel paper, or general intangible that is assigned, except insofar as the account, chattel paper, or general intangible itself creates a security interest (as often is the case with chattel paper). Thus, Article 2, and not this Article, determines whether a seller of goods makes or effectively disclaims warranties, even if the sale is secured. Similarly, other law, and not this Article, determines the effectiveness of an account debtor's undertaking to pay notwithstanding, and not to assert, any defenses or claims against an assignor–e.g., a "hell-or-high-water" provision in the underlying agreement that is assigned. If other law gives effect to this undertaking, then, under principles of *nemo dat*, the undertaking would be enforceable by

the assignee (secured party). If other law prevents the assignor from enforcing the undertaking, this section nevertheless might permit the assignee to do so. The right of the assignee to enforce would depend upon whether, under the particular facts, the account debtor's undertaking fairly could be construed as an agreement that falls within the scope of this section and whether the assignee meets the requirements of this section.

5. **Relationship to Federal Trade Commission Rule.** Subsection (d) is new. It applies to rights evidenced by a record that is required to contain, but does not contain, the notice set forth in Federal Trade Commission Rule 433, 16 C.F.R. Part 433 (the "Holder-in-Due–Course Regulations"). Under this subsection, an assignee of such a record takes subject to the consumer account debtor's claims and defenses to the same extent as it would have if the writing had contained the required notice. Thus, subsection (d) effectively renders waiver-of-defense clauses ineffective in the transactions with consumers to which it applies.

6. **Relationship to Other Law.** Like former Section 9–206(1), this section takes no position on the enforceability of waivers of claims and defenses by consumer account debtors, leaving that question to other law. However, the reference to "law other than this article" in subsection (e) encompasses administrative rules and regulations; the reference in former Section 9–206(1) that it replaces ("statute or decision") arguably did not.

This section does not displace other law that gives effect to a non-consumer account debtor's agreement not to assert defenses against an assignee, even if the agreement would not qualify under subsection (b). See subsection (f). It validates, but does not invalidate, agreements made by a non-consumer account debtor. This section also does not displace other law to the extent that the other law permits an assignee, who takes an assignment with notice of a claim of a property or possessory right, a defense, or a claim in recoupment, to enforce an account debtor's agreement not to assert claims and defenses against the assignor (e.g., a "hell-or-high-water" agreement). See Comment 4. It also does not displace an assignee's right to assert that an account debtor is estopped from asserting a claim or defense. Nor does this section displace other law with respect to waivers of potential future claims and defenses that are the subject of an agreement between the account debtor and the assignee. Finally, it does not displace Section 1–107, concerning waiver of a breach that allegedly already has occurred.

§ 9–404.   Rights Acquired by Assignee; Claims and Defenses Against Assignee.

(a) **[Assignee's rights subject to terms, claims, and defenses; exceptions.]** Unless an account debtor has made an enforceable agreement not to assert defenses or claims, and subject to subsections (b) through (e), the rights of an assignee are subject to:

(1) all terms of the agreement between the account debtor and assignor and any defense or claim in recoupment arising from the transaction that gave rise to the contract; and

(2) any other defense or claim of the account debtor against the assignor which accrues before the account debtor receives a notification of the assignment authenticated by the assignor or the assignee.

(b) **[Account debtor's claim reduces amount owed to assignee.]** Subject to subsection (c) and except as otherwise provided in subsection (d), the claim of an account debtor against an assignor may be asserted against an assignee under subsection (a) only to reduce the amount the account debtor owes.

(c) **[Rule for individual under other law.]** This section is subject to law other than this article which establishes a different rule for an account debtor who is an individual and who incurred the obligation primarily for personal, family, or household purposes.

(d) **[Omission of required statement in consumer transaction.]** In a consumer transaction, if a record evidences the account debtor's obligation, law other than this article requires that the record include a statement to the effect that the account debtor's recovery against an assignee with respect to claims and defenses against the assignor may not exceed amounts paid by the account debtor under the record, and the record does not include such a statement, the extent to which a claim of an account debtor against the assignor may be asserted against an assignee is determined as if the record included such a statement.

(e) **[Inapplicability to health-care-insurance receivable.]** This section does not apply to an assignment of a health-care-insurance receivable.

Official Comment

1. **Source.** Former Section 9–318(1).

2. **Purpose; Rights of Assignee in General.** Subsection (a), like former Section 9–318(1), provides that an assignee generally takes an assignment subject to defenses and claims of an account debtor. Under subsection (a)(1), if the account debtor's defenses on an assigned claim arise from the transaction that gave rise to the contract with the assignor, it makes no difference whether the defense or claim accrues before or after the account debtor is notified of the assignment. Under subsection (a)(2), the assignee takes subject to other defenses or claims only if they accrue before the account debtor has been notified of the assignment. Of course, an account debtor may waive its right to assert defenses or claims against an assignee under Section 9–403 or other applicable law. Subsection (a) tracks Section 3–305(a)(3) more closely than its predecessor.

3. **Limitation on Affirmative Claims.** Subsection (b) is new. It limits the claim that the account debtor may assert against an assignee. Borrowing from Section 3–305(a)(3) and cases construing former Section 9–318, subsection (b) generally does not afford the account debtor the right to an affirmative recovery from an assignee.

4. **Consumer Account Debtors; Relationship to Federal Trade Commission Rule.** Subsections (c) and (d) also are new. Subsection (c) makes clear that the rules of this section are subject to other law establishing special rules for consumer account debtors. An "account debtor who is an individual" as used in subsection (c) includes individuals who are jointly or jointly and severally obligated. Subsection (d) applies to rights evidenced by a record that is required to contain, but does not contain, the notice set forth in Federal Trade Commission Rule 433, 16 C.F.R. Part 433 (the "Holder-in-Due–Course Regulations"). Under subsection (d), a consumer account debtor has the same right to an affirmative recovery from an assignee of such a record as the consumer would have had against the assignee had the record contained the required notice.

5. **Scope; Application to "Account Debtor."** This section deals only with the rights and duties of "account debtors"—and for the most part only with account debtors on accounts, chattel paper, and payment intangibles. Subsection (e) provides that the obligation of an insurer with respect to a health-care-insurance receivable is governed by other law. References in this section to an "account debtor" include account debtors on collateral that is proceeds. Neither this section nor any other provision of this Article,

including Sections 9–408 and 9–409, provides analogous regulation of the rights and duties of other obligors on collateral, such as the maker of a negotiable instrument (governed by Article 3), the issuer of or nominated person under a letter of credit (governed by Article 5), or the issuer of a security (governed by Article 8). Article 9 leaves those rights and duties untouched; however, Section 9–409 deals with the special case of letters of credit. When chattel paper is composed in part of a negotiable instrument, the obligor on the instrument is not an "account debtor," and Article 3 governs the rights of the assignee of the chattel paper with respect to the issues that this section addresses. See, e.g., Section 3–601 (dealing with discharge of an obligation to pay a negotiable instrument).

§ 9–405. Modification of Assigned Contract.

(a) **[Effect of modification on assignee.]** A modification of or substitution for an assigned contract is effective against an assignee if made in good faith. The assignee acquires corresponding rights under the modified or substituted contract. The assignment may provide that the modification or substitution is a breach of contract by the assignor. This subsection is subject to subsections (b) through (d).

(b) **[Applicability of subsection (a).]** Subsection (a) applies to the extent that:

(1) the right to payment or a part thereof under an assigned contract has not been fully earned by performance; or

(2) the right to payment or a part thereof has been fully earned by performance and the account debtor has not received notification of the assignment under Section 9–406(a).

(c) **[Rule for individual under other law.]** This section is subject to law other than this article which establishes a different rule for an account debtor who is an individual and who incurred the obligation primarily for personal, family, or household purposes.

(d) **[Inapplicability to health-care-insurance receivable.]** This section does not apply to an assignment of a health-care-insurance receivable.

Official Comment

1. **Source.** Former Section 9–318(2).

807

2. **Modification of Assigned Contract.** The ability of account debtors and assignors to modify assigned contracts can be important, especially in the case of government contracts and complex contractual arrangements (e.g., construction contracts) with respect to which modifications are customary. Subsections (a) and (b) provide that good-faith modifications of assigned contracts are binding against an assignee to the extent that (i) the right to payment has not been fully earned or (ii) the right to payment has been earned and notification of the assignment has not been given to the account debtor. Former Section 9–318(2) did not validate modifications of fully-performed contracts under any circumstances, whether or not notification of the assignment had been given to the account debtor. Subsection (a) protects the interests of assignees by (i) limiting the effectiveness of modifications to those made in good faith, (ii) affording the assignee with corresponding rights under the contract as modified, and (iii) recognizing that the modification may be a breach of the assignor's agreement with the assignee.

3. **Consumer Account Debtors.** Subsection (c) is new. It makes clear that the rules of this section are subject to other law establishing special rules for consumer account debtors.

4. **Account Debtors on Health-Care-Insurance Receivables.** Subsection (d) also is new. It provides that this section does not apply to an assignment of a health-care-insurance receivable. The obligation of an insurer with respect to a health-care-insurance receivable is governed by other law.

§ 9–406. Discharge of Account Debtor; Notification of Assignment; Identification and Proof of Assignment; Restrictions on Assignment of Accounts, Chattel Paper, Payment Intangibles, and Promissory Notes Ineffective.

(a) **[Discharge of account debtor; effect of notification.]** Subject to subsections (b) through (i), an account debtor on an account, chattel paper, or a payment intangible may discharge its obligation by paying the assignor until, but not after, the account debtor receives a notification, authenticated by the assignor or the assignee, that the amount due or to become due has been assigned and that payment is to be made to the assignee. After receipt of the notification, the account debtor may discharge its obligation by paying the assignee and may not discharge the obligation by paying the assignor.

(b) **[When notification ineffective.]** Subject to subsection (h), notification is ineffective under subsection (a):

(1) if it does not reasonably identify the rights assigned;

(2) to the extent that an agreement between an account debtor and a seller of a payment intangible limits the account debtor's duty to pay a person other than the seller and the limitation is effective under law other than this article; or

(3) at the option of an account debtor, if the notification notifies the account debtor to make less than the full amount of any installment or other periodic payment to the assignee, even if:

(A) only a portion of the account, chattel paper, or payment intangible has been assigned to that assignee;

(B) a portion has been assigned to another assignee; or

(C) the account debtor knows that the assignment to that assignee is limited.

(c) **[Proof of assignment.]** Subject to subsection (h), if requested by the account debtor, an assignee shall seasonably furnish reasonable proof that the assignment has been made. Unless the assignee complies, the account debtor may discharge its obligation by paying the assignor, even if the account debtor has received a notification under subsection (a).

(d) **[Term restricting assignment generally ineffective.]** Except as otherwise provided in subsection (e) and Sections 2A–303 and 9–407, and subject to subsection (h), a term in an agreement between an account debtor and an assignor or in a promissory note is ineffective to the extent that it:

(1) prohibits, restricts, or requires the consent of the account debtor or person obligated on the promissory note to the assignment or transfer of, or the creation, attachment, perfection, or enforcement of a security interest in, the account, chattel paper, payment intangible, or promissory note; or

(2) provides that the assignment or transfer or the creation, attachment, perfection, or enforcement of the security interest may give rise to a default, breach, right of recoup-

ment, claim, defense, termination, right of termination, or remedy under the account, chattel paper, payment intangible, or promissory note.

(e) **[Inapplicability of subsection (d) to certain sales.]** Subsection (d) does not apply to the sale of a payment intangible or promissory note.

(f) **[Legal restrictions on assignment generally ineffective.]** Except as otherwise provided in Sections 2A–303 and 9–407 and subject to subsections (h) and (i), a rule of law, statute, or regulation that prohibits, restricts, or requires the consent of a government, governmental body or official, or account debtor to the assignment or transfer of, or creation of a security interest in, an account or chattel paper is ineffective to the extent that the rule of law, statute, or regulation:

(1) prohibits, restricts, or requires the consent of the government, governmental body or official, or account debtor to the assignment or transfer of, or the creation, attachment, perfection, or enforcement of a security interest in the account or chattel paper; or

(2) provides that the assignment or transfer or the creation, attachment, perfection, or enforcement of the security interest may give rise to a default, breach, right of recoupment, claim, defense, termination, right of termination, or remedy under the account or chattel paper.

(g) **[Subsection (b)(3) not waivable.]** Subject to subsection (h), an account debtor may not waive or vary its option under subsection (b)(3).

(h) **[Rule for individual under other law.]** This section is subject to law other than this article which establishes a different rule for an account debtor who is an individual and who incurred the obligation primarily for personal, family, or household purposes.

(i) **[Inapplicability to health-care-insurance receivable.]** This section does not apply to an assignment of a health-care-insurance receivable.

(j) **[Section prevails over specified inconsistent law.]** This section prevails over any inconsistent provisions of the following statutes, rules, and regulations:

[List here any statutes, rules, and regulations containing provisions inconsistent with this section.]

Legislative Note: States that amend statutes, rules, and regulations to remove provisions inconsistent with this section need not enact subsection (j)

As amended in 1999 and 2000.

Official Comment

1. **Source.** Former Section 9–318(3), (4).

2. **Account Debtor's Right to Pay Assignor Until Notification.** Subsection (a) provides the general rule concerning an account debtor's right to pay the assignor until the account debtor receives appropriate notification. The revision makes clear that once the account debtor receives the notification, the account debtor cannot discharge its obligation by paying the assignor. It also makes explicit that payment to the assignor before notification, or payment to the assignee after notification, discharges the obligation. No change in meaning from former Section 9–318 is intended. Nothing in this section conditions the effectiveness of a notification on the identity of the person who gives it. An account debtor that doubts whether the right to payment has been assigned may avail itself of the procedures in subsection (c). See Comment 4.

An effective notification under subsection (a) must be authenticated. This requirement normally could be satisfied by sending notification on the notifying person's letterhead or on a form on which the notifying person's name appears. In each case the printed name would be a symbol adopted by the notifying person for the purpose of identifying the person and adopting the notification. See Section 9–102 (defining "authenticate").

Subsection (a) applies only to account debtors on accounts, chattel paper, and payment intangibles. (Section 9–102 defines the term "account debtor" more broadly, to include those obligated on all general intangibles.) Although subsection (a) is more precise than its predecessor, it probably does not change the rule that applied under former Article 9. Former Section 9–318(3) referred to the account debtor's obligation to "pay," indicating that the subsection was limited to account debtors on accounts, chattel paper, and other payment obligations.

3. **Limitations on Effectiveness of Notification.** Subsection (b) contains some special rules concerning the effectiveness of a notification under subsection (a).

Subsection (b)(1) tracks former Section 9–318(3) by making ineffective a notification that does not reasonably identify the rights assigned. A reasonable identification need not identify the right to payment with specificity, but what is reasonable also is not left to the arbitrary decision of the account debtor. If an account debtor has doubt as to the adequacy of a notification, it may not be safe in disregarding the notification unless it notifies the assignee with reasonable promptness as to the respects in which the account debtor considers the notification defective.

Subsection (b)(2), which is new, applies only to sales of payment intangibles. It makes a notification ineffective to the extent that other law gives effect to an agreement between an account debtor and a seller of a payment intangible that limits the account debtor's duty to pay a person other than the seller. Payment intangibles are substantially less fungible than accounts and chattel paper. In some (e.g., commercial bank loans), account debtors customarily and legitimately expect that they will not be required to pay any person other than the financial institution that has advanced funds.

It has become common in financing transactions to assign interests in a single obligation to more than one assignee. Requiring an account debtor that owes a single obligation to make multiple payments to multiple assignees would be unnecessarily burdensome. Thus, under subsection (b)(3), an account debtor that is notified to pay an assignee less than the full amount of any installment or other periodic payment has the option to treat the notification as ineffective, ignore the notice, and discharge the assigned obligation by paying the assignor. Some account debtors may not realize that the law affords them the right to ignore certain notices of assignment with impunity. By making the notification ineffective at the account debtor's option, subsection (b)(3) permits an account debtor to pay the assignee in accordance with the notice and thereby to satisfy its obligation *pro tanto*. Under subsection (g), the rights and duties created by subsection (b)(3) cannot be waived or varied.

4. **Proof of Assignment.** Subsection (c) links payment with discharge, as in subsection (a). It follows former Section 9–318(3) in referring to the right of the account debtor to pay the assignor if the requested proof of assignment is not seasonably forthcoming. Even if the proof is not forthcoming, the notification of assignment would remain effective, so that, in the absence of reasonable proof of the assignment, the account debtor could discharge the obligation by paying either the assignee or the assignor. Of course, if the assignee did not in fact receive an assignment, the

account debtor cannot discharge its obligation by paying a putative assignee who is a stranger. The observations in Comment 3 concerning the reasonableness of an identification of a right to payment also apply here. An account debtor that questions the adequacy of proof submitted by an assignee would be well advised to promptly inform the assignee of the defects.

An account debtor may face another problem if its obligation becomes due while the account debtor is awaiting reasonable proof of the assignment that it has requested from the assignee. This section does not excuse the account debtor from timely compliance with its obligations. Consequently, an account debtor that has received a notification of assignment and who has requested reasonable proof of the assignment may discharge its obligation by paying the assignor at the time (or even earlier if reasonably necessary to avoid risk of default) when a payment is due, even if the account debtor has not yet received a response to its request for proof. On the other hand, after requesting reasonable proof of the assignment, an account debtor may not discharge its obligation by paying the assignor substantially in advance of the time that the payment is due unless the assignee has failed to provide the proof seasonably.

5. **Contractual Restrictions on Assignment.** Former Section 9–318(4) rendered ineffective an agreement between an account debtor and an assignor which prohibited assignment of an account (whether outright or to secure an obligation) or prohibited a security assignment of a general intangible for the payment of money due or to become due. Subsection (d) essentially follows former Section 9–318(4), but expands the rule of free assignability to chattel paper (subject to Sections 2A–303 and 9–407) and promissory notes and explicitly overrides both restrictions and prohibitions of assignment. The policies underlying the ineffectiveness of contractual restrictions under this section build on common-law developments that essentially have eliminated legal restrictions on assignments of rights to payment as security and other assignments of rights to payment such as accounts and chattel paper. Any that might linger for accounts and chattel paper are addressed by new subsection (f). See Comment 6.

Former Section 9–318(4) did not apply to a sale of a payment intangible (as described in the former provision, "a general intangible for money due or to become due") but did apply to an assignment of a payment intangible for security. Subsection (e) continues this approach and also makes subsection (d) inapplicable to sales of promissory notes. Section 9–408 addresses anti-assignment clauses with respect to sales of payment intangibles and promissory notes.

Like former Section 9–318(4), subsection (d) provides that anti-assignment clauses are "ineffective." The quoted term means that the clause is of no effect whatsoever; the clause does not prevent the assignment from taking effect between the parties and the prohibited assignment does not constitute a default under the agreement between the account debtor and assignor. However, subsection (d) does not override terms that do not directly prohibit, restrict, or require consent to an assignment but which might, nonetheless, present a practical impairment of the assignment. Properly read, however, subsection (d) reaches only covenants that prohibit, restrict, or require consents to assignments; it does not override all terms that might "impair" an assignment in fact.

Example: Buyer enters into an agreement with Seller to buy equipment that Seller is to manufacture according to Buyer's specifications. Buyer agrees to make a series of prepayments during the construction process. In return, Seller agrees to set aside the prepaid funds in a special account and to use the funds solely for the manufacture of the designated equipment. Seller also agrees that it will not assign any of its rights under the sale agreement with Buyer. Nevertheless, Seller grants to Secured Party a security interest in its accounts. Seller's anti-assignment agreement is ineffective under subsection (d); its agreement concerning the use of prepaid funds, which is not a restriction or prohibition on assignment, is not. However, if Secured Party notifies Buyer to make all future payments directly to Secured Party, Buyer will be obliged to do so under subsection (a) if it wishes the payments to discharge its obligation. Unless Secured Party releases the funds to Seller so that Seller can comply with its use-of-funds covenant, Seller will be in breach of that covenant.

In the example, there appears to be a plausible business purpose for the use-of-funds covenant. However, a court may conclude that a covenant with no business purpose other than imposing an impediment to an assignment actually is a direct restriction that is rendered ineffective by subsection (d).

6. **Legal Restrictions on Assignment.** Former Section 9–318(4), like subsection (d) of this section, addressed only contractual restrictions on assignment. The former section was grounded on the reality that legal, as opposed to contractual, restrictions on assignments of rights to payment had largely disappeared. New subsection (f) codifies this principle of free assign-ability for accounts and chattel paper. For the most part the discussion of contractual restrictions in Comment 5 applies as well to legal restrictions rendered ineffective under subsection (f).

7. **Multiple Assignments.** This section, like former Section 9–318, is not a complete codification of the law of assignments of rights to payment. In particular, it is silent concerning many of the ramifications for an account debtor in cases of multiple assignments of the same right. For example, an assignor might assign the same receivable to multiple assignees (which assignments could be either inadvertent or wrongful). Or, the assignor could assign the receivable to assignee–1, which then might re-assign it to assignee–2, and so forth. The rights and duties of an account debtor in the face of multiple assignments and in other circumstances not resolved in the statutory text are left to the common-law rules. See, e.g., Restatement (2d), Contracts §§ 338(3), 339. The failure of former Article 9 to codify these rules does not appear to have caused problems.

8. **Consumer Account Debtors.** Subsection (h) is new. It makes clear that the rules of this section are subject to other law establishing special rules for consumer account debtors.

9. **Account Debtors on Health–Care–Insurance Receivables.** Subsection (i) also is new. The obligation of an insurer with respect to a health-care-insurance receivable is governed by other law. Section 9–408 addresses contractual and legal restrictions on the assignment of a health-care-insurance receivable.

§ 9–407. Restrictions on Creation or Enforcement of Security Interest in Leasehold Interest or in Lessor's Residual Interest.

(a) **[Term restricting assignment generally ineffective.]** Except as otherwise provided in subsection (b), a term in a lease agreement is ineffective to the extent that it:

(1) prohibits, restricts, or requires the consent of a party to the lease to the assignment or transfer of, or the creation, attachment, perfection, or enforcement of a security interest in an interest of a party under the lease contract or in the lessor's residual interest in the goods; or

(2) provides that the assignment or transfer or the creation, attachment, perfection, or enforcement of the security interest may give rise to a default, breach, right of recoup-

ment, claim, defense, termination, right of termination, or remedy under the lease.

(b) **[Effectiveness of certain terms.]** Except as otherwise provided in Section 2A–303(7), a term described in subsection (a)(2) is effective to the extent that there is:

(1) a transfer by the lessee of the lessee's right of possession or use of the goods in violation of the term; or

(2) a delegation of a material performance of either party to the lease contract in violation of the term.

(c) **[Security interest not material impairment.]** The creation, attachment, perfection, or enforcement of a security interest in the lessor's interest under the lease contract or the lessor's residual interest in the goods is not a transfer that materially impairs the lessee's prospect of obtaining return performance or materially changes the duty of or materially increases the burden or risk imposed on the lessee within the purview of Section 2A–303(4) unless, and then only to the extent that, enforcement actually results in a delegation of material performance of the lessor.

As amended in 1999.

Official Comment

1. **Source.** Section 2A–303.

2. **Restrictions on Assignment Generally Ineffective.** Under subsection (a), as under former Section 2A–303(3), a term in a lease agreement which prohibits or restricts the creation of a security interest generally is ineffective. This reflects the general policy of Section 9–406(d) and former Section 9–318(4). This section has been conformed in several respects to analogous provisions in Sections 9–406, 9–408, and 9–409, including the substitution of "ineffective" for "not enforceable" and the substitution of *"assignment or transfer of, or the"** creation, attachment, perfection, or enforcement of a security interest" for "creation or enforcement of a security interest."

3. **Exceptions for Certain Transfers and Delegations.** Subsection (b) provides exceptions to the general ineffectiveness of restrictions under subsection (a). A term that otherwise is ineffective under subsection (a)(2) is effective to the extent that a lessee

* Amendments in italics approved by the Permanent Editorial Board for Uniform Commercial Code October 20, 1999.

transfers its right to possession and use of goods or if either party delegates material performance of the lease contract in violation of the term. However, under subsection (c), as under former Section 2A–303(3), a lessor's creation of a security interest in its interest in a lease contract or its residual interest in the leased goods is not a material impairment under Section 2A–303(4) (former Section 2A–303(5)), absent an actual delegation of the lessor's material performance. The terms of the lease contract determine whether the lessor, in fact, has any remaining obligations to perform. If it does, it is then necessary to determine whether there has been an actual delegation of "material performance." See Section 2A–303, Comments 3 and 4.

As amended in 1999.

§ 9–408. Restrictions on Assignment of Promissory Notes, Health-Care-Insurance Receivables, and Certain General Intangibles Ineffective.

(a) **[Term restricting assignment generally ineffective.]** Except as otherwise provided in subsection (b), a term in a promissory note or in an agreement between an account debtor and a debtor which relates to a health-care-insurance receivable or a general intangible, including a contract, permit, license, or franchise, and which term prohibits, restricts, or requires the consent of the person obligated on the promissory note or the account debtor to, the assignment or transfer of, or creation, attachment, or perfection of a security interest in, the promissory note, health-care-insurance receivable, or general intangible, is ineffective to the extent that the term:

(1) would impair the creation, attachment, or perfection of a security interest; or

(2) provides that the assignment or transfer or the creation, attachment, or perfection of the security interest may give rise to a default, breach, right of recoupment, claim, defense, termination, right of termination, or remedy under the promissory note, health-care-insurance receivable, or general intangible.

(b) **[Applicability of subsection (a) to sales of certain rights to payment.]** Subsection (a) applies to a security interest in a payment intangible or promissory note only if the security interest arises out of a sale of the payment intangible or promissory note.

(c) **[Legal restrictions on assignment generally ineffective.]** A rule of law, statute, or regulation that prohibits, restricts, or requires the consent of a government, governmental body or official, person obligated on a promissory note, or account debtor to the assignment or transfer of, or creation of a security interest in, a promissory note, health-care-insurance receivable, or general intangible, including a contract, permit, license, or franchise between an account debtor and a debtor, is ineffective to the extent that the rule of law, statute, or regulation:

(1) would impair the creation, attachment, or perfection of a security interest; or

(2) provides that the assignment or transfer or the creation, attachment, or perfection of the security interest may give rise to a default, breach, right of recoupment, claim, defense, termination, right of termination, or remedy under the promissory note, health-care-insurance receivable, or general intangible.

(d) **[Limitation on ineffectiveness under subsections (a) and (c).]** To the extent that a term in a promissory note or in an agreement between an account debtor and a debtor which relates to a health-care-insurance receivable or general intangible or a rule of law, statute, or regulation described in subsection (c) would be effective under law other than this article but is ineffective under subsection (a) or (c), the creation, attachment, or perfection of a security interest in the promissory note, health-care-insurance receivable, or general intangible:

(1) is not enforceable against the person obligated on the promissory note or the account debtor;

(2) does not impose a duty or obligation on the person obligated on the promissory note or the account debtor;

(3) does not require the person obligated on the promissory note or the account debtor to recognize the security interest, pay or render performance to the secured party, or accept payment or performance from the secured party;

(4) does not entitle the secured party to use or assign the debtor's rights under the promissory note, health-care-insurance receivable, or general intangible, including any related information or materials furnished to the debtor in the transaction giving rise to the promissory note, health-care-insurance receivable, or general intangible;

(5) does not entitle the secured party to use, assign, possess, or have access to any trade secrets or confidential information of the person obligated on the promissory note or the account debtor; and

(6) does not entitle the secured party to enforce the security interest in the promissory note, health-care-insurance receivable, or general intangible.

(e) **[Section prevails over specified inconsistent law.]** This section prevails over any inconsistent provisions of the following statutes, rules, and regulations:

[List here any statutes, rules, and regulations containing provisions inconsistent with this section.]

Legislative Note: States that amend statutes, rules, and regulations to remove provisions inconsistent with this section need not enact subsection (e).

As amended in 1999.

Official Comment

1. **Source.** New.

2. **Free Assignability.** This section makes ineffective any attempt to restrict the assignment of a general intangible, health-care-insurance receivable, or promissory note, whether the restriction appears in the terms of a promissory note or the agreement between an account debtor and a debtor (subsection (a)) or in a rule of law, including a statute or governmental rule or regulation (subsection (c)). This result allows the creation, attachment, and perfection of a security interest in a general intangible, such as an agreement for the nonexclusive license of software, as well as sales of certain receivables, such as a health-care-insurance receivable (which is an "account"), payment intangible, or promissory note, without giving rise to a default or breach by the assignor or from triggering a remedy of the account debtor or person obligated on a promissory note. This enhances the ability of certain debtors

to obtain credit. On the other hand, subsection (d) protects the other party—the "account debtor" on a general intangible or the person obligated on a promissory note—from adverse effects arising from the security interest. It leaves the account debtor's or obligated person's rights and obligations unaffected in all material respects if a restriction rendered ineffective by subsection (a) or (c) would be effective under law other than Article 9.

Example 1: A term of an agreement for the nonexclusive license of computer software prohibits the licensee from assigning any of its rights as licensee with respect to the software. The agreement also provides that an attempt to assign rights in violation of the restriction is a default entitling the licensor to terminate the license agreement. The licensee, as debtor, grants to a secured party a security interest in its rights under the license and in the computers in which it is installed. Under this section, the term prohibiting assignment and providing for a default upon an attempted assignment is ineffective to prevent the creation, attachment, or perfection of the security interest or entitle the licensor to terminate the license agreement. However, under subsection (d), the secured party (absent the licensor's agreement) is not entitled to enforce the license or to use, assign, or otherwise enjoy the benefits of the licensed software, and the licensor need not recognize (or pay any attention to) the secured party. Even if the secured party takes possession of the computers on the debtor's default, the debtor would remain free to remove the software from the computer, load it on another computer, and continue to use it, if the license so permits. If the debtor does not remove the software, other law may require the secured party to remove it before disposing of the computer. Disposition of the software with the computer could violate an effective prohibition on enforcement of the security interest. See subsection (d).

3. **Nature of Debtor's Interest.** Neither this section nor any other provision of this Article determines whether a debtor has a property interest. The definition of the term "security interest" provides that it is an "interest in personal property." See Section 1–201(37). Ordinarily, a debtor can create a security interest in collateral only if it has "rights in the collateral." See Section 9–203(b). Other law determines whether a debtor has a property interest ("rights in the collateral") and the nature of that interest. For example, the nonexclusive license addressed in Example 1 may not create any property interest whatsoever in the intellectual property (e.g., copyright) that underlies the license and that effectively enables the licensor

to grant the license. The debtor's property interest may be confined solely to its interest in the promises made by the licensor in the license agreement (e.g., a promise not to sue the debtor for its use of the software).

4. **Scope: Sales of Payment Intangibles and Other General Intangibles; Assignments Unaffected by this Section.** Subsections (a) and (c) render ineffective restrictions on assignments only "to the extent" that the assignments restrict the "creation, attachment, or perfection of a security interest," including sales of payment intangibles and promissory notes. This section does not render ineffective a restriction on an assignment that does not create a security interest. For example, if the debtor in Comment 2, Example 1 purported to assign the license to another entity that would use the computer software itself, other law would govern the effectiveness of the anti-assignment provisions.

Subsection (a) applies to a security interest in payment intangibles only if the security interest arises out of sale of the payment intangibles. Contractual restrictions directed to security interests in payment intangibles which secure an obligation are subject to Section 9–406(d). Subsection (a) also deals with sales of promissory notes which also create security interests. See Section 9–109(a). Subsection (c) deals with all security interests in payment intangibles or promissory notes, whether or not arising out of a sale.

Subsection (a) does not render ineffective any term, and subsection (c) does not render ineffective any law, statute or regulation, that restricts outright sales of general intangibles other than payment intangibles. They deal only with restrictions on security interests. The only sales of general intangibles that create security interests are sales of payment intangibles.

5. **Terminology: "Account Debtor"; "Person Obligated on a Promissory Note."** This section uses the term "account debtor" as it is defined in Section 9–102. The term refers to the party, other than the debtor, to a general intangible, including a permit, license, franchise, or the like, and the person obligated on a health-care-insurance receivable, which is a type of account. The definition of "account debtor" does not limit the term to persons who are obligated to *pay* under a general intangible. Rather, the term includes all persons who are obligated on a general intangible, including those who are obligated to render performance in exchange for payment. In some cases, e.g., the creation of a security interest in a franchisee's rights under a franchise agreement, the principal payment obligation may be owed *by* the debtor (franchisee) *to*

the account debtor (franchisor). This section also refers to a "person obligated on a promissory note," inasmuch as those persons do not fall within the definition of "account debtor."

Example 2: A licensor and licensee enter into an agreement for the nonexclusive license of computer software. The licensee's interest in the license agreement is a general intangible. If the licensee grants to a secured party a security interest in its rights under the license agreement, the licensee is the debtor and the licensor is the account debtor. On the other hand, if the licensor grants to a secured party a security interest in its right to payment (an account) under the license agreement, the licensor is the debtor and the licensee is the account debtor. (This section applies to the security interest in the general intangible but not to the security interest in the account, which is not a health-care-insurance receivable.)

6. **Effects on Account Debtors and Persons Obligated on Promissory Notes.** Subsections (a) and (c) affect two classes of persons. These subsections affect account debtors on general intangibles and health-care-insurance receivables and persons obligated on promissory notes. Subsection (c) also affects governmental entities that enact or determine rules of law. *However, subsection (d) ensures that these affected persons are not affected adversely.* That provision removes any burdens or adverse effects on these persons for which any rational basis could exist to restrict the effectiveness of an assignment or to exercise any remedies. For this reason, the effects of subsections (a) and (c) are immaterial insofar as those persons are concerned.

Subsection (a) does not override terms that do not directly prohibit, restrict, or require consent to an assignment but which might, nonetheless, present a practical impairment of the assignment. Properly read, however, this section, like Section 9–406(d), reaches only covenants that prohibit, restrict, or require consents to assignments; it does not override all terms that might "impair" an assignment in fact.

Example 3: A licensor and licensee enter into an agreement for the nonexclusive license of valuable business software. The license agreement includes terms (i) prohibiting the licensee from assigning its rights under the license, (ii) prohibiting the licensee from disclosing to anyone certain information relating to the software and the licensor, and (iii) deeming prohibited assignments and prohibited disclosures to be defaults. The licensee wishes to obtain financing and, in exchange, is willing to grant a

security interest in its rights under the license agreement. The secured party, reasonably, refuses to extend credit unless the licensee discloses the information that it is prohibited from disclosing under the license agreement. The secured party cannot determine the value of the proposed collateral in the absence of this information. Under this section, the terms of the license prohibiting the assignment (grant of the security interest) and making the assignment a default are ineffective. However, the non-disclosure covenant is not a term that prohibits the assignment or creation of a security interest in the license. Consequently, the nondisclosure term is enforceable even though the *practical* effect is to restrict the licensee's ability to use its rights under the license agreement as collateral.

The nondisclosure term also would be effective in the factual setting of Comment 2, Example 1. If the secured party's possession of the computers loaded with software would put it in a position to discover confidential information that the debtor was prohibited from disclosing, the licensor should be entitled to enforce its rights against the secured party. Moreover, the licensor could have required the debtor to obtain the secured party's agreement that (i) it would immediately return all copies of software loaded on the computers and that (ii) it would not examine or otherwise acquire any information contained in the software. This section does not prevent an account debtor from protecting by agreement its independent interests that are unrelated to the "creation, attachment, or perfection" of a security interest. In Example 1, moreover, the secured party is not in possession of copies of software by virtue of its security interest or in connection with enforcing its security interest *in the debtor's license of the software.* Its possession is incidental to its possession of the computers, in which it has a security interest. Enforcing against the secured party a restriction relating to the software in no way interferes with its security interest in the computers.

7. **Effect in Assignor's Bankruptcy.** This section could have a substantial effect if the assignor enters bankruptcy. Roughly speaking, Bankruptcy Code Section 552 invalidates security interests in property acquired after a bankruptcy petition is filed, except to the extent that the postpetition property constitutes proceeds of prepetition collateral.

Example 4: A debtor is the owner of a cable television franchise that, under applicable law, cannot be assigned without the consent of the municipal franchisor. A lender wishes to extend credit to the debtor, provided that the credit is secured by the debtor's "going business" value. To secure the loan, the debtor grants a security interest in all its existing and after-acquired property. The franchise represents the principal value of the business. The municipality refuses to consent to any assignment for collateral purposes. If other law were given effect, the security interest in the franchise would not attach; and if the debtor were to enter bankruptcy and sell the business, the secured party would receive but a fraction of the business's value. Under this section, however, the security interest would attach to the franchise. As a result, the security interest would attach to the proceeds of any sale of the franchise while a bankruptcy is pending. However, this section would protect the interests of the municipality by preventing the secured party from enforcing its security interest to the detriment of the municipality.

8. **Effect Outside of Bankruptcy.** The principal effects of this section will take place outside of bankruptcy. Compared to the relatively few debtors that enter bankruptcy, there are many more that do not. By making available previously unavailable property as collateral, this section should enable debtors to obtain additional credit. For purposes of determining whether to extend credit, under some circumstances a secured party may ascribe value to the collateral to which its security interest has attached, even if this section precludes the secured party from enforcing the security interest without the agreement of the account debtor or person obligated on the promissory note. This may be the case where the secured party sees a likelihood of obtaining that agreement in the future. This may also be the case where the secured party anticipates that the collateral will give rise to a type of proceeds as to which this section would not apply.

Example 5: Under the facts of Example 4, the debtor does not enter bankruptcy. Perhaps in exchange for a fee, the municipality agrees that the debtor may transfer the franchise to a buyer. As consideration for the transfer, the debtor receives from the buyer its check for part of the purchase price and its promissory note for the balance. The security interest attaches to the check and promissory note as proceeds. See Section 9–315(a)(2). This section does not apply to the security interest in the check, which is not a promissory note, health-care-insurance receivable, or general intangible. Nor does it apply to the security interest in the promissory note, inasmuch as it was not sold to the secured party.

9. **Contrary Federal Law.** This section does not override federal law to the contrary. However, it does reflect an important policy judgment that should provide a template for future federal law reforms.

§ 9–409. Restrictions on Assignment of Letter-of-Credit Rights Ineffective.

(a) **[Term or law restricting assignment generally ineffective.]** A term in a letter of credit or a rule of law, statute, regulation, custom, or practice applicable to the letter of credit which prohibits, restricts, or requires the consent of an applicant, issuer, or nominated person to a beneficiary's assignment of or creation of a security interest in a letter-of-credit right is ineffective to the extent that the term or rule of law, statute, regulation, custom, or practice:

(1) would impair the creation, attachment, or perfection of a security interest in the letter-of-credit right; or

(2) provides that the assignment or the creation, attachment, or perfection of the security interest may give rise to a default, breach, right of recoupment, claim, defense, termination, right of termination, or remedy under the letter-of-credit right.

(b) **[Limitation on ineffectiveness under subsection (a).]** To the extent that a term in a letter of credit is ineffective under subsection (a) but would be effective under law other than this article or a custom or practice applicable to the letter of credit, to the transfer of a right to draw or otherwise demand performance under the letter of credit, or to the assignment of a right to proceeds of the letter of credit, the creation, attachment, or perfection of a security interest in the letter-of-credit right:

(1) is not enforceable against the applicant, issuer, nominated person, or transferee beneficiary;

(2) imposes no duties or obligations on the applicant, issuer, nominated person, or transferee beneficiary; and

(3) does not require the applicant, issuer, nominated person, or transferee beneficiary to recognize the security interest, pay or render performance to the secured party, or accept payment or other performance from the secured party.

As amended in 1999.

Official Comment

1. **Source.** New.

2. **Purpose and Relevance.** This section, patterned on Section 9–408, limits the effectiveness of attempts to restrict the creation, attachment, or perfection of a security interest in letter-of-credit rights, whether the restriction appears in the letter of credit or a rule of law, custom, or practice applicable to the letter of credit. It protects the creation, attachment, and perfection of a security interest while preventing these events from giving rise to a default or breach by the assignor or from triggering a remedy or defense of the issuer or other person obligated on a letter of credit. Letter-of-credit rights are a type of supporting obligation. See Section 9–102. Under Sections 9–203 and 9–308, a security interest in a supporting obligation attaches and is perfected automatically if the security interest in the supported obligation attaches and is perfected. See Section 9–107, Comment 5. The automatic attachment and perfection under Article 9 would be anomalous or misleading if, under other law (e.g., Article 5), a restriction on transfer or assignment were effective to block attachment and perfection.

3. **Relationship to Letter-of-Credit Law.** Although restrictions on an assignment of a letter of credit are ineffective to prevent creation, attachment, and perfection of a security interest, subsection (b) protects the issuer and other parties from any adverse effects of the security interest by preserving letter-of-credit law and practice that limits the right of a beneficiary to transfer its right to draw or otherwise demand performance (Section 5–112) and limits the obligation of an issuer or nominated person to recognize a beneficiary's assignment of letter-of-credit proceeds (Section 5–114). Thus, this section's treatment of letter-of-credit rights differs from this Article's treatment of instruments and investment property. Moreover, under Section 9–109(c)(4), this Article does not apply to the extent that the rights of a transferee beneficiary or nominated person are independent and superior under Section 5–114, thereby preserving the "independence principle" of letter-of-credit law.

PART 5

FILING

[SUBPART 1. FILING OFFICE; CONTENTS AND EFFECTIVENESS OF FINANCING STATEMENT]

§ 9–501. Filing Office.

(a) **[Filing offices.]** Except as otherwise provided in subsection (b), if the local law of this State governs perfection of a security interest or agricultural lien, the office in which to file a financing statement to perfect the security interest or agricultural lien is:

(1) the office designated for the filing or recording of a record of a mortgage on the related real property, if:

(A) the collateral is as-extracted collateral or timber to be cut; or

(B) the financing statement is filed as a fixture filing and the collateral is goods that are or are to become fixtures; or

(2) the office of [ ] [or any office duly authorized by [ ]], in all other cases, including a case in which the collateral is goods that are or are to become fixtures and the financing statement is not filed as a fixture filing.

(b) **[Filing office for transmitting utilities.]** The office in which to file a financing statement to perfect a security interest in collateral, including fixtures, of a transmitting utility is the office of [ ]. The financing statement also constitutes a fixture filing as to the collateral indicated in the financing statement which is or is to become fixtures.

Legislative Note: The State should designate the filing office where the brackets appear. The filing office may be that of a governmental official (e.g., the Secretary of State) or a private party that maintains the State's filing system.

Official Comment

1. **Source.** Derived from former Section 9–401.

2. **Where to File.** Subsection (a) indicates where in a given State a financing statement is to be filed. Former Article 9 afforded each State three alternative approaches, depending on the extent to which the State desires central filing (usually with the Secretary of State), local filing (usually with a county office), or both. As Comment 1 to former Section 9–401 observed,

"The principal advantage of state-wide filing is ease of access to the credit information which the files exist to provide. Consider for example the national distributor who wishes to have current information about the credit standing of the thousands of persons he sells to on credit. The more completely the files are centralized on a state-wide basis, the easier and cheaper it becomes to procure credit information; the more the files are scattered in local filing units, the more burdensome and costly." Local filing increases the net costs of secured transactions also by increasing uncertainty and the number of required filings. Any benefit that local filing may have had in the 1950's is now insubstantial. Accordingly, this Article dictates central filing for most situations, while retaining local filing for real-estate-related collateral and special filing provisions for transmitting utilities.

3. **Minerals and Timber.** Under subsection (a)(1), a filing in the office where a record of a mortgage on the related real property would be filed will perfect a security interest in as-extracted collateral. Inasmuch as the security interest does not attach until extraction, the filing continues to be effective after extraction. A different result occurs with respect to timber to be cut, however. Unlike as-extracted collateral, standing timber may be goods before it is cut. See Section 9–102 (defining "goods"). Once cut, however, it is no longer timber *to be* cut, and the filing in the real-property-mortgage office ceases to be effective. The timber then becomes ordinary goods, and filing in the office specified in subsection (a)(2) is necessary for perfection. Note also that after the timber is cut the law of the debtor's location, not the location of the timber, governs perfection under Section 9–301.

4. **Fixtures.** There are two ways in which a secured party may file a financing statement to perfect a security interest in goods that are or are to become fixtures. It may file in the Article 9 records, as with most other goods. See subsection (a)(2). Or it may file the financing statement as a "fixture filing," defined in Section 9–102, in the office in which a record of a mortgage on the related real property would be filed. See subsection(a)(1)(B).

5. **Transmitting Utilities.** The usual filing rules do not apply well for a transmitting utility (defined in Section 9–102). Many pre-UCC statutes provided special filing rules for railroads and in some cases for other public utilities, to avoid the requirements for filing with legal descriptions in every county in which such debtors had property. Former Section 9–401(5) recreated and broadened these provisions, and subsection (b) follows this approach. The nature of the debtor

will inform persons searching the record as to where to make a search.

§ 9–502. Contents of Financing Statement; Record of Mortgage as Financing Statement; Time of Filing Financing Statement.

(a) **[Sufficiency of financing statement.]** Subject to subsection (b), a financing statement is sufficient only if it:

(1) provides the name of the debtor;

(2) provides the name of the secured party or a representative of the secured party; and

(3) indicates the collateral covered by the financing statement.

(b) **[Real-property-related financing statements.]** Except as otherwise provided in Section 9–501(b), to be sufficient, a financing statement that covers as-extracted collateral or timber to be cut, or which is filed as a fixture filing and covers goods that are or are to become fixtures, must satisfy subsection (a) and also:

(1) indicate that it covers this type of collateral;

(2) indicate that it is to be filed [for record] in the real property records;

(3) provide a description of the real property to which the collateral is related [sufficient to give constructive notice of a mortgage under the law of this State if the description were contained in a record of the mortgage of the real property]; and

(4) if the debtor does not have an interest of record in the real property, provide the name of a record owner.

(c) **[Record of mortgage as financing statement.]** A record of a mortgage is effective, from the date of recording, as a financing statement filed as a fixture filing or as a financing statement covering as-extracted collateral or timber to be cut only if:

(1) the record indicates the goods or accounts that it covers;

(2) the goods are or are to become fixtures related to the real property described in the record or the collateral is related to the real property described in the record and is as-extracted collateral or timber to be cut;

(3) the record satisfies the requirements for a financing statement in this section other than an indication that it is to be filed in the real property records; and

(4) the record is [duly] recorded.

(d) **[Filing before security agreement or attachment.]** A financing statement may be filed before a security agreement is made or a security interest otherwise attaches.

Legislative Note: Language in brackets is optional. Where the State has any special recording system for real property other than the usual grantor-grantee index (as, for instance, a tract system or a title registration or Torrens system) local adaptations of subsection (b) and Section 9–519(d) and (e) may be necessary. See, e.g., Mass. Gen. Laws Chapter 106, Section 9–410.

Official Comment

1. **Source.** Former Section 9–402(1), (5), (6).

2. **"Notice Filing."** This section adopts the system of "notice filing." What is required to be filed is not, as under pre-UCC chattel mortgage and conditional sales acts, the security agreement itself, but only a simple record providing a limited amount of information (financing statement). The financing statement may be filed before the security interest attaches or thereafter. See subsection (d). See also Section 9–308(a) (contemplating situations in which a financing statement is filed before a security interest attaches).

The notice itself indicates merely that a person may have a security interest in the collateral indicated. Further inquiry from the parties concerned will be necessary to disclose the complete state of affairs. Section 9–210 provides a statutory procedure under which the secured party, at the debtor's request, may be required to make disclosure. However, in many cases, information may be forthcoming without the need to resort to the formalities of that section.

Notice filing has proved to be of great use in financing transactions involving inventory, accounts, and chattel paper, because it obviates the necessity of refiling on each of a series of transactions in a continuing arrangement under which the collateral changes from day to day. However, even in the case of filings that do not necessarily involve a series of transactions (e.g., a loan secured by a single item of equipment), a financing statement is effective to encompass transactions under a security agreement not in existence and not contemplated at the time the notice was filed, if the indication of collateral in the financing statement is sufficient to cover the collateral concerned. Similarly, a financing statement is effective to cover after-acquired property of the type indicated and to perfect with respect to future advances under security agreements, regardless of whether after-acquired property or future advances are mentioned in the financing statement and even if not in the contemplation of the parties at the time the financing statement was authorized to be filed.

3. **Debtor's Signature; Required Authorization.** Subsection (a) sets forth the simple formal requirements for an effective financing statement. These requirements are: (1) the debtor's name; (2) the name of a secured party or representative of the secured party; and (3) an indication of the collateral.

Whereas former Section 9–402(1) required the debtor's signature to appear on a financing statement, this Article contains no signature requirement. The elimination of the signature requirement facilitates paperless filing. (However, as PEB Commentary No. 15 indicates, a paperless financing statement was sufficient under former Article 9.) Elimination of the signature requirement also makes the exceptions provided by former Section 9–402(2) unnecessary.

The fact that this Article does not require that an authenticating symbol be contained in the public record does not mean that all filings are authorized. Rather, Section 9–509(a) entitles a person to file an initial financing statement, an amendment that adds collateral, or an amendment that adds a debtor only if the debtor authorizes the filing, and Section 9–509(d) entitles a person other than the debtor to file a termination statement only if the secured party of record authorizes the filing. Of course, a filing has legal effect only to the extent it is authorized. See Section 9–510.

Law other than this Article, including the law with respect to ratification of past acts, generally determines whether a person has the requisite authority to file a record under this Article. See Sections 1–103 and 9–509, Comment 3. However, under Section 9–509(b), the debtor's authentication of (or becoming bound by) a security agreement *ipso facto* constitutes the debtor's authorization of the filing of a financing statement covering the collateral described in the security agreement. The secured party need not obtain a separate authorization.

Section 9–625 provides a remedy for unauthorized filings. Making an unauthorized filing also may give rise to civil or criminal liability under other law. In addition, this Article contains provisions that assist in the discovery of unauthorized filings and the amelioration of their practical effect. For example, Section 9–

518 provides a procedure whereby a person may add to the public record a statement to the effect that a financing statement indexed under the person's name was wrongfully filed, and Section 9–509(d) entitles any person to file a termination statement if the secured party of record fails to comply with its obligation to file or send one to the debtor, the debtor authorizes the filing, and the termination statement so indicates. However, the filing office is neither obligated nor permitted to inquire into issues of authorization. See Section 9–520(a).

4. **Certain Other Requirements.** Subsection (a) deletes other provisions of former Section 9–402(1) because they seems unwise (real-property description for financing statements covering crops), unnecessary (adequacy of copies of financing statements), or both (copy of security agreement as financing statement). In addition, the filing office must reject a financing statement lacking certain other information formerly required as a condition of perfection (e.g., an address for the debtor or secured party). See Sections 9–516(b), 9–520(a). However, if the filing office accepts the record, it is effective nevertheless. See Section 9–520(c).

5. **Real-Property-Related Filings.** Subsection (b) contains the requirements for financing statements filed as fixture filings and financing statements covering timber to be cut or minerals and minerals-related accounts constituting as-extracted collateral. A description of the related real property must be sufficient to reasonably identify it. See Section 9–108. This formulation rejects the view that the real property description must be by metes and bounds, or otherwise conforming to traditional real-property practice in conveyancing, but, of course, the incorporation of such a description by reference to the recording data of a deed, mortgage or other instrument containing the description should suffice under the most stringent standards. The proper test is that a description of real property must be sufficient so that the financing statement will fit into the real-property search system and be found by a real-property searcher. Under the optional language in subsection (b)(3), the test of adequacy of the description is whether it would be adequate in a record of a mortgage of the real property. As suggested in the Legislative Note, more detail may be required if there is a tract indexing system or a land registration system.

If the debtor does not have an interest of record in the real property, a real-property-related financing statement must show the name of a record owner, and Section 9–519(d) requires the financing statement to be indexed in the name of that owner. This requirement also enables financing statements covering as-extracted collateral or timber to be cut and financing statements filed as fixture filings to fit into the real-property search system.

6. **Record of Mortgage Effective as Financing Statement.** Subsection (c) explains when a record of a mortgage is effective as a financing statement filed as a fixture filing or to cover timber to be cut or as-extracted collateral. Use of the term "record of a mortgage" recognizes that in some systems the record actually filed is not the record pursuant to which a mortgage is created. Moreover, "mortgage" is defined in Section 9–102 as an "interest in real property," not as the record that creates or evidences the mortgage or the record that is filed in the public recording systems. A record creating a mortgage may also create a security interest with respect to fixtures (or other goods) in conformity with this Article. A single agreement creating a mortgage on real property and a security interest in chattels is common and useful for certain purposes. Under subsection (c), the recording of the record evidencing a mortgage (if it satisfies the requirements for a financing statement) constitutes the filing of a financing statement as to the fixtures (but not, of course, as to other goods). Section 9–515(g) makes the usual five-year maximum life for financing statements inapplicable to mortgages that operate as fixture filings under Section 9–502(c). Such mortgages are effective for the duration of the real-property recording.

Of course, if a combined mortgage covers chattels that are not fixtures, a regular financing statement filing is necessary with respect to the chattels, and subsection (c) is inapplicable. Likewise, a financing statement filed as a "fixture filing" is not effective to perfect a security interest in personal property other than fixtures.

In some cases it may be difficult to determine whether goods are or will become fixtures. Nothing in this Part prohibits the filing of a "precautionary" fixture filing, which would provide protection in the event goods are determined to be fixtures. The fact of filing should not be a factor in the determining whether goods are fixtures. Cf. Section 9–505(b).

§ 9–503. Name of Debtor and Secured Party.

(a) **[Sufficiency of debtor's name.]** A financing statement sufficiently provides the name of the debtor:

(1) if the debtor is a registered organization, only if the financing statement provides the name of the debtor indicated on the public record of the debtor's jurisdiction of

organization which shows the debtor to have been organized;

(2) if the debtor is a decedent's estate, only if the financing statement provides the name of the decedent and indicates that the debtor is an estate;

(3) if the debtor is a trust or a trustee acting with respect to property held in trust, only if the financing statement:

(A) provides the name specified for the trust in its organic documents or, if no name is specified, provides the name of the settlor and additional information sufficient to distinguish the debtor from other trusts having one or more of the same settlors; and

(B) indicates, in the debtor's name or otherwise, that the debtor is a trust or is a trustee acting with respect to property held in trust; and

(4) in other cases:

(A) if the debtor has a name, only if it provides the individual or organizational name of the debtor; and

(B) if the debtor does not have a name, only if it provides the names of the partners, members, associates, or other persons comprising the debtor.

(b) **[Additional debtor-related information.]** A financing statement that provides the name of the debtor in accordance with subsection (a) is not rendered ineffective by the absence of:

(1) a trade name or other name of the debtor; or

(2) unless required under subsection (a)(4)(B), names of partners, members, associates, or other persons comprising the debtor.

(c) **[Debtor's trade name insufficient.]** A financing statement that provides only the debtor's trade name does not sufficiently provide the name of the debtor.

(d) **[Representative capacity.]** Failure to indicate the representative capacity of a secured party or representative of a secured party does not affect the sufficiency of a financing statement.

(e) **[Multiple debtors and secured parties.]** A financing statement may provide the name of more than one debtor and the name of more than one secured party.

Official Comment

1. **Source.** Subsections (a)(4)(A), (b), and (c) derive from former Section 9–402(7); otherwise, new.

2. **Debtor's Name.** The requirement that a financing statement provide the debtor's name is particularly important. Financing statements are indexed under the name of the debtor, and those who wish to find financing statements search for them under the debtor's name. Subsection (a) explains what the debtor's name is for purposes of a financing statement. If the debtor is a "registered organization" (defined in Section 9–102 so as to ordinarily include corporations, limited partnerships, and limited liability companies), then the debtor's name is the name shown on the public records of the debtor's "jurisdiction of organization" (also defined in Section 9–102). Subsections (a)(2) and (a)(3) contain special rules for decedent's estates and common-law trusts. (Subsection (a)(1) applies to business trusts that are registered organizations.)

Subsection (a)(4)(A) essentially follows the first sentence of former Section 9–402(7). Section 1–201(28) defines the term "organization," which appears in subsection (a)(4), very broadly, to include all legal and commercial entities as well as associations that lack the status of a legal entity. Thus, the term includes corporations, partnerships of all kinds, business trusts, limited liability companies, unincorporated associations, personal trusts, governments, and estates. If the organization has a name, that name is the correct name to put on a financing statement. If the organization does not have a name, then the financing statement should name the individuals or other entities who comprise the organization.

Together with subsections (b) and (c), subsection (a) reflects the view prevailing under former Article 9 that the actual individual or organizational name of the debtor on a financing statement is both necessary and sufficient, whether or not the financing statement provides trade or other names of the debtor and, if the debtor has a name, whether or not the financing statement provides the names of the partners, members, or associates who comprise the debtor.

Note that, even if the name provided in an initial financing statement is correct, the filing office nevertheless must reject the financing statement if it does not identify an individual debtor's last name (e.g., if it is not clear whether the debtor's name is Perry Mason or Mason Perry). See Section 9–516(b)(3)(C).

3. Secured Party's Name. New subsection (d) makes clear that when the secured party is a representative, a financing statement is sufficient if it names the secured party, whether or not it indicates any representative capacity. Similarly, a financing statement that names a representative of the secured party is sufficient, even if it does not indicate the representative capacity.

Example: Debtor creates a security interest in favor of Bank X, Bank Y, and Bank Z, but not to their representative, the collateral agent (Bank A). The collateral agent is not itself a secured party. See Section 9–102. Under Sections 9–502(a) and 9–503(d), however, a financing statement is effective if it names as secured party Bank A and not the actual secured parties, even if it omits Bank A's representative capacity.

Each person whose name is provided in an initial financing statement as the name of the secured party or representative of the secured party is a secured party of record. See Section 9–511.

4. Multiple Names. Subsection (e) makes explicit what is implicit under former Article 9: a financing statement may provide the name of more than one debtor and secured party. See Section 1–102(5)(a) (words in the singular include the plural). With respect to records relating to more than one debtor, see Section 9–520(d). With respect to financing statements providing the name of more than one secured party, see Sections 9–509(e) and 9–510(b).

§ 9–504. Indication of Collateral.

A financing statement sufficiently indicates the collateral that it covers if the financing statement provides:

(1) a description of the collateral pursuant to Section 9–108; or

(2) an indication that the financing statement covers all assets or all personal property.

As amended in 1999.

Official Comment

1. **Source.** Former Section 9–402(1).

2. **Indication of Collateral.** To comply with Section 9–502(a), a financing statement must "indicate" the collateral it covers. A financing statement sufficiently indicates collateral claimed to be covered by the financing statement if it satisfies the purpose of conditioning perfection on the filing of a financing statement, i.e., if it provides notice that a person may have a security interest in the collateral claimed. See Section

9–502, Comment 2. In particular, an indication of collateral that would have satisfied the requirements of former Section 9–402(1) (i.e., "a statement indicating the types, or describing the items, of collateral") suffices under Section 9502(a). An indication may satisfy the requirements of Section 9–502(a), even if it would not have satisfied the requirements of former Section 9–402(1).

This section provides two safe harbors. Under paragraph (1), a "description" of the collateral (as the term is explained in Section 9–108) suffices as an indication for purposes of the sufficiency of a financing statement.

Debtors sometimes create a security interest in all, or substantially all, of their assets. To accommodate this practice, paragraph (2) expands the class of sufficient collateral references to embrace "an indication that the financing statement covers all assets or all personal property." If the property in question belongs to the debtor and is personal property, any searcher will know that the property is covered by the financing statement. Of course, regardless of its breadth, a financing statement has no effect with respect to property indicated but to which a security interest has not attached. Note that a broad statement of this kind (e.g., "all debtor's personal property") would not be a sufficient "description" for purposes of a security agreement. See Sections 9–203(b)(3)(A), 9–108. It follows that a somewhat narrower description than "all assets," e.g., "all assets other than automobiles," is sufficient for purposes of this section, even if it does not suffice for purposes of a security agreement.

As amended in 2000.

§ 9–505. Filing and Compliance With Other Statutes and Treaties for Consignments, Leases, Other Bailments, and Other Transactions.

(a) **[Use of terms other than "debtor" and "secured party."]** A consignor, lessor, or other bailor of goods, a licensor, or a buyer of a payment intangible or promissory note may file a financing statement, or may comply with a statute or treaty described in Section 9–311(a), using the terms "consignor", "consignee", "lessor", "lessee", "bailor", "bailee", "licensor", "licensee", "owner", "registered owner", "buyer", "seller", or words of similar import, instead of the terms "secured party" and "debtor".

(b) **[Effect of financing statement under subsection (a).]** This part applies to the filing of a financing statement under subsection (a) and, as appropriate, to compliance that is equivalent to filing a financing statement under Section 9–311(b), but the filing or compliance is not of itself a factor in determining whether the collateral secures an obligation. If it is determined for another reason that the collateral secures an obligation, a security interest held by the consignor, lessor, bailor, licensor, owner, or buyer which attaches to the collateral is perfected by the filing or compliance.

Official Comment

1. **Source.** Former Section 9–408.

2. **Precautionary Filing.** Occasionally, doubts arise concerning whether a transaction creates a relationship to which this Article or its filing provisions apply. For example, questions may arise over whether a "lease" of equipment in fact creates a security interest or whether the "sale" of payment intangibles in fact secures an obligation, thereby requiring action to perfect the security interest. This section, which derives from former Section 9–408, affords the option of filing of a financing statement with appropriate changes of terminology but without affecting the substantive question of classification of the transaction.

3. **Changes from Former Section 9–408.** This section expands the rule of Section 9–408 to embrace more generally other bailments and transactions, as well as sales transactions, primarily sales of payment intangibles and promissory notes. It provides the same benefits for compliance with a statute or treaty described in Section 9–311(a) that former Section 9–408 provided for filing, in connection with the use of terms such as "lessor," "consignor," etc. The references to "owner" and "registered owner" are intended to address, for example, the situation where a putative lessor is the registered owner of an automobile covered by a certificate of title and the transaction is determined to create a security interest. Although this section provides that the security interest is perfected, the relevant certificate-of-title statute may expressly provide to the contrary or may be ambiguous. If so, it may be necessary or advisable to amend the certificate-of-title statute to ensure that perfection of the security interest will be achieved.

As does Section 1–201, former Article 9 referred to transactions, including leases and consignments, "intended as security." This misleading phrase created the erroneous impression that the parties to a transaction can dictate how the law will classify it (e.g., as a bailment or as a security interest) and thus affect the rights of third parties. This Article deletes the phrase wherever it appears. Subsection (b) expresses the principle more precisely by referring to a security interest that "secures an obligation."

4. **Consignments.** Although a "true" consignment is a bailment, the filing and priority provisions of former Article 9 applied to "true" consignments. See former Sections 2–326(3), 9–114. A consignment "intended as security" created a security interest that was in all respects subject to former Article 9. This Article subsumes most true consignments under the rubric of "security interest." See Sections 9–102 (definition of "consignment"), 9–109(a)(4), 1–201(37) (definition of "security interest"). Nevertheless, it maintains the distinction between a (true) "consignment," as to which only certain aspects of Article 9 apply, and a so-called consignment that actually "secures an obligation," to which Article 9 applies in full. The revisions to this section reflect the change in terminology.

§ 9–506.   Effect of Errors or Omissions.

(a) **[Minor errors and omissions.]** A financing statement substantially satisfying the requirements of this part is effective, even if it has minor errors or omissions, unless the errors or omissions make the financing statement seriously misleading.

(b) **[Financing statement seriously misleading.]** Except as otherwise provided in subsection (c), a financing statement that fails sufficiently to provide the name of the debtor in accordance with Section 9–503(a) is seriously misleading.

(c) **[Financing statement not seriously misleading.]** If a search of the records of the filing office under the debtor's correct name, using the filing office's standard search logic, if any, would disclose a financing statement that fails sufficiently to provide the name of the debtor in accordance with Section 9–503(a), the name provided does not make the financing statement seriously misleading.

(d) **["Debtor's correct name."]** For purposes of Section 9–508(b), the "debtor's correct name" in subsection (c) means the correct name of the new debtor.

Official Comment

1. **Source.** Former Section 9–402(8).

2. **Errors.** Like former Section 9–402(8), subsection (a) is in line with the policy of this Article to

simplify formal requisites and filing requirements. It is designed to discourage the fanatical and impossibly refined reading of statutory requirements in which courts occasionally have indulged themselves. Subsection (a) provides the standard applicable to indications of collateral. Subsections (b) and (c), which are new, concern the effectiveness of financing statements in which the debtor's name is incorrect. Subsection (b) contains the general rule: a financing statement that fails sufficiently to provide the debtor's name in accordance with Section 9–503(a) is seriously misleading as a matter of law. Subsection (c) provides an exception: If the financing statement nevertheless would be discovered in a search under the debtor's correct name, using the filing office's standard search logic, if any, then as a matter of law the incorrect name does not make the financing statement seriously misleading. A financing statement that is seriously misleading under this section is ineffective even if it is disclosed by (i) using a search logic other than that of the filing office to search the official records, or (ii) using the filing office's standard search logic to search a data base other than that of the filing office.

In addition to requiring the debtor's name and an indication of the collateral, Section 9–502(a) requires a financing statement to provide the name of the secured party or a representative of the secured party. Inasmuch as searches are not conducted under the secured party's name, and no filing is needed to continue the perfected status of security interest after it is assigned, an error in the name of the secured party or its representative will not be seriously misleading. However, in an appropriate case, an error of this kind may give rise to an estoppel in favor of a particular holder of a conflicting claim to the collateral. See Section 1–103.

3. **New Debtors.** Subsection (d) provides that, in determining the extent to which a financing statement naming an original debtor is effective against a new debtor, the sufficiency of the financing statement should be tested against the name of the new debtor.

§ 9–507. Effect of Certain Events on Effectiveness of Financing Statement.

(a) **[Disposition.]** A filed financing statement remains effective with respect to collateral that is sold, exchanged, leased, licensed, or otherwise disposed of and in which a security interest or agricultural lien continues, even if the secured party knows of or consents to the disposition.

(b) **[Information becoming seriously misleading.]** Except as otherwise provided in sub-section (c) and Section 9–508, a financing statement is not rendered ineffective if, after the financing statement is filed, the information provided in the financing statement becomes seriously misleading under Section 9–506.

(c) **[Change in debtor's name.]** If a debtor so changes its name that a filed financing statement becomes seriously misleading under Section 9–506:

(1) the financing statement is effective to perfect a security interest in collateral acquired by the debtor before, or within four months after, the change; and

(2) the financing statement is not effective to perfect a security interest in collateral acquired by the debtor more than four months after the change, unless an amendment to the financing statement which renders the financing statement not seriously misleading is filed within four months after the change.

Official Comment

1. **Source.** Former Section 9–402(7).

2. **Scope of Section.** This section deals with situations in which the information in a proper financing statement becomes inaccurate after the financing statement is filed. Compare Section 9–338, which deals with situations in which a financing statement contains a particular kind of information concerning the debtor (i.e., the information described in Section 9–516(b)(5)) that is incorrect at the time it is filed.

3. **Post-Filing Disposition of Collateral.** Under subsection (a), a financing statement remains effective even if the collateral is sold or otherwise disposed of. This subsection clarifies the third sentence of former Section 9–402(7) by providing that a financing statement remains effective following the disposition of collateral only when the security interest or agricultural lien continues in that collateral. This result is consistent with the conclusion of PEB Commentary No. 3. Normally, a security interest does continue after disposition of the collateral. See Section 9–315(a). Law other than this Article determines whether an agricultural lien survives disposition of the collateral.

As a consequence of the disposition, the collateral may be owned by a person other than the debtor against whom the financing statement was filed. Under subsection (a), the secured party remains perfected even if it does not correct the public record. For this reason, any person seeking to determine whether a debtor owns collateral free of security interests must inquire as to the debtor's source of title and, if circumstances seem to require it, search in the name of a former owner. Subsection (a) addresses only the sufficiency of the information contained in the financing statement. A disposition of collateral may result in loss of perfection for other reasons. See Section 9–316.

Example: Dee Corp. is an Illinois corporation. It creates a security interest in its equipment in favor of Secured Party. Secured Party files a proper financing statement in Illinois. Dee Corp. sells an item of equipment to Bee Corp., a Pennsylvania corporation, subject to the security interest. The security interest continues, see Section 9–315(a), and remains perfected, see Section 9–507(a), notwithstanding that the financing statement is filed under "D" (for Dee Corp.) and not under "B." However, because Bee Corp. is located in Pennsylvania and not Illinois, see Section 9–307, unless Secured Party perfects under Pennsylvania law within one year after the transfer, its security interest will become unperfected and will be deemed to have been unperfected against purchasers of the collateral. See Section 9–316.

4. **Other Post–Filing Changes.** Subsection (b) provides that, as a general matter, post-filing changes that render a financing statement inaccurate and seriously misleading have no effect on a financing statement. The financing statement remains effective. It is subject to two exceptions: Section 9–508 and Section 9–507(c). Section 9–508 addresses the effectiveness of a financing statement filed against an original debtor when a new debtor becomes bound by the original debtor's security agreement. It is discussed in the Comments to that section. Section 9–507(c) addresses a "pure" change of the debtor's name, i.e., a change that does not implicate a new debtor. It clarifies former Section 9–402(7). If a name change renders a filed financing statement seriously misleading, the financing statement, unless amended to provide the debtor's new correct name, is effective only to perfect a security interest in collateral acquired by the debtor before, or within four months after, the change. If an amendment that provides the new correct name is filed within four months after the change, the financing statement as amended would be effective also with respect to collateral acquired more than four months after the change. If an amendment that provides the new correct name is filed more than four months after the change, the financing statement as amended would be effective also with respect to collateral acquired more than four months after the change, but only from the time of the filing of the amendment.

§ 9–508. Effectiveness of Financing Statement if New Debtor Becomes Bound by Security Agreement.

(a) **[Financing statement naming original debtor.]** Except as otherwise provided in this section, a filed financing statement naming an original debtor is effective to perfect a security interest in collateral in which a new debtor has or acquires rights to the extent that the financing statement would have been effective had the original debtor acquired rights in the collateral.

(b) **[Financing statement becoming seriously misleading.]** If the difference between the name of the original debtor and that of the new debtor causes a filed financing statement that is effective under subsection (a) to be seriously misleading under Section 9–506:

(1) the financing statement is effective to perfect a security interest in collateral acquired by the new debtor before, and within four months after, the new debtor becomes bound under Section 9–203(d); and

(2) the financing statement is not effective to perfect a security interest in collateral acquired by the new debtor more than four months after the new debtor becomes bound under Section 9–203(d) unless an initial financing statement providing the name of the new debtor is filed before the expiration of that time.

(c) **[When section not applicable.]** This section does not apply to collateral as to which a filed financing statement remains effective against the new debtor under Section 9–507(a).

Official Comment

1. **Source.** New.

2. **The Problem.** Section 9–203(d) and (e) and this section deal with situations where one party (the "new debtor") becomes bound as debtor by a security agreement entered into by another person (the "original debtor"). These situations often arise as a consequence of changes in business structure. For example, the original debtor may be an individual debtor who operates a business as a sole proprietorship and then incorporates it. Or, the original debtor may be a corporation that is merged into another corporation. Under both former Article 9 and this Article, collateral that is transferred in the course of the incorporation or merg-

er normally would remain subject to a perfected security interest. See Sections 9-315(a), 9-507(a). Former Article 9 was less clear with respect to whether an after-acquired property clause in a security agreement signed by the original debtor would be effective to create a security interest in property acquired by the new corporation or the merger survivor and, if so, whether a financing statement filed against the original debtor would be effective to perfect the security interest. This section and Sections 9-203(d) and (e) are a clarification.

3. **How New Debtor Becomes Bound.** Normally, a security interest is unenforceable unless the debtor has authenticated a security agreement describing the collateral. See Section 9-203(b). New Section 9-203(e) creates an exception, under which a security agreement entered into by one person is effective with respect to the property of another. This exception comes into play if a "new debtor" becomes bound as debtor by a security agreement entered into by another person (the "original debtor"). (The quoted terms are defined in Section 9-102.) If a new debtor does become bound, then the security agreement entered into by the original debtor satisfies the security-agreement requirement of Section 9-203(b)(3) as to existing or after-acquired property of the new debtor to the extent the property is described in the security agreement. In that case, no other agreement is necessary to make a security interest enforceable in that property. See Section 9-203(e).

Section 9-203(d) explains when a new debtor becomes bound by an original debtor's security agreement. Under Section 9-203(d)(1), a new debtor becomes bound as debtor if, by contract or operation of other law, the security agreement becomes effective to create a security interest in the new debtor's property. For example, if the applicable corporate law of mergers provides that when A Corp merges into B Corp, B Corp becomes a debtor under A Corp's security agreement, then B Corp would become bound as debtor following such a merger. Similarly, B Corp would become bound as debtor if B Corp contractually assumes A's obligations under the security agreement.

Under certain circumstances, a new debtor becomes bound for purposes of this Article even though it would not be bound under other law. Under Section 9-203(d)(2), a new debtor becomes bound when, by contract or operation of other law, it (i) becomes obligated not only for the secured obligation but also generally for the obligations of the original debtor and (ii) acquires or succeeds to substantially all the assets of the original debtor. For example, some corporate laws provide that, when two corporations merge, the surviving corporation succeeds to the assets of its merger partner and "has all liabilities" of both corporations. In the case where, for example, A Corp merges into B Corp (and A Corp ceases to exist), some people have questioned whether A Corp's grant of a security interest in its existing and after-acquired property becomes a "liability" of B Corp, such that B Corp's existing and after-acquired property becomes subject to a security interest in favor of A Corp's lender. Even if corporate law were to give a negative answer, under Section 9-203(d)(2), B Corp would become bound for purposes of Section 9-203(e) and this section. The "substantially all of the assets" requirement of Section 9-203(d)(2) excludes sureties and other secondary obligors as well as persons who become obligated through veil piercing and other non-successorship doctrines. In most cases, it will exclude successors to the assets and liabilities of a division of a debtor.

4. **When Financing Statement Effective Against New Debtor.** Subsection (a) provides that a filing against the original debtor generally is effective to perfect a security interest in collateral that a new debtor has at the time it becomes bound by the original debtor's security agreement and collateral that it acquires after the new debtor becomes bound. Under subsection (b), however, if the filing against the original debtor is seriously misleading as to the new debtor's name, the filing is effective as to collateral acquired by the new debtor more than four months after the new debtor becomes bound only if a person files during the four-month period an initial financing statement providing the name of the new debtor. Compare Section 9-507(c) (four-month period of effectiveness with respect to collateral acquired by a debtor after the debtor changes its name). Moreover, if the original debtor and the new debtor are located in different jurisdictions, a filing against the original debtor would not be effective to perfect a security interest in collateral that the new debtor acquires or has acquired from a person other than the original debtor. See Example 5, Section 9-316, Comment 2.

5. **Transferred Collateral.** This section does not apply to collateral transferred by the original debtor to a new debtor. See subsection (c). Under those circumstances, the filing against the original debtor continues to be effective until it lapses or perfection is lost for another reason. See sections 9-316, 9-507(a).

6. **Priority.** Section 9-326 governs the priority contest between a secured creditor of the original debtor and a secured creditor of the new debtor.

As amended in 2000.

§ 9–509. Persons Entitled to File a Record.

(a) **[Person entitled to file record.]** A person may file an initial financing statement, amendment that adds collateral covered by a financing statement, or amendment that adds a debtor to a financing statement only if:

(1) the debtor authorizes the filing in an authenticated record or pursuant to subsection (b) or (c); or

(2) the person holds an agricultural lien that has become effective at the time of filing and the financing statement covers only collateral in which the person holds an agricultural lien.

(b) **[Security agreement as authorization.]** By authenticating or becoming bound as debtor by a security agreement, a debtor or new debtor authorizes the filing of an initial financing statement, and an amendment, covering:

(1) the collateral described in the security agreement; and

(2) property that becomes collateral under Section 9–315(a)(2), whether or not the security agreement expressly covers proceeds.

(c) **[Acquisition of collateral as authorization.]** By acquiring collateral in which a security interest or agricultural lien continues under Section 9–315(a)(1), a debtor authorizes the filing of an initial financing statement, and an amendment, covering the collateral and property that becomes collateral under Section 9–315(a)(2).

(d) **[Person entitled to file certain amendments.]** A person may file an amendment other than an amendment that adds collateral covered by a financing statement or an amendment that adds a debtor to a financing statement only if:

(1) the secured party of record authorizes the filing; or

(2) the amendment is a termination statement for a financing statement as to which the secured party of record has failed to file or send a termination statement as required by Section 9–513(a) or (c), the debtor authorizes the filing, and the termination statement indicates that the debtor authorized it to be filed.

(e) **[Multiple secured parties of record.]** If there is more than one secured party of record for a financing statement, each secured party of record may authorize the filing of an amendment under subsection (d).

As amended in 2000.

Official Comment

1. **Source.** New.

2. **Scope and Approach of This Section.** This section collects in one place most of the rules determining whether a record may be filed. Section 9–510 explains the extent to which a filed record is effective. Under these sections, the identity of the person who effects a filing is immaterial. The filing scheme contemplated by this Part does not contemplate that the identity of a "filer" will be a part of the searchable records. This is consistent with, and a necessary aspect of, eliminating signatures or other evidence of authorization from the system. (Note that the 1972 amendments to this Article eliminated the requirement that a financing statement contain the signature of the secured party.) As long as the appropriate person authorizes the filing, or, in the case of a termination statement, the debtor is entitled to the termination, it is insignificant whether the secured party or another person files any given record. The question of authorization is one for the court, not the filing office. However, a filing office may choose to employ authentication procedures in connection with electronic communications, e.g., to verify the identity of a filer who seeks to charge the filing fee.

3. **Unauthorized Filings.** Records filed in the filing office do not require signatures for their effectiveness. Subsection (a)(1) substitutes for the debtor's signature on a financing statement the requirement that the debtor authorize in an authenticated record the filing of an initial financing statement or an amendment that adds collateral. Also, under subsection (a)(1), if an amendment adds a debtor, the debtor who is added must authorize the amendment. A person who files an unauthorized record in violation of subsection (a)(1) is liable under Section 9–625(b) and (e) for actual and statutory damages. Of course, a filed financing statement is ineffective to perfect a security interest if the filing is not authorized. See Section 9–510(a). Law other than this Article, including the law with respect to ratification of past acts, generally determines whether a person has the requisite authority to file a record under this section. See Sections 1–103, 9–502, Comment 3. This Article applies to other issues, such as the priority of a security interest perfected by the filing of a financing statement.

4. *Ipso Facto* **Authorization.** Under subsection (b), the authentication of a security agreement *ipso facto* constitutes the debtor's authorization of the filing of a financing statement covering the collateral described in the security agreement. The secured party need not obtain a separate authorization. Similarly, a new debtor's becoming bound by a security agreement *ipso facto* constitutes the new debtor's authorization of the filing of a financing statement covering the collateral described in the security agreement by which the new debtor has become bound. And, under subsection (c), the acquisition of collateral in which a security interest continues after disposition under Section 9–315(a)(1) *ipso facto* constitutes an authorization to file an initial financing statement againt the person who acquired the collateral. The authorization to file an initial financing statement also constitutes an authorization to file a record covering actual proceeds of the original collateral, even if the security agreement is silent as to proceeds.

Example 1: Debtor authenticates a security agreement creating a security interest in Debtor's inventory in favor of Secured Party. Secured Party files a financing statement covering inventory and accounts. The financing statement is authorized insofar as it covers inventory and unauthorized insofar as it covers accounts. (Note, however, that the financing statement will be effective to perfect a security interest in accounts constituting proceeds of the inventory to the same extent as a financing statement covering only inventory.)

Example 2: Debtor authenticates a security agreement creating a security interest in Debtor's inventory in favor of Secured Party. Secured Party files a financing statement covering inventory. Debtor sells some inventory, deposits the buyer's payment into a deposit account, and withdraws the funds to purchase equipment. As long as the equipment can be traced to the inventory, the security interest continues in the equipment. See Section 9–315(a)(2). However, because the equipment was acquired with cash proceeds, the financing statement becomes ineffective to perfect the security interest in the equipment on the 21st day after the security interest attaches to the equipment unless Secured Party continues perfection beyond the 20–day period by filing a financing statement against the equipment or amending the filed financing statement to cover equipment. See Section 9–315(d). Debtor's authentication of the security agreement authorizes the filing of an initial financing statement or amendment covering the equipment, which is "property that becomes collater-al under Section 9–315(a)(2)." See Section 9–509(b)(2).

5. **Agricultural Liens.** Under subsection (a)(2), the holder of an agricultural lien may file a financing statement covering collateral subject to the lien without obtaining the debtor's authorization. Because the lien arises as matter of law, the debtor's consent is not required. A person who files an unauthorized record in violation of this subsection is liable under Section 9–625(e) for a statutory penalty and damages.

6. **Amendments; Termination Statements Authorized by Debtor.** Most amendments may not be filed unless the secured party of record, as determined under Section 9–511, authorizes the filing. See subsection (d)(1). However, under subsection (d)(2), the authorization of the secured party of record is not required for the filing of a termination statement if the secured party of record failed to send or file a termination statement as required by Section 9–513, the debtor authorizes it to be filed, and the termination statement so indicates.

7. **Multiple Secured Parties of Record.** Subsection (e) deals with multiple secured parties of record. It permits each secured party of record to authorize the filing of amendments. However, Section 9–510(b) protects the rights and powers of one secured party of record from the effects of filings made by another secured party of record. See Section 9–510, Comment 3.

8. **Successor to Secured Party of Record.** A person may succeed to the powers of the secured party of record by operation of other law, e.g., the law of corporate mergers. In that case, the successor has the power to authorize filings within the meaning of this section.

§ 9–510.   Effectiveness of Filed Record.

(a) **[Filed record effective if authorized.]** A filed record is effective only to the extent that it was filed by a person that may file it under Section 9–509.

(b) **[Authorization by one secured party of record.]** A record authorized by one secured party of record does not affect the financing statement with respect to another secured party of record.

(c) **[Continuation statement not timely filed.]** A continuation statement that is not filed within the six-month period prescribed by Section 9–515(d) is ineffective.

Official Comment

1. **Source.** New.

2. **Ineffectiveness of Unauthorized or Over-broad Filings.** Subsection (a) provides that a filed financing statement is effective only to the extent it was filed by a person entitled to file it.

Example 1: Debtor authorizes the filing of a financing statement covering inventory. Under Section 9–509, the secured party may file a financing statement covering only inventory; it may not file a financing statement covering other collateral. The secured party files a financing statement covering inventory and equipment. This section provides that the financing statement is effective only to the extent the secured party may file it. Thus, the financing statement is effective to perfect a security interest in inventory but ineffective to perfect a security interest in equipment.

3. **Multiple Secured Parties of Record.** Section 9–509(e) permits any secured party of record to authorize the filing of most amendments. Subsection (b) of this section prevents a filing authorized by one secured party of record from affecting the rights and powers of another secured party of record without the latter's consent.

Example 2: Debtor creates a security interest in favor of A and B. The filed financing statement names A and B as the secured parties. An amendment deleting some collateral covered by the financing statement is filed pursuant to B's authorization. Although B's security interest in the deleted collateral becomes unperfected, A's security interest remains perfected in all the collateral.

Example 3: Debtor creates a security interest in favor of A and B. The financing statement names A and B as the secured parties. A termination statement is filed pursuant to B's authorization. Although the effectiveness of the financing statement terminates with respect to B's security interest, A's rights are unaffected. That is, the financing statement continues to be effective to perfect A's security interest.

4. **Continuation Statements.** A continuation statement may be filed only within the six months immediately before lapse. See Section 9–515(d). The filing office is obligated to reject a continuation statement that is filed outside the six-month period. See Sections 9–520(a), 9–516(b)(7). Subsection (c) provides that if the filing office fails to reject a continuation statement that is not filed in a timely manner, the continuation statement is ineffective nevertheless.

§ 9–511. Secured Party of Record.

(a) **[Secured party of record.]** A secured party of record with respect to a financing statement is a person whose name is provided as the name of the secured party or a representative of the secured party in an initial financing statement that has been filed. If an initial financing statement is filed under Section 9–514(a), the assignee named in the initial financing statement is the secured party of record with respect to the financing statement.

(b) **[Amendment naming secured party of record.]** If an amendment of a financing statement which provides the name of a person as a secured party or a representative of a secured party is filed, the person named in the amendment is a secured party of record. If an amendment is filed under Section 9–514(b), the assignee named in the amendment is a secured party of record.

(c) **[Amendment deleting secured party of record.]** A person remains a secured party of record until the filing of an amendment of the financing statement which deletes the person.

Official Comment

1. **Source.** New.

2. **Secured Party of Record.** This new section explains how the secured party of record is to be determined. If SP–1 is named as the secured party in an initial financing statement, it is the secured party of record. Similarly, if an initial financing statement reflects a total assignment from SP–0 to SP–1, then SP–1 is the secured party of record. See subsection (a). If, subsequently, an amendment is filed assigning SP–1's status to SP–2, then SP–2 becomes the secured party of record in place of SP–1. The same result obtains if a subsequent amendment deletes the reference to SP–1 and substitutes therefor a reference to SP–2. If, however, a subsequent amendment adds SP–2 as a secured party but does not purport to remove SP–1 as a secured party, then SP–2 and SP–1 each is a secured party of record. See subsection (b). An amendment purporting to remove the only secured party of record without providing a successor is ineffective. See Section 9–512(e). At any point in time, all effective records that comprise a financing statement must be examined to determine the person or persons that have the status of secured party of record.

3. **Successor to Secured Party of Record.** Application of other law may result in a person succeed-

ing to the powers of a secured party of record. For example, if the secured party of record (A) merges into another corporation (B) and the other corporation (B) survives, other law may provide that B has all of A's powers. In that case, B is authorized to take all actions under this Part that A would have been authorized to take. Similarly, acts taken by a person who is authorized under generally applicable principles of agency to act on behalf of the secured party of record are effective under this Part.

§ 9–512. Amendment of Financing Statement.

[Alternative A]

(a) **[Amendment of information in financing statement.]** Subject to Section 9–509, a person may add or delete collateral covered by, continue or terminate the effectiveness of, or, subject to subsection (e), otherwise amend the information provided in, a financing statement by filing an amendment that:

(1) identifies, by its file number, the initial financing statement to which the amendment relates; and

(2) if the amendment relates to an initial financing statement filed [or recorded] in a filing office described in Section 9–501(a)(1), provides the information specified in Section 9–502(b).

[Alternative B]

(a) **[Amendment of information in financing statement.]** Subject to Section 9–509, a person may add or delete collateral covered by, continue or terminate the effectiveness of, or, subject to subsection (e), otherwise amend the information provided in, a financing statement by filing an amendment that:

(1) identifies, by its file number, the initial financing statement to which the amendment relates; and

(2) if the amendment relates to an initial financing statement filed [or recorded] in a filing office described in Section 9–501(a)(1), provides the date [and time] that the initial financing statement was filed [or recorded] and the information specified in Section 9–502(b).

[End of Alternatives]

(b) **[Period of effectiveness not affected.]** Except as otherwise provided in Section 9–515, the filing of an amendment does not extend the period of effectiveness of the financing statement.

(c) **[Effectiveness of amendment adding collateral.]** A financing statement that is amended by an amendment that adds collateral is effective as to the added collateral only from the date of the filing of the amendment.

(d) **[Effectiveness of amendment adding debtor.]** A financing statement that is amended by an amendment that adds a debtor is effective as to the added debtor only from the date of the filing of the amendment.

(e) **[Certain amendments ineffective.]** An amendment is ineffective to the extent it:

(1) purports to delete all debtors and fails to provide the name of a debtor to be covered by the financing statement; or

(2) purports to delete all secured parties of record and fails to provide the name of a new secured party of record.

Legislative Note: States whose real-estate filing offices require additional information in amendments and cannot search their records by both the name of the debtor and the file number should enact Alternative B to Sections 9–512(a), 9–518(b), 9–519(f) and 9–522(a).

Official Comment

1. **Source.** Former 9–402(4).

2. **Changes to Financing Statements.** This section addresses changes to financing statements, including addition and deletion of collateral. Although termination statements, assignments, and continuation statements are types of amendment, this Article follows former Article 9 and contains separate sections containing additional provisions applicable to particular types of amendments. See Section 9–513 (termination statements); 9–514 (assignments); 9–515 (continuation statements). One should not infer from this separate treatment that this Article requires a separate amendment to accomplish each change. Rather, a single amendment would be legally sufficient to, e.g., add collateral and continue the effectiveness of the financing statement.

3. **Amendments.** An amendment under this Article may identify only the information contained in a financing statement that is to be changed; alternative-

ly, it may take the form of an amended and restated financing statement. The latter would state, for example, that the financing statement "is amended and restated to read as follows: . . ." References in this Part to an "amended financing statement" are to a financing statement as amended by an amendment using either technique.

This section revises former Section 9–402(4) to permit secured parties of record to make changes in the public record without the need to obtain the debtor's signature. However, the filing of an amendment that adds collateral or adds a debtor must be authorized by the debtor or it will not be effective. See Sections 9–509(a), 9–510(a).

4. **Amendment Adding Debtor.** An amendment that adds a debtor is effective, provided that the added debtor authorizes the filing. See Section 9–509(a). However, filing an amendment adding a debtor to a previously filed financing statement affords no advantage over filing an initial financing statement against that debtor and may be disadvantageous. With respect to the added debtor, for purposes of determining the priority of the security interest, the time of filing is the time of the filing of the amendment, not the time of the filing of the initial financing statement. See subsection (d). However, the effectiveness of the financing statement lapses with respect to added debtor at the time it lapses with respect to the original debtor. See subsection (b).

5. **Deletion of All Debtors or Secured Parties of Record.** Subsection (e) assures that there will be a debtor and secured party of record for every financing statement.

> **Example:** A filed financing statement names A and B as secured parties of record and covers inventory and equipment. An amendment deletes equipment and purports to delete A and B as secured parties of record without adding a substitute secured party. The amendment is ineffective to the extent it purports to delete the secured parties of record but effective with respect to the deletion of collateral. As a consequence, the financing statement, as amended, covers only inventory, but A and B remain as secured parties of record.

§ 9–513. Termination Statement.

(a) **[Consumer goods.]** A secured party shall cause the secured party of record for a financing statement to file a termination statement for the financing statement if the financing statement covers consumer goods and:

(1) there is no obligation secured by the collateral covered by the financing statement and no commitment to make an advance, incur an obligation, or otherwise give value; or

(2) the debtor did not authorize the filing of the initial financing statement.

(b) **[Time for compliance with subsection (a).]** To comply with subsection (a), a secured party shall cause the secured party of record to file the termination statement:

(1) within one month after there is no obligation secured by the collateral covered by the financing statement and no commitment to make an advance, incur an obligation, or otherwise give value; or

(2) if earlier, within 20 days after the secured party receives an authenticated demand from a debtor.

(c) **[Other collateral.]** In cases not governed by subsection (a), within 20 days after a secured party receives an authenticated demand from a debtor, the secured party shall cause the secured party of record for a financing statement to send to the debtor a termination statement for the financing statement or file the termination statement in the filing office if:

(1) except in the case of a financing statement covering accounts or chattel paper that has been sold or goods that are the subject of a consignment, there is no obligation secured by the collateral covered by the financing statement and no commitment to make an advance, incur an obligation, or otherwise give value;

(2) the financing statement covers accounts or chattel paper that has been sold but as to which the account debtor or other person obligated has discharged its obligation;

(3) the financing statement covers goods that were the subject of a consignment to the debtor but are not in the debtor's possession; or

(4) the debtor did not authorize the filing of the initial financing statement.

(d) **[Effect of filing termination statement.]** Except as otherwise provided in Section 9–510, upon the filing of a termination statement with the filing office, the financing statement to which the termination statement relates ceases to be effective. Except as otherwise provided in Section 9–510, for purposes of Sections 9–519(g), 9–522(a), and 9–523(c), the filing with the filing office of a termination statement relating to a financing statement that indicates that the debtor is a transmitting utility also causes the effectiveness of the financing statement to lapse.

As amended in 2000.

Official Comment

1. **Source.** Former Section 9–404.

2. **Duty to File or Send.** This section specifies when a secured party must cause the secured party of record to file or send to the debtor a termination statement for a financing statement. Because most financing statements expire in five years unless a continuation statement is filed (Section 9–515), no compulsion is placed on the secured party to file a termination statement unless demanded by the debtor, except in the case of consumer goods. Because many consumers will not realize the importance to them of clearing the public record, an affirmative duty is put on the secured party in that case. But many purchase-money security interests in consumer goods will not be filed, except for motor vehicles. See Section 9–309(1). Under Section 9–311(b), compliance with a certificate-of-title statute is "equivalent to the filing of a financing statement under this article." Thus, this section applies to a certificate of title unless the section is superseded by a certificate-of-title statute that contains a specific rule addressing a secured party's duty to cause a notation of a security interest to be removed from a certificate of title. In the context of a certificate of title, however, the secured party could comply with this section by causing the removal itself or providing the debtor with documentation sufficient to enable the debtor to effect the removal.

Subsections (a) and (b) apply to a financing statement covering consumer goods. Subsection (c) applies to other financing statements. Subsection (a) and (c) each makes explicit what was implicit under former Article 9: If the debtor did not authorize the filing of a financing statement in the first place, the secured party of record should file or send a termination statement. The liability imposed upon a secured party that fails to comply with subsection (a) or (c) is identical to that imposed for the filing of an unauthorized financing statement or amendment. See Section 9–625(e).

3. **"Bogus" Filings.** A secured party's duty to send a termination statement arises when the secured party "receives" an authenticated demand from the debtor. In the case of an unauthorized financing statement, the person named as debtor in the financing statement may have no relationship with the named secured party and no reason to know the secured party's address. Inasmuch as the address in the financing statement is "held out by [the person named as secured party in the financing statement] as the place for receipt of such communications [i.e., communications relating to security interests]," the putative secured party is deemed to have "received" a notification delivered to that address. See Section 1–201(26). If a termination statement is not forthcoming, the person named as debtor itself may authorize the filing of a termination statement, which will be effective if it indicates that the person authorized it to be filed. See Sections 9–509(d)(2), 9–510(c).

4. **Buyers of Receivables.** Applied literally, former Section 9–404(1) would have required many buyers of receivables to file a termination statement immediately upon filing a financing statement because "there is no outstanding secured obligation and no commitment to make advances, incur obligations, or otherwise give value." Subsections (c)(1) and (2) remedy this problem. While the security interest of a buyer of accounts or chattel paper (B–1) is perfected, the debtor is not deemed to retain an interest in the sold receivables and thus could transfer no interest in them to another buyer (B–2) or to a lien creditor (LC). However, for purposes of determining the rights of the debtor's creditors and certain purchasers of accounts or chattel paper from the debtor, while B–1's security interest is unperfected, the debtor-seller is deemed to have rights in the sold receivables, and a competing security interest or judicial lien may attach to those rights. See Sections 9–318, 9–109, Comment 5. Suppose that B–1's security interest in certain accounts and chattel paper is perfected by filing, but the effectiveness of the financing statement lapses. Both before and after lapse, B–1 collects some of the receivables. After lapse, LC acquires a lien on the accounts and chattel paper. B–1's unperfected security interest in the accounts and chattel paper is subordinate to LC's rights. See Section 9–317(a)(2). But collections on accounts and chattel paper are not "accounts" or "chattel paper." Even if B–1's security interest in the accounts and chattel paper is or becomes unperfected, neither the debtor nor LC acquires rights to the collections that B–1 collects (and owns) before LC acquires a lien.

5. **Effect of Filing.** Subsection (d) states the effect of filing a termination statement: the related financing statement ceases to be effective. If one of several secured parties of record files a termination statement,

subsection (d) applies only with respect to the rights of the person who authorized the filing of the termination statement. See Section 9–510(b). The financing statement remains effective with respect to the rights of the others. However, even if a financing statement is *terminated* (and thus no longer is effective) with respect to all secured parties of record, the financing statement, including the termination statement, will remain of record until at least one year after it *lapses* with respect to all secured parties of record. See Section 9–519(g).

§ 9–514. Assignment of Powers of Secured Party of Record.

(a) **[Assignment reflected on initial financing statement.]** Except as otherwise provided in subsection (c), an initial financing statement may reflect an assignment of all of the secured party's power to authorize an amendment to the financing statement by providing the name and mailing address of the assignee as the name and address of the secured party.

(b) **[Assignment of filed financing statement.]** Except as otherwise provided in subsection (c), a secured party of record may assign of record all or part of its power to authorize an amendment to a financing statement by filing in the filing office an amendment of the financing statement which:

(1) identifies, by its file number, the initial financing statement to which it relates;

(2) provides the name of the assignor; and

(3) provides the name and mailing address of the assignee.

(c) **[Assignment of record of mortgage.]** An assignment of record of a security interest in a fixture covered by a record of a mortgage which is effective as a financing statement filed as a fixture filing under Section 9–502(c) may be made only by an assignment of record of the mortgage in the manner provided by law of this State other than [the Uniform Commercial Code].

Official Comment

1. **Source.** Former Section 9–405.

2. **Assignments.** This section provides a permissive device whereby a secured party of record may effectuate an assignment of its power to affect a financing statement. It may also be useful for a secured party

who has assigned all or part of its security interest or agricultural lien and wishes to have the fact noted of record, so that inquiries concerning the transaction would be addressed to the assignee. See Section 9–502, Comment 2. Upon the filing of an assignment, the assignee becomes the "secured party of record" and may authorize the filing of a continuation statement, termination statement, or other amendment. Note that under Section 9–310(c) no filing of an assignment is required as a condition of continuing the perfected status of the security interest against creditors and transferees of the original debtor. However, if an assignment is not filed, the assignor remains the secured party of record, with the power (even if not the right) to authorize the filing of effective amendments. See Sections 9–511(c), 9–509(d).

Where a record of a mortgage is effective as a financing statement filed as a fixture filing (Section 9–502(c)), then an assignment of record of the security interest may be made only in the manner in which an assignment of record of the mortgage may be made under local real-property law.

3. **Comparison to Prior Law.** Most of the changes reflected in this section are for clarification or to embrace medium-neutral drafting. As a general matter, this section preserves the opportunity given by former Section 9–405 to assign a security interest of record in one of two different ways. Under subsection (a), a secured party may assign all of its power to affect a financing statement by naming an assignee in the initial financing statement. The secured party of record may accomplish the same result under subsection (b) by making a subsequent filing. Subsection (b) also may be used for an assignment of only some of the secured party of record's power to affect a financing statement, e.g., the power to affect the financing statement as it relates to particular items of collateral or as it relates to an undivided interest in a security interest in all the collateral. An initial financing statement may not be used to change the secured party of record under these circumstances. However, an amendment adding the assignee as a secured party of record may be used.

§ 9–515. Duration and Effectiveness of Financing Statement; Effect of Lapsed Financing Statement.

(a) **[Five-year effectiveness.]** Except as otherwise provided in subsections (b), (e), (f), and (g), a filed financing statement is effective for a period of five years after the date of filing.

(b) **[Public-finance or manufactured-home transaction.]** Except as otherwise provided in subsections (e), (f), and (g), an initial financing statement filed in connection with a public-finance transaction or manufactured-home transaction is effective for a period of 30 years after the date of filing if it indicates that it is filed in connection with a public-finance transaction or manufactured-home transaction.

(c) **[Lapse and continuation of financing statement.]** The effectiveness of a filed financing statement lapses on the expiration of the period of its effectiveness unless before the lapse a continuation statement is filed pursuant to subsection (d). Upon lapse, a financing statement ceases to be effective and any security interest or agricultural lien that was perfected by the financing statement becomes unperfected, unless the security interest is perfected otherwise. If the security interest or agricultural lien becomes unperfected upon lapse, it is deemed never to have been perfected as against a purchaser of the collateral for value.

(d) **[When continuation statement may be filed.]** A continuation statement may be filed only within six months before the expiration of the five-year period specified in subsection (a) or the 30–year period specified in subsection (b), whichever is applicable.

(e) **[Effect of filing continuation statement.]** Except as otherwise provided in Section 9–510, upon timely filing of a continuation statement, the effectiveness of the initial financing statement continues for a period of five years commencing on the day on which the financing statement would have become ineffective in the absence of the filing. Upon the expiration of the five-year period, the financing statement lapses in the same manner as provided in subsection (c), unless, before the lapse, another continuation statement is filed pursuant to subsection (d). Succeeding continuation statements may be filed in the same manner to continue the effectiveness of the initial financing statement.

(f) **[Transmitting utility financing statement.]** If a debtor is a transmitting utility and a filed financing statement so indicates, the financing statement is effective until a termination statement is filed.

(g) **[Record of mortgage as financing statement.]** A record of a mortgage that is effective as a financing statement filed as a fixture filing under Section 9–502(c) remains effective as a financing statement filed as a fixture filing until the mortgage is released or satisfied of record or its effectiveness otherwise terminates as to the real property.

Official Comment

1. **Source.** Former Section 9–403(2), (3), (6).

2. **Period of Financing Statement's Effectiveness.** Subsection (a) states the general rule: a financing statement is effective for a five-year period unless its effectiveness is continued under this section or terminated under Section 9–513. Subsection (b) provides that if the financing statement relates to a public-finance transaction or a manufactured-home transaction and so indicates, the financing statement is effective for 30 years. These financings typically extend well beyond the standard, five-year period. Under subsection (f), a financing statement filed against a transmitting utility remains effective indefinitely, until a termination statement is filed. Likewise, under subsection (g), a mortgage effective as a fixture filing remains effective until its effectiveness terminates under real-property law.

3. **Lapse.** When the period of effectiveness under subsection (a) or (b) expires, the effectiveness of the financing statement lapses. The last sentence of subsection (c) addresses the effect of lapse. The deemed retroactive unperfection applies only with respect to purchasers for value; unlike former Section 9–403(2), it does not apply with respect to lien creditors.

Example 1: SP–1 and SP–2 both hold security interests in the same collateral. Both security interests are perfected by filing. SP–1 filed first and has priority under Section 9–322(a)(1). The effectiveness of SP–1's filing lapses. As long as SP–2's security interest remains perfected thereafter, SP–2 is entitled to priority over SP–1's security interest, which is deemed never to have been perfected as against a purchaser for value (SP–2). See Section 9–322(a)(2).

Example 2: SP holds a security interest perfected by filing. On July 1, LC acquires a judicial lien on the collateral. Two weeks later, the effectiveness of the financing statement lapses. Although the security interest becomes unperfected upon lapse, it was perfected when LC acquired its lien. Accordingly, notwithstanding the lapse, the perfected security interest has priority over the rights of LC, who is not a purchaser. See Section 9–317(a)(2).

4. **Effect of Debtor's Bankruptcy.** Under former Section 9–403(2), lapse was tolled if the debtor entered bankruptcy or another insolvency proceeding. Nevertheless, being unaware that insolvency proceedings had

been commenced, filing offices routinely removed records from the files as if lapse had not been tolled. Subsection (c) deletes the former tolling provision and thereby imposes a new burden on the secured party: to be sure that a financing statement does not lapse during the debtor's bankruptcy. The secured party can prevent lapse by filing a continuation statement, even without first obtaining relief from the automatic stay. See Bankruptcy Code Section 362(b)(3). Of course, if the debtor enters bankruptcy before lapse, the provisions of this Article with respect to lapse would be of no effect to the extent that federal bankruptcy law dictates a contrary result (e.g., to the extent that the Bankruptcy Code determines rights as of the date of the filing of the bankruptcy petition).

5. **Continuation Statements.** Subsection (d) explains when a continuation statement may be filed. A continuation statement filed at a time other than that prescribed by subsection (d) is ineffective, see Section 9–510(c), and the filing office may not accept it. See Sections 9–520(a), 9–516(b). Subsection (e) specifies the effect of a continuation statement and provides for successive continuation statements.

§ 9–516. What Constitutes Filing; Effectiveness of Filing.

(a) **[What constitutes filing.]** Except as otherwise provided in subsection (b), communication of a record to a filing office and tender of the filing fee or acceptance of the record by the filing office constitutes filing.

(b) **[Refusal to accept record; filing does not occur.]** Filing does not occur with respect to a record that a filing office refuses to accept because:

(1) the record is not communicated by a method or medium of communication authorized by the filing office;

(2) an amount equal to or greater than the applicable filing fee is not tendered;

(3) the filing office is unable to index the record because:

(A) in the case of an initial financing statement, the record does not provide a name for the debtor;

(B) in the case of an amendment or correction statement, the record:

(i) does not identify the initial financing statement as required by Section 9–512 or 9–518, as applicable; or

(ii) identifies an initial financing statement whose effectiveness has lapsed under Section 9–515;

(C) in the case of an initial financing statement that provides the name of a debtor identified as an individual or an amendment that provides a name of a debtor identified as an individual which was not previously provided in the financing statement to which the record relates, the record does not identify the debtor's last name; or

(D) in the case of a record filed [or recorded] in the filing office described in Section 9–501(a)(1), the record does not provide a sufficient description of the real property to which it relates;

(4) in the case of an initial financing statement or an amendment that adds a secured party of record, the record does not provide a name and mailing address for the secured party of record;

(5) in the case of an initial financing statement or an amendment that provides a name of a debtor which was not previously provided in the financing statement to which the amendment relates, the record does not:

(A) provide a mailing address for the debtor;

(B) indicate whether the debtor is an individual or an organization; or

(C) if the financing statement indicates that the debtor is an organization, provide:

(i) a type of organization for the debtor;

(ii) a jurisdiction of organization for the debtor; or

(iii) an organizational identification number for the debtor or indicate that the debtor has none;

(6) in the case of an assignment reflected in an initial financing statement under Section 9–514(a) or an amendment filed under Section 9–514(b), the record does not provide a name and mailing address for the assignee; or

(7) in the case of a continuation statement, the record is not filed within the six-month period prescribed by Section 9–515(d).

(c) **[Rules applicable to subsection (b).]** For purposes of subsection (b):

(1) a record does not provide information if the filing office is unable to read or decipher the information; and

(2) a record that does not indicate that it is an amendment or identify an initial financing statement to which it relates, as required by Section 9–512, 9–514, or 9–518, is an initial financing statement.

(d) **[Refusal to accept record; record effective as filed record.]** A record that is communicated to the filing office with tender of the filing fee, but which the filing office refuses to accept for a reason other than one set forth in subsection (b), is effective as a filed record except as against a purchaser of the collateral which gives value in reasonable reliance upon the absence of the record from the files.

Official Comment

1. **Source.** Subsection (a): former Section 9–403(1); the remainder is new.

2. **What Constitutes Filing.** Subsection (a) deals generically with what constitutes filing of a record, including an initial financing statement and amendments of all kinds (e.g., assignments, termination statements, and continuation statements). It follows former Section 9–403(1), under which either acceptance of a record by the filing office or presentation of the record and tender of the filing fee constitutes filing.

3. **Effectiveness of Rejected Record.** Subsection (b) provides an exclusive list of grounds upon which the filing office may reject a record. See Section 9–520(a). Although some of these grounds would also be grounds for rendering a filed record ineffective (e.g., an initial financing statement does not provide a name for the debtor), many others would not be (e.g., an initial financing statement does not provide a mailing address for the debtor or secured party of record). Neither this section nor Section 9–520 requires or authorizes the filing office to determine, or even consider, the accuracy of information provided in a record. For example, the State A filing office may not reject under subsection (b)(5)(C) an initial financing statement indicating that the debtor is a State A corporation and providing a three-digit organizational identification number, even if all State A organizational identification numbers contain at least five digits and two letters. Some organizations that are not registered organizations

(such as foreign corporations) have a readily determinable jurisdiction of organization. When that is not the case, with respect to an organization that is not a registered organization, for purposes of this section, the debtor's jurisdiction of organization is any jurisdiction that bears a reasonable relation to the debtor, such as the jurisdiction stated in any organizational document or agreement for the debtor as the jurisdiction under whose law the organization is formed or as the jurisdiction whose law is the governing law, or the jurisdiction in which the debtor is located under Section 9–307(b) (i.e., its place of business or its chief executive office). Thus, for purposes of this section, more than one jurisdiction may qualify as the debtor's jurisdiction of organization. See Comment 9.

A financing statement or other record that is communicated to the filing office but which the filing office refuses to accept provides no public notice, regardless of the reason for the rejection. However, this section distinguishes between records that the filing office rightfully rejects and those that it wrongfully rejects. A filer is able to prevent a rightful rejection by complying with the requirements of subsection (b). No purpose is served by giving effect to records that justifiably never find their way into the system, and subsection (b) so provides.

Subsection (d) deals with the filing office's unjustified refusal to accept a record. Here, the filer is in no position to prevent the rejection and as a general matter should not be prejudiced by it. Although wrongfully rejected records generally are effective, subsection (d) contains a special rule to protect a third-party purchaser of the collateral (e.g., a buyer or competing secured party) who gives value in reliance upon the apparent absence of the record from the files. As against a person who searches the public record and reasonably relies on what the public record shows, subsection (d) imposes upon the filer the risk that a record failed to make its way into the filing system because of the filing office's wrongful rejection of it. (Compare Section 9–517, under which a mis-indexed financing statement is fully effective.) This risk is likely to be small, particularly when a record is presented electronically, and the filer can guard against this risk by conducting a post-filing search of the records. Moreover, Section 9–520(b) requires the filing office to give prompt notice of its refusal to accept a record for filing.

4. **Method or Medium of Communication.** Rejection pursuant to subsection (b)(1) for failure to communicate a record properly should be understood to mean noncompliance with procedures relating to security, authentication, or other communication-relat-

ed requirements that the filing office may impose. Subsection (b)(1) does not authorize a filing office to impose additional substantive requirements. See Section 9–520, Comment 2.

5. **Address for Secured Party of Record.** Under subsection (b)(4) and Section 9–520(a), the lack of a mailing address for the secured party of record requires the filing office to reject an initial financing statement. The failure to include an address for the secured party of record no longer renders a financing statement ineffective. See Section 9–502(a). The function of the address is not to identify the secured party of record but rather to provide an address to which others can send required notifications, e.g., of a purchase-money security interest in inventory or of the disposition of collateral. Inasmuch as the address shown on a filed financing statement is an "address that is reasonable under the circumstances," a person required to send a notification to the secured party may satisfy the requirement by sending a notification to that address, even if the address is or becomes incorrect. See Section 9–102 (definition of "send"). Similarly, because the address is "held out by [the secured party] as the place for receipt of such communications [i.e., communications relating to security interests]," the secured party is deemed to have received a notification delivered to that address. See Section 1–201(26).

6. **Uncertainty Concerning Individual Debtor's Last Name.** Subsection (b)(3)(C) requires the filing office to reject an initial financing statement or amendment adding an individual debtor if the office cannot index the record because it does not identify the debtor's last name (e.g., it is unclear whether the debtor's name is Elton John or John Elton).

7. **Inability of Filing Office to Read or Decipher Information.** Under subsection (c)(1), if the filing office cannot read or decipher information, the information is not provided by a record for purposes of subsection (b).

8. **Classification of Records.** For purposes of subsection (b), a record that does not indicate it is an amendment or identify an initial financing statement to which it relates is deemed to be an initial financing statement. See subsection (c)(2).

9. **Effectiveness of Rejectable But Unrejected Record.** Section 9–520(a) requires the filing office to refuse to accept an initial financing statement for a reason set forth in subsection (b). However, if the filing office accepts such a financing statement nevertheless, the financing statement generally is effective if it complies with the requirements of Section 9–502(a) and

(b). See Section 9–520(c). Similarly, an otherwise effective financing statement generally remains so even though the information in the financing statement becomes incorrect. See Section 9–507(b). (Note that if the information required by subsection (b)(5) is incorrect when the financing statement is filed, Section 9–338 applies.)

§ 9–517. Effect of Indexing Errors.

The failure of the filing office to index a record correctly does not affect the effectiveness of the filed record.

Official Comment

1. **Source.** New.

2. **Effectiveness of Mis–Indexed Records.** This section provides that the filing office's error in misindexing a record does not render ineffective an otherwise effective record. As did former Section 9–401, this section imposes the risk of filing-office error on those who search the files rather than on those who file.

§ 9–518. Claim Concerning Inaccurate or Wrongfully Filed Record.

(a) **[Correction statement.]** A person may file in the filing office a correction statement with respect to a record indexed there under the person's name if the person believes that the record is inaccurate or was wrongfully filed.

[Alternative A]

(b) **[Sufficiency of correction statement.]** A correction statement must:

(1) identify the record to which it relates by the file number assigned to the initial financing statement to which the record relates;

(2) indicate that it is a correction statement; and

(3) provide the basis for the person's belief that the record is inaccurate and indicate the manner in which the person believes the record should be amended to cure any inaccuracy or provide the basis for the person's belief that the record was wrongfully filed.

[Alternative B]

(b) **[Sufficiency of correction statement.]** A correction statement must:

(1) identify the record to which it relates by:

   (A) the file number assigned to the initial financing statement to which the record relates; and

   (B) if the correction statement relates to a record filed [or recorded] in a filing office described in Section 9–501(a)(1), the date [and time] that the initial financing statement was filed [or recorded] and the information specified in Section 9–502(b);

(2) indicate that it is a correction statement; and

(3) provide the basis for the person's belief that the record is inaccurate and indicate the manner in which the person believes the record should be amended to cure any inaccuracy or provide the basis for the person's belief that the record was wrongfully filed.

[End of Alternatives]

(c) **[Record not affected by correction statement.]** The filing of a correction statement does not affect the effectiveness of an initial financing statement or other filed record.

Legislative Note: States whose real-estate filing offices require additional information in amendments and cannot search their records by both the name of the debtor and the file number should enact Alternative B to Sections 9–512(a), 9–518(b), 9–519(f) and 9–522(a).

Official Comment

1. **Source.** New.

2. **Correction Statements.** Former Article 9 did not afford a nonjudicial means for a debtor to correct a financing statement or other record that was inaccurate or wrongfully filed. Subsection (a) affords the debtor the right to file a correction statement. Among other requirements, the correction statement must provide the basis for the debtor's belief that the public record should be corrected. See subsection (b). These provisions, which resemble the analogous remedy in the Fair Credit Reporting Act, 15 U.S.C. § 1681i, afford an aggrieved person the opportunity to state its position on the public record. They do not permit an aggrieved person to change the legal effect of the public record. Thus, although a filed correction statement becomes part of the "financing statement," as defined in Section 9–102, the filing does not affect the effectiveness of the initial financing statement or any other filed record. See subsection (c).

This section does not displace other provisions of this Article that impose liability for making unauthorized filings or failing to file or send a termination statement (see Section 9–625(e)), nor does it displace any available judicial remedies.

3. **Resort to Other Law.** This Article cannot provide a satisfactory or complete solution to problems caused by misuse of the public records. The problem of "bogus" filings is not limited to the UCC filing system but extends to the real-property records, as well. A summary judicial procedure for correcting the public record and criminal penalties for those who misuse the filing and recording systems are likely to be more effective and put less strain on the filing system than provisions authorizing or requiring action by filing and recording offices.

[SUBPART 2. DUTIES AND OPERATION OF FILING OFFICE]

§ 9–519. Numbering, Maintaining, and Indexing Records; Communicating Information Provided in Records.

(a) **[Filing office duties.]** For each record filed in a filing office, the filing office shall:

(1) assign a unique number to the filed record;

(2) create a record that bears the number assigned to the filed record and the date and time of filing;

(3) maintain the filed record for public inspection; and

(4) index the filed record in accordance with subsections (c), (d), and (e).

(b) **[File number.]** A file number [assigned after January 1, 2002,] must include a digit that:

(1) is mathematically derived from or related to the other digits of the file number; and

(2) aids the filing office in determining whether a number communicated as the file number includes a single-digit or transpositional error.

(c) [**Indexing: general.**] Except as otherwise provided in subsections (d) and (e), the filing office shall:

(1) index an initial financing statement according to the name of the debtor and index all filed records relating to the initial financing statement in a manner that associates with one another an initial financing statement and all filed records relating to the initial financing statement; and

(2) index a record that provides a name of a debtor which was not previously provided in the financing statement to which the record relates also according to the name that was not previously provided.

(d) [**Indexing: real-property-related financing statement.**] If a financing statement is filed as a fixture filing or covers as-extracted collateral or timber to be cut, [it must be filed for record and] the filing office shall index it:

(1) under the names of the debtor and of each owner of record shown on the financing statement as if they were the mortgagors under a mortgage of the real property described; and

(2) to the extent that the law of this State provides for indexing of records of mortgages under the name of the mortgagee, under the name of the secured party as if the secured party were the mortgagee thereunder, or, if indexing is by description, as if the financing statement were a record of a mortgage of the real property described.

(e) [**Indexing: real-property-related assignment.**] If a financing statement is filed as a fixture filing or covers as-extracted collateral or timber to be cut, the filing office shall index an assignment filed under Section 9–514(a) or an amendment filed under Section 9–514(b):

(1) under the name of the assignor as grantor; and

(2) to the extent that the law of this State provides for indexing a record of the assignment of a mortgage under the name of the assignee, under the name of the assignee.

[**Alternative A**]

(f) [**Retrieval and association capability.**] The filing office shall maintain a capability:

(1) to retrieve a record by the name of the debtor and by the file number assigned to the initial financing statement to which the record relates; and

(2) to associate and retrieve with one another an initial financing statement and each filed record relating to the initial financing statement.

[**Alternative B**]

(f) [**Retrieval and association capability.**] The filing office shall maintain a capability:

(1) to retrieve a record by the name of the debtor and:

(A) if the filing office is described in Section 9–501(a)(1), by the file number assigned to the initial financing statement to which the record relates and the date [and time] that the record was filed [or recorded]; or

(B) if the filing office is described in Section 9–501(a)(2), by the file number assigned to the initial financing statement to which the record relates; and

(2) to associate and retrieve with one another an initial financing statement and each filed record relating to the initial financing statement.

[**End of Alternatives**]

(g) [**Removal of debtor's name.**] The filing office may not remove a debtor's name from the index until one year after the effectiveness of a financing statement naming the debtor lapses under Section 9–515 with respect to all secured parties of record.

(h) [**Timeliness of filing office performance.**] The filing office shall perform the acts required by subsections (a) through (e) at the time and in the manner prescribed by filing-office rule, but not later than two business days after the filing office receives the record in question.

[(i) [**Inapplicability to real-property-related filing office.**] Subsection[s] [(b)] [and] [(h)] do[es] not apply to a filing office described in Section 9–501(a)(1).]

Legislative Notes:

1. States whose filing offices currently assign file numbers that include a verification number, commonly known as a "check digit," or can implement this requirement before the effective date of this Article should omit the bracketed language in subsection (b).

2. In States in which writings will not appear in the real property records and indices unless actually recorded the bracketed language in subsection (d) should be used.

3. States whose real-estate filing offices require additional information in amendments and cannot search their records by both the name of the debtor and the file number should enact Alternative B to Sections 9–512(a), 9–518(b), 9–519(f) and 9–522(a).

4. A State that elects not to require real-estate filing offices to comply with either or both of subsections (b) and (h) may adopt an applicable variation of subsection (i) and add "Except as otherwise provided in subsection (i)," to the appropriate subsection or subsections.

Official Comment

1. **Source.** Former Sections 9–403(4), (7), 9–405(2).

2. **Filing Office's Duties.** Subsections (a) through (e) set forth the duties of the filing office with respect to filed records. Subsection (h), which is new, imposes a minimum standard of performance for those duties. Prompt indexing is crucial to the effectiveness of any filing system. An accepted but un-indexed record affords no public notice. Subsection (f) requires the filing office to maintain appropriate storage and retrieval facilities, and subsection (g) contains minimum requirements for the retention of records.

3. **File Number.** Subsection (a)(1) requires the filing office to assign a unique number to each filed record. That number is the "file number" only if the record is an initial financing statement. See Section 9–102.

4. **Time of Filing.** Subsection (a)(2) and Section 9–523 refer to the "date and time" of filing. The statutory text does not contain any instructions to a filing office as to how the time of filing is to be determined. The method of determining or assigning a time of filing is an appropriate matter for filing-office rules to address.

5. **Related Records.** Subsections (c) and (f) are designed to ensure that an initial financing statement and all filed records relating to it are associated with one another, indexed under the name of the debtor,

and retrieved together. To comply with subsection (f), a filing office (other than a real-property recording office in a State that enacts subsection (f), Alternative B) must be capable of retrieving records in each of two ways: by the name of the debtor and by the file number of the initial financing statement to which the record relates.

6. **Prohibition on Deleting Names from Index.** This Article contemplates that the filing office will not delete the name of a debtor from the index until at least one year passes after the effectiveness of the financing statement lapses as to all secured parties of record. See subsection (g). This rule applies even if the filing office accepts an amendment purporting to delete or modify the name of a debtor or terminate the effectiveness of the financing statement. If an amendment provides a modified name for a debtor, the amended name should be added to the index, see subsection (c)(2), but the pre-amendment name should remain in the index.

Compared to former Article 9, the rule in subsection (g) increases the amount of information available to those who search the public records. The rule also contemplates that searchers—not the filing office—will determine the significance and effectiveness of filed records.

§ 9–520. Acceptance and Refusal to Accept Record.

(a) **[Mandatory refusal to accept record.]** A filing office shall refuse to accept a record for filing for a reason set forth in Section 9–516(b) and may refuse to accept a record for filing only for a reason set forth in Section 9–516(b).

(b) **[Communication concerning refusal.]** If a filing office refuses to accept a record for filing, it shall communicate to the person that presented the record the fact of and reason for the refusal and the date and time the record would have been filed had the filing office accepted it. The communication must be made at the time and in the manner prescribed by filing-office rule but [, in the case of a filing office described in Section 9–501(a)(2),] in no event more than two business days after the filing office receives the record.

(c) **[When filed financing statement effective.]** A filed financing statement satisfying Section 9–502(a) and (b) is effective, even if the filing office is required to refuse to accept it for filing under subsection (a). However, Section 9–

338 applies to a filed financing statement providing information described in Section 9–516(b)(5) which is incorrect at the time the financing statement is filed.

(d) **[Separate application to multiple debtors.]** If a record communicated to a filing office provides information that relates to more than one debtor, this part applies as to each debtor separately.

Legislative Note: A State that elects not to require real-property filing offices to comply with subsection (b) should include the bracketed language.

Official Comment

1. **Source.** New.

2. **Refusal to Accept Record for Filing.** In some States, filing offices considered themselves obligated by former Article 9 to review the form and content of a financing statement and to refuse to accept those that they determine are legally insufficient. Some filing offices imposed requirements for or conditions to filing that do not appear in the statute. Under this section, the filing office is not expected to make legal judgments and is not permitted to impose additional conditions or requirements.

Subsection (a) both prescribes and limits the bases upon which the filing office must and may reject records by reference to the reasons set forth in Section 9–516(b). For the most part, the bases for rejection are limited to those that prevent the filing office from dealing with a record that it receives—because some of the requisite information (e.g., the debtor's name) is missing or cannot be deciphered, because the record is not communicated by a method (e.g., it is MIME-rather than UU-encoded) or medium (e.g., it is written rather than electronic) that the filing office accepts, or because the filer fails to tender an amount equal to or greater than the filing fee.

3. **Consequences of Accepting Rejectable Record.** Section 9–516(b) includes among the reasons for rejecting an initial financing statement the failure to give certain information that is not required as a condition of effectiveness. In conjunction with Section 9–516(b)(5), this section requires the filing office to refuse to accept a financing statement that is legally sufficient to perfect a security interest under Section 9–502 but does not contain a mailing address for the debtor, does not disclose whether the debtor is an individual or an organization (e.g., a partnership or corporation) or, if the debtor is an organization, does not give certain specified information concerning the organization. The information required by Section 9–516(b)(5) assists searchers in weeding out "false positives," i.e., records that a search reveals but which do not pertain to the debtor in question. It assists filers by helping to ensure that the debtor's name is correct and that the financing statement is filed in the proper jurisdiction.

If the filing office accepts a financing statement that does not give this information at all, the filing is fully effective. Section 9–520(c). The financing statement also generally is effective if the information is given but is incorrect; however, Section 9–338 affords protection to buyers and holders of perfected security interests who gives value in reasonable reliance upon the incorrect information.

4. **Filing Office's Duties with Respect to Rejected Record.** Subsection (b) requires the filing office to communicate the fact of rejection and the reason therefor within a fixed period of time. Inasmuch as a rightfully rejected record is ineffective and a wrongfully rejected record is not fully effective, prompt communication concerning any rejection is important.

5. **Partial Effectiveness of Record.** Under subsection (d), the provisions of this Part apply to each debtor separately. Thus, a filing office may reject an initial financing statement or other record as to one named debtor but accept it as to the other.

Example: An initial financing statement is communicated to the filing office. The financing statement names two debtors, John Smith and Jane Smith. It contains all of the information described in Section 9–516(b)(5) with respect to John but lacks some of the information with respect to Jane. The filing office must accept the financing statement with respect to John, reject it with respect to Jane, and notify the filer of the rejection.

§ 9–521. Uniform Form of Written Financing Statement and Amendment.

(a) **[Initial financing statement form.]** A filing office that accepts written records may not refuse to accept a written initial financing statement in the following form and format except for a reason set forth in Section 9–516(b):

UCC FINANCING STATEMENT
FOLLOW INSTRUCTIONS (front and back) CAREFULLY

A. NAME & PHONE OF CONTACT AT FILER [optional]

B. SEND ACKNOWLEDGMENT TO:　(Name and Address)

THE ABOVE SPACE IS FOR FILING OFFICE USE ONLY

1. DEBTOR'S EXACT FULL LEGAL NAME - insert only one debtor name (1a or 1b) - do not abbreviate or combine names

1a. ORGANIZATION'S NAME			
OR	1b. INDIVIDUAL'S LAST NAME	FIRST NAME	MIDDLE NAME	SUFFIX

1c. MAILING ADDRESS	CITY	STATE	POSTAL CODE	COUNTRY

1d. TAX ID #:　SSN OR EIN	ADD'L INFO RE ORGANIZATION DEBTOR	1e. TYPE OF ORGANIZATION	1f. JURISDICTION OF ORGANIZATION	1g. ORGANIZATIONAL ID #, if any
				☐ NONE

2. ADDITIONAL DEBTOR'S EXACT FULL LEGAL NAME - insert only one debtor name (2a or 2b) - do not abbreviate or combine names

2a. ORGANIZATION'S NAME			
OR	2b. INDIVIDUAL'S LAST NAME	FIRST NAME	MIDDLE NAME	SUFFIX

2c. MAILING ADDRESS	CITY	STATE	POSTAL CODE	COUNTRY

2d. TAX ID #:　SSN OR EIN	ADD'L INFO RE ORGANIZATION DEBTOR	2e. TYPE OF ORGANIZATION	2f. JURISDICTION OF ORGANIZATION	2g. ORGANIZATIONAL ID #, if any
				☐ NONE

3. SECURED PARTY'S NAME (or NAME of TOTAL ASSIGNEE of ASSIGNOR S/P) - insert only one secured party name (3a or 3b)

3a. ORGANIZATION'S NAME			
OR	3b. INDIVIDUAL'S LAST NAME	FIRST NAME	MIDDLE NAME	SUFFIX

3c. MAILING ADDRESS	CITY	STATE	POSTAL CODE	COUNTRY

4. This FINANCING STATEMENT covers the following collateral:

5. ALTERNATIVE DESIGNATION (if applicable):	LESSEE/LESSOR	CONSIGNEE/CONSIGNOR	BAILEE/BAILOR	SELLER/BUYER	AG. LIEN	NON-UCC FILING

6. ☐ This FINANCING STATEMENT is to be filed [for record] (or recorded) in the REAL ESTATE RECORDS.　Attach Addendum [if applicable]	7. Check to REQUEST SEARCH REPORT(S) on Debtor(s) [ADDITIONAL FEE]　[optional]	All Debtors	Debtor 1	Debtor 2

8. OPTIONAL FILER REFERENCE DATA

NATIONAL UCC FINANCING STATEMENT (FORM UCC1) (REV. 07/29/98)

UCC FINANCING STATEMENT ADDENDUM

FOLLOW INSTRUCTIONS (front and back) CAREFULLY

9. NAME OF FIRST DEBTOR (1a or 1b) ON RELATED FINANCING STATEMENT

9a. ORGANIZATION'S NAME		

OR

9b. INDIVIDUAL'S LAST NAME	FIRST NAME	MIDDLE NAME,SUFFIX

10.MISCELLANEOUS:

THE ABOVE SPACE IS FOR FILING OFFICE USE ONLY

11. ADDITIONAL DEBTOR'S EXACT FULL LEGAL NAME - Insert only one name (11a or 11b) - do not abbreviate or combine names

11a. ORGANIZATION'S NAME			

OR

11b. INDIVIDUAL'S LAST NAME	FIRST NAME	MIDDLE NAME	SUFFIX

11c. MAILING ADDRESS	CITY	STATE	POSTAL CODE	COUNTRY

11d. TAX ID #: SSN OR EIN	ADD'L INFO RE ORGANIZATION DEBTOR	11e. TYPE OF ORGANIZATION	11f. JURISDICTION OF ORGANIZATION	11g. ORGANIZATIONAL ID #, if any	NONE

12. ☐ ADDITIONAL SECURED PARTY'S or ☐ ASSIGNOR S/P'S NAME - insert only one name (12a or 12b)

12a. ORGANIZATION'S NAME			

OR

12b. INDIVIDUAL'S LAST NAME	FIRST NAME	MIDDLE NAME	SUFFIX

12c. MAILING ADDRESS	CITY	STATE	POSTAL CODE	COUNTRY

13. This FINANCING STATEMENT covers ☐ timber to be cut or ☐ as-extracted collateral, or is filed as a ☐ fixture filing.

14. Description of real estate:

16. Additional collateral description:

15. Name and address of a RECORD OWNER of above-described real estate (if Debtor does not have a record interest):

17. Check only if applicable and check only one box.

Debtor is a ☐ Trust or ☐ Trustee acting with respect to property held in trust or ☐ Decedent's Estate

18. Check only if applicable and check only one box.

☐ Debtor is a TRANSMITTING UTILITY

☐ Filed in connection with a Manufactured-Home Transaction — effective 30 years

☐ Filed in connection with a Public-Finance Transaction — effective 30 years

NATIONAL UCC FINANCING STATEMENT ADDENDUM (FORM UCC1Ad) (REV. 07/29/98)

843

(b) [**Amendment form.**] A filing office that accepts written records may not refuse to accept a written record in the following form and format except for a reason set forth in Section 9–516(b):

UCC FINANCING STATEMENT AMENDMENT

FOLLOW INSTRUCTIONS (front and back) CAREFULLY

A. NAME & PHONE OF CONTACT AT FILER [optional]

B. SEND ACKNOWLEDGMENT TO: (Name and Address)

THE ABOVE SPACE IS FOR FILING OFFICE USE ONLY

1a. INITIAL FINANCING STATEMENT FILE #

1b. This FINANCING STATEMENT AMENDMENT is to be filed [for record] (or recorded) in the REAL ESTATE RECORDS.

2. ☐ TERMINATION: Effectiveness of the Financing Statement identified above is terminated with respect to security interest(s) of the Secured Party authorizing this Termination Statement.

3. ☐ CONTINUATION: Effectiveness of the Financing Statement identified above with respect to security interest(s) of the Secured Party authorizing this Continuation Statement is continued for the additional period provided by applicable law.

4. ☐ ASSIGNMENT (full or partial): Give name of assignee in item 7a or 7b and address of assignee in item 7c; and also give name of assignor in item 9.

5. AMENDMENT (PARTY INFORMATION): This Amendment affects ☐ Debtor or ☐ Secured Party of record. Check only one of these two boxes.
Also check one of the following three boxes and provide appropriate information in items 6 and/or 7.
☐ CHANGE name and/or address ☐ DELETE name ☐ ADD name

6. CURRENT RECORD INFORMATION:
6a. ORGANIZATION'S NAME

OR 6b. INDIVIDUAL'S LAST NAME | FIRST NAME | MIDDLE NAME | SUFFIX

7. CHANGED (NEW) OR ADDED INFORMATION:
7a. ORGANIZATION'S NAME

OR 7b. INDIVIDUAL'S LAST NAME | FIRST NAME | MIDDLE NAME | SUFFIX

7c. MAILING ADDRESS | CITY | STATE | POSTAL CODE | COUNTRY

7d. TAX ID #: SSN OR EIN | ADD'L INFO RE ORGANIZATION DEBTOR | 7e. TYPE OF ORGANIZATION | 7f. JURISDICTION OF ORGANIZATION | 7g. ORGANIZATIONAL ID #, if any ☐ NONE

8. AMENDMENT (COLLATERAL CHANGE): check only one box.
Describe collateral ☐ deleted or ☐ added, or give entire ☐ restated collateral description, or describe collateral ☐ assigned.

9. NAME OF SECURED PARTY OF RECORD AUTHORIZING THIS AMENDMENT (name of assignor, if this is an Assignment). If this is an Amendment authorized by a Debtor which adds collateral or adds the authorizing Debtor, or if this is a Termination authorized by a Debtor, check here ☐ and enter name of DEBTOR authorizing this Amendment.
9a. ORGANIZATION'S NAME

OR 9b. INDIVIDUAL'S LAST NAME | FIRST NAME | MIDDLE NAME | SUFFIX

10. OPTIONAL FILER REFERENCE DATA

NATIONAL UCC FINANCING STATEMENT AMENDMENT (FORM UCC3) (REV. 07/29/98)

UCC FINANCING STATEMENT AMENDMENT ADDENDUM

FOLLOW INSTRUCTIONS (front and back) CAREFULLY

11. INITIAL FINANCING STATEMENT FILE # (same as item 1a on Amendment form)

12. NAME OF PARTY AUTHORIZING THIS AMENDMENT (same as item 9 on Amendment form)

12a. ORGANIZATION'S NAME

OR | 12b. INDIVIDUAL'S LAST NAME | FIRST NAME | MIDDLE NAME,SUFFIX

13. Use this space for additional information

THE ABOVE SPACE IS FOR FILING OFFICE USE ONLY

NATIONAL UCC FINANCING STATEMENT AMENDMENT ADDENDUM (FORM UCC3Ad) (REV. 07/29/98)

Official Comment

1. **Source.** New.

2. **"Safe Harbor" Written Forms.** Although Section 9–520 limits the bases upon which the filing office can refuse to accept records, this section provides sample written forms that must be accepted in every filing office in the country, as long as the filing office's rules permit it to accept written communications. By completing one of the forms in this section, a secured party can be certain that the filing office is obligated to accept it.

The forms in this section are based upon national financing statement forms that were in use under former Article 9. Those forms were developed over an extended period and reflect the comments and suggestions of filing officers, secured parties and their counsel, and service companies. The formatting of those forms and of the ones in this section has been designed to reduce error by both filers and filing offices.

A filing office that accepts written communications may not reject, on grounds of form or format, a filing using these forms. Although filers are not required to use the forms, they are encouraged and can be expected to do so, inasmuch as the forms are well designed and avoid the risk of rejection on the basis of form or format. As their use expands, the forms will rapidly become familiar to both filers and filing-office personnel. Filing offices may and should encourage the use of these forms by declaring them to be the "standard" (but not exclusive) forms for each jurisdiction, albeit without in any way suggesting that alternative forms are unacceptable.

The multi-purpose form in subsection (b) covers changes with respect to the debtor, the secured party, the collateral, and the status of the financing statement (termination and continuation). A single form may be used for several different types of amendments at once (e.g., both to change a debtor's name and continue the effectiveness of the financing statement).

§ 9–522. Maintenance and Destruction of Records.

[Alternative A]

(a) **[Post-lapse maintenance and retrieval of information.]** The filing office shall maintain a record of the information provided in a filed financing statement for at least one year after the effectiveness of the financing statement has lapsed under Section 9–515 with respect to all secured parties of record. The record must be retrievable by using the name of the debtor and

by using the file number assigned to the initial financing statement to which the record relates.

[Alternative B]

(a) **[Post-lapse maintenance and retrieval of information.]** The filing office shall maintain a record of the information provided in a filed financing statement for at least one year after the effectiveness of the financing statement has lapsed under Section 9–515 with respect to all secured parties of record. The record must be retrievable by using the name of the debtor and:

(1) if the record was filed [or recorded] in the filing office described in Section 9–501(a)(1), by using the file number assigned to the initial financing statement to which the record relates and the date [and time] that the record was filed [or recorded]; or

(2) if the record was filed in the filing office described in Section 9–501(a)(2), by using the file number assigned to the initial financing statement to which the record relates.

[End of Alternatives]

(b) **[Destruction of written records.]** Except to the extent that a statute governing disposition of public records provides otherwise, the filing office immediately may destroy any written record evidencing a financing statement. However, if the filing office destroys a written record, it shall maintain another record of the financing statement which complies with subsection (a).

Legislative Note: States whose real-estate filing offices require additional information in amendments and cannot search their records by both the name of the debtor and the file number should enact Alternative B to Sections 9–512(a), 9–518(b), 9–519(f) and 9–522(a).

Official Comment

1. **Source.** Former Section 9–403(3), revised substantially.

2. **Maintenance of Records.** Section 9–523 requires the filing office to provide information concerning certain lapsed financing statements. Accordingly, subsection (a) requires the filing office to maintain a record of the information in a financing statement for at least one year after lapse. During that time, the filing office may not delete any information with re-

spect to a filed financing statement; it may only add information. This approach relieves the filing office from any duty to determine whether to substitute or delete information upon receipt of an amendment. It also assures searchers that they will receive all information with respect to financing statements filed against a debtor and thereby be able themselves to determine the state of the public record.

The filing office may maintain this information in any medium. Subsection (b) permits the filing office immediately to destroy written records evidencing a financing statement, provided that the filing office maintains another record of the information contained in the financing statement as required by subsection (a).

§ 9–523. Information From Filing Office; Sale or License of Records.

(a) [**Acknowledgment of filing written record.**] If a person that files a written record requests an acknowledgment of the filing, the filing office shall send to the person an image of the record showing the number assigned to the record pursuant to Section 9–519(a)(1) and the date and time of the filing of the record. However, if the person furnishes a copy of the record to the filing office, the filing office may instead:

(1) note upon the copy the number assigned to the record pursuant to Section 9–519(a)(1) and the date and time of the filing of the record; and

(2) send the copy to the person.

(b) [**Acknowledgment of filing other record.**] If a person files a record other than a written record, the filing office shall communicate to the person an acknowledgment that provides:

(1) the information in the record;

(2) the number assigned to the record pursuant to Section 9–519(a)(1); and

(3) the date and time of the filing of the record.

(c) [**Communication of requested information.**] The filing office shall communicate or otherwise make available in a record the following information to any person that requests it:

(1) whether there is on file on a date and time specified by the filing office, but not a date earlier than three business days before the filing office receives the request, any financing statement that:

(A) designates a particular debtor [or, if the request so states, designates a particular debtor at the address specified in the request];

(B) has not lapsed under Section 9–515 with respect to all secured parties of record; and

(C) if the request so states, has lapsed under Section 9–515 and a record of which is maintained by the filing office under Section 9–522(a);

(2) the date and time of filing of each financing statement; and

(3) the information provided in each financing statement.

(d) [**Medium for communicating information.**] In complying with its duty under subsection (c), the filing office may communicate information in any medium. However, if requested, the filing office shall communicate information by issuing [its written certificate] [a record that can be admitted into evidence in the courts of this State without extrinsic evidence of its authenticity].

(e) [**Timeliness of filing office performance.**] The filing office shall perform the acts required by subsections (a) through (d) at the time and in the manner prescribed by filing-office rule, but not later than two business days after the filing office receives the request.

(f) [**Public availability of records.**] At least weekly, the [insert appropriate official or governmental agency] [filing office] shall offer to sell or license to the public on a nonexclusive basis, in bulk, copies of all records filed in it under this part, in every medium from time to time available to the filing office.

Legislative Notes:

1. States whose filing office does not offer the additional service of responding to search requests limited to a particular address should omit the bracketed language in subsection (c)(1)(A).

2. A State that elects not to require real-estate filing offices to comply with either or both of subsections (e) and (f) should specify in the appro-

priate subsection(s) only the filing office described in Section 9–501(a)(2).

Official Comment

1. **Source.** Former Section 9–407; subsections (d) and (e) are new.

2. **Filing Office's Duty to Provide Information.** Former Section 9–407, dealing with obtaining information from the filing office, was bracketed to suggest to legislatures that its enactment was optional. Experience has shown that the method by which interested persons can obtain information concerning the public records should be uniform. Accordingly, the analogous provisions of this Article are not in brackets.

Most of the other changes from former Section 9–407 are for clarification, to embrace medium-neutral drafting, or to impose standards of performance on the filing office.

3. **Acknowledgments of Filing.** Subsections (a) and (b) require the filing office to acknowledge the filing of a record. Under subsection (a), the filing office is required to acknowledge the filing of a written record only upon request of the filer. Subsection (b) requires the filing office to acknowledge the filing of a non-written record even in the absence of a request from the filer.

4. **Response to Search Request.** Subsection (c)(3) requires the filing office to provide "the information contained in each financing statement" to a person who requests it. This requirement can be satisfied by providing copies, images, or reports. The requirement does not in any manner inhibit the filing office from also offering to provide less than all of the information (presumably for a lower fee) to a person who asks for less. Thus, subsection (c) accommodates the practice of providing only the type of record (e.g., initial financing statement, continuation statement), number assigned to the record, date and time of filing, and names and addresses of the debtor and secured party when a requesting person asks for no more (i.e., when the person does not ask for copies of financing statements). In contrast, the filing office's obligation under subsection (b) to provide an acknowledgment containing "the information contained in the record" is not defined by a customer's request. Thus unless the filer stipulates otherwise, to comply with subsection (b) the filing office's acknowledgment must contain all of the information in a record.

Subsection (c) assures that a minimum amount of information about filed records will be available to the public. It does not preclude a filing office from offering additional services.

5. **Lapsed and Terminated Financing Statements.** This section reflects the policy that terminated financing statements will remain part of the filing office's data base. The filing office may remove from the data base only lapsed financing statements, and then only when at least a year has passed after lapse. See Section 9–519(g). Subsection (c)(1)(C) requires a filing office to conduct a search and report as to lapsed financing statements that have not been removed from the data base, when requested.

6. **Search by Debtor's Address.** Subsection (c)(1)(A) contemplates that, by making a single request, a searcher will receive the results of a search of the entire public record maintained by any given filing office. Addition of the bracketed language in subsection (c)(1)(A) would permit a search report limited to financing statements showing a particular address for the debtor, but only if the search request is so limited. With or without the bracketed language, this subsection does not permit the filing office to compel a searcher to limit a request by address.

7. **Medium of Communication; Certificates.** Former Article 9 provided that the filing office respond to a request for information by providing a certificate. The principle of medium-neutrality would suggest that the statute not require a written certificate. Subsection (d) follows this principle by permitting the filing office to respond by communicating "in any medium." By permitting communication "in any medium," subsection (d) is not inconsistent with a system in which persons other than filing office staff conduct searches of the filing office's (computer) records.

Some searchers find it necessary to introduce the results of their search into evidence. Because official written certificates might be introduced into evidence more easily than official communications in another medium, subsection (d) affords States the option of requiring the filing office to issue written certificates upon request. The alternative bracketed language in subsection (d) recognizes that some States may prefer to permit the filing office to respond in another medium, as long as the response can be admitted into evidence in the courts of that State without extrinsic evidence of its authenticity.

8. **Performance Standard.** The utility of the filing system depends on the ability of searchers to get current information quickly. Accordingly, subsection (e) requires that the filing office respond to a request for information no later than two business days after it receives the request. The information contained in the response must be current as of a date no earlier than

three business days before the filing office receives the request. See subsection (c)(1). The failure of the filing office to comply with performance standards, such as subsection (e), has no effect on the private rights of persons affected by the filing of records.

9. **Sales of Records in Bulk.** Subsection (f), which is new, mandates that the appropriate official or the filing office sell or license the filing records to the public in bulk, on a nonexclusive basis, in every medium available to the filing office. The details of implementation are left to filing-office rules.

§ 9–524.   Delay by Filing Office.

Delay by the filing office beyond a time limit prescribed by this part is excused if:

(1) the delay is caused by interruption of communication or computer facilities, war, emergency conditions, failure of equipment, or other circumstances beyond control of the filing office; and

(2) the filing office exercises reasonable diligence under the circumstances.

Official Comment

Source. New; derived from Section 4–109.

§ 9–525.   Fees.

(a) **[Initial financing statement or other record: general rule.]** Except as otherwise provided in subsection (e), the fee for filing and indexing a record under this part, other than an initial financing statement of the kind described in subsection (b), is [the amount specified in subsection (c), if applicable, plus]:

(1) $[X] if the record is communicated in writing and consists of one or two pages;

(2) $[2X] if the record is communicated in writing and consists of more than two pages; and

(3) $[½X] if the record is communicated by another medium authorized by filing-office rule.

(b) **[Initial financing statement: public-finance and manufactured-housing transactions.]** Except as otherwise provided in subsection (e), the fee for filing and indexing an initial financing statement of the following kind is [the amount specified in subsection (c), if applicable, plus]:

(1) $_____ if the financing statement indicates that it is filed in connection with a public-finance transaction;

(2) $_____ if the financing statement indicates that it is filed in connection with a manufactured-home transaction.

[Alternative A]

(c) **[Number of names.]** The number of names required to be indexed does not affect the amount of the fee in subsections (a) and (b).

[Alternative B]

(c) **[Number of names.]** Except as otherwise provided in subsection (e), if a record is communicated in writing, the fee for each name more than two required to be indexed is $_____.

[End of Alternatives]

(d) **[Response to information request.]** The fee for responding to a request for information from the filing office, including for [issuing a certificate showing] [communicating] whether there is on file any financing statement naming a particular debtor, is:

(1) $_____ if the request is communicated in writing; and

(2) $_____ if the request is communicated by another medium authorized by filing-office rule.

(e) **[Record of mortgage.]** This section does not require a fee with respect to a record of a mortgage which is effective as a financing statement filed as a fixture filing or as a financing statement covering as-extracted collateral or timber to be cut under Section 9–502(c). However, the recording and satisfaction fees that otherwise would be applicable to the record of the mortgage apply.

Legislative Notes:

1. To preserve uniformity, a State that places the provisions of this section together with statutes setting fees for other services should do so without modification.

2. A State should enact subsection (c), Alternative A, and omit the bracketed language in subsections (a) and (b) unless its indexing system entails a substantial additional cost when indexing additional names.

As amended in 2000.

Official Comment

1. **Source.** Various sections of former Part 4.

2. **Fees.** This section contains all fee requirements for filing, indexing, and responding to requests for information. Uniformity in the fee structure (but not necessarily in the amount of fees) makes this Article easier for secured parties to use and reduces the likelihood that a filed record will be rejected for failure to pay at least the correct amount of the fee. See Section 9–516(b)(2).

The costs of processing electronic records are less than those with respect to written records. Accordingly, this section mandates a lower fee as an incentive to file electronically and imposes the additional charge (if any) for multiple debtors only with respect to written records. When written records are used, this Article encourages the use of the uniform forms in Section 9–521. The fee for filing these forms should be no greater than the fee for other written records.

To make the relevant information included in a filed record more accessible once the record is found, this section mandates a higher fee for longer written records than for shorter ones. Finally, recognizing that financing statements naming more than one debtor are most often filed against a husband and wife, any additional charge for multiple debtors applies to records filed with respect to more than two debtors, rather than with respect to more than one.

§ 9–526. Filing–Office Rules.

(a) **[Adoption of filing-office rules.]** The [insert appropriate governmental official or agency] shall adopt and publish rules to implement this article. The filing-office rules must be[:

(1)] consistent with this article[; and

(2) adopted and published in accordance with the [insert any applicable state administrative procedure act]].

(b) **[Harmonization of rules.]** To keep the filing-office rules and practices of the filing office in harmony with the rules and practices of filing offices in other jurisdictions that enact substantially this part, and to keep the technology used by the filing office compatible with the technology used by filing offices in other jurisdictions that enact substantially this part, the [insert appropriate governmental official or agency], so far as is consistent with the purposes, policies, and

provisions of this article, in adopting, amending, and repealing filing-office rules, shall:

(1) consult with filing offices in other jurisdictions that enact substantially this part; and

(2) consult the most recent version of the Model Rules promulgated by the International Association of Corporate Administrators or any successor organization; and

(3) take into consideration the rules and practices of, and the technology used by, filing offices in other jurisdictions that enact substantially this part.

Official Comment

1. **Source.** New; subsection (b) derives in part from the Uniform Consumer Credit Code (1974).

2. **Rules Required.** Operating a filing office is a complicated business, requiring many more rules and procedures than this Article can usefully provide. Subsection (a) requires the adoption of rules to carry out the provisions of Article 9. The filing-office rules must be consistent with the provisions of the statute and adopted in accordance with local procedures. The publication requirement informs secured parties about filing-office practices, aids secured parties in evaluating filing-related risks and costs, and promotes regularity of application within the filing office.

3. **Importance of Uniformity.** In today's national economy, uniformity of the policies and practices of the filing offices will reduce the costs of secured transactions substantially. The International Association of Corporate Administrators (IACA), referred to in subsection (b), is an organization whose membership includes filing officers from every State. These individuals are responsible for the proper functioning of the Article 9 filing system and have worked diligently to develop model filing-office rules, with a view toward efficiency and uniformity.

Although uniformity is an important desideratum, subsection (a) affords considerable flexibility in the adoption of filing-office rules. Each State may adopt a version of subsection (a) that reflects the desired relationship between the statewide filing office described in Section 9–501(a)(2) and the local filing offices described in Section 9–501(a)(1) and that takes into account the practices of its filing offices. Subsection (a) need not designate a single official or agency to adopt rules applicable to all filing offices, and the rules applicable to the statewide filing office need not be identical to those applicable to the local filing office. For example, subsection (a) might provide for the statewide filing office to adopt filing-office rules, and, if not prohibited by other law, the filing office might adopt one set of rules for itself and another for local offices. Or, subsection (a) might designate one official or agency to adopt rules for the statewide filing office and another to adopt rules for local filing offices.

§ 9–527. Duty to Report.

The [insert appropriate governmental official or agency] shall report [annually on or before _____] to the [Governor and Legislature] on the operation of the filing office. The report must contain a statement of the extent to which:

(1) the filing-office rules are not in harmony with the rules of filing offices in other jurisdictions that enact substantially this part and the reasons for these variations; and

(2) the filing-office rules are not in harmony with the most recent version of the Model Rules promulgated by the International Association of Corporate Administrators, or any successor organization, and the reasons for these variations.

Official Comment

1. **Source.** New; derived in part from the Uniform Consumer Credit Code (1974).

2. **Duty to Report.** This section is designed to promote compliance with the standards of performance imposed upon the filing office and with the requirement that the filing office's policies, practices, and technology be consistent and compatible with the policies, practices, and technology of other filing offices.

PART 6

DEFAULT

[SUBPART 1. DEFAULT AND ENFORCEMENT OF SECURITY INTEREST]

§ 9–601. Rights After Default; Judicial Enforcement; Consignor or Buyer of Accounts, Chattel Paper, Payment Intangibles, or Promissory Notes.

(a) **[Rights of secured party after default.]** After default, a secured party has the rights provided in this part and, except as otherwise provided in Section 9–602, those provided by agreement of the parties. A secured party:

(1) may reduce a claim to judgment, foreclose, or otherwise enforce the claim, security interest, or agricultural lien by any available judicial procedure; and

(2) if the collateral is documents, may proceed either as to the documents or as to the goods they cover.

(b) **[Rights and duties of secured party in possession or control.]** A secured party in possession of collateral or control of collateral under Section 7–106, 9–104, 9–105, 9–106, or 9–107 has the rights and duties provided in Section 9–207.

(c) **[Rights cumulative; simultaneous exercise.]** The rights under subsections (a) and (b) are cumulative and may be exercised simultaneously.

(d) **[Rights of debtor and obligor.]** Except as otherwise provided in subsection (g) and Section 9–605, after default, a debtor and an obligor have the rights provided in this part and by agreement of the parties.

(e) **[Lien of levy after judgment.]** If a secured party has reduced its claim to judgment, the lien of any levy that may be made upon the collateral by virtue of an execution based upon the judgment relates back to the earliest of:

(1) the date of perfection of the security interest or agricultural lien in the collateral;

(2) the date of filing a financing statement covering the collateral; or

(3) any date specified in a statute under which the agricultural lien was created.

(f) **[Execution sale.]** A sale pursuant to an execution is a foreclosure of the security interest or agricultural lien by judicial procedure within the meaning of this section. A secured party may purchase at the sale and thereafter hold the collateral free of any other requirements of this article.

(g) **[Consignor or buyer of certain rights to payment.]** Except as otherwise provided in

Section 9–607(c), this part imposes no duties upon a secured party that is a consignor or is a buyer of accounts, chattel paper, payment intangibles, or promissory notes.

As amended in 2003.

Official Comment

1. **Source.** Former Section 9–501(1), (2), (5).

2. **Enforcement: In General.** The rights of a secured party to enforce its security interest in collateral after the debtor's default are an important feature of a secured transaction. (Note that the term "rights," as defined in Section 1–201, includes "remedies.") This Part provides those rights as well as certain limitations on their exercise for the protection of the defaulting debtor, other creditors, and other affected persons. However, subsections (a) and (d) make clear that the rights provided in this Part do not exclude other rights provided by agreement.

3. **When Remedies Arise.** Under subsection (a) the secured party's rights arise "[a]fter default." As did former Section 9–501, this Article leaves to the agreement of the parties the circumstances giving rise to a default. This Article does not determine whether a secured party's post-default conduct can constitute a waiver of default in the face of an agreement stating that such conduct shall not constitute a waiver. Rather, it continues to leave to the parties' agreement, as supplemented by law other than this Article, the determination whether a default has occurred or has been waived. See Section 1–103.

4. **Possession of Collateral; Section 9–207.** After a secured party takes possession of collateral following a default, there is no longer any distinction between a security interest that before default was nonpossessory and a security interest that was possessory before default, as under a common-law pledge. This Part generally does not distinguish between the rights of a secured party with a nonpossessory security interest and those of a secured party with a possessory security interest. However, Section 9–207 addresses rights and duties with respect to collateral in a secured party's possession. Under subsection (b) of this section, Section 9–207 applies not only to possession before default but also to possession after default. Subsection (b) also has been conformed to Section 9–207, which, unlike former Section 9–207, applies to secured parties having control of collateral.

5. **Cumulative Remedies.** Former Section 9–501(1) provided that the secured party's remedies were cumulative, but it did not explicitly provide whether the remedies could be exercised simultaneously. Subsection (c) permits the simultaneous exercise of remedies if the secured party acts in good faith. The liability scheme of Subpart 2 affords redress to an aggrieved debtor or obligor. Moreover, permitting the simultaneous exercise of remedies under subsection (c) does not override any non-UCC law, including the law of tort and statutes regulating collection of debts, under which the simultaneous exercise of remedies in a particular case constitutes abusive behavior or harassment giving rise to liability.

6. **Judicial Enforcement.** Under subsection (a) a secured party may reduce its claim to judgment or foreclose its interest by any available procedure outside this Article under applicable law. Subsection (e) generally follows former Section 9–501(5). It makes clear that any judicial lien that the secured party may acquire against the collateral effectively is a continuation of the original security interest (if perfected) and not the acquisition of a new interest or a transfer of property on account of a preexisting obligation. Under former Section 9–501(5), the judicial lien was stated to relate back to the date of perfection of the security interest. Subsection (e), however, provides that the lien relates back to the earlier of the date of filing or the date of perfection. This provides a secured party who enforces a security interest by judicial process with the benefit of the "first-to-file-or-perfect" priority rule of Section 9–322(a)(1).

7. **Agricultural Liens.** Part 6 provides parallel treatment for the enforcement of agricultural liens and security interests. Because agricultural liens are statutory rather than consensual, this Article does draw a few distinctions between these liens and security interests. Under subsection (e), the statute creating an agricultural lien would govern whether and the date to which an execution lien relates back. Section 9–606 explains when a "default" occurs in the agricultural lien context.

8. **Execution Sales.** Subsection (f) also follows former Section 9–501(5). It makes clear that an execution sale is an appropriate method of foreclosure contemplated by this Part. However, the sale is governed by other law and not by this Article, and the limitations under Section 9–610 on the right of a secured party to purchase collateral do not apply.

9. **Sales of Receivables; Consignments.** Subsection (g) provides that, except as provided in Section 9–607(c), the duties imposed on secured parties do not apply to buyers of accounts, chattel paper, payment intangibles, or promissory notes. Although denominated "secured parties," these buyers own the entire interest in the property sold and so may enforce their

rights without regard to the seller ("debtor") or the seller's creditors. Likewise, a true consignor may enforce its ownership interest under other law without regard to the duties that this Part imposes on secured parties. Note, however, that Section 9–615 governs cases in which a consignee's secured party (other than a consignor) is enforcing a security interest that is senior to the security interest (i.e., ownership interest) of a true consignor.

§ 9–602. Waiver and Variance of Rights and Duties.

Except as otherwise provided in Section 9–624, to the extent that they give rights to a debtor or obligor and impose duties on a secured party, the debtor or obligor may not waive or vary the rules stated in the following listed sections:

(1) Section 9–207(b)(4)(C), which deals with use and operation of the collateral by the secured party;

(2) Section 9–210, which deals with requests for an accounting and requests concerning a list of collateral and statement of account;

(3) Section 9–607(c), which deals with collection and enforcement of collateral;

(4) Sections 9–608(a) and 9–615(c) to the extent that they deal with application or payment of noncash proceeds of collection, enforcement, or disposition;

(5) Sections 9–608(a) and 9–615(d) to the extent that they require accounting for or payment of surplus proceeds of collateral;

(6) Section 9–609 to the extent that it imposes upon a secured party that takes possession of collateral without judicial process the duty to do so without breach of the peace;

(7) Sections 9–610(b), 9–611, 9–613, and 9–614, which deal with disposition of collateral;

(8) Section 9–615(f), which deals with calculation of a deficiency or surplus when a disposition is made to the secured party, a person related to the secured party, or a secondary obligor;

(9) Section 9–616, which deals with explanation of the calculation of a surplus or deficiency;

(10) Sections 9–620, 9–621, and 9–622, which deal with acceptance of collateral in satisfaction of obligation;

(11) Section 9–623, which deals with redemption of collateral;

(12) Section 9–624, which deals with permissible waivers; and

(13) Sections 9–625 and 9–626, which deal with the secured party's liability for failure to comply with this article.

Official Comment

1. **Source.** Former Section 9–501(3).

2. **Waiver: In General.** Section 1–102(3) addresses which provisions of the UCC are mandatory and which may be varied by agreement. With exceptions relating to good faith, diligence, reasonableness, and care, immediate parties, as between themselves, may vary its provisions by agreement. However, in the context of rights and duties after default, our legal system traditionally has looked with suspicion on agreements that limit the debtor's rights and free the secured party of its duties. As stated in former Section 9–501, Comment 4, "no mortgage clause has ever been allowed to clog the equity of redemption." The context of default offers great opportunity for overreaching. The suspicious attitudes of the courts have been grounded in common sense. This section, like former Section 9–501(3), codifies this long-standing and deeply rooted attitude. The specified rights of the debtor and duties of the secured party may not be waived or varied except as stated. Provisions that are not specified in this section are subject to the general rules in Section 1–102(3).

3. **Nonwaivable Rights and Duties.** This section revises former Section 9–501(3) by restricting the ability to waive or modify additional specified rights and duties: (i) duties under Section 9–207(b)(4)(C), which deals with the use and operation of consumer goods, (ii) the right to a response to a request for an accounting, concerning a list of collateral, or concerning a statement of account (Section 9–210), (iii) the duty to collect collateral in a commercially reasonable manner (Section 9–607), (iv) the implicit duty to refrain from a breach of the peace in taking possession of collateral under Section 9–609, (v) the duty to apply noncash proceeds of collection or disposition in a commercially reasonable manner (Sections 9–608 and 9–615), (vi) the right to a special method of calculating a surplus or deficiency in certain dispositions to a secured party, a person related to secured party, or a secondary obligor

(Section 9–615), (vii) the duty to give an explanation of the calculation of a surplus or deficiency (Section 9–616), (viii) the right to limitations on the effectiveness of certain waivers (Section 9–624), and (ix) the right to hold a secured party liable for failure to comply with this Article (Sections 9–625 and 9–626). For clarity and consistency, this Article uses the term "waive or vary" instead of "renounc[e] or modify[]," which appeared in former Section 9–504(3).

This section provides generally that the specified rights and duties "may not be waived or varied." However, it does not restrict the ability of parties to agree to settle, compromise, or renounce claims for past conduct that may have constituted a violation or breach of those rights and duties, even if the settlement involves an express "waiver."

4. **Waiver by Debtors and Obligors.** The restrictions on waiver contained in this section apply to obligors as well as debtors. This resolves a question under former Article 9 as to whether secondary obligors, assuming that they were "debtors" for purposes of former Part 5, were permitted to waive, under the law of suretyship, rights and duties under that Part.

5. **Certain Post–Default Waivers.** Section 9–624 permits post-default waivers in limited circumstances. These waivers must be made in agreements that are authenticated. Under Section 1–201, an "'agreement' means the bargain of the parties in fact." In considering waivers under Section 9–624 and analogous agreements in other contexts, courts should carefully scrutinize putative agreements that appear in records that also address many additional or unrelated matters.

§ 9–603. Agreement on Standards Concerning Rights and Duties.

(a) **[Agreed standards.]** The parties may determine by agreement the standards measuring the fulfillment of the rights of a debtor or obligor and the duties of a secured party under a rule stated in Section 9–602 if the standards are not manifestly unreasonable.

(b) **[Agreed standards inapplicable to breach of peace.]** Subsection (a) does not apply to the duty under Section 9–609 to refrain from breaching the peace.

Official Comment

1. **Source.** Former Section 9–501(3).

2. **Limitation on Ability to Set Standards.** Subsection (a), like former Section 9–501(3), permits the parties to set standards for compliance with the rights

and duties under this Part if the standards are not "manifestly unreasonable." Under subsection (b), the parties are not permitted to set standards measuring fulfillment of the secured party's duty to take collateral without breaching the peace.

§ 9–604. Procedure if Security Agreement Covers Real Property or Fixtures.

(a) **[Enforcement: personal and real property.]** If a security agreement covers both personal and real property, a secured party may proceed:

(1) under this part as to the personal property without prejudicing any rights with respect to the real property; or

(2) as to both the personal property and the real property in accordance with the rights with respect to the real property, in which case the other provisions of this part do not apply.

(b) **[Enforcement: fixtures.]** Subject to subsection (c), if a security agreement covers goods that are or become fixtures, a secured party may proceed:

(1) under this part; or

(2) in accordance with the rights with respect to real property, in which case the other provisions of this part do not apply.

(c) **[Removal of fixtures.]** Subject to the other provisions of this part, if a secured party holding a security interest in fixtures has priority over all owners and encumbrancers of the real property, the secured party, after default, may remove the collateral from the real property.

(d) **[Injury caused by removal.]** A secured party that removes collateral shall promptly reimburse any encumbrancer or owner of the real property, other than the debtor, for the cost of repair of any physical injury caused by the removal. The secured party need not reimburse the encumbrancer or owner for any diminution in value of the real property caused by the absence of the goods removed or by any necessity of replacing them. A person entitled to reimbursement may refuse permission to remove until the secured party gives adequate assurance for the performance of the obligation to reimburse.

Official Comment

1. **Source.** Former Sections 9–501(4), 9–313(8).

2. **Real–Property–Related Collateral.** The collateral in many transactions consists of both real and personal property. In the interest of simplicity, speed, and economy, subsection (a), like former Section 9–501(4), permits (but does not require) the secured party to proceed as to both real and personal property in accordance with its rights and remedies with respect to the real property. Subsection (a) also makes clear that a secured party who exercises rights under Part 6 with respect to personal property does not prejudice any rights under real-property law.

This Article does not address certain other real-property-related problems. In a number of States, the exercise of remedies by a creditor who is secured by both real property and non-real property collateral is governed by special legal rules. For example, under some anti-deficiency laws, creditors risk loss of rights against personal property collateral if they err in enforcing their rights against the real property. Under a "one-form-of-action" rule (or rule against splitting a cause of action), a creditor who judicially enforces a real property mortgage and does not proceed in the same action to enforce a security interest in personalty may (among other consequences) lose the right to proceed against the personalty. Although statutes of this kind create impediments to enforcement of security interests, this Article does not override these limitations under other law.

3. **Fixtures.** Subsection (b) is new. It makes clear that a security interest in fixtures may be enforced either under real-property law or under any of the applicable provisions of Part 6, including sale or other disposition either before or after removal of the fixtures (see subsection (c)). Subsection (b) also serves to overrule cases holding that a secured party's only remedy after default is the removal of the fixtures from the real property. See, e.g., *Maplewood Bank & Trust v. Sears, Roebuck & Co.*, 625 A.2d 537 (N.J. Super. Ct. App. Div. 1993).

Subsection (c) generally follows former Section 9–313(8). It gives the secured party the right to remove fixtures under certain circumstances. A secured party whose security interest in fixtures has priority over owners and encumbrancers of the real property may remove the collateral from the real property. However, subsection (d) requires the secured party to reimburse any owner (other than the debtor) or encumbrancer for the cost of repairing any physical injury caused by the removal. This right to reimbursement is implemented by the last sentence of subsection (d), which gives the owner or encumbrancer a right to security or indemnity as a condition for giving permission to remove.

§ 9–605. Unknown Debtor or Secondary Obligor.

A secured party does not owe a duty based on its status as secured party:

(1) to a person that is a debtor or obligor, unless the secured party knows:

(A) that the person is a debtor or obligor;

(B) the identity of the person; and

(C) how to communicate with the person; or

(2) to a secured party or lienholder that has filed a financing statement against a person, unless the secured party knows:

(A) that the person is a debtor; and

(B) the identity of the person.

Official Comment

1. **Source.** New.

2. **Duties to Unknown Persons.** This section relieves a secured party from duties owed to a debtor or obligor, if the secured party does not know about the debtor or obligor. Similarly, it relieves a secured party from duties owed to a secured party or lienholder who has filed a financing statement against the debtor, if the secured party does not know about the debtor. For example, a secured party may be unaware that the original debtor has sold the collateral subject to the security interest and that the new owner has become the debtor. If so, the secured party owes no duty to the new owner (debtor) or to a secured party who has filed a financing statement against the new owner. This section should be read in conjunction with the exculpatory provisions in Section 9–628. Note that it relieves a secured party not only from duties arising under this Article but also from duties arising under other law by virtue of the secured party's status as such under this Article, unless the other law otherwise provides.

§ 9–606. Time of Default for Agricultural Lien.

For purposes of this part, a default occurs in connection with an agricultural lien at the time the secured party becomes entitled to enforce the lien in accordance with the statute under which it was created.

Official Comment

1. **Source.** New.

2. **Time of Default.** Remedies under this Part become available upon the debtor's "default." See Sec-

tion 9–601. This section explains when "default" occurs in the agricultural-lien context. It requires one to consult the enabling statute to determine when the lienholder is entitled to enforce the lien.

§ 9–607. Collection and Enforcement by Secured Party.

(a) **[Collection and enforcement generally.]** If so agreed, and in any event after default, a secured party:

(1) may notify an account debtor or other person obligated on collateral to make payment or otherwise render performance to or for the benefit of the secured party;

(2) may take any proceeds to which the secured party is entitled under Section 9–315;

(3) may enforce the obligations of an account debtor or other person obligated on collateral and exercise the rights of the debtor with respect to the obligation of the account debtor or other person obligated on collateral to make payment or otherwise render performance to the debtor, and with respect to any property that secures the obligations of the account debtor or other person obligated on the collateral;

(4) if it holds a security interest in a deposit account perfected by control under Section 9–104(a)(1), may apply the balance of the deposit account to the obligation secured by the deposit account; and

(5) if it holds a security interest in a deposit account perfected by control under Section 9–104(a)(2) or (3), may instruct the bank to pay the balance of the deposit account to or for the benefit of the secured party.

(b) **[Nonjudicial enforcement of mortgage.]** If necessary to enable a secured party to exercise under subsection (a)(3) the right of a debtor to enforce a mortgage nonjudicially, the secured party may record in the office in which a record of the mortgage is recorded:

(1) a copy of the security agreement that creates or provides for a security interest in the obligation secured by the mortgage; and

(2) the secured party's sworn affidavit in recordable form stating that:

(A) a default has occurred; and

(B) the secured party is entitled to enforce the mortgage nonjudicially.

(c) **[Commercially reasonable collection and enforcement.]** A secured party shall proceed in a commercially reasonable manner if the secured party:

(1) undertakes to collect from or enforce an obligation of an account debtor or other person obligated on collateral; and

(2) is entitled to charge back uncollected collateral or otherwise to full or limited recourse against the debtor or a secondary obligor.

(d) **[Expenses of collection and enforcement.]** A secured party may deduct from the collections made pursuant to subsection (c) reasonable expenses of collection and enforcement, including reasonable attorney's fees and legal expenses incurred by the secured party.

(e) **[Duties to secured party not affected.]** This section does not determine whether an account debtor, bank, or other person obligated on collateral owes a duty to a secured party.

Official Comment

1. **Source.** Former Section 9–502; subsections (b), (d), and (e) are new.

2. **Collections: In General.** Collateral consisting of rights to payment is not only the most liquid asset of a typical debtor's business but also is property that may be collected without any interruption of the debtor's business This situation is far different from that in which collateral is inventory or equipment, whose removal may bring the business to a halt. Furthermore, problems of valuation and identification, present with collateral that is tangible personal property, frequently are not as serious in the case of rights to payment and other intangible collateral. Consequently, this section, like former Section 9–502, recognizes that financing through assignments of intangibles lacks many of the complexities that arise after default in other types of financing. This section allows the assignee to liquidate collateral by collecting whatever may become due on the collateral, whether or not the method of collection contemplated by the security arrangement before default was direct (i.e., payment by the account debtor to the assignee, "notification" financing) or indirect (i.e., payment by the account debtor to the assignor, "nonnotification" financing).

3. **Scope.** The scope of this section is broader than that of former Section 9–502. It applies not only to collections from account debtors and obligors on instruments but also to enforcement more generally against all persons obligated on collateral. It explicitly provides for the secured party's enforcement of the debtor's rights in respect of the account debtor's (and other third parties') obligations and for the secured party's enforcement of supporting obligations with respect to those obligations. (Supporting obligations are components of the collateral under Section 9–203(f).) The rights of a secured party under subsection (a) include the right to enforce claims that the debtor may enjoy against others. For example, the claims might include a breach-of-warranty claim arising out of a defect in equipment that is collateral or a secured party's action for an injunction against infringement of a patent that is collateral. Those claims typically would be proceeds of original collateral under Section 9–315.

4. **Collection and Enforcement Before Default.** Like Part 6 generally, this section deals with the rights and duties of secured parties following default. However, as did former Section 9–502 with respect to collection rights, this section also applies to the collection and enforcement rights of secured parties even if a default has not occurred, as long as the debtor has so agreed. It is not unusual for debtors to agree that secured parties are entitled to collect and enforce rights against account debtors prior to default.

5. **Collections by Junior Secured Party.** A secured party who holds a security interest in a right to payment may exercise the right to collect and enforce under this section, even if the security interest is subordinate to a conflicting security interest in the same right to payment. Whether the junior secured party has priority in the collected proceeds depends on whether the junior secured party qualifies for priority as a purchaser of an instrument (e.g., the account debtor's check) under Section 9–330(d), as a holder in due course of an instrument under Sections 3–305 and 9–331(a), or as a transferee of money under Section 9–332(a). See Sections 9–330, Comment 7; 9–331, Comment 5; and 9–332.

6. **Relationship to Rights and Duties of Persons Obligated on Collateral.** This section permits a secured party to collect and enforce obligations included in collateral in its capacity as a secured party. It is not necessary for a secured party first to become the owner of the collateral pursuant to a disposition or acceptance. However, the secured party's rights, as between it and the debtor, to collect from and enforce collateral against account debtors and others obligated on collateral under subsection (a) are subject to Section 9–341, Part 4, and other applicable law. *Neither this section nor former Section 9–502 should be understood to regulate the duties of an account debtor or other person obligated on collateral.* Subsection (e) makes this explicit. For example, the secured party may be unable to exercise the debtor's rights under an instrument if the debtor is in possession of the instrument, or under a non-transferable letter of credit if the debtor is the beneficiary. Unless a secured party has control over a letter-of-credit right and is entitled to receive payment or performance from the issuer or a nominated person under Article 5, its remedies with respect to the letter-of-credit right may be limited to the recovery of any identifiable proceeds from the debtor. This section establishes only the baseline rights of the secured party *vis-a-vis the debtor*—the secured party is entitled to enforce and collect after default and earlier if so agreed.

7. **Deposit Account Collateral.** Subsections (a)(4) and (5) set forth the self-help remedy for a secured party whose collateral is a deposit account. Subsection (a)(4) addresses the rights of a secured party that is the bank with which the deposit account is maintained. That secured party automatically has control of the deposit account under Section 9–104(a)(1). After default, and otherwise if so agreed, the bank/secured party may apply the funds on deposit to the secured obligation.

If a security interest of a third party is perfected by control (Section 9–104(a)(2) or (a)(3)), then after default, and otherwise if so agreed, the secured party may instruct the bank to pay out the funds in the account. If the third party has control under Section 9–104(a)(3), the depositary institution is obliged to obey the instruction because the secured party is its customer. See Section 4–401. If the third party has control under Section 9–104(a)(2), the control agreement determines the depositary institution's obligation to obey.

If a security interest in a deposit account is unperfected, or is perfected by filing by virtue of the proceeds rules of Section 9–315, the depositary institution ordinarily owes no obligation to obey the secured party's instructions. See Section 9–341. To reach the funds without the debtor's cooperation, the secured party must use an available judicial procedure.

8. **Rights Against Mortgagor of Real Property.** Subsection (b) addresses the situation in which the collateral consists of a mortgage note (or other obligation secured by a mortgage on real property). After the debtor's (mortgagee's) default, the secured party (assignee) may wish to proceed with a nonjudicial

foreclosure of the mortgage securing the note but may be unable to do so because it has not become the assignee of record. The assignee/secured party may not have taken a recordable assignment at the commencement of the transaction (perhaps the mortgage note in question was one of hundreds assigned to the secured party as collateral). Having defaulted, the mortgagee may be unwilling to sign a recordable assignment. This section enables the secured party (assignee) to become the assignee of record by recording in the applicable real-property records the security agreement and an affidavit certifying default. Of course, the secured party's rights derive from those of its debtor. Subsection (b) would not entitle the secured party to proceed with a foreclosure unless the mortgagor also were in default or the debtor (mortgagee) otherwise enjoyed the right to foreclose.

9. **Commercial Reasonableness.** Subsection (c) provides that the secured party's collection and enforcement rights under subsection (a) must be exercised in a commercially reasonable manner. These rights include the right to settle and compromise claims against the account debtor. The secured party's failure to observe the standard of commercial reasonableness could render it liable to an aggrieved person under Section 9–625, and the secured party's recovery of a deficiency would be subject to Section 9–626. Subsection (c) does not apply if, as is characteristic of most sales of accounts, chattel paper, payment intangibles, and promissory notes, the secured party (buyer) has no right of recourse against the debtor (seller) or a secondary obligor. However, if the secured party does have a right of recourse, the commercial-reasonableness standard applies to collection and enforcement even though the assignment to the secured party was a "true" sale. The obligation to proceed in a commercially reasonable manner arises because the collection process affects the extent of the seller's recourse liability, not because the seller retains an interest in the sold collateral (the seller does not). Concerning classification of a transaction, see Section 9–109, Comment 4.

10. **Attorney's Fees and Legal Expenses.** The phrase "reasonable attorney's fees and legal expenses," which appears in subsection (d), includes only those fees and expenses incurred in proceeding against account debtors or other third parties. The secured party's right to recover these expenses from the collections arises automatically under this section. The secured party also may incur other attorney's fees and legal expenses in proceeding against the debtor or obligor. Whether the secured party has a right to recover those fees and expenses depends on whether the debtor or obligor has agreed to pay them, as is the case with respect to attorney's fees and legal expenses under Sections 9–608(a)(1)(A) and 9–615(a)(1). The parties also may agree to allocate a portion of the secured party's overhead to collection and enforcement under subsection (d) or Section 9–608(a).

As amended in 2000.

§ 9–608. Application of Proceeds of Collection or Enforcement; Liability for Deficiency and Right to Surplus.

(a) **[Application of proceeds, surplus, and deficiency if obligation secured.]** If a security interest or agricultural lien secures payment or performance of an obligation, the following rules apply:

(1) A secured party shall apply or pay over for application the cash proceeds of collection or enforcement under Section 9–607 in the following order to:

(A) the reasonable expenses of collection and enforcement and, to the extent provided for by agreement and not prohibited by law, reasonable attorney's fees and legal expenses incurred by the secured party;

(B) the satisfaction of obligations secured by the security interest or agricultural lien under which the collection or enforcement is made; and

(C) the satisfaction of obligations secured by any subordinate security interest in or other lien on the collateral subject to the security interest or agricultural lien under which the collection or enforcement is made if the secured party receives an authenticated demand for proceeds before distribution of the proceeds is completed.

(2) If requested by a secured party, a holder of a subordinate security interest or other lien shall furnish reasonable proof of the interest or lien within a reasonable time. Unless the holder complies, the secured party need not comply with the holder's demand under paragraph (1)(C).

(3) A secured party need not apply or pay over for application noncash proceeds of collection and enforcement under Section 9–607 unless the failure to do so would be commercially unreasonable. A secured party

that applies or pays over for application noncash proceeds shall do so in a commercially reasonable manner.

(4) A secured party shall account to and pay a debtor for any surplus, and the obligor is liable for any deficiency.

(b) **[No surplus or deficiency in sales of certain rights to payment.]** If the underlying transaction is a sale of accounts, chattel paper, payment intangibles, or promissory notes, the debtor is not entitled to any surplus, and the obligor is not liable for any deficiency.

As amended in 2000.

Official Comment

1. **Source.** Subsection (a) is new; subsection (b) derives from former Section 9–502(2).

2. **Modifications of Prior Law.** Subsections (a) and (b) modify former Section 9–502(2) by explicitly providing for the application of proceeds recovered by the secured party in substantially the same manner as provided in Section 9–615(a) and (e) for dispositions of collateral.

3. **Surplus and Deficiency.** Subsections (a)(4) and (b) omit, as unnecessary, the references contained in former Section 9–502(2) to agreements varying the baseline rules on surplus and deficiency. The parties are always free to agree that an obligor will not be liable for a deficiency, even if the collateral secures an obligation, and that an obligor is liable for a deficiency, even if the transaction is a sale of receivables. For parallel provisions, see Section 9–615(d) and (e).

4. **Noncash Proceeds.** Subsection (a)(3) addresses the situation in which an enforcing secured party receives noncash proceeds.

Example: An enforcing secured party receives a promissory note from an account debtor who is unable to pay an account when it is due. The secured party accepts the note in exchange for extending the date on which the account debtor's obligation is due. The secured party may wish to credit its debtor (the assignor) with the principal amount of the note upon receipt of the note, but probably will prefer to credit the debtor only as and when the note is paid.

Under subsection (a)(3), the secured party is under no duty to apply the note or its value to the outstanding obligation unless its failure to do so would be commercially unreasonable. If the secured party does apply the note to the outstanding obligation, however, it must do so in a commercially reasonable manner. The parties may provide for the method of application of noncash proceeds by agreement, if the method is not manifestly unreasonable. See Section 9–603. This section does not explain when the failure to apply noncash proceeds would be commercially unreasonable; it leaves that determination to case-by-case adjudication. In the example, the secured party appears to have accepted the account debtor's note in order to increase the likelihood of payment and decrease the likelihood that the account debtor would dispute its obligation. Under these circumstances, it may well be commercially reasonable for the secured party to credit its debtor's obligations only as and when cash proceeds are collected from the account debtor, especially given the uncertainty that attends the account debtor's eventual payment. For an example of a secured party's receipt of noncash proceeds in which it may well be commercially unreasonable for the secured party to delay crediting its debtor's obligations with the value of noncash proceeds, see Section 9–615, Comment 3.

When the secured party is not required to "apply or pay over for application noncash proceeds," the proceeds nonetheless remain collateral subject to this Article. If the secured party were to dispose of them, for example, appropriate notification would be required (see Section 9–611), and the disposition would be subject to the standards provided in this Part (see Section 9–610). Moreover, a secured party in possession of the noncash proceeds would have the duties specified in Section 9–207.

5. **No Effect on Priority of Senior Security Interest.** The application of proceeds required by subsection (a) does not affect the priority of a security interest in collateral which is senior to the interest of the secured party who is collecting or enforcing collateral under Section 9–607. Although subsection (a) imposes a duty to apply proceeds to the enforcing secured party's expenses and to the satisfaction of the secured obligations owed to it and to subordinate secured parties, that duty applies only among the enforcing secured party and those persons. Concerning the priority of a junior secured party who collects and enforces collateral, see Section 9–607, Comment 5.

§ 9–609. Secured Party's Right to Take Possession After Default.

(a) **[Possession; rendering equipment unusable; disposition on debtor's premises.]** After default, a secured party:

(1) may take possession of the collateral; and

(2) without removal, may render equipment unusable and dispose of collateral on a debtor's premises under Section 9–610.

(b) **[Judicial and nonjudicial process.]** A secured party may proceed under subsection (a):

(1) pursuant to judicial process; or

(2) without judicial process, if it proceeds without breach of the peace.

(c) **[Assembly of collateral.]** If so agreed, and in any event after default, a secured party may require the debtor to assemble the collateral and make it available to the secured party at a place to be designated by the secured party which is reasonably convenient to both parties.

Official Comment

1. **Source.** Former Section 9–503.

2. **Secured Party's Right to Possession.** This section follows former Section 9–503 and earlier uniform legislation. It provides that the secured party is entitled to take possession of collateral after default.

3. **Judicial Process; Breach of Peace.** Subsection (b) permits a secured party to proceed under this section without judicial process if it does so "without breach of the peace." Although former Section 9–503 placed the same condition on a secured party's right to take possession of collateral, subsection (b) extends the condition to the right provided in subsection (a)(2) as well. Like former Section 9–503, this section does not define or explain the conduct that will constitute a breach of the peace, leaving that matter for continuing development by the courts. In considering whether a secured party has engaged in a breach of the peace, however, courts should hold the secured party responsible for the actions of others taken on the secured party's behalf, including independent contractors engaged by the secured party to take possession of collateral.

This section does not authorize a secured party who repossesses without judicial process to utilize the assistance of a law-enforcement officer. A number of cases have held that a repossessing secured party's use of a law-enforcement officer without benefit of judicial process constituted a failure to comply with former Section 9–503.

4. **Damages for Breach of Peace.** Concerning damages that may be recovered based on a secured party's breach of the peace in connection with taking possession of collateral, see Section 9–625, Comment 3.

5. **Multiple Secured Parties.** More than one secured party may be entitled to take possession of collateral under this section. Conflicting rights to possession among secured parties are resolved by the priority rules of this Article. Thus, a senior secured party is entitled to possession as against a junior claimant. Non–UCC law governs whether a junior secured party in possession of collateral is liable to the senior in conversion. Normally, a junior who refuses to relinquish possession of collateral upon the demand of a secured party having a superior possessory right to the collateral would be liable in conversion.

6. **Secured Party's Right to Disable and Dispose of Equipment on Debtor's Premises.** In the case of some collateral, such as heavy equipment, the physical removal from the debtor's plant and the storage of the collateral pending disposition may be impractical or unduly expensive. This section follows former Section 9–503 by providing that, in lieu of removal, the secured party may render equipment unusable or may dispose of collateral on the debtor's premises. Unlike former Section 9–503, however, this section explicitly conditions these rights on the debtor's default. Of course, this section does not validate unreasonable action by a secured party. Under Section 9–610, all aspects of a disposition must be commercially reasonable.

7. **Debtor's Agreement to Assemble Collateral.** This section follows former Section 9–503 also by validating a debtor's agreement to assemble collateral and make it available to a secured party at a place that the secured party designates. Similar to the treatment of agreements to permit collection prior to default under Section 9–607 and former 9–502, however, this section validates these agreements whether or not they are conditioned on the debtor's default. For example, a debtor might agree to make available to a secured party, from time to time, any instruments or negotiable documents that the debtor receives on account of collateral. A court should not infer from this section's validation that a debtor's agreement to assemble and make available collateral would not be enforceable under other applicable law.

8. **Agreed Standards.** Subject to the limitation imposed by Section 9–603(b), this section's provisions concerning agreements to assemble and make available collateral and a secured party's right to disable equipment and dispose of collateral on a debtor's premises are likely topics for agreement on standards as contemplated by Section 9–603.

§ 9–610. Disposition of Collateral After Default.

(a) **[Disposition after default.]** After default, a secured party may sell, lease, license, or otherwise dispose of any or all of the collateral in its present condition or following any commercially reasonable preparation or processing.

(b) **[Commercially reasonable disposition.]** Every aspect of a disposition of collateral, including the method, manner, time, place, and other terms, must be commercially reasonable. If commercially reasonable, a secured party may dispose of collateral by public or private proceedings, by one or more contracts, as a unit or in parcels, and at any time and place and on any terms.

(c) **[Purchase by secured party.]** A secured party may purchase collateral:

(1) at a public disposition; or

(2) at a private disposition only if the collateral is of a kind that is customarily sold on a recognized market or the subject of widely distributed standard price quotations.

(d) **[Warranties on disposition.]** A contract for sale, lease, license, or other disposition includes the warranties relating to title, possession, quiet enjoyment, and the like which by operation of law accompany a voluntary disposition of property of the kind subject to the contract.

(e) **[Disclaimer of warranties.]** A secured party may disclaim or modify warranties under subsection (d):

(1) in a manner that would be effective to disclaim or modify the warranties in a voluntary disposition of property of the kind subject to the contract of disposition; or

(2) by communicating to the purchaser a record evidencing the contract for disposition and including an express disclaimer or modification of the warranties.

(f) **[Record sufficient to disclaim warranties.]** A record is sufficient to disclaim warranties under subsection (e) if it indicates "There is no warranty relating to title, possession, quiet enjoyment, or the like in this disposition" or uses words of similar import.

Official Comment

1. **Source.** Former Section 9–504(1), (3)

2. **Commercially Reasonable Dispositions.** Subsection (a) follows former Section 9–504 by permitting a secured party to dispose of collateral in a commercially reasonable manner following a default. Although subsection (b) permits both public and private dispositions, "every aspect of a disposition ... must be commercially reasonable." This section encourages private dispositions on the assumption that they frequently will result in higher realization on collateral for the benefit of all concerned. Subsection (a) does not restrict dispositions to sales; collateral may be sold, leased, licensed, or otherwise disposed. Section 9–627 provides guidance for determining the circumstances under which a disposition is "commercially reasonable."

3. **Time of Disposition.** This Article does not specify a period within which a secured party must dispose of collateral. This is consistent with this Article's policy to encourage private dispositions through regular commercial channels. It may, for example, be prudent not to dispose of goods when the market has collapsed. Or, it might be more appropriate to sell a large inventory in parcels over a period of time instead of in bulk. Of course, under subsection (b) every aspect of a disposition of collateral must be commercially reasonable. This requirement explicitly includes the "method, manner, time, place and other terms." For example, if a secured party does not proceed under Section 9–620 and holds collateral for a long period of time without disposing of it, and if there is no good reason for not making a prompt disposition, the secured party may be determined not to have acted in a "commercially reasonable" manner. See also Section 1–203 (general obligation of good faith).

4. **Pre-Disposition Preparation and Processing.** Former Section 9–504(1) appeared to give the secured party the choice of disposing of collateral either "in its then condition or following any commercially reasonable preparation or processing." Some courts held that the "commercially reasonable" standard of former Section 9–504(3) nevertheless could impose an affirmative duty on the secured party to process or prepare the collateral prior to disposition. Subsection (a) retains the substance of the quoted language. Although courts should not be quick to impose a duty of preparation or processing on the secured party, subsection (a) does not grant the secured party the right to dispose of the collateral "in its then condition" under *all* circumstances. A secured party may not dispose of collateral "in its then condition" when, taking into account the costs and probable benefits of preparation or processing and the fact that the secured party would be advancing the costs at its risk,

it would be commercially unreasonable to dispose of the collateral in that condition.

5. **Disposition by Junior Secured Party.** Disposition rights under subsection (a) are not limited to first-priority security interests. Rather, any secured party as to whom there has been a default enjoys the right to dispose of collateral under this subsection. The exercise of this right by a secured party whose security interest is subordinate to that of another secured party does not of itself constitute a conversion or otherwise give rise to liability in favor of the holder of the senior security interest. Section 9–615 addresses application of the proceeds of a disposition by a junior secured party. Under Section 9–615(a), a junior secured party owes no obligation to apply the proceeds of disposition to the satisfaction of obligations secured by a senior security interest. Section 9–615(g) builds on this general rule by protecting certain juniors from claims of a senior concerning cash proceeds of the disposition. Even if a senior were to have a non-Article 9 claim to proceeds of a junior's disposition, Section 9–615(g) would protect a junior that acts in good faith and without knowledge that its actions violate the rights of a senior party. Because the disposition by a junior would not cut off a senior's security interest or other lien (see Section 9–617), in many (probably most) cases the junior's receipt of the cash proceeds would not violate the rights of the senior.

The holder of a senior security interest is entitled, by virtue of its priority, to take possession of collateral from the junior secured party and conduct its own disposition, provided that the senior enjoys the right to take possession of the collateral from the debtor. See Section 9–609. The holder of a junior security interest normally must notify the senior secured party of an impending disposition. See Section 9–611. Regardless of whether the senior receives a notification from the junior, the junior's disposition does not of itself discharge the senior's security interest. See Section 9–617. Unless the senior secured party has authorized the disposition free and clear of its security interest, the senior's security interest ordinarily will survive the disposition by the junior and continue under Section 9–315(a). If the senior enjoys the right to repossess the collateral from the debtor, the senior likewise may recover the collateral from the transferee.

When a secured party's collateral is encumbered by another security interest or other lien, one of the claimants may seek to invoke the equitable doctrine of marshaling. As explained by the Supreme Court, that doctrine "rests upon the principle that a creditor having two funds to satisfy his debt, may not by his application of them to his demand, defeat another creditor, who may resort to only one of the funds." *Meyer v. United States*, 375 U.S. 233, 236 (1963), quoting *Sowell v. Federal Reserve Bank*, 268 U.S. 449, 456–57 (1925). The purpose of the doctrine is "to prevent the arbitrary action of a senior lienor from destroying the rights of a junior lienor or a creditor having less security." Id. at 237. Because it is an equitable doctrine, marshaling "is applied only when it can be equitably fashioned as to all of the parties" having an interest in the property. Id. This Article leaves courts free to determine whether marshaling is appropriate in any given case. See Section 1–103.

6. **Security Interests of Equal Rank.** Sometimes two security interests enjoy the same priority. This situation may arise by contract, e.g., pursuant to "equal and ratable" provisions in indentures, or by operation of law. See Section 9–328(6). This Article treats a security interest having equal priority like a senior security interest in many respects. Assume, for example, that SP–X and SP–Y enjoy equal priority, SP–W is senior to them, and SP–Z is junior. If SP–X disposes of the collateral under this section, then (i) SP–W's and SP–Y's security interests survive the disposition but SP–Z's does not, see Section 9–617, and (ii) neither SP–W nor SP–Y is entitled to receive a distribution of proceeds, but SP–Z is. See Section 9–615(a)(3).

When one considers the ability to obtain possession of the collateral, a secured party with equal priority is unlike a senior secured party. As the senior secured party, SP–W should enjoy the right to possession as against SP–X. See Section 9–609, Comment 5. If SP–W takes possession and disposes of the collateral under this section, it is entitled to apply the proceeds to satisfy its secured claim. SP–Y, however, should not have such a right to take possession from SP–X; otherwise, once SP–Y took possession from SP–X, SP–X would have the right to get possession from SP–Y, which would be obligated to redeliver possession to SP–X, and so on. Resolution of this problem is left to the parties and, if necessary, the courts.

7. **Public vs. Private Dispositions.** This Part maintains two distinctions between "public" and other dispositions: (i) the secured party may buy at the former, but normally not at the latter (Section 9–610(c)), and (ii) the debtor is entitled to notification of "the time and place of a public disposition" and notification of "the time after which" a private disposition or other intended disposition is to be made (Section 9–613(1)(E)). It does not retain the distinction under former Section 9–504(4), under which transferees in a noncomplying public disposition could lose protection

more easily than transferees in other noncomplying dispositions. Instead, Section 9–617(b) adopts a unitary standard. Although the term is not defined, as used in this Article, a "public disposition" is one at which the price is determined after the public has had a meaningful opportunity for competitive bidding. "Meaningful opportunity" is meant to imply that some form of advertisement or public notice must precede the sale (or other disposition) and that the public must have access to the sale (disposition).

8. **Investment Property.** Dispositions of investment property may be regulated by the federal securities laws. Although a "public" disposition of securities under this Article may implicate the registration requirements of the Securities Act of 1933, it need not do so. A disposition that qualifies for a "private placement" exemption under the Securities Act of 1933 nevertheless may constitute a "public" disposition within the meaning of this section. Moreover, the "commercially reasonable" requirements of subsection (b) need not prevent a secured party from conducting a foreclosure sale without the issuer's compliance with federal registration requirements.

9. **"Recognized Market."** A "recognized market," as used in subsection (c) and Section 9–611(d), is one in which the items sold are fungible and prices are not subject to individual negotiation. For example, the New York Stock Exchange is a recognized market. A market in which prices are individually negotiated or the items are not fungible is not a recognized market, even if the items are the subject of widely disseminated price guides or are disposed of through dealer auctions.

10. **Relevance of Price.** While not itself sufficient to establish a violation of this Part, a low price suggests that a court should scrutinize carefully all aspects of a disposition to ensure that each aspect was commercially reasonable. Note also that even if the disposition is commercially reasonable, Section 9–615(f) provides a special method for calculating a deficiency or surplus if (i) the transferee in the disposition is the secured party, a person related to the secured party, or a secondary obligor, and (ii) the amount of proceeds of the disposition is significantly below the range of proceeds that a complying disposition to a person other than the secured party, a person related to the secured party, or a secondary obligor would have brought.

11. **Warranties.** Subsection (d) affords the transferee in a disposition under this section the benefit of any title, possession, quiet enjoyment, and similar warranties that would have accompanied the disposition by operation of non-Article 9 law had the disposition been conducted under other circumstances. For example, the Article 2 warranty of title would apply to a sale of goods, the analogous warranties of Article 2A would apply to a lease of goods, and any common-law warranties of title would apply to dispositions of other types of collateral. See, e.g., Restatement (2d), Contracts § 333 (warranties of assignor).

Subsection (e) explicitly provides that these warranties can be disclaimed either under other applicable law or by communicating a record containing an express disclaimer. The record need not be written, but an oral communication would not be sufficient. See Section 9–102 (definition of "record"). Subsection (f) provides a sample of wording that will effectively exclude the warranties in a disposition under this section, whether or not the exclusion would be effective under non-Article 9 law.

The warranties incorporated by subsection (d) are those relating to "title, possession, quiet enjoyment, and the like." Depending on the circumstances, a disposition under this section also may give rise to other statutory or implied warranties, e.g., warranties of quality or fitness for purpose. Law other than this Article determines whether such other warranties apply to a disposition under this section. Other law also determines issues relating to disclaimer of such warranties. For example, a foreclosure sale of a car by a car dealer could give rise to an implied warranty of merchantability (Section 2–314) unless effectively disclaimed or modified (Section 2–316).

This section's approach to these warranties conflicts with the former Comment to Section 2–312. This Article rejects the baseline assumption that commercially reasonable dispositions under this section are out of the ordinary commercial course or peculiar. The Comment to Section 2–312 has been revised accordingly.

§ 9–611.   Notification Before Disposition of Collateral.

(a) **["Notification date."]** In this section, "notification date" means the earlier of the date on which:

(1) a secured party sends to the debtor and any secondary obligor an authenticated notification of disposition; or

(2) the debtor and any secondary obligor waive the right to notification.

(b) **[Notification of disposition required.]** Except as otherwise provided in subsection (d), a secured party that disposes of collateral under Section 9–610 shall send to the persons specified in subsection (c) a reasonable authenticated notification of disposition.

(c) **[Persons to be notified.]** To comply with subsection (b), the secured party shall send an authenticated notification of disposition to:

(1) the debtor;

(2) any secondary obligor; and

(3) if the collateral is other than consumer goods:

(A) any other person from which the secured party has received, before the notification date, an authenticated notification of a claim of an interest in the collateral;

(B) any other secured party or lienholder that, 10 days before the notification date, held a security interest in or other lien on the collateral perfected by the filing of a financing statement that:

(i) identified the collateral;

(ii) was indexed under the debtor's name as of that date; and

(iii) was filed in the office in which to file a financing statement against the debtor covering the collateral as of that date; and

(C) any other secured party that, 10 days before the notification date, held a security interest in the collateral perfected by compliance with a statute, regulation, or treaty described in Section 9–311(a).

(d) **[Subsection (b) inapplicable: perishable collateral; recognized market.]** Subsection (b) does not apply if the collateral is perishable or threatens to decline speedily in value or is of a type customarily sold on a recognized market.

(e) **[Compliance with subsection (c)(3)(B).]** A secured party complies with the requirement for notification prescribed by subsection (c)(3)(B) if:

(1) not later than 20 days or earlier than 30 days before the notification date, the secured party requests, in a commercially reasonable manner, information concerning financing statements indexed under the debtor's name in the office indicated in subsection (c)(3)(B); and

(2) before the notification date, the secured party:

(A) did not receive a response to the request for information; or

(B) received a response to the request for information and sent an authenticated notification of disposition to each secured party or other lienholder named in that response whose financing statement covered the collateral.

Official Comment

1. **Source.** Former Section 9–504(3).

2. **Reasonable Notification.** This section requires a secured party who wishes to dispose of collateral under Section 9–610 to send "a reasonable authenticated notification of disposition" to specified interested persons, subject to certain exceptions. The notification must be reasonable as to the manner in which it is sent, its timeliness (i.e., a reasonable time before the disposition is to take place), and its content. See Sections 9–612 (timeliness of notification), 9–613 (contents of notification generally), 9–614 (contents of notification in consumer-goods transactions).

3. **Notification to Debtors and Secondary Obligors.** This section imposes a duty to send notification of a disposition not only to the debtor but also to any secondary obligor. Subsections (b) and (c) resolve an uncertainty under former Article 9 by providing that secondary obligors (sureties) are entitled to receive notification of an intended disposition of collateral, regardless of who created the security interest in the collateral. If the surety created the security interest, it would be the debtor. If it did not, it would be a secondary obligor. (This Article also resolves the question of the secondary obligor's ability to waive, pre-default, the right to notification—waiver generally is not permitted. See Section 9–602.) Section 9–605 relieves a secured party from any duty to send notification to a debtor or secondary obligor unknown to the secured party.

Under subsection (b), the principal obligor (borrower) is not always entitled to notification of disposition.

Example: Behnfeldt borrows on an unsecured basis, and Bruno grants a security interest in her car to secure the debt. Behnfeldt is a primary obligor, not a secondary obligor. As such, she is not entitled to notification of disposition under this section.

4. **Notification to Other Secured Parties.** Prior to the 1972 amendments to Article 9, former Section

9–504(3) required the enforcing secured party to send reasonable notification of the disposition:

> except in the case of consumer goods to any other person who has a security interest in the collateral and who has duly filed a financing statement indexed in the name of the debtor in this State or who is known by the secured party to have a security interest in the collateral.

The 1972 amendments eliminated the duty to give notice to secured parties other than those from whom the foreclosing secured party had received written notice of a claim of an interest in the collateral.

Many of the problems arising from dispositions of collateral encumbered by multiple security interests can be ameliorated or solved by informing all secured parties of an intended disposition and affording them the opportunity to work with one another. To this end, subsection (c)(3)(B) expands the duties of the foreclosing secured party to include the duty to notify (and the corresponding burden of searching the files to discover) certain competing secured parties. The subsection imposes a search burden that in some cases may be greater than the pre–1972 burden on foreclosing secured parties but certainly is more modest than that faced by a new secured lender.

To determine who is entitled to notification, the foreclosing secured party must determine the proper office for filing a financing statement as of a particular date, measured by reference to the "notification date," as defined in subsection (a). This determination requires reference to the choice-of-law provisions of Part 3. The secured party must ascertain whether any financing statements covering the collateral and indexed under the debtor's name, as the name existed as of that date, in fact were filed in that office. The foreclosing secured party generally need not notify secured parties whose effective financing statements have become more difficult to locate because of changes in the location of the debtor, proceeds rules, or changes in the debtor's name.

Under subsection (c)(3)(C), the secured party also must notify a secured party who has perfected a security interest by complying with a statute or treaty described in Section 9–311(a), such as a certificate-of-title statute.

Subsection (e) provides a "safe harbor" that takes into account the delays that may be attendant to receiving information from the public filing offices. It provides, generally, that the secured party will be deemed to have satisfied its notification duty under subsection (c)(3)(B) if it requests a search from the proper office at least 20 but not more than 30 days before sending notification to the debtor and if it also sends a notification to all secured parties (and other lienholders) reflected on the search report. The secured party's duty under subsection (c)(3)(B) also will be satisfied if the secured party requests but does not receive a search report before the notification is sent to the debtor. Thus, if subsection (e) applies, a secured party who is entitled to notification under subsection (c)(3)(B) has no remedy against a foreclosing secured party who does not send the notification. The foreclosing secured party has complied with the notification requirement. Subsection (e) has no effect on the requirements of the other paragraphs of subsection (c). For example, if the foreclosing secured party received a notification from the holder of a conflicting security interest in accordance with subsection (c)(3)(A) but failed to send to the holder a notification of the disposition, the holder of the conflicting security interest would have the right to recover any loss under Section 9–625(b).

5. **Authentication Requirement.** Subsections (b) and (c) explicitly provide that a notification of disposition must be "authenticated." Some cases read former Section 9–504(3) as validating oral notification.

6. **Second Try.** This Article leaves to judicial resolution, based upon the facts of each case, the question whether the requirement of "reasonable notification" requires a "second try," i.e., whether a secured party who sends notification and learns that the debtor did not receive it must attempt to locate the debtor and send another notification.

7. **Recognized Market; Perishable Collateral.** New subsection (d) makes it clear that there is no obligation to give notification of a disposition in the case of perishable collateral or collateral customarily sold on a recognized market (e.g., marketable securities). Former Section 9–504(3) might be read (incorrectly) to relieve the secured party from its duty to notify a debtor but not from its duty to notify other secured parties in connection with dispositions of such collateral.

8. **Failure to Conduct Notified Disposition.** Nothing in this Article prevents a secured party from electing not to conduct a disposition after sending a notification. Nor does this Article prevent a secured party from electing to send a revised notification if its plans for disposition change. This assumes, however, that the secured party acts in good faith, the revised notification is reasonable, and the revised plan for disposition and any attendant delay are commercially reasonable.

9. **Waiver.** A debtor or secondary obligor may waive the right to notification under this section only by a post-default authenticated agreement. See Section 9–624(a).

§ 9–612. Timeliness of Notification Before Disposition of Collateral.

(a) **[Reasonable time is question of fact.]** Except as otherwise provided in subsection (b), whether a notification is sent within a reasonable time is a question of fact.

(b) **[10-day period sufficient in non-consumer transaction.]** In a transaction other than a consumer transaction, a notification of disposition sent after default and 10 days or more before the earliest time of disposition set forth in the notification is sent within a reasonable time before the disposition.

Official Comment

1. **Source.** New.

2. **Reasonable Notification.** Section 9–611(b) requires the secured party to send a "reasonable authenticated notification." Under that section, as under former Section 9–504(3), one aspect of a reasonable notification is its timeliness. This generally means that the notification must be sent at a reasonable time in advance of the date of a public disposition or the date after which a private disposition is to be made. A notification that is sent so near to the disposition date that a notified person could not be expected to act on or take account of the notification would be unreasonable.

3. **Timeliness of Notification: Safe Harbor.** The 10–day notice period in subsection (b) is intended to be a "safe harbor" and not a minimum requirement. To qualify for the "safe harbor" the notification must be sent after default. A notification also must be sent in a commercially reasonable manner. See Section 9–611(b) ("reasonable authenticated notification"). These requirements prevent a secured party from taking advantage of the "safe harbor" by, for example, giving the debtor a notification at the time of the original extension of credit or sending the notice by surface mail to a debtor overseas.

§ 9–613. Contents and Form of Notification Before Disposition of Collateral: General.

Except in a consumer-goods transaction, the following rules apply:

(1) The contents of a notification of disposition are sufficient if the notification:

(A) describes the debtor and the secured party;

(B) describes the collateral that is the subject of the intended disposition;

(C) states the method of intended disposition;

(D) states that the debtor is entitled to an accounting of the unpaid indebtedness and states the charge, if any, for an accounting; and

(E) states the time and place of a public disposition or the time after which any other disposition is to be made.

(2) Whether the contents of a notification that lacks any of the information specified in paragraph (1) are nevertheless sufficient is a question of fact.

(3) The contents of a notification providing substantially the information specified in paragraph (1) are sufficient, even if the notification includes:

(A) information not specified by that paragraph; or

(B) minor errors that are not seriously misleading.

(4) A particular phrasing of the notification is not required.

(5) The following form of notification and the form appearing in Section 9–614(3), when completed, each provides sufficient information:

NOTIFICATION OF DISPOSITION OF COLLATERAL

To: [*Name of debtor, obligor, or other person to which the notification is sent*]

From: [*Name, address, and telephone number of secured party*]

Name of Debtor(s): [*Include only if debtor(s) are not an addressee*]

[*For a public disposition:*]
We will sell [or lease or license, *as applicable*] the [*describe collateral*] [to the highest qualified bidder] in public as follows:

Day and Date: _____

Time: _____

Place: _____

[For a private disposition:]

We will sell [or lease or license, *as applicable*] the [*describe collateral*] privately sometime after [*day and date*].

You are entitled to an accounting of the unpaid indebtedness secured by the property that we intend to sell [or lease or license, *as applicable*] [for a charge of $_____]. You may request an accounting by calling us at [*telephone number*]

[End of Form]

As amended in 2000.

Official Comment

1. **Source.** New.

2. **Contents of Notification.** To comply with the "reasonable authenticated notification" requirement of Section 9–611(b), the contents of a notification must be reasonable. Except in a consumer-goods transaction, the contents of a notification that includes the information set forth in paragraph (1) are sufficient as a matter of law, unless the parties agree otherwise. (The reference to "time" of disposition means here, as it did in former Section 9–504(3), not only the hour of the day but also the date.) Although a secured party may choose to include additional information concerning the transaction or the debtor's rights and obligations, no additional information is required unless the parties agree otherwise. A notification that lacks some of the information set forth in paragraph (1) nevertheless may be sufficient if found to be reasonable by the trier of fact, under paragraph (2). A properly completed sample form of notification in paragraph (5) or in Section 9–614(a)(3) is an example of a notification that would contain the information set forth in paragraph (1). Under paragraph (4), however, no particular phrasing of the notification is required.

§ 9–614. Contents and Form of Notification Before Disposition of Collateral: Consumer-Goods Transaction.

In a consumer-goods transaction, the following rules apply:

(1) A notification of disposition must provide the following information:

(A) the information specified in Section 9–613(1);

(B) a description of any liability for a deficiency of the person to which the notification is sent;

(C) a telephone number from which the amount that must be paid to the secured party to redeem the collateral under Section 9–623 is available; and

(D) a telephone number or mailing address from which additional information concerning the disposition and the obligation secured is available.

(2) A particular phrasing of the notification is not required.

(3) The following form of notification, when completed, provides sufficient information:

[*Name and address of secured party*]

[*Date*]

NOTICE OF OUR PLAN TO SELL PROPERTY

[*Name and address of any obligor who is also a debtor*]

Subject: [*Identification of Transaction*]

We have your [*describe collateral*], because you broke promises in our agreement.

[*For a public disposition:*]
We will sell [*describe collateral*] at public sale. A sale could include a lease or license. The sale will be held as follows:

Date: _____

Time: _____

Place: _____

You may attend the sale and bring bidders if you want.

[*For a private disposition:*]
We will sell [*describe collateral*] at private sale sometime after [*date*]. A sale could include a lease or license.

The money that we get from the sale (after paying our costs) will reduce the amount you owe. If we get less money than you owe, you [*will or will not, as applicable*] still owe us the difference. If we get more money than you owe, you will get the extra money, unless we must pay it to someone else.

You can get the property back at any time before we sell it by paying us the full amount you owe (not just the past due payments), including our expenses. To learn the exact amount you must pay, call us at [*telephone number*].

If you want us to explain to you in writing how we have figured the amount that you owe us, you may call us at [*telephone number*] [or write us at [*secured party's address*]] and request a written explanation. [We will charge you $for the explanation if we sent you another written explanation of the amount you owe us within the last six months.]

If you need more information about the sale call us at [*telephone number*] [or write us at [*secured party's address*]].

We are sending this notice to the following other people who have an interest in [*describe collateral*] or who owe money under your agreement:

[*Names of all other debtors and obligors, if any*]

[End of Form]

(4) A notification in the form of paragraph (3) is sufficient, even if additional information appears at the end of the form.

(5) A notification in the form of paragraph (3) is sufficient, even if it includes errors in information not required by paragraph (1), unless the error is misleading with respect to rights arising under this article.

(6) If a notification under this section is not in the form of paragraph (3), law other than this article determines the effect of including information not required by paragraph (1).

Official Comment

1. **Source.** New.

2. **Notification in Consumer–Goods Transactions.** Paragraph (1) sets forth the information required for a reasonable notification in a consumer-goods transaction. A notification that lacks any of the information set forth in paragraph (1) is insufficient as a matter of law. Compare Section 9–613(2), under which the trier of fact may find a notification to be sufficient even if it lacks some information listed in paragraph (1) of that section.

3. **Safe-Harbor Form of Notification; Errors in Information.** Although paragraph (2) provides that a particular phrasing of a notification is not required, paragraph (3) specifies a safe-harbor form that, when properly completed, satisfies paragraph (1). Paragraphs

(4), (5), and (6) contain special rules applicable to erroneous and additional information. Under paragraph (4), a notification in the safe-harbor form specified in paragraph (3) is not rendered insufficient if it contains additional information at the end of the form. Paragraph (5) provides that non-misleading errors in information contained in a notification are permitted if the safe-harbor form is used *and if the errors are in information not required by paragraph (1)*. Finally, if a notification is in a form other than the paragraph (3) safe-harbor form, other law determines the effect of including in the notification information other than that required by paragraph (1).

§ 9–615. Application of Proceeds of Disposition; Liability for Deficiency and Right to Surplus.

(a) **[Application of proceeds.]** A secured party shall apply or pay over for application the cash proceeds of disposition under Section 9–610 in the following order to:

(1) the reasonable expenses of retaking, holding, preparing for disposition, processing, and disposing, and, to the extent provided for by agreement and not prohibited by law, reasonable attorney's fees and legal expenses incurred by the secured party;

(2) the satisfaction of obligations secured by the security interest or agricultural lien under which the disposition is made;

(3) the satisfaction of obligations secured by any subordinate security interest in or other subordinate lien on the collateral if:

(A) the secured party receives from the holder of the subordinate security interest or other lien an authenticated demand for proceeds before distribution of the proceeds is completed; and

(B) in a case in which a consignor has an interest in the collateral, the subordinate security interest or other lien is senior to the interest of the consignor; and

(4) a secured party that is a consignor of the collateral if the secured party receives from the consignor an authenticated demand for proceeds before distribution of the proceeds is completed.

(b) **[Proof of subordinate interest.]** If requested by a secured party, a holder of a subordinate security interest or other lien shall furnish reasonable proof of the interest or lien within a reasonable time. Unless the holder does so, the secured party need not comply with the holder's demand under subsection (a)(3).

(c) **[Application of noncash proceeds.]** A secured party need not apply or pay over for application noncash proceeds of disposition under Section 9–610 unless the failure to do so would be commercially unreasonable. A secured party that applies or pays over for application noncash proceeds shall do so in a commercially reasonable manner.

(d) **[Surplus or deficiency if obligation secured.]** If the security interest under which a disposition is made secures payment or performance of an obligation, after making the payments and applications required by subsection (a) and permitted by subsection (c):

(1) unless subsection (a)(4) requires the secured party to apply or pay over cash proceeds to a consignor, the secured party shall account to and pay a debtor for any surplus; and

(2) the obligor is liable for any deficiency.

(e) **[No surplus or deficiency in sales of certain rights to payment.]** If the underlying transaction is a sale of accounts, chattel paper, payment intangibles, or promissory notes:

(1) the debtor is not entitled to any surplus; and

(2) the obligor is not liable for any deficiency.

(f) **[Calculation of surplus or deficiency in disposition to person related to secured party.]** The surplus or deficiency following a disposition is calculated based on the amount of proceeds that would have been realized in a disposition complying with this part to a transferee other than the secured party, a person related to the secured party, or a secondary obligor if:

(1) the transferee in the disposition is the secured party, a person related to the secured party, or a secondary obligor; and

(2) the amount of proceeds of the disposition is significantly below the range of proceeds that a complying disposition to a person other than the secured party, a person

related to the secured party, or a secondary obligor would have brought.

(g) **[Cash proceeds received by junior secured party.]** A secured party that receives cash proceeds of a disposition in good faith and without knowledge that the receipt violates the rights of the holder of a security interest or other lien that is not subordinate to the security interest or agricultural lien under which the disposition is made:

(1) takes the cash proceeds free of the security interest or other lien;

(2) is not obligated to apply the proceeds of the disposition to the satisfaction of obligations secured by the security interest or other lien; and

(3) is not obligated to account to or pay the holder of the security interest or other lien for any surplus.

As amended in 2000.

Official Comment

1. **Source.** Former Section 9–504(1), (2).

2. **Application of Proceeds.** This section contains the rules governing application of proceeds and the debtor's liability for a deficiency following a disposition of collateral. Subsection (a) sets forth the basic order of application. The proceeds are applied first to the expenses of disposition, second to the obligation secured by the security interest that is being enforced, and third, in the specified circumstances, to interests that are subordinate to that security interest.

Subsections (a) and (d) also address the right of a consignor to receive proceeds of a disposition by a secured party whose interest is senior to that of the consignor. Subsection (a) requires the enforcing secured party to pay excess proceeds first to subordinate secured parties or lienholders whose interests are senior to that of a consignor and, finally, to a consignor. Inasmuch as a consignor is the owner of the collateral, secured parties and lienholders whose interests are junior to the consignor's interest will not be entitled to any proceeds. In like fashion, under subsection (d)(1) the debtor is not entitled to a surplus when the enforcing secured party is required to pay over proceeds to a consignor.

3. **Noncash Proceeds.** Subsection (c) addresses the application of noncash proceeds of a disposition, such as a note or lease. The explanation in Section 9–608, Comment 4, generally applies to this subsection.

Example: A secured party in the business of selling or financing automobiles takes possession of collateral (an automobile) following its debtor's default. The secured party decides to sell the automobile in a private disposition under Section 9–610 and sends appropriate notification under Section 9–611. After undertaking its normal credit investigation and in accordance with its normal credit policies, the secured party sells the automobile on credit, on terms typical of the credit terms normally extended by the secured party in the ordinary course of its business. The automobile stands as collateral for the remaining balance of the price. The noncash proceeds received by the secured party are chattel paper. The secured party may wish to credit its debtor (the assignor) with the principal amount of the chattel paper or may wish to credit the debtor only as and when the payments are made on the chattel paper by the buyer.

Under subsection (c), the secured party is under no duty to apply the noncash proceeds (here, the chattel paper) or their value to the secured obligation unless its failure to do so would be commercially unreasonable. If a secured party elects to apply the chattel paper to the outstanding obligation, however, it must do so in a commercially reasonable manner. The facts in the example indicate that it would be commercially unreasonable for the secured party to fail to apply the value of the chattel paper to the original debtor's secured obligation. Unlike the example in Comment 4 to Section 9–608, the noncash proceeds received in this example are of the type that the secured party regularly generates in the ordinary course of its financing business in nonforeclosure transactions. The original debtor should not be exposed to delay or uncertainty in this situation. Of course, there will be many situations that fall between the examples presented in the Comment to Section 9–608 and in this Comment. This Article leaves their resolution to the court based on the facts of each case.

One would expect that where noncash proceeds are or may be material, the secured party and debtor would agree to more specific standards in an agreement entered into before or after default. The parties may agree to the method of application of noncash proceeds if the method is not manifestly unreasonable. See Section 9–603.

When the secured party is not required to "apply or pay over for application noncash proceeds," the proceeds nonetheless remain collateral subject to this Article. See Section 9–608, Comment 4.

4. **Surplus and Deficiency.** Subsection (d) deals with surplus and deficiency. It revises former Section 9–504(2) by imposing an explicit requirement that the secured party "pay" the debtor for any surplus, while retaining the secured party's duty to "account." Inasmuch as the debtor may not be an obligor, subsection (d) provides that the obligor (not the debtor) is liable for the deficiency. The special rule governing surplus and deficiency when receivables have been sold likewise takes into account the distinction between a debtor and an obligor. Subsection (d) also addresses the situation in which a consignor has an interest that is subordinate to the security interest being enforced.

5. **Collateral Under New Ownership.** When the debtor sells collateral subject to a security interest, the original debtor (creator of the security interest) is no longer a debtor inasmuch as it no longer has a property interest in the collateral; the buyer is the debtor. See Section 9–102. As between the debtor (buyer of the collateral) and the original debtor (seller of the collateral), the debtor (buyer) normally would be entitled to the surplus following a disposition. Subsection (d) therefore requires the secured party to pay the surplus to the debtor (buyer), not to the original debtor (seller) with which it has dealt. But, because this situation typically arises as a result of the debtor's wrongful act, this Article does not expose the secured party to the risk of determining ownership of the collateral. If the secured party does not know about the buyer and accordingly pays the surplus to the original debtor, the exculpatory provisions of this Article exonerate the secured party from liability to the buyer. See Sections 9–605, 9–628(a), (b). If a debtor sells collateral *free* of a security interest, as in a sale to a buyer in ordinary course of business (see Section 9–320(a)), the property is no longer collateral and the buyer is not a debtor.

6. **Certain "Low-Price" Dispositions.** Subsection (f) provides a special method for calculating a deficiency or surplus when the secured party, a person related to the secured party (defined in Section 9–102), or a secondary obligor acquires the collateral at a foreclosure disposition. It recognizes that when the foreclosing secured party or a related party is the transferee of the collateral, the secured party sometimes lacks the incentive to maximize the proceeds of disposition. As a consequence, the disposition may comply with the procedural requirements of this Article (e.g., it is conducted in a commercially reasonable manner following reasonable notice) but nevertheless fetch a low price.

Subsection (f) adjusts for this lack of incentive. If the proceeds of a disposition of collateral to a secured party, a person related to the secured party, or a secondary obligor are "significantly below the range of proceeds that a complying disposition to a person other than the secured party, a person related to the secured party, or a secondary obligor would have brought," then instead of calculating a deficiency (or surplus) based on the actual net proceeds, the calculation is based upon the amount that would have been received in a commercially reasonable disposition to a person other than the secured party, a person related to the secured party, or a secondary obligor. Subsection (f) thus rejects the view that the secured party's receipt of such a price necessarily constitutes noncompliance with Part 6. However, such a price may suggest the need for greater judicial scrutiny. See Section 9-610, Comment 10.

7. **"Person Related To."** Section 9-102 defines "person related to." That term is a key element of the system provided in subsection (f) for low-price dispositions. One part of the definition applies when the secured party is an individual, and the other applies when the secured party is an organization. The definition is patterned closely on the corresponding definition in Section 1.301(32) of the Uniform Consumer Credit Code.

§ 9-616. Explanation of Calculation of Surplus or Deficiency.

(a) **[Definitions.]** In this section:

(1) "Explanation" means a writing that:

(A) states the amount of the surplus or deficiency;

(B) provides an explanation in accordance with subsection (c) of how the secured party calculated the surplus or deficiency;

(C) states, if applicable, that future debits, credits, charges, including additional credit service charges or interest, rebates, and expenses may affect the amount of the surplus or deficiency; and

(D) provides a telephone number or mailing address from which additional information concerning the transaction is available.

(2) "Request" means a record:

(A) authenticated by a debtor or consumer obligor;

(B) requesting that the recipient provide an explanation; and

(C) sent after disposition of the collateral under Section 9-610.

(b) **[Explanation of calculation.]** In a consumer-goods transaction in which the debtor is entitled to a surplus or a consumer obligor is liable for a deficiency under Section 9-615, the secured party shall:

(1) send an explanation to the debtor or consumer obligor, as applicable, after the disposition and:

(A) before or when the secured party accounts to the debtor and pays any surplus or first makes written demand on the consumer obligor after the disposition for payment of the deficiency; and

(B) within 14 days after receipt of a request; or

(2) in the case of a consumer obligor who is liable for a deficiency, within 14 days after receipt of a request, send to the consumer obligor a record waiving the secured party's right to a deficiency.

(c) **[Required information.]** To comply with subsection (a)(1)(B), a writing must provide the following information in the following order:

(1) the aggregate amount of obligations secured by the security interest under which the disposition was made, and, if the amount reflects a rebate of unearned interest or credit service charge, an indication of that fact, calculated as of a specified date:

(A) if the secured party takes or receives possession of the collateral after default, not more than 35 days before the secured party takes or receives possession; or

(B) if the secured party takes or receives possession of the collateral before default or does not take possession of the collateral, not more than 35 days before the disposition;

(2) the amount of proceeds of the disposition;

(3) the aggregate amount of the obligations after deducting the amount of proceeds;

(4) the amount, in the aggregate or by type, and types of expenses, including expenses of retaking, holding, preparing for disposition, processing, and disposing of the col-

lateral, and attorney's fees secured by the collateral which are known to the secured party and relate to the current disposition;

(5) the amount, in the aggregate or by type, and types of credits, including rebates of interest or credit service charges, to which the obligor is known to be entitled and which are not reflected in the amount in paragraph (1); and

(6) the amount of the surplus or deficiency.

(d) **[Substantial compliance.]** A particular phrasing of the explanation is not required. An explanation complying substantially with the requirements of subsection (a) is sufficient, even if it includes minor errors that are not seriously misleading.

(e) **[Charges for responses.]** A debtor or consumer obligor is entitled without charge to one response to a request under this section during any six-month period in which the secured party did not send to the debtor or consumer obligor an explanation pursuant to subsection (b)(1). The secured party may require payment of a charge not exceeding $25 for each additional response.

Official Comment

1. **Source.** New.

2. **Duty to Send Information Concerning Surplus or Deficiency.** This section reflects the view that, in every consumer-goods transaction, the debtor or obligor is entitled to know the amount of a surplus or deficiency and the basis upon which the surplus or deficiency was calculated. Under subsection (b)(1), a secured party is obligated to provide this information (an "explanation," defined in subsection (a)(1)) no later than the time that it accounts for and pays a surplus or the time of its first written attempt to collect the deficiency. The obligor need not make a request for an accounting in order to receive an explanation. A secured party who does not attempt to collect a deficiency in writing or account for and pay a surplus has no obligation to send an explanation under subsection (b)(1) and, consequently, cannot be liable for noncompliance.

A debtor or secondary obligor need not wait until the secured party commences written collection efforts in order to receive an explanation of how a deficiency or surplus was calculated. Subsection (b)(2) obliges the secured party to send an explanation within 14 days

after it receives a "request" (defined in subsection (a)(2)).

3. **Explanation of Calculation of Surplus or Deficiency.** Subsection (c) contains the requirements for how a calculation of a surplus or deficiency must be explained in order to satisfy subsection (a)(1)(B). It gives a secured party some discretion concerning rebates of interest or credit service charges. The secured party may include these rebates in the aggregate amount of obligations secured, under subsection (c)(1), or may include them with other types of rebates and credits under subsection (c)(5). Rebates of interest or credit service charges are the only types of rebates for which this discretion is provided. If the secured party provides an explanation that includes rebates of precomputed interest, its explanation must so indicate. The expenses and attorney's fees to be described pursuant to subsection (c)(4) are those relating to the most recent disposition, not those that may have been incurred in connection with earlier enforcement efforts and which have been resolved by the parties.

4. **Liability for Noncompliance.** A secured party who fails to comply with subsection (b)(2) is liable for any loss caused plus $500. See Section 9–625(b), (c), (e)(6). A secured party who fails to send an explanation under subsection (b)(1) is liable for any loss caused plus, if the noncompliance was "part of a pattern, or consistent with a practice of noncompliance," $500. See Section 9–625(b), (c), (e)(5). However, a secured party who fails to comply with this section is not liable for statutory minimum damages under Section 9–625(c)(2). See Section 9–628(d).

§ 9–617. Rights of Transferee of Collateral.

(a) **[Effects of disposition.]** A secured party's disposition of collateral after default:

(1) transfers to a transferee for value all of the debtor's rights in the collateral;

(2) discharges the security interest under which the disposition is made; and

(3) discharges any subordinate security interest or other subordinate lien [other than liens created under [cite acts or statutes providing for liens, if any, that are not to be discharged]].

(b) **[Rights of good-faith transferee.]** A transferee that acts in good faith takes free of the rights and interests described in subsection (a), even if the secured party fails to comply with this article or the requirements of any judicial proceeding.

(c) **[Rights of other transferee.]** If a transferee does not take free of the rights and interests described in subsection (a), the transferee takes the collateral subject to:

(1) the debtor's rights in the collateral;

(2) the security interest or agricultural lien under which the disposition is made; and

(3) any other security interest or other lien.

Official Comment

1. **Source.** Former Section 9–504(4).

2. **Title Taken by Good–Faith Transferee.** Subsection (a) sets forth the rights acquired by persons who qualify under subsection (b)—transferees who act in good faith. Such a person is a "transferee," inasmuch as a buyer at a foreclosure sale does not meet the definition of "purchaser" in Section 1–201 (the transfer is not, vis-a-vis the debtor, "voluntary"). By virtue of the expanded definition of the term "debtor" in Section 9–102, subsection (a) makes clear that the ownership interest of a person who bought the collateral subject to the security interest is terminated by a subsequent disposition under this Part. Such a person is a debtor under this Article. Under former Article 9, the result arguably was the same, but the statute was less clear. Under subsection (a), a disposition normally discharges the security interest being foreclosed and any subordinate security interests and other liens.

A disposition has the effect specified in subsection (a), even if the secured party fails to comply with this Article. An aggrieved person (e.g., the holder of a subordinate security interest to whom a notification required by Section 9–611 was not sent) has a right to recover any loss under Section 9–625(b).

3. **Unitary Standard in Public and Private Dispositions.** Subsection (b) now contains a unitary standard that applies to transferees in both private and public dispositions—acting in good faith. However, this change from former Section 9–504(4) should not be interpreted to mean that a transferee acts in good faith even though it has knowledge of defects or buys in collusion, standards applicable to public dispositions under the former section. Properly understood, those standards were specific examples of the absence of good faith.

4. **Title Taken by Nonqualifying Transferee.** Subsection (c) specifies the consequences for a transferee who does not qualify for protection under subsections (a) and (b) (i.e., a transferee who does not act in

good faith). The transferee takes subject to the rights of the debtor, the enforcing secured party, and other security interests or other liens.

§ 9–618.   Rights and Duties of Certain Secondary Obligors.

(a) **[Rights and duties of secondary obligor.]** A secondary obligor acquires the rights and becomes obligated to perform the duties of the secured party after the secondary obligor:

(1) receives an assignment of a secured obligation from the secured party;

(2) receives a transfer of collateral from the secured party and agrees to accept the rights and assume the duties of the secured party; or

(3) is subrogated to the rights of a secured party with respect to collateral.

(b) **[Effect of assignment, transfer, or subrogation.]** An assignment, transfer, or subrogation described in subsection (a):

(1) is not a disposition of collateral under Section 9–610; and

(2) relieves the secured party of further duties under this article.

Official Comment

1. **Source.** Former Section 9–504(5).

2. **Scope of This Section.** Under this section, assignments of secured obligations and other transactions (regardless of form) that function like assignments of secured obligations are not dispositions to which Part 6 applies. Rather, they constitute assignments of rights and (occasionally) delegations of duties. Application of this section may require an investigation into the agreement of the parties, which may not be reflected in the words of the repurchase agreement (e.g., when the agreement requires a recourse party to "purchase the collateral" but contemplates that the purchaser will then conduct an Article 9 foreclosure disposition).

This section, like former Section 9–504(5), does not constitute a general and comprehensive rule for allocating rights and duties upon assignment of a secured obligation. Rather, it applies only in situations involving a secondary obligor described in subsection (a). In other contexts, the agreement of the parties and applicable law other than Article 9 determine whether the assignment imposes upon the assignee any duty to the debtor and whether the assignor retains its duties to the debtor after the assignment.

Subsection (a)(1) applies when there has been an assignment of an obligation that is secured at the time it is assigned. Thus, if a secondary obligor acquires the collateral at a disposition under Section 9–610 and simultaneously or subsequently discharges the unsecured deficiency claim, subsection (a)(1) is not implicated. Similarly, subsection (a)(3) applies only when the secondary obligor is subrogated to the secured party's rights with respect to collateral. Thus, this subsection will not be implicated if a secondary obligor discharges the debtor's unsecured obligation for a post-disposition deficiency. Similarly, if the secured party disposes of some of the collateral and the secondary obligor thereafter discharges the remaining obligation, subsection (a) applies only with respect to rights and duties concerning the remaining collateral, and, under subsection (b), the subrogation is not a disposition *of the remaining collateral*.

As discussed more fully in Comment 3, a secondary obligor may receive a transfer of collateral in a disposition under Section 9–610 in exchange for a payment that is applied against the secured obligation. However, a secondary obligor who pays and receives a transfer of collateral does not necessarily become subrogated to the rights of the secured party as contemplated by subsection (a)(3). Only to the extent the secondary obligor makes a payment in satisfaction of its secondary obligation would it become subrogated. To the extent its payment constitutes the price of the collateral in a Section 9–610 disposition by the secured party, the secondary obligor would not be subrogated. Thus, if the amount paid by the secondary obligor for the collateral in a Section 9–610 disposition is itself insufficient to discharge the secured obligation, but the secondary obligor makes an additional payment that satisfies the remaining balance, the secondary obligor would be subrogated to the secured party's deficiency claim. However, the duties of the secured party *as such* would have come to an end with respect to that collateral. In some situations the capacity in which the payment is made may be unclear. Accordingly, the parties should in their relationship provide clear evidence of the nature and circumstances of the payment by the secondary obligor.

3. **Transfer of Collateral to Secondary Obligor.** It is possible for a secured party to transfer collateral to a secondary obligor in a transaction that is a disposition under Section 9–610 and that establishes a surplus or deficiency under Section 9–615. Indeed, this Article includes a special rule, in Section 9–615(f), for establishing a deficiency in the case of some disposi-

tions to, *inter alia*, secondary obligors. This Article rejects the view, which some may have ascribed to former Section 9–504(5), that a transfer of collateral to a recourse party can *never* constitute a disposition of collateral which discharges a security interest. Inasmuch as a secured party could itself buy collateral at its own public sale, it makes no sense to prohibit a recourse party ever from buying at the sale.

4. **Timing and Scope of Obligations.** Under subsection (a), a recourse party acquires rights and incurs obligations only "after" one of the specified circumstances occurs. This makes clear that when a successor assignee, transferee, or subrogee becomes obligated it does not assume any liability for earlier actions or inactions of the secured party whom it has succeeded unless it agrees to do so. Once the successor becomes obligated, however, it is responsible for complying with the secured party's duties thereafter. For example, if the successor is in possession of collateral, then it has the duties specified in Section 9–207.

Under subsection (b), the same event (assignment, transfer, or subrogation) that gives rise to rights to, and imposes obligations on, a successor relieves its predecessor of any further duties under this Article. For example, if the security interest is enforced after the secured obligation is assigned, the assignee—but not the assignor—has the duty to comply with this Part. Similarly, the assignment does not excuse the assignor from liability for failure to comply with duties that arose before the event or impose liability on the assignee for the assignor's failure to comply.

§ 9–619. Transfer of Record or Legal Title.

(a) [**"Transfer statement."**] In this section, "transfer statement" means a record authenticated by a secured party stating:

(1) that the debtor has defaulted in connection with an obligation secured by specified collateral;

(2) that the secured party has exercised its post-default remedies with respect to the collateral;

(3) that, by reason of the exercise, a transferee has acquired the rights of the debtor in the collateral; and

(4) the name and mailing address of the secured party, debtor, and transferee.

(b) [**Effect of transfer statement.**] A transfer statement entitles the transferee to the transfer of record of all rights of the debtor in the collateral specified in the statement in any official filing, recording, registration, or certificate-of-title system covering the collateral. If a transfer statement is presented with the applicable fee and request form to the official or office responsible for maintaining the system, the official or office shall:

(1) accept the transfer statement;

(2) promptly amend its records to reflect the transfer; and

(3) if applicable, issue a new appropriate certificate of title in the name of the transferee.

(c) [**Transfer not a disposition; no relief of secured party's duties.**] A transfer of the record or legal title to collateral to a secured party under subsection (b) or otherwise is not of itself a disposition of collateral under this article and does not of itself relieve the secured party of its duties under this article.

Official Comment

1. **Source.** New.

2. **Transfer of Record or Legal Title.** Potential buyers of collateral that is covered by a certificate of title (e.g., an automobile) or is subject to a registration system (e.g., a copyright) typically require as a condition of their purchase that the certificate or registry reflect their ownership. In many cases, this condition can be met only with the consent of the record owner. If the record owner is the debtor and, as may be the case after the default, the debtor refuses to cooperate, the secured party may have great difficulty disposing of the collateral.

Subsection (b) provides a simple mechanism for obtaining record or legal title, for use primarily when other law does not provide one. Of course, use of this mechanism will not be effective to clear title to the extent that subsection (b) is preempted by federal law. Subsection (b) contemplates a transfer of record or legal title to a third party, following a secured party's exercise of its disposition or acceptance remedies under this Part, as well as a transfer by a debtor to a secured party prior to the secured party's exercise of those remedies. Under subsection (c), a transfer of record or legal title (under subsection (b) or under other law) to a secured party prior to the exercise of those remedies merely puts the secured party in a position to pass legal or record title to a transferee at foreclosure. A secured party who has obtained record or legal title retains its duties with respect to enforcement of its

security interest, and the debtor retains its rights as well.

3. **Title-Clearing Systems Under Other Law.** Applicable non-UCC law (e.g., a certificate-of-title statute, federal registry rules, or the like) may provide a means by which the secured party may obtain or transfer record or legal title for the purpose of a disposition of the property under this Article. The mechanism provided by this section is in addition to any title-clearing provision under law other than this Article.

§ 9–620. Acceptance of Collateral in Full or Partial Satisfaction of Obligation; Compulsory Disposition of Collateral.

(a) [**Conditions to acceptance in satisfaction.**] Except as otherwise provided in subsection (g), a secured party may accept collateral in full or partial satisfaction of the obligation it secures only if:

(1) the debtor consents to the acceptance under subsection (c);

(2) the secured party does not receive, within the time set forth in subsection (d), a notification of objection to the proposal authenticated by:

(A) a person to which the secured party was required to send a proposal under Section 9–621; or

(B) any other person, other than the debtor, holding an interest in the collateral subordinate to the security interest that is the subject of the proposal;

(3) if the collateral is consumer goods, the collateral is not in the possession of the debtor when the debtor consents to the acceptance; and

(4) subsection (e) does not require the secured party to dispose of the collateral or the debtor waives the requirement pursuant to Section 9–624.

(b) [**Purported acceptance ineffective.**] A purported or apparent acceptance of collateral under this section is ineffective unless:

(1) the secured party consents to the acceptance in an authenticated record or sends a proposal to the debtor; and

(2) the conditions of subsection (a) are met.

(c) **[Debtor's consent.]** For purposes of this section:

(1) a debtor consents to an acceptance of collateral in partial satisfaction of the obligation it secures only if the debtor agrees to the terms of the acceptance in a record authenticated after default; and

(2) a debtor consents to an acceptance of collateral in full satisfaction of the obligation it secures only if the debtor agrees to the terms of the acceptance in a record authenticated after default or the secured party:

(A) sends to the debtor after default a proposal that is unconditional or subject only to a condition that collateral not in the possession of the secured party be preserved or maintained;

(B) in the proposal, proposes to accept collateral in full satisfaction of the obligation it secures; and

(C) does not receive a notification of objection authenticated by the debtor within 20 days after the proposal is sent.

(d) **[Effectiveness of notification.]** To be effective under subsection (a)(2), a notification of objection must be received by the secured party:

(1) in the case of a person to which the proposal was sent pursuant to Section 9–621, within 20 days after notification was sent to that person; and

(2) in other cases:

(A) within 20 days after the last notification was sent pursuant to Section 9–621; or

(B) if a notification was not sent, before the debtor consents to the acceptance under subsection (c).

(e) **[Mandatory disposition of consumer goods.]** A secured party that has taken possession of collateral shall dispose of the collateral pursuant to Section 9–610 within the time specified in subsection (f) if:

(1) 60 percent of the cash price has been paid in the case of a purchase-money security interest in consumer goods; or

(2) 60 percent of the principal amount of the obligation secured has been paid in the case of a non-purchase-money security interest in consumer goods.

(f) **[Compliance with mandatory disposition requirement.]** To comply with subsection (e), the secured party shall dispose of the collateral:

(1) within 90 days after taking possession; or

(2) within any longer period to which the debtor and all secondary obligors have agreed in an agreement to that effect entered into and authenticated after default.

(g) **[No partial satisfaction in consumer transaction.]** In a consumer transaction, a secured party may not accept collateral in partial satisfaction of the obligation it secures.

Official Comment

1. **Source.** Former Section 9–505.

2. **Overview.** This section and the two sections following deal with strict foreclosure, a procedure by which the secured party acquires the debtor's interest in the collateral without the need for a sale or other disposition under Section 9–610. Although these provisions derive from former Section 9–505, they have been entirely reorganized and substantially rewritten. The more straightforward approach taken in this Article eliminates the fiction that the secured party always will present a "proposal" for the retention of collateral and the debtor will have a fixed period to respond. By eliminating the need (but preserving the possibility) for proceeding in that fashion, this section eliminates much of the awkwardness of former Section 9–505. It reflects the belief that strict foreclosures should be encouraged and often will produce better results than a disposition for all concerned.

Subsection (a) sets forth the conditions necessary to an effective acceptance (formerly, retention) of collateral in full or partial satisfaction of the secured obligation. Section 9–621 requires in addition that a secured party who wishes to proceed under this section notify certain other persons who have or claim to have an interest in the collateral. Unlike the failure to meet the conditions in subsection (a), under Section 9–622(b) the failure to comply with the notification requirement of Section 9–621 does not render the acceptance of collateral ineffective. Rather, the acceptance can take effect notwithstanding the secured party's noncompliance. A person to whom the required notice was not sent has the right to recover damages under Section 9–625(b). Section 9–622(a) sets forth the effect of an acceptance of collateral.

3. **Conditions to Effective Acceptance.** Subsection (a) contains the conditions necessary to the effectiveness of an acceptance of collateral. Subsection (a)(1) requires the debtor's consent. Under subsections (c)(1) and (c)(2), the debtor may consent by agreeing to the acceptance in writing after default. Subsection (c)(2) contains an alternative method by which to satisfy the debtor's-consent condition in subsection (a)(1). It follows the proposal-and-objection model found in former Section 9–505: The debtor consents if the secured party sends a proposal to the debtor and does not receive an objection within 20 days. Under subsection (c)(1), however, that silence is not deemed to be consent with respect to acceptances in partial satisfaction. Thus, a secured party who wishes to conduct a "partial strict foreclosure" must obtain the debtor's agreement in a record authenticated after default. In all other respects, the conditions necessary to an effective partial strict foreclosure are the same as those governing acceptance of collateral in full satisfaction. (But see subsection (g), prohibiting partial strict foreclosure of a security interest in consumer transactions.)

The time when a debtor consents to a strict foreclosure is significant in several circumstances under this section and the following one. See Sections 9–620(a)(1), (d)(2), 9–621(a)(1), (a)(2), (a)(3). For purposes of determining the time of consent, a debtor's conditional consent constitutes consent.

Subsection (a)(2) contains the second condition to the effectiveness of an acceptance under this section—the absence of a timely objection from a person holding a junior interest in the collateral or from a secondary obligor. Any junior party—secured party or lienholder—is entitled to lodge an objection to a proposal, even if that person was not entitled to notification under Section 9–621. Subsection (d), discussed below, indicates when an objection is timely.

Subsections (a)(3) and (a)(4) contain special rules for transactions in which consumers are involved. See Comment 12.

4. **Proposals.** Section 9–102 defines the term "proposal." It is necessary to send a "proposal" to the debtor only if the debtor does not agree to an acceptance in an authenticated record as described in subsection (c)(1) or (c)(2). Section 9–621(a) determines whether it is necessary to send a proposal to third parties. A proposal need not take any particular form as long as it sets forth the terms under which the secured party is willing to accept collateral in satisfaction. A proposal to accept collateral should specify the amount (or a means of calculating the amount, such as by including a per diem accrual figure) of the secured obligations to be satisfied, state the conditions (if any) under which the proposal may be revoked, and describe any other applicable conditions. Note, however, that a conditional proposal generally requires the debtor's agreement in order to take effect. See subsection (c).

5. **Secured Party's Agreement; No "Constructive" Strict Foreclosure.** The conditions of subsection (a) relate to actual or implied consent by the debtor and any secondary obligor or holder of a junior security interest or lien. To ensure that the debtor cannot unilaterally cause an acceptance of collateral, subsection (b) provides that compliance with these conditions is necessary but not sufficient to cause an acceptance of collateral. Rather, under subsection (b), acceptance does not occur unless, in addition, the secured party consents to the acceptance in an authenticated record or sends to the debtor a proposal. For this reason, a mere delay in collection or disposition of collateral does not constitute a "constructive" strict foreclosure. Instead, delay is a factor relating to whether the secured party acted in a commercially reasonable manner for purposes of Section 9–607 or 9–610. A debtor's voluntary surrender of collateral to a secured party and the secured party's acceptance of possession of the collateral does not, of itself, necessarily raise an implication that the secured party intends or is proposing to accept the collateral in satisfaction of the secured obligation under this section.

6. **When Acceptance Occurs.** This section does not impose any formalities or identify any steps that a secured party must take in order to accept collateral once the conditions of subsections (a) and (b) have been met. Absent facts or circumstances indicating a contrary intention, the fact that the conditions have been met provides a sufficient indication that the secured party has accepted the collateral on the terms to which the secured party has consented or proposed and the debtor has consented or failed to object. Following a proposal, acceptance of the collateral normally is automatic upon the secured party's becoming bound and the time for objection passing. As a matter of good business practice, an enforcing secured party may wish to memorialize its acceptance following a proposal, such as by notifying the debtor that the strict foreclosure is effective or by placing a written record to that effect in its files. The secured party's agreement to accept collateral is self-executing and cannot be breached. The secured party is bound by its agreement to accept collateral and by any proposal to which the debtor consents.

7. **No Possession Requirement.** This section eliminates the requirement in former Section 9–505

that the secured party be "in possession" of collateral. It clarifies that intangible collateral, which cannot be possessed, may be subject to a strict foreclosure under this section. However, under subsection (a)(3), if the collateral is consumer goods, acceptance does not occur unless the debtor is not in possession.

8. **When Objection Timely.** Subsection (d) explains when an objection is timely and thus prevents an acceptance of collateral from taking effect. An objection by a person to which notification was sent under Section 9–621 is effective if it is received by the secured party within 20 days from the date the notification was sent to that person. Other objecting parties (i.e., third parties who are not entitled to notification) may object at any time within 20 days after the last notification is sent under Section 9–621. If no such notification is sent, third parties must object before the debtor agrees to the acceptance in writing or is deemed to have consented by silence. The former may occur any time after default, and the latter requires a 20–day waiting period. See subsection (c).

9. **Applicability of Other Law.** This section does not purport to regulate all aspects of the transaction by which a secured party may become the owner of collateral previously owned by the debtor. For example, a secured party's acceptance of a motor vehicle in satisfaction of secured obligations may require compliance with the applicable motor vehicle certificate-of-title law. State legislatures should conform those laws so that they mesh well with this section and Section 9–610, and courts should construe those laws and this section harmoniously. A secured party's acceptance of collateral in the possession of the debtor also may implicate statutes dealing with a seller's retention of possession of goods sold.

10. **Accounts, Chattel Paper, Payment Intangibles, and Promissory Notes.** If the collateral is accounts, chattel paper, payment intangibles, or promissory notes, then a secured party's acceptance of the collateral in satisfaction of secured obligations would constitute a sale to the secured party. That sale normally would give rise to a new security interest (the ownership interest) under Sections 1–201(37) and 9–109. In the case of accounts and chattel paper, the new security interest would remain perfected by a filing that was effective to perfect the secured party's original security interest. In the case of payment intangibles or promissory notes, the security interest would be perfected when it attaches. See Section 9–309. However, the procedures for acceptance of collateral under this section satisfy all necessary formalities and a new security agreement authenticated by the debtor would not be necessary.

11. **Role of Good Faith.** Section 1–203 imposes an obligation of good faith on a secured party's enforcement under this Article. This obligation may not be disclaimed by agreement. See Section 1–102. Thus, a proposal and acceptance made under this section in bad faith would not be effective. For example, a secured party's proposal to accept marketable securities worth $1,000 in full satisfaction of indebtedness in the amount of $100, made in the hopes that the debtor might inadvertently fail to object, would be made in bad faith. On the other hand, in the normal case proposals and acceptances should be not second-guessed on the basis of the "value" of the collateral involved. Disputes about valuation or even a clear excess of collateral value over the amount of obligations satisfied do not necessarily demonstrate the absence of good faith.

12. **Special Rules in Consumer Cases.** Subsection (e) imposes an obligation on the secured party to dispose of consumer goods under certain circumstances. Subsection (f) explains when a disposition that is required under subsection (e) is timely. An effective acceptance of collateral cannot occur if subsection (e) requires a disposition unless the debtor waives this requirement pursuant to Section 9–624(b). Moreover, a secured party who takes possession of collateral and unreasonably delays disposition violates subsection (e), if applicable, and may also violate Section 9–610 or other provisions of this Part. Subsection (e) eliminates as superfluous the express statutory reference to "conversion" found in former Section 9–505. Remedies available under other law, including conversion, remain available under this Article in appropriate cases. See Sections 1–103, 1–106.

Subsection (g) prohibits the secured party in consumer transactions from accepting collateral in partial satisfaction of the obligation it secures. If a secured party attempts an acceptance in partial satisfaction in a consumer transaction, the attempted acceptance is void.

§ 9–621. Notification of Proposal to Accept Collateral.

(a) **[Persons to which proposal to be sent.]** A secured party that desires to accept collateral in full or partial satisfaction of the obligation it secures shall send its proposal to:

(1) any person from which the secured party has received, before the debtor consented to the acceptance, an authenticated notifi-

cation of a claim of an interest in the collateral;

(2) any other secured party or lienholder that, 10 days before the debtor consented to the acceptance, held a security interest in or other lien on the collateral perfected by the filing of a financing statement that:

(A) identified the collateral;

(B) was indexed under the debtor's name as of that date; and

(C) was filed in the office or offices in which to file a financing statement against the debtor covering the collateral as of that date; and

(3) any other secured party that, 10 days before the debtor consented to the acceptance, held a security interest in the collateral perfected by compliance with a statute, regulation, or treaty described in Section 9–311(a).

(b) **[Proposal to be sent to secondary obligor in partial satisfaction.]** A secured party that desires to accept collateral in partial satisfaction of the obligation it secures shall send its proposal to any secondary obligor in addition to the persons described in subsection (a).

Official Comment

1. **Source.** Former Section 9–505.

2. **Notification Requirement.** Subsection (a) specifies three classes of competing claimants to whom the secured party must send notification of its proposal: (i) those who notify the secured party that they claim an interest in the collateral, (ii) holders of certain security interests and liens who have filed against the debtor, and (iii) holders of certain security interests who have perfected by compliance with a statute (including a certificate-of-title statute), regulation, or treaty described in Section 9–311(a). With regard to (ii), see Section 9–611, Comment 4. Subsection (b) also requires notification to any secondary obligor if the proposal is for acceptance in partial satisfaction.

Unlike Section 9–611, this section contains no "safe harbor," which excuses an enforcing secured party from notifying certain secured parties and other lienholders. This is because, unlike Section 9–610, which requires that a disposition of collateral be commercially reasonable, Section 9–620 permits the debtor and secured party to set the amount of credit the debtor will

receive for the collateral subject only to the requirement of good faith. An effective acceptance discharges subordinate security interests and other subordinate liens. See Section 9–622. If collateral is subject to several liens securing debts much larger than the value of the collateral, the debtor may be disinclined to refrain from consenting to an acceptance by the holder of the senior security interest, even though, had the debtor objected and the senior disposed of the collateral under Section 9–610, the collateral may have yielded more than enough to satisfy the senior security interest (but not enough to satisfy all the liens). Accordingly, this section imposes upon the enforcing secured party the risk of the filing office's errors and delay. The holder of a security interest who is entitled to notification under this section but does not receive it has the right to recover under Section 9–625(b) any loss resulting from the enforcing secured party's noncompliance with this section.

§ 9–622.   Effect of Acceptance of Collateral.

(a) **[Effect of acceptance.]** A secured party's acceptance of collateral in full or partial satisfaction of the obligation it secures:

(1) discharges the obligation to the extent consented to by the debtor;

(2) transfers to the secured party all of a debtor's rights in the collateral;

(3) discharges the security interest or agricultural lien that is the subject of the debtor's consent and any subordinate security interest or other subordinate lien; and

(4) terminates any other subordinate interest.

(b) **[Discharge of subordinate interest notwithstanding noncompliance.]** A subordinate interest is discharged or terminated under subsection (a), even if the secured party fails to comply with this article.

Official Comment

1. **Source.** New.

2. **Effect of Acceptance.** Subsection (a) specifies the effect of an acceptance of collateral in full or partial satisfaction of the secured obligation. The acceptance to which it refers is an effective acceptance. If a purported acceptance is ineffective under Section 9–620, e.g., because the secured party receives a timely objection from a person entitled to notification, then neither this subsection nor subsection (b) applies. Paragraph

(1) expresses the fundamental consequence of accepting collateral in full or partial satisfaction of the secured obligation—the obligation is discharged to the extent consented to by the debtor. Unless otherwise agreed, the obligor remains liable for any deficiency. Paragraphs (2) through (4) indicate the effects of an acceptance on various property rights and interests. Paragraph (2) follows Section 9–617(a) in providing that the secured party acquires "all of a debtor's rights in the collateral." Under paragraph (3), the effect of strict foreclosure on holders of junior security interests and other liens is the same regardless of whether the collateral is accepted in full or partial satisfaction of the secured obligation: all junior encumbrances are discharged. Paragraph (4) provides for the termination of other subordinate interests.

Subsection (b) makes clear that subordinate interests are discharged under subsection (a) regardless of whether the secured party complies with this Article. Thus, subordinate interests are discharged regardless of whether a proposal was required to be sent or, if required, was sent. However, a secured party's failure to send a proposal or otherwise to comply with this Article may subject the secured party to liability under Section 9–625.

§ 9–623. Right to Redeem Collateral.

(a) **[Persons that may redeem.]** A debtor, any secondary obligor, or any other secured party or lienholder may redeem collateral.

(b) **[Requirements for redemption.]** To redeem collateral, a person shall tender:

(1) fulfillment of all obligations secured by the collateral; and

(2) the reasonable expenses and attorney's fees described in Section 9–615(a)(1).

(c) **[When redemption may occur.]** A redemption may occur at any time before a secured party:

(1) has collected collateral under Section 9–607;

(2) has disposed of collateral or entered into a contract for its disposition under Section 9–610; or

(3) has accepted collateral in full or partial satisfaction of the obligation it secures under Section 9–622.

Official Comment

1. **Source.** Former Section 9–506.

2. **Redemption Right.** Under this section, as under former Section 9–506, the debtor or another secured party may redeem collateral as long as the secured party has not collected (Section 9–607), disposed of or contracted for the disposition of (Section 9–610), or accepted (Section 9–620) the collateral. Although this section generally follows former Section 9–506, it extends the right of redemption to holders of nonconsensual liens. To redeem the collateral a person must tender fulfillment of all obligations secured, plus certain expenses. If the entire balance of a secured obligation has been accelerated, it would be necessary to tender the entire balance. A tender of fulfillment obviously means more than a new promise to perform an existing promise. It requires payment in full of all monetary obligations then due and performance in full of all other obligations then matured. If unmatured secured obligations remain, the security interest continues to secure them (i.e., as if there had been no default).

3. **Redemption of Remaining Collateral Following Partial Enforcement.** Under Section 9–610 a secured party may make successive dispositions of portions of its collateral. These dispositions would not affect the debtor's, another secured party's, or a lienholder's right to redeem the remaining collateral.

4. **Effect of "Repledging."** Section 9–207 generally permits a secured party having possession or control of collateral to create a security interest in the collateral. As explained in the Comments to that section, the debtor's right (as opposed to its practical ability) to redeem collateral is not affected by, and does not affect, the priority of a security interest created by the debtor's secured party.

§ 9–624. Waiver.

(a) **[Waiver of disposition notification.]** A debtor or secondary obligor may waive the right to notification of disposition of collateral under Section 9–611 only by an agreement to that effect entered into and authenticated after default.

(b) **[Waiver of mandatory disposition.]** A debtor may waive the right to require disposition of collateral under Section 9–620(e) only by an agreement to that effect entered into and authenticated after default.

(c) **[Waiver of redemption right.]** Except in a consumer-goods transaction, a debtor or secondary obligor may waive the right to redeem collateral under Section 9–623 only by an agreement to that effect entered into and authenticated after default.

Official Comment

1. **Source.** Former Sections 9–504(3), 9–505, 9–506.

2. **Waiver.** This section is a limited exception to Section 9–602, which generally prohibits waiver by debtors and obligors. It makes no provision for waiver of the rule prohibiting a secured party from buying at its own private disposition. Transactions of this kind are equivalent to "strict foreclosures" and are governed by Sections 9–620, 9–621, and 9–622.

[SUBPART 2. NONCOMPLIANCE WITH ARTICLE]

§ 9–625. Remedies for Secured Party's Failure to Comply With Article.

(a) **[Judicial orders concerning noncompliance.]** If it is established that a secured party is not proceeding in accordance with this article, a court may order or restrain collection, enforcement, or disposition of collateral on appropriate terms and conditions.

(b) **[Damages for noncompliance.]** Subject to subsections (c), (d), and (f), a person is liable for damages in the amount of any loss caused by a failure to comply with this article. Loss caused by a failure to comply may include loss resulting from the debtor's inability to obtain, or increased costs of, alternative financing.

(c) **[Persons entitled to recover damages; statutory damages in consumer-goods transaction.]** Except as otherwise provided in Section 9–628:

(1) a person that, at the time of the failure, was a debtor, was an obligor, or held a security interest in or other lien on the collateral may recover damages under subsection (b) for its loss; and

(2) if the collateral is consumer goods, a person that was a debtor or a secondary obligor at the time a secured party failed to comply with this part may recover for that failure in any event an amount not less than the credit service charge plus 10 percent of the principal amount of the obligation or the time-price differential plus 10 percent of the cash price.

(d) **[Recovery when deficiency eliminated or reduced.]** A debtor whose deficiency is eliminated under Section 9–626 may recover damages for the loss of any surplus. However, a debtor or secondary obligor whose deficiency is eliminated or reduced under Section 9–626 may not otherwise recover under subsection (b) for noncompliance with the provisions of this part relating to collection, enforcement, disposition, or acceptance.

(e) **[Statutory damages: noncompliance with specified provisions.]** In addition to any damages recoverable under subsection (b), the debtor, consumer obligor, or person named as a debtor in a filed record, as applicable, may recover $500 in each case from a person that:

(1) fails to comply with Section 9–208;

(2) fails to comply with Section 9–209;

(3) files a record that the person is not entitled to file under Section 9–509(a);

(4) fails to cause the secured party of record to file or send a termination statement as required by Section 9–513(a) or (c);

(5) fails to comply with Section 9–616(b)(1) and whose failure is part of a pattern, or consistent with a practice, of noncompliance; or

(6) fails to comply with Section 9–616(b)(2).

(f) **[Statutory damages: noncompliance with Section 9–210.]** A debtor or consumer obligor may recover damages under subsection (b) and, in addition, $500 in each case from a person that, without reasonable cause, fails to comply with a request under Section 9–210. A recipient of a request under Section 9–210 which never claimed an interest in the collateral or obligations that are the subject of a request under that section has a reasonable excuse for failure to comply with the request within the meaning of this subsection.

(g) **[Limitation of security interest: noncompliance with Section 9–210.]** If a secured party fails to comply with a request regarding a list of collateral or a statement of account under Section 9–210, the secured party may claim a security interest only as shown in the list or statement included in the request as against a person that is reasonably misled by the failure.

As amended in 2000.

Official Comment

1. **Source.** Former Section 9–507.

2. **Remedies for Noncompliance; Scope.** Subsections (a) and (b) provide the basic remedies afforded to those aggrieved by a secured party's failure to comply with this Article. Like all provisions that create liability, they are subject to Section 9–628, which should be read in conjunction with Section 9–605. The principal limitations under this Part on a secured party's right to enforce its security interest against collateral are the requirements that it proceed in good faith (Section 1–203), in a commercially reasonable manner (Sections 9–607 and 9–610), and, in most cases, with reasonable notification (Sections 9–611 through 9–614). Following former Section 9–507, under subsection (a) an aggrieved person may seek injunctive relief, and under subsection (b) the person may recover damages for losses caused by noncompliance. Unlike former Section 9–507, however, subsections (a) and (b) are not limited to noncompliance with provisions of this Part of Article 9. Rather, they apply to noncompliance with any provision of this Article. The change makes this section applicable to noncompliance with Sections 9–207 (duties of secured party in possession of collateral), 9–208 (duties of secured party having control over deposit account), 9–209 (duties of secured party if account debtor has been notified of an assignment), 9–210 (duty to comply with request for accounting, etc.), 9–509(a) (duty to refrain from filing unauthorized financing statement), and 9–513(a) or (c) (duty to provide termination statement). Subsection (a) also modifies the first sentence of former Section 9–507(1) by adding the references to "collection" and "enforcement." Subsection (c)(2), which gives a minimum damage recovery in consumer-goods transactions, applies only to noncompliance with the provisions of this Part.

3. **Damages for Noncompliance with This Article.** Subsection (b) sets forth the basic remedy for failure to comply with the requirements of this Article: a damage recovery in the amount of loss caused by the noncompliance. Subsection (c) identifies who may recover under subsection (b). It affords a remedy to any aggrieved person who is a debtor or obligor. However, a principal obligor who is not a debtor may recover damages only for noncompliance with Section 9–616, inasmuch as none of the other rights and duties in this Article run in favor of such a principal obligor. Such a principal obligor could not suffer any loss or damage on account of noncompliance with rights or duties of which it is not a beneficiary. Subsection (c) also affords a remedy to an aggrieved person who holds a competing security interest or other lien, regardless of whether the aggrieved person is entitled to notification under Part 6. The remedy is available even to holders of senior security interests and other liens. The exercise of this remedy is subject to the normal rules of pleading and proof. A person who has delegated the duties of a secured party but who remains obligated to perform them is liable under this subsection. The last sentence of subsection (d) eliminates the possibility of double recovery or other over-compensation arising out of a reduction or elimination of a deficiency under Section 9–626, based on noncompliance with the provisions of this Part relating to collection, enforcement, disposition, or acceptance. Assuming no double recovery, a debtor whose deficiency is eliminated under Section 9–626 may pursue a claim for a surplus. Because Section 9–626 does not apply to consumer transactions, the statute is silent as to whether a double recovery or other over-compensation is possible in a consumer transaction.

Damages for violation of the requirements of this Article, including Section 9–609, are those reasonably calculated to put an eligible claimant in the position that it would have occupied had no violation occurred. See Section 1–106. Subsection (b) supports the recovery of actual damages for committing a breach of the peace in violation of Section 9–609, and principles of tort law supplement this subsection. See Section 1–103. However, to the extent that damages in tort compensate the debtor for the same loss dealt with by this Article, the debtor should be entitled to only one recovery.

4. **Minimum Damages in Consumer–Goods Transactions.** Subsection (c)(2) provides a minimum, statutory, damage recovery for a debtor and secondary obligor in a consumer-goods transaction. It is patterned on former Section 9–507(1) and is designed to ensure that every noncompliance with the requirements of Part 6 in a consumer-goods transaction results in liability, regardless of any injury that may have resulted. Subsection (c)(2) leaves the treatment of statutory damages as it was under former Article 9. A secured party is not liable for statutory damages under this subsection more than once with respect to any one secured obligation (see Section 9–628(e)), nor is a secured party liable under this subsection for failure to comply with Section 9–616 (see Section 9–628(d)).

Following former Section 9–507(1), this Article does not include a definition or explanation of the terms "credit service charge," "principal amount," "time-price differential," or "cash price," as used in subsection (c)(2). It leaves their construction and application to the court, taking into account the subsection's purpose of providing a minimum recovery in consumer-goods transactions.

5. **Supplemental Damages.** Subsections (e) and (f) provide damages that supplement the recovery, if any, under subsection (b). Subsection (e) imposes an additional $500 liability upon a person who fails to comply with the provisions specified in that subsection, and subsection (f) imposes like damages on a person who, without reasonable excuse, fails to comply with a request for an accounting or a request regarding a list of collateral or statement of account under Section 9–210. However, under subsection (f), a person has a reasonable excuse for the failure if the person never claimed an interest in the collateral or obligations that were the subject of the request.

6. **Estoppel.** Subsection (g) limits the extent to which a secured party who fails to comply with a request regarding a list of collateral or statement of account may claim a security interest.

§ 9–626. Action in Which Deficiency or Surplus Is in Issue.

(a) **[Applicable rules if amount of deficiency or surplus in issue.]** In an action arising from a transaction, other than a consumer transaction, in which the amount of a deficiency or surplus is in issue, the following rules apply:

(1) A secured party need not prove compliance with the provisions of this part relating to collection, enforcement, disposition, or acceptance unless the debtor or a secondary obligor places the secured party's compliance in issue.

(2) If the secured party's compliance is placed in issue, the secured party has the burden of establishing that the collection, enforcement, disposition, or acceptance was conducted in accordance with this part.

(3) Except as otherwise provided in Section 9–628, if a secured party fails to prove that the collection, enforcement, disposition, or acceptance was conducted in accordance with the provisions of this part relating to collection, enforcement, disposition, or acceptance, the liability of a debtor or a secondary obligor for a deficiency is limited to an amount by which the sum of the secured obligation, expenses, and attorney's fees exceeds the greater of:

(A) the proceeds of the collection, enforcement, disposition, or acceptance; or

(B) the amount of proceeds that would have been realized had the noncomplying secured party proceeded in accordance with the provisions of this part relating to collection, enforcement, disposition, or acceptance.

(4) For purposes of paragraph (3)(B), the amount of proceeds that would have been realized is equal to the sum of the secured obligation, expenses, and attorney's fees unless the secured party proves that the amount is less than that sum.

(5) If a deficiency or surplus is calculated under Section 9–615(f), the debtor or obligor has the burden of establishing that the amount of proceeds of the disposition is significantly below the range of prices that a complying disposition to a person other than the secured party, a person related to the secured party, or a secondary obligor would have brought.

(b) **[Non-consumer transactions; no inference.]** The limitation of the rules in subsection (a) to transactions other than consumer transactions is intended to leave to the court the determination of the proper rules in consumer transactions. The court may not infer from that limitation the nature of the proper rule in consumer transactions and may continue to apply established approaches.

Official Comment

1. **Source.** New.

2. **Scope.** The basic damage remedy under Section 9–625(b) is subject to the special rules in this section for transactions other than consumer transactions. This section addresses situations in which the amount of a deficiency or surplus is in issue, i.e., situations in which the secured party has collected, enforced, disposed of, or accepted the collateral. It contains special rules applicable to a determination of the amount of a deficiency or surplus. Because this section affects a person's liability for a deficiency, it is subject to Section 9–628, which should be read in conjunction with Section 9–605. The rules in this section apply only to noncompliance in connection with the "collection, enforcement, disposition, or acceptance" under Part 6. For other types of noncompliance with Part 6, the

general liability rule of Section 9–625(b)—recovery of actual damages—applies. Consider, for example, a repossession that does not comply with Section 9–609 for want of a default. The debtor's remedy is under Section 9–625(b). In a proper case, the secured party also may be liable for conversion under non-UCC law. If the secured party thereafter disposed of the collateral, however, it would violate Section 9–610 at that time, and this section would apply.

3. **Rebuttable Presumption Rule.** Subsection (a) establishes the rebuttable presumption rule for transactions other than consumer transactions. Under paragraph (1), the secured party need not prove compliance with the relevant provisions of this Part as part of its prima facie case. If, however, the debtor or a secondary obligor raises the issue (in accordance with the forum's rules of pleading and practice), then the secured party bears the burden of proving that the collection, enforcement, disposition, or acceptance complied. In the event the secured party is unable to meet this burden, then paragraph (3) explains how to calculate the deficiency. Under this rebuttable presumption rule, the debtor or obligor is to be credited with the greater of the actual proceeds of the disposition or the proceeds that would have been realized had the secured party complied with the relevant provisions. If a deficiency remains, then the secured party is entitled to recover it. The references to "the secured obligation, expenses, and attorney's fees" in paragraphs (3) and (4) embrace the application rules in Sections 9–608(a) and 9–615(a).

Unless the secured party proves that compliance with the relevant provisions would have yielded a smaller amount, under paragraph (4) the amount that a complying collection, enforcement, or disposition would have yielded is deemed to be equal to the amount of the secured obligation, together with expenses and attorney's fees. Thus, the secured party may not recover any deficiency unless it meets this burden.

4. **Consumer Transactions.** Although subsection (a) adopts a version of the rebuttable presumption rule for transactions other than consumer transactions, with certain exceptions Part 6 does not specify the effect of a secured party's noncompliance in consumer transactions. (The exceptions are the provisions for the recovery of damages in Section 9–625.) Subsection (b) provides that the limitation of subsection (a) to transactions other than consumer transactions is intended to leave to the court the determination of the proper rules in consumer transactions. It also instructs the court not to draw any inference from the limitation as to the proper rules for consumer transactions and

leaves the court free to continue to apply established approaches to those transactions.

Courts construing former Section 9–507 disagreed about the consequences of a secured party's failure to comply with the requirements of former Part 5. Three general approaches emerged. Some courts have held that a noncomplying secured party may not recover a deficiency (the "absolute bar" rule). A few courts held that the debtor can offset against a claim to a deficiency all damages recoverable under former Section 9–507 resulting from the secured party's noncompliance (the "offset" rule). A plurality of courts considering the issue held that the noncomplying secured party is barred from recovering a deficiency unless it overcomes a rebuttable presumption that compliance with former Part 5 would have yielded an amount sufficient to satisfy the secured debt. In addition to the nonuniformity resulting from court decisions, some States enacted special rules governing the availability of deficiencies.

5. **Burden of Proof When Section 9–615(f) Applies.** In a non-consumer transaction, subsection (a)(5) imposes upon a debtor or obligor the burden of proving that the proceeds of a disposition are so low that, under Section 9–615(f), the actual proceeds should not serve as the basis upon which a deficiency or surplus is calculated. Were the burden placed on the secured party, then debtors might be encouraged to challenge the price received in every disposition to the secured party, a person related to the secured party, or a secondary obligor.

6. **Delay in Applying This Section.** There is an inevitable delay between the time a secured party engages in a noncomplying collection, enforcement, disposition, or acceptance and the time of a subsequent judicial determination that the secured party did not comply with Part 6. During the interim, the secured party, believing that the secured obligation is larger than it ultimately is determined to be, may continue to enforce its security interest in collateral. If some or all of the secured indebtedness ultimately is discharged under this section, a reasonable application of this section would impose liability on the secured party for the amount of any excess, unwarranted recoveries but would not make the enforcement efforts wrongful.

§ 9–627. Determination of Whether Conduct Was Commercially Reasonable.

(a) **[Greater amount obtainable under other circumstances; no preclusion of commercial reasonableness.]** The fact that a greater amount could have been obtained by a collection, enforcement, disposition, or acceptance at a different time or in a different method from that selected by the secured party is not of itself sufficient to preclude the secured party from establishing that the collection, enforcement, disposition, or acceptance was made in a commercially reasonable manner.

(b) **[Dispositions that are commercially reasonable.]** A disposition of collateral is made in a commercially reasonable manner if the disposition is made:

(1) in the usual manner on any recognized market;

(2) at the price current in any recognized market at the time of the disposition; or

(3) otherwise in conformity with reasonable commercial practices among dealers in the type of property that was the subject of the disposition.

(c) **[Approval by court or on behalf of creditors.]** A collection, enforcement, disposition, or acceptance is commercially reasonable if it has been approved:

(1) in a judicial proceeding;

(2) by a bona fide creditors' committee;

(3) by a representative of creditors; or

(4) by an assignee for the benefit of creditors.

(d) **[Approval under subsection (c) not necessary; absence of approval has no effect.]** Approval under subsection (c) need not be obtained, and lack of approval does not mean that the collection, enforcement, disposition, or acceptance is not commercially reasonable.

Official Comment

1. **Source.** Former Section 9–507(2).

2. **Relationship of Price to Commercial Reasonableness.** Some observers have found the notion contained in subsection (a) (derived from former Section 9–507(2)) (the fact that a better price could have been obtained does not establish lack of commercial reasonableness) to be inconsistent with that found in Section 9–610(b) (derived from former Section 9–504(3)) (every aspect of the disposition, including its terms, must be commercially reasonable). There is no such inconsistency. While not itself sufficient to establish a violation of this Part, a low price suggests that a court should scrutinize carefully all aspects of a disposition to ensure that each aspect was commercially reasonable.

The law long has grappled with the problem of dispositions of personal and real property which comply with applicable procedural requirements (e.g., advertising, notification to interested persons, etc.) but which yield a price that seems low. This Article addresses that issue in Section 9–615(f). That section applies only when the transferee is the secured party, a person related to the secured party, or a secondary obligor. It contains a special rule for calculating a deficiency or surplus in a complying disposition that yields a price that is "significantly below the range of proceeds that a complying disposition to a person other than the secured party, a person related to the secured party, or a secondary obligor would have brought."

3. **Determination of Commercial Reasonableness; Advance Approval.** It is important to make clear the conduct and procedures that are commercially reasonable and to provide a secured party with the means of obtaining, by court order or negotiation with a creditors' committee or a representative of creditors, advance approval of a proposed method of enforcement as commercially reasonable. This section contains rules that assist in that determination and provides for advance approval in appropriate situations. However, none of the specific methods of disposition specified in subsection (b) is required or exclusive.

4. **"Recognized Market."** As in Sections 9–610(c) and 9–611(d), the concept of a "recognized market" in subsections (b)(1) and (2) is quite limited; it applies only to markets in which there are standardized price quotations for property that is essentially fungible, such as stock exchanges.

§ 9–628. Nonliability and Limitation on Liability of Secured Party; Liability of Secondary Obligor.

(a) **[Limitation of liability of secured party for noncompliance with article.]** Unless a secured party knows that a person is a debtor or obligor, knows the identity of the person, and knows how to communicate with the person:

(1) the secured party is not liable to the person, or to a secured party or lienholder that has filed a financing statement against the person, for failure to comply with this article; and

(2) the secured party's failure to comply with this article does not affect the liability of the person for a deficiency.

(b) **[Limitation of liability based on status as secured party.]** A secured party is not liable because of its status as secured party:

(1) to a person that is a debtor or obligor, unless the secured party knows:

(A) that the person is a debtor or obligor;

(B) the identity of the person; and

(C) how to communicate with the person; or

(2) to a secured party or lienholder that has filed a financing statement against a person, unless the secured party knows:

(A) that the person is a debtor; and

(B) the identity of the person.

(c) **[Limitation of liability if reasonable belief that transaction not a consumer-goods transaction or consumer transaction.]** A secured party is not liable to any person, and a person's liability for a deficiency is not affected, because of any act or omission arising out of the secured party's reasonable belief that a transaction is not a consumer-goods transaction or a consumer transaction or that goods are not consumer goods, if the secured party's belief is based on its reasonable reliance on:

(1) a debtor's representation concerning the purpose for which collateral was to be used, acquired, or held; or

(2) an obligor's representation concerning the purpose for which a secured obligation was incurred.

(d) **[Limitation of liability for statutory damages.]** A secured party is not liable to any person under Section 9–625(c)(2) for its failure to comply with Section 9–616.

(e) **[Limitation of multiple liability for statutory damages.]** A secured party is not liable under Section 9–625(c)(2) more than once with respect to any one secured obligation.

Official Comment

1. **Source.** New.

2. **Exculpatory Provisions.** Subsections (a), (b), and (c) contain exculpatory provisions that should be read in conjunction with Section 9–605. Without this group of provisions, a secured party could incur liability to unknown persons and under circumstances that would not allow the secured party to protect itself. The broadened definition of the term "debtor" underscores the need for these provisions.

If a secured party reasonably, but mistakenly, believes that a consumer transaction or consumer-goods transaction is a non-consumer transaction or non-consumer-goods transaction, and if the secured party's belief is based on its reasonable reliance on a representation of the type specified in subsection (c)(1) or (c)(2), then this Article should be applied as if the facts reasonably believed and the representation reasonably relied upon were true. For example, if a secured party reasonably believed that a transaction was a non-consumer transaction and its belief was based on reasonable reliance on the debtor's representation that the collateral secured an obligation incurred for business purposes, the secured party is not liable to any person, and the debtor's liability for a deficiency is not affected, because of any act or omission of the secured party which arises out of the reasonable belief. Of course, if the secured party's belief is not reasonable or, even if reasonable, is not based on reasonable reliance on the debtor's representation, this limitation on liability is inapplicable.

3. **Inapplicability of Statutory Damages to Section 9–616.** Subsection (d) excludes noncompliance with Section 9–616 entirely from the scope of statutory damage liability under Section 9–625(c)(2).

4. **Single Liability for Statutory Minimum Damages.** Subsection (e) ensures that a secured party will incur statutory damages only once in connection with any one secured obligation.

As amended in 2000.

PART 7

TRANSITION

§ 9–701. Effective Date.

This [Act] takes effect on July 1, 2001.

Official Comment

A uniform law as complex as Article 9 necessarily gives rise to difficult problems and uncertainties during the transition to the new law. As is customary for uniform laws, this Article is based on the general assumption that all States will have enacted substantially identical versions. While always important, uniformity is essential to the success of this Article. If former Article 9 is in effect in some jurisdictions, and this Article is in effect in others, horrendous complications may arise. For example, the proper place in which to file to perfect a security interest (and thus the status of a particular security interest as perfected or unperfected) would depend on whether the matter was litigated in a State in which former Article 9 was in effect or a State in which this Article was in effect. Accordingly, this section contemplates that States will adopt a uniform effective date for this Article. Any one State's failure to adopt the uniform effective date will greatly increase the cost and uncertainty surrounding the transition.

Other problems arise from transactions and relationships that were entered into under former Article 9 or under non-UCC law and which remain outstanding on the effective date of this Article. The difficulties arise primarily because this Article expands the scope of former Article 9 to cover additional types of collateral and transactions and because it provides new methods of perfection for some types of collateral, different priority rules, and different choice-of-law rules governing perfection and priority. This Section and the other sections in this Part address primarily this second set of problems.

§ 9–702. Savings Clause.

(a) **[Pre-effective-date transactions or liens.]** Except as otherwise provided in this part, this [Act] applies to a transaction or lien within its scope, even if the transaction or lien was entered into or created before this [Act] takes effect.

(b) **[Continuing validity.]** Except as otherwise provided in subsection (c) and Sections 9–703 through 9–709:

(1) transactions and liens that were not governed by [former Article 9], were validly entered into or created before this [Act] takes effect, and would be subject to this [Act] if they had been entered into or created after this [Act] takes effect, and the rights, duties, and interests flowing from those transactions and liens remain valid after this [Act] takes effect; and

(2) the transactions and liens may be terminated, completed, consummated, and enforced as required or permitted by this

[Act] or by the law that otherwise would apply if this [Act] had not taken effect.

(c) **[Pre-effective-date proceedings.]** This [Act] does not affect an action, case, or proceeding commenced before this [Act] takes effect.

As amended in 2000.

Official Comment

1. **Pre–Effective–Date Transactions.** Subsection (a) contains the general rule that this Article applies to transactions, security interests, and other liens within its scope (see Section 9–109), even if the transaction or lien was entered into or created before the effective date. Thus, secured transactions entered into under former Article 9 must be terminated, completed, consummated, and enforced under this Article. Subsection (b) is an exception to the general rule. It applies to valid, pre-effective-date transactions and liens that were not governed by former Article 9 but would be governed by this Article if they had been entered into or created after this Article takes effect. Under subsection (b), these valid transactions, such as the creation of agricultural liens and security interests in commercial tort claims, retain their validity under this Article and may be terminated, completed, consummated, and enforced under this Article. However, these transactions also may be terminated, completed, consummated, and enforced by the law that otherwise would apply had this Article not taken effect.

2. **Judicial Proceedings Commenced Before Effective Date.** As is usual in transition provisions, subsection (c) provides that this Article does not affect litigation pending on the effective date.

§ 9–703. Security Interest Perfected Before Effective Date.

(a) **[Continuing priority over lien creditor: perfection requirements satisfied.]** A security interest that is enforceable immediately before this [Act] takes effect and would have priority over the rights of a person that becomes a lien creditor at that time is a perfected security interest under this [Act] if, when this [Act] takes effect, the applicable requirements for enforceability and perfection under this [Act] are satisfied without further action.

(b) **[Continuing priority over lien creditor: perfection requirements not satisfied.]** Except as otherwise provided in Section 9–705, if, immediately before this [Act] takes effect, a security interest is enforceable and would have priority over the rights of a person that becomes a lien creditor at that time, but the applicable requirements for enforceability or perfection under this [Act] are not satisfied when this [Act] takes effect, the security interest:

(1) is a perfected security interest for one year after this [Act] takes effect;

(2) remains enforceable thereafter only if the security interest becomes enforceable under Section 9–203 before the year expires; and

(3) remains perfected thereafter only if the applicable requirements for perfection under this [Act] are satisfied before the year expires.

Official Comment

1. **Perfected Security Interests Under Former Article 9 and This Article.** This section deals with security interests that are perfected (i.e., that are enforceable and have priority over the rights of a lien creditor) under former Article 9 or other applicable law immediately before this Article takes effect. Subsection (a) provides, not surprisingly, that if the security interest would be a perfected security interest under this Article (i.e., if the transaction satisfies this Article's requirements for enforceability (attachment) and perfection), no further action need be taken for the security interest to be a perfected security interest.

2. **Security Interests Enforceable and Perfected Under Former Article 9 but Unenforceable or Unperfected Under This Article.** Subsection (b) deals with security interests that are enforceable and perfected under former Article 9 or other applicable law immediately before this Article takes effect but do not satisfy the requirements for enforceability (attachment) or perfection under this Article. Except as otherwise provided in Section 9–705, these security interests are perfected security interests for one year after the effective date. If the security interest satisfies the requirements for attachment and perfection within that period, the security interest remains perfected thereafter. If the security interest satisfies only the requirements for attachment within that period, the security interest becomes unperfected at the end of the one-year period.

Example 1: A pre-effective-date security agreement in a consumer transaction covers "all securities accounts." The security interest is properly perfected. The collateral description was adequate under former Article 9 (see former Section 9–115(3)) but is insufficient under this Article (see Section 9–

108(e)(2)). Unless the debtor authenticates a new security agreement describing the collateral other than by "type" (or Section 9–203(b)(3) otherwise is satisfied) within the one-year period following the effective date, the security interest becomes unenforceable at the end of that period.

Other examples under former Article 9 or other applicable law that may be effective as attachment or enforceability steps but may be ineffective under this Article include an oral agreement to sell a payment intangible or possession by virtue of a notification to a bailee under former Section 9–305. Neither the oral agreement nor the notification would satisfy the revised Section 9–203 requirements for attachment.

Example 2: A pre-effective-date possessory security interest in instruments is perfected by a bailee's receipt of notification under former 9–305. The bailee has not, however, acknowledged that it holds for the secured party's benefit under revised Section 9–313. Unless the bailee authenticates a record acknowledging that it holds for the secured party (or another appropriate perfection step is taken) within the one-year period following the effective date, the security interest becomes unperfected at the end of that period.

3. **Interpretation of Pre–Effective–Date Security Agreements.** Section 9–102 defines "security agreement" as "an agreement that creates or provides for a security interest." Under Section 1–201(3), an "agreement" is a "bargain of the parties in fact." If parties to a pre-effective-date security agreement describe the collateral by using a term defined in former Article 9 in one way and defined in this Article in another way, in most cases it should be presumed that the bargain of the parties contemplated the meaning of the term under former Article 9.

Example 3: A pre-effective-date security agreement covers "all accounts" of a debtor. As defined under former Article 9, an "account" did not include a right to payment for lottery winnings. These rights to payment are "accounts" under this Article, however. The agreement of the parties presumptively created a security interest in "accounts" as defined in former Article 9. A different result might be appropriate, for example, if the security agreement explicitly contemplated future changes in the Article 9 definitions of types of collateral—e.g., " 'Accounts' means 'accounts' as defined in the UCC Article 9 of [State X], *as that definition may be amended from time to time*." Whether a different approach is appropriate in any given case depends on the bargain of the parties, as determined by applying ordinary principles of contract construction.

§ 9–704. Security Interest Unperfected Before Effective Date.

A security interest that is enforceable immediately before this [Act] takes effect but which would be subordinate to the rights of a person that becomes a lien creditor at that time:

(1) remains an enforceable security interest for one year after this [Act] takes effect;

(2) remains enforceable thereafter if the security interest becomes enforceable under Section 9–203 when this [Act] takes effect or within one year thereafter; and

(3) becomes perfected:

(A) without further action, when this [Act] takes effect if the applicable requirements for perfection under this [Act] are satisfied before or at that time; or

(B) when the applicable requirements for perfection are satisfied if the requirements are satisfied after that time.

Official Comment

This section deals with security interests that are enforceable but unperfected (i.e., subordinate to the rights of a person who becomes a lien creditor) under former Article 9 or other applicable law immediately before this Article takes effect. These security interests remain enforceable for one year after the effective date, and thereafter if the appropriate steps for attachment under this Article are taken before the one-year period expires. (This section's treatment of enforceability is the same as that of Section 9–703.) The security interest becomes a perfected security interest on the effective date if, at that time, the security interest satisfies the requirements for perfection under this Article. If the security interest does not satisfy the requirements for perfection until sometime thereafter, it becomes a perfected security interest at that later time.

Example: A security interest has attached under former Article 9 but is unperfected because the filed financing statement covers "all of debtor's personal property" and controlling case law in the applicable jurisdiction has determined that this identification of collateral in a financing statement is insufficient. Upon the effective date of this Article, the financing statement becomes sufficient under Section 9–504(2). On that date the security interest becomes perfected. (This assumes, of course, that the financ-

ing statement is filed in the proper filing office under this Article.)

§ 9–705. Effectiveness of Action Taken Before Effective Date.

(a) **[Pre-effective-date action; one-year perfection period unless reperfected.]** If action, other than the filing of a financing statement, is taken before this [Act] takes effect and the action would have resulted in priority of a security interest over the rights of a person that becomes a lien creditor had the security interest become enforceable before this [Act] takes effect, the action is effective to perfect a security interest that attaches under this [Act] within one year after this [Act] takes effect. An attached security interest becomes unperfected one year after this [Act] takes effect unless the security interest becomes a perfected security interest under this [Act] before the expiration of that period.

(b) **[Pre-effective-date filing.]** The filing of a financing statement before this [Act] takes effect is effective to perfect a security interest to the extent the filing would satisfy the applicable requirements for perfection under this [Act].

(c) **[Pre-effective-date filing in jurisdiction formerly governing perfection.]** This [Act] does not render ineffective an effective financing statement that, before this [Act] takes effect, is filed and satisfies the applicable requirements for perfection under the law of the jurisdiction governing perfection as provided in [former Section 9–103]. However, except as otherwise provided in subsections (d) and (e) and Section 9–706, the financing statement ceases to be effective at the earlier of:

(1) the time the financing statement would have ceased to be effective under the law of the jurisdiction in which it is filed; or

(2) June 30, 2006.

(d) **[Continuation statement.]** The filing of a continuation statement after this [Act] takes effect does not continue the effectiveness of the financing statement filed before this [Act] takes effect. However, upon the timely filing of a continuation statement after this [Act] takes effect and in accordance with the law of the jurisdiction governing perfection as provided in Part 3, the effectiveness of a financing statement filed in the same office in that jurisdiction before this [Act] takes effect continues for the period provided by the law of that jurisdiction.

(e) **[Application of subsection (c)(2) to transmitting utility financing statement.]** Subsection (c)(2) applies to a financing statement that, before this [Act] takes effect, is filed against a transmitting utility and satisfies the applicable requirements for perfection under the law of the jurisdiction governing perfection as provided in [former Section 9–103] only to the extent that Part 3 provides that the law of a jurisdiction other than the jurisdiction in which the financing statement is filed governs perfection of a security interest in collateral covered by the financing statement.

(f) **[Application of Part 5.]** A financing statement that includes a financing statement filed before this [Act] takes effect and a continuation statement filed after this [Act] takes effect is effective only to the extent that it satisfies the requirements of Part 5 for an initial financing statement.

Official Comment

1. **General.** This section addresses primarily the situation in which the perfection step is taken under former Article 9 or other applicable law before the effective date of this Article, but the security interest does not attach until after that date.

2. **Perfection Other Than by Filing.** Subsection (a) applies when the perfection step is a step other than the filing of a financing statement. If the step that would be a valid perfection step under former Article 9 or other law is taken before this Article takes effect, and if a security interest attaches within one year after this Article takes effect, then the security interest becomes a perfected security interest upon attachment. However, the security interest becomes unperfected one year after the effective date unless the requirements for attachment and perfection under this Article are satisfied within that period.

3. **Perfection by Filing: Ineffective Filings Made Effective.** Subsection (b) deals with financing statements that were filed under former Article 9 and which would not have perfected a security interest under the former Article (because, e.g., they did not accurately describe the collateral or were filed in the wrong place), but which would perfect a security interest under this Article. Under subsection (b), such a financing statement is effective to perfect a security interest to the extent it complies with this Article. Subsection (b) applies regardless of the reason for the

filing. For example, a secured party need not wait until the effective date to respond to the change this Article makes with respect to the jurisdiction whose law governs perfection of certain security interests. Rather, a secured party may wish to prepare for this change by filing a financing statement before the effective date in the jurisdiction whose law governs perfection under this Article. When this Article takes effect, the filing becomes effective to perfect a security interest (assuming the filing satisfies the perfection requirements of this Article). Note, however, that Section 9–706 determines whether a financing statement filed before the effective date operates to continue the effectiveness of a financing statement filed in another office before the effective date.

4. **Perfection by Filing: Change in Applicable Law or Filing Office.** Subsection (c) provides that a financing statement filed in the proper jurisdiction under former Section 9–103 remains effective for all purposes, despite the fact that this Article would require filing of a financing statement in a different jurisdiction or in a different office in the same jurisdiction. This means that, during the early years of this Article's effectiveness, it may be necessary to search not only in the filing office of the jurisdiction whose law governs perfection under this Article but also (if different) in the jurisdiction(s) and filing office(s) designated by Article 9. To limit this burden, subsection (c) provides that a financing statement filed in the jurisdiction determined by former Section 9–103 becomes ineffective at the earlier of the time it would become ineffective under the law of that jurisdiction or June 30, 2006. The June 30, 2006, limitation addresses some nonuniform versions of former Article 9 that extended the effectiveness of a financing statement beyond five years. Note that a financing statement filed before the effective date may remain effective beyond June 30, 2006, if subsection (d) (concerning continuation statements) or (e) (concerning transmitting utilities) or Section 9–706 (concerning initial financing statements that operate to continue pre-effective-date financing statements) so provides.

Subsection (c) is an exception to Section 9–703(b). Under the general rule in Section 9–703(b), a security interest that is enforceable and perfected on the effective date of this Article is a perfected security interest for one year after this Article takes effect, even if the security interest is not enforceable under this Article and the applicable requirements for perfection under this Article have not been met. However, in some cases subsection (c) may shorten the one-year period of perfection; in others, if the security interest is enforceable under Section 9–203, it may extend the period of perfection.

Example 1: On July 3, 1996, D, a State X corporation, creates a security interest in certain manufacturing equipment located in State Y. On July 6, 1996, SP perfects a security interest in the equipment under former Article 9 by filing in the office of the State Y Secretary of State. See former Section 9–103(1)(b). This Article takes effect in States X and Y on July 1, 2001. Under Section 9–705(c), the financing statement remains effective until it lapses in July 2001. See former Section 9–403. Had SP continued the effectiveness of the financing statement by filing a continuation statement in State Y under former Article 9 before July 1, 2001, the financing statement would have remained effective to perfect the security interest through June 30, 2006. See subsection (c)(2). Alternatively, SP could have filed an initial financing statement in State X under subsection (b) or Section 9–706 before the State Y financing statement lapsed. Had SP done so, the security interest would have remained perfected without interruption until the State X financing statement lapsed.

5. **Continuing Effectiveness of Filed Financing Statement.** A financing statement filed before the effective date of this Article may be continued only by filing in the State and office designated by this Article. This result is accomplished in the following manner: Subsection (d) indicates that, as a general matter, a continuation statement filed after the effective date of this Article does not continue the effectiveness of a financing statement filed under the law designated by former Section 9–103. Instead, an initial financing statement must be filed under Section 9–706. The second sentence of subsection (d) contains an exception to the general rule. It provides that a continuation statement is effective to continue the effectiveness of a financing statement filed before this Article takes effect if this Article prescribes not only the same jurisdiction but also the same filing office.

Example 2: On November 8, 2000, D, a State X corporation, creates a security interest in certain manufacturing equipment located in State Y. On November 15, 2000, SP perfects a security interest in the equipment under former Article 9 by filing in office of the State Y Secretary of State. See former Section 9–103(1)(b). This Article takes effect in States X and Y on July 1, 2001. Under Section 9–705(c), the financing statement ceases to be effective in November, 2005, when it lapses. See Section 9–515. Under this Article, the law of D's location (State X, see Section 9–307) governs perfection. See Section 9–301. Thus, the filing of a continuation statement

in State Y after the effective date would not continue the effectiveness of the financing statement. See subsection (d). However, the effectiveness of the financing statement could be continued under Section 9–706.

Example 3: The facts are as in Example 2, except that D is a State Y corporation. Assume State Y adopted former Section 9–401(1) (second alternative). State Y law governs perfection under Part 3 of this Article. (See Sections 9–301, 9–307.) Under the second sentence of subsection (d), the timely filing of a continuation statement in accordance with the law of State Y continues the effectiveness of the financing statement.

Example 4: The facts are as in Example 3, except that the collateral is equipment used in farming operations and, in accordance with former Section 9–401(1) (second alternative) as enacted in State Y, the financing statement was filed in State Y, in the office of the Shelby County Recorder of Deeds. Under this Article, a continuation statement must be filed in the office of the State Y Secretary of State. See Section 9–501(a)(2). Under the second sentence of subsection (d), the timely filing of a continuation statement in accordance with the law of State Y operates to continue a pre-effective-date financing statement only if the continuation statement is filed in the same office as the financing statement. Accordingly, the continuation statement is not effective in this case, but the financing statement may be continued under Section 9–706.

Example 5: The facts are as in Example 3, except that State Y enacted former Section 9–401(1) (third alternative). As required by former Section 9–401(1), SP filed financing statements in both the office of the State Y Secretary of State and the office of the Shelby County Recorder of Deeds. Under this Article, a continuation statement must be filed in the office of the State Y Secretary of State. See Section 9–501(a)(2). The timely filing of a continuation statement in that office after this Article takes effect would be effective to continue the effectiveness of the financing statement (and thus continue the perfection of the security interest), even if the financing statement filed with the County Recorder lapses.

6. **Continuation Statements.** In some cases, this Article reclassifies collateral covered by a financing statement filed under former Article 9. For example, collateral consisting of the right to payment for real property sold would be a "general intangible" under the former Article but an "account" under this Article. To continue perfection under those circumstances, a

continuation statement must comply with the normal requirements for a continuation statement. See Section 9–515. In addition, the pre-effective-date financing statement and continuation statement, taken together, must satisfy the requirements of this Article concerning the sufficiency of the debtor's name, secured party's name, and indication of collateral. See subsection (f).

Example 6: A pre-effective-date financing statement covers "all general intangibles" of a debtor. As defined under former Article 9, a "general intangible," would include rights to payment for lottery winnings. These rights to payment are "accounts" under this Article, however. A post-effective-date continuation statement will not continue the effectiveness of the pre-effective-date financing statement with respect to lottery winnings unless it amends the indication of collateral covered to include lottery winnings (e.g., by adding "accounts," "rights to payment for lottery winnings," or the like). If the continuation statement does not amend the indication of collateral, the continuation statement will be effective to continue the effectiveness of the financing statement only with respect to "general intangibles" as defined in this Article.

Example 7: The facts are as in Example 6, except that the pre-effective-date financing statement covers "all accounts and general intangibles." Even though rights to payment for lottery winnings are "general intangibles" under former Article 9 and "accounts" under this Article, a post-effective-date continuation statement would continue the effectiveness of the pre-effective-date financing statement with respect to lottery winnings. There would be no need to amend the indication of collateral covered, inasmuch as the indication ("accounts") satisfies the requirements of this Article.

As amended in 2000.

§ 9–706. When Initial Financing Statement Suffices to Continue Effectiveness of Financing Statement.

(a) **[Initial financing statement in lieu of continuation statement.]** The filing of an initial financing statement in the office specified in Section 9–501 continues the effectiveness of a financing statement filed before this [Act] takes effect if:

(1) the filing of an initial financing statement in that office would be effective to perfect a security interest under this [Act];

(2) the pre-effective-date financing statement was filed in an office in another State or another office in this State; and

(3) the initial financing statement satisfies subsection (c).

(b) **[Period of continued effectiveness.]** The filing of an initial financing statement under subsection (a) continues the effectiveness of the pre-effective-date financing statement:

(1) if the initial financing statement is filed before this [Act] takes effect, for the period provided in [former Section 9–403] with respect to a financing statement; and

(2) if the initial financing statement is filed after this [Act] takes effect, for the period provided in Section 9–515 with respect to an initial financing statement.

(c) **[Requirements for initial financing statement under subsection (a).]** To be effective for purposes of subsection (a), an initial financing statement must:

(1) satisfy the requirements of Part 5 for an initial financing statement;

(2) identify the pre-effective-date financing statement by indicating the office in which the financing statement was filed and providing the dates of filing and file numbers, if any, of the financing statement and of the most recent continuation statement filed with respect to the financing statement; and

(3) indicate that the pre-effective-date financing statement remains effective.

Official Comment

1. **Continuation of Financing Statements Not Filed in Proper Filing Office Under This Article.** This section deals with continuing the effectiveness of financing statements that are filed in the proper State and office under former Article 9, but which would be filed in the wrong State or in the wrong office of the proper State under this Article. Section 9–705(d) provides that, under these circumstances, filing a continuation statement after the effective date of this Article in the office designated by former Article 9 would not be effective. This section provides the means by which the effectiveness of such a financing statement can be continued if this Article governs perfection under the applicable choice-of-law rule: filing an initial financing statement in the office specified by Section 9–501.

Although it has the effect of continuing the effectiveness of a pre-effective-date financing statement, an initial financing statement described in this section is not a continuation statement. Rather, it is governed by the rules applicable to initial financing statements. (However, the debtor need not authorize the filing. See Section 9–708.) Unlike a continuation statement, the initial financing statement described in this section may be filed any time during the effectiveness of the pre-effective-date financing statement—even before this Article is enacted—and not only within the six months immediately prior to lapse. In contrast to a continuation statement, which extends the lapse date of a filed financing statement for five years, the initial financing statement has its own lapse date, which bears no relation to the lapse date of the pre-effective-date financing statement whose effectiveness the initial financing statement continues. See subsection (b).

As subsection (a) makes clear, the filing of an initial financing statement under this section *continues* the effectiveness of a pre-effective-date financing statement. If the effectiveness of a pre-effective-date financing statement lapses before the initial financing statement is filed, the effectiveness of the pre-effective-date financing statement cannot be continued. Rather, unless the security interest is perfected otherwise, there will be a period during which the security interest is unperfected before becoming perfected again by the filing of the initial financing statement under this section.

If an initial financing statement is filed under this section before the effective date of this Article, it takes effect when this Article takes effect (assuming that it is ineffective under former Article 9). Note, however, that former Article 9 determines whether the filing office is obligated to accept such an initial financing statement. For the reason given in the preceding paragraph, an initial financing statement filed before the effective date of this Article does not continue the effectiveness of a pre-effective-date financing statement unless the latter remains effective on the effective date of this Article. Thus, for example, if the effectiveness of the pre-effective-date financing statement lapses before this Article takes effect, the initial financing statement would not continue its effectiveness.

2. Requirements of Initial Financing Statement Filed in Lieu of Continuation Statement. Subsection (c) sets forth the requirements for the initial financing statement under subsection (a). These requirements are needed to inform searchers that the initial financing statement operates to continue a financing statement filed elsewhere and to enable searchers to locate and discover the attributes of the other financing statement. A single initial financing statement may continue the effectiveness of more than one financing statement filed before this Article's effective date. See Section 1–102(5)(a) (words in the singular include the plural). If a financing statement has been filed in more than one office in a given jurisdiction, as may be the case if the jurisdiction had adopted former Section 9–401(1), third alternative, then an identification of the filing in the central filing office suffices for purposes of subsection (c)(2). If under this Article the collateral is of a type different from its type under former Article 9—as would be the case, e.g., with a right to payment of lottery winnings (a "general intangible" under former Article 9 and an "account" under this Article), then subsection (c) requires that the initial financing statement indicate the type under this Article.

As amended in 2000.

§ 9–707. Amendment of Pre-Effective-Date Financing Statement.

(a) ["**Pre-effective-date financing statement**".] In this section, "Pre-effective-date financing statement" means a financing statement filed before this [Act] takes effect.

(b) [**Applicable law.**] After this [Act] takes effect, a person may add or delete collateral covered by, continue or terminate the effectiveness of, or otherwise amend the information provided in, a pre-effective-date financing statement only in accordance with the law of the jurisdiction governing perfection as provided in Part 3. However, the effectiveness of a pre-effective-date financing statement also may be terminated in accordance with the law of the jurisdiction in which the financing statement is filed.

(c) [**Method of amending: general rule.**] Except as otherwise provided in subsection (d), if the law of this State governs perfection of a security interest, the information in a pre-effective-date financing statement may be amended after this [Act] takes effect only if:

(1) the pre-effective-date financing statement and an amendment are filed in the office specified in Section 9–501;

(2) an amendment is filed in the office specified in Section 9–501 concurrently with, or after the filing in that office of, an initial financing statement that satisfies Section 9–706(c); or

(3) an initial financing statement that provides the information as amended and satisfies Section 9–706(c) is filed in the office specified in Section 9–501.

(d) **[Method of amending: continuation.]** If the law of this State governs perfection of a security interest, the effectiveness of a pre-effective-date financing statement may be continued only under Section 9–705(d) and (f) or 9–706.

(e) **[Method of amending: additional termination rule.]** Whether or not the law of this State governs perfection of a security interest, the effectiveness of a pre-effective-date financing statement filed in this State may be terminated after this [Act] takes effect by filing a termination statement in the office in which the pre-effective-date financing statement is filed, unless an initial financing statement that satisfies Section 9–706(c) has been filed in the office specified by the law of the jurisdiction governing perfection as provided in Part 3 as the office in which to file a financing statement.

As added in 2000.

Official Comment

1. **Scope of This Section.** This section addresses post-effective-date amendments to pre-effective-date financing statements.

2. **Applicable Law.** Determining how to amend a pre-effective-date financing statement requires one first to determine the jurisdiction whose law applies. Subsection (b) provides that, as a general matter, post-effective-date amendments to pre-effective-date financing statements are effective only if they are accomplished in accordance with the substantive (or local) law of the jurisdiction governing perfection under Part 3 of this Article. However, under certain circumstances, the effectiveness of a financing statement may be terminated in accordance with the substantive law of the jurisdiction in which the financing statement is filed. See Comment 5, below.

Example 1: D is a corporation organized under the law of State Y. It owns equipment located in State X. Under former Article 9, SP properly perfected a security interest in the equipment by filing a financing statement in State X. Under this Article, the law of State Y governs perfection of the security interest. See Sections 9–301, 9–307. After this Article takes effect, SP wishes to amend the financing statement to reflect a change in D's name. Under subsection (b), the financing statement may be amended in

accordance with the law of State Y, i.e., in accordance with subsection (c) as enacted in State Y.

Example 2: The facts are as in Example 1, except that SP wishes to terminate the effectiveness of the State X filing. The first sentence of subsection (b) provides that the financing statement may be terminated after the effective date of this Article in accordance with the law of State Y, i.e., in accordance with subsection (c) as enacted in State Y. However, the second sentence provides that the financing statement also may be terminated in accordance with the law of the jurisdiction in which it is filed, i.e., in accordance with subsection (e) as enacted in State X. If the pre-effective-date financing statement is filed in the jurisdiction whose law governs perfection (here, State Y), then both sentences would designate the law of State Y as applicable to the termination of the financing statement. That is, the financing statement could be terminated in accordance with subsection (c) or (e) as enacted in State Y.

3. **Method of Amending.** Subsection (c) provides three methods of effectuating a post-effective-date amendment to a pre-effective-date financing statement. Under subsection (c)(1), if the financing statement is filed in the jurisdiction and office determined by this Article, then an effective amendment may be filed in the same office.

Example 3: D is a corporation organized under the law of State Z. It owns equipment located in State Z. Before the effective date of this Article, SP perfected a security interest in the equipment by filing in two offices in State Z, a local filing office and the office of the Secretary of State. See former Section 9–401(1) (third alternative). State Z enacts this Article and specifies in Section 9–501 that a financing statement covering equipment is to be filed in the office of the Secretary of State. SP wishes to assign its power as secured party of record. Under subsection (b), the substantive law of State Z applies. Because the pre-effective-date financing statement is filed in the office specified in subsection (c)(1) as enacted by State Z, SP may effectuate the assignment by filing an amendment under Section 9–514 with the office of the Secretary of State. SP need not amend the local filing, and the priority of the security interest perfected by the filing of the financing statement would not be affected by the failure to amend the local filing.

If a pre-effective-date financing statement is filed in an office other than the one specified by Section 9–501 of the relevant jurisdiction, then ordinarily an amendment filed in that office is ineffective. (Subsection (e) provides an exception for termination statements.) Rather, the amendment must be effectuated by a filing in the jurisdiction and office determined by this Article. That filing may consist of an initial financing statement followed by an amendment, an initial financing statement together with an amendment, or an initial financing statement that indicates the information provided in the financing statement, as amended. Subsection (c)(2) encompasses the first two options; subsection (c)(3) contemplates the last. In each instance, the initial financing statement must satisfy Section 9–706(c).

4. **Continuation.** Subsection (d) refers to the two methods by which a secured party may continue the effectiveness of a pre-effective-date financing statement under this Part. The Comments to Sections 9–705 and 9–706 explain these methods.

5. **Termination.** The effectiveness of a pre-effective-date financing statement may be terminated pursuant to subsection (c). This section also provides an alternative method for accomplishing this result: filing a termination statement in the office in which the financing statement is filed. The alternative method becomes unavailable once an initial financing statement that relates to the pre-effective-date financing statement and satisfies Section 9–706(c) is filed in the jurisdiction and office determined by this Article.

Example 4: The facts are as in Example 1, except that SP wishes to terminate a financing statement filed in State X. As explained in Example 1, the financing statement may be amended in accordance with the law of the jurisdiction governing perfection under this Article, i.e., in accordance with the substantive law of State Y. As enacted in State Y, subsection (c)(1) is inapplicable because the financing statement was not filed in the State Y filing office specified in Section 9–501. Under subsection (c)(2), the financing statement may be amended by filing in the State Y filing office an initial financing statement followed by a termination statement. The filing of an initial financing statement together with a termination statement also would be legally sufficient under subsection (c)(2), but Section 9–512(a)(1) may render this method impractical. The financing statement also may be amended under subsection (c)(3), but the resulting initial financing statement is likely to be very confusing. In each instance, the initial financing statement must satisfy Section 9–706(c). Applying the law of State Y, subsection (e) is inapplicable, because the financing statement was not filed in "this State," i.e., State Y.

This section affords another option to SP. Subsection (b) provides that the effectiveness of a financing statement may be terminated either in accordance with the law of the jurisdiction governing perfection (here, State Y) or in accordance with the substantive law of the jurisdiction in which the financing statement is filed (here, State X). Applying the law of State X, the financing statement is filed in "this State," i.e., State X, and subsection (e) applies. Accordingly, the effectiveness of the financing statement can be terminated by filing a termination statement in the State X office in which the financing statement is filed, unless an initial financing statement that relates to the financing statement and satisfies Section 9–706(c) as enacted in State X has been filed in the jurisdiction and office determined by this Article (here, the State Y filing office).

As amended in 2000.

§ 9–708.   Persons Entitled to File Initial Financing Statement or Continuation Statement.

A person may file an initial financing statement or a continuation statement under this part if:

(1) the secured party of record authorizes the filing; and

(2) the filing is necessary under this part:

(A) to continue the effectiveness of a financing statement filed before this [Act] takes effect; or

(B) to perfect or continue the perfection of a security interest.

As amended in 2000.

Official Comment

This section permits a secured party to file an initial financing statement or continuation statement necessary under this Part to continue the effectiveness of a financing statement filed before this Article takes effect or to perfect or otherwise continue the perfection of a security interest. Because a filing described in this section typically operates to continue the effectiveness of a financing statement whose filing the debtor already has authorized, this section does not require authorization from the debtor.

§ 9–709.   Priority.

(a) **[Law governing priority.]** This [Act] determines the priority of conflicting claims to collateral. However, if the relative priorities of the claims were established before this [Act] takes effect, [former Article 9] determines priority.

(b) **[Priority if security interest becomes enforceable under Section 9–203.]** For purposes of Section 9–322(a), the priority of a security interest that becomes enforceable under Section 9–203 of this [Act] dates from the time this [Act] takes effect if the security interest is perfected under this [Act] by the filing of a financing statement before this [Act] takes effect which would not have been effective to perfect the security interest under [former Article 9]. This subsection does not apply to conflicting security interests each of which is perfected by the filing of such a financing statement.

As amended in 2000.

Official Comment

1. **Law Governing Priority.** Ordinarily, this Article determines the priority of conflicting claims to collateral. However, when the relative priorities of the claims were established before this Article takes effect, former Article 9 governs.

Example 1: In 1999, SP–1 obtains a security interest in a right to payment for goods sold ("account"). SP–1 fails to file a financing statement. This Article takes effect on July 1, 2001. Thereafter, on August 1, 2001, D creates a security interest in the same account in favor of SP–2, who files a financing statement. This Article determines the relative priorities of the claims. SP–2's security interest has priority under Section 9–322(a)(1).

Example 2: In 1999, SP–1 obtains a security interest in a right to payment for goods sold ("account"). SP–1 fails to file a financing statement. In 2000, D creates a security interest in the same account in favor of SP–2, who likewise fails to file a financing statement. This Article takes effect on July 1, 2001. Because the relative priorities of the security interests were established before the effective date of this Article, former Article 9 governs priority, and SP–1's security interest has priority under former Section 9–312(5)(b).

Example 3: The facts are as in Example 2, except that, on August 1, 2001, SP–2 files a proper financing statement under this Article. Until August 1, 2001, the relative priorities of the security interests were established before the effective date of this Article, as in Example 2. However, by taking the affirmative step of filing a financing statement, SP–2 established anew the relative priority of the conflict-

ing claims after the effective date. Thus, this Article determines priority. SP–2's security interest has priority under Section 9–322(a)(1).

As Example 3 illustrates, relative priorities that are "established" before the effective date do not necessarily remain unchanged following the effective date. Of course, unlike priority contests among unperfected security interests, some priorities are established permanently, e.g., the rights of a buyer of property who took free of a security interest under former Article 9.

One consequence of the rule in subsection (a) is that the mere taking effect of this Article does not of itself adversely affect the priority of conflicting claims to collateral.

Example 4: In 1999, SP–1 obtains a security interest in a right to payment for lottery winnings (a "general intangible" as defined in former Article 9 but an "account" as defined in this Article). SP–1's security interest is unperfected because its filed financing statement covers only "accounts." In 2000, D creates a security interest in the same right to payment in favor of SP–2, who files a financing statement covering "accounts and general intangibles." Before this Article takes effect on July 1, 2001, SP–2's perfected security interest has priority over SP–1's unperfected security interest under former 9–312(5). Because the relative priorities of the security interests were established before the effective date of this Article, former Article 9 continues to govern priority after this Article takes effect. Thus, SP–2's priority is not adversely affected by this Article's having taken effect.

Note that were this Article to govern priority, SP–2 would become subordinated to SP–1 under Section 9–322(a)(1), even though nothing changes other than this Article's having taken effect. Under Section 9–704, SP–1's security interest would become perfected; the financing statement covering "accounts" adequately covers the lottery winnings and complies with the other perfection requirements of this Article, e.g., it is filed in the proper office.

Example 5: In 1999, SP–1 obtains a security interest in a right to payment for lottery winnings—a "general intangible" (as defined under former Article 9). SP–1's security interest is unperfected because its filed financing statement covers only "accounts." In 2000, D creates a security interest in the same right to payment in favor of SP–2, who makes the same mistake and also files a financing statement covering only "accounts." Before this Article takes effect on July 1, 2001, SP–1's unperfected

security interest has priority over SP–2's unperfected security interest, because SP–1's security interest was the first to attach. See former Section 9–312(5)(b). Because the relative priorities of the security interests were established before the effective date of this Article, former Article 9 continues to govern priority after this Article takes effect. Although Section 9–704 makes both security interests perfected for purposes of this Article, both are unperfected under former Article 9, which determines their relative priorities.

2. **Financing Statements Ineffective Under Former Article 9 but Effective Under This Article.** If this Article determines priority, subsection (b) may apply. It deals with the case in which a filing that occurs before the effective date of this Article would be ineffective to perfect a security interest under former Article 9 but effective under this Article. For purposes of Section 9–322(a), the priority of a security interest that attaches after this Article takes effect and is perfected in this manner dates from the time this Article takes effect.

Example 6: In 1999, SP–1 obtains a security interest in D's existing and after-acquired instruments and files a financing statement covering "instruments." In 2000, D grants a security interest in its existing and after-acquired accounts in favor of SP–2, who files a financing statement covering "accounts." After this Article takes effect on July 1, 2001, one of D's account debtors gives D a negotiable note to evidence its obligation to pay an overdue account. Under the first-to-file-or-perfect rule in Section 9–322(a), SP–1 would have priority in the instrument, which constitutes SP–2's proceeds. SP–1's filing in 1999 was earlier than SP–2's in 2000. However, subsection (b) provides that, for purposes of Section 9–322(a), SP–1's priority dates from the time this Article takes effect (July 1, 2001). Under Section 9–322(b), SP–2's priority with respect to the proceeds (instrument) dates from its filing as to the original collateral (accounts). Accordingly, SP–2's security interest would be senior.

Subsection (b) does not apply to conflicting security interests each of which is perfected by a pre-effective-date filing that was not effective under former Article 9 but is effective under this Article.

Example 7: In 1999, SP–1 obtains a security interest in D's existing and after-acquired instruments and files a financing statement covering "instruments." In 2000, D grants a security interest in its existing and after-acquired instruments in favor of SP–2, who files a financing statement covering "instruments." After this Article takes effect on July 1, 2001, one of D's account debtors gives D a negotiable note to evidence its obligation to pay an overdue account. Under the first-to-file-or-perfect rule in Section 9–322(a), SP–1 would have priority in the instrument. Both filings are effective under this Article, see Section 9–705(b), and SP–1's filing in 1999 was earlier than SP–2's in 2000. Subsection (b) does not change this result.

APPENDIX A

REVISED UCC ARTICLE 1 (2001)

CONFORMING AMENDMENTS TO OTHER ARTICLES

Section

2–103. Definitions and Index of Definitions.

2–202. Final Written Expression: Parol or Extrinsic Evidence

2–208. Course of Performance or Practical Construction

2A–103. Definitions and Index of Definitions

2A–207. Course of Performance or Practical Construction

2A–501. Default: Procedure

2A–518. Cover; Substitute Goods

2A–519. Lessee's Damages for Non-delivery, Repudiation, Default and Breach of Warranty in Regard to Accepted Goods

Section

2A–527. Lessor's Rights to Dispose of Goods

2A–528. Lessor's Damages for Non-acceptance, Failure to Pay, Repudiation, or Other Default

3–103. Definitions

4–104. Definitions and Index of Definitions

4A–105. Other Definitions

4A–106. Time Payment Order is Received

4A–204. Refund of Payment and Duty of Customer to Report with Respect to Unauthorized Payment Order

5–103. Scope

8–102. Definitions

9–102. Definitions and Index of Definitions

---

§ 2–103. Definitions and Index of Definitions.

(1) In this Article unless the context otherwise requires

(a) "Buyer" means a person who buys or contracts to buy goods.

(b) [Reserved.] "Good faith" in the case of a merchant means honesty in fact and the observance of reasonable commercial standards of fair dealing in the trade.

(c) "Receipt" of goods means taking physical possession of them.

(d) "Seller" means a person who sells or contracts to sell goods.

* * *

§ 2–202. Final Written Expression: Parol or Extrinsic Evidence.

Terms with respect to which the confirmatory memoranda of the parties agree or which are otherwise set forth in a writing intended by the parties as a final expression of their agreement with respect to such terms as are included therein may not be contradicted by evidence of any prior agreement or of a contemporaneous oral agreement but may be explained or supplemented

(a) by course of performance, course of dealing, or usage of trade (Section 1–205 1–303) or by course of performance (Section 2–208); and

(b) by evidence of consistent additional terms unless the court finds the writing to have been intended also as a complete and exclusive statement of the terms of the agreement.

Official Comment

* * *

Cross References:

Point 3: Sections 1–205 1–303, 2–207, 2–302 and 2–316.

Definitional Cross References:

"Agreed" and "agreement". Section 1–201.

"Course of dealing". Section 1–205 1–303.

"Course of performance". Section 1–303.

"Partyies". Section 1–201.
"Term". Section 1–201.
"Usage of trade". Section ~~1–205~~ 1–303.
"Written" and "writing". Section 1–201.

§ 2–208. ~~Course~~ ~~of~~ ~~Performance~~ ~~or~~ ~~Practical~~ ~~Construction.~~

~~(1) Where the contract for sale involves repeated occasions for performance by either party with knowledge of the nature of the performance and opportunity for objection to it by the other, any course of performance accepted or acquiesced in without objection shall be relevant to determine the meaning of the agreement.~~

~~(2) The express terms of the agreement and any such course of performance, as well as any course of dealing and usage of trade, shall be construed whenever reasonable as consistent with each other; but when such construction is unreasonable, express terms shall control course of performance and course of performance shall control both course of dealing and usage of trade (Section 1–205).~~

~~(3) Subject to the provisions of the next section on modification and waiver, such course of performance shall be relevant to show a waiver or modification of any term inconsistent with such course of performance.~~

~~Official Comment~~

~~Prior Uniform Statutory Provision: No such general provision but concept of this section recognized by terms such as "course of dealing", "the circumstances of the case," "the conduct of the parties," etc., in Uniform Sales Act.~~

~~Purposes:~~

~~1. The parties themselves know best what they have meant by their words of agreement and their action under that agreement is the best indication of what that meaning was. This section thus rounds out the set of factors which determines the meaning of the "agreement" and therefore also of the "unless otherwise agreed" qualification to various provisions of this Article.~~

~~2. Under this section a course of performance is always relevant to determine the meaning of the agreement. Express mention of course of performance elsewhere in this Article carries no contrary implication when there is a failure to refer to it in other sections.~~

~~3. Where it is difficult to determine whether a particular act merely sheds light on the meaning of the~~ ~~agreement or represents a waiver of a term of the agreement, the preference is in favor of "waiver" whenever such construction, plus the application of the provisions on the reinstatement of rights waived (see Section 2–209), is needed to preserve the flexible character of commercial contracts and to prevent surprise or other hardship.~~

~~4. A single occasion of conduct does not fall within the language of this section but other sections such as the ones on silence after acceptance and failure to specify particular defects can affect the parties' rights on a single occasion (see Sections 2–605 and 2–607).~~

~~Cross References:~~

~~Point 1: Section 1–201.~~
~~Point 2: Section 2–202.~~
~~Point 3: Sections 2–209, 2–601 and 2–607.~~
~~Point 4: Sections 2–605 and 2–607.~~

§ 2A–103. Definitions and Index of Definitions.

* * *

(3) The following definitions in other Articles apply to this Article:

"Account". Section 9–102(a)(2).

"Between merchants". Section 2–104(3).

"Buyer". Section 2–103(1)(a).

"Chattel paper". Section 9–102(a)(11).

"Consumer goods". Section 9–102(a)(23).

"Document". Section 9–102(a)(30).

"Entrusting". Section 2–403(3).

"General intangible". Section 9–102(a)(42).

~~"Good faith". Section 2–103(1)(b).~~

"Instrument". Section 9–102(a)(47).

"Merchant". Section 2–104(1).

"Mortgage". Section 9–102(a)(55).

"Pursuant to commitment". Section 9–102(a)(68).

"Receipt". Section 2–103(1)(c).

"Sale". Section 2–106(1).

"Sale on approval". Section 2–326.

"Sale or return". Section 2–326.

"Seller". Section 2–103(1)(d).

* * *

Official Comment

(a) "Buyer in ordinary course of business". Section 1–201(b)(9).

* * *

(h) "Goods". Section 9–105(1)(h) 9–102(a)(44). See Section 2A–103(3) for reference to the definition of "Account", "Chattel paper", "Document", "General intangibles" and "Instrument". See Section 2A–217 for determination of the time and manner of identification.

* * *

(j) "Lease". New. There are several reasons to codify the law with respect to leases of goods. An analysis of the case law as it applies to leases of goods suggests at least several significant issues to be resolved by codification. First and foremost is the definition of a lease. It is necessary to define lease to determine whether a transaction creates a lease or a security interest disguised as a lease. If the transaction creates a security interest disguised as a lease, the transaction will be governed by the Article on Secured Transactions (Article 9) and the lessor will be required to file a financing statement or take other action to perfect its interest in the goods against third parties. There is no such requirement with respect to leases under the common law and, except with respect to leases of fixtures (Section 2A–309), this Article imposes no such requirement. Yet the distinction between a lease and a security interest disguised as a lease is not clear from the case law at the time of the promulgation of this Article. DeKoven, *Leases of Equipment: Puritan Leasing Company v. August, A Dangerous Decision,* 12 U.S.F. L.Rev. 257 (1978).

At common law a lease of personal property is a bailment for hire. While there are several definitions of bailment for hire, all require a thing to be let and a price for the letting. Thus, in modern terms and as provided in this definition, a lease is created when the lessee agrees to furnish consideration for the right to the possession and use of goods over a specified period of time. Mooney, *Personal Property Leasing: A Challenge,* 36 Bus.Law. 1605, 1607 (1981). Further, a lease is neither a sale (Section 2–106(1)) nor a retention or creation of a security interest (Sections 1–201(37)(b)(35) and 1–203). Due to extensive litigation to distinguish true leases from security interests, an amendment to former Section 1–201(37) (now codified as Section 1–203) was has been promulgated with this Article to create a sharper distinction.

This section as well as Section 1–201(37) 1–203 must be examined to determine whether the transaction in question creates a lease or a security interest. The following hypotheticals indicate the perimeters of the issue. Assume that A has purchased a number of copying machines, new, for $1,000 each; the machines have an estimated useful economic life of three years. A advertises that the machines are available to rent for a minimum of one month and that the monthly rental is $100.00. A intends to enter into leases where A provides all maintenance, without charge to the lessee. Further, the lessee will rent the machine, month to month, with no obligation to renew. At the end of the lease term the lessee will be obligated to return the machine to A's place of business. This transaction qualifies as a lease under the first half of the definition, for the transaction includes a transfer by A to a prospective lessee of possession and use of the machine for a stated term, month to month. The machines are goods (Section 2A–103(1)(h)). The lessee is obligated to pay consideration in return, $100.00 for each month of the term.

However, the second half of the definition provides that a sale or a security interest is not a lease. Since there is no passing of title, there is no sale. Sections 2A–103(3) and 2–106(1). Under pre-Act security law this transaction would have created a bailment for hire or a true lease and not a conditional sale. *Da Rocha v. Macomber*, 330 Mass. 611, 614–15, 116 N.E.2d 139, 142 (1953). Under Section 1–201(37) 1–203, as amended with the promulgation of this Article, the same result would follow. While the lessee is obligated to pay rent for the one month term of the lease, one of the other four conditions of the second paragraph of Section 1–201(37) Section 1–203(b) must be met and none is. The term of the lease is one month and the economic life of the machine is 36 months; thus, subparagraph (a) of Section 1–201(37) Section 1–203(b)(1) is not now satisfied. Considering the amount of the monthly rent, absent economic duress or coercion, the lessee is not bound either to renew the lease for the remaining economic life of the goods or to become the owner. If the lessee did lease the machine for 36 months, the lessee would have paid the lessor $3,600 for a machine that could have been purchased for $1,000; thus, subparagraph (b) of Section 1–201(37) Section 1–203(b)(2) is not satisfied. Finally, there are no options; thus, subparagraphs (c3) and (d4) of Section 1–201(37) 1–203(b) are not satisfied. This transaction creates a lease, not a security interest. However, with each renewal of the lease the facts and circumstances at the time of each renewal must be examined to determine if that conclusion remains accurate, as it is possible that a transaction that first creates a lease, later creates a security interest.

Assume that the facts are changed and that A requires each lessee to lease the goods for 36 months, with no right to terminate. Under pre-Act security law this transaction would have created a conditional sale, and not a bailment for hire or true lease. *Hervey v. Rhode Island Locomotive Works*, 93 U.S. 664, 672–73 (1876). Under this subsection, and Section 1–203 1–201(37), as amended with the inclusion of this Article in the Act, the same result would follow. The lessee's obligation for the term is not subject to termination by the lessee and the term is equal to the economic life of the machine.

Between these extremes there are many transactions that can be created. Some of the transactions have were not been properly categorized by the courts in applying the 1978 and earlier Official Texts of former Section 1–201(37). This subsection, together with Section 1–203 1–201(37), as amended with the promulgation of this Article, draws a brighter line, which should create a clearer signal to the professional lessor and lessee.

(k) "Lease agreement". This definition is derived from the first sentence of Section 1–201(b)(3). Because the definition of lease is broad enough to cover future transfers, lease agreement includes an agreement contemplating a current or subsequent transfer. Thus it was not necessary to make an express reference to an agreement for the future lease of goods (Section 2–106(1)). This concept is also incorporated in the definition of lease contract. Note that the definition of lease does not include transactions in ordinary building materials that are incorporated into an improvement on land. Section 2A–309(2).

The provisions of this Article, if applicable, determine whether a lease agreement has legal consequences; otherwise the law of bailments and other applicable law determine the same. Sections 2A–103(4) and 1–103.

(l) "Lease contract". This definition is derived from the definition of contract in Section 1–201(11)(b)(12). Note that a lease contract may be for the future lease of goods, since this notion is included in the definition of lease.

* * *

(o) "Lessee in ordinary course of business". Section 1–201(b)(9).

* * *

(u) "Present value". New. Authorities agree that present value should be used to determine fairly the damages payable by the lessor or the lessee on default.

E.g., Taylor v. Commercial Credit Equip. Corp., 170 Ga.App. 322, 316 S.E.2d 788 (1984). Present value is defined to mean an amount that represents the discounted value as of a date certain of one or more sums payable in the future. This is a function of the economic principle that a dollar today is more valuable to the holder than a dollar payable in two years. While there is no question as to the principle, reasonable people would differ as to the rate of discount to apply in determining the value of that future dollar today. To minimize litigation, this Article allows the parties to specify the discount or interest rate, if the rate was not manifestly unreasonable at the time the transaction was entered into. In all other cases, the interest rate will be a commercially reasonable rate that takes into account the facts and circumstances of each case, as of the time the transaction was entered into.

(v) "Purchase". Section 1–201(32)(b)(29). This definition omits the reference to lien contained in the definition of purchase in Article 1 (Section 1–201(32)(b)(29)). This should not be construed to exclude consensual liens from the definition of purchase in this Article; the exclusion was mandated by the scope of the definition of lien in Section 2A–103(1)(r). Further, the definition of purchaser in this Article adds a reference to lease; as purchase is defined in Section 1–201(32)(b)(29) to include any other voluntary transaction creating an interest in property, this addition is not substantive.

* * *

§ 2A–207. Course of Performance or Practical Construction.

(1) If a lease contract involves repeated occasions for performance by either party with knowledge of the nature of the performance and opportunity for objection to it by the other, any course of performance accepted or acquiesced in without objection is relevant to determine the meaning of the lease agreement.

(2) The express terms of a lease agreement and any course of performance, as well as any course of dealing and usage of trade, must be construed whenever reasonable as consistent with each other; but if that construction is unreasonable, express terms control course of performance, course of performance controls both course of dealing and usage of trade, and course of dealing controls usage of trade.

(3) Subject to the provisions of Section 2A–208 on modification and waiver, course of perform-

ance is relevant to show a waiver or modification of any term inconsistent with the course of performance.

Official Comment

Uniform Statutory Source: Sections 2-208 and 1-205(4).

Changes: Revised to reflect leasing practices and terminology, except that subsection (2) was further revised to make the subsection parallel the provisions of Section 1-205(4) by adding that course of dealing controls usage of trade.

Purposes: The section should be read in conjunction with Section 2A-208. In particular, although a specific term may control over course of performance as a matter of lease construction under subsection (2), subsection (3) allows the same course of dealing to show a waiver or modification, if Section 2A-208 is satisfied.

Cross References:

Sections 1-205(4), 2-208 and 2A-208.

Definitional Cross References:

"Course of dealing". Section 1-205.
"Knowledge". Section 1-201(25).
"Lease agreement". Section 2A-103(1)(k).
"Lease contract". Section 2A-103(1)(l).
"Party". Section 1-201(29).
"Term". Section 1-201(42).
"Usage of trade". Section 1-205.

§ 2A–501. Default: Procedure.

* * *

(4) Except as otherwise provided in Section ~~1-106(1)~~ 1-305(a) or this Article or the lease agreement, the rights and remedies referred to in subsections (2) and (3) are cumulative.

* * *

Official Comment

Uniform Statutory Source: Former Section 9-501 (now codified as Sections 9-601 through 9-604).

* * *

2. Subsection (2) is a version of the first sentence of Section ~~9-501(1)~~ 9-601(a), revised to reflect leasing terminology.

3. Subsection (3), an expansive version of the second sentence of Section ~~9-501(1)~~ 9-601(a), lists the procedures that may be followed by the party seeking

enforcement; in effect, the scope of the procedures listed in subsection (3) is consistent with the scope of the procedures available to the foreclosing secured party.

4. Subsection (4) establishes that the parties' rights and remedies are cumulative. DeKoven, *Leases of Equipment: Puritan Leasing Company v. August, A Dangerous Decision*, 12 U.S.F.L.Rev. 257, 276–80 (1978). Cumulation, and largely unrestricted selection, of remedies is allowed in furtherance of the general policy of the Commercial Code, stated in Section ~~1-106~~ 1-305, that remedies be liberally administered to put the aggrieved party in as good a position as if the other party had fully performed. Therefore, cumulation of, or selection among, remedies is available to the extent necessary to put the aggrieved party in as good a position as it would have been in had there been full performance. However, cumulation of, or selection among, remedies is not available to the extent that the cumulation or selection would put the aggrieved party in a better position than it would have been in had there been full performance by the other party.

5. Section ~~9-501(3)~~ 9-602, which, among other things, states that certain rules, to the extent they give rights to the debtor and impose duties on the secured party, may not be waived or varied, ~~was~~ is not incorporated in this Article. Given the significance of freedom of contract in the development of the common law as it applies to bailments for hire and the lessee's lack of an equity of redemption, there ~~was~~ is no reason to impose that restraint.

Cross References:

Sections ~~1-106~~ 1-305, 2A-508, 2A-523, Article 9, especially Sections ~~9-501(1)~~ 9-601 and ~~9-501(3)~~ 9-602.

Definitional Cross References:

* * *

"Party". Section 1-201~~(29)~~(b)(26).
"Remedy". Section 1-201~~(34)~~(b)(32).
"Rights". Section 1-201~~(36)~~(b)(34).

§ 2A–518. Cover; Substitute Goods.

* * *

(2) Except as otherwise provided with respect to damages liquidated in the lease agreement (Section 2A–504) or otherwise determined pursuant to agreement of the parties (Sections ~~1-102(3)~~ 1-302 and 2A–503), if a lessee's cover is by a lease agreement substantially similar to the

original lease agreement and the new lease agreement is made in good faith and in a commercially reasonable manner, the lessee may recover from the lessor as damages (i) the present value, as of the date of the commencement of the term of the new lease agreement, of the rent under the new lease agreement applicable to that period of the new lease term which is comparable to the then remaining term of the original lease agreement minus the present value as of the same date of the total rent for the then remaining lease term of the original lease agreement, and (ii) any incidental or consequential damages, less expenses saved in consequence of the lessor's default.

* * *

Official Comment

* * *

1. Subsection (1) allows the lessee to take action to fix its damages after default by the lessor. Such action may consist of the lease of goods. The decision to cover is a function of commercial judgment, not a statutory mandate replete with sanctions for failure to comply. Cf. Section 9–507 9–625.

Cross References:

Sections 2–712(1), 2A–519 and 9–507 9–625.

Definitional Cross References:

"Agreement". Section 1–201(b)(3).
"Contract". Section 1–201(11)(b)(12).
"Good faith". Sections 1–201(b)(20) 1–201(19) and 2–103(1)(b).
"Goods". Section 2A–103(1)(h).
"Lease". Section 2A–103(1)(j).
"Lease agreement". Section 2A–103(1)(k).
"Lease contract". Section 2A–103(1)(l).
"Lessee". Section 2A–103(1)(n).
"Lessor". Section 2A–103(1)(p).
"Party". Section 1–201(29)(b)(26).
"Present value". Section 2A–103(1)(u) 1–201(b)(28).
"Purchase". Section 2A–103(1)(v).

§ 2A–519. Lessee's Damages for Non–Delivery, Repudiation, Default, and Breach of Warranty in Regard to Accepted Goods.

(1) Except as otherwise provided with respect to damages liquidated in the lease agreement (Section 2A–504) or otherwise determined pursuant to agreement of the parties (Sections 1–102(3) 1–302 and 2A–503), if a lessee elects not to cover or a lessee elects to cover and the cover is by lease agreement that for any reason does not qualify for treatment under Section 2A–518(2), or is by purchase or otherwise, the measure of damages for non-delivery or repudiation by the lessor or for rejection or revocation of acceptance by the lessee is the present value, as of the date of the default, of the then market rent minus the present value as of the same date of the original rent, computed for the remaining lease term of the original lease agreement, together with incidental and consequential damages, less expenses saved in consequence of the lessor's default.

* * *

Official Comment

* * *

Definitional Cross References:

"Conforming". Section 2A–103(1)(d).
"Delivery". Section 1–201(14)(b)(15).
"Goods". Section 2A–103(1)(h).
"Lease". Section 2A–103(1)(j).
"Lease agreement". Section 2A–103(1)(k).
"Lessee". Section 2A–103(1)(n).
"Lessor". Section 2A–103(1)(p).
"Notification". Section 1–201(26) 1–202.
"Present value". Section 2A–103(1)(u) 1–201(b)(28).
"Value". Section 1–201(44) 1–204.

§ 2A–527. Lessor's Rights to Dispose of Goods.

* * *

(2) Except as otherwise provided with respect to damages liquidated in the lease agreement (Section 2A–504) or otherwise determined pursuant to agreement of the parties (Sections 1–102(3) 1–302 and 2A–503), if the disposition is by lease agreement substantially similar to the original lease agreement and the new lease agreement is made in good faith and in a commercially reasonable manner, the lessor may recover from the lessee as damages (i) accrued and unpaid rent as of the date of the commencement of the term of the new lease agreement, (ii) the present value, as of the same date, of the total rent for the then remaining lease term of the original lease

agreement minus the present value, as of the same date, of the rent under the new lease agreement applicable to that period of the new lease term which is comparable to the then remaining term of the original lease agreement, and (iii) any incidental damages allowed under Section 2A–530, less expenses saved in consequence of the lessee's default.

* * *

Official Comment

* * *

1. Subsection (1), a revised version of the first sentence of subsection 2–706(1), allows the lessor the right to dispose of goods after a statutory or other material default by the lessee (even if the goods remain in the lessee's possession—Section 2A–525(2)), after the lessor refuses to deliver or takes possession of the goods, or, if agreed, after other contractual default. The lessor's decision to exercise this right is a function of a commercial judgment, not a statutory mandate replete with sanctions for failure to comply. Cf. Section 9–507 9–625. As the owner of the goods, in the case of a lessor, or as the prime lessee of the goods, in the case of a sublessor, compulsory disposition of the goods is inconsistent with the nature of the interest held by the lessor or the sublessor and is not necessary because the interest held by the lessee or the sublessee is not protected by a right of redemption under the common law or this Article. Subsection 2A–527(5).

2. The rule for determining the measure of damages recoverable by the lessor against the lessee is a function of several variables. If the lessor has elected to effect disposition under subsection (1) and such disposition is by lease that qualifies under subsection (2), the measure of damages set forth in subsection (2) will apply, absent agreement to the contrary. Sections 2A–504, 2A–103(4) and 1–102(3) 1–302.

* * *

Cross References:

Sections 1–102(3) 1–302, 2–706(1), 2–706(5), 2–706(6), 2A–103(4), 2A–304(1), 2A–504, 2A–507(2), 2A–523(1)(e), 2A–525(2), 2A–527(5), 2A–528 and 9–507 9–625.

Definitional Cross References:

"Buyer" and "Buying". Section 2–103(1)(a).
"Delivery". Section 1–201(14)(b)(15).
"Good faith". Sections 1–201(b)(20)1–201(19) and 2–103(1)(b).

"Goods". Section 2A–103(1)(h).
"Lease". Section 2A–103(1)(j).
"Lease contract". Section 2A–103(1)(l).
"Lessee". Section 2A–103(1)(n).
"Lessor". Section 2A–103(1)(p).
"Present value". Section 2A–103(1)(u) 1–201(b)(28).
"Rights". Section 1–201(36)(b)(34).
"Sale". Section 2–106(1).
"Security interest". Sections 1–201(37)(b)(35) and 1–203.
"Value". Section 1–201(44) 1–204.

§ 2A–528. Lessor's Damages for Non-Acceptance, Failure to Pay, Repudiation, or Other Default.

(1) Except as otherwise provided with respect to damages liquidated in the lease agreement (Section 2A–504) or otherwise determined pursuant to agreement of the parties (Sections 1–102(3) 1–302 and 2A–503), if a lessor elects to retain the goods or a lessor elects to dispose of the goods and the disposition is by lease agreement that for any reason does not qualify for treatment under Section 2A–527(2), or is by sale or otherwise, the lessor may recover from the lessee as damages for a default of the type described in Section 2A–523(1) or 2A–523(3)(a), or, if agreed, for other default of the lessee, (i) accrued and unpaid rent as of the date of default if the lessee has never taken possession of the goods, or, if the lessee has taken possession of the goods, as of the date the lessor repossesses the goods or an earlier date on which the lessee makes a tender of the goods to the lessor, (ii) the present value as of the date determined under clause (i) of the total rent for the then remaining lease term of the original lease agreement minus the present value as of the same date of the market rent at the place where the goods are located computed for the same lease term, and (iii) any incidental damages allowed under Section 2A–530, less expenses saved in consequence of the lessee's default.

* * *

Official Comment

* * *

1. Subsection (1), a substantially revised version of Section 2–708(1), states the basic rule governing the measure of lessor's damages for a default described in

Section 2A–523(1) or (3)(a), and, if agreed, for a contractual default. This measure will apply if the lessor elects to retain the goods (whether undelivered, returned by the lessee, or repossessed by the lessor after acceptance and default by the lessee) or if the lessor's disposition does not qualify under subsection 2A–527(2). Section 2A–527(3). Note that under some of these conditions, the lessor may recover damages from the lessee pursuant to the rule set forth in Section 2A–529. There is no sanction for disposition that does not qualify under subsection 2A–527(2). Application of the rule set forth in this section is subject to agreement to the contrary. Sections 2A–504, 2A–103(4) and ~~1–102(3)~~ 1–302.

* * *

Cross References:

Sections ~~1–102(3)~~ 1–302, 2–708, 2A–103(1)(u), 2A–402, 2A–504, 2A–507, 2A–527(2) and 2A–529.

Definitional Cross References:

"Agreement". Section 1–201(b)(3).
"Goods". Section 2A–103(1)(h).
"Lease". Section 2A–103(1)(j).
"Lease agreement". Section 2A–103(1)(k).
"Lessee". Section 2A–103(1)(n).
"Lessor". Section 2A–103(1)(p).
"Party". Section 1–201~~(29)~~(b)(26).
"Present value". Section ~~2A–103(1)(u)~~ 1–201(b)(28).
"Sale". Section 2–106(1).

§ 3–103. Definitions.

(a) In this Article:

* * *

(4) ~~"Good faith" means honesty in fact and the observance of reasonable commercial standards of fair dealing.~~ [reserved]

* * *

(10) "Prove" with respect to a fact means to meet the burden of establishing the fact (Section 1–201(b)(8)).

* * *

Official Comment

* * *

~~4. Subsection (a)(4) introduces a definition of good faith to apply to Articles 3 and 4. Former Articles 3 and 4 used the definition in Section 1–201(19). The definition in subsection (a)(4) is consistent with the~~ ~~definitions of good faith applicable to Articles 2, 2A, 4, and 4A. The definition requires not only honesty in fact but also "observance of reasonable commercial standards of fair dealing." Although fair dealing is a broad term that must be defined in context, it is clear that it is concerned with the fairness of conduct rather than the care with which an act is performed. Failure to exercise ordinary care in conducting a transaction is an entirely different concept than failure to deal fairly in conducting the transaction. Both fair dealing and ordinary care, which is defined in Section 3–103(a)(7), are to be judged in the light of reasonable commercial standards, but those standards in each case are directed to different aspects of commercial conduct.~~

5̲4. Subsection (a)(7) is a definition of ordinary care which is applicable not only to Article 3 but to Article 4 as well. See Section 4–104(c). The general rule is stated in the first sentence of subsection (a)(7) and it applies both to banks and to persons engaged in businesses other than banking. Ordinary care means observance of reasonable commercial standards of the relevant businesses prevailing in the area in which the person is located. The second sentence of subsection (a)(7) is a particular rule limited to the duty of a bank to examine an instrument taken by a bank for processing for collection or payment by automated means. This particular rule applies primarily to Section 4–406 and it is discussed in Comment 4 to that section. Nothing in Section 3–103(a)(7) is intended to prevent a customer from proving that the procedures followed by a bank are unreasonable, arbitrary, or unfair.

6̲5. In subsection (c) reference is made to a new definition of "bank" in amended Article 4.

§ 4–104. Definitions and Index of Definitions.

* * *

(c) The following definitions in other Articles apply to this Article:

* * *

~~"Good faith" Section 3–103.~~

* * *

§ 4A–105. Other Definitions.

(a) In this Article:

* * *

(6) ~~"Good faith" means honesty in fact and the observance of reasonable commercial standards of fair dealing.~~ [reserved]

(7) "Prove" with respect to a fact means to meet the burden of establishing the fact (Section 1–201(b)(8)).

* * *

§ 4A–106. Time Payment Order is Received.

(a) The time of receipt of a payment order or communication cancelling or amending a payment order is determined by the rules applicable to receipt of a notice stated in Section ~~1–201(27)~~ 1–202. A receiving bank may fix a cut-off time or times on a funds-transfer business day for the receipt and processing of payment orders and communications cancelling or amending payment orders. Different cut-off times may apply to payment orders, cancellations, or amendments, or to different categories of payment orders, cancellations, or amendments. A cut-off time may apply to senders generally or different cut-off times may apply to different senders or categories of payment orders. If a payment order or communication cancelling or amending a payment order is received after the close of a funds-transfer business day or after the appropriate cut-off time on a funds-transfer business day, the receiving bank may treat the payment order or communication as received at the opening of the next funds-transfer business day.

* * *

Official Comment

The time that a payment order is received by a receiving bank usually defines the payment date or the execution date of a payment order. Section 4A–401 and Section 4A–301. The time of receipt of a payment order, or communication cancelling or amending a payment order is defined in subsection (a) by reference to the rules stated in Section ~~1–201(27)~~ 1–202. Thus, time of receipt is determined by the same rules that determine when a notice is received. Time of receipt, however, may be altered by a cut-off time.

§ 4A–204. Refund of Payment and Duty of Customer to Report with Respect to Unauthorized Payment Order.

* * *

(b) Reasonable time under subsection (a) may be fixed by agreement as stated in Section ~~1–204(1)~~ 1–302(b), but the obligation of a receiving bank to refund payment as stated in subsection (a) may not otherwise be varied by agreement.

§ 5–103. Scope.

* * *

(c) With the exception of this subsection, subsections (a) and (d), Sections 5–102(a)(9) and (10), 5–106(d), and 5–114(d), and except to the extent prohibited in Sections ~~1–102(3)~~ 1–302 and 5–117(d), the effect of this article may be varied by agreement or by a provision stated or incorporated by reference in an undertaking. A term in an agreement or undertaking generally excusing liability or generally limiting remedies for failure to perform obligations is not sufficient to vary obligations prescribed by this article.

* * *

Official Comment

* * *

2. Like all of the provisions of the Uniform Commercial Code, Article 5 is supplemented by Section 1–103 and, through it, by many rules of statutory and common law. Because this article is quite short and has no rules on many issues that will affect liability with respect to a letter of credit transaction, law beyond Article 5 will often determine rights and liabilities in letter of credit transactions. Even within letter of credit law, the article is far from comprehensive; it deals only with "certain" rights of the parties. Particularly with respect to the standards of performance that are set out in Section 5–108, it is appropriate for the parties and the courts to turn to customs and practice such as the Uniform Customs and Practice for Documentary Credits, currently published by the International Chamber of Commerce as I.C.C. Pub. No. 500 (hereafter UCP). Many letters of credit specifically adopt the UCP as applicable to the particular transaction. Where the UCP are adopted but conflict with Article 5 and except where variation is prohibited, the UCP terms are permissible contractual modifications under Sections ~~1–102(3)~~ 1–302 and 5–103(c). See Section 5–116(c). Normally Article 5 should not be considered to conflict with practice except when a rule explicitly stated in the UCP or other practice is different from a rule explicitly stated in Article 5.

[remainder of comment 2 is unchanged]

* * *

§ 8–102. Definitions.

(a) In this Article:

* * *

(10) [reserved] ~~"Good faith," for purposes of the obligation of good faith in the performance or enforcement of contracts or duties within this Article, means honesty in fact and the observance of reasonable commercial standards of fair dealing.~~

* * *

Official Comment

* * *

10. "Good faith." ~~Good faith is defined in Article 8 for purposes of the application to Article 8 of~~ Section 1–203, ~~which~~ provides that "Every contract or duty within ~~this Act~~ [the Uniform Commercial Code] imposes an obligation of good faith in its performance or enforcement." Section 1–201(b)(20) defines "good faith" as "honesty in fact and the observance of reasonable commercial standards of fair dealing." ~~The sole function of the good faith definition in Revised Article 8 is to give content to the Section 1–203 obligation as it applies to contracts and duties that are governed by Article 8. The standard is one of "reasonable commercial standards of fair dealing."~~ The reference to commercial standards makes clear that assessments of conduct are to be made in light of the commercial setting. The substantive rules of Article 8 have been drafted to take account of the commercial circumstances of the securities holding and processing system. For example, Section 8–115 provides that a securities intermediary acting on an effective entitlement order, or a broker or other agent acting as a conduit in a securities transaction, is not liable to an adverse claimant, unless the claimant obtained legal process or the intermediary acted in collusion with the wrongdoer. This, and other similar provisions, see Sections 8–404 and 8–503(e), do not depend on notice of adverse claims, because it would impair rather than advance the interest of investors in having a sound and efficient securities clearance and settlement system to require intermediaries to investigate the propriety of the transactions they are processing. The good faith obligation does not supplant the standards of conduct established in provisions of this kind.

In Revised Article 8, the definition of good faith is not germane to the question whether a purchaser takes free from adverse claims. The rules on such questions as whether a purchaser who takes in suspicious circumstances is disqualified from protected purchaser status are treated not as an aspect of good faith but directly in the rules of Section 8–105 on notice of adverse claims.

* * *

Definitional Cross References:

"Agreement". Section 1–201(b)(3).
"Bank". Section 1–201(b)(4).
"Person". Section 1–201~~(30)~~(b)(27).
"Send". Section 1–201~~(38)~~(b)(36).
"Signed". Section 1–201~~(39)~~(b)(37).
"Writing". Section 1–201~~(46)~~(b)(43).

§ 9–102. Definitions and Index of Definitions.

(a) **[Article 9 definitions.]** In this article:

* * *

(43) [reserved] ~~"Good faith" means honesty in fact and the observance of reasonable commercial standards of fair dealing.~~

* * *

Official Comment

* * *

3. **Definitions Relating to Creation of a Security Interest.**

* * *

b. **"Security Agreement."** The definition of "security agreement" is substantially the same as under former Section 9–105–an agreement that creates or provides for a security interest. However, the term frequently was used colloquially in former Article 9 to refer to the document or writing that contained a debtor's security agreement. This Article eliminates that usage, reserving the term for the more precise meaning specified in the definition.

Whether an agreement creates a security interest depends not on whether the parties intend that the law *characterize* the transaction as a security interest but rather on whether the transaction falls within the definition of "security interest" in Section 1–201. Thus, an agreement that the parties characterize as a "lease" of goods may be a "security agreement," notwithstanding the parties' stated intention that the law treat the transaction as a lease and not as a secured transaction. See Section 1–203.

* * *

14. **Consignment-Related Definitions: "Consignee"; "Consignment"; "Consignor."** The definition of "consignment" excludes, in subparagraphs (B) and (C), transactions for which filing would be inappropriate or of insufficient benefit to justify the costs. A consignment excluded from the application of this Article by one of those subparagraphs may still be a true consignment; however, it is governed by non-Article 9 law. The definition also excludes, in subparagraph (D), what have been called "consignments intended for security." These "consignments" are not bailments but secured transactions. Accordingly, all of Article 9 applies to them. See Sections 1–201(37)(b)(35), 9–109(a)(1). The "consignor" is the person who delivers goods to the "consignee" in a consignment.

The definition of "consignment" requires that the goods be delivered "to a merchant for the purpose of sale." If the goods are delivered for another purpose as

well, such as milling or processing, the transaction is a consignment nonetheless because a purpose of the delivery is "sale." On the other hand, if a merchant-processor-bailee will not be selling the goods itself but will be delivering to buyers to which the owner-bailor agreed to sell the goods, the transaction would not be a consignment.

* * *

16. **"Document."** The definition of "document" is unchanged in substance from the corresponding definitions in former Section 9–105. See Section 1–201(15)(b)(16) and Comment 1516.

* * *

19. **"Good Faith."** This Article expands the definition of "good faith" to include "the observance of reasonable commercial standards of fair dealing." The definition in this section applies when the term is used in this Article, and the same concept applies in the context of this Article for purposes of the obligation of good faith imposed by Section 1–203. See subsection (c).

APPENDIX B

REVISED UCC ARTICLE 7 (2003)

CONFORMING AMENDMENTS TO OTHER ARTICLES

AMENDMENTS TO UNIFORM COMMERCIAL CODE ARTICLE 1
ALTERNATIVE A

Legislative Note: These amendments should be adopted in the event a state has not yet adopted Revised Article 1 as approved in 2001.

§ 1–201. General Definitions.

Subject to additional definitions contained in the subsequent Articles of this Act which are applicable to specific Articles or Parts thereof, and unless the context otherwise requires, in this Act:

* * *

(5) "Bearer" means a person in control of a negotiable electronic document of title or a ~~the~~ person in possession of an instrument, a negotiable tangible document of title, or a certificated security payable to bearer or indorsed in blank.

(6) "Bill of lading" means a document of title evidencing the receipt of goods for shipment issued by a person engaged in the business of directly or indirectly transporting or forwarding goods. The term does not include a warehouse receipt~~, and includes an airbill. "Airbill" means a document serving for air transportation as a bill of lading does for marine or rail transportation, and includes an air consignment note or air waybill~~.

* * *

~~(10) "Conspicuous": A term or clause is conspicuous when it is so written that a reasonable person against whom it is to operate ought to have noticed it. A printed heading in capitals (as: NON-NEGOTIABLE BILL OF LADING) is conspicuous. Language in the body of a form is "conspicuous" if it is in larger or other contrasting type or color. But in a telegram any stated~~ ~~term is "conspicuous". Whether a term or clause is "conspicuous" or not is for decision by the court.~~

(10) "Conspicuous", with reference to a term, means so written, displayed, or presented that a reasonable person against which it is to operate ought to have noticed it. Whether a term is "conspicuous" or not is a decision for the court. Conspicuous terms include the following:

(A) a heading in capitals equal to or greater in size than the surrounding text, or in contrasting type, font, or color to the surrounding text of the same or lesser size; and

(B) language in the body of a record or display in larger type than the surrounding text, or in contrasting type, font, or color to the surrounding text of the same size, or set off from surrounding text of the same size by symbols or other marks that call attention to the language.

* * *

(14) "Delivery" with respect to an electronic document of title means voluntary transfer of control and with respect to instruments, tangible documents of title, chattel paper, or certificated securities means voluntary transfer of possession.

(15) "Document of title" ~~includes bill of lading, dock warrant, dock receipt, warehouse receipt or order for the delivery of goods, and also any other~~ means a record (i) that ~~document which~~ in the regular course of business or financing is treated as adequately evidencing that the person in possession or control of the record ~~it~~ is entitled to receive, control, hold, and dispose of the record ~~document~~ and the goods ~~it~~ the record covers and (ii) that purports to be issued by or addressed to a bailee and to cover goods in the bailee's possession which are either identified or

are fungible portions of an identified mass. The term includes a bill of lading, transport document, dock warrant, dock receipt, warehouse receipt, and order for delivery of goods. ~~To be a document of title, a document must purport to be issued by or addressed to a bailee and purport to cover goods in the bailee's possession which are either identified or are fungible portions of an identified mass.~~ An electronic document of title means a document of title evidenced by a record consisting of information stored in an electronic medium. A tangible document of title means a document of title evidenced by a record consisting of information that is inscribed on a tangible medium.

* * *

(20) ~~"Holder," with respect to a negotiable instrument, means the person in possession if the instrument is payable to bearer or, in the case of an instrument payable to an identified person, if the identified person is in possession. "Holder" with respect to a document of title means the person in possession if the goods are deliverable to bearer or to the order of the person in possession.~~

"Holder" means:

(A) the person in possession of a negotiable instrument that is payable either to bearer or to an identified person that is the person in possession;

(B) the person in possession of a negotiable tangible document of title if the goods are deliverable either to bearer or to the order of the person in possession; or

(C) the person in control of a negotiable electronic document of title.

* * *

(25) Subject to subsection (27), a ~~A~~ person has "notice" of a fact if the person ~~when~~

(a) ~~he~~ has actual knowledge of it; ~~or~~

(b) ~~he~~ has received a notice or notification of it; or

(c) from all the facts and circumstances known to ~~him~~ the person at the time in question, ~~he~~ has reason to know that it exists.

A person "knows" or has "knowledge" of a fact when the person ~~he~~ has actual knowledge of it.

"Discover" or "learn" or a word or phrase of similar import refers to knowledge rather than to reason to know. The time and circumstances under which a notice or notification may cease to be effective are not determined by this Act.

(26) A person "notifies" or "gives" a notice or notification to another person by taking such steps as may be reasonably required to inform the other person in ordinary course, whether or not ~~such other~~ the other person actually comes to know of it. Subject to subsection (27), a ~~A~~ person "receives" a notice or notification when

(a) it comes to ~~his~~ that person's attention; or

(b) it is duly delivered in a form reasonable under the circumstances at the place of business through which the contract was made or at another location ~~any other place~~ held out by that person ~~him~~ as the place for receipt of such communications.

(27) Notice, knowledge, or a notice or notification received by an organization is effective for a particular transaction from the time when it is brought to the attention of the individual conducting that transaction, and in any event, from the time when it would have been brought to the individual's ~~his~~ attention if the organization had exercised due diligence. An organization exercises due diligence if it maintains reasonable routines for communicating significant information to the person conducting the transaction and there is reasonable compliance with the routines. Due diligence does not require an individual acting for the organization to communicate information unless such communication is part of the individual's ~~his~~ regular duties or the individual ~~unless he~~ has reason to know of the transaction and that the transaction would be materially affected by the information.

* * *

(38) ~~"Send" in connection with any writing or notice means to deposit in the mail or deliver for transmission by any other usual means of communication with postage or cost of transmission provided for and properly addressed and in the case of an instrument to an address specified thereon or otherwise agreed, or if there be none to any address reasonable under the circumstances. The receipt of any writing or notice~~

within the time at which it would have arrived if properly sent has the effect of a proper signing.

(38) "Send" in connection with a writing, record, or notice means:

(A) to deposit in the mail or deliver for transmission by any other usual means of communication with postage or cost of transmission provided for and properly addressed and, in the case of an instrument, to an address specified thereon or otherwise agreed, or if there be none to any address reasonable under the circumstances; or

(B) in any other way to cause to be received any record or notice within the time it would have arrived if properly sent.

* * *

(45) "Warehouse receipt" means a document of title receipt issued by a person engaged in the business of storing goods for hire.

Official Comment

* * *

5. "Bearer". From Section 191, Uniform Negotiable Instruments Law. The prior definition has been broadened. The term bearer applies to negotiable documents of title and has been broadened to include a person in control of an electronic negotiable document of title. Control of an electronic document of title is defined in Article 7 (Section 7–106).

6. "Bill of Lading". See similar definitions in Section 1, Uniform Bills of Lading Act. The definition has been enlarged to include freight forwarders' bills and bills issued by contract carriers as well as those issued by common carriers. The definition of airbill is new. A bill of lading is one type of document of title as defined in subsection (15). This definition should be read in conjunction with the definition of carrier in Article 7 (Section 7–102).

* * *

10. "Conspicuous". New. This is intended to indicate some of the methods of making a term attention-calling. But the test is whether attention can reasonably be expected to be called to it. This definition states the general standard that to be conspicuous a term ought to be noticed by a reasonable person. Whether a term is conspicuous is an issue for the court. Subparagraphs (A) and (B) set out several methods for making a term conspicuous. Requiring that a

term be conspicuous blends a notice function (the term ought to be noticed) and a planning function (giving guidance to the party relying on the term regarding how that result can be achieved). Although these paragraphs indicate some of the methods for making a term attention-calling, the test is whether attention can reasonably be expected to be called to it. The statutory language should not be construed to permit a result that is inconsistent with that test.

* * *

14. "Delivery". Section 76, Uniform Sales Act, Section 191, Uniform Negotiable Instruments Law, Section 58, Uniform Warehouse Receipts Act and Section 53, Uniform Bills of Lading Act. The definition has been revised to accommodate electronic documents of title. Control of an electronic document of title is defined in Article 7 (Section 7–106).

15. "Document of title". From Section 76, Uniform Sales Act, but rephrased to eliminate certain ambiguities. This definition makes explicit Thus, by making it explicit that the obligation or designation of a third party as "bailee" is essential to a document, this definition and clearly rejects any such result as obtained in Hixson v. Ward, 254 Ill.App. 505 (1929), which treated a conditional sales contract as a document of title. Also the definition is left open so that new types of documents may be included, including documents which gain commercial recognition in the international arena. See UNCITRAL Draft Instrument on the Carriage of Goods by Sea. It is unforeseeable what documents may one day serve the essential purpose now filled by warehouse receipts and bills of lading. Truck transport has already opened up problems which do not fit the patterns of practice resting upon the assumption that a draft can move through banking channels faster than the goods themselves can reach their destination. There lie ahead air transport and such probabilities as teletype transmission of what may some day be regarded commercially as "Documents of Title". The definition is stated in terms of the function of the documents with the intention that any document which gains commercial recognition as accomplishing the desired result shall be included within its scope. Fungible goods are adequately identified within the language of the definition by identification of the mass of which they are a part.

Dock warrants were within the Sales Act definition of document of title apparently for the purpose of recognizing a valid tender by means of such paper. In current commercial practice a dock warrant or receipt is a kind of interim certificate issued by steamship shipping companies upon delivery of the goods at the dock, entitling a designated person ~~to have issued to him at the company's office~~ to be issued a bill of lading. The receipt itself is invariably nonnegotiable in form although it may indicate that a negotiable bill is to be forthcoming. Such a document is not within the general compass of the definition, although trade usage may in some cases entitle such paper to be treated as a document of title. If the dock receipt actually represents a storage obligation undertaken by the shipping company, then it is a warehouse receipt within this Section regardless of the name given to the instrument.

The goods must be "described", but the description may be by marks or labels and may be qualified in such a way as to disclaim personal knowledge of the issuer regarding contents or condition. However, baggage and parcel checks and similar "tokens" of storage which identify stored goods only as those received in exchange for the token are not covered by this Article. The definition is broad enough to include an airway bill.

A document of title may be either tangible or electronic. Tangible documents of title should be construed to mean traditional paper documents. Electronic documents of title are documents that are stored in an electronic medium instead of in tangible form. The concept of an electronic medium should be construed liberally to include electronic, digital, magnetic, optical, electromagnetic, or any other current or similar emerging technologies. As to reissuing a document of title in an alternative medium, see Article 7, Section 7–105. Control for electronic documents of title is defined in Article 7 (Section 7–106).

* * *

19. "Good faith". See Section 76(2), Uniform Sales Act; Section 58(2), Uniform Warehouse Receipts Act; Section 53(2), Uniform Bills of Lading Act; Section 22(2), Uniform Stock Transfer Act. "Good faith", whenever it is used in the Code, means at least what is here stated. In certain Articles, by specific provision, additional requirements are made applicable. See, e.g., Secs. 2–103(1)(b), ~~7–404~~. To illustrate, in the Article on Sales, Section 2–103, good faith is expressly defined as including in the case of a merchant observance of reasonable commercial standards of fair dealing in the trade, so that throughout that Article wherever a merchant appears in the case an inquiry into his observance of such standards is necessary to determine his good faith.

20. "Holder". See similar definitions in Section 191, Uniform Negotiable Instruments Law; Section 58,

Uniform Warehouse Receipts Act; Section 53, Uniform Bills of Lading Act. The definition has been amended to provide for electronic negotiable documents of title.

* * *

25. ~~"Notice". New. Compare N.I.L. Sec. 56. Under the definition a person has notice when he has received a notification of the fact in question. But by the last sentence the act leaves open the time and circumstances under which notice or notification may cease to be effective. Therefore such cases as Graham v. White-Phillips Co., 296 U.S. 27, 56 S.Ct. 21, 80 L.Ed. 20 (1935), are not overruled.~~

26. ~~"Notifies". New. This is the word used when the essential fact is the proper dispatch of the notice, not its receipt. Compare "Send". When the essential fact is the other party's receipt of the notice, that is stated. The second sentence states when a notification is received.~~

27. ~~New. This makes clear that reason to know, knowledge, or a notification, although "received" for instance by a clerk in Department A of an organization, is effective for a transaction conducted in Department B only from the time when it was or should have been communicated to the individual conducting that transaction.~~

A person has notice of a fact when, inter alia, the person has received a notification of the fact in question. The word "notifies" is used when the essential fact is the proper dispatch of the notice, not its receipt. Compare "send." When the essential fact is the other party's receipt of the notice, that is stated. Subsection (26) states when a notification is received. Subsection (27) makes clear that notice, knowledge, or a notification, although "received," for instance, by a clerk in Department A of an organization, is effective for a transaction conducted in Department B only from the time when it was or should have been communicated to the individual conducting that transaction.

* * *

38. "Send". New. Compare "notifies". The definition of send has been modified to allow for electronic dispatch.

* * *

45. "Warehouse receipt". See Section 76(1), Uniform Sales Act; Section 1, Uniform Warehouse Receipts Act. Receipts issued by a field warehouse are included, provided the warehouseman and the depositor of the goods are different persons. The definition makes clear

that the receipt must qualify as a document of title under subsection (15).

ALTERNATIVE B

Legislative Note: These amendments should be used if the jurisdiction has enacted or is enacting at the same time as this Act the provisions of Revised Article 1 as approved in 2001 .

§ 1–201.   General Definitions.

* * *

(b) Subject to definitions contained in other articles of [the Uniform Commercial Code] that apply to particular articles or parts thereof:

* * *

(5) "Bearer" means a person in control of a negotiable electronic document of title or a person in possession of a negotiable instrument, negotiable tangible document of title, or certificated security that is payable to bearer or indorsed in blank.

(6) "Bill of lading" means a document of title evidencing the receipt of goods for shipment issued by a person engaged in the business of directly or indirectly transporting or forwarding goods. The term does not include a warehouse receipt.

* * *

(15) "Delivery", with respect to an electronic document of title means voluntary transfer of control and with respect to an instrument, a tangible document of title, or chattel paper, means voluntary transfer of possession.

(16) "Document of title" ~~includes bill of lading, dock warrant, dock receipt, warehouse receipt or order for the delivery of goods, and also any other~~ means a record (i) that ~~document which~~ in the regular course of business or financing is treated as adequately evidencing that the person in possession or control of the record ~~it~~ is entitled to receive, control, hold, and dispose of the record ~~document~~ and the goods ~~it~~ the record covers and (ii) that purports to be issued by or addressed to a bailee and to cover goods in the bailee's

possession which are either identified or are fungible portions of an identified mass. The term includes a bill of lading, transport document, dock warrant, dock receipt, warehouse receipt, and order for delivery of goods. ~~To be a document of title, a document must purport to be issued by or addressed to a bailee and purport to cover goods in the bailee's possession which are either identified or are fungible portions of an identified mass.~~ An electronic document of title means a document of title evidenced by a record consisting of information stored in an electronic medium. A tangible document of title means a document of title evidenced by a record consisting of information that is inscribed on a tangible medium.

* * *

(21) "Holder" means:

(A) the person in possession of a negotiable instrument that is payable either to bearer or to an identified person that is the person in possession; ~~or~~

(B) the person in possession of a negotiable tangible document of title if the goods are deliverable either to bearer or to the order of the person in possession; or

(C) the person in control of a negotiable electronic document of title.

* * *

(42) "Warehouse receipt" means a document of title ~~receipt~~ issued by a person engaged in the business of storing goods for hire.

Official Comment

5. "Bearer". Unchanged, except in one respect, from former section 1–201, which was derived from Section 191, Uniform Negotiable Instruments Law. The term bearer applies to negotiable documents of title and has been broadened to include a person in control of an electronic negotiable document of title. Control of an electronic document of title is defined in Article 7 (Section 7–106).

6. "Bill of Lading". Derived from former Section 1–201. The reference to, and definition of, an "airbill" has been deleted as no longer necessary. A bill of

914

lading is one type of document of title as defined in subsection (16). This definition should be read in conjunction with the definition of carrier in Article 7 (Section 7–102).

* * *

15. "Delivery". Derived from former Section 1–201. The reference to certificated securities has been deleted in light of the more specific treatment of the matter in Section 8–301. The definition has been revised to accommodate electronic documents of title. Control of an electronic document of title is defined in Article 7 (Section 7–106).

16. "Document of title". Unchanged Derived from former Section 1–201, which was derived from Section 76, Uniform Sales Act. This definition makes explicit Thus, by making it explicit that the obligation or designation of a third party as "bailee" is essential to a document of title, this definition and clearly rejects any such result as obtained in Hixson v. Ward, 254 Ill.App. 505 (1929), which treated a conditional sales contract as a document of title. Also the definition is left open so that new types of documents may be included, including documents which gain commercial recognition in the international arena. See UNCITRAL Draft Instrument on the Carriage of Goods By Sea. It is unforeseeable what documents may one day serve the essential purpose now filled by warehouse receipts and bills of lading. Truck transport has already opened up problems which do not fit the patterns of practice resting upon the assumption that a draft can move through banking channels faster than the goods themselves can reach their destination. There lie ahead air transport and such probabilities as teletype transmission of what may some day be regarded commercially as "Documents of Title". The definition is stated in terms of the function of the documents with the intention that any document which gains commercial recognition as accomplishing the desired result shall be included within its scope. Fungible goods are adequately identified within the language of the definition by identification of the mass of which they are a part.

Dock warrants were within the Sales Act definition of document of title apparently for the purpose of recognizing a valid tender by means of such paper. In current commercial practice a dock warrant or receipt is a kind of interim certificate issued by steamship shipping companies upon delivery of the goods at the dock, entitling a designated person to have issued to him at the company's office to be issued a bill of lading. The receipt itself is invariably nonnegotiable in form although it may indicate that a negotiable bill is to be forthcoming. Such a document is not within the general compass of the definition, although trade usage may in some cases entitle such paper to be treated as a document of title. If the dock receipt actually represents a storage obligation undertaken by the shipping company, then it is a warehouse receipt within this Section regardless of the name given to the instrument.

The goods must be "described", but the description may be by marks or labels and may be qualified in such a way as to disclaim personal knowledge of the issuer regarding contents or condition. However, baggage and parcel checks and similar "tokens" of storage which identify stored goods only as those received in exchange for the token are not covered by this Article. The definition is broad enough to include an airway bill.

A document of title may be either tangible or electronic. Tangible documents of title should be construed to mean traditional paper documents. Electronic documents of title are documents that are stored in an electronic medium instead of in tangible form. The concept of an electronic medium should be construed liberally to include electronic, digital, magnetic, optical, electromagnetic, or any other current or similar emerging technologies. As to reissuing a document of title in an alternative medium, see Article 7, Section 7–105. Control for electronic documents of title is defined in Article 7 (Section 7–106).

* * *

21. "Holder". Derived from former Section 1–201. The definition has been reorganized for clarity and amended to provide for electronic negotiable documents of title.

* * *

42. "Warehouse receipt". Unchanged Derived from former Section 1–201, which was derived from Section 76(1), Uniform Sales Act; Section 1, Uniform Warehouse Receipts Act. Receipts issued by a field warehouse are included, provided the warehouseman and the depositor of the goods are different persons. The definition makes clear that the receipt must qualify as a document of title under subsection (16).

AMENDMENTS TO UNIFORM COMMERCIAL CODE ARTICLE 2

Legislative Note: These amendments should be adopted in the event a state has not yet adopted Amended Article 2 as approved in 2003.

§ 2–103. Definitions and Index of Definitions.

* * *

(3) "Control" as provided in Section 7–106 and the following definitions in other Articles apply to this Article:

"Check". Section 3–104.

"Consignee". Section 7–102.

"Consignor". Section 7–102.

"Consumer Goods". Section 9–102.

"Dishonor". Section 3–502.

"Draft". Section 3–104.

Official Comment

* * *

2. "Receipt" must be distinguished from delivery particularly in regard to the problems arising out of shipment of goods, whether or not the contract calls for making delivery by way of documents of title, since the seller may frequently fulfill his obligations to "deliver" even though the buyer may never "receive" the goods. Delivery with respect to documents of title is defined in Article 1 and requires transfer of physical delivery of a tangible document of title and transfer of control of an electronic document of title. Otherwise the many divergent incidents of delivery are handled incident by incident.

§ 2–104. Definitions: "Merchant"; "Between Merchants"; "Financing Agency".

* * *

(2) "Financing agency" means a bank, finance company or other person who in the ordinary course of business makes advances against goods or documents of title or who by arrangement with either the seller or the buyer intervenes in ordinary course to make or collect payment due or claimed under the contract for sale, as by purchasing or paying the seller's draft or making advances against it or by merely taking it for collection whether or not documents of title accompany or are associated with the draft. "Financing agency" includes also a bank or other person who similarly intervenes between persons who are in the position of seller and buyer in respect to the goods (Section 2–707).

* * *

§ 2–308. Absence of Specified Place for Delivery.

Official Comment

3. Where "customary banking channels" call only for due notification by the banker that the documents are available on hand, leaving the buyer himself to see to the physical receipt of the goods, tender at the buyer's address is not required under paragraph (c). But that paragraph merely eliminates the possibility of a default by the seller if "customary banking channels" have been properly used in giving notice to the buyer. Where the bank has purchased a draft accompanied by or associated with documents or has undertaken its collection on behalf of the seller, Part 5 of Article 4 spells out its duties and relations to its customer. Where the documents move forward under a letter of credit the Article on Letters of Credit spells out the duties and relations between the bank, the seller and the buyer. Delivery in relationship to either tangible or electronic documents of title is defined in Article 1, Section 1–201.

§ 2–310. Open Time for Payment or Running of Credit; Authority to Ship Under Reservation.

Unless otherwise agreed

(a) payment is due at the time and place at which the buyer is to receive the goods even though the place of shipment is the place of delivery; and

(b) if the seller is authorized to send the goods he may ship them under reservation, and may tender the documents of title, but the buyer may inspect the goods after their arrival before payment is due unless such inspection is inconsistent with the terms of the contract (Section 2–513); and

(c) if delivery is authorized and made by way of documents of title otherwise than by subsection (b) then payment is due regardless of where the goods are to be received (i) at the time and place at which the buyer is to receive delivery of the tangible documents or (ii) at the time the buyer is to receive delivery of the electronic documents and at the seller's place of business or if none, the seller's residence ~~regardless of where the goods are to be received~~; and

(d) where the seller is required or authorized to ship the goods on credit the credit period runs from the time of shipment but post-dating the invoice or delaying its dispatch will correspondingly delay the starting of the credit period.

Official Comment

* * *

2. Paragraph (b) while providing for inspection by the buyer before he pays, protects the seller. He is not required to give up possession of the goods until he has received payment, where no credit has been contemplated by the parties. The seller may collect through a bank by a sight draft against an order bill of lading "hold until arrival; inspection allowed." The obligations of the bank under such a provision are set forth in Part 5 of Article 4. Under subsection (c), in the absence of a credit term, the seller is permitted to ship under reservation and if he does payment is then due where and when the buyer is to receive delivery of the tangible documents of title. In the case of an electronic document of title, payment is due when the buyer is to receive delivery of the electronic document and at the seller's place of business, or if none, the seller's residence. Delivery as to documents of title is stated in Article 1, Section 1–201.

3. Unless otherwise agreed, the place for the ~~receipt~~ delivery of the documents and payment is the buyer's city but the time for payment is only after arrival of the goods, since under paragraph (b), and Sections 2–512 and 2–513 the buyer is under no duty to pay prior to inspection. Tender of a document of title requires that the seller be ready, willing and able to transfer possession of a tangible document of title or control of an electronic document of title to the buyer.

* * *

§ 2–320. C.I.F. and C. & F. Terms.

Official Comment

* * *

5. The seller is given the option of paying or providing for the payment of freight. He has no option to ship "freight collect" unless the agreement so provides. The rule of the common law that the buyer need not pay the freight if the goods do not arrive is preserved.

Unless the shipment has been sent "freight collect" the buyer is entitled to receive documentary evidence that he is not obligated to pay the freight; the seller is therefore required to obtain a receipt "showing that the freight has been paid or provided for." The usual notation ~~in the appropriate space~~ on the bill of lading that the freight has been prepaid is a sufficient receipt, as at common law. The phrase "provided for" is intended to cover the frequent situation in which the carrier extends credit to a shipper for the freight on successive shipments and receives periodical payments of the accrued freight charges from him.

* * *

11. The buyer needs all of the documents required under a C.I.F. contract, in due form and, if a tangible document of title, with necessary endorsements, so that before the goods arrive he may deal with them by negotiating the documents or may obtain prompt possession of the goods after their arrival. If the goods are lost or damaged in transit the documents are necessary to enable him promptly to assert his remedy against the carrier or insurer. The seller is therefore obligated to do what is mercantilely reasonable in the circumstances and should make every reasonable exertion to send forward the documents as soon as possible after the shipment. The requirement that the documents be forwarded with "commercial promptness" expresses a more urgent need for action than that suggested by the phrase "reasonable time".

* * *

§ 2–323. Form of Bill of Lading Required in Overseas Shipment; "Overseas".

(1) Where the contract contemplates overseas shipment and contains a term C.I.F. or C. & F. or F.O.B. vessel, the seller unless otherwise agreed must obtain a negotiable bill of lading stating that the goods have been loaded in board or, in the case of a term C.I.F. or C. & F., received for shipment.

(2) Where in a case within subsection (1) a tangible bill of lading has been issued in a set of parts, unless otherwise agreed if the documents are not to be sent from abroad the buyer may demand tender of the full set; otherwise only one part of the bill of lading need be tendered. Even if the agreement expressly requires a full set

(a) due tender of a single part is acceptable within the provisions of this Article on cure of improper delivery (subsection (1) of Section 2–508); and

(b) even though the full set is demanded, if the documents are sent from abroad the person tendering an incomplete set may nevertheless require payment upon furnishing an indemnity which the buyer in good faith deems adequate.

* * *

Official Comment

* * *

2. Subsection (2) deals with the problem of bills of lading covering deep water shipments, issued not as a single bill of lading but in a set of parts, each part referring to the other parts and the entire set constituting in commercial practice and at law a single bill of lading. Commercial practice in international commerce is to accept and pay against presentation of the first part of a set if the part is sent from overseas even though the contract of the buyer requires presentation of a full set of bills of lading provided adequate indemnity for the missing parts is forthcoming. In accord with the amendment to Section 7–304, bills of lading in a set are limited to tangible bills.

* * *

§ 2–401. Passing of Title; Reservation for Security; Limited Application of This Section.

Each provision of this Article with regard to the rights, obligations and remedies of the seller, the buyer, purchasers or other third parties applies irrespective of title to the goods except where the provision refers to such title. Insofar as situations are not covered by the other provisions of this Article and matters concerning title become material the following rules apply:

(1) Title to goods cannot pass under a contract for sale prior to their identification to the contract (Section 2–501), and unless otherwise explicitly agreed the buyer acquires by their identification a special property as limited by this Act. Any retention or reservation by the seller of the title (property) in goods shipped or delivered to the buyer is limited in effect to a reservation of a security interest. Subject to these provisions and to the provisions of the Article on Secured Transactions (Article 9), title to goods passes from the

seller to the buyer in any manner and on any conditions explicitly agreed on by the parties.

(2) Unless otherwise explicitly agreed title passes to the buyer at the time and place at which the seller completes his performance with reference to the physical delivery of the goods, despite any reservation of a security interest and even though a document of title is to be delivered at a different time or place; and in particular and despite any reservation of a security interest by the bill of lading

(a) if the contract requires or authorizes the seller to send the goods to the buyer but does not require him to deliver them at destination, title passes to the buyer at the time and place of shipment; but

(b) if the contract requires delivery at destination, title passes on tender there.

(3) Unless otherwise explicitly agreed where delivery is to be made without moving the goods,

(a) if the seller is to deliver a tangible document of title, title passes at the time when and the place where he delivers such documents and if the seller is to deliver an electronic document of title, title passes when the seller delivers the document; or

(b) if the goods are at the time of contracting already identified and no documents of title are to be delivered, title passes at the time and place of contracting.

(4) A rejection or other refusal by the buyer to receive or retain the goods, whether or not justified, or a justified revocation of acceptance revests title to the goods in the seller. Such revesting occurs by operation of law and is not a "sale".

Official Comment

* * *

4. The factual situations in subsections (2) and (3) upon which passage of title turn actually base the test upon the time when the seller has finally committed himself in regard to specific goods. Thus in a "shipment" contract he commits himself by the act of making the shipment. If shipment is not contemplated subsection (3) turns on the seller's final commitment, i.e. the delivery of documents or the making of the contract. As to delivery of an electronic document of title, see definition of delivery in Article 1, Section 1–

201. This Article does not state a rule as to the place of title passage as to goods covered by an electronic document of title.

§ 2–403. Power to Transfer; Good Faith Purchase of Goods; "Entrusting".

Official Comment

* * *

2. The many particular situations in which a buyer in ordinary course of business from a dealer has been protected against reservation of property or other hidden interest are gathered by subsections (2)-(4) into a single principle protecting persons who buy in ordinary course out of inventory. Consignors have no reason to complain, nor have lenders who hold a security interest in the inventory, since the very purpose of goods in inventory is to be turned into cash by sale. The principle is extended in subsection (3) to fit with the abolition of the old law of "cash sale" by subsection (1)(c). It is also freed from any technicalities depending on the extended law of larceny; such extension of the concept of theft to include trick, particular types of fraud, and the like is for the purpose of helping conviction of the offender; it has no proper application to the long-standing policy of civil protection of buyers from persons guilty of such trick or fraud. Finally, the policy is extended, in the interest of simplicity and sense, to any entrusting by a bailor; this is in consonance with the explicit provisions of Section 7–205 on the powers of a warehouseman who is also in the business of buying and selling fungible goods of the kind he warehouses stores. As to entrusting by a secured party, subsection (2) is limited by the more specific provisions of Section 9–320, which deny protection to a person buying farm products from a person engaged in farming operations.

* * *

§ 2–503. Manner of Seller's Tender of Delivery.

* * *

(4) Where goods are in the possession of a bailee and are to be delivered without being moved

(a) tender requires that the seller either tender a negotiable document of title covering such goods or procure acknowledgment by the bailee of the buyer's right to possession of the goods; but

(b) tender to the buyer of a non-negotiable document of title or of a written direction to record directing the bailee to deliver is sufficient tender unless the buyer seasonably objects, and except as otherwise provided in Article 9 receipt by the bailee of notification of the buyer's rights fixes those rights as against the bailee and all third persons; but risk of loss of the goods and of any failure by the bailee to honor the non-negotiable document of title or to obey the direction remains on the seller until the buyer has had a reasonable time to present the document or direction, and a refusal by the bailee to honor the document or to obey the direction defeats the tender.

(5) Where the contract requires the seller to deliver documents

(a) he must tender all such documents in correct form, except as provided in this Article with respect to bills of lading in a set (subsection (2) of Section 2–323); and

(b) tender through customary banking channels is sufficient and dishonor of a draft accompanying or associated with the documents constitutes non-acceptance or rejection.

Official Comment

1. The major general rules governing the manner of proper or due tender of delivery are gathered in this section. The term "tender" is used in this Article in two different senses. In one sense it refers to "due tender" which contemplates an offer coupled with a present ability to fulfill all the conditions resting on the tendering party and must be followed by actual performance if the other party shows himself ready to proceed. Unless the context unmistakably indicates otherwise this is the meaning of "tender" in this Article and the occasional addition of the word "due" is only for clarity and emphasis. At other times it is used to refer to an offer of goods or documents under a contract as if in fulfillment of its conditions even though there is a defect when measured against the contract obligation. Used in either sense, however, "tender" connotes such performance by the tendering party as puts the other party in default if he fails to proceed in some manner. These concepts of tender would apply to tender of either tangible or electronic documents of title.

* * *

7. Under subsection (5) documents are never "required" except where there is an express contract term or it is plainly implicit in the peculiar circumstances of the case or in a usage of trade. Documents may, of course, be "authorized" although not required, but such cases are not within the scope of this subsection. When documents are required, there are three main requirements of this subsection: (1) "All": each required document is essential to a proper tender; (2) "Such": the documents must be the ones actually required by the contract in terms of source and substance; (3) "Correct form": All documents must be in correct form. These requirements apply to both tangible and electronic documents of title. When tender is made through customary banking channels, a draft may accompany or be associated with a document of title. The language has been broadened to allow for drafts to be associated with an electronic document of title. Compare Section 2–104(2) definition of financing agency.

When a prescribed document cannot be procured, a question of fact arises under the provision of this Article on substituted performance as to whether the agreed manner of delivery is actually commercially impracticable and whether the substitute is commercially reasonable.

§ 2–505. Seller's Shipment Under Reservation.

(1) Where the seller has identified goods to the contract by or before shipment:

(a) his procurement of a negotiable bill of lading to his own order or otherwise reserves in him a security interest in the goods. His procurement of the bill to the order of a financing agency or of the buyer indicates in addition only the seller's expectation of transferring that interest to the person named.

(b) a non-negotiable bill of lading to himself or his nominee reserves possession of the goods as security but except in a case of conditional delivery (subsection (2) of Section 2–507) a non-negotiable bill of lading naming the buyer as consignee reserves no security interest even though the seller retains possession or control of the bill of lading.

(2) When shipment by the seller with reservation of a security interest is in violation of the contract for sale it constitutes an improper contract for transportation within the preceding section but impairs neither the rights given to the buyer by shipment and identification of the goods to the contract nor the seller's powers as a holder of a negotiable document of title.

Official Comment

* * *

5. Under subsection (2) an improper reservation by the seller which would constitute a breach in no way impairs such of the buyer's rights as result from identification of the goods. The security title reserved by the seller under subsection (1) does not protect his holding retaining possession or control of the document or the goods for the purpose of exacting more than is due him under the contract.

§ 2–506. Rights of Financing Agency.

* * *

(2) The right to reimbursement of a financing agency which has in good faith honored or purchased the draft under commitment to or authority from the buyer is not impaired by subsequent discovery of defects with reference to any relevant document which was apparently regular on its face.

Official Comment

* * *

5. The deletion of the language "on its face" from subsection (2) is designed to accommodate electronic documents of title without changing the requirement of regularity of the document.

§ 2–509. Risk of Loss in The Absence of Breach.

* * *

(2) Where the goods are held by a bailee to be delivered without being moved, the risk of loss passes to the buyer

(a) on his receipt of possession or control of a negotiable document of title covering the goods; or

(b) on acknowledgment by the bailee of the buyer's right to possession of the goods; or

(c) after his receipt of possession or control of a non-negotiable document of title or other

~~written~~ direction to deliver <u>in a record</u>, as provided in subsection (4)(b) of Section 2–503.

* * *

Official Comment

* * *

4. Where the agreement provides for delivery of the goods as between the buyer and seller without removal from the physical possession of a bailee, the provisions on manner of tender of delivery apply on the point of transfer of risk. Due delivery of a negotiable document of title covering the goods or acknowledgment by the bailee that he holds for the buyer completes the "delivery" and passes the risk. <u>See definition of delivery in Article 1, Section 1–201 and the definition of control in Article 7, Section 7–106.</u>

* * *

§ 2–513. Buyer's Right to Inspection of the Goods.

Official Comment

* * *

5. In the case of payment against documents, subsection (3) requires payment before inspection, since shipping documents against which payment is to be made will commonly ~~arrive and~~ be tendered while the goods are still in transit. This Article recognizes no exception in any peculiar case in which the goods happen to arrive before the documents <u>are tendered</u>. However, where by the agreement payment is to await the arrival of the goods, inspection before payment becomes proper since the goods are then "available for inspection."

Where by the agreement the documents are ~~to be held~~ <u>to be tendered after</u> ~~until~~ arrival <u>of the goods</u>, the buyer is entitled to inspect before payment since the goods are then "available for inspection". Proof of usage is not necessary to establish this right, but if inspection before payment is disputed the contrary must be established by usage or by an explicit contract term to that effect.

For the same reason, that the goods are available for inspection, a term calling for payment against storage documents or a delivery order does not normally bar the buyer's right to inspection before payment under subsection (3)(b). This result is reinforced by the buyer's right under subsection (1) to inspect goods which have been appropriated with notice to him.

* * *

§ 2–605. Waiver of Buyer's Objections by Failure to Particularize.

* * *

(2) Payment against documents made without reservation of rights precludes recovery of the payment for defects apparent ~~on the face of~~ <u>in</u> the documents.

Official Comment

* * *

4. Subsection (2) applies to the particular case of documents the same principle which the section on effects of acceptance applies to the case of goods. The matter is dealt with in this section in terms of "waiver" of objections rather than of right to revoke acceptance, partly to avoid any confusion with the problems of acceptance of goods and partly because defects in documents which are not taken as grounds for rejection are generally minor ones. The only defects concerned in the present subsection are defects in the documents which are apparent. ~~on their face.~~ <u>This rule applies to both tangible and electronic documents of title.</u> Where payment is required against the documents they must be inspected before payment, and the payment then constitutes acceptance of the documents. Under the section dealing with this problem, such acceptance of the documents does not constitute an acceptance of the goods or impair any options or remedies of the buyer for their improper delivery. Where the documents are delivered without requiring such contemporary action as payment from the buyer, the reason of the next section on what constitutes acceptance of goods, applies. Their acceptance by non-objection is therefore postponed until after a reasonable time for their inspection. In either situation, however, the buyer "waives" only ~~what is~~ <u>the defects</u> apparent ~~on the face of~~ <u>in</u> the documents.

§ 2–705. Seller's Stoppage of Delivery in Transit or Otherwise.

* * *

(2) As against such buyer the seller may stop delivery until

(a) receipt of the goods by the buyer; or

(b) acknowledgment to the buyer by any bailee of the goods except a carrier that the bailee holds the goods for the buyer; or

(c) such acknowledgment to the buyer by a carrier by reshipment or as a warehouse-man; or

(d) negotiation to the buyer of any negotiable document of title covering the goods.

(3)(a) To stop delivery the seller must so notify as to enable the bailee by reasonable diligence to prevent delivery of the goods.

(b) After such notification the bailee must hold and deliver the goods according to the directions of the seller but the seller is liable to the bailee for any ensuing charges or damages.

(c) If a negotiable document of title has been issued for goods the bailee is not obliged to obey a notification to stop until surrender of possession or control of the document.

(d) A carrier who has issued a non-negotiable bill of lading is not obliged to obey a notification to stop received from a person other than the consignor.

Official Comment

* * *

3. A diversion of a shipment is not a "reshipment" under subsection (2)(c) when it is merely an incident to the original contract of transportation. Nor is the procurement of "exchange bills" of lading which change only the name of the consignee to that of the buyer's local agent but do not alter the destination of a reshipment.

Acknowledgment by the carrier as a "warehouse-man" within the meaning of this Article requires a contract of a truly different character from the original shipment, a contract not in extension of transit but as a warehouseman.

4. Subsection (3)(c) makes the bailee's obedience of a notification to stop conditional upon the surrender of possession or control of any outstanding negotiable document.

* * *

AMENDMENTS TO UNIFORM COMMERCIAL CODE ARTICLE 2A

Legislative Note: These amendments should be used if the jurisdiction has not yet adopted Amended Article 2A as approved in 2003.

§ 2A–103. Definitions and Index of Definitions.

(1) In this Article unless the context otherwise requires:

(a) "Buyer in ordinary course of business" means a person who in good faith and without knowledge that the sale to him [or her] is in violation of the ownership rights or security interest or leasehold interest of a third party in the goods, buys in ordinary course from a person in the business of selling goods of that kind but does not include a pawnbroker. "Buying" may be for cash or by exchange of other property or on secured or unsecured credit and includes receiving acquiring goods or documents of title under a pre-existing contract for sale but does not include a transfer in bulk or as security for or in total or partial satisfaction of a money debt.

* * *

(o) "Lessee in ordinary course of business" means a person who in good faith and without knowledge that the lease to him [or her] is in violation of the ownership rights or security interest or leasehold interest of a third party in the goods, leases in ordinary course from a person in the business of selling or leasing goods of that kind but does not include a pawnbroker. "Leasing" may be for cash or by exchange of other property or on secured or unsecured credit and includes receiving acquiring goods or documents of title under a pre-existing lease contract but does not include a transfer in bulk or as security for or in total or partial satisfaction of a money debt.

* * *

§ 2A–514. Waiver of Lessee's Objections.

* * *

(2) A lessee's failure to reserve rights when paying rent or other consideration against documents precludes recovery of the payment for defects apparent on the face of in the documents.

§ 2A–526. Lessor's Stoppage of Delivery in Transit or Otherwise.

* * *

(2) In pursuing its remedies under subsection (1), the lessor may stop delivery until

(a) receipt of the goods by the lessee;

(b) acknowledgment to the lessee by any bailee of the goods, except a carrier, that the bailee holds the goods for the lessee; or

(c) such an acknowledgment to the lessee by a carrier via reshipment or as a warehouse-man.

* * *

AMENDMENTS TO UNIFORM COMMERCIAL CODE ARTICLE 4

§ 4–104. Definitions and Index of Definitions.

* * *

(c) "Control" as provided in Section 7–106 and the following definitions in other Articles apply to this Article:

"Acceptance" Section 3–409

"Alteration" Section 3–407

"Cashier's check" Section 3–104

"Certificate of deposit" Section 3–104

"Certified check" Section 3–409

"Check" Section 3–104

"Good faith" Section 3–103

"Holder in due course" Section 3–302

"Instrument" Section 3–104

"Notice of dishonor" Section 3–503

"Order" Section 3–103

"Ordinary care" Section 3–103

"Person entitled to enforce" Section 3–301

"Presentment" Section 3–501

"Promise" Section 3–103

"Prove" Section 3–103

"Teller's check" Section 3–104

"Unauthorized signature" Section 3–403

Official Comment

* * *

5. Paragraph (a)(6): "Documentary draft" applies even though the documents do not accompany the draft but are to be received by the drawee or other payor before acceptance or payment of the draft. Documents may be either in electronic or tangible form. See Article 5, Section 5–102, Comment 2 and Article 1, Section 1–201 (definition of "document of title").

* * *

§ 4–210. Security Interest of Collecting Bank in Items, Accompanying Documents and Proceeds.

(a) A collecting bank has a security interest in an item and any accompanying documents or the proceeds of either:

(1) in case of an item deposited in an account, to the extent to which credit given for the item has been withdrawn or applied;

(2) in case of an item for which it has given credit available for withdrawal as of right, to the extent of the credit given, whether or not the credit is drawn upon or there is a right of charge-back; or

(3) if it makes an advance on or against the item.

(b) If credit given for several items received at one time or pursuant to a single agreement is withdrawn or applied in part, the security interest remains upon all the items, any accompanying documents or the proceeds of either. For the purpose of this section, credits first given are first withdrawn.

(c) Receipt by a collecting bank of a final settlement for an item is a realization on its security interest in the item, accompanying documents, and proceeds. So long as the bank does not receive final settlement for the item or give up possession of the item or possession or control of the accompanying documents for purposes other than collection, the security interest continues to that extent and is subject to Article 9, but:

(1) no security agreement is necessary to make the security interest enforceable (Section 9–203(b)(3)(A));

(2) no filing is required to perfect the security interest; and

(3) the security interest has priority over conflicting perfected security interests in the item, accompanying documents, or proceeds.

§ 4–501. Handling of Documentary Drafts; Duty to Send for Presentment and to Notify Customer of Dishonor.

* * *

Official Comment

This section states the duty of a bank handling a documentary draft for a customer. "Documentary draft" is defined in Section 4–104. The duty stated exists even if the bank has bought the draft. This is because to the customer the draft normally represents an underlying commercial transaction, and if that is not going through as planned the customer should know it promptly. An electronic document of title may be presented through allowing access to the document or delivery of the document. Article 1, Section 1–201 (definition of "delivery").

§ 4–503. Responsibility of Presenting Bank for Documents and Goods; Report of Reasons for Dishonor; Referee in Case of Need.

* * *

Official Comment

1. This section states the rules governing, in the absence of instructions, the duty of the presenting bank in case either of honor or of dishonor of a documentary draft. The section should be read in connection with Section 2–514 on when documents are deliverable on acceptance, when on payment. In the case of a dishonor of the draft, the bank, subject to Section 4–504, must return possession or control of the documents to its principal.

2. If the draft is drawn under a letter of credit, Article 5 controls. See Sections 5–109 through 5–114.

AMENDMENTS TO UNIFORM COMMERCIAL CODE ARTICLE 5

§ 5–102. Definitions.

* * *

Official Comment

* * *

2. The definition of "document" contemplates and facilitates the growing recognition of electronic and other nonpaper media as "documents," however, for the time being, data in those media constitute documents only in certain circumstances. For example, a facsimile received by an issuer would be a document only if the letter of credit explicitly permitted it, if the standard practice authorized it and the letter did not prohibit it, or the agreement of the issuer and beneficiary permitted it. The fact that data transmitted in a nonpaper (unwritten) medium can be recorded on paper by a recipient's computer printer, facsimile machine, or the like does not under current practice render the data so transmitted a "document." A facsimile or S.W.I.F.T. message received directly by the issuer is in an electronic medium when it crosses the boundary of the issuer's place of business. One wishing to make a presentation by facsimile (an electronic medium) will have to procure the explicit agreement of the issuer (assuming that the standard practice does not authorize it). Article 5 contemplates that electronic documents may be presented under a letter of credit and the provisions of this Article should be read to apply to electronic documents as well as tangible documents. An electronic document of title is delivered through the voluntary transfer of control. Article 1, Section 1–201 (definition of "delivery"). See Article 7, Section 7–106 on control of an electronic document. Where electronic transmissions are authorized neither by the letter of credit nor by the practice, the beneficiary may transmit the data electronically to its agent who may be able to put it in written form and make a conforming presentation. Cf. Article 7, Section 7–105 on reissuing an electronic document in a tangible medium.

* * *

§ 5–108. Issuer's Rights and Obligations.

* * *

Official Comment

* * *

2.   Section 5–108(a) balances the need of the issuer for time to examine the documents against the possibility that the examiner (at the urging of the applicant or for fear that it will not be reimbursed) will take excessive time to search for defects. What is a "reasonable time" is not extended to accommodate an issuer's procuring a waiver from the applicant. See Article 14c of the UCP.

Under both the UCC and the UCP the issuer has a reasonable time to honor or give notice. The outside limit of that time is measured in business days under the UCC and in banking days under the UCP, a difference that will rarely be significant. Neither business nor banking days are defined in Article 5, but a court may find useful analogies in Regulation CC, 12 CFR 229.2, in state law outside of the Uniform Commercial Code, and in Article 4.

Examiners must note that the seven-day period is not a safe harbor. The time within which the issuer must give notice is the lesser of a reasonable time or seven business days. Where there are few documents (as, for example, with the mine run standby letter of credit), the reasonable time would be less than seven days. If more than a reasonable time is consumed in examination, no timely notice is possible. What is a "reasonable time" is to be determined by examining the behavior of those in the business of examining documents, mostly banks. Absent prior agreement of the issuer, one could not expect a bank issuer to examine documents while the beneficiary waited in the lobby if the normal practice was to give the documents to a person who had the opportunity to examine those together with many others in an orderly process. That the applicant has not yet paid the issuer or that the applicant's account with the issuer is insufficient to cover the amount of the draft is not a basis for extension of the time period.

This section does not preclude the issuer from contacting the applicant during its examination; however, the decision to honor rests with the issuer, and it has no duty to seek a waiver from the applicant or to notify the applicant of receipt of the documents. If the issuer dishonors a conforming presentation, the beneficiary will be entitled to the remedies under Section 5–111, irrespective of the applicant's views.

Even though the person to whom presentation is made cannot conduct a reasonable examination of documents within the time after presentation and before the expiration date, presentation establishes the parties' rights. The beneficiary's right to honor or the issuer's right to dishonor arises upon presentation at the place provided in the letter of credit even though it might take the person to whom presentation has been made several days to determine whether honor or dishonor is the proper course. The issuer's time for honor or giving notice of dishonor may be extended or shortened by a term in the letter of credit. The time for the issuer's performance may be otherwise modified or waived in accordance with Section 5–106.

The issuer's time to inspect runs from the time of its "receipt of documents." Documents are considered to be received only when they are received at the place specified for presentation by the issuer or other party to whom presentation is made. "Receipt of documents" when documents of title are presented must be read in light of the definition of "delivery" in Article 1, Section 1–201 and the definition of "presentment" in Section 5–102(a)(12).

Failure of the issuer to act within the time permitted by subsection (b) constitutes dishonor. Because of the preclusion in subsection (c) and the liability that the issuer may incur under Section 5–111 for wrongful dishonor, the effect of such a silent dishonor may ultimately be the same as though the issuer had honored, i.e., it may owe damages in the amount drawn but unpaid under the letter of credit.

* * *

13.   The last clause of Section 5–108(i)(5) deals with a special case in which the fraud is not committed by the beneficiary, but is committed by a stranger to the transaction who forges the beneficiary's signature. If the issuer pays against documents on which a required signature of the beneficiary is forged, it remains liable to the true beneficiary. This principle is applicable to both electronic and tangible documents.

* * *

§ 5–113.   Transfer by Operation of Law.

* * *

Official Comment

This section affirms the result in Pastor v. Nat. Republic Bank of Chicago, 76 Ill.2d 139, 390 N.E.2d 894 (Ill. 1979) and Federal Deposit Insurance Co. v. Bank of Boulder, 911 F.2d 1466 (10th Cir. 1990). Both electronic and tangible documents may be signed.

An issuer's requirements for recognition of a successor's status might include presentation of a certificate of merger, a court order appointing a bankruptcy trustee or receiver, a certificate of appointment as bankruptcy trustee, or the like. The issuer is entitled to rely upon such documents which on their face demonstrate that presentation is made by a successor of a beneficiary. It is not obliged to make an independent investigation to determine the fact of succession.

AMENDMENTS TO UNIFORM COMMERCIAL CODE ARTICLE 8

§ 8–103. Rules for Determining Whether Certain Obligations and Interests are Securities or Financial Assets.

* * *

(g) A document of title is not a financial asset unless Section 8–102(a)(9)(iii) applies.

Official Comment

* * *

8. Subsection (g) allows a document of title to be a financial asset and thus subject to the indirect holding system rules of Part 5 only to the extent that the intermediary and the person entitled under the document agree to do so. This is to prevent the inadvertent application of the Part 5 rules to intermediaries who may hold either electronic or tangible documents of title.

AMENDMENTS TO UNIFORM COMMERCIAL CODE ARTICLE 9

§ 9–102. Definitions and Index of Definitions.

(a) [Article 9 definitions.] In this article:

* * *

(30) "Document" means a document of title or a receipt of the type described in Section 7–201(2) 7–201(b).

* * *

(b) [Definitions in other articles.] "Control" as provided in Section 7–106 and the following definitions in other articles apply to this article:

"Applicant". Section 5–102.

"Beneficiary". Section 5–102.

"Broker". Section 8–102.

"Certificated security". Section 8–102.

"Check". Section 3–104.

"Clearing corporation". Section 8–102.

"Contract for sale". Section 2–106.

"Customer". Section 4–104.

"Entitlement holder". Section 8–102.

"Financial asset". Section 8–102.

"Holder in due course". Section 3–302.

"Issuer" (with respect to a letter of credit or letter-of-credit right). Section 5–102.

"Issuer" (with respect to a security). Section 8–201.

"Issuer" (with respect to documents of title). Section 7–102.

"Lease". Section 2A–103.

"Lease agreement". Section 2A–103.

"Lease contract". Section 2A–103.

"Leasehold interest". Section 2A–103.

"Lessee". Section 2A–103.

"Lessee in ordinary course of business". Section 2A–103.

"Lessor". Section 2A–103.

"Lessor's residual interest". Section 2A–103.

"Letter of credit". Section 5–102.

"Merchant". Section 2–104.

"Negotiable instrument". Section 3–104.

"Nominated person". Section 5–102.

"Note". Section 3–104.

"Proceeds of a letter of credit". Section 5–114.

"Prove". Section 3–103.

"Sale". Section 2–106.

"Securities account". Section 8–501.

"Securities intermediary". Section 8–102.

"Security". Section 8–102.

"Security certificate". Section 8–102.

"Security entitlement". Section 8–102.

"Uncertificated security". Section 8–102.

Official Comment

* * *

16. **"Document."** The definition of "document" is unchanged in substance from the corresponding definitions in former Section 9–105. incorporates both tangible and electronic documents of title. See Section 1–201(15)[1–201(b)16] and Comment 15 [16].

Legislative Note: Former Article 1 defined document of title in section 1–201(15) and accompanying comment 15. Revised Article 1 defines document of title in Section 1–201(b)(16) and accompanying comment 16. Cross references should be adapted depending upon which version of Article 1 is in force in the jurisdiction.

§ 9–203. Attachment and Enforceability of Security Interest; Proceeds; Supporting Obligations; Formal Requisites.

* * *

(b) **[Enforceability.]** Except as otherwise provided in subsections (c) through (i), a security interest is enforceable against the debtor and third parties with respect to the collateral only if :

(1) value has been given;

(2) the debtor has rights in the collateral or the power to transfer rights in the collateral to a secured party; and

(3) one of the following conditions is met:

(A) the debtor has authenticated a security agreement that provides a description of the collateral and, if the security interest covers timber to be cut, a description of the land concerned;

(B) the collateral is not a certificated security and is in the possession of the secured party under Section 9–313 pursuant to the debtor's security agreement;

(C) the collateral is a certificated security in registered form and the security certificate has been delivered to the secured party under Section 8–301 pursuant to the debtor's security agreement; or

(D) the collateral is deposit accounts, electronic chattel paper, investment property, or letter-of-credit rights, or electronic documents, and the secured party has control under Section 7–106, 9–104, 9–105, 9–106, or 9–107 pursuant to the debtor's security agreement.

* * *

Official Comment

* * *

4. **Possession, Delivery, or Control Pursuant to Security Agreement.** The other alternatives in subsection (b)(3) dispense with the requirement of an authenticated security agreement and provide alternative evidentiary tests. Under paragraph (3)(B), the secured party's possession substitutes for the debtor's authentication under paragraph (3)(A) if the secured party's possession is "pursuant to the debtor's security agreement." That phrase refers to the debtor's agreement to the secured party's possession for the purpose of creating a security interest. The phrase should not be confused with the phrase "debtor has authenticated a security agreement," used in paragraph (3)(A), which contemplates the debtor's authentication of a record. In the unlikely event that possession is obtained without the debtor's agreement, possession would not suffice as a substitute for an authenticated security agreement. However, once the security interest has become enforceable and has attached, it is not impaired by the fact that the secured party's possession is maintained without the agreement of a subsequent debtor (e.g., a transferee). Possession as contemplated by Section 9–313 is possession for purposes of subsection (b)(3)(B), even though it may not constitute possession "pursuant to the debtor's agreement" and consequently might not serve as a substitute for an authenticated security agreement under subsection (b)(3)(A). Subsection (b)(3)(C) provides that delivery of a certificated security to the secured party under Section 8–301 pursuant to the debtor's security agreement is sufficient as a substitute for an authenticated security agreement. Similarly, under subsection (b)(3)(D), control of investment property, a deposit

account, electronic chattel paper, ~~or~~ a letter-of-credit right, or electronic documents satisfies the evidentiary test if control is pursuant to the debtor's security agreement.

* * *

§ 9–207. Rights and Duties of Secured Party Having Possession or Control of Collateral.

* * *

(c) **[Duties and rights when secured party in possession or control.]** Except as otherwise provided in subsection (d), a secured party having possession of collateral or control of collateral under Section 7–106, 9–104, 9–105, 9–106, or 9–107:

(1) may hold as additional security any proceeds, except money or funds, received from the collateral;

(2) shall apply money or funds received from the collateral to reduce the secured obligation, unless remitted to the debtor; and

(3) may create a security interest in the collateral.

* * *

§ 9–208. Additional Duties of Secured Party Having Control of Collateral.

(a) **[Applicability of section.]** This section applies to cases in which there is no outstanding secured obligation and the secured party is not committed to make advances, incur obligations, or otherwise give value.

(b) **[Duties of secured party after receiving demand from debtor.]** Within 10 days after receiving an authenticated demand by the debtor:

(1) a secured party having control of a deposit account under Section 9–104(a)(2) shall send to the bank with which the deposit account is maintained an authenticated statement that releases the bank from any further obligation to comply with instructions originated by the secured party;

(2) a secured party having control of a deposit account under Section 9–104(a)(3) shall:

(A) pay the debtor the balance on deposit in the deposit account; or

(B) transfer the balance on deposit into a deposit account in the debtor's name;

(3) a secured party, other than a buyer, having control of electronic chattel paper under Section 9–105 shall:

(A) communicate the authoritative copy of the electronic chattel paper to the debtor or its designated custodian;

(B) if the debtor designates a custodian that is the designated custodian with which the authoritative copy of the electronic chattel paper is maintained for the secured party, communicate to the custodian an authenticated record releasing the designated custodian from any further obligation to comply with instructions originated by the secured party and instructing the custodian to comply with instructions originated by the debtor; and

(C) take appropriate action to enable the debtor or its designated custodian to make copies of or revisions to the authoritative copy which add or change an identified assignee of the authoritative copy without the consent of the secured party;

(4) a secured party having control of investment property under Section 8–106(d)(2) or 9–106(b) shall send to the securities intermediary or commodity intermediary with which the security entitlement or commodity contract is maintained an authenticated record that releases the securities intermediary or commodity intermediary from any further obligation to comply with entitlement orders or directions originated by the secured party; ~~and~~

(5) a secured party having control of a letter-of-credit right under Section 9–107 shall send to each person having an unfulfilled obligation to pay or deliver proceeds of the letter of credit to the secured party an authenticated release from any further obligation to pay or deliver proceeds of the letter of credit to the secured party; and

(6) a secured party having control of an electronic document shall:

(A) give control of the electronic document to the debtor or its designated custodian;

(B) if the debtor designates a custodian that is the designated custodian with which the authoritative copy of the electronic document is maintained for the secured party, communicate to the custodian an authenticated record releasing the designated custodian from any further obligation to comply with instructions originated by the secured party and instructing the custodian to comply with instructions originated by the debtor; and

(C) take appropriate action to enable the debtor or its designated custodian to make copies of or revisions to the authoritative copy which add or change an identified assignee of the authoritative copy without the consent of the secured party.

Official Comment

* * *

2. **Scope and Purpose.** This section imposes duties on a secured party who has control of a deposit account, electronic chattel paper, investment property, ~~or~~ a letter-of-credit right, or electronic documents of title. The duty to terminate the secured party's control is analogous to the duty to file a termination statement, imposed by Section 9–513. Under subsection (a), it applies only when there is no outstanding secured obligation and the secured party is not committed to give value. The requirements of this section can be varied by agreement under Section 1–102(3). For example, a debtor could by contract agree that the secured party may comply with subsection (b) by releasing control more than 10 days after demand. Also, duties under this section should not be read to conflict with the terms of the collateral itself. For example, if the collateral is a time deposit account, subsection (b)(2) should not require a secured party with control to make an early withdrawal of the funds (assuming that were possible) in order to pay them over to the debtor or put them in an account in the debtor's name.

* * *

§ 9–301. Law Governing Perfection and Priority of Security Interests.

Except as otherwise provided in Sections 9–303 through 9–306, the following rules determine the law governing perfection, the effect of perfection or nonperfection, and the priority of a security interest in collateral:

(1) Except as otherwise provided in this section, while a debtor is located in a jurisdiction, the local law of that jurisdiction governs perfection, the effect of perfection or nonperfection, and the priority of a security interest in collateral.

(2) While collateral is located in a jurisdiction, the local law of that jurisdiction governs perfection, the effect of perfection or nonperfection, and the priority of a possessory security interest in that collateral.

(3) Except as otherwise provided in paragraph (4), while tangible negotiable documents, goods, instruments, money, or tangible chattel paper is located in a jurisdiction, the local law of that jurisdiction governs:

(A) perfection of a security interest in the goods by filing a fixture filing;

(B) perfection of a security interest in timber to be cut; and

(C) the effect of perfection or nonperfection and the priority of a nonpossessory security interest in the collateral.

(4) The local law of the jurisdiction in which the wellhead or minehead is located governs perfection, the effect of perfection or nonperfection, and the priority of a security interest in as-extracted collateral.

Official Comment

* * *

5. **Law Governing Perfection: Exceptions.** The general rule is subject to several exceptions. It does not apply to goods covered by a certificate of title (see Section 9–303), deposit accounts (see Section 9–304), investment property (see Section 9–305), or letter-of-credit rights (see Section 9–306). Nor does it apply to possessory security interests, i.e., security interests that the secured party has perfected by taking possession of the collateral (see paragraph (2)), security interests perfected by filing a fixture filing (see subparagraph (3)(A)), security interests in timber to be cut (subparagraph (3)(B)), or security interests in as-extracted collateral (see paragraph (4)).

a. **Possessory Security Interests.** Paragraph (2) applies to possessory security interests and provides that perfection is governed by the local law of the jurisdiction in which the collateral is located. This is the rule of former Section 9–103(1)(b), except paragraph (2) eliminates the troublesome "last event" test of former law.

The distinction between nonpossessory and possessory security interests creates the potential for the same jurisdiction to apply two different choice-of-law rules to determine perfection in the same collateral. For example, were a secured party in possession of an instrument or a tangible document to relinquish possession in reliance on temporary perfection, the applicable law immediately would change from that of the location of the collateral to that of the location of the debtor. The applicability of two different choice-of-law rules for perfection is unlikely to lead to any material practical problems. The perfection rules of one Article 9 jurisdiction are likely to be identical to those of another. Moreover, under paragraph (3), the relative priority of competing security interests in tangible collateral is resolved by reference to the law of the jurisdiction in which the collateral is located, regardless of how the security interests are perfected.

* * *

7. **Law Governing Effect of Perfection and Priority: Goods, Documents, Instruments, Money, Negotiable Documents, and Tangible Chattel Paper.** Under former Section 9–103, the law of a single jurisdiction governed both questions of perfection and those of priority. This Article generally adopts that approach. See paragraph (1). But the approach may create problems if the debtor and collateral are located in different jurisdictions. For example, assume a security interest in equipment located in Pennsylvania is perfected by filing in Illinois, where the debtor is located. If the law of the jurisdiction in which the debtor is located were to govern priority, then the priority of an execution lien on goods located in Pennsylvania would be governed by rules enacted by the Illinois legislature.

To address this problem, paragraph (3)(C) divorces questions of perfection from questions of "the effect of perfection or nonperfection and the priority of a security interest." Under paragraph (3)(C), the rights of competing claimants to tangible collateral are resolved by reference to the law of the jurisdiction in which the collateral is located. A similar bifurcation applied to security interests in investment property under former Section 9–103(6). See Section 9–305.

Paragraph (3)(C) applies the law of the situs to determine priority only with respect to goods (including fixtures), instruments, money, tangible negotiable documents, and tangible chattel paper. Compare former Section 9–103(1), which applied the law of the location of the collateral to documents, instruments, and "ordinary" (as opposed to "mobile") goods. This Article does not distinguish among types of goods. The ordinary/mobile goods distinction appears to address concerns about where to file and search, rather than concerns about priority. There is no reason to preserve this distinction under the bifurcated approach.

Particularly serious confusion may arise when the choice-of-law rules of a given jurisdiction result in each of two competing security interests in the same collateral being governed by a different priority rule. The potential for this confusion existed under former Section 9–103(4) with respect to chattel paper: Perfection by possession was governed by the law of the location of the paper, whereas perfection by filing was governed by the law of the location of the debtor. Consider the mess that would have been created if the language or interpretation of former Section 9–308 were to differ in the two relevant States, or if one of the relevant jurisdictions (e.g., a foreign country) had not adopted Article 9. The potential for confusion could have been exacerbated when a secured party perfected both by taking possession in the State where the collateral is located (State A) and by filing in the State where the debtor is located (State B)—a common practice for some chattel paper financers. By providing that the law of the jurisdiction in which the collateral is located governs priority, paragraph (3) substantially diminishes this problem.

* * *

§ 9–308. When Security Interest or Agricultural Lien Is Perfected; Continuity of Perfection.

Official Comment

* * *

4. **Continuous Perfection.** The following example illustrates the operation of subsection (c):

Example 1: Debtor, an importer, creates a security interest in goods that it imports and the documents of title that cover the goods. The secured party, Bank, takes possession of a tangible negotiable bill of lading covering certain imported goods and thereby perfects its security interest in the bill of lading and the goods. See Sections 9–313(a), 9–

312(c)(1). Bank releases the bill of lading to the debtor for the purpose of procuring the goods from the carrier and selling them. Under Section 9–312(f), Bank continues to have a perfected security interest in the document and goods for 20 days. Bank files a financing statement covering the collateral before the expiration of the 20–day period. Its security interest now continues perfected for as long as the filing is good.

If the successive stages of Bank's security interest succeed each other without an intervening gap, the security interest is "perfected continuously," and the date of perfection is when the security interest first became perfected (i.e., when Bank received possession of the tangible bill of lading). If, however, there is a gap between stages—for example, if Bank does not file until after the expiration of the 20–day period specified in Section 9–312(f) and leaves the collateral in the debtor's possession—then, the chain being broken, the perfection is no longer continuous. The date of perfection would now be the date of filing (after expiration of the 20–day period). Bank's security interest would be vulnerable to any interests arising during the gap period which under Section 9–317 take priority over an unperfected security interest.

* * *

§ 9–310. **When Filing Required to Perfect Security Interest or Agricultural Lien; Security Interests and Agricultural Liens to Which Filing Provisions Do Not Apply.**

* * *

(b) **[Exceptions: filing not necessary.]** The filing of a financing statement is not necessary to perfect a security interest:

(1) that is perfected under Section 9–308(d), (e), (f), or (g);

(2) that is perfected under Section 9–309 when it attaches;

(3) in property subject to a statute, regulation, or treaty described in Section 9–311(a);

(4) in goods in possession of a bailee which is perfected under Section 9–312(d)(1) or (2);

(5) in certificated securities, documents, goods, or instruments which is perfected without filing, control, or possession under Section 9–312(e), (f), or (g);

(6) in collateral in the secured party's possession under Section 9–313;

(7) in a certificated security which is perfected by delivery of the security certificate to the secured party under Section 9–313;

(8) in deposit accounts, electronic chattel paper, electronic documents, investment property, or letter-of-credit rights which is perfected by control under Section 9–314;

(9) in proceeds which is perfected under Section 9–315; or

(10) that is perfected under Section 9–316.

* * *

§ 9–312. **Perfection of Security Interests in Chattel Paper, Deposit Accounts, Documents, Goods Covered by Documents, Instruments, Investment Property, Letter–of–Credit Rights, and Money; Perfection by Permissive Filing; Temporary Perfection Without Filing or Transfer of Possession.**

* * *

(e) **[Temporary perfection: new value.]** A security interest in certificated securities, negotiable documents, or instruments is perfected without filing or the taking of possession or control for a period of 20 days from the time it attaches to the extent that it arises for new value given under an authenticated security agreement.

* * *

Official Comment

* * *

3. **Chattel Paper; Negotiable Documents.** Subsection (a) further provides that filing is available as a method of perfection for security interests in chattel paper and negotiable documents. Tangible chattel paper is sometimes delivered to the assignee, and sometimes left in the hands of the assignor for collection. Subsection (a) allows the assignee to perfect its security interest by filing in the latter case. Alternatively, the assignee may perfect by taking possession. See Section 9–313(a). An assignee of electronic chattel paper may perfect by taking control. See Sections 9–314(a), 9–105. The security interest of an assignee who takes possession or control may qualify for priority

over a competing security interest perfected by filing. See Section 9–330.

Negotiable documents may be, and usually are, delivered to the secured party. See Article 1, Section 1–201 (definition of "delivery"). The secured party's taking possession of a tangible document or control of an electronic document will suffice as a perfection step. See Sections 9–313(a), 9–314 and 7–106. However, as is the case with chattel paper, a security interest in a negotiable document may be perfected by filing.

* * *

7. **Goods Covered by Document of Title.** Subsection (c) applies to goods in the possession of a bailee who has issued a negotiable document covering the goods. Subsection (d) applies to goods in the possession of a bailee who has issued a nonnegotiable document of title, including a document of title that is "non-negotiable" under Section 7–104. Section 9–313 governs perfection of a security interest in goods in the possession of a bailee who has not issued a document of title.

Subsection (c) clarifies the perfection and priority rules in former Section 9–304(2). Consistently with the provisions of Article 7, subsection (c) takes the position that, as long as a negotiable document covering goods is outstanding, title to the goods is, so to say, locked up in the document. Accordingly, a security interest in goods covered by a negotiable document may be perfected by perfecting a security interest in the document. The security interest also may be perfected by another method, e.g., by filing. The priority rule in subsection (c) governs only priority between (i) a security interest in goods which is perfected by perfecting in the document and (ii) a security interest in the goods which becomes perfected by another method while the goods are covered by the document.

Example 1: While wheat is in a grain elevator and covered by a negotiable warehouse receipt, Debtor creates a security interest in the wheat in favor of SP–1 and SP–2. SP–1 perfects by filing a financing statement covering "wheat." Thereafter, SP–2 perfects by filing a financing statement describing the warehouse receipt. Subsection (c)(1) provides that SP–2's security interest is perfected. Subsection (c)(2) provides that SP–2's security interest is senior to SP–1's.

Example 2: The facts are as in Example 1, but SP–1's security interest attached and was perfected before the goods were delivered to the grain elevator. Subsection (c)(2) does not apply, because SP–1's security interest did not become perfected during the time that the wheat was in the possession of a bailee.

Rather, the first-to-file-or-perfect priority rule applies. See Sections 9–322 and 7–503.

A secured party may become "a holder to whom a negotiable document of title has been duly negotiated" under Section 7–501. If so, the secured party acquires the rights specified by Article 7. Article 9 does not limit those rights, which may include the right to priority over an earlier-perfected security interest. See Section 9–331(a).

Subsection (d) takes a different approach to the problem of goods covered by a nonnegotiable document. Here, title to the goods is not looked on as being locked up in the document, and the secured party may perfect its security interest directly in the goods by filing as to them. The subsection provides two other methods of perfection: issuance of the document in the secured party's name (as consignee of a straight bill of lading or the person to whom delivery would be made under a non-negotiable warehouse receipt) and receipt of notification of the secured party's interest by the bailee. Perfection under subsection (d) occurs when the bailee receives notification of the secured party's interest in the goods, regardless of who sends the notification. Receipt of notification is effective to perfect, regardless of whether the bailee responds. Unlike former Section 9–304(3), from which it derives, subsection (d) does not apply to goods in the possession of a bailee who has not issued a document of title. Section 9–313(c) covers that case and provides that perfection by possession as to goods not covered by a document requires the bailee's acknowledgment.

8. **Temporary Perfection Without Having First Otherwise Perfected.** Subsection (e) follows former Section 9–304(4) in giving perfected status to security interests in certificated securities, instruments, and negotiable documents for a short period (reduced from 21 to 20 days, which is the time period generally applicable in this Article), although there has been no filing and the collateral is in the debtor's possession or control. The 20–day temporary perfection runs from the date of attachment. There is no limitation on the purpose for which the debtor is in possession, but the secured party must have given "new value" (defined in Section 9–102) under an authenticated security agreement.

9. **Maintaining Perfection After Surrendering Possession.** There are a variety of legitimate reasons—many of them are described in subsections (f) and (g)—why certain types of collateral must be released temporarily to a debtor. No useful purpose would be served by cluttering the files with records of such exceedingly short term transactions.

Subsection (f) affords the possibility of 20–day perfection in negotiable documents and goods in the possession of a bailee but not covered by a negotiable document. Subsection (g) provides for 20–day perfection in certificated securities and instruments. These subsections derive from former Section 9–305(5). However, the period of temporary perfection has been reduced from 21 to 20 days, which is the time period generally applicable in this Article, and "enforcement" has been added in subsection (g) as one of the special and limited purposes for which a secured party can release an instrument or certificated security to the debtor and still remain perfected. The period of temporary perfection runs from the date a secured party who already has a perfected security interest turns over the collateral to the debtor. There is no new value requirement, but the turnover must be for one or more of the purposes stated in subsection (f) or (g). The 20–day period may be extended by perfecting as to the collateral by another method before the period expires. However, if the security interest is not perfected by another method until after the 20–day period expires, there will be a gap during which the security interest is unperfected.

Temporary perfection extends only to the negotiable document or goods under subsection (f) and only to the certificated security or instrument under subsection (g). It does not extend to proceeds. If the collateral is sold, the security interest will continue in the proceeds for the period specified in Section 9–315.

Subsections (f) and (g) deal only with perfection. Other sections of this Article govern the priority of a security interest in goods after surrender of possession or control of the document covering them. In the case of a purchase-money security interest in inventory, priority may be conditioned upon giving notification to a prior inventory financer. See Section 9–324.

§ 9–313. When Possession by or Delivery to Secured Party Perfects Security Interest Without Filing.

(a) [Perfection by possession or delivery.] Except as otherwise provided in subsection (b), a secured party may perfect a security interest in tangible negotiable documents, goods, instruments, money, or tangible chattel paper by taking possession of the collateral. A secured party may perfect a security interest in certificated securities by taking delivery of the certificated securities under Section 8–301.

* * *

Official Comment

* * *

2. **Perfection by Possession.** As under the common law of pledge, no filing is required by this Article to perfect a security interest if the secured party takes possession of the collateral. See Section 9–310(b)(6).

This section permits a security interest to be perfected by the taking of possession only when the collateral is goods, instruments, tangible negotiable documents, money, or tangible chattel paper. Accounts, commercial tort claims, deposit accounts, investment property, letter-of-credit rights, letters of credit, and oil, gas, or other minerals before extraction are excluded. (But see Comment 6, below, regarding certificated securities.) A security interest in accounts and payment intangibles—property not ordinarily represented by any writing whose delivery operates to transfer the right to payment—may under this Article be perfected only by filing. This rule would not be affected by the fact that a security agreement or other record described the assignment of such collateral as a "pledge." Section 9–309(2) exempts from filing certain assignments of accounts or payment intangibles which are out of the ordinary course of financing. These exempted assignments are perfected when they attach. Similarly, under Section 9–309(3), sales of payment intangibles are automatically perfected.

§ 9–314. Perfection by Control.

(a) [Perfection by control.] A security interest in investment property, deposit accounts, letter-of-credit rights, or electronic chattel paper, or electronic documents may be perfected by control of the collateral under Section 7–106, 9–104, 9–105, 9–106, or 9–107.

(b) [Specified collateral: time of perfection by control; continuation of perfection.] A security interest in deposit accounts, electronic chattel paper, or letter-of-credit rights, or electronic documents is perfected by control under Section 7–106, 9–104, 9–105, or 9–107 when the secured party obtains control and remains perfected by control only while the secured party retains control.

(c) [Investment property: time of perfection by control; continuation of perfection.] A security interest in investment property is perfected by control under Section 9–106 from the time the secured party obtains control and remains perfected by control until:

(1) the secured party does not have control; and

(2) one of the following occurs:

(A) if the collateral is a certificated security, the debtor has or acquires possession of the security certificate;

(B) if the collateral is an uncertificated security, the issuer has registered or registers the debtor as the registered owner; or

(C) if the collateral is a security entitlement, the debtor is or becomes the entitlement holder.

Official Comment

* * *

2. **Control.** This section provides for perfection by control with respect to investment property, deposit accounts, letter-of-credit rights, and electronic chattel paper, and electronic documents. For explanations of how a secured party takes control of these types of collateral, see Sections 9–104 through 9–107 and Section 7–106. Subsection (b) explains when a security interest is perfected by control and how long a security interest remains perfected by control. Like Section 9–313(d) and for the same reasons, subsection (b) makes no reference to the doctrine of "relation back." See Section 9–313, Comment 5. As to an electronic document that is reissued in a tangible medium, Section 7–105, a secured party that is perfected by control in the electronic document should file as to the document before relinquishing control in order to maintain continuous perfection in the document. See Section 9–308.

§ 9–317. Interests That Take Priority Over or Take Free of Security Interest or Agricultural Lien.

* * *

(b) **[Buyers that receive delivery.]** Except as otherwise provided in subsection (e), a buyer, other than a secured party, of tangible chattel paper, tangible documents, goods, instruments, or a security certificate takes free of a security interest or agricultural lien if the buyer gives value and receives delivery of the collateral without knowledge of the security interest or agricultural lien and before it is perfected.

(c) **[Lessees that receive delivery.]** Except as otherwise provided in subsection (e), a lessee of goods takes free of a security interest or agricultural lien if the lessee gives value and receives delivery of the collateral without knowledge of the security interest or agricultural lien and before it is perfected.

(d) **[Licensees and buyers of certain collateral.]** A licensee of a general intangible or a buyer, other than a secured party, of accounts, electronic chattel paper, electronic documents, general intangibles, or investment property other than a certificated security takes free of a security interest if the licensee or buyer gives value without knowledge of the security interest and before it is perfected.

* * *

Official Comment

* * *

6. **Purchasers Other Than Secured Parties.** Subsections (b), (c), and (d) afford priority over an unperfected security interest to certain purchasers (other than secured parties) of collateral. They derive from former Sections 9–301(1)(c), 2A–307(2), and 9–301(d). Former Section 9–301(1)(c) and (1)(d) provided that unperfected security interests are "subordinate" to the rights of certain purchasers. But, as former Comment 9 suggested, the practical effect of subordination in this context is that the purchaser takes free of the security interest. To avoid any possible misinterpretation, subsections (b) and (d) of this section use the phrase "takes free."

Subsection (b) governs goods, as well as intangibles of the type whose transfer is effected by physical delivery of the representative piece of paper (tangible chattel paper, tangible documents, instruments, and security certificates). To obtain priority, a buyer must both give value and receive delivery of the collateral without knowledge of the existing security interest and before perfection. Even if the buyer gave value without knowledge and before perfection, the buyer would take subject to the security interest if perfection occurred before physical delivery of the collateral to the buyer. Subsection (c) contains a similar rule with respect to lessees of goods. Note that a lessee of goods in ordinary course of business takes free of all security interests created by the lessor, even if perfected. See Section 9–321.

Normally, there will be no question when a buyer of tangible chattel paper, tangible documents, instruments, or security certificates "receives delivery" of the property. See Section 1–201 (defining "delivery"). However, sometimes a buyer or lessee of goods, such as complex machinery, takes delivery of the goods in stages and completes assembly at its own location. Under those circumstances, the buyer or lessee "receives delivery" within the meaning of subsections (b) and (c) when, after an inspection of the portion of the goods remaining with the seller or lessor, it would be apparent to a potential lender to the seller or lessor that another person might have an interest in the goods.

The rule of subsection (b) obviously is not appropriate where the collateral consists of intangibles and there is no representative piece of paper whose physical delivery is the only or the customary method of transfer. Therefore, with respect to such intangibles (accounts, electronic chattel paper, <u>electronic documents,</u> general intangibles, and investment property other than certificated securities), subsection (d) gives priority to any buyer who gives value without knowledge, and before perfection, of the security interest. A licensee of a general intangible takes free of an unperfected security interest in the general intangible under the same circumstances. Note that a licensee of a general intangible in ordinary course of business takes rights under a nonexclusive license free of security interests created by the licensor, even if perfected. See Section 9–321.

Unless Section 9–109 excludes the transaction from this Article, a buyer of accounts, chattel paper, payment intangibles, or promissory notes is a "secured party" (defined in Section 9–102), and subsections (b) and (d) do not determine priority of the security interest created by the sale. Rather, the priority rules generally applicable to competing security interests apply. See Section 9–322.

* * *

§ 9–322. Priorities Among Conflicting Security Interests in and Agricultural Liens on Same Collateral.

Official Comment

* * *

Example 3: On October 1, A acquires a temporarily perfected (20–day) security interest, unfiled, in a <u>tangible</u> negotiable document in the debtor's possession under Section 9–312(e). On October 5, B files and thereby perfects a security interest that previously had attached to the same document. On October 10, A files. A has priority, even after the 20–day period expires, regardless of whether A knows of B's security interest when A files. A was the first to perfect and maintained continuous perfection or filing since the start of the 20–day period. However, the perfection of A's security interest extends only "to the extent it arises for new value given." To the extent A's security interest secures advances made by A beyond the 20–day period, its security interest would be subordinate to B's, inasmuch as B was the first to file.

* * *

8. **Proceeds of Non–Filing Collateral: Non–Temporal Priority.** Subsection (c)(2) provides a baseline priority rule for proceeds of non-filing collateral which applies if the secured party has taken the steps required for non-temporal priority over a conflicting security interest in non-filing collateral (e.g., control, in the case of deposit accounts, letter-of-credit rights, ~~and~~ investment property, <u>and in some cases, electronic negotiable documents, section 9–331</u>). This rule determines priority in proceeds of non-filing collateral whether or not there exists an actual conflicting security interest in the original non-filing collateral. Under subsection (c)(2), the priority in the original collateral continues in proceeds if the security interest in proceeds is perfected and the proceeds are cash proceeds or non-filing proceeds "of the same type" as the original collateral. As used in subsection (c)(2), "type" means a type of collateral defined in the Uniform Commercial Code and should be read broadly. For example, a security is "of the same type" as a security entitlement (i.e., investment property), and a promissory note is "of the same type" as a draft (i.e., an instrument).

* * *

§ 9–323. Future Advances.

Official Comment

* * *

Example 2: On October 1, A acquires a temporarily perfected (20–day) security interest, unfiled, in a <u>tangible</u> negotiable document in the debtor's possession under Section 9–312(e) or (f). The security interest secures an advance made on that day as well as future advances. On October 5, B files and thereby perfects a security interest that previously had attached to the same document. On October 8, A makes an additional advance. On October 10, A files. Under Section 9–322(a)(1), because A was the first to perfect and maintained continuous perfection or filing since the start of the 20–day period, A has priority, even after the 20–day period expires. See Section 9–322, Comment 4, Example 3. However, under this section, for purposes of Section 9–322(a)(1), to the extent A's security interest secures the October 8 advance, the security interest was perfected on October 8. Inasmuch as B perfected on October 5, B has priority over the October 8 advance.

* * *

§ 9–338. Priority of Security Interest or Agricultural Lien Perfected by Filed Financing Statement Providing Certain Incorrect Information.

If a security interest or agricultural lien is perfected by a filed financing statement providing information described in Section 9–516(b)(5) which is incorrect at the time the financing statement is filed:

(1) the security interest or agricultural lien is subordinate to a conflicting perfected security interest in the collateral to the extent that the holder of the conflicting security interest gives

value in reasonable reliance upon the incorrect information; and

(2) a purchaser, other than a secured party, of the collateral takes free of the security interest or agricultural lien to the extent that, in reasonable reliance upon the incorrect information, the purchaser gives value and, in the case of tangible chattel paper, tangible documents, goods, instruments, or a security certificate, receives delivery of the collateral.

§ 9–601. Rights After Default; Judicial Enforcement; Consignor or Buyer of Accounts, Chattel Paper, Payment Intangibles, or Promissory Notes.

* * *

(b) **[Rights and duties of secured party in possession or control.]** A secured party in possession of collateral or control of collateral under Section 7–106, 9–104, 9–105, 9–106, or 9–107 has the rights and duties provided in Section 9–207.

* * *

APPENDIX C

UNREVISED UCC ARTICLE 1 (2000)

Set forth below are the text and Official Comments of Article 1 as they existed prior to revision in 2001.

2003 amendments (Article 7 revision) . . . . *Appendix B*
2005 amendments . . . . *Appendix J*

ARTICLE 1
GENERAL PROVISIONS

PART 1.   SHORT TITLE, CONSTRUCTION, APPLICATION AND SUBJECT MATTER OF THE ACT

Section
1–101.   Short Title.
1–102.   Purposes; Rules of Construction; Variation by Agreement.
1–103.   Supplementary General Principles of Law Applicable.
1–104.   Construction Against Implicit Repeal.
1–105.   Territorial Application of the Act; Parties' Power to Choose Applicable Law.
1–106.   Remedies to Be Liberally Administered.
1–107.   Waiver or Renunciation of Claim or Right After Breach.
1–108.   Severability.
1–109.   Section Captions.

PART 2.   GENERAL DEFINITIONS AND PRINCIPLES OF INTERPRETATION

1–201.   General Definitions.
1–202.   Prima Facie Evidence by Third Party Documents.
1–203.   Obligation of Good Faith.
1–204.   Time; Reasonable Time; "Seasonably".
1–205.   Course of Dealing and Usage of Trade.
1–206.   Statute of Frauds for Kinds of Personal Property Not Otherwise Covered.
1–207.   Performance or Acceptance Under Reservation of Rights.
1–208.   Option to Accelerate at Will.
1–209.   Subordinated Obligations.

PART 1

SHORT TITLE, CONSTRUCTION, APPLICATION AND SUBJECT MATTER OF THE ACT

§ 1–101.   Short Title.

This Act shall be known and may be cited as Uniform Commercial Code.

Official Comment

Each Article of the Code (except this Article and Article 10) may also be cited by its own short title.

See Sections 2–101, 3–101, 4–101, 5–101, 6–101, 7–101, 8–101 and 9–101.

937

§ 1–102. Purposes; Rules of Construction; Variation by Agreement.

(1) This Act shall be liberally construed and applied to promote its underlying purposes and policies.

(2) Underlying purposes and policies of this Act are

(a) to simplify, clarify and modernize the law governing commercial transactions;

(b) to permit the continued expansion of commercial practices through custom, usage and agreement of the parties;

(c) to make uniform the law among the various jurisdictions.

(3) The effect of provisions of this Act may be varied by agreement, except as otherwise provided in this Act and except that the obligations of good faith, diligence, reasonableness and care prescribed by this Act may not be disclaimed by agreement but the parties may by agreement determine the standards by which the performance of such obligations is to be measured if such standards are not manifestly unreasonable.

(4) The presence in certain provisions of this Act of the words "unless otherwise agreed" or words of similar import does not imply that the effect of other provisions may not be varied by agreement under subsection (3).

(5) In this Act unless the context otherwise requires

(a) words in the singular number include the plural, and in the plural include the singular;

(b) words of the masculine gender include the feminine and the neuter, and when the sense so indicates words of the neuter gender may refer to any gender.

Official Comment

Prior Uniform Statutory Provision: Section 74, Uniform Sales Act; Section 57, Uniform Warehouse Receipts Act; Section 52, Uniform Bills of Lading Act; Section 19, Uniform Stock Transfer Act; Section 18, Uniform Trust Receipts Act.

Changes: Rephrased and new material added.

Purposes of Changes:

1. Subsections (1) and (2) are intended to make it clear that:

This Act is drawn to provide flexibility so that, since it is intended to be a semi-permanent piece of legislation, it will provide its own machinery for expansion of commercial practices. It is intended to make it possible for the law embodied in this Act to be developed by the courts in the light of unforeseen and new circumstances and practices. However, the proper construction of the Act requires that its interpretation and application be limited to its reason.

Courts have been careful to keep broad acts from being hampered in their effects by later acts of limited scope. Pacific Wool Growers v. Draper & Co., 158 Or. 1, 73 P.2d 1391 (1937), and compare Section 1–104. They have recognized the policies embodied in an act as applicable in reason to subject-matter which was not expressly included in the language of the act, Commercial Nat. Bank of New Orleans v. Canal-Louisiana Bank & Trust Co., 239 U.S. 520, 36 S.Ct. 194, 60 L.Ed. 417 (1916) (bona fide purchase policy of Uniform Warehouse Receipts Act extended to case not covered but of equivalent nature). They have done the same where reason and policy so required, even where the subject-matter had been intentionally excluded from the act in general. Agar v. Orda, 264 N.Y. 248, 190 N.E. 479 (1934) (Uniform Sales Act change in seller's remedies applied to contract for sale of choses in action even though the general coverage of that Act was intentionally limited to goods "other than things in action.") They have implemented a statutory policy with liberal and useful remedies not provided in the statutory text. They have disregarded a statutory limitation of remedy where the reason of the limitation did not apply. Fiterman v. J. N. Johnson & Co., 156 Minn. 201, 194 N.W. 399 (1923) (requirement of return of the goods as a condition to rescission for breach of warranty; also, partial rescission allowed). Nothing in this Act stands in the way of the continuance of such action by the courts.

The Act should be construed in accordance with its underlying purposes and policies. The text of each section should be read in the light of the purpose and policy of the rule or principle in question, as also of the Act as a whole, and the application of the language should be construed narrowly or broadly, as the case may be, in conformity with the purposes and policies involved.

2. Subsection (3) states affirmatively at the outset that freedom of contract is a principle of the Code: "the effect" of its provisions may be varied by "agreement." The meaning of the statute itself must be found in its text, including its definitions, and in appropriate extrinsic aids; it cannot be varied by agreement. But the Code seeks to avoid the type of

interference with evolutionary growth found in Manhattan Co. v. Morgan, 242 N.Y. 38, 150 N.E. 594 (1926). Thus private parties cannot make an instrument negotiable within the meaning of Article 3 except as provided in Section 3–104; nor can they change the meaning of such terms as "bona fide purchaser," "holder in due course," or "due negotiation," as used in this Act. But an agreement can change the legal consequences which would otherwise flow from the provisions of the Act. "Agreement" here includes the effect given to course of dealing, usage of trade and course of performance by Sections 1–201, 1–205 and 2–208; the effect of an agreement on the rights of third parties is left to specific provisions of this Act and to supplementary principles applicable under the next section. The rights of third parties under Section 9–317 when a security interest is unperfected, for example, cannot be destroyed by a clause in the security agreement.

This principle of freedom of contract is subject to specific exceptions found elsewhere in the Act and to the general exception stated here. The specific exceptions vary in explicitness: the statute of frauds found in Section 2–201, for example, does not explicitly preclude oral waiver of the requirement of a writing, but a fair reading denies enforcement to such a waiver as part of the "contract" made unenforceable; Section 9–602, on the other hand, is quite explicit. Under the exception for "the obligations of good faith, diligence, reasonableness and care prescribed by this Act," provisions of the Act prescribing such obligations are not to be disclaimed. However, the section also recognizes the prevailing practice of having agreements set forth standards by which due diligence is measured and explicitly provides that, in the absence of a showing that the standards manifestly are unreasonable, the agreement controls. In this connection, Section 1–205 incorporating into the agreement prior course of dealing and usages of trade is of particular importance.

3. Subsection (4) is intended to make it clear that, as a matter of drafting, words such as "unless otherwise agreed" have been used to avoid controversy as to whether the subject matter of a particular section does or does not fall within the exceptions to subsection (3), but absence of such words contains no negative implication since under subsection (3) the general and residual rule is that the effect of all provisions of the Act may be varied by agreement.

4. Subsection (5) is modelled on 1 U.S.C. Section 1 and New York General Construction Law Sections 22 and 35.

§ 1–103. Supplementary General Principles of Law Applicable.

Unless displaced by the particular provisions of this Act, the principles of law and equity, including the law merchant and the law relative to capacity to contract, principal and agent, estoppel, fraud, misrepresentation, duress, coercion, mistake, bankruptcy, or other validating or invalidating cause shall supplement its provisions.

Official Comment

Prior Uniform Statutory Provision: Sections 2 and 73, Uniform Sales Act; Section 196, Uniform Negotiable Instruments Act; Section 56, Uniform Warehouse Receipts Act; Section 51, Uniform Bills of Lading Act; Section 18, Uniform Stock Transfer Act; Section 17, Uniform Trust Receipts Act.

Changes: Rephrased, the reference to "estoppel" and "validating" being new.

Purposes of Changes:

1. While this section indicates the continued applicability to commercial contracts of all supplemental bodies of law except insofar as they are explicitly displaced by this Act, the principle has been stated in more detail and the phrasing enlarged to make it clear that the "validating", as well as the "invalidating" causes referred to in the prior uniform statutory provisions, are included here. "Validating" as used here in conjunction with "invalidating" is not intended as a narrow word confined to original validation, but extends to cover any factor which at any time or in any manner renders or helps to render valid any right or transaction.

2. The general law of capacity is continued by express mention to make clear that section 2 of the old Uniform Sales Act (omitted in this Act as stating no matter not contained in the general law) is also consolidated in the present section. Hence, where a statute limits the capacity of a non-complying corporation to sue, this is equally applicable to contracts of sale to which such corporation is a party.

3. The listing given in this section is merely illustrative; no listing could be exhaustive. Nor is the fact that in some sections particular circumstances have led to express reference to other fields of law intended at any time to suggest the negation of the general application of the principles of this section.

§ 1–104. Construction Against Implicit Repeal.

This Act being a general act intended as a unified coverage of its subject matter, no part of it shall be deemed to be impliedly repealed by subsequent legislation if such construction can reasonably be avoided.

Official Comment

Prior Uniform Statutory Provision: None.

Purposes:

To express the policy that no Act which bears evidence of carefully considered permanent regulative intention should lightly be regarded as impliedly repealed by subsequent legislation. This Act, carefully integrated and intended as a uniform codification of permanent character covering an entire "field" of law, is to be regarded as particularly resistant to implied repeal. See Pacific Wool Growers v. Draper & Co., 158 Or. 1, 73 P.2d 1391 (1937).

§ 1-105. Territorial Application of the Act; Parties' Power to Choose Applicable Law.

(1) Except as provided hereafter in this section, when a transaction bears a reasonable relation to this state and also to another state or nation the parties may agree that the law either of this state or of such other state or nation shall govern their rights and duties. Failing such agreement this Act applies to transactions bearing an appropriate relation to this state.

(2) Where one of the following provisions of this Act specifies the applicable law, that provision governs and a contrary agreement is effective only to the extent permitted by the law (including the conflict of laws rules) so specified:

Rights of creditors against sold goods. Section 2-402.

Applicability of the Article on Leases. Sections 2A-105 and 2A-106.

Applicability of the Article on Bank Deposits and Collections. Section 4-102.

Governing law in the Article on Funds Transfers. Section 4A-507.

Letters of Credit. Section 5-116.

Bulk sales subject to the Article on Bulk Sales. Section 6-103.

[If a state adopts the repealer of Article 6—Bulk Transfers (Alternative A), there should not be any item relating to bulk transfers. If, however, a state adopts revised Article 6—Bulk Sales (Alternative B),

then the item relating to bulk sales should read as set out ante.]

Applicability of the Article on Investment Securities. Section 8-110.

Law governing perfection, the effect of perfection or nonperfection, and the priority of security interests and agricultural liens. Sections 9-301 through 9-307.

As amended in 1972, 1987, 1988, 1989, 1994, 1995, and 1999.

Official Comment

Prior Uniform Statutory Provision: None.

Purposes:

1. Subsection (1) states affirmatively the right of the parties to a multi-state transaction or a transaction involving foreign trade to choose their own law. That right is subject to the firm rules stated in the five sections listed in subsection (2), and is limited to jurisdictions to which the transaction bears a "reasonable relation." In general, the test of "reasonable relation" is similar to that laid down by the Supreme Court in Seeman v. Philadelphia Warehouse Co., 274 U.S. 403, 47 S.Ct. 626, 71 L.Ed. 1123 (1927). Ordinarily the law chosen must be that of a jurisdiction where a significant enough portion of the making or performance of the contract is to occur or occurs. But an agreement as to choice of law may sometimes take effect as a shorthand expression of the intent of the parties as to matters governed by their agreement, even though the transaction has no significant contact with the jurisdiction chosen.

2. Where there is no agreement as to the governing law, the Act is applicable to any transaction having an "appropriate" relation to any state which enacts it. Of course, the Act applies to any transaction which takes place in its entirety in a state which has enacted the Act. But the mere fact that suit is brought in a state does not make it appropriate to apply the substantive law of that state. Cases where a relation to the enacting state is not "appropriate" include, for example, those where the parties have clearly contracted on the basis of some other law, as where the law of the place of contracting and the law of the place of contemplated performance are the same and are contrary to the law under the Code.

3. Where a transaction has significant contacts with a state which has enacted the Act and also with other jurisdictions, the question what relation is "appropriate" is left to judicial decision. In deciding that

question, the court is not strictly bound by precedents established in other contexts. Thus a conflict-of-laws decision refusing to apply a purely local statute or rule of law to a particular multi-state transaction may not be valid precedent for refusal to apply the Code in an analogous situation. Application of the Code in such circumstances may be justified by its comprehensiveness, by the policy of uniformity, and by the fact that it is in large part a reformulation and restatement of the law merchant and of the understanding of a business community which transcends state and even national boundaries. Compare Global Commerce Corp. v. Clark-Babbitt Industries, Inc., 239 F.2d 716, 719 (2d Cir. 1956). In particular, where a transaction is governed in large part by the Code, application of another law to some detail of performance because of an accident of geography may violate the commercial understanding of the parties.

4. The Act does not attempt to prescribe choice-of-law rules for states which do not enact it, but this section does not prevent application of the Act in a court of such a state. Common-law choice of law often rests on policies of giving effect to agreements and of uniformity of result regardless of where suit is brought. To the extent that such policies prevail, the relevant considerations are similar in such a court to those outlined above.

5. Subsection (2) spells out essential limitations on the parties' right to choose the applicable law. Especially in Article 9 parties taking a security interest or asked to extend credit which may be subject to a security interest must have sure ways to find out whether and where to file and where to look for possible existing filings.

6. Sections 9–301 through 9–307 should be consulted as to the rules for perfection of security interests and agricultural liens, the effect of perfection and nonperfection, and priority.

As amended in 1999.

§ 1–106. Remedies to Be Liberally Administered.

(1) The remedies provided by this Act shall be liberally administered to the end that the aggrieved party may be put in as good a position as if the other party had fully performed but neither consequential or special nor penal damages may be had except as specifically provided in this Act or by other rule of law.

(2) Any right or obligation declared by this Act is enforceable by action unless the provision declaring it specifies a different and limited effect.

Official Comment

Prior Uniform Statutory Provision: Subsection (1)—none; Subsection (2)—Section 72, Uniform Sales Act.

Changes: Reworded.

Purposes of Changes and New Matter: Subsection (1) is intended to effect three things:

1. First, to negate the unduly narrow or technical interpretation of some remedial provisions of prior legislation by providing that the remedies in this Act are to be liberally administered to the end stated in the section. Second, to make it clear that compensatory damages are limited to compensation. They do not include consequential or special damages, or penal damages; and the Act elsewhere makes it clear that damages must be minimized. Cf. Sections 1–203, 2–706(1), and 2–712(2). The third purpose of subsection (1) is to reject any doctrine that damages must be calculable with mathematical accuracy. Compensatory damages are often at best approximate: they have to be proved with whatever definiteness and accuracy the facts permit, but no more. Cf. Section 2–204(3).

2. Under subsection (2) any right or obligation described in this Act is enforceable by court action, even though no remedy may be expressly provided, unless a particular provision specifies a different and limited effect. Whether specific performance or other equitable relief is available is determined not by this section but by specific provisions and by supplementary principles. Cf. Sections 1–103, 2–716.

3. "Consequential" or "special" damages and "penal" damages are not defined in terms in the Code, but are used in the sense given them by the leading cases on the subject.

Cross References:

Sections 1–103, 1–203, 2–204(3), 2–701, 2–706(1), 2–712(2) and 2–716.

Definitional Cross References:

"Action". Section 1–201.
"Aggrieved party". Section 1–201.
"Party". Section 1–201.
"Remedy". Section 1–201.
"Rights". Section 1–201.

§ 1–107. Waiver or Renunciation of Claim or Right After Breach.

Any claim or right arising out of an alleged breach can be discharged in whole or in part without consideration by a written waiver or renunciation signed and delivered by the aggrieved party.

Official Comment

Prior Uniform Statutory Provision: Compare Section 1, Uniform Written Obligations Act; Sections 119(3), 120(2) and 122, Uniform Negotiable Instruments Law.

Purposes:

This section makes consideration unnecessary to the effective renunciation or waiver of rights or claims arising out of an alleged breach of a commercial contract where such renunciation is in writing and signed and delivered by the aggrieved party. Its provisions, however, must be read in conjunction with the section imposing an obligation of good faith. (Section 1–203). There may, of course, also be an oral renunciation or waiver sustained by consideration but subject to Statute of Frauds provisions and to the section of Article 2 on Sales dealing with the modification of signed writings (Section 2–209). As is made express in the latter section this Act fully recognizes the effectiveness of waiver and estoppel.

Cross References:

Sections 1–203, 2–201 and 2–209. And see Section 2–719.

Definitional Cross References:

"Aggrieved party". Section 1–201.

"Rights". Section 1–201.
"Signed". Section 1–201.
"Written". Section 1–201.

§ 1–108. Severability.

If any provision or clause of this Act or application thereof to any person or circumstances is held invalid, such invalidity shall not affect other provisions or applications of the Act which can be given effect without the invalid provision or application, and to this end the provisions of this Act are declared to be severable.

Official Comment

This is the model severability section recommended by the National Conference of Commissioners on Uniform State Laws for inclusion in all acts of extensive scope.

Definitional Cross Reference:

"Person". Section 1–201.

§ 1–109. Section Captions.

Section captions are parts of this Act.

Official Comment

Prior Uniform Statutory Provision: None.

Purposes:

To make explicit in all jurisdictions that section captions are a part of the text of this Act and not mere surplusage.

As amended in 1999.

PART 2

GENERAL DEFINITIONS AND PRINCIPLES OF INTERPRETATION

§ 1–201. General Definitions.

Subject to additional definitions contained in the subsequent Articles of this Act which are applicable to specific Articles or Parts thereof, and unless the context otherwise requires, in this Act:

(1) "Action" in the sense of a judicial proceeding includes recoupment, counterclaim, set-off, suit in equity and any other proceedings in which rights are determined.

(2) "Aggrieved party" means a party entitled to resort to a remedy.

(3) "Agreement" means the bargain of the parties in fact as found in their language or by implication from other circumstances including course of dealing or usage of trade or course of performance as provided in this Act (Sections 1–205, 2–208, and 2A–207). Whether an agreement has legal consequences is determined by the provisions of this Act, if applicable; other-

wise by the law of contracts (Section 1–103). (Compare "Contract".)

(4) "Bank" means any person engaged in the business of banking.

(5) "Bearer" means the person in possession of an instrument, document of title, or certificated security payable to bearer or indorsed in blank.

(6) "Bill of lading" means a document evidencing the receipt of goods for shipment issued by a person engaged in the business of transporting or forwarding goods, and includes an airbill. "Airbill" means a document serving for air transportation as a bill of lading does for marine or rail transportation, and includes an air consignment note or air waybill.

(7) "Branch" includes a separately incorporated foreign branch of a bank.

(8) "Burden of establishing" a fact means the burden of persuading the triers of fact that the existence of the fact is more probable than its non-existence.

(9) "Buyer in ordinary course of business" means a person that buys goods in good faith,without knowledge that the sale violates the rights of another person in the goods, and in the ordinary course from a person, other than a pawnbroker, in the business of selling goods of that kind. A person buys goods in the ordinary course if the sale to the person comports with the usual or customary practices in the kind of business in which the seller is engaged or with the seller's own usual or customary practices. A person that sells oil, gas, or other minerals at the wellhead or minehead is a person in the business of selling goods of that kind. A buyer in ordinary course of business may buy for cash, by exchange of other property, or on secured or unsecured credit, and may acquire goods or documents of title under a pre-existing contract for sale. Only a buyer that takes possession of the goods or has a right to recover the goods from the seller under Article 2 may be a buyer in ordinary course of business. A person that acquires goods in a transfer in bulk or as security for or in total or partial satisfaction of a money debt is not a buyer in ordinary course of business.

(10) "Conspicuous": A term or clause is conspicuous when it is so written that a reasonable person against whom it is to operate ought to have noticed it. A printed heading in capitals (as: NON-NEGOTIABLE BILL OF LADING) is conspicu-ous. Language in the body of a form is "conspicuous" if it is in larger or other contrasting type or color. But in a telegram any stated term is "conspicuous". Whether a term or clause is "conspicuous" or not is for decision by the court.

(11) "Contract" means the total legal obligation which results from the parties' agreement as affected by this Act and any other applicable rules of law. (Compare "Agreement".)

(12) "Creditor" includes a general creditor, a secured creditor, a lien creditor and any representative of creditors, including an assignee for the benefit of creditors, a trustee in bankruptcy, a receiver in equity and an executor or administrator of an insolvent debtor's or assignor's estate.

(13) "Defendant" includes a person in the position of defendant in a cross-action or counterclaim.

(14) "Delivery" with respect to instruments, documents of title, chattel paper, or certificated securities means voluntary transfer of possession.

(15) "Document of title" includes bill of lading, dock warrant, dock receipt, warehouse receipt or order for the delivery of goods, and also any other document which in the regular course of business or financing is treated as adequately evidencing that the person in possession of it is entitled to receive, hold and dispose of the document and the goods it covers. To be a document of title a document must purport to be issued by or addressed to a bailee and purport to cover goods in the bailee's possession which are either identified or are fungible portions of an identified mass.

(16) "Fault" means wrongful act, omission or breach.

(17) "Fungible" with respect to goods or securities means goods or securities of which any unit is, by nature or usage of trade, the equivalent of any other like unit. Goods which are not fungible shall be deemed fungible for the purposes of this Act to the extent that under a particular agreement or document unlike units are treated as equivalents.

(18) "Genuine" means free of forgery or counterfeiting.

(19) "Good faith" means honesty in fact in the conduct or transaction concerned.

(20) "Holder," with respect to a negotiable instrument, means the person in possession if the instrument is payable to bearer or, in the case of an instrument payable to an identified person, if the identified person is in possession. "Holder" with respect to a document of title means the person in possession if the goods are deliverable to bearer or to the order of the person in possession.

(21) To "honor" is to pay or to accept and pay, or where a credit so engages to purchase or discount a draft complying with the terms of the credit.

(22) "Insolvency proceedings" includes any assignment for the benefit of creditors or other proceedings intended to liquidate or rehabilitate the estate of the person involved.

(23) A person is "insolvent" who either has ceased to pay his debts in the ordinary course of business or cannot pay his debts as they become due or is insolvent within the meaning of the federal bankruptcy law.

(24) "Money" means a medium of exchange authorized or adopted by a domestic or foreign government and includes a monetary unit of account established by an intergovernmental organization or by agreement between two or more nations.

(25) A person has "notice" of a fact when

(a) he has actual knowledge of it; or

(b) he has received a notice or notification of it; or

(c) from all the facts and circumstances known to him at the time in question he has reason to know that it exists.

A person "knows" or has "knowledge" of a fact when he has actual knowledge of it. "Discover" or "learn" or a word or phrase of similar import refers to knowledge rather than to reason to know. The time and circumstances under which a notice or notification may cease to be effective are not determined by this Act.

(26) A person "notifies" or "gives" a notice or notification to another by taking such steps as may be reasonably required to inform the other in ordinary course whether or not such other actually comes to know of it. A person "receives" a notice or notification when

(a) it comes to his attention; or

(b) it is duly delivered at the place of business through which the contract was made or at any other place held out by him as the place for receipt of such communications.

(27) Notice, knowledge or a notice or notification received by an organization is effective for a particular transaction from the time when it is brought to the attention of the individual conducting that transaction, and in any event from the time when it would have been brought to his attention if the organization had exercised due diligence. An organization exercises due diligence if it maintains reasonable routines for communicating significant information to the person conducting the transaction and there is reasonable compliance with the routines. Due diligence does not require an individual acting for the organization to communicate information unless such communication is part of his regular duties or unless he has reason to know of the transaction and that the transaction would be materially affected by the information.

(28) "Organization" includes a corporation, government or governmental subdivision or agency, business trust, estate, trust, partnership or association, two or more persons having a joint or common interest, or any other legal or commercial entity.

(29) "Party", as distinct from "third party", means a person who has engaged in a transaction or made an agreement within this Act.

(30) "Person" includes an individual or an organization (See Section 1–102).

(31) "Presumption" or "presumed" means that the trier of fact must find the existence of the fact presumed unless and until evidence is introduced which would support a finding of its non-existence.

(32) "Purchase" includes taking by sale, discount, negotiation, mortgage, pledge, lien, security interest, issue or re-issue, gift or any other voluntary transaction creating an interest in property.

(33) "Purchaser" means a person who takes by purchase.

(34) "Remedy" means any remedial right to which an aggrieved party is entitled with or without resort to a tribunal.

(35) "Representative" includes an agent, an officer of a corporation or association, and a

trustee, executor or administrator of an estate, or any other person empowered to act for another.

(36) "Rights" includes remedies.

(37) "Security interest" means an interest in personal property or fixtures which secures payment or performance of an obligation. The term also includes any interest of a consignor and a buyer of accounts, chattel paper, a payment intangible, or a promissory note in a transaction that is subject to Article 9. The special property interest of a buyer of goods on identification of those goods to a contract for sale under Section 2–401 is not a "security interest", but a buyer may also acquire a "security interest" by complying with Article 9. Except as otherwise provided in Section 2–505, the right of a seller or lessor of goods under Article 2 or 2A to retain or acquire possession of the goods is not a "security interest", but a seller or lessor may also acquire a "security interest" by complying with Article 9. The retention or reservation of title by a seller of goods notwithstanding shipment or delivery to the buyer (Section 2–401) is limited in effect to a reservation of a "security interest".

Whether a transaction creates a lease or security interest is determined by the facts of each case; however, a transaction creates a security interest if the consideration the lessee is to pay the lessor for the right to possession and use of the goods is an obligation for the term of the lease not subject to termination by the lessee, and

(a) the original term of the lease is equal to or greater than the remaining economic life of the goods,

(b) the lessee is bound to renew the lease for the remaining economic life of the goods or is bound to become the owner of the goods,

(c) the lessee has an option to renew the lease for the remaining economic life of the goods for no additional consideration or nominal additional consideration upon compliance with the lease agreement, or

(d) the lessee has an option to become the owner of the goods for no additional consideration or nominal additional consideration upon compliance with the lease agreement.

A transaction does not create a security interest merely because it provides that

(a) the present value of the consideration the lessee is obligated to pay the lessor for the right to possession and use of the goods is substantially equal to or is greater than the fair market value of the goods at the time the lease is entered into,

(b) the lessee assumes risk of loss of the goods, or agrees to pay taxes, insurance, filing, recording, or registration fees, or service or maintenance costs with respect to the goods,

(c) the lessee has an option to renew the lease or to become the owner of the goods,

(d) the lessee has an option to renew the lease for a fixed rent that is equal to or greater than the reasonably predictable fair market rent for the use of the goods for the term of the renewal at the time the option is to be performed, or

(e) the lessee has an option to become the owner of the goods for a fixed price that is equal to or greater than the reasonably predictable fair market value of the goods at the time the option is to be performed.

For purposes of this subsection (37):

(x) Additional consideration is not nominal if (i) when the option to renew the lease is granted to the lessee the rent is stated to be the fair market rent for the use of the goods for the term of the renewal determined at the time the option is to be performed, or (ii) when the option to become the owner of the goods is granted to the lessee the price is stated to be the fair market value of the goods determined at the time the option is to be performed. Additional consideration is nominal if it is less than the lessee's reasonably predictable cost of performing under the lease agreement if the option is not exercised;

(y) "Reasonably predictable" and "remaining economic life of the goods" are to be determined with reference to the facts and circumstances at the time the transaction is entered into; and

(z) "Present value" means the amount as of a date certain of one or more sums payable in the future, discounted to the date certain. The discount is determined by the interest rate specified by the parties if the rate is not manifestly unreasonable at the time the transaction is entered into; otherwise, the discount is determined by a commercially reasonable rate that takes into account the facts and circumstances of each case at the time the transaction was entered into.

(38) "Send" in connection with any writing or notice means to deposit in the mail or deliver for transmission by any other usual means of communication with postage or cost of transmission provided for and properly addressed and in the case of an instrument to an address specified thereon or otherwise agreed, or if there be none to any address reasonable under the circumstances. The receipt of any writing or notice within the time at which it would have arrived if properly sent has the effect of a proper sending.

(39) "Signed" includes any symbol executed or adopted by a party with present intention to authenticate a writing.

(40) "Surety" includes guarantor.

(41) "Telegram" includes a message transmitted by radio, teletype, cable, any mechanical method of transmission, or the like.

(42) "Term" means that portion of an agreement which relates to a particular matter.

(43) "Unauthorized" signature means one made without actual, implied, or apparent authority and includes a forgery.

(44) "Value". Except as otherwise provided with respect to negotiable instruments and bank collections (Sections 3–303, 4–210 and 4–211) a person gives "value" for rights if he acquires them

(a) in return for a binding commitment to extend credit or for the extension of immediately available credit whether or not drawn upon and whether or not a chargeback is provided for in the event of difficulties in collection; or

(b) as security for or in total or partial satisfaction of a pre-existing claim; or

(c) by accepting delivery pursuant to a pre-existing contract for purchase; or

(d) generally, in return for any consideration sufficient to support a simple contract.

(45) "Warehouse receipt" means a receipt issued by a person engaged in the business of storing goods for hire.

(46) "Written" or "writing" includes printing, typewriting or any other intentional reduction to tangible form.

As amended in 1962, 1972, 1977, 1987, 1990, 1994 and 1999.

Official Comment

Prior Uniform Statutory Provision, Changes and New Matter:

1. "Action". See similar definitions in Section 191, Uniform Negotiable Instruments Law; Section 76, Uniform Sales Act; Section 58, Uniform Warehouse Receipts Act; Section 53, Uniform Bills of Lading Act. The definition has been rephrased and enlarged.

2. "Aggrieved party". New.

3. "Agreement". New. As used in this Act the word is intended to include full recognition of usage of trade, course of dealing, course of performance and the surrounding circumstances as effective parts thereof, and of any agreement permitted under the provisions of this Act to displace a stated rule of law.

4. "Bank". See Section 191, Uniform Negotiable Instruments Law.

5. "Bearer". From Section 191, Uniform Negotiable Instruments Law. The prior definition has been broadened.

6. "Bill of Lading". See similar definitions in Section 1, Uniform Bills of Lading Act. The definition has been enlarged to include freight forwarders' bills and bills issued by contract carriers as well as those issued by common carriers. The definition of airbill is new.

7. "Branch". New.

8. "Burden of establishing a fact". New.

9. "Buyer in ordinary course of business". From Section 1, Uniform Trust Receipts Act. The definition has been expanded to make clear the type of person protected. Its major significance lies in Section 2–403 and in the Article on Secured Transactions (Article 9).

The first sentence of paragraph (9) makes clear that a buyer from a pawnbroker cannot be a buyer in ordinary course of business. The second sentence tracks Section 6–102(1)(m). It explains what it means to buy "in the ordinary course." The penultimate sentence prevents a buyer that does not have the right to possession as against the seller from being a buyer in ordinary course of business. Concerning when a buyer obtains possessory rights, see Sections 2–502 and 2–716. However, the penultimate sentence is not intended to affect a buyer's status as a buyer in ordinary course of business in cases (such as a "drop shipment") involving delivery by the seller to a person buying from the buyer or a donee from the buyer. The requirement relates to whether *as against the seller* the buyer or one taking through the buyer has possessory rights.

10. "Conspicuous". New. This is intended to indicate some of the methods of making a term attention-calling. But the test is whether attention can reasonably be expected to be called to it.

11. "Contract". New. But see Sections 3 and 71, Uniform Sales Act.

12. "Creditor". New.

13. "Defendant". From Section 76, Uniform Sales Act. Rephrased.

14. "Delivery". Section 76, Uniform Sales Act, Section 191, Uniform Negotiable Instruments Law, Section 58, Uniform Warehouse Receipts Act and Section 53, Uniform Bills of Lading Act.

15. "Document of title". From Section 76, Uniform Sales Act, but rephrased to eliminate certain ambiguities. Thus, by making it explicit that the obligation or designation of a third party as "bailee" is essential to a document of title, this definition clearly rejects any such result as obtained in Hixson v. Ward, 254 Ill.App. 505 (1929), which treated a conditional sales contract as a document of title. Also the definition is left open so that new types of documents may be included. It is unforeseeable what documents may one day serve the essential purpose now filled by warehouse receipts and bills of lading. Truck transport has already opened up problems which do not fit the patterns of practice resting upon the assumption that a draft can move through banking channels faster than the goods themselves can reach their destination. There lie ahead air transport and such probabilities as teletype transmission of what may some day be regarded commercially as "Documents of Title". The definition is stated in terms of the function of the documents with the intention that any document which gains commercial recognition as accomplishing the desired result shall be included within its scope. Fungible goods are adequately identified within the language of the definition by identification of the mass of which they are a part.

Dock warrants were within the Sales Act definition of document of title apparently for the purpose of recognizing a valid tender by means of such paper. In

current commercial practice a dock warrant or receipt is a kind of interim certificate issued by steamship companies upon delivery of the goods at the dock, entitling a designated person to have issued to him at the company's office a bill of lading. The receipt itself is invariably nonnegotiable in form although it may indicate that a negotiable bill is to be forthcoming. Such a document is not within the general compass of the definition, although trade usage may in some cases entitle such paper to be treated as a document of title. If the dock receipt actually represents a storage obligation undertaken by the shipping company, then it is a warehouse receipt within this Section regardless of the name given to the instrument.

The goods must be "described", but the description may be by marks or labels and may be qualified in such a way as to disclaim personal knowledge of the issuer regarding contents or condition. However, baggage and parcel checks and similar "tokens" of storage which identify stored goods only as those received in exchange for the token are not covered by this Article.

The definition is broad enough to include an airway bill.

16. "Fault". From Section 76, Uniform Sales Act.

17. "Fungible". See Sections 5, 6 and 76, Uniform Sales Act; Section 58, Uniform Warehouse Receipts Act. Fungibility of goods "by agreement" has been added for clarity and accuracy. ~~As to securities, see Section 8–107 and Comment.~~ *Amendment approved by the Permanent Editorial Board for Uniform Commercial Code November 4, 1995.*

18. "Genuine". New.

19. "Good faith". See Section 76(2), Uniform Sales Act; Section 58(2), Uniform Warehouse Receipts Act; Section 53(2), Uniform Bills of Lading Act; Section 22(2), Uniform Stock Transfer Act. "Good faith", whenever it is used in the Code, means at least what is here stated. In certain Articles, by specific provision, additional requirements are made applicable. See, e.g., Secs. 2–103(1)(b), 7–404. To illustrate, in the Article on Sales, Section 2–103, good faith is expressly defined as including in the case of a merchant observance of reasonable commercial standards of fair dealing in the trade, so that throughout that Article wherever a merchant appears in the case an inquiry into his observance of such standards is necessary to determine his good faith.

20. "Holder". See similar definitions in Section 191, Uniform Negotiable Instruments Law; Section 58, Uniform Warehouse Receipts Act; Section 53, Uniform Bills of Lading Act.

21. "Honor". New.

22. "Insolvency proceedings". New.

23. "Insolvent". Section 76(3), Uniform Sales Act. The three tests of insolvency—"ceased to pay his debts in the ordinary course of business," "cannot pay his debts as they become due," and "insolvent within the meaning of the federal bankruptcy law"—are expressly set up as alternative tests and must be approached from a commercial standpoint.

24. "Money". Section 6(5), Uniform Negotiable Instruments Law. The test adopted is that of sanction of government, whether by authorization before issue or adoption afterward, which recognizes the circulating medium as a part of the official currency of that government. The narrow view that money is limited to legal tender is rejected.

25. "Notice". New. Compare N.I.L. Sec. 56. Under the definition a person has notice when he has received a notification of the fact in question. But by the last sentence the act leaves open the time and circumstances under which notice or notification may cease to be effective. Therefore such cases as Graham v. White-Phillips Co., 296 U.S. 27, 56 S.Ct. 21, 80 L.Ed. 20 (1935), are not overruled.

26. "Notifies". New. This is the word used when the essential fact is the proper dispatch of the notice, not its receipt. Compare "Send". When the essential fact is the other party's receipt of the notice, that is stated. The second sentence states when a notification is received.

27. New. This makes clear that reason to know, knowledge, or a notification, although "received" for instance by a clerk in Department A of an organization, is effective for a transaction conducted in Department B only from the time when it was or should have been communicated to the individual conducting that transaction.

28. "Organization". This is the definition of every type of entity or association, excluding an individual, acting as such. Definitions of "person" were included in Section 191, Uniform Negotiable Instruments Law; Section 76, Uniform Sales Act; Section 58, Uniform Warehouse Receipts Act; Section 53, Uniform Bills of Lading Act; Section 22, Uniform Stock Transfer Act; Section 1, Uniform Trust Receipts Act. The definition of "organization" given here includes a number of entities or associations not specifically mentioned in prior definition of "person", namely, government, governmental subdivision or agency, business trust, trust and estate.

29. "Party". New. Mention of a party includes, of course, a person acting through an agent. However, where an agent comes into opposition or contrast to his principal, particular account is taken of that situation.

30. "Person". See Comment to definition of "Organization". The reference to Section 1–102 is to subsection (5) of that section.

31. "Presumption". New.

32. "Purchase". Section 58, Uniform Warehouse Receipts Act; Section 76, Uniform Sales Act; Section 53, Uniform Bills of Lading Act; Section 22, Uniform Stock Transfer Act; Section 1, Uniform Trust Receipts Act. Rephrased. With the addition of taking "by . . . security interest," the revised definition makes explicit what formerly was implicit.

33. "Purchaser". Section 58, Uniform Warehouse Receipts Act; Section 76, Uniform Sales Act; Section 53, Uniform Bills of Lading Act; Section 22, Uniform Stock Transfer Act; Section 1, Uniform Trust Receipts Act. Rephrased.

34. "Remedy". New. The purpose is to make it clear that both remedy and rights (as defined) include those remedial rights of "self help" which are among the most important bodies of rights under this Act, remedial rights being those to which an aggrieved party can resort on his own motion.

35. "Representative". New.

36. "Rights". New. See Comment to "Remedy".

37. "Security Interest". See Section 1, Uniform Trust Receipts Act. The definition of "security interest" was revised in connection with the promulgation of Article 2A and also to take account of the expanded scope of Article 9 as revised in the 1998 Official Text. It includes the interest of a consignor and the interest of a buyer of accounts, chattel paper, payment intangibles, or promissory notes. See Section 9–109. It also makes clear that, with certain exceptions, in rem rights of sellers and lessors under Articles 2 and 2A are not "security interests." Among the rights that are not security interests are the right to withhold delivery under Section 2–702(1), 2–703(a), or 2A–525, the right to stop delivery under Section 2–705 or 2A–526, and the right to reclaim under Section 2–507(2) or 2–702(2).

One of the reasons it was decided to codify the law with respect to leases was to resolve an issue that has created considerable confusion in the courts: what is a lease? The confusion exists, in part, due to the last two sentences of the definition of security interest in the 1978 Official Text of the Act. Section 1–201(37). The confusion is compounded by the rather considerable change in the federal, state and local tax laws and accounting rules as they relate to leases of goods. The answer is important because the definition of lease determines not only the rights and remedies of the parties to the lease but also those of third parties. If a transaction creates a lease and not a security interest, the lessee's interest in the goods is limited to its leasehold estate; the residual interest in the goods belongs to the lessor. This has significant implications to the lessee's creditors. "On common law theory, the lessor, since he has not parted with title, is entitled to full protection against the lessee's creditors and trustee in bankruptcy ...." 1 G. Gilmore, *Security Interests in Personal Property* § 3.6, at 76 (1965).

Under pre-Act chattel security law there was generally no requirement that the lessor file the lease, a financing statement, or the like, to enforce the lease agreement against the lessee or any third party; the Article on Secured Transactions (Article 9) did not change the common law in that respect. Coogan, Leasing and the Uniform Commercial Code, in *Equipment Leasing—Leveraged Leasing* 681, 700 n.25, 729 n.80 (2d ed.1980). The Article on Leases (Article 2A) has not changed the law in that respect, except for leases of fixtures. Section 2A–309. An examination of the common law will not provide an adequate answer to the question of what is a lease. The definition of security interest in Section 1–201(37) of the 1978 Official Text of the Act provides that the Article on Secured Transactions (Article 9) governs security interests disguised as leases, *i.e.*, leases intended as security; however, the definition is vague and outmoded.

Lease is defined in Article 2A as a transfer of the right to possession and use of goods for a term, in return for consideration. Section 2A–103(1)(j). The definition continues by stating that the retention or creation of a security interest is not a lease. Thus, the task of sharpening the line between true leases and security interests disguised as leases continues to be a function of this section.

The first paragraph of this definition is a revised version of the first five sentences of the 1978 Official Text of Section 1–201(37). The changes are modest in that they make a style change in the fourth sentence and delete the reference to lease in the fifth sentence. The balance of this definition is new, although it preserves elements of the last two sentences of the prior definition. The focus of the changes was to draw a sharper line between leases and security interests disguised as leases to create greater certainty in commercial transactions.

Prior to this amendment, Section 1–201(37) provided that whether a lease was intended as security (*i.e.*, a security interest disguised as a lease) was to be determined from the facts of each case; however, (a) the inclusion of an option to purchase did not itself make the lease one intended for security, and (b) an agreement that upon compliance with the terms of the lease the lessee would become, or had the option to become, the owner of the property for no additional consideration, or for a nominal consideration, did make the lease one intended for security.

Reference to the intent of the parties to create a lease or security interest has led to unfortunate results. In discovering intent, courts have relied upon factors that were thought to be more consistent with sales or loans than leases. Most of these criteria, however, are as applicable to true leases as to security interests. Examples include the typical net lease provisions, a purported lessor's lack of storage facilities or its character as a financing party rather than a dealer in goods. Accordingly, amended Section 1–201(37) deletes all reference to the parties' intent.

The second paragraph of the new definition is taken from Section 1(2) of the Uniform Conditional Sales Act (act withdrawn 1943), modified to reflect current leasing practice. Thus, reference to the case law prior to this Act will provide a useful source of precedent. Gilmore, *Security Law, Formalism and Article 9*, 47 Neb.L.Rev. 659, 671 (1968). Whether a transaction creates a lease or a security interest continues to be determined by the facts of each case. The second paragraph further provides that a transaction creates a security interest if the lessee has an obligation to continue paying consideration for the term of the lease, if the obligation is not terminable by the lessee (thus correcting early statutory gloss, *e.g., In re Royer's Bakery, Inc.*, 1 U.C.C. Rep.Serv. (Callaghan) 342 (Bankr.E.D.Pa.1963)) and if one of four additional tests is met. The first of these four tests, subparagraph (a), is that the original lease term is equal to or greater than the remaining economic life of the goods. The second of these tests, subparagraph (b), is that the lessee is either bound to renew the lease for the remaining economic life of the goods or to become the owner of the goods. *In re Gehrke Enters.*, 1 Bankr. 647, 651–52 (Bankr.W.D.Wis.1979). The third of these tests, subparagraph (c), is whether the lessee has an option to renew the lease for the remaining economic life or the goods for no additional consideration or for nominal additional consideration, which is defined later in this section. *In re Celeryvale Transp.*, 44 Bankr. 1007, 1014–15 (Bankr.E.D.Tenn.1984). The fourth of these tests, subparagraph (d), is whether the lessee has an option to become the owner of the goods for no additional consideration or for nominal additional consideration. All of these tests focus on economics, not the intent of the parties. *In re Berge,* 32 Bankr. 370, 371–73 (Bankr.W.D.Wis.1983).

The focus on economics is reinforced by the next paragraph, which is new. It states that a transaction does not create a security interest merely because the transaction has certain characteristics listed therein. Subparagraph (a) has no statutory derivative; it states that a full payout lease does not *per se* create a security interest. *Rushton v. Shea,* 419 F.Supp. 1349, 1365 (D.Del.1976). Subparagraph (b) provides the same regarding the provisions of the typical net lease. *Compare All-States Leasing Co. v. Ochs,* 42 Or.App. 319, 600 P.2d 899 (Ct.App.1979) *with In re Tillery,* 571 F.2d 1361 (5th Cir.1978). Subparagraph (c) restates and expands the provisions of former Section 1–201(37) to make clear that the option can be to buy or renew. Subparagraphs (d) and (e) treat fixed price options and provide that fair market value must be determined at the time the transaction is entered into. *Compare Arnold Mach. Co. v. Balls,* 624 P.2d 678 (Utah 1981) *with Aoki v. Shepherd Mach. Co.,* 665 F.2d 941 (9th Cir.1982).

The relationship of the second paragraph of this subsection to the third paragraph of this subsection deserves to be explored. The fixed price purchase option provides a useful example. A fixed price purchase option in a lease does not of itself create a security interest. This is particularly true if the fixed price is equal to or greater than the reasonably predictable fair market value of the goods at the time the option is to be performed. A security interest is created only if the option price is nominal and the conditions stated in the introduction to the second paragraph of this subsection are met. There is a set of purchase options whose fixed price is less than fair market value but greater than nominal that must be determined on the facts of each case to ascertain whether the transaction in which the option is included creates a lease or a security interest.

It was possible to provide for various other permutations and combinations with respect to options to purchase and renew. For example, this section could have stated a rule to govern the facts of *In re Marhoefer Packing Co.,* 674 F.2d 1139 (7th Cir.1982). This was not done because it would unnecessarily complicate the definition. Further development of this rule is left to the courts.

The fourth paragraph provides definitions and rules of construction.

38.   "Send". New. Compare "notifies".

39.   "Signed". New. The inclusion of authentication in the definition of "signed" is to make clear that as the term is used in this Act a complete signature is not necessary. Authentication may be printed, stamped or written; it may be by initials or by thumbprint. It may be on any part of the document and in appropriate cases may be found in a billhead or letterhead. No catalog of possible authentications can be complete and the court must use common sense and commercial experience in passing upon these matters. The question always is whether the symbol was executed or adopted by the party with present intention to authenticate the writing.

40.   "Surety". New.

41.   "Telegram". New.

42.   "Term". New.

43.   Under the former version of § 1–201(43), it was not clear whether a reference to an "unauthorized signature" in Articles 3 and 4 applied to indorsements. The words "or indorsement" are deleted so that references to "unauthorized signature" in § 3–406 and elsewhere will unambiguously refer to any signature.

44.   "Value". See Sections 25, 26, 27, 191, Uniform Negotiable Instruments Law; Section 76, Uniform Sales Act; Section 53, Uniform Bills of Lading Act; Section 58, Uniform Warehouse Receipts Act; Section 22(1), Uniform Stock Transfer Act; Section 1, Uniform Trust Receipts Act. All the Uniform Acts in the commercial law field (except the Uniform Conditional Sales Act) have carried definitions of "value". All those definitions provided that value was any consideration sufficient to support a simple contract, including the taking of property in satisfaction of or as security for a pre-existing claim. Subsections (a), (b) and (d) in substance continue the definitions of "value" in the earlier acts. Subsection (c) makes explicit that "value" is also given in a third situation: where a buyer by taking delivery under a pre-existing contract converts a contingent into a fixed obligation.

This definition is not applicable to Articles 3 and 4, but the express inclusion of immediately available credit as value follows the separate definitions in those Articles. See Sections 4–208, 4–209, 3–303. A bank or other financing agency which in good faith makes advances against property held as collateral becomes a bona fide purchaser of that property even though provision may be made for charge-back in case of trouble. Checking credit is "immediately available" within the meaning of this section if the bank would be subject to an action for slander of credit in case checks drawn against the credit were dishonored, and when a charge-back is not discretionary with the bank, but may only be made when difficulties in collection arise in connection with the specific transaction involved.

45. "Warehouse receipt". See Section 76(1), Uniform Sales Act; Section 1, Uniform Warehouse Receipts Act. Receipts issued by a field warehouse are included, provided the warehouseman and the depositor of the goods are different persons.

46. "Written" or "writing". This is a broadening of the definition contained in Section 191 of the Uniform Negotiable Instruments Law.

As amended in 1999.

§ 1-202. Prima Facie Evidence by Third Party Documents.

A document in due form purporting to be a bill of lading, policy or certificate of insurance, official weigher's or inspector's certificate, consular invoice, or any other document authorized or required by the contract to be issued by a third party shall be prima facie evidence of its own authenticity and genuineness and of the facts stated in the document by the third party.

Official Comment

Prior Uniform Statutory Provision: None.

Purposes:

1. This section is designed to supply judicial recognition for documents which have traditionally been relied upon as trustworthy by commercial men.

2. This section is concerned only with documents which have been given a preferred status by the parties themselves who have required their procurement in the agreement and for this reason the applicability of the section is limited to actions arising out of the contract which authorized or required the document. The documents listed are intended to be illustrative and not all inclusive.

3. The provisions of this section go no further than establishing the documents in question as prima facie evidence and leave to the court the ultimate determination of the facts where the accuracy or authenticity of the documents is questioned. In this connection the section calls for a commercially reasonable interpretation.

Definitional Cross References:

"Bill of lading". Section 1-201.
"Contract". Section 1-201.

"Genuine". Section 1-201.

§ 1-203. Obligation of Good Faith.

Every contract or duty within this Act imposes an obligation of good faith in its performance or enforcement.

Official Comment

Prior Uniform Statutory Provision: None.

Purposes:

This section sets forth a basic principle running throughout this Act. The principle involved is that in commercial transactions good faith is required in the performance and enforcement of all agreements or duties. Particular applications of this general principle appear in specific provisions of the Act such as the option to accelerate at will (Section 1-208), the right to cure a defective delivery of goods (Section 2-508), the duty of a merchant buyer who has rejected goods to effect salvage operations (Section 2-603), substituted performance (Section 2-614), and failure of presupposed conditions (Section 2-615). The concept, however, is broader than any of these illustrations and applies generally, as stated in this section, to the performance or enforcement of every contract or duty within this Act. It is further implemented by Section 1-205 on course of dealing and usage of trade. This section does not support an independent cause of action for failure to perform or enforce in good faith. Rather, this section means that a failure to perform or enforce, in good faith, a specific duty or obligation under the contract, constitutes a breach of that contract or makes unavailable, under the particular circumstances, a remedial right or power. This distinction makes it clear that the doctrine of good faith merely directs a court towards interpreting contracts within the commercial context in which they are created, performed, and enforced, and does not create a separate duty of fairness and reasonableness which can be independently breached. See PEB Commentary No. 10, dated February 10, 1994 [Appendix V, infra].

It is to be noted that under the Sales Article definition of good faith (Section 2-103), contracts made by a merchant have incorporated in them the explicit standard not only of honesty in fact (Section 1-201), but also of observance by the merchant of reasonable commercial standards of fair dealing in the trade.

Cross References:

Sections 1-201; 1-205; 1-208; 2-103; 2-508; 2-603; 2-614; 2-615.

Definitional Cross References:

"Contract". Section 1–201.
"Good faith". Sections 1–201; 2–103.

§ 1–204.   Time; Reasonable Time; "Seasonably".

(1) Whenever this Act requires any action to be taken within a reasonable time, any time which is not manifestly unreasonable may be fixed by agreement.

(2) What is a reasonable time for taking any action depends on the nature, purpose and circumstances of such action.

(3) An action is taken "seasonably" when it is taken at or within the time agreed or if no time is agreed at or within a reasonable time.

Official Comment

Prior Uniform Statutory Provision: Compare Section 193, Uniform Negotiable Instruments Law.

Purposes:

1. Subsection (1) recognizes that nothing is stronger evidence of a reasonable time than the fixing of such time by a fair agreement between the parties. However, provision is made for disregarding a clause which whether by inadvertence or overreaching fixes a time so unreasonable that it amounts to eliminating all remedy under the contract. The parties are not required to fix the most reasonable time but may fix any time which is not obviously unfair as judged by the time of contracting.

2. Under the section, the agreement which fixes the time need not be part of the main agreement, but may occur separately. Notice also that under the definition of "agreement" (Section 1–201) the circumstances of the transaction, including course of dealing or usages of trade or course of performance may be material. On the question what is a reasonable time these matters will often be important.

Definitional Cross Reference:

"Agreement". Section 1–201.

§ 1–205.   Course of Dealing and Usage of Trade.

(1) A course of dealing is a sequence of previous conduct between the parties to a particular transaction which is fairly to be regarded as establishing a common basis of understanding for interpreting their expressions and other conduct.

(2) A usage of trade is any practice or method of dealing having such regularity of observance in a place, vocation or trade as to justify an expectation that it will be observed with respect to the transaction in question. The existence and scope of such a usage are to be proved as facts. If it is established that such a usage is embodied in a written trade code or similar writing the interpretation of the writing is for the court.

(3) A course of dealing between parties and any usage of trade in the vocation or trade in which they are engaged or of which they are or should be aware give particular meaning to and supplement or qualify terms of an agreement.

(4) The express terms of an agreement and an applicable course of dealing or usage of trade shall be construed wherever reasonable as consistent with each other; but when such construction is unreasonable express terms control both course of dealing and usage of trade and course of dealing controls usage of trade.

(5) An applicable usage of trade in the place where any part of performance is to occur shall be used in interpreting the agreement as to that part of the performance.

(6) Evidence of a relevant usage of trade offered by one party is not admissible unless and until he has given the other party such notice as the court finds sufficient to prevent unfair surprise to the latter.

Official Comment

Prior Uniform Statutory Provision: No such general provision but see Sections 9(1), 15(5), 18(2), and 71, Uniform Sales Act.

Purposes: This section makes it clear that:

1. This Act rejects both the "lay-dictionary" and the "conveyancer's" reading of a commercial agreement. Instead the meaning of the agreement of the parties is to be determined by the language used by them and by their action, read and interpreted in the light of commercial practices and other surrounding circumstances. The measure and background for interpretation are set by the commercial context, which may explain and supplement even the language of a formal or final writing.

2. Course of dealing under subsection (1) is restricted, literally, to a sequence of conduct between the parties previous to the agreement. However, the pro-

visions of the Act on course of performance make it clear that a sequence of conduct after or under the agreement may have equivalent meaning. (Section 2–208.)

3. "Course of dealing" may enter the agreement either by explicit provisions of the agreement or by tacit recognition.

4. This Act deals with "usage of trade" as a factor in reaching the commercial meaning of the agreement which the parties have made. The language used is to be interpreted as meaning what it may fairly be expected to mean to parties involved in the particular commercial transaction in a given locality or in a given vocation or trade. By adopting in this context the term "usage of trade" this Act expresses its intent to reject those cases which see evidence of "custom" as representing an effort to displace or negate "established rules of law". A distinction is to be drawn between mandatory rules of law such as the Statute of Frauds provisions of Article 2 on Sales whose very office is to control and restrict the actions of the parties, and which cannot be abrogated by agreement, or by a usage of trade, and those rules of law (such as those in Part 3 of Article 2 on Sales) which fill in points which the parties have not considered and in fact agreed upon. The latter rules hold "unless otherwise agreed" but yield to the contrary agreement of the parties. Part of the agreement of the parties to which such rules yield is to be sought for in the usages of trade which furnish the background and give particular meaning to the language used, and are the framework of common understanding controlling any general rules of law which hold only when there is no such understanding.

5. A usage of trade under subsection (2) must have the "regularity of observance" specified. The ancient English tests for "custom" are abandoned in this connection. Therefore, it is not required that a usage of trade be "ancient or immemorial", "universal" or the like. Under the requirement of subsection (2) full recognition is thus available for new usages and for usages currently observed by the great majority of decent dealers, even though dissidents ready to cut corners do not agree. There is room also for proper recognition of usage agreed upon by merchants in trade codes.

6. The policy of this Act controlling explicit unconscionable contracts and clauses (Sections 1–203, 2–302) applies to implicit clauses which rest on usage of trade and carries forward the policy underlying the ancient requirement that a custom or usage must be "reasonable". However, the emphasis is shifted. The very fact of commercial acceptance makes out a prima facie case that the usage is reasonable, and the burden is no longer on the usage to establish itself as being reasonable. But the anciently established policing of usage by the courts is continued to the extent necessary to cope with the situation arising if an unconscionable or dishonest practice should become standard.

7. Subsection (3), giving the prescribed effect to usages of which the parties "are or should be aware", reinforces the provision of subsection (2) requiring not universality but only the described "regularity of observance" of the practice or method. This subsection also reinforces the point of subsection (2) that such usages may be either general to trade or particular to a special branch of trade.

8. Although the terms in which this Act defines "agreement" include the elements of course of dealing and usage of trade, the fact that express reference is made in some sections to those elements is not to be construed as carrying a contrary intent or implication elsewhere. Compare Section 1–102(4).

9. In cases of a well established line of usage varying from the general rules of this Act where the precise amount of the variation has not been worked out into a single standard, the party relying on the usage is entitled, in any event, to the minimum variation demonstrated. The whole is not to be disregarded because no particular line of detail has been established. In case a dominant pattern has been fairly evidenced, the party relying on the usage is entitled under this section to go to the trier of fact on the question of whether such dominant pattern has been incorporated into the agreement.

10. Subsection (6) is intended to insure that this Act's liberal recognition of the needs of commerce in regard to usage of trade shall not be made into an instrument of abuse.

Cross References:

Point 1: Sections 1–203, 2–104 and 2–202.
Point 2: Section 2–208.
Point 4: Section 2–201 and Part 3 of Article 2.
Point 6: Sections 1–203 and 2–302.
Point 8: Sections 1–102 and 1–201.
Point 9: Section 2–204(3).

Definitional Cross References:

"Agreement". Section 1–201.
"Contract". Section 1–201.
"Party". Section 1–201.
"Term". Section 1–201.

§ 1–206. Statute of Frauds for Kinds of Personal Property Not Otherwise Covered.

(1) Except in the cases described in subsection (2) of this section a contract for the sale of personal property is not enforceable by way of action or defense beyond five thousand dollars in amount or value of remedy unless there is some writing which indicates that a contract for sale has been made between the parties at a defined or stated price, reasonably identifies the subject matter, and is signed by the party against whom enforcement is sought or by his authorized agent.

(2) Subsection (1) of this section does not apply to contracts for the sale of goods (Section 2–201) nor of securities (Section 8–113) nor to security agreements (Section 9–203).

As amended in 1994.

Official Comment

Prior Uniform Statutory Provision: Section 4, Uniform Sales Act (which was based on Section 17 of the Statute of 29 Charles II).

Changes: Completely rewritten by this and other sections.

Purposes: To fill the gap left by the Statute of Frauds provisions for goods (Section 2–201), ~~securities (Section 8–319),~~ and security interests (Section 9–203). As to securities, see Section 8–113. The Uniform Sales Act covered the sale of "choses in action"; the principal gap relates to sale of ~~the~~ "general intangibles" that are not "payment intangibles" (as those terms are defined in Section 9–102) and to transactions excluded from Article 9 by Section 9–109(d). The informality normal to such transactions is recognized by lifting the limit for oral transactions to $5,000. In such transactions there is often no standard of practice by which to judge, and values can rise or drop without warning; troubling abuses are avoided when the dollar limit is exceeded by requiring that the subject-matter be reasonably identified in a signed writing which indicates that a contract for sale has been made at a defined or stated price. *Amendments approved by the Permanent Editorial Board for Uniform Commercial Code November 4, 1995.*

Definitional Cross References:

"Action". Section 1–201.
"Agreement". Section 1–201.
"Contract". Section 1–201.
"Contract for sale". Section 2–106.
"Goods". Section 2–105.

"Party". Section 1–201.
"Sale". Section 2–106.
"Signed". Section 1–201.
"Writing". Section 1–201.

§ 1–207. Performance or Acceptance Under Reservation of Rights.

(1) A party who, with explicit reservation of rights performs or promises performance or assents to performance in a manner demanded or offered by the other party does not thereby prejudice the rights reserved. Such words as "without prejudice", "under protest" or the like are sufficient.

(2) Subsection (1) does not apply to an accord and satisfaction.

As amended in 1990.

Official Comment

1. This section provides machinery for the continuation of performance along the lines contemplated by the contract despite a pending dispute, by adopting the mercantile device of going ahead with delivery, acceptance, or payment "without prejudice," "under protest," "under reserve," "with reservation of all our rights," and the like. All of these phrases completely reserve all rights within the meaning of this section. The section therefore contemplates that limited as well as general reservations and acceptance by a party may be made "subject to satisfaction of our purchaser," "subject to acceptance by our customers," or the like.

2. This section does not add any new requirement of language of reservation where not already required by law, but merely provides a specific measure on which a party can rely as that party makes or concurs in any interim adjustment in the course of performance. It does not affect or impair the provisions of this Act such as those under which the buyer's remedies for defect survive acceptance without being expressly claimed if notice of the defects is given within a reasonable time. Nor does it disturb the policy of those cases which restrict the effect of a waiver of a defect to reasonable limits under the circumstances, even though no such reservation is expressed.

The section is not addressed to the creation or loss of remedies in the ordinary course of performance but rather to a method of procedure where one party is claiming as of right something which the other believes to be unwarranted.

3. Judicial authority was divided on the issue of whether former Section 1–207 (present subsection (1))

applied to an accord and satisfaction. Typically the cases involved attempts to reach an accord and satisfaction by use of a check tendered in full satisfaction of a claim. Subsection (2) of revised Section 1–207 resolves this conflict by stating that Section 1–207 does not apply to an accord and satisfaction. Section 3–311 of revised Article 3 governs if an accord and satisfaction is attempted by tender of a negotiable instrument as stated in that section. If Section 3–311 does not apply, the issue of whether an accord and satisfaction has been effected is determined by the law of contract. Whether or not Section 3–311 applies, Section 1–207 has no application to an accord and satisfaction.

§ 1–208. Option to Accelerate at Will.

A term providing that one party or his successor in interest may accelerate payment or performance or require collateral or additional collateral "at will" or "when he deems himself insecure" or in words of similar import shall be construed to mean that he shall have power to do so only if he in good faith believes that the prospect of payment or performance is impaired. The burden of establishing lack of good faith is on the party against whom the power has been exercised.

Official Comment
Prior Uniform Statutory Provision: None.

Purposes:

The increased use of acceleration clauses either in the case of sales on credit or in time paper or in security transactions has led to some confusion in the cases as to the effect to be given to a clause which seemingly grants the power of an acceleration at the whim and caprice of one party. This Section is intended to make clear that despite language which can be so construed and which further might be held to make the agreement void as against public policy or to make the contract illusory or too indefinite for enforcement, the clause means that the option is to be exercised only in the good faith belief that the prospect of payment or performance is impaired.

Obviously this section has no application to demand instruments or obligations whose very nature permits call at any time with or without reason. This section applies only to an agreement or to paper which in the first instance is payable at a future date.

Definitional Cross References:

"Burden of establishing". Section 1–201.

"Good faith". Section 1–201.
"Party". Section 1–201.
"Term". Section 1–201.

§ 1–209. Subordinated Obligations.

An obligation may be issued as subordinated to payment of another obligation of the person obligated, or a creditor may subordinate his right to payment of an obligation by agreement with either the person obligated or another creditor of the person obligated. Such a subordination does not create a security interest as against either the common debtor or a subordinated creditor. This section shall be construed as declaring the law as it existed prior to the enactment of this section and not as modifying it. Added 1966.

Note: *This new section is proposed as an optional provision to make it clear that a subordination agreement does not create a security interest unless so intended.*

Official Comment
Source: New York.

Prior Uniform Statutory Provision: None.

Reason for Change: The drafting history of Article 9 makes it clear that there was no intention to cover agreements by which the rights of one unsecured creditor are subordinated to the rights of another unsecured creditor of a common debtor. Nevertheless, since in insolvency proceedings dividends otherwise payable to a subordinated creditor are turned over to the superior creditor, fears have been expressed that a subordination agreement might be treated as a "security agreement" creating a "security interest" in property of the subordinated creditor, and that inappropriate provisions of Article 9 might be applied. This optional section is intended to allay such fears by making an explicit declaration that a subordination agreement does not of itself create a security interest. Nothing in this section prevents the creation of a security interest in such a case when the parties to the agreement so intend.

Purposes:

1. Billions of dollars of subordinated debt are held by the public and by institutional investors. Commonly, the subordinated debt is subordinated on issue or acquisition and is evidenced by an investment security or by a negotiable or non-negotiable note. Debt is also sometimes subordinated after it arises, either by agreement between the subordinating creditor and the debtor, by agreement between two creditors of the same

debtor, or by agreement of all three parties. The subordinated creditor may be a stockholder or other "insider" interested in the common debtor; the subordinated debt may consist of accounts or other rights to payment not evidenced by any instrument. All such cases are included in the terms "subordinated obligation," "subordination," and "subordinated creditor."

2. Subordination agreements are enforceable between the parties as contracts; and in the bankruptcy of the common debtor dividends otherwise payable to the subordinated creditor are turned over to the superior creditor. This "turn-over" practice has on occasion been explained in terms of "equitable lien," "equitable assignment," or "constructive trust," but whatever the label the practice is essentially an equitable remedy and does not mean that there is a transaction "intended to create a security interest," a "sale of accounts, contract rights or chattel paper," or a "security interest created by contract," within the meaning of Section 9–102. On the other hand, nothing in this section prevents one creditor from assigning his rights to another creditor of the same debtor in such a way as to create a security interest within Article 9, where the parties so intend.

3. The last sentence of this section is intended to negate any implication that the section changes the law. It is intended to be declaratory of pre-existing law. Both the history and the text of Article 9 make it clear that it was not intended to cover subordination agreements. The provisions of Section 9–203 for authentication by the "debtor" would be entirely unworkable if read to require authentication by public

holders of subordinated investment securities. The priorities, filing provisions and remedies on default provided by Article 9 would also be largely inappropriate in many situations. The precautionary language of Section 9–339 preserving subordination of priority by agreement between secured parties points to the conclusion that similar arrangements among unsecured lenders are not covered unless otherwise within the scope of the Article.

4. The enforcement of subordination agreements is largely left to supplementary principles under Section 1–103. If the subordinated debt is evidenced by an investment security, Section 8–202(1) a certificated security, Section 8–202(a) authorizes enforcement against purchasers on terms stated or referred to on the security certificate. If the fact of subordination is noted on a negotiable instrument, a holder under Sections 3–302 and 3–306 is subject to the term because notice precludes him from taking free of the subordination. Sections 3–302(3)(a), 3–306 and 8–317 severely limit the rights of levying creditors of a subordinated creditor in such cases. *Amendments approved by the Permanent Editorial Board for Uniform Commercial Code November 4, 1995.*

Definitional Cross References:

"Agreement". Section 1–201.
"Creditor". Section 1–201.
"Debtor". Section 9–102(a)(28).
"Person". Section 1–201.
"Rights". Section 1–201.
"Security interest". Section 1–201.

APPENDIX D

UNAMENDED UCC ARTICLE 2 (2000)

Set forth below are the text and Official Comments of Article 2 as they existed prior to amendment in 2001 and 2003.

2001 amendments (Article 1 revision) .... *Appendix A*
2003 amendments .... *Appendix F*
2003 amendments (Article 7 revision) .... *Appendix B*
2005 amendments .... *Appendix J*

ARTICLE 2

SALES

PART 1. SHORT TITLE, GENERAL
CONSTRUCTION AND SUBJECT
MATTER

Section
2–101. Short Title.
2–102. Scope; Certain Security and Other Transactions Excluded From This Article.
2–103. Definitions and Index of Definitions.
2–104. Definitions: "Merchant"; "Between Merchants"; "Financing Agency".
2–105. Definitions: Transferability; "Goods"; "Future" Goods; "Lot"; "Commercial Unit".
2–106. Definitions: "Contract"; "Agreement"; "Contract for Sale"; "Sale"; "Present Sale"; "Conforming" to Contract; "Termination"; "Cancellation".
2–107. Goods to Be Severed From Realty: Recording.

PART 2. FORM, FORMATION
AND READJUSTMENT OF
CONTRACT

2–201. Formal Requirements; Statute of Frauds.
2–202. Final Written Expression: Parol or Extrinsic Evidence.
2–203. Seals Inoperative.
2–204. Formation in General.
2–205. Firm Offers.

Section
2–206. Offer and Acceptance in Formation of Contract.
2–207. Additional Terms in Acceptance or Confirmation.
2–208. [Reserved.]
2–209. Modification, Rescission and Waiver.
2–210. Delegation of Performance; Assignment of Rights.

PART 3. GENERAL OBLIGATION AND
CONSTRUCTION OF CONTRACT

2–301. General Obligations of Parties.
2–302. Unconscionable Contract or Clause.
2–303. Allocation or Division of Risks.
2–304. Price Payable in Money, Goods, Realty, or Otherwise.
2–305. Open Price Term.
2–306. Output, Requirements and Exclusive Dealings.
2–307. Delivery in Single Lot or Several Lots.
2–308. Absence of Specified Place for Delivery.
2–309. Absence of Specific Time Provisions; Notice of Termination.
2–310. Open Time for Payment or Running of Credit; Authority to Ship Under Reservation.
2–311. Options and Cooperation Respecting Performance.

Section

2–312. Warranty of Title and Against Infringement; Buyer's Obligation Against Infringement.

2–313. Express Warranties by Affirmation, Promise, Description, Sample.

2–314. Implied Warranty: Merchantability; Usage of Trade.

2–315. Implied Warranty: Fitness for Particular Purpose.

2–316. Exclusion or Modification of Warranties.

2–317. Cumulation and Conflict of Warranties Express or Implied.

2–318. Third Party Beneficiaries of Warranties Express or Implied.

2–319. F.O.B. and F.A.S. Terms.

2–320. C.I.F. and C. & F. Terms.

2–321. C.I.F. or C. & F.: "Net Landed Weights"; "Payment on Arrival"; Warranty of Condition on Arrival.

2–322. Delivery "Ex-Ship".

2–323. Form of Bill of Lading Required in Overseas Shipment; "Overseas".

2–324. "No Arrival, No Sale" Term.

2–325. "Letter of Credit" Term; "Confirmed Credit".

2–326. Sale on Approval and Sale or Return; Consignment Sales and Rights of Creditors.

2–327. Special Incidents of Sale on Approval and Sale or Return.

2–328. Sale by Auction.

PART 4. TITLE, CREDITORS AND GOOD FAITH PURCHASERS

2–401. Passing of Title; Reservation for Security; Limited Application of This Section.

2–402. Rights of Seller's Creditors Against Sold Goods.

2–403. Power to Transfer; Good Faith Purchase of Goods; "Entrusting".

PART 5. PERFORMANCE

2–501. Insurable Interest in Goods; Manner of Identification of Goods.

2–502. Buyer's Right to Goods on Seller's Insolvency.

2–503. Manner of Seller's Tender of Delivery.

2–504. Shipment by Seller.

2–505. Seller's Shipment Under Reservation.

2–506. Rights of Financing Agency.

2–507. Effect of Seller's Tender; Delivery on Condition.

Section

2–508. Cure by Seller of Improper Tender or Delivery; Replacement.

2–509. Risk of Loss in the Absence of Breach.

2–510. Effect of Breach on Risk of Loss.

2–511. Tender of Payment by Buyer; Payment by Check.

2–512. Payment by Buyer Before Inspection.

2–513. Buyer's Right to Inspection of Goods.

2–514. When Documents Deliverable on Acceptance; When on Payment.

2–515. Preserving Evidence of Goods in Dispute.

PART 6. BREACH, REPUDIATION AND EXCUSE

2–601. Buyer's Rights on Improper Delivery.

2–602. Manner and Effect of Rightful Rejection.

2–603. Merchant Buyer's Duties as to Rightfully Rejected Goods.

2–604. Buyer's Options as to Salvage of Rightfully Rejected Goods.

2–605. Waiver of Buyer's Objections by Failure to Particularize.

2–606. What Constitutes Acceptance of Goods.

2–607. Effect of Acceptance; Notice of Breach; Burden of Establishing Breach After Acceptance; Notice of Claim or Litigation to Person Answerable Over.

2–608. Revocation of Acceptance in Whole or in Part.

2–609. Right to Adequate Assurance of Performance.

2–610. Anticipatory Repudiation.

2–611. Retraction of Anticipatory Repudiation.

2–612. "Installment Contract"; Breach.

2–613. Casualty to Identified Goods.

2–614. Substituted Performance.

2–615. Excuse by Failure of Presupposed Conditions.

2–616. Procedure on Notice Claiming Excuse.

PART 7. REMEDIES

2–701. Remedies for Breach of Collateral Contracts Not Impaired.

2–702. Seller's Remedies on Discovery of Buyer's Insolvency.

2–703. Seller's Remedies in General.

2–704. Seller's Right to Identify Goods to the Contract Notwithstanding Breach or to Salvage Unfinished Goods.

2–705. Seller's Stoppage of Delivery in Transit or Otherwise.

2–706. Seller's Resale Including Contract for Resale.

2–707. "Person in the Position of a Seller".

2–708. Seller's Damages for Non-acceptance or Repudiation.

Section
2–709. Action for the Price.
2–710. Seller's Incidental Damages.
2–711. Buyer's Remedies in General; Buyer's Security Interest in Rejected Goods.
2–712. "Cover"; Buyer's Procurement of Substitute Goods.
2–713. Buyer's Damages for Non-delivery or Repudiation.
2–714. Buyer's Damages for Breach in Regard to Accepted Goods.
2–715. Buyer's Incidental and Consequential Damages.
2–716. Buyer's Right to Specific Performance or Replevin.

Section
2–717. Deduction of Damages From the Price.
2–718. Liquidation or Limitation of Damages; Deposits.
2–719. Contractual Modification or Limitation of Remedy.
2–720. Effect of "Cancellation" or "Rescission" on Claims for Antecedent Breach.
2–721. Remedies for Fraud.
2–722. Who Can Sue Third Parties for Injury to Goods.
2–723. Proof of Market Price: Time and Place.
2–724. Admissibility of Market Quotations.
2–725. Statute of Limitations in Contracts for Sale.

PART 1

SHORT TITLE, GENERAL CONSTRUCTION AND SUBJECT MATTER

§ 2–101. Short Title.

This Article shall be known and may be cited as Uniform Commercial Code—Sales.

Official Comment

This Article is a complete revision and modernization of the Uniform Sales Act which was promulgated by the National Conference of Commissioners on Uniform State Laws in 1906 and has been adopted in 34 states and Alaska, the District of Columbia and Hawaii.

The coverage of the present Article is much more extensive than that of the old Sales Act and extends to the various bodies of case law which have been developed both outside of and under the latter.

The arrangement of the present Article is in terms of contract for sale and the various steps of its performance. The legal consequences are stated as following directly from the contract and action taken under it without resorting to the idea of when property or title passed or was to pass as being the determining factor. The purpose is to avoid making practical issues between practical men turn upon the location of an intangible something, the passing of which no man can prove by evidence and to substitute for such abstractions proof of words and actions of a tangible character.

§ 2–102. Scope; Certain Security and Other Transactions Excluded From This Article.

Unless the context otherwise requires, this Article applies to transactions in goods; it does not apply to any transaction which although in the form of an unconditional contract to sell or present sale is intended to operate only as a security transaction nor does this Article impair or repeal any statute regulating sales to consumers, farmers or other specified classes of buyers.

Official Comment

Prior Uniform Statutory Provision: Section 75, Uniform Sales Act.

Changes: Section 75 has been rephrased.

Purposes of Changes and New Matter: To make it clear that:

The Article leaves substantially unaffected the law relating to purchase money security such as conditional sale or chattel mortgage though it regulates the general sales aspects of such transactions. "Security transaction" is used in the same sense as in the Article on Secured Transactions (Article 9).

Cross Reference:

Article 9.

Definitional Cross References:

"Contract". Section 1–201.
"Contract for sale". Section 2–106.
"Present sale". Section 2–106.
"Sale". Section 2–106.

§ 2–103. Definitions and Index of Definitions.

(1) In this Article unless the context otherwise requires

(a) "Buyer" means a person who buys or contracts to buy goods.

(b) "Good faith" in the case of a merchant means honesty in fact and the observance of reasonable commercial standards of fair dealing in the trade.

(c) "Receipt" of goods means taking physical possession of them.

(d) "Seller" means a person who sells or contracts to sell goods.

(2) Other definitions applying to this Article or to specified Parts thereof, and the sections in which they appear are:

"Acceptance". Section 2–606.

"Banker's credit". Section 2–325.

"Between merchants". Section 2–104.

"Cancellation". Section 2–106(4).

"Commercial unit". Section 2–105.

"Confirmed credit". Section 2–325.

"Conforming to contract". Section 2–106.

"Contract for sale". Section 2–106.

"Cover". Section 2–712.

"Entrusting". Section 2–403.

"Financing agency". Section 2–104.

"Future goods". Section 2–105.

"Goods". Section 2–105.

"Identification". Section 2–501.

"Installment contract". Section 2–612.

"Letter of Credit". Section 2–325.

"Lot". Section 2–105.

"Merchant". Section 2–104.

"Overseas". Section 2–323.

"Person in position of seller". Section 2–707.

"Present sale". Section 2–106.

"Sale". Section 2–106.

"Sale on approval". Section 2–326.

"Sale or return". Section 2–326.

"Termination". Section 2–106.

(3) The following definitions in other Articles apply to this Article:

"Check". Section 3–104.

"Consignee". Section 7–102.

"Consignor". Section 7–102.

"Consumer goods". Section 9–102.

"Dishonor". Section 3–502.

"Draft". Section 3–104.

(4) In addition Article 1 contains general definitions and principles of construction and interpretation applicable throughout this Article.

As amended in 1994 and 1999.

Official Comment

Prior Uniform Statutory Provision: Subsection (1): Section 76, Uniform Sales Act.

Changes:

The definitions of "buyer" and "seller" have been slightly rephrased, the reference in Section 76 of the prior Act to "any legal successor in interest of such person" being omitted. The definition of "receipt" is new.

Purposes of Changes and New Matter:

1. The phrase "any legal successor in interest of such person" has been eliminated since Section 2–210 of this Article, which limits some types of delegation of performance on assignment of a sales contract, makes it clear that not every such successor can be safely included in the definition. In every ordinary case, however, such successors are as of course included.

2. "Receipt" must be distinguished from delivery particularly in regard to the problems arising out of shipment of goods, whether or not the contract calls for making delivery by way of documents of title, since the seller may frequently fulfill his obligations to "deliver" even though the buyer may never "receive" the goods. Delivery with respect to documents of title is defined in Article 1 and requires transfer of physical delivery. Otherwise the many divergent incidents of delivery are handled incident by incident.

Cross References:

Point 1: See Section 2–210 and Comment thereon.
Point 2: Section 1–201.

Definitional Cross Reference:

"Person". Section 1–201.

§ 2–104. Definitions: "Merchant"; "Between Merchants"; "Financing Agency".

(1) "Merchant" means a person who deals in goods of the kind or otherwise by his occupation holds himself out as having knowledge or skill peculiar to the practices or goods involved in the transaction or to whom such knowledge or skill may be attributed by his employment of an agent or broker or other intermediary who by his occupation holds himself out as having such knowledge or skill.

(2) "Financing agency" means a bank, finance company or other person who in the ordinary course of business makes advances against goods or documents of title or who by arrangement with either the seller or the buyer intervenes in ordinary course to make or collect payment due or claimed under the contract for sale, as by purchasing or paying the seller's draft or making advances against it or by merely taking it for collection whether or not documents of title accompany the draft. "Financing agency" includes also a bank or other person who similarly intervenes between persons who are in the position of seller and buyer in respect to the goods (Section 2–707).

(3) "Between merchants" means in any transaction with respect to which both parties are chargeable with the knowledge or skill of merchants.

Official Comment

Prior Uniform Statutory Provision: None. But see Sections 15(2), (5), 16(c), 45(2) and 71, Uniform Sales Act, and Sections 35 and 37, Uniform Bills of Lading Act for examples of the policy expressly provided for in this Article.

Purposes:

1. This Article assumes that transactions between professionals in a given field require special and clear rules which may not apply to a casual or inexperienced seller or buyer. It thus adopts a policy of expressly stating rules applicable "between merchants" and "as against a merchant", wherever they are needed instead of making them depend upon the circumstances of each case as in the statutes cited above. This section lays the foundation of this policy by defining those who are to be regarded as professionals or "merchants" and by stating when a transaction is deemed to be "between merchants".

2. The term "merchant" as defined here roots in the "law merchant" concept of a professional in business. The professional status under the definition may be based upon specialized knowledge as to the goods, specialized knowledge as to business practices, or specialized knowledge as to both and which kind of specialized knowledge may be sufficient to establish the merchant status is indicated by the nature of the provisions.

The special provisions as to merchants appear only in this Article and they are of three kinds. Sections 2–201(2), 2–205, 2–207 and 2–209 dealing with the statute of frauds, firm offers, confirmatory memoranda and modification rest on normal business practices which are or ought to be typical of and familiar to any person in business. For purposes of these sections almost every person in business would, therefore, be deemed to be a "merchant" under the language "who ... by his occupation holds himself out as having knowledge or skill peculiar to the practices ... involved in the transaction ..." since the practices involved in the transaction are non-specialized business practices such as answering mail. In this type of provision, banks or even universities, for example, well may be "merchants." But even these sections only apply to a merchant in his mercantile capacity; a lawyer or bank president buying fishing tackle for his own use is not a merchant.

On the other hand, in Section 2–314 on the warranty of merchantability, such warranty is implied only "if the seller is a merchant with respect to goods of that kind." Obviously this qualification restricts the implied warranty to a much smaller group than everyone who is engaged in business and requires a professional status as to particular kinds of goods. The exception in Section 2–402(2) for retention of possession by a merchant-seller falls in the same class; as does Section 2–403(2) on entrusting of possession to a merchant "who deals in goods of that kind".

A third group of sections includes 2–103(1)(b), which provides that in the case of a merchant "good faith" includes observance of reasonable commercial standards of fair dealing in the trade; 2–327(1)(c), 2–603 and 2–605, dealing with responsibilities of merchant buyers to follow seller's instructions, etc.; 2–509 on risk of loss, and 2–609 on adequate assurance of performance. This group of sections applies to persons who are merchants under either the "practices" or the "goods" aspect of the definition of merchant.

3. The "or to whom such knowledge or skill may be attributed by his employment of an agent or broker . . ." clause of the definition of merchant means that even persons such as universities, for example, can come within the definition of merchant if they have regular purchasing departments or business personnel who are familiar with business practices and who are equipped to take any action required.

Cross References:

Point 1: See Sections 1–102 and 1–203.
Point 2: See Sections 2–314, 2–315 and 2–320 to 2–325, of this Article, and Article 9.

Definitional Cross References:

"Bank". Section 1–201.
"Buyer". Section 2–103.
"Contract for sale". Section 2–106.
"Document of title". Section 1–201.
"Draft". Section 3–104.
"Goods". Section 2–105.
"Person". Section 1–201.
"Purchase". Section 1–201.
"Seller". Section 2–103.

§ 2–105. Definitions: Transferability; "Goods"; "Future" Goods; "Lot"; "Commercial Unit".

(1) "Goods" means all things (including specially manufactured goods) which are movable at the time of identification to the contract for sale other than the money in which the price is to be paid, investment securities (Article 8) and things in action. "Goods" also includes the unborn young of animals and growing crops and other identified things attached to realty as described in the section on goods to be severed from realty (Section 2–107).

(2) Goods must be both existing and identified before any interest in them can pass. Goods which are not both existing and identified are "future" goods. A purported present sale of future goods or of any interest therein operates as a contract to sell.

(3) There may be a sale of a part interest in existing identified goods.

(4) An undivided share in an identified bulk of fungible goods is sufficiently identified to be sold although the quantity of the bulk is not determined. Any agreed proportion of such a bulk or any quantity thereof agreed upon by number, weight or other measure may to the extent of the seller's interest in the bulk be sold to the buyer who then becomes an owner in common.

(5) "Lot" means a parcel or a single article which is the subject matter of a separate sale or delivery, whether or not it is sufficient to perform the contract.

(6) "Commercial unit" means such a unit of goods as by commercial usage is a single whole for purposes of sale and division of which materially impairs its character or value on the market or in use. A commercial unit may be a single article (as a machine) or a set of articles (as a suite of furniture or an assortment of sizes) or a quantity (as a bale, gross, or carload) or any other unit treated in use or in the relevant market as a single whole.

Official Comment

Prior Uniform Statutory Provision: Subsections (1), (2), (3) and (4)—Sections 5, 6 and 76, Uniform Sales Act; Subsections (5) and (6)—none.

Changes: Rewritten.

Purposes of Changes and New Matter:

1. Subsection (1) on "goods": The phraseology of the prior uniform statutory provision has been changed so that:

The definition of goods is based on the concept of movability and the term "chattels personal" is not used. It is not intended to deal with things which are not fairly identifiable as movables before the contract is performed.

Growing crops are included within the definition of goods since they are frequently intended for sale. The concept of "industrial" growing crops has been abandoned, for under modern practices fruit, perennial hay, nursery stock and the like must be brought within the scope of this Article. The young of animals are also included expressly in this definition since they, too, are frequently intended for sale and may be contracted for before birth. The period of gestation of domestic animals is such that the provisions of the section on identification can apply as in the case of crops to be planted. The reason of this definition also leads to the inclusion of a wool crop or the like as "goods" subject to identification under this Article.

The exclusion of "money in which the price is to be paid" from the definition of goods does not mean that foreign currency which is included in the definition of money may not be the subject matter of a sales transaction. Goods is intended to cover the sale of money when money is being treated as a commodity but not to include it when money is the medium of payment.

As to contracts to sell timber, minerals, or structures to be removed from the land Section 2–107(1) (Goods to be severed from Realty: recording) controls.

The use of the word "fixtures" is avoided in view of the diversity of definitions of that term. This Article in including within its scope "things attached to realty" adds the further test that they must be capable of severance without material harm thereto. As between the parties any identified things which fall within that definition become "goods" upon the making of the contract for sale.

"Investment securities" are expressly excluded from the coverage of this Article. It is not intended by this exclusion, however, to prevent the application of a particular section of this Article by analogy to securities (as was done with the Original Sales Act in Agar v. Orda, 264 N.Y. 248, 190 N.E. 479, 99 A.L.R. 269 (1934)) when the reason of that section makes such application sensible and the situation involved is not covered by the Article of this Act dealing specifically with such securities (Article 8).

2. References to the fact that a contract for sale can extend to future or contingent goods and that ownership in common follows the sale of a part interest have been omitted here as obvious without need for expression; hence no inference to negate these principles should be drawn from their omission.

3. Subsection (4) does not touch the question of how far an appropriation of a bulk of fungible goods may or may not satisfy the contract for sale.

4. Subsections (5) and (6) on "lot" and "commercial unit" are introduced to aid in the phrasing of later sections.

5. The question of when an identification of goods takes place is determined by the provisions of Section 2–501 and all that this section says is what kinds of goods may be the subject of a sale.

Cross References:

Point 1: Sections 2–107, 2–201, 2–501 and Article 8.
Point 5: Section 2–501.
See also Section 1–201.

Definitional Cross References:

"Buyer". Section 2–103.
"Contract". Section 1–201.
"Contract for sale". Section 2–106.
"Fungible". Section 1–201.
"Money". Section 1–201.
"Present sale". Section 2–106.
"Sale". Section 2–106.
"Seller". Section 2–103.

§ 2–106. Definitions: "Contract"; "Agreement"; "Contract for Sale"; "Sale"; "Present Sale"; "Conforming" to Contract; "Termination"; "Cancellation".

(1) In this Article unless the context otherwise requires "contract" and "agreement" are limited to those relating to the present or future sale of goods. "Contract for sale" includes both a present sale of goods and a contract to sell goods at a future time. A "sale" consists in the passing of title from the seller to the buyer for a price (Section 2–401). A "present sale" means a sale which is accomplished by the making of the contract.

(2) Goods or conduct including any part of a performance are "conforming" or conform to the contract when they are in accordance with the obligations under the contract.

(3) "Termination" occurs when either party pursuant to a power created by agreement or law puts an end to the contract otherwise than for its breach. On "termination" all obligations which are still executory on both sides are discharged but any right based on prior breach or performance survives.

(4) "Cancellation" occurs when either party puts an end to the contract for breach by the other and its effect is the same as that of "termination" except that the cancelling party also retains any remedy for breach of the whole contract or any unperformed balance.

Official Comment

Prior Uniform Statutory Provision: Subsection (1)—Section 1(1) and (2), Uniform Sales Act; Subsection (2)—none, but subsection generally continues policy of Sections 11, 44 and 69, Uniform Sales Act; Subsections (3) and (4)—none.

Changes: Completely rewritten.

Purposes of Changes and New Matter:

1. Subsection (1): "Contract for sale" is used as a general concept throughout this Article, but the rights of the parties do not vary according to whether the transaction is a present sale or a contract to sell unless the Article expressly so provides.

2. Subsection (2): It is in general intended to continue the policy of requiring exact performance by the seller of his obligations as a condition to his right to require acceptance. However, the seller is in part safeguarded against surprise as a result of sudden technicality on the buyer's part by the provisions of Section 2–508 on seller's cure of improper tender or delivery. Moreover usage of trade frequently permits commercial leeways in performance and the language of the agreement itself must be read in the light of such custom or usage and also, prior course of dealing, and in a long term contract, the course of performance.

3. Subsections (3) and (4): These subsections are intended to make clear the distinction carried forward throughout this Article between termination and cancellation.

Cross References:

Point 2: Sections 1–203, 1–205, 2–208 and 2–508.

Definitional Cross References:

"Agreement". Section 1–201.
"Buyer". Section 2–103.
"Contract". Section 1–201.
"Goods". Section 2–105.
"Party". Section 1–201.
"Remedy". Section 1–201.
"Rights". Section 1–201.
"Seller". Section 2–103.

§ 2–107. Goods to Be Severed From Realty: Recording.

(1) A contract for the sale of minerals or the like (including oil and gas) or a structure or its materials to be removed from realty is a contract for the sale of goods within this Article if they are to be severed by the seller but until severance a purported present sale thereof which is not effective as a transfer of an interest in land is effective only as a contract to sell.

(2) A contract for the sale apart from the land of growing crops or other things attached to realty and capable of severance without material harm thereto but not described in subsection (1) or of timber to be cut is a contract for the sale of goods within this Article whether the subject matter is to be severed by the buyer or by the seller even though it forms part of the realty at the time of contracting, and the parties can by identification effect a present sale before severance.

(3) The provisions of this section are subject to any third party rights provided by the law relating to realty records, and the contract for sale may be executed and recorded as a document transferring an interest in land and shall then constitute notice to third parties of the buyer's rights under the contract for sale.

As amended in 1972.

Official Comment

Prior Uniform Statutory Provision: See Section 76, Uniform Sales Act on prior policy; Section 7, Uniform Conditional Sales Act.

Purposes:

1. Subsection (1). Notice that this subsection applies only if the minerals or structures "are to be severed by the seller". If the buyer is to sever, such transactions are considered contracts affecting land and all problems of the Statute of Frauds and of the recording of land rights apply to them. Therefore, the Statute of Frauds section of this Article does not apply to such contracts though they must conform to the Statute of Frauds affecting the transfer of interests in land.

2. Subsection (2). "Things attached" to the realty which can be severed without material harm are goods within this Article regardless of who is to effect the severance. The word "fixtures" has been avoided because of the diverse definitions of this term, the test of "severance without material harm" being substituted.

The provision in subsection (3) for recording such contracts is within the purview of this Article since it is a means of preserving the buyer's rights under the contract of sale.

3. The security phases of things attached to or to become attached to realty are dealt with in the Article on Secured Transactions (Article 9) and it is to be noted that the definition of goods in that Article differs from the definition of goods in this Article.

However, both Articles treat as goods growing crops and also timber to be cut under a contract of severance.

Cross References:

Point 1: Section 2–201.
Point 2: Section 2–105.

Point 3: Article 9 and Section 9–102(a)(44).

Definitional Cross References:

"Buyer". Section 2–103.

"Contract". Section 1–201.

"Contract for sale". Section 2–106.

"Goods". Section 2–105.

"Party". Section 1–201.

"Present sale". Section 2–106.

"Rights". Section 1–201.

"Seller". Section 2–103.

PART 2

FORM, FORMATION AND READJUSTMENT OF CONTRACT

§ 2–201. Formal Requirements; Statute of Frauds.

(1) Except as otherwise provided in this section a contract for the sale of goods for the price of $500 or more is not enforceable by way of action or defense unless there is some writing sufficient to indicate that a contract for sale has been made between the parties and signed by the party against whom enforcement is sought or by his authorized agent or broker. A writing is not insufficient because it omits or incorrectly states a term agreed upon but the contract is not enforceable under this paragraph beyond the quantity of goods shown in such writing.

(2) Between merchants if within a reasonable time a writing in confirmation of the contract and sufficient against the sender is received and the party receiving it has reason to know its contents, it satisfies the requirements of subsection (1) against such party unless written notice of objection to its contents is given within 10 days after it is received.

(3) A contract which does not satisfy the requirements of subsection (1) but which is valid in other respects is enforceable

(a) if the goods are to be specially manufactured for the buyer and are not suitable for sale to others in the ordinary course of the seller's business and the seller, before notice of repudiation is received and under circumstances which reasonably indicate that the goods are for the buyer, has made either a substantial beginning of their manufacture or commitments for their procurement; or

(b) if the party against whom enforcement is sought admits in his pleading, testimony or otherwise in court that a contract for sale was made, but the contract is not enforceable under this provision beyond the quantity of goods admitted; or

(c) with respect to goods for which payment has been made and accepted or which have been received and accepted (Sec. 2–606).

Official Comment

Prior Uniform Statutory Provision: Section 4, Uniform Sales Act (which was based on Section 17 of the Statute of 29 Charles II).

Changes: Completely rephrased; restricted to sale of goods. See also Sections 1–206, 8–319 and 9–203.

Purposes of Changes: The changed phraseology of this section is intended to make it clear that:

1. The required writing need not contain all the material terms of the contract and such material terms as are stated need not be precisely stated. All that is required is that the writing afford a basis for believing that the offered oral evidence rests on a real transaction. It may be written in lead pencil on a scratch pad. It need not indicate which party is the buyer and which the seller. The only term which must appear is the quantity term which need not be accurately stated but recovery is limited to the amount stated. The price, time and place of payment or delivery, the general quality of the goods, or any particular warranties may all be omitted.

Special emphasis must be placed on the permissibility of omitting the price term in view of the insistence of some courts on the express inclusion of this term even where the parties have contracted on the basis of a published price list. In many valid contracts for sale the parties do not mention the price in express terms, the buyer being bound to pay and the seller to accept a reasonable price which the trier of the fact may well be trusted to determine. Again, frequently the price is not mentioned since the parties have based their agreement on a price list or catalogue known to both of them and this list serves as an efficient safeguard against perjury. Finally, "market" prices and valuations that are current in the vicinity constitute a similar check. Thus if the price is not stated in the memorandum it can normally be supplied without danger of fraud. Of course if the "price" consists of goods rather than money the quantity of goods must be stated.

Only three definite and invariable requirements as to the memorandum are made by this subsection. First, it must evidence a contract for the sale of goods; second, it must be "signed", a word which includes any authentication which identifies the party to be charged; and third, it must specify a quantity.

2. "Partial performance" as a substitute for the required memorandum can validate the contract only for the goods which have been accepted or for which payment has been made and accepted.

Receipt and acceptance either of goods or of the price constitutes an unambiguous overt admission by both parties that a contract actually exists. If the court can make a just apportionment, therefore, the agreed price of any goods actually delivered can be recovered without a writing or, if the price has been paid, the seller can be forced to deliver an apportionable part of the goods. The overt actions of the parties make admissible evidence of the other terms of the contract necessary to a just apportionment. This is true even though the actions of the parties are not in themselves inconsistent with a different transaction such as a consignment for resale or a mere loan of money.

Part performance by the buyer requires the delivery of something by him that is accepted by the seller as such performance. Thus, part payment may be made by money or check, accepted by the seller. If the agreed price consists of goods or services, then they must also have been delivered and accepted.

3. Between merchants, failure to answer a written confirmation of a contract within ten days of receipt is tantamount to a writing under subsection (2) and is sufficient against both parties under subsection (1). The only effect, however, is to take away from the party who fails to answer the defense of the Statute of Frauds; the burden of persuading the trier of fact that a contract was in fact made orally prior to the written confirmation is unaffected. Compare the effect of a failure to reply under Section 2–207.

4. Failure to satisfy the requirements of this section does not render the contract void for all purposes, but merely prevents it from being judicially enforced in favor of a party to the contract. For example, a buyer who takes possession of goods as provided in an oral contract which the seller has not meanwhile repudiated, is not a trespasser. Nor would the Statute of Frauds provisions of this section be a defense to a third person who wrongfully induces a party to refuse to perform an oral contract, even though the injured party cannot maintain an action for damages against the party so refusing to perform.

5. The requirement of "signing" is discussed in the comment to Section 1–201.

6. It is not necessary that the writing be delivered to anybody. It need not be signed or authenticated by both parties but it is, of course, not sufficient against one who has not signed it. Prior to a dispute no one can determine which party's signing of the memorandum may be necessary but from the time of contracting each party should be aware that to him it is signing by the other which is important.

7. If the making of a contract is admitted in court, either in a written pleading, by stipulation or by oral statement before the court, no additional writing is necessary for protection against fraud. Under this section it is no longer possible to admit the contract in court and still treat the Statute as a defense. However, the contract is not thus conclusively established. The admission so made by a party is itself evidential against him of the truth of the facts so admitted and of nothing more; as against the other party, it is not evidential at all.

Cross References:

See Sections 1–201, 2–202, 2–207, 2–209 and 2–304.

Definitional Cross References:

"Action". Section 1–201.
"Between merchants". Section 2–104.
"Buyer". Section 2–103.
"Contract". Section 1–201.
"Contract for sale". Section 2–106.
"Goods". Section 2–105.
"Notice". Section 1–201.
"Party". Section 1–201.
"Reasonable time". Section 1–204.
"Sale". Section 2–106.
"Seller". Section 2–103.

§ 2–202. Final Written Expression: Parol or Extrinsic Evidence.

Terms with respect to which the confirmatory memoranda of the parties agree or which are otherwise set forth in a writing intended by the parties as a final expression of their agreement with respect to such terms as are included therein may not be contradicted by evidence of any prior agreement or of a contemporaneous oral agreement but may be explained or supplemented

(a) by course of dealing, or usage of trade (Section 1–205) or by course of performance (Section 2–208); and

(b) by evidence of consistent additional terms unless the court finds the writing to have been intended also as a complete and exclusive statement of the terms of the agreement.

Official Comment

Prior Uniform Statutory Provisions: None.

Purposes:

1. This section definitely rejects:

(a) Any assumption that because a writing has been worked out which is final on some matters, it is to be taken as including all the matters agreed upon;

(b) The premise that the language used has the meaning attributable to such language by rules of construction existing in the law rather than the meaning which arises out of the commercial context in which it was used; and

(c) The requirement that a condition precedent to the admissibility of the type of evidence specified in paragraph (a) is an original determination by the court that the language used is ambiguous.

2. Paragraph (a) makes admissible evidence of course of dealing, usage of trade and course of performance to explain or supplement the terms of any writing stating the agreement of the parties in order that the true understanding of the parties as to the agreement may be reached. Such writings are to be read on the assumption that the course of prior dealings between the parties and the usages of trade were taken for granted when the document was phrased. Unless carefully negated they have become an element of the meaning of the words used. Similarly, the course of actual performance by the parties is considered the best indication of what they intended the writing to mean.

3. Under paragraph (b) consistent additional terms, not reduced to writing, may be proved unless the court finds that the writing was intended by both parties as a complete and exclusive statement of all the terms. If the additional terms are such that, if agreed upon, they would certainly have been included in the document in the view of the court, then evidence of their alleged making must be kept from the trier of fact.

Cross References:

Point 3: Sections 1–205, 2–207, 2–302 and 2–316.

Definitional Cross References:

"Agreed" and "agreement". Section 1–201.
"Course of dealing". Section 1–205.
"Course of performance". Section 1–208.
"Parties". Section 1–201.
"Term". Section 1–201.
"Usage of trade". Section 1–205.
"Written" and "writing". Section 1–201.

§ 2–203.   Seals Inoperative.

The affixing of a seal to a writing evidencing a contract for sale or an offer to buy or sell goods does not constitute the writing a sealed instrument and the law with respect to sealed instruments does not apply to such a contract or offer.

Official Comment

Prior Uniform Statutory Provision: Section 3, Uniform Sales Act.

Changes: Portion pertaining to "seals" rewritten.

Purposes of Changes:

1. This section makes it clear that every effect of the seal which relates to "sealed instruments" as such is wiped out insofar as contracts for sale are concerned. However, the substantial effects of a seal, except extension of the period of limitations, may be had by appropriate drafting as in the case of firm offers (see Section 2–205).

2. This section leaves untouched any aspects of a seal which relate merely to signatures or to authentication of execution and the like. Thus, a statute providing that a purported signature gives prima facie evidence of its own authenticity or that a signature gives prima facie evidence of consideration is still applicable to sales transactions even though a seal may be held to be a signature within the meaning of such a statute. Similarly, the authorized affixing of a corporate seal bearing the corporate name to a contractual writing purporting to be made by the corporation may have effect as a signature without any reference to the law of sealed instruments.

Cross Reference:

Point 1: Section 2–205.

Definitional Cross References:

"Contract for sale". Section 2–106.
"Goods". Section 2–105.
"Writing". Section 1–201.

§ 2–204.   Formation in General.

(1) A contract for sale of goods may be made in any manner sufficient to show agreement, including conduct by both parties which recognizes the existence of such a contract.

(2) An agreement sufficient to constitute a contract for sale may be found even though the moment of its making is undetermined.

(3) Even though one or more terms are left open a contract for sale does not fail for indefiniteness if the parties have intended to make a contract and there is a reasonably certain basis for giving an appropriate remedy.

Official Comment

Prior Uniform Statutory Provision: Sections 1 and 3, Uniform Sales Act.

Changes: Completely rewritten by this and other sections of this Article.

Purposes of Changes:

Subsection (1) continues without change the basic policy of recognizing any manner of expression of agreement, oral, written or otherwise. The legal effect of such an agreement is, of course, qualified by other provisions of this Article.

Under subsection (1) appropriate conduct by the parties may be sufficient to establish an agreement. Subsection (2) is directed primarily to the situation where the interchanged correspondence does not disclose the exact point at which the deal was closed, but the actions of the parties indicate that a binding obligation has been undertaken.

Subsection (3) states the principle as to "open terms" underlying later sections of the Article. If the parties intend to enter into a binding agreement, this subsection recognizes that agreement as valid in law, despite missing terms, if there is any reasonably certain basis for granting a remedy. The test is not certainty as to what the parties were to do nor as to the exact amount of damages due the plaintiff. Nor is the fact that one or more terms are left to be agreed upon enough of itself to defeat an otherwise adequate agreement. Rather, commercial standards on the point of "indefiniteness" are intended to be applied, this Act making provision elsewhere for missing terms needed for performance, open price, remedies and the like.

The more terms the parties leave open, the less likely it is that they have intended to conclude a binding agreement, but their actions may be frequently conclusive on the matter despite the omissions.

Cross References:

Subsection (1): Sections 1–103, 2–201 and 2–302.
Subsection (2): Sections 2–205 through 2–209.
Subsection (3): See Part 3.

Definitional Cross References:

"Agreement". Section 1–201.
"Contract". Section 1–201.
"Contract for sale". Section 2–106.
"Goods". Section 2–105.
"Party". Section 1–201.
"Remedy". Section 1–201.
"Term". Section 1–201.

§ 2–205.   Firm Offers.

An offer by a merchant to buy or sell goods in a signed writing which by its terms gives assurance that it will be held open is not revocable, for lack of consideration, during the time stated or if no time is stated for a reasonable time, but in no event may such period of irrevocability exceed three months; but any such term of assurance on a form supplied by the offeree must be separately signed by the offeror.

Official Comment

Prior Uniform Statutory Provision: Sections 1 and 3, Uniform Sales Act.

Changes: Completely rewritten by this and other sections of this Article.

Purposes of Changes:

1. This section is intended to modify the former rule which required that "firm offers" be sustained by consideration in order to bind, and to require instead that they must merely be characterized as such and expressed in signed writings.

2. The primary purpose of this section is to give effect to the deliberate intention of a merchant to make a current firm offer binding. The deliberation is shown in the case of an individualized document by the merchant's signature to the offer, and in the case of an offer included on a form supplied by the other party to the transaction by the separate signing of the particular clause which contains the offer. "Signed" here also includes authentication but the reasonableness of the authentication herein allowed must be determined in the light of the purpose of the section. The circumstances surrounding the signing may justify something

less than a formal signature or initialing but typically the kind of authentication involved here would consist of a minimum of initialing of the clause involved. A handwritten memorandum on the writer's letterhead purporting in its terms to "confirm" a firm offer already made would be enough to satisfy this section, although not subscribed, since under the circumstances it could not be considered a memorandum of mere negotiation and it would adequately show its own authenticity. Similarly, an authorized telegram will suffice, and this is true even though the original draft contained only a typewritten signature. However, despite settled courses of dealing or usages of the trade whereby firm offers are made by oral communication and relied upon without more evidence, such offers remain revocable under this Article since authentication by a writing is the essence of this section.

3. This section is intended to apply to current "firm" offers and not to long term options, and an outside time limit of three months during which such offers remain irrevocable has been set. The three month period during which firm offers remain irrevocable under this section need not be stated by days or by date. If the offer states that it is "guaranteed" or "firm" until the happening of a contingency which will occur within the three month period, it will remain irrevocable until that event. A promise made for a longer period will operate under this section to bind the offeror only for the first three months of the period but may of course be renewed. If supported by consideration it may continue for as long as the parties specify. This section deals only with the offer which is not supported by consideration.

4. Protection is afforded against the inadvertent signing of a firm offer when contained in a form prepared by the offeree by requiring that such a clause be separately authenticated. If the offer clause is called to the offeror's attention and he separately authenticates it, he will be bound; Section 2–302 may operate, however, to prevent an unconscionable result which otherwise would flow from other terms appearing in the form.

5. Safeguards are provided to offer relief in the case of material mistake by virtue of the requirement of good faith and the general law of mistake.

Cross References:

Point 1: Section 1–102.
Point 2: Section 1–102.
Point 3: Section 2–201.
Point 5: Section 2–302.

Definitional Cross References:

"Goods". Section 2–105.
"Merchant". Section 2–104.
"Signed". Section 1–201.
"Writing". Section 1–201.

§ 2–206. Offer and Acceptance in Formation of Contract.

(1) Unless otherwise unambiguously indicated by the language or circumstances

(a) an offer to make a contract shall be construed as inviting acceptance in any manner and by any medium reasonable in the circumstances;

(b) an order or other offer to buy goods for prompt or current shipment shall be construed as inviting acceptance either by a prompt promise to ship or by the prompt or current shipment of conforming or non-conforming goods, but such a shipment of non-conforming goods does not constitute an acceptance if the seller seasonably notifies the buyer that the shipment is offered only as an accommodation to the buyer.

(2) Where the beginning of a requested performance is a reasonable mode of acceptance an offeror who is not notified of acceptance within a reasonable time may treat the offer as having lapsed before acceptance.

Official Comment

Prior Uniform Statutory Provision: Sections 1 and 3, Uniform Sales Act.

Changes: Completely rewritten in this and other sections of this Article.

Purposes of Changes: To make it clear that:

1. Any reasonable manner of acceptance is intended to be regarded as available unless the offeror has made quite clear that it will not be acceptable. Former technical rules as to acceptance, such as requiring that telegraphic offers be accepted by telegraphed acceptance, etc., are rejected and a criterion that the acceptance be "in any manner and by any medium reasonable under the circumstances," is substituted. This section is intended to remain flexible and its applicability to be enlarged as new media of communication develop or as the more time-saving present day media come into general use.

2. Either shipment or a prompt promise to ship is made a proper means of acceptance of an offer looking

to current shipment. In accordance with ordinary commercial understanding the section interprets an order looking to current shipment as allowing acceptance either by actual shipment or by a prompt promise to ship and rejects the artificial theory that only a single mode of acceptance is normally envisaged by an offer. This is true even though the language of the offer happens to be "ship at once" or the like. "Shipment" is here used in the same sense as in Section 2–504; it does not include the beginning of delivery by the seller's own truck or by messenger. But loading on the seller's own truck might be a beginning of performance under subsection (2).

3. The beginning of performance by an offeree can be effective as acceptance so as to bind the offeror only if followed within a reasonable time by notice to the offeror. Such a beginning of performance must unambiguously express the offeree's intention to engage himself. For the protection of both parties it is essential that notice follow in due course to constitute acceptance. Nothing in this section however bars the possibility that under the common law performance begun may have an intermediate effect of temporarily barring revocation of the offer, or at the offeror's option, final effect in constituting acceptance.

4. Subsection (1)(b) deals with the situation where a shipment made following an order is shown by a notification of shipment to be referable to that order but has a defect. Such a non-conforming shipment is normally to be understood as intended to close the bargain, even though it proves to have been at the same time a breach. However, the seller by stating that the shipment is non-conforming and is offered only as an accommodation to the buyer keeps the shipment or notification from operating as an acceptance.

Definitional Cross References:

"Buyer". Section 2–103.
"Conforming". Section 2–106.
"Contract". Section 1–201.
"Goods". Section 2–105.
"Notifies". Section 1–201.
"Reasonable time". Section 1–204.

§ 2–207. Additional Terms in Acceptance or Confirmation.

(1) A definite and seasonable expression of acceptance or a written confirmation which is sent within a reasonable time operates as an acceptance even though it states terms additional to or different from those offered or agreed upon, un-

less acceptance is expressly made conditional on assent to the additional or different terms.

(2) The additional terms are to be construed as proposals for addition to the contract. Between merchants such terms become part of the contract unless:

(a) the offer expressly limits acceptance to the terms of the offer;

(b) they materially alter it; or

(c) notification of objection to them has already been given or is given within a reasonable time after notice of them is received.

(3) Conduct by both parties which recognizes the existence of a contract is sufficient to establish a contract for sale although the writings of the parties do not otherwise establish a contract. In such case the terms of the particular contract consist of those terms on which the writings of the parties agree, together with any supplementary terms incorporated under any other provisions of this Act.

Official Comment

Prior Uniform Statutory Provision: Sections 1 and 3, Uniform Sales Act.

Changes: Completely rewritten by this and other sections of this Article.

Purposes of Changes:

1. This section is intended to deal with two typical situations. The one is the written confirmation, where an agreement has been reached either orally or by informal correspondence between the parties and is followed by one or both of the parties sending formal memoranda embodying the terms so far as agreed upon and adding terms not discussed. The other situation is offer and acceptance, in which a wire or letter expressed and intended as an acceptance or the closing of an agreement adds further minor suggestions or proposals such as "ship by Tuesday," "rush," "ship draft against bill of lading inspection allowed," or the like. A frequent example of the second situation is the exchange of printed purchase order and acceptance (sometimes called "acknowledgment") forms. Because the forms are oriented to the thinking of the respective drafting parties, the terms contained in them often do not correspond. Often the seller's form contains terms different from or additional to those set forth in the buyer's form. Nevertheless, the parties proceed with the transaction. [Comment 1 was amended in 1966.]

2. Under this Article a proposed deal which in commercial understanding has in fact been closed is recognized as a contract. Therefore, any additional matter contained in the confirmation or in the acceptance falls within subsection (2) and must be regarded as a proposal for an added term unless the acceptance is made conditional on the acceptance of the additional or different terms. [Comment 2 was amended in 1966.]

3. Whether or not additional or different terms will become part of the agreement depends upon the provisions of subsection (2). If they are such as materially to alter the original bargain, they will not be included unless expressly agreed to by the other party. If, however, they are terms which would not so change the bargain they will be incorporated unless notice of objection to them has already been given or is given within a reasonable time.

4. Examples of typical clauses which would normally "materially alter" the contract and so result in surprise or hardship if incorporated without express awareness by the other party are: a clause negating such standard warranties as that of merchantability or fitness for a particular purpose in circumstances in which either warranty normally attaches; a clause requiring a guaranty of 90% or 100% deliveries in a case such as a contract by cannery, where the usage of the trade allows greater quantity leeways; a clause reserving to the seller the power to cancel upon the buyer's failure to meet any invoice when due; a clause requiring that complaints be made in a time materially shorter than customary or reasonable.

5. Examples of clauses which involve no element of unreasonable surprise and which therefore are to be incorporated in the contract unless notice of objection is seasonably given are: a clause setting forth and perhaps enlarging slightly upon the seller's exemption due to supervening causes beyond his control, similar to those covered by the provision of this Article on merchant's excuse by failure of presupposed conditions or a clause fixing in advance any reasonable formula of proration under such circumstances; a clause fixing a reasonable time for complaints within customary limits, or in the case of a purchase for sub-sale, providing for inspection by the sub-purchaser; a clause providing for interest on overdue invoices or fixing the seller's standard credit terms where they are within the range of trade practice and do not limit any credit bargained for; a clause limiting the right of rejection for defects which fall within the customary trade tolerances for acceptance "with adjustment" or otherwise limiting remedy in a reasonable manner (see Sections 2–718 and 2–719).

6. If no answer is received within a reasonable time after additional terms are proposed, it is both fair and commercially sound to assume that their inclusion has been assented to. Where clauses on confirming forms sent by both parties conflict each party must be assumed to object to a clause of the other conflicting with one on the confirmation sent by himself. As a result the requirement that there be notice of objection which is found in subsection (2) is satisfied and the conflicting terms do not become a part of the contract. The contract then consists of the terms originally expressly agreed to, terms on which the confirmations agree, and terms supplied by this Act, including subsection (2). The written confirmation is also subject to Section 2–201. Under that section a failure to respond permits enforcement of a prior oral agreement; under this section a failure to respond permits additional terms to become part of the agreement. [Comment 6 was amended in 1966.]

7. In many cases, as where goods are shipped, accepted and paid for before any dispute arises, there is no question whether a contract has been made. In such cases, where the writings of the parties do not establish a contract, it is not necessary to determine which act or document constituted the offer and which the acceptance. See Section 2–204. The only question is what terms are included in the contract, and subsection (3) furnishes the governing rule. [Comment 7 was added in 1966.]

Cross References:

See generally Section 2–302.
Point 5: Sections 2–513, 2–602, 2–607, 2–609, 2–612, 2–614, 2–615, 2–616, 2–718 and 2–719.
Point 6: Sections 1–102 and 2–104.

Definitional Cross References:

"Between merchants". Section 2–104.
"Contract". Section 1–201.
"Notification". Section 1–201.
"Reasonable time". Section 1–204.
"Seasonably". Section 1–204.
"Send". Section 1–201.
"Term". Section 1–201.
"Written". Section 1–201.

§ 2–208. Course of Performance or Practical Construction.

(1) Where the contract for sale involves repeated occasions for performance by either party with knowledge of the nature of the performance and opportunity for objection to it by the other,

any course of performance accepted or acquiesced in without objection shall be relevant to determine the meaning of the agreement.

(2) The express terms of the agreement and any such course of performance, as well as any course of dealing and usage of trade, shall be construed whenever reasonable as consistent with each other; but when such construction is unreasonable, express terms shall control course of performance and course of performance shall control both course of dealing and usage of trade (Section 1–205).

(3) Subject to the provisions of the next section on modification and waiver, such course of performance shall be relevant to show a waiver or modification of any term inconsistent with such course of performance.

Official Comment

Prior Uniform Statutory Provision: No such general provision but concept of this section recognized by terms such as "course of dealing", "the circumstances of the case," "the conduct of the parties," etc., in Uniform Sales Act.

Purposes:

1. The parties themselves know best what they have meant by their words of agreement and their action under that agreement is the best indication of what that meaning was. This section thus rounds out the set of factors which determines the meaning of the "agreement" and therefore also of the "unless otherwise agreed" qualification to various provisions of this Article.

2. Under this section a course of performance is always relevant to determine the meaning of the agreement. Express mention of course of performance elsewhere in this Article carries no contrary implication when there is a failure to refer to it in other sections.

3. Where it is difficult to determine whether a particular act merely sheds light on the meaning of the agreement or represents a waiver of a term of the agreement, the preference is in favor of "waiver" whenever such construction, plus the application of the provisions on the reinstatement of rights waived (see Section 2–209), is needed to preserve the flexible character of commercial contracts and to prevent surprise or other hardship.

4. A single occasion of conduct does not fall within the language of this section but other sections such as the ones on silence after acceptance and failure to specify particular defects can affect the parties' rights on a single occasion (see Sections 2–605 and 2–607).

§ 2–209. Modification, Rescission and Waiver.

(1) An agreement modifying a contract within this Article needs no consideration to be binding.

(2) A signed agreement which excludes modification or rescission except by a signed writing cannot be otherwise modified or rescinded, but except as between merchants such a requirement on a form supplied by the merchant must be separately signed by the other party.

(3) The requirements of the statute of frauds section of this Article (Section 2–201) must be satisfied if the contract as modified is within its provisions.

(4) Although an attempt at modification or rescission does not satisfy the requirements of subsection (2) or (3) it can operate as a waiver.

(5) A party who has made a waiver affecting an executory portion of the contract may retract the waiver by reasonable notification received by the other party that strict performance will be required of any term waived, unless the retraction would be unjust in view of a material change of position in reliance on the waiver.

Official Comment

Prior Uniform Statutory Provision: Subsection (1)—Compare Section 1, Uniform Written Obligations Act; Subsections (2) to (5)—none.

Purposes of Changes and New Matter:

1. This section seeks to protect and make effective all necessary and desirable modifications of sales contracts without regard to the technicalities which at present hamper such adjustments.

2. Subsection (1) provides that an agreement modifying a sales contract needs no consideration to be binding.

However, modifications made thereunder must meet the test of good faith imposed by this Act. The effective use of bad faith to escape performance on the original contract terms is barred, and the extortion of a "modification" without legitimate commercial reason is ineffective as a violation of the duty of good faith. Nor can a mere technical consideration support a modification made in bad faith.

The test of "good faith" between merchants or as against merchants includes "observance of reasonable commercial standards of fair dealing in the trade" (Section 2–103), and may in some situations require an objectively demonstrable reason for seeking a modification. But such matters as a market shift which makes performance come to involve a loss may provide such a reason even though there is no such unforeseen difficulty as would make out a legal excuse from performance under Sections 2–615 and 2–616.

3. Subsections (2) and (3) are intended to protect against false allegations of oral modifications. "Modification or rescission" includes abandonment or other change by mutual consent, contrary to the decision in Green v. Doniger, 300 N.Y. 238, 90 N.E.2d 56 (1949); it does not include unilateral "termination" or "cancellation" as defined in Section 2–106.

The Statute of Frauds provisions of this Article are expressly applied to modifications by subsection (3). Under those provisions the "delivery and acceptance" test is limited to the goods which have been accepted, that is, to the past. "Modification" for the future cannot therefore be conjured up by oral testimony if the price involved is $500.00 or more since such modification must be shown at least by an authenticated memo. And since a memo is limited in its effect to the quantity of goods set forth in it there is safeguard against oral evidence.

Subsection (2) permits the parties in effect to make their own Statute of Frauds as regards any future modification of the contract by giving effect to a clause in a signed agreement which expressly requires any modification to be by signed writing. But note that if a consumer is to be held to such a clause on a form supplied by a merchant it must be separately signed.

4. Subsection (4) is intended, despite the provisions of subsections (2) and (3), to prevent contractual provisions excluding modification except by a signed writing from limiting in other respects the legal effect of the parties' actual later conduct. The effect of such conduct as a waiver is further regulated in subsection (5).

Cross References:

Point 1: Section 1–203.
Point 2: Sections 1–201, 1–203, 2–615 and 2–616.
Point 3: Sections 2–106, 2–201 and 2–202.
Point 4: Sections 2–202 and 2–208.

Definitional Cross References:

"Agreement". Section 1–201.
"Between merchants". Section 2–104.
"Contract". Section 1–201.
"Notification". Section 1–201.
"Signed". Section 1–201.

"Term". Section 1–201.
"Writing". Section 1–201.

§ 2–210. Delegation of Performance; Assignment of Rights.

(1) A party may perform his duty through a delegate unless otherwise agreed or unless the other party has a substantial interest in having his original promisor perform or control the acts required by the contract. No delegation of performance relieves the party delegating of any duty to perform or any liability for breach.

(2) Except as otherwise provided in Section 9–406, unless otherwise agreed, all rights of either seller or buyer can be assigned except where the assignment would materially change the duty of the other party, or increase materially the burden or risk imposed on him by his contract, or impair materially his chance of obtaining return performance. A right to damages for breach of the whole contract or a right arising out of the assignor's due performance of his entire obligation can be assigned despite agreement otherwise.

(3) The creation, attachment, perfection, or enforcement of a security interest in the seller's interest under a contract is not a transfer that materially changes the duty of or increases materially the burden or risk imposed on the buyer or impairs materially the buyer's chance of obtaining return performance within the purview of subsection (2) unless, and then only to the extent that, enforcement actually results in a delegation of material performance of the seller. Even in that event, the creation, attachment, perfection, and enforcement of the security interest remain effective, but (i) the seller is liable to the buyer for damages caused by the delegation to the extent that the damages could not reasonably be prevented by the buyer, and (ii) a court having jurisdiction may grant other appropriate relief, including cancellation of the contract for sale or an injunction against enforcement of the security interest or consummation of the enforcement.

(4) Unless the circumstances indicate the contrary a prohibition of assignment of "the contract" is to be construed as barring only the delegation to the assignee of the assignor's performance.

(5) An assignment of "the contract" or of "all my rights under the contract" or an assignment in similar general terms is an assign-

ment of rights and unless the language or the circumstances (as in an assignment for security) indicate the contrary, it is a delegation of performance of the duties of the assignor and its acceptance by the assignee constitutes a promise by him to perform those duties. This promise is enforceable by either the assignor or the other party to the original contract.

(6) The other party may treat any assignment which delegates performance as creating reasonable grounds for insecurity and may without prejudice to his rights against the assignor demand assurances from the assignee (Section 2–609).

As amended in 1999.

Official Comment

Prior Uniform Statutory Provision: None.

Purposes:

1. Generally, this section recognizes both delegation of performance and assignability as normal and permissible incidents of a contract for the sale of goods.

2. Delegation of performance, either in conjunction with an assignment or otherwise, is provided for by subsection (1) where no substantial reason can be shown as to why the delegated performance will not be as satisfactory as personal performance.

3. Under subsection (2) rights which are no longer executory such as a right to damages for breach may be assigned although the agreement prohibits assignment. In such cases no question of delegation of any performance is involved. Subsection (2) is subject to Section 9–406, which makes rights to payment for goods sold ("accounts"), whether or not earned, freely alienable notwithstanding a contrary agreement or rule of law.

4. The nature of the contract or the circumstances of the case, however, may bar assignment of the contract even where delegation of performance is not involved. This Article and this section are intended to clarify this problem, particularly in cases dealing with output requirement and exclusive dealing contracts. In the first place the section on requirements and exclusive dealing removes from the construction of the original contract most of the "personal discretion" element by substituting the reasonably objective standard of good faith operation of the plant or business to be supplied. Secondly, the section on insecurity and assurances, which is specifically referred to in subsection (5) of this section, frees the other party from the doubts and uncertainty which may afflict him under an assignment of the character in question by permitting him to demand adequate assurance of due performance without which he may suspend his own performance. Subsection (5) is not in any way intended to limit the effect of the section on insecurity and assurances and the word "performance" includes the giving of orders under a requirements contract. Of course, in any case where a material personal discretion is sought to be transferred, effective assignment is barred by subsection (2).

5. Subsection (4) lays down a general rule of construction distinguishing between a normal commercial assignment, which substitutes the assignee for the assignor both as to rights and duties, and a financing assignment in which only the assignor's rights are transferred.

This Article takes no position on the possibility of extending some recognition or power to the original parties to work out normal commercial readjustments of the contract in the case of financing assignments even after the original obligor has been notified of the assignment. This question is dealt with in the Article on Secured Transactions (Article 9).

6. Subsection (5) recognizes that the non-assigning original party has a stake in the reliability of the person with whom he has closed the original contract, and is, therefore, entitled to due assurance that any delegated performance will be properly forthcoming.

7. This section is not intended as a complete statement of the law of delegation and assignment but is limited to clarifying a few points doubtful under the case law. Particularly, neither this section nor this Article touches directly on such questions as the need or effect of notice of the assignment, the rights of successive assignees, or any question of the form of an assignment, either as between the parties or as against any third parties. Some of these questions are dealt with in Article 9.

Cross References:

Point 3: Articles 5 and 9.
Point 4: Sections 2–306 and 2–609.
Point 5: Article 9, Sections 9–402, 9–404, 9–405, and 9–406.
Point 7: Article 9.

Definitional Cross References:

"Agreement". Section 1–201.
"Buyer". Section 2–103.
"Contract". Section 1–201.
"Party". Section 1–201.
"Rights". Section 1–201.

"Seller". Section 2–103.

"Term". Section 1–201.

As amended in 1999.

PART 3

GENERAL OBLIGATION AND CONSTRUCTION OF CONTRACT

§ 2–301. General Obligations of Parties.

The obligation of the seller is to transfer and deliver and that of the buyer is to accept and pay in accordance with the contract.

Official Comment

Prior Uniform Statutory Provision: Sections 11 and 41, Uniform Sales Act.

Changes: Rewritten.

Purposes of Changes:

This section uses the term "obligation" in contrast to the term "duty" in order to provide for the "condition" aspects of delivery and payment insofar as they are not modified by other sections of this Article such as those on cure of tender. It thus replaces not only the general provisions of the Uniform Sales Act on the parties' duties, but also the general provisions of that Act on the effect of conditions. In order to determine what is "in accordance with the contract" under this Article usage of trade, course of dealing and performance, and the general background of circumstances must be given due consideration in conjunction with the lay meaning of the words used to define the scope of the conditions and duties.

Cross References:

Section 1–106. See also Sections 1–205, 2–208, 2–209, 2–508 and 2–612.

Definitional Cross References:

"Buyer". Section 2–103.

"Contract". Section 1–201.

"Party". Section 1–201.

"Seller". Section 2–103.

§ 2–302. Unconscionable Contract or Clause.

(1) If the court as a matter of law finds the contract or any clause of the contract to have been unconscionable at the time it was made the court may refuse to enforce the contract, or it may enforce the remainder of the contract with-out the unconscionable clause, or it may so limit the application of any unconscionable clause as to avoid any unconscionable result.

(2) When it is claimed or appears to the court that the contract or any clause thereof may be unconscionable the parties shall be afforded a reasonable opportunity to present evidence as to its commercial setting, purpose and effect to aid the court in making the determination.

Official Comment

Prior Uniform Statutory Provision: None.

Purposes:

1. This section is intended to make it possible for the courts to police explicitly against the contracts or clauses which they find to be unconscionable. In the past such policing has been accomplished by adverse construction of language, by manipulation of the rules of offer and acceptance or by determinations that the clause is contrary to public policy or to the dominant purpose of the contract. This section is intended to allow the court to pass directly on the unconscionability of the contract or particular clause therein and to make a conclusion of law as to its unconscionability. The basic test is whether, in the light of the general commercial background and the commercial needs of the particular trade or case, the clauses involved are so one-sided as to be unconscionable under the circumstances existing at the time of the making of the contract. Subsection (2) makes it clear that it is proper for the court to hear evidence upon these questions. The principle is one of the prevention of oppression and unfair surprise (Cf. Campbell Soup Co. v. Wentz, 172 F.2d 80, 3d Cir. 1948) and not of disturbance of allocation of risks because of superior bargaining power. The underlying basis of this section is illustrated by the results in cases such as the following:

Kansas City Wholesale Grocery Co. v. Weber Packing Corporation, 93 Utah 414, 73 P.2d 1272 (1937), where a clause limiting time for complaints was held inapplicable to latent defects in a shipment of catsup which could be discovered only by microscopic analysis; Hardy v. General Motors Acceptance Corporation, 38 Ga. App. 463, 144 S.E. 327 (1928), holding that a disclaimer of warranty clause applied only to express warranties, thus letting in a fair implied warranty; Andrews Bros. v. Singer & Co. (1934 CA) 1 K.B. 17, holding that where a car with substantial mileage was delivered instead of a "new" car, a disclaimer of warranties, including those "implied," left unaffected an "express obligation" on the description, even though the Sale of Goods Act called such an implied warranty; New Prague Flouring Mill Co. v. G. A. Spears, 194 Iowa 417, 189 N.W. 815 (1922), holding that a clause permitting the seller, upon the buyer's failure to supply shipping instructions, to cancel, ship, or allow delivery date to be indefinitely postponed 30 days at a time by the inaction, does not indefinitely postpone the date of measuring damages for the buyer's breach, to the seller's advantage; and Kansas Flour Mills Co. v. Dirks, 100 Kan. 376, 164 P. 273 (1917), where under a similar clause in a rising market the court permitted the buyer to measure his damages for non-delivery at the end of only one 30 day postponement; Green v. Arcos, Ltd. (1931 CA) 47 T.L.R. 336, where a blanket clause prohibiting rejection of shipments by the buyer was restricted to apply to shipments where discrepancies represented merely mercantile variations; Meyer v. Packard Cleveland Motor Co., 106 Ohio St. 328, 140 N.E. 118 (1922), in which the court held that a "waiver" of all agreements not specified did not preclude implied warranty of fitness of a rebuilt dump truck for ordinary use as a dump truck; Austin Co. v. J. H. Tillman Co., 104 Or. 541, 209 P. 131 (1922), where a clause limiting the buyer's remedy to return was held to be applicable only if the seller had delivered a machine needed for a construction job which reasonably met the contract description; Bekkevold v. Potts, 173 Minn. 87, 216 N.W. 790, 59 A.L.R. 1164 (1927), refusing to allow warranty of fitness for purpose imposed by law to be negated by clause excluding all warranties "made" by the seller; Robert A. Munroe & Co. v. Meyer (1930) 2 K.B. 312, holding that the warranty of description overrides a clause reading "with all faults and defects" where adulterated meat not up to the contract description was delivered.

2. Under this section the court, in its discretion, may refuse to enforce the contract as a whole if it is permeated by the unconscionability, or it may strike any single clause or group of clauses which are so tainted or which are contrary to the essential purpose of the agreement, or it may simply limit unconscionable clauses so as to avoid unconscionable results.

3. The present section is addressed to the court, and the decision is to be made by it. The commercial evidence referred to in subsection (2) is for the court's consideration, not the jury's. Only the agreement which results from the court's action on these matters is to be submitted to the general triers of the facts.

Definitional Cross Reference:

"Contract". Section 1–201.

§ 2–303.   Allocation or Division of Risks.

Where this Article allocates a risk or a burden as between the parties "unless otherwise agreed", the agreement may not only shift the allocation but may also divide the risk or burden.

Official Comment

Prior Uniform Statutory Provision: None.

Purposes:

1. This section is intended to make it clear that the parties may modify or allocate "unless otherwise agreed" risks or burdens imposed by this Article as they desire, always subject, of course, to the provisions on unconscionability.

Compare Section 1–102(4).

2. The risk or burden may be divided by the express terms of the agreement or by the attending circumstances, since under the definition of "agreement" in this Act the circumstances surrounding the transaction as well as the express language used by the parties enter into the meaning and substance of the agreement.

Cross References:

Point 1: Sections 1–102, 2–302.
Point 2: Section 1–201.

Definitional Cross References:

"Party". Section 1–201.
"Agreement". Section 1–201.

§ 2–304.   Price   Payable   in   Money, Goods, Realty, or Otherwise.

(1) The price can be made payable in money or otherwise. If it is payable in whole or in part in goods each party is a seller of the goods which he is to transfer.

(2) Even though all or part of the price is payable in an interest in realty the transfer of the goods and the seller's obligations with reference to them are subject to this Article, but not

the transfer of the interest in realty or the transferor's obligations in connection therewith.

Official Comment

Prior Uniform Statutory Provision: Subsections (2) and (3) of Section 9, Uniform Sales Act.

Changes: Rewritten.

Purposes of Changes:

1. This section corrects the phrasing of the Uniform Sales Act so as to avoid misconstruction and produce greater accuracy in commercial result. While it continues the essential intent and purpose of the Uniform Sales Act it rejects any purely verbalistic construction in disregard of the underlying reason of the provisions.

2. Under subsection (1) the provisions of this Article are applicable to transactions where the "price" of goods is payable in something other than money. This does not mean, however, that this whole Article applies automatically and in its entirety simply because an agreed transfer of title to goods is not a gift. The basic purposes and reasons of the Article must always be considered in determining the applicability of any of its provisions.

3. Subsection (2) lays down the general principle that when goods are to be exchanged for realty, the provisions of this Article apply only to those aspects of the transaction which concern the transfer of title to goods but do not affect the transfer of the realty since the detailed regulation of various particular contracts which fall outside the scope of this Article is left to the courts and other legislation. However, the complexities of these situations may be such that each must be analyzed in the light of the underlying reasons in order to determine the applicable principles. Local statutes dealing with realty are not to be lightly disregarded or altered by language of this Article. In contrast, this Article declares definite policies in regard to certain matters legitimately within its scope though concerned with real property situations, and in those instances the provisions of this Article control.

Cross References:

Point 1: Section 1–102.
Point 3: Sections 1–102, 1–103, 1–104 and 2–107.

Definitional Cross References:

"Goods". Section 2–105.
"Money". Section 1–201.
"Party". Section 1–201.
"Seller". Section 2–103.

§ 2–305. Open Price Term.

(1) The parties if they so intend can conclude a contract for sale even though the price is not settled. In such a case the price is a reasonable price at the time for delivery if

  (a) nothing is said as to price; or

  (b) the price is left to be agreed by the parties and they fail to agree; or

  (c) the price is to be fixed in terms of some agreed market or other standard as set or recorded by a third person or agency and it is not so set or recorded.

(2) A price to be fixed by the seller or by the buyer means a price for him to fix in good faith.

(3) When a price left to be fixed otherwise than by agreement of the parties fails to be fixed through fault of one party the other may at his option treat the contract as cancelled or himself fix a reasonable price.

(4) Where, however, the parties intend not to be bound unless the price be fixed or agreed and it is not fixed or agreed there is no contract. In such a case the buyer must return any goods already received or if unable so to do must pay their reasonable value at the time of delivery and the seller must return any portion of the price paid on account.

Official Comment

Prior Uniform Statutory Provision: Sections 9 and 10, Uniform Sales Act.

Changes: Completely rewritten.

Purposes of Changes:

1. This section applies when the price term is left open on the making of an agreement which is nevertheless intended by the parties to be a binding agreement. This Article rejects in these instances the formula that "an agreement to agree is unenforceable" if the case falls within subsection (1) of this section, and rejects also defeating such agreements on the ground of "indefiniteness". Instead this Article recognizes the dominant intention of the parties to have the deal continue to be binding upon both. As to future performance, since this Article recognizes remedies such as cover (Section 2–712), resale (Section 2–706) and specific performance (Section 2–716) which go beyond any mere arithmetic as between contract price and market price, there is usually a "reasonably certain

basis for granting an appropriate remedy for breach" so that the contract need not fail for indefiniteness.

2. Under some circumstances the postponement of agreement on price will mean that no deal has really been concluded, and this is made express in the preamble of subsection (1) ("The parties *if they so intend*") and in subsection (4). Whether or not this is so is, in most cases, a question to be determined by the trier of fact.

3. Subsection (2), dealing with the situation where the price is to be fixed by one party rejects the uncommercial idea that an agreement that the seller may fix the price means that he may fix any price he may wish by the express qualification that the price so fixed must be fixed in good faith. Good faith includes observance of reasonable commercial standards of fair dealing in the trade if the party is a merchant. (Section 2–103). But in the normal case a "posted price" or a future seller's or buyer's "given price," "price in effect," "market price," or the like satisfies the good faith requirement.

4. The section recognizes that there may be cases in which a particular person's judgment is not chosen merely as a barometer or index of a fair price but is an essential condition to the parties' intent to make any contract at all. For example, the case where a known and trusted expert is to "value" a particular painting for which there is no market standard differs sharply from the situation where a named expert is to determine the grade of cotton, and the difference would support a finding that in the one the parties did not intend to make a binding agreement if that expert were unavailable whereas in the other they did so intend. Other circumstances would of course affect the validity of such a finding.

5. Under subsection (3), wrongful interference by one party with any agreed machinery for price fixing in the contract may be treated by the other party as a repudiation justifying cancellation, or merely as a failure to take cooperative action thus shifting to the aggrieved party the reasonable leeway in fixing the price.

6. Throughout the entire section, the purpose is to give effect to the agreement which has been made. That effect, however, is always conditioned by the requirement of good faith action which is made an inherent part of all contracts within this Act. (Section 1–203).

Cross References:

Point 1: Sections 2–204(3), 2–706, 2–712 and 2–716.
Point 3: Section 2–103.

Point 5: Sections 2–311 and 2–610.
Point 6: Section 1–203.

Definitional Cross References:

"Agreement". Section 1–201.
"Burden of establishing". Section 1–201.
"Buyer". Section 2–103.
"Cancellation". Section 2–106.
"Contract". Section 1–201.
"Contract for sale". Section 2–106.
"Fault". Section 1–201.
"Goods". Section 2–105.
"Party". Section 1–201.
"Receipt of goods". Section 2–103.
"Seller". Section 2–103.
"Term". Section 1–201.

§ 2–306. Output, Requirements and Exclusive Dealings.

(1) A term which measures the quantity by the output of the seller or the requirements of the buyer means such actual output or requirements as may occur in good faith, except that no quantity unreasonably disproportionate to any stated estimate or in the absence of a stated estimate to any normal or otherwise comparable prior output or requirements may be tendered or demanded.

(2) A lawful agreement by either the seller or the buyer for exclusive dealing in the kind of goods concerned imposes unless otherwise agreed an obligation by the seller to use best efforts to supply the goods and by the buyer to use best efforts to promote their sale.

Official Comment

Prior Uniform Statutory Provision: None.

Purposes:

1. Subsection (1) of this section, in regard to output and requirements, applies to this specific problem the general approach of this Act which requires the reading of commercial background and intent into the language of any agreement and demands good faith in the performance of that agreement. It applies to such contracts of nonproducing establishments such as dealers or distributors as well as to manufacturing concerns.

2. Under this Article, a contract for output or requirements is not too indefinite since it is held to mean the actual good faith output or requirements of the particular party. Nor does such a contract lack mutuality of obligation since, under this section, the party

who will determine quantity is required to operate his plant or conduct his business in good faith and according to commercial standards of fair dealing in the trade so that his output or requirements will approximate a reasonably foreseeable figure. Reasonable elasticity in the requirements is expressly envisaged by this section and good faith variations from prior requirements are permitted even when the variation may be such as to result in discontinuance. A shut-down by a requirements buyer for lack of orders might be permissible when a shut-down merely to curtail losses would not. The essential test is whether the party is acting in good faith. Similarly, a sudden expansion of the plant by which requirements are to be measured would not be included within the scope of the contract as made but normal expansion undertaken in good faith would be within the scope of this section. One of the factors in an expansion situation would be whether the market price had risen greatly in a case in which the requirements contract contained a fixed price. Reasonable variation of an extreme sort is exemplified in Southwest Natural Gas Co. v. Oklahoma Portland Cement Co., 102 F.2d 630 (C.C.A.10, 1939). This Article takes no position as to whether a requirements contract is a provable claim in bankruptcy.

3. If an estimate of output or requirements is included in the agreement, no quantity unreasonably disproportionate to it may be tendered or demanded. Any minimum or maximum set by the agreement shows a clear limit on the intended elasticity. In similar fashion, the agreed estimate is to be regarded as a center around which the parties intend the variation to occur.

4. When an enterprise is sold, the question may arise whether the buyer is bound by an existing output or requirements contract. That question is outside the scope of this Article, and is to be determined on other principles of law. Assuming that the contract continues, the output or requirements in the hands of the new owner continue to be measured by the actual good faith output or requirements under the normal operation of the enterprise prior to sale. The sale itself is not grounds for sudden expansion or decrease.

5. Subsection (2), on exclusive dealing, makes explicit the commercial rule embodied in this Act under which the parties to such contracts are held to have impliedly, even when not expressly, bound themselves to use reasonable diligence as well as good faith in their performance of the contract. Under such contracts the exclusive agent is required, although no express commitment has been made, to use reasonable effort and due diligence in the expansion of the market or the promotion of the product, as the case may be.

The principal is expected under such a contract to refrain from supplying any other dealer or agent within the exclusive territory. An exclusive dealing agreement brings into play all of the good faith aspects of the output and requirement problems of subsection (1). It also raises questions of insecurity and right to adequate assurance under this Article.

Cross References:

Point 4: Section 2–210.
Point 5: Sections 1–203 and 2–609.

Definitional Cross References:

"Agreement". Section 1–201.
"Buyer". Section 2–103.
"Contract for sale". Section 2–106.
"Good faith". Section 1–201.
"Goods". Section 2–105.
"Party". Section 1–201.
"Term". Section 1–201.
"Seller". Section 2–103.

§ 2–307. Delivery in Single Lot or Several Lots.

Unless otherwise agreed all goods called for by a contract for sale must be tendered in a single delivery and payment is due only on such tender but where the circumstances give either party the right to make or demand delivery in lots the price if it can be apportioned may be demanded for each lot.

Official Comment

Prior Uniform Statutory Provision: Section 45(1), Uniform Sales Act.

Changes: Rewritten and expanded.

Purposes of Changes:

1. This section applies where the parties have not specifically agreed whether delivery and payment are to be by lots and generally continues the essential intent of original Act, Section 45(1) by assuming that the parties intended delivery to be in a single lot.

2. Where the actual agreement or the circumstances do not indicate otherwise, delivery in lots is not permitted under this section and the buyer is properly entitled to reject for a deficiency in the tender, subject to any privilege in the seller to cure the tender.

3. The "but" clause of this section goes to the case in which it is not commercially feasible to deliver or to receive the goods in a single lot as for example, where a

contract calls for the shipment of ten carloads of coal and only three cars are available at a given time. Similarly, in a contract involving brick necessary to build a building the buyer's storage space may be limited so that it would be impossible to receive the entire amount of brick at once, or it may be necessary to assemble the goods as in the case of cattle on the range, or to mine them.

In such cases, a partial delivery is not subject to rejection for the defect in quantity alone, if the circumstances do not indicate a repudiation or default by the seller as to the expected balance or do not give the buyer ground for suspending his performance because of insecurity under the provisions of Section 2–609. However, in such cases the undelivered balance of goods under the contract must be forthcoming within a reasonable time and in a reasonable manner according to the policy of Section 2–503 on manner of tender of delivery. This is reinforced by the express provisions of Section 2–608 that if a lot has been accepted on the reasonable assumption that its nonconformity will be cured, the acceptance may be revoked if the cure does not seasonably occur. The section rejects the rule of Kelly Construction Co. v. Hackensack Brick Co., 91 N.J.L. 585, 103 A. 417, 2 A.L.R. 685 (1918) and approves the result in Lynn M. Ranger, Inc. v. Gildersleeve, 106 Conn. 372, 138 A. 142 (1927) in which a contract was made for six carloads of coal then rolling from the mines and consigned to the seller but the seller agreed to divert the carloads to the buyer as soon as the car numbers became known to him. He arranged a diversion of two cars and then notified the buyer who then repudiated the contract. The seller was held to be entitled to his full remedy for the two cars diverted because simultaneous delivery of all of the cars was not contemplated by either party.

4. Where the circumstances indicate that a party has a right to delivery in lots, the price may be demanded for each lot if it is apportionable.

Cross References:

Point 1: Section 1–201.
Point 2: Sections 2–508 and 2–601.
Point 3: Sections 2–503, 2–608 and 2–609.

Definitional Cross References:

"Contract for sale". Section 2–106.
"Goods". Section 2–105.
"Lot". Section 2–105.
"Party". Section 1–201.
"Rights". Section 1–201.

§ 2–308. Absence of Specified Place for Delivery.

Unless otherwise agreed

(a) the place for delivery of goods is the seller's place of business or if he has none his residence; but

(b) in a contract for sale of identified goods which to the knowledge of the parties at the time of contracting are in some other place, that place is the place for their delivery; and

(c) documents of title may be delivered through customary banking channels.

Official Comment

Prior Uniform Statutory Provision: Paragraphs (a) and (b)—Section 43(1), Uniform Sales Act; Paragraph (c)—none.

Changes: Slight modification in language.

Purposes of Changes and New Matter:

1. Paragraphs (a) and (b) provide for those noncommercial sales and for those occasional commercial sales where no place or means of delivery has been agreed upon by the parties. Where delivery by carrier is "required or authorized by the agreement", the seller's duties as to delivery of the goods are governed not by this section but by Section 2–504.

2. Under paragraph (b) when the identified goods contracted for are known to both parties to be in some location other than the seller's place of business or residence, the parties are presumed to have intended that place to be the place of delivery. This paragraph also applies (unless, as would be normal, the circumstances show that delivery by way of documents is intended) to a bulk of goods in the possession of a bailee. In such a case, however, the seller has the additional obligation to procure the acknowledgment by the bailee of the buyer's right to possession.

3. Where "customary banking channels" call only for due notification by the banker that the documents are on hand, leaving the buyer himself to see to the physical receipt of the goods, tender at the buyer's address is not required under paragraph (c). But that paragraph merely eliminates the possibility of a default by the seller if "customary banking channels" have been properly used in giving notice to the buyer. Where the bank has purchased a draft accompanied by documents or has undertaken its collection on behalf of the seller, Part 5 of Article 4 spells out its duties and relations to its customer. Where the documents move

forward under a letter of credit the Article on Letters of Credit spells out the duties and relations between the bank, the seller and the buyer.

4. The rules of this section apply only "unless otherwise agreed." The surrounding circumstances, usage of trade, course of dealing and course of performance, as well as the express language of the parties, may constitute an "otherwise agreement".

Cross References:

Point 1: Sections 2–504 and 2–505.
Point 2: Section 2–503.
Point 3: Section 2–512, Articles 4, Part 5, and 5.

Definitional Cross References:

"Contract for sale". Section 2–106.
"Delivery". Section 1–201.
"Document of title". Section 1–201.
"Goods". Section 2–105.
"Party". Section 1–201.
"Seller". Section 2–103.

§ 2–309. Absence of Specific Time Provisions; Notice of Termination.

(1) The time for shipment or delivery or any other action under a contract if not provided in this Article or agreed upon shall be a reasonable time.

(2) Where the contract provides for successive performances but is indefinite in duration it is valid for a reasonable time but unless otherwise agreed may be terminated at any time by either party.

(3) Termination of a contract by one party except on the happening of an agreed event requires that reasonable notification be received by the other party and an agreement dispensing with notification is invalid if its operation would be unconscionable.

Official Comment

Prior Uniform Statutory Provision: Subsection (1)—see Sections 43(2), 45(2), 47(1) and 48, Uniform Sales Act, for policy continued under this Article; Subsection (2)—none; Subsection (3)—none.

Changes: Completely different in scope.

Purposes of Changes and New Matter:

1. Subsection (1) requires that all actions taken under a sales contract must be taken within a reasonable time where no time has been agreed upon. The reasonable time under this provision turns on the

criteria as to "reasonable time" and on good faith and commercial standards set forth in Sections 1–203, 1–204 and 2–103. It thus depends upon what constitutes acceptable commercial conduct in view of the nature, purpose and circumstances of the action to be taken. Agreement as to a definite time, however, may be found in a term implied from the contractual circumstances, usage of trade or course of dealing or performance as well as in an express term. Such cases fall outside of this subsection since in them the time for action is "agreed" by usage.

2. The time for payment, where not agreed upon, is related to the time for delivery; the particular problems which arise in connection with determining the appropriate time of payment and the time for any inspection before payment which is both allowed by law and demanded by the buyer are covered in Section 2–513.

3. The facts in regard to shipment and delivery differ so widely as to make detailed provision for them in the text of this Article impracticable. The applicable principles, however, make it clear that surprise is to be avoided, good faith judgment is to be protected, and notice or negotiation to reduce the uncertainty to certainty is to be favored.

4. When the time for delivery is left open, unreasonably early offers of or demands for delivery are intended to be read under this Article as expressions of desire or intention, requesting the assent or acquiescence of the other party, not as final positions which may amount without more to breach or to create breach by the other side. See Sections 2–207 and 2–609.

5. The obligation of good faith under this Act requires reasonable notification before a contract may be treated as breached because a reasonable time for delivery or demand has expired. This operates both in the case of a contract originally indefinite as to time and of one subsequently made indefinite by waiver.

When both parties let an originally reasonable time go by in silence, the course of conduct under the contract may be viewed as enlarging the reasonable time for tender or demand of performance. The contract may be terminated by abandonment.

6. Parties to a contract are not required in giving reasonable notification to fix, at peril of breach, a time which is in fact reasonable in the unforeseeable judgment of a later trier of fact. Effective communication of a proposed time limit calls for a response, so that failure to reply will make out acquiescence. Where objection is made, however, or if the demand is merely

for information as to when goods will be delivered or will be ordered out, demand for assurances on the ground of insecurity may be made under this Article pending further negotiations. Only when a party insists on undue delay or on rejection of the other party's reasonable proposal is there a question of flat breach under the present section.

7. Subsection (2) applies a commercially reasonable view to resolve the conflict which has arisen in the cases as to contracts of indefinite duration. The "reasonable time" of duration appropriate to a given arrangement is limited by the circumstances. When the arrangement has been carried on by the parties over the years, the "reasonable time" can continue indefinitely and the contract will not terminate until notice.

8. Subsection (3) recognizes that the application of principles of good faith and sound commercial practice normally call for such notification of the termination of a going contract relationship as will give the other party reasonable time to seek a substitute arrangement. An agreement dispensing with notification or limiting the time for the seeking of a substitute arrangement is, of course, valid under this subsection unless the results of putting it into operation would be the creation of an unconscionable state of affairs.

9. Justifiable cancellation for breach is a remedy for breach and is not the kind of termination covered by the present subsection.

10. The requirement of notification is dispensed with where the contract provides for termination on the happening of an "agreed event." "Event" is a term chosen here to contrast with "option" or the like.

Cross References:

Point 1: Sections 1–203, 1–204 and 2–103.
Point 2: Sections 2–320, 2–321, 2–504, and 2–511 through 2–514.
Point 5: Section 1–203.
Point 6: Section 2–609.
Point 7: Section 2–204.
Point 9: Sections 2–106, 2–318, 2–610 and 2–703.

Definitional Cross References:

"Agreement". Section 1–201.
"Contract". Section 1–201.
"Notification". Section 1–201.
"Party". Section 1–201.
"Reasonable time". Section 1–204.
"Termination". Section 2–106.

§ 2–310. Open Time for Payment or Running of Credit; Authority to Ship Under Reservation.

Unless otherwise agreed

(a) payment is due at the time and place at which the buyer is to receive the goods even though the place of shipment is the place of delivery; and

(b) if the seller is authorized to send the goods he may ship them under reservation, and may tender the documents of title, but the buyer may inspect the goods after their arrival before payment is due unless such inspection is inconsistent with the terms of the contract (Section 2–513); and

(c) if delivery is authorized and made by way of documents of title otherwise than by subsection (b) then payment is due at the time and place at which the buyer is to receive the documents regardless of where the goods are to be received; and

(d) where the seller is required or authorized to ship the goods on credit the credit period runs from the time of shipment but postdating the invoice or delaying its dispatch will correspondingly delay the starting of the credit period.

Official Comment

Prior Uniform Statutory Provision: Sections 42 and 47(2), Uniform Sales Act.

Changes: Completely rewritten in this and other sections.

Purposes of Changes: This section is drawn to reflect modern business methods of dealing at a distance rather than face to face. Thus:

1. Paragraph (a) provides that payment is due at the time and place "the buyer is to receive the goods" rather than at the point of delivery except in documentary shipment cases (paragraph (c)). This grants an opportunity for the exercise by the buyer of his preliminary right to inspection before paying even though under the delivery term the risk of loss may have previously passed to him or the running of the credit period has already started.

2. Paragraph (b) while providing for inspection by the buyer before he pays, protects the seller. He is not required to give up possession of the goods until he has received payment, where no credit has been contemplated by the parties. The seller may collect through a bank by a sight draft against an order bill of lading "hold until arrival; inspection allowed." The obli-

gations of the bank under such a provision are set forth in Part 5 of Article 4. In the absence of a credit term, the seller is permitted to ship under reservation and if he does payment is then due where and when the buyer is to receive the documents.

3. Unless otherwise agreed, the place for the receipt of the documents and payment is the buyer's city but the time for payment is only after arrival of the goods, since under paragraph (b), and Sections 2–512 and 2–513 the buyer is under no duty to pay prior to inspection.

4. Where the mode of shipment is such that goods must be unloaded immediately upon arrival, too rapidly to permit adequate inspection before receipt, the seller must be guided by the provisions of this Article on inspection which provide that if the seller wishes to demand payment before inspection, he must put an appropriate term into the contract. Even requiring payment against documents will not of itself have this desired result if the documents are to be held until the arrival of the goods. But under (b) and (c) if the terms are C.I.F., C.O.D., or cash against documents payment may be due before inspection.

5. Paragraph (d) states the common commercial understanding that an agreed credit period runs from the time of shipment or from that dating of the invoice which is commonly recognized as a representation of the time of shipment. The provision concerning any delay in sending forth the invoice is included because such conduct results in depriving the buyer of his full notice and warning as to when he must be prepared to pay.

Cross References:

Generally: Part 5.
Point 1: Section 2–509.
Point 2: Sections 2–505, 2–511, 2–512, 2–513 and Article 4.
Point 3: Sections 2–308(b), 2–512 and 2–513.
Point 4: Section 2–513(3)(b).

Definitional Cross References:

"Buyer". Section 2–103.
"Delivery". Section 1–201.
"Document of title". Section 1–201.
"Goods". Section 2–105.
"Receipt of goods". Section 2–103.
"Seller". Section 2–103.
"Send". Section 1–201.
"Term". Section 1–201.

§ 2–311. Options and Cooperation Respecting Performance.

(1) An agreement for sale which is otherwise sufficiently definite (subsection (3) of Section 2–204) to be a contract is not made invalid by the fact that it leaves particulars of performance to be specified by one of the parties. Any such specification must be made in good faith and within limits set by commercial reasonableness.

(2) Unless otherwise agreed specifications relating to assortment of the goods are at the buyer's option and except as otherwise provided in subsections (1)(c) and (3) of Section 2–319 specifications or arrangements relating to shipment are at the seller's option.

(3) Where such specification would materially affect the other party's performance but is not seasonably made or where one party's cooperation is necessary to the agreed performance of the other but is not seasonably forthcoming, the other party in addition to all other remedies

(a) is excused for any resulting delay in his own performance; and

(b) may also either proceed to perform in any reasonable manner or after the time for a material part of his own performance treat the failure to specify or to cooperate as a breach by failure to deliver or accept the goods.

Official Comment

Prior Uniform Statutory Provision: None.

Purposes:

1. Subsection (1) permits the parties to leave certain detailed particulars of performance to be filled in by either of them without running the risk of having the contract invalidated for indefiniteness. The party to whom the agreement gives power to specify the missing details is required to exercise good faith and to act in accordance with commercial standards so that there is no surprise and the range of permissible variation is limited by what is commercially reasonable. The "agreement" which permits one party so to specify may be found as well in a course of dealing, usage of trade, or implication from circumstances as in explicit language used by the parties.

2. Options as to assortment of goods or shipping arrangements are specifically reserved to the buyer and seller respectively under subsection (2) where no other arrangement has been made. This section rejects the test which mechanically and without regard to

usage or the purpose of the option gave the option to the party "first under a duty to move" and applies instead a standard commercial interpretation to these circumstances. The "unless otherwise agreed" provision of this subsection covers not only express terms but the background and circumstances which enter into the agreement.

3. Subsection (3) applies when the exercise of an option or cooperation by one party is necessary to or materially affects the other party's performance, but it is not seasonably forthcoming; the subsection relieves the other party from the necessity for performance or excuses his delay in performance as the case may be. The contract-keeping party may at his option under this subsection proceed to perform in any commercially reasonable manner rather than wait. In addition to the special remedies provided, this subsection also reserves "all other remedies". The remedy of particular importance in this connection is that provided for insecurity. Request may also be made pursuant to the obligation of good faith for a reasonable indication of the time and manner of performance for which a party is to hold himself ready.

4. The remedy provided in subsection (3) is one which does not operate in the situation which falls within the scope of Section 2–614 on substituted performance. Where the failure to cooperate results from circumstances set forth in that Section, the other party is under a duty to proffer or demand (as the case may be) substitute performance as a condition to claiming rights against the noncooperating party.

Cross References:

Point 1: Sections 1–201, 2–204 and 1–203.
Point 3: Sections 1–203 and 2–609.
Point 4: Section 2–614.

Definitional Cross References:

"Agreement". Section 1–201.
"Buyer". Section 2–103.
"Contract for sale". Section 2–106.
"Goods". Section 2–105.
"Party". Section 1–201.
"Remedy". Section 1–201.
"Seasonably". Section 1–204.
"Seller". Section 2–103.

§ 2–312. Warranty of Title and Against Infringement; Buyer's Obligation Against Infringement.

(1) Subject to subsection (2) there is in a contract for sale a warranty by the seller that

(a) the title conveyed shall be good, and its transfer rightful; and

(b) the goods shall be delivered free from any security interest or other lien or encumbrance of which the buyer at the time of contracting has no knowledge.

(2) A warranty under subsection (1) will be excluded or modified only by specific language or by circumstances which give the buyer reason to know that the person selling does not claim title in himself or that he is purporting to sell only such right or title as he or a third person may have.

(3) Unless otherwise agreed a seller who is a merchant regularly dealing in goods of the kind warrants that the goods shall be delivered free of the rightful claim of any third person by way of infringement or the like but a buyer who furnishes specifications to the seller must hold the seller harmless against any such claim which arises out of compliance with the specifications.

Official Comment

Prior Uniform Statutory Provision: Section 13, Uniform Sales Act.

Changes: Completely rewritten, the provisions concerning infringement being new.

Purposes of Changes:

1. Subsection (1) makes provision for a buyer's basic needs in respect to a title which he in good faith expects to acquire by his purchase, namely, that he receive a good, clean title transferred to him also in a rightful manner so that he will not be exposed to a lawsuit in order to protect it.

The warranty extends to a buyer whether or not the seller was in possession of the goods at the time the sale or contract to sell was made.

The warranty of quiet possession is abolished. Disturbance of quiet possession, although not mentioned specifically, is one way, among many, in which the breach of the warranty of title may be established.

The "knowledge" referred to in subsection 1(b) is actual knowledge as distinct from notice.

2. The provisions of this Article requiring notification to the seller within a reasonable time after the buyer's discovery of a breach apply to notice of a breach of the warranty of title, where the seller's breach was innocent. However, if the seller's breach was in bad faith he cannot be permitted to claim that

he has been misled or prejudiced by the delay in giving notice. In such case the "reasonable" time for notice should receive a very liberal interpretation. Whether the breach by the seller is in good or bad faith Section 2–725 provides that the cause of action accrues when the breach occurs. Under the provisions of that section the breach of the warranty of good title occurs when tender of delivery is made since the warranty is not one which extends to "future performance of the goods."

3. When the goods are part of the seller's normal stock and are sold in his normal course of business, it is his duty to see that no claim of infringement of a patent or trademark by a third party will mar the buyer's title. A sale by a person other than a dealer, however, raises no implication in its circumstances of such a warranty. Nor is there such an implication when the buyer orders goods to be assembled, prepared or manufactured on his own specifications. If, in such a case, the resulting product infringes a patent or trademark, the liability will run from buyer to seller. There is, under such circumstances, a tacit representation on the part of the buyer that the seller will be safe in manufacturing according to the specifications, and the buyer is under an obligation in good faith to indemnify him for any loss suffered.

4. This section rejects the cases which recognize the principle that infringements violate the warranty of title but deny the buyer a remedy unless he has been expressly prevented from using the goods. Under this Article "eviction" is not a necessary condition to the buyer's remedy since the buyer's remedy arises immediately upon receipt of notice of infringement; it is merely one way of establishing the fact of breach.

5. Subsection (2) recognizes that sales by sheriffs, executors, certain foreclosing lienors and persons similarly situated may be so out of the ordinary commercial course that their peculiar character is immediately apparent to the buyer and therefore no personal obligation is imposed upon the seller who is purporting to sell only an unknown or limited right. This subsection does not touch upon and leaves open all questions of restitution arising in such cases, when a unique article so sold is reclaimed by a third party as the rightful owner.

Foreclosure sales under Article 9 are another matter. Section 9–610 provides that a disposition of collateral under that section includes warranties such as those imposed by this section on a voluntary disposition of property of the kind involved. Consequently, unless properly excluded under subsection (2) or under the special provisions for exclusion in Section 9–610, a disposition under Section 9–610 of collateral consisting of goods includes the warranties imposed by subsection (1) and, if applicable, subsection (3).

6. The warranty of subsection (1) is not designated as an "implied" warranty, and hence is not subject to Section 2–316(3). Disclaimer of the warranty of title is governed instead by subsection (2), which requires either specific language or the described circumstances.

Cross References:

Point 1: Section 2–403.
Point 2: Sections 2–607 and 2–725.
Point 3: Section 1–203.
Point 4: Sections 2–609 and 2–725.
Point 6: Section 2–316.

Definitional Cross References:

"Buyer". Section 2–103.
"Contract for sale". Section 2–106.
"Goods". Section 2–105.
"Person". Section 1–201.
"Right". Section 1–201.
"Seller". Section 2–103.

As amended in 1999.

§ 2–313. Express Warranties by Affirmation, Promise, Description, Sample.

(1) Express warranties by the seller are created as follows:

(a) Any affirmation of fact or promise made by the seller to the buyer which relates to the goods and becomes part of the basis of the bargain creates an express warranty that the goods shall conform to the affirmation or promise.

(b) Any description of the goods which is made part of the basis of the bargain creates an express warranty that the goods shall conform to the description.

(c) Any sample or model which is made part of the basis of the bargain creates an express warranty that the whole of the goods shall conform to the sample or model.

(2) It is not necessary to the creation of an express warranty that the seller use formal words such as "warrant" or "guarantee" or that he have a specific intention to make a warranty, but an affirmation merely of the value of the goods or a statement purporting to be merely the seller's opinion or commendation of the goods does not create a warranty.

Official Comment

Prior Uniform Statutory Provision: Sections 12, 14 and 16, Uniform Sales Act.

Changes: Rewritten.

Purposes of Changes: To consolidate and systematize basic principles with the result that:

1. "Express" warranties rest on "dickered" aspects of the individual bargain, and go so clearly to the essence of that bargain that words of disclaimer in a form are repugnant to the basic dickered terms. "Implied" warranties rest so clearly on a common factual situation or set of conditions that no particular language or action is necessary to evidence them and they will arise in such a situation unless unmistakably negated.

This section reverts to the older case law insofar as the warranties of description and sample are designated "express" rather than "implied".

2. Although this section is limited in its scope and direct purpose to warranties made by the seller to the buyer as part of a contract for sale, the warranty sections of this Article are not designed in any way to disturb those lines of case law growth which have recognized that warranties need not be confined either to sales contracts or to the direct parties to such a contract. They may arise in other appropriate circumstances such as in the case of bailments for hire, whether such bailment is itself the main contract or is merely a supplying of containers under a contract for the sale of their contents. The provisions of Section 2–318 on third party beneficiaries expressly recognize this case law development within one particular area. Beyond that, the matter is left to the case law with the intention that the policies of this Act may offer useful guidance in dealing with further cases as they arise.

3. The present section deals with affirmations of fact by the seller, descriptions of the goods or exhibitions of samples, exactly as any other part of a negotiation which ends in a contract is dealt with. No specific intention to make a warranty is necessary if any of these factors is made part of the basis of the bargain. In actual practice affirmations of fact made by the seller about the goods during a bargain are regarded as part of the description of those goods; hence no particular reliance on such statements need be shown in order to weave them into the fabric of the agreement. Rather, any fact which is to take such affirmations, once made, out of the agreement requires clear affirmative proof. The issue normally is one of fact.

4. In view of the principle that the whole purpose of the law of warranty is to determine what it is that the seller has in essence agreed to sell, the policy is adopted of those cases which refuse except in unusual circumstances to recognize a material deletion of the seller's obligation. Thus, a contract is normally a contract for a sale of something describable and described. A clause generally disclaiming "all warranties, express or implied" cannot reduce the seller's obligation with respect to such description and therefore cannot be given literal effect under Section 2–316.

This is not intended to mean that the parties, if they consciously desire, cannot make their own bargain as they wish. But in determining what they have agreed upon good faith is a factor and consideration should be given to the fact that the probability is small that a real price is intended to be exchanged for a pseudo-obligation.

5. Paragraph (1)(b) makes specific some of the principles set forth above when a description of the goods is given by the seller.

A description need not be by words. Technical specifications, blueprints and the like can afford more exact description than mere language and if made part of the basis of the bargain goods must conform with them. Past deliveries may set the description of quality, either expressly or impliedly by course of dealing. Of course, all descriptions by merchants must be read against the applicable trade usages with the general rules as to merchantability resolving any doubts.

6. The basic situation as to statements affecting the true essence of the bargain is no different when a sample or model is involved in the transaction. This section includes both a "sample" actually drawn from the bulk of goods which is the subject matter of the sale, and a "model" which is offered for inspection when the subject matter is not at hand and which has not been drawn from the bulk of the goods.

Although the underlying principles are unchanged, the facts are often ambiguous when something is shown as illustrative, rather than as a straight sample. In general, the presumption is that any sample or model just as any affirmation of fact is intended to become a basis of the bargain. But there is no escape from the question of fact. When the seller exhibits a sample purporting to be drawn from an existing bulk, good faith of course requires that the sample be fairly drawn. But in mercantile experience the mere exhibition of a "sample" does not of itself show whether it is merely intended to "suggest" or to "be" the character of the subject-matter of the contract. The question is whether the seller has so acted with reference to the sample as to make him responsible that the whole shall have at least the values shown by it. The circumstances aid in answering this question. If the sample has been drawn from an existing bulk, it must be regarded as describing values of the goods contracted for unless it is accompanied by an unmistakable denial of such responsibility. If, on the other hand, a model of merchandise not on hand is offered, the mercantile presumption that it has become a literal description of the subject matter is not so strong, and particularly so if modification on the buyer's initiative impairs any feature of the model.

7. The precise time when words of description or affirmation are made or samples are shown is not material. The sole question is whether the language or samples or models are fairly to be regarded as part of the contract. If language is used after the closing of the deal (as when the buyer when taking delivery asks and receives an additional assurance), the warranty becomes a modification, and need not be supported by consideration if it is otherwise reasonable and in order (Section 2–209).

8. Concerning affirmations of value or a seller's opinion or commendation under subsection (2), the basic question remains the same: What statements of the seller have in the circumstances and in objective judgment become part of the basis of the bargain? As indicated above, all of the statements of the seller do so unless good reason is shown to the contrary. The provisions of subsection (2) are included, however, since common experience discloses that some statements or predictions cannot fairly be viewed as entering into the bargain. Even as to false statements of value, however, the possibility is left open that a remedy may be provided by the law relating to fraud or misrepresentation.

Cross References:

Point 1: Section 2–316.
Point 2: Sections 1–102(3) and 2–318.
Point 3: Section 2–316(2)(b).
Point 4: Section 2–316.
Point 5: Sections 1–205(4) and 2–314.
Point 6: Section 2–316.
Point 7: Section 2–209.
Point 8: Section 1–103.

Definitional Cross References:

"Buyer". Section 2–103.
"Conforming". Section 2–106.
"Goods". Section 2–105.
"Seller". Section 2–103.

§ 2–314. Implied Warranty: Merchantability; Usage of Trade.

(1) Unless excluded or modified (Section 2–316), a warranty that the goods shall be mer-

chantable is implied in a contract for their sale if the seller is a merchant with respect to goods of that kind. Under this section the serving for value of food or drink to be consumed either on the premises or elsewhere is a sale.

(2) Goods to be merchantable must be at least such as

(a) pass without objection in the trade under the contract description; and

(b) in the case of fungible goods, are of fair average quality within the description; and

(c) are fit for the ordinary purposes for which such goods are used; and

(d) run, within the variations permitted by the agreement, of even kind, quality and quantity within each unit and among all units involved; and

(e) are adequately contained, packaged, and labeled as the agreement may require; and

(f) conform to the promise or affirmations of fact made on the container or label if any.

(3) Unless excluded or modified (Section 2–316) other implied warranties may arise from course of dealing or usage of trade.

Official Comment

Prior Uniform Statutory Provision: Section 15(2), Uniform Sales Act.

Changes: Completely rewritten.

Purposes of Changes: This section, drawn in view of the steadily developing case law on the subject, is intended to make it clear that:

1. The seller's obligation applies to present sales as well as to contracts to sell subject to the effects of any examination of specific goods. (Subsection (2) of Section 2–316). Also, the warranty of merchantability applies to sales for use as well as to sales for resale.

2. The question when the warranty is imposed turns basically on the meaning of the terms of the agreement as recognized in the trade. Goods delivered under an agreement made by a merchant in a given line of trade must be of a quality comparable to that generally acceptable in that line of trade under the description or other designation of the goods used in the agreement. The responsibility imposed rests on any merchant-seller, and the absence of the words

"grower or manufacturer or not" which appeared in Section 15(2) of the Uniform Sales Act does not restrict the applicability of this section.

3. A specific designation of goods by the buyer does not exclude the seller's obligation that they be fit for the general purposes appropriate to such goods. A contract for the sale of second-hand goods, however, involves only such obligation as is appropriate to such goods for that is their contract description. A person making an isolated sale of goods is not a "merchant" within the meaning of the full scope of this section and, thus, no warranty of merchantability would apply. His knowledge of any defects not apparent on inspection would, however, without need for express agreement and in keeping with the underlying reason of the present section and the provisions on good faith, impose an obligation that known material but hidden defects be fully disclosed.

4. Although a seller may not be a "merchant" as to the goods in question, if he states generally that they are "guaranteed" the provisions of this section may furnish a guide to the content of the resulting express warranty. This has particular significance in the case of second-hand sales, and has further significance in limiting the effect of fine-print disclaimer clauses where their effect would be inconsistent with large-print assertions of "guarantee".

5. The second sentence of subsection (1) covers the warranty with respect to food and drink. Serving food or drink for value is a sale, whether to be consumed on the premises or elsewhere. Cases to the contrary are rejected. The principal warranty is that stated in subsections (1) and (2)(c) of this section.

6. Subsection (2) does not purport to exhaust the meaning of "merchantable" nor to negate any of its attributes not specifically mentioned in the text of the statute, but arising by usage of trade or through case law. The language used is "must be at least such as . . .," and the intention is to leave open other possible attributes of merchantability.

7. Paragraphs (a) and (b) of subsection (2) are to be read together. Both refer, as indicated above, to the standards of that line of the trade which fits the transaction and the seller's business. "Fair average" is a term directly appropriate to agricultural bulk products and means goods centering around the middle belt of quality, not the least or the worst that can be understood in the particular trade by the designation, but such as can pass "without objection." Of course a fair percentage of the least is permissible but the goods are not "fair average" if they are all of the least or worst quality possible under the description. In cases of doubt as to what quality is intended, the price at which a merchant closes a contract is an excellent index of the nature and scope of his obligation under the present section.

8. Fitness for the ordinary purposes for which goods of the type are used is a fundamental concept of the present section and is covered in paragraph (c). As stated above, merchantability is also a part of the obligation owing to the purchaser for use. Correspondingly, protection, under this aspect of the warranty, of the person buying for resale to the ultimate consumer is equally necessary, and merchantable goods must therefore be "honestly" resalable in the normal course of business because they are what they purport to be.

9. Paragraph (d) on evenness of kind, quality and quantity follows case law. But precautionary language has been added as a remainder of the frequent usages of trade which permit substantial variations both with and without an allowance or an obligation to replace the varying units.

10. Paragraph (e) applies only where the nature of the goods and of the transaction require a certain type of container, package or label. Paragraph (f) applies, on the other hand, wherever there is a label or container on which representations are made, even though the original contract, either by express terms or usage of trade, may not have required either the labelling or the representation. This follows from the general obligation of good faith which requires that a buyer should not be placed in the position of reselling or using goods delivered under false representations appearing on the package or container. No problem of extra consideration arises in this connection since, under this Article, an obligation is imposed by the original contract not to deliver mislabeled articles, and the obligation is imposed where mercantile good faith so requires and without reference to the doctrine of consideration.

11. Exclusion or modification of the warranty of merchantability, or of any part of it, is dealt with in the section to which the text of the present section makes explicit precautionary references. That section must be read with particular reference to its subsection (4) on limitation of remedies. The warranty of merchantability, wherever it is normal, is so commonly taken for granted that its exclusion from the contract is a matter threatening surprise and therefore requiring special precaution.

12. Subsection (3) is to make explicit that usage of trade and course of dealing can create warranties and that they are implied rather than express warranties and thus subject to exclusion or modification under

Section 2–316. A typical instance would be the obligation to provide pedigree papers to evidence conformity of the animal to the contract in the case of a pedigreed dog or blooded bull.

13. In an action based on breach of warranty, it is of course necessary to show not only the existence of the warranty but the fact that the warranty was broken and that the breach of the warranty was the proximate cause of the loss sustained. In such an action an affirmative showing by the seller that the loss resulted from some action or event following his own delivery of the goods can operate as a defense. Equally, evidence indicating that the seller exercised care in the manufacture, processing or selection of the goods is relevant to the issue of whether the warranty was in fact broken. Action by the buyer following an examination of the goods which ought to have indicated the defect complained of can be shown as matter bearing on whether the breach itself was the cause of the injury.

Cross References:

Point 1: Section 2–316.
Point 3: Sections 1–203 and 2–104.
Point 5: Section 2–315.
Point 11: Section 2–316.
Point 12: Sections 1–201, 1–205 and 2–316.

Definitional Cross References:

"Agreement". Section 1–201.
"Contract". Section 1–201.
"Contract for sale". Section 2–106.
"Goods". Section 2–105.
"Merchant". Section 2–104.
"Seller". Section 2–103.

§ 2–315. Implied Warranty: Fitness for Particular Purpose.

Where the seller at the time of contracting has reason to know any particular purpose for which the goods are required and that the buyer is relying on the seller's skill or judgment to select or furnish suitable goods, there is unless excluded or modified under the next section an implied warranty that the goods shall be fit for such purpose.

Official Comment

Prior Uniform Statutory Provision: Section 15(1), (4), (5), Uniform Sales Act.

Changes: Rewritten.

Purposes of Changes:

1. Whether or not this warranty arises in any individual case is basically a question of fact to be determined by the circumstances of the contracting. Under this section the buyer need not bring home to the seller actual knowledge of the particular purpose for which the goods are intended or of his reliance on the seller's skill and judgment, if the circumstances are such that the seller has reason to realize the purpose intended or that the reliance exists. The buyer, of course, must actually be relying on the seller.

2. A "particular purpose" differs from the ordinary purpose for which the goods are used in that it envisages a specific use by the buyer which is peculiar to the nature of his business whereas the ordinary purposes for which goods are used are those envisaged in the concept of merchantability and go to uses which are customarily made of the goods in question. For example, shoes are generally used for the purpose of walking upon ordinary ground, but a seller may know that a particular pair was selected to be used for climbing mountains.

A contract may of course include both a warranty of merchantability and one of fitness for a particular purpose.

The provisions of this Article on the cumulation and conflict of express and implied warranties must be considered on the question of inconsistency between or among warranties. In such a case any question of fact as to which warranty was intended by the parties to apply must be resolved in favor of the warranty of fitness for particular purpose as against all other warranties except where the buyer has taken upon himself the responsibility of furnishing the technical specifications.

3. In connection with the warranty of fitness for a particular purpose the provisions of this Article on the allocation or division of risks are particularly applicable in any transaction in which the purpose for which the goods are to be used combines requirements both as to the quality of the goods themselves and compliance with certain laws or regulations. How the risks are divided is a question of fact to be determined, where not expressly contained in the agreement, from the circumstances of contracting, usage of trade, course of performance and the like, matters which may constitute the "otherwise agreement" of the parties by which they may divide the risk or burden.

4. The absence from this section of the language used in the Uniform Sales Act in referring to the seller, "whether he be the grower or manufacturer or not," is not intended to impose any requirement that the seller

be a grower or manufacturer. Although normally the warranty will arise only where the seller is a merchant with the appropriate "skill or judgment," it can arise as to non-merchants where this is justified by the particular circumstances.

5. The elimination of the "patent or other trade name" exception constitutes the major extension of the warranty of fitness which has been made by the cases and continued in this Article. Under the present section the existence of a patent or other trade name and the designation of the article by that name, or indeed in any other definite manner, is only one of the facts to be considered on the question of whether the buyer actually relied on the seller, but it is not of itself decisive of the issue. If the buyer himself is insisting on a particular brand he is not relying on the seller's skill and judgment and so no warranty results. But the mere fact that the article purchased has a particular patent or trade name is not sufficient to indicate nonreliance if the article has been recommended by the seller as adequate for the buyer's purposes.

6. The specific reference forward in the present section to the following section on exclusion or modification of warranties is to call attention to the possibility of eliminating the warranty in any given case. However it must be noted that under the following section the warranty of fitness for a particular purpose must be excluded or modified by a conspicuous writing.

Cross References:

Point 2: Sections 2–314 and 2–317.
Point 3: Section 2–303.
Point 6: Section 2–316.

Definitional Cross References:

"Buyer". Section 2–103.
"Goods". Section 2–105.
"Seller". Section 2–103.

§ 2–316. Exclusion or Modification of Warranties.

(1) Words or conduct relevant to the creation of an express warranty and words or conduct tending to negate or limit warranty shall be construed wherever reasonable as consistent with each other; but subject to the provisions of this Article on parol or extrinsic evidence (Section 2–202) negation or limitation is inoperative to the extent that such construction is unreasonable.

(2) Subject to subsection (3), to exclude or modify the implied warranty of merchantability

or any part of it the language must mention merchantability and in case of a writing must be conspicuous, and to exclude or modify any implied warranty of fitness the exclusion must be by a writing and conspicuous. Language to exclude all implied warranties of fitness is sufficient if it states, for example, that "There are no warranties which extend beyond the description on the face hereof."

(3) Notwithstanding subsection (2)

(a) unless the circumstances indicate otherwise, all implied warranties are excluded by expressions like "as is", "with all faults" or other language which in common understanding calls the buyer's attention to the exclusion of warranties and makes plain that there is no implied warranty; and

(b) when the buyer before entering into the contract has examined the goods or the sample or model as fully as he desired or has refused to examine the goods there is no implied warranty with regard to defects which an examination ought in the circumstances to have revealed to him; and

(c) an implied warranty can also be excluded or modified by course of dealing or course of performance or usage of trade.

(4) Remedies for breach of warranty can be limited in accordance with the provisions of this Article on liquidation or limitation of damages and on contractual modification of remedy (Sections 2–718 and 2–719).

Official Comment

Prior Uniform Statutory Provision: None. See sections 15 and 71, Uniform Sales Act.

Purposes:

1. This section is designed principally to deal with those frequent clauses in sales contracts which seek to exclude "all warranties, express or implied." It seeks to protect a buyer from unexpected and unbargained language of disclaimer by denying effect to such language when inconsistent with language of express warranty and permitting the exclusion of implied warranties only by conspicuous language or other circumstances which protect the buyer from surprise.

2. The seller is protected under this Article against false allegations of oral warranties by its provisions on parol and extrinsic evidence and against unauthorized representations by the customary "lack of authority"

clauses. This Article treats the limitation or avoidance of consequential damages as a matter of limiting remedies for breach, separate from the matter of creation of liability under a warranty. If no warranty exists, there is of course no problem of limiting remedies for breach of warranty. Under subsection (4) the question of limitation of remedy is governed by the sections referred to rather than by this section.

3. Disclaimer of the implied warranty of merchantability is permitted under subsection (2), but with the safeguard that such disclaimers must mention merchantability and in case of a writing must be conspicuous.

4. Unlike the implied warranty of merchantability, implied warranties of fitness for a particular purpose may be excluded by general language, but only if it is in writing and conspicuous.

5. Subsection (2) presupposes that the implied warranty in question exists unless excluded or modified. Whether or not language of disclaimer satisfies the requirements of this section, such language may be relevant under other sections to the question whether the warranty was ever in fact created. Thus, unless the provisions of this Article on parol and extrinsic evidence prevent, oral language of disclaimer may raise issues of fact as to whether reliance by the buyer occurred and whether the seller had "reason to know" under the section on implied warranty of fitness for a particular purpose.

6. The exceptions to the general rule set forth in paragraphs (a), (b) and (c) of subsection (3) are common factual situations in which the circumstances surrounding the transaction are in themselves sufficient to call the buyer's attention to the fact that no implied warranties are made or that a certain implied warranty is being excluded.

7. Paragraph (a) of subsection (3) deals with general terms such as "as is," "as they stand," "with all faults," and the like. Such terms in ordinary commercial usage are understood to mean that the buyer takes the entire risk as to the quality of the goods involved. The terms covered by paragraph (a) are in fact merely a particularization of paragraph (c) which provides for exclusion or modification of implied warranties by usage of trade.

8. Under paragraph (b) of subsection (3) warranties may be excluded or modified by the circumstances where the buyer examines the goods or a sample or model of them before entering into the contract. "Examination" as used in this paragraph is not synonymous with inspection before acceptance or at any other time after the contract has been made. It goes rather

to the nature of the responsibility assumed by the seller at the time of the making of the contract. Of course if the buyer discovers the defect and uses the goods anyway, or if he unreasonably fails to examine the goods before he uses them, resulting injuries may be found to result from his own action rather than proximately from a breach of warranty. See Sections 2–314 and 2–715 and comments thereto.

In order to bring the transaction within the scope of "refused to examine" in paragraph (b), it is not sufficient that the goods are available for inspection. There must in addition be a demand by the seller that the buyer examine the goods fully. The seller by the demand puts the buyer on notice that he is assuming the risk of defects which the examination ought to reveal. The language "refused to examine" in this paragraph is intended to make clear the necessity for such demand.

Application of the doctrine of "caveat emptor" in all cases where the buyer examines the goods regardless of statements made by the seller is, however, rejected by this Article. Thus, if the offer of examination is accompanied by words as to their merchantability or specific attributes and the buyer indicates clearly that he is relying on those words rather than on his examination, they give rise to an "express" warranty. In such cases the question is one of fact as to whether a warranty of merchantability has been expressly incorporated in the agreement. Disclaimer of such an express warranty is governed by subsection (1) of the present section.

The particular buyer's skill and the normal method of examining goods in the circumstances determine what defects are excluded by the examination. A failure to notice defects which are obvious cannot excuse the buyer. However, an examination under circumstances which do not permit chemical or other testing of the goods would not exclude defects which could be ascertained only by such testing. Nor can latent defects be excluded by a simple examination. A professional buyer examining a product in his field will be held to have assumed the risk as to all defects which a professional in the field ought to observe, while a nonprofessional buyer will be held to have assumed the risk only for such defects as a layman might be expected to observe.

9. The situation in which the buyer gives precise and complete specifications to the seller is not explicitly covered in this section, but this is a frequent circumstance by which the implied warranties may be excluded. The warranty of fitness for a particular purpose would not normally arise since in such a situation

there is usually no reliance on the seller by the buyer. The warranty of merchantability in such a transaction, however, must be considered in connection with the next section on the cumulation and conflict of warranties. Under paragraph (c) of that section in case of such an inconsistency the implied warranty of merchantability is displaced by the express warranty that the goods will comply with the specifications. Thus, where the buyer gives detailed specifications as to the goods, neither of the implied warranties as to quality will normally apply to the transaction unless consistent with the specifications.

Cross References:

Point 2: Sections 2-202, 2-718 and 2-719.
Point 7: Sections 1-205 and 2-208.

Definitional Cross References:

"Agreement". Section 1-201.
"Buyer". Section 2-103.
"Contract". Section 1-201.
"Course of dealing". Section 1-205.
"Goods". Section 2-105.
"Remedy". Section 1-201.
"Seller". Section 2-103.
"Usage of trade". Section 1-205.

§ 2-317. Cumulation and Conflict of Warranties Express or Implied.

Warranties whether express or implied shall be construed as consistent with each other and as cumulative, but if such construction is unreasonable the intention of the parties shall determine which warranty is dominant. In ascertaining that intention the following rules apply:

(a) Exact or technical specifications displace an inconsistent sample or model or general language of description.

(b) A sample from an existing bulk displaces inconsistent general language of description.

(c) Express warranties displace inconsistent implied warranties other than an implied warranty of fitness for a particular purpose.

Official Comment

Prior Uniform Statutory Provision: On cumulation of warranties see Sections 14, 15, and 16, Uniform Sales Act.

Changes: Completely rewritten into one section.

Purposes of Changes:

1. The present section rests on the basic policy of this Article that no warranty is created except by some conduct (either affirmative action or failure to disclose) on the part of the seller. Therefore, all warranties are made cumulative unless this construction of the contract is impossible or unreasonable.

This Article thus follows the general policy of the Uniform Sales Act except that in case of the sale of an article by its patent or trade name the elimination of the warranty of fitness depends solely on whether the buyer has relied on the seller's skill and judgment; the use of the patent or trade name is but one factor in making this determination.

2. The rules of this section are designed to aid in determining the intention of the parties as to which of inconsistent warranties which have arisen from the circumstances of their transaction shall prevail. These rules of intention are to be applied only where factors making for an equitable estoppel of the seller do not exist and where he has in perfect good faith made warranties which later turn out to be inconsistent. To the extent that the seller has led the buyer to believe that all of the warranties can be performed, he is estopped from setting up any essential inconsistency as a defense.

3. The rules in subsections (a), (b) and (c) are designed to ascertain the intention of the parties by reference to the factor which probably claimed the attention of the parties in the first instance. These rules are not absolute but may be changed by evidence showing that the conditions which existed at the time of contracting make the construction called for by the section inconsistent or unreasonable.

Cross Reference:

Point 1: Section 2-315.

Definitional Cross Reference:

"Party". Section 1-201.

§ 2-318. Third Party Beneficiaries of Warranties Express or Implied.

Note: *If this Act is introduced in the Congress of the United States this section should be omitted. (States to select one alternative.)*

Alternative A

A seller's warranty whether express or implied extends to any natural person who is in the family or household of his buyer or who is a guest in his home if it is reasonable to expect that such person may use, consume or be affected by the goods and who is injured in person by breach of the warranty. A seller may not exclude or limit the operation of this section.

Alternative B

A seller's warranty whether express or implied extends to any natural person who may reasonably be expected to use, consume or be affected by the goods and who is injured in person by breach of the warranty. A seller may not exclude or limit the operation of this section.

Alternative C

A seller's warranty whether express or implied extends to any person who may reasonably be expected to use, consume or be affected by the goods and who is injured by breach of the warranty. A seller may not exclude or limit the operation of this section with respect to injury to the person of an individual to whom the warranty extends.

As amended in 1966.

Official Comment

Prior Uniform Statutory Provision: None.

Purposes:

1. The last sentence of this section does not mean that a seller is precluded from excluding or disclaiming a warranty which might otherwise arise in connection with the sale provided such exclusion or modification is permitted by Section 2–316. Nor does that sentence preclude the seller from limiting the remedies of his own buyer and of any beneficiaries, in any manner provided in Sections 2–718 or 2–719. To the extent that the contract of sale contains provisions under which warranties are excluded or modified, or remedies for breach are limited, such provisions are equally operative against beneficiaries of warranties under this section. What this last sentence forbids is exclusion of liability by the seller to the persons to whom the warranties which he has made to his buyer would extend under this section.

2. The purpose of this section is to give certain beneficiaries the benefit of the same warranty which the buyer received in the contract of sale, thereby freeing any such beneficiaries from any technical rules as to "privity." It seeks to accomplish this purpose without any derogation of any right or remedy resting on negligence. It rests primarily upon the merchant-

seller's warranty under this Article that the goods sold are merchantable and fit for the ordinary purposes for which such goods are used rather than the warranty of fitness for a particular purpose. Implicit in the section is that any beneficiary of a warranty may bring a direct action for breach of warranty against the seller whose warranty extends to him [As amended in 1966].

3. The first alternative expressly includes as beneficiaries within its provisions the family, household and guests of the purchaser. Beyond this, the section in this form is neutral and is not intended to enlarge or restrict the developing case law on whether the seller's warranties, given to his buyer who resells, extend to other persons in the distributive chain.

The second alternative is designed for states where the case law has already developed further and for those that desire to expand the class of beneficiaries. The third alternative goes further, following the trend of modern decisions as indicated by Restatement of Torts 2d § 402A (Tentative Draft No. 10, 1965) in extending the rule beyond injuries to the person [As amended in 1966].

Cross References:

Point 1: Sections 2–316, 2–718 and 2–719.
Point 2: Section 2–314.

Definitional Cross References:

"Buyer". Section 2–103.
"Goods". Section 2–105.
"Seller". Section 2–103.

§ 2–319. F.O.B. and F.A.S. Terms.

(1) Unless otherwise agreed the term F.O.B. (which means "free on board") at a named place, even though used only in connection with the stated price, is a delivery term under which

(a) when the term is F.O.B. the place of shipment, the seller must at that place ship the goods in the manner provided in this Article (Section 2–504) and bear the expense and risk of putting them into the possession of the carrier; or

(b) when the term is F.O.B. the place of destination, the seller must at his own expense and risk transport the goods to that place and there tender delivery of them in the manner provided in this Article (Section 2–503);

(c) when under either (a) or (b) the term is also F.O.B. vessel, car or other vehicle, the seller must in addition at his own expense and risk load the goods on board. If the term is F.O.B. vessel the buyer must name the vessel and in an appropriate case the seller must comply with the provisions of this Article on the form of bill of lading (Section 2–323).

(2) Unless otherwise agreed the term F.A.S. vessel (which means "free alongside") at a named port, even though used only in connection with the stated price, is a delivery term under which the seller must

(a) at his own expense and risk deliver the goods alongside the vessel in the manner usual in that port or on a dock designated and provided by the buyer; and

(b) obtain and tender a receipt for the goods in exchange for which the carrier is under a duty to issue a bill of lading.

(3) Unless otherwise agreed in any case falling within subsection (1)(a) or (c) or subsection (2) the buyer must seasonably give any needed instructions for making delivery, including when the term is F.A.S. or F.O.B. the loading berth of the vessel and in an appropriate case its name and sailing date. The seller may treat the failure of needed instructions as a failure of cooperation under this Article (Section 2–311). He may also at his option move the goods in any reasonable manner preparatory to delivery or shipment.

(4) Under the term F.O.B. vessel or F.A.S. unless otherwise agreed the buyer must make payment against tender of the required documents and the seller may not tender nor the buyer demand delivery of the goods in substitution for the documents.

Official Comment

Prior Uniform Statutory Provision: None.

Purposes:

1. This section is intended to negate the uncommercial line of decision which treats an "F.O.B." term as "merely a price term." The distinctions taken in subsection (1) handle most of the issues which have on occasion led to the unfortunate judicial language just referred to. Other matters which have led to sound results being based on unhappy language in regard to F.O.B. clauses are dealt with in this Act by Section 2–311(2) (seller's option re arrangements relating to shipment) and Sections 2–614 and 615 (substituted performance and seller's excuse).

2. Subsection (1)(c) not only specifies the duties of a seller who engages to deliver "F.O.B. vessel," or the like, but ought to make clear that no agreement is soundly drawn when it looks to reshipment from San Francisco or New York, but speaks merely of "F.O.B." the place.

3. The buyer's obligations stated in subsection (1)(c) and subsection (3) are, as shown in the text, obligations of cooperation. The last sentence of subsection (3) expressly, though perhaps unnecessarily, authorizes the seller, pending instructions, to go ahead with such preparatory moves as shipment from the interior to the named point of delivery. The sentence presupposes the usual case in which instructions "fail"; a prior repudiation by the buyer, giving notice that breach was intended, would remove the reason for the sentence, and would normally bring into play, instead, the second sentence of Section 2–704, which duly calls for lessening damages.

4. The treatment of "F.O.B. vessel" in conjunction with F.A.S. fits, in regard to the need for payment against documents, with standard practice and case-law; but "F.O.B. vessel" is a term which by its very language makes express the need for an "on board" document. In this respect, that term is stricter than the ordinary overseas "shipment" contract (C.I.F., etc., Section 2–320).

Cross References:

Sections 2–311(3), 2–323, 2–503 and 2–504.

Definitional Cross References:

"Agreed". Section 1–201.
"Bill of lading". Section 1–201.
"Buyer". Section 2–103.
"Goods". Section 2–105.
"Seasonably". Section 1–204.
"Seller". Section 2–103.
"Term". Section 1–201.

§ 2–320.   C.I.F. and C. & F. Terms.

(1) The term C.I.F. means that the price includes in a lump sum the cost of the goods and the insurance and freight to the named destination. The term C. & F. or C.F. means that the price so includes cost and freight to the named destination.

(2) Unless otherwise agreed and even though used only in connection with the stated price and destination, the term C.I.F. destination or its

equivalent requires the seller at his own expense and risk to

    (a) put the goods into the possession of a carrier at the port for shipment and obtain a negotiable bill or bills of lading covering the entire transportation to the named destination; and

    (b) load the goods and obtain a receipt from the carrier (which may be contained in the bill of lading) showing that the freight has been paid or provided for; and

    (c) obtain a policy or certificate of insurance, including any war risk insurance, of a kind and on terms then current at the port of shipment in the usual amount, in the currency of the contract, shown to cover the same goods covered by the bill of lading and providing for payment of loss to the order of the buyer or for the account of whom it may concern; but the seller may add to the price the amount of the premium for any such war risk insurance; and

    (d) prepare an invoice of the goods and procure any other documents required to effect shipment or to comply with the contract; and

    (e) forward and tender with commercial promptness all the documents in due form and with any indorsement necessary to perfect the buyer's rights.

(3) Unless otherwise agreed the term C. & F. or its equivalent has the same effect and imposes upon the seller the same obligations and risks as a C.I.F. term except the obligation as to insurance.

(4) Under the term C.I.F. or C. & F. unless otherwise agreed the buyer must make payment against tender of the required documents and the seller may not tender nor the buyer demand delivery of the goods in substitution for the documents.

Official Comment

Prior Uniform Statutory Provisions: None.

Purposes: To make it clear that:

1. The C.I.F. contract is not a destination but a shipment contract with risk of subsequent loss or damage to the goods passing to the buyer upon shipment if the seller has properly performed all his obligations with respect to the goods. Delivery to the carrier is delivery to the buyer for purposes of risk and "title". Delivery of possession of the goods is accomplished by delivery of the bill of lading, and upon tender of the required documents the buyer must pay the agreed price without awaiting the arrival of the goods and if they have been lost or damaged after proper shipment he must seek his remedy against the carrier or insurer. The buyer has no right of inspection prior to payment or acceptance of the documents.

2. The seller's obligations remain the same even though the C.I.F. term is "used only in connection with the stated price and destination".

3. The insurance stipulated by the C.I.F. term is for the buyer's benefit, to protect him against the risk of loss or damage to the goods in transit. A clause in a C.I.F. contract "insurance—for the account of sellers" should be viewed in its ordinary mercantile meaning that the sellers must pay for the insurance and not that it is intended to run to the seller's benefit.

4. A bill of lading covering the entire transportation from the port of shipment is explicitly required but the provision on this point must be read in the light of its reason to assure the buyer of as full protection as the conditions of shipment reasonably permit, remembering always that this type of contract is designed to move the goods in the channels commercially available. To enable the buyer to deal with the goods while they are afloat the bill of lading must be one that covers only the quantity of goods called for by the contract. The buyer is not required to accept his part of the goods without a bill of lading because the latter covers a larger quantity, nor is he required to accept a bill of lading for the whole quantity under a stipulation to hold the excess for the owner. Although the buyer is not compelled to accept either goods or documents under such circumstances he may of course claim his rights in any goods which have been identified to his contract.

5. The seller is given the option of paying or providing for the payment of freight. He has no option to ship "freight collect" unless the agreement so provides. The rule of the common law that the buyer need not pay the freight if the goods do not arrive is preserved.

Unless the shipment has been sent "freight collect" the buyer is entitled to receive documentary evidence that he is not obligated to pay the freight; the seller is therefore required to obtain a receipt "showing that the freight has been paid or provided for." The usual notation in the appropriate space on the bill of lading that the freight has been prepaid is a sufficient receipt, as at common law. The phrase "provided for" is intended to cover the frequent situation in which the carrier extends credit to a shipper for the freight on successive shipments and receives periodical payments of the accrued freight charges from him.

6. The requirement that unless otherwise agreed the seller must procure insurance "of a kind and on terms then current at the port for shipment in the usual amount, in the currency of the contract, sufficiently shown to cover the same goods covered by the bill of lading", applies to both marine and war risk insurance. As applied to marine insurance, it means such insurance as is usual or customary at the port for shipment with reference to the particular kind of goods involved, the character and equipment of the vessel, the route of the voyage, the port of destination and any other considerations that affect the risk. It is the substantial equivalent of the ordinary insurance in the particular trade and on the particular voyage and is subject to agreed specifications of type or extent of coverage. The language does not mean that the insurance must be adequate to cover all risks to which the goods may be subject in transit. There are some types of loss or damage that are not covered by the usual marine insurance and are excepted in bills of lading or in applicable statutes from the causes of loss or damage for which the carrier or the vessel is liable. Such risks must be borne by the buyer under this Article.

Insurance secured in compliance with a C.I.F. term must cover the entire transportation of the goods to the named destination.

7. An additional obligation is imposed upon the seller in requiring him to procure customary war risk insurance at the buyer's expense. This changes the common law on the point. The seller is not required to assume the risk of including in the C.I.F. price the cost of such insurance, since it often fluctuates rapidly, but is required to treat it simply as a necessary for the buyer's account. What war risk insurance is "current" or usual turns on the standard forms of policy or rider in common use.

8. The C.I.F. contract calls for insurance covering the value of the goods at the time and place of shipment and does not include any increase in market value during transit or any anticipated profit to the buyer on a sale by him.

The contract contemplates that before the goods arrive at their destination they may be sold again and again on C.I.F. terms and that the original policy of insurance and bill of lading will run with the interest in the goods by being transferred to each successive buyer. A buyer who becomes the seller in such an intermediate contract for sale does not thereby, if his sub-buyer knows the circumstances, undertake to insure the goods again at an increased price fixed in the new contract or to cover the increase in price by additional insurance, and his buyer may not reject the documents on the ground that the original policy does not cover such higher price. If such a sub-buyer desires additional insurance he must procure it for himself.

Where the seller exercises an option to ship "freight collect" and to credit the buyer with the freight against the C.I.F. price, the insurance need not cover the freight since the freight is not at the buyer's risk. On the other hand, where the seller prepays the freight upon shipping under a bill of lading requiring prepayment and providing that the freight shall be deemed earned and shall be retained by the carrier "ship and/or cargo lost or not lost," or using words of similar import, he must procure insurance that will cover the freight, because notwithstanding that the goods are lost in transit the buyer is bound to pay the freight as part of the C.I.F. price and will be unable to recover it back from the carrier.

9. Insurance "for the account of whom it may concern" is usual and sufficient. However, for a valid tender the policy of insurance must be one which can be disposed of together with the bill of lading and so must be "sufficiently shown to cover the same goods covered by the bill of lading". It must cover separately the quantity of goods called for by the buyer's contract and not merely insure his goods as part of a larger quantity in which others are interested, a case provided for in American mercantile practice by the use of negotiable certificates of insurance which are expressly authorized by this section. By usage these certificates are treated as the equivalent of separate policies and are good tender under C.I.F. contracts. The term "certificate of insurance", however, does not of itself include certificates or "cover notes" issued by the insurance broker and stating that the goods are covered by a policy. Their sufficiency as substitutes for policies will depend upon proof of an established usage or course of dealing. The present section rejects the English rule that not only brokers' certificates and "cover notes" but also certain forms of American insurance certificates are not the equivalent of policies and are not good tender under a C.I.F. contract.

The seller's failure to tender a proper insurance document is waived if the buyer refuses to make payment on other and untenable grounds at a time when proper insurance could have been obtained and tendered by the seller if timely objection had been made. Even a failure to insure on shipment may be cured by seasonable tender of a policy retroactive in effect; e.g., one insuring the goods "lost or not lost." The provisions of this Article on cure of improper tender and on waiver of buyer's objections by silence are applicable to insurance tenders under a C.I.F. term. Where there is no waiver by the buyer as described above, however, the fact that the goods arrive safely does not cure the seller's breach of his obligations to insure them and tender to the buyer a proper insurance document.

10. The seller's invoice of the goods shipped under a C.I.F. contract is regarded as a usual and necessary document upon which reliance may properly be placed. It is the document which evidences points of description, quality and the like which do not readily appear in other documents. This Article rejects those statements to the effect that the invoice is a usual but not a necessary document under a C.I.F. term.

11. The buyer needs all of the documents required under a C.I.F. contract, in due form and with necessary endorsements, so that before the goods arrive he may deal with them by negotiating the documents or may obtain prompt possession of the goods after their arrival. If the goods are lost or damaged in transit the documents are necessary to enable him promptly to assert his remedy against the carrier or insurer. The seller is therefore obligated to do what is mercantilely reasonable in the circumstances and should make every reasonable exertion to send forward the documents as soon as possible after the shipment. The requirement that the documents be forwarded with "commercial promptness" expresses a more urgent need for action than that suggested by the phrase "reasonable time".

12. Under a C.I.F. contract the buyer, as under the common law, must pay the price upon tender of the required documents without first inspecting the goods, but his payment in these circumstances does not constitute an acceptance of the goods nor does it impair his right of subsequent inspection or his options and remedies in the case of improper delivery. All remedies and rights for the seller's breach are reserved to him. The buyer must pay before inspection and assert his remedy against the seller afterward unless the nonconformity of the goods amounts to a real failure of consideration, since the purpose of choosing this form of contract is to give the seller protection against the buyer's unjustifiable rejection of the goods at a distant port of destination which would necessitate taking possession of the goods and suing the buyer there.

13. A valid C.I.F. contract may be made which requires part of the transportation to be made on land and part on the sea, as where the goods are to be brought by rail from an inland point to a seaport and thence transported by vessel to the named destination under a "through" or combination bill of lading issued by the railroad company. In such a case shipment by rail from the inland point within the contract period is a timely shipment notwithstanding that the loading of the goods on the vessel is delayed by causes beyond the seller's control.

14. Although subsection (2) stating the legal effects of the C.I.F. term is an "unless otherwise agreed" provision, the express language used in an agreement is frequently a precautionary, fuller statement of the normal C.I.F. terms and hence not intended as a departure or variation from them. Moreover, the dominant outlines of the C.I.F. term are so well understood commercially that any variation should, whenever reasonably possible, be read as falling within those dominant outlines rather than as destroying the whole meaning of a term which essentially indicates a contract for proper shipment rather than one for delivery at destination. Particularly careful consideration is necessary before a printed form or clause is construed to mean agreement otherwise and where a C.I.F. contract is prepared on a printed form designed for some other type of contract, the C.I.F. terms must prevail over printed clauses repugnant to them.

15. Under subsection (4) the fact that the seller knows at the time of the tender of the documents that the goods have been lost in transit does not affect his rights if he has performed his contractual obligations. Similarly, the seller cannot perform under a C.I.F. term by purchasing and tendering landed goods.

16. Under the C. & F. term, as under the C.I.F. term, title and risk of loss are intended to pass to the buyer on shipment. A stipulation in a C. & F. contract that the seller shall effect insurance on the goods and charge the buyer with the premium (in effect that he shall act as the buyer's agent for that purpose) is entirely in keeping with the pattern. On the other hand, it often happens that the buyer is in a more advantageous position than the seller to effect insurance on the goods or that he has in force an "open" or "floating" policy covering all shipments made by him or to him, in either of which events the C. & F. term is adequate without mention of insurance.

17. It is to be remembered that in a French contract the term "C.A.F." does not mean "Cost and Freight" but has exactly the same meaning as the term "C.I.F." since it is merely the French equivalent of that term. The "A" does not stand for "and" but for "assurance" which means insurance.

Cross References:

Point 4: Section 2–323.

Point 6: Section 2–509(1)(a).

Point 9: Sections 2–508 and 2–605(1)(a).

Point 12: Sections 2–321(3), 2–512 and 2–513(3) and Article 5.

Definitional Cross References:

"Bill of lading". Section 1–201.

"Buyer". Section 2–103.

"Contract". Section 1–201.

"Goods". Section 2–105.

"Rights". Section 1–201.

"Seller". Section 2–103.

"Term". Section 1–201.

§ 2–321. C.I.F. or C. & F.: "Net Landed Weights"; "Payment on Arrival"; Warranty of Condition on Arrival.

Under a contract containing a term C.I.F. or C. & F.

(1) Where the price is based on or is to be adjusted according to "net landed weights", "delivered weights", "out turn" quantity or quality or the like, unless otherwise agreed the seller must reasonably estimate the price. The payment due on tender of the documents called for by the contract is the amount so estimated, but after final adjustment of the price a settlement must be made with commercial promptness.

(2) An agreement described in subsection (1) or any warranty of quality or condition of the goods on arrival places upon the seller the risk of ordinary deterioration, shrinkage and the like in transportation but has no effect on the place or time of identification to the contract for sale or delivery or on the passing of the risk of loss.

(3) Unless otherwise agreed where the contract provides for payment on or after arrival of the goods the seller must before payment allow such preliminary inspection as is feasible; but if the goods are lost delivery of the documents and payment are due when the goods should have arrived.

Official Comment

Prior Uniform Statutory Provision: None.

Purposes:

This section deals with two variations of the C.I.F. contract which have evolved in mercantile practice but are entirely consistent with the basic C.I.F. pattern.

Subsections (1) and (2), which provide for a shift to the seller of the risk of quality and weight deterioration during shipment, are designed to conform the law to the best mercantile practice and usage without changing the legal consequences of the C.I.F. or C. & F. term as to the passing of marine risks to the buyer at the point of shipment. Subsection (3) provides that where under the contract documents are to be presented for payment after arrival of the goods, this amounts merely to a postponement of the payment under the C.I.F. contract and is not to be confused with the "no arrival, no sale" contract. If the goods are lost, delivery of the documents and payment against them are due when the goods should have arrived. The clause for payment on or after arrival is not to be construed as such a condition precedent to payment that if the goods are lost in transit the buyer need never pay and the seller must bear the loss.

Cross Reference:

Section 2–324.

Definitional Cross References:

"Agreement". Section 1–201.

"Contract". Section 1–201.

"Delivery". Section 1–201.

"Goods". Section 2–105.

"Seller". Section 2–103.

"Term". Section 1–201.

§ 2–322. Delivery "Ex-Ship".

(1) Unless otherwise agreed a term for delivery of goods "ex-ship" (which means from the carrying vessel) or in equivalent language is not restricted to a particular ship and requires delivery from a ship which has reached a place at the named port of destination where goods of the kind are usually discharged.

(2) Under such a term unless otherwise agreed

(a) the seller must discharge all liens arising out of the carriage and furnish the buyer with a direction which puts the carrier under a duty to deliver the goods; and

(b) the risk of loss does not pass to the buyer until the goods leave the ship's tackle or are otherwise properly unloaded.

Official Comment

Prior Uniform Statutory Provision: None.

Purposes:

1. The delivery term, "ex-ship", as between seller and buyer, is the reverse of the f.a.s. term covered.

2. Delivery need not be made from any particular vessel under a clause calling for delivery "ex-ship", even though a vessel on which shipment is to be made originally is named in the contract, unless the agreement by appropriate language, restricts the clause to delivery from a named vessel.

3. The appropriate place and manner of unloading at the port of destination depend upon the nature of the goods and the facilities and usages of the port.

4. A contract fixing a price "ex-ship" with payment "cash against documents" calls only for such documents as are appropriate to the contract. Tender of a delivery order and of a receipt for the freight after the arrival of the carrying vessel is adequate. The seller is not required to tender a bill of lading as a document of title nor is he required to insure the goods for the buyer's benefit, as the goods are not at the buyer's risk during the voyage.

Cross Reference:

Point 1: Section 2–319(2).

Definitional Cross References:

"Buyer". Section 2–103.
"Goods". Section 2–105.
"Seller". Section 2–103.
"Term". Section 1–201.

§ 2–323. Form of Bill of Lading Required in Overseas Shipment; "Overseas".

(1) Where the contract contemplates overseas shipment and contains a term C.I.F. or C. & F. or F.O.B. vessel, the seller unless otherwise agreed must obtain a negotiable bill of lading stating that the goods have been loaded in board or, in the case of a term C.I.F. or C. & F., received for shipment.

(2) Where in a case within subsection (1) a bill of lading has been issued in a set of parts, unless otherwise agreed if the documents are not to be sent from abroad the buyer may demand tender of the full set; otherwise only one part of the bill of lading need be tendered. Even if the agreement expressly requires a full set

(a) due tender of a single part is acceptable within the provisions of this Article on cure of improper delivery (subsection (1) of Section 2–508); and

(b) even though the full set is demanded, if the documents are sent from abroad the person tendering an incomplete set may nevertheless require payment upon furnishing an indemnity which the buyer in good faith deems adequate.

(3) A shipment by water or by air or a contract contemplating such shipment is "overseas" insofar as by usage of trade or agreement it is subject to the commercial, financing or shipping practices characteristic of international deep water commerce.

Official Comment

Prior Uniform Statutory Provision: None.

Purposes:

1. Subsection (1) follows the "American" rule that a regular bill of lading indicating delivery of the goods at the dock for shipment is sufficient, except under a term "F.O.B. vessel." See Section 2–319 and comment thereto.

2. Subsection (2) deals with the problem of bills of lading covering deep water shipments, issued not as a single bill of lading but in a set of parts, each part referring to the other parts and the entire set constituting in commercial practice and at law a single bill of lading. Commercial practice in international commerce is to accept and pay against presentation of the first part of a set if the part is sent from overseas even though the contract of the buyer requires presentation of a full set of bills of lading provided adequate indemnity for the missing parts is forthcoming.

This subsection codifies that practice as between buyer and seller. Article 5 (Section 5–113) authorizes banks presenting drafts under letters of credit to give indemnities against the missing parts, and this subsection means that the buyer must accept and act on such indemnities if he in good faith deems them adequate. But neither this subsection nor Article 5 decides whether a bank which has issued a letter of credit is similarly bound. The issuing bank's obligation under a letter of credit is independent and depends on its own terms. See Article 5.

Cross References:

Sections 2–508(2), 5–113.

Definitional Cross References:

"Bill of lading". Section 1–201.
"Buyer". Section 2–103.

"Contract". Section 1–201.
"Delivery". Section 1–201.
"Financing agency". Section 2–104.
"Person". Section 1–201.
"Seller". Section 2–103.
"Send". Section 1–201.
"Term". Section 1–201.

§ 2-324. "No Arrival, No Sale" Term.

Under a term "no arrival, no sale" or terms of like meaning, unless otherwise agreed,

(a) the seller must properly ship conforming goods and if they arrive by any means he must tender them on arrival but he assumes no obligation that the goods will arrive unless he has caused the non-arrival; and

(b) where without fault of the seller the goods are in part lost or have so deteriorated as no longer to conform to the contract or arrive after the contract time, the buyer may proceed as if there had been casualty to identified goods (Section 2–613).

Official Comment

Prior Uniform Statutory Provision: None.

Purposes:

1. The "no arrival, no sale" term in a "destination" overseas contract leaves risk of loss on the seller but gives him an exemption from liability for non-delivery. Both the nature of the case and the duty of good faith require that the seller must not interfere with the arrival of the goods in any way. If the circumstances impose upon him the responsibility for making or arranging the shipment, he must have a shipment made despite the exemption clause. Further, the shipment made must be a conforming one, for the exemption under a "no arrival, no sale" term applies only to the hazards of transportation and the goods must be proper in all other respects.

The reason of this section is that where the seller is reselling goods bought by him as shipped by another and this fact is known to the buyer, so that the seller is not under any obligation to make the shipment himself, the seller is entitled under the "no arrival, no sale" clause to exemption from payment of damages for non-delivery if the goods do not arrive or if the goods which actually arrive are non-conforming. This does not extend to sellers who arrange shipment by their own agents, in which case the clause is limited to casualty due to marine hazards. But sellers who make known that they are contracting only with respect to what will be delivered to them by parties over whom they assume no control are entitled to the full quantum of the exemption.

2. The provisions of this Article on identification must be read together with the present section in order to bring the exemption into application. Until there is some designation of the goods in a particular shipment or on a particular ship as being those to which the contract refers there can be no application of an exemption for their non-arrival.

3. The seller's duty to tender the agreed or declared goods if they do arrive is not impaired because of their delay in arrival or by their arrival after transshipment.

4. The phrase "to arrive" is often employed in the same sense as "no arrival, no sale" and may then be given the same effect. But a "to arrive" term, added to a C.I.F. or C. & F. contract, does not have the full meaning given by this section to "no arrival, no sale". Such a "to arrive" term is usually intended to operate only to the extent that the risks are not covered by the agreed insurance and the loss or casualty is due to such uncovered hazards. In some instances the "to arrive" term may be regarded as a time of payment term, or, in the case of the reselling seller discussed in point 1 above, as negating responsibility for conformity of the goods, if they arrive, to any description which was based on his good faith belief of the quality. Whether this is the intention of the parties is a question of fact based on all the circumstances surrounding the resale and in case of ambiguity the rules of Sections 2–316 and 2–317 apply to preclude dishonor.

5. Paragraph (b) applies where goods arrive impaired by damage or partial loss during transportation and makes the policy of this Article on casualty to identified goods applicable to such a situation. For the term cannot be regarded as intending to give the seller an unforeseen profit through casualty; it is intended only to protect him from loss due to causes beyond his control.

Cross References:

Point 1: Section 1–203.
Point 2: Section 2–501(a) and (c).
Point 5: Section 2–613.

Definitional Cross References:

"Buyer". Section 2–103.
"Conforming". Section 2–106.
"Contract". Section 1–201.
"Fault". Section 1–201.
"Goods". Section 2–105.

"Sale". Section 2–106.
"Seller". Section 2–103.
"Term". Section 1–201.

§ 2–325. "Letter of Credit" Term; "Confirmed Credit".

(1) Failure of the buyer seasonably to furnish an agreed letter of credit is a breach of the contract for sale.

(2) The delivery to seller of a proper letter of credit suspends the buyer's obligation to pay. If the letter of credit is dishonored, the seller may on seasonable notification to the buyer require payment directly from him.

(3) Unless otherwise agreed the term "letter of credit" or "banker's credit" in a contract for sale means an irrevocable credit issued by a financing agency of good repute and, where the shipment is overseas, of good international repute. The term "confirmed credit" means that the credit must also carry the direct obligation of such an agency which does business in the seller's financial market.

Official Comment

Prior Uniform Statutory Provision: None.

Purposes: To express the established commercial and banking understanding as to the meaning and effects of terms calling for "letters of credit" or "confirmed credit":

1. Subsection (2) follows the general policy of this Article and Article 3 (Section 3–802) on conditional payment, under which payment by check or other short-term instrument is not ordinarily final as between the parties if the recipient duly presents the instrument and honor is refused. Thus the furnishing of a letter of credit does not substitute the financing agency's obligation for the buyer's, but the seller must first give the buyer reasonable notice of his intention to demand direct payment from him.

2. Subsection (3) requires that the credit be irrevocable and be a prime credit as determined by the standing of the issuer. It is not necessary, unless otherwise agreed, that the credit be a negotiation credit; the seller can finance himself by an assignment of the proceeds under Section 5–116(2).

3. The definition of "confirmed credit" is drawn on the supposition that the credit is issued by a bank which is not doing direct business in the seller's financial market; there is no intention to require the obligation of two banks both local to the seller.

Cross References:

Sections 2–403, 2–511(3) and 3–802 and Article 5.

Definitional Cross References:

"Buyer". Section 2–103.
"Contract for sale". Section 2–106.
"Draft". Section 3–104.
"Financing agency". Section 2–104.
"Notifies". Section 1–201.
"Overseas". Section 2–323.
"Purchaser". Section 1–201.
"Seasonably". Section 1–204.
"Seller". Section 2–103.
"Term". Section 1–201.

§ 2–326. Sale on Approval and Sale or Return; Rights of Creditors.

(1) Unless otherwise agreed, if delivered goods may be returned by the buyer even though they conform to the contract, the transaction is

   (a) a "sale on approval" if the goods are delivered primarily for use, and

   (b) a "sale or return" if the goods are delivered primarily for resale.

(2) Goods held on approval are not subject to the claims of the buyer's creditors until acceptance; goods held on sale or return are subject to such claims while in the buyer's possession.

(3) Any "or return" term of a contract for sale is to be treated as a separate contract for sale within the statute of frauds section of this Article (Section 2–201) and as contradicting the sale aspect of the contract within the provisions of this Article on parol or extrinsic evidence (Section 2–202).

As amended in 1999.

Official Comment

Prior Uniform Statutory Provision: Section 19(3), Uniform Sales Act.

Changes: Completely rewritten in this and the succeeding section.

Purposes of Changes: To make it clear that:

1. Both a "sale on approval" and a "sale or return" should be distinguished from other types of transactions with which they frequently have been confused. A "sale on approval," sometimes also called a sale "on trial" or "on satisfaction," deals with a contract under which the seller undertakes a risk in order to satisfy its

prospective buyer with the appearance or performance of the goods that are sold. The goods are delivered to the proposed purchaser but they remain the property of the seller until the buyer accepts them. The price has already been agreed. The buyer's willingness to receive and test the goods is the consideration for the seller's engagement to deliver and sell. A "sale or return," on the other hand, typically is a sale to a merchant whose unwillingness to buy is overcome by the seller's engagement to take back the goods (or any commercial unit of goods) in lieu of payment if they fail to be resold. A sale or return is a present sale of goods which may be undone at the buyer's option. Accordingly, subsection (2) provides that goods delivered on approval are not subject to the prospective buyer's creditors until acceptance, and goods delivered in a sale or return are subject to the buyer's creditors while in the buyer's possession.

These two transactions are so strongly delineated in practice and in general understanding that every presumption runs against a delivery to a consumer being a "sale or return" and against a delivery to a merchant for resale being a "sale on approval."

2. The right to return goods for failure to conform to the contract of sale does not make the transaction a "sale on approval" or "sale or return" and has nothing to do with this section or Section 2–327. This section is not concerned with remedies for breach of contract. It deals instead with a power given by the contract to turn back the goods even though they are wholly as warranted. This section nevertheless presupposes that a contract for sale is contemplated by the parties, although that contract may be of the particular character that this section addresses (i.e., a sale on approval or a sale or return).

If a buyer's obligation as a buyer is conditioned not on its personal approval but on the article's passing a described objective test, the risk of loss by casualty pending the test is properly the seller's and proper return is at its expense. On the point of "satisfaction" as meaning "reasonable satisfaction" when an industrial machine is involved, this Article takes no position.

3. Subsection (3) resolves a conflict in the pre-UCC case law by recognizing that an "or return" provision is so definitely at odds with any ordinary contract for sale of goods that if a written agreement is involved the "or return" term must be contained in a written memorandum. The "or return" aspect of a sales contract must be treated as a separate contract under the Statute of Frauds section and as contradicting the sale insofar as questions of parol or extrinsic evidence are concerned.

4. Certain true consignment transactions were dealt with in former Sections 2–326(3) and 9–114. These provisions have been deleted and have been replaced by new provisions in Article 9. See, e.g., Sections 9–109(a)(4); 9–103(d); 9–319.

Cross References:

Point 2: Article 9.
Point 3: Sections 2–201 and 2–202.

Definitional Cross References:

"Between merchants". Section 2–104.
"Buyer". Section 2–103.
"Conform". Section 2–106.
"Contract for sale". Section 2–106.
"Creditor". Section 1–201.
"Goods". Section 2–105.
"Sale". Section 2–106.
"Seller". Section 2–103.

As amended in 1999 and 2000.

§ 2–327. Special Incidents of Sale on Approval and Sale or Return.

(1) Under a sale on approval unless otherwise agreed

(a) although the goods are identified to the contract the risk of loss and the title do not pass to the buyer until acceptance; and

(b) use of the goods consistent with the purpose of trial is not acceptance but failure seasonably to notify the seller of election to return the goods is acceptance, and if the goods conform to the contract acceptance of any part is acceptance of the whole; and

(c) after due notification of election to return, the return is at the seller's risk and expense but a merchant buyer must follow any reasonable instructions.

(2) Under a sale or return unless otherwise agreed

(a) the option to return extends to the whole or any commercial unit of the goods while in substantially their original condition, but must be exercised seasonably; and

(b) the return is at the buyer's risk and expense.

Official Comment

Prior Uniform Statutory Provision: Section 19(3), Uniform Sales Act.

Changes: Completely rewritten in preceding and this section.

Purposes of Changes: To make it clear that:

1. In the case of a sale on approval:

If all of the goods involved conform to the contract, the buyer's acceptance of part of the goods constitutes acceptance of the whole. Acceptance of part falls outside the normal intent of the parties in the "on approval" situation and the policy of this Article allowing partial acceptance of a defective delivery has no application here. A case where a buyer takes home two dresses to select one commonly involves two distinct contracts; if not, it is covered by the words "unless otherwise agreed".

2. In the case of a sale or return, the return of any unsold unit merely because it is unsold is the normal intent of the "sale or return" provision, and therefore the right to return for this reason alone is independent of any other action under the contract which would turn on wholly different considerations. On the other hand, where the return of goods is for breach, including return of items resold by the buyer and returned by the ultimate purchasers because of defects, the return procedure is governed not by the present section but by the provisions on the effects and revocation of acceptance.

3. In the case of a sale on approval the risk rests on the seller until acceptance of the goods by the buyer, while in a sale or return the risk remains throughout on the buyer.

4. Notice of election to return given by the buyer in a sale on approval is sufficient to relieve him of any further liability. Actual return by the buyer to the seller is required in the case of a sale or return contract. What constitutes due "giving" of notice, as required in "on approval" sales, is governed by the provisions on good faith and notice. "Seasonable" is used here as defined in Section 1–204. Nevertheless, the provisions of both this Article and of the contract on this point must be read with commercial reason and with full attention to good faith.

Cross References:

Point 1: Sections 2–501, 2–601 and 2–603.
Point 2: Sections 2–607 and 2–608.
Point 4: Sections 1–201 and 1–204.

Definitional Cross References:

"Agreed". Section 1–201.
"Buyer". Section 2–103.
"Commercial unit". Section 2–105.
"Conform". Section 2–106.

"Contract". Section 1–201.
"Goods". Section 2–105.
"Merchant". Section 2–104.
"Notifies". Section 1–201.
"Notification". Section 1–201.
"Sale on approval". Section 2–326.
"Sale or return". Section 2–326.
"Seasonably". Section 1–204.
"Seller". Section 2–103.

§ 2–328. Sale by Auction.

(1) In a sale by auction if goods are put up in lots each lot is the subject of a separate sale.

(2) A sale by auction is complete when the auctioneer so announces by the fall of the hammer or in other customary manner. Where a bid is made while the hammer is falling in acceptance of a prior bid the auctioneer may in his discretion reopen the bidding or declare the goods sold under the bid on which the hammer was falling.

(3) Such a sale is with reserve unless the goods are in explicit terms put up without reserve. In an auction with reserve the auctioneer may withdraw the goods at any time until he announces completion of the sale. In an auction without reserve, after the auctioneer calls for bids on an article or lot, that article or lot cannot be withdrawn unless no bid is made within a reasonable time. In either case a bidder may retract his bid until the auctioneer's announcement of completion of the sale, but a bidder's retraction does not revive any previous bid.

(4) If the auctioneer knowingly receives a bid on the seller's behalf or the seller makes or procures such a bid, and notice has not been given that liberty for such bidding is reserved, the buyer may at his option avoid the sale or take the goods at the price of the last good faith bid prior to the completion of the sale. This subsection shall not apply to any bid at a forced sale.

Official Comment

Prior Uniform Statutory Provision: Section 21, Uniform Sales Act.

Changes: Completely rewritten.

Purposes of Changes: To make it clear that:

1. The auctioneer may in his discretion either reopen the bidding or close the sale on the bid on which the hammer was falling when a bid is made at that

moment. The recognition of a bid of this kind by the auctioneer in his discretion does not mean a closing in favor of such a bidder, but only that the bid has been accepted as a continuation of the bidding. If recognized, such a bid discharges the bid on which the hammer was falling when it was made.

2. An auction "with reserve" is the normal procedure. The crucial point, however, for determining the nature of an auction is the "putting up" of the goods. This Article accepts the view that the goods may be withdrawn before they are actually "put up," regardless of whether the auction is advertised as one without reserve, without liability on the part of the auction announcer to persons who are present. This is subject to any peculiar facts which might bring the case within the "firm offer" principle of this Article, but an offer to persons generally would require unmistakable language in order to fall within that section. The prior announcement of the nature of the auction either as

with reserve or without reserve will, however, enter as an "explicit term" in the "putting up" of the goods and conduct thereafter must be governed accordingly. The present section continues the prior rule permitting withdrawal of bids in auctions both with and without reserve; and the rule is made explicit that the retraction of a bid does not revive a prior bid.

Cross Reference:

Point 2: Section 2–205.

Definitional Cross References:

"Buyer". Section 2–103.
"Good faith". Section 1–201.
"Goods". Section 2–105.
"Lot". Section 2–105.
"Notice". Section 1–201.
"Sale". Section 2–106.
"Seller". Section 2–103.

PART 4

TITLE, CREDITORS AND GOOD FAITH PURCHASERS

§ 2–401. Passing of Title; Reservation for Security; Limited Application of This Section.

Each provision of this Article with regard to the rights, obligations and remedies of the seller, the buyer, purchasers or other third parties applies irrespective of title to the goods except where the provision refers to such title. Insofar as situations are not covered by the other provisions of this Article and matters concerning title become material the following rules apply:

(1) Title to goods cannot pass under a contract for sale prior to their identification to the contract (Section 2–501), and unless otherwise explicitly agreed the buyer acquires by their identification a special property as limited by this Act. Any retention or reservation by the seller of the title (property) in goods shipped or delivered to the buyer is limited in effect to a reservation of a security interest. Subject to these provisions and to the provisions of the Article on Secured Transactions (Article 9), title to goods passes from the seller to the buyer in any manner and on any conditions explicitly agreed on by the parties.

(2) Unless otherwise explicitly agreed title passes to the buyer at the time and place at which the seller completes his performance with

reference to the physical delivery of the goods, despite any reservation of a security interest and even though a document of title is to be delivered at a different time or place; and in particular and despite any reservation of a security interest by the bill of lading

(a) if the contract requires or authorizes the seller to send the goods to the buyer but does not require him to deliver them at destination, title passes to the buyer at the time and place of shipment; but

(b) if the contract requires delivery at destination, title passes on tender there.

(3) Unless otherwise explicitly agreed where delivery is to be made without moving the goods,

(a) if the seller is to deliver a document of title, title passes at the time when and the place where he delivers such documents; or

(b) if the goods are at the time of contracting already identified and no documents are to be delivered, title passes at the time and place of contracting.

(4) A rejection or other refusal by the buyer to receive or retain the goods, whether or not justified, or a justified revocation of acceptance re-

vests title to the goods in the seller. Such re-vesting occurs by operation of law and is not a "sale".

Official Comment

Prior Uniform Statutory Provision: See generally, Sections 17, 18, 19 and 20, Uniform Sales Act.

Purposes: To make it clear that:

1. This Article deals with the issues between seller and buyer in terms of step by step performance or non-performance under the contract for sale and not in terms of whether or not "title" to the goods has passed. That the rules of this section in no way alter the rights of either the buyer, seller or third parties declared elsewhere in the Article is made clear by the preamble of this section. This section, however, in no way intends to indicate which line of interpretation should be followed in cases where the applicability of "public" regulation depends upon a "sale" or upon location of "title" without further definition. The basic policy of this Article that known purpose and reason should govern interpretation cannot extend beyond the scope of its own provisions. It is therefore necessary to state what a "sale" is and when title passes under this Article in case the courts deem any public regulation to incorporate the defined term of the "private" law.

2. "Future" goods cannot be the subject of a present sale. Before title can pass the goods must be identified in the manner set forth in Section 2-501. The parties, however, have full liberty to arrange by specific terms for the passing of title to goods which are existing.

3. The "special property" of the buyer in goods identified to the contract is excluded from the definition of "security interest"; its incidents are defined in provisions of this Article such as those on the rights of the seller's creditors, on good faith purchase, on the buyer's right to goods on the seller's insolvency, and on the buyer's right to specific performance or replevin.

4. The factual situations in subsections (2) and (3) upon which passage of title turn actually base the test upon the time when the seller has finally committed himself in regard to specific goods. Thus in a "ship-ment" contract he commits himself by the act of making the shipment. If shipment is not contemplated subsection (3) turns on the seller's final commitment, i.e. the delivery of documents or the making of the contract.

Cross References:

Point 2: Sections 2-102, 2-501 and 2-502.
Point 3: Sections 1-201, 2-402, 2-403, 2-502 and 2-716.

Definitional Cross References:

"Agreement". Section 1-201.
"Bill of lading". Section 1-201.
"Buyer". Section 2-103.
"Contract". Section 1-201.
"Contract for sale". Section 2-106.
"Delivery". Section 1-201.
"Document of title". Section 1-201.
"Good faith". Section 2-103.
"Goods". Section 2-105.
"Party". Section 1-201.
"Purchaser". Section 1-201.
"Receipt" of goods. Section 2-103.
"Remedy". Section 1-201.
"Rights". Section 1-201.
"Sale". Section 2-106.
"Security interest". Section 1-201.
"Seller". Section 2-103.
"Send". Section 1-201.

§ 2-402. Rights of Seller's Creditors Against Sold Goods.

(1) Except as provided in subsections (2) and (3), rights of unsecured creditors of the seller with respect to goods which have been identified to a contract for sale are subject to the buyer's rights to recover the goods under this Article (Sections 2-502 and 2-716).

(2) A creditor of the seller may treat a sale or an identification of goods to a contract for sale as void if as against him a retention of possession by the seller is fraudulent under any rule of law of the state where the goods are situated, except that retention of possession in good faith and current course of trade by a merchant-seller for a commercially reasonable time after a sale or identification is not fraudulent.

(3) Nothing in this Article shall be deemed to impair the rights of creditors of the seller

(a) under the provisions of the Article on Secured Transactions (Article 9); or

(b) where identification to the contract or delivery is made not in current course of trade but in satisfaction of or as security for a pre-existing claim for money, security or the like and is made under circumstances which under any rule of law of the state where the goods are situated would apart from this Article constitute the transaction a fraudulent transfer or voidable preference.

Official Comment

Prior Uniform Statutory Provision: Subsection (2)—Section 26, Uniform Sales Act; Subsections (1) and (3)—none.

Changes: Rephrased.

Purposes of Changes and New Matter: To avoid confusion on ordinary issues between current sellers and buyers and issues in the field of preference and hindrance by making it clear that:

1. Local law on questions of hindrance of creditors by the seller's retention of possession of the goods are outside the scope of this Article, but retention of possession in the current course of trade is legitimate. Transactions which fall within the law's policy against improper preferences are reserved from the protection of this Article.

2. The retention of possession of the goods by a merchant seller for a commercially reasonable time after a sale or identification in current course is exempted from attack as fraudulent. Similarly, the provisions of subsection (3) have no application to identification or delivery made in the current course of trade, as measured against general commercial understanding of what a "current" transaction is.

Definitional Cross References:

"Contract for sale". Section 2–106.
"Creditor". Section 1–201.
"Good faith". Section 2–103.
"Goods". Section 2–105.
"Merchant". Section 2–104.
"Money". Section 1–201.
"Reasonable time". Section 1–204.
"Rights". Section 1–201.
"Sale". Section 2–106.
"Seller". Section 2–103.

§ 2–403.　Power to Transfer; Good Faith Purchase of Goods; "Entrusting".

(1) A purchaser of goods acquires all title which his transferor had or had power to transfer except that a purchaser of a limited interest acquires rights only to the extent of the interest purchased. A person with voidable title has power to transfer a good title to a good faith purchaser for value. When goods have been delivered under a transaction of purchase the purchaser has such power even though

(a) the transferor was deceived as to the identity of the purchaser, or

(b) the delivery was in exchange for a check which is later dishonored, or

(c) it was agreed that the transaction was to be a "cash sale", or

(d) the delivery was procured through fraud punishable as larcenous under the criminal law.

(2) Any entrusting of possession of goods to a merchant who deals in goods of that kind gives him power to transfer all rights of the entruster to a buyer in ordinary course of business.

(3) "Entrusting" includes any delivery and any acquiescence in retention of possession regardless of any condition expressed between the parties to the delivery or acquiescence and regardless of whether the procurement of the entrusting or the possessor's disposition of the goods have been such as to be larcenous under the criminal law.

[*Publisher's Editorial Note: If a state adopts the repealer of Article 6—Bulk Transfers (Alternative A), subsec. (4) should read as follows:*]

(4) The rights of other purchasers of goods and of lien creditors are governed by the Articles on Secured Transactions (Article 9) and Documents of Title (Article 7).

[*Publisher's Editorial Note: If a state adopts Revised Article 6—Bulk Sales (Alternative B), subsec. (4) should read as follows:*]

(4) The rights of other purchasers of goods and of lien creditors are governed by the Articles on Secured Transactions (Article 9), Bulk Sales (Article 6) and Documents of Title (Article 7).

As amended in 1988.

For material relating to the changes made in text in 1988, see section 3 of Alternative A (Repealer of Article 6—Bulk Transfers) and Conforming Amendment to Section 2–403 following end of Alternative B (Revised Article 6—Bulk Sales).

Official Comment

Prior Uniform Statutory Provision: Sections 20(4), 23, 24, 25, Uniform Sales Act; Section 9, especially 9(2), Uniform Trust Receipts Act; Section 9, Uniform Conditional Sales Act.

Changes: Consolidated and rewritten.

Purposes of Changes: To gather together a series of prior uniform statutory provisions and the case-law thereunder and to state a unified and simplified policy on good faith purchase of goods.

1. The basic policy of our law allowing transfer of such title as the transferor has is generally continued and expanded under subsection (1). In this respect the provisions of the section are applicable to a person taking by any form of "purchase" as defined by this Act. Moreover the policy of this Act expressly providing for the application of supplementary general principles of law to sales transactions wherever appropriate joins with the present section to continue unimpaired all rights acquired under the law of agency or of apparent agency or ownership or other estoppel, whether based on statutory provisions or on case law principles. The section also leaves unimpaired the powers given to selling factors under the earlier Factors Acts. In addition subsection (1) provides specifically for the protection of the good faith purchaser for value in a number of specific situations which have been troublesome under prior law.

On the other hand, the contract of purchase is of course limited by its own terms as in a case of pledge for a limited amount or of sale of a fractional interest in goods.

2. The many particular situations in which a buyer in ordinary course of business from a dealer has been protected against reservation of property or other hidden interest are gathered by subsections (2)–(4) into a single principle protecting persons who buy in ordinary course out of inventory. Consignors have no reason to complain, nor have lenders who hold a security interest in the inventory, since the very purpose of goods in inventory is to be turned into cash by sale.

The principle is extended in subsection (3) to fit with the abolition of the old law of "cash sale" by subsection (1)(c). It is also freed from any technicalities depending on the extended law of larceny; such extension of the concept of theft to include trick, particular types of fraud, and the like is for the purpose of helping conviction of the offender; it has no proper application to the long-standing policy of civil protection of buyers from persons guilty of such trick or fraud. Finally, the policy is extended, in the interest of simplicity and sense, to any entrusting by a bailor; this is in consonance with the explicit provisions of Section 7–205 on the powers of a warehouseman who is also in the business of buying and selling fungible goods of the kind he warehouses. As to entrusting by a secured party, subsection (2) is limited by the more specific provisions of Section 9–320, which deny protection to a person buying farm products from a person engaged in farming operations.

3. The definition of "buyer in ordinary course of business" (Section 1–201) is effective here and preserves the essence of the healthy limitations engrafted by the case-law on the older statutes. The older loose concept of good faith and wide definition of value combined to create apparent good faith purchasers in many situations in which the result outraged common sense; the court's solution was to protect the original title especially by use of "cash sale" or of over-technical construction of the enabling clauses of the statutes. But such rulings then turned into limitations on the proper protection of buyers in the ordinary market. Section 1–201(9) cuts down the category of buyer in ordinary course in such fashion as to take care of the results of the cases, but with no price either in confusion or in injustice to proper dealings in the normal market.

4. Except as provided in subsection (1), the rights of purchasers other than buyers in ordinary course are left to the Articles on Secured Transactions, Documents of Title, and Bulk Sales.

Cross References:

Point 1: Sections 1–103 and 1–201.
Point 2: Sections 1–201, 2–402, 7–205 and 9–320.
Points 3 and 4: Sections 1–102, 1–201, 2–104, 2–707 and Articles 6, 7 and 9.

Definitional Cross References:

"Buyer in ordinary course of business". Section 1–201.
"Good faith". Sections 1–201 and 2–103.
"Goods". Section 2–105.
"Person". Section 1–201.
"Purchaser". Section 1–201.
"Signed". Section 1–201.
"Term". Section 1–201.
"Value". Section 1–201.

PART 5

PERFORMANCE

§ 2–501. Insurable Interest in Goods; Manner of Identification of Goods.

(1) The buyer obtains a special property and an insurable interest in goods by identification of existing goods as goods to which the contract refers even though the goods so identified are non-conforming and he has an option to return or reject them. Such identification can be made at any time and in any manner explicitly agreed to by the parties. In the absence of explicit agreement identification occurs

(a) when the contract is made if it is for the sale of goods already existing and identified;

(b) if the contract is for the sale of future goods other than those described in paragraph (c), when goods are shipped, marked or otherwise designated by the seller as goods to which the contract refers;

(c) when the crops are planted or otherwise become growing crops or the young are conceived if the contract is for the sale of unborn young to be born within twelve months after contracting or for the sale of crops to be harvested within twelve months or the next normal harvest season after contracting whichever is longer.

(2) The seller retains an insurable interest in goods so long as title to or any security interest in the goods remains in him and where the identification is by the seller alone he may until default or insolvency or notification to the buyer that the identification is final substitute other goods for those identified.

(3) Nothing in this section impairs any insurable interest recognized under any other statute or rule of law.

Official Comment

Prior Uniform Statutory Provision: See Sections 17 and 19, Uniform Sales Act.

Purposes:

1. The present section deals with the manner of identifying goods to the contract so that an insurable interest in the buyer and the rights set forth in the next section will accrue. Generally speaking, identification may be made in any manner "explicitly agreed to" by the parties. The rules of paragraphs (a), (b) and (c) apply only in the absence of such "explicit agreement".

2. In the ordinary case identification of particular existing goods as goods to which the contract refers is unambiguous and may occur in one of many ways. It is possible, however, for the identification to be tentative or contingent. In view of the limited effect given to identification by this Article, the general policy is to resolve all doubts in favor of identification.

3. The provision of this section as to "explicit agreement" clarifies the present confusion in the law of sales which has arisen from the fact that under prior uniform legislation all rules of presumption with reference to the passing of title or to appropriation (which in turn depended upon identification) were regarded as subject to the contrary intention of the parties or of the party appropriating. Such uncertainty is reduced to a minimum under this section by requiring "explicit agreement" of the parties before the rules of paragraphs (a), (b) and (c) are displaced—as they would be by a term giving the buyer power to select the goods. An "explicit" agreement, however, need not necessarily be found in the terms used in the particular transaction. Thus, where a usage of the trade has previously been made explicit by reduction to a standard set of "rules and regulations" currently incorporated by reference into the contracts of the parties, a relevant provision of those "rules and regulations" is "explicit" within the meaning of this section.

4. In view of the limited function of identification there is no requirement in this section that the goods be in deliverable state or that all of the seller's duties with respect to the processing of the goods be completed in order that identification occur. For example, despite identification the risk of loss remains on the seller under the risk of loss provisions until completion of his duties as to the goods and all of his remedies remain dependent upon his not defaulting under the contract.

5. Undivided shares in an identified fungible bulk, such as grain in an elevator or oil in a storage tank, can be sold. The mere making of the contract with reference to an undivided share in an identified fungible bulk is enough under subsection (a) to effect an

identification if there is no explicit agreement otherwise. The seller's duty, however, to segregate and deliver according to the contract is not affected by such an identification but is controlled by other provisions of this Article.

6. Identification of crops under paragraph (c) is made upon planting only if they are to be harvested within the year or within the next normal harvest season. The phrase "next normal harvest season" fairly includes nursery stock raised for normally quick "harvest," but plainly excludes a "timber" crop to which the concept of a harvest "season" is inapplicable.

Paragraph (c) is also applicable to a crop of wool or the young of animals to be born within twelve months after contracting. The product of a lumbering, mining or fishing operation, though seasonal, is not within the concept of "growing". Identification under a contract for all or part of the output of such an operation can be effected early in the operation.

Cross References:

Point 1: Section 2–502.
Point 4: Sections 2–509, 2–510 and 2–703.
Point 5: Sections 2–105, 2–308, 2–503 and 2–509.
Point 6: Sections 2–105(1), 2–107(1) and 2–402.

Definitional Cross References:

"Agreement". Section 1–201.
"Contract". Section 1–201.
"Contract for sale". Section 2–106.
"Future goods". Section 2–105.
"Goods". Section 2–105.
"Notification". Section 1–201.
"Party". Section 1–201.
"Sale". Section 2–106.
"Security interest". Section 1–201.
"Seller". Section 2–103.

§ 2–502. Buyer's Right to Goods on Seller's Insolvency.

(1) Subject to subsections (2) and (3) and even though the goods have not been shipped a buyer who has paid a part or all of the price of goods in which he has a special property under the provisions of the immediately preceding section may on making and keeping good a tender of any unpaid portion of their price recover them from the seller if:

(a) in the case of goods bought for personal, family, or household purposes, the seller repudiates or fails to deliver as required by the contract; or

(b) in all cases, the seller becomes insolvent within ten days after receipt of the first installment on their price.

(2) The buyer's right to recover the goods under subsection (1)(a) vests upon acquisition of a special property, even if the seller had not then repudiated or failed to deliver.

(3) If the identification creating his special property has been made by the buyer he acquires the right to recover the goods only if they conform to the contract for sale.

As amended in 1999.

Official Comment

Prior Uniform Statutory Provision: Compare Sections 17, 18 and 19, Uniform Sales Act.

Purposes:

1. This section gives an additional right to the buyer as a result of identification of the goods to the contract in the manner provided in Section 2–501. The buyer is given a right to recover the goods, conditioned upon making and keeping good a tender of any unpaid portion of the price, in two limited circumstances. First, the buyer may recover goods bought for personal, family, or household purposes if the seller repudiates the contract or fails to deliver the goods. Second, in any case, the buyer may recover the goods if the seller becomes insolvent within 10 days after the seller receives the first installment on their price. The buyer's right to recover the goods under this section is an exception to the usual rule, under which the disappointed buyer must resort to an action to recover damages.

2. The question of whether the buyer also acquires a security interest in identified goods and has rights to the goods when insolvency takes place after the ten-day period provided in this section depends upon compliance with the provisions of the Article on Secured Transactions (Article 9).

3. Under subsection (2), the buyer's right to recover consumer goods under subsection (1)(a) vests upon acquisition of a special property, which occurs upon identification of the goods to the contract. See Section 2–501. Inasmuch as a secured party normally acquires no greater rights in its collateral that its debtor had or had power to convey, see Section 2–403(1) (first sentence), a buyer who acquires a right to recover under this section will take free of a security interest created by the seller if it attaches to the goods after the goods have been identified to the contract. The buyer will

take free, even if the buyer does not buy in ordinary course and even if the security interest is perfected. Of course, to the extent that the buyer pays the price after the security interest attaches, the payments will constitute proceeds of the security interest.

4. Subsection (3) is included to preclude the possibility of unjust enrichment, which would exist if the buyer were permitted to recover goods even though they were greatly superior in quality or quantity to that called for by the contract for sale.

Cross References:

Point 1: Sections 1–201 and 2–702.
Point 2: Article 9.

Definitional Cross References:

"Buyer". Section 2–103.
"Conform". Section 2–106.
"Contract for sale". Section 2–106.
"Goods". Section 2–105.
"Insolvent". Section 1–201.
"Rights". Section 1–201.
"Seller". Section 2–103.

As amended in 1999.

§ 2–503. Manner of Seller's Tender of Delivery.

(1) Tender of delivery requires that the seller put and hold conforming goods at the buyer's disposition and give the buyer any notification reasonably necessary to enable him to take delivery. The manner, time and place for tender are determined by the agreement and this Article, and in particular

(a) tender must be at a reasonable hour, and if it is of goods they must be kept available for the period reasonably necessary to enable the buyer to take possession; but

(b) unless otherwise agreed the buyer must furnish facilities reasonably suited to the receipt of the goods.

(2) Where the case is within the next section respecting shipment tender requires that the seller comply with its provisions.

(3) Where the seller is required to deliver at a particular destination tender requires that he comply with subsection (1) and also in any appropriate case tender documents as described in subsections (4) and (5) of this section.

(4) Where goods are in the possession of a bailee and are to be delivered without being moved

(a) tender requires that the seller either tender a negotiable document of title covering such goods or procure acknowledgment by the bailee of the buyer's right to possession of the goods; but

(b) tender to the buyer of a non-negotiable document of title or of a written direction to the bailee to deliver is sufficient tender unless the buyer seasonably objects, and receipt by the bailee of notification of the buyer's rights fixes those rights as against the bailee and all third persons; but risk of loss of the goods and of any failure by the bailee to honor the non-negotiable document of title or to obey the direction remains on the seller until the buyer has had a reasonable time to present the document or direction, and a refusal by the bailee to honor the document or to obey the direction defeats the tender.

(5) Where the contract requires the seller to deliver documents

(a) he must tender all such documents in correct form, except as provided in this Article with respect to bills of lading in a set (subsection (2) of Section 2–323); and

(b) tender through customary banking channels is sufficient and dishonor of a draft accompanying the documents constitutes non-acceptance or rejection.

Official Comment

Prior Uniform Statutory Provision: See Sections 11, 19, 20, 43(3) and (4), 46 and 51, Uniform Sales Act.

Changes: The general policy of the above sections is continued and supplemented but subsection (3) changes the rule of prior section 19(5) as to what constitutes a "destination" contract and subsection (4) incorporates a minor correction as to tender of delivery of goods in the possession of a bailee.

Purposes of Changes:

1. The major general rules governing the manner of proper or due tender of delivery are gathered in this section. The term "tender" is used in this Article in two different senses. In one sense it refers to "due tender" which contemplates an offer coupled with a present ability to fulfill all the conditions resting on

the tendering party and must be followed by actual performance if the other party shows himself ready to proceed. Unless the context unmistakably indicates otherwise this is the meaning of "tender" in this Article and the occasional addition of the word "due" is only for clarity and emphasis. At other times it is used to refer to an offer of goods or documents under a contract as if in fulfillment of its conditions even though there is a defect when measured against the contract obligation. Used in either sense, however, "tender" connotes such performance by the tendering party as puts the other party in default if he fails to proceed in some manner.

2. The seller's general duty to tender and deliver is laid down in Section 2–301 and more particularly in Section 2–507. The seller's right to a receipt if he demands one and receipts are customary is governed by Section 1–205. Subsection (1) of the present section proceeds to set forth two primary requirements of tender: first, that the seller "put and hold conforming goods at the buyer's disposition" and, second, that he "give the buyer any notice reasonably necessary to enable him to take delivery."

In cases in which payment is due and demanded upon delivery the "buyer's disposition" is qualified by the seller's right to retain control of the goods until payment by the provision of this Article on delivery on condition. However, where the seller is demanding payment on delivery he must first allow the buyer to inspect the goods in order to avoid impairing his tender unless the contract for sale is on C.I.F., C.O.D., cash against documents or similar terms negating the privilege of inspection before payment.

In the case of contracts involving documents the seller can "put and hold conforming goods at the buyer's disposition" under subsection (1) by tendering documents which give the buyer complete control of the goods under the provisions of Article 7 on due negotiation.

3. Under paragraph (a) of subsection (1) usage of the trade and the circumstances of the particular case determine what is a reasonable hour for tender and what constitutes a reasonable period of holding the goods available.

4. The buyer must furnish reasonable facilities for the receipt of the goods tendered by the seller under subsection (1), paragraph (b). This obligation of the buyer is no part of the seller's tender.

5. For the purposes of subsections (2) and (3) there is omitted from this Article the rule under prior uniform legislation that a term requiring the seller to pay the freight or cost of transportation to the buyer is equivalent to an agreement by the seller to deliver to the buyer or at an agreed destination. This omission is with the specific intention of negating the rule, for under this Article the "shipment" contract is regarded as the normal one and the "destination" contract as the variant type. The seller is not obligated to deliver at a named destination and bear the concurrent risk of loss until arrival, unless he has specifically agreed so to deliver or the commercial understanding of the terms used by the parties contemplates such delivery.

6. Paragraph (a) of subsection (4) continues the rule of the prior uniform legislation as to acknowledgment by the bailee. Paragraph (b) of subsection (4) adopts the rule that between the buyer and the seller the risk of loss remains on the seller during a period reasonable for securing acknowledgment of the transfer from the bailee, while as against all other parties the buyer's rights are fixed as of the time the bailee receives notice of the transfer.

7. Under subsection (5) documents are never "required" except where there is an express contract term or it is plainly implicit in the peculiar circumstances of the case or in a usage of trade. Documents may, of course, be "authorized" although not required, but such cases are not within the scope of this subsection. When documents are required, there are three main requirements of this subsection: (1) "All": each required document is essential to a proper tender; (2) "Such": the documents must be the ones actually required by the contract in terms of source and substance; (3) "Correct form": All documents must be in correct form.

When a prescribed document cannot be procured, a question of fact arises under the provision of this Article on substituted performance as to whether the agreed manner of delivery is actually commercially impracticable and whether the substitute is commercially reasonable.

Cross References:

Point 2: Sections 1–205, 2–301, 2–310, 2–507 and 2–513 and Article 7.
Point 5: Sections 2–308, 2–310 and 2–509.
Point 7: Section 2–614(1).
Specific matters involving tender are covered in many additional sections of this Article. See Sections 1–205, 2–301, 2–306 to 2–319, 2–321(3), 2–504, 2–507(2), 2–511(1), 2–513, 2–612 and 2–614.

Definitional Cross References:

"Agreement". Section 1–201.
"Bill of lading". Section 1–201.

"Buyer". Section 2–103.
"Conforming". Section 2–106.
"Contract". Section 1–201.
"Delivery". Section 1–201.
"Dishonor". Section 3–508.
"Document of title". Section 1–201.
"Draft". Section 3–104.
"Goods". Section 2–105.
"Notification". Section 1–201.
"Reasonable time". Section 1–204.
"Receipt" of goods. Section 2–103.
"Rights". Section 1–201.
"Seasonably". Section 1–204.
"Seller". Section 2–103.
"Written". Section 1–201.

§ 2–504. Shipment by Seller.

Where the seller is required or authorized to send the goods to the buyer and the contract does not require him to deliver them at a particular destination, then unless otherwise agreed he must

(a) put the goods in the possession of such a carrier and make such a contract for their transportation as may be reasonable having regard to the nature of the goods and other circumstances of the case; and

(b) obtain and promptly deliver or tender in due form any document necessary to enable the buyer to obtain possession of the goods or otherwise required by the agreement or by usage of trade; and

(c) promptly notify the buyer of the shipment.

Failure to notify the buyer under paragraph (c) or to make a proper contract under paragraph (a) is a ground for rejection only if material delay or loss ensues.

Official Comment

Prior Uniform Statutory Provision: Section 46, Uniform Sales Act.

Changes: Rewritten.

Purposes of Changes: To continue the general policy of the prior uniform statutory provision while incorporating certain modifications with respect to the requirement that the contract with the carrier be made expressly on behalf of the buyer and as to the necessity of giving notice of the shipment to the buyer, so that:

1. The section is limited to "shipment" contracts as contrasted with "destination" contracts or contracts for delivery at the place where the goods are located.

The general principles embodied in this section cover the special cases of F.O.B. point of shipment contracts and C.I.F. and C. & F. contracts. Under the preceding section on manner of tender of delivery, due tender by the seller requires that he comply with the requirements of this section in appropriate cases.

2. The contract to be made with the carrier under paragraph (a) must conform to all express terms of the agreement, subject to any substitution necessary because of failure of agreed facilities as provided in the later provision on substituted performance. However, under the policies of this Article on good faith and commercial standards and on buyer's rights on improper delivery, the requirements of explicit provisions must be read in terms of their commercial and not their literal meaning. This policy is made express with respect to bills of lading in a set in the provision of this Article on form of bills of lading required in overseas shipment.

3. In the absence of agreement, the provision of this Article on options and cooperation respecting performance gives the seller the choice of any reasonable carrier, routing and other arrangements. Whether or not the shipment is at the buyer's expense the seller must see to any arrangements, reasonable in the circumstances, such as refrigeration, watering of live stock, protection against cold, the sending along of any necessary help, selection of specialized cars and the like for paragraph (a) is intended to cover all necessary arrangements whether made by contract with the carrier or otherwise. There is, however, a proper relaxation of such requirements if the buyer is himself in a position to make the appropriate arrangements and the seller gives him reasonable notice of the need to do so. It is an improper contract under paragraph (a) for the seller to agree with the carrier to a limited valuation below the true value and thus cut off the buyer's opportunity to recover from the carrier in the event of loss, when the risk of shipment is placed on the buyer by his contract with the seller.

4. Both the language of paragraph (b) and the nature of the situation it concerns indicate that the requirement that the seller must obtain and deliver promptly to the buyer in due form any document necessary to enable him to obtain possession of the goods is intended to cumulate with the other duties of the seller such as those covered in paragraph (a).

In this connection, in the case of pool car shipments a delivery order furnished by the seller on the pool car consignee, or on the carrier for delivery out of a larger quantity, satisfies the requirements of paragraph (b) unless the contract requires some other form of document.

5. This Article, unlike the prior uniform statutory provision, makes it the seller's duty to notify the buyer of shipment in all cases. The consequences of his failure to do so, however, are limited in that the buyer may reject on this ground only where material delay or loss ensues.

A standard and acceptable manner of notification in open credit shipments is the sending of an invoice and in the case of documentary contracts is the prompt forwarding of the documents as under paragraph (b) of this section. It is also usual to send on a straight bill of lading but this is not necessary to the required notification. However, should such a document prove necessary or convenient to the buyer, as in the case of loss and claim against the carrier, good faith would require the seller to send it on request.

Frequently the agreement expressly requires prompt notification as by wire or cable. Such a term may be of the essence and the final clause of paragraph (c) does not prevent the parties from making this a particular ground for rejection. To have this vital and irreparable effect upon the seller's duties, such a term should be part of the "dickered" terms written in any "form," or should otherwise be called seasonably and sharply to the seller's attention.

6. Generally, under the final sentence of the section, rejection by the buyer is justified only when the seller's dereliction as to any of the requirements of this section in fact is followed by material delay or damage. It rests on the seller, so far as concerns matters not within the peculiar knowledge of the buyer, to establish that his error has not been followed by events which justify rejection.

Cross References:

Point 1: Sections 2–319, 2–320 and 2–503(2).
Point 2: Sections 1–203, 2–323(2), 2–601 and 2–614(1).
Point 3: Section 2–311(2).
Point 5: Section 1–203.

Definitional Cross References:

"Agreement". Section 1–201.
"Buyer". Section 2–103.
"Contract". Section 1–201.
"Delivery". Section 1–201.
"Goods". Section 2–105.
"Notifies". Section 1–201.
"Seller". Section 2–103.
"Send". Section 1–201.
"Usage of trade". Section 1–205.

§ 2–505. Seller's Shipment Under Reservation.

(1) Where the seller has identified goods to the contract by or before shipment:

(a) his procurement of a negotiable bill of lading to his own order or otherwise reserves in him a security interest in the goods. His procurement of the bill to the order of a financing agency or of the buyer indicates in addition only the seller's expectation of transferring that interest to the person named.

(b) a non-negotiable bill of lading to himself or his nominee reserves possession of the goods as security but except in a case of conditional delivery (subsection (2) of Section 2–507) a non-negotiable bill of lading naming the buyer as consignee reserves no security interest even though the seller retains possession of the bill of lading.

(2) When shipment by the seller with reservation of a security interest is in violation of the contract for sale it constitutes an improper contract for transportation within the preceding section but impairs neither the rights given to the buyer by shipment and identification of the goods to the contract nor the seller's powers as a holder of a negotiable document.

Official Comment

Prior Uniform Statutory Provision: Section 20(2), (3), (4), Uniform Sales Act.

Changes: Completely rephrased, the "powers" of the parties in cases of reservation being emphasized primarily rather than the "rightfulness" of reservation.

Purposes of Changes: To continue in general the policy of the prior uniform statutory provision with certain modifications of emphasis and language, so that:

1. The security interest reserved to the seller under subsection (1) is restricted to securing payment or performance by the buyer and the seller is strictly limited in his disposition and control of the goods as against the buyer and third parties. Under this Article, the provision as to the passing of interest expressly applies "despite any reservation of security title" and also provides that the "rights, obligations and remedies" of the parties are not altered by the incidence of

title generally. The security interest, therefore, must be regarded as a means given to the seller to enforce his rights against the buyer which is unaffected by and in turn does not affect the location of title generally. The rules set forth in subsection (1) are not to be altered by any apparent "contrary intent" of the parties as to passing of title, since the rights and remedies of the parties to the contract of sale, as defined in this Article, rest on the contract and its performance or breach and not on stereotyped presumptions as to the location of title.

This Article does not attempt to regulate local procedure in regard to the effective maintenance of the seller's security interest when the action is in replevin by the buyer against the carrier.

2. Every shipment of identified goods under a negotiable bill of lading reserves a security interest in the seller under subsection (1) paragraph (a).

It is frequently convenient for the seller to make the bill of lading to the order of a nominee such as his agent at destination, the financing agency to which he expects to negotiate the document or the bank issuing a credit to him. In many instances, also, the buyer is made the order party. This Article does not deal directly with the question as to whether a bill of lading made out by the seller to the order of a nominee gives the carrier notice of any rights which the nominee may have so as to limit its freedom or obligation to honor the bill of lading in the hands of the seller as the original shipper if the expected negotiation fails. This is dealt with in the Article on Documents of Title (Article 7).

3. A non-negotiable bill of lading taken to a party other than the buyer under subsection (1) paragraph (b) reserves possession of the goods as security in the seller but if he seeks to withhold the goods improperly the buyer can tender payment and recover them.

4. In the case of a shipment by non-negotiable bill of lading taken to a buyer, the seller, under subsection (1) retains no security interest or possession as against the buyer and by the shipment he *de facto* loses control as against the carrier except where he rightfully and effectively stops delivery in transit. In cases in which the contract gives the seller the right to payment against delivery, the seller, by making an immediate demand for payment, can show that his delivery is conditional, but this does not prevent the buyer's power to transfer full title to a sub-buyer in ordinary course or other purchaser under Section 2–403.

5. Under subsection (2) an improper reservation by the seller which would constitute a breach in no way impairs such of the buyer's rights as result from identification of the goods. The security title reserved by the seller under subsection (1) does not protect his holding of the document or the goods for the purpose of exacting more than is due him under the contract.

Cross References:

Point 1: Section 1–201.
Point 2: Article 7.
Point 3: Sections 2–501(2) and 2–504.
Point 4: Sections 2–403, 2–507(2) and 2–705.
Point 5: Sections 2–310, 2–319(4), 2–320(4), 2–501 and 2–502 and Article 7.

Definitional Cross References:

"Bill of lading". Section 1–201.
"Buyer". Section 2–103.
"Consignee". Section 7–102.
"Contract". Section 1–201.
"Contract for sale". Section 2–106.
"Delivery". Section 1–201.
"Financing agency". Section 2–104.
"Goods". Section 2–105.
"Holder". Section 1–201.
"Person". Section 1–201.
"Security interest". Section 1–201.
"Seller". Section 2–103.

§ 2–506. Rights of Financing Agency.

(1) A financing agency by paying or purchasing for value a draft which relates to a shipment of goods acquires to the extent of the payment or purchase and in addition to its own rights under the draft and any document of title securing it any rights of the shipper in the goods including the right to stop delivery and the shipper's right to have the draft honored by the buyer.

(2) The right to reimbursement of a financing agency which has in good faith honored or purchased the draft under commitment to or authority from the buyer is not impaired by subsequent discovery of defects with reference to any relevant document which was apparently regular on its face.

Official Comment

Prior Uniform Statutory Provision: None.

Purposes:

1. "Financing agency" is broadly defined in this Article to cover every normal instance in which a party aids or intervenes in the financing of a sales transaction. The term as used in subsection (1) is not in any

sense intended as a limitation and covers any other appropriate situation which may arise outside the scope of the definition.

2. "Paying" as used in subsection (1) is typified by the letter of credit, or "authority to pay" situation in which a banker, by arrangement with the buyer or other consignee, pays on his behalf a draft for the price of the goods. It is immaterial whether the draft is formally drawn on the party paying or his principal, whether it is a sight draft paid in cash or a time draft "paid" in the first instance by acceptance, or whether the payment is viewed as absolute or conditional. All of these cases constitute "payment" under this subsection. Similarly, "purchasing for value" is used to indicate the whole area of financing by the seller's banker, and the principle of subsection (1) is applicable without any niceties of distinction between "purchase," "discount," "advance against collection" or the like. But it is important to notice that the only right to have the draft honored that is acquired is that *against the buyer*; if any right against any one else is claimed it will have to be under some separate obligation of that other person. A letter of credit does not necessarily protect *purchasers* of drafts. See Article 5. And for the relations of the parties to documentary drafts see Part 5 of Article 4.

3. Subsection (1) is made applicable to payments or advances against a draft which "relates to" a shipment of goods and this has been chosen as a term of maximum breadth. In particular the term is intended to cover the case of a draft against an invoice or against a delivery order. Further, it is unnecessary that there be an explicit assignment of the invoice attached to the draft to bring the transaction within the reason of this subsection.

4. After shipment, "the rights of the shipper in the goods" are merely security rights and are subject to the buyer's right to force delivery upon tender of the price. The rights acquired by the financing agency are similarly limited and, moreover, if the agency fails to procure any outstanding negotiable document of title, it may find its exercise of these rights hampered or even defeated by the seller's disposition of the document to a third party. This section does not attempt to create any new rights in the financing agency against the carrier which would force the latter to honor a stop order from the agency, a stranger to the shipment, or any new rights against a holder to whom a document of title has been duly negotiated under Article 7.

Cross References:

Point 1: Section 2-104(2) and Article 4.

Point 2: Part 5 of Article 4, and Article 5.

Point 4: Sections 2-501 and 2-502(1) and Article 7.

Definitional Cross References:

"Buyer". Section 2-103.

"Document of title". Section 1-201.

"Draft". Section 3-104.

"Financing agency". Section 2-104.

"Good faith". Section 2-103.

"Goods". Section 2-105.

"Honor". Section 1-201.

"Purchase". Section 1-201.

"Rights". Section 1-201.

"Value". Section 1-201.

§ 2-507. Effect of Seller's Tender; Delivery on Condition.

(1) Tender of delivery is a condition to the buyer's duty to accept the goods and, unless otherwise agreed, to his duty to pay for them. Tender entitles the seller to acceptance of the goods and to payment according to the contract.

(2) Where payment is due and demanded on the delivery to the buyer of goods or documents of title, his right as against the seller to retain or dispose of them is conditional upon his making the payment due.

Official Comment

Prior Uniform Statutory Provision: See Sections 11, 41, 42 and 69, Uniform Sales Act.

Purposes:

1. Subsection (1) continues the policies of the prior uniform statutory provisions with respect to tender and delivery by the seller. Under this Article the same rules in these matters are applied to present sales and to contracts for sale. But the provisions of this subsection must be read within the framework of the other sections of this Article which bear upon the question of delivery and payment.

2. The "unless otherwise agreed" provision of subsection (1) is directed primarily to cases in which payment in advance has been promised or a letter of credit term has been included. Payment "according to the contract" contemplates immediate payment, payment at the end of an agreed credit term, payment by a time acceptance or the like. Under this Act, "contract" means the total obligation in law which results from the parties' agreement including the effect of this Article. In this context, therefore, there must be considered the effect in law of such provisions as those on

means and manner of payment and on failure of agreed means and manner of payment.

3. Subsection (2) deals with the effect of a conditional delivery by the seller and in such a situation makes the buyer's "right as against the seller" conditional upon payment. These words are used as words of limitation to conform with the policy set forth in the bona fide purchase sections of this Article. Should the seller after making such a conditional delivery fail to follow up his rights, the condition is waived. This subsection (2) codifies the cash seller's right of reclamation which is in the nature of a lien. There is no specific time limit for a cash seller to exercise the right of reclamation. However, the right will be defeated by delay causing prejudice to the buyer, waiver, estoppel, or ratification of the buyer's right to retain possession. Common law rules and precedents governing such principles are applicable (Section 1–103). If third parties are involved, Section 2–403(1) protects good faith purchasers. See PEB Commentary No. 1, dated March 10, 1990 [Appendix V, infra].

Cross References:

Point 1: Sections 2–310, 2–503, 2–511, 2–601 and 2–711 to 2–713.
Point 2: Sections 1–201, 2–511 and 2–614.
Point 3: Sections 2–401, 2–403, and 2–702(1)(b).

Definitional Cross References:

"Buyer". Section 2–103.
"Contract". Section 1–201.
"Delivery". Section 1–201.
"Document of title". Section 1–201.
"Goods". Section 2–105.
"Rights". Section 1–201.
"Seller". Section 2–103.

§ 2–508. Cure by Seller of Improper Tender or Delivery; Replacement.

(1) Where any tender or delivery by the seller is rejected because non-conforming and the time for performance has not yet expired, the seller may seasonably notify the buyer of his intention to cure and may then within the contract time make a conforming delivery.

(2) Where the buyer rejects a non-conforming tender which the seller had reasonable grounds to believe would be acceptable with or without money allowance the seller may if he seasonably notifies the buyer have a further reasonable time to substitute a conforming tender.

Official Comment

Prior Uniform Statutory Provision: None.

Purposes:

1. Subsection (1) permits a seller who has made a non-conforming tender in any case to make a conforming delivery within the contract time upon seasonable notification to the buyer. It applies even where the seller has taken back the non-conforming goods and refunded the purchase price. He may still make a good tender within the contract period. The closer, however, it is to the contract date, the greater is the necessity for extreme promptness on the seller's part in notifying of his intention to cure, if such notification is to be "seasonable" under this subsection.

The rule of this subsection, moreover, is qualified by its underlying reasons. Thus if, after contracting for June delivery, a buyer later makes known to the seller his need for shipment early in the month and the seller ships accordingly, the "contract time" has been cut down by the supervening modification and the time for cure of tender must be referred to this modified time term.

2. Subsection (2) seeks to avoid injustice to the seller by reason of a surprise rejection by the buyer. However, the seller is not protected unless he had "reasonable grounds to believe" that the tender would be acceptable. Such reasonable grounds can lie in prior course of dealing, course of performance or usage of trade as well as in the particular circumstances surrounding the making of the contract. The seller is charged with commercial knowledge of any factors in a particular sales situation which require him to comply strictly with his obligations under the contract as, for example, strict conformity of documents in an overseas shipment or the sale of precision parts or chemicals for use in manufacture. Further, if the buyer gives notice either implicitly, as by a prior course of dealing involving rigorous inspections, or expressly, as by the deliberate inclusion of a "no replacement" clause in the contract, the seller is to be held to rigid compliance. If the clause appears in a "form" contract evidence that it is out of line with trade usage or the prior course of dealing and was not called to the seller's attention may be sufficient to show that the seller had reasonable grounds to believe that the tender would be acceptable.

3. The words "a further reasonable time to substitute a conforming tender" are intended as words of limitation to protect the buyer. What is a "reasonable time" depends upon the attending circumstances. Compare Section 2–511 on the comparable case of a seller's surprise demand for legal tender.

4. Existing trade usages permitting variations without rejection but with price allowance enter into the agreement itself as contractual limitations of remedy and are not covered by this section.

Cross References:

Point 2: Section 2–302.
Point 3: Section 2–511.
Point 4: Sections 1–205 and 2–721.

Definitional Cross References:

"Buyer". Section 2–103.
"Conforming". Section 2–106.
"Contract". Section 1–201.
"Money". Section 1–201.
"Notifies". Section 1–201.
"Reasonable time". Section 1–204.
"Seasonably". Section 1–204.
"Seller". Section 2–103.

§ 2–509. Risk of Loss in the Absence of Breach.

(1) Where the contract requires or authorizes the seller to ship the goods by carrier

(a) if it does not require him to deliver them at a particular destination, the risk of loss passes to the buyer when the goods are duly delivered to the carrier even though the shipment is under reservation (Section 2–505); but

(b) if it does require him to deliver them at a particular destination and the goods are there duly tendered while in the possession of the carrier, the risk of loss passes to the buyer when the goods are there duly so tendered as to enable the buyer to take delivery.

(2) Where the goods are held by a bailee to be delivered without being moved, the risk of loss passes to the buyer

(a) on his receipt of a negotiable document of title covering the goods; or

(b) on acknowledgment by the bailee of the buyer's right to possession of the goods; or

(c) after his receipt of a non-negotiable document of title or other written direction to deliver, as provided in subsection (4)(b) of Section 2–503.

(3) In any case not within subsection (1) or (2), the risk of loss passes to the buyer on his receipt of the goods if the seller is a merchant; other-wise the risk passes to the buyer on tender of delivery.

(4) The provisions of this section are subject to contrary agreement of the parties and to the provisions of this Article on sale on approval (Section 2–327) and on effect of breach on risk of loss (Section 2–510).

Official Comment

Prior Uniform Statutory Provision: Section 22, Uniform Sales Act.

Changes: Rewritten, subsection (3) of this section modifying prior law.

Purposes of Changes: To make it clear that:

1. The underlying theory of these sections on risk of loss is the adoption of the contractual approach rather than an arbitrary shifting of the risk with the "property" in the goods. The scope of the present section, therefore, is limited strictly to those cases where there has been no breach by the seller. Where for any reason his delivery or tender fails to conform to the contract, the present section does not apply and the situation is governed by the provisions on effect of breach on risk of loss.

2. The provisions of subsection (1) apply where the contract "requires or authorizes" shipment of the goods. This language is intended to be construed parallel to comparable language in the section on shipment by seller. In order that the goods be "duly delivered to the carrier" under paragraph (a) a contract must be entered into with the carrier which will satisfy the requirements of the section on shipment by the seller and the delivery must be made under circumstances which will enable the seller to take any further steps necessary to a due tender. The underlying reason of this subsection does not require that the shipment be made after contracting, but where, for example, the seller buys the goods afloat and later diverts the shipment to the buyer, he must identify the goods to the contract before the risk of loss can pass. To transfer the risk it is enough that a proper shipment and a proper identification come to apply to the same goods although, aside from special agreement, the risk will not pass retroactively to the time of shipment in such a case.

3. Whether the contract involves delivery at the seller's place of business or at the situs of the goods, a merchant seller cannot transfer risk of loss and it remains upon him until actual receipt by the buyer, even though full payment has been made and the

buyer has been notified that the goods are at his disposal. Protection is afforded him, in the event of breach by the buyer, under the next section.

The underlying theory of this rule is that a merchant who is to make physical delivery at his own place continues meanwhile to control the goods and can be expected to insure his interest in them. The buyer, on the other hand, has no control of the goods and it is extremely unlikely that he will carry insurance on goods not yet in his possession.

4. Where the agreement provides for delivery of the goods as between the buyer and seller without removal from the physical possession of a bailee, the provisions on manner of tender of delivery apply on the point of transfer of risk. Due delivery of a negotiable document of title covering the goods or acknowledgment by the bailee that he holds for the buyer completes the "delivery" and passes the risk.

5. The provisions of this section are made subject by subsection (4) to the "contrary agreement" of the parties. This language is intended as the equivalent of the phrase "unless otherwise agreed" used more frequently throughout this Act. "Contrary" is in no way used as a word of limitation and the buyer and seller are left free to readjust their rights and risks as declared by this section in any manner agreeable to them. Contrary agreement can also be found in the circumstances of the case, a trade usage or practice, or a course of dealing or performance.

Cross References:

Point 1: Section 2–510(1).
Point 2: Sections 2–503 and 2–504.
Point 3: Sections 2–104, 2–503 and 2–510.
Point 4: Section 2–503(4).
Point 5: Section 1–201.

Definitional Cross References:

"Agreement". Section 1–201.
"Buyer". Section 2–103.
"Contract". Section 1–201.
"Delivery". Section 1–201.
"Document of title". Section 1–201.
"Goods". Section 2–105.
"Merchant". Section 2–104.
"Party". Section 1–201.
"Receipt" of goods. Section 2–103.
"Sale on approval". Section 2–326.
"Seller". Section 2–103.

§ 2–510. Effect of Breach on Risk of Loss.

(1) Where a tender or delivery of goods so fails to conform to the contract as to give a right of rejection the risk of their loss remains on the seller until cure or acceptance.

(2) Where the buyer rightfully revokes acceptance he may to the extent of any deficiency in his effective insurance coverage treat the risk of loss as having rested on the seller from the beginning.

(3) Where the buyer as to conforming goods already identified to the contract for sale repudiates or is otherwise in breach before risk of their loss has passed to him, the seller may to the extent of any deficiency in his effective insurance coverage treat the risk of loss as resting on the buyer for a commercially reasonable time.

Official Comment

Prior Uniform Statutory Provision: None.

Purposes: To make clear that:

1. Under subsection (1) the seller by his individual action cannot shift the risk of loss to the buyer unless his action conforms with all the conditions resting on him under the contract.

2. The "cure" of defective tenders contemplated by subsection (1) applies only to those situations in which the seller makes changes in goods already tendered, such as repair, partial substitution, sorting out from an improper mixture and the like since "cure" by repossession and new tender has no effect on the risk of loss of the goods originally tendered. The seller's privilege of cure does not shift the risk, however, until the cure is completed.

Where defective documents are involved a cure of the defect by the seller or a waiver of the defects by the buyer will operate to shift the risk under this section. However, if the goods have been destroyed prior to the cure or the buyer is unaware of their destruction at the time he waives the defect in the documents, the risk of the loss must still be borne by the seller, for the risk shifts only at the time of cure, waiver of documentary defects or acceptance of the goods.

3. In cases where there has been a breach of the contract, if the one in control of the goods is the aggrieved party, whatever loss or damage may prove to be uncovered by his insurance falls upon the contract breaker under subsections (2) and (3) rather than upon him. The word "effective" as applied to insurance coverage in those subsections is used to meet the case of supervening insolvency of the insurer. The "deficiency" referred to in the text means such deficiency in

the insurance coverage as exists without subrogation. This section merely distributes the risk of loss as stated and is not intended to be disturbed by any subrogation of an insurer.

Cross Reference:

Section 2–509.

Definitional Cross References:

"Buyer". Section 2–103.
"Conform". Section 2–106.
"Contract for sale". Section 2–106.
"Goods". Section 2–105.
"Seller". Section 2–103.

§ 2–511. Tender of Payment by Buyer; Payment by Check.

(1) Unless otherwise agreed tender of payment is a condition to the seller's duty to tender and complete any delivery.

(2) Tender of payment is sufficient when made by any means or in any manner current in the ordinary course of business unless the seller demands payment in legal tender and gives any extension of time reasonably necessary to procure it.

(3) Subject to the provisions of this Act on the effect of an instrument on an obligation (Section 3–310), payment by check is conditional and is defeated as between the parties by dishonor of the check on due presentment.

As amended in 1994.

Official Comment

Prior Uniform Statutory Provision: Section 42, Uniform Sales Act.

Changes: Rewritten by this section and Section 2–507.

Purposes of Changes:

1. The requirement of payment against delivery in subsection (1) is applicable to non-commercial sales generally and to ordinary sales at retail although it has no application to the great body of commercial contracts which carry credit terms. Subsection (1) applies also to documentary contracts in general and to contracts which look to shipment by the seller but contain no term on time and manner of payment, in which situations the payment may, in proper case, be demanded against delivery of appropriate documents.

In the case of specific transactions such as C.O.D. sales or agreements providing for payment against

documents, the provisions of this subsection must be considered in conjunction with the special sections of the Article dealing with such terms. The provision that tender of payment is a condition to the seller's duty to tender and complete "any delivery" integrates this section with the language and policy of the section on delivery in several lots which call for separate payment. Finally, attention should be directed to the provision on right to adequate assurance of performance which recognizes, even before the time for tender, an obligation on the buyer not to impair the seller's expectation of receiving payment in due course.

2. Unless there is agreement otherwise the concurrence of the conditions as to tender of payment and tender of delivery requires their performance at a single place or time. This Article determines that place and time by determining in various other sections the place and time for tender of delivery under various circumstances and in particular types of transactions. The sections dealing with time and place of delivery together with the section on right to inspection of goods answer the subsidiary question as to when payment may be demanded before inspection by the buyer.

3. The essence of the principle involved in subsection (2) is avoidance of commercial surprise at the time of performance. The section on substituted performance covers the peculiar case in which legal tender is not available to the commercial community.

4. Subsection (3) is concerned with the rights and obligations as between the parties to a sales transaction when payment is made by check. This Article recognizes that the taking of a seemingly solvent party's check is commercially normal and proper and, if due diligence is exercised in collection, is not to be penalized in any way. The conditional character of the payment under this section refers only to the effect of the transaction "as between the parties" thereto and does not purport to cut into the law of "absolute" and "conditional" payment as applied to such other problems as the discharge of sureties or the responsibilities of a drawee bank which is at the same time an agent for collection.

The phrase "by check" includes not only the buyer's own but any check which does not effect a discharge under Article 3 (Section 3–802). Similarly the reason of this subsection should apply and the same result should be reached where the buyer "pays" by sight draft on a commercial firm which is financing him.

5. Under subsection (3) payment by check is defeated if it is not honored upon due presentment. This

corresponds to the provisions of article on Commercial Paper. (Section 3–802). But if the seller procures certification of the check instead of cashing it, the buyer is discharged. (Section 3–411).

6. Where the instrument offered by the buyer is not a payment but a credit instrument such as a note or a check post-dated by even one day, the seller's acceptance of the instrument insofar as third parties are concerned, amounts to a delivery on credit and his remedies are set forth in the section on buyer's insolvency. As between the buyer and the seller, however, the matter turns on the present subsection and the section on conditional delivery and subsequent dishonor of the instrument gives the seller rights on it as well as for breach of the contract for sale.

Cross References:

Point 1: Sections 2–307, 2–310, 2–320, 2–325, 2–503, 2–513 and 2–609.
Point 2: Sections 2–307, 2–310, 2–319, 2–322, 2–503, 2–504 and 2–513.
Point 3: Section 2–614.
Point 5: Article 3, esp. Sections 3–802 and 3–411.
Point 6: Sections 2–507, 2–702, and Article 3.

Definitional Cross References:

"Buyer". Section 2–103.
"Check". Section 3–104.
"Dishonor". Section 3–508.
"Party". Section 1–201.
"Reasonable time". Section 1–204.
"Seller". Section 2–103.

§ 2–512. Payment by Buyer Before Inspection.

[1995 Amendments to text indicated by strikeout and underline]

(1) Where the contract requires payment before inspection non-conformity of the goods does not excuse the buyer from so making payment unless

(a) the non-conformity appears without inspection; or

(b) despite tender of the required documents the circumstances would justify injunction against honor under ~~the provisions of~~ this Act (Section ~~5–114~~ 5–109(b)).

(2) Payment pursuant to subsection (1) does not constitute an acceptance of goods or impair the buyer's right to inspect or any of his remedies.

As amended in 1995.

Official Comment

Prior Uniform Statutory Provision: None, but see Sections 47 and 49, Uniform Sales Act.

Purposes:

1. Subsection (1) of the present section recognizes that the essence of a contract providing for payment before inspection is the intention of the parties to shift to the buyer the risks which would usually rest upon the seller. The basic nature of the transaction is thus preserved and the buyer is in most cases required to pay first and litigate as to any defects later.

2. "Inspection" under this section is an inspection in a manner reasonable for detecting defects in goods whose surface appearance is satisfactory.

3. Clause (a) of this subsection states an exception to the general rule based on common sense and normal commercial practice. The apparent non-conformity referred to is one which is evident in the mere process of taking delivery.

4. Clause (b) is concerned with contracts for payment against documents and incorporates the general clarification and modification of the case law contained in the section on excuse of a financing agency. Section 5–109(b).

5. Subsection (2) makes explicit the general policy of the Uniform Sales Act that the payment required before inspection in no way impairs the buyer's remedies or rights in the event of a default by the seller. The remedies preserved to the buyer are all of his remedies, which include as a matter of reason the remedy for total non-delivery after payment in advance.

The provision on performance or acceptance under reservation of rights does not apply to the situations contemplated here in which payment is made in due course under the contract and the buyer need not pay "under protest" or the like in order to preserve his rights as to defects discovered upon inspection.

6. This section applies to cases in which the contract requires payment before inspection either by the express agreement of the parties or by reason of the effect in law of that contract. The present section must therefore be considered in conjunction with the provision on right to inspection of goods which sets forth the instances in which the buyer is not entitled to inspection before payment.

Cross References:

Point 4: Article 5.

Point 5: Section 1–207.

Point 6: Section 2–513(3).

Definitional Cross References:

"Buyer". Section 2–103.

"Conform". Section 2–106.

"Contract". Section 1–201.

"Financing agency". Section 2–104.

"Goods". Section 2–105.

"Remedy". Section 1–201.

"Rights". Section 1–201.

§ 2–513. Buyer's Right to Inspection of Goods.

(1) Unless otherwise agreed and subject to subsection (3), where goods are tendered or delivered or identified to the contract for sale, the buyer has a right before payment or acceptance to inspect them at any reasonable place and time and in any reasonable manner. When the seller is required or authorized to send the goods to the buyer, the inspection may be after their arrival.

(2) Expenses of inspection must be borne by the buyer but may be recovered from the seller if the goods do not conform and are rejected.

(3) Unless otherwise agreed and subject to the provisions of this Article on C.I.F. contracts (subsection (3) of Section 2–321), the buyer is not entitled to inspect the goods before payment of the price when the contract provides

(a) for delivery "C.O.D." or on other like terms; or

(b) for payment against documents of title, except where such payment is due only after the goods are to become available for inspection.

(4) A place or method of inspection fixed by the parties is presumed to be exclusive but unless otherwise expressly agreed it does not postpone identification or shift the place for delivery or for passing the risk of loss. If compliance becomes impossible, inspection shall be as provided in this section unless the place or method fixed was clearly intended as an indispensable condition failure of which avoids the contract.

Official Comment

Prior Uniform Statutory Provisions: Section 47(2), (3), Uniform Sales Act.

Changes: Rewritten, Subsections (2) and (3) being new.

Purposes of Changes and New Matter: To correspond in substance with the prior uniform statutory provision and to incorporate in addition some of the results of the better case law so that:

1. The buyer is entitled to inspect goods as provided in subsection (1) unless it has been otherwise agreed by the parties. The phrase "unless otherwise agreed" is intended principally to cover such situations as those outlined in subsections (3) and (4) and those in which the agreement of the parties negates inspection before tender of delivery. However, no agreement by the parties can displace the entire right of inspection except where the contract is simply for the sale of "this thing." Even in a sale of boxed goods "as is" inspection is a right of the buyer, since if the boxes prove to contain some other merchandise altogether the price can be recovered back; nor do the limitations of the provision on effect of acceptance apply in such a case.

2. The buyer's right of inspection is available to him upon tender, delivery or appropriation of the goods with notice to him. Since inspection is available to him on tender, where payment is due against delivery he may, unless otherwise agreed, make his inspection before payment of the price. It is also available to him after receipt of the goods and so may be postponed after receipt for a reasonable time. Failure to inspect before payment does not impair the right to inspect after receipt of the goods unless the case falls within subsection (4) on agreed and exclusive inspection provisions. The right to inspect goods which have been appropriated with notice to the buyer holds whether or not the sale was by sample.

3. The buyer may exercise his right of inspection at any reasonable time or place and in any reasonable manner. It is not necessary that he select the most appropriate time, place or manner to inspect or that his selection be the customary one in the trade or locality. Any reasonable time, place or manner is available to him and the reasonableness will be determined by trade usages, past practices between the parties and the other circumstances of the case.

The last sentence of subsection (1) makes it clear that the place of arrival of shipped goods is a reasonable place for their inspection.

4. Expenses of an inspection made to satisfy the buyer of the seller's performance must be assumed by the buyer in the first instance. Since the rule provides merely for an allocation of expense there is no policy to prevent the parties from providing otherwise in the agreement. Where the buyer would normally bear the

expenses of the inspection but the goods are rightly rejected because of what the inspection reveals, demonstrable and reasonable costs of the inspection are part of his incidental damage caused by the seller's breach.

5. In the case of payment against documents, subsection (3) requires payment before inspection, since shipping documents against which payment is to be made will commonly arrive and be tendered while the goods are still in transit. This Article recognizes no exception in any peculiar case in which the goods happen to arrive before the documents. However, where by the agreement payment is to await the arrival of the goods, inspection before payment becomes proper since the goods are then "available for inspection."

Where by the agreement the documents are to be held until arrival the buyer is entitled to inspect before payment since the goods are then "available for inspection". Proof of usage is not necessary to establish this right, but if inspection before payment is disputed the contrary must be established by usage or by an explicit contract term to that effect.

For the same reason, that the goods are available for inspection, a term calling for payment against storage documents or a delivery order does not normally bar the buyer's right to inspection before payment under subsection (3)(b). This result is reinforced by the buyer's right under subsection (1) to inspect goods which have been appropriated with notice to him.

6. Under subsection (4) an agreed place or method of inspection is generally held to be intended as exclusive. However, where compliance with such an agreed inspection term becomes impossible, the question is basically one of intention. If the parties clearly intend that the method of inspection named is to be a necessary condition without which the entire deal is to fail, the contract is at an end if that method becomes impossible. On the other hand, if the parties merely seek to indicate a convenient and reliable method but do not intend to give up the deal in the event of its failure, any reasonable method of inspection may be substituted under this Article.

Since the purpose of an agreed place of inspection is only to make sure at that point whether or not the goods will be thrown back, the "exclusive" feature of the named place is satisfied under this Article if the buyer's failure to inspect there is held to be an acceptance with the knowledge of such defects as inspection would have revealed within the section on waiver of buyer's objections by failure to particularize. Revocation of the acceptance is limited to the situations stated in the section pertaining to that subject. The reason-

able time within which to give notice of defects within the section on notice of breach begins to run from the point of the "acceptance."

7. Clauses on time of inspection are commonly clauses which limit the time in which the buyer must inspect and give notice of defects. Such clauses are therefore governed by the section of this Article which requires that such a time limitation must be reasonable.

8. Inspection under this Article is not to be regarded as a "condition precedent to the passing of title" so that risk until inspection remains on the seller. Under subsection (4) such an approach cannot be sustained. Issues between the buyer and seller are settled in this Article almost wholly by special provisions and not by the technical determination of the locus of the title. Thus "inspection as a condition to the passing of title" becomes a concept almost without meaning. However, in peculiar circumstances inspection may still have some of the consequences hitherto sought and obtained under that concept.

9. "Inspection" under this section has to do with the buyer's check-up on whether the seller's performance is in accordance with a contract previously made and is not to be confused with the "examination" of the goods or of a sample or model of them at the time of contracting which may affect the warranties involved in the contract.

Cross References:

Generally: Sections 2–310(b), 2–321(3) and 2–606(1)(b).
    Point 1: Section 2–607.
    Point 2: Sections 2–501 and 2–502.
    Point 4: Section 2–715.
    Point 5: Section 2–321(3).
    Point 6: Sections 2–606 to 2–608.
    Point 7: Section 1–204.
    Point 8: Comment to Section 2–401.
    Point 9: Section 2–316(3)(b).

Definitional Cross References:

"Buyer". Section 2–103.
"Conform". Section 2–106.
"Contract". Section 1–201.
"Contract for sale". Section 2–106.
"Document of title". Section 1–201.
"Goods". Section 2–105.
"Party". Section 1–201.
"Presumed". Section 1–201.
"Reasonable time". Section 1–204.
"Rights". Section 1–201.
"Seller". Section 2–103.

"Send". Section 1-201.
"Term". Section 1-201.

§ 2-514. When Documents Deliverable on Acceptance; When on Payment.

Unless otherwise agreed documents against which a draft is drawn are to be delivered to the drawee on acceptance of the draft if it is payable more than three days after presentment; otherwise, only on payment.

Official Comment

Prior Uniform Statutory Provision: Section 41, Uniform Bills of Lading Act.

Changes: Rewritten.

Purposes of Changes: To make the provision one of general application so that:

1. It covers any document against which a draft may be drawn, whatever may be the form of the document, and applies to interpret the action of a seller or consignor insofar as it may affect the rights and duties of any buyer, consignee or financing agency concerned with the paper. Supplementary or corresponding provisions are found in Sections 4-503 and 5-112.

2. An "arrival" draft is a sight draft within the purpose of this section.

Cross References:

Point 1: See Sections 2-502, 2-505(2), 2-507(2), 2-512, 2-513, 2-607 concerning protection of rights of buyer and seller, and 4-503 and 5-112 on delivery of documents.

Definitional Cross References:

"Delivery". Section 1-201.
"Draft". Section 3-104.

§ 2-515. Preserving Evidence of Goods in Dispute.

In furtherance of the adjustment of any claim or dispute

(a) either party on reasonable notification to the other and for the purpose of ascertaining the facts and preserving evidence has the right to inspect, test and sample the goods including such of them as may be in the possession or control of the other; and

(b) the parties may agree to a third party inspection or survey to determine the conformity or condition of the goods and may agree that the findings shall be binding upon them in any subsequent litigation or adjustment.

Official Comment

Prior Uniform Statutory Provision: None.

Purposes:

1. To meet certain serious problems which arise when there is a dispute as to the quality of the goods and thereby perhaps to aid the parties in reaching a settlement, and to further the use of devices which will promote certainty as to the condition of the goods, or at least aid in preserving evidence of their condition.

2. Under paragraph (a), to afford either party an opportunity for preserving evidence, whether or not agreement has been reached, and thereby to reduce uncertainty in any litigation and, in turn perhaps, to promote agreement.

Paragraph (a) does not conflict with the provisions on the seller's right to resell rejected goods or the buyer's similar right. Apparent conflict between these provisions which will be suggested in certain circumstances is to be resolved by requiring prompt action by the parties. Nor does paragraph (a) impair the effect of a term for payment before inspection. Short of such defects as amount to fraud or substantial failure of consideration, non-conformity is neither an excuse nor a defense to an action for non-acceptance of documents. Normally, therefore, until the buyer has made payment, inspected and rejected the goods, there is no occasion or use for the rights under paragraph (a).

3. Under paragraph (b), to provide for third party inspection upon the agreement of the parties, thereby opening the door to amicable adjustments based upon the findings of such third parties.

The use of the phrase "conformity or condition" makes it clear that the parties' agreement may range from a complete settlement of all aspects of the dispute by a third party to the use of a third party merely to determine and record the condition of the goods so that they can be resold or used to reduce the stake in controversy. "Conformity", at one end of the scale of possible issues, includes the whole question of interpretation of the agreement and its legal effect, the state of the goods in regard to quality and condition, whether any defects are due to factors which operate at the risk of the buyer, and the degree of non-conformity where that may be material. "Condition", at the other end of the scale, includes nothing but the degree of damage or deterioration which the goods show. Paragraph (b) is intended to reach any point in the gamut which the parties may agree upon.

The principle of the section on reservation of rights reinforces this paragraph in simplifying such adjustments as the parties wish to make in partial settlement while reserving their rights as to any further points. Paragraph (b) also suggests the use of arbitration, where desired, of any points left open, but nothing in this section is intended to repeal or amend any statute governing arbitration. Where any question arises as to the extent of the parties' agreement under the paragraph, the presumption should be that it was meant to extend only to the relation between the contract description and the goods as delivered, since that is what a craftsman in the trade would normally be expected to report upon. Finally, a written and authenticated report of inspection or tests by a third party, whether or not sampling has been practicable, is entitled to be admitted as evidence under this Act, for it is a third party document.

Cross References:

Point 2: Sections 2–513(3), 2–706 and 2–711(2) and Article 5.

Point 3: Sections 1–202 and 1–207.

Definitional Cross References:

"Conform". Section 2–106.
"Goods". Section 2–105.
"Notification". Section 1–201.
"Party". Section 1–201.

PART 6

BREACH, REPUDIATION AND EXCUSE

§ 2–601. Buyer's Rights on Improper Delivery.

Subject to the provisions of this Article on breach in installment contracts (Section 2–612) and unless otherwise agreed under the sections on contractual limitations of remedy (Sections 2–718 and 2–719), if the goods or the tender of delivery fail in any respect to conform to the contract, the buyer may

(a) reject the whole; or

(b) accept the whole; or

(c) accept any commercial unit or units and reject the rest.

Official Comment

Prior Uniform Statutory Provision: No one general equivalent provision but numerous provisions, dealing with situations of non-conformity where buyer may accept or reject, including Sections 11, 44 and 69(1), Uniform Sales Act.

Changes: Partial acceptance in good faith is recognized and the buyer's remedies on the contract for breach of warranty and the like, where the buyer has returned the goods after transfer of title, are no longer barred.

Purposes of Changes: To make it clear that:

1. A buyer accepting a non-conforming tender is not penalized by the loss of any remedy otherwise open to him. This policy extends to cover and regulate the acceptance of a part of any lot improperly tendered in any case where the price can reasonably be apportioned. Partial acceptance is permitted whether the part of the goods accepted conforms or not. The only limitation on partial acceptance is that good faith and commercial reasonableness must be used to avoid undue impairment of the value of the remaining portion of the goods. This is the reason for the insistence on the "commercial unit" in paragraph (c). In this respect, the test is not only what unit has been the basis of contract, but whether the partial acceptance produces so materially adverse an effect on the remainder as to constitute bad faith.

2. Acceptance made with the knowledge of the other party is final. An original refusal to accept may be withdrawn by a later acceptance if the seller has indicated that he is holding the tender open. However, if the buyer attempts to accept, either in whole or in part, after his original rejection has caused the seller to arrange for other disposition of the goods, the buyer must answer for any ensuing damage since the next section provides that any exercise of ownership after rejection is wrongful as against the seller. Further, he is liable even though the seller may choose to treat his action as acceptance rather than conversion, since the damage flows from the misleading notice. Such arrangements for resale or other disposition of the goods by the seller must be viewed as within the normal contemplation of a buyer who has given notice of rejection. However, the buyer's attempts in good faith to dispose of defective goods where the seller has failed to give instructions within a reasonable time are not to be regarded as an acceptance.

Cross References:

Sections 2–602(2)(a), 2–612, 2–718 and 2–719.

Definitional Cross References:

"Buyer". Section 2–103.
"Commercial unit". Section 2–105.
"Conform". Section 2–106.
"Contract". Section 1–201.
"Goods". Section 2–105.
"Installment contract". Section 2–612.
"Rights". Section 1–201.

§ 2–602. Manner and Effect of Rightful Rejection.

(1) Rejection of goods must be within a reasonable time after their delivery or tender. It is ineffective unless the buyer seasonably notifies the seller.

(2) Subject to the provisions of the two following sections on rejected goods (Sections 2–603 and 2–604),

(a) after rejection any exercise of ownership by the buyer with respect to any commercial unit is wrongful as against the seller; and

(b) if the buyer has before rejection taken physical possession of goods in which he does not have a security interest under the provisions of this Article (subsection (3) of Section 2–711), he is under a duty after rejection to hold them with reasonable care at the seller's disposition for a time sufficient to permit the seller to remove them; but

(c) the buyer has no further obligations with regard to goods rightfully rejected.

(3) The seller's rights with respect to goods wrongfully rejected are governed by the provisions of this Article on Seller's remedies in general (Section 2–703).

Official Comment

Prior Uniform Statutory Provision: Section 50, Uniform Sales Act.

Changes: Rewritten.

Purposes of Changes: To make it clear that:

1. A tender or delivery of goods made pursuant to a contract of sale, even though wholly non-conforming, requires affirmative action by the buyer to avoid acceptance. Under subsection (1), therefore, the buyer is given a reasonable time to notify the seller of his rejection, but without such seasonable notification his rejection is ineffective. The sections of this Article dealing with inspection of goods must be read in connection with the buyer's reasonable time for action under this subsection. Contract provisions limiting the time for rejection fall within the rule of the section on "Time" and are effective if the time set gives the buyer a reasonable time for discovery of defects. What constitutes a due "notifying" of rejection by the buyer to the seller is defined in Section 1–201.

2. Subsection (2) lays down the normal duties of the buyer upon rejection, which flow from the relationship of the parties. Beyond his duty to hold the goods with reasonable care for the buyer's [seller's] disposition, this section continues the policy of prior uniform legislation in generally relieving the buyer from any duties with respect to them, except when the circumstances impose the limited obligation of salvage upon him under the next section.

3. The present section applies only to rightful rejection by the buyer. If the seller has made a tender which in all respects conforms to the contract, the buyer has a positive duty to accept and his failure to do so constitutes a "wrongful rejection" which gives the seller immediate remedies for breach. Subsection (3) is included here to emphasize the sharp distinction between the rejection of an improper tender and the non-acceptance which is a breach by the buyer.

4. The provisions of this section are to be appropriately limited or modified when a negotiation is in process.

Cross References:

Point 1: Sections 1–201, 1–204(1) and (3), 2–512(2), 2–513(1) and 2–606(1)(b).
Point 2: Section 2–603(1).
Point 3: Section 2–703.

Definitional Cross References:

"Buyer". Section 2–103.
"Commercial unit". Section 2–105.
"Goods". Section 2–105.
"Merchant". Section 2–104.
"Notifies". Section 1–201.
"Reasonable time". Section 1–204.
"Remedy". Section 1–201.
"Rights". Section 1–201.
"Seasonably". Section 1–204.
"Security interest". Section 1–201.
"Seller". Section 2–103.

§ 2–603. Merchant Buyer's Duties as to Rightfully Rejected Goods.

(1) Subject to any security interest in the buyer (subsection (3) of Section 2–711), when the seller has no agent or place of business at the market of rejection a merchant buyer is under a duty after rejection of goods in his possession or control to follow any reasonable instructions received from the seller with respect to the goods and in the absence of such instructions to make reasonable efforts to sell them for the seller's account if they are perishable or threaten to decline in value speedily. Instructions are not reasonable if on demand indemnity for expenses is not forthcoming.

(2) When the buyer sells goods under subsection (1), he is entitled to reimbursement from the seller or out of the proceeds for reasonable expenses of caring for and selling them, and if the expenses include no selling commission then to such commission as is usual in the trade or if there is none to a reasonable sum not exceeding ten per cent on the gross proceeds.

(3) In complying with this section the buyer is held only to good faith and good faith conduct hereunder is neither acceptance nor conversion nor the basis of an action for damages.

Official Comment

Prior Uniform Statutory Provision: None.

Purposes:

1. This section recognizes the duty imposed upon the merchant buyer by good faith and commercial practice to follow any reasonable instructions of the seller as to reshipping, storing, delivery to a third party, reselling or the like. Subsection (1) goes further and extends the duty to include the making of reasonable efforts to effect a salvage sale where the value of the goods is threatened and the seller's instructions do not arrive in time to prevent serious loss.

2. The limitations on the buyer's duty to resell under subsection (1) are to be liberally construed. The buyer's duty to resell under this section arises from commercial necessity and thus is present only when the seller has "no agent or place of business at the market of rejection". A financing agency which is acting in behalf of the seller in handling the documents rejected by the buyer is sufficiently the seller's agent to lift the burden of salvage resale from the buyer. (See provisions of Sections 4–503 and 5–112 on bank's duties with respect to rejected documents.) The buyer's duty to resell is extended only to goods in his "possession or control", but these are intended as words of wide, rather than narrow, import. In effect, the measure of the buyer's "control" is whether he can practically effect control without undue commercial burden.

3. The explicit provisions for reimbursement and compensation to the buyer in subsection (2) are applicable and necessary only where he is not acting under instructions from the seller. As provided in subsection (1) the seller's instructions to be "reasonable" must on demand of the buyer include indemnity for expenses.

4. Since this section makes the resale of perishable goods an affirmative duty in contrast to a mere right to sell as under the case law, subsection (3) makes it clear that the buyer is liable only for the exercise of good faith in determining whether the value of the goods is sufficiently threatened to justify a quick resale or whether he has waited a sufficient length of time for instructions, or what a reasonable means and place of resale is.

5. A buyer who fails to make a salvage sale when his duty to do so under this section has arisen is subject to damages pursuant to the section on liberal administration of remedies.

Cross References:

Point 2: Sections 4–503 and 5–112.
Point 5: Section 1–106. Compare generally section 2–706.

Definitional Cross References:

"Buyer". Section 2–103.
"Good faith". Section 1–201.
"Goods". Section 2–105.
"Merchant". Section 2–104.
"Security interest". Section 1–201.
"Seller". Section 2–103.

§ 2–604. Buyer's Options as to Salvage of Rightfully Rejected Goods.

Subject to the provisions of the immediately preceding section on perishables if the seller gives no instructions within a reasonable time after notification of rejection the buyer may store the rejected goods for the seller's account or reship them to him or resell them for the seller's account with reimbursement as provided in the preceding section. Such action is not acceptance or conversion.

Official Comment

Prior Uniform Statutory Provision: None.

Purposes:

The basic purpose of this section is twofold: on the one hand it aims at reducing the stake in dispute and on the other at avoiding the pinning of a technical "acceptance" on a buyer who has taken steps towards realization on or preservation of the goods in good faith. This section is essentially a salvage section and the buyer's right to act under it is conditioned upon (1) non-conformity of the goods, (2) due notification of rejection to the seller under the section on manner of rejection, and (3) the absence of any instructions from the seller which the merchant-buyer has a duty to follow under the preceding section.

This section is designed to accord all reasonable leeway to a rightfully rejecting buyer acting in good faith. The listing of what the buyer may do in the absence of instructions from the seller is intended to be not exhaustive but merely illustrative. This is not a "merchant's" section and the options are pure options given to merchant and nonmerchant buyers alike. The merchant-buyer, however, may in some instances be under a duty rather than an option to resell under the provisions of the preceding section.

Cross References:

Sections 2-602(1), and 2-603(1) and 2-706.

Definitional Cross References:

"Buyer". Section 2-103.
"Notification". Section 1-201.
"Reasonable time". Section 1-204.
"Seller". Section 2-103.

§ 2-605. Waiver of Buyer's Objections by Failure to Particularize.

(1) The buyer's failure to state in connection with rejection a particular defect which is ascertainable by reasonable inspection precludes him from relying on the unstated defect to justify rejection or to establish breach

    (a) where the seller could have cured it if stated seasonably; or

    (b) between merchants when the seller has after rejection made a request in writing for a full and final written statement of all defects on which the buyer proposes to rely.

(2) Payment against documents made without reservation of rights precludes recovery of the payment for defects apparent on the face of the documents.

Official Comment

Prior Uniform Statutory Provision: None.

Purposes:

1. The present section rests upon a policy of permitting the buyer to give a quick and informal notice of defects in a tender without penalizing him for omissions in his statement, while at the same time protecting a seller who is reasonably misled by the buyer's failure to state curable defects.

2. Where the defect in a tender is one which could have been cured by the seller, a buyer who merely rejects the delivery without stating his objections to it is probably acting in commercial bad faith and seeking to get out of a deal which has become unprofitable. Subsection (1)(a), following the general policy of this Article which looks to preserving the deal wherever possible, therefore insists that the seller's right to correct his tender in such circumstances be protected.

3. When the time for cure is past, subsection (1)(b) makes it plain that a seller is entitled upon request to a final statement of objections upon which he can rely. What is needed is that he make clear to the buyer exactly what is being sought. A formal demand under paragraph (b) will be sufficient in the case of a merchant-buyer.

4. Subsection (2) applies to the particular case of documents the same principle which the section on effects of acceptance applies to the case of goods. The matter is dealt with in this section in terms of "waiver" of objections rather than of right to revoke acceptance, partly to avoid any confusion with the problems of acceptance of goods and partly because defects in documents which are not taken as grounds for rejection are generally minor ones. The only defects concerned in the present subsection are defects in the documents which are apparent on their face. Where payment is required against the documents they must be inspected before payment, and the payment then constitutes acceptance of the documents. Under the section dealing with this problem, such acceptance of the documents does not constitute an acceptance of the goods or impair any options or remedies of the buyer for their improper delivery. Where the documents are delivered without requiring such contemporary action as payment from the buyer, the reason of the next section on what constitutes acceptance of goods, applies. Their acceptance by non-objection is therefore postponed until after a reasonable time for their in-

spection. In either situation, however, the buyer "waives" only what is apparent on the face of the documents.

Cross References:

Point 2: Section 2–508.
Point 4: Sections 2–512(2), 2–606(1)(b), 2–607(2).

Definitional Cross References:

"Between merchants". Section 2–104.
"Buyer". Section 2–103.
"Seasonably". Section 1–204.
"Seller". Section 2–103.
"Writing" and "written". Section 1–201.

§ 2–606. What Constitutes Acceptance of Goods.

(1) Acceptance of goods occurs when the buyer
(a) after a reasonable opportunity to inspect the goods signifies to the seller that the goods are conforming or that he will take or retain them in spite of their non-conformity; or
(b) fails to make an effective rejection (subsection (1) of Section 2–602), but such acceptance does not occur until the buyer has had a reasonable opportunity to inspect them; or
(c) does any act inconsistent with the seller's ownership; but if such act is wrongful as against the seller it is an acceptance only if ratified by him.

(2) Acceptance of a part of any commercial unit is acceptance of that entire unit.

Official Comment

Prior Uniform Statutory Provision: Section 48, Uniform Sales Act.

Changes: Rewritten, the qualification in paragraph (c) and subsection (2) being new; otherwise the general policy of the prior legislation is continued.

Purposes of Changes and New Matter: To make it clear that:

1. Under this Article "acceptance" as applied to goods means that the buyer, pursuant to the contract, takes particular goods which have been appropriated to the contract as his own, whether or not he is obligated to do so, and whether he does so by words, action, or silence when it is time to speak. If the goods conform to the contract, acceptance amounts only to the performance by the buyer of one part of his legal obligation.

2. Under this Article acceptance of goods is always acceptance of identified goods which have been appropriated to the contract or are appropriated by the contract. There is no provision for "acceptance of title" apart from acceptance in general, since acceptance of title is not material under this Article to the detailed rights and duties of the parties. (See Section 2–401). The refinements of the older law between acceptance of goods and of title become unnecessary in view of the provisions of the sections on effect and revocation of acceptance, on effects of identification and on risk of loss, and those sections which free the seller's and buyer's remedies from the complications and confusions caused by the question of whether title has or has not passed to the buyer before breach.

3. Under paragraph (a), payment made after tender is always one circumstance tending to signify acceptance of the goods but in itself it can never be more than one circumstance and is not conclusive. Also, a conditional communication of acceptance always remains subject to its expressed conditions.

4. Under paragraph (c), any action taken by the buyer, which is inconsistent with his claim that he has rejected the goods, constitutes an acceptance. However, the provisions of paragraph (c) are subject to the sections dealing with rejection by the buyer which permit the buyer to take certain actions with respect to the goods pursuant to his options and duties imposed by those sections, without effecting an acceptance of the goods. The second clause of paragraph (c) modifies some of the prior case law and makes it clear that "acceptance" in law based on the wrongful act of the acceptor is acceptance only as against the wrongdoer and then only at the option of the party wronged.

In the same manner in which a buyer can bind himself, despite his insistence that he is rejecting or has rejected the goods, by an act inconsistent with the seller's ownership under paragraph (c), he can obligate himself by a communication of acceptance despite a prior rejection under paragraph (a). However, the sections on buyer's rights on improper delivery and on the effect of rightful rejection, make it clear that after he once rejects a tender, paragraph (a) does not operate in favor of the buyer unless the seller has re-tendered the goods or has taken affirmative action indicating that he is holding the tender open. See also Comment 2 to Section 2–601.

5. Subsection (2) supplements the policy of the section on buyer's rights on improper delivery, recognizing the validity of a partial acceptance but insisting

that the buyer exercise this right only as to whole commercial units.

Cross References:

Point 2: Sections 2–401, 2–509, 2–510, 2–607, 2–608 and Part 7.

Point 4: Sections 2–601 through 2–604.

Point 5: Section 2–601.

Definitional Cross References:

"Buyer". Section 2–103.
"Commercial unit". Section 2–105.
"Goods". Section 2–105.
"Seller". Section 2–103.

§ 2–607. Effect of Acceptance; Notice of Breach; Burden of Establishing Breach After Acceptance; Notice of Claim or Litigation to Person Answerable Over.

(1) The buyer must pay at the contract rate for any goods accepted.

(2) Acceptance of goods by the buyer precludes rejection of the goods accepted and if made with knowledge of a non-conformity cannot be revoked because of it unless the acceptance was on the reasonable assumption that the non-conformity would be seasonably cured but acceptance does not of itself impair any other remedy provided by this Article for non-conformity.

(3) Where a tender has been accepted

(a) the buyer must within a reasonable time after he discovers or should have discovered any breach notify the seller of breach or be barred from any remedy; and

(b) if the claim is one for infringement or the like (subsection (3) of Section 2–312) and the buyer is sued as a result of such a breach he must so notify the seller within a reasonable time after he receives notice of the litigation or be barred from any remedy over for liability established by the litigation.

(4) The burden is on the buyer to establish any breach with respect to the goods accepted.

(5) Where the buyer is sued for breach of a warranty or other obligation for which his seller is answerable over

(a) he may give his seller written notice of the litigation. If the notice states that the seller may come in and defend and that if the seller does not do so he will be bound

in any action against him by his buyer by any determination of fact common to the two litigations, then unless the seller after seasonable receipt of the notice does come in and defend he is so bound.

(b) if the claim is one for infringement or the like (subsection (3) of Section 2–312) the original seller may demand in writing that his buyer turn over to him control of the litigation including settlement or else be barred from any remedy over and if he also agrees to bear all expense and to satisfy any adverse judgment, then unless the buyer after seasonable receipt of the demand does turn over control the buyer is so barred.

(6) The provisions of subsections (3), (4) and (5) apply to any obligation of a buyer to hold the seller harmless against infringement or the like (subsection (3) of Section 2–312).

Official Comment

Prior Uniform Statutory Provision: Subsection (1)—Section 41, Uniform Sales Act; Subsections (2) and (3)—Sections 49 and 69, Uniform Sales Act.

Changes: Rewritten.

Purposes of Changes: To continue the prior basic policies with respect to acceptance of goods while making a number of minor though material changes in the interest of simplicity and commercial convenience so that:

1. Under subsection (1), once the buyer accepts a tender the seller acquires a right to its price on the contract terms. In cases of partial acceptance, the price of any part accepted is, if possible, to be reasonably apportioned, using the type of apportionment familiar to the courts in quantum valebant cases, to be determined in terms of "the contract rate," which is the rate determined from the bargain in fact (the agreement) after the rules and policies of this Article have been brought to bear.

2. Under subsection (2) acceptance of goods precludes their subsequent rejection. Any return of the goods thereafter must be by way of revocation of acceptance under the next section. Revocation is unavailable for a non-conformity known to the buyer at the time of acceptance, except where the buyer has accepted on the reasonable assumption that the non-conformity would be seasonably cured.

3. All other remedies of the buyer remain unimpaired under subsection (2). This is intended to include the buyer's full rights with respect to future installments despite his acceptance of any earlier nonconforming installment.

4. The time of notification is to be determined by applying commercial standards to a merchant buyer. "A reasonable time" for notification from a retail consumer is to be judged by different standards so that in his case it will be extended, for the rule of requiring notification is designed to defeat commercial bad faith, not to deprive a good faith consumer of his remedy.

The content of the notification need merely be sufficient to let the seller know that the transaction is still troublesome and must be watched. There is no reason to require that the notification which saves the buyer's rights under this section must include a clear statement of all the objections that will be relied on by the buyer, as under the section covering statements of defects upon rejection (Section 2–605). Nor is there reason for requiring the notification to be a claim for damages or of any threatened litigation or other resort to a remedy. The notification which saves the buyer's rights under this Article need only be such as informs the seller that the transaction is claimed to involve a breach, and thus opens the way for normal settlement through negotiation.

5. Under this Article various beneficiaries are given rights for injuries sustained by them because of the seller's breach of warranty. Such a beneficiary does not fall within the reason of the present section in regard to discovery of defects and the giving of notice within a reasonable time after acceptance, since he has nothing to do with acceptance. However, the reason of this section does extend to requiring the beneficiary to notify the seller that an injury has occurred. What is said above, with regard to the extended time for reasonable notification from the lay consumer after the injury is also applicable here; but even a beneficiary can be properly held to the use of good faith in notifying, once he has had time to become aware of the legal situation.

6. Subsection (4) unambiguously places the burden of proof to establish breach on the buyer after acceptance. However, this rule becomes one purely of procedure when the tender accepted was non-conforming and the buyer has given the seller notice of breach under subsection (3). For subsection (2) makes it clear that acceptance leaves unimpaired the buyer's right to be made whole, and that right can be exercised by the buyer not only by way of cross-claim for damages, but also by way of recoupment in diminution or extinction of the price.

7. Subsections (3)(b) and (5)(b) give a warrantor against infringement an opportunity to defend or compromise third-party claims or be relieved of his liability. Subsection (5)(a) codifies for all warranties the practice of voucher to defend. Compare Section 3–803. Subsection (6) makes these provisions applicable to the buyer's liability for infringement under Section 2–312.

8. All of the provisions of the present section are subject to any explicit reservation of rights.

Cross References:

Point 1: Section 1–201.
Point 2: Section 2–608.
Point 4: Sections 1–204 and 2–605.
Point 5: Section 2–318.
Point 6: Section 2–717.
Point 7: Sections 2–312 and 3–803.
Point 8: Section 1–207.

Definitional Cross References:

"Burden of establishing". Section 1–201.
"Buyer". Section 2–103.
"Conform". Section 2–106.
"Contract". Section 1–201.
"Goods". Section 2–105.
"Notifies". Section 1–201.
"Reasonable time". Section 1–204.
"Remedy". Section 1–201.
"Seasonably". Section 1–204.

§ 2–608. Revocation of Acceptance in Whole or in Part.

(1) The buyer may revoke his acceptance of a lot or commercial unit whose non-conformity substantially impairs its value to him if he has accepted it

(a) on the reasonable assumption that its non-conformity would be cured and it has not been seasonably cured; or

(b) without discovery of such non-conformity if his acceptance was reasonably induced either by the difficulty of discovery before acceptance or by the seller's assurances.

(2) Revocation of acceptance must occur within a reasonable time after the buyer discovers or should have discovered the ground for it and before any substantial change in condition of the goods which is not caused by their own defects. It is not effective until the buyer notifies the seller of it.

(3) A buyer who so revokes has the same rights and duties with regard to the goods involved as if he had rejected them.

Official Comment

Prior Uniform Statutory Provision: Section 69(1)(d), (3), (4) and (5), Uniform Sales Act.

Changes: Rewritten.

Purposes of Changes: To make it clear that:

1. Although the prior basic policy is continued, the buyer is no longer required to elect between revocation of acceptance and recovery of damages for breach. Both are now available to him. The non-alternative character of the two remedies is stressed by the terms used in the present section. The section no longer speaks of "rescission," a term capable of ambiguous application either to transfer of title to the goods or to the contract of sale and susceptible also of confusion with cancellation for cause of an executed or executory portion of the contract. The remedy under this section is instead referred to simply as "revocation of acceptance" of goods tendered under a contract for sale and involves no suggestion of "election" of any sort.

2. Revocation of acceptance is possible only where the non-conformity substantially impairs the value of the goods to the buyer. For this purpose the test is not what the seller had reason to know at the time of contracting; the question is whether the non-conformity is such as will in fact cause a substantial impairment of value to the buyer though the seller had no advance knowledge as to the buyer's particular circumstances.

3. "Assurances" by the seller under paragraph (b) of subsection (1) can rest as well in the circumstances or in the contract as in explicit language used at the time of delivery. The reason for recognizing such assurances is that they induce the buyer to delay discovery. These are the only assurances involved in paragraph (b). Explicit assurances may be made either in good faith or bad faith. In either case any remedy accorded by this Article is available to the buyer under the section on remedies for fraud.

4. Subsection (2) requires notification of revocation of acceptance within a reasonable time after discovery of the grounds for such revocation. Since this remedy will be generally resorted to only after attempts at adjustment have failed, the reasonable time period should extend in most cases beyond the time in which notification of breach must be given, beyond the time for discovery of non-conformity after acceptance and beyond the time for rejection after tender. The parties may by their agreement limit the time for notification under this section, but the same sanctions and considerations apply to such agreements as are discussed in the comment on manner and effect of rightful rejection.

5. The content of the notice under subsection (2) is to be determined in this case as in others by considerations of good faith, prevention of surprise, and reasonable adjustment. More will generally be necessary than the mere notification of breach required under the preceding section. On the other hand the requirements of the section on waiver of buyer's objections do not apply here. The fact that quick notification of trouble is desirable affords good ground for being slow to bind a buyer by his first statement. Following the general policy of this Article, the requirements of the content of notification are less stringent in the case of a non-merchant buyer.

6. Under subsection (2) the prior policy is continued of seeking substantial justice in regard to the condition of goods restored to the seller. Thus the buyer may not revoke his acceptance if the goods have materially deteriorated except by reason of their own defects. Worthless goods, however, need not be offered back and minor defects in the articles reoffered are to be disregarded.

7. The policy of the section allowing partial acceptance is carried over into the present section and the buyer may revoke his acceptance, in appropriate cases, as to the entire lot or any commercial unit thereof.

Cross References:

Point 3: Section 2–721.
Point 4: Sections 1–204, 2–602 and 2–607.
Point 5: Sections 2–605 and 2–607.
Point 7: Section 2–601.

Definitional Cross References:

"Buyer". Section 2–103.
"Commercial unit". Section 2–105.
"Conform". Section 2–106.
"Goods". Section 2–105.
"Lot". Section 2–105.
"Notifies". Section 1–201.
"Reasonable time". Section 1–204.
"Rights". Section 1–201.
"Seasonably". Section 1–204.
"Seller". Section 2–103.

§ 2–609. Right to Adequate Assurance of Performance.

(1) A contract for sale imposes an obligation on each party that the other's expectation of

receiving due performance will not be impaired. When reasonable grounds for insecurity arise with respect to the performance of either party the other may in writing demand adequate assurance of due performance and until he receives such assurance may if commercially reasonable suspend any performance for which he has not already received the agreed return.

(2) Between merchants the reasonableness of grounds for insecurity and the adequacy of any assurance offered shall be determined according to commercial standards.

(3) Acceptance of any improper delivery or payment does not prejudice the aggrieved party's right to demand adequate assurance of future performance.

(4) After receipt of a justified demand failure to provide within a reasonable time not exceeding thirty days such assurance of due performance as is adequate under the circumstances of the particular case is a repudiation of the contract.

Official Comment

Prior Uniform Statutory Provision: See Sections 53, 54(1)(b), 55 and 63(2), Uniform Sales Act.

Purposes:

1. The section rests on the recognition of the fact that the essential purpose of a contract between commercial men is actual performance and they do not bargain merely for a promise, or for a promise plus the right to win a lawsuit and that a continuing sense of reliance and security that the promised performance will be forthcoming when due, is an important feature of the bargain. If either the willingness or the ability of a party to perform declines materially between the time of contracting and the time for performance, the other party is threatened with the loss of a substantial part of what he has bargained for. A seller needs protection not merely against having to deliver on credit to a shaky buyer, but also against having to procure and manufacture the goods, perhaps turning down other customers. Once he has been given reason to believe that the buyer's performance has become uncertain, it is an undue hardship to force him to continue his own performance. Similarly, a buyer who believes that the seller's deliveries have become uncertain cannot safely wait for the due date of performance when he has been buying to assure himself of materials for his current manufacturing or to replenish his stock of merchandise.

2. Three measures have been adopted to meet the needs of commercial men in such situations. First, the aggrieved party is permitted to suspend his own performance and any preparation therefor, with excuse for any resulting necessary delay, until the situation has been clarified. "Suspend performance" under this section means to hold up performance pending the outcome of the demand, and includes also the holding up of any preparatory action. This is the same principle which governs the ancient law of stoppage and seller's lien, and also of excuse of a buyer from prepayment if the seller's actions manifest that he cannot or will not perform. (Original Act, Section 63(2).)

Secondly, the aggrieved party is given the right to require adequate assurance that the other party's performance will be duly forthcoming. This principle is reflected in the familiar clauses permitting the seller to curtail deliveries if the buyer's credit becomes impaired, which when held within the limits of reasonableness and good faith actually express no more than the fair business meaning of any commercial contract.

Third, and finally, this section provides the means by which the aggrieved party may treat the contract as broken if his reasonable grounds for insecurity are not cleared up within a reasonable time. This is the principle underlying the law of anticipatory breach, whether by way of defective part performance or by repudiation. The present section merges these three principles of law and commercial practice into a single theory of general application to all sales agreements looking to future performance.

3. Subsection (2) of the present section requires that "reasonable" grounds and "adequate" assurance as used in subsection (1) be defined by commercial rather than legal standards. The express reference to commercial standards carries no connotation that the obligation of good faith is not equally applicable here.

Under commercial standards and in accord with commercial practice, a ground for insecurity need not arise from or be directly related to the contract in question. The law as to "dependence" or "independence" of promises within a single contract does not control the application of the present section.

Thus a buyer who falls behind in "his account" with the seller, even though the items involved have to do with separate and legally distinct contracts, impairs the seller's expectation of due performance. Again, under the same test, a buyer who requires precision parts which he intends to use immediately upon delivery, may have reasonable grounds for insecurity if he discovers that his seller is making defective deliveries of such parts to other buyers with similar needs.

Thus, too, in a situation such as arose in Jay Dreher Corporation v. Delco Appliance Corporation, 93 F.2d 275 (C.C.A.2, 1937), where a manufacturer gave a dealer an exclusive franchise for the sale of his product but on two or three occasions breached the exclusive dealing clause, although there was no default in orders, deliveries or payments under the separate sales contract between the parties, the aggrieved dealer would be entitled to suspend his performance of the contract for sale under the present section and to demand assurance that the exclusive dealing contract would be lived up to. There is no need for an explicit clause tying the exclusive franchise into the contract for the sale of goods since the situation itself ties the agreements together.

The nature of the sales contract enters also into the question of reasonableness. For example, a report from an apparently trustworthy source that the seller had shipped defective goods or was planning to ship them would normally give the buyer reasonable grounds for insecurity. But when the buyer has assumed the risk of payment before inspection of the goods, as in a sales contract on C.I.F. or similar cash against documents terms, that risk is not to be evaded by a demand for assurance. Therefore no ground for insecurity would exist under this section unless the report went to a ground which would excuse payment by the buyer.

4. What constitutes "adequate" assurance of due performance is subject to the same test of factual conditions. For example, where the buyer can make use of a defective delivery, a mere promise by a seller of good repute that he is giving the matter his attention and that the defect will not be repeated, is normally sufficient. Under the same circumstances, however, a similar statement by a known corner-cutter might well be considered insufficient without the posting of a guaranty or, if so demanded by the buyer, a speedy replacement of the delivery involved. By the same token where a delivery has defects, even though easily curable, which interfere with easy use by the buyer, no verbal assurance can be deemed adequate which is not accompanied by replacement, repair, money-allowance, or other commercially reasonable cure.

A fact situation such as arose in Corn Products Refining Co. v. Fasola, 94 N.J.L. 181, 109 A. 505 (1920) offers illustration both of reasonable grounds for insecurity and "adequate" assurance. In that case a contract for the sale of oils on 30 days' credit, 2% off for payment within 10 days, provided that credit was to be extended to the buyer only if his financial responsibility was satisfactory to the seller. The buyer had been in the habit of taking advantage of the discount but at the same time that he failed to make his customary 10 day payment, the seller heard rumors, in fact false, that the buyer's financial condition was shaky. Thereupon, the seller demanded cash before shipment or security satisfactory to him. The buyer sent a good credit report from his banker, expressed willingness to make payments when due on the 30 day terms and insisted on further deliveries under the contract. Under this Article the rumors, although false, were enough to make the buyer's financial condition "unsatisfactory" to the seller under the contract clause. Moreover, the buyer's practice of taking the cash discounts is enough, apart from the contract clause, to lay a commercial foundation for suspicion when the practice is suddenly stopped. These matters, however, go only to the justification of the seller's demand for security, or his "reasonable grounds for insecurity".

The adequacy of the assurance given is not measured as in the type of "satisfaction" situation affected with intangibles, such as in personal service cases, cases involving a third party's judgment as final, or cases in which the whole contract is dependent on one party's satisfaction, as in a sale on approval. Here, the seller must exercise good faith and observe commercial standards. This Article thus approves the statement of the court in James B. Berry's Sons Co. of Illinois v. Monark Gasoline & Oil Co., Inc., 32 F.2d 74 (C.C.A.8, 1929), that the seller's satisfaction under such a clause must be based upon reason and must not be arbitrary or capricious; and rejects the purely personal "good faith" test of the Corn Products Refining Co. case, which held that in the seller's sole judgment, if for *any* reason he was dissatisfied, he was entitled to revoke the credit. In the absence of the buyer's failure to take the 2% discount as was his custom, the banker's report given in that case would have been "adequate" assurance under this Act, regardless of the language of the "satisfaction" clause. However, the seller is reasonably entitled to feel insecure at a sudden expansion of the buyer's use of a credit term, and should be entitled either to security or to a satisfactory explanation.

The entire foregoing discussion as to adequacy of assurance by way of explanation is subject to qualification when repeated occasions for the application of this section arise. This Act recognizes that repeated delinquencies must be viewed as cumulative. On the other hand, commercial sense also requires that if repeated claims for assurance are made under this section, the basis for these claims must be increasingly obvious.

5. A failure to provide adequate assurance of performance and thereby to re-establish the security of

expectation, results in a breach only "by repudiation" under subsection (4). Therefore, the possibility is continued of retraction of the repudiation under the section dealing with that problem, unless the aggrieved party has acted on the breach in some manner.

The thirty day limit on the time to provide assurance is laid down to free the question of reasonable time from uncertainty in later litigation.

6. Clauses seeking to give the protected party exceedingly wide powers to cancel or readjust the contract when ground for insecurity arises must be read against the fact that good faith is a part of the obligation of the contract and not subject to modification by agreement and includes, in the case of a merchant, the reasonable observance of commercial standards of fair dealing in the trade. Such clauses can thus be effective to enlarge the protection given by the present section to a certain extent, to fix the reasonable time within which requested assurance must be given, or to define adequacy of the assurance in any commercially reasonable fashion. But any clause seeking to set up arbitrary standards for action is ineffective under this Article. Acceleration clauses are treated similarly in the Articles on Commercial Paper and Secured Transactions.

Cross References:

Point 3: Section 1–203.
Point 5: Section 2–611.
Point 6: Sections 1–203 and 1–208 and Articles 3 and 9.

Definitional Cross References:

"Aggrieved party". Section 1–201.
"Between merchants". Section 2–104.
"Contract". Section 1–201.
"Contract for sale". Section 2–106.
"Party". Section 1–201.
"Reasonable time". Section 1–204.
"Rights". Section 1–201.
"Writing". Section 1–201.

§ 2–610.   Anticipatory Repudiation.

When either party repudiates the contract with respect to a performance not yet due the loss of which will substantially impair the value of the contract to the other, the aggrieved party may

(a) for a commercially reasonable time await performance by the repudiating party; or

(b) resort to any remedy for breach (Section 2–703 or Section 2–711), even though he has notified the repudiating party that he

would await the latter's performance and has urged retraction; and

(c) in either case suspend his own performance or proceed in accordance with the provisions of this Article on the seller's right to identify goods to the contract notwithstanding breach or to salvage unfinished goods (Section 2–704).

Official Comment

Prior Uniform Statutory Provision: See Sections 63(2) and 65, Uniform Sales Act.

Purposes: To make it clear that:

1. With the problem of insecurity taken care of by the preceding section and with provision being made in this Article as to the effect of a defective delivery under an installment contract, anticipatory repudiation centers upon an overt communication of intention or an action which renders performance impossible or demonstrates a clear determination not to continue with performance.

Under the present section when such a repudiation substantially impairs the value of the contract, the aggrieved party may at any time resort to his remedies for breach, or he may suspend his own performance while he negotiates with, or awaits performance by, the other party. But if he awaits performance beyond a commercially reasonable time he cannot recover resulting damages which he should have avoided.

2. It is not necessary for repudiation that performance be made literally and utterly impossible. Repudiation can result from action which reasonably indicates a rejection of the continuing obligation. And, a repudiation automatically results under the preceding section on insecurity when a party fails to provide adequate assurance of due future performance within thirty days after a justifiable demand therefor has been made. Under the language of this section, a demand by one or both parties for more than the contract calls for in the way of counter-performance is not in itself a repudiation nor does it invalidate a plain expression of desire for future performance. However, when under a fair reading it amounts to a statement of intention not to perform except on conditions which go beyond the contract, it becomes a repudiation.

3. The test chosen to justify an aggrieved party's action under this section is the same as that in the section on breach in installment contracts—namely the substantial value of the contract. The most useful test of substantial value is to determine whether material inconvenience or injustice will result if the aggrieved

party is forced to wait and receive an ultimate tender minus the part or aspect repudiated.

4. After repudiation, the aggrieved party may immediately resort to any remedy he chooses provided he moves in good faith (see Section 1–203). Inaction and silence by the aggrieved party may leave the matter open but it cannot be regarded as misleading the repudiating party. Therefore the aggrieved party is left free to proceed at any time with his options under this section, unless he has taken some positive action which in good faith requires notification to the other party before the remedy is pursued.

Cross References:

> Point 1: Sections 2–609 and 2–612.
> Point 2: Section 2–609.
> Point 3: Section 2–612.
> Point 4: Section 1–203.

Definitional Cross References:

> "Aggrieved party". Section 1–201.
> "Contract". Section 1–201.
> "Party". Section 1–201.
> "Remedy". Section 1–201.

§ 2–611. Retraction of Anticipatory Repudiation.

(1) Until the repudiating party's next performance is due he can retract his repudiation unless the aggrieved party has since the repudiation cancelled or materially changed his position or otherwise indicated that he considers the repudiation final.

(2) Retraction may be by any method which clearly indicates to the aggrieved party that the repudiating party intends to perform, but must include any assurance justifiably demanded under the provisions of this Article (Section 2–609).

(3) Retraction reinstates the repudiating party's rights under the contract with due excuse and allowance to the aggrieved party for any delay occasioned by the repudiation.

Official Comment

Prior Uniform Statutory Provision: None.

Purposes: To make it clear that:

1. The repudiating party's right to reinstate the contract is entirely dependent upon the action taken by the aggrieved party. If the latter has cancelled the contract or materially changed his position at any time

after the repudiation, there can be no retraction under this section.

2. Under subsection (2) an effective retraction must be accompanied by any assurances demanded under the section dealing with right to adequate assurance. A repudiation is of course sufficient to give reasonable ground for insecurity and to warrant a request for assurance as an essential condition of the retraction. However, after a timely and unambiguous expression of retraction, a reasonable time for the assurance to be worked out should be allowed by the aggrieved party before cancellation.

Cross Reference:

> Point 2: Section 2–609.

Definitional Cross References:

> "Aggrieved party". Section 1–201.
> "Cancellation". Section 2–106.
> "Contract". Section 1–201.
> "Party". Section 1–201.
> "Rights". Section 1–201.

§ 2–612. "Installment Contract"; Breach.

(1) An "installment contract" is one which requires or authorizes the delivery of goods in separate lots to be separately accepted, even though the contract contains a clause "each delivery is a separate contract" or its equivalent.

(2) The buyer may reject any installment which is non-conforming if the non-conformity substantially impairs the value of that installment and cannot be cured or if the non-conformity is a defect in the required documents; but if the non-conformity does not fall within subsection (3) and the seller gives adequate assurance of its cure the buyer must accept that installment.

(3) Whenever non-conformity or default with respect to one or more installments substantially impairs the value of the whole contract there is a breach of the whole. But the aggrieved party reinstates the contract if he accepts a non-conforming installment without seasonably notifying of cancellation or if he brings an action with respect only to past installments or demands performance as to future installments.

Official Comment

Prior Uniform Statutory Provision: Section 45(2), Uniform Sales Act.

Changes: Rewritten.

Purposes of Changes: To continue prior law but to make explicit the more mercantile interpretation of many of the rules involved, so that:

1. The definition of an installment contract is phrased more broadly in this Article so as to cover installment deliveries tacitly authorized by the circumstances or by the option of either party.

2. In regard to the apportionment of the price for separate payment this Article applies the more liberal test of what can be apportioned rather than the test of what is clearly apportioned by the agreement. This Article also recognizes approximate calculation or apportionment of price subject to subsequent adjustment. A provision for separate payment for each lot delivered ordinarily means that the price is at least roughly calculable by units of quantity, but such a provision is not essential to an "installment contract." If separate acceptance of separate deliveries is contemplated, no generalized contrast between wholly "entire" and wholly "divisible" contracts has any standing under this Article.

3. This Article rejects any approach which gives clauses such as "each delivery is a separate contract" their legalistically literal effect. Such contracts nonetheless call for installment deliveries. Even where a clause speaks of "a separate contract for all purposes", a commercial reading of the language under the section on good faith and commercial standards requires that the singleness of the document and the negotiation, together with the sense of the situation, prevail over any uncommercial and legalistic interpretation.

4. One of the requirements for rejection under subsection (2) is non-conformity substantially impairing the value of the installment in question. However, an installment agreement may require accurate conformity in quality as a condition to the right to acceptance if the need for such conformity is made clear either by express provision or by the circumstances. In such a case the effect of the agreement is to define explicitly what amounts to substantial impairment of value impossible to cure. A clause requiring accurate compliance as a condition to the right to acceptance must, however, have some basis in reason, must avoid imposing hardship by surprise and is subject to waiver or to displacement by practical construction.

Substantial impairment of the value of an installment can turn not only on the quality of the goods but also on such factors as time, quantity, assortment, and the like. It must be judged in terms of the normal or specifically known purposes of the contract. The defect in required documents refers to such matters as the absence of insurance documents under a C.I.F. contract, falsity of a bill of lading, or one failing to show shipment within the contract period or to the contract destination. Even in such cases, however, the provisions on cure of tender apply if appropriate documents are readily procurable.

5. Under subsection (2) an installment delivery must be accepted if the non-conformity is curable and the seller gives adequate assurance of cure. Cure of non-conformity of an installment in the first instance can usually be afforded by an allowance against the price, or in the case of reasonable discrepancies in quantity either by a further delivery or a partial rejection. This Article requires reasonable action by a buyer in regard to discrepant delivery and good faith requires that the buyer make any reasonable minor outlay of time or money necessary to cure an overshipment by severing out an acceptable percentage thereof. The seller must take over a cure which involves any material burden; the buyer's obligation reaches only to cooperation. Adequate assurance for purposes of subsection (2) is measured by the same standards as under the section on right to adequate assurance of performance.

6. Subsection (3) is designed to further the continuance of the contract in the absence of an overt cancellation. The question arising when an action is brought as to a single installment only is resolved by making such action waive the right to cancellation. This involves merely a defect in one or more installments, as contrasted with the situation where there is a true repudiation within the section on anticipatory repudiation. Whether the non-conformity in any given installment justifies cancellation as to the future depends, not on whether such non-conformity indicates an intent or likelihood that the future deliveries will also be defective, but whether the non-conformity substantially impairs the value of the whole contract. If only the seller's security in regard to future installments is impaired, he has the right to demand adequate assurances of proper future performance but has not an immediate right to cancel the entire contract. It is clear under this Article, however, that defects in prior installments are cumulative in effect, so that acceptance does not wash out the defect "waived." Prior policy is continued, putting the rule as to buyer's default on the same footing as that in regard to seller's default.

7. Under the requirement of seasonable notification of cancellation under subsection (3), a buyer who accepts a non-conforming installment which substantially impairs the value of the entire contract should

properly be permitted to withhold his decision as to whether or not to cancel pending a response from the seller as to his claim for cure or adjustment. Similarly, a seller may withhold a delivery pending payment for prior ones, at the same time delaying his decision as to cancellation. A reasonable time for notifying of cancellation, judged by commercial standard under the section on good faith, extends of course to include the time covered by any reasonable negotiation in good faith. However, during this period the defaulting party is entitled, on request, to know whether the contract is still in effect, before he can be required to perform further.

Cross References:

Point 2: Sections 2–307 and 2–607.
Point 3: Section 1–203.
Point 5: Sections 2–208 and 2–609.
Point 6: Section 2–610.

Definitional Cross References:

"Action". Section 1–201.
"Aggrieved party". Section 1–201.
"Buyer". Section 2–103.
"Cancellation". Section 2–106.
"Conform". Section 2–106.
"Contract". Section 1–201.
"Lot". Section 2–105.
"Notifies". Section 1–201.
"Seasonably". Section 1–204.
"Seller". Section 2–103.

§ 2–613. Casualty to Identified Goods.

Where the contract requires for its performance goods identified when the contract is made, and the goods suffer casualty without fault of either party before the risk of loss passes to the buyer, or in a proper case under a "no arrival, no sale" term (Section 2–324) then

(a) if the loss is total the contract is avoided; and

(b) if the loss is partial or the goods have so deteriorated as no longer to conform to the contract the buyer may nevertheless demand inspection and at his option either treat the contract as avoided or accept the goods with due allowance from the contract price for the deterioration or the deficiency in quantity but without further right against the seller.

Official Comment

Prior Uniform Statutory Provision: Sections 7 and 8, Uniform Sales Act.

Changes: Rewritten, the basic policy being continued but the test of a "divisible" or "indivisible" sale or contract being abandoned in favor of adjustment in business terms.

Purposes of Changes:

1. Where goods whose continued existence is presupposed by the agreement are destroyed without fault of either party, the buyer is relieved from his obligation but may at his option take the surviving goods at a fair adjustment. "Fault" is intended to include negligence and not merely wilful wrong. The buyer is expressly given the right to inspect the goods in order to determine whether he wishes to avoid the contract entirely or to take the goods with a price adjustment.

2. The section applies whether the goods were already destroyed at the time of contracting without the knowledge of either party or whether they are destroyed subsequently but before the risk of loss passes to the buyer. Where under the agreement, including of course usage of trade, the risk has passed to the buyer before the casualty, the section has no application. Beyond this, the essential question in determining whether the rules of this section are to be applied is whether the seller has or has not undertaken the responsibility for the continued existence of the goods in proper condition through the time of agreed or expected delivery.

3. The section on the term "no arrival, no sale" makes clear that delay in arrival, quite as much as physical change in the goods, gives the buyer the options set forth in this section.

Cross Reference:

Point 3: Section 2–324.

Definitional Cross References:

"Buyer". Section 2–103.
"Conform". Section 2–106.
"Contract". Section 1–201.
"Fault". Section 1–201.
"Goods". Section 2–105.
"Party". Section 1–201.
"Rights". Section 1–201.
"Seller". Section 2–103.

§ 2–614. Substituted Performance.

(1) Where without fault of either party the agreed berthing, loading, or unloading facilities

fail or an agreed type of carrier becomes unavailable or the agreed manner of delivery otherwise becomes commercially impracticable but a commercially reasonable substitute is available, such substitute performance must be tendered and accepted.

(2) If the agreed means or manner of payment fails because of domestic or foreign governmental regulation, the seller may withhold or stop delivery unless the buyer provides a means or manner of payment which is commercially a substantial equivalent. If delivery has already been taken, payment by the means or in the manner provided by the regulation discharges the buyer's obligation unless the regulation is discriminatory, oppressive or predatory.

Official Comment

Prior Uniform Statutory Provision: None.

Purposes:

1. Subsection (1) requires the tender of a commercially reasonable substituted performance where agreed to facilities have failed or become commercially impracticable. Under this Article, in the absence of specific agreement, the normal or usual facilities enter into the agreement either through the circumstances, usage of trade or prior course of dealing.

This section appears between Section 2–613 on casualty to identified goods and the next section on excuse by failure of presupposed conditions, both of which deal with excuse and complete avoidance of the contract where the occurrence or non-occurrence of a contingency which was a basic assumption of the contract makes the expected performance impossible. The distinction between the present section and those sections lies in whether the failure or impossibility of performance arises in connection with an incidental matter or goes to the very heart of the agreement. The differing lines of solution are contrasted in a comparison of International Paper Co. v. Rockefeller, 161 App.Div. 180, 146 N.Y.S. 371 (1914) and Meyer v. Sullivan, 40 Cal.App. 723, 181 P. 847 (1919). In the former case a contract for the sale of spruce to be cut from a particular tract of land was involved. When a fire destroyed the trees growing on that tract the seller was held excused since performance was impossible. In the latter case the contract called for delivery of wheat "f.o.b. Kosmos Steamer at Seattle." The war led to cancellation of that line's sailing schedule after space had been duly engaged and the buyer was held entitled to demand substituted delivery at the warehouse on the line's loading dock. Under this Article,

of course, the seller would also be entitled, had the market gone the other way, to make a substituted tender in that manner.

There must, however, be a true commercial impracticability to excuse the agreed to performance and justify a substituted performance. When this is the case a reasonable substituted performance tendered by either party should excuse him from strict compliance with contract terms which do not go to the essence of the agreement.

2. The substitution provided in this section as between buyer and seller does not carry over into the obligation of a financing agency under a letter of credit, since such an agency is entitled to performance which is plainly adequate on its face and without need to look into commercial evidence outside of the documents. See Article 5, especially Sections 5–102, 5–103, 5–109, 5–110, 5–114.

3. Under subsection (2) where the contract is still executory on both sides, the seller is permitted to withdraw unless the buyer can provide him with a commercially equivalent return despite the governmental regulation. Where, however, only the debt for the price remains, a larger leeway is permitted. The buyer may pay in the manner provided by the regulation even though this may not be commercially equivalent provided that the regulation is not "discriminatory, oppressive or predatory."

Cross Reference:

Point 2: Article 5.

Definitional Cross References:

"Buyer". Section 2–103.
"Fault". Section 1–201.
"Party". Section 1–201.
"Seller". Section 2–103.

§ 2–615. Excuse by Failure of Presupposed Conditions.

Except so far as a seller may have assumed a greater obligation and subject to the preceding section on substituted performance:

(a) Delay in delivery or non-delivery in whole or in part by a seller who complies with paragraphs (b) and (c) is not a breach of his duty under a contract for sale if performance as agreed has been made impracticable by the occurrence of a contingency the non-occurrence of which was a basic assumption on which the contract was made or by compliance in good faith with any applicable foreign or domestic governmental regulation or order whether or not it later proves to be invalid.

(b) Where the causes mentioned in paragraph (a) affect only a part of the seller's capacity to perform, he must allocate production and deliveries among his customers but may at his option include regular customers not then under contract as well as his own requirements for further manufacture. He may so allocate in any manner which is fair and reasonable.

(c) The seller must notify the buyer seasonally that there will be delay or non-delivery and, when allocation is required under paragraph (b), of the estimated quota thus made available for the buyer.

Official Comment

Prior Uniform Statutory Provision: None.

Purposes:

1. This section excuses a seller from timely delivery of goods contracted for, where his performance has become commercially impracticable because of unforeseen supervening circumstances not within the contemplation of the parties at the time of contracting. The destruction of specific goods and the problem of the use of substituted performance on points other than delay or quantity, treated elsewhere in this Article, must be distinguished from the matter covered by this section.

2. The present section deliberately refrains from any effort at an exhaustive expression of contingencies and is to be interpreted in all cases sought to be brought within its scope in terms of its underlying reason and purpose.

3. The first test for excuse under this Article in terms of basic assumption is a familiar one. The additional test of commercial impracticability (as contrasted with "impossibility," "frustration of performance" or "frustration of the venture") has been adopted in order to call attention to the commercial character of the criterion chosen by this Article.

4. Increased cost alone does not excuse performance unless the rise in cost is due to some unforeseen contingency which alters the essential nature of the performance. Neither is a rise or a collapse in the market in itself a justification, for that is exactly the type of business risk which business contracts made at fixed prices are intended to cover. But a severe shortage of raw materials or of supplies due to a contingency such as war, embargo, local crop failure, unforeseen shutdown of major sources of supply or the like, which either causes a marked increase in cost or altogether prevents the seller from securing supplies necessary to his performance, is within the contemplation of this section. (See Ford & Sons, Ltd., v. Henry Leetham & Sons, Ltd., 21 Com.Cas. 55 (1915, K.B.D.).)

5. Where a particular source of supply is exclusive under the agreement and fails through casualty, the present section applies rather than the provision on destruction or deterioration of specific goods. The same holds true where a particular source of supply is shown by the circumstances to have been contemplated or assumed by the parties at the time of contracting. (See Davis Co. v. Hoffmann-LaRoche Chemical Works, 178 App.Div. 855, 166 N.Y.S. 179 (1917) and International Paper Co. v. Rockefeller, 161 App.Div. 180, 146 N.Y.S. 371 (1914).) There is no excuse under this section, however, unless the seller has employed all due measures to assure himself that his source will not fail. (See Canadian Industrial Alcohol Co., Ltd., v. Dunbar Molasses Co., 258 N.Y. 194, 179 N.E. 383, 80 A.L.R. 1173 (1932) and Washington Mfg. Co. v. Midland Lumber Co., 113 Wash. 593, 194 P. 777 (1921).)

In the case of failure of production by an agreed source for causes beyond the seller's control, the seller should, if possible, be excused since production by an agreed source is without more a basic assumption of the contract. Such excuse should not result in relieving the defaulting supplier from liability nor in dropping into the seller's lap an unearned bonus of damages over. The flexible adjustment machinery of this Article provides the solution under the provision on the obligation of good faith. A condition to his making good the claim of excuse is the turning over to the buyer of his rights against the defaulting source of supply to the extent of the buyer's contract in relation to which excuse is being claimed.

6. In situations in which neither sense nor justice is served by either answer when the issue is posed in flat terms of "excuse" or "no excuse," adjustment under the various provisions of this Article is necessary, especially the sections on good faith, on insecurity and assurance and on the reading of all provisions in the light of their purposes, and the general policy of this Act to use equitable principles in furtherance of commercial standards and good faith.

7. The failure of conditions which go to convenience or collateral values rather than to the commercial practicability of the main performance does not

amount to a complete excuse. However, good faith and the reason of the present section and of the preceding one may properly be held to justify and even to require any needed delay involved in a good faith inquiry seeking a readjustment of the contract terms to meet the new conditions.

8. The provisions of this section are made subject to assumption of greater liability by agreement and such agreement is to be found not only in the expressed terms of the contract but in the circumstances surrounding the contracting, in trade usage and the like. Thus the exemptions of this section do not apply when the contingency in question is sufficiently foreshadowed at the time of contracting to be included among the business risks which are fairly to be regarded as part of the dickered terms, either consciously or as a matter of reasonable, commercial interpretation from the circumstances. (See Madeirense Do Brasil, S.A. v. Stulman-Emrick Lumber Co., 147 F.2d 399 (C.C.A., 2 Cir., 1945).) The exemption otherwise present through usage of trade under the present section may also be expressly negated by the language of the agreement. Generally, express agreements as to exemptions designed to enlarge upon or supplant the provisions of this section are to be read in the light of mercantile sense and reason, for this section itself sets up the commercial standard for normal and reasonable interpretation and provides a minimum beyond which agreement may not go.

Agreement can also be made in regard to the consequences of exemption as laid down in paragraphs (b) and (c) and the next section on procedure on notice claiming excuse.

9. The case of a farmer who has contracted to sell crops to be grown on designated land may be regarded as falling either within the section on casualty to identified goods or this section, and he may be excused, when there is a failure of the specific crop, either on the basis of the destruction of identified goods or because of the failure of a basic assumption of the contract.

Exemption of the buyer in the case of a "requirements" contract is covered by the "Output and Requirements" section both as to assumption and allocation of the relevant risks. But when a contract by a manufacturer to buy fuel or raw material makes no specific reference to a particular venture and no such reference may be drawn from the circumstances, commercial understanding views it as a general deal in the general market and not conditioned on any assumption of the continuing operation of the buyer's plant. Even when notice is given by the buyer that the supplies are needed to fill a specific contract of a normal commercial kind, commercial understanding does not see such a supply contract as conditioned on the continuance of the buyer's further contract for outlet. On the other hand, where the buyer's contract is in reasonable commercial understanding conditioned on a definite and specific venture or assumption as, for instance, a war procurement subcontract known to be based on a prime contract which is subject to termination, or a supply contract for a particular construction venture, the reason of the present section may well apply and entitle the buyer to the exemption.

10. Following its basic policy of using commercial practicability as a test for excuse, this section recognizes as of equal significance either a foreign or domestic regulation and disregards any technical distinctions between "law," "regulation," "order" and the like. Nor does it make the present action of the seller depend upon the eventual judicial determination of the legality of the particular governmental action. The seller's good faith belief in the validity of the regulation is the test under this Article and the best evidence of his good faith is the general commercial acceptance of the regulation. However, governmental interference cannot excuse unless it truly "supervenes" in such a manner as to be beyond the seller's assumption of risk. And any action by the party claiming excuse which causes or colludes in inducing the governmental action preventing his performance would be in breach of good faith and would destroy his exemption.

11. An excused seller must fulfill his contract to the extent which the supervening contingency permits, and if the situation is such that his customers are generally affected he must take account of all in supplying one. Subsections (a) and (b), therefore, explicitly permit in any proration a fair and reasonable attention to the needs of regular customers who are probably relying on spot orders for supplies. Customers at different stages of the manufacturing process may be fairly treated by including the seller's manufacturing requirements. A fortiori, the seller may also take account of contracts later in date than the one in question. The fact that such spot orders may be closed at an advanced price causes no difficulty, since any allocation which exceeds normal past requirements will not be reasonable. However, good faith requires, when prices have advanced, that the seller exercise real care in making his allocations, and in case of doubt his contract customers should be favored and supplies prorated evenly among them regardless of price. Save for the extra care thus required by changes in the market, this section seeks to leave every reasonable business leeway to the seller.

Cross References:

Point 1: Sections 2–613 and 2–614.
Point 2: Section 1–102.
Point 5: Sections 1–203 and 2–613.
Point 6: Sections 1–102, 1–203 and 2–609.
Point 7: Section 2–614.
Point 8: Sections 1–201, 2–302 and 2–616.
Point 9: Sections 1–102, 2–306 and 2–613.

Definitional Cross References:

"Between merchants". Section 2–104.
"Buyer". Section 2–103.
"Contract". Section 1–201.
"Contract for sale". Section 2–106.
"Good faith". Section 1–201.
"Merchant". Section 2–104.
"Notifies". Section 1–201.
"Seasonably". Section 1–201.
"Seller". Section 2–103.

§ 2–616. Procedure on Notice Claiming Excuse.

(1) Where the buyer receives notification of a material or indefinite delay or an allocation justified under the preceding section he may by written notification to the seller as to any delivery concerned, and where the prospective deficiency substantially impairs the value of the whole contract under the provisions of this Article relating to breach of installment contracts (Section 2–612), then also as to the whole,

   (a) terminate and thereby discharge any unexecuted portion of the contract; or

   (b) modify the contract by agreeing to take his available quota in substitution.

(2) If after receipt of such notification from the seller the buyer fails so to modify the contract within a reasonable time not exceeding thirty days the contract lapses with respect to any deliveries affected.

(3) The provisions of this section may not be negated by agreement except in so far as the seller has assumed a greater obligation under the preceding section.

Official Comment

Prior Uniform Statutory Provision: None.

Purposes:

This section seeks to establish simple and workable machinery for providing certainty as to when a supervening and excusing contingency "excuses" the delay, "discharges" the contract, or may result in a waiver of the delay by the buyer. When the seller notifies, in accordance with the preceding section, claiming excuse, the buyer may acquiesce, in which case the contract is so modified. No consideration is necessary in a case of this kind to support such a modification. If the buyer does not elect so to modify the contract, he may terminate it and under subsection (2) his silence after receiving the seller's claim of excuse operates as such a termination. Subsection (3) denies effect to any contract clause made in advance of trouble which would require the buyer to stand ready to take delivery whenever the seller is excused from delivery by unforeseen circumstances.

Cross References:

Point 1: Sections 2–209 and 2–615.

Definitional Cross References:

"Buyer". Section 2–103.
"Contract". Section 1–201.
"Installment contract". Section 2–612.
"Notification". Section 1–201.
"Reasonable time". Section 1–204.
"Seller". Section 2–103.
"Termination". Section 2–106.
"Written". Section 1–201.

PART 7

REMEDIES

§ 2–701. Remedies for Breach of Collateral Contracts Not Impaired.

Remedies for breach of any obligation or promise collateral or ancillary to a contract for sale are not impaired by the provisions of this Article.

Official Comment

Prior Uniform Statutory Provision: None.

Purposes:

Whether a claim for breach of an obligation collateral to the contract for sale requires separate trial to avoid confusion of issues is beyond the scope of this Article; but contractual arrangements which as a business matter enter vitally into the contract should be considered a part thereof in so far as cross-claims or defenses are concerned.

Definitional Cross References:

"Contract for sale". Section 2–106.
"Remedy". Section 1–201.

§ 2–702.　Seller's Remedies on Discovery of Buyer's Insolvency.

(1) Where the seller discovers the buyer to be insolvent he may refuse delivery except for cash including payment for all goods theretofore delivered under the contract, and stop delivery under this Article (Section 2–705).

(2) Where the seller discovers that the buyer has received goods on credit while insolvent he may reclaim the goods upon demand made within ten days after the receipt, but if misrepresentation of solvency has been made to the particular seller in writing within three months before delivery the ten day limitation does not apply. Except as provided in this subsection the seller may not base a right to reclaim goods on the buyer's fraudulent or innocent misrepresentation of solvency or of intent to pay.

(3) The seller's right to reclaim under subsection (2) is subject to the rights of a buyer in ordinary course or other good faith purchaser under this Article (Section 2–403). Successful reclamation of goods excludes all other remedies with respect to them.

As amended in 1966.

Official Comment

Prior Uniform Statutory Provision: Subsection (1)—Sections 53(1)(b), 54(1)(c) and 57, Uniform Sales Act; Subsection (2)—none; Subsection (3)—Section 76(3), Uniform Sales Act.

Changes: Rewritten, the protection given to a seller who has sold on credit and has delivered goods to the buyer immediately preceding his insolvency being extended.

Purposes of Changes and New Matter: To make it clear that:

1. The seller's right to withhold the goods or to stop delivery except for cash when he discovers the buyer's insolvency is made explicit in subsection (1) regardless of the passage of title, and the concept of stoppage has been extended to include goods in the

possession of any bailee who has not yet attorned to the buyer.

2. Subsection (2) takes as its base line the proposition that any receipt of goods on credit by an insolvent buyer amounts to a tacit business misrepresentation of solvency and therefore is fraudulent as against the particular seller. This Article makes discovery of the buyer's insolvency and demand within a ten day period a condition of the right to reclaim goods on this ground. The ten day limitation period operates from the time of receipt of the goods.

An exception to this time limitation is made when a written misrepresentation of solvency has been made to the particular seller within three months prior to the delivery. To fall within the exception the statement of solvency must be in writing, addressed to the particular seller and dated within three months of the delivery.

3. Because the right of the seller to reclaim goods under this section constitutes preferential treatment as against the buyer's other creditors, subsection (3) provides that such reclamation bars all his other remedies as to the goods involved. As amended 1966.

Cross References:

Point 1: Sections 2–401 and 2–705.
Compare Section 2–502.

Definitional Cross References:

"Buyer". Section 2–103.
"Buyer in ordinary course of business". Section 1–201.
"Contract". Section 1–201.
"Good faith". Section 1–201.
"Goods". Section 2–105.
"Insolvent". Section 1–201.
"Person". Section 1–201.
"Purchaser". Section 1–201.
"Receipt" of goods. Section 2–103.
"Remedy". Section 1–201.
"Rights". Section 1–201.
"Seller". Section 2–103.
"Writing". Section 1–201.

§ 2–703.　Seller's Remedies in General.

Where the buyer wrongfully rejects or revokes acceptance of goods or fails to make a payment due on or before delivery or repudiates with respect to a part or the whole, then with respect to any goods directly affected and, if the breach is of the whole contract (Section 2–612), then also with respect to the whole undelivered balance, the aggrieved seller may

  (a) withhold delivery of such goods;

  (b) stop delivery by any bailee as hereafter provided (Section 2–705);

  (c) proceed under the next section respecting goods still unidentified to the contract;

  (d) resell and recover damages as hereafter provided (Section 2–706);

  (e) recover damages for non-acceptance (Section 2–708) or in a proper case the price (Section 2–709);

  (f) cancel.

Official Comment

Prior Uniform Statutory Provision: No comparable index section. See Section 53, Uniform Sales Act.

Purposes:

1. This section is an index section which gathers together in one convenient place all of the various remedies open to a seller for any breach by the buyer. This Article rejects any doctrine of election of remedy as a fundamental policy and thus the remedies are essentially cumulative in nature and include all of the available remedies for breach. Whether the pursuit of one remedy bars another depends entirely on the facts of the individual case.

2. The buyer's breach which occasions the use of the remedies under this section may involve only one lot or delivery of goods, or may involve all of the goods which are the subject matter of the particular contract. The right of the seller to pursue a remedy as to all the goods when the breach is as to only one or more lots is covered by the section on breach in installment contracts. The present section deals only with the remedies available after the goods involved in the breach have been determined by that section.

3. In addition to the typical case of refusal to pay or default in payment, the language in the preamble, "fails to make a payment due," is intended to cover the dishonor of a check on due presentment, or the non-acceptance of a draft, and the failure to furnish an agreed letter of credit.

4. It should also be noted that this Act requires its remedies to be liberally administered and provides that any right or obligation which it declares is enforceable by action unless a different effect is specifically prescribed (Section 1–106).

Cross References:

Point 2: Section 2–612.
Point 3: Section 2–325.
Point 4: Section 1–106.

Definitional Cross References:

"Aggrieved party". Section 1–201.
"Buyer". Section 2–103.
"Cancellation". Section 2–106.
"Contract". Section 1–201.
"Goods". Section 2–105.
"Remedy". Section 1–201.
"Seller". Section 2–103.

§ 2–704. Seller's Right to Identify Goods to the Contract Notwithstanding Breach or to Salvage Unfinished Goods.

(1) An aggrieved seller under the preceding section may

  (a) identify to the contract conforming goods not already identified if at the time he learned of the breach they are in his possession or control;

  (b) treat as the subject of resale goods which have demonstrably been intended for the particular contract even though those goods are unfinished.

(2) Where the goods are unfinished an aggrieved seller may in the exercise of reasonable commercial judgment for the purposes of avoiding loss and of effective realization either complete the manufacture and wholly identify the goods to the contract or cease manufacture and resell for scrap or salvage value or proceed in any other reasonable manner.

Official Comment

Prior Uniform Statutory Provision: Sections 63(3) and 64(4), Uniform Sales Act.

Changes: Rewritten, the seller's rights being broadened.

Purposes of Changes:

1. This section gives an aggrieved seller the right at the time of breach to identify to the contract any conforming finished goods, regardless of their resalability, and to use reasonable judgment as to completing unfinished goods. It thus makes the goods available for resale under the resale section, the seller's primary remedy, and in the special case in which resale is not practicable, allows the action for the price which would

then be necessary to give the seller the value of his contract.

2. Under this Article the seller is given express power to complete manufacture or procurement of goods for the contract unless the exercise of reasonable commercial judgment as to the facts as they appear at the time he learns of the breach makes it clear that such action will result in a material increase in damages. The burden is on the buyer to show the commercially unreasonable nature of the seller's action in completing manufacture.

Cross References:

Sections 2–703 and 2–706.

Definitional Cross References:

"Aggrieved party". Section 1–201.
"Conforming". Section 2–106.
"Contract". Section 1–201.
"Goods". Section 2–105.
"Rights". Section 1–201.
"Seller". Section 2–103.

§ 2–705. Seller's Stoppage of Delivery in Transit or Otherwise.

(1) The seller may stop delivery of goods in the possession of a carrier or other bailee when he discovers the buyer to be insolvent (Section 2–702) and may stop delivery of carload, truckload, planeload or larger shipments of express or freight when the buyer repudiates or fails to make a payment due before delivery or if for any other reason the seller has a right to withhold or reclaim the goods.

(2) As against such buyer the seller may stop delivery until

(a) receipt of the goods by the buyer; or

(b) acknowledgment to the buyer by any bailee of the goods except a carrier that the bailee holds the goods for the buyer; or

(c) such acknowledgment to the buyer by a carrier by reshipment or as warehouseman; or

(d) negotiation to the buyer of any negotiable document of title covering the goods.

(3)(a) To stop delivery the seller must so notify as to enable the bailee by reasonable diligence to prevent delivery of the goods.

(b) After such notification the bailee must hold and deliver the goods according to the di-rections of the seller but the seller is liable to the bailee for any ensuing charges or damages.

(c) If a negotiable document of title has been issued for goods the bailee is not obliged to obey a notification to stop until surrender of the document.

(d) A carrier who has issued a non-negotiable bill of lading is not obliged to obey a notification to stop received from a person other than the consignor.

Official Comment

Prior Uniform Statutory Provision: Sections 57–59, Uniform Sales Act; see also Sections 12, 14 and 42, Uniform Bills of Lading Act and Sections 9, 11 and 49, Uniform Warehouse Receipts Act.

Changes: This section continues and develops the above sections of the Uniform Sales Act in the light of the other uniform statutory provisions noted.

Purposes: To make it clear that:

1. Subsection (1) applies the stoppage principle to other bailees as well as carriers.

It also expands the remedy to cover the situations, in addition to buyer's insolvency, specified in the subsection. But since stoppage is a burden in any case to carriers, and might be a very heavy burden to them if it covered all small shipments in all these situations, the right to stop for reasons other than insolvency is limited to carload, truckload, planeload or larger shipments. The seller shipping to a buyer of doubtful credit can protect himself by shipping C.O.D.

Where stoppage occurs for insecurity it is merely a suspension of performance, and if assurances are duly forthcoming from the buyer the seller is not entitled to resell or divert.

Improper stoppage is a breach by the seller if it effectively interferes with the buyer's right to due tender under the section on manner of tender of delivery. However, if the bailee obeys an unjustified order to stop he may also be liable to the buyer. The measure of his obligation is dependent on the provisions of the Documents of Title Article (Section 7–303). Subsection 3(b) therefore gives him a right of indemnity as against the seller in such a case.

2. "Receipt by the buyer" includes receipt by the buyer's designated representative, the subpurchaser, when shipment is made direct to him and the buyer himself never receives the goods. It is entirely proper under this Article that the seller, by making such

direct shipment to the sub-purchaser, be regarded as acquiescing in the latter's purchase and as thus barred from stoppage of the goods as against him.

As between the buyer and the seller, the latter's right to stop the goods at any time until they reach the place of final delivery is recognized by this section.

Under subsection (3)(c) and (d), the carrier is under no duty to recognize the stop order of a person who is a stranger to the carrier's contract. But the seller's right as against the buyer to stop delivery remains, whether or not the carrier is obligated to recognize the stop order. If the carrier does obey it, the buyer cannot complain merely because of that circumstance; and the seller becomes obligated under subsection (3)(b) to pay the carrier any ensuing damages or charges.

3. A diversion of a shipment is not a "reshipment" under subsection (2)(c) when it is merely an incident to the original contract of transportation. Nor is the procurement of "exchange bills" of lading which change only the name of the consignee to that of the buyer's local agent but do not alter the destination of a reshipment.

Acknowledgment by the carrier as a "warehouseman" within the meaning of this Article requires a contract of a truly different character from the original shipment, a contract not in extension of transit but as a warehouseman.

4. Subsection (3)(c) makes the bailee's obedience of a notification to stop conditional upon the surrender of any outstanding negotiable document.

5. Any charges or losses incurred by the carrier in following the seller's orders, whether or not he was obligated to do so, fall to the seller's charge.

6. After an effective stoppage under this section the seller's rights in the goods are the same as if he had never made a delivery.

Cross References:

Sections 2–702 and 2–703.
Point 1: Sections 2–503 and 2–609, and Article 7.
Point 2: Section 2–103 and Article 7.

Definitional Cross References:

"Buyer". Section 2–103.
"Contract for sale". Section 2–106.
"Document of title". Section 1–201.
"Goods". Section 2–105.
"Insolvent". Section 1–201.
"Notification". Section 1–201.
"Receipt" of goods. Section 2–103.

"Rights". Section 1–201.
"Seller". Section 2–103.

§ 2–706. Seller's Resale Including Contract for Resale.

(1) Under the conditions stated in Section 2–703 on seller's remedies, the seller may resell the goods concerned or the undelivered balance thereof. Where the resale is made in good faith and in a commercially reasonable manner the seller may recover the difference between the resale price and the contract price together with any incidental damages allowed under the provisions of this Article (Section 2–710), but less expenses saved in consequence of the buyer's breach.

(2) Except as otherwise provided in subsection (3) or unless otherwise agreed resale may be at public or private sale including sale by way of one or more contracts to sell or of identification to an existing contract of the seller. Sale may be as a unit or in parcels and at any time and place and on any terms but every aspect of the sale including the method, manner, time, place and terms must be commercially reasonable. The resale must be reasonably identified as referring to the broken contract, but it is not necessary that the goods be in existence or that any or all of them have been identified to the contract before the breach.

(3) Where the resale is at private sale the seller must give the buyer reasonable notification of his intention to resell.

(4) Where the resale is at public sale

(a) only identified goods can be sold except where there is a recognized market for a public sale of futures in goods of the kind; and

(b) it must be made at a usual place or market for public sale if one is reasonably available and except in the case of goods which are perishable or threaten to decline in value speedily the seller must give the buyer reasonable notice of the time and place of the resale; and

(c) if the goods are not to be within the view of those attending the sale the notification of sale must state the place where the goods are located and provide for their reasonable inspection by prospective bidders; and

(d) the seller may buy.

(5) A purchaser who buys in good faith at a resale takes the goods free of any rights of the original buyer even though the seller fails to comply with one or more of the requirements of this section.

(6) The seller is not accountable to the buyer for any profit made on any resale. A person in the position of a seller (Section 2–707) or a buyer who has rightfully rejected or justifiably revoked acceptance must account for any excess over the amount of his security interest, as hereinafter defined (subsection (3) of Section 2–711).

Official Comment

Prior Uniform Statutory Provision: Section 60, Uniform Sales Act.

Changes: Rewritten.

Purposes of Changes: To simplify the prior statutory provision and to make it clear that:

1. The only condition precedent to the seller's right of resale under subsection (1) is a breach by the buyer within the section on the seller's remedies in general or insolvency. Other meticulous conditions and restrictions of the prior uniform statutory provision are disapproved by this Article and are replaced by standards of commercial reasonableness. Under this section the seller may resell the goods after any breach by the buyer. Thus, an anticipatory repudiation by the buyer gives rise to any of the seller's remedies for breach, and to the right of resale. This principle is supplemented by subsection (2) which authorizes a resale of goods which are not in existence or were not identified to the contract before the breach.

2. In order to recover the damages prescribed in subsection (1) the seller must act "in good faith and in a commercially reasonable manner" in making the resale. This standard is intended to be more comprehensive than that of "reasonable care and judgment" established by the prior uniform statutory provision. Failure to act properly under this section deprives the seller of the measure of damages here provided and relegates him to that provided in Section 2–708.

Under this Article the seller resells by authority of law, in his own behalf, for his own benefit and for the purpose of fixing his damages. The theory of a seller's agency is thus rejected.

3. If the seller complies with the prescribed standard of duty in making the resale, he may recover from the buyer the damages provided for in subsection (1). Evidence of market or current prices at any particular time or place is relevant only on the question of whether the seller acted in a commercially reasonable manner in making the resale.

The distinction drawn by some courts between cases where the title had not passed to the buyer and the seller had resold as owner, and cases where the title had passed and the seller had resold by virtue of his lien on the goods, is rejected.

4. Subsection (2) frees the remedy of resale from legalistic restrictions and enables the seller to resell in accordance with reasonable commercial practices so as to realize as high a price as possible in the circumstances. By "public" sale is meant a sale by auction. A "private" sale may be effected by solicitation and negotiation conducted either directly or through a broker. In choosing between a public and private sale the character of the goods must be considered and relevant trade practices and usages must be observed.

5. Subsection (2) merely clarifies the common law rule that the time for resale is a reasonable time after the buyer's breach, by using the language "commercially reasonable." What is such a reasonable time depends upon the nature of the goods, the condition of the market and the other circumstances of the case; its length cannot be measured by any legal yardstick or divided into degrees. Where a seller contemplating resale receives a demand from the buyer for inspection under the section of preserving evidence of goods in dispute, the time for resale may be appropriately lengthened.

On the question of the place for resale, subsection (2) goes to the ultimate test, the commercial reasonableness of the seller's choice as to the place for an advantageous resale. This Article rejects the theory that the seller is required to resell at the agreed place for delivery and that a resale elsewhere can be permitted only in exceptional cases.

6. The purpose of subsection (2) being to enable the seller to dispose of the goods to the best advantage, he is permitted in making the resale to depart from the terms and conditions of the original contract for sale to any extent "commercially reasonable" in the circumstances.

7. The provision of subsection (2) that the goods need not be in existence to be resold applies when the buyer is guilty of anticipatory repudiation of a contract for future goods, before the goods or some of them have come into existence. In such a case the seller may exercise the right of resale and fix his damages by "one or more contracts to sell" the quantity of conforming future goods affected by the repudiation. The companion provision of subsection (2) that resale may

be made although the goods were not identified to the contract prior to the buyer's breach, likewise contemplates an anticipatory repudiation by the buyer but occurring after the goods are in existence. If the goods so identified conform to the contract, their resale will fix the seller's damages quite as satisfactorily as if they had been identified before the breach.

8. Where the resale is to be by private sale, subsection (3) requires that reasonable notification of the seller's intention to resell must be given to the buyer. The length of notification of a private sale depends upon the urgency of the matter. Notification of the time and place of this type of sale is not required.

Subsection (4)(b) requires that the seller give the buyer reasonable notice of the time and place of a public resale so that he may have an opportunity to bid or to secure the attendance of other bidders. An exception is made in the case of goods "which are perishable or threaten to decline speedily in value."

9. Since there would be no reasonable prospect of competitive bidding elsewhere, subsection (4) requires that a public resale "must be made at a usual place or market for public sale if one is reasonably available;" i.e., a place or market which prospective bidders may reasonably be expected to attend. Such a market may still be "reasonably available" under this subsection, though at a considerable distance from the place where the goods are located. In such a case the expense of transporting the goods for resale is recoverable from the buyer as part of the seller's incidental damages under subsection (1). However, the question of availability is one of commercial reasonableness in the circumstances and if such "usual" place or market is not reasonably available, a duly advertised public resale may be held at another place if it is one which prospective bidders may reasonably be expected to attend, as distinguished from a place where there is no demand whatsoever for goods of the kind.

Paragraph (a) of subsection (4) qualifies the last sentence of subsection (2) with respect to resales of unidentified and future goods at public sale. If conforming goods are in existence the seller may identify them to the contract after the buyer's breach and then resell them at public sale. If the goods have not been identified, however, he may resell them at public sale only as "future" goods and only where there is a recognized market for public sale of futures in goods of the kind.

The provisions of paragraph (c) of subsection (4) are intended to permit intelligent bidding.

The provision of paragraph (d) of subsection (4) permitting the seller to bid and, of course, to become

the purchaser, benefits the original buyer by tending to increase the resale price and thus decreasing the damages he will have to pay.

10. This Article departs in subsection (5) from the prior uniform statutory provision in permitting a good faith purchaser at resale to take a good title as against the buyer even though the seller fails to comply with the requirements of this section.

11. Under subsection (6), the seller retains profit, if any, without distinction based on whether or not he had a lien since this Article divorces the question of passage of title to the buyer from the seller's right of resale or the consequences of its exercise. On the other hand, where "a person in the position of a seller" or a buyer acting under the section on buyer's remedies, exercises his right of resale under the present section he does so only for the limited purpose of obtaining cash for his "security interest" in the goods. Once that purpose has been accomplished any excess in the resale price belongs to the seller to whom an accounting must be made as provided in the last sentence of subsection (6).

Cross References:

Point 1: Sections 2–610, 2–702 and 2–703.
Point 2: Section 1–201.
Point 3: Sections 2–708 and 2–710.
Point 4: Section 2–328.
Point 8: Section 2–104.
Point 9: Section 2–710.
Point 11: Sections 2–401, 2–707 and 2–711(3).

Definitional Cross References:

"Buyer". Section 2–103.
"Contract". Section 1–201.
"Contract for sale". Section 2–106.
"Good faith". Section 2–103.
"Goods". Section 2–105.
"Merchant". Section 2–104.
"Notification". Section 1–201.
"Person in position of seller". Section 2–707.
"Purchase". Section 1–201.
"Rights". Section 1–201.
"Sale". Section 2–106.
"Security interest". Section 1–201.
"Seller". Section 2–103.

§ 2–707. "Person in the Position of a Seller".

(1) A "person in the position of a seller" includes as against a principal an agent who has paid or become responsible for the price of goods

on behalf of his principal or anyone who otherwise holds a security interest or other right in goods similar to that of a seller.

(2) A person in the position of a seller may as provided in this Article withhold or stop delivery (Section 2–705) and resell (Section 2–706) and recover incidental damages (Section 2–710).

Official Comment

Prior Uniform Statutory Provision: Section 52(2), Uniform Sales Act.

Changes: Rewritten.

Purposes of Changes: To make it clear that:

In addition to following in general the prior uniform statutory provision, the case of a financing agency which has acquired documents by honoring a letter of credit for the buyer or by discounting a draft for the seller has been included in the term "a person in the position of a seller."

Cross Reference:

Article 5, Section 2–506.

Definitional Cross References:

"Consignee". Section 7–102.
"Consignor". Section 7–102.
"Goods". Section 2–105.
"Security interest". Section 1–201.
"Seller". Section 2–103.

2–708. Seller's Damages for Non-acceptance or Repudiation.

(1) Subject to subsection (2) and to the provisions of this Article with respect to proof of market price (Section 2–723), the measure of damages for non-acceptance or repudiation by the buyer is the difference between the market price at the time and place for tender and the unpaid contract price together with any incidental damages provided in this Article (Section 2–710), but less expenses saved in consequence of the buyer's breach.

(2) If the measure of damages provided in subsection (1) is inadequate to put the seller in as good a position as performance would have done then the measure of damages is the profit (including reasonable overhead) which the seller would have made from full performance by the buyer, together with any incidental damages provided in this Article (Section 2–710), due allowance for costs reasonably incurred and due credit for payments or proceeds of resale.

Official Comment

Prior Uniform Statutory Provision: Section 64, Uniform Sales Act.

Changes: Rewritten.

Purposes of Changes: To make it clear that:

1. The prior uniform statutory provision is followed generally in setting the current market price at the time and place for tender as the standard by which damages for non-acceptance are to be determined. The time and place of tender is determined by reference to the section on manner of tender of delivery, and to the sections on the effect of such terms as FOB, FAS, CIF, C & F, Ex Ship and No Arrival, No Sale.

In the event that there is no evidence available of the current market price at the time and place of tender, proof of a substitute market may be made under the section on determination and proof of market price. Furthermore, the section on the admissibility of market quotations is intended to ease materially the problem of providing competent evidence.

2. The provision of this section permitting recovery of expected profit including reasonable overhead where the standard measure of damages is inadequate, together with the new requirement that price actions may be sustained only where resale is impractical, are designed to eliminate the unfair and economically wasteful results arising under the older law when fixed price articles were involved. This section permits the recovery of lost profits in all appropriate cases, which would include all standard priced goods. The normal measure there would be list price less cost to the dealer or list price less manufacturing cost to the manufacturer. It is not necessary to a recovery of "profit" to show a history of earnings, especially of a new venture is involved.

3. In all cases the seller may recover incidental damages.

Cross References:

Point 1: Sections 2–319 through 2–324, 2–503, 2–723 and 2–724.
Point 2: Section 2–709.
Point 3: Section 2–710.

Definitional Cross References:

"Buyer". Section 2–103.
"Contract". Section 1–201.
"Seller". Section 2–103.

§ 2–709. Action for the Price.

(1) When the buyer fails to pay the price as it becomes due the seller may recover, together with any incidental damages under the next section, the price

(a) of goods accepted or of conforming goods lost or damaged within a commercially reasonable time after risk of their loss has passed to the buyer; and

(b) of goods identified to the contract if the seller is unable after reasonable effort to resell them at a reasonable price or the circumstances reasonably indicate that such effort will be unavailing.

(2) Where the seller sues for the price he must hold for the buyer any goods which have been identified to the contract and are still in his control except that if resale becomes possible he may resell them at any time prior to the collection of the judgment. The net proceeds of any such resale must be credited to the buyer and payment of the judgment entitles him to any goods not resold.

(3) After the buyer has wrongfully rejected or revoked acceptance of the goods or has failed to make a payment due or has repudiated (Section 2–610), a seller who is held not entitled to the price under this section shall nevertheless be awarded damages for non-acceptance under the preceding section.

Official Comment

Prior Uniform Statutory Provision: Section 63, Uniform Sales Act.

Changes: Rewritten, important commercially needed changes being incorporated.

Purposes of Changes: To make it clear that:

1. Neither the passing of title to the goods nor the appointment of a day certain for payment is now material to a price action.

2. The action for the price is now generally limited to those cases where resale of the goods is impracticable except where the buyer has accepted the goods or where they have been destroyed after risk of loss has passed to the buyer.

3. This section substitutes an objective test by action for the former "not readily resalable" standard. An action for the price under subsection (1)(b) can be sustained only after a "reasonable effort to resell" the goods "at reasonable price" has actually been made or where the circumstances "reasonably indicate" that such an effort will be unavailing.

4. If a buyer is in default not with respect to the price, but on an obligation to make an advance, the seller should recover not under this section for the price as such, but for the default in the collateral (though coincident) obligation to finance the seller. If the agreement between the parties contemplates that the buyer will acquire, on making the advance, a security interest in the goods, the buyer on making the advance has such an interest as soon as the seller has rights in the agreed collateral. See Section 9–204.

5. "Goods accepted" by the buyer under subsection (1)(a) include only goods as to which there has been no justified revocation of acceptance, for such a revocation means that there has been a default by the seller which bars his rights under this section. "Goods lost or damaged" are covered by the section on risk of loss. "Goods identified to the contract" under subsection (1)(b) are covered by the section on identification and the section on identification notwithstanding breach.

6. This section is intended to be exhaustive in its enumeration of cases where an action for the price lies.

7. If the action for the price fails, the seller may nonetheless have proved a case entitling him to damages for non-acceptance. In such a situation, subsection (3) permits recovery of those damages in the same action.

Cross References:

Point 4: Section 1–106.
Point 5: Sections 2–501, 2–509, 2–510 and 2–704.
Point 7: Section 2–708.

Definitional Cross References:

"Action". Section 1–201.
"Buyer". Section 2–103.
"Conforming". Section 2–106.
"Contract". Section 1–201.
"Goods". Section 2–105.
"Seller". Section 2–103.

§ 2–710. Seller's Incidental Damages.

Incidental damages to an aggrieved seller include any commercially reasonable charges, expenses or commissions incurred in stopping delivery, in the transportation, care and custody of goods after the buyer's breach, in connection with return or resale of the goods or otherwise resulting from the breach.

Official Comment

Prior Uniform Statutory Provision: See Sections 64 and 70, Uniform Sales Act.

Purposes: To authorize reimbursement of the seller for expenses reasonably incurred by him as a result of the buyer's breach. The section sets forth the principal normal and necessary additional elements of damage flowing from the breach but intends to allow all commercially reasonable expenditures made by the seller.

Definitional Cross References:

"Aggrieved party". Section 1–201.
"Buyer". Section 2–103.
"Goods". Section 2–105.
"Seller". Section 2–103.

§ 2–711. Buyer's Remedies in General; Buyer's Security Interest in Rejected Goods.

(1) Where the seller fails to make delivery or repudiates or the buyer rightfully rejects or justifiably revokes acceptance then with respect to any goods involved, and with respect to the whole if the breach goes to the whole contract (Section 2–612), the buyer may cancel and whether or not he has done so may in addition to recovering so much of the price as has been paid

(a) "cover" and have damages under the next section as to all the goods affected whether or not they have been identified to the contract; or

(b) recover damages for non-delivery as provided in this Article (Section 2–713).

(2) Where the seller fails to deliver or repudiates the buyer may also

(a) if the goods have been identified recover them as provided in this Article (Section 2–502); or

(b) in a proper case obtain specific performance or replevy the goods as provided in this Article (Section 2–716).

(3) On rightful rejection or justifiable revocation of acceptance a buyer has a security interest in goods in his possession or control for any payments made on their price and any expenses reasonably incurred in their inspection, receipt, transportation, care and custody and may hold such goods and resell them in like manner as an aggrieved seller (Section 2–706).

Official Comment

Prior Uniform Statutory Provision: No comparable index section; Subsection (3)—Section 69(5), Uniform Sales Act.

Changes: The prior uniform statutory provision is generally continued and expanded in Subsection (3).

Purposes of Changes and New Matter:

1. To index in this section the buyer's remedies, subsection (1) covering those remedies permitting the recovery of money damages, and subsection (2) covering those which permit reaching the goods themselves. The remedies listed here are those available to a buyer who has not accepted the goods or who has justifiably revoked his acceptance. The remedies available to a buyer with regard to goods finally accepted appear in the section dealing with breach in regard to accepted goods. The buyer's right to proceed as to all goods when the breach is as to only some of the goods is determined by the section on breach in installment contracts and by the section on partial acceptance.

Despite the seller's breach, proper retender of delivery under the section on cure of improper tender or replacement can effectively preclude the buyer's remedies under this section, except for any delay involved.

2. To make it clear in subsection (3) that the buyer may hold and resell rejected goods if he has paid a part of the price or incurred expenses of the type specified. "Paid" as used here includes acceptance of a draft or other time negotiable instrument or the signing of a negotiable note. His freedom of resale is coextensive with that of a seller under this Article except that the buyer may not keep any profit resulting from the resale and is limited to retaining only the amount of the price paid and the costs involved in the inspection and handling of the goods. The buyer's security interest in the goods is intended to be limited to the items listed in subsection (3), and the buyer is not permitted to retain such funds as he might believe adequate for his damages. The buyer's right to cover, or to have damages for non-delivery, is not impaired by his exercise of his right of resale.

3. It should also be noted that this Act requires its remedies to be liberally administered and provides that any right or obligation which it declares is enforceable by action unless a different effect is specifically prescribed (Section 1–106).

Cross References:

Point 1: Sections 2–508, 2–601(c), 2–608, 2–612 and 2–714.

Point 2: Section 2–706.
Point 3: Section 1–106.

Definitional Cross References:

"Aggrieved party". Section 1–201.
"Buyer". Section 2–103.
"Cancellation". Section 2–106.
"Contract". Section 1–201.
"Cover". Section 2–712.
"Goods". Section 2–105.
"Notifies". Section 1–201.
"Receipt" of goods. Section 2–103.
"Remedy". Section 1–201.
"Security interest". Section 1–201.
"Seller". Section 2–103.

§ 2–712. "Cover"; Buyer's Procurement of Substitute Goods.

(1) After a breach within the preceding section the buyer may "cover" by making in good faith and without unreasonable delay any reasonable purchase of or contract to purchase goods in substitution for those due from the seller.

(2) The buyer may recover from the seller as damages the difference between the cost of cover and the contract price together with any incidental or consequential damages as hereinafter defined (Section 2–715), but less expenses saved in consequence of the seller's breach.

(3) Failure of the buyer to effect cover within this section does not bar him from any other remedy.

Official Comment

Prior Uniform Statutory Provision: None.

Purposes:

1. This section provides the buyer with a remedy aimed at enabling him to obtain the goods he needs thus meeting his essential need. This remedy is the buyer's equivalent of the seller's right to resell.

2. The definition of "cover" under subsection (1) envisages a series of contracts or sales, as well as a single contract or sale; goods not identical with those involved but commercially usable as reasonable substitutes under the circumstances of the particular case; and contracts on credit or delivery terms differing from the contract in breach, but again reasonable under the circumstances. The test of proper cover is whether at the time and place the buyer acted in good faith and in a reasonable manner, and it is immaterial that hindsight may later prove that the method of cover used was not the cheapest or most effective.

The requirement that the buyer must cover "without unreasonable delay" is not intended to limit the time necessary for him to look around and decide as to how he may best effect cover. The test here is similar to that generally used in this Article as to reasonable time and seasonable action.

3. Subsection (3) expresses the policy that cover is not a mandatory remedy for the buyer. The buyer is always free to choose between cover and damages for non-delivery under the next section.

However, this subsection must be read in conjunction with the section which limits the recovery of consequential damages to such as could not have been obviated by cover. Moreover, the operation of the section on specific performance of contracts for "unique" goods must be considered in this connection for availability of the goods to the particular buyer for his particular needs is the test for that remedy and inability to cover is made an express condition to the right of the buyer to replevy the goods.

4. This section does not limit cover to merchants, in the first instance. It is the vital and important remedy for the consumer buyer as well. Both are free to use cover: the domestic or non-merchant consumer is required only to act in normal good faith while the merchant buyer must also observe all reasonable commercial standards of fair dealing in the trade, since this falls within the definition of good faith on his part.

Cross References:

Point 1: Section 2–706.
Point 2: Section 1–204.
Point 3: Sections 2–713, 2–715 and 2–716.
Point 4: Section 1–203.

Definitional Cross References:

"Buyer". Section 2–103.
"Contract". Section 1–201.
"Good faith". Section 2–103.
"Goods". Section 2–105.
"Purchase". Section 1–201.
"Remedy". Section 1–201.
"Seller". Section 2–103.

§ 2–713. Buyer's Damages for Non-delivery or Repudiation.

(1) Subject to the provisions of this Article with respect to proof of market price (Section 2–723), the measure of damages for non-delivery or repudiation by the seller is the difference between the market price at the time when the

buyer learned of the breach and the contract price together with any incidental and consequential damages provided in this Article (Section 2–715), but less expenses saved in consequence of the seller's breach.

(2) Market price is to be determined as of the place for tender or, in cases of rejection after arrival or revocation of acceptance, as of the place of arrival.

Official Comment

Prior Uniform Statutory Provision: Section 67(3), Uniform Sales Act.

Changes: Rewritten.

Purposes of Changes: To clarify the former rule so that:

1. The general baseline adopted in this section uses as a yardstick the market in which the buyer would have obtained cover had he sought that relief. So the place for measuring damages is the place of tender (or the place of arrival if the goods are rejected or their acceptance is revoked after reaching their destination) and the crucial time is the time at which the buyer learns of the breach.

2. The market or current price to be used in comparison with the contract price under this section is the price for goods of the same kind and in the same branch of trade.

3. When the current market price under this section is difficult to prove the section on determination and proof of market price is available to permit a showing of a comparable market price or, where no market price is available, evidence of spot sale prices is proper. Where the unavailability of a market price is caused by a scarcity of goods of the type involved, a good case is normally made for specific performance under this Article. Such scarcity conditions, moreover, indicate that the price has risen and under the section providing for liberal administration of remedies, opinion evidence as to the value of the goods would be admissible in the absence of a market price and a liberal construction of allowable consequential damages should also result.

4. This section carries forward the standard rule that the buyer must deduct from his damages any expenses saved as a result of the breach.

5. The present section provides a remedy which is completely alternative to cover under the preceding section and applies only when and to the extent that the buyer has not covered.

Cross References:

Point 3: Sections 1–106, 2–716 and 2–723.
Point 5: Section 2–712.

Definitional Cross References:

"Buyer". Section 2–103.
"Contract". Section 1–201.
"Seller". Section 2–103.

§ 2–714. Buyer's Damages for Breach in Regard to Accepted Goods.

(1) Where the buyer has accepted goods and given notification (subsection (3) of Section 2–607) he may recover as damages for any nonconformity of tender the loss resulting in the ordinary course of events from the seller's breach as determined in any manner which is reasonable.

(2) The measure of damages for breach of warranty is the difference at the time and place of acceptance between the value of the goods accepted and the value they would have had if they had been as warranted, unless special circumstances show proximate damages of a different amount.

(3) In a proper case any incidental and consequential damages under the next section may also be recovered.

Official Comment

Prior Uniform Statutory Provision: Section 69(6) and (7), Uniform Sales Act.

Changes: Rewritten.

Purposes of Changes:

1. This section deals with the remedies available to the buyer after the goods have been accepted and the time for revocation of acceptance has gone by. In general this section adopts the rule of the prior uniform statutory provision for measuring damages where there has been a breach of warranty as to goods accepted, but goes further to lay down an explicit provision as to the time and place for determining the loss.

The section on deduction of damages from price provides an additional remedy for a buyer who still owes part of the purchase price, and frequently the two remedies will be available concurrently. The buyer's failure to notify of his claim under the section on effects of acceptance, however, operates to bar his remedies under either that section or the present section.

2. The "non-conformity" referred to in subsection (1) includes not only breaches of warranties but also any failure of the seller to perform according to his obligations under the contract. In the case of such non-conformity, the buyer is permitted to recover for his loss "in any manner which is reasonable."

3. Subsection (2) describes the usual, standard and reasonable method of ascertaining damages in the case of breach of warranty but it is not intended as an exclusive measure. It departs from the measure of damages for non-delivery in utilizing the place of acceptance rather than the place of tender. In some cases the two may coincide, as where the buyer signifies his acceptance upon the tender. If, however, the non-conformity is such as would justify revocation of acceptance, the time and place of acceptance under this section is determined as of the buyer's decision not to revoke.

4. The incidental and consequential damages referred to in subsection (3), which will usually accompany an action brought under this section, are discussed in detail in the comment on the next section.

Cross References:

Point 1: Compare Section 2–711; Sections 2–607 and 2–717.
Point 2: Section 2–106.
Point 3: Sections 2–608 and 2–713.
Point 4: Section 2–715.

Definitional Cross References:

"Buyer". Section 2–103.
"Conform". Section 2–106.
"Goods". Section 1–201.
"Notification". Section 1–201.
"Seller". Section 2–103.

§ 2–715. Buyer's Incidental and Consequential Damages.

(1) Incidental damages resulting from the seller's breach include expenses reasonably incurred in inspection, receipt, transportation and care and custody of goods rightfully rejected, any commercially reasonable charges, expenses or commissions in connection with effecting cover and any other reasonable expense incident to the delay or other breach.

(2) Consequential damages resulting from the seller's breach include

(a) any loss resulting from general or particular requirements and needs of which the seller at the time of contracting had reason to know and which could not reasonably be prevented by cover or otherwise; and

(b) injury to person or property proximately resulting from any breach of warranty.

Official Comment

Prior Uniform Statutory Provisions: Subsection (2)(b)—Sections 69(7) and 70, Uniform Sales Act.

Changes: Rewritten.

Purposes of Changes and New Matter:

1. Subsection (1) is intended to provide reimbursement for the buyer who incurs reasonable expenses in connection with the handling of rightfully rejected goods or goods whose acceptance may be justifiably revoked, or in connection with effecting cover where the breach of the contract lies in non-conformity or non-delivery of the goods. The incidental damages listed are not intended to be exhaustive but are merely illustrative of the typical kinds of incidental damage.

2. Subsection (2) operates to allow the buyer, in an appropriate case, any consequential damages which are the result of the seller's breach. The "tacit agreement" test for the recovery of consequential damages is rejected. Although the older rule at common law which made the seller liable for all consequential damages of which he had "reason to know" in advance is followed, the liberality of that rule is modified by refusing to permit recovery unless the buyer could not reasonably have prevented the loss by cover or otherwise. Subparagraph (2) carries forward the provisions of the prior uniform statutory provision as to consequential damages resulting from breach of warranty, but modifies the rule by requiring first that the buyer attempt to minimize his damages in good faith, either by cover or otherwise.

3. In the absence of excuse under the section on merchant's excuse by failure of presupposed conditions, the seller is liable for consequential damages in all cases where he had reason to know of the buyer's general or particular requirements at the time of contracting. It is not necessary that there be a conscious acceptance of an insurer's liability on the seller's part, nor is his obligation for consequential damages limited to cases in which he fails to use due effort in good faith.

Particular needs of the buyer must generally be made known to the seller while general needs must rarely be made known to charge the seller with knowledge.

Any seller who does not wish to take the risk of consequential damages has available the section on contractual limitation of remedy.

4. The burden of proving the extent of loss incurred by way of consequential damage is on the buyer, but the section on liberal administration of remedies rejects any doctrine of certainty which requires almost mathematical precision in the proof of loss. Loss may be determined in any manner which is reasonable under the circumstances.

5. Subsection (2)(b) states the usual rule as to breach of warranty, allowing recovery for injuries "proximately" resulting from the breach. Where the injury involved follows the use of goods without discovery of the defect causing the damage, the question of "proximate" cause turns on whether it was reasonable for the buyer to use the goods without such inspection as would have revealed the defects. If it was not reasonable for him to do so, or if he did in fact discover the defect prior to his use, the injury would not proximately result from the breach of warranty.

6. In the case of sale of wares to one in the business of reselling them, resale is one of the requirements of which the seller has reason to know within the meaning of subsection (2)(a).

Cross References:

Point 1: Section 2–608.
Point 3: Sections 1–203, 2–615 and 2–719.
Point 4: Section 1–106.

Definitional Cross References:

"Cover". Section 2–712.
"Goods". Section 1–201.
"Person". Section 1–201.
"Receipt" of goods. Section 2–103.
"Seller". Section 2–103.

§ 2–716. Buyer's Right to Specific Performance or Replevin.

(1) Specific performance may be decreed where the goods are unique or in other proper circumstances.

(2) The decree for specific performance may include such terms and conditions as to payment of the price, damages, or other relief as the court may deem just.

(3) The buyer has a right of replevin for goods identified to the contract if after reasonable effort he is unable to effect cover for such goods or the circumstances reasonably indicate that such effort will be unavailing or if the goods have been shipped under reservation and satisfaction of the security interest in them has been made or tendered. In the case of goods bought for personal, family, or household purposes, the buyer's right of replevin vests upon acquisition of a special property, even if the seller had not then repudiated or failed to deliver.

As amended in 1999.

Official Comment

Prior Uniform Statutory Provision: Section 68, Uniform Sales Act.

Changes: Rephrased.

Purposes of Changes: To make it clear that:

1. The present section continues in general prior policy as to specific performance and injunction against breach. However, without intending to impair in any way the exercise of the court's sound discretion in the matter, this Article seeks to further a more liberal attitude than some courts have shown in connection with the specific performance of contracts of sale.

2. In view of this Article's emphasis on the commercial feasibility of replacement, a new concept of what are "unique" goods is introduced under this section. Specific performance is no longer limited to goods which are already specific or ascertained at the time of contracting. The test of uniqueness under this section must be made in terms of the total situation which characterizes the contract. Output and requirements contracts involving a particular or peculiarly available source or market present today the typical commercial specific performance situation, as contrasted with contracts for the sale of heirlooms or priceless works of art which were usually involved in the older cases. However, uniqueness is not the sole basis of the remedy under this section for the relief may also be granted "in other proper circumstances" and inability to cover is strong evidence of "other proper circumstances".

3. The legal remedy of replevin is given to the buyer in cases in which cover is reasonably unavailable and goods have been identified to the contract. This is in addition to the buyer's right to recover identified goods under Section 2–502. For consumer goods, the buyer's right to replevin vests upon the buyer's acquisition of a special property, which occurs upon identification of the goods to the contract. See Section 2–501. Inasmuch as a secured party normally acquires no

greater rights in its collateral that its debtor had or had power to convey, see Section 2-403(1) (first sentence), a buyer who acquires a right of replevin under subsection (3) will take free of a security interest created by the seller if it attaches to the goods after the goods have been identified to the contract. The buyer will take free, even if the buyer does not buy in ordinary course and even if the security interest is perfected. Of course, to the extent that the buyer pays the price after the security interest attaches, the payments will constitute proceeds of the security interest.

4. This section is intended to give the buyer rights to the goods comparable to the seller's rights to the price.

5. If a negotiable document of title is outstanding, the buyer's right of replevin relates of course to the document not directly to the goods. See Article 7, especially Section 7-602.

Cross References:

Point 3: Section 2-502.
Point 4: Section 2-709.
Point 5: Article 7.

Definitional Cross References:

"Buyer". Section 2-103.
"Goods". Section 1-201.
"Rights". Section 1-201.

As amended in 1999.

§ 2-717. Deduction of Damages From the Price.

The buyer on notifying the seller of his intention to do so may deduct all or any part of the damages resulting from any breach of the contract from any part of the price still due under the same contract.

Official Comment

Prior Uniform Statutory Provision: See Section 69(1)(a), Uniform Sales Act.

Purposes:

1. This section permits the buyer to deduct from the price damages resulting from any breach by the seller and does not limit the relief to cases of breach of warranty as did the prior uniform statutory provision. To bring this provision into application the breach involved must be of the same contract under which the price in question is claimed to have been earned.

2. The buyer, however, must give notice of his intention to withhold all or part of the price if he wishes to avoid a default within the meaning of the section on insecurity and right to assurances. In conformity with the general policies of this Article, no formality of notice is required and any language which reasonably indicates the buyer's reason for holding up his payment is sufficient.

Cross Reference:

Point 2: Section 2-609.

Definitional Cross References:

"Buyer". Section 2-103.
"Notifies". Section 1-201.

§ 2-718. Liquidation or Limitation of Damages; Deposits.

(1) Damages for breach by either party may be liquidated in the agreement but only at an amount which is reasonable in the light of the anticipated or actual harm caused by the breach, the difficulties of proof of loss, and the inconvenience or nonfeasibility of otherwise obtaining an adequate remedy. A term fixing unreasonably large liquidated damages is void as a penalty.

(2) Where the seller justifiably withholds delivery of goods because of the buyer's breach, the buyer is entitled to restitution of any amount by which the sum of his payments exceeds

(a) the amount to which the seller is entitled by virtue of terms liquidating the seller's damages in accordance with subsection (1), or

(b) in the absence of such terms, twenty per cent of the value of the total performance for which the buyer is obligated under the contract or $500, whichever is smaller.

(3) The buyer's right to restitution under subsection (2) is subject to offset to the extent that the seller establishes

(a) a right to recover damages under the provisions of this Article other than subsection (1), and

(b) the amount or value of any benefits received by the buyer directly or indirectly by reason of the contract.

(4) Where a seller has received payment in goods their reasonable value or the proceeds of their resale shall be treated as payments for the

purposes of subsection (2); but if the seller has notice of the buyer's breach before reselling goods received in part performance, his resale is subject to the conditions laid down in this Article on resale by an aggrieved seller (Section 2–706).

Official Comment

Prior Uniform Statutory Provision: None.

Purposes:

1. Under subsection (1) liquidated damage clauses are allowed where the amount involved is reasonable in the light of the circumstances of the case. The subsection sets forth explicitly the elements to be considered in determining the reasonableness of a liquidated damage clause. A term fixing unreasonably large liquidated damages is expressly made void as a penalty. An unreasonably small amount would be subject to similar criticism and might be stricken under the section on unconscionable contracts or clauses.

2. Subsection (2) refuses to recognize a forfeiture unless the amount of the payment so forfeited represents a reasonable liquidation of damages as determined under subsection (1). A special exception is made in the case of small amounts (20% of the price or $500, whichever is smaller) deposited as security. No distinction is made between cases in which the payment is to be applied on the price and those in which it is intended as security for performance. Subsection (2) is applicable to any deposit or down or part payment. In the case of a deposit or turn in of goods resold before the breach, the amount actually received on the resale is to be viewed as the deposit rather than the amount allowed the buyer for the trade in. However, if the seller knows of the breach prior to the resale of the goods turned in, he must make reasonable efforts to realize their true value, and this is assured by requiring him to comply with the conditions laid down in the section on resale by an aggrieved seller.

Cross References:

Point 1: Section 2–302.
Point 2: Section 2–706.

Definitional Cross References:

"Aggrieved party". Section 1–201.
"Agreement". Section 1–201.
"Buyer". Section 2–103.
"Goods". Section 2–105.
"Notice". Section 1–201.
"Party". Section 1–201.
"Remedy". Section 1–201.
"Seller". Section 2–103.

"Term". Section 1–201.

§ 2–719. Contractual Modification or Limitation of Remedy.

(1) Subject to the provisions of subsections (2) and (3) of this section and of the preceding section on liquidation and limitation of damages,

(a) the agreement may provide for remedies in addition to or in substitution for those provided in this Article and may limit or alter the measure of damages recoverable under this Article, as by limiting the buyer's remedies to return of the goods and repayment of the price or to repair and replacement of non-conforming goods or parts; and

(b) resort to a remedy as provided is optional unless the remedy is expressly agreed to be exclusive, in which case it is the sole remedy.

(2) Where circumstances cause an exclusive or limited remedy to fail of its essential purpose, remedy may be had as provided in this Act.

(3) Consequential damages may be limited or excluded unless the limitation or exclusion is unconscionable. Limitation of consequential damages for injury to the person in the case of consumer goods is prima facie unconscionable but limitation of damages where the loss is commercial is not.

Official Comment

Prior Uniform Statutory Provision: None.

Purposes:

1. Under this section parties are left free to shape their remedies to their particular requirements and reasonable agreements limiting or modifying remedies are to be given effect.

However, it is of the very essence of a sales contract that at least minimum adequate remedies be available. If the parties intend to conclude a contract for sale within this Article they must accept the legal consequence that there be at least a fair quantum of remedy for breach of the obligations or duties outlined in the contract. Thus any clause purporting to modify or limit the remedial provisions of this Article in an unconscionable manner is subject to deletion and in that event the remedies made available by this Article are applicable as if the stricken clause had never existed. Similarly, under subsection (2), where an apparently fair and reasonable clause because of circumstances fails in its purpose or operates to deprive either party of the substantial value of the bargain, it must give way to the general remedy provisions of this Article.

2. Subsection (1)(b) creates a presumption that clauses prescribing remedies are cumulative rather than exclusive. If the parties intend the term to describe the sole remedy under the contract, this must be clearly expressed.

3. Subsection (3) recognizes the validity of clauses limiting or excluding consequential damages but makes it clear that they may not operate in an unconscionable manner. Actually such terms are merely an allocation of unknown or undeterminable risks. The seller in all cases is free to disclaim warranties in the manner provided in Section 2–316.

Cross References:

Point 1: Section 2–302.
Point 3: Section 2–316.

Definitional Cross References:

"Agreement". Section 1–201.
"Buyer". Section 2–103.
"Conforming". Section 2–106.
"Contract". Section 1–201.
"Goods". Section 2–105.
"Remedy". Section 1–201.
"Seller". Section 2–103.

§ 2–720. Effect of "Cancellation" or "Rescission" on Claims for Antecedent Breach.

Unless the contrary intention clearly appears, expressions of "cancellation" or "rescission" of the contract or the like shall not be construed as a renunciation or discharge of any claim in damages for an antecedent breach.

Official Comment

Prior Uniform Statutory Provision: None.

Purpose:

This section is designed to safeguard a person holding a right of action from any unintentional loss of rights by the ill-advised use of such terms as "cancellation", "rescission", or the like. Once a party's rights have accrued they are not to be lightly impaired by concessions made in business decency and without intention to forego them. Therefore, unless the cancellation of a contract expressly declares that it is

"without reservation of rights", or the like, it cannot be considered to be a renunciation under this section.

Cross Reference:

Section 1–107.

Definitional Cross References:

"Cancellation". Section 2–106.
"Contract". Section 1–201.

§ 2–721. Remedies for Fraud.

Remedies for material misrepresentation or fraud include all remedies available under this Article for non-fraudulent breach. Neither rescission or a claim for rescission of the contract for sale nor rejection or return of the goods shall bar or be deemed inconsistent with a claim for damages or other remedy.

Official Comment

Prior Uniform Statutory Provision: None.

Purposes: To correct the situation by which remedies for fraud have been more circumscribed than the more modern and mercantile remedies for breach of warranty. Thus the remedies for fraud are extended by this section to coincide in scope with those for non-fraudulent breach. This section thus makes it clear that neither rescission of the contract for fraud nor rejection of the goods bars other remedies unless the circumstances of the case make the remedies incompatible.

Definitional Cross References:

"Contract for sale". Section 2–106.
"Goods". Section 1–201.
"Remedy". Section 1–201.

§ 2–722. Who Can Sue Third Parties for Injury to Goods.

Where a third party so deals with goods which have been identified to a contract for sale as to cause actionable injury to a party to that contract

(a) a right of action against the third party is in either party to the contract for sale who has title to or a security interest or a special property or an insurable interest in the goods; and if the goods have been destroyed or converted a right of action is also in the party who either bore the risk of loss under the contract for sale or has since the injury assumed that risk as against the other;

(b) if at the time of the injury the party plaintiff did not bear the risk of loss as against the other party to the contract for sale and there is no arrangement between them for disposition of the recovery, his suit or settlement is, subject to his own interest, as a fiduciary for the other party to the contract;

(c) either party may with the consent of the other sue for the benefit of whom it may concern.

Official Comment

Prior Uniform Statutory Provision: None.

Purposes: To adopt and extend somewhat the principle of the statutes which provide for suit by the real party in interest. The provisions of this section apply only after identification of the goods. Prior to that time only the seller has a right of action. During the period between identification and final acceptance (except in the case of revocation of acceptance) it is possible for both parties to have the right of action. Even after final acceptance both parties may have the right of action if the seller retains possession or otherwise retains an interest.

Definitional Cross References:

"Action". Section 1–201.
"Buyer". Section 2–103.
"Contract for sale". Section 2–106.
"Goods". Section 2–105.
"Party". Section 1–201.
"Rights". Section 1–201.
"Security interest". Section 1–201.

§ 2–723. Proof of Market Price: Time and Place.

(1) If an action based on anticipatory repudiation comes to trial before the time for performance with respect to some or all of the goods, any damages based on market price (Section 2–708 or Section 2–713) shall be determined according to the price of such goods prevailing at the time when the aggrieved party learned of the repudiation.

(2) If evidence of a price prevailing at the times or places described in this Article is not readily available the price prevailing within any reasonable time before or after the time de-

scribed or at any other place which in commercial judgment or under usage of trade would serve as a reasonable substitute for the one described may be used, making any proper allowance for the cost of transporting the goods to or from such other place.

(3) Evidence of a relevant price prevailing at a time or place other than the one described in this Article offered by one party is not admissible unless and until he has given the other party such notice as the court finds sufficient to prevent unfair surprise.

Official Comment

Prior Uniform Statutory Provision: None.

Purposes: To eliminate the most obvious difficulties arising in connection with the determination of market price, when that is stipulated as a measure of damages by some provision of this Article. Where the appropriate market price is not readily available the court is here granted reasonable leeway in receiving evidence of prices current in other comparable markets or at other times comparable to the one in question. In accordance with the general principle of this Article against surprise, however, a party intending to offer evidence of such a substitute price must give suitable notice to the other party.

This section is not intended to exclude the use of any other reasonable method of determining market price or of measuring damages if the circumstances of the case make this necessary.

Definitional Cross References:

"Action". Section 1–201.
"Aggrieved party". Section 1–201.
"Goods". Section 2–105.
"Notifies". Section 1–201.
"Party". Section 1–201.
"Reasonable time". Section 1–204.
"Usage of trade". Section 1–205.

§ 2–724. Admissibility of Market Quotations.

Whenever the prevailing price or value of any goods regularly bought and sold in any established commodity market is in issue, reports in official publications or trade journals or in newspapers or periodicals of general circulation published as the reports of such market shall be admissible in evidence. The circumstances of the preparation of such a report may be shown to affect its weight but not its admissibility.

Official Comment

Prior Uniform Statutory Provision: None.

Purposes: To make market quotations admissible in evidence while providing for a challenge of the material by showing the circumstances of its preparation.

No explicit provision as to the weight to be given to market quotations is contained in this section, but such quotations, in the absence of compelling challenge, offer an adequate basis for a verdict.

Market quotations are made admissible when the price or value of goods traded "in any established market" is in issue. The reason of the section does not require that the market be closely organized in the manner of a produce exchange. It is sufficient if transactions in the commodity are frequent and open enough to make a market established by usage in which one price can be expected to affect another and in which an informed report of the range and trend of prices can be assumed to be reasonably accurate.

This section does not in any way intend to limit or negate the application of similar rules of admissibility to other material, whether by action of the courts or by statute. The purpose of the present section is to assure a minimum of mercantile administration in this important situation and not to limit any liberalizing trend in modern law.

Definitional Cross Reference:

"Goods". Section 2–105.

§ 2–725. Statute of Limitations in Contracts for Sale.

(1) An action for breach of any contract for sale must be commenced within four years after the cause of action has accrued. By the original agreement the parties may reduce the period of limitation to not less than one year but may not extend it.

(2) A cause of action accrues when the breach occurs, regardless of the aggrieved party's lack of knowledge of the breach. A breach of warranty occurs when tender of delivery is made, except that where a warranty explicitly extends to future performance of the goods and discovery of the breach must await the time of such performance the cause of action accrues when the breach is or should have been discovered.

(3) Where an action commenced within the time limited by subsection (1) is so terminated as to leave available a remedy by another action for the same breach such other action may be commenced after the expiration of the time limited and within six months after the termination of the first action unless the termination resulted from voluntary discontinuance or from dismissal for failure or neglect to prosecute.

(4) This section does not alter the law on tolling of the statute of limitations nor does it apply to causes of action which have accrued before this Act becomes effective.

Official Comment

Prior Uniform Statutory Provision: None.

Purposes: To introduce a uniform statute of limitations for sales contracts, thus eliminating the jurisdictional variations and providing needed relief for concerns doing business on a nationwide scale whose contracts have heretofore been governed by several different periods of limitation depending upon the state in which the transaction occurred. This Article takes sales contracts out of the general laws limiting the time for commencing contractual actions and selects a four year period as the most appropriate to modern business practice. This is within the normal commercial record keeping period.

Subsection (1) permits the parties to reduce the period of limitation. The minimum period is set at one year. The parties may not, however, extend the statutory period.

Subsection (2), providing that the cause of action accrues when the breach occurs, states an exception where the warranty extends to future performance.

Subsection (3) states the saving provision included in many state statutes and permits an additional short period for bringing new actions, where suits begun within the four year period have been terminated so as to leave a remedy still available for the same breach.

Subsection (4) makes it clear that this Article does not purport to alter or modify in any respect the law on tolling of the Statute of Limitations as it now prevails in the various jurisdictions.

Definitional Cross References:

"Action". Section 1–201.
"Aggrieved party". Section 1–201.
"Agreement". Section 1–201.
"Contract for sale". Section 2–106.
"Goods". Section 2–105.

"Party". Section 1–201.
"Remedy". Section 1–201.

"Term". Section 1–201.
"Termination". Section 2–106.

APPENDIX E

UNAMENDED UCC ARTICLE 2A (2000)

Set forth below are the text and Official Comments of Article 2A as they existed prior to amendment in in 2001 and 2003.

2001 amendments (Article 1 revision) ....*Appendix A*
2003 amendments ....*Appendix F*
2003 amendments (Article 7 revision) ....*Appendix B*
2005 amendments ....*Appendix J*

ARTICLE 2A
LEASES

PART 1.   GENERAL PROVISIONS

Section
2A–101.   Short Title.
2A–102.   Scope.
2A–103.   Definitions and Index of Definitions.
2A–104.   Leases Subject to Other Law.
2A–105.   Territorial Application of Article to Goods Covered by Certificate of Title.
2A–106.   Limitation on Power of Parties to Consumer Lease to Choose Applicable Law and Judicial Forum.
2A–107.   Waiver or Renunciation of Claim or Right After Default.
2A–108.   Unconscionability.
2A–109.   Option to Accelerate at Will.

PART 2.   FORMATION AND CONSTRUCTION OF LEASE CONTRACT

2A–201.   Statute of Frauds.
2A–202.   Final Written Expression: Parol or Extrinsic Evidence.
2A–203.   Seals Inoperative.
2A–204.   Formation in General.
2A–205.   Firm Offers.
2A–206.   Offer and Acceptance in Formation of Lease Contract.
2A–207.   [Reserved.]
2A–208.   Modification, Rescission and Waiver.
2A–209.   Lessee Under Finance Lease as Beneficiary of Supply Contract.

Section
2A–210.   Express Warranties.
2A–211.   Warranties Against Interference and Against Infringement; Lessee's Obligation Against Infringement.
2A–212.   Implied Warranty of Merchantability.
2A–213.   Implied Warranty of Fitness for Particular Purpose.
2A–214.   Exclusion or Modification of Warranties.
2A–215.   Cumulation and Conflict of Warranties Express or Implied.
2A–216.   Third-Party Beneficiaries of Express and Implied Warranties.
2A–217.   Identification.
2A–218.   Insurance and Proceeds.
2A–219.   Risk of Loss.
2A–220.   Effect of Default on Risk of Loss.
2A–221.   Casualty to Identified Goods.

PART 3.   EFFECT OF LEASE CONTRACT

2A–301.   Enforceability of Lease Contract.
2A–302.   Title to and Possession of Goods.
2A–303.   Alienability of Party's Interest Under Lease Contract or of Lessor's Residual Interest in Goods; Delegation of Performance; Transfer of Rights.
2A–304.   Subsequent Lease of Goods by Lessor.
2A–305.   Sale or Sublease of Goods by Lessee.
2A–306.   Priority of Certain Liens Arising by Operation of Law.

Section

2A–307. Priority of Liens Arising by Attachment or Levy on, Security Interests in, and Other Claims to Goods.

2A–308. Special Rights of Creditors.

2A–309. Lessor's and Lessee's Rights When Goods Become Fixtures.

2A–310. Lessor's and Lessee's Rights When Goods Become Accessions.

2A–311. Priority Subject to Subordination.

Section

A. IN GENERAL

Section

2A–501. Default: Procedure.

2A–502. Notice After Default.

2A–503. Modification or Impairment of Rights and Remedies.

2A–504. Liquidation of Damages.

2A–505. Cancellation and Termination and Effect of Cancellation, Termination, Rescission, or Fraud on Rights and Remedies.

2A–506. Statute of Limitations.

2A–507. Proof of Market Rent: Time and Place.

B. DEFAULT BY LESSOR

2A–508. Lessee's Remedies.

2A–509. Lessee's Rights on Improper Delivery; Rightful Rejection.

2A–510. Installment Lease Contracts: Rejection and Default.

2A–511. Merchant Lessee's Duties as to Rightfully Rejected Goods.

2A–512. Lessee's Duties as to Rightfully Rejected Goods.

2A–513. Cure by Lessor of Improper Tender or Delivery; Replacement.

2A–514. Waiver of Lessee's Objections.

2A–515. Acceptance of Goods.

2A–516. Effect of Acceptance of Goods; Notice of Default; Burden of Establishing Default After Acceptance; Notice of

PART 4. PERFORMANCE OF LEASE CONTRACT: REPUDIATED, SUBSTITUTED AND EXCUSED

2A–401. Insecurity: Adequate Assurance of Performance.

2A–402. Anticipatory Repudiation.

2A–403. Retraction of Anticipatory Repudiation.

2A–404. Substituted Performance.

2A–405. Excused Performance.

2A–406. Procedure on Excused Performance.

2A–407. Irrevocable Promises: Finance Leases.

PART 5. DEFAULT

Section

Claim or Litigation to Person Answerable Over.

2A–517. Revocation of Acceptance of Goods.

2A–518. Cover; Substitute Goods.

2A–519. Lessee's Damages for Non-delivery, Repudiation, Default, and Breach of Warranty in Regard to Accepted Goods.

2A–520. Lessee's Incidental and Consequential Damages.

2A–521. Lessee's Right to Specific Performance or Replevin.

2A–522. Lessee's Right to Goods on Lessor's Insolvency.

C. DEFAULT BY LESSEE

2A–523. Lessor's Remedies.

2A–524. Lessor's Right to Identify Goods to Lease Contract.

2A–525. Lessor's Right to Possession of Goods.

2A–526. Lessor's Stoppage of Delivery in Transit or Otherwise.

2A–527. Lessor's Rights to Dispose of Goods.

2A–528. Lessor's Damages for Non-acceptance, Failure to Pay, Repudiation, or Other Default.

2A–529. Lessor's Action for the Rent.

2A–530. Lessor's Incidental Damages.

2A–531. Standing to Sue Third Parties for Injury to Goods.

2A–532. Lessor's Rights to Residual Interest.

National Conference of Commissioners on Uniform State Laws

REPORTER

Ronald DeKoven, New York, New York

DRAFTING COMMITTEE

CHAIRMAN

Edward I. Cutler, Tampa, Florida

MEMBERS

FOREWORD

Article 2A of the Uniform Commercial Code, along with Conforming Amendments to Articles 1 and 9, is presented, upon the recommendation of the Permanent Editorial Board for the Uniform Commercial Code, by the National Conference of Commissioners on Uniform State Laws and the American Law Institute. It represents a major development in commercial law, addressing a type of business transaction, the leasing of personal property, that has long existed. Under present law, transactions of this type are governed partly by common law principles relating to personal property, partly by principles relating to real estate leases, and partly by reference to Articles 2 and 9 of the Uniform Commercial Code, dealing with Sales and Secured Transactions respectively. The legal rules and concepts derived from these sources imperfectly fit a transaction that involves personal property rather than realty, and a lease rather than either a sale or a security interest as such. A statute directly addressing the personal property lease is therefore appropriate.

Such a statute has become especially appropriate with the exponential expansion of the number and scale of personal property lease transactions. Article 2A will apply to transactions involving billions of dollars annually. It will apply to consumer's rental of automobiles or do-it-yourself equipment, on the one hand, and to leases of such items as commercial aircraft (to the extent not preempted by federal law) and industrial machinery, on the other. The text recognizes the differences between consumer and business leasing, while resting upon concepts that apply generally to any personal property lease transactions.

The final product represents an important undertaking of the Conference and the Institute. It has proceeded, following recommendations by the Conference's Study Committee in 1981, through preparation and review by the Conference's Drafting Committee first of a proposed free-standing Uniform Personal Property Leasing Act, which was approved by the Conference, and later of Article 2A, which proceeded through the Permanent Editorial Board, the Executive Committee of the Conference, the Conference, and the Council of the Institute and the Annual Meeting of the members of the Institute. Carrying the text through these several stages has required coordination of somewhat different procedures, and continued patience and mutual forbearance. At the same time, the text has been subjected to analysis and criticism from many points of view and thereby steadily improved.

The resulting product borrows from both Articles 2 and 9. These existing Articles of the Uniform Commercial Code have certain imperfections revealed by the long experience since their adoption. Article 2A cannot overcome those imperfections but seeks to minimize their significance as applied to leases. More fundamentally, there is important conceptual dissonance between Article 2 and Article 9. The formulation of Article 2A takes Articles 2 and 9 as they are for the time being and hence has required careful adjustment to this dissonance.

The drafting task has been complicated both as a matter of substance and as a matter of process. The Reporter, Ronald DeKoven, has been a master of substance and a steady and receptive principal in the process. We join with the Conference and the Institute in expressing our admiration and appreciation for his contribution to this important field of law.

Geoffrey C. Hazard, Jr., *Chairman* Permanent Editorial Board for the Uniform Commercial Code

October 1, 1987

PART 1

GENERAL PROVISIONS

§ 2A–101. Short Title.

This Article shall be known and may be cited as the Uniform Commercial Code—Leases.

Official Comment

Rationale for Codification:

There are several reasons for codifying the law with respect to leases of goods. An analysis of the case law as it applies to leases of goods suggests at least three significant issues to be resolved by codification. First, what is a lease? It is necessary to define lease to determine whether a transaction creates a lease or a security interest disguised as a lease. If the transaction creates a security interest disguised as a lease, the lessor will be required to file a financing statement or take other action to perfect its interest in the goods against third parties. There is no such requirement with respect to leases. Yet the distinction between a lease and a security interest disguised as a lease is not clear. Second, will the lessor be deemed to have made warranties to the lessee? If the transaction is a sale the express and implied warranties of Article 2 of the Uniform Commercial Code apply. However, the warranty law with respect to leases is uncertain. Third, what remedies are available to the lessor upon the lessee's default? If the transaction is a security interest disguised as a lease, the answer is stated in Part 5 of the Article on Secured Transactions (Article 9). There is no clear answer with respect to leases.

There are reasons to codify the law with respect to leases of goods in addition to those suggested by a review of the reported cases. The answer to this important question should not be limited to the issues raised in these cases. Is it not also proper to determine the remedies available to the lessee upon the lessor's default? It is, but that issue is not reached through a review of the reported cases. This is only one of the many issues presented in structuring, negotiating and documenting a lease of goods.

Statutory Analogue:

After it was decided to proceed with the codification project, the drafting committee of the National Conference of Commissioners on Uniform State Laws looked for a statutory analogue, gradually narrowing the focus to the Article on Sales (Article 2) and the Article on Secured Transactions (Article 9). A review of the literature with respect to the sale of goods reveals that Article 2 is predicated upon certain assumptions: Parties to the sales transaction frequently are without counsel; the agreement of the parties often is oral or evidenced by scant writings; obligations between the parties are bilateral; applicable law is influenced by the need to preserve freedom of contract. A review of the literature with respect to personal property security law reveals that Article 9 is predicated upon very different assumptions: Parties to a secured transaction regularly are represented by counsel; the agreement of the parties frequently is reduced to a writing, extensive in scope; the obligations between the parties are essentially unilateral; and applicable law seriously limits freedom of contract.

The lease is closer in spirit and form to the sale of goods than to the creation of a security interest. While parties to a lease are sometimes represented by counsel and their agreement is often reduced to a writing, the obligations of the parties are bilateral and the common law of leasing is dominated by the need to preserve freedom of contract. Thus the drafting committee concluded that Article 2 was the appropriate statutory analogue.

Issues: The drafting committee then identified and resolved several issues critical to codification:

Scope: The scope of the Article was limited to leases (Section 2A–102). There was no need to include leases intended as security, *i.e.*, security interests disguised as leases, as they are adequately treated in Article 9. Further, even if leases intended as security were included, the need to preserve the distinction would remain, as policy suggests treatment significantly different from that accorded leases.

Definition of Lease: Lease was defined to exclude leases intended as security (Section 2A–103(1)(j)). Given the litigation to date a revised definition of security interest was suggested for inclusion in the Act. (Section 1–201(37)). This revision sharpens the distinction between leases and security interests disguised as leases.

Filing: The lessor was not required to file a financing statement against the lessee or take any other action to protect the lessor's interest in the goods (Section 2A–301). The refined definition of security interest will more clearly signal the need to file to potential lessors of goods. Those lessors who are concerned will file a protective financing statement (Section 9–505).

Warranties: All of the express and implied warranties of the Article on Sales (Article 2) were included (Sections 2A–210 through 2A–216), revised to reflect differences in lease transactions. The lease of goods is sufficiently similar to the sale of goods to justify this decision. Further, many courts have reached the same decision.

Certificate of Title Laws: Many leasing transactions involve goods subject to certificate of title statutes. To avoid conflict with those statutes, this Article is subject to them (Section 2A–104(1)(a)).

Consumer Leases: Many leasing transactions involve parties subject to consumer protection statutes or decisions. To avoid conflict with those laws this Article is subject to them to the extent provided in (Section 2A–104(1)(c) and (2)). Further, certain consumer protections have been incorporated in the Article.

Finance Leases: Certain leasing transactions substitute the supplier of the goods for the lessor as the party responsible to the lessee with respect to warranties and the like. The definition of finance lease (Section 2A–103(1)(g)) was developed to describe these transactions. Various sections of the Article implement the substitution of the supplier for the lessor, including Sections 2A–209 and 2A–407. No attempt was made to fashion a special rule where the finance lessor is an affiliate of the supplier of goods; this is to be developed by the courts, case by case.

Sale and Leaseback: Sale and leaseback transactions are becoming increasingly common. A number of state statutes treat transactions where possession is retained by the seller as fraudulent *per se* or *prima facie* fraudulent. That position is not in accord with modern practice and thus is changed by the Article "if the buyer bought for value and in good faith" (Section 2A–308(3)).

Remedies: The Article has not only provided for lessor's remedies upon default by the lessee (Sections 2A–523 through 2A–531), but also for lessee's remedies upon default by the lessor (Sections 2A–508 through 2A–522). This is a significant departure from Article 9, which provides remedies only for the secured party upon default by the debtor. This difference is compelled by the bilateral nature of the obligations between the parties to a lease.

Damages: Many leasing transactions are predicated on the parties' ability to stipulate an appropriate measure of damages in the event of default. The rule with respect to sales of goods (Section 2–718) is not sufficiently flexible to accommodate this practice. Consistent with the common law emphasis upon freedom to contract, the Article has created a revised rule that allows greater flexibility with respect to leases of goods (Section 2A–504(1)).

History:

This Article is a revision of the Uniform Personal Property Leasing Act, which was approved by the National Conference of Commissioners on Uniform State Laws in August, 1985. However, it was believed that the subject matter of the Uniform Personal Property Leasing Act would be better treated as an article of this Act. Thus, although the Conference promulgated the Uniform Personal Property Leasing Act as a Uniform Law, activity was held in abeyance to allow time to restate the Uniform Personal Property Leasing Act as Article 2A.

In August, 1986 the Conference approved and recommended this Article (including conforming amendments to Article 1 and Article 9) for promulgation as an amendment to this Act. In December, 1986 the Council of the American Law Institute approved and recommended this Article (including conforming amendments to Article 1 and Article 9), with official comments, for promulgation as an amendment to this Act. In March, 1987 the Permanent Editorial Board for the Uniform Commercial Code approved and recommended this Article (including conforming amendments to Article 1 and Article 9), with official comments, for promulgation as an amendment to this Act. In May, 1987 the American Law Institute approved and recommended this Article (including conforming amendments to Article 1 and Article 9), with official comments, for promulgation as an amendment to this Act. In August, 1987 the Conference confirmed its approval of the final text of this Article.

Upon its initial promulgation, Article 2A was rapidly enacted in several states, was introduced in a number of other states, and underwent bar association, law revision commission and legislative study in still further states. In that process debate emerged, principally sparked by the study of Article 2A by the California Bar Association, California's non-uniform amendments to Article 2A, and articles appearing in a symposium on Article 2A published after its promulgation in the Alabama Law Review. The debate chiefly centered on whether Article 2A had struck the proper balance or was clear enough concerning the ability of a lessor to grant a security interest in its leasehold interest and in the residual, priority between a secured party and the lessee, and the lessor's remedy structure under Article 2A.

This debate over issues on which reasonable minds could and did differ began to affect the enactment effort for Article 2A in a deleterious manner. Consequently, the Standby Committee for Article 2A, composed predominantly of the former members of the drafting committee, reviewed the legislative actions and studies in the various states, and opened a dialogue with the principal proponents of the non-uniform amendments. Negotiations were conducted in conjunction with, and were facilitated by, a study of the uniform Article and the non-uniform Amendments by the New York Law Revision Commission. Ultimately, a consensus was reached, which has been approved by the membership of the Conference, the Permanent Editorial Board, and the Council of the Institute. Rapid and uniform enactment of Article 2A is expected as a result of the completed amendments. The Article 2A experience reaffirms the essential viability of the procedures of the Conference and the Institute for creating and updating uniform state law in the commercial law area.

Relationship of Article 2A to Other Articles:

The Article on Sales provided a useful point of reference for codifying the law of leases. Many of the provisions of that Article were carried over, changed to reflect differences in style, leasing terminology or leasing practices. Thus, the official comments to those sections of Article 2 whose provisions were carried over are incorporated by reference in Article 2A, as well; further, any case law interpreting those provisions should be viewed as persuasive but not binding on a court when deciding a similar issue with respect to leases. Any change in the sequence that has been made when carrying over a provision from Article 2 should be viewed as a matter of style, not substance. This is not to suggest that in other instances Article 2A did not also incorporate substantially revised provisions of Article 2, Article 9 or otherwise where the revision was driven by a concern over the substance; but for the lack of a mandate, the drafting committee might well have made the same or a similar change in the statutory analogue. Those sections in Article 2A include Sections 2A–104, 2A–105, 2A–106, 2A–108(2) and (4), 2A–109(2), 2A–208, 2A–214(2) and (3)(a), 2A–216, 2A–303, 2A–306, 2A–503, 2A–504(3)(b), 2A–506(2), and 2A–515. For lack of relevance or significance not all of the provisions of Article 2 were incorporated in Article 2A.

This codification was greatly influenced by the fundamental tenet of the common law as it has developed with respect to leases of goods: freedom of the parties to contract. Note that, like all other Articles of this Act, the principles of construction and interpretation contained in Article 1 are applicable throughout Article 2A (Section 2A–103(4)). These principles include the ability of the parties to vary the effect of the provisions of Article 2A, subject to certain limitations including those that relate to the obligations of good faith, diligence, reasonableness and care (Section 1–102(3)). Consistent with those principles no negative inference is to be drawn by the episodic use of the phrase "unless otherwise agreed" in certain provisions of Article 2A. Section 1–102(4). Indeed, the contrary is true, as the general rule in the Act, including this Article, is that the effect of the Act's provisions may be varied by agreement. Section 1–102(3). This conclusion follows even where the statutory analogue contains the phrase and the correlative provision in Article 2A does not.

§ 2A–102.   Scope.

This Article applies to any transaction, regardless of form, that creates a lease.

Official Comment

Uniform Statutory Source: Former Section 9–102(1) (now codified as Section 9–109). Throughout this Article, unless otherwise stated, references to "Section" are to other sections of this Act.

Changes: Substantially revised.

Purposes: This Article governs transactions as diverse as the lease of a hand tool to an individual for a few hours and the leveraged lease of a complex line of industrial equipment to a multi-national organization for a number of years.

To achieve that end it was necessary to provide that this Article applies to any transaction, regardless of form, that creates a lease. Since lease is defined as a transfer of an interest in goods (Section 2A–103(1)(j)) and goods is defined to include fixtures (Section 2A–103(1)(h)), application is limited to the extent the transaction relates to goods, including fixtures. Further, since the definition of lease does not include a sale (Section 2–106(1)) or retention or creation of a security interest (Section 1–201(37)), application is further limited; sales and security interests are governed by other Articles of this Act.

Finally, in recognition of the diversity of the transactions to be governed, the sophistication of many of the parties to these transactions, and the common law tradition as it applies to the bailment for hire or lease, freedom of contract has been preserved. DeKoven, Proceedings After Default by the Lessee Under a True Lease of Equipment, in 1C P. Coogan, W. Hogan, D. Vagts, *Secured Transactions Under the Uniform Commercial Code*, § 29B.02[2] (1986). Thus, despite the extensive regulatory scheme established by this Article, the parties to a lease will be able to create private rules to govern their transaction. Sections 2A–103(4) and 1–102(3). However, there are special rules in this Article governing consumer leases, as well as other state and federal statutes, that may further limit freedom of contract with respect to consumer leases.

A court may apply this Article by analogy to any transaction, regardless of form, that creates a lease of personal property other than goods, taking into account the expressed intentions of the parties to the transaction and any differences between a lease of goods and a lease of other property. Such application has precedent as the provisions of the Article on Sales (Article 2) have been applied by analogy to leases of goods. *E.g.*, Hawkland, *The Impact of the Uniform Commercial Code on Equipment Leasing*, 1972 Ill.L.F. 446; Murray, *Under the Spreading Analogy of Article 2 of the Uniform Commercial Code*, 39 Fordham L.Rev. 447 (1971). Whether such application would be appropriate for other bailments of personal property, gratuitous or for hire, should be determined by the facts of each case. *See Mieske v. Bartell Drug Co.*, 92 Wash.2d 40, 46–48, 593 P.2d 1308, 1312 (1979).

Further, parties to a transaction creating a lease of personal property other than goods, or a bailment of personal property may provide by agreement that this Article applies. Upholding the parties' choice is consistent with the spirit of this Article.

Cross References:

Sections 1–102(3), 1–201(37), Article 2, esp. Section 2–106(1), and Sections 2A–103(1)(h), 2A–103(1)(j) and 2A–103(4).

Definitional Cross Reference:

"Lease". Section 2A–103(1)(j).

§ 2A–103. Definitions and Index of Definitions.

(1) In this Article unless the context otherwise requires:

(a) "Buyer in ordinary course of business" means a person who in good faith and without knowledge that the sale to him [or her] is in violation of the ownership rights or security interest or leasehold interest of a third party in the goods buys in ordinary course from a person in the business of selling goods of that kind but does not include a pawnbroker. "Buying" may be for cash or by exchange of other property or on secured or unsecured credit and includes receiving goods or documents of title under a pre-existing contract for sale but does not include a transfer in bulk or as security for or in total or partial satisfaction of a money debt.

(b) "Cancellation" occurs when either party puts an end to the lease contract for default by the other party.

(c) "Commercial unit" means such a unit of goods as by commercial usage is a single whole for purposes of lease and division of which materially impairs its character or value on the market or in use. A commercial unit may be a single article, as a machine, or a set of articles, as a suite of furniture or a line of machinery, or a quantity, as a gross or carload, or any other unit treated in use or in the relevant market as a single whole.

(d) "Conforming" goods or performance under a lease contract means goods or performance that are in accordance with the obligations under the lease contract.

(e) "Consumer lease" means a lease that a lessor regularly engaged in the business of leasing or selling makes to a lessee who is an individual and who takes under the lease primarily for a personal, family, or household purpose [, if the total payments to be made under the lease contract, excluding payments for options to renew or buy, do not exceed $_____].

(f) "Fault" means wrongful act, omission, breach, or default.

(g) "Finance lease" means a lease with respect to which:

(i) the lessor does not select, manufacture, or supply the goods;

(ii) the lessor acquires the goods or the right to possession and use of the goods in connection with the lease; and

(iii) one of the following occurs:

(A) the lessee receives a copy of the contract by which the lessor acquired the goods or the right to possession and use of the goods before signing the lease contract;

(B) the lessee's approval of the contract by which the lessor acquired the goods or the right to possession and use of the goods is a condition to effectiveness of the lease contract;

(C) the lessee, before signing the lease contract, receives an accurate and complete statement designating the promises and warranties, and any disclaimers of warranties, limitations or modifications of remedies, or liquidated damages, including those of a third party, such as the manufacturer of the goods, provided to the lessor by the person supplying the goods in connection with or as part of the contract by which the lessor acquired the goods or the right to possession and use of the goods; or

(D) if the lease is not a consumer lease, the lessor, before the lessee signs the lease contract, informs the lessee in writing (a) of the identity of the person supplying the goods to the lessor, unless the lessee has selected that person and directed the lessor to acquire the goods or the right to possession

and use of the goods from that person, (b) that the lessee is entitled under this Article to the promises and warranties, including those of any third party, provided to the lessor by the person supplying the goods in connection with or as part of the contract by which the lessor acquired the goods or the right to possession and use of the goods, and (c) that the lessee may communicate with the person supplying the goods to the lessor and receive an accurate and complete statement of those promises and warranties, including any disclaimers and limitations of them or of remedies.

(h) "Goods" means all things that are movable at the time of identification to the lease contract, or are fixtures (Section 2A–309), but the term does not include money, documents, instruments, accounts, chattel paper, general intangibles, or minerals or the like, including oil and gas, before extraction. The term also includes the unborn young of animals.

(i) "Installment lease contract" means a lease contract that authorizes or requires the delivery of goods in separate lots to be separately accepted, even though the lease contract contains a clause "each delivery is a separate lease" or its equivalent.

(j) "Lease" means a transfer of the right to possession and use of goods for a term in return for consideration, but a sale, including a sale on approval or a sale or return, or retention or creation of a security interest is not a lease. Unless the context clearly indicates otherwise, the term includes a sublease.

(k) "Lease agreement" means the bargain, with respect to the lease, of the lessor and the lessee in fact as found in their language or by implication from other circumstances including course of dealing or usage of trade or course of performance as provided in this Article. Unless the context clearly indicates otherwise, the term includes a sublease agreement.

(l) "Lease contract" means the total legal obligation that results from the lease agreement as affected by this Article and any other applicable rules of law. Unless the context clearly indicates otherwise, the term includes a sublease contract.

(m) "Leasehold interest" means the interest of the lessor or the lessee under a lease contract.

(n) "Lessee" means a person who acquires the right to possession and use of goods under a lease. Unless the context clearly indicates otherwise, the term includes a sublessee.

(o) "Lessee in ordinary course of business" means a person who in good faith and without knowledge that the lease to him [or her] is in violation of the ownership rights or security interest or leasehold interest of a third party in the goods, leases in ordinary course from a person in the business of selling or leasing goods of that kind but does not include a pawnbroker. "Leasing" may be for cash or by exchange of other property or on secured or unsecured credit and includes receiving goods or documents of title under a pre-existing lease contract but does not include a transfer in bulk or as security for or in total or partial satisfaction of a money debt.

(p) "Lessor" means a person who transfers the right to possession and use of goods under a lease. Unless the context clearly indicates otherwise, the term includes a sublessor.

(q) "Lessor's residual interest" means the lessor's interest in the goods after expiration, termination, or cancellation of the lease contract.

(r) "Lien" means a charge against or interest in goods to secure payment of a debt or performance of an obligation, but the term does not include a security interest.

(s) "Lot" means a parcel or a single article that is the subject matter of a separate lease or delivery, whether or not it is sufficient to perform the lease contract.

(t) "Merchant lessee" means a lessee that is a merchant with respect to goods of the kind subject to the lease.

(u) "Present value" means the amount as of a date certain of one or more sums payable in the future, discounted to the date certain. The discount is determined by the interest rate specified by the parties if the rate was not manifestly unreasonable at the time the transaction was entered into; otherwise, the discount is determined by a commercially reasonable rate that takes into account the facts and circumstances of each case at the time the transaction was entered into.

(v) "Purchase" includes taking by sale, lease, mortgage, security interest, pledge, gift, or any other voluntary transaction creating an interest in goods.

(w) "Sublease" means a lease of goods the right to possession and use of which was acquired by the lessor as a lessee under an existing lease.

(x) "Supplier" means a person from whom a lessor buys or leases goods to be leased under a finance lease.

(y) "Supply contract" means a contract under which a lessor buys or leases goods to be leased.

(z) "Termination" occurs when either party pursuant to a power created by agreement or law puts an end to the lease contract otherwise than for default.

(2) Other definitions applying to this Article and the sections in which they appear are:

"Accessions". Section 2A–310(1).

"Construction mortgage". Section 2A–309(1)(d).

"Encumbrance". Section 2A–309(1)(e).

"Fixtures". Section 2A–309(1)(a).

"Fixture filing". Section 2A–309(1)(b).

"Purchase money lease". Section 2A–309(1)(c).

(3) The following definitions in other Articles apply to this Article:

"Account". Section 9–102(a)(2).

"Between merchants". Section 2–104(3).

"Buyer". Section 2–103(1)(a).

"Chattel paper". Section 9–102(a)(11).

"Consumer goods". Section 9–102(a)(23).

"Document". Section 9–102(a)(30).

"Entrusting". Section 2–403(3).

"General intangible". Section 9–102(a)(42).

"Good Faith". Section 2–103(1)(b).

"Instrument". Section 9–102(a)(47).

"Merchant". Section 2–104(1).

"Mortgage". Section 9–102(a)(55).

"Pursuant to commitment". Section 9–102(a)(68).

"Receipt". Section 2–103(1)(c).

"Sale". Section 2–106(1).

"Sale on approval". Section 2–326.

"Sale or return". Section 2–326.

"Seller". Section 2–103(1)(d).

(4) In addition Article 1 contains general definitions and principles of construction and interpretation applicable throughout this Article.

As amended in 1990, 1999 and 2001.

Official Comment

(a) "Buyer in ordinary course of business". Section 1–201(9).

(b) "Cancellation". Section 2–106(4). The effect of a cancellation is provided in Section 2A–505(1).

(c) "Commercial unit". Section 2–105(6).

(d) "Conforming". Section 2–106(2).

(e) "Consumer lease". New. This Article includes a subset of rules that applies only to consumer leases. Sections 2A–106, 2A–108(2), 2A–108(4), 2A–109(2), 2A–221, 2A–309, 2A–406, 2A–407, 2A–504(3)(b), and 2A–516(3)(b).

For a transaction to qualify as a consumer lease it must first qualify as a lease. Section 2A–103(1)(j). Note that this Article regulates the transactional elements of a lease, including a consumer lease; consumer protection statutes, present and future, and existing consumer protection decisions are unaffected by this Article. Section 2A–104(1)(c) and (2). Of course, Article 2A as state law also is subject to federal consumer protection law.

This definition is modeled after the definition of consumer lease in the Consumer Leasing Act, 15 U.S.C. § 1667 (1982), and in the Unif. Consumer Credit Code § 1.301(14), 7A U.L.A. 43 (1974). However, this definition of consumer lease differs from its models in several respects: the lessor can be a person

regularly engaged either in the business of leasing or of selling goods, the lease need not be for a term exceeding four months, a lease primarily for an agricultural purpose is not covered, and whether there should be a limitation by dollar amount and its amount is left up to the individual states.

This definition focuses on the parties as well as the transaction. If a lease is within this definition, the lessor must be regularly engaged in the business of leasing or selling, and the lessee must be an individual, not an organization; note that a lease to two or more individuals having a common interest through marriage or the like is not excluded as a lease to an organization under Section 1–201(28). The lessee must take the interest primarily for a personal, family or household purpose. If required by the enacting state, total payments under the lease contract, excluding payments for options to renew or buy, cannot exceed the figure designated.

(f) "Fault". Section 1–201(16).

(g) "Finance Lease". New. This Article includes a subset of rules that applies only to finance leases. Sections 2A–209, 2A–211(2), 2A–212(1), 2A–213, 2A–219(1), 2A–220(1)(a), 2A–221, 2A–405(c), 2A–407, 2A–516(2) and 2A–517(1)(a) and (2).

For a transaction to qualify as a finance lease it must first qualify as a lease. Section 2A–103(1)(j). Unless the lessor is comfortable that the transaction will qualify as a finance lease, the lease agreement should include provisions giving the lessor the benefits created by the subset of rules applicable to the transaction that qualifies as a finance lease under this Article.

A finance lease is the product of a three party transaction. The supplier manufactures or supplies the goods pursuant to the lessee's specification, perhaps even pursuant to a purchase order, sales agreement or lease agreement between the supplier and the lessee. After the prospective finance lease is negotiated, a purchase order, sales agreement, or lease agreement is entered into by the lessor (as buyer or prime lessee) or an existing order, agreement or lease is assigned by the lessee to the lessor, and the lessor and the lessee then enter into a lease or sublease of the goods. Due to the limited function usually performed by the lessor, the lessee looks almost entirely to the supplier for representations, covenants and warranties. If a manufacturer's warranty carries through, the lessee may also look to that. Yet, this definition does not restrict the lessor's function solely to the supply of funds; if the lessor undertakes or performs other functions, express warranties, covenants and the common law will protect the lessee.

This definition focuses on the transaction, not the status of the parties; to avoid confusion it is important to note that in other contexts, *e.g.*, tax and accounting, the term finance lease has been used to connote different types of lease transactions, including leases that are disguised secured transactions. M. Rice, *Equipment Financing*, 62–71 (1981). A lessor who is a merchant with respect to goods of the kind subject to the lease may be a lessor under a finance lease. Many leases that are leases back to the seller of goods (Section 2A–308(3)) will be finance leases. This conclusion is easily demonstrated by a hypothetical. Assume that B has bought goods from C pursuant to a sales contract. After delivery to and acceptance of the goods by B, B negotiates to sell the goods to A and simultaneously to lease the goods back from A, on terms and conditions that, we assume, will qualify the transaction as a lease. Section 2A–103(1)(j). In documenting the sale and lease back, B assigns the original sales contract between B, as buyer, and C, as seller, to A. A review of these facts leads to the conclusion that the lease from A to B qualifies as a finance lease, as all three conditions of the definition are satisfied. Subparagraph (i) is satisfied as A, the lessor, had nothing to do with the selection, manufacture, or supply of the equipment. Subparagraph (ii) is satisfied as A, the lessor, bought the equipment at the same time that A leased the equipment to B, which certainly is in connection with the lease. Finally, subparagraph (iii)(A) is satisfied as A entered into the sales contract with B at the same time that A leased the equipment back to B. B, the lessee, will have received a copy of the sales contract in a timely fashion.

Subsection (i) requires the lessor to remain outside the selection, manufacture and supply of the goods; that is the rationale for releasing the lessor from most of its traditional liability. The lessor is not prohibited from possession, maintenance or operation of the goods, as policy does not require such prohibition. To insure the lessee's reliance on the supplier, and not on the lessor, subsection (ii) requires that the goods (where the lessor is the buyer of the goods) or that the right to possession and use of the goods (where the lessor is the prime lessee and the sublessor of the goods) be acquired in connection with the lease (or sublease) to qualify as a finance lease. The scope of the phrase "in connection with" is to be developed by the courts, case by case. Finally, as the lessee generally relies almost entirely upon the supplier for representations and covenants, and upon the supplier or a manufacturer, or both, for warranties with respect to

the goods, subsection (iii) requires that one of the following occur: (A) the lessee receive a copy of the supply contract before signing the lease contract; (B) the lessee's approval of the supply contract is a condition to the effectiveness of the lease contract; (C) the lessee receive a statement describing the promises and warranties and any limitations relevant to the lessee before signing the lease contract; or (D) before signing the lease contract and except in a consumer lease, the lessee receive a writing identifying the supplier (unless the supplier was selected and required by the lessee) and the rights of the lessee under Section 2A–209, and advising the lessee a statement of promises and warranties is available from the supplier. Thus, even where oral supply orders or computer placed supply orders are compelled by custom and usage the transaction may still qualify as a finance lease if the lessee approves the supply contract before the lease contract is effective and such approval was a condition to the effectiveness of the lease contract. Moreover, where the lessor does not want the lessee to see the entire supply contract, including price information, the lessee may be provided with a separate statement of the terms of the supply contract relevant to the lessee; promises between the supplier and the lessor that do not affect the lessee need not be included. The statement can be a restatement of those terms or a copy of portions of the supply contract with the relevant terms clearly designated. Any implied warranties need not be designated, but a disclaimer or modification of remedy must be designated. A copy of any manufacturer's warranty is sufficient if that is the warranty provided. However, a copy of any Regulation M disclosure given pursuant to 12 C.F.R. § 213.4(g) concerning warranties in itself is not sufficient since those disclosures need only briefly identify express warranties and need not include any disclaimer of warranty.

If a transaction does not qualify as a finance lease, the parties may achieve the same result by agreement; no negative implications are to be drawn if the transaction does not qualify. Further, absent the application of special rules (fraud, duress, and the like), a lease that qualifies as a finance lease and is assigned by the lessor or the lessee to a third party does not lose its status as a finance lease under this Article. Finally, this Article creates no special rule where the lessor is an affiliate of the supplier; whether the transaction qualifies as a finance lease will be determined by the facts of each case.

(h) "Goods". Section 9–102(a)(44). See Section 2A–103(3) for reference to the definition of "Account", "Chattel paper", "Document", "General intangibles" and "Instrument". See Section 2A–217 for determination of the time and manner of identification.

(i) "Installment lease contract". Section 2–612(1).

(j) "Lease". New. There are several reasons to codify the law with respect to leases of goods. An analysis of the case law as it applies to leases of goods suggests at least several significant issues to be resolved by codification. First and foremost is the definition of a lease. It is necessary to define lease to determine whether a transaction creates a lease or a security interest disguised as a lease. If the transaction creates a security interest disguised as a lease, the transaction will be governed by the Article on Secured Transactions (Article 9) and the lessor will be required to file a financing statement or take other action to perfect its interest in the goods against third parties. There is no such requirement with respect to leases under the common law and, except with respect to leases of fixtures (Section 2A–309), this Article imposes no such requirement. Yet the distinction between a lease and a security interest disguised as a lease is not clear from the case law at the time of the promulgation of this Article. DeKoven, *Leases of Equipment: Puritan Leasing Company v. August, A Dangerous Decision*, 12 U.S.F. L.Rev. 257 (1978).

At common law a lease of personal property is a bailment for hire. While there are several definitions of bailment for hire, all require a thing to be let and a price for the letting. Thus, in modern terms and as provided in this definition, a lease is created when the lessee agrees to furnish consideration for the right to the possession and use of goods over a specified period of time. Mooney, *Personal Property Leasing: A Challenge*, 36 Bus.Law. 1605, 1607 (1981). Further, a lease is neither a sale (Section 2–106(1)) nor a retention or creation of a security interest (Section 1–201(37)). Due to extensive litigation to distinguish true leases from security interests, an amendment to Section 1–201(37) has been promulgated with this Article to create a sharper distinction.

This section as well as Section 1–201(37) must be examined to determine whether the transaction in question creates a lease or a security interest. The following hypotheticals indicate the perimeters of the issue. Assume that A has purchased a number of copying machines, new, for $1,000 each; the machines have an estimated useful economic life of three years. A advertises that the machines are available to rent for a minimum of one month and that the monthly rental is $100.00. A intends to enter into leases where A provides all maintenance, without charge to the lessee. Further, the lessee will rent the machine, month to month, with no obligation to renew. At the end of the lease term the lessee will be obligated to return the machine to A's place of business. This transaction qualifies as a lease under the first half of the definition, for the transaction includes a transfer by A to a prospective lessee of possession and use of the machine for a stated term, month to month. The machines are goods (Section 2A–103(1)(h)). The lessee is obligated to pay consideration in return, $100.00 for each month of the term.

However, the second half of the definition provides that a sale or a security interest is not a lease. Since there is no passing of title, there is no sale. Sections 2A–103(3) and 2–106(1). Under pre-Act security law this transaction would have created a bailment for hire or a true lease and not a conditional sale. *Da Rocha v. Macomber*, 330 Mass. 611, 614–15, 116 N.E.2d 139, 142 (1953). Under Section 1–201(37), as amended with the promulgation of this Article, the same result would follow. While the lessee is obligated to pay rent for the one month term of the lease, one of the other four conditions of the second paragraph of Section 1–201 (37) must be met and none is. The term of the lease is one month and the economic life of the machine is 36 months; thus, subparagraph (a) of Section 1–201(37) is not now satisfied. Considering the amount of the monthly rent, absent economic duress or coercion, the lessee is not bound either to renew the lease for the remaining economic life of the goods or to become the owner. If the lessee did lease the machine for 36 months, the lessee would have paid the lessor $3,600 for a machine that could have been purchased for $1,000; thus, Section 1–201(37)(b) is not satisfied. Finally, there are no options; thus, subparagraphs (c) and (d) of Section 1–201(37) are not satisfied. This transaction creates a lease, not a security interest. However, with each renewal of the lease the facts and circumstances at the time of each renewal must be examined to determine if that conclusion remains accurate, as it is possible that a transaction that first creates a lease, later creates a security interest.

Assume that the facts are changed and that A requires each lessee to lease the goods for 36 months, with no right to terminate. Under pre-Act security law this transaction would have created a conditional sale, and not a bailment for hire or true lease. *Hervey v. Rhode Island Locomotive Works*, 93 U.S. 664, 672–73 (1876). Under this subsection, and Section 1–201(37), as amended with the inclusion of this Article in the Act, the same result would follow. The lessee's obligation for the term is not subject to termination by the lessee and the term is equal to the economic life of the machine.

Between these extremes there are many transactions that can be created. Some of the transactions have not been properly categorized by the courts in applying the 1978 and earlier Official Texts of Section 1–201(37). This subsection, together with Section 1–201(37) as amended with the promulgation of this Article, draws a brighter line, which should create a clearer signal to the professional lessor and lessee.

(k) "Lease agreement". This definition is derived from the first sentence of Section 1–201(3). Because the definition of lease is broad enough to cover future transfers, lease agreement includes an agreement contemplating a current or subsequent transfer. Thus it was not necessary to make an express reference to an agreement for the future lease of goods (Section 2–106(1)). This concept is also incorporated in the definition of lease contract. Note that the definition of lease does not include transactions in ordinary building materials that are incorporated into an improvement on land. Section 2A–309(2).

The provisions of this Article, if applicable, determine whether a lease agreement has legal consequences; otherwise the law of bailments and other applicable law determine the same. Sections 2A–103(4) and 1–103.

(*l*) "Lease contract". This definition is derived from the definition of contract in Section 1–201(11). Note that a lease contract may be for the future lease of goods, since this notion is included in the definition of lease.

(m) "Leasehold interest". New.

(n) "Lessee". New.

(o) "Lessee in ordinary course of business". Section 1–201(9).

(p) "Lessor". New.

(q) "Lessor's residual interest". New.

(r) "Lien". New. This term is used in Section 2A–307 (Priority of Liens Arising by Attachment or Levy on, Security Interests in, and Other Claims to Goods).

(s) "Lot". Section 2–105(5).

(t) "Merchant lessee". New. This term is used in Section 2A–511 (Merchant Lessee's Duties as to Rightfully Rejected Goods). A person may satisfy the requirement of dealing in goods of the kind subject to the lease as lessor, lessee, seller, or buyer.

(u) "Present value". New. Authorities agree that present value should be used to determine fairly the damages payable by the lessor or the lessee on default. *E.g., Taylor v. Commercial Credit Equip. Corp.,* 170 Ga.App. 322, 316 S.E.2d 788 (1984). Present value is defined to mean an amount that represents the discounted value as of a date certain of one or more sums payable in the future. This is a function of the economic principle that a dollar today is more valuable to the holder than a dollar payable in two years. While there is no question as to the principle, reasonable people would differ as to the rate of discount to apply in determining the value of that future dollar today. To minimize litigation, this Article allows the parties to specify the discount or interest rate, if the rate was not manifestly unreasonable at the time the transaction was entered into. In all other cases, the interest rate will be a commercially reasonable rate that takes into account the facts and circumstances of each case, as of the time the transaction was entered into.

(v) "Purchase". Section 1–201(32). This definition omits the reference to lien contained in the definition of purchase in Article 1 (Section 1–201(32)). This should not be construed to exclude consensual liens from the definition of purchase in this Article; the exclusion was mandated by the scope of the definition of lien in Section 2A–103(1)(r). Further, the definition of purchaser in this Article adds a reference to lease; as purchase is defined in Section 1–201(32) to include any other voluntary transaction creating an interest in property, this addition is not substantive.

(w) "Sublease". New.

(x) "Supplier". New.

(y) "Supply contract". New.

(z) "Termination". Section 2–106(3). The effect of a termination is provided in Section 2A–505(2).

As amended in 1999.

§ 2A–104. Leases Subject to Other Law.

(1) A lease, although subject to this Article, is also subject to any applicable:

(a) certificate of title statute of this State: (list any certificate of title statutes covering automobiles, trailers, mobile homes, boats, farm tractors, and the like);

(b) certificate of title statute of another jurisdiction (Section 2A–105); or

(c) consumer protection statute of this State, or final consumer protection decision of a court of this State existing on the effective date of this Article.

(2) In case of conflict between this Article, other than Sections 2A–105, 2A–304(3), and 2A–

305(3), and a statute or decision referred to in subsection (1), the statute or decision controls.

(3) Failure to comply with an applicable law has only the effect specified therein.

As amended in 1990.

Official Comment

Uniform Statutory Source: Former Sections 9–203(4) and 9–302(3)(b) and (c) (now codified as Sections 9–201 and 9–311(a)(2) and (3)).

Changes: Substantially revised.

Purposes:

1. This Article creates a comprehensive scheme for the regulation of transactions that create leases. Section 2A–102. Thus, the Article supersedes all prior legislation dealing with leases, except to the extent set forth in this Section.

2. Subsection (1) states the general rule that a lease, although governed by the scheme of this Article, also may be governed by certain other applicable laws. This may occur in the case of a consumer lease. Section 2A–103(1)(e). Those laws may be state statutes existing prior to enactment of Article 2A or passed afterward. In this case, it is desirable for this Article to specify which statute controls. Or the law may be a pre-existing consumer protection decision. This Article preserves such decisions. Or the law may be a statute of the United States. Such a law controls without any statement in this Article under applicable principles of preemption.

An illustration of a statute of the United States that governs consumer leases is the Consumer Leasing Act, 15 U.S.C. §§ 1667–1667(e) (1982) and its implementing regulation, Regulation M, 12 C.F.R. § 213 (1986); the statute mandates disclosures of certain lease terms, delimits the liability of a lessee in leasing personal property, and regulates the advertising of lease terms. An illustration of a state statute that governs consumer leases and which if adopted in the enacting state prevails over this Article is the Unif. Consumer Credit Code, which includes many provisions similar to those of the Consumer Leasing Act, e.g. Unif. Consumer Credit Code §§ 3.202, 3.209, 3.401, 7A U.L.A. 108–09, 115, 125 (1974), as well as provisions in addition to those of the Consumer Leasing Act, e.g., Unif. Consumer Credit Code §§ 5.109–.111, 7A U.L.A. 171–76 (1974) (the right to cure a default). Such statutes may define consumer lease so as to govern transactions within and without the definition of consumer lease under this Article.

3. Under subsection (2), subject to certain limited exclusions, in case of conflict a statute or a decision described in subsection (1) prevails over this Article. For example, a provision like Unif. Consumer Credit Code § 5.112, 7A U.L.A. 176 (1974), limiting self-help repossession, prevails over Section 2A–525(3). A consumer protection decision rendered after the effective date of this Article may supplement its provisions. For example, in relation to Article 9 a court might conclude that an acceleration clause may not be enforced against an individual debtor after late payments have been accepted unless a prior notice of default is given. To the extent the decision establishes a general principle applicable to transactions other than secured transactions, it may supplement Section 2A–502.

4. Consumer protection in lease transactions is primarily left to other law. However, several provisions of this Article do contain special rules that may not be varied by agreement in the case of a consumer lease. E.g., Sections 2A–106, 2A–108, and 2A–109(2). Were that not so, the ability of the parties to govern their relationship by agreement together with the position of the lessor in a consumer lease too often could result in a one-sided lease agreement.

5. In construing this provision the reference to statute should be deemed to include applicable regulations. A consumer protection decision is "final" on the effective date of this Article if it is not subject to appeal on that date or, if subject to appeal, is not later reversed on appeal. Of course, such a decision can be overruled by a later decision or superseded by a later statute.

Cross References:

Sections 2A–103(1)(e), 2A–106, 2A–108, 2A–109(2) and 2A–525(3).

Definitional Cross Reference:

"Lease". Section 2A–103(1)(j).

§ 2A–105. Territorial Application of Article to Goods Covered by Certificate of Title.

Subject to the provisions of Sections 2A–304(3) and 2A–305(3), with respect to goods covered by a certificate of title issued under a statute of this State or of another jurisdiction, compliance and the effect of compliance or noncompliance with a certificate of title statute are governed by the law (including the conflict of laws rules) of the jurisdiction issuing the certificate until the earlier of (a) surrender of the certificate, or (b) four months after the goods are removed from that jurisdiction and thereafter until a new certificate of title is issued by another jurisdiction.

Official Comment

Uniform Statutory Source: Former Section 9–103(2)(a) and (b) (now codified as Sections 9–303 and 9–316).

Changes: Substantially revised. The provisions of the last sentence of former Section 9–103(2)(b) were not incorporated as they are superfluous in this context. The provisions of former Section 9–103(2)(d) were not incorporated because the problems dealt with are adequately addressed by this section and Sections 2A–304(3) and 305(3).

Purposes: The new certificate referred to in (b) must be permanent, not temporary. Generally, the lessor or creditor whose interest is indicated on the most recently issued certificate of title will prevail over interests indicated on certificates issued previously by other jurisdictions. This provision reflects a policy that it is reasonable to require holders of interests in goods covered by a certificate of title to police the goods or risk losing their interests when a new certificate of title is issued by another jurisdiction.

Cross References:

Sections 2A–304(3) and 2A–305(3); former Sections 9–103(2)(b) and 9–103(2)(d) (now codified as Sections 9–303, 9–316, and 9–337).

Definitional Cross Reference:

"Goods". Section 2A–103(1)(h).

§ 2A–106. Limitation on Power of Parties to Consumer Lease to Choose Applicable Law and Judicial Forum.

(1) If the law chosen by the parties to a consumer lease is that of a jurisdiction other than a jurisdiction in which the lessee resides at the time the lease agreement becomes enforceable or within 30 days thereafter or in which the goods are to be used, the choice is not enforceable.

(2) If the judicial forum chosen by the parties to a consumer lease is a forum that would not otherwise have jurisdiction over the lessee, the choice is not enforceable.

Official Comment

Uniform Statutory Source: Unif. Consumer Credit Code § 1.201(8), 7A U.L.A. 36 (1974).

Changes: Substantially revised.

Purposes: There is a real danger that a lessor may induce a consumer lessee to agree that the applicable law will be a jurisdiction that has little effective consumer protection, or to agree that the applicable forum will be a forum that is inconvenient for the lessee in the event of litigation. As a result, this section invalidates these choice of law or forum clauses, except where the law chosen is that of the state of the consumer's residence or where the goods will be kept, or the forum chosen is one that otherwise would have jurisdiction over the lessee.

Subsection (1) limits potentially abusive choice of law clauses in consumer leases. The 30-day rule in subsection (1) was suggested by former Section 9–103(1)(c). This section has no effect on choice of law clauses in leases that are not consumer leases. Such clauses would be governed by other law.

Subsection (2) prevents enforcement of potentially abusive jurisdictional consent clauses in consumer leases. By using the term judicial forum, this section does not limit selection of a nonjudicial forum, such as arbitration. This section has no effect on choice of forum clauses in leases that are not consumer leases; such clauses are, as a matter of current law, "prima facie valid". *The Bremen v. Zapata Off-Shore Co.*, 407 U.S. 1, 10 (1972). Such clauses would be governed by other law, including the Model Choice of Forum Act (1968).

Cross Reference:

Former Section 9–103(1)(c).

Definitional Cross References:

"Consumer lease". Section 2A–103(1)(e).
"Lease agreement". Section 2A–103(1)(k).
"Lessee". Section 2A–103(1)(n).
"Goods". Section 2A–103(1)(h).
"Party". Section 1–201(29).

§ 2A–107. Waiver or Renunciation of Claim or Right After Default.

Any claim or right arising out of an alleged default or breach of warranty may be discharged in whole or in part without consideration by a written waiver or renunciation signed and delivered by the aggrieved party.

Official Comment

Uniform Statutory Source: Section 1–107.

Changes: Revised to reflect leasing practices and terminology. This clause is used throughout the official comments to this Article to indicate the scope of change in the provisions of the Uniform Statutory Source included in the section; these changes range from one extreme, *e.g.*, a significant difference in practice (a warranty as to merchantability is not implied in a finance lease (Section 2A–212)) to the other extreme, *e.g.*, a modest difference in style or terminology (the transaction governed is a lease not a sale (Section 2A–203 2A–103 *)).

Cross References:

Sections 2A–203 2A–103 * and 2A–212.

Definitional Cross References:

"Aggrieved party". Section 1–201(2).
"Delivery". Section 1–201(14).
"Rights". Section 1–201(36).
"Signed". Section 1–201(39).
"Written". Section 1–201(46).

* *Previous incorrect cross reference corrected by Permanent Editorial Board action November 1992.*

§ 2A–108. Unconscionability.

(1) If the court as a matter of law finds a lease contract or any clause of a lease contract to have been unconscionable at the time it was made the court may refuse to enforce the lease contract, or it may enforce the remainder of the lease contract without the unconscionable clause, or it may so limit the application of any unconscionable clause as to avoid any unconscionable result.

(2) With respect to a consumer lease, if the court as a matter of law finds that a lease contract or any clause of a lease contract has been induced by unconscionable conduct or that unconscionable conduct has occurred in the collection of a claim arising from a lease contract, the court may grant appropriate relief.

(3) Before making a finding of unconscionability under subsection (1) or (2), the court, on its own motion or that of a party, shall afford the parties a reasonable opportunity to present evidence as to the setting, purpose, and effect of the lease contract or clause thereof, or of the conduct.

(4) In an action in which the lessee claims unconscionability with respect to a consumer lease:

(a) If the court finds unconscionability under subsection (1) or (2), the court shall award reasonable attorney's fees to the lessee.

(b) If the court does not find unconscionability and the lessee claiming unconscionability has brought or maintained an action he [or she] knew to be groundless, the court shall award reasonable attorney's fees to the party against whom the claim is made.

(c) In determining attorney's fees, the amount of the recovery on behalf of the claimant under subsections (1) and (2) is not controlling.

Official Comment

Uniform Statutory Source: Section 2–302 and Unif. Consumer Credit Code § 5.108, 7A U.L.A. 167–69 (1974).

Changes: Subsection (1) is taken almost verbatim from the provisions of Section 2–302(1). Subsection (2) is suggested by the provisions of Unif. Consumer Credit Code § 5.108(1), (2), 7A U.L.A. 167 (1974). Subsection (3), taken from the provisions of Section 2–302(2), has been expanded to cover unconscionable conduct. Unif. Consumer Credit Code § 5.108(3), 7A U.L.A. 167 (1974). The provision for the award of attorney's fees to consumers, subsection (4), covers unconscionability under subsection (1) as well as (2). Subsection (4) is modeled on the provisions of Unif. Consumer Credit Code § 5.108(6), 7A U.L.A. 169 (1974).

Purposes: Subsections (1) and (3) of this section apply the concept of unconscionability reflected in the provisions of Section 2–302 to leases. *See Dillman & Assocs. v. Capitol Leasing Co.*, 110 Ill.App.3d 335, 342, 442 N.E.2d 311, 316 (App.Ct.1982). Subsection (3) omits the adjective "commercial" found in subsection 2–302(2) because subsection (3) is concerned with all leases and the relevant standard of conduct is determined by the context.

The balance of the section is modeled on the provisions of Unif. Consumer Credit Code § 5.108, 7A U.L.A. 167–69 (1974). Thus subsection (2) recognizes that a consumer lease or a clause in a consumer lease may not itself be unconscionable but that the agreement would never have been entered into if unconscionable means had not been employed to induce the consumer to agree. To make a statement to induce the consumer to lease the goods, in the expectation of invoking an integration clause in the lease to exclude the statement's admissibility in a subsequent dispute, may be unconscionable. Subsection (2) also provides a consumer remedy for unconscionable conduct, such as using or threatening to use force or violence, in the collection of a claim arising from a lease contract. These provisions are not exclusive. The remedies of this section are in addition to remedies otherwise available for the same conduct under other law, for example, an action in tort for abusive debt collection or under another statute of this State for such conduct. The reference to appropriate relief in subsection (2) is intended to foster liberal administration of this remedy. Sections 2A–103(4) and 1–106(1).

Subsection (4) authorizes an award of reasonable attorney's fees if the court finds unconscionability with respect to a consumer lease under subsection (1) or (2). Provision is also made for recovery by the party against whom the claim was made if the court does not find unconscionability and does find that the consumer knew the action to be groundless. Further, subsection (4)(b) is independent of, and thus will not override, a term in the lease agreement that provides for the payment of attorney's fees.

Cross References:

Sections 1–106(1), 2–302 and 2A–103(4).

Definitional Cross References:

"Action". Section 1–201(1).
"Consumer lease". Section 2A–103(1)(e).
"Lease contract". Section 2A–103(1)(l).
"Lessee". Section 2A–103(1)(n).
"Party". Section 1–201(29).

§ 2A–109. Option to Accelerate at Will.

(1) A term providing that one party or his [or her] successor in interest may accelerate payment or performance or require collateral or additional collateral "at will" or "when he [or she] deems himself [or herself] insecure" or in words of similar import must be construed to mean that he [or she] has power to do so only if he [or she]

in good faith believes that the prospect of payment or performance is impaired.

(2) With respect to a consumer lease, the burden of establishing good faith under subsection (1) is on the party who exercised the power; otherwise the burden of establishing lack of good faith is on the party against whom the power has been exercised.

Official Comment

Uniform Statutory Source: Section 1–208 and Unif. Consumer Credit Code § 5.109(2), 7A U.L.A. 171 (1974).

Purposes: Subsection (1) reflects modest changes in style to the provisions of the first sentence of Section 1–208.

Subsection (2), however, reflects a significant change in the provisions of the second sentence of Section 1–208 by creating a new rule with respect to a consumer lease. A lease provision allowing acceleration at the will of the lessor or when the lessor deems itself insecure is of critical importance to the lessee. In a consumer lease it is a provision that is not usually agreed to by the parties but is usually mandated by the lessor. Therefore, where its invocation depends not on specific criteria but on the discretion of the lessor, its use should be regulated to prevent abuse. Subsection (1) imposes a duty of good faith upon its exercise. Subsection (2) shifts the burden of establishing good faith to the lessor in the case of a consumer lease, but not otherwise.

Cross Reference:

Section 1–208.

Definitional Cross References:

"Burden of establishing". Section 1–201(8).
"Consumer lease". Section 2A–103(1)(e).
"Good faith". Sections 1–201(19) and 2–103(1)(b).
"Party". Section 1–201(29).
"Term". Section 1–201(42).

PART 2

FORMATION AND CONSTRUCTION OF LEASE CONTRACT

§ 2A–201. Statute of Frauds.

(1) A lease contract is not enforceable by way of action or defense unless:

(a) the total payments to be made under the lease contract, excluding payments for op-

tions to renew or buy, are less than $1,000; or

(b) there is a writing, signed by the party against whom enforcement is sought or by that party's authorized agent, sufficient to indicate that a lease contract has been made between the parties and to describe the goods leased and the lease term.

(2) Any description of leased goods or of the lease term is sufficient and satisfies subsection (1)(b), whether or not it is specific, if it reasonably identifies what is described.

(3) A writing is not insufficient because it omits or incorrectly states a term agreed upon, but the lease contract is not enforceable under subsection (1)(b) beyond the lease term and the quantity of goods shown in the writing.

(4) A lease contract that does not satisfy the requirements of subsection (1), but which is valid in other respects, is enforceable:

(a) if the goods are to be specially manufactured or obtained for the lessee and are not suitable for lease or sale to others in the ordinary course of the lessor's business, and the lessor, before notice of repudiation is received and under circumstances that reasonably indicate that the goods are for the lessee, has made either a substantial beginning of their manufacture or commitments for their procurement;

(b) if the party against whom enforcement is sought admits in that party's pleading, testimony or otherwise in court that a lease contract was made, but the lease contract is not enforceable under this provision beyond the quantity of goods admitted; or

(c) with respect to goods that have been received and accepted by the lessee.

(5) The lease term under a lease contract referred to in subsection (4) is:

(a) if there is a writing signed by the party against whom enforcement is sought or by that party's authorized agent specifying the lease term, the term so specified;

(b) if the party against whom enforcement is sought admits in that party's pleading, testimony, or otherwise in court a lease term, the term so admitted; or

(c) a reasonable lease term.

Official Comment

Uniform Statutory Source: Section 2–201; former Sections 9–203(1) and 9–110 (now codified as Sections 9–203(b) and 9–108).

Changes: This section is modeled on Section 2–201, with changes to reflect the differences between a lease contract and a contract for the sale of goods. In particular, subsection (1)(b) adds a requirement that the writing "describe the goods leased and the lease term", borrowing that concept, with revisions, from the provisions of former Section 9–203(1)(a) (now codified as Section 9–203(b)(3)(A)). Subsection (2), relying on the statutory analogue in former Section 9–110 (now codified as Section 9–108), sets forth the minimum criterion for satisfying that requirement.

Purposes: The changes in this section conform the provisions of Section 2–201 to custom and usage in lease transactions. Section 2–201(2), stating a special rule between merchants, was not included in this section as the number of such transactions involving leases, as opposed to sales, was thought to be modest. Subsection (4) creates no exception for transactions where payment has been made and accepted. This represents a departure from the analogue, Section 2–201(3)(c). The rationale for the departure is grounded in the distinction between sales and leases. Unlike a buyer in a sales transaction, the lessee does not tender payment in full for goods delivered, but only payment of rent for one or more months. It was decided that, as a matter of policy, this act of payment is not a sufficient substitute for the required memorandum. Subsection (5) was needed to establish the criteria for supplying the lease term if it is omitted, as the lease contract may still be enforceable under subsection (4).

Cross References:

Sections 2–201, 9–108 and 9–203(b)(3)(A).

Definitional Cross References:

"Action". Section 1–201(1).
"Agreed". Section 1–201(3).
"Buying". Section 2A–103(1)(a).
"Goods". Section 2A–103(1)(h).
"Lease". Section 2A–103(1)(j).
"Lease contract". Section 2A–103(1)(l).
"Lessee". Section 2A–103(1)(n).
"Lessor". Section 2A–103(1)(p).
"Notice". Section 1–201(25).
"Party". Section 1–201(29).
"Sale". Section 2–106(1).
"Signed". Section 1–201(39).
"Term". Section 1–201(42).
"Writing". Section 1–201(46).

§ 2A–202. Final Written Expression: Parol or Extrinsic Evidence.

Terms with respect to which the confirmatory memoranda of the parties agree or which are otherwise set forth in a writing intended by the parties as a final expression of their agreement with respect to such terms as are included therein may not be contradicted by evidence of any prior agreement or of a contemporaneous oral agreement but may be explained or supplemented:

  (a) by course of dealing or usage of trade or by course of performance; and

  (b) by evidence of consistent additional terms unless the court finds the writing to have been intended also as a complete and exclusive statement of the terms of the agreement.

Official Comment

Uniform Statutory Source: Section 2–202.

Definitional Cross References:

"Agreement". Section 1–201(3).
"Course of dealing". Section 1–205.
"Party". Section 1–201(29).
"Term". Section 1–201(42).
"Usage of trade". Section 1–205.
"Writing". Section 1–201(46).

§ 2A–203. Seals Inoperative.

The affixing of a seal to a writing evidencing a lease contract or an offer to enter into a lease contract does not render the writing a sealed instrument and the law with respect to sealed instruments does not apply to the lease contract or offer.

Official Comment

Uniform Statutory Source: Section 2–203.

Changes: Revised to reflect leasing practices and terminology.

Definitional Cross References:

"Lease contract". Section 2A–103(1)(*l*).
"Writing". Section 1–201(46).

§ 2A–204. Formation in General.

(1) A lease contract may be made in any manner sufficient to show agreement, including conduct by both parties which recognizes the existence of a lease contract.

(2) An agreement sufficient to constitute a lease contract may be found although the moment of its making is undetermined.

(3) Although one or more terms are left open, a lease contract does not fail for indefiniteness if the parties have intended to make a lease contract and there is a reasonably certain basis for giving an appropriate remedy.

Official Comment

Uniform Statutory Source: Section 2–204.

Changes: Revised to reflect leasing practices and terminology.

Definitional Cross References:

"Agreement". Section 1–201(3).
"Lease contract". Section 2A–103(1)(*l*).
"Party". Section 1–201(29).
"Remedy". Section 1–201(34).
"Term". Section 1–201(42).

§ 2A–205. Firm Offers.

An offer by a merchant to lease goods to or from another person in a signed writing that by its terms gives assurance it will be held open is not revocable, for lack of consideration, during the time stated or, if no time is stated, for a reasonable time, but in no event may the period of irrevocability exceed 3 months. Any such term of assurance on a form supplied by the offeree must be separately signed by the offeror.

Official Comment

Uniform Statutory Source: Section 2–205.

Changes: Revised to reflect leasing practices and terminology.

Definitional Cross References:

"Goods". Section 2A–103(1)(h).
"Lease". Section 2A–103(1)(j).
"Merchant". Section 2–104(1).
"Person". Section 1–201(30).
"Reasonable time". Section 1–204(1) and (2).
"Signed". Section 1–201(39).
"Term". Section 1–201(42).
"Writing". Section 1–201(46).

§ 2A–206. Offer and Acceptance in Formation of Lease Contract.

(1) Unless otherwise unambiguously indicated by the language or circumstances, an offer to make a lease contract must be construed as invit-

ing acceptance in any manner and by any medium reasonable in the circumstances.

(2) If the beginning of a requested performance is a reasonable mode of acceptance, an offeror who is not notified of acceptance within a reasonable time may treat the offer as having lapsed before acceptance.

Official Comment

Uniform Statutory Source: Section 2–206(1)(a) and (2).

Changes: Revised to reflect leasing practices and terminology.

Definitional Cross References:

"Lease contract". Section 2A–103(1)(*l*).
"Notifies". Section 1–201(26).
"Reasonable time". Section 1–204(1) and (2).

§ 2A–207. Course of Performance or Practical Construction.

(1) If a lease contract involves repeated occasions for performance by either party with knowledge of the nature of the performance and opportunity for objection to it by the other, any course of performance accepted or acquiesced in without objection is relevant to determine the meaning of the lease agreement.

(2) The express terms of a lease agreement and any course of performance, as well as any course of dealing and usage of trade, must be construed whenever reasonable as consistent with each other; but if that construction is unreasonable, express terms control course of performance, course of performance controls both course of dealing and usage of trade, and course of dealing controls usage of trade.

(3) Subject to the provisions of Section 2A–208 on modification and waiver, course of performance is relevant to show a waiver or modification of any term inconsistent with the course of performance.

Official Comment

Uniform Statutory Source: Sections 2–208 and 1–205(4).

Changes: Revised to reflect leasing practices and terminology, except that subsection (2) was further revised to make the subsection parallel the provisions of Section 1–205(4) by adding that course of dealing controls usage of trade.

Purposes: The section should be read in conjunction with Section 2A–208. In particular, although a specific term may control over course of performance as a matter of lease construction under subsection (2), subsection (3) allows the same course of dealing to show a waiver or modification, if Section 2A–208 is satisfied.

Cross References:

Sections 1–205(4), 2–208 and 2A–208.

Definitional Cross References:

"Course of dealing". Section 1–205.
"Knowledge". Section 1–201(25).
"Lease agreement". Section 2A–103(1)(k).
"Lease contract". Section 2A–103(1)(*l*).
"Party". Section 1–201(29).
"Term". Section 1–201(42).
"Usage of trade". Section 1–205.

§ 2A–208. Modification, Rescission and Waiver.

(1) An agreement modifying a lease contract needs no consideration to be binding.

(2) A signed lease agreement that excludes modification or rescission except by a signed writing may not be otherwise modified or rescinded, but, except as between merchants, such a requirement on a form supplied by a merchant must be separately signed by the other party.

(3) Although an attempt at modification or rescission does not satisfy the requirements of subsection (2), it may operate as a waiver.

(4) A party who has made a waiver affecting an executory portion of a lease contract may retract the waiver by reasonable notification received by the other party that strict performance will be required of any term waived, unless the retraction would be unjust in view of a material change of position in reliance on the waiver.

Official Comment

Uniform Statutory Source: Section 2–209.

Changes: Revised to reflect leasing practices and terminology, except that the provisions of subsection 2–209(3) were omitted.

Purposes: Section 2–209(3) provides that "the requirements of the statute of frauds section of this Article (Section 2–201) must be satisfied if the contract as modified is within its provisions." This provision was not incorporated as it is unfair to allow an oral modification to make the entire lease contract unenforceable, *e.g.* if the modification takes it a few dollars over the dollar limit. At the same time, the problem could not be solved by providing that the lease contract would still be enforceable in its pre-modification state (if it then satisfied the statute of frauds) since in some cases that might be worse than no enforcement at all. Resolution of the issue is left to the courts based on the facts of each case.

Cross References:

Sections 2–201 and 2–209.

Definitional Cross References:

"Agreement". Section 1–201(3).
"Between merchants". Section 2–104(3).
"Lease agreement". Section 2A–103(1)(k).
"Lease contract". Section 2A–103(1)(*l*).
"Merchant". Section 2–104(1).
"Notification". Section 1–201(26).
"Party". Section 1–201(29).
"Signed". Section 1–201(39).
"Term". Section 1–201(42).
"Writing". Section 1–201(46).

§ 2A–209. Lessee Under Finance Lease as Beneficiary of Supply Contract.

(1) The benefit of a supplier's promises to the lessor under the supply contract and of all warranties, whether express or implied, including those of any third party provided in connection with or as part of the supply contract, extends to the lessee to the extent of the lessee's leasehold interest under a finance lease related to the supply contract, but is subject to the terms of the warranty and of the supply contract and all defenses or claims arising therefrom.

(2) The extension of the benefit of a supplier's promises and of warranties to the lessee (Section 2A–209(1)) does not: (i) modify the rights and obligations of the parties to the supply contract, whether arising therefrom or otherwise, or (ii) impose any duty or liability under the supply contract on the lessee.

(3) Any modification or rescission of the supply contract by the supplier and the lessor is effective between the supplier and the lessee unless, before the modification or rescission, the supplier has received notice that the lessee has entered into a finance lease related to the supply contract. If the modification or rescission is effective between the supplier and the lessee, the

lessor is deemed to have assumed, in addition to the obligations of the lessor to the lessee under the lease contract, promises of the supplier to the lessor and warranties that were so modified or rescinded as they existed and were available to the lessee before modification or rescission.

(4) In addition to the extension of the benefit of the supplier's promises and of warranties to the lessee under subsection (1), the lessee retains all rights that the lessee may have against the supplier which arise from an agreement between the lessee and the supplier or under other law.

As amended in 1990.

Official Comment

Uniform Statutory Source: None.

Changes: This section is modeled on former Section 9–318 (now codified as Sections 9–404 through 9–406), the Restatement (Second) of Contracts §§ 302–315 (1981), and leasing practices. *See Earman Oil Co. v. Burroughs Corp.*, 625 F.2d 1291, 1296–97 (5th Cir. 1980).

Purposes:

1. The function performed by the lessor in a finance lease is extremely limited. Section 2A–103(1)(g). The lessee looks to the supplier of the goods for warranties and the like or, in some cases as to warranties, to the manufacturer if a warranty made by that person is passed on. That expectation is reflected in subsection (1), which is self-executing. As a matter of policy, the operation of this provision may not be excluded, modified or limited; however, an exclusion, modification, or limitation of any term of the supply contract or warranty, including any with respect to rights and remedies, and any defense or claim such as a statute of limitations, effective against the lessor as the acquiring party under the supply contract, is also effective against the lessee as the beneficiary designated under this provision. For example, the supplier is not precluded from excluding or modifying an express or implied warranty under a supply contract. Sections 2–312(2) and 2–316, or Section 2A–214. Further, the supplier is not precluded from limiting the rights and remedies of the lessor and from liquidating damages. Sections 2–718 and 2–719 or Sections 2A–503 and 2A–504. If the supply contract excludes or modifies warranties, limits remedies, or liquidates damages with respect to the lessor, such provisions are enforceable against the lessee as beneficiary. Thus, only selective discrimination against the beneficiaries designated under this section is precluded, i.e., exclusion of the

supplier's liability to the lessee with respect to warranties made to the lessor. This section does not affect the development of other law with respect to products liability.

2. Enforcement of this benefit is by action. Sections 2A-103(4) and 1-106(2).

3. The benefit extended by these provisions is not without a price, as this Article also provides in the case of a finance lease that is not a consumer lease that the lessee's promises to the lessor under the lease contract become irrevocable and independent upon the lessee's acceptance of the goods. Section 2A-407.

4. Subsection (2) limits the effect of subsection (1) on the supplier and the lessor by preserving, notwithstanding the transfer of the benefits of the supply contract to the lessee, all of the supplier's and the lessor's rights and obligations with respect to each other and others; it further absolves the lessee of any duties with respect to the supply contract that might have been inferred from the extension of the benefits thereof.

5. Subsections (2) and (3) also deal with difficult issues related to modification or rescission of the supply contract. Subsection (2) states a rule that determines the impact of the statutory extension of benefit contained in subsection (1) upon the relationship of the parties to the supply contract and, in a limited respect, upon the lessee. This statutory extension of benefit, like that contained in Sections 2A-216 and 2-318, is not a modification of the supply contract by the parties. Thus, subsection (3) states the rules that apply to a modification or rescission of the supply contract by the parties. Subsection (3) provides that a modification or rescission is not effective between the supplier and the lessee if, before the modification or rescission occurs, the supplier received notice that the lessee has entered into the finance lease. On the other hand, if the modification or rescission is effective, then to the extent of the modification or rescission of the benefit or warranty, the lessor by statutory dictate assumes an obligation to provide to the lessee that which the lessee would otherwise lose. For example, assume a reduction in an express warranty from four years to one year. No prejudice to the lessee may occur if the goods perform as agreed. If, however, there is a breach of the express warranty after one year and before four years pass, the lessor is liable. A remedy for any prejudice to the lessee because of the bifurcation of the lessee's recourse resulting from the action of the supplier and the lessor is left to resolution by the courts based on the facts of each case.

6. Subsection (4) makes it clear that the rights granted to the lessee by this section do not displace any rights the lessee otherwise may have against the supplier.

Cross References:

Sections 2A-103(1)(g), 2A-407, 9-404, 9-405 and 9-406.

Definitional Cross References:

"Action". Section 1-201(1).
"Finance lease". Section 2A-103(1)(g).
"Leasehold interest". Section 2A-103(1)(m).
"Lessee". Section 2A-103(1)(n).
"Lessor". Section 2A-103(1)(p).
"Notice". Section 1-201(25).
"Party". Section 1-201(29).
"Rights". Section 1-201(36).
"Supplier". Section 2A-103(1)(x).
"Supply contract". Section 2A-103(1)(y).
"Term". Section 1-201(42).

§ 2A-210.   Express Warranties.

(1) Express warranties by the lessor are created as follows:

(a) Any affirmation of fact or promise made by the lessor to the lessee which relates to the goods and becomes part of the basis of the bargain creates an express warranty that the goods will conform to the affirmation or promise.

(b) Any description of the goods which is made part of the basis of the bargain creates an express warranty that the goods will conform to the description.

(c) Any sample or model that is made part of the basis of the bargain creates an express warranty that the whole of the goods will conform to the sample or model.

(2) It is not necessary to the creation of an express warranty that the lessor use formal words, such as "warrant" or "guarantee," or that the lessor have a specific intention to make a warranty, but an affirmation merely of the value of the goods or a statement purporting to be merely the lessor's opinion or commendation of the goods does not create a warranty.

Official Comment

Uniform Statutory Source: Section 2-313.

Changes: Revised to reflect leasing practices and terminology.

Purposes: All of the express and implied warranties of the Article on Sales (Article 2) are included in this Article, revised to reflect the differences between a sale of goods and a lease of goods. Sections 2A–210 through 2A–216. The lease of goods is sufficiently similar to the sale of goods to justify this decision. Hawkland, *The Impact of the Uniform Commercial Code on Equipment Leasing*, 1972 Ill.L.F. 446, 459–60. Many state and federal courts have reached the same conclusion.

Value of the goods, as used in subsection (2), includes rental value.

Cross References:

Article 2, esp. Section 2–313, and Sections 2A–210 through 2A–216.

Definitional Cross References:

"Conforming". Section 2A–103(1)(d).
"Goods". Section 2A–103(1)(h).
"Lessee". Section 2A–103(1)(n).
"Lessor". Section 2A–103(1)(p).
"Value". Section 1–201(44).

§ 2A–211. Warranties Against Interference and Against Infringement; Lessee's Obligation Against Infringement.

(1) There is in a lease contract a warranty that for the lease term no person holds a claim to or interest in the goods that arose from an act or omission of the lessor, other than a claim by way of infringement or the like, which will interfere with the lessee's enjoyment of its leasehold interest.

(2) Except in a finance lease there is in a lease contract by a lessor who is a merchant regularly dealing in goods of the kind a warranty that the goods are delivered free of the rightful claim of any person by way of infringement or the like.

(3) A lessee who furnishes specifications to a lessor or a supplier shall hold the lessor and the supplier harmless against any claim by way of infringement or the like that arises out of compliance with the specifications.

Official Comment

Uniform Statutory Source: Section 2–312.

Changes: This section is modeled on the provisions of Section 2–312, with modifications to reflect the limited

interest transferred by a lease contract and the total interest transferred by a sale. Section 2–312(2), which is omitted here, is incorporated in Section 2A–214. The warranty of quiet possession was abolished with respect to sales of goods. Section 2–312 official comment 1. Section 2A–211(1) reinstates the warranty of quiet possession with respect to leases. Inherent in the nature of the limited interest transferred by the lease—the right to possession and use of the goods—is the need of the lessee for protection greater than that afforded to the buyer. Since the scope of the protection is limited to claims or interests that arose from acts or omissions of the lessor, the lessor will be in position to evaluate the potential cost, certainly a far better position than that enjoyed by the lessee. Further, to the extent the market will allow, the lessor can attempt to pass on the anticipated additional cost to the lessee in the guise of higher rent.

Purposes: General language was chosen for subsection (1) that expresses the essence of the lessee's expectation: with an exception for infringement and the like, no person holding a claim or interest that arose from an act or omission of the lessor will be able to interfere with the lessee's use and enjoyment of the goods for the lease term. Subsection (2), like other similar provisions in later sections, excludes the finance lessor from extending this warranty; with few exceptions (Sections 2A–210 and 2A–211(1)), the lessee under a finance lease is to look to the supplier for warranties and the like or, in some cases as to warranties, to the manufacturer if a warranty made by that person is passed on. Subsections (2) and (3) are derived from Section 2–312(3). These subsections, as well as the analogue, should be construed so that applicable principles of law and equity supplement their provisions. Sections 2A–103(4) and 1–103.

Cross References:

Sections 2–312, 2–312(1), 2–312(2), 2–312 official comment 1, 2A–210, 2A–211(1) and 2A–214.

Definitional Cross References:

"Delivery". Section 1–201(14).
"Finance lease". Section 2A–103(1)(g).
"Goods". Section 2A–103(1)(h).
"Lease". Section 2A–103(1)(j).
"Lease contract". Section 2A–103(1)(*l*).
"Leasehold interest". Section 2A–103(1)(m).
"Lessee". Section 2A–103(1)(n).
"Lessor". Section 2A–103(1)(p).
"Merchant". Section 2–104(1).
"Person". Section 1–201(30).
"Supplier". Section 2A–103(1)(x).

§ 2A-212. Implied Warranty of Merchantability.

(1) Except in a finance lease, a warranty that the goods will be merchantable is implied in a lease contract if the lessor is a merchant with respect to goods of that kind.

(2) Goods to be merchantable must be at least such as

(a) pass without objection in the trade under the description in the lease agreement;

(b) in the case of fungible goods, are of fair average quality within the description;

(c) are fit for the ordinary purposes for which goods of that type are used;

(d) run, within the variation permitted by the lease agreement, of even kind, quality, and quantity within each unit and among all units involved;

(e) are adequately contained, packaged, and labeled as the lease agreement may require; and

(f) conform to any promises or affirmations of fact made on the container or label.

(3) Other implied warranties may arise from course of dealing or usage of trade.

Official Comment

Uniform Statutory Source: Section 2–314.

Changes: Revised to reflect leasing practices and terminology. *E.g., Glenn Dick Equip. Co. v. Galey Constr., Inc.,* 97 Idaho 216, 225, 541 P.2d 1184, 1193 (1975) (implied warranty of merchantability (Article 2) extends to lease transactions).

Definitional Cross References:

"Conforming". Section 2A–103(1)(d).
"Course of dealing". Section 1–205.
"Finance lease". Section 2A–103(1)(g).
"Fungible". Section 1–201(17).
"Goods". Section 2A–103(1)(h).
"Lease agreement". Section 2A–103(1)(k).
"Lease contract". Section 2A–103(1)(*l*).
"Lessor". Section 2A–103(1)(p).
"Merchant". Section 2–104(1).
"Usage of trade". Section 1–205.

§ 2A-213. Implied Warranty of Fitness for Particular Purpose.

Except in a finance lease, if the lessor at the time the lease contract is made has reason to know of any particular purpose for which the goods are required and that the lessee is relying on the lessor's skill or judgment to select or furnish suitable goods, there is in the lease contract an implied warranty that the goods will be fit for that purpose.

Official Comment

Uniform Statutory Source: Section 2–315.

Changes: Revised to reflect leasing practices and terminology. *E.g., All-States Leasing Co. v. Bass,* 96 Idaho 873, 879, 538 P.2d 1177, 1183 (1975) (implied warranty of fitness for a particular purpose (Article 2) extends to lease transactions).

Definitional Cross References:

"Finance lease". Section 2A–103(1)(g).
"Goods". Section 2A–103(1)(h).
"Knows". Section 1–201(25).
"Lease contract". Section 2A–103(1)(*l*).
"Lessee". Section 2A–103(1)(n).
"Lessor". Section 2A–103(1)(p).

§ 2A-214. Exclusion or Modification of Warranties.

(1) Words or conduct relevant to the creation of an express warranty and words or conduct tending to negate or limit a warranty must be construed wherever reasonable as consistent with each other; but, subject to the provisions of Section 2A–202 on parol or extrinsic evidence, negation or limitation is inoperative to the extent that the construction is unreasonable.

(2) Subject to subsection (3), to exclude or modify the implied warranty of merchantability or any part of it the language must mention "merchantability", be by a writing, and be conspicuous. Subject to subsection (3), to exclude or modify any implied warranty of fitness the exclusion must be by a writing and be conspicuous. Language to exclude all implied warranties of fitness is sufficient if it is in writing, is conspicuous and states, for example, "There is no warranty that the goods will be fit for a particular purpose".

(3) Notwithstanding subsection (2), but subject to subsection (4),

(a) unless the circumstances indicate otherwise, all implied warranties are excluded by expressions like "as is," or "with all faults," or by other language that in common understanding calls the lessee's attention to the exclusion of warranties and makes plain that there is no implied warranty, if in writing and conspicuous;

(b) if the lessee before entering into the lease contract has examined the goods or the sample or model as fully as desired or has refused to examine the goods, there is no implied warranty with regard to defects that an examination ought in the circumstances to have revealed; and

(c) an implied warranty may also be excluded or modified by course of dealing, course of performance, or usage of trade.

(4) To exclude or modify a warranty against interference or against infringement (Section 2A–211) or any part of it, the language must be specific, be by a writing, and be conspicuous, unless the circumstances, including course of performance, course of dealing, or usage of trade, give the lessee reason to know that the goods are being leased subject to a claim or interest of any person.

Official Comment

Uniform Statutory Source: Sections 2–316 and 2–312(2).

Changes: Subsection (2) requires that a disclaimer of the warranty of merchantability be conspicuous and in writing as is the case for a disclaimer of the warranty of fitness; this is contrary to the rule stated in Section 2–316(2) with respect to the disclaimer of the warranty of merchantability. This section also provides that to exclude or modify the implied warranty of merchantability, fitness or against interference or infringement the language must be in writing and conspicuous. There are, however, exceptions to the rule. *E.g.,* course of dealing, course of performance, or usage of trade may exclude or modify an implied warranty. Section 2A–214(3)(c). The analogue of Section 2–312(2) has been moved to subsection (4) of this section for a more unified treatment of disclaimers; there is no policy with respect to leases of goods that would justify continuing certain distinctions found in the Article on Sales (Article 2) regarding the treatment of the disclaimer of various warranties. *Compare* Sections 2–312(2) and 2–316(2). Finally, the example of a disclaimer of the implied warranty of fitness stated in subsection (2) differs from the analogue stated in Sec-

tion 2–316(2); this example should promote a better understanding of the effect of the disclaimer.

Purposes: These changes were made to reflect leasing practices. *E.g., FMC Finance Corp. v. Murphree,* 632 F.2d 413, 418 (5th Cir.1980) (disclaimer of implied warranty under lease transactions must be conspicuous and in writing). The omission of the provisions of Section 2–316(4) was not substantive. Sections 2A–503 and 2A–504.

Cross References:

Article 2, esp. Sections 2–312(2) and 2–316, and Sections 2A–503 and 2A–504.

Definitional Cross References:

"Conspicuous". Section 1–201(10).
"Course of dealing". Section 1–205.
"Fault". Section 2A–103(1)(f).
"Goods". Section 2A–103(1)(h).
"Knows". Section 1–201(25).
"Lease". Section 2A–103(1)(j).
"Lease contract". Section 2A–103(1)(l).
"Lessee". Section 2A–103(1)(n).
"Person". Section 1–201(30).
"Usage of trade". Section 1–205.
"Writing". Section 1–201(46).

§ 2A–215. Cumulation and Conflict of Warranties Express or Implied.

Warranties, whether express or implied, must be construed as consistent with each other and as cumulative, but if that construction is unreasonable, the intention of the parties determines which warranty is dominant. In ascertaining that intention the following rules apply:

(a) Exact or technical specifications displace an inconsistent sample or model or general language of description.

(b) A sample from an existing bulk displaces inconsistent general language of description.

(c) Express warranties displace inconsistent implied warranties other than an implied warranty of fitness for a particular purpose.

Official Comment

Uniform Statutory Source: Section 2–317.

Definitional Cross Reference:

"Party". Section 1–201(29).

§ 2A–216. Third-Party Beneficiaries of Express and Implied Warranties.

ALTERNATIVE A

A warranty to or for the benefit of a lessee under this Article, whether express or implied, extends to any natural person who is in the family or household of the lessee or who is a guest in the lessee's home if it is reasonable to expect that such person may use, consume, or be affected by the goods and who is injured in person by breach of the warranty. This section does not displace principles of law and equity that extend a warranty to or for the benefit of a lessee to other persons. The operation of this section may not be excluded, modified, or limited, but an exclusion, modification, or limitation of the warranty, including any with respect to rights and remedies, effective against the lessee is also effective against any beneficiary designated under this section.

ALTERNATIVE B

A warranty to or for the benefit of a lessee under this Article, whether express or implied, extends to any natural person who may reasonably be expected to use, consume, or be affected by the goods and who is injured in person by breach of the warranty. This section does not displace principles of law and equity that extend a warranty to or for the benefit of a lessee to other persons. The operation of this section may not be excluded, modified, or limited, but an exclusion, modification, or limitation of the warranty, including any with respect to rights and remedies, effective against the lessee is also effective against the beneficiary designated under this section.

ALTERNATIVE C

A warranty to or for the benefit of a lessee under this Article, whether express or implied, extends to any person who may reasonably be expected to use, consume, or be affected by the goods and who is injured by breach of the warranty. The operation of this section may not be excluded, modified, or limited with respect to injury to the person of an individual to whom the warranty extends, but an exclusion, modification, or limitation of the warranty, including any with respect to rights and remedies, effective against

the lessee is also effective against the beneficiary designated under this section.

Official Comment

Uniform Statutory Source: Section 2–318.

Changes: The provisions of Section 2–318 have been included in this section, modified in two respects: first, to reflect leasing practice, including the special practices of the lessor under a finance lease; second, to reflect and thus codify elements of the official comment to Section 2–318 with respect to the effect of disclaimers and limitations of remedies against third parties.

Purposes: Alternative A is based on the 1962 version of Section 2–318 and is least favorable to the injured person as the doctrine of privity imposed by other law is abrogated to only a limited extent. Alternatives B and C are based on later additions to Section 2–318 and are more favorable to the injured person. In determining which alternative to select, the state legislature should consider making its choice parallel to the choice it made with respect to Section 2–318, as interpreted by the courts.

The last sentence of each of Alternatives A, B and C does not preclude the lessor from excluding or modifying an express or implied warranty under a lease. Section 2A–214. Further, that sentence does not preclude the lessor from limiting the rights and remedies of the lessee and from liquidating damages. Sections 2A–503 and 2A–504. If the lease excludes or modifies warranties, limits remedies for breach, or liquidates damages with respect to the lessee, such provisions are enforceable against the beneficiaries designated under this section. However, this last sentence forbids selective discrimination against the beneficiaries designated under this section, *i.e.*, exclusion of the lessor's liability to the beneficiaries with respect to warranties made by the lessor to the lessee.

Other law, including the Article on Sales (Article 2), may apply in determining the extent to which a warranty to or for the benefit of the lessor extends to the lessee and third parties. This is in part a function of whether the lessor has bought or leased the goods.

This Article does not purport to change the development of the relationship of the common law, with respect to products liability, including strict liability in tort (as restated in Restatement (Second) of Torts, § 402A (1965)), to the provisions of this Act. *Compare Cline v. Prowler Indus. of Maryland*, 418 A.2d 968 (Del.1980) and *Hawkins Constr. Co. v. Matthews Co.*, 190 Neb. 546, 209 N.W.2d 643 (1973) with *Dippel v. Sciano*, 37 Wis.2d 443, 155 N.W.2d 55 (1967).

Cross References:

Article 2, esp. Section 2–318, and Sections 2A–214, 2A–503 and 2A–504.

Definitional Cross References:

"Goods". Section 2A–103(1)(h).
"Lessee". Section 2A–103(1)(n).
"Person". Section 1–201(30).
"Remedy". Section 1–201(34).
"Rights". Section 1–201(36).

§ 2A–217. Identification.

Identification of goods as goods to which a lease contract refers may be made at any time and in any manner explicitly agreed to by the parties. In the absence of explicit agreement, identification occurs:

(a) when the lease contract is made if the lease contract is for a lease of goods that are existing and identified;

(b) when the goods are shipped, marked, or otherwise designated by the lessor as goods to which the lease contract refers, if the lease contract is for a lease of goods that are not existing and identified; or

(c) when the young are conceived, if the lease contract is for a lease of unborn young of animals.

Official Comment

Uniform Statutory Source: Section 2–501.

Changes: This section, together with Section 2A–218, is derived from the provisions of Section 2–501, with changes to reflect lease terminology; however, this section omits as irrelevant to leasing practice the treatment of special property.

Purposes: With respect to subsection (b) there is a certain amount of ambiguity in the reference to when goods are designated, *e.g.*, when the lessor is both selling and leasing goods to the same lessee/buyer and has marked goods for delivery but has not distinguished between those related to the lease contract and those related to the sales contract. As in Section 2–501(1)(b), this issue has been left to be resolved by the courts, case by case.

Cross References:

Sections 2–501 and 2A–218.

Definitional Cross References:

"Agreement". Section 1–201(3).

"Goods". Section 2A–103(1)(h).
"Lease". Section 2A–103(1)(j).
"Lease contract". Section 2A–103(1)(*l*).
"Lessor". Section 2A–103(1)(p).
"Party". Section 1–201(29).

§ 2A–218. Insurance and Proceeds.

(1) A lessee obtains an insurable interest when existing goods are identified to the lease contract even though the goods identified are nonconforming and the lessee has an option to reject them.

(2) If a lessee has an insurable interest only by reason of the lessor's identification of the goods, the lessor, until default or insolvency or notification to the lessee that identification is final, may substitute other goods for those identified.

(3) Notwithstanding a lessee's insurable interest under subsections (1) and (2), the lessor retains an insurable interest until an option to buy has been exercised by the lessee and risk of loss has passed to the lessee.

(4) Nothing in this section impairs any insurable interest recognized under any other statute or rule of law.

(5) The parties by agreement may determine that one or more parties have an obligation to obtain and pay for insurance covering the goods and by agreement may determine the beneficiary of the proceeds of the insurance.

Official Comment

Uniform Statutory Source: Section 2–501.

Changes: This section, together with Section 2A–217, is derived from the provisions of Section 2–501, with changes and additions to reflect leasing practices and terminology.

Purposes: Subsection (2) states a rule allowing substitution of goods by the lessor under certain circumstances, until default or insolvency of the lessor, or until notification to the lessee that identification is final. Subsection (3) states a rule regarding the lessor's insurable interest that, by virtue of the difference between a sale and a lease, necessarily is different from the rule stated in Section 2–501(2) regarding the seller's insurable interest. For this purpose the option to buy shall be deemed to have been exercised by the lessee when the resulting sale is closed, not when the lessee gives notice to the lessor. Further, subsection (5) is new and reflects the common practice of shifting the responsibility and cost of insuring the goods between the parties to the lease transaction.

Cross References:

Sections 2–501, 2–501(2) and 2A–217.

Definitional Cross References:

"Agreement". Section 1–201(3).
"Buying". Section 2A–103(1)(a).
"Conforming". Section 2A–103(1)(d).
"Goods". Section 2A–103(1)(h).
"Insolvent". Section 1–201(23).
"Lease contract". Section 2A–103(1)(*l*).
"Lessee". Section 2A–103(1)(n).
"Lessor". Section 2A–103(1)(p).
"Notification". Section 1–201(26).
"Party". Section 1–201(29).

§ 2A–219.   Risk of Loss.

(1) Except in the case of a finance lease, risk of loss is retained by the lessor and does not pass to the lessee. In the case of a finance lease, risk of loss passes to the lessee.

(2) Subject to the provisions of this Article on the effect of default on risk of loss (Section 2A–220), if risk of loss is to pass to the lessee and the time of passage is not stated, the following rules apply:

  (a) If the lease contract requires or authorizes the goods to be shipped by carrier

    (i) and it does not require delivery at a particular destination, the risk of loss passes to the lessee when the goods are duly delivered to the carrier; but

    (ii) if it does require delivery at a particular destination and the goods are there duly tendered while in the possession of the carrier, the risk of loss passes to the lessee when the goods are there duly so tendered as to enable the lessee to take delivery.

  (b) If the goods are held by a bailee to be delivered without being moved, the risk of loss passes to the lessee on acknowledgment by the bailee of the lessee's right to possession of the goods.

  (c) In any case not within subsection (a) or (b), the risk of loss passes to the lessee on the lessee's receipt of the goods if the lessor, or, in the case of a finance lease, the supplier,

is a merchant; otherwise the risk passes to the lessee on tender of delivery.

Official Comment

Uniform Statutory Source: Section 2–509(1) through (3).

Changes: Subsection (1) is new. The introduction to subsection (2) is new, but subparagraph (a) incorporates the provisions of Section 2–509(1); subparagraph (b) incorporates the provisions of Section 2–509(2) only in part, reflecting current practice in lease transactions.

Purposes: Subsection (1) states rules related to retention or passage of risk of loss consistent with current practice in lease transactions. The provisions of subsection (4) of Section 2–509 are not incorporated as they are not necessary. This section does not deal with responsibility for loss caused by the wrongful act of either the lessor or the lessee.

Cross References:

Sections 2–509(1), 2–509(2) and 2–509(4).

Definitional Cross References:

"Delivery". Section 1–201(14).
"Finance lease". Section 2A–103(1)(g).
"Goods". Section 2A–103(1)(h).
"Lease contract". Section 2A–103(1)(*l*).
"Lessee". Section 2A–103(1)(n).
"Lessor". Section 2A–103(1)(p).
"Merchant". Section 2–104(1).
"Receipt". Section 2–103(1)(c).
"Rights". Section 1–201(36).
"Supplier". Section 2A–103(1)(x).

§ 2A–220.   Effect of Default on Risk of Loss.

(1) Where risk of loss is to pass to the lessee and the time of passage is not stated:

  (a) If a tender or delivery of goods so fails to conform to the lease contract as to give a right of rejection, the risk of their loss remains with the lessor, or, in the case of a finance lease, the supplier, until cure or acceptance.

  (b) If the lessee rightfully revokes acceptance, he [or she], to the extent of any deficiency in his [or her] effective insurance coverage, may treat the risk of loss as having remained with the lessor from the beginning.

(2) Whether or not risk of loss is to pass to the lessee, if the lessee as to conforming goods already identified to a lease contract repudiates or is otherwise in default under the lease contract, the lessor, or, in the case of a finance lease, the supplier, to the extent of any deficiency in his [or her] effective insurance coverage may treat the risk of loss as resting on the lessee for a commercially reasonable time.

Official Comment

Uniform Statutory Source: Section 2–510.

Changes: Revised to reflect leasing practices and terminology. The rule in Section (1)(b) does not allow the lessee under a finance lease to treat the risk of loss as having remained with the supplier from the beginning. This is appropriate given the limited circumstances under which the lessee under a finance lease is allowed to revoke acceptance. Section 2A–517 and Section 2A–516 official comment.

Definitional Cross References:

"Conforming". Section 2A–103(1)(d).
"Delivery". Section 1–201(14).
"Finance lease". Section 2A–103(1)(g).
"Goods". Section 2A–103(1)(h).
"Lease contract". Section 2A–103(1)(l).
"Lessee". Section 2A–103(1)(n).
"Lessor". Section 2A–103(1)(p).
"Reasonable time". Section 1–204(1) and (2).
"Rights". Section 1–201(36).
"Supplier". Section 2A–103(1)(x).

§ 2A–221. Casualty to Identified Goods.

If a lease contract requires goods identified when the lease contract is made, and the goods suffer casualty without fault of the lessee, the lessor or the supplier before delivery, or the goods suffer casualty before risk of loss passes to the lessee pursuant to the lease agreement or Section 2A–219, then:

(a) if the loss is total, the lease contract is avoided; and

(b) if the loss is partial or the goods have so deteriorated as to no longer conform to the lease contract, the lessee may nevertheless demand inspection and at his [or her] option either treat the lease contract as avoided or, except in a finance lease that is not a consumer lease, accept the goods with due allowance from the rent payable for the balance of the lease term for the deterioration or the deficiency in quantity but without further right against the lessor.

Official Comment

Uniform Statutory Source: Section 2–613.

Changes: Revised to reflect leasing practices and terminology.

Purpose: Due to the vagaries of determining the amount of due allowance (Section 2–613(b)), no attempt was made in subsection (b) to treat a problem unique to lease contracts and installment sales contracts: determining how to recapture the allowance, *e.g.*, application to the first or last rent payments or allocation, *pro rata*, to all rent payments.

Cross References:

Section 2–613.

Definitional Cross References:

"Conforming". Section 2A–103(1)(d).
"Consumer lease". Section 2A–103(1)(e).
"Delivery". Section 1–201(14).
"Fault". Section 2A–103(1)(f).
"Finance lease". Section 2A–103(1)(g).
"Goods". Section 2A–103(1)(h).
"Lease". Section 2A–103(1)(j).
"Lease agreement". Section 2A–103(1)(k).
"Lease contract". Section 2A–103(1)(l).
"Lessee". Section 2A–103(1)(n).
"Lessor". Section 2A–103(1)(p).
"Rights". Section 1–201(36).
"Supplier". Section 2A–103(1)(x).

PART 3

EFFECT OF LEASE CONTRACT

§ 2A–301. Enforceability of Lease Contract.

Except as otherwise provided in this Article, a lease contract is effective and enforceable according to its terms between the parties, against purchasers of the goods and against creditors of the parties.

Official Comment

Uniform Statutory Source: Former Section 9–201 (now codified as Section 9–201).

Changes: The first sentence of former Section 9–201 was incorporated, modified to reflect leasing terminology. The second sentence of former Section 9–201 was eliminated as not relevant to leasing practices.

Purposes:

1. This section establishes a general rule regarding the validity and enforceability of a lease contract. The lease contract is effective and enforceable between the parties and against third parties. Exceptions to this general rule arise where there is a specific rule to the contrary in this Article. Enforceability is, thus, dependent upon the lease contract meeting the requirements of the Statute of Frauds provisions of Section 2A–201. Enforceability is also a function of the lease contract conforming to the principles of construction and interpretation contained in the Article on General Provisions (Article 1). Section 2A–103(4).

2. The effectiveness or enforceability of the lease contract is not dependent upon the lease contract or any financing statement or the like being filed or recorded; however, the priority of the interest of a lessor of fixtures with respect to the interests of certain third parties in such fixtures is subject to the provisions of the Article on Secured Transactions (Article 9). Section 2A–309. Prior to the adoption of this Article filing or recording was not required with respect to leases, only leases intended as security. The definition of security interest, as amended concurrently with the adoption of this Article, more clearly delineates leases and leases intended as security and thus signals the need to file. Section 1–201(37). Those lessors who are concerned about whether the transaction creates a lease or a security interest will continue to file a protective financing statement. Section 9–505. Coogan, Leasing and the Uniform Commercial Code, in *Equipment Leasing-Leveraged Leasing* 681, 744–46 (2d ed. 1980).

3. **Hypothetical:**

(a) In construing this section it is important to recognize its relationship to other sections in this Article. This is best demonstrated by reference to a hypothetical. Assume that on February 1 A, a manufacturer of combines and other farm equipment, leased a fleet of six combines to B, a corporation engaged in the business of farming, for a 12 month term. Under the lease agreement between A and B, A agreed to defer B's payment of the first two months' rent to April 1. On March 1 B recognized that it would need only four combines and thus subleased two combines to C for an 11 month term.

(b) This hypothetical raises a number of issues that are answered by the sections contained in this part. Since lease is defined to include sublease (Section 2A–103(1)(j) and (w)), this section provides that the prime lease between A and B and the sublease between B and C are enforceable in accordance with their terms, except as otherwise provided in this Article; that exception, in this case, is one of considerable scope.

(c) The separation of ownership, which is in A, and possession, which is in B with respect to four combines and which is in C with respect to two combines, is not relevant. Section 2A–302. A's interest in the six combines cannot be challenged simply because A parted with possession to B, who in turn parted with possession of some of the combines to C. Yet it is important to note that by the terms of Section 2A–302 this conclusion is subject to change if otherwise provided in this Article.

(d) B's entering the sublease with C raises an issue that is treated by this part. In a dispute over the leased combines A may challenge B's right to sublease. The rule is permissive as to transfers of interests under a lease contract, including subleases. Section 2A–303(2). However, the rule has two significant qualifications. If the prime lease contract between A and B prohibits B from subleasing the combines, or makes such a sublease an event of default, Section 2A–303(2) applies; thus, while B's interest under the prime lease may be transferred under the sublease to C, A may have a remedy pursuant to Section 2A–303(5). Absent a prohibition or default provision in the prime lease contract A might be able to argue that the sublease to C materially increases A's risk; thus, while B's interest under the prime lease may be transferred under the sublease to C, A may have a remedy pursuant to Section 2A–303(5). Section 2A–303(5)(b)(ii).

(e) Resolution of this issue is also a function of the section dealing with the sublease of goods by a prime lessee (Section 2A–305). Subsection (1) of Section 2A–305, which is subject to the rules of Section 2A–303 stated above, provides that C takes subject to the interest of A under the prime lease between A and B. However, there are two exceptions. First, if B is a merchant (Sections 2A–103(3) and 2–104(1)) dealing in goods of that kind and C is a sublessee in the ordinary course of business (Sections 2A–103(1)(o) and 2A–103(1)(n)), C takes free of the prime lease between A and B. Second, if B has rejected the six combines under the prime lease with A, and B disposes of the goods by sublease to C, C takes free of the prime lease if C can establish good faith. Section 2A-511(4).

(f) If the facts of this hypothetical are expanded and we assume that the prime lease obligated B to maintain the combines, an additional issue may be presented. Prior to entering the sublease, B, in satisfaction of its maintenance covenant, brought the two combines that it desired to sublease to a local independent dealer of A's. The dealer did the requested work for B. C inspected the combines on the dealer's lot after the work was completed. C signed the sublease with B two days later. C, however, was prevented from taking delivery of the two combines as B refused to pay the dealer's invoice for the repairs. The dealer furnished the repair service to B in the ordinary course of the dealer's business. If under applicable law the dealer has a lien on repaired goods in the dealer's possession, the dealer's lien will take priority over B's and C's interests and also should take priority over A's interest, depending upon the terms of the lease contract and the applicable law. Section 2A-306.

(g) Now assume that C is in financial straits and one of C's creditors obtains a judgment against C. If the creditor levies on C's subleasehold interest in the two combines, who will prevail? Unless the levying creditor also holds a lien covered by Section 2A-306, discussed above, the judgment creditor will take its interest subject to B's rights under the sublease and A's rights under the prime lease. Section 2A-307(1). The hypothetical becomes more complicated if we assume that B is in financial straits and B's creditor holds the judgment. Here the judgment creditor takes subject to the sublease unless the lien attached to the two combines before the sublease contract became enforceable. Section 2A-307(2)(a). However, B's judgment creditor cannot prime A's interest in the goods because, with respect to A, the judgment creditor is a creditor of B in its capacity as lessee under the prime lease between A and B. Thus, here the judgment creditor's interest is subject to the lease between A and B. Section 2A-307(1).

(h) Finally, assume that on April 1 B is unable to pay A the deferred rent then due under the prime lease, but that C is current in its payments under the sublease from B. What effect will B's default under the prime lease between A and B have on C's rights under the sublease between B and C? Section 2A-301 provides that a lease contract is effective against the creditors of either party. Since a lease contract includes a sublease contract (Section 2A-103(1)(*l*)), the sublease contract between B and C arguably could be enforceable against A, a prime lessor who has extended unsecured credit to B, the prime lessee/sublessor, if the sublease contract meets the requirements of Section 2A-201. However, the rule stated in Section 2A-301 is subject to other provisions in this Article. Under Section 2A-305, C, as sublessee, would take subject to the prime lease contract in most cases. Thus, B's default under the prime lease will in most cases lead to A's recovery of the goods from C. Section 2A-523. A and C could provide otherwise by agreement. Section 2A-311. C's recourse will be to assert a claim for damages against B. Sections 2A-211(1) and 2A-508.

4. **Relationship Between Sections:**

(a) As the analysis of the hypothetical demonstrates, Part 3 of the Article focuses on issues that relate to the enforceability of the lease contract (Sections 2A-301, 2A-302 and 2A-303) and to the priority of various claims to the goods subject to the lease contract (Sections 2A-304, 2A-305, 2A-306, 2A-307, 2A-308, 2A-309, 2A-310, and 2A-311).

(b) This section states a general rule of enforceability, which is subject to specific rules to the contrary stated elsewhere in the Article. Section 2A-302 negates any notion that the separation of title and possession is fraudulent as a rule of law. Finally, Section 2A-303 states rules with respect to the transfer of the lessor's interest (as well as the residual interest in the goods) or the lessee's interest under the lease contract. Qualifications are imposed as a function of various issues, including whether the transfer is the creation or enforcement of a security interest or one that is material to the other party to the lease contract. In addition, a system of rules is created to deal with the rights and duties among assignor, assignee and the other party to the lease contract.

(c) Sections 2A-304 and 2A-305 are twins that deal with good faith transferees of goods subject to the lease contract. Section 2A-304 creates a set of rules with respect to transfers by the lessor of goods subject to a lease contract; the transferee considered is a subsequent lessee of the goods. The priority dispute covered here is between the subsequent lessee and the original lessee of the goods (or persons claiming through the original lessee). Section 2A-305 creates a set of rules with respect to transfers by the lessee of goods subject to a lease contract; the transferees considered are buyers of the goods or sublessees of the goods. The priority dispute covered here is between the transferee and the lessor of the goods (or persons claiming through the lessor).

(d) Section 2A–306 creates a rule with respect to priority disputes between holders of liens for services or materials furnished with respect to goods subject to a lease contract and the lessor or the lessee under that contract. Section 2A–307 creates a rule with respect to priority disputes between the lessee and creditors of the lessor and priority disputes between the lessor and creditors of the lessee.

(e) Section 2A–308 creates a series of rules relating to allegedly fraudulent transfers and preferences. The most significant rule is that set forth in subsection (3) which validates sale-leaseback transactions if the buyer-lessor can establish that he or she bought for value and in good faith.

(f) Sections 2A–309 and 2A–310 create a series of rules with respect to priority disputes between various third parties and a lessor of fixtures or accessions, respectively, with respect thereto.

(g) Finally, Section 2A–311 allows parties to alter the statutory priorities by agreement.

Cross References:

Article 1, especially Section 1–201(37), and Sections 2–104(1), 2A–103(1)(j), 2A–103(1)(l), 2A–103(1)(n), 2A–103(1)(o) and 2A–103(1)(w), 2A–103(3), 2A–103(4), 2A–201, 2A–301 through 2A–303, 2A–303(2), 2A–303(5), 2A–304 through 2A–307, 2A–307(1), 2A–307(2)(a), 2A–308 through 2A–311, 2A–508, 2A–511(4), 2A–523, Article 9, especially Sections 9–201 and 9–505.

Definitional Cross References:

"Creditor". Section 1–201(12).
"Goods". Section 2A–103(1)(h).
"Lease contract". Section 2A–103(1)(l).
"Party". Section 1–201(29).
"Purchaser". Section 1–201(33).
"Term". Section 1–201(42).

§ 2A–302. Title to and Possession of Goods.

Except as otherwise provided in this Article, each provision of this Article applies whether the lessor or a third party has title to the goods, and whether the lessor, the lessee, or a third party has possession of the goods, notwithstanding any statute or rule of law that possession or the absence of possession is fraudulent.

Official Comment

Uniform Statutory Source: Former Section 9–202 (now codified as Section 9–202).

Changes: Former Section 9–202 was modified to reflect leasing terminology and to clarify the law of leases with respect to fraudulent conveyances or transfers.

Purposes: The separation of ownership and possession of goods between the lessor and the lessee (or a third party) has created problems under certain fraudulent conveyance statutes. *See, e.g., In re Ludlum Enters.,* 510 F.2d 996 (5th Cir. 1975); *Suburbia Fed. Sav. & Loan Ass'n v. Bel-Air Conditioning Co.,* 385 So.2d 1151 (Fla.Dist.Ct.App.1980). This section provides, among other things, that separation of ownership and possession *per se* does not affect the enforceability of the lease contract. Sections 2A–301 and 2A–308.

Cross References:

Sections 2A–301, 2A–308 and 9–202.

Definitional Cross References:

"Goods". Section 2A–103(1)(h).
"Lessee". Section 2A–103(1)(n).
"Lessor". Section 2A–103(1)(p).

§ 2A–303. Alienability of Party's Interest Under Lease Contract or of Lessor's Residual Interest in Goods; Delegation of Performance; Transfer of Rights.

(1) As used in this section, "creation of a security interest" includes the sale of a lease contract that is subject to Article 9, Secured Transactions, by reason of Section 9–109(a)(3).

(2) Except as provided in subsection (3) and Section 9–407, a provision in a lease agreement which (i) prohibits the voluntary or involuntary transfer, including a transfer by sale, sublease, creation or enforcement of a security interest, or attachment, levy, or other judicial process, of an interest of a party under the lease contract or of the lessor's residual interest in the goods, or (ii) makes such a transfer an event of default, gives rise to the rights and remedies provided in subsection (4), but a transfer that is prohibited or is an event of default under the lease agreement is otherwise effective.

(3) A provision in a lease agreement which (i) prohibits a transfer of a right to damages for default with respect to the whole lease contract or of a right to payment arising out of the

transferor's due performance of the transferor's entire obligation, or (ii) makes such a transfer an event of default, is not enforceable, and such a transfer is not a transfer that materially impairs the prospect of obtaining return performance by, materially changes the duty of, or materially increases the burden or risk imposed on, the other party to the lease contract within the purview of subsection (4).

(4) Subject to subsection (3) and Section 9–407:

(a) if a transfer is made which is made an event of default under a lease agreement, the party to the lease contract not making the transfer, unless that party waives the default or otherwise agrees, has the rights and remedies described in Section 2A–501(2);

(b) if paragraph (a) is not applicable and if a transfer is made that (i) is prohibited under a lease agreement or (ii) materially impairs the prospect of obtaining return performance by, materially changes the duty of, or materially increases the burden or risk imposed on, the other party to the lease contract, unless the party not making the transfer agrees at any time to the transfer in the lease contract or otherwise, then, except as limited by contract, (i) the transferor is liable to the party not making the transfer for damages caused by the transfer to the extent that the damages could not reasonably be prevented by the party not making the transfer and (ii) a court having jurisdiction may grant other appropriate relief, including cancellation of the lease contract or an injunction against the transfer.

(5) A transfer of "the lease" or of "all my rights under the lease", or a transfer in similar general terms, is a transfer of rights and, unless the language or the circumstances, as in a transfer for security, indicate the contrary, the transfer is a delegation of duties by the transferor to the transferee. Acceptance by the transferee constitutes a promise by the transferee to perform those duties. The promise is enforceable by either the transferor or the other party to the lease contract.

(6) Unless otherwise agreed by the lessor and the lessee, a delegation of performance does not relieve the transferor as against the other party of any duty to perform or of any liability for default.

(7) In a consumer lease, to prohibit the transfer of an interest of a party under the lease contract or to make a transfer an event of default, the language must be specific, by a writing, and conspicuous.

As amended in 1990 and 1999.

Official Comment

Uniform Statutory Source: Section 2–210; former Section 9–311 (now codified as Section 9–401).

Changes: The provisions of Section 2–210 and former Section 9–311 were incorporated in this section, with substantial modifications to reflect leasing terminology and practice and to harmonize the principles of the respective provisions, i.e. limitations on delegation of performance on the one hand and alienability of rights on the other. In addition, unlike Section 2–210 which deals only with voluntary transfers, this section deals with involuntary as well as voluntary transfers. Moreover, the principle of former Section 9–318(4) (now codified as Section 9–406) denying effectiveness to contractual terms prohibiting assignments of receivables due and to become due also is implemented.

Purposes:

1. Subsection (2) states a rule, consistent with Section 9–401(b), that voluntary and involuntary transfers of an interest of a party under the lease contract or of the lessor's residual interest, including by way of the creation or enforcement of a security interest, are effective, notwithstanding a provision in the lease agreement prohibiting the transfer or making the transfer an event of default. Although the transfers are effective, the provision in the lease agreement is nevertheless enforceable, but only as provided in subsection (4). Under subsection (4) the prejudiced party is limited to the remedies on "default under the lease contract" in this Article and, except as limited by this Article, as provided in the lease agreement, if the transfer has been made an event of default. Section 2A–501(2). Usually, there will be a specific provision to this effect or a general provision making a breach of a covenant an event of default. In those cases where the transfer is prohibited, but not made an event of default, the prejudiced party may recover damages; or, if the damage remedy would be ineffective adequately to protect that party, the court can order cancellation of the lease contract or enjoin the transfer. This rule that such provisions generally are enforceable is subject to

subsection (3) and Section 9–407, which make such provisions unenforceable in certain instances.

2. Under Section 9–407, a provision in a lease agreement which prohibits the creation or enforcement of a security interest, including sales of lease contracts subject to Article 9 (Section 9–109(a)(3)), or makes it an event of default is generally not enforceable, reflecting the policy of Section 9–406 and former Section 9–318(4).

3. Subsection (3) is based upon Section 2–210(2) and Section 9–406. It makes unenforceable a prohibition against transfers of certain rights to payment or a provision making the transfer an event of default. It also provides that such transfers do not materially impair the prospect of obtaining return performance by, materially change the duty of, or materially increase the burden or risk imposed on, the other party to the lease contract so as to give rise to the rights and remedies stated in subsection (4). Accordingly, a transfer of a right to payment cannot be prohibited or made an event of default, or be one that materially impairs performance, changes duties or increases risk, if the right is already due or will become due without further performance being required by the party to receive payment. Thus, a lessor can transfer the right to future payments under the lease contract, including by way of a grant of a security interest, and the transfer will not give rise to the rights and remedies stated in subsection (4) if the lessor has no remaining performance under the lease contract. The mere fact that the lessor is obligated to allow the lessee to remain in possession and to use the goods as long as the lessee is not in default does not mean that there is remaining performance on the part of the lessor. Likewise, the fact that the lessor has potential liability under a "non-operating" lease contract for breaches of warranty does not mean that there is remaining performance. In contrast, the lessor would have remaining performance under a lease contract requiring the lessor to regularly maintain and service the goods or to provide "upgrades" of the equipment on a periodic basis in order to avoid obsolescence. The basic distinction is between a mere potential duty to respond which is not remaining performance, and an affirmative duty to render stipulated performance. Although the distinction may be difficult to draw in some cases, it is instructive to focus on the difference between "operating" and "non-operating" leases as generally understood in the marketplace. Even if there is remaining performance under a lease contract, a transfer for security of a right to payment that is made an event of default or that is in violation of a prohibition against transfer does not give rise to the rights and remedies under subsection (4) if

it does not constitute an actual delegation of a material performance under Section 9–407.

4. The application of either the rule of Section 9–407 or the rule of subsection (3) to the grant by the lessor of a security interest in the lessor's right to future payment under the lease contract may produce the same result. Both provisions generally protect security transfers by the lessor in particular because the creation by the lessor of a security interest or the enforcement of that interest generally will not prejudice the lessee's rights if it does not result in a delegation of the lessor's duties. To the contrary, the receipt of loan proceeds or relief from the enforcement of an antecedent debt normally should enhance the lessor's ability to perform its duties under the lease contract. Nevertheless, there are circumstances where relief might be justified. For example, if ownership of the goods is transferred pursuant to enforcement of a security interest to a party whose ownership would prevent the lessee from continuing to possess the goods, relief might be warranted. See 49 U.S.C. § 1401(a) and (b) which places limitations on the operation of aircraft in the United States based on the citizenship or corporate qualification of the registrant.

5. Relief on the ground of material prejudice when the lease agreement does not prohibit the transfer or make it an event of default should be afforded only in extreme circumstances, considering the fact that the party asserting material prejudice did not insist upon a provision in the lease agreement that would protect against such a transfer.

6. Subsection (4) implements the rule of subsection (2). Subsection (2) provides that, even though a transfer is effective, a provision in the lease agreement prohibiting it or making it an event of default may be enforceable as provided in subsection (4). See Brummund v. First National Bank of Clovis, 656 P.2d 884, 35 U.C.C. Rep.Serv. (Callaghan) 1311 (N.Mex.1983), stating the analogous rule for Section 9–311. If the transfer prohibited by the lease agreement is made an event of default, then, under subsection (4)(a), unless the default is waived or there is an agreement otherwise, the aggrieved party has the rights and remedies referred to in Section 2A–501(2), viz. those in this Article and, except as limited in the Article, those provided in the lease agreement. In the unlikely circumstance that the lease agreement prohibits the transfer without making a violation of the prohibition an event of default or, even if there is no prohibition against the transfer, and the transfer is one that materially impairs performance, changes duties, or increases risk (for example, a sublease or assignment to a party using the goods improperly or for an illegal

purpose), then subsection (4)(b) is applicable. In that circumstance, unless the party aggrieved by the transfer has otherwise agreed in the lease contract, such as by assenting to a particular transfer or to transfers in general, or agrees in some other manner, the aggrieved party has the right to recover damages from the transferor and a court may, in appropriate circumstances, grant other relief, such as cancellation of the lease contract or an injunction against the transfer.

7. If a transfer gives rise to the rights and remedies provided in subsection (4), the transferee as an alternative may propose, and the other party may accept, adequate cure or compensation for past defaults and adequate assurance of future due performance under the lease contract. Subsection (4) does not preclude any other relief that may be available to a party to the lease contract aggrieved by a transfer subject to an enforceable prohibition, such as an action for interference with contractual relations.

8. Subsection (7) requires that a provision in a consumer lease prohibiting a transfer, or making it an event of default, must be specific, written and conspicuous. See Section 1–201(10). This assists in protecting a consumer lessee against surprise assertions of default.

9. Subsection (5) is taken almost verbatim from the provisions of Section 2–210(5). The subsection states a rule of construction that distinguishes a commercial assignment, which substitutes the assignee for the assignor as to rights and duties, and an assignment for security or financing assignment, which substitutes the assignee for the assignor only as to rights. Note that the assignment for security or financing assignment is a subset of all security interests. Security interest is defined to include "any interest of a buyer of ... chattel paper". Section 1–201(37). Chattel paper is defined to include a lease. Section 9–102. Thus, a buyer of leases is the holder of a security interest in the leases. That conclusion should not influence this issue, as the policy is quite different. Whether a buyer of leases is the holder of a commercial assignment, or an assignment for security or financing assignment should be determined by the language of the assignment or the circumstances of the assignment.

Cross References:

Sections 1–201(11), 1–201(37), 2–210, 2A–401, 9–102(a)(11), 9–109(a)(3), 9–406, and 9–407.

Definitional Cross References:

"Agreed" and "Agreement". Section 1–201(3).
"Conspicuous". Section 1–201(10).
"Goods". Section 2A–103(1)(h).

"Lease". Section 2A–103(1)(j).
"Lease contract". Section 2A–103(1)(l).
"Lessee". Section 2A–103(1)(n).
"Lessor". Section 2A–103(1)(p).
"Lessor's residual interest". Section 2A–103(1)(q).
"Notice". Section 1–201(25).
"Party". Section 1–201(29).
"Person". Section 1–201(30).
"Reasonable time". Section 1–204(1) and (2).
"Rights". Section 1–201(36).
"Term". Section 1–201(42).
"Writing". Section 1–201(46).

As amended in 1999.

§ 2A–304. Subsequent Lease of Goods by Lessor.

(1) Subject to Section 2A–303, a subsequent lessee from a lessor of goods under an existing lease contract obtains, to the extent of the leasehold interest transferred, the leasehold interest in the goods that the lessor had or had power to transfer, and except as provided in subsection (2) and Section 2A–527(4), takes subject to the existing lease contract. A lessor with voidable title has power to transfer a good leasehold interest to a good faith subsequent lessee for value, but only to the extent set forth in the preceding sentence. If goods have been delivered under a transaction of purchase, the lessor has that power even though:

(a) the lessor's transferor was deceived as to the identity of the lessor;

(b) the delivery was in exchange for a check which is later dishonored;

(c) it was agreed that the transaction was to be a "cash sale"; or

(d) the delivery was procured through fraud punishable as larcenous under the criminal law.

(2) A subsequent lessee in the ordinary course of business from a lessor who is a merchant dealing in goods of that kind to whom the goods were entrusted by the existing lessee of that lessor before the interest of the subsequent lessee became enforceable against that lessor obtains, to the extent of the leasehold interest transferred, all of that lessor's and the existing lessee's rights to the goods, and takes free of the existing lease contract.

(3) A subsequent lessee from the lessor of goods that are subject to an existing lease contract and are covered by a certificate of title issued under a statute of this State or of another jurisdiction takes no greater rights than those provided both by this section and by the certificate of title statute.

As amended in 1990.

Official Comment

Uniform Statutory Source: Section 2–403.

Changes: While Section 2–403 was used as a model for this section, the provisions of Section 2–403 were significantly revised to reflect leasing practices and to integrate this Article with certificate of title statutes.

Purposes:

1. This section must be read in conjunction with, as it is subject to, the provisions of Section 2A–303, which govern voluntary and involuntary transfers of rights and duties under a lease contract, including the lessor's residual interest in the goods.

2. This section must also be read in conjunction with Section 2–403. This section and Section 2A–305 are derived from Section 2–403, which states a unified policy on good faith purchases of goods. Given the scope of the definition of purchaser (Section 1–201(33)), a person who bought goods to lease as well as a person who bought goods subject to an existing lease from a lessor will take pursuant to Section 2–403. Further, a person who leases such goods from the person who bought them should also be protected under Section 2–403, first because the lessee's rights are derivative and second because the definition of purchaser should be interpreted to include one who takes by lease; no negative implication should be drawn from the inclusion of lease in the definition of purchase in this Article. Section 2A–103(1)(v).

3. There are hypotheticals that relate to an entrustee's unauthorized lease of entrusted goods to a third party that are outside the provisions of Sections 2–403, 2A–304 and 2A–305. Consider a sale of goods by M, a merchant, to B, a buyer. After paying for the goods B allows M to retain possession of the goods as B is short of storage. Before B calls for the goods M leases the goods to L, a lessee. This transaction is not governed by Section 2–403(2) as L is not a buyer in the ordinary course of business. Section 1–201(9). Further, this transaction is not governed by Section 2A–304(2) as B is not an existing lessee. Finally, this transaction is not governed by Section 2A–305(2) as B is not M's lessor. Section 2A–307(2) resolves the potential dispute between B, M and L. By virtue of B's entrustment of the goods to M and M's lease of the goods to L, B has a cause of action against M under the common law. Sections 2A–103(4) and 1–103. *See, e.g.,* Restatement (Second) of Torts §§ 222A–243. Thus, B is a creditor of M. Sections 2A–103(4) and 1–201(12). Section 2A–307(2) provides that B, as M's creditor, takes subject to M's lease to L. Thus, if L does not default under the lease, L's enjoyment and possession of the goods should be undisturbed. However, B is not without recourse. B's action should result in a judgment against M providing, among other things, a turnover of all proceeds arising from M's lease to L, as well as a transfer of all of M's right, title and interest as lessor under M's lease to L, including M's residual interest in the goods. Section 2A–103(1)(q).

4. Subsection (1) states a rule with respect to the leasehold interest obtained by a subsequent lessee from a lessor of goods under an existing lease contract. The interest will include such leasehold interest as the lessor has in the goods as well as the leasehold interest that the lessor had the power to transfer. Thus, the subsequent lessee obtains unimpaired all rights acquired under the law of agency, apparent agency, ownership or other estoppel, whether based upon statutory provisions or upon case law principles. Sections 2A–103(4) and 1–103. In general, the subsequent lessee takes subject to the existing lease contract, including the existing lessee's rights thereunder. Furthermore, the subsequent lease contract is, of course, limited by its own terms, and the subsequent lessee takes only to the extent of the leasehold interest transferred thereunder.

5. Subsection (1) further provides that a lessor with voidable title has power to transfer a good leasehold interest to a good faith subsequent lessee for value. In addition, subsections (1)(a) through (d) provide specifically for the protection of the good faith subsequent lessee for value in a number of specific situations which have been troublesome under prior law.

6. The position of an existing lessee who entrusts leased goods to its lessor is not distinguishable from the position of other entrusters. Thus, subsection (2) provides that the subsequent lessee in the ordinary course of business takes free of the existing lease contract between the lessor entrustee and the lessee entruster, if the lessor is a merchant dealing in goods of that kind. Further, the subsequent lessee obtains all of the lessor entrustee's and the lessee entruster's rights to the goods, but only to the extent of the leasehold interest transferred by the lessor entrustee. Thus, the lessor entrustee retains the residual interest

in the goods. Section 2A–103(1)(q). However, entrustment by the existing lessee must have occurred before the interest of the subsequent lessee became enforceable against the lessor. Entrusting is defined in Section 2–403(3) and that definition applies here. Section 2A–103(3).

7. Subsection (3) states a rule with respect to a transfer of goods from a lessor to a subsequent lessee where the goods are subject to an existing lease and covered by a certificate of title. The subsequent lessee's rights are no greater than those provided by this section and the applicable certificate of title statute, including any applicable case law construing such statute. Where the relationship between the certificate of title statute and Section 2–403, the statutory analogue to this section, has been construed by a court, that construction is incorporated here. Sections 2A–103(4) and 1–102(1) and (2). The better rule is that the certificate of title statutes are in harmony with Section 2–403 and thus would be in harmony with this section. *E.g.*, *Atwood Chevrolet-Olds v. Aberdeen Mun. School Dist.*, 431 So.2d 926, 928 (Miss.1983); *Godfrey v. Gilsdorf*, 476 P.2d 3, 6, 86 Nev. 714, 718 (1970); *Martin v. Nager*, 192 N.J.Super. 189, 197–98, 469 A.2d 519, 523 (Super.Ct.Ch.Div.1983). Where the certificate of title statute is silent on this issue of transfer, this section will control.

Cross References:

Sections 1–102, 1–103, 1–201(33), 2–403, 2A–103(1)(v), 2A–103(3), 2A–103(4), 2A–303 and 2A–305.

Definitional Cross References:

"Agreed". Section 1–201(3).
"Delivery". Section 1–201(14).
"Entrusting". Section 2–403(3).
"Good faith". Sections 1–201(19) and 2–103(1)(b).
"Goods". Section 2A–103(1)(h).
"Lease". Section 2A–103(1)(j).
"Lease contract". Section 2A–103(1)(*l*).
"Leasehold interest". Section 2A–103(1)(m).
"Lessee". Section 2A–103(1)(n).
"Lessee in the ordinary course of business". Section 2A–103(1)(*o*).
"Lessor". Section 2A–103(1)(p).
"Merchant". Section 2–104(1).
"Purchase". Section 2A–103(1)(v).
"Rights". Section 1–201(36).
"Value". Section 1–201(44).

§ 2A–305. Sale or Sublease of Goods by Lessee.

(1) Subject to the provisions of Section 2A–303, a buyer or sublessee from the lessee of goods under an existing lease contract obtains, to the extent of the interest transferred, the leasehold interest in the goods that the lessee had or had power to transfer, and except as provided in subsection (2) and Section 2A–511(4), takes subject to the existing lease contract. A lessee with a voidable leasehold interest has power to transfer a good leasehold interest to a good faith buyer for value or a good faith sublessee for value, but only to the extent set forth in the preceding sentence. When goods have been delivered under a transaction of lease the lessee has that power even though:

(a) the lessor was deceived as to the identity of the lessee;

(b) the delivery was in exchange for a check which is later dishonored; or

(c) the delivery was procured through fraud punishable as larcenous under the criminal law.

(2) A buyer in the ordinary course of business or a sublessee in the ordinary course of business from a lessee who is a merchant dealing in goods of that kind to whom the goods were entrusted by the lessor obtains, to the extent of the interest transferred, all of the lessor's and lessee's rights to the goods, and takes free of the existing lease contract.

(3) A buyer or sublessee from the lessee of goods that are subject to an existing lease contract and are covered by a certificate of title issued under a statute of this State or of another jurisdiction takes no greater rights than those provided both by this section and by the certificate of title statute.

Official Comment

Uniform Statutory Source: Section 2–403.

Changes: While Section 2–403 was used as a model for this section, the provisions of Section 2–403 were significantly revised to reflect leasing practice and to integrate this Article with certificate of title statutes.

Purposes: This section, a companion to Section 2A–304, states the rule with respect to the leasehold interest obtained by a buyer or sublessee from a lessee of goods under an existing lease contract. *Cf.* Section 2A–304 official comment. Note that this provision is consistent with existing case law, which prohibits the bailee's transfer of title to a good faith purchaser for value under Section 2–403(1). *Rohweder v. Aberdeen Product. Credit Ass'n*, 765 F.2d 109 (8th Cir. 1985).

Subsection (2) is also consistent with existing case law. *American Standard Credit, Inc. v. National Cement Co.*, 643 F.2d 248, 269–70 (5th Cir. 1981); *but cf. Exxon Co., U.S.A. v. TLW Computer Indus.*, 37 U.C.C.Rep.Serv. (Callaghan) 1052, 1057–58 (D.Mass. 1983). Unlike Section 2A–304(2), this subsection does not contain any requirement with respect to the time that the goods were entrusted to the merchant. In Section 2A–304(2) the competition is between two customers of the merchant lessor; the time of entrusting was added as a criterion to create additional protection to the customer who was first in time: the existing lessee. In subsection (2) the equities between the competing interests were viewed as balanced.

There appears to be some overlap between Section 2–403(2) and Section 2A–305(2) with respect to a buyer in the ordinary course of business. However, an examination of this Article's definition of buyer in the ordinary course of business (Section 2A–103(1)(a)) makes clear that this reference was necessary to treat entrusting in the context of a lease.

Subsection (3) states a rule of construction with respect to a transfer of goods from a lessee to a buyer or sublessee, where the goods are subject to an existing lease and covered by a certificate of title. *Cf.* Section 2A–304 official comment.

Cross References:

Sections 2–403, 2A–103(1)(a), 2A–304 and 2A–305(2).

Definitional Cross References:

"Buyer". Section 2–103(1)(a).
"Buyer in the ordinary course of business". Section 2A–103(1)(a).
"Delivery". Section 1–201(14).
"Entrusting". Section 2–403(3).
"Good faith". Sections 1–201(19) and 2–103(1)(b).
"Goods". Section 2A–103(1)(h).
"Lease". Section 2A–103(1)(j).
"Lease contract". Section 2A–103(1)(*l*).
"Leasehold interest." Section 2A–103(1)(m).
"Lessee". Section 2A–103(1)(n).
"Lessee in the ordinary course of business". Section 2A–103(1)(o).
"Lessor". Section 2A–103(1)(p).
"Merchant". Section 2–104(1).
"Rights". Section 1–201(36).
"Sale". Section 2–106(1).
"Sublease". Section 2A–103(1)(w).
"Value". Section 1–201(44).

§ 2A–306. Priority of Certain Liens Arising by Operation of Law.

If a person in the ordinary course of his [or her] business furnishes services or materials with respect to goods subject to a lease contract, a lien upon those goods in the possession of that person given by statute or rule of law for those materials or services takes priority over any interest of the lessor or lessee under the lease contract or this Article unless the lien is created by statute and the statute provides otherwise or unless the lien is created by rule of law and the rule of law provides otherwise.

Official Comment

Uniform Statutory Source: Former Section 9–310 (now codified as Section 9–333).

Changes: The approach reflected in the provisions of former Section 9–310 was included, but revised to conform to leasing terminology and to expand the exception to the special priority granted to protected liens to cover liens created by rule of law as well as those created by statute.

Purposes: This section should be interpreted to allow a qualified lessor or a qualified lessee to be the competing lienholder if the statute or rule of law so provides. The reference to statute includes applicable regulations and cases; these sources must be reviewed in resolving a priority dispute under this section.

Cross Reference:

Section 9–333.

Definitional Cross References:

"Goods". Section 2A–103(1)(h).
"Lease contract". Section 2A–103(1)(*l*).
"Lessee". Section 2A–103(1)(n).
"Lessor". Section 2A–103(1)(p).
"Lien". Section 2A–103(1)(r).
"Person". Section 1–201(30).

§ 2A–307. Priority of Liens Arising by Attachment or Levy on, Security Interests in, and Other Claims to Goods.

(1) Except as otherwise provided in Section 2A–306, a creditor of a lessee takes subject to the lease contract.

(2) Except as otherwise provided in subsection (3) and in Sections 2A–306 and 2A–308, a creditor of a lessor takes subject to the lease contract unless the creditor holds a lien that attached to

the goods before the lease contract became enforceable.

(3) Except as otherwise provided in Sections 9–317, 9–321, and 9–323, a lessee takes a leasehold interest subject to a security interest held by a creditor of the lessor.

As amended in 1990 and 1999.

Official Comment

Uniform Statutory Source: None for subsection (1). The remainder of the Section was derived from former Sections 9–301 (now codified as Section 9–317) and 9–307(1) and (3) (now codified as Sections 9–320(a) and 9–323), respectively, and was substantially rewritten in conjunction with the 1998 revisions of Article 9.

Changes: The provisions of former Sections 9–301 and 9–307(1) and (3) were incorporated, and modified to reflect leasing terminology and the basic concepts reflected in this Article.

1998 Changes: Many of the substantive provisions of this Section were moved to Article 9 in conjunction with the 1998 revisions of Article 9.

Purposes:

1. Subsection (1) states a general rule of priority that a creditor of the lessee takes subject to the lease contract. The term lessee (Section 2A–103(1)(n)) includes sublessee. Therefore, this subsection not only covers disputes between the prime lessor and a creditor of the prime lessee but also disputes between the prime lessor, or the sublessor, and a creditor of the sublessee. Section 2A–301 official comment 3(g). Further, by using the term creditor (Section 1–201(12)), this subsection will cover disputes with a general creditor, a secured creditor, a lien creditor and any representative of creditors. Section 2A–103(4).

2. Subsection (2) states a general rule of priority that a creditor of a lessor takes subject to the lease contract. Note the discussion above with regard to the scope of these rules. Section 2A–301 official comment 3(g). Thus, the section will not only cover disputes between the prime lessee and a creditor of the prime lessor but also disputes between the prime lessee, or the sublessee, and a creditor of the sublessor.

3. To take priority over the lease contract, and the interests derived therefrom, the creditor must come within the exception stated in subsection (2) or within one of the provisions of Article 9 mentioned in subsection (3). Subsection (2) provides that where the creditor holds a lien (Section 2A–103(1)(r)) that attached before the lease contract became enforceable (Section

2A–301), the creditor does not take subject to the lease. Subsection (3) provides that a lessee takes its leasehold interest subject to a security interest except as otherwise provided in Sections 9–317, 9–321, or 9–323.

4. The rules of this section operate in favor of whichever party to the lease contract may enforce it, even if one party perhaps may not, e.g., under Section 2A–201(1)(b).

Cross References:

Sections 1–201(12), 1–201(25), 1–201(37), 1–201(44), 2A–103(1)(n), 2A–103(1)(o), 2A–103(1)(r), 2A–103(4), 2A–201(1)(b), 2A–301 official comment 3(g), Article 9, especially Sections 9–317, 9–321 and 9–323.

Definitional Cross References:

"Creditor". Section 1–201(12).
"Goods". Section 2A–103(1)(h).
"Knowledge" and "Knows". Section 1–201(25).
"Lease". Section 2A–103(1)(j).
"Lease contract". Section 2A–103(1)(l).
"Leasehold interest". Section 2A–103(1)(m).
"Lessee". Section 2A–103(1)(n).
"Lessee in the ordinary course of business". Section 2A–103(1)(o).
"Lessor". Section 2A–103(1)(p).
"Lien". Section 2A–103(1)(r).
"Party". Section 1–201(29).
"Pursuant to commitment". Section 2A–103(3).
"Security interest". Section 1–201(37).

As amended in 1999.

§ 2A–308. Special Rights of Creditors.

(1) A creditor of a lessor in possession of goods subject to a lease contract may treat the lease contract as void if as against the creditor retention of possession by the lessor is fraudulent under any statute or rule of law, but retention of possession in good faith and current course of trade by the lessor for a commercially reasonable time after the lease contract becomes enforceable is not fraudulent.

(2) Nothing in this Article impairs the rights of creditors of a lessor if the lease contract (a) becomes enforceable, not in current course of trade but in satisfaction of or as security for a pre-existing claim for money, security, or the like, and (b) is made under circumstances which under any statute or rule of law apart from this Article would constitute the transaction a fraudulent transfer or voidable preference.

(3) A creditor of a seller may treat a sale or an identification of goods to a contract for sale as void if as against the creditor retention of possession by the seller is fraudulent under any statute or rule of law, but retention of possession of the goods pursuant to a lease contract entered into by the seller as lessee and the buyer as lessor in connection with the sale or identification of the goods is not fraudulent if the buyer bought for value and in good faith.

Official Comment

Uniform Statutory Source: Section 2–402(2) and (3)(b).

Changes: Rephrased and new material added to conform to leasing terminology and practice.

Purposes: Subsection (1) states a general rule of avoidance where the lessor has retained possession of goods if such retention is fraudulent under any statute or rule of law. However, the subsection creates an exception under certain circumstances for retention of possession of goods for a commercially reasonable time after the lease contract becomes enforceable.

Subsection (2) also preserves the possibility of an attack on the lease by creditors of the lessor if the lease was made in satisfaction of or as security for a pre-existing claim, and would constitute a fraudulent transfer or voidable preference under other law.

Finally, subsection (3) states a new rule with respect to sale-leaseback transactions, *i.e.,* transactions where the seller sells goods to a buyer but possession of the goods is retained by the seller pursuant to a lease contract between the buyer as lessor and the seller as lessee. Notwithstanding any statute or rule of law that would treat such retention as fraud, whether *per se, prima facie,* or otherwise, the retention is not fraudulent if the buyer bought for value (Section 1–201(44)) and in good faith (Sections 1–201(19) and 2–103(1)(b)). Section 2A–103(3) and (4). This provision overrides Section 2–402(2) to the extent it would otherwise apply to a sale-leaseback transaction.

Cross References:

Sections 1–201(19), 1–201(44), 2–402(2) and 2A–103(4).

Definitional Cross References:

"Buyer". Section 2–103(1)(a).
"Contract". Section 1–201(11).
"Creditor". Section 1–201(12).
"Good faith". Sections 1–201(19) and 2–103(1)(b).

"Goods". Section 2A–103(1)(h).
"Lease contract". Section 2A–103(1)(l).
"Lessee". Section 2A–103(1)(n).
"Lessor". Section 2A–103(1)(p).
"Money". Section 1–201(24).
"Reasonable time". Section 1–204(1) and (2).
"Rights". Section 1–201(36).
"Sale". Section 2–106(1).
"Seller". Section 2–103(1)(d).
"Value". Section 1–201(44).

§ 2A–309. Lessor's and Lessee's Rights When Goods Become Fixtures.

(1) In this section:

(a) goods are "fixtures" when they become so related to particular real estate that an interest in them arises under real estate law;

(b) a "fixture filing" is the filing, in the office where a record of a mortgage on the real estate would be filed or recorded, of a financing statement covering goods that are or are to become fixtures and conforming to the requirements of Section 9–502(a) and (b);

(c) a lease is a "purchase money lease" unless the lessee has possession or use of the goods or the right to possession or use of the goods before the lease agreement is enforceable;

(d) a mortgage is a "construction mortgage" to the extent it secures an obligation incurred for the construction of an improvement on land including the acquisition cost of the land, if the recorded writing so indicates; and

(e) "encumbrance" includes real estate mortgages and other liens on real estate and all other rights in real estate that are not ownership interests.

(2) Under this Article a lease may be of goods that are fixtures or may continue in goods that become fixtures, but no lease exists under this Article of ordinary building materials incorporated into an improvement on land.

(3) This Article does not prevent creation of a lease of fixtures pursuant to real estate law.

(4) The perfected interest of a lessor of fixtures has priority over a conflicting interest of an encumbrancer or owner of the real estate if:

(a) the lease is a purchase money lease, the conflicting interest of the encumbrancer or owner arises before the goods become fixtures, the interest of the lessor is perfected by a fixture filing before the goods become fixtures or within ten days thereafter, and the lessee has an interest of record in the real estate or is in possession of the real estate; or

(b) the interest of the lessor is perfected by a fixture filing before the interest of the encumbrancer or owner is of record, the lessor's interest has priority over any conflicting interest of a predecessor in title of the encumbrancer or owner, and the lessee has an interest of record in the real estate or is in possession of the real estate.

(5) The interest of a lessor of fixtures, whether or not perfected, has priority over the conflicting interest of an encumbrancer or owner of the real estate if:

(a) the fixtures are readily removable factory or office machines, readily removable equipment that is not primarily used or leased for use in the operation of the real estate, or readily removable replacements of domestic appliances that are goods subject to a consumer lease, and before the goods become fixtures the lease contract is enforceable; or

(b) the conflicting interest is a lien on the real estate obtained by legal or equitable proceedings after the lease contract is enforceable; or

(c) the encumbrancer or owner has consented in writing to the lease or has disclaimed an interest in the goods as fixtures; or

(d) the lessee has a right to remove the goods as against the encumbrancer or owner. If the lessee's right to remove terminates, the priority of the interest of the lessor continues for a reasonable time.

(6) Notwithstanding subsection (4)(a) but otherwise subject to subsections (4) and (5), the interest of a lessor of fixtures, including the lessor's residual interest, is subordinate to the conflicting interest of an encumbrancer of the real estate under a construction mortgage recorded before the goods become fixtures if the goods become fixtures before the completion of the construction. To the extent given to refinance a construction mortgage, the conflicting interest of an encumbrancer of the real estate under a mortgage has this priority to the same extent as the encumbrancer of the real estate under the construction mortgage.

(7) In cases not within the preceding subsections, priority between the interest of a lessor of fixtures, including the lessor's residual interest, and the conflicting interest of an encumbrancer or owner of the real estate who is not the lessee is determined by the priority rules governing conflicting interests in real estate.

(8) If the interest of a lessor of fixtures, including the lessor's residual interest, has priority over all conflicting interests of all owners and encumbrancers of the real estate, the lessor or the lessee may (i) on default, expiration, termination, or cancellation of the lease agreement but subject to the agreement and this Article, or (ii) if necessary to enforce other rights and remedies of the lessor or lessee under this Article, remove the goods from the real estate, free and clear of all conflicting interests of all owners and encumbrancers of the real estate, but the lessor or lessee must reimburse any encumbrancer or owner of the real estate who is not the lessee and who has not otherwise agreed for the cost of repair of any physical injury, but not for any diminution in value of the real estate caused by the absence of the goods removed or by any necessity of replacing them. A person entitled to reimbursement may refuse permission to remove until the party seeking removal gives adequate security for the performance of this obligation.

(9) Even though the lease agreement does not create a security interest, the interest of a lessor of fixtures, including the lessor's residual interest, is perfected by filing a financing statement as a fixture filing for leased goods that are or are to become fixtures in accordance with the relevant provisions of the Article on Secured Transactions (Article 9).

As amended in 1990 and 1999.

Official Comment

Uniform Statutory Source: Former Section 9–313.

Changes: Revised to reflect leasing terminology and to add new material.

Purposes:

1. While former Section 9–313 (now codified as Sections 9–334 and 9–604) provided a model for this section, certain provisions were substantially revised.

2. Section 2A–309(1)(c), which is new, defines purchase money lease to exclude leases where the lessee had possession or use of the goods or the right thereof before the lease agreement became enforceable. This term is used in subsection (4)(a) as one of the conditions that must be satisfied to obtain priority over the conflicting interest of an encumbrancer or owner of the real estate.

3. Section 2A–309(4), which states one of several priority rules found in this section, deletes reference to office machines and the like (former Section 9–313(4)(c) (now codified as Section 9–334(e)(2)(A))) as well as certain liens (former Section 9–313(4)(d) (now codified as Section 9–334(e)(3))). However, these items are included in subsection (5), another priority rule that is more permissive than the rule found in subsection (4) as it applies whether or not the interest of the lessor is perfected. In addition, subsection (5)(a) expands the scope of the provisions of former Section 9–313(4)(c) (now codified as Section 9–334(e)(2)(A)) to include readily removable equipment not primarily used or leased for use in the operation of real estate; the qualifier is intended to exclude from the expanded rule equipment integral to the operation of real estate, *e.g.*, heating and air conditioning equipment.

4. The rule stated in subsection (7) is more liberal than the rule stated in former Section 9–313(7) (now codified as Section 9–334(c)) in that issues of priority not otherwise resolved in this subsection are left for resolution by the priority rules governing conflicting interests in real estate, as opposed to the former Section 9–313(7) (now codified as Section 9–334(c)) automatic subordination of the security interest in fixtures. Note that, for the purpose of this section, where the interest of an encumbrancer or owner of the real estate is paramount to the interest of the lessor, the latter term includes the residual interest of the lessor.

5. The rule stated in subsection (8) is more liberal than the rule stated in former Section 9–313(8) (now codified as Section 9–604) in that the right of removal is extended to both the lessor and the lessee and the occasion for removal includes expiration, termination or cancellation of the lease agreement, and enforcement of rights and remedies under this Article, as well as default. The new language also provides that upon removal the goods are free and clear of conflicting interests of owners and encumbrancers of the real estate.

6. Finally, subsection (9) provides a mechanism for the lessor of fixtures to perfect its interest by filing a financing statement under the provisions of the Article on Secured Transactions (Article 9), even though the lease agreement does not create a security interest. Section 1–201(37). The relevant provisions of Article 9 must be interpreted permissively to give effect to this mechanism as it implicitly expands the scope of Article 9 so that its filing provisions apply to transactions that create a lease of fixtures, even though the lease agreement does not create a security interest. This mechanism is similar to that provided in Section 2–326(3)(c) for the seller of goods on consignment, even though the consignment is not "intended as security". Section 1–201(37). Given the lack of litigation with respect to the mechanism created for consignment sales, this new mechanism should prove effective.

Cross References:

Sections 1–201(37), 2A–309(1)(c), 2A–309(4), Article 9, especially Sections 9–334, 9–604 and 9–505.

Definitional Cross References:

"Agreed". Section 1–201(3).
"Cancellation". Section 2A–103(1)(b).
"Conforming". Section 2A–103(1)(d).
"Consumer lease". Section 2A–103(1)(e).
"Goods". Section 2A–103(1)(h).
"Lease". Section 2A–103(1)(j).
"Lease agreement". Section 2A–103(1)(k).
"Lease contract". Section 2A–103(1)(*l*).
"Lessee". Section 2A–103(1)(n).
"Lessor". Section 2A–103(1)(p).
"Lien". Section 2A–103(1)(r).
"Mortgage". Section 9–102(a)(55).
"Party". Section 1–201(29).
"Person". Section 1–201(30).
"Reasonable time". Section 1–204(1) and (2).
"Remedy". Section 1–201(34).
"Rights". Section 1–201(36).
"Security interest". Section 1–201(37).
"Termination". Section 2A–103(1)(z).
"Value". Section 1–201(44).
"Writing". Section 1–201(46).

§ 2A–310. Lessor's and Lessee's Rights When Goods Become Accessions.

(1) Goods are "accessions" when they are installed in or affixed to other goods.

(2) The interest of a lessor or a lessee under a lease contract entered into before the goods became accessions is superior to all interests in the whole except as stated in subsection (4).

(3) The interest of a lessor or a lessee under a lease contract entered into at the time or after the goods became accessions is superior to all subsequently acquired interests in the whole except as stated in subsection (4) but is subordinate to interests in the whole existing at the time the lease contract was made unless the holders of such interests in the whole have in writing consented to the lease or disclaimed an interest in the goods as part of the whole.

(4) The interest of a lessor or a lessee under a lease contract described in subsection (2) or (3) is subordinate to the interest of

(a) a buyer in the ordinary course of business or a lessee in the ordinary course of business of any interest in the whole acquired after the goods became accessions; or

(b) a creditor with a security interest in the whole perfected before the lease contract was made to the extent that the creditor makes subsequent advances without knowledge of the lease contract.

(5) When under subsections (2) or (3) and (4) a lessor or a lessee of accessions holds an interest that is superior to all interests in the whole, the lessor or the lessee may (a) on default, expiration, termination, or cancellation of the lease contract by the other party but subject to the provisions of the lease contract and this Article, or (b) if necessary to enforce his [or her] other rights and remedies under this Article, remove the goods from the whole, free and clear of all interests in the whole, but he [or she] must reimburse any holder of an interest in the whole who is not the lessee and who has not otherwise agreed for the cost of repair of any physical injury but not for any diminution in value of the whole caused by the absence of the goods removed or by any necessity for replacing them. A person entitled to reimbursement may refuse permission to remove until the party seeking removal gives adequate security for the performance of this obligation.

Official Comment

Uniform Statutory Source: Former Section 9–314 (now codified as Section 9–335).

Changes: Revised to reflect leasing terminology and to add new material.

Purposes: Subsection (1) defines "accessions." Subsection (2) adds leasing terminology to the priority rule that applies when the lease is entered into before the goods become accessions. Subsection (3) adds leasing terminology to the priority rule that applies when the lease is entered into on or after the goods become accessions.

Subsection (4) creates two exceptions to the priority rules stated in subsections (2) and (3).

Finally, subsection (5) is modeled on the provisions of former Section 9–314(4) (now codified as Section 9–335(d) and (e)) with respect to removal of accessions, restated to reflect the parallel changes in Section 2A–309(8).

Neither this section nor Section 9–335 governs where the accession to the goods is not subject to the interest of a lessor or a lessee under a lease contract and is not subject to the interest of a secured party under a security agreement. This issue is to be resolved by the courts, case by case.

Cross References:

Sections 2A–309(8), 9–102(a)(1), 9–335.

Definitional Cross References:

"Agreed". Section 1–201(3).
"Buyer in the ordinary course of business". Section 2A–103(1)(a).
"Cancellation". Section 2A–103(1)(b).
"Creditor". Section 1–201(12).
"Goods". Section 2A–103(1)(h).
"Holder". Section 1–201(20).
"Knowledge". Section 1–201(25).
"Lease". Section 2A–103(1)(j).
"Lease contract". Section 2A–103(1)(*l*).
"Lessee". Section 2A–103(1)(n).
"Lessee in the ordinary course of business". Section 2A–103(1)(*o*).
"Lessor". Section 2A–103(1)(p).
"Party". Section 1–201(29).
"Person". Section 1–201(30).
"Remedy". Section 1–201(34).
"Rights". Section 1–201(36).
"Security interest". Section 1–201(37).
"Termination". Section 2A–103(1)(z).
"Value". Section 1–201(44).
"Writing". Section 1–201(46).

§ 2A–311.   Priority Subject to Subordination.

Nothing in this Article prevents subordination by agreement by any person entitled to priority.

As added in 1990.

Official Comment

Uniform Statutory Source: Former Section 9–316 (now codified as Section 9–339).

Purposes: The several preceding sections deal with questions of priority. This section is inserted to make it entirely clear that a person entitled to priority may effectively agree to subordinate the claim. Only the person entitled to priority may make such an agreement: the rights of such a person cannot be adversely affected by an agreement to which that person is not a party.

Cross References:

Sections 1–102 and 2A–304 through 2A–310.
Definitional Cross References:
"Agreement". Section 1–201(3).
"Person". Section 1–201(30).

PART 4

PERFORMANCE OF LEASE CONTRACT: REPUDIATED, SUBSTITUTED AND EXCUSED

§ 2A–401.   Insecurity: Adequate Assurance of Performance.

(1) A lease contract imposes an obligation on each party that the other's expectation of receiving due performance will not be impaired.

(2) If reasonable grounds for insecurity arise with respect to the performance of either party, the insecure party may demand in writing adequate assurance of due performance. Until the insecure party receives that assurance, if commercially reasonable the insecure party may suspend any performance for which he [or she] has not already received the agreed return.

(3) A repudiation of the lease contract occurs if assurance of due performance adequate under the circumstances of the particular case is not provided to the insecure party within a reasonable time, not to exceed 30 days after receipt of a demand by the other party.

(4) Between merchants, the reasonableness of grounds for insecurity and the adequacy of any assurance offered must be determined according to commercial standards.

(5) Acceptance of any nonconforming delivery or payment does not prejudice the aggrieved party's right to demand adequate assurance of future performance.

Official Comment

Uniform Statutory Source: Section 2–609.

Changes: Revised to reflect leasing practices and terminology. Note that in the analogue to subsection (3) (Section 2–609(4)), the adjective "justified" modifies demand. The adjective was deleted here as unnecessary, implying no substantive change.

Definitional Cross References:

"Aggrieved party". Section 1–201(2).
"Agreed". Section 1–201(3).
"Between merchants". Section 2–104(3).
"Conforming". Section 2A–103(1)(d).
"Delivery". Section 1–201(14).
"Lease contract". Section 2A–103(1)(*l*).
"Party". Section 1–201(29).
"Reasonable time". Section 1–204(1) and (2).
"Receipt". Section 2–103(1)(c).
"Rights". Section 1–201(36).
"Writing". Section 1–201(46).

§ 2A–402.   Anticipatory Repudiation.

If either party repudiates a lease contract with respect to a performance not yet due under the lease contract, the loss of which performance will substantially impair the value of the lease contract to the other, the aggrieved party may:

(a) for a commercially reasonable time, await retraction of repudiation and performance by the repudiating party;

(b) make demand pursuant to Section 2A–401 and await assurance of future performance adequate under the circumstances of the particular case; or

(c) resort to any right or remedy upon default under the lease contract or this Article, even though the aggrieved party has notified the repudiating party that the aggrieved party would await the repudiating party's performance and assurance and has urged retraction. In addition, whether or not the aggrieved party is pursuing one of the foregoing remedies, the aggrieved party may suspend performance or, if the aggrieved party is the lessor, proceed in accordance with the provisions of this Article on the lessor's right to identify goods to the lease contract notwithstanding default or to salvage unfinished goods (Section 2A–524).

Official Comment

Uniform Statutory Source: Section 2–610.

Changes: Revised to reflect leasing practices and terminology.

Definitional Cross References:

"Aggrieved party". Section 1–201(2).
"Goods". Section 2A–103(1)(h).
"Lease contract". Section 2A–103(1)(*l*).
"Lessor". Section 2A–103(1)(p).
"Notifies". Section 1–201(26).
"Party". Section 1–201(29).
"Reasonable time". Section 1–204(1) and (2).
"Remedy". Section 1–201(34).
"Rights". Section 1–201(36).
"Value". Section 1–201(44).

§ 2A–403. Retraction of Anticipatory Repudiation.

(1) Until the repudiating party's next performance is due, the repudiating party can retract the repudiation unless, since the repudiation, the aggrieved party has cancelled the lease contract or materially changed the aggrieved party's position or otherwise indicated that the aggrieved party considers the repudiation final.

(2) Retraction may be by any method that clearly indicates to the aggrieved party that the repudiating party intends to perform under the lease contract and includes any assurance demanded under Section 2A–401.

(3) Retraction reinstates a repudiating party's rights under a lease contract with due excuse and allowance to the aggrieved party for any delay occasioned by the repudiation.

Official Comment

Uniform Statutory Source: Section 2–611.

Changes: Revised to reflect leasing practices and terminology. Note that in the analogue to subsection (2) (Section 2–611(2)) the adjective "justifiably" modifies demanded. The adjective was deleted here (as it was in Section 2A–401) as unnecessary, implying no substantive change.

Definitional Cross References:

"Aggrieved party". Section 1–201(2).
"Cancellation". Section 2A–103(1)(b).
"Lease contract". Section 2A–103(1)(*l*).
"Party". Section 1–201(29).
"Rights". Section 1–201(36).

§ 2A–404. Substituted Performance.

(1) If without fault of the lessee, the lessor and the supplier, the agreed berthing, loading, or unloading facilities fail or the agreed type of carrier becomes unavailable or the agreed manner of delivery otherwise becomes commercially impracticable, but a commercially reasonable substitute is available, the substitute performance must be tendered and accepted.

(2) If the agreed means or manner of payment fails because of domestic or foreign governmental regulation:

(a) the lessor may withhold or stop delivery or cause the supplier to withhold or stop delivery unless the lessee provides a means or manner of payment that is commercially a substantial equivalent; and

(b) if delivery has already been taken, payment by the means or in the manner provided by the regulation discharges the lessee's obligation unless the regulation is discriminatory, oppressive, or predatory.

Official Comment

Uniform Statutory Source: Section 2–614.

Changes: Revised to reflect leasing practices and terminology.

Definitional Cross References:

"Agreed". Section 1–201(3).
"Delivery". Section 1–201(14).
"Fault". Section 2A–103(1)(f).
"Lessee". Section 2A–103(1)(n).
"Lessor". Section 2A–103(1)(p).
"Supplier". Section 2A–103(1)(x).

§ 2A–405. Excused Performance.

Subject to Section 2A–404 on substituted performance, the following rules apply:

(a) Delay in delivery or nondelivery in whole or in part by a lessor or a supplier who complies with paragraphs (b) and (c) is not a default under the lease contract if performance as agreed has been made impracticable by the occurrence of a contingency the nonoccurrence of which was a basic assumption on which the lease contract was made or by compliance in good faith with any applicable foreign or domestic governmental regulation or order, whether or not the regulation or order later proves to be invalid.

(b) If the causes mentioned in paragraph (a) affect only part of the lessor's or the supplier's capacity to perform, he [or she] shall allocate production and deliveries among his [or her] customers but at his [or her] option may include regular customers not then under contract for sale or lease as well as his [or her] own requirements for further manufacture. He [or she] may so allocate in any manner that is fair and reasonable.

(c) The lessor seasonally shall notify the lessee and in the case of a finance lease the supplier seasonally shall notify the lessor and the lessee, if known, that there will be delay or nondelivery and, if allocation is required under paragraph (b), of the estimated quota thus made available for the lessee.

Official Comment

Uniform Statutory Source: Section 2–615.

Changes: Revised to reflect leasing practices and terminology.

Definitional Cross References:

"Agreed". Section 1–201(3).
"Contract". Section 1–201(11).
"Delivery". Section 1–201(14).
"Finance lease". Section 2A–103(1)(g).
"Good faith". Sections 1–201(19) and 2–103(1)(b).
"Knows". Section 1–201(25).
"Lease". Section 2A–103(1)(j).
"Lease contract". Section 2A–103(1)(*l*).
"Lessee". Section 2A–103(1)(n).
"Lessor". Section 2A–103(1)(p).
"Notifies". Section 1–201(26).
"Sale". Section 2–106(1).
"Seasonably". Section 1–204(3).
"Supplier". Section 2A–103(1)(x).

§ 2A–406. Procedure on Excused Performance.

(1) If the lessee receives notification of a material or indefinite delay or an allocation justified under Section 2A–405, the lessee may by written notification to the lessor as to any goods involved, and with respect to all of the goods if under an installment lease contract the value of the whole lease contract is substantially impaired (Section 2A–510):

(a) terminate the lease contract (Section 2A–505(2)); or

(b) except in a finance lease that is not a consumer lease, modify the lease contract by accepting the available quota in substitution, with due allowance from the rent payable for the balance of the lease term for the deficiency but without further right against the lessor.

(2) If, after receipt of a notification from the lessor under Section 2A–405, the lessee fails so to modify the lease agreement within a reasonable time not exceeding 30 days, the lease contract lapses with respect to any deliveries affected.

Official Comment

Uniform Statutory Source: Section 2–616(1) and (2).

Changes: Revised to reflect leasing practices and terminology. Note that subsection 1(a) allows the lessee under a lease, including a finance lease, the right to terminate the lease for excused performance (Sections 2A–404 and 2A–405). However, subsection 1(b), which allows the lessee the right to modify the lease for excused performance, excludes a finance lease that is not a consumer lease. This exclusion is compelled by the same policy that led to codification of provisions with respect to irrevocable promises. Section 2A–407.

Definitional Cross References:

"Consumer lease". Section 2A–103(1)(e).
"Delivery". Section 1–201(14).
"Finance lease". Section 2A–103(1)(g).
"Goods". Section 2A–103(1)(h).
"Installment lease contract". Section 2A–103(1)(i).
"Lease agreement". Section 2A–103(1)(k).
"Lease contract". Section 2A–103(1)(*l*).
"Lessee". Section 2A–103(1)(n).
"Lessor". Section 2A–103(1)(p).
"Notice". Section 1–201(25).
"Reasonable time". Section 1–204(1) and (2).

"Receipt". Section 2–103(1)(c).
"Rights". Section 1–201(36).
"Termination". Section 2A–103(1)(z).
"Value". Section 1–201(44).
"Written". Section 1–201(46).

§ 2A–407. Irrevocable Promises: Finance Leases.

(1) In the case of a finance lease that is not a consumer lease the lessee's promises under the lease contract become irrevocable and independent upon the lessee's acceptance of the goods.

(2) A promise that has become irrevocable and independent under subsection (1):

(a) is effective and enforceable between the parties, and by or against third parties including assignees of the parties; and

(b) is not subject to cancellation, termination, modification, repudiation, excuse, or substitution without the consent of the party to whom the promise runs.

(3) This section does not affect the validity under any other law of a covenant in any lease contract making the lessee's promises irrevocable and independent upon the lessee's acceptance of the goods.

As amended in 1990.

Official Comment

Uniform Statutory Source: None.

Purposes:

1. This section extends the benefits of the classic "hell or high water" clause to a finance lease that is not a consumer lease. This section is self-executing; no special provision need be added to the contract. This section makes covenants in a finance lease irrevocable and independent due to the function of the finance lessor in a three party relationship: the lessee is looking to the supplier to perform the essential covenants and warranties. Section 2A–209. Thus, upon the lessee's acceptance of the goods the lessee's promises to the lessor under the lease contract become irrevocable and independent. The provisions of this section remain subject to the obligation of good faith (Sections 2A–103(4) and 1–203), and the lessee's revocation of acceptance (Section 2A–517).

2. The section requires the lessee to perform even if the lessor's performance after the lessee's acceptance is not in accordance with the lease contract; the lessee may, however, have and pursue a cause of action

against the lessor, e.g., breach of certain limited warranties (Sections 2A–210 and 2A–211(1)). This is appropriate because the benefit of the supplier's promises and warranties to the lessor under the supply contract and, in some cases, the warranty of a manufacturer who is not the supplier, is extended to the lessee under the finance lease. Section 2A–209. Despite this balance, this section excludes a finance lease that is a consumer lease. That a consumer be obligated to pay notwithstanding defective goods or the like is a principle that is not tenable under case law (Unico v. Owen, 50 N.J. 101, 232 A.2d 405 (1967)), state statute (Unif.Consumer Credit Code §§ 3.403–.405, 7A U.L.A. 126–31 (1974)), or federal statute (15 U.S.C. § 1666i (1982)).

3. The relationship of the three parties to a transaction that qualifies as a finance lease is best demonstrated by a hypothetical. A, the potential lessor, has been contacted by B, the potential lessee, to discuss the lease of an expensive line of equipment that B has recently placed an order for with C, the manufacturer of such goods. The negotiation is completed and A, as lessor, and B, as lessee, sign a lease of the line of equipment for a 60-month term. B, as buyer, assigns the purchase order with C to A. If this transaction creates a lease (Section 2A–103(1)(j)), this transaction should qualify as a finance lease. Section 2A–103(1)(g).

4. The line of equipment is delivered by C to B's place of business. After installation by C and testing by B, B accepts the goods by signing a certificate of delivery and acceptance, a copy of which is sent by B to A and C. One year later the line of equipment malfunctions and B falls behind in its manufacturing schedule.

5. Under this Article, because the lease is a finance lease, no warranty of fitness or merchantability is extended by A to B. Sections 2A–212(1) and 2A–213. Absent an express provision in the lease agreement, application of Section 2A–210 or Section 2A–211(1), or application of the principles of law and equity, including the law with respect to fraud, duress, or the like (Sections 2A–103(4) and 1–103), B has no claim against A. B's obligation to pay rent to A continues as the obligation became irrevocable and independent when B accepted the line of equipment (Section 2A–407(1)). B has no right of set-off with respect to any part of the rent still due under the lease. Section 2A–508(6). However, B may have another remedy. Despite the lack of privity between B and C (the purchase order with C having been assigned by B to A), B may have a claim against C. Section 2A–209(1).

6. This section does not address whether a "hell or high water" clause, *i.e.*, a clause that is to the effect of this section, is enforceable if included in a finance lease that is a consumer lease or a lease that is not a finance lease. That issue will continue to be determined by the facts of each case and other law which this section does not affect. Sections 2A–104, 2A–103(4), 9–403 and 9–404. However, with respect to finance leases that are not consumer leases courts have enforced "hell or high water" clauses. *In re O.P.M. Leasing Servs.*, 21 Bankr. 993, 1006 (Bankr.S.D.N.Y.1982).

7. Subsection (2) further provides that a promise that has become irrevocable and independent under subsection (1) is enforceable not only between the parties but also against third parties. Thus, the finance lease can be transferred or assigned without disturbing enforceability. Further, subsection (2) also provides that the promise cannot, among other things, be cancelled or terminated without the consent of the lessor.

Cross References:

Sections 1–103, 1–203, 2A–103(1)(g), 2A–103(1)(j), 2A–103(4), 2A–104, 2A–209, 2A–209(1), 2A–210, 2A–211(1), 2A–212(1), 2A–213, 2A–517(1)(b), 9–403 and 9–404.

Definitional Cross References:

"Cancellation". Section 2A–103(1)(b).
"Consumer lease". Section 2A–103(1)(e).
"Finance lease". Section 2A–103(1)(g).
"Goods". Section 2A–103(1)(h).
"Lease contract". Section 2A–103(1)(*l*).
"Lessee". Section 2A–103(1)(n).
"Party". Section 1–201(29).
"Termination". Section 2A–103(1)(z).

PART 5

DEFAULT

A. IN GENERAL

§ 2A–501.   Default: Procedure.

(1) Whether the lessor or the lessee is in default under a lease contract is determined by the lease agreement and this Article.

(2) If the lessor or the lessee is in default under the lease contract, the party seeking enforcement has rights and remedies as provided in this Article and, except as limited by this Article, as provided in the lease agreement.

(3) If the lessor or the lessee is in default under the lease contract, the party seeking enforcement may reduce the party's claim to judgment, or otherwise enforce the lease contract by self-help or any available judicial procedure or nonjudicial procedure, including administrative proceeding, arbitration, or the like, in accordance with this Article.

(4) Except as otherwise provided in Section 1–106(1) or this Article or the lease agreement, the rights and remedies referred to in subsections (2) and (3) are cumulative.

(5) If the lease agreement covers both real property and goods, the party seeking enforcement may proceed under this Part as to the goods, or under other applicable law as to both the real property and the goods in accordance with that party's rights and remedies in respect of the real property, in which case this Part does not apply.

As amended in 1990 and 2001.

Official Comment

Uniform Statutory Source: Former Section 9–501 (now codified as Sections 9–601 through 9–604).

Changes: Substantially revised.

Purposes:

1. Subsection (1) is new and represents a departure from the Article on Secured Transactions (Article 9) as the subsection makes clear that whether a party to the lease agreement is in default is determined by this Article as well as the agreement. Sections 2A–508 and 2A–523. It further departs from Article 9 in recognizing the potential default of either party, a function of the bilateral nature of the obligations between the parties to the lease contract.

2. Subsection (2) is a version of the first sentence of Section 9–601(a), revised to reflect leasing terminology.

3. Subsection (3), an expansive version of the second sentence of Section 9–601(a), lists the procedures that may be followed by the party seeking enforcement; in effect, the scope of the procedures listed in subsection (3) is consistent with the scope of the procedures available to the foreclosing secured party.

4. Subsection (4) establishes that the parties' rights and remedies are cumulative. DeKoven, *Leases of Equipment: Puritan Leasing Company v. August, A Dangerous Decision*, 12 U.S.F.L.Rev. 257, 276–80 (1978). Cumulation, and largely unrestricted selection, of remedies is allowed in furtherance of the general policy of the Commercial Code, stated in Section 1–106, that remedies be liberally administered to put the aggrieved party in as good a position as if the other party had fully performed. Therefore, cumulation of, or selection among, remedies is available to the extent necessary to put the aggrieved party in as good a position as it would have been in had there been full performance. However, cumulation of, or selection among, remedies is not available to the extent that the cumulation or selection would put the aggrieved party in a better position than it would have been in had there been full performance by the other party.

5. Section 9–602, which, among other things, states that certain rules, to the extent they give rights to the debtor and impose duties on the secured party, may not be waived or varied, is not incorporated in this Article. Given the significance of freedom of contract in the development of the common law as it applies to bailments for hire and the lessee's lack of an equity of redemption, there is no reason to impose that restraint.

Cross References:

Sections 1–106, 2A–508, 2A–523, Article 9, especially Sections 9–601 and 9–602.

Definitional Cross References:

"Goods". Section 2A–103(1)(h).
"Lease agreement". Section 2A–103(1)(k).
"Lease contract". Section 2A–103(1)(*l*).
"Lessee". Section 2A–103(1)(n).
"Lessor". Section 2A–103(1)(p).
"Party". Section 1–201(29).
"Remedy". Section 1–201(34).
"Rights". Section 1–201(36).

§ 2A–502. Notice After Default.

Except as otherwise provided in this Article or the lease agreement, the lessor or lessee in default under the lease contract is not entitled to notice of default or notice of enforcement from the other party to the lease agreement.

Official Comment

Uniform Statutory Source: None.

Purposes: This section makes clear that absent agreement to the contrary or provision in this Article to the contrary, *e.g.*, Section 2A–516(3)(a), the party in default is not entitled to notice of default or enforcement. While a review of Part 5 of Article 9 leads to the same conclusion with respect to giving notice of default to the debtor, it is never stated. Although Article 9 requires notice of disposition and strict foreclosure, the different scheme of lessors' and lessees' rights and remedies developed under the common law, and codified by this Article, generally does not require notice of enforcement; furthermore, such notice is not mandated by due process requirements. However, certain sections of this Article do require notice. *E.g.*, Section ~~2A–517(2)~~ 2A–517(4) *.

Cross References:

Sections 2A–516(3)(a), ~~2A–517(2)~~ 2A–517(4) *, and Article 9, esp. Part 5.

Definitional Cross References:

"Lease agreement". Section 2A–103(1)(k).
"Lease contract". Section 2A–103(1)(*l*).
"Lessee". Section 2A–103(1)(n).
"Lessor". Section 2A–103(1)(p).
"Notice". Section 1–201(25).
"Party". Section 1–201(29).

* *Previous incorrect cross reference corrected by Permanent Editorial Board action, November 1992.*

§ 2A–503. Modification or Impairment of Rights and Remedies.

(1) Except as otherwise provided in this Article, the lease agreement may include rights and remedies for default in addition to or in substitution for those provided in this Article and may limit or alter the measure of damages recoverable under this Article.

(2) Resort to a remedy provided under this Article or in the lease agreement is optional unless the remedy is expressly agreed to be exclusive. If circumstances cause an exclusive or limited remedy to fail of its essential purpose, or provision for an exclusive remedy is unconscionable, remedy may be had as provided in this Article.

(3) Consequential damages may be liquidated under Section 2A–504, or may otherwise be limited, altered, or excluded unless the limitation, alteration, or exclusion is unconscionable. Limitation, alteration, or exclusion of consequential damages for injury to the person in the case of

consumer goods is prima facie unconscionable but limitation, alteration, or exclusion of damages where the loss is commercial is not prima facie unconscionable.

(4) Rights and remedies on default by the lessor or the lessee with respect to any obligation or promise collateral or ancillary to the lease contract are not impaired by this Article.

As amended in 1990.

Official Comment

Uniform Statutory Source: Sections 2–719 and 2–701.

Changes: Rewritten to reflect lease terminology and to clarify the relationship between this section and Section 2A–504.

Purposes:

1. A significant purpose of this Part is to provide rights and remedies for those parties to a lease who fail to provide them by agreement or whose rights and remedies fail of their essential purpose or are unenforceable. However, it is important to note that this implies no restriction on freedom to contract. Sections 2A–103(4) and 1–102(3). Thus, subsection (1), a revised version of the provisions of Section 2–719(1), allows the parties to the lease agreement freedom to provide for rights and remedies in addition to or in substitution for those provided in this Article and to alter or limit the measure of damages recoverable under this Article. Except to the extent otherwise provided in this Article (e.g., Sections 2A–105, 106 and 108(1) and (2)), this Part shall be construed neither to restrict the parties' ability to provide for rights and remedies or to limit or alter the measure of damages by agreement, nor to imply disapproval of rights and remedy schemes other than those set forth in this Part.

2. Subsection (2) makes explicit with respect to this Article what is implicit in Section 2–719 with respect to the Article on Sales (Article 2): if an exclusive remedy is held to be unconscionable, remedies under this Article are available. Section 2–719 official comment 1.

3. Subsection (3), a revision of Section 2–719(3), makes clear that consequential damages may also be liquidated. Section 2A–504(1).

4. Subsection (4) is a revision of the provisions of Section 2–701. This subsection leaves the treatment of default with respect to obligations or promises collateral or ancillary to the lease contract to other law.

Sections 2A–103(4) and 1–103. An example of such an obligation would be that of the lessor to the secured creditor which has provided the funds to leverage the lessor's lease transaction; an example of such a promise would be that of the lessee, as seller, to the lessor, as buyer, in a sale-leaseback transaction.

Cross References:

Sections 1–102(3), 1–103, Article 2, especially Sections 2–701, 2–719, 2–719(1), 2–719(3), 2–719 official comment 1, and Sections 2A–103(4), 2A–105, 2A–106, 2A–108(1), 2A–108(2), and 2A–504.

Definitional Cross References:

"Agreed". Section 1–201(3).
"Consumer goods". Section 9–102(a)(23).
"Lease agreement". Section 2A–103(1)(k).
"Lease contract". Section 2A–103(1)(l).
"Lessee". Section 2A–103(1)(n).
"Lessor". Section 2A–103(1)(p).
"Person". Section 1–201(30).
"Remedy". Section 1–201(34).
"Rights". Section 1–201(36).

§ 2A–504.   Liquidation of Damages.

(1) Damages payable by either party for default, or any other act or omission, including indemnity for loss or diminution of anticipated tax benefits or loss or damage to lessor's residual interest, may be liquidated in the lease agreement but only at an amount or by a formula that is reasonable in light of the then anticipated harm caused by the default or other act or omission.

(2) If the lease agreement provides for liquidation of damages, and such provision does not comply with subsection (1), or such provision is an exclusive or limited remedy that circumstances cause to fail of its essential purpose, remedy may be had as provided in this Article.

(3) If the lessor justifiably withholds or stops delivery of goods because of the lessee's default or insolvency (Section 2A–525 or 2A–526), the lessee is entitled to restitution of any amount by which the sum of his [or her] payments exceeds:

(a) the amount to which the lessor is entitled by virtue of terms liquidating the lessor's damages in accordance with subsection (1); or

(b) in the absence of those terms, 20 percent of the then present value of the total rent the lessee was obligated to pay for the balance of the lease term, or, in the case of a consumer lease, the lesser of such amount or $500.

(4) A lessee's right to restitution under subsection (3) is subject to offset to the extent the lessor establishes:

(a) a right to recover damages under the provisions of this Article other than subsection (1); and

(b) the amount or value of any benefits received by the lessee directly or indirectly by reason of the lease contract.

Official Comment

Uniform Statutory Source: Sections 2–718(1), (2), (3) and 2–719(2).

Changes: Substantially rewritten.

Purposes: Many leasing transactions are predicated on the parties' ability to agree to an appropriate amount of damages or formula for damages in the event of default or other act or omission. The rule with respect to sales of goods (Section 2–718) may not be sufficiently flexible to accommodate this practice. Thus, consistent with the common law emphasis upon freedom to contract with respect to bailments for hire, this section has created a revised rule that allows greater flexibility with respect to leases of goods.

Subsection (1), a significantly modified version of the provisions of Section 2–718(1), provides for liquidation of damages in the lease agreement at an amount or by a formula. Section 2–718(1) does not by its express terms include liquidation by a formula; this change was compelled by modern leasing practice. Subsection (1), in a further expansion of Section 2–718(1), provides for liquidation of damages for default as well as any other act or omission.

A liquidated damages formula that is common in leasing practice provides that the sum of lease payments past due, accelerated future lease payments, and the lessor's estimated residual interest, less the net proceeds of disposition (whether by sale or re-lease) of the leased goods is the lessor's damages. Tax indemnities, costs, interest and attorney's fees are also added to determine the lessor's damages. Another common liquidated damages formula utilizes a periodic depreciation allocation as a credit to the aforesaid amount in mitigation of a lessor's damages. A third formula provides for a fixed number of periodic payments as a means of liquidating damages. Stipulated loss or stipulated damage schedules are also common. Whether these formulae are enforceable will be determined in the context of each case by applying a standard of reasonableness in light of the harm anticipated when the formula was agreed to. Whether the inclusion of these formulae will affect the classification of the transaction as a lease or a security interest is to be determined by the facts of each case. Section 1–201(37). E.g., In re Noack, 44 Bankr. 172, 174–75 (Bankr.E.D.Wis.1984).

This section does not incorporate two other tests that under sales law determine enforceability of liquidated damages, i.e., difficulties of proof of loss and inconvenience or nonfeasibility of otherwise obtaining an adequate remedy. The ability to liquidate damages is critical to modern leasing practice; given the parties' freedom to contract at common law, the policy behind retaining these two additional requirements here was thought to be outweighed. Further, given the expansion of subsection (1) to enable the parties to liquidate the amount payable with respect to an indemnity for loss or diminution of anticipated tax benefits resulted in another change: the last sentence of Section 2–718(1), providing that a term fixing unreasonably large liquidated damages is void as a penalty, was also not incorporated. The impact of local, state and federal tax laws on a leasing transaction can result in an amount payable with respect to the tax indemnity many times greater than the original purchase price of the goods. By deleting the reference to unreasonably large liquidated damages the parties are free to negotiate a formula, restrained by the rule of reasonableness in this section. These changes should invite the parties to liquidate damages. Peters, *Remedies for Breach of Contracts Relating to the Sale of Goods Under the Uniform Commercial Code: A Roadmap for Article Two*, 73 Yale L.J. 199, 278 (1963).

Subsection (2), a revised version of Section 2–719(2), provides that if the liquidated damages provision is not enforceable or fails of its essential purpose, remedy may be had as provided in this Article.

Subsection (3)(b) of this section differs from subsection (2)(b) of Section 2–718; in the absence of a valid liquidated damages amount or formula the lessor is permitted to retain 20 percent of the present value of the total rent payable under the lease. The alternative limitation of $500 contained in Section 2–718 is deleted as unrealistically low with respect to a lease other than a consumer lease.

Cross References:

Sections 1–201(37), 2–718, 2–718(1), 2–718(2)(b) and 2–719(2).

Definitional Cross References:

"Consumer lease". Section 2A–103(1)(e).

"Delivery". Section 1–201(14).

"Goods". Section 2A–103(1)(h).

"Insolvent". Section 1–201(23).

"Lease agreement". Section 2A–103(1)(k).

"Lease contract". Section 2A–103(1)(*l*).

"Lessee". Section 2A–103(1)(n).

"Lessor". Section 2A–103(1)(p).

"Lessor's residual interest". Section 2A–103(1)(q).

"Party". Section 1–201(29).

"Present value". Section 2A–103(1)(u).

"Remedy". Section 1–201(34).

"Rights". Section 1–201(36).

"Term". Section 1–201(42).

"Value". Section 1–201(44).

§ 2A–505. Cancellation and Termination and Effect of Cancellation, Termination, Rescission, or Fraud on Rights and Remedies.

(1) On cancellation of the lease contract, all obligations that are still executory on both sides are discharged, but any right based on prior default or performance survives, and the cancelling party also retains any remedy for default of the whole lease contract or any unperformed balance.

(2) On termination of the lease contract, all obligations that are still executory on both sides are discharged but any right based on prior default or performance survives.

(3) Unless the contrary intention clearly appears, expressions of "cancellation," "rescission," or the like of the lease contract may not be construed as a renunciation or discharge of any claim in damages for an antecedent default.

(4) Rights and remedies for material misrepresentation or fraud include all rights and remedies available under this Article for default.

(5) Neither rescission nor a claim for rescission of the lease contract nor rejection or return of the goods may bar or be deemed inconsistent with a claim for damages or other right or remedy.

Official Comment

Uniform Statutory Source: Sections 2–106(3) and (4), 2–720 and 2–721.

Changes: Revised to reflect leasing practices and terminology.

Definitional Cross References:

"Cancellation". Section 2A–103(1)(b).

"Goods". Section 2A–103(1)(h).

"Lease contract". Section 2A–103(1)(*l*).

"Party". Section 1–201(29).

"Remedy". Section 1–201(34).

"Rights". Section 1–201(36).

"Termination". Section 2A–103(1)(z).

§ 2A–506. Statute of Limitations.

(1) An action for default under a lease contract, including breach of warranty or indemnity, must be commenced within 4 years after the cause of action accrued. By the original lease contract the parties may reduce the period of limitation to not less than one year.

(2) A cause of action for default accrues when the act or omission on which the default or breach of warranty is based is or should have been discovered by the aggrieved party, or when the default occurs, whichever is later. A cause of action for indemnity accrues when the act or omission on which the claim for indemnity is based is or should have been discovered by the indemnified party, whichever is later.

(3) If an action commenced within the time limited by subsection (1) is so terminated as to leave available a remedy by another action for the same default or breach of warranty or indemnity, the other action may be commenced after the expiration of the time limited and within 6 months after the termination of the first action unless the termination resulted from voluntary discontinuance or from dismissal for failure or neglect to prosecute.

(4) This section does not alter the law on tolling of the statute of limitations nor does it apply to causes of action that have accrued before this Article becomes effective.

Official Comment

Uniform Statutory Source: Section 2–725.

Changes: Substantially rewritten.

Purposes: Subsection (1) does not incorporate the limitation found in Section 2–725(1) prohibiting the parties from extending the period of limitation. Breach of warranty and indemnity claims often arise in a lease transaction; with the passage of time such claims often diminish or are eliminated. To encourage the parties to commence litigation under these circumstances makes little sense.

Subsection (2) states two rules for determining when a cause of action accrues. With respect to default, the rule of Section 2–725(2) is not incorporated in favor of a more liberal rule of the later of the date when the default occurs or when the act or omission on which it is based is or should have been discovered. With respect to indemnity, a similarly liberal rule is adopted.

Cross References:

Sections 2–725(1) and 2–725(2).

Definitional Cross References:

"Action". Section 1–201(1).
"Aggrieved party". Section 1–201(2).
"Lease contract". Section 2A–103(1)(*l*).
"Party". Section 1–201(29).
"Remedy". Section 1–201(34).
"Termination". Section 2A–103(1)(z).

§ 2A–507. Proof of Market Rent: Time and Place.

(1) Damages based on market rent (Section 2A–519 or 2A–528) are determined according to the rent for the use of the goods concerned for a lease term identical to the remaining lease term of the original lease agreement and prevailing at the times specified in Sections 2A–519 and 2A–528.

(2) If evidence of rent for the use of the goods concerned for a lease term identical to the remaining lease term of the original lease agreement and prevailing at the times or places described in this Article is not readily available, the rent prevailing within any reasonable time before or after the time described or at any other place or for a different lease term which in commercial judgment or under usage of trade would serve as a reasonable substitute for the one described may be used, making any proper allowance for the difference, including the cost of transporting the goods to or from the other place.

(3) Evidence of a relevant rent prevailing at a time or place or for a lease term other than the one described in this Article offered by one party is not admissible unless and until he [or she] has given the other party notice the court finds sufficient to prevent unfair surprise.

(4) If the prevailing rent or value of any goods regularly leased in any established market is in issue, reports in official publications or trade journals or in newspapers or periodicals of general circulation published as the reports of that market are admissible in evidence. The circumstances of the preparation of the report may be shown to affect its weight but not its admissibility.

As amended in 1990.

Official Comment

Uniform Statutory Source: Sections 2–723 and 2–724.

Changes: Revised to reflect leasing practices and terminology. Sections 2A–519 and 2A–528 specify the times as of which market rent is to be determined.

Definitional Cross References:

"Goods". Section 2A–103(1)(h).
"Lease". Section 2A–103(1)(j).
"Lease agreement". Section 2A–103(1)(k).
"Notice". Section 1–201(25).
"Party". Section 1–201(29).
"Reasonable time". Section 1–204(1) and (2).
"Usage of trade". Section 1–205.
"Value". Section 1–201(44).

B. DEFAULT BY LESSOR

§ 2A–508. Lessee's Remedies.

(1) If a lessor fails to deliver the goods in conformity to the lease contract (Section 2A–509) or repudiates the lease contract (Section 2A–402), or a lessee rightfully rejects the goods (Section 2A–509) or justifiably revokes acceptance of the goods (Section 2A–517), then with respect to any goods involved, and with respect to all of the goods if under an installment lease contract the value of the whole lease contract is substantially impaired (Section 2A–510), the lessor is in default under the lease contract and the lessee may:

(a) cancel the lease contract (Section 2A–505(1));

(b) recover so much of the rent and security as has been paid and is just under the circumstances;

(c) cover and recover damages as to all goods affected whether or not they have been identified to the lease contract (Sections 2A–518 and 2A–520), or recover damages for nondelivery (Sections 2A–519 and 2A–520);

(d) exercise any other rights or pursue any other remedies provided in the lease contract.

(2) If a lessor fails to deliver the goods in conformity to the lease contract or repudiates the lease contract, the lessee may also:

(a) if the goods have been identified, recover them (Section 2A–522); or

(b) in a proper case, obtain specific performance or replevy the goods (Section 2A–521).

(3) If a lessor is otherwise in default under a lease contract, the lessee may exercise the rights and pursue the remedies provided in the lease contract, which may include a right to cancel the lease, and in Section 2A–519(3).

(4) If a lessor has breached a warranty, whether express or implied, the lessee may recover damages (Section 2A–519(4)).

(5) On rightful rejection or justifiable revocation of acceptance, a lessee has a security interest in goods in the lessee's possession or control for any rent and security that has been paid and any expenses reasonably incurred in their inspection, receipt, transportation, and care and custody and may hold those goods and dispose of them in good faith and in a commercially reasonable manner, subject to Section 2A–527(5).

(6) Subject to the provisions of Section 2A–407, a lessee, on notifying the lessor of the lessee's intention to do so, may deduct all or any part of the damages resulting from any default under the lease contract from any part of the rent still due under the same lease contract.

As amended in 1990.

Official Comment

Uniform Statutory Source: Sections 2–711 and 2–717.

Changes: Substantially rewritten.

Purposes:

1. This section is an index to Sections 2A–509 through 522 which set out the lessee's rights and remedies after the lessor's default. The lessor and the lessee can agree to modify the rights and remedies available under this Article; they can, among other things, provide that for defaults other than those specified in subsection (1) the lessee can exercise the rights and remedies referred to in subsection (1); and they can create a new scheme of rights and remedies triggered by the occurrence of the default. Sections 2A–103(4) and 1–102(3).

2. Subsection (1), a substantially rewritten version of the provisions of Section 2–711(1), lists three cumulative remedies of the lessee where the lessor has failed to deliver conforming goods or has repudiated the contract, or the lessee has rightfully rejected or justifiably revoked. Sections 2A–501(2) and (4). Subsection (1) also allows the lessee to exercise any contractual remedy. This Article rejects any general doctrine of election of remedy. To determine if one remedy bars another in a particular case is a function of whether the lessee has been put in as good a position as if the lessor had fully performed the lease agreement. Use of multiple remedies is barred only if the effect is to put the lessee in a better position than it would have been in had the lessor fully performed under the lease. Sections 2A–103(4), 2A–501(4), and 1–106(1). Subsection (1)(b), in recognition that no bright line can be created that would operate fairly in all installment lease cases and in recognition of the fact that a lessee may be able to cancel the lease (revoke acceptance of the goods) after the goods have been in use for some period of time, does not require that all lease payments made by the lessee under the lease be returned upon cancellation. Rather, only such portion as is just of the rent and security payments made may be recovered. If a defect in the goods is discovered immediately upon tender to the lessee and the goods are rejected immediately, then the lessee should recover all payments made. If, however, for example, a 36–month equipment lease is terminated in the 12th month because the lessor has materially breached the contract by failing to perform its maintenance obligations, it may be just to return only a small part or none of the rental payments already made.

3. Subsection (2), a version of the provisions of Section 2–711(2) revised to reflect leasing terminology, lists two alternative remedies for the recovery of the goods by the lessee; however, each of these remedies is cumulative with respect to those listed in subsection (1).

4. Subsection (3) is new. It covers defaults which do not deprive the lessee of the goods and which are not so serious as to justify rejection or revocation of acceptance under subsection (1). It also covers defaults for which the lessee could have rejected or revoked acceptance of the goods but elects not to do so and retains the goods. In either case, a lessee which retains the goods is entitled to recover damages as stated in Section 2A–519(3). That measure of damages is "the loss resulting in the ordinary course of events from the lessor's default as determined in any

manner that is reasonable together with incidental and consequential damages, less expenses saved in consequence of the lessor's breach.''

5. Subsection (1)(d) and subsection (3) recognize that the lease agreement may provide rights and remedies in addition to or different from those which Article 2A provides. In particular, subsection (3) provides that the lease agreement may give the remedy of cancellation of the lease for defaults by the lessor that would not otherwise be material defaults which would justify cancellation under subsection (1). If there is a right to cancel, there is, of course, a right to reject or revoke acceptance of the goods.

6. Subsection (4) is new and merely adds to the completeness of the index by including a reference to the lessee's recovery of damages upon the lessor's breach of warranty; such breach may not rise to the level of a default by the lessor justifying revocation of acceptance. If the lessee properly rejects or revokes acceptance of the goods because of a breach of warranty, the rights and remedies are those provided in subsection (1) rather than those in Section 2A-519(4).

7. Subsection (5), a revised version of the provisions of Section 2-711(3), recognizes, on rightful rejection or justifiable revocation, the lessee's security interest in goods in its possession and control. Former Section 9-113 (now codified as Section 9-110), which recognized security interests arising under the Article on Sales (Article 2), was amended with the adoption of this Article to reflect the security interests arising under this Article. Pursuant to Section 2A-511(4), a purchaser who purchases goods from the lessee in good faith takes free of any rights of the lessor, or in the case of a finance lease, the supplier. Such goods, however, must have been rightfully rejected and disposed of pursuant to Section 2A-511 or 2A-512. However, Section 2A-517(5) provides that the lessee will have the same rights and duties with respect to goods where acceptance has been revoked as with respect to goods rejected. Thus, Section 2A-511(4) will apply to the lessee's disposition of such goods.

8. Pursuant to Section 2A-527(5), the lessee must account to the lessor for the excess proceeds of such disposition, after satisfaction of the claim secured by the lessee's security interest.

9. Subsection (6), a slightly revised version of the provisions of Section 2-717, sanctions a right of set-off by the lessee, subject to the rule of Section 2A-407 with respect to irrevocable promises in a finance lease that is not a consumer lease, and further subject to an enforceable ''hell or high water'' clause in the lease agreement. Section 2A-407 official comment. No at-

tempt is made to state how the set-off should occur; this is to be determined by the facts of each case.

10. There is no special treatment of the finance lease in this section. Absent supplemental principles of law and equity to the contrary, in the case of most finance leases, following the lessee's acceptance of the goods, the lessee will have no rights or remedies against the lessor, because the lessor's obligations to the lessee are minimal. Sections 2A-210 and 2A-211(1). Since the lessee will look to the supplier for performance, this is appropriate. Section 2A-209.

Cross References:

Sections 1-102(3), 1-103, 1-106(1), Article 2, especially Sections 2-711, 2-717 and Sections 2A-103(4), 2A-209, 2A-210, 2A-211(1), 2A-407, 2A-501(2), 2A-501(4), 2A-509 through 2A-522, 2A-511(3), 2A-517(5), 2A-527(5) and Section 9-110.

Definitional Cross References:

"Conforming". Section 2A-103(1)(d).
"Delivery". Section 1-201(14).
"Good faith". Sections 1-201(19) and 2-103(1)(b).
"Goods". Section 2A-103(1)(h).
"Installment lease contract". Section 2A-103(1)(i).
"Lease contract". Section 2A-103(1)(l).
"Lessee". Section 2A-103(1)(n).
"Lessor". Section 2A-103(1)(p).
"Notifies". Section 1-201(26).
"Receipt". Section 2-103(1)(c).
"Remedy". Section 1-201(34).
"Rights". Section 1-201(36).
"Security interest". Section 1-201(37).
"Value". Section 1-201(44).

§ 2A-509. Lessee's Rights on Improper Delivery; Rightful Rejection.

(1) Subject to the provisions of Section 2A-510 on default in installment lease contracts, if the goods or the tender or delivery fail in any respect to conform to the lease contract, the lessee may reject or accept the goods or accept any commercial unit or units and reject the rest of the goods.

(2) Rejection of goods is ineffective unless it is within a reasonable time after tender or delivery of the goods and the lessee seasonably notifies the lessor.

Official Comment

Uniform Statutory Source: Sections 2-601 and 2-602(1).

Changes: Revised to reflect leasing practices and terminology.

Definitional Cross References:

"Commercial unit". Section 2A–103(1)(c).
"Conforming". Section 2A–103(1)(d).
"Delivery". Section 1–201(14).
"Goods". Section 2A–103(1)(h).
"Installment lease contract". Section 2A–103(1)(i).
"Lease contract". Section 2A–103(1)(*l*).
"Lessee". Section 2A–103(1)(n).
"Lessor". Section 2A–103(1)(p).
"Notifies". Section 1–201(26).
"Reasonable time". Section 1–204(1) and (2).
"Rights". Section 1–201(36).
"Seasonably". Section 1–204(3).

§ 2A–510. Installment Lease Contracts: Rejection and Default.

(1) Under an installment lease contract a lessee may reject any delivery that is nonconforming if the nonconformity substantially impairs the value of that delivery and cannot be cured or the nonconformity is a defect in the required documents; but if the nonconformity does not fall within subsection (2) and the lessor or the supplier gives adequate assurance of its cure, the lessee must accept that delivery.

(2) Whenever nonconformity or default with respect to one or more deliveries substantially impairs the value of the installment lease contract as a whole there is a default with respect to the whole. But, the aggrieved party reinstates the installment lease contract as a whole if the aggrieved party accepts a nonconforming delivery without seasonably notifying of cancellation or brings an action with respect only to past deliveries or demands performance as to future deliveries.

Official Comment

Uniform Statutory Source: Section 2–612.

Changes: Revised to reflect leasing practices and terminology.

Definitional Cross References:

"Action". Section 1–201(1).
"Aggrieved party". Section 1–201(2).
"Cancellation". Section 2A–103(1)(b).
"Conforming". Section 2A–103(1)(d).
"Delivery". Section 1–201(14).
"Installment lease contract". Section 2A–103(1)(i).

"Lessee". Section 2A–103(1)(n).
"Lessor". Section 2A–103(1)(p).
"Notifies". Section 1–201(26).
"Seasonably". Section 1–204(3).
"Supplier". Section 2A–103(1)(x).
"Value". Section 1–201(44).

§ 2A–511. Merchant Lessee's Duties as to Rightfully Rejected Goods.

(1) Subject to any security interest of a lessee (Section 2A–508(5)), if a lessor or a supplier has no agent or place of business at the market of rejection, a merchant lessee, after rejection of goods in his [or her] possession or control, shall follow any reasonable instructions received from the lessor or the supplier with respect to the goods. In the absence of those instructions, a merchant lessee shall make reasonable efforts to sell, lease, or otherwise dispose of the goods for the lessor's account if they threaten to decline in value speedily. Instructions are not reasonable if on demand indemnity for expenses is not forthcoming.

(2) If a merchant lessee (subsection (1)) or any other lessee (Section 2A–512) disposes of goods, he [or she] is entitled to reimbursement either from the lessor or the supplier or out of the proceeds for reasonable expenses of caring for and disposing of the goods and, if the expenses include no disposition commission, to such commission as is usual in the trade, or if there is none, to a reasonable sum not exceeding 10 percent of the gross proceeds.

(3) In complying with this section or Section 2A–512, the lessee is held only to good faith. Good faith conduct hereunder is neither acceptance or conversion nor the basis of an action for damages.

(4) A purchaser who purchases in good faith from a lessee pursuant to this section or Section 2A–512 takes the goods free of any rights of the lessor and the supplier even though the lessee fails to comply with one or more of the requirements of this Article.

Official Comment

Uniform Statutory Source: Sections 2–603 and 2–706(5).

Changes: Revised to reflect leasing practices and terminology. This section, by its terms, applies to merchants as well as others. Thus, in construing the section it is important to note that under this Act the term good faith is defined differently for merchants (Section 2–103(1)(b)) than for others (Section 1–201(19)). Section 2A–103(3) and (4).

Definitional Cross References:

"Action". Section 1–201(1).
"Good faith". Sections 1–201(19) and 2–103(1)(b).
"Goods". Section 2A–103(1)(h).
"Lease". Section 2A–103(1)(j).
"Lessee". Section 2A–103(1)(n).
"Lessor". Section 2A–103(1)(p).
"Merchant lessee". Section 2A–103(1)(t).
"Purchaser". Section 1–201(33).
"Rights". Section 1–201(36).
"Security interest". Section 1–201(37).
"Supplier". Section 2A–103(1)(x).
"Value". Section 1–201(44).

§ 2A–512. Lessee's Duties as to Rightfully Rejected Goods.

(1) Except as otherwise provided with respect to goods that threaten to decline in value speedily (Section 2A–511) and subject to any security interest of a lessee (Section 2A–508(5)):

(a) the lessee, after rejection of goods in the lessee's possession, shall hold them with reasonable care at the lessor's or the supplier's disposition for a reasonable time after the lessee's seasonable notification of rejection;

(b) if the lessor or the supplier gives no instructions within a reasonable time after notification of rejection, the lessee may store the rejected goods for the lessor's or the supplier's account or ship them to the lessor or the supplier or dispose of them for the lessor's or the supplier's account with reimbursement in the manner provided in Section 2A–511; but

(c) the lessee has no further obligations with regard to goods rightfully rejected.

(2) Action by the lessee pursuant to subsection (1) is not acceptance or conversion.

Official Comment

Uniform Statutory Source: Sections 2–602(2)(b) and (c) and 2–604.

Changes: Substantially rewritten.

Purposes: The introduction to subsection (1) references goods that threaten to decline in value speedily

and not perishables, the reference in Section 2–604, the statutory analogue. This is a change in style, not substance, as the first phrase includes the second. Subparagraphs (a) and (c) are revised versions of the provisions of Section 2–602(2)(b) and (c). Subparagraph (a) states the rule with respect to the lessee's treatment of goods in its possession following rejection; subparagraph (b) states the rule regarding such goods if the lessor or supplier then fails to give instructions to the lessee. If the lessee performs in a fashion consistent with subparagraphs (a) and (b), subparagraph (c) exonerates the lessee.

Cross References:

Sections 2–602(2)(b), 2–602(2)(c) and 2–604.

Definitional Cross References:

"Action". Section 1–201(1).
"Goods". Section 2A–103(1)(h).
"Lessee". Section 2A–103(1)(n).
"Lessor". Section 2A–103(1)(p).
"Notification". Section 1–201(26).
"Reasonable time". Section 1–204(1) and (2).
"Seasonably". Section 1–204(3).
"Security interest". Section 1–201(37).
"Supplier". Section 2A–103(1)(x).
"Value". Section 1–201(44).

§ 2A–513. Cure by Lessor of Improper Tender or Delivery; Replacement.

(1) If any tender or delivery by the lessor or the supplier is rejected because nonconforming and the time for performance has not yet expired, the lessor or the supplier may seasonably notify the lessee of the lessor's or the supplier's intention to cure and may then make a conforming delivery within the time provided in the lease contract.

(2) If the lessee rejects a nonconforming tender that the lessor or the supplier had reasonable grounds to believe would be acceptable with or without money allowance, the lessor or the supplier may have a further reasonable time to substitute a conforming tender if he [or she] seasonably notifies the lessee.

Official Comment

Uniform Statutory Source: Section 2–508.

Changes: Revised to reflect leasing practices and terminology.

Definitional Cross References:

"Conforming".   Section 2A–103(1)(d).
"Delivery".   Section 1–201(14).
"Lease contract".   Section 2A–103(1)(*l*).
"Lessee".   Section 2A–103(1)(n).
"Lessor".   Section 2A–103(1)(p).
"Money".   Section 1–201(24).
"Notifies".   Section 1–201(26).
"Reasonable time".   Section 1–204(1) and (2).
"Seasonably".   Section 1–204(3).
"Supplier".   Section 2A–103(1)(x).

§ 2A–514.   Waiver of Lessee's Objections.

(1) In rejecting goods, a lessee's failure to state a particular defect that is ascertainable by reasonable inspection precludes the lessee from relying on the defect to justify rejection or to establish default:

(a) if, stated seasonably, the lessor or the supplier could have cured it (Section 2A–513); or

(b) between merchants if the lessor or the supplier after rejection has made a request in writing for a full and final written statement of all defects on which the lessee proposes to rely.

(2) A lessee's failure to reserve rights when paying rent or other consideration against documents precludes recovery of the payment for defects apparent on the face of the documents.

Official Comment

Uniform Statutory Source: Section 2–605.

Changes: Revised to reflect leasing practices and terminology.

Purposes: The principles applicable to the commercial practice of payment against documents (subsection 2) are explained in official comment 4 to Section 2–605, the statutory analogue to this section.

Cross Reference:

Section 2–605 official comment 4.

Definitional Cross References:

"Between merchants".   Section 2–104(3).
"Goods".   Section 2A–103(1)(h).
"Lessee".   Section 2A–103(1)(n).
"Lessor".   Section 2A–103(1)(p).
"Rights".   Section 1–201(36).
"Seasonably".   Section 1–204(3).

"Supplier".   Section 2A–103(1)(x).
"Writing".   Section 1–201(46).

§ 2A–515.   Acceptance of Goods.

(1) Acceptance of goods occurs after the lessee has had a reasonable opportunity to inspect the goods and

(a) the lessee signifies or acts with respect to the goods in a manner that signifies to the lessor or the supplier that the goods are conforming or that the lessee will take or retain them in spite of their nonconformity; or

(b) the lessee fails to make an effective rejection of the goods (Section 2A–509(2)).

(2) Acceptance of a part of any commercial unit is acceptance of that entire unit.

Official Comment

Uniform Statutory Source: Section 2–606.

Changes: The provisions of Section 2–606(1)(a) were substantially rewritten to provide that the lessee's conduct may signify acceptance. Further, the provisions of Section 2–606(1)(c) were not incorporated as irrelevant given the lessee's possession and use of the leased goods.

Cross References:

Sections 2–606(1)(a) and 2–606(1)(c).

Definitional Cross References:

"Commercial unit".   Section 2A–103(1)(c).
"Conforming".   Section 2A–103(1)(d).
"Goods".   Section 2A–103(1)(h).
"Lessee".   Section 2A–103(1)(n).
"Lessor".   Section 2A–103(1)(p).
"Supplier".   Section 2A–103(1)(x).

§ 2A–516.   Effect of Acceptance of Goods; Notice of Default; Burden of Establishing Default After Acceptance; Notice of Claim or Litigation to Person Answerable Over.

(1) A lessee must pay rent for any goods accepted in accordance with the lease contract, with due allowance for goods rightfully rejected or not delivered.

(2) A lessee's acceptance of goods precludes rejection of the goods accepted. In the case of a finance lease, if made with knowledge of a non-

conformity, acceptance cannot be revoked because of it. In any other case, if made with knowledge of a nonconformity, acceptance cannot be revoked because of it unless the acceptance was on the reasonable assumption that the nonconformity would be seasonably cured. Acceptance does not of itself impair any other remedy provided by this Article or the lease agreement for nonconformity.

(3) If a tender has been accepted:

(a) within a reasonable time after the lessee discovers or should have discovered any default, the lessee shall notify the lessor and the supplier, if any, or be barred from any remedy against the party not notified;

(b) except in the case of a consumer lease, within a reasonable time after the lessee receives notice of litigation for infringement or the like (Section 2A–211) the lessee shall notify the lessor or be barred from any remedy over for liability established by the litigation; and

(c) the burden is on the lessee to establish any default.

(4) If a lessee is sued for breach of a warranty or other obligation for which a lessor or a supplier is answerable over the following apply:

(a) The lessee may give the lessor or the supplier, or both, written notice of the litigation. If the notice states that the person notified may come in and defend and that if the person notified does not do so that person will be bound in any action against that person by the lessee by any determination of fact common to the two litigations, then unless the person notified after seasonable receipt of the notice does come in and defend that person is so bound.

(b) The lessor or the supplier may demand in writing that the lessee turn over control of the litigation including settlement if the claim is one for infringement or the like (Section 2A–211) or else be barred from any remedy over. If the demand states that the lessor or the supplier agrees to bear all expense and to satisfy any adverse judgment, then unless the lessee after seasonable receipt of the demand does turn over control the lessee is so barred.

(5) Subsections (3) and (4) apply to any obligation of a lessee to hold the lessor or the supplier harmless against infringement or the like (Section 2A–211).

As amended in 1990.

Official Comment

Uniform Statutory Source: Section 2–607.

Changes: Substantially revised.

Purposes:

1. Subsection (2) creates a special rule for finance leases, precluding revocation if acceptance is made with knowledge of nonconformity with respect to the lease agreement, as opposed to the supply agreement; this is not inequitable as the lessee has a direct claim against the supplier. Section 2A–209(1). Revocation of acceptance of a finance lease is permitted if the lessee's acceptance was without discovery of the nonconformity (with respect to the lease agreement, not the supply agreement) and was reasonably induced by the lessor's assurances. Section 2A–517(1)(b). Absent exclusion or modification, the lessor under a finance lease makes certain warranties to the lessee. Sections 2A–210 and 2A–211(1). Revocation of acceptance is not prohibited even after the lessee's promise has become irrevocable and independent. Section 2A–407 official comment. Where the finance lease creates a security interest, the rule may be to the contrary. *General Elec. Credit Corp. of Tennessee v. Ger-Beck Mach. Co.*, 806 F.2d 1207 (3rd Cir. 1986).

2. Subsection (3)(a) requires the lessee to give notice of default, within a reasonable time after the lessee discovered or should have discovered the default. In a finance lease, notice may be given either to the supplier, the lessor, or both, but remedy is barred against the party not notified. In a finance lease, the lessor is usually not liable for defects in the goods and the essential notice is to the supplier. While notice to the finance lessor will often not give any additional rights to the lessee, it would be good practice to give the notice since the finance lessor has an interest in the goods. Subsection (3)(a) does not use the term finance lease, but the definition of supplier is a person from whom a lessor buys or leases goods to be leased under a finance lease. Section 2A–103(1)(x). Therefore, there can be a "supplier" only in a finance lease. Subsection (4) applies similar notice rules as to lessors and suppliers if a lessee is sued for a breach of warranty or other obligation for which a lessor or supplier is answerable over.

3. Subsection (3)(b) requires the lessee to give the lessor notice of litigation for infringement or the like. There is an exception created in the case of a consumer lease. While such an exception was considered for a finance lease, it was not created because it was not necessary—the lessor in a finance lease does not give a warranty against infringement. Section 2A–211(2). Even though not required under subsection (3)(b), the lessee who takes under a finance lease should consider giving notice of litigation for infringement or the like to the supplier, because the lessee obtains the benefit of the suppliers' promises subject to the suppliers' defenses or claims. Sections 2A–209(1) and 2–607(3)(b).

Cross References:

Sections 2–607(3)(b), 2A–103(1)(x), 2A–209(1), 2A–210, 2A–211(1), 2A–211(2), 2A–407 official comment and 2A–517(1)(b).

Definitional Cross References:

"Action". Section 1–201(1).
"Agreement". Section 1–201(3).
"Burden of establishing". Section 1–201(8).
"Conforming". Section 2A–103(1)(d).
"Consumer lease". Section 2A–103(1)(e).
"Delivery". Section 1–201(14).
"Discover". Section 1–201(25).
"Finance lease". Section 2A–103(1)(g).
"Goods". Section 2A–103(1)(h).
"Knowledge". Section 1–201(25).
"Lease agreement". Section 2A–103(1)(k).
"Lease contract". Section 2A–103(1)(*l*).
"Lessee". Section 2A–103(1)(n).
"Lessor". Section 2A–103(1)(p).
"Notice". Section 1–201(25).
"Notifies". Section 1–201(26).
"Person". Section 1–201(30).
"Reasonable time". Section 1–204(1) and (2).
"Receipt". Section 2–103(1)(c).
"Remedy". Section 1–201(34).
"Seasonably". Section 1–204(3).
"Supplier". Section 2A–103(1)(x).
"Written". Section 1–201(46).

§ 2A–517. Revocation of Acceptance of Goods.

(1) A lessee may revoke acceptance of a lot or commercial unit whose nonconformity substantially impairs its value to the lessee if the lessee has accepted it:

  (a) except in the case of a finance lease, on the reasonable assumption that its noncon-

formity would be cured and it has not been seasonably cured; or

  (b) without discovery of the nonconformity if the lessee's acceptance was reasonably induced either by the lessor's assurances or, except in the case of a finance lease, by the difficulty of discovery before acceptance.

(2) Except in the case of a finance lease that is not a consumer lease, a lessee may revoke acceptance of a lot or commercial unit if the lessor defaults under the lease contract and the default substantially impairs the value of that lot or commercial unit to the lessee.

(3) If the lease agreement so provides, the lessee may revoke acceptance of a lot or commercial unit because of other defaults by the lessor.

(4) Revocation of acceptance must occur within a reasonable time after the lessee discovers or should have discovered the ground for it and before any substantial change in condition of the goods which is not caused by the nonconformity. Revocation is not effective until the lessee notifies the lessor.

(5) A lessee who so revokes has the same rights and duties with regard to the goods involved as if the lessee had rejected them.

As amended in 1990.

Official Comment

Uniform Statutory Source: Section 2–608.

Changes: Revised to reflect leasing practices and terminology. Note that in the case of a finance lease the lessee retains a limited right to revoke acceptance. Sections 2A–517(1)(b) and 2A–516 official comment. New subsections (2) and (3) added.

Purposes:

1. The section states the situations under which the lessee may return the goods to the lessor and cancel the lease. Subsection (2) recognizes that the lessor may have continuing obligations under the lease and that a default as to those obligations may be sufficiently material to justify revocation of acceptance of the leased items and cancellation of the lease by the lessee. For example, a failure by the lessor to fulfill its obligation to maintain leased equipment or to supply other goods which are necessary for the operation of the leased equipment may justify revocation of acceptance and cancellation of the lease.

2. Subsection (3) specifically provides that the lease agreement may provide that the lessee can revoke

acceptance for defaults by the lessor which in the absence of such an agreement might not be considered sufficiently serious to justify revocation. That is, the parties are free to contract on the question of what defaults are so material that the lessee can cancel the lease.

Cross Reference:

Section 2A–516 official comment.

Definitional Cross References:

"Commercial unit". Section 2A–103(1)(c).
"Conforming". Section 2A–103(1)(d).
"Discover". Section 1–201(25).
"Finance lease". Section 2A–103(1)(g).
"Goods". Section 2A–103(1)(h).
"Lessee". Section 2A–103(1)(n).
"Lessor". Section 2A–103(1)(p).
"Lot". Section 2A–103(1)(s).
"Notifies". Section 1–201(26).
"Reasonable time". Section 1–204(1) and (2).
"Rights". Section 1–201(36).
"Seasonably". Section 1–204(3).
"Value". Section 1–201(44).

§ 2A–518. Cover; Substitute Goods.

(1) After a default by a lessor under the lease contract of the type described in Section 2A–508(1), or, if agreed, after other default by the lessor, the lessee may cover by making any purchase or lease of or contract to purchase or lease goods in substitution for those due from the lessor.

(2) Except as otherwise provided with respect to damages liquidated in the lease agreement (Section 2A–504) or otherwise determined pursuant to agreement of the parties (Sections 1–102(3) and 2A–503), if a lessee's cover is by a lease agreement substantially similar to the original lease agreement and the new lease agreement is made in good faith and in a commercially reasonable manner, the lessee may recover from the lessor as damages (i) the present value, as of the date of the commencement of the term of the new lease agreement, of the rent under the new lease agreement applicable to that period of the new lease term which is comparable to the then remaining term of the original lease agreement minus the present value as of the same date of the total rent for the then remaining lease term of the original lease agreement, and (ii) any incidental or consequential damages, less ex-

penses saved in consequence of the lessor's default.

(3) If a lessee's cover is by lease agreement that for any reason does not qualify for treatment under subsection (2), or is by purchase or otherwise, the lessee may recover from the lessor as if the lessee had elected not to cover and Section 2A–519 governs.

As amended in 1990.

Official Comment

Uniform Statutory Source: Section 2–712.

Changes: Substantially revised.

Purposes:

1. Subsection (1) allows the lessee to take action to fix its damages after default by the lessor. Such action may consist of the lease of goods. The decision to cover is a function of commercial judgment, not a statutory mandate replete with sanctions for failure to comply. *Cf.* Section 9–625.

2. Subsection (2) states a rule for determining the amount of lessee's damages provided that there is no agreement to the contrary. The lessee's damages will be established using the new lease agreement as a measure if the following three criteria are met: (i) the lessee's cover is by lease agreement, (ii) the lease agreement is substantially similar to the original lease agreement, and (iii) such cover was effected in good faith, and in a commercially reasonable manner. Thus, the lessee will be entitled to recover from the lessor the present value, as of the date of commencement of the term of the new lease agreement, of the rent under the new lease agreement applicable to that period which is comparable to the then remaining term of the original lease agreement less the present value of the rent reserved for the remaining term under the original lease, together with incidental or consequential damages less expenses saved in consequence of the lessor's default. Consequential damages may include loss suffered by the lessee because of deprivation of the use of the goods during the period between the default and the acquisition of the goods under the new lease agreement. If the lessee's cover does not satisfy the criteria of subsection (2), Section 2A–519 governs.

3. Two of the three criteria to be met by the lessee are familiar, but the concept of the new lease agreement being substantially similar to the original lease agreement is not. Given the many variables facing a party who intends to lease goods and the rapidity of change in the market place, the policy decision was made not to draft with specificity. It was thought

unwise to seek to establish certainty at the cost of fairness. Thus, the decision of whether the new lease agreement is substantially similar to the original will be determined case by case.

4. While the section does not draw a bright line, it is possible to describe some of the factors that should be considered in finding that a new lease agreement is substantially similar to the original. First, the goods subject to the new lease agreement should be examined. For example, in a lease of computer equipment the new lease might be for more modern equipment. However, it may be that at the time of the lessor's breach it was not possible to obtain the same type of goods in the market place. Because the lessee's remedy under Section 2A–519 is intended to place the lessee in essentially the same position as if he had covered, if goods similar to those to have been delivered under the original lease are not available, then the computer equipment in this hypothetical should qualify as a commercially reasonable substitute. *See* Section 2–712(1).

5. Second, the various elements of the new lease agreement should also be examined. Those elements include the presence or absence of options to purchase or release; the lessor's representations, warranties and covenants to the lessee, as well as those to be provided by the lessee to the lessor; and the services, if any, to be provided by the lessor or by the lessee. All of these factors allocate cost and risk between the lessor and the lessee and thus affect the amount of rent to be paid. If the differences between the original lease and the new lease can be easily valued, it would be appropriate for a court to adjust the difference in rental to take account of the difference between the two leases, find that the new lease is substantially similar to the old lease, and award cover damages under this section. If, for example, the new lease requires the lessor to insure the goods in the hands of the lessee, while the original lease required the lessee to insure, the usual cost of such insurance could be deducted from the rent due under the new lease before determining the difference in rental between the two leases.

6. Having examined the goods and the agreement, the test to be applied is whether, in light of these comparisons, the new lease agreement is substantially similar to the original lease agreement. These findings should not be made with scientific precision, as they are a function of economics, nor should they be made independently with respect to the goods and each element of the agreement, as it is important that a sense of commercial judgment pervade the finding. To establish the new lease as a proper measure of damage under subsection (2), these factors, taken as a whole,

must result in a finding that the new lease agreement is substantially similar to the original.

7. A new lease can be substantially similar to the original lease even though its term extends beyond the remaining term of the original lease, so long as both (a) the lease terms are commercially comparable (e.g., it is highly unlikely that a one-month rental and a five-year lease would reflect similar commercial realities), and (b) the court can fairly apportion a part of the rental payments under the new lease to that part of the term of the new lease which is comparable to the remaining lease term under the original lease. Also, the lease term of the new lease may be comparable to the term of the original lease even though the beginning and ending dates of the two leases are not the same. For example, a two-month lease of agricultural equipment for the months of August and September may be comparable to a two-month lease running from the 15th of August to the 15th of October if in the particular location two-month leases beginning on August 15th are basically interchangeable with two-month leases beginning August 1st. Similarly, the term of a one-year truck lease beginning on the 15th of January may be comparable to the term of a one-year truck lease beginning January 2d. If the lease terms are found to be comparable, the court may base cover damages on the entire difference between the costs under the two leases.

Cross References:

Sections 2–712(1), 2A–519 and 9–625.

Definitional Cross References:

"Agreement". Section 1–201(3).
"Contract". Section 1–201(11).
"Good faith". Section 1–201(19) and 2–103(1)(b).
"Goods". Section 2A–103(1)(h).
"Lease". Section 2A–103(1)(j).
"Lease agreement". Section 2A–103(1)(k).
"Lease contract". Section 2A–103(1)(*l*).
"Lessee". Section 2A–103(1)(n).
"Lessor". Section 2A–103(1)(p).
"Party". Section 1–201(29).
"Present value". Section 2A–103(1)(u).
"Purchase". Section 2A–103(1)(v).

§ 2A–519. Lessee's Damages for Non-delivery, Repudiation, Default, and Breach of Warranty in Regard to Accepted Goods.

(1) Except as otherwise provided with respect to damages liquidated in the lease agreement (Section 2A–504) or otherwise determined pursu-

ant to agreement of the parties (Sections 1–102(3) and 2A–503), if a lessee elects not to cover or a lessee elects to cover and the cover is by lease agreement that for any reason does not qualify for treatment under Section 2A–518(2), or is by purchase or otherwise, the measure of damages for non-delivery or repudiation by the lessor or for rejection or revocation of acceptance by the lessee is the present value, as of the date of the default, of the then market rent minus the present value as of the same date of the original rent, computed for the remaining lease term of the original lease agreement, together with incidental and consequential damages, less expenses saved in consequence of the lessor's default.

(2) Market rent is to be determined as of the place for tender or, in cases of rejection after arrival or revocation of acceptance, as of the place of arrival.

(3) Except as otherwise agreed, if the lessee has accepted goods and given notification (Section 2A–516(3)), the measure of damages for non-conforming tender or delivery or other default by a lessor is the loss resulting in the ordinary course of events from the lessor's default as determined in any manner that is reasonable together with incidental and consequential damages, less expenses saved in consequence of the lessor's default.

(4) Except as otherwise agreed, the measure of damages for breach of warranty is the present value at the time and place of acceptance of the difference between the value of the use of the goods accepted and the value if they had been as warranted for the lease term, unless special circumstances show proximate damages of a different amount, together with incidental and consequential damages, less expenses saved in consequence of the lessor's default or breach of warranty.

As amended in 1990.

Official Comment

Uniform Statutory Source: Sections 2–713 and 2–714.

Changes: Substantially revised.

Purposes:

1. Subsection (1), a revised version of the provisions of Section 2–713(1), states the basic rule governing the measure of lessee's damages for non-delivery or repudiation by the lessor or for rightful rejection or revocation of acceptance by the lessee. This measure will apply, absent agreement to the contrary, if the lessee does not cover or if the cover does not qualify under Section 2A–518. There is no sanction for cover that does not qualify.

2. The measure of damage is the present value, as of the date of default, of the market rent for the remaining term of the lease less the present value of the original rent for the remaining term of the lease, plus incidental and consequential damages less expenses saved in consequence of the default. Note that the reference in Section 2A–519(1) is to the date of default not to the date of an event of default. An event of default under a lease agreement becomes a default under a lease agreement only after the expiration of any relevant period of grace and compliance with any notice requirements under this Article and the lease agreement. American Bar Foundation, *Commentaries on Indentures*, § 5–1, at 216–217 (1971). Section 2A–501(1). This conclusion is also a function of whether, as a matter of fact or law, the event of default has been waived, suspended or cured. Sections 2A–103(4) and 1–103.

3. Subsection (2), a revised version of the provisions of Section 2–713(2), states the rule with respect to determining market rent.

4. Subsection (3), a revised version of the provisions of Section 2–714(1) and (3), states the measure of damages where goods have been accepted and acceptance is not revoked. The subsection applies both to defaults which occur at the inception of the lease and to defaults which occur subsequently, such as failure to comply with an obligation to maintain the leased goods. The measure in essence is the loss, in the ordinary course of events, flowing from the default.

5. Subsection (4), a revised version of the provisions of Section 2–714(2), states the measure of damages for breach of warranty. The measure in essence is the present value of the difference between the value of the goods accepted and of the goods if they had been as warranted.

6. Subsections (1), (3) and (4) specifically state that the parties may by contract vary the damages rules stated in those subsections.

Cross References:

Sections 2–713(1), 2–713(2), 2–714 and Section 2A–518.

Definitional Cross References:

"Conforming". Section 2A–103(1)(d).

"Delivery". Section 1–201(14).
"Goods". Section 2A–103(1)(h).
"Lease". Section 2A–103(1)(j).
"Lease agreement". Section 2A–103(1)(k).
"Lessee". Section 2A–103(1)(n).
"Lessor". Section 2A–103(1)(p).
"Notification". Section 1–201(26).
"Present value". Section 2A–103(1)(u).
"Value". Section 1–201(44).

§ 2A–520. Lessee's Incidental and Consequential Damages.

(1) Incidental damages resulting from a lessor's default include expenses reasonably incurred in inspection, receipt, transportation, and care and custody of goods rightfully rejected or goods the acceptance of which is justifiably revoked, any commercially reasonable charges, expenses or commissions in connection with effecting cover, and any other reasonable expense incident to the default.

(2) Consequential damages resulting from a lessor's default include:

(a) any loss resulting from general or particular requirements and needs of which the lessor at the time of contracting had reason to know and which could not reasonably be prevented by cover or otherwise; and

(b) injury to person or property proximately resulting from any breach of warranty.

Official Comment

Uniform Statutory Source: Section 2–715.

Changes: Revised to reflect leasing terminology and practices.

Purposes: Subsection (1), a revised version of the provisions of Section 2–715(1), lists some examples of incidental damages resulting from a lessor's default; the list is not exhaustive. Subsection (1) makes clear that it applies not only to rightful rejection, but also to justifiable revocation.

Subsection (2), a revised version of the provisions of Section 2–715(2), lists some examples of consequential damages resulting from a lessor's default; the list is not exhaustive.

Cross References:

Section 2–715.

Definitional Cross References:

"Goods". Section 2A–103(1)(h).

"Knows". Section 1–201(25).
"Lessee". Section 2A–103(1)(n).
"Lessor". Section 2A–103(1)(p).
"Person". Section 1–201(30).
"Receipt". Section 2–103(1)(c).

§ 2A–521. Lessee's Right to Specific Performance or Replevin.

(1) Specific performance may be decreed if the goods are unique or in other proper circumstances.

(2) A decree for specific performance may include any terms and conditions as to payment of the rent, damages, or other relief that the court deems just.

(3) A lessee has a right of replevin, detinue, sequestration, claim and delivery, or the like for goods identified to the lease contract if after reasonable effort the lessee is unable to effect cover for those goods or the circumstances reasonably indicate that the effort will be unavailing.

Official Comment

Uniform Statutory Source: Section 2–716.

Changes: Revised to reflect leasing practices and terminology, and to expand the reference to the right of replevin in subsection (3) to include other similar rights of the lessee.

Definitional Cross References:

"Delivery". Section 1–201(14).
"Goods". Section 2A–103(1)(h).
"Lease contract". Section 2A–103(1)(l).
"Lessee". Section 2A–103(1)(n).
"Rights". Section 1–201(36).
"Term". Section 1–201(42).

§ 2A–522. Lessee's Right to Goods on Lessor's Insolvency.

(1) Subject to subsection (2) and even though the goods have not been shipped, a lessee who has paid a part or all of the rent and security for goods identified to a lease contract (Section 2A–217) on making and keeping good a tender of any unpaid portion of the rent and security due under the lease contract may recover the goods identified from the lessor if the lessor becomes insolvent within 10 days after receipt of the first installment of rent and security.

(2) A lessee acquires the right to recover goods identified to a lease contract only if they conform to the lease contract.

Official Comment

Uniform Statutory Source: Section 2–502.

Changes: Revised to reflect leasing practices and terminology.

Definitional Cross References:

"Conforming". Section 2A–103(1)(d).
"Goods". Section 2A–103(1)(h).
"Insolvent". Section 1–201(23).
"Lease contract". Section 2A–103(1)(l).
"Lessee". Section 2A–103(1)(n).
"Lessor". Section 2A–103(1)(p).
"Receipt". Section 2–103(1)(c).
"Rights". Section 1–201(36).

C. DEFAULT BY LESSEE

§ 2A–523. Lessor's Remedies.

(1) If a lessee wrongfully rejects or revokes acceptance of goods or fails to make a payment when due or repudiates with respect to a part or the whole, then, with respect to any goods involved, and with respect to all of the goods if under an installment lease contract the value of the whole lease contract is substantially impaired (Section 2A–510), the lessee is in default under the lease contract and the lessor may:

(a) cancel the lease contract (Section 2A–505(1));

(b) proceed respecting goods not identified to the lease contract (Section 2A–524);

(c) withhold delivery of the goods and take possession of goods previously delivered (Section 2A–525);

(d) stop delivery of the goods by any bailee (Section 2A–526);

(e) dispose of the goods and recover damages (Section 2A–527), or retain the goods and recover damages (Section 2A–528), or in a proper case recover rent (Section 2A–529);

(f) exercise any other rights or pursue any other remedies provided in the lease contract.

(2) If a lessor does not fully exercise a right or obtain a remedy to which the lessor is entitled under subsection (1), the lessor may recover the loss resulting in the ordinary course of events from the lessee's default as determined in any reasonable manner, together with incidental damages, less expenses saved in consequence of the lessee's default.

(3) If a lessee is otherwise in default under a lease contract, the lessor may exercise the rights and pursue the remedies provided in the lease contract, which may include a right to cancel the lease. In addition, unless otherwise provided in the lease contract:

(a) if the default substantially impairs the value of the lease contract to the lessor, the lessor may exercise the rights and pursue the remedies provided in subsections (1) or (2); or

(b) if the default does not substantially impair the value of the lease contract to the lessor, the lessor may recover as provided in subsection (2).

As amended in 1990.

Official Comment

Uniform Statutory Source: Section 2–703.

Changes: Substantially revised.

Purposes:

1. Subsection (1) is an index to Sections 2A–524 through 2A–531 and states that the remedies provided in those sections are available for the defaults referred to in subsection (1): wrongful rejection or revocation of acceptance, failure to make a payment when due, or repudiation. In addition, remedies provided in the lease contract are available. Subsection (2) sets out a remedy if the lessor does not pursue to completion a right or actually obtain a remedy available under subsection (1), and subsection (3) sets out statutory remedies for defaults not specifically referred to in subsection (1). Subsection (3) provides that, if any default by the lessee other than those specifically referred to in subsection (1) is material, the lessor can exercise the remedies provided in subsection (1) or (2); otherwise the available remedy is as provided in subsection (3). A lessor who has brought an action seeking or has nonjudicially pursued one or more of the remedies available under subsection (1) may amend so as to claim or may nonjudicially pursue a remedy under subsection (2) unless the right or remedy first chosen has been pursued to an extent actually inconsistent with the new course of action. The intent of the

provision is to reject the doctrine of election of remedies and to permit an alteration of course by the lessor unless such alteration would actually have an effect on the lessee that would be unreasonable under the circumstances. Further, the lessor may pursue remedies under both subsections (1) and (2) unless doing so would put the lessor in a better position than it would have been in had the lessee fully performed.

2. The lessor and the lessee can agree to modify the rights and remedies available under the Article; they can, among other things, provide that for defaults other than those specified in subsection (1) the lessor can exercise the rights and remedies referred to in subsection (1), whether or not the default would otherwise be held to substantially impair the value of the lease contract to the lessor; they can also create a new scheme of rights and remedies triggered by the occurrence of the default. Sections 2A–103(4) and 1–102(3).

3. Subsection (1), a substantially rewritten version of Section 2–703, lists various cumulative remedies of the lessor where the lessee wrongfully rejects or revokes acceptance, fails to make a payment when due, or repudiates. Section 2A–501(2) and (4). The subsection also allows the lessor to exercise any contractual remedy.

4. This Article rejects any general doctrine of election of remedy. Whether, in a particular case, one remedy bars another, is a function of whether lessor has been put in as good a position as if the lessee had fully performed the lease contract. Multiple remedies are barred only if the effect is to put the lessor in a better position than it would have been in had the lessee fully performed under the lease. Sections 2A–103(4), 2A–501(4), and 1–106(1).

5. **Hypothetical:** To better understand the application of subparagraphs (a) through (e), it is useful to review a hypothetical. Assume that A is a merchant in the business of selling and leasing new bicycles of various types. B is about to engage in the business of subleasing bicycles to summer residents of and visitors to an island resort. A, as lessor, has agreed to lease 60 bicycles to B. While there is one master lease, deliveries and terms are staggered. 20 bicycles are to be delivered by A to B's island location on June 1; the term of the lease of these bicycles is four months. 20 bicycles are to be delivered by A to B's island location on July 1; the term of the lease of these bicycles is three months. Finally, 20 bicycles are to be delivered by A to B's island location on August 1; the term of the lease of these bicycles is two months. B is obligated to pay rent to A on the 15th day of each month during the term for the lease. Rent is $50 per month,

per bicycle. B has no option to purchase or release and must return the bicycles to A at the end of the term, in good condition, reasonable wear and tear excepted. Since the retail price of each bicycle is $400 and bicycles used in the retail rental business have a useful economic life of 36 months, this transaction creates a lease. Sections 2A–103(1)(j) and 1–201(37).

6. A's current inventory of bicycles is not large. Thus, upon signing the lease with B in February, A agreed to purchase 60 new bicycles from A's principal manufacturer, with special instructions to drop ship the bicycles to B's island location in accordance with the delivery schedule set forth in the lease.

7. The first shipment of 20 bicycles was received by B on May 21. B inspected the bicycles, accepted the same as conforming to the lease and signed a receipt of delivery and acceptance. However, due to poor weather that summer, business was terrible and B was unable to pay the rent due on June 15. Pursuant to the lease A sent B notice of default and proceeded to enforce his rights and remedies against B.

8. A's counsel first advised A that under Section 2A–510(2) and the terms of the lease B's failure to pay was a default with respect to the whole. Thus, to minimize A's continued exposure, A was advised to take possession of the bicycles. If A had possession of the goods A could refuse to deliver. Section 2A–525(1). However, the facts here are different. With respect to the bicycles in B's possession, A has the right to take possession of the bicycles, without breach of the peace. Section 2A–525(2). If B refuses to allow A access to the bicycles, A can proceed by action, including replevin or injunctive relief.

9. With respect to the 40 bicycles that have not been delivered, this Article provides various alternatives. First, assume that 20 of the remaining 40 bicycles have been manufactured and delivered by the manufacturer to a carrier for shipment to B. Given the size of the shipment, the carrier was using a small truck for the delivery and the truck had not yet reached the island ferry when the manufacturer (at the request of A) instructed the carrier to divert the shipment to A's place of business. A's right to stop delivery is recognized under these circumstances. Section 2A–526(1). Second, assume that the 20 remaining bicycles were in the process of manufacture when B defaulted. A retains the right (as between A as lessor and B as lessee) to exercise reasonable commercial judgment whether to complete manufacture or to dispose of the unfinished goods for scrap. Since A is not the manufacturer and A has a binding contract to buy the bicycles, A elected to allow the manufacturer to

complete the manufacture of the bicycles, but instructed the manufacturer to deliver the completed bicycles to A's place of business.   Section 2A–524(2).

10.   Thus, so far A has elected to exercise the remedies referred to in subparagraphs (b) through (d) in subsection (1).   None of these remedies bars any of the others because A's election and enforcement merely resulted in A's possession of the bicycles.   Had B performed A would have recovered possession of the bicycles.   Thus A is in the process of obtaining the benefit of his bargain.   Note that A could exercise any other rights or pursue any other remedies provided in the lease contract (Section 2A–523(1)(f)), or elect to recover his loss due to the lessee's default under Section 2A–523(2).

11.   A's counsel next would determine what action, if any, should be taken with respect to the goods.   As stated in subparagraph (e) and as discussed fully in Section 2A–527(1) the lessor may, but has no obligation to, dispose of the goods by a substantially similar lease (indeed, the lessor has no obligation whatsoever to dispose of the goods at all) and recover damages based on that action, but lessor will not be able to recover damages which put it in a better position than performance would have done, nor will it be able to recover damages for losses which it could have reasonably avoided.   In this case, since A is in the business of leasing and selling bicycles, A will probably inventory the 60 bicycles for its retail trade.

12.   A's counsel then will determine which of the various means of ascertaining A's damages against B are available.   Subparagraph (e) catalogues each relevant section.   First, under Section 2A–527(2) the amount of A's claim is computed by comparing the original lease between A and B with any subsequent lease of the bicycles but only if the subsequent lease is substantially similar to the original lease contract.   While the section does not define this term, the official comment does establish some parameters.   If, however, A elects to lease the bicycles to his retail trade, it is unlikely that the resulting lease will be substantially similar to the original, as leases to retail customers are considerably different from leases to wholesale customers like B.   If, however, the leases were substantially similar, the damage claim is for accrued and unpaid rent to the beginning of the new lease, plus the present value as of the same date, of the rent reserved under the original lease for the balance of its term less the present value as of the same date of the rent reserved under the replacement lease for a term comparable to the balance of the term of the original lease, together with incidental damages less expenses saved in consequence of the lessee's default.

13.   If the new lease is not substantially similar or if A elects to sell the bicycles or to hold the bicycles, damages are computed under Section 2A–528 or 2A–529.

14.   If A elects to pursue his claim under Section 2A–528(1) the damage rule is the same as that stated in Section 2A–528(2) except that damages are measured from default if the lessee never took possession of the goods or from the time when the lessor did or could have regained possession and that the standard of comparison is not the rent reserved under a substantially similar lease entered into by the lessor but a market rent, as defined in Section 2A–507.   Further, if the facts of this hypothetical were more elaborate A may be able to establish that the measure of damage under subsection (1) is inadequate to put him in the same position that B's performance would have, in which case A can claim the present value of his lost profits.

15.   Yet another alternative for computing A's damage claim against B which will be available in some situations is recovery of the present value, as of entry of judgment, of the rent for the then remaining lease term under Section 2A–529.   However, this formulation is not available if the goods have been repossessed or tendered back to A.   For the 20 bicycles repossessed and the remaining 40 bicycles, A will be able to recover the present value of the rent only if A is unable to dispose of them, or circumstances indicate the effort will be unavailing.   If A has prevailed in an action for the rent, at any time up to collection of a judgment by A against B, A might dispose of the bicycles.   In such case A's claim for damages against B is governed by Section 2A–527 or 2A–528.   Section 2A–529(3).   The resulting recalculation of claim should reduce the amount recoverable by A against B and the lessor is required to cause an appropriate credit to be entered against the earlier judgment.   However, the nature of the post-judgment proceedings to resolve this issue, and the sanctions for a failure to comply, if any, will be determined by other law.

16.   Finally, if the lease agreement had so provided pursuant to subparagraph (f), A's claim against B would not be determined under any of these statutory formulae, but pursuant to a liquidated damages clause.   Section 2A–504(1).

17.   These various methods of computing A's damage claim against B are alternatives subject to Section 2A–501(4).   However, the pursuit of any one of these alternatives is not a bar to, nor has it been barred by, A's earlier action to obtain possession of the 60 bicy-

cles. These formulae, which vary as a function of an overt or implied mitigation of damage theory, focus on allowing A a recovery of the benefit of his bargain with B. Had B performed, A would have received the rent as well as the return of the 60 bicycles at the end of the term.

18. Finally, A's counsel should also advise A of his right to cancel the lease contract under subparagraph (a). Section 2A-505(1). Cancellation will discharge all existing obligations but preserve A's rights and remedies.

19. Subsection (2) recognizes that a lessor who is entitled to exercise the rights or to obtain a remedy granted by subsection (1) may choose not to do so. In such cases, the lessor can recover damages as provided in subsection (2). For example, for non-payment of rent, the lessor may decide not to take possession of the goods and cancel the lease, but rather to merely sue for the unpaid rent as it comes due plus lost interest or other damages "determined in any reasonable manner." Subsection (2) also negates any loss of alternative rights and remedies by reason of having invoked or commenced the exercise or pursuit of any one or more rights or remedies.

20. Subsection (3) allows the lessor access to a remedy scheme provided in this Article as well as that contained in the lease contract if the lessee is in default for reasons other than those stated in subsection (1). Note that the reference to this Article includes supplementary principles of law and equity, *e.g.*, fraud, misrepresentation and duress. Sections 2A-103(4) and 1-103.

21. There is no special treatment of the finance lease in this section. Absent supplementary principles of law to the contrary, in most cases the supplier will have no rights or remedies against the defaulting lessee. Section 2A-209(2)(ii). Given that the supplier will look to the lessor for payment, this is appropriate. However, there is a specific exception to this rule with respect to the right to identify goods to the lease contract. Section 2A-524(2). The parties are free to create a different result in a particular case. Sections 2A-103(4) and 1-102(3).

Cross References:

Sections 1-102(3), 1-103, 1-106(1), 1-201(37), 2-703, 2A-103(1)(j), 2A-103(4), 2A-209(2)(ii), 2A-501(4), 2A-504(1), 2A-505(1), 2A-507, 2A-510(2), 2A-524 through 2A-531, 2A-524(2), 2A-525(1), 2A-525(2), 2A-526(1), 2A-527(1), 2A-527(2), 2A-528(1) and 2A-529(3).

Definitional Cross References:

"Delivery". Section 1-201(14).
"Goods". Section 2A-103(1)(h).
"Installment lease contract". Section 2A-103(1)(i).
"Lease contract". Section 2A-103(1)(*l*).
"Lessee". Section 2A-103(1)(n).
"Lessor". Section 2A-103(1)(p).
"Remedy". Section 1-201(34).
"Rights". Section 1-201(36).
"Value". Section 1-201(44).

§ 2A-524. Lessor's Right to Identify Goods to Lease Contract.

(1) After default by the lessee under the lease contract of the type described in Section 2A-523(1) or 2A-523(3)(a) or, if agreed, after other default by the lessee, the lessor may:

(a) identify to the lease contract conforming goods not already identified if at the time the lessor learned of the default they were in the lessor's or the supplier's possession or control; and

(b) dispose of goods (Section 2A-527(1)) that demonstrably have been intended for the particular lease contract even though those goods are unfinished.

(2) If the goods are unfinished, in the exercise of reasonable commercial judgment for the purposes of avoiding loss and of effective realization, an aggrieved lessor or the supplier may either complete manufacture and wholly identify the goods to the lease contract or cease manufacture and lease, sell, or otherwise dispose of the goods for scrap or salvage value or proceed in any other reasonable manner.

As amended in 1990.

Official Comment

Uniform Statutory Source: Section 2-704.

Changes: Revised to reflect leasing practices and terminology.

Purposes: The remedies provided by this section are available to the lessor (i) if there has been a default by the lessee which falls within Section 2A-523(1) or 2A-523(3)(a), or (ii) if there has been any other default for which the lease contract gives the lessor the remedies provided by this section. Under "(ii)", the lease contract may give the lessor the remedies of identification and disposition provided by this section in various ways. For example, a lease provision might specifically refer to the remedies of identification and disposition, or it might refer to this section by number (*i.e.*, 2A–524), or it might do so by a more general reference such as "all rights and remedies provided by Article 2A for default by the lessee."

Definitional Cross References:

"Aggrieved party". Section 1–201(2).
"Conforming". Section 2A–103(1)(d).
"Goods". Section 2A–103(1)(h).
"Learn". Section 1–201(25).
"Lease". Section 2A–103(1)(j).
"Lease contract". Section 2A–103(1)(*l*).
"Lessor". Section 2A–103(1)(p).
"Rights". Section 1–201(36).
"Supplier". Section 2A–103(1)(x).
"Value". Section 1–201(44).

§ 2A–525. Lessor's Right to Possession of Goods.

(1) If a lessor discovers the lessee to be insolvent, the lessor may refuse to deliver the goods.

(2) After a default by the lessee under the lease contract of the type described in Section 2A–523(1) or 2A–523(3)(a) or, if agreed, after other default by the lessee, the lessor has the right to take possession of the goods. If the lease contract so provides, the lessor may require the lessee to assemble the goods and make them available to the lessor at a place to be designated by the lessor which is reasonably convenient to both parties. Without removal, the lessor may render unusable any goods employed in trade or business, and may dispose of goods on the lessee's premises (Section 2A–527).

(3) The lessor may proceed under subsection (2) without judicial process if it can be done without breach of the peace or the lessor may proceed by action.

As amended in 1990.

Official Comment

Uniform Statutory Source: Section 2–702(1) and former Section 9–503 (now codified as Section 9–609).

Changes: Substantially revised.

Purposes:

1. Subsection (1), a revised version of the provisions of Section 2–702(1), allows the lessor to refuse to deliver goods if the lessee is insolvent. Note that the provisions of Section 2–702(2), granting the unpaid seller certain rights of reclamation, were not incorporated in this section. Subsection (2) made this unnecessary.

2. Subsection (2), a revised version of the provisions of former Section 9–503 (now codified as Section 9–609), allows the lessor, on a Section 2A–523(1) or 2A–523(3)(a) default by the lessee, the right to take possession of or reclaim the goods. Also, the lessor can contract for the right to take possession of the goods for other defaults by the lessee. Therefore, since the lessee's insolvency is an event of default in a standard lease agreement, subsection (2) is the functional equivalent of Section 2–702(2). Further, subsection (2) sanctions the classic crate and delivery clause obligating the lessee to assemble the goods and to make them available to the lessor. Finally, the lessor may leave the goods in place, render them unusable (if they are goods employed in trade or business), and dispose of them on the lessee's premises.

3. Subsection (3), a revised version of the provisions of former Section 9–503 (now codified as Section 9–609), allows the lessor to proceed under subsection (2) without judicial process, absent breach of the peace, or by action. Sections 2A–501(3), 2A–103(4) and 1–201(1). In the appropriate case action includes injunctive relief. *Clark Equip. Co. v. Armstrong Equip. Co.,* 431 F.2d 54 (5th Cir.1970), *cert. denied,* 402 U.S. 909 (1971). This Section, as well as a number of other Sections in this Part, are included in the Article to codify the lessor's common law right to protect the lessor's reversionary interest in the goods. Section 2A–103(1)(q). These Sections are intended to supplement and not displace principles of law and equity with respect to the protection of such interest. Sections 2A–103(4) and 1–103. Such principles apply in many instances, *e.g.,* loss or damage to goods if risk of loss passes to the lessee, failure of the lessee to return goods to the lessor in the condition stipulated in the lease, and refusal of the lessee to return goods to the lessor after termination or cancellation of the lease. See also Section 2A–532.

Cross References:

Sections 1–106(2), 2–702(1), 2–702(2), 2A–103(4), 2A–501(3), 2A–532 and 9–609.

Definitional Cross References:

"Action". Section 1–201(1).
"Delivery". Section 1–201(14).
"Discover". Section 1–201(25).
"Goods". Section 2A–103(1)(h).
"Insolvent". Section 1–201(23).
"Lease contract". Section 2A–103(1)(*l*).
"Lessee". Section 2A–103(1)(n).

"Lessor". Section 2A–103(1)(p).
"Party". Section 1–201(29).
"Rights". Section 1–201(36).

§ 2A–526. Lessor's Stoppage of Delivery in Transit or Otherwise.

(1) A lessor may stop delivery of goods in the possession of a carrier or other bailee if the lessor discovers the lessee to be insolvent and may stop delivery of carload, truckload, planeload, or larger shipments of express or freight if the lessee repudiates or fails to make a payment due before delivery, whether for rent, security or otherwise under the lease contract, or for any other reason the lessor has a right to withhold or take possession of the goods.

(2) In pursuing its remedies under subsection (1), the lessor may stop delivery until

(a) receipt of the goods by the lessee;

(b) acknowledgment to the lessee by any bailee of the goods, except a carrier, that the bailee holds the goods for the lessee; or

(c) such an acknowledgment to the lessee by a carrier via reshipment or as warehouseman.

(3)(a) To stop delivery, a lessor shall so notify as to enable the bailee by reasonable diligence to prevent delivery of the goods.

(b) After notification, the bailee shall hold and deliver the goods according to the directions of the lessor, but the lessor is liable to the bailee for any ensuing charges or damages.

(c) A carrier who has issued a nonnegotiable bill of lading is not obliged to obey a notification to stop received from a person other than the consignor.

Official Comment

Uniform Statutory Source: Section 2–705.

Changes: Revised to reflect leasing practices and terminology.

Definitional Cross References:

"Bill of lading". Section 1–201(6).
"Delivery". Section 1–201(14).
"Discover". Section 1–201(25).
"Goods". Section 2A–103(1)(h).
"Insolvent". Section 1–201(23).
"Lease contract". Section 2A–103(1)(l).

"Lessee". Section 2A–103(1)(n).
"Lessor". Section 2A–103(1)(p).
"Notifies" and "Notification". Section 1–201(26).
"Person". Section 1–201(30).
"Receipt". Section 2–103(1)(c).
"Remedy". Section 1–201(34).
"Rights". Section 1–201(36).

§ 2A–527. Lessor's Rights to Dispose of Goods.

(1) After a default by a lessee under the lease contract of the type described in Section 2A–523(1) or 2A–523(3)(a) or after the lessor refuses to deliver or takes possession of goods (Section 2A–525 or 2A–526), or, if agreed, after other default by a lessee, the lessor may dispose of the goods concerned or the undelivered balance thereof by lease, sale, or otherwise.

(2) Except as otherwise provided with respect to damages liquidated in the lease agreement (Section 2A–504) or otherwise determined pursuant to agreement of the parties (Sections 1–102(3) and 2A–503), if the disposition is by lease agreement substantially similar to the original lease agreement and the new lease agreement is made in good faith and in a commercially reasonable manner, the lessor may recover from the lessee as damages (i) accrued and unpaid rent as of the date of the commencement of the term of the new lease agreement, (ii) the present value, as of the same date, of the total rent for the then remaining lease term of the original lease agreement minus the present value, as of the same date, of the rent under the new lease agreement applicable to that period of the new lease term which is comparable to the then remaining term of the original lease agreement, and (iii) any incidental damages allowed under Section 2A–530, less expenses saved in consequence of the lessee's default.

(3) If the lessor's disposition is by lease agreement that for any reason does not qualify for treatment under subsection (2), or is by sale or otherwise, the lessor may recover from the lessee as if the lessor had elected not to dispose of the goods and Section 2A–528 governs.

(4) A subsequent buyer or lessee who buys or leases from the lessor in good faith for value as a result of a disposition under this section takes the goods free of the original lease contract and any rights of the original lessee even though the

lessor fails to comply with one or more of the requirements of this Article.

(5) The lessor is not accountable to the lessee for any profit made on any disposition. A lessee who has rightfully rejected or justifiably revoked acceptance shall account to the lessor for any excess over the amount of the lessee's security interest (Section 2A–508(5)).

As amended in 1990.

Official Comment

Uniform Statutory Source: Section 2–706(1), (5) and (6).

Changes: Substantially revised.

Purposes:

1. Subsection (1), a revised version of the first sentence of subsection 2–706(1), allows the lessor the right to dispose of goods after a statutory or other material default by the lessee (even if the goods remain in the lessee's possession—Section 2A–525(2)), after the lessor refuses to deliver or takes possession of the goods, or, if agreed, after other contractual default. The lessor's decision to exercise this right is a function of a commercial judgment, not a statutory mandate replete with sanctions for failure to comply. Cf. Section 9–625. As the owner of the goods, in the case of a lessor, or as the prime lessee of the goods, in the case of a sublessor, compulsory disposition of the goods is inconsistent with the nature of the interest held by the lessor or the sublessor and is not necessary because the interest held by the lessee or the sublessee is not protected by a right of redemption under the common law or this Article. Subsection 2A–527(5).

2. The rule for determining the measure of damages recoverable by the lessor against the lessee is a function of several variables. If the lessor has elected to effect disposition under subsection (1) and such disposition is by lease that qualifies under subsection (2), the measure of damages set forth in subsection (2) will apply, absent agreement to the contrary. Sections 2A–504, 2A–103(4) and 1–102(3).

3. The lessor's damages will be established using the new lease agreement as a measure if the following three criteria are satisfied: (i) the lessor disposed of the goods by lease, (ii) the lease agreement is substantially similar to the original lease agreement, and (iii) such disposition was in good faith, and in a commercially reasonable manner. Thus, the lessor will be entitled to recover from the lessee the accrued and unpaid rent as of the date of commencement of the term of the new lease, and the present value, as of the same date, of the rent, under the original lease for the then remaining term less the present value as of the same date of the rent under the new lease agreement applicable to the period of the new lease comparable to the remaining term under the original lease, together with incidental damages less expenses saved in consequence of the lessee's default. If the lessor's disposition does not satisfy the criteria of subsection (2), the lessor may calculate its claim against the lessee pursuant to Section 2A–528. Section 2A–523(1)(e).

4. Two of the three criteria to be met by the lessor are familiar, but the concept of the new lease agreement that is substantially similar to the original lease agreement is not. Given the many variables facing a party who intends to lease goods and the rapidity of change in the market place, the policy decision was made not to draft with specificity. It was thought unwise to seek to establish certainty at the cost of fairness. The decision of whether the new lease agreement is substantially similar to the original will be determined case by case.

5. While the section does not draw a bright line, it is possible to describe some of the factors that should be considered in a finding that a new lease agreement is substantially similar to the original. The various elements of the new lease agreement should be examined. Those elements include the options to purchase or release; the lessor's representations, warranties and covenants to the lessee as well as those to be provided by the lessee to the lessor; and the services, if any, to be provided by the lessor or by the lessee. All of these factors allocate cost and risk between the lessor and the lessee and thus affect the amount of rent to be paid. These findings should not be made with scientific precision, as they are a function of economics, nor should they be made independently, as it is important that a sense of commercial judgment pervade the finding. See Section 2A–507(2). To establish the new lease as a proper measure of damage under subsection (2), these various factors, taken as a whole, must result in a finding that the new lease agreement is substantially similar to the original. If the differences between the original lease and the new lease can be easily valued, it would be appropriate for a court to find that the new lease is substantially similar to the old lease, adjust the difference in the rent between the two leases to take account of the differences, and award damages under this section. If, for example, the new lease requires the lessor to insure the goods in the hands of the lessee, while the original lease required the lessee to insure, the usual cost of such insurance could be deducted from rent due under the new lease

before the difference in rental between the two leases is determined.

6. The following hypothetical illustrates the difficulty of providing a bright line. Assume that A buys a jumbo tractor for $1 million and then leases the tractor to B for a term of 36 months. The tractor is delivered to and is accepted by B on May 1. On June 1 B fails to pay the monthly rent to A. B returns the tractor to A, who immediately releases the tractor to C for a term identical to the term remaining under the lease between A and B. All terms and conditions under the lease between A and C are identical to those under the original lease between A and B, except that C does not provide any property damage or other insurance coverage, and B agreed to provide complete coverage. Coverage is expensive and difficult to obtain. It is a question of fact whether it is so difficult to adjust the recovery to take account of the difference between the two leases as to insurance that the second lease is not substantially similar to the original.

7. A new lease can be substantially similar to the original lease even though its term extends beyond the remaining term of the original lease, so long as both (a) the lease terms are commercially comparable (e.g., it is highly unlikely that a one-month rental and a five-year lease would reflect similar realities), and (b) the court can fairly apportion a part of the rental payments under the new lease to that part of the term of the new lease which is comparable to the remaining lease term under the original lease. Also, the lease term of the new lease may be comparable to the remaining term of the original lease even though the beginning and ending dates of the two leases are not the same. For example, a two-month lease of agricultural equipment for the months of August and September may be comparable to a two-month lease running from the 15th of August to the 15th of October if in the particular location two-month leases beginning on August 15th are basically interchangeable with two-month leases beginning August 1st. Similarly, the term of a one-year truck lease beginning on the 15th of January may be comparable to the term of a one-year truck lease beginning January 2d. If the lease terms are found to be comparable, the court may base cover damages on the entire difference between the costs under the two leases.

8. Subsection (3), which is new, provides that if the lessor's disposition is by lease that does not qualify under subsection (2), or is by sale or otherwise, Section 2A–528 governs.

9. Subsection (4), a revised version of subsection 2–706(5), applies to protect a subsequent buyer or lessee

who buys or leases from the lessor in good faith and for value, pursuant to a disposition under this section. Note that by its terms, the rule in subsection 2A–304(1), which provides that the subsequent lessee takes subject to the original lease contract, is controlled by the rule stated in this subsection.

10. Subsection (5), a revised version of subsection 2–706(6), provides that the lessor is not accountable to the lessee for any profit made by the lessor on a disposition. This rule follows from the fundamental premise of the bailment for hire that the lessee under a lease of goods has no equity of redemption to protect.

Cross References:

Sections 1–102(3), 2–706(1), 2–706(5), 2–706(6), 2A–103(4), 2A–304(1), 2A–504, 2A–507(2), 2A–523(1)(e), 2A–525(2), 2A–527(5), 2A–528 and 9–625.

Definitional Cross References:

"Buyer" and "Buying". Section 2–103(1)(a).
"Delivery". Section 1–201(14).
"Good faith". Section 1–201(19) and 2–103(1)(b).
"Goods". Section 2A–103(1)(h).
"Lease". Section 2A–103(1)(j).
"Lease contract". Section 2A–103(1)(*l*).
"Lessee". Section 2A–103(1)(n).
"Lessor". Section 2A–103(1)(p).
"Present value". Section 2A–103(1)(u).
"Right". Section 1–201(36).
"Sale". Section 2–106(1).
"Security interest". Sections 1–201(37).
"Value". Section 1–201(44).

§ 2A–528. Lessor's Damages for Non-acceptance, Failure to Pay, Repudiation, or Other Default.

(1) Except as otherwise provided with respect to damages liquidated in the lease agreement (Section 2A–504) or otherwise determined pursuant to agreement of the parties (Sections 1–102(3) and 2A–503), if a lessor elects to retain the goods or a lessor elects to dispose of the goods and the disposition is by lease agreement that for any reason does not qualify for treatment under Section 2A–527(2), or is by sale or otherwise, the lessor may recover from the lessee as damages for a default of the type described in Section 2A–523(1) or 2A–523(3)(a), or, if agreed, for other default of the lessee, (i) accrued and unpaid rent as of the date of default if the lessee has never taken possession of the goods, or, if the lessee has taken possession of the goods, as of the date the lessor repossesses the goods or an earli-

er date on which the lessee makes a tender of the goods to the lessor, (ii) the present value as of the date determined under clause (i) of the total rent for the then remaining lease term of the original lease agreement minus the present value as of the same date of the market rent at the place where the goods are located computed for the same lease term, and (iii) any incidental damages allowed under Section 2A–530, less expenses saved in consequence of the lessee's default.

(2) If the measure of damages provided in subsection (1) is inadequate to put a lessor in as good a position as performance would have, the measure of damages is the present value of the profit, including reasonable overhead, the lessor would have made from full performance by the lessee, together with any incidental damages allowed under Section 2A–530, due allowance for costs reasonably incurred and due credit for payments or proceeds of disposition.

As amended in 1990.

Official Comment

Uniform Statutory Source: Section 2–708.

Changes: Substantially revised.

Purposes:

1. Subsection (1), a substantially revised version of Section 2–708(1), states the basic rule governing the measure of lessor's damages for a default described in Section 2A–523(1) or (3)(a), and, if agreed, for a contractual default. This measure will apply if the lessor elects to retain the goods (whether undelivered, returned by the lessee, or repossessed by the lessor after acceptance and default by the lessee) or if the lessor's disposition does not qualify under subsection 2A–527(2). Section 2A–527(3). Note that under some of these conditions, the lessor may recover damages from the lessee pursuant to the rule set forth in Section 2A–529. There is no sanction for disposition that does not qualify under subsection 2A–527(2). Application of the rule set forth in this section is subject to agreement to the contrary. Sections 2A–504, 2A–103(4) and 1–102(3).

2. If the lessee has never taken possession of the goods, the measure of damage is the accrued and unpaid rent as of the date of default together with the present value, as of the date of default, of the original rent for the remaining term of the lease less the present value as of the same date of market rent, and

incidental damages, less expenses saved in consequence of the default. Note that the reference in Section 2A–528(1)(i) and (ii) is to the date of default not to the date of an event of default. An event of default under a lease agreement becomes a default under a lease agreement only after the expiration of any relevant period of grace and compliance with any notice requirements under this Article and the lease agreement. American Bar Foundation, *Commentaries on Indentures,* § 5–1, at 216–217 (1971). Section 2A–501(1). This conclusion is also a function of whether, as a matter of fact or law, the event of default has been waived, suspended or cured. Sections 2A–103(4) and 1–103. If the lessee has taken possession of the goods, the measure of damages is the accrued and unpaid rent as of the earlier of the time the lessor repossesses the goods or the time the lessee tenders the goods to the lessor plus the difference between the present value, as of the same time, of the rent under the lease for the remaining lease term and the present value, as of the same time, of the market rent.

3. Market rent will be computed pursuant to Section 2A–507.

4. Subsection (2), a somewhat revised version of the provisions of subsection 2–708(2), states a measure of damages which applies if the measure of damages in subsection (1) is inadequate to put the lessor in as good a position as performance would have. The measure of damage is the lessor's profit, including overhead, together with incidental damages, with allowance for costs reasonably incurred and credit for payments or proceeds of disposition. In determining the amount of due credit with respect to proceeds of disposition a proper value should be attributed to the lessor's residual interest in the goods. Sections 2A–103(1)(q) and 2A–507(4).

5. In calculating profit, a court should include any expected appreciation of the goods, *e.g.* the foal of a leased brood mare. Because this subsection is intended to give the lessor the benefit of the bargain, a court should consider any reasonable benefit or profit expected by the lessor from the performance of the lease agreement. *See Honeywell, Inc. v. Lithonia Lighting, Inc.,* 317 F.Supp. 406, 413 (N.D.Ga.1970); *Locks v. Wade,* 36 N.J.Super. 128, 131, 114 A.2d 875, 877 (Super.Ct.App.Div.1955). Further, in calculating profit the concept of present value must be given effect. *Taylor v. Commercial Credit Equip. Corp.,* 170 Ga.App. 322, 316 S.E.2d 788 (Ct.App.1984). *See generally* Section 2A–103(1)(u).

Cross References:

Sections 1–102(3), 2–708, 2A–103(1)(u), 2A–402, 2A–504, 2A–507, 2A–527(2) and 2A–529.

Definitional Cross References:

"Agreement". Section 1–201(3).
"Goods". Section 2A–103(1)(h).
"Lease". Section 2A–103(1)(j).
"Lease agreement". Section 2A–103(1)(k).
"Lessee". Section 2A–103(1)(n).
"Lessor". Section 2A–103(1)(p).
"Party". Section 1–201(29).
"Present value". Section 2A–103(1)(u).
"Sale". Section 2–106(1).

§ 2A–529. Lessor's Action for the Rent.

(1) After default by the lessee under the lease contract of the type described in Section 2A–523(1) or 2A–523(3)(a) or, if agreed, after other default by the lessee, if the lessor complies with subsection (2), the lessor may recover from the lessee as damages:

(a) for goods accepted by the lessee and not repossessed by or tendered to the lessor, and for conforming goods lost or damaged within a commercially reasonable time after risk of loss passes to the lessee (Section 2A–219), (i) accrued and unpaid rent as of the date of entry of judgment in favor of the lessor, (ii) the present value as of the same date of the rent for the then remaining lease term of the lease agreement, and (iii) any incidental damages allowed under Section 2A–530, less expenses saved in consequence of the lessee's default; and

(b) for goods identified to the lease contract if the lessor is unable after reasonable effort to dispose of them at a reasonable price or the circumstances reasonably indicate that effort will be unavailing, (i) accrued and unpaid rent as of the date of entry of judgment in favor of the lessor, (ii) the present value as of the same date of the rent for the then remaining lease term of the lease agreement, and (iii) any incidental damages allowed under Section 2A–530, less expenses saved in consequence of the lessee's default.

(2) Except as provided in subsection (3), the lessor shall hold for the lessee for the remaining lease term of the lease agreement any goods that have been identified to the lease contract and are in the lessor's control.

(3) The lessor may dispose of the goods at any time before collection of the judgment for damages obtained pursuant to subsection (1). If the disposition is before the end of the remaining lease term of the lease agreement, the lessor's recovery against the lessee for damages is governed by Section 2A–527 or Section 2A–528, and the lessor will cause an appropriate credit to be provided against a judgment for damages to the extent that the amount of the judgment exceeds the recovery available pursuant to Section 2A–527 or 2A–528.

(4) Payment of the judgment for damages obtained pursuant to subsection (1) entitles the lessee to the use and possession of the goods not then disposed of for the remaining lease term of and in accordance with the lease agreement.

(5) After default by the lessee under the lease contract of the type described in Section 2A–523(1) or Section 2A–523(3)(a) or, if agreed, after other default by the lessee, a lessor who is held not entitled to rent under this section must nevertheless be awarded damages for non-acceptance under Section 2A–527 or Section 2A–528.

As amended in 1990.

Official Comment

Uniform Statutory Source: Section 2–709.

Changes: Substantially revised.

Purposes:

1. Absent a lease contract provision to the contrary, an action for the full unpaid rent (discounted to present value as of the time of entry of judgment as to rent due after that time) is available as to goods not lost or damaged only if the lessee retains possession of the goods or the lessor is or apparently will be unable to dispose of them at a reasonable price after reasonable effort. There is no general right in a lessor to recover the full rent from the lessee upon holding the goods for the lessee. If the lessee tenders goods back to the lessor, and the lessor refuses to accept the tender, the lessor will be limited to the damages it would have suffered had it taken back the goods. The rule in Article 2 that the seller can recover the price of accepted goods is rejected here. In a lease, the lessor always has a residual interest in the goods which the lessor usually realizes upon at the end of a lease term by either sale or a new lease. Therefore, it is not a substantial imposition on the lessor to require it to

take back and dispose of the goods if the lessee chooses to tender them back before the end of the lease term: the lessor will merely do earlier what it would have done anyway, sell or relet the goods. Further, the lessee will frequently encounter substantial difficulties if the lessee attempts to sublet the goods for the remainder of the lease term. In contrast to the buyer who owns the entire interest in goods and can easily dispose of them, the lessee is selling only the right to use the goods under the terms of the lease and the sublessee must assume a relationship with the lessor. In that situation, it is usually more efficient to eliminate the original lessee as a middleman by allowing the lessee to return the goods to the lessor who can then redispose of them.

2. In some situations even where possession of the goods is reacquired, a lessor will be able to recover as damages the present value of the full rent due, not under this section, but under 2A–528(2) which allows a lost profit recovery if necessary to put the lessor in the position it would have been in had the lessee performed. Following is an example of such a case. A is a lessor of construction equipment and maintains a substantial inventory. B leases from A a backhoe for a period of two weeks at a rental of $1,000. After three days, B returns the backhoe and refuses to pay the rent. A has five backhoes in inventory, including the one returned by B. During the next 11 days after the return by B of the backhoe, A rents no more than three backhoes at any one time and, therefore, always has two on hand. If B had kept the backhoe for the full rental period, A would have earned the full rental on that backhoe, plus the rental on the other backhoes it actually did rent during that period. Getting this backhoe back before the end of the lease term did not enable A to make any leases it would not otherwise have made. The only way to put A in the position it would have been in had the lessee fully performed is to give the lessor the full rentals. A realized no savings at all because the backhoe was returned early and might even have incurred additional expense if it was paying for parking space for equipment in inventory. A has no obligation to relet the backhoe for the benefit of B rather than leasing that backhoe or any other in inventory for its own benefit. Further, it is probably not reasonable to expect A to dispose of the backhoe by sale when it is returned in an effort to reduce damages suffered by B. Ordinarily, the loss of a two-week rental would not require A to reduce the size of its backhoe inventory. Whether A would similarly be entitled to full rentals as lost profit in a one-year lease of a backhoe is a question of fact: in any event the lessor, subject to mitigation of damages rules, is enti-

tled to be put in as good a position as it would have been had the lessee fully performed the lease contract.

3. Under subsection (2) a lessor who is able and elects to sue for the rent due under a lease must hold goods not lost or damaged for the lessee. Subsection (3) creates an exception to the subsection (2) requirement. If the lessor disposes of those goods prior to collection of the judgment (whether as a matter of law or agreement), the lessor's recovery is governed by the measure of damages in Section 2A–527 if the disposition is by lease that is substantially similar to the original lease, or otherwise by the measure of damages in Section 2A–528. Section 2A–523 official comment.

4. Subsection (4), which is new, further reinforces the requisites of Subsection (2). In the event the judgment for damages obtained by the lessor against the lessee pursuant to subsection (1) is satisfied, the lessee regains the right to use and possession of the remaining goods for the balance of the original lease term; a partial satisfaction of the judgment creates no right in the lessee to use and possession of the goods.

5. The relationship between subsections (2) and (4) is important to understand. Subsection (2) requires the lessor to hold for the lessee identified goods in the lessor's possession. Absent agreement to the contrary, whether in the lease or otherwise, under most circumstances the requirement that the lessor hold the goods for the lessee for the term will mean that the lessor is not allowed to use them. Sections 2A–103(4) and 1–203. Further, the lessor's use of the goods could be viewed as a disposition of the goods that would bar the lessor from recovery under this section, remitting the lessor to the two preceding sections for a determination of the lessor's claim for damages against the lessee.

6. Subsection (5), the analogue of subsection 2–709(3), further reinforces the thrust of subsection (3) by stating that a lessor who is held not entitled to rent under this section has not elected a remedy; the lessor must be awarded damages under Sections 2A–527 and 2A–528. This is a function of two significant policies of this Article—that resort to a remedy is optional, unless expressly agreed to be exclusive (Section 2A–503(2)) and that rights and remedies provided in this Article generally are cumulative. (Section 2A–501(2) and (4)).

Cross References:

Sections 1–203, 2–709, 2–709(3), 2A–103(4), 2A–501(2), 2A–501(4), 2A–503(2), 2A–504, 2A–523(1)(e), 2A–525(2), 2A–527, 2A–528 and 2A–529(2).

Definitional Cross References:

"Action". Section 1–201(1).
"Conforming". Section 2A–103(1)(d).
"Goods". Section 2A–103(1)(h).
"Lease". Section 2A–103(1)(j).
"Lease agreement". Section 2A–103(1)(k).
"Lease contract". Section 2A–103(1)(l).
"Lessee". Section 2A–103(1)(n).
"Lessor". Section 2A–103(1)(p).
"Present value". Section 2A–103(1)(u).
"Reasonable time". Section 1–204(1) and (2).

§ 2A–530. Lessor's Incidental Damages.

Incidental damages to an aggrieved lessor include any commercially reasonable charges, expenses, or commissions incurred in stopping delivery, in the transportation, care and custody of goods after the lessee's default, in connection with return or disposition of the goods, or otherwise resulting from the default.

Official Comment

Uniform Statutory Source: Section 2–710.

Changes: Revised to reflect leasing practices and terminology.

Definitional Cross References:

"Aggrieved party". Section 1–201(2).
"Delivery". Section 1–201(14).
"Goods". Section 2A–103(1)(h).
"Lessee". Section 2A–103(1)(n).
"Lessor". Section 2A–103(1)(p).

§ 2A–531. Standing to Sue Third Parties for Injury to Goods.

(1) If a third party so deals with goods that have been identified to a lease contract as to cause actionable injury to a party to the lease contract (a) the lessor has a right of action against the third party, and (b) the lessee also has a right of action against the third party if the lessee:

(i) has a security interest in the goods;

(ii) has an insurable interest in the goods; or

(iii) bears the risk of loss under the lease contract or has since the injury assumed

that risk as against the lessor and the goods have been converted or destroyed.

(2) If at the time of the injury the party plaintiff did not bear the risk of loss as against the other party to the lease contract and there is no arrangement between them for disposition of the recovery, his [or her] suit or settlement, subject to his [or her] own interest, is as a fiduciary for the other party to the lease contract.

(3) Either party with the consent of the other may sue for the benefit of whom it may concern.

Official Comment

Uniform Statutory Source: Section 2–722.

Changes: Revised to reflect leasing practices and terminology.

Definitional Cross References:

"Action". Section 1–201(1).
"Goods". Section 2A–103(1)(h).
"Lease contract". Section 2A–103(1)(l).
"Lessee". Section 2A–103(1)(n).
"Lessor". Section 2A–103(1)(p).
"Party". Section 1–201(29).
"Rights". Section 1–201(36).
"Security interest". Section 1–201(37).

§ 2A–532. Lessor's Rights to Residual Interest.

In addition to any other recovery permitted by this Article or other law, the lessor may recover from the lessee an amount that will fully compensate the lessor for any loss of or damage to the lessor's residual interest in the goods caused by the default of the lessee.

As added in 1990.

Official Comment

Uniform Statutory Source: None.

Purposes: This section recognizes the right of the lessor to recover under this Article (as well as under other law) from the lessee for failure to comply with the lease obligations as to the condition of leased goods when returned to the lessor, for failure to return the goods at the end of the lease, or for any other default which causes loss or injury to the lessor's residual interest in the goods.

APPENDIX F

2003 AMENDMENTS TO UCC ARTICLES 2 & 2A

In strikethrough/underline format

Pre–2001 Article 2 .... *Appendix D*
Pre–2001 Article 2A.. *Appendix E*
2003 amendments (Article 7 revision) .... *Appendix B*
2005 amendments .... *Appendix J*

DRAFTING COMMITTEE TO AMEND UNIFORM COMMERCIAL CODE ARTICLE 2, SALES, AND ARTICLE 2A, LEASES

The Committee acting for the National Conference of Commissioners on Uniform State Laws and the American Law Institute in preparing Amendments to Uniform Commercial Code Article 2 is as follows:

BORIS AUERBACH, 332 Ardon Ln., Wyoming, OH 45215, *Chair*

MARION W. BENFIELD, JR., 10 Overlook Circle, New Braunfels, TX 78132

AMELIA H. BOSS, Temple University, School of Law, 1719 N. Broad St., Philadelphia, PA 19122, *The American Law Institute Representative*

NEIL B. COHEN, Brooklyn Law School, Room 904A, 250 Joralemon St., Brooklyn, NY 11201, *The American Law Institute Representative*

HENRY DEEB GABRIEL, JR., Loyola University, School of Law, 526 Pine St., New Orleans, LA 70118, *National Conference Reporter*

BYRON D. SHER, California State Senate, State Capitol, Suite 2082, Sacramento, CA 95814

JAMES J. WHITE, University of Michigan Law School, 625 S. State St., Room 300, Ann Arbor, MI 48109–1215

LINDA J. RUSCH, Hamline University School of Law, 1536 Hewitt Ave., St. Paul, MN 55104, *Associate Reporter from 1996–1999*

RICHARD E. SPEIDEL, Northwestern University, School of Law, 357 E. Chicago Ave., Chicago, IL 60611, *Reporter from 1991–1999*

EX OFFICIO

K. KING BURNETT, P.O. Box 910, Salisbury, MD 21803–0910, *President*

LANI LIU EWART, Alii Pl., Suite 1800, 1099 Alakea St., Honolulu, HI 96813, *Division Chair*

AMERICAN BAR ASSOCIATION ADVISOR

THOMAS J. McCARTHY, 7 Southview Path, Chadds Ford, PA 19317–9179

EXECUTIVE DIRECTOR

WILLIAM H. HENNING, University of Alabama, School of Law, Box 870382, Tuscaloosa, AL 35487–0382, *Executive Director*

WILLIAM J. PIERCE, 1505 Roxbury Road, Ann Arbor, MI 48104, *Executive Director Emeritus*

PREFATORY NOTE

After over a decade of analysis and discussion, a set of amendments to Article 2 has been adopted. For the most part, the changes update the article to accommodate electronic commerce, which is desirable to avoid questions of interrelation with federal law, and also to reflect the development of business practices, changes in other law, and to resolve some interpretive difficulties of practical significance. The amendments reflect the fact that, overall, Article 2 continues to serve well. This is largely a result of the approach of the Article, which relies to a large extent on the ability of the parties to adapt its provisions by agreement, including course of performance, course of dealing and usage of trade, and on the courts to apply the provisions sensibly. A summary of the amendments includes:

Good Faith

Consistent with the other articles of the Uniform Commercial Code, other than Article 5, the definition of good faith, which is in Section 2–103(1)(j), is amended to cover both "honesty in fact and observance of reasonable commercial standards of fair dealing".

Scope

Although the scope of Article 2 remains unchanged, three amendments affect its application. First, "information," which is an undefined term, is excluded from the definition of "goods" in Section 2–103(1)(k). Second, the subject matter of "foreign exchange transactions," a term defined in Section 2–103(1)(i) in a manner that distinguishes transactions crediting and debiting trading balances from transactions for the physical exchange of money, is also excluded from the definition of "goods." Finally, Section 2–108 addresses the relationship between Article 2 and other laws relating to transactions in goods.

Electronic Commerce

There are a number of changes designed to accommodate electronic commerce. These include the change of the term "writing" to "record" throughout the article, a redefinition of the terms "sign" and "conspicuous", and definitions and use of the new terms "electronic," "electronic agent," and "electronic record".

Section 2–204, which is concerned with formation generally, has been amended to provide that a contract may be formed by the interaction of electronic agents or the interaction of an individual and an electronic agent. New Section 2–211 provides that a record, signature, or contract cannot be denied legal effect and enforceability merely because it is electronic in form. New Section 2–212 provides a rule to determine whether an electronic record or electronic signature is attributable to a person. New Section 2–213 provides that if receipt of an electronic communication has a legal effect, that effect is not changed merely because no individual is aware of the receipt. This section also provides that re-

ceipt of an electronic communication does not establish the content of the communication.

Formation and Terms

The statute-of-frauds provision, contained in Section 2–201, has been amended to change the jurisdictional amount from $500 to $5,000 to reflect over 50 years of inflation. The exception for admissions in court has been broadened to include out-of-court admissions "under oath." The amended section also implicitly recognizes the application of nonstatutory exceptions such as promissory estoppel. The section also expressly excludes application of a statute-of-frauds provision from other law which is predicated on the passage of time.

Section 2–202, which sets out the rules on parol or extrinsic evidence, has been amended to clarify that a finding of ambiguity is not a prerequisite to an admission of evidence of a course of dealing, course of performance, or usage of trade for the purpose of explaining a term.

Section 2–207 has been thoroughly revised. The section no longer addresses issues of offer and acceptance. The principle that a definite and seasonable expression of acceptance on terms other than those of the offer may operate as an acceptance, which was contained previously in Section 2–207(1), has been moved to Section 2–206(3), and Section 2–207 is now only concerned with the terms of the contract. Section 2–207 applies to all contracts, not just those formed by a "battle of the forms". The amended section now provides that terms that appear in the records of both parties, terms to which both parties agree, and supplemental terms under the UCC constitute the contract.

Former Sections 2–319 through 2–324 that dealt with shipping and delivery have been deleted. Those sections dealt with standard shipping terms in a manner inconsistent with modern commercial usage.

Clarifying what was unclear in the prior law, Section 2–503 now provides that, when goods are in the bailee's possession and are to be delivered without movement by tender of delivery, a bailee's acknowledgment must be to the buyer. This section now explicitly provides that the effect of a bailee's receipt of notice on third-party rights is subject to Article 9. Section 2–504 has also been changed to clarify that compliance with the requirements for a shipping contract requires a seller to put "conforming" goods in the carrier's possession.

Section 2–513 now provides explicitly that the parties may by agreement fix a standard of inspection, and Section 2–309 now provides explicitly that the parties may by agreement specify a standard for the nature and timing of a notice of termination.

Sections 2–325, 2–506, and 2–514 have been amended to coordinate with Article 5.

Warranties

Section 2–312 has been amended to bring into the text what was formerly in the comments; that is, the warranty of title is breached if the sale "unreasonably exposes the buyer to litigation because of a colorable claim or interest in the goods."

Section 2–313, which is subject to Section 2–318, has been amended to make it clear that the section applies only to parties in privity. The section has also been amended to provide that a "remedial promise," which is defined in Section 2–103(1)(n) as a promise by a seller to repair, replace, or refund upon the happening of an agreed event, is enforceable without reference to the basis-of-the-bargain test. "Remedial promise" as a distinct category of promise was created to deal with a statute-of-limitations problem. New Section 2–725(2)(c) provides that a cause of action accrues if a remedial promise is not performed when performance is due.

New Sections 2–313A and 2–313B, which are also subject to Section 2–318, create statutory obligations in the nature of express warranties that run directly from a seller to a remote purchaser that is not in privity. Each section applies only to "new goods or goods sold or leased as new goods in a transaction of purchase in the normal chain of distribution," excludes liability for statements that are mere opinion, permits the seller to modify or limit remedies as long as the modification or limitation is provided to the remote purchaser at or before the time of purchase, and excludes recovery for consequential damages in the form of lost profits. Liability under Section 2–313A arises only if the seller "makes an affirmation of fact or promise that relates to the goods, provides a description that relates to the goods, or makes a remedial promise," the affirmation, promise, description or re-

medial promise is "in a record packaged with or accompanying the goods," and the seller "reasonably expects the record to be, and the record is, furnished to the remote purchaser." Section 2–313B differs from Section 2–313A in that it is predicated on an affirmation of fact, promise, description or remedial promise made "in advertising or a similar communication to the public." In addition to the tests for liability set forth in Section 2–313A, under Section 2–313B the remote purchaser must also enter into the transaction "with knowledge of and with the expectation that the goods will conform to the affirmation of fact, promise, or description, or that the seller will perform the remedial promise."

Section 2–316, which deals with the exclusion or modification of warranties, has been amended to provide that a disclaimer of the implied warranty of merchantability in a consumer contract, which is defined in Section 2–103(1)(d) as a contract between a merchant seller and a consumer, must be in a record, must be conspicuous, and must use understandable language that states "[T]he seller undertakes no responsibility for the quality of the goods except as otherwise provided in this contract." The section as amended also provides that a disclaimer of the implied warranty of fitness for a particular purpose in a consumer contract must be in a record, be conspicuous, and use understandable language that states "[T]he seller assumes no responsibility that the goods will be fit for any particular purpose for which you may be buying these goods, except as otherwise provided in this contract." The amendments also now provide that an "as is" or "with all faults" disclaimer in a consumer contract must be conspicuously set forth in a record if the consumer contract is evidenced by a record. The amended section also clarifies that a buyer's refusal to inspect must be predicated on a demand by the seller.

Section 2–318 retains the three alternatives of the former article but is revised to extend to the class of persons designated in each alternative the benefits of remedial promises and statutory obligations in the nature of express warranties under Sections 2–313A and 2–313B.

Performance and Breach

Several provisions on acceptance, rejection, and revocation of acceptance have been amended.

The test for rejection of a single installment in Section 2–612 is now consistent with the test for revocation of acceptance under Section 2–608. The test is that the installment may be rejected if the installment's value to the buyer is substantially impaired. Section 2–602 has been amended to clarify that the buyer must take reasonable care of the goods in both rightful and wrongful rejection cases. Sections 2–602 and 2–608 have been amended in light of many cases to provide that a buyer's reasonable use of goods after rejection or revocation of acceptance is not an acceptance of the goods, but the buyer may be obligated to pay for the value of the use to the buyer. Unreasonable use remains wrongful against the seller and is an acceptance if ratified.

Section 2–508 has been revised to provide that, in a nonconsumer contract, the seller has a right to cure if the buyer justifiably revokes acceptance under Section 2–608(2). The section now predicates the right to cure on good-faith performance by the seller and, when the time for performance has expired, on the cure being appropriate and timely under the circumstances. Another amendment to this section imposes liability on the seller for the buyer's reasonable expenses caused by the breach and subsequent cure.

Section 2–605 has been amended to provide that a buyer that fails to state with particularity a defect ascertainable by reasonable inspection that justifies revocation of acceptance suffers the same consequences as a buyer that similarly fails to particularize a defect in connection with a rejection. The particularity requirement applies only if the seller has a right to cure the defect, not merely the ability to cure. Failure to state a defect with particularity bars the buyer from predicating a rightful rejection or justifiable revocation of acceptance on the defect but no longer bars the buyer from using the defect to establish breach. Section 2–607 has been amended to provide that failure to give timely notice of breach in the case of accepted goods bars a remedy only to the extent the seller is prejudiced by the untimely notice.

Section 2–509, which governs risk of loss, has been amended to provide that if the goods are to be delivered through a bailee and tender is based on notification to the bailee, for risk of loss to pass, the bailee must acknowledge to the buyer that the buyer has a right to possess the goods. In the case of a noncarrier, nonbailee delivery, the section has been amended so that risk of loss for both merchant and nonmerchant passes upon the buyer's receipt of the goods.

The terminology in the excuse provisions; Sections 2–614 through 2–616, has been changed to govern all performance issues and not just delivery issues.

Remedies

Sections 2–703 and 2–711 contain a comprehensive indexing, respectively, of seller's and buyer's remedies.

A credit seller's right to reclaim the goods under Section 2–702 has been changed to provide that demand must be made within a "reasonable time" based on the circumstances instead of the former fixed period of 10 days after delivery or a longer reasonable time if there has been a misrepresentation of solvency. A cash seller's right to reclaim goods under Section 2–507 is now parallel to the credit seller's right under Section 2–702.

For a stoppage in transit in cases other than insolvency, Section 2–705 has been broadened by eliminating the requirement that the goods be by the "carload, truckload, planeload or larger shipments of express or freight" as this is no longer necessary due to modern tracking technology.

The amendments incorporate the change to Section 2–502(1) that were promulgated as part of the revision of Article 9 which provide a consumer buyer with a right to possession if the seller repudiates or fails to deliver the goods as required by the contract. The vesting rule of subsection (2) has been broadened to cover all rights of buyer under the section. The change to Section 2–716 promulgated as part of the revision of Article 9 is also included in the amendments with the vesting rule in this section broadened so that it applies to all buyers that seek replevin. In addition, Section 2–716 has been expanded to give courts discretion in nonconsumer contracts to enforce the parties' agreement for specific performance unless the sole remaining obligation is the payment of money.

Several provisions governing sellers' damages have been clarified or amended. Section 2–706 now explicitly provides that a seller's failure to resell in accordance with the section does not bar the seller from other remedies. Under Section 2–707, the remedies available to a person in the position of a seller include all remedies available to sellers generally. Under Section 2–708, the market price of goods in the case of an anticipatory repudiation is measured at the "expiration of a commercially reasonable time after the seller learned of the repudiation" and Section 2–723 has been amended to be consistent. Section 2–708(2) now explicitly provides that the lost-profit measure of damages is available when the resale remedy is not adequate and the troublesome language in former 2–708(2) that provided for "due allowance for costs reasonably incurred and due credit for payments or proceeds of resale" has been deleted. Moreover, sellers may now recover consequential damages in nonconsumer contracts subject to a test set out in Section 2–710(2) that parallels the test for buyers' consequential damages in Section 2–715(2)(a). Sellers may not recover consequential damages in consumer contracts.

Consistent with Section 2–708(1), Section 2–713 on buyers' market damages has been amended to provide that the market price in the case of an anticipatory repudiation is measured at the "expiration of a commercially reasonable time after the seller learned of the repudiation." The market price in cases other than anticipatory repudiation is now measured at the time for tender.

Section 2–718 has been amended to provide that, in a nonconsumer contract, the test for enforceability of a liquidated damage clause is limited to the reasonableness of the clause in light of the actual or anticipated harm. The former language that indicated that a clause that provided for an unreasonably large amount of liquidated damages was void as a penalty has been deleted because it might cause some to infer, incorrectly, that a clause setting an unreasonably small amount of liquidated damages cannot constitute a penalty. Language has also been added to clarify that the enforceability of a clause that limits remedies is to be determined under Section 2–719.

Section 2–718(3) has been amended to expand a buyer's right to restitution of the price paid to all circumstances in which the seller stops performance because of the buyer's breach or insolvency. The statutory liquidated-damages

deduction from the breaching buyer's restitution remedy has also been eliminated.

The general limitations period of Section 2–725(1) has been amended from a flat four years to "one year after the breach was or should have been discovered, but no longer than five years after the right of action accrued." The limitation period may not be reduced in a consumer contract. In addition to retaining the accrual rules from current law, the section now provides specific accrual rules for breach by repudiation, breach of a remedial promise, a claim over (indemnity), breach of a warranty of title, breach of a warranty against infringement, and breach of a statutory obligation arising under Section 2–313A or Section 2–313B.

A Note Regarding the CISG

When parties enter into an agreement for the international sale of goods, because the United States is a party to the United Nations Convention on Contracts for the International Sale of Goods (CISG), the Convention may be the applicable law. Since many of the provisions of the CISG appear similar to provisions of Article 2, the committee drafting the amendments considered making references in the Official Comments to provisions in the CISG. However, upon reflection, it was decided that this would not be done because the inclusion of such references might suggest a greater similarity between Article 2 and the CISG than in fact exists.

The principle concern was the possibility of an inappropriate use of cases decided under one law to interpret provisions of the other law. This type of interpretation is contrary to the mandate of both the Uniform Commercial Code and the CISG. Specifically, Section 1–103(b) of the Code directs courts to interpret it in light of its common-law history. This was an underlying principle in original Article 2, and these amendments do not change this in any way. On the other hand, the CISG specifically directs courts to interpret its provisions in light of international practice with the goal of achieving international uniformity. *See* CISG art. 7. This approach specifically eschews the use of domestic law, such as Article 2, as a basis for interpretation.

AMENDMENTS TO ARTICLE 2–SALES

PART 1

SHORT TITLE, GENERAL CONSTRUCTION AND SUBJECT MATTER

§ 2–103. Definitions and Index of Definitions.

(1) In this article unless the context otherwise requires:

(a) "Buyer" means a person ~~who~~ that buys or contracts to buy goods.

(b) "Conspicuous", with reference to a term, means so written, displayed, or presented that a reasonable person against which it is to operate ought to have noticed it. A term in an electronic record intended to evoke a response by an electronic agent is conspicuous if it is presented in a form that would enable a reasonably configured electronic agent to take it into account or react to it without review of the record by an individual. Whether a term is "conspicuous" or not is a decision for the court. Conspicuous terms include the following:

(i) for a person:

(A) a heading in capitals equal to or greater in size than the surrounding text, or in contrasting type, font, or color to the surrounding text of the same or lesser size; and

(B) language in the body of a record or display in larger type than the surrounding text, or in contrasting type, font, or color to the surrounding text of the same size, or set off from surrounding text of the same size by symbols or other marks that call attention to the language; and

(ii) for a person or an electronic agent, a term that is so placed in a record or display that the person or electronic agent may not proceed without taking action with respect to the particular term.

(c) "Consumer" means an individual who buys or contracts to buy goods that, at the time of contracting, are intended by the individual to be used primarily for personal, family, or household purposes.

(d) "Consumer contract" means a contract between a merchant seller and a consumer.

(e) "Delivery" means the voluntary transfer of physical possession or control of goods.

(f) "Electronic" means relating to technology having electrical, digital, magnetic, wireless, optical, electromagnetic, or similar capabilities.

(g) "Electronic agent" means a computer program or an electronic or other automated means used independently to initiate an action or respond to electronic records or performances in whole or in part, without review or action by an individual.

(h) "Electronic record" means a record created, generated, sent, communicated, received, or stored by electronic means.

(i) "Foreign exchange transaction" means a transaction in which one party agrees to deliver a quantity of a specified money or unit of account in consideration of the other party's agreement to deliver another quantity of a different money or unit of account either currently or at a future date, and in which delivery is to be through funds transfer, book entry accounting, or other form of payment order, or other agreed means to transfer a credit balance. The term includes a transaction of this type involving two or more moneys and spot, forward, option, or other products derived from underlying moneys and any combination of these transactions. The term does not include a transaction involving two or more moneys in which one or both of the parties is obligated to make physical delivery, at the time of contracting or in the future, of banknotes, coins, or other form of legal tender or specie.

[(j) Reserved]

[(j) "Good faith" means honesty in fact and the observance of reasonable commercial standards of fair dealing .]

Legislative Note: The definition of "good faith" should not be adopted if the jurisdiction has enacted this definition as part of Article 1.

(k) "Goods" means all things that are movable at the time of identification to a contract for sale. The term includes future goods, specially manufactured goods, the unborn young of animals, growing crops, and other identified things attached to realty as described in Section 2–107. The term does not include information, the money in which the price is to be paid, investment securities under Article 8, the subject matter of foreign exchange transactions, or choses in action.

(l) "Receipt of goods" means taking physical possession of goods.

(m) "Record" means information that is inscribed on a tangible medium or that is stored in an electronic or other medium and is retrievable in perceivable form.

Legislative Note: The definition of "record" should not be adopted if the jurisdiction has enacted revised Article 1.

(n) "Remedial promise" means a promise by the seller to repair or replace goods or to refund all or part of the price of goods upon the happening of a specified event.

(d) (o) "Seller" means a person who that sells or contracts to sell goods.

(p) "Sign" means, with present intent to authenticate or adopt a record:

(i) to execute or adopt a tangible symbol; or

(ii) to attach to or logically associate with the record an electronic sound, symbol, or process.

(2) Other definitions applying to this Article or to specified Parts thereof, and the sections in which they appear are:

"Acceptance". Section 2–606.
"Banker's credit". Section 2–325
"Between merchants". Section 2–104.
"Cancellation". Section 2–106(4).
"Commercial unit". Section 2–105.
"Confirmed credit". Section 2–325
"Conforming to contract". Section 2–106.
"Contract for sale". Section 2–106.
"Cover". Section 2–712.
"Entrusting". Section 2–403.
"Financing agency". Section 2–104.
"Future goods". Section 2–105.
"Goods". Section 2–103.
"Identification". Section 2–501.
"Installment contract". Section 2–612.
"Letter of credit". Section 2–325
"Lot". Section 2–105.
"Merchant". Section 2–104.
"Overseas". Section 2–323
"Person in position of seller". Section 2–707.
"Present sale". Section 2–106.
"Sale". Section 2–106.

"Sale on approval". Section 2–326.
"Sale or return". Section 2–326.
"Termination". Section 2–106.

(3) "Control" as provided in Section 7–106 The and the following definitions in other Articles apply to this Article:

"Check". Section 3–104(f).
"Consignee". Section 7–102(3)
"Consignor". Section 7–102(4)
"Consumer goods". Section 9–102(a)(23).
"Dishonor". Section 3–502.
"Draft". Section 3–104(e).
"Honor". Section 5–102(a)(8).
"Injunction against honor". Section 5–109(b).
"Letter of credit". Section 5–102(a)(10).

(4) In addition Article 1 contains general definitions and principles of construction and interpretation applicable throughout this Article.

§ 2–104. Definitions: "Merchant"; "Between Merchants"; "Financing Agency".

(1) "Merchant" means a person who that deals in goods of the kind or otherwise by his occupation holds himself out holds itself out by occupation as having knowledge or skill peculiar to the practices or goods involved in the transaction or to whom which such the knowledge or skill may be attributed by his the person's employment of an agent or broker or other intermediary who by his occupation holds himself out that holds itself out by occupation as having such the knowledge or skill.

(2) "Financing agency" means a bank, finance company, or other person who that in the ordinary course of business makes advances against goods or documents of title or who that by arrangement with either the seller or the buyer intervenes in ordinary course to make or collect payment due or claimed under the contract for sale, as by purchasing or paying the seller's draft or making advances against it or by merely taking it for collection whether or not documents of title accompany or are associated with the draft. "Financing agency" The term includes also a bank or other person who that similarly intervenes between persons who that are in the position of seller and buyer in respect to the goods (Section 2–707).

(3) "Between merchants" means in any transaction with respect to which both parties are chargeable with the knowledge or skill of merchants.

§ 2–105. Definitions: Transferability; "Goods"; "Future" Goods; "Lot"; "Commercial Unit".

(1) ~~"Goods" means all things (including specially manufactured goods) which are movable at the time of identification to the contract for sale other than the money in which the price is to be paid, investment securities (Article 8) and things in action. "Goods" also includes the unborn young of animals and growing crops and other identified things attached to realty as described in the section on goods to be severed from realty (Section 2–107).~~

~~(2)~~ (1) Goods must be both existing and identified before any interest in them ~~can~~ may pass. Goods ~~which~~ that are not both existing and identified are "future" goods. A purported present sale of future goods or of any interest therein operates as a contract to sell.

~~(3)~~ (2) There may be a sale of a part interest in existing identified goods.

~~(4)~~ (3) An undivided share in an identified bulk of fungible goods is sufficiently identified to be sold although the quantity of the bulk is not determined. Any agreed proportion of ~~such a~~ the bulk or any quantity thereof agreed upon by number, weight, or other measure may to the extent of the seller's interest in the bulk be sold to the buyer ~~who~~ that then becomes an owner in common.

~~(5)~~ (4) "Lot" means a parcel or a single article which is the subject matter of a separate sale or delivery, whether or not it is sufficient to perform the contract.

~~(6)~~ (5) "Commercial unit" means such a unit of goods as by commercial usage is a single whole for purposes of sale and division of which materially impairs its character or value on the market or in use. A commercial unit may be a single article (as a machine) or a set of articles (as a suite of furniture or an assortment of sizes) or a quantity (as a bale, gross, or carload) or any other unit treated in use or in the relevant market as a single whole.

PART 2

FORM, FORMATION, TERMS AND READJUSTMENT OF CONTRACT; ELECTRONIC CONTRACTING

§ 2–201. Formal Requirements; Statute of Frauds.

(1) ~~Except as otherwise provided in this section a~~ A contract for the sale of goods for the price of ~~$500~~ $5,000 or more is not enforceable by way of action or defense unless there is some ~~writing~~ record sufficient to indicate that a contract for sale has been made between the parties and signed by the party against ~~whom~~ which enforcement is sought or by ~~his~~ the party's authorized agent or broker. A ~~writing~~ record is not insufficient because it omits or incorrectly states a term agreed upon, but the contract is not enforceable under this ~~paragraph~~ subsection beyond the quantity of goods shown in ~~such~~ the ~~writing~~ record.

(2) Between merchants if within a reasonable time a ~~writing~~ record in confirmation of the contract and sufficient against the sender is received and the party receiving it has reason to know its contents, it satisfies the requirements of subsection (1) against ~~such party~~ the recipient unless ~~written~~ notice of objection to its contents is given in a record within 10 days after it is received.

(3) A contract ~~which~~ that does not satisfy the requirements of subsection (1) but which is valid in other respects is enforceable:

(a) if the goods are to be specially manufactured for the buyer and are not suitable for sale to others in the ordinary course of the seller's business and the seller, before notice of repudiation is received and under circumstances ~~which~~ that reasonably indicate that the goods are for the buyer, has made either a substantial beginning of their manufacture or commitments for their procurement; ~~or~~

(b) if the party against ~~whom~~ which enforcement is sought admits in ~~his~~ the party's pleading, or in the party's testimony or otherwise ~~in court~~ under oath that a contract for sale was made, but the contract is not enforceable under this ~~provision~~ paragraph beyond the quantity of goods admitted; or

(c) with respect to goods for which payment has been made and accepted or which have been received and accepted (Sec. 2–606).

(4) A contract that is enforceable under this section is not unenforceable merely because it is not capable of being performed within one year or any other period after its making.

§ 2–202. Final ~~Written~~ Expression in a Record: Parol or Extrinsic Evidence.

(1) Terms with respect to which the confirmatory ~~memoranda~~ records of the parties agree or which are otherwise set forth in a ~~writing~~ record intended by the parties as a final expression of their agreement with respect to such terms as are included therein may not be contradicted by evidence of any prior agreement or of a contemporaneous oral agreement but may be ~~explained or~~ supplemented by evidence of:

(a) ~~by course of dealing or usage of trade (Section 1–205) or by course of performance (Section 2–208)~~ course of performance, course of dealing, or usage of trade (Section 1–303); and

(b) ~~by evidence of~~ consistent additional terms unless the court finds the ~~writing~~ record to have been intended also as a complete and exclusive statement of the terms of the agreement.

(2) Terms in a record may be explained by evidence of course of performance, course of dealing, or usage of trade without a preliminary determination by the court that the language used is ambiguous.

Legislative Note: The cross-references in subsection (1)(a) should not be changed if the jurisdiction has not adopted revised Article 1.

§ 2–203. Seals Inoperative.

The affixing of a seal to a ~~writing~~ record evidencing a contract for sale or an offer to buy or sell goods does not constitute the ~~writing~~ record a sealed ~~instrument and the~~ instrument. The law with respect to sealed instruments does not apply to such a contract or offer.

§ 2–204. Formation in General.

(1) A contract for sale of goods may be made in any manner sufficient to show agreement, including offer and acceptance, conduct by both parties which recognizes the existence of ~~such~~ a contract, the interaction of electronic agents, and the interaction of an electronic agent and an individual.

(2) An agreement sufficient to constitute a contract for sale may be found even ~~though~~ if the moment of its making is undetermined.

(3) Even ~~though~~ if one or more terms are left open, a contract for sale does not fail for indefiniteness if the parties have intended to make a contract and there is a reasonably certain basis for giving an appropriate remedy.

(4) Except as otherwise provided in Sections 2–211 through 2–213, the following rules apply:

(a) A contract may be formed by the interaction of electronic agents of the parties, even if no individual was aware of or reviewed the electronic agents' actions or the resulting terms and agreements.

(b) A contract may be formed by the interaction of an electronic agent and an individual acting on the individual's own behalf or for another person. A contract is formed if the individual takes actions that the individual is free to refuse to take or makes a statement, and the individual has reason to know that the actions or statement will:

(i) cause the electronic agent to complete the transaction or performance; or

(ii) indicate acceptance of an offer, regardless of other expressions or actions by the individual to which the electronic agent cannot react.

§ 2–205. Firm Offers.

An offer by a merchant to buy or sell goods in a signed ~~writing which~~ record that by its terms gives assurance that it will be held open is not revocable, for lack of consideration, during the time stated or if no time is stated for a reasonable time, but in no event may ~~such~~ the period of irrevocability exceed three ~~months, but any~~ months. Any such term of assurance ~~on a form~~ in a form supplied by the offeree must be separately signed by the offeror.

§ 2–206. Offer and Acceptance in Formation of Contract.

(1) Unless otherwise unambiguously indicated by the language or circumstances:

(a) an offer to make a contract shall be construed as inviting acceptance in any manner and by any medium reasonable in the circumstances;

(b) an order or other offer to buy goods for prompt or current shipment shall be construed as inviting acceptance either by a prompt promise to ship or by the prompt or current shipment of conforming or ~~non-conforming~~ nonconforming goods, but ~~such a~~ the shipment of ~~non-conforming~~ nonconforming goods ~~does not constitute~~ is not an acceptance if the seller seasonably notifies the buyer that the shipment is offered only as an accommodation to the buyer.

(2) ~~Where~~ If the beginning of a requested performance is a reasonable mode of acceptance, an offeror ~~who~~ that is not notified of acceptance within a reasonable time may treat the offer as having lapsed before acceptance.

(3) A definite and seasonable expression of acceptance in a record operates as an acceptance even if it contains terms additional to or different from the offer.

§ 2-207. Additional Terms in Acceptance or Terms of Contract; Effect of Confirmation.

(1) ~~A definite and seasonable expression of acceptance or a written confirmation which is sent within a reasonable time operates as an acceptance even though it states terms additional to or different from those offered or agreed upon, unless acceptance is expressly made conditional on assent to the additional or different terms.~~

(2) ~~The additional terms are to be construed as proposals for addition to the contract. Between merchants such terms become part of the contract unless:~~

~~(a) the offer expressly limits acceptance to the terms of the offer;~~

~~(b) they materially alter it; or~~

~~(c) notification of objection to them has already been given or is given within a reasonable time after notice of them is received.~~

(3) ~~Conduct by both parties which recognizes the existence of a contract is sufficient to establish a contract for sale although the writings of the parties do not otherwise establish a contract. In such case the terms of the particular contract consist of those terms on which the writings of the parties agree, together with any supplemen-~~ ~~tary terms incorporated under any other provisions of this Act.~~

Subject to Section 2-202, if (i) conduct by both parties recognizes the existence of a contract although their records do not otherwise establish a contract, (ii) a contract is formed by an offer and acceptance, or (iii) a contract formed in any manner is confirmed by a record that contains terms additional to or different from those in the contract being confirmed, the terms of the contract are:

(a) terms that appear in the records of both parties;

(b) terms, whether in a record or not, to which both parties agree; and

(c) terms supplied or incorporated under any provision of this Act.

§ 2-208. ~~Course of Performance on Practical Construction~~ Reserved.

(1) ~~Where the contract for sale involves repeated occasions for performance by either party with knowledge of the nature of the performance and opportunity for objection to it by the other, any course of performance accepted or acquiesced in without objection shall be relevant to determine the meaning of the agreement.~~

(2) ~~The express terms of the agreement and any such course of performance, as well as any course of dealing and usage of trade, shall be construed whenever reasonable as consistent with each other; but when such construction is unreasonable, express terms shall control course of performance and course of performance shall control both course of dealing and usage of trade (Section 1-205).~~

(3) ~~Subject to the provisions of the next section on modification and waiver, such course of performance shall be relevant to show a waiver or modification of any term inconsistent with such course of performance.~~

Legislative Note: This section should not be repealed if the jurisdiction has not adopted revised Article 1.

§ 2-209. Modification; Rescission and Waiver.

(1) An agreement modifying a contract within this Article needs no consideration to be binding.

(2) ~~A signed agreement~~ An agreement in a signed record which excludes modification or re-

scission except by a signed ~~writing cannot~~ record may not be otherwise modified or rescinded, but except as between merchants such a requirement ~~on a form~~ in a form supplied by the merchant must be separately signed by the other party.

(3) The requirements of ~~the statute of frauds section of this Article (Section 2–201)~~ Section 2–201 must be satisfied if the contract as modified is within its provisions.

(4) Although an attempt at modification or rescission does not satisfy the requirements of subsection (2) or (3)_, it ~~can~~ may operate as a waiver.

(5) A party ~~who~~ that has made a waiver affecting an executory portion of ~~the~~ a contract may retract the waiver by reasonable notification received by the other party that strict performance will be required of any term waived, unless the retraction would be unjust in view of a material change of position in reliance on the waiver.

§ 2–210. Delegation of Performance; Assignment of Rights.

~~(1) A party may perform his duty through a delegate unless otherwise agreed or unless the other party has a substantial interest in having his original promisor perform or control the acts required by the contract. No delegation of performance relieves the party delegating of any duty to perform or any liability for breach.~~

~~(2) Except as otherwise provided in Section 9–406, unless otherwise agreed, all rights of either seller or buyer can be assigned except where the assignment would materially change the duty of the other party, or increase materially the burden or risk imposed on him by his contract, or impair materially his chance of obtaining return performance. A right to damages for breach of the whole contract or a right arising out of the assignor's due performance of his entire obligation can be assigned despite agreement otherwise.~~

~~(3) The creation, attachment, perfection, or enforcement of a security interest in the seller's interest under a contract is not a transfer that materially changes the duty of or increases materially the burden or risk imposed on the buyer or impairs materially the buyer's chance of obtaining return performance within the purview of subsection (2) unless, and then only to the extent that, enforcement actually results in a delegation~~

~~of material performance of the seller. Even in that event, the creation, attachment, perfection, and enforcement of the security interest remain effective, but (i) the seller is liable to the buyer for damages caused by the delegation to the extent that the damages could not reasonably be prevented by the buyer, and (ii) a court having jurisdiction may grant other appropriate relief, including cancellation of the contract for sale or an injunction against enforcement of the security interest or consummation of the enforcement.~~

~~(4) An assignment of "the contract" or of "all my rights under the contract" or an assignment in similar general terms is an assignment of rights and unless the language or the circumstances (as in an assignment for security) indicate the contrary, it is a delegation of performance of the duties of the assignor and its acceptance by the assignee constitutes a promise by him to perform those duties. This promise is enforceable by either the assignor or the other party to the original contract.~~

~~(5) The other party may treat any assignment which delegates performance as creating reasonable grounds for insecurity and may without prejudice to his rights against the assignor demand assurances from the assignee (Section 2–609).~~

(1) If the seller or buyer assigns rights under a contract, the following rules apply:

(a) Subject to paragraph (b) and except as otherwise provided in Section 9–406 or as otherwise agreed, all rights of the seller or the buyer may be assigned unless the assignment would materially change the duty of the other party, increase materially the burden or risk imposed on that party by the contract, or impair materially that party's chance of obtaining return performance. A right to damages for breach of the whole contract or a right arising out of the assignor's due performance of its entire obligation may be assigned despite an agreement otherwise.

(b) The creation, attachment, perfection, or enforcement of a security interest in the seller's interest under a contract is not an assignment that materially changes the duty of or materially increases the burden or risk imposed on the buyer or materially impairs the buyer's chance of obtaining return performance under paragraph (a) unless, and only to the extent that, enforcement of the security interest results in a delegation of a material performance of the seller. Even in that event, the creation, attachment, perfection, and enforcement of the security interest remain effective. However, the seller is liable to the buyer for damages caused by the delegation to the extent that the damages could not reasonably be prevented by the buyer, and a court may grant other appropriate relief, including cancellation of the contract or an injunction against enforcement of the security interest or consummation of the enforcement.

(2) If the seller or buyer delegates performance of its duties under a contract, the following rules apply:

(a) A party may perform its duties through a delegate unless otherwise agreed or unless the other party has a substantial interest in having the original promisor perform or control the acts required by the contract. Delegation of performance does not relieve the delegating party of any duty to perform or liability for breach.

(b) Acceptance of a delegation of duties by the assignee constitutes a promise to perform those duties. The promise is enforceable by either the assignor or the other party to the original contract.

(c) The other party may treat any delegation of duties as creating reasonable grounds for insecurity and may without prejudice to its rights against the assignor demand assurances from the assignee under Section 2–609.

(d) A contractual term prohibiting the delegation of duties otherwise delegable under paragraph (a) is enforceable, and an attempted delegation is not effective.

(3) An assignment of "the contract" or of "all my rights under the contract" or an assignment in similar general terms is an assignment of rights and unless the language or the circumstances, as in an assignment for security, indicate the contrary, it is also a delegation of performance of the duties of the assignor.

(4) Unless the circumstances indicate the contrary, a prohibition of assignment of "the contract" is to be construed as barring only the delegation to the assignee of the assignor's performance.

PART 3

GENERAL OBLIGATION AND CONSTRUCTION OF CONTRACT

§ 2–302. Unconscionable Contract or Clause Term.

(1) If the court as a matter of law finds the contract or any clause term of the contract to have been unconscionable at the time it was made, the court may refuse to enforce the contract, or it may enforce the remainder of the contract without the unconscionable clause term, or it may so limit the application of any unconscionable clause term as to avoid any unconscionable result.

(2) When If it is claimed or appears to the court that the contract or any clause term thereof may be unconscionable, the parties shall be afforded a reasonable opportunity to present evidence as to its commercial setting, purpose, and effect to aid the court in making the determination.

§ 2–304. Price Payable in Money, Goods, Realty, or Otherwise.

(1) The price can may be made payable in money or otherwise. If it is payable in whole or in part in goods, each party is a seller of the goods which he that the party is to transfer.

(2) Even though if all or part of the price is payable in an interest in realty real property the transfer of the goods, and the seller's obligations with reference to them are subject to this Article, but not the transfer of the interest in realty real property or the transferor's obligations in connection therewith.

§ 2–305. Open Price Term.

(1) The parties if they so intend can may conclude a contract for sale even though if the price is not settled. In such a case the price is a reasonable price at the time for delivery if:

(a) nothing is said as to price; or

(b) the price is left to be agreed by the parties and they fail to agree; or

(c) the price is to be fixed in terms of some agreed market or other standard as set or recorded by a third person or agency and it is not so set or recorded.

(2) A price to be fixed by the seller or by the buyer means a price ~~for him to fix~~ to be fixed in good faith.

(3) ~~When~~ If a price left to be fixed otherwise than by agreement of the parties fails to be fixed through fault of one party, the other may at ~~his~~ the party's option treat the contract as canceled or ~~himself~~ the party may fix a reasonable price.

(4) ~~Where~~ If, however, the parties intend not to be bound unless the price ~~be~~ is fixed or agreed and it is not fixed or agreed, there is no contract. In such a case the buyer must return any goods already received or if unable ~~so~~ to do so must pay their reasonable value at the time of delivery and the seller must return any portion of the price paid on account.

§ 2–308. Absence of Specified Place for Delivery.

Unless otherwise agreed:

(a) the place for delivery of goods is the seller's place of business or if ~~he has~~ none, ~~his~~ the seller's residence; but

(b) in a contract for sale of identified goods ~~which~~ that to the knowledge of the parties at the time of contracting are in some other place, that place is the place for their delivery; and

(c) documents of title may be delivered through customary banking channels.

§ 2–309. Absence of Specific Time Provisions; Notice of Termination.

(1) The time for shipment or delivery or any other action under a contract if not provided in this Article or agreed upon shall be a reasonable time.

(2) ~~Where~~ If the contract provides for successive performances but is indefinite in duration, it is valid for a reasonable time but unless otherwise agreed may be terminated at any time by either party.

(3) Termination of a contract by one party except on the happening of an agreed event requires that reasonable notification be received by the other party and an agreement dispensing

with notification is invalid if its operation would be unconscionable. A term specifying standards for the nature and timing of notice is enforceable if the standards are not manifestly unreasonable.

§ 2–310. Open Time for Payment or Running of Credit; Authority to Ship under Reservation.

Unless otherwise agreed:

(a) payment is due at the time and place at which the buyer is to receive the goods even though the place of shipment is the place of delivery; ~~and~~

(b) if the seller is required or authorized to send the goods, ~~he~~ the seller may ship them under reservation, and may tender the documents of title, but the buyer may inspect the goods after their arrival before payment is due unless ~~such~~ the inspection is inconsistent with the terms of the contract (Section 2–513); ~~and~~

(c) if tender of delivery is ~~authorized and~~ agreed to be made by way of documents of title otherwise than by ~~subsection~~ paragraph (b), then payment is due regardless of where the goods are to be received (i) at the time and place at which the buyer is to receive delivery of the tangible documents, or (ii) at the time the buyer is to receive delivery of the electronic documents and at the seller's place of business or if none, the seller's residence ~~regardless of where the goods are to be received~~; and

(d) ~~where~~ if the seller is required or authorized to ship the goods on credit, the credit period runs from the time of shipment but ~~post-dating~~ postdating the invoice or delaying its dispatch will correspondingly delay the starting of the credit period.

§ 2–311. Options and Cooperation Respecting Performance.

(1) An agreement for sale which is otherwise sufficiently definite ~~(Subsection (3) of Section 2–204)~~ (Section 2–204(3)) to be a contract is not made invalid by the fact that it leaves particulars of performance to be specified by one of the parties. Any such specification must be made in good faith and within limits set by commercial reasonableness.

(2) Unless otherwise agreed, specifications relating to assortment of the goods are at the

buyer's option and ~~except as otherwise provided in subsections (1)(c) and (3) of Section 2-319~~ specifications or arrangements relating to shipment are at the seller's option.

(3) ~~Where such~~ If the specification would materially affect the other party's performance but ~~is~~ not seasonably made or ~~where~~ if one party's cooperation is necessary to the agreed performance of the other but is not seasonably forthcoming, the other party in addition to all other remedies:

(a) is excused for any resulting delay in ~~his own~~ that party's performance; and

(b) may also either proceed to perform in any reasonable manner or after the time for a material part of ~~his~~ that party's ~~own~~ performance treat the failure to specify or to cooperate as a breach by failure to deliver or accept the goods.

§ 2-312. Warranty of Title and Against Infringement; Buyer's Obligation Against Infringement.

(1) Subject to subsection ~~(2)~~(3), there is in a contract for sale a warranty by the seller that:

(a) the title conveyed shall be ~~good,~~ good and its transfer rightful and shall not unreasonably expose the buyer to litigation because of any colorable claim to or interest in the goods; and

(b) the goods shall be delivered free from any security interest or other lien or encumbrance of which the buyer at the time of contracting has no knowledge.

~~(2) A warranty under subsection (1) will be excluded or modified only by specific language or by circumstances which give the buyer reason to know that the person selling does not claim title in himself or that it is purporting to sell only such right or title as it or a third person may have.~~

~~(3) Unless otherwise agreed a seller who is a merchant regularly dealing in goods of the kind warrants that the goods shall be delivered free of the rightful claim of any third person by way of infringement or the like but a buyer who furnishes specifications to the seller must hold the seller harmless against any such claim which arises out of compliance with the specifications.~~

(2) Unless otherwise agreed, a seller that is a merchant regularly dealing in goods of the kind warrants that the goods shall be delivered free of the rightful claim of any third person by way of infringement or the like but a buyer that furnishes specifications to the seller must hold the seller harmless against any such claim that arises out of compliance with the specifications.

(3) A warranty under this section may be disclaimed or modified only by specific language or by circumstances that give the buyer reason to know that the seller does not claim title, that the seller is purporting to sell only the right or title as the seller or a third person may have, or that the seller is selling subject to any claims of infringement or the like.

§ 2-313. Express Warranties by Affirmation, Promise, Description, Sample; Remedial Promise.

(1) In this section, "immediate buyer" means a buyer that enters into a contract with the seller.

~~(1)~~ (2) Express warranties by the seller to the immediate buyer are created as follows:

(a) Any affirmation of fact or promise made by the seller ~~to the buyer~~ which relates to the goods and becomes part of the basis of the bargain creates an express warranty that the goods shall conform to the affirmation or promise.

(b) Any description of the goods which is made part of the basis of the bargain creates an express warranty that the goods shall conform to the description.

(c) Any sample or model ~~which~~ that is made part of the basis of the bargain creates an express warranty that the whole of the goods shall conform to the sample or model.

~~(2)~~ (3) It is not necessary to the creation of an express warranty that the seller use formal words such as "warrant" or "guarantee" or that ~~he~~ the seller have a specific intention to make a warranty, but an affirmation merely of the value of the goods or a statement purporting to be merely the seller's opinion or commendation of the goods does not create a warranty.

(4) Any remedial promise made by the seller to the immediate buyer creates an obligation that the promise will be performed upon the happening of the specified event.

§ 2-313A. Obligation to Remote Purchaser Created by Record Packaged With or Accompanying Goods.

(1) In this section:

(a) "Immediate buyer" means a buyer that enters into a contract with the seller.

(b) "Remote purchaser" means a person that buys or leases goods from an immediate buyer or other person in the normal chain of distribution.

(2) This section applies only to new goods and goods sold or leased as new goods in a transaction of purchase in the normal chain of distribution.

(3) If in a record packaged with or accompanying the goods the seller makes an affirmation of fact or promise that relates to the goods, provides a description that relates to the goods, or makes a remedial promise, and the seller reasonably expects the record to be, and the record is, furnished to the remote purchaser, the seller has an obligation to the remote purchaser that:

(a) the goods will conform to the affirmation of fact, promise, or description unless a reasonable person in the position of the remote purchaser would not believe that the affirmation of fact, promise, or description created an obligation; and

(b) the seller will perform the remedial promise.

(4) It is not necessary to the creation of an obligation under this section that the seller use formal words such as "warrant" or "guarantee" or that the seller have a specific intention to undertake an obligation, but an affirmation merely of the value of the goods or a statement purporting to be merely the seller's opinion or commendation of the goods does not create an obligation.

(5) The following rules apply to the remedies for breach of an obligation created under this section:

(a) The seller may modify or limit the remedies available to the remote purchaser if the modification or limitation is furnished to the remote purchaser no later than the time of purchase or if the modification or limitation is contained in the record that contains the affirmation of fact, promise, or description.

(b) Subject to a modification or limitation of remedy, a seller in breach is liable for incidental or consequential damages under Section 2–715, but not for lost profits.

(c) The remote purchaser may recover as damages for breach of a seller's obligation arising under subsection (3) the loss resulting in the ordinary course of events as determined in any reasonable manner.

(6) An obligation that is not a remedial promise is breached if the goods did not conform to the affirmation of fact, promise, or description creating the obligation when the goods left the seller's control.

§ 2–313B. Obligation to Remote Purchaser Created by Communication to the Public.

(1) In this section:

(a) "Immediate buyer" means a buyer that enters into a contract with the seller.

(b) "Remote purchaser" means a person that buys or leases goods from an immediate buyer or other person in the normal chain of distribution.

(2) This section applies only to new goods and goods sold or leased as new goods in a transaction of purchase in the normal chain of distribution.

(3) If in an advertisement or a similar communication to the public a seller makes an affirmation of fact or promise that relates to the goods, provides a description that relates to the goods, or makes a remedial promise, and the remote purchaser enters into a transaction of purchase with knowledge of and with the expectation that the goods will conform to the affirmation of fact, promise, or description, or that the seller will perform the remedial promise, the seller has an obligation to the remote purchaser that:

(a) the goods will conform to the affirmation of fact, promise, or description unless a reasonable person in the position of the remote purchaser would not believe that the affirmation of fact, promise, or description created an obligation; and

(b) the seller will perform the remedial promise.

(4) It is not necessary to the creation of an obligation under this section that the seller use formal words such as "warrant" or "guarantee" or that the seller have a specific intention to undertake an obligation, but an affirmation merely of the value of the goods or a statement purporting to be merely the seller's opinion or commendation of the goods does not create an obligation.

(5) The following rules apply to the remedies for breach of an obligation created under this section:

(a) The seller may modify or limit the remedies available to the remote purchaser if the modification or limitation is furnished to the remote purchaser no later than the time of purchase. The modification or limitation may be furnished as part of the communication that contains the affirmation of fact, promise, or description.

(b) Subject to a modification or limitation of remedy, a seller in breach is liable for incidental or consequential damages under Section 2–715, but not for lost profits.

(c) The remote purchaser may recover as damages for breach of a seller's obligation arising under subsection (3) the loss resulting in the ordinary course of events as determined in any reasonable manner.

(6) An obligation that is not a remedial promise is breached if the goods did not conform to the affirmation of fact, promise, or description creating the obligation when the goods left the seller's control.

§ 2–314. Implied Warranty: Merchantability; Usage of Trade.

(1) Unless excluded or modified (Section 2–316), a warranty that the goods shall be merchantable is implied in a contract for their sale if the seller is a merchant with respect to goods of that kind. Under this section the serving for value of food or drink to be consumed either on the premises or elsewhere is a sale.

(2) Goods to be merchantable must be at least such as:

(a) pass without objection in the trade under the contract description; and

(b) in the case of fungible goods, are of fair average quality within the description; and

(c) are fit for the ordinary purposes for which such goods of that description are used; and

(d) run, within the variations permitted by the agreement, of even kind, quality and quantity within each unit and among all units involved; and

(e) are adequately contained, packaged, and labeled as the agreement may require; and

(f) conform to the promise or affirmations of fact made on the container or label if any.

(3) Unless excluded or modified (Section 2–316) other implied warranties may arise from course of dealing or usage of trade.

§ 2–316. Exclusion or Modification of Warranties.

(1) Words or conduct relevant to the creation of an express warranty and words or conduct tending to negate or limit warranty shall be construed wherever reasonable as consistent with each other; but subject to the provisions of this Article on parol or extrinsic evidence (Section 2–202) Section 2–202, negation or limitation is inoperative to the extent that such construction is unreasonable.

(2) Subject to subsection (3), to exclude or modify the implied warranty of merchantability or any part of it in a consumer contract the language must be in a record, be conspicuous, and state "The seller undertakes no responsibility for the quality of the goods except as otherwise provided in this contract," and in any other contract the language must mention merchantability and in case of a writing record must be conspicuous, and to. Subject to subsection (3), to exclude or modify the implied warranty of fitness, the exclusion must be by a writing in a record and be conspicuous. Language to exclude all implied warranties of fitness in a consumer contract must state "The seller assumes no responsibility that the goods will be fit for any particular purpose for which you may be buying these goods, except as otherwise provided in the contract," and in any other contract the language is sufficient if it states, for example, that "There are no warranties which that extend beyond the description on the face hereof." Language that satisfies the requirements of this subsection for the exclusion or modification of a warranty in a consumer contract also satisfies the requirements for any other contract.

(3) Notwithstanding subsection (2):

(a) unless the circumstances indicate otherwise, all implied warranties are excluded by expressions like "as is", "with all faults" or other language which that in common understanding calls the buyer's attention to the exclusion of warranties and, makes plain that there is no implied warranty, and, in a consumer contract evidenced by a record, is set forth conspicuously in the record; and

(b) when if the buyer before entering into the contract has examined the goods or the sample or model as fully as he desired or has refused to examine the goods after a demand by the seller there is no implied warranty with regard to defects ~~which~~ that an examination ~~ought~~ in the circumstances ~~to~~ should have revealed to ~~him~~ the buyer; and

(c) an implied warranty ~~can~~ may also be excluded or modified by course of dealing or course of performance or usage of trade.

(4) Remedies for breach of warranty ~~can~~ may be limited in accordance with ~~the provisions of this article on liquidation or limitation of damages and on contractual modification of remedy (Sections 2–718 and 2–719)~~ Sections 2–718 and 2–719.

§ 2–318. ~~Third Party~~ Third-party Beneficiaries of Warranties ~~Express or Implied~~ and Obligations.

(1) In this section:

(a) "Immediate buyer" means a buyer that enters into a contract with the seller.

(b) "Remote purchaser" means a person that buys or leases goods from an immediate buyer or other person in the normal chain of distribution.

Alternative A to subsection (2)

(2) ~~A seller's warranty whether express or implied extends to any natural person who is in the family or household of his buyer or who is a guest in his home if it is reasonable to expect that such person may use, consume or be affected by the goods and who is injured in person by breach of the warranty.~~ A seller's warranty to an immediate buyer, whether express or implied, a seller's remedial promise to an immediate buyer, or a seller's obligation to a remote purchaser under Section 2–313A or 2–313B extends to any individual who is in the family or household of the immediate buyer or the remote purchaser or who is a guest in the home of either if it is reasonable to expect that the person may use, consume, or be affected by the goods and who is injured in person by breach of the warranty, remedial promise, or obligation. A seller may not exclude or limit the operation of this section.

Alternative B to subsection (2)

(2) ~~A seller's warranty whether express or implied extends to any natural person who may reasonably be expected to use, consume or be affected by the goods and who is injured in person by breach of the warranty.~~ A seller's warranty to an immediate buyer, whether express or implied, a seller's remedial promise to an immediate buyer, or a seller's obligation to a remote purchaser under Section 2–313A or 2–313B extends to any individual who may reasonably be expected to use, consume, or be affected by the goods and who is injured in person by breach of the warranty, remedial promise, or obligation. A seller may not exclude or limit the operation of this section.

Alternative C to subsection (2)

(2) ~~A seller's warranty whether express or implied extends to any person who may reasonably be expected to use, consume or be affected by the goods and who is injured by breach of the warranty.~~ A seller's warranty to an immediate buyer, whether express or implied, a seller's remedial promise to an immediate buyer, or a seller's obligation to a remote purchaser under Section 2–313A or 2–313B extends to any person that may reasonably be expected to use, consume, or be affected by the goods and that is injured by breach of the warranty, remedial promise, or obligation. A seller may not exclude or limit the operation of this section with respect to injury to the person of an individual to whom the warranty, remedial promise, or obligation extends.

§ 2–319. F.O.B. and F.A.S. Terms Reserved.

~~(1) Unless otherwise agreed the term F.O.B. (which means "free on board") at a named place, even though used only in connection with the stated price, is a delivery term under which~~

~~(a) when the term is F.O.B. the place of shipment, the seller must at that place ship the goods in the manner provided in this Article (Section 2–504) and bear the expense and risk of putting them into the possession of the carrier; or~~

~~(b) when the term is F.O.B. the place of destination, the seller must at his own expense and risk transport the goods to that place and there tender delivery of them in the manner provided in this Article (Section 2–503);~~

~~(c) when under either (a) or (b) the term is also F.O.B. vessel, car or other vehicle, the seller must in addition at his own expense and risk load the goods on board. If the term is F.O.B. vessel the buyer must name the vessel and in an appropriate case the seller must comply with the provisions of this Article on the form of bill of lading (Section 2–323).~~

(2) Unless otherwise agreed the term F.A.S. vessel (which means "free alongside") at a named port, even though used only in connection with the stated price, is a delivery term under which the seller must

(a) at his own expense and risk deliver the goods alongside the vessel in the manner usual in that port or on a dock designated and provided by the buyer; and

(b) obtain and tender a receipt for the goods in exchange for which the carrier is under a duty to issue a bill of lading.

(3) Unless otherwise agreed in any case falling within subsection (1)(a) or(c) or subsection (2) the buyer must seasonably give any needed instructions for making delivery, including when the term is F.A.S. or F.O.B. the loading berth of the vessel and in an appropriate case its name and sailing date. The seller may treat the failure of needed instructions as a failure of cooperation under this Article (Section 2–311). He may also at his option move the goods in any reasonable manner preparatory to delivery or shipment.

(4) Under the term F.O.B. vessel or F.A.S. unless otherwise agreed the buyer must make payment against tender of the required documents and the seller may not tender nor the buyer demand delivery of the goods in substitution for the documents.

§ 2–320.   C.I.F. AND C. & F. Terms Reserved.

(1) The term C.I.F. means that the price includes in a lump sum the cost of the goods and the insurance and freight to the named destination. The term C. & F. or C.F. means that the price so includes cost and freight to the named destination.

(2) Unless otherwise agreed and even though used only in connection with the stated price and destination, the term C.I.F. destination or its equivalent requires the seller at his own expense and risk to

(a) put the goods into the possession of a carrier at the port for shipment and obtain a negotiable bill or bills of lading covering the entire transportation to the named destination; and

(b) load the goods and obtain a receipt from the carrier (which may be contained in the bill of lading) showing that the freight has been paid or provided for; and

(c) obtain a policy or certificate of insurance, including any war risk insurance, of a kind and on terms then current at the port of shipment in the usual amount, in the currency of the contract, shown to cover the same goods covered by the bill of lading and providing for payment of loss to the order of the buyer or for the account of whom it may concern; but the seller may add to the price the amount of the premium for any such war risk insurance; and

(d) prepare an invoice of the goods and procure any other documents required to effect shipment or to comply with the contract; and

(e) forward and tender with commercial promptness all the documents in due form and with any indorsement necessary to perfect the buyer's rights.

(3) Unless otherwise agreed the term C. & F. or its equivalent has the same effect and imposes upon the seller the same obligations and risks as a C.I.F. term except the obligation as to insurance.

(4) Under the term C.I.F. or C. & F. unless otherwise agreed the buyer must make payment against tender of the required documents and the seller may not tender nor the buyer demand delivery of the goods in substitution for the documents.

§ 2–321.   C.I.F. OR C. & F.: "Net Landed Weights"; "Payment on Arrival"; Warranty of Condition on Arrival Reserved.

Under a contract containing a term C.I.F. or C. & F.

(1) Where the price is based on or is to be adjusted according to "net landed weights", "delivered weights", "out turn" quantity or quality or the like, unless otherwise agreed the seller must reasonably estimate the price. The payment due on tender of the documents called for by the contract is the amount so estimated, but after final adjustment of the price a settlement must be made with commercial promptness.

(2) An agreement described in subsection (1) or any warranty of quality or condition of the goods on arrival places upon the seller the risk of ordinary deterioration, shrinkage and the like in transportation but has no effect on the place or time of identification to the contract for sale or delivery or on the passing of the risk of loss.

(3) Unless otherwise agreed where the contract provides for payment on or after arrival of the goods the seller must before payment allow such preliminary inspection as is feasible; but if the goods are lost delivery of the documents and payment are due when the goods should have arrived.

§ 2–322. Delivery "Ex-ship" Reserved.

(1) Unless otherwise agreed a term for delivery of goods "ex-ship" (which means from the carrying vessel) or in equivalent language is not restricted to a particular ship and requires delivery from a ship which has reached a place at the named port of destination where goods of the kind are usually discharged.

(2) Under such a term unless otherwise agreed

(a) the seller must discharge all liens arising out of the carriage and furnish the buyer with a direction which puts the carrier under a duty to deliver the goods; and

(b) the risk of loss does not pass to the buyer until the goods leave the ship's tackle or are otherwise properly unloaded.

§ 2–323. Form of Bill of Lading Required in Overseas Shipment; "Overseas" Reserved.

(1) Where the contract contemplates overseas shipment and contains a term C.I.F. or C. & F. or F.O.B. vessel, the seller unless otherwise agreed must obtain a negotiable bill of lading stating that the goods have been loaded in board or, in the case of a term C.I.F. or C. & F., received for shipment.

(2) Where in a case within subsection (1) a bill of lading has been issued in a set of parts, unless otherwise agreed if the documents are not to be sent from abroad the buyer may demand tender of the full set; otherwise only one part of the bill of lading need be tendered. Even if the agreement expressly requires a full set

(a) due tender of a single part is acceptable within the provisions of this Article on cure of improper delivery (subsection (1) of Section 2–508); and

(b) even though the full set is demanded, if the documents are sent from abroad the person tendering an incomplete set may nevertheless require payment upon furnishing an indemnity which the buyer in good faith deems adequate.

(3) A shipment by water or by air or a contract contemplating such shipment is "overseas" insofar as by usage of trade or agreement it is subject to the commercial, financing or shipping practices characteristic of international deep water commerce.

§ 2–324. "No Arrival, No Sale" Term Reserved.

Under a term "no arrival, no sale" or terms of like meaning, unless otherwise agreed,

(a) the seller must properly ship conforming goods and if they arrive by any means he must tender them on arrival but he assumes no obligation that the goods will arrive unless he has caused the non-arrival; and

(b) where without fault of the seller the goods are in part lost or have so deteriorated as no longer to conform to the contract or arrive after the contract time, the buyer may proceed as if there had been casualty to identified goods (Section 2–613).

§ 2–325. "Letter of Credit" Term; "Confirmed Credit" Failure to Pay by Agreed Letter of Credit.

(1) Failure of the buyer seasonably to furnish an agreed letter of credit is a breach of the contract for sale.

(2) The delivery to seller of a proper letter of credit suspends the buyer's obligation to pay. If the letter of credit is dishonored, the seller may on seasonable notification to the buyer require payment directly from him.

(3) Unless otherwise agreed the term "letter of credit" or "banker's credit" in a contract for sale means an irrevocable credit issued by a financing agency of good repute and, where the shipment is overseas, of good international repute. The term "confirmed credit" means that the credit must also carry the direct obligation of such an agency which does business in the seller's financial market.

If the parties agree that the primary method of payment will be by letter of credit, the following rules apply:

(a) The buyer's obligation to pay is suspended by seasonable delivery to the seller of a letter of credit issued or confirmed by a financing agency of good repute in which the issuer and any confirmer undertake to pay against presentation of documents that evidence delivery of the goods.

(b) Failure of a party seasonably to furnish a letter of credit as agreed is a breach of the contract for sale.

(c) If the letter of credit is dishonored or repudiated, the seller, on seasonable notification, may require payment directly from the buyer.

§ 2–326. Sale on Approval and Sale or Return; ~~Consignment Sales and Rights of Creditors.~~

(1) Unless otherwise agreed, if delivered goods may be returned by the buyer even ~~though~~ if they conform to the contract, the transaction is:

(a) a "sale on approval" if the goods are delivered primarily for ~~use,~~ use; and

(b) a "sale or return" if the goods are delivered primarily for resale.

(2) Goods held on approval are not subject to the claims of the buyer's creditors until acceptance; goods held on sale or return are subject to such claims while in the buyer's possession.

(3) Any "or return" term of a contract for sale is to be treated as a separate contract for sale ~~within the statute of frauds section of this Article (Section 2–201)~~ under Section 2–201 and as contradicting the sale aspect of the contract ~~within the provisions of this Article on parol or extrinsic evidence (Section 2–202)~~ under Section 2–202.

§ 2–328. Sale by Auction.

(1) In a sale by auction, if goods are put up in lots, each lot is the subject of a separate sale.

(2) A sale by auction is complete when the auctioneer so announces by the fall of the hammer or in other customary manner. ~~Where~~ If a bid is made ~~while the hammer is falling in acceptance of~~ during the process of completing the sale but before a prior bid is accepted, the auctioneer ~~may in his~~ has discretion to reopen the bidding

or to declare the goods sold under the prior bid ~~on which the hammer was falling~~.

(3) ~~Such a sale is with reserve unless the goods are in explicit terms put up without reserve. In an auction with reserve the auctioneer may withdraw the goods at any time until he announces completion of the sale. In an auction without reserve, after the auctioneer calls for bids on an article or lot, that article or lot cannot be withdrawn unless no bid is made within a reasonable time. In either case a bidder may retract his bid until the auctioneer's announcement of completion of the sale, but a bidder's retraction does not revive any previous bid.~~ A sale by auction is subject to the seller's right to withdraw the goods unless at the time the goods are put up or during the course of the auction it is announced in express terms that the right to withdraw the goods is not reserved. In an auction in which the right to withdraw the goods is reserved, the auctioneer may withdraw the goods at any time until completion of the sale is announced by the auctioneer. In an auction in which the right to withdraw the goods is not reserved, after the auctioneer calls for bids on an article or lot, the article or lot may not be withdrawn unless no bid is made within a reasonable time. In either case a bidder may retract a bid until the auctioneer's announcement of completion of the sale, but a bidder's retraction does not revive any previous bid.

(4) If the auctioneer knowingly receives a bid on the seller's behalf or the seller makes or procures such a bid, and notice has not been given that liberty for such bidding is reserved, the buyer may at ~~his~~ the buyer's option avoid the sale or take the goods at the price of the last ~~good faith~~ good-faith bid prior to the completion of the sale. This subsection shall not apply to any bid at ~~a forced sale~~ an auction required by law.

PART 4

TITLE, CREDITORS, AND GOOD–FAITH PURCHASERS

§ 2–401. Passing of Title; Reservation for Security; Limited Application of this Section.

Each provision of this Article with regard to the rights, obligations, and remedies of the seller,

the buyer, purchasers, or other third parties applies irrespective of title to the goods except where the provision refers to such title. Insofar as situations are not covered by the other provisions of this Article and matters concerning title become material, the following rules apply:

(1) Title to goods cannot pass under a contract for sale prior to their identification to the contract (Section 2–501), and unless otherwise explicitly agreed, the buyer acquires by their identification a special property as limited by this Act. Any retention or reservation by the seller of the title (property) in goods shipped or delivered to the buyer is limited in effect to a reservation of a security interest. Subject to these provisions and to ~~the provisions of the Article on Secured Transactions (Article 9)~~ Article 9, title to goods passes from the seller to the buyer in any manner and on any conditions explicitly agreed on by the parties.

(2) Unless otherwise explicitly agreed title passes to the buyer at the time and place at which the seller completes ~~his~~ performance with reference to the ~~physical~~ delivery of the goods, despite any reservation of a security interest and even ~~though~~ if a document of title is to be delivered at a different time or place; and in particular and despite any reservation of a security interest by the bill of lading:

(a) if the contract requires or authorizes the seller to send the goods to the buyer but does not require ~~him~~ the seller to deliver them at destination, title passes to the buyer at the time and place of shipment; but

(b) if the contract requires delivery at destination, title passes on tender there.

(3) Unless otherwise explicitly agreed, ~~where~~ if delivery is to be made without moving the ~~goods,~~ goods:

(a) if the seller is to deliver a tangible document of title, title passes at the time when and the place where ~~he~~ the seller delivers ~~such documents~~ the document, and if the seller is to deliver an electronic document of title, title passes when the seller delivers the document; or

(b) if the goods are at the time of contracting already identified and no documents of title are to be delivered, title passes at the time and place of contracting.

(4) A rejection or other refusal by the buyer to receive or retain the goods, whether or not justified, or a justified revocation of acceptance revests title to the goods in the seller. Such revesting occurs by operation of law and is not a "sale".

§ 2–402. Rights of Seller's Creditors Against Sold Goods.

(1) Except as provided in subsections (2) and (3), rights of unsecured creditors of the seller with respect to goods ~~which~~ that have been identified to a contract for sale are subject to the buyer's rights to recover the goods under ~~this Article (Sections 2–502 and 2–716)~~ Sections 2–502 and 2–716.

(2) A creditor of the seller may treat a sale or an identification of goods to a contract for sale as void if as against ~~him~~ the creditor a retention of possession by the seller is fraudulent under any rule of law of the state where the goods are ~~situated, except that~~ situated. However, retention of possession in good faith and current course of trade by a merchant-seller for a commercially reasonable time after a sale or identification is not fraudulent.

(3) ~~Nothing~~ Except as otherwise provided in Section 2–403(2), nothing in this Article shall be deemed to impair the rights of creditors of the seller:

(a) under ~~the provisions of the Article on Secured Transactions (Article 9)~~ Article 9; or

(b) ~~where~~ if identification to the contract or delivery is made not in current course of trade but in satisfaction of or as security for a ~~pre-existing~~ preexisting claim for money, security, or the like and is made under circumstances ~~which~~ that under any rule of law of the state where the goods are situated would apart from this Article constitute the transaction a fraudulent transfer or voidable preference.

§ 2–403. Power to Transfer; Good Faith Purchase of Goods; "Entrusting".

(1) A purchaser of goods acquires all title ~~which his~~ that the purchaser's transferor had or had power to transfer except that a purchaser of a limited interest acquires rights only to the extent of the interest purchased. A person with voidable title has power to transfer a good title to a ~~good faith~~ good-faith purchaser for value. ~~When~~ If goods have been delivered under a transaction of purchase, the purchaser has such power even ~~though~~ if:

(a) the transferor was deceived as to the identity of the ~~purchaser, or~~ purchaser;

(b) the delivery was in exchange for a check ~~which~~ that is later ~~dishonored, or~~ dishonored;

(c) it was agreed that the transaction was to be a "cash ~~sale",~~ sale"; or

(d) the delivery was procured through criminal fraud ~~punishable as larcenous under the criminal law~~.

(2) Any entrusting ~~of possession~~ of goods to a merchant ~~who~~ that deals in goods of that kind gives ~~him~~ the merchant power to transfer ~~all rights of the entruster~~ all of the entruster's rights to the goods and to transfer the goods free of any interest of the entruster to a buyer in ordinary course of business.

(3) "Entrusting" includes any delivery and any acquiescence in retention of possession regardless of any condition expressed between the parties to the delivery or acquiescence and regardless of whether the procurement of the entrusting or the possessor's disposition of the goods ~~have been such as to be larcenous~~ was punishable under the criminal law.

[*Legislative Note: If a state adopts the repealer of Article 6—Bulk Transfers (Alternative A), subsection (4) should read as follows:*]

(4) The rights of other purchasers of goods and of lien creditors are governed by ~~the Articles on Secured Transactions (Article 9) and Documents of Title (Article 7)~~ Articles 7 and 9.

[*Legislative Note: If a state adopts revised Article 6—Bulk Sales (Alternative B), subsection (4) should read as follows:*]

(4) The rights of other purchasers of goods and of lien creditors are governed by ~~the Articles on Secured Transactions (Article 9), Bulk Sales (Article 6) and Documents of Title (Article 7)~~ Articles 6, 7, and 9.

PART 5

PERFORMANCE

§ 2–501. Insurable Interest in Goods; Manner of Identification of Goods.

(1) The buyer obtains a special property and an insurable interest in goods by identification of existing goods as goods to which the contract refers even ~~though~~ if the goods so identified are ~~non-conforming~~ nonconforming and ~~he~~ the buyer has an option to return or reject them. Such identification ~~can~~ may be made at any time and in any manner explicitly agreed to by the parties. In the absence of explicit agreement identification occurs:

(a) when the contract is made if it is for the sale of goods already existing and identified;

(b) if the contract is for the sale of future goods other than those described in paragraph (c), when goods are shipped, marked, or otherwise designated by the seller as goods to which the contract refers;

(c) when the crops are planted or otherwise become growing crops or the young are conceived if the contract is for the sale of unborn young to be born within ~~twelve~~ 12 months after contracting or for the sale of crops to be harvested within ~~twelve~~ 12 months or the next normal harvest season after contracting whichever is longer.

(2) The seller retains an insurable interest in goods so long as title to or any security interest in the goods remains in ~~him and where~~ the seller. If the identification is by the seller alone, ~~he~~ the seller may until default or insolvency or notification to the buyer that the identification is final substitute other goods for those identified.

(3) Nothing in this section impairs any insurable interest recognized under any other statute or rule of law.

§ 2–502. Buyer's Right to Goods on Seller's Insolvency, Repudiation, or Failure to Deliver.

(1) Subject to subsections (2) and (3) and even ~~though~~ if the goods have not been shipped, a buyer ~~who~~ that has paid a part or all of the price of goods in which ~~he~~ the buyer has a special property under ~~the provisions of the immediately preceding section~~ Section 2–501 may on making and keeping good a tender of any unpaid portion of their price recover them from the seller if:

(a) in the case of goods bought ~~for personal, family, or household purposes~~ by a consumer, the seller repudiates or fails to deliver as required by the contract; or

(b) in all cases, the seller becomes insolvent within 10 days after receipt of the first installment on their price.

(2) The buyer's right to recover the goods under subsection (1) vests upon acquisition of a special property, even if the seller had not then repudiated or failed to deliver.

(3) If the identification creating ~~his~~ a special property has been made by ~~the buyer he~~ the buyer, the buyer acquires the right to recover the goods only if they conform to the contract for sale.

§ 2–503. Manner of Seller's Tender of Delivery.

(1) Tender of delivery requires that the seller put and hold conforming goods at the buyer's disposition and give the buyer any notification reasonably necessary to enable ~~him~~ the buyer to take delivery. The manner, time, and place for tender are determined by the agreement and this Article, and in particular:

(a) tender must be at a reasonable hour, and if it is of goods they must be kept available for the period reasonably necessary to enable the buyer to take possession; but

(b) unless otherwise agreed the buyer must furnish facilities reasonably suited to the receipt of the goods.

(2) ~~Where~~ If the case is within ~~the next section respecting shipment~~ Section 2–504, tender requires that the seller comply with its provisions.

(3) ~~Where~~ If the seller is required to deliver at a particular destination, tender requires that ~~he~~ the seller comply with subsection (1) and also in any appropriate case tender documents as described in subsections (4) and (5) of this section.

(4) ~~Where~~ If goods are in the possession of a bailee and are to be delivered without being moved:

(a) tender requires that the seller either tender a negotiable document of title covering such goods or procure acknowledgment by the bailee to the buyer of the buyer's right to possession of the goods; but

(b) tender to the buyer of a ~~non-negotiable~~ nonnegotiable document of title or of ~~a written direction to~~ a record directing the bailee to deliver is sufficient tender unless the buyer seasonably objects, and except as otherwise provided in Article 9 receipt by the bailee of notification of the buyer's rights fixes those rights as against the bailee and all third persons; but risk of loss of the goods and of any failure by the bailee to

honor the ~~non-negotiable~~ nonnegotiable document of title or to obey the direction remains on the seller until the buyer has had a reasonable time to present the document or ~~direction, and a refusal~~ direction. Refusal by the bailee to honor the document or to obey the direction defeats the tender.

(5) ~~Where~~ If the contract requires the seller to deliver documents:

(a) ~~he~~ the seller must tender all such documents in correct form~~, except as provided in this Article with respect to bills of lading in a set (subsection (2) of Section 2–323)~~; and

(b) tender through customary banking channels is sufficient and dishonor of a draft accompanying or associated with the documents constitutes ~~non-acceptance~~ nonacceptance or rejection.

§ 2–504. Shipment by Seller.

~~Where~~ If the seller is required or authorized to send the goods to the buyer and the contract does not require ~~him~~ the seller to deliver them at a particular destination, then unless otherwise agreed ~~he~~ the seller must:

(a) put ~~the~~ conforming goods in the possession of ~~such~~ a carrier and make ~~such~~ a proper contract for their transportation, ~~as may be reasonable~~ having regard to the nature of the goods and other circumstances of the case; ~~and~~

(b) obtain and promptly deliver or tender in due form any document necessary to enable the buyer to obtain possession of the goods or otherwise required by the agreement or by usage of trade; and

(c) promptly notify the buyer of the shipment.

Failure to notify the buyer under paragraph (c) or to make a proper contract under paragraph (a) is a ground for rejection only if material delay or loss ensues.

§ 2–505. Seller's Shipment under Reservation.

(1) ~~Where~~ If the seller has identified goods to the contract by or before shipment:

(a) ~~his~~ The seller's procurement of a negotiable bill of lading to ~~his~~ the seller's own order or otherwise reserves in ~~him~~ the seller a security interest in the goods. ~~His~~ The seller's procurement of the bill to the order of a financing agency or of the buyer indicates in addition only the seller's expectation of transferring that interest to the person named.

(b) ~~a non-negotiable~~ A nonnegotiable bill of lading to ~~himself~~ the seller or ~~his~~ the seller's nominee reserves possession of the goods as ~~security but~~ security. However, ~~except in a case of conditional delivery~~ unless a seller has a right to reclaim the goods under ~~(subsection (2) of Section 2-507)~~ Section 2–507(2) a ~~non-negotiable~~ nonnegotiable bill of lading naming the buyer as consignee reserves no security interest even ~~though~~ if the seller retains possession or control of the bill of lading.

(2) ~~When~~ If shipment by the seller with reservation of a security interest is in violation of the contract for sale, it constitutes an improper contract for transportation ~~within the preceding section~~ under Section 2–504 but impairs neither the rights given to the buyer by shipment and identification of the goods to the contract nor the seller's powers as a holder of a negotiable document of title.

§ 2–506. Rights of Financing Agency.

(1) ~~A~~ Except as otherwise provided in Article 5, a financing agency by paying or purchasing for value a draft ~~which~~ that relates to a shipment of goods acquires to the extent of the payment or purchase and in addition to its own rights under the draft and any document of title securing it any rights of the shipper in the goods including the right to stop delivery and the shipper's right to have the draft honored by the buyer.

(2) The right to reimbursement of a financing agency ~~which~~ that has in good faith honored or purchased the draft under commitment to or authority from the buyer is not impaired by subsequent discovery of defects with reference to any relevant document ~~which~~ that was apparently regular ~~on its face~~.

§ 2–507. Effect of Seller's Tender; Delivery on Condition.

(1) Tender of delivery is a condition to the buyer's duty to accept the goods and, unless otherwise agreed, to ~~his~~ the buyer's duty to pay for them. Tender entitles the seller to acceptance of the goods and to payment according to the contract.

(2) ~~Where~~ If payment is due and demanded on the delivery to the buyer of goods or documents

of title, ~~his right as against the seller to retain or dispose of them is conditional upon his making the payment due~~ the seller may reclaim the goods delivered upon a demand made within a reasonable time after the seller discovers or should have discovered that payment was not made.

(3) The seller's right to reclaim under subsection (2) is subject to the rights of a buyer in ordinary course of business or other good-faith purchaser for value under Section 2–403.

§ 2–508. Cure by Seller of Improper Tender or Delivery; Replacement.

~~(1) Where any tender or delivery by the seller is rejected because non-conforming and the time for performance has not yet expired, the seller may seasonably notify the buyer of his intention to cure and may then within the contract time make a conforming delivery.~~

~~(2) Where the buyer rejects a non-conforming tender which the seller had reasonable grounds to believe would be acceptable with or without money allowance the seller may if he seasonably notifies the buyer have a further reasonable time to substitute a conforming tender.~~

(1) If the buyer rejects goods or a tender of delivery under Section 2–601 or 2–612 or, except in a consumer contract, justifiably revokes acceptance under Section 2–608(1)(b) and the agreed time for performance has not expired, a seller that has performed in good faith, upon seasonable notice to the buyer and at the seller's own expense, may cure the breach of contract by making a conforming tender of delivery within the agreed time. The seller shall compensate the buyer for all of the buyer's reasonable expenses caused by the seller's breach of contract and subsequent cure.

(2) If the buyer rejects goods or a tender of delivery under Section 2–601 or 2–612 or, except in a consumer contract, justifiably revokes acceptance under Section 2–608(1)(b) and the agreed time for performance has expired, a seller that has performed in good faith, upon seasonable notice to the buyer and at the seller's own expense, may cure the breach of contract, if the cure is appropriate and timely under the circumstances, by making a tender of conforming goods. The seller shall compensate the buyer for all of

the buyer's reasonable expenses caused by the seller's breach of contract and subsequent cure.

§ 2–509. Risk of Loss in the Absence of Breach.

(1) ~~Where~~ If the contract requires or authorizes the seller to ship the goods by carrier:

(a) if it does not require ~~him~~ the seller to deliver them at a particular destination, the risk of loss passes to the buyer when the goods are ~~duly~~ delivered to the carrier even ~~though~~ if the shipment is under reservation (Section 2–505); but

(b) if it does require ~~him~~ the seller to deliver them at a particular destination and the goods are there ~~duly~~ tendered while in the possession of the carrier, the risk of loss passes to the buyer when the goods are there ~~duly~~ so tendered as to enable the buyer to take delivery.

(2) ~~Where~~ If the goods are held by a bailee to be delivered without being moved, the risk of loss passes to the buyer:

(a) on ~~his~~ the buyer's receipt of possession or control of a negotiable document of title covering the goods; ~~or~~

(b) on acknowledgment by the bailee to the buyer of the buyer's right to possession of the goods; or

(c) after ~~his~~ the buyer's receipt of possession or control of a ~~non-negotiable~~ nonnegotiable document of title or other ~~written~~ direction to deliver in a record, as provided in ~~subsection (4)(b) of~~ Section 2–503(4)(b).

(3) In any case not within subsection (1) or (2), the risk of loss passes to the buyer on ~~his~~ the buyer's receipt of the goods ~~if the seller is a merchant; otherwise the risk passes to the buyer on tender of delivery~~.

(4) The provisions of this section are subject to contrary agreement of the parties and to ~~the provisions of this Article on sale on approval (Section 2–327) and on effect of breach on risk of loss (Section 2–510)~~ Sections 2–327 and 2–510.

§ 2–510. Effect of Breach on Risk of Loss.

(1) ~~Where~~ If a tender or delivery of goods so fails to conform to the contract as to give a right of rejection, the risk of their loss remains on the seller until cure or acceptance.

(2) ~~Where~~ If the buyer rightfully revokes acceptance, ~~he~~ the buyer may to the extent of any deficiency in ~~his~~ the buyer's effective insurance coverage treat the risk of loss as having rested on the seller from the beginning.

(3) ~~Where~~ If the buyer as to conforming goods already identified to the contract for sale repudiates or is otherwise in breach before risk of their loss has passed to ~~him~~ the buyer, the seller may to the extent of any deficiency in ~~his~~ the seller's effective insurance coverage treat the risk of loss as resting on the buyer for a commercially reasonable time.

§ 2–512. Payment by Buyer Before Inspection.

(1) ~~Where~~ If the contract requires payment before inspection, ~~non-conformity~~ nonconformity of the goods does not excuse the buyer from so making payment unless:

(a) the ~~non-conformity~~ nonconformity appears without inspection; or

(b) despite tender of the required documents the circumstances would justify injunction against honor under this Act (Section 5–109(b)).

(2) Payment pursuant to subsection (1) does not constitute an acceptance of goods or impair the buyer's right to inspect or any of ~~his~~ the buyer's remedies.

§ 2–513. Buyer's Right to Inspection of Goods.

(1) Unless otherwise agreed and subject to subsection (3), ~~where~~ if goods are tendered or delivered or identified to the contract for sale, the buyer has a right before payment or acceptance to inspect them at any reasonable place and time and in any reasonable manner. ~~When~~ If the seller is required or authorized to send the goods to the buyer, the inspection may be after their arrival.

(2) Expenses of inspection must be borne by the buyer but may be recovered from the seller if the goods do not conform and are rejected.

(3) Unless otherwise agreed ~~and subject to the provisions of this Article on C.I.F. contracts (subsection (3) of Section 2–321)~~, the buyer is not entitled to inspect the goods before payment of the price ~~when~~ if the contract provides:

(a) for delivery ~~"C.O.D." or on other like terms~~ on terms that under applicable course of performance, course of dealing, or usage of trade are interpreted to preclude inspection before payment; or

(b) for payment against documents of title, except where ~~such~~ the payment is due only after the goods are to become available for inspection.

(4) A place ~~or method~~ , method, or standard of inspection fixed by the parties is presumed to be exclusive, but unless otherwise expressly agreed it does not postpone identification or shift the place for delivery or for passing the risk of loss. If compliance becomes impossible, inspection shall be as provided in this section unless the place ~~or~~ ~~method~~ , method, or standard fixed was clearly intended as an indispensable condition failure of which avoids the contract.

§ 2-514. When Documents Deliverable on Acceptance; When on Payment.

Unless otherwise agreed and except as otherwise provided in Article 5, documents against which a draft is drawn are to be delivered to the drawee on acceptance of the draft if it is payable more than three days after presentment; otherwise, only on payment.

PART 6

BREACH, REPUDIATION, AND EXCUSE

§ 2-601. Buyer's Rights on Improper Delivery.

Subject to ~~the provisions of this Article on breach in installment contracts (Section 2-612)~~ Sections 2-504 and 2-612, and unless otherwise agreed under ~~the sections on contractual limitations of remedy (Sections 2-718 and 2-719)~~ Sections 2-718 and 2-719, if the goods or the tender of delivery fail in any respect to conform to the contract, the buyer may:

(a) reject the whole; ~~or~~

(b) accept the whole; or

(c) accept any commercial unit or units and reject the rest.

§ 2-602. Manner and Effect of ~~Rightful~~ Rejection.

(1) Rejection of goods must be within a reasonable time after their delivery or tender. It is ineffective unless the buyer seasonably notifies the seller.

(2) Subject to ~~the provisions of the two following sections on rejected goods (Sections 2-603 and 2-604),~~ Sections 2-603, 2-604, and Section 2-608(4):

(a) after rejection any exercise of ownership by the buyer with respect to any commercial unit is wrongful as against the seller; and

(b) if the buyer has before rejection taken physical possession of goods in which ~~he~~ the buyer does not have a security interest under ~~the provisions of this Article (subsection (3) of Section 2-711)~~ Section 2-711(3), ~~he~~ the buyer is under a duty after rejection to hold them with reasonable care at the seller's disposition for a time sufficient to permit the seller to remove them; but

(c) the buyer has no further obligations with regard to goods rightfully rejected.

(3) The seller's rights with respect to goods wrongfully rejected are governed by the provisions of this Article on Seller's remedies in general (Section 2-703).

§ 2-603. Merchant Buyer's Duties as to ~~Rightfully~~ Rejected Goods.

(1) Subject to any security interest in the buyer ~~(subsection (3) of Section 2-711)~~ under Section 2-711(3), ~~when~~ if the seller has no agent or place of business at the market of rejection, a merchant buyer is under a duty after rejection of goods in ~~his~~ the buyer's possession or control to follow any reasonable instructions received from the seller with respect to the goods and in the absence of such instructions to make reasonable efforts to sell them for the seller's account if they are perishable or threaten to decline in value speedily. ~~Instructions~~ In the case of a rightful rejection, instructions are not reasonable if on demand indemnity for expenses is not forthcoming.

(2) ~~When~~ If the buyer sells goods under subsection (1) following a rightful rejection, ~~he~~ the buyer is entitled to reimbursement from the seller or out of the proceeds for reasonable expenses of caring for and selling them, and if the ex-

penses include no selling commission then to such commission as is usual in the trade or if there is none to a reasonable sum not exceeding ten 10 per cent on the gross proceeds.

(3) In complying with this section the buyer is held only to good faith and good faith good-faith conduct hereunder under this section is neither acceptance nor conversion nor the basis of an action for damages.

§ 2–604. Buyer's Options as to Salvage of Rightfully Rejected Goods.

Subject to the provisions of the immediately preceding section Section 2–603 on perishables, if the seller gives no instructions within a reasonable time after notification of rejection, the buyer may store the rejected goods for the seller's account or reship them to him the seller or resell them for the seller's account with reimbursement as provided in the preceding section Section 2–603. Such action is not acceptance or conversion.

§ 2–605. Waiver of Buyer's Objections by Failure to Particularize.

(1) The A buyer's failure to state in connection with rejection a particular defect or in connection with revocation of acceptance a defect that justifies revocation which is ascertainable by reasonable inspection precludes him the buyer from relying on the unstated defect to justify rejection or to establish breach revocation of acceptance if the defect is ascertainable by reasonable inspection:

(a) where if the seller had a right to cure the defect and could have cured it if stated seasonably; or

(b) between merchants, when if the seller has after rejection or revocation of acceptance made a request in writing a record and for a full and final written statement in a record of all defects on which the buyer proposes to rely.

(2) Payment A buyer's payment against documents tendered to the buyer made without reservation of rights precludes recovery of the payment for defects apparent on the face of in the documents.

§ 2–606. What Constitutes Acceptance of Goods.

(1) Acceptance of goods occurs when the buyer:

(a) after a reasonable opportunity to inspect the goods signifies to the seller that the goods are conforming or that he the buyer will take or retain them in spite of their non-conformity nonconformity;

(b) fails to make an effective rejection (subsection (1) of Section 2–602) under Section 2–602(1), but such acceptance does not occur until the buyer has had a reasonable opportunity to inspect them; or

(c) Subject to Section 2–608(4), does any act inconsistent with the seller's ownership but if such act is wrongful as against the seller it is an acceptance only if ratified by him.

(2) Acceptance of a part of any commercial unit is acceptance of that entire unit.

§ 2–607. Effect of Acceptance; Notice of Breach; Burden of Establishing Breach after Acceptance; Notice of Claim or Litigation to Person Answerable Over.

(1) The buyer must pay at the contract rate for any goods accepted.

(2) Acceptance of goods by the buyer precludes rejection of the goods accepted and if made with knowledge of a non-conformity cannot nonconformity may not be revoked because of it unless the acceptance was on the reasonable assumption that the non-conformity nonconformity would be seasonably cured, but acceptance does not of itself impair any other remedy provided by this Article for non-conformity nonconformity.

(3) Where If a tender has been accepted:

(a) the buyer must within a reasonable time after he the buyer discovers or should have discovered any breach notify the seller of breach or be barred from any remedy., but failure to give timely notice bars the buyer from a remedy only to the extent that the seller is prejudiced by the failure; and

(b) if the claim is one for infringement or the like (subsection (3) of Section 2–312) under Section 2–312(2) and the buyer is sued as a result of such a breach, he the buyer must so notify the seller within a reasonable time after he the buyer receives notice of the litigation or be barred from any remedy over for liability established by the litigation.

(4) The burden is on the buyer to establish any breach with respect to the goods accepted.

(5) ~~Where~~ If the buyer is sued for indemnity, breach of a warranty, or other obligation for which ~~his seller~~ another party is answerable over:

(a) ~~he~~ the buyer may give ~~his seller~~ the other party ~~written~~ notice of the ~~litigation. If litigation~~ in a record, and if the notice states that the ~~seller~~ other party may come in and defend and that if the ~~seller~~ other party does not do so ~~he~~ the other party will be bound in any action against ~~him~~ the other party by ~~his~~ the buyer by any determination of fact common to the two litigations, then unless the ~~seller~~ other party after seasonable receipt of the notice does come in and defend ~~he~~ the other party is so bound.

(b) if the claim is one for infringement or the like ~~(subsection (3) of Section 2–312)~~ under Section 2–312(2), the original seller may demand in ~~writing~~ a record that ~~his~~ its buyer turn over to ~~him~~ it control of the litigation including settlement or else be barred from any remedy over and if ~~he~~ it also agrees to bear all expense and to satisfy any adverse judgment, ~~then~~ the buyer is ~~so barred~~ unless the buyer after seasonable receipt of the demand does turn over control ~~the buyer is so barred~~.

(6) ~~The provisions of subsections~~ Subsections (3), (4), and (5) apply to any obligation of a buyer to hold the seller harmless against infringement or the like ~~(subsection (3) of Section 2–312)~~ under Section 2–312(2).

§ 2–608. Revocation of Acceptance in Whole or in Part.

(1) ~~The~~ A buyer may revoke ~~his~~ acceptance of a lot or commercial unit whose ~~non-conformity~~ nonconformity substantially impairs its value to ~~him~~ the buyer if ~~he~~ the buyer has accepted it:

(a) on the reasonable assumption that its ~~non-conformity~~ nonconformity would be cured and it has not been seasonably cured; or

(b) without discovery of ~~such non-conformity~~ the nonconformity if ~~his~~ the buyer's acceptance was reasonably induced either by the difficulty of discovery before acceptance or by the seller's assurances.

(2) Revocation of acceptance must occur within a reasonable time after the buyer discovers or should have discovered the ground for it and before any substantial change in condition of the goods which is not caused by their own defects. ~~It~~

The revocation is not effective until the buyer notifies the seller of it.

(3) A buyer ~~who~~ that so revokes has the same rights and duties with regard to the goods involved as if ~~he~~ the buyer had rejected them.

(4) If a buyer uses the goods after a rightful rejection or justifiable revocation of acceptance, the following rules apply:

(a) Any use by the buyer that is unreasonable under the circumstances is wrongful as against the seller and is an acceptance only if ratified by the seller.

(b) Any use of the goods that is reasonable under the circumstances is not wrongful as against the seller and is not an acceptance, but in an appropriate case the buyer is obligated to the seller for the value of the use to the buyer.

§ 2–609. Right to Adequate Assurance of Performance.

(1) A contract for sale imposes an obligation on each party that the other's expectation of receiving due performance will not be impaired. ~~When~~ If reasonable grounds for insecurity arise with respect to the performance of either party, the other may ~~in writing~~ demand in a record adequate assurance of due performance and until ~~he~~ the party receives the assurance may if commercially reasonable suspend any performance for which ~~he~~ it has not already received the agreed return.

(2) Between merchants, the reasonableness of grounds for insecurity and the adequacy of any assurance offered shall be determined according to commercial standards.

(3) Acceptance of any improper delivery or payment does not prejudice the aggrieved party's right to demand adequate assurance of future performance.

(4) After receipt of a justified demand, failure to provide within a reasonable time not exceeding ~~thirty~~ 30 days such assurance of due performance as is adequate under the circumstances of the particular case is a repudiation of the contract.

§ 2–610. Anticipatory Repudiation.

(1) ~~When~~ If either party repudiates the contract with respect to a performance not yet due the loss of which will substantially impair the

value of the contract to the other, the aggrieved party may:

(a) for a commercially reasonable time await performance by the repudiating party; or

(b) resort to any remedy for breach (Section 2–703 or Section 2–711), even ~~though he~~ if the aggrieved party has notified the repudiating party that ~~he~~ it would await the latter's performance and has urged retraction; and

(c) in either case suspend ~~his own~~ performance or proceed in accordance with the provisions of this Article on the seller's right to identify goods to the contract notwithstanding breach or to salvage unfinished goods (Section 2–704).

(2) Repudiation includes language that a reasonable person would interpret to mean that the other party will not or cannot make a performance still due under the contract or voluntary, affirmative conduct that would appear to a reasonable person to make a future performance by the other party impossible.

§ 2–611. Retraction of Anticipatory Repudiation.

(1) Until the repudiating party's next performance is due, ~~he can~~ that party may retract ~~his~~ the repudiation unless the aggrieved party has since the repudiation canceled or materially changed ~~his~~ position or otherwise indicated that ~~he considers~~ the repudiation is final.

(2) Retraction may be by any method ~~which~~ that clearly indicates to the aggrieved party that the repudiating party intends to perform, but must include any assurance justifiably demanded under ~~the provisions of this Article (Section 2–609)~~ Section 2–609.

(3) Retraction reinstates the repudiating party's rights under the contract with due excuse and allowance to the aggrieved party for any delay occasioned by the repudiation.

§ 2–612. "Installment Contract"; Breach.

(1) An "installment contract" is one ~~which~~ that requires or authorizes the delivery of goods in separate lots to be separately accepted, even ~~though~~ if the contract contains a clause "each delivery is a separate contract" or its equivalent.

(2) The buyer may reject any installment ~~which~~ that is ~~non-conforming~~ nonconforming if the ~~non-conformity~~ nonconformity substantially

impairs the value of that installment ~~and cannot be cured~~ to the buyer or if the ~~non-conformity~~ nonconformity is a defect in the required ~~documents; but~~ documents. However, if the ~~non-conformity~~ nonconformity does not fall within subsection (3) and the seller gives adequate assurance of its cure the buyer must accept that installment.

(3) ~~Whenever non-conformity~~ If nonconformity or default with respect to one or more installments substantially impairs the value of the whole contract, there is a breach of the whole. But the aggrieved party reinstates the contract if ~~he~~ the party accepts a ~~non-conforming~~ nonconforming installment without seasonably notifying of cancellation or if ~~he~~ the party brings an action with respect only to past installments or demands performance as to future installments.

§ 2–613. Casualty to Identified Goods.

~~Where~~ If the contract requires for its performance goods identified when the contract is made, and the goods suffer casualty without fault of either party before the risk of loss passes to the buyer, ~~or in a proper case under a "no arrival, no sale" term (Section 2–324)~~ then:

(a) if the loss is total the contract is ~~avoided~~ terminated; and

(b) if the loss is partial or the goods have so deteriorated ~~as~~ that they no longer ~~to~~ conform to the contract, the buyer may nevertheless demand inspection and at ~~his~~ the buyer's option either treat the contract as ~~avoided~~ terminated or accept the goods with due allowance from the contract price for the deterioration or the deficiency in quantity but without further right against the seller.

§ 2–614. Substituted Performance.

(1) ~~Where~~ If without fault of either party the agreed berthing, loading, or unloading facilities fail or an agreed type of carrier becomes unavailable or the agreed manner of ~~delivery~~ performance otherwise becomes commercially impracticable but a commercially reasonable substitute is available, ~~such~~ the substitute performance must be tendered and accepted.

(2) If the agreed means or manner of payment fails because of domestic or foreign governmental regulation, the seller may withhold or stop deliv-

ery unless the buyer provides a means or manner of payment which is commercially a substantial equivalent. If delivery has already been taken, payment by the means or in the manner provided by the regulation discharges the buyer's obligation unless the regulation is discriminatory, oppressive, or predatory.

§ 2–615. Excuse by Failure of Presupposed Conditions.

Except ~~so far as~~ to the extent that a seller may have assumed a greater obligation and subject to ~~the preceding section on substituted performance~~ Section 2–614:

(a) Delay in ~~delivery or non-delivery~~ performance or nonperformance in whole or in part by a seller ~~who~~ that complies with paragraphs (b) and (c) is not a breach of ~~his~~ the seller's duty under a contract for sale if performance as agreed has been made impracticable by the occurrence of a contingency the ~~non-occurrence~~ nonoccurrence of which was a basic assumption on which the contract was made or by compliance in good faith with any applicable foreign or domestic governmental regulation or order whether or not it later proves to be invalid.

(b) ~~Where~~ If the causes mentioned in paragraph (a) affect only a part of the seller's capacity to perform, ~~he~~ the seller must allocate production and deliveries among ~~his~~ its customers but may at ~~his~~ its option include regular customers not then under contract as well as ~~his~~ its own requirements for further manufacture. ~~He~~ The seller may so allocate in any manner ~~which~~ that is fair and reasonable.

(c) The seller must notify the buyer seasonably that there will be delay or nonperformance ~~nondelivery~~ and, ~~when~~ if allocation is required under paragraph (b), of the estimated quota thus made available for the buyer.

§ 2–616. Procedure on Notice Claiming Excuse.

(1) ~~Where the~~ If a buyer receives notification of a material or indefinite delay or an allocation justified under ~~the preceding section he~~ Section 2–615, the buyer may by ~~written~~ notification in a record to the seller as to any ~~delivery~~ performance concerned, and ~~where~~ if the prospective deficiency substantially impairs the value of the whole contract under ~~the provisions of this Article relating to breach of installment contracts (Section 2–612)~~ Section 2–612, then also as to the ~~whole,~~ whole:

(a) terminate and thereby discharge any unexecuted portion of the contract; or

(b) modify the contract by agreeing to take ~~his~~ the buyer's available quota in substitution.

(2) If after receipt of ~~such~~ notification from the seller the buyer fails ~~so~~ to modify the contract within a reasonable time not exceeding ~~thirty~~ 30 days, the contract ~~lapses~~ is terminated with respect to any ~~deliveries~~ performance affected.

(3) The provisions of this section may not be negated by agreement except in so far as the seller has assumed a greater obligation under ~~the preceding section~~ Section 2–615.

PART 7

REMEDIES

§ 2–702. Seller's Remedies on Discovery of Buyer's Insolvency.

(1) ~~Where~~ If the seller discovers ~~the buyer to be~~ that the buyer is insolvent, ~~he~~ the seller may refuse delivery except for cash including payment for all goods theretofore delivered under the contract, and stop delivery under ~~this Article (Section 2–705)~~ Section 2–705.

(2) ~~Where~~ If the seller discovers that the buyer has received goods on credit while insolvent, ~~he~~ the seller may reclaim the goods upon demand made within ~~ten days~~ a reasonable time after the buyer's receipt of the goods, ~~but if misrepresentation of solvency has been made to the particular seller in writing within three months before delivery the ten day limitation does not apply.~~ Except as provided in this subsection, the seller may not base a right to reclaim goods on the buyer's fraudulent or innocent misrepresentation of solvency or of intent to pay.

(3) The seller's right to reclaim under subsection (2) is subject to the rights of a buyer in ordinary course of business or other good-faith

purchaser for value under ~~this Article (Section 2–403)~~ Section 2–403. Successful reclamation of goods excludes all other remedies with respect to them.

§ 2–703. Seller's Remedies in General.

~~Where the buyer wrongfully rejects or revokes acceptance of goods or fails to make a payment due on or before delivery or repudiates with respect to a part or the whole, then with respect to any goods directly affected and, if the breach is of the whole contract (Section 2–612), then also with respect to the whole undelivered balance, the aggrieved seller may~~

~~(a) withhold delivery of such goods;~~

~~(b) stop delivery by any bailee as hereafter provided (Section 2–705);~~

~~(c) proceed under the next section respecting goods still unidentified to the contract;~~

~~(d) resell and recover damages as hereafter provided (Section 2–706);~~

~~(e) recover damages for non-acceptance (Section 2–708) or in a proper case the price (Section 2–709);~~

~~(f) cancel.~~

(1) A breach of contract by the buyer includes the buyer's wrongful rejection or wrongful attempt to revoke acceptance of goods, wrongful failure to perform a contractual obligation, failure to make a payment when due, and repudiation.

(2) If the buyer is in breach of contract the seller, to the extent provided for by this Act or other law, may:

(a) withhold delivery of the goods;

(b) stop delivery of the goods under Section 2–705;

(c) proceed under Section 2–704 with respect to goods unidentified to the contract or unfinished;

(d) reclaim the goods under Section 2–507(2) or 2–702(2);

(e) require payment directly from the buyer under Section 2–325(c);

(f) cancel;

(g) resell and recover damages under Section 2–706;

(h) recover damages for nonacceptance or repudiation under Section 2–708(1);

(i) recover lost profits under Section 2–708(2);

(j) recover the price under Section 2–709;

(k) obtain specific performance under Section 2–716;

(*l*) recover liquidated damages under Section 2–718;

(m) in other cases, recover damages in any manner that is reasonable under the circumstances.

(3) If the buyer becomes insolvent, the seller may:

(a) withhold delivery under Section 2–702(1);

(b) stop delivery of the goods under Section 2–705;

(c) reclaim the goods under Section 2–702(2).

§ 2–704. Seller's Right to Identify Goods to the Contract Notwithstanding Breach or to Salvage Unfinished Goods.

(1) An aggrieved seller ~~under the preceding section may,~~ may in an appropriate case involving breach by the buyer:

(a) identify to the contract conforming goods not already identified if at the time ~~he~~ the seller learned of the breach ~~they~~ the goods are in ~~his~~ the seller's possession or control;

(b) treat as the subject of resale goods ~~which~~ that have demonstrably been intended for the particular contract even ~~though~~ if those goods are unfinished.

(2) ~~Where~~ If the goods are unfinished, an aggrieved seller may in the exercise of reasonable commercial judgment for the purposes of avoiding loss and of effective realization either complete the manufacture and wholly identify the goods to the contract or cease manufacture and resell for scrap or salvage value or proceed in any other reasonable manner.

§ 2–705. Seller's Stoppage of Delivery in Transit or Otherwise.

(1) ~~The~~ A seller may stop delivery of goods in the possession of a carrier or other bailee ~~when he~~ if the seller discovers the buyer to be insolvent (Section 2–702) ~~and may stop delivery of carload, truckload, planeload or larger shipments of express or freight~~ or ~~when~~ if the buyer repudiates or fails to make a payment due before delivery or if for any other reason the seller has a right to withhold or reclaim the goods.

(2) As against such buyer the seller may stop delivery until:

(a) receipt of the goods by the buyer; ~~or~~

(b) acknowledgment to the buyer by any bailee of the goods, except a carrier, that the bailee holds the goods for the buyer; or

(c) such acknowledgment to the buyer by a carrier by reshipment or as ~~warehouseman~~ warehouse; or

(d) negotiation to the buyer of any negotiable document of title covering the goods.

(3)(a) To stop delivery the seller must so notify as to enable the bailee by reasonable diligence to prevent delivery of the goods.

(b) After such notification the bailee must hold and deliver the goods according to the directions of the seller but the seller is liable to the bailee for any ensuing charges or damages.

(c) If a negotiable document of title has been issued for goods, the bailee is not obliged to obey a notification to stop until surrender of possession or control of the document.

(d) A carrier ~~who~~ that has issued a ~~non-negotiable~~ nonnegotiable bill of lading is not obliged to obey a notification to stop received from a person other than the consignor.

§ 2-706.   Seller's Resale Including Contract for Resale.

(1) ~~Under the conditions stated in Section 2-703 on seller's remedies~~ In an appropriate case involving breach by the buyer, the seller may resell the goods concerned or the undelivered balance thereof. ~~Where~~ If the resale is made in good faith and in a commercially reasonable manner, the seller may recover the difference between the contract price and the resale price ~~and the contract price~~ together with any incidental or consequential damages allowed under ~~the provisions of this Article (Section 2-710)~~ Section 2-710, but less expenses saved in consequence of the buyer's breach.

(2) Except as otherwise provided in subsection (3) or unless otherwise agreed, resale may be at public or private sale including sale by way of one or more contracts to sell or of identification to an existing contract of the seller. Sale may be as a unit or in parcels and at any time and place, and on any terms, but every aspect of the sale including the method, manner, time, place and terms must be commercially reasonable. The resale must be reasonably identified as referring to the broken contract, but it is not necessary that the goods be in existence or that any or all of them have been identified to the contract before the breach.

(3) ~~Where~~ If the resale is at private sale, the seller must give the buyer reasonable notification of ~~his~~ an intention to resell.

(4) ~~Where~~ If the resale is at public sale:

(a) only identified goods ~~can~~ may be sold ~~except where~~ unless there is a recognized market for a public sale of futures in goods of the kind; ~~and~~

(b) it must be made at a usual place or market for public sale if one is reasonably available and except in the case of goods which are perishable or threaten to decline in value speedily the seller must give the buyer reasonable notice of the time and place of the resale; ~~and~~

(c) if the goods are not to be within the view of those attending the sale, the notification of sale must state the place where the goods are located and provide for their reasonable inspection by prospective bidders; and

(d) the seller may buy.

(5) A purchaser ~~who~~ that buys in good faith at a resale takes the goods free of any rights of the original buyer even ~~though~~ if the seller fails to comply with one or more of the requirements of this section.

(6) The seller is not accountable to the buyer for any profit made on any resale. A person in the position of a seller (Section 2-707) or a buyer ~~who~~ that has rightfully rejected or justifiably revoked acceptance must account for any excess over the amount of ~~his~~ the buyer's security interest, ~~as hereinafter defined (subsection (3) of Section 2-711)~~ under Section 2-711(3).

(7) Failure of a seller to resell under this section does not bar the seller from any other remedy.

§ 2-707.   "Person in the Position of a Seller".

(1) A "person in the position of a seller" includes as against a principal an agent ~~who~~ that has paid or become responsible for the price of goods on behalf of ~~his~~ the principal or ~~anyone~~ a person ~~who~~ that otherwise holds a security interest or other right in goods similar to that of a seller.

(2) A person in the position of a seller ~~may as provided in this Article~~ withhold or stop delivery ~~(Section 2-705)~~ and resell ~~(Section 2-706)~~ and

recover incidental damages (Section 2–710) has the same remedies as a seller under this Article.

§ 2–708. Seller's Damages for ~~Non-acceptance~~ Nonacceptance or Repudiation.

(1) Subject to subsection (2) and to ~~the provisions of this Article with respect to proof of market price (Section 2–723)~~ Section 2–723:

(a) the measure of damages for ~~non-acceptance or repudiation~~ nonacceptance by the buyer is the difference between the contract price and the market price at the time and place for tender ~~and the unpaid contract price~~ together with any incidental or consequential damages provided in ~~this Article (Section 2–710)~~ Section 2–710, but less expenses saved in consequence of the buyer's ~~breach.~~ breach; and

(b) the measure of damages for repudiation by the buyer is the difference between the contract price and the market price at the place for tender at the expiration of a commercially reasonable time after the seller learned of the repudiation, but no later than the time stated in paragraph (a), together with any incidental or consequential damages provided in Section 2–710, less expenses saved in consequence of the buyer's breach.

(2) If the measure of damages provided in subsection (1) or in Section 2–706 is inadequate to put the seller in as good a position as performance would have ~~done then~~ done, the measure of damages is the profit (including reasonable overhead) ~~which~~ that the seller would have made from full performance by the buyer, together with any incidental or consequential damages provided in this Article (Section 2–710), ~~due allowance for costs reasonably incurred and due credit for payments or proceeds of resale.~~

§ 2–709. Action for the Price.

(1) ~~When~~ If the buyer fails to pay the price as it becomes due, the seller may recover, together with any incidental or consequential damages under ~~the next section~~ Section 2–710, the price:

(a) of goods accepted or of conforming goods lost or damaged within a commercially reasonable time after risk of their loss has passed to the buyer; and

(b) of goods identified to the contract if the seller is unable after reasonable effort to resell them at a reasonable price or the circumstances reasonably indicate that such effort will be unavailing.

(2) ~~Where~~ If the seller sues for the price, ~~he~~ the seller must hold for the buyer any goods ~~which~~ that have been identified to the contract and are still in ~~his~~ the seller's ~~control except that~~ control. However, if resale becomes possible, ~~he~~ the seller may resell them at any time prior to the collection of the judgment. The net proceeds of any such resale must be credited to the buyer, and payment of the judgment entitles ~~him~~ the buyer to any goods not resold.

(3) After the buyer has wrongfully rejected or revoked acceptance of the goods or has failed to make a payment due or has repudiated (Section 2–610), a seller ~~who~~ that is held not entitled to the price under this section shall nevertheless be awarded damages for ~~non-acceptance~~ nonacceptance under ~~the preceding section~~ Section 2–708.

§ 2–710. Seller's Incidental and Consequential Damages.

(1) Incidental damages to an aggrieved seller include any commercially reasonable charges, expenses or commissions incurred in stopping delivery, in the transportation, care, and custody of goods after the buyer's breach, in connection with return or resale of the goods or otherwise resulting from the breach.

(2) Consequential damages resulting from the buyer's breach include any loss resulting from general or particular requirements and needs of which the buyer at the time of contracting had reason to know and which could not reasonably be prevented by resale or otherwise.

(3) In a consumer contract, a seller may not recover consequential damages from a consumer.

§ 2–711. Buyer's Remedies in General; Buyer's Security Interest in Rejected Goods.

(1) ~~Where the seller fails to make delivery or repudiates or the buyer rightfully rejects or justifiably revokes acceptance then with respect to any goods involved, and with respect to the whole if the breach goes to the whole contract (Section 2–612), the buyer may cancel and whether or not he has done so may in addition to recovering so much of the price as has been paid~~

(a) "cover" and have damages under the next section as to all the goods affected whether or not they have been identified to the contract; or

(b) recover damages for non-delivery as provided in this Article (Section 2–713).

(2) Where the seller fails to deliver or repudiates the buyer may also

(a) if the goods have been identified recover them as provided in this Article (Section 2–502); or

(b) in a proper case obtain specific performance or replevy the goods as provided in this Article (Section 2–716).

(1) A breach of contract by the seller includes the seller's wrongful failure to deliver or to perform a contractual obligation, making of a nonconforming tender of delivery or performance, and repudiation.

(2) If the seller is in breach of contract under subsection (1), the buyer, to the extent provided for by this Act or other law, may:

(a) in the case of rightful cancellation, rightful rejection, or justifiable revocation of acceptance, recover so much of the price as has been paid;

(b) deduct damages from any part of the price still due under Section 2–717;

(c) cancel;

(d) cover and have damages under Section 2–712 as to all goods affected whether or not they have been identified to the contract;

(e) recover damages for nondelivery or repudiation under Section 2–713;

(f) recover damages for breach with regard to accepted goods or breach with regard to a remedial promise under Section 2–714;

(g) recover identified goods under Section 2–502;

(h) obtain specific performance or obtain the goods by replevin or similar remedy under Section 2–716;

(i) recover liquidated damages under Section 2–718;

(j) in other cases, recover damages in any manner that is reasonable under the circumstances.

(3) On rightful rejection or justifiable revocation of acceptance a buyer has a security interest in goods in his the buyer's possession or control for any payments made on their price and any expenses reasonably incurred in their inspection, receipt, transportation, care and custody and may hold such goods and resell them in like manner as an aggrieved seller (Section 2–706).

§ 2–712. "Cover"; Buyer's Procurement of Substitute Goods.

(1) After a breach within the preceding section If the seller wrongfully fails to deliver or repudiates or the buyer rightfully rejects or justifiably revokes acceptance, the buyer may "cover" by making in good faith and without unreasonable delay any reasonable purchase of or contract to purchase goods in substitution for those due from the seller.

(2) The A buyer may recover from the seller as damages the difference between the cost of cover and the contract price together with any incidental or consequential damages as hereinafter defined (Section 2–715) under Section 2–715, but less expenses saved in consequence of the seller's breach.

(3) Failure of the buyer to effect cover within this section does not bar him the buyer from any other remedy.

§ 2–713. Buyer's Damages for Non-delivery Nondelivery or Repudiation.

(1) Subject to the provisions of this Article with respect to proof of market price (Section 2–723), Section 2–723, if the seller wrongfully fails to deliver or repudiates or the buyer rightfully rejects or justifiably revokes acceptance:

(a) the measure of damages for non-delivery or repudiation in the case of wrongful failure to deliver by the seller or rightful rejection or justifiable revocation of acceptance by the buyer is the difference between the market price at the time when the buyer learned of the breach for tender under the contract and the contract price together with any incidental and or consequential damages provided in this Article (Section 2–715) under Section 2–715, but less expenses saved in consequence of the seller's breach. breach; and

(b) the measure of damages for repudiation by the seller is the difference between the market price at the expiration of a commercially reasonable time after the buyer learned of the repudiation, but no later than the time stated in paragraph (a), and the contract price together with any incidental or consequential damages provided in this Article (Section 2–715), less expenses saved in consequence of the seller's breach.

(2) Market price is to be determined as of the place for tender or, in cases of rejection after arrival or revocation of acceptance, as of the place of arrival.

§ 2–714. Buyer's Damages for Breach in Regard to Accepted Goods.

(1) ~~Where~~ If the buyer has accepted goods and given notification ~~(subsection (3) of Section 2–607) he~~ pursuant to Section 2–607(3), the buyer may recover as damages for any ~~non-conformity~~ nonconformity of tender the loss resulting in the ordinary course of events from the seller's breach as determined in any reasonable manner ~~which is reasonable~~.

(2) The measure of damages for breach of warranty is the difference at the time and place of acceptance between the value of the goods accepted and the value they would have had if they had been as warranted, unless special circumstances show proximate damages of a different amount.

(3) In a proper case any incidental and consequential damages under ~~the next section~~ Section 2–715 may also be recovered.

§ 2–716. ~~Buyer's Right to~~ Specific Performance ~~Or;~~ Buyer's Right to Replevin.

(1) Specific performance may be decreed ~~where~~ if the goods are unique or in other proper circumstances. In a contract other than a consumer contract, specific performance may be decreed if the parties have agreed to that remedy. However, even if the parties agree to specific performance, specific performance may not be decreed if the breaching party's sole remaining contractual obligation is the payment of money.

(2) The decree for specific performance may include such terms and conditions as to payment of the price, damages, or other relief as the court may deem just.

(3) The buyer has a right of replevin or similar remedy for goods identified to the contract if after reasonable effort ~~he~~ the buyer is unable to effect cover for such goods or the circumstances reasonably indicate that such effort will be unavailing or if the goods have been shipped under reservation and satisfaction of the security interest in them has been made or tendered. ~~In the case of goods bought for personal, family, or~~

~~household purposes, the buyer's right of replevin vests upon acquisition of a special property, even if the seller had not then repudiated or failed to deliver.~~

(4) The buyer's right under subsection (3) vests upon acquisition of a special property, even if the seller had not then repudiated or failed to deliver.

§ 2–717. Deduction of Damages from the Price.

The buyer on notifying the seller of ~~his~~ the intention to do so may deduct all or any part of the damages resulting from any breach of the contract from any part of the price still due under the same contract.

§ 2–718. Liquidation or Limitation of Damages; Deposits.

(1) Damages for breach by either party may be liquidated in the agreement but only at an amount ~~which~~ that is reasonable in the light of the anticipated or actual harm caused by the breach and, in a consumer contract, the difficulties of proof of loss, and the inconvenience or nonfeasibility of otherwise obtaining an adequate remedy. ~~A term fixing unreasonably large liquidated damages is void as a penalty.~~ Section 2–719 determines the enforceability of a term that limits but does not liquidate damages.

(2) ~~Where~~ If the seller justifiably withholds delivery of goods or stops performance because of the buyer's breach or insolvency, the buyer is entitled to restitution of any amount by which the sum of ~~his~~ the buyer's payments exceeds ~~(a)~~ the amount to which the seller is entitled by virtue of terms liquidating the seller's damages in accordance with subsection (1)~~, or (b) in the absence of such terms, twenty per cent of the value of the total performance for which the buyer is obligated under the contract or $500, whichever is smaller~~.

(3) The buyer's right to restitution under subsection (2) is subject to offset to the extent that the seller establishes:

(a) a right to recover damages under the provisions of this Article other than subsection ~~(1)~~, (1); and

1171

(b) the amount or value of any benefits received by the buyer directly or indirectly by reason of the contract.

(4) ~~Where~~ If a seller has received payment in goods, their reasonable value or the proceeds of their resale shall be treated as payments for the purposes of subsection ~~(2); but~~ (2). However, if the seller has notice of the buyer's breach before reselling goods received in part performance, ~~his~~ the resale is subject to the conditions ~~laid down in~~ of this Article on resale by an aggrieved seller (Section 2-706).

§ 2-722. Who ~~Can~~ May Sue Third Parties for Injury to Goods.

~~Where~~ If a third party so deals with goods ~~which~~ that have been identified to a contract for sale as to cause actionable injury to a party to that contract:

(a) a right of action against the third party is in either party to the contract for sale ~~who~~ that has title to or a security interest or a special property or an insurable interest in the ~~goods;~~ goods, and if the goods have been destroyed or converted, a right of action is also in the party ~~who~~ that either bore the risk of loss under the contract for sale or has since the injury assumed that risk as against the other;

(b) if at the time of the injury the party plaintiff did not bear the risk of loss as against the other party to the contract for sale and there is no arrangement between them for disposition of the recovery, ~~his~~ the party plaintiff's suit or settlement is, subject to ~~his~~ its own interest, as a fiduciary for the other party to the contract; and

(c) either party may with the consent of the other sue for the benefit of whom it may concern.

§ 2-723. Proof of Market: Time and Place.

~~(1) If an action based on anticipatory repudiation comes to trial before the time for performance with respect to some or all of the goods, any damages based on market price (Section 2-708 or Section 2-713) shall be determined according to the price of such goods prevailing at the time when the aggrieved party learned of the repudiation.~~

~~(2)~~ (1) If evidence of a price prevailing at the times or places described in this Article is not readily available, the price prevailing within any reasonable time before or after the time described or at any other place ~~which~~ that in commercial judgment or under usage of trade would serve as a reasonable substitute for the one described may be used, making any proper allowance for the cost of transporting the goods to or from ~~such~~ the other place.

~~(3)~~ (2) Evidence of a relevant price prevailing at a time or place other than the one described in this Article offered by one party is not admissible unless and until ~~he~~ the party has given the other party such notice as the court finds sufficient to prevent unfair surprise.

§ 2-724. Admissibility of Market Quotations.

~~Whenever~~ If the prevailing price or value of any goods regularly bought and sold in any established commodity market is in issue, reports in official publications or trade journals or in newspapers ~~or periodicals~~ , periodicals or other means of communication in ~~of~~ general circulation published as the reports of ~~such~~ the market ~~shall be~~ are admissible in evidence. The circumstances of the preparation of such a report may be shown to affect its weight but not its admissibility.

§ 2-725. Statute of Limitations in Contracts for Sale.

~~(1) An action for breach of any contract for sale must be commenced within four years after the cause of action has accrued. By the original agreement the parties may reduce the period of limitation to not less than one year but may not extend it.~~

~~(2) A cause of action accrues when the breach occurs, regardless of the aggrieved party's lack of knowledge of the breach. A breach of warranty occurs when tender of delivery is made, except that where a warranty explicitly extends to future performance of the goods and discovery of the breach must await the time of such performance the cause of action accrues when the breach is or should have been discovered.~~

(1) Except as otherwise provided in this section, an action for breach of any contract for sale must be commenced within the later of four years after the right of action has accrued under subsection (2) or (3) or one year after the breach was or should have been discovered, but no long-

er than five years after the right of action accrued. By the original agreement the parties may reduce the period of limitation to not less than one year but may not extend it. However, in a consumer contract, the period of limitation may not be reduced.

(2) Except as otherwise provided in subsection (3), the following rules apply:

(a) Except as otherwise provided in this subsection, a right of action for breach of a contract accrues when the breach occurs, even if the aggrieved party did not have knowledge of the breach.

(b) For breach of a contract by repudiation, a right of action accrues at the earlier of when the aggrieved party elects to treat the repudiation as a breach or when a commercially reasonable time for awaiting performance has expired.

(c) For breach of a remedial promise, a right of action accrues when the remedial promise is not performed when performance is due.

(d) In an action by a buyer against a person that is answerable over to the buyer for a claim asserted against the buyer, the buyer's right of action against the person answerable over accrues at the time the claim was originally asserted against the buyer.

(3) If a breach of a warranty arising under Section 2–312, 2–313(2), 2–314, or 2–315, or a breach of an obligation, other than a remedial promise, arising under Section 2–313A or 2–313B, is claimed, the following rules apply:

(a) Except as otherwise provided in paragraph (c), a right of action for breach of a warranty arising under Section 2–313(2), 2–314, or 2–315 accrues when the seller has tendered delivery to the immediate buyer, as defined in Section 2–313, and has completed performance of any agreed installation or assembly of the goods.

(b) Except as otherwise provided in paragraph (c), a right of action for breach of an obligation, other than a remedial promise, arising under Section 2–313A or 2–313B accrues when the remote purchaser, as defined in Section 2–313A or 2–313B, receives the goods.

(c) If a warranty arising under Section 2–313(2) or an obligation, other than a remedial promise, arising under Section 2–313A or 2–313B explicitly extends to future performance of the goods and discovery of the breach must await the time for performance, the right of action accrues when the immediate buyer as defined in Section 2–313 or the remote purchaser as defined in Section 2–313A or 2–313B discovers or should have discovered the breach.

(d) A right of action for breach of warranty arising under Section 2–312 accrues when the aggrieved party discovers or should have discovered the breach. However, an action for breach of the warranty of noninfringement may not be commenced more than six years after tender of delivery of the goods to the aggrieved party.

(3) (4) ~~Where~~ If an action commenced within the time limited by subsection (1) is so terminated as to leave available a remedy by another action for the same breach, ~~such~~ the other action may be commenced after the expiration of the time limited and within six months after the termination of the first action unless the termination resulted from voluntary discontinuance or from dismissal for failure or neglect to prosecute.

(4) (5) This section does not alter the law on tolling of the statute of limitations nor does it apply to causes of action ~~which have~~ that accrued before this Act becomes effective.

AMENDMENTS TO ARTICLE 2A–LEASES

PART 1

GENERAL PROVISIONS

§ 2A–101.   Short Title.

The text for this section was not amended in 2003.

§ 2A–103.   Definitions and Index of Definitions.

(1) In this Article, unless the context otherwise requires:

(a) ~~"Buyer in ordinary course of business" means a person who in good faith and without knowledge that the sale to him [or her] is in violation of the ownership rights or security interest or leasehold interest of a third party in the goods buys in ordinary course from a person in the business of selling goods of that kind but does not include a pawnbroker. "Buying" may be for cash or by exchange of other property or on secured or unsecured credit and includes receiving goods or documents of title under a preexisting contract for sale but does not include a transfer in bulk or as security for or in total or partial satisfaction of a money debt.~~

~~(b)~~ (a) "Cancellation" occurs when either party puts an end to the lease contract for default by the other party.

~~(c)~~ (b) "Commercial unit" means such a unit of goods as by commercial usage is a single whole for purposes of lease and division of which materially impairs its character or value on the market or in use. A commercial unit may be a single article, as a machine, or a set of articles, as a suite of furniture or a line of machinery, or a quantity, as a gross or carload, or any other unit treated in use or in the relevant market as a single whole.

~~(d)~~ (c) "Conforming" goods or performance under a lease contract means goods or performance that are in accordance with the obligations under the lease contract.

(d) "Conspicuous", with reference to a term, means so written, displayed, or presented that a reasonable person against which it is to operate ought to have noticed it. A term in an electronic record intended to evoke a response by an electronic agent is conspicuous if it is presented in a form that would enable a reasonably configured electronic agent to take it into account or react to it without review of the record by an individual. Whether a term is "conspicuous" or not is a decision for the court. Conspicuous terms include the following:

(i) for a person:

(A) a heading in capitals equal to or greater in size than the surrounding text, or in contrasting type, font, or color to the surrounding text of the same or lesser size; and

(B) language in the body of a record or display in larger type than the surrounding text, or in contrasting type, font, or color to the surrounding text of the same size, or set off from surrounding text of the same size by symbols or other marks that call attention to the language; and

(ii) for a person or an electronic agent, a term that is so placed in a record or display that the person or electronic agent cannot proceed without taking action with respect to the particular term.

(e) "Consumer" means an individual who leases or contracts to lease goods that, at the time of contracting, are intended by the individual to be used primarily for personal, family, or household purposes.

~~(e)~~ (f) "Consumer lease" means a lease that a lessor regularly engaged in the business of leasing or selling makes to ~~a lessee who is an individual and who takes under the lease primarily for a personal, family, or household purpose [, if the total payments to be made under the lease contract, excluding payments for options to renew or buy, do not exceed $_____]~~ a consumer.

Legislative Note: Present Article 2A has a bracketed provision allowing States to insert a dollar cap on leases designated as consumer leases, amended Article 2 defines "consumer contract" and does not include a dollar cap in the definition. Some States have not included a dol-

lar cap in present Article 2A and States which have adopted a dollar cap have stated varying amounts. If a State wishes to include a dollar cap, the cap should be inserted here. Any cap probably should be set high enough to bring within the definition most automobile leasing transactions for personal, family, or household use.

(g) "Delivery" means the voluntary transfer of physical possession or control of goods.

(h) "Electronic" means relating to technology having electrical, digital, magnetic, wireless, optical, electromagnetic, or similar capabilities.

(i) "Electronic agent" means a computer program or an electronic or other automated means used independently to initiate an action or respond to electronic records or performances in whole or in part, without review or action by an individual.

(j) "Electronic record" means a record created, generated, sent, communicated, received, or stored by electronic means.

(f) (k) "Fault" means wrongful act, omission, breach, or default.

(g) "Finance lease" means a lease with respect to which:

(i) the lessor does not select, manufacture, or supply the goods;

(ii) the lessor acquires the goods or the right to possession and use of the goods in connection with the lease; and

(iii) one of the following occurs:

(A) the lessee receives a copy of the contract by which the lessor acquired the goods or the right to possession and use of the goods before signing the lease contract;

(B) the lessee's approval of the contract by which the lessor acquired the goods or the right to possession and use of the goods is a condition to effectiveness of the lease contract;

(C) the lessee, before signing the lease contract, receives an accurate and complete statement designating the promises and warranties, and any disclaimers of warranties, limitations or modifications of remedies, or liquidated damages, including those of a third party, such as the manufacturer of the goods, provided to the lessor by the person supplying the goods in connection with or as part of the contract by which the lessor acquired the goods or the right to possession and use of the goods; or

(D) if the lease is not a consumer lease, the lessor, before the lessee signs the lease contract, informs the lessee in writing (a) of the identity of the person supplying the goods to the lessor, unless the lessee has selected that person and directed the lessor to acquire the goods or the right to possession and use of the goods from that person, (b) that the lessee is entitled under this Article to the promises and warranties, including those of any third party, provided to the lessor by the person supplying the goods in connection with or as part of the contract by which the lessor acquired the goods or the right to possession and use of the goods, and (c) that the lessee may communicate with the person supplying the goods to the lessor and receive an accurate and complete statement of those promises and warranties, including any disclaimers and limitations of them or of remedies.

(*l*) "Finance lease" means a lease with respect to which:

(i) the lessor does not select, manufacture, or supply the goods;

(ii) the lessor acquires the goods or the right to possession and use of the goods in connection with the lease or, in the case of goods that have been leased previously by the lessor and are not being leased to a consumer, in connection with another lease; and

(iii) one of the following occurs:

(A) the lessee receives a copy of the agreement by which the lessor acquired, or proposes to acquire, the goods or the right to possession and use of the goods before signing the lease agreement;

(B) the lessee's approval of the agreement or of the general contractual terms under which the lessor acquired or proposes to acquire the goods or the right to possession and use of the goods is a condition to the effectiveness of the lease contract;

(C) the lessee, before signing the lease agreement, receives an accurate and complete statement designating the promises and warranties, and any disclaimers of warranties, limitations or modifications of remedies, or liquidated damages, including those of a third party, such as the manufacturer of the goods, provided to the lessor by the person supplying the goods in connection with or as part of the contract by which the lessor acquired the goods or the right to possession and use of the goods; or

(D) if the lease is not a consumer lease, before the lessee signs the lease agreement, the lessor informs the lessee in a record:

(I) of the identity of the person supplying the goods to the lessor, unless the lessee has selected that person and directed the lessor to acquire the goods or the right to possession and use of the goods from that person;

(II) that the lessee is entitled under this article to the promises and warranties, including those of any third party, provided to the lessor by the person supplying the goods in connection with or as part of the contract by which the lessor acquired the goods or the right to possession and use of the goods; and

(III) that the lessee may communicate with the person supplying the goods to the lessor and receive an accurate and complete statement of those promises and warranties, including any disclaimers and limitations of them, or a statement of remedies.

(m) "Good faith" means honesty in fact and the observance of reasonable commercial standards of fair dealing.

Legislative Note: Definition (m) should not be adopted if the jurisdiction has enacted the equivalent provision in the 2001 Revised Article 1.

(h) (n) "Goods" means all things that are movable at the time of identification to a lease contract or that are fixtures (Section 2A–309) but the term does not include money, documents, instruments, accounts, chattel paper, general intangibles, or minerals and the like, including oil and gas, before extraction. The term includes future goods, specially manufactured goods, and the unborn young of animals. The term does not include information, the money in which the price is to be paid, investment securities under Article 8, or choses in action. The term also includes the unborn young of animals.

(i) (o) "Installment lease contract" means a lease contract that authorizes or requires the delivery of goods in separate lots to be separately accepted, even though the lease contract contains a clause "each delivery is a separate lease" or its equivalent.

(j) (p) "Lease" means a transfer of the right to possession and use of goods for a term period in return for consideration, but a sale, including a sale on approval or a sale or return, or retention or creation of a security interest, or license of information is not a lease. Unless the context

clearly indicates otherwise, the term includes a sublease.

(k) (q) "Lease agreement", as distinguished from "lease contract", means the bargain, with respect to the lease, of the lessor and the lessee in fact as found in their language or inferred by implication from other circumstances including course of performance, course of dealing , or usage of trade dealing or usage of trade or course of performance as provided in Section 1–303. this Article. Unless the context clearly indicates otherwise, the term includes a sublease agreement.

(l) (r) "Lease contract", as distinguished from "lease agreement", means the total legal obligation that results from the lease agreement as determined by the [Uniform Commercial Code] as supplemented by affected by this Article and any other applicable rules of law. Unless the context clearly indicates otherwise, the term includes a sublease contract.

(m) (s) "Leasehold interest" means the interest of the lessor or the lessee under a lease contract.

(n) (t) "Lessee" means a person who that acquires the right to possession and use of goods under a lease. Unless the context clearly indicates otherwise, the term includes a sublessee.

(o) "Lessee in ordinary course of business" means a person who in good faith and without knowledge that the lease to him [or her] is in violation of the ownership rights or security interest or leasehold interest of a third party in the goods, leases in ordinary course from a person in the business of selling or leasing goods of that kind but does not include a pawnbroker. "Leasing" may be for cash or by exchange of other property or on secured or unsecured credit and includes receiving goods or documents of title under a pre-existing lease contract but does not include a transfer in bulk or as security for or in total or partial satisfaction of a money debt.

(u) "Lessee in ordinary course of business" means a person that leases goods in good faith, without knowledge that the lease violates the rights of another person, and in the ordinary course from a person, other than a pawnbroker, in the business of selling or leasing goods of that kind. A person leases in ordinary course if the lease to the person comports with the usual or customary practices in the kind of business in which the lessor is engaged or with the lessor's own usual or customary practices. A lessee in ordinary course of business may lease for cash, by exchange of other property, or on secured or unsecured credit, and may acquire goods or documents of title under a preexisting lease contract. Only a lessee that takes possession of the goods or has a right to recover the goods from the lessor under this article may be a lessee in ordinary course of business. A person that acquires goods in a transfer in bulk or as security for or in total or partial satisfaction of a money debt is not a lessee in ordinary course of business.

(p) (v) "Lessor" means a person who that transfers the right to possession and use of goods under a lease. Unless the context clearly indicates otherwise, the term includes a sublessor.

(q) (w) "Lessor's residual interest" means the lessor's interest in the goods after expiration, termination, or cancellation of the lease contract.

(r) (x) "Lien" means a charge against or interest in goods to secure payment of a debt or performance of an obligation., but the The term does not include a security interest.

(s) (y) "Lot" means a parcel or a single article that is the subject matter of a separate lease or delivery, whether or not it is sufficient to perform the lease contract.

(t) (z) "Merchant lessee" means a lessee that is a merchant with respect to goods of the kind subject to the lease.

(u) (aa) "Present value" means the amount as of a date certain of one or more sums payable in the future, discounted to the date certain by use of either an interest rate specified by the parties if that rate is not manifestly unreasonable at the time the transaction is entered into or, if an interest rate is not so specified, a commercially reasonable rate that takes into account the facts and circumstances at the time the transaction is entered into The discount is determined by the interest rate specified by the parties if the rate was not manifestly unreasonable at the time the transaction was entered into; otherwise, the discount is determined by a commercially reasonable rate that takes into account the facts and circumstances of each case at the time the transaction was entered into.

Legislative Note: Definition (aa) should not be adopted if the jurisdiction has enacted the equivalent provision in the 2001 Revised Article 1.

(v) (bb) "Purchase" includes taking by sale, lease, mortgage, security interest, pledge, gift, or any other voluntary transaction creating an interest in goods.

Legislative Note: Definition (bb) should not be adopted if the jurisdiction has enacted the equivalent provision in the 2001 Revised Article 1.

(cc) "Record" means information that is inscribed on a tangible medium or that is stored in an electronic or other medium and is retrievable in perceivable form.

Legislative Note: Definition (cc) should not be adopted if the jurisdiction has enacted the equivalent provision in the 2001 Revised Article 1.

(dd) "Sign" means, with present intent to authenticate or adopt a record,

(i) to execute or adopt a tangible symbol; or

(ii) to attach to or logically associate with the record an electronic sound, symbol, or process.

(w) (ee) "Sublease" means a lease of goods the right to possession and use of which was acquired by the lessor as a lessee under an existing lease.

(x) (ff) "Supplier" means a person from whom which a lessor buys or leases goods to be leased under a finance lease.

(y) (gg) "Supply contract" means a contract under which a lessor buys or leases goods to be leased.

(z) (hh) "Termination" occurs when either party pursuant to a power created by agreement or law puts an end to the lease contract otherwise than for default.

(2) Other definitions applying to this Article and the sections in which they appear are:

"Accessions". Section 2A–310(1).

"Construction mortgage". Section 2A–309(1)(d).

"Encumbrance". Section 2A–309(1)(e).

"Fixtures". Section 2A–309(1)(a).

"Fixture filing". Section 2A–309(1)(b).

"Purchase money lease". Section 2A–309(1)(c).

(3) The following definitions in other Articles apply to this Article:

"Account". Section 9–102(a)(2).

"Between merchants". Section 2–104(3).

"Buyer". Section 2–103(1)(a).

"Chattel Paper". Section 9–102(a)(11).

"Consumer goods". Section 102(a)(23) 9–109(1).

"Document". Section 9–102(a)(30).

"Entrusting". Section 2–403(3).

"General intangible". Section 9–102(a)(42).

"Good faith". Section 2-103(1)(b).

"Instrument". Section 9-102(a)(47).

"Letter of credit". Section 5-102(a)(10).

"Merchant". Section 2-104(1).

"Mortgage". Section 9-102(a)(55).

"Pursuant to Commitment". Section 9-102(a)(68).

"Receipt of goods". Section 2-103(1)(c).

"Sale". Section 2-106(1).

"Sale on approval". Section 2-326.

"Sale or return". Section 2-326.

"Seller". Section 2-103(1)(d)(n).

(4) In addition Article 1 contains general definitions and principles of construction and interpretation applicable throughout this Article.

§ 2A-104.   Leases Subject to Other Law.

(1) A lease, although subject to this Article, is also subject to any applicable:

(a) certificate of title statute of this State: ([list any certificate of title statutes covering automobiles, trailers, mobile homes, boats, farm tractors, or and the like);]

(b) certificate of title statute of another jurisdiction (Section 2A-105); or

(c) consumer protection statute of this State, or final consumer protection decision of a court of this State existing on the effective date of this Article rule of law that establishes a different rule for consumers.

(2) To the extent there is a In case of conflict between this Article, other than Sections 2A-105, 2A-304(3), and 2A-305(3), and a statute or decision law referred to in subsection (1), that law governs the statute or decision controls.

(3) Failure to comply with an applicable law has only the effect specified therein For purposes of this Article, failure to comply with a law referred to in subsection (1) has only the effect specified in that law.

(4) This article modifies, limits, and supersedes the federal Electronic Signatures in Global and National Commerce Act, 15 U.S.C. Section 7001 et seq., except that nothing in this article modifies, limits, or supersedes Section 7001(c) of that Act or authorizes electronic delivery of any of the notices described in Section 7003(b) of that Act.

§ 2A-105.   Territorial Application of Article to Goods Covered by Certificate of Title.

Subject to the provisions of Sections 2A-304(3) and 2A-305(3), with respect to goods covered by a certificate of title issued under a statute of this State or of another jurisdiction, compliance and the effect of compliance or noncompliance with a certificate of title statute are governed by the law (including the conflict of laws rules) of the jurisdiction issuing the certificate until the earlier of (a) surrender of the certificate, or (b) four months after the goods are removed from that jurisdiction and thereafter until a new certificate of title is issued by another jurisdiction.

(1) This section applies to goods covered by a certificate of title, even if there is no other relationship between the jurisdiction under whose certificate of title the goods are covered and the goods or the lessee or lessor.

(2) Goods become covered by a certificate of title when a valid application for the certificate of title and the application fee are delivered to the appropriate authority. Goods cease to be covered by a certificate of title at the earlier of the time the certificate of title ceases to be effective under the law of the issuing jurisdiction or the time the goods become covered subsequently by a certificate of title issued by another jurisdiction.

(3) Subject to Sections 2A-304(3) and 2A-305(3), with respect to goods covered by a certificate of title under a statute of this State or of another jurisdiction, compliance and the effect of compliance or noncompliance with the certificate-of-title statute are governed by the local law of the jurisdiction whose certificate of title covers the goods from the time the goods become covered by the certificate until the goods cease to be covered by the certificate of title.

§ 2A-106.   Limitation on Power of Parties to Consumer Lease to Choose Applicable Law and Judicial Forum.

The text for this section was not amended in 2003.

§ 2A-107.   Waiver or Renunciation of Claim or Right after Default.

Any A claim or right arising out of an alleged default or breach of warranty may be discharged in whole or in part without consideration by ~~a written waiver or renunciation signed and delivered by~~ the aggrieved party in a signed record.

§ 2A–108. Unconscionability.

* * *

(4) In an action in which the lessee claims unconscionability with respect to a consumer lease:

(a) If the court finds unconscionability under subsection (1) or (2), the court shall award reasonable attorney's fees to the lessee.

(b) If the court does not find unconscionability and the lessee claiming unconscionability has brought or maintained an action ~~he [or she]~~ the lessee knew to be groundless, the court shall award reasonable attorney's fees to the party against ~~whom~~ which the claim is made.

§ 2A–109. Option to Accelerate at Will.

(1) A term providing that one party or ~~his [or her]~~ that party's successor in interest may accelerate payment or performance or require collateral or additional collateral "at will" or "when ~~he [or she]~~ the party deems ~~himself [or herself]~~ itself insecure" or ~~in~~ words of similar import ~~must be construed to~~ means that ~~he [or she]~~ the party has power to do so only if ~~he [or she]~~ that party in good faith believes that the prospect of payment or performance is impaired.

(2) With respect to a consumer lease, the burden of establishing good faith under subsection (1) is on the party ~~who~~ that has exercised the power; otherwise the burden of establishing lack of good faith is on the party against ~~whom~~ which the power has been exercised.

PART 2

FORMATION AND CONSTRUCTION OF LEASE CONTRACT; ELECTRONIC CONTRACTING

§ 2A–201. Statute of Frauds.

(1) A lease contract is not enforceable by way of action or defense unless:

(a) the total payments to be made under the lease contract, excluding payments for options to renew or buy, are less than $1,000; or

(b) there is a ~~writing~~ record, signed by the party against ~~whom~~ which enforcement is sought or by that party's authorized agent, sufficient to indicate that a lease contract has been made between the parties and to describe the goods leased and the lease term.

(2) Any description of leased goods or of the lease term is sufficient and satisfies subsection (1)(b), whether or not it is specific, if it reasonably identifies what is described.

(3) A ~~writing~~ record is not insufficient because it omits or incorrectly states a term agreed upon, but the lease contract is not enforceable under subsection (1)(b) beyond the lease term and the quantity of goods shown in the ~~writing~~ record.

(4) A lease contract that does not satisfy the requirements of subsection (1), but which is valid in other respects, is enforceable:

(a) if the goods are to be specially manufactured or obtained for the lessee and are not suitable for lease or sale to others in the ordinary course of the lessor's business, and the lessor, before notice of repudiation is received and under circumstances that reasonably indicate that the goods are for the lessee, has made either a substantial beginning of their manufacture or commitments for their procurement;

(b) if the party against ~~whom~~ which enforcement is sought admits in ~~that~~ the party's pleading, ~~testimony or otherwise in court~~ or in the party's testimony or otherwise under oath that a lease contract was made, but the lease contract is not enforceable under this ~~provision~~ paragraph beyond the quantity of goods admitted; or

(c) with respect to goods that have been received and accepted by the lessee.

(5) The lease term under a lease contract referred to in subsection (4) is:

(a) if there is a ~~writing~~ record signed by the party against ~~whom~~ which enforcement is sought or by that party's authorized agent specifying the lease term, the term so specified;

(b) if the party against ~~whom~~ which enforcement is sought admits in ~~that~~ the party's pleading, ~~testimony or otherwise in court~~ or in the party's testimony or otherwise under oath a lease term, the term so admitted; or

(c) a reasonable lease term.

(6) A lease contract that is enforceable under this section is not unenforceable merely because it is not capable of being performed within one year or any other period after its making.

§ 2A–202.   Final ~~Written~~ Expression in a Record: Parol or Extrinsic Evidence.

(1) Terms with respect to which the confirmatory memoranda of the parties agree or which are otherwise set forth in a ~~writing~~ record intended by the parties as a final expression of their agreement with respect to such terms as are included therein may not be contradicted by evidence of any prior agreement or of a contemporaneous oral agreement but may be ~~explained or~~ supplemented by evidence of :

(a) ~~by course of dealing or usage of trade or by course of performance~~ course of performance, course of dealing, or usage of trade (Section 1–303); and

(b) ~~by evidence of~~ consistent additional terms unless the court finds the ~~writing~~ record to have been intended also as a complete and exclusive statement of the terms of the agreement.

(2) Terms in a record may be explained by evidence of course of performance, course of dealing, or usage of trade without a preliminary determination by the court that the language used is ambiguous.

§ 2A–203.   Seals Inoperative.

The affixing of a seal to a ~~writing~~ record evidencing a lease contract or an offer to enter into a lease contract does not render the ~~writing~~ record a sealed instrument and the law with respect to sealed instruments does not apply to the lease contract or offer.

§ 2A–204.   Formation in General.

(1) A lease contract may be made in any manner sufficient to show agreement, including offer and acceptance, conduct by both parties which recognizes the existence of a lease contract, the interaction of electronic agents, and the interaction of an electronic agent and an individual.

(2) An agreement sufficient to constitute a lease contract may be found although the moment of its making is undetermined.

(3) Even if ~~Although~~ one or more terms are left open, a lease contract does not fail for indefiniteness if the parties have intended to make a lease contract and there is a reasonably certain basis for giving an appropriate remedy.

(4) Except as otherwise provided in Sections 2A–222 through 2A–224, the following rules apply:

(a) A lease contract may be formed by the interaction of electronic agents of the parties, even if no individual was aware of or reviewed the electronic agents' actions or the resulting terms and agreements.

(b) A lease contract may be formed by the interaction of an electronic agent and an individual acting on the individual's own behalf or for another person. A lease contract is formed if the individual takes actions that the individual is free to refuse to take or makes a statement, and the individual has reason to know that the actions or statement will:

(i) cause the electronic agent to complete the transaction or performance; or

(ii) indicate acceptance of an offer, regardless of other expressions or actions by the individual to which the electronic agent cannot react.

§ 2A–205.   Firm Offers.

An offer by a merchant to lease goods to or from another person in a signed ~~writing~~ record that by its terms gives assurance it will be held open is not revocable, for lack of consideration, during the time stated or, if no time is stated, for a reasonable time, but in no event may the period of irrevocability exceed three ~~3~~ months. Any such term of assurance ~~on a form~~ in a form supplied by the offeree must be separately signed by the offeror.

§ 2A–208.   Modification, Rescission and Waiver.

(1) An agreement modifying a lease contract needs no consideration to be binding.

(2) A signed lease agreement that excludes modification or rescission except by a signed ~~writing~~ record may not be otherwise modified or

rescinded, but, except as between merchants, such a requirement ~~on a form~~ in a form supplied by a merchant must be separately signed by the other party.

(3) Although an attempt at modification or rescission does not satisfy the requirements of subsection (2), it may operate as a waiver.

(4) A party ~~who~~ that has made a waiver affecting an executory portion of a lease contract may retract the waiver by reasonable notification received by the other party that strict performance will be required of any term waived, unless the retraction would be unjust in view of a material change of position in reliance on the waiver.

§ 2A-211. Warranties Against Interference and Against Infringement; Lessee's Obligation Against Infringement.

~~(1) There is in a lease contract a warranty that for the lease term no person holds a claim to or interest in the goods that arose from an act or omission of the lessor, other than a claim by way of infringement or the like, which will interfere with the lessee's enjoyment of its leasehold interest.~~

~~(2) Except in a finance lease there is in a lease contract by a lessor who is a merchant regularly dealing in goods of the kind a warranty that the goods are delivered free of the rightful claim of any person by way of infringement or the like.~~

~~(3) A lessee who furnishes specifications to a lessor or a supplier shall hold the lessor and the supplier harmless against any claim by way of infringement or the like that arises out of compliance with the specifications.~~

(1) Except in a finance lease, a lessor in a lease contract warrants that, except for claims by any person by way of infringement or the like, for the duration of the lease no person holds:

(a) a claim to or interest in the goods not attributable to the lessee's own act or omission which will interfere with the lessee's enjoyment of its leasehold interest; or

(b) a colorable claim to or interest in the goods which will unreasonably expose the lessee to litigation.

(2) A finance lessor warrants that, except for claims by way of infringement or the like, for the duration of the lease no person holds:

(a) a claim or interest in the goods that arose from an act or omission of the lessor which will

interfere with the lessee's enjoyment of its leasehold interest; or

(b) a colorable claim to or interest in the goods that arose from an act or omission of the lessor which will unreasonably expose the lessee to litigation.

(3) Except in a finance lease, a lessor that is a merchant regularly dealing in goods of the kind warrants that the goods will be delivered free of the rightful claim of a third party by way of infringement or the like. However, a lessee that furnishes specifications to a lessor or a supplier holds the lessor and the supplier harmless against any claim of infringement or the like that arises out of compliance with the specifications.

(4) A warranty under this section may be excluded or modified only by specific language that is conspicuous and contained in a record, or by circumstances, including course of performance, course of dealing, or usage of trade, that give the lessee reason to know that the lessor purports to transfer only such right as the lessor or a third party may have, or that it is leasing subject to any claims of infringement or the like.

§ 2A-212. Implied Warranty of Merchantability.

(1) Except in a finance lease, a warranty that the goods will be merchantable is implied in a lease contract if the lessor is a merchant with respect to goods of that kind.

(2) Goods to be merchantable must be at least such as

(a) pass without objection in the trade under the description in the lease agreement;

(b) in the case of fungible goods, are of fair average quality within the description;

(c) are fit for the ordinary purposes for which goods of that ~~type~~ description are used;

(d) run, within the variation permitted by the lease agreement, of even kind, quality, and quantity within each unit and among all units involved;

(e) are adequately contained, packaged, and labeled as the lease agreement may require; and

(f) conform to any promises or affirmations of fact made on the container or label.

(3) Other implied warranties may arise from course of dealing or usage of trade.

§ 2A–214. Exclusion or Modification of Warranties.

(1) Words or conduct relevant to the creation of an express warranty and words or conduct tending to negate or limit a warranty must be construed wherever reasonable as consistent with each other; but, subject to ~~the provisions of~~ Section 2A–202 ~~on parol or extrinsic evidence~~, negation or limitation is inoperative to the extent that the construction is unreasonable.

(2) Subject to subsection (3), to exclude or modify the implied warranty of merchantability or any part of it the language must be in a record and be conspicuous. In a consumer lease the language must state "The lessor undertakes no responsibility for the quality of the goods except as otherwise provided in this contract," and in any other contract the language must mention "merchantability" ~~be by a writing, and be conspicuous~~. Subject to subsection (3), to exclude or modify ~~any~~ the implied warranty of fitness the exclusion must be ~~by a writing~~ in a record and be conspicuous. Language to exclude all implied warranties of fitness in a consumer lease must state "The lessor assumes no responsibility that the goods will be fit for any particular purpose for which you may be leasing these goods, except as otherwise provided in the contract," and in any other contract the language is sufficient if it ~~is in writing, is conspicuous and~~ states, for example, that "There ~~is~~ are no ~~warranty~~ warranties that ~~the goods will be fit for a particular purpose~~ extend beyond the description on the face hereof." Language that satisfies the requirements of this subsection for a consumer lease also satisfies its requirements for any other lease contract.

(3) Notwithstanding subsection (2):~~, but subject to subsection (4)~~

(a) unless the circumstances indicate otherwise, all implied warranties are excluded by expressions like "as is", "with all faults", or ~~by~~ other language that in common understanding calls the lessee's attention to the exclusion of warranties and makes plain that there is no implied warranty, if in ~~writing~~ a record and conspicuous;

(b) if the lessee before entering into the lease contract has examined the goods or the sample or model as fully as desired or has refused to examine the goods, after a demand by the lessor there is no implied warranty with regard to defects that an examination ought in the circumstances to have revealed to the lessee; and

(c) an implied warranty may also be excluded or modified by course of dealing, or course of performance, or usage of trade.

(4) Remedies for breach of warranty can be limited in accordance with Section 2A–503 and 2A–504.

~~(4) To exclude or modify a warranty against interference or against infringement (Section 2A–211) or any part of it, the language must be specific, be by a writing, and be conspicuous, unless the circumstances, including course of performance, course of dealing, or usage of trade, give the lessee reason to know that the goods are being leased subject to a claim or interest of any person.~~

§ 2A–219. Risk of Loss.

(1) Except in the case of a finance lease, risk of loss is retained by the lessor and does not pass to the lessee. In the case of a finance lease, risk of loss passes to the lessee.

(2) Subject to ~~the provisions of this Article on the effect of default on risk of loss~~ (Section 2A–220), if risk of loss is to pass to the lessee and the time of passage is not stated, the following rules apply:

(a) If the lease contract requires or authorizes the goods to be shipped by carrier

(i) and it does not require delivery at a particular destination, the risk of loss passes to the lessee when the goods are ~~duly~~ delivered to the carrier; but

(ii) if it does require delivery at a particular destination and the goods are there ~~duly~~ tendered while in the possession of the carrier, the risk of loss passes to the lessee when the goods are there ~~duly~~ so tendered as to enable the lessee to take delivery.

(b) If the goods are held by a bailee to be delivered without being moved, the risk of loss passes to the lessee on acknowledgment by the bailee to the lessee of the lessee's right to possession of the goods.

(c) In any case not within subsection (a) or (b), the risk of loss passes to the lessee on the lessee's receipt of the goods ~~if the lessor, or, in the case of a finance lease, the supplier, is a merchant; otherwise the risk passes to the lessee on tender of delivery~~.

§ 2A–220.   Effect of Default on Risk of Loss.

(1) Where risk of loss is to pass to the lessee and the time of passage is not stated:

(a) If a tender or delivery of goods so fails to conform to the lease contract as to give a right of rejection, the risk of their loss remains with the lessor, or, in the case of a finance lease, the supplier, until cure or acceptance.

(b) If the lessee rightfully revokes acceptance, he [or she] the lessee, to the extent of any deficiency in his [or her] its effective insurance coverage, may treat the risk of loss as having remained with the lessor from the beginning.

(2) Whether or not risk of loss is to pass to the lessee, if the lessee as to conforming goods already identified to a lease contract repudiates or is otherwise in default under the lease contract, the lessor, or, in the case of a finance lease, the supplier, to the extent of any deficiency in his [or her] its effective insurance coverage may treat the risk of loss as resting on the lessee for a commercially reasonable time.

§ 2A–221.   Casualty to Identified Goods.

If a lease contract requires goods identified when the lease contract is made, and the goods suffer casualty without fault of the lessee, the lessor or the supplier before delivery, or the goods suffer casualty before risk of loss passes to the lessee pursuant to the lease agreement or Section 2A–219, then:

(a) if the loss is total, the lease contract is avoided terminated; and

(b) if the loss is partial or the goods have so deteriorated as to no longer conform to the lease contract, the lessee may nevertheless demand inspection and at the lessee's his [or her] option either treat the lease contract as avoided terminated or, except in a finance lease that is not a consumer lease, accept the goods with due allowance from the rent payable for the balance of the lease term for the deterioration or the deficiency in quantity but without further right against the lessor.

PART 3

EFFECT OF LEASE CONTRACT

§ 2A–303.   Alienability of Party's Interest under Lease Contract or of Lessor's Residual Interest in Goods; Delegation of Performance; Transfer of Rights.

(1) As used in this section, "creation of a security interest" includes the sale of a lease contract that is subject to Article 9, Secured Transactions, by reason of Section 9–109(a)(3).

(2) Except as provided in subsection (3) and Section 9–407, a provision in a lease agreement which (i) prohibits the voluntary or involuntary transfer, including a transfer by sale, sublease, creation or enforcement of a security interest, or attachment, levy, or other judicial process, of an interest of a party under the lease contract or of the lessor's residual interest in the goods, or (ii) makes such a transfer an event of default, gives rise to the rights and remedies provided in subsection (5), but a transfer that is prohibited or is an event of default under the lease agreement is otherwise effective.

(3) A provision in a lease agreement which (i) prohibits a transfer of a right to damages for default with respect to the whole lease contract or of a right to payment arising out of the transferor's due performance of the transferor's entire obligation, or (ii) makes such a transfer an event of default, is not enforceable, and such a transfer is not a transfer that materially impairs the prospect of obtaining return performance by, materially changes the duty of, or materially increases the burden or risk imposed on, the other party to the lease contract within the purview of subsection (4).

(4) Subject to subsection (3) and Section 9–407:

(a) if a transfer is made which is made an event of default under a lease agreement, the party to the lease contract not making the transfer, unless that party waives the default or otherwise agrees, has the rights and remedies described in Section 2A–501(2);

(b) if paragraph (a) is not applicable and if a transfer is made that (i) is prohibited under a lease agreement or (ii) materially impairs the prospect of obtaining return performance by, materially changes the duty of, or materially increases the burden or risk imposed on, the other party to the lease contract, unless the party not making the transfer agrees at any time to the transfer in the lease contract or otherwise, then, except as limited by contract, (i) the transferor is liable to the party not making the transfer for damages caused by the transfer to the extent that the damages could not reasonably be prevented by the party not making the transfer and (ii) a court having jurisdiction may grant other appropriate relief, including cancellation of the lease contract or an injunction against the transfer.

(2) Subject to subsection (3) and except as otherwise provided in Section 9–407 or as otherwise agreed, a provision in a lease agreement which (i) prohibits the voluntary or involuntary transfer, including a transfer by sale, sublease, creation or enforcement of a security interest, or attachment, levy, or other judicial process, of an interest of a party under the lease contract or of the lessor's residual interest in the goods, or (ii) makes such a transfer an event of default, gives rise to the rights and remedies provided in subsection (4). However, a transfer that is prohibited or is an event of default under the lease agreement is otherwise effective.

(3) A provision in a lease agreement which (i) prohibits a transfer of a right to damages for default with respect to the whole lease contract or of a right to payment arising out of the transferor's due performance of the transferor's entire obligation, or (ii) makes such a transfer an event of default, is not enforceable, and such a transfer is not a transfer that materially impairs the prospect of obtaining return performance by, materially changes the duty of, or materially increases the burden or risk imposed on, the other party to the lease contract within subsection (4).

(4) Subject to subsection (3) and Section 9–407:

(a) if a transfer is made that is an event of default under a lease agreement, the party to the lease contract not making the transfer, unless that party waives the default or otherwise agrees, has the rights and remedies described in Section 2A–501(2);

(b) if paragraph (a) is not applicable and if a transfer is made that (i) is prohibited under a lease agreement or (ii) materially impairs the prospect of obtaining return performance by, ma-

terially changes the duty of, or materially increases the burden or risk imposed on, the other party to the lease contract, unless the party not making the transfer agrees at any time to the transfer in the lease contract or otherwise, then, except as limited by contract, (i) the transferor is liable to the party not making the transfer for damages caused by the transfer to the extent that the damages could not reasonably be prevented by the party not making the transfer and (ii) a court having jurisdiction may grant other appropriate relief, including cancellation of the lease contract or an injunction against the transfer.

(5) A transfer of "the lease" or of "all my rights under the lease", or a transfer in similar general terms, is a transfer of rights and, unless the language or the circumstances, as in a transfer for security, indicate the contrary, the transfer is a delegation of duties by the transferor to the transferee. Acceptance by the transferee constitutes a promise by the transferee to perform those duties. The promise is enforceable by either the transferor or the other party to the lease contract.

(6) Unless otherwise agreed by the lessor and the lessee, a delegation of performance does not relieve the transferor as against the other party of any duty to perform or of any liability for default.

(7) In a consumer lease, to prohibit the transfer of an interest of a party under the lease contract or to make a transfer an event of default, the language must be specific, by a ~~writing~~ record, and conspicuous.

§ 2A–304. Subsequent Lease of Goods by Lessor.

(1) Subject to Section 2A–303, a subsequent lessee from a lessor of goods under an existing lease contract obtains, to the extent of the leasehold interest transferred, the leasehold interest in the goods that the lessor had or had power to transfer, and except as provided in subsection (2) and Section 2A–527(4), takes subject to the existing lease contract. A lessor with voidable title has power to transfer a good leasehold interest to a good faith subsequent lessee for value, but only to the extent set forth in the preceding sentence. If goods have been delivered under a transaction

of purchase, the lessor has that power even if though:

(a) the lessor's transferor was deceived as to the identity of the lessor;

(b) the delivery was in exchange for a check which is later dishonored;

(c) it was agreed that the transaction was to be a "cash sale"; or

(d) the delivery was procured through ~~fraud punishable as larcenous under the criminal law~~ criminal fraud.

(2) A subsequent lessee in ~~the~~ ordinary course of business from a lessor ~~who~~ that is a merchant dealing in goods of that kind to ~~whom~~ which the goods were entrusted by the existing lessee of that lessor before the interest of the subsequent lessee became enforceable against that lessor obtains, to the extent of the leasehold interest transferred, all of that lessor's and the existing lessee's rights to the goods, and takes free of the existing lease contract.

(3) A subsequent lessee from the lessor of goods that are subject to an existing lease contract and are covered by a certificate of title issued under a statute of this State or of another jurisdiction takes no greater rights than those provided both by this section and by the certificate of title statute.

§ 2A–305. Sale or Sublease of Goods by Lessee.

(1) Subject to ~~the provisions of~~ Section 2A–303, a buyer or sublessee from the lessee of goods under an existing lease contract obtains, to the extent of the interest transferred, the leasehold interest in the goods that the lessee had or had power to transfer, and except as provided in subsection (2) and Section 2A–511(4), takes subject to the existing lease contract. A lessee with a voidable leasehold interest has power to transfer a good leasehold interest to a good faith buyer for value or a good faith sublessee for value, but only to the extent set forth in the preceding sentence. If ~~When~~ goods have been delivered under a transaction of lease the lessee has that power even if though:

(a) the lessor was deceived as to the identity of the lessee;

(b) the delivery was in exchange for a check which is later dishonored; or

(c) the delivery was procured through ~~fraud punishable as larcenous under the criminal law~~ criminal fraud.

(2) A buyer in ~~the~~ ordinary course of business or a sublessee in ~~the~~ ordinary course of business from a lessee ~~who~~ that is a merchant dealing in goods of that kind to ~~whom~~ which the goods were entrusted by the lessor obtains, to the extent of the interest transferred, all of the lessor's and lessee's rights to the goods, and takes free of the existing lease contract.

(3) A buyer or sublessee from the lessee of goods that are subject to an existing lease contract and are covered by a certificate of title issued under a statute of this State or of another jurisdiction takes no greater rights than those provided both by this section and by the certificate of title statute.

§ 2A–306. Priority of Certain Liens Arising by Operation of Law.

If a person in the ordinary course of ~~his [or her]~~ its business furnishes services or materials with respect to goods subject to a lease contract, a lien upon those goods in the possession of that person given by statute or rule of law for those materials or services takes priority over any interest of the lessor or lessee under the lease contract or this Article unless the lien is created by statute and the statute provides otherwise or unless the lien is created by rule of law and the rule of law provides otherwise.

§ 2A–307. Priority of Liens Arising by Attachment or Levy On, Security Interests In, and Other Claims to Goods.

~~(1) Except as otherwise provided in Section 2A–306, a creditor of a lessee takes subject to the lease contract.~~

~~(2) Except as otherwise provided in subsection (3) and in Sections 2A–306 and 2A–308, a creditor of a lessor takes subject to the lease contract unless the creditor holds a lien that attached to the goods before the lease contract became enforceable.~~

(1) Except as otherwise provided in Section 2A–306, a creditor of a lessee takes subject to the lease contract.

(2) Except as otherwise provided in subsection (3) and Sections 2A–306 and 2A–308, a creditor of a lessor takes subject to the lease contract

unless the creditor holds a lien that attached to the goods before the lease contract became enforceable.

(3) Except as otherwise provided in Sections 9–317, 9–321, and 9–323, a lessee takes a leasehold interest subject to a security interest held by a creditor of the lessor.

§ 2A–309. Lessor's and Lessee's Rights When Goods Become Fixtures.

(1) In this section:

(a) goods are "fixtures" if ~~when~~ they become so related to particular real property ~~estate~~ that an interest in them arises under real ~~estate~~ property law;

(b) a "fixture filing" is the filing, in the office where a ~~record of a~~ mortgage on the real property ~~estate~~ would be filed or recorded, of a financing statement covering goods that are or are to become fixtures and conforming to the requirements of Section 9–502(a) and (b);

(c) a lease is a "purchase money lease" unless the lessee has possession or use of the goods or the right to possession or use of the goods before the lease agreement is enforceable;

(d) a mortgage is a "construction mortgage" to the extent it secures an obligation incurred for the construction of an improvement on land, including the acquisition cost of the land, if ~~the recorded writing~~ a recorded record of the mortgage so indicates; and

(e) "encumbrance" includes real property ~~estate~~ mortgages and other liens on real property ~~estate~~ and all other rights in real property ~~estate~~ that are not ownership interests.

(2) Under this Article a lease may be of goods that are fixtures or may continue in goods that become fixtures, but no lease exists under this Article of ordinary building materials incorporated into an improvement on land.

(3) This Article does not prevent creation of a lease of fixtures pursuant to real ~~estate~~ property law.

(4) The perfected interest of a lessor of fixtures has priority over a conflicting interest of an encumbrancer or owner of the real property ~~estate~~ if:

(a) the lease is a purchase money lease, the conflicting interest of the encumbrancer or owner arises before the goods become fixtures, the interest of the lessor is perfected by a fixture filing before the goods become fixtures or within 10 ~~ten~~ days thereafter, and the lessee has an interest of record in the real property ~~estate~~ or is in possession of the real property ~~estate~~; or

(b) the interest of the lessor is perfected by a fixture filing before the interest of the encumbrancer or owner is of record, the lessor's interest has priority over any conflicting interest of a predecessor in title of the encumbrancer or owner, and the lessee has an interest of record in the real property ~~estate~~ or is in possession of the real property ~~estate~~.

(5) The interest of a lessor of fixtures, whether or not perfected, has priority over the conflicting interest of an encumbrancer or owner of the real property ~~estate~~ if:

(a) the fixtures are readily removable factory or office machines, readily removable equipment that is not primarily used or leased for use in the operation of the real property ~~estate~~, or readily removable replacements of domestic appliances that are goods subject to a consumer lease, and before the goods become fixtures the lease contract is enforceable; or

(b) the conflicting interest is a lien on the real property ~~estate~~ obtained by legal or equitable proceedings after the lease contract is enforceable; or

(c) the encumbrancer or owner has consented in ~~writing~~ a record to the lease or has disclaimed an interest in the goods as fixtures; or

(d) ~~the lessee has a right to remove the goods as against the encumbrancer or owner. If the lessee's right to remove terminates, the priority of the interest of the lessor continues for a reasonable time~~ the lessee has a right to remove the goods as against the encumbrancer or owner, but if the lessee's right to remove terminates, the priority of the interest of the lessor continues for a reasonable time.

(6) Notwithstanding subsection (4)(a) but otherwise subject to subsections (4) and (5), the interest of a lessor of fixtures, including the lessor's residual interest, is subordinate to the conflicting interest of an encumbrancer of the real property ~~estate~~ under a construction mortgage recorded before the goods become fixtures if the goods become fixtures before the completion of the construction. To the extent given to refinance a construction mortgage, the conflicting interest of an encumbrancer of the real property

estate under a mortgage has this priority to the same extent as the encumbrancer of the real property estate under the construction mortgage.

(7) In cases not within the preceding subsections In cases not covered by subsections (3) through (6), priority between the interest of a lessor of fixtures, including the lessor's residual interest, and the conflicting interest of an encumbrancer or owner of the real property estate who that is not the lessee is determined by the priority rules governing conflicting interests in real property estate.

(8) If the interest of a lessor of fixtures, including the lessor's residual interest, has priority over all conflicting interests of all owners and encumbrancers of the real property estate, the lessor or the lessee may (i) on default, expiration, termination, or cancellation of the lease agreement but subject to the agreement and this Article, or (ii) if necessary to enforce other rights and remedies of the lessor or lessee under this Article, remove the goods from the real property estate, free and clear of all conflicting interests of all owners and encumbrancers of the real property estate, but the lessor or lessee must reimburse any encumbrancer or owner of the real property estate who that is not the lessee and who that has not otherwise agreed for the cost of repair of any physical injury, but not for any diminution in value of the real property estate caused by the absence of the goods removed or by any necessity of replacing them. A person entitled to reimbursement may refuse permission to remove until the party seeking removal gives adequate security for the performance of this obligation.

(9) Even if though the lease agreement does not create a security interest, the interest of a lessor of fixtures, including the lessor's residual interest, is perfected by filing a financing statement as a fixture filing for leased goods that are or are to become fixtures in accordance with the relevant provisions of the Article on Secured Transactions (Article 9).

§ 2A–310. Lessor's and Lessee's Rights When Goods Become Accessions.

(1) Goods are "accessions" when they are installed in or affixed to other goods.

(2) The interest of a lessor or a lessee under a lease contract entered into before the goods became accessions is superior to all interests in the whole except as stated in subsection (4).

(3) The interest of a lessor or a lessee under a lease contract entered into at the time or after the goods became accessions is superior to all subsequently acquired interests in the whole except as stated in subsection (4) but is subordinate to interests in the whole existing at the time the lease contract was made unless the holders of such interests in the whole have in writing a record consented to the lease or disclaimed an interest in the goods as part of the whole.

(4) The interest of a lessor or a lessee under a lease contract described in subsection (2) or (3) is subordinate to the interest of

(a) a buyer in the ordinary course of business or a lessee in the ordinary course of business of any interest in the whole acquired after the goods became accessions; or

(b) a creditor with a security interest in the whole perfected before the lease contract was made to the extent that the creditor makes subsequent advances without knowledge of the lease contract.

(5) When under subsections (2) or (3) and (4) a lessor or a lessee of accessions holds an interest that is superior to all interests in the whole, the lessor or the lessee may (a) on default, expiration, termination, or cancellation of the lease contract by the other party but subject to the provisions of the lease contract and this Article, or (b) if necessary to enforce his [or her] other rights and remedies under this Article, remove the goods from the whole, free and clear of all interests in the whole, but he [or she] the lessor or the lessee must reimburse any holder of an interest in the whole who is not the lessee and who has not otherwise agreed for the cost of repair of any physical injury but not for any diminution in value of the whole caused by the absence of the goods removed or by any necessity for replacing them. A person entitled to reimbursement may refuse permission to remove until the party seeking removal gives adequate security for the performance of this obligation.

PART 4

PERFORMANCE OF LEASE CONTRACT: REPUDIATED, SUBSTITUTED AND EXCUSED

§ 2A–401. Insecurity: Adequate Assurance of Performance.

(1) A lease contract imposes an obligation on each party that the other's expectation of receiving due performance will not be impaired.

(2) If reasonable grounds for insecurity arise with respect to the performance of either party, the insecure party may demand in ~~writing~~ a record adequate assurance of due performance. Until the insecure party receives that assurance, if commercially reasonable the insecure party may suspend any performance for which ~~he [or she]~~ the insecure party has not already received the agreed return.

* * *

§ 2A–402. Anticipatory Repudiation.

(1) If either party repudiates a lease contract with respect to a performance not yet due under the lease contract, the loss of which performance will substantially impair the value of the lease contract to the other, the aggrieved party may:

(a) for a commercially reasonable time, await retraction of repudiation and performance by the repudiating party;

(b) make demand pursuant to Section 2A–401 and await assurance of future performance adequate under the circumstances of the particular case; or

(c) resort to any right or remedy upon default under the lease contract or this Article, even if ~~though~~ the aggrieved party has notified the repudiating party that the aggrieved party would await the repudiating party's performance and assurance and has urged retraction. In addition, whether or not the aggrieved party is pursuing one of the foregoing remedies, the aggrieved party may suspend performance or, if the aggrieved party is the lessor, proceed in accordance with the provisions of this Article on the lessor's right to identify goods to the lease contract notwithstanding default or to salvage unfinished goods under ~~(Section 2A–524)~~.

(2) Repudiation includes language that a reasonable person would interpret to mean that the other person will not or cannot make a performance still due under the contract or voluntary, affirmative conduct that would appear to a reasonable party to make a future performance by the other party impossible.

§ 2A–404. Substituted Performance.

(1) If without fault of the lessee, the lessor and the supplier, the agreed berthing, loading, or unloading facilities fail or the agreed type of carrier becomes unavailable or the agreed manner of ~~delivery~~ performance otherwise becomes commercially impracticable, but a commercially reasonable substitute is available, the substitute performance must be tendered and accepted.

* * *

§ 2A–405. Excused Performance.

Subject to Section 2A–404 on substituted performance, the following rules apply:

(a) Delay in ~~delivery or nondelivery~~ performance or nonperformance in whole or in part by a lessor or a supplier ~~who~~ that complies with paragraphs (b) and (c) is not a default under the lease contract if performance as agreed has been made impracticable by the occurrence of a contingency the nonoccurrence of which was a basic assumption on which the lease contract was made or by compliance in good faith with any applicable foreign or domestic governmental regulation or order, whether or not the regulation or order later proves to be invalid.

(b) If the causes mentioned in paragraph (a) affect only part of the lessor's or the supplier's capacity to perform, ~~he [or she]~~ the lessor or supplier shall allocate production and deliveries among ~~his [or her]~~ customers but at ~~his [or her]~~ the lessor's or supplier's option may include regular customers not then under contract for sale or lease as well as ~~his [or her]~~ the lessor's or supplier's own requirements for further manufacture. ~~He [or she]~~ The lessor or supplier may so allocate in any manner that is fair and reasonable.

(c) The lessor seasonally shall notify the lessee and in the case of a finance lease the supplier seasonally shall notify the lessor and the lessee, if known, that there will be delay or ~~nondelivery~~ nonperformance and, if allocation is required under paragraph (b), of the estimated quota thus made available for the lessee.

§ 2A–406. Procedure on Excused Performance.

(1) If the lessee receives notification of a material or indefinite delay or an allocation justified under Section 2A–405, the lessee may by ~~written~~ notification in a record to the lessor as to any goods involved, and with respect to all of the goods if under an installment lease contract the value of the whole lease contract is substantially impaired (Section 2A–510):

(a) terminate the lease contract (Section 2A–505(2)); or

(b) except in a finance lease that is not a consumer lease, modify the lease contract by accepting the available quota in substitution, with due allowance from the rent payable for the balance of the lease term for the deficiency but without further right against the lessor.

(2) If, after receipt of a notification from the lessor under Section 2A–405, the lessee fails so to modify the lease agreement within a reasonable time not exceeding 30 days, the lease contract ~~lapses~~ is terminated with respect to any ~~deliveries~~ performance affected.

PART 5

DEFAULT

A. IN GENERAL

§ 2A–504. Liquidation of Damages.

(1) Damages payable by either party for default, or any other act or omission, including indemnity for loss or diminution of anticipated tax benefits or loss or damage to lessor's residual interest, may be liquidated in the lease agreement but only at an amount or by a formula that is reasonable in light of the then anticipated harm caused by the default or other act or omission. Section 2A–503 determines the enforceability of a term that limits but does not liquidate damages.

(2) If the lease agreement provides for liquidation of damages, and such provision does not comply with subsection (1), or such provision is an exclusive or limited remedy that circumstances cause to fail of its essential purpose, remedy may be had as provided in this Article.

(3) If the lessor justifiably withholds or stops delivery of goods because of the lessee's default or insolvency (Section 2A–525 or 2A–526), the lessee is entitled to restitution of any amount by which the sum of his [or her] payments exceeds:

(a) the amount to which the lessor is entitled by virtue of terms liquidating the lessor's damages in accordance with subsection (1); or

(b) in the absence of those terms, 20 percent of the then present value of the total rent the lessee was obligated to pay for the balance of the lease term, or, in the case of a consumer lease, the lesser of such amount or $500.

(3) If the lessor justifiably withholds delivery of goods or stops performance because of the lessee's default or insolvency, the lessee is entitled to restitution of any amount by which the sum of the lessee's payments exceeds the amount to which the lessor is entitled by virtue of terms liquidating the lessor's damages in accordance with subsection (1).

(4) A lessee's right to restitution under subsection (3) is subject to offset to the extent the lessor establishes:

(a) a right to recover damages under the provisions of this Article other than subsection (1); and

(b) the amount or value of any benefits received by the lessee directly or indirectly by reason of the lease contract.

§ 2A–506. Statute of Limitations.

(1) An action for default under a lease contract, including breach of warranty or indemnity, must be commenced within four % x4 ~~years after the cause of action accrued.~~ By the original lease contract the parties may reduce the period of limitation to not less than one year ~~Except in a consumer lease or an action for indemnity, the~~

original lease agreement may reduce the period of limitations to not less than one year.

* * *

B. DEFAULT BY LESSOR

§ 2A–508. Lessee's Remedies.

(1) If a lessor fails to deliver the goods in conformity to the lease contract (Section 2A–509) or repudiates the lease contract (Section 2A–402), or a lessee rightfully rejects the goods (Section 2A–509) or justifiably revokes acceptance of the goods (Section 2A–517), then with respect to any goods involved, and with respect to all of the goods if under an installment lease contract the value of the whole lease contract is substantially impaired (Section 2A–510), the lessor is in default under the lease contract and the lessee may:

(a) cancel the lease contract (Section 2A–505(1));

(b) recover so much of the rent and security as has been paid and is just under the circumstances;

(c) cover and recover damages as to all goods affected whether or not they have been identified to the lease contract (Sections 2A–518 and 2A–520), or recover damages for nondelivery (Sections 2A–519 and 2A–520);

(d) exercise any other rights or pursue any other remedies provided in the lease contract.

(2) If a lessor fails to deliver the goods in conformity to the lease contract or repudiates the lease contract, the lessee may also:

(a) if the goods have been identified, recover them (Section 2A–522); or

(b) in a proper case, obtain specific performance or replevy the goods (Section 2A–521).

(1) If a lessor fails to deliver the goods in conformity to the lease contract or repudiates the contract, or a lessee rightfully rejects the goods or justifiably revokes acceptance of the goods, the lessor is in default under the lease contract, and the lessee may do one or more of the following:

(a) cancel the lease contract under Section 2A–505(1);

(b) recover so much of the rent and security as has been paid and is just under the circumstances;

(c) cover and obtain damages under Section 2A–518;

(d) recover damages for nondelivery under Section 2A–519(1);

(e) if an acceptance of goods has not been justifiably revoked, recover damages for default with regard to accepted goods under Section 2A–519(3) and (4);

(f) enforce a security interest under subsection (4);

(g) recover identified goods under Section 2A–522;

(h) obtain specific performance or obtain the goods by replevin or similar remedy under Section 2A–507A;

(i) recover liquidated damages under Section 2A–504;

(j) enforce limited remedies under Section 2A–503;

(k) exercise any other right or pursue any other remedy as provided in the lease contract.

(3) (2) If a lessor is otherwise in default under a lease contract, the lessee may exercise the rights and pursue the remedies provided in the lease contract, which may include a right to cancel the lease, and in Section 2A–519(3).

(4) (3) If a lessor has breached a warranty, whether express or implied, the lessee may recover damages (Section 2A–519(4)).

(5) (4) On rightful rejection or justifiable revocation of acceptance, a lessee has a security interest in goods in the lessee's possession or control for any rent and security that has been paid and any expenses reasonably incurred in their inspection, receipt, transportation, and care and custody and may hold those goods and dispose of them in good faith and in a commercially reasonable manner, subject to Section 2A–527(5).

(6) (5) Subject to the provisions of Section 2A–407, a lessee, on notifying the lessor of the lessee's intention to do so, may deduct all or any part of the damages resulting from any default under the lease contract from any part of the rent still due under the same lease contract.

§ 2A–509. Lessee's Rights on Improper Delivery; Rightful Manner and Effect of Rejection.

(1) Subject to the provisions of Section 2A–510 on default in installment lease contracts, if the goods or the tender or delivery fail in any respect to conform to the lease contract, the lessee may

~~reject or accept the goods or accept any commer-~~
~~cial unit or units and reject the rest of the goods.~~

~~(2) Rejection of goods is ineffective unless it is~~
~~within a reasonable time after tender or delivery~~
~~of the goods and the lessee seasonably notifies~~
~~the lessor.~~

(1) Subject to Sections 2A–503, 2A–504, and 2A–510, if the goods or the tender of delivery fail in any respect to conform to the contract, the lessee may:

(a) reject the whole;

(b) accept the whole; or

(c) accept any commercial unit or units and reject the rest.

(2) Rejection of goods must be within a reasonable time after their delivery or tender. It is ineffective unless the lessee seasonably notifies the lessor or supplier.

(3) Subject to Sections 2A–511, 2A–512, and 2A–517(6):

(a) after rejection any use by the lessee with respect to any commercial unit is wrongful as against the lessor or supplier; and

(b) if the lessee has before rejection taken physical possession of goods in which the lessee does not have a security interest under Section 2A–508(4), the lessee is under a duty after rejection to hold them with reasonable care at the lessor's or supplier's disposition for a time sufficient to permit the lessor or supplier to remove them; but

(c) the lessee has no further obligations with regard to goods rightfully rejected.

(d) The lessor's or supplier's remedies with respect to goods wrongfully rejected are governed by Section 2A–523.

* * *

§ 2A–510. Installment Lease Contracts: Rejection and Default.

(1) Under an installment lease contract a lessee may reject any delivery that is nonconforming if the nonconformity substantially impairs the value of that delivery to the lessee ~~and cannot be cured~~ or the nonconformity is a defect in the required documents; but if the nonconformity does not fall within subsection (2) and the lessor or the supplier gives adequate assurance of its cure, the lessee must accept that delivery.

(2) If ~~Whenever~~ a nonconformity or default with respect to one or more deliveries substan-

tially impairs the value of the installment lease contract as a whole there is a default with respect to the whole. But, the aggrieved party reinstates the installment lease contract as a whole if the aggrieved party accepts a nonconforming delivery without seasonably notifying of cancellation or brings an action with respect only to past deliveries or demands performance as to future deliveries.

§ 2A–511. Merchant Lessee's Duties as to ~~Rightfully~~ Rejected Goods.

(1) Subject to any security interest of a lessee (Section 2A–508(4)~~(5)~~), if a lessor or a supplier has no agent or place of business at the market of rejection, a merchant lessee, after rejection of goods in ~~his [or her]~~ the lessee's possession or control, shall follow any reasonable instructions received from the lessor or the supplier with respect to the goods. In the absence of those instructions, a merchant lessee shall make reasonable efforts to sell, lease, or otherwise dispose of the goods for the lessor's account if they threaten to decline in value speedily. ~~Instructions~~ In the case of a rightful rejection instructions are not reasonable if on demand indemnity for expenses is not forthcoming.

(2) If a merchant lessee (subsection (1)) or any other lessee (Section 2A–512) disposes of goods following a rightful rejection, ~~he [or she]~~ the lessee is entitled to reimbursement either from the lessor or the supplier or out of the proceeds for reasonable expenses of caring for and disposing of the goods and, if the expenses include no disposition commission, to such commission as is usual in the trade, or if there is none, to a reasonable sum not exceeding 10 percent of the gross proceeds.

(3) In complying with this section or Section 2A–512, the lessee is held only to good faith. Good faith conduct hereunder is neither acceptance or conversion nor the basis of an action for damages.

(4) A purchaser ~~who~~ that purchases in good faith from a lessee pursuant to this section or Section 2A–512 takes the goods free of any rights of the lessor and the supplier even if ~~though~~ the lessee fails to comply with one or more of the requirements of this Article.

* * *

§ 2A–512. Lessee's Duties as to Rightfully Rejected Goods.

(1) Except as otherwise provided with respect to goods that threaten to decline in value speedily (Section 2A–511) and subject to any security interest of a lessee (Section 2A–508(4)),

(a) the lessee, after rejection of goods in the lessee's possession, shall hold them with reasonable care at the lessor's or the supplier's disposition for a reasonable time after the lessee's seasonable notification of rejection;

(b) if the lessor or the supplier gives no instructions within a reasonable time after notification of rejection, the lessee may store the rejected goods for the lessor's or the supplier's account or ship them to the lessor or the supplier or dispose of them for the lessor's or the supplier's account with reimbursement in the manner provided in Section 2A–511; but

(c) the lessee has no further obligations with regard to goods rightfully rejected.

(1) If the lessor or the supplier gives no instructions within a reasonable time after notification of rejection, the lessee may store the rejected goods for the lessor's or the supplier's account or ship them to the lessor or the supplier or dispose of them for the lessor's or the supplier's account with reimbursement in the manner provided in Section 2A–511.

(2) Action by the lessee pursuant to subsection (1) is not acceptance or conversion.

§ 2A–513. Cure by Lessor of Improper Tender or Delivery; Replacement.

(1) If any tender or delivery by the lessor or the supplier is rejected because nonconforming and the time for performance has not yet expired, the lessor or the supplier may seasonably notify the lessee of the lessor's or the supplier's intention to cure and may then make a conforming delivery within the time provided in the lease contract.

(2) If the lessee rejects a nonconforming tender that the lessor or the supplier had reasonable grounds to believe would be acceptable with or without money allowance, the lessor or the supplier may have a further reasonable time to substitute a conforming tender if he [or she] seasonably notifies the lessee.

(1) If the lessee rejects goods or a tender of delivery under Section 2A–509 or 2A–510 or,

except in a consumer contract, justifiably revokes acceptance under Section 2A–517(1)(b) and the agreed time for performance has not expired, a lessor or a supplier that has performed in good faith, upon seasonable notice to the lessee, and at the lessor's or supplier's own expense, may cure the default by making a conforming tender of delivery within the agreed time. The lessor or supplier shall compensate the lessee for all of the lessee's reasonable expenses caused by the lessor's or supplier's default and subsequent cure.

(2) If the lessee rejects goods or a tender of delivery under Section 2A–509 or 2A–510 or, except in a consumer lease, justifiably revokes acceptance under Section 2A–517(1)(b) and the agreed time for performance has expired, a lessor or supplier that has performed in good faith may, upon seasonable notice to the lessee and at the lessor's or supplier's own expense, cure the default, if the cure is appropriate and timely under the circumstances, by making a tender of conforming goods. The lessor or supplier shall compensate the lessee for all of the lessee's reasonable expenses caused by the lessor's or supplier's default and subsequent cure.

§ 2A–514. Waiver of Lessee's Objections.

(1) In rejecting goods, a lessee's failure to state a particular defect that is ascertainable by reasonable inspection precludes the lessee from relying on the defect to justify rejection or to establish default:

(a) if, stated seasonably, the lessor or the supplier could have cured it (Section 2A–513); or

(b) between merchants if the lessor or the supplier after rejection has made a request in writing for a full and final written statement of all defects on which the lessee proposes to rely.

(1) A lessee's failure to state in connection with rejection a particular defect or in connection with revocation of acceptance a defect that justifies revocation precludes the lessee from relying on the unstated defect to justify rejection or revocation of acceptance if the defect is

ascertainable by reasonable inspection

(a) if the lessor or supplier had a right to cure the defect and could have cured it if stated seasonably; or

(b) between merchants if the lessor or the supplier after rejection or revocation of acceptance has made a request in a record for a full and final statement in a record of all defects on which the lessee proposes to rely.

(2) A lessee's failure to reserve rights when paying rent or other consideration against documents precludes recovery of the payment for defects apparent in ~~on the face of~~ the documents.

§ 2A–515. Acceptance of Goods.

(1) ~~Acceptance of goods occurs after the lessee has had a reasonable opportunity to inspect the goods and~~

(a) ~~the lessee signifies or acts with respect to the goods in a manner that signifies to the lessor or the supplier that the goods are conforming or that the lessee will take or retain them in spite of their nonconformity; or~~

(b) ~~the lessee fails to make an effective rejection of the goods (Section 2A–509(2)).~~

(1) Acceptance of goods occurs when the lessee:

(a) after a reasonable opportunity to inspect the goods signifies to the lessor or supplier that the goods are conforming or will be taken or retained in spite of their nonconformity;

(b) fails to make an effective rejection under Section 2A–509(2), but such acceptance does not occur until the lessee has had a reasonable opportunity to inspect them; or

(c) subject to Section 2A–517(6), uses the goods in any manner that is inconsistent with the lessor's or supplier's rights.

(2) Acceptance of a part of any commercial unit is acceptance of that entire unit.

§ 2A–516. Effect of Acceptance of Goods; Notice of Default; Burden of Establishing Default after Acceptance; Notice of Claim or Litigation to Person Answerable over.

(1) A lessee must pay rent for any goods accepted in accordance with the lease contract, ~~with due allowance for goods rightfully rejected or not delivered.~~

(2) A lessee's acceptance of goods precludes rejection of the goods accepted. In the case of a finance lease, if made with knowledge of a nonconformity, acceptance may not ~~cannot~~ be revoked because of it. In any other case, if made with knowledge of a nonconformity, acceptance may not ~~cannot~~ be revoked because of it unless

the acceptance was on the reasonable assumption that the nonconformity would be seasonably cured. Acceptance does not of itself impair any other remedy provided by this Article or the lease agreement for nonconformity.

(3) If a tender has been accepted:

(a) within a reasonable time after the lessee discovers or should have discovered any default, the lessee shall notify the lessor and the supplier, if any~~;, or be barred from any remedy against the party not notified~~ however, failure to give timely notice bars the lessee from a remedy only to the extent that the lessor or supplier is prejudiced by the failure;

(b) except in the case of a consumer lease, within a reasonable time after the lessee receives notice of litigation for infringement or the like (Section 2A–211) the lessee shall notify the lessor or be barred from any remedy over for liability established by the litigation; and

(c) the burden is on the lessee to establish any default.

(4) If a lessee is sued for indemnity, breach of a warranty or other obligation for which ~~a lessor or a supplier~~ another party is answerable over the following rules apply:

(a) The lessee may give ~~the lessor or the supplier, or both, written~~ the other party notice of the litigation in a record. If the notice states that the person notified may come in and defend and that if the person notified does not do so that person will be bound in any action against that person by the lessee by any determination of fact common to the two litigations, then unless the person notified after seasonable receipt of the notice does come in and defend that person is so bound.

(b) The ~~lessor or the supplier~~ other party may demand in ~~writing~~ a record that the lessee turn over control of the litigation including settlement if the claim is one for infringement or the like (Section 2A–211) or else be barred from any remedy over. If the demand states that the ~~lessor or the supplier~~ other party agrees to bear all expense and to satisfy any adverse judgment, then unless the lessee after seasonable receipt of the demand does turn over control the lessee is so barred.

(5) Subsections (3) and (4) apply to any obligation of a lessee to hold the lessor or the suppli-

er harmless against infringement or the like (Section 2A-211).

§ 2A-517. Revocation of Acceptance of Goods.

* * *

(5) A lessee ~~who~~ that so revokes has the same rights and duties with regard to the goods involved as if the lessee had rejected them.

(6) If a lessee uses the goods after a rightful rejection or justifiable revocation of acceptance, the following rules apply:

(a) Any use by the lessee which is unreasonable under the circumstances is wrongful as against the lessor or supplier and is an acceptance only if ratified by the lessor or supplier under Section 2-515(1)(c).

(b) Any use of the goods which is reasonable under the circumstances is not wrongful as against the lessor or supplier and is not an acceptance, but in an appropriate case the lessee shall be obligated to the lessor or supplier for the value of the use to the lessee.

§ 2A-522. Lessee's Right to Goods on Lessor's Insolvency.

(1) Subject to subsection (2) and even if ~~though~~ the goods have not been shipped, a lessee ~~who~~ that has paid a part or all of the rent and security for goods identified to a lease contract (Section 2A-217) on making and keeping good a tender of any unpaid portion of the rent and security due under the lease contract may recover the goods identified from the lessor if ~~the lessor becomes insolvent within 10 days after receipt of the first installment of rent and security.~~

(a) in the case of goods leased by a consumer, the lessor repudiates or fails to deliver as required by the lease contract; or

(b) in all cases, the lessor becomes insolvent within 10 days after receipt of the first installment on their rent and security.

(2) A lessee acquires the right to recover goods identified to a lease contract only if they conform to the lease contract.

C. DEFAULT BY LESSEE

§ 2A-523. Lessor's Remedies.

~~(1) If a lessee wrongfully rejects or revokes acceptance of goods or fails to make a payment~~ ~~when due or repudiates with respect to a part or the whole, then, with respect to any goods involved, and with respect to all of the goods if under an installment lease contract the value of the whole lease contract is substantially impaired (Section 2A-510), the lessee is in default under the lease contract and the lessor may:~~

~~(a) cancel the lease contract (Section 2A-505(1));~~

~~(b) proceed respecting goods not identified to the lease contract (Section 2A-524);~~

~~(c) withhold delivery of the goods and take possession of goods previously delivered (Section 2A-525);~~

~~(d) stop delivery of the goods by any bailee (Section 2A-526);~~

~~(e) dispose of the goods and recover damages (Section 2A-527), or retain the goods and recover damages (Section 2A-528), or in a proper case recover rent (Section 2A-529);~~

~~(f) exercise any other rights or pursue any other remedies provided in the lease contract.~~

(1) If the lessee wrongfully rejects or attempts to revoke acceptance of goods or fails to make a payment when due or repudiates with respect to a part or the whole, the lessee is in default under the lease contract with respect to any goods involved and the lessor may do one or more of the following:

(a) withhold delivery of the goods and take possession of goods previously delivered under Section 2A-525;

(b) stop delivery of the goods by any carrier or bailee under Section 2A-526;

(c) proceed under Section 2A-524 with respect to goods still unidentified to the lease contract or unfinished;

(d) obtain specific performance under Section 2A-507A or recover the rent under Section 2A-529;

(e) dispose of the goods and recover damages under Section 2A-527 or retain the goods and recover damages under Section 2A-528;

(f) cancel the lease contract under Section 2A-505(1);

(g) recover liquidated damages under Section 2A-504;

(h) enforce limited remedies under Section 2A-503;

(i) exercise any other rights or pursue any other remedies provided in the lease agreement.

(2) If a lessee becomes insolvent but is not in default of the lease contract under subsections (1) or (4), the lessor may:

(a) refuse to deliver the goods under Section 2A–525(1);

(b) take possession of the goods under Section 2A–525(2);

(c) stop delivery of the goods by any bailee or carrier under Section 2A–526(1).

(2) (3) If a lessor does not fully exercise a right or obtain a remedy to which the lessor is entitled under subsection (1), the lessor may recover the loss resulting in the ordinary course of events from the lessee's default as determined in any reasonable manner, together with incidental or consequential damages allowed under Section 2A–530, less expenses saved in consequence of the lessee's default.

(3) (4) If a lessee is otherwise in default under a lease contract, the lessor may exercise the rights and pursue the remedies provided in the lease contract, which may include a right to cancel the lease. In addition, unless otherwise provided in the lease contract:

(a) if the default substantially impairs the value of the lease contract to the lessor, the lessor may exercise the rights and pursue the remedies provided in subsections (1) or (2); or

(b) if the default does not substantially impair the value of the lease contract to the lessor, the lessor may recover as provided in subsection (2).

§ 2A–526. Lessor's Stoppage of Delivery in Transit or Otherwise.

(1) A lessor may stop delivery of goods in the possession of a carrier or other bailee if the lessor discovers the lessee to be insolvent and may stop delivery of carload, truckload, planeload, or larger shipments of express or freight if or if the lessee repudiates or fails to make a payment due before delivery, whether for rent, security or otherwise under the lease contract, or for any other reason the lessor has a right to withhold or take possession of the goods.

(2) In pursuing its remedies under subsection (1), the lessor may stop delivery until

(a) receipt of the goods by the lessee;

(b) acknowledgment to the lessee by any bailee of the goods, except a carrier, that the bailee holds the goods for the lessee; or

(c) such an acknowledgment to the lessee by a carrier via reshipment or as a warehouseman.

(3)(a) To stop delivery, a lessor shall so notify as to enable the bailee by reasonable diligence to prevent delivery of the goods.

(b) After notification, the bailee shall hold and deliver the goods according to the directions of the lessor, but the lessor is liable to the bailee for any ensuing charges or damages.

(c) A carrier who that has issued a nonnegotiable bill of lading is not obliged to obey a notification to stop received from a person other than the consignor.

§ 2A–527. Lessor's Rights to Dispose of Goods.

(1) After a default by a lessee under the lease contract of the type described in Section 2A–523(1) or 2A–523(3)(4)(a) or after the lessor refuses to deliver or takes possession of goods (Section 2A–525 or 2A–526), or, if agreed, after other default by a lessee, the lessor may dispose of the goods concerned or the undelivered balance thereof by lease, sale, or otherwise.

(2) Except as otherwise provided with respect to damages liquidated in the lease agreement (Section 2A–504) or otherwise determined pursuant to agreement of the parties (Section 1–102(3) 1–302 and 2A–503), if the disposition is by lease agreement substantially similar to the original lease agreement and the new lease agreement is made in good faith and in a commercially reasonable manner, the lessor may recover from the lessee as damages (i) accrued and unpaid rent as of the date of the commencement of the term of the new lease agreement, (ii) the present value, as of the same date, of the total rent for the then remaining lease term of the original lease agreement minus the present value, as of the same date, of the rent under the new lease agreement applicable to that period of the new lease term which is comparable to the then remaining term of the original lease agreement, and (iii) any incidental or consequential damages allowed under Section 2A–530, less expenses saved in consequence of the lessee's default.

(3) If the lessor's disposition is by lease agreement that for any reason does not qualify for

treatment under subsection (2), or is by sale or otherwise, the lessor may recover from the lessee as if the lessor had elected not to dispose of the goods and Section 2A–528 governs.

(4) A subsequent buyer or lessee ~~who~~ that buys or leases from the lessor in good faith for value as a result of a disposition under this section takes the goods free of the original lease contract and any rights of the original lessee even if ~~though~~ the lessor fails to comply with one or more of the requirements of this Article.

(5) The lessor is not accountable to the lessee for any profit made on any disposition. A lessee ~~who~~ that has rightfully rejected or justifiably revoked acceptance shall account to the lessor for any excess over the amount of the lessee's security interest (Section 2A–508~~(5)~~(4)).

Legislative Note: The cross-reference in subsection (2) should not be changed if the jurisdiction has not adopted the 2001 Revised Article 1.

§ 2A–528. Lessor's Damages for Non-acceptance, Failure to Pay, Repudiation, or Other Default.

(1) Except as otherwise provided with respect to damages liquidated in the lease agreement (Section 2A–504) or otherwise determined pursuant to agreement of the parties (Sections 1–302 and 2A–503), if a lessor elects to retain the goods or a lessor elects to dispose of the goods and the disposition is by lease agreement that for any reason does not qualify for treatment under Section 2A–527(2), or is by sale or otherwise, the lessor may recover from the lessee as damages for a default of the type described in Section 2A–523(1) or 2A–523~~(3)~~(4)(a), or, if agreed, for other default of the lessee, (i) accrued and unpaid rent as of the date of default if the lessee has never taken possession of the goods, or, if the lessee has taken possession of the goods, as of the date the lessor repossesses the goods or an earlier date on which the lessee makes a tender of the goods to the lessor, (ii) the present value as of the date determined under clause (i) of the total rent for the then remaining lease term of the original lease agreement minus the present value as of the same date of the market rent at the place where the goods are located computed for the same lease term, and (iii) any incidental or consequential damages allowed under Section

2A–530, less expenses saved in consequence of the lessee's default.

(2) If the measure of damages provided in subsection (1) is inadequate to put a lessor in as good a position as performance would have, the measure of damages is the present value of the profit, including reasonable overhead, the lessor would have made from full performance by the lessee, together with any incidental or consequential damages allowed under Section 2A–530~~, due allowance for costs reasonably incurred and due credit for payments or proceeds of disposition~~.

§ 2A–529. Lessor's Action for the Rent.

(1) After default by the lessee under the lease contract of the type described in Section 2A–523(1) or 2A–523~~(3)~~(4)(a) or, if agreed, after other default by the lessee, if the lessor complies with subsection (2), the lessor may recover from the lessee as damages:

(a) for goods accepted by the lessee and not repossessed by or tendered to the lessor, and for conforming goods lost or damaged within a commercially reasonable time after risk of loss passes to the lessee (Section 2A–219), (i) accrued and unpaid rent as of the date of entry of judgment in favor of the lessor, (ii) the present value as of the same date of the rent for the then remaining lease term of the lease agreement, and (iii) any incidental or consequential damages allowed under Section 2A–530, less expenses saved in consequence of the lessee's default; and

(b) for goods identified to the lease contract if the lessor is unable after reasonable effort to dispose of them at a reasonable price or the circumstances reasonably indicate that effort will be unavailing, (i) accrued and unpaid rent as of the date of entry of judgment in favor of the lessor, (ii) the present value as of the same date of the rent for the then remaining lease term of the lease agreement, and (iii) any incidental or consequential damages allowed under Section 2A–530, less expenses saved in consequence of the lessee's default.

(2) Except as provided in subsection (3), the lessor shall hold for the lessee for the remaining lease term of the lease agreement any goods that have been identified to the lease contract and are in the lessor's control.

(3) The lessor may dispose of the goods at any time before collection of the judgment for damages obtained pursuant to subsection (1). If the disposition is before the end of the remaining lease term of the lease agreement, the lessor's recovery against the lessee for damages is governed by Section 2A–527 or ~~Section~~ 2A–528, and the lessor will cause an appropriate credit to be provided against a judgment for damages to the extent that the amount of the judgment exceeds the recovery available pursuant to Section 2A–527 or 2A–528.

(4) Payment of the judgment for damages obtained pursuant to subsection (1) entitles the lessee to the use and possession of the goods not then disposed of for the remaining lease term of and in accordance with the lease agreement.

(5) After default by the lessee under the lease contract of the type described in Section 2A–523(1) or ~~Section~~ 2A–523~~(3)~~(4)(a) or, if agreed, after other default by the lessee, a lessor ~~who~~ that is held not entitled to rent under this section must nevertheless be awarded damages for non-acceptance under Section 2A–527 or ~~Section~~ 2A–528.

§ 2A–530. Lessor's Incidental and Consequential Damages.

(1) Incidental damages to an aggrieved lessor include any commercially reasonable charges, expenses, or commissions incurred in stopping delivery, in the transportation, care and custody of goods after the lessee's default, in connection with return or disposition of the goods, or otherwise resulting from the default.

(2) Consequential damages resulting from a lessee's default include any loss resulting from general or particular requirements and needs of which the lessee at the time of contracting had reason to know and which could not reasonably be prevented by disposition under Section 2A–527 or otherwise.

(3) In a consumer lease contract, a lessor may not recover consequential damages from a consumer.

§ 2A–531. Standing to Sue Third Parties for Injury to Goods.

(1) If a third party so deals with goods that have been identified to a lease contract as to cause actionable injury to a party to the lease contract (a) the lessor has a right of action against the third party, and (b) the lessee also has a right of action against the third party if the lessee:

~~(i)~~(a) has a security interest in the goods;

~~(ii)~~(b) has an insurable interest in the goods; or

~~(iii)~~(c) bears the risk of loss under the lease contract or has since the injury assumed that risk as against the lessor and the goods have been converted or destroyed.

(2) If at the time of the injury the party plaintiff did not bear the risk of loss as against the other party to the lease contract and there is no arrangement between them for disposition of the recovery, ~~his [or her]~~ the party plaintiff's suit or settlement, subject to ~~his [or her]~~ the party plaintiff's own interest, is as a fiduciary for the other party to the lease contract.

(3) Either party with the consent of the other may sue for the benefit of ~~whom~~ which it may concern.

APPENDIX I

UNREVISED UCC ARTICLE 7 (2002)

ARTICLE 7

WAREHOUSE RECEIPTS, BILLS OF LADING AND OTHER DOCUMENTS OF TITLE

PART 1. GENERAL

Section
7-101. Short Title.
7-102. Definitions and Index of Definitions.
7-103. Relation of Article to Treaty, Statute, Tariff, Classification or Regulation.

Section
7-104. Negotiable and Non-negotiable Warehouse Receipt, Bill of Lading or Other Document of Title.
7-105. Construction Against Negative Implication.

PART 2. WAREHOUSE RECEIPTS: SPECIAL PROVISIONS

Section
7-201. Who May Issue a Warehouse Receipt; Storage Under Government Bond.
7-202. Form of Warehouse Receipt; Essential Terms; Optional Terms.
7-203. Liability for Non-receipt or Misdescription.
7-204. Duty of Care; Contractual Limitation of Warehouseman's Liability.
7-205. Title Under Warehouse Receipt Defeated in Certain Cases.

Section
7-206. Termination of Storage at Warehouseman's Option.
7-207. Goods Must Be Kept Separate; Fungible Goods.
7-208. Altered Warehouse Receipts.
7-209. Lien of Warehouseman.
7-210. Enforcement of Warehouseman's Lien.

PART 3. BILLS OF LADING: SPECIAL PROVISIONS

Section
7-301. Liability for Non-receipt or Misdescription; "Said to Contain"; "Shipper's Load and Count"; Improper Handling.
7-302. Through Bills of Lading and Similar Documents.
7-303. Diversion; Reconsignment; Change of Instructions.

Section
7-304. Bills of Lading in a Set.
7-305. Destination Bills.
7-306. Altered Bills of Lading.
7-307. Lien of Carrier.
7-308. Enforcement of Carrier's Lien.
7-309. Duty of Care; Contractual Limitation of Carrier's Liability.

PART 4. WAREHOUSE RECEIPTS AND BILLS OF LADING: GENERAL OBLIGATIONS

Section
7-401. Irregularities in Issue of Receipt or Bill or Conduct of Issuer.

Section
7-402. Duplicate Receipt or Bill; Overissue.

Section
7–403. Obligation of Warehouseman or Carrier to Deliver; Excuse.

Section
7–404. No Liability for Good Faith Delivery Pursuant to Receipt or Bill.

Section

PART 5. WAREHOUSE RECEIPTS AND BILLS OF
LADING: NEGOTIATION AND TRANSFER

Section
7–501. Form of Negotiation and Requirements of "Due Negotiation".
7–502. Rights Acquired by Due Negotiation.
7–503. Document of Title to Goods Defeated in Certain Cases.
7–504. Rights Acquired in the Absence of Due Negotiation; Effect of Diversion; Seller's Stoppage of Delivery.
7–505. Indorser Not a Guarantor for Other Parties.

Section
7–506. Delivery Without Indorsement: Right to Compel Indorsement.
7–507. Warranties on Negotiation or Transfer of Receipt or Bill.
7–508. Warranties of Collecting Bank as to Documents.
7–509. Receipt or Bill: When Adequate Compliance With Commercial Contract.

Section

PART 6. WAREHOUSE RECEIPTS AND BILLS OF
LADING: MISCELLANEOUS PROVISIONS

Section
7–601. Lost and Missing Documents.
7–602. Attachment of Goods Covered by a Negotiable Document.

Section
7–603. Conflicting Claims; Interpleader.

PART 1

GENERAL

§ 7–101. Short Title.

This Article shall be known and may be cited as Uniform Commercial Code—Documents of Title.

Official Comment

This Article is a consolidation and revision of the Uniform Warehouse Receipts Act and the Uniform Bills of Lading Act, and embraces also the provisions of the Uniform Sales Act relating to negotiation of documents of title.

The only substantial omissions of material covered in the previous uniform acts are the criminal provisions found in the Warehouse Receipts and Bills of Lading acts. These criminal provisions are inappropriate to a Commercial Code, and for the most part duplicate portions of the ordinary criminal law relating to frauds.

The Article does not attempt to define the tort liability of bailees, except to hold certain classes of bailees to a minimum standard of reasonable care. For important classes of bailees, liabilities in case of loss, damage or destruction, as well as other legal questions associated with particular documents of title, are governed by federal statutes, international treaties, and in some cases regulatory state laws, which supersede the provisions of this Article in case of inconsistency. See Section 7–103.

§ 7–102. Definitions and Index of Definitions.

(1) In this Article, unless the context otherwise requires:

(a) "Bailee" means the person who by a warehouse receipt, bill of lading or other document of title acknowledges possession of goods and contracts to deliver them.

(b) "Consignee" means the person named in a bill to whom or to whose order the bill promises delivery.

(c) "Consignor" means the person named in a bill as the person from whom the goods have been received for shipment.

(d) "Delivery order" means a written order to deliver goods directed to a warehouseman, carrier or other person who in the ordinary course of business issues warehouse receipts or bills of lading.

(e) "Document" means document of title as defined in the general definitions in Article 1 (Section 1–201).

(f) "Goods" means all things which are treated as movable for the purposes of a contract of storage or transportation.

(g) "Issuer" means a bailee who issues a document except that in relation to an unaccepted delivery order it means the person who orders the possessor of goods to deliver. Issuer includes any person for whom an agent or employee purports to act in issuing a document if the agent or employee has real or apparent authority to issue documents, notwithstanding that the issuer received no goods or that the goods were misdescribed or that in any other respect the agent or employee violated his instructions.

(h) "Warehouseman" is a person engaged in the business of storing goods for hire.

(2) Other definitions applying to this Article or to specified Parts thereof, and the sections in which they appear are:

"Duly negotiate". Section 7–501.

"Person entitled under the document". Section 7–403(4).

(3) Definitions in other Articles applying to this Article and the sections in which they appear are:

"Contract for sale". Section 2–106.

"Overseas". Section 2–323.

"Receipt" of goods. Section 2–103.

(4) In addition Article 1 contains general definitions and principles of construction and interpretation applicable throughout this Article.

Official Comment

Prior Uniform Statutory Provision: Section 76, Uniform Sales Act; Section 58, Uniform Warehouse Receipts Act; Sections 1 and 53, Uniform Bills of Lading Act.

Changes: Applicable definitions from the uniform acts have been consolidated and revised; definition of delivery order is new.

Purposes of Changes and New Matter:

1. "Bailee" was not defined in the old uniform acts. It is used in this Article as a blanket term to designate carriers, warehousemen and others who normally issue documents of title on the basis of goods which they have received. The definition does not, however, require actual possession of the goods. If a bailee acknowledges possession when he does not have it he is bound by sections of this Article which declare the "bailee's" obligations. (See definition of "Issuer" in this section and Sections 7–203 and 7–301 on liability in case of non-receipt.)

2. The definition of warehouse receipt contained in the general definitions section of this Act (Section 1–201) eliminates the requirement of the Uniform Warehouse Receipts Act that the issuing warehouseman be "lawfully engaged" in business. The warehouseman's compliance with applicable state regulations such as the filing of a bond has no bearing on the substantive issues dealt with in this Article. Certainly the issuer's violations of law should not diminish his responsibility on documents he has put in commercial circulation. The Uniform Warehouse Receipts Act requirement that the warehouseman be engaged "for profit" has also been eliminated in view of the existence of state operated and co-operative warehouses. But it is still essential that the business be storing goods "for hire" (Section 1–201 and this section). A person does not become a warehouseman by storing his own goods.

3. Delivery orders, which were included without qualification in the Uniform Sales Act definition of document of title, must be treated differently in this consolidation of provisions from the three uniform acts. When a delivery order has been accepted by the bailee it is for practical purposes indistinguishable from a warehouse receipt. Prior to such acceptance there is no basis for imposing obligations on the bailee other than the ordinary obligation of contract which the bailee may have assumed to the depositor of the goods.

Cross References:

Point 1: Sections 7–203 and 7–301.

Point 2: Sections 1–201 and 7–203.

See general comment to document of title in Section 1–201.

Definitional Cross References:

"Bill of lading". Section 1–201.
"Contract". Section 1–201.
"Contract for sale". Section 2–106.
"Delivery". Section 1–201.
"Document of title". Section 1–201.
"Person". Section 1–201.
"Purchase". Section 1–201.
"Receipt of goods". Section 2–103.
"Right". Section 1–201.
"Warehouse receipt". Section 1–201.
"Written". Section 1–201.

§ 7–103. Relation of Article to Treaty, Statute, Tariff, Classification or Regulation.

To the extent that any treaty or statute of the United States, regulatory statute of this State or tariff, classification or regulation filed or issued pursuant thereto is applicable, the provisions of this Article are subject thereto.

Official Comment

Prior Uniform Statutory Provision: None.

Purposes:

1. To make clear what would of course be true without the Section, that applicable Federal law is paramount.

2. To make clear also that *regulatory* state statutes (such as those fixing or authorizing a commission to fix rates and prescribe services, authorizing different charges for goods of different values, and limiting liability for loss to the declared value on which the charge was based) are not affected by the Article and are controlling on the matters which they cover. Notice that the reference is not only to such statutes, but to tariffs, classifications and regulations filed or issued pursuant to them.

Cross References:

Sections 7–201, 7–202, 7–204, 7–206, 7–309, 7–401, and 7–403.

Definitional Cross Reference:

"Bill of lading". Section 1–201.

§ 7–104. Negotiable and Non-negotiable Warehouse Receipt, Bill of Lading or Other Document of Title.

(1) A warehouse receipt, bill of lading or other document of title is negotiable

   (a) if by its terms the goods are to be delivered to bearer or to the order of a named person; or

   (b) where recognized in overseas trade, if it runs to a named person or assigns.

(2) Any other document is non-negotiable. A bill of lading in which it is stated that the goods are consigned to a named person is not made negotiable by a provision that the goods are to be delivered only against a written order signed by the same or another named person.

Official Comment

Prior Uniform Statutory Provision: Sections 27 and 76, Uniform Sales Act; Sections 2, 3, 4, and 5, Uniform Warehouse Receipts Act; Sections 2, 3, 4, 5 and 53, Uniform Bills of Lading Act.

Changes: Consolidated and rewritten.

Purposes of Changes:

This Article deals with a class of commercial paper representing commodities in storage or transportation. This "commodity paper" is to be distinguished from what might be called "money paper" dealt with in the Article of this Act on Commercial Paper (Article 3) and "investment paper" dealt with in the Article of this Act on Investment Securities (Article 8). The class of "commodity paper" is designated "document of title" following the terminology of the Uniform Sales Act Section 76. Section 1–201. The distinctions between negotiable and nonnegotiable documents in this section makes the most important subclassification employed in the Article, in that the holder of negotiable documents may acquire more rights than his transferor had (See Section 7–502).

A document of title is negotiable only if it satisfies this section. "Deliverable on proper indorsement and surrender of this receipt" will not render a document negotiable. Bailees often include such provisions as a means of insuring return of non-negotiable receipts for record purposes. Such language may be regarded as insistence by the bailee upon a particular kind of receipt in connection with delivery of the goods. Subsections (1)(a) and (2) make it clear that a document is not negotiable which provides for delivery to order or bearer only if written instructions to that effect are given by a named person.

Cross Reference:

Section 7–502.

Definitional Cross References:

"Bearer". Section 1–201.
"Bill of lading". Section 1–201.
"Delivery". Section 1–201.
"Document of title". Section 1–201.
"Overseas". Section 2–323.
"Person". Section 1–201.
"Warehouse receipt". Section 1–201.

§ 7–105. Construction Against Negative Implication.

The omission from either Part 2 or Part 3 of this Article of a provision corresponding to a provision made in the other Part does not imply that a corresponding rule of law is not applicable.

Official Comment

Prior Uniform Statutory Provision: None.

Purposes:

To avoid any impairment, for example, of any common-law right of indemnity a warehouseman may have corresponding to Section 7–301(5), or of any contractual security interest a carrier might have corresponding to Section 7–209(2).

Cross References:

Parts 2 and 3 of Article 7.

PART 2

WAREHOUSE RECEIPTS: SPECIAL PROVISIONS

§ 7–201. Who May Issue a Warehouse Receipt; Storage Under Government Bond.

(1) A warehouse receipt may be issued by any warehouseman.

(2) Where goods including distilled spirits and agricultural commodities are stored under a statute requiring a bond against withdrawal or a license for the issuance of receipts in the nature of warehouse receipts, a receipt issued for the goods has like effect as a warehouse receipt even though issued by a person who is the owner of the goods and is not a warehouseman.

Official Comment

Prior Uniform Statutory Provision: Section 1, Uniform Warehouse Receipts Act.

Changes: Provision added to cover storage under government bond or under licensing statute.

Purposes:

It is not intended by reenactment of subsection (1) to repeal any provisions of special licensing or other statutes regulating who may become a warehouseman. See Section 10–103. Subsection (2) covers receipts issued by the owner for whiskey or other goods stored in bonded warehouses under such statutes as 26 U.S.C. Chapter 26. Limitations on the transfer of the receipts and criminal sanctions for violation of such limitations are not impaired. Section 7–103. Compare Section 7–401(d) on the liability of the issuer in such cases.

Cross References:

Sections 7–103, 7–401, 10–103.

Definitional Cross References:

"Warehouse receipt". Section 1–201.
"Warehouseman". Section 7–102.

§ 7–202. Form of Warehouse Receipt; Essential Terms; Optional Terms.

(1) A warehouse receipt need not be in any particular form.

(2) Unless a warehouse receipt embodies within its written or printed terms each of the following, the warehouseman is liable for damages caused by the omission to a person injured thereby:

(a) the location of the warehouse where the goods are stored;

(b) the date of issue of the receipt;

(c) the consecutive number of the receipt;

(d) a statement whether the goods received will be delivered to the bearer, to a specified person, or to a specified person or his order;

(e) the rate of storage and handling charges, except that where goods are stored under a field warehousing arrangement a statement of that fact is sufficient on a non-negotiable receipt;

(f) a description of the goods or of the packages containing them;

(g) the signature of the warehouseman, which may be made by his authorized agent;

(h) if the receipt is issued for goods of which the warehouseman is owner, either solely or jointly or in common with others, the fact of such ownership; and

(i) a statement of the amount of advances made and of liabilities incurred for which the warehouseman claims a lien or security interest (Section 7–209). If the precise amount of such advances made or of such liabilities incurred is, at the time of the issue of the receipt, unknown to the warehouseman or to his agent who issues it, a statement of the fact that advances have been made or liabilities incurred and the purpose thereof is sufficient.

(3) A warehouseman may insert in his receipt any other terms which are not contrary to the provisions of this Act and do not impair his obligation of delivery (Section 7–403) or his duty of care (Section 7–204). Any contrary provisions shall be ineffective.

Official Comment

Prior Uniform Statutory Provision: Section 2, Uniform Warehouse Receipts Act.

Changes: Exemption for field warehouse receipts added in subsection (2)(e).

Purposes:

To make clear that the formal requirements of the Uniform Warehouse Receipts Act are continued but not to displace particular legislation requiring other or different specifications of form, see Sections 7–103 and 10–103. This section does not require that a receipt be issued but states formal requirements for those which are issued.

Cross References:

Sections 7–103 and 10–103.

Definitional Cross References:

"Bearer". Section 1–201.

"Delivery". Section 1–201.

"Goods". Section 7–102.

"Person". Section 1–201.

"Security interest". Section 1–201.

"Term". Section 1–201.

"Warehouse receipt". Section 1–201.

"Warehouseman". Section 7–102.

"Written". Section 1–201.

§ 7–203. Liability for Non-receipt or Misdescription.

A party to or purchaser for value in good faith of a document of title other than a bill of lading relying in either case upon the description therein of the goods may recover from the issuer damages caused by the non-receipt or misdescription of the goods, except to the extent that the document conspicuously indicates that the issuer does not know whether any part or all of the goods in fact were received or conform to the description, as where the description is in terms of marks or labels or kind, quantity or condition, or the receipt or description is qualified by "contents, condition and quality unknown", "said to contain" or the like, if such indication be true, or the party or purchaser otherwise has notice.

Official Comment

Prior Uniform Statutory Provision: Section 20, Uniform Warehouse Receipts Act.

Changes: New section confined to problem of non-receipt and misdescription.

Purposes of Changes and New Matter:

This section is a simplified restatement of existing law as to the method by which a bailee may avoid responsibility for the accuracy of descriptions which are made by or in reliance upon information furnished by the depositor. The issuer is liable on documents issued by an agent, contrary to instructions of his principal, without receiving goods. No disclaimer of the latter liability is permitted.

Cross References:

Sections 7–301 and 7–203.

Definitional Cross References:

"Conspicuous". Section 1–201.

"Document". Section 7–102.

"Document of title". Section 1–201.

"Goods". Section 7–102.

"Issuer". Section 7–102.

"Notice". Section 1–201.

"Party". Section 1–201.
"Purchaser". Section 1–201.
"Receipt of goods". Section 2–103.
"Value". Section 1–201.

§ 7–204. Duty of Care; Contractual Limitation of Warehouseman's Liability.

(1) A warehouseman is liable for damages for loss of or injury to the goods caused by his failure to exercise such care in regard to them as a reasonably careful man would exercise under like circumstances but unless otherwise agreed he is not liable for damages which could not have been avoided by the exercise of such care.

(2) Damages may be limited by a term in the warehouse receipt or storage agreement limiting the amount of liability in case of loss or damage, and setting forth a specific liability per article or item, or value per unit of weight, beyond which the warehouseman shall not be liable; provided, however, that such liability may on written request of the bailor at the time of signing such storage agreement or within a reasonable time after receipt of the warehouse receipt be increased on part or all of the goods thereunder, in which event increased rates may be charged based on such increased valuation, but that no such increase shall be permitted contrary to a lawful limitation of liability contained in the warehouseman's tariff, if any. No such limitation is effective with respect to the warehouseman's liability for conversion to his own use.

(3) Reasonable provisions as to the time and manner of presenting claims and instituting actions based on the bailment may be included in the warehouse receipt or tariff.

(4) This section does not impair or repeal . . .

Note: *Insert in subsection (4) a reference to any statute which imposes a higher responsibility upon the warehouseman or invalidates contractual limitations which would be permissible under this Article.*

Official Comment

Prior Uniform Statutory Provision: Sections 3 and 21, Uniform Warehouse Receipts Act.

Changes: Consolidated and rewritten; material on limitation of remedy is new.

Purposes of Changes:

The old uniform acts provided that receipts could not contain terms impairing the obligation of reasonable care. Whether this is violated by a stipulation that in case of loss the bailee's liability is limited to stated amounts has been much controverted. The section is intended to eliminate that controversy by setting forth the conditions under which liability is so limited. However, as subsection (4) makes clear, the states as well as the federal government may supplement this section with more rigid standards of responsibility for some or all bailees.

Cross References:

Sections 7–103 and 10–103.

Definitional Cross References:

"Action". Section 1–201.
"Agreed". Section 1–201.
"Goods". Section 7–102.
"Reasonable time". Section 1–204.
"Sign". Section 1–201.
"Term". Section 1–201.
"Value". Section 1–201.
"Warehouse receipt". Section 1–201.
"Warehouseman". Section 7–102.
"Written". Section 1–201.

§ 7–205. Title Under Warehouse Receipt Defeated in Certain Cases.

A buyer in the ordinary course of business of fungible goods sold and delivered by a warehouseman who is also in the business of buying and selling such goods takes free of any claim under a warehouse receipt even though it has been duly negotiated.

Official Comment

Prior Uniform Statutory Provision: None.

Purposes:

The typical case covered by this section is that of the warehouseman-dealer in grain, and the substantive question at issue is whether in case the warehouseman becomes insolvent the receipt holders shall be able to trace and recover grain shipped to farmers and other purchasers from the elevator. This was possible under the old acts, although courts were eager to find estoppels to prevent it. The practical difficulty of tracing fungible grain means that the preservation of this theoretical right adds little to the commercial acceptability of negotiable grain receipts, which really circulate on the credit of the warehouseman. Moreover, on default of the warehouseman, the receipt holders at least share in what grain remains, whereas retaking the grain from a good faith cash purchaser reduces him completely to the status of general creditor in a situation where there was very little he could do to guard against the loss. Compare 15 U.S.C. Section 714p, enacted in 1955.

Cross References:

Sections 2–403 and 9–320.

Definitional Cross References:

"Buyer in ordinary course of business". Section 1–201.
"Delivery". Section 1–201.
"Duly negotiate". Section 7–501.
"Fungible" goods. Section 1–201.
"Goods". Section 7–102.
"Value". Section 1–201.
"Warehouse receipt". Section 1–201.
"Warehouseman". Section 7–102.

§ 7–206. Termination of Storage at Warehouseman's Option.

(1) A warehouseman may on notifying the person on whose account the goods are held and any other person known to claim an interest in the goods require payment of any charges and removal of the goods from the warehouse at the termination of the period of storage fixed by the document, or, if no period is fixed, within a stated period not less than thirty days after the notification. If the goods are not removed before the date specified in the notification, the warehouseman may sell them in accordance with the provisions of the section on enforcement of a warehouseman's lien (Section 7–210).

(2) If a warehouseman in good faith believes that the goods are about to deteriorate or decline in value to less than the amount of his lien within the time prescribed in subsection (1) for notification, advertisement and sale, the warehouseman may specify in the notification any reasonable shorter time for removal of the goods and in case the goods are not removed, may sell them at public sale held not less than one week after a single advertisement or posting.

(3) If as a result of a quality or condition of the goods of which the warehouseman had no notice at the time of deposit the goods are a hazard to other property or to the warehouse or to persons, the warehouseman may sell the goods at public or private sale without advertisement

on reasonable notification to all persons known to claim an interest in the goods. If the warehouseman after a reasonable effort is unable to sell the goods he may dispose of them in any lawful manner and shall incur no liability by reason of such disposition.

(4) The warehouseman must deliver the goods to any person entitled to them under this Article upon due demand made at any time prior to sale or other disposition under this section.

(5) The warehouseman may satisfy his lien from the proceeds of any sale or disposition under this section but must hold the balance for delivery on the demand of any person to whom he would have been bound to deliver the goods.

Official Comment

Prior Uniform Statutory Provision: Section 34, Uniform Warehouse Receipts Act.

Changes: Rewritten and expanded to define the warehouseman's right to terminate the storage not only where the goods are perishable or hazardous as in Uniform Warehouse Receipts Act, Section 34, but also for any other reason including decline in value of the goods imperilling the warehouseman's security for charges.

Purposes of Changes:

1. Most warehousing is for an indefinite term, the bailor being entitled to delivery on reasonable demand. It is necessary to define the warehouseman's power to terminate the bailment, since it would be commercially intolerable to allow warehousemen to order removal of the goods on short notice. The thirty day period provided where the document does not carry its own period of termination corresponds to commercial practice of computing rates on a monthly basis. The right to terminate under subsection (1) includes a right to require payment of "any charges", but does not depend on the existence of unpaid charges.

2. In permitting expeditious disposition of perishable and hazardous goods Uniform Warehouse Receipts Act, Section 34, made no distinction between cases where the warehouseman knowingly undertook to store such goods and cases where the goods were discovered to be of that character subsequent to storage. The former situation presents no such emergency as justifies the summary power of removal and sale. Subsections (2) and (3) distinguish between the two situations.

3. Protection of his lien is the only interest which the warehouseman has to justify summary sale of

perishable goods which are not hazardous. This same interest must be recognized when the stored goods, although not perishable, decline in market value to a point which threatens the warehouseman's security.

4. The right to order removal of stored goods is subject to provisions of the public warehousing laws of some states forbidding warehousemen from discriminating among customers. Nor does the section relieve the warehouseman of any obligation under the states laws to secure the approval of a public official before disposing of deteriorating goods. Such *regulatory* statutes and the regulations under them remain in force and operative. Sections 7–103, 10–103.

Cross References:

Sections 7–103, 7–403, 10–103.

Definitional Cross References:

"Delivery". Section 1–201.
"Document". Section 7–102.
"Good faith". Section 1–201.
"Goods". Section 7–102.
"Notice". Section 1–201.
"Notification". Section 1–201.
"Person". Section 1–201.
"Reasonable time". Section 1–204.
"Value". Section 1–201.
"Warehouseman". Section 7–102.

§ 7–207. Goods Must Be Kept Separate; Fungible Goods.

(1) Unless the warehouse receipt otherwise provides, a warehouseman must keep separate the goods covered by each receipt so as to permit at all times identification and delivery of those goods except that different lots of fungible goods may be commingled.

(2) Fungible goods so commingled are owned in common by the persons entitled thereto and the warehouseman is severally liable to each owner for that owner's share. Where because of overissue a mass of fungible goods is insufficient to meet all the receipts which the warehouseman has issued against it, the persons entitled include all holders to whom overissued receipts have been duly negotiated.

Official Comment

Prior Uniform Statutory Provision: Sections 22, 23 and 24, Uniform Warehouse Receipts Act.

Changes: Consolidated and revised; holders of overissued receipts permitted to share in mass of fungible goods.

Purposes of Changes:

No change of substance is made other than the explicit statement that holders to whom overissued receipts have been duly negotiated shall share in a mass of fungible goods. Where individual ownership interests are merged into claims on a common fund, as is necessarily the case with fungible goods, there is no policy reason for discriminating between successive purchasers of similar claims.

Definitional Cross References:

"Delivery". Section 1–201.
"Duly negotiate". Section 7–501.
"Fungible" goods. Section 1–201.
"Goods". Section 7–102.
"Holder". Section 1–201.
"Person". Section 1–201.
"Warehouse receipt". Section 1–201.
"Warehouseman". Section 7–102.

§ 7–208. Altered Warehouse Receipts.

Where a blank in a negotiable warehouse receipt has been filled in without authority, a purchaser for value and without notice of the want of authority may treat the insertion as authorized. Any other unauthorized alteration leaves any receipt enforceable against the issuer according to its original tenor.

Official Comment

Prior Uniform Statutory Provision: Section 13, Uniform Warehouse Receipts Act.

Changes: Generally revised and simplified; explicit treatment of the situation where a blank in an executed document is filled without authority.

Purposes of Changes:

1. The execution of warehouse receipts in blank is a dangerous practice. As between the issuer and an innocent purchaser the risks should clearly fall on the former.

2. An unauthorized alteration whether made with or without fraudulent intent does not relieve the issuer of his liability on the warehouse receipt as originally executed. The unauthorized alteration itself is of course ineffective against the warehouseman.

Definitional Cross References:

"Issuer". Section 7–102.

"Notice". Section 1–201.
"Purchaser". Section 1–201.
"Value". Section 1–201.
"Warehouse receipt". Section 1–201.

§ 7–209. Lien of Warehouseman.

(1) A warehouseman has a lien against the bailor on the goods covered by a warehouse receipt or on the proceeds thereof in his possession for charges for storage or transportation (including demurrage and terminal charges), insurance, labor, or charges present or future in relation to the goods, and for expenses necessary for preservation of the goods or reasonably incurred in their sale pursuant to law. If the person on whose account the goods are held is liable for like charges or expenses in relation to other goods whenever deposited and it is stated in the receipt that a lien is claimed for charges and expenses in relation to other goods, the warehouseman also has a lien against him for such charges and expenses whether or not the other goods have been delivered by the warehouseman. But against a person to whom a negotiable warehouse receipt is duly negotiated a warehouseman's lien is limited to charges in an amount or at a rate specified on the receipt or if no charges are so specified then to a reasonable charge for storage of the goods covered by the receipt subsequent to the date of the receipt.

(2) The warehouseman may also reserve a security interest against the bailor for a maximum amount specified on the receipt for charges other than those specified in subsection (1), such as for money advanced and interest. Such a security interest is governed by the Article on Secured Transactions (Article 9).

(3)(a) A warehouseman's lien for charges and expenses under subsection (1) or a security interest under subsection (2) is also effective against any person who so entrusted the bailor with possession of the goods that a pledge of them by him to a good faith purchaser for value would have been valid but is not effective against a person as to whom the document confers no right in the goods covered by it under Section 7–503.

(b) A warehouseman's lien on household goods for charges and expenses in relation to the goods under subsection (1) is also effective against all persons if the depositor was the legal possessor of the goods at the time of deposit. "Household goods" means furniture, furnishings and personal effects used by the depositor in a dwelling.

(4) A warehouseman loses his lien on any goods which he voluntarily delivers or which he unjustifiably refuses to deliver.

As amended in 1966.

Official Comment

Prior Uniform Statutory Provision: Sections 27 through 32, Uniform Warehouse Receipts Act.

Changes: Rewritten.

Purposes of Changes:

1. Subsection (1) defines the warehouseman's statutory lien. A specific lien attaches automatically, without express notation on the receipt, to goods stored under a non-negotiable receipt. That lien is limited to the usual charges arising out of a storage transaction; by notation on the receipt it can be made a general lien extending to like charges in relation to other goods. The same rules apply where the receipt is negotiable, except that as against a holder by due negotiation the lien is limited to the amount or rate specified on the receipt, or, if none is specified, to a reasonable charge for storage of the specific goods after the date of the receipt.

2. Subsection (2) provides for a security interest based upon agreement. Such a security interest arises out of relations between the parties other than bailment for storage or transportation, as where the bailee assumes the role of financer or performs a manufacturing operation, extending credit in reliance upon the goods covered by the receipt. Such a security interest is not a statutory lien. Compare Sections 9–109 and 9–333. It is governed in all respects by Article 9, except that subsection (2) requires that the receipt specify a maximum amount and limits the security interest to the amount specified.

3. Subsections (1) and (2) validate the lien and security interest "against the bailor." As against third parties, subsection (3)(a) continues the rule under the prior uniform statutory provision that to validate the lien the owner must have entrusted the goods to the depositor, and that the circumstances must be such that a pledge by the depositor to a good faith purchaser for value would have been valid. Thus the owner's interest will not be subjected to a lien or security interest arising out of a deposit of his goods by a thief.

The warehouseman may be protected because of the actual, implied or apparent authority of the depositor, because of a Factor's Act, or because of other circumstances which would protect a bona fide pledgee, unless those circumstances are denied effect under Section 7–503. Where the third party is the holder of a security interest, the rights of the warehouseman depend on the priority given to a hypothetical bona fide pledgee by Article 9, particularly Section 9–322. Thus the special priority granted to statutory liens by Section 9–333 does not apply to liens under subsection (1) of this section, since subsection (3) "expressly provides otherwise" within the meaning of Section 9–333. As to household goods, however, subsection (3)(b) makes the warehouseman's lien "for charges and expenses in relation to the goods" effective against all persons if the depositor was the legal possessor. The purpose of the exception is to permit the warehouseman to accept household goods for storage in sole reliance on the value of the goods themselves, especially in situations of family emergency. [This paragraph was amended in 1966].

4. It is unnecessary to state here, as in Uniform Warehouse Receipts Act 31, that a bailee with a valid lien need not deliver until the lien is satisfied. Section 7–403 provides that a person demanding delivery under a document must be prepared to satisfy the bailee's lien.

5. Where goods have been stored under a nonnegotiable warehouse receipt and are sold by the person to whom the receipt has been issued, frequently the goods are not withdrawn by the new owner. The obligations of the seller of the goods in this situation are set forth in Section 2–503(4) on tender of delivery and include procurement of an acknowledgment by the bailee of the buyer's right to possession of the goods. If a new receipt is requested, such an acknowledgment can be withheld until storage charges have been paid or provided for. The statutory lien for charges on the goods sold, granted by the first sentence of subsection (1), continues valid unless the bailee gives it up. But once a new receipt is issued to the buyer, the buyer becomes "the person on whose account the goods are held" under the second sentence of subsection (1); unless he undertakes liability for charges in relation to other goods stored by the seller, there is no general lien against the buyer for such charges. Of course, the bailee may preserve the general lien in such a case either by an arrangement by which the buyer "is liable for" such charges, or by reserving a security interest under subsection (2).

Cross References:

Point 2: Sections 9–109 and 9–333.
Point 3: Sections 7–503, 9–333 and 9–322.
Point 4: Section 7–403.
Point 5: Section 2–503.

Definitional Cross References:

"Deliver". Section 1–201.
"Document". Section 7–102.
"Goods". Section 7–102.
"Money". Section 1–201.
"Person". Section 1–201.
"Purchaser". Section 1–201.
"Right". Section 1–201.
"Security interest". Section 1–201.
"Value". Section 1–201.
"Warehouse receipt". Section 1–201.
"Warehouseman". Section 7–102.

§ 7–210. Enforcement of Warehouseman's Lien.

(1) Except as provided in subsection (2), a warehouseman's lien may be enforced by public or private sale of the goods in block or in parcels, at any time or place and on any terms which are commercially reasonable, after notifying all persons known to claim an interest in the goods. Such notification must include a statement of the amount due, the nature of the proposed sale and the time and place of any public sale. The fact that a better price could have been obtained by a sale at a different time or in a different method from that selected by the warehouseman is not of itself sufficient to establish that the sale was not made in a commercially reasonable manner. If the warehouseman either sells the goods in the usual manner in any recognized market therefor, or if he sells at the price current in such market at the time of his sale, or if he has otherwise sold in conformity with commercially reasonable practices among dealers in the type of goods sold, he has sold in a commercially reasonable manner. A sale of more goods than apparently necessary to be offered to insure satisfaction of the obligation is not commercially reasonable except in cases covered by the preceding sentence.

(2) A warehouseman's lien on goods other than goods stored by a merchant in the course of his business may be enforced only as follows:

(a) All persons known to claim an interest in the goods must be notified.

(b) The notification must be delivered in person or sent by registered or certified letter to the last known address of any person to be notified.

(c) The notification must include an itemized statement of the claim, a description of the goods subject to the lien, a demand for payment within a specified time not less than ten days after receipt of the notification, and a conspicuous statement that unless the claim is paid within that time the goods will be advertised for sale and sold by auction at a specified time and place.

(d) The sale must conform to the terms of the notification.

(e) The sale must be held at the nearest suitable place to that where the goods are held or stored.

(f) After the expiration of the time given in the notification, an advertisement of the sale must be published once a week for two weeks consecutively in a newspaper of general circulation where the sale is to be held. The advertisement must include a description of the goods, the name of the person on whose account they are being held, and the time and place of the sale. The sale must take place at least fifteen days after the first publication. If there is no newspaper of general circulation where the sale is to be held, the advertisement must be posted at least ten days before the sale in not less than six conspicuous places in the neighborhood of the proposed sale.

(3) Before any sale pursuant to this section any person claiming a right in the goods may pay the amount necessary to satisfy the lien and the reasonable expenses incurred under this section. In that event the goods must not be sold, but must be retained by the warehouseman subject to the terms of the receipt and this Article.

(4) The warehouseman may buy at any public sale pursuant to this section.

(5) A purchaser in good faith of goods sold to enforce a warehouseman's lien takes the goods free of any rights of persons against whom the lien was valid, despite noncompliance by the warehouseman with the requirements of this section.

(6) The warehouseman may satisfy his lien from the proceeds of any sale pursuant to this section but must hold the balance, if any, for delivery on demand to any person to whom he would have been bound to deliver the goods.

(7) The rights provided by this section shall be in addition to all other rights allowed by law to a creditor against his debtor.

(8) Where a lien is on goods stored by a merchant in the course of his business the lien may be enforced in accordance with either subsection (1) or (2).

(9) The warehouseman is liable for damages caused by failure to comply with the requirements for sale under this section and in case of willful violation is liable for conversion.

As amended in 1962.

Official Comment

Prior Uniform Statutory Provision: Section 33, Uniform Warehouse Receipts Act.

Changes: Rewritten; simplified foreclosure proceeding provided for all liens other than warehousemen's lien in non-commercial storage.

Purposes of Changes:

1. Subsection (1) makes "commercial reasonableness" the standard for foreclosure proceedings in all cases except non-commercial storage with a warehouseman. The latter category embraces principally storage of household goods by private owners; and for such cases the detailed provisions as to notification, publication and public sale, found in Section 33 of the Uniform Warehouse Receipts Act are retained in subsection (2). The swifter, more flexible procedure of subsection (1) is appropriate to commercial storage. Compare seller's power of resale on breach by buyer under the provisions of the Article on Sales (Section 2–706).

2. The provisions of subsections (4) and (5) permitting the bailee to bid at public sales and confirming the title of purchasers at foreclosure sales are designed to secure more bidding and better prices.

Cross Reference:

Section 7–403.

Definitional Cross References:

"Bill of lading". Section 1–201.
"Conspicuous". Section 1–201.
"Creditor". Section 1–201.
"Delivery". Section 1–201.

"Document". Section 7–102.
"Good faith". Section 1–201.
"Goods". Section 7–102.
"Notification". Section 1–201.
"Notifies". Section 1–201.

"Person". Section 1–201.
"Purchaser". Section 1–201.
"Rights". Section 1–201.
"Term". Section 1–201.
"Warehouseman". Section 7–102.

PART 3

BILLS OF LADING: SPECIAL PROVISIONS

§ 7–301. Liability for Non-receipt or Misdescription; "Said to Contain"; "Shipper's Load and Count"; Improper Handling.

(1) A consignee of a non-negotiable bill who has given value in good faith or a holder to whom a negotiable bill has been duly negotiated relying in either case upon the description therein of the goods, or upon the date therein shown, may recover from the issuer damages caused by the misdating of the bill or the non-receipt or misdescription of the goods, except to the extent that the document indicates that the issuer does not know whether any part or all of the goods in fact were received or conform to the description, as where the description is in terms of marks or labels or kind, quantity, or condition or the receipt or description is qualified by "contents or condition of contents of packages unknown", "said to contain", "shipper's weight, load and count" or the like, if such indication be true.

(2) When goods are loaded by an issuer who is a common carrier, the issuer must count the packages of goods if package freight and ascertain the kind and quantity if bulk freight. In such cases "shipper's weight, load and count" or other words indicating that the description was made by the shipper are ineffective except as to freight concealed by packages.

(3) When bulk freight is loaded by a shipper who makes available to the issuer adequate facilities for weighing such freight, an issuer who is a common carrier must ascertain the kind and quantity within a reasonable time after receiving the written request of the shipper to do so. In such cases "shipper's weight" or other words of like purport are ineffective.

(4) The issuer may by inserting in the bill the words "shipper's weight, load and count" or other words of like purport indicate that the goods were loaded by the shipper; and if such statement be true the issuer shall not be liable for damages caused by the improper loading. But their omission does not imply liability for such damages.

(5) The shipper shall be deemed to have guaranteed to the issuer the accuracy at the time of shipment of the description, marks, labels, number, kind, quantity, condition and weight, as furnished by him; and the shipper shall indemnify the issuer against damage caused by inaccuracies in such particulars. The right of the issuer to such indemnity shall in no way limit his responsibility and liability under the contract of carriage to any person other than the shipper.

Official Comment

Prior Uniform Statutory Provision: Section 23, Uniform Bills of Lading Act.

Changes: Rewritten in part.

Purposes of Changes:

1. The provision as to misdating in subsection (1) conforms to the policy of the amendment to the Federal Bills of Lading Act by 44 Stat. 1450 (1927), as amended 49 U.S.C. Section 102, after the holding in Browne v. Union Pac. R. Co., 113 Kan. 726, 216 P. 299 (1923), affirmed on other grounds 267 U.S. 255, 45 S.Ct. 315, 69 L.Ed. 601 (1925). Subsections (2) and (3) conform to the policy of the Federal Bills of Lading Act, 49 U.S.C. Sections 100, 101, and the laws of several states. See, e.g., N.Y.Pers.Prop.Law Section 209; Report of N.Y. Law Revision Commission, N.Y.Leg.Doc. (1941) No. 65(F).

2. The language of the old Uniform Act suggested that a carrier is ordinarily liable for damage caused by improper loading, but may relieve himself of liability by disclosing on the bill that shipper actually loaded. A more accurate statement of the law is that the carrier is not liable for losses caused by act or default of the shipper, which would include improper loading. There is some question whether under present law a carrier is liable even to a good faith purchaser of a negotiable bill for such losses, if the shipper's faulty

loading in fact caused the loss. It is this doubtful liability which subsection (4) permits the carrier to bar by disclosure of shipper's loading. There is no implication that decisions such as Modern Tool Corp. v. Pennsylvania R. Co., 100 F.Supp. 595 (D.N.J.1951), are disapproved.

3. This section is a simplified restatement of existing law as to the method by which a bailee may avoid responsibility for the accuracy of descriptions which are made by or in reliance upon information furnished by the depositor or shipper. The issuer is liable on documents issued by an agent, contrary to instructions of his principal, without receiving goods. No disclaimer of this liability is permitted since it is not a matter either of the care of the goods or their description.

4. The shipper's erroneous report to the carrier concerning the goods may cause damage to the carrier. Subsection (5) therefore provides appropriate indemnity.

Cross References:

Sections 7–203 and 7–309.

Definitional Cross References:

"Bill of lading". Section 1–201.
"Consignee". Section 7–102.
"Document". Section 7–102.
"Duly negotiate". Section 7–501.
"Good faith". Section 1–201.
"Goods". Section 7–102.
"Holder". Section 1–201.
"Issuer". Section 7–102.
"Notice". Section 1–201.
"Party". Section 1–201.
"Purchaser". Section 1–201.
"Receipt of goods". Section 2–103.
"Value". Section 1–201.

§ 7–302. Through Bills of Lading and Similar Documents.

(1) The issuer of a through bill of lading or other document embodying an undertaking to be performed in part by persons acting as its agents or by connecting carriers is liable to anyone entitled to recover on the document for any breach by such other persons or by a connecting carrier of its obligation under the document but to the extent that the bill covers an undertaking to be performed overseas or in territory not contiguous to the continental United States or an undertaking including matters other than trans-portation this liability may be varied by agreement of the parties.

(2) Where goods covered by a through bill of lading or other document embodying an undertaking to be performed in part by persons other than the issuer are received by any such person, he is subject with respect to his own performance while the goods are in his possession to the obligation of the issuer. His obligation is discharged by delivery of the goods to another such person pursuant to the document, and does not include liability for breach by any other such persons or by the issuer.

(3) The issuer of such through bill of lading or other document shall be entitled to recover from the connecting carrier or such other person in possession of the goods when the breach of the obligation under the document occurred, the amount it may be required to pay to anyone entitled to recover on the document therefor, as may be evidenced by any receipt, judgment, or transcript thereof, and the amount of any expense reasonably incurred by it in defending any action brought by anyone entitled to recover on the document therefor.

Official Comment

Prior Uniform Statutory Provision: None.

Purposes:

1. The purpose of this section is to subject the initial carrier under a through bill to suit for breach of the contract of carriage by any connecting carrier and to make it clear that any such connecting carrier holds the goods on terms which are defined by the document of title even though such connecting carrier did not issue the document. Since the connecting carrier does hold on the terms of the document, it must honor a proper demand for delivery or a diversion order just as the original bailee would have to. Similarly it has the benefits of the excuses for nondelivery and limitations of liability provided for the original bailee. Unlike the original bailee-issuer, the connecting carrier's responsibility is limited to the period while the goods are in its possession. The section is patterned generally after the Interstate Commerce Act, but does not impose any obligation to issue through bills.

2. The reference to documents other than through bills looks to the possibility that multi-purpose documents may come into use, e.g., combination warehouse receipts and bills of lading.

3. Where the obligations or standards applicable to different parties bound by a document of title are different, the initial carrier's responsibility for portions of the journey not on its own lines will be determined by the standards appropriate to the connecting carrier. Thus a land carrier issuing a through bill of lading involving water carriage at a later stage will have the benefit of the water carrier's immunity from liability for negligence of its servants in navigating the vessel, where the law provides such an immunity for water carriers and the loss occurred while the goods were in the water carrier's possession.

4. Under Subsection (1) the issuer of a through bill of lading may become liable for the fault of another person. Subsection (3) gives it appropriate rights of recourse.

Definitional Cross References:

"Agreement". Section 1–201.
"Bailee". Section 7–102.
"Bill of lading". Section 1–201.
"Delivery". Section 1–201.
"Document". Section 7–102.
"Goods". Section 7–102.
"Issuer". Section 7–102.
"Overseas". Section 2–323.
"Party". Section 1–201.
"Person". Section 1–201.

§ 7–303. Diversion; Reconsignment; Change of Instructions.

(1) Unless the bill of lading otherwise provides, the carrier may deliver the goods to a person or destination other than that stated in the bill or may otherwise dispose of the goods on instructions from

(a) the holder of a negotiable bill; or

(b) the consignor on a non-negotiable bill notwithstanding contrary instructions from the consignee; or

(c) the consignee on a non-negotiable bill in the absence of contrary instructions from the consignor, if the goods have arrived at the billed destination or if the consignee is in possession of the bill; or

(d) the consignee on a non-negotiable bill if he is entitled as against the consignor to dispose of them.

(2) Unless such instructions are noted on a negotiable bill of lading, a person to whom the bill is duly negotiated can hold the bailee according to the original terms.

Official Comment

Prior Uniform Statutory Provision: None.

Purposes:

1. The old Acts contained no reference to diversion, a very common commercial practice which defeats delivery to the consignee originally named in a bill of lading. The carrier was protected under the heading of "justified delivery" if the substituted consignee who received delivery was "a person lawfully entitled to possession of the goods." Cf. subsection (1)(d). This in turn depended on whether the person ordering the diversion was the owner of the goods or empowered to dispose of them, which again might depend upon whether under sales law title had passed from the consignor-seller to the consignee-buyer. The carrier is plainly not in a position to decide such questions when directed by the person with whom it has contracted for transportation to change the destination of the goods in transit. Carriers may as a business matter be willing to accept instructions from consignees in which case, as under the old uniform acts, the carrier will be liable for misdelivery if the consignee was not the owner or otherwise empowered to dispose of the goods. The section imposes no duty on carriers to undertake diversion; it is of course subject to the provisions of filed tariffs. Section 7–103.

2. It should be noted that the section provides only an immunity for carriers against liability for "misdelivery." It does not, for example, defeat the title to the goods which the consignee-buyer may have acquired from the consignor-seller upon delivery of the goods to the carrier under a non-negotiable bill of lading. Thus if the carrier, upon instructions from the consignor, returns the goods to him, the consignee may recover the goods from the consignor or his insolvent estate. However, under certain circumstances, the consignee's title may be defeated by diversion of the goods in transit to a different consignee.

Cross References:

Point 2: Sections 7–403 and 7–504(3).

Definitional Cross References:

"Bailee". Section 7–102.
"Bill of lading". Section 1–201.
"Consignee". Section 7–102.
"Consignor". Section 7–102.
"Delivery". Section 1–201.
"Goods". Section 7–102.

"Holder". Section 1–201.
"Notice". Section 1–201.
"Person". Section 1–201.
"Purchaser". Section 1–201.
"Term". Section 1–201.

§ 7–304. Bills of Lading in a Set.

(1) Except where customary in overseas transportation, a bill of lading must not be issued in a set of parts. The issuer is liable for damages caused by violation of this subsection.

(2) Where a bill of lading is lawfully drawn in a set of parts, each of which is numbered and expressed to be valid only if the goods have not been delivered against any other part, the whole of the parts constitute one bill.

(3) Where a bill of lading is lawfully issued in a set of parts and different parts are negotiated to different persons, the title of the holder to whom the first due negotiation is made prevails as to both the document and the goods even though any later holder may have received the goods from the carrier in good faith and discharged the carrier's obligation by surrender of his part.

(4) Any person who negotiates or transfers a single part of a bill of lading drawn in a set is liable to holders of that part as if it were the whole set.

(5) The bailee is obliged to deliver in accordance with Part 4 of this Article against the first presented part of a bill of lading lawfully drawn in a set. Such delivery discharges the bailee's obligation on the whole bill.

Official Comment

Prior Uniform Statutory Provision: Section 6, Uniform Bills of Lading Act.

Changes: This section adds to existing legislation, which merely prohibits bills in a set in ordinary domestic trade, a statement of the legal effect of a lawfully issued set.

Purposes of Changes:

The statement of the legal effect of a lawfully issued set is in accord with existing commercial law relating to maritime and other overseas bills. This law has been codified in the Hague and Warsaw Conventions and in the Carriage of Goods by Sea Act, the provisions of which would ordinarily govern in situations where bills in a set are recognized by this Article.

Cross Reference:

Section 10–103.

Definitional Cross References:

"Bailee". Section 7–102.
"Bill of lading". Section 7–102.
"Delivery". Section 1–201.
"Document". Section 7–102.
"Duly negotiate". Section 7–501.
"Good faith". Section 1–201.
"Goods". Section 7–102.
"Holder". Section 1–201.
"Issuer". Section 7–102.
"Overseas". Section 2–323.
"Person". Section 1–201.
"Receipt of goods". Section 2–103.

§ 7–305. Destination Bills.

(1) Instead of issuing a bill of lading to the consignor at the place of shipment a carrier may at the request of the consignor procure the bill to be issued at destination or at any other place designated in the request.

(2) Upon request of anyone entitled as against the carrier to control the goods while in transit and on surrender of any outstanding bill of lading or other receipt covering such goods, the issuer may procure a substitute bill to be issued at any place designated in the request.

Official Comment

Prior Uniform Statutory Provision: None.

Purposes:

This proposal is designed to facilitate the use of order bills in connection with fast shipments. Use of order bills on high speed shipments is impeded by the fact that the goods may arrive at destination before the documents, so that no one is ready to take delivery from the carrier. This is especially inconvenient for carriers by truck and air, who do not have terminal facilities where shipments can be held to await consignee's appearance. Order bills would be useful to take advantage of bank collection. This may be preferable to C.O.D. shipment in which the carrier, e.g. a truck driver, is the collecting and remitting agent. Financing of shipments under this plan would be handled as follows: seller at San Francisco delivers the goods to an airline with instructions to issue a bill in New York to a named bank. Seller receives a receipt embodying this undertaking to issue a destination bill. Airline wires its New York freight agent to issue the bill as instructed by the seller. Seller wires the New

York bank a draft on buyer. New York bank indorses the bill to buyer when he honors the draft. Normally seller would act through his own bank in San Francisco, which would extend him credit in reliance on the airline's contract to deliver a bill to the order of its New York correspondent. This section is entirely permissive; it imposes no duty to issue such bills. Whether a connecting carrier will act as issuing agent is left to agreement between carriers.

Definitional Cross References:

"Bill of lading". Section 1–201.
"Consignor". Section 7–102.
"Goods". Section 7–102.
"Issuer". Section 7–102.
"Receipt of goods". Section 2–103.

§ 7–306. Altered Bills of Lading.

An unauthorized alteration or filling in of a blank in a bill of lading leaves the bill enforceable according to its original tenor.

Official Comment

Prior Uniform Statutory Provision: Section 16, Uniform Bills of Lading Act.

Changes: Generally revised and simplified; explicit treatment of the situation where a blank in an executed document is filled without authority.

Purposes of Changes:

An unauthorized alteration whether made with or without fraudulent intent does not relieve the issuer of his liability on the document as originally executed. Uniform Warehouse Receipts Act 13 excused the issuer from any liability to a fraudulent alterer, other than the liability to deliver the goods according to the terms of the original document. It is difficult to conceive what liability the draftsman intended to excuse. Uniform Bills of Lading Act 16 contains no such excuse provision, and is followed in this respect in the present section. Uniform Bills of Lading Act 16 characterizes an unauthorized alteration as "void" but apparently nothing more was intended than that the alteration did not change the obligation of the issuer. This is sufficiently covered by the terms of this Section. Moreover cases are conceivable in which an alteration would not be "void"; for example, an alteration made by common consent of a transferor and transferee of a document might evidence an enforceable contract between them. The same rule is made applicable to the filling in of blanks, a matter on which the prior Acts were silent.

Definitional Cross References:

"Bill of lading". Section 1–201.
"Issuer". Section 7–102.

§ 7–307. Lien of Carrier.

(1) A carrier has a lien on the goods covered by a bill of lading for charges subsequent to the date of its receipt of the goods for storage or transportation (including demurrage and terminal charges) and for expenses necessary for preservation of the goods incident to their transportation or reasonably incurred in their sale pursuant to law. But against a purchaser for value of a negotiable bill of lading a carrier's lien is limited to charges stated in the bill or the applicable tariffs, or if no charges are stated then to a reasonable charge.

(2) A lien for charges and expenses under subsection (1) on goods which the carrier was required by law to receive for transportation is effective against the consignor or any person entitled to the goods unless the carrier had notice that the consignor lacked authority to subject the goods to such charges and expenses. Any other lien under subsection (1) is effective against the consignor and any person who permitted the bailor to have control or possession of the goods unless the carrier had notice that the bailor lacked such authority.

(3) A carrier loses his lien on any goods which he voluntarily delivers or which he unjustifiably refuses to deliver.

Official Comment

Prior Uniform Statutory Provision: Sections 27 through 32, Uniform Warehouse Receipts Act.

Changes: Rewritten; lien extended to carrier. Lien of common carrier validated unless carrier had notice that consignor lacked authority to subject the goods to charges and expenses. Where the carrier is not required by law to receive the goods for transportation, lien validated against anyone who permitted the bailor to have possession even if he had no real or apparent authority.

Purposes of Changes:

The section is intended to give carriers a specific statutory lien for charges and expenses similar to that given to warehousemen by the first sentence of Section 7–209. But since carriers do not commonly claim a lien for charges in relation to other goods or lend money on the security of goods in their hands, provisions for a general lien or a security interest similar to those in Section 7–209(1) and (2) are omitted. See Comment to Section 7–105. Since the lien given by this section is specific, and the storage or transportation often preserves or increases the value of the goods, subsection (2) validates the lien against anyone who permitted the bailor to have possession of the goods. Where the carrier is required to receive the goods for transportation, the owner's interest may be subjected to charges and expenses arising out of deposit of his goods by a thief. Cf. Section 9–333. The crucial mental element is the carrier's knowledge or reason to know of the bailor's lack of authority.

Cross References:

Sections 7–209, 9–109 and 9–333.

Definitional Cross References:

"Bill of lading". Section 1–201.
"Consignor". Section 7–102.
"Delivery". Section 1–201.
"Goods". Section 7–102.
"Person". Section 1–201.
"Purchaser". Section 1–201.
"Value". Section 1–201.

§ 7–308. Enforcement of Carrier's Lien.

(1) A carrier's lien may be enforced by public or private sale of the goods, in block or in parcels, at any time or place and on any terms which are commercially reasonable, after notifying all persons known to claim an interest in the goods. Such notification must include a statement of the amount due, the nature of the proposed sale and the time and place of any public sale. The fact that a better price could have been obtained by a sale at a different time or in a different method from that selected by the carrier is not of itself sufficient to establish that the sale was not made in a commercially reasonable manner. If the carrier either sells the goods in the usual manner in any recognized market therefor or if he sells at the price current in such market at the time of his sale or if he has otherwise sold in conformity with commercially reasonable practices among dealers in the type of goods sold he has sold in a commercially reasonable manner. A sale of more goods than apparently necessary to be offered to ensure satisfaction of the obligation is not commercially reasonable except in cases covered by the preceding sentence.

(2) Before any sale pursuant to this section any person claiming a right in the goods may pay the amount necessary to satisfy the lien and the reasonable expenses incurred under this section. In that event the goods must not be sold, but must be retained by the carrier subject to the terms of the bill and this Article.

(3) The carrier may buy at any public sale pursuant to this section.

(4) A purchaser in good faith of goods sold to enforce a carrier's lien takes the goods free of any rights of persons against whom the lien was valid, despite noncompliance by the carrier with the requirements of this section.

(5) The carrier may satisfy his lien from the proceeds of any sale pursuant to this section but must hold the balance, if any, for delivery on demand to any person to whom he would have been bound to deliver the goods.

(6) The rights provided by this section shall be in addition to all other rights allowed by law to a creditor against his debtor.

(7) A carrier's lien may be enforced in accordance with either subsection (1) or the procedure set forth in subsection (2) of Section 7–210.

(8) The carrier is liable for damages caused by failure to comply with the requirements for sale under this section and in case of willful violation is liable for conversion.

Official Comment

Prior Uniform Statutory Provision: Section 33, Uniform Warehouse Receipts Act.

Changes: Rewritten; provisions extended to carriers' liens; simplified foreclosure proceeding provided.

Purposes of Changes:

This section is intended to give the carrier an enforcement procedure of his lien coextensive with that given the warehousemen in cases other than those covering noncommercial storage by him. See Comment to Section 7–210.

Cross Reference:

Section 7–210.

Definitional Cross References:

"Bill of lading". Section 1–201.
"Creditor". Section 1–201.
"Delivery". Section 1–201.
"Good faith". Section 1–201.
"Goods". Section 7–102.

"Notification". Section 1–201.
"Notifies". Section 1–201.
"Person". Section 1–201.
"Purchaser". Section 1–201.
"Rights". Section 1–201.
"Term". Section 1–201.

§ 7–309. Duty of Care; Contractual Limitation of Carrier's Liability.

(1) A carrier who issues a bill of lading whether negotiable or non-negotiable must exercise the degree of care in relation to the goods which a reasonably careful man would exercise under like circumstances. This subsection does not repeal or change any law or rule of law which imposes liability upon a common carrier for damages not caused by its negligence.

(2) Damages may be limited by a provision that the carrier's liability shall not exceed a value stated in the document if the carrier's rates are dependent upon value and the consignor by the carrier's tariff is afforded an opportunity to declare a higher value or a value as lawfully provided in the tariff, or where no tariff is filed he is otherwise advised of such opportunity; but no such limitation is effective with respect to the carrier's liability for conversion to its own use.

(3) Reasonable provisions as to the time and manner of presenting claims and instituting actions based on the shipment may be included in a bill of lading or tariff.

Official Comment

Prior Uniform Statutory Provision: Section 3, Uniform Bills of Lading Act.

Changes: Consolidated and rewritten.

Purposes of Changes:

The old uniform act provided that bills of lading could not contain terms impairing the obligation of reasonable care. Whether this is violated by a stipulation that in case of loss the bailee's liability is limited to stated amounts has been much controverted. For interstate rail transportation the matter is settled by the Carmack Amendment to the Interstate Commerce Act (See 49 U.S.C.A. § 20(11)). The present section is a generalized version of the Interstate Commerce Act provisions. The obligation of due care is radically qualified, in the case of maritime bills and international airbills, by federal legislation and treaty. All this special legislation would remain in effect even if Congress enacts this Code, including the present Article. See Section 7–103.

Subsection (1) does not impair any rule of law imposing the liability of an insurer on a common carrier in intrastate commerce. Subsection (2), however, applies to such liability as well as to liability based on negligence. The entire section is subject under Section 7–103 to applicable provisions in filed tariffs, such as the common disclaimer of responsibility for undeclared articles of extraordinary value, hidden from view. Tariffs which lawfully provide a maximum unit value beyond which goods are not taken fall within the same principle, and are expressly covered by the words "value as lawfully provided in the tariff."

Cross Reference:

Section 7–103.

Definitional Cross References:

"Action". Section 1–201.
"Bill of lading". Section 1–201.
"Consignor". Section 7–102.
"Document". Section 7–102.
"Goods". Section 7–102.
"Value". Section 1–201.

PART 4

WAREHOUSE RECEIPTS AND BILLS OF LADING: GENERAL OBLIGATIONS

§ 7–401. Irregularities in Issue of Receipt or Bill or Conduct of Issuer.

The obligations imposed by this Article on an issuer apply to a document of title regardless of the fact that

(a) the document may not comply with the requirements of this Article or of any other law or regulation regarding its issue, form or content; or

(b) the issuer may have violated laws regulating the conduct of his business; or

(c) the goods covered by the document were owned by the bailee at the time the document was issued; or

(d) the person issuing the document does not come within the definition of warehouseman if it purports to be a warehouse receipt.

Official Comment

Prior Uniform Statutory Provision: Section 20, Uniform Warehouse Receipts Act; Section 23, Uniform Bills of Lading Act.

Changes: Most of the material is new; the uniform act sections cited deal only with non-receipt and misdescription.

Purposes of Changes and New Matter:

The bailee's liability on his document despite non-receipt or misdescription of the goods is affirmed in Sections 7–203 and 7–301. The purpose of this section is to make it clear that regardless of irregularities a document which falls within the definition of document of title imposes on the issuer the obligations stated in this Article. For example, a bailee will not be permitted to avoid his obligation to deliver the goods (Section 7–403) or his obligation of due care with respect to them (Sections 7–204 and 7–309) by taking the position that no valid "document" was issued because he failed to file a statutory bond or did not pay stamp taxes or did not disclose the place of storage in the document. Sanctions against violations of statutory or administrative duties with respect to documents should be limited to revocation of license or other measures prescribed by the regulation imposing the duty. As to the continuing vitality of regulations, in addition to those found in this Article, of documents of title, see Sections 7–103 and 10–103.

Cross References:

Sections 7–103, 7–203, 7–204, 7–301, 7–309 and 10–103.

Definitional Cross References:

"Bailee". Section 7–102.
"Document". Section 7–102.
"Document of title". Section 1–201.
"Goods". Section 7–102.
"Issuer". Section 7–102.
"Person". Section 1–201.
"Warehouse receipt". Section 1–201.
"Warehouseman". Section 7–102.

§ 7–402. Duplicate Receipt or Bill; Overissue.

Neither a duplicate nor any other document of title purporting to cover goods already represented by an outstanding document of the same issuer confers any right in the goods, except as provided in the case of bills in a set, overissue of documents for fungible goods and substitutes for lost, stolen or destroyed documents. But the issuer is liable for damages caused by his overissue or failure to identify a duplicate document as such by conspicuous notation on its face.

Official Comment

Prior Uniform Statutory Provision: Section 6, Uniform Warehouse Receipts Act; Section 7, Uniform Bills of Lading Act.

Changes: Consolidated and rewritten.

Purposes of Changes:

1. This section treats a duplicate which is not properly identified as such like any other overissue of documents: a purchaser of such a document acquires no title but only a cause of action for damages against the person who made his deception possible, except in the cases noted in the section. But parts of a bill lawfully issued in a set of parts are not "overissue" (Section 7–304). Of course, if the issuer has clearly indicated that a document is a duplicate so that no one can be deceived by it, and in fact the duplicate is a correct copy of the original, the warehouseman is not liable for preparing and delivering such a duplicate copy.

2. The section applies to nonnegotiable documents to the extent of providing an action for damages for one who acquires an unmarked duplicate from a transferor who knew the facts and would therefore himself have had no cause of action against the issuer of the duplicate. Ordinarily the transferee of a nonnegotiable document acquires only the rights of his transferor.

3. Overissue is defined so as to exclude the common situation where two valid documents of different issuers are outstanding for the same goods at the same time. Thus freight forwarders commonly issue bills of lading to their customers for small shipments to be combined into carload shipments for which the railroad will issue a bill of lading to the forwarder. So also a warehouse receipt may be outstanding against goods, and the holder of the receipt may issue delivery orders against the same goods. In these cases dealings with the subsequently issued documents may be effective to transfer title; e.g. negotiation of a delivery order will effectively transfer title in the ordinary case where no dishonesty has occurred and the goods are available to satisfy the orders. Section 7–503 provides for cases of conflict between documents of different issuers.

Cross References:

Point 1: Sections 7–207, 7–304, and 7–601.
Point 3: Section 7–503.

Definitional Cross References:

"Bill of lading". Section 1–201.
"Conspicuous". Section 1–201.
"Document". Section 7–102.
"Document of title". Section 1–201.
"Fungible" goods. Section 1–201.
"Goods". Section 7–102.
"Issuer". Section 7–102.
"Right". Section 1–201.

§ 7–403. Obligation of Warehouseman or Carrier to Deliver; Excuse.

(1) The bailee must deliver the goods to a person entitled under the document who complies with subsections (2) and (3), unless and to the extent that the bailee establishes any of the following:

(a) delivery of the goods to a person whose receipt was rightful as against the claimant;

(b) damage to or delay, loss or destruction of the goods for which the bailee is not liable [, but the burden of establishing negligence in such cases is on the person entitled under the document];

Note: *The brackets in (1)(b) indicate that State enactments may differ on this point without serious damage to the principle of uniformity.*

(c) previous sale or other disposition of the goods in lawful enforcement of a lien or on warehouseman's lawful termination of storage;

(d) the exercise by a seller of his right to stop delivery pursuant to the provisions of the Article on Sales (Section 2–705);

(e) a diversion, reconsignment or other disposition pursuant to the provisions of this Article (Section 7–303) or tariff regulating such right;

(f) release, satisfaction or any other fact affording a personal defense against the claimant;

(g) any other lawful excuse.

(2) A person claiming goods covered by a document of title must satisfy the bailee's lien where the bailee so requests or where the bailee is prohibited by law from delivering the goods until the charges are paid.

(3) Unless the person claiming is one against whom the document confers no right under Sec. 7–503(1), he must surrender for cancellation or notation of partial deliveries any outstanding negotiable document covering the goods, and the bailee must cancel the document or conspicuously note the partial delivery thereon or be liable to any person to whom the document is duly negotiated.

(4) "Person entitled under the document" means holder in the case of a negotiable document, or the person to whom delivery is to be made by the terms of or pursuant to written instructions under a non-negotiable document.

Official Comment

Prior Uniform Statutory Provision: Sections 8 through 12, 16 and 19, Uniform Warehouse Receipts Act; Sections 11 through 15, 19 and 22, Uniform Bills of Lading Act.

Changes: Consolidated and rewritten.

Purposes of Changes:

1. The general and primary purpose of this revision is to simplify the statement of the bailee's obligation on the document. The interrelations of the separate sections of the old uniform acts dealing with "obligation to deliver," "justification in delivering," and "liability for misdelivery" are obscure. The present section is constructed on the basis of stating what previous deliveries or other circumstances operate to excuse the bailee's normal obligation on the document. Accordingly, "justified" deliveries under the old uniform acts now find their place as "excuse" under subsection (1). Unjustified deliveries, i.e., "misdeliveries" under the old acts, are simply omitted from the list of excuses, thus permitting the normal obligation on the document to be asserted.

2. The principal case covered by subsection (1)(a) is delivery to a person whose title is paramount to the rights represented by the document. For example, if a thief deposits stolen goods in a warehouse and takes a negotiable receipt, the warehouseman is not liable on the receipt if he has surrendered the goods to the true owner, even though the receipt is held by a good faith purchaser. See Section 7–503(1). However, if the owner entrusted the goods to a person with power of

disposition, and that person deposited the goods and took a negotiable document, the owner's receipt would not be rightful as against a holder to whom the negotiable document was duly negotiated, and delivery to the owner would not give the bailee a defense against such a holder. See Sections 7–502(1)(b), 7–503(1)(a).

3. Subsection (1)(b) amounts to a cross reference to all the tort law that determines the varying responsibilities and standards of care applicable to commercial bailees. A restatement of this tort law would be beyond the scope of this Act. Much of the applicable law as to responsibility of bailees for the preservation of the goods and limitation of liability in case of loss has been codified for particular classes of bailees in interstate and foreign commerce by federal legislation and treaty and for intrastate carriers and other bailees by the regulatory state laws preserved by Section 7–103. In the absence of governing legislation the common law will prevail subject to the minimum standard of reasonable care prescribed by Sections 7–204 and 7–309 of this Article. The optional language in subsection (1)(b) states the rule laid down for interstate carriers in many federal cases. State decisions are in conflict as to both carriers and warehousemen. Particular states may prefer to adopt the federal rule.

4. Subsection (2) eliminates the implication of the old uniform acts that a request for delivery must be accompanied by a formal tender of the amount of the charges due. Rather, the bailee must request payment of the amount of his lien when asked to deliver, and only in case this request is refused is he justified in declining to deliver because of nonpayment of charges. Where delivery without payment is forbidden by law, the request is treated as implicit. Such a prohibition reflects a policy of uniformity to prevent discrimination by failure to request payment in particular cases.

5. Subsection (3) states the obvious duty of a bailee to take up a negotiable document or note partial deliveries conspicuously thereon, and the result of failure in that duty. It is subject to only one exception, that stated in subsection 1(a) of this section and in Section 7–503(1). It is limited to cases of delivery to a claimant; it has no application, for example, where goods held under a negotiable document are lawfully sold to enforce the bailee's lien.

Cross References:

Point 2: Sections 7–502 and 7–503.
Point 3: Sections 7–103, 7–204, 7–309 and 10–103.
Point 5: Section 7–503(1).

Definitional Cross References:

"Bailee". Section 7–102.

"Conspicuous". Section 1–201.
"Delivery". Section 1–201.
"Document". Section 7–102.
"Document of title". Section 1–201.
"Duly negotiate". Section 7–501.
"Goods". Section 7–102.
"Person". Section 1–201.
"Receipt of goods". Section 2–103.
"Right". Section 1–201.
"Terms". Section 1–201.
"Warehouseman". Section 7–102.
"Written". Section 1–201.

§ 7–404. No Liability for Good Faith Delivery Pursuant to Receipt or Bill.

A bailee who in good faith including observance of reasonable commercial standards has received goods and delivered or otherwise disposed of them according to the terms of the document of title or pursuant to this Article is not liable therefor. This rule applies even though the person from whom he received the goods had no authority to procure the document or to dispose of the goods and even though the person to whom he delivered the goods had no authority to receive them.

Official Comment

Prior Uniform Statutory Provision: Section 10, Uniform Warehouse Receipts Act; Section 13, Uniform Bills of Lading Act.

Changes: Consolidated and rewritten.

Purposes of Changes:

The generalized test of good faith and observance of reasonable commercial standards is substituted for the attempts to particularize what constitutes good faith in the cited sections of the old uniform acts. The section states explicitly what is perhaps an implication from the old acts that the common law rule of "innocent conversion" by unauthorized "intermeddling" with another's property is inapplicable to the operations of commercial carriers and warehousemen, who in good faith and with reasonable observance of commercial standards perform obligations which they have assumed and which generally they are under a legal compulsion to assume. The section applies to delivery to a fraudulent holder of a valid document as well as to delivery to the holder of an invalid document.

Definitional Cross References:

"Bailee". Section 7–102.

"Delivery". Section 1–201.
"Document of title". Section 1–201.
"Good faith". Section 1–201.
"Goods". Section 7–102.

"Person". Section 1–201.
"Receipt of goods". Section 2–103.
"Term". Section 1–201.

PART 5

WAREHOUSE RECEIPTS AND BILLS OF LADING: NEGOTIATION AND TRANSFER

§ 7–501. Form of Negotiation and Requirements of "Due Negotiation".

(1) A negotiable document of title running to the order of a named person is negotiated by his indorsement and delivery. After his indorsement in blank or to bearer any person can negotiate it by delivery alone.

(2)(a) A negotiable document of title is also negotiated by delivery alone when by its original terms it runs to bearer.

(b) When a document running to the order of a named person is delivered to him the effect is the same as if the document had been negotiated.

(3) Negotiation of a negotiable document of title after it has been indorsed to a specified person requires indorsement by the special indorsee as well as delivery.

(4) A negotiable document of title is "duly negotiated" when it is negotiated in the manner stated in this section to a holder who purchases it in good faith without notice of any defense against or claim to it on the part of any person and for value, unless it is established that the negotiation is not in the regular course of business or financing or involves receiving the document in settlement or payment of a money obligation.

(5) Indorsement of a non-negotiable document neither makes it negotiable nor adds to the transferee's rights.

(6) The naming in a negotiable bill of a person to be notified of the arrival of the goods does not limit the negotiability of the bill nor constitute notice to a purchaser thereof of any interest of such person in the goods.

Official Comment

Prior Uniform Statutory Provision: Sections 28, 29, 31, 32 and 38, Uniform Sales Act; Sections 37, 38, 39, 40 and 47, Uniform Warehouse Receipts Act; Sections 9, 28, 29, 30, 31 and 38, Uniform Bills of Lading Act.

Changes: Consolidated and rewritten.

Purposes of Changes:

1. In general this section is intended to clarify the language of the old acts and to restate the effect of the better decisions thereunder. An important new concept is added, however, in the requirement of "regular course of business or financing" to effect the "due negotiation" which will transfer greater rights than those held by the person negotiating. The foundation of the mercantile doctrine of good faith purchase for value has always been, as shown by the case situations, the furtherance and protection of the regular course of trade. The reason for allowing a person, in bad faith or in error, to convey away rights which are not his own has from the beginning been to make possible the speedy handling of that great run of commercial transactions which are patently usual and normal.

There are two aspects to the usual and normal course of mercantile dealings, namely, the person making the transfer and the nature of the transaction itself. The first question which arises is: Is the transferor a person with whom it is reasonable to deal as having full powers? In regard to documents of title the only holder whose possession appears, commercially, to be in order is almost invariably a person in the trade. No commercial purpose is served by allowing a tramp or a professor to "duly negotiate" an order bill of lading for hides or cotton not his own, and since such a transfer is obviously not in the regular course of business, it is excluded from the scope of the protection of subsection (4).

The second question posed by the "regular course" qualification is: Is the transaction one which is normally proper to pass full rights without inquiry, even though the transferor himself may not have such rights to pass, and even though he may be acting in breach of duty? In raising this question the "regular course" criterion has the further advantage of limiting the effective wrongful disposition to transactions whose protection will really further trade. Obviously, the snapping up of goods for quick resale at a price suspiciously below the market deserves no protection as a matter of policy: it is also clearly outside the range of regular course.

Any notice from the face of the document sufficient to put a merchant on inquiry as to the "regular course" quality of the transaction will frustrate a "due negotiation". Thus irregularity of the document on its face or unexplained staleness of a bill of lading may appropriately be recognized as negating a negotiation in "regular" course.

A pre-existing claim constitutes value, and "due negotiation" does not require "new value." A usual and ordinary transaction in which documents are received as security for credit previously extended may be in "regular" course, even though there is a demand for additional collateral because the creditor "deems himself insecure." But the matter has moved out of the regular course of financing if the debtor is thought to be insolvent, the credit previously extended is in effect cancelled, and the creditor snatches a plank in the shipwreck under the guise of a demand for additional collateral. Where a money debt is "paid" in commodity paper, any question of "regular" course disappears, as the case is explicitly excepted from "due negotiation".

2. Negotiation under this section may be made by any holder no matter how he acquired possession of the document. The present section follows in this respect the Uniform Bills of Lading Act and amendments of the original Uniform Sales Act and Uniform Warehouse Receipts Act proposed by the Commissioners on Uniform State Laws in 1922.

3. Subsection (2)(b) makes explicit a matter upon which the intent of the old acts was clear but the language somewhat obscure: a negotiation results from a delivery to a banker or buyer to whose order the document has been taken by the person making the bailment. There is no presumption of irregularity in such a negotiation; it may very well be in "regular course."

4. This Article does not contain any provision creating a presumption of due negotiation to, and full rights in, a holder of a document of title akin to that created by Sections 16, 24 and 59 of the Negotiable Instruments Law. But the reason of the provisions of this Act (Section 1–202) on the prima facie authenticity and accuracy of third party documents, joins with the reason of the present section to work such a presumption in favor of any person who has power to make a due negotiation. It would not make sense for this Act to authorize a purchaser to indulge the presumption of

regularity if the courts were not also called upon to do so.

Cross References:

Point 1: Sections 7–502 and 7–503.
Point 2: Section 7–502.

Definitional Cross References:

"Bearer". Section 1–201.
"Delivery". Section 1–201.
"Document". Section 7–102.
"Document of title". Section 1–201.
"Good faith". Section 1–201.
"Holder". Section 1–201.
"Notice". Section 1–201.
"Person". Section 1–201.
"Purchase". Section 1–201.
"Rights". Section 1–201.
"Term". Section 1–201.
"Value". Section 1–201.

§ 7–502. Rights Acquired by Due Negotiation.

(1) Subject to the following section and to the provisions of Section 7–205 on fungible goods, a holder to whom a negotiable document of title has been duly negotiated acquires thereby:

(a) title to the document;

(b) title to the goods;

(c) all rights accruing under the law of agency or estoppel, including rights to goods delivered to the bailee after the document was issued; and

(d) the direct obligation of the issuer to hold or deliver the goods according to the terms of the document free of any defense or claim by him except those arising under the terms of the document or under this Article. In the case of a delivery order the bailee's obligation accrues only upon acceptance and the obligation acquired by the holder is that the issuer and any indorser will procure the acceptance of the bailee.

(2) Subject to the following section, title and rights so acquired are not defeated by any stoppage of the goods represented by the document or by surrender of such goods by the bailee, and are not impaired even though the negotiation or any prior negotiation constituted a breach of duty or even though any person has been deprived of possession of the document by misrep-

resentation, fraud, accident, mistake, duress, loss, theft or conversion, or even though a previous sale or other transfer of the goods or document has been made to a third person.

Official Comment

Prior Uniform Statutory Provision: Sections 20(4), 25, 33, 38 and 62, Uniform Sales Act; Sections 41, 47, 48 and 49, Uniform Warehouse Receipts Act; Sections 32, 38, 39, 40 and 42, Uniform Bills of Lading Act.

Changes: Rewritten.

Purposes of Changes:

1. The several necessary qualifications of the broad principle that the holder of a document acquired in a due negotiation is the owner of the document and the goods have been brought together in the next section.

2. Subsection (1)(c) covers the case of "feeding" of a duly negotiated document by subsequent delivery to the bailee of such goods as the document falsely purported to cover; the bailee in such case is estopped as against the holder of the document.

3. The explicit statement in subsection (1)(d) of the bailee's direct obligation to the holder precludes the defense, sometimes successfully asserted under the old acts, that the document in question was "spent" after the carrier had delivered the goods to a previous holder. But the holder is subject to such defenses as nonnegligent destruction even though not apparent on the face of the document, and the bailee's obligation is of course subject to lawful provisions in filed classifications and tariffs. See Sections 7–103, 7–403. The sentence on delivery orders applies only to delivery orders in negotiable form which have been duly negotiated. On delivery orders, see also Section 7–503(2) and Comment.

4. Subsection (2) condenses and continues the law of a number of sections of the prior acts which gave full effect to the issuance or due negotiation of a negotiable document. The subsection adds nothing to the effect of the rules stated in subsection (1), but it has been included since such explicit references were relied upon under the prior acts to preserve the rights of a purchaser by due negotiation unimpaired. The listing is not exhaustive. Only those matters have been repeated in this subsection which were explicitly reserved in the prior acts except in the case of stoppage in transit. Here, the language has been broadened to include "any stoppage" lest an inference be drawn that a stoppage of the goods before or after transit might cut off or otherwise impair the purchaser's rights.

Cross References:

Sections 7–103, 7–205, 7–403 and 7–503.

Definitional Cross References:

"Bailee". Section 7–102.
"Delivery". Section 1–201.
"Delivery order". Section 7–102.
"Document". Section 7–102.
"Document of title". Section 1–201.
"Duly negotiate". Section 7–501.
"Fungible". Section 1–201.
"Goods". Section 7–102.
"Holder". Section 1–201.
"Issuer". Section 7–102.
"Person". Section 1–201.
"Rights". Section 1–201.
"Term". Section 1–201.
"Warehouse receipt". Section 1–201.

§ 7–503. Document of Title to Goods Defeated in Certain Cases.

(1) A document of title confers no right in goods against a person who before issuance of the document had a legal interest or a perfected security interest in them and who neither

(a) delivered or entrusted them or any document of title covering them to the bailor or his nominee with actual or apparent authority to ship, store or sell or with power to obtain delivery under this Article (Section 7–403) or with power of disposition under this Act (Sections 2–403 and 9–320) or other statute or rule of law; nor

(b) acquiesced in the procurement by the bailor or his nominee of any document of title.

(2) Title to goods based upon an unaccepted delivery order is subject to the rights of anyone to whom a negotiable warehouse receipt or bill of lading covering the goods has been duly negotiated. Such a title may be defeated under the next section to the same extent as the rights of the issuer or a transferee from the issuer.

(3) Title to goods based upon a bill of lading issued to a freight forwarder is subject to the rights of anyone to whom a bill issued by the freight forwarder is duly negotiated; but delivery by the carrier in accordance with Part 4 of this Article pursuant to its own bill of lading discharges the carrier's obligation to deliver.

As amended in 1999.

Official Comment

Prior Uniform Statutory Provision: Section 33, Uniform Sales Act; Section 41, Uniform Warehouse Receipts Act; Section 32, Uniform Bills of Lading Act.

Changes: Subsection (1) narrows, as compared to the cited sections, the occasions for defeating the document holder's title.

Purposes of Changes:

1. In general it may be said that the title of a purchaser by due negotiation prevails over almost any interest in the goods which existed prior to the procurement of the document of title if the possession of the goods by the person obtaining the document derived from any action by the prior claimant which introduced the goods into the stream of commerce or carried them along that stream. A thief of the goods cannot indeed by shipping or storing them to his own order acquire power to transfer them to a good faith purchaser. Nor can a tenant or mortgagor defeat any rights of a landlord or mortgagee which have been perfected under the local law merely by wrongfully shipping or storing a portion of the crop or other goods. However, "acquiescence" by the landlord or tenant does not require active consent under subsection (1)(b) and knowledge of the likelihood of storage or shipment with no objection or effort to control it is sufficient to defeat his rights as against one who takes by "due" negotiation of a negotiable document.

On the other hand, where goods are delivered to a factor for sale, even though the factor has made no advances and is limited in his duty to sell for cash, the goods are "entrusted" to him "with actual ... authority ... to sell" under subsection (1)(a), and if he procures a negotiable document of title he can transfer the owner's interest to a purchaser by due negotiation. Further, where the factor is in the business of selling, goods entrusted to him simply for safekeeping or storage may be entrusted under circumstances which give him "apparent authority to ship, store or sell" under subsection (1)(a), or power of disposition under Section 2–403, 7–205 or 9–320, or under a statute such as the earlier Factors Acts, or under a rule of law giving effect to apparent ownership. See Section 1–103.

Persons having an interest in goods also frequently deliver or entrust them to agents or servants other than factors for the purpose of shipping or warehousing or under circumstances reasonably contemplating such action. Rounding out the case law development under the prior Acts, this Act is clear that such persons assume full risk that the agent to whom the goods are so delivered may ship or store in breach of duty, take a document to his own order and then proceed to misap-

propriate it. This Act makes no distinction between possession or mere custody in such situations and finds no exception in the case of larceny by a bailee or the like. The safeguard in such situations lies in the requirement that a due negotiation can occur only "in the regular course of business or financing" and that the purchase be in good faith and without notice. See Section 7–501. Documents of title have no market among the commercially inexperienced and the commercially experienced do not take them without inquiry from persons known to be truck drivers or petty clerks even though such persons purport to be operating in their own names.

Again, where the seller allows a buyer to receive goods under a contract for sale, though as a "conditional delivery" or under "cash sale" terms and on explicit agreement for immediate payment, the buyer thereby acquires power to defeat the seller's interest by transfer of the goods to certain good faith purchasers. See Section 2–403. Both in policy and under the language of subsection (1)(a) that same power must be extended to accomplish the same result if the buyer procures a negotiable document of title to the goods and duly negotiates it.

2. Under subsection (1) a delivery order issued by a person having no right in or power over the goods is ineffective unless the owner acts as provided in subsection (1)(a) or (b). Thus the rights of a transferee of a non-negotiable warehouse receipt can be defeated by a delivery order subsequently issued by the transferor only if the transferee "delivers or entrusts" to the "person procuring" the delivery order or "acquiesces" in his procurement. Similarly, a second delivery order issued by the same issuer for the same goods will ordinarily be subject to the first, both under this section and under Section 7–402. After a delivery order is validly issued but before it is accepted, it may nevertheless be defeated under subsection (2) in much the same way that the rights of a transferee may be defeated under Section 7–504. For example, a buyer in ordinary course from the issuer may defeat the rights of the holder of a prior delivery order if the bailee receives notification of the buyer's rights before notification of the holder's rights. Section 7–504(2)(b). But an accepted delivery order has the same effect as a document issued by the bailee.

3. Under subsection (3) a bill of lading issued to a freight forwarder is subordinated to the freight forwarder's certificate, since the bill on its face gives notice of the fact that a freight forwarder is in the picture and has in all probability issued a certificate.

But the carrier is protected in following the terms of its own bill of lading.

Cross References:

Point 1: Sections 2–403, 7–205, 7–501, 9–320, and 9–331.

Point 2: Sections 7–402 and 7–504.

Point 3: Sections 7–402, 7–403 and 7–404.

Definitional Cross References:

"Bill of lading". Section 1–201.

"Contract for sale". Section 2–106.

"Delivery". Section 1–201.

"Delivery order". Section 7–102.

"Document". Section 7–102.

"Document of title". Section 1–201.

"Duly negotiate". Section 7–501.

"Goods". Section 7–102.

"Person". Section 1–201.

"Right". Section 1–201.

"Warehouse receipt". Section 1–201.

§ 7–504. Rights Acquired in the Absence of Due Negotiation; Effect of Diversion; Seller's Stoppage of Delivery.

(1) A transferee of a document, whether negotiable or non-negotiable, to whom the document has been delivered but not duly negotiated, acquires the title and rights which his transferor had or had actual authority to convey.

(2) In the case of a non-negotiable document, until but not after the bailee receives notification of the transfer, the rights of the transferee may be defeated

(a) by those creditors of the transferor who could treat the sale as void under Section 2–402; or

(b) by a buyer from the transferor in ordinary course of business if the bailee has delivered the goods to the buyer or received notification of his rights; or

(c) as against the bailee by good faith dealings of the bailee with the transferor.

(3) A diversion or other change of shipping instructions by the consignor in a non-negotiable bill of lading which causes the bailee not to deliver to the consignee defeats the consignee's title to the goods if they have been delivered to a buyer in ordinary course of business and in any event defeats the consignee's rights against the bailee.

(4) Delivery pursuant to a non-negotiable document may be stopped by a seller under Section 2–705, and subject to the requirement of due notification there provided. A bailee honoring the seller's instructions is entitled to be indemnified by the seller against any resulting loss or expense.

Official Comment

Prior Uniform Statutory Provision: Section 34, Uniform Sales Act; Sections 41(b) and 42, Uniform Warehouse Receipts Act; Sections 32(b) and 33, Uniform Bills of Lading Act.

Changes: Generally rewritten; Subsection (3) is new.

Purposes of Changes and New Matter:

1. Under the general principles controlling negotiable documents, it is clear that in the absence of due negotiation a transferor cannot convey greater rights than he himself has, even when the negotiation is formally perfect. This section recognizes the transferor's power to transfer rights which he himself has or has "actual authority to convey." Thus, where a negotiable document of title is being transferred the operation of the principle of estoppel is not recognized, as contrasted with situations involving the transfer of the goods themselves. (Compare Section 2–403 on good faith purchase of goods.)

A necessary part of the price for the protection of regular dealings with negotiable documents of title is an insistence that no dealing which is in any way irregular shall be recognized as a good faith purchase of the document or of any rights pertaining to it. So, where the transfer of a negotiable document fails as a negotiation because a requisite indorsement is forged or otherwise missing, the purchaser in good faith and for value may be in the anomalous position of having less rights, in part, than if he had purchased the goods themselves. True, his rights are not subject to defeat by attachment of the goods or surrender of them to his transferor [Contrast subsection (2)]; but on the other hand, he cannot acquire enforceable rights to control or receive the goods over the bailee's objection merely by giving notice to the bailee. Similarly, a consignee who makes payment to his consignor against a straight bill of lading can thereby acquire the position of a good faith purchaser of goods under provisions of the Article of this Act on Sales (Section 2–403), whereas the same payment made in good faith against an unindorsed order bill would not have such effect. The appropriate remedy of a purchaser in such a situation is to regularize his status by compelling indorsement of the document (see Section 7–506).

2. As in the case of transfer—as opposed to "due negotiation"—of negotiable documents, subsection (1) empowers the transferor of a nonnegotiable document to transfer only such rights as he himself has or has "actual authority" to convey. In contrast to situations involving the goods themselves the operation of estoppel or agency principles is not here recognized to enable the transferor to convey greater rights than he actually has. Subsection (2) makes it clear, however, that the transferee of a nonnegotiable document may acquire rights greater in some respects than those of his transferor by giving notice of the transfer to the bailee.

3. Subsection (3) is in part a reiteration of the carrier's immunity from liability if it honors instructions of the consignor to divert, but there is added a provision protecting the title of the substituted consignee if the latter is a buyer in ordinary course of business. A typical situation would be where a manufacturer, having shipped a lot of standardized goods to A on nonnegotiable bill of lading, diverts the goods to customer B who pays for them. Under orthodox passage-of-title-by-appropriation doctrine A might reclaim the goods from B. However, no consideration of commercial policy supports this involvement of an innocent third party in the default of the manufacturer on his contract to A; and the common commercial practice of diverting goods in transit suggests a trade understanding in accordance with this subsection.

4. Subsection (4) gives the carrier an express right to indemnity where he honors a seller's request to stop delivery.

5. Section 1–201(27) gives the bailee protection, if due diligence is exercised, similar to that found in the third paragraph of Section 33, Uniform Bills of Lading Act, where the bailee's organization has not had time to act on a notification.

Cross References:

Point 1: Sections 2–403 and 7–506.
Point 2: Section 2–403.
Point 3: Sections 7–303 and 7–403(1)(e).
Point 4: Sections 2–705 and 7–403(1)(d).

Definitional Cross References:

"Bailee". Section 7–102.
"Bill of lading". Section 1–201.
"Buyer in ordinary course of business". Section 1–201.
"Consignee". Section 7–102.
"Consignor". Section 7–102.
"Creditor". Section 1–201.
"Delivery". Section 1–201.

"Document". Section 7–102.
"Duly negotiate". Section 7–501.
"Good faith". Section 1–201.
"Goods". Section 7–102.
"Honor". Section 1–201.
"Notification". Section 1–201.
"Purchaser". Section 1–201.
"Rights". Section 1–201.

§ 7–505. Indorser Not a Guarantor for Other Parties.

The indorsement of a document of title issued by a bailee does not make the indorser liable for any default by the bailee or by previous indorsers.

Official Comment

Prior Uniform Statutory Provision: Section 37, Uniform Sales Act; Section 45, Uniform Warehouse Receipts Act; Section 36, Uniform Bills of Lading Act.

Changes: No substantial change.

Purposes of Changes:

The indorsement of a document of title is generally understood to be directed towards perfecting the transferee's rights rather than towards assuming additional obligations. The language of the present section, however, does not preclude the one case in which an indorsement given for value guarantees future action, namely, that in which the bailee has not yet become liable upon the document at the time of the indorsement. Under such circumstances the indorser, of course, engages that appropriate honor of the document by the bailee will occur. See Section 7–502(1)(d) as to negotiable delivery orders. However, even in such a case, once the bailee attorns to the transferee, the indorser's obligation has been fulfilled and the policy of this section excludes any continuing obligation on the part of the indorser for the bailee's ultimate actual performance.

Cross Reference:

Section 7–502.

Definitional Cross References:

"Bailee". Section 7–102.
"Document of title". Section 1–201.
"Party". Section 1–201.

§ 7–506. Delivery Without Indorsement: Right to Compel Indorsement.

The transferee of a negotiable document of title has a specifically enforceable right to have his transferor supply any necessary indorsement but the transfer becomes a negotiation only as of the time the indorsement is supplied.

Official Comment

Prior Uniform Statutory Provision: Section 35, Uniform Sales Act; Section 43, Uniform Warehouse Receipts Act; Section 34, Uniform Bills of Lading Act.

Changes: Consolidated and rewritten; former requirement that transfer be "for value" eliminated.

Purposes of Changes:

1. From a commercial point of view the intention to transfer a negotiable document of title which requires an indorsement for its transfer, is incompatible with an intention to withhold such indorsement and so defeat the effective use of the document. This position is sustained by the absence of any reported case applying the prior provisions in almost forty years of decisions. Further, the preceding section and the Comment thereto make it clear that an indorsement generally imposes no responsibility on the indorser.

2. Although this section provides that delivery of a document of title without the necessary indorsement is effective as a transfer, the transferee, of course, has not regularized his position until such indorsement is supplied. Until this is done he cannot claim rights under due negotiation within the requirements of this Article (subsection (4) of Section 7–501) on "due negotiation". Similarly, despite the transfer to him of his transferor's title, he cannot demand the goods from the bailee until the negotiation has been completed and the document is in proper form for surrender. See Section 7–403(3).

Cross References:

Point 1: Section 7–505.
Point 2: Sections 7–501(4) and 7–403(2).

Definitional Cross References:

"Document of title". Section 1–201.
"Rights". Section 1–201.

§ 7–507. Warranties on Negotiation or Transfer of Receipt or Bill.

Where a person negotiates or transfers a document of title for value otherwise than as a mere intermediary under the next following section, then unless otherwise agreed he warrants to his immediate purchaser only in addition to any warranty made in selling the goods

  (a) that the document is genuine; and

  (b) that he has no knowledge of any fact which would impair its validity or worth; and

  (c) that his negotiation or transfer is rightful and fully effective with respect to the title to the document and the goods it represents.

Official Comment

Prior Uniform Statutory Provision: Section 36, Uniform Sales Act; Section 44, Uniform Warehouse Receipts Act; Section 35, Uniform Bills of Lading Act.

Changes: Consolidated and rewritten without change in policy.

Purposes of Changes:

1. This section omits provisions of the prior acts on warranties as to the goods as unnecessary and incomplete. It is unnecessary because such warranties derive from the contract of sale and not from the transfer of the documents. The fact that transfer of control occurs by way of a document of title does not limit or displace the ordinary obligations of a seller. The former provision, moreover, was incomplete because it did not expressly include all of the warranties which might rest upon a seller under such circumstances. This Act handles the problem by means of the precautionary reference to "any warranty made in selling the goods." If the transfer of documents attends or follows the making of a contract for the sale of goods, the general obligations on warranties as to the goods (Sections 2–312 through 2–318) are brought to bear as well as the special warranties under this section.

2. The limited warranties of a delivering or collecting intermediary are stated in Section 7–508.

Cross References:

Point 1: Sections 2–312 through 2–318.
Point 2: Section 7–508.

Definitional Cross References:

"Document". Section 7–102.
"Document of title". Section 1–201.
"Genuine". Section 1–201.
"Goods". Section 7–102.
"Person". Section 1–201.
"Purchaser". Section 1–201.
"Value". Section 1–201.

§ 7–508. Warranties of Collecting Bank as to Documents.

A collecting bank or other intermediary known to be entrusted with documents on behalf of another or with collection of a draft or other claim against delivery of documents warrants by such delivery of the documents only its own good faith and authority. This rule applies even though the intermediary has purchased or made advances against the claim or draft to be collected.

Official Comment

Prior Uniform Statutory Provision: None.

Purposes:

1. To state the limited warranties given with respect to the documents accompanying a documentary draft.

2. In warranting its authority a bank only warrants its authority from its transferor. See Section 4–203. It does not warrant the genuineness or effectiveness of the document. Compare Section 7–507.

3. Other duties and rights of banks handling documentary drafts for collection are stated in Article 4, Part 5.

Cross References:

Sections 4–203 and 7–507, 4–501 through 4–504.

Definitional Cross References:

"Collecting bank". Section 4–105.
"Delivery". Section 1–201.

"Document". Section 7–102.
"Draft". Section 5–103.
"Good faith". Section 1–201.

§ 7–509. Receipt or Bill: When Adequate Compliance With Commercial Contract.

The question whether a document is adequate to fulfill the obligations of a contract for sale or the conditions of a credit is governed by the Articles on Sales (Article 2) and on Letters of Credit (Article 5).

Official Comment

Prior Uniform Statutory Provision: None.

Purposes:

To cross-refer to the Articles of this Act which deal with the substantive issues of the type of document of title required under the contract entered into by the parties.

Cross References:

Articles 2 and 5.

Definitional Cross References:

"Contract for sale". Section 2–106.
"Document". Section 7–102.

PART 6

WAREHOUSE RECEIPTS AND BILLS OF LADING: MISCELLANEOUS PROVISIONS

§ 7–601. Lost and Missing Documents.

(1) If a document has been lost, stolen or destroyed, a court may order delivery of the goods or issuance of a substitute document and the bailee may without liability to any person comply with such order. If the document was negotiable the claimant must post security approved by the court to indemnify any person who may suffer loss as a result of non-surrender of the document. If the document was not negotiable, such security may be required at the discretion of the court. The court may also in its discretion order payment of the bailee's reasonable costs and counsel fees.

(2) A bailee who without court order delivers goods to a person claiming under a missing negotiable document is liable to any person injured thereby, and if the delivery is not in good faith becomes liable for conversion. Delivery in good faith is not conversion if made in accordance with a filed classification or tariff or, where no classification or tariff is filed, if the claimant posts security with the bailee in an amount at least double the value of the goods at the time of posting to indemnify any person injured by the delivery who files a notice of claim within one year after the delivery.

Official Comment

Prior Uniform Statutory Provision: Section 14, Uniform Warehouse Receipts Act; Section 17, Uniform Bills of Lading Act.

Changes: General Revision. Principal innovations include: affirmation of bailee's privilege to deliver to claimant without resort to judicial proceedings if the bailee acts in good faith and is willing to take the full risk of loss in case the lost document turns up in the hands of an innocent purchaser; explicit authorization to the court to order bailee to issue a substitute document rather than make physical delivery of the goods; inclusion of "stolen" as well as lost documents; extension of section to non-negotiable documents.

Purposes of Changes: The purposes of the changes insofar as they are not self-evident are as follows:

1. As to bailee's privilege to deliver without court order, doubt had arisen as to the propriety of such action under Section 54 of the Uniform Warehouse Receipts Act, which made it a crime to deliver goods covered by negotiable receipts without taking up the receipts "except in the cases provided for in Section 14" (the lost receipts section). This has been interpreted by one court as exempting from criminal liability only if the judicial procedure of Section 14 was followed. Dahl v. Winter-Truesdell-Diercks Co., 61 N.D. 84, 237 N.W. 202 (1931). Although the criminal provisions are not being re-enacted in this Act (and the Uniform Bills of Lading Act never did include such a criminal provision), it seems advisable to clarify the legality of the well established commercial practice of bailees to make delivery where they are satisfied that the claimant is the person entitled under a lost document. Since the bailee remains liable on the document in such cases, he will usually insist that the claimant provide an indemnity bond.

2. The old acts provide only for compulsory delivery of goods; this Section provides also for compulsory issuance of a substitute document. If continuance of the bailment is desirable there is no reason to require the goods to be withdrawn and redeposited in order to secure a negotiable document. The present acts would probably be so interpreted. Section 20 of the Federal Warehouse Act and some state laws expressly require issuance of a new receipt on proof of loss and posting of bond.

3. Claimants on non-negotiable instruments are permitted to avail themselves of this procedure because straight bills of lading sometimes contain provisions that the goods shall not be delivered except upon production of the bill. If the carrier should choose to insist upon production of the bill, the consignee should have some means of compelling delivery on satisfactory proof of entitlement.

Ordinarily no security would be necessary to indemnify a bailee in delivering to the person named in a non-negotiable document. But disputes as to negotiability may arise, in which case if there is a reasonable doubt on the point the bailee should be protected against the possibility that the missing document would, in the hands of an innocent purchaser for value, be held negotiable.

4. It seems unnecessary to state, as do the present acts, that the court shall act "on satisfactory proof of such loss or destruction." The right of action created by the section is conditioned on a document being lost, stolen or destroyed. Plaintiff must of course bring himself within the section. There is nothing in the language of the old acts to suggest that they intended to impose anything but the normal burden of proof on the plaintiff in such proceedings.

5. Subsection (2) makes it clear that after delivery without court order the bailee remains liable for actual damages. Liability for conversion is provided where the delivery is dishonest, but excluded where a filed classification or tariff is followed in good faith, or where the described bond is posted in good faith and no classification or tariff is filed. Liability for conversion in other cases is left to judicial decision.

Definitional Cross References:

"Bailee". Section 7–102.
"Bill of lading". Section 1–201.
"Delivery". Section 1–201.
"Document". Section 7–102.
"Good faith". Section 1–201.
"Goods". Section 7–102.
"Person". Section 1–201.
"Warehouse receipt". Section 1–201.
"Warehouseman". Section 7–102.

§ 7–602.　Attachment of Goods Covered by a Negotiable Document.

Except where the document was originally issued upon delivery of the goods by a person who had no power to dispose of them, no lien attaches by virtue of any judicial process to goods in the possession of a bailee for which a negotiable document of title is outstanding unless the document be first surrendered to the bailee or its negotiation enjoined, and the bailee shall not be compelled to deliver the goods pursuant to process until the document is surrendered to him or impounded by the court. One who purchases the document for value without notice of the process or injunction takes free of the lien imposed by judicial process.

Official Comment

Prior Uniform Statutory Provisions: Section 25, Uniform Warehouse Receipts Act; Section 24, Uniform Bills of Lading Act.

Changes: Consolidated and rewritten.

Purposes of Changes:

1. The purpose of the section is to protect the bailee from conflicting claims of the document holder and the judgment creditors of the person who deposited the goods. The rights of the former prevail unless, in effect, the judgment creditors immobilize the negotiable document. However, if the document was issued upon deposit of the goods by a person who had no power to dispose of the goods so that the document is ineffective to pass title, judgment liens are valid to the extent of the debtor's interest in the goods.

2. The last sentence covers the possibility that the holder of a document who has been enjoined from negotiating it will violate the injunction by negotiating to an innocent purchaser for value. In such case the lien will be defeated.

Cross Reference:

Point 1: Section 7–503.

Definitional Cross References:

"Bailee". Section 7–102.
"Delivery". Section 1–201.
"Document". Section 7–102.
"Goods". Section 7–102.
"Notice". Section 1–201.
"Person". Section 1–201.
"Purchase". Section 1–201.
"Value". Section 1–201.

§ 7–603. Conflicting Claims; Interpleader.

If more than one person claims title or possession of the goods, the bailee is excused from delivery until he has had a reasonable time to ascertain the validity of the adverse claims or to bring an action to compel all claimants to interplead and may compel such interpleader, either in defending an action for non-delivery of the goods, or by original action, whichever is appropriate.

Official Comment

Prior Uniform Statutory Provision: Sections 16 and 17, Uniform Warehouse Receipts Act; Sections 20 and 21, Uniform Bills of Lading Act.

Changes: Consolidation without substantial change.

Purposes of Changes:

The section enables a bailee faced with conflicting claims to the goods to compel the claimants to litigate their claims with each other rather than with him.

Definitional Cross References:

"Action". Section 1–201.
"Bailee". Section 7–102.
"Delivery". Section 1–201.
"Goods". Section 7–102.
"Person". Section 1–201.
"Reasonable time". Section 1–204.

APPENDIX J

2005 AMENDMENTS TO UNIFORM COMMERCIAL CODE

---

§ 1–201. General Definitions.

The text for this section was not amended in 2005.

Official Comment

* * *

20. "Good faith." Former Section 1–201(19) defined "good faith" simply as honesty in fact; the definition contained no element of commercial reasonableness. Initially, that definition applied throughout the Code with only one exception. Former Section 2–103(1)(b) provided that, "~~in this Article . . . good faith~~ in that Article, " 'good faith' in the case of a merchant means honesty in fact and the observance of reasonable commercial standards of fair dealing in the trade." This alternative definition was limited in applicability ~~in three ways,~~ though, because it applied only to transactions within the scope of Article 2 and it applied only to merchants. ~~First, it applied only to transactions within the scope of Article 2. Second, it applied only to merchants. Third, strictly construed it applied only to uses of the phrase "good faith" *in Article 2*; thus, so construed it would not define "good faith" for its most important use-the obligation of good faith imposed by former Section 1–203.~~

Over time, however, amendments to the Uniform Commercial Code brought the Article 2 merchant concept of good faith (subjective honesty and objective commercial reasonableness) into other Articles. First, Article 2A explicitly incorporated the Article 2 standard. See Section 2A–103(7). Then, other Articles broadened the applicability of that standard by adopting it for all parties rather than just for merchants. *See, e.g.,* Sections 3–103(a)(4), 4A–105(a)(6), 7–102(a)(6), 8–102(a)(10), and 9–102(a)(43). Finally, Articles 2 and 2A were amended so as to apply the standard to non-merchants as well as merchants. See Sections 2–103(1)(j), 2A–103(1)(m). All of these definitions are comprised of two elements–honesty in fact *and* the observance of reasonable commercial standards of fair dealing. Only revised Article 5 defines "good faith" solely in terms of subjective honesty, and only Article 6 ~~and Article 7 are~~ (in the few states that have not chosen to delete the Article) is without ~~definitions~~ a definition of good faith. (It should be noted that, while revised Article 6 did not define good faith, Comment 2 to revised Section 6–102 states that "this Article adopts the definition of 'good faith' in Article 1 in all cases, even when the buyer is a merchant.") ~~Given these developments, it is appropriate to move the broader definition of "good faith" to Article 1. Of course, this definition is subject to the applicability of the narrower definition in revised Article 5.~~

Thus, the definition of "good faith" in this section merely confirms what has been the case for a number of years as Articles of the UCC have been amended or revised–the obligation of "good faith," applicable in each Article, is to be interpreted in the context of all Articles except for Article 5 as including both the subjective element of honesty in fact and the objective element of the observance of reasonable commercial standards of fair dealing. As a result, both the subjective and objective elements are part of the standard of "good faith," whether that obligation is specifically referenced in another Article of the Code (other than Article 5) or is provided by this Article.

Of course, as noted in the statutory text, the definition of "good faith" in this section does not apply when the narrower definition of "good faith" in revised Article 5 is applicable.

As noted above, the definition of "good faith" in this section requires not only honesty in fact but also "observance of reasonable commercial standards of fair dealing." Although "fair dealing" is a broad term that must be defined in context, it is clear that it is concerned with the fairness of conduct rather than the care with which an act is performed. This is an entirely different concept than whether a party exercised ordinary care in conducting a transaction. Both concepts are to be determined in the light of reasonable commercial standards, but those standards in each case are directed to different aspects of commercial conduct. See e.g., Sections 3–103(a)(9) and 4–104(c) and Comment 4 to Section 3–103.

* * *

1230

§ 2–103(2). Definitions and Index of Definitions.

(1) In this article unless the context otherwise requires:

* * *

(e) "Delivery" means, with respect to goods, the voluntary transfer of physical possession or control of goods.

* * *

(2) Other definitions applying to this Article or to specified Parts thereof, and the sections in which they appear are:

"Acceptance". Section 2–606.
"Between merchants". Section 2–104.
"Cancellation". Section 2–106(4).
"Commercial unit". Section 2–105.
"Conforming to contract". Section 2–106.
"Contract for sale". Section 2–106.
"Cover". Section 2–712.
"Entrusting". Section 2–403.
"Financing agency". Section 2–104.
"Future goods". Section 2–105.
"Goods". Section 2–103.
"Identification". Section 2–501.
"Installment contract". Section 2–612.
"Lot". Section 2–105.
"Merchant". Section 2–104.
"Person in position of seller". Section 2–707.
"Present sale". Section 2–106.
"Sale". Section 2–106.
"Sale on approval". Section 2–326.
"Sale or return". Section 2–326.
"Termination". Section 2–106.

* * *

§ 2–207. Terms of Contract; Effect of Confirmation.

Official Comment

1. This section applies to all contracts for the sale of goods, and it is not limited only to those contracts where there has been a "battle of forms." The references in this section to contracts formed by offer and acceptance includes, inter alia, contracts formed by the interaction of electronic agents and by the interaction of an electronic agent and an individual. See section 2–204(1).

* * *

§ 2–703. Seller's Remedies in General.

* * *

(2) If the buyer is in breach of contract the seller, to the extent provided for by this Act or other law, may:

(a) withhold delivery of the goods under Section 2–703(4);

* * *

(f) cancel under Section 2–703(4);

* * *

(4) If the buyer wrongfully rejects or revokes acceptance of goods, fails to make a payment when due, or repudiates with respect to a part or the whole, with respect to any goods directly affected and, if the breach is of the whole contract (Section 2–612), with respect to the whole undelivered balance, the aggrieved seller may

(a) withhold delivery of such goods; or

(b) cancel.

§ 2–711. Buyer's Remedies in General; Buyer's Security Interest in Rejected Goods.

* * *

(2) If the seller is in breach of contract under subsection (1), the buyer, to the extent provided for by this Act or other law, may:

(a) in the case of rightful cancellation, rightful rejection, or justifiable revocation of acceptance, recover so much of the price as has been paid;

(b) deduct damages from any part of the price still due under Section 2–717;

(c) cancel under Section 2–711(4);

* * *

(3) On rightful rejection or justifiable revocation of acceptance a buyer has a security interest in goods in the buyer's possession or control for any payments made on their price and any expenses reasonably incurred in their inspection, receipt, transportation, care and custody and may hold such goods and resell them in a like manner as an aggrieved seller (Section 2–706).

(4) If the seller fails to make delivery or repudiates or the buyer rightfully rejects or justifiably revokes acceptance, with respect to any goods involved and with respect to the whole if the breach goes to the whole contract (Section 2–612), the buyer may cancel.

§ 2A–101.   Short Title.

The text for this section was not amended in 2005.

Official Comment

* * *

Warranties

Because of the manner in which leased goods are promoted and distributed–for example, lessors generally do not engage in mass-market advertising aimed at, or make representations in materials to be delivered to, remote lessees–amended Article 2A does not contain provisions analogous to Sections 2–313A and 2–313B of amended Article 2. Though nothing in this Article precludes, in an appropriate case, the application of the principles contained in those sections to a lease transaction, a lessor is responsible only for the lessor's representations and those of the lessor's agents and the lessor is not for the representations made by a third party, such as the supplier or manufacturer of the goods. In addition, a lessee may have the right as a "remote purchaser" under Article 2 to assert claims under Sections 2A–313A 2–313A and 2–313B directly against a manufacturer or supplier that has engaged in advertising.

* * *

§ 2A–103.   Definitions and Index of Definitions.

The text for this section was not amended in 2005.

Official Comment

* * *

(g) For a transaction to qualify as a finance lease it must first qualify as a lease. Unless the lessor is comfortable that the transaction will qualify as a finance lease, the lease agreement should include provisions giving the lessor the benefits created by the subset of rules applicable to the transaction that qualifies as a finance lease under this Article.

A finance lease is the product of a three party transaction. The supplier manufactures or supplies the goods pursuant to the lessee's specification, perhaps even pursuant to a purchase order, sales agreement or lease agreement between the supplier and the lessee. After the prospective finance lease is negotiated, a purchase order, sales agreement, or lease agreement is entered into by the lessor (as buyer or prime lessee) or an existing order, agreement or lease is assigned by the lessee to the lessor, and the lessor and the lessee then enter into a lease or sublease of the goods. Due to the limited function usually performed by the lessor, the lessee looks almost entirely to the supplier for representations, covenants and warranties. If a manufacturer's warranty carries through, the lessee may also look to that. Yet, this definition does not restrict the lessor's function solely to the supply of funds; if the lessor undertakes or performs other functions, express warranties, covenants and the common law will protect the lessee.

This definition focuses on the transaction, not the status of the parties; to avoid confusion it is important to note that in other contexts, *e.g.*, tax and accounting, the term finance lease has been used to connote different types of lease transactions, including leases that are disguised secured transactions. M. Rice, *Equipment Financing*, 62–71 (1981). A lessor who is a merchant with respect to goods of the kind subject to the lease may be a lessor under a finance lease. Many leases that are leases back to the seller of goods (Section 2A–308(3)) will be finance leases. This conclusion is easily demonstrated by a hypothetical. Assume that B has bought goods from C pursuant to a sales contract. After delivery to and acceptance of the goods by B, B negotiates to sell the goods to A and simultaneously to lease the goods back from A, on terms and conditions that, we assume, will qualify the transaction as a lease. In documenting the sale and lease back, B assigns the original sales contract between B, as buyer, and C, as seller, to A. A review of these facts leads to the conclusion that the lease from A to B qualifies as a finance lease, as all three conditions of the definition are satisfied. Subparagraph (A) (i) is satisfied as A, the lessor, had nothing to do with the selection, manufacture, or supply of the equipment. Subparagraph (B) (ii) is satisfied as A, the lessor, bought the equipment at the same time that A leased the equipment to B, which certainly is in connection with the lease. Finally, subparagraph (C)(I) (iii)(A) is satisfied as A entered into the sales contract with B at the same time that A leased the equipment back to B. B, the lessee, will have received a copy of the sales contract in a timely fashion.

Subsection (A) Subparagraph (i) requires the lessor to remain outside the selection, manufacture and supply of the goods; that is the rationale for releasing the lessor from most of its traditional liability. The lessor is not prohibited from possession, maintenance or operation of the goods, as policy does not require such prohibition. To insure the lessee's reliance on the supplier, and not on the lessor, subsection (B) subparagraph (ii) requires that the goods (where the lessor is the buyer of the goods) or that the right to possession and use of the goods (where the lessor is the prime lessee and the sublessor of the goods) be acquired in connection with the lease (or sublease) to qualify as a finance lease. The scope of the phrase "in connection with" is to be developed by the courts, case by case. Finally, as the lessee generally relies almost entirely upon the supplier for representations and covenants, and upon the supplier or a manufacturer, or both, for warranties with respect to the goods, subsection (C) subparagraph (iii) requires that one of the following occur: (A) the lessee receive a copy of the supply contract before signing the lease contract; (B) the lessee's approval of the supply contract is a condition to the effectiveness of the lease contract; (C) the lessee receive a statement describing the promises and warranties and any limitations relevant to the lessee before signing the lease contract; or (D) before signing the lease contract and except in a consumer lease, the lessee receive a writing identifying the supplier (unless the supplier was selected and required by the lessee) and the rights of the lessee under Section 2A–303, and advising the lessee a statement of promises and warranties is available from the supplier. Thus, even where oral supply orders or computer placed supply orders are compelled by custom and usage the transaction may still qualify as a finance lease if the lessee approves the supply contract before the lease contract is effective and such approval was a condition to the effectiveness of the lease contract. Moreover, where the lessor does not want the lessee to see the entire supply contract, including price information, the lessee may be provided with a separate statement of the terms of the supply contract relevant to the lessee; promises between the supplier and the lessor that do not affect the lessee need not be included. The statement can be a restatement of those terms or a copy of portions of the supply contract with the relevant terms clearly designated. Any implied warranties need not be designated, but a disclaimer or modification of remedy must be designated. A copy of any manufacturer's warranty is sufficient if that is the warranty provided. However, a copy of any Regulation M disclosure given pursuant to 12 C.F.R. § 213.4(g) concerning warranties in itself is not sufficient since those disclosures need only brief-ly identify express warranties and need not include any disclaimer of warranty.

Under subsections (B) and (C) subparagraphs (ii) and (iii), except when the new lease is to a consumer lessee, a finance lessor can have that status on releasing the property after it is returned from an original lease. However, in that case, the other elements required for the lease to be a finance lessee must be complied with.

* * *

§ 2A–211. Warranties Against Interference and Against Infringement; Lessee's Obligation Against Infringement.

* * *

(4) A warranty under this section may be excluded or modified only by specific language that is conspicuous and contained in a record, or by circumstances, including course of performance, course of dealing, or usage of trade, that give the lessee reason to know that the lessor purports to transfer only such right as the lessor or a third party may have is leasing the goods subject to a claim or interest of any person, or that it is leasing subject to any claims of infringement or the like.

§ 2A–501. Default: Procedure.

* * *

(4) Except as otherwise provided in Section 1–106(1) Section 1–305(a) or this Article or the lease agreement, the rights and remedies referred to in subsections (2) and (3) are cumulative.

* * *

§ 2A–507A. Right to Specific Performance or Replevin or the Like.

* * *

(3) A lessee has a right of replevin or similar remedy for goods identified to the lease contract if after reasonable effort the lessee is unable to effect cover for those goods or the circumstances reasonably indicate that the effort will be unavailing or if the goods have been shipped under

~~reservation and satisfaction of the security interest in them has been made or tendered~~.

§ 2A–508. Lessee's Remedies.

* * *

(1) If a lessor fails to deliver the goods in conformity to the lease contract or repudiates the contract, or a lessee rightfully rejects the goods or justifiably revokes acceptance of the goods, the lessor is in default under the lease contract, and the lessee may do one or more of the following:

(a) cancel the lease contract ~~under Section 2A–505(1)~~;

* * *

§ 2A–509. Lessee's Rights on Improper Delivery; Manner and Effect of Rejection.

The text for this section was not amended in 2005.

Official Comment

* * *

3. Elimination of the word "rightful" in the title makes it clear that a ~~buyer~~ lessee can effectively reject goods even though the rejection is wrongful and constitutes a breach. The word ~~"rightful"~~ "rightfully" has also been deleted from the titles to Section 2A–511 and 2A–512.

* * *

§ 2A–514. Waiver of Lessee's Objections.

* * *

(2) A lessee's failure to reserve rights when paying rent or other consideration against documents presented to the lessee precludes recovery of the payment for defects apparent in the documents.

§ 2A–517. Revocation of Acceptance of Goods.

* * *

(6) If a lessee uses the goods after a rightful rejection or justifiable revocation of acceptance, the following rules apply:

(a) Any use by the lessee which is unreasonable under the circumstances is wrongful as against the lessor or supplier and is an acceptance only if ratified by the lessor or supplier ~~under Section 2–515(1)(c)~~.

(b) Any use of the goods which is reasonable under the circumstances is not wrongful as against the lessor or supplier and is not an acceptance, but in an appropriate case the lessee shall be obligated to the lessor or supplier for the value of the use to the lessee.

Official Comment

* * *

3. Subsection (6) deals with the problem of post-rejection or revocation use of the goods. If the lessee's use after an effective rejection or a justified revocation of acceptance is unreasonable under the circumstances, it is inconsistent with the rejection or revocation of acceptance and is wrongful as against the lessor. This gives the lessor the option of ratifying the use, thereby treating it as an acceptance, or pursuing a non-Code remedy for conversion.

If the lessee's use is reasonable under the circumstances, the lessee's actions cannot be treated as an acceptance. The lessee must, in appropriate circumstances, compensate the lessor for the value of the use of the goods to the lessee. Determining the appropriate level of compensation requires a consideration of the lessee's particular circumstances and should take into account the defective condition of the goods. There may be circumstances, such as where the use is solely for the purpose of protecting the lessee's security interest in the goods, where no compensation is due the lessor. In other circumstances, the lessor's right to compensation must be netted out against any right of the lessee to damages.

* * *

§ 2A–523. Lessor's Remedies.

(1) If the lessee wrongfully rejects or attempts to revoke acceptance of goods or fails to make a payment when due or repudiates with respect to a part or the whole, the lessee is in default under the lease contract with respect to any goods

involved and the lessor may do one or more of the following:

* * *

(f) cancel the lease contract ~~under Section 2A–505(1)~~;

* * *

§ 2A–524. Lessor's Right to Identify Goods to Lease Contract.

(1) After default by the lessee under the lease contract of the type described in Section 2A–523(1) or ~~2A–523(3)(a)~~ 2A–523(4)(a) or, if agreed, after other default by the lessee, the lessor may:

(a) identify to the lease contract conforming goods not already identified if at the time the lessor learned of the default they were in the lessor's or the supplier's possession or control; and

(b) dispose of goods (Section 2A–527(1)) that demonstrably have been intended for the particular lease contract even though those goods are unfinished.

* * *

§ 2A–525. Lessor's Right to Possession of Goods.

* * *

(2) After a default by the lessee under the lease contract of the type described in Section 2A–523(1) or ~~2A–523(3)(a)~~ 2A–523(4)(a) or, if agreed, after other default by the lessee, the lessor has the right to take possession of the goods. If the lease contract so provides, the lessor may require the lessee to assemble the goods and make them available to the lessor at a place to be designated by the lessor which is reasonably convenient to both parties. Without removal, the lessor may render unusable any goods employed in trade or business, and may dispose of goods on the lessee's premises (Section 2A–527).

* * *

§ 3–405. Employer's Responsibility for Fraudulent Indorsement by Employee.

The text for this section was not amended in 2005.

Official Comment

1. Section 3–405 is addressed to fraudulent indorsements made by an employee with respect to instruments with respect to which the employer has given responsibility to the employee. It covers two categories of fraudulent indorsements: indorsements made in the name of the employer to instruments payable to the employer and indorsements made in the name of payees of instruments issued by the employer. This section applies to instruments generally but normally the instrument will be a check. Section 3–405 adopts the principle that the risk of loss for fraudulent indorsements by employees who are entrusted with responsibility with respect to checks should fall on the employer rather than the bank that takes the check or pays it, if the bank was not negligent in the transaction. Section 3–405 is based on the belief that the employer is in a far better position to avoid the loss by care in choosing employees, in supervising them, and in adopting other measures to prevent forged indorsements on instruments payable to the employer or fraud in the issuance of instruments in the name of the employer. If the bank failed to exercise ordinary care, subsection (b) allows the employer to shift loss to the bank to the extent the bank's failure to exercise ordinary care contributed to the loss. "Ordinary care" is defined in ~~Section 3–103(a)(7)~~ Section 3–103(a)(9). The provision applies regardless of whether the employer is negligent.

* * *

§ 9–325. Priority of Security Interests in Transferred Collateral.

The text for this section was not amended in 2005.

Official Comment

* * *

6. **Unusual Situations.** The appropriateness of the rule of subsection (a) is most apparent when it works to subordinate security interests having priority under the basic priority rules of Section 9–322(a) or the purchase-money priority rules of Section 9–324. The rule also works properly when applied to the security interest of a buyer under Section 2–711(3) or a lessee under Section 2A–508(5). However, subsection (a) may provide an inappropriate resolution of the "double debtor" problem in some of the wide variety of other contexts in which the problem may arise. Al-

though subsection (b) limits the application of subsection (a) to those cases in which subordination is known to be appropriate, courts should apply the rule in other settings, if necessary to promote the underlying purposes and policies of the Uniform Commercial Code. See ~~Section 1–102(1)~~ Section 1–103(a).

APPENDIX K

PEB COMMENTARY: #1, #10

CONTENTS

PEB Resolution on Purposes, Standards and Procedures for PEB Commentary to the UCC
PEB Commentary No. 1, Section 2–507(2)
PEB Commentary No. 10, Section 1–203

PEB RESOLUTION ON PURPOSES, STANDARDS AND PROCEDURES FOR PEB COMMENTARY TO THE UCC

1. The Permanent Editorial Board (PEB), in accordance with the standards and procedures set out in this resolution of March 14, 1987, and the authority given in the agreement between the American Law Institute and the National Conference of Commissioners on Uniform State Laws dated July 31, 1986, will issue supplemental commentary on the Uniform Commercial Code (UCC) from time to time.

a. The supplemental commentary of the PEB generally will be known as *PEB Commentary,* to distinguish it from the Official Comments to the UCC, and will be preserved separately from the Official Comments.

b. The underlying purposes and policies of the *PEB Commentary* are those specified in UCC § 1–102(2). A *PEB Commentary* should come within one or more of the following specific purposes, which should be made apparent at the inception of the Commentary: (1) to resolve an ambiguity in the UCC by restating more clearly what the PEB considers to be the legal rule; (2) to state a preferred resolution of an issue on which judicial opinion or scholarly writing diverges; (3) to elaborate on the application of the UCC where the statute and/or the Official Comment leaves doubt as to inclusion or exclusion of, or application to, particular circumstances or transactions; (4) consistent with UCC § 1–102(2)(b), to apply the principles of the UCC to new or changed circumstances; (5) to clarify or elaborate upon the operation of the UCC as it relates to other statutes (such as the Bankruptcy Code and various federal and state consumer protection statutes) and general principles of law and equity pursuant to UCC § 1–103; or (6) to otherwise improve the operation of the UCC.

c. The format of the *PEB Commentary* normally will consist of an identification of the issue, a discussion concerning the possible resolutions of the issue to be addressed, and a statement of the view of the PEB as to how the issue should be resolved. On a carefully selected basis supplemental commentary may be issued as an identified supplement to the Official Comments, in which case it generally should take the form of a brief exposition modeled substantially on the form and style of the Official Comments.

d. Topics for *PEB Commentary* will be selected periodically by the PEB from suggestions, accompanied by supporting reasons, made by PEB members and by other persons. *PEB Commentary* may be issued whether or not a perceived issue has been litigated or is in litigation, and whether or not the position taken by the PEB accords with the weight of authority on the issue. The number of topics and topics that are chosen at any given time will be determined by the PEB weighing criteria appropriate under the circumstances, which may include the practical importance of the issue, the absence of other means of resolution, the time and effort to be involved in the preparation of the *PEB Commentary,* the extent to which the *PEB Commentary* is likely to be successful in addressing an issue, whether it is known to the PEB that the topic of the *PEB Commentary* is in specific litigation and, if so, the probable impact upon that litigation, and the availability of resources. However, normally no *PEB Commentary* should be begun with respect to a UCC Article that is undergoing amendment or initial promulgation except upon consultation with and concurrence of the study or drafting committee for such amendment or initial promulgation. Moreover, except in extraordinary cases and in the case of *PEB Commentary* identified as specific supplements to Official Comments, an Official Comment, as opposed to the text of the UCC, should not be the specific subject of *PEB Commentary.*

e. For a variety of reasons, topics initially identified by the PEB for *PEB Commen-*

tary and advisors' drafts of *PEB Commentary* (discussed in paragraph 2 below) may not result in the final approval of *PEB Commentary*. Such reasons might include the failure of a consensus to emerge on the substance of an issue or a conclusion that the issue would better be treated by a change in the UCC Official Text. No inference should be drawn from, and no weight should be accorded to, any withdrawal of an advisor's draft or any failure to proceed with a *PEB Commentary* on any particular topic.

2. The process by which *PEB Commentary* is prepared and issued by the PEB should be flexible, but usually should include:

a. periodic publication of the topics under consideration by the PEB with a request for comment by interested persons by a stated date as to whether any listed topic should be deleted or a related topic added and as to the appropriate resolution of the issues presented by the topics under consideration;

b. selection of one or more appropriate advisers, who are not members of the PEB, to review any comments submitted by inter-

ested persons and other relevant materials and to prepare a tentative adviser's draft of the proposed *PEB Commentary;*

c. publication of the adviser's draft of the *PEB Commentary,* after supervisory review of the PEB, soliciting comments by interested persons by a stated date on the substance and style of the work;

d. approval by the PEB of the substance and style of the *PEB Commentary* as finally submitted by the adviser(s) and comments submitted by interested persons or, when warranted, the withdrawal of the proposal with the reasons for withdrawal stated; and

e. periodic publication of such *PEB Commentary* as is approved by the PEB on a regular schedule.

Approval by the PEB of *PEB Commentary* shall be by three quarters of the members of the PEB voting on the *Commentary.* The manner of publication of *PEB Commentary* by the PEB will be in accordance with procedures formulated under a resolution related to that subject generally.

PEB COMMENTARY NO. 1
SECTION 2–507(2)
(March 10, 1990)

ISSUE

A cash seller has the right to be paid upon delivery of goods and, if not paid, to reclaim the goods. This right is codified by § 2–507(2). Payment may be made by a check, but such payment is conditional and defeated by dishonor of the check giving rise to the seller's right of reclamation. Comment 3 to § 2–507(2) states:

"Subsection (2) deals with the effect of a conditional delivery by the seller and in such a situation makes the buyer's 'right as against the seller' conditional upon payment. These words are used as words of limitation to conform with the policy set forth in the bona fide purchase sections of this Article. Should the seller after making such a conditional delivery fail to follow up his rights, the

condition is waived. *The provision of this Article for a ten day limit within which the seller may reclaim goods delivered on credit to an insolvent buyer is also applicable here."* (emphasis supplied)

If the payment is tendered by check, the seller payee will only learn that the check has been or will be dishonored *after* the goods are delivered. The seller will gain this information either by learning from the bank where the check was deposited that it had been dishonored by the payor bank; or, sometimes by inquiring directly of the payor bank and being told that there is no such account or there is an account but with insufficient funds to cover the check. Oftentimes, the seller may not learn of the dishonor or anticipated dishonor until more than ten days after delivery of the goods.[1] Does the reference in the Comment to the requirement of § 2–702(2) requiring a credit seller to demand reclamation of the goods "within ten days after the receipt" mean that the cash seller also loses the right of reclamation where demand is made more than ten days after delivery of the goods, even though the seller did not learn of the dishonor before then?

DISCUSSION

The cash seller's right of reclamation was a common law remedy in the nature of a lien. "The ground upon which an unpaid seller is allowed a lien and kindred remedies is the inherent injustice of depriving him of goods with which he has not finally parted where it is evident that he has not been paid or will not be paid the price for them when it is due." Williston, *Sales*, 99 (1948).

The "cash sale" is expressly mentioned in the voidable title provision of § 2–403(1)(c) (along with payment by check (§ 2–403(1)(b))), but the right of reclamation is not specifically mentioned. Instead, it is implicit in § 2–507(2) and § 2–511(3). As noted by the First Circuit in Szabo v. Vinton Motors, 630 F.2d 1, 3, 29 UCC Rep.Serv. (Callaghan) 737 (1st Cir.1980):

"Although the right of such a cash seller to reclaim goods sold in a 'bad check' transaction is not specifically set forth in the Code provisions, [footnote omitted] such a reclamation right is inherent in 2–507(2) and 2–511(3) of the Code, Mass. Gen. Laws ch. 106, §§ 2–507(2), 2–511(3). In re Mort Co., 208 F.Supp. 309, 310 [1 UCC Rep. 166] (ED Pa.1962); In re Helms Veneer Corp., 287 F.Supp. 840, 845–46 [5 UCC Rep. 977, 983–4] (WD Va.1968). See generally Mann & Phillips, The Cash Seller Under the Uniform Commercial Code, 20 B.C.L.Rev. 370, 375–84 (1979). Section 2–507(2) makes a buyer's 'right as against the seller to retain or dispose of [the goods] . . . conditional upon his

making the payment due.' Section 2–511(3), in turn, provides that 'payment by check is conditional and is defeated as between the parties by dishonor of the check on due presentment.' Taking these two Code provisions together, the clear implication is that a buyer cannot retain and, conversely, a seller has the right to reclaim goods sold in a cash transaction if the buyer's check is dishonored.

"The existence of the cash seller's right to reclaim is further supported, and limited, by Comment 3 to section 2–507:

"[quotation omitted]

"The reference in the last sentence of Comment 3 is to the limitation contained in § 2–702(2) requiring a credit seller to reclaim goods within ten days of receipt. See note 1 supra. Based on this reference, courts have invariably held that a cash seller must make a demand for the return of the goods within ten days after the goods are received by the buyer. E.g., In re Samuels & Co., 526 F.2d 1238, 1245 (5th Cir.) (en banc), cert. denied 429 U.S. 834 (1976); In re Helms Veneer Corp., supra, at 846 *** [footnote omitted]."

See also Dugan, *Cash Sellers Under Articles 2 and 9 of the UCC*, 8 UCC L.J. 330, 345–349 (1976).

Szabo, which represents the majority view by reason of the Comment, went on to hold that the seller's right of reclamation is lost if demand is made more than ten days after delivery of the goods:

"Appellee urges us to disregard the limitation contained in Comment 3 on the ground that it directly contradicts the language of the Code. Although official Code Comments do not have the force of law, they are helpful in explaining the Code provisions and their purpose is to promote uniformity in construction. Mass.Gen. Laws ch. 106, Comment to Title; Thompson v. United States,

---

1. This problem should become less significant under Federal Reserve Board Regulation CC, 12 CFR Part 229, issued pursuant to the Expedited Funds Availability Act, 12 USC Section 4001 et seq. Under Section 229.30, the payor bank has a duty to effect an "expeditious return" of the check and if the check is for $2,500 or more, Section 229.33 requires that it provide notice of non-payment that is received by the depositary bank by 4:00 P.M. on the second business day following the banking day on which the check was presented; and that the depositary bank send notice to its customer by midnight of the banking day following its receipt of the notice or within a reasonable longer time.

408 F.2d 1075, 1084 n. 15 (8th Cir.1969). See generally Skilton, Some Comments on the Comments to the Uniform Commercial Code, 1966 Wisc.L.Rev. 597. It has been stated that the Official Comments 'are powerful dicta.' In re Yale Express System, Inc., 370 F.2d 433, 437 (2d Cir.1966). Nevertheless, it is the Code provisions and not the Comments which control. We do not, however, accept appellee's argument that there is a direct conflict between the cash sale provisions of the Code and Comment 3 to § 2–507. As noted above, Comment 3 supports a reclamation right which is only implicit in §§ 2–507(2) and 2–511(3), and limits that right by reference to another Code provision, § 2–702(2), dealing with credit sales. Comment 3 does not contradict, but merely complements and explains the Code. We decline to disregard it." (630 F.2d at 3–4).

The Eighth Circuit, however, rejected *Szabo* in Burk v. Emmick, 637 F.2d 1172, 29 UCC Rep. Serv. (Callaghan) 1489 (8th Cir.1980):

"We reject this reasoning. In our view, it would tend to coerce the cash seller who reasonably expects the buyer to tender payment at delivery to go through the cautious motions of a credit seller dealing with an economically unstable buyer. This we are not prepared to do...." (637 F.2d at 1175 n. 6).

"Our holding is quite limited. We determine that as between the seller and the buyer, where a cash seller reclaims goods sold to a breaching buyer, the only limitation imposed upon the seller's right is a reasonableness requirement...." (637 F.2d at 1176).

There is nothing in the language of § 2–507(2) supporting the imposition of the "ten day limit" mentioned in Comment 3. At common law, there was no specific time limitation. Rather, an attempt to reclaim after excessive delay would be defeated by doctrines such as waiver, estoppel, or ratification of the buyer's property interest. See, e.g., Frech v. Lewis, 218 Pa. 141, 67 A. 45 (1907). Under § 1–103, common law principles supplement Code provisions, unless "displaced by the particular provisions." Proper implementation of this doctrine compels the conclusion that the codification of the "cash sale" concept implicit in § 2–507(2), without any mention of a time limit, means that common law rules governing enforcement are still applicable. Indeed, the third sentence of Comment 3 is consistent with this interpretation in referring to waiver where a seller fails "to follow up his rights." The cases which, even though they rely on Comment 3, impose a ten day limit, must be considered to have reached an improper result. There is no need to impose a specific time limitation for enforcement of a cash seller's right of reclamation. The common law rules defeating the right where there is delay resulting in prejudice to the buyer adequately cover instances where only the seller and buyer are involved: If the rights of third parties are implicated § 2–403(1)(b) and (c) protect good faith purchasers.

CONCLUSION

There is no justification for barring the cash seller's right or remedy of reclamation before discovery of non-payment. There is no specific time limit for a cash seller to exercise the right of reclamation. The right may be exercised as long as there has not been an excessive delay causing inequitable prejudice to the buyer. Common law rules and precedents governing such circumstances are applicable.

The last sentence of Official Comment 3 to § 2–507 is deleted as inappropriate and replaced by the following:

... This subsection (2) codifies the cash seller's right of reclamation which is in the nature of a lien. There is no specific time limit for a cash seller to exercise the right of reclamation. However, the right will be defeated by delay causing prejudice to the buyer, waiver, estoppel, or ratification of the buyer's right to retain possession. Common law rules and precedents governing such principles are applicable (Section 1–103). If third parties are involved, Section 2–403(1) protects good faith purchasers. See PEB Commentary No. 1, dated March 10, 1990.

PEB COMMENTARY NO. 10
SECTION 1–203
(February 10, 1994)

ISSUE

Section 1–203 provides that "Every contract or duty within this Act imposes an obligation of good faith in its performance or enforcement." [1] While this concept applies generally to every contract, it finds particular expression throughout the Code. For example, out of over 400 Code provisions, more than 50 sections make specific reference to "good faith." [2]

The meaning of "good faith" varies with the context. Sometimes the context is as a standard of performance or enforcement; other times the context is that of good faith purchase. [3] This Commentary deals only with good faith performance or enforcement of a right or duty under a contract that is within the Code.

In the context in which the obligation of good faith functions as the standard of contract performance or enforcement, can the failure to meet this standard support a cause of action where no other basis for a cause of action exists? This Commentary examines this question in order to promote a uniform understanding of what it means to say that a general obligation of good faith is imposed on every contracting party. In so doing, several principles are discussed.

1. This does not mean that the obligation of good faith as defined in the Code will necessarily apply to all aspects of the same transaction. As written, the scope of § 1–203 is co-extensive with the Code's coverage. For example, if a loan agreement that provides for an Article 9 security interest also contains financial covenants which are not governed by the Code, § 1–203 would apply to the former and the general law of contracts would apply to the latter. See, e.g., Restatement, Second, Contracts § 205 (1981).

2. Farnsworth, *Good Faith Performance and Commercial Reasonableness Under the Uniform Commercial Code*, 30 U.Chi.L.Rev. 666, 667 (1963).

3. See, e.g., UCC §§ 2–403 (good faith purchaser); 3–302 (holder in due course); 9–307 (buyer in the ordinary course of business). On the distinction between the doctrines of good faith performance and good faith purchase, see generally id.

4. This sparse definition found in Article 1 is expanded elsewhere in the Code for purposes of particular Articles.

DISCUSSION

1. Good Faith, Commercial Expectations, and the Concept of Agreement

Section 1–201(19) defines good faith as "honesty in fact in the conduct or transaction concerned." [4] Commentators have said that this general requirement of good faith sets a "subjective" standard, [5] while the particularized definitions elsewhere also create an additional "objective" standard of the observance of reasonable commercial standards of fair dealing. This Commentary applies with equal force to both standards of good faith.

The principal author of the Code, Karl Llewellyn, recognized that parties develop expectations over time against the background of commercial practices and that if commercial law fails to account for those practices, it will cut against the parties' actual expectations. In an unpublished commentary on the Proposed Final Draft of the Uniform Revised Sales Act, Llewellyn had this to say about good faith:

No inconsistency of language and background exists merely because the words used mean something different to an outsider than they do to the merchants who used that language in the light of the commercial background against which they contracted. This is the necessary result of applying commer-

See, e.g., §§ 2–103(1)(b); 2A–103(2); 3–103(a)(4); 4–104(c); 4A–105(a)(6). This expanded definition "is concerned with the fairness of conduct rather than the care with which an act is performed." UCC § 3–103, Comment 4.

5. See Aronstein, *Good Faith Performance of Security Agreements: The Liability of Corporate Managers*, 120 U.Pa.L.Rev. 1, 31 (1971) ("Good faith [as] defined in § 1–201(19) ... [has] been historically construed as applying only to the actor's subjective state of mind."); Braucher, *The Legislative History of the Uniform Commercial Code*, 58 Colum.L.Rev. 798, 812 (1958) (describing the test of good faith in § 1–201(19) as a "subjective" test, sometimes known as the rule of "the pure heart and empty head"); Lawrence, *The Prematurely Reported Demise of the Perfect Tender Rule*, 35 U.Kan.L.Rev. 557, 571 (1987) ("Good faith is a subjective term meaning 'honesty in fact in the contract or transaction concerned.' ").

cial standards and principles of good faith to the agreement.... Moreover, where the commercial background normally gives to a term in question some breadth of meaning so that it describes a range of acceptable tolerances rather than a sharp-edged single line of action, any attempted narrowing of this meaning by one party is so unusual as not likely to be expected or perceived by the other. Therefore, attention must be called to a desire to contract at material variance from the accepted commercial pattern of contract or use of language. Thus, this Act rejects any "surprise" variation from the fair and normal meaning of the agreement.[6]

Explaining the doctrine of good faith in such terms is thus a recognition that, as expressed in the Code, it serves as a directive to protect the reasonable expectations of the contracting parties. The general imperative that the reasonable expectations of the parties are the measure of the good faith of each suggests that good faith is a concept with conceptual content related to that of agreement.

The Code definition of "Agreement" reads: "Agreement" means the bargain of the parties in fact as found in their language or by implication from other circumstances including course of dealing or usage of trade or course of performance as provided in this Act (Sections 1–205 and 2–208).[7]

The agreement of the parties consists of more than their language alone. In elaborating on this theme, Comment 3 to § 1–201 emphasizes that "the word [agreement] is intended to include full recognition of usage of trade, course of dealing, *course of performance* and the surrounding circumstances as effective parts thereof...." (emphasis added).[8]

"Course of dealing" is defined as follows:

A course of dealing is a sequence of previous conduct between the parties to a particular transaction which is fairly to be regarded as establishing a common basis of understanding for interpreting their expressions and other conduct.[9]

"Usage of trade" is defined as follows:

A usage of trade is any practice or method of dealing having such regularity of observance in a place, vocation or trade as to justify an expectation that it will be observed with respect to the transaction in question. The existence and scope of such a usage are to be proved as facts. If it is established that such a usage is embodied in a written trade code or similar writing the interpretation of the writing is for the court.[10]

"Course of performance" is defined as follows:

Where the contract for sale involves repeated occasions for performance by either party with knowledge of the nature of the performance and opportunity for objection to it by the other, any course of performance accepted or acquiesced in without objection shall be

---

6. The Karl Llewellyn Papers, The University of Chicago Law Library, File J.X.2.K. 1, 9, *reprinted in* D. Patterson, *Good Faith and Lender Liability* 217 (1990).

7. UCC § 1–201(3). Furthermore, Comment 1 to § 1–205 ("Course of Dealing and Usage of Trade") reinforces this definition by stating:

This Act rejects both the "lay-dictionary" and the "conveyancer's" reading of a commercial agreement. Instead the meaning of the agreement of the parties is to be determined by the language used by them and by their action, read and interpreted in the light of commercial practices and other surrounding circumstances. The measure and background for interpretation are set by the commercial context, which may explain and supplement even the language of a formal or final writing.

8. This Commentary recognizes the fact that course of performance is defined in Articles 2 and 2A and was originally not a part of the general definition of "Agreement" in Article 1. The concept is included here as an element of the agreement of the parties because there

exists no plausible justification for excluding it. This view is strongly supported by Comments 1 and 2 to § 2–208. Comment 2, in particular, emphasizes that "a course of performance is always relevant to determine the meaning of the agreement." See also Westinghouse Credit Corp. v. Shelton, 645 F.2d 869, 31 UCC Rep.Serv. (Callaghan) 410 (10th Cir.1981) (course of performance may also be used for discerning the meaning of "Agreement" in Article 9).

The Restatement, Second, of Contracts does not reflect the Code's isolation of course of performance in Articles 2 and 2A. The Restatement provides that all four elements—express terms, course of dealing, course of performance, and usage of trade—are all elements of the meaning of "contract." See Restatement, Second, Contracts § 203. In fact, § 202(4) states that "any course of performance accepted or acquiesced in without objection is given great weight in the interpretation of the agreement."

9. UCC § 1–205(1).

10. UCC § 1–205(2).

relevant to determine the meaning of the agreement.[11]

In addition to two definitional sections, § 1–205 contains two additional methodological sections which direct how express terms, course of dealing, and usage of trade are to be synthesized:

(3) A course of dealing between parties and any usage of trade in the vocation or trade in which they are engaged or of which they are or should be aware give particular meaning to and supplement or qualify terms of an agreement.

(4) The express terms of an agreement and an applicable course of dealing or usage of trade shall be construed wherever reasonable as consistent with each other; but when such construction is unreasonable express terms control both course of dealing and usage of trade and course of dealing controls usage of trade.[12]

At this juncture it is important to recognize that one acts in good faith relative to the agreement of the parties. To decide the question whether a party has acted in good faith, a court must first ascertain the substance of the parties' agreement.

The performance and enforcement of agreements in a manner consistent with the reasonable expectations of the parties is in keeping with the broadest understanding of contract doctrine.[13] The Code is consistent with this tradition of thought. However, the Code's concept of agreement broadens the sources for determining the meaning of the parties' agreement. The concept of agreement is not limited to the terms of the parties' writing: it includes a variety of elements, all of which must be synthesized.

Under § 1–205(4), the initial interpretive effort is to read all the terms as consistent with one another. Only when this is impossible does the interpreter then move to a lexical ordering of the terms, with express terms at the head of the list. Cases which make no attempt to reconcile the various terms before according priority to express terms in the construction of the parties' agreement must be considered to have proceeded improperly.[14] The better application of § 1–205(4), and the issues of interpretation which are central to it, is illustrated in cases like *Nanakuli Paving & Rock Co. v. Shell Oil Co.*, 664 F.2d 772, 32 UCC Rep.Serv. (Callaghan) 1025 (9th Cir. 1981) (upholding a finding that the written price term in an asphalt supply contract was qualified by a trade practice requiring suppliers to delay price increases for jobs on which buyers have already bid). Accordingly, in order to answer the question, "Has a party performed or enforced a contractual right or duty in good faith?", the

---

11. UCC § 2–208(1). This definition is duplicated in § 2A–207(1).

12. UCC § 1–205(3)–(4). The connection between § 1–205 and good faith is made explicit in the Comment to § 1–203, wherein it is stated that the obligation of good faith "is further implemented by Section 1–205 on course of dealing and usage of trade."

The interpretational priorities set forth in § 1–205 are, with the added inclusion of course of performance, duplicated in § 2–208(2). That section states as follows:

The express terms of the agreement and any such course of performance, as well as any course of dealing and usage of trade, shall be construed whenever reasonable as consistent with each other; but when such construction is unreasonable, express terms shall control course of performance and course of performance shall control both course of dealing and usage of trade (Section 1–205).

See also UCC § 2A–207(2).

13. See 3 A. Corbin, *Corbin on Contracts* § 570 (West Supp.1993).

If the purpose of contract law is to enforce the reasonable expectations of parties induced by promises, then at some point it becomes necessary for courts to look to the substance rather than to the form of the agreement, and to hold that substance controls over form. What courts are doing here, whether calling the process "implication" of promises, or interpreting the requirements of "good faith," as the current fashion may be, is but a recognition that the parties occasionally have understandings or expectations that were so fundamental that they did not need to negotiate about those expectations. When the court "implies a promise" or holds that "good faith" requires a party not to violate those expectations, it is recognizing that sometimes silence says more than words, and it is understanding its duty to the spirit of the bargain is higher than its duty to the technicalities of the language.

Id. Reiter & Swan, Contracts and the Protection of Reasonable Expectations, in *Studies in Contract Law* 1, 11 (B. Reiter & J. Swan eds. 1980) ("[T]hroughout the law of contract, a striving to protect reasonable expectations is visible. . . .").

14. See, e.g., Southern Concrete Servs. v. Mableton Contractors, Inc., 407 F.Supp. 581, 19 UCC Rep.Serv. (Callaghan) 79 (N.D.Ga.1975), aff'd mem., 569 F.2d 1154 (5th Cir.1978); Division of Triple T Serv. v. Mobil Oil Corp., 304 N.Y.S.2d 191, 6 UCC Rep.Serv. (Callaghan) 1011 (Sup.Ct.1969).

content of the parties' agreement must first be determined.[15]

2. UCC § 1–203 Does Not Create an Independent Cause of Action

The inherent flaw in the view that § 1–203 supports an independent cause of action is the belief that the obligation of good faith has an existence which is conceptually separate from the underlying agreement. As the above discussion demonstrates, however, this is an incorrect view of the duty. "A party cannot simply 'act in good faith.' One acts in good faith relative to the agreement of the parties. Thus the real question is 'What is the Agreement of the parties?' "[16] Put differently, good faith merely directs attention to the parties' reasonable expectations; it is not an independent source from which rights and duties evolve.[17] The language of § 1–203 itself makes this quite clear by providing that the obligation to perform or enforce in good faith extends only to the rights and duties resulting from the parties' contract. The term "contract" is, in turn, defined as "the total legal obligation which results from the parties' *agreement* . . . ."[18] Consequently, resort to principles of law or equity outside the Code are not appropriate to create rights, duties, and liabilities inconsistent with those stated in the Code.[19] For example, a breach of a contract or duty within the Code arising from a failure to act in good faith does not give rise to a claim for punitive damages unless specifically permitted.[20]

CONCLUSION

Section 1–203 does not support a cause of action where no other basis for a cause of action exists.

The concept of Agreement permeates the entirety of the Code. For example, § 9–105(1)(*l*) incorporates the Article 1 concept of Agreement directly into Article 9. The "agreement of the parties" cannot be read off the face of a document, but must be discerned against the background of actual commercial practice. Not only does the Code recognize "the reasonable practices and standards of the commercial community . . . [as] an appropriate source of legal obligation,"[21] but it also rejects the "premise that the language used [by the parties] has the meaning attributable to [it] by rules of construction existing in the law rather than the meaning which arises out of the commercial context in which it was used."[22] The correct perspective on the meaning of good faith performance and enforcement is the Agreement of the parties. The critical question is, "Has 'X' acted in good faith with respect to the performance or enforcement of some right or duty under the terms of the Agreement?" It is therefore wrong to conclude that as long as the agreement allows a party to do something, it is under all terms and conditions permissible. Such a conclusion overlooks completely the distinction between merely performing or enforcing a right or duty under an

---

15. For a non-Code decision which is consistent with this approach, see Southwest Savings and Loan Association v. Sunamp Systems, Inc., 838 P.2d 1314 (Ariz.App. 1992) (holding that inquiry does not stop with recognition that lender had general authority in written loan agreement to take the particular action, but inquiry extends to whether lender exercised that authority "for a reason beyond the risks" assumed by borrower in loan agreement, or beyond borrower's "justified expectations," in the context of how a reasonable lender might act).

16. Patterson, *supra*, at 143. Good faith is sometimes the basis of an implied term to fill a gap or deal with an omitted case, e.g., the duty of cooperation frequently imposed on a party whose cooperation is essential and not unreasonably burdensome; or, the duty to give notice within a reasonable time of some important fact of which the other party would otherwise be unaware. See § 2–309(3) and Comment 8; 2 Farnsworth on Contracts §§ 7.17, 7.17a (1990). A breach of such duties gives rise to a cause of action for breach of the contract of which the implied term becomes a part. Although such a cause of action arguably has the same practical content as a cause of action based upon a purported breach of § 1–203, there

is an important methodological difference in that this Commentary requires, in the case of contracts within the Code, that the focus be upon the Agreement of the parties and their reasonable expectations.

17. Cases reaching this conclusion include Management Assistance, Inc. v. Computer Dimensions, Inc., 546 F.Supp. 666 (N.D.Ga.1982), *aff'd* 747 F.2d 708 (11th Cir. 1984), and Chandler v. Hunter, 340 So.2d 818, 21 UCC Rep.Serv. (Callaghan) 484 (Ala.Civ.App.1976). A contrary conclusion was reached in Reid v. Key Bank of Southern Maine, Inc., 821 F.2d 9, 3 UCC Rep.Serv.2d (Callaghan) 1665 (1st Cir.1987).

18. UCC § 1–201(11) (emphasis supplied).

19. See UCC § 1–103.

20. See UCC § 1–106(1).

21. Kastely, *Stock Equipment for the Bargain in Fact: Trade Usage, "Express Terms," and Consistency Under Section 1–205 of the Uniform Commercial Code*, 64 N.C.L.Rev. 777, 780 (1986).

22. UCC § 2–202, Comment 1.

agreement on the one hand and, on the other hand, doing so in a way that recognizes that the agreement should be interpreted in a manner consistent with the reasonable expectations of the parties in the light of the commercial conditions existing in the context under scrutiny. The latter is the correct approach. Examples are: (1) Is it reasonable for a buyer in a particular locale or trade to expect that an express quantity term in a contract is "not really" a quantity term, but a mere projection to be adjusted according to market forces?[23]; (2) Does a party to a sales contract that permits discretionary termination have the right to expect that the decision whether to terminate will be made on the basis of sound business criteria?

The Official Comment to § 1–203 is amended by adding the following language at the end of the first paragraph:

23. See Columbia Nitrogen Corp. v. Royster Co., 451 F.2d 3, 9 UCC Rep.Serv. (Callaghan) 977 (4th Cir.1971).

This section does not support an independent cause of action for failure to perform or enforce in good faith. Rather, this section means that a failure to perform or enforce, in good faith, a specific duty or obligation under the contract, constitutes a breach of that contract or makes unavailable, under the particular circumstances, a remedial right or power. This distinction makes it clear that the doctrine of good faith merely directs a court towards interpreting contracts within the commercial context in which they are created, performed, and enforced, and does not create a separate duty of fairness and reasonableness which can be independently breached. See PEB Commentary No. 10, dated February 10, 1994.

UNIFORM ELECTRONIC TRANSACTIONS ACT (1999)*

January 20, 2000

Sec.
1. Short Title
2. Definitions
3. Scope
4. Prospective Application
5. Use of Electronic Records and Electronic Signatures; Variation By Agreement
6. Construction and Application
7. Legal Recognition of Electronic Records, Electronic Signatures, and Electronic Contracts
8. Provision of Information in Writing; Presentation of Records
9. Attribution and Effect of Electronic Record and Electronic Signature
10. Effect of Change or Error

Sec.
11. Notarization and Acknowledgment
12. Retention of Electronic Records; Originals
13. Admissibility in Evidence
14. Automated Transaction
15. Time and Place of Sending and Receipt
16. Transferable Records
17. Creation and Retention of Electronic Records and Conversion of Written Records By Governmental Agencies
18. Acceptance and Distribution of Electronic Records by Governmental Agencies
19. Interoperability
20. Severability Clause
21. Effective Date

UNIFORM ELECTRONIC TRANSACTIONS ACT (1999)

PREFATORY NOTE

With the advent of electronic means of communication and information transfer, business models and methods for doing business have evolved to take advantage of the speed, efficiencies, and cost benefits of electronic technologies. These developments have occurred in the face of existing legal barriers to the legal efficacy of records and documents which exist solely in electronic media. Whether the legal requirement that information or an agreement or contract must be contained or set forth in a pen and paper writing derives from a statute of frauds affecting the enforceability of an agreement, or from a record retention statute that calls for keeping the paper record of a transaction, such legal requirements raise real barriers to the effective use of electronic media.

One striking example of electronic barriers involves so called check retention statutes in every State. A study conducted by the Federal Reserve Bank of Boston identified more than 2500 different state laws which require the retention of canceled checks by the issuers of those checks. These requirements not only impose burdens on the issuers, but also effectively restrain the ability of banks handling the checks to automate the process. Although check truncation is validated under the Uniform Commercial Code, if the bank's customer must store the canceled paper check, the bank will not be able to deal with the item through electronic transmission of the information. By establishing the equivalence of an electronic record of the information, the Uniform Electronic Transactions Act (UETA) removes these barriers without affecting the underlying legal rules and requirements.

It is important to understand that the purpose of the UETA is to remove barriers to electronic commerce by validating and effectuating electronic records and signatures. It is NOT a general contracting statute–the substantive rules of contracts remain unaffected by UETA. Nor is it a digital signature statute. To the extent that a State has a Digital Signature Law, the UETA is designed to support and compliment that statute.

* Reproduced by permission of the National Conference of Commissioners on Uniform State Laws

A. Scope of the Act and Procedural Approach. The scope of this Act provides coverage which sets forth a clear framework for covered transactions, and also avoids unwarranted surprises for unsophisticated parties dealing in this relatively new media. The clarity and certainty of the scope of the Act have been obtained while still providing a solid legal framework that allows for the continued development of innovative technology to facilitate electronic transactions.

With regard to the general scope of the Act, the Act's coverage is inherently limited by the definition of "transaction." The Act does not apply to *all* writings and signatures, but only to electronic records and signatures relating to a transaction, defined as those interactions between people relating to business, commercial and governmental affairs. In general, there are few writing or signature requirements imposed by law on many of the "standard" transactions that had been considered for exclusion. A good example relates to trusts, where the general rule on creation of a trust imposes no formal writing requirement. Further, the writing requirements in other contexts derived from governmental filing issues. For example, real estate transactions were considered potentially troublesome because of the need to file a deed or other instrument for protection against third parties. Since the efficacy of a real estate purchase contract, or even a deed, between the parties is not affected by any sort of filing, the question was raised why these transactions should not be validated by this Act if done via an electronic medium. No sound reason was found. Filing requirements fall within Sections 17–19 on governmental records. An exclusion of all real estate transactions would be particularly unwarranted in the event that a State chose to convert to an electronic recording system, as many have for Article 9 financing statement filings under the Uniform Commercial Code.

The exclusion of specific Articles of the Uniform Commercial Code reflects the recognition that, particularly in the case of Articles 5, 8 and revised Article 9, electronic transactions were addressed in the specific contexts of those revision processes. In the context of Articles 2 and 2A the UETA provides the vehicle for assuring that such transactions may be accomplished and effected via an electronic medium. At such time as Articles 2 and 2A are revised the extent of coverage in those Articles/Acts may make application of this Act as a gap-filling law desirable. Similar considerations apply to the recently promulgated Uniform Computer Information Transactions Act ("UCITA").

The need for certainty as to the scope and applicability of this Act is critical, and makes any sort of a broad, general exception based on notions of inconsistency with existing writing and signature requirements unwise at best. The uncertainty inherent in leaving the applicability of the Act to judicial construction of this Act with other laws is unacceptable if electronic transactions are to be facilitated.

Finally, recognition that the paradigm for the Act involves two willing parties conducting a transaction electronically, makes it necessary to expressly provide that some form of acquiescence or intent on the part of a person to conduct transactions electronically is necessary before the Act can be invoked. Accordingly, Section 5 specifically provides that the Act only applies between parties that have agreed to conduct transactions electronically. In this context, the construction of the term agreement must be broad in order to assure that the Act applies whenever the circumstances show the parties intention to transact electronically, regardless of whether the intent rises to the level of a formal agreement.

B. Procedural Approach. Another fundamental premise of the Act is that it be minimalist and procedural. The general efficacy of existing law in an electronic context, so long as biases and barriers to the medium are removed, validates this approach. The Act defers to existing substantive law. Specific areas of deference to other law in this Act include: (1) the meaning and effect of "sign" under existing law, (2) the method and manner of displaying, transmitting and formatting information in Section 8, (3) rules of attribution in Section 9, and (4) the law of mistake in Section 10.

The Act's treatment of records and signatures demonstrates best the minimalist approach that has been adopted. Whether a record is attributed to a person is left to law outside this Act. Whether an electronic signature has any effect is left to the surrounding circumstances and other law. These provisions are salutary directives to assure that records and signatures will be treated in the same manner, under currently existing law, as written records and manual signatures.

The deference of the Act to other substantive law does not negate the necessity of setting forth rules and standards for using electronic media. The Act expressly validates electronic records, signatures and contracts. It provides for the use of electronic records and information for retention purposes, providing certainty in an area with great potential in cost savings and efficiency. The Act makes clear that the actions of machines ("electronic agents") programmed and used by people will bind the user of the machine, regardless of whether human review of a particular transaction has occurred. It specifies the standards for sending and receipt of electronic records, and it allows for innovation in financial services through the implementation of transferable records. In these ways the Act permits electronic transactions to be accomplished with certainty under existing substantive rules of law.

§ 1. Short Title.

This [Act] may be cited as the Uniform Electronic Transactions Act.

§ 2. Definitions.

In this [Act]:

(1) "Agreement" means the bargain of the parties in fact, as found in their language or inferred from other circumstances and from rules, regulations, and procedures given the effect of agreements under laws otherwise applicable to a particular transaction.

(2) "Automated transaction" means a transaction conducted or performed, in whole or in part, by electronic means or electronic records, in which the acts or records of one or both parties are not reviewed by an individual in the ordinary course in forming a contract, performing under an existing contract, or fulfilling an obligation required by the transaction.

(3) "Computer program" means a set of statements or instructions to be used directly or indirectly in an information processing system in order to bring about a certain result.

(4) "Contract" means the total legal obligation resulting from the parties' agreement as affected by this [Act] and other applicable law.

(5) "Electronic" means relating to technology having electrical, digital, magnetic, wireless, optical, electromagnetic, or similar capabilities.

(6) "Electronic agent" means a computer program or an electronic or other automated means used independently to initiate an action or respond to electronic records or performances in whole or in part, without review or action by an individual.

(7) "Electronic record" means a record created, generated, sent, communicated, received, or stored by electronic means.

(8) "Electronic signature" means an electronic sound, symbol, or process attached to or logically associated with a record and executed or adopted by a person with the intent to sign the record.

(9) "Governmental agency" means an executive, legislative, or judicial agency, department, board, commission, authority, institution, or instrumentality of the federal government or of a State or of a county, municipality, or other political subdivision of a State.

(10) "Information" means data, text, images, sounds, codes, computer programs, software, databases, or the like.

(11) "Information processing system" means an electronic system for creating, generating, sending, receiving, storing, displaying, or processing information.

(12) "Person" means an individual, corporation, business trust, estate, trust, partnership, limited liability company, association, joint venture, governmental agency, public corporation, or any other legal or commercial entity.

(13) "Record" means information that is inscribed on a tangible medium or that is stored in an electronic or other medium and is retrievable in perceivable form.

(14) "Security procedure" means a procedure employed for the purpose of verifying that an electronic signature, record, or performance is that of a specific person or for detecting changes or errors in the information in an electronic record. The term includes a procedure that requires the use of algorithms or other codes, identifying words or numbers, encryption, or callback or other acknowledgment procedures.

(15) "State" means a State of the United States, the District of Columbia, Puerto Rico, the United States Virgin Islands, or any territory or insular possession subject to the jurisdiction of the United States. The term includes an Indian tribe or band, or Alaskan native village, which is recognized by federal law or formally acknowledged by a State.

(16) "Transaction" means an action or set of actions occurring between two or more persons relating to the conduct of business, commercial, or governmental affairs.

Sources: UNCITRAL Model Law on Electronic Commerce; Uniform Commercial Code; Uniform Computer Information Transactions Act; Restatement 2d Contracts.

Comment

1. **"Agreement."** Whether the parties have reached an agreement is determined by their express language and all surrounding circumstances. The Restatement 2d Contracts § 3 provides that, "An agreement is a manifestation of mutual assent on the part of two or more persons." See also Restatement 2d Contracts, Section 2, Comment b. The Uniform Commercial Code specifically includes in the circumstances from which an agreement may be inferred "course of performance, course of dealing and usage of trade . . ." as defined in the UCC. Although the definition of agreement in this Act does not make specific reference to usage of trade and other party conduct, this definition is not intended to affect the construction of the parties' agreement under the substantive law applicable to a particular transaction. Where that law takes account of usage and conduct in informing the terms of the parties' agreement, the usage or conduct would be relevant as "other circumstances" included in the definition under this Act.

Where the law applicable to a given transaction provides that system rules and the like constitute part of the agreement of the parties, such rules will have the same effect in determining the parties agreement under this Act. For example, UCC Article 4 (Section 4–103(b)) provides that Federal Reserve regulations and operating circulars and clearinghouse rules have the effect of agreements. Such agreements by law properly would be included in the definition of agreement in this Act.

The parties' agreement is relevant in determining whether the provisions of this Act have been varied by agreement. In addition, the parties' agreement may

establish the parameters of the parties' use of electronic records and signatures, security procedures and similar aspects of the transaction. See Model Trading Partner Agreement, 45 Business Lawyer Supp. Issue (June 1990). See Section 5(b) and Comments thereto.

2. **"Automated Transaction."** An automated transaction is a transaction performed or conducted by electronic means in which machines are used without human intervention to form contracts and perform obligations under existing contracts. Such broad coverage is necessary because of the diversity of transactions to which this Act may apply.

As with electronic agents, this definition addresses the circumstance where electronic records may result in action or performance by a party although no human review of the electronic records is anticipated. Section 14 provides specific rules to assure that where one or both parties do not review the electronic records, the resulting agreement will be effective.

The critical element in this definition is the lack of a human actor on one or both sides of a transaction. For example, if one orders books from Bookseller.com through Bookseller's website, the transaction would be an automated transaction because Bookseller took and confirmed the order via its machine. Similarly, if Automaker and supplier do business through Electronic Data Interchange, Automaker's computer, upon receiving information within certain pre-programmed parameters, will send an electronic order to supplier's computer. If Supplier's computer confirms the order and processes the shipment because the order falls within pre-programmed parameters in Supplier's computer, this would be a fully automated transaction. If, instead, the Supplier relies on a human employee to review, accept, and process the Buyer's order, then only the Automaker's side of the transaction would be automated. In either case, the entire transaction falls within this definition.

3. **"Computer program."** This definition refers to the functional and operating aspects of an electronic, digital system. It relates to operating instructions used in an electronic system such as an electronic agent. (See definition of "Electronic Agent.")

4. **"Electronic."** The basic nature of most current technologies and the need for a recognized, single term warrants the use of "electronic" as the defined term. The definition is intended to assure that the Act will be applied broadly as new technologies develop. The term must be construed broadly in light of developing technologies in order to fulfill the purpose of this Act to validate commercial transactions regardless of the medium used by the parties. Current legal require-

ments for "writings" can be satisfied by almost any tangible media, whether paper, other fibers, or even stone. The purpose and applicability of this Act covers intangible media which are technologically capable of storing, transmitting and reproducing information in human perceivable form, but which lack the tangible aspect of paper, papyrus or stone.

While not all technologies listed are technically "electronic" in nature (e.g., optical fiber technology), the term "electronic" is the most descriptive term available to describe the majority of current technologies. For example, the development of biological and chemical processes for communication and storage of data, while not specifically mentioned in the definition, are included within the technical definition because such processes operate on electromagnetic impulses. However, whether a particular technology may be characterized as technically "electronic," i.e., operates on electromagnetic impulses, should not be determinative of whether records and signatures created, used and stored by means of a particular technology are covered by this Act. This Act is intended to apply to all records and signatures created, used and stored by any medium which permits the information to be retrieved in perceivable form.

5. **"Electronic agent."** This definition establishes that an electronic agent is a machine. As the term "electronic agent" has come to be recognized, it is limited to a tool function. The effect on the party using the agent is addressed in the operative provisions of the Act (e.g., Section 14)

An electronic agent, such as a computer program or other automated means employed by a person, is a tool of that person. As a general rule, the employer of a tool is responsible for the results obtained by the use of that tool since the tool has no independent volition of its own. However, an electronic agent, by definition, is capable within the parameters of its programming, of initiating, responding or interacting with other parties or their electronic agents once it has been activated by a party, without further attention of that party.

While this Act proceeds on the paradigm that an electronic agent is capable of performing only within the technical strictures of its preset programming, it is conceivable that, within the useful life of this Act, electronic agents may be created with the ability to act autonomously, and not just automatically. That is, through developments in artificial intelligence, a computer may be able to "learn through experience, modify the instructions in their own programs, and even devise new instructions." Allen and Widdison, "Can Computers Make Contracts?" *9 Harv. J.L. & Tech 25*

(Winter, 1996). If such developments occur, courts may construe the definition of electronic agent accordingly, in order to recognize such new capabilities.

The examples involving Bookseller.com and Automaker in the Comment to the definition of Automated Transaction are equally applicable here. Bookseller acts through an electronic agent in processing an order for books. Automaker and the supplier each act through electronic agents in facilitating and effectuating the just-in-time inventory process through EDI.

6. **"Electronic record."** An electronic record is a subset of the broader defined term "record." It is any record created, used or stored in a medium other than paper (see definition of electronic). The defined term is also used in this Act as a limiting definition in those provisions in which it is used.

Information processing systems, computer equipment and programs, electronic data interchange, electronic mail, voice mail, facsimile, telex, telecopying, scanning, and similar technologies all qualify as electronic under this Act. Accordingly information stored on a computer hard drive or floppy disc, facsimiles, voice mail messages, messages on a telephone answering machine, audio and video tape recordings, among other records, all would be electronic records under this Act.

7. **"Electronic signature."** The idea of a signature is broad and not specifically defined. Whether any particular record is "signed" is a question of fact. Proof of that fact must be made under other applicable law. This Act simply assures that the signature may be accomplished through electronic means. No specific technology need be used in order to create a valid signature. One's voice on an answering machine may suffice if the requisite intention is present. Similarly, including one's name as part of an electronic mail communication also may suffice, as may the firm name on a facsimile. It also may be shown that the requisite intent was not present and accordingly the symbol, sound or process did not amount to a signature. One may use a digital signature with the requisite intention, or one may use the private key solely as an access device with no intention to sign, or otherwise accomplish a legally binding act. In any case the critical element is the intention to execute or adopt the sound or symbol or process for the purpose of signing the related record.

The definition requires that the signer execute or adopt the sound, symbol, or process with the intent to sign the record. The act of applying a sound, symbol or process to an electronic record could have differing meanings and effects. The consequence of the act and the effect of the act as a signature are determined under other applicable law. However, the essential attribute of a signature involves applying a sound, symbol or process with an intent to do a legally significant act. It is that intention that is understood in the law as a part of the word "sign", without the need for a definition.

This Act establishes, to the greatest extent possible, the equivalency of electronic signatures and manual signatures. Therefore the term "signature" has been used to connote and convey that equivalency. The purpose is to overcome unwarranted biases against electronic methods of signing and authenticating records. The term "authentication," used in other laws, often has a narrower meaning and purpose than an electronic signature as used in this Act. However, an authentication under any of those other laws constitutes an electronic signature under this Act.

The precise effect of an electronic signature will be determined based on the surrounding circumstances under Section 9(b).

This definition includes as an electronic signature the standard webpage click through process. For example, when a person orders goods or services through a vendor's website, the person will be required to provide information as part of a process which will result in receipt of the goods or services. When the customer ultimately gets to the last step and clicks "I agree," the person has adopted the process and has done so with the intent to associate the person with the record of that process. The actual effect of the electronic signature will be determined from all the surrounding circumstances, however, the person adopted a process which the circumstances indicate s/he intended to have the effect of getting the goods/services and being bound to pay for them. The adoption of the process carried the intent to do a legally significant act, the hallmark of a signature.

Another important aspect of this definition lies in the necessity that the electronic signature be linked or logically associated with the record. In the paper world, it is assumed that the symbol adopted by a party is attached to or located somewhere in the same paper that is intended to be authenticated, e.g., an allonge firmly attached to a promissory note, or the classic signature at the end of a long contract. These tangible manifestations do not exist in the electronic environment, and accordingly, this definition expressly provides that the symbol must in some way be linked to, or connected with, the electronic record being signed. This linkage is consistent with the regulations promul-

gated by the Food and Drug Administration. 21 CFR Part 11 (March 20, 1997).

A digital signature using public key encryption technology would qualify as an electronic signature, as would the mere inclusion of one's name as a part of an e-mail message–so long as in each case the signer executed or adopted the symbol with the intent to sign.

8. **"Governmental agency."** This definition is important in the context of optional Sections 17–19.

9. **"Information processing system."** This definition is consistent with the UNCITRAL Model Law on Electronic Commerce. The term includes computers and other information systems. It is principally used in Section 15 in connection with the sending and receiving of information. In that context, the key aspect is that the information enter a system from which a person can access it.

10. **"Record."** This is a standard definition designed to embrace all means of communicating or storing information except human memory. It includes any method for storing or communicating information, including "writings." A record need not be indestructible or permanent, but the term does not include oral or other communications which are not stored or preserved by some means. Information that has not been retained other than through human memory does not qualify as a record. As in the case of the terms "writing" or "written," the term "record" does not establish the purposes, permitted uses or legal effect which a record may have under any particular provision of substantive law. ABA Report on Use of the Term "Record," October 1, 1996.

11. **"Security procedure."** A security procedure may be applied to verify an electronic signature, verify the identity of the sender, or assure the informational integrity of an electronic record. The definition does not identify any particular technology. This permits the use of procedures which the parties select or which are established by law. It permits the greatest flexibility among the parties and allows for future technological development.

The definition in this Act is broad and is used to illustrate one way of establishing attribution or content integrity of an electronic record or signature. The use of a security procedure is not accorded operative legal effect, through the use of presumptions or otherwise, by this Act. In this Act, the use of security procedures is simply one method for proving the source or content of an electronic record or signature.

A security procedure may be technologically very sophisticated, such as an asymmetric cryptographic system. At the other extreme the security procedure may be as simple as a telephone call to confirm the identity of the sender through another channel of communication. It may include the use of a mother's maiden name or a personal identification number (PIN). Each of these examples is a method for confirming the identity of a person or accuracy of a message.

12. **"Transaction."** The definition has been limited to actions between people taken in the context of business, commercial or governmental activities. The term includes all interactions between people for business, commercial, including specifically consumer, or governmental purposes. However, the term does not include unilateral or non-transactional actions. As such it provides a structural limitation on the scope of the Act as stated in the next section.

It is essential that the term commerce and business be understood and construed broadly to include commercial and business transactions involving individuals who may qualify as "consumers" under other applicable law. If Alice and Bob agree to the sale of Alice's car to Bob for $2000 using an internet auction site, that transaction is fully covered by this Act. Even if Alice and Bob each qualify as typical "consumers" under other applicable law, their interaction is a transaction in commerce. Accordingly their actions would be related to commercial affairs, and fully qualify as a transaction governed by this Act.

Other transaction types include:

1. A single purchase by an individual from a retail merchant, which may be accomplished by an order from a printed catalog sent by facsimile, or by exchange of electronic mail.

2. Recurring orders on a weekly or monthly basis between large companies which have entered into a master trading partner agreement to govern the methods and manner of their transaction parameters.

3. A purchase by an individual from an online internet retail vendor. Such an arrangement may develop into an ongoing series of individual purchases, with security procedures and the like, as a part of doing ongoing business.

4. The closing of a business purchase transaction via facsimile transmission of documents or even electronic mail. In such a transaction, all parties may participate through electronic conferencing technologies. At the appointed time all electronic records are executed electronically and transmitted to the other party. In such a case, the electronic records and

electronic signatures are validated under this Act, obviating the need for "in person" closings.

A transaction must include interaction between two or more persons. Consequently, to the extent that the execution of a will, trust, or a health care power of attorney or similar health care designation does not involve another person and is a unilateral act, it would not be covered by this Act because not occurring as a part of a transaction as defined in this Act. However, this Act *does* apply to all electronic records and signatures *related* to a transaction, and so does cover, for example, internal auditing and accounting records related to a transaction.

§ 3. Scope

(a) Except as otherwise provided in subsection (b), this [Act] applies to electronic records and electronic signatures relating to a transaction.

(b) This [Act] does not apply to a transaction to the extent it is governed by:

    (1) a law governing the creation and execution of wills, codicils, or testamentary trusts;

    (2) [The Uniform Commercial Code other than Sections 1–107 and 1–206, Article 2, and Article 2A];

    (3) [the Uniform Computer Information Transactions Act]; and

    (4) [other laws, if any, identified by State].

(c) This [Act] applies to an electronic record or electronic signature otherwise excluded from the application of this [Act] under subsection (b) to the extent it is governed by a law other than those specified in subsection (b).

(d) A transaction subject to this [Act] is also subject to other applicable substantive law.

See Legislative Note below, following Comment.

Comment

1. The scope of this Act is inherently limited by the fact that it only applies to transactions related to business, commercial (including consumer) and governmental matters. Consequently, transactions with no relation to business, commercial or governmental transactions would not be subject to this Act. Unilaterally generated electronic records and signatures which are not part of a transaction also are not covered by this Act. See Section 2, Comment 12.

2. This Act affects the medium in which information, records and signatures may be presented and

retained under current legal requirements. While this Act covers all electronic records and signatures which are used in a business, commercial (including consumer) or governmental transaction, the operative provisions of the Act relate to requirements for writings and signatures under other laws. Accordingly, the exclusions in subsection (b) focus on those legal rules imposing certain writing and signature requirements which will *not* be affected by this Act.

3. The exclusions listed in subsection (b) provide clarity and certainty regarding the laws which are and are not affected by this Act. This section provides that transactions subject to specific laws are unaffected by this Act and leaves the balance subject to this Act.

4. Paragraph (1) excludes wills, codicils and testamentary trusts. This exclusion is largely salutary given the unilateral context in which such records are generally created and the unlikely use of such records in a transaction as defined in this Act (i.e., actions taken by two or more persons in the context of business, commercial or governmental affairs). Paragraph (2) excludes all of the Uniform Commercial Code other than UCC Sections 1–107 and 1–206, and Articles 2 and 2A. This Act does not apply to the excluded UCC articles, whether in "current" or "revised" form. The Act does apply to UCC Articles 2 and 2A and to UCC Sections 1–107 and 1–206.

5. Articles 3, 4 and 4A of the UCC impact payment systems and have specifically been removed from the coverage of this Act. The check collection and electronic fund transfer systems governed by Articles 3, 4 and 4A involve systems and relationships involving numerous parties beyond the parties to the underlying contract. The impact of validating electronic media in such systems involves considerations beyond the scope of this Act. Articles 5, 8 and 9 have been excluded because the revision process relating to those Articles included significant consideration of electronic practices. Paragraph 4 provides for exclusion from this Act of the Uniform Computer Information Transactions Act (UCITA) because the drafting process of that Act also included significant consideration of electronic contracting provisions.

6. The very limited application of this Act to Transferable Records in Section 16 does not affect payment systems, and the section is designed to apply to a transaction only through express agreement of the parties. The exclusion of Articles 3 and 4 will not affect the Act's coverage of Transferable Records. Section 16 is designed to allow for the development of systems which will provide "control" as defined in Section 16. Such control is necessary as a substitute for the idea of

possession which undergirds negotiable instrument law. The technology has yet to be developed which will allow for the possession of a unique electronic token embodying the rights associated with a negotiable promissory note. Section 16's concept of control is intended as a substitute for possession.

The provisions in Section 16 operate as free standing rules, establishing the rights of parties using Transferable Records *under this Act*. The references in Section 16 to UCC Sections 3–302, 7–501, and 9–308 (R9–330(d)) are designed to incorporate the substance of those provisions into this Act for the limited purposes noted in Section 16(c). Accordingly, an electronic record which is also a Transferable Record, would not be used for purposes of a transaction governed by Articles 3, 4, or 9, but would be an electronic record used for purposes of a transaction governed by Section 16. However, it is important to remember that those UCC Articles will still apply to the transferable record in their own right. Accordingly any other substantive requirements, e.g., method and manner of perfection under Article 9, must be complied with under those other laws. See Comments to Section 16.

7. This Act does apply, *in toto*, to transactions under unrevised Articles 2 and 2A. There is every reason to validate electronic contracting in these situations. Sale and lease transactions do not implicate broad systems beyond the parties to the underlying transaction, such as are present in check collection and electronic funds transfers. Further sales and leases generally do not have as far reaching effect on the rights of third parties beyond the contracting parties, such as exists in the secured transactions system. Finally, it is in the area of sales, licenses and leases that electronic commerce is occurring to its greatest extent today. To exclude these transactions would largely gut the purpose of this Act.

In the event that Articles 2 and 2A are revised and adopted in the future, UETA will only apply to the extent provided in those Acts.

8. An electronic record/signature may be used for purposes of more than one legal requirement, or may be covered by more than one law. Consequently, it is important to make clear, despite any apparent redundancy, in subsection (c) that an electronic record used for purposes of a law which is *not* affected by this Act under subsection (b) may nonetheless be used and validated for purposes of other laws not excluded by subsection (b). For example, this Act does not apply to an electronic record of a check when used for purposes of a transaction governed by Article 4 of the Uniform Commercial Code, i.e., the Act does not validate so-

called electronic checks. However, for purposes of check retention statutes, the same electronic record of the check is covered by this Act, so that retention of an electronic image/record of a check will satisfy such retention statutes, so long as the requirements of Section 12 are fulfilled.

In another context, subsection (c) would operate to allow this Act to apply to what would appear to be an excluded transaction under subsection (b). For example, Article 9 of the Uniform Commercial Code applies generally to any transaction that creates a security interest in personal property. However, Article 9 excludes landlord's liens. Accordingly, although this Act excludes from its application transactions subject to Article 9, this Act would apply to the creation of a landlord lien if the law otherwise applicable to landlord's liens did not provide otherwise, because the landlord's lien transaction is excluded from Article 9.

9. Additional exclusions under subparagraph (b)(4) should be limited to laws which govern electronic records and signatures which may be used in transactions as defined in Section 2(16). Records used unilaterally, or which do not relate to business, commercial (including consumer), or governmental affairs are not governed by this Act in any event, and exclusion of laws relating to such records may create unintended inferences about whether other records and signatures are covered by this Act.

It is also important that additional exclusions, if any, be incorporated under subsection (b)(4). As noted in Comment 8 above, an electronic record used in a transaction excluded under subsection (b), e.g., a check used to pay one's taxes, will nonetheless be validated for purposes of other, non-excluded laws under subsection (c), e.g., the check when used as proof of payment. It is critical that additional exclusions, if any, be incorporated into subsection (b) so that the salutary effect of subsection (c) apply to validate those records in other, non-excluded transactions. While a legislature may determine that a particular notice, such as a utility shutoff notice, be provided to a person in writing on paper, it is difficult to see why the utility should not be entitled to use electronic media for storage and evidentiary purposes.

Legislative Note Regarding Possible Additional Exclusions under Section 3(b)(4).

The following discussion is derived from the Report dated September 21, 1998 of The Task Force on State Law Exclusions (the "Task Force") presented to the Drafting Committee. After consideration of the Report, the Drafting Committee determined that exclusions other than those specified in the Act were not warrant-

ed. In addition, other inherent limitations on the applicability of the Act (the definition of transaction, the requirement that the parties acquiesce in the use of an electronic format) also militate against additional exclusions. Nonetheless, the Drafting Committee recognized that some legislatures may wish to exclude additional transactions from the Act, and determined that guidance in some major areas would be helpful to those legislatures considering additional areas for exclusion.

Because of the overwhelming number of references in state law to writings and signatures, the following list of possible transactions is not exhaustive. However, they do represent those areas most commonly raised during the course of the drafting process as areas that might be inappropriate for an electronic medium. It is important to keep in mind however, that the Drafting Committee determined that exclusion of these additional areas was not warranted.

1. **Trusts** (other than testamentary trusts). Trusts can be used for both business and personal purposes. By virtue of the definition of transaction, trusts used outside the area of business and commerce would not be governed by this Act. With respect to business or commercial trusts, the laws governing their formation contain few or no requirements for paper or signatures. Indeed, in most jurisdictions trusts of any kind may be created orally. Consequently, the Drafting Committee believed that the Act should apply to any transaction where the law leaves to the parties the decision of whether to use a writing. Thus, in the absence of legal requirements for writings, there is no sound reason to exclude laws governing trusts from the application of this Act.

2. **Powers of Attorney.** A power of attorney is simply a formalized type of agency agreement. In general, no formal requirements for paper or execution were found to be applicable to the validity of powers of attorney.

Special health powers of attorney have been established by statute in some States. These powers may have special requirements under state law regarding execution, acknowledgment and possibly notarization. In the normal case such powers will not arise in a transactional context and so would not be covered by this Act. However, even if such a record were to arise in a transactional context, this Act operates simply to remove the barrier to the use of an electronic medium, and preserves other requirements of applicable substantive law, avoiding any necessity to exclude such laws from the operation of this Act. Especially in light of the provisions of Sections 8 and 11, the substantive requirements under such laws will be preserved and may be satisfied in an electronic format.

3. **Real Estate Transactions.** It is important to distinguish between the efficacy of paper documents involving real estate between the parties, as opposed to their effect on third parties. As between the parties it is unnecessary to maintain existing barriers to electronic contracting. There are no unique characteristics to contracts relating to real property as opposed to other business and commercial (including consumer) contracts. Consequently, the decision whether to use an electronic medium for their agreements should be a matter for the parties to determine. Of course, to be effective against third parties state law generally requires filing with a governmental office. Pending adoption of electronic filing systems by States, the need for a piece of paper to file to perfect rights against third parties, will be a consideration for the parties. In the event notarization and acknowledgment are required under other laws, Section 11 provides a means for such actions to be accomplished electronically.

With respect to the requirements of government filing, those are left to the individual States in the decision of whether to adopt and implement electronic filing systems. (See optional Sections 17–19.) However, government recording systems currently require paper deeds including notarized, manual signatures. Although California and Illinois are experimenting with electronic filing systems, until such systems become widespread, the parties likely will choose to use, at the least, a paper deed for filing purposes. Nothing in this Act precludes the parties from selecting the medium best suited to the needs of the particular transaction. Parties may wish to consummate the transaction using electronic media in order to avoid expensive travel. Yet the actual deed may be in paper form to assure compliance with existing recording systems and requirements. The critical point is that nothing in this Act prevents the parties from selecting paper or electronic media for all or part of their transaction.

4. **Consumer Protection Statutes.** Consumer protection provisions in state law often require that information be disclosed or provided to a consumer in writing. Because this Act does apply to such transactions, the question of whether such laws should be specifically excluded was considered. Exclusion of consumer transactions would eliminate a huge group of commercial transactions which benefit consumers by enabling the efficiency of the electronic medium. Commerce over the internet is driven by consumer demands and concerns and must be included.

At the same time, it is important to recognize the protective effects of many consumer statutes. Consumer statutes often require that information be provided in writing, or may require that the consumer separately sign or initial a particular provision to evidence that the consumer's attention was brought to the provision. Subsection (1) requires electronic records to be retainable by a person whenever the law requires information to be delivered in writing. The section imposes a significant burden on the sender of information. The sender must assure that the information system of the recipient is compatible with, and capable of retaining the information sent by, the sender's system. Furthermore, nothing in this Act permits the avoidance of legal requirements of separate signatures or initialing. The Act simply permits the signature or initialing to be done electronically.

Other consumer protection statutes require (expressly or implicitly) that certain information be presented in a certain manner or format. Laws requiring information to be presented in particular fonts, formats or in similar fashion, as well as laws requiring conspicuous displays of information are preserved. Section 8(b)(3) specifically preserves the applicability of such requirements in an electronic environment. In the case of legal requirements that information be presented or appear conspicuous, the determination of what is conspicuous will be left to other law. Section 8 was included to specifically preserve the protective functions of such disclosure statutes, while at the same time allowing the use of electronic media if the substantive requirements of the other laws could be satisfied in the electronic medium.

Formatting and separate signing requirements serve a critical purpose in much consumer protection legislation, to assure that information is not slipped past the unsuspecting consumer. Not only does this Act not disturb those requirements, it preserves those requirements. In addition, other bodies of substantive law continue to operate to allow the courts to police any such bad conduct or overreaching, e.g., unconscionability, fraud, duress, mistake and the like. These bodies of law remain applicable regardless of the medium in which a record appears.

The requirement that both parties agree to conduct a transaction electronically also prevents the imposition of an electronic medium on unwilling parties See Section 5(b). In addition, where the law requires inclusion of specific terms or language, those requirements are preserved broadly by Section 5(e).

Requirements that information be sent to, or received by, someone have been preserved in Section 15.

As in the paper world, obligations to send do not impose any duties on the sender to assure receipt, other than reasonable methods of dispatch. In those cases where receipt is required legally, Sections 5, 8, and 15 impose the burden on the sender to assure delivery to the recipient if satisfaction of the legal requirement is to be fulfilled.

The preservation of existing safeguards, together with the ability to opt out of the electronic medium entirely, demonstrate the lack of any need generally to exclude consumer protection laws from the operation of this Act. Legislatures may wish to focus any review on those statutes which provide for post-contract formation and post-breach notices to be in paper. However, any such consideration must also balance the needed protections against the potential burdens which may be imposed. Consumers and others will not be well served by restrictions which preclude the employment of electronic technologies sought and desired by consumers.

§ 4. Prospective Application.

This [Act] applies to any electronic record or electronic signature created, generated, sent, communicated, received, or stored on or after the effective date of this [Act].

Comment

This section makes clear that the Act only applies to validate electronic records and signatures which arise subsequent to the effective date of the Act. Whether electronic records and electronic signatures arising before the effective date of this Act are valid is left to other law.

§ 5. Use of Electronic Records and Electronic Signatures; Variation by Agreement.

(a) This [Act] does not require a record or signature to be created, generated, sent, communicated, received, stored, or otherwise processed or used by electronic means or in electronic form.

(b) This [Act] applies only to transactions between parties each of which has agreed to conduct transactions by electronic means. Whether the parties agree to conduct a transaction by electronic means is determined from the context and surrounding circumstances, including the parties' conduct.

(c) A party that agrees to conduct a transaction by electronic means may refuse to conduct other transactions by electronic means. The right granted by this subsection may not be waived by agreement.

(d) Except as otherwise provided in this [Act], the effect of any of its provisions may be varied by agreement. The presence in certain provisions of this [Act] of the words "unless otherwise agreed", or words of similar import, does not imply that the effect of other provisions may not be varied by agreement.

(e) Whether an electronic record or electronic signature has legal consequences is determined by this [Act] and other applicable law.

Comment

This section limits the applicability of this Act to transactions which parties have agreed to conduct electronically. Broad interpretation of the term agreement is necessary to assure that this Act has the widest possible application consistent with its purpose of removing barriers to electronic commerce.

1. This section makes clear that this Act is intended to facilitate the use of electronic means, but does not require the use of electronic records and signatures. This fundamental principle is set forth in subsection (a) and elaborated by subsections (b) and (c), which require an intention to conduct transactions electronically and preserve the right of a party to refuse to use electronics in any subsequent transaction.

2. The paradigm of this Act is two willing parties doing transactions electronically. It is therefore appropriate that the Act is voluntary and preserves the greatest possible party autonomy to refuse electronic transactions. The requirement that party agreement be found from all the surrounding circumstances is a limitation on the scope of this Act.

3. If this Act is to serve to facilitate electronic transactions, it must be applicable under circumstances not rising to a full fledged contract to use electronics. While absolute certainty can be accomplished by obtaining an explicit contract before relying on electronic transactions, such an explicit contract should not be necessary before one may feel safe in conducting transactions electronically. Indeed, such a requirement would itself be an unreasonable barrier to electronic commerce, at odds with the fundamental purpose of this Act. Accordingly, the requisite agreement, express or implied, must be determined from all available circumstances and evidence.

4. Subsection (b) provides that the Act applies to transactions in which the parties have agreed to conduct the transaction electronically. In this context it is

essential that the parties' actions and words be broadly construed in determining whether the requisite agreement exists. Accordingly, the Act expressly provides that the party's agreement is to be found from all circumstances, including the parties' conduct. The critical element is the intent of a party to conduct a transaction electronically. Once that intent is established, this Act applies. See Restatement 2d Contracts, Sections 2, 3, and 19.

Examples of circumstances from which it may be found that parties have reached an agreement to conduct transactions electronically include the following:

A. Automaker and supplier enter into a Trading Partner Agreement setting forth the terms, conditions and methods for the conduct of business between them electronically.

B. Joe gives out his business card with his business e-mail address. It may be reasonable, under the circumstances, for a recipient of the card to infer that Joe has agreed to communicate electronically for business purposes. However, in the absence of additional facts, it would not necessarily be reasonable to infer Joe's agreement to communicate electronically for purposes outside the scope of the business indicated by use of the business card.

C. Sally may have several e-mail addresses—home, main office, office of a non-profit organization on whose board Sally sits. In each case, it may be reasonable to infer that Sally is willing to communicate electronically with respect to business related to the business/purpose associated with the respective e-mail addresses. However, depending on the circumstances, it may not be reasonable to communicate with Sally for purposes other than those related to the purpose for which she maintained a particular e-mail account.

D. Among the circumstances to be considered in finding an agreement would be the time when the assent occurred relative to the timing of the use of electronic communications. If one orders books from an on-line vendor, such as Bookseller.com, the intention to conduct that transaction and to receive any correspondence related to the transaction electronically can be inferred from the conduct. Accordingly, as to information related to that transaction it is reasonable for Bookseller to deal with the individual electronically.

The examples noted above are intended to focus the inquiry on the party's agreement to conduct a transaction electronically. Similarly, if two people are at a meeting and one tells the other to send an e-mail to confirm a transaction–the requisite agreement under subsection (b) would exist. In each case, the use of a business card, statement at a meeting, or other evidence of willingness to conduct a transaction electronically must be viewed in light of all the surrounding circumstances with a view toward broad validation of electronic transactions.

5. Just as circumstances may indicate the existence of agreement, express or implied from surrounding circumstances, circumstances may also demonstrate the absence of true agreement. For example:

A. If Automaker, Inc. were to issue a recall of automobiles via its Internet website, it would not be able to rely on this Act to validate that notice in the case of a person who never logged on to the website, or indeed, had no ability to do so, notwithstanding a clause in a paper purchase contract by which the buyer agreed to receive such notices in such a manner.

B. Buyer executes a standard form contract in which an agreement to receive all notices electronically in set forth on page 3 in the midst of other fine print. Buyer has never communicated with Seller electronically, and has not provided any other information in the contract to suggest a willingness to deal electronically. Not only is it unlikely that any but the most formalistic of agreements may be found, but nothing in this Act prevents courts from policing such form contracts under common law doctrines relating to contract formation, unconscionability and the like.

6. Subsection (c) has been added to make clear the ability of a party to refuse to conduct a transaction electronically, even if the person has conducted transactions electronically in the past. The effectiveness of a party's refusal to conduct a transaction electronically will be determined under other applicable law in light of all surrounding circumstances. Such circumstances must include an assessment of the transaction involved.

A party's right to decline to act electronically under a specific contract, on the ground that each action under that contract amounts to a separate "transaction," must be considered in light of the purpose of the contract and the action to be taken electronically. For example, under a contract for the purchase of goods, the giving and receipt of notices electronically, as provided in the contract, should not be viewed as discreet transactions. Rather such notices amount to separate actions which are part of the "transaction" of purchase evidenced by the contract. Allowing one party to require a change of medium in the middle of the transaction evidenced by that contract is not the purpose of this subsection. Rather this subsection is intended to preserve the party's right to conduct the next purchase in a non-electronic medium.

7. Subsection (e) is an essential provision in the overall scheme of this Act. While this Act validates and effectuates electronic records and electronic signatures, the legal effect of such records and signatures is left to existing substantive law outside this Act except in very narrow circumstances. See, e.g., Section 16. Even when this Act operates to validate records and signatures in an electronic medium, it expressly preserves the substantive rules of other law applicable to such records. See, e.g., Section 11.

For example, beyond validation of records, signatures and contracts based on the medium used, Section 7 (a) and (b) should not be interpreted as establishing the legal effectiveness of any given record, signature or contract. Where a rule of law requires that the record contain minimum substantive content, the legal effect of such a record will depend on whether the record meets the substantive requirements of other applicable law.

Section 8 expressly preserves a number of legal requirements in currently existing law relating to the presentation of information in writing. Although this Act now would allow such information to be presented in an electronic record, Section 8 provides that the other substantive requirements of law must be satisfied in the electronic medium as well.

§ 6. Construction and Application.

This [Act] must be construed and applied:

(1) to facilitate electronic transactions consistent with other applicable law;

(2) to be consistent with reasonable practices concerning electronic transactions and with the continued expansion of those practices; and

(3) to effectuate its general purpose to make uniform the law with respect to the subject of this [Act] among States enacting it.

Comment

1. The purposes and policies of this Act are

(a) to facilitate and promote commerce and governmental transactions by validating and authorizing the use of electronic records and electronic signatures;

(b) to eliminate barriers to electronic commerce and governmental transactions resulting from uncer-

tainties relating to writing and signature requirements;

(c) to simplify, clarify and modernize the law governing commerce and governmental transactions through the use of electronic means;

(d) to permit the continued expansion of commercial and governmental electronic practices through custom, usage and agreement of the parties;

(e) to promote uniformity of the law among the States (and worldwide) relating to the use of electronic and similar technological means of effecting and performing commercial and governmental transactions;

(f) to promote public confidence in the validity, integrity and reliability of electronic commerce and governmental transactions; and

(g) to promote the development of the legal and business infrastructure necessary to implement electronic commerce and governmental transactions.

2. This Act has been drafted to permit flexible application consistent with its purpose to validate electronic transactions. The provisions of this Act validating and effectuating the employ of electronic media allow the courts to apply them to new and unforeseen technologies and practices. As time progresses, it is anticipated that what is new and unforeseen today will be commonplace tomorrow. Accordingly, this legislation is intended to set a framework for the validation of media which may be developed in the future and which demonstrate the same qualities as the electronic media contemplated and validated under this Act.

§ 7. Legal Recognition of Electronic Records, Electronic Signatures, and Electronic Contracts.

(a) A record or signature may not be denied legal effect or enforceability solely because it is in electronic form.

(b) A contract may not be denied legal effect or enforceability solely because an electronic record was used in its formation.

(c) If a law requires a record to be in writing, an electronic record satisfies the law.

(d) If a law requires a signature, an electronic signature satisfies the law.

Source: UNCITRAL Model Law on Electronic Commerce, Articles 5, 6, and 7.

Comment

1. This section sets forth the fundamental premise of this Act: namely, that the medium in which a record, signature, or contract is created, presented or retained does not affect it's legal significance. Subsections (a) and (b) are designed to eliminate the single element of medium as a reason to deny effect or enforceability to a record, signature, or contract. The fact that the information is set forth in an electronic, as opposed to paper, record is irrelevant.

2. Under Restatement 2d Contracts Section 8, a contract may have legal effect and yet be unenforceable. Indeed, one circumstance where a record or contract may have effect but be unenforceable is in the context of the Statute of Frauds. Though a contract may be unenforceable, the records may have collateral effects, as in the case of a buyer that insures goods purchased under a contract unenforceable under the Statute of Frauds. The insurance company may not deny a claim on the ground that the buyer is not the owner, though the buyer may have no direct remedy against seller for failure to deliver. See Restatement 2d Contracts, Section 8, Illustration 4.

While this section would validate an electronic record for purposes of a statute of frauds, if an agreement to conduct the transaction electronically cannot reasonably be found (See Section 5(b)) then a necessary predicate to the applicability of this Act would be absent and this Act would not validate the electronic record. Whether the electronic record might be valid under other law is not addressed by this Act.

3. Subsections (c) and (d) provide the positive assertion that electronic records and signatures satisfy legal requirements for writings and signatures. The provisions are limited to requirements in laws that a record be in writing or be signed. This section does not address requirements imposed by other law in addition to requirements for writings and signatures See, e.g., Section 8.

Subsections (c) and (d) are particularized applications of subsection (a). The purpose is to validate and effectuate electronic records and signatures as the equivalent of writings, subject to all of the rules applicable to the efficacy of a writing, except as such other rules are modified by the more specific provisions of this Act.

Illustration 1: A sends the following e-mail to B: "I hereby offer to buy widgets from you, delivery next Tuesday. /s/ A." B responds with the following e-mail: "I accept your offer to buy widgets for delivery next Tuesday. /s/ B." The e-mails may not be denied effect solely because they are electronic. In addition, the e-mails do qualify as records under the Statute of Frauds. However, because there is no quantity stated in either record, the parties' agreement would be unenforceable under existing UCC Section 2–201(1).

Illustration 2: A sends the following e-mail to B: "I hereby offer to buy 100 widgets for $1000, delivery next Tuesday. /s/ A." B responds with the following e-mail: "I accept your offer to purchase 100 widgets for $1000, delivery next Tuesday. /s/ B." In this case the analysis is the same as in Illustration 1 except that here the records otherwise satisfy the requirements of UCC Section 2–201(1). The transaction may not be denied legal effect solely because there is not a pen and ink "writing" or "signature".

4. Section 8 addresses additional requirements imposed by other law which may affect the legal effect or enforceability of an electronic record in a particular case. For example, in Section 8(a) the legal requirement addressed is *the provision of information* in writing. The section then sets forth the standards to be applied in determining whether the provision of information by an electronic record is the equivalent of the provision of information in writing. The requirements in Section 8 are in addition to the bare validation that occurs under this section.

5. Under the substantive law applicable to a particular transaction within this Act, the legal effect of an electronic record may be separate from the issue of whether the record contains a signature. For example, where notice must be given as part of a contractual obligation, the effectiveness of the notice will turn on whether the party provided the notice regardless of whether the notice was signed (See Section 15). An electronic record attributed to a party under Section 9 and complying with the requirements of Section 15 would suffice in that case, notwithstanding that it may not contain an electronic signature.

§ 8. Provision of Information in Writing; Presentation of Records.

(a) If parties have agreed to conduct a transaction by electronic means and a law requires a person to provide, send, or deliver information in writing to another person, the requirement is satisfied if the information is provided, sent, or delivered, as the case may be, in an electronic record capable of retention by the recipient at the time of receipt. An electronic record is not capable of retention by the recipient if the sender or its information processing system inhibits the ability of the recipient to print or store the electronic record.

(b) If a law other than this [Act] requires a record (i) to be posted or displayed in a certain manner, (ii) to be sent, communicated, or transmitted by a specified method, or (iii) to contain information that is formatted in a certain manner, the following rules apply:

(1) The record must be posted or displayed in the manner specified in the other law.

(2) Except as otherwise provided in subsection (d)(2), the record must be sent, communicated, or transmitted by the method specified in the other law.

(3) The record must contain the information formatted in the manner specified in the other law.

(c) If a sender inhibits the ability of a recipient to store or print an electronic record, the electronic record is not enforceable against the recipient.

(d) The requirements of this section may not be varied by agreement, but:

(1) to the extent a law other than this [Act] requires information to be provided, sent, or delivered in writing but permits that requirement to be varied by agreement, the requirement under subsection (a) that the information be in the form of an electronic record capable of retention may also be varied by agreement; and

(2) a requirement under a law other than this [Act] to send, communicate, or transmit a record by [first-class mail, postage prepaid] [regular United States mail], may be varied by agreement to the extent permitted by the other law.

Source: Canadian–Uniform Electronic Commerce Act

Comment

1. This section is a savings provision, designed to assure, consistent with the fundamental purpose of this Act, that otherwise applicable substantive law will not be overridden by this Act. The section makes clear that while the pen and ink provisions of such other law may be satisfied electronically, nothing in this Act vitiates the other requirements of such laws. The section addresses a number of issues related to disclosures and notice provisions in other laws.

2. This section is independent of the prior section. Section 7 refers to legal requirements for a writing. This section refers to legal requirements for the provision of information in writing or relating to the method or manner of presentation or delivery of information. The section addresses more specific legal requirements of other laws, provides standards for satisfying the more particular legal requirements, and defers to other law for satisfaction of requirements under those laws.

3. Under subsection (a), to meet a requirement of other law that information be provided in writing, the recipient of an electronic record of the information must be able to get to the electronic record and read it, and must have the ability to get back to the information in some way at a later date. Accordingly, the section requires that the electronic record be capable of retention for later review.

The section specifically provides that any inhibition on retention imposed by the sender or the sender's system will preclude satisfaction of this section. Use of technological means now existing or later developed which prevents the recipient from retaining a copy the information would result in a determination that information has not been provided under subsection (a). The policies underlying laws requiring the provision of information in writing warrant the imposition of an additional burden on the sender to make the information available in a manner which will permit subsequent reference. A difficulty does exist for senders of information because of the disparate systems of their recipients and the capabilities of those systems. However, in order to satisfy the *legal requirement* of other law to make information available, the sender must assure that the recipient receives and can retain the information. However, it is left for the courts to determine whether the sender has complied with this subsection if evidence demonstrates that it is something peculiar the recipient's system which precludes subsequent reference to the information.

4. Subsection (b) is a savings provision for laws which provide for the means of delivering or displaying information and which are not affected by the Act. For example, if a law requires delivery of notice by first class US mail, that means of delivery would not be affected by this Act. The information to be delivered may be provided on a disc, i.e., in electronic form, but the particular means of delivery must still be via the US postal service. Display, delivery and formatting requirements will continue to be applicable to electronic records and signatures. If those legal requirements can be satisfied in an electronic medium, e.g., the

information can be presented in the equivalent of 20 point bold type as required by other law, this Act will validate the use of the medium, leaving to the other applicable law the question of whether the particular electronic record meets the other legal requirements. If a law requires that particular records be delivered together, or attached to other records, this Act does not preclude the delivery of the records together in an electronic communication, so long as the records are connected or associated with each other in a way determined to satisfy the other law.

5. Subsection (c) provides incentives for senders of information to use systems which will not inhibit the other party from retaining the information. However, there are circumstances where a party providing certain information may wish to inhibit retention in order to protect intellectual property rights or prevent the other party from retaining confidential information about the sender. In such cases inhibition is understandable, but if the sender wishes to enforce the record in which the information is contained, the sender may not inhibit its retention by the recipient. Unlike subsection (a), subsection (c) applies in all transactions and simply provides for unenforceability against the recipient. Subsection (a) applies only where another law imposes the writing requirement, and subsection (a) imposes a broader responsibility on the sender to assure retention capability by the recipient.

6. The protective purposes of this section justify the non-waivability provided by subsection (d). However, since the requirements for sending and formatting and the like are imposed by other law, to the extent other law permits waiver of such protections, there is no justification for imposing a more severe burden in an electronic environment.

§ 9. Attribution and Effect of Electronic Record and Electronic Signature.

(a) An electronic record or electronic signature is attributable to a person if it was the act of the person. The act of the person may be shown in any manner, including a showing of the efficacy of any security procedure applied to determine the person to which the electronic record or electronic signature was attributable.

(b) The effect of an electronic record or electronic signature attributed to a person under subsection (a) is determined from the context and surrounding circumstances at the time of its creation, execution, or adoption, including the parties' agreement, if any, and otherwise as provided by law.

Comment

1. Under subsection (a), so long as the electronic record or electronic signature resulted from a person's action it will be attributed to that person–the legal effect of that attribution is addressed in subsection (b). This section does not alter existing rules of law regarding attribution. The section assures that such rules will be applied in the electronic environment. A person's actions include actions taken by human agents of the person, as well as actions taken by an electronic agent, i.e., the tool, of the person. Although the rule may appear to state the obvious, it assures that the record or signature is not ascribed to a machine, as opposed to the person operating or programing the machine.

In each of the following cases, both the electronic record and electronic signature would be attributable to a person under subsection (a):

A. The person types his/her name as part of an e-mail purchase order;

B. The person's employee, pursuant to authority, types the person's name as part of an e-mail purchase order;

C. The person's computer, programmed to order goods upon receipt of inventory information within particular parameters, issues a purchase order which includes the person's name, or other identifying information, as part of the order.

In each of the above cases, law other than this Act would ascribe both the signature and the action to the person if done in a paper medium. Subsection (a) expressly provides that the same result will occur when an electronic medium is used.

2. Nothing in this section affects the use of a signature as a device for attributing a record to a person. Indeed, a signature is often the primary method for attributing a record to a person. In the foregoing examples, once the electronic signature is attributed to the person, the electronic record would also be attributed to the person, unless the person established fraud, forgery, or other invalidating cause. However, a signature is not the only method for attribution.

3. The use of facsimile transmissions provides a number of examples of attribution using information other than a signature. A facsimile may be attributed to a person because of the information printed across the top of the page that indicates the machine from which it was sent. Similarly, the transmission may contain a letterhead which identifies the sender. Some cases have held that the letterhead actually constituted a signature because it was a symbol adopted by the

sender with intent to authenticate the facsimile. However, the signature determination resulted from the necessary finding of intention in that case. Other cases have found facsimile letterheads NOT to be signatures because the requisite intention was not present. The critical point is that with or without a signature, information within the electronic record may well suffice to provide the facts resulting in attribution of an electronic record to a particular party.

In the context of attribution of records, normally the content of the record will provide the necessary information for a finding of attribution. It is also possible that an established course of dealing between parties may result in a finding of attribution Just as with a paper record, evidence of forgery or counterfeiting may be introduced to rebut the evidence of attribution.

4. Certain information may be present in an electronic environment that does not appear to attribute but which clearly links a person to a particular record. Numerical codes, personal identification numbers, public and private key combinations all serve to establish the party to whom an electronic record should be attributed. Of course security procedures will be another piece of evidence available to establish attribution.

The inclusion of a specific reference to security procedures as a means of proving attribution is salutary because of the unique importance of security procedures in the electronic environment. In certain processes, a technical and technological security procedure may be the best way to convince a trier of fact that a particular electronic record or signature was that of a particular person. In certain circumstances, the use of a security procedure to establish that the record and related signature came from the person's business might be necessary to overcome a claim that a hacker intervened. The reference to security procedures is not intended to suggest that other forms of proof of attribution should be accorded less persuasive effect. It is also important to recall that the particular strength of a given procedure does not affect the procedure's status as a security procedure, but only affects the weight to be accorded the evidence of the security procedure as tending to establish attribution.

5. This section does apply in determining the effect of a ''click-through'' transaction. A ''click-through'' transaction involves a process which, if executed with an intent to ''sign,'' will be an electronic signature. See definition of Electronic Signature. In the context of an anonymous ''click-through,'' issues of proof will be paramount. This section will be relevant to establish that the resulting electronic record is attributable to a particular person upon the requisite proof, including security procedures which may track the source of the click-through.

6. Once it is established that a record or signature is attributable to a particular party, the effect of a record or signature must be determined in light of the context and surrounding circumstances, including the parties' agreement, if any. Also informing the effect of any attribution will be other legal requirements considered in light of the context. Subsection (b) addresses the effect of the record or signature once attributed to a person.

§ 10. Effect of Change or Error.

If a change or error in an electronic record occurs in a transmission between parties to a transaction, the following rules apply:

(1) If the parties have agreed to use a security procedure to detect changes or errors and one party has conformed to the procedure, but the other party has not, and the nonconforming party would have detected the change or error had that party also conformed, the conforming party may avoid the effect of the changed or erroneous electronic record.

(2) In an automated transaction involving an individual, the individual may avoid the effect of an electronic record that resulted from an error made by the individual in dealing with the electronic agent of another person if the electronic agent did not provide an opportunity for the prevention or correction of the error and, at the time the individual learns of the error, the individual:

(A) promptly notifies the other person of the error and that the individual did not intend to be bound by the electronic record received by the other person;

(B) takes reasonable steps, including steps that conform to the other person's reasonable instructions, to return to the other person or, if instructed by the other person, to destroy the consideration received, if any, as a result of the erroneous electronic record; and

(C) has not used or received any benefit or value from the consideration, if any, received from the other person.

(3) If neither paragraph (1) nor paragraph (2) applies, the change or error has the effect

provided by other law, including the law of mistake, and the parties' contract, if any.

(4) Paragraphs (2) and (3) may not be varied by agreement.

Source: Restatement 2d Contracts, Sections 152–155.

Comment

1. This section is limited to changes and errors occurring in transmissions between parties–whether person-person (paragraph 1) or in an automated transaction involving an individual and a machine (paragraphs 1 and 2). The section focuses on the effect of changes and errors occurring when records are exchanged between parties. In cases where changes and errors occur in contexts other than transmission, the law of mistake is expressly made applicable to resolve the conflict.

The section covers both changes and errors. For example, if Buyer sends a message to Seller ordering 100 widgets, but Buyer's information processing system changes the order to 1000 widgets, a "change" has occurred between what Buyer transmitted and what Seller received. If on the other hand, Buyer typed in 1000 intending to order only 100, but sent the message before noting the mistake, an error would have occurred which would also be covered by this section.

2. Paragraph (1) deals with any transmission where the parties have agreed to use a security procedure to detect changes and errors. It operates against the non-conforming party, i.e., the party in the best position to have avoided the change or error, regardless of whether that person is the sender or recipient. The source of the error/change is not indicated, and so both human and machine errors/changes would be covered. With respect to errors or changes that would not be detected by the security procedure even if applied, the parties are left to the general law of mistake to resolve the dispute.

3. Paragraph (1) applies only in the situation where a security procedure would detect the error/change but one party fails to use the procedure and does not detect the error/change. In such a case, consistent with the law of mistake generally, the record is made avoidable at the instance of the party who took all available steps to avoid the mistake. See Restatement 2d Contracts Sections 152–154.

Making the erroneous record avoidable by the conforming party is consistent with Sections 153 and 154 of the Restatement 2d Contracts because the non-conforming party was in the best position to avoid the

problem, and would bear the risk of mistake. Such a case would constitute mistake by one party. The mistaken party (the conforming party) would be entitled to avoid any resulting contract under Section 153 because s/he does not have the risk of mistake and the non-conforming party had reason to know of the mistake.

4. As with paragraph (1), paragraph (2), when applicable, allows the mistaken party to avoid the effect of the erroneous electronic record. However, the subsection is limited to human error on the part of an individual when dealing with the electronic agent of the other party. In a transaction between individuals there is a greater ability to correct the error before parties have acted on it. However, when an individual makes an error while dealing with the electronic agent of the other party, it may not be possible to correct the error before the other party has shipped or taken other action in reliance on the erroneous record.

Paragraph (2) applies only to errors made by individuals. If the error results from the electronic agent, it would constitute a system error. In such a case the effect of that error would be resolved under paragraph (1) if applicable, otherwise under paragraph (3) and the general law of mistake.

5. The party acting through the electronic agent/machine is given incentives by this section to build in safeguards which enable the individual to prevent the sending of an erroneous record, or correct the error once sent. For example, the electronic agent may be programmed to provide a "confirmation screen" to the individual setting forth all the information the individual initially approved. This would provide the individual with the ability to prevent the erroneous record from ever being sent. Similarly, the electronic agent might receive the record sent by the individual and then send back a confirmation which the individual must again accept before the transaction is completed. This would allow for correction of an erroneous record. In either case, the electronic agent would "provide an opportunity for prevention or correction of the error," *and the subsection would not apply.* Rather, the affect of any error is governed by other law.

6. Paragraph (2) also places additional requirements on the mistaken individual before the paragraph may be invoked to avoid an erroneous electronic record. The individual must take prompt action to advise the other party of the error and the fact that the individual did not intend the electronic record. Whether the action is prompt must be determined from all the circumstances including the individual's ability to

contact the other party. The individual should advise the other party both of the error and of the lack of intention to be bound (i.e., avoidance) by the electronic record received. Since this provision allows avoidance by the mistaken party, that party should also be required to expressly note that it is seeking to avoid the electronic record, i.e., lacked the intention to be bound.

Second, restitution is normally required in order to undo a mistaken transaction. Accordingly, the individual must also return or destroy any consideration received, adhering to instructions from the other party in any case. This is to assure that the other party retains control over the consideration sent in error.

Finally, and most importantly in regard to transactions involving intermediaries which may be harmed because transactions cannot be unwound, the individual cannot have received any benefit from the transaction. This section prevents a party from unwinding a transaction after the delivery of value and consideration which cannot be returned or destroyed. For example, if the consideration received is information, it may not be possible to avoid the benefit conferred. While the information itself could be returned, mere access to the information, or the ability to redistribute the information would constitute a benefit precluding the mistaken party from unwinding the transaction. It may also occur that the mistaken party receives consideration which changes in value between the time of receipt and the first opportunity to return. In such a case restitution cannot be made adequately, and the transaction would not be avoidable. In each of the foregoing cases, under subparagraph (2)(c), the individual would have received the benefit of the consideration and would NOT be able to avoid the erroneous electronic record under this section.

7. In all cases not covered by paragraphs (1) or (2), where error or change to a record occur, the parties contract, or other law, specifically including the law of mistake, applies to resolve any dispute. In the event that the parties' contract and other law would achieve different results, the construction of the parties' contract is left to the other law. If the error occurs in the context of record retention, Section 12 will apply. In that case the standard is one of accuracy and retrievability of the information.

8. Paragraph (4) makes the error correction provision in paragraph (2) and the application of the law of mistake in paragraph (3) non-variable. Paragraph (2) provides incentives for parties using electronic agents to establish safeguards for individuals dealing with them. It also avoids unjustified windfalls to the individual by erecting stringent requirements before the indi-

vidual may exercise the right of avoidance under the paragraph. Therefore, there is no reason to permit parties to avoid the paragraph by agreement. Rather, parties should satisfy the paragraph's requirements.

§ 11. Notarization and Acknowledgment.

If a law requires a signature or record to be notarized, acknowledged, verified, or made under oath, the requirement is satisfied if the electronic signature of the person authorized to perform those acts, together with all other information required to be included by other applicable law, is attached to or logically associated with the signature or record.

Comment

This section permits a notary public and other authorized officers to act electronically, effectively removing the stamp/seal requirements. However, the section does not eliminate any of the other requirements of notarial laws, and consistent with the entire thrust of this Act, simply allows the signing and information to be accomplished in an electronic medium.

For example, Buyer wishes to send a notarized Real Estate Purchase Agreement to Seller via e-mail. The notary must appear in the room with the Buyer, satisfy him/herself as to the identity of the Buyer, and swear to that identification. All that activity must be reflected as part of the electronic Purchase Agreement and the notary's electronic signature must appear as a part of the electronic real estate purchase contract.

As another example, Buyer seeks to send Seller an affidavit averring defects in the products received. A court clerk, authorized under state law to administer oaths, is present with Buyer in a room. The Clerk administers the oath and includes the statement of the oath, together with any other requisite information, in the electronic record to be sent to the Seller. Upon administering the oath and witnessing the application of Buyer's electronic signature to the electronic record, the Clerk also applies his electronic signature to the electronic record. So long as all substantive requirements of other applicable law have been fulfilled and are reflected in the electronic record, the sworn electronic record of Buyer is as effective as if it had been transcribed on paper.

§ 12. Retention of Electronic Records; Originals.

(a) If a law requires that a record be retained, the requirement is satisfied by retaining an electronic record of the information in the record which:

(1) accurately reflects the information set forth in the record after it was first generated in its final form as an electronic record or otherwise; and

(2) remains accessible for later reference.

(b) A requirement to retain a record in accordance with subsection (a) does not apply to any information the sole purpose of which is to enable the record to be sent, communicated, or received.

(c) A person may satisfy subsection (a) by using the services of another person if the requirements of that subsection are satisfied.

(d) If a law requires a record to be presented or retained in its original form, or provides consequences if the record is not presented or retained in its original form, that law is satisfied by an electronic record retained in accordance with subsection (a).

(e) If a law requires retention of a check, that requirement is satisfied by retention of an electronic record of the information on the front and back of the check in accordance with subsection (a).

(f) A record retained as an electronic record in accordance with subsection (a) satisfies a law requiring a person to retain a record for evidentiary, audit, or like purposes, unless a law enacted after the effective date of this [Act] specifically prohibits the use of an electronic record for the specified purpose.

(g) This section does not preclude a governmental agency of this State from specifying additional requirements for the retention of a record subject to the agency's jurisdiction.

Source: UNCITRAL Model Law On Electronic Commerce Articles 8 and 10.

Comment

1. This section deals with the serviceability of electronic records as retained records and originals. So long as there exists reliable assurance that the electronic record accurately reproduces the information, this section continues the theme of establishing the functional equivalence of electronic and paper-based records. This is consistent with Fed.R.Evid. 1001(3) and Unif.R.Evid. 1001(3) (1974). This section assures that information stored electronically will remain effective for all audit, evidentiary, archival and similar purposes.

2. In an electronic medium, the concept of an original document is problematic. For example, as one drafts a document on a computer the "original" is either on a disc or the hard drive to which the document has been initially saved. If one periodically saves the draft, the fact is that at times a document may be first saved to disc then to hard drive, and at others vice versa. In such a case the "original" may change from the information on the disc to the information on the hard drive. Indeed, it may be argued that the "original" exists solely in RAM and, in a sense, the original is destroyed when a "copy" is saved to a disc or to the hard drive. In any event, in the context of record retention, the concern focuses on the integrity of the information, and not with its "originality."

3. Subsection (a) requires accuracy and the ability to access at a later time. The requirement of accuracy is derived from the Uniform and Federal Rules of Evidence. The requirement of continuing accessibility addresses the issue of technology obsolescence and the need to update and migrate information to developing systems. It is not unlikely that within the span of 5–10 years (a period during which retention of much information is required) a corporation may evolve through one or more generations of technology. More to the point, this technology may be incompatible with each other necessitating the reconversion of information from one system to the other.

For example, certain operating systems from the early 1980's, e.g., memory typewriters, became obsolete with the development of personal computers. The information originally stored on the memory typewriter would need to be converted to the personal computer system in a way meeting the standards for accuracy contemplated by this section. It is also possible that the medium on which the information is stored is less stable. For example, information stored on floppy discs is generally less stable, and subject to a greater threat of disintegration, that information stored on a computer hard drive. In either case, the continuing accessibility issue must be satisfied to validate information stored by electronic means under this section.

This section permits parties to convert original written records to electronic records for retention so long as the requirements of subsection (a) are satisfied. Accordingly, in the absence of specific requirements to retain written records, written records may be destroyed once saved as electronic records satisfying the requirements of this section.

The subsection refers to the information contained in an electronic record, rather than relying on the term electronic record, as a matter of clarity that the critical aspect in retention is the information itself. What information must be retained is determined by the purpose for which the information is needed. If the addressing and pathway information regarding an e-mail is relevant, then that information should also be retained. However if it is the substance of the e-mail that is relevant, only that information need be retained. Of course, wise record retention would include all such information since what information will be relevant at a later time will not be known.

4. Subsections (b) and (c) simply make clear that certain ancillary information or the use of third parties, does not affect the serviceability of records and information retained electronically. Again, the relevance of particular information will not be known until that information is required at a subsequent time.

5. Subsection (d) continues the theme of the Act as validating electronic records as originals where the law requires retention of an original. The validation of electronic records and electronic information as originals is consistent with the Uniform Rules of Evidence. See Uniform Rules of Evidence 1001(3), 1002, 1003 and 1004.

6. Subsection (e) specifically addresses particular concerns regarding check retention statutes in many jurisdictions. A Report compiled by the Federal Reserve Bank of Boston identifies hundreds of state laws which require the retention or production of original canceled checks. Such requirements preclude banks and their customers from realizing the benefits and efficiencies related to truncation processes otherwise validated under current law. The benefits to banks and their customers from electronic check retention are effectuated by this provision.

7. Subsections (f) and (g) generally address other record retention statutes. As with check retention, all businesses and individuals may realize significant savings from electronic record retention. So long as the standards in Section 12 are satisfied, this section permits all parties to obtain those benefits. As always the government may require records in any medium, however, these subsections require a governmental agency to specifically identify the types of records and requirements that will be imposed.

§ 13. Admissibility in Evidence.

In a proceeding, evidence of a record or signature may not be excluded solely because it is in electronic form.

Source: UNCITRAL Model Law on Electronic Commerce Article 9.

Comment

Like Section 7, this section prevents the nonrecognition of electronic records and signatures solely on the ground of the media in which information is presented.

Nothing in this section relieves a party from establishing the necessary foundation for the admission of an electronic record. See Uniform Rules of Evidence 1001(3), 1002, 1003 and 1004.

§ 14. Automated Transaction.

In an automated transaction, the following rules apply:

(1) A contract may be formed by the interaction of electronic agents of the parties, even if no individual was aware of or reviewed the electronic agents' actions or the resulting terms and agreements.

(2) A contract may be formed by the interaction of an electronic agent and an individual, acting on the individual's own behalf or for another person, including by an interaction in which the individual performs actions that the individual is free to refuse to perform and which the individual knows or has reason to know will cause the electronic agent to complete the transaction or performance.

(3) The terms of the contract are determined by the substantive law applicable to it.

Source: UNCITRAL Model Law on Electronic Commerce Article 11.

Comment

1. This section confirms that contracts can be formed by machines functioning as electronic agents for parties to a transaction. It negates any claim that lack of human intent, at the time of contract formation, prevents contract formation. When machines are involved, the requisite intention flows from the programing and use of the machine. As in other cases, these are salutary provisions consistent with the fundamental purpose of the Act to remove barriers to electronic transactions while leaving the substantive law, e.g., law of mistake, law of contract formation, unaffected to the greatest extent possible.

2. The process in paragraph (2) validates an anonymous click-through transaction. It is possible that an anonymous click-through process may simply result in no recognizable legal relationship, e.g., A goes to a person's website and acquires access without in any way identifying herself, or otherwise indicating agreement or assent to any limitation or obligation, and the owner's site grants A access. In such a case no legal relationship has been created.

On the other hand it may be possible that A's actions indicate agreement to a particular term. For example, A goes to a website and is confronted by an initial screen which advises her that the information at this site is proprietary, that A may use the information for her own personal purposes, but that, by clicking below, A agrees that any other use without the site owner's permission is prohibited. If A clicks "agree" and downloads the information and then uses the information for other, prohibited purposes, should not A be bound by the click? It seems the answer properly should be, and would be, yes.

If the owner can show that the only way A could have obtained the information was from his website, and that the process to access the subject information required that A must have clicked the "I agree" button after having the ability to see the conditions on use, A has performed actions which A was free to refuse, which A knew would cause the site to grant her access, i.e., "complete the transaction." The terms of the resulting contract will be determined under general contract principles, but will include the limitation on A's use of the information, as a condition precedent to granting her access to the information.

3. In the transaction set forth in Comment 2, the record of the transaction also will include an electronic signature. By clicking "I agree" A adopted a process with the intent to "sign," i.e., bind herself to a legal obligation, the resulting record of the transaction. If a "signed writing" were required under otherwise applicable law, this transaction would be enforceable. If a "signed writing" were not required, it may be sufficient to establish that the electronic record is attributable to A under Section 9. Attribution may be shown in any manner reasonable including showing that, of necessity, A could only have gotten the information through the process at the website.

§ 15. Time and Place of Sending and Receipt.

(a) Unless otherwise agreed between the sender and the recipient, an electronic record is sent when it:

(1) is addressed properly or otherwise directed properly to an information processing system that the recipient has designated or uses for the purpose of receiving electronic records or information of the type sent and from which the recipient is able to retrieve the electronic record;

(2) is in a form capable of being processed by that system; and

(3) enters an information processing system outside the control of the sender or of a person that sent the electronic record on behalf of the sender or enters a region of the information processing system designated or used by the recipient which is under the control of the recipient.

(b) Unless otherwise agreed between a sender and the recipient, an electronic record is received when:

(1) it enters an information processing system that the recipient has designated or uses for the purpose of receiving electronic records or information of the type sent and from which the recipient is able to retrieve the electronic record; and

(2) it is in a form capable of being processed by that system.

(c) Subsection (b) applies even if the place the information processing system is located is different from the place the electronic record is deemed to be received under subsection (d).

(d) Unless otherwise expressly provided in the electronic record or agreed between the sender and the recipient, an electronic record is deemed to be sent from the sender's place of business and to be received at the recipient's place of business. For purposes of this subsection, the following rules apply:

(1) If the sender or recipient has more than one place of business, the place of business of that person is the place having the closest relationship to the underlying transaction.

(2) If the sender or the recipient does not have a place of business, the place of business is the sender's or recipient's residence, as the case may be.

(e) An electronic record is received under subsection (b) even if no individual is aware of its receipt.

(f) Receipt of an electronic acknowledgment from an information processing system described in subsection (b) establishes that a record was received but, by itself, does not establish that the content sent corresponds to the content received.

(g) If a person is aware that an electronic record purportedly sent under subsection (a), or purportedly received under subsection (b), was not actually sent or received, the legal effect of the sending or receipt is determined by other applicable law. Except to the extent permitted by the other law, the requirements of this subsection may not be varied by agreement.

Source: UNCITRAL Model Law on Electronic Commerce Article 15.

Comment

1. This section provides default rules regarding when and from where an electronic record is sent and when and where an electronic record is received. This section does not address the efficacy of the record that is sent or received. That is, whether a record is unintelligible or unusable by a recipient is a separate issue from whether that record was sent or received. The effectiveness of an illegible record, whether it binds any party, are questions left to other law.

2. Subsection (a) furnishes rules for determining when an electronic record is sent. The effect of the sending and its import are determined by other law once it is determined that a sending has occurred.

In order to have a proper sending, the subsection requires that information be properly addressed or otherwise directed to the recipient. In order to send within the meaning of this section, there must be specific information which will direct the record to the intended recipient. Although mass electronic sending is not precluded, a general broadcast message, sent to systems rather than individuals, would not suffice as a sending.

The record will be considered sent once it leaves the control of the sender, or comes under the control of the recipient. Records sent through e-mail or the internet will pass through many different server systems. Accordingly, the critical element when more than one system is involved is the loss of control by the sender.

However, the structure of many message delivery systems is such that electronic records may actually never leave the control of the sender. For example, within a university or corporate setting, e-mail sent within the system to another faculty member is technically not out of the sender's control since it never leaves the organization's server. Accordingly, to qualify as a sending, the e-mail must arrive at a point where the recipient has control. This section does not address the effect of an electronic record that is thereafter "pulled back," e.g., removed from a mailbox. The analog in the paper world would be removing a letter from a person's mailbox. As in the case of providing information electronically under Section 8, the recipient's ability to receive a message should be judged from the perspective of whether the sender has done any action which would preclude retrieval. This is especially the case in regard to sending, since the sender must direct the record to a system designated or used by the recipient.

3. Subsection (b) provides simply that when a record enters the system which the recipient has designated or uses and to which it has access, in a form capable of being processed by that system, it is received. Keying receipt to a system accessible by the recipient removes the potential for a recipient leaving messages with a server or other service in order to avoid receipt. However, the section does not resolve the issue of how the sender proves the time of receipt.

To assure that the recipient retains control of the place of receipt, subsection (b) requires that the system be specified or used by the recipient, and that the system be used or designated for the type of record being sent. Many people have multiple e-mail addresses for different purposes. Subsection (b) assures that recipients can designate the e-mail address or system to be used in a particular transaction. For example, the recipient retains the ability to designate a home e-mail for personal matters, work e-mail for official business, or a separate organizational e-mail solely for the business purposes of that organization. If A sends B a notice at his home which relates to business, it may not be deemed received if B designated his business address as the sole address for business purposes. Whether actual knowledge upon seeing it at home would qualify as receipt is determined under the otherwise applicable substantive law.

4. Subsections (c) and (d) provide default rules for determining where a record will be considered to have been sent or received. The focus is on the place of business of the recipient and not the physical location of the information processing system, which may bear absolutely no relation to the transaction between the parties. It is not uncommon for users of electronic commerce to communicate from one State to another without knowing the location of information systems through which communication is operated. In addition, the location of certain communication systems may

change without either of the parties being aware of the change. Accordingly, where the place of sending or receipt is an issue under other applicable law, e.g., conflict of laws issues, tax issues, the relevant location should be the location of the sender or recipient and not the location of the information processing system.

Subsection (d) assures individual flexibility in designating the place from which a record will be considered sent or at which a record will be considered received. Under subsection (d) a person may designate the place of sending or receipt unilaterally in an electronic record. This ability, as with the ability to designate by agreement, may be limited by otherwise applicable law to places having a reasonable relationship to the transaction.

5. Subsection (e) makes clear that receipt is not dependent on a person having notice that the record is in the person's system. Receipt occurs when the record reaches the designated system whether or not the recipient ever retrieves the record. The paper analog is the recipient who never reads a mail notice.

6. Subsection (f) provides legal certainty regarding the effect of an electronic acknowledgment. It only addresses the fact of receipt, not the quality of the content, nor whether the electronic record was read or "opened."

7. Subsection (g) limits the parties' ability to vary the method for sending and receipt provided in subsections (a) and (b), when there is a legal requirement for the sending or receipt. As in other circumstances where legal requirements derive from other substantive law, to the extent that the other law permits variation by agreement, this Act does not impose any additional requirements, and provisions of this Act may be varied to the extent provided in the other law.

§ 16. Transferable Records.

(a) In this section, "transferable record" means an electronic record that:

(1) would be a note under [Article 3 of the Uniform Commercial Code] or a document under [Article 7 of the Uniform Commercial Code] if the electronic record were in writing; and

(2) the issuer of the electronic record expressly has agreed is a transferable record.

(b) A person has control of a transferable record if a system employed for evidencing the transfer of interests in the transferable record reliably establishes that person as the person to which the transferable record was issued or transferred.

(c) A system satisfies subsection (b), and a person is deemed to have control of a transferable record, if the transferable record is created, stored, and assigned in such a manner that:

(1) a single authoritative copy of the transferable record exists which is unique, identifiable, and, except as otherwise provided in paragraphs (4), (5), and (6), unalterable;

(2) the authoritative copy identifies the person asserting control as:

(A) the person to which the transferable record was issued; or

(B) if the authoritative copy indicates that the transferable record has been transferred, the person to which the transferable record was most recently transferred;

(3) the authoritative copy is communicated to and maintained by the person asserting control or its designated custodian;

(4) copies or revisions that add or change an identified assignee of the authoritative copy can be made only with the consent of the person asserting control;

(5) each copy of the authoritative copy and any copy of a copy is readily identifiable as a copy that is not the authoritative copy; and

(6) any revision of the authoritative copy is readily identifiable as authorized or unauthorized.

(d) Except as otherwise agreed, a person having control of a transferable record is the holder, as defined in [Section 1–201(20) of the Uniform Commercial Code], of the transferable record and has the same rights and defenses as a holder of an equivalent record or writing under [the Uniform Commercial Code], including, if the applicable statutory requirements under [Section 3–302(a), 7–501, or 9–308 of the Uniform Commercial Code] are satisfied, the rights and defenses of a holder in due course, a holder to which a negotiable document of title has been duly negotiated, or a purchaser, respectively. Delivery, possession, and indorsement are not required to obtain or exercise any of the rights under this subsection.

(e) Except as otherwise agreed, an obligor under a transferable record has the same rights and defenses as an equivalent obligor under equivalent records or writings under [the Uniform Commercial Code].

(f) If requested by a person against which enforcement is sought, the person seeking to enforce the transferable record shall provide reasonable proof that the person is in control of the transferable record. Proof may include access to the authoritative copy of the transferable record and related business records sufficient to review the terms of the transferable record and to establish the identity of the person having control of the transferable record.

Source: Revised Article 9, Section 9–105.

Comment

1. Paper negotiable instruments and documents are unique in the fact that a tangible token–a piece of paper–actually embodies intangible rights and obligations. The extreme difficulty of creating a unique electronic token which embodies the singular attributes of a paper negotiable document or instrument dictates that the rules relating to negotiable documents and instruments not be simply amended to allow the use of an electronic record for the requisite paper writing. However, the desirability of establishing rules by which business parties might be able to acquire some of the benefits of negotiability in an electronic environment is recognized by the inclusion of this section on Transferable Records.

This section provides legal support for the creation, transferability and enforceability of electronic note and document equivalents, as against the issuer/obligor. The certainty created by the section provides the requisite incentive for industry to develop the systems and processes, which involve significant expenditures of time and resources, to enable the use of such electronic documents.

The importance of facilitating the development of systems which will permit electronic equivalents is a function of cost, efficiency and safety for the records. The storage cost and space needed for the billions of paper notes and documents is phenomenal. Further, natural disasters can wreak havoc on the ability to meet legal requirements for retaining, retrieving and delivering paper instruments. The development of electronic systems meeting the rigorous standards of this section will permit retention of copies which reflect the same integrity as the original. As a result storage, transmission and other costs will be reduced, while security and the ability to satisfy legal requirements governing such paper records will be enhanced.

Section 16 provides for the creation of an electronic record which may be controlled by the holder, who in turn may obtain the benefits of holder in due course and good faith purchaser status. If the benefits and efficiencies of electronic media are to be realized in this industry it is essential to establish a means by which transactions involving paper promissory notes may be accomplished completely electronically. Particularly as other aspects of such transactions are accomplished electronically, the drag on the transaction of requiring a paper note becomes evident. In addition to alleviating the logistical problems of generating, storing and retrieving paper, the mailing and transmission costs associated with such transactions will also be reduced.

2. The definition of transferable record is limited in two significant ways. First, only the equivalent of paper promissory notes and paper documents of title can be created as transferable records. Notes and Documents of Title do not impact the broad systems that relate to the broader payments mechanisms related, for example, to checks. Impacting the check collection system by allowing for "electronic checks" has ramifications well beyond the ability of this Act to address. Accordingly, this Act excludes from its scope transactions governed by UCC Articles 3 and 4. The limitation to promissory note equivalents in Section 16 is quite important in that regard because of the ability to deal with many enforcement issues by contract without affecting such systemic concerns.

Second, not only is Section 16 limited to electronic records which would qualify as negotiable promissory notes or documents if they were in writing, but the issuer of the electronic record must expressly agree that the electronic record is to be considered a transferable record. The definition of transferable record as "an electronic record that ... the issuer of the electronic record expressly has agreed is a transferable record" indicates that the electronic record itself will likely set forth the issuer's agreement, though it may be argued that a contemporaneous electronic or written record might set forth the issuer's agreement. However, conversion of a paper note issued as such would not be possible because the issuer would not be the issuer, in such a case, of an electronic record. The purpose of such a restriction is to assure that transferable records can only be created at the time of issuance by the obligor. The possibility that a paper note might be converted to an electronic record and then intentionally destroyed, and the effect of such action, was not intended to be covered by Section 16.

The requirement that the obligor expressly agree in the electronic record to its treatment as a transferable record does not otherwise affect the characterization of a transferable record (i.e., does not affect what would be a paper note) because it is a statutory condition. Further, it does not obligate the issuer to undertake to do any other act than the payment of the obligation evidenced by the transferable record. Therefore, it does not make the transferable record "conditional" within the meaning of Section 3–104(a)(3) of the Uniform Commercial Code.

3. Under Section 16 acquisition of "control" over an electronic record serves as a substitute for "possession" in the paper analog. More precisely, "control" under Section 16 serves as the substitute for delivery, indorsement and possession of a negotiable promissory note or negotiable document of title. Section 16(b) allows control to be found so long as "a system employed for evidencing the transfer of interests in the transferable record reliably establishes [the person claiming control] as the person to which the transferable record was issued or transferred." The key point is that a system, whether involving third party registry or technological safeguards, must be shown to reliably establish the identity of *the* person entitled to payment. Section 16(c) then sets forth a safe harbor list of very strict requirements for such a system. The specific provisions listed in Section 16(c) are derived from Section 105 of Revised Article 9 of the Uniform Commercial Code. Generally, the transferable record must be unique, identifiable, and except as specifically permitted, unalterable. That "authoritative copy" must (i) identify the person claiming control as the person to whom the record was issued or most recently transferred, (ii) be maintained by the person claiming control or its designee, and (iii) be unalterable except with the permission of the person claiming control. In addition any copy of the authoritative copy must be readily identifiable as a copy and all revisions must be readily identifiable as authorized or unauthorized.

The control requirements may be satisfied through the use of a trusted third party registry system. Such systems are currently in place with regard to the transfer of securities entitlements under Article 8 of the Uniform Commercial Code, and in the transfer of cotton warehouse receipts under the program sponsored by the United States Department of Agriculture. This Act would recognize the use of such a system so long as the standards of subsection (c) were satisfied. In addition, a technological system which met such exacting standards would also be permitted under Section 16.

For example, a borrower signs an electronic record which would be a promissory note or document if it were paper. The borrower specifically agrees in the electronic record that it will qualify as a transferable record under this section. The lender implements a newly developed technological system which dates, encrypts, and stores all the electronic information in the transferable record in a manner which lender can demonstrate reliably establishes lender as the person to which the transferable record was issued. In the alternative, the lender may contract with a third party to act as a registry for all such transferable records, retaining records establishing the party to whom the record was issued and all subsequent transfers of the record. An example of this latter method for assuring control is the system established for the issuance and transfer of electronic cotton warehouse receipts under 7 C.F.R. section 735 et seq.

Of greatest importance in the system used is the ability to securely and demonstrably be able to transfer the record to others in a manner which assures that only one "holder" exists. The need for such certainty and security resulted in the very stringent standards for a system outlined in subsection (c). A system relying on a third party registry is likely the most effective way to satisfy the requirements of subsection (c) that the transferable record remain unique, identifiable and unalterable, while also providing the means to assure that the transferee is clearly noted and identified.

It must be remembered that Section 16 was drafted in order to provide sufficient legal certainty regarding the rights of those in control of such electronic records, that legal incentives would exist to warrant the development of systems which would establish the requisite control. During the drafting of Section 16, representatives from the Federal Reserve carefully scrutinized the impact of any electronicization of any aspect of the national payment system. Section 16 represents a compromise position which, as noted, serves as a bridge pending more detailed study and consideration of what legal changes, if any, are necessary or appropriate in the context of the payment systems impacted. Accordingly, Section 16 provides limited scope for the attainment of important rights derived from the concept of negotiability, in order to permit the development of systems which will satisfy its strict requirements for control.

4. It is important to note what the section does not provide. Issues related to enforceability against intermediate transferees and transferors (i.e., indorser liability under a paper note), warranty liability that would attach in a paper note, and issues of the effect of taking a transferable record on the underlying obligation, are NOT addressed by this section. Such matters must be addressed, if at all, by contract between

and among the parties in the chain of transmission and transfer of the transferable record. In the event that such matters are not addressed by the contract, the issues would need to be resolved under otherwise applicable law. Other law may include general contract principles of assignment and assumption, or may include rules from Article 3 of the Uniform Commercial Code applied by analogy.

For example, Issuer agrees to pay a debt by means of a transferable record issued to A. Unless there is agreement between issuer and A that the transferable record "suspends" the underlying obligation (see Section 3–310 of the Uniform Commercial Code), A would not be prevented from enforcing the underlying obligation without the transferable record. Similarly, if A transfers the transferable record to B by means granting B control, B may obtain holder in due course rights against the obligor/issuer, but B's recourse against A would not be clear unless A agreed to remain liable under the transferable record. Although the rules of Article 3 may be applied by analogy in an appropriate context, in the absence of an express agreement in the transferable record or included by applicable system rules, the liability of the transferor would not be clear.

5. Current business models exist which rely for their efficacy on the benefits of negotiability. A principal example, and one which informed much of the development of Section 16, involves the mortgage backed securities industry. Aggregators of commercial paper acquire mortgage secured promissory notes following a chain of transfers beginning with the origination of the mortgage loan by a mortgage broker. In the course of the transfers of this paper, buyers of the notes and lenders/secured parties for these buyers will intervene. For the ultimate purchaser of the paper, the ability to rely on holder in due course and good faith purchaser status creates the legal security necessary to issue its own investment securities which are backed by the obligations evidenced by the notes purchased. Only through their HIDC status can these purchasers be assured that third party claims will be barred. Only through their HIDC status can the end purchaser avoid the incredible burden of requiring and assuring that each person in the chain of transfer has waived any and all defenses to performance which may be created during the chain of transfer.

6. This section is a stand-alone provision. Although references are made to specific provisions in Article 3, Article 7, and Article 9 of the Uniform Commercial Code, these provisions are incorporated into this Act and made the applicable rules for purposes of this Act. The rights of parties to transferable records are established under subsections (d) and (e). Subsection (d) provides rules for determining the rights of a party in control of a transferable record. The subsection makes clear that the rights are determined under this section, and not under other law, by incorporating the rules on the manner of acquisition into this statute. The last sentence of subsection (d) is intended to assure that requirements related to notions of possession, which are inherently inconsistent with the idea of an electronic record, are not incorporated into this statute.

If a person establishes control, Section 16(d) provides that that person is the "holder" of the transferable record which is equivalent to a holder of an analogous paper negotiable instrument. More importantly, if the person acquired control in a manner which would make it a holder in due course of an equivalent paper record, the person acquires the rights of a HIDC. The person in control would therefore be able to enforce the transferable record against the obligor regardless of intervening claims and defenses. However, by pulling these rights into Section 16, this Act does NOT validate the wholesale electrification of promissory notes under Article 3 of the Uniform Commercial Code.

Further, it is important to understand that a transferable record under Section 16, while having no counterpart under Article 3 of the Uniform Commercial Code, would be an "account," "general intangible," or "payment intangible" under Article 9 of the Uniform Commercial Code. Accordingly, two separate bodies of law would apply to that asset of the obligee. A taker of the transferable record under Section 16 may acquire purchaser rights under Article 9 of the Uniform Commercial Code, however, those rights may be defeated by a trustee in bankruptcy of a prior person in control unless perfection under Article 9 of the Uniform Commercial Code by filing is achieved. If the person in control also takes control in a manner granting it holder in due course status, of course that person would take free of any claim by a bankruptcy trustee or lien creditor.

7. Subsection (e) accords to the obligor of the transferable record rights equal to those of an obligor under an equivalent paper record. Accordingly, unless a waiver of defense clause is obtained in the electronic record, or the transferee obtains HDC rights under subsection (d), the obligor has all the rights and defenses available to it under a contract assignment. Additionally, the obligor has the right to have the payment noted or otherwise included as part of the electronic record.

8. Subsection (f) grants the obligor the right to have the transferable record and other information made available for purposes of assuring the correct person to pay. This will allow the obligor to protect its

interest and obtain the defense of discharge by payment or performance. This is particularly important because a person receiving subsequent control under the appropriate circumstances may well qualify as a holder in course who can enforce payment of the transferable record.

9. Section 16 is a singular exception to the thrust of this Act to simply validate electronic media used in commercial transactions. Section 16 actually provides a means for expanding electronic commerce. It provides certainty to lenders and investors regarding the enforceability of a new class of financial services. It is hoped that the legal protections afforded by Section 16 will engender the development of technological and business models which will permit realization of the significant cost savings and efficiencies available through electronic transacting in the financial services industry. Although only a bridge to more detailed consideration of the broad issues related to negotiability in an electronic context, Section 16 provides the impetus for that broader consideration while allowing continuation of developing technological and business models.

[§ 17.　Creation and Retention of Electronic Records and Conversion of Written Records by Governmental Agencies.

[Each governmental agency] [The [designated state officer]] of this State shall determine whether, and the extent to which, [it] [a governmental agency] will create and retain electronic records and convert written records to electronic records.]

Comment

See Comments following Section 19.

[§ 18.　Acceptance and Distribution of Electronic Records by Governmental Agencies.

(a) Except as otherwise provided in Section 12(f), [each governmental agency] [the [designated state officer]] of this State shall determine whether, and the extent to which, [it] [a governmental agency] will send and accept electronic records and electronic signatures to and from other persons and otherwise create, generate, communicate, store, process, use, and rely upon electronic records and electronic signatures.

(b) To the extent that a governmental agency uses electronic records and electronic signatures under subsection (a), the [governmental agency] [designated state officer], giving due consideration to security, may specify:

(1) the manner and format in which the electronic records must be created, generated, sent, communicated, received, and stored and the systems established for those purposes;

(2) if electronic records must be signed by electronic means, the type of electronic signature required, the manner and format in which the electronic signature must be affixed to the electronic record, and the identity of, or criteria that must be met by, any third party used by a person filing a document to facilitate the process;

(3) control processes and procedures as appropriate to ensure adequate preservation, disposition, integrity, security, confidentiality, and auditability of electronic records; and

(4) any other required attributes for electronic records which are specified for corresponding nonelectronic records or reasonably necessary under the circumstances.

(c) Except as otherwise provided in Section 12(f), this [Act] does not require a governmental agency of this State to use or permit the use of electronic records or electronic signatures.]

Source: Illinois Act Section 25–101; Florida Electronic Signature Act, Chapter 96–324, Section 7 (1996).

Comment

See Comments following Section 19.

[§ 19.　Interoperability.

The [governmental agency] [designated officer] of this State which adopts standards pursuant to Section 18 may encourage and promote consistency and interoperability with similar requirements adopted by other governmental agencies of this and other States and the federal government and nongovernmental persons interacting with governmental agencies of this State. If appropriate, those standards may specify differing levels of standards from which governmental agencies of this State may choose in implementing the most appropriate standard for a particular application.]

Source: Illinois Act Section 25–115.

See Legislative Note below, following Comment.

Comment

1. Sections 17–19 have been bracketed as optional provisions to be considered for adoption by each State. Among the barriers to electronic commerce are barriers which exist in the use of electronic media by state governmental agencies–whether among themselves or in external dealing with the private sector. In those circumstances where the government acts as a commercial party, e.g., in areas of procurement, the general validation provisions of this Act will apply. That is to say, the government must agree to conduct transactions electronically with vendors and customers of government services.

However, there are other circumstances when government ought to establish the ability to proceed in transactions electronically. Whether in regard to records and communications within and between governmental agencies, or with respect to information and filings which must be made with governmental agencies, these sections allow a State to establish the ground work for such electronicization.

2. The provisions in Sections 17–19 are broad and very general. In many States they will be unnecessary because enacted legislation designed to facilitate governmental use of electronic records and communications is in place. However, in many States broad validating rules are needed and desired. Accordingly, this Act provides these sections as a baseline.

Of paramount importance in all States however, is the need for States to assure that whatever systems and rules are adopted, the systems established are compatible with the systems of other governmental agencies and with common systems in the private sector. A very real risk exists that implementation of systems by myriad governmental agencies and offices may create barriers because of a failure to consider compatibility, than would be the case otherwise.

3. The provisions in Section 17–19 are broad and general to provide the greatest flexibility and adaptation to the specific needs of the individual States. The differences and variations in the organization and structure of governmental agencies mandates this approach. However, it is imperative that each State always keep in mind the need to prevent the erection of barriers through appropriate coordination of systems and rules within the parameters set by the State.

4. Section 17 authorizes state agencies to use electronic records and electronic signatures generally for intra-governmental purposes, and to convert written records and manual signatures to electronic records and electronic signatures. By its terms the section gives enacting legislatures the option to leave the decision to use electronic records or convert written records and signatures to the governmental agency or assign that duty to a designated state officer. It also authorizes the destruction of written records after conversion to electronic form.

5. Section 18 broadly authorizes state agencies to send and receive electronic records and signatures in dealing with non-governmental persons. Again, the provision is permissive and not obligatory (see subsection (c)). However, it does provide specifically that with respect to electronic records used for evidentiary purposes, Section 12 will apply unless a particular agency expressly opts out.

6. Section 19 is the most important section of the three. It requires governmental agencies or state officers to take account of consistency in applications and interoperability to the extent practicable when promulgating standards. This section is critical in addressing the concern that inconsistent applications may promote barriers greater than currently exist. Without such direction the myriad systems that could develop independently would be new barriers to electronic commerce, not a removal of barriers. The key to interoperability is flexibility and adaptability. The requirement of a single system may be as big a barrier as the proliferation of many disparate systems.

Legislative Note Regarding Adoption of Sections 17–19

1. Sections 17–19 are optional sections for consideration by individual legislatures for adoption, and have been bracketed to make this clear. The inclusion or exclusion of Sections 17–19 will not have a detrimental impact on the uniformity of adoption of this Act, so long as Sections 1–16 are adopted uniformly as presented. In some States Sections 17–19 will be unnecessary because legislation is already in place to authorize and implement government use of electronic media. However, the general authorization provided by Sections 17–19 may be critical in some States which desire to move forward in this area.

2. In the event that a state legislature chooses to adopt Sections 17–19, a number of issues must be addressed:

A. Is the general authorization to adopt electronic media, provided by Sections 17–19 sufficient for the needs of the particular jurisdiction, or is more detailed and specific authorization necessary? This determination may be affected by the decision regarding the appropriate entity or person to oversee implementation of the use of electronic media (See next paragraph). Sections 17–19 are broad and general in the authorization granted. Certainly greater specificity can be added subsequent to adoption of these sections. The question for the legislature is whether greater direction and specificity is needed at this time. If so, the legislature should not enact Sections 17–19 at this time.

B. Assuming a legislature decides to enact Sections 17–19, what entity or person should oversee implementation of the government's use of electronic media? As noted in each of Sections 17–19, again by brackets, a choice must be made regarding the entity to make critical decisions regarding the systems and rules which will govern the use of electronic media by the State. Each State will need to consider its particular structure and administration in making this determination. However, legislatures are strongly encouraged to make compatibility and interoperability considerations paramount in making this determination.

C. Finally, a decision will have to be made regarding the process by which coordination of electronic systems will occur between the various branches of state government and among the various levels of government within the State. Again this will require consideration of the unique situation in each State.

3. If a State chooses not to enact Sections 17–19, UETA Sections 1–16 will still apply to governmental entities when acting as a "person" engaging in "transactions" within its scope. The definition of transaction includes "governmental affairs." Of course, like any other party, the circumstances surrounding a transaction must indicate that the governmental actor has agreed to act electronically (See Section 5(b)), but otherwise all the provisions of Sections 1–16 will apply to validate the use of electronic records and signatures in transactions involving governmental entities.

If a State does choose to enact Sections 17–19, Sections 1–16 will continue to apply as above. In addition, Sections 17–19 will provide authorization for intra-governmental uses of electronic media. Finally, Sections 17–19 provide a broader authorization for the State to develop systems and procedures for the use of electronic media in its relations with non-governmental entities and persons.

§ 20.   Severability Clause.

If any provision of this [Act] or its application to any person or circumstance is held invalid, the invalidity does not affect other provisions or applications of this [Act] which can be given effect without the invalid provision or application, and to this end the provisions of this [Act] are severable.

§ 21.   Effective Date.

This [Act] takes effect [   ].

UNITED NATIONS CONVENTION ON CONTRACTS FOR THE INTERNATIONAL SALE OF GOODS (1980)* (CISG)

THE STATES PARTIES TO
THIS CONVENTION

BEARING IN MIND the broad objectives in the resolutions adopted by the sixth special session of the General Assembly of the United Nations on the establishment of a New International Economic Order,

CONSIDERING that the development of international trade on the basis of equality and mutual benefit is an important element in promoting friendly relations among States,

BEING OF THE OPINION that the adoption of uniform rules which govern contracts for the international sale of goods and take into account the different social, economic and legal systems would contribute to the removal of legal barriers in international trade and promote the development of international trade,

HAVE AGREED as follows:

PART I. SPHERE OF APPLICATION AND GENERAL PROVISIONS

CHAPTER I. SPHERE OF APPLICATION

Article 1

(1) This Convention applies to contracts of sale of goods between parties whose places of business are in different States:

(a) when the States are Contracting States; or

(b) when the rules of private international law lead to the application of the law of a Contracting State.

(2) The fact that the parties have their places of business in different States is to be disregarded whenever this fact does not appear either from the contract or from any dealings between, or from information disclosed by, the parties at any time before or at the conclusion of the contract.

(3) Neither the nationality of the parties nor the civil or commercial character of the parties or of the contract is to be taken into consideration in determining the application of this Convention.

[The United States has declared a reservation under Article 95, and therefore is not bound by Article 1(1)(b).]

Article 2

This Convention does not apply to sales:

(a) of goods bought for personal, family or household use, unless the seller, at any time before or at the conclusion of the contract, neither knew nor ought to have known that the goods were bought for any such use;

(b) by auction;

* [This Convention (CISG) was prepared by the United Nations Commission on International Trade Law (UNCITRAL) and issued for signature through a United Nations Diplomatic Conference in Vienna in 1980. As its Final Clauses (Articles 89–101) indicate, CISG became effective as a multilateral treaty on January 1, twelve months after ten nations ratified it. On December 11, 1986, China, Italy and the United States became the ninth, tenth, and eleventh nations to ratify the Convention. Thus, CISG became effective within its scope of application (see Article 1) on January 1, 1988. It will govern all international sales contracts within Article 1 concluded after that date, although the parties may expressly "opt out" of its coverage under Article 6.]

Through May 1, 2006, CISG has been ratified by, and entered into force in, Argentina, Australia, Austria, Belarus, Belgium, Bosnia-Herzegovina, Bulgaria, Burundi, Canada, Chile, China (PRC), Colombia, Croatia, Cuba, Cyprus, Czech Republic, Denmark, Ecuador, Egypt, Estonia, Finland, France, Gabon, Georgia, Germany, Greece, Guinea, Honduras, Hungary, Iceland, Iraq, Israel, Italy, Kyrgstan, Latvia, Lesotho, Liberia, Lithuania, Luxembourg, Mauritania, Mexico, Republic of Moldova, Mongolia, Netherlands, New Zealand, Norway, Paraguay, Peru, Poland, Republic of Korea, Romania, the Russian Federation, Saint Vincent & Grenadines, Singapore, Slovakia, Slovenia, Spain, Sweden, Switzerland, Syria, Uganda, Ukraine, United States of America, Uruguay, Uzbekistan, Yugoslavia, and Zambia.

(c) on execution or otherwise by authority of law;

(d) of stocks, shares, investment securities, negotiable instruments or money;

(e) of ships, vessels, hovercraft or aircraft;

(f) of electricity.

Article 3

(1) Contracts for the supply of goods to be manufactured or produced are to be considered sales unless the party who orders the goods undertakes to supply a substantial part of the materials necessary for such manufacture or production.

(2) This Convention does not apply to contracts in which the preponderant part of the obligations of the party who furnishes the goods consists in the supply of labour or other services.

Article 4

This Convention governs only the formation of the contract of sale and the rights and obligations of the seller and the buyer arising from such a contract. In particular, except as otherwise expressly provided in this Convention, it is not concerned with:

(a) the validity of the contract or of any of its provisions or of any usage;

(b) the effect which the contract may have on the property in the goods sold.

Article 5

This Convention does not apply to the liability of the seller for death or personal injury caused by the goods to any person.

Article 6

The parties may exclude the application of this Convention or, subject to Article 12, derogate from or vary the effect of any of its provisions.

CHAPTER II. GENERAL PROVISIONS

Article 7

(1) In the interpretation of this Convention, regard is to be had to its international character and to the need to promote uniformity in its ⁚⁚⁚ʳᵗⁱᵒⁿ and the observance of good faith in ⁚ʳaltrade.

(2) Questions concerning matters governed by this Convention which are not expressly settled in it are to be settled in conformity with the general principles on which it is based or, in the absence of such principles, in conformity with the law applicable by virtue of the rules of private international law.

Article 8

(1) For the purposes of this Convention statements made by and other conduct of a party are to be interpreted according to his intent where the other party knew or could not have been unaware what that intent was.

(2) If the preceding paragraph is not applicable, statements made by and other conduct of a party are to be interpreted according to the understanding that a reasonable person of the same kind as the other party would have had in the same circumstances.

(3) In determining the intent of a party or the understanding a reasonable person would have had, due consideration is to be given to all relevant circumstances of the case including the negotiations, any practices which the parties have established between themselves, usages and any subsequent conduct of the parties.

Article 9

(1) The parties are bound by any usage to which they have agreed and by any practices which they have established between themselves.

(2) The parties are considered, unless otherwise agreed, to have impliedly made applicable to their contract or its formation a usage of which the parties knew or ought to have known and which in international trade is widely known to, and regularly observed by, parties to contracts of the type involved in the particular trade concerned.

Article 10

For the purposes of this Convention:

(a) if a party has more than one place of business, the place of business is that which has the closest relationship to the contract and its performance, having regard to the circumstances known to or contemplated by the parties at any time before or at the conclusion of the contract;

(b) if a party does not have a place of business, reference is to be made to his habitual residence.

Article 11

A contract of sale need not be concluded in or evidenced by writing and is not subject to any other requirement as to form. It may be proved by any means, including witnesses.

Article 12

Any provision of article 11, article 29 or Part II of this Convention that allows a contract of sale or its modification or termination by agreement or any offer, acceptance or other indication of intention to be made in any form other than in writing does not apply where any party has his place of business in a Contracting State which has made a declaration under article 96 of this Convention. The parties may not derogate from or vary the effect of this article.

Article 13

For the purposes of this Convention "writing" includes telegram and telex.

PART II. FORMATION OF THE CONTRACT

Article 14

(1) A proposal for concluding a contract addressed to one or more specific persons constitutes an offer if it is sufficiently definite and indicates the intention of the offeror to be bound in case of acceptance. A proposal is sufficiently definite if it indicates the goods and expressly or implicitly fixes or makes provision for determining the quantity and the price.

(2) A proposal other than one addressed to one or more specific persons is to be considered merely as an invitation to make offers, unless the contrary is clearly indicated by the person making the proposal.

Article 15

(1) An offer becomes effective when it reaches the offeree.

(2) An offer, even if it is irrevocable, may be withdrawn if the withdrawal reaches the offeree before or at the same time as the offer.

Article 16

(1) Until a contract is concluded an offer may be revoked if the revocation reaches the offeree before he has dispatched an acceptance.

(2) However, an offer cannot be revoked:

(a) if it indicates, whether by stating a fixed time for acceptance or otherwise, that it is irrevocable; or

(b) if it was reasonable for the offeree to rely on the offer as being irrevocable and the offeree has acted in reliance on the offer.

Article 17

An offer, even if it is irrevocable, is terminated when a rejection reaches the offeror.

Article 18

(1) A statement made by or other conduct of the offeree indicating assent to an offer is an acceptance. Silence or inactivity does not in itself amount to acceptance.

(2) An acceptance of an offer becomes effective at the moment the indication of assent reaches the offeror. An acceptance is not effective if the indication of assent does not reach the offeror within the time he has fixed or, if no time is fixed, within a reasonable time, due account being taken of the circumstances of the transaction, including the rapidity of the means of communication employed by the offeror. An oral offer must be accepted immediately unless the circumstances indicate otherwise.

(3) However, if, by virtue of the offer or as a result of practices which the parties have established between themselves or of usage, the offeree may indicate assent by performing an act, such as one relating to the dispatch of the goods or payment of the price, without notice to the offeror, the acceptance is effective at the moment the act is performed, provided that the act is performed within the period of time laid down in the preceding paragraph.

Article 19

(1) A reply to an offer which purports to be an acceptance but contains additions, limitations or other modifications is a rejection of the offer and constitutes a counter-offer.

(2) However, a reply to an offer which purports to be an acceptance but contains additional

or different terms which do not materially alter the terms of the offer constitutes an acceptance, unless the offeror, without undue delay, objects orally to the discrepancy or dispatches a notice to that effect. If he does not so object, the terms of the contract are the terms of the offer with the modifications contained in the acceptance.

(3) Additional or different terms relating, among other things, to the price, payment, quality and quantity of the goods, place and time of delivery, extent of one party's liability to the other or the settlement of disputes are considered to alter the terms of the offer materially.

Article 20

(1) A period of time for acceptance fixed by the offeror in a telegram or a letter begins to run from the moment the telegram is handed in for dispatch or from the date shown on the letter or, if no such date is shown, from the date shown on the envelope. A period of time for acceptance fixed by the offeror by telephone, telex or other means of instantaneous communication, begins to run from the moment that the offer reaches the offeree.

(2) Official holidays or non-business days occurring during the period for acceptance are included in calculating the period. However, if a notice of acceptance cannot be delivered at the address of the offeror on the last day of the period because that day falls on an official holiday or a non-business day at the place of business of the offeror, the period is extended until the first business day which follows.

Article 21

(1) A late acceptance is nevertheless effective as an acceptance if without delay the offeror orally so informs the offeree or dispatches a notice to that effect.

(2) If a letter or other writing containing a late acceptance shows that it has been sent in such circumstances that if its transmission had been normal it would have reached the offeror in due time, the late acceptance is effective as an acceptance unless, without delay, the offeror orally informs the offeree that he considers his offer as ~~lapsed~~ or dispatches a notice to that ef-

Article 22

An acceptance may be withdrawn if the withdrawal reaches the offeror before or at the same time as the acceptance would have become effective.

Article 23

A contract is concluded at the moment when an acceptance of an offer becomes effective in accordance with the provisions of this Convention.

Article 24

For the purposes of this Part of the Convention, an offer, declaration of acceptance or any other indication of intention "reaches" the addressee when it is made orally to him or delivered by any other means to him personally, to his place of business or mailing address or, if he does not have a place of business or mailing address, to his habitual residence.

PART III.   SALE OF GOODS
CHAPTER I.   GENERAL PROVISIONS
Article 25

A breach of contract committed by one of the parties is fundamental if it results in such detriment to the other party as substantially to deprive him of what he is entitled to expect under the contract, unless the party in breach did not foresee and a reasonable person of the same kind in the same circumstances would not have foreseen such a result.

Article 26

A declaration of avoidance of the contract is effective only if made by notice to the other party.

Article 27

Unless otherwise expressly provided in this Part of the Convention, if any notice, request or other communication is given or made by a party in accordance with this Part and by means appropriate in the circumstances, a delay or error in the transmission of the communication or its failure to arrive does not deprive that party of the right to rely on the communication.

Article 28

If, in accordance with the provisions of this Convention, one party is entitled to require performance of any obligation by the other party, a court is not bound to enter a judgment for specific performance unless the court would do so under its own law in respect of similar contracts of sale not governed by this Convention.

Article 29

(1) A contract may be modified or terminated by the mere agreement of the parties.

(2) A contract in writing which contains a provision requiring any modification or termination by agreement to be in writing may not be otherwise modified or terminated by agreement. However, a party may be precluded by his conduct from asserting such a provision to the extent that the other party has relied on that conduct.

CHAPTER II. OBLIGATIONS OF THE SELLER

Article 30

The seller must deliver the goods, hand over any documents relating to them and transfer the property in the goods, as required by the contract and this Convention.

SECTION I.

DELIVERY OF THE GOODS AND HANDING OVER OF DOCUMENTS

Article 31

If the seller is not bound to deliver the goods at any other particular place, his obligation to deliver consists:

(a) if the contract of sale involves carriage of the goods—in handing the goods over to the first carrier for transmission to the buyer;

(b) if, in cases not within the preceding subparagraph, the contract relates to specific goods, or unidentified goods to be drawn from a specific stock or to be manufactured or produced, and at the time of the conclusion of the contract the parties knew that the goods were at, or were to be manufactured or produced at, a particular place—in placing the goods at the buyer's disposal at that place;

(c) in other cases—in placing the goods at the buyer's disposal at the place where the seller had his place of business at the time of the conclusion of the contract.

Article 32

(1) If the seller, in accordance with the contract or this Convention, hands the goods over to a carrier and if the goods are not clearly identified to the contract by markings on the goods, by shipping documents or otherwise, the seller must give the buyer notice of the consignment specifying the goods.

(2) If the seller is bound to arrange for carriage of the goods, he must make such contracts as are necessary for carriage to the place fixed by means of transportation appropriate in the circumstances and according to the usual terms for such transportation.

(3) If the seller is not bound to effect insurance in respect of the carriage of the goods, he must, at the buyer's request, provide him with all available information necessary to enable him to effect such insurance.

Article 33

The seller must deliver the goods:

(a) if a date is fixed by or determinable from the contract, on that date;

(b) if a period of time is fixed by or determinable from the contract, at any time within that period unless circumstances indicate that the buyer is to choose a date; or

(c) in any other case, within a reasonable time after the conclusion of the contract.

Article 34

If the seller is bound to hand over documents relating to the goods, he must hand them over at the time and place and in the form required by the contract. If the seller has handed over documents before that time, he may, up to that time, cure any lack of conformity in the documents, if the exercise of this right does not cause the buyer unreasonable inconvenience or unreasonable expense. However, the buyer retains any right to claim damages as provided for in this Convention.

SECTION II.

CONFORMITY OF THE GOODS AND THIRD PARTY CLAIMS

Article 35

(1) The seller must deliver goods which are of the quantity, quality and description required by the contract and which are contained or packaged in the manner required by the contract.

(2) Except where the parties have agreed otherwise, the goods do not conform with the contract unless they;

(a) are fit for the purposes for which goods of the same description would ordinarily be used;

(b) are fit for any particular purpose expressly or impliedly made known to the seller at the time of the conclusion of the contract, except where the circumstances show that the buyer did not rely, or that it was unreasonable for him to rely, on the seller's skill and judgement;

(c) possess the qualities of goods which the seller has held out to the buyer as a sample or model;

(d) are contained or packaged in the manner usual for such goods or, where there is no such manner, in a manner adequate to preserve and protect the goods.

(3) The seller is not liable under subparagraphs (a) to (d) of the preceding paragraph for any lack of conformity of the goods if at the time of the conclusion of the contract the buyer knew or could not have been unaware of such lack of conformity.

Article 36

(1) The seller is liable in accordance with the contract and this Convention for any lack of conformity which exists at the time when the risk passes to the buyer, even though the lack of conformity becomes apparent only after that time.

(2) The seller is also liable for any lack of conformity which occurs after the time indicated in the preceding paragraph and which is due to a breach of any of his obligations, including a breach of any guarantee that for a period of time the goods will remain fit for their ordinary pur~~for~~ some particular purpose or will retain ~~qu~~alities or characteristics.

Article 37

If the seller has delivered goods before the date for delivery, he may, up to that date, deliver any missing part or make up any deficiency in the quantity of the goods delivered, or deliver goods in replacement of any non-conforming goods delivered or remedy any lack of conformity in the goods delivered, provided that the exercise of this right does not cause the buyer unreasonable inconvenience or unreasonable expense. However, the buyer retains any right to claim damages as provided for in this Convention.

Article 38

(1) The buyer must examine the goods, or cause them to be examined, within as short a period as is practicable in the circumstances.

(2) If the contract involves carriage of the goods, examination may be deferred until after the goods have arrived at their destination.

(3) If the goods are redirected in transit or redispatched by the buyer without a reasonable opportunity for examination by him and at the time of the conclusion of the contract the seller knew or ought to have known of the possibility of such redirection or redispatch, examination may be deferred until after the goods have arrived at the new destination.

Article 39

(1) The buyer loses the right to rely on a lack of conformity of the goods if he does not give notice to the seller specifying the nature of the lack of conformity within a reasonable time after he has discovered it or ought to have discovered it.

(2) In any event, the buyer loses the right to rely on a lack of conformity of the goods if he does not give the seller notice thereof at the latest within a period of two years from the date on which the goods were actually handed over to the buyer, unless this time-limit is inconsistent with a contractual period of guarantee.

Article 40

The seller is not entitled to rely on the provisions of articles 38 and 39 if the lack of conformity relates to facts of which he knew or could not have been unaware and which he did not disclose to the buyer.

Article 41

The seller must deliver goods which are free from any right or claim of a third party, unless the buyer agreed to take the goods subject to that right or claim. However, if such right or claim is based on industrial property or other intellectual property, the seller's obligation is governed by article 42.

Article 42

(1) The seller must deliver goods which are free from any right or claim of a third party based on industrial property or other intellectual property, of which at the time of the conclusion of the contract the seller knew or could not have been unaware, provided that the right or claim is based on industrial property or other intellectual property:

(a) under the law of the State where the goods will be resold or otherwise used, if it was contemplated by the parties at the time of the conclusion of the contract that the goods would be resold or otherwise used in that State; or

(b) in any other case, under the law of the State where the buyer has his place of business.

(2) The obligation of the seller under the preceding paragraph does not extend to cases where:

(a) at the time of the conclusion of the contract the buyer knew or could not have been unaware of the right or claim; or

(b) the right or claim results from the seller's compliance with technical drawings, designs, formulae or other such specifications furnished by the buyer.

Article 43

(1) The buyer loses the right to rely on the provisions of article 41 or article 42 if he does not give notice to the seller specifying the nature of the right or claim of the third party within a reasonable time after he has become aware or ought to have become aware of the right or claim.

(2) The seller is not entitled to rely on the provisions of the preceding paragraph if he knew of the right or claim of the third party and the nature of it.

Article 44

Notwithstanding the provisions of paragraph (1) of article 39 and paragraph (1) of article 43, the buyer may reduce the price in accordance with article 50 or claim damages, except for loss of profit, if he has a reasonable excuse for his failure to give the required notice.

SECTION III.

REMEDIES FOR BREACH OF CONTRACT BY THE SELLER

Article 45

(1) If the seller fails to perform any of his obligations under the contract or this Convention, the buyer may:

(a) exercise the rights provided in articles 46 to 52;

(b) claim damages as provided in articles 74 to 77.

(2) The buyer is not deprived of any right he may have to claim damages by exercising his right to other remedies.

(3) No period of grace may be granted to the seller by a court or arbitral tribunal when the buyer resorts to a remedy for breach of contract.

Article 46

(1) The buyer may require performance by the seller of his obligations unless the buyer has resorted to a remedy which is inconsistent with this requirement.

(2) If the goods do not conform with the contract, the buyer may require delivery of substitute goods only if the lack of conformity constitutes a fundamental breach of contract and a request for substitute goods is made either in conjunction with notice given under article 39 or within a reasonable time thereafter.

(3) If the goods do not conform with the contract, the buyer may require the seller to remedy the lack of conformity by repair, unless this is unreasonable having regard to all the circumstances. A request for repair must be made either in conjunction with notice given under article 39 or within a reasonable time thereafter.

Article 47

(1) The buyer may fix an additional period of time of reasonable length for performance by the seller of his obligations.

(2) Unless the buyer has received notice from the seller that he will not perform within the period so fixed, the buyer may not, during that period, resort to any remedy for breach of contract. However, the buyer is not deprived thereby of any right he may have to claim damages for delay in performance.

Article 48

(1) Subject to article 49, the seller may, even after the date for delivery, remedy at his own expense any failure to perform his obligations, if he can do so without unreasonable delay and without causing the buyer unreasonable inconvenience or uncertainty of reimbursement by the seller of expenses advanced by the buyer. However, the buyer retains any right to claim damages as provided for in this Convention.

(2) If the seller requests the buyer to make known whether he will accept performance and the buyer does not comply with the request within a reasonable time, the seller may perform within the time indicated in his request. The buyer may not, during that period of time, resort to any remedy which is inconsistent with performance by the seller.

(3) A notice by the seller that he will perform within a specified period of time is assumed to include a request, under the preceding paragraph, that the buyer make known his decision.

(4) A request or notice by the seller under paragraph (2) or (3) of this article is not effective unless received by the buyer.

Article 49

(1) The buyer may declare the contract avoided:

(a) if the failure by the seller to perform any of his obligations under the contract or this Convention amounts to a fundamental breach of contract; or

(b) in case of non-delivery, if the seller does not deliver the goods within the additional ___ ___ time fixed by the buyer in accordance ___ agraph (1) of article 47 or declares that he will not deliver within the period so fixed.

(2) However, in cases where the seller has delivered the goods, the buyer loses the right to declare the contract avoided unless he does so:

(a) in respect of late delivery, within a reasonable time after he has become aware that delivery has been made;

(b) in respect of any breach other than late delivery, within a reasonable time:

(i) after he knew or ought to have known of the breach;

(ii) after the expiration of any additional period of time fixed by the buyer in accordance with paragraph (1) of article 47, or after the seller has declared that he will not perform his obligations within such an additional period; or

(iii) after the expiration of any additional period of time indicated by the seller in accordance with paragraph (2) of article 48, or after the buyer has declared that he will not accept performance.

Article 50

If the goods do not conform with the contract and whether or not the price has already been paid, the buyer may reduce the price in the same proportion as the value that the goods actually delivered had at the time of the delivery bears to the value that conforming goods would have had at that time. However, if the seller remedies any failure to perform his obligations in accordance with article 37 or article 48 or if the buyer refuses to accept performance by the seller in accordance with those articles, the buyer may not reduce the price.

Article 51

(1) If the seller delivers only a part of the goods or if only a part of the goods delivered is in conformity with the contract, articles 46 to 50 apply in respect of the part which is missing or which does not conform.

(2) The buyer may declare the contract avoided in its entirety only if the failure to make delivery completely or in conformity with the contract amounts to a fundamental breach of the contract.

Article 52

(1) If the seller delivers the goods before the date fixed, the buyer may take delivery or refuse to take delivery.

(2) If the seller delivers a quantity of goods greater than that provided for in the contract, the buyer may take delivery or refuse to take delivery of the excess quantity. If the buyer takes delivery of all or part of the excess quantity, he must pay for it at the contract rate.

CHAPTER III. OBLIGATIONS OF THE BUYER

Article 53

The buyer must pay the price for the goods and take delivery of them as required by the contract and this Convention.

SECTION I.
PAYMENT OF THE PRICE
Article 54

The buyer's obligation to pay the price includes taking such steps and complying with such formalities as may be required under the contract or any laws and regulations to enable payment to be made.

Article 55

Where a contract has been validly concluded but does not expressly or implicitly fix or make provision for determining the price, the parties are considered, in the absence of any indication to the contrary, to have impliedly made reference to the price generally charged at the time of the conclusion of the contract for such goods sold under comparable circumstances in the trade concerned.

Article 56

If the price if fixed according to the weight of the goods, in case of doubt it is to be determined by the net weight.

Article 57

(1) If the buyer is not bound to pay the price at any other particular place, he must pay it to the seller:

(a) at the seller's place of business; or

(b) if the payment is to be made against the handing over of the goods or of documents, at the place where the handing over takes place.

(2) The seller must bear any increase in the expenses incidental to payment which is caused by a change in his place of business subsequent to the conclusion of the contract.

Article 58

(1) If the buyer is not bound to pay the price at any other specific time, he must pay it when the seller places either the goods or documents controlling their disposition at the buyer's disposal in accordance with the contract and this Convention. The seller may make such payment a condition for handing over the goods or documents.

(2) If the contract involves carriage of the goods, the seller may dispatch the goods on terms whereby the goods, or documents controlling their disposition, will not be handed over to the buyer except against payment of the price.

(3) The buyer is not bound to pay the price until he has had an opportunity to examine the goods, unless the procedures for delivery or payment agreed upon by the parties are inconsistent with his having such an opportunity.

Article 59

The buyer must pay the price on the date fixed by or determinable from the contract and this Convention without the need for any request or compliance with any formality on the part of the seller.

SECTION II.
TAKING DELIVERY
Article 60

The buyer's obligation to take delivery consists:

(a) in doing all the acts which could reasonably be expected of him in order to enable the seller to make delivery; and

(b) in taking over the goods.

SECTION III.
REMEDIES FOR BREACH OF CONTRACT BY THE BUYER
Article 61

(1) If the buyer fails to perform any of his obligations under the contract or this Convention, the seller may:

(a) exercise the rights provided in articles 62 to 65;

(b) claim damages as provided in articles 74 to 77.

(2) The seller is not deprived of any right he may have to claim damages by exercising his right to other remedies.

(3) No period of grace may be granted to the buyer by a court or arbitral tribunal when the seller resorts to a remedy for breach of contract.

Article 62

The seller may require the buyer to pay the price, take delivery or perform his other obligations, unless the seller has resorted to a remedy which is inconsistent with this requirement.

Article 63

(1) The seller may fix an additional period of time of reasonable length for performance by the buyer of his obligations.

(2) Unless the seller has received notice from the buyer that he will not perform within the period so fixed, the seller may not, during that period, resort to any remedy for breach of contract. However, the seller is not deprived thereby of any right he may have to claim damages for delay in performance.

Article 64

(1) The seller may declare the contract avoided:

(a) if the failure by the buyer to perform any of his obligations under the contract or this Convention amounts to a fundamental breach of contract; or

(b) if the buyer does not, within the additional period of time fixed by the seller in accordance with paragraph (1) of article 63, perform his obligation to pay the price or take delivery of the goods, or if he declares that he will not do so within the period so fixed.

(2) However, in cases where the buyer has paid the price, the seller loses the right to declare the contract avoided unless he does so:

(a) in respect of late performance by the ~~fore the seller has become aware that~~ ~~nce has been rendered; or~~

(b) in respect of any breach other than late performance by the buyer, within a reasonable time:

(i) after the seller knew or ought to have known of the breach; or

(ii) after the expiration of any additional period of time fixed by the seller in accordance with paragraph (1) of article 63, or after the buyer has declared that he will not perform his obligations within such an additional period.

Article 65

(1) If under the contract the buyer is to specify the form, measurement or other features of the goods and he fails to make such specification either on the date agreed upon or within a reasonable time after receipt of a request from the seller, the seller may, without prejudice to any other rights he may have, make the specification himself in accordance with the requirements of the buyer that may be known to him.

(2) If the seller makes the specification himself, he must inform the buyer of the details thereof and must fix a reasonable time within which the buyer may make a different specification. If, after receipt of such a communication, the buyer fails to do so within the time so fixed, the specification made by the seller is binding.

CHAPTER IV. PASSING OF RISK
Article 66

Loss of or damage to the goods after the risk has passed to the buyer does not discharge him from his obligation to pay the price, unless the loss or damage is due to an act or omission of the seller.

Article 67

(1) If the contract of sale involves carriage of the goods and the seller is not bound to hand them over at a particular place, the risk passes to the buyer when the goods are handed over to the first carrier for transmission to the buyer in accordance with the contract of sale. If the seller is bound to hand the goods over to a carrier at a particular place, the risk does not pass to the buyer until the goods are handed over to the carrier at that place. The fact that the seller is authorized to retain documents controlling the disposition of the goods does not affect the passage of the risk.

(2) Nevertheless, the risk does not pass to the buyer until the goods are clearly identified to the contract, whether by markings on the goods, by shipping documents, by notice given to the buyer or otherwise.

Article 68

The risk in respect of goods sold in transit passes to the buyer from the time of the conclusion of the contract. However, if the circumstances so indicate, the risk is assumed by the buyer from the time the goods were handed over to the carrier who issued the documents embodying the contract of carriage. Nevertheless, if at the time of the conclusion of the contract of sale the seller knew or ought to have known that the goods had been lost or damaged and did not disclose this to the buyer, the loss or damage is at the risk of the seller.

Article 69

(1) In cases not within articles 67 and 68, the risk passes to the buyer when he takes over the goods or, if he does not do so in due time, from the time when the goods are placed at his disposal and he commits a breach of contract by failing to take delivery.

(2) However, if the buyer is bound to take over the goods at a place other than a place of business of the seller, the risk passes when delivery is due and the buyer is aware of the fact that the goods are placed at his disposal at that place.

(3) If the contract relates to goods not then identified, the goods are considered not to be placed at the disposal of the buyer until they are clearly identified to the contract.

Article 70

If the seller had committed a fundamental breach of contract, articles 67, 68 and 69 do not impair the remedies available to the buyer on account of the breach.

CHAPTER V. PROVISIONS COMMON TO THE OBLIGATIONS OF THE SELLER AND OF THE BUYER
SECTION I.
ANTICIPATORY BREACH AND INSTALMENT CONTRACTS
Article 71

(1) A party may suspend the performance of his obligations if, after the conclusion of the contract, it becomes apparent that the other party will not perform a substantial part of his obligations as a result of:

(a) a serious deficiency in his ability to perform or in his creditworthiness; or

(b) his conduct in preparing to perform or in performing the contract.

(2) If the seller has already dispatched the goods before the grounds described in the preceding paragraph become evident, he may prevent the handing over of the goods to the buyer even though the buyer holds a document which entitles him to obtain them. The present paragraph relates only to the rights in the goods as between the buyer and the seller.

(3) A party suspending performance, whether before or after dispatch of the goods, must immediately give notice of the suspension to the other party and must continue with performance if the other party provides adequate assurance of his performance.

Article 72

(1) If prior to the date for performance of the contract it is clear that one of the parties will commit a fundamental breach of contract, the other party may declare the contract avoided.

(2) If time allows, the party intending to declare the contract avoided must give reasonable notice to the other party in order to permit him to provide adequate assurance of his performance.

(3) The requirements of the preceding paragraph do not apply if the other party has declared that he will not perform his obligations.

Article 73

(1) In the case of a contract for delivery of goods by instalments, if the failure of one party to perform any of his obligations in respect of any instalment constitutes a fundamental breach of contract with respect to that instalment, the other party may declare the contract avoided with respect to that instalment.

(2) If one party's failure to perform any of his obligations in respect of any instalment gives the other party good grounds to conclude that a

fundamental breach of contract will occur with respect to future instalments, he may declare the contract avoided for the future, provided that he does so within a reasonable time.

(3) A buyer who declares the contract avoided in respect of any delivery may, at the same time, declare it avoided in respect of deliveries already made or of future deliveries if, by reason of their interdependence, those deliveries could not be used for the purpose contemplated by the parties at the time of the conclusion of the contract.

SECTION II.
DAMAGES
Article 74

Damages for breach of contract by one party consist of a sum equal to the loss, including loss of profit, suffered by the other party as a consequence of the breach. Such damages may not exceed the loss which the party in breach foresaw or ought to have foreseen at the time of the conclusion of the contract, in the light of the facts and matters of which he then knew or ought to have known, as a possible consequence of the breach of contract.

Article 75

If the contract is avoided and if, in a reasonable manner and within a reasonable time after avoidance, the buyer has bought goods in replacement or the seller has resold the goods, the party claiming damages may recover the difference between the contract price and the price in the substitute transaction as well as any further damages recoverable under article 74.

Article 76

(1) If the contract is avoided and there is a current price for the goods, the party claiming damages may, if he has not made a purchase or resale under article 75, recover the difference between the price fixed by the contract and the current price at the time of avoidance as well as any further damages recoverable under article 74. If, however, the party claiming damages has avoided the contract after taking over the goods, the current price at the time of such taking over shall be applied instead of the current price at the time of avoidance.

(2) For the purpose of the preceding paragraph, the current price is the price prevailing at the place where delivery of the goods should have been made or, if there is no current price at that place, the price at such other place as serves as a reasonable substitute, making due allowance for differences in the cost of transporting the goods.

Article 77

A party who relies on a breach of contract must take such measures as are reasonable in the circumstances to mitigate the loss, including loss of profit, resulting from the breach. If he fails to take such measures, the party in breach may claim a reduction in the damages in the amount by which the loss should have been mitigated.

SECTION III.
INTEREST
Article 78

If a party fails to pay the price or any other sum that is in arrears, the other party is entitled to interest on it, without prejudice to any claim for damages recoverable under article 74.

SECTION IV.
EXEMPTIONS
Article 79

(1) A party is not liable for a failure to perform any of his obligations if he proves that the failure was due to an impediment beyond his control and that he could not reasonably be expected to have taken the impediment into account at the time of the conclusion of the contract or to have avoided or overcome it or its consequences.

(2) If the party's failure is due to the failure by a third person whom he has engaged to perform the whole or a part of the contract, that party is exempt from liability only if:

(a) he is exempt under the preceding paragraph; and

(b) the person whom he has so engaged would be so exempt if the provisions of that paragraph were applied to him.

(3) The exemption provided by this article has effect for the period during which the impediment exists.

(4) The party who fails to perform must give notice to the other party of the impediment and its effects on his ability to perform. If the notice is not received by the other party within a reasonable time after the party who fails to perform knew or ought to have known of the impediment, he is liable for damages resulting from such non-receipt.

(5) Nothing in this article prevents either party from exercising any right other than to claim damages under this Convention.

Article 80

A party may not rely on a failure of the other party to perform, to the extent that such failure was caused by the first party's act or omission.

SECTION V.

EFFECTS OF AVOIDANCE

Article 81

(1) Avoidance of the contract releases both parties from their obligations under it, subject to any damages which may be due. Avoidance does not affect any provision of the contract for the settlement of disputes or any other provision of the contract governing the rights and obligations of the parties consequent upon the avoidance of the contract.

(2) A party who has performed the contract either wholly or in part may claim restitution from the other party of whatever the first party has supplied or paid under the contract. If both parties are bound to make restitution, they must do so concurrently.

Article 82

(1) The buyer loses the right to declare the contract avoided or to require the seller to deliver substitute goods if it is impossible for him to make restitution of the goods substantially in the condition in which he received them.

(2) The preceding paragraph does not apply:

(a) if the impossibility of making restitution of the goods or of making restitution of the goods substantially in the condition in which the buyer received them is not due to his act or omission;

(b) if the goods or part of the goods have perished or deteriorated as a result of the examination provided for in article 38; or

(c) if the goods or part of the goods have been sold in the normal course of business or have been consumed or transformed by the buyer in the course of normal use before he discovered or ought to have discovered the lack of conformity.

Article 83

A buyer who has lost the right to declare the contract avoided or to require the seller to deliver substitute goods in accordance with article 82 retains all other remedies under the contract and this Convention.

Article 84

(1) If the seller is bound to refund the price, he must also pay interest on it, from the date on which the price was paid.

(2) The buyer must account to the seller for all benefits which he has derived from the goods or part of them:

(a) if he must make restitution of the goods or part of them; or

(b) if it is impossible for him to make restitution of all or part of the goods or to make restitution of all or part of the goods substantially in the condition in which he received them, but he has nevertheless declared the contract avoided or required the seller to deliver substitute goods.

SECTION VI.

PRESERVATION OF THE GOODS

Article 85

If the buyer is in delay in taking delivery of the goods or, where payment of the price and delivery of the goods are to be made concurrently, if he fails to pay the price, and the seller is either in possession of the goods or otherwise able to control their disposition, the seller must take such steps as are reasonable in the circumstances to preserve them. He is entitled to retain them until he has been reimbursed his reasonable expenses by the buyer.

Article 86

(1) If the buyer has received the goods and intends to exercise any right under the contract or this Convention to reject them, he must take

such steps to preserve them as are reasonable in the circumstances. He is entitled to retain them until he has been reimbursed his reasonable expenses by the seller.

(2) If goods dispatched to the buyer have been placed at his disposal at their destination and he exercises the right to reject them, he must take possession of them on behalf of the seller, provided that this can be done without payment of the price and without unreasonable inconvenience or unreasonable expense. This provision does not apply if the seller or a person authorized to take charge of the goods on his behalf is present at the destination. If the buyer takes possession of the goods under this paragraph, his rights and obligations are governed by the preceding paragraph.

Article 87

A party who is bound to take steps to preserve the goods may deposit them in a warehouse of a third person at the expense of the other party provided that the expense incurred is not unreasonable.

Article 88

(1) A party who is bound to preserve the goods in accordance with article 85 or 86 may sell them by any appropriate means if there has been an unreasonable delay by the other party in taking possession of the goods or in taking them back or in paying the price or the cost of preservation, provided that reasonable notice of the intention to sell has been given to the other party.

(2) If the goods are subject to rapid deterioration or their preservation would involve unreasonable expense, a party who is bound to preserve the goods in accordance with article 85 or 86 must take reasonable measures to sell them. To the extent possible he must give notice to the other party of his intention to sell.

(3) A party selling the goods has the right to retain out of the proceeds of sale an amount equal to the reasonable expenses of preserving the goods and of selling them. He must account to the other party for the balance.

PART IV. FINAL PROVISIONS
Article 89

The Secretary-General of the United Nations is hereby designated as the depositary for this Convention.

Article 90

This Convention does not prevail over any international agreement which has already been or may be entered into and which contains provisions concerning the matters governed by this Convention, provided that the parties have their places of business in States parties to such agreement.

Article 91

(1) This Convention is open for signature at the concluding meeting of the United Nations Conference on Contracts for the International Sale of Goods and will remain open for signature by all States at the Headquarters of the United Nations, New York until 30 September 1981.

(2) This Convention is subject to ratification, acceptance or approval by the signatory States.

(3) This Convention is open for accession by all States which are not signatory States as from the date it is open for signature.

(4) Instruments of ratification, acceptance, approval and accession are to be deposited with the Secretary-General of the United Nations.

Article 92

(1) A Contracting State may declare at the time of signature, ratification, acceptance, approval or accession that it will not be bound by Part II of this Convention or that it will not be bound by Part III of this Convention.

(2) A Contracting State which makes a declaration in accordance with the preceding paragraph in respect of Part II or Part III of this Convention is not to be considered a Contracting State within paragraph (1) of article 1 of this Convention in respect of matters governed by the Part to which the declaration applies.

Article 93

(1) If a Contracting State has two or more territorial units in which, according to its constitution, different systems of law are applicable in relation to the matters dealt with in this Convention, it may, at the time of signature, ratification, acceptance, approval or accession, declare that this Convention is to extend to all its territorial units or only to one or more of them, and may

amend its declaration by submitting another declaration at any time.

(2) These declarations are to be notified to the depositary and are to state expressly the territorial units to which the Convention extends.

(3) If, by virtue of a declaration under this article, this Convention extends to one or more but not all of the territorial units of a Contracting State, and if the place of business of a party is located in that State, this place of business, for the purposes of this Convention, is considered not to be in a Contracting State, unless it is in a territorial unit to which the Convention extends.

(4) If a Contracting State makes no declaration under paragraph (1) of this article, the Convention is to extend to all territorial units of that State.

Article 94

(1) Two or more Contracting States which have the same or closely related legal rules on matters governed by this Convention may at any time declare that the Convention is not to apply to contracts of sale or to their formation where the parties have their places of business in those States. Such declarations may be made jointly or by reciprocal unilateral declarations.

(2) A Contracting State which has the same or closely related legal rules on matters governed by this Convention as one or more non-Contracting States may at any time declare that the Convention is not to apply to contracts of sale or to their formation where the parties have their places of business in those States.

(3) If a State which is the object of a declaration under the preceding paragraph subsequently becomes a Contracting State, the declaration made will, as from the date on which the Convention enters into force in respect of the new Contracting State, have the effect of a declaration made under paragraph (1), provided that the new Contracting State joins in such declaration or makes a reciprocal unilateral declaration.

Article 95

Any State may declare at the time of the deposit of its instrument of ratification, acceptance, approval or accession that it will not be bound by subparagraph (1)(b) of article 1 of this Convention.

[The United States has declared a reservation to CISG under Article 95].

Article 96

A Contracting State whose legislation requires contracts of sale to be concluded in or evidenced by writing may at any time make a declaration in accordance with article 12 that any provision of article 11, article 29, or Part II of this Convention, that allows a contract of sale or its modification or termination by agreement or any offer, acceptance, or other indication of intention to be made in any form other than in writing, does not apply where any party has his place of business in that State.

Article 97

(1) Declarations made under this Convention at the time of signature are subject to confirmation upon ratification, acceptance or approval.

(2) Declarations and confirmations of declarations are to be in writing and be formally notified to the depositary.

(3) A declaration takes effect simultaneously with the entry into force of this Convention in respect of the State concerned. However, a declaration of which the depositary receives formal notification after such entry into force takes effect on the first day of the month following the expiration of six months after the date of its receipt by the depositary. Reciprocal unilateral declarations under article 94 take effect on the first day of the month following the expiration of six months after the receipt of the latest declaration by the depositary.

(4) Any State which makes a declaration under this Convention may withdraw it at any time by a formal notification in writing addressed to the depositary. Such withdrawal is to take effect on the first day of the month following the expiration of six months after the date of the receipt of the notification by the depositary.

(5) A withdrawal of a declaration made under article 94 renders inoperative, as from the date on which the withdrawal takes effect, any reciprocal declaration made by another State under that article.

Article 98

No reservations are permitted except those expressly authorized in this Convention.

Article 99

(1) This Convention enters into force, subject to the provisions of paragraph (6) of this article, on the first day of the month following the expiration of twelve months after the date of deposit of the tenth instrument of ratification, acceptance, approval or accession, including an instrument which contains a declaration made under article 92.

(2) When a State ratifies, accepts, approves or accedes to this Convention after the deposit of the tenth instrument of ratification, acceptance, approval or accession, this Convention, with the exception of the Part excluded, enters into force in respect of that State, subject to the provisions of paragraph (6) of this article, on the first day of the month following the expiration of twelve months after the date of the deposit of its instrument of ratification, acceptance, approval or accession.

(3) A State which ratifies, accepts, approves or accedes to this Convention and is a party to either or both the Convention relating to a Uniform Law on the Formation of Contracts for the International Sale of Goods done at The Hague on 1 July 1964 (1964 Hague Formation Convention) and the Convention relating to a Uniform Law on the International Sale of Goods done at The Hague on 1 July 1964 (1964 Hague Sales Convention) shall at the same time denounce, as the case may be, either or both the 1964 Hague Sales Convention and the 1964 Hague Formation Convention by notifying the Government of the Netherlands to that effect.

(4) A State party to the 1964 Hague Sales Convention which ratifies, accepts, approves or accedes to the present Convention and declares or has declared under article 92 that it will not be bound by Part II of this Convention shall at the time of ratification, acceptance, approval or accession denounce the 1964 Hague Sales Convention by notifying the Government of the Netherlands to that effect.

(5) A State party to the 1964 Hague Formation Convention which ratifies, accepts, approves or accedes to the present Convention and declares or has declared under article 92 that it will not be bound by Part III of this Convention shall at the time of ratification, acceptance, approval or accession denounce the 1964 Hague Formation Convention by notifying the Government of the Netherlands to that effect.

(6) For the purpose of this article, ratifications, acceptances, approvals and accessions in respect of this Convention by States parties to the 1964 Hague Formation Convention or to the 1964 Hague Sales Convention shall not be effective until such denunciations as may be required on the part of those States in respect of the latter two Conventions have themselves become effective. The depositary of this Convention shall consult with the Government of the Netherlands, as the depositary of the 1964 Convention, so as to ensure necessary co-ordination in this respect.

Article 100

(1) This Convention applies to the formation of a contract only when the proposal for concluding the contract is made on or after the date when the Convention enters into force in respect of the Contracting States referred to in subparagraph (1)(a) or the Contracting State referred to in subparagraph (1)(b) of article 1.

(2) This Convention applies only to contracts concluded on or after the date when the Convention enters into force in respect of the Contracting States referred to in subparagraph (1)(a) or the Contracting State referred to in subparagraph (1)(b) of article 1.

Article 101

(1) A Contracting State may denounce this Convention, or Part II or Part III of the Convention, by a formal notification in writing addressed to the depositary.

(2) The denunciation takes effect on the first day of the month following the expiration of twelve months after the notification is received by the depositary. Where a longer period for the denunciation to take effect is specified in the notification, the denunciation takes effect upon the expiration of such longer period after the notification is received by the depositary.

ELECTRONIC SIGNATURES IN GLOBAL AND NATIONAL COMMERCE ACT (ESIGN)

15 U.S.C.A. §§ 7001–7031

Current through April 9, 2007; P.L. 110–17

TABLE OF CONTENTS

Subchapter I—Electronic Records and Signatures in Commerce

Sec.
7001. General Rule of Validity.
7002. Exemption to Preemption.
7003. Specific Exceptions.
7004. Applicability to Federal and State Governments.
7005. Studies.
7006. Definitions.

Subchapter II—Transferable Records

7021. Transferable Records.

Subchapter III—Promotion of International Electronic Commerce.

7031. Principles Governing the Use of Electronic Signatures in International Transactions.

---

§ 7001. General Rule of Validity

(a) In general

Notwithstanding any statute, regulation, or other rule of law (other than this subchapter and subchapter II of this chapter), with respect to any transaction in or affecting interstate or foreign commerce—

(1) a signature, contract, or other record relating to such transaction may not be denied legal effect, validity, or enforceability solely because it is in electronic form; and

(2) a contract relating to such transaction may not be denied legal effect, validity, or enforceability solely because an electronic signature or electronic record was used in its formation.

(b) Preservation of rights and obligations

This subchapter does not—

(1) limit, alter, or otherwise affect any requirement imposed by a statute, regulation, or rule of law relating to the rights and obligations of persons under such statute, regulation, or rule of law other than a requirement that contracts or other records be written, signed, or in nonelectronic form; or

(2) require any person to agree to use or accept electronic records or electronic signatures, other than a governmental agency with respect to a record other than a contract to which it is a party.

(c) Consumer disclosures

(1) Consent to electronic records

Notwithstanding subsection (a), if a statute, regulation, or other rule of law requires that information relating to a transaction or transactions in or affecting interstate or foreign commerce be provided or made available to a consumer in writing, the use of an electronic record to provide or make available (whichever is required) such information satisfies the requirement that such information be in writing if—

(A) the consumer has affirmatively consented to such use and has not withdrawn such consent;

(B) the consumer, prior to consenting, is provided with a clear and conspicuous statement—

(i) informing the consumer of (I) any right or option of the consumer to have the record provided or made available on paper or in nonelectronic form, and (II)

1293

the right of the consumer to withdraw the consent to have the record provided or made available in an electronic form and of any conditions, consequences (which may include termination of the parties' relationship), or fees in the event of such withdrawal;

(ii) informing the consumer of whether the consent applies (I) only to the particular transaction which gave rise to the obligation to provide the record, or (II) to identified categories of records that may be provided or made available during the course of the parties' relationship;

(iii) describing the procedures the consumer must use to withdraw consent as provided in clause (i) and to update information needed to contact the consumer electronically; and

(iv) informing the consumer (I) how, after the consent, the consumer may, upon request, obtain a paper copy of an electronic record, and (II) whether any fee will be charged for such copy;

(C) the consumer—

(i) prior to consenting, is provided with a statement of the hardware and software requirements for access to and retention of the electronic records; and

(ii) consents electronically, or confirms his or her consent electronically, in a manner that reasonably demonstrates that the consumer can access information in the electronic form that will be used to provide the information that is the subject of the consent; and

(D) after the consent of a consumer in accordance with subparagraph (A), if a change in the hardware or software requirements needed to access or retain electronic records creates a material risk that the consumer will not be able to access or retain a subsequent electronic record that was the subject of the consent, the person providing the electronic record—

(i) provides the consumer with a statement of (I) the revised hardware and software requirements for access to and retention of the electronic records, and (II) the

right to withdraw consent without the imposition of any fees for such withdrawal and without the imposition of any condition or consequence that was not disclosed under subparagraph (B)(i); and

(ii) again complies with subparagraph (C).

(2) Other rights

(A) Preservation of consumer protections

Nothing in this subchapter affects the content or timing of any disclosure or other record required to be provided or made available to any consumer under any statute, regulation, or other rule of law.

(B) Verification or acknowledgment

If a law that was enacted prior to this chapter expressly requires a record to be provided or made available by a specified method that requires verification or acknowledgment of receipt, the record may be provided or made available electronically only if the method used provides verification or acknowledgment of receipt (whichever is required).

(3) Effect of failure to obtain electronic consent or confirmation of consent

The legal effectiveness, validity, or enforceability of any contract executed by a consumer shall not be denied solely because of the failure to obtain electronic consent or confirmation of consent by that consumer in accordance with paragraph (1)(C)(ii).

(4) Prospective effect

Withdrawal of consent by a consumer shall not affect the legal effectiveness, validity, or enforceability of electronic records provided or made available to that consumer in accordance with paragraph (1) prior to implementation of the consumer's withdrawal of consent. A consumer's withdrawal of consent shall be effective within a reasonable period of time after receipt of the withdrawal by the provider of the record. Failure to comply with paragraph (1)(D) may, at the election of the consumer, be treated as a withdrawal of consent for purposes of this paragraph.

(5) Prior consent

This subsection does not apply to any records that are provided or made available to a consumer who has consented prior to the effective date of this subchapter to receive such records in electronic form as permitted by any statute, regulation, or other rule of law.

(6) Oral communications

An oral communication or a recording of an oral communication shall not qualify as an electronic record for purposes of this subsection except as otherwise provided under applicable law.

(d) Retention of contracts and records

(1) Accuracy and accessibility

If a statute, regulation, or other rule of law requires that a contract or other record relating to a transaction in or affecting interstate or foreign commerce be retained, that requirement is met by retaining an electronic record of the information in the contract or other record that—

(A) accurately reflects the information set forth in the contract or other record; and

(B) remains accessible to all persons who are entitled to access by statute, regulation, or rule of law, for the period required by such statute, regulation, or rule of law, in a form that is capable of being accurately reproduced for later reference, whether by transmission, printing, or otherwise.

(2) Exception

A requirement to retain a contract or other record in accordance with paragraph (1) does not apply to any information whose sole purpose is to enable the contract or other record to be sent, communicated, or received.

(3) Originals

If a statute, regulation, or other rule of law requires a contract or other record relating to a transaction in or affecting interstate or foreign commerce to be provided, available, or retained in its original form, or provides consequences if the contract or other record is not provided, available, or retained in its original form, that statute, regulation, or rule of law is satisfied by an electronic record that complies with paragraph (1).

(4) Checks

If a statute, regulation, or other rule of law requires the retention of a check, that requirement is satisfied by retention of an electronic record of the information on the front and back of the check in accordance with paragraph (1).

(e) Accuracy and ability to retain contracts and other records

Notwithstanding subsection (a), if a statute, regulation, or other rule of law requires that a contract or other record relating to a transaction in or affecting interstate or foreign commerce be in writing, the legal effect, validity, or enforceability of an electronic record of such contract or other record may be denied if such electronic record is not in a form that is capable of being retained and accurately reproduced for later reference by all parties or persons who are entitled to retain the contract or other record.

(f) Proximity

Nothing in this subchapter affects the proximity required by any statute, regulation, or other rule of law with respect to any warning, notice, disclosure, or other record required to be posted, displayed, or publicly affixed.

(g) Notarization and acknowledgment

If a statute, regulation, or other rule of law requires a signature or record relating to a transaction in or affecting interstate or foreign commerce to be notarized, acknowledged, verified, or made under oath, that requirement is satisfied if the electronic signature of the person authorized to perform those acts, together with all other information required to be included by other applicable statute, regulation, or rule of law, is attached to or logically associated with the signature or record.

(h) Electronic agents

A contract or other record relating to a transaction in or affecting interstate or foreign commerce may not be denied legal effect, validity, or enforceability solely because its formation, creation, or delivery involved the action of one or more electronic agents so long as the action of any such electronic agent is legally attributable to the person to be bound.

(i) Insurance

It is the specific intent of the Congress that this subchapter and subchapter II of this chapter apply to the business of insurance.

(j) Insurance agents and brokers

An insurance agent or broker acting under the direction of a party that enters into a contract by means of an electronic record or electronic signature may not be held liable for any deficiency in the electronic procedures agreed to by the parties under that contract if—

(1) the agent or broker has not engaged in negligent, reckless, or intentional tortious conduct;

(2) the agent or broker was not involved in the development or establishment of such electronic procedures; and

(3) the agent or broker did not deviate from such procedures.

§ 7002. Exemption to Preemption

(a) In general

A State statute, regulation, or other rule of law may modify, limit, or supersede the provisions of section 7001 of this title with respect to State law only if such statute, regulation, or rule of law—

(1) constitutes an enactment or adoption of the Uniform Electronic Transactions Act as approved and recommended for enactment in all the States by the National Conference of Commissioners on Uniform State Laws in 1999, except that any exception to the scope of such Act enacted by a State under section 3(b)(4) of such Act shall be preempted to the extent such exception is inconsistent with this subchapter or subchapter II of this chapter, or would not be permitted under paragraph (2)(A)(ii) of this subsection; or

(2)(A) specifies the alternative procedures or requirements for the use or acceptance (or both) of electronic records or electronic signatures to establish the legal effect, validity, or enforceability of contracts or other records, if—

(i) such alternative procedures or requirements are consistent with this subchapter and subchapter II of this chapter; and

(ii) such alternative procedures or requirements do not require, or accord greater legal status or effect to, the implementation or application of a specific technology or technical specification for performing the functions of creating, storing, generating, receiving, communicating, or authenticating electronic records or electronic signatures; and

(B) if enacted or adopted after June 30, 2000, makes specific reference to this chapter.

(b) Exceptions for actions by States as market participants

Subsection (a)(2)(A)(ii) shall not apply to the statutes, regulations, or other rules of law governing procurement by any State, or any agency or instrumentality thereof.

(c) Prevention of circumvention

Subsection (a) does not permit a State to circumvent this subchapter or subchapter II of this chapter through the imposition of nonelectronic delivery methods under section 8(b)(2) of the Uniform Electronic Transactions Act.

§ 7003. Specific Exceptions

(a) Excepted requirements

The provisions of section 7001 of this title shall not apply to a contract or other record to the extent it is governed by—

(1) a statute, regulation, or other rule of law governing the creation and execution of wills, codicils, or testamentary trusts;

(2) a State statute, regulation, or other rule of law governing adoption, divorce, or other matters of family law; or

(3) the Uniform Commercial Code, as in effect in any State, other than sections 1–107 and 1–206 and Articles 2 and 2A.

(b) Additional exceptions

The provisions of section 7001 of this title shall not apply to—

(1) court orders or notices, or official court documents (including briefs, pleadings, and other writings) required to be executed in connection with court proceedings;

(2) any notice of—

(A) the cancellation or termination of utility services (including water, heat, and power);

(B) default, acceleration, repossession, foreclosure, or eviction, or the right to cure, under a credit agreement secured by, or a rental agreement for, a primary residence of an individual;

(C) the cancellation or termination of health insurance or benefits or life insurance benefits (excluding annuities); or

(D) recall of a product, or material failure of a product, that risks endangering health or safety; or

(3) any document required to accompany any transportation or handling of hazardous materials, pesticides, or other toxic or dangerous materials.

(c) Review of exceptions

(1) Evaluation required

The Secretary of Commerce, acting through the Assistant Secretary for Communications and Information, shall review the operation of the exceptions in subsections (a) and (b) to evaluate, over a period of 3 years, whether such exceptions continue to be necessary for the protection of consumers. Within 3 years after June 30, 2000, the Assistant Secretary shall submit a report to the Congress on the results of such e valuation.

(2) Determinations

If a Federal regulatory agency, with respect to matter within its jurisdiction, determines after notice and an opportunity for public comment, and publishes a finding, that one or more such exceptions are no longer necessary for the protection of consumers and eliminating such exceptions will not increase the material risk of harm to consumers, such agency may extend the application of section 7001 of this title to the exceptions identified in such finding.

§ 7004. Applicability to Federal and State Governments

(a) Filing and access requirements

Subject to subsection (c)(2), nothing in this subchapter limits or supersedes any requirement by a Federal regulatory agency, self-regulatory organization, or State regulatory agency that records be filed with such agency or organization in accordance with specified standards or formats.

(b) Preservation of existing rulemaking authority

(1) Use of authority to interpret

Subject to paragraph (2) and subsection (c), a Federal regulatory agency or State regulatory agency that is responsible for rulemaking under any other statute may interpret section 7001 of this title with respect to such statute through—

(A) the issuance of regulations pursuant to a statute; or

(B) to the extent such agency is authorized by statute to issue orders or guidance, the issuance of orders or guidance of general applicability that are publicly available and published (in the Federal Register in the case of an order or guidance issued by a Federal regulatory agency).

This paragraph does not grant any Federal regulatory agency or State regulatory agency authority to issue regulations, orders, or guidance pursuant to any statute that does not authorize such issuance.

(2) Limitations on interpretation authority

Notwithstanding paragraph (1), a Federal regulatory agency shall not adopt any regulation, order, or guidance described in paragraph (1), and a State regulatory agency is preempted by section 101 from adopting any regulation, order, or guidance described in paragraph (1), unless—

(A) such regulation, order, or guidance is consistent with section 7001 of this title;

(B) such regulation, order, or guidance does not add to the requirements of such section; and

(C) such agency finds, in connection with the issuance of such regulation, order, or guidance, that—

(i) there is a substantial justification for the regulation, order, or guidance;

(ii) the methods selected to carry out that purpose—

(I) are substantially equivalent to the requirements imposed on records that are not electronic records; and

(II) will not impose unreasonable costs on the acceptance and use of electronic records; and

(iii) the methods selected to carry out that purpose do not require, or accord greater legal status or effect to, the implementation or application of a specific technology or technical specification for performing the functions of creating, storing, generating, receiving, communicating, or authenticating electronic records or electronic signatures.

(3) Performance standards

(A) Accuracy, record integrity, accessibility

Notwithstanding paragraph (2)(C)(iii), a Federal regulatory agency or State regulatory agency may interpret section 7001(d) of this title to specify performance standards to assure accuracy, record integrity, and accessibility of records that are required to be retained. Such performance standards may be specified in a manner that imposes a requirement in violation of paragraph (2)(C)(iii) if the requirement (i) serves an important governmental objective; and (ii) is substantially related to the achievement of that objective. Nothing in this paragraph shall be construed to grant any Federal regulatory agency or State regulatory agency authority to require use of a particular type of software or hardware in order to comply with section 7001(d) of this title.

(B) Paper or printed form

Notwithstanding subsection (c)(1), a Federal regulatory agency or State regulatory agency may interpret section 7001(d) of this title to require retention of a record in a tangible printed or paper form if—

(i) there is a compelling governmental interest relating to law enforcement or national security for imposing such requirement; and

(ii) imposing such requirement is essential to attaining such interest.

(4) Exceptions for actions by Government as market participant

Paragraph (2)(C)(iii) shall not apply to the statutes, regulations, or other rules of law governing procurement by the Federal or any State government, or any agency or instrumentality thereof.

(c) Additional limitations

(1) Reimposing paper prohibited

Nothing in subsection (b) (other than paragraph (3)(B) thereof) shall be construed to grant any Federal regulatory agency or State regulatory agency authority to impose or reimpose any requirement that a record be in a tangible printed or paper form.

(2) Continuing obligation under Government Paperwork Elimination Act

Nothing in subsection (a) or (b) relieves any Federal regulatory agency of its obligations under the Government Paperwork Elimination Act (title XVII of Public Law 105–277).

(d) Authority to exempt from consent provision

(1) In general

A Federal regulatory agency may, with respect to matter within its jurisdiction, by regulation or order issued after notice and an opportunity for public comment, exempt without condition a specified category or type of record from the requirements relating to consent in section 7001(c) of this title if such exemption is necessary to eliminate a substantial burden on electronic commerce and will not increase the material risk of harm to consumers.

(2) Prospectuses

Within 30 days after June 30, 2000, the Securities and Exchange Commission shall issue a regulation or order pursuant to paragraph (1) exempting from section 7001(c) of this title any records that are required to be provided in order to allow advertising, sales literature, or other information concerning a security issued by an investment company that is registered under the Investment Company Act of 1940, or concerning the issuer thereof, to be excluded from the definition of a prospectus under section 77b(a)(10)(A) of this title.

(e) Electronic letters of agency

The Federal Communications Commission shall not hold any contract for telecommunications service or letter of agency for a preferred carrier change, that otherwise complies with the Commission's rules, to be legally ineffective, invalid, or unenforceable solely because an electronic record or electronic signature was used in its formation or authorization.

§ 7005. Studies

(a) Delivery

Within 12 months after June 30, 2000, the Secretary of Commerce shall conduct an inquiry regarding the effectiveness of the delivery of electronic records to consumers using electronic mail as compared with delivery of written records via the United States Postal Service and private express mail services. The Secretary shall submit a report to the Congress regarding the results of such inquiry by the conclusion of such 12–month period.

(b) Study of electronic consent

Within 12 months after June 30, 2000, the Secretary of Commerce and the Federal Trade Commission shall submit a report to the Congress evaluating any benefits provided to consumers by the procedure required by section 7001(c)(1)(C)(ii) of this title; any burdens imposed on electronic commerce by that provision; whether the benefits outweigh the burdens; whether the absence of the procedure required by section 7001(c)(1)(C)(ii) of this title would increase the incidence of fraud directed against consumers; and suggesting any revisions to the provision deemed appropriate by the Secretary and the Commission. In conducting this evaluation, the Secretary and the Commission shall solicit comment from the general public, consumer representatives, and electronic commerce businesses.

§ 7006. Definitions

For purposes of this subchapter:

(1) Consumer

The term "consumer" means an individual who obtains, through a transaction, products or services which are used primarily for personal, family, or household purposes, and also means the legal representative of such an individual.

(2) Electronic

The term "electronic" means relating to technology having electrical, digital, magnetic, wireless, optical, electromagnetic, or similar capabilities.

(3) Electronic agent

The term "electronic agent" means a computer program or an electronic or other automated means used independently to initiate an action or respond to electronic records or performances in whole or in part without review or action by an individual at the time of the action or response.

(4) Electronic record

The term "electronic record" means a contract or other record created, generated, sent, communicated, received, or stored by electronic means.

(5) Electronic signature

The term "electronic signature" means an electronic sound, symbol, or process, attached to or logically associated with a contract or other record and executed or adopted by a person with the intent to sign the record.

(6) Federal regulatory agency

The term "Federal regulatory agency" means an agency, as that term is defined in section 552(f) of Title 5.

(7) Information

The term "information" means data, text, images, sounds, codes, computer programs, software, databases, or the like.

(8) Person

The term "person" means an individual, corporation, business trust, estate, trust, partnership, limited liability company, association, joint venture, governmental agency, public corporation, or any other legal or commercial entity.

(9) Record

The term "record" means information that is inscribed on a tangible medium or that is stored in an electronic or other medium and is retrievable in perceivable form.

(10) Requirement

The term "requirement" includes a prohibition.

(11) Self-regulatory organization

The term "self-regulatory organization" means an organization or entity that is not a Federal regulatory agency or a State, but that is under the supervision of a Federal regulatory agency and is authorized under Federal law to adopt and administer rules applicable to its members that are enforced by such organization or entity, by a Federal regulatory agency, or by another self-regulatory organization.

(12) State

The term "State" includes the District of Columbia and the territories and possessions of the United States.

(13) Transaction

The term "transaction" means an action or set of actions relating to the conduct of business, consumer, or commercial affairs between two or more persons, including any of the following types of conduct—

(A) the sale, lease, exchange, licensing, or other disposition of (i) personal property, including goods and intangibles, (ii) services, and (iii) any combination thereof; and

(B) the sale, lease, exchange, or other disposition of any interest in real property, or any combination thereof.

Subchapter II—Transferable Records

§ 7021.   Transferable Records

(a) Definitions

For purposes of this section:
(1) Transferable record
The term "transferable record" means an electronic record that—

(A) would be a note under Article 3 of the Uniform Commercial Code if the electronic record were in writing;

(B) the issuer of the electronic record expressly has agreed is a transferable record; and

(C) relates to a loan secured by real property.

A transferable record may be executed using an electronic signature.

(2) Other definitions
The terms "electronic record", "electronic signature", and "person" have the same meanings provided in section 7006 of this title.

(b) Control

A person has control of a transferable record if a system employed for evidencing the transfer of interests in the transferable record reliably establishes that person as the person to which the transferable record was issued or transferred.

(c) Conditions

A system satisfies subsection (b), and a person is deemed to have control of a transferable record, if the transferable record is created, stored, and assigned in such a manner that—

(1) a single authoritative copy of the transferable record exists which is unique, identifiable, and, except as otherwise provided in paragraphs (4), (5), and (6), unalterable;

(2) the authoritative copy identifies the person asserting control as—

(A) the person to which the transferable record was issued; or

(B) if the authoritative copy indicates that the transferable record has been transferred, the person to which the transferable record was most recently transferred;

(3) the authoritative copy is communicated to and maintained by the person asserting control or its designated custodian;

(4) copies or revisions that add or change an identified assignee of the authoritative copy can be made only with the consent of the person asserting control;

(5) each copy of the authoritative copy and any copy of a copy is readily identifiable as a copy that is not the authoritative copy; and

(6) any revision of the authoritative copy is readily identifiable as authorized or unauthorized.

(d) Status as holder

Except as otherwise agreed, a person having control of a transferable record is the holder, as defined in section 1–201(20) of the Uniform Commercial Code, of the transferable record and has the same rights and defenses as a holder of an equivalent record or writing under the Uniform Commercial Code, including, if the applicable statutory requirements under section 3–302(a),

9–308, or revised section 9–330 of the Uniform Commercial Code are satisfied, the rights and defenses of a holder in due course or a purchaser, respectively. Delivery, possession, and endorsement are not required to obtain or exercise any of the rights under this subsection.

(e) Obligor rights

Except as otherwise agreed, an obligor under a transferable record has the same rights and defenses as an equivalent obligor under equivalent records or writings under the Uniform Commercial Code.

(f) Proof of control

If requested by a person against which enforcement is sought, the person seeking to enforce the transferable record shall provide reasonable proof that the person is in control of the transferable record. Proof may include access to the authoritative copy of the transferable record and related business records sufficient to review the terms of the transferable record and to establish the identity of the person having control of the transferable record.

(g) UCC references

For purposes of this subsection, all references to the Uniform Commercial Code are to the Uniform Commercial Code as in effect in the jurisdiction the law of which governs the transferable record.

Subchapter III—Promotion of International Electronic Commerce

§ 7031. Principles Governing the Use of Electronic Signatures in International Transactions

(a) Promotion of electronic signatures

(1) Required actions
The Secretary of Commerce shall promote the acceptance and use, on an international basis, of electronic signatures in accordance with the principles specified in paragraph (2) and in a manner consistent with section 7001 of this title. The Secretary of Commerce shall take all actions necessary in a manner consistent with such principles to eliminate or reduce, to the maximum extent possible, the impediments to commerce in electronic signatures, for the purpose of facilitating the development of interstate and foreign commerce.

(2) Principles
The principles specified in this paragraph are the following:

(A) Remove paper-based obstacles to electronic transactions by adopting relevant principles from the Model Law on Electronic Commerce adopted in 1996 by the United Nations Commission on International Trade Law.

(B) Permit parties to a transaction to determine the appropriate authentication technologies and implementation models for their transactions, with assurance that those technologies and implementation models will be recognized and enforced.

(C) Permit parties to a transaction to have the opportunity to prove in court or other proceedings that their authentication approaches and their transactions are valid.

(D) Take a nondiscriminatory approach to electronic signatures and authentication methods from other jurisdictions.

(b) Consultation

In conducting the activities required by this section, the Secretary shall consult with users and providers of electronic signature products and services and other interested persons.

(c) Definitions

As used in this section, the terms "electronic record" and "electronic signature" have the same meanings provided in section 7006 of this title.

MAGNUSON–MOSS WARRANTY—FEDERAL TRADE COMMISSION IMPROVEMENT ACT

15 U.S.C.A. §§ 2301–2312

Current through April 9, 2007; P.L. 110–17

TITLE I. CONSUMER PRODUCT WARRANTIES

Sec.
101. Definitions.
102. Warranty provisions.
103. Designation of warranties.
104. Federal minimum standards for warranty.
105. Full and limited warranting of a consumer product.
106. Service contracts.

Sec.
107. Designation of representatives.
108. Limitation on disclaimer of implied warranties.
109. Commission rules.
110. Remedies.
111. Effect on other laws.
112. Effective date.

§ 101. Definitions [15 U.S.C.A. § 2301]

For the purposes of this title:

(1) The term "consumer product" means any tangible personal property which is distributed in commerce and which is normally used for personal, family, or household purposes (including any such property intended to be attached to or installed in any real property without regard to whether it is so attached or installed).

(2) The term "Commission" means the Federal Trade Commission.

(3) The term "consumer" means a buyer (other than for purposes of resale) of any consumer product, any person to whom such product is transferred during the duration of an implied or written warranty (or service contract) applicable to the product, and any other person who is entitled by the terms of such warranty (or service contract) or under applicable State law to enforce against the warrantor (or service contractor) the obligations of the warranty (or service contract).

(4) The term "supplier" means any person engaged in the business of making a consumer product directly or indirectly available to consumers.

(5) The term "warrantor" means any supplier or other person who gives or offers to give a written warranty or who is or may be obligated under an implied warranty.

(6) The term "written warranty" means—

(A) any written affirmation of fact or written promise made in connection with the sale of a consumer product by a supplier to a buyer which relates to the nature of the material or workmanship and affirms or promises that such material or workmanship is defect free or will meet a specified level of performance over a specified period of time, or

(B) any undertaking in writing in connection with the sale by a supplier of a consumer product to refund, repair, replace, or take other remedial action with respect to such product in the event that such product fails to meet the specifications set forth in the undertaking,

which written affirmation, promise, or undertaking becomes part of the basis of the bargain between a supplier and a buyer for purposes other than resale of such product.

(7) The term "implied warranty" means an implied warranty arising under State law (as modified by sections 108 and 104(a)) in connection with the sale by a supplier of a consumer product.

(8) The term "service contract" means a contract in writing to perform, over a fixed period of time or for a specified duration, services relating to the maintenance or repair (or both) of a consumer product.

(9) The term "reasonable and necessary maintenance" consists of those operations (A) which the consumer reasonably can be expected to perform or have performed and (B) which are necessary to keep any consumer product performing its intended function and operating at a reasonable level of performance.

(10) The term "remedy" means whichever of the following actions the warrantor elects:

(A) repair,

(B) replacement, or

(C) refund;

except that the warrantor may not elect refund unless (i) the warrantor is unable to provide replacement and repair is not commercially practicable or cannot be timely made, or (ii) the consumer is willing to accept such refund.

(11) The term "replacement" means furnishing a new consumer product which is identical or reasonably equivalent to the warranted consumer product.

(12) The term "refund" means refunding the actual purchase price (less reasonable depreciation based on actual use where permitted by rules of the Commission).

(13) The term "distributed in commerce" means sold in commerce, introduced or delivered for introduction into commerce, or held for sale or distribution after introduction into commerce.

(14) The term "commerce" means trade, traffic, commerce, or transportation—

(A) between a place in a State and any place outside thereof, or

(B) which affects trade, traffic, commerce, or transportation described in subparagraph (A).

(15) The term "State" means a State, the District of Columbia, the Commonwealth of Puerto Rico, the Virgin Islands, Guam, the Canal Zone, or American Samoa. The term "State law" includes a law of the United States applicable only to the District of Columbia or only to a territory or possession of the United States; and the term "Federal law" excludes any State law.

§ 102. Warranty provisions [15 U.S.C.A. § 2302]

(a) In order to improve the adequacy of information available to consumers, prevent deception, and improve competition in the marketing of consumer products, any warrantor warranting a consumer product to a consumer by means of a written warranty shall, to the extent required by rules of the Commission, fully and conspicuously disclose in simple and readily understood language the terms and conditions of such warranty. Such rules may require inclusion in the written warranty of any of the following items among others:

(1) The clear identification of the names and addresses of the warrantors.

(2) The identity of the party or parties to whom the warranty is extended.

(3) The products or parts covered.

(4) A statement of what the warrantor will do in the event of a defect, malfunction, or failure to conform with such written warranty—at whose expense—and for what period of time.

(5) A statement of what the consumer must do and expenses he must bear.

(6) Exceptions and exclusions from the terms of the warranty.

(7) The step-by-step procedure which the consumer should take in order to obtain performance of any obligation under the warranty, including the identification of any person or class of persons authorized to perform the obligations set forth in the warranty.

(8) Information respecting the availability of any informal dispute settlement procedure of-

fered by the warrantor and a recital, where the warranty so provides, that the purchaser may be required to resort to such procedure before pursuing any legal remedies in the courts.

(9) A brief, general description of the legal remedies available to the consumer.

(10) The time at which the warrantor will perform any obligations under the warranty.

(11) The period of time within which, after notice of a defect, malfunction, or failure to conform with the warranty, the warrantor will perform any obligations under the warranty.

(12) The characteristics or properties of the products, or parts thereof, that are not covered by the warranty.

(13) The elements of the warranty in words or phrases which would not mislead a reasonable, average consumer as to the nature or scope of the warranty.

(b)(1)(A) The Commission shall prescribe rules requiring that the terms of any written warranty on a consumer product be made available to the consumer (or prospective consumer) prior to the sale of the product to him.

(B) The Commission may prescribe rules for determining the manner and form in which information with respect to any written warranty of a consumer product shall be clearly and conspicuously presented or displayed so as not to mislead the reasonable, average consumer, when such information is contained in advertising, labeling, point-of-sale material, or other representations in writing.

(2) Nothing in this chapter (other than paragraph (3) of this subsection) shall be deemed to authorize the Commission to prescribe the duration of written warranties given or to require that a consumer product or any of its components be warranted.

(3) The Commission may prescribe rules for extending the period of time a written warranty or service contract is in effect to correspond with any period of time in excess of a reasonable period (not less than 10 days) during which the consumer is deprived of the use of such consumer product by reason of failure of the product to conform with the written warranty or by reason of the failure of the warrantor (or service contractor) to carry out such warranty (or service contract) within the peri-

od specified in the warranty (or service contract).

(c) No warrantor of a consumer product may condition his written or implied warranty of such product on the consumer's using, in connection with such product, any article or service (other than article or service provided without charge under the terms of the warranty) which is identified by brand, trade, or corporate name; except that the prohibition of this subsection may be waived by the Commission if—

(1) the warrantor satisfies the Commission that the warranted product will function properly only if the article or service so identified is used in connection with the warranted product, and

(2) the Commission finds that such a waiver is in the public interest.

The Commission shall identify in the Federal Register, and permit public comment on, all applications for waiver of the prohibition of this subsection, and shall publish in the Federal Register its disposition of any such application, including the reasons therefor.

(d) The Commission may by rule devise detailed substantive warranty provisions which warrantors may incorporate by reference in their warranties.

(e) The provisions of this section apply only to warranties which pertain to consumer products actually costing the consumer more than $5.

§ 103. Designation of warranties [15 U.S.C.A. § 2303]

(a) Any warrantor warranting a consumer product by means of a written warranty shall clearly and conspicuously designate such warranty in the following manner, unless exempted from doing so by the Commission pursuant to subsection (c) of this section:

(1) If the written warranty meets the Federal minimum standards for warranty set forth in section 104 of this Act, then it shall be conspicuously designated a "full (statement of duration) warranty".

(2) If the written warranty does not meet the Federal minimum standards for warranty set forth in section 104 of this Act, then it shall

be conspicuously designated a "limited warranty".

(b) Sections 102, 103, and 104 shall not apply to statements or representations which are similar to expressions of general policy concerning customer satisfaction and which are not subject to any specific limitations.

(c) In addition to exercising the authority pertaining to disclosure granted in section 102 of this Title, the Commission may by rule determine when a written warranty does not have to be designated either "full (statement of duration)" or "limited" in accordance with this section.

(d) The provisions of subsections (a) and (c) of this section apply only to warranties which pertain to consumer products actually costing the consumer more than $10 and which are not designated "full (statement of duration) warranties".

§ 104. Federal minimum standards for warranty [15 U.S.C.A. § 2304]

(a) In order for a warrantor warranting a consumer product by means of a written warranty to meet the Federal minimum standards for warranty—

(1) such warrantor must as a minimum remedy such consumer product within a reasonable time and without charge, in the case of a defect, malfunction, or failure to conform with such written warranty;

(2) notwithstanding section 108(b), such warrantor may not impose any limitation on the duration of any implied warranty on the product;

(3) such warrantor may not exclude or limit consequential damages for breach of any written or implied warranty on such product, unless such exclusion or limitation conspicuously appears on the face of the warranty; and

(4) if the product (or a component part thereof) contains a defect or malfunction after a reasonable number of attempts by the warrantor to remedy defects or malfunctions in such product, such warrantor must permit the consumer to elect either a refund for, or replacement without charge of, such product or part (as the case may be). The Commission may by rule specify for purposes of this paragraph, what constitutes a reasonable number of attempts to remedy particular kinds of defects or malfunctions under different circumstances. If the warrantor replaces a component part of a consumer product, such replacement shall include installing the part in the product without charge.

(b)(1) In fulfilling the duties under subsection (a) respecting a written warranty, the warrantor shall not impose any duty other than notification upon any consumer as a condition of securing remedy of any consumer product which malfunctions, is defective, or does not conform to the written warranty, unless the warrantor has demonstrated in a rulemaking proceeding, or can demonstrate in an administrative or judicial enforcement proceeding (including private enforcement), or in an informal dispute settlement proceeding, that such a duty is reasonable.

(2) Notwithstanding paragraph (1), a warrantor may require, as a condition to replacement of, or refund for, any consumer product under subsection (a), that such consumer product shall be made available to the warrantor free and clear of liens and other encumbrances, except as otherwise provided by rule or order of the Commission in cases in which such a requirement would not be practicable.

(3) The Commission may, by rule define in detail the duties set forth in section 104(a) of this Act and the applicability of such duties to warrantors of different categories of consumer products with "full (statement of duration)" warranties.

(4) The duties under subsection (a) extend from the warrantor to each person who is a consumer with respect to the consumer product.

(c) The performance of the duties under subsection (a) of this section shall not be required of the warrantor if he can show that the defect, malfunction, or failure of any warranted consumer product to conform with a written warranty, was caused by damage (not resulting from defect or malfunction) while in the possession of the consumer, or unreasonable use (including failure to provide reasonable and necessary maintenance).

(d) For purposes of this section and of section 102(c), the term "without charge" means that the warrantor may not assess the consumer for any costs the warrantor or his representatives incur in connection with the required remedy of a warranted consumer product. An obligation under subsection (a)(1)(A) to remedy without charge does not necessarily require the warrantor to compensate the consumer for incidental expenses; however, if any incidental expenses are incurred because the remedy is not made within a reasonable time or because the warrantor imposed an unreasonable duty upon the consumer as a condition of securing remedy, then the consumer shall be entitled to recover reasonable incidental expenses which are so incurred in any action against the warrantor.

(e) If a supplier designates a warranty applicable to a consumer product as a "full (statement of duration)" warranty, then the warranty on such product shall, for purposes of any action under section 110(d) or under any State law, be deemed to incorporate at least the minimum requirements of this section and rules prescribed under this section.

§ 105. Full and limited warranting of a consumer product [15 U.S.C.A. § 2305]

Nothing in this title shall prohibit the selling of a consumer product which has both full and limited warranties if such warranties are clearly and conspicuously differentiated.

§ 106. Service contracts [15 U.S.C.A. § 2306]

(a) The Commission may prescribe by rule the manner and form in which the terms and conditions of service contracts shall be fully, clearly, and conspicuously disclosed.

(b) Nothing in this title shall be construed to prevent a supplier or warrantor from entering into a service contract with the consumer in addition to or in lieu of a written warranty if such contract fully, clearly, and conspicuously discloses its terms and conditions in simple and readily understood language.

§ 107. Designation of representatives [15 U.S.C.A. § 2307]

Nothing in this title shall be construed to prevent any warrantor from designating representatives to perform duties under the written or implied warranty: *Provided*, That such warrantor shall make reasonable arrangements for compensation of such designated representatives, but no such designation shall relieve the warrantor of his direct responsibilities to the consumer or make the representative a cowarrantor.

§ 108. Limitation on disclaimer of implied warranties [15 U.S.C.A. § 2308]

(a) No supplier may disclaim or modify (except as provided in subsection (b)) any implied warranty to a consumer with respect to such consumer product if (1) such supplier makes any written warranty to the consumer with respect to such consumer product, or (2) at the time of sale, or within 90 days thereafter, such supplier enters into a service contract with the consumer which applies to such consumer product.

(b) For purposes of this title (other than section 104(a)(2)), implied warranties may be limited in duration to the duration of a written warranty of reasonable duration, if such limitation is conscionable and is set forth in clear and unmistakable language and prominently displayed on the face of the warranty.

(c) A disclaimer, modification, or limitation made in violation of this section shall be ineffective for purposes of this title and State law.

§ 109. Commission rules [15 U.S.C.A. § 2309]

(a) Any rule prescribed under this title shall be prescribed in accordance with section 553 of title 5, United States Code; except that the Commission shall give interested persons an opportunity for oral presentations of data, views, and arguments, in addition to written submissions. A transcript shall be kept of any oral presentation. Any such rule shall be subject to judicial review under section 18(e) of the Federal Trade Commission Act (as amended by section 202 of this Act) in the same manner as rules prescribed under section 18(a)(1)(B) of such Act, except that section 18(e)(3)(B) of such Act shall not apply.

(b) The Commission shall initiate within one year after the date of enactment of this Act a rulemaking proceeding dealing with warranties and warranty practices in connection with the sale of used motor vehicles; and, to the extent necessary to supplement the protections offered the consumer by this title, shall prescribe rules dealing with such warranties and practices. In prescribing rules under this subsection, the Commission may exercise any authority it may have under this title, or other law, and in addition it may require disclosure that a used motor vehicle is sold without any warranty and specify the form and content of such disclosure.

§ 110.   Remedies [15 U.S.C.A. § 2310]

(a)(1) Congress hereby declares it to be its policy to encourage warrantors to establish procedures whereby consumer disputes are fairly and expeditiously settled through informal dispute settlement mechanisms.

(2) The Commission shall prescribe rules setting forth minimum requirements for any informal dispute settlement procedure which is incorporated into the terms of a written warranty to which any provision of this title applies. Such rules shall provide for participation in such procedure by independent or governmental entities.

(3) One or more warrantors may establish an informal dispute settlement procedure which meets the requirements of the Commission's rules under paragraph (2). If—

(A) a warrantor establishes such a procedure,

(B) such procedure, and its implementation, meets the requirements of such rules, and

(C) he incorporates in a written warranty a requirement that the consumer resort to such procedure before pursuing any legal remedy under this section respecting such warranty,

then (i) the consumer may not commence a civil action (other than a class action) under subsection (d) of this section unless he initially resorts to such procedure; and (ii) a class of consumers may not proceed in a class action under subsection (d) except to the extent the court determines necessary to establish the representative capacity of the named plaintiffs, unless the named plaintiffs (upon notifying the defendant that they are named plaintiffs in a class action with respect to a warranty obligation) initially resort to such procedure. In the case of such a class action which is brought in a district court of the United States, the representative capacity of the named plaintiffs shall be established in the application

of rule 23 of the Federal Rules of Civil Procedure. In any civil action arising out of a warranty obligation and relating to a matter considered in such a procedure, any decision in such procedure shall be admissible in evidence.

(4) The Commission on its own initiative may, or upon written complaint filed by any interested person shall, review the bona fide operation of any dispute settlement procedure resort to which is stated in a written warranty to be a prerequisite to pursuing a legal remedy under this section. If the Commission finds that such procedure or its implementation fails to comply with the requirements of the rules under paragraph (2), the Commission may take appropriate remedial action under any authority it may have under this title or any other provision of law.

(5) Until rules under paragraph (2) take effect, this subsection shall not affect the validity of any informal dispute settlement procedure respecting consumer warranties, but in any action under subsection (d), the court may invalidate any such procedure if it finds that such procedure is unfair.

(b) It shall be a violation of section 5(a)(1) of the Federal Trade Commission Act (15 U.S.C. 45(a)(1)) for any person to fail to comply with any requirement imposed on such person by this title (or a rule thereunder) or to violate any prohibition contained in this title (or a rule thereunder).

(c)(1) The district courts of the United States shall have jurisdiction of any action brought by the Attorney General (in his capacity as such), or by the Commission by any of its attorneys designated by it for such purpose, to restrain (A) any warrantor from making a deceptive warranty with respect to a consumer product, or (B) any person from failing to comply with any requirement imposed on such person by or pursuant to this title or from violating any prohibition contained in this title. Upon proper showing that, weighing the equities and considering the Commission's or Attorney General's likelihood of ultimate success, such action would be in the public interest and after notice to the defendant, a temporary restraining order or preliminary injunction may be granted without bond. In the case of an action brought by the Commission, if a complaint under section 5 of the Federal Trade

Commission Act is not filed within such period (not exceeding 10 days) as may be specified by the court after the issuance of the temporary restraining order or preliminary injunction, the order or injunction shall be dissolved by the court and be of no further force and effect. Any suit shall be brought in the district in which such person resides or transacts business. Whenever it appears to the court that the ends of justice require that other persons should be parties in the action, the court may cause them to be summoned whether or not they reside in the district in which the court is held, and to that end process may be served in any district.

(2) For the purposes of this subsection, the term "deceptive warranty" means (A) a written warranty which (i) contains an affirmation, promise, description, or representation which is either false or fraudulent, or which, in light of all of the circumstances, would mislead a reasonable individual exercising due care; or (ii) fails to contain information which is necessary in light of all of the circumstances, to make the warranty not misleading to a reasonable individual exercising due care; or (B) a written warranty created by the use of such terms as "guaranty" or "warranty", if the terms and conditions of such warranty so limit its scope and application as to deceive a reasonable individual.

(d)(1) Subject to subsections (a)(3) and (e), a consumer who is damaged by the failure of a supplier, warrantor, or service contractor to comply with any obligation under this title, or under a written warranty, implied warranty, or service contract, may bring suit for damages and other legal and equitable relief—

(A) in any court of competent jurisdiction in any State or the District of Columbia; or

(B) in an appropriate district court of the United States, subject to paragraph (3) of this subsection.

(2) If a consumer finally prevails in any action brought under paragraph (1) of this subsection, he may be allowed by the court to recover as part of the judgment a sum equal to the aggregate amount of cost and expenses (including attorneys' fees based on actual time expended) determined by the court to have been reasonably incurred by the plaintiff for or in connection with the commencement and prosecution of such action, unless the court in its discretion shall determine that such an award of attorneys' fees would be inappropriate.

(3) No claim shall be cognizable in a suit brought under paragraph (1)(B) of this subsection—

(A) if the amount in controversy of any individual claim is less than the sum or value of $25;

(B) if the amount in controversy is less than the sum or value of $50,000 (exclusive of interests and costs) computed on the basis of all claims to be determined in this suit; or

(C) if the action is brought as a class action, and the number of named plaintiffs is less than one hundred.

(e) No action (other than a class action or an action respecting a warranty to which subsection (a)(3) applies) may be brought under subsection (d) for failure to comply with any obligation under any written or implied warranty or service contract, and a class of consumers may not proceed in a class action under such subsection with respect to such a failure except to the extent the court determines necessary to establish the representative capacity of the named plaintiffs, unless the person obligated under the warranty or service contract is afforded a reasonable opportunity to cure such failure to comply. In the case of such a class action (other than a class action respecting a warranty to which subsection (a)(3) applies) brought under subsection (d) for breach of any written or implied warranty or service contract, such reasonable opportunity will be afforded by the named plaintiffs and they shall at that time notify the defendant that they are acting on behalf of the class. In the case of such a class action which is brought in a district court of the United States, the representative capacity of the named plaintiffs shall be established in the application of rule 23 of the Federal Rules of Civil Procedure.

(f) For purposes of this section, only the warrantor actually making a written affirmation of fact, promise, or undertaking shall be deemed to have created a written warranty, and any rights arising thereunder may be enforced under this section only against such warrantor and no other person.

§ 111. Effect on other laws [15 U.S.C.A. § 2311]

(a)(1) Nothing contained in this title shall be construed to repeal, invalidate, or supersede the Federal Trade Commission Act (15 U.S.C. 41 et seq.) or any statute defined therein as an Antitrust Act.

(2) Nothing in this title shall be construed to repeal, invalidate, or supersede the Federal Seed Act (7 U.S.C. 1551–1611) and nothing in this title shall apply to seed for planting.

(b)(1) Nothing in this title shall invalidate or restrict any right or remedy of any consumer under State law or any other Federal law.

(2) Nothing in this title (other than sections 108 and 104(a)(2) and (4)) shall (A) affect the liability of, or impose liability on, any person for personal injury, or (B) supersede any provision of State law regarding consequential damages for injury to the person or other injury.

(c)(1) Except as provided in subsection (b) and in paragraph (2) of this subsection, a State requirement—

(A) which relates to labeling or disclosure with respect to written warranties or performance thereunder;

(B) which is within the scope of an applicable requirement of sections 102, 103, and 104 (and rules implementing such sections), and

(C) which is not identical to a requirement of section 102, 103, or 104 (or a rule thereunder),

shall not be applicable to written warranties complying with such sections (or rules thereunder).

(2) If, upon application of an appropriate State agency, the Commission determines (pursuant to rules issued in accordance with section 109) that any requirement of such State covering any transaction to which this title applies (A) affords protection to consumers greater than the requirements of this title and (B) does not unduly burden interstate commerce, then such State requirement shall be applicable (notwithstanding the provisions of paragraph (1) of this subsection) to the extent specified in such determination for so long as the State administers and enforces effectively any such greater requirement.

(d) This title (other than section 102(c)) shall be inapplicable to any written warranty the making or content of which is otherwise governed by Federal law. If only a portion of a written warranty is so governed by Federal law, the remaining portion shall be subject to this title.

§ 112. Effective date [15 U.S.C.A. § 2312]

(a) Except as provided in subsection (b) of this section, this title shall take effect 6 months after the date of its enactment but shall not apply to consumer products manufactured prior to such date.

(b) Section 102(a) shall take effect 6 months after the final publication of rules respecting such section; except that the Commission, for good cause shown, may postpone the applicability of such sections until one year after such final publication in order to permit any designated classes of suppliers to bring their written warranties into compliance with rules promulgated pursuant to this title.

(c) The Commission shall promulgate rules for initial implementation of this title as soon as possible after the date of enactment of this Act but in no event later than one year after such date.

MAGNUSON–MOSS
WARRANTY ACT
REGULATIONS

---

16 C.F.R. Parts 700–703

Current through April 5, 2007; 72 F.R. 16983

TITLE 16.   COMMERCIAL PRACTICES REGULATIONS

PART 700. INTERPRETATIONS OF MAGNUSON–MOSS WARRANTY ACT

Sec.
700.1   Products covered.
700.2   Date of manufacture.
700.3   Written warranty.
700.4   Parties "actually making" a written warranty.
700.5   Expressions of general policy.
700.6   Designation of warranties.
700.7   Use of warranty registration cards.
700.8   Warrantor's decision as final.
700.9   Duty to install under a full warranty.
700.10 Section 102(c).
700.11 Written warranty, service contract, and insurance distinguished for purposes of compliance under the Act.
700.12 Effective date of 16 CFR, Parts 701 and 702.

PART 701. DISCLOSURE OF WRITTEN CONSUMER PRODUCT WARRANTY TERMS AND CONDITIONS

701.1   Definitions.

Sec.
701.2   Scope.
701.3   Written warranty terms.
701.4   Owner registration cards.

PART 702. PRE–SALE AVAILABILITY OF WRITTEN WARRANTY TERMS

702.1   Definitions.
702.2   Scope.
702.3   Pre-sale availability of written warranty terms.

PART 703. INFORMAL DISPUTE SETTLEMENT PROCEDURES

703.1   Definitions.
703.2   Duties of warrantor.

MINIMUM REQUIREMENTS OF THE MECHANISM

703.3   Mechanism organization.
703.4   Qualification of members.
703.5   Operation of the Mechanism.
703.6   Recordkeeping.
703.7   Audits.
703.8   Openness of records and proceedings.

PART 700

INTERPRETATIONS OF MAGNUSON–MOSS WARRANTY ACT

§ 700.1 Products covered.

(a) The Act applies to written warranties on tangible personal property which is normally used for personal, family, or household purposes. This definition includes property which is intended to be attached to or installed in any real property without regard to whether it is so attached or installed. This means that a product is a "consumer product" if the use of that type of product is not uncommon. The percentage of sales or the use to which a product is put by any individual buyer is not determinative. For example, products such as automobiles and typewriters which are used for both personal and commercial purposes come within the definition of consumer product. Where it is unclear whether a particular product is covered under the definition of consumer product, any ambiguity will be resolved in favor of coverage.

(b) Agricultural products such as farm machinery, structures and implements used in the business or occupation of farming are not covered by the Act where their personal, family, or household use is uncommon. However, those agricultural products normally used for personal or household gardening (for example, to produce goods for personal consumption, and not for resale) are consumer products under the Act.

(c) The definition of "Consumer product" limits the applicability of the Act to personal property, "including any such property intended to be attached to or installed in any real property without regard to whether it is so attached or installed." This provision brings under the Act separate items of equipment attached to real property, such as air conditioners, furnaces, and water heaters.

(d) The coverage of separate items to equipment attached to real property includes, but is not limited to, appliances and other thermal, mechanical, and electrical equipment. (It does not extend to the wiring, plumbing, ducts and other items which are integral component parts of the structure.) State law would classify many such products as fixtures to, and therefore a part of, realty. The statutory definition is designed to bring such products under the Act regardless of whether they may be considered fixtures under state law.

(e) The coverage of building materials which are not separate items of equipment is based on the nature of the purchase transaction. An analysis of the transaction will determine whether the goods are real or personal property. The numerous products which go into the construction of a consumer dwelling are all consumer products when sold "over the counter," as by hardware and building supply retailers. This is also true where a consumer contracts for the purchase of such materials in connection with the improvement, repair, or modification of a home (for example, paneling, dropped ceilings, siding, roofing, storm windows, remodeling). However, where such products are at the time of sale integrated into the structure of a dwelling they are not consumer products as they cannot be practically distinguished from realty. Thus, for example, the beams, wallboard, wiring, plumbing, windows, roofing, and other structural components of a dwelling are not consumer products when they are sold as part of real estate covered by a written warranty.

(f) In the case where a consumer contracts with a builder to construct a home, a substantial addition to a home, or other realty (such as a garage or an in-ground swimming pool) the building materials to be used are not consumer products. Although the materials are separately identifiable at the time the contract is made, it is the intention of the parties to contract for the construction of realty which will integrate the component materials. Of course, as noted above, any separate items of equipment to be attached to such realty are consumer products under the Act.

(g) Certain provisions of the Act apply only to products actually costing the consumer more than a specified amount. Section 103 applies to consumer products actually costing the consumer more than $10, excluding tax. The $10 minimum will be interpreted to include multiple-packaged items which may individually sell for less than $10, but which have been packaged in a manner that does not permit breaking the package to purchase an item or items at a price less than $10. Thus, a written warranty on a dozen items packaged and priced for sale at $12 must be designated, even though identical items may be offered in smaller quantities at under $10. This interpretation applies in the same manner to the minimum dollar limits in section 102 and rules promulgated under that section.

(h) Warranties or replacement parts and components used to repair consumer products are covered; warranties on services are not covered. Therefore, warranties which apply solely to a repairer's workmanship in performing repairs are not subject to the Act. Where a written agreement warrants both the parts provided to effect a repair and the workmanship in making that repair, the warranty must comply with the Act and the rules thereunder.

(i) The Act covers written warranties on consumer products "distributed in commerce" as that term is defined in section 101(3). Thus, by its terms the Act arguably applies to products exported to foreign jurisdictions. However, the public interest would not be served by the use of Commission resources to enforce the Act with respect to such products. Moreover, the legislative intent to apply the requirements of the Act to such products is not sufficiently clear to justify such an extraordinary result. The Commission does not contemplate the enforcement of the Act with respect to consumer products exported to foreign jurisdictions. Products exported for sale at military post exchanges remain subject to the same enforcement standards as products sold within the United States, its territories and possessions.

§ 700.2   Date of manufacture.

Section 112 of the Act provides that the Act shall apply only to those consumer products manufactured after July 4, 1975. When a consumer purchases repair of a consumer product the date of manufacture of any replacement parts used is the measuring date for determining coverage under the Act. The date of manufacture of the consumer product being repaired is in this instance not relevant. Where a consumer pur-

chases or obtains on an exchange basis a rebuilt consumer product, the date that the rebuilding process is completed determines the Act's applicability.

§ 700.3   Written warranty.

(a) The Act imposes specific duties and liabilities on suppliers who offer written warranties on consumer products. Certain representations, such as energy efficiency ratings for electrical appliances, care labeling of wearing apparel, and other product information disclosures may be express warranties under the Uniform Commercial Code. However, these disclosures alone are not written warranties under this Act. Section 101(6) provides that a written affirmation of fact or a written promise of a specified level of performance must relate to a specified period of time in order to be considered a "written warranty." [1] A product information disclosure without a specified time period to which the disclosure relates is therefore not a written warranty. In addition, section 111(d) exempts from the Act (except section 102(c)) any written warranty the making or content of which is required by federal law. The Commission encourages the disclosure of product information which is not deceptive and which may benefit consumers, and will not construe the Act to impede information disclosure in product advertising or labeling.

(b) Certain terms, or conditions, of sale of a consumer product may not be "written warranties" as that term is defined in Section 101(6), and should not be offered or described in a manner that may deceive consumers as to their enforceability under the Act. For example, a seller of consumer products may give consumers an unconditional right to revoke acceptance of goods within a certain number of days after delivery without regard to defects or failure to meet a specified level of performance. Or a seller may permit consumers to return products for any reason for credit toward purchase of another item. Such terms of sale taken alone are not written warranties under the Act. Therefore, suppliers should avoid any characterization of such terms of sale as warranties. The use of such terms as "free trial period" and "trade-in

---

1. A "written warranty" is also created by a written affirmation of fact or a written promise that the product is

defect free, or by a written undertaking of remedial action within the meaning of § 101(6)(B).

credit policy" in this regard would be appropriate. Furthermore, such terms of sale should be stated separately from any written warranty. Of course, the offering and performance of such terms of sale remain subject to section 5 of the Federal Trade Commission Act, 15 U.S.C. 45.

(c) The Magnuson-Moss Warranty Act generally applies to written warranties covering consumer products. Many consumer products are covered by warranties which are neither intended for, nor enforceable by, consumers. A common example is a warranty given by a component supplier to a manufacturer of consumer products. (The manufacturer may, in turn, warrant these components to consumers.) The component supplier's warranty is generally given solely to the product manufacturer, and is neither intended to be conveyed to the consumer nor brought to the consumer's attention in connection with the sale. Such warranties are not subject to the Act, since a written warranty under section 101(6) of the Act must become "part of the basis of the bargain between a supplier and a buyer for purposes other than resale." However, the Act applies to a component supplier's warranty in writing which is given to the consumer. An example is a supplier's written warranty to the consumer covering a refrigerator that is sold installed in a boat or recreational vehicle. The supplier of the refrigerator relies on the boat or vehicle assembler to convey the written agreement to the consumer. In this case, the supplier's written warranty is to a consumer, and is covered by the Act.

§ 700.4 Parties "actually making" a written warranty.

Section 110(f) of the Act provides that only the supplier "actually making" a written warranty is liable for purposes of FTC and private enforcement of the Act. A supplier who does no more than distribute or sell a consumer product covered by a written warranty offered by another person or business and which identifies that person or business as the warrantor is not liable for failure of the written warranty to comply with the Act or rules thereunder. However, other actions and written and oral representations of such a supplier in connection with the offer or sale of a warranted product may obligate that supplier under the Act. If under state law the supplier is deemed to have "adopted" the written

affirmation of fact, promise, or undertaking, the supplier is also obligated under the Act. Suppliers are advised to consult state law to determine those actions and representations which may make them co-warrantors, and therefore obligated under the warranty of the other person or business.

§ 700.5 Expressions of general policy.

(a) Under section 103(b), statements or representations of general policy concerning customer satisfaction which are not subject to any specific limitation need not be designated as full or limited warranties, and are exempt from the requirements of sections 102, 103, and 104 of the Act and rules thereunder. However, such statements remain subject to the enforcement provisions of section 110 of the Act, and to section 5 of the Federal Trade Commission Act, 15 U.S.C. 45.

(b) The section 103(b) exemption applies only to general policies not to those which are limited to specific consumer products manufactured or sold by the supplier offering such a policy. In addition, to qualify for an exemption under section 103(b) such policies may not be subject to any specific limitations. For example, policies which have an express limitation of duration or a limitation of the amount to be refunded are not exempted. This does not preclude the imposition of reasonable limitations based on the circumstances in each instance a consumer seeks to invoke such an agreement. For instance, a warrantor may refuse to honor such an expression of policy where a consumer has used a product for 10 years without previously expressing any dissatisfaction with the product. Such a refusal would not be a specific limitation under this provision.

§ 700.6 Designation of warranties.

(a) Section 103 of the Act provides that written warranties on consumer products manufactured after July 4, 1975, and actually costing the consumer more than $10, excluding tax, must be designated either "Full (statement of duration) Warranty" or "Limited Warranty". Warrantors may include a statement of duration in a limited warranty designation. The designation or designations should appear clearly and conspicuously as a caption, or prominent title, clearly separated from the text of the warranty. The full (statement of duration) warranty and limited warranty are the exclusive designations permitted under the Act, unless a specific exception is created by rule.

(b) Section 104(b)(4) states that "the duties under subsection (a) (of section 104) extend from the warrantor to each person who is a consumer with respect to the consumer product." Section 101(3) defines a consumer as "a buyer (other than for purposes of resale) of any consumer product, any person to whom such product is transferred during the duration of an implied or written warranty (or service contract) applicable to the product ...." Therefore, a full warranty may not expressly restrict the warranty rights of a transferee during its stated duration. However, where the duration of a full warranty is defined solely in terms of first purchaser ownership there can be no violation of section 104(b)(4), since the duration of the warranty expires, by definition, at the time of transfer. No rights of a subsequent transferee are cut off as there is no transfer of ownership "during the duration of (any) warranty." Thus, these provisions do not preclude the offering of a full warranty with its duration determined exclusively by the period during which the first purchaser owns the product, or uses it in conjunction with another product. For example, an automotive battery or muffler warranty may be designated as "full warranty for as long as you own your car." Because this type of warranty leads the consumer to believe that proof of purchase is not needed so long as he or she owns the product a duty to furnish documentary proof may not be reasonably imposed on the consumer under this type of warranty. The burden is on the warrantor to prove that a particular claimant under this type of warranty is not the original purchaser or owner of the product. Warrantors or their designated agents may, however, ask consumers to state or affirm that they are the first purchaser of the product.

§ 700.7　Use of warranty registration cards.

(a) Under section 104(b)(1) of the Act a warrantor offering a full warranty may not impose on consumers any duty other than notification of a defect as a condition of securing remedy of the defect or malfunction, unless such additional

duty can be demonstrated by the warrantor to be reasonable. Warrantors have in the past stipulated the return of a "warranty registration" or similar card. By "warranty registration card" the Commission means a card which must be returned by the consumer shortly after purchase of the product and which is stipulated or implied in the warranty to be a condition precedent to warranty coverage and performance.

(b) A requirement that the consumer return a warranty registration card or a similar notice as a condition of performance under a full warranty is an unreasonable duty. Thus, a provision such as, "This warranty is void unless the warranty registration card is returned to the warrantor" is not permissible in a full warranty, nor is it permissible to imply such a condition in a full warranty.

(c) This does not prohibit the use of such registration cards where a warrantor suggests use of the card as one possible means of proof of the date the product was purchased. For example, it is permissible to provide in a full warranty that a consumer may fill out and return a card to place on file proof of the date the product was purchased. Any such suggestion to the consumer must include notice that failure to return the card will not affect rights under the warranty, so long as the consumer can show in a reasonable manner the date the product was purchased. Nor does this interpretation prohibit a seller from obtaining from purchasers at the time of sale information requested by the warrantor.

§ 700.8　Warrantor's decision as final.

A warrantor shall not indicate in any written warranty or service contract either directly or indirectly that the decision of the warrantor, service contractor, or any designated third party is final or binding in any dispute concerning the warranty or service contract. Nor shall a warrantor or service contractor state that it alone shall determine what is a defect under the agreement. Such statements are deceptive since section 110(d) of the Act gives state and federal courts jurisdiction over suits for breach of warranty and service contract.

§ 700.9　Duty to install under a full warranty.

Under section 101(a)(1) of the Act, the remedy under a full warranty must be provided to the consumer without charge. If the warranted product has utility only when installed, a full warranty must provide such installation without charge regardless of whether or not the consumer originally paid for installation by the warrantor or his agent. However, this does not preclude the warrantor from imposing on the consumer a duty to remove, return, or reinstall where such duty can be demonstrated by the warrantor to meet the standard of reasonableness under section 104(b)(1).

§ **700.10** Section 102(c).

(a) Section 102(c) prohibits tying arrangements that condition coverage under a written warranty on the consumer's use of an article or service identified by brand, trade, or corporate name unless that article or service is provided without charge to the consumer.

(b) Under a limited warranty that provides only for replacement of defective parts and no portion of labor charges, section 102(c) prohibits a condition that the consumer use only service (labor) identified by the warrantor to install the replacement parts. A warrantor or his designated representative may not provide parts under the warranty in a manner which impedes or precludes the choice by the consumer of the person or business to perform necessary labor to install such parts.

(c) No warrantor may condition the continued validity of a warranty on the use of only authorized repair service and/or authorized replacement parts for non-warranty service and maintenance. For example, provisions such as, "This warranty is void if service is performed by anyone other than an authorized 'ABC' dealer and all replacement parts must be genuine 'ABC' parts," and the like, are prohibited where the service or parts are not covered by the warranty. These provisions violate the Act in two ways. First, they violate the section 102(c) ban against tying arrangements. Second, such provisions are deceptive under section 110 of the Act, because a warrantor cannot, as a matter of law, avoid liability under a written warranty where a defect is unrelated to the use by a consumer of "unauthorized" articles or service. This does not preclude a warrantor from expressly excluding liability for defects or damage caused by such "unauthorized" articles or service; nor does it preclude

the warrantor from denying liability where the warrantor can demonstrate that the defect or damage was so caused.

§ **700.11** Written warranty, service contract, and insurance distinguished for purposes of compliance under the Act.

(a) The Act recognizes two types of agreements which may provide similar coverage of consumer products, the written warranty, and the service contract. In addition, other agreements may meet the statutory definitions of either "written warranty" or "service contract," but are sold and regulated under state law as contracts of insurance. One example is the automobile breakdown insurance policies sold in many jurisdictions and regulated by the state as a form of casualty insurance. The McCarran-Ferguson Act, 15 U.S.C. 1011 et seq., precludes jurisdiction under federal law over "the business of insurance" to the extent an agreement is regulated by state law as insurance. Thus, such agreements are subject to the Magnuson-Moss Warranty Act only to the extent they are not regulated in a particular state as the business of insurance.

(b) "Written warranty" and "service contract" are defined in sections 101(6) and 101(8) of the Act, respectively. A written warranty must be "part of the basis of the bargain." This means that it must be conveyed at the time of sale of the consumer product and the consumer must not give any consideration beyond the purchase price of the consumer product in order to benefit from the agreement. It is not a requirement of the Act that an agreement obligate a supplier of the consumer product to a written warranty, but merely that it be part of the basis of the bargain between a supplier and a consumer. This contemplates written warranties by third-party non-suppliers.

(c) A service contract under the Act must meet the definitions of section 101(8). An agreement which would meet the definition of written warranty in section 101(6)(A) or (B) but for its failure to satisfy the basis of the bargain test is a service contract. For example, an agreement which calls for some consideration in addition to the purchase price of the consumer product, or which is entered into at some date after the purchase of the consumer product to which it applies, is a service contract. An agreement which relates only to the performance of maintenance and/or inspection services and which is not an undertaking, promise, or affirmation with respect to a specified level of performance, or that the product is free of defects in materials or workmanship, is a service contract. An agreement to perform periodic cleaning and inspection of a product over a specified period of time, even when offered at the time of sale and without charge to the consumer, is an example of such a service contract.

§ 700.12   Effective date of 16 CFR, Parts 701 and 702.

The Statement of Basis and Purpose of the final rules promulgated on December 31, 1975, provides that Parts 701 and 702 will become effective one year after the date of promulgation, December 31, 1976. The Commission intends this to mean that these rules apply only to written warranties on products manufactured after December 31, 1976.

PART 701

DISCLOSURE OF WRITTEN CONSUMER PRODUCT WARRANTY TERMS AND CONDITIONS

§ 701.1   Definitions.

(a) "The Act" means the Magnuson-Moss Warranty Federal Trade Commission Improvement Act, 15 U.S.C. 2301, et seq.

(b) "Consumer product" means any tangible personal property which is distributed in commerce and which is normally used for personal, family, or household purposes (including any such property intended to be attached to or installed in any real property without regard to whether it is so attached or installed). Products which are purchased solely for commercial or industrial use are excluded solely for purposes of this Part.

(c) "Written warranty" means—

(1) any written affirmation of fact or written promise made in connection with the sale of a consumer product by a supplier to a buyer which relates to the nature of the material or workmanship and affirms or promises that such material or workmanship is defect free or will meet a specified level of performance over a specified period of time, or

(2) any undertaking in writing in connection with the sale by a supplier of a consumer product to refund, repair, replace, or take other remedial action with respect to such product in the event that such product fails to meet the specifications set forth in the undertaking, which written affirmation, promise or undertaking becomes part of the basis of the bargain between a supplier and a buyer for purposes other than resale of such product.

(d) "Implied warranty" means an implied warranty arising under State law (as modified by secs. 104(a) and 108 of the Act) in connection with the sale by a supplier of a consumer product.

(e) "Remedy" means whichever of the following actions the warrantor elects:

(1) repair,

(2) replacement, or

(3) refund; except that the warrantor may not elect refund unless:

(i) the warrantor is unable to provide replacement and repair is not commercially practicable or cannot be timely made, or

(ii) the consumer is willing to accept such refund.

(f) "Supplier" means any person engaged in the business of making a consumer product directly or indirectly available to consumers.

(g) "Warrantor" means any supplier or other person who gives or offers to give a written warranty.

(h) "Consumer" means a buyer (other than for purposes of resale or use in the ordinary course of the buyer's business) of any consumer product, any person to whom such product is transferred during the duration of an implied or written warranty applicable to the product, and any other such person who is entitled by the terms of such warranty or under applicable State law to enforce against the warrantor the obligations of the warranty.

(i) "On the face of the warranty" means—

(1) where the warranty is a single sheet with printing on both sides of the sheet or where the warranty is comprised of more than one sheet, the page on which the warranty text begins;

(2) where the warranty is included as part of a larger document, such as a use and care manual, the page in such document on which the warranty text begins.

§ 701.2 Scope.

The regulations in this part establish requirements for warrantors for disclosing the terms and conditions of written warranties on consumer products actually costing the consumer more than $15.00.

§ 701.3 Written warranty terms.

(a) Any warrantor warranting to a consumer by means of a written warranty a consumer product actually costing the consumer more than $15.00 shall clearly and conspicuously disclose in a single document in simple and readily understood language, the following items of information:

(1) The identity of the party or parties to whom the written warranty is extended, if the enforceability of the written warranty is limited to the original consumer purchaser or is otherwise limited to persons other than every consumer owner during the term of the warranty;

(2) A clear description and identification of products, or parts, or characteristics, or components or properties covered by and where necessary for clarification, excluded from the warranty;

(3) A statement of what the warrantor will do in the event of a defect, malfunction or failure to conform with the written warranty, including the items or services the warrantor will pay for or provide, and, where necessary for clarification, those which the warrantor will not pay for or provide;

(4) The point in time or event on which the warranty term commences, if different from the purchase date, and the time period or other measurement of warranty duration;

(5) A step-by-step explanation of the procedure which the consumer should follow in order to obtain performance of any warranty obligation, including the persons or class of persons authorized to perform warranty obligations. This in-

cludes the name(s) of the warrantor(s), together with: the mailing address(es) of the warrantor(s), and/or the name or title and the address of any employee or department of the warrantor responsible for the performance of warranty obligations, and/or a telephone number which consumers may use without charge to obtain information on warranty performance;

(6) Information respecting the availability of an informal dispute settlement mechanism elected by the warrantor in compliance with Part 703 of this subchapter;

(7) Any limitations on the duration of implied warranties, disclosed on the face of the warranty as provided in Section 108 of the Act, accompanied by the following statement:

Some states do not allow limitations on how long an implied warranty lasts, so the above limitation may not apply to you.

(8) Any exclusions of or limitations on relief such as incidental or consequential damages, accompanied by the following statement, which may be combined with the statement required in sub-paragraph (7) above:

Some states do not allow the exclusion or limitation of incidental or consequential damages, so the above limitation or exclusion may not apply to you.

(9) A statement in the following language:

This warranty gives you specific legal rights, and you may also have other rights which vary from state to state.

(b) Paragraph (a)(1)–(9) of this Section shall not be applicable with respect to statements of general policy on emblems, seals or insignias issued by third parties promising replacement or refund if a consumer product is defective, which statements contain no representation or assurance of the quality or performance characteristics of the product; provided that (1) the disclosures required by paragraph (a)(1)–(9) are published by such third parties in each issue of a publication with a general circulation, and (2) such disclosures are provided free of charge to any consumer upon written request.

§ 701.4 Owner registration cards.

When a warrantor employs any card such as an owner's registration card, a warranty registration card, or the like, and the return of such card is a condition precedent to warranty coverage and performance, the warrantor shall disclose this fact in the warranty. If the return of such card reasonably appears to be a condition precedent to warranty coverage and performance, but is not such a condition, that fact shall be disclosed in the warranty.

PART 702

PRE–SALE AVAILABILITY OF WRITTEN WARRANTY TERMS

§ 702.1   Definitions.

(a) "The Act" means the Magnuson-Moss Warranty Federal Trade Commission Improvement Act, 15 U.S.C. 2301, et seq.

(b) "Consumer product" means any tangible personal property which is distributed in commerce and which is normally used for personal, family, or household purposes (including any such property intended to be attached to or installed in any real property without regard to whether it is so attached or installed). Products which are purchased solely for commercial or industrial use are excluded solely for purposes of this Part.

(c) "Written warranty" means—

(1) any written affirmation of fact or written promise made in connection with the sale of a consumer product by a supplier to a buyer which relates to the nature of the material or workmanship and affirms or promises that such material or workmanship is defect free or will meet a specified level of performance over a specified period of time, or

(2) any undertaking in writing in connection with the sale by a supplier of a consumer product to refund, repair, replace, or take other remedial action with respect to such product in the event that such product fails to meet the specifications set forth in the undertaking, which written affirmation, promise or undertaking becomes part of the basis of the bargain between a supplier and a buyer for purposes other than resale of such product.

(d) "Warrantor" means any supplier or other person who gives or offers to give a written warranty.

(e) "Seller" means any person who sells or offers for sale for purposes other than resale or use in the ordinary course of the buyer's business any consumer product.

(f) "Supplier" means any person engaged in the business of making a consumer product directly or indirectly available to consumers.

§ 702.2   Scope.

The regulations in this part establish requirements for sellers and warrantors for making the terms of any written warranty on a consumer product available to the consumer prior to sale.

§ 702.3   Pre-sale availability of written warranty terms.

The following requirements apply to consumer products actually costing the consumer more than $15.00:

(a) *Duties of seller.* Except as provided in paragraphs (c) through (d) of this section, the seller of a consumer product with a written warranty shall make a text of the warranty readily available for examination by the prospective buyer by:

(1) Displaying it in close proximity to the warranted product, or

(2) Furnishing it upon request prior to sale and placing signs reasonably calculated to elicit the prospective buyer's attention in prominent locations in the store or department advising such prospective buyers of the availability of warranties upon request.

(b) *Duties of the warrantor.* (1) A warrantor who gives a written warranty warranting to a consumer a consumer product actually costing the consumer more than $15.00 shall:

(i) Provide sellers with warranty materials necessary for such sellers to comply with the requirements set forth in paragraph (a) of this section, by the use of one or more by the following means:

(A) Providing a copy of the written warranty with every warranted consumer product; and/or

(B) Providing a tag, sign, sticker, label, decal or other attachment to the product, which contains the full text of the written warranty; and/or

(C) Printing on or otherwise attaching the text of the written warranty to the package, carton, or other container if that package, carton or other container is normally used for display purposes. If the warrantor elects this option a copy of the written warranty must also accompany the warranted product; and/or

(D) Providing a notice, sign, or poster disclosing the text of a consumer product warranty.

If the warrantor elects this option, a copy of the written warranty must also accompany each warranted product.

(ii) Provide catalog, mail order, and door-to-door sellers with copies of written warranties necessary for such sellers to comply with the requirements set forth in paragraphs (c) and (d) of this section.

(2) Sub-paragraph (1) of this paragraph (b) shall not be applicable with respect to statements of general policy on emblems, seals or insignias issued by third parties promising replacement or refund if a consumer product is defective, which statements contain no representation or assurance of the quality or performance characteristics of the product; provided that (i) the disclosures required by 701.3(a)(1)–(9) are published by such third parties in each issue of a publication with a general circulation, and (ii) such disclosures are provided free of charge to any consumer upon written request.

(c) *Catalog and Mail Order Sales.* (1) For purposes of this paragraph:

(i) "Catalog or mail order sales", means any offer for sale, or any solicitation for an order for a consumer product with a written warranty, which includes instructions for ordering the product which do not require a personal visit to the seller's establishment.

(ii) "Close conjunction" means on the page containing the description of the warranted product, or on the page facing that page.

(2) Any seller who offers for sale to consumers consumer products with written warranties by means of a catalog or mail order solicitation shall:

(i) clearly and conspicuously disclose in such catalog or solicitation in close conjunction to the description of warranted product, or in an information section of the catalog or solicitation clearly referenced, including a page number, in close conjunction to the description of the warranted product, *either*:

(A) the full text of the written warranty; or

(B) that the written warranty can be obtained free upon specific written request, and the address where such warranty can be obtained. If this option is elected, such seller shall promptly provide a copy of any written warranty requested by the consumer.

(d) *Door-to-door sales.* (1) For purposes of this paragraph:

(i) "Door-to-door sale" means a sale of consumer products in which the seller or his representative personally solicits the sale, including those in response to or following an invitation by a buyer, and the buyer's agreement to offer to purchase is made at a place other than the place of business of the seller.

(ii) "Prospective buyer" means an individual solicited by a door-to-door seller to buy a consumer product who indicates sufficient interest in that consumer product or maintains sufficient contact with the seller for the seller reasonably to conclude that the person solicited is considering purchasing the product.

(2) Any seller who offers for sale to consumers consumer products with written warranties by means of door-to-door sales shall, prior to the consummation of the sale, disclose the fact that the sales representative has copies of the warranties for the warranted products being offered for sale, which may be inspected by the prospective buyer at any time during the sales presentation. Such disclosure shall be made orally and shall be included in any written materials shown to prospective buyers.

PART 703

INFORMAL DISPUTE SETTLEMENT PROCEDURES

§ 703.1 Definitions.

(a) "The Act" means the Magnuson-Moss Warranty—Federal Trade Commission Improvement Act, 15 U.S.C. 2301, et seq.

(b) "Consumer product" means any tangible personal property which is distributed in commerce and which is normally used for personal, family, or household purposes (including any such property intended to be attached to or installed in any real property without regard to whether it is so attached or installed).

(c) "Written warranty" means:

(1) Any written affirmation of fact or written promise made in connection with the sale of a consumer product by a supplier to a buyer which relates to the nature of the material or workmanship and affirms or promises that such material or workmanship is defect free or will meet a specified level of performance over a specified period of time, or

(2) Any undertaking in writing in connection with the sale by a supplier of a consumer product to refund, repair, replace, or take other remedial action with respect to such product in the event that such product fails to meet the specifications set forth in the undertaking, which written affirmation, promise or undertaking becomes part of the basis of the bargain between a supplier and a buyer for purposes other than resale of such product.

(d) "Warrantor" means any person who given or offers to give a written warranty which incorporates an informal dispute settlement mechanism.

(e) "Mechanism" means an informal dispute settlement procedure which is incorporated into the terms of a written warranty to which any provision of Title I of the Act applies, as provided in Section 110 of the Act.

(f) "Members" means the person or persons within a Mechanism actually deciding disputes.

(g) "Consumer" means a buyer (other than for purposes of resale) of any consumer product, any person to whom such product is transferred during the duration of a written warranty applicable to the product, and any other person who is entitled by the terms of such warranty or under

applicable state law to enforce against the warrantor the obligations of the warranty.

(h) "On the face of the warranty" means:

(1) If the warranty is a single sheet with printing on both sides of the sheet, or if the warranty is comprised of more than one sheet, the page on which the warranty text begins;

(2) If the warranty is included as part of a longer document, such as a use and care manual, the page in such document on which the warranty text begins.

§ 703.2 Duties of warrantor.

(a) The warrantor shall not incorporate into the terms of a written warranty a Mechanism that fails to comply with the requirements contained in §§ 703.3–703.8 of this part. This paragraph shall not prohibit a warrantor from incorporating into the terms of a written warranty the step-by-step procedure which the consumer should take in order to obtain performance of any obligation under the warranty as described in section 102(a)(7) of the Act and required by Part 701 of this subchapter.

(b) The warrantor shall disclose clearly and conspicuously at least the following information on the face of the written warranty:

(1) A statement of the availability of the informal dispute settlement mechanism;

(2) The name and address of the Mechanism, or the name and a telephone number of the Mechanism which consumers may use without charge;

(3) A statement of any requirement that the consumer resort to the Mechanism before exercising rights or seeking remedies created by Title I of the Act; together with the disclosure that if a consumer chooses to seek redress by pursuing rights and remedies not created by Title I of the Act, resort to the Mechanism would not be required by any provision of the Act; and

(4) A statement, if applicable, indicating where further information on the Mechanism can be found in materials accompanying the product, as provided in § 703.2(c) of this section.

1320

(c) The warrantor shall include in the written warranty or in a separate section of materials accompanying the product, the following information:

(1) Either (i) a form addressed to the Mechanism containing spaces requesting the information which the Mechanism may require for prompt resolution of warranty disputes; or (ii) a telephone number of the Mechanism which consumers may use without charge;

(2) The name and address of the Mechanism;

(3) A brief description of Mechanism procedures;

(4) The time limits adhered to by the Mechanism; and

(5) The types of information which the Mechanism may require for prompt resolution of warranty disputes.

(d) The warrantor shall take steps reasonably calculated to make consumers aware of the Mechanism's existence at the time consumers experience warranty disputes. Nothing contained in paragraphs (b), (c), or (d) of this section shall limit the warrantor's option to encourage consumers to seek redress directly from the warrantor as long as the warrantor does not expressly require consumers to seek redress directly from the warrantor. The warrantor shall proceed fairly and expeditiously to attempt to resolve all disputes submitted directly to the warrantor.

(e) Whenever a dispute is submitted directly to the warrantor, the warrantor shall, within a reasonable time, decide whether, and to what extent, it will satisfy the consumer, and inform the consumer of its decision. In its notification to the consumer of its decision, the warrantor shall include the information required in § 703.2(b) and (c) of this section.

(f) The warrantor shall:

(1) Respond fully and promptly to reasonable requests by the Mechanism for information relating to disputes;

(2) Upon notification of any decision of the Mechanism that would require action on the part of the warrantor, immediately notify the Mechanism whether, and to what extent, warrantor will abide by the decision; and

(3) Perform any obligations it has agreed to.

(g) The warrantor shall act in good faith in determining whether, and to what extent, it will abide by a Mechanism decision.

(h) The warrantor shall comply with any reasonable requirements imposed by the Mechanism to fairly and expeditiously resolve warranty disputes.

MINIMUM REQUIREMENTS OF THE MECHANISM

§ 703.3 Mechanism organization.

(a) The Mechanism shall be funded and competently staffed at a level sufficient to ensure fair and expeditious resolution of all disputes, and shall not charge consumers any fee for use of the Mechanism.

(b) The warrantor and the sponsor of the Mechanism (if other than the warrantor) shall take all steps necessary to ensure that the Mechanism, and its members and staff, are sufficiently insulated from the warrantor and the sponsor, so that the decisions of the members and the performance of the staff are not influenced by either the warrantor or the sponsor. Necessary steps shall include, at a minimum, committing funds in advance, basing personnel decisions solely on merit, and not assigning conflicting warrantor or sponsor duties to Mechanism staff persons.

(c) The Mechanism shall impose any other reasonable requirements necessary to ensure that the members and staff act fairly and expeditiously in each dispute.

§ 703.4 Qualification of members.

(a) No member deciding a dispute shall be:

(1) A party to the dispute, or an employee or agent of a party other than for purposes of deciding disputes; or

(2) A person who is or may become a party in any legal action, including but not limited to class actions, relating to the product or complaint in dispute, or an employee or agent of such person other than for purposes of deciding disputes. For purposes of this paragraph (a) a person shall not be considered a "party" solely because he or she acquires or owns an interest in a party solely for investment, and the acquisition or ownership of an interest which is offered to the general public shall be prima facie evidence

of its acquisition or ownership solely for investment.

(b) When one or two members are deciding a dispute, all shall be persons having no direct involvement in the manufacture, distribution, sale or service of any product. When three or more members are deciding a dispute, at least two-thirds shall be persons having no direct involvement in the manufacture, distribution, sale or service of any product. "Direct involvement" shall not include acquiring or owning an interest solely for investment, and the acquisition or ownership of an interest which is offered to the general public shall be prima facie evidence of its acquisition or ownership solely for investment. Nothing contained in this section shall prevent the members from consulting with any persons knowledgeable in the technical, commercial or other areas relating to the product which is the subject of the dispute.

(c) Members shall be persons interested in the fair and expeditious settlement of consumer disputes.

§ 703.5   Operation of the Mechanism.

(a) The Mechanism shall establish written operating procedures which shall include at least those items specified in paragraphs (b) through (j) of this section. Copies of the written procedures shall be made available to any person upon request.

(b) Upon notification of a dispute, the Mechanism shall immediately inform both the warrantor and the consumer of receipt of the dispute.

(c) The Mechanism shall investigate, gather and organize all information necessary for a fair and expeditious decision in each dispute. When any evidence gathered by or submitted to the Mechanism raises issues relating to the number of repair attempts, the length of repair periods, the possibility of unreasonable use of the product, or any other issues relevant in light of Title I of the Act (or rules thereunder), including issues relating to consequential damages, or any other remedy under the Act (or rules thereunder), the Mechanism shall investigate these issues. When information which will or may be used in the decision, submitted by one party, or a consultant under § 703.4(b) of this part, or any other source tends to contradict facts submitted by the other party, the Mechanism shall clearly, accurately, and completely disclose to both parties the contradictory information (and its source) and shall provide both parties an opportunity to explain or rebut the information and to submit additional materials. The Mechanism shall not require any information not reasonably necessary to decide the dispute.

(d) If the dispute has not been settled, the Mechanism shall, as expeditiously as possible but at least within 40 days of notification of the dispute, except as provided in paragraph (e) of this section:

(1) Render a fair decision based on the information gathered as described in paragraph (c) of this section, and on any information submitted at an oral presentation which conforms to the requirements of paragraph (f) of this section (A decision shall include any remedies appropriate under the circumstances, including repair, replacement, refund, reimbursement for expenses, compensation for damages, and any other remedies available under the written warranty or the Act (or rules thereunder); and a decision shall state a specified reasonable time for performance);

(2) Disclose to the warrantor its decision and the reasons therefor;

(3) If the decision would require action on the part of the warrantor, determine whether, and to what extent, warrantor will abide by its decision; and

(4) Disclose to the consumer its decision, the reasons therefor, warrantor's intended actions (if the decision would require action on the part of the warrantor), and the information described in paragraph (g) of this section. For purposes of this paragraph (d) a dispute shall be deemed settled when the Mechanism has ascertained from the consumer that:

(i) The dispute has been settled to the consumer's satisfaction; and

(ii) the settlement contains a specified reasonable time for performance.

(e) The Mechanism may delay the performance of its duties under paragraph (d) of this section beyond the 40 day time limit;

(1) Where the period of delay is due solely to failure of a consumer to provide promptly his or her name and address, brand name and model number of the product involved, and a statement

as to the nature of the defect or other complaint; or

(2) For a 7 day period in those cases where the consumer has made no attempt to seek redress directly from the warrantor.

(f) The Mechanism may allow an oral presentation by a party to a dispute (or a party's representative) only if:

(1) Both warrantor and consumer expressly agree to the presentation;

(2) Prior to agreement the Mechanism fully discloses to the consumer the following information:

(i) That the presentation by either party will take place only if both parties so agree, but that if they agree, and one party fails to appear at the agreed upon time and place, the presentation by the other party may still be allowed;

(ii) That the members will decide the dispute whether or not an oral presentation is made;

(iii) The proposed date, time and place for the presentation; and

(iv) A brief description of what will occur at the presentation including, if applicable, parties' rights to bring witnesses and/or counsel; and

(3) Each party has the right to be present during the other party's oral presentation. Nothing contained in this paragraph (b) of this section shall preclude the Mechanism from allowing an oral presentation by one party, if the other party fails to appear at the agreed upon time and place, as long as all of the requirements of this paragraph have been satisfied.

(g) The Mechanism shall inform the consumer, at the time of disclosure required in paragraph (d) of this section that:

(1) If he or she is dissatisfied with its decision or warrantor's intended actions, or eventual performance, legal remedies, including use of small claims court, may be pursued;

(2) The Mechanism's decision is admissible in evidence as provided in section 110(a)(3) of the Act; and

(3) The consumer may obtain, at reasonable cost, copies of all Mechanism records relating to the consumer's dispute.

(h) If the warrantor has agreed to perform any obligations, either as part of a settlement agreed

to after notification to the Mechanism of the dispute or as a result of a decision under paragraph (d) of this section, the Mechanism shall ascertain from the consumer within 10 working days of the date for performance whether performance has occurred.

(i) A requirement that a consumer resort to the Mechanism prior to commencement of an action under section 110(d) of the Act shall be satisfied 40 days after notification to the Mechanism of the dispute or when the Mechanism completes all of its duties under paragraph (d) of this section, whichever occurs sooner. Except that, if the Mechanism delays performance of its paragraph (d) of this section duties as allowed by paragraph (e) of this section, the requirement that the consumer initially resort to the Mechanism shall not be satisfied until the period of delay allowed by paragraph (e) of this section has ended.

(j) Decisions of the Mechanism shall not be legally binding on any person. However, the warrantor shall act in good faith, as provided in § 703.2(g) of this part. In any civil action arising out of a warranty obligation and relating to a matter considered by the Mechanism, any decision of the Mechanism shall be admissible in evidence, as provided in section 110(a)(3) of the Act.

§ 703.6 Recordkeeping.

(a) The Mechanism shall maintain records on each dispute referred to it which shall include:

(1) Name, address and telephone number of the consumer;

(2) Name, address, telephone number and contact person of the warrantor;

(3) Brand name and model number of the product involved;

(4) The date of receipt of the dispute and the date of disclosure to the consumer of the decision;

(5) All letters or other written documents submitted by either party;

(6) All other evidence collected by the Mechanism relating to the dispute, including summaries of relevant and material portions of telephone calls and meetings between the Mechanism and any other person (including consultants described in § 703.4(b) of this part);

(7) A summary of any relevant and material information presented by either party at an oral presentation;

(8) The decision of the members including information as to date, time and place of meeting, and the identity of members voting; or information on any other resolution;

(9) A copy of the disclosure to the parties of the decision;

(10) A statement of the warrantor's intended action(s);

(11) Copies of follow-up letters (or summaries of relevant and material portions of follow-up telephone calls) to the consumer, and responses thereto; and

(12) Any other documents and communications (or summaries of relevant and material portions of oral communications) relating to the dispute.

(b) The Mechanism shall maintain an index of each warrantor's disputes grouped under brand name and subgrouped under product model.

(c) The Mechanism shall maintain an index for each warrantor as will show:

(1) All disputes in which the warrantor has promised some performance (either by settlement or in response to a Mechanism decision) and has failed to comply; and

(2) All disputes in which the warrantor has refused to abide by a Mechanism decision.

(d) The Mechanism shall maintain an index as will show all disputes delayed beyond 40 days.

(e) The Mechanism shall compile semi-annually and maintain statistics which show the number and percent of disputes in each of the following categories:

(1) Resolved by staff of the Mechanism and warrantor has complied;

(2) Resolved by staff of the Mechanism, time for compliance has occurred, and warrantor has not complied;

(3) Resolved by staff of the Mechanism and time for compliance has not yet occurred;

(4) Decided by members and warrantor has complied;

(5) Decided by members, time for compliance has occurred, and warrantor has not complied;

(6) Decided by members and time for compliance has not yet occurred;

(7) Decided by members adverse to the consumer;

(8) No jurisdiction;

(9) Decision delayed beyond 40 days under § 703.5(e)(1) of this part;

(10) Decision delayed beyond 40 days under § 703.5(e)(2) of this part;

(11) Decision delayed beyond 40 days for any other reason; and

(12) Pending decision.

(f) The Mechanism shall retain all records specified in paragraphs (a) through (e) of this section for at least 4 years after final disposition of the dispute.

§ 703.7 Audits.

(a) The Mechanism shall have an audit conducted at least annually, to determine whether the Mechanism and its implementation are in compliance with this part. All records of the Mechanism required to be kept under § 703.6 of this part shall be available for audit.

(b) Each audit provided for in paragraph (a) of this section shall include at a minimum the following:

(1) Evaluation of warrantors' efforts to make consumers aware of the Mechanism's existence as required in § 703.2(d) of this part;

(2) Review of the indexes maintained pursuant to § 703.6(b), (c), and (d) of this part; and

(3) Analysis of a random sample of disputes handled by the Mechanism to determine the following:

(i) Adequacy of the Mechanism's complaint and other forms, investigation, mediation and follow-up efforts, and other aspects of complaint handling; and

(ii) Accuracy of the Mechanism's statistical compilations under § 703.6(e) of this part. (For purposes of this subparagraph "analysis" shall include oral or written contact with the consumers involved in each of the disputes in the random sample.)

(c) A report of each audit under this section shall be submitted to the Federal Trade Commission, and shall be made available to any person at reasonable cost. The Mechanism may direct its auditor to delete names of parties to disputes, and identity of products involved, from the audit report.

(d) Auditors shall be selected by the Mechanism. No auditor may be involved with the

Mechanism as a warrantor, sponsor or member, or employee or agent thereof, other than for purposes of the audit.

§ 703.8 Openness of records and proceedings.

(a) The statistical summaries specified in § 703.6(e) of this part shall be available to any person for inspection and copying.

(b) Except as provided under paragraphs (a) and (e) of this section, and paragraph (c) of § 703.7 of this part, all records of the Mechanism may be kept confidential, or made available only on such terms and conditions, or in such form, as the Mechanism shall permit.

(c) The policy of the Mechanism with respect to records made available at the Mechanism's option shall be set out in the procedures under § 703.5(a) of this part; the policy shall be applied uniformly to all requests for access to or copies of such records.

(d) Meetings of the members to hear and decide disputes shall be open to observers on reasonable and nondiscriminatory terms. The identity of the parties and products involved in disputes need not be disclosed at meetings.

(e) Upon request the Mechanism shall provide to either party to a dispute:

(1) Access to all records relating to the dispute; and

(2) Copies of any records relating to the dispute, at reasonable cost.

(f) The Mechanism shall make available to any person upon request, information relating to the qualifications of Mechanism staff and members.

†